Principles of
GERIATRIC MEDICINE
AND GERONTOLOGY

Principles of
GERIATRIC MEDICINE AND GERONTOLOGY

Second Edition

William R. Hazzard, M.D.

Professor of Medicine and Chairman
Department of Internal Medicine
Bowman Gray School of Medicine of Wake Forest University
Winston-Salem, North Carolina

Reubin Andres, M.D.

Clinical Director
National Institute on Aging, NIH
Professor, Department of Medicine
The Johns Hopkins University
Gerontology Research Center at Francis Scott Key Medical Center
Baltimore, Maryland

Edwin L. Bierman, M.D.

Professor of Medicine
Head, Division of Metabolism, Endocrinology and Nutrition
University of Washington School of Medicine
Seattle, Washington

John P. Blass, M.D.

Burke Professor of Neurology and Medicine
Cornell University Medical College
Director, Dementia Research Service
The Burke Rehabilitation Center
White Plains, New York

McGraw-Hill Information Services Company
HEALTH PROFESSIONS DIVISION

New York St. Louis San Francisco Colorado Springs
Auckland Bogotá Caracas Hamburg Lisbon London Madrid Mexico Milan Montreal
New Delhi Paris San Juan São Paulo Singapore Sydney Tokyo Toronto

PRINCIPLES OF GERIATRIC MEDICINE AND GERONTOLOGY

1234567890 HALHAL 89432109

ISBN 0-07-027500-9

This book was set in Caledonia by York Graphic Services, Inc.
The editors were Avé McCracken and Bruce Williams;
the production supervisor was Clare Stanley;
the cover was designed by Edward R. Schultheis;
the index was prepared by Alexandra Nickerson.
Arcata Graphics/Halliday was printer and binder.

Library of Congress Cataloging-in-Publication Data
Principles of geriatric medicine and gerontology / editors, William R.
  Hazzard . . . [et al.].—2nd ed.
     p. cm.
   Rev. ed. of: Principles of geriatric medicine/[edited by] Reubin
Andres, Edwin L. Bierman, William R. Hazzard. c1985.
   Includes bibliographies and index.
   ISBN 0-07-027500-9:
   1. Geriatrics. I. Hazzard, William R., date. II. Principles
of geriatric medicine.
   [DNLM: 1. Geriatrics.   WT 100 P9575]
RC952.P752   1990
618.97—dc20
DNLM/DLC   89-12510

CONTENTS

CONTRIBUTORS, xiii

PREFACE, xxiii

INTRODUCTION: THE PRACTICE OF GERIATRIC MEDICINE, xxv

1
PRINCIPLES OF GERONTOLOGY

1	BIOLOGICAL MECHANISMS OF AGING: AN OVERVIEW *Vincent J. Cristofalo*	3
2	EVOLUTIONARY PERSPECTIVE OF HUMAN LONGEVITY *Richard G. Cutler*	15
3	GENETICS OF HUMAN DISEASE, LONGEVITY, AND AGING *George M. Martin and Mitchell S. Turker*	22
4	THE SEX DIFFERENTIAL IN LONGEVITY *William R. Hazzard*	37
5	NUTRITION AND AGING *John E. Morley*	48
6	CLINICAL IMMUNOLOGY *William H. Adler and James E. Nagel*	60
7	ONCOLOGY AND AGING: GENERAL PRINCIPLES OF CANCER IN THE ELDERLY *Harvey Jay Cohen*	72
8	EXERCISE IN OLDER PEOPLE: CARDIOVASCULAR AND METABOLIC ADAPTATIONS *Jerome L. Fleg and Andrew P. Goldberg*	85
9	PERSONALITY AND AGING *Paul T. Costa, Jr., and Robert R. McCrae*	101
10	SEXUALITY AND AGING *Julian M. Davidson*	108
11	SOCIOLOGY OF AGING *George L. Maddox*	115
12	RISK FACTORS FOR MORBIDITY AND MORTALITY IN OLDER POPULATIONS: AN EPIDEMIOLOGIC APPROACH *Trudy L. Bush, Susan R. Miller, Michael H. Criqui, and* *Elizabeth Barrett-Connor*	125

13 TOWARD SUCCESSFUL AGING: LIMITATION OF THE
MORBIDITY ASSOCIATED WITH "NORMAL" AGING   138
John W. Rowe

14 LONG-LIVED POPULATIONS (EXTREME OLD AGE)   142
Alexander Leaf

15 THE EPIDEMIOLOGY AND DEMOGRAPHY OF AGING   146
Deborah J. Moritz and Adrian M. Ostfeld

16 HEALTH CARE IMPLICATIONS OF AN AGING POPULATION   157
L. Gregory Pawlson

17 PREVENTIVE GERONTOLOGY: STRATEGIES FOR ATTENUATION
OF THE CHRONIC DISEASES OF AGING   167
Edwin L. Bierman and William R. Hazzard

2

PRINCIPLES OF GERIATRICS

18 CLINICAL EVALUATION OF THE ELDERLY PATIENT   175
Richard W. Besdine

19 THE TEAM APPROACH TO GERIATRIC CARE   184
Conn J. Foley, Leslie S. Libow, and Fred B. Charatan

20 HEALTH PROMOTION AND DISEASE PREVENTION   192
Linda P. Fried

21 CLINICAL PHARMACOLOGY   201
Robert E. Vestal

22 DIFFERENCE IN THE PRESENTATION OF DISEASE   212
George Rosenthal and Knight Steel

23 COMPREHENSIVE FUNCTIONAL ASSESSMENT (CFA)
IN EVERYDAY PRACTICE   218
Marsha Duke Fretwell

24 NEUROPSYCHIATRIC ASSESSMENT   224
Lissy F. Jarvik and John P. Blass

25 SOCIAL FACTORS IN CARE: THE ELDERLY PATIENT'S FAMILY   232
Elaine M. Brody

26 ALTERATIONS OF LABORATORY FINDINGS   241
H. Malcolm Hodkinson

27 ACUTE HOSPITAL CARE FOR FRAIL OLDER PATIENTS   247
Marsha Duke Fretwell

28 SURGERY IN THE ELDERLY   254
Ronnie Ann Rosenthal and Dana K. Andersen

29 ANESTHESIA FOR THE ELDERLY PATIENT   270
Raymond C. Roy

30 PAIN MANAGEMENT IN THE ELDERLY   281
Kathleen M. Foley

31 ENTERAL/PARENTERAL ALIMENTATION   296
Edward W. Lipkin

32 GERONTOLOGICAL NURSING 304
Evelynn Clark Gioiella

33 TRANSITIONAL REHABILITATION: AN APPROACH
TO THE PATIENT WITH A NEW DISABILITY 312
Leo M. Cooney, Jr.

34 REHABILITATION OF THE GERIATRIC PATIENT 319
Kenneth Brummel-Smith

35 NURSING HOME CARE 331
Joseph G. Ouslander

36 COMMUNITY-BASED LONG-TERM CARE: THE DILEMMA
OF QUALITY AND COST 349
Thomas E. Finucane and John R. Burton

37 THE CARE OF THE DYING PATIENT 354
Elizabeth Cobbs and Joanne Lynn

38 THE LEGAL ASPECTS OF GERIATRIC MEDICINE:
PLANNING AND PROTECTION 362
J. Dinsmore Adams, Jr., and Constance P. Carden

39 ETHICAL ISSUES IN GERIATRIC CARE 367
Robert A. Pearlman

3

DISEASES OF THE ORGAN SYSTEMS

40 AGING OF HUMAN SKIN 383
Arthur K. Balin

41 THE ORAL CAVITY 413
Bruce J. Baum and Jonathan A. Ship

42 THE EYE 422
Einar Stefánsson

43 AUDITORY AND VESTIBULAR DYSFUNCTION IN AGING 432
Thomas S. Rees and Larry G. Duckert

SECTION A The Cardiovascular System

44 ALTERATIONS IN CIRCULATORY FUNCTION 445
Edward G. Lakatta and Gary Gerstenblith

45 AGING AND ATHEROSCLEROSIS 458
Edwin L. Bierman

46 DISORDERS OF THE HEART 466
Gary Gerstenblith and Edward G. Lakatta

47 PERIPHERAL VASCULAR DISEASE 476
Brian L. Thiele and D. Eugene Strandness, Jr.

48 HYPERTENSION 485
William B. Applegate

SECTION B   The Respiratory System

49   AGING OF THE RESPIRATORY SYSTEM   499
     Melvyn S. Tockman

50   PNEUMONIA   509
     John G. Bartlett

51   TUBERCULOSIS: A SPECIAL PROBLEM IN THE ELDERLY   518
     William W. Stead and Asim K. Dutt

52   CHRONIC AIRWAYS OBSTRUCTION AND RESPIRATORY FAILURE   526
     Peter B. Terry

53   INTERSTITIAL LUNG DISEASE, HYPERSENSITIVITY PNEUMONITIS,
     AND PULMONARY VASCULAR DISEASE IN THE ELDERLY   538
     Brian P. Zehr and Gary W. Hunninghake

54   LUNG CANCER   548
     Melvyn S. Tockman and Wilmot C. Ball, Jr.

SECTION C   The Renal System and Urinary Tract

55   AGING CHANGES IN RENAL FUNCTION   555
     Laurence H. Beck and John M. Burkart

56   RENAL DISEASES IN THE ELDERLY   565
     John M. Burkart and Laurence H. Beck

57   DISORDERS OF THE PROSTATE   582
     Charles B. Brendler

SECTION D   The Gastrointestinal System

58   AGING OF THE GASTROINTESTINAL SYSTEM   593
     James B. Nelson and Donald O. Castell

59   DISORDERS OF THE ESOPHAGUS   609
     Wallace C. Wu and Joel E. Richter

60   DISORDERS OF THE STOMACH AND DUODENUM   619
     Robert M. Kerr

61   HEPATOBILIARY DISORDERS   631
     John H. Gilliam III

62   PANCREATIC DISORDERS   640
     John H. Gilliam III

63   COLONIC DISORDERS   645
     Lawrence J. Cheskin and Marvin M. Schuster

SECTION E   The Hematologic System

64   AGING OF THE HEMATOPOIETIC SYSTEM   655
     David A. Lipschitz

65 ANEMIA IN THE ELDERLY 662
David A. Lipschitz

66 WHITE CELL DISORDERS 669
Robert L. Capizzi, Bayard L. Powell, and Julia M. Cruz

67 PLATELETS AND ARTERIAL THROMBOSIS 679
Laurence A. Harker

68 COAGULATION DISORDERS, VENOUS THROMBOSIS,
AND ANTITHROMBOTIC THERAPY 692
Arthur R. Thompson

SECTION F   The Endocrine and Metabolic Systems

69 AGING OF THE ENDOCRINE SYSTEM 705
L. Cass Terry and Jeffrey B. Halter

70 THYROID DISEASES 719
Robert I. Gregerman

71 DIABETES MELLITUS IN THE ELDERLY 739
Andrew P. Goldberg, Reubin Andres, and Edwin L. Bierman

72 MORTALITY AND OBESITY: THE RATIONALE FOR
AGE-SPECIFIC HEIGHT-WEIGHT TABLES 759
Reubin Andres

73 AGING AND PLASMA LIPOPROTEINS 767
Norman E. Miller

74 THE MENOPAUSE AND ESTROGEN REPLACEMENT THERAPY 777
Mikal Janelle Odom, Bruce R. Carr, and Paul C. MacDonald

75 BREAST DISEASES OF ELDERLY WOMEN 789
Roger E. Moe

SECTION G   Disorders of Bone and Mineral Metabolism

76 CALCIUM AND BONE HOMEOSTASIS WITH AGING 799
Marius E. Kraenzlin, John C. Jennings, and David J. Baylink

77 OSTEOPOROSIS 813
Charles H. Chestnut III

78 OSTEOMALACIA 826
David J. Baylink

79 HYPERPARATHYROIDISM IN THE ELDERLY 837
Kenneth W. Lyles

80 PAGET'S DISEASE OF BONE 843
Frederick R. Singer

SECTION H   The Muscle and Joint Systems

81 AGING AND THE MUSCULOSKELETAL SYSTEM 849
David Hamerman

82 POLYMYALGIA RHEUMATICA AND GIANT CELL ARTERITIS   861
    William J. Arnold

83 POLYMYOSITIS AND DERMATOMYOSITIS   865
    William J. Arnold

84 RHEUMATOID ARTHRITIS   869
    M. E. Csuka and James S. Goodwin

85 OSTEOARTHRITIS   880
    Walter H. Ettinger, Jr., and Maradee A. Davis

86 GOUT AND CHONDROCALCINOSIS (PSEUDOGOUT)   889
    J. Edwin Seegmiller

87 AMYLOID   897
    Evan Calkins and John R. Wright

SECTION I The Nervous System

88   NEUROCHEMISTRY OF THE AGING HUMAN BRAIN   905
     Judes Poirier and Caleb E. Finch

89   COGNITION AND AGING   913
     Marilyn S. Albert

90   DELIRIUM (ACUTE CONFUSIONAL STATES)   920
     Zbigniew J. Lipowski

91   STROKE IN THE ELDERLY   926
     Christopher Power and Vladimir Hachinski

92   ALZHEIMER'S DISEASE   934
     Richard Mayeux

93   LESS COMMON DEMENTIAS   949
     Peter J. Whitehouse and Douglas J. Lanska

94   PARKINSON'S DISEASE   954
     Lucien J. Cote and Margaret Henly

95   OTHER DEGENERATIVE DISORDERS OF THE NERVOUS SYSTEM   964
     John P. Blass and Donald L. Price

96   SPINE DISEASE   970
     John C. Morris

97   PERIPHERAL NEUROPATHIES   977
     Reid Taylor and Walter G. Bradley

98   CENTRAL NERVOUS SYSTEM INFECTIONS   983
     William G. Gardner and Joseph P. Myers

99   HEAD INJURY (INCLUDING SUBDURAL HEMATOMA)   990
     Dennis G. Vollmer and Howard M. Eisenberg

100 SEIZURES AND EPILEPSY   999
     John W. Miller and James A. Ferrendelli

101 INTRACRANIAL NEOPLASMS   1004
     Jerome B. Posner

102 DEPRESSION   1010
     Dan Blazer

103 PARAPHRENIAS AND OTHER PSYCHOSES 1019
Leila B. Laitman and Kenneth L. Davis

104 AGING OF THE CHRONICALLY NEUROPSYCHOLOGICALLY IMPAIRED 1026
Steven R. Gambert

105 CHEMICAL DEPENDENCY IN THE ELDERLY 1030
Patricia P. Barry

106 PERSONALITY DISORDERS IN THE ELDERLY 1036
Jacobo E. Mintzer, Margarita Lermo, and Carl Eisdorfer

107 PSYCHOTHERAPY AND PSYCHOPHARMACOLOGY 1045
Kimberly A. Sherrill and Burton V. Reifler

4

GERIATRIC SYNDROMES AND SPECIAL PROBLEMS

108 APPROACH TO THE DIAGNOSIS AND TREATMENT OF THE
INFECTED OLDER ADULT 1055
Thomas T. Yoshikawa

109 DIZZINESS AND SYNCOPE 1062
Palmi V. Jonsson and Lewis A. Lipsitz

110 DISORDERS OF FLUID AND ELECTROLYTE BALANCE 1079
Kenneth M. Davis and Kenneth L. Minaker

111 DISORDERS OF TEMPERATURE REGULATION 1084
Itamar B. Abrass

112 SYNDROMES OF ALTERED MENTAL STATE 1089
Marshal F. Folstein and Susan E. Folstein

113 FATIGUE, FAILURE TO THRIVE, WEIGHT LOSS, AND CACHEXIA 1102
Roy B. Verdery

114 DISORDERED SLEEP IN THE ELDERLY 1109
Edward F. Haponik

115 URINARY INCONTINENCE 1123
Joseph G. Ouslander

116 FECAL INCONTINENCE 1143
Lawrence J. Cheskin and Marvin M. Schuster

117 IMPOTENCE 1146
Stanley G. Korenman

118 EATING AND SWALLOWING DISORDERS 1155
Donald O. Castell

119 CONSTIPATION 1161
Lawrence J. Cheskin and Marvin M. Schuster

120 DIARRHEA IN THE ELDERLY 1168
William B. Greenough III and Richard G. Bennett

121 HERPES ZOSTER 1177
Arthur K. Balin

122 GAIT DISORDERS 1183
William C. Koller and Sander L. Glatt

123 FALLS   1192
     Mary E. Tinetti

124 HIP FRACTURES   1200
     Thomas W. Jackson and Kenneth W. Lyles

125 PRESSURE ULCERS   1204
     Richard M. Allman

126 PREDICTING FUNCTIONAL OUTCOME IN OLDER PEOPLE   1212
     Mark E. Williams and Thomas V. Jones

     INDEX   1223

CONTRIBUTORS

Itamar B. Abrass, M.D. [111]
Professor of Medicine
Head, Division of Gerontology and Geriatric Medicine
University of Washington
Harborview Medical Center
Seattle, Washington

J. Dinsmore Adams, Jr. [38]
Webster and Sheffield
New York, New York

William H. Adler, M.D. [6]
Chief, Clinical Immunology
Gerontology Research Center
National Institute on Aging
Baltimore, Maryland

Marilyn S. Albert, Ph.D. [89]
Departments of Psychiatry and Neurology
Massachusetts General Hospital
Boston, Massachusetts

Richard M. Allman, M.D. [125]
Department of Medicine
University of Alabama at Birmingham
Birmingham, Alabama

Dana K. Andersen, M.D. [28]
Associate Professor of Surgery and Medicine
State University of New York Downstate Medical Center
Brooklyn, New York

Reubin Andres, M.D. [71, 72]
Clinical Director
National Institute on Aging (NIH)
Professor, Department of Medicine
The Johns Hopkins University
Gerontology Research Center at Francis Scott Key Medical
    Center
Baltimore, Maryland

William B. Applegate, M.D., M.P.H. [48]
Professor of Medicine and Preventive Medicine
College of Medicine
University of Tennessee, Memphis
Memphis, Tennessee

Numbers in brackets refer to chapter numbers.

William J. Arnold, M.D., [82, 83]
Clinical Associate Professor of Medicine
University of Illinois College of Medicine
Chicago, Illinois
Chairman, Department of Medicine
Lutheran General Hospital
Park Ridge, Illinois

Arthur K. Balin, M.D., Ph.D. [40, 121]
Assistant Professor
Laboratory For Investigative Dermatology
The Rockefeller University
New York, New York

Wilmot C. Ball, Jr., M.D. [54]
Associate Professor of Medicine
The Johns Hopkins University School of Medicine
Baltimore, Maryland

Elizabeth Barrett-Conner, M.D. [12]
Professor and Chair
Department of Community and Family Medicine
University of California, San Diego
La Jolla, California

Patricia P. Barry, M.D., M.P.H. [105]
Chief, Section of Geriatrics
Division of General Medicine
Department of Medicine
University of Miami School of Medicine
Miami, Florida

John G. Bartlett, M.D. [50]
Professor of Medicine
Chief, Division of Infectious Diseases
The Johns Hopkins University School of Medicine
Baltimore, Maryland

Bruce J. Baum, D.M.D., Ph.D. [41]
Chief, Clinical Investigations and Patient Care Branch
National Institute of Dental Research
Bethesda, Maryland

David J. Baylink, M.D. [76, 78]
Distinguished Professor of Medicine
Loma Linda University School of Medicine
Chief, Mineral Metabolism
Jerry L. Pettis Veterans Administration Hospital
Loma Linda, California

Laurence H. Beck, M.D. [55, 56]
Chairman, Department of General Medicine
Geisinger Medical Center
Danville, Pennsylvania

Richard G. Bennett, M.D. [120]
Assistant Professor of Medicine
Division of Geriatric Medicine
The Johns Hopkins University School of Medicine
Francis Scott Key Medical Center
Baltimore, Maryland

Richard W. Besdine, M.D. [18]
Travelers Professor of Geriatrics and Gerontology
Director, Travelers Center on Aging
Associate Professor of Medicine, Community Medicine and
    Family Medicine
University of Connecticut School of Medicine
Farmington, Connecticut

Edwin L. Bierman, M.D. [17, 45, 71]
Professor of Medicine
Head, Division of Metabolism, Endocrinology and Nutrition
University of Washington School of Medicine
Seattle, Washington

John P. Blass, M.D., Ph.D. [24, 95]
Burke Professor of Neurology and Medicine
Cornell University Medical College
Director, Dementia Research Service
The Burke Rehabilitation Center
White Plains, New York

Dan Blazer, M.D., Ph.D. [102]
Professor of Psychiatry
Director, Affective Disorders Program
Department of Psychiatry
Duke University Medical Center
Durham, North Carolina

Walter G. Bradley, D.M., F.R.C.P. [97]
Department of Neurology
University of Vermont College of Medicine
Burlington, Vermont

Charles B. Brendler, M.D. [57]
Associate Professor of Urology
The Johns Hopkins University School of Medicine
Baltimore, Maryland

Elaine M. Brody [25]
Associate Director of Research
Philadelphia Geriatric Center
Philadelphia, Pennsylvania

Kenneth Brummel-Smith, M.D. [34]
Associate Professor of Clinical Family Medicine
Director, Section on Geriatrics
Department of Family Medicine
University of Southern California School of Medicine
Los Angeles, California

Co-Chief, Clinical Gerontology Service
Rancho Los Amigos Medical Center
Downey, California

John M. Burkart, M.D. [55, 56]
Assistant Professor of Medicine
Department of Medicine, Section on Nephrology
Bowman Gray School of Medicine of Wake Forest
    University
Winston-Salem, North Carolina

John R. Burton, M.D. [36]
Associate Professor of Medicine and Clinical Director,
    Division of Geriatric Medicine and Gerontology
The Johns Hopkins University School of Medicine
Director of Geriatric Medicine
Francis Scott Key Medical Center
Baltimore, Maryland

Trudy L. Bush, Ph.D., M.H.S. [12]
Associate Professor
Department of Epidemiology
The Johns Hopkins University School of Hygiene and
    Public Health
Baltimore, Maryland

Evan Calkins, M.D. [87]
Professor of Medicine
State University of New York at Buffalo
Veterans Administration Medical Center
Buffalo, New York

Robert L. Capizzi, M.D. [66]
Department of Medicine
Bowman Gray School of Medicine of Wake Forest
    University
Winston-Salem, North Carolina

Constance P. Carden [38]
Senior Attorney
Legal Services for the Elderly
New York, New York

Bruce R. Carr, M.D. [74]
Professor and Director of Reproductive Endocrinology
Department of Obstetrics and Gynecology
University of Texas Southwestern Medical Center
Dallas, Texas

Donald O. Castell, M.D. [58, 118]
Chief, Gastroenterology and Hepatology Section
Jefferson Medical College
Philadelphia, Pennsylvania

Fred B. Charatan, M.D. [19]
Clinical Director
Central Islip Psychiatric Center
Central Islip, New York

Lawrence J. Cheskin, M.D. [63, 116, 119]
Assistant Professor of Medicine
The Johns Hopkins University School of Medicine
Baltimore, Maryland

Charles H. Chesnut III, M.D. [77]
Professor, Medicine and Radiology
University of Washington School of Medicine
Seattle, Washington

Elizabeth Cobbs, M.D. [37]
Assistant Professor
Department of Medicine
Division of Geriatric Medicine
The George Washington University Medical Center
Washington, D.C.

Harvey Jay Cohen, M.D. [7]
Director, Geriatric Research Education and Clinical Center,
    Veterans Administration Medical Center, and Center
    for the Study of Aging and Human Development
Duke University Medical Center
Durham, North Carolina

Leo M. Cooney, Jr., M.D. [33]
Humana Foundation Professor of Geriatric Medicine
Yale University School of Medicine
New Haven, Connecticut

Paul T. Costa, Jr., M.D., Ph.D. [9]
Gerontology Research Center
National Institute on Aging
Baltimore, Maryland

Lucien J. Cote, M.D. [94]
Department of Neurology
College of Physicians and Surgeons
Columbia University
New York, New York

Michael H. Criqui, M.D., M.P.H. [12]
Professor of Community and Family Medicine and Professor
    of Medicine, Division of Epidemiology
University of California, San Diego
La Jolla, California

Vincent J. Cristofalo, Ph.D. [1]
Professor of Animal Biology
Professor and Director, Center for the Study of Aging
University of Pennsylvania and The Wistar Institute of
    Anatomy and Biology
Philadelphia, Pennsylvania

Julia M. Cruz, M.D. [66]
Department of Medicine
Bowman Gray School of Medicine of Wake Forest
    University
Winston-Salem, North Carolina

M. E. Csuka, M.D. [84]
Department of Medicine

Medical College of Wisconsin
Milwaukee, Wisconsin

Richard G. Cutler, M.D. [2]
Gerontology Research Center
National Institute on Aging
Baltimore, Maryland

Julian M. Davidson, Ph.D. [10]
Department of Physiology
Stanford University
Stanford, California

Kenneth L. Davis, M.D. [103]
Professor and Chairman
Department of Psychiatry
Mt. Sinai School of Medicine
New York, New York

Kenneth M. Davis, M.D. [110]
Instructor of Medicine
Division on Aging
Harvard Medical School
Boston, Massachusetts

Maradee A. Davis, Ph.D., M.P.H. [85]
Associate Professor
Department of Epidemiology and International Health
University of California at San Francisco
San Francisco, California

Larry G. Duckert, M.D., Ph.D. [43]
Professor of Otolaryngology
University of Washington School of Medicine
Seattle, Washington

Asim K. Dutt, M.D. [51]
Chief of Medical Service
Alvin York Memorial Veterans Administration Hospital
Murfreesboro, Tennessee

Carl Eisdorfer, Ph.D., M.D. [106]
Department of Psychiatry
University of Miami School of Medicine
Miami, Florida

Howard M. Eisenberg, M.D. [99]
Professor and Chief
Division of Neurosurgery
The University of Texas Medical Branch
Galveston, Texas

Walter H. Ettinger, Jr., M.D. [85]
Associate Professor
Department of Medicine
Bowman Gray School of Medicine of Wake Forest
    University
Winston-Salem, North Carolina

James A. Ferrendelli, M.D. [100]
Seay Professor of Clinical Neuropharmacology

Departments of Pharmacology and Neurology
Washington University School of Medicine
St. Louis, Missouri

Caleb E. Finch, Ph.D. [88]
Professor, Neurobiology of Aging
Ethel Percy Andrus Gerontology Center
University of Southern California
Los Angeles, California

Thomas E. Finucane, M.D. [36]
Assistant Professor of Medicine
The Johns Hopkins University School of Medicine
Director, Elder House Call Program
Francis Scott Key Medical Center
Baltimore, Maryland

Jerome L. Fleg, M.D. [8]
Laboratory of Cardiovascular Science
Gerontology Research Center
Baltimore, Maryland

Conn J. Foley, M.D. [19]
Medical Director
Jewish Institute of Geriatric Care
New Hyde Park, New York

Kathleen M. Foley, M.D. [30]
Professor of Neurology and Pharmacology
Cornell University Medical College
Chief, Pain Service, Department of Neurology
Memorial Sloan-Kettering Cancer Center
New York, New York

Marshal F. Folstein, M.D. [112]
Eugene Meyer III Professor of Psychiatry and Medicine
Director, Division of General Hospital Psychiatry
Department of Psychiatry
The Johns Hopkins University School of Medicine
Baltimore, Maryland

Susan E. Folstein, M.D. [112]
Associate Professor of Psychiatry, Pediatrics, and Medicine
Director, Division of Psychiatric Genetics
The Johns Hopkins University School of Medicine
Baltimore, Maryland

Marsha Duke Fretwell, M.D. [23, 27]
Assistant Professor of Medicine
Head, Department of Geriatrics Program in Medicine
Brown University
Roger Williams General Hospital
Providence, Rhode Island

Linda P. Fried, M.D., M.P.H. [20]
Henry J. Kaiser Family Foundation Faculty Scholar in
    General Internal Medicine
Assistant Professor of Medicine and Epidemiology
Director, The Johns Hopkins Geriatric Assessment Center
Baltimore, Maryland

Steven R. Gambert, M.D. [104]
Professor of Medicine
Director, Center for Aging
New York Medical College
Valhalla, New York

William G. Gardner, M.D. [98]
Professor of Medicine
Northeastern Ohio Universities College of Medicine
Division of Infectious Diseases
Akron General Medical Center
Akron, Ohio

Gary Gerstenblith, M.D. [44, 46]
Associate Professor of Medicine
Cardiology Division
The Johns Hopkins Hospital
Baltimore, Maryland

John H. Gilliam III, M.D. [61, 62]
Department of Medicine
Bowman Gray School of Medicine of Wake Forest
    University
Winston-Salem, North Carolina

Evelynn Clark Gioiella, R.N., Ph.D. [32]
Dean, Hunter-Bellevue School of Nursing
Hunter College of the City University of New York
New York, New York

Sander L. Glatt, M.D. [122]
Department of Neurology
University of Kansas Medical Center
Kansas City, Kansas

Andrew P. Goldberg, M.D. [8, 71]
Associate Professor
Department of Medicine
Division of Geriatrics
The Johns Hopkins University School of Medicine
Francis Scott Key Medical Center
Baltimore, Maryland

James S. Goodwin, M.D. [84]
Department of Medicine
University of Wisconsin School of Medicine
Sinai Samaritan Geriatrics Institute
Milwaukee, Wisconsin

William B. Greenough III, M.D. [120]
Professor of Medicine
The Johns Hopkins University School of Medicine
Division of Geriatric Medicine
Francis Scott Key Medical Center
Baltimore, Maryland

Robert I. Gregerman, M.D. [70]
Professor of Medicine
The Johns Hopkins University School of Medicine
Head, Division of Endocrinology and Metabolism

Francis Scott Key Medical Center
Guest Scientist
Gerontology Research Center
Baltimore, Maryland

Vladimir Hachinski, M.D., F.R.C.P. (C), D.Sc. (Med.) [91]
Professor of Neurology
Department of Clinical Neurological Sciences
University of Western Ontario
Director, Stroke and Aging Research
The John P. Robarts Research Institute
London, Ontario, Canada

Jeffrey B. Halter, M.D. [69]
Professor of Internal Medicine
Chief, Division of Geriatric Medicine
University of Michigan
Director, Geriatric Research Education and Clinical Center
Veterans Administration Medical Center
Ann Arbor, Michigan

David Hamerman, M.D. [81]
Department of Medicine, Montefiore Medical Center
Albert Einstein College of Medicine
Bronx, New York

Edward F. Haponik, M.D. [114]
Professor of Medicine
Clinical Director of Pulmonary/Critical Care Section
Department of Medicine
Bowman Gray School of Medicine of Wake Forest
    University
Winston-Salem, North Carolina

Laurence A. Harker, M.D. [67]
Blomeyer Professor of Medicine
Director of Hematology/Oncology
Emory University School of Medicine
Atlanta, Georgia

William R. Hazzard, M.D. [4, 17]
Professor of Medicine and Chairman
Department of Internal Medicine
Bowman Gray School of Medicine of Wake Forest
    University
Winston-Salem, North Carolina

Margaret Henly, R.P.T. [94]
Department of Rehabilitation Medicine
Columbia University Neurological Institute
New York, New York

H. Malcolm Hodkinson, D.M., F.R.C.P. [26]
Barlow Professor of Geriatric Medicine
Department of Geriatric Medicine
University College and Middlesex School of Medicine
University College, London
St. Pancras Hospital
London, England

Gary W. Hunninghake, M.D. [53]
Professor of Medicine
Director of Pulmonary Medicine
University of Iowa College of Medicine
Iowa City, Iowa

Thomas W. Jackson, M.D. [124]
Associate
Department of Medicine, Geriatric Division
Duke University Medical Center
Durham, North Carolina

Lissy F. Jarvik, M.D., Ph.D. [24]
Department of Psychiatry and Biobehavioral Sciences
University of California, Los Angeles
Psychogeriatric Unit, West Los Angeles
Veterans Administration Medical Center, Brentwood
    Division
Los Angeles, California

John C. Jennings, M.D. [76]
Associate Professor of Medicine
Loma Linda University School of Medicine
Chief, Endocrinology and Metabolism
Jerry L. Pettis Veterans Administration Hospital
Loma Linda, California

Thomas V. Jones, M.D. [126]
Program On Aging
University of North Carolina School of Medicine
Chapel Hill, North Carolina

Palmi V. Jonsson, M.D. [109]
Research Fellow Division on Aging
Harvard Medical School
Boston, Massachusetts

Robert M. Kerr, M.D. [60]
Gastroenterology Section
Department of Medicine
Bowman Gray School of Medicine of Wake Forest
    University
Winston-Salem, North Carolina

William C. Koller, M.D., Ph.D. [122]
Department of Neurology
University of Kansas Medical Center
Kansas City, Kansas

Stanley G. Korenman, M.D. [117]
Professor of Medicine
Associate Dean for Educational Development
UCLA School of Medicine
Los Angeles, California

Marius E. Kraenzlin, M.D. [76]
Endocrine Practice
Basle, Switzerland

Leila B. Laitman, M.D. [103]
Department of Psychiatry

Mount Sinai School of Medicine
New York, New York

Edward G. Lakatta, M.D. [44, 46]
Professor of Medicine
The Johns Hopkins University School of Medicine
Professor of Physiology
University of Maryland School of Medicine
Chief, Laboratory of Cardiovascular Science
Gerontology Research Center
National Institute on Aging
National Institutes of Health
Baltimore, Maryland

Douglas J. Lanska, M.D. [93]
Alzheimer's Disease Center
University Hospitals of Cleveland
Cleveland, Ohio

Alexander Leaf, M.D. [14]
Chairman
Ridley Watts Professor of Preventive Medicine and
    Professor of Medicine
Harvard Medical School
Boston, Massachusetts

Margarita Lermo, M.D. [106]
Assistant Professor
Department of Psychiatry
University of Miami School of Medicine
Miami, Florida

Leslie S. Libow, M.D. [19]
Chief of Medical Services
The Jewish Home and Hospital for the Aged
New York, New York

Edward W. Lipkin, M.D., Ph.D. [31]
Assistant Professor of Medicine
Division of Metabolism, Endocrinology, and Nutrition
University of Washington School of Medicine
Seattle, Washington

**Zbigniew J. Lipowski, M.D., F.R.C.P. (C), Br. Med.
    (Hon.) [90]**
Professor of Psychiatry
University of Toronto
Toronto, Ontario, Canada

David A. Lipschitz, M.D. [64, 65]
McClellan Veterans Administration Medical Center and
    Geriatric Research Education and Clinical Center
Little Rock, Arkansas

Lewis A. Lipsitz, M.D. [109]
Assistant Professor of Medicine
Harvard Medical School
Director of Education and Clinical Research
Hebrew Rehabilitation Center for Aged
Boston, Massachusetts

Kenneth W. Lyles, M.D. [79, 124]
Assistant Professor
Department of Medicine
Duke University Medical Center
Geriatric Research Education and Clinical Center
Veterans Administration Medical Center
Durham, North Carolina

Joanne Lynn, M.D. [37]
Assistant Professor
Division of Geriatric Medicine
The George Washington University Medical Center
Washington, D.C.

Paul C. MacDonald, M.D. [74]
Professor
Director of the Cecil H. and Ida Green Center for
    Reproductive Biology Sciences
University of Texas Southwestern Medical Center
Dallas, Texas

George L. Maddox, Ph.D. [11]
Center for Studies on Aging
Duke University Medical Center
Durham, North Carolina

George M. Martin, M.D. [3]
Professor of Pathology
Director, Alzheimer's Disease Research Center
University of Washington
Seattle, Washington

Richard Mayeux, M.D. [92]
Associate Professor
College of Physicians and Surgeons
Columbia University Neurological Institute
New York, New York

Robert R. McRae, M.D. [9]
Gerontology Research Center
National Institute on Aging
Baltimore, Maryland

John W. Miller, M.D., Ph.D. [100]
Assistant Professor
Department of Neurology
Washington University School of Medicine
St. Louis, Missouri

Norman E. Miller, M.D., D.Sc. [73]
Section on Endocrinology and Metabolism
Department of Medicine
Bowman Gray School of Medicine of Wake Forest
    University
Winston-Salem, North Carolina

Susan R. Miller, M.P.H. [12]
Research Program Coordinator
Department of Health Policy and Management
The Johns Hopkins University School of Hygiene and
    Public Health
Baltimore, Maryland

Kenneth L. Minaker, M.D. [110]
Assistant Professor of Medicine
Division on Aging, Harvard Medical School
Joint Department of Medicine
Beth Israel and Brigham and Women's Hospitals
Director, Geriatric Research Education and Clinical Center
Veterans Administration Medical Center
Brockton, West Roxbury
Boston, Massachusetts

Jacobo E. Mintzer, M.D. [106]
Assistant Clinical Professor
Department of Psychiatry
Director of Geriatric Psychiatry
University of Miami School of Medicine
Miami, Florida

Roger E. Moe, M.D. [75]
Associate Professor of Surgery
The Breast Clinic
University Hospital
University of Washington School of Medicine
Seattle, Washington

Deborah J. Moritz, Ph.D. [15]
Postdoctoral Fellow
Department of Epidemiology and Public Health
Yale University School of Medicine
New Haven, Connecticut

John E. Morley, M.D. [5]
Professor of Medicine
UCLA School of Medicine
Los Angeles, California
Director of Geriatric Research Education and Clinical
    Center
Sepulveda Veterans Administration Medical Center
Sepulveda, California

John C. Morris, M.D. [96]
Assistant Professor of Neurology
Washington University School of Medicine
Associate Chief of Neurology
The Jewish Hospital at Washington University Medical
    Center
St. Louis, Missouri

Joseph P. Myers, M.D. [98]
Associate Professor of Medicine
Northeastern Ohio Universities College of Medicine
Division of Infectious Diseases
Akron General Medical Center
Akron, Ohio

James E. Nagel, M.D. [6]
Gerontology Research Center
National Institute on Aging
Baltimore, Maryland

James B. Nelson, M.D. [58]
Department of Medicine
Bowman Gray School of Medicine of Wake Forest
    University
Winston-Salem, North Carolina

Mikal Janelle Odom, M.D. [74]
Assistant Professor
Department of Obstetrics and Gynecology
University of Texas Southwestern Medical Center
Dallas, Texas

Adrian M. Ostfeld, M.D. [15]
Lauder Professor of Epidemiology and Public Health
Yale University School of Medicine
New Haven, Connecticut

Joseph G. Ouslander, M.D. [35, 115]
Medical Director, Victory Village
Jewish Homes for the Aging of Greater Los Angeles
Multicampus Division of Geriatric Medicine and
    Gerontology
UCLA School of Medicine
Los Angeles, California

L. Gregory Pawlson, M.D., M.P.H. [16]
George Washington University Medical Center
Washington, D.C.

Robert A. Pearlman, M.D., M.P.H. [39]
Associate Professor
Departments of Medicine and Health Services
University of Washington
Seattle Veterans Administration Medical Center
Seattle, Washington

Judes Poirier, Ph.D. [88]
Research Associate
Department of Neurobiology
University of Southern California
Los Angeles, California

Jerome B. Posner, M.D. [101]
Department of Neurology
Cornell University Medical College
Memorial Sloan-Kettering Cancer Center
New York, New York

Bayard L. Powell, M.D. [66]
Department of Medicine
Bowman Gray School of Medicine of Wake Forest
    University
Winston-Salem, North Carolina

Christopher Power, M.D. [91]
Department of Clinical Neurological Sciences
University Hospital
London, Ontario, Canada

Donald L. Price, M.D. [95]
Departments of Pathology, Neurology and Neuroscience

The Johns Hopkins University School of Medicine
Baltimore, Maryland

Thomas S. Rees, Ph.D. [43]
Associate Professor of Otolaryngology
Department of Otolaryngology
University of Washington School of Medicine
Seattle, Washington

Burton V. Reifler, M.D. [107]
Professor and Chairman
Department of Psychiatry
Bowman Gray School of Medicine of Wake Forest
    University
Winston-Salem, North Carolina

Joel E. Richter, M.D. [59]
Professor of Medicine
University of Alabama at Birmingham
Birmingham, Alabama

George Rosenthal, M.D. [22]
Assistant Professor of Medicine
Boston University Medical Center
The University Hospital Home Medical Service
Boston, Massachusetts

Ronnie Ann Rosenthal, M.D. [28]
Assistant Professor of Surgery
State University of New York Health Science Center
Brooklyn, New York

John W. Rowe, M.D. [13]
President
Mount Sinai Medical Center
The Mount Sinai Hospital
New York, New York

Raymond C. Roy, M.D. [29]
Associate Professor and Vice-Chairman
Department of Anesthesia
Bowman Gray School of Medicine of Wake Forest
    University
Winston-Salem, North Carolina

Marvin M. Schuster, M.D. [63, 116, 119]
Professor of Medicine
The Johns Hopkins University School of Medicine
Baltimore, Maryland

J. Edwin Seegmiller, M.D. [86]
Professor of Medicine
Director, Institute for Research on Aging
University of California, San Diego
La Jolla, California

Kimberly A. Sherrill, M.D. [107]
Department of Psychiatry
Bowman Gray School of Medicine of Wake Forest
    University
Winston-Salem, North Carolina

Jonathan A. Ship, D.M.D. [41]
Staff Fellow, Clinical Investigations and Patient Care
    Branch
National Institute of Dental Research
Bethesda, Maryland

Frederick R. Singer, M.D. [80]
Director Bone Center
Cedars Sinai Medical Center
Visiting Professor of Medicine
UCLA School of Medicine
Los Angeles, California

William W. Stead, M.D. [51]
Professor of Medicine
University of Arkansas Medical School
Director, Tuberculosis Program
Arkansas Department of Health
Little Rock, Arkansas

Knight Steel, M.D. [22]
Professor of Medicine
Chief, Geriatrics Section
Boston University Medical Center
Director, The University Hospital Home Medical Services
Boston, Massachusetts

Einar Stefánsson, M.D., Ph.D. [42]
Assistant Professor
Department of Ophthalmology
Duke University Medical Center
Durham, North Carolina

D. Eugene Strandness, Jr., M.D. [47]
Professor of Surgery
Department of Surgery
University of Washington School of Medicine
Seattle, Washington

Reid Taylor, M.D. [97]
Mountain Neurological Center
Asheville, North Carolina

L. Cass Terry, M.D., Ph.D. [69]
Professor and Chairman, Department of Neurology
Professor of Physiology
Medical College of Wisconsin
Froedtert Memorial Lutheran Hospital
Milwaukee, Wisconsin

Peter B. Terry, M.D. [52]
Associate Professor of Medicine
The Johns Hopkins University School of Medicine
Francis Scott Key Medical Center
Baltimore, Maryland

Brian L. Thiele, M.D. [47]
Professor of Surgery
Milton S. Hershey Medical Center
Pennsylvania State University
Hershey, Pennsylvania

Arthur R. Thompson, M.D., Ph.D. [68]
Professor of Medicine
University of Washington School of Medicine
Director, Coagulation Laboratories
Puget Sound Blood Center
Seattle, Washington

Mary E. Tinetti, M.D. [123]
Associate Professor of Medicine
Yale University School of Medicine
New Haven, Connecticut

Melvyn S. Tockman, M.D., Ph.D. [49, 54]
Associate Professor of Environmental Health Sciences
The Johns Hopkins University School of Hygiene and
    Public Health
Baltimore, Maryland

Mitchell S. Turker, Ph.D. [3]
Assistant Professor of Pathology
Department of Pathology and Lucille P. Markey Cancer
    Center
University of Kentucky
Lexington, Kentucky

Roy B. Verdery, Ph.D., M.D. [113]
Department of Internal Medicine
Bowman Gray School of Medicine of Wake Forest
    University
Winston-Salem, North Carolina

Robert E. Vestal, M.D. [21]
Professor of Medicine and Adjunct Professor of
    Pharmacology
University of Washington
Seattle, Washington
Associate Chief of Staff for Research and Development
Chief, Clinical Pharmacology and Gerontology Research
    Unit
Veterans Administration Medical Center
Boise, Idaho

Dennis G. Vollmer, M.D. [99]
Assistant Professor
Division of Neurosurgery
University of North Carolina
Chapel Hill, North Carolina

Peter J. Whitehouse, M.D., Ph.D. [93]
Associate Professor of Neurology
Director, Division of Behavioral Neurology
Case Western Reserve University
Director, Alzheimer's Disease Center
University Hospitals of Cleveland
Cleveland, Ohio

Mark E. Williams, M.D. [126]
Director, Program on Aging
University of North Carolina School of Medicine
Chapel Hill, North Carolina

John R. Wright, M.D. [87]
Professor and Chairman
Department of Pathology
State University of New York at Buffalo
Buffalo, New York

Wallace C. Wu, M.B.B.S. [59]
Professor of Medicine
Bowman Gray School of Medicine of Wake Forest
    University
Winston-Salem, North Carolina

Thomas T. Yoshikawa, M.D. [108]
Adjunct Professor of Health Care Sciences
George Washington University
Clinical Professor of Medicine
Georgetown University
Assistant Chief Medical Director
Office of Geriatrics and Extended Care
Department of Veterans Affairs
Washington, D.C.

Brain P. Zehr, M.D. [53]
Fort Wayne Pulmonary Consultants, Inc.
Fort Wayne, Indiana

PREFACE

The "graying of America" in the late twentieth century has stimulated the academic medical establishment to address the health care needs of a burgeoning elderly population. Adding to the problem of meeting these needs is the relative neglect of the study of aging in the elderly until the past decade or so, as reflected by the paucity of research in the aging process and instruction of medical students and postgraduate and practicing physicians in gerontology and geriatric medicine. The response of academic medicine to the challenge has clearly begun and is gathering momentum. Pressures from both public and private sectors have led medical and other schools in the health sciences to define goals and introduce instructional, research, and service programs. Medical students, residents, fellows, and practicing physicians are participating in a wide variety of educational programs in gerontology and geriatric medicine. A benchmark in this trend toward increasing recognition of the validity and importance of geriatrics was the awarding of the certificate of added qualifications in geriatrics to over 2000 internists and family practitioners following their successful passing of the first geriatrics examination jointly developed by the American Board of Internal Medicine and the American Board of Family Practice in 1988. In support of this accelerating educational movement has been the development of a growing number of journals, other periodicals, and textbooks, including the present, second edition of *Principles of Geriatric Medicine and Gerontology*.

For the student wishing to master the state-of-the-art knowledge of geriatric medicine and gerontology, this textbook provides information both in breadth and in depth relevant to the understanding and care of the aging patient. It has been substantially expanded in the second edition, with the addition of over 50 chapters and the complete rewriting of the vast majority of the remainder. As with the first edition, the book begins with chapters outlining the principles of gerontology (the study of aging). These span the spectrum from the genome through the epidemiology of aging and the implications of that epidemiology for the health care of a progressively aging population. Part 2 follows with chapters devoted to the principles of geriatrics (the care of the elderly). This section, greatly expanded from the first edition, presents the information, both practical and

theoretical, that defines geriatric medicine. New elements in this edition include chapters devoted to clinical evaluation of the elderly patient, altered presentations of disease in the elderly, comprehensive functional assessment, special aspects of the care of elderly patients in the hospital and in transition between hospital and long-term care or home-based care, specific aspects of rehabilitation in the elderly, nursing home care, and community-based care. Other added features include chapters on ethical, legal, and financial issues, management of pain, enteral/parenteral alimentation, and a primer on gerontological nursing for the geriatrician.

Next, Part 3 gives information in depth on the diseases of the organ systems in the elderly. The organization of this part represents an altered strategy from that of the first edition; that is, the information is now medically comprehensive enough so that no other companion textbook is necessary to supplement the material. Thus, the chapters in Part 3 are divided into sections according to organ system, are more self-sufficient, and are presented in greater depth with more extensive bibliographies. In addition, organ systems not discussed in the first edition are presented herein: the eye, auditory and vestibular systems, and, notably, a greatly increased attention to diseases of the nervous system. Nineteen chapters relating to the nervous system, coordinated by our new editor, John P. Blass, are included.

Finally, an almost entirely new Part 4 covering geriatric syndromes and special problems concludes this volume. Here the authors deal with those presentations and constellations of findings and problems that are of central importance to geriatric medicine. Issues such as syncope, dehydration, failure to thrive, sleep disorders, impotence, incontinence, gait disorders, falls, hip fractures, and pressure ulcers are presented in detail. This section should therefore prove of immediate, practical value to the medical student or physician caring for the elderly.

Thus, the second edition of *Principles of Geriatric Medicine and Gerontology* is larger, more comprehensive, more integrative, and more detailed in its approach to the understanding and care of the elderly patient.

Assembling this volume has been an exciting project. The editors are grateful not only to the contributors for their monumental efforts but also to our own supporters, including the editorial staff at McGraw-Hill, notably Avé McCracken and Bruce Williams. The secretarial/editorial staff for the four editors included Jeanette Robertson, Amy Sentell, Alyce Craft, and Kathleen Smidebush for Dr. Hazzard at Wake Forest University/Bowman Gray School of Medicine; Ellen Meyer for Dr. Bierman at the University of Washington; Jerlline Muller for Dr. Andres at the Gerontology Research Center/Francis Scott Key Medical Center; and Carol Montanaro for Dr. Blass at Burke Rehabilitation Center/Cornell Westchester Division. Finally, special recognition is due to Ellen B. Hazzard, Chief Editorial Assistant, whose

special efforts kept this complicated and geographically dispersed project on track.

As the disciplines of gerontology and geriatric medicine are growing daily both quantitatively and qualitatively, this textbook reflects a work in progress, and the editors look forward to working continually to keep readers apace of new developments in these exciting fields.

WILLIAM R. HAZZARD
REUBIN ANDRES
EDWIN L. BIERMAN
JOHN P. BLASS

INTRODUCTION: THE PRACTICE OF GERIATRIC MEDICINE

The changing distribution of the American population by age which has characterized the latter half of the twentieth century (often called the "graying of America" or "the demographic imperative") has given special meaning to the interrelated disciplines of gerontology and geriatric medicine and an urgency to the mastery of both by physicians and other health care practitioners. For the purposes of this text we shall define *gerontology* as the study of aging, *geriatrics* as the health and social care of the elderly, and *geriatric medicine* as that subdiscipline within geriatrics specifically devoted to the medical care of the elderly.

Geriatric medicine can be described by the nature of its clientele, elderly patients, and the characteristics of its practitioners and their activities. Its clientele has been traditionally defined by demographers, insurers, and employers as those over the age of 65. In those nations where geriatric medicine has emerged as a distinct specialty, the age of 75 is more often employed, with flexibility about that age depending upon the specific age of the patient in question and the capacity of the geriatric health care system to meet his or her specific needs. Hence, in such countries, geriatricians may care for certain chronically disabled patients even below age 65. It is clear that those over 75 years of age, however, have generally accumulated the multiple problems which distinguish the elderly. Perhaps no age definition is truly desirable given the variable rates of aging and disease accumulation by different persons. As this area of interest expands, however, geriatricians must often define and defend their specific area of expertise. To the question as to "What is the typical geriatric patient?", this author responds, "Think of your oldest, sickest, most complicated and frail patient."

Such a patient encompasses the problems most often encountered by the geriatrician. He or, more frequently, she often presents with multiple disabilities, covert as well as overt. Thus while signs and symptoms might suggest, for example, pneumonia as in the younger patient, limited physiologic reserves in multiple systems may lead to complications and all too often a cascade of complications vastly reducing the remaining life span of the patient. The elderly patient often also presents atypically; e.g., infection may present without fever, myocardial infarction without pain, or hyperthyroidism without evidence of hypermetabolism. This aspect of geriatric practice is often overdrawn, however, nor are there many conditions which present uniquely in the elderly (e.g., polymyalgia rheumatica is rare except in the geriatric patient). Thus these atypical presentations and diseases are unusual even in the elderly and do not comprise a large fraction of the practice of the geriatrician. More demanding of the physician's time are the chronic, progressive, only partially reversible problems which are typical in the elderly patient once the health care system is encountered. Management of such enduring problems defines geriatric medicine as primary care medicine in the elderly in this nation, as opposed to the role of consultant that has been reserved for the geriatrician in countries such as the United Kingdom, where geriatrics has been defined as a hospital-based specialty. Another characteristic of geriatric practice in the U.S. health care system is overlap among and necessary consideration of multiple dimensions of the patient's life, which are the rule in defining the presentation of impairment or the ability to live with the disability that is imposed. Thus, multidisciplinary assessment is essential, emphasizing not only physical and mental parameters but also social, economic, and most importantly, functional measures. Therapeutic planning must be similarly multidimensional, and multiple persons become involved. Health practitioners from numerous fields, notably medicine, psychiatry, neurology, nursing, social work, dentistry, pharmacy, rehabilitation medicine, and the related therapies, occupational, physical, recreational, must collaborate with supporters, especially friends and family, in assisting patients to maximize their independence for as long as possible in whatever setting they may reside. In this circumstance, the physician is usually called upon to be a team leader, administrator, and coordinator. Specific medical expertise is crucial, but diplomacy and clear definition of spheres of responsibility and tasks to be performed are essential. Leadership in a corporate sense rather than the image of the solo practitioner of old is a distinguishing characteristic of the modern geriatrician.

The coincidence of multiple problems in the elderly patient often produces blurring of diagnostic categories, and nonspecific presentations and courses are common. This has led some to define geriatric medicine by its emphasis upon specific problem complexes ("The 5 I's"): Iatrogenic disease, (mental) Incompetence, Incontinence, Immobility, and Impaired homeostasis. Each of these syndromes is dealt with in detail elsewhere in this volume and thus no summary will be attempted here. However, their mastery is essential to the successful practice of geriatric medicine. Of the five, perhaps iatrogenic disease is of greatest concern to the geriatrician, given the primary role of the physician in its genesis. In this regard it would appear that the therapeutic ratio for almost any modality of diagnosis or therapy narrows in the elderly and may even become negative. This appears especially true for pharmacological interventions, and the tendency for multiple problems to be treated with multiple drugs compounds that risk in exponential fashion. Thus a cardinal principle of geriatric medicine, especially when the course of a patient turns suddenly for the worse, is to ask first, "What have I done to the patient?" rather than what the environment or the given disease process has done.

A final cardinal feature of disease and disability in the elderly is their tendency to be chronic and often progressive. Thus the primary care physician caring for the elderly patient becomes an expert in the management of chronic disease across the spectrum of levels of health care, including long-term institutional care. In this practice the geriatrician learns to use the dimension of time in the diagnostic and treatment process perhaps more than his or her acute care colleague. This may both reduce risk by minimizing aggressive and invasive diagnostic efforts and also allow the constant tailoring of therapy to the changing needs of the patient through time. A subjective estimate of the time remaining in the patient's life is also constantly kept in mind. A major proportion of the geriatrician's efforts are devoted to those in the final stages of life. Some, such as those with terminal malignancies, are clearly dying; the courses of others, when a terminal cause is not evident, are not so clearly capable of delineation. Given that a substantial fraction of the total health care resources consumed by an individual during his or her lifetime is expended in the final year,

the geriatrician must also bear in mind the inordinate cost of the care delivered under his or her direction. Questions of life and death, of the efficacy, risk, and ethics of diagnosis and treatment are a major concern of the geriatrician, and he or she must continuously consult with the patient, supporters, and other members of the health care team (on occasion including clergy, lawyers, ethicists) as to the wisdom or folly of therapeutic efforts. The geriatrician must always bear in mind that prolongation of the dying process is to be avoided, while preservation of comfort and dignity is a primary goal. Inherent in these considerations is the special role of patience and humility in the make-up of the consummate geriatrician. Given that the upper limit of the human life span is relatively fixed and that most patients will be approaching that limit, the geriatrician must respect a limited ability to intervene when that barrier is approached. Thus art and compassion are the essence of geriatric medicine, and wisdom plays a greater role in its practice than technical knowledge or skill.

In what ways is gerontology related to geriatric medicine? An appreciation of the aging process in all its stages is of both theoretical and practical importance to the geriatrician. Knowledge of the multiple dimensions of physiological decline which precede the presentation of the elderly patient is essential to the geriatrician. Appreciation of the interaction of these declines with specific diseases will help define the course of individual patients. The art of individualizing such knowledge to the given patient combines a subjective assessment of the point in that person's life course at which the encounter with the health care system has taken place and a clinical estimate of the trajectory of the patient's future course and its remediable and irremediable components. When to intervene with all the technology and resources of the health care system and when to observe and support without resorting to that technology is critical to the practice of expert geriatric medicine. Finally, appreciation of the areas of physiology and psychology which do not decline or which become stronger by virtue of time and the aging process is also important to the geriatrician. The elderly are themselves an enormous resource in their own health care and the care of others, and the knowledge and trust built between the physician and the elderly patient constitute an important resource in both the diagnostic and therapeutic processes.

Given these characteristics of elderly patients and their physicians, just who should practice geriatric medicine? It would appear most likely that in the pluralistic health care system prevailing in the United States that the majority of geriatric medicine will be practiced by generalists, be they family physicians or internists. A small proportion of such physicians may choose to devote all of their practice to the care of the elderly. Another minority may elect to obtain additional training through continuing medical education, preceptorships in divisions of geriatric medicine, or through fellowship training which emphasizes those aspects of medicine especially pertinent to the care of the elderly. However, to define geriatric medicine as a narrow specialty to be practiced only by those with specific training therein would be to both overwhelm the extant geriatric training programs and also ignore the enormous existing resource in the form of well-trained and experienced generalists within the medical profession. To assure that all physicians will be prepared to meet the demands that the demographic imperative will place upon their professional capabilities, the principles of gerontology and geriatric medicine should be incorporated within all levels of the medical school and postgraduate and continuing education curricula, especially those for the internist, family physician, psychiatrist, neurologist, and physiatrist. Indeed, no physician, even the pediatrician or obstetrician (whose patients' lives are likely to be affected by the expanding burden of care for elderly family them-

selves), should lack such knowledge. Hence this text is directed toward students of medicine at all levels, given the increasing attention to the health care needs of the elderly which will be brought about by their growing proportion and absolute numbers within our population, their greater vulnerability to disease and disability, and the greater per capita expenditure of health care resources on their behalf. The charge to physicians of the future is clear: *care* for your elderly patients, in every sense of this word. To do otherwise would be to neglect a basic challenge to the medical profession. This text is assembled to assist the physician in meeting that challenge by presenting in one volume the current body of knowledge regarding the aging process and its implications to the care of the elderly, in so doing also serving to lend credibility and respect to the practice of geriatric medicine.

WILLIAM R. HAZZARD

Principles of
GERIATRIC MEDICINE
AND GERONTOLOGY

Part One
PRINCIPLES
OF GERONTOLOGY

Chapter 1

BIOLOGICAL MECHANISMS OF AGING: AN OVERVIEW

Vincent J. Cristofalo

How old would you be if you didn't know how old you was?
Satchel Paige

INTRODUCTION TO THE BIOLOGY OF AGING

The study of the biology of aging has a long and picturesque history. It is probably no surprise to the reader that in ancient literature Aristotle addressed the questions of aging. He discussed life span and theories of aging and catalogued the maximum longevities for a variety of species. Later, Galen and then Roger Bacon contributed to the ancient and medieval literature on the subject.

In the Renaissance period Francis Bacon wrote *History of Life and Death,* in which he made the depressing observation that "men of age object too much, consult too long, adventure too little, repent too soon and seldom drive business home to the full period but content themselves with a mediocrity of success."[1] A monograph by Joseph Freeman[1] presents a fascinating review of the history of aging research over the last 2500 years.

Various authors describe the modern era of aging research as beginning anywhere from the turn of the twentieth century to about 1950. For example, in 1908, Elie Metchnikoff received the Nobel Prize for his many contributions to biology and to the study of aging. He introduced the concept that aging was caused by the continuous absorption of toxins from intestinal bacteria, an idea neither proven nor completely discredited at this writing.

Comfort[2] regards the modern period of gerontology as having begun about 1950, when systematic studies which described the aging phenotype in terms of physi-

ology, biochemistry, and cell morphology were carried out. This advance in experimental approaches might have been expected to lead to a theoretical development of the field with an increasing focus on better defined, experimentally testable hypotheses. Actually that did not occur, at least not to any great extent. Even now the various theories of aging are often presented as independent ideas which do not carry the theoretical formulation of the field forward.

One of the two major groups of theories about aging is called by Comfort "Fundamentalist" and depends on some aspects of "wear and tear."[3] This group of theories includes the pathological formulation which attributes aging to specific tissues (e.g., nervous, endocrine, vascular, connective tissue, and so forth).

The other general group of theories views aging as an epiphenomenon. Environmental insults from, for example, toxins, cosmic rays, and gravity are thought to be the basis for aging. Additional theories which bear separate mention but which could be (arguably) forced into one of the above two categories include various development theories which view aging as a continuum with development and morphogenesis[4] and others which relate aging to such factors as energy depletion[5] and cessation of somatic cell growth.[6]

More specific modern versions of these general theories have involved the immune system, the neuroendocrine system, random mutation in somatic cells, failures in DNA repair, errors in protein synthesis, accumulation of toxic products, random damage from free radicals, and others. Unfortunately, even at this more specific level, each author's zeal for his own theory has caused each theory to be presented to the exclusion of others, resulting in more harm than good to the field. I would emphasize that these theories, however classified, are not mutually exclusive, are global in nature, and suffer from the unfortunate attempt to identify *the* cause, mechanism, or basis for aging. Aging is not one thing and probably does not have a single cause. All could be, at least in part, correct. What is more, the changes that occur with age may be interdependent. Aging need not depend on a single mechanism. The major mechanisms regulating the aging rate in fixed postmitotic cells may be different from those operating in renewable tissues. The combination of environmental damage and intrinsic processes further obscures the fundamental mechanisms operating.

In the United States prior to 1940, most studies on aging focused on longevity rather than on senescence. The goal was prolonging human life, and a variety of means, many of which could be described as bizarre, were advocated to reach that goal. Things changed, however, in 1939, with publication of the first edition of Cowdry's *Problems of Aging*.[7] Cowdry was a well-respected pathologist and cancer researcher, and he was able to recruit scientists of the caliber of the biochemist A. Baird Hastings and the physiologist A. J. Carlson to contribute chapters to his book. Nathan Shock (personal communication, see below) has suggested that this publication marks the beginning of the modern scientific era of gerontology.

In the United States since 1940, the history of research on aging is intimately connected to the history of the National Institutes of Health program on aging and to the eventual establishment of the National Institute on Aging. After the publication of the first volume of *Problems of Aging* by Cowdry, The Josiah Macy foundation supported a number of conferences to discuss the biology of aging. In 1940, the Surgeon General of the United States authorized the establishment of a unit on aging to focus on the physiological phenomena underlying the chronic diseases of old age. This unit was financed by the Macy Foundation.

In 1941, the National Heart Institute of the National Institutes of Health took over support of this unit. Nathan W. Shock, then Assistant Professor of Physiology at the University of California, Berkeley, was asked to head the unit, which was moved to the campus of the Baltimore (MD) City Hospital. This Gerontology Research Center is the largest research institution in the Western hemisphere devoted entirely to aging.

The National Institutes of Health extramural research program on aging developed over the years, first in the National Heart Institute and then in the National Institute of Child Health and Human Development. The National Institute on Aging was established by legislation passed in 1974. Largely through the rapid growth of this institute and the explosion in the knowledge base and technology of modern biology, there is now a substantial and rapidly expanding effort in the biology of aging.

The increasing maturity of aging research did not come easily, however. Historically and even today many competent scientists have carefully avoided being identified with this area of research, in part because both the ancient and modern history of aging research has had far more than its share of workers of questionable integrity and limited talent. So, in the minds of many, the field is tainted and lacks the glorious history of such areas as microbiology and nuclear physics. In addition, many scientists have ignored research on the biology of aging because they see it as either addressing a "non-question" or one not currently answerable. Obviously aging depends on an enormous number of variables and causes, and no clear focus has emerged. However, modern biology cannot realistically ignore a process which occurs with essentially the same scenario in the somatic cells of virtually all eukaryotes. Nor can biology avoid the challenge of observations such as, for example, the differing trajectories in aging of the mouse and human. These organisms have very similar physiologies and nearly identical quantities of DNA and yet complete what we call their maximum life spans in a chronological time period that differs by about 30-fold. This observation points to a highly conserved mechanism that runs at a variable rate.

For the biologist, the compelling attraction of aging is the challenge of discovering how so fundamental and universal a biological property works. To the geriatrician* the outcome of a better understanding of the process of aging means an improved armamentarium of treatments and strategies for improving the quality of life of elderly people.

In this introductory chapter I will attempt to review, evaluate, and categorize the most prominent theories of aging and the status of research in aging at this time. The reader is no doubt aware that this review cannot be comprehensive, given the large amount of information available. However, I believe that this formulation of current theories and knowledge will provide both a review of modern research on aging and a basic framework for understanding and critically evaluating the later, more detailed chapters, which discuss clinical observations and strategies.

OBSERVATIONS ON AGING

No discussion of the theories of aging can begin without a brief review of the observations and correlations associated with the aging process. Although aging has intrigued scientists throughout recorded history, we do not know a great deal about the nature of the mechanisms involved. This is not only because good work in this area has been limited but also because the problem

*Most authors use the term *geriatrics* to refer to the care of elderly people. The term *gerontology* refers to the study of aging.

itself is intrinsically difficult. The myriad of aging scenarios and trajectories that occur in nature, the different combinations of environmental and intrinsic changes, the lack of measurable waypoints or biomarkers to define the kinetics of the process of aging, and the lack of an endpoint other than death all serve to obscure any unifying principles.

Even a good general definition of aging is difficult to frame. It is clear that aging is characterized by an increasing vulnerability to environmental change. A consequence of this is that increasing chronological age brings with it an increasing probability of dying. In fact, a mathematical approach to biological aging is to contrast this increased probability of dying as a function of time with nonbiological processes of deterioration (such as radioactive decay), in which the fraction of the population dying (decaying) is constant over time. Some biologists argue that the survivorship kinetics of biological aging may be an artifact of civilization, domestication, and zoos. In nature, populations of animals (including humans) only recently began to live long enough to show the characteristic kinetics of biological aging. Most species in the wild are killed by predators or die from accidents long before they have a chance to show the increasing vulnerability that characterizes biological aging. In essence, the survival curve of wild populations resemble those of radioactive decay.

A related question is why the biological aging process characteristic of protected populations should occur at all in nature. If we think of aging as a genetically programmed, purposeful process, in which vulnerability to the environment increases with time, then we must consider how evolution would have selected for such a process. Why should evolution select for a negative property? Rose[8] has reviewed the development of evolutionary thought on aging. Perhaps the most attractive set of ideas have been proposed by Medawar[9] and Williams.[10] Both argue that optimization of reproduction is what is selected for. Medawar pointed out that deleterious genes associated with senescence may be delayed until the postreproductive period. Williams introduced the idea of antagonistic pleiotropy, which states that genes expressed early in life and associated with optimization of fecundity have deleterious effects later in life. Thus, aging may be the price we pay for mechanisms which assure successful reproduction. Sacher[11] and Cutler[12] have argued that the important question is not why we grow old, but why we live as long as we do. Successful reproduction would not require the organism to live to a very old age. In dealing with the question of "why longevity" Sacher makes a distinction between semelparous and iteroparous organisms. Semelparous organisms, such as annual plants and the Pacific salmon, die after a single reproductive effort. Sacher has argued that this rapid aging, which is tightly coupled to a single reproductive event, may represent a kind of programmed

aging which is directly dependent on reproduction. However, for iteroparous organisms, evolutionary success requires repeated reproduction, so senescence has no positive role. Rather, stability of the organism, in a changing environment, is the selection factor. Thus the study of "longevity assurance genes" might be more productive. A comparative study of iteroparous species with different maximum life span potentials might lead to the identification of these putative longevity assurance genes.

I see no reason to believe that ideas about selection for senescence (e.g., antagonistic pleiotropy) are in any way in conflict with the concept of longevity assurance genes. One can envision, for example, that to have genes which assure physiological stability through the major reproductive period, we must pay the price of senescence.* Perhaps, for example, mechanisms which reduce the probability of neoplastic transformation may do so by suppressing the plasticity of gene expression in the organism. This is, of course, a completely speculative notion but one which I think many biologists would find attractive.

Another confounding problem in understanding aging is the fact that there is a vast spectrum of aging changes. The process of aging is probably multifactorial in its regulation; however, it is virtually impossible to tell which changes are primary to a senescence-regulated event and which are secondary.

Finally, a confusion exists between aging, disease, and dying. Aging characteristically brings a loss in homeostasis and, with it, vulnerability to disease. Some diseases cause death. For too long now death has been used as the endpoint measurement of aging. However, death can occur from many causes, some of which are related to the aging process only secondarily and, in some cases, not at all. Aging does not occur in all species or in all organisms of the same species in exactly the same way: while one tissue may be losing functional capacity (aging, senescence) rapidly, others may be quite "young" functionally and indeed never get a chance to age. Death of the organism reflects the failure of a cell or tissue type (for example, the vascular system in humans) on which the entire organism depends. To understand biological processes and mechanisms of aging, we need to dissect the scenario of aging tissue by tissue and species by species.

Chronological age is also a much less useful and definitive measure of functional capacity than we would like. Satchel Paige summarized this concept (see quote on title page) in his response to repeated questions about his age as he pitched his way into baseball's major leagues at an age estimated to be somewhere between 40

*Most authors use the term *aging* as a general term to include all periods in the life history. *Senescence*, on the other hand, usually refers to postmaturational physiological deterioration. Both terms are imprecise.

and 50 years. A number of attempts have been made to establish criteria for biological age in humans (see, for example, Ref. 12a); however, at this time, no test battery has been presented which adequately evaluates the fitness of an individual. For the clinician/geriatrician, chronological age must be viewed critically as a criterion of biological age.

CHARACTERISTICS OF AGING

Amidst all these confusing attributes, a set of characteristics of aging can be identified in mammals:

1. Increased mortality with age after maturation.[13]
2. Well-documented changes in the chemical composition of the body with age. These changes have been studied primarily in mammals and include a decrease in lean body mass and an increase in fat. Also characteristic are increases in lipofuscin pigment (age pigment) in certain tissues and increased cross-linking in matrix molecules such as collagen.[13]
3. A broad spectrum of progressive deteriorative changes, demonstrated both in cross-sectional and longitudinal studies.[14]
4. Reduced ability to respond adaptively to environmental change (perhaps the hallmark of aging). This can be demonstrated at all levels from molecule to organism.[15] Thus, the changes of age are not so much the resting pulse rate or the fasting serum glucose but the ability to return these parameters to normal after a physiological stress such as running up three flights of stairs or eating a meal high in carbohydrates.
5. A very well-documented but very poorly understood increased vulnerability to many diseases with age.[14]

The broad spectrum of deteriorative physiological changes with aging mentioned above includes changes in glomerular filtration rate, maximal heart rate, vital capacity, and other measures of functional capacity. Based on cross-sectional studies, these capacities decline in a roughly linear way from about age 30 on.[14] Mortality from various causes, including diseases, however, increases exponentially with age.[16] The curves showing the increase in mortality from each of the various causes trace a more or less parallel slope. Thus, if one does not die in old age from the most common cause of death in old age, then one will die shortly thereafter from the second or third or fourth most common cause. Demographers have estimated that if all atherosclerosis and neoplasia were eliminated as causes of death in the population of the United States, this would only add about 10 years to the average life span.[17] In the absence of those two causes, death would come from the numerous other diseases or conditions for which mortality increases ex-

ponentially with age. This, I believe, further emphasizes the point that fundamental changes which occur in cells and tissues with age underlie the age-associated increase in vulnerability to diseases. Thought of in this way, aging is a process which is quite distinct from disease. The fundamental changes of aging can be thought of as providing the substratum in which the age-associated diseases can flourish.

THEORIES OF AGING

There is currently no adequate theory of biological aging. The fact that there is no adequate theory of biological aging has done nothing to discourage the proliferation of theories. Historically, one of the major problems in gerontology is the ease and frequency with which new theories have appeared. Even now some researchers view aging as "a thing" that happens rather than as a period in the life history of organisms which begins at maturity (or at conception) and lasts for the rest of the life span. Our view of aging should be the same as our view of development. During both processes numerous primary and secondary changes occur. Some changes are caused by the environment; others seem to be programmed and directed from within the body. Understanding aging and formulating coherent, testable hypotheses require that these various aspects of aging be separated from each other and examined critically.

A review of the literature shows that different authors have used different classification systems for the theories of aging. All are useful and all have inherent difficulties. One effective way to present this information is to group the multiplicity of theories into two classes according to their fundamental conceptual basis and then describe prominent examples of both of these classes. I remind the reader that this classification is operational only and that neither the classes of theories nor the theories themselves are mutually exclusive.

STOCHASTIC THEORIES

The first class of theories can be described as stochastic theories. In this formulation, aging is caused by the accumulation of "insults" from the environment. The insults eventually reach a level incompatible with life. The most prominent specific example of this class of theories is the Somatic Mutation Theory of Aging.[18,19] This theory was given impetus following World War II and the increased research activity in radiation biology. The theory states that mutations (genetic damage), presumably resulting from background radiation and perhaps radiomimetic agents, will accumulate and eventually produce functional failure and, ultimately, death. The major experimental support for this theory was derived from the well-documented observation that exposure to ionizing radiation shortens life span. Szilard[19] argued that "hits" from radiation were recessive, that two hits were required to inactivate a given locus, and that this must occur in a sufficient number of cells for the damage to be expressed. Curtis and Miller[20] gathered support for this view in their comparison of chromosome aberrations in dividing cells in the livers of old mice. They found a higher frequency of these abnormalities in short-lived strains compared with long-lived strains. These data represent probably the major experimental support for the somatic mutation theory. However, the results of this study have been controversial.

On the other hand, there are a number of arguments against the somatic mutation theory. For one thing, on logical grounds, life span shortening by radiation does not define whether the mechanism for this life span shortening bears any relationship to the normal mechanism of aging. One can envision numerous treatments which would shorten life span but are not related to normal aging. The pitfalls inherent in using death as an endpoint for aging (see above) are eminently obvious in this example.

Second, there are experiments which argue directly against somatic mutation. For example, if the theory were correct, inbred animals would have a longer life span than outbred animals since inbred animals would be homologous at most genetic loci and thus more resistant to random damage. In fact the reverse is true, as exemplified in the well-known phenomenon of hybrid vigor and in the fact that for both mice and *Drosophila*, inbreeding shortens life span.[21]

Perhaps the most compelling experiments to address somatic mutation are those of Clark and Rubin on the hymenopteran wasp *Habrobracon*.[22] In studies on radiation effects and life span which compared haploid and diploid animals, these workers showed that although the haploid animals were much more sensitive to ionizing radiation, when the animals were not irradiated, both haploids and diploids had the same life span. This observation is very difficult to reconcile with the classical formulation of the somatic mutation theory of aging. Although direct experiments on this theory have been few over the past decade or so, more modern formulations of somatic mutation theory have yet to be examined. For example, the possibility of mobile genes or gene splicing, which could occur randomly in aging and which could account for changing gene expression, has not been examined with the techniques of modern biology. Perhaps such mechanisms could be important not only in the limitation of life span but in the speciation process which is somehow coupled to changes in maximum life span potential. In any case, a reexamination of this theory in light of modern molecular genetics seems worthwhile.

A second example of a stochastic theory is the error theory. This theory, first articulated (in this form) by Orgel,[23] proposes that, although random errors in protein synthesis may occur, the error-containing protein molecule will be turned over and the next copy will be error-free. However, if the error-containing protein is one which is involved in synthesis of the genetic material or in the protein synthesizing machinery, then this molecule could cause further errors so that the number of error-containing proteins would expand to result in an "error crisis," which would be incompatible with proper function and life. An early fundamental test of this theory as it applies to human cell cultures was carried out by Ryan et al.,[24] in which WI-38 cells[25] were fed, early in their life span, with two amino acid analogues, *p*-fluorophenylalanine and ethionine. In one set of cells, the analogues were given at obviously toxic levels, which stopped proliferation and killed many cells. At the end of one week, the analogues were removed and the cells were fed with fresh medium and cultured by normal procedures throughout their proliferative life span. Presumably, the surviving cells had accumulated large amounts of these analogues into their proteins. Certainly sufficient errors should have been present to generate an aging crisis.

In the companion experiment sister cultures were fed with very low doses of these analogues throughout the life span. No toxic effects were observed, and the proliferation rate of the cells was identical to that of control, untreated cells. Addition of ^{14}C-labeled analogues at the same molar concentration to sister flasks documented that, at this concentration, the analogues were incorporated into protein. Thus, after a number of transfers the cells would have numerous error-containing proteins.

The results showed that both the short-term, high-dose cultures and the long-term, low-dose cultures had essentially the same replicative life spans. This result seemed irreconcilable with the error theory as stated for cell cultures. However, the theory had basic appeal to biochemists because of its apparently straightforward testability through the detection of missynthesized proteins. Despite numerous reports of altered proteins in aging,[26] no direct evidence of age-dependent missynthesis has yet been obtained. Altered proteins do occur in aging cells and tissues; however, at present it seems that the fidelity of the protein synthesizing machinery does not decrease with age, rather the capacity of the protein removal machinery in old cells is compromised (see reviews by Rothstein,[27] Gracy,[28] Oliver,[29] and others). It may follow that the accumulation of altered functionally important proteins could impair physiologic capacity.

Another correlate of error theories in general is the notion that the ability to repair damage to the genetic material is somehow associated with aging or the rate of aging. Hart and Setlow[30] obtained evidence that the ability to repair ultraviolet damage to DNA in cell cultures derived from a variety of species of different maximum life spans was directly correlated with maximum life span potential. Although the idea that differences in DNA repairability provide the basis for the differences in species life span is attractive, current experimental support for this idea remains inconclusive.[31] Probably if DNA repair capability is involved in the determination of maximum life span, it is more likely to be site-specific than generalized.

A related theory is based on cross-linking in macromolecules. Although cross-linking is not restricted to proteins (DNA, for example, can cross-link), most experimental attention has been paid to collagen and elastin since these molecules are accessible, do not readily turn over, and show increased cross-linking with age. The major proponents of this theory have been Kohn[32] and Bjorksten.[33] The core of the idea is that these matrix molecules comprise over 20 percent of mammalian body weight. Since cross-linking increases with age, the vital physiological processes which occur in a bed of matrix molecules will not be able to proceed as effectively. The concepts underlying this theory are probably overly simplistic. It is true that collagen shows increasing cross-links. However, there is much more to matrix molecule metabolism than simply cross-linking. Some collagen types are replaced by other collagen types in development and aging. Also, cross-linking is a process of maturation for which increased cross-linking at some sites leads to improved function, while at other sites it leads to impaired function.[34] A great deal still needs to be learned about these matrix molecules. Today, few if any researchers view collagen cross-linking as a major underlying cause of aging.

DEVELOPMENT-GENETIC THEORIES

Development-genetic theories consider the process of aging to be part of a continuum with development, genetically controlled and programmed. Resistance to the idea of an aging process which is continuous with and probably operating through the same mechanisms as development derives from two sources. One has to do with the earlier discussed selection for aging mechanisms through evolution. The second results from an intuitive sense that the diverse scenarios and trajectories of aging are not likely to be controlled by a process whose mechanisms regulate the very precise processes of development. I believe this negative view really derives from the notion that death is the relevant endpoint for aging and that the regulation of aging depends on a single process.

Another dimension is whether aging is controlled by genetic processes. There is really no question that environmental factors can regulate or modify mortality and probably even aging rates in the very broad sense. It is clear, for example, that what we call skin aging is accelerated by exposure to the sun. Overall, however,

most gerontologists agree that maximum life span and aging rate are regulated intrinsically. The major evidence in support of this view derives from the species specificity of maximum life span. Variation in life span is far greater among species than within species. Since maximum life span breeds true and is a species characteristic, it must be genetically determined. Further evidence for the genetic basis of aging and maximal life span comes from the recognition of genetic disease of precocious aging. Martin and Turker (Chap. 3) discuss in detail the genetics of aging and these genetic progeroid syndromes. Hutchinson-Guilford syndrome, the "classic" progeria, Werner's syndrome, and Down's syndrome are probably the best known of these diseases. Although the precise and complete scenario of human aging is not replicated at an accelerated rate in individuals with these diseases, many of the commonly recognized aging changes occur more rapidly. Thus, these diseases may turn out to be important probes of aging.

At the familial level, studies comparing the longevity of monozygotic and dizygotic twins and nontwin siblings have shown a remarkable similarity between monozygotic twins that is not demonstrated in the other two groups.[35,36] Interestingly, this similarity can be observed in human fibroblast cell cultures from monozygotic twins, which show a much greater similarity of behavior and replicative life span than nontwin, age-matched controls.[37]

Unfortunately, the interpretation of all these findings is not completely clear. One can, for example, argue that genetics governs susceptibility to certain fatal diseases but not to aging per se. Alternatively, what could be inherited is a certain "vigor" that protects against the development of susceptibility to a wide variety of diseases. Although in some specific cases the former mechanism can be recognized, in many more cases it is not possible to distinguish between the two. In any case there is ample circumstantial evidence for genetically controlled mechanisms of aging which could operate in a way similar to developmental processes, although there is no direct evidence that this is so.

We shall consider four examples of development-genetic theories: the first group can be collected under the general heading of neuroendocrine theories of aging.[38] This group of theories regards functional decrements in neurons and their associated hormones as central to the aging process. Given the major integrative role of the neuroendocrine system in physiology, this is an attractive approach. An important version of this theory proposes that the hypothalamic, pituitary, adrenal axis is the master timekeeper for the organism and the primary regulator of the aging process. Functional changes in this system are accompanied by or regulate functional decrements throughout the organism.

The cascade effect of functional decrements in the

hypothalamus, for example, and their potential sequelae are evident. The neuroendocrine system regulates early development, growth, puberty, the control of the reproductive system, metabolism, and in part the activities of all the major organ systems in the body. Several lines of evidence have accumulated which support the neuroendocrine theory. For example, in aging male and female rats the decline in reproductive capacity is due to a decline in the release of gonadotropin-releasing hormone by the hypothalamus, which may be due, in turn, to a decline in the activity of hypothalamic catecholamines.[39] Similarly it has been shown that pulsatile growth hormone release declines with age in rats. Both of these changes would have profound effects upon general functional capacity. Other studies have suggested loss of neurons in discrete brain areas[40] and loss of responsiveness to neutrotransmitters.

Another aspect of the neuroendocrine basis of aging depends on the role of pituitary hormones and the effect of hypophysectomy.[41,42] When rats were hypophysectomized and the known hormones of the hypophysis were replaced, the animals lived longer. Denckla[42] has shown that aged rats have a lower minimal O_2 consumption and a reduced increase in O_2 consumption in response to T_4. This effect is abolished with hypophysectomy and hormone replacement. Denckla concluded that this finding provided evidence for the presence of a previously undescribed pituitary hormone called "decreasing oxygen consumption hormone" (DECO), which probably begins to be elaborated at puberty under stimulation by thyroid hormones. DECO is proposed to be responsible for the decreasing oxygen consumption observed in aging and the reduced effort of thyroid hormone in aging. This substance has been referred to as a "death hormone." Although it is an intriguing idea, no such hormone has been demonstrated. The potential for artifact here is high. For example, if the strain of animals used typically gets pituitary tumors, then the increasing average life span after removal of the pituitary gland is probably due to the prevention of this specific cancer. Hypophysectomy could also prevent or delay the appearance of a variety of other tumors. In the absence of the identification of a specific hormone and careful studies which compare age-associated pathology in hypophysectomized and control animals, Denckla's observation must be viewed with caution.

The importance of neuroendocrine research cannot be overemphasized. However, critics point out that *the master timekeeper of aging, the neuroendocrine system*, lacks universality. Many organisms which (superficially?) age with a scenario very similar to that of higher vertebrates have no complex neuroendocrine system. It can also be argued that the changes which occur in the neuroendocrine system are fundamental changes and occur in all tissues. Aging of the brain, however, produces

additional secondary effects which, although not fundamental to aging, contribute to the development of the overall aging phenotype. Certainly the study of aging in the neuroendocrine system can tell us a great deal about the aging of the organism. What it can tell us about the regulation of aging at a more fundamental level remains to be determined.

A second theory in this class of development-genetic aging theories is referred to as the theory of Intrinsic Mutagenesis. This idea was first proposed by Burnet[43] and is an attempt to reconcile stochastic theories of aging with the genetic regulation of maximum life span. Burnet suggests that each species is endowed with a specific genetic constitution which regulates the fidelity of the genetic material and its replication. The degree of fidelity regulates the rate of appearance of mutations or errors and, thus, the life span. Alternatively, we can envision a case in which new "fidelity regulators" appear at different stages in an animal's life history. Each successive set of regulators could have diminished capacity, thus allowing an increase in mutational events. Although there is no substantial evidence to support this theory, it is attractive, and various methods of mutation analysis can be used to test its validity.

Another aspect of intrinsic mutagenesis is concerned with the increase in DNA excision repair associated with maximal life span.[30] There is also evidence that the fidelity of DNA polymerase may diminish with age,[44–46] but the data in support of both these findings are at present controversial.

Finally, in this section on intrinsic mutagenesis, the role of DNA methylation as a regulatory factor in aging bears mention. For example, diploid fibroblasts in culture are unable to maintain a constant level of 5-methyl cytosine,[47–49] and in other systems DNA methylation patterns have been linked to X chromosome inactivation-reactivation.[50] These ideas are potentially important but require more thorough testing before a reliable body of evidence will emerge.

A third development-genetic theory is the Immunological Theory of Aging. This theory, as proposed by Walford,[51] is based on two observations: (1) that the functional capacity of the immune system declines with age, as seen in reduced T-cell function[52] and in reduced resistance to infectious disease, and (2) that the fidelity of the immune system declines with age, as evidenced by the striking age-associated increase in autoimmune disease. Walford[53] has related these immune system changes to the genes of the major histocompatibility complex in rats and mice. Congenic animals which differ only at the major histocompatibility locus appear to have different maximal life spans, suggesting that life span is regulated (in part at least) by this locus. Interestingly, this locus also regulates superoxide dismutase and mixed-function oxidase levels, a finding which relates the immunologic theory of aging to the free radical theory of aging.

As with the neuroendocrine theory, the immunologic theory is very attractive. The immune system has a major integrative role and is clearly of the utmost importance in health maintenance. On the other hand, the role of the major histocompatibility complex is difficult to interpret since, for example, life span differences could be due simply to the prevention of specific diseases. The same caveat can be leveled at the immunologic theory as at the neuroendocrine theory. The lack of universality of the complex immune system as we know it in mammals suggests that its role is important in health and life span determinations. However, it is difficult to defend its role as the primary timekeeper in the biology of all organisms. Similarly, the inability to distinguish between primary and secondary effects on aging and the possibility that changes in the immune system are no different from changes in other cell types makes interpretation of this theory difficult. Further research in this very active area should help to clarify the significance of this theory.

The fourth example of development-genetic theory has to do with free radicals. This theory, usually attributed to Harman,[54,55] proposes that most aging changes are due to damage caused by radicals. Free radicals are atoms or molecules with an unpaired electron. Chemically they are highly reactive species which are generated commonly in single electron transfer reactions of metabolism. Free radicals are rapidly destroyed by protective enzyme systems such as superoxide dismutase. Presumably (according to the theory), however, some free radicals escape destruction and cause damage which accumulates in important biological structures. This accumulation of damage eventually interferes with function and ultimately causes death. In cells the most common free radical is superoxide and the molecules produced by its interactions. Common reactions involving oxygen and superoxide are

$$O_2 + e \longrightarrow O_2^- \cdot \quad \text{(superoxide radical)}$$

$$2H^+ + O_2 + O_2^- \cdot \xrightarrow[\text{dismutase}]{\text{superoxide}} O_2 + H_2O_2$$

$$2H_2O_2 \xrightarrow{\text{catalase}} 2H_2O + O_2$$

or

$$H_2O_2 + 2GSH \xrightarrow[\text{peroxidase}]{\text{glutathione}} H_2O + GSSG$$

When excess O_2 is present, the Haber-Weiss reaction can take place, yielding the highly reactive hydroxyl radical.

$$O_2 + H_2O_2 \longrightarrow OH^- \cdot + O_2$$

Examples of free radical damage which might occur include the peroxidation of lipids. Lipofuscin, an "age pigment," accumulates in aging cells and may be the oxidation product of free radical action upon polyunsaturated fatty acids. Autoxidation of lipids by free radical pathways may lead to the information of hydroperoxides, which then decompose to products such as ethane and pentane.

This is a very appealing theory since it provides a mechanism for aging that does not depend on tissue-specific action but is fundamental to all aerobic tissues. Although this theory has an aspect of random damage, it was not included with the stochastic theories because some observations about free radicals and aging are more suggestive of the development-genetic theory.

For example, the German physiologist Rubner[5] determined that for a series of mammals, the bigger the animal, the lower its metabolic rate. The adaptive significance of this is that as animals get larger, their surface-to-volume ratio changes, resulting in a reduction in the animal's ability to dissipate the heat produced in metabolic reactions. Thus, a high metabolic rate could cause serious overheating in a large animal. Rubner proposed, however, that metabolism per se caused damage to the organism.

Others[56] observed that, for a limited group of mammals, life span is more or less a direct function of body size. Bigger homoiotherms, by and large, live longer, suggesting an inverse relationship between metabolic rate and life span. (Actually, the relationship is most precise if body size is modified by a factor for brain size.) Thus, investigators have speculated that each species is capable of burning a given number of calories in its lifetime. Those species that burn them rapidly live a short time; for those that burn them more slowly, life span is extended.

Since metabolic rate is related directly to free radical generation and inversely to life span, it is reasonable to hypothesize that the rate of free radical production is in some way related to life span determination or to senescence. Evidence to support this view is primarily circumstantial. For example, superoxide dismutase specific activity in the liver appears to be directly proportional to species maximum life span.[57] Similarly, proponents point to the observation made for rats and mice that caloric restriction can increase mean and maximal life span by approximately 50 percent. This remains the only method known for extending the life span of warm-blooded animals and has evoked a great deal of interest. The notion had been that caloric restriction lowers metabolic rate and thus free radical production. However, Masoro[58] has shown that the specific metabolic rate of calorically restricted rats appears to be the same as those fed ad libitum. Of course, this does not diminish the significance of the observation on dietary restriction and life span extension but only complicates its interpretation.

Caloric restriction and its effect on life span extension is perhaps one of the most promising probes of the mechanism of aging. Caloric restriction may exert its effectiveness through the neuroendocrine system, since Everitt et al.[59] have shown a striking similarity between dietary restriction and hypophysectomy (see above).

A very simple extrapolation of the free radical theory of aging leads to the conclusion that active individuals would have a shorter life span than nonactive individuals. Similarly, vigorous exercise would be a life-shortening activity. There is no evidence to support this view. In addition to all the intuitively known beneficial effects of exercise, Paffenberger and colleagues[60] have shown that (within limits) greater caloric expenditure is positively associated with increasing length of life and health span in humans. A caveat here, as with other statements, is that exercise could have beneficial effects in preventing disease (presumably cardiovascular disease) while at the same time accelerating aging through increased free radical generation. However, the disease prevention aspects could completely obscure the free radical effects.

The evidence derived from attempts at direct testing of the free radical theory is difficult to interpret. The results of feeding antioxidants to mice or rats are unclear, since the observed small increases in life span could not be attributed to the reduction of free radicals and, in fact, in some cases were most likely attributable to caloric restriction. Experiments by Balin et al.[61] using human cell cultures showed that, separately or in combination, α-tocopherol (vitamin E) and a reduced partial pressure of oxygen (49 mmHg) did not extend the replicative cell life span. The observation is very difficult to reconcile with the effect of free radicals on aging. On the other hand, using cell culture models, others have shown important effects of free radicals on cell transformation and neoplasia. Overall, despite its appeal, the specific role of free radicals in aging will be difficult to define. The concept that free radicals represent a single basic cause of aging on which other aging changes depend is, I believe, unlikely to be correct.

THE CELLULAR BASIS OF AGING

Most of our discussion, thus far, has dealt with aging at the organismic level. However, the cell is the fundamental living unit, and I would like to conclude with a discussion of aging at the cellular level. From an historical point of view the concept of aging as a cell-based phenomenon is comparatively new. Most of the theories deal with the integrative functioning of the organism. The concept that aging is somehow a supracellular phenomenon operating at the level of integrative function is well entrenched in this field. To examine the question of cell versus organismic aging, we must go back in history. The nineteenth century embryologist Weissman, for example, appears to be the first biologist to emphasize the distinction between somatic cells which become se-

nescent, and germ cells, which do not. Weissman proposed that aging was the price somatic cells paid for their differentiation. He was also probably the first to suggest that the failure of somatic cells to replicate indefinitely limited the life span of the individual. This view was brought into serious question by the experiments of Alexis Carrel and co-workers at the Rockefeller University who, beginning with experiments in 1911, were able to keep chick heart cells growing continuously in culture until 1945, when Carrel retired and terminated the experiment.[62–64] Since 34 years is longer than the life span of the chicken, this was considered compelling evidence that individual cells were immortal. This work and the concepts emanating from it dominated biology, especially gerontology, for the first half of this century. The accepted view was that aging was not a characteristic of cells. Isolated cells were immortal; it was the tissues that were involved in the aging process.

In the late 1950s and early 1960s, Hayflick and Moorhead were developing methods to detect what they believed to be latent human tumor viruses in normal human cells. Their approach required that normal human cells be grown in tissue culture. Then, under these sterile conditions, they tried to detect the putative latent tumor viruses. They were unsuccessful. However, during the course of this work, they noticed that a period of rapid and vigorous cellular proliferation was consistently followed by a period of decline in proliferative activity during which the cells acquired characteristics reminiscent of senescent cells in vivo, and the apparent senescence was followed finally by the death of the cultures. Swim and Parker[65] and perhaps others had made this same observation previously, but Hayflick and Moorhead, with extraordinary insight, recognized the process as senescence in culture. They proposed a new view, namely, that aging was a cellular as well as an organismic phenomenon and that perhaps the loss in functional capacity of the aging individual reflected the summation of the loss of critical functional capacities of individual cells. This interpretation has changed our understanding of the process of aging and altered the direction and interpretation of aging research.[25,66]

Repeated attempts to replicate and verify the early experiments of Carrel et al. have been uniformly unsuccessful,[67] and there is no documented explanation for the apparent near-immortality of their cells. The opinion among scientists is that there was artifactual introduction of fresh young cells into the culture at regular intervals.

In other experiments on human cells, Hayflick and Moorhead[66] were able to show that a deteriorative change in the cells was not dependent on environmental influences; rather, it was intrinsic to the cells. They also addressed the generality of this phenomenon and pointed out that unless transformation occurred at some point in the life history of the cells, senescence always resulted. Transformation can occur at any point in the life history; and if transformation occurs, the cells acquire a constellation of abnormal characteristics, including chromosomal abnormalities and an indefinite life span—properties of tumor cells.

Finally, if we examine the relationship between the cellular aging phenomenon in culture and aging of the individual, we find first that this general scenario of in vitro aging is not specific to fibroblasts but has been demonstrated also in smooth muscle cells, endothelial cells, glial cells, and lymphocytes. A number of changes that take place during in vitro senescence are reminiscent of changes which occur in vivo in aging. Cell culture studies have also shown that the replicative life span of cells in culture is inversely related to the age of the donor[68,69] and directly related to the maximum life span of the species.[70] These observations are usually taken as evidence of the relationships between in vivo and in vitro aging. However, this is an oversimplification. What these observations show is that aging in vivo is expressed in culture. It is not clear that the observed cellular aging in culture actually contributes to what we recognize as the in vivo aging phenotype of the organism. There is no reason to believe that the in vitro replicative life span of mesenchymal cells is important in determining the life span of the organism. On the other hand, living things maintain their functional capacity over long periods through processes of repair and replacement, both of which involve proliferation of mesenchymal cells. The whole issue of proliferative homeostasis must be evaluated in terms of the ability of the organism to respond successfully to environmental stress through carefully regulated replication.

Of course, mechanistically, the aging of proliferating mesenchymal cells may be quite different from that of fixed postmitotic cells or reverting postmitotic cells. Perhaps these cells in culture are not significant in determining the life span of the organism. However, it is not life span but rather the mechanism regulating the process of aging that is of interest. By any definition of aging, these normal cells in culture undergo aging processes. There is a gradual failure in functional capacity—in this case proliferative capacity—and the cells show changes similar to changes in vivo.

Cellular aging under controlled environmental conditions and in the absence of tissue- and cell-type interactions has profound implications for the theories of biological aging. The results suggest that, underlying the effects of various proposed "master timekeeping" systems, cells contain individual "clocks" that ultimately limit their life span. Senescence in these cells seem to be driven by replications, not by sidereal time. The concept is a complicated one because studies of the life spans of individual clones and subclones of human cells suggest that genetic death for individual cells is a stochastic event.

One way to envision the organism's aging scenario is that each cell type has its own aging trajectory. Death occurs when the capacity for homeostasis in the most rapidly aging component of the organism falls below the level necessary to maintain itself. This causes death of that cell type and terminates the aging trajectory of the organism even though other cell systems within the organism may be quite vigorous.

If we are to understand the mechanisms by which aging (as distinct from the more complicated issue of life span) is regulated, then careful dissection of changes that occur at the cell level will be important. Each cell and tissue type must be examined in the absence of interactive systems and the mechanisms of regulation determined. This is a very exciting time in biology because the tools to do this at the most fundamental level are now available. The ultimate synthesis of the findings from these many lines of research will determine the future of the quality of human life.

REFERENCES

1. Freeman JT: *Aging: Its History and Literature.* New York, Humana Science Press, 1979.
2. Comfort A: *The Biology of Senescence*, 3d ed. New York, Elsevier, 1979.
3. Pearl R: *The Rate of Living.* New York, Vropfu, 1928.
4. Warthin AS: *Old Age, the Major Revolution: The Philosophy and Pathology of the Aging Process.* New York, Hoeber, 1929.
5. Rubner M: *Das Problem der Lebensdaver und Seine Beziebungen zum Wachstum und Ernabrung.* Munich, Oldenbourg, 1908.
6. Weissman A: *Uber die Dauer des Lebens.* Jena, 1882.
7. Cowdry EV: *Problems of Aging.* New York, Williams & Wilkins, 1939.
8. Rose MR: *Evolutionary Biology of Senescence.* Boston, Oxford University Press, 1989.
9. Medawar PB: *An Unsolved Problem of Biology.* London, HK Lewis, 1952.
10. Williams GC: Pleiotropy, natural selection and the evolution of senescence. *Evolution* 11:398, 1957.
11. Sacher GA: Molecular versus systemic theories on the genesis of aging. *Exp Gerontol* 3:265, 1968.
12. Cutler RG: Evolution of human longevity: A critical overview. *Mech Ageing Dev* 9:337, 1979.
12a. Dean W: *Biological Aging Measurement, Clinical Applications.* Los Angeles, Center for Bio-Gerontology, 1988.
13. Strehler BL: *Time, Cells and Aging*, 2d ed. New York, Academic Press, 1977.
14. Shock NW: Longitudinal studies of aging in humans, in Finch CE, Schneider EL (eds): *Handbook of the Biology of Aging*, 2d ed. New York, Van Nostrand Reinhold, 1985, p 721.
15. Adelman RC: Hormone interaction during aging, in Schimke RT (ed): *Biological Mechanism in Aging.* Washington, Department of Health and Human Services, 1980, p 686.

16. Kohn RR: Extracellular aging, in Kohn RR (ed): *Principles of Mammalian Aging*. Engelwood Cliffs, NJ, Prentice-Hall, 1971.

17. Greville TNE: US life tables by cause of death: 1969–1971. US Decennial Life Tables for 1969–71 1:5, 1976.

18. Failla G: The aging process and carcinogenesis. *Ann NY Acad Sci* 71:1124, 1958.

19. Szilard L: On the nature of the aging process. *Proc Natl Acad Sci USA* 45:30, 1959.

20. Curtis HF, Miller K: Chromosome aberrations in lower cells of guinea pigs. *J Gerontol* 26:292, 1971.

21. Maynard-Smith J: Review lecturer on senescence: I. The causes of aging. *Proc R Soc Lond [Biol]* 157:115, 1962.

22. Clark AM, Rubin MA: The modification by X-irradiation of the life span of haploid and diploid *Habrobracon*. *Radiat Res* 15:244, 1961.

23. Orgel LE: The maintenance of the accuracy of protein synthesis and its relevance to aging. *Proc Natl Acad Sci USA* 49:517, 1963.

24. Ryan JM et al: Error accumulation and aging in human diploid cells. *J Gerontol* 29:616, 1974.

25. Hayflick L: The limited in vitro lifetime of human diploid cell strains. *Exp Cell Res* 37:614, 1965.

26. Holliday R, Tarrant GM: Altered enzymes in ageing human fibroblasts. *Nature* 238:26, 1972.

27. Rothstein M: Age-related changes in enzyme levels and enzyme properties, in Rothstein M (ed): *Review of Biological Research in Aging*, vol 1. New York, Alan Liss, 1985, p 421.

28. Gracy RW et al: Impaired protein degradation may account for the accumulation of "abnormal" proteins in aging cells, in Adelman RC, Dekker EE (eds): *Modification of Proteins During Aging*. New York, Alan Liss, 1985, p 1.

29. Oliver CN et al: Age-related alterations of enzymes may involve mixed-function oxidation reactions, in Adelman RC, Dekker EE (eds): *Modification of Proteins During Aging*. New York, Alan Liss, 1985, p 39.

30. Hart RW, Setlow RB: Correlation between DNA excision repair and life span in a number of mammalian species. *Proc Natl Acad Sci USA* 71:2169, 1974.

31. Tice RB, Setlow RB: DNA repair and replication in aging organisms and cells, in Finch CE, Schneider EL (eds): *Handbook of the Biology of Aging*, 2d ed. New York, Van Nostrand Rheinhold, 1985, p 173.

32. Kohn RR: *Principles of Mammalian Aging*, 2d ed. Englewood Cliffs, NJ, Prentice-Hall, 1978.

33. Bjorksten J: Cross linkage and the aging process, in Rothstein M (ed): *Theoretical Aspects of Aging*. New York, Academic Press, 1974, p 43.

34. Hall DA: *The Aging of Connective Tissue*. New York, Academic Press, 1976.

35. Kallman JF, Jarvik LF: Twin data on genetic variations in resistance to tuberculosis, in Gedda L (ed): *Genetica Della Tuberculosi e Dei Tumori*. Rome, Gregorio Mendel Inst, 1957, p 15.

36. Jarvik LF et al: Survival trends in a senescent twin population. *Am J Hum Genet* 12:170, 1960.

37. Ryan JM: A comparison of the proliferative and replicative life span kinetics of cell cultures derived from monozygotic twins. *In Vitro* 17:20, 1981.

38. Finch CE, Landfield PW: Neuroendocrine and autonomic functions in aging mammals, in Finch CE, Schneider EL (eds): *Handbook of the Biology of Aging*, 2d ed. New York, Van Nostrand Reinhold, 1985, p 567.

39. Wise PM: Aging of the female reproductive system. *Rev Biol Res Aging* 1:15, 1983.

40. Brody H, Jayashankar N: Anatomical changes in the nervous system, in Finch CE, Hayflick L (eds): *Handbook of the Biology of Aging*. New York, Van Nostrand Reinhold, 1977, p 214.

41. Everitt AV: The hypothalamic pituitary control of aging and age-related pathology. *Exp Gerontol* 8:265, 1973.

42. Denckla WD: Role of the pituitary and thyroid glands in the decline of minimal O_2 consumption with age. *J Clin Invest* 53:572, 1974.

43. Burnet M: *Intrinsic Mutagenesis: A Genetic Approach for Aging*. New York, Wiley, 1974.

44. Linn S et al: Decreased fidelity of DNA polymerase activity isolated from aging human fibroblasts. *Proc Natl Acad Sci USA* 13:2818, 1976.

45. Murray V, Holliday R: Increased error frequency of DNA polymerases from senescent human fibroblasts. *J Mol Biol* 146:55, 1981.

46. Krauss SW, Linn S: Studies of DNA polymerases alpha and beta from cultured human cells in various replicative states. *J Cell Physiol* 126:99, 1986.

47. Wilson VL, Jones PA: DNA methylation decreases in aging but not in immortal cells. *Science* 220:1054, 1983.

48. Holliday R: Strong effects of 5-azacytidine on the in vitro lifespan of human diploid fibroblasts. *Exp Cell Res* 166:543, 1986.

49. Fairweather S et al: The in vitro lifespan of MRC-5 cells is shortened by 5 azacytidine induced demethylation. *Exp Cell Res* 168:153, 1987.

50. Wareham VA et al: Age related reactivation of an X-linked gene. *Nature* 327:725, 1987.

51. Walford RL et al: Immunopathology of aging, in Eisdorfer C (ed): *Ann Rev Gerontol Ger*. New York, Springer, 1981, p 3.

52. Walford R: *The Immunologic Theory of Aging*. Copenhagen, Munksgaard, 1969.

53. Walford, RL: Multigene families, histocompatibility system, transformation, meiosis, stem cells and DNA repair. *Mech Ageing Dev* 9:19, 1979.

54. Harman, D: Aging: A theory based on free radical and radiation chemistry. *J Gerontol* 11:298, 1956.

55. Harman, D: The aging process. *Proc Natl Acad Sci USA* 78:7124, 1981.

56. Sacher GA, Duffy PH: Genetic relation of life span to metabolic rate for inbred mouse strains and their hybrids. *Fed Proc* 38:184, 1979.

57. Tolmasoff JM et al: Superoxide dismutase: Correlation with life span and specific metabolic rate in primate species. *Proc Natl Acad Sci USA* 77:2777, 1980.

58. Masoro EJ: Metabolism, in Finch CE, Schneider EL (eds): *Handbook of the Biology of Aging*, 2d ed. New York, Van Nostrand Reinhold, 1985, p 540.

59. Everitt AV et al: The effects of hypophysectomy and continuous food restriction, begun at ages 70 and 400 days, on collagen aging, proteinuria, incidence of pathology and longevity in the male rat. *Mech Ageing Dev* 12:161, 1980.

60. Paffenberger RS: Physical activity, all-cause mortality, and longevity of college alumni. *N Engl J Med* 314(10):605, 1986.

61. Balin AK et al: The effect of oxygen and vitamin E on the life span of human diploid cells. *J Cell Biol* 74:58, 1978.

62. Carrel A, Burrows MT: On the physiochemical regulation of the growth of tissues. *J Exp Med* 13:562, 1911.

63. Carrel A: On the permanent life of tissues outside the organism. *J Exp Med* 15:516, 1912.

64. Carrel A: Present condition of a strain of connective tissue twenty-eight months old. *J Exp Med* 20:1, 1914.

65. Swim HE, Parker RF: Culture characteristics of human fibroblasts propagated serially. *Am J Hyg* 45:20, 1957.

66. Hayflick L, Moorhead PS: The serial cultivation of human diploid cell strains. *Exp Cell Res* 25:585, 1961.

67. Gey GO et al: Long-term growth of chicken fibroblasts on a collagen substrate. *Exp Cell Res* 84:63, 1974.

68. Martin GM et al: Replication lifespan of cultivated human cells: Effects of damage, tissue, and genotype. *Lab Invest* 23:86, 1970.

69. Schneider EL, Mitsui Y: The relationship between in vitro cellular aging and in vivo human age. *Proc Natl Acad Sci USA* 73:3584, 1976.

70. Rohme D: Evidence for a relationship between longevity of mammalian species and lifespan of normal fibroblasts in vitro and erythrocytes in vivo. *Proc Natl Acad Sci USA* 78:3584, 1981.

Chapter 2

EVOLUTIONARY PERSPECTIVE OF HUMAN LONGEVITY

Richard G. Cutler

A characteristic not commonly appreciated concerning human biology is that human beings are the longest-lived of all mammalian species. This characteristic appears to be largely due to an unusually slow intrinsic aging rate of essentially all physiological processes and is accordingly an inherent genetic characteristic. Another interesting longevity characteristic is that humans have the largest metabolic energy capacity of all mammals. This parameter is called *life span energy potential (LEP)* and represents the average energy consumed over life span per body weight. While most mammalian species from mouse to elephant have LEP values in the range of 200–300 kcal/g, human values run about 800–900 kcal/g. Thus, human longevity appears unusually high, both in chronological time as well as metabolic energy usage.

An understanding of the biological basis of human longevity could uncover unique characteristics important to general health maintenance and longevity. One approach to attaining such knowledge has been an evolutionary and comparative approach. Mammalian species represent an evolutionary and biologically related group in which the qualitative nature of their biology, including their aging processes, is remarkably similar. In spite of these similarities, a wide range (about 30-fold) of life spans exists among the different mammalian species. Thus, it appears that substantial differences in physiological aging rates exist.

An evolutionary and comparative study of mammalian species leads naturally to such questions as to why aging occurs, why different species have different life spans and aging rates, and what role longevity may play in determining the evolutionary success of an organism.[1,2] Attempts to answer such questions are helpful in developing rational experimental approaches and hypotheses for the study of aging of all animal species and, in particular, the search for the unique biological characteristics that determine human longevity.[1–6]

COMPARATIVE STUDIES ON AGING AND LONGEVITY

MAXIMUM LIFE SPAN POTENTIAL AND AGING RATE

The life span of a mammalian species is dependent on two major factors: the intensity of its exogenous environmental factors and its endogenous aging rate. A survival curve is a convenient means of illustrating and measuring the interaction of these two factors. This curve is constructed of data determining the percentage survival of a population as time passes until the last individual dies. Typical curves for human populations in different historical periods are shown in Fig. 2-1. The 50 percent survival value is frequently used to measure the life span of the population. It is sometimes termed *life span expectancy.* The different 50 percent survival values shown in this figure are thought to be largely due to differences in the frequencies of early childhood deaths, infectious diseases, and general nutrition and not to differences in the intrinsic aging rates of the individuals making up these populations. This conclusion is based on evidence that (1) those persons who have lower-than-normal life spans are usually found to die of specific diseases not likely related to the aging processes and (2) the maximum life span potential of the different human populations is found to be remarkably constant and independent of a wide-ranging difference in 50 percent survival life span (see Fig. 2-1).

15

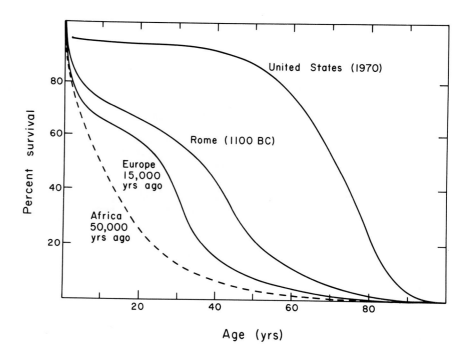

Maximum life span potential (MLSP) represents a statistical estimate of the maximum life span characteristic of a species where most exogenous environmental hazards have been removed. It is obtained from survival curve data and represents the point where percent survival reaches zero. In Fig. 2-1, MLSP would be about 100 years. In human beings and in a few other mammalian species (largely mice, rats, and a few primate species) where MLSP has been estimated under a wide range of environmental hazard conditions, MLSP has been found to be remarkably constant and independent of the 50 percent survival of the population. In addition, comparative survival data of different mammalian species living in captivity, where most environmental hazards are eliminated, have shown that the different MLSPs that are found are largely independent of nutritional differences and other minor environmental factors.[4,8,9] Thus, MLSP appears to be largely a genetic characteristic of a species, and 50 percent survival is largely a characteristic of both environmental hazards and a species' innate MLSP.

The *aging rate of an organism* generally refers to its overall average rate of loss of general physiological health or vigor. Specific biological functions that determine the general health status of an animal are found to decrease at widely different rates among the various mammalian species. The limited amount of comparative data available on the biological aging rates of different mammalian species having different MLSPs indicates that an inverse correlation exists between these two parameters.[4] That is, species having higher MLSPs also have lower biological aging rates of most of their common physiological characteristics. These comparative

data have led to the conclusions that mammalian species (1) age qualitatively in a similar manner, (2) undergo wide differences in biological aging rates, and (3) have an inverse correlation of their biological aging rate with MLSP.[4,9,10] Thus, MLSP appears to reflect reasonably well the physiological aging rate of an organism, and it is accordingly generally used in this manner for comparative purposes.

LONGEVITY IN THE WILD AND IN CAPTIVITY

Typical survival curves for species living in the wild or in their natural ecological niche are found to be declining exponential curves rather than the squared sigmoidal curves, as is typical for animals living in captivity and for present-day human populations.[2,3] A comparison of the known aging rate (or MLSP) of a species and its probability of survival in the wild indicates that few individuals in the wild ever reach the chronological age where their biological performance is seriously affected by biological aging. In addition, survival data for birds, small rodents, fish, and a few nonhuman primate species in the wild indicate that their mortality rate is inversely correlated with their MLSP.

A similar case is found for the human where, for most of human history, percentage survival also followed an exponentially declining curve. Survival values in different historical epochs (Table 2-1) show that, until recent times, by age 30 to 40 years half the population had died; the MLSP has, however, remained close to 100 years, as would be expected if human beings had not changed significantly in their species characteristic aging rate.[7,12,13]

TABLE 2-1
Human Mortality Rate under Different Environmental Conditions

Time Period	Approximate Age at 50% Survival, Year	Approximate Maximum Life Span Potential, Year
Wurm (about 60,000–30,000 years ago)	29	69–77
Upper Paleolithic (about 30,000–12,000 years ago)	32	95
Mesolithic (about 12,000–10,000 years ago)	31	95
Neolithic Anatolian (about 10,000–8000 years ago)	38	95
Classic Greece (1100 B.C.–1 A.D.)	35	95
Classic Rome (753 B.C.–476 A.D.)	32	95
England (1276 A.D.)	48	95
England (1376–1400)	38	95
United States (1900–1902)	61.5	95
United States (1950)	70.0	95
United States (1970)	72.5	95

SOURCE: Some of the data taken from Deevey.[11]

In natural populations in the wild, few individuals live to the age at which senescence begins to seriously lower performance capacity. However, the comparatively recent increase in the 50 percent survival for humans from about 30 to 40 years to the present value of about 70 years without a corresponding increase in MLSP has resulted in a substantial increase in the percentage of individuals over the age of 30 to 40 years that are in various phases of declining health and vigor due to biological aging processes. It is apparent that modern

human populations are living older longer—not *younger* longer.

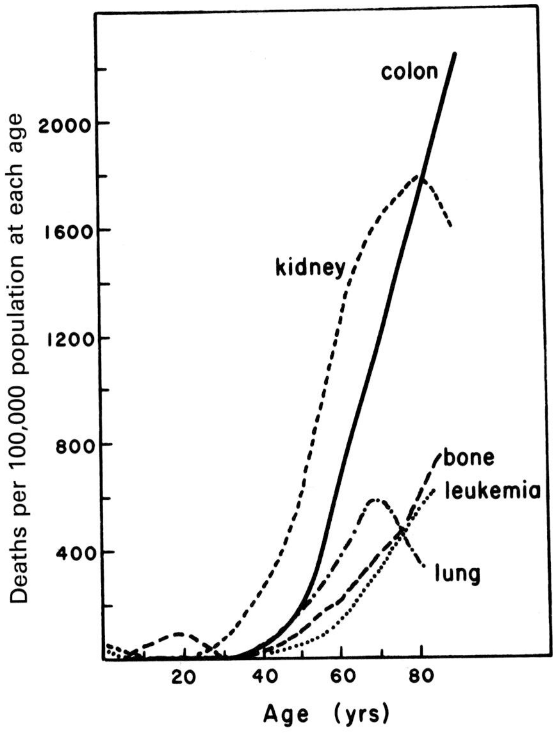

Aging to the extent we find it in today's population is clearly not an effect of natural selection but an artifact of our culture and civilization by its success in lowering exogenous environmental hazards. Cross-sectional studies of human populations suggest that humankind has evolved the capacity to maintain optimum health and vigor up to the age of 30 to 40 years before decline becomes evident. It is therefore significant that this age level was the normal life span of most individuals for most of human history. This inference is supported also by observing the time-dependent onset frequencies of various types of human dysfunctions and diseases. For example, in Fig. 2-2 it is seen that deaths due to a number of different types of cancer do not increase significantly until the age of about 30 to 40 years.[14,15] In different species, this same age-dependent onset frequency curve is found, but where rate of increase is inversely related to a species' MLSP. Thus, probability of cancer is not only age-dependent but also aging rate–dependent. Such data suggest a possible common mechanism for many different types of cancer with those processes causing aging.

The characteristic aging rate of a species appears to represent that value at which a further decrease would provide no significant advantage in species' survival (as opposed to individual survival) or reproductive value. Take, for example, the field mouse, which has an MLSP of about 3 years. The aging process for this species runs at such a rate that general performance is not significantly affected until it reaches the age of about 1 year. However, in the wild, few of these mice ever reach the age of 1 year. This is not because old mice are preferentially killed or eliminated by predators. Instead, the exponential-declining nature of their survival curve indicates that the probability of their death remains constant

FIGURE 2-2
Onset frequency of fatal human cancer as a function of age. (*From Kohn.*[14])

throughout their life span and is therefore largely independent of chronological or biological age. Thus, for the field mouse under its natural ecological environmental conditions, there would be little reproductive advantage for this species if it had the biological potential to maintain good health and vigor for, say, 10 years if few individuals rarely survived up to the age of 1 year. This would be particularly true if a biological cost is required to achieve a longer life span (such as higher enzyme levels). Thus, longer life span had no advantage and consequently did not evolve. For many different species, including mammals, fish, and birds, it is generally found that MLSP is inversely related to the intensity of the environmental hazards of their natural ecological niche. Such data help to explain why different MLSPs exist among the various species. Thus, a possible reason why human health begins to decline significantly after the age of 30 to 40 years appears to be simply that human beings through most of their history could not live much past that age, even if aging were completely eliminated, and therefore there was no evolutionary advantage to evolve mechanisms to reduce the aging rate further.

A major factor, then, that appears to have influenced the MLSP of mammalian species is the intensity of that species' natural environmental hazards in which it evolved. In this sense, MLSP appears to be an independently evolving characteristic of a species and not a byproduct of longevity-related properties. A species' MLSP appears to have evolved through the principles of natural selection for the purpose of reducing senescence from the population to an insignificant level. This is why one seldom finds old or senescent animals in the wild, only in captivity.

These comparative data counter the concept that aging evolved as a positive selective characteristic. For example, aging has been proposed to be the result of specific aging or death genes or of a genetic program of aging for the good of the species, such as removing the old to make room for the young[2,16–18] or for evolutionary selection to operate. Our analysis indicates, however, that there appears to be no need for a positive endogenous means to have evolved to cause the senescence or death of an organism in view of the normally intense natural hazards that appear always to have existed. In fact, the major problem for most species is survival—not too much survival. In this regard, no beneficial biological function of aging or senescence has ever been demonstrated for any organism.

These results have led to the important conclusion that if aging is not somehow an active or positive selective characteristic, then its cause must be passive in nature. That is, aging is the result of living. Examples would be normal by-products of development or metabolism having short-term benefits but long-term aging effects. Furthermore, instead of aging genes or a genetic program of aging, it appears that longevity genes or a

genetic program of longevity has evolved as the positive characteristic on which natural selection has operated.[10,19] In this regard, MLSP does not appear to have been limited to further increases by some intrinsic biological inadequacy but by lack of selective pressure. Taking this viewpoint, the reason the field mouse has an MLSP of only 3 years does not appear to be a result of some type of inherent biological limitation which somehow prevents this species from having a much higher MLSP but simply because a higher MLSP would not improve its reproductive or its survival value.

EVOLUTION OF LONGEVITY IN PRIMATE SPECIES

Primate species have MLSPs ranging from about 10 to 13 years for the tree shrews to about 95 to 115 years for humans (Table 2-2). The human being clearly has the highest MLSP of all primate species and indeed of all mammalian species. Comparative physiological and pathological data indicate that the qualitative nature of aging processes in primates is remarkably similar. We can therefore estimate that a difference of about eightfold in the aging rate of the same types of aging processes exists within the primate family. This eightfold difference in aging rates among the living primate species has evolved from a single common ancestral species over the last 70 million years. Thus, MLSP clearly evolved during primate evolution, where the complex qualitative nature of aging processes appear to be remarkably uniform and independent of MLSP.

It is clear that aging processes are highly complex and involve much of the genetic and biochemical characteristics of an organism. It is not obvious, however, what the genetic or biochemical complexities may be which govern aging rates. However, by estimating how fast a given primate characteristic has evolved, it is possible to assess the genetic and biological complexity involved in determining this particular species' characteristics. This evolutionary approach has been taken to estimate the genetic and biological complexity of the processes involved in governing human longevity.[20,23]

The basis of such a study is dependent on an estimation of MLSPs of extinct primate species. MLSP can be estimated for living mammalian species by knowing only their body and brain weights.[9,22] Representative calculations are shown in Table 2-2. Because MLSP can be reasonably estimated for living primate species and indeed for all mammalian species by use of this formula, it was considered reasonable that MLSP could also be estimated for extinct species by this same formula.

By utilizing estimates of brain and body weights taken from the fossils of extinct primate species, MLSP has been calculated for about 20 extinct primate species.[20,23] The results indicated that MLSP has steadily increased during the evolution of the primate species.[20]

TABLE 2-2
Prediction of Maximum Life Span Potential for Some Common Mammalian Species

Common Name	Cranial Capacity, cm²	Body Weight, kg	Maximum Life Span Potential, Year	
			Observed*	Predicted†
Nonprimate Species				
Pigmy shrew	0.11	0.0053	1.5	1.8
Field mouse	0.45	0.0226	3.5	3.2
Opossum	7.65	5.0	7.0	5.8
Mongolian horse	587	260	46	38
Camel	570	450	30	33
Cow	423	465	30	27
Giraffe	680	529	34	35
Elephant (India)	5045	2347	70	89
Mountain lion	154	54	19	23
Domestic dog	79	13.4	20	21
Primate Species				
Tree shrew	4.3	0.275	7	7.7
Marmoset	9.8	0.413	15	12
Squirrel monkey	24.8	0.63	21	20
Rhesus monkey	106	8.7	29	27
Baboon	179	16	36	33
Gibbon	104	5.5	32	30
Orangutan	420	69	50	41
Gorilla	550	140	40	42
Chimpanzee	410	49	45	43
Human beings	1446	65	95	92

*These data from Cutler.[20,21]
†The equation used to calculate maximum life span potential (MLSP) was formulated by Sacher[22] and is
$MLSP = (brain\ wt,\ g)^{0.636} (body\ wt,\ g)^{-0.225}$ (see Refs. 9, 22).

A similar result has been found for nonprimate mammalian species.[21] Along the hominid ancestral-descendant sequence leading to the human, MLSP was found to increase at an ever-increasing rate over the past 70 million years. The increase in MLSP found for the hominid species over a 1.5-million-year period is shown in Fig. 2-3. A maximum rate of about 14 years of increased MLSP per 100,000 years was found to occur about 100,000 years ago. Shortly after this period of hominid evolution, the rate of increase of MLSP suddenly dropped to zero with the appearance of *Homo sapiens* for reasons yet to be fully explained.

This rate of increase of MLSP during hominid evolution is unusually high compared with other biological characteristics and has some far-reaching implications as to the genetic and biological complexity of the functions governing the intrinsic aging rate of the human.[20,23] If the qualitative nature of aging in the different living primates is indeed as similar as it appears to be, then this similarity is also likely to hold for the different extinct primates. Thus, the increase in MLSP, as was predicted by these calculations, would imply a uniform decrease in the aging rate of most physiological functions, resulting in a uniform prolongation of general health and vigor.

A number of different factors influence how fast a given biological characteristic can evolve. Some of these factors are the number of individuals in the evolving population, the genetic mutational load that can be tolerated in the germ cells, and the intrinsic mutation rate of the germ cells. Other limiting factors are the many possible biological trade-offs that frequently exist between the gain of one characteristic and the loss of another. However, one of the most limiting factors is the number of genes involved or the number of genetic alterations required in determining a characteristic, the slower this characteristic would be expected to evolve.

On calculating an upper limit of how many genetic alterations are likely to have occurred during the evolution of longevity in the hominid species 100,000 years ago, it was estimated as an upper limit that about one alteration per gene, making up 0.6 percent of the genome, was involved.[23] This represents a considerable amount of genetic change, but clearly the biological basis governing the human aging rate does not appear to involve most of the genes in the organism, and it also does not appear to be as complex as the aging process per se. Instead, the human life span appears to be dependent on the expression of a relatively small fraction of the total number of genes in the cell. This and other comparative evidence had led to the prediction that genes exist which

FIGURE 2-3

Rate of increase in longevity (maximum life span MLSP) along the hominid ancestral-descendant sequence leading to the human. ○, MLSP; ●, rate of change in MLSP per million years. *(From Cutler.[23])*

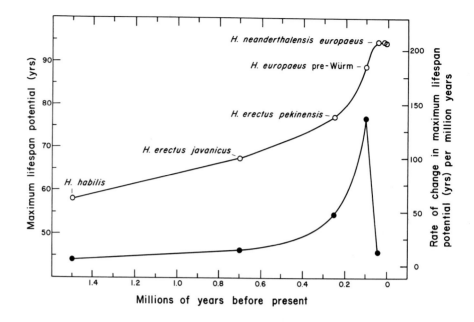

have unusually high influence on determining MLSP. Such genes are called *longevity-determinant genes.*

This result contrasts to another hypothesis in which human longevity is predicted to depend on the processes causing or resulting in aging and is the result of complex interactions of most of the genes and/or biological processes of the organism. This high level of complexity is probably true for the aging processes, which are indeed extraordinarily complex, but it appears now that biochemically separate and far less complex processes may be involved in governing the human life span as well as the life span of other primate and nonprimate mammalian species.

Genetic and biochemical studies concerning the mechanisms of speciation are consistent with these findings.[24-27] Mammalian species are found to be remarkably similar to one another, from the molecular to the physiological levels. For example, no major cellular or biochemical differences have yet been identified between human and chimpanzee; nevertheless a twofold difference exists in their aging rates.[20,25] In addition, the rate of morphological changes leading to the appearance of new species appears to be independent of the rate of accumulation of DNA mutations or of the appearance of new proteins. Instead, these changes correlated best with the changes in concentrations of previously existing enzymes. These types of studies have led to the concept that speciation may be the result of a difference in timing and the extent of expression of a common set of structural genes found in all mammalian species. Thus, speciation may involve genetic changes involving mainly regulatory genes that regulate the timing and degree of expression of structural genes.[28,29]

This model of speciation fits well with the genetic processes that appear to govern species' longevity. Longevity-determinant genes would exist that are similar in all mammalian species, including human beings, and MLSP would be largely a result of differences in the timing and extent of expression of these longevity-determinant genes as controlled by a relatively few regulatory genes. Thus, the genetic basis governing longevity and the general health maintenance of the entire mammalian organism may be largely governed by biological processes that are orders of magnitude less complex than the diseases and other dysfunctions commonly associated with aging.[12,23,28,29] According to this model, human beings would not be expected to have qualitative biochemical or tissue differences to account for their unusually long life span, but simply more or less of the same components existing in all mammalian species. Experimental work in testing this hypothesis is currently under way in a number of laboratories, searching for potential longevity-determinant genes using both nonprimate as well as primate species[30] and in selecting for long-lived progeny in *Drosophila* populations.[5,6]

SUMMARY AND CONCLUSION

From a comparative and evolutionary perspective of aging and longevity in the primate species, it appears that key longevity-determinant processes exist which govern the length of time general good health and vigor are to be maintained. This concept is based largely on the extraordinarily high biological similarities that exist between different mammalian species having substantial differences in aging rates and on the evidence that the recent evolution of human longevity appears to have occurred very rapidly. Longevity-determinant processes in different mammalian species may consist of a common set of defense mechanisms protecting the organism against the long-term effects of common types of toxic by-products of metabolism, growth, and development.

Much of the supporting evidence for the existence of longevity-determinant processes is of a preliminary nature, and much more experimental data are required in this relatively new area of research. Nevertheless, this work has opened up a new field of research investigating the biological basis of human longevity. The merit of such research is that if specific longevity-determinant processes do exist, new approaches may become possible in the prevention and treatment of age-related dysfunctions and diseases.

REFERENCES

1. Sacher GA: Longevity, aging and death: An evolutionary perspective. *Gerontologist* 18:112, 1978.
2. Williams GC: Pleiotropy, natural selection, and the evolution of senescence. *Evolution* 11:398, 1957.
3. Medawar PB: *The Uniqueness of the Individual.* London, Methuen, 1957.
4. Cutler RG: Evolutionary biology of aging and longevity in mammalian species, in Johnson JE (ed): *Aging and Cell Function.* New York, Plenum Press, 1984, p 1.
5. Rose MR: The evolution of animal senescence. *Can J Zool* 62:1661, 1984.
6. Luckinbill LS, Graves JL, Reed AH, Koetsawang S: Localizing genes that defer senescence in *Drosophila melanogaster. Heredity* 60:367, 1988.
7. Acsádi G, Nemeskéri J: *History of Human Lifespan and Mortality.* Budapest, Akadémiai Kiadó, 1970.
8. Finch CE: Comparative biology of senescence: Some evolutionary and developmental considerations, in *Animal Models for Biomedical Research* IV. Washington, National Academy of Sciences, 1971, p 47.
9. Sacher GA: Life table modification and life prolongation, in Finch CE, Hayflick L (eds): *Handbook of the Biology of Aging.* New York, Van Nostrand Reinhold, 1977, p 582.
10. Cutler RG: Transcription of reiterated DNA sequence classes throughout the life span of the mouse, in Strehler BL (ed): *Advances in Gerontology Research.* New York, Academic Press, 1972, vol 4, p 219.
11. Deevy ES: The human population. *Sci Am* 203:195, 1960.
12. Cutler RG: Evolutionary biology of senescence, in Behnke JA, Finch CE, Moment GB (eds): *The Biology of Aging.* New York, Plenum Press, 1978, p 311.
13. Cutler RG: Evolution of human longevity, in Borek C, Fenoglio CM, King DW (eds): *Advances in Pathobiology 7. Aging, Cancer and Cell Membranes.* New York, Thieme-Stratton, 1980, p 43.
14. Kohn RR: *Principles of Mammalian Aging.* Englewood Cliffs, NJ, Prentice-Hall, 1978.
15. Dix D, Cohen P: On the role of aging in cancer incidence. *J Theor Biol* 83:163, 1980.
16. Kirkwood TBL, Holliday R: The evolution of aging and longevity. *Proc R Soc Lond (Biol)* 205:531, 1979.
17. Hayflick L: The cellular basis for biological aging, in Finch CE, Hayflick L (eds): *Handbook of the Biology of Aging.* New York, Van Nostrand Reinhold, 1977, p 159.
18. Denckla WE: A time to die. *Life Sci* 16:31, 1975.
19. Sacher GA: Maturation and longevity in relation to cranial capacity in hominid evolution, in Tuttle R (ed): *Antecedents of Man and After,* vol 1: *Primates: Functional Morphology and Evolution.* The Hague, Mouton, 1975, p 419.
20. Cutler RG: Evolution of longevity in primates. *J Hum Evol* 5:169, 1976.
21. Cutler RG: Evolution of longevity in ungulates and carnivores. *Gerontology* 25:69, 1979.
22. Sacher GA: Relation of lifespan to brain and body weight in mammals, in *Ciba Found Colloq Ageing,* Wolstenholme GEW, O'Connor CM (eds): *The Lifespan of Animals.* London, Churchill, 1959, vol 5, p 115.
23. Cutler RG: Evolution of human longevity and the genetic complexity governing aging rate. *Proc Natl Acad Sci USA* 72:4664, 1975.
24. Brown WT: Human mutations affecting aging—A review. *Mech Ageing Dev* 9:325, 1979.
25. King MC, Wilson AC: Evolution at two levels in humans and chimpanzees. *Science* 188:107, 1976.
26. Wilson AC et al: Biochemical evolution. *Annu Rev Biochem* 46:573, 1977.
27. Wilson AC: Gene regulation in evolution, in Ayala FJ (ed): *Molecular Evolution.* Sunderland, Mass, Sinauer Associated, 1976, p 225.
28. Cutler RG: Longevity is determined by specific genes: Testing the hypothesis, in Adelman, RC, Roth GS (eds): *Testing the Theories of Aging.* Boca Raton, Fla, CRC Press, 1982, p 25.
29. Cutler RG: Antioxidants, aging and longevity, in Pryor WA (ed): *Free Radicals in Biology.* New York, Academic Press, 1984, vol. 6, p 371.
30. Cutler RG: Aging and oxygen radicals, in Taylor AE, Matalon S, Ward PA (eds): *Physiology of Oxygen Radicals.* Bethesda, Md, American Physiological Society, 1986, p 251.

Chapter 3

GENETICS OF HUMAN DISEASE, LONGEVITY, AND AGING

George M. Martin and Mitchell S. Turker

The physician may be called upon to respond to a variety of questions concerning the relationships between human genetics and the pathobiology of aging. While some questions are of purely theoretical interest, others have important implications for patient management. In this review, we shall deal with examples of both categories of questions. We shall begin with an overview of some basic issues regarding genetics and aging, several of which are dealt with, from different points of view, in other chapters. This overview will lead naturally into a discussion of the human progeroid syndromes.

Although most of this chapter is concerned with the effects of aging on human *somatic cells*, we shall conclude with a brief consideration of the clinically and biologically important topic of the effects of parental age upon reproductive performance, in which the focus is upon qualitative aspects of the *germ line*.

A major thesis of this chapter is that, to a considerable extent, future progress in geriatric medicine is likely to be coupled to progress in basic and medical genetics. A few basic terms of genetics have been defined in the body of the text. For those seeking a more comprehensive glossary, we suggest the works of King and Stansfield[1] and Rieger et al.[2]

SOME BASIC CONSIDERATIONS OF GENETICS AND AGING

MAXIMUM LIFE SPAN POTENTIAL AS A CONSTITUTIONAL FEATURE OF SPECIATION

When a new species evolves, an array of phenotypic variations appears involving intrinsic or constitutional properties including qualitative and quantitative alterations

in development, maturational structure and function, and the pattern of aging. A given species thus can be characterized by a maximum life span *potential* (MLSP), resulting from the *most* optimal nature–nurture (gene–environment) interaction so far observed for that parameter with large populations of randomly mating individuals. For humans, this potential life span would appear to be at least 115 years.[3] With increasing population size, improvements in disease prevention and management, and increasing genetic and environmental diversity, somewhat greater documented occurrences of maximum longevity may yet be observed under natural conditions. For *Mus musculus* (the common laboratory or house mouse), the MLSP of cohorts of under a thousand or so is of the order of 4 years.[4] Obviously, if we are to understand the genetic basis for such striking differences in life span potential, we shall have to understand the molecular genetic basis of speciation, about which little is known. The immediate concern of the physician, however, is not with *interspecific* genetic differences as the basis of MLSP, but with the genetic contribution to longevity and to age-related disorders within his own species.

HERITABILITY OF LONGEVITY

When one considers the complex interactions of each person's set of genes involved in the determination of life span, combined with multiple differences in environmental factors influencing their expression, it is clear why attempts to examine the heritability of longevity in humans are tenuous at best. Even studies with inbred strains of research mice, whose environment and genetic variability can be reasonably controlled, are confounded by complex survival and disease patterns.[5] How then are we to assess the impact of a single gene, or a given set of genes, on longevity of humans?

A logical approach is to examine aging in monozygotic twins, since their genetic constitutions, with the exception of those genes whose final structures are developmentally regulated (e.g., immunoglobin genes), are identical. A comparison of aging in such twin pairs with dizygotic twin pairs indicated that the intrapair difference in the age of death was smaller for the monozygotic twins than for the dizygotic twins (14.5 vs. 18.6 years). Perhaps the more salient point, however, is the large mean difference in the age of death in both cases,[6,7] suggesting a role for environmental factors. Classic examples of environmental factors influencing aspects of aging in humans include alcohol,[8] smoking,[9] and exposure to sun.[10] In rodents, caloric restriction is known to increase longevity and to delay the onset of age-related diseases.[11] A novel observation of the influence of environment on mortality was that male prisoners in French jails had lower mortality rates for all types of natural deaths than males in the general French population.[12]

A second approach, used at times in this chapter, is to examine in different kindreds the expression of a single mutant allele (an *allele* is simply an alternative form of a gene) associated with an age-related onset of clinical symptoms. This approach has allowed us to conclude that a number of family-specific traits interact with the mutant allele to influence the age of disease onset. This approach, however, offers little information concerning the functions of these heritable traits, although a suggestion by Finch[13] to explain late-onset Huntington's disease is presented later in this chapter.

A third approach is to search for "private markers"[14] in persons with unusual longevities, such as nonagenerians and centenarians. In a recent study of such populations, a positive correlation for HLA-DR1 and a negative correlation for HLA-DRw9 was found.[15] The presence of HLA-DRw9 has been positively correlated with the presence of autoimmune antibodies. The appearance of these antibodies increases as a function of age.[16] A genetic study of purported high-longevity populations in the Georgian Republic of the Soviet Union failed to find any significant deviation in the observed genotypic frequencies from those predicted by the Hardy-Weinberg equation for the red-cell enzyme markers adenylate kinase, esterase D, phosphoglucomutase I, acid phosphotase, 6-phosphogluconate dehydrogenase, glutamate pyruvate transaminase, phosphoglycolate phosphatase, phosphoexose isomerase, and the serum proteins haptoglobin, Gc-component, and transferrin.[17] (The Hardy-Weinberg expression describes the genotypic equilibrium produced by a static gene pool. In a large, randomly mating population, both the gene frequencies and the genotype frequencies are constant from generation to generation in the absence of mutations, migration, or selection.)

A fourth approach is to search for genetic polymorphisms that may be present in families with unusual susceptibility to some age-related alteration. One potential example is genetic variation for the alpha$_1$-antitrypsin locus. This locus codes for a glycoprotein that inhibits neutrophil elastase, a proteolytic enzyme capable of degrading multiple components of connective tissue. Approximately 30 different genetic variants have been described with the normal M type being found at a gene frequency of 0.9. Other variants include S and Z, with gene frequencies of 0.02 to 0.04 and 0.01 to 0.02, respectively. MZ and SZ heterozygotes are prone to develop chronic obstructive pulmonary disease as they age,[14] with a variable age of onset; clinically evident emphysema is commonly not observable until after age 50.[18,19] In the latter study, the oldest apparent heterozygote studied who exhibited pulmonary dysfunction was a 70-year-old male with a positive smoking history.

A final approach attempts to determine the heritability of longevity in nonmammalian model systems.[20] For example, an excellent series of experiments has been carried out with the nematode *Caenorhabditis elegans* in which the component of life span variation due to genetic rather than environmental factors was estimated to be as high as 50 percent and as low as 20 percent. A single mutant locus has been identified which confers a significantly increased longevity. Another interesting system involves maternal inheritance of senescence in the ascomycete fungus *Podospora anserina*. A maternal component for longevity in humans has also been reported.[21,22]

ESTIMATE OF THE NUMBER OF GENETIC LOCI INVOLVED IN AGING IN HUMANS

There have been two general approaches to the question of the number of genetic loci involved in aging in humans. Sacher[23] and Cutler[24] estimated the rates of evolution of MLSP from hominoid precursors. Judging from the known rates of amino acid substitutions in proteins, Sacher concluded: "If on the order of a few hundred loci were involved in the transition from *Australopithecus* to *Homo sapiens*, then a considerably smaller number of genes might be able to effect notable improvements in general vigor or intelligence in an evolutionarily natural way." Cutler concluded: "Assuming 4×10^4 genes per genome, it is predicted that about 250 genes or 0.6% of the total functional genes have received base substitutions leading to one or more adaptive amino-acid changes in 10,000 generations of hominid evolution." These interesting and ingenious estimates suggest that a comparatively small proportion of genes are of crucial importance in modulating life span potential. The relative importance of various potential genetic mechanisms of hominid evolution, however, have not yet been established. It is conceivable that point mutations played a comparatively minor role compared to chromosomal rearrangements.[25–27] The latter have the potential, via position effects, to regulate the extent of expression of many hundreds or thousands of genes.

The second approach involved a determination of the proportion of the known spontaneous genetic variation in man that has the potential to modulate one or more aspects of the senescent phenotype or that involves loci thought to be of significance to the pathobiology of aging.[28] An example of the latter would be the locus controlling the extent of inducibility of aryl hydrocarbon hydroxylase enzymes (mixed function oxidases) which can convert premutagenic and precarcinogenic compounds to proximal mutagens and carcinogens. Examples of loci that have the potential to modulate the rates of development of certain components of the senescent phenotype are given in a later section of this chapter that deals with human progeroid syndromes. It was concluded that the probable upper limit for the proportion of the human genome of relevance to the pathobiology of aging is approximately 7 percent. Assuming an upper limit of about 100,000 informational genes in humans, this would give up to 7000 loci, different alleles of which could differentially modulate the rates of development of particular subsets of the senescent phenotype. The majority of the loci identified, however, certainly could not be assumed to regularly influence major aspects of the phenotype in most individuals. A reasonable crude estimate would be that perhaps only 1 percent of the total might eventually be characterized as major aging genes, giving about 70 such genes.[28] It remains to be seen how far such crude estimates are from reality. It is important to realize, however, that given the number of possible permutations and combinations, even as few as 70 major genes can result in an extraordinarily rich variety of aging phenotypes. Consider the fact, for example, that with the amount of genetic variation already known for the major histocompatibility complex of humans (at least 30 alleles at each of the major [A and B] subloci, 7 or 8 at the C sublocus, and at least 10 at the D region), there is enough information to code for up to a billion unique phenotypes.[29,30] When we add to this equation the vast number of possibilities of different interactions with humanity's ever-changing and enormously varied environment, one has to conclude that no two human beings, even identical twins, have ever aged or will ever age in precisely the same fashion.

SEX DIFFERENCES IN LONGEVITY

There is as yet no evidence that the MLSP of human females is greater than that of human males. The cur-

rently best-accepted longevity record (113 years and 100 days) is, as a matter of fact, held by a male.[3] There is ample evidence, however, that other life-table parameters, such as mean life span and average life expectancy, indicate greater longevity for most females. Early on in life males are at a numerical advantage, with approximately 115 males conceived for each 100 females. By birth, this ratio has dropped to somewhere between 105 and 100 and continues to drop until age 30, at which age the sex ratio is equal.[31] In each successive age group, the surviving female cohort increasingly outnumbers the corresponding surviving male cohort until by age 65, 84 percent of females compared with 70 percent of males are still alive.[32] There are several arguments that indicate an important genetic contribution to this phenomenon which, to an increasing degree, poses serious social problems for the more advanced societies. First of all, preferential survival of the female is observed not only in the United States, but also in all the advanced societies.[32] Such a finding could, of course, be largely attributable to common elements in the environment and lifestyle. This possibility will be addressed at the end of this section. A more persuasive argument is that the bulk of the evidence, although still incomplete,[3] seems to indicate that the female advantage is widespread among the animal kingdom.[33] An even more cogent argument, however, would depend upon documentation that it was not femaleness per se that was correlated with enhanced survival, but rather a sex chromosomal constitution that was *homogametic*. In humans and other mammals, the female is homogametic, having two X chromosomes that segregate during meiosis. The mammalian male is *heterogametic* since he has one X chromosome and one Y chromosome, each of his sperm bearing either one or the other. Thus, the male is at a potential disadvantage, in that sex-linked recessive alleles would be expressed. Although there is good evidence for dosage compensation in the female via inactivation during early development of one of her two X chromosomes,[34] such inactivation is random and clonally inherited so that she is in effect a fine-grained somatic mosaic. Since, on the average, only half of her cells would be transcribing information from the X chromosome bearing a given recessive mutation, many such mutations (for example, the classic hemophilias and a rare sex-linked recessive form of parkinsonism)[35] are in fact not expressed. It is, furthermore, important to note that not *all* X-linked genes are subject to complete inactivation in the human female. A well-documented example is the gene coding for steroid sulfatase,[36,37] a deficiency of which results in a sex-linked skin disorder, ichthyosis vulgaris.

Recent evidence indicates that in mice a particular locus on the inactivated X chromosome may be reactivated during aging.[38] If such observations can be generalized for the case of multiple X-linked loci and other mammalian species (an initial study indicates that it may *not* obtain for a different locus on the human X chromosome),[39] this could create, via abnormal gene dosage, an actual disadvantage for the female.

Differences in longevity have also been attributed to genes located on the Y chromosome. An Amish kindred has been identified in which the men are missing a portion of the long arm of the Y chromosome and outlive their wives by 5 years (82.3 vs. 77.4 years).[31]

The limited data available indicate that there is no dosage compensation for sex-linked loci in avian species.[40] Therefore, one might expect the homogametic sex to exhibit a survival advantage, in that unfavorable recessive alleles would not be expressed (with the reservation that such advantages might be countered, in part, by inappropriate gene expression associated with reactivation). In birds, the male is the homogametic sex. Do male birds thus tend to have greater life spans? If so, then we will have provided an important test of the genetic hypothesis for the female advantage in our species. Most of the old data on this subject are not of much use, as they deal with very small numbers of birds and mainly measure short-term survival.[33] Reasonable, although still incomplete data are available for Japanese quail (*Coturnix coturnix japonica*),[41] and these life tables quite clearly point to a substantially greater life span for males.

Finally, it is important to consider that sex differences in longevity reflect a complex interaction of biological, behavioral, and sociocultural characteristics. In societies where men and women share similar lifestyles, such as the society of a kibbutz in Israel, the difference in life span between males and females is lessened.[42] Similarly, it has been shown that the difference in the mean age of death between male and female Seventh-Day Adventists, whose adherents do not smoke and have relatively prudent diets (i.e., low-fat, high-fiber), is relatively small.[43] In both of the above cases, however, the women still outlive the men. Therefore, intrinsic biological differences cannot be ignored. For example, it has been postulated that the more efficient metabolism of lipoproteins by women may be due to their higher levels of estrogen.[44] Combined with differences in lifestyle in most cultures, these biological factors may be critical in determining a shorter life span for men than women. Such differences might include greater male exposure, in some societies, to ethanol[45] and to tobacco smoke.[46] These important issues are dealt with in greater detail elsewhere in this text.

GENE ACTION AND AGING

What might be the mechanisms whereby heredity influences MLSP and the rates of aging in various tissues and organs? Most of what can be said about this most crucial of all gerontological questions remains in the realm of speculation; however, we can certainly begin to see areas in which further research is likely to prove productive.

It is convenient, first of all, to consider two broad domains of gene action—one related to the *development* of the organism and the other related to the *maintenance* of the structural and functional integrity of the mature organism. These two are clearly related, as a failure of proper development of a given system must certainly cause subsequent difficulties for the maintenance system designed for it. Hutchinson-Gilford syndrome, which is described in a later section, may reflect this relationship. Although various genetic systems will be described in this chapter in which apparently normal development is followed by late onset of disease, it should be noted that more than 90 percent of genetic diseases are expressed prior to the onset of puberty.[47] Changes in the rate of development may have played important roles in evolution, as a slowing of this rate, a process sometimes referred to as "fetalization," has been postulated as an important mechanism in the evolution of primates.[48,49]

Genetic control of the kinetics of cellular proliferation must also be considered in the domain of maintenance of structure and function. It is now well-established that cultures of human and other animal diploid somatic cells from embryos and adults undergo a process of clonal attenuation,[50,51] whereby there is a gradual and variable loss of the growth potential of all individual clones of cells. This restriction of growth potential is often referred to as the "Hayflick limit" after the scientist who first quantitatively documented the phenomenon.[52] Such processes can be assumed to be taking place in vivo and must surely be under genetic control. The implication is that differential gene action could lead to differential degrees of cellular reserve and, ultimately, tissue atrophy among various subjects. The situation is surely much more complicated, however. While tissue atrophy is a common observation in senescent mammals, a major aspect of the senescent phenotype is in fact an inappropriate and multifocal *proliferation* of many somatic cell types.[27] It is possible that such age-related hyperplasias play important roles in the pathogenesis of cancer and of atherosclerosis.[27,53]

Most of the current research on gene action and the maintenance of structure and function in adult organisms, however, focuses upon the concept of "longevity assurance genes."[54,55] The function of such genes is presumed to be the maintenance of appropriate gene expression throughout the life span. Thus, those who advocate the free-radical theory of aging[56] would argue that the genes controlling the baseline activities and the efficiency of induction of the enzymes that protect cells from free-radical-mediated injury are of seminal importance. Among these are the genes for cytoplasmic and mitochondrial forms of superoxide dismutase, hydrogen peroxidase, catalase, glutathione peroxidase, and glutathione reductase. Comparable lists of genes can be devised for other theories of aging. For the intrinsic mutagenesis theory,[57] the several DNA-dependent DNA polymerases would be most prominent, since the basic idea is that the enzymes of long-lived organisms copy DNA more faithfully than those of short-lived organisms, thus minimizing the accumulation of somatic mutations. DNA repair enzymes would also figure prominently. For the protein synthesis error-catastrophe theory,[58] the key genes would be those that are responsible for the accuracy of gene transcription and gene translation as well as those that control the synthesis of proteolytic enzymes capable of recognizing and of degrading abnormal proteins. A number of laboratories have now reported the accumulation of abnormal proteins with aging, which is largely attributable to post-transcriptional modifications and to impaired protein degradation[59]; an important role for biosynthetic errors has not been established.[60]

A recent theory has suggested that age-related nonmutational changes in gene expression may be of critical importance,[61] including changes in DNA methylation patterns. Increased DNA methylation has been linked to X-chromosome inactivation and to changes in gene expression for autosomal loci. Therefore, age-related alterations in DNA methylase and a putative mechanism to remove methylated bases may also have important consequences.

An important approach to testing these theories would be to examine the various gene products in detail, comparing those from species of various MLSPs. Moreover, it would be useful to determine if such gene products are altered (i.e., mutant) or if they exhibit normal amino acid sequences with abnormal post-translational modifications. A study such as this should also determine if the gene products are expressed at appropriate times and in appropriate cell types. Another approach is to investigate the pathogenetic mechanisms responsible for putative progeroid and "antiprogeroid" syndromes. We shall now turn our attention to certain of these entities in humans.

GENETIC SYNDROMES THAT MODULATE ASPECTS OF THE SENESCENT PHENOTYPE

PROGEROID SYNDROMES

The suffix *-oid* (a term borrowed from the Greek language meaning "like" or "resembling") is among the most venerable and popular linguistic tools of pathologists, who use it to communicate their uncertainty regarding a diagnostic or descriptive term. For example, Virchow coined the term *amyloid* ("like starch") because

such tissue deposits stain purple when treated with iodine and sulfuric acid.[62] To what extent the various *progeroid* ("like premature senility") syndromes prove useful as model systems for various aspects of the senescent phenotype, or as probes of the pathogenesis of various age-related disorders, awaits further research. However, any clues which can provide a molecular understanding of unusual pathways—leading, for example, to accumulations of lipofuscins, amyloids, or paired helical filaments—can provide us with the keys to the discovery of the usual pathways.

Segmental Progeroid Syndromes

While there is no single hereditary disorder that brings forward in time all of the signs and symptoms of aging, there are several which appear to involve multiple aspects; hence the term *segmental progeroid syndrome*.[28]

WERNER'S SYNDROME Werner's syndrome (WS) represents an important segmental progeroid syndrome because of its potential to link a specific biochemical lesion with the pathogenesis of several of the major age-related disorders of humans including cancer, osteoporosis, diabetes, and cataracts.[63,64] An extensive compilation of research concerning WS was published in 1985.[64]

In contrast to the Hutchinson-Gilford "progeria of childhood" syndrome (discussed later), the Mendelian pattern of inheritance in WS is well-understood.[65–67] Since it is an autosomal recessive, WS is highly likely to be attributable to a deficiency of a single enzyme, as is the case with typical recessive orders of metabolism.[68] As is the case with other recessive disorders, the frequency of consanguineous marriages is elevated among the parents of patients with WS. Since the proportion of such marriages is inversely related to the frequency of the recessive genes in the population, calculations can be made of the frequencies of WS heterozygotes (about 1 to 5 per thousand) and homozygotes (about 1 to 25 per million).[65] For the total Japanese population (about 110 million), a theoretical calculation has been made of 1000 to 5000 total cases, although only 162 living cases were documented between 1961 and 1982.[67]

As noted above, heterozygotes show no evidence of expression, save for the possibility of premature graying of the hair and a recent suggestion of an increased susceptibility to cancer; these are far from established, however. Homozygotes appear to be normal at birth and during childhood, although probably they tend to be smaller than unaffected sibs. A few patients, however, have exhibited symptoms such as graying hair, skin changes, and cataracts as early as 6 to 8 years of age.[67] The first obvious signal of a clinical problem is the failure to undergo the usual adolescent growth spurt. Graying of the hair, some loss of hair, and atrophic changes of the skin (sometimes described as being similar to scleroderma) appear during the early twenties. The voice takes on a peculiar high-pitched, weak, and squeaky quality, the cause of which is not well-understood but which may be associated with atrophy and/or hypoplasia of the laryngeal skeletal muscles and/or other laryngeal structures; the morphology of the latter can vary substantially, however. By about age 30, the patient may consult an ophthalmologist because of visual symptoms. The combination of short stature, gray hair, atrophic skin, high-pitched voice, and cataracts should prompt the ophthalmologist to make a diagnosis of WS, but unfortunately such a diagnosis is seldom thought about. A great deal more research is needed to define better the type of cataracts associated with WS, but it is thought that there is a predilection for posterior and subcapsular localizations not typical of ordinary senile cataracts. By the mid-thirties, skin atrophy and an apparently disproportionate loss of subcutaneous fat of the limbs is often associated with chronic leg ulcers. Diabetes mellitus and progressive osteoporosis (especially of the distal limbs) begin to be evident. X rays show soft-tissue calcifications; these result from deposits in peripheral arteries (medical calcinosis), tendons, ligaments, and various soft tissues. There is also a striking degree of calcification of heart valve rings. Fertility for both males and females is reduced; this reduction is associated with severe hyalinization of seminiferous tubules in the male (the histological picture being that of normal senescent males) and loss of primary follicles in the ovaries of the female. Death typically occurs in the late forties from either degenerative vascular disease (atherosclerosis, arteriolosclerosis, and medial calcinosis) or neoplasia. Estimates of the frequency of neoplasms among patients have varied from 5.6 percent to 10 percent. The neoplasms may include common age-related cancers, such as carcinoma of the prostate and carcinoma of the colon, but there is a disproportionately higher frequency of tumors of mesenchymal origin and of rare types of neoplasms. Meningiomas appear to be particularly frequent. It will be of great importance to confirm and extend a report of a relatively high incidence of cancer among sibs of the Japanese patients with WS (4.2 percent versus an estimate of 0.11 percent for the general Japanese populations).[69] A final clinical-pathological point to be stressed is that there is no clinical or histopathological evidence of accelerated aging within the central nervous system (CNS).[28]

There are several reasons for believing that WS predominantly results from an abnormality in the metabolism of mesenchymal cells:

1. A great deal of the pathology can be explained by a primary involvement of mesenchymal derivatives.
2. Cultures of fibroblast-like cells from the skin of WS

patients have sharply diminished replicative potentials in comparison to age-matched controls[70]; they may also exhibit an intrinsically diminished rate of DNA synthesis.[71,72] In addition to an increased non-cycling fraction in WS fibroblast cultures, there is an increase in the duration of S-phase when compared with normal fibroblasts. Moreover, the distance between replicon units is increased, suggesting a decrease in the frequency of replicon initiation.[73]

3. There is an excessive urinary excretion of hyaluronic acid and increased amounts of glycosaminoglycans in cultured cells.[74]

The fact that there is an accelerated aging of these somatic cells in vitro, of course, suggests that the basic biochemical defect is expressed in cultured cells. A thorough cytogenetic analysis of fibroblast cultures from WS patients has prompted the classification of WS as a chromosomal instability syndrome.[75] These cells show a propensity to undergo reciprocal translocations, deletions, and inversions, resulting in a large variety of pseudodiploid cells (variegated translocation mosaicism). The distribution of the chromosomal breaks responsible for these various lesions is not random, there being several characteristic "hot spots" within the chromosomes. Similar rearrangements have also been reported in B-cell-derived lymphoblastoid cells lines.[76] There is also evidence that such rearrangements occur in skin fibroblasts and lymphocytes in vivo.[77]

A recent finding of potential importance is that SV-40-transformed WS fibroblast cell lines exhibit a mutator phenotype when compared with similarly transformed fibroblasts from non-WS persons.[78] The relationship between this mutator phenotype and chromosomal instability remains to be determined, but it is quite possible that they are both a result of the primary WS defect. This appears to be the case for Bloom's syndrome (BS), which has been associated with a deficiency in DNA ligase I.[79,80] BS patients are characterized by low birth weight, telangiectatic cutaneous lesions, immunodeficiency, and a predisposition to develop a variety of cancers.[81,82] At the cellular level, BS is characterized by a mutator phenotype,[83,84] chromosomal instability (expressed as a high frequency of sister-chromatid exchange), and a reduced growth potential in vitro. The common cellular phenotypes observed in WS and BS raise the possibility that the WS genetic defect may also involve a DNA-replication or repair-related enzyme.

HUTCHINSON-GILFORD SYNDROME[85,86] Hutchinson and Gilford were both pediatricians, which should help us to remember that the syndrome they described was "progeria of childhood," in contrast to the generally later onset of WS; but often Hutchinson-Gilford syndrome is simply referred to as "progeria." In addition to quite clear-cut clinical-pathological differences between these two progeroid syndromes, there is evidence that they also have different Mendelian modes of inheritance. In contrast to the situation in WS, there is no evidence of consanguinity among parents of children with progeria, and there is a low frequency of reoccurrence in families. Moreover, fathers of patients with progeria tend to be older than expected. These three facts suggest that progeria is most likely a sporadic autosomal dominant.[86] It is apparently even rarer than WS, with a frequency in the general population of approximately 1 in 8 million.[86] As of 1986 there were only 20 known living cases of progeria. These patients and their families meet for one week each year in a gathering sponsored by the Sunshine Foundation of Philadelphia.

Patients at birth are usually considered to be normal infants, which sets progeria apart from the "neonatal progeroid syndrome" (Wiedemann-Rautenstrauch syndrome) in which depletion of subcutaneous fat, sparse hair, small size, and progeroid facies are quite obvious at birth. In Hutchinson-Gilford patients, profound growth retardation is evident within a year after birth, and there is so little hair and subcutaneous fat over the scalp that the scalp veins become remarkably prominent; patients have been described as having a "plucked-bird" appearance. Nonetheless, patients have normal to above-normal intelligence. Dentition is delayed and abnormal and the bones become demineralized; particularly striking is the thinning and partial resorption of the distal ends of the clavicles and the distal phalanges. Coxa valga results in a "horse-riding" stance and a shuffling, wide-based gait. The skin is sclerodermatous and the nails are dystrophic. The voice is weak and high-pitched. As in WS, there is no evidence of CNS pathology. Despite an initial report to the contrary, semiquantitative studies of the extent of lipofuscin pigment accumulation in the CNS show no differences from controls. A significant increase (approximately 14-fold) in the excretion of hyaluronic acid has been reported in patients. Hyaluronic acid is believed to inhibit angiogenesis, whereas its degradation products are believed to promote it; it was suggested that this alteration may be critical in the pathogenesis of the progeria phenotype.[86]

Geriatricians are justifiably skeptical of the designation of "progeria," as the clinical picture is more that of a failure of development than of an accelerated postmaturational failure. However, the accompanying atherosclerosis, often leading to myocardial infarction and death in the early teens,[87] makes this syndrome a high priority for intensive research. As far as can be discerned, the histological picture and distribution cannot be distinguished from the usual age-related atherosclerosis. Other cardiovascular degenerative changes include calcification of heart rings, cardiomyopathy, arteriolosclerosis, and arterial aneurysms.[87,88] As mentioned

earlier, Hutchinson-Gilford syndrome might be an example of a failure to develop normally compounded by a subsequent failure of maintenance systems.

A variety of research has been undertaken on the assumption that the biochemical lesion of progeria is expressed in cultivated somatic cells. There is in fact some evidence for a relatively decreased replicative life span of skin fibroblast-like cells, but this does not yet have firm statistical underpinning comparable to the studies performed on cells from patients with WS. An increase in hyaluronic acid excretion in cultured cells, perhaps due to a decrease in degradation, has been reported.[86] Fibroblast-like cells in culture also exhibit a six- to ninefold increase in tropoelastin production (both at the protein and mRNA levels), further evidence of a biochemical aberration in mesenchymal cells.[89]

ATAXIA TELANGIECTASIA[90–92] Patients with ataxia telangiectasia (AT), an autosomal, recessively inherited disorder, develop a progressive cerebellar ataxia in early childhood and are typically confined to a wheelchair by the time of adolescence. Whereas ordinary human subjects exhibit a gradual loss of Purkinje's cells as they age, with about a 25 percent loss by the tenth decade,[93] this cell loss is vastly accelerated in AT patients. Other clinical features include additional degenerative neuropathological changes, including cerebral cortical cell loss, immunological defects, premature graying of hair, a high propensity to develop tumors, increased levels of serum alpha-fetoprotein, and glucose intolerance.[92] Most AT patients who do not die from cancer will eventually succumb to chronic pulmonary disease.[94] Exposed skin and skin subjected to friction undergo premature atrophic changes, together with hyper- and hypopigmentation and telangiectasia. Hypogonadism is striking, with depletion of ovarian follicles and testicular atrophy. Consistent with the immunological deficiency, the thymus is described as hypoplastic or even absent. Approximately 10 to 15 percent of AT patients develop cancers, of which approximately half are lymphoreticular neoplasms and leukemia.[95] Chromosomal instability in lymphocytes is another hallmark of AT, with translocations involving chromosomes 7 and 14 being particularly noted in AT leukemias.[92]

Although AT is listed as an autosomal recessive, some aspects of the phenotype may be expressive in heterozygotes, thereby indicating a degree of autosomal dominance. Evidence has been presented indicating that heterozygotes have an increased susceptibility to develop neoplasms, and it has been suggested that such individuals may comprise more than 5 percent of all persons dying from cancer before the age of 45.[96] AT heterozygotes also appear to have an increased incidence of ischemic heart disease at comparatively young ages.[94]

The clinical observation that homozygotes are extremely susceptible to ionizing radiation has led to an active line of research aimed at elucidating possible deficiency in an enzyme necessary for the repair of radiation-induced damage. Although cultured cells from these patients exhibit enhanced sensitivity to x-ray damage, the underlying enzymatic deficiency for AT has not been determined. The possibility exists that a complex pathway may be involved for the AT phenotype, such as a recombinational pathway.[97] Painter and Young have proposed that the mutation(s) may involve structural abnormalities in the packaging of DNA.[98] The fact that there are at least five complementation groups[99,100] indicates that at least five different genes are involved and is consistent with the idea of a complex pathway whose function is disrupted in AT.

DOWN'S SYNDROME Down's syndrome (DS) was listed as a leading candidate as a segmental progeroid syndrome,[28] with symptoms including premature graying of hair and hair loss, and premature increases in tissue lipofuscin, neurodegenerative changes,[101] autoimmunity, degenerative vascular disease, and cataracts.[86] Perhaps the most striking observation concerning DS is that 96 to 98 percent of autopsied patients over the age of 40 demonstrate the characteristic changes of senile dementia of Alzheimer's type (SDAT), i.e., neuritic plaques with amyloid cores and neurofibrillary tangles. This morphological relationship has been strengthened by the chemical demonstration that the amyloid fibrils found in the affected brains of both disorders are identical.[102] Age-matched control patients with non-DS forms of mental retardation exhibited a frequency of plaques and tangles of 14 percent (a surprisingly high figure, but still some sevenfold less than that observed in DS subjects).[103] Despite the morphological appearance of SDAT, however, progressive intellectual deterioration is not necessarily observed in elderly DS patients.[104,105] Such deterioration, however, might be difficult to document.

The underlying genetic defect for DS is trisomy for at least a portion of the long arm of chromosome 21 (band 21q22).[86] The overall incidence of DS is approximately 1 in 700 to 1000 live births. The risk of progeny with DS rises steeply with increasing maternal age, beginning at around age 35. After the age of 45 the incidence can reach as high as 1 in 35 births.[16]

To better understand the biochemical expression of DS, investigators have mapped a number of specific genes and anonymous DNA fragments to chromosome 21.[86] This includes the cytosolic form of superoxide dismutase (SOD), the DS and SDAT form of amyloid, and the S100 calcium-binding protein. This latter gene maps to band 21q22.[106] Several hypotheses have been proposed to explain the relationship between trisomy 21 and DS, most speculating a disruption in normal gene

activity by an increase in expression in a subset of genes.[107] An intriguing hypothesis is that the 50 percent increase in SOD results in an increase in hydrogen peroxide formation and therefore an elevated level of free radicals. This hypothesis predicts an increase in the inducible enzyme glutathione peroxidase in the cells of DS patients, which has in fact been observed.[108] A novel approach to studying the relationship between increased expression for chromosome 21 gene products and specific DS phenotypes is to overexpress one or more of its genes in transgenic mice. This approach has now been implemented for the case of SOD[109]; the transgenic animals have not yet lived long enough to provide a full evaluation of the effects of such changes in gene dosage.

OTHER SEGMENTAL PROGEROID SYNDROMES
Martin has listed other hereditary disorders deserving of further investigation as models for the study of genetic control of multiple aspects of the senescent phenotype.[28] Two of them (familial cervical lipodysplasia and the Seip syndrome) are of special interest because they were initially identified as a result of a deliberate search for conditions characterized by aberrations in the amounts and/or distributions of adipose tissue.

In addition to DS, two other constitutional aneuploidies (the Klinefelter and Turner syndromes) were cited as exhibiting multiple features suggestive of premature aging, thus underscoring the importance of abnormalities in gene dosage. Myotonic dystrophy (Steinert disease) was also mentioned in a list of the 10 leading candidates of segmental progeroid syndromes. The mapping of this disorder to chromosome 19 may facilitate the identification of linked DNA probes.[110]

Unimodal Progeroid Syndromes

Equally important conceptually are a group of hereditary disorders that accelerate predominantly a particular aspect of the senescent phenotype. Investigations of such genetic diseases[111] provide the potential for a more fine-grained analysis of the biochemical genetic basis of various aspects of aging. We can give here only a few examples.

FAMILIAL HYPERCHOLESTEROLEMIA[112,113] Familial hypercholesterolemia (FH) results from a variety of mutations (including unequal crossing over, deletion, duplication, and base-pair substitution) in the gene coding for the cell surface receptor controlling the degradation of low-density lipoprotein (LDL).[114] The structure of the LDL receptor gene, which contains several repeated regions, has contributed to the marked diversity of mutant genotypes. Although not usually thought about in the context of accelerated aging, it is apparent that the predominant feature of this disorder, premature atherosclerosis, would qualify it as a unimodal progeroid syndrome. Quantitative evidence that atherosclerosis can be considered as a marker of aging in humans came from extensive population studies in humans.[53,115] While the rate of increase in the lesions varies substantially among different geographic-ethnic groups, all populations studied so far show steady (typically linear) age-related increments. FH heterozygotes, who are present at a frequency of approximately 1 individual out of 500, exhibit various symptoms in an age-dependent manner. Hypercholesterolemia is present virtually from birth. Arcus corneae and tendon xanthomas appear in the latter part of the second decade, with each being present in about half of the patients by the third decade. Coronary heart disease appears by the fourth decade. Homozygotes are far more severely affected, with all of the above symptoms present in childhood; most die before the age of 30 from myocardial infarction. Therefore, FH is not a true autosomal dominant disease. Homozygotes are simply more severely affected than heterozygotes. FH is likely to serve as a prototype of unimodal progeroid syndromes because of the detailed molecular understanding of its pathogenesis and genetic defects. It is also a model because it has illustrated how an in-depth analysis of a relevant inborn error of metabolism can open up an entire area of cell and molecular biology of crucial importance to gerontology—in this case, the field of lipoprotein receptors and transport.

HEREDITARY AMYLOIDOSIS[62] *Amyloidosis* is a generic term for a heterogeneous group of conditions associated with the multifocal accumulations of various types of polypeptides having certain physical-chemical commonalities. A hallmark of these amyloid proteins is their apple-green appearance when stained with congo red and examined with polarized light. Excluding the common amyloid of SDAT and DS and a distinct form found in cerebral amyloid angiopathy,[116] many of the other described forms of hereditary amyloidosis result from distinct mutations in a single protein (transthyretin). Other amyloid proteins include cystatin C, apolipoprotein, and calcitonin. The genetics of inheritance and clinical manifestations of hereditary mutation in transthyretin will be considered in this section. Other forms of age-related amyloidosis will be considered in another chapter.

Most hereditary forms of amyloidosis are inherited as autosomal dominant diseases with virtually 100 percent penetrance (i.e., all carriers of a single copy of the mutant gene develop some degree of deposition of amyloid in their tissues as they age). The recent identification of DNA markers for specific mutant proteins has allowed the unambiguous identification of both the mutant and wild-type alleles in affected individuals. Since affected homozygotes have not been identified, how-

ever, it cannot yet be stated that hereditary amyloidosis is a true autosomal dominant disease. This form of hereditary amyloidosis is due to one of a variety of amino acid substitutions in the transthyretin protein. This molecule is normally found as a tetramer. Transthyretin has been mapped to chromosome 18.[117] It functions as a transport protein for thyroxin and retinol. It is believed that one or more mutant molecules will allow the molecule to participate in the formation of an amyloid fibril. At least six separate mutant forms of transthyretin have been identified, each having a specific tissue distribution (for summary, see Benson[62]). One specific mutation, leading to a substitution of methionine for valine at position 30, has been observed in certain families in Portugal, Japan, Sweden, Italy, Greece, England, and the United States. A founder effect (i.e., the establishment of a new population by a single individual or a few individuals) has been postulated for the occurrence of the mutation in some of these families. In the affected English and American kindreds, this mutation invariably produces cardiomyopathy, whereas the affected Swedish individuals usually suffer severe kidney disease. In an elegant utilization of the mutant protein sequences, it was possible to deduce novel restriction enzyme sites in some of the mutant transthyretin genes.[118,119] Therefore, molecular probes are now available to allow prenatal detection and carrier determination for some of the affected kindreds.

The transthyretin form of hereditary amyloidosis has been proposed as a model for late-onset genetic disease[62] for several reasons. First, by using the DNA markers to identify children with the mutant form of transthyretin, it has been possible to demonstrate that their tissues are unaffected during childhood. Since penetrance is virtually 100 percent, it is clear that these individuals will eventually become affected. Therefore, age-related events will eventually allow the fibrils to accumulate. In this regard it is useful to recall that a variety of altered proteins are normally found to accumulate with aging.[60] Perhaps this process also contributes to the accumulation of mutant transthyretin molecules. Second, the various mutant forms of transthyretin have different ages of onset in affected individuals, ranging from the twenties (mutation involving position 30) to approximately age 60 (mutation involving position 60). This effect may be partially related to the third and most intriguing observation: the identical mutation at position 30, in addition to having different tissue distributions, will also have different ages of onset in different kindreds. In the Portuguese family, the age of onset will often occur in the twenties,[120] whereas it occurs after age 30 and as late as age 47 in a Japanese family.[121] These latter two observations, combined with the various patterns of tissue distributions, strongly suggest that other family-associated gene products (i.e., "private markers")[14] will interact with the mutant transthyretin to produce this marked heterogeneity of age onset and tissue distribution.

FAMILIAL ALZHEIMER'S DISEASE By 1979 some 50 families had been reported in which there was evidence of a hereditary basis for the emergence of a familial form of dementia of the Alzheimer type (FAD), including 47 families in which there was at least one histologically confirmed case.[122] (The pathology of Alzheimer's disease will be described in a separate chapter.) In many such pedigrees, the best interpretation is that a single autosomal dominant gene segregates, leading to a high probability that dementia will be expressed if the subject bearing the mutant allele lives long enough. Research into the molecular biology and genetics of SDAT and FAD has increased at a rapid rate in the 1980s, leading to a number of significant observations.[123] The gene coding for a protein with properties of a cell membrane receptor, a portion of which forms the amyloid found in the brains of SDAT, FAD, and DS patients, has been cloned and localized to chromosome 21, most likely in the region bordering between 21q21 and 21q22.[124,125] As discussed previously, this region has been implicated in the DS phenotype. For some European pedigrees, the FAD gene has also been localized to chromosome 21,[126] although it does not segregate with the amyloid gene.[125,127] This FAD gene has been tentatively mapped to 22q21. This observation of nonlinkage dashed early hopes that a mutant form of this amyloid gene would prove to be the underlying genetic defect of FAD.

The recent report of five American pedigrees with FAD, all of whom can be traced back to a small region of Russia inhabited by Volga Germans, may provide a unique opportunity to examine a founder effect for FAD.[128] For these pedigrees it is assumed that a single autosomal dominant FAD gene was inherited from a common ancestor. Significantly, the FAD gene(s) in seven Volga German families (two were added since the initial report), as well as seven additional kindreds, was not found to be linked to the chromosome 21q21 region discussed previously.[129] Therefore, there now exists the distinct possibility that FAD may actually represent two or more genetic defects.

Assuming that there is a common FAD gene for the Volga Germans, these families are instructive in demonstrating both heterogeneity and homogeneity of expression for FAD. The age of disease onset was found to range from 50.6 to 63.1 years for the seven families[129]; however, if the age of onset for two outlying families are excluded, the range for mean age of onset becomes 54.3 to 58.0 years. In one family the standard deviation was only one year, indicating a remarkable homogeneity for age of onset. For the seven non-Volga German families examined, the mean age of onset ranged from 41.1 to

77.7 years of age. Until more information is available concerning the nature of the FAD gene(s) in these families, however, it will be difficult to assess the potential interactions between the FAD gene(s) and other familial private markers that might influence expression.

HUNTINGTON'S DISEASE[107,130] Huntington's disease (HD) is a progressive neurodegenerative disorder characterized by both motor abnormalities (chorea and athetosis) and intellectual deterioration. These symptoms result from premature neuronal death, particularly for the neurons of the basal ganglia.[130] Selective, regional neuronal death also occurs during normal aging.[131]

HD is inherited as an autosomal dominant with a mean age of onset between 35 and 44 years.[132] The disease then follows a 10 to 20 year period of progression leading to death. Both juvenile onset (before the age of 20) and very late onset (after 60 years of age) have been reported. Progression of juvenile onset is characteristically rapid, whereas very late onset patients have relatively mild symptoms. Juvenile onset is often associated with paternal inheritance of the HD gene.[13,133] HD has been mapped to chromosome 4 and a diagnostic polymorphic DNA marker linked to the disease has been described.[130] This marker has allowed the unambiguous observation that some HD patients in a large Venezuelan kindred are homozygous carriers. Such patients are clinically indistinguishable from heterozygotes, proof that HD is a true autosomal dominant.[134] This represents the first such demonstration in human subjects.[135] As for the case of FAD, an examination of age-of-onset heterogeneity for HD has determined greater variation between families than within families.[132] These observations led to the conclusion that both the age of onset and age of death for HD patients are partially determined by nonallelic modifying factors. Such factors were also detected in nonaffected siblings.[133] One possibility offered by Finch is that genes that modulate the expression of age-related neural degeneration interact with the HD gene to cause accelerated cell death.[13] This hypothesis predicts that nonaffected siblings of late-onset individuals would show comparatively slow rates of age-related neuronal loss.

ANTIGEROID SYNDROMES

In at least a proportion of cases, once one has identified a genetic locus at which mutation can lead to a progeroid syndrome, there could exist alleles at that locus that lead to comparable *anti*progeroid syndromes. Expression of such genes would conceivably inhibit a particular aging process. "Antioncogenes" (tumor suppressor loci) have been recently discovered which appear to inhibit the formation of specific tumors.[136] For example, it is known that a deficiency of one of a group of proteins involved in the excision repair of DNA following ultraviolet injury to the skin can lead to an accelerated aging of sun-exposed regions of skin, as manifested by severe senile elastosis,[137] basophilic degeneration of collagen,[137] and a spectacular increase in the rates of development of various age-related epidermal neoplasms, including basal cell carcinomas, squamous cell carcinomas, and malignant melanomas.[138] These genetic disorders, collectively referred to as "xeroderma pigmentosum,"[138] could readily be regarded as unimodal progeroid syndromes, in that they typically result in an accelerated aging limited to sun-exposed skin.[111] (Neurological involvement may be confined to certain subtypes and, in any case, may represent developmental lesions rather than postmaturational aging lesions.) A reasonable proposition is that certain alleles at these loci might lead to enhancement of the efficiency and fidelity of such DNA repair, so that, even in the face of a long life span and more than the usual exposure to ultraviolet light, the probability of developing *those* types of age-related changes of the skin would be greatly diminished.

Neonatal familial hyperalphalipoproteinemia and hypobetalipoproteinemia may represent examples of unimodal antigeroid syndromes.[139,140] Affected individuals have elevations of high-density lipoproteins. At least in some pedigrees, this elevation may be associated with reduced cardiac mortality and morbidity and prolonged life expectancy, presumably by virtue of the ability of high-density lipoproteins to mediate mobilization of cholesterol from the arterial wall and hence to diminish the rate of development of atherosclerosis. Although these neonatal conditions were originally thought to be inherited by an individual as a simple autosomal dominant, recent studies suggest a polygenic determination[141] and question the generality of a relationship to enhanced life expectancy.[142]

PARENTAL AGE AND MUTATION

PATERNAL AGE AND POINT MUTATION

Since the normal male remains fertile throughout most of his life span, the quality of his gametes provides an important bioassay of the effects of age upon the rate of genetic mutations. For dominant mutations with complete penetrance, such calculations can be determined directly and provide clear evidence that older fathers are more likely to sire children bearing certain types of deleterious mutations.[143] For example, for the case of achondroplasia, the risk for a father in his late forties may be up to nine times that for a father in his mid-twenties. The absolute risk, however, remains comparatively

small for the ages so far studied (mainly lower than age 50); for the case of achondroplasia, the mutation rate in the general population is of the order of one mutant per 100,000 gametes.[143] This relatively mild impact of paternal age is in contrast to the clinically significant problem of the increase in the risk of chromosomal aneuploidy with advanced maternal age, as described below.

It is of considerable theoretical interest that some dominant mutations do not increase in incidence with advancing paternal age; examples include osteogenesis imperfecta, neurofibromatosis, and tuberous sclerosis. Vogel has argued that such mutations may derive from mechanisms other than point mutation—for example, from insertional types of mutagenesis.[144]

MATERNAL AGE AND ANEUPLOIDY

Knowledge of this subject is now of medical and legal importance, as a physician may be subject to a malpractice suit if he or she fails to inform pregnant patients who will deliver when they are over the age of 35 ("advanced maternal age") of the availability of prenatal tests for chromosomally abnormal fetuses. With the exception of the classic variety of the Turner syndrome (45,X), all of the major aneuploid syndromes that are compatible with a live birth dramatically increase in frequency as a function of advancing maternal age and, to a more limited extent, as a function of advancing paternal age.[145] For example, the frequency of births of infants with trisomy 21 (Down's syndrome) for a 20-year-old mother is about 1 in 2000; for mothers over the age of 45, the frequency is about 1 in 35. A cytogenetic analysis of over 2200 spontaneous abortions has also revealed an age-related increase for trisomy for most of the human chromosomes. For those chromosomes in which an increase was noted, the increased frequency was usually modest until approximately 32 to 33 years of age, after which the frequencies of trisomic abortuses increased dramatically. An unusual pattern for chromosome 16 was observed, the increase being linear after age 20. Trisomies for the A + B group chromosomes showed little or no increase with maternal age, nor did sex chromosome monosomy or polyploidy.[146] These various patterns, of course, reflect the combined forces of etiologic factors and selective abortion. The usual explanation is that the probability of meiotic nondisjunction increases as a function of maternal age. The observation, in mice, that the number of chromosomal chiasmata (sites of prolonged association of homologous chromosomes, where crossing-over takes place) declines with maternal age could be interpreted as support for this hypothesis.[147]

Additional experiments with mice have demonstrated that unilateral ovariectomy, which leads to a premature loss of fecundity, caused an earlier-than-normal rise in aneuploidy in embryos examined at 3.5 days. The authors concluded that biological rather than chronological age of the reproductive system was the determining factor in the increase in aneuploidy and suggested that unilateral ovariectomy in women might be an additional risk factor for Down's syndrome.[148]

A number of theories have been proposed to explain the association between maternal age and trisomy. Possibilities include decay of spindle components during the prolonged meiotic prophase, environmental insults, dissolution of the nucleolus, or predetermination of trisomy by the order of formation of oocytes during development.[148] An additional hypothesis to explain an increase in Down's syndrome with maternal age, termed *relaxed selection*, proposes that a putative mechanism to spontaneously abort chromosomally abnormal embryos begins to fail with age.[149,150] In addition to an increase in the percentage of live-birth trisomies with maternal age, however, there is an increase in the percentage of spontaneously aborted trisomies. Moreover, the ratio of live-births to spontaneously aborted trisomies decreases with age,[146] in contradiction to the predictions of this theory.

REFERENCES

1. King RC, Stansfield WA: *A Dictionary of Genetics*. New York, Oxford, Oxford University Press, 1985.
2. Rieger R et al: *Glossary of Genetics and Cytogenetics*. Berlin, Heidelberg, New York, Springer-Verlag, 1976.
3. Comfort A: *The Biology of Senescence*. New York, Elsevier, 1979.
4. Committee on Animal Models for Research on Aging: *Mammalian Models for Research on Aging*. Washington, National Academy, 1981.
5. Gelman R et al: Murine chromosomal regions correlated with longevity. *Genetics* 118:693, 1988.
6. Jarvik LF et al: Survival trends in senescent twin populations. *Am J Hum Genet* 12:170, 1960.
7. Hauge M et al: The Danish twin register. *Acta Genet Med Gemellol* 17:315, 1968.
8. Leber WR, Parsons OA: Premature aging and alcoholism. *Int J Addict* 17:61, 1982.
9. Read RC: Systemic effects of smoking. *Am J Surg* 148:706, 1984.
10. Kligman LH: Photoaging: Manifestations, prevention, and treatment. *Dermatol Clin* 4:517, 1986.
11. Masoro EJ: Minireview: Food restriction in rodents: An evaluation of its role in the study of aging. *J Gerontol* 43:B59, 1988.
12. Clavel F et al: Decreased mortality among male prisoners. *Lancet* 2:1012, 1987.
13. Finch CE: The relationships of aging changes in the basal ganglia to manifestations of Huntington's chorea. *Ann Neurol* 7:406, 1980.
14. Martin GM: Constitutional genetic markers of aging. *Exp Gerontol* 23:257, 1988.
15. Takata H et al: Influence of major histocompatibility complex region genes on human longevity in Okinawan-Japanese centenarians and nonagenerians. *Lancet* 2:824, 1987.
16. Martin GM: Interactions of aging and environmental agents: The gerontological perspective, in Baker SR, Rogul M (eds): *Environmental Toxicity and the Aging Processes*. New York, Alan R. Liss, 1987, p 25.
17. Lelashvili NG, Dalakishvili SM: Genetic study of high longevity index populations. *Mech Ageing Dev* 28:261, 1984.
18. Lieberman J: Heterozygous and homozygous alpha₁-antitrypsin deficiency in patients with pulmonary emphysema. *N Engl J Med* 281:279, 1969.
19. Stevens PM et al: Pathophysiology of hereditary emphysema. *Ann Intern Med* 74:672, 1971.
20. Martin GM, Turker MS: Model systems for the genetic analysis of mechanisms of aging. *J Gerontol* 43:B33, 1988.
21. Jalavisto E: Inheritance of longevity according to Finnish and Swedish genealogies. *Ann Med Intern Fenniae* 40:263, 1951.
22. Abbott MH et al: The familial component in longevity. A study of offspring of nonagenarians: II. Preliminary analysis of the completed study. *Johns Hopkins Med J* 134:1, 1974.
23. Sacher GA: Maturation and longevity in relation to cranial capacity in hominid evolution, in Tuttle R (ed): *Antecedents of Man and After*, vol 1, *Primates: Functional Morphology and Evolution*. The Hague, Mouton, 1975, p 417.
24. Cutler RG: Evolution of human longevity and the genetic complexity governing aging rate. *Proc Natl Acad Sci USA* 72:4664, 1975.
25. Wilson AC et al: Biochemical evolution. *Annu Rev Biochem* 46:573, 1977.
26. Bush GL et al: Rapid speciation and chromosomal evolution in mammals. *Proc Natl Acad Sci USA* 74:3942, 1977.
27. Martin GM: Genetic and evolutionary aspects of aging. *Fed Proc* 38:1962, 1979.
28. Martin GM: Genetic syndromes in man with potential relevance to the pathobiology of aging, in Bergsma D, Harrison DE (eds): *Genetic Effects on Aging. Birth Defects: Original Article Series*, vol XIV, no 1. New York, Alan R Liss, 1978, p 5.
29. Bodmer WF et al (eds): Histocompatibility Testing 1977, *Report of the 7th International Workshop and Conference*. Copenhagen, Munksgaard, 1978.
30. Stern C: *Principles of Human Genetics*, 2d ed. San Francisco, WH Freeman, 1960.
31. Holden C: Why do women live longer than men? *Science* 238:158, 1987.
32. Brody JA, Brock DB: Epidemiologic and statistical characteristics of the United States elderly population, in Finch CE, Schneider EL (eds): *Handbook of the Biology of Aging*, 2d ed. New York, Van Nostrand Reinhold, 1985, p 3.
33. Hamilton JB: The role of testicular secretions as indicated by the effects of castration in man and the short lifespan associated with maleness. *Recent Prog Horm Res* 3:257, 1948.
34. Lyon MF: Possible mechanisms of X chromosome inactivation. *Nature* 232:229, 1971.
35. Johnston AW, McKusick VA: Sex-linked recessive inheritance in spastic paraplegia and Parkinsonism. *Proc Second Int Congr Hum Genet* 3:1652, 1961.

36. Shapiro LJ et al: Non-inactivation of an X-chromosome locus in man. *Science* 204:1224, 1979.

37. Migeon BR et al: Differential expression of steroid sulfatase locus on active and inactive human X chromosomes. *Nature* 299:838, 1982.

38. Wareham KA et al: Age-related reactivation of an X-linked gene. *Nature* 327:725, 1987.

39. Migeon BR et al: Effects of ageing on reactivation of the human X-linked HPRT locus. *Nature* 335:93, 1988.

40. Cock AG: Dosage compensation and sex-chromatin in nonmammals. *Genet Res* 5:354, 1964.

41. Cherkin A, Eckardt MJ: Effects of dimethylaminoethanol upon life-span and behavior of aged Japanese quail. *J Gerontol* 32:38, 1977.

42. Leviatan V, Cohen J: Gender differences in life expectancy among kibbutz members. *Soc Sci Med* 21:545, 1985.

43. Berkel J, de Waard F: Mortality pattern and life expectancy of Seventh-Day Adventists in the Netherlands. *Int J Epidemiol* 12:455, 1983.

44. Hazzard WR: Biological basis of the sex differential in longevity. *J Am Geriatr Soc* 34:455, 1986.

45. McDonnel R, Maynard A: Estimation of life years lost from alcohol-related premature death. *Alcohol Alcohol* 20:435, 1985.

46. Holden C: Can smoking explain the ultimate gender gap? *Science* 221:1034, 1983.

47. Childs B, Schriver CR: Age at onset and causes of disease. *Perspect Biol Med* 29:437, 1986.

48. Bolk L: The part played by the endocrine glands in the evolution of man. *Lancet* 2:588, 1921.

49. Gould S: *Ontogeny and Phylogeny.* Cambridge, MA, Harvard University Press, 1977.

50. Martin GM et al: Clonal selection, attenuation and differentiation in an *in-vitro* model of hyperplasia. *Am J Pathol* 74:137, 1974.

51. Smith JR, Whitney RG: Intraclonal variation in proliferative potential of human diploid fibroblasts: Stochastic mechanism for cellular aging. *Science* 207:82, 1980.

52. Hayflick L, Moorhead PS: The serial cultivation of human diploid cell strains. *Exp Cell Res* 25:585, 1961.

53. Martin G et al: Senescence and vascular disease, in Cristofalo VJ, Roberts J, Adelman RC (eds): *Explorations in Aging.* New York, Plenum Press. *Adv Exp Med Biol* 61:163, 1975.

54. Cutler RG: On the nature of aging and life maintenance processes, in Cutler RG (ed): *Interdisciplinary Topics in Gerontology,* vol 9. Basel, Karger, 1976, p 83.

55. Sacher GA: Longevity, aging and death: An evolutionary perspective. *Gerontologist* 18:112, 1978.

56. Harman D: The aging process. *Proc Natl Acad Sci USA* 78:7124, 1981.

57. Burnet M: *Intrinsic Mutagenesis: A Genetic Approach to Ageing.* New York, John Wiley & Sons, 1974.

58. Orgel LE: The maintenance of the accuracy of protein synthesis and its relevance to ageing. *Proc Natl Acad Sci USA* 49:517, 1963.

59. Gracy RW et al: Impaired protein degradation may account for the accumulation of "abnormal" proteins in aging cells, in Adelman RC, Dekker EE (eds): *Modifications of Proteins during Aging,* vol 7. New York, Alan R. Liss, 1985, p 1.

60. Tollefsbol TO, Cohen HJ: Role of protein molecular and metabolic aberrations in aging, in the physiological decline of the aged, and in age-associated diseases. *J Am Geriatr Soc* 34:282, 1986.

61. Holliday R: The inheritance of epigenetic defects. *Science* 238:163, 1987.

62. Benson, MD: Hereditary amyloidosis-disease entity and clinical model. *Hosp Pract* 23(3):165, 1988.

63. Salk D: Werner's syndrome: A review of recent research with an analysis of connective tissue metabolism, growth control of cultured cells, and chromosomal aberrations. *Hum Genet* 62:1, 1982.

64. Salk D et al: *Werner's Syndrome and Human Aging.* New York, Plenum Press, 1985.

65. Epstein CJ et al: Werner's syndrome: A review of its symptomatology, natural history, pathologic features, genetics, and relationship to the natural aging process. *Medicine* 45:177, 1966.

66. Epstein CJ et al: Werner's syndrome: A review of its symptomatology, natural history, pathologic features, genetics, and relationship to the natural aging process, in Salk D, Fujiwara Y, Martin GM (eds): *Werner's Syndrome and Human Aging.* New York, Plenum Press, 1985, p 57.

67. Goto M et al: Clinical, demographic and genetic aspects of the Werner syndrome in Japan, in Salk D, Fujiwara Y, Martin GM (eds): *Werner's Syndrome and Human Aging.* New York, Plenum, 1985, p 245.

68. Stanbury JB et al: *The Metabolic Basis of Inherited Disease,* 4th ed. New York, McGraw-Hill, 1978.

69. Goto M et al: Family analysis of Werner's syndrome: A survey of 42 Japanese families with a review of the literature. *Clin Genet* 19:8, 1981.

70. Martin GM et al: Replicative life-span of cultivated human cells. Effects of donor's age, tissue, and genotype. *Lab Invest* 23:86, 1970.

71. Fujiwara Y et al: A retarded rate of DNA replication and normal level of DNA repair in Werner's syndrome fibroblasts in culture. *J Cell Physiol* 92:365, 1977.

72. Fujiwara Y et al: Abnormal fibroblast aging and DNA replication in the Werner syndrome, in Salk D, Fujiwara Y, Martin GM (eds): *Werner's Syndrome and Human Aging.* New York, Plenum Press, 1985, p 459.

73. Hanaoka F et al: Autoradiographic studies of DNA replication in Werner's syndrome cells, in Salk D, Fujiwara Y, Martin GM (eds): *Werner's Syndrome and Human Aging.* New York, Plenum Press, 1985, p 439.

74. Tajima T et al: The increase of glycosaminoglycan synthesis and accumulation on the cell surface of cultured skin fibroblasts in Werner's syndrome. *Exp Pathol* 20:221, 1981.

75. Salk D et al: Cytogenetics of Werner's syndrome cultured skin fibroblasts: Variegated translocation mosaicism. *Cytogenet Cell Genet* 30:92, 1981.

76. Schonberg S et al: Werner's syndrome: Proliferation in vitro of clones of cells bearing chromosome translocations. *Am J Hum Genet* 36:387, 1984.

77. Salk D et al: Growth characteristics of Werner syndrome cells in vitro, in Salk D, Fujiwara Y, Martin GM (eds): *Werner's Syndrome and Human Aging.* New York, Plenum Press, 1985, p 305.

78. Fukuchi K et al: Elevated spontaneous mutation rate in

SV40-transformed Werner syndrome fibroblast cell lines. *Somatic Cell Mol Genet* 11:303, 1985.

79. Chan JYH et al: Altered DNA ligase I activity in Bloom's syndrome cells. *Nature* 325:357, 1987.

80. Willis AE, Lindahl T: DNA ligase I deficiency in Bloom's syndrome. *Nature* 325:355, 1987.

81. Carter DM: Human diseases characterized by heritable DNA instability. *Birth Defects* 17:117, 1981.

82. German J et al: Bloom's syndrome XI. Progress report for 1983. *Clin Genet* 25:166, 1984.

83. Vijayalaxmi et al: Bloom's syndrome: Evidence for an increased mutation frequency in vivo. *Science* 221:851, 1983.

84. Warren ST et al: Elevated spontaneous mutation rate in Bloom syndrome fibroblasts. *Proc Natl Acad Sci USA* 78:3133, 1981.

85. DeBusk F: The Hutchinson-Gilford progeria syndrome. *J Pediatr* 80:697, 1972.

86. Brown WT: Genetic aspects of aging in humans. *Rev Biol Res Aging* 3:77, 1987.

87. Baker PB: Cardiovascular abnormalities in progeria. Case report and review of the literature. *Arch Pathol Lab Med* 105:384, 1981.

88. Green LN: Progeria with carotid artery aneurysms: Report of a case. *Arch Neurol* 38:659, 1981.

89. Sephel GC et al: Increased elastin production by progeria skin fibroblasts is controlled by the steady-state levels of elastin mRNA. *J Invest Dermatol* 90:643, 1988.

90. Paterson MC, Smith PJ: Ataxia talangiectasia: An inherited human disorder involving hypersensitivity to ionizing radiation and related DNA-damaging chemicals. *Ann Rev Genet* 13:291, 1979.

91. Gatti RA, Swift M (eds): *Ataxia-Telangiectasia: Genetics, Neuropathology, and Immunology of a Degenerative Disease of Childhood.* KROC Found Ser 19:XX, 1985.

92. McKinnon PJ: Ataxia-telangiectasia: An inherited disorder of ionizing radiation sensitivity in man. *Hum Genet* 75:197, 1987.

93. Hall TC et al: Variations in the human Purkinje cell population according to age and sex. *Neuropathol Appl Neurobiol* 1:267, 1975.

94. Swift M: Genetics and epidemiology of ataxia-telangiectasia. *KROC Found Ser* 19:133, 1985.

95. Boder E: Ataxia-telangiectasia: An overview. *KROC Found Ser* 19:1, 1985.

96. Swift M et al: Malignant neoplasms in the families of patients with ataxia-telangiectasia. *Cancer Res* 36:209, 1976.

97. Russo G et al: Molecular analysis of a t(7;14)(q35;q32) chromosome translocation in a T cell leukemia of a patient with ataxia-telangiectasia. *Cell* 53:137, 1988.

98. Painter RB, Young BR: Radiosensitivity in ataxia-telangiectasia: A new explanation. *Proc Natl Acad Sci USA* 77:7315, 1980.

99. Murnane JP, Painter RB: Complementation of the effects in DNA synthesis in irradiated and unirradiated ataxia-telangiectasia cells. *Proc Natl Acad Sci USA* 79:1960, 1982.

100. Jaspers NGJ, Bootsma D: Genetic heterogeneity in ataxia-telangiectasia studied by cell fusion. *Proc Natl Acad Sci USA* 79:2641, 1982.

101. Coyle JT et al: The neurobiological consequences of Down syndrome. *Brain Res Bull* 16:773, 1986.

102. Glenner GG, Wong CW: Alzheimer's disease and Down's syndrome: Sharing of a unique cerebrovascular amyloid fibril protein. *Biochem Biophys Res Commun* 122:1131, 1984.

103. Wright AF, Whalley LJ: Genetics, ageing, and dementia. *Br J Psychiatry* 145:20, 1984.

104. Hewitt KE et al: Ageing in Down's syndrome. *Br J Psychiatry* 147:58, 1985.

105. Silverstein AB et al: Effects of age on the adaptive behavior of institutionalized individuals with Down syndrome. *Am J Ment Defic* 90:659, 1986.

106. Allore R et al: Gene encoding the beta subunit of S100 protein is on chromosome 21: Implications for Down syndrome. *Science* 239:1311, 1988.

107. Farrer LA et al: Genetic neurodegenerative disease models for human aging. *Rev Biol Res Aging* 3:163, 1987.

108. Sinet PM: Metabolism of oxygen derivatives in Down's syndrome. *Ann NY Acad Sci* 396:83, 1982.

109. Epstein CJ et al: Transgenic mice with increased Cu/Zn-superoxide dismutase activity: Animal model of dosage effects in Down syndrome. *Proc Natl Acad Sci USA* 84:8044, 1987.

110. Davies KE et al: Molecular analysis of human muscular dystrophies. *Muscle Nerve* 10:191, 1987.

111. Martin GM: Syndromes of accelerated aging. *Natl Cancer Inst Monogr* 60:241, 1982.

112. Goldstein JL, Brown MS: The LDL receptor defect in familial hypercholesterolemia. Implications for pathogenesis and therapy. *Med Clin North Am* 66:335, 1982.

113. Goldstein JL, Brown MS: Familial hypercholesterolemia, in Stanbury JB, Wyngaarden JB, Frederickson DS, Goldstein JL, Brown MS (eds): *The Metabolic Basis of Inherited Disease*, 5th ed. New York, McGraw-Hill, 1983, p 672.

114. Lehrman MA et al: Duplication of seven exons in LDL receptor gene caused by Alu-Alu recombination in a subject with familial hypercholesterolemia. *Cell* 48:827, 1987.

115. Eggen DA, Solberg LA: Variations of atherosclerosis with age. *Lab Invest* 18:571, 1968.

116. Vinters HV: Cerebral amyloid angiopathy: A critical review. *Stroke* 18:311, 1987.

117. Wallace MR et al: Localization of the human prealbumin gene to chromosome 18. *Biochem Biophys Res Commun* 129:753, 1985.

118. Wallace MR et al: Molecular detection of carriers of hereditary amyloidosis in a Swedish-American family. *Am J Med Genet* 25:335, 1986.

119. Wallace MR et al: Biochemical and molecular genetic characterization of a new variant prealbumin associated with hereditary amyloidosis. *J Clin Invest* 78:6, 1986.

120. Saraiva MJM et al: Amyloid fibril protein in familial amyloidotic polyneuropathy, Portuguese type. *J Clin Invest* 74:104, 1984.

121. Araki S et al: Polyneuritic amyloidosis in a Japanese family. *Arch Neurol* 18:593, 1968.

122. Cook RH et al: Studies in aging of the brain: IV. Familial Alzheimer disease: Relation to transmissible dementia, aneuploidy, and microtubular defects. *Neurology* 29:1402, 1979.

123. Glenner GG: Alzheimer's disease: Its proteins and genes. *Cell* 52:307, 1988.

124. Tanzi RE et al: Amyloid beta protein gene: cDNA, mRNA distribution, and genetic linkage near the Alzheimer locus. *Science* 235:880, 1987.

125. Van Broekhoven C et al: Failure of familial Alzheimer's disease to segregate with the A4-amyloid gene in several European families. *Nature* 329:153, 1987.

126. St. George-Hyslop PH et al: The genetic defect causing familial Alzheimer's disease maps on chromosome 21. *Science* 235:885, 1987.

127. Tanzi RE et al: The genetic defect in familial Alzheimer's disease is not tightly linked to the amyloid beta-protein gene. *Nature* 329:156, 1987.

128. Bird TD et al: Familial Alzheimer's disease in American descendants of the Volga Germans: Probable genetic founder effect. *Ann Neurol* 23:25, 1988.

129. Schellenberg GD et al: Absence of linkage of chromosome 21q21 markers to familial Alzheimer's disease. *Science* 241:1507, 1988.

130. Gusella JF et al: A polymorphic DNA marker genetically linked to Huntington's disease. *Nature* 306:234, 1983.

131. Martin GM: Cellular aging—Postreplicative cells: A review. Part II. *Am J Pathol* 89:513, 1977.

132. Pericak-Vance MA et al: Age-of-onset heterogeneity in Huntington disease families. *Am J Med Genet* 14:49, 1983.

133. Farrer LA et al: The natural history of Huntington disease: Possible role of "aging genes." *Am J Med Genet* 18:115, 1984.

134. Wexler NS et al: Homozygotes for Huntington's disease. *Nature* 326:194, 1987.

135. Pauli RM: Dominance and homozygosity in man. *Am J Med Genet* 16:455, 1983.

136. Knudson AG Jr: Genetic oncodemes and antioncogenes, in Harris CC (ed): *Biochemical and Molecular Epidemiology of Cancer*, UCLA Symposia on Molecular and Cellular Biology, vol 40. New York, Alan R. Liss, 1986, p 127.

137. Montgomery H: *Dermatopathology*, vol 1. New York, Harper & Row, 1967, p 125.

138. Robbins JH et al: Xeroderma pigmentosum. An inherited disease with sun sensitivity, multiple cutaneous neoplasms, and abnormal DNA repair. *Ann Intern Med* 80:221, 1974.

139. Glueck CJ et al: Familial hyper-alpha-lipoproteinemia: Studies in eighteen kindreds. *Metabolism* 24:1243, 1975.

140. Glueck CJ et al: Longevity syndromes: Familial hypobeta and familial hyperalpha lipoproteinemia. *J Lab Clin Med* 88:941, 1976.

141. Iselius L, Lalouel JM: Complex segregation analysis of hyperalphalipoproteinemia. *Metabolism* 31:521, 1982.

142. Heckers H et al: Hyper-alpha-lipoproteinemia and hypo-beta-lipoproteinemia are not markers for a high life expectancy. Serum lipid and lipoprotein findings in 103 randomly selected nonagenarians. *Gerontology* 28:176, 1982.

143. Vogel F et al: Spontaneous mutation in man. *Adv Hum Genet* 5:223, 1975.

144. Vogel F: Aging and reproductive performance: Models for the study of age-related chromosomal and point mutations. Paternal age and point mutations, in Schimke RT (ed): *Biological Mechanisms in Aging*. Bethesda, MD, DHHS (NIH) 81-2194, 1981, p 55.

145. Kram D, Schneider EL: Parental-age effects: Increased frequencies of genetically abnormal offspring, in Schneider EL (ed): *The Genetics of Aging*. New York, Plenum, 1978, p 225.

146. Hassold T, Chiu P: Maternal age-specific rates of numerical chromosomal abnormalities with specific reference to trisomy. *Hum Genet* 70:11, 1985.

147. Henderson SA, Edwards RG: Chiasma frequency and maternal age in mammals. *Nature* 218:22, 1968.

148. Brook JD et al: Maternal ageing and aneuploid embryos—Evidence from the mouse that biological age and not chronological age is the important influence. *Hum Genet* 66:41, 1984.

149. Erickson JD: Down syndrome, paternal age, maternal age and birth order. *Ann Hum Genet* 41:289, 1978.

150. Sved JA, Sandler L: Relation of maternal age effect in Down syndrome to nondisjunction, in del la Cruz FF, Gerald PS (eds): *Trisomy 21 (Down Syndrome). Research Perspective*. Baltimore, University Park Press, 1981, p 95.

GENERAL READING

Bergsma D, Harrison DE (ed): *Genetic Effects on Aging, Birth Defects: Original Article Series*, vol XIV, no 1. New York, Alan R. Liss, 1978.

Holliday R (ed): *Genes, Proteins, and Cellular Aging*. New York, Van Nostrand Reinhold, 1986.

Lints FA: *Genetics and Ageing*. Basel, S. Karger, 1978.

Rose MR: *Evolutionary Biology of Senescence* (in preparation).

Rothstein M (ed): *Review of Biological Research in Aging*, vol 3. New York, Alan R. Liss, 1987.

Schneider EL (ed): *The Genetics of Aging*. New York, Plenum Press, 1978.

Sohol RS, Birnbaum LS, Cutler RG (eds): *Molecular Biology of Aging: Gene Stability and Gene Expression*, vol 29. New York, Raven Press, 1985.

Chapter 4

THE SEX DIFFERENTIAL IN LONGEVITY

William R. Hazzard

A visit to almost any long-term-care facility (excepting those of the Veterans Administration) will prompt the same question from even the most casual observer: "Where are the men?" This treatise will attempt to answer this intriguing question on the basis of both practical and theoretical considerations, though the data base for the speculations and conclusions is only now beginning to be assembled.

DIMENSIONS OF THE SEX DIFFERENTIAL IN LONGEVITY

The sex differential for longevity at birth in contemporary American society is between 7 and 8 years (Table 4-1). This can be contrasted with that in this country at the beginning of the twentieth century, when the nation was largely undeveloped, and in developing nations today, with expected longevity at birth being almost equal between the sexes in both circumstances. Thus the sex differential in longevity has arisen historically as a by-product of socioeconomic and industrial development together with increasing longevity of both sexes attribut-

able to improved educational levels, nutrition, housing, sanitation, public health, etc. Except for a dip at the time of influenza epidemic in 1918, the sex ratio in mortality figure in the United States has risen progressively throughout the twentieth century (Fig. 4-1), only recently appearing to reach a plateau.[1] To a certain extent this reflects the improved status of females that accompanies socioeconomic development (less sex discrimination in access to food and health care during childhood, better prenatal and obstetrical care, increased employment opportunities, etc). This allows a greater propor-

TABLE 4-1
Average Life Expectancy at Given Ages for Adult Whites, United States, 1980, Presented by Sex

	Life Expectancy, years		Male/Female Ratio, %
	Male	Female	
At birth	70.7	78.1	90.5
At 60 years	17.5	22.4	78.1
At 65 years	14.2	18.5	76.8
At 70 years	11.3	14.8	76.4
At 75 years	8.8	11.5	76.5
At 80 years	6.7	8.6	77.0
At 85 years	5.0	6.3	79.4

SOURCE: From Wylie, Ref. 2.

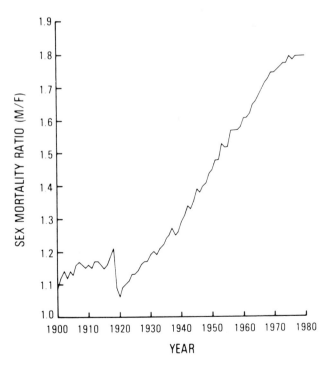

FIGURE 4-1
Sex mortality ratio (M/F), United States 1900–1980. Based on mortality rates age-adjusted to the 1940 total US population. (*From Wingard D*, Ref.1)

tion of girls born to escape the hazards of growth, development, and childbearing and to survive into middle and old age, when the chronic diseases that preferentially afflict men progressively dominate the list of causes of death.

When in the life cycle does the greater mortality of males begin? Apparently at conception (Fig. 4-2), when the ratio of male to female zygotes may be as high as 170 to 100 (for reasons that are unclear, Y-bearing sperm are far more likely to fertilize an egg than those with the X chromosome). At 10 to 12 weeks, the sex ratio among abortuses is approximately 130:100. By birth this has declined to 106:100. Parity between the sexes is reached near adolescence. At all points beyond that era, females outnumber males, and since the sex ratio at any given age is the cumulative result of the sex ratio in mortality at all previous ages, the gender gap grows progressively throughout the remainder of the life span. This is in spite of a progressive *decrease* in the absolute difference in remaining longevity between the sexes,[2] which declines to just over 1 year at age 85 (Table 4-1) (this may

be a minimum estimate, however, since a man who has survived to age 85 may be considerably hardier than a woman survivor of the same age). Interestingly, the ratio between the sexes in average remaining longevity is relatively constant beyond middle age, the man having 75 to 80 percent of the expected longevity of the woman of comparable age.

The sex ratio in long-term care facilities is thus due in part to the sex ratio in survival to advanced ages (which is approximately 3:2). However, the dependency (reflecting primarily marital) status of elderly woman is also a major contributor: about 80 percent of men over 65 are married, and although 40 percent of women over 65 are married, the majority are widows, and the ratio of widows to widowers is 4:1. Thus the elderly man requiring social and health care support is likely to have the help and company of his wife (who is also usually younger and more vigorous), whereas the elderly woman requiring such care is much less likely to have an able spouse in attendance, and long-term institutional care is thus a far more likely outcome.

FIGURE 4-2
Mortality rates by sex, US 1976. (*Compiled from data presented in Gee EM, Veevers JE: Accelerating sex differentials in mortality: An analysis of contributing factors. Social Biology 30:75, 1984.*)

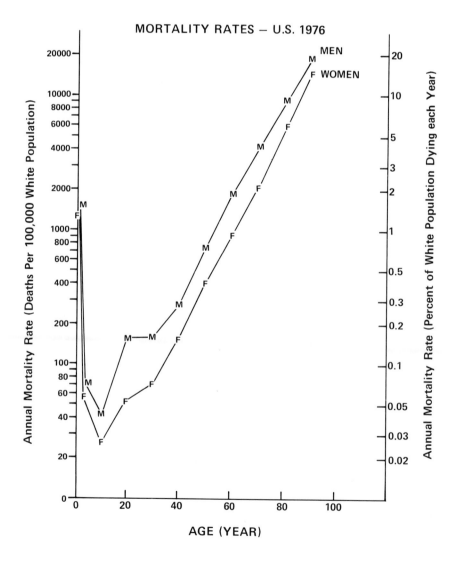

BIOLOGICAL BASIS OF THE SEX DIFFERENTIAL IN LONGEVITY

The greater longevity of females than males appears to have a fundamental biological basis. Studies of comparative zoology suggest that greater female longevity is virtually universal. Only when strains are inbred for lethal diseases selectively afflicting females does this general rule of zoology not apply, e.g., murine strains inbred for systemic lupus erythematosus in females. Thus it is logical to examine genetics to search for the basis of the sex differential in longevity.

To date, however, this approach has been largely unrewarding, whether at the level of molecular or population genetics. Clearly the burden of reduced longevity represented by all the known X-linked recessive disorders can account for but a tiny fraction of the sex differential in longevity. Studies of the Y chromosome (which bears but a few identified genes) and of the X chromosome have also thus far not yielded clues as to the greater hardiness of the XX genotype (there is no evidence for reactivation of the X chromosome inactivated by lyonization at the time of fertilization to replace X chromosome DNA damaged later in life, for instance). Further, studies (admittedly preliminary) of somatic cell longevity (population doublings or plating efficiency in culture) have failed to identify greater inherent longevity or hardiness of those with the XX genotype. Nevertheless, the possibility of a genetic basis for greater female longevity remains both an attractive hypothesis and an investigative opportunity.

Another line of investigation also bears consideration. A basic principle of gerontology holds that because decline in no single organ system is sufficient to account for the upper limit of the human life span, one should examine the function of integrating systems for decreased efficiencies with aging that may produce a synergistic effect among other systems, leading to a terminal cascade ending in death by a maximum of 120 years. Specifically, these effects might occur in the neural, endocrine, or immune systems or at linkages among the three.

On superficial examination this approach is highly attractive to explain the sex differential in longevity in both nonhuman and human species. Clearly there are major sex differentials in behavior, evident in both veterinary and human medicine, and preliminary anatomical evidence suggests sexual dimorphism in the human brain very early in life. Clear-cut sex differentials exist in areas of both normal intellectual function (e.g., a majority of boys perform better than girls on mathematical tasks and a majority of girls better than boys on verbal tests of the Scholastic Aptitude Test) and abnormal psychological performance (a pronounced male predilection is evident for such disorders as stuttering, hyperactivity/ inattention, and dyslexia). It thus seems logical to hypothesize that the sex differential in behavior that underlies much of the sex differential in the major causes of death across the life span (see below) has as its root cause a sex differential in the neuroendocrine system, perhaps based in turn upon sexual dimorphism in sex steroid secretion at critical periods in development—intrauterine, infancy, and adolescence. However, perhaps because such an approach seems overly simplistic and becomes entangled in the long-standing scientific struggle between "nature versus nurture" and "culture versus biology," this area of investigation remains curiously unpursued, reflecting the historical gulf in communication between social and biological scientists that only recently has begun to be bridged.[1,3] That the sex hormones confer a sex differential in the risk factors to the major chronic diseases of middle and old age is incontrovertible, however, and this evidence constitutes the major thrust of this treatise (see below).

Equally as attractive (and equally as scientifically neglected) is the possibility that a sex differential in immune regulation (also likely conferred by the sex differential in sex hormones) underlies the sex differential in longevity. Most research and clinical evidence to date have focused upon the greater vulnerability of women than men to most of the autoimmune diseases (rheumatoid arthritis, systemic lupus erythematosus, and autoimmune thyroiditis are three notable examples) and to the rise in titer of many autoantibodies that accompanies aging. Indeed, such evidence of immune dysfunction may underlie the substantial female excess in many of the chronic diseases across the adult life span that account for greater *morbidity* among women (without commensurate increases in mortality), arthritis being the prime example. Put another way, there is no set of diseases that increase mortality that are more common in women than men other than the autoimmune disorders (save for those virtually unique to the female such as breast cancer). However, the collective prevalence of such disorders is not sufficient to narrow even slightly the overall sex differential in longevity.

Less clear-cut, but potentially more relevant to that differential, is what has been considered the other side of the coin of immunology, isoimmune regulation (the recognition of and reaction to foreign antigens), the declining function of which has been advanced as a fundamental theory of aging.[4] Here—though this is poorly documented—males may be at a disadvantage. Clearly males are at increased risk of death from infection across the entire life span, and the greater vulnerability of men than women to death from cancer may reflect a greater impairment in immune surveillance (this, too, is confounded by the sex differential in traditional "male behaviors" that increase risk of oncogenesis). Overall, however, like the sex differentials in neuroendocrinology, the sex differential in immunology has been largely unexplored, though preliminary results suggesting modulation of immune function by certain sex steroids are intriguing.[5,6]

CAUSE-SPECIFIC SEX DIFFERENTIALS IN MORTALITY

A more empirical approach to the sex differential in human longevity begins with inspection of the sex ratio in longevity across the life span (Figure 4-3). This configuration, with a peak of about 3:1 at age 20 and a dome of about 2:1 in late middle age, is seen not only in the United States but also in nearly all developed nations.[1]

Inspection of the sex ratio in the leading causes of death (Table 4-2) readily allows grouping of these causes into those that are common in adolescence and young adulthood—dominated by violence and the risks of a youthful lifestyle—and those that are prevalent in middle and old age, the chronic and progressive "degenerative" diseases of complex etiology. In the first group neurobehavioral sex differentials are clearly causative—"macho" behavior involving considerable risk being the most obvious factor increasing male vulnerability. Once again, however, the possibility that such behavior is determined at least in part by hormonal factors should not be dismissed, though modification—exaggeration or dampening—by sociocultural forces is clearly important. This risk-taking behavior also extends to sex differentials in drug abuse and sexual practices, with consequences that could have a dramatic impact upon the sex differential in longevity if the AIDS epidemic continues to affect men overwhelmingly more than women.

The causality of the diseases clustered under the dome of greater male mortality in later life is certain to prove multifactorial. An attractive hypothesis advanced principally by social scientists has, as with the spike in youth, focused upon behavioral-cultural factors. Men in Western societies have traditionally adopted lifestyles of greater risk to health: more miles driven, more alcohol consumed, more cigarettes smoked, less focus upon health promotion and disease prevention. Men have also traditionally made fewer visits to physicians and taken fewer prescription drugs. These latter phenomena have tended to confound the issue of gender and health: Women have greater morbidity (often reported in terms of encounters with the health care system), but men have greater mortality.[2] The bases for these sex differentials in health behavior have been widely investigated (though with relatively little correlation with quantitative biomarkers of disease risk or measurements of sex hormone transport or effects) and have been recently reviewed elsewhere.[1,3]

The behavior with greatest potential impact upon

the sex differential in longevity—and that behavior currently in greatest flux—relates to cigarette smoking. Cigarette smoking became fashionable in this country in the twentieth century and until recently was predominantly a masculine habit, reinforced by the encouragement of cigarette smoking during the World Wars. And the clear parallel of increases in male cigarette smoking and to the sex ratio in mortality cannot be ignored. Indeed, it has been estimated by consensus that the historical sex differential in cigarette smoking behavior may account for as much as four years of the seven-year differential in expected longevity at birth.[7]

In this context it is relevant to examine recent trends in cigarette smoking in both sexes and parallel trends in mortality rates from cigarette-smoking-related diseases. Cigarette smoking reached its peak prevalence in the United States shortly after World War II, when nearly half the adult population were smokers. At that time not only did more men than women smoke but also heavy cigarette use was far more prevalent in men. From that point through the present cigarette smoking has declined, a decline that has accelerated progressively since the landmark Surgeon General's *Report on Smoking and Health* in 1963, the first clear public statement linking cigarette smoking to lung cancer and other diseases. Initially the decline in smoking appeared to be greater in men than in women, but by the late 1960s women were also giving up smoking. The decline was most notable among those over 35 years of age in both sexes. Hence by 1974, when the decline in coronary heart disease (CHD) mortality first received public attention (the "epidemic" having reached its peak about

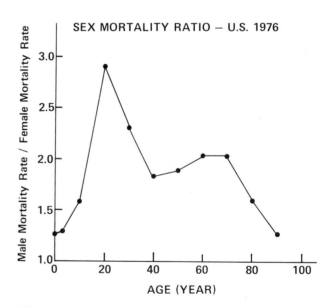

FIGURE 4-3
Sex mortality ratio, US 1976. (*Compiled from data presented in Gee EM, Veevers JE: Accelerating sex differentials in mortality: An analysis of contributing factors. Social Biology 30:75, 1984.*)

TABLE 4-2
Sex-specific Mortality Rates and Sex Differentials for the 12 Leading Causes of Death, United States, 1980*

Cause	Age-adjusted Mortality Rate†		Sex Ratio (M/F)	Sex Difference (M-F)
	Males	Females		
Diseases of the heart	280.4	140.3	1.99	140.1
Malignant neoplasms	165.5	109.2	1.51	56.3
Respiratory system	59.7	18.3	3.43	41.4
Cerebrovascular diseases	44.9	37.6	1.19	7.3
Accidents	64.0	21.8	2.93	42.2
Motor vehicle	34.3	11.8	2.90	22.5
Other	29.6	10.0	2.96	19.6
Chronic obstructive pulmonary disease	26.1	8.9	2.93	17.2
Pneumonia and influenza	17.4	9.8	1.77	7.6
Diabetes mellitus	10.2	10.0	1.02	0.2
Cirrhosis of the liver	17.1	7.9	2.16	9.2
Atherosclerosis	6.6	5.0	1.32	1.6
Suicide	18.0	5.4	3.33	12.6
Homicide	17.4	4.5	3.86	12.9
Certain causes in infancy	11.1	8.7	1.27	2.4
All causes	777.2	432.6	1.79	344.6

*Rank based on number of deaths.
†Per 100,000, direct standardization to the 1940 total U.S. population.
SOURCE: Calculated from data from the National Center for Health Statistics, 1983.

1963, coincident with the Surgeon General's report), a significant proportion of that decrease was attributed to the decline in cigarette smoking.[8] Interestingly, the relative decline in coronary disease mortality (which has continued to progress to the present) has been equivalent between the sexes, mortality among women declining by the same percentage (approximately 35 percent) as among men (the decline among women was shown actually to have begun far earlier, however). Nevertheless, because the absolute levels of CHD mortality were much higher in men, their absolute decrease in CHD deaths has been greater. Similarly, because the absolute level of cigarette smoking in men was higher than in women, their absolute reduction in cigarette "consumption" has been greater. Hence recent trends have shown a decrease in the difference in the number of CHD deaths in men versus women in parallel with the decrease in the number of cigarettes smoked by men as opposed to women. And, ominously, the sex differentials in certain clear-cut consequences of chronic cigarette abuse such as lung cancer (which recently surpassed breast cancer as the most common cause of cancer-related death in women), chronic obstructive lung disease, and peptic ulcer disease appear to have narrowed in recent years. Finally, the recent plateau in the previously escalating sex ratio in total mortality (Fig. 4-1) may reflect these changing patterns of cigarette smoking behavior between the sexes. Indeed, if working women adopt (or retain) the heavy cigarette smoking behavior

historically characteristic of men, a popular hypothesis related to changing lifestyles of women in the second half of the twentieth century may be borne out; namely, that the increased participation of women in the work force characteristic of this era (and their penetration into work domains traditionally dominated by men) will result in increased female mortality from diseases traditionally considered masculine, and a consequent narrowing in the sex differential in longevity will occur. Suffice it to summarize here the extant (but clearly imperfect and premature) data on this contentious subject: To date there is no evidence to suggest that women working outside the home suffer increased morbidity or mortality; quite to the contrary, employed women clearly enjoy improved health, with fewer days of disability and fewer physician visits than nonemployed women.[3] Just as clearly, however, these trends will bear close surveillance as the full impact through time of changing lifestyles between the genders becomes evident over the next several decades.

THE SEX DIFFERENTIAL IN ATHEROSCLEROSIS: THE DOMINANT FACTOR

Review of the leading causes of death (Table 4-2) clearly places atherosclerosis at the center of any consideration of the sex differential in longevity. It has been estimated, for instance, that elimination of atherosclerotic disease in its various manifestations, notably coronary heart disease, cerebrovascular disease, and peripheral arterial disease, could add more than 10 years to average longevity above age 65 in the United States,[9] raising the mean age at death to over 85 years. Furthermore, by deferring death among men beyond late middle age, reduction in the sex ratio in mortality and narrowing between the sexes (and between marriage partners) in their ages at death would be by-products. Reference to Table 4-2 allows estimation of the potential reduction in the sex differential in mortality were these leading causes of death to be eliminated; it is readily apparent that elimination of atherosclerosis-related deaths would reduce the sex differential in longevity by nearly half, close to that potentially achievable through elimination of all the other leading causes combined.

While sex differentials may exist in the most basic aspects of atherogenesis (e.g., arterial intimal integrity or other aspects of arterial wall biology), all such possibilities are but speculative at the present. A more practical approach is to review the traditional atherosclerosis risk factors as to possible sex differentials across the life span. Population studies (e.g., Tecumseh) suggest at least subtle differentials. Median systolic and diastolic blood pressure levels are lower in women than in men until middle age, when a crossover occurs such that hypertension (especially isolated systolic hypertension) is more common in older women than in men. After administration of oral glucose, blood sugar levels show a similar pattern. By contrast, blood lipids (cholesterol and triglyceride) change with age in a biphasic pattern, increasing in both sexes (albeit at lower levels in women that in men) until middle age and declining thereafter. Except for the abrupt increase in cholesterol levels in women beyond age 50, these changes in blood lipid levels (and the increase in blood pressure and in glycemic levels after administration of glucose in the first half of adult life only) have been thought to be mediated by changes in relative body weight (Fig. 4-4). These increases normally continue until middle age, when a plateau is reached. A decline during old age follows (the continued increase in blood pressure and blood glucose beyond middle age require a different explanation). Close inspection of these curves reveals subtly different patterns in men as opposed to women: the increases from ages 20 to 50 are concave downward in men and convex downward in women, the middle-age-weight plateau being achieved approximately a decade later in women than in men (during the sixties rather than the fifties). Thus a slower accretion of weight and a later achievement of peak weight in women than in men may explain in part the more favorable cardiovascular risk profiles of women prior to age 50 and the infrequency of coronary heart disease in women prior to that age, a benefit that may carry over into the succeeding era by virtue of the slower rate of atherogenesis in women to that point.

The sex differential in regional patterns of weight gain is another possible explanation of lower cardiovascular risk in women, a topic of intense contemporary investigation (see Chap. 72). Women prototypically gain

FIGURE 4-4
Median plasma cholesterol (Chol), triglyceride (TG), and relative body weight values as a function of age in Tecumseh (cholesterol and relative weights) and Stockholn (TG) community studies. (*Reprinted with permission from Williams RDH (ed): Textbook of Endocrinology, 5th ed. Philadelphia, Saunders, 1974.*)

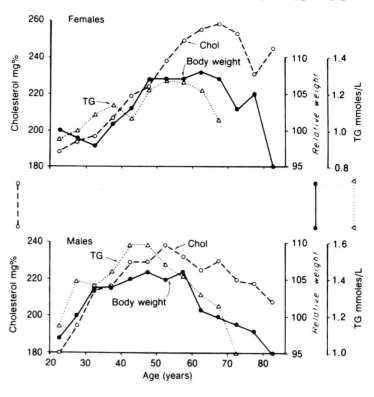

adipose mass during adulthood preferentially about the hips and buttocks (so-called "lower body," "pear-shaped," or "gynoid" obesity), while men add fat about the waist ("upper body," "apple-shaped," or "android" obesity). The latter has been shown to confer extra cardiovascular risk, exaggerating the known interaction between relative body weight and the traditional risk factors in population studies such as in Framingham. Moreover, women who atypically demonstrate upper body obesity have cardiovascular risk profiles (and relative sex steroid patterns) resembling those of men and are at substantially increased risk of type II diabetes mellitus (perhaps by virtue of increased insulin resistance and compensatory hyperinsulinism conferred by their relative androgenicity). This topic is of special interest in a review of the sex differential in longevity, given that diabetes mellitus is the one clear exception to the rule of greater male mortality (Table 4-2). Diabetes is, in fact, a relatively more ominous disease in women than in men, since it eliminates the relative immunity to death enjoyed by women in other spheres.

Additional insight into the sex differential in atherosclerotic disease may be afforded by inspection of the sex ratio in cardiovascular mortality across the adult life span (Fig. 4-5). This demonstrates a major decline with advancing age, from greater than 5:1 at age 35 to approximately 1.2:1 at age 85 (it never dips below unity). Thus

the pattern is far from static. Viewed from another perspective, women enjoy approximately a 10-year relative immunity to cardiovascular disease compared with their male counterparts (the rate in women 55 to 64 being equivalent to that in men 45 to 54, for instance).[10] This immunity is even evident in the presence of a major monogenic disorder vastly accelerating atherogenesis [heterozygous familial hypercholesterolemia, in which a simply inherited approximately 50 percent reduction in low-density lipoprotein (LDL) receptors results in twice normal LDL cholesterol levels]. Women with this disorder, present in about 1 in 500 in the American population, develop clinical atherosclerosis approximately a decade later than their similarly affected male siblings.[10]

A further clue to the mechanisms of this protection is afforded in the greater incidence of ischemic heart disease in pre- versus postmenopausal women of comparable age (who are still at lower risk than men of the same age, however).[10] This suggests that the differential sex hormone status of premenopausal women may underlie their relative immunity to cardiovascular disease.

To consider this further, it becomes appropriate to review the hierarchy of cardiovascular risk factors by gender in middle and old age.[11] This clearly identifies the high-density lipoprotein (HDL) cholesterol as the most powerful risk factor (albeit in a negative, protective fashion), followed by the LDL cholesterol, positively

FIGURE 4-5
Linear sex ratio (M/F) in cardiovascular mortality, coronary and hypertensive, US, by age and race, 1955. (*From Furman RH: Coronary heart disease and the menopause, in Ryan KJ, Gibson DC (eds): Menopause and Aging, DHEW(NIH)73-319, 1973.*)

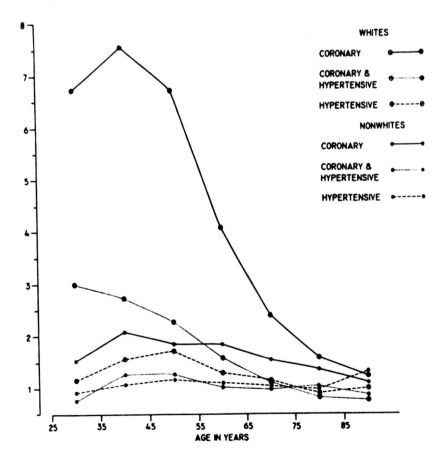

associated with risk, and the other traditional factors. Of note, triglyceride levels and relative body weight each appear to be positively associated with cardiovascular disease only in women and only on univariate analysis, but this disappears in both instances on multivariate analysis. This reflects the inverse relationships between HDL cholesterol and both triglyceride and relative body weight. Thus obese, hypertriglyceridemic women may be at increased cardiovascular risk if their HDL cholesterol levels are depressed; if, however, their HDL levels remain normal in the presence of obesity and hypertriglyceridemia, they remain at normal risk.

Next let us review in detail mean population levels of LDL cholesterol, HDL cholesterol, and the LDL/HDL ratio (a convenient index of net lipid–associated risk) across the adult life span to determine whether sex differentials in these levels may account for the sex differential in cardiovascular risk (Fig. 4-6). In so doing we shall pay particular attention to the periods of greatest change in sex hormone status—adolescence and the perimenopausal era. These data from the 11-population hyperlipidemia prevalence surveys of the Lipid Research Clinics in the 1970s[12] reveal distinct differences between the genders. First, lipid levels are equivalent in both sexes until puberty. At that time (and in parallel with the Tanner scale of pubertal development), HDL levels decline in boys, average levels remaining lower in men than in women throughout the adult life span. Thus it would seem most likely that androgens physiologically suppress HDL levels (and, if estrogens have the opposite effect, androgens exert the more powerful action). Second, with regard to LDL, whereas mean levels rise in both sexes between puberty and the menopause, they remain substantially lower in women than in men until the menopausal era, when they rise significantly, average levels in postmenopausal women exceeding those in men of comparable age. These trends in women seem most likely to be attributable to the effects of estrogen in premenopausal women and the lack of estrogen beyond the menopause. Third, because the continuing differential in HDL levels exceeds that in LDL in the postmenopausal era, the mean LDL/HDL ratio remains higher in men than in women beyond the menopause, but the magnitude of the differential is lower among older persons.

Thus (1) the adult male/female ratio in cardiovascular disease is greater than unity at all ages, but it declines with advancing age; (2) the adult male/female ratio in LDL/HDL is greater than unity at all ages, but it, too, declines with advancing age coincident with lesser estrogen secretion by postmenopausal women. Given these parallel trends, a simplistic hypothesis emerges, namely, that the sex differential in sex hormone secretion determines the sex differential in longevity in Western societies.

Can this, however, account for the entire sex differ-

ential in atherosclerosis? Not entirely, it would appear, yet nevertheless for a substantial fraction. Thus, in the lower three quintiles of the ratio of the total cholesterol to HDL (as an approximation of the LDL/HDL) in the Framingham study, women at a given ratio were still at lower risk than men.[11] However, in the upper two quintiles of this ratio (in which the majority of cardiovascular events were clustered), women were at equivalent risk with men.

Direct evidence linking sex hormone status with LDL or HDL levels has been hard to obtain, however; no study to date clearly links plasma levels of testosterone, the several estrogens, or progesterone with plasma

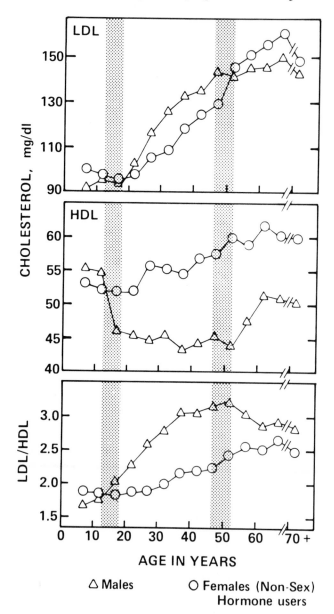

FIGURE 4-6
Median North American population high-density lipoprotein (HDL) cholesterol, low-density lipoprotein (LDL) cholesterol, and the ratio between the two versus age in white subjects. (*Data from Lipid Research Clinic Prevalence Survey.*)

levels of the lipoproteins [levels of the sex hormone–binding globulin (SHBG), reflecting the net effects of both androgens and estrogens upon sex hormone transport, probably represents the most promising index].

The most compelling evidence to date, lying in the association of exogenous sex hormone therapy with alterations in mean lipoprotein lipid levels, is far from persuasive.[13] In the same Lipid Research Clinics surveys (Fig. 4-7), postmenopausal women taking estrogen replacement therapy (overwhelmingly consisting of Premarin, 0.625 or 1.25 mg daily) had higher HDL and lower LDL levels than those not taking estrogens. Contrasting patterns were evident in premenopausal women taking combination oral contraceptives: Their mean LDL cholesterol levels were higher than in women not taking exogenous hormones, presumably reflecting the androgenic effects of the progestational components, usually derived from 19-nor-testosterone, while average HDL levels were unaffected. Closer analysis of the latter data, however,[14] revealed that women taking oral contraceptives with a high estrogen/(androgenic) progestin ratio had increased average HDL levels, whereas those consuming combinations with a low estrogen/progestin ratio had decreased average HDL levels compared to those in women not taking these oral contraceptives. Other less clearly population-based studies have shown similar results.[15]

These effects of exogenous estrogens have been confirmed in recent carefully controlled metabolic studies of postmenopausal women maintained on a diet of constant composition enriched in cholesterol content 84 days, in the middle 28 days of which ethinyl estradiol in a dosage averaging 0.06 mg/day was added.[16] These studies revealed rapid, reproducible, and dramatic changes in blood lipids with estrogen: average triglyceride levels rose (by 57 percent), total and LDL cholesterol levels fell (by 13 and 26 percent, respectively), and HDL levels rose (by 21 percent, albeit somewhat more sluggishly), the latter rising selectively in the more cholesterol-rich, buoyant, putatively more antiatherogenic HDL$_2$ subfraction (by 42 percent). The mean LDL/HDL ratio in these women declined by nearly 40 percent, from 2.5 to 1.5 (a current threshold for concern regarding therapy is 3.0). All changes were rapidly reversed upon estrogen withdrawal. Mean levels of the carrier apolipoproteins changed in the expected fashion: apo B fell, as did apo E, whereas apo A-I increased. Of potential mechanistic significance, the level of hepatic triglyceride lipase (HTGL), an enzyme released into plasma by heparin and thought to represent a potential mediator of HDL catabolism, declined abruptly on estrogen, consistent with limited studies[17] showing retarded HDL removal during estrogen (other studies have suggested increased apo A-I synthesis.[18]

The other side of the story, also relying on exogenous hormone administration, is seen in persons taking androgenic anabolic steroids.[27–29] One such study[19] of postmenopausal osteoporotic women disclosed the dramatic effects of stanozolol in a therapeutic dosage of 6 mg/day: LDL rose (by 21 percent), and HDL declined (by 53 percent), and the mean LDL/HDL ratio rose from 2.5 to 6.8, the latter clearly in the range of theoretically high risk. Moreover, the HDL$_2$ cholesterol fraction fell most dramatically (by 85 percent). HDL$_3$ cholesterol and apo A-I and A-II levels also declined, but more modestly. Of mechanistic implication was the concomitant, dramatic increase in average HTGL levels after administration of heparin in these women, consistent with accelerated HDL catabolism demonstrated in a separate study of volunteers taking stanozolol.[20] A third study from this laboratory[21] traced daily trends in HDL$_2$, HDL$_3$, and postheparin HTGL early during the course of stanozolol therapy: After stanozolol therapy, the HTGL rose within 24 h, peaking in 4 days, whereas HDL$_2$ began to decline only after 72 h (HDL$_3$ remained unchanged for 10 days). These results are also consistent

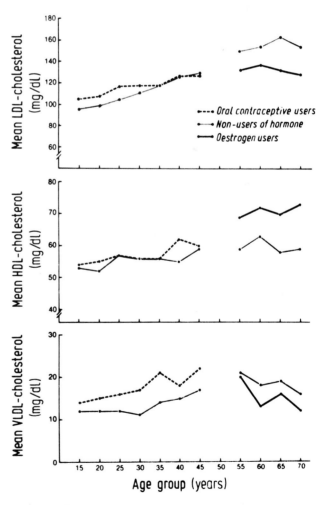

FIGURE 4-7
Plasma lipoprotein cholesterol levels in users and nonusers of oral contraceptives and estrogens. (*Reprinted with permission from Wallace RB et al: Altered plasma lipid and lipoprotein levels associated with oral contraceptive and oestrogen use. Lancet 2:11, 1979.*)

with a causative role of stanozolol-induced changes in HTGL in lowering HDL$_2$ levels. Of note, average levels of HTGL after heparin administration were lower in women than in men in population studies, which also confirmed the higher levels of HDL in women than in men, specifically HDL$_2$.[22]

A detailed study of a single volunteer confirmed those effects of ethinyl estradiol and stanozolol[17]: estrogen dramatically and reproducibly raised HDL and lowered LDL cholesterol levels; stanozolol exerted opposite effects. Interestingly, the LDL and HDL levels of this woman were the same on the combination of both drugs as they were off both hormones.

Thus, exogenous estrogens and androgens produce changes in lipoprotein lipids which are at least a *caricature* of those in men and women under physiological conditions. Estrogens lower LDL and raise HDL (selectively HDL$_2$), while androgens raise LDL and lower HDL (selectively HDL$_2$). The mechanism of the fall in LDL (and in apo B and E levels) with estrogens is likely to relate to enhanced LDL (apo B and apo E) receptor function directly demonstrated in animals treated with estrogens[23,24] (and implied acceleration of LDL removal); whether androgens down-regulate the LDL receptor in reciprocal fashion is unknown. The mechanism of the increase in HDL with estrogen is likely to reflect retarded HDL catabolism (though increased synthesis is also likely), perhaps mediated by induced reduction in HTGL activity; androgens in mirror-image fashion lower HDL and induce increases in HTGL activity, which may accelerate HDL catabolism.

Whether these pharmacological effects of sex steroids are relevant to the physiological effects of such hormones upon lipoprotein lipids, much less upon the sex differential in cardiovascular risk and longevity, is speculative. As noted, simple measurements of the sex hormones and their binding protein do not provide a clear pattern of the expected correlations with lipoprotein lipids.

The effects of sex hormones upon those lipids are also not likely to account for the entire sex differential in cardiovascular disease. Indeed, two important paradoxes remain. First, men with premature myocardial infarctions have been reported to have *increased*, not decreased, estrogen levels.[25] Whether such hyperestrogenism is generally characteristic of men with premature atherosclerosis is not clear, however, and, more importantly, it has yet to be demonstrated that hyperestrogenism in such men *precedes* their atherosclerotic event. More importantly, estrogen given to men in middle and early old age has been associated with *increased*, not decreased, cardiovascular events. In a VA cooperative study of older men with noninvasive prostatic carcinoma, estrogen increased the death rate, attributable to a rise in cardiovascular deaths.[26] Estrogen

(Premarin in a high dosage of 5.0 mg) also increased recurrent myocardial infarction (despite lowering cholesterol levels) in the Coronary Drug Project, a secondary prevention trial.[27] These results have led to caution in the possible translation of favorable estrogen-induced LDL/HDL changes into widespread use of estrogens, especially in men, since "what is good for the goose may *not* be good for the gander."

What may resolve this paradox? While the following explanation has not been tested experimentally, it seems likely that other, relatively well-established effects of estrogen may be particularly hazardous for those with advanced (but perhaps preclinical) atherosclerosis, notably the increased tendency to thrombosis (with increased coagulation factors and decreased anticoagulation factors such as antithrombin III). Thus the woman with atherogenesis retarded by lifelong, especially premenopausal sex hormone secretion may be at little risk to superimposed thrombosis from exogenous estrogens, whereas the man with advanced atherosclerosis, based in part upon long-standing androgenic effects upon lipoprotein metabolism, may suffer a coronary thrombosis during estrogen treatment even while his LDL is being lowered and his HDL raised by the hormone.

Finally, a comment regarding the potential cardiovascular effects of the current widespread postmenopausal sex steroid replacement therapy (covered elsewhere in Chaps. 74 and 77, the latter with special reference to preservation of bone mineral content). A clear majority of epidemiological studies have shown reduced cardiovascular mortality (by more than 50 percent) in postmenopausal women taking estrogen replacement therapy.[28,29] The well-known increased risk of endometrial carcinoma in such women (with intact uteri) dictates cyclic progestational therapy to avoid the risks of unopposed estrogen treatment. Perhaps fortuitously, the progestin currently in widest use (and reported to nullify such risk) is medroxyprogesterone acetate (Provera), a weakly androgenic progestin (not a 19-nor-testosterone derivative) that has no measurable effects upon lipoprotein lipids (and, of mechanistic interest, does not affect HTGL levels after heparin administration).[30] This theory would suggest manifold benefits of such postmenopausal estrogen-progestin treatment: less osteoporosis and, of greatest impact upon longevity, reduced atherosclerosis.

Perhaps unfortunately, widespread application of such regimens might prolong female longevity and further widen the sex differential in mortality. Fortunately, however, newer approaches to the prevention of atherosclerosis are now widely available and are being intensely promoted—early detection and control of hypertension, prevention and cessation of cigarette smoking, and early detection and treatment of hypercholesterolemia by diet and drugs. These approaches offer relatively more benefits to men, given their greater risk to atherosclerosis, than to women, and hence if widely accepted and practiced continuously by men should serve to narrow the sex differential in atherosclerosis and longevity in Western society.

REFERENCES

1. Wingard DL: The sex differential in morbidity, mortality and lifestyle. *Ann Rev Public Health* 5:433, 1984.
2. Wylie CM: Contrasts in the health of elderly men and women: An analysis of recent data for whites in the United States. *J Am Geriatr Soc*, 32:670, 1984.
3. Nathanson CA, Lorenz G: Women and health: the social dimensions of biomedical data, in Giele JZ (ed): *Women in the Middle Years*. New York, Wiley, 1982, pp 37.
4. Walford RL: *The Immunologic Theory of Aging*. Copenhagen, Munkgaard, 1969.
5. Lakita RG: Sex steroids and autoimmune disease. *Arth Rheum* 28:121, 1985.
6. Sthoeger ZM, Chiorazzi N, Lahita RG: Regulation of the immune response by sex steroids. In vitro effects of estradiol and testosterone on pokeweed-nitrogen induced human B cell differentiation. *J Immunol* 141:91, 1988.
7. Holden C: Can smoking explain the ultimate gender gap? *Science* 221:1034, 1983.
8. Stern MP: The recent decline in ischemic heart disease mortality. *Ann Intern Med* 91:630, 1979.
9. Brock DB, Brody JA: Statistical and epidemiological characteristics, in *Principles of Geriatric Medicine*. Andres R, Bierman E, Hazzard W (eds): McGraw-Hill, New York, chap 6, 1984.
10. Sullivan JL: The sex differential in ischemic heart disease. *Persp Biol Med* 26:657, 1983.
11. Kannel WB, Brand FN: Cardiovascular risk factors in the elderly, in Andres R, Bierman E, Hazzard W, (eds): *Principles of Geriatric Medicine*. McGraw-Hill, New York, Chap 10, 1984.
12. The Lipid Research Clinics: *Population Studies Data Book*. vol I. *The Prevalence Study*. DHHS (NIH) 80:1527, 1980.
13. Godsland IF, Wynn V, Crook D, Miller NE: Sex, plasma lipoproteins, and atherosclerosis: prevailing assumptions and outstanding questions. *Am Heart J* 114: 1467, 1987.
14. Knopp RH, Walden CE, Wahl PW et al: Oral contraceptive and postmenopausal estrogen effects on lipoprotein triglyceride and cholesterol in an adult female population: Relationships to estrogen and progestin potency. *J Clin Endocrinol Metab* 53:1123, 1981.
15. Bradley DD, Wingard J, Petit DB, Krauss RM, Ramcharan S: Serum high density lipoprotein cholesterol in women using oral contraceptives, estrogens, and progestins. *N Engl J Med* 299:17, 1978.
16. Applebaum-Bowden D, Hazzard W, McLean P et al: Estrogen reduces LDL cholesterol on high cholesterol diet in post-menopausal women (abstract). *Arteriosclerosis* 2; 415A, 1982.
17. Hazzard WR, Haffner SM, Kushwaha RS et al: Preliminary report: Kinetic studies on the modulation of high-density lipoprotein, apolipoprotein, and subfraction metabolism by sex steroids in a post-menopausal woman. *Metabolism* 33:779, 1984.
18. Schaefer EJ, Foster DM, Zech LA, Lingren FT, Brewer HB, Levy RI: The effects of estrogen administration on plasma lipoprotein metabolism in premenopausal females. *J Clin Endocrinol Metab* 57:262, 1983.
19. Taggart H McA, Applebaum-Bowden D, Haffner S et al: Reduction in high density lipoproteins by anabolic steroid (stanozolol) therapy for post-menopausal osteoporosis. *Metabolism* 31:1147, 1982.
20. Haffner SM, Kushwaha RS, Foster DM et al: Studies on the metabolic mechanism of reduced high density lipoproteins during anabolic steroid therapy. *Metabolism* 32:413, 1983.
21. Applebaum-Bowden D, Haffner S, Hazzard WR: The dyslipoproteinemia of anabolic steroid therapy: Increase in hepatic triglyceride lipase precedes the decrease in high density lipoprotein$_2$ cholesterol. *Metabolism* 36:949, 1987.
22. Applebaum-Bowden D, Haffner SM, Wahl PW et al: Post-heparin plasma triglyceride lipase: Relationships with very low density lipoprotein triglyceride and high density lipoprotein$_2$ cholesterol. *Arteriosclerosis* 5:273, 1985.
23. Windler E, Kovanen Y, Chao S, Brown MS, Hand RJ, Goldstein JL: The estradiol simulated lipoprotein receptor of rat liver: A binding site that mediates the uptake of rat lipoproteins containing apoproteins B & E. *J Biol Chem* 255:10464, 1980.
24. Ma PT, Yamamoto T, Goldstein JL, Brown MS: Increased mRNA for low density lipoprotein receptor in liver of rabbits treated with 17-alpha ethinyl estradiol. *Proc Natl Acad Sci USA* 83:792, 1986.
25. Phillips GB: Evidence for hyperestrogenaemia as a risk factor for myocardial infarction in men. *Lancet* 2:14, 1976.
26. The Veterans Administration Cooperative Urological Research Group: Treatment and survival of patients with cancer of the prostrate. *Surg Gynecol Obstet* 124:1011, 1967.
27. Coronary Drug Project Research Group. The coronary drug project: Initial findings leading to modifications of research protocol. *JAMA* 214:1301, 1970.
28. Bush TL, Barrett-Connor E: Noncontraceptive estrogen use and cardiovascular disease. *Epidemiol Rev* 7:80, 1985.
29. Bush TL, Barrett-Connor E, Cowan LD, Criqui MH, Wallace RB, Suchindran CM, Tysoler HA, Rifkind BM: Cardiovascular mortality and noncontraceptive use of estrogen in women: Results from the Lipid Research Clinics Program Follow-up Study. *Circulation* 75:1102, 1987.
30. Tikkanen MJ, Nikkila EA, Kuusi T, Sipinen S: Reduction of plasma high density lipoprotein and cholesterol and increase of postheparin plasma hepatic lipase activity during progestin treatment. *Clin Chim Acta* 115:63, 1981.

Chapter 5

NUTRITION AND AGING

John E. Morley

With advancing age and the occurrence of concomitant illness there is an increased risk of developing nutritional deficiencies. It is now widely recognized that there is a need to compress the period of morbidity experienced by the elderly, and there is an increasing need to place emphasis on preventive gerontology. Altered nutritional status is associated with the pathogenesis of a number of common diseases of the elderly (Table 5-1); thus, it would appear that nutritional modulation represents one possible approach to successful aging.

Animal studies of the role of nutrition in aging have examined the ability of nutritional intervention to prolong the maximal life span. In the 1930s and early 1940s, McCay and colleagues found that nutritional deprivation delays maturation and increases the life span of rats.[1,2] These studies extended earlier studies completed by Osborne and Mendel[3] in 1915. Subsequently, dietary restriction has been demonstrated to extend life span in a variety of species. Restriction of total caloric intake appears to be more important than the restriction of any particular macronutrient. The mechanism of the effect of caloric restriction is unknown. One theory has suggested that overeating results in an increased generation of free radicals that accelerates the aging process. Alternatively, numerous studies have shown that nutrients can modulate gene expression, suggesting that some of these gene products may play a role in the onset of senescence.

In humans there is little evidence that a Spartan lifestyle will prolong existence. It is the self-indulgent, overnourished people of the developed Western nations, rather than the undernourished Third World residents, who have the longest life spans. Support for the notion that the Spartan ethic prolongs life span originally came from studies of three isolated communities in Georgia, Russia; Vilacambamba, Equador; and the Himalayan mountains. Early studies suggested that many individuals in these communities lived well into their 100s. However, careful investigations of these communities have shown that the alleged longevity of their residents was based on an inability to count correctly and on community mythology (see Chap. 14).

Multiple studies have shown that both being underweight and being overweight increase the risk of death[4] (see Chap. 72). While originally it was claimed that the increased risks of mortality in underweight subjects were related to cigarette smoking, two recent studies showed that the increased mortality risk associated with underweight is also present in subjects who do not smoke.[5,6] It also needs to be recognized that lower-body fat deposition ("gynoid") is much less likely to be associated with increased mortality, increased risk of coronary artery disease, or cerebrovascular accidents than is midriff fat deposition.

TABLE 5-1
Putative Role of Nutrients in the Pathogenesis of Some Diseases in the Elderly

Nutritional Problem	Disease
Protein-calorie malnutrition	Immune deficiency; anemia; fatigue; increased infection; dementia, bed sores
Hypodipsia	Dehydration; orthostatic hypotension; hypernatremia
Excessive calorie intake	Obesity; hypertension; Type II diabetes mellitus
Decreased calcium and vitamin D intake and decreased sun exposure	Osteopenia; hip fractures
Low-fiber diets	Diverticulitis; constipation
High-fiber diets	Volvulus
Zinc deficiency	Immune deficiency; anorexia; poor wound healing
Folate and vitamin B_{12} deficiency	Anemia; dementia
Iron deficiency	Anemia
Selenium deficiency	Cancer; ? myopathy
Vitamin A excess	Hypercalcemia
Excess sodium intake	Hypertension; cerebrovascular accidents

PROTEIN-CALORIE MALNUTRITION

According to the Health and Nutrition Examination Survey (HANES), up to 16 percent of Americans over the age of 65 ingest less than 1000 calories a day.[7] Of elderly persons in acute care hospitals, 17 to 65 percent suffer from malnutrition.[8,9] Some degree of inadequate nutrition is present in 26 to 59 percent of institutionalized elderly patients.[10,11] According to one study, protein-energy malnutrition was present in 50 percent of patients with Alzheimer's disease or multi-infarct dementia, and the population had a mean reference weight of 82 percent of ideal body weight.[12] In a study of medical outpatients over the age of 70, we found that 9 percent were underweight and 5 percent had albumin levels less than 3.5 g/dl. From this recounting of statistics, it is clear that the elderly are particularly vulnerable to protein-calorie malnutrition.

NUTRITIONAL ASSESSMENT

In our experience, many of the elderly with a marginal caloric intake lose weight but manage to maintain their serum albumin at normal levels. They present with a picture similar to that seen in marasmic children. Serum albumin levels are maintained by a combination of a minimal caloric intake supplemented by protein from muscle. These patients tend to have moderate-to-severe weight loss and are usually below 90 percent of average body weight; in some cases patients weigh less than 80 percent of average body weight. Therefore, we feel that the best nutritional indicators are height and weight and a documented history of weight loss. At present, we prefer to use the Master's tables of average weight instead of the Metropolitan Life Insurance Tables, as the Master's tables are adjusted in 5-year increments for the elderly.[13] On the whole, an older person should weigh more for any given height than should a younger person because there is a reduction in height of approximately 1.2 cm for each 20-year period after the age of 40. Other age-adjusted weight tables are those prepared by Reuben Andres from the Metropolitan Life Insurance Tables for subjects aged 60 to 70 years[14] and the recently published weight ranges from the Framingham study[6] (see Chap. 12). As the Framingham data have been correlated with mortality, they may represent the best approximation of ideal body weight for the elderly. Bed- or wheelchair-bound patients whose height cannot be obtained should have arm length measured to obtain weight values from tables that match appropriate weight with arm length.[15]

When the serum albumin level falls below 3.5 g/dl, visceral protein depletion is present. Levels of albumin below 3.0 g/dl represent an extremely poor prognostic sign in the elderly and justify rapid and intensive intervention (see Chap. 31). It should be remembered that going to the recumbent position will cause up to a 0.5 g/dl fall in serum albumin level because of fluid redistribution. Thus, truly healthy ambulatory elderly should not have albumin levels below 4.0 g/dl. Population studies in healthy elderly have suggested that albumin levels either do not fall or decline minimally with advancing age.

Midarm muscle circumference has been used as an index of muscle loss. Studies performed in New Zealand have reported that this measurement is a useful predictor of subsequent mortality in the elderly.[16] Triceps muscle circumference and subscapular skin-fold thickness can be used to approximate adipose tissue mass. In men, subscapular measurement appears to be more accurate, while in women the triceps muscle provides the better measurement. If these anthropomorphic measurements are used, it is essential that the values be compared to age-adjusted values.

In our experience, the short-lived proteins, i.e., transferrin, retinol-binding protein, and prealbumin, play little role in the assessment of protein-calorie malnutrition. These proteins may have some use as acute measures of protein repletion (see Chap. 31). Similarly, anergy occurs commonly in the elderly even when protein-calorie malnutrition is not present, making skin testing a relatively poor indicator of nutritional status. Low cholesterol levels are an indicator of protein-calorie malnutrition and have been correlated with mortality in the long-term care setting.[17] A total lymphocyte count of less than 1500/cm^3 has also been used as a sign of malnutrition. Somatomedin C levels fall with advancing age. However, Rudman et al.[18] have found that even lower levels are present in malnourished elderly.

Overall, we recommend that the cost-effective initial nutritional assessment in the elderly consist of a history of weight loss, a measurement of height and weight, and a test of serum albumin levels.

TREATABLE CAUSES OF MALNUTRITION

Table 5-2 lists the causes of malnutrition identified in hospitalized patients.[19,20] It is important to recognize that many of these causes are treatable.

While depression occurs less commonly in the elderly, it is often missed or overlooked by those providing care. Up to 40 percent of patients in nursing homes have some degree of depression. Bereavement is a particularly common precipitant of anorexia associated with depression in the elderly. Depressed older patients are more likely to have major weight loss than depressed younger patients.[21] The anorexia associated with depression is most probably due to the increased activation of hypothalamic corticotropin-releasing factor (CRF), which has been shown to be a potent anorectic agent in

TABLE 5-2
Treatable Causes of Malnutrition

Depression
Drugs (e.g., digoxin)
Intestinal ischemia
Esophageal candidiasis
Physical factors
Zinc deficiency
Metabolic causes (e.g., hyperthyroidism, hyperparathyroidism)
Chronic obstructive pulmonary disease
Malabsorption syndromes

animals.[22] The anorexia and weight loss associated with depression often respond well to low-dose antidepressant therapy. When a depressed patient is severely malnourished, vigorous therapy, including electroconvulsive therapy, if necessary, should be considered.

Drug side effects are a common cause of anorexia. For example, up to one-fourth of patients over age 70 who take digoxin develop anorexia.[23]

Esophageal candidiasis may be persistent in an elderly patient and requires lifetime treatment. Many institutionalized elderly patients eat in a nonerect position, which often causes aspiration of food and produces a conditioned aversion to eating. This problem can be resolved by taking care to see that the patient is in an upright position while eating. Intestinal ischemia can present as early satiety or a feeling of bloating. It responds well to either nitrates or calcium channel antagonists.

Zinc deficiency can cause anorexia, although it is rare to find an elderly patient whose anorexia is *primarily* due to zinc deficiency. In most cases, zinc deficiency is a secondary cause of anorexia in patients who have reduced caloric intake for other reasons. Both diuretics and diabetes mellitus can cause hyperzincuria, which can produce a borderline zinc status.[24]

The classical metabolic cause of weight loss is hyperthyroidism. It should be remembered that atypical presentations (apathetic hyperthyroidism) are not rare in older subjects. In addition, malnutrition leads to a reduction in triiodothyronine (T_3) levels. Thus, a severely malnourished patient who fails to show the typically low T_3 levels of the euthyroid sick syndrome may, in fact, have inappropriately elevated T_3 levels that suggest hyperthyroidism. Hyperparathyroidism and other causes of hypercalcemia may result in anorexia.

Severe weight loss is a common problem in patients with chronic obstructive pulmonary disease. Many of these patients become severely short of breath with the effort of eating. The provision of multiple small meals may result in beneficial weight gain in a number of these patients.

THE ANOREXIA OF AGING

In approximately one-fourth of elderly patients with significant weight loss, no obvious cause can be identified. In some of these patients social factors, such as poverty, a need for help with food shopping and preparation, and the lack of socialization at meals, are key elements; in others, no social problems are identifiable. Recently, a number of case reports have appeared describing a variant of anorexia nervosa occurring in patients over 60 years old.[25,26] This condition is characterized by dramatic weight loss associated with the patient's refusal to eat an adequate diet and a disturbance of body image. In our experience, a number of patients in nursing homes use food refusal to manipulate staff in an attempt to regain their locus of control.

Whether a true syndrome of age-associated anorexia exists remains controversial. However, human and animal studies have suggested that a number of age-related changes exist which would be expected to lead to a reduced calorie intake in the elderly (Table 5-3).

The decrease in metabolic rate and reduced activity are well documented to occur with advancing age and clearly represent a physiological reason for reduced calorie intake. In addition, some reduction in chemical senses appears to be a universal concomitant of aging. Gustatory papillae begin to atrophy in females in the early forties and in males in the fifties. There are approximately 250 taste buds in each circumvallate papilla in young adults, while individuals between 75 and 84 years of age have less than 100 taste buds in each circumvallate papilla.[27] Taste thresholds increase with advancing age, but it is controversial whether the changes are of sufficient magnitude to produce a marked effect on food intake.[28] There are marked changes in olfaction in older subjects, as well. Schiffman[29] has demonstrated the inability of older subjects to recognize blended foods, predominantly due to a decrease in odor detection.

TABLE 5-3
Causes of the Anorexia of Aging

Decreased demand
  Lower metabolic rate
  Reduced activity
Decreased hedonic qualities
  Taste
  Smell
  Vision
Decreased feeding drive
  Neurotransmitters (e.g., decreased endogenous opioid effect)
  Nutritional factors (e.g., zinc deficiency)
Increased activity of satiety factors
  Cholecystokinin

It is now well-recognized that the endogenous opioid peptide, dynorphin, plays a role in producing the feeding drive.[30] Recently, rodent studies have demonstrated a marked attenuation of this opioid feeding-drive system in older animals.[31] Termination of a meal is brought about by the release of a number of gastrointestinal hormones as food passes through the gastrointestinal tract. Silver et al.[32] have demonstrated that old animals have an enhanced sensitivity to the action of the satiety peptide, cholecystokinin. This excessive action of cholecystokinin could explain the early satiety which is seen in some older subjects who are losing weight.

PATHOLOGICAL CAUSES OF WEIGHT LOSS IN THE ELDERLY

Weight loss is common in association with dementia. Dementia can lead to indifference to food, failure to remember to eat, failure to recognize the need to eat, and behavioral abnormalities, such as holding food in the mouth and apraxia. Severely demented patients require help with feeding, and one study[33] found that 99 minutes a day was spent feeding demented patients at home, while only 18 minutes was spent on feeding similar patients in nursing homes. Whether malnutrition in patients with Alzheimer's disease is due to decreased food intake or increased metabolism is controversial. Sandman et al.[12] found marked protein-calorie malnutrition in patients with Alzheimer's disease despite a mean daily energy intake of over 2000 calories. Patients with Alzheimer's disease have reduced levels of neuropeptide Y and norepinephrine in the central nervous system. Both of these neurotransmitters have been shown to play a role in initiating feeding in animals.[28]

Cachectin (tumor necrosis factor) is released from macrophages when subjects are exposed to infection or cancer[34] (see Chap. 113). Cachectin inhibits lipogenic enzymes[35] and also causes anorexia.[36] A number of nursing home patients have repeated bouts of infection and appear to lose weight out of proportion to their decrease in food intake. It is possible that in these patients cachectin plays a causative role in the excessive weight loss.

Ectopic hormone production in association with neoplasms occurs commonly in older subjects and may precede the overt development of signs and symptoms of cancer. A number of peptides produced by tumors, e.g., bombesin and calcitonin, are potent anorectic agents. Thus, ectopic production of peptides needs to be considered in the differential diagnosis of malnutrition and weight loss in aging.

The factors involved in the anorexia of the elderly are summarized in Fig. 5-1.

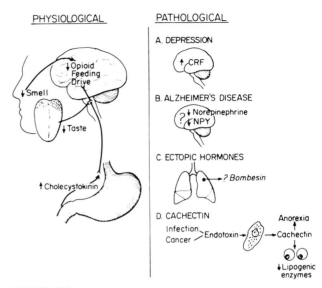

FIGURE 5-1
Factors involved in the pathogenesis of anorexia in the elderly. (*Reproduced with permission from Morley and Silver.*[28])

COMPARISON BETWEEN THE EFFECTS OF PROTEIN-CALORIE MALNUTRITION AND AGING

There are a number of similarities between the aging process and protein-calorie malnutrition (Table 5-4).[37] In addition, in some cases the changes attributed to aging, e.g., decreased albumin, may, in fact, be due to poor nutritional intake. However, in most cases the changes associated with aging are not due to malnutrition, although malnutrition can clearly exacerbate the changes associated with normal aging. Also, the changes due to malnutrition may be reversible with institution of proper nutritional support and thus need to be distinguished from those associated with aging. Failure to recognize malnutrition in the elderly can have serious effects on morbidity and mortality, as is illustrated in Fig. 5-2, which shows the classical course of malnutrition in the elderly.

MACRONUTRIENTS

PROTEINS

Aging is associated with a reduction in lean body mass and a reduction in protein intake. In Sweden, 70-year-olds were demonstrated to lose 1 kg of lean body mass over the subsequent 5 years of life.[38] The recommended daily allowance (RDA) for protein is 0.8 g protein per kg body weight. Early studies suggested that this amount of protein or even less was sufficient to maintain nitrogen balance in the elderly.[39,40] More recently, Uauy et al.[41] and Gersovitz et al.[42] both found that some elderly sub-

TABLE 5-4
Comparison between the Effects of Aging and Protein-Calorie Malnutrition

Parameter	Effect of Age*	Malnutrition
Lean body mass	↓	↓
Adipose tissue	↑	↓
Basal metabolic rate	↓	↓
Albumin	N or (↓)	↓
Somatomedin C	↓	↓
Skeletal muscle mass/strength	↓	↓
Cardiac output	N or (↓)	↓
Maximum breathing capacity	↓	↓
Glomerular filtration rate	↓	↓
Glucose clearance	↓	↓
Hematocrit	N	↓
Bone mass	↓	↓
Intestinal mucosal mass	↓	↓
Drug metabolism	↓	↓
Immune function		
Cell-mediated immunity	↓	↓
T-cells	↓	↓
Blastic response to mitogen stimulation	↓	↓
Natural killer cells	N or ↑	↓
Antibodies	↓	↓
Autoantibodies	↑	N
Granulocyte response to infection	↓	↓
Cognition	↓	↓

*N, no change; ↓, decrease; ↑, increase. A symbol in parentheses suggests that the change is due to disease, rather than to aging per se.

jects with minor chronic diseases required a greater protein intake than the recommended 0.8 g/kg/day. Studies in the United States and Britain have suggested that on the whole, healthy elderly ingest approximately 1 g protein/kg/day.[43] However, subjects with chronic diseases who may, in fact, require a greater protein intake are likely to ingest less protein. Further, there is an emerging controversy regarding high-protein diets and the risk of acceleration of chronic renal disease.

With aging, there are slight decreases in both whole-body protein synthesis and protein degradation rates.[44,45] Gersovitz et al.[42] found that albumin synthesis rates were slightly lower in old than in young subjects, but old subjects failed to adapt to a decreased protein intake by reducing albumin synthesis. In healthy elderly, serum albumin levels are maintained, but minor degrees of illness can lead to depressed levels of serum albumin in many elderly.[46]

Levels of essential amino acids, such as valine, methionine, isoleucine, leucine, phenylalanine, and lysine, are lower in older human subjects than in young adults.[47] Whether there is a true increase in essential amino acid requirements with aging is controversial. Essential amino acid requirements can be met in most adults by approximately 20 percent of their total protein intake, making it extremely unlikely for elderly adults to have essential amino acid deficiency.

LIPIDS

Serum cholesterol and triglyceride levels increase with age as does the proportion of total adipose tissue.[24] In the old old (over age 80), cholesterol and low-density lipoprotein (LDL) levels fall in comparison to levels of LDL in people between ages 60 and 79.[48] This reduction in lipid levels with extreme advanced age either could be associated with the removal by coronary heart disease of many of those with elevated cholesterol levels

FIGURE 5-2
Classical course of malnutrition in an elderly individual.

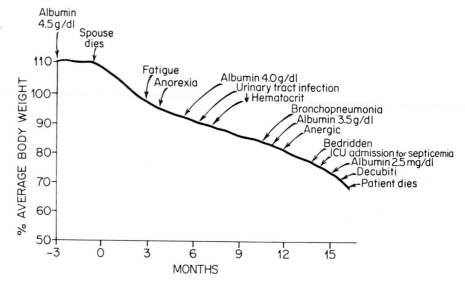

from the population distribution or could be secondary to the fact that many long-lived individuals come from kindreds with familial hypobeta- or hyperalphalipoproteinemia.[24] In addition, high-density lipoprotein (HDL) cholesterol levels tend to be higher in older individuals than in middle-aged individuals in cross-sectional studies.[49] Finally, the predictive value of cholesterol levels for the development of cardiovascular disease is markedly attenuated in subjects over 70 years of age.[50]

Obesity remains a problem in the elderly population, with one-fourth to one-half being 20 percent or more overweight.[24] While underweight is a major problem of the elderly, we cannot afford to ignore the problem of overweight which is also associated with increased mortality in all but the very old.[4] Even in nursing home situations, overweight is associated with excess mortality.[11] It needs to be remembered that lower-body fat distribution is associated with a much lower incidence of cardiovascular and cerebrovascular accidents (and death) than is midriff obesity. Surgery for obesity is not recommended for patients over 60 years old. Exercise is an important intervention for obese older subjects and should be tried at the same time as moderate calorie restriction.

CARBOHYDRATES

There are no specific requirements for carbohydrates in the elderly except as a component of total energy intake. Nonabsorbable carbohydrates (i.e., fiber) do influence nutritional considerations in the elderly. The enzymes necessary for the breakdown of dietary fiber are not present in the human digestive tract. Dietary fiber increases peristalsis and decreases intestinal transit time; hence, increased intake of dietary fiber may alleviate constipation. However, it needs to be remembered that dietary fiber in bedfast individuals is constipating and can lead to megacolon and sigmoid volvulus. In institutionalized individuals, dietary fiber prescriptions should be limited to those patients who are ambulatory. Soluble dietary fiber may also smooth the glycemic response to a meal, preventing major swings in postprandial glucose levels. Dietary fiber may bind trace elements, leading to a decrease in absorption. While in most subjects on an adequate diet this does not represent a problem, in those with borderline nutritional status an increase in dietary fiber may result in trace element deficiencies. While small increases in dietary fiber (5 g/day) are often well tolerated by the elderly, increases approaching amounts recommended for younger adults (20 g/day) are poorly tolerated. An increase in dietary fiber intake must always be accompanied by an increase in fluid intake.

WATER AND HYPODIPSIA

Water is the most essential of all elements. As stressed by Watkin[51]:

> The primacy of water in the management of illnesses and accidents among the old deserves the greatest of deference. Altogether too many older persons arrive in the emergency rooms near death, not for the lack of proper medications or even nursing care at home, but for the lack of knowledge that proper hydration is an ever-present requirement of good health.

Water comprises approximately two-thirds of the body weight and is found in intracellular compartments (41 percent of body weight); interstitial compartments (trapped between connective tissue—15 percent of body weight); and in the form of plasma, lymph, and spinal fluid (9 percent of body weight). With advancing age, there is slow chronic dehydration. There is a decreased ability of renal tubules to recycle the water filtered by the renal glomerulae.[52] In addition, the colon is a major site for water reabsorption from the feces. Decreased dietary fiber intake by the elderly leads to less water being delivered to the colon trapped in hydrophilic vegetable fibers to allow for colonic reabsorption.

Dehydration is the most common cause of fluid and electrolyte disturbance in the elderly. The regulation of serum osmolality is dependent on water intake normally driven by thirst and on renal excretion of solute-free water. Abnormalities in the secretion and effectiveness of both arginine vasopressin and atrial natriuretic factor with aging interact with deteriorating renal function to place the elderly individual in a precarious balance as far as renal free water excretion is concerned. Diuretic administration may further aggravate the free water loss.

Hypodipsia has been clearly documented to occur in elderly individuals even when they are obviously in a position to request and obtain water. In some cases, this hypodipsia appears to be related to cerebrovascular disease. In other cases, environmental conditions, such as the presence of water at the bedside but just out of reach of the disabled individual, represents a major barrier to obtaining adequate amounts of fluids. Phillips et al.[53] have clearly demonstrated that after overnight water deprivation, older males are less thirsty in comparison to younger males and fail to drink sufficient water to correct their water deficit. In preliminary studies in rodents, we have found that older mice fail to show the obligatory increase in water intake normally associated with food ingestion. The reasons for the failure of older individuals to recognize a water need are unclear. The reduced baroreceptor sensitivity seen with aging could be partly responsible, as the baroreceptor may fail to signal the presence of hypovolemia. Older subjects also report that their mouths feel less dry with dehydration, suggesting that oropharyngeal factors may play a role in the decreased thirst recognition seen with aging.

Extracellular fluid loss in the elderly produces a number of effects classically thought to be associated with aging. These include weight loss; sunken eyes due to loss of retro-orbital fat; stiff joints due to decreased synovial fluid secretion; constipation; xerostomia; xeropthalmia; dry, scaly, loose skin; apathy; depression; and cognitive disturbances. In addition, fluid loss can lead to decreased urine volume and breakdown of body reserves to produce endogenous water from fats and carbohydrates.

Active management of water metabolism is essential in the elderly. Geriatricians believe that the development of dehydration in elderly patients in hospitals or nursing homes reflects inadequate medical and nursing care. Admission to hospital often places elderly subjects in a "water desert," where water appears to be readily available but is, in fact, rarely within reach of the individual.[54] A water desert requires a water prescription. The fluid prescription for the elderly patient, a major part of the therapeutic armamentarium, needs to be delivered with the same care as is given to the administration of other life-preserving drugs. Care needs to be taken to write the water prescription with an awareness of the patient's overall electrolyte status. The syndrome of inappropriate antidiuretic hormone secretion, which is commonly present in debilitated elderly, requires water restriction rather than water repletion. We suggest that for all elderly in whom there is no contraindication a minimum water prescription on admission to a hospital or a long-term care setting should consist of an additional one liter of fluid per day.

TRACE ELEMENTS

ZINC

Zinc was demonstrated to be an essential nutrient in 1934. The RDA for zinc is 15 mg (229 μmol) per day. Most of the elderly ingest less than the RDA, with the average daily intake being 107 to 198 μmol/day in home-dwelling elderly and as little as 53 to 81 μmol/day in patients in nursing homes.[55] Metabolic balance studies have suggested that the RDA is a gross overestimation of the amount of zinc necessary for healthy elderly subjects to maintain zinc balance and that levels around 137 μmol/day are adequate. However, in housebound elderly, levels between 51 to 149 μmol/day resulted in a negative zinc balance.[56]

The major determinant of zinc balance is calorie intake. With the exception of oysters, no food has an especially high zinc content. All subjects who ingest less than 1000 calories a day are at risk for zinc deficiency. In addition, administration of pharmacological doses of iron

and calcium can interfere with the absorption of zinc, as can high-fiber diets and phytates. There is a mild impairment of zinc absorption with advancing age. In addition, diabetes mellitus and diuretic use cause zinc wastage in the urine. Overall serum, bone, and kidney zinc concentrations decrease with advancing age, while leukocyte zinc concentrations appear to be maintained. The alterations in zinc metabolism that occur with age are summarized in Fig. 5-3.

Zinc deficiency produces many abnormalities which are similar to those changes attributed to normal aging (Table 5-5).[57] These abnormalities include anorexia, dysgeusia, T-cell deficiencies, poor wound healing, decreased vision, impotence, and carbohydrate abnormalities. Animal studies have clearly established that zinc deficiency produces anorexia. While zinc deficiency in humans is associated with taste abnormalities, as is aging, zinc replacement has not been shown to reverse the dysgeusia of the elderly. Much evidence has suggested that zinc deficiency causes poor wound healing in animals, and zinc replacement has been demonstrated to accelerate healing of peripheral vascular ulcers in patients with a low serum zinc level. No good controlled study of the efficacy of zinc in the treatment of decubiti has been published, although zinc supplementation is widely advocated, especially for the malnourished with bed sores. Zinc is co-secreted with insulin; however, no studies have convincingly shown a role for zinc in the pathogenesis of the hyperglycemia of aging. A number of animal studies have shown that zinc deficiency leads to hypogonadism, and preliminary studies have shown that a small subgroup of older impotent subjects may have zinc deficiency and that their impotence may be reversed by pharmacological zinc supplementation.[58]

Zinc is necessary for adequate T-cell function. Low serum zinc levels in the elderly are associated with anergy and a poor postimmunization antibody response to influenza vaccine.[59,60] Zinc replacement improves cellu-

TABLE 5-5
Comparison between Zinc Deficiency and Aging

	Zinc Deficiency	*Aging*
Anorexia	Yes	Common
Dysgeusia	Yes	Yes
T-cell abnormalities	Yes	Yes
Wound healing	Poor	Zinc enhances healing of peripheral vascular ulcers.
Impotence/hypo-gonadism	Yes	Yes
Carbohydrate metabolism	Impaired	Impaired
Age-related macular degeneration	?	Zinc slows rate of progression.

FIGURE 5-3
The effects of aging, drugs, and disease on
zinc balance.

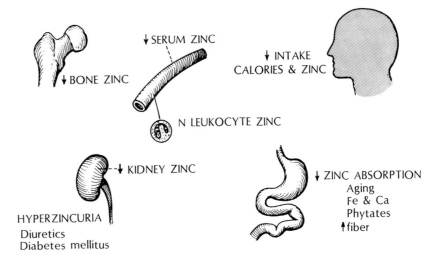

lar immunity in the elderly,[61,62] in diabetic patients with low serum zinc,[63] and in patients with lung cancer.[64]

Zinc plays a key role in the metabolism of the retina, and the highest concentration of zinc in the body is found in the retinal pigment epithelium-choroid complex. Age-related macular degeneration is an important cause of visual loss in older individuals. Recently, Newsome et al.[65] found in a placebo-controlled, double-blind study that oral zinc treatment delayed the development of significant visual loss as compared to the onset of significant loss seen in placebo-treated subjects.

Toxic effects with zinc administration are rare. Large pharmacological doses of zinc decrease HDL cholesterol levels and will also decrease T-cell activity. The sulfate in zinc sulfate causes gastrointestinal irritation, so zinc sulfate should be administered with meals. Zinc gluconate does not cause gastric upset but is more expensive than zinc sulfate.

SELENIUM

As a constituent of glutathione peroxidase, selenium plays a role in the system that prevents the accumulation of lipid peroxides and free radicals, which damage cell membranes and macromolecules, including DNA. Free radical generation may play a role in the pathogenesis of the aging process.

There is no evidence that serum selenium levels fall with advancing age[66] in the United States. Selenium levels in hair fall slightly with advancing age.[67] Selenium levels in humans correlate more closely with the selenium content of the soil than with advancing age. Two studies have demonstrated low serum selenium levels and reduced activity of glutathione perioxidase in elderly nursing home patients who are being tube fed.[68,69]

Selenium deficiency has been associated with a painful myopathy and nail changes in patients on total parenteral nutrition. Young children in selenium-defi-

cient areas develop a cardiomyopathy (Keshan disease). Whether selenium deficiency can aggravate heart disease in the elderly is unknown. Selenium deficiency has been associated with impaired cellular and humoral immune response.

There is some evidence that low selenium intake may be associated with increased cancer risk.[70] A case-controlled prospective study demonstrated marked increases in cancer risk when serum selenium levels were depressed.[71] This risk of cancer was magnified when vitamin E levels were also depressed. Numerous animal studies have shown that high selenium levels retard the development of cancer. An in vitro study of irradiated cells found that both selenium and vitamin E, acting at different sites, could attenuate the radiation-induced damage.

In adults, a daily intake of 50 to 200 μg of selenium has been recommended. The maximum safe daily dose is estimated to be between 350 and 700 μg. Signs of selenium toxicity include a garlic odor on the breath, fingernail changes, hepatotoxicity, and a peripheral neuropathy. Selenium supplementation should be considered in elderly who are being tube fed.

CHROMIUM

Animal studies have shown that chromium deficiency results in hyperglycemia, hypercholesterolemia, and corneal opacities.[72] The bioactive form of chromium is complexed with a dinicotinic acid/glutathione complex which is termed *glucose tolerance factor*. Tissue chromium levels decline with advancing age. The role of chromium deficiency in the pathogenesis of the hyperglycemia of aging in humans is controversial, with some studies supporting a minor role and others rejecting it. A recent, well-controlled study in 16 patients over the age of 65 found that chromium given with nicotinic acid resulted in a 15 percent decrease in the integrated glucose area in response to a glucose load.[73] However the clinical significance of such observations is not clear. The RDA for chromium is 50 to 200 μg per day, which is probably higher than the amount needed to maintain chromium balance in healthy elderly individuals.

OTHER TRACE ELEMENTS

The role of calcium is discussed in detail in Chap. 77. Overall, it is estimated that the elderly should ingest 1 to 1.5 g of calcium daily. Manganese deficiency can lead to abnormal bone and cartilage formation and impaired glucose tolerance.[74] There is no evidence that serum manganese concentrations are altered with aging. Tissue concentrations of cobalt, which functions as an integral part of the vitamin B_{12} molecule, do not alter with age. Silicon is involved in the maintenance of the structural integrity of bone and connective tissue. Silicon levels have been found to decline in the tissues of rodents and humans with advancing age. Patients with severe atherosclerosis have decreased silicon levels in the arterial walls.

Copper is an important cofactor in numerous enzymatic reactions, including the cross-linking of collagen and elastin, the superoxidase dismutase reaction, and the conversion of norepinephrine to dopamine. Copper is also involved in iron absorption and mobilization. Copper deficiency increases serum cholesterol levels in rats.[75] Plasma copper levels appear to increase with advancing age.

The RDA for iron is 10 mg. The HANES study showed that daily intakes of iron for American men averaged 14 mg and for elderly women, 10 mg.[24] A study in New Mexico showed that one-third of the elderly ingested less than 10 mg of iron per day. Insufficient iron stores are present in approximately 5 percent of older subjects. Serum ferritin increases in the majority of elderly, as do bone marrow iron stores. Liver iron stores are unchanged in elderly males and increased in females following cessation of menstruation. Iron absorption is unaltered with advancing age.

VITAMINS

The RDA for vitamins is outdated and provides little allowance for age-related differences. There is evidence that the 1980 RDA is too low for vitamins B_6, B_{12}, and D and too high for folate and vitamin A. There is accumulating data on the vitamin intake of the elderly population. In one survey, one-fourth of healthy elderly had dietary intakes of vitamins B_6, D, E, and folacin less than 50 percent of the RDA, and vitamin B_{12} intake was only 75 percent of the RDA.[76] Based on data from the HANES study, it was estimated that 10 percent of the elderly have vitamin intakes below two-thirds of the

RDA.[43] Intake of vitamin A and water-soluble vitamins was particularly poor. On the other hand, 57 percent of healthy elderly men and 61 percent of healthy elderly women surveyed in Albuquerque, New Mexico, were taking one or more vitamin or mineral supplements.[76]

VITAMIN C

There is much evidence that plasma, leukocyte, and platelet vitamin C levels decline with advancing age.[24] As there is no evidence that vitamin C absorption is altered with aging, this decline must be attributed to decreased intake. Ascorbate levels below 0.2 mg/dl (a level at which clinical evidence of scurvy is liable to develop) were present in 1.9 percent of elderly subjects.

Encouraged by the proclamations (and longevity) of Linus Pauling, many people have taken megadoses of vitamin C to protect against upper respiratory tract infections and neoplasms. In a Southern California retirement community, 67 percent of residents were taking vitamin C supplements and 6 percent were taking 2 g or more of vitamin C daily.[77]

Surveys of the literature have concluded that taking megadoses of vitamin C is neither worth the effort nor the risk. Table 5-6 summarizes the major risks associated with megadose vitamin C ingestion. In particular, physicians need to be careful not to withdraw vitamin C suddenly from patients undergoing surgery (some of whom are taking 20 to 40 g of vitamin C per day) as these patients are at risk for developing rebound scurvy. Vitamin C should be withdrawn for at least 3 days before testing stools for occult blood. Recently, we have seen diabetic patients taking greater than 10 g of vitamin C daily; the vitamin C interferes with the measurement of serum glucose in these patients, resulting in inappropriate alterations in the insulin dosage.

VITAMIN A

The major functions of vitamin A are in dark adaptation, hemoglobin synthesis, and maintenance of epithelial integrity. While aging is associated with a significant decline in the light threshold, this decline is not correlated with the serum vitamin A levels and is not reversed by vitamin A supplementation.[78] The classic sign of vitamin

TABLE 5-6
Side Effects of Megadoses of Vitamin C

Rebound scurvy
False-negative fecal occult blood disease
Altered urine and serum glucose measurements
Oxalic acid renal calculi
Reduced vitamin B_{12} absorption
Excessive absorption of dietary iron
Hemolytic anemia (glucose-6-phosphate dehydrogenase
    deficiency)

A deficiency, follicular hyperkeratosis, while seen in the elderly, is more often related to poor hygiene than to vitamin A deficiency. Vitamin A and retinol-binding protein levels do not fall with age. As a person ages, vitamin A is more rapidly absorbed from the intestine, and the liver takes up vitamin A less adequately from the circulation. These changes are protective of the vitamin A stores in the elderly. Vitamin A deficiency may be present in a few institutionalized elderly, alcoholics, those with malabsorption syndromes, and patients taking drugs that interfere with vitamin A absorption (such as mineral oil, neomycin, or cholestyramine). Overall, a vitamin A intake of 600 to 700 μg a day should be sufficient to prevent vitamin A deficiency in the elderly.

Epidemiologic studies have suggested that a high intake of foods containing vitamin A or its precursor, beta-carotene, may be protective against lung cancer.[79] If a patient insists on taking vitamin A or beta-carotene for this purpose, beta-carotene is to be preferred, as the body can efficiently prevent excessive production of vitamin A from the beta-carotene. Beta-carotene produces a yellow discoloration of the skin without ictal sclera. Hypothyroidism can lead to elevated circulating beta-carotene levels.

Vitamin A is the second most commonly consumed nutritional supplement. Vitamin A toxicity occurs after long-term ingestion of 50,000 IU or more per day. Toxic effects of vitamin A include malaise, headaches, liver dysfunction, leukopenia, and hypercalcemia. It would seem that vitamin A should not be included in geriatric multivitamin supplements.

VITAMIN E

Vitamin E is a series of compounds consisting of 6-hydroxychromane with a 16-carbon isoprenoid side chain. The most important of these compounds is alpha-tocopherol. The need for vitamin E is dependent on the diet, with much higher levels being necessary if the diet is rich in polyunsaturated fats. Vitamin E is necessary for the action of glutathione peroxidase which prevents the formation of the hydroxyl radical. Vitamin E has also been used in the treatment of intermittent claudication.[80] In the healthy elderly, there is no change in plasma alpha-tocopherol and a slight decline in gamma-tocopherol.[81] Platelet levels of alpha- and gamma-tocopherol decline with age. Lower levels of tocopherols have been reported in sick elderly, while diabetes mellitus appears to raise vitamin E levels.[82]

VITAMIN K

Hazell and Baloch[83] have found that 74 percent of older subjects have an abnormal thrombotest for coagulation factors and that this abnormality can be reversed by oral administration of vitamin K. Relative vitamin K deficiency may explain the increased sensitivity of older humans to warfarin.

B VITAMINS

Thiamine intake is less than two-thirds of the RDA in nearly 50 percent of elderly.[43] Measurements of blood thiamine, red blood cell transaminase, thiamine pyrophosphate, and urinary thiamine excretion have all suggested that approximately 10 percent of elderly have a borderline thiamine status. Excessive alcohol intake in a malnourished individual represents the classic situation in which thiamine deficiency develops. In addition, glucose infusion may precipitate thiamine deficiency, as thiamine is an essential cofactor for entry into the Krebs cycle. It should also be remembered that in a malnourished individual thiamine administration may increase glucose metabolism and precipitate hypoglycemia.

The elderly often have borderline riboflavin (vitamin B$_{12}$) and pyridoxine (B$_6$) status. No changes in niacin status have been demonstrated in the elderly. Folate intakes of 100 μg/day (one-fourth of the RDA) appear to be adequate to maintain folate balance in the elderly. Folate deficiency (less than 3 μg/ml of blood) occurs in 3 to 7 percent of free-living elderly. Pantothenic acid (blood- and protein-bound) declines with advancing age. Biotin levels have been reported to be unchanged or decreased with advancing age.

Vitamin B$_{12}$ deficiency (i.e., pernicious anemia) is usually due to loss of intrinsic factor. However, the increasing prevalence of hypo- and achlorhydria due to atrophic gastritis with advancing age will decrease B$_{12}$ absorption by not adequately freeing B$_{12}$ bound to protein and by allowing the development of bacterial overgrowth. B$_{12}$ intakes appear to be reduced in many elderly, and serum B$_{12}$ levels below 150 pg/ml increase in the elderly.

Overall, the elderly appear to be in borderline B-vitamin status. For this reason, it is not unreasonable for an elderly individual to take a B-vitamin supplement, particularly if calorie intake has been reduced.

DRUG–NUTRIENT INTERACTIONS

In the elderly with borderline nutritional status, the addition of a drug can result in nutritional decompensation. Multiple drugs, including digoxin, theophylline, hydrochlorthiazide, nonsteroidal anti-inflammatory agents, and triamterene, can result in anorexia, while allopurinol, clindamycin, and antihistamines can lead to hypogeusia. Isoniazid can produce both vitamin B$_6$ and niacin deficiency (pellagra). Mineral oil can impair the absorption of vitamins A, D, and K. Hydralazine can result in B$_6$ deficiency. Tetracycline reduces the absorption of calcium and iron. Folate deficiency occurs with anticonvulsants, triamterene, and trimethoprim. Anticonvulsants also impair vitamin D absorption and increase the requirement for vitamin K. Salicylates decrease the uptake of vitamin C by platelets and leukocytes and can result in iron-deficiency anemia and hypoprothrombinemia secondary to interfering with vitamin K metabolism. Diuretics can lead to zinc deficiency.

On the other hand, foods can interfere with drug effects. Vitamin K–containing foods, such as cabbage and broccoli, can interfere with the anticoagulant activity of warfarin sodium. Coadministration of food can reduce drug absorption of a number of drugs, such as cephalosporins, penicillin, and sulfadiazine, while in other cases it may reduce first-pass hepatic metabolism, resulting in increased drug availability (e.g., with propranolol and spironolactone).

REFERENCES

1. McCay L et al: The effect of retarded growth upon the length of life span and upon the ultimate body size. *J Nutr* 10:63, 1935.
2. McCay L et al: Retarded growth, life span, ultimate body size and age changes in the albino rat after feeding diets restricted in calories. *J Nutr* 18:1, 1939.
3. Osborne TB, Mendel LB: The resumption of growth after long continued failure to grow. *J Biol Chem* 23:439, 1915.
4. Andres R: Effect of obesity on total mortality. *Int J Obes* 4:381, 1980.
5. Feinleib M: Epidemiology of obesity in relation to health hazzards. *Ann Intern Med* 103:1019, 1985.
6. Harris T et al: Body mass index and mortality among nonsmoking older persons. The Framingham Heart Study. *JAMA* 259:1522, 1988.
7. Abraham S et al: Dietary intake of persons 1–74 years of age in the United States. Advance data from Vital and Health Statistics of the National Center for Health Statistics, No. 6. Rockville, Maryland, Health Resources Administration, Public Health Service, March 30, 1977.
8. Hill GL et al: Malnutrition in surgical patients. *Lancet* 1:689, 1977.
9. Bienia R et al: Malnutrition in the hospitalized geriatric patient. *J Am Geriatr Soc* 30:433, 1982.
10. Pinchofsky-Devin GD, Kaminski MV: Correlation of pressure sores and nutritional status. *J Am Geriatr Soc* 34:435, 1986.
11. Silver AJ et al: Nutritional status in an academic nursing home. *J Am Geriatr Soc* 36:487, 1988.
12. Sandman PO et al: Nutritional status and dietary intake in institutionalized patients with Alzheimer's disease and multiinfarct dementia. *J Am Geriatr Soc* 35:31, 1987.
13. Master A, Lasser R: Tables of average weight and height of Americans aged 65–94 years. *JAMA* 172:658, 1960.
14. Andres R et al: Impact of age on weight goals. *Ann Intern Med* 103:1030, 1985.
15. Mitchell C, Lipschitz D: Arm length measurement as an alternative to height in nutritional assessment of the elderly. *J Parenter Enteral Nutr* 6:226, 1982.
16. Friedman PJ et al: Prospective trial of a new diagnostic criterion for severe wasting malnutrition in the elderly. *Age Ageing* 14:149, 1985.
17. Rudman D et al: Antecedents of death in the men of a Veterans Administration nursing home. *J Am Geriatr Soc* 35:496, 1987.
18. Rudman D et al: Hyposomatomedinemia in the nursing home patient. *J Am Geriatr Soc* 34:427, 1986.
19. Marton et al: Involuntary weight loss: Diagnostic and prognostic significance. *Ann Intern Med* 95:568, 1981.
20. Rabinowitz M et al: Unintentional weight loss. *Arch Intern Med* 146:186, 1986.
21. Blazer D et al: Major depression with melancholia: A comparison of middle-aged and elderly adults. *J Am Geriatr Soc* 35:927, 1987.
22. Morley JE, Levine AS: Corticotropin-releasing factor, grooming and ingestive behavior. *Life Sci* 31:1459, 1982.
23. Bowman K et al: Is maintenance digoxin necessary in geriatric patients? *Acta Med Scand* 210:493, 1981.
24. Morley JE: Nutritional status of the elderly. *Am J Med* 81:679, 1986.
25. Romell MD, Brown N: Anorexia nervosa in a 67-year-old woman. *Postgrad Med J* 64:48, 1988.
26. Price WA et al: Anorexia nervosa in the elderly. *J Am Geriatr Soc* 33:213, 1985.
27. Arey LB et al: The numerical and topographical relations of taste buds to human circumvallate papillae throughout the life span. *Anat Rec* 64 (suppl 1):9, 1936.
28. Morley JE, Silver AS: Anorexia in the elderly. *Neurobiol Aging* 9:9, 1988.
29. Schiffman S: Food recognition by the elderly. *J Gerontol* 32:586, 1977.
30. Morley JE et al: Opioid modulation of appetite. *Neurosci Biobehav Rev* 7:281, 1983.
31. Gosnell BA et al: The effects of aging on opioid modulation of feeding in rats. *Life Sci* 32:2793, 1983.
32. Silver AJ et al: Effect of gastrointestinal peptides on ingestion in young and old mice. *Peptides* 9:221, 1988.
33. Hu T et al: Evaluation of the costs of caring for the senile demented elderly: A pilot study. *Gerontologist* 26:158, 1986.
34. Morley JE et al: The effect of vagotomy on the satiety effects of neuropeptides and naloxone. *Life Sci* 30:1943, 1982.
35. Torti FM et al: A macrophage factor inhibits adipocyte gene expression: An *in-vitro* model of cachexia. *Science* 229:867, 1985.
36. Wei H et al: Cachectin mediates suppressed food intake and anemia during chronic administration. *Fed Proc* 46:1339A, 1987.
37. Dworkin BM: Nutritional support of the geriatric patient, in Gambert SR (ed): *Contemporary Geriatric Medicine*, vol 2. New York, Plenum, 1986, p 375.
38. Steen GB et al: Body composition at 70 and 75 years of age: A longitudinal population study. *J Clin Exp Gerontol* 1:185, 1979.
39. Cheng AHR et al: Comparative nitrogen balance study between young and aged adults using three levels of protein intake from a combination of wheat-soy-milk mixture. *Am J Clin Nutr* 31:12, 1978.
40. Zanni E et al: Protein requirements of elderly men. *J Nutr* 109:513, 1979.

41. Uauy R et al: Human protein requirements: Nitrogen balance response to graded levels of egg protein in elderly men and women. *Am J Clin Nutr* 31:779, 1978.

42. Gersovitz M et al: Human protein requirements: Assessment of the adequacy of the current recommended dietary allowance for dietary protein in elderly men and women. *Am J Clin Nutr* 35:6, 1982.

43. Munro HN et al: Nutritional requirements of the elderly. *Annu Rev Nutr* 7:23, 1987.

44. Young VR: Impact of aging on protein metabolism, in Armbrecht HJ, Prendergast JM, Coe RM (eds): *Nutritional Intervention in the Aging Process*. New York, Springer Verlag, 1984, p 27.

45. Golden MHN, Waterlow JC: Total protein synthesis in elderly people: A comparison of the results with 15-N glycine and 14-C leucine. *Clin Sci* 53:227, 1977.

46. Mitchell CO, Lipschitz DA: The effect of age and sex on the routinely used measurements to assess the nutritional status of hospitalized patients. *Am J Clin Nutr* 36:340, 1982.

47. Ackermann PG, Kheim T: Plasma amino acids in young and older human subjects. *Clin Chem* 10:32, 1964.

48. Nicholson J et al: Lipid and lipoprotein distributions in octo- and nonagenarians. *Metabolism* 28:51, 1979.

49. U.S. Department of Health and Human Services, Public Health Service, National Institutes of Health, Lipid Metabolism Branch, NHLBI: The Lipid Research Clinics, Population Studies Data Book, vol 1. NIH 80:1527, Bethesda, MD, 1980.

50. Leupker RV: Detection and treatment of hypercholesterolemia in the older adult. *Geriatr Med Today* 7(5):48, 1988.

51. Watkin DM: *Handbook of Nutrition, Health and Aging*. Park Ridge, New Jersey, Noyes Publications, 1983.

52. Massler M: Water needs in the elderly, in Watson RR (ed): *CRC Handbook of Nutrition in the Aged*. Boca Raton, Florida, CRC Press, 1986, p 195.

53. Phillips PA et al: Reduced thirst after water deprivation in healthy elderly men. *N Engl J Med* 311:753, 1984.

54. Lye M: Electrolyte disorders in the elderly. *J Clin Endocrinol Metab* 13:377, 1984.

55. Bunker VW et al: Assessment of zinc and copper status of healthy elderly people using metabolic balance studies and measurement of leukocyte concentrations. *Am J Clin Nutr* 40:1096, 1984.

56. Bunker VW et al: Metabolic balance studies for zinc and copper in housebound elderly people and the relationship between zinc balance and leukocyte zinc concentrations. *Am J Clin Nutr* 46:353, 1987.

57. Morley JE et al: UCLA Grand Rounds: Nutrition and the elderly. *J Am Geriatr Soc* 34:823, 1986.

58. Morley JE, Levine AS: Involvement of dynorphin and the kappa opioid receptor in feeding. *Peptides* 4:797, 1983.

59. Bogden JD et al: Zinc and immunocompetence in the elderly: Baseline data on zinc nutriture and immunity in unsupplemented subjects. *Am J Clin Nutr* 46:101, 1987.

60. Steidemann M, Harrell I: Relation of immunocompetence to selected nutrients in elderly women. *Nutr Rep Int* 21:931, 1980.

61. Duchateau J et al: Beneficial effects of oral zinc supplementation on the immune response of old people. *Am J Med* 70:1001, 1981.

62. Wagner PA et al: Zinc nutriture and cell-mediated immunity in the aged. *Int J Vitam Nutr Res* 53:94, 1983.

63. Niewoehner CB et al: The role of zinc supplementation in Type II diabetes mellitus. *Am J Med* 81:63, 1986.

64. Allen JI et al: The association between urinary zinc excretion and lymphocyte dysfunction in patients with lung cancer. *Am J Med* 79:209, 1985.

65. Newsome DA et al: Oral zinc in macular degeneration. *Arch Ophthalmol* 106:192, 1988.

66. Lane HW et al: Blood selenium and glutathione peroxidase levels and dietary selenium of free-living and institutionalized elderly subjects. *Proc Soc Exp Biol Med* 173:87, 1983.

67. Ganapathy SN, Thimaya S: Selenium in the aged, in Watson RR (ed): *CRC Handbook of Nutrition in the Aged*. Boca Raton, Florida, CRC Press, 1986, p 111.

68. Feller AG et al: Subnormal concentrations of serum selenium and plasma carnitine in chronically tube-fed patients. *Am J Clin Nutr* 45:476, 1987.

69. Gellert SA, Woldseth R: Trace element analysis as part of the nutritional assessment of geriatric patients. *Nutr Res* (suppl I):217, 1985.

70. Clark LC, Coombs GF Jr: Selenium compounds and the prevention of cancer: Research needs and public health implications. *J Nutr* 116:170, 1986.

71. Salomen JT et al: Association between serum selenium and risk of cancer. *Am J Epidemiol* 120:342, 1984.

72. Mooradian AD, Morley JE: Micronutrient status in diabetes mellitus. *Am J Clin Nutr* 45:877, 1987.

73. Urberg M, Zemel MB: Evidence for synergism between chromium and nicotinic acid in the control of glucose tolerance in elderly humans. *Metabolism* 36:896, 1987.

74. Udipi SA, Watson RR: Trace element requirements of the elderly, in Watson RR (ed): *CRC Handbook of Nutrition in the Aged*. Boca Raton, Florida, CRC Press, 1986, p 145.

75. Klevay LM: Hypercholesterolemia in rats produced by an increase in the ratio of zinc to copper ingested. *Am J Clin Nutr* 26:1060, 1973.

76. Garry PJ, Goodwin JS: Nutritional status in a healthy elderly population: Dietary and supplemental intakes. *Am J Clin Nutr* 36:319, 1982.

77. Gray GE et al: Dietary intake and nutrient supplement use in a Southern California retirement community. *Am J Clin Nutr* 38:122, 1983.

78. Birren JE et al: The relation of structural changes of the eye and vitamin A elevation of the light threshold in later life. *J Exp Psychol* 40:260, 1950.

79. Willett WC et al: Relation of serum vitamin A and E carotenoids to the risk of cancer. *N Engl J Med* 310:430, 1984.

80. Clein LJ et al: The use of tocopherol in the treatment of intermittent claudication. *Can Med Assoc J* 86:215, 1961; 87:538, 1962.

81. Vatassery GT: Changes in vitamin E concentrations in human plasma and platelets with age. *J Am Coll Nutr* 4:369, 1983.

82. Vatassery GT et al: Vitamin E in plasma and platelets of human diabetic patients and control subjects. *Am J Clin Nutr* 37:641, 1983.

83. Hazell K, Baloch KH: Vitamin K deficiency in the elderly. *Gerontol Clin* 12:10, 1970.

Chapter 6

CLINICAL IMMUNOLOGY

William H. Adler and James E. Nagel

The immune system provides a crucial mechanism for an individual's interaction with his or her environment. It is therefore necessary that this physiologic system be very adaptable so that it can respond to a variety of interacting external and internal factors. One factor that has a profound effect on immune function and host defense mechanisms is age. The determination of the effects of age on immune function and the mechanisms by which age can influence or alter these functions is difficult. This is so because many external factors, such as nutrition, environmental pollution, chemicals, and perhaps ultraviolet irradiation as well as factors unique to the individual, such as genetics, prior illness, influences of the neuroendocrine and endocrine systems, and anatomic variations, can alter immune function. For these reasons, it is difficult to isolate the role of age as a variable having an influence in a particular individual. It is also a well-established generalization that physiologic functions show high variability among individuals regardless of age. Furthermore, for most variables, interpopulation variability increases with age. As with other physiologic systems, one can find among even the oldest old some individuals with levels of immune function similar to that seen in much younger individuals. However, in general, with aging there are increasing numbers of individuals with decreased levels of function.

To the clinician faced with the care of an elderly patient, the conservative assumption is that one is dealing with an individual with an immunodeficiency and defective host defense mechanisms resulting in an increased chance of developing an infectious disease and having a greater morbidity and mortality due to that disease. These underlying problems often markedly affect the outcome of many illnesses that have an age-related increased incidence, such as emphysema, postoperative infections, urinary tract infections, bowel inflammation, and infections in areas with decreased blood perfusion. Behavioral or lifestyle variables, such as smoking, stress, alcohol abuse, drug abuse, and obesity, throughout a lifetime can also influence the incidence, morbidity, and mortality of diseases associated with aging.

In spite of the interactions and multifactorial cause–effect relationships between immune function and other factors, it has been possible to determine the effects of age on immune function by studying individuals who either are free of known illness or who have only minor diseases known to have no significant influences on immune function.

Perhaps the most convincing data that support the hypothesis that the immune system and host defense mechanisms decline in function with age are those associated with the data concerning morbidity and mortality from infectious illnesses. In most infectious illnesses there is an age-associated increase in morbidity and mortality. Most studies show high morbidity and mortality in the neonatal period, which then decline during the pre-teen, teenage, and early adult years. However, after sexual maturity has been reached there is a gradual increase in morbidity and mortality from infectious diseases that continues into the oldest age groups. In the oldest groups there is also a decrease in responsiveness to antibiotic therapy, probably because of defective or compromised immune or nonimmune host defense mechanisms.[1,2] These age-related changes in morbidity and mortality can be seen with meningitis, empyema, tuberculosis, pneumococcal pneumonia, influenza, AIDS, and bacteremia from any cause.

The age at which mortality and morbidity from infectious illnesses begin to increase occurs during the time when the thymus begins to involute. The thymus is crucial in the development of the immune system, and it is reasonable to associate this involution with an eventual down-regulation of immune function. The problems in linking thymic involution with immune dysfunction is that many of the cells in the immune system have very long life spans (decades) that make the onset of a clinically significant immunodeficiency a variable, time-related event. The concept of "using up" immunocompetent cells, which could be accelerated by life events such as stress, alcohol, smoking, and infection, may help to explain the variations in levels of immunocompetency in the population.

Data that describe the immunodeficiency associated with aging have utilized elderly individuals, some of whom are ambulatory healthy individuals and others nursing home residents or individuals in other chronic care medical facilities. The results obtained on these populations differ, although it is interesting to note the similarities of some data. Since clinicians must deal with both healthy and ill elderly patients, it is important to recognize the various changes in immune function that occur in these diverse populations. However, if the effects of age per se on immune function are to be ascertained, it is necessary to select study subjects who are not ill. In general, the differences in measures of immune function for healthy versus ill elderly individuals is less a matter of losses in specific activities than of differing degrees of loss in the same areas. The one system in the immune network which is most influenced by age is the T-cell system.[3] This would be expected if thymic involution has a long-term effect, since the development of immunocompetence depends on the presence of a functioning thymus. The T-cell system is of paramount importance in regulation of the immune response and in the development of cell-mediated immune responses. The effects of a failure in this system is quite important, as has been dramatically shown in the AIDS epidemic.

Very little data are available on longitudinal changes in immune function with age. It is very difficult to design a longitudinal immunology study because so many facets of the immune response are either very recently described or are still in the process of being defined and changed. There probably is not one immune function assay that could be predicted as being both valid today and valid in 20 or 30 years. Therefore, most studies are cross-sectional only, and the natural history of the developing immune deficiency is unknown.

ORGANIZATION OF THE IMMUNE SYSTEM

The immune system is one part of the host defense mechanism that includes a variety of both cells and serum factors. This complexity provides adaptability so that individuals can deal effectively with their environment. While specific defenses against pathogens, acquired from previous natural exposure or through immunization, are generally more effective in protecting an individual, there are nonspecific host defenses that are also important in providing protection. This protection from illness requires a complex interaction of many separate components of the host defense system. Before considering specific age-related defects in these systems, it would be useful to review the components of the host defense system that contribute to the maintenance of health.

A primary consideration in the interaction between a pathogen and host in determining whether the host will become ill and die is the element of time. Generally, nonspecific defense systems in a healthy individual are always ready to function and require minimal time before they are fully effective. In contrast, an immune reaction takes time. If the individual encounters a pathogen for the first time, the infection can be well-established before there is an adequate immune response. The immune response, if adequate, can in most cases limit the infection, leading to the recovery of the patient. However, if the response is inadequate, the infection will progress, become chronic, and possibly cause death. An immunization procedure which precedes contact with the pathogen provides protective antibody and antigensensitive cells that will be present at the time of later contact with the pathogen and can prevent or attenuate the infection. It is the element of time which may be the most important consideration in the discussion of an age-related immunodeficiency. Since this type of deficiency is usually one of degree, rather than an absolute, it is difficult to envision what half-normal levels of function may mean. It could be argued that with a lower level of function than seen in young adults, an elderly person could be infected with fewer organisms or that the pathogens would have a longer period of time to establish themselves prior to the onset of an effective immune response. It is well established that both morbidity and mortality for most infectious illnesses are increased in the elderly age group. However, a defective immune response is not the sole cause of this finding. The first lines of host defense, granulocytes, complement, acute phase reactants, natural killer cells, and fixed and circulating macrophage/monocytes, are important in the early contact with a pathogen. They are also important in combating an established infection until an immune response is fully developed. Cytotoxic antibody, lytic destruction of the pathogen, and phagocytosis of antibody-coupled (opsonized) pathogens are all important. The role of granulocytes in this process can not be overemphasized. Diseases such as agranulocytosis, chronic granulomatous disease, and Chédiak-Higashi syndrome, in which there is defective granulocyte function, demonstrate that normal T- and B-lymphocyte function on its own is ineffective in preventing or eliminating a bacterial infection. Individuals with deficiencies in specific complement components also have difficulty with infections despite the presence of normal cellular immune function.

Our knowledge of the role of nonspecific and specific host defenses in disease prevention is in large measure the result of studying infectious diseases. In most cases an individual, usually a child, who has demonstrated a propensity for repeatedly developing serious or unusual infectious illnesses has been found to lack a critical component of the host defense system. This differs from the problems in geriatric medicine since a complete lack of a factor or cell or antibody is generally not the usual situation. Since there are extensive interactions within the immune system among cells, antibodies, growth factors, inflammatory molecules, complement, and reticuloendothelial tissues, it is difficult to establish a direct cause-and-effect relationship between a change (usually decrease) of some function and a disease. Because of this and the fact that the basic causes of immune function changes in the elderly are unknown, it is difficult to recommend therapy for reconstitution or augmentation of any part of the host defense system. Much of the knowledge linking the fields of immunology, host defense, and aging is descriptive, and the mechanisms of age-related change remain obscure. Before detailing the changes seen in immune function in the aging individual, we will review important features of normal immune function and host defense mechanisms.

NORMAL IMMUNE FUNCTION AND HOST DEFENSE MECHANISMS

The immune system relies on the functioning of cells in certain tissues in the body, such as the lymph nodes, spleen, bone marrow, tonsils, and thymus, as well as in localized lymphoid tissue associated with the respiratory and gastrointestinal tract. These tissues are composed of cells that either provide regulatory function or cell-mediated immunity or differentiate into antibody-forming plasma cells. Many lymphocytes, mostly of the "T" (thymus-derived) series, also circulate in the peripheral blood and in lymph channels, traveling throughout the body and trafficking through the solid lymphoid tissue. Regional lymphoid tissue (the lymph nodes) responds rapidly to antigens introduced into its region. As soon as 5 seconds after introduction of an antigen into the foot pad of a rabbit, the antigen can be found in the lymph node draining that region. The architecture of lymph node and splenic tissue is distinct and depends on the subtypes of the lymphocytes present in these tissues. The two major subclasses of lymphocytes are T cells and B cells. The T cells reside in interstitial reticular areas, while the B cells are found in germinal centers. The T lymphocytes, which depend on thymic influence for their differentiation and development from precursor to immunocompetent units, can be further subdivided into function subclasses based on identifiable membrane markers (Table 6-1). The subclasses include inducer/helper cells and suppressive/cytotoxic cells. These classifications can have some overlap depending on the functional assays employed. B cells can also be subdivided based on their stage of development, so that precursor, activated, immunoglobulin-synthesizing, and memory B cells are all identifiable stages in the B-cell cycle. Furthermore, immunoglobulin-synthesizing cells can be subclassified by the types of light chains and heavy chains being synthesized. The membrane markers and membrane and cytoplasmic immunoglobulin can be

TABLE 6-1
Cell Surface Markers

Antigen Cluster	Other Names	Cell Types	Specificity
CD2	OKT11, Leu 5b, 9.6, T11, LFA-2	Thymocytes, T cells	SRBC (sheep red blood cell) receptor
CD3	OKT3, Leu 4, T3	T cells, thymocytes	Associated with T-cell receptor
CD4	OKT4, Leu 3, T4	T cells, thymocytes	Helper/inducer T cells
CD8	OKT8, Leu 2, T8	T cells, thymocytes	Cytotoxic/suppressor T cells
CD5	OKT1, Leu 1, T1 T101, 10.2	T cells	
CD16	Leu 11, 3G8	NK cells, neutrophils	Fc IgG receptor
CD19	B4, Leu 12	B cells	
CD20	B1, Leu 16	B cells	
CD25	Tac B1.49.9 7G7/B1	Lymphoblasts	p55 IL-2 receptor subunit
	HNK-1, Leu 7	Large granular lymphocytes (NK cells)	
	TCR-1, WT31	T cells, thymocytes	α/β T-cells antigen receptor

identified using monoclonal antibodies. Serum antibody and immunoprotein can also be identified using various methods that utilize antisera, radial diffusion, radio-immunoassay, enzyme-linked immunosorbent assay (ELISA), and solid-state immunoassays.

Another subset of lymphoid cells which carry unique membrane markers is also associated with a specific functional assay. This group consists of the natural killer (NK) cells. These cells have the ability to lyse tumor cell lines in vitro without the necessity for a preceding immunization procedure. The role of NK cells in host defense is still uncertain, but there are reports that they can kill some bacteria, again without a requirement for a preceding immunization. How these cells recognize a target as a tumor cell or a foreign organism without membrane immunoglobulin, Fc receptors, or T-cell antigen receptors is still unknown, but the in vitro assay for NK cell activity clearly shows that they have this ability.

The cells in the immune system can interact with each other either through cell contact or through the release of factors which can modulate their activity. These factors can supply obligatory signals for cellular differentiation or proliferation or they can facilitate the development of immunocompetency in concert with other factors or antigen. In many cases the cells which respond to a factor will express membrane receptors for the factor as part of a development or activation process. It is possible to assay factor production, receptor expression, mRNA accumulation for the factor and its receptor, and the modulation of the receptor complex of the cell membrane. It is also possible to determine the membrane expression of structures associated with cellular activation, as well as the changes in RNA/DNA content which occur as the cell enters the division cycle. Using molecular biology techniques it is possible to determine the rearrangement of the genes for the T-cell antigen receptor and for the immunoglobulin molecule, which are crucial steps in the differentiation of both T and B cells respectively. A listing of the various factors inducing immune-cell differentiation can be found in Table 6-2.

The initiation of an immune response requires the recognition of an antigen by immunocompetent lymphocytes. The recognition may require both a T cell and a B cell, as well as an accessory cell (monocyte/macrophage) which functions in the presentation of the antigen. The T cell may recognize a separate binding site (epitope) on the whole antigen (usually larger than that recognized by the B cell). After the recognition step, there is an activation process which involves the intracellular transduction of signals to the cytoplasm and nucleus. This results in the up-regulation of mRNAs for several proto-oncogenes and receptor components and the expression of new molecules on the cell membrane. Some of these structures are involved with the recognition of the B cell

by the T cell, while others function as high-affinity receptors for growth factors. The activated T cell may release newly synthesized factors which result in an expansion of the clone of T cells that recognize the antigen to form a specific clone, while other factors influence the development of B cells into antibody-synthesizing units. The control of this response is dependent on several elements: the amount and type of antigen administered, the activity of T helper and suppressor cells, the synthesis of anti-idiotypic antibody, the number of antigen-sensitive cells involved in the response (which is most important in secondary response), and the presence of inflammatory molecules, such as endotoxin and interferon. As antigen is depleted, and the anti-idiotype network expands, the response subsides, leaving an expanded population of memory cells, mostly B cells, which are ready to respond in an accelerated fashion to the next contact with the same or related antigen.

Other host defenses besides the immune reaction also depend on cellular and protein factors. The cells involved with the first line of defense are granulocytes

TABLE 6-2
Growth and Differentiation Factors

	Other Names	Function
Interleukin 1α	Lymphocyte-activating factor (LAF)	T-cell activation, B-cell growth and differentiation
Interleukin 1β		
Interleukin 2	T-cell growth factor (TCGF)	T cell and monocyte growth and differentiation
Interleukin 3	Colony-stimulating factor (CSF)	Growth and differentiation of hemopoietic stem cells
Interleukin 4	B cell–stimulating factor (BSF-1) B-cell growth factor (BCGF-1)	B-cells and mast cell activation, growth, and differentiation; induce Ig synthesis
Interleukin 5	T cell–replacing factor (TRF) B-cell growth factor (BCGF-2)	Eosinophil growth and differentiation
Interleukin 6	B cell–stimulating factor 2 (BSF-2) Interferon β₂ (IFNβ₂)	T-cell activation, B-cell Ig synthesis
Interleukin 7	Lymphopoetin-1 (LP-1)	Differentiation and maintenance of B-cell precursors

and monocytic cells with membrane receptors (Fc receptors) for immunoprotein (usually IgG). Both types of cells have the ability to phagocytose organisms, but the granulocytes can function in the absence of antibody to the organism, while the monocytes are better able to function if they encounter an antibody-coated organism. Along with phagocytosis there is a burst in metabolic activity and the release of cytoplasmic enzymes which lead to the destruction of the organism. Granulocytes are very efficient in this activity and provide the most important first-line defense against infection.

The role of allergic reactions in host defense and in particular in immune reaction is not fully known. In certain parasitic diseases an allergic response to the parasite may participate in the initiation of an inflammatory response which may be beneficial. The immediate reactivity to an antigen with the release of a variety of very potent chemical mediators would putatively be an effective immune reaction, but most information on the allergic system demonstrates that this reactivity is against nonpathogen-associated antigens and the inflammatory response and the mediators themselves cause disease.

Another system with a questionable role in providing protection is the secretory immune system mediated through the immunoprotein IgA. While the IgA immunoprotein and IgA-type antibody can be found in tears, saliva, milk, gastrointestinal secretions, and pulmonary tract secretions, it is still not clear what benefit they provide. In ataxia-telangiectasia, a condition with an associated immune deficit, there is a lack of IgA. However, in 11 percent of the population there is also a deficiency of IgA with no clinical signs or symptoms of an immune deficiency. The consideration of the efficacy of the IgA (secretory IgA) system is connected to the development of topical vaccines that are administered by aerosol and are meant to provide local immunity. While it has been shown that specific IgA antibody can be induced in this manner, there is still debate as to the efficacy of this antibody in preventing illness. A major consideration in determining the role of IgA is that it does not fix complement and therefore cannot provide a lytic or opsonization component for dealing with a pathogen. On the other hand, there are data that show that aerosol vaccines, which induce local IgA antibody responses, do provide protection. This is an important area for research on vaccine development for the elderly.

The immune system, since it is an adaptive system, not only interacts with various components in itself but also, as a physiologic system, is influenced by other systems within and outside of the individual. Sorting out the role of aging in the decline of immune function seen during a life span of an individual requires careful analysis of the individual for the presence of confounding factors. With this in mind, the following section will detail what is known about the changes seen in immune function with aging.

ASSESSMENT OF IMMUNE FUNCTION IN THE ELDERLY

Since the first edition of this text, there has been an unprecedented growth in knowledge of immunologic mechanisms. However, with few exceptions, studies of age-related changes in immune function continue to be primarily descriptive rather than mechanistic. While this has produced an increased knowledge of both the scope and magnitude of the alterations, the mechanism(s) responsible for age-associated defects in immune function remain unknown. Because of this lack of information about the underlying pathogenesis at the biochemical and molecular level, it is sometimes difficult to evaluate immunosenescence and to advocate therapeutic strategies.

Assays of immune function, like other diagnostic laboratory examinations, vary in their usefulness in the clinical care of patients. Some tests are useful for diagnosis or for monitoring the progress of a disease, while others serve mainly a research function. Because older individuals often have complex, multisystem medical problems, their laboratory results frequently fall outside the range of normal for young persons and raise the question as to whether the values truly represent "disease." Because clinicians are aware that numerous diseases are accompanied by or produce altered immune function, the clinical use of costly immunologic testing has increased. However, it should be kept in mind that relatively few diseases, especially among the elderly, have a primary immunologic etiology. Another widespread problem is that as the complexity and sophistication of many laboratory tests increase, in-depth laboratory studies of immune function are not, even in major medical centers, readily available to the clinician or interpretable by him or her. Further, many in vitro tests of immune function take considerable time to perform, especially if they involve tissue culture. This means that the results of these assays are frequently not available for use in clinical diagnosis or management for several days, or perhaps weeks. However, considerable useful information regarding the adequacy of an elderly individual's immune system can be obtained from several widely available laboratory studies (Table 6-3). Additional studies, usually directed toward precisely identifying the etiology of a defect found through use of the widely available tests, are done in the research laboratory (Table 6-4).

Preliminary evaluation of immune function begins with the determination of the number of immunocompetent cells in an individual's peripheral circulation. While the total number of peripheral blood white blood cells, as well as the total numbers of the major morphologic components, including lymphocytes, monocytes, and neutrophils, appear to be remarkably stable throughout the adult life span, two points deserve mention. First, longitudinal studies indicate that the number of leukocytes in a particular individual is unique and relatively constant during adult life. When studied over a 25-year span, most healthy individuals display little fluctuation in their total white cell count or in the number of lymphocytes. While some healthy individuals consistently maintain baseline white counts of 10,000 to 12,000 cells/mm^3, other equally healthy persons have counts in the range of 3000 to 4000 cells/mm^3. Second, there appears to be a subtle yet definite decrease in the number of circulating lymphoid cells during the few years immediately preceding death.[4] This is a decrease (from the norm of a particular individual) that occurs before any overt signs of terminal illness can be appreciated. The subtlety of this finding does not make it clinically useful to predict mortality, but it is a point that certainly deserves recognition when interpreting lymphocyte data in the elderly.

One useful technique to determine immune function in vivo is the delayed hypersensitivity skin reaction that develops in sensitized individuals 12 to 48 hours after an intradermal injection of antigens such as purified protein derivative (PPD), streptokinase-streptodornase (SKSD), *Candida*, or *Trichophyton*. While the information that this test provides concerning cell-mediated immunity (CMI) and T-cell function is unquestionably useful, the actual performance of the test frequently creates a number of practical difficulties. With the exception of PPD, the clinician often finds that appropriate and clinically approved delayed hypersensitivity skin-testing materials are not readily available. While preparations of *Candida* and *Trichophyton* can be obtained from companies marketing materials for allergy diagnosis and therapy, the performance of these antigens varies widely by manufacturer and lot number. Additionally,

intradermal injection of the antigen is often difficult in elderly persons with thin, easily traumatized skin. Even when applied by experienced individuals using fine, short bevel needles, it is not uncommon in elderly individuals to inject subcutaneously or to cause hematoma formation, which makes reading the reaction difficult and possibly invalid. Recently a disposable plastic puncture device (Multitest CMI) preloaded with seven standardized antigens has become available. This device has been extensively evaluated[5,6] in all adult age groups and appears to be a solution to many of the problems previously mentioned.

Useful data regarding delayed hypersensitivity reactivity in normal elderly individuals are difficult to obtain because the results of many studies from the 1960s and 1970s are significantly influenced by patient selection. Recent studies using multiple standardized antigens indicate that while the area of induration decreases with age, total anergy is uncommon even in quite elderly persons. Nonreactivity to tuberculin now appears to be commonplace among persons admitted to nursing homes, a finding that differs significantly from earlier generations.[7]

Age-related alterations in the number and/or function of T lymphocytes is unquestionably the most widely studied area of immunosenescence and has been the topic of several recent reviews.[8,9] In general, results in this area are characterized by a lack of consensus as to precisely what changes occur. Perhaps the most influential factor accounting for the different results in studies of CMI and aging is related to the selection criteria for the study population. The health status of participants in various studies ranges from uncategorized nursing home residents to persons studied on multiple visits over many years[10] to individuals chosen on the basis of rigid clinical

TABLE 6-3
Readily Available Tests of Immune Function

1. Complete blood count and differential
2. Quantitative immunoglobulins (IgG, IgA, IgM)
3. T-cell function (in vivo) intradermal skin testing for delayed hypersensitivity responses
4. B-cell function:
   Antibody titers to common pathogens or vaccine antigens (i.e., rubella, rubeola, polio, influenza, diphtheria, tetanus)
   Isohemagglutinins
   Response to immunization (pre- and post-immunization antibody titers)
5. Complement activity and quantification:
   C3
   CH$_{50}$
6. Granulocyte function:
   Nitroblue tetrazolium (NBT) dye reduction
   Bacterial killing (in vitro)
   Phagocytic ability
7. Determine if antibody to HIV present

TABLE 6-4
Assays of Immune Function Available in a Research Setting

1. Enumerate T-cell subpopulations with monoclonal antibodies.
2. Enumerate NK cells with monoclonal antibodies and assay NK cell activity against K562 cell line.
3. Assay cytotoxic T-cell activity.
4. Determine proliferative ability of lymphocytes following activation with mitogens (PHA, Con A, PWM), allogeneic cells (MLC), or monoclonal antibody (anti-CD3).
5. Assay lymphokine production (IL-1, IL-2, IL-3, IL-4, IL-5, IL-6, IL-7) by activated cells.
6. Quantify mRNA for cell membrane receptors and lymphokines.
7. Determine immunoglobulin gene rearrangement in B cells.
8. Assay thymic hormones.
9. Evaluate B-lymphocyte membrane markers (IgM, IgD, IgG, IgA, Fc receptors, C3, EBV).
10. Measure IgG subclasses and κ/λ ratio.

and laboratory criteria such as those associated with the SENIEUR protocol of Eurage.[11]

Earlier laboratory methods that relied on techniques such as rosetting with sheep erythrocytes to identify and quantify T lymphocytes and T-cell subsets have now been replaced by immunofluorescence with monoclonal antibodies that identify developmental and functional markers on T cells. The recent introduction into the laboratory of flow cytometers with multicolor analysis capabilities, which permit the simultaneous use of two, three, or more monoclonal antibodies, provides the ability to identify very small subpopulations of immunocompetent cells phenotypically. There are now perhaps 100 commercial and an indeterminate number of noncommercial, anti-human T-cell monoclonal antibodies, many with similar specificities, available for clinical research, diagnosis, or therapy. The once widely used commercial designations, such as OKT and Leu, should now be abandoned in favor of a system developed by the International Workshop of Human Leukocyte Differentiation Antigens[12] that groups the antibodies and the cells that they identify into functional groups or antigen clusters designated by cluster designation (CD) numbers (Table 6-1). While the identification and quantification of cell populations with individual monoclonal antibodies have become commonplace in modern clinical practice, especially in oncology and the diagnosis of AIDS, the value of this information in the evaluation of the elderly generally remains unproven. Recent studies in our laboratory indicate a high degree of positive correlation between the representation of CD3+ cells in the peripheral blood and an individual's ability to make antibody in vivo.

There is a slight decrease with age in the absolute number of T cells bearing the CD3 antigen, the general marker for mature T lymphocytes.[13,14] The changes in the functional subsets which account for this decline remain uncertain—both CD4+ helper/inducer and CD8+ cytotoxic/suppressor cell populations have been variously reported to increase and to decrease with age.[10,15,16] Recent research has complicated this point by making it clear that both the CD4+ and CD8+ T-cell populations are functionally heterogeneous. One proposed explanation of the decreased proportion of CD3+ cells is that elderly persons have a defect in T-cell maturation that results in a disproportionate representation of circulating immature CD3− T cells in their peripheral blood.[17] This idea has not been totally excluded, but examination of other markers of T-cell maturation has generally failed to confirm this hypothesis.[18] The overwhelmingly predominant technique to assess the function of T cells continues to be mitogen reactivity. The ability of peripheral blood T lymphocytes to proliferate following activation with plant lectins such as phytohemagglutinin or concanavalin A, monoclonal anti-

bodies such as anti-CD3, or allogeneic cells (MLC) decreases with advancing age.[3,19,20] Although they are a minority in each population, some apparently healthy young individuals respond quite poorly, and some robust elderly persons respond very well. The mitogen assay is very sensitive to the presence of concurrent illness. This makes assay results obtained at a single point in time on a clinically ill patient of dubious value in establishing the level of the individual's T-cell function.

Since the decline in T-cell function with age is preceded by the involution of the thymus, it is attractive to hypothesize that these events are associated, although there is presently no direct evidence that this is the case. Thymic involution begins during adolescence and progresses fairly rapidly, so that almost complete involution is present at an age when no significant change in T-cell numbers in the peripheral blood of humans or in the solid lymphoreticular tissues of mice can be appreciated. Present data relating thymic-hormone levels (α and β thymosins, facteur thymique serique [FTS], thymopoietin, thymopentin) to age indicate that the levels decrease with age and become undetectable after the age of 50 to 60 years old.[21,22] While the administration of various thymic-hormone preparations to mice appears to be capable of enhancing or restoring immunocompetence to T-cell populations,[23-25] the results in clinical studies, while encouraging, have not been dramatic or resulted in clinically significant alterations in immune function in aged humans.[26] Additional research is needed, emphasizing higher dosages and/or longer-term administration schedules, to evaluate the potential of thymic hormones or factors in the rejuvenation or maintenance of the immune system of the elderly.

The mechanisms underlying the age-associated decrease in the proliferative ability of T cells continue to remain elusive. While elderly individuals synthesize and respond less to the proliferation-inducing lymphokine interleukin 2 (IL-2),[27] this protein is clearly only a symptom rather than a cause of the problem. The addition of even large quantities of exogenous IL-2 does not fully reconstitute in vitro proliferative ability, and studies of IL-2 receptors indicate that the proliferating cells from both young and old persons have similar numbers of signal-transducing high-affinity IL-2 receptors.[28] While age-related changes in the amount of IL-2 mRNAs have been reported,[29] this defect appears more closely linked to an inability to respond to a particular activation stimulus, rather than to a genetic incapacity to produce IL-2. The defect of T cells from elderly humans is really an inability of a portion of the cells to be activated since, once activated, the T lymphocytes from both young and old proliferate similarly. With this in mind, research is shifting toward the investigation of cell activation, which, unlike proliferation that involves a myriad of signals and biochemical processes, is likely controlled by a single, possibly unique, on-off signal. Research areas being actively pursued in search of an activation defect include modifications of transmembrane signal transmission via intracellular second messengers such as the protein kinases and inositol lipid metabolites, changes in intracellular calcium and pH, defects in the expression or control of regulatory protoncogenes, and alterations in guanine nucleotide-binding regulatory proteins (G-proteins).

For the clinician, evaluation of B-cell function is best accomplished by quantitative measurement of serum immunoglobulin levels by either radial immunodiffusion or nephelometry. Additionally, quantification of antibody titers to common bacteria or viruses (e.g. tetanus, measles, pneumococcus) and isohemagglutinins can provide useful information about the individual's ability to make specific antibody. Age-related changes in serum levels of various immunoglobulins have been reported, although the significance is difficult to establish since all studies are cross-sectional and various exclusionary selection criteria have been applied to the participants. Available data indicate that serum levels of IgM and IgD decrease modestly with age, while serum and secretory IgA values rise.[30] Although there is not universal agreement on the subject, serum IgG levels appear to increase slightly with age, which could be due to the effects on mean values of a few elderly individuals with monoclonal gammopathies. IgE declines sharply with age in atopic individuals, possibly partially accounting for the decline in pollen- and dander-induced allergic symptoms observed in the elderly. Despite these decreases, serum IgG, A, and M remain well above the levels generally considered to represent an immunodeficiency.

Available information indicates that both primary and, to a lesser degree, secondary specific antibody responses decrease with age. The mechanism responsible for this decrease is likely related to decreased helper T-cell activity as well as defective B-cell responsiveness. Whatever the etiology, two important clinical considerations are that booster injections of common vaccines are certainly more effective when administered at an age when immune function remains fairly normal, and single-dose immunization of elderly persons may not produce the expected rises in protective antibody.

In the elderly it is not unusual to find a monoclonal immunoglobulin (M-component) present in the serum.[31] This monoclonal serum immunoprotein is thought to arise through a series of events that involves both a deregulation of normal cell differentiation and chronic antigenic stimulation. During this process a cell of the B-lymphocyte lineage escapes normal control at the pre-plasma-cell stage and is driven to terminal differentiation by chronic antigen stimulation. The finding of a monoclonal immunoglobulin spike has been given a variety of generally interchangeable names, including *monoclonal gammopathy*, *paraproteinemia*, *plasma cell dyscrasia*, and *dysproteinemia*. Whatever one chooses to term the homogeneous immunoglobulin, they produce a family of clinical diseases that includes multiple myeloma (monoclonal IgG, A, D, E or light chain), Waldenström's macroglobulinemia (monoclonal IgM), primary amyloidosis (polymerized light-chain fragments), and heavy-chain disease (IgG, A, or M heavy chains with F_d region deleted). While there is an increased incidence of these monoclonal B-cell neoplasms in the elderly, it is also not uncommon to detect high levels of monoclonal serum immunoglobulin without the associated findings of recurrent infections, anemia, hyperviscosity, lymphadenopathy, hepatosplenomegaly, renal failure, lytic bone lesions, or hypercalcemia. Whereas high levels of monoclonal immunoglobulin in the young and middle-aged adult are almost certainly indicative of a neoplastic process, older individuals may have homogeneous serum immunoprotein without apparent serious disease. This condition, formerly termed benign monoclonal gammopathy (BMG), is now generally referred to as monoclonal gammopathy of uncertain significance (MGUS).[32] It is actually more common in the elderly than is multiple myeloma. While the lack of physical findings and negative laboratory studies (<2 g/dl M-component, no Bence Jones proteins in the urine, <5 percent bone marrow plasmacytosis, and a thymidine labelling index <1 percent) usually permits MGUS to be recognized, approximately 10 percent of cases eventually (usually within the first year) display neoplastic behavior. Another point to be kept in mind is that immunoglobulin catabolism is regulated by serum immunoglobulin levels. As a result, individuals with large M-components, particularly of the IgG class, are often frankly hypogammaglobulinemic in respect to the normal types of functioning serum immunoglobulin.

In addition to monoclonal gammopathies, many studies have noted that the serum from 10 to 15 percent of elderly individuals contains some type of autoimmune antibodies. These autoantibodies in the elderly are additional evidence of disordered T-cell immunoregulation, since terminal B-cell differentiation is controlled by a balance between suppressor and helper T cells that recognize self-antigens. While autoantibodies to DNA, IgG, thyroid tissue, gastric parietal cells, erythrocytes, lymphocytes, cardiolipids, and cytoskeletal proteins may be found in the elderly, it remains uncertain as to whether the incidence of autoantibodies other than anti-IgG specific IgM (i.e., rheumatoid factor) is greater than that found in younger individuals.[33] The important clinical consideration is that the presence of autoantibodies in the elderly is seldom associated with manifestations of autoimmune disease. The frequent finding among the elderly of serum autoantibodies is the basis of the "autoimmune theory of aging," in which these antibodies are thought to be involved with *causing* the aging process. Based on Burnet's clonal selection theory, the hypothesis proposes that autoantibodies cause aging through immune complex, and antibody-induced and immune complex–induced tissue damage. While disease from failure to eliminate so-called "forbidden clones" that produce self-directed antibodies is certainly worth consideration, present knowledge of the function of the immune system makes this concept outdated. While previously the receptor for self was postulated as the cause of autoimmune disease, present models (also based on Jerne's network theory) implicate the receptor for self as a regulator that restrains potentially disease-causing T and B lymphocytes that are spontaneously and randomly generated by the immune system.

There is considerable current interest in a specific type of autoantibody. The unique portions of the variable region of the immunoglobulin molecule (the region responsible for antigen binding) is called the idiotype, and antibodies reactive with this region are called anti-idiotype antibodies. Formation of autologous anti-idiotype is clearly part of the normal immune response, and it appears likely that these antibodies function as an off signal for antibody synthesis.[34] It is easily recognized that if there is a defect in idiotype–anti-idiotype interaction, B-cell hyperreactivity will result. Anti-idiotype antibodies also appear important in the pathogenesis of many clinical autoimmune diseases.[35]

While there may be the impression that all components of the immune system deteriorate with advancing age, this is not universally the case. NK cells, Fc receptor–positive large granular lymphocytes, are recognized as having an effector role in immune surveillance against tumor- and virus-infected cells and in the regulation of hematopoiesis. Unlike T-cell proliferative responses, NK-cell function does not show any age-related defect. In fact, NK activity appears to be slightly enhanced in persons over 80 years of age.[36,37] Additionally, the number of cells expressing the Leu 7 and CD16 antigens, phenotypic markers for NK cells, are maintained with advancing age.[38] However, there is evidence that gender, cigarette smoking, and alcohol consumption all influence the level of NK-cell activity, variables which could influence the interpretation of assay results.

As previously outlined, granulocytes play an important role in host defense against disease. Even in individuals who are hypogammaglobulinemic, normal phagocytic cell function prevents the development of most bacterial diseases. In general, there must be a profound decrease in the number of granulocytes, to perhaps less than 10 percent of normal, before an increased susceptibility to infection is apparent. The number of granulocytes in the peripheral blood does not change with age, and neither do assays of granulocyte metabolic or bacte-

ricidal activity. Decreased phagocytic ability by a portion of the granulocytes of the elderly has been reported[39]; however, this defect does not appear to have clinical significance.

Monocytes and macrophages, especially as secretors of bioactive immunoregulatory proteins, play important roles in many diverse types of immune reactions.[40] Long-recognized as the secretor of IL-1 or endogenous pyrogen, other important lymphokines such as IL-2 and tumor necrosis factor are also products of the macrophage. Unfortunately, the effects of aging on monocyte/macrophage function remain largely unstudied, although it is reasonable to infer from both clinical observations (decreased fever response in the elderly) and the research laboratory (alterations in cell growth and proliferation) that these cells have age-associated defects.

It can be readily appreciated that there are a large number of defects, many of which may not be relevant to patient care, found in the immune system of elderly persons. The more generally agreed-upon changes are summarized in Fig. 6-1 and Table 6-5.

AUGMENTATION OF THE IMMUNE RESPONSE

With the realization that the immune system of an elderly individual is not functioning at the same level seen in young people, it is a natural step to consider procedures for augmenting that response. Most clinical procedures that have been developed for modulating immune activity are those that involve down-regulation of responsiveness (immunosuppression). This can be seen with the therapy for allergic conditions, organ transplantation, and autoimmune disorders. This area of therapy has become quite effective and comprises a range of

TABLE 6-5
Summary of Immune Function and Aging

1. Decreased production of thymic hormones
2. Diminished in vitro production of and responsiveness to IL-2
3. Decreased cell proliferation in response to mitogenic stimulation
4. Decreased cell-mediated cytotoxicity
5. Enhanced cellular sensitivity to prostaglandin E_2
6. Increased synthesis of anti-idiotype antibodies
7. Decreased levels of specific antibody response
8. Increased presence of autoimmune antibodies
9. Increased incidence of serum monoclonal immunoproteins
10. No change in NK cell function
11. No change in number of peripheral blood B lymphocytes
12. Diminished delayed hypersensitivity
13. No change in numbers of peripheral blood lymphocytes

agents which can interfere with T-cell function, protein synthesis, and in the production of the mediators that cause an inflammatory response. Unfortunately, there are fewer agents available which augment an immune response, and none is used on a routine basis in a clinical setting.

The reason for this lack of an appropriate agent is related to the need for an agent that has a well-defined effective function and no side effects that would be harmful. For example, if one wished to augment T-cell activity, then one must consider if all T cells were to be stimulated, or just a helper or suppressor subset, or just those cells with specificity to one antigen in particular. As a general T-cell stimulant, one could consider IL-2 as an appropriate agent. However, IL-2 would be able to augment only those cells which had already responded to an activation signal. Furthermore, in vitro experiments have shown that IL-2 cannot reconstitute T-cell responses of some of the cells of the elderly donors. There are cells from the elderly which do not respond to either an activation signal or to IL-2. Finally, in vivo studies in cancer patients have shown that the administration of large doses IL-2 has routinely been accompanied by significant, potentially life-threatening, side effects.

If one wished to augment B-cell activity these same problems would be present. Which B cells? All of them or just specific clones? And what if anti-idiotype clones were also activated? The transformation of specific clones of B cells results in multiple myeloma. Anti-idiotype antibodies down-regulate a response rather than promote it. What would be the effect of the activation of clones of B cells which would make antibody against self-antigens, an autoimmune antibody?

While there have been many cell growth factors described, most are a long way from being even remotely considered as therapeutic agents. Despite this, the use of a nonspecific agent for the promotion of T-cell development, such as thymic hormone, remains an attractive consideration. The idea that with age-related thymic involution there is a loss of a mechanism for continuing T-cell development conceptually, at least, makes sense. The problem is that at present there is still no clear-cut evidence that any thymic-hormone preparation has an in vivo effect of any sort in humans or experimental animals. There are mechanisms for augmenting a specific immune response. The use of adjuvants has been shown to be effective in augmenting an immune response to specific antigens given at the same time. This strategy may be useful in designing vaccines for use in the elderly but would not be useful as a general "tonic" for the immune system since they work by expanding a specific antigen-sensitive clone of cells. On an experimental basis, vaccines which are given with IL-2, or

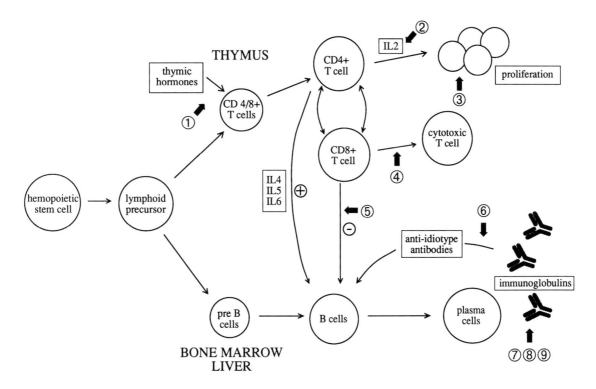

Age-Associated Defects in Lymphoid Cells

FIGURE 6-1
The effect of age on the T- and B-cell development and function. Numbers on figure refer to Table 6-5.

which are the products of recombinant technology in which the IL-2 gene is coupled to the gene for the antigen and the whole package is transfected into the cells of the animal, have been shown to be effective in T cell-deficient nude mice in allowing a normal immune response to proceed. These procedures may also be useful for designing vaccines but again do not provide a general reconstituting force.

Another important consideration is whether one wishes to reconstitute an immune system or if it is better to consider maintaining that system and preventing it from declining in activity. There is clinical experience in which an immune deficiency may spontaneously correct itself. This has been seen in the DiGeorge syndrome in children. In some cases the correction of function has been accompanied by severe disease that resembles an autoimmune phenomenon. It may be that during the period of immunodeficiency there is an establishment of viral infections which promotes the development of cell surface viral antigens. Upon the return of T-cell function, these cells are destroyed, and there is a severe illness associated with this process. There is evidence in experimental animals to support this hypothesis. Therefore, it is probably better to consider mechanisms to prevent the decline in immune function and maintain the function in later life than to consider reconstitution. In considering how to maintain function throughout life, it is best to list those possibilities which are already available and those which would be ideal. The ideal agents would function to provide a continuous supply of immunocompetent T cells throughout life. These agents do not exist. Transplantation of fetal thymus tissue into adults will not work in a human population, although there is evidence in syngeneic mice that such a procedure is effective.[41] The maintenance of an ideal diet may be the best beneficial procedure available but even then there are difficulties. In the first place there is no generally accepted definition of a "good" diet. In experimental animals there is evidence to show that extension of life span is associated with caloric restriction.[42] However, controlled studies of lifelong caloric restriction in man probably cannot be carried out and thus have not been correlated with life extension. The routine administration of vaccines against common pathogens such as the pneumococcus and influenza virus should be beneficial. This will become even more efficacious when better vaccines, specifically designed for use in the elderly population, are available.

In summary, the immune system is a complicated interplay of many different cells and factors. At this time there is no experimentally verified way to forestall deterioration or to reconstitute lost function of the immune system. Future work in this area will need to focus on these issues in order to understand what parts of the system need help and how to do it without producing disease.

REFERENCES

1. Finland M, Barnes MW: Acute bacterial meningitis at Boston City Hospital during 12 selected years, 1935–1972. *J Infect Dis* 136:400, 1977.
2. Couch RB et al: Influenza: Its control in persons and populations. *J Infect Dis* 153:431, 1986.
3. Adler WH, Takiguchi T, Smith RT: Effect of age upon primary alloantigen recognition by mouse spleen cells. *J Immunol* 107:1357, 1971.
4. Bender BS et al: Absolute peripheral blood lymphocyte count and subsequent mortality in elderly men: The Baltimore Longitudinal Study of Aging. *J Am Geriatr Soc* 34:649, 1986.
5. Knicker WT et al: Multitest CMI for standardized measurement of delayed cutaneous hypersensitivity and cell-mediated immunity: Normal values and proposed scoring system for healthy adults in the USA. *Ann Allergy* 52:75, 1984.
6. Marrie TJ, Johnson S, Durant H: Cell-mediated immunity of healthy adult Nova Scotians in various age groups compared with nursing home and hospitalized senior citizens. *J Allergy Clin Immunol* 81:836, 1988.
7. Stead WW et al: Tuberculosis as an endemic and nosocomial infection among the elderly in nursing homes. *N Engl J Med* 312:1483, 1985.
8. Jones KH, Ennist DL: Mechanisms of age-related changes in cell-mediated immunity. *Rev Biol Res Aging* 2:155, 1985.
9. Gottesman SRS: Changes in T-cell-mediated immunity with age: An update. *Rev Biol Res Aging* 3:96, 1987.
10. Nagel JE: Immunology. *Rev Biol Res Aging* 1:103, 1983.
11. Ligthart GJ et al: Admission criteria for immuno-gerontological studies in man: The SENIEUR protocol. *Mech Ageing Dev* 28:47, 1984.
12. Haynes GF: Summary of T cell studies performed during the Second International Workshop and Conference on Human Leukocyte Differentiation Antigens, in Reinherz EL et al (eds): *Leukocyte Typing II*, vol 1, *Human T Lymphocytes*. New York, Springer-Verlag, 1984, pp 3–30.
13. Nagel JE, Chrest FJ, Adler WH: Enumeration of T-lymphocyte subsets by monoclonal antibodies in young and aged humans. *J Immunol* 127:2086, 1981.
14. Nagel JE et al: Monoclonal antibody analysis of T-lymphocyte subsets in young and aged adults. *Immunol Commun* 12: 223, 1983.
15. Mascart-Lemone F et al: Characterization of immunoregulatory T lymphocytes during aging by monoclonal antibodies. *Clin Exp Immunol* 48:148, 1982.
16. Traill KN et al: Age-related changes in lymphocyte subset populations, surface differentiation antigen density and plasma membrane fluidity: Application of the Eurage SENIEUR protocol admission criteria. *Mech Ageing Dev* 33:39, 1985.
17. Hallgren HM, Jackola DR, O'Leary JJ: Unusual pattern of surface marker expression on peripheral lymphocytes from aged humans suggestive of a population of less differentiated cells. *J Immunol* 131:191, 1983.
18. Jensen TL et al: Do immature T cells accumulate in advanced age? *Mech Ageing Dev* 33:237, 1986.
19. Makinodan T, Adler WH: The effects of aging on the differentiation and proliferation potentials of cells of the immune system. *Fed Proc* 34:153, 1975.

20. Nagel JE, Chrest FJ, Adler WH: Activity of 12-O-tetradecanoyl phorbol-13-acetate on peripheral blood lymphocytes from young and elderly adults. *Clin Exp Immunol* 49:217, 1982.

21. Lewis VM et al: Age, thymic involution and circulating thymic hormone activity. *J Clin Endocrinol Metab* 47:145, 1978.

22. Naylor PH et al: Immunochemical studies of thymosin; radioimmunoassay for thymosin β_4. *Immunopharmacology* 7:9, 1984.

23. Bach JF: Thymic hormones: Biochemistry, and biological and clinical activities. *Annu Rev Pharmacol Toxicol* 17:281, 1977.

24. Frasca D, Garavini M, Doria G: Recovery of T cell functions in aged mice injected with synthetic thymosin α_1. *Cell Immunol* 72:384, 1982.

25. Frasca D, Adorini L, Doria G: Enhancement of helper and suppressor T cell activities by thymosin α_1 in old mice. *Immunopharmacology* 10:41, 1985.

26. Barcellini W et al: *In vivo* immunopotentiating activity of thymopentin in aging humans: Modulation of IL-2 receptor expression. *Clin Immunol Immunopathol* 48:140, 1988.

27. Gillis S et al: Immunological studies of aging: Decreased production of and response to T cell growth factor by lymphocytes from aged humans. *J Clin Invest* 67:937, 1981.

28. Nagel JE et al: Effect of age on the human high affinity interleukin 2 receptor of phytohemagglutinin-stimulated peripheral blood lymphocytes. *Clin Exp Immunol* 75:286, 1989.

29. Nagel JE et al: Decreased proliferation, interleukin 2 synthesis, and interleukin 2 receptor expression is accompanied by decreased mRNA expression in phytohemagglutinin-stimulated cells from elderly donors. *J Clin Invest* 81:1096, 1988.

30. Buckley CE III, Dorsey FC: Effect of aging on human serum immunoglobulin concentrations. *J Immunol* 105:964, 1970.

31. Radl J et al: Immunoglobulin patterns in humans over 95 years of age. *Clin Exp Immunol* 22:84, 1975.

32. Kyle RA: Monoclonal gammopathy of undetermined significance: Natural history in 241 cases. *Am J Med* 64:814, 1978.

33. Silvestris F et al: Discrepancy in the expression of autoantibodies in healthy aged individuals. *Clin Immunol Immunopathol* 35:234, 1985.

34. Geha RS: Regulation of the immune response by idiotypic-antiidiotypic interactions. *N Engl J Med* 305:25, 1981.

35. Schoenfeld Y, Schwartz RS: Immunologic and genetic factors in autoimmune diseases. *N Engl J Med* 311:1019, 1984.

36. Nagel JE, Collins GC, Adler WH: Spontaneous or natural killer cytotoxicity of K562 erythroleukemic cells in normal patients. *Cancer Res* 41:2284, 1981.

37. Krishnaraj R, Blandford G: Age-associated alteration in human natural killer cells. I. Increased activity as per conventional and kinetic analysis. *Clin Immunol Immunopathol* 45:268, 1987.

38. Bender BS, Chrest FJ, Adler WH: Phenotypic expression of natural killer cell associated membrane antigens and cytolytic function of purified blood cells from different aged humans. *J Clin Lab Immunol* 21:31, 1986.

39. Nagel JE et al: Oxidative metabolism and bactericidal capacity of polymorphonuclear leukocytes from normal young and aged adults. *J Gerontol* 37:529, 1986.

40. Unanue E, Allen PM: The basis for the immunoregulatory role of macrophages and other accessory cells. *Science* 236:551, 1987.

41. Kirokawa K, Albright JW, Makinodan T: Restoration of impaired immune function in aging animals. II. Effect of syngeneic thymus and bone marrow grafts. *Clin Immunol Immunopathol* 5:371, 1976.

42. Weindruch R, Gottesman SRS, Walford RL: Modification of age-related immune decline in mice dietarily restricted from or after midadulthood. *Proc Natl Acad Sci USA* 79:898, 1982.

Chapter 7

ONCOLOGY AND AGING: GENERAL PRINCIPLES OF CANCER IN THE ELDERLY

Harvey Jay Cohen

This chapter will discuss many of the general relationships of oncology and aging. It will focus on the epidemiologic, basic etiologic, and biological relationships between the processes of aging and neoplasia, and the generalizable aspects of management of malignant disease in the elderly patient. This chapter will also discuss clinical management of individual malignancies only as an example of general principles. The approach to specific malignancies will be covered in subsequent chapters related to the appropriate organ system.

It is now well-recognized that cancer is a major problem for elderly individuals.[1,2] It is the second leading cause of death after heart disease in the United States, and one-half of all cancers occur in the 11 percent of the population over the age of 65.[3,4] What may not be as well appreciated is the magnitude of the problem for the elderly individual as well as for the physicians caring for this population. If one examines incidence and mortality data obtained from the National Cancer Institute's Surveillance, Epidemiology, and End Results (SEER) Program (Fig. 7-1),[5] one sees that the total cancer incidence rises progressively through the middle years and then falls off in the later years. However, the age-specific cancer incidence rises progressively throughout the age range. Thus, while the rate of increase diminishes somewhat in the oldest age groups, the risk of developing cancer continues to rise for an individual throughout life. Since the number of people in this country above the age of 65 is rising rapidly and the oldest of the old—i.e., over the age of 85—are increasing at the greatest rate, geriatricians, generalists, and internists will be encountering increasing numbers of elderly individuals with cancer in their practices.

Not only does cancer occur at an increased rate in older individuals, it makes a significant impact on such people's lives, both from the standpoint of increasing morbidity as well as mortality. Thus, as Fig. 7-1 also demonstrates, the age-specific cancer mortality continues to rise as a function of age, as does incidence. In support of this observation is the report from the SEER Program that five-year survivals for most types of cancer decrease with advancing age.[6]

Though the overall pattern for the incidence of age-specific cancer shows a rise with age, this is not uniform for individual cancers. Moreover, for some malignancies there has been an apparent decrease in incidence in people over the age of 80. This may be due to a number of factors, including underreporting or a natural selection which would allow the less cancer-prone population to survive. However, cohort effects may have the most significant impact.[7] Figure 7-2A demonstrates age-specific annual cancer incidence rate from the SEER Program with a fall in incidence in the oldest age groups for both prostate and lung cancer. Figure 7-2B shows data corrected for certain known risk factors. Thus, for prostate cancer when only men are considered in the base population at risk, the incidence continues to rise into the oldest age groups. For lung cancer, an apparent decrease in lung cancer incidence in the older age groups might be explained by a smaller high-risk population because of decreased prevalence of smoking in the older age groups. When data derived from the Lung Cancer Early Detection Project[8] for annual cancer incidence in male smokers over the age of 45 are used, one notes a continuing increase into advanced age. There is little change in the case of colorectal cancer because the entire

FIGURE 7-1
Comparison of age with the percent of total cancer incidence and mortality versus the age-specific cancer incidence and mortality. Data compiled from the SEER Program, 1973–1977, all areas except Puerto Rico. (*From Crawford and Cohen, Clin Geriatr Med 3:419, 1987.*[7])

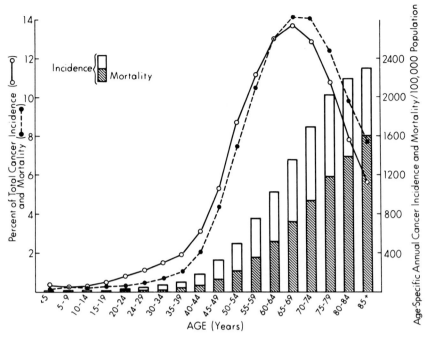

population appears to be at risk while for women with breast cancer, as for men with prostate cancer, the incidence continues to rise slowly into advanced age. For other gynecologic malignancies there does appear to be a decrease, perhaps due to different interactions of hormonal status and neoplasia in hormonally responsive target organs.

Other types of patterns in age-specific incidence may also be seen.[7] Thus, for example, Hodgkin's disease has a distinct bimodal distribution in incidence with a peak both in the early years and another peak after late

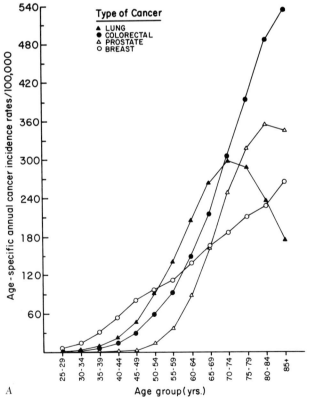

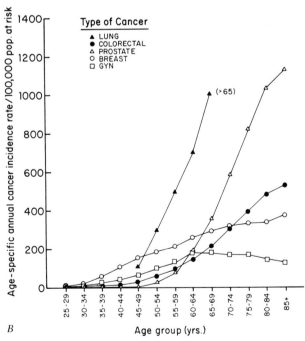

FIGURE 7-2
A. Age-specific annual cancer incidence rates, SEER Program, all races, both sexes, 1978–1981. *B.* Age- and population-specific annual cancer incidence rates. Tabulated from the SEER Program, 1978–1981: colorectal, all races, both sexes; prostate, males only; breast and gynecologic, females only. Compiled from Lung Cancer Early Detection Program: lung cancer, male smokers only. (*From Crawford and Cohen, Clin Geriatr Med 3:419, 1987.*[7])

middle age. This has led to the suggestion that there actually may be two different diseases involved, one in the young individual and one in the older, but that they assume similar morphologic features, so that with current technologies we are unable to tell them apart. This impression is further substantiated by the markedly different response to treatment obtained for younger and older groups of individuals with this disease. On the other hand, the most common leukemias and lymphomas in the elderly are those derived from the B-lymphocyte arm of the immune system. These, including chronic lymphocytic leukemia and multiple myeloma, rise dramatically in incidence throughout life with the great majority of these disorders found in elderly individuals. Whether this dramatic relationship is due to an enhanced susceptibility of the B lymphocyte to neoplastic transformation in older individuals is a question relevant to the entire issue of the relationship between the aging process and the neoplastic process—a subject which will be considered next.

RELATIONSHIP OF AGING AND NEOPLASIA

It is difficult to discuss a relationship between two processes, both of which are incompletely understood at this time, i.e., aging (senescence) and neoplastic transformation. In order to explore the relationship, however, we must first briefly describe the current understanding of the process of carcinogenesis. Figure 7-3 shows the current concept of the multistep nature of cancer development which includes the major stages of initiation, promotion, and progression.[7,9] The first stage of cancer development is known as *initiation*. In this process, chemical or physical carcinogens, or certain viruses, cause a change in the cell that predisposes it to a subsequent malignant transformation. This change appears to be an irreversible lesion in the genomic DNA of a stem cell, that may remain stable for a long period of time. It is not clear whether such an initiated cell can be recognized clinically, but certain disorders such as preleukemia, or carcinoma-in-situ may be a manifestation of this phenomenon.

The next stage of carcinogenesis is called *promotion* and involves a proliferative phase. *Promoters* are agents which can induce mitogenesis, or cell division, in an initiated cell. Whereas it appears that a single initiating event is sufficient to begin the process, promotion appears to be most successful when it is repetitive. This may occur shortly after initiation, or after a prolonged delay, and appears to be dose-dependent as well as reversible. For this reason researchers believe that cessation of cigarette smoking (containing both initiators and promoters) reduces the incidence of cancer in former smokers compared to those who continue to smoke.

The final stage of cancer development in this model is *progression*. This is actually multiphasic itself, and involves the transformation of a cell from a premalignant to a malignant state, the potential clonal evolution of a subset of such cells, and the potential development of metastasis. The latter two phenomena are quite important and have led to the concept of tumor cell heterogeneity. While we believe that tumors arise from a single "clone of cells," tumor cells are genetically more unstable than normal cells yielding progeny with variable proliferative and metastatic potential. Thus, not all cells within a given tumor are the same. Clinically, this may explain such diversity as variable chemosensitivity of tumor cells, the selection of resistant cells and the differential behavior of different metastatic lesions compared with the original tumor and with other metastatic lesions, and the sometimes unpredictable behavior of a particular cancer.

In recent years we have also begun to appreciate the potential role of cellular genetics in neoplastic evolution.[10,11] Oncogenes, or cancer genes, were initially described as viral genes capable of transforming normal cells to malignant ones. It was subsequently found that these viral oncogenes had normal cellular counterparts, i.e., a normal cellular gene important to the physiologic regulation of cellular processes. It is now felt that such

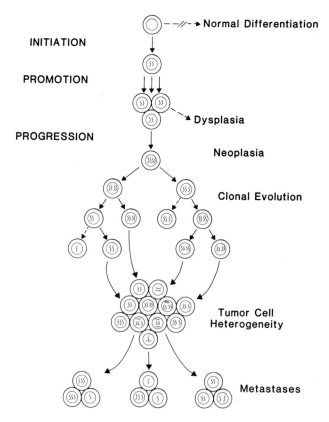

FIGURE 7-3
Stages of carcinogenesis. (*From Crawford and Cohen, Clin Geriatr Med 3:424, 1987.[7]*)

genes have the potential of causing malignant transformation of a normal cell, if the genetic information is altered or expressed inappropriately, as with the application of mutagenic or carcinogenic stimuli as noted in the previous section. Though it is not clear what the precise interaction of oncogenes is with other aspects of the carcinogenic process, they may also play a role during the latter stages of progression of neoplasia.

Two major families of oncogenes have been described called the *ras-like* and *myc-like* oncogenes. Ras acts at a cytoplasmic level to promote transduction of growth-promoting signals, while myc acts at a nuclear level and increases the sensitivity of cells to exogenous growth factors.[12] Increased cellular oncogenic expression has been noted in many tumors and can be mimicked experimentally by altering the DNA encoding for the oncogene, usually at or near the promoter. Thus, it is possible that the chromosomal damage noted in neoplasia during the initiation and promotion phases, if it occurred near the region of an oncogene, could result in transformation and clonal evolution of the cancer. The evolution noted in Burkitt's lymphoma, and chronic granulocytic leukemia may be examples of this process. It is likely that the expression of more than one oncogene is necessary to cause transformation.

More recently the existence of another class of genes has been proposed in which the loss of gene function is associated with oncogenesis.[13,14] This class of genes, which give rise to tumors by a loss of function, has been termed *recessive oncogenes, cancer suppressor genes,* or *antioncogenes.* Since we might expect mutations to more easily result in the loss of function rather than in an enhancement of function postulated in the case of oncogenes, alterations in such cancer suppressor genes may play an important role in the neoplastic process.

How then might the aging process influence the process of neoplastic transformation to result in the markedly increased rates of cancer in older people?[15,16] General aspects of the aging process have been covered in Chap. 1, and only certain specific aspects relevant to the process under discussion will be reiterated here. The types of theories which appear relevant to an explanation of the striking epidemiologic relationship are given in Table 7-1. First, it is possible that aging simply allows the time necessary for the accumulation of cellular

TABLE 7-1
Cancer: Aging Theories

1. Longer duration of carcinogenic exposure
2. Increased susceptibility of cells to carcinogens
3. Decreased ability to repair DNA
4. Oncogene activation or amplification; tumor suppressor gene loss
5. Decreased immune surveillance

events to develop into a clinical neoplasm. There is evidence for age-related accumulation and expression of genetic damage.[7,15] Somatic mutations are felt to occur at the rate of approximately 1 in 10^6 cell divisions with approximately 10^{16} cell divisions occurring in a lifetime of a human being. The passage of time alone, however, is not likely to explain the phenomenon, since the time for a mutated cell to become a malignant cell and then subsequently to become a detectable tumor has been estimated to be approximately 10 to 30 percent of the maximum life span for a given species, which may vary from just a few years to over 100 years. Second, there may be altered susceptibility of aging cells to a given amount of carcinogenic exposure. Data in this area are somewhat contradictory.[7,16] In some cases the incidence of skin tumors in mice produced with benzpyrene has been more related to dose than to age while in other models accelerated carcinogenesis as a function of age has been demonstrated, as for example, when dimethylbenzanthracene (DMBA) was applied to skin grafts for young and old mice.[15] In addition, an age-related increase in sensitivity of lymphocytes to cell cycle arrest and chromosome damage after radiation has been demonstrated.[17] It is also possible that there are alterations in carcinogen metabolism with age, but the findings from such studies have also been contradictory.[18] Third, it is possible that damage once initiated is more difficult to repair in older cells. A number of studies have demonstrated decreased DNA repair as a function of age following damage by carcinogens as well as for radiation.[7,19] Such repair failures may also be reflected in increased karyotypic abnormalities in aged normal cells as well as in older patients with neoplastic disease. Fourth, oncogene activation or amplification might be increased in the older host resulting in either increased initiation or promotion or in differential clonal evolution. Though evidence is currently limited, there have been observations of increased amplification of protooncogenes and their products, in aging fibroblasts in vitro as well as evidence for increased c-myc transcript levels in the livers of aging mice.[20,21] Alternatively such factors as genetic alterations or DNA damage could lead to inactivation of cancer suppressor genes. Finally, a decrease in immune surveillance, or immunosenescence, could contribute to the increased incidence. This phenomenon has been described in detail in Chap. 6. However, with respect to tumor-related immunity, there is a considerable amount of evidence for a loss of tumor-specific immunity with progressive age in animal models.[7,22] This includes the altered capacity of old mice to reject transplanted tumors, the close relationship between susceptibility to malignant melanomas and the rate of age-related T-cell-dependent immune function decline, and the ability by immunopharmacologic manipulation to increase age-depressed tumoricidal immune function and to decrease the incidence of spontaneous tumors. The evidence linking such data to age-associated immune deficiency and the rise of cancer incidence in humans, however, is mainly circumstantial.

Probably the explanation for the increased incidence of neoplasia that occurs with advancing age in humans will be multifactorial and will include a number of these factors as well as others yet to be discovered. It is also likely that through research at the basic level concerning the interactions of these two processes we will learn a great deal about the fundamental basis of each. Such information will hopefully enhance our ability to engage in prevention at the primary and secondary levels. Such approaches are currently limited to general suggestions, including decreasing contact with carcinogens such as tobacco smoke, dietary moderation, and preliminary trials of chemotherapeutic prevention.[7] All these appear applicable to older adults as well as the young.

CLINICAL PRESENTATIONS AND DISEASE BEHAVIOR

SCREENING IN ASYMPTOMATIC INDIVIDUALS

The situations in which periodic routine screening are recommended for all individuals regardless of age are relatively few. In general, although there is some variation in the recommendations of different organizations, the American Cancer Society guidelines for screening of asymptomatic individuals appears to be a reasonable baseline for decision making.[23] It should be recognized that when applied to the elderly, especially those over 75, such information is largely empirically derived.[24] These recommendations are directed at mass screening of populations. When applied to individuals within a physician's office or other practice, they serve only as general guidelines for decisions which may be modified by many other factors. The current guidelines of the American Cancer Society relevant to the older adult are shown in Table 7-2. These guidelines generally provide information concerning the age at which to initiate screening and the age at which to increase the frequency of screening (in middle age), based in part upon the rapidly rising incidence of neoplasia described earlier in this chapter. However, most of these recommendations do not directly address alterations in strategy for people at more advanced ages. The American Cancer Society recommends screening for only four tumor types: colorectal cancer, breast cancer, cervical cancer, and prostate cancer. Recommendations for colorectal cancer and prostate cancer are relatively straightforward, with prostate cancer covered by the recommended yearly digital rectal

examination. Breast cancer screening likewise should be a lifelong activity. There are potential problems regarding the widespread use of mammography in the elderly related to the availability of facilities and trained personnel. There are alterations in fat and glandular patterns of breast tissue which may influence interpretations (Chap. 75). Moreover, in the current cohort of elderly individuals, many women over the age of 65 have not had baseline mammograms, making comparisons diffi-

TABLE 7-2
ACS Guidelines for Early Detection of Cancer in People without Symptoms, Applicable to the Older Adult

Should include the procedures below plus health counseling (such as tips on quitting cigarettes) and examinations for cancers of the thyroid, testes, prostate, mouth, ovaries, skin, and lymph nodes. (Some people are at higher risk for certain cancers and may need to have tests more frequently. Risk factors are indicated.)

Breast

Examination by doctor every year, self-examination every month. Mammogram every year after 50. Between ages 40 and 50, mammogram every 1 to 2 years. (Higher risk for breast cancer: Personal or family history of breast cancer, never had children, first child after 30.)

Uterus

Pelvic examination every year.

Cervix

All women who are, or have been, sexually active, or have reached age 18 years, should have an annual Pap test and pelvic examination. After a woman has had three or more consecutive satisfactory normal annual examinations, the Pap test may be performed less frequently at the discretion of her physician. (Higher risk for cervical cancer: Early age at first intercourse, multiple sex partners)

Endometrium

Endometrial tissue sample at menopause if at risk. (Higher risk for endometrial cancer: Infertility, obesity, failure of ovulation, abnormal uterine bleeding, estrogen therapy.)

Colon and Rectum

Digital rectal examination every year after age 40, stool blood test every year after age 50, proctoscopic examination—after two initial negative tests 1 year apart—every 3 to 5 years after age 50. (Higher risk for colorectal cancer: Personal or family history of colon or rectal cancer, personal or family history of polyps in the colon or rectum, ulcerative colitis.)

Source: Adapted from Refs. 23 and 25.

cult. The most controversial recommendations however, have been those directed toward cervical cancer and the Pap test. The effectiveness of this screening modality is widely accepted. Controversy has centered more around the frequency of testing required, and whether testing could be suspended at either a certain age or after a certain number of negative tests. Recommendations have varied substantially. The earlier position of the American Cancer Society was that for women over 40, testing could be performed up to every 3 years following two initially negative tests a year apart. Based on the data that, for people undergoing such screening, the risk of cervical cancer in women over the age 65 was extremely small, it had been felt that the screening would no longer be necessary after this age. There were two major problems with this line of reasoning: First, it subsequently became clear that many women over the age of 40 and into the more elderly range had not received initial Pap smears and would still be at high risk, but would not be screened because of the assumption that they had been previously screened. Second, there was concern that if Pap smears were not performed, yearly pelvic examination for the possibility of uterine cancer would also not be performed. This would adversely affect the very population at highest risk for development of this malignancy. After extensive study of this situation, a new American Cancer Society guideline for detection of cervical cancer in asymptomatic women has been proposed.[25] This appears to be a consensus position which should adequately address the issue, and states that "all women who are, or who have been, sexually active, or have reached age 18 years, have an annual Pap test and pelvic examination. After a woman has three or more consecutive satisfactory normal annual examinations, the Pap test may be performed less frequently at the discretion of her physician." It is to be noted that this recommendation has no specific upper-age limitation, and the discussion of these recommendations contains a reminder that "mature women—those over 65—also require testing." This is considered to be critical if such women have not had a history of regular Pap testing in their younger years. Thus, we would recommend that for the older patient whose history of previous screening is not clear, Pap testing be done until the recommendations have been fulfilled.

For one of the most common malignancies in both sexes, i.e., lung cancer, specific mass screening is not recommended. This is based on lack of demonstrated cost-benefit efficacy, even in high-risk smoking groups.[26] However, with the relatively few elderly patients involved in the large screening trials on which these recommendations have been based and given the very high cancer incidence in the older smoker and recent evidence (to be described later) that this malignancy may present at an earlier stage in older pa-

tients, there exists some rationale for the potential usefulness of screening in individual patients in the older age group.

Despite these widely disseminated recommendations, many individuals do not follow them.[27] This appears to relate to both physician- and patient-derived factors. Despite the increased risk of cancer in the older age group, such individuals appear to avail themselves of routine screening even less frequently than their younger counterparts.[28] The physician, and other health care professionals in a position to do so, should ensure that the older individual is aware of the importance of screening, that the opportunity for such examinations is provided, and that fears and anxieties about these tests are allayed to as great an extent as possible.

INITIAL PRESENTATION

As an extension of the screening concept, the goal for initial cancer detection is to make the diagnosis as early as possible with the hope that treatment at the earliest stages of disease would yield the best survival rates. Therefore, attention to symptoms that may herald the onset of the neoplastic process, by both patient and physician, is of great importance. Though information on "warning signs of cancer" has been widely disseminated by the American Cancer Society and others, it is often ignored. This may be due in part to a lack of knowledge of what the implications of such warning signs are. Indeed some studies have indicated that the elderly know less about potential cancer symptoms and their significance than young individuals, which might lead to a delay in presentation.[29] Another factor that might interfere with early diagnosis is what might be called "cancer symptom confusion"; that is, not the specific failure to know that a particular symptom might indicate a neoplastic process but a tendency to write off the symptom as simply another change due to the aging process. Examples of such possibilities are listed in Table 7-3. Physicians and patients alike may be prone to such assumptions and should be alerted to the fact that a new symptom or a change in symptoms should be appropriately pursued in the elderly individual.

Current evidence suggests that once having noticed a symptom that appears to be related to cancer, older individuals do not delay appreciably in seeking medical help. Thus, in both a study of a Rhode Island population and a population-based study in New Mexico, older individuals were no more likely than younger ones to delay seeking medical attention once the symptom was noted.[29,30] Physicians, however, may be guilty of delaying further diagnostic pursuits in elderly patients. In one study of factors affecting the delay in the ultimate diagnosis of breast cancer, there was somewhat of a longer

TABLE 7-3
Cancer Symptom Confusion

Symptom or Sign	Possible Malignancy	Aging "Explanation"
Increase in skin pigment	Melanoma, squamous cell	"Age spots"
Rectal bleeding	Colon/rectum	Hemmorhoids
Constipation	Rectal	"Old age"
Dyspnea	Lung	Getting old, out of shape
Decrease in urinary stream	Prostate	"Dribbling"—BPH
Breast contour change	Breast	"Normal" atrophy, fibrosis
Fatigue	Metastatic or other	Loss of energy due to "aging"
Bone pain	Metastatic or other	Arthritis: "aches and pains of aging"

delay in diagnosis from the time of presentation for older patients than for younger, but the greatest part of this delay was due to factors for which the physician was responsible rather than those for which patients were responsible.[31] Part of the problem may lie in a failure to recognize some of the new signs and symptoms in patients with multiple disease processes. It is easy to attribute such symptoms as anorexia, weight loss, or decrease in performance status to social or psychological changes. The increasing prevalence of processes, such as anemia in the elderly, may lower the index of suspicion for attributing the factor to a new specific neoplastic process. The remarkable age-related increase in cancer incidence described above should be sufficient to maintain vigilance in this regard, though it must be balanced by judgment concerning the risk/benefit ratio for diagnostic evaluations in individual patients depending on their other medical status. Thus, the initial discovery of a new symptom in a previously totally well, active 80-year-old may be pursued rather differently than a similar discovery in a severely demented, bedbound, individual with severe congestive heart failure, diabetes, and pulmonary failure.

BIOLOGIC BEHAVIOR OF TUMORS IN THE ELDERLY HOST

The effect of the aging process on the clinical course of cancer—or to put it another way, whether cancer behaves differently in the older individual—is not clearcut. While the SEER data noted previously suggested that in many cancers the 5-year survival rate is lower for older people, it is possible that this is related more to comorbid disease and other factors rather than simply to aging per se. On the other hand, there is a widespread belief that cancers may behave more indolently in the elderly. These are important issues since they may affect decisions regarding treatment to a considerable degree. In fact there is both clinical and experimental evidence to support both sides of this issue, and it is likely that there is a spectrum of responses dependent upon initial tumor types as well as individual host status. One indicator of the phenomenon is the extent of disease at presentation. For most cancers examined there has been no consistent difference in the stage of disease or presentation for different age groups.[29] For those which have been determined, the directions are not always the same.[32] Thus, for malignant melanoma, older patients have been consistently found to have more advanced-stage local disease with deeper penetrating lesions at presentation.[33,34] For breast cancer, some studies show a greater proportion of older patients with distant metastatic spread at presentation,[35] while for lung cancer the opposite has been found, and older patients have been noted to present with localized disease in a greater proportion of cases.[36,37] Uterine and cervical cancers have in some cases been noted to be later in the course of disease at presentation in older individuals.[32] Of course, even these differences might be related to such phenomena as delay in the patient's presenting for diagnosis (which does not appear to be the case), delay in pursuing the diagnosis, and/or intensity of diagnostic endeavors, or on the other hand a greater chance for a serendipitous finding because of more frequent visits to physicians.

Another biological factor that may influence behavior in neoplasia in differently aged hosts is the histologic subtype of the tumor. Thus, while thyroid cancer overall appears to behave more aggressively in the older host, it is also true that a larger proportion of thyroid neoplasia in the elderly is made up by anaplastic carcinoma which at any age has more aggressive behavior.[38,39] In addition, however, there may be a poorer overall prognosis for older individuals with thyroid cancer even independent of histologic type.[40] Similarly, for malignant melanoma while there is an increased proportion of older people who have melanomas of poor prognostic histologic type and location at presentation, older individuals have a poorer prognosis for survival than do younger ones independent of this phenomenon even for localized disease.[34] Similarly, for lung cancer the increased proportion of elderly patients with squamous carcinoma of the lung—which is the histologic subset most likely to present as localized disease—partially, but not completely, explains some of the findings noted above.[41,42,43] Such biological differences may be manifested in other ways, as in the case of breast cancer, where older women have an increased frequency of estrogen-receptor-positive breast cancer probably related to hormonal influences of the postmenopausal state.[44] Since estrogen receptor positivity is associated with better prognosis, with more slowly growing tumors, and with longer disease-free survivals, this phenomenon, rather than age per se, might explain the reason why the cancer appears to behave more indolently in an older individual.[45]

MANAGEMENT

This section will examine the utility of the major modalities of cancer treatment in the elderly individual. The use of such modalities is heavily conditioned by the initial decision-making process, i.e., whether to screen, whether to pursue diagnostic workups, whether to treat at all, and how intensively to treat. In such decisions the physician is often placed in the position of weighing benefits versus risks of diagnostic and therapeutic interventions. This is as it should be, and the physician should take into account the various biological, psychological, and social factors involved in the patient's well-being. Of great importance in this regard is the patient's own assessment of the value of both quantity and quality of potential survival during and after the treatment for malignancy. In this process there is a clear need to individualize such decisions, and a decision made for a "wellderly" patient may be appropriately different than for a "frailderly" patient. Currently it would appear that age bias in diagnostic and treatment decisions for older patients with cancer does exist. Thus, it has been reported that despite the presentation of older patients with higher proportion of localized lung cancer, such patients more infrequently received potentially curative surgical therapy.[37] Though this study did not address the appropriateness of such decisions, another study of patients with breast cancer did, and revealed that older women with breast cancer received appropriate therapy, be it surgical, hormonal, chemotherapy, etc., less frequently than did younger women.[46] Other studies have

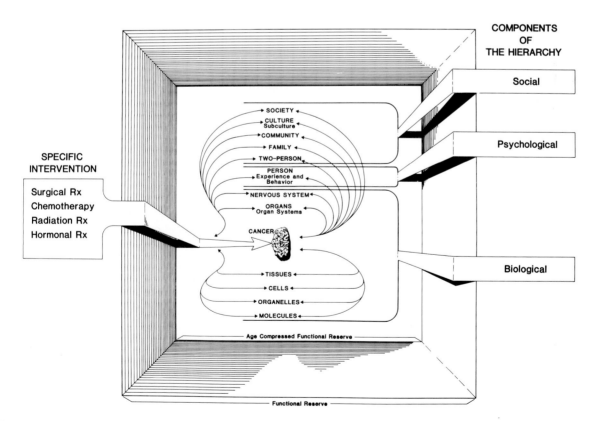

FIGURE 7-4
Comprehensive Geriatric Model. [*From Cohen and DeMaria: Comprehensive cancer care: Special problems of the elderly, in Laszlo (ed): Physician's Guide to Cancer Care Complications. New York and Basel, Marcel Dekker, 1986.[50]*]

confirmed these variations in treatment decisions on the basis of the patient's age.[47-49] Differences in decisions may be entirely appropriate in certain situations but must be based on specific individualized patient information not on categorical decisions made on the basis of chronological age.

We have proposed one framework in which the general aspects of such decision making can be considered for the individual patient.[50] This is shown in Fig. 7-4, and is called the Comprehensive Geriatric Model. It graphically presents a number of the concepts critical to the care of the elderly, i.e., the fact that there is a decreased functional reserve and, as an extension of Engel's Bio-Psycho-Social Model, that all these various aspects of the individual's background must be taken into account when making decisions about the new process—i.e., the cancer. Thus, each of these levels, e.g., biological or psychological, can create interactions which influence both the cancer and the host, and likewise any intervention directed at the cancer may influence both the cancer and each of these levels of the host's function. Conversely, each of these levels of function, when compromised by the aging process or other comorbid diseases, may influence the ability to deliver these various interventions. Thus, in a sense, a conceptual checklist is presented in which a four-way street of various interacting factors can be systematically considered when making such decisions. In this concept, chronological age per se plays a role only by having defined the potentially decreased functional reserve in any of these areas that the older patients may exhibit, but once this is factored into the system, subsequent decisions are dependent more upon those capabilities actually still remaining in the social, psychological, and biological spheres for the individual patient. We would suggest that such considerations be the ones that more directly weigh upon subsequent management decisions for utilization of diagnostic as well as therapeutic technologies for the elderly patient with cancer.

MAJOR THERAPEUTIC MODALITIES

SURGERY

Surgery and other invasive procedures are frequently involved in initial diagnostic as well as therapeutic approaches to the elderly patient with cancer. The general aspects of surgery in the elderly will be discussed thoroughly in Chap. 28. Suffice it to say here that a number of studies have demonstrated that cancer surgery may be accomplished in elderly patients with mortality and morbidity rates which are similar in many cases to those for younger patients and appears to be conditioned more by the extent of comorbid disease and declines in measurable physiologic functions, than chronological age. In

comparing potential alternative modalities, it is well to remember that the acute and time-limited stress of surgery may be preferable to many older patients than the more chronic or protracted courses of therapy frequently involved in radiation therapy and/or chemotherapy.

RADIATION THERAPY

Radiation therapy is used in the treatment of malignancies with both curative and palliative intent.[51] In an attempt to cure local or regional disease, since both radiation therapy or surgery might be considered, one must consider whether the cure rate is equivalent and whether there are differences in morbidity or mortality between the procedures that would cause one to favor one over the other. Radiation therapy has the advantage of having no appreciable acute mortality; it is generally not contraindicated by associated medical conditions; and it may allow maintenance of function of the organ in which the tumor arises. For example, for an elderly person, radiating laryngeal carcinoma and maintaining speech, rather than requiring the learning of laryngeal speech postoperatively may be of considerable advantage. On the other hand, radiation treatment frequently involves a protracted course of therapy.

Radiation therapy is also utilized as an effective adjunct to surgery and/or chemotherapy. For those surgical procedures with high operative mortality, utilizing adjunct radiation therapy to reduce the degree of surgery required may be especially attractive to an elderly patient. The results for adjunct radiation therapy and approaches such as quadrantectomy in breast cancer or lymph node excision in head or neck cancer have been demonstrated to be equivalent to more extensive surgical procedures.[51,52] Palliatively radiation therapy can be extremely effective in providing relief from pain from bone metastases, the effects of brain metastases, control of local obstructive symptoms, and spinal cord compromise. Such treatments can frequently be delivered in courses of 1 to 2 weeks' duration rather than the longer courses of therapy that may be more difficult to tolerate. However, short courses of high-dose radiation may be associated with a higher incidence of acute side effects. The results of treatment, as well as the incidence of complications, are highly dependent upon the technology available and its correct application. Thus, the frequency of complications is directly related to excessive target volume dose and the volume of tissue radiated. Megavoltage equipment, such as the linear accelerator and cobalt-60, are more penetrating than older orthovoltage conventional x rays, thus sparing the skin when treating deep-seated malignancies. The linear accelerator which has very high output, straight-beam edges, and excellent localizability is the most desirable and has been associated with improved therapeutic responses. Thus, for example, in prostate cancer, local recurrences occurred in only 10 percent of those patients treated with 6-MeV, or greater, equipment, but in those treated with cobalt machines recurrence was 20 percent. Similarly, there were fewer recurrences for both cervical cancer and Hodgkin's disease in treatment facilities utilizing a linear accelerator rather than a cobalt unit.[53]

The side effects of therapy may create problems for the older patient. The radiation effect on normal tissue is said to be enhanced approximately 10 to 15 percent in the elderly.[54] Logically, those organs with more marked physiologic decline would be at greatest risk. Radiation to the oral pharynx and oral cavity can produce a loss of taste, dryness of mucous membranes, and involution of salivary glands which when combined with a precarious nutritional intake in a frail and elderly individual might be lethal, or certainly contribute a considerable amount of morbidity, if not recognized. Moreover, if daily treatment is tolerated poorly due to nausea or weakness, treatment may be compromised because of the decreased daily doses, patient's unscheduled absences, or decrease in the total planned dose. Since radiation therapy is frequently used in the treatment of lung cancer, pulmonary complications may be of particular importance. In one study, severe radiation pneumonitis was noted more frequently in elderly individuals than in younger ones regardless of field size and other therapies.[55] Alterations in schedule can be made, and still deliver potential curative radiation therapy to older individuals. This must be done with care, however; although decreasing the daily fraction has not been shown to be detrimental to local control of neck and head cancer, split-dose schedules have been associated with significantly lower control rates for some tumor sites.[51,53]

CHEMO- AND HORMONAL THERAPY

A thorough discussion of the principles of pharmacology in the elderly can be found in Chap. 21. There have been few direct studies of the effect of age on the pharmacokinetics of orally or parenterally administered chemotherapeutic agents.[56] There has been no clear demonstration of differences in the responsiveness of malignant cells per se to chemotherapy in the older versus younger host. The delivery of equivalent doses of the drug to the tumor site, however, may be conditioned by the alterations in pharmacokinetics and pharmacodynamics which may be seen in the elderly individual.

The potential for response and degree of toxicity for various regimens in elderly patients appears to constitute a spectrum depending predominantly upon the aggressiveness of the therapeutic regimen. The major limiting factor for most drugs is bone marrow reserve. Decreased reserve capacity has been demonstrated both in experimental animals and humans,[57,58] but clinical

toxicity would depend upon the degree to which this is stressed. Other toxicities, such as pulmonary toxicity from bleomycin, cardiotoxicity of doxorubicin, and peripheral nerve toxicity of vincristine, also appear to be increased somewhat, though, again, depending upon the aggressiveness of the regimen.[56] Thus, in one clinical study of treatment for metastatic lung, breast, and colorectal carcinoma, the responses of the elderly patients were equivalent to those of the younger with no substantial increase in toxicity.[59] For these relatively unaggressive treatment regimens, excessive toxicity was seen with only two drugs. One was methotrexate. For this drug however, apparently age-related excesses in toxicity have been shown to be more related to, and limitable by adjustment for, decrements in renal function.[60] The other drug was methyl-CCNU which may have rather profound and long-lasting effects on marrow stem cells. However, in another treatment trial of combination chemotherapy of a moderately aggressive nature for multiple myeloma, including another bischlorethylnitrosourea (BCNU), equivalent success rates in terms of response and survival were obtained for elderly patients with no increase in bone marrow or other toxicities.[61]

When one considers somewhat more aggressive combination chemotherapy, such as for small-cell carcinoma of the lung, equivalent response rates have been obtained for older individuals, but this has come at the cost of increased marrow toxicity.[62] Likewise, multiagent chemotherapy approaches for Hodgkin's disease and for non-Hodgkin's lymphoma have been associated with markedly increased toxicity, increased numbers of early deaths, and therefore decreased survival for elderly patients.[63–67] This phenomenon is seen to the maximal extent in elderly patients treated with the most aggressive regimens for acute nonlymphocytic leukemia, wherein excessive early treatment-related deaths severely constrain the use of such approaches.[68–70]

For the hormonally responsive cancers, such as prostate cancer and breast cancer, hormonal therapy is purported to be at least as good in elderly patients as it is in younger patients, and it may be actively employed alone or in combination with other modalities for effective palliative treatment.[53]

When approaching decisions about chemotherapy in treating the elderly patient, the clinician must use those modalities which in the prescribed dosages have acceptable responses with acceptable levels of toxicity, while in the case of those tumor types which require extremely aggressive therapy, the physician must seek modifications and new approaches in order to achieve lower levels of toxicity for the results achieved. In making these decisions, an effective dialogue between the patient and physician will be critically important. We must be wary of the phenomenon of "risk aversion" leading to underdosing, where, in an attempt to avoid toxicities, we effectively abrogate any chance of a therapeutic response. Such a phenomenon may explain the initial reports of the failure of adjunct chemotherapy for breast cancer to have an effect in elderly women.[71] Upon reanalysis of this information, it appears that no effect had been seen in those elderly women who had lower than the prescribed dosage of adjunct therapy, presumably in an attempt to avoid toxicities, while in those older women who had received equivalent doses of therapy as the younger women, an equal effect was noted.

SUPPORTIVE CARE

The effects of cancer and its treatment may be devastating to elderly patients and may require substantial supportive care.[72] The goal of such therapy is to maximize the ability of patients to tolerate the treatment as well as the disease. Underlying problems requiring symptomatic relief need to be actively sought by the physician since elderly patients more frequently underreport their symptoms. Many of the specific aspects of supportive care will be covered in other chapters and are only mentioned here to stress their importance for the management of the elderly cancer patient. These include the extreme importance of effective pain management discussed in Chap. 30, maintenance of appropriate nutritional support discussed in Chap. 31, the supportive role of nursing discussed in Chap. 32, the importance of patient, physician, and family discussions concerning decisions regarding terminal care and other issues discussed in Chaps. 37 and 39, and utility of hospice care discussed in Chap. 37.

One complication frequently seen in treatment of the cancer patient, i.e., nausea and vomiting, has not been discussed elsewhere. These side effects can seriously compromise the ability to deliver effective chemotherapy, and they create a considerable degree of morbidity. It is interesting that elderly patients appear to experience less nausea and vomiting than younger ones.[73] Nevertheless, it is wise to attempt to prevent this occurrence in the first place and correct it where possible. Patients should be kept well-hydrated, and an attempt should be made to eliminate environmental factors, such as food and other odors, which may trigger vomiting. Oral feedings with dry bland foods are generally well tolerated, but high-protein diets are not. Antiemetic drugs may be required for control.[73–75] Phenothiazines have been the mainstay of antiemetic therapy. The elderly appear to be more susceptible to the side effects of these drugs, including excessive sedation, hypertension, and extrapyramidal reactions. Benzodiazepines, such as lorazepam, may be useful in preventing anticipatory nausea and vomiting, which is a conditioned response in patients with previous chemotherapy reactions. For very severely emetogenic chemotherapy,

such as cis-platinum, metoclopramide has proved to be effective, and steroids may be beneficial when utilized in combination with other antiemetics. Though cannabinols (THC) may be effective agents in the control of nausea, the profound sedation and dysphoria sometimes seen in the elderly preclude their general utility.

Elderly patients may be particularly predisposed to constipation, especially as a side effect of such drugs as vincristine, and both preventive and treatment approaches to this problem should be borne in mind at all times. Because of the bone marrow suppressive effects of most cancer chemotherapies, significant cytopenias may result and should be treated with blood products. Because of decreased functional reserve, as well as other comorbid processes, maintenance of an effective and appropriate hemoglobin level should be approached with prophylactic and maintenance transfusion during the period of cytopenia.

Thus, cancer is a disease seen with great frequency in elderly patients. The relationship of cancer to aging poses a challenge to our scientific understanding of these processes as well as to our clinical approach to the elderly patient. Further research will be required to resolve the former,[76] but a systematic, logically developed diagnostic and treatment plan can produce effective and gratifying results in the latter.

REFERENCES

1. Crawford J, Cohen HJ: Aging and neoplasia. *Annu Rev Gerontol Geriatr*, 4:3, 1984.
2. Lipschitz DA et al: Cancer in the elderly: Basic science and clinical aspects. *Ann Intern Med* 102:218, 1985.
3. Baranovsky A, Myers MH: Cancer incidence and survival in patients 65 years of age and older. *CA* 36:26, 1986.
4. Cancer statistics, 1988. *CA* 38:6, 1988.
5. Young JL et al: Surveillance, epidemiology, and end results: Incidence and mortality data, 1973–1977. *Natl Cancer Inst Monogr* 57:1981.
6. Ries LG et al: Cancer patient survival: Surveillance, epidemiology, and end results program, 1973–79. *J Natl Cancer Inst* 70:693, 1983.
7. Crawford J, Cohen HJ: Relationship of cancer and aging. *Clin Geriatr Med* 3:419, 1987.
8. Melamed MR et al: Screening for lung cancer: Results of the Memorial Sloan Kettering study in New York. *Chest* 86:44, 1984.
9. Farber E: The multistep nature of cancer development. *Cancer Res* 44:4217, 1984.
10. Bishop JM: The molecular genetics of cancer. *Science* 235:305, 1987.
11. Croce CM: Chromosomal translocations, oncogenes, and B-cell tumors. *Hosp Pract* 204:41, 1985.
12. Klein G, Klein E: Conditioned tumorigenicity of activated oncogenes. *Cancer Res* 46:3211, 1986.
13. Klein G: The approaching era of the tumor suppressor genes. *Science* 238:1539, 1987.

14. Friend SH et al: Oncogenes and tumor-suppressing genes. *N Engl J Med* 318:618, 1988.

15. Ebbesen P: Cancer and normal aging. *Mech Ageing Dev* 25:269, 1984.

16. Macieira-Coelho A: Review article cancer and aging. *Exp Gerontol* 21:483, 1986.

17. Staiano-Coico L et al: Increased sensitivity of lymphocytes from people over 65 to cell cycle arrest and chromosomal damage. *Science* 219:1335, 1983.

18. Birnbaum LS: Age-related changes in carcinogen metabolism. *J Am Geriatr Soc* 35:51, 1987.

19. Neidermuller H: Age dependency of DNA repair in rats after DNA damage by carcinogens. *Mech Ageing Dev* 19:259, 1982.

20. Srivastava A et al: C-Ha-ras-1 protooncogene amplification and overexpression during the limited replicative life span of normal human fibroblasts. *J Biocommun* 260:6404, 1985.

21. Matocha MF et al: Selective elevation of c-myc transcript levels in the liver of the aging Fischer-344 rat. *Biochem Biophys Res Commun* 147:1, 1987.

22. Makinodan T et al: Age-associated immunodeficiency and cancer, in Mathe G, Reizenstein P (eds): *Pathophysiological Aspects of Cancer Epidemiology.* Elmsford, NY, Pergamon Press, 1985.

23. American Cancer Society: Guidelines for the cancer-related checkup: Recommendations and rationale. *CA* 30:4, 1980.

24. List ND: Perspectives in cancer screening in the elderly. *Clin Geriatr Med* 3:433, 1987.

25. Fink DJ: Change in American Cancer Society checkup guidelines for detection of cervical cancer. *CA* 38:127, 1988.

26. Early Lung Cancer Cooperative Study: Early lung cancer detection: Summary and conclusions. *Am Rev Respir Dis* 130:565, 1984.

27. Hayward RA et al: Who gets screened for cervical and breast cancer? *Arch Intern Med* 148:1177, 1988.

28. Brown JT, Hulka GS: Screening mammography in the elderly: A case-control study. *J Gen Int Med* 3:126, 1988.

29. Mor V: Malignant disease and the elderly, in *1988 Research and the Ageing Population.* Wiley, Chichester (Ciba Foundation Symposium 134), p 160.

30. Samet JM et al: Delay in seeking care for cancer symptoms: A population-based study of elderly New Mexicans. *J Natl Cancer Inst* 80:432, 1988.

31. Robinson E et al: Factors affecting delay in diagnosis of breast cancer: Relationship of delay of disease. *Isr J Med Sci* 22:333, 1986.

32. Goodwin JS et al: Stage at diagnosis of cancer varies with the age of the patient. *J Am Geriatr Soc* 43:20, 1986.

33. Levine J et al: Correlation of thickness of superficial spreading malignant melanomas and ages of patients. *J Dermatol Surg Oncol* 7:311, 1981.

34. Cohen HJ et al: Malignant melanoma in the elderly. *J Clin Oncol* 5:100, 1987.

35. Allen C et al: Breast cancer in the elderly: Current patterns of care. *J Am Geriatr Soc* 34:637, 1986.

36. DeMaria LC, Cohen HJ: Characteristics of lung cancer in elderly patients. *J Gerontol* 452:540, 1987.

37. O'Rourke M et al: Age trends of lung cancer stage at diagnosis: Implications for lung cancer screening in the elderly. *JAMA* 258:921, 1987.

38. Cady R: Risk factor analysis in differentiated thyroid cancer. *Cancer* 43:810, 1979.

39. Schelfhout LJDM et al: Multivariate analysis of survival in differentiated thyroid cancer: The prognostic significance of the age factor. *Eur J Cancer* 24(2):331, 1988.

40. Joensuu H et al: Survival and prognostic factors in thyroid carcinoma. *Acta Radiol [Oncol]* 25 (1986) Fasc 4–6, 243.

41. Teeter SM et al: Lung carcinoma in the elderly population: Influence of histology on the inverse relationship of stage to age. *Cancer* 60:1331, 1987.

42. O'Rourke MA, Crawford J: Lung cancer in the elderly. *Clin Geriatr Med* 3:595, 1987.

43. Dodds L et al: A population based study of lung cancer incidence trends by histologic type, 1974–81. *J Natl Cancer Inst* 76:21, 1986.

44. McCarty KS Jr et al: Relationship of age and menopausal status to estrogen receptor content in primary carcinoma of the breast. *Ann Surg* 197:123, 1983.

45. Cox EB: Breast cancer in the elderly. Cancer II: Specific neoplasms. *Clin Geriatr Med* 695, 1987.

46. Greenfield S et al: Patterns of care related to age of breast cancer patients. *JAMA* 257:2766, 1987.

47. Greenberg ER et al: Social and economic factors in the choice of lung cancer treatment. *N Engl J Med* 318:612, 1988.

48. Chu J et al: The effect of age on the care of women with breast cancer in community hospitals. *J Gerontol* 42:185, 1987.

49. Wetle T: Age as a risk factor for inadequate treatment. *JAMA* 258:516, 1987.

50. Cohen HJ, DeMaria L: Comprehensive cancer care: Special problems of the elderly, in Laszlo J (ed): *Physician's Guide to Cancer Care Complications.* New York and Basel, Marcel Dekker, 1986.

51. Crocker I, Prosnitz L: Radiation therapy of the elderly. *Clin Geriatr Med* 3:473, 1987.

52. Parsons J et al: The influence of excisional or incisional biopsy of metastatic neck nodes on the management of head and neck cancer. *Int J Radiat Oncol Biol Phys* 11:1447, 1985.

53. Hertler AA et al: Cancer in the elderly, in Ham R (ed): *Geriatric Medicine Annual, 1988–89.* Medical Economics Books, Oradell, NJ.

54. Gunn WG: Radiation therapy for the aging patient. *Cancer* 30:337, 1980.

55. Koga K et al: Age factor relevant to the development of radiation pneumonitis in radiotherapy of lung cancer. *Int J Radiat Oncol Biol Phys* 14:367, 1988.

56. Hutchins LF, Lipschitz DA: Cancer, clinical pharmacology and aging. *Clin Geriatr Med* 3:483, 1987.

57. Rothstein G et al: Kinetic evaluation of the pool sizes and proliferative response of neutrophils in bacterially challenged aging mice. *Blood* 70:1836, 1987.

58. Lipschitz DA et al: Effect of age on hematopoiesis in man. *Blood* 63: 502, 1984.

59. Begg CB, Carbone PP: Clinical trials and drug toxicity in the elderly. *Cancer* 52:1986, 1983.

60. Gelman RS, Taylor SG: Cyclophosphamide, methotrexate, and 5-fluorouracil chemotherapy in women more than 65 years old with advanced breast cancer: The elimination of age trends in toxicity by using doses based on creatinine clearance. *J Clin Oncol* 2:1404, 1984.

61. Cohen HJ, Bartolucci A: Influence of age on response to

treatment and survival in mutliple myeloma. *J Am Geriatr Soc* 31:272, 1983.

62. Poplin E et al: Small cell carcinoma of the lung: Influence of age on treatment outcome. *Cancer Treat Rep* 71:291, 1987.

63. Armitage JO, Potter JF: Aggressive chemotherapy for diffuse histiocytic lymphoma in the elderly: Increased complications with advancing age. *J Am Geriatr Soc* 32:269, 1984.

64. Dixon DO et al: Effect of age on therapeutic outcome in advanced diffuse histiocytic lymphoma: The Southwest Oncology Group experience. *J Clin Oncol* 4:295, 1986.

65. Connors JM: Infusions, age, and drug dosages: Learning about large-cell lymphoma. *J Clin Oncol* 6:407, 1988.

66. Peterson BA et al: Effect of age on therapeutic response and survival in advanced Hodgkin's disease. *Cancer Treat Rep* 66:889, 1982.

67. Solal-Celigny P et al: Age as the main prognostic factor in adult aggressive non-Hodgkin's lymphoma. *Am J Med* 83:1075, 1987.

68. Arlin AZ, Clarkson BD: The treatment of acute nonlymphoblastic leukemia in adults. *Adv Intern Med* 28:303, 1983.

69. Kahn SB et al: Full dose versus attenuated dose daunorubicin, cytosine arabinoside, and 6-thioguanine in the treatment of actue nonlymphocytic leukemia in the elderly. *J Clin Oncol* 2: 865, 1984.

70. Walters RS et al: Intensive treatment of acute leukemia in adults 70 years of age and older. *Cancer* 60:149, 1987.

71. Bonadonna G, Valagussa P: Dose-response effect of adjuvant chemotherapy in breast cancer. *N Engl J Med* 304:10, 1981.

72. Dugan SO, Scallion LM: Nursing care of elderly persons throughout the cancer experience: A quality of life framework. *Clin Geriatr Med* 3:517, 1987.

73. Triozzi PL et al: Supportive care of the patient with cancer. *Clin Geriatr Med* 3:505, 1987.

74. Laszlo J: *Antiemetics and Cancer Chemotherapy.* Baltimore, Williams and Wilkins, 1983.

75. Laszlo J et al: Lorazepam in cancer patients treated with cisplatin: A drug having antiemetic, amnesic, and anxiolytic effects. *J Clin Oncol* 3:864, 1985.

76. McCachren SS, Cohen HJ: Cancer, in Cooper RL, Goldman JM, Harbin TJ (eds): *Aging and Environmental Toxicology.* Baltimore, Johns Hopkins University Press, 1989.

Chapter 8

EXERCISE IN OLDER PEOPLE: CARDIOVASCULAR AND METABOLIC ADAPTATIONS

Jerome L. Fleg and Andrew P. Goldberg

Advancing age is accompanied by a progressive decline in the functional capacity of multiple organ systems. Among the more prominent changes are declines in maximal cardiorespiratory performance,[1-4] a loss of muscle and bone mass,[4-6] and a deterioration in glucose (see Refs. 7 and 8 and Chap. 71) and lipid homeostasis (see Chap. 73). Although the variability in these functions found among older individuals of similar chronologic age can be attributed in part to genetic differences in the aging process, at least two other factors may adversely affect functional capacity in humans. The first and most obvious cause for a decline in function is the development of disease. For example, coronary artery disease significantly alters cardiovascular structure and function (see Chaps. 44 and 45); diabetes mellitus affects the function of multiple organs, including the brain, kidneys, eyes, nerves, pancreas, and liver (Chap. 71); and cancer may affect one or several organs (see Chap. 7). The second factor to which functional declines may be attributed is a more subtle process that is related to an individual's physical conditioning.

Prolonged immobilization results in numerous untoward physiologic changes, including a decline in exercise capacity,[9,10] muscle mass and strength,[11] bone density,[12] plasma volume,[13] and glucose tolerance,[14] as well

as deterioration in high-density lipoprotein and triglyceride metabolism.[15] Even short periods of physical inactivity have dramatic effects on insulin sensitivity.[16] Indeed, this profile of physiologic changes parallels many of the changes attributed to the aging process. Though most older persons are not confined to bed rest, a striking decrease in physical activity occurs over the life span. In active community-dwelling participants in the Baltimore Longitudinal Study of Aging (BLSA), caloric expenditure for physical activity diminished progressively between the third and eighth decades (Fig. 8-1).[17] Similarly, numerous surveys document that the percent of older subjects participating in vigorous athletic pursuits is much lower than the percent of younger adults doing so. Thus, many of the physiologic declines with advancing age might be due, at least in part, to age-associated declines in physical activity, rather than to aging per se.

In this chapter, we discuss the interactions between physical-conditioning status and the physiologic changes which often accompany the aging process. First, we review the principles of exercise physiology, including the difference between isotonic (i.e., aerobic, or oxygen-utilizing) exercise and isometric (i.e., anaerobic, or non–oxygen-utilizing) exercise and the way age affects the physiologic responses to these distinct forms of exercise. Then we address several important issues: Can older sedentary individuals be physically trained? To what extent? Does regular exercise training decrease the

The authors are indebted to Mrs. Beverly Eldrett for her typing and editing skills. The research reported was supported by NIH grants 1 PO1 AG04402-05, 1 R01 AG07660-01, 5 MO1 RR02719-03, and NIA intramural funds.

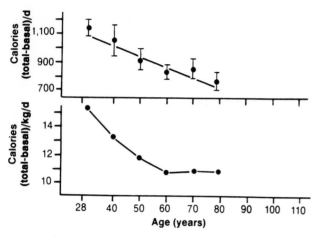

FIGURE 8-1
Effect of age on the average daily caloric expenditure for physical activity in volunteers from the Baltimore Longitudinal Study of Aging. Whether expressed as calories per day (*top*) or calories per kg body weight per day (*bottom*), a noteworthy reduction with age is observed. (*From McGandy et al.* [17])

"aging" of the cardiovascular system? Can such exercise improve or attenuate declines in glucose homeostasis, lipid metabolism, and bone density in older people? Can habitual exercise decrease morbidity and mortality from cardiovascular disease? When possible we will distinguish the salutary effects of physical fitness, indexed as maximal aerobic capacity or $\dot{V}O_{2\,max}$, from those health benefits derived from the reduction in body fat, reduced intake of dietary fat and cholesterol, cessation of cigarette smoking, and heightened awareness of good health habits, which often occur concomitantly in individuals with high levels of physical fitness. In addressing these issues, it is our goal to provide a framework for the practitioner to consider incorporating exercise as a preventive and therapeutic modality for older patients.

MAXIMAL AEROBIC CAPACITY IN THE ELDERLY

It is widely recognized that maximal athletic performance for a wide variety of sports declines with advancing age, usually beginning in the third or fourth decade. In the laboratory, the most effective method of assessing overall aerobic fitness is the measurement of maximal oxygen consumption ($\dot{V}O_{2\,max}$) during treadmill or bicycle exercise.[18] $\dot{V}O_{2\,max}$, the product of cardiac output and systemic arteriovenous oxygen difference, represents the maximal ability of the cardiovascular system to deliver oxygenated blood to the periphery and the capacity for exercising muscle and other tissues to extract oxygen from the blood. In a given individual, $\dot{V}O_{2\,max}$ is highly reproducible and is not altered by the involvement of additional muscles once 50 to 60 percent of the

muscle mass is exercised. These features, as well as the relative noninvasiveness of the $\dot{V}O_{2\,max}$ test, make $\dot{V}O_{2\,max}$ an excellent overall measure of cardiovascular fitness.

One of the most consistent findings in gerontological research is the age-related decline in $\dot{V}O_{2\,max}$, which averages 5 to 10 percent per decade between ages 25 and 75 (Fig. 8-2). Because the decline in $\dot{V}O_{2\,max}$ with age parallels the decline in work capacity, it is not caused by an increase in the metabolic efficiency of older persons. At a given treadmill exercise stress or work load, in fact, older people may demonstrate a slightly higher level of oxygen consumption than younger people, perhaps owing to their reduction in the efficiency of walking.

Until recently, the belief was nearly universal that the age-associated decline in $\dot{V}O_{2\,max}$ was secondary to a decrease in maximal cardiac output,[19,20] which resulted from a progressive decline in maximal heart rate and, to a lesser extent, from a decrease in stroke volume with age at maximal exertion. This concept of an obligatory decrease in maximal cardiac output with age has been

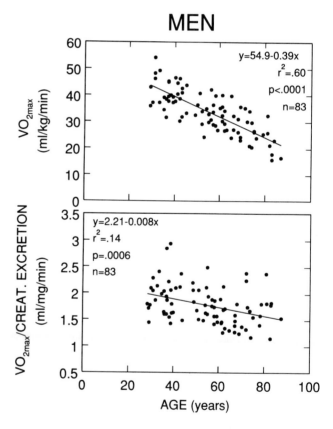

FIGURE 8-2
(*Top*) Maximal oxygen consumption ($\dot{V}O_{2\,max}$) per kg body weight as a function of age in healthy nonobese male participants from the Baltimore Longitudinal Study. A decline of nearly 10% per decade is observed. (*Bottom*) $\dot{V}O_{2\,max}$ normalized for urinary creatinine excretion and plotted as a function of age in the same men as above. Expressed in this manner, the decline in $\dot{V}O_{2\,max}$ is now attenuated to only 4.5% per decade. (*From Fleg and Lakatta.* [4])

challenged by a recent study in healthy subjects from the BLSA, rigorously screened by exercise thallium scintigraphy to exclude significant but asymptomatic coronary artery disease.[21] As discussed in greater detail elsewhere (Chap. 44), cardiac output during maximal exertion on a bicycle in these volunteers showed only a slight, statistically nonsignificant decrease with age. The age-related decline in maximal heart rate was compensated by an increase in stroke volume, mediated in turn by a greater augmentation of left ventricular end-diastolic volume (i.e., a greater reliance on the Frank-Starling mechanism). It is therefore possible that much of the decline in cardiac output with age in prior studies was due to unrecognized coronary artery disease and, perhaps, to physical deconditioning.

CENTRAL VERSUS PERIPHERAL DETERMINANTS OF $\dot{V}O_2$ MAX

Indirect evidence exists that some of the decline in $\dot{V}O_2$ max with advancing age is due to peripheral factors, i.e., a reduction in the arteriovenous oxygen difference. For example, in BLSA volunteers, maximal cycle workload (and presumably peak $\dot{V}O_2$ max achieved) decreased with age despite the maintenance of cardiac output, suggesting an age-related decrease in arteriovenous oxygen difference.[21] Additional evidence is derived from both cross-sectional[22] and longitudinal studies[23] in which a higher $\dot{V}O_2$ max in older trained subjects was mediated primarily by an augmented arteriovenous oxygen difference, with only a minimal difference in cardiac output. Future studies in which $\dot{V}O_2$ max and cardiac output are measured in a large sample across a broad age range are needed to determine precisely the relative roles of central (cardiac output) versus peripheral (arteriovenous oxygen difference) factors in the age-associated decline in $\dot{V}O_2$ max.

Viewed in another context, part of the age-related decline in $\dot{V}O_2$ max may derive from changes in body composition with aging. Although $\dot{V}O_2$ max is usually expressed per kilogram of body weight, it is actually the exercising muscles that consume over 90 percent of the oxygen during strenuous aerobic exercise. In 184 healthy, nonobese BLSA volunteers, total body muscle mass was estimated from 24-hour urinary creatinine excretion and found to decline approximately 6 percent per decade in both sexes.[4] When $\dot{V}O_2$ max was expressed relative to muscle mass, rather than to total body weight, the proportion of the $\dot{V}O_2$ max decline attributable to age decreased from 60 percent to 14 percent in men and from 50 percent to 14 percent in women (Fig. 8-2). These findings suggest that strategies to preserve muscle mass may also help to lessen the magnitude of the decline in $\dot{V}O_2$ max during aging.

PHYSIOLOGIC ADAPTATIONS IN AEROBICALLY CONDITIONED OLDER ATHLETES

Is there evidence that regular aerobic exercise training actually attenuates the 10 percent per decade decline in $\dot{V}O_2$ max normally seen with advancing age? Cross-sectional studies have consistently found a decrease in $\dot{V}O_2$ max of 0.40 to 0.50 ml/kg · min/year in men and 0.20 to 0.35 ml/kg · min/year in women.[3,24] In general, these studies show no clear differences in the rate of change in $\dot{V}O_2$ max with aging between active and sedentary populations. However, when the $\dot{V}O_2$ max in endurance-trained male athletes aged 19 to 27 years was compared to that of athletes aged 50 to 72 years who were matched to the younger athletes for both training habits and performance in the same event at a similar age, the $\dot{V}O_2$ max of the older athletes averaged only 15 percent less than that of the matched younger athletes.[1] Assuming that the two groups had similar $\dot{V}O_2$ max levels in their third decade, extrapolation of these data suggests an estimated decline in $\dot{V}O_2$ max of 5 percent per decade in these older highly trained men, approximately one-half the rate of decline reported in sedentary populations.[3]

Given the inherent biases of cross-sectional studies, particularly the potential for selective survival in older age groups, longitudinal studies offer a more rigorous approach to the study of the long-term effects of regular physical activity on age-related changes in $\dot{V}O_2$ max. In 40 men ages 40 to 72, Dehn and Bruce[3] reported that those who jogged the equivalent of 3 miles weekly had less of a decrease in $\dot{V}O_2$ max than did their sedentary peers (0.56 vs. 1.62 ml/kg · min/year). However, the entire difference in $\dot{V}O_2$ max could be attributed to an accelerated decline in the sedentary group, mediated by a significant weight gain, rather than to a greater absolute reduction in maximal oxygen consumption.

Kasch et al. have performed longitudinal studies in a group of 15 men engaged in vigorous aerobic exercise training over a 20-year span from age 45 to 65.[25] Throughout this period, the men exercised 3.0 to 3.6 times per week at 77 to 84 percent of maximal heart-rate reserve (defined as maximal heart rate − resting heart rate) for approximately 1 hour per session. $\dot{V}O_2$ max declined from 44.4 to 38.9 ml/kg · min or 12.4 percent over these two decades for an average decline of only 0.27 ml/kg · min/year (Fig. 8-3). However, there was a mean weight loss of 3.4 kg in these men over the 20 years. Thus, if $\dot{V}O_2$ max is expressed in liters/min instead of kg/min, the decline in $\dot{V}O_2$ max would be 16.3 percent rather than 12.4 percent, or about 8 percent per decade. This value lies midway between the decline of 10 percent per decade usually quoted for sedentary populations and the 5 percent decline deduced by Heath et al.[1] in highly conditioned older men.

FIGURE 8-3
Effect of two decades of regular aerobic exercise on the age-related decline in $\dot{V}_{O_2\,max}$ in men whose initial mean age was 45 years. Compared with two sets of pooled data in sedentary men, the regular exercisers show a blunted rate of decline in $\dot{V}_{O_2\,max}$. (*Adapted from Kasch et al.*[25])

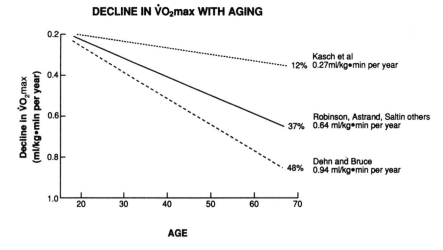

DECLINE IN $\dot{V}_{O_2}$max WITH AGING

Kasch et al
12% 0.27ml/kg•min per year

Robinson, Astrand, Saltin others
37% 0.64 ml/kg•min per year

Dehn and Bruce
48% 0.94 ml/kg•min per year

Decline in $\dot{V}_{O_2}$max (ml/kg•min per year)

AGE

Possibly the best data available for examining whether habitual exercise slows the age-associated decline in $\dot{V}_{O_2\,max}$ come from a study which evaluated 24 runners over a 10-year period from an initial mean age of 52 to 62 years.[26] Although all of the men maintained their running mileage over the decade, half of the men maintained their original running speed, while the other half reduced their pace by 1.5 min/mile. Body weight remained nearly constant in both groups. While the group which reduced training intensity experienced a 13 percent reduction in $\dot{V}_{O_2\,max}$ (from 52.5 to 45.9 ml/kg · min), the group which maintained training intensity experienced only a 2 percent loss of $\dot{V}_{O_2\,max}$ (from 54.2 to 53.3 ml/kg · min) over the decade. These compelling data suggest that the decline in maximal aerobic capacity with advancing age can be attenuated markedly by maintaining both a high intensity and quantity of physical activity. However, the possible contributions of genetic factors to these processes cannot be disregarded.

EFFECTS OF AEROBIC EXERCISE TRAINING IN SEDENTARY OLDER PEOPLE

Given the reality that most older Americans have not followed a regimen of vigorous aerobic activity throughout their adult lives, a more practical question is "Can sedentary older men and women derive a significant training effect from an aerobic exercise program?" The hallmark of such a training effect would be an increase in $\dot{V}_{O_2\,max}$, both in absolute terms and per kilogram of body weight. Until the past decade, the available data suggested that healthy individuals older than 60 years of age could not increase their $\dot{V}_{O_2\,max}$ in response to an endurance exercise training stimulus. Several recent investigations convincingly refute this notion. $\dot{V}_{O_2\,max}$ estimated from responses to submaximal exercise were found by DeVries to increase approximately 10 percent after 42 weeks of calisthenics, jogging, and aquatics in 112 men whose mean age was 70.[27] In men averaging 63

years of age and exercising at 70 percent of heart-rate reserve for 1 year, Thomas et al.[28] reported increases in directly measured $\dot{V}_{O_2\,max}$ of 12 percent. Several other studies[28–33] have reported increases in peak $\dot{V}_{O_2}$ measured during cycle ergometry, in older subjects who participated in 8 to 52 weeks of training (Fig. 8-4).

In the most comprehensive study to date, a 6-month walking program at 40 percent of heart-rate reserve increased $\dot{V}_{O_2\,max}$ by 12 percent in 11 healthy men

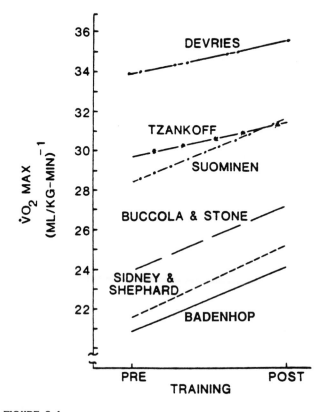

DEVRIES

TZANKOFF

SUOMINEN

BUCCOLA & STONE

SIDNEY & SHEPHARD

BADENHOP

$\dot{V}_{O_2}$ MAX (ML/KG-MIN)$^{-1}$

PRE — POST
TRAINING

FIGURE 8-4
Changes in $\dot{V}_{O_2\,max}$ resulting from aerobic exercise training programs in subjects older than age 60. In general, the lower the initial fitness level, the greater the improvement with training. (*Adapted from Badenhop et al.*[33])

and women ages 65 ± 3.[23] Six additional months of higher-intensity exercise at 80 to 85 percent of heart-rate reserve raised $\dot{V}O_2$ max an additional 18 percent and reduced percent body fat (Fig. 8-5) This increase in $\dot{V}O_2$ max was mediated primarily through an increase in the maximal arteriovenous oxygen difference, with little change in the indirectly calculated maximal cardiac output. There were significant improvement in pulmonary function with training,[34] suggesting that some of the in-

crease in maximal oxygen consumption may have been mediated by improved gas exchange, although pulmonary responses were probably not a limiting factor for $\dot{V}O_2$ max at baseline. Insulin sensitivity and lipoprotein lipid levels only improved after the high-intensity regimen (Fig. 8-6).[35] The results of these investigations suggest that healthy sedentary older individuals are capable of achieving relative increases of $\dot{V}O_2$ max comparable to those of younger subjects.[23,34,35] It is not yet clear, how-

FIGURE 8-5
The cardiovascular and body composition effects of 6 months of low-intensity training (40% of heart-rate reserve) followed by 6 months of high-intensity training (80–85% of heart-rate reserve) were examined in 11 sedentary older men and women. Baseline characteristics of subjects undergoing exercise training and their sedentary age-matched controls are shown in A. There were significant increases in $\dot{V}O_2$ max after each phase of training (B) but percent body fat decreased significantly only after the 6 months of high-intensity training (C). (*Adapted from Seals et al.*[23,35])

A. SUBJECT CHARACTERISTICS

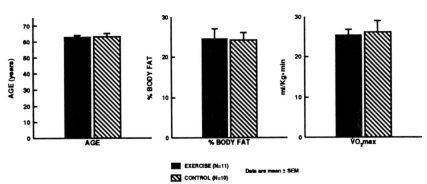

B. $\dot{V}O_2$ max

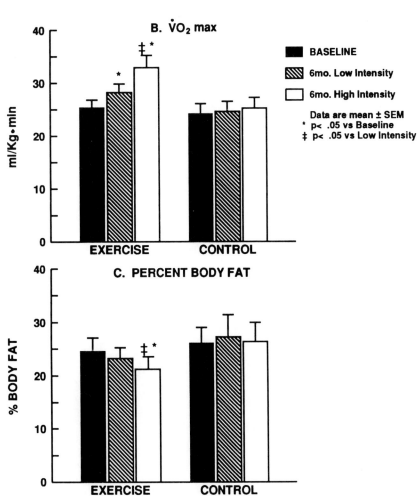

C. PERCENT BODY FAT

A. GLUCOSE METABOLISM

ORAL GLUCOSE TOLERANCE

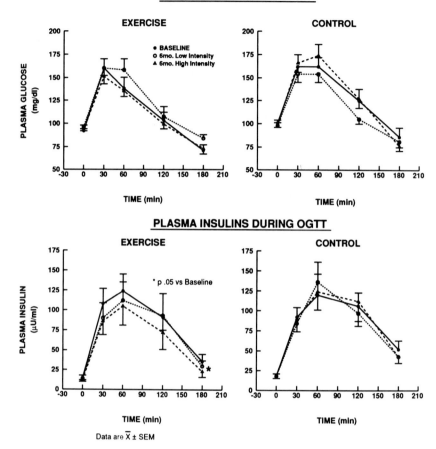

PLASMA INSULINS DURING OGTT

Data are $\overline{X} \pm$ SEM

B. LIPOPROTEIN LIPIDS

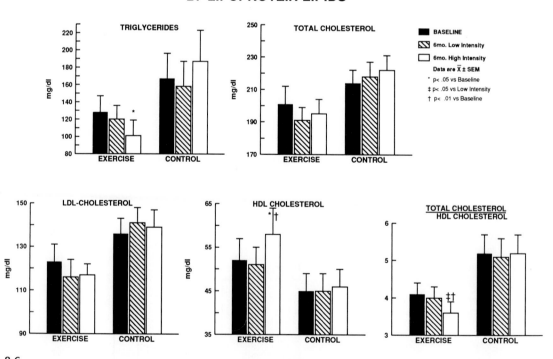

FIGURE 8-6

Six months of low-intensity training did not affect glucose or lipoprotein lipid metabolism. However, after 6 months of high-intensity training, there was a significant improvement in insulin sensitivity without change in glucose tolerance ($p < .05$, Fig. A). Six months of high-intensity training also resulted in a significant decline in plasma triglyceride levels ($p < .05$), an increase in high-density lipoprotein (HDL) cholesterol ($p < .05$), and a reduction in the plasma total to HDL cholesterol ratio ($p < .01$, Fig. B). (*Adapted from Seals et al.*[35])

ever, whether individuals substantially older than 70 years can increase their $\dot{V}O_{2\,max}$ in response to vigorous aerobic exercise training.

In younger subjects, training intensities in excess of 60 to 70 percent of $\dot{V}O_{2\,max}$ are generally required to elicit an increase in $\dot{V}O_{2\,max}$. In older, sedentary individuals, training at an intensity as low as 40 percent of $\dot{V}O_{2\,max}$ elicits increases in $\dot{V}O_{2\,max}$.[23,35] The lower relative training threshold for older individuals may be a result of their lower initial $\dot{V}O_{2\,max}$ rather than aging per se, since the training intensity needed to augment $\dot{V}O_{2\,max}$ is inversely proportional to the $\dot{V}O_{2\,max}$ at the start of training. Despite the increase of $\dot{V}O_{2\,max}$ elicited at these lower work intensities, other physiologic variables, such as body weight, body composition, percent body fat, plasma blood lipids, glucose tolerance, and insulin sensitivity, did not seem to improve until the older subjects trained at higher work intensities.[35]

ISOMETRIC EXERCISE CAPACITY IN THE ELDERLY

The prior discussion has been limited to age-associated changes in aerobic exercise. However, many tasks performed in everyday life, such as lifting, pushing, or pulling against a fixed resistance, involve primarily isometric or static exercise, characterized by the development of tension within a muscle without a significant change in the length of its fibers. In contrast to aerobic exercise, isometric activities are primarily anaerobic and are measured as strength, i.e., the quantity of weight which can be lifted, pushed, or pulled in   fashion.

MUSCLE STRUCTURE AND FUNCTION WITH AGING

A number of studies have confirmed an age-related loss in maximal isometric strength. Between the ages of 30 and 80, this loss is approximately 40 percent in the leg and back muscles and 30 percent in the arm muscles[36] (Fig. 8-7). These declines in strength seem to parallel both the age-associated decrease in total body muscle mass as well as the decrease in muscle cross-sectional area.[37] Thus, strength per unit of muscle area remains relatively constant over the age span. The loss of strength with age appears to follow a curvilinear pattern, with gradual acceleration of loss occurring in later years. It has been postulated that the faster decline in the legs and back versus the arms is a result of the fact that leg and back muscles are utilized less frequently than arm muscles in the daily activities of older people.

Histologically, the decline in muscle cross-sectional area with age appears to be due primarily to a loss of muscle fiber number, rather than fiber size. In one study, the muscle fiber count in vastus lateralis was 364,000 in men ages 70 to 73, as compared to 478,000 in men ages 19 to 37 years old, reflecting a decrease of 24 percent.[38] Only minor changes in muscle fiber size occur during adult life until the seventh decade; after that age, the cross-sectional area of fast-twitch fibers, the fibers primarily involved in isometric work, seems to decline by 5 to 10 percent.[39] The area of slow-twitch fibers, involved primarily in aerobic work, appears to remain nearly constant until the eighth decade of life.

Accompanying the loss of muscle fiber number with advancing age is a decline in the number of functioning motor units in both upper and lower extremities.[40,41] The remaining motor units appear to enlarge, suggesting that they include more muscle fibers. This loss of motor units appears to parallel a loss of motor neurons in the nervous system. Some of the muscle fibers without innervation may necrose, while others may become reinnervated, suggesting that muscle fibers undergo dynamic reorganization across the age span.

Considering the anatomic and neurophysiologic age-associated changes in skeletal muscle described above, an obvious question is whether such "aged muscle" can hypertrophy and increase in strength in response to a training stimulus. Several studies suggest that such adaptations can occur. In men 69 to 74 years old, an increase in quadriceps muscle strength of 9 to 22

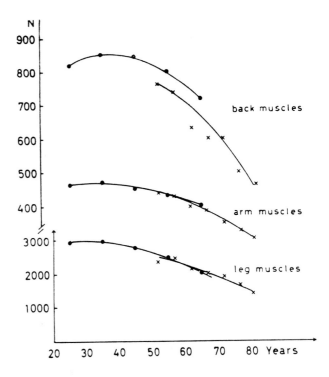

FIGURE 8-7
Age-associated changes in maximal isometric strength, in newtons, in three different muscle groups. Declines occur with age in all three muscle groups but are most pronounced in individuals over the age of 50. (*From Asmussen.*[37])

percent and an enlargement in the relative area of fast-twitch fibers occurred during 12 weeks of strength training.[42] The increase in fiber size also appeared to be associated with an increase in the recruitment of motor units. Recently, Frontera et al.[43] demonstrated sizeable increases in both strength and muscle areas (measured by computerized tomographic scanning) in men 60 to 72 years old, after a 12-week program of strength training. Thus, the trainability of skeletal muscle in response to an isometric stimulus persists even into older age. Since many activities of daily living, such as rising from a chair or climbing stairs, depend on muscular strength, such training has the potential to enhance the daily functional capacity of older individuals.

CARDIOVASCULAR RESPONSES TO ISOMETRIC EXERCISE

The hemodynamic responses to isometric exercise consist of modest increases in heart rate and cardiac output, relatively large increases in both systolic and diastolic blood pressure, and little or no change in systemic vascular resistance.[44] Evaluation of age-associated changes in hemodynamic response to isometric exercise have been limited largely to heart rate and blood pressure. As with aerobic exercise, there is a blunted cardioacceleration to isometric handgrip with advancing age, both at maximal and submaximal effort.[45] In contrast, the increase in systolic blood pressure during handgrip is augmented with age, while the rise in diastolic blood pressure appears to be unaffected.[45] Systolic time intervals, an indirect index of cardiac contractility, demonstrated an increase in pre-ejection period in older men and a reduction in pre-ejection period in young men, suggesting impaired contractility in the former groups.[45] The dependence of systolic time intervals on loading conditions, however, and the absence of blood pressure measurements in that study, hamper interpretation of these data. The availability of accurate noninvasive imaging techniques should allow better characterization of the changes in left ventricular responses to isometric exercise with aging.

METABOLIC FUNCTION IN THE ELDERLY

There is a great deal of variability in the deterioration in glucose, lipoprotein, and bone-mineral metabolism which commonly occurs in older individuals. The differences in metabolic function among older people may reflect genetic heterogeneity in rates of aging, yet it is more likely that some of this diversity is the effect of secondary processes which often accompany aging. There are numerous secondary factors which can ad-

versely affect metabolic function over the human life span. These include obesity, improper diet, physical inactivity, cigarette smoking, chronic disease, malnutrition and/or medications affecting nutrient absorption, blood flow to tissues, fluid and electrolyte balance, and central nervous system function. Some of these secondary processes, especially inappropriate dietary intake, cigarette smoking, obesity, and physical inactivity, may be modifiable, suggesting that it may be possible to retard or even prevent some of the declines in metabolic function previously attributed to aging.

The worsening of glucose and lipoprotein metabolism with aging predisposes older people to develop diabetes and hyperlipidemia (Chaps. 71 and 73). These metabolic diseases increase the risk of coronary artery disease, the leading cause of death in older Americans (Chap. 45). In several autopsy series, coronary artery disease was present in 40 to 60 percent of unselected subjects dying in the seventh decade and beyond, even though only approximately one-half of these individuals were symptomatic during life. Nearly 50 percent of all deaths in the United States are related to cardiovascular disease. Approximately two-thirds of individuals reaching age 65 will die of cardiovascular disease, while the next most frequent disease group, cancer, accounts for only 15 percent of deaths. In 1984, heart attacks accounted for 600,000 of 1 million cardiovascular deaths. Not only is cardiovascular disease the major cause of death in the United States, but it is also the major cause of morbidity. The acute and chronic cost for medical care related to cardiovascular disease is nearly 60 billion dollars annually. Successful prevention of coronary artery disease and other complications of atherosclerosis would be expected to prolong life by 10 to 15 years in a healthy 65-year-old, far in excess of the aggregate life extension predicted from all other major causes of death in the United States combined.[46]

Osteopenia is common in older populations and is due to a generalized reduction in bone mass called osteoporosis.[6] Osteoporosis contributes to some 1.3 million bone fractures per year in people over 45 years of age. An additional 15 to 20 percent of women aged 60 to 80 years will suffer a Colles' fracture. On the basis of x-ray evidence, one-third of women and one-sixth of men will have suffered a hip fracture by age 90, leading to death in 12 and 20 percent of those cases, respectively, and to long-term nursing care for those who survive. Epidemiologic surveys suggest that of a total of 150,000 hip fractures a year, 75 percent will be in women over the age of 70. The short- and long-term direct costs for treatment of osteoporosis and its consequences approach 1 and 8 billion dollars, respectively.[47]

If physical inactivity is a significant determinant of the decline in glucose and lipoprotein metabolism and loss of bone mass with aging, then interventions which increase exercise habits and raise maximal aerobic capacity may improve organ function, reduce metabolic risk factors for coronary artery and peripheral vascular disease, reduce osteoporosis and the incidence of fractures in the elderly, and lower the morbidity and mortality associated with these conditions. This might prolong the survival and improve the quality of life in older people. The profound effects of physical conditioning on glucose and lipoprotein metabolism and body composition is well-recognized in younger and middle-aged individuals; however, the long-term effects of endurance exercise training on glucose, lipoprotein, and bone-mineral metabolism have not been conclusively determined in older populations.

AGING, PHYSICAL ACTIVITY, AND GLUCOSE METABOLISM

Numerous studies indicate there is a slight age-related increase after maturity in fasting plasma glucose levels in healthy older individuals (1 mg/dl per decade). This small increase in fasting glucose levels is accompanied, however, by a striking 10 mg per decade increase in plasma glucose levels 2 hours after the ingestion of a drink containing 40 g glucose per square meter body surface area.[48,49] These higher postprandial glucose levels usually are associated with an increase in plasma insulin levels, suggesting that a decrease in insulin sensitivity, rather than a reduction in insulin secretion, is responsible for the deterioration in glucose tolerance with aging. Glucose clamp studies demonstrate that at submaximal insulin concentrations, both glucose disposal and the suppressability of hepatic glucose production are reduced in older subjects, despite normal insulin-receptor function and number (see Refs. 7 and 8 and Chap. 71). Tissue responsiveness to insulin, defined as glucose disposal at maximal insulin concentrations, is normal in some older subjects and reduced in others, depending on an individual's degree of glucose intolerance and severity of hyperinsulinemia.[50] These results suggest that in some older people there may be a defect in insulin action distal to the insulin receptor (i.e., a post-receptor binding defect) that is responsible for the decline in insulin sensitivity with aging. The presence of an in vivo decline in the maximal capacity for glucose uptake during hyperinsulinemia, despite minimal change in affinity for glucose during hyperglycemia, suggests that there also may be a defect in the number and/or activity of glucose transporters in older people.[51,52]

There are several studies which suggest that the ingestion of a high-carbohydrate diet will normalize glucose in older individuals[53]; when healthy, lean, older individuals are matched to younger individuals for body weight and activity status, glucose tolerance and insulin sensitivity are comparable.[54,55] Furthermore, interventions of endurance exercise training[35] (Fig. 8-6B) and weight loss[56] will improve insulin sensitivity and glucose tolerance in older people. Other possible mechanisms could be responsible for the hyperinsulinemia and glucose intolerance with aging, including elevated plasma concentrations of norepinephrine and other counter-regulatory hormones which impair insulin secretion and action,[57] a defective second phase of insulin secretion in response to intravenous glucose,[58] and chronic diseases.[59]

Regular physical activity and a high $\dot{V}O_{2\,max}$ are associated with increased insulin sensitivity in younger or middle-aged normal individuals and with improvements in insulin sensitivity and/or glucose tolerance in obese subjects, type II diabetics, and older individuals.[59-61] The ability of regular physical activity to increase insulin sensitivity and improve glucose tolerance suggests that the sedentary lifestyle and low aerobic capacity of many older individuals may be partially responsible for the decline in glucose tolerance and reduction in insulin sensitivity in response to oral glucose seen with aging.[35,59,61] That regular physical activity of just 1-week duration, without change in body weight, was sufficient to improve glucose tolerance and increase insulin sensitivity in middle-aged individuals suggests that such a program may have comparable effects in older subjects. However, the observation that the improvements in metabolic function only occurred when there was a concomitant decline in percent body fat during the period of intense physical activity[35,63,64] (Fig. 8-6) suggests that weight loss and changes in adipose tissue metabolism during exercise may be as important as the increase in $\dot{V}O_{2\,max}$ in mediating improvements in metabolic function. However, it is not clear whether or not similar changes would have occurred without a change in percent fat if a low-intensity exercise program had been continued for 6 additional months or if the food intake had been increased sufficiently to prevent weight loss. Collectively these results suggest that physical conditioning and weight loss may have complementary and perhaps synergistic physiologic effects on metabolic function, and both may be effective in reducing the risk of this population for developing type II diabetes and hyperlipidemia.[65,66] This finding could have major public health implications for reducing morbidity and mortality from diabetes and atherosclerosis in older people who tend to be overweight and sedentary.

Results from studies in master athletes, i.e., older individuals who train regularly, maintain high levels of maximal oxygen consumption, and compete in local and national athletic events,[1] suggest that intense, regular aerobic physical activity may protect against age-related declines of glucose tolerance, insulin sensitivity, and lipoprotein lipids (Figs. 8-8 and 8-9). However, a high $\dot{V}O_{2\,max}$ and low percent body fat are closely related,

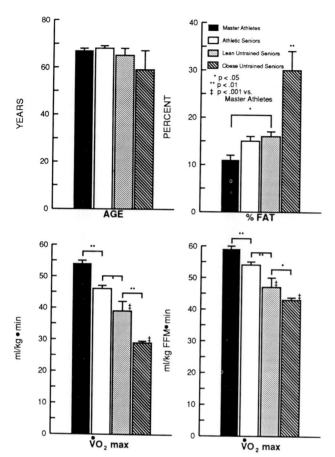

FIGURE 8-8

Healthy, athletic older men (Athletic Seniors, *n* = 11) and active, lean, untrained, older men (Lean Untrained Seniors, *n* = 10) were matched as closely as possible to healthy, highly conditioned master athletes (Master Athletes, *n* = 12) for age and percent body fat to determine the effects of regular physical conditioning on lipoprotein and glucose metabolism. An active, obese group of untrained men (Obese Untrained Seniors, *n* = 15) of comparable age were selected to determine the effects of obesity on metabolic function in older men. The ages of the men were comparable, but percent fat was significantly higher in the Lean Untrained Seniors than the Master Athletes ($p < .05$); the obese men had a higher percentage of body fat than all the other groups had. $\dot{V}O_{2\ max}$ differed significantly among all the groups when expressed both per kg body weight and per kg fat-free mass to normalize oxygen consumption for differences in body composition.

perhaps via genetic processes and environmental influences; hence, it is often difficult to distinguish the relationship of physical-conditioning status to glucose tolerance and insulin sensitivity independent from body composition and dietary habits in older individuals. In only one study was consideration given to the effects of $\dot{V}O_{2\ max}$ and percent body fat on glucose metabolism in older individuals[54]; our data (Fig. 8-8 and 8-9) support the findings of Seals et al.[54,67] that maintenance of a high level of physical conditioning is associated with lipoprotein lipid profiles, glucose tolerance, and insulin sensitivity comparable to those of healthy active younger subjects. There are no longitudinal studies which have

examined the effects of changing both physical-conditioning status and body fat on the mechanisms regulating glucose metabolism in older people.

The heightened incidence of insulin resistance, impaired glucose tolerance, and non-insulin-dependent diabetes mellitus in middle-aged and older individuals, and the potential for modification of these states by physical conditioning, increases the significance of determining whether or not regular exercise can reverse or attenuate the glucose intolerance and hyperinsulinemia seen in older type II diabetics.[66,67] Results of endurance exercise training programs in middle-aged type II diabetics suggest that exercise may be a valuable intervention for older sedentary individuals with mild glucose tolerance and insulin resistance.[66,68,69] This possibility is reinforced by a recent study in which 7 days of endurance exercise training did not significantly change $\dot{V}O_{2\ max}$ but significantly improved insulin sensitivity and glucose tolerance in type II diabetics.[62] This finding suggests that regular physical activity with or without an increase in $\dot{V}O_{2\ max}$ may be beneficial for older type II diabetics.

It is not known whether or not the improvements in glucose metabolism which have been attributed to exercise training in cross-sectional studies and demonstrated longitudinally in a few reports in young and middle-aged subjects can be demonstrated prospectively in older overweight individuals with limited capacity for physical activity. It is possible that older individuals who have been inactive for prolonged periods may not be able to exercise intensely enough to improve muscle metabolism sufficiently to increase insulin sensitivity with exercise training. Furthermore, the risks of cardiac events, orthopedic injury, falls, and dehydration for overexertion may exceed the benefits of endurance training in some older people. These issues need to be addressed in future research examining the importance of regular physical activity and exercise training for the promotion of health in older populations.[59]

AGING, PHYSICAL ACTIVITY, AND LIPOPROTEIN METABOLISM

Aging is often associated with a rise in fasting plasma total and low-density lipoprotein (LDL) cholesterol from the third to sixth decade, followed by a decline (Chap. 73). The ratio of high-density lipoprotein (HDL) cholesterol to total cholesterol falls by 30 to 50 percent during the same period before plateauing. Triglyceride levels tend to rise across the age span. Some of these relationships may vary in cross-sectional studies of older populations; however, in general there seems to be an increase in the variability of lipid levels with aging such that some selected older people actually display lipoprotein lipid levels comparable to those of younger individuals. These findings are supported by studies in older master athletes whose levels of HDL cholesterol, triglyceride, and LDL cholesterol were found to be comparable to those of athletic younger individuals, while plasma triglyceride and LDL were lower and HDL levels were higher than untrained, less active, age- and weight-matched as well as obese peers.[67] This suggests that physical conditioning and maintenance of low body fat may prevent some of the age-related deterioration in lipoprotein lipid metabolism.

Secondary aging processes, such as increasing body weight, physical inactivity, and chronic disease, have significant deleterious effects on lipoprotein metabolism. Obesity, deconditioning, chronic renal disease, and diabetes mellitus cause a significant decline in lipoprotein metabolism, as manifested by elevations in total cholesterol and triglyceride and by reductions in HDL cholesterol levels.[70] Diets high in cholesterol and saturated fat increase LDL cholesterol levels, while diabetes mellitus, end-stage renal disease, obesity, and physical inactivity usually cause hyperlipidemia and low HDL cholesterol levels. Abnormal lipoprotein lipid profiles (and glucose metabolism) in some older individuals may also be caused by coexistent chronic disease and the use of certain medications, such as thiazide diuretics, beta blockers, corticosteroids, androgens, and progestins, to treat them (Chap. 73).

The mechanisms responsible for the occurrence of lipoprotein lipid abnormalities and their long-term consequences in older people are not known. There is also little known about the processes governing the metabolic relationships among lipoproteins in older individu-

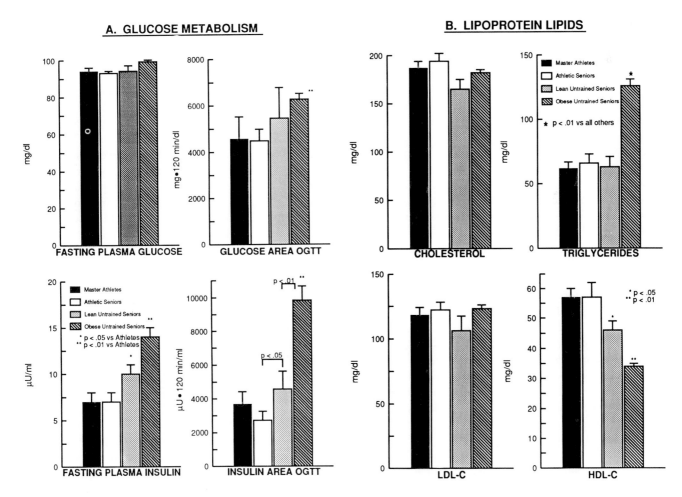

FIGURE 8-9
Fasting plasma glucose levels were comparable in the Master Athletes and Athletic Seniors (athletes) and untrained men (**A**). All of the men had normal oral glucose tolerance tests (OGTT). However, plasma glucose levels during the OGTT were significantly higher in the Obese Untrained Seniors than in both groups of athletes ($p < .01$, Fig.A), despite the fact that fasting insulin levels and the rise in insulin during the OGTT were significantly higher in the Obese Untrained Men than in both groups of the athletes as well as the Lean Untrained Men (Fig. **A**). Plasma triglyceride levels were significantly higher in the Obese Untrained Seniors, while total- and low-density lipoprotein cholesterol (LDL-C) levels did not differ among the groups (Fig. **B**). Plasma high-density lipoprotein cholesterol (HDL-C) levels were lowest in the Obese Untrained Seniors ($p < .01$ vs. athletes and Lean Untrained Men) and significantly higher in the two groups of athletes than in the Lean Untrained Seniors ($p < .05$, Fig.B).

als; hence, the metabolic effects of nonpharmacologic interventions (e.g., weight loss, diet change, and exercise) and pharmacologic interventions (e.g., hypolipidemic drugs) on lipoproteins in older people with dyslipidemia are uncertain. Furthermore, there is no prospective information about the long-term effects of such interventions with respect to overall morbidity, adverse side effects, or the mortality progression of atherosclerosis in the elderly.

The roles of hepatic and intestinal lipoprotein synthesis and secretion, tissue receptor- and nonreceptor-mediated lipoprotein metabolism, and lipoprotein lipase (LPL), hepatic lipase, and lecithin-cholesterol acyltransferase (LCAT) in the regulation of lipoprotein metabolism have not been evaluated in the elderly. LPL, the rate-limiting enzyme in the clearance of triglyceride from plasma, regulates the formation of HDL, while hepatic lipase is involved in the catabolism of the HDL_2 subspecies and chylomicron remnants. LCAT, the plasma cholesterol–esterifying enzyme, plays a central role in the regulation of cholesterol transport, lipid exchange, and the formation of HDL in humans. How each of these enzymes acts to regulate lipoprotein lipids in older individuals is not known, but studies in younger and middle-aged subjects suggest that physical conditioning improves triglyceride clearance and increases HDL formation by increasing LPL and LCAT and reducing hepatic lipase activity; conversely, obesity is associated with a reduced triglyceride clearance and HDL formation, increased endogenous triglyceride synthesis, and elevated hepatic lipase activity.[70,71]

The composition of the diet also affects lipoprotein metabolism. Whereas high-carbohydrate diets tend to lower HDL and LDL and raise triglyceride, high-fat diets increase total and LDL cholesterol, raise triglyceride, and (possibly) increase the HDL_2 subspecies. While several studies have examined the effects of diet and exercise on lipoprotein metabolism and postprandial lipoprotein lipid levels in younger healthy subjects, these relationships have not been examined in older people. If the deposition of lipoproteins in the vascular wall could be delayed or prevented in older people by physical conditioning,[59] the progression of atherosclerosis would be slowed, thus reducing the incidence of myocardial infarction and stroke and prolonging survival of older people[72] (see Chaps. 45 and 73).

AGING, PHYSICAL ACTIVITY, AND BONE MINERAL METABOLISM

There are two main types of osteoporosis in older individuals: type I, which becomes clinically significant at time of menopause in women, and type II, which occurs in individuals over 70 years of age.[6] Type I, or menopausal osteoporosis, is characterized by the excessive and disproportionate trabecular bone loss due to estrogen deficiency. It affects 5 to 10 percent of women in early menopause and increases depending on the presence of other risk factors for osteopenia. Type II osteopenia has elements of both osteoporosis and osteomalacia, hence the name *osteopenia* is probably more appropriate for this type of osteoporosis. Type II osteopenia occurs in over 50 percent of older women and about 25 percent of older men[73] and involves both trabecular and cortical bone. Fractures in type II osteopenia occur in both the hip and the vertebrae. Primary aging is considered to be a major factor in the loss of skeletal bone in type II osteopenia, but the effects of estrogen deficiency (i.e., the menopause) in women, vitamin D deficiency, physical inactivity, inadequate calcium intake, renal disease, decreased osteoblastic activity, increased parathyroid hormone, cigarette smoking, alcohol, and caffeine in the pathogenesis of osteopenia with aging are unclear.[74]

In women, vertebral bone mass begins to decline at the age of 20 and continues thereafter in a linear fashion.[73] Bone mass in the appendicular skeleton does not decrease in either men or women until age 50; in women the decline in appendicular bone mass is accelerated between ages 51 and 65 and decelerates after age 65. By age 65, one-half of women have a bone mass below the 90th percentile and are considered to have asymptomatic osteoporosis. It is estimated that bone-mineral density decreases by 40 percent in the lumbar space and by 50 percent in the femoral neck region in women between ages 60 and 80. The most common fractures within 5 or more years after the menopause are "crush type" fractures of the lumbar vertebrae and Colles' fractures of the distal radius. The decline in bone density and the development of osteopenia associated with aging, especially in women, are similar to the changes in bone seen with prolonged inactivity and restriction to bed rest, as observed in individuals with hip fractures. A number of cross-sectional studies suggest that bone loss can be attenuated by heightened physical activity,[75–79] and several prospective studies demonstrate that postmenopausal women who exercise regularly gain bone mass.[80,81]

There are no firm data to quantify the amount and duration of physical activity required to prevent or ameliorate osteopenia in normal, healthy older individuals. While osteopenia increases with aging, especially in women, it is not known whether there is a causal relationship between the age-related decline in muscle mass with the decline in bone-mineral mass with aging, independent of the degree of physical activity. If such a relationship existed, it would probably be under hormonal regulation, but there is limited information about the roles of growth hormone, somatomedin-C, sex steroids, insulin, parathyroid hormone, and calcitonin in the pathogenesis of the decline in skeletal mass, as well as muscle mass, with aging.

Physical activity that involves moderate weight bearing and isometric stress, especially walking and strength training, seem best for increasing muscle and bone mass, while flexion exercises are not recommended since they can contribute to compression of osteoporotic vertebrae.[82] Results of several studies confirm that weight-bearing activities increase bone and muscle mass more effectively than regular high-intensity aerobic physical activity. It is possible that maintenance of adequate muscle mass during aging by obligatory weight bearing, as of a large torso in the case of overweight individuals, may protect from osteoporosis; indeed, several studies suggest that muscular, strong, and often obese older individuals are less prone to osteopenia than lean subjects.[83] This indicates that gravitational stress on the skeleton may be essential for maintenance of musculoskeletal mass. In an industrialized society, motorized transport substitutes for regular walking and other types of physical activity which might improve muscle strength and bone density. A number of cross-sectional studies suggest that bone loss in both premenopausal and postmenopausal women can be attenuated by physical exercise and heightened fitness levels.[79–81] If the development of osteoporosis can be delayed until the menopause, then perhaps the institution of estrogen replacement would effectively retard the development of significant osteoporosis. A multifaceted approach in postmenopausal women consisting of estrogen therapy supplemented with simultaneous weight-bearing exercise, adequate calcium and vitamin D intake, reduction in alcohol intake, and elimination of cigarette smoking might act synergistically to prevent osteopenia and its consequences in older women.

EXERCISE IN THE PREVENTION OF CORONARY ARTERY DISEASE WITH AGING

An extensive body of epidemiologic data implicates physical inactivity as a risk factor for morbidity and mortality from coronary artery disease. A recent review of 43 studies yielded a median risk ratio of 1.9 for physical inactivity and coronary artery disease, a ratio of similar magnitude to that for either elevated systolic blood pressure, smoking, or hypercholesterolemia.[84] More disturbing is the fact that 59 percent of Americans do not perform regular exercise (defined as three or more sessions per week of longer than 20 minutes each)[84]; the percentage of physically inactive older people is undoubtedly higher.

Using leisure-time activity questionnaires in a 6- to 10-year follow-up of nearly 17,000 Harvard alumni ages 35 to 74, Paffenbarger et al.[85] noted a 64 percent reduction in nonfatal and fatal myocardial infarction in men expending 2000 kcals per week as compared to men with lower weekly energy expenditures. The magnitude of the reduction in coronary events in men 65 to 74 years old was similar to that in younger individuals. Strenuous sports, as well as walking and stair climbing, were all associated with a reduced risk for a coronary event. After 12 to 16 years of follow-up, alumni ages 60 to 84 at the highest activity level had one-half the risk of all-cause mortality of those at the lowest activity levels; in comparison, the relative risk in alumni aged 35 ot 49 was 0.79, demonstrating that the protective effect on all-cause mortality was actually greater in the elderly group than in younger groups.[86] For walking, 2000 kcals per week would require approximately 21 miles of walking, i.e., 3 miles per day, a level achievable by most older people. Other studies also suggest that even the low levels of physical exertion in activities such as gardening may reduce the incidence of coronary events.[87] Additional research is needed to better define the threshold and nature of the dose-response relationship for physical activity to reduce coronary morbidity and mortality in older people.

EXERCISE PRESCRIPTION FOR OLDER PEOPLE

Because coronary and peripheral vascular disease, as well as pulmonary, musculoskeletal, and neurologic dysfunction, are common in older people, involvement in programs of physical activity should be preceded by a thorough physical examination with special attention to the cardiovascular system, lungs, extremities, and neurologic function. Exercise capacity should be determined during a physician-administered treadmill exercise test with electrocardiographic, blood pressure, and symptom monitoring to identify patients with myocardial ischemia, exercise-induced arrhythmias, hypertensive responses, or automatic dysfunction causing vascular and central nervous system instability during exercise. The risks for adverse physiologic (cardiovascular, pulmonary, metabolic, neurologic, and musculoskeletal) responses during exercise training are best determined during this test. Individuals with abnormal exercise tests should be referred for further evaluation to a medical specialist in the area of dysfunction.

The exercise prescription should be based on the older individual's functional capacity, as determined by physical examination, medical history, and the results of the exercise test. If oxygen consumption can be measured during the stress test, functional capacity can be expressed in ml oxygen consumed/kg · min and related to heart rate. The low and high points of optimal range of exercise intensity can be defined by the heart rates at 50 percent and 85 percent of the functional capacity, respectively. The energy expenditure for most physical activities is calculated in METs (1 MET = resting oxygen consumption = 3.5 ml/kg · min or 1 kcal/kg · h) and can be extrapolated to a safe range of exercise intensity, usually 4 to 7 METs, for most older individuals who display no cardiovascular limitations during maximal exercise testing.

The relative levels of effort can be easily related to heart rate; the target heart rate during exercise is calculated as the training intensity or percentage of functional capacity times the heart rate reserve plus the resting heart rate. The target heart rate is usually monitored during exercise sessions as an index of training intensity. It is also worthwhile to monitor the subjective perceived exertion in older individuals during exercise testing and training, using a visual analog scale in which a rating of 6 is the least and 20 the most intense effort.[88] In people over 65 years of age, the exercise test should be reviewed by a cardiologist, and advice should be sought from an exercise physiologist in designing the prescription for physical exercise training.

Initial physical activity should be supervised and progression undertaken in a slow, sequential manner to ensure that the individual's exercise capacity is not exceeded, injury is prevented, and cardiovascular responses (heart rate and blood pressure) are appropriate. Aerobic activities involving large muscle groups (walking, swimming, stationary bicycling, and jogging) are the preferred types of exercise because their energy costs (METs) are usually well-defined, and these activities enhance cardiopulmonary capacity and metabolic function to the greatest extent. The progression of exercise training intensity and duration should be slow, with frequent monitoring and reassessment of exercise capacity on the treadmill with electrocardiographic monitoring if hemodynamic instability develops. Training sessions should be held at least 3 days per week. Each session should include a 5- to 10-minute warm-up and stretching period, approximately 30 minutes of aerobic exercise, and 5 to 10 minutes of cool-down time.

A program of isometric exercises using low resistance weights at relatively high repetitions can complement an aerobic exercise program by increasing strength and muscle tone and perhaps attenuating the age-associated decline in muscle mass. Such an isometric regimen may be performed in conjunction with the aerobic exercise sessions or performed on separate days. Activities associated with straining and breath-holding, such as low-repetition, strenuous isometric exercises, whether performed with free weights or a weight machine, are undesirable because they may raise blood pressure excessively and increase risk of retinal detachment, vitreous hemorrhage, stroke, and myocardial ischemia.

Compliance and avoidance of injury are the major problems in maintaining an exercise program at any age.

Older people fear injury during exercise, and caution is recommended to avoid this complication by prescribing a slow progression of exercise intensity, frequency, and duration. Rarely does an older person return to a program following an injury precipitated during exercise. Attention to adequate warm-up, choice of an orthopedically suitable form of exercise, and proper footwear will minimize the risk of injury. The use of behavior modification techniques in conjunction with the exercise program may improve the outcome, but prolonged adherence varies directly with the intensity of the follow-up program. Peer interaction, a socially desirable environment, frequent telephone contact by the therapist, and regular health maintenance meetings seem to produce the greatest success.

CONCLUDING REMARKS

Although a large body of knowledge has accumulated over the last decade on the systemic effects and therapeutic benefits of exercise training, the vast majority of the data have been derived from younger and middle-aged individuals. Recent studies suggest, however, that many of the declines in cardiovascular and metabolic function seen with advancing age may be mediated to a large degree by age-associated decreases in physical activity and accompanying changes in body composition, rather than by aging per se. There is also growing evidence that these age-associated declines in aerobic capacity, lipid and glucose metabolism, and bone density are related to the higher prevalence of coronary artery and generalized vascular disease, diabetes, and fractures among older people. Several recent studies, albeit mostly of a cross-sectional nature, have demonstrated the possibility that some older people may be able to derive major physiologic benefits from regular physical exercise, including an augmented maximal oxygen capacity, greater strength, lower plasma LDL cholesterol and triglyceride levels, higher plasma HDL cholesterol, better glucose tolerance, and denser bones. These benefits, if substantiated by large-scale longitudinal investigation in heterogeneous elderly populations, could have major public health implications for older Americans.

REFERENCES

1. Heath et al: A physiological comparison of young and older endurance athletes. *J Appl Physiol* 51:634, 1981.
2. Astrand I: Aerobic work capacity in men and women with special reference to age. *Acta Physiol Scand* 169:1, 1960.
3. Dehn MM, Bruce RA: Longitudinal variation in maximal oxygen intake with age and activity. *J Appl Physiol* 33:805, 1972.

4. Fleg JL, Lakatta EG: Role of muscle loss in the age-associated decline of maximal aerobic capacity. *J Appl Physiol* 65:1147, 1988.

5. Tzankoff SP, Norris HA: Effect of muscle mass decrease on age-related BMR changes. *J Appl Physiol* 43:1001, 1977.

6. Riggs BL, Melton LJ: Involutional osteoporosis. *N Engl J Med* 314:1676, 1986.

7. Rowe JW et al: Characterization of the insulin resistance of aging. *J Clin Invest* 71:1581, 1983.

8. Chen M et al: Pathogenesis of age-related glucose intolerance in man: Insulin resistance and decreased B-cell function. *J Clin Endocrinol Metab* 60:13, 1985.

9. Convertino VA et al: Bedrest-induced peak VO₂ reduction associated with age, gender and aerobic capacity. *Aviat Space Environ Med* 57:17, 1986.

10. Saltin B et al: Response to exercise after bedrest and after training. *Circulation* 37(suppl VII)1, 1968.

11. Coyle EF et al: Time course of loss of adaptations after stopping prolonged intense endurance training. *J Appl Physiol* 57:1857, 1984.

12. Donaldson CL et al: Effect of prolonged bedrest on bone mineral. *Metabolism* 19:1071, 1970.

13. Chobanian AV et al: The metabolic and hemodynamic effects of prolonged bedrest in normal subjects. *Circulation* 49:551, 1974.

14. Dolkas CB, Greenleaf JE: Insulin and glucose responses during bedrest with isotonic and isometric exercise. *J Appl Physiol* 43:1033, 1977.

15. Wood PD, Haskell WL: The effect of exercise on plasma high density lipoproteins. *Lipids* 14:417, 1979.

16. King DS et al: Effects of exercise and lack of exercise on insulin sensitivity and responsiveness. *J Appl Physiol* 64:1942, 1980.

17. McGandy et al: Nutrient intakes and energy expenditures in men of different ages. *J Gerontol* 21:581, 1966.

18. Rowell LB: Human cardiovascular adjustments to exercise and thermal stress. *Physiol Rev* 54:75, 1974.

19. Strandell T: Circulatory studies on healthy old men. With special reference to the limitation of the maximal physical working capacity. *Acta Med Scand* 175(suppl 414):2, 1964.

20. Julius S et al: Influence of age on the hemodynamic response to exercise. *Circulation* 36:222, 1967.

21. Rodeheffer RJ et al: Exercise cardiac output is maintained with advancing age in healthy human subjects: Cardiac dilation in increased stroke volume compensate for a diminished heart rate. *Circulation* 69:203, 1984.

22. Fleg JL et al: Central versus peripheral adaptations in highly trained seniors. *Physiologist* 32:A518. 1988.

23. Seals DR et al: Endurance training in older men and women. I. Cardiovascular response to exercise. *J Appl Physiol* 57:1024, 1984.

24. Buskirk ER, Hodgson JL: Age and aerobic power: The rate of change in men and women. *Fed Proc* 46:1824, 1987.

25. Kasch FW et al: A longitudinal study of cardiovascular stability in active men aged 45 to 65 years. *Physician Sports Med* 16:117, 1988.

26. Pollock ML et al: Effect of age and training on aerobic capacity and body composition of master athletes. *J Appl Physiol* 62:725, 1987.

27. DeVries HA: Physiological effects of an exercise training regimen upon men aged 52–88. *J Gerontol* 25:325, 1970.

28. Thomas SG et al: Determinants of the training response in elderly men. *Med Sci Sports Exerc* 17:667, 1985.

29. Tzankoff SP et al: Physiological adjustments to work in older men as affected by physical training. *J Appl Physiol* 33:346, 1972.

30. Buccola VA, Stone WL: Effects of jogging and cycling programs on physiological and personality variables in aged men. *Res Q* 46:134, 1975.

31. Suominen H et al: Effects of eight weeks physical training on muscle and connective tissue of the m. vastus lateralis in 69-year-old men and women. *J Gerontol* 32:33, 1977.

32. Sidney KH, Shephard RJ: Frequency and intensity of exercise training for elderly subjects. *Med Sci Sports Exerc* 10:125, 1978.

33. Badenhop DT et al: Physiological adjustments to higher- or lower-intensity exercise in elders. *Med Sci Sports Exerc* 15:496, 1983.

34. Yerg JE et al: The effect of endurance exercise training on ventilatory function in older individuals. *J Appl Physiol* 58:791, 1985.

35. Seals DR et al: Effects of endurance exercise training on glucose tolerance and plasma lipid levels in older men and women. *JAMA* 252:645, 1984.

36. Asmussen E, Heebill-Nielsen K: Isometric muscle strength of adult men and women. *Comm Danish Natl Assoc Infant Paralysis* 11, 1961.

37. Asmussen E: Aging and exercise, in Horvath SM, Yousef MK (eds): *Environmental Physiology: Aging, Heat and Altitude*. North Holland, Elsevier, 1980, p 419.

38. Lexell J et al: Distribution of different fibre types in human skeletal muscles. 2. A study of cross-sections of whole m. vastus laterales. *Acta Phys Scand* 117:115, 1982.

39. Grimby G, Saltin B: The aging muscle. *Clin Physiol* 3:209, 1983.

40. Campbell MJ et al: Physiological changes in aging muscles. *J Neurol Neurosurg Psychiatry* 36:174, 1973.

41. Brown WF: A method for estimating the number of motor units in thenar muscles and the changes in motor unit count with aging. *J Neurol Neurosurg Psychiatry* 35:845, 1972.

42. Aniansson A, Gustafsson E: Physical training in elderly man with special reference to quadriceps muscle strength and morphology. *Clin Physiol* 1:87, 1981.

43. Frontera WR et al: Strength conditioning in older men: Skeletal muscle hypertrophy and improved function. *J Appl Physiol* 64:1038, 1988.

44. Kino M et al: Effect of age on responses to isometric exercise. *Am Heart J* 90:575, 1975.

45. Petrofsky JS et al: Comparison of physiological responses of women and men to isometric exercise. *J Appl Physiol* 38:863, 1975.

46. TNE Greville: US decennial life tables for 1961–71. National Center for Health Statistics, USPHS. "US Life Tables by Cause of Death: 1969–1971," 1:5, 1976.

47. Owen RA et al: The national cost of acute care of hip fractures associated with osteoporosis. *Clin Orthop* 150:172, 1980.

48. Andres R: Aging and diabetes. *Med Clin North Am* 55:835, 1971.

49. Davidson MB: The effect of aging on carbohydrate metabolism: A comprehensive review and practical approach to the problem, in Korenman SG (ed): *Endocrinology Aspects of Aging.* New York, Elsevier, 1982, p 231.

50. Fink RI et al: Mechanisms of insulin resistance with aging. *J Clin Invest* 71:1523, 1983.

51. Fink RI et al: The effect of aging on glucose mediated glucose disposal and glucose transport. *J Clin Invest* 77:2034, 1986.

52. Fink RI et al: The role of the glucose transport system in the postreceptor defect in insulin action associated with human aging. *J Clin Endocrinol Metab* 58:721, 1984.

53. Chen M et al: The role of the dietary carbohydrate in the decreased glucose tolerance of the elderly. *J Am Geriatr Soc* 35:417, 1987.

54. Seals DR et al: Glucose tolerance in young and older athletes and sedentary men. *J Appl Physiol* 56:1521, 1984.

55. Pacini G et al: Insulin sensitivity and beta cell responsivity are not decreased in elderly subjects with normal OGTT. *J Am Geriatr Soc* 36:317, 1988.

56. Coon PJ et al: Effects of body composition and exercise capacity on glucose tolerance, insulin and lipoprotein lipids in older men: A cross-sectional and longitudinal intervention study. *Metabolism,* 1989, in press.

57. Rowe J, Troen BR: Sympathetic nervous system and aging in man. *Endocr Rev* 1:167, 1980.

58. Chen M et al: Pathogenesis of age-related glucose intolerance in man: Insulin resistance and decreased β-cell function. *J Clin Endocrinol Metab* 60:13, 1985.

59. Goldberg AP: Health promotion and aging: Physical exercise, in Abdellah FG, Moor, SR (eds): *Surgeon Generals Workshop.* DHHS/PHS, 1987, p C-1.

60. Schneider SH et al: Atherosclerosis and physical activity. *Diabetes Metab Rev* 1:513, 1986.

61. Koivisto VA et al: Physical training and insulin sensitivity. *Diabetes Metab Rev* 1:445, 1986.

62. Rogers MA et al: Improvement in glucose tolerance after 1 wk of exercise in patients with NIDDM. *Diabetes Care* 11:613, 1988.

63. Wood et al: Increased exercise level and plasma lipoprotein concentrations: A one-year, randomized controlled study in sedentary middle-aged men. *Metabolism* 32:31, 1983.

64. Wood PD et al: Changes in plasma lipids and lipoproteins in overweight men during weight loss through dieting as compared to exercise. *N Engl J Med* 319:1173, 1988.

65. Goldberg AP, Coon PJ: Non-insulin dependent diabetes mellitus in the elderly. *Endocrinol Metab Clin North Am* 16:843, 1987.

66. Holloszy JO et al: Effects of exercise on glucose tolerance and insulin resistance. *Acta Med Scand [Suppl]* 711:55, 1986.

67. Seals DR et al: Elevated high density lipoprotein cholesterol levels in older endurance athletes. *Am J Cardiol* 54:390, 1984.

68. Schneider SH et al: Studies of the mechanisms of improved glucose control during regular exercise in type II (non-insulin dependent diabetes. *Diabetologia* 26:355, 1984.

69. Bogardus L et al: Effects of physical training and diet therapy on carbohydrate metabolism in patients with glucose intolerance and non-insulin-dependent diabetes mellitus. *Diabetes* 33:311, 1984.

70. Brunzell JD: Pathophysiologic approach to hyperlipidemia, in Schwartz, TB, Ryan WG (eds): *Yearbook of Endocrinology.* Chicago, Yearbook Medical Publishers, 1984, p 11.

71. Patsch JR: Metabolic aspects of subfractions of serum lipoproteins, in Carlson LA, Pernow B (eds): *Metabolic Risk Factors in Ischemic Cardiovascular Disease.* New York, Raven Press, 1982, p 123.

72. Rowe, JW, Kahn RL: Human aging: Usual and successful. *Science* 237:143, 1987.

73. Gallagher JC et al: Epidemiology of fractures of the proximal femur in Rochester, Minnesota. *Clin Orthop* 150:163, 1980.

74. Williams AR et al: Effect of weight, smoking and estrogen use on the risk of hip and forearm fractures in postmenopausal women. *Obstet Gynecol* 60:695, 1982.

75. Riggs BL et al: Differential changes in bone mineral density of the appendicular and axial skeleton with aging: Relationship to spinal osteoporosis. *J Clin Invest* 67:328, 1981.

76. Aloia JF et al: Skeletal mass and body composition in marathon runners. *Metabolism* 27:1793, 1978.

77. Brewer V et al: Role of exercise in the prevention of involutional bone loss. *Med Sci Sports Exerc* 15:545, 1983.

78. Pocock NA et al: Physical fitness is a major determinant of femoral neck and lumbar spine bone density. *J Clin Invest* 78:618, 1986.

79. Aloia JF: Premenopausal bone mass is related to physical activity. *Arch Intern Med* 148:121, 1988.

80. Krolner B et al: Physical exercise as a prophylaxis against involutional vertebral bone loss, a controlled trial. *Clin Sci* 64:541, 1983.

81. Smith EL et al: Physical activity and calcium: Modalities for bone mineral increase in aged women. *Med Sci Sports Exerc* 13:60, 1981.

82. Osteoporosis: Consensus Conference. *JAMA* 252:799, 1984.

83. Sinaki M: Relationship between bone mineral density of spine and strength of back extensors in healthy postmenopausal women. *Mayo Clin Proc* 61:116, 1986.

84. Behavior Epidemiology and Evaluation Branch, CDC: Protective effect of physical activity on coronary heart disease. *Morbidity and Mortality World Report* 36:426, 1987.

85. Paffenbarger RS et al: Physical activity as an index of heart attack risk in college alumni. *Am J Epidemiol* 108:161, 1978.

86. Paffenbarger RS et al: Physical activity, all-cause mortality and longevity of college alumni. *N Engl J Med* 314:605, 1986.

87. Sallis JF et al: Moderate intensity physical activity and cardiovascular risk factors: The Stanford five-city project. *Prev Med* 15:561, 1986.

88. Borg GAV: Psychophysical basis of perceived exertion. *Med Sci Sports Exerc* 14:377, 1982.

Chapter 9

PERSONALITY AND AGING

Paul T. Costa, Jr., and Robert R. McCrae

Aging is devalued in our society, and physicians are not immune to the negative stereotypes. It is widely believed that older individuals are hypochondriacs, prone to depression, and unable to adapt to change,[1] and some of these generalizations appear to be confirmed by clinical experience. When, however, standardized measures of personality are used in unselected samples, the influence of age on personality is seen to be very slight. A more objective view of personality in aging men and women can provide a more informed basis for dealing with older patients. This chapter provides an overview of recent research on age and personality and discusses some of the implications most relevant to geriatric medicine.

A DEFINITION OF PERSONALITY

Psychiatry is the medical specialty most directly concerned with personality, and psychiatric approaches to personality have traditionally been dominated by psychoanalytic concepts like id, ego, and superego. Both psychopathology and normal personality were discussed in terms of instinctual impulses and unconscious defensive processes. Because the major determinants of personality were thought to be unconscious, the individual's own conception of himself or herself could not be trusted as a source of data: A skilled clinician, perhaps using inkblots or other projective tests, was seen as the only legitimate judge of personality.

In the past few decades the psychoanalytic position has fallen out of favor with most personality psychologists, and psychiatrists have also begun to adopt alternative views.[2] Self-report instruments have shown their utility in thousands of applications, and a recent review[3] comparing self-reports with expert ratings found that the former were equal or superior to the latter in predicting a variety of important criteria. Psychometric sophistica-

tion has also increased over the years, and self-report measures of anxiety,[4] depression,[5] and symptoms of personality disorders[6] are now widely used as part of the comprehensive psychiatric evaluation of individuals. Personality ratings, whether from experts or from acquaintances or family members, remain an important adjunct to self-reports.

When questionnaire data collected from large samples of subjects become the focus of psychological study, the definition of personality changes. Instead of evidence of internal conflict, symbolic distortion, and neurotic defense, researchers look for consistent patterns of response that distinguish one individual from another. Personality *traits*—characteristic emotional, interpersonal, experiential, and motivational styles—emerge as the basic elements of personality.[7,8]

In their extreme form, personality traits are readily recognizable on even casual observation. In clinical practice, some individuals are silent and reserved; they take the medical interview with great seriousness. Others are talkative, informal, and light-hearted. Again, some patients chronically minimize their medical problems, while others complain long and loud about relatively minor symptoms. Inferences about personality are almost inevitable in these cases. It is, however, essential to note that behavior in the special situation of a visit to a physician or hospital may not be characteristic of the individual. Standard psychological tests, perhaps taken at home, would provide a much better guide to the individual and could set in context the particular reactions seen by the physician during an examination.

THE FIVE-FACTOR MODEL

The English language contains thousands of words to describe individuals, and psychologists have created hundreds of scales to measure theoretically important traits. The clinician or researcher is faced with the problem of selecting the most appropriate of these, and until recently there was little basis for the selection. Several independent lines of research[9-12] have now begun to converge on the five-factor model of personality, according to which most traits can be seen as aspects of Neuroticism, Extraversion, Openness, Agreeableness, or Conscientiousness. Table 9-1 gives examples of some of the adjectives that characterize these five broad domains of personality. The same dimensions have been found in analyses of questionnaire scale and adjective checklists,[12] in self-reports and observer ratings,[13] in men and women, and in English and other languages.[14] These five factors appear to be fundamental to the description of normal personality and form a comprehensive basis for systematic research and assessment.

PERSONALITY AND AGING: STABILITY OR CHANGE?

Throughout most of history, adulthood has been considered a kind of plateau between the growth of childhood and the decline of old age. Erikson's work on psychosocial development[15] signaled a new approach, in which theorists began to look for ways in which individuals continued to develop across the life span. A wide range of theories were proposed: Age might bring increased introversion and inferiority,[16] growth and maturity,[17] or a reversal of sex-role-linked characteristics.[18] Elaborate theories of stages of adult development have been advanced,[19] and the view that individuals undergo a period of tumultuous personal reassessment around age 40—the so-called "midlife crisis"—has become the conventional wisdom. These theories often conflict with one another, but all concur in suggesting that the period of adulthood is not a plateau, but a period of dynamic growth and change in personality.

MEAN-LEVEL DIFFERENCES IN PERSONALITY TRAITS

When put to empirical test, however, a very different picture emerges. The theories described would suggest that, on the average, predictable changes in personality traits should occur with age and that, other things being equal, these changes should appear as mean-level differences in cross-sectional studies. Early cross-sectional studies on small samples yielded a variety of small and inconsistent results.[20] However, when short scales measuring the three dimensions of Neuroticism, Extraversion, and Openness to Experience were examined in a national sample with more than 10,000 respondents, the results were clear.[21] As Fig. 9-1 shows, there is very little difference in these three aspects of personality for adults between the ages of 25 and 75. There are statistically significant declines in all three traits, but they are quite small in magnitude. Further, there is no evidence that personality scores are different for individuals around the time of the hypothesized "midlife crisis," or around the age of retirement, as might be suggested by some role-based theories of personality.

Regardless of the sample, all cross-sectional studies are limited by the confounding of generational differences with age differences. The small age differences seen in Fig. 9-1, for example, might be due to changes in patterns of child rearing over the past century. For that reason, the results of longitudinal studies in which the same individuals are retested at different ages are particularly important. A number of longitudinal studies have reported analyses of longitudinal changes using a variety of standard personality instruments.[22-25] Although changes between adolescence and adulthood are often

TABLE 9-1
Examples of Traits from the Five Personality Factors

Factor	Characteristic	
	Low Scorer	High Scorer
Neuroticism	Calm	Worrying
	Even-tempered	Temperamental
	Self-satisfied	Self-pitying
	Comfortable	Self-conscious
	Unemotional	Emotional
	Hardy	Vulnerable
Extraversion	Reserved	Affectionate
	Loner	Joiner
	Quiet	Talkative
	Passive	Active
	Sober	Fun-loving
	Unfeeling	Passionate
Openness	Down-to-earth	Imaginative
	Uncreative	Creative
	Conventional	Original
	Prefers routine	Prefers variety
	Uncurious	Curious
	Conservative	Liberal
Agreeableness	Ruthless	Soft-hearted
	Suspicious	Trusting
	Stingy	Generous
	Antagonistic	Acquiescent
	Critical	Lenient
	Irritable	Good-natured
Conscientiousness	Negligent	Conscientious
	Lazy	Hard-working
	Disorganized	Well-organized
	Late	Punctual
	Aimless	Ambitious
	Quitting	Persevering

SOURCE: From Costa PT Jr, McCrae RR: Personality stability and its implications for clinical psychology. *Clin Psychol Rev* 6:407, 1986.

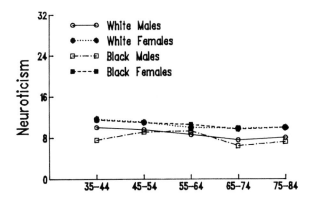

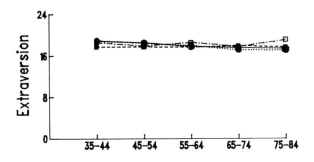

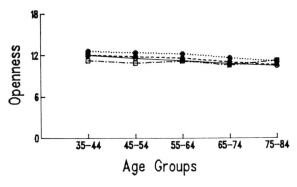

FIGURE 9-1
Mean levels of neuroticism, extraversion, and openness to experience for 10-year age groups of white men, black men, white women, and black women, aged from 35 to 84 years. *(From Costa et al., 1986.[21])*

seen,[23] and occasional age changes are reported for older adults—e.g., a small decline in activity level[22]—the great majority of studies report little or no change in the average level of personality traits after about age 30. Some of the studies include individuals tested up to age 90; again, there is no consistent evidence of change in the average level of most personality traits even in advanced age.

STABILITY OF INDIVIDUAL DIFFERENCES

The fact that average levels of a variable do not change over time does not necessarily mean that the variable is constant within the individual: For some people the variable may have increased, while for others, it declined. Indeed, one of the oldest theories of personality development[26] held that such complementary changes should be seen, as each individual developed in late life the aspects of personality that had been dormant in early life. Cross-sectional studies cannot speak to these issues, but longitudinal research can. The degree to which individuals maintain the same relative order is assessed by the correlation coefficient; positive correlations imply stability of individual differences, whereas low or negative correlations suggest that there have been substantial changes in the individual over the retest interval.

A recent study[25] addressed this question using the NEO Personality Inventory,[27] a questionnaire measure of the five-factor model. Self-report data from a 6-year retest were available for 398 men and women, initially aged 25 to 84, on the Neuroticism, Extraversion, and Openness scales; 3-year retest data were available for 360 men and women on the Agreeableness and Conscientiousness scales. Retest correlations ranged from .63 to .83, and equally high correlations were found for younger and older subjects, and for men and women. These correlations are almost as high as the short-term retest reliability of the scales and strongly suggest that all five of the major dimensions of personality are highly stable in adulthood.

It has sometimes been argued that such high stability might be due to a crystallized self-concept[28]; that is, individuals may develop a picture of themselves early in life and retain this image despite actual changes in personality. One way to test this hypothesis is by examining stability or change in descriptions made by external observers. Spouse ratings of Neuroticism, Extraversion, and Openness were available for 89 men and 79 women. The 6-year stability coefficients ranged from .68 to .83, again supporting the view that individual differences in personality are highly stable.

These findings are consistent with a large body of longitudinal results, using a variety of personality tests in diverse samples and over intervals of up to 30 years.[29–32] Studies of adolescents traced into adulthood show somewhat lower levels of stability,[23,33] but there is clear evidence of at least some continuity in personality from childhood on. Combined with the evidence of little or no change in mean levels, these studies suggest that by about age 30, men and women have attained their adult personality, and—barring therapeutic interventions or catastrophic events or illnesses—they maintain these characteristics for the rest of their lives.

These findings make it necessary to reexamine many of the popular theories of aging. Some people are prone to experience periods of personal crisis, and when they are at midlife, the crisis is likely to take the form of concerns over career choice, impending physical declines, and discontent with marriage. A period of personal problems during these years may resemble the legendary midlife crisis, but only a small portion of the population is likely to experience such a crisis.[34] Higher levels of neuroticism predispose individuals to have crises at all ages.[35] Again, Erikson's famous stages of adult life may represent meaningful changes in social roles and expectations, but they do not imply changes in the underlying personality of the individuals.

SOME IMPLICATIONS OF PERSONALITY STABILITY

Gerontologists sometimes assume that gerontology is the study of what changes with age; if personality does not change, why study personality and aging? This is surely a narrow view of the field. The question the gerontologist really asks is "What happens to a variable as individuals age?" And if the answer is "It remains constant," that is a potentially important finding in itself. When age changes are found, the next questions are "What mechanisms are responsible for the change" and "How might interventions affect the rate of change?" The stability of personality suggests different but equally basic questions: How does personality remain stable despite changes in social roles, cognitive and physical declines, and the accumulation of a lifetime of experience? What kind of interventions would be needed to alter undesirable aspects of personality?

In a broader context, the stability of personality is important to gerontology and geriatrics because personality itself is important in many areas of life. Personality profoundly affects psychological well-being and morale,[36] vocational choices,[37] methods of coping,[38] interpersonal relations,[39] and health perceptions and health behaviors.[40,41] Knowing that these effects are likely to persist throughout adulthood provides a deeper perspective on all these areas.

IMPLICATIONS FOR THE INDIVIDUAL

The finding that personality is generally stable in adulthood is often viewed with dismay by humanistic psychologists and others who would prefer to imagine limitless possibilities for human growth. Conversely, it is welcomed by those who fear that age must bring depression, isolation, and rigidity. Clearly, how one evaluates the fact depends on one's expectations; it also depends on how satisfied one is with one's current personality. Individuals who are well-adjusted and happy should be pleased to learn that they are likely to remain so. Those who are less happy with themselves should learn to accept the fact that they are likely to remain unhappy unless they take concrete steps, including perhaps professional counseling, to change themselves. The mere passage of time is unlikely to improve their condition.

The stability of personality traits, styles, and motives contributes to the individual's sense of identity and gives continuity and coherence to the course of adult life. Stable individual differences provide a basis for realistic long-term planning. Students would not go through the rigors of medical school unless they believed that their interest in medicine would persist. People would not marry without some faith that the spouse would retain the characteristics that are now found to be so lovable. How could people meaningfully plan for a peaceful or an exciting or a productive retirement if they were unsure whether they would continue to prefer tranquility or adventure or achievement? Age stereotypes provide a poor basis for future planning. At all ages, the range of individual differences is large, and men and women preserve their individuality throughout old age.

IMPLICATIONS FOR PSYCHIATRY

Other chapters in this volume are devoted to a discussion of psychiatric conditions and their diagnosis and treatment in the elderly. It should be pointed out, however, that the distinction between normal personality traits and psychiatric conditions is often one of degree.[2] Personality disorders, in particular, can be viewed as maladaptive forms of familiar traits, and one focus of contemporary research is on linking DSM-III Axis II disorders with the five-factor model of normal personality.[42] Anxiety and depression are also clinical conditions that may reflect lifelong predispositions to experience these affects.

Findings on the stability of personality are therefore relevant to the diagnosis of psychiatric conditions in the elderly. Psychiatric problems may be reactions to recent stressors like bereavement, reflections of organic pathology, or continuations of lifelong patterns of maladjustment, but they are not likely to be attributable to aging itself. Depression, in particular, is not an inevitable or even common[43] feature of normal aging and should be regarded as a mental health problem in individuals of any age.

Against the background of normative constancy, marked changes in personality may be indicative of pathology. For example, uncharacteristic behavior may be the first sign of senile dementia noticed by family members.[44] Apparent changes in personality might also be due to sensory problems or to reactions to medication; any marked change should alert the physician to the need for a careful evaluation.

A word on prognosis is also appropriate. Historically, psychiatrists were reluctant to undertake therapy with the elderly both because the shortness of remaining life did not seem to justify it and because the elderly were believed to be unable to benefit. An increasing number of geropsychiatrists[45] and psychotherapists[46] dispute both these claims, and research suggests that older individuals are able to adapt even to the most stressful events. Although death of a spouse is associated with a slightly higher risk of mortality in the year following bereavement,[47] the great majority of widows and widowers continue their lives and, in the long run, show little or no evidence of psychological impairment.[48] Older men and women show a remarkable degree of psychological resilience.

IMPLICATIONS FOR MEDICAL EVALUATION AND TREATMENT

For many years, the chief relevance of personality to physicians was believed to be its etiological significance in certain diseases. Specific intrapsychic conflicts[49] were thought to give rise to particular forms of pathology, but these views have found little empirical support.[50] The Type A behavior pattern, which was officially recognized by the National Heart Lung and Blood Institute as a risk factor for coronary heart disease (CHD) a few years ago,[51] has in subsequent studies failed to predict CHD morbidity or mortality.[52] However, there is some evidence that one aspect of the Type A pattern, antagonistic hostility,[53] is a predictor of CHD, and this may explain why early studies using global measures of Type A found significant associations. Although it is widely believed that anger, anxiety, and depression are etiological factors in the development of coronary artery disease, cancer, and a variety of other illnesses,[54] the evidence at present is very mixed, and critical interpretations cast doubt on the link between these aspects of personality and objective indicators of disease.[41] Psychosomatic medicine continues to be an important, if controversial, topic for research, and one which presupposes the stability of personality: If traits were not chronic conditions, they would be unlikely to exert much long-term effect on physical health. Finally, it should be pointed out that the five-factor model of personality offers a comprehensive framework in which links between personality and disease can be systematically assessed.[55]

Whatever the role of personality in objective medical conditions, there is little doubt that the dimension of Neuroticism plays a prominent role in subjective health status. Individuals high in Neuroticism—that is, people who are characteristically anxious, frustrated, depressed, and unable to cope with stress—consistently report more medical complaints and make a disproportionate number of visits to physicians and medical clinics.[40] In the extreme, these individuals are considered hypochondriacs, but the same phenomenon—the magnification of minor pains or other physical sensations as signs of disease—can be seen in psychiatrically normal individuals high in Neuroticism.[40]

The association of medical complaints with Neuroticism and the stability of Neuroticism across the adult life span together suggest that styles of reporting symptoms should themselves be stable, and longitudinal studies generally confirm this hypothesis. Total physical complaints on the Cornell Medical Index showed a 6-year stability coefficient of .74 in a sample of 386 men in the Baltimore Longitudinal Study of Aging,[40] and analyses of mean-level changes showed predictable increases in cardiovascular, genitourinary, and sensory systems, but no consistent changes in other systems. Subjects higher in Neuroticism showed higher scores on all physical and psychiatric sections, regardless of age.

There are two conclusions to be drawn from these findings. First, the widespread belief that individuals become hypochondriacs as they age is not supported. The increased use of medical treatment by older men and women is a rational response to their greater objective health problems, and somatic complaints should never be discounted simply because the patient is old.

Second, physicians should be aware that there are enduring individual differences in styles of perceiving, recalling, and reporting medical symptoms. Knowing the individual's personality traits and history of reporting symptoms can give insight into current complaints. Individuals high in Neuroticism may exaggerate reports of pain, leading to inappropriate diagnoses[41]; in these cases, more extensive objective testing may be indicated. Individuals particularly low in Neuroticism also require special attention, because they may be inclined to minimize problems, and they may not encounter the routine screenings that frequent clinic visitors experience.[56] In this way, the early signs of disease may be missed.

Although there has been less research on the relevance of the other four dimensions of personality to health behavior, there is reason to suspect that they, too, will be important. Patients high in Openness to Experience may be more inquisitive and more willing to try novel approaches to therapy; however, they may also be less deferential to medical authority and more likely to seek a second opinion. The dimension of Conscientiousness is of particular interest in regard to health practices. Conscientious patients should be better able to maintain diet and exercise regimens and more scrupulous about taking medications as prescribed. Patients who are very low in Conscientiousness may need extra motivation and monitoring on the part of the physician.

SUMMARY

Personality can be defined in terms of enduring individual differences in emotional, interpersonal, experiential, attitudinal, and motivational styles. Five major domains of personality have been identified: Neuroticism, Extraversion, Openness, Agreeableness, and Conscientiousness. Despite the popularity of theories of adult development, both large-scale cross-sectional studies and longitudinal research demonstrate that personality traits in all five domains are highly stable after about age 30. Enduring dispositions give a sense of identity to the individual and provide a basis for future planning. The stability of normal personality traits provides a context for the evaluation of psychiatric disorders, which may reflect recent stressors or organic pathology, or may instead be continuations of lifelong patterns of maladjustment. The five-factor model provides a basis for systematic research in psychosomatic medicine, and knowledge of personality traits can assist the physician in the interpretation of somatic complaints at all ages.

REFERENCES

1. Friedman SA et al: *The Doctors' Guide to Growing Older.* New York, New American Library, 1980.
2. McHugh PR, Slavney PR: *The Perspectives of Psychiatry.* Baltimore, Johns Hopkins University Press, 1983.
3. Shrauger JS, Osberg TM: The relative accuracy of self-predictions and judgments by others in psychological assessment. *Psychol Bull* 90:322, 1981.
4. Spielberger CD et al: *Manual for the State-Trait Anxiety Inventory.* Palo Alto, CA: Consulting Psychologists Press, 1983.
5. Zung WW: A self-report depression scale. *Arch Gen Psychiatry* 12:63, 1965.
6. Millon T: *Millon Clinical Multiaxial Inventory Manual,* 3d ed. Minneapolis, Interpretive Scoring Systems, 1983.
7. McCrae RR, Costa PT Jr: *Emerging Lives, Enduring Dispositions: Personality in Adulthood.* Boston, Little, Brown, 1984.
8. Hogan R et al: Traits, tests, and personality research. *Am Psychol* 32:255, 1977.
9. Digman JM, Inouye J: Further specification of the five robust factors of personality. *J Pers Soc Psychol* 50:116, 1986.
10. Goldberg LR: Language and individual differences: The search for universals in personality lexicons, in Wheeler L (ed): *Review of Personality and Social Psychology.* Hillsdale, NJ, Lawrence Erlbaum Associates, 1981, vol 2, p 141.
11. Hogan RT: "Socioanalytic Theory of Personality," in Page MM (ed): *1982 Nebraska Symposium on Motivation: Personality—Current Theory and Research.* Lincoln, NE: University of Nebraska Press, 1983, p 55.
12. McCrae RR, Costa PT Jr: Updating Norman's "adequate taxonomy": Intelligence and personality dimensions in natural language and in questionnaires. *J Pers Soc Psychol* 49:710, 1985.
13. McCrae RR, Costa PT Jr: Validation of the five-factor model across instruments and observers. *J Pers Soc Psychol* 52:81, 1987.
14. John OP et al: Better than the alphabet: Taxonomies of personality-descriptive terms in English, Dutch, and German, in Bonarius HJC et al (eds): *Personality Psychology in Europe: Theoretical and Empirical Developments.* Lisse, Switzerland, Swets & Zeitlinger, 1984, p 83.
15. Erikson EH: *Childhood and Society.* New York, Norton, 1950.
16. Neugarten BL: *Personality in Middle and Later Life.* New York, Atherton, 1964.
17. Vaillant GE: *Adaptation to Life.* Boston, Little, Brown, 1977.
18. Gutmann DL: An exploration of ego configurations in middle and later life, in Neugarten BL (ed): *Personality in Middle and Later Life.* New York, Atherton, 1964, p. 114.
19. Levinson DJ et al: *The Seasons of a Man's Life.* New York, Knopf, 1978.
20. Neugarten BL: Personality and aging, in Birren JE, Schaie KW (eds): *Handbook of the Psychology of Aging,* 1st ed. New York, Van Nostrand Reinhold, 1977, p 626.
21. Costa PT Jr et al: Cross-sectional studies of personality in a national sample: 2. Stability in neuroticism, extraversion, and openness. *Psychol Aging* 1:144, 1986.
22. Douglas K, Arenberg D: Age changes, cohort differences, and cultural change on the Guilford-Zimmerman Temperament Survey. *J Gerontol* 33:737, 1978.
23. Mortimer JT et al: Persistence and change in development: The multidimensional self-concept, in Baltes PB, Brim OG Jr (eds): *Life-Span Development and Behavior.* New York, Academic Press, 1982, vol 4, p 264.
24. Siegler IC et al: Cross-sequential analysis of adult personality. *Dev Psychol* 15:350, 1979.
25. Costa PT Jr, McCrae RR: Personality in adulthood: A six-year longitudinal study of self-reports and spouse ratings on the NEO Personality Inventory. *J Pers Soc Psychol* 54:853, 1988.
26. Jung CG: *Psychological Types.* Princeton, NJ, Princeton University Press, 1923/1971.
27. Costa PT Jr, McCrae RR: *The NEO Personality Inventory Manual.* Odessa, FL, Psychological Assessment Resources, 1985.
28. McCrae RR, Costa PT Jr: Self-concept and the stability of personality: Cross-sectional comparisons of self-reports and ratings. *J Pers Soc Psychol* 43:1282, 1982.
29. Costa PT Jr et al: Enduring dispositions in adult males. *J Pers Soc Psychol* 38:793, 1980.
30. Leon GR et al: Personality stability and change over a 30 year period—middle age to old age. *J Consult Clin Psychol* 47:517, 1979.
31. Conley JJ: Longitudinal stability of personality traits: A multitrait-multimethod-multioccasion analysis. *J Pers Soc Psychol* 49:1266, 1985.
32. Woodruff, D: The role of memory in personality continuity: A 25 year follow-up. *Exp Aging Res* 9:31, 1983.
33. Helson R, Moane G: Personality change in women from college to midlife. *J Pers Soc Psychol* 53:176, 1987.
34. Farrell MP, Rosenberg SD: *Men at Midlife.* Boston, Auburn House, 1981.
35. Costa PT Jr, McCrae RR: Objective personality assessment, in Storandt M et al (eds): *The Clinical Psychology of Aging.* New York, Plenum Press, 1978, p 119.
36. Costa PT Jr, McCrae RR: Personality as a lifelong determinant of well-being, in Malatesta C, Izard C (eds): *Affective Processes in Adult Development and Aging.* Beverly Hills, CA, Sage, 1984, p 141.
37. Costa PT Jr et al: Personality and vocational interests in an adult sample. *J Appl Psychol* 69:390, 1984.

38. McCrae RR, Costa PT Jr: Personality, coping, and coping effectiveness in an adult sample. *J Pers* 54:385, 1986.

39. Wiggins JS: A psychological taxonomy of trait-descriptive terms: The interpersonal domain. *J Pers Soc Psychol* 37:395, 1979.

40. Costa PT Jr, McCrae RR: Hypochondriasis, neuroticism, and aging: When are somatic complaints unfounded? *Am Psychol* 40:19, 1985.

41. Costa PT Jr, McCrae RR: Neuroticism, somatic complaints, and disease: Is the bark worse than the bite? *J Pers* 55:299, 1987.

42. Wiggins JS: "How Interpersonal Are the MMPI Personality Disorder Scales?" in *Current Research in MMPI Personality Disorder Scales*. Symposium conducted at the Annual Convention of the American Psychological Association, New York, September 1987.

43. Costa PT Jr et al: Personality variable in the NHANES-I followup, in Cornoni-Huntley J et al (eds): *Health Status and Well-being of the Elderly: National Health and Nutrition Examination I-Epidemiologic Followup Survey*. New York, Oxford University Press, in press.

44. Raskind MA, Storrie MC: The organic mental disorders, in Busse EW, Blazer DG (eds): *Handbook of Geriatric Psychiatry*. New York, Van Nostrand Reinhold, 1980, p 305.

45. Ruskin PE: Geropsychiatric consultation in a university hospital: A report on 67 referrals. *Am J Psychiatry* 412:333, 1985.

46. Thompson LW et al: Comparative effectiveness of psychotherapies for depressed elders. *J Consult Clin Psychol* 55:385, 1987.

47. Stroebe M, Stroebe W: *Bereavement and Health*. New York, Cambridge University Press, 1987.

48. McCrae RR, Costa PT Jr: Psychological resilience among widowed men and women: A 10-year followup of a national sample. *J Soc Issues*, 44:129, 1988.

49. Alexander F: *Psychosomatic Medicine*. New York, Norton, 1950.

50. Luborsky L et al: Onset conditions for psychosomatic symptoms: A comparative review of immediate observation with retrospective research. *Psychosom Med* 35:187, 1973.

51. Cooper T et al: Coronary-prone behavior and coronary heart disease: A critical review. *Circulation* 263:1199, 1981.

52. Costa PT Jr et al: Hostility, agreeableness-antagonism, and coronary heart disease. *Holistic Med* 2:161, 1987.

53. Costa PT Jr et al: Agreeableness vs. antagonism: Explication of a potential risk factor for CHD, in Siegman A, Dembroski TM (eds): *In Search of Coronary-Prone Behavior*. Hillsdale, NJ, Lawrence Erlbaum Associates, in press.

54. Friedman HS, Booth-Kewley S: The "disease-prone personality": A metanalytic view of the construct. *Am Psychol* 42:539, 1987.

55. Costa PT Jr, McCrae RR: Personality assessment in psychosomatic medicine: Value of a trait taxonomy, in Fava GA, Wise TN (eds): *Advances in Psychosomatic Medicine*, vol 17: *Research Paradigms in Psychosomatic Medicine*. Basel, Karger, 1987, p 71.

56. Berglund G et al: Personality and reporting of symptoms in normo- and hypertensive 50 year old males. *J Psychosom Res* 19:139, 1975.

Chapter 10

SEXUALITY AND AGING

Julian M. Davidson

Vigorous sexuality is normally regarded as an attribute of youth, yet history and literature record many prodigies of sexual survivorship such as the birth of the patriarch Isaac when Abraham was 120 and Sarah 80 years of age. More instructive than exceptional cases, however, is the poorly recognized fact that active sexuality continues in a rather high proportion of men and women advanced in age. In a recent survey of approximately 80 men and 80 women over the age of 80 living in northern California residences for the aged, 63 percent of the men reported having sexual intercourse "at least several times a year," as did 30 percent of the women.[1] It should be understood that interpretations of these data are subject to the extremely lopsided availability of the two sexes in this age bracket; in these residences, there was a male to female ratio of 1:6. Moreover, these individuals spent their formative years in a period of history noted for its prudery and official antagonism toward nonprocreative sex. Writings from the seventies emphasizing the prevalence of and promoting the importance of sexuality in the aged should lead to increased expectations on the part of those otherwise prone to accept sexual senility.[2,3]

It is important for the physician to know what changes to expect in the sexual side of life as men and women age. This chapter deals both with these changes and with the difficult problem of the biological etiology of sexual aging, the future solution to which should provide a basis for therapeutic measures.

ANALYSIS AND ASSESSMENT OF HUMAN SEXUALITY

In medical writings, sexual function is all too often dealt with as a unidimensional continuum extending from hypersexuality to impotence or frigidity. This tendency, common among both medical practitioners and clinical researchers, is deleterious both to patient care and med-

The author's work on aging is supported by NIH grant AG1437.

ical progress. A first and vital step in the assessment process is to distinguish between two categories of sexuality, libido and potency, and to use standardized definitions.[4]

Libido will be defined for present purposes as the sum of the affective-cognitive processes which impel a person to engage in sexual behavior. The libido of an individual can be assessed by careful elicitation of information on sexual desires and fantasies and the enjoyment of sex. In animal research, analogous data may be obtained by measuring sexual motivation as reflected in the tendency to initiate mating, isolated from consummatory behavior which is influenced by potency factors. *Potency* can be defined as the capacity to respond to sexual stimuli (exogenous or endogenous), based on specific physiological responses in both sexes. These responses can be assessed in the laboratory, and the validity of the assessment depends in part on the degree to which it can be isolated from libido factors. Thus the capacity for genital vasocongestive responses, in the presumed absence of known psychogenic influences, is now often measured by evaluating nocturnal penile tumescence (NPT), which is largely an accompaniment of rapid eye movement (REM) sleep. The evaluation is performed in sleep laboratories or carried out with portable monitors used by the patient at home. Not yet used clinically, but potentially available, is the assessment of vaginal vasomotor changes during sleep,[5] a physiological measure analogous to NPT in men.

Methods for eliciting and quantitatively assessing genital vasocongestion in the waking state, as well as for assessing physiological manifestations of orgasm, are available in the research laboratory[6] but are seldom used for clinical testing. The various extragenital responses to sexual arousal and orgasm (blood pressure increase, electrodermal responses, etc.) are of more dubious utility and significance since they have not yet been shown to have specific patterns distinguishing them from responses to nonsexual emotions.

Sexual sensations, i.e., subjective awareness of feelings associated with sexual arousal and activity, belong somewhere between the categories of libido and potency. They are conscious phenomena, yet are manifested in physiological activation of sensory receptors and thus have the potential of being assessed quantitatively by psychophysical measurement.

THE AGING MALE

Support for a biological basis of sexual decline in aging derives from the finding of similar changes in aging males of the various animal species which have been studied. Though a decline in frequency of sexual activity is invariably present in aging animals, the elements of sexual behavior affected by aging differ among different species.[7,8] The effects of aging on sexual behavior in the human's closest "relatives," the nonhuman primates, have received very little study. Phoenix and coworkers have, however, discovered a marked decrement in sexual activity in rhesus monkeys over 20 years of age.[9] While the authors emphasize the decrease in sexual motivation (libido) as the major sexual aspect affected by age, decreases in potency were not specifically investigated. In human males, on the other hand, several studies have claimed that age-related decline has a greater impact on potency than on libido.[10-13] This latter phenomenon is responsible for the development of a libido-potency gap, often a source of distress in aging men.

Although there are no complete longitudinal investigations in men, cross-sectional studies convincingly demonstrate a steady decline in sexual activity from a peak frequency of "sexual outlet" (orgasmic activity of any sort) which, according to Kinsey's monumental study,[10] occurs in late adolescence. However, these changes do not become of medical importance until the decline becomes manifest in true sexual dysfunction. In fact, the Kinsey data do not show a significant increase in the incidence of impotence until the seventh decade of life.

The common effects of aging on potency involve both erection and ejaculation/orgasm, though erectile changes are clinically more important as presenting complaints. A laboratory study, using electronic monitoring of changes in penile dimensions, found that the rate of erection in response to erotic films was six times slower in men aged 48 to 65 than in others aged 19 to 30 years.[14] Though this difference could have been exaggerated by a "cohort effect," a progressive age-related decline in erectile capacity is also indicated by quantitative decreases in NPT.[15,16]

The effects of aging on ejaculation and orgasm were described by Masters and Johnson.[17] They reported (albeit without systematic quantitative data) decreases in strength and frequency of contractions of the pelvic striated muscles that have the effect of reducing the force of expulsion of semen. These contractions seem to be correlated with the orgasmic "altered state of consciousness,"[4] so that changes of this sort may be associated with a decreased intensity of the subjective experience of orgasm in aging men. An important change in orgasmic function is the increase in the post-ejaculatory refractory time period during which men are completely or relatively unresponsive; this increases typically from a few minutes in adolescence to several days in old age. In addition, a latency to orgasm is experienced which is related to the reputed decline in "ejaculatory demand,"[17] due presumably to a decreased sensitivity of the ejaculatory mechanism—a phenomenon also found in experimental animals.[7,8] The resulting increased orgasmic control entails one of the few sexual bonuses of aging in men—a decline in premature ejaculation—while other sexual dysfunctions become more prevalent with advancing age.

In line with the general blunting of sensory function in aging there is a specific decrease in penile sensitivity, which has been demonstrated in terms of increased thresholds to vibrotactile and electric stimulation of the penis.[18,19] The extent to which this change affects the sexual life of the aging male (i.e., its clinical importance) has not been established.

From a clinical point of view, it cannot be stressed too much that the normal decline in sexual performance of the aging male should not be considered as pathologic. For the most part, changes in quantity and quality of sexual life can be accepted without major complaint, especially when the couple is amenable to altering styles of sexual interaction to accommodate with the constraints of age (see "Therapy").

ANDROGEN LEVEL AND MALE SEXUAL SENESCENCE

Although the mechanism of the behavioral action of androgen is still unclear,[20] clinical experience and double-blind experimental studies demonstrate the importance of testosterone in maintaining the sexuality of men,[21-23] as is the case in other species.[24] Thus the fact that blood levels of testosterone decline along with sexual function in the aging male population compels serious consideration of the hypothesis that geriatric sexual hypofunction is a direct result of reduced androgen levels.

What is the evidence that behavioral changes are, in fact, related to aging changes, rather than both types of change being independent correlates of the aging process? In a survey of 220 men aged 41 to 93 years, data on sexuality were collected by a simple questionnaire, and hormone levels were measured in a simultaneously obtained blood sample.[13] As reported in previous investigations, there was a significant decrease in circulating testosterone level, and, because sex hormone-binding globulin increased, a greater decrease was found in calculated free testosterone. In addition, mean increases of about 100 percent in follicle-stimulating hormone (FSH) and luteinizing hormone (LH) were found, but estradiol and prolactin levels were unchanged in these population samples. Statistical analysis demonstrated that only a small part of the variance in sexual function could be attributed to changes in free testosterone level, and none to changes in total testosterone. Thus, the aging decline in sexuality has to be explained largely by other factors (presently unknown). Likewise, in selected populations of aging men in which testosterone levels did not significantly decline, the usual decreases in sexual behavior were found.[25]

Finding no decrease in total free testosterone in aging men selected for optimal physical and mental health and high socioeconomic-educational level, Harman and Tsitouras proposed that the age-related decrease in testosterone results from disease.[26] However, there is no direct evidence to support this view; partial correlation analysis indicated that disease was not an important factor in the changes in testosterone level found in the Stanford study.[13]

Finally, it should be noted that the "male climacteric"—a relatively rapid-onset hypogonadal condition associated with sexual dysfunction—is a rare condition which has not been well characterized. It is thus not to be compared in importance with the universal female climacteric, which depletes gonadal hormones and eliminates the menstrual cycle.

One caveat about the conclusion that testosterone is not responsible for sexual decline comes from studies of frequent blood sampling throughout the day and night.[27] They show that aging men have a blunting of the diurnal variation in serum testosterone and a decrease in free testosterone levels. The possibility therefore arises that the pattern of diurnal release of testosterone may be relevant to geriatric sexual aging. As yet, however, this hypothesis has not been proved.

OTHER CAUSES OF MALE DECLINE

Since declining androgen can, at this time, explain only a small part of the sexual decline in men, alternative hypotheses, albeit speculative, deserve mention. First, sexual decline, like other brain-related disabilities of aging, may have to do with failure of cerebral monoamine function, that is, the monoaminergic pathways in the brain. Such pathways have been implicated in the sexual behavior of animals,[28] and they become depleted

with age.[7] Various central nervous system (CNS) neuropeptides can also be considered as candidates for the role of mediators of sexual aging. In rats, age-related changes in LHRH and endorphin have been implicated in the sexual decline of animals.[29]

A second hypothesis is the possibility of age-related changes in the sensitivity of relevant target cells to the effects of androgen. There may be decline in the number, affinity, or other characteristics of androgen receptors or a decline in other aspects of the mechanism of androgen action on relevant cells as yet unidentified in humans. That aging male rats are behaviorally less sensitive to testosterone has been demonstrated in quantitative replacement therapy experiments; even high pharmacological levels of testosterone could not restore to the aging rat the degree of sexual vigor found in the young adult rat.[8] At the peripheral cellular level there are some indications of a decreased effectiveness of androgen acting on genital tissues in old age.[30,31] In aging men, change in responsiveness of sexual behavior to testosterone has not yet been demonstrated in adequately controlled studies.

While the inevitable sexual changes of age need not result in perceived dysfunction, specific age-dependent conditions can catapult the aging man into clinical dysfunction. One of these factors is depression, which is correlated with both low testosterone levels and sexual dysfunction. Statistical analysis indicates, however, that depression-induced hypogonadism is not responsible for the normal sexual deficits of age.[32] Another source of sexual dysfunction in aging is the widespread use of antihypertensive and psychotropic drugs. The incidence of hypertension increases considerably with advancing age, as does the prevalence of significant depressive symptomatology. (A related hazard to the aging population is noncompliance with antihypertension medication.)

THE AGING FEMALE

Biological and medical aspects of sexual behavior have been studied much less in women than in men or in female animals. This neglect extends to clinical interest in women's sexual health and, to a degree, stems from the traditionally submissive sexual role of the female, i.e., the perceived role of the woman as a receptacle for the more complex and vulnerable male apparatus. Because of this neglect, for example, we know much less about medication-induced dysfunction in women than in men. It is, however, well documented that women undergo significant decreases in sexual function in their fifties and further decreases thereafter.[10–12] The parameters of sexuality most often investigated in aging women have been the incidence and degree of activity and interest (drive), but age affects most of, if not all of, the major elements of female sexuality, encompassing declines in both libido and "potency." What is not so clear is the extent to which these changes are due to causes intrinsic to the woman and, particularly, whether they are of biological origin, rather than resulting from sociocultural constraints.

In the Duke University cross-sectional and longitudinal studies of the 1950s and 1960s, women of 50 to 69 years of age most frequently attributed the responsibility for cessation of coitus to loss of their husband's sexual capacity and/or lack of interest.[33] The husbands attributed their own sexual decline to factors within themselves. Among sociocultural factors operating to decrease sexual activity in aging widows are the paucity of older males, taboos against extramarital sex, and the popular view of older women as being sexually unattractive. Furthermore, the decrease in coital activity does appear to be replaced, to some extent at least, by masturbation.[34] Thus it appears that factors extrinsic to the aging woman may play a crucial role in the decline of her sexual activity.

THE EFFECTS OF MENOPAUSE

Since the major age-related changes in the adult female reproductive and sexual function appear to span the period of menopause, it is important to consider the contribution of this dramatic event to the sexual decline of aging, which was not adequately assessed in the earlier well-known studies.[10–12] In a more recent study of 800 Swedish women, strong evidence was provided to support the important role of menopause in sexual aging.[35] In this population, evidence was adduced that the sexual decline in activity, interest, and orgasmic frequency, occurring between the fifth and sixth decades of life, were not due to the "husband effect." In addition, however, comparison of pre- and postmenopausal women indicates that changes in these parameters reported between 46 and 54 years of age were due to menopause and not to aging per se.

Yet despite the statistical-epidemiological evidence, it is not possible to predict the impact of menopause on a woman's sexuality. Some women are unaffected, some show a sexual decline, and still others experience an enhancement of sexual activity and/or satisfaction. Such enhancement may be due to the removal of the fear of conception, whether or not birth control was previously used.[10,36] An ongoing longitudinal study of menopause, however, confirms the view that negative effects are the most common. Twenty women completed a detailed questionnaire on sexuality on several occasions over a period of several months before the last menstrual period, and the same procedure was repeated after menstruation ceased.[37] Significantly lower ratings were ob-

tained postmenopausally on self-assessment of sexual enjoyment, arousal, and frequency of sexual thoughts, but not on self-assessment of sexual activity.

THE HORMONAL FACTOR IN WOMEN

It is generally accepted that as women have evolved they have developed a considerable degree of "emancipation" from sexual behavior that is dependent on ovarian hormones, as exemplified by their maintenance of sexuality throughout the phases of the menstrual cycle and beyond menopause. The extent of this evolutionary development has not been definitively evaluated. Many studies have claimed fluctuations in sexuality that relate to certain stages of the menstrual cycle. That these claims are contradictory is less important in the present context than the fact that postmenopausally, estrogen and progesterone levels are consistently below those found at almost all stages of the menstrual cycle. Decreased sexual function is not a universal complaint in postmenopausal women, but this sexual variability could be due to individual variance in postmenopausal steroid levels and/or sensitivity to hormonal effects.[38]

What is the evidence for such a role of hormones in women? Consider the well-known anatomical effects of postmenopausal ovarian steroid deprivation. Prominent among these is atrophic vaginitis. This condition involves a thinning of the vaginal walls and atrophic changes in the labia, with reduction in fatty tissue deposits. During sexual activity, there is decreased vaginal lubrication, as well as decreased tumescence of the glans clitoridis. In addition, the involuted uterus is reported to show lessened elevation during sexual arousal and the os cervix to be less dilated.[17]

Quantitative laboratory data have indicated significant changes in vaginal structure and function in older postmenopausal women, as measured by a lowered volume of secretions and of electrical potential difference across the vaginal mucosa, as well as by an elevated pH level.[39] It is not known whether these changes result from menopause per se or are simply effects of aging. In one study, decreased vasocongestion in the unstimulated state of the vaginal wall increased gradually over a 24-month period of estrogen therapy.[40] More directly relevant to sexuality are measures of genital response in actual conditions of sexual arousal. Morrell et al. used photoplethysmographic assessment of vaginal blood flow when sexual arousal was produced by erotic film and fantasy. The response (which is analogous to erection in men) was significantly lower in older, postmenopausal women (mean age 57 years) than in younger, cycling subjects (mean age 31 years). This effect was apparently due to menopause rather than to the difference in ages between the two groups, as demonstrated by the high responsiveness of a group of older women (mean age 51) still having regular menstrual cycles.[41]

What remains unclear is the extent to which these anatomical and physiological changes, related to genital sexual response, are of clinical importance, i.e., how much they may result in sexual dysfunction or at least diminish the quality of sexual experience. In the previously mentioned study, for instance, the older women with diminished sexual response were not sexually dysfunctional, nor did their subjective assessment of degree of sexual arousal in response to the film or fantasy differ from that of the younger women.[41] The emerging field of medical sexology has not yet provided clinical norms for genital response as assessed in the laboratory.

The most definitive approach to the question of hormonal etiology in the sexual changes of middle-aged women is to determine whether menopausal deficiencies in both potency and libido can be restored by ovarian steroid replacement therapy. A number of studies have addressed this issue with varying degrees of superficiality and thoroughness, but no definitive data on laboratory-assessed sexual response are yet available. In one double-blind investigation, estrogen decreased the incidence of self-reported vaginal dryness, though no improvement was found in frequency of coitus, masturbation, orgasm, or sexual satisfaction.[42] In another study, estrogen reportedly increased the frequency of sexual activity and enhanced orgasmic capacity.[43] A thorough double-blind study dealt with estrogen and estrogen-progesterone replacement therapy after hysterectomy/ovariectomy for benign disorders.[44] Synthetic estrogen, but not synthetic progestin, improved sexual desire, enjoyment, and orgasmic frequency. No significant differences were observed in coital frequency or sexual response.

An important, still-unresolved question is the extent to which the potential beneficial effects of estrogen on libido or other elements of sexuality may be mediated by enhancement of mood, including reduced depression.[45] Nevertheless, whatever is the proximate mechanism of these effects, the above results suggest that postmenopausal sexual dysfunction can be ascribed at least in part to estrogen deficiency, making estrogen therapy a rational treatment of sexual dysfunction symptoms, in addition to its other well-known medical benefits. Since it is established that the simultaneous daily administration of progestational agents protects against the danger of estrogen-induced endometriosis, it is relevant that Dennerstein et al. found only mild and borderline deleterious effects of daily progestin treatment on sexual function.[44] Moreover, the commonly used mode of treatment requires only brief, periodic progesterone supplementation,[46] which is not likely to interfere significantly with the benefits of estrogen on sexuality. It should be noted that topical administration of estrogen in vaginal creams has not yet been shown to confer any protective effect against adverse systemic effects of estrogen because this route of administration results in blood levels at least as high as levels resulting from oral administration.[47]

ANDROGEN IN WOMEN

A widespread belief among some clinicians and investigators is that androgen, rather than estrogen, is the hormone of major importance in maintaining female sexuality. As usually stated, the assumption is that this androgen is largely of adrenal origin.[48,49] While the early view was not yet supported by adequate data, several groups have more recently reported beneficial use of estrogen-androgen combinations for sexual dysfunction (along with other symptoms) in the postmenopausal woman.[50,51] Apart from the absence of well-controlled studies, such use presents questions of rationale. For example, adrenal androgen levels are not greatly affected by menopause, and effects of administered testosterone in women could be mediated by its aromatization to estrogen in peripheral tissues. On the other hand, since estrogen stimulates adrenocortical secretion, the possibility that effects of estrogen replacement therapy could be mediated by increased adrenal androgen needs to be considered.

The most impressive data on the role of androgen are those of Sherwin et al.[52,53] This double-blind crossover study compared prospective sexual data resulting from injection of estradiol and testosterone esters, separately and together, in women hysterectomized and bilaterally oophorectomized for reasons other than cancer. In addition, a premenopausal unoperated group and an operated group were given placebo. The results showed a clear advantage to testosterone and the combined dose of estrogen and androgen, which specifically improved libido-motivational aspects of sexuality (arousal, desire, and fantasy). Interestingly, these are the same measures primarily stimulated by testosterone in men. Problematic in Sherwin's studies has been the supraphysiologic levels of serum testosterone.

One caveat is that since the Sherwin studies included only women who had undergone surgical menopause, the results may not reflect changes that would occur in natural menopause, because of its less rapid changes in endocrine status and the residual production of gonadal steroids.[54] Two recent double-blind studies of the effects of estrogen and progestin[55] and of estrogen and testosterone[56] used women who had experienced natural menopause. Physiologically measured sexual response was unaffected by the hormone treatments in these studies, and only few slight changes in sexual functioning were statistically significant.

A fairly common view is that continued sexual activity in earlier life contributes to maintenance of adequate sexual functioning in older men and women, with the implication that there is a causal relationship between the two.[17,57] This idea is, however, supported only by data of more or less an anecdotal nature and by correlations shown between sexual activity in old age and level of past sexual activity or interest in earlier adulthood. Such correlations have been interpreted as a result of the tendency for individuals to maintain "consistency of lifestyle."[33]

THERAPY

When sexual decline in aging presents as a problem, behaviorally oriented counseling is advisable for both men and women, preferably in conjoint marital therapy, as developed by Masters and Johnson.[48] Treatment should be aimed at developing adjustments to specified age-related physiological conditions such as erectile hypofunction, dyspareunia, or failure of lubrication. In the latter case, simple lubricating jellies can be helpful.

Therapy may include learning new techniques of lovemaking, including increased emphasis on noncoital activity, self or partner masturbation, and stressing of nonorgasmic sex when necessary (e.g., when physiologic orgasmic dysfunction is suspected). Often therapy should contain an educational component to align expectations with age-appropriate norms or to combat anxiety due to discrepancies between the two. On the other hand, the therapist may have to combat stereotypic attitudes implying that sex and "old age" are morally or medically inconsistent.

Hormone replacement therapy, widely used in postmenopausal women for nonsexual indications, should eliminate problems stemming primarily from estrogen deprivation of the genitopelvic tissues and will likely eliminate some problems of cerebral origin.

At present there is no established rationale for the use of androgen treatment in men, except for frankly hypogonadal men, in which case injection of 200 mg testosterone enanthate at 2-week intervals is recommended. Local application of the hormone, presently uncommon, will likely increase.

In light of the findings of Sherwin et al., there is now more rational justification for hormone replacement therapy with testosterone in women. The dose should be adjusted to prevent virilization. The indication for such treatment would be loss of libido.

REFERENCES

1. Bretschneider J, McCoy NM: Sexual interest and behavior in healthy 80- to 102-years-olds. *Arch Sex Behav* 17:109, 1988.
2. Burnside IM: *Sexuality and Aging.* Los Angeles, University of Southern California Press, 1974.
3. Solnick RL: *Sexuality and Aging.* Los Angeles, University of Southern California Press, 1978.
4. Davidson JM: The psychobiology of sexual experience, in Davidson JM, Davidson RJ (eds): *The Psychobiology of Consciousness.* New York, Plenum, 1980, p 271.
5. Abel G: A woman's vaginal responses during REM sleep. *J Sex Marital Ther* 5:5, 1979.
6. Rosen R, Beck G: *Sexual Psychophysiology.* New York, Guilford Press, 1988.
7. Davidson JM et al: The sexual psychoendocrinology of aging, in Meites J (ed): *Neuroendocrinology of Aging.* New York, Plenum, 1983, pp 221–258.
8. Gray GD et al: Sexual behavior and testosterone in middle-aged male rats. *Endocrinology* 109:1597, 1981.
9. Phoenix CH et al: Sexual behavior in aging male rhesus monkeys, in Chiarelli B (ed): *Advanced Views on Primate Biology.* Heidelberg, Springer-Verlag, 1983, p 95.
10. Kinsey AC et al: *Sexual Behavior in the Human Male.* Philadelphia, Saunders, 1948.
11. Verwoerdt A et al: Sexual behavior in senescence—changes in sexual activity and interest of aging men and women. *J Geriatr Psychiatry* 2:163, 1969.
12. Verwoerdt A et al: Sexual behavior in senescence. *Geriatrics* 24:137, 1969.
13. Davidson JM et al: Hormonal changes in sexual function in aging men. *J Clin Endocrinol Metab* 57:71, 1983.
14. Solnick RL: Age and male erectile responsiveness. *Arch Sex Behav* 6:1, 1977.
15. Kahn E et al: The sleep characteristics of the normal aged male. *J Nerv Ment Dis* 148:477, 1969.
16. Karacan I et al: Some characteristics of nocturnal penile tumescence in elderly males. *J Gerontol* 27:39, 1972.
17. Masters WH, Johnson VC: *Human Sexual Response.* Boston, Little, Brown, 1966.
18. Edwards AE, Husted JR: Penile sensitivity, age and sexual behavior. *J Clin Psychol* 32:697, 1976.
19. Rowland DL et al: Penile and finger sensory thresholds in aging and diabetic impotence. *Arch Sex Behav* 18:1, 1989.
20. Davidson JM et al: Hormonal replacement and sexuality in men. *J Clin Endocrinol Metab* 11:599, 1982.
21. Davidson JM et al: Effects of androgen on sexual behavior in hypogonadal men. *J Clin Endocrinol Metab* 48:955, 1979.
22. Skakkebaek NE et al: Androgen replacement with oral testosterone undecanoate in hypogonadal men: A double-blind controlled study. *Clin Endocrinol* 14:49, 1980.
23. Luisi M: Double-blind group comparative study of testosterone undecanoate and mesterolone in hypogonadal male patients. *J Endocrinol Invest* 3:305, 1980.
24. Davidson JM: Neuro-hormonal bases of male sexual behavior, in Greep RO (ed): *Reproductive Physiology II, International Review of Physiology.* Baltimore, University Park Press, 1977, vol 13, pp 225–254.
25. Tsitouras PD et al: Relationship of serum testosterone to sexual activity in healthy elderly men. *J Gerontol* 37:288, 1982.
26. Harman SM, Tsitouras PD: Reproductive hormones in aging men. I. Measurement of sex steroids, basal luteinizing hormone and Leydig cell response to human chorionic gonadotropin. *J Clin Endocrinol Metab* 51:35, 1980.
27. Bremner WJ, Vitiello MV, Prinz PN: Loss of circadian rhythmicity in blood testosterone levels with aging in normal men. *J Clin Endocrinol Metab* 56:1278, 1983.

28. Bitran D, Hull EM: Pharmacologic analysis of male rat sexual behavior. *Neurosci Biobehav Rev* 11:365, 1987.

29. Dorsa DM et al: Immunoreactive-beta-endorphin and LHRH levels in the brains of aged male rats with impaired sex behavior. *Neurobiol Aging* 5:115, 1984.

30. Wilson JD: Testosterone metabolism in skin. *17 Symp Dtsch Ges Endokrinol*. Berlin, Springer-Verlag, 1971, p 11.

31. Desleypere JP et al: Aging and tissue androgens. *J Clin Endocrinol Metab* 53:430, 1981.

32. Yesavage JA et al: Plasma testosterone, depression, sexuality and age. *Biol Psychiatry* 20:199, 1985.

33. Pfeiffer E et al: Sexual behavior in middle life. *Am J Psychiatry* 128:1262, 1978.

34. Christenson CV, Gagnon JH: Sexual behavior in a group of older women. *J Gerontol* 20:351, 1965.

35. Hallstrom T: Sexuality in the climacteric. *Clin Obstet Gynecol* 4:227, 1977.

36. Christenson CV, Johnson HB: Sexual patterns in a group of older, never married women. *J Geriatr Psychiatry* 6:80, 1973.

37. McCoy N et al: Relationship among sexual behavior, hot flashes and hormone levels in perimenopausal women. *Arch Sex Behav* 14:385, 1985.

38. Chakravarti S et al: Relation between plasma hormone profiles, symptoms and response to oestrogen treatment in women approaching the menopause. *Br Med J* 1:983, 1979.

39. Semmens JP, Wagner G: Estrogen deprivation and vaginal function in postmenopausal women. *JAMA* 248:445, 1982.

40. Semmens JP et al: Effects of estrogen therapy on vaginal physiology during menopause. *Obstet Gynec* 66:15, 1985.

41. Morrell MJ et al: The influence of age and ovulatory status on sexual arousability in women. *Am J Obstet Gynecol* 148:66, 1984.

42. Campbell S: Double blind psychometric studies on the effects of natural estrogens on postmenopausal women, in Campbell S (ed): *The Management of the Menopause and Post-menopausal Years*. Lancaster, PA, MTP Press, 1976, pp 149–158.

43. Fedor-Freybergh P: The influence of oestrogens on the well being and mental performance in climacteric and post-menopausal women. *Acta Obstet Gynecol Scand* (Suppl) 64:1977.

44. Dennerstein L et al: Hormones and sexuality: Effect of estrogen and progestogen. *Obstet Gynecol* 56:316, 1980.

45. Cullberg J: Mood changes and menstrual symptoms with different gestagen/estrogen combinations. *Acta Psychiatr Scand* (Suppl) 236, 1972.

46. Gambrell DR Jr: The prevention of endometrial cancer in postmenopausal women with progestogens. *Maturitas* 1:107, 1978.

47. Studd J et al: The climacteric. *Clin Obstet Gynecol* 4:3, 1977.

48. Waxenberg SE et al: The role of hormones in human behavior: I. Changes in female sexuality after adrenalectomy. *J Clin Endocrinol Metab* 19:193, 1959.

49. Schon M, Sutherland AM: The role of hormones in human behavior: III. Changes in female sexuality after hypophysectomy. *J Clin Endocrinol Metab* 20:833, 1960.

50. Gambrell RD: The menopause: Benefits and risks of estrogen-progestogen replacement therapy. *Fertil Steril* 37:457, 1982.

51. Greenblatt RB, Perez DH: Problems of libido in the elderly, in Greenblatt RB, Mahesh VB, McDonough PG (eds): *The Menopausal Syndrome*. New York, Medcom Press, 1974, pp 95–101.

52. Sherwin BB, Gelfand MM, Brender W: Androgen enhances sexual motivation in females: A prospective cross-over study of sex steroid administration in the surgical menopause. *Psychosom Med* 47:339, 1985.

53. Sherwin BB, Gelfand MM: The role of androgen in the maintenance of sexual functioning in oophorectomized women. *Psychosom Med* 49:397, 1987.

54. Davidson JM: Menopause, sexuality and hormones: A critical survey, in Dennerstein L, Fraser I (eds): *Hormones and Behaviour*. Amsterdam, Elsevier, 1986, pp 561–572.

55. Myers LS, Morokoff PJ: Physiological and subjective sexual arousal in pre- and postmenopausal women and postmenopausal women taking replacement therapy. *Psychophysiology* 23:283, 1986.

56. Myers LS, Davidson JM: Unpublished data, 1988.

57. Martin CE: Factors affecting sexual functioning in 60–79 year old married males. *Arch Sex Behav* 10:399, 1981.

Chapter 11

SOCIOLOGY OF AGING

George L. Maddox

The perspective of gerontologists and geriatricians on the processes and outcomes of human aging has been persistently and distinctively multidisciplinary and action-oriented over the history of these relatively new fields of inquiry and practice. Four decades of research and scholarship have reinforced the perceived utility of studying aging as a synergistic product of interacting biological, behavioral, and social factors. Each type of factor is known to be diverse and, to a degree yet to be fully determined, modifiable. Gerontologists and geriatricians have, however, already illustrated in research and demonstrations the relevance of a venerable maxim of experimental and clinical sciences: If you want to understand something, try to change it.

In gerontology and geriatrics, the understanding required for realistic and responsible testing of the modifiability of aging processes and outcomes necessarily involves not only the research of biological scientists but also the research of behavioral and social scientists. Commitment among gerontologists and geriatricians to the intellectual interdependence of the specific disciplines which share an interest in human aging remains deep and persistent, as illustrated by the multidisciplinary structure of The Gerontological Society of America and its major scientific journals. Research and scholarship in the social sciences generally, and in sociology in particular, have continued to complement the work of biological gerontologists and geriatricians who themselves tend to perceive and acknowledge that, in understanding human development, biology reveals what is possible in human life, not just what is necessary.

Four propositions that summarize a contemporary sociological perspective in aging outline the argument which will be developed in this chapter:

1. The well-documented diversity of aging processes and outcomes can be satisfactorily explained only by inclusion of contextual factors external to individuals; the material and social resources available to and differentially distributed by societies constitute key externalities affecting human development over the life course.

2. In human development, past does tend to be prologue. Consequently, the roots of differential aging are found early in the life course and suggest the wisdom of identifying and assessing early in life the risks factors not only for survival but also for well-being in later life.

3. The potential for modifying the processes and outcomes of aging by social policy is suggested generally by the observed effects of social resource allocations on morbidity, mortality, and well-being in later life and specifically by the demonstrable beneficial effects of particular public policy initiatives.

4. Public policy intended to shape the future of how one ages may be usefully informed by scientific information; but, in the final analysis, effective public policy regarding aging tends to reflect and reinforce the dominant values and preferences of society and the political feasibility of the particular policy proposals regarding the distribution of resources across the life course.

Critical overviews of gerontological research underlying these propositions are conveniently summarized in two recent articles by Rowe and Kahn[1] and by Maddox.[2] These articles, in turn, reference a large and diverse multidisciplinary literature relevant to this chapter. Additionally, *The Annual Review of Gerontology and Geriatrics*[3] focuses specifically on documenting and discussing the theoretical issues, and it illustrates a wide variety of practical implications of diversity in the processes and experience of human aging from the perspective of economists, epidemiologists, sociologists, and public policy analysts.

DIVERSITY IN AGING

Scientific research, as normally practiced and taught, places considerable emphasis on empirically derived succinct generalizations about various phenomena under study and, consequently, tends to be reductionistic. Although scientific investigators are aware that every statistical mean summarizing a complex array of values in a data set inexorably has a companion estimate of variance around the mean, measures of central tendency appear to be more interesting and memorable than measures of dispersion in reports of scientific inquiry. The neglect of measures of dispersion reflects in part a concern that variance may be attributable to errors in measurement as well as real substantive differences in the phenomena observed. While measurement error is a legitimate concern, there is no longer reason to doubt substantial intraspecies diversity in the processes and outcomes of aging among all animals or that the diversity in human aging explained by contextual factors external to the individual is substantial.

SOCIETIES ARE NATURAL EXPERIMENTS

Societies are large-scale natural experiments in the effects of differential availability and allocation of material and social resources on the processes and outcomes of aging. These effects appear at three different levels: *macro*, *meso*, and *micro*.[4]

Macrosocial Effects

Macrosocial effects can be illustrated in at least two ways. One illustration focuses on implications of the distinction between societies which are more or less developed. The other notes the implications of socioeconomic differentiation within a society.

DIFFERENTIAL RESOURCES Both historical and contemporary demographic and epidemiologic evidence document (see Chap. 15) convincingly that survival to old age as an average expectation at birth is a recent achievement. This is an achievement explained initially by the differential ability of societies to provide a stable supply of food and water and the basic elements of public sanitation and, more recently, by advances in medical sciences which have increased age-specific life expectancy in adulthood generally and specifically for individuals 80 years and older. In the United States in the twentieth century, the average life expectancy at birth increased from about 50 years in 1900 to the mid-70s in 1985—a demographic achievement not far behind those of the world's leaders, the Nordic countries and Japan. Average life expectancy at birth in the United States in the 1980s was 74.7 years overall, and 71.9 years for white

males, 78.7 years for white females. Even at age 85, age-specific expected years of life remaining were estimated to be 6.0–5.1 for white males, 6.4 years for white females.[5] Such achievements cannot be taken for granted. In a few developing nations average life expectancy continues to be about where the United States was at the turn of the century. Estimated life expectancy for all less developed nations in 1980 was, for example, 55 years and, specifically for Africa, 48.6 years. Average life expectancy at birth for all countries of the world in the year 2000 is now estimated to be only 63.9 years.[6]

The differential success of societies in achieving long life as an average expectation continues to be reflected dramatically in the contemporary distinction between less and more developed nations and the availability of the essential resources which this distinction implies. Patterns of disease and illness are expectedly different in developing and developed nations. The epidemiology of a developing nation documents that one is most likely to experience nutritional deprivation or acute, epidemic disease typically of viral or bacterial origin; the epidemiology of a developed nation (Chap. 15) is, in contrast, likely to highlight chronic disease to involve the gradual deterioration and failure of one or another biological system and to be influenced by behavior and lifestyle characteristics.[4]

SOCIOECONOMIC DIFFERENTIATION Differential availability of resources occurs within as well as between societies. Within a given society, even if adequate resources to meet overall societal needs are assumed to be available, material and social resources are not inevitably distributed equally. In fact, the evidence indicates that unequal distribution of resources within a society in relation to socioeconomic status is the norm. The rationale for observed unequal distribution is found in societal values and preferences regarding rules of equity. All societies generate systems of differential rewards of goods, status, honor, and power. The process and outcome of consensual differences about distribution of resources is what is meant by social stratification. In any society, to be at the top of the system of stratification means more than the prospects of having access to material and social rewards such as prestigious occupation, higher pay, and a maximum degree of self-determination. These rewards, in turn, change patterns of morbidity and mortality in a favorable direction and increase the prospects of perceived well-being in later life. Social status continues, given such correlates, to be one of the most powerful predictor variables in epidemiologic research.[7] Growing old poor, uneducated, and socially isolated clearly is not the same as growing old rich, educated, and socially integrated.

The ingenuity of social groups to differentiate members for purposes of special treatment does not end with general status differentiation. Social groups can and do differentiate individuals complexly on the basis of race, nationality, or religion or simply as male or female. Growing old as a member of a racial or ethnic minority or as a member of a majority group in a society typically is quite different. Life expectancy at birth varied by as much as 6 years for minority and majority individuals in the United States in 1985. For women, who appear to be biologically programmed for longer life than males, the fact that women have an elevated risk for poverty is explained better socially than biologically.[3]

The relationship between the distribution of social resources and differential outcomes of aging has been demonstrated with special effectiveness in a Canadian study by Wilkins and Adams.[8] In this study, the authors develop the concepts of *health expectancy* (i.e., disability-free life expectancy at birth) and *quality-adjusted life expectancy* (i.e., a weighted measure to indicate the probability of capacity for self-care in a noninstitutional setting) and apply these to the experience of Canada; for similar evidence from the United States, see Katz.[9] These concepts make an important distinction differentiating living personally and socially satisfying and adequate living from simply surviving. Table 11-1 summarizes important illustrations of diversity of aging outcomes in relation to both income level and residence in a poor versus a middle-class neighborhood. The almost 5-year average differential in life expectancy at birth between those with lowest and highest income is overshadowed by the even larger income-related differentials in quality-adjusted life expectancy (7.7 years) and disability-free life expectancy (11 years). Residential location, which by implication adds adequate housing and

degree of social integration to income as predictors, also has the expected effect on survival. Life expectancy at birth is 9.1 years greater for those residing in a middle-class neighborhood in contrast to those in a poor neighborhood. The differential favoring those in a middle-class neighborhood for quality-adjusted life expectancy is 10.8 years and for disability-free years, 13.3. The effects of socioeconomic status on survival and quality of life are consistently less dramatic for females than males. Socioeconomic factors modify the persistent effects of biological differences on survival and also have an effect on the quality-adjusted life expectancy of females.

In sum, whether one survives into later life and how one grows old are substantially affected by external macrosocial factors. The operation of these factors is illustrated both through the effectiveness with which a society controls its food supply and sanitation and through its internal allocation of resources in terms of implicit and explicit values and related social policy regarding the perceived differential worth of individuals.

Mesosocial Effects

At the mesosocial level, societies are also natural experiments in the effects of alternative institutionalized arrangements for providing and maintaining income in adulthood, delivering health care, and structuring living environments. The social roles traditionally allocated to women and the effects of this allocation on economic security in later life illustrate this point particularly well. Angela O'Rand[10] in a comparative analysis of the incomes of older women and men in both the United States and Sweden documents the inferior economic

TABLE 11-1
Life Expectancy, Disability-Free Expectancy, and Quality-Adjusted Life Expectancy at Birth in Years by Gender, Income Level, and Socioeconomic Status of Residential Area, Canada, 1978

Quartile	Life Expectancy			Disability-Free Expectancy			Quality-Adjusted Expectancy		
	M	F	Total	M	F	Total	M	F	Total
Income Level									
Lowest	67.1	76.6	71.9	50.0	59.9	54.9	59.4	69.7	64.6
Second	70.1	77.6	73.8	57.9	61.8	59.9	64.8	71.1	68.0
Third	70.9	78.5	74.7	61.1	64.3	62.7	66.8	72.7	69.8
Fourth	72.0	79.0	75.5	62.6	63.5	63.1	68.1	72.8	70.5
Highest	73.4	79.4	76.4	64.3	67.5	65.9	69.7	74.8	72.3
Residential Neighborhood									
Poor	61.4	70.9	66.1	49.2	54.0	51.6	56.1	63.9	60.0
Middle-class	72.2	78.2	75.2	62.9	66.9	64.9	68.2	73.5	70.8

SOURCE: From Wilkins R, Adams O: *Healthfulness of Life: A Unified View of Mortality, Institutionalization and Non-institutionalized Disability Research.* Montreal, Institute for Research in Public Policy, 1978.

outcomes for older women compared to older men in both societies and explains why this outcome is observed. The explanation reflects similar institutional arrangements in both societies regarding family responsibility, careers within the workplace, and public policy regarding the indexing of pension income to income during the working years. In both societies, although more so in the United States than in Sweden, women have continued to have more extensive responsibilities than men for child rearing. These responsibilities, in turn, affect entry into and continuation in the workforce, influence career advancement and related income, and determine the probability of working in industries likely to provide additional private pensions in retirement. Consequently, women in both societies tend to have lower average incomes in retirement than men. Gender in a society, then, has social connotations for economic security as well as for survival. Social roles related to gender become proxies for shared understandings about social obligations which, as they are met, have consequences for careers and the level of resources available in the postretirement years. Therefore, explanation of differential incomes for older men and women is found substantially in a society's preferred institutional arrangements.

The effects of preferred societal arrangements for organizing and financing health care are also easily illustrated with evidence from the experience of older adults in North America (see also Chap. 16). In critical reviews of a large body of empirical evidence about the health and health care of older adults, Wolinsky and Arnold[11] and Shapiro[12] have documented the incorrectness of generalizations such as "older adults have poor health and high rates of health care utilization." In fact, a minority of older adults have a disabling chronic illness and only a relatively small proportion of them have extraordinarily high rates of utilization, particularly in the last year of life. These elevated rates of disability and care utilization of a subpopulation and the related high health care costs generated are a reflection not only of age-related biological decrement but also of public policy which ensures that chronic and particularly terminal illnesses will be treated in the high-technology environments of hospitals or some other institutional setting. In societies whose populations are aging, these policy decisions ensure that large concentrations of older adults in high-cost medical settings will achieve very high social visibility, particularly if the treatment involves public expenditure. Consequently, a society's institutional arrangements which determine where older adults are treated, what kind of care they receive, and who pays for that care contribute significantly to whether a population is really concerned about population aging and the expressed nature of that concern. Medicare and medicaid legislation in the United States in 1965 literally laid the groundwork for creating in the private sector a new component of the health care industry—the nursing home.

This industry has come to dominate thinking about long-term care to the degree that long-term care is inappropriately, even if inadvertently, equated with nursing home care.

The National Long Term Care Survey (see Manton[13]) provides the estimate that in 1984, 5.5 percent of persons 65 and older in the United States were institutionalized, primarily in nursing homes. But, this survey also reinforces other evidence which documents the diversity of older adults as the risk of disability increases. More than twice the proportion of impaired elderly who are institutionalized continue to reside in communities in spite of high levels of disabilities similar to those observed among institutionalized persons. Whether disabled elderly persons continue to live in a community or move to an institution is obviously not simply a matter of the presence or absence of disability, although level of disability is demonstrably an important factor. Other factors which affect the risk of whether one is institutionalized include marital status, living arrangements, socioeconomic status, and public policy regarding institutionalization. One finds that, holding the level of disability constant, women are more likely to be institutionalized than men, in part because women are more likely than men to be single or widowed and to live alone. The shorter average life expectancy of men increases the likelihood that a spouse will provide care. As one surveys across societies where older impaired individuals currently live out their lives, the effects of alternative living arrangements, socioeconomic status, and public policy are also evident. Canada and a number of countries in Western Europe, which include long-term care as a basic component of their national health financing schemes, have relatively high rates of disabled older adults in special settings.[14] The United States, as a matter of policy, has concentrated on nursing homes for impaired older adults rather than a continuum of sheltered housing environments or community-based care and has required nonindigent individuals to pay for long-term care (as distinct from relatively brief posthospital care). Consequently, long-term care in the United States tends for all practical purposes to be equated with nursing home care. In 1985, 55 percent of the national total of $35.2 million spent on nursing home care in the United States was paid by individuals. Of the 47 percent of the total paid by federal and state governments, the great majority (42 of the 47 percent) was paid by medicaid in behalf of persons qualifying as indigent either prior to institutionalization or as a result of depletion of private resources following extended personal payment for care.[15] Informed observers speculate that current long-term care policy in the United States is likely to continue because of the estimate of high cost of public financing and lack of clear national consensus about the balance of public–private financing of long-term care.[16] Neither the United States nor Canada has developed a continuum of special housing for disabled older adults of the kind found in the United Kingdom, Sweden, Norway, or the Netherlands where from 9 to 11 percent of older adults are housed in specially designed and managed group quarters in addition to nursing homes.

Similarly, whether an older adult receives care from health professionals who have received special training in geriatrics and in settings which emphasize the special problems of older adults reflects public policy and related societal investments in gerontological and geriatric programs. The United Kingdom and Sweden have had designated medical consultants and special assessment units in geriatrics for several decades. In the United States both federal agencies and private foundations have increased their investment in promoting geriatrics as a subspecialty in medicine and psychiatry and as a specialty in nursing and social work more recently.[17] In short, the type of person who responds to the health and welfare needs of older adults, the competence of such a caregiver, and the locale of the service are all functions of social preferences and public policy.

Microsocial Effects

Microsocial factors affecting the processes and outcomes of aging are illustrated when individuals are easily observed in the various milieus recognizable in everyday life. Irving Rosow[18] summarized a broad range of early research on the effects of milieu in its most common form—residential location and living arrangement—on the well-being of older adults (see also Lawton[19]). Specifically Rosow hypothesized that in a society inclined to prejudice toward aging and discrimination toward the aged, older adults would lack positive models of adaptation to aging. His research suggested that age and socioeconomic homogeneity of neighborhoods increased the probability of supportive interaction and, in turn, perceived well-being of older adults. While this conclusion suggested to some observers an unacceptable argument for age segregation, Rosow's sociological point is valid: The meaning of and responses to aging are not independent of one's social milieu. Powell Lawton and Lucille Nahemow[20] generalized Rosow's basic point in the development of the concept of person–environment fitting—that is, the matching of personal capabilities and preferences with the demands and opportunities of different milieus. The observed competence of an older adult from this perspective is substantially dependent on the types and levels of competences expected or required in a particular milieu and the compensatory resources available to reduce the effects of impairments. Lawton and Nahemow argued that milieus can be both over- and underdemanding and can provide many or few compensatory aids.

The research of Rudolph Moos,[21] an environmental psychologist, also addresses the issue of person–environment fitting in a useful way by analyzing physical, social, and organizational milieus in terms of their positive or negative contributions to therapeutic outcomes. His analysis of the behavioral consequences of physical as well as organizational barriers in institutional settings makes a point that is now becoming better understood in our society as we have become sensitive about the kinds of modifiable barriers which make ordinary personal and interpersonal behavior difficult if not impossible. That is, different milieus in which older adults live are differentially handicapping for individuals with the same level of impairment and disability. For example, Judith Rodin and colleagues[22] have written about long-term care environments which encourage personal disengagement from personal responsibility for self-care and exaggerate dependency. This sort of institutionalized encouragement to disengage from self-care responsibility is well-known in care settings which may define the good resident as passive, nondemanding, and compliant. Rodin's research (see also Arnetz[23]) indicates there are behavioral techniques for increasing the appropriate self-reliance of disabled older adults. Having demonstrated that the potential personal initiative is greater than one may observe, Rodin's work suggests, but answers only implicitly, the next question: If the level of dependency or self-care is manipulable and dependent on the presence or absence of stimuli and incentives in the milieu, then the construction of appropriately stimulating milieus should be a function of the training of caregivers, the philosophy of care among caregivers, and of organizational policies which affect the selection and supervision of caregivers.

CONTINUITIES OF THE LIFE COURSE

The importance of the milieus in which individuals age provides a transition to the second basic proposition of this chapter. Aging processes illustrate important continuities in the way individuals interact with milieus as they age. This person–milieu interaction creates not only recognizable biographies but also patterns of behavior and lifestyle which affect survival and well-being. There are discontinuities and surprises in processes of aging. But longitudinal research in aging has demonstrated repeatedly that the best predictor of a variable in aging is the value of that variable at an earlier time. For example, research in the social sciences on patterns of physical and social activity in adulthood demonstrates that even as levels of activity tend to decline with age, individuals who are rank-ordered on the basis of levels and types of activity tend to hold their rank in relation to peers over time. Similarly, the perception of subjective well-being among adults as excellent or poor tends to remain fairly stable in the later years even though the components of well-being may change. That is, two basic components of well-being—affect (happiness) and satisfaction (realized expectations)—may reflect a changing balance with age so that age-related declines in positive affect may be countered by increases in the sense of satisfaction with life accomplishments to achieve the observed continuity of perceived well-being in later life.[2]

RISK FACTORS AND COHORTS

Two concepts widely used by demographers and epidemiologists are particularly useful in illustrating continuities in the human life course. These concepts are risk factor and cohort. The concept *risk factor* has been popularized in discussions of the etiology of cardiovascular disease. The argument proceeds like this: If one smokes cigarettes; indulges in a diet that includes large quantities of salt, sugar, and fat; ignores the importance of exercise; and handles stress poorly, over time the probability (risk) of cardiovascular illness increases. This sort of argument has interesting sociological implications. The factors most commonly identified which reportedly change the probability of an unwanted outcome are all related to learned, socially reinforced behaviors. Cumulatively these behaviors may pattern as healthy or unhealthy lifestyles reflecting shared, reinforced preferences for living. It is worth noting that research evidence indicates that unhealthy lifestyles are more commonly found in persons of lower socioeconomic status and that, in at least some surveys, older adults tend to display relatively healthy lifestyles.[24] The latter observation may reflect the probability that surveyed older adults have survived in part because their lifestyles are healthy. In any case, discussion of risk factors for survival and well-being reminds one that one's past behavior is a prologue to one's later years.

The second concept of interest is *cohort*. This concept has been introduced by demographers and social scientists to take account of the expected differential experience of individuals born at different times. The timing of birth possibly exposes individuals to distinctively different environmental circumstances, events, or milieus initially and over the course of their development. Eras characterized by overpopulation, war, or economic depression immediately come to mind. The concept also permits the possibility of intracohort variation occasioned by socioeconomic or other social differences affecting person–milieu interaction over the life course (see Ref. 25). To be born in a less developed nation in contrast to a developed nation has easily understandable implications for survival because "less developed" in this case is a proxy for levels of public sanitation, food and water supplied, and health care which are known to predict survival. Similarly, to be born into a family of lower rather than higher socioeconomic status at a point in time in a particular society is associated with a higher probability of minimal education, low income, and social isolation. Or, in contrast, individuals born in the United States in the mid-1920s have been appropriately characterized as one of the most advantaged cohorts in human history. Born at the beginning of a depression, this cohort was relatively small. And, assuming that most would survive the Second World War, their small number inherited a milieu of postwar affluence in which they competed with great success for extensive social and economic resources such as education, income, housing, and eventually public policies intended to secure their retirement income and health care. This cohort of adults are the parents of the Baby Boomers, a very large cohort which succeeded their affluent parents, inherited much more intense competition for social resources, and predictably exhibited elevated rates of social maladjustment (see, e.g., Ref. 26). For worse as well as for better, members of cohorts interact with milieus in the process of development in ways which generate identifiable differences in the problems encountered and the personal and social responses developed.

Several important practical implications of understanding risk factors and cohorts follow. One is that late life is best understood as a later but continuous part of the human life course. The processes and experience of aging do not occur in a vacuum. Individuals as the result of circumstances of birth (e.g., born in a developing or developed country, born in lower or higher socioeconomic status) will age and experience their aging differently. Second, different learned patterns of behavior and lifestyles developed and continued over the life course change the probabilities of survival and well-being in later life. If learned behavior can be presumed to be modifiable, one thinks of potentially beneficial interventions to modify aging processes. The modification of unhealthy lifestyles and the promotion of healthy lifestyles not just in adulthood but also early in life would appear sensible in the interest of well-being in later life. From this perspective, discussions of generational equity which suggest that older adults are being supported at the expense of children as though the distribution is only a matter of equity miss an important point. The social and economic deprivation of children has predictable long-range implications for the aging of future cohorts. The benefits of reducing risk factors early in life by avoiding exposure to dangerous drugs, improving the diet, increasing the amount of exercise, and managing stress more effectively seem obvious enough. One needs, however, to add that equally powerful or more powerful factors affecting well-being over the entire life course are social and societal in origin—ignorance, poverty, and social isolation. These social factors affect the processes of aging and the experience of aging as powerfully as the biomedical and lifestyle factors more frequently discussed. These social factors in aging are also demonstrably modifiable by public policy.

MODIFIABILITY OF AGING PROCESSES

Scientific investigation, as it is normally taught and practiced, we reiterate, emphasizes the search for predictable relationships between variables and, in seeking economical explanations, tends to be reductionistic. Biological theories of aging have tended, for example, to conceptualize aging processes of decline which are intrinsic and hence inevitable. The issue of differential rates of age-related biological change and the explanation of these differences has received less attention. The observed differences in aging processes and the experience of aging are precisely what we have stressed in this chapter. We have stressed them because we believe the observed differences are the outcome of a synergistic interaction of internal biological potential and the activation of this potential through interaction with the externalities we index as milieu, the social resources and institutional arrangements for meeting needs, and the distribution of social and material resources available to and distributed within a society.

In an earlier literature, gerontologists and geriatricians attempted to distinguish between primary and secondary aging. This distinction was meant to differentiate intrinsic biological forces of development from those aspects of development affected by externalities. This, we argue, is a false dichotomy rejected by both contemporary biology and the social sciences. In the contemporary view, biology specifies what genetic potential makes possible in various contexts, not just what genetic structure makes necessary. The social sciences, in turn, index and trace the consequences of the exposure of individuals and cohorts of individuals to different milieus over the course of development.

A first obvious move away from the perception of necessary biological process of decline in gerontology and geriatrics was evident at least a decade ago with the emergence of what might be called "therapeutic optimism." This designation was meant to contrast with an earlier orientation designated "therapeutic nihilism" which focused on a biology of inevitable decline[4] or as Row and Kahn[1] observe, one needs to distinguish between "usual" and "successful aging" as research has increasingly demonstrated that later life is not adequately characterized as a period of uniform decline in biological and related functional capacities (see also Ref. 13).

James Fries was among the first not only to stress the potential for modifying aging processes but also to mix theoretical conjecture with bits of evidence to sug-gest that modification of aging processes have been occurring[27]; for a review of critiques, see Ref. 28. Fries's controversial argument is worth noting briefly because it sheds light on the inadequacy of current evidence about aging processes. His argument had two parts: The first part conjectured that the biological limits of human survival would on average turn out to be about 85 years. Demographic evidence suggests this conjecture is wrong. Age-specific life expectancy is continuing to drift upward even at very advanced ages. Fries's second proposition is that, on theoretical grounds, one might expect a variety of purposive biological and social interventions to delay both the onset of disabling illness and death. Hence, if life expectancy does not increase so as to offset the expected delay in onset of disabling illness, future cohorts of older individuals will display more active years and fewer disabled years in the later years. This optimistic conclusion runs far beyond any available evidence since no country currently has the series of epidemiologic evidence required to answer the question. Katz and colleagues[9] have shown how such a conceptualization can be applied using longitudinal data from Massachusetts; Wilkins and Adams[8] have illustrated promising analyses of survey data on health and functional performance in Canada.

Beyond whether Fries is correct or not, there are data from longitudinal studies of functional capacity for self-care in later life to indicate that significant minorities of functionally disabled older adults indicate improved functional status over a period of 2 years (e.g., see Manton[13]). But again we do not yet have adequate time series data to demonstrate a significant delay in the onset of disabling chronic disease or incapacity for self-care.

The beneficial effects of a variety of social and societal interventions on the quality of life in later adulthood have been suggested and sometimes effectively demonstrated. The health benefits of not smoking cigarettes in particular or cessation of all forms of smoking is now well documented and widely known. Access to adequate social and material resources change the risk of morbidity and mortality favorably whether one is comparing less developed nations which do or do not experience development or comparing socioeconomically deprived individuals who do or do not receive economic, health, and social interventions. There is every reason to expect what one now observes worldwide, as adequate food, water, and sanitation are increasingly available worldwide, and this is that life expectancy at birth and age-specific life expectancy in adults will continue to increase in all societies. This achievement, sometimes referred to as the "First Revolution in Health," ensures the necessity in every society of a Second Revolution as populations age and chronic disease replaces acute disease as a primary health concern. This Second Revolution in health must focus on lifestyle and environmental issues, which are so central to the understanding of and in the response to age-related chronic impairments, disabilities, and handicaps.[4]

At the mesosocial level of intervention, public policy to modify institutional arrangements for income and access to health care has been demonstrably affected in beneficial ways in the United States in the past two decades.[29–31,11] And at the microsocial level of milieu and lifestyle modification, the available evidence indicates that promoting healthy lifestyles has apparently been increasingly effective in achieving beneficial change among at least educated adults (e.g., Berkman[24]). The effects of public policy regarding income maintenance in later adulthood is a story of successful public policy, although the success is far from complete.

Table 11-2 illustrates how social security policy in the United States has reduced poverty among older adults in less than two decades. The reduction is sufficient to produce a rate of poverty among older adults which is slightly below that of children. This fact has activated some expressed concern about generational equity. There is no obvious answer to questions about generational equity, and it is more appropriate here to note the limited success of national income policy for older women in the United States. For older unmarried women in 1984, 20.6 percent were in poverty. For elderly persons with one or more limitations in activities of daily living (ADL), 34.1 percent were poor and another 27.6 percent "near poor." Women were found to be two and a half times more likely than men to be poor or near poor.[32]

The upshot of such evidence of modifiability of the experience of aging is that in gerontology and geriatrics, a reaffirmation of a venerable maxim of clinical and experimental science is observed: If you want to understand something, try to change it. The benefits of aerobic exercise on cardiovascular efficiency and possibly the mood of older adults has been suggested[33]; the possible

restoration of some cognitive functioning through retraining illustrated[34]; and increased self-respect and greater personal responsibility for self-care through modest behavioral interventions demonstrated.[22] Lifestyles affect risks for survival and quality of life.[24] The social milieus of housing, living arrangements, and neighborhoods affect the sense of well-being and the effective expression of independence in later life.[22]

The demonstrated potential for change indicates a realistic basis for optimism without, however, indicating the feasible and reasonable limits of change in aging processes. We also do not have a sense of the limits of desirable change even when change is feasible. In any case, what is feasible is a scientific question. What is desirable is an ethical and political question. Whether we should expect, following Fries, to compress morbidity and to what degree we should expect to compress it is clearly debatable, and the issue will continue to be debated, particularly in the absence of definitive evidence. But there is no question that public policy in regard to sanitation and institutional arrangements for income maintenance, health care, and housing, and the demonstrably beneficial modification of milieus to enhance functioning of older adults have had profoundly beneficial effects on both the objective and subjective well-being of older adults, not only in the United States but in all developed nations.

THE IMPORTANCE OF PUBLIC POLICY

The fourth proposition follows inevitably from the validity of the first three: Societal consensus about allocating resources over the life course affects how individuals age and experience their aging. Resource availability and allocation affect functional capacity and perceived well-being as well as survival. Institutional arrangements affect who wins and who loses in gaining access to income, health care, and the amenities of lifestyle which make growing old a very different experience for the rich and the poor, for the socially integrated and the isolated elderly, for the informed and the ignorant.

In this chapter the focus on the externalities involved in understanding how we grow older has important practical implications for geriatric physicians and, more generally, for all geriatric practitioners. First, observed diversity cautions practitioners to be wary about generalizations regarding the elderly. Contemporary older adults literally are not what they were or will be. This is an obvious implication of the concept of cohort differences discussed above. The changing probability of cohorts of individuals developing and aging differently are obvious enough. Yet the pressure to simplify our thinking about aging processes and aging persons with

TABLE 11-2
Proportion of the Elderly Below Selected Income Thresholds, 1969–1986

Year	*The Poverty Threshold*	*125% of Poverty*	*150% of Poverty*
1969	25.1	35.2	43.3
1975	15.3	25.4	34.9
1980	15.7	25.7	34.4
1983	14.1	22.5	30.2
1986	12.4	20.5	28.0

SOURCE: From Moon M: The economic situation of older Americans: Emerging wealth and continuing hardship, in Maddox G, Lawton P (eds): *Varieties in Aging, Annual Review of Gerontology and Geriatrics.* New York, Springer, 1988, vol 8, chap 4.

facile stereotypes is persistently powerful. Stereotyping encourages inappropriate projection of personal, socially reinforced expectations about later life. "What do you expect at your age?" clinicians may ask an older patient or client even when they probably do not have a large and definitive factual basis for answering that question. Factual evidence indicates that there would have to be many different answers to that question.

But there is an even more significant reason for gerontological and geriatric practitioners to study how externalities affect aging processes and the experience of aging. Kane and Kane[35] in their comparative study of long-term care in three Canadian provinces noted the persistent tension between two competing perspectives on long-term care: One is that the disabling functional impairments of later life are most adequately viewed as the domain of medicine and hospitals, although with some need for social interventions. The competing perspective is that geriatric care is more adequately perceived as basically a social process best pursued in a community setting with appropriate assistance from health practitioners. The attractiveness of these alternative viewpoints and the probability of acting on one or the other is very much dependent on sociocultural values and how the preferences related to these values are embedded in the training of professional caregivers and the expectations of laypersons.

In the United States, in fact in Western industrial countries generally, the care of older adults has been primarily a medical affair and resources have been concentrated in the institutional context of hospitals and nursing homes. Experienced geriatricians, one suspects, recognize that one of their greatest and necessary skills may be as a care manager who takes into consideration the reality that the externalities of income, housing, and social support have a great deal to do with determining well-being in later life. But different societies are clearly pursuing with more or less confidence and vigor quite different facets of issues and problems related to the aging of populations.[17] For example, the United Kingdom and Sweden have maintained strong medically oriented and hospital-based geriatricians. Both are advanced welfare states with well-developed income maintenance programs for older citizens, established traditions of integrated social and medical services and a broad range of alternative housing other than nursing homes for dependent elderly. Geriatric care in Britain and Sweden is unambiguously primarily the responsibility of the public sector.

The United States, in contrast to the United Kingdom and Sweden, has continued to assert the private sector's primacy in responsibility for aging populations, particularly in regard to health care. This has continued to be the case even as public investment in geriatric care has escalated upward in the past two decades. Public policy regarding geriatric care remains ambiguous and without obvious consensus, however, regarding the preferred mix of public and private responsibility. Certainly there is no evidence of political interest in a national health service or a national health insurance system or in the systematic integration of health and social services. Issues related to long-term care illustrate the ambiguities and ambivalence in the United States regarding public policy regarding geriatric care.

Even though relatively high cost nursing homes have not ensured quality care, no consensus has emerged for alternatives to the institutionalization of dependent older adults. Community-based care has not emerged as more than a theoretically cost-effective alternative to institutionalization[36] because no politically acceptable alternative to a fragmented health and welfare system has been identified. Consequently, long-term care remains the last great risk of life that has remained inadequately insured even for most middle-and upper-income individuals.[37] In 1985 slightly more than half of expenditures for long-term care were paid for privately. Most of the public sector payment for care (42 of 47 percent) was provided by medicaid, clearly a public welfare mechanism in the United States. In the late 1980s legislation ostensibly creating protection against catastrophic illness in later life proved to be protection against acute medical illness in hospital settings. This financial risk is demonstrably secondary to the much greater financial risk of the average older adult for long-term care in a nursing home setting in 1988 at an average cost of $22,000 per year.

A recent analysis of researchers at The Brookings Institution[16] reaches a pessimistic conclusion regarding a change of national public policy regarding long-term care in the United States. Under realistic assumptions about the current and future cost of care and personal economic resources of adults, no more than 30 to 40 percent of adults will be able to afford to insure long-term care adequately. The great majority (60 to 70 percent) will have to depend on public provision of care, a provision which The Brookings researchers conclude is likely to continue to be the existing medicaid procedure requiring certification of indigence as a condition of eligibility.

Attention to long-term care is not given with the intention to view with alarm the current situation in the United States or to suggest an easy solution. The point rather is to make clear that a basic issue in care and welfare in later life remains a matter of achieving political consensus regarding objectives and responsibilities and the related political will to act on that consensus. The future of welfare in later life will, for better or worse, be invented by thoughtful political action or inherited by default. It is not "Nature" so much as the preferences of effective political groups in a society which determine how populations grow older and deal with their aging and how health and welfare institutions serving older adults are staffed and managed.

REFERENCES

1. Rowe J, Kahn R: Human aging: Usual and successful. *Science* 237:143, 1987.
2. Maddox GL: Aging differently. *Gerontologist* 27:5:557, 1987.
3. Maddox G, Lawton P: *Varieties in Aging: Annual Review of Gerontology and Geriatrics*, vol 8. New York, Springer, 1988.
4. Maddox GL: Modifying the social environment, in Holland W et al (eds): *Oxford Textbook of Public Health*, vol 2. London, Oxford University Press, 1985.
5. Metropolitan Life: New longevity record in the United States, *Statistical bulletin*, July-September 1988, p 10.
6. Myers G: Aging and worldwide population change, in Binstock R, Shanas E (eds): *Handbook of Aging and the Social Sciences*, 2nd ed. New York, Van Nostrand Reinhold, 1985, p 173.
7. Syme SL, Berkman LF: Social class, susceptibility and sickness. *Am J Epidemiol* 104:1, 1976.
8. Wilkins R, Adams O: *Healthfulness of Life: A Unified View of Mortality, Institutionalization and Non-institutionalized Disability Research*. Montreal, Institute for Research in Public Policy, 1978.
9. Katz S et al: Active life expectancy. *N Engl J Med* 309:1218, 1983.
10. O'Rand A: Covergence, institutionalization and bifurcation: Gender and the pension acquisition process, in Maddox G, Lawton P (eds): *Varieties in Aging: Annual Review of Gerontology and Geriatrics*. New York, Springer, 1988, vol 8, chap 5.
11. Wolinsky F, Arnold L: A different perspective on health and health service utilization, in Maddox G, Lawton P (eds): *Varieties in Aging: Annual Review of Gerontology and Geriatrics*. New York, Springer, 1988, vol 8, chap 3.
12. Shapiro E: The relevance of research on aging to policy making and planning: Evidence from the Manitoba longitudinal studies of aging, in Brody J, Maddox G (eds): *Epidemiology and Aging*. New York, Springer, 1988, chap 11, p 167.
13. Manton K: Planning long-term care for heterogeneous populations, in Maddox G, Lawton P (eds): *Varieties in Aging: Annual Review of Gerontology and Geriatrics*. New York, Springer, 1988, vol 8, chap 8.
14. Rabin D, Stockton P: *Long Term Care for the Elderly: A Factbook*. New York, Oxford University Press, 1987, chap 12.
15. Swan J et al: State medicaid reimbursement for nursing homes, 1978–86. *Health Care Financ Rev* 9:3:33, 1988.
16. Rivlin A et al: Insuring long-term care, in Maddox G, Lawton P (eds): *Varieties in Aging: Annual Review of Gerontology and Geriatrics*. New York, Springer, 1988, vol 8, chap 9.
17. Eisdorfer C, Maddox G: *The Role of Hospitals in Geriatric Care*. New York, Springer, 1988.
18. Rosow I: *Social Integration of the Aged*. New York, The Free Press, 1967.
19. Lawton P: Housing and living environments of older people, in Binstock R, Shanas E (eds): *Handbook of Aging and the Social Sciences*, 2nd ed. New York, Van Nostrand Reinhold, 1985, p 450.
20. Lawton P, Nahemow L: Ecology and the aging process, in Eisdorfer C, Lawton P (eds): *Psychology of Adult Development and Aging*. Washington, American Psychological Association, 1973.
21. Moos R: Specialized living arrangements for older people, *J Soc Issues* 36:75, 1980.
22. Rodin J et al: The construct of control, in Lawton P, Maddox G (eds): *Annual Review of Gerontology and Geriatrics*. New York, Springer, 1985, vol 5, chap 1, p 3.
23. Arnetz B: Interaction of biomedical and psychosocial factors in research on aging, in Lawton P, Maddox G (eds): *Annual Review of Gerontology and Geriatrics*. New York, Springer, 1985, vol 5, chap 2, p 56.
24. Berkman L: The changing and heterogeneous nature of aging and longevity: A social and biomedical perspective, in Maddox G, Lawton P (eds): *Varieties in Aging: Annual Review of Gerontology and Geriatrics*. New York, Springer, 1988, vol 8, chap 2.
25. Maddox G, Campbell R: Scope, concepts and methods in the study of aging, in Binstock R, Shanas E (eds): *Handbook of Aging and the Social Sciences*, 2nd ed. New York, Van Nostrand Reinhold, 1985, p 3.
26. Easterlin R: *Birth and Fortune*. New York, Basic Books, 1980.
27. Fries J: Aging, natural death, and the compression of morbidity. *N Engl J Med* 303:130, 1980.
28. White L et al: Epidemiology of aging, in Eisdorfer C (ed): *Annual Review of Gerontology and Geriatrics*. New York, Springer, 1986, vol 6, chap 6.
29. Clark R, Maddox G et al: *The Economic Well-being of the Elderly*. Baltimore, Johns Hopkins University Press, 1984.
30. Moon M: The economic situation of older Americans: Emerging wealth and continuing hardship, in Maddox G, Lawton P (eds): *Varieties in Aging: Annual Review of Gerontology and Geriatrics*. New York, Springer, 1988, vol 8, chap 4.
31. Chen Y-P: Better options for work and retirement: Some suggestions for improving economic security mechanisms for old age, in Maddox G, Lawton P (eds): *Varieties in Aging: Annual Review of Gerontology and Geriatrics*. New York, Springer, 1988, vol 8, chap 7.
32. Commonwealth Fund: *Medicare's Poor: A Report of the Commission on Elderly People Living Alone*. New York, November 20, 1987.
33. Blumenthal J et al: Psychological and physiological effects of physical conditioning on the elderly. *J Psychosom Res* 26:5:505, 1982.
34. Schaie W, Willis S: Can decline in intellectual functioning be reversed? *Dev Psychol* 22:223, 1986.
35. Kane R, Kane R: *A Will and a Way: What the United States Can Learn from Canada about Caring for the Elderly*. New York, Columbia University Press, 1985.
36. Maddox GL: The continuum of care: Movement toward the community, in Busse E, Blazer D (eds): *Handbook of Geriatric Psychiatry*. New York, Van Nostrand Reinhold, 1980.
37. Somers AR: Insurance for long-term care. *N Engl J Med* 317:23, 1982.

Chapter 12

RISK FACTORS FOR MORBIDITY AND MORTALITY IN OLDER POPULATIONS: AN EPIDEMIOLOGIC APPROACH

Trudy L. Bush, Susan R. Miller, Michael H. Criqui, and Elizabeth Barrett-Connor

This chapter discusses risk factors for morbidity (nonfatal conditions and disability) and mortality in older persons. *Risk factors* may be defined as innate or acquired characteristics of individuals which are associated with an increased likelihood of a disease or condition. Of particular importance are those factors which are amenable to change and/or treatment, since it may be possible to alter the risk of morbid and mortal events by altering the risk factor.

It may be argued that the identification of risk factors for mortality in older individuals is less important than in younger persons, since it is possible only to delay death. The biologic limit to the human life span now appears to be around 100 years of age. However, our goal as physicians and public health practitioners is to postpone death, enabling more persons to live out their full life spans, that is, to prevent the deaths occurring in individuals in their seventh and eighth decades.

Perhaps even more important than the potential to delay death is the potential to delay or even avoid morbidity and disability. Consequently, the identification of risk factors for nonfatal conditions associated with serious sequelae may, in the long run, enable older persons to live out that full life span in good health. Even if we are unable to extend life, the prevention of morbid events,

including impairments, disabilities, and handicaps, is a most worthy goal.

Until recently, the principal purpose of identifying risk factors has been to prevent "premature" mortality and morbidity, with the definition of a premature event as one which occurs in persons younger than 60 years of age. Thus, the majority of major studies on antecedents of coronary heart disease, cancers, and other common conditions has included primarily middle-aged individuals as participants. Few studies have looked exclusively or even primarily at antecedents of fatal and nonfatal events in older people.

Nevertheless, there is a growing recognition that the old definition of a "premature" event is outdated. In the last two decades the marked decline in death rates from coronary heart disease and stroke in persons over 65 years of age provided empirical evidence that mortality can be delayed in the oldest individuals. It may be argued now that a conservative definition of a "premature" death is one that occurs before age 75.

Conventional wisdom holds that traditional risk factors for morbidity and mortality (e.g., smoking, elevated blood pressure, elevated serum cholesterol) are less important, or even unimportant, in older persons. The implication of this "wisdom" is that there is little personal or public health benefit to be gained by modifying risk factors in older people. However, this view, that conventional risk factors are unimportant determinants of disease and disability in older persons, has been inferred from information which is both dated and limited.

As an example, many studies have found no association between smoking and mortality in older adults. However, these reports have failed to consider that the negative results may represent methodologic problems of survivorship bias or a cohort effect. That is, smoking and mortality may appear not to be associated in older people because insufficient numbers of older persons who had smoked survived into old age, or because too few older persons smoked.

In this chapter we examine known and suspected risk factors for coronary heart disease, stroke, cancer, and fractures in older people. These specific conditions were chosen because they are (1) common in older individuals; (2) the major causes of death and of functional disability in older persons; and (3) associated with significant health care costs. In addition, risk factors for these conditions have been identified in younger individuals, and modification of these risk factors results in a reduced risk of death/morbidity in younger people.

Currently there is no consensus on the definition of older persons, although individuals 65 years and older are, by convention, considered to be older. Thus, most of the data presented in this chapter will be from studies of individuals 65 years of age and older. Of necessity, however, some of the data discussed here will be from studies of individuals over 55 or 60 years of age.

AGE AND SEX AS RISK FACTORS

AGE

Chronologic age is the most consistent and robust predictor of morbidity and mortality in both sexes across the entire life span. In other words, the age of an individual is the best indicator of his or her risk of dying and/or of having a chronic disease or disability.

Figure 12-1 presents all-cause death rates by 5-year age groups for men and women in the United States in 1984.[1] (Mortality data on persons older than 84 years of age are not available in 5-year increments.) As evident from this figure, there is an exponential increase in mortality with increasing chronologic age. This association of age with mortality is consistent across the entire age span, with each 5-year increase in age associated with an approximately 50 percent increased risk of death.

An increase in disability and morbidity is also associated with increasing chronologic age. Figure 12-2 presents the proportion of the noninstitutionalized elderly population having difficulty performing selected activi-

ties of daily living by age groups.[2] As can be seen in this figure, the prevalence of all disabilities is higher at each successive age; each 10-year increase in age is associated with a 50 to 100 percent increase in the prevalence of a specific disability.

The percent of older persons with selected chronic conditions and sensory impairments (loss of hearing or visual acuity) by age is presented in Fig. 12-3. These data, from a geriatric screening program located in Dunedin, Florida (the Florida Geriatric Research Program), clearly indicate that increasing age is associated with higher prevalence of morbid conditions. The burden of morbid conditions by age is underestimated, however, since comorbidity (the presence of multiple chronic conditions) also increases with increasing age.

SEX

Next to chronologic age, an individual's sex is the most important predictor of mortality. Men at every age, even the oldest ages, have mortality rates 60 to 80 percent higher than women (Fig. 12-4). On average, death rates in women lag behind those in men by approximately 8 years.

A common misconception is that the female advantage in mortality is rapidly lost after menopause, and that at advanced ages women "catch up" to men vis à vis their mortality experiences. However, the data do not support this thesis. Younger women (in their forties and fifties) have mortality rates about 45 percent lower than men of the same ages; in postmenopausal women in their sixties and seventies, mortality rates also are 45 percent lower than similarly aged men. Even at the oldest ages (i.e., 85 years and older), women have death rates 22 percent lower than men.[1]

While female sex is protective against death at the older ages, this same protection is not afforded for disabilities and morbidity (Figs. 12-5 and 12-6). Compared to men of similar ages, women over 65 years of age have more difficulty performing more activities of daily living. For example, as seen in Fig. 12-5, women have more difficulty walking, bathing, dressing, going outside, getting out of a bed or chair, and using a toilet than do men.[2]

Likewise, women do not have any apparent advantage in actual burden of disease. As demonstrated by data from the Florida Geriatric Research Program (Fig. 12-6), women and men have about an equal prevalence of diabetes, sensory deprivation, and gastrointestinal problems, men are somewhat more likely than women to have cardiovascular diseases and cancer, and women are more likely to have bone and joint conditions and hypertension.

In summary, both age and sex are consistent and immutable risk factors for mortality across the entire life

FIGURE 12-1
Death rates by age, United States, 1984.

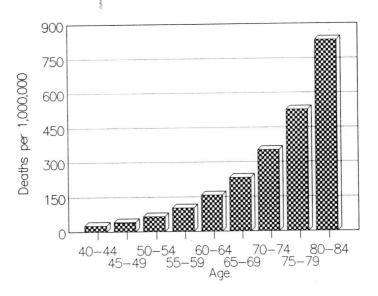

FIGURE 12-2
Percent of older persons with difficulty doing daily activities, by age.

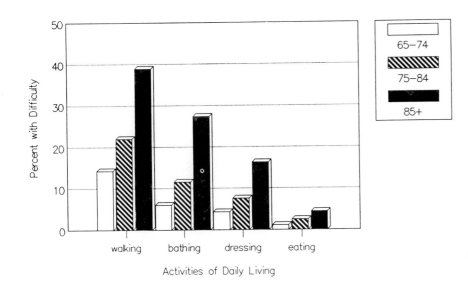

FIGURE 12-3
Percent of older persons with selected chronic conditions, by age.

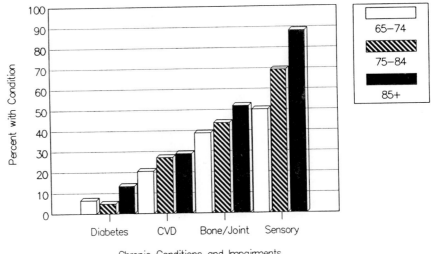

127

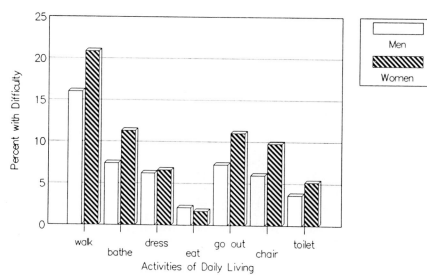

Men

Women

FIGURE 12-4
Death rates by sex and age, United States, 1984.

FIGURE 12-5
Percent of older persons with difficulty doing daily activities, by sex.

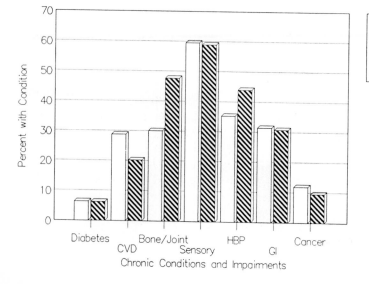

FIGURE 12-6
Percent of older persons with selected chronic conditions, by sex.

128

span, including old age. Increasing age is associated with increasing risk of death, with the risk increasing exponentially by age for each sex. However, at every age, females have a clear advantage compared to males. Nonetheless, older women tend to have somewhat greater disability than older men and about the same burden of chronic conditions.

RISK FACTORS FOR SELECTED CONDITIONS

CORONARY HEART DISEASE

Coronary heart disease (CHD) is the major killer of older people,[1] accounting for 31 percent of all deaths in both men and women over 65 years of age. CHD also accounts for significant health costs and is a major cause of disability in older people. The prevalence of CHD and limitations in activities as a result of the disease have been increasing during the past two decades.[2,3] As a result of the aging of the entire population, a 40 percent increase in the prevalence and cost of CHD by the beginning of the new century is expected.[4]

However, since the mid-1960s, mortality from CHD has been declining at all ages, including the oldest ages.[2] Even in recent years (between 1979 and 1984), there has been a substantial decline in coronary deaths in older people (Table 12-1). This recent decline is substantial (7 percent) in those over 85 years and in the younger elderly (65–74 years) (13 percent). This evidence suggests that both medical interventions and changes in lifestyle may have contributed to this decline in mortality.[5]

These observations of decreasing CHD mortality in the elderly are compatible with the thesis that risk factors and risk factor changes can impact on the risk of CHD mortality even at the oldest ages. A growing body of evidence suggests that CHD is not an inevitable expression of normal senescence but is a disease process in persons of all ages (see Chapter 46). Some data from earlier studies suggested that the traditional risk factors for CHD were weaker at the advanced ages. However, even if this were the case (i.e., that a risk factor demonstrated a lesser relative effect in older ages), the high prevalence of risk factors and the high incidence of CHD

at older ages would mean that the absolute impact of risk factor reduction could be greater in that age range.[6] Further, there is mounting evidence, reviewed below, that risk factors which predict CHD in midlife also predict CHD at the older ages.[7–10]

Lipids and Lipoproteins

In younger individuals, total cholesterol, high-density lipoproteins (HDL), and low-density lipoproteins (LDL) are all major predictors of CHD. However, in older individuals the data are both limited and conflicting. The prevalence of hyperlipidemia is lower in older people, which may reflect (1) a survivorship effect (persons with hyperlipidemia on average die younger); (2) a cohort effect (persons born earlier in the century have lower lipid levels); or (3) an effect of other illnesses on lipid levels. Thus, many of the studies which have evaluated lipids as predictors of CHD in older people have insufficient power to detect a lipid effect.

TOTAL SERUM CHOLESTEROL Data from three large prospective studies, the Framingham Study,[7] Rancho Bernardo,[10] and the Lipid Research Clinics' (LRC) Follow-Up Study[9] suggest that total cholesterol continues to be a risk factor for coronary heart disease in individuals over 65 years of age. Other studies have also demonstrated that elevated cholesterol levels are associated with an increased risk of CHD in persons over 60 years of age.[8,11] However, older and smaller studies have not demonstrated a positive association.[12–14]

In the Framingham study, total cholesterol was statistically significantly associated with an increased risk of CHD in older women. In that 30-year follow-up, women who had total cholesterol levels over 295 mg/dl had CHD rates approximately 75 percent higher than women with cholesterol levels less than 205 mg/dl. Although the association between total cholesterol and CHD in the Framingham men was not statistically significant, men with clearly elevated total cholesterol levels (over 295 mg/dl) had CHD rates over 70 percent higher than men with more desirable levels (under 205 mg/dl).

Total cholesterol levels were significantly predictive of CHD mortality among men and women aged 65 to 79 years in the Rancho Bernardo study.[10] Men and women in the highest quintile of cholesterol had death rates 40 to 50 percent higher than those in the lowest quintile.

In the LRC Program Follow-Up Study, total cholesterol levels were significantly predictive of subsequent CHD mortality in both men and women over 65 years of age. Among the men, each 20 mg/dl increase in total cholesterol was associated with a 17 percent increased risk of CHD death. Among the older women the associa-

TABLE 12-1
Percent Decline in Mortality from Ischemic Heart Disease 1979–1984 by Age and Sex

Age	Men	Women
65–74	−15.8%	− 9.7%
75–84	−10.3%	−11.6%
85+	− 7.4%	− 6.6%

tion was somewhat stronger, with each 20 mg/dl increase in total cholesterol associated with a 29 percent increased risk of CHD mortality.

HDL AND LDL CHOLESTEROL Data from both the Framingham and LRC studies support the thesis that HDL and LDL cholesterol are significant determinants of CHD in elderly persons. In Framingham participants between the ages of 50 and 82 years, HDL cholesterol was strongly and inversely associated with risk of developing CHD in both men and women.[15] In this same cohort, LDL cholesterol was positively and significantly associated with CHD incidence in both men and women. For both sexes HDL was the stronger predictor of CHD.

In the LRC study, LDL was positively and significantly associated with CHD death in both older men and women; an increase of 20 mg/dl of LDL cholesterol was associated with a 17 percent increased risk of CHD death in older men and a 32 percent increased risk of CHD death in older women. However, HDL was only significantly associated with CHD death in women.

Smoking

The adverse health consequences of smoking are clearly established in younger individuals. However, the health effects of smoking in older persons are less well defined. The prevalence of smoking is lowest in the oldest ages, which may be partly explained by a survivorship effect. Nonetheless, recent estimates indicate that 20 percent of elderly men and 13 percent of elderly women currently smoke. Among these men and women, 53 percent and 21 percent, respectively, are former smokers.[2]

Currently, cigarette smoking is a major risk factor for cardiovascular disease mortality and morbidity in both men and women under 65 years of age. Further, there is clear evidence of a dose–response association between number of cigarettes smoked and risk of CHD at these ages.[7,8,16]

Among older people, the association between smoking and CHD is less clear. In the Framingham study there was no significant association between smoking and CHD incidence in men or women aged 65 to 94 years, although older men smoking more than two packs a day had CHD rates 40 percent higher than nonsmokers.[7] Several other large studies (American Cancer Society and the Canadian Veterans Study) also found no significantly increased risk among older smokers.

In contrast, other studies have reported an increased risk of CHD in older smokers, although the findings are not always concordant by sex. Results from the British Physicians Study indicated that smoking clearly increased the risk of CHD among female physicians of all ages; however, smoking was not a predictor for CHD in the older male physicians. Likewise, elderly women living in Massachusetts who smoked had an increased risk of death compared to nonsmokers; among men there was no association between smoking and mortality.[17] An analysis of pilot data from the Systolic Hypertension in the Elderly Program (SHEP) found that smoking was a significant predictor of first cardiovascular event, myocardial infarction, and sudden death.[18] And, in a large prospective study of over 2500 poor men aged 65 and 74 years, current smokers compared to exsmokers or to those who had never smoked had a 52 percent excess risk of CHD death.[19]

Hypertension

High blood pressure is very common in people over 65 years of age in the United States; 41 percent of women and 33 percent of men aged 65 to 74 years and 48 percent of women and 29 percent of men over 75 years reported hypertension (systolic > 160 mmHg and/or diastolic > 95 mmHg).[2] Isolated systolic hypertension (systolic > 160 mmHg and diastolic < 90 mmHg) is seen less frequently and has been estimated to occur in 7 percent of older persons.[20]

Unlike other risk factors for CHD in the elderly, the evidence regarding hypertension as a risk factor for CHD at older ages is strong. Elevations of both systolic and diastolic blood pressures are associated with an increased risk of CHD in both men and women. In the Framingham study, for example, men and women 65 to 94 years with systolic pressures > 180 mmHg had risk of CHD 300 to 400 percent higher than those with systolic pressures < 120 mmHg. Likewise, men and women with diastolic pressures > 105 mmHg had a risk of CHD nearly 200 to 300 percent higher than those with diastolic pressures < 75 mmHg.[7] Other studies in different populations generally support the Framingham results.[8,21] However, a recent study from Finland suggests that after age 85, lower blood pressure may be associated with an increased risk of cardiovascular death.[22]

Isolated systolic hypertension also appears to be associated with a significantly increased risk of CHD. Framingham participants aged 55 to 74 years with isolated systolic hypertension had a 200 to 500 percent excess risk of cardiovascular death during a 2-year follow-up.[23] The 1979 Build and Blood Pressure Study reported that insured persons with isolated systolic hypertension had mortality rates 51 percent higher than normotensive individuals.[24] Additionally, a cohort study of upper middle class individuals living in California found a 200 to 300 percent increased risk of cardiovascular death among those persons 60 years or older with isolated systolic hypertension.[25]

There is also a body of evidence suggesting that

treating diastolic hypertension in older persons reduces the risk of CHD. Data from both the U.S.-based Hypertension Detection and Follow-up Program and the Australian Nation Blood Pressure Study show that antihypertensive therapy in persons 60 to 69 years of age significantly reduces the risk of cardiovascular morbidity and mortality.[26,27] Additionally, the European Working Party on High Blood Pressure in the Elderly Trial reported a 38 percent reduction of fatal cardiac events among persons over 60 years of age randomized to antihypertensive therapy.[28] However, one large ($N = 884$) randomized trial in persons 60 to 79 years found no benefit of antihypertensive therapy in preventing coronary disease, although a significant reduction in stroke was observed.[29]

It is currently unknown whether treating isolated systolic hypertension in older people will result in a reduction of their risk of CHD. An ongoing trial in the United States (the Systolic Hypertension in the Elderly Program) is designed to answer this question.

Physical Activity

A recent review of the effects of physical activity on disease risk concluded that habitual exercise was inversely related to the risk of CHD at all ages.[30] Further, it was suggested that the elderly, as a group, might benefit significantly by increasing their levels of habitual physical activity. Unfortunately, most of the data on physical activity and CHD risk in both younger and older persons come from observational studies. Thus, it remains uncertain whether physical activity appears beneficial for CHD because healthier people are more likely to exercise, or if physical activity prevents CHD.

Physical activity has been found to be inversely related to CHD risk in older individuals in several (but not all) studies. In the Alameda County study, in which persons 60 to 94 years of age were followed for 17 years, a relatively crude measure of physical activity, i.e., "having little leisure time for physical activity," was significantly associated with the risk of death.[31]

Similarly, in a study of Harvard alumni, the risk of death decreased with increasing levels of exercise, even at the oldest ages (70–84 years) and after adjusting for preexisting illness.[32] However, not all studies have demonstrated a protective effect of physical activity. In a 5-year follow-up study of people over 65 years in Massachusetts, physical activity did not predict risk of death or CHD once preexisting illnesses were considered.[17]

Physical activity could impact directly on the risk of CHD or could effect the occurrence of CHD by altering other CHD risk factors. One study reported that older people who exercised were more likely to be nonsmokers and to have better weight control than more sedentary people.[33] In a large group of men over 60 years of age, both serum cholesterol and blood pressure were inversely related to leisure time activity.[34] Physical activity has also been associated with improvement in glucose tolerance, insulin resistance, and neuropsychological functioning in older individuals.[35–37]

There is also evidence suggesting that older people, even those who had been previously sedentary, can become conditioned by a regular exercise program.[35] One report of 112 men 52 to 87 years of age found significant improvement in several physiologic measures, particularly oxygen transport capacity, after as little as 6 weeks of vigorous training.[38] Another study found significant improvements in maximum work load and maximum oxygen uptake in eight women and four men (mean age, 71 years) who trained for 3 months on a bicycle ergometer.[39] Further, there is some agreement among cardiologists that exercise training (cardiac rehabilitation) is appropriate for older persons with clinical manifestations of CHD.[40–42] However, this view remains controversial.[43]

Obesity

The positive association between overweight, obesity, and risk of CHD is generally accepted for younger individuals.[44] However, the association between overweight, obesity, and CHD in older persons is less well studied and remains controversial.[45,46]

In 597 nonsmoking men and 1126 nonsmoking women over 65 years of age followed for up to 23 years in the Framingham study,[47] the risk of cardiovascular mortality among the heaviest was increased. Women with body mass greater than the 70th percentile had about twice the risk of dying from cardiovascular disease than women whose body mass was between the 30th and 49th percentile. In men, an increase in body mass was also associated with a 40 percent increased risk of cardiovascular death; only the results in women were statistically significant.

These results are compared to a very large Norwegian study, which reported on the association between body mass and mortality among men and women aged 65 and older ($N = 236,000$).[48] Among the men, a slightly increased risk of death (approximately 10 percent) was seen for those whose body mass index (BMI) was greater than 29 kg/m^2. Among the younger women (65 to 79 years), an increased risk of mortality (approximately 15 percent) was observed for those whose BMI was greater than 31 kg/m^2. However, there was no association between BMI and risk of death in the oldest women (those over 80 years of age).

In a follow-up study of very old persons (over 85 years) living in Finland, BMI was found to be negatively associated with subsequent risk of mortality.[49] The lowest 5-year mortality rate was seen in the group of persons with a BMI greater than 30 kg/m^2, leading the authors to conclude that "moderate overweight may . . . be a sign of good health."

In all three studies cited above, thinness was strongly associated with subsequent risk of death in older persons. In Framingham, the thinnest men and women were nearly twice as likely to die from cardiovascular disease than more "normal" sized (30th < BMI < 49th percentile) persons. Likewise in the Norwegian study, men with a BMI less than 21 kg/m^2 and women with a BMI less than 23 kg/m^2 were at an increased risk of death. In the Finnish study, the highest 5-year mortality rates were observed for persons with a BMI less than 20 kg/m^2. These results support the hypothesis that there is a U-shaped association between body mass and mortality in older people.

Estrogen Use

In virtually all published studies, estrogen replacement therapy appears to protect against the development of fatal and nonfatal CHD among older women. However, of the two published reports from the Framingham Study, one shows no effect of estrogen use on CHD risk in women over 60,[50] and the other shows a slight increased risk.[51] In two large prospective studies[52,53] unopposed estrogen therapy was associated with a dramatic (greater than 50 percent) reduction in risk of CHD in women over 70 years of age. It has been suggested that estrogen-altered lipoprotein fractions account for much of the protective effect of estrogen use.

STROKE

Cerebrovascular disease is primarily a disease of older individuals.[54] The death rates from stroke increase exponentially with age and are higher in men than in women

TABLE 12-2
Percent Decline in Mortality from Stroke 1979–1984 by Age and Sex

Age	Men	Women
65–74	−23.2%	−20.8%
75–84	−22.1%	−20.4%
85+	−17.9%	−16.5%

(Fig. 12-7). Stroke is the third leading cause of mortality in older Americans, accounting for more than 150,000 deaths each year. Nonfatal strokes are common (7 percent of persons over 65 have had a stroke) and may be associated with significant disability.[55]

Stroke mortality has been declining in the United States since as early as 1915. The downward trend had remained relatively constant until the early 1970s, when the rates began to decline even more steeply.[56] This decline in stroke mortality has continued up to 1984 (the latest date for which data are available) and is seen for both men and women at all ages (Table 12-2). The identification and treatment of hypertensive persons has been suggested to account for most of the observed decline.[56]

Hypertension

Both diastolic and isolated systolic hypertension increase the risk of stroke. Further, the risk of stroke increases almost linearly for all levels of systolic and diastolic pressures.[56] Most observational studies find that individuals with systolic blood pressures over 160 mmHg and/or diastolic pressures over 95 mmHg have a two- to threefold increased risk of stroke compared to normotensive individuals.

Treatment of hypertension in the elderly has been demonstrated to reduce the risk of stroke. In the Euro-

FIGURE 12-7
Death rates from stroke, United States, 1984, by sex and age group.

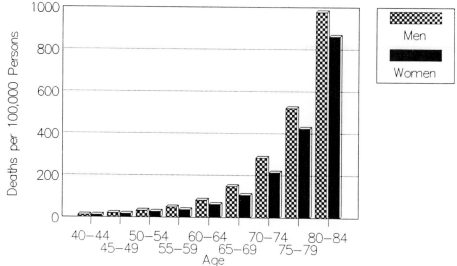

pean Working Party on High Blood Pressure in the Elderly Trial, cerebrovascular mortality was reduced 32 percent in the treated group compared to controls.[28] In a second randomized trial, fatal strokes were reduced to 30 percent, and all strokes (fatal and nonfatal) were reduced 58 percent in the group treated for their hypertension.[29]

Diabetes

Clinical diabetes is also a suspected risk factor for stroke, although the data are not consistent. Results from the Framingham study indicate that diabetic compared to nondiabetic individuals have over twice the risk of stroke. Data from the Chicago Stroke Study also found a significantly increased risk of stroke (approximately 65 percent) among diabetic persons.[57] Of particular concern are individuals who have both hypertension and diabetes. The risk of stroke in these persons is approximately six times that in individuals with neither risk factor.[55]

Other Factors

Other risk factors for atherosclerosis, including smoking, serum lipids and lipoproteins, exercise, personality characteristics, and obesity, have not been shown to be consistent predictors of stroke. While hypertension appears to be the strongest predictor of stroke occurrence, the decline in stroke mortality seen in this country occurred long before effective antihypertensive therapy was available. This latter observation suggests additional risk factors, perhaps dietary ones, are influencing the occurrence of stroke. Two dietary candidates include sodium intake (hypothesized to be positively associated

with hypertension) and potassium intake (shown to be negatively associated with stroke occurrence).[58]

CANCER

Cancers are the second leading cause of mortality in older persons, accounting for almost 20 percent of all deaths in individuals over 65 years of age. Although only 12 percent of the U.S. population is over 65 years of age, 65 percent of all cancer fatalities occur in this group.[1] Unfortunately, relatively few studies have specifically examined risk factors for cancers in elderly individuals.

Risk factors for cancer at all ages include smoking, diet, environmental exposures, and family history. However, the most important risk factors for cancer in older persons are probably smoking and diet.[59] The most commonly occurring tumors in older persons are lung, colon, and breast. Thus, the risk factors briefly reviewed below (smoking and diet) are somewhat specific to these tumor sites.

Smoking

It has been suggested that 25 to 35 percent of all cancers occurring in the United States are the result of cigarette smoking, with the majority of these tumors being cancer of the lung. Further, lung cancers occur most frequently in older people; 60 percent of all lung cancer deaths occur in persons over 65 years of age (Fig. 12-8). In men over 65 years of age, smoking is associated with a 12-fold increased risk of lung cancer.[60] Among older women, the risk of lung cancer in smokers compared to nonsmokers ranges from a three- to fivefold excess risk.[61]

Smoking has also been shown to be significantly associated with tumors of other sites in older men. Compared to nonsmokers, men smoking cigarettes had ex-

FIGURE 12-8
Death rates from lung cancer, United States, 1984, by sex and age group.

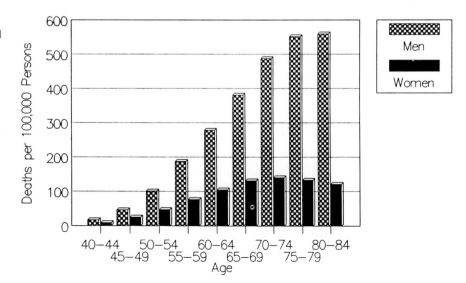

cess risk for dying from kidney cancer (relative risk [RR] = 1.6), bladder cancer (RR = 3.0), esophageal cancer (RR = 1.7), cancer of the larynx (RR = 9.0), and cancer of the buccal cavity (RR = 2.9).[60]

Diet

Many nutrients have been suggested to increase or decrease the risk of cancer.[62,63] These nutrients include fiber, vitamin C, vitamin A and retinoids, vitamin E, trace minerals, alcohol, and fats. Again, very few studies have specifically looked at dietary factors as predictors of death in older persons.

One study, however, reported on 1271 residents of Massachusetts over 65 years of age who were followed for 5 years.[64] Persons in the highest quintile of intake of green and yellow vegetables had a significantly reduced risk for all cancer mortality (RR = 0.3) and all cause mortality (RR = 0.5) compared to persons in the lowest quintile. The authors attribute this apparent protective effect to the provitamin A content of the vegetables. In contrast, another study found no association between vitamin supplementation and mortality in a group of health-conscious older people.[65]

It has been suggested that dietary fat increases the risk for both colon cancer and breast cancers.[62,63] However, the epidemiologic data on the association between fat intake and these tumors in humans are inconsistent.

For colon cancer, there is reason to suspect an association with fat intake for two reasons. The animal studies are remarkably consistent, as animals fed increased amounts of saturated and unsaturated fats and cholesterol all had increased rates of colon tumors.[62,63] Second, individuals at high risk of colon cancer, with colon cancer, and with colonic polyps all have increased fecal concentrations of bile acids, which are the by-products of diets high in fat and which act as tumor promoters.[62,63]

The evidence linking dietary fat to breast cancer in humans is not well studied, although there are extensive animal data which would support such an hypothesis. However, most of the evidence which points toward a causal role for dietary fat in the pathogenesis of breast cancer (vis à vis a hormonal mechanism) appears to be limited to premenopausal women.[62,63]

FALLS, FRACTURES, AND OSTEOPOROSIS

Fractures are a significant cause of morbidity and mortality in older persons. The two most commonly occurring fractures in older persons are hip and vertebral. Falls are a major risk factor for these fractures, and by themselves are associated with risk of increased morbidity (restricted activity, soft tissue injury, nursing home admissions) and mortality. Falls account for the majority of deaths related to injuries in aged persons, and are the sixth leading cause of death in persons over 65 years of age.[66]

Risk Factors for Falls

About 30 percent of community dwelling elderly persons fall each year,[67–69] and between 2 and 6 percent of all falls are associated with a fracture.[67,70] Approximately 24 percent of fallers incur serious injury.[67] Women appear to be twice as likely to fall as men.[69,71]

One of the most consistent predictors of falls appears to be sedative use[67,69,72]; in one longitudinal study, the risk of falling was 28 times higher in persons using sedatives than in individuals not using them.[67] Other risk factors for falls include environmental hazards such as poor lighting, worn carpet, and electric cords.[66,70] It has been suggested that between 35 and 50 percent of home falls are associated with accidents or environmental causes.[70]

Other identified risk factors for falls include cognitive impairment (a fivefold excess risk), disabilities of the lower extremities (a fourfold excess risk), palmomental reflex (a threefold excess risk), abnormalities of balance and gait (a twofold excess risk), and foot problems (a twofold excess risk).[67] There also appears to be a dose–response association between number of risk factors for falling and the risk of falling.[67]

Osteoporosis and Fractures

As noted, fractures are a serious problem in older individuals. It has been estimated that one-third of women over 65 years of age will have vertebral fractures.[73] Hip fracture, which increases dramatically with age, leads to death in 12 to 20 percent of cases; an additional 25 percent of hip fracture patients require long-term nursing home care and ultimately 50 percent are unable to walk without help.[74]

Osteoporosis is considered the major risk factor for fracture. The epidemiologic determinants of osteoporosis include advanced age, female sex, geographic location, white race, and estrogen deficiency.[74] Some researchers have suggested that calcium consumption is inversely associated with risk of osteoporosis and fracture.[75,76] Smoking, high alcohol consumption, and lean body mass have also been suggested to increase the risk of osteoporosis and fracture.[75]

Physical activity has also been suggested as a protective risk factor for bone loss and fracture. In an extensive review, exercise was clearly shown to increase bone mass in the elderly.[75] In the Florida Geriatric Research Program, men and women walking at least one mile three or more times per week had a reduced risk of subsequent fracture (RR = 0.5 in men and 0.6 in women).[77]

Perhaps the most potent predictor of osteoporosis

and osteoporotic fracture in women is estrogen deficiency. One study has found that estrogen deficiency and not age per se is responsible for the loss of bone mass which occurs in the two decades after menopause.[78] Further, estrogen replacement therapy in peri- and postmenopausal women is a powerful determinant of bone loss and fracture risk.[74,79,80] It has been estimated that 50 percent of hip fractures (not to mention fractures of other sites) could be prevented by a more widespread use of estrogen therapy.[81]

SUMMARY AND CONCLUSIONS

In this chapter we have briefly reviewed risk factors for the major causes of death and disability in older persons. We are limited in any definitive conclusions we may want to draw about most of the factors addressed here simply because of the paucity of studies of risk factors in older people. However, two general points have emerged.

First, there is good evidence that disease in older people is not the inevitable consequence of biologic aging, but is in fact a pathological process with identifiable risk factors. Thus, the potential exists to modify the occurrence of disease in older people by modifying their risk factor profiles. Most of the risk factors for death and morbidity which operate at midlife also continue to predict events at the advanced ages. This suggests that general hygienic interventions such as improved diet, smoking cessation, weight control, and exercise could improve the health of older people.

Second, there is direct evidence that therapeutic interventions in older persons can reduce morbidity and mortality. Clearly, pharmacologic treatment of hypertension leads to a reduced risk of stroke and possibly CHD, and the use of estrogen replacement therapy probably reduces the risk of CHD and fracture. Whether other therapeutic interventions such as pharmacologic treatment of hyperlipidemia are effective in this age group remains to be seen, although there is no compelling reason to suppose that this would not be the case.

In summary, there is sufficient evidence at this time to encourage primary prevention of disease in older persons by hygienic measures and, if appropriate, with pharmacologic treatments. Such measures will prevent "premature mortality" and enable persons to live healthier lives.

REFERENCES

1. National Center for Health Statistics: *Vital Statistics of the United States, 1984*, Vol. II, Mortality, Parts A and B, DHHS Pub No. (PHS) 87-1122 and 87-1114, Public Health Service. Washington, Government Printing Office, 1987.
2. National Center for Health Statistics, Havlik RJ et al: *Health Statistics on Older Persons, United States, 1986.* Vital and Health Statistics, Series 3, No. 25, DHHS Pub. No. (PHS) 87-1409, Public Health Service. Washington, Government Printing Office, 1987.
3. Verbrugge L: Longer life but worsening health? Trends in health and mortality of middle-aged and older persons. *Milband Mem Fund Q* 62:475, 1984.
4. Weinstein MC et al: Forecasting coronary heart disease incidence, mortality, and cost: The coronary heart disease policy model. *Am J Public Health* 77:1417, 1987.
5. Gillum R et al: Decline in coronary heart disease mortality. Old questions and new facts. *Am J Med* 76:1055, 1984.
6. Rose G: Strategy of prevention: Lessons from cardiovascular disease. *Br Med J* 282:1847, 1981.
7. Kannel W et al: Primary risk factors for coronary heart disease in the elderly: The Framingham study, in Wenger N et al (eds): *Coronary Heart Disease in the Elderly: Working Conference on the Recognition and Management of Coronary Heart Disease in the Elderly.* New York, Elsevier, 1986.
8. The Pooling Project Research Group: Relationship of blood pressure, serum cholesterol, smoking habit, relative weight, and ECG abnormalities to incidence of major coronary events: Final report of the Pooling Project. *J Chronic Dis* 31:201, 1978.
9. Bush TL et al: Total and LDL cholesterol as predictors of CHD death in elderly men: The Lipid Research Clinics' Program Follow-Up Study. *CVD Epidemiol Newslett* 43:22, 1988.
10. Barrett-Connor E et al: Ischemic heart disease risk factors after age 50. *J Chronic Dis* 37:903, 1984.
11. Abramson JH et al: Risk markers for mortality among elderly men: A community study in Jerusalem. *J Chronic Dis* 35:565, 1982.
12. Shanoff HM et al: Studies of male survivors of myocardial infarction: XII. Relation of serum lipids and lipoproteins to survival over a 10-year period. *Can Med Assoc J* 103:927, 1970.
13. Leren P: The Oslo diet-heart study: Eleven-year report. *Circulation* 42:935, 1970.
14. Friedman GD et al: Kaiser-Permanente epidemiologic study of myocardial infarction: Study design and results for standard risk factors. *Am J Epidemiol* 99:101, 1974.
15. Kannel WB et al: Prevention of cardiovascular disease in the elderly. *J Am Coll Cardiol* 10:25A, 1987.
16. Criqui MH et al: Lipoproteins as mediators for the effects of alcohol consumption and cigarette smoking on cardiovascular mortality: Results from the Lipid Research Clinics' Follow-Up Study. *Am J Epidemiol* 126:629, 1987.
17. Branch LG et al: Personal health practices and mortality among the elderly. *Am J Publ Health* 74:1126. 1984.
18. Siegel D et al: Predictors of cardiovascular events and mortality in the Systolic Hypertension in the Elderly pilot project. *Am J Epidemiol* 126:385, 1987.
19. Jajick CL et al: Smoking and coronary heart disease mortality in the elderly. *JAMA* 252:2831, 1984.
20. Curb JD et al: Isolated systolic hypertension in 14 communities. *Am J Epidemiol* 121:362, 1985.

21. Chapman JM et al: The interrelationship of serum cholesterol, hypertension, body weight, and risk of coronary disease. The results of the first ten years of follow-up in the Los Angeles Heart Study. *J Chronic Dis* 17:933, 1964.

22. Mattila K et al: Blood pressure and five year survival in the very old. *Brit Med J* 296:887, 1988.

23. Kannel WB: Implications of Framingham study data for treatment of hypertension: Impact of other risk factors, in Laragh JH et al (eds): *Frontiers in Hypertension Research*. New York, Springer-Verlag, 1981.

24. *Build Study 1979*. Chicago, Society of Actuaries and the Association of Life Insurance Medical Directors of America, 1980.

25. Garland C et al: Isolated systolic hypertension and mortality after age 60 years: A prospective population-based study. *Am J Epidemiol* 118:365, 1983.

26. Hypertension Detection and Follow-up Program Cooperative Group: Five-year findings of the Hypertension Detection and Follow-up Program: II. Mortality by race, sex, and age. *JAMA* 242:2572, 1979.

27. National Heart Foundation of Australia: Treatment of mild hypertension in the elderly: Report by the Management Committee. *Med J Aust* 2:398, 1981.

28. Amery A et al: Mortality and morbidity results from the European Working Party on High Blood Pressure in the Elderly Trial. *Lancet* 1:1349, 1985.

29. Coope J et al: Randomised trial of treatment of hypertension in elderly patients in primary care. *Br Med J* 293:1145, 1986.

30. Siscovick DS et al: The disease-specific benefits and risks of physical activity and exercise. *Public Health Rep* 100:180, 1985.

31. Kaplan GA et al: Mortality among the elderly in the Alameda County Study: Behavioral and demographic risk factors. *Am J Public Health* 77:307, 1987.

32. Paffenbarger RS et al: Physical activity, all-cause mortality, and longevity of college alumni. *N Engl J Med* 314:605, 1986.

33. Blair SN et al: Relationships between exercise or physical activity and other health behaviors. *Pub Health Rep* 100:172, 1985.

34. Hickey N et al: Study of coronary risk factors related to physical activity in 15,171 men. *Br Med J* 3:507, 1975.

35. Fitzgerald PL: Exercise for the elderly. *Med Clin N Am* 69:189, 1985.

36. Rowe JW et al: Human aging: Usual and successful. *Science* 237:143, 1987.

37. Dustman RE et al: Aerobic exercise training and improved neuropsychological function of older individuals. *Neurobiol Aging* 5:35, 1984.

38. deVries HA: Physiological effects of an exercise training regimen upon men aged 52–88. *J Gerontol* 25:325, 1970.

39. Haber P et al: Effects in elderly people 67–76 years of age of three-month endurance training on a bicycle ergometer. *Eur Heart J* 5(Suppl E):37, 1984.

40. Oldridge NB et al: Cardiac rehabilitation after myocardial infarction. Combined experience of randomized clinical trials. *JAMA* 260:945, 1988.

41. Herd JA: Management of coronary heart disease in the elderly: Education and rehabilitation, in Wenger N et al (eds): *Coronary Heart Disease in the Elderly. Working Conference on the Recognition and Management of Coronary Heart Disease in the Elderly*. New York, Elsevier, 1986.

42. Williams MA et al: Early exercise training in patients older than age 65 years compared with that in younger patients after acute myocardial infarction or coronary artery bypass grafting. *Am J Cardiol* 55:263, 1985.

43. Froelicher C: Exercise testing and training. New York, LeJacq, 1982.

44. Kannel WB et al: Physiological and medical concomitants of obesity: The Framingham Study, in Bray GA (ed): *Obesity in America*, DHEW Pub. No. (NIH) 79-359. Washington, Government Printing Office, 1979.

45. Jarret RJ et al: Weight and mortality in the Whitehall study. *Br Med J* 285:535, 1982.

46. Andres R et al: Impact of age on weight goals. *Ann Intern Med* 103:1030, 1985.

47. Harris T et al: Body mass index and mortality among nonsmoking older persons. *JAMA* 259:1520, 1988.

48. Waaler HT: Height, weight and mortality: The Norwegian experience. *Acta Med Scand [Suppl]* 679:1, 1984.

49. Mattila K et al: Body mass index and mortality in the elderly. *Br Med J* 292:867, 1986.

50. Eaker ED et al: Coronary heart disease and its risk factors among women in the Framingham Study, in Eaker ED (ed): *Coronary Heart Disease in Women*, proceedings of an N.I.H. Workshop, Haymarket Doyma, New York, 1987, pp 123–130.

51. Wilson PWF et al: Postmenopausal estrogen use, cigarette smoking, and cardiovascular morbidity in women over 50. *N Engl J Med* 313:1308. 1985.

52. Bush TL et al: Cardiovascular mortality and non-contraceptive use of estrogen in women: Results from the Lipid Research Clinics' Program Follow-up Study. *Circulation* 75:1102, 1987.

53. Henderson BE et al: Estrogen use and cardiovascular disease. *Am J Obstet Gynecol* 154:1181, 1986.

54. Weinfeld FD: The national survey of stroke. National Institute of Neurological and Communicative Disorders and Stroke. *Stroke* 12(Suppl):I1, 1981.

55. Smith W: Cardiovascular disease. A profile of health and disease in America. *Facts on File*, New York, 1987.

56. Ostfeld AM: A review of stroke epidemiology. *Epidemiol Rev* 2:136, 1980.

57. Ostfeld AM et al: Epidemiology of stroke in an elderly welfare population. *Am J Public Health* 64:450, 1974.

58. Khaw K-T et al: Dietary potassium and stroke-associated mortality. A 12-year prospective population study. *N Engl J Med* 316:235, 1987.

59. Balducci L et al: Nutrition, cancer, and aging: An annotated review: I. Diet, carcinogenesis, and aging. *J Am Geriatr Soc* 34:127, 1986.

60. Hammond EC: Smoking in relation to the death rates of one million men and women. *Natl Cancer Inst Monogr* 19:126, 1966.

61. Garfinkel L, Stellman SD: Smoking and lung cancer in women: Findings in a prospective study. *Cancer Res* 48:6951, 1988.

62. Willett WC et al: Diet and cancer—an overview (first of two parts). *N Engl J Med* 310:633, 1984.

63. Willett WC et al: Diet and cancer—an overview (second of two parts). *N Engl J Med* 310:697, 1984

64. Colditz GA et al: Increased green and yellow vegetable intake and lowered cancer deaths in an elderly population. *Am J Clin Nutr* 41:32, 1985.

65. Enstrom JE et al: Mortality among health-conscious elderly Californians. *Proc Natl Acad Sci* 79:6023, 1982.

66. Baker SL: The preventability of falls, in Gray JAM (ed): *Prevention of Disease in the Elderly.* New York, Churchill Livingstone, 1985, pp 114–129.

67. Tinetti ME et al: Risk factors for falls among elderly persons living in the community. *N Engl J Med* 319:1701, 1988.

68. Campbell AJ et al: Falls in old age: A study of frequency and related clinical factors. *Age Ageing* 10:264, 1981.

69. Prudham D, Evans JG: Factors associated with falls in the elderly: A community study. *Age Ageing* 10:141, 1981.

70. Rubenstein LZ et al: Falls and instability in the elderly. *J Am Geriatr Soc* 36:266, 1988.

71. Perry BC: Falls among the elderly: A review of the methods and conclusions of epidemiologic studies. *J Am Geriatr Soc* 30:367, 1982.

72. Ray WA et al: Psychotropic drug use and the risk of hip fracture. *N Engl J Med* 316:363, 1987.

73. Riggs BL et al: Osteoporosis and age-related fracture syndromes, in *Research and the Ageing Population.* Chichester, Wiley (Ciba Foundation Symposium 134), 1988, pp 129–142.

74. Cummings SR et al: Osteoporosis and osteoporotic fractures. *Epidemiol Rev* 7:178, 1985.

75. Rodysill KJ: Postmenopausal osteoporosis—intervention and prophylaxis. A review. *J Chronic Dis* 40:743, 1987.

76. Holbrook TL et al: Dietary calcium and risk of hip fracture: 14-year prospective population study. *Lancet* 2:1046, 1988.

77. Sorock GS et al: Physical activity and fracture risk in a free-living elderly cohort. *J Gerontol* 43:M134, 1988.

78. Richelson LS et al: Relative contributions of aging and estrogen deficiency to postmenopausal bone loss. *N Engl J Med* 311:1273, 1984.

79. Kiel DP et al: Hip fracture and the use of estrogens in postmenopausal women. The Framingham Study. *N Engl J Med* 317:1169, 1987.

80. Lindsay R. Prevention of osteoporosis, in Gray JAM(ed): *Prevention of Disease in the Elderly.* New York, Churchill Livingstone, 1985.

81. Brody JA et al: Diseases and disorders of aging: An hypothesis. *J Chron Dis* 39:871, 1986.

Chapter 13

TOWARD SUCCESSFUL AGING: LIMITATION OF THE MORBIDITY ASSOCIATED WITH "NORMAL" AGING

John W. Rowe

Rapid increases in the number and proportion of elderly people and their high use of health care resources has enhanced interest in geriatrics. Substantial research efforts are targeted on the organization and financing of acute and long-term geriatric health care. Unfortunately, little interest and few initiatives have focused on health promotion and disease prevention in old age. This neglect represents a risky, short-sighted strategy since increases in life span over this century have set the stage for increases in active health span and decreases in morbidity.[1]

Traditionally, issues related to the elderly have been stratified into the categories of "pathologic aging" and "normal aging." Pathologic aging issues include aspects of diseases that occur either solely or disproportionately in the elderly. The health promotion and disease prevention initiatives that have been launched in geriatrics have focused primarily on these disease-related issues. Thus, the major targets have been osteoporosis, cardiac disease and stroke, falling, and so on. The factors guiding such studies, and the progress made to date, are outlined in later chapters in this textbook.

Studies of normal aging are concerned with the physiologic and biochemical changes that occur with aging in the absence of disease. The rationale for this approach emphasizes that the physiologic changes that accompany aging may influence the presentation of disease, its response to treatment, and the complications that ensue. Carefully conducted cross-sectional and longitudinal studies have demonstrated major effects of age on a number of clinically relevant variables, including pulmonary function, renal function, and immune function.[2,3]

SUCCESSFUL AND USUAL AGING

Certain limitations are common to many of the prior studies of the physiology of aging. While they have generally excluded individuals whose results may have been contaminated by the effects of disease, they have often fallen far short of taking into account many factors, such as diet, exercise, body composition, alcohol and tobacco use, and psychosocial factors, which may have a major modifying influence on the aging process. Additionally, they have neglected the substantial physiologic heterogeneity among older people and have implied that the physiologic changes that occur in older individuals in the absence of disease are harmless and do not carry significant risk. In short, the tendency to define these changes as "normal" suggests that they might represent the natural state of affairs and thus should not or cannot be modified.

These limitations of prior physiologic studies outlined above suggest the value of an additional conceptual distinction within the category of "normal aging." While many important physiologic variables show substantial average losses with advancing age, an important characteristic of such age-group data is the substantial variability within groups and the fact that, in many cases, the variance increases with advancing age in physiological factors.[4] In data sets that show substantial average decline with age, one can often find older persons with minimal physiologic loss, or none at all, when compared to the average decline of their younger counterparts. These people might be viewed as having aged *successfully* with regard to the particular variable under study, while individuals with substantial physiologic decrements would represent *usual aging*. People who demonstrate little or no loss in a constellation of physiologic functions might be regarded as more broadly successful in physiologic terms and might be said to demonstrate a physiologic condition approximating a "pure aging syndrome." They, in combination with people who show the typical nonpathologic age-linked losses that I propose to designate as "usual" aging, constitute the heterogeneous category of "normal (i.e., nonpathologic) aging."[5]

The value of the distinction between usual and successful aging is linked to recent findings about blood pressure, body weight, and serum cholesterol levels, as well as other age-related changes discussed below: while they may be usual in the populations in which they have most frequently been studied, they represent significant risk factors for adverse outcome such as cardiovascular disease. Moreover, such changes which have been interpreted as age-intrinsic are turning out to be usual in prosperous industrial countries but not in pastoral or traditional agriculture societies. Thus it seems that the effect of age per se may often be exaggerated in that factors of diet, exercise, nutrition, and the like may have been underestimated or ignored as potential modifiers of the intrinsic aging process. If so, the prospects for avoidance or even reversal of functional age-associated loss are vastly improved, and the stage is set for initiatives of health promotion and disease prevention in old age focusing on *physiologic* rather than pathologic age-associated changes. The research evidence that bears on the distinction between usual and successful aging for two physiologic characteristics—carbohydrate intolerance of aging and osteopenia—will be briefly reviewed below.[6]

AGING AND CARBOHYDRATE METABOLISM

Evidence now indicates that the carbohydrate intolerance of aging carries substantial risk in the usual-but-not-yet-diseased state and holds the promise of substantial modifiability. It has been known for over six decades

that advancing age is associated with impaired capacity to metabolize glucose.[7] Results of oral or intravenous glucose tolerance tests show a remarkable increase in the mean 2-hour blood sugar level with advancing age and substantial increase in the variability of the results in successive age groups. Many older individuals metabolize glucose as well as their average younger counterparts do, while others show marked declines in this physiologic function. Resistance to the effect of insulin on peripheral tissues appears to play a major role in the genesis of the glucose intolerance of aging, which is associated with progressive increases in postprandial insulin levels.[8]

Studies focusing on age-associated postprandial hyperinsulinemia, the hallmark of insulin resistance, have shown increases in insulin levels to be a significant independent contributor to the incidence of death from coronary heart disease. Regarding glucose levels, a recent report from the Honolulu Heart Program evaluated the 12-year risk of stroke in 690 diabetics and 6908 nondiabetics free of stroke at study entry.[9] Diabetes was clearly associated with increased risk of stroke, as expected. Additionally, among nondiabetics the risk of stroke was markedly age-related and was significantly higher for those with serum glucose levels in the 80th percentile than for those with levels in the 20th percentile.

Recent studies have attempted to clarify which components of age-associated alterations in carbohydrate tolerance are related to aging per se (age-determined) and which components might be related to other factors (age-associated) which are extrinsic to the aging process. In Italian factory workers age 22 to 73 years, Zavaroni and colleagues evaluated the relevant contributions of obesity, physical activity, family history, diabetes, and the use of diabetogenic drugs to the age-related increases of glucose in insulin levels after an oral glucose tolerance test.[10] The initial strong statistical correlation between age and postprandial glucose and insulin levels became much weaker when the effects of exercise, diet, and drugs were taken into account. Ultimately the correlation between glucose and age was limited to marginal statistical significance, and the effect of age on insulin levels was no longer demonstrable. These findings suggest that much of the carbohydrate intolerance of aging may be related to factors other than normal biological aging per se. These studies fit nicely with recent physiologic studies showing that well-structured exercise programs in elderly glucose intolerant individuals can markedly improve glucose metabolism and reduce circulating insulin levels. The emerging data suggest that modifications in diet or exercise may substantially blunt the emergence in old age of carbohydrate intolerance and insulin resistance and their attendant risk of cardiovascular disease.

AGING AND OSTEOPOROSIS

Aging is associated with a progressive decline in bone density in both males and females after maturity. Osteoporosis is of major importance in the elderly—by age 65 one-third of women will have vertebral fractures and by age 80 one-third of women and one-sixth of men will have suffered hip fracture.[11] Although it has long been recognized that osteoporosis is a process with multiple possible causes which varies a great deal among older people, aging itself is generally considered a major factor in the loss of skeletal integrity. In a reconceptualization of the origins of osteoporosis, Riggs and Melton[11] indicate three separate general contributors to *bone loss:* the effects of intrinsic aging; the effects of menopause; and a third component representing "extrinsic factors" which are present to a variable degree in the population and contribute to the remarkable variance in bone density among the elderly. These preventable external risk factors include cigarette smoking, heavy alcohol intake, and inadequate calcium intake.

In addition to identifying several potential modifiable contributors to the emergence of osteopenia, studies now suggest that bone loss can be blunted in advancing age by institution of moderate exercise programs.[11] Thus, emergence of osteoporosis as a common, crippling, and expensive geriatric disorder, previously considered to represent the normal aging process, is variable and influenced by aging and nonaging factors. The marked reductions in bone density associated with usual aging may in large part be preventable or modifiable.

These examples of glucose intolerance and osteopenia can be matched by similar analyses in areas of age-related physiologic change, including declines in skin function, cognition, lung and immune functions, and others. The effects of the aging process itself have been exaggerated, and the modifying effects of diet, exercise, personal habits, and psychosocial factors have been underestimated. Within the category of normal aging a distinction can be made between usual aging, in which extrinsic factors heighten the effects of aging alone, and successful aging, in which extrinsic factors play a neutral or positive role. Research is needed on the risks associated with usual aging, and strategies to modify them should help to elucidate how a transition from usual to successful aging can be facilitated.

Thus, emerging evidence suggests that health promotion initiatives in geriatrics take two general forms. The first is an initiative targeted toward shifting an increasing proportion of elderly into the category of "successful aging" in order to decrease the morbidity associated with usual aging. The focus of these initiatives is on physiologic alterations that are age-related and are due to extrinsic factors rather than to the intrinsic aging process. The second aspect of gerontological health promo-

tion focuses on pathologic aging and aims to decrease the emergence of disease or, in the presence of age, to decrease morbidity. The relationship of these two aspects of geriatric health promotion is depicted in Fig. 13-1. In this figure the curve furthest to the right displays the current age-specific mortality experience of the United States. This rather rectangular curve is typical for developed nations. The next curve, labeled "Disability," depicts the portion of the population at any age without disability. With advancing age the proportion of disabled individuals in the population increases rather dramatically. The next curve, labeled "Disease," represents a theoretical estimate of the increasing emergence with advancing age of specific disease processes such as cardiac disease, dementia, osteoporosis, and hypertension. As can be clearly seen at any given age, the portion of individuals who are diseased and still living can be divided into those who have developed disability from their disease and those who have not yet developed disability. The major aim of health promotion efforts targeting pathologic aging is to compress the emergence of disease and disease-related disability further toward the end of life, i.e., to shift the disease and disability curves to the right so that they approximate the mortality curve. The final curve on Fig. 13-1, labeled "Risk," provides a theoretical estimate of the portion of the nondiseased population at any age that has developed physiologic age-related changes which carry considerable risk and thus might be considered to be usual aging. Thus the population below the disease curve can be broken into a population further below the risk curve (i.e., those who are aging successfully) and a larger population of individuals who lie between the risk and disease curves who might be said to demonstrate usual aging. The goal of geriatric health promotion efforts aimed at successful aging would be to shift this risk curve associated with physiologic aspects of aging further to the right by decreasing the impact of extrinsic age-associated factors.

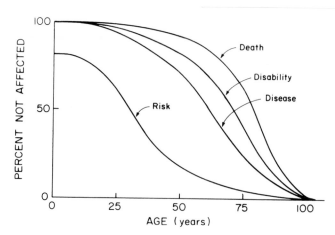

FIGURE 13-1
Relationship between risk of usual aging and pathology.

REFERENCES

1. Rowe JW: Aging reconsidered: Strategies to promote health and prevent disease in old age. *Q J Med* 249:1, 1988.
2. Rowe JW: Health care of the elderly. *N Engl J Med* 312:827, 1985.
3. Shock NW et al: *Normal Human Aging: The Baltimore Longitudinal Study of Aging.* Washington, DC, U.S. Department of Health and Human Services, 1984.
4. Rowe JW: Systolic hypertension in the elderly. *N Engl J Med* 309:1246, 1983.
5. Rowe JW, Kahn RL: Human aging: Usual and successful. *Science* 237:143, 1987.
6. Waldron I et al: Cross-cultural variation in blood pressure: A quantitative analysis of the relationships of blood pressure to cultural characteristics, salt consumption and body weight. *Soc Sci Med* 16:419, 1982.
7. Minaker KL, Meneilly et al: *Handbook of the Biology of Aging.* New York, Van Nostrand Reinhold, 1985, pp. 433–456.
8. Davidson MB: The effect of aging on carbohydrate metabolism. *Metabolism* 28:688, 1979.
9. Abbott RD et al: Diabetes and the risk of stroke: The Honolulu Heart Program. *JAMA* 257:949, 1987.
10. Zavaroni I et al: Effect of age and environmental factors on glucose tolerance and insulin secretion in a worker population. *J Am Geriatr Soc* 34:271, 1986.
11. Riggs BL et al: Involutional osteoporosis. *N Engl J Med* 314:1676, 1986.

Chapter 14

LONG-LIVED POPULATIONS (EXTREME OLD AGE)

Alexander Leaf

When we are healthy and the world seems good to us, the thought of death is generally very remote. We have a sense of personal immortality. Death is for the others but not for us. We reject and fear that which we cannot comprehend; death and the hereafter remain major mysteries despite the age-old teachings and assurances of many religions.

In view of these considerations it is not surprising that in our culture, as in many past ones, there has been great interest in unusual longevity. The fountain of youth has been long sought after, and, though it still eludes us, any claims that purport its existence, whether innocent or fraudulent, receive much public attention.

Literature past and present abounds in claims of unusual longevity. The Book of Genesis provides the most extravagant claims, if taken literally. Methuselah was the oldest of the biblical patriarchs, living to 969 years, but Adam and five of his direct descendants survived over 900 years. Claims of similar remarkable longevity appear in the legends of other cultures.

In modern times claims of unusual longevity have stemmed from the Caucasus in southern U.S.S.R., the small state of Hunza in the Karakoram mountains at the tip of West Pakistan, and the Ecuadorian village of Vilcabamba in the Andes. I had the opportunity in 1970 and 1974 to visit these three places and examine the alleged supercentenarians there. These are backward areas according to our view of modern societies. Each is an agrarian community where nearly everyone works long hours on the rugged hillsides to eke a living from the meager soil. Living is characterized by much physical labor, sparse vegetarian diets, and a closely knit supportive social structure. It is also characterized by poor sanitation, infectious diseases, high infant mortality, illiter-

acy, and lack of modern medical care. Nevertheless there are old people for whom their neighbors claim unusual longevity. The claims made locally have in several instances been further extended by western visitors.

In 1970 I was especially interested to visit Vilcabamba in Ecuador since its inhabitants were Spanish-speaking and Catholic. The local church held the baptismal records and other documents from which ages were verified, I was assured. When I was first introduced to Miguel Carpio, I was told he was the oldest living citizen of the valley and aged 121. Since the Ecuadorian physicians accompanying us claimed to have checked the documents, I did not then question this stated age. Four years later, however, I returned to Vilcabamba to obtain blood, skin, and urine samples from the old people to study. On this return visit I was again introduced to Miguel Carpio but told now that he was 132 years old! Even I became suspicious at this claim and insisted on seeing the baptismal certificate for Miguel Carpio. Unfortunately no documentation could be found—a fire allegedly destroyed some of the records. (At least the first seven pages of the earliest book of birth records had been torn out. This book, which started on June 17, 1852, had as its first entry, after the missing seven pages, birth number 54 of the year 1863.)

Micaela Quezada's case is another which typifies the difficulties encountered in determining ages. She claimed to be 106 years old. I had seen her baptismal record prominently underscored by local officials in the book of birth records. She was born in 1870 and it was then 1974, so the documented age of 104 was not too inconsistent with her claim of 106 years. However, on questioning, we found her father's name to be Benino Quezada and her mother's, Maria de los Angeles Men-

142

dietta. A return visit to the baptismal records revealed that the Micaela Quezada listed there as born in 1870 had parents named Juan Quezada and Maria Mercedes Patino. This revelation was quite disconcerting since clearly the entry in the baptismal record was of a person with different parents from our living Micaela Quezada. When confronted directly by these facts, Senorita Quezada said, "Oh, yes, of course, that's my cousin who lived in San Pedro [a village some 3 mi away]. She was older than me and died thirty or forty years ago." Thus we had been misled by accepting a baptismal record which our Ecuadorian friends had mistaken for that of the living Micaela Quezada. Since the same names were used repeatedly, one must make certain that the name in the baptismal record is of the same generation as that of the living person.

In 1971, following our first visit, a census was taken at our request by the Instituto Nacional de Estatistica of Ecuador which recorded a total population for Vilcabamba of 819, with nine individuals over the age of 100 years. Subsequent to my visits Drs. Richard Mazess and Sylvia Forman have returned to Vilcabamba and painstakingly worked out the genealogy and actual ages of the inhabitants of this village. They found no one to be 100 years of age.[1] Miguel Carpio died according to their study at the ripe age of 93. Even the unusual 11.4 percent of villagers that the census found to be over 60 years of age in comparison with the 4.5 percent for rural Ecuador generally they were able to ascribe to the in-migration of a few elders and the departure from the valley of a larger number of young people and not to unusual longevity. Mazess and Forman have produced an informa-

tive chart comparing the stated age of the adult population of Vilcabamba against their actual ages obtained from church and civil documents, etc. (see Fig. 14-1). To the age of 70 there is good correspondence between stated and actual ages. Above age 70, however, the stated ages exceeded the actual ages by some 10 to 20 percent.

The reasons for the exaggeration of ages in Vilcabamba differ from those in the other cultures visited. Clearly the old people do not benefit by being accorded higher status because of their ages. They appeared to be a singularly neglected lot despite the fuss made over their ages. The main reason for the exaggeration, however, proved not to be subtle.

On my first visit to Vilcabamba the trip from Loja was a rough, long 36 miles by four-wheel jeep. On my return 4 years later a surfaced road connected the two villages. When I arrived I was embarrassed to be greeted by the local band and the governor who hailed me as the economic savior of this depressed region. Pointing to a few elders, he proclaimed, "These are our oil wells!"

Despite my own stated skepticism regarding the extreme ages claimed for the Vilcabamba elders and the careful and thorough study of Mazess and Forman, in 1978 when Mazess and I cosponsored a meeting at the National Institutes of Health, to which all investigators of Vilcabamba were invited, it was surprising to see how some clung to the myths of supercentenarians. At that date a Japanese group was negotiating with the authorities in Vilcabamba to build a high-rise hotel so that wealthy Americans could fly down for a weekend of lon-

FIGURE 14-1
The relationship of actual ages documented from church and other records to the stated ages of the inhabitants of Vilcabamba, Ecuador. *(Data from Mazess and Forman.[1])*

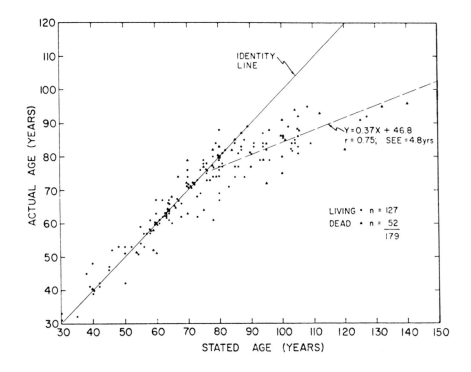

gevity. An American entrepreneur and his Ecuadorian spouse were starting a bottle works to bottle and sell water from Vilcabamba's stream.

Thus, even when confronted with the facts, a myth dies hard. The economic interests to perpetuate it in Vilcabamba are considerable. Nevertheless, I remain puzzled by the account of the master of one Yankee clipper ship, Captain Coggeshall,[2] who wrote in 1851 of his visit to a locale which must have been quite close to Vilcabamba. He described the salubrious nature of that area and his visit to several elderly, one of whom he records as 111 years of age. What was the incentive for exaggerating ages in those days?

In the Caucasus and in Hunza the potential documentation of ages proved to be quite different than in Ecuador.[3,4] In Hunza I was introduced to Tulah Beg in 1972 and told by the then Mir—the king—that Tulah Beg was 110 years old. The next oldest person was a 105-year-old male and the other old people were in their nineties or eighties, I was told. The population of the state of Hunza was then estimated by the Mir to be about 40,000 persons. But there had been no census, and no records documented the statements of this English-educated ruler. In fact, the spoken language is Burasheski, which differs from any other language, I learned, because of the extreme geographic isolation of this community and lack of communication with the outside world over many centuries. Hidden among the towering peaks of the majestic Karakoram mountains, generations had lived in splendid isolation without even a written language to document events, past or present. The word of the Mir serves in lieu of such records. The old people were held in considerable esteem here as judged by the existence of a Council of Elders who advised the Mir in matters of state. Also during the frequent festivals, the public dances were led by an elder—a feature which did not contribute to the vivacity of the dancing.

In the low Caucasus Mountains of Georgian Russia exaggeration of ages takes on a modern record. There many old people are claimed to be over 100, with the official record claimed by the Soviet press for Shirali Mislimov of 168 years at the time of his death, September 1973, in the village of Barzavu in Azerbaijan, west of the Caspian Sea. His and the ages of many other supercentenarians must be exaggerated. There are no written records to document birth dates of any of these old people. This portion of the U.S.S.R. has had a stormy history up until recent times with the land changing hands between Turks and Russians. The frequent wars uprooted the population of that area repeatedly, making civil record-keeping impossible. Many churches with their records have been closed or destroyed. Thus, there is no written documentation of the extreme ages.

The Russian-born geneticist Dr. Zhores A. Med-

vedev has done much to debunk the claims of extreme old age in the Caucasus.[5] He has pointed out that internal passports and other Soviet documents go back only to 1932, at which time the data were obtained by oral interviews with no documentation of authenticity. The census is taken the same way. Thus these current official documents prove very little in regard to ages.

In the United States, despite recent figures[6] showing that the age group over 85 years is the most rapidly growing segment of our population by percentage, there are major uncertainties regarding the numbers of centenarians even here. Raw census figures showed 4447 centenarians in 1950, 10,369 in 1960, and 106,441 in 1970.[7] But these figures are based on simple assertions of those interviewed or on the claims of relatives and friends, just as in the U.S.S.R. In fact, a comment in the Appendix to the 1970 census states[8]:

> The number of persons shown as 100 years old and over in the 1970 census is overstated, apparently because of misunderstanding by some persons in filling the age portion of the census questionnaire. This kind of reporting error appears to have affected the count of persons 100 years and over in varying degrees in all of the States. Available evidence suggests that the true number of persons 100 years old and over in the United States does not exceed several thousand and is possibly less than 5000, as compared with the tabulated figures 106,441.

According to Social Security figures of 1970, there were only 6200 recipients of benefits who were 100 years old or over. This latter number would yield a figure of three centenarians per 100,000 in the United States, which is the same as the figure for Japan, where birth records have been carefully maintained for the past 110 years. From the raw census figures for 1970 we get, by contrast, 52 centenarians per 100,000, which is not too different than the figures I had obtained for Georgia, U.S.S.R., of 39 and for Azerbaijan of 84 per 100,000.[4] As stated, there are sufficient reasons to doubt both the U.S.S.R. figures and our own raw census figures.

To date, in the absence of written birth records, there has been no certain means of ascertaining human age. There is no physiologic function that changes at the same rate with time in all persons. It is common knowledge that some individuals "age" early while others preserve youthful characteristics into advanced ages. But some means of dating people, as objects of greater antiquity may be dated with ^{14}C measurements, would provide an objective means to determine ages in the absence of adequate written records. Recently such a method of chemical dating has been proposed and tested by Helfman and Bada.[9] Their ingenious method of objectively determining age is based on the well-known fact that the body can utilize only L-amino acids with which to synthesize proteins. With time, however, these L-amino acids racemize back to their equilibrium ratio of

D- to L-isomers. This racemization is a first-order reaction dependent only upon time and temperature. Since body temperature stays quite constant during life and the rate of racemization at 37°C is known, the age can be calculated from the observed D- to L-amino acid ratio in tissues. However, the problem is to obtain a protein that is laid down in the body early in life and does not turn over. Such proteins are found in the dentine of teeth and the lens of the eye. Determining the ratio of D- to L-aspartic acid in these tissues allows an estimate of age within a 10 percent error. Because of the scarcity of teeth among the very elderly and the unavailability of lens protein, this method has not yet been tested on the alleged supercentenarians. It is encouraging that a method has been developed and is being tested which could provide the objective test to the verbal claims of extreme ages—provided a tooth is available to sample!

The natural limit of the human life span has been estimated in several ways. Fries[10] uses the rate at which life expectancy at various ages is increasing to calculate the point at which the curves intersect. As examples of this method he makes two calculations. (1) Over the first eight decades of this century average life expectancy from birth increased at the rate of 0.33 years per year of the century, and life expectancy from age 65 has increased by 0.05 years per year. These curves intersect in the year 2009, at a mean age at death of 82.4 years. (2) During the most recent decade average life expectancy from birth has continued to increase 0.33 years per year and life expectancy at age 65 has increased at 0.12 years per year. These curves intersect in the year 2018 at a mean age at death of 85.6 years. From such calculations it is estimated that our life span has a finite limit of 85 ± 10 years.

The extremes of age are thus simply the tail of the Gaussian distribution about this mean figure of 85. The total number of deaths in the United States in 1975 of individuals 85 and older was 280,077. The number of deaths at 96 to 100 was 1392, at 101 through 105 was 186, and at 106 through 110 was 28.[11,12] A person reaching the age of 85 has only 1 chance in 10,000 of reaching the age of 110.

There has been no extension of the limit of the life span; only the proportion of the population who are reaching the apparent biologic limit of some 85 ± 10 years is increasing. About two decades ago several gerontologists were predicting a large quantum increase in the upper limit of the human life span. They based these predictions on expectations that the new science of gerontology would provide sufficient understanding of the nature of the aging process to allow interventions that would stop or significantly retard the process. As the trials of vitamin E, other antioxidants, hormones, etc., have failed to prolong life of experimental animals, fewer and fewer predictions of a prolonged life are being made by responsible investigators. Though a biological limit to the human life span is being recognized which is independent of disease, the increase of 20 to 40 percent in the life span that McCay[13,14] obtained in rats on a calorically restricted diet and the 8- to 15-year life span of queen bees fed royal jelly in contrast to genetically identical siblings who survive only a year will continue to fire the human imagination with the hope that some environmental manipulation may comparably affect the limit of human survival. So far this has not occurred.

REFERENCES

1. Mazess RB, Forman SH: Longevity and age exaggeration in Vilcabamba, Ecuador. *J Gerontol* 34:94, 1979.
2. Coggeshall G: *Voyages to Various Parts of the World Made between the Years 1799 and 1844.* New York, Appleton, 1951.
3. Leaf A, Lannois J: Search for the oldest people. *Natl Geographic* 143:93, 1973.
4. Leaf A: *Youth in Old Age.* New York, McGraw-Hill, 1975, p 233.
5. Medvedev ZA: Caucasus and Altay longevity—a biological or social problem. *Gerontologist* 14:381, 1974.
6. "Population Profile of the United States, 1980." US Department of Commerce, Bureau of the Census, p 9.
7. "1970 Census of Population," vol 1, "Characteristics of the Population," pt I, United States Summary, sect 1, Table 50. US Department of Commerce publication.
8. "1970 Census of Population," vol 1, "Characteristics of the Population," pt I, United States Summary, sect 2, Appendix B, App. 15. US Department of Commerce publication.
9. Helfman PM, Bada JL: Aspartic acid racemization in dentine as a measure of aging. *Nature* 262:279, 1976.
10. Fries JF: Aging, natural death and the compression of morbidity. *N Engl J Med* 303:130, 1980.
11. "Vital Statistics of the United States 1977," vol 2, sect 5, National Center for Health Statistics, Hyattsville, MD, DHEW Publication PHS 80-1104, 1980.
12. National Center for Health Statistics: "Health in the United States 1978," Office of the Assistant Secretary, Public Health Service, Hyattsville, MD, DHEW Publication PHS 78-1232.
13. McCay CM et al: Retarded growth, life span, ultimate body size and age changes in the albino rat after feeding diets restricted in calories. *J Nutr* 18:1, 1939.
14. McCay CM, in Lansing AI (ed): *Problems of Ageing.* Baltimore, Williams & Wilkins, 1952.

Chapter 15

THE EPIDEMIOLOGY AND DEMOGRAPHY OF AGING

Deborah J. Moritz and Adrian M. Ostfeld

The age composition of the U.S. population has changed substantially during the twentieth century. The size of the elderly population (arbitrarily defined as ages 65 and over) has increased dramatically and is expected to continue to increase well into the next century.[1,2]

The purpose of this chapter is to present a broad overview of current knowledge of demographic trends and health conditions among members of the U.S. population age 65 and over. Data have been drawn primarily from four sources: (1) population estimates and projections prepared by the U.S. Bureau of the Census, (2) national surveys conducted by the National Center for Health Statistics, (3) the Established Populations for Epidemiologic Studies in the Elderly (EPESE) sponsored by the National Institute on Aging, and (4) the National Cancer Survey and the Surveillance Epidemiology and End Results (SEER) program. These data should be considered with two caveats. First, all computations and conclusions are based upon summary statistics. The population 65 and over is a large and diverse group, however, and there is considerable heterogeneity in the manner in which people age.[3,4] Second, there are certain limitations inherent in studies restricted to populations age 65 and over. These limitations are that (1) conclusions are based upon the select portion of the population healthy enough to survive to age 65; and (2) it is difficult to identify aspects of the aging process occurring before the onset of "old age" that may play important roles in health and well-being in later life. (These issues are discussed in more detail in Ref. 5.)

DEMOGRAPHY

In 1987, there were approximately 30 million people age 65 and over living in the United States, 12.2 percent of the total population (Table 15-1). This represents a substantial increase since the turn of the century, when only 4 percent of the population was aged 65 and over. Population projections suggest that the size of the elderly population will continue to increase over the next 60 years, reaching 67 million or 22 percent of the total population, by the year 2040.[2] Further, the elderly population is itself aging. In 1987 the age distribution of the elderly population was as follows: 59 percent age 65 to 74, 31 percent age 75 to 84, and 10 percent age 85 and over. By 2040, the proportion of the elderly population age 65 and over (the "oldest old") is expected to reach 19 percent (13 million individuals), whereas the proportion 65 to 74 will decline to 44 percent.[6] The oldest-old segment is the frailest group, with the greatest health care needs.

The age composition of a population is determined by rates of fertility, mortality, and migration. When fertility rates decline, the result is always an increase in the elderly proportion of the population. However, a decline in mortality rates leads to an increase in the elderly proportion of the population only when the decline is concentrated at older ages.[2,7] The increase in the elderly proportion of the population to date is principally due to a decline in fertility. Although mortality rates in the elderly have been decreasing since about 1940, these de-

TABLE 15-1
Estimates of the U.S. Population 65 Years and Over by Age, Sex, and Race, 1987 (in thousands)

	Total Population All Ages*	65 Years and Over*				
		Number	Percent of Total	65–74	75–84	85+
All races						
Men and women combined	243,915	29,835	12.2	17,668	9,301	2,867
Men	118,987	12,119	5.0	7,824	3,489	806
Women	124,928	17,716	7.3	9,844	5,811	2,061
White						
Men	100,920	10,905	4.5	7,028	3,154	723
Women	105,267	15,960	6.5	8,788	5,284	1,887
Nonwhite						
Men	18,067	1,214	0.5	796	335	83
Women	19,661	1,756	0.7	1,055	527	174

*Numbers may not add to totals due to rounding.
SOURCE: United States population estimates, by age, sex, and race: 1980 to 1987, in *Current Population Reports*, ser P-25, no 1022. Washington, U.S. Bureau of the Census, Government Printing Office, 1988.

creases have led to an increase in the elderly proportion of the population only since 1968, when such declines started to be concentrated at the older ages. Numerical projections presented in this chapter will not be affected by future changes in fertility, since all individuals who will be 65 and over in the year 2040 have already been born. However, if mortality rates decrease more rapidly than expected, the elderly population could grow at an even faster rate than anticipated.[8,9]

SEX DISTRIBUTION

In 1987 the majority of the population over 65 (59 percent) was female and the male-to-female ratio decreased with increasing age (Table 15-1). At ages 65 to 74 there were 80 males for every 100 females, whereas at ages 85 and over, there were only 39 males for every 100 females. The deficit of men relative to women is a reflection of the progressive effects of higher mortality rates for males than for females at all ages.[2] The deficit of elderly men is a relatively recent phenomenon. Only 50 years ago, there were equal numbers of men and women age 65 and over. Census Bureau projections indicate that the ratio of men to women will continue to fall over the next few decades.

RACE DISTRIBUTION

Elderly nonwhite* men and women comprised only a very small proportion of the total population in 1987 (0.5 and 0.7 percent, respectively). As compared to whites, a substantially smaller proportion of nonwhites were aged

*Most of the nonwhites (about 83 percent) were black.

65 and over (8 versus 13 percent). This difference is attributed to both higher fertility rates and higher mortality rates at ages lower than 65 among nonwhites.[2]

SOCIAL AND ECONOMIC VARIABLES

EDUCATION

Educational attainment in the elderly is well below that of younger populations. In 1985 approximately 45 percent of individuals age 75 and over had discontinued their formal education at eighth grade or earlier, as compared to 14 percent of the population 25 and older. About 40 percent of the group aged 75 and older had completed high school, as compared to 74 percent of individuals aged 25 and over. Black elderly individuals had considerably lower educational levels than did white elderly individuals.[10]

The educational gap between elderly and younger cohorts has been narrowing over the last 30 years, and is expected to continue to diminish. Census Bureau projections indicate that by the year 2000, 64 percent of the population age 65 and over will have completed high school, as compared to 80 percent of the 25 and over population.[2]

LABOR FORCE PARTICIPATION AND INCOME

The majority of elderly individuals are not in the labor force (i.e., currently working or looking for work). In 1987, 16 percent of men and 7 percent of women age 65 and over participated in the labor force.[11] These figures reflect a substantial downward trend since 1955, when 40 percent of men and 11 percent of women 65 and older worked.[2]

Consistent with the low rates of labor participation are the generally low income levels among the elderly. In 1986, median incomes for elderly men and women were approximately $11,500 and $6,500, respectively.[12] White men tend to have the highest median incomes and black women the lowest. In 1986, four out of every five elderly black women had incomes less than $7000, as compared to about half of white women, half of black men, and one-fourth of white men. Although income levels remain quite low in the elderly, they more than doubled between 1951 and 1981 (in 1981 dollars).[13]

DEPENDENCY RATIO

One way to determine how age contributes to economic and social trends is to examine *dependency ratios* which measure the size of some "dependent" segment of the population relative to the size of some "productive" group.[14] As indicated in Table 15-2, the ratio of the 65-and-over population to the 18- to 64-year-old population (societal-aged dependency ratio) has increased steadily since 1930 and is expected to continue increasing into the middle of the next century. These changes imply that working people face an increasing burden in supporting the elderly population. Note that familial-aged dependency ratios are expected to increase substantially, although less steadily. As a result of declining fertility rates and the entry of women into the labor force, elderly individuals of the future will have fewer children to care for them than elderly individuals today.[15,16]

MARITAL STATUS AND LIVING ARRANGEMENTS

Elderly women are much more likely than elderly men to be widowed and to live alone (Table 15-3). In 1985, 41 percent of women age 65 and over lived alone, as compared to 15 percent of elderly men.[17] Elderly black individuals were more likely to be widowed than were elderly whites, although the sex differences far outweighed the race differences. Several factors account for the sex differences in widowhood. The most important factor is the higher mortality of men as compared to women. This is compounded by the tendency of women to marry men who are older than themselves. In addition, widowers have higher rates of remarriage than do widows.[2]

INSTITUTIONALIZATION

In 1985, the proportion of the elderly population living in nursing homes was just under 5 percent.[18,19] The proportion in nursing homes increased with age, was higher among women than men, and was higher among whites than in nonwhites (Fig. 15-1). Among the 1.3 million elderly individuals living in nursing homes in 1985, 45 percent were aged 85 and over, as compared to just 16 percent who were ages 65 to 74. The majority were women (75 percent) and white (93 percent).

While the proportion of the elderly population in nursing homes has remained fairly constant since 1973 (when the first National Nursing Home Survey was conducted), the number of elderly individuals in nursing homes has increased from 960,000 during the period 1973–1974 to 1.3 million in 1985.[18] This increase is pri-

TABLE 15-2
Societal- and Familial-Aged Dependency Ratios 1930 to 2030

	Societal-Aged Dependency Ratio	Familial-Aged Dependency Ratios	
	Population 65 and over ×100	*Population 65–79* ×100	*Population 85 and over*
Year*	Population 18–64	Population 45–49	Population 65–69
1930	9.1	82	10
1940	10.9	95	10
1950	13.4	166	12
1960	16.8	129	15
1970	17.6	135	20
1980	18.6	185	26
1990	20.7	174	35
2000	21.2	126	56
2010	21.9	126	58
2020	28.7	220	44
2030	36.9	241	49

*Figures for 1930 to 1980 are estimates; those for 1990 to 2030 are projections. Projections are taken from middle series.
SOURCE: Demographic and socioecomomic aspects of aging in the United States, in *Current Population Reports*, ser P-23, no 138. Washington, U.S. Bureau of the Census, Government Printing Office, 1984.

TABLE 15-3
Marital Status and Living Arrangements in the Population 65 and Over by Sex and Age, 1985

	Marital Status				*Living Arrangements*			
	Percent Married	*Percent Widowed*	*Percent Never Married*	*Percent Separated or Divorced*	*Percent Living Alone*	*Percent Living with Spouse*	*Percent Living with Other Relatives*	*Percent Living with Nonrelatives Only*
Men								
65–74	79.5	9.3	5.2	6.0	12.0	78.9	6.2	2.9
75+	68.6	22.7	5.3	3.4	19.9	67.4	9.9	2.9
Women								
65–74	49.9	38.9	4.4	6.9	35.0	49.1	14.0	1.9
75+	23.4	67.7	6.2	2.7	49.9	22.8	24.8	2.5

SOURCE: Marital status and living arrangements: March 1985, in *Current Population Reports*, ser P-20, no 410. Washington, U.S. Bureau of the Census, Government Printing Office, 1986.

marily a result of the aging of the elderly population. Seventy-six percent of the increase in the number of elderly individuals living in U.S. nursing homes between 1977 and 1985 can be accounted for by the group 85 and over.[19]

While the proportion of elderly individuals living in nursing homes at any one time is fairly low, a much larger proportion of individuals will spend at least some time in a nursing home.[20,21] A substantial proportion of individuals who enter nursing homes do so in order to recuperate from specific illnesses, such as hip fractures or acute myocardial infarctions, and eventually will return to the community.

The most likely explanation for the higher risk of institutionalization for women, as compared to men, is the greater probability of being a widow and living alone. A number of studies have suggested that living alone predicts institutionalization and, conversely, that the presence of caregiving family can prevent institutionalization.[21–23] The reasons for the lower rates of in-

stitutionalization among blacks are less clear since blacks are not less likely (and perhaps are more likely) than whites to suffer from the types of conditions requiring intensive nursing care.[24]

GEOGRAPHIC DISTRIBUTION

In 1987 in the United States, the seven states with the largest populations together accounted for about 45 percent of the elderly population: New York, California, Florida, Pennsylvania, Texas, Illinois, and Ohio. California, New York, and Florida each had over 2 million individuals age 65 and over in 1987; the other four states each had over 1 million elderly inhabitants.[25] At 17.8 percent, the proportion of the population ages 65 and over is larger in Florida than in any other state. Estimates of net migration between 1970 and 1980 indicate movement away from the Middle Atlantic and East North Central states and into the South and West, in particular to Florida, Texas, Arizona, California, and Nevada.[2–13]

FIGURE 15-1
Percent of population 65 and over living in nursing homes by age, race, and sex, 1985. [*Health Statistics on Older Persons, United States, 1986. National Center for Health Statistics, DHHS (PHS) 87-1409. Washington, Government Printing Office, 1987.*]

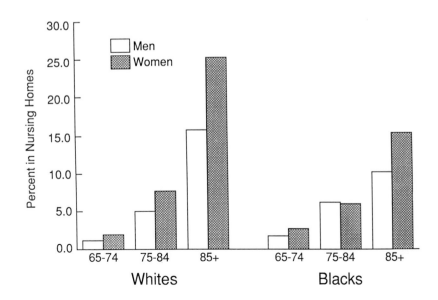

As compared to younger populations, elderly groups move very little. Between 1975 and 1979, only about 4 percent of the 65-and-over population moved across state lines, as compared to 9 percent of the population age 5 and over. Eighty-three percent remained in the same house during this time period. In 1981, the majority of the elderly population (about two-thirds) lived in metropolitan areas, with approximately half living outside of central cities.

EPIDEMIOLOGY

MORTALITY AND MORBIDITY

Mortality rates in the population 65 and over have decreased substantially since 1940 (Fig. 15-2). As a result of this decline, life expectancy at age 65 increased from 12.8 years in 1940 to 16.7 years in 1985 (Table 15-4). The decline has been fairly steady, with the exception of the period between 1954 and 1968 when mortality rates in the elderly were relatively stable.[2,26] Mortality data from 1980 to 1985 suggest that the rate of decline may be decelerating.

At the turn of the century, life expectancy at age 65 was only slightly longer (0.7 years) for women than for men. By 1985, however, life expectancy for 65-year-old women was 4 years greater than for 65-year-old men (Table 15-4). Census Bureau estimates predict that in the year 2050, 65-year-old women will live 6 years longer than 65-year-old men.[2] It is generally believed that the steady increase in the sex differential since 1900 can be attributed to decreasing mortality rates for diseases affecting women of all ages (i.e., maternal mortality and cancer of the cervix and uterus) and increasing mortality rates for diseases more common in men (i.e., lung cancer and cardiovascular disease). After 1968, cardiovascular disease mortality decreased in both men and women, but the rate of decrease was greater for women, thereby contributing to a widening sex differential.[27] Note that (1) the sex differential in longevity narrows beyond age 65 years and (2) mortality rates for males are higher than mortality rates for females starting at birth.[27,28] Thus, it is likely that the major basis of the sex differential in longevity occurs before old age.[28]

Throughout most of the life course, mortality rates are higher and life expectancy is shorter for nonwhites than for whites. This racial differential is usually attributed to socioeconomic differences.[1,29] At age 65 the differential narrows (Table 15-4), and by age 80, life expectancy is longer for nonwhites than for whites. Although reasons for this "crossover effect" are not well understood, it has been consistently observed in U.S. vital statistics data since 1900 and in community-dwelling samples of elderly individuals.[30] Vital statistics data indicate the existence of a black-white crossover for each of the major causes of death.[2,31] The most commonly proposed explanation, although not fully satisfactory, is that selective survival leads to a nonwhite elderly population that is relatively more robust than the elderly white population (discussed further in Ref. 30).

PRINCIPAL CAUSES OF DEATH IN THE ELDERLY

The leading causes of death have changed considerably since the early part of the century. In 1900, five of the ten leading causes of death were infectious diseases. In 1985, only pneumonia and influenza ranked in the top ten causes of death; together these accounted for only 4 percent of mortality in persons 65 and over (Table 15-5). The percentage of deaths due to pneumonia or influenza was 2 percent in those 65 to 74 years of age, 4 percent at ages 75 to 84, and 7 percent in the oldest old.

FIGURE 15-2
Age-adjusted death rates for persons 65 years of age and over by sex, 1940–1978. (Reprinted from Ref. 26, with permission.)

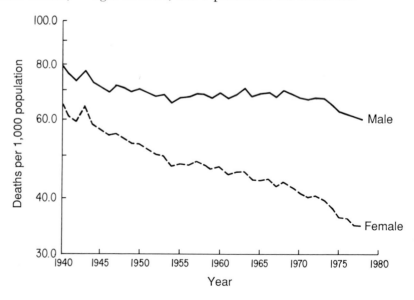

TABLE 15-4
Average Life Expectancy at Birth, at Age 65, and at Age 80 by Race and Sex, 1900–
1985

	1900–1902	1939–1941	1954	1968	1985
At birth					
All groups combined	49.2	63.6	69.6	70.2	74.7
White males	48.2	62.8	67.4	67.5	71.9
Nonwhite males	32.5	52.3	61.0	60.1	67.2
White females	51.1	67.3	73.6	74.9	78.7
Nonwhite females	35.0	55.6	65.8	67.5	75.0
At age 65					
All groups combined	11.9	12.8	14.4	14.6	16.7
White males	11.5	12.1	13.1	12.8	14.6
Nonwhite males	10.4	12.2	13.5	12.1	14.0
White females	12.2	13.6	15.7	16.4	18.7
Nonwhite females	11.4	13.9	15.7	15.1	17.6
At age 80					
All groups combined	5.3	5.7	6.9	6.8	8.1
White males	5.1	5.4	6.3	6.2	6.8
Nonwhite males	5.1	6.6	9.1	8.7	7.2
White females	5.5	5.9	7.0	7.0	8.7
Nonwhite females	6.5	8.0	10.1	9.3	8.9

SOURCE: *Vital Statistics of the U.S., 1985*, vol II, sec 6, Life Tables, DHHS (PHS) 88-1104. Washington, National Center for Health Statistics, Government Printing Office, 1988.

TABLE 15-5
Annual Death Rates for the 10 Leading Causes of Death for Ages 65 and
Over, by Age: 1985 (Deaths per 100,000 Population)

Causes of Death, in Rank Order	65 Years and Over	65 to 74 Years	75 to 84 Years	85 Years and Over
All causes	5,153	2,839	6,445	15,480
1. Diseases of the heart	2,173	1,081	2,713	7,275
2. Malignant neoplasms	1,047	838	1,281	1,592
3. Cerebrovascular diseases	464	171	606	1,838
4. Chronic obstructive pulmonary diseases and allied conditions	212	148	292	360
5. Pneumonia and influenza	206	58	241	1,024
6. Diabetes mellitus	96	60	128	215
7. Accidents				
Motor vehicle	22	18	28	26
All other	66	33	80	228
8. Atherosclerosis	80	17	82	466
9. Nephritis, nephrotic syndrome, and nephrosis	61	28	78	214
10. Septicemia	47	22	62	160

SOURCE: Advance report of final mortality statistics, 1985, in Monthly Vital Statistics Report, 36(5) (suppl), August 1987c. Washington, National Center for Health Statistics.

HEART DISEASE

Heart disease has been the leading cause of death in the total population and in the elderly throughout the second half of this century. In 1985, diseases of the heart, cerebrovascular disease, and atherosclerosis ranked first, third, and eighth, respectively, as causes of death (Table 15-5). In that year, diseases of the heart accounted for 620,000 deaths (42 percent of all mortality) in the elderly. Together, cardiovascular diseases (CVD) accounted for 775,000 deaths (53 percent of all mortality) in individuals 65 and over.[32] Rates of heart disease mortality increased sharply with age (Table 15-5) and were higher in men than women in all age groups above age 65. The sex ratio for heart disease mortality decreased from 2.1 at ages 65 to 74 to 1.5 at ages 75 to 84 to 1.2 at ages 85 and over. White men age 65 and over had higher rates of mortality from diseases of the heart than did black men, whereas there were no substantial race differences among women. Black men and women had higher rates of cerebrovascular disease mortality than did white men and women.[18]

Because diseases of the heart are responsible for such a large number of deaths in the United States, trends in mortality from heart disease determine to a large extent trends in all-cause mortality.[6,26] Since 1968 there has been a marked decline in heart disease mortality among all sex-age-race groups.[33,34] Between 1968 and 1980, the decline in coronary heart disease (the leading cause of heart disease deaths) was greater for elderly women than for elderly men.[35,36] This sex differential may be changing. Between 1980 and 1982, the declines were fairly similar for elderly men and women. From 1982 to 1985, the greatest decline (9.7 percent) was experienced by 65- to 74-year-old men. Mortality rates from stroke have also declined substantially since 1973.

Although *rates* of mortality from CVD have been declining rapidly, this has not always translated into a decline in *numbers* of deaths from CVD. In Connecticut, for example, although coronary heart disease mortality rates in the oldest old decreased between 1970 and 1981, the number of individuals age 85 and over who died from coronary heart disease increased from 1761 to 2829.[37] This apparent anomaly arose because the population 85 and older grew faster than the number of deaths. Despite declining overall mortality rates there remains much work to do in CVD prevention and treatment.

The reasons for the rapid decline in CVD mortality are not well established. Although it has been argued that technological advances such as coronary care units and coronary bypass surgery are at least partly responsible, data supporting this view are sparse. Risk-factor reductions, such as declines in hypertension, cigarette smoking, and fat consumption, can more readily account for the rapid decline in CVD mortality than can advances in technology (discussed in more detail in Refs. 38 and 39).

CANCER

Among individuals 65 and over, cancer is the second leading cause of death (Table 15-5). Rates of cancer mortality increase with age, although the rate of increase is much smaller than for CVD mortality. In 1985, there were approximately 300,000 deaths from cancer in the elderly, accounting for 20 percent of mortality. While the percentage of deaths due to heart disease increased with age, the percentage of deaths due to cancer decreased from 30 percent at ages 65 to 74, to 20 percent at ages 75 to 84, and to 10 percent at ages 85 and over. In the oldest old, cancer was the third leading cause of death; cerebrovascular disease ranked second. In contrast to CVD mortality, cancer mortality has increased over time, although only slightly.

The relationship between age and cancer mortality varies substantially for different cancer sites. For example, rates of lung cancer mortality peak between ages 70 and 79 and then decline. By contrast, rates of colon and breast cancer continue to increase through ages 85 and above. In 1985, the most common causes of cancer mortality among elderly men were cancer of the lung, colon, and prostate. Among elderly women, the leading causes of cancer death were cancer of the lung, breast, and colon.[40]

Age, race, and sex interact in a complex manner to influence rates of cancer incidence and case fatality. While a detailed exploration of these interrelationships is beyond the scope of this chapter, data on breast cancer are described to illustrate the complexity. At ages lower than 40, breast cancer incidence and mortality are higher in black women than in white women. At ages 40 and above, breast cancer incidence is higher in white women. However, the case fatality rate is greater for black women and, as a result, mortality rates are fairly similar for black and white women. Some, but not all, cancer sites show similar patterns.[41]

Rates of incidence and case fatality for a number of cancer sites are higher in blacks than in whites. Reasons for these racial differences are not well understood. Proposed explanations include (1) higher rates of alcohol consumption and cigarette smoking among blacks, (2) different dietary customs, (3) genetic factors, and (4) different occupational exposures. Additional hypothesized reasons for the differences in mortality include (1) detection of cancer at later stages in blacks, (2) different attitudes toward cancer treatment, and (3) histologic differences in tumor types. (See Refs. 42 and 43 for a more detailed discussion.)

CHRONIC CONDITIONS AND FUNCTIONING

Most diseases common to elderly individuals are not unique to them. However, because the incidence and prevalence of many chronic conditions increase with age, elderly people are more likely than younger people to suffer from multiple coexisting conditions. Further, when they become acutely ill, they experience more disability and more restricted activity days than do other groups of adults.[44] Table 15-6 shows the lifetime prevalence of several common chronic conditions among participants in the Established Populations for Epidemiologic Studies in the Elderly (EPESE). The EPESE project includes studies of noninstitutionalized persons age 65 and over living in three communities: East Boston, Massachusetts; Iowa and Washington Counties, Iowa; and New Haven, Connecticut.* The study populations were first identified in 1982 and participants have been recontacted annually up to the present time (1989). The goals of the project are (1) to determine the incidence and prevalence of chronic diseases and disability in community-dwelling elderly populations and (2) to identify risk factors for chronic diseases, disability, mortality, hospitalization, and institutionalization.[24] Hypertension was the most commonly reported condition in the EPESE populations, occurring in about 35 percent of males (slightly higher in New Haven) and 50 percent of females. With the exceptions of hip fracture and sensory impairments, most conditions did not increase with age. As would be expected, history of myocardial infarction was more common in men than in women, although sex differences leveled off in the oldest groups. In New Haven (the only site with substantial numbers of black participants), black women were more likely than white women to report a history of hypertension, diabetes, myocardial infarction, or stroke. Black men were less likely to report a history of cancer or myocardial infarction than were white men. Inferences regarding race or sex differences must be drawn cautiously since both sex and race influence survival to age 65.

FUNCTIONING

Functioning is a critical indicator of health and well-being in older populations, perhaps even more important than the presence of specific diseases. Impairments in physical and cognitive functioning predict both mortality and institutionalization among the elderly.[22,44a,45] Functional limitations can negatively influence the health and well-being of the impaired elder and of members of his or her family.[46,47]

*A fourth site in Durham County, North Carolina, was added in 1984.

TABLE 15-6
Percent Reporting Lifetime History of Selected Chronic Conditions by Sex, Race, and Location among EPESE Participants, 1982

Condition	E. Boston		Iowa		New Haven*	
	Men	Women	Men	Women	Men	Women
Myocardial infarction	15.1	10.0	22.1	9.4	16.0	9.7
Stroke	6.3	4.2	7.8	6.1	8.4	6.7
Diabetes	16.7	15.8	13.2	11.1	13.8	14.8
Hypertension	34.0	48.7	35.1	49.6	40.1	52.5
Hip fracture	3.6	3.9	2.4	5.5	3.1	4.6
Cancer	10.9	17.6	14.7	15.6	10.2	16.3
Impaired vision†	10.8	14.6	5.5	7.3	8.4	10.7
Impaired hearing‡	11.0	8.7	13.6	11.4	11.7	11.1

*Numbers and percentages are population estimates, projected from sample data.
†Cannot read ordinary newspaper print.
‡Cannot hear a normal voice in a quiet room.
SOURCE: Cornoni-Huntley J, Brock DB, Ostfeld AM, Taylor JO, Wallace RS (eds): *Established Populations for Epidemiologic Study in the Elderly* (DHHS) (NIH) 86-2443. Washington, Government Printing Office, 1986.

PHYSICAL FUNCTIONING

Physical functioning can be assessed in a variety of ways, although there is no single ideal method.[48,49] Participants in the EPESE studies were asked a series of 15 questions drawn from previously standardized questionnaires.[50-52] As would be expected of community-dwelling samples of the population (as opposed to nursing home samples), limitations in activities of daily living (ADLs), which generally indicate an inability to live independently, were fairly uncommon in the EPESE populations. Of the seven ADLs measured (walking across a room, dressing, eating, bathing, using the toilet, grooming, and transferring), the most commonly reported limitations across all three sites were walking across a room (reported by about 10 percent of participants) and bathing (reported by about 9 percent of participants). By contrast, the prevalence of one or more ADL limitations has been reported to be as high as 92 percent in nursing home inhabitants.[19] Disability in gross mobility was more common than were ADL limitations. For example, about 25 percent of participants (across all sites) said they were unable to walk half a mile. In general, the prevalence of both ADL limitations and mobility disability increased with age and was greater in women than in men. The New Haven data indicate a higher prevalence of disability among nonwhites than among whites, particularly in women.[24]

COGNITIVE FUNCTIONING

It is quite difficult to diagnose dementing disorders in the community and, consequently, prevalence and incidence have not been well established. (Methodological difficulties are discussed in more detail in Refs. 53, 53a, and 54.) Brief mental status questionnaires, such as Pfeiffer's Short Portable Mental Status Questionnaire[55] or Folstein's Mini-Mental State Exam,[55a] are frequently used to screen for dementing disorders in community samples. When interpreting scores on brief mental status tests, it is important to recognize (1) that poor scores indicate an increased probability that a dementing disorder is present, but screening test scores alone do not measure presence of a disorder, and (2) that education influences test performance, with poorly educated people making more errors.[55-57] It is not known whether education (or some correlate of education) is a risk factor for impaired cognitive functioning or a biasing factor. Alternatively, it is possible that the validity of mental status exams with regard to a "true" diagnosis of dementia varies by level of education (see Refs. 58, 59, and 60 for a further discussion of this issue).

The most commonly cited prevalence estimates among individuals age 65 and over are 4 to 5 percent for severe dementia and 10 to 12 percent for mild-to-moderate dementia.[45,61] The largest proportion of cases (50 to 75 percent) have Alzheimer's disease.[62] The second most common cause of dementia in the elderly is multiinfarct dementia, accounting for some 15 to 25 percent of presenting cases.[62,63] Prevalence and incidence rates for the dementias rise sharply with age. Prevalence starts at about 1 percent at age 60 and then doubles approximately every 5 years, reaching 32 percent at age 85.[62] Reports of annual incidence rates range from 1.1/1000 to 15.6/1000.[64-66] Data from the National Nursing Home Survey suggest that among inhabitants of nursing homes about 47 percent have some sort of dementing disorder.[19]

SOCIAL TIES

It is well accepted that the maintenance of social connections has an important association with health and well-being.[67,68] Although it has been proposed that the presence of social ties influences health to a greater extent in older than in younger populations, there is not much empirical evidence supporting this view.[5,69] Older and younger populations differ in that (1) older people are less likely to maintain extensive contacts from many sources,[5] and their networks tend to be somewhat more

limited[70,71]; (2) elderly people are more likely to experience life changes, such as widowhood and involuntary relocation, which have a profound impact on their social relations; and (3) the relative importance of specific social connections may vary with age. As an illustration of the third point, consider the association between marriage and mortality: It is well known that in younger populations marriage decreases the risk of mortality.[72,73] A number of recent studies, however, suggest that marriage loses its potency as a protective factor in older populations, whereas ties with friends and relatives are more powerful predictors of mortality in older than in younger age groups.[74-76] It may be that marital status does not predict mortality in older ages because not having a spouse is a more normative (and therefore less stressful) experience for elderly persons (in particular for women) than for younger groups.

To summarize, the elderly population of tomorrow will consist of individuals who are older and more likely to be female than the elderly population of today. As a consequence, the proportion of the elderly population living alone will increase, while the proportion participating in the labor force will decrease. The elderly of tomorrow will be better educated and will therefore be more demanding and sophisticated health care consumers. Because the number and proportion of elderly individuals in the total population will increase, so too will the number and proportion of individuals suffering from cognitive and physical impairments increase. In order to improve the lives of tomorrow's elderly and to decrease the societal burden of care for this burgeoning segment of the population, we must strive to identify those factors, both biological and psychosocial, that lead to "successful aging," and develop and evaluate new forms of aggregating and caring for the elderly.

REFERENCES

1. Siegel JS: Recent and prospective demographic trends for the elderly population and some implications for health care, in Haynes SG, Feinleib M (eds): *Second Conference on the Epidemiology of Aging*, DHHS (NIH) 80-969. Washington, Government Printing Office, 1980.
2. Demographic and socioeconomic aspects of aging in the United States, *Current Population Reports*, ser P-23, no 138. Washington, US Bureau of the Census, Government Printing Office, 1984.
3. Eisdorfer C: Some variables relating to longevity in humans, in Ostfeld AM, Gibson DC (eds): *Epidemiology of Aging*. DHEW(NIH) 77-711. Washington, Government Printing Office, 1977.
4. Berkman LF: The changing and heterogeneous nature of aging and longevity: A social and biomedical perspective. *Ann Rev Gerontol Geriatr*, 1988, in press.

5. Kasl SV, Berkman LF: Psychosocial influences on health status of the elderly: The perspective of social epidemiology, in McGaugh JL, Kiesler SB (eds): *Aging: Biology and Behavior*. New York, Academic Press, 1981, p 345.

6. Guralnik JM, Fitzsimmons SC: Aging in America: A demographic perspective. *Geriatr Cardiol* 4:175, 1986.

7. Deming MB, Cutler NE: Demography of the aged, in Woodruff DS, Birren JE (eds): *Aging Scientific Perspective and Social Issues*, 2d ed. Belmont, CA, Wadsworth, 1983, p 18.

8. Kart CS, Metress EK, Metress S: *Aging Health and Society*. Boston, Jones and Bartlett, 1988.

9. Vaupel JW, Gowan AE: Passage to Methuselah: Some demographic consequences of continued progress against mortality. *Am J Public Health* 76:430, 1986.

10. Educational attainment in the United States: March 1982 to 1985, *Current Population Reports*, ser P-20, no 415. Washington, US Bureau of the Census, Government Printing Office, 1987.

11. *Employment and Earnings, March 1987*. Washington, U.S. Department of Labor, Bureau of Labor Statistics, Government Printing Office, 1987.

12. Money income of households, families, and persons in the United States: 1986, *Current Population Reports*, ser P-60, no 159. Washington, US Bureau of the Census Government Printing Office, 1988a.

13. America in transition: An aging society, *Current Population Reports*, ser P-23, no 128. Washington, US Bureau of the Census, Government Printing Office, 1983.

14. Mausner JS, Bahn A: *Epidemiology, An Introductory Text*. Philadelphia, Saunders, 1974.

15. Aizenberg R, Treas J: The family in late life: Psychosocial and demographic considerations, in Birren JE, Schaie KW (eds): *Handbook of the Psychology of Aging*. New York, Van Nostrand Reinhold, 1985, p 169.

16. Serow WJ, Sly DF: The demography of current and future aging cohorts, in Institute of Medicine (eds): *The Social and Built Environment in an Older Society*. Washington, National Academy Press, 1988, p 42.

17. Marital status and living arrangements: March 1985, *Current Population Reports*, ser P-20, no 410. Washington, US Bureau of the Census, Government Printing Office, 1986.

18. *Health Statistics on Older Persons United States, 1986*. DHHS (PHS) 87-1409. Washington, National Center for Health Statistics, Government Printing Office, 1987.

19. *Use of Nursing Homes by the Elderly: Preliminary Data from the 1985 National Nursing Home Survey*, Advancedata 135. Washington, National Center for Health Statistics, Government Printing Office, 1987.

20. Kastenbaum RE, Candy SE: The 4% fallacy: Many die where few have lived, in Kastenbaum RE (ed): *Old Age on the New Scene*. New York, Springer, 1981, p 262.

21. Palmore E: Total chance of institutionalization among the aged. *Gerontologist* 16:504, 1976.

22. Branch LG, Jette AM: A prospective study of long-term care institutionalization among the aged. *Am J Public Health* 72:1373, 1982.

23. Shanas E: The family as a social support system in old age. *Gerontologist* 19:169, 1979.

24. Cornoni-Huntley J, Brock DB, Ostfeld AM, Taylor JO, Wallace RB (eds): *Established Populations for Epidemiologic Studies of the Elderly*. DHHS (NIH) 86-2443.

25. State population and household estimates, with age, sex, and components of change: 1981–1987, *Current Population Reports*, ser P-25, no 1024. US Bureau of the Census, Washington, Government Printing Office, 1988b.

26. Fingerhut LA, Rosenberg HM: Mortality in the elderly, in *Health, U.S. 1981*. National Center for Health Statistics, DHHS (PHS) 82-1232. Washington, Government Printing Office, 1981.

27. Wingard DL: The sex differential in morbidity, mortality, and lifestyle. *Ann Rev Public Health* 5:433, 1984.

28. Hazzard WR: Biological basis of the sex differential in longevity. *J Am Geriatr Soc* 34:455, 1986.

29. Kitagawa EM, Hauser PM: *Differential Mortality in the United States*. Cambridge, Harvard University Press, 1973.

30. Wing S, Manton KG, Stallard E, Hames C, Tyroler HA: The black/white mortality crossover: Investigation in a community-based study. *J Gerontol* 40:78, 1985.

31. Manton KG, Poss SS, Wing S: The black/white mortality crossover: Investigation from the perspective of the components of aging. *Gerontologist* 19:291, 1979.

32. Advance Report of Final Mortality Statistics, 1985, *Monthly Vital Statistics Report* 36(5) (suppl) August 1987. Washington, National Center for Health Statistics.

33. Feinlieb M, Gillum RF: Coronary heart disease in the elderly—The magnitude of the problem in the United States, in Wenger NK, Furberg CD, Pitt E (eds): *The NHLBI Working Conference on the Recognition and Management of Coronary Heart Disease in the Elderly*. New York, Elsevier Science, 1986.

34. Rosenberg HM, Klebba MA: Trends in cardiovascular mortality with focus on ischemic heart disease: U.S., 1950–1976. *Proceedings of the Conference on Declining Cardiovascular Mortality*. NHLBI, HEW (NIH) 79-1610, 1979.

35. Fredman L, Haynes S: An epidemiologic profile of the elderly, in Phillips HT, Gaylord SA (eds): *Aging and Public Health*. New York, Springer, p 1, 1985.

36. Changes in Mortality Among the Elderly: United States, 1940–1978 (suppl to 1980). *Vital Health Stat* [3] no 22a, DHHS (PHS) 84-1406a. Washington, National Center for Health Statistics, Government Printing Office, 1984.

37. Ostfeld AM: The potential for primary prevention of coronary heart disease in the elderly, in Wenger NK, Furberg CD, Pitt E (eds): *Coronary Heart Disease in the Elderly*. New York, Elsevier, 1986a, p 117.

38. Ostfeld AM: Cardiovascular disease, in Aiken LH, Mechanic D (eds): *Applications of Social Science to Clinical Medicine and Health Policy*. New Brunswick, NJ, Rutgers University Press, 1986b, p 129.

39. Levy RI: The decline in cardiovascular disease mortality. *Ann Rev Public Health* 2:49, 1981.

40. *Annual Cancer Statistics Review Including Cancer Trends: 1950–1985*. Washington, U.S. Department of Health and Human Services, Government Printing Office, 1988.

41. *Cancer Among Blacks and Other Minorities: Statistical Profiles*. DHHS (NIH) 86-2785. Washington, U.S. Department of Health and Human Services, Government Printing Office, 1986.

42. *Cancer in the Economically Disadvantaged*, special report prepared by the Subcommittee on Cancer in the

Economically Disadvantaged. Washington, American Cancer Society, 1986.

43. Hill LT: Cancer—the behavioral dimension: An interaction of lifestyle and disease, in Parron D, Solomon F, Jenkins CD (eds): *Behavior Health Risks, and Social Disadvantage*. Washington, Institute of Medicine, National Academy Press, 1982.

44. Estes EH: Health experience in the elderly, in Busse EW, Pfeiffer E (eds): *Behavior and Adaptation in Late Life*. Boston, Little, Brown, 1977, p 99.

44a. Guralnik J, Farmer M, Branch L, Wolz M, Wolf P: The joint effects of cognitive and physical disability in the Framingham Heart Study. *Gerontologist* 27 (special issue), p 60A, 1987.

45. Schneck MK, Reisberg B, Ferris SH: An overview of current concepts of Alzheimer's disease. *Am J Psychiat* 139:165, 1982.

46. Horowitz A: Family caregiving to the frail elderly. *Ann Rev Gerontol Geriatr* 5:194, 1985.

47. Moritz DJ, Kasl SV, Berkman LF: The health impact of living with a cognitively impaired elderly spouse: Depressive symptoms and social functioning. *J Gerontol Soc Sci* 44:S17, 1989.

48. Fillenbaum GG: *The Well-Being of the Elderly: Approaches to Multidimensional Assessment*. Geneva, World Health Organization Offset publication 84, 1984.

49. Kane RA, Kane RL: *Assessing the Elderly. A Practical Guide to Measurement*. Lexington, MA, Lexington Books, 1981.

50. Katz S, Downs TD, Cash HR et al: Progress in the development of an index of ADL. *Gerontologist* 10:20, 1970.

51. Nagi SZ: An epidemiology of disability among adults in the U.S. *Milbank Mem Fund Q* 54:439, 1976.

52. Rosow I, Breslau N: A Gutman Health Scale for the aged. *J Gerontol* 21:556, 1966.

53. Gruenberg E: Epidemiology of senile dementia, in Schoenberg B (ed): *Adv Neurol* 19:437, 1978.

53a. Henderson AS: The epidemiology of Alzheimer's disease. *Br Med Bull* 42:3, 1986.

54. Mortimer JA, Schuman LM, French LR: Epidemiology of Dementing Illness, in Mortimer JA, Schuman LM (eds): *The Epidemiology of Dementia*. New York, Oxford University Press, 1981.

55. Pfeiffer E: A short portable mental status questionnaire for the assessment of organic brain deficit in elderly patients. *J Am Geriatr Soc* 23:433, 1975.

55a. Folstein M, Folstein S, McHugh P: "Mini-mental state": A practical method for grading the cognitive state of patients for the clinician. *J Psychiat Res* 12:189, 1975.

56. Anthony JC, LeResche L, Niaz V, VonKorff MR, Fostein MF: Limits of the "mini-mental state" as a screening test for dementia and delirium among hospitalized patients. *Psychol Med* 12:397, 1982.

57. Holzer CE, Tischler GL, Leaf PL, Myers JK: An epidemiologic assessment of cognitive impairment in a community population. *Res Community Mental Health* 4:3, 1984.

58. Berkman LF: The association between educational attainment and mental status examinations: Of etiologic significance for senile dementia or not? *J Chron Dis* 39:171, 1986.

59. Gurland BJ: The borderland of dementia: The influence of sociocultural characteristics on rates of dementia occurring in the senium, in Miller NB, Cohen GD (eds): *Clinical Aspects of Alzheimer's Disease and Senile Dementia*. New York, Raven Press, 1981.

60. Kittner SJ, White LR, Farmer ME, Wolz M, Kaplan E, Moes E, Brody JA, Feinleib M: Methodological issues in screening for dementia: The problem of education adjustment. *J Chron Dis* 39:163, 1986.

61. Katzman R: Alzheimer's disease. *N Engl J Med* 314:964, 1986.

62. White L, Cartwright W, Cornoni-Huntley J, Brock D: Geriatric epidemiology. *Ann Rev Gerontol Geriatr* 6:215, 1986.

63. Cohen D, Eisdorfer C: Risk factors in later life dementia, in *Senile Dementia Outlook for the Future*. New York, Alan R. Liss, 1984, p 221.

64. Kay DWK, Bergmann K: Epidemiology of mental disorders among the aged in the community, in Birren JE, Sloane RB (eds): *Handbook of Mental Health and Aging*. Englewood Cliffs, NJ, Prentice-Hall, 1980, p 34.

65. Sayetta RB: Rates of senile dementia—Alzheimer's type in the Baltimore Longitudinal Study. *J Chron Dis* 39:271, 1986.

66. Sluss TK, Gruenberg EM, Kramer M: The use of longitudinal studies in the investigation of risk factors for senile dementia—Alzheimer type, in Mortimer JA, Schuman LM (eds): *The Epidemiology of Dementia*. New York, Oxford University Press, 1981, p 132.

67. House JS, Landis KR, Umberson D: Social relationships and health. *Science* 241:540, 1988.

68. Cassel J: The contribution of the social environment to host resistance. The Fourth Wade Hampton Frost Lecture. *Am J Epidemiol* 104:107, 1976.

68a. Berkman LF: The relationship of social support to morbidity and mortality, in Cohen S, Syme SL (eds): *Social Support and Health*. Orlando, FL, Academic Press, 1985, p 243.

69. Minkler M: Social support and health of the elderly, in Cohen S, Syme SL (eds): *Social Support and Health*. Orlando, FL, Academic Press, 1985, p 199.

70. Kahn RL: Aging and social support, in Riley MW (ed): *Aging from Birth to Death: Interdisciplinary Perspectives*. Boulder, CO, Westview Press, 1979, p 77.

71. Steuve A, Fischer CS: *Social Networks and Older Women*, working paper 292, University of California, Berkeley, prepared for the Workshop on Older Women, National Institute on Aging, Washington, September 14–16, 1978. Berkeley, CA, Institute of Urban and Regional Development, University of California, 1978.

72. Berkman LF, Syme SL: Social networks, host resistance, and mortality: A nine-year follow-up study of Alameda County residents. *Am J Epidemiol* 109:186, 1979.

73. House JS, Robbins C, Metzner HL: The association of social relationships and activities with mortality: Prospective evidence from the Tecumseh Community Health Study. *Am J Epidemiol* 116:123, 1982.

74. Blazer DG: Social support and mortality in an elderly community population. *Am J Epidemiol* 115:684, 1982.

75. Schoenbach VJ, Kaplan BH, Fredman L et al: Social ties and mortality in Evans County, Georgia. *Am J Epidemiol* 123:577, 1986.

76. Seeman TE, Kaplan GA, Knudsen L, Cohen R, Guralnik J: Social network ties and mortality among the elderly in the Alameda County Study. *Am J Epidemiol* 126:714, 1987.

Chapter 16

HEALTH CARE IMPLICATIONS OF AN AGING POPULATION

L. Gregory Pawlson

Despite the magnitude of the demographic changes outlined in Chap. 15, the impact of those changes on the utilization, cost, financing, and delivery of health services is only slowly being recognized. The large number of "baby boomers" entering the work force over the last 15 years has significantly reduced the apparent effect of enhanced longevity on the use and cost of services. The most pronounced effect of the baby-boomer phenomenon has been to dilute the burden of increasing cost of health care of retirees by spreading the financing over a larger base. Even so, the public origin of financing for a significant proportion of the care of those over 65 and the gradual realization of the eventual effect of the aging of the baby-boom generation itself have resulted in increasing attention to this area.[1,2] In this chapter we will explore in depth the effect of the changing age structure of our population on the utilization, costs, and financing of health care. Then we will briefly examine the related areas of quality assessment, service organization, and manpower. In each area, we will first examine changes which appear to be related to the aging of our population over the last 20 years together with current patterns and then attempt to ascertain what changes are likely over the next 50 to 75 years. The reader is cautioned that projections of more than a year or two in the future are subject to errors that multiply with time and do not take into account "catastrophic" changes that can and often do occur.

UTILIZATION

Both the absolute amount and rates of utilization of health care services are important in understanding the impact of changes in the population on the need for health care.[4,5] Table 16-1 provides information on the utilization of different types of health services by age. Clearly, the age dependency of nursing home and home care utilization is greater than that of hospital use, with physician use varying the least. However, recent trends seem to indicate an increasing rate of visits to physicians by the elderly, with steady or declining rates of use of nursing homes and hospitals. Data on home care use is so inadequate as to prevent an accurate determination of trends in this area, except for the postacute services provided as part of the Medicare benefit. Even here, the accuracy is questionable because of changes in the way the benefit has been defined by the Health Care Financing Administration (HCFA).

One of the most difficult issues in projecting future use is to predict whether past changes in rates will increase, decrease, or stabilize, especially in those instances where rates appear to be highly variable. Our projections for utilization in the period from 1990 to 2050 (Fig. 16-1) are based on the assumption of stable rates. In essence, these projections tell us what utilization would be today if our current population had the demographic structure we will have at various times in the

157

TABLE 16-1
Utilization of Health Services

	Hospital Bed Days/1000*	Physician Office Visits per Year[†]	Nursing Home Admissions/1000[‡]	Home Care Use per 1000 Medicare Enrollees[§]
15–44	600	4.3	0.2	
45–64	1100	5.2	2.4	
65–74	2850	6.4	14.0	21
75–84	4450	6.4	66.0	46
> 85	5525	6.8	170.0	68
Percent of Change				
< 65 to > 65	500%	35%	6000%	
65–74 to > 85	94%	6%	1200%	225%

SOURCE: *National Center for Health Statistice; advance data no. 140 September 1987. [†] National Center for Health Statistice; series 10 no. 144 1980. [‡] Reference 5 (adapted from page 87). [§] Health Care Financing Administration: Health Care Financing Program Statistics—1984. (This underestimates the use and differences since only Medicare reimbursed home care services are recorded.)

future. The years between 2010 and 2040 pose an especially interesting challenge to our health care system. Even when expressed in terms of absolute number and rates for the entire population, taking into account the reduction in the number of persons under 65 that will occur in the period, hospital utilization increases by 65 percent in absolute terms and 22 percent in days per 1000, and nursing home use by 200 percent and 100 percent, respectively.

While the aging of the population may be of considerable importance in the future, it has accounted for less than 10 percent of the increase in utilization in the past 25 years. The Rand Health Insurance Study[6] provides evidence that decreases in deductibles and copayments or covering deductibles and coinsurance with "supplemental" private insurance (as is common with Medicare) are likely to increase utilization. Another factor that has not been widely studied is the effect of the increasing relative wealth of the elderly as compared to that of the younger population on health care utilization. Most studies have suggested that medical care utilization varies considerably with income. Since 1965 the number of elderly living under the poverty line has decreased by 50 percent and the average income of households headed by persons over 65 has increased in relation to the average for those under 65. Educational level, another factor known to be related to increased utilization of health services, is also increasing with each new cohort of persons over 65. Another factor that may be increasing health care utilization is the increasing supply of physicians in the United States. While there is still controversy as to whether physicians can "induce" demand in health services, it seems likely that easier access to the services of physicians results in increased use of those services. Our changing attitudes toward aging and older

persons and the increasing political power of nearly 30 million retirees may also be contributing to the increasing use of medical care services in this age group. Finally, despite a few studies indicating that targeted geriatric services can decrease the utilization of some services, most of the attempts to reduce the use of nursing home or hospital admissions have resulted in markedly increased ambulatory visits to physicians, home care, and other ancillary services with no overall reductions in expenditures.

As-yet-unanticipated technologies that may cure or control chronic illnesses, further changes in family structure and function, or changes in the absolute and relative wealth of future cohorts of elderly are all factors that

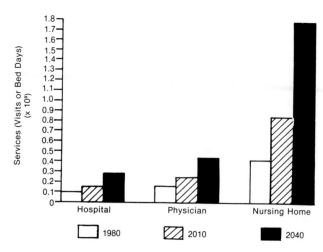

FIGURE 16-1
Growth in health care services for persons over 65, 1980–2040.

could affect the use of health services in the future. It is instructive to note that our history over the last 25 years is toward ever-increasing per capita use of health care services for those over 65.

The increasing knowledge and concerns about the causes of increased utilization may eventually have an impact on utilization itself. For example, the studies of variation in the use of medical services have shown that the rate of some surgical procedures varies by over 100 percent in comparable health service areas.[7-9] A more recent study from researchers at the Rand Corporation found a 50 to 200 percent variation in the rates of some procedures (carotid enarterectomy, coronary arteriogram, and endoscopy) in different large areas (states).[10] In addition, the study found that the proportion of procedures that were judged by an expert panel to have been done for appropriate reasons was only in the 30 to 50 percent range. Moreover, only a small part of the differences in appropriateness were explained by the variations of the utilization rates in different areas. If utilization and costs continue to rise, these and similar studies will accelerate efforts to reduce utilization rates by eliminating procedures that are ineffective.[11] Another area of inquiry is whether alteration in the use of one service can reduce the use of other more costly services. It has been shown that intensified home care services can reduce the rate of nursing home utilization. Unfortunately, overall costs may actually increase, although the "Social HMO" demonstration project may provide us with better information in this area. Other programs such as preadmission screening of nursing home applicants have been implemented with varying success.[13]

COSTS

The term *cost* is used in a variety of contexts with confusing results. In this text we will use it in the sense of denoting the product of volume and prices of inputs needed to produce health care services. The term *expenditures* will be used to refer to the amount paid by individuals or insurance for services.

CAUSES OF INCREASING EXPENDITURES

Expenditures for medical care in the aggregate are the product of utilization by service category and price. In the case of expenditures for persons over 65—even if there were neither inflation in the general or medical care economy nor new technologies—the increased utilization due to demographic changes would result in increased costs. However, our experience in this country over the last 25 years is that there has been marked inflation in the medical care sector that has consistently out-

paced that in the economy in general, and a plethora of expensive new technologies has been developed. Expenditures for medical care services for those over 65 have increased at an accelerating pace (Fig. 16-2).[14,15] An analysis of the causes of increased expenditures in the Medicare program reveals that only a small proportion (about 8 percent) of the increase has been due to increases in the numbers of Medicare enrollees. In the 10 years from 1975 to 1984, general inflation in the economy accounted for nearly 50 percent of the total rise in Medicare expenditures.[15] However, over the past 3 years, the marked reduction in general inflation, continued inflation in medical care prices, and increases in service volume and intensity explain a far-greater proportion (nearly 75 percent) of the continued rise in expenditures.

Some of the reasons for increased volume or intensity of services per Medicare enrollee were discussed in the preceding section. An additional factor is new technologies that add to, rather than replace, existing services. For example, the use of thallium scans as an adjunct to the diagnosis and management of angina has not produced a concomitant reduction in the use of electrocardiograms or coronary arteriograms. Most new technologies also increase costs through a factor termed *intensity of service*. For example, in the hospital treatment of myocardial infarction, multiple new technologies have been added in the treatment of such patients, including both diagnostic and monitoring devices (e.g., radionuclide scanning and pulmonary wedge pressure monitoring) and therapeutic modalities (coronary angioplasty or bypass). These new technologies result in increases in the "intensity" and costs of a given service (in our example, the service is hospital treatment for myocardial in-

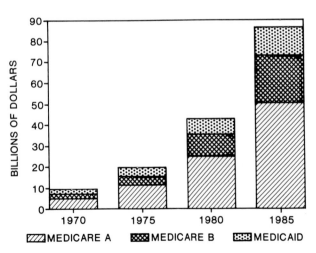

FIGURE 16-2
Medicare and Medicaid expenditures for persons 65 and older.

farction).[16] In addition, the specialized personnel needed to provide some of these technologies further accelerate hospital labor costs.

Another factor which appears to have contributed to increasing expenditures for medical care services for older persons is the reimbursement structure of Medicare. Prior to 1983, hospitals were reimbursed on the basis of their costs (i.e., the amount they reported spending in providing health services). Further, there were few, if any, controls on the appropriateness of admissions or on the length of stay. This resulted in an incentive for hospitals to acquire expensive new technologies and to allow increased labor costs since the costs could simply be "passed on" to Medicare for reimbursement. In addition, the "costs" that were recognized included costs of depreciation of capital (including that acquired through charity or government grants) and the costs of graduate medical education. Many felt that a reasonable portion of the increase in Medicare expenditures for hospital services was a result of the cost-based reimbursement system.[17] The radical change of incentives and controls on admissions imposed by the prospective payment system (PPS) using diagnosis-related groupings (DRGs) and the use of peer review organizations (PROs) has resulted in a reduction of both length of stay and admissions. While most observers agree that expenditures for hospital services have increased at a slower rate than they otherwise may have, some of the "savings" have been displaced by concurrent increases in the use of ambulatory services such as outpatient surgery and home care.

Physician reimbursement under Medicare has also come under increasing scrutiny, especially since Medicare expenditures in this area have been rising more rapidly than virtually any other sector except home care. Based on past experience, it is clear that both volume of services and price paid must be addressed if overall expenditures for services by physicians are to be controlled.[18]

DISTRIBUTION OF EXPENDITURES

The distribution of the use of health care services and expenditures for these services by those over 65 is highly skewed.[4,19,20]. The skewness is especially marked for care in a nursing home, somewhat less so for hospital care, and least, but still substantially, for physician and drug costs. It has been shown, for example, that only 10 percent of Medicare enrollees account for over 70 percent of the overall program expenditures. At the other extreme, approximately 35 percent of Medicare enrollees have no reimbursable expenses in a given year.[15] Even in the group of persons over 85, there are still over 20 percent who do not expend Medicare funds. Data from the National Medical Care Utilization and Expend-

iture Survey (NMCUES) from 1980 provide us with information about the distribution of all direct expenditures (except for premiums for Medicare or private insurance) from all sources for those elderly residing in the community.[4] Persons who resided in the community for less than the full year (i.e., those who died or were institutionalized), while representing only 5 percent of the group, accounted for 22 percent of total expenditures. Of those residing in the community for the full year, 12 percent incurred expenses of more than $3000 and accounted for nearly 60 percent of all expenditures. Thus, 17 percent of the overall group accounted for over 80 percent of the expenditures. Other analyses have focused on expenditures for care in the last year of life. The 5.9 percent of Medicare patients who die each year account for nearly 30 percent of total program expenditures. Within the group of decedents, less than 6 percent account for nearly 30 percent of the expenditures (this 0.4 percent of Medicare recipients account for over 10 percent of total program costs).[21] However, since people who die tend to be sick (and vice versa) and since it is difficult to predict who is going to die, it is not clear how these observations may be useful in addressing the problem of cost increases. Clearly, a major portion of expenditures are concentrated in a relatively small number of older persons. As we shall see, the skewness also has important implications for financing care for the elderly.

FUTURE TREND IN EXPENDITURES

Barring a major depression, increases in costs of health care and expenditures for this care will continue.[5] Indeed, it is likely that increases may be even greater in the years ahead than they have been in the recent past. The development of low-risk, high-cost procedures such as magnetic resonance imaging (MRI) is likely to further increase the rate of expenditures since the MRI can be applied in situations of low marginal benefit.[22] This is especially true in older persons where there is a high prevalence of disease but a high risk of complication from more invasive procedures. Furthermore, many of the trends cited, such as increasing wealth and educational attainment of the elderly, enhanced supply of physicians (and perhaps of geriatricians), and the development of new, but "additive" costly technologies are likely to continue in the future.

It should be noted that increases in expenditures and utilization for medical care services for the elderly are not inherently undesirable. Like some cost-containment efforts directed toward the elderly, it may actively result in just shifting costs or reducing services.[23,24] Indeed, some of the shift has occurred because we have delayed the onset of disease from the preretirement years to the postretirement years, something that seems very desirable. However, as medical care expenditures for those over 65 continue to rise as a proportion of the gross national product (GNP), questions as to whether the benefits that we gain for additional health services for our older citizens are comparable in value to those that would be gained by investing more in areas such as perinatal care, education, highway improvement, defense, or energy research will intensify. This is especially true because of the way in which we currently finance the care of our older citizens, a topic addressed in the next section.

FINANCING

The continuing conflict in our society between the values of ensuring reasonable access for all to health care and our history of favoring "free enterprise" and private insurance over government programs and social insurance have been nowhere more manifest than in decisions concerning the financing of health care for our elderly and disabled citizens. Since the current system of financing health care for the elderly has grown with no coherent plan, it is not surprising that the sources of financing are fragmented and inconsistent from service to service (Fig. 16-3) and among different socioeconomic groups. We will consider each of the major financing mechanisms beginning with the public programs.

In 1965, prior to the implementation of Medicare, over 25 percent of those 65 and over had incomes below the federal poverty line. While about 60 percent had some form of private insurance for hospital care, many of those policies were inadequate. Thus, a significant proportion of the elderly were forced to rely on charity or

were denied access to care. The growing effectiveness and resultant increased cost of hospital care gave a major impetus toward recognition of the need for more comprehensive insurance. In part because the elderly were a less significant political force in 1965 than they are today, it was necessary in proposing a social insurance program to make major concessions to hospitals and physicians. These concessions formed the basis of some of the cost and utilization problems which followed the implementation of the Medicare program.

The financing of the Medicare program is dichotomous because the program itself was put together from at least two separate and largely unrelated concepts.[25] Medicare Part A, which covers the hospital and rehabilitation-oriented skilled nursing home and home care was modeled after the social security program. Funds from a specially designated portion of the social security tax are placed in a separate trust fund (the Hospital Trust Fund) from which payments to providers are disbursed. Participation in the program is linked with social security and is essentially mandatory. The tie to the concepts of the social security system is important for a variety of reasons. Social security is viewed by many as an entitlement which is guaranteed on retirement for those who have contributed to the program during their working years. A key element is that, while there is some linkage between benefits per month and preretirement income, there is no direct link between the actual amounts contributed to the program and any benefit received. Thus, in reality, both the social security program and Part A of Medicare are transfers of income from those currently employed to pay for benefits for those who are retired.

By contrast, Part B of the Medicare program was introduced by the AMA and the Republican members of

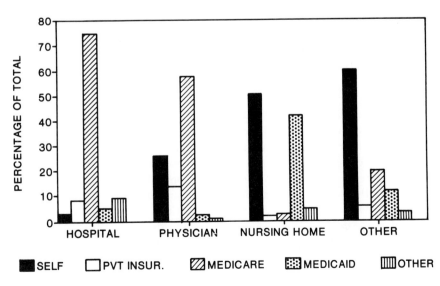

FIGURE 16-3
Source of payment for health care services for persons 65 and older.

Congress opposed to social insurance as an alternative to Medicare Part A.[25] It was originally funded 50 percent from general tax revenues and 50 percent from a premium paid by participants and was and remains a voluntary program. The use of general tax revenues reflected the problem that, with the large proportion of elderly below the poverty line in 1965, many individuals would not be able to afford the premiums necessary to fund the entire program. Because of the rapid rise in the costs of Part B and the growing political power of the elderly, the proportion of costs covered by the Part B premium has declined to less than 25 percent of total costs.[12]

The Medicaid program has become an important element in the financing of health care for the elderly largely by default. Like Medicare Part B, Medicaid was originally formulated as an alternative to a universal social health insurance program.[25] It was reasoned that if the government financed the care of the poor, the rest of the population would be enrolled through the workplace or could afford to purchase private insurance or to pay directly for health care. With relatively little notice, long-term care in the form of a rather comprehensive nursing home benefit and a more limited home care benefit were included as an element of the joint state-federal Medicaid program. Because of an absence of private long-term care insurance, a lack of Medicare coverage for long-term care, and the "deinstitutionalization" and release of many older persons with dementia that had been housed in state-financed mental hospitals, the Medicaid program quickly became the codominant (with self-pay) form of financing for nursing home care. In 1986, Medicaid provided financing for approximately 42 percent of long-term care expenditures with self-pay accounting for 50 percent, private insurance for 1 percent, Medicare for 3 percent, and other sources (such as the Veterans Administration) for another 4 percent (Fig. 16-3).

Medicaid financing of long-term care for the older person presents a number of difficult problems. Since Medicaid is financed by a combination of general tax revenues from the federal government and state tax revenues, to the extent that those taxes are based on wages or income of workers, they will be affected by changing demographics. Further, the income and asset levels permitted and the benefits provided vary widely from state to state. Many older persons find it humiliating to have to impoverish themselves by income and asset depletion to qualify for the program. Other older persons with substantial assets or income have evaded this necessity by transferring income and assets to other family members, further subverting the intent of Medicaid as a welfare program for the poor.[26]

Private insurance has played a rather uncertain role in the financing of health care for retired persons in this country. In the period before the development of Medicare and Medicaid, private insurance coverage for re- tirees was constrained by the high prevalence of poverty among the elderly and relatively small number of employers providing health insurance to their retirees. With the emergence of the political and economic power of retirees (and especially those in the 55- to 70-year-old group) there was a proliferation of both self-purchased and employer-sponsored private insurance. The self-purchase insurance often took the form of "Medigap" coverage, that is coverage of the "gaps" in the Medicare program. By 1987, nearly 70 percent of the Medicare-covered population had some form of Medigap coverage.[14] Most of the policies covered some or all of the Medicare physician and hospital deductible and copay, and a few covered areas such as prescription drugs which were not addressed by the Medicare program. However, there are still major gaps in coverage, the most notable being in long-term care. For example, while private insurance finances about 10 percent of hospital expenses and 25 percent of physician's fees, it accounts for less than 1 percent of long-term care expenses (Fig. 16-3).

In addition, there is evidence of what some feel is exploitation of the elderly by a few private insurers. While those policies actually labeled "Medicare supplemental" have to adhere to certain specified principles, others do not. As a result, there are older persons who have purchased multiple policies with overlapping coverages and policies that return less than 50 cents per dollar of premium in the form of benefits paid to the policyholders. In most cases the most flagrant abuses appear to emanate from policies sold directly to individuals via the mail or door-to-door merchandizing. Finally the focus of many Medigap policies on first-dollar coverage of deductibles and copayments may result in overutilization of some services.[27]

While avoiding some of the problems of policies sold to individuals, private insurance provided by former employers shares the problem of offering policies of limited scope, often directed to first-dollar coverage. Coverage of retiree health benefits is largely confined to large manufacturing sector employers, who offered what in the short term was a relatively inexpensive benefit, often to mollify unions or to encourage early retirement. However, the cumulative burden of these retiree health benefits presents a major long-range fiscal crisis for many of these businesses. Because of tax laws, only a small portion of the benefits can be funded in advance. With time and increasing longevity, the number of retirees increases and the cost of these benefits per unit of production rises as a consequence. At present and long before the adverse demographics of the period 2020–2050, the unfunded retiree health benefits of some corporations exceed their net worth. Cost shifting by Medicare has added to the problem, and many corporations have serious concerns as to the long-range effects of this obligation. Attempts to reduce benefits to current retirees have been largely unsuccessful due to legal opinions which, in effect, limit the reductions to future retirees.[28]

The problems resulting from the pattern of use and benefits provided in the public programs and private insurance are most apparent when we consider the distribution of payments made by individuals for uninsured expenses (Fig. 16-3). These problems include the following:

1. Prior to the enactment of the "catastrophic"-cost Medicare expansion in 1988, the limit on the number of days of hospital care and the presence of a copayment which increased as the use of hospital days increased in Medicare Part A, elderly persons with prolonged high-cost hospitalization often paid a higher proportion of their expenses as out-of-pocket payment than did those with less severe illness.[14]
2. Some older persons face high out-of-pocket expenses because of the provision in Medicare Part B that allows physicians (but not hospitals or home care agencies) the option of billing the patient the difference between what Medicare deemed to be its "allowable" charge and what the physician actually charges.[14]
3. Because of lack of insurance coverage for certain items like prescription drugs or chronic long-term care, those with the need for these services account for nearly 80 percent of those with high levels of out-of-pocket expenses.[29]

These variations in the sources of financing for different types and intensities of services have produced a very uneven pattern of out-of-pocket expenses for older persons. An especially vexatious problem is that not only the absolute amount, but also the proportion of expenses that are paid directly by the "victim" actually increases with very high cost illness. Thus, persons who have the most severe illness often have self-pay expenses that are "catastrophic," either in absolute terms (for example greater than $10,000) or in relative terms (costs which exceed 20 percent of income). Most affected are individuals with incomes or assets too high to qualify for Medicaid but too low to afford adequate private insurance. While the average out-of-pocket expenses of the elderly are approximately $1500 or slightly more than one-quarter of total expenses, this average, like many others, is very misleading. Twelve percent of the elderly had self-pay expenses of more than $500 per year, and those who did averaged nearly $5000 and accounted for nearly 50 percent of all self-pay expenditures. By contrast, the nearly 75 percent of enrollees who do not incur hospital or long-term care expenses average less than $700 per year for all self-pay expenses including premiums for private insurance and Medicare Part B.[4]

Several demographic changes will have a major impact on the current financing mechanisms. The trends toward increasing educational level and earlier retirement substantially reduce the ratio between time in the work force and time prior to work-force entry or in retirement. This, together with increasing longevity and the graying of the baby-boom generation, will have a dramatic effect on programs such as Medicare Part A which rely on transfers of income from those in the work force to retirees. Reliance on general tax revenues is less affected, although a substantial portion of the income and benefits received by retirees, such as half of the social security benefit, is not subject to federal or state income tax. This problem will be most acute during the period from 2010 until 2060 when the ratio of persons in the work force to retirees will be less than two to one, as compared to four to one at present, or nearly eight to one in 1932 when social security was implemented. Given the increased costs of health care for retirees due just to the size of population, this would translate into a need for a three- to fourfold increase in the 2.9 percent (1.45 percent each for employer and employee) social security tax currently used to fund Medicare Part A. (Note that this assumes no future expansion of Medicare benefits.)

The marked reduction in poverty among the elderly between 1965 and 1988 have led some to suggest that the elderly should pay a greater share of either current or future health care costs.[30] Incomes among the elderly show an almost bimodal distribution with the largest proportion (nearly 50 percent) clustered below one and one-half times the poverty level ($10,000 in 1988) and a small but growing population with incomes over $25,000 per year. Attempting to increase the share paid by the elderly by increasing direct self-pay (i.e., uncovered, copay, or deductible) expenses seems self-defeating, since as was noted, those who are very old are often the most ill, and have low to moderate incomes, and they already face a staggering burden of self-financed health care costs.

Congress has recently passed a major expansion of Medicare that would eliminate the large and repeated deductibles and copays under Medicare Part A. The mechanism for financing this Medicare "catastrophic" insurance signifies a major turning point in the financing of Medicare. Recognizing some of the economic gains of the elderly and the fact that the new benefit eliminates the need for some Medigap insurance and reduces the aggregate out-of-pocket expenses of the elderly, the entire cost of financing the new benefits will be borne by the elderly themselves. Increasing the Part B premium to cover the full cost of the benefits was problematic since the premium, currently at nearly $300 per year, is already difficult for some non-Medicaid-eligible, poor elderly to afford. Recognition of the uneven distribution of income of the elderly led to the proposal to fund a portion of the benefits by a premium which varies based on taxable income. Whether this will lead to the use of other taxes which, in contrast to the social security tax, either include or are focused exclusively on retirees as a means of financing health care for the elderly, remains to be seen. Such revenue sources might include allowing the full amount of social security benefits to be treated as taxable income, increasing the rate or lowering the exclusion (currently at $600,000) of the tax on estates, or including the value of tax-supported health care benefits as taxable income.

The growing recognition of the need to provide adequate and equitable financing for long-term care is an area that will require careful consideration of both current need and future demographics. The use of a public social insurance program such as Medicare Part A, which relies largely on the employed population to fund retiree benefits, will further add to the problems of health care financing which face this country in the period from 2020 to 2050. The use of private insurance, which is essentially a form of prepayment (i.e., reserves are set aside now to cover future expenses), is on the surface an attractive option.[31] However, it is not clear that many persons in their forties or fifties will be willing to pay premiums of several hundred dollars a year for an event that is most likely to occur 30 to 40 years later. In addition, because of the fear among private insurance companies of assuming what could be an almost open-ended risk at a time far in the future, essentially all currently available long-term-care policies limit benefits to a set total payout or a flat amount per month. Given our past history of inflation it is unclear how much protection a $50/day benefit might provide 30 years hence. Finally, due to the problem of adverse selection, the cost of long-term-care insurance to those already at high risk of needing such care is beyond the means of the vast majority of such individuals. Other solutions that have been advanced include full public financing through a Medicare expansion financed by increased social security taxes[32] and a more limited expansion financed by estate tax and an income-related premium and existing Medicaid revenues to fund a public program that would provide coverage for high-cost, chronic nursing home care and home care. The latter program would be augmented by private insurance purchased by employee groups at or prior to the time of retirement.[33]

HEALTH CARE PERSONNEL AND ORGANIZATION

Implicit in the discussion of the use of health care resources by our aging population is the issue of the distribution of the health care work force. Obviously, in the case of the need for physicians having a greater proportion of our population over 65, this means a higher relative demand for internists and ophthalmologists and a lower relative demand for pediatricians and obstetricians. While a number of sources have predicted a relative surplus of physicians in the future, the earlier projections did not take into account the apparent increases in the rate of physician utilization by those over 65 or the differential impact of a higher average age within the over-65 group on demand.[34] What role the emergence of geriatric medicine as a specialty, subspecialty, or area of "additional qualifications" will have is unclear. Estimates of the "need" for geriatricians are highly subjective and are dependent on assumptions about the amount of direct patient care assumed by geriatricians—whether the care will be in the form of consultation or primary care and whether patients will actually prefer the care offered by geriatric specialists to that supplied by general internists or family practitioners. Assumptions about supply hinge on how much interest medical students and house staff have or will develop in the area of geriatric medicine and reimbursement issues and on what training opportunities are available in the area.[35]

Given the large differences in the utilization of nursing homes, hospitals, and home care by our older population, the demand for professional nurses, for allied health personnel, and for those who assist in personal care is likely to increase substantially. The problem in nursing is likely to be especially critical given the substantial and growing shortage of nursing personnel at all levels and the seemingly low appeal of chronic care nursing, especially in nursing homes. The efforts at controlling the costs of nursing home and home care are likely to conflict with the need to increase nursing and allied health salaries to attract more persons into these fields. It is probable that we will see the emergence of new types of providers in these areas as well as redistribution of tasks to those in lower-paying positions. How such changes will affect the access to care or the cost and quality of health services for the elderly is unclear.

The cost and diversity of health care services required by some older persons is also beginning to have an impact on the organization of health services in this country. While the original intent of Medicare was to ensure access for the elderly to the existing health care system, a number of observers have begun to question whether older persons, most especially those with severe chronic disease and functional impairments, might not benefit from a more organized health care system. The impetus for this experimentation has come mostly from efforts to control costs. However, in some instances, the innovation has resulted in better outcomes, but at the same or even greater costs than the baseline situation. Geriatric assessment and management, life care at home, and the social health maintenance organizations are just a few examples that have been advanced.

The growth of consumer, industry, or government-based organized care systems such as HMOs and PPOs (preferred provider organizations) oriented toward the older member is a trend that is also likely to continue. It is important to remember, however, that at present a smaller proportion of those over 65 are enrolled in such organizations than persons under 65. This is not surprising given the tendency of those with chronic illness to stay with their usual source of care. It is likely that future cohorts of retired persons will be more favorably disposed toward alternative forms of practice since more of them will have had direct experience with those alternatives during their years of employment. Whether organized practices can indeed better-serve the needs of the elderly is unproved both in the health care research community as well as in the minds of the older population.

QUALITY OF CARE

The impact of our aging population on considerations of the quality and distribution of health care is less obvious than the impact on utilization, cost, and financing. Yet, what we consider "quality" care is dependent on the type and purpose of the care being rendered. To take an extreme example, it is foolish to measure the quality of care in a hospice by mortality rates or the number of years of survival. Even in the acute-care setting, the quality of care of persons with chronic illness and markedly limited life expectancy is more difficult to discern and measure than quality measures for the treatment of a young person with appendicitis. The problem is especially marked in the area of long-term-care services. The excellent monograph by Kane and Kane[36] provides an extensive discussion of the difficult task of assigning a value and determining the quality of long-term-care services. The need to develop and test quality monitoring measures that accurately define and efficiently and effectively measure changes in functional ability, attitudes, moods, and overall quality of life is paramount.

Despite the difficulty, the growing numbers of older individuals in nursing homes and home care settings will force us into better definitions and standards of quality of care in those areas. The formation of organizations such as the National Citizens Coalition for Nursing Home Reform and the passage of legislation setting higher standards for nursing home care is one evidence of this demand.

COST-QUALITY TRADE-OFFS AND ALLOCATION OF HEALTH CARE

The issues of what constitute quality of care and how to place a value on care for elderly persons are hidden elements in most debates about cost. Since the dollars that are spent by individuals and by society in providing health care benefits for the elderly presumably could be used in other ways, it is appropriate for our society to ask questions about the quality and value of the services received by the elderly in relation to other goods and services. As we have a larger proportion of our population in the age group where the need for health care services is high, with costs that exceed the ability of the individual (or the elderly as a group) to pay, these questions will become more pressing.

Our task becomes even greater when we try to compare the benefits of providing a more humane dying process in a hospice as opposed to providing prenatal education, a liver transplant, or the use of a pediatric neonatal intensive care unit. While some commentators have been concerned with possible "rationing," it would seem that their concerns are misplaced. Rationing already occurs. We do not send every patient with a headache for a CT scan, and we do not provide a heart transplant for a patient dying from congestive heart failure who is 85 and demented. The question is not whether we should or should not ration health care, but rather at what level we ration, what criteria are used to ration, and whether the rationing is implicit or explicit. In considering the value of a service to the elderly, it is important that we avoid overt age biases and base our choices on criteria such as life expectancy or severity of chronic illness that are applicable to broader groups. In the final analysis, an important measure of the humaneness of our society is the equity and openness of the processes by which we decide how to address the problem of health care for our older citizens.

REFERENCES

1. Mechanic D: Cost containment and the quality of medical care: Rationing strategies in an era of constrained resources. *Milbank Mem Fund Q* 63(3):453, 1985.
2. Aaron HJ, Schwartz WB: *The Painful Prescription: Rationing Health Care.* Washington, Brookings Institute, 1984.
3. Blumenthal D et al: Special report—The future of medicare. *N Engl J Med* 314(11):722, 1986.
4. Kovar MG: Expenditures for the medical care of elderly people living in the community in 1980. *Milbank Mem Fund Q* 64(1):100, 1986.
5. Division of National Cost Estimates, Office of the Actuary, Health Care Financing Administration: National health expenditures, 1986–2000. *Health Care Financ Rev* 8(4):1, summer 1987.
6. *Med Care* supplement 24(9): September 1986.
7. Pasley B et al: Geographic variations in elderly hospital and surgical discharge rates, New York State. *Am J Public Health* 77(6):6, 679, 1987.
8. McPherson K et al: Small-area variations in the use of common surgical procedures: An international compari-

son of New England, England, and Norway. *N Engl J Med* 307(21):1310, 1982.

9. Greenspan AM et al: Incidence of unwarranted implantation of permanent cardiac pacemakers in a large medical population. *N Engl J Med* 318(3):158, 1988.

10. Chassin MR et al: Does inappropriate use explain geographic variations in the use of health care services? *JAMA* 258(18):2533, 1987.

11. Wennberg JE: Dealing with medical practice variations: a proposal for action. *Health Aff (Millwood)* summer 1984, p 6.

12. Leutz W et al: Targeting expanded care to the aged: Early SHMO experience. *Gerontologist* 28(1):4, 1988.

13. Polich CL, Iversen LH: State preadmission screening programs for controlling utilization of long-term care. *Health Care Financ Rev* 9(1):43, fall 1987.

14. Christensen S et al: Acute health care costs for the aged Medicare population: Overview and policy options. *Milbank Mem Fund Q* 65(3):397, 1987.

15. Gornick M et al: Twenty years of Medicare and Medicaid: Covered populations, use of benefits, and program expenditures. *Health Care Financ Rev* (annual supplement) 1985, p 13.

16. Sawitz E et al: The use of in-hospital physician services for acute myocardial infarction—Changes in volume and complexity over time. *JAMA* 259(16):2419, 1988.

17. Freeland MS, Schendler CE: Health spending in the 1980's: Integration of clinical practice patterns with management. *Health Care Financ Rev* 5(3):1, spring 1984.

18. "Medicare Physician Payment: An Agenda for Reform," *Annual Report to Congress*, Physician Payment Review Commission, March 1, 1987.

19. Roos NP, Shapiro E: The Manitoba longitudinal study on aging—Preliminary findings on health care utilization by the elderly. *Med Care* 19(6):644, 1981.

20. Roos NP et al: Aging and the demand for health services: Which aged and whose demand? *Gerontologist* 24(1):31, 1984.

21. Riley G et al: The use and costs of Medicare services by cause of death. *Inquiry* 24:233, fall 1987.

22. Kent DL, Larson EB: Magnetic resonance imaging of the brain and spine—Is clinical efficacy established after the first decade? *Ann Intern Med* 108(3):402, 1988.

23. Schwartz WB: The inevitable failure of current cost-containment strategies—Why they can provide only temporary relief. *JAMA* 257(2):220, 1987.

24. Estes CL: Cost containment and the elderly: Conflict or challenge? *J Am Geriatr Soc* 36(1):68, 1988.

25. Cohen WJ: Reflections on enactment of Medicare and Medicaid. *Health Care Financ Rev* (annual supplement) 6:3, 1985.

26. Spitz B: Controlling nursing home costs, in Blendon RJ, Moloney TW (eds): *New Approach to the Medicaid Crisis*. New York, F&S Press, 1982.

27. "An Aging Society—Meeting the Needs of the Elderly While Responding to Rising Federal Costs," *Report to the Chairman, Subcommittee on Intergovernmental Relations and Human Resources, Committee on Government Operations, House of Representatives*. Washington, HRD-86-135, U.S. General Accounting Office, September 1986.

28. Birnbaum H, Reilly H: Retiree health care costs demand attention. *Business Health*, March 1988, p 28.

29. Rice T, Gabel J: Protecting the elderly against high health care costs. *Health Affairs*, fall 1986, p 5.

30. Longman P: Justice between generations. *The Atlantic Monthly*, June 1985, p 73.

31. Task Force on Long-Term Health Care Policies, U.S. Department of Health and Human Services: *Report to Congress and the Secretary*. Washington, September 21, 1987.

32. Rivlin AM, Weiner J: *Caring for the Disabled Elderly: Who Will Pay*. Washington, Brookings Institute, 1988.

33. Pawlson LG: Financing Long-Term Care: An Insurance-Based Approach. *J Am Geriatr Soc*, in press.

34. Schwartz WB et al: Why there will be little or no physician surplus between now and the year 2000. *N Engl J Med* 318(14):892, April 7, 1988.

35. Vivell S et al: Medical education responds to the 20th century's success story. *J Am Geriatr Soc* 35(12):1107, 1987.

36. Kane RL, Kane RA: *Values and Long-Term Care*. Lexington, MA, Heath, 1982.

Chapter 17

PREVENTIVE GERONTOLOGY: STRATEGIES FOR ATTENUATION OF THE CHRONIC DISEASES OF AGING

Edwin L. Bierman and William R. Hazzard

The most striking feature of disorders afflicting individuals in old age is the progressive emergence of chronic diseases. These "diseases of aging" (or, more accurately, time-related diseases), such as atherosclerotic coronary or cerebrovascular disease, osteoarthritis, hypertension, chronic lung disease, and non-insulin-dependent diabetes mellitus, tend to be highly prevalent in Westernized societies. Characteristically, they remain subclinical for long periods, reaching the clinical horizon (i.e., onset of symptoms) sometime during "middle age" or "old age."

Since these chronic diseases require time for their expression, and time is inextricably linked to aging, prevention or attenuation of the chronic diseases of aging should be the ultimate goal of medical practice in the interests of a healthy, vigorous, and satisfying old age. It must be stressed, however, that this most often requires intervention during middle age or earlier. Thus, given the fact that the upper limit of life span is fixed, prevention of the chronic diseases of old age can be defined as a delay in the onset of their clinical expression until the upper limit of the human life span is reached. A practical consequence and a realistic goal for many of the chronic diseases discussed in this chapter is the shortening of the period of symptoms and disability that exists between the delayed onset of the disease and the upper limit of the human life span (the "compression of morbidity").[1] However, at the present time we are far from this goal. Since the number of very old individuals is increasing and life expectancy is increasing,[2] it appears that the average period of disability is also lengthening and chronic diseases will probably occupy a larger proportion of the life span unless multiple preventive strategies are instituted on a broad scale. This has implications for both individual health and health care policy, since, if current trends continue, the fastest growing segment of the population (i.e., the group over age 85) is the one most susceptible to chronic diseases.[2]

The chronic disorders of the elderly are, as a rule, multifactorial in etiology. They result from complex, interacting forces, both genetic and environmental, linked to the variable rate of biological aging in individuals who may share in common only their chronological age. Since preventive genetics is not currently practical, and intervention to slow the rate of intrinsic aging remains only a future possibility, the primary strategy for prevention must be an alteration of the environmental factors that contribute to chronic disease.

Unfortunately, possible measures for prevention or

attenuation of chronic diseases of old age (Table 17-1) require, during middle age or earlier, the personal rejection of many aspects of a way of life which is still accepted by the majority of individuals in Westernized societies. Considerations of personal freedom of choice, lack of conclusive proof (in many instances) of cause and effect (i.e., that a modification of lifestyle will, in fact, prevent or attenuate a chronic disease), and powerful social and economic forces leave the burden of modification of a popular way of life on the individual and his or her supporters, including the physician. Thus, while a multifaceted strategy designed to defer or totally prevent the common disorders of old age through lifestyle modification in middle age can be articulated (Table 17-1), putting such a strategy into place requires determination and an ethic of self-denial in the interest of future health, which is a mind-set at odds with common contemporary lifestyles. However, the recent inroads into the social acceptability and public perceptions of cigarette smoking in the United States suggest that important aspects of lifestyle can be modified across all segments of the population.

TABLE 17-1
Common Chronic Diseases of Aging Potentially Modifiable in Middle Age through Personal Changes in Lifestyle

Disorder	*Preventive Strategy*
Hypertension	Reduction of dietary sodium
	Reduction of body weight
Atherosclerotic cardiovascular disease (CAD; stroke)	Treatment of hypertension
	Cessation of cigarette smoking
	Reduction of body weight
	Reduction of dietary fat and cholesterol
	Increased aerobic exercise
Cancer	Cessation of cigarette smoking
	Reduction of dietary fat
	Reduction of salt- or smoke-cured food intake
	Minimization of radiation exposure
Chronic obstructive pulmonary disease	Cessation of cigarette smoking
Diabetes mellitus (type II)	Reduction of body weight
	Diet consistent with atherosclerosis prevention
Osteoporosis	Maintenance of dietary calcium
	Regular exercise
	Cessation of cigarette smoking
Osteoarthritis	Reduction of body weight
Cholelithiasis	Reduction of body weight*

*Gallstones may be precipitated during active weight loss; this may be prevented by concurrent ursochenodeoxycholic acid treatment.

CIGARETTE SMOKING

The adverse health consequences of cigarette smoking and, to a much lesser extent, cigar and pipe smoking are well documented in terms of their associations with chronic bronchopulmonary disease, atherosclerotic coronary heart disease, and peripheral arterial insufficiency, aside from their clear role in the pathogenesis of bronchogenic, oral, and other cancers. Cigarette smoking is the most important cause of chronic obstructive pulmonary disease among adults in the United States; even younger smokers have demonstrable reduction in pulmonary function. From the standpoint of preventive strategy, evidence is accumulating that cessation or appreciable reduction of cigarette smoking can decrease morbidity from these chronic diseases.[3] Progress in overcoming this single most clear-cut threat to health in middle and old age has been substantial, even to the extent that young smokers have decreased per capita cigarette consumption in recent years. Starting with the unequivocal message from the scientific community that smoking may be dangerous to health, there has been progressive social pressure to curb smoking on an individual and population-wide basis. The dramatic progress of the past two decades in this most difficult campaign justifies optimism that other lifestyle modifications once considered unpopular and peculiar may become widespread, a current example being the popularity of running and other aerobic exercise.

OBESITY

Among the multiplicity of factors involved in the causation of chronic diseases, obesity, clearly present when an individual is more than 30 percent above the age-, height-, and sex-specific population average, is a most potent risk factor (see Chap. 72). Excess morbidity in such individuals is attributable mainly to atherosclerotic disorders, hypertension and its complications, cholelithiasis, endometrial cancer, and diabetes mellitus.[4] With regard to atherosclerosis in particular, obesity is associated with at least six identifiable risk factors; i.e., hypertension, non-insulin-dependent diabetes mellitus, hyperinsulinemia, hypercholesterolemia, hypertriglyceridemia, and reduced high-density lipoprotein (HDL) cholesterol levels. It is now appreciated that there are two major types of obesity, central (abdominal or "android") and peripheral (lower-body or "gynoid"). The obesity-linked risk factors for atherosclerotic coronary heart disease are associated with only one type, abdominal obesity,[5] simply estimated as the waist/hip circumference ratio. It has been suggested that measures to attenuate the effects of obesity in predisposing to atherosclerosis should be focused on those individuals with abdominal obesity (those with the "middle-age spread," reflecting excessive weight gain after age 25, and those who have a family history of familial combined hyperlipidemia or non-insulin-dependent diabetes).[6] Abdominal obesity should be amenable to the preventive strategy of long-term caloric restriction and increased energy expenditure through regular exercise. However, this lifestyle change is not easy to make in an environment in which food is readily available, attractive, and convenient, and in which labor-saving devices and automation continue to proliferate. Nevertheless, the recent popularity of voluntary aerobic exercise programs suggests that social forces may encourage an increase in energy expenditure and thus help attenuate or prevent adult-onset adiposity and its long-term sequelae. Regular aerobic exercise in adult life also may contribute its own benefits to maintenance of cardiovascular health in the elderly.[7]

ATHEROSCLEROSIS

Other dietary modifications are also attractive as preventive strategies during the middle years. Reduction of dietary sodium may be very effective among the (unknown proportion of) individuals in the population whose blood pressure is sensitive to variations in dietary sodium intake. Reduction of dietary fat (particularly saturated fat and cholesterol) to 30 percent of total calories or less has been associated with lowered plasma levels of cholesterol and triglyceride, and these, in turn, are associated with reduced atherosclerotic risk (see Chap. 45). In addition, reduction of calorically dense fat-rich foods may make caloric restriction easier. While not all skeptics have been convinced of the efficacy of this preventive strategy, and individual variation in response will remain great, such a personal program of dietary modification appears safe and hygienic, and recent statistics in food consumption in the United States suggest a population-wide secular trend in the direction of these alterations.

CANCER

Partly as a result of a comprehensive study by the National Research Council,[8] it has become apparent that many common cancers may be influenced by diet. The evidence was deemed strong enough to warrant recommendation of dietary modifications designed to reduce the risks of developing these malignancies. Such measures include reduction of total fat intake (both saturated and unsaturated) to about 30 percent of daily calories,

increased ingestion of fruits, vegetables, and whole-grain cereal products (especially those high in vitamin C and carotene, which is converted in the body to vitamin A), marked reduction of intake of salt-cured, salt-pickled, and smoked foods, and alcohol drinking in moderation. Although it is clearly not possible to design a diet that protects all people from all forms of cancer, the clear associations from epidemiological studies would seem to warrant a dietary preventive strategy for cancer which is remarkably similar to that suggested for atherosclerosis prevention.

OSTEOPOROSIS

Dietary modifications during the middle years and earlier may also influence the development of osteoporosis. A lifelong increase in calcium intake, especially among white and Asian females, who are at greatest risk, appears to be warranted. When translated into particular foodstuffs, conflicts may be produced in the achievement of certain goals. For example, though milk is a rich source of calcium and protein, it is also high in saturated fat and calories. Modified foods such as low-fat or skim milk in this example, may represent appropriate compromises. The interaction with other aspects of lifestyle modification should also be recognized: exercise enhances lean body mass (including bony mineral) retention; avoidance of cigarette smoking appears to defer menopause by several years, and, hence, the important effect of endogenous estrogens upon bone mineral content is prolonged.

ALCOHOL

The watchword in regard to alcohol is *moderation*. Clearly alcoholic cirrhosis and the other morbid sequelae of alcohol excess can be prevented by lifelong abstinence. There can be no alcoholism without alcohol. However, despite the burden to the population represented by all the adverse associations with alcohol abuse, there is little current enthusiasm for revival of the Eighteenth Amendment; to the contrary, the per capita consumption of alcohol has steadily increased in recent decades. This has coincided with epidemiological evidence of minimal mortality being associated with modest alcohol intake, not with abstinence.[9] This "protective effect" of alcohol appears to be mediated principally by a reduction in cardiovascular disease mortality among those imbibing modestly. This relationship holds despite the inclusion of an important subset of hypertensives whose high blood pressure is induced by alcohol. While the exact mechanism of the apparent protective effect of moderate alcohol intake remains unclear, a possible link may be the connection between alcohol intake and serum HDL cholesterol levels[10] in a manner suggesting a dose–response effect and demonstrable in controlled metabolic studies. Above a weekly intake of about 10 to 15 oz of alcohol (one to two drinks per day), however, the mortality rate climbs rapidly, and any potential benefits in the cardiovascular realm are outweighed by adverse effects all too familiar to the clinician. Thus the decision as to whether to drink alcohol is a personal one and should depend on the ability of the individual to drink only in moderation. That this decision is a difficult one is suggested by the close correlation demonstrated in many societies between the average per capita alcohol consumption and the prevalence of alcohol-related diseases and costs, both personal and societal.[11]

DISCUSSION AND CONCLUSIONS

Life involves a continuing series of choices. As improvements in standard of living and associated changes in the environment make death in childhood uncommon, these choices increasingly relate to the future health of those who will survive into middle and old age. While advances in medical technology would clearly seem to have contributed to the decline in many diseases, it is generally accepted that changes, often subtle, in lifestyle and the environment have had the greatest impact upon the prevalence and incidence of the major diseases of adulthood: The decline in tuberculosis preceded the advent of specific antimicrobial agents; the decrease in rheumatic heart disease has been more clearly related to better housing than to penicillin; most recently, the decline in cardiovascular mortality is more attributable to changing patterns of diet, cigarette smoking, and the diagnosis and treatment of hypertension than to acute coronary care or coronary artery bypass surgery or angioplasty.

From the perspective of the epidemiologist the greatest impact upon the burden of chronic disease in the population can be made through widespread adherence to the guidelines for the prevention of these diseases detailed earlier. This is perhaps best achieved through public education, utilizing the talents and technology of those in the communications media and perhaps involving physicians only in a supportive capacity as role models and sources of expertise. Such mass preventive strategies require acceptance of differential benefit on the part of the participants in such a program: Since all are not at equal risk, all will not derive equal benefit, and many will incur only marginal advantage over their less compliant counterparts. Some, in fact, will still suffer premature coronary disease, cancer, osteoporosis, and other chronic illnesses which this strategy is designed to prevent. In this connection, quantification of

potential benefit through individualized risk factor assessment and prescription of specific lifestyle modifications will involve the physician in an important professional role. The physician will also remain a critical supporter of the afflicted whether or not a prevention strategy has been part of the patient's lifestyle. The two approaches—mass versus individualized intervention strategies—are often mutually reinforcing, the physician (and his or her team) having only to reinforce the tenets of prevention already known to the patient by the time of their medical encounter.

This should not suggest that all is known in this area. Clearly this is not the case, and future research will disclose surprises (e.g., reduced osteoporosis among persons taking thiazide diuretics) as well as quantify risk/benefit ratios and clarify mechanisms. An important element of such research, highlighted in the current focus on cholesterol, is the timing of such preventive strategies: When should they begin? In childhood? Young adulthood? Middle age? And, equally important, when should they cease, if ever? Should hypercholesterolemia be treated in old age? Clearly there will come a time in each person's life when the benefit of such treatment will no longer justify the effort and perhaps even the risk. Thus *preventive gerontology* must be distinguished from *preventive geriatrics* (the subject of Chap. 20), which focuses on health maintenance/disease prevention once old age has been reached. And the balanced application of both will be a hallmark of "successful aging" (see Chap. 13).

Research must also address behavioral issues related to the barriers to compliance and improved techniques of "behavioral modification." Nevertheless the direction of future trends is clear: What has happened already in developed nations, the near elimination of death in childhood and that related to childbearing, is likely to be followed by a reduction in morbidity and premature death from atherosclerosis and, it is to be hoped, other chronic diseases of middle and old age as well. When this occurs, the dream of "rectangularization" of the human survival curve and its possible corollary, "the compression of morbidity," will have been achieved, and death from "old age" (multiple, interacting, perhaps nonspecific causes) will once again achieve respectability and prominence.

REFERENCES

1. Fries J: Aging, natural death, and the compression of morbidity. *N Engl J Med* 303:130, 1980.
2. Schneider EL, Brody JA: Sounding board: Aging, natural death, and the compression of morbidity: Another view. *N Engl J Med* 309:854, 1983.
3. Friedman GD et al: Mortality in cigarette smokers and quitters. *N Engl J Med* 304:1407, 1981.

4. Lew EA, Garfinkel L: Variation in mortality by weight among 750,000 men and women. *J Chron Dis* 32:563, 1979.

5. Stern MP, Haffner SM: Body fat distribution and hyperinsulinemia as risk factors for diabetes and cardiovascular disease. *Arteriosclerosis* 6:123, 1986.

6. Brunzell J: Obesity and coronary heart disease, a targeted approach. *Arteriosclerosis* 4:180, 1984.

7. Larson EB, Bruce RA: Health benefits of exercise in an aging society. *Arch Intern Med* 147:353, 1987.

8. Committee of Diet, Nutrition and Cancer: Assembly of Life Sciences, National Research Council: *Diet, Nutrition, and Cancer*. Washington, National Academy Press, 1982.

9. Friedman GD, Siegelaub AB: Alcohol and mortality: The ten year Kaiser-Permanente experience. *Ann Intern Med* 95:139, 1981.

10. Ernst N et al: The association of plasma high-density lipoprotein cholesterol with dietary intake and alcohol consumption. *Circulation* 62(suppl IV):31, 1980.

11. Gordis E, Dole VP, Ashley MJ: Regulation of alcohol consumption. *Am J Med* 74:322, 1983.

Part Two
PRINCIPLES OF GERIATRICS

Chapter 18

CLINICAL EVALUATION OF THE ELDERLY PATIENT

Richard W. Besdine

Clinical contact with the elderly patient is an event that is both commonplace and extraordinarily variable. Most physicians and other health professionals interact with and evaluate older persons daily, and the practice of medicine itself is rapidly becoming dominated by geriatric care. As clinicians prepare themselves to assess elderly persons, negative attitudes are still prevalent based on anticipation of prolonged and frustrating histories, a longer time for patients to undress and dress, extensive and vague complaints, difficulty establishing a diagnosis, less predictable outcomes of treatment, and complexity in getting paid for services. Not surprisingly, quality of care received by older persons in all settings has been found to be inferior to that received by younger persons.[1]

Beyond the demographic and fiscal imperatives driving our health care system to geriatrics, what attractions are there in geriatric care for the physician and other health professionals? Our aged patients define the future for us and link the past with the present. More concrete and pertinent, successfully managing disease and disability in older persons is more difficult and intellectually challenging, and gratification for successful caregiving is similarly greater. There has been extraordinary growth of knowledge in all areas related to aging over the past two decades, and centers of excellence in clinical geriatric care, solidly based on robust research and education programs, have developed in a dozen or more universities nationwide.

Although there is certainly need for more research to improve geriatric care, abundant relevant data now exist, and new knowledge is accumulating rapidly. This knowledge base is the intellectual frontier in geriatrics and must be integrated into diagnosis and treatment for the elderly. Basic information about normal human aging allows us to approach the patient with an understanding of cardiac output, kidney function, blood pressure, ventilatory capacity, immune function, and glucose metabolism in the healthy old person. When illness coincides with these and other age-related changes, the classic parallel lines of normal human biology and disease converge in the elderly patient. The need for detailed understanding of normal aging and its influence on disease is obvious when we consider the potential for confusion in evaluating a sick old person. Abnormalities not found in younger healthy individuals are discovered, but correctly assigning the observed differences to normal aging or disease cannot be done without detailed knowledge of normal aging, geriatric medicine, and their complex interactions. Uncertainty can produce two equally dangerous consequences. First, age-related changes erroneously attributed to disease will generate interventions that will likely be ineffective and may even do harm. Second, disease may be mistaken for normal aging and be neglected, resulting in progression of a once-treatable underlying disease. A third and worst outcome is the shunning of elderly patients by clinicians, frustrated and discouraged by aged patients whose multiple problems have both disease and age-related components.

Yet another crucial dimension has been added to the consideration of morbidity and its management in the elderly in relation to how we define "normal" changes of aging. It has become apparent that within the group of normal or healthy older persons, a spectrum of risk can be identified for future morbid events, and those with the least risk, based on genetics, life style, diet, and personal health practices, are most likely to age successfully (Chap. 13). Full understanding of the malleability of the many risks for "unsuccessful aging" is crucial to clinical approaches to the older patient as health promotion and disease prevention (Chap. 20) become more and more possible in old age. This chapter first addresses those principles in geriatric medicine relevant to evaluation of the older patient, and then deals with the specifics of history taking and physical examination.

PRINCIPLES OF EVALUATION

BEHAVIOR DURING ILLNESS

Behavior of the Patient

Behavior of the patient is influenced by a variety of social, ethnic, psychological and clinical phenomena, including perceived severity of illness, degree of disruption of daily life, alternatives to explain symptoms (denial), and the availability of care.[2,3] Since old age further alters the phenomena which influence health and illness behavior, we must examine the impact of aging on behavior during illness.

SELF-PERCEPTION OF HEALTH Although perceived personal health is dependent upon health status itself and on the presence and severity of disease, the peer group in which the patient lives and functions and its norms and expectations concerning health also may have major effects. A healthy octogenarian living independently in her own apartment in a social network of similarly robust elders is likely to evaluate a disabling condition as far more serious than her twin sister living in a nursing home. As people age, their health expectations appear to diminish independent of health status. In one study, although more diseases were reported by 75- to 84-year-olds than by 65- to 74-year-olds, the older group gave more positive evaluations of their overall health status.[4] Older people who underestimate disease are obviously at risk for neglect of treatment. This process of overestimating healthiness is sometimes called "normalization" and makes the patient attribute dysfunction to a transient or external occurrence rather than to disease. Accordingly, a fall is attributed to a loose rug or a moved table, or to the fatigue, poor vision, or clumsiness that "just happens when you get old." In addition, older people tend to underestimate the severity or gravity of disease when finally acknowledging illness. Angina may be explained away as muscle strain of household activity, and losing one's way in the shopping mall may be thought to be caused by poor eyesight. Interactions with physicians in the past, in which complaints may have been trivialized, also may influence self-evaluation of health and may cause delay in seeking care. The expectation of disability and functional decline in late life is likely to result in underemphasis of the severity of symptoms and delay in treatment for improvable conditions. One recent study comparing the appraisal of personal health between middle-aged and elderly persons found substantially more pessimism among the old, even after controlling for objective health status; and the elderly also showed a stronger association between depressive symptoms and perceived poor health than did the middle-aged.[5] Thus attitudes of helplessness, and consequent inaction regarding health, appear to characterize older persons.

Underreporting of Symptoms

It has been widely acknowledged that legitimate symptoms heralding serious, but often treatable, disease are concealed or at least not reported by elderly patients. In the 1950s and 1960s, several pioneer Scottish geriatricians screened older individuals, evaluating their health status, in the community.[6,7] These and subsequent corroborating studies documented substantial new illnesses and disability among elderly persons who were enrolled in the British National Health Service, which seemed adequate to deliver satisfactory care. Each older person had an identified physician, and care was provided without charge. And yet new problems were identified repeatedly, not obscure or tangential problems, requiring elaborate workup and yielding little patient benefit, but instead, common and treatable illnesses. The lists included congestive heart failure, correctable hearing and vision deficits, tuberculosis, urinary dysfunction, anemia, bronchitis, claudication, cancers, nutritional deficiencies, uncontrolled diabetes, immobility from foot problems, oral disease preventing eating, dementia, and depression.

A U.S. study in the 1950s found that nearly 90 percent of older individuals had experienced symptoms in the previous 30 days, but only 30 percent had sought care or advice from their doctors.[8] When asked to identify the person they would go to if sudden sickness arose, nearly 90 percent named a relative and fewer than 10 percent named a physician. One-third of their relatives, when questioned, thought that the patients were not getting sufficient medical care and thought that the older persons viewed symptoms as normal for their ages. Other American studies of symptom reporting by older persons living in the community revealed persistent minimizing of complaints.[9] Overall, less than 1 percent of 2000 symptoms were reported to any health professional. A substudy of a selected list of 20 key symptoms, identified as potentially most serious, also revealed serious underreporting. More than half of all symptoms were not reported to a health professional. The usual confidant was a family member, and when symptoms were unreported, explanations included "no big deal," "nobody cares," "nothing can be done about it," or "don't want to bother people."

Another study of health attitudes and behavior found that the oldest people had the highest baseline levels of health-promoting behavior, but were least likely to act when experiencing symptoms of serious illness.[10] Mild symptoms were usually attributed to age alone by individuals of all ages, but all symptoms (brief severe, brief mild, and chronic mild) were increasingly attributed to aging by those of increasing age. Symptoms attributed to aging usually evoked one of the following responses: (1) waiting and watching, (2) accepting the symptoms, (3) denying or minimizing the threat, or (4) postponing or avoiding medical attention.

Older people perceive and comprehend pain, malaise, and disability adequately, but do not report symptoms and thus do not get evaluation and treatment. A common explanation for nonreporting is the belief by the patient that old age itself brings irremediable functional decline and "feeling sick." This "ageist" view of gerontology makes it likely that older persons experiencing the same symptoms that bring middle-aged patients to the doctor will not seek care, will silently suffer as disease progresses, and will be burdened with the functional losses of untreated illness. Normal old age is usually characterized by good health and independent function, and occasionally, successful aging illustrates a vigor and vitality we can all hope and work for (Chap. 13); but ignorance of the knowledge base in aging makes it likely that elders and their doctors will continue to expect decline and dysfunction. The Scottish aphorism is that sick old people are sick because they are sick, not because they are old. Although decline in some biologic functions accompanies normal human aging, these declines and their functional impact are gradual; and their impact is further softened by the decades over which they occur and by remaining, if shrinking, physiologic reserve. Major functional decline occurring abruptly in an already aged person should be assumed to be caused by disease, not aging. In addition to ageism, depression or dementia also can disrupt accurate reporting of symptoms. The increasing prevalence of cognitive loss in old age interferes with detection of disease in two ways. First, demented patients complain less specifically, and second, they also tend to be evaluated less enthusiastically even when they do complain.

Documentation of underreporting of symptoms by the elderly seems contrary to the clinical saw that older persons are often hypochondriacal. Many practitioners and house officers are quick to describe elderly patients who try their patience and goodwill with endless complaints and "doctor shopping," driven by trivial or nonexistent illness. Yet at least one good study reports that the complaining and hypochondriacal old person appears to be one more unverifiable myth among our beliefs about aging.[11] Not only are older people less often hypochondriacs than the middle-aged, but also, when the elderly patient does complain, disease is found at the root of the complaint more often than in younger nonhypochondriacal patients.[12]

BEHAVIOR OF DISEASE

Multiple Disease Processes

One characteristic of illness in old age highly relevant to patient evaluation which puts elderly patients at risk for functional decline due to late disease detection is the presence of multiple disease processes. Several or numerous concurrent diseases in one old person, who either is not obviously sick or who is being treated for a separate disorder, can devastate health and functional status. An early Scottish study of persons in the community over 65 found nearly 3.5 major problems in each individual.[7] Among elderly patients being admitted to hospitals, six disease conditions were discovered per person.[13] An American nursing home survey identified the most common problems coexisting in elderly residents (Table 18-1).[14]

The presence of multiple disease processes is dangerous to the well-being of older patients in at least two important ways. First, diseases unidentified or ignored can interact with the diagnostic evaluation or treatment of the current illness and produce iatrogenic harm—a disease-treatment interaction. For example, an old man with congestive heart failure who is begun on potent diuretics without consideration of glucose intolerance, hyperuricemia, prostatism, or frail gait of early parkinsonism is more likely to be harmed than helped by the intravenous dose of furosemide given "to get things going in the right direction."

Second, disease-disease interactions occur when unidentified diseases interact adversely with one another to the detriment of the patient. These interactions are especially common and harmful in frail elderly patients, who are likely to suffer major functional losses which may remain, even after appropriate management of eventually detected illness. For example, an 86-year-old woman with arthritic knees, poor vision, and slow

TABLE 18-1
Common Coexisting Conditions in the Elderly

1.	Congestive heart failure	9.	Urinary incontinence
2.	Depression	10.	Vascular insufficiency
3.	Dementia	11.	Constipation
4.	Chronic renal failure	12.	Diabetes
5.	Angina pectoris	13.	Sensory deficits
6.	Osteoarthritis	14.	Sleep disturbance
7.	Osteoporosis	15.	Adverse drug reactions
8.	Gait disorders	16.	Anemia

gait gets a urinary tract infection (UTI) and urinates on the floor while walking to the bathroom; she slips and falls, fractures her osteoporotic hip, and succumbs to a postoperative myocardial infarction. Her problem list of (1) degenerative joint disease, (2) gait disorder, (3) atrophic vaginitis, (4) osteoporosis, (5) cataracts, and (6) coronary artery disease had never been assembled or considered by her physician, who thought of her as a "typical old woman." Her gait had never been considered for support with a cane, her cataracts had not been evaluated for surgery, her vaginitis had not been identified or treated with estrogens for comfort or reduction of UTI risk, and her osteoporosis had not been considered for treatment. The late and retrospective diagnosis of remediable problems which have produced permanent functional deficits is a discouraging but preventable part of geriatric care.

The number of problems per person is directly proportional to age, and rises to more than ten or even two dozen in the oldest and frailest, especially in the nursing home. When all problems are not identified and carefully considered, diagnostic procedures or treatment may do iatrogenic harm, as the intervention disrupts the already impaired function in an organ with undiscovered disease: the disease-treatment adverse interaction. The apparently stable patient with occult multiple diseases is also at high risk for decline. Korenchevsky[15] noted the dangers of unattended multiple diseases in the uncomplaining elderly patient resulting from disease-disease adverse interactions. Undetected, untreated problems in several organ systems or tissues interact with one another to further impair the previously diseased but compensated physiologic function. One can imagine a "domino effect" which creates an irreversible concatenation of functional losses leading to infirmity, dependence, and, if uninterrupted, death.

Chronicity of Disease

The prevalence of chronic disease is directly proportional to age, and chronic disease is defined as any condition lasting more than 3 months.[16] Eighty percent of Americans over 65 years of age have at least one chronic disease, and many have several. Some individuals grow old with chronic illnesses acquired in earlier years, but for many, chronic disease first appears late in life and may interact with age-related decrements resulting in accelerated loss of organ reserve. Chronic diseases account for most deaths over age 65, and heart disease, accounting for nearly half of all deaths at these ages, is most common. Diseases of the heart, malignant neoplasms, and cerebrovascular diseases cause nearly 80 percent of deaths among older persons.

The high prevalence of chronic disease among older persons is a major determinant of health care use, and over 80 percent of all health care resources in the United States are devoted to chronic conditions.[17] As the elderly population increases, chronic disease will become more common and disability even more prevalent. In addition, successful management of chronic disease requires sensitive and accurate assessment of functional status initially and over time. And physicians caring for the chronically ill must emphasize caring rather than curing. Efforts concentrating on management, functional improvement, and postponing deterioration are most relevant to chronic disease.

Functional Loss in the Elderly

Functional loss is the final common pathway for many disorders in the elderly. Functional impairment means decreased ability to meet one's own needs and is measured by assessing the activities of daily living (ADL), including mobility, eating, toileting, dressing, and grooming, and by assessing the instrumental activities of daily living (IADL), including housekeeping, cooking, shopping, banking, and driving or using public transportation. In addition, objective assessments of cognition and behavior and of social, economic, and emotional states are required to document health-related function of older persons. Unlike young persons, when elderly individuals get sick, the first sign of new illness or reactivated chronic disease is uncommonly a single, specific complaint which helps to localize the organ system or tissue in which the disease occurs. Instead, elderly persons often present when ill with one or more nonspecific problems, which themselves are manifestations of impaired function (see Ref. 18 and Table 18-2). These problems quickly impair independence in the previously self-sufficient elderly person without necessarily producing obvious, typical signs of illness by most lay and even general professional standards.

Why disease presents first with functional loss in old patients, usually in organ systems unrelated to the locus of illness, is not well understood. It appears that disruption of homeostasis by *any* disease is likely to be expressed in the most vulnerable, most delicately balanced systems in previously independent, functional elderly persons. And these most vulnerable systems, or weakest links, are likely to fail and produce problems of ADL or

TABLE 18-2
Functional Presentations of Illness

1. Stopping eating or drinking
2. Falling
3. Urinary incontinence
4. Dizziness
5. Acute confusion
6. New onset, or worsening of previously mild, dementia
7. Weight loss
8. Failure to thrive

IADL function rather than the usual classic signs and symptoms of disease. Thus, difficulties in mobility, cognition, continence, and nutrition are frequently the first manifestations of disease in an old person, regardless of the organ system or tissue in which the disease resides. Progressive restriction of the ability to maintain homeostasis, or the occurrence of "homeostenosis," is an important physiologic principle of biologic aging.[3]

The lesson for health care providers, family members, and elders themselves is that deterioration of functional independence in active, previously unimpaired elders is an early and subtle sign of untreated illness; and quality of life can be maintained only by rapid and thorough clinical evaluation when such functional impairments develop. These disease-generated functional impairments in old people are usually treatable and improvable, but detection and evaluation are essential steps before treatment can be initiated.[7] Since disease is likely to present with abrupt impairment of function in elderly individuals, functional assessment allows for early detection and thus intervention during the beginning phases of active illness (Chap. 23).

Active Life Expectancy

Important to an understanding of disease in old age is the concept of active life expectancy (ALE). Using a modification of the Katz ADL index[19] and life-table techniques, calculations were made of remaining years of independence, or ALE, for noninstitutionalized older persons.[20] Dependency was defined by degree of assistance needed with activities of daily living. Years of ALE declined with increasing age, as expected, shrinking from 10 years for persons 65 to 70 years of age, to less than 3 years for those 85 and above. ALE was lower at all ages for the poor elderly. Although net years of ALE were similar for men and women at most ages, the greater longevity of women means that the percent of life spent without dependency was greater for men at each 5-year interval. Beyond its utility in predicting the need for services and in furthering research on the condition of older persons, the concept of ALE allows us to consider the impact of an intervention on active life rather than on longevity alone. For the first time, predictive data can be collected on disability and its onset associated with increasing life expectancy.

Relationship of Function and Disease

A major component of medical education is mastering the clinical signs and symptoms associated with specific disease conditions. The poor correlation between functional disability (both type and severity) and the disease problem list commonly encountered in elderly patients demands an additional dimension of assessment. Since the burdens of disease and functional loss are both pro-

portional to age, it is often assumed that the length of an old person's problem list predicts the kind and intensity of functional disability. But a long problem list does not necessarily produce major loss of function; rather, independent and vigorous older persons often have remarkably long lists of serious problems. Likewise, individuals with short or even single-item problem lists may be severely disabled. Another common error is to assume that the type of disability is determined by the site of disease, so that immobility originates in musculoskeletal or neurologic disorders, confusion arises from brain disease, and incontinence stems from urinary tract problems. This apparently logical disease causality, usually valid in younger patients, does not hold in the elderly. Instead, especially vulnerable systems are likely to decompensate from the systemic impact of disease anywhere in the body.

EXAMINATION OF THE PATIENT

Evaluation of the older person requires modification and supplementation of the usual doctor-patient interaction for the young and middle-aged person if success and gratification are to be obtained. Different components of the history and physical examination need to be emphasized, and the physical environment and interpretation of laboratory data (see Chap. 26) require attention as well. Perhaps most important, comprehensive functional assessment must be coupled with the usual medical evaluation strategies (see Chap. 23).

THE SETTING

The setting in which assessment occurs should be modified in anticipation of frequent problems among older persons. Sensory impairments, physical discomfort, and communication difficulties require a considerate and individualized approach to every patient, regardless of age, but there are general principles useful to the physician caring for large numbers of older patients.

Beginning the interview by reassuring the person and by carefully introducing yourself to establish a friendly relationship is usually worthwhile and productive, and often older persons are comforted by a gentle touch on the hand or arm during conversation. The interview and examining rooms should be especially free of extraneous noise to allow communication and prevent distraction for patients with the common hearing impairment of presbycusis. Your words should be spoken clearly, with your body directly facing and on a level with the patient to allow lip reading and other visual clues. Speaking loudly is often helpful and necessary to communicate with a hearing-impaired older person. Since the prevalence of hearing loss exceeds 50 percent among patients over age 65, one should be prepared to speak up or to use a speaking tube. However, not all older persons are hard of hearing, and so it makes sense to ask about hearing at the outset rather than shouting unnecessarily throughout the interview. If hearing impairment requires raising the voice, and the deficit is due to presbycusis, which causes selective high tone loss, volume of speech should be increased in the lower frequency range rather than the high range in which most of us tend to raise our voices. Presbycusis causes poor perception of consonants, and in addition to speaking louder, exaggerated consonant articulation is also helpful. Most relevant, the physician should ask whether the patient has a hearing aid, if it works, and if it has been brought along. A reminder about bringing a hearing aid or any other prosthetic to the doctor's office before the visit is most useful of all.

Since visual impairment is also common among the elderly, adequate lighting is important both for safety and accurate perception by the patient. It is estimated that over age 65, two-thirds of the light which reaches the retina at age 20 is blocked by yellowing of the lens. Shadows can make the room dangerous for the aged patient, but very bright light, especially from above, can be painful following cataract extraction without lens implantation. Because aging eyes accommodate less well, the physician should never be backlighted. As with the hearing aid, glasses should be brought to and worn at the doctor's office.

Safety and comfort require that consideration be given to equipment used in the examination. Chairs of adequate height to allow easy sitting and arising are essential. The examining table should be of a height and size so as not to endanger an unsteady, small older person in the process of mounting, dismounting, or being examined. Gowns should not be difficult to manage for people with arthritic joints and should be short enough that an elderly woman under five feet will not step on the hem and perhaps fall. Allowing sufficient time for undressing and dressing again after examination is essential, but the physician need not wait around for the patient. Since patients are years and often decades older than their physicians and nurses, formal address as Mr., Miss, Mrs., or Ms. should be used unless the patient indicates a preference for first names. At no time should the impersonal generic "Dear" be used.

THE HISTORY

It has been said that the patient will try to tell us the diagnosis if only we will listen. Yet gathering an adequate history is more complex and time-consuming in the elderly, not only because they have had more time to accumulate disease, but also because disease is more common in the aged. In addition, more aspects of everyday life become relevant to health care in old age, and must be discussed. Besides conducting the patient interview and gleaning data from previous medical records, friends and family members and other physicians and health professionals who have participated in the care of the patient should be contacted as part of the history. Although family members can make important contributions to the history, reliance on the family or allowing them to dominate the evaluation interferes with assessment of the patient's view of the problem and of the physician's perception of cognition and emotion. Intellectual impairment, mild or severe, is not a reason to skip the history. Demented patients often are able to describe symptoms and response to therapy. The patient should be seen alone first unless there is outright refusal. Only after the patient is interviewed should the family join or be seen separately. A well-intentioned family member should not be the director of the patient's visit to the doctor.

Substantial preliminary data can be gathered before the physician sees the patient, and that information can be used to direct the doctor's history. Although standard history-taking forms have been found unsatisfactory for use with typical problems of elderly patients,[21] no consensus has been reached to recommend a specific geriatric history form. The chief complaint rarely adequately illuminates the complexity of disease in the elderly. Often one cannot even identify a single chief complaint in an older person who has deteriorated. Multiple disease problems and accumulated chronic disease generally produce numerous chronic and fluctuating unrelated complaints in the older person. Clinical decompensation from recrudescent chronic disease or a new acute problem is characterized by a cascade of symptoms in several organ systems, usually accompanied by disruption of psychosocial and economic balance of the old person. Multiple presenting complaints or identified problems are often dominated by functional losses, which have been called nonspecific (Table 18-2). Different complaints originate in different problems, and the law of parsimony, or Occam's razor, rarely applies to elderly patients. Even if a single presenting complaint can be identified in a decompensated older person, that complaint is less useful in narrowing the differential, leading to a separate literature on altered presentation of disease (Chap. 22). Each complaint, whether a major complaint or not, is likely to have its own "history of present illness," and each is best enumerated separately.

Family history can usually be abbreviated in older persons, though current data on heredity of Alzheimer's disease and its relationship to Down's syndrome is a notable exception. Social history must include information not usually collected in younger individuals. The social relationships with friends and family play a major role in the overall well-being and mental health of older persons, and have been shown to correlate with survival and health.[22] Inventory of resources in the neighborhood and home, including friends, family, and clergy, is needed to determine what kind and intensity of disability can be managed in the community. Services currently used and safety in the home should be documented. In view of health care costs, resources and insurance coverage should be listed. Diet history is relevant for most older individuals, especially when disease management includes food restriction or diet alteration that could interfere with nutrition, for example, with conditions such as diabetes, hypertension, ulcer disease, or congestive heart failure. Although polio, pertussis, and diphtheria immunization histories are not relevant in older persons, pneumococcal, influenza and tetanus status is important.

Sexual history is often omitted entirely by otherwise conscientious physicians, either through discomfort or mistaken assumptions about sexuality and aging (Chap. 10). An open-ended initial question will often be sufficient ("Tell me about your sex life") as long as an understanding and neutral attitude is taken in the interview. More specific questions about libido, masturbation, partners, frequency, function (or dysfunction), pain, and satisfaction can be asked as needed. It is becoming clear that the major cause of impotence in old men is not psychological, but rather organic disease (Ref. 23 and Chap. 117).

Although drug lists appear regularly in an older person's medical record, believing them to be accurate and complete can be dangerous. Drugs may be duplicated when the patient visits multiple physicians not known to one another, and treatment may be neglected if we assume that all listed medications are still being taken. The most reliable medication lists come from physically inspecting and inquiring about all drugs in the patient's possession. The patient and family should be asked to bring all medications to the doctor's office or to the hospital at the time of admission. With all containers laid out, both prescription and over-the-counter drugs, the physician can inquire of the patient which are taken, for what symptoms, and at what intervals. Discrepancies (one kind of noncompliance) are common at any age, but occur more often and with worse consequences in older patients (Chap. 21).

Finally, gathering historical information from sources other than the patient often assumes greater importance in geriatric medicine. Family members, friends, neighbors, landlords, and other health and social professionals, clergy—any of these may provide information crucial to both diagnosis and management. Tenacity in the pursuit of such information is a mark of the excellent geriatrician.

PHYSICAL EXAMINATION

Although the increased disease burden found in older patients would be expected to consume more time for an adequate physical examination, less time is actually allocated to older patients in physician encounters.[24] There are aspects of the physical examination that do require special attention in older patients, but care must be taken not to make physicians feel that a great deal more must be done and a great deal more time spent in examining the patient. In fact, most discourses on the special features of the physical examination in older individuals describe diseases to be found by the *usual* thorough examination which should be performed in patients of any age. Herein are noted only those maneuvers which require special attention in older patients or findings which have different meaning in the elderly.

Vital signs deserve emphasis. Blood pressure measurements are best done with the patient lying quietly for at least 10 minutes and then standing for at least 3 minutes to exclude postural hypotension.[25] Note should be made of whether the patient becomes symptomatic or not upon standing, and any blood pressure or pulse change should likewise be recorded. Because presence and degree of orthostatic drop may be proportional to height of systolic blood pressure, the presence of hypertension, with or without hypotensive drug treatment, should not exclude postural recordings.[26] Since older persons are particularly vulnerable to accidental hypothermia, low normal temperature recordings must be verified with appropriate low-reading thermometers. If disease presentation suggests or is consistent with hypothermia, a low-reading thermometer should be used whether screening temperature is normal or not (Chap. 111). Since infections in the elderly often present with less fever than in the young, and occasionally patients are afebrile (or even, paradoxically, hypothermic), clinical suspicion about level of temperature and infection should be high for the older patient. Pulse is routinely recorded in all patients, but the frequent baroreflex blunting found in older persons makes it useful to note whether and how much cardioacceleration occurs if blood pressure falls upon standing (Chap. 44). Height measurement is rarely important other than for calculation of body surface area or body mass index (BMI, kg/m^2), but elderly patients should be weighed under similar conditions at each medical evaluation. Measurement of weight is essential in following nutritional and fluid status, and it is vital to remember that involuntary weight loss in older patients is generally ominous.[27]

Aged skin frequently reveals multiple abnormalities (Chap. 40). Turgor is difficult to judge because of age and disease-related loss of supporting subcutaneous tissue and wrinkling, but the lateral aspect of the cheek may be a more reliable site for evaluation. Subtle evidence of pressure- and sore-prone areas should be sought, including hyperpigmentation and hyperkeratosis. The smallest areas of pressure-induced breakdown should cause concern for two reasons. First, one pressure sore generally heralds others to come; and second, most pressure sores are cone-shaped with the point at the skin and the much larger base in subcutaneous tissue or underlying muscle.

A few aspects of the head and neck exam merit emphasis in older persons. Arcus senilis, often cited in the past as a marker of premature cardiovascular disease, loses its clinical significance with advancing age (generally above 50) and in fact for the elderly is frequently a result of depigmentation within the iris associated with normal aging.[28] Although glaucoma is the second leading cause of blindness in America, and increasingly common with age, measurement of normal intraocular pressure by Schiotz tonometry may not exclude disease, due to the considerable diurnal variation in this pressure. Thus, funduscopic exam and testing for visual field loss are at least as important in screening, especially in those at high risk.[29] Temporal arteries should be palpated routinely for evidence of thickening or tenderness whether or not the patient complains, since temporal arteritis can be vague and unusual in its presentations. Carotid bruits should be noted and followed over time, but their presence correlates more strongly with generalized atherosclerosis and coronary insufficiency than with cerebrovascular symptoms.[30] The oral cavity should be examined carefully and, when relevant, both with dentures in place to check for comfort and fit and also after dentures have been removed to detect sores or possibly cancerous lesions. Diseased teeth and adequacy of saliva should be noted, as relevant to nutrition.

Deferring breast or pelvic examination in an elderly woman is indefensible in view of the increased incidence of malignancy in both tissues. A palpable ovary 10 years after menopause should raise the suspicion of tumor.[31] Genital and rectal examination in men and women provide excellent opportunities to assess bowel and bladder function, as well as the presence of impaction or more ominous rectal lesions. Atrophic vaginitis, urethritis, cystocele/rectocele, uterine prolapse, and evidence of incontinence are generally easily detected. Pelvic exam and Papanicolaou smear should be done at least every 2 years in elderly women with intact uteri.[31,32]

Cardiac and pulmonary examinations are much the same in older and younger persons, but certain findings require different interpretations in older persons. Systolic ejection murmurs occur more often than not in people over age 70 and generally are due to hemodynamically insignificant aortic valve sclerosis. These murmurs are crescendo-decrescendo and usually no louder than grade 2/6. Grade 3/6 or louder murmurs or the presence of symptoms such as exertional syncope or angina in the presence of any murmur should provoke an echocardiogram and possibly cardiology consultation. Clinical markers of hemodynamically important aortic stenosis, such as quiet or absent S_2 or dampened pulse upstroke, may be "falsely normal" because of elevated blood pressure or stiff arteries, respectively.

Careful neurologic examination is crucial given the frequent occurrence of primary neurologic diseases in older persons and the common expression of other illnesses through secondary dysfunction in the nervous system. Mental status testing by a reasonably sensitive standard screening instrument is mandatory in assessing older individuals with or without complaints, both to establish baseline norms and to detect abnormalities requiring further workup (Chap. 24). Symmetrical diminution or disappearance of gag reflex and vibratory sensation in the toes are commonly isolated age-related changes and should not, in isolation, be attributed to disease. Frontal release signs, often touted as evidence of dementing disease, have been shown to occur with normal aging and are not correlated with cognitive impairment.[33]

REFERENCES

1. Siu AL: The quality of medical care received by older persons. *J Am Geriatr Soc* 35:104, 1987.
2. Mechanic D: *Medical Sociology*, 2nd ed. New York, Free Press, 1978.
3. Besdine RW et al: Health and illness behaviors in elder veterans, in Wetle T, Rowe JW (eds): *Older Veterans: Linking VA and Community Resources.* Cambridge, Harvard University Press, 1984.
4. Ferraro K: Self-ratings of health among the old and the old-old. *J Health Soc Behav* 21:377, 1980.
5. Levkoff SE et al: Differences in the appraisal of health between aged and middle-aged adults. *J Gerontol* 42:114, 1987.
6. Anderson WF: "The Prevention of Illness in the Elderly: The Rutherglen Experiment in Medicine in Old Age," *Proceedings of a conference held at the Royal College of Physicians of London.* London, Pitman, 1966.
7. Williamson J et al: Old people at home: Their unreported needs. *Lancet* 1:1117, 1964.
8. Shanas E: *The Health of Older People.* Cambridge, Harvard University Press, 1961.
9. Brody EM: Tomorrow and tomorrow and tomorrow: Toward squaring the suffering curve, in Gaitz CM et al (eds): *Aging 2000: Our Health Care Destiny.* New York, Springer-Verlag, vol II, 1985.
10. Leventhal EA, Prohaska TR: Age, symptom interpretation and health behavior. *J Am Geriatr Soc* 34:185, 1986.
11. Costa PT Jr, McCrae RR: Somatic complaints in males as a function of age and neuroticism: A longitudinal analysis. *J Behav Med* 3:245, 1980.
12. Stenback A et al: Illness and health behavior in septuagenarians. *Gerontologist* 33:57, 1978.
13. Wilson LA et al: Multiple disorders in the elderly. *Lancet* 2:841, 1962.
14. Besdine RW: Approach to the elderly patient, in Rowe JW, Besdine RW (eds): *Geriatric Medicine*, 2d ed. Boston, Little Brown, 1988.
15. Korenchevsky V: *Physiological and Pathological Aging.* New York, Basel/Karger, 1961.

16. Jack S, Ries P (eds): Current estimates from the National Health Interview Survey, United States, 1979. *Vital Health Stat* ser 10:136, DHHS (PHS) 81-1564. National Center for Health Statistics, Washington, April 1981.

17. Cluff LF: Chronic disease, function and quality of care. *J Chronic Dis* 34:299, 1981.

18. Besdine RW: Geriatric medicine: An overview. *Ann Rev Gerontol Geriatr* 1:135, 1980.

19. Katz S et al: Studies of illness in the aged. The index of ADL: A standardized measure of biological and psychosocial function. *JAMA* 185:94, 1963.

20. Katz S et al: Active life expectancy. *N Engl J Med* 309:1218, 1983.

21. Kerzner LJ et al: History-taking forms and the care of geriatric patients. *J Med Ed* 57:376, 1982.

22. Berkman LF: Social networks, support, and health: Taking the next step forward. *Am J Epidemiol* 123:559, 1986.

23. Davis SS et al: Evaluation of impotence in old men. *West J Med* 142:499, 1985.

24. Keeler EB et al: Effect of patient age on duration of medical encounters with physicians. *Med Care* 20:1101, 1982.

25. Lipsitz LA: Syncope in the elderly patient. *Hosp Pract* 21:33, 1986.

26. MacLennan WJ et al: Postural hyptension in old age: Is it a disorder of the nervous system or blood vessels? *Age Ageing* 9:25, 1980.

27. Marton KI et al: Involuntary weight loss: Diagnostic and prognostic significance. *Ann Intern Med* 95:568, 1981.

28. Editorial. *Lancet* February 18, 1984, p 376.

29. Eddy DM: The value of screening for glaucoma with tonometry. *Surv Ophthalmol* 28(3):194, 1983.

30. Heyman A et al: Risk of stroke in asymptomatic persons with cervical arterial bruits. *N Engl J Med* 302:838, 1980.

31. Barber HRK: *Perimenopausal and Geriatric Gynecology.* New York, Macmillan, 1988.

32. Gunby P: Compromise reached on suggested intervals between Pap tests. *JAMA* 244:1411, 1980.

33. Basavaraju NG et al: Primative reflexes and perceptual sensory tests in the elderly—Their usefulness in dementia. *J Chronic Dis* 34:367, 1981.

Chapter 19

THE TEAM APPROACH TO GERIATRIC CARE

Conn J. Foley, Leslie S. Libow, and Fred B. Charatan

The *team* and the *team approach* are central concepts and components of geriatric clinical practice.[1,2] However, as distinct from other aspects of geriatric care, the elements, efficacy, and long-term benefits of the team approach are not well defined.

In a recent review of geriatric team assessment, Rubenstein[3] determined that team-managed patients appear, in general, to achieve equal or better results than control patients provided with traditional care and that the team approach was more likely to facilitate desired outcomes. In contrast, Williams[4] did not find specific benefit from outpatient team evaluations, and Saltz et al.[5] reported that a randomized controlled study of an inpatient geriatric consultation team demonstrated no benefit to patients who were followed up 6 months after discharge. Reasons suggested for these differences include inappropriate comparison groups or weak treatment options. We suggest another reason.

In most studies of geriatric team effectiveness, "the team," as if it were a well-described and understood instrument, is said to be in place. Instead the studies focus on the health care program, the variables and the outcomes are identified, while the mechanism by which the team operates is ill-defined. There is usually no delineation of an educational process or of quality controls which might have been applied to the team's activities. This lack of description of any calibration or standardization, of reliability or reproducibility, reflects our view that, in reality, little or no attention is given to the mechanical functioning or accuracy of the instrument, namely the team, whose efficacy is being studied.

The areas of oversights are addressed in part in this chapter by highlighting specific aspects of team function which can be defined, taught, refined, measured, and studied.

THE TEAM: THE TECHNOLOGY OF GERIATRICS

The team is "the instrument" of geriatrics. It should be regarded as a specific tool or technology within geriatric medicine, which can be compared to the endoscopes of the gastroenterologist or the catheter laboratory of the cardiologist. The team, viewed as a technology, can be evaluated, its productivity measured, and, where validated and its value recognized, it can be reimbursed by third parties as is the case for other medical technologies. The procedures and practices which constitute the use of the team as an instrument have been documented in specific areas of medical practice such as in psychiatry,[6-8] where the team approach is recognized as integral to much of its practice. The psychiatric and social work[9] literature on the team emphasizes the need to appreciate and understand the nature of group focus on patient care and the need for the group to be aware of the internal dynamics of its team effort; specifically the group must focus on its own team process. In contrast, the geriatric literature gives little formal recognition to the complicated nature of teams.

THE CONCEPT OF TEAM

A geriatric health care team is identified as a group of professionals with diverse training and skills who meld together their joint expertise for the benefit of the individual patient or client and who provide support for the individual members who constitute the team. The geriatric problems confronted include assessment, establishment of a comprehensive data base, the development of therapeutic strategies and management interventions, care plans, discharge planning, and follow-up.[10] The internal or organizational problems which the group must confront include the establishment, development, maintenance, and support of itself as a team in addition to assurance of its own efficiency.

A team's or group's effectiveness is measured first by its capacity to get its assigned or assumed work completed and second by its ability to manage itself as an independent group of people. This requires team cohesion, which is achieved through the team's commitment to interdisciplinary cooperation for patient care. The challenge is to develop a collaborative and effective team whose output is greater in sum than the contribution of its individual members.

CONTROVERSY ON THE NATURE OF TEAMS

TEAM FORMAT

A review of team literature[10–16] identifies the following diverse team formats, namely teams structured as or described as being inter/intra/multi-disciplinary or professional. There is no uniformity in the definition of these teams. Geriatric teams are generally identified as being of multidisciplinary composition and as functioning as an interdisciplinary entity.

DIVERSITY OF PROFESSIONAL RESPONSIBILITY

For the physician the nature of his responsibility toward an individual patient should be a clear responsibility for the total health care of that patient, namely the medical, psychological, and social components, and not just a focus on disease.[17] There is, however, a wide range of interpretation of this concept, from that of a surgeon or organ subspecialist to that of a primary care generalist or family practitioner. There is little disagreement among physicians that they enter a formal contract with their patient which mandates significant professional, ethical, and legal responsibilities.[18,19] On the other hand, the social worker is also a member of the interdisciplinary team and has a perception of and training in a different type of relationship. Psychiatric social workers frequently have significant primary care involvement with their patients (or clients), often serving as their primary therapists. The care they provide is under the supervision of, or in conjunction with, psychiatrists who prescribe psychotropic medications and who may review the therapy provided. Medical social workers, on the other hand, in most instances have little or no primary therapeutic patient care involvement. Their responsibilities to their clients may be to facilitate discharge from

institutions, arrange for placement, and act as ombudsmen, case managers, counselors, or resource finders. Thus, within defined professions the training, perceptions, scope of practice, accepted responsibilities, and, ultimately, the focus of individual members of a profession may be quite diversified.

TEAM COMPOSITION AND MEMBERSHIP

The composition of the team is yet another area where there is lack of agreement. In general, there is a core team consisting of physician, nurse, and social worker. Other professionals who extend the team may include a rehabilitation therapist,[20] an activities therapist, a dietician, a clergyman, an administrator, and students (Table 19-1). Whether these additional members are permanent, card-holding members of the team with voting or veto power is ill-defined and generally situation-specific. Consultants may assist teams, but their involvement is variable and is generally of very short duration.

Documentation on team membership generally ignores the role of the patient and the patient's family as participants. It is well recognized in standard ambulatory geriatric practice that it is usual to have the older patient accompanied by relatives, typically a spouse or daughter. Thus, it is appropriate at times to incorporate the family as team members, and much time may have to be assigned to discussions with them. This is not only reasonable but often necessary, since members of the family have access to information pertinent to decision making and they will have to be included, usually as caregivers, into the ongoing plan of care.

We suggest that an understanding of the components of a team's operation, as listed in Table 19-2, can

TABLE 19-1
Typical Members of the Core and Extended Geriatric Team for the Institutionalized or Ambulatory Patient

Core Clinical Members

Nurse
Physician
Social Worker

Extended Membership (variable)

Family	Occupational therapist
Nurse's aide	Physical therapist
Psychiatrist	Speech therapist
Psychologist	Audiologist
Podiatrist	Physiatrist
Dietician	Activities therapist
Administrator	Clergy/ethicist
Consultants	Students

TABLE 19-2
The Team: How To Operate, Maintain, and Repair

Goals/objectives
Education of team members
Role expectations
   Internal
   External
Communication patterns
Leadership
Decision making
Norms
Conflict management/negotiation

lead to successful use of the team as a tool or technology and that a focus on areas such as leadership, decision making, and conflict management can also act as reasonable parameters by which team effectiveness can be measured.

THE TEAM: HOW TO OPERATE, MAINTAIN, AND REPAIR

GOALS AND OBJECTIVES

The development and achievement of therapeutic goals is the reason for a team's existence, even if the goal sometimes is "no intervention," since this is an active decision requiring considerable knowledge and resolve. It is important to understand how these goals are set and who is responsible for the decision that the identified goals are appropriate to a particular patient.[21]

For the physician working in a geriatric team, the difficulties in establishing goals may create special challenges. The team must develop a plan of care, specific components of management must be defined, and time frames for the completion of interventions must be identified and met. The physician may feel distressed by organizational and governmental requirements to justify care, to identify the quality of the care provided, and to document integration with other team members. It is, nonetheless, a prerequisite of team goal setting that the physician as a team member accept with enthusiasm, rather than with negativity, these external requirements which may appear to limit physician independence, autonomy, and perceived superiority. In reality, these stipulations may improve the care rendered by physicians in selected situations.

Clarity of goals is an important consideration in geriatrics since the scope of responsibility and the nature of the problems addressed are much more global and frequently more challenging than in many areas of medical practice.[23] It is clear, for example, that in the case of the surgical team, where the goal is to perform surgery, that it is the surgeon who as the team leader defines the chain of command which permits the surgery to be accom-plished, the specific nature of the surgery to be undertaken, the sequence of steps to complete the surgery, and the time frame for its completion.

Final goals do not necessarily have to be defined as exclusive or all encompassing endpoints, but they can be formulated as a direction to be taken or as a general objective toward which the team will direct its best efforts. A vagueness in the final goal does not preclude clarity in defining the sequential steps or subgoals leading to it. These components of goal setting should be formally documented as a record of the team's endeavors. They should be developed as clear measures or markers which permit recognition of stepwise progress along a path toward final goal achievement.

Subgoals must be reasonable and appropriate. But when established, they must be understood and openly recognized to present a degree of difficulty. They should not be so demanding that they cannot be attained within a few days. Such an orchestrated challenge assures a good likelihood of success which will be accompanied by a true sense of achievement. The reward is excellent morale for staff and patient and enthusiasm to advance to the next step and ultimately to levels of attainment which might not have been thought to be possible.

It may be much more challenging for a geriatric team, than for a surgical team, for example, to identify specific goals and steps in the management of an 80-year-old patient with multiple medical diagnoses. Such a patient may require innumerable therapeutic interventions, may be depressed, have cognitive decline, limited finances, and have lived alone or have family who are unavailable or uninvolved. There can be much role negotiation or argument in deciding who will assume responsibility for defining goals under these circumstances and for deciding on the members who will participate in completing assignments necessary in the achievement of these goals.

The goals which teams set must be judged for appropriateness in relationship to the goals of the organization within which that team functions, the personal goals of professional staff, and the attitudes of each staff member toward the patient and toward other team members. It must be recognized that individual team members develop goals in relationship to their own personal, professional, or social goals.[22] Excessive personal involvement or investment may result in an overprotective stance and a limitation on the patient's ability to achieve maximal independence.

EDUCATION OF TEAM MEMBERS
Health

It is impossible to discuss team goals in geriatric practice without reflecting on the concept of health in late life. Health is not simply the absence of disease or illness, but is a state of psychological, emotional, and social well-being. It is important for team members to reflect on what constitutes the differences between good health and poor health; wellness as against sickness, illness, or disease; independence versus dependence; and good function rather than dysfunction. An older patient's perception of these issues and thus their goals may be quite different from those of the team. The disruptions which can be caused by misunderstandings of these concepts between the team and patients and among team members is both a stimulus to teams and a threat to their effective function. Each of these areas requires specific evaluation and discussion if the group hopes to move toward unison and consensus on actions.[24]

Diseases and Problems of Old Age

The health challenges of old age can, as suggested, be categorized as medical, psychological, or social. Another grouping allows these categories to be further refined. Specifically, there are clearly defined diseases such as pneumonia, urinary tract infections, depression, diabetes, cancer, and hypertension, all conditions which exist in younger individuals, but whose prevalence increases significantly in the elderly. The apparent simple increase in frequency of certain diagnoses established in later life belies the complicated nature of these diseases. The symptoms, signs, natural history, prognosis, and options for treatment and management are decidedly different.

Problem complexes found predominantly in later life are no less complicated and challenging than its diseases. These complexes are typified by cognitive decline, falls, incontinence, dependence, and loss of function. For a team to have general familiarity with these conditions is not sufficient. It must have specific expertise in their management.

The different time course for evaluation, treatment, and management of problem complexes must also be appreciated and is generally measured in weeks to months rather than in the minutes to hours of the acute care setting. Prevention too is an essential concept and must be accepted as a goal to be achieved by team interventions.

Provision of Health Care Services

The regulations, economics, barriers, and opportunities of the health care system as they relate to the elderly, whether community or institutionally based, should be understood. The team must have access or organizational links to the multiple sites where the elderly can be provided with care. Furthermore, the team should have some ongoing responsibility for assuring accuracy and specificity throughout the continuum of geriatric care.

Comprehensive Assessment

A responsibility of the team, whether in the office, the home, the hospital, or the long-term care institution, is to capture, in an organized manner, a comprehensive data base on each patient. The time and resources consumed by a team when a comprehensive assessment is undertaken are significant and should be allocated with discretion. Not all patients should have comprehensive assessment; for example, it may be inappropriate for patients for whom limited therapeutic intervention is the most reasonable management. Nonetheless, in the case of older persons it is imperative that team members understand geriatric assessment, the evaluation of mental status, the nature of long-term and chronic disabling conditions, the issues related to multiple functional disabilities, the overlap of multiple pathologies, and the judicious use of medications to treat these conditions. The group evaluation is directed toward a functional assessment or a complete bio-psychosocial evaluation, sometimes also defined as a socioeconomic, psychological, and physical evaluation. Having completed discipline-specific evaluations, the team must have the ability to integrate individual members' assessments and to develop reasonable and rational goals. These goals should have both short- and long-term components for each one of a patient's deficits, problems, or diagnoses.

Team Approach

The body of knowledge which constitutes interdisciplinary group function must be provided to team members. This can be achieved both in didactic sessions and as practical demonstrations by well-functioning teams who can act as role models. Teams must be required to take time to review and revise their group process with a view to improving their overall efficiency.

ROLE EXPECTATIONS
Externally Imposed

The individual team member is a member of several groups identified as reference groups. Each of these reference groups has expectations of its members which influence that person's behavior. The external organization around a team may impose goals, rules, time frames for action, limitations of responsibility, and leadership. The expectations of the external reference groups or organization and those of the core group of which the person is a member can be ambiguous, in conflict, or create overload. An individual team member thus has multiple loyalties potentially producing significant behavioral constraints.

Internally Generated Role Expectations

Role expectations are the behaviors expected of a person in a given situation and are based on social and professional standards of conformity.[25]

Team members have their own internally generated set of role expectations both for other team members and for themselves. These expectations are frequently not explicitly stated but become obvious when they act to facilitate or inhibit a team's function. In geriatrics the team structure is less well defined and its goals are more complex and global than are those of many other health care teams. Such relative lack of definition can lead to the following:

> *Role ambiguity:* The extent to which these role expectations are not defined or communicated.
>
> *Role conflict:* The extent to which these role expectations are not compatible with or are in conflict with one another or with the individual or among team members.
>
> *Role overload:* The extent to which an individual might not be able to meet the multiple expectations they confront in geriatrics.

Factors Contributing to Role Expectations

Role expectations take their effect at the personal level. Some of the factors which contribute to these expectations include the following:

1. Personal and professional self-image.
2. The perception of how one is seen by others. This perception is frequently incorrect and inaccurate.
3. Expectation of one's own profession in the setting in which a team finds itself and team members' expectations of how a health professional similar to themselves would act and relate to others in that setting.
4. The level of understanding of the professional code skill and responsibilities of colleagues. This understanding is frequently flawed, obscured, and biased. It might be typified by lack of understanding of the significant training in psychology required of most occupational therapists. Lacking this understanding, many team members might have discomfort in assigning a psychotherapeutic responsibility to an occupational therapist although that therapist is both trained and capable of assuming some such responsibility.

An example of the potential pressures imposed by both internal and external forces on a geriatric clinician might include being one of the following:

1. Manager of the health care team

2. A subordinate to an attending or supervising physician
3. Member of a group of peers
4. Member of a geriatric division
5. Member of a hospital staff

Behavioral Roles of Team Members

Individual role expectations create specific behavioral manifestations which are relatively easily categorized and can be recognized. These behaviors can be grouped into individual roles, group building and maintenance roles, and group task roles.

Individual or Self-Promoting Personality Roles

Aggressor
Blocker
Recognition seeker
Self-confessor
Dominator
Help seeker
Special interest pleader
Joker/humorist

Although potentially inhibiting, these behaviors can also move the team toward effectiveness and improved function.[26]

A second area of individual team member contribution is in the area of group building and maintenance of rules and reflect a dynamic contribution to the team.[27]

Group Building and Maintenance Rules

Encourager
Harmonizer
Compromiser
Gate keeper and expediter
Standard setter
Observer/commentator
Follower

Group task roles are the functions of management[28,29] performed by team members.

Group Task Roles

1. Initiator-contributor
2. Information securer
3. Opinion securer
4. Information giver
5. Opinion giver
6. Elaborator
7. Coordinator
8. Orientor

9. Evaluator-critic
10. Energizer
11. Procedural technician
12. Recorder

COMMUNICATION PATTERNS

The availability of information which is both accurate and timely is central to problem solving and decision making. Communication must be effective for this to occur. There must be a free flow of information among team members.[23]

Communication is an active process. There is a dynamic two-directional flow relationship between the transmitter and the listener[30] which can easily be disrupted. If it is distracting, attention and communication will be impaired. Team members must ensure that their contributions are heard, understood, and integrated. They have to personally concentrate on and try to assimilate the contributions of others. The setting or environment where the team meets is also important.

LEADERSHIP

For teams to function efficiently, the group must have many individual acts of leadership. There is not necessarily "one leader." There are usually many leaders who act in such varied roles as initiators, facilitators, or encouragers. This does not suggest, however, that good groups are leaderless, rather that all groups must have significant internal leadership strengths. Formal titular leadership is generally imposed by the organization within which the team operates and is an example of the intrusion of external reference groups on the role expectations of individual team members and on the overall functioning or performance of that team.

DECISION MAKING

Teams are required to take actions. To do this, decisions must be made. Examples of decision making include decisions which are:

1. Unanimous
2. Consensus
3. Majority vote
4. Unilateral (authority rule)
5. By default (lack of group response)

Each of these decision-making approaches may be appropriate under certain conditions. Each has different consequences. For example, there is significant potential lack of commitment to implementation when a unilateral decision has been made.

It is not necessary that the entire group come together to make all decisions as a group. It is generally reasonable that those who have the relevant information and who will have to effect or carry out a task be given the responsibility for decision making. There are two important components: one, obtaining the relevant information, and two, implementing the decision.[31] In general, the more information available to and the greater the agreement among the individuals responsible for completing the assignment, the more likely it is that the task will be done efficiently and happily.

NORMS

Norms are those unwritten and often untested rules which govern or attempt to govern the behavior of people within a group. Norms, in an abstract, but nonetheless explicit manner, attempt to define and constrain behavior into categories which are either good or bad, acceptable or unacceptable. For an individual to be accepted as a functioning member of a group, that individual must comply with the group norms.[32] Norms, which often come into existence for reasons which are often unclear, begin to assume the importance of laws, and, as with laws, infractions meet with punishment. There is generally a consensus that norms should not be questioned. They take upon themselves the quality of immutability, often culminating in statements to the effect that "It's the way we do it!" A mode or method of operation is not to be questioned and for those who violate, the results may be serious, ranging from quiet uneasiness among the group to gentle but joking reminders of what is expected and acceptable. Recalcitrance as viewed by the team results in the team effectively ignoring, excluding, or ultimately expelling the errant member not just psychologically but physically. The need for conflict management becomes an imperative.[33]

CONFLICT MANAGEMENT AND NEGOTIATION

The complex nature of the interactions between team members will inevitably result in disagreements or conflicts. The approaches to managing conflict include ignoring it, smoothing it over, allowing one person to force a decision, creating a compromise, confronting all the realities of the conflict including facts and feelings, and attempting to develop an innovative solution.

To be effective, it is necessary that the team agree that one of its primary internal goals be that conflict management will be an open and purposeful activity. The group must charge itself with the responsibility of both solving a problem involving disagreeing parties and getting those adversary members to accept and live with their differences without compromising overall team function. The objective and goal which must be accepted by all team members is one which requires openness for individuals to deal with a conflict and a stated commitment to move a conflict problem on a rapid time frame to a resolution.[33]

TEAM CARE OF THE AGED

Teams provide care to older persons in many diverse settings:

Selected Sites or Locations

Community	Institutional
Community care team	Hospital
Home care team	Nursing home
Home care hospice	Day hospital
Senior center	Respite center
Day treatment center	Outpatient department

Within these settings, many different specific teams exist:

Specific Clinical Care Teams

> Admission team
> Patient care team
> Stroke rehabilitation team
> Decubitus ulcer team
> Pain management team
> Discharge team

There are larger programmatic areas which have broader team responsibilities:

Special Program Teams

> Continuity of care team
> Hospice team
> Geropsychiatry team
> Consultation service
> Rehabilitation service

The team skills acquired and used in the clinical setting have applicability to many administrative situations:

Extended Organizational Teams

> Medical board committee
> Medical staff committee
> Bylaws committee
> Morbidity/mortality committee
> Research committee
> Human subjects review committee
> Medical records committee
> Ethics committee

ADMINISTRATIVE AND ORGANIZATIONAL TEAM PROBLEMS

COMPLEX ROLES OF THE GERIATRICIAN

Within teams that provide a broad range of services, particularly in those which focus on the multiple problems of the elderly, the role of the physician may become uncertain. For the geriatrician, there can be significant ambiguity and conflict of role. Role creation and role negotiation is a major component of the geriatrician's activities.

The geriatrician must have significant skill in the management of committees and must understand the nature, structure, and complexity of organizations. Such skills are not taught in medical school or residency programs and are only more recently being offered as a component of geriatric fellowship training. But the training and experience gleaned from the clinical team setting is often directly applicable to the management challenges within organizations.

PROGRAM DEVELOPMENT

The development of health care programs requires that the geriatrician have skills in problem solving, personnel management, health care planning, organizational management, and marketing. Strong team management skills are necessary for success in all of these areas. The necessary strengths are skills in communication; insight into group dynamics; understanding of the team decision-making process; strong people management skills and a facility to resolve conflicts; the skills of leadership either by authority, affiliation, or both; and the ability to negotiate roles for increasing levels of authority and responsibility. For geriatricians these skills are often developed first in the setting of the clinical team.

HEALTH SYSTEM CHALLENGES TO THE TEAM

Under the diagnosis-related group (DRG) system, the concerns which must be addressed by the team include alternative level of care, discharge planning, and fiscal responsibility. The problems shift from clinical skills to issues of reimbursement, utilization review, level of care criteria, patient responses, and provider response. This requires that there be formal team understanding and agreement upon the goals for admission, discharge planning, and for utilization review. Thus, an understanding of these global organizational issues must be brought to small core teams involved with individual patients. Health system issues for teams now become quality of care and quality of life for patients, effectiveness, productivity, efficiency, cost consciousness, and cost constraining efforts and ethical dilemmas.

For the geriatrician, current health system issues are those of credentialing, scope of practice, and remuneration for cognitive rather than procedural interventions. Whether functions of the team emerge as an appropriately reimbursed technology remains to be determined!

SUMMARY

This chapter has focused on the specific components of team function within the geriatric health care system. Health professionals generally receive minimal training in the specifics of team care. Furthermore, little time is given to assuring quality in the process by which professionals provide team care. Clinicians believe that the geriatric team has both utility and effectiveness. If the current oversights in team process are addressed and resolved, then studies may demonstrate that this belief is correct.

REFERENCES

1. Rao DB: The team approach to integrated care of the elderly. *Geriatrics* 32:88, 1977.
2. Libow LS: General concepts of geriatric medicine, in Libow LS, Sherman FT (eds): *The Core of Geriatric Medicine.* St. Louis, Mosby, 1981, p 2.
3. Rubenstein LZ: Geriatric assessment. *Clin Geriatr Med* 3:1-15, 1987.
4. Williams, ME: Outpatient geriatric evaluation. *Clin Geriatr Med* 3:175, 1987.
5. Saltz CC, McVey LJ, Becker PM, Feussner JR, Cohen HJ: Impact of a geriatric consultation team on discharge placement and report hospitalization. *Gerontologist* 28(3):344, 1988.
6. Bepko RA: Problems facing multidisciplinary teams in a large psychiatric facility. *Clin Gerontol* 2(3):64, 1984.
7. Goldberg RJ, Tull R, Sullivan N, et al: Defining discipline roles in consultation psychiatry: The multidisciplinary team approach to psychosocial oncology. *Gen Hosp Psychiatry* 6:17, 1984.
8. Berkman B, Campion E, Swagerty E, et al: Geriatric consultation team: Alternate approach to social work discharge planning. *J Gerontol Soc* 5:77, 1983.
9. Maguire GH (ed.): *Care of the Elderly: A Health Team Approach.* Boston/Toronto, Little, Brown, 1985.
10. Ducanis AJ, Golin AK: *The Interdisciplinary Health Care Team: A Handbook.* Germantown, MD, Aspen Systems Corporation, 1979.
11. Horwitz JJ: *Team Practice and the Specialist.* Springfield, Ill, Charles C Thomas, 1970.
12. Barber JH, Kratz CR: *Towards Team Care.* New York, Churchill Livingstone, 1980.
13. Tichy MK: *Health Care Teams: An Annotated Bibliography.* New York, Praeger, 1974.
14. Halstead LS: Team care in chronic illness: A critical review of the literature of the past 25 years. *Arch Phys Med Rehabil* 57:507, 1976.
15. Kane RA: Interprofessional teamwork. Manpower monograph, No. 8, Syracuse University, School of Social Work, Syracuse, New York, 1975.
16. Gosselin JY: The team approach: For or against the patient? *Canada's Mental Health* 31:23, 1983.
17. Haug MR (ed.): *Elderly Patients and Their Doctors.* New York, Springer, 1981.
18. Wright IS: The role of the primary physician in the care of elderly patients. *Bull NY Acad Med* 54:639, 1977.
19. Cole KD, Campbell LJ: Interdisciplinary team training for occupational therapists. *Phys Occup Ther Geriatr* 4(4):69.
20. Dawes PL: The nurses' aide and the team approach in the nursing home. *J Geriatr Psychiatry* 14:265, 1981.
21. Kane RA: Teams: Thoughts from the bleachers. *Health Soc Work* 7:2, 1982.
22. Clarfield AM: Multidisciplinary teams: Common goals and communication. *Clin Gerontol* 3(2):38, 1984.
23. Bloom BS, Soper KA: Health and medical care for the elderly and aged population: The state of the evidence. *J Am Geriatr Soc* 28:451, 1980.
24. Brink TL: Multi-disciplinary team success: The role of mutual respect. *Clin Gerontol* 2(3):73, 1984.
25. Farrell MP, Heinemann GD, Schmitt MH: Informal roles, rituals, and styles of humor in interdisciplinary health care teams: Their relationship to stages of group development. Proceedings of the International Conference on Small Group Dynamics, 1986, Harvard University, in Polley RB, Schneider JF (eds): *International Journal of Small Group Research*, Vol. 2, No. 2, 1986.
26. Feiger SM, Schmitt MH: Collegiality in interdisciplinary health teams: Its measurement and its effects. *Soc Sci Med* 13A:217, 1979.
27. Thomas B, Royer J: Problems in evaluating the team approach to primary care, in *Policy Issues in the Team Approach to Primary Health Care Delivery*, Conference proceedings. Iowa City, University of Iowa, Health Services Research Center, 1977, pp 157–179.
28. Gaitz CM: The coordinator; an essential member of a multidisciplinary team delivering health care services to aged persons. *Gerontologist* autumn 1970, pp 217–220.
29. Pena JJ: The team approach to patient management: A supervisor's responsibility. *Health Care Supervisor* 3(2):52, 1985.
30. Pearson PH: The interdisciplinary team process, or the professionals' Tower of Babel. *Dev Med Child Neurol* 25:390, 1983.
31. Rubin IM, Plovnick MS, Fry RE: *Improving the Coordination of Care: A Program for Health Team Development.* Cambridge, MA, Ballinger Publishing Co., 1975.
32. Rubin IM, Plovnick MS, Fry RE: *Managing Human Resources in Health Care Organizations: An Applied Approach.* Virginia, Reston, 1978.
33. Lowe JI, Kerranen M: Conflict in teamwork: Understanding roles and relationships. *Soc Work Health Care* 3:323, 1978.

Chapter 20

HEALTH PROMOTION AND DISEASE PREVENTION

Linda P. Fried

Increasing recognition that the diseases associated with aging are not inevitable components of normal aging provides a conceptual base for the role of preventive health care for the elderly, as well as for younger persons. The high burden of illness in older persons, coupled with increased life expectancy and staggering health care costs, compel the need for effective prevention in this age group. To impact on this burden of illness, intervention in the care of the elderly should focus not only on disease prevention but also, and especially, on preventing the unnecessary morbidity and disability resulting from diseases already present and on maintenance of quality of life. The goals for a geriatric preventive health care strategy need to be based on both analysis of where the predominant threats to health and functioning lie for older persons and on which beneficial outcomes are most meaningful to the older individual and to society.

Morbidity and mortality in the elderly are now primarily due to chronic diseases (in developed countries), with arthritis, hypertension, heart disease, and hearing impairment ranking first through fourth in prevalence and occurring in 47, 42, 31, and 29 percent, respectively, of noninstitutionalized persons 65 years and older in the United States.[1] Heart disease, cancer, and stroke together account for 75 percent of all deaths among persons 65 years and older and are responsible for about 20 percent of doctor visits, 40 percent of hospital days, and 50 percent of all days spent in bed.[2] The rate of chronic diseases is substantially higher for persons 65 years and older than for those age 45 to 64, and continues to increase with advancing age. Four out of five persons 65 years and over have one or more chronic diseases.[2] Each disease is, of course, associated with its specific morbidity, and the severity of this morbidity is directly associated with the potential benefit from its prevention.

The core of geriatrics is an understanding that illness in older persons often is highly complex, being a result of not just the physical disease itself, but also of the effect of disease and comorbidity on functioning, frequently aggravated by physiologic vulnerabilities, adverse effects of environment, loss of social support, and decline in financial resources associated with increasing age,[3] as well as the psychological status of the individual. Forty percent of community-dwelling people 65 years and over in the United States report limitations in their ability to carry on their usual activities, primarily as a result of chronic disease.[4] It has been reported that 41 percent of these women and 15 percent of these men 65 and over live alone, and more than 28 percent subsist below the U.S. poverty level, the latter compared with 22 percent of persons 45 to 64 years of age.[2] To be effective in older persons, preventive care must incorporate interventions that take into account the multiple dimensions that impact on health.

The broad spectrum of health issues in the elderly includes the onset of new disease, both chronic and acute; the morbidity and comorbidity of disease already present; and the consequences of chronic disease, including functional decrements, disability, dependency, hospitalization, institutionalization, and death, as well as (often superimposed) acute illnesses and injuries. The types of preventive approaches needed in order to decrease the burden of illness in the elderly throughout this range parallels this spectrum. These approaches include primary prevention, defined as prevention of the onset of disease; secondary prevention, defined as early intervention to arrest the progress of disease, including screening to detect early disease; and tertiary prevention, defined as measures to minimize the effect(s) of disease, already present, on the level of independence and activity.[5]

The goals for these three types of prevention differ. Primary and secondary prevention are focused, respectively, on the prevention, or on the early detection and treatment, of disease. Tertiary prevention, on the other hand, reflects the major goals of geriatric medicine, being directed at the maintenance of function in the presence of disease, the prevention of disease-specific morbidity, disability, and dependency, and improving the quality of life. For older persons, preventive efforts can have a major impact, potentially, in the areas of tertiary and secondary prevention, as well as in the prevention of acute illnesses and injuries. The latter is especially true for the "old-old" population, 75 years of age and above.

The appropriate types of prevention are tailored to the individual, based on factors such as age, the nature and extent of the illness and risk factors present, and the personal needs and living situation. For example, while all older persons may benefit from improvement of health habits (see Table 20-1), other preventive interventions are more appropriate for some specific subgroups of the elderly than for others; e.g., rehabilitation as a tertiary preventive strategy may be indicated after a stroke,[6] while persons with recurrent falls, urinary incontinence, functional dependency, or cognitive decline constitute a group at high risk for institutionalization and in need of tertiary prevention targeted to this risk.[7,20] In fact, the appropriateness and effectiveness of prevention depends on the identification of the risk characteristics of the individual or group. For older persons, because of the broad spectrum of health problems, risk characteristics can range from exposure to a contagious disease (e.g., tuberculosis or influenza, especially in a long-term-care setting), to the presence of a chronic disease putting the person at risk for disability or injury, to the constellation of factors in a frail elderly person which constitute risk for loss of functional autonomy. Thus, for older persons in particular, risk profiles include not just the risk factors for a disease, but for the entire range of potential adverse outcomes, including morbidity, disability, loss of autonomy, institutionalization, hospitalization, and death (also see Chaps. 12, 15, and 23).

PRACTICING PREVENTION

SETTINGS AND APPROACHES

The effectiveness of types of preventive health care in the elderly varies according to the setting. Thus, national programs have been targeted at educating older persons as to the value of improving health habits.[8] Community-based screening can be directed at identifying persons with risk factors for a particular adverse outcome, including stroke, osteoporosis, or falls. The office-based setting of clinical practice provides its own special opportunities for preventive health care. Combining knowledge of the individual patient with both a periodic health examination for primary prevention and detection of asymptomatic disease (see below) and with a case-finding strategy (defined as screening for problems amenable to preventive health care at the time of an office visit for other illnesses, as well as the follow-up of such findings) to identify specific risk characteristics or early disease or disability, the physician has the opportunity to target the potentially most effective preventive strategies for the individual. For example, a case-finding strategy would include early identification of geriatric conditions—such as urinary incontinence, periodontal disease, falls, hearing and visual impairment, and depression—which carry a high morbidity and which are seriously underdiagnosed and yet are amenable to treatment.

In the context of the office-based setting for prevention, the approach to prevention also varies by the patient's characteristics, including age group. Preventive health care recommendations for "young-old" (65 to 74 years) and "old-old" (75+ years) persons vary to some extent, particularly in the increased focus on tertiary prevention of loss of functional autonomy with increasing age.

Overall, because of a lack of randomized controlled trials demonstrating efficacy for specific preventive interventions for the elderly,[9] current recommendations are based on a combination of scientific evidence and clinical consensus. Randomized controlled trials to establish benefit have only been completed for influenza immunization and for the treatment of diastolic hypertension.[9] While there is substantial clinical evidence to support the current recommendations (described below), a more refined set of recommendations needs to be based on evaluation of the causal relationship between each factor and its adverse outcome, the alterability of the causal factor, the demonstration of improved outcomes with earlier intervention rather than later, and the efficacy and effectiveness of interventions in specific settings and specific subgroups of individuals.[10,11] In addition, given that the average person of age 65 can expect to live another 15 years,[12] there is a clear need for further development and testing of the components of a geriatric preventive health care program that will maximize quality of life and ability to function.

RECOMMENDATIONS FOR PREVENTIVE HEALTH CARE

Since 1975, recommendations for preventive health care practice by means of age group-specific periodic health examinations have emanated from four different

TABLE 20-1
Clinician-Based Preventive Health Care for Persons 65 Years and Older:
Recommended Periodic Health Evaluations and Frequency

	Recommendations as to Frequency
Primary and Secondary Prevention	
Education	Every 4 years[17,18]
Accident prevention	
Use of seat belts	
Self-examination of the skin, oral cavity, breast, testes	
Reporting of postmenopausal bleeding	
Health habit promotion	
Exercise	
Nutrition	
Obesity	Every 4 years, or as needed[17,18]
Daily oral hygiene	
Sleep	
Medication use	
Disease prevention	
Cholesterol screening	Every 4 years[15]
	Every 4 years through age 70[17,18]
Immunization	
Influenza	Every year[9]
Pneumococcus	One time only[17]
Tetanus booster	Every 10 years[13,17,18]
Dental checkups:	
Periodontal disease	
Dental caries	Annually[13]
Screening for early disease	
Hearing impairment	Detection of high-risk group by history taking[16]
Hypertension screening	Blood pressure measurement every 1[15] or 2 years[11,13]
Hypothyroidism	Clinical examination every 2 years[13]
Breast cancer	Breast exam annually[14,15,17,18]
	Mammogram annually through age 80[14,15,17,18]
Cervical cancer	Pap smear: Every 5 years[13]; every 2 years through age 70[17,18]; every 3 years[58]
Colorectal cancer	Rectal exam annually[14] or biannually[15]
	Stool for occult blood, annually[13,14,17,18] or biannually[15]
	Sigmoidoscopy every 4 years[19]
Oral cancer	Oral exam annually after age 75[13]
Skin cancer	Inspection and counseling; frequency as indicated by clinical judgment[13]
Malnutrition	Assessment biannually age 65–74, annually age 75+[13]
High-risk groups: Screen for	As indicated by clinical judgment[13]
Tuberculosis[13]	
Cancer of the bladder[13]	
Tertiary Prevention	
Progressive incapacity with aging	Assessment of physical, social, and psychological function; preferably with home visit: every 2 years, 65–74; every year, 75+[13]

groups[10,13–15] and have subsequently been updated[16–18] and summarized by the American College of Physicians.[19] These recommendations are for the "minimal preventive measures to be taken on behalf of apparently well, asymptomatic persons at low medical risk"[19] in the context of an office visit scheduled for this purpose at preset intervals. For low-risk groups, and for all older persons, these recommendations constitute the minimal preventive health care practice. They are not sufficient for many individuals and need to be supplemented with additional preventive measures targeted to the health status and conditions of the person, including screening for conditions prevalent with increased age, but not included in the periodic health examination recommendations.

As the initial approach to preventive health care in the elderly, these basic recommendations can be summarized by the types of prevention as well as by the suggested periodicity of screening for persons 65 to 74 and 75+ years of age. This section will outline the contents of the periodic health examination in these age groups (see Table 20-1; note that the recommendations by the different authors vary) and will then supplement this with the areas in which geriatric case-finding preventive strategies have potential for maintaining the health and functional status of older persons.

HEALTH HABITS

In general, the recommendations by Frame[17,18] are that patients' health habits be formally evaluated at least every 4 years, or as needed, and that the physician provide counseling on health habit modification. While data on the impact of health habit changes for persons 65 and older are lacking, it can be inferred from data in younger persons that health habit improvement is likely to be associated with risk reduction in the elderly as well.[20] The health habits recommended for evaluation are discussed selectively below.

CIGARETTE SMOKING

This is one of the seven harmful habits predictive of overall mortality,[21] as well as a risk factor for hypertension, stroke, atherosclerosis, myocardial infarction, lung cancer, and chronic obstructive pulmonary disease. It has been demonstrated that the acute effects of smoking can be reversible, as has been shown in studies demonstrating that incidence of myocardial infarction declines after smoking cessation.[22–24] From 17 to 22 percent of men and women 65 to 74 years are current smokers.[4] Recommendations as to whether screening is effective or indicated vary. However, based on the preceding data, the clinician should employ a case-finding approach, and, when indicated, counsel smokers to quit.

LACK OF EXERCISE

Lack of exercise has been shown to be a risk factor for overall mortality,[21] and may be a risk factor for the development of coronary heart disease, stroke, and osteoporosis. It also appears that inactivity in older persons contributes to declines in functional ability, possibly related to decreased muscle strength, endurance, coordination, flexibility, range of motion, and, especially, max-

imal exercise tolerance (aerobic capacity).[25] It is possible to improve these parameters and to decrease risk of falling[26] in elderly persons by regular exercise regimens. For all these reasons, the physician should evaluate parameters representing fitness and frequency of exercise, including walking, climbing stairs, lifting, activities of daily living, participation in a regular exercise program, and the percent of time spent seated or in bed. Based on this information, it is recommended that the physician counsel each patient individually regarding an exercise program tailored to his or her current abilities and limitations.

IMPROPER DIET

While the prevalence of undernutrition in the elderly is unknown in the United States, it is known that undernutrition (fewer than three meals per day) is a risk factor for mortality.[21] Clearly, certain groups are at higher risk for undernutrition, including those elderly persons who have severe chronic illness and/or functional decrements that limit their food purchasing or preparation abilities, who live alone, who have severe dental or periodontal disease or ill-fitting dentures affecting appetite and poor intake, who are depressed or cognitively impaired, or who have financial constraints on their ability to purchase adequate amounts of food.

The converse of this high-risk group are obese persons. It is estimated that 25 percent of women 75 to 84 years of age are obese. Obesity appears to be an independent risk factor for osteoarthritis[27] and glucose intolerance,[28] and may be a risk factor for total and cardiovascular disease mortality in the elderly, although the strength of obesity as an independent risk factor for the latter decreases with age.[29–31]

The goal of the clinical appraisal is to identify these high-risk groups, in part by asking (1) the number of meals eaten per day and (2) the ability to prepare or purchase food. In addition, the clinician should screen for eating habits that increase the risk of specific diseases—including coronary heart disease (cholesterol and sodium intake), hypertension (sodium intake), and colorectal cancer (fiber)—and that contribute to morbid obesity.

ALCOHOL ABUSE

It is estimated that approximately 10 percent of community-dwelling persons 65 years and older are alcohol abusers. This is a serious problem in terms of day-to-day functioning as well as a risk factor for hypertension, stroke, and alcohol-related diseases. Alcohol abuse is also a major cause of 15 to 20 percent of nursing home admissions, 10 percent of hospital admissions, and 5 to 15 percent of medical outpatient visits among elderly persons. Alcohol abuse is a strong risk factor for suicide, falls, and motor vehicle accidents.[25] Therefore, although not recommended as part of the periodic health examination, the clinician should apply a case-finding approach as indicated and seek information on the quantity, frequency, and types (alcohol spirits, cough medicines) of alcohol use and screen for markers of alcoholism that include depression, social isolation, personal neglect, injuries, falls, and moving-vehicle accidents.

INADEQUATE SLEEP

Lack of adequate sleep, like the other health habits, has been shown to be a risk factor for total mortality.[21] In addition, older persons experience a high frequency of sleep disturbances which can affect their functional ability and mental health status, as well as the ability of caretakers to provide care. Finally, sleep disturbances can often be manifestations of other underlying problems which are potentially treatable, including depression, sleep apnea, and dementia.[32] For these reasons, the periodic health examination must include evaluation for sleep disturbances, expanding, where appropriate, to identify the number of hours of sleep per night, and whether specific disturbances exist such as difficulty falling asleep, early-morning awakening, or regular daytime napping that may affect ability to sleep at night.

PRIMARY AND SECONDARY PREVENTION

Primary and secondary intervention by the physician on behalf of the elderly includes screening for risk factors and early detection of disease and disability.

IMMUNIZATION

Influenza and bacterial pneumonia are, together, the fifth leading cause of death in persons 65 years and older in the United States. Further, they account for substantial numbers of hospital admissions as well as bed days.[33] Influenza vaccine has been shown to be 60 to 70 percent effective in reducing mortality and hospital admissions in the elderly.[34,35] Despite this, less than half of persons 65 years and over are receiving influenza immunization.[20] As a high-risk group for influenza, all persons 65 and over should receive annual vaccination in the fall or early winter.

Pneumococcal disease causes 25 percent of all cases of pneumonia. The incidence and mortality associated with pneumococcal pneumonia increases with age.[25] Recent data indicate that the vaccine may be as much as 60 to 70 percent effective in preventing pneumococcal infections in persons 55 to 60 years of age and older.[36]

Based on such data, it appears reasonable to administer the new 23-valent pneumococcal vaccine to all persons 65 and over. It should be given one time only.

Tetanus has an 80 percent mortality rate in the elderly, as well as having the highest incidence among the elderly.[25] Although a tetanus-diphtheria booster injection needs to be given only once every 10 years, 50 to 70 percent of elderly persons lack protective serum levels for tetanus antitoxin due to infrequent vaccinations.[37,38] It is recommended that physicians routinely determine the date of the most recent tetanus-diphtheria booster and that this be repeated every 10 years.

TOTAL CHOLESTEROL

Serum cholesterol has been shown to be an independent risk factor for coronary heart disease in young and middle-aged adults.[39] Recent data from the Lipid Research Clinics study indicate that 30 percent of persons 65 years of age and over have elevated total cholesterol and that cholesterol level is strongly related to cardiovascular disease mortality.[40] Given that cardiovascular disease affects 50 percent of those ages 70 and over[20] and that in younger persons the cholesterol level is modifiable by dietary changes, the periodic health examination should include screening for elevated total cholesterol in persons 65 and older.[15,17,18] This screening provides a basis for identifying those persons needing more detailed evaluation of cardiovascular disease risk and those needing specific dietary counseling or more aggressive therapy.

DENTAL AND PERIODONTAL DISEASE

Diseases of the teeth and gums are highly prevalent in the elderly and are associated with high morbidity, and yet both are preventable. Periodontal disease is the major cause of tooth loss.[41] It also causes decreased appetite and loss of taste sensation.[42] Loss of teeth affects eating ability, as well as appearance, self-esteem, and social participation.[20] Over 45 percent of persons 65 to 74 years were totally edentulous, among persons surveyed in the 1971–74 Health and Nutrition Examination Survey.[43] In that same survey, 25 percent needed full dentures, 8 percent needed repair of dentures or bridges, and 23 percent needed repair of bridges or partials. It is estimated that almost one-third of the population is likely to lose remaining teeth between the ages of 50 and 70, primarily because of periodontal disease.[41] Because of the high prevalence and significant health and functional status-related problems of tooth loss, and particularly because it is preventable, it is important to include a screening exam and referral process for dental disease in the preventive health care evaluation.[13]

HEARING IMPAIRMENT

It has been estimated that hearing loss severe enough to produce disability is present in up to 25 percent of persons 65 and older and in 50 percent of persons 85+ years.[44] Only 8 percent of persons 65 years and over in the United States report using a hearing aid.[45] Hearing loss is a risk factor for social isolation, withdrawal, disorientation, depression, paranoia, and loss of functional independence.[46–48] Data are lacking as to the potential effectiveness of hearing aids in decreasing the disability resulting from hearing loss. However, it has been pointed out that lack of reimbursement for hearing screening as well as hearing aids has limited the ability to evaluate the improvements that would result.[20] The Canadian Task Force recommends that screening for detection of early hearing impairment is efficacious, and should be done during the periodic health examination or during office visits for other reasons.[16]

HYPERTENSION

The risk of stroke varies directly with a person's blood pressure.[49] At 75 years and older, 60 to 70 percent of stroke events occurred in hypertensives in the Framingham Study population.[50] The prevalence of hypertension ($\geq$ 140/90 mmHg) is estimated to be 64 percent in persons 65 to 74 years, with a higher prevalence in blacks (76 percent) than in whites (63 percent).[51] Antihypertensive therapy decreases the cardiovascular sequelae of hypertension in persons up to 70 years of age[20]; data on older groups are not currently available. However, based on these data, screening for hypertension in the elderly appears to be an effective approach to stroke prevention.[50] The national goal directed at control of elevated blood pressure is to have 60 percent of the affected population (including the elderly) attain a persistent level of 140/90 mmHg or lower by 1990.[44] The clinical screening evaluation includes measurement of three seated blood pressures, following the standardized guidelines of the American Heart Association (1980). For further details regarding detection and management of hypertension, see Chap. 48.

BREAST CANCER SCREENING

Until recently, breast cancer was the most frequent cancer-related cause of death among women 55 to 74 years of age. It is now slightly exceeded by lung cancer.[52] Among women 75 years and above, breast cancer is the second-highest cancer-related cause of death. A randomized controlled trial on the efficacy of breast cancer screening with clinical examination of the breast and mammography demonstrated an initial 30 percent reduction in breast cancer mortality and a somewhat smaller decrease over a longer follow-up period.[53] The efficacy of screening has been replicated in other studies. Recommendations for annual screening with physical examination and mammography by the American Cancer Society (ACS)[54] and the National Cancer Institute (NCI)[55] include women over 65 years of age (see Table 20-1). The NCI objectives for increasing the levels of participation in screening by the years 1990 and 2000 cover the situation among women through 70 years of age. Above that age, a checkup depends on the individual and her overall health status. The ACS has no upper age limit for breast cancer checkups. It is proposed that provision be made for annual checkup with these two modalities in the expectation that participation will be greatest at ages 65 to 70 years.

CERVICAL CANCER SCREENING

Since cervical cancer is a relatively slow growing tumor, examination with a Pap (Papanicolaou cytologic) smear and pelvic examination are effective tools for early detection. Half the women over 65 have never gone for the Pap test or have not had one for 3 years or more. This compares to less than 20 percent of women aged 30 to 44 years.[56] Older women have poorer survival rates from cervical cancer largely because they present in more advanced stages with more extensive disease.[57]

The American Cancer Society no longer recommends an upper age limit on Pap smear screening.[58] The National Cancer Institute recommends routine Pap smear tests at least once every 3 years. The American Cancer Society recommends that screening less frequently than annually be considered only after two negative annual tests. These qualifiers indicate that Pap smears more frequently than every 3 years may be required.

COLORECTAL CANCER

Five percent of persons 65 years and over develop cancer of the colon.[25] Colorectal cancer is the second most frequent cause of cancer deaths in persons over age 75. Early detection of localized cancer yields a highly improved 67 percent, 5-year survival rate, compared to 36 percent in nonlocalized cancer.[59] However, only 41 percent of such cancers are detected at such a localized state. Although research is still under way to test the efficacy of the guaiac test for fecal occult blood, it is generally agreed that it is advisable to include this test as part of the annual periodic health evaluation. This inexpensive procedure detects fecal blood, often associated with asymptomatic colon cancer.[60]

TERTIARY PREVENTION

Substantial disability occurs in older persons as a result of chronic diseases, as described previously. While decrements in functioning are often associated with loss of functional independence, it appears that early and appropriate supportive interventions can improve the ability of the individual to continue to function autonomously.[20] It is well accepted that rehabilitative therapy has significant impact in restoring or maintaining functional ability in a number of conditions, especially for persons who are recovering from strokes, hip fractures, or amputation or who are limited by degenerative joint disease, visual and hearing impairment, or cardiac and pulmonary disease.

Tertiary preventive efforts, directed at maintenance of functional autonomy and quality of life in the presence of disease that has already manifested itself, involve evaluation of physical and cognitive impairments as well as the impact of environment and the capabilities of family and social services in the community to compensate for deficits. Because of the burden associated with functional loss, the Canadian Task Force,[13] as well as many others (see Chap. 23), recommend that physical, social, and psychological function be assessed biannually for persons aged 65 to 74, and annually for those 75 years and older. Preferably, this screening would include home visits. In addition, a comprehensive geriatric assessment using a multidisciplinary team has been shown to be effective as a tertiary preventive strategy, whether for prevention of functional loss[61] or of other adverse outcomes including nursing home placement.[62]

CASE FINDING

The high prevalence of chronic diseases and the many conditions associated with aging, and their potential for prevention, necessitate that the physician supplement these periodic health examination recommendations with a case-finding approach. During visits for other purposes, the physician should therefore screen for the conditions outlined in Table 20-2. Each of these is discussed in detail elsewhere in this text. Many of these conditions will not come to light unless the appropriate information is sought from the patient by the physician.[63]

SUMMARY

The role of prevention in the health care of older persons has assumed increasing importance with the recognition of the high burden of illness currently associated with increased life expectancy. The overwhelming goal for

TABLE 20-2
Secondary and Tertiary Prevention:
Screening for Geriatric Conditions

Confusion, disorientation
Dementia
Dependency, loss of autonomy
Depression
Drug side effects, overdosage, and interactions
Environmental risk, safety
Falls
Immobilization (unnecessary)
Incontinence
Instrumentation
Podiatric problems
Risk aversion causing unnecessary dependency
Visual impairment

effective prevention is to decrease the unnecessary morbidity and disability now associated with aging. This will be accomplished both through the active use of recommended prevention practices and the future development and testing of new interventions consonant with a geriatric preventive health care program.

REFERENCES

1. Moss AJ, Parsons VL: Current estimates from the National Health Interview Survey, United States, 1985. National Center for Health Statistics, *Vital Health Stat* ser 10:160, DHHS (PHS) 86-1588, Sept. 1986.
2. *Aging America: Trends and Projections, 1987–88.* Washington, U.S. Senate Special Committee on Aging in conjunction with the American Association of Retired Persons, the Federal Council on Aging, and the U.S. Administration on Aging.
3. Evans JG: Prevention of age-associated loss of autonomy: Epidemiological approaches. *J Chronic Dis* 37:353, 1984.
4. Havlik RJ, Liu BM, Kovar MG et al: Health statistics on older persons, United States, 1986. *Vital Health Stat* National Center for Health Statistics, ser 25, DHHS (PHS) 87-1409, June 1987.
5. The John E. Fogarty International Center for Advanced Study in the Health Sciences, National Institutes of Health and the American College of Preventive Medicine: Task force reports. Prodist, *Prev Med* 258, 1976.
6. Lehmann JF, Delateur BJ, Fowler RS et al: Stroke: Does rehabilitation affect outcome? *Arch Phys Med Rehabil* 56:375, 1975.
7. Keene JS, Anderson CA: Hip fractures in the elderly: Discharge predictions with a functional rating scale. *JAMA* 248:564, 1982.
8. *Healthy Older People Program: A final report,* Office of Disease Prevention and Health Promotion, Public Health Service Washington, 1988.
9. Sackett DL: Preventive geriatric medicine. *Primary Care* 9:3, 1982.
10. Frame PS, Carlson SJ: A critical review of periodic health

screening using specific screening criterias. *J Fam Pract* 2:29, 123, 190, 283, 1975.

11. Fried LP, Bush TL: Morbidity as the focus of prevention in the elderly. *Epidemiol Rev* 10:48, 1988.

12. Rabin DL, Stockton P: *Long-Term Care for the Elderly: A Fact Book.* New York, Oxford University Press, 1987, p 8.

13. Canadian Task Force on the Periodic Health Examination: The periodic health examination. *Can Med Assoc J* 121:1193, 1979.

14. American Cancer Society: ACS report on the cancer-related health checkup. *CA* 30:194, 1980.

15. Breslow L, Somers AR: The lifetime health monitoring program: Practical approach to preventive medicine. *N Engl J Med* 296: 601, 1977.

16. Canadian Task Force on the Periodic Health Examination. Update: the periodic health examination. *Can Med Assoc J* 130:1276, 1984.

17. Frame PS. A critical review of adult health maintenance. *J Fam Pract* 22:341, 417, 511, 1986.

18. Frame PS. A critical review of adult health maintenance. *J Fam Pract* 23:29, 1986.

19. Medical Practice Committee, American College of Physicians: Periodic health examination: Guide for designing individualized preventive health care in the asymptomatic patient. *Ann Intern Med* 94:729, 1981.

20. Kane RL, Kane RA, Arnold SB: Prevention and the elderly: Risk factors. *Health Serv Res* 19:973, 1985.

21. Wingard D, Berkman L, Brand R: A multivariate analysis of health practices: A nine-year mortality follow-up of the Alameda County study. *Am J Epidemiol* 116(5)765, 1982.

22. Rosenberg L, Kaufman DW, Helmrich SP, Shapiro S: The risk of myocardial infarction after quitting smoking in men under 55 years of age. *N Engl J Med* 313:1511, 1985.

23. Gordon T, Kannel WB, McGee D: Death and coronary attacks in men after giving up cigarette smoking. *Lancet* 8(10):1345, 1974.

24. Jajich CL, Ostfeld AM, Freeman DH: Smoking and coronary heart disease mortality in the elderly. *JAMA* 252(20):2831, 1984.

25. Stults BM: Preventive health care for the elderly. *West J Med* 141:832, 1984.

26. Fitzgerald PL: Exercise for the elderly. *Med Clin North Am* 69:189, 1985.

27. Davis MA, Ettinger WH, Neuhaus JM, Hauck WW: Sex differences in osteoarthritis of the knee: The role of obesity. *Am J Epidemiol* 127:1019, 1988.

28. Gordon T, Castelli WP, Hjortland NC, Kannel WB, Dawber TR: Diabetes, blood lipids, and the role of obesity in coronary heart disease risk for women—The Framingham Study. *Ann Intern Med* 87:393, 1977.

29. Keys A, Aravanis C, Blackburn H, Van Buchem FSP, Buzina R, Djordjevic BS, Fidanza F, Karvonen MJ, Menotti A, Puddu V, Taylor HL: Coronary heart disease: Overweight and obesity as risk factors. *Ann Intern Med* 77:15, 1972.

30. Heyden S, Hames CG, Bartel A, Cassel JC, Tyroler HA, Cornoni JC: Weight and weight history in relation to cerebrovascular and ischemic heart disease. *Arch Intern Med* 128:956, 1971.

31. Hubert MB, Feinleib M, McNamara PM, Castelli WP: Obesity as an independent risk factor for cardiovascular disease: A 26-year follow-up of participants in the Fram-

ingham Heart Study. *Circulation* 67(5):968, 1983.

32. Pressman MR, Fry JM: What is normal sleep in the elderly? *Clin Geriatr Med* 4:71, 1988.

33. Moss AJ, Parsons VL: Current Estimates from the National Health Interview Survey, United States, 1985. *Vital Health Stat* 10:160, DHHS (PHS) 86-1588. Washington, Public Health Service, National Center for Health Statistics, September 1986.

34. Schoenbaum SC: Immunization, in Glechman RA, Gantz NM (eds): *Infections in the Elderly.* Boston, Little, Brown, 1983, p 63.

35. Barker WH, Mullooly JP: Influenza vaccination of elderly persons—Reduction in pneumonia and influenza hospitalization and deaths. *JAMA* 244:2547, 1980.

36. Sims RV, Steinmann WC, McCronville JH, King LR, Zwick WC, Schwartz JS: The clinical effectiveness of pneumococcal vaccine in the elderly. *Ann Intern Med* 108:653, 1988.

37. Crossley K, Irvine P, Warren JB et al: Tetanus and diphtheria immunity in urban Minnesota adults. *JAMA* 242:2298, 1979.

38. Russell LB: *Evaluating Preventive Care: Report on a Workshop.* Washington, The Brookings Institute, 1987.

39. Pooling Project Research Group: "Relationship of blood pressure, serum cholesterol, smoking habit, relative weight and elderly abnormalities to incidence of major coronary events," *Final report of pooling project.* American Heart Association Monograph 60, Dallas, 1978.

40. Bush TL, Criqui MH, Cohn R et al: Do lipids/lipoproteins predict cardiovascular death in old people? *CVD Epidemiol Newsletter* 35:33, 1984.

41. Gron P: Preventive dental health program for the elderly: Rationale and preliminary findings. *Spec Care Dent* 2:129, 1981.

42. Wayler AH, Kapur KK, Feldman RS, Chauncy HH: Effects of age and dentition status on measures of food acceptability. *J Gerontol* 37:294, 1982.

43. Basic data on dental examination findings of persons 1–74 years, United States, 1971–1974. *Vital Health Stat*, ser II:214. Washington, National Center for Health Statistics, DHHS (PHS), 1979.

44. Fisch L: Special senses: The aging auditory system, in Brocklehurst JC (ed): *Textbook of Geriatric Medicine and Gerontology*, 2d ed. Edinburgh, Churchill Livingstone, 1978, p 276.

45. *Health, United States, 1986.* DHHS (PHS) 87-1232. Washington, National Center for Health Statistics, 1986.

46. Mader S: Hearing impairment in elderly persons. *J Am Geriatr Soc* 32:548, 1984.

47. Gilhome-Herbst K, Humphrey C: Hearing impairment and mental state in the elderly living at home. *Br Med J* 281:903, 1980.

48. Eastwood MR, Corbin S, Reed M: Hearing impairment and paraphrenia. *Otolaryngol* 10:306, 1981.

49. *1987 Stroke Facts.* Dallas, American Heart Association, 1987.

50. Klag MJ, Whelton PK: Prevention of blood pressure-related complications in the elderly: Is case-finding of hypertensives an adequate approach? *Second Annual Meeting of the American Society of Hypertension*, New York, May 1987.

51. Working Group on Hypertension in the Elderly: Statement on hypertension in the elderly. *JAMA* 256:70, 1986.

52. Silverberg E, Lubera J: *Cancer Statistics*. New York, American Cancer Society, 1987.

53. Shapiro S, Venet W, Strax P, Venet L, Roeser R: Selection, follow-up and analysis in the Health Insurance Plan Study: A randomized trial with breast cancer screening. National Cancer Institute Monograph 67, 1983.

54. American Cancer Society: Mammography: Two statements of the American Cancer Society. *CA* 33:4, 1983.

55. National Cancer Institute: *Cancer Control Objectives for the Nation: 1985–2000*. DHHS (PHS) 86-2880, no 2, 1986.

56. Havlik RJ, Liu BM, Kovar MG et al: Health statistics on older persons—United States, 1986. Washington, National Center for Health Statistics. *Vital Health Stat* ser 25, DHHS (PHS) 87-1409, June 1987.

57. Axtrell LM, Asire AJ, Meyers MH: *Cancer Patient Survival Report 5, 1976*. A report from the Cancer Surveillance Epidemiologic and End Results (SEER) Program. Bethesda, MD, National Cancer Institute.

58. Fink DJ: Change in American Cancer Society checkup guidelines for detection of cervical cancer. *CA* 38:127, 1988.

59. Sherlock P, Winawer SJ: Detection and diagnosis of colorectal cancer in older persons, in Yancik R (ed): *Perspectives on Prevention and Treatment of Cancer in the Elderly*. New York, Raven Press, 1983.

60. American Cancer Society: Guidelines for cancer-related check-ups. *CA* 30:194, 1980.

61. Rubenstein LZ, Josephson KR, Wieland GD et al: Effectiveness of a geriatric evaluation unit: A randomized clinical trial. *N Engl J Med* 311:1664, 1984.

62. Williams TF. Comprehensive functional assessment: An overview. *J Am Geriatr Soc* 31:637, 1983.

63. Anderson F. The effects of screening on the quality of life after seventy. *J R Coll Physicians* (London) 10:161, 1976.

Chapter 21

CLINICAL PHARMACOLOGY

Robert E. Vestal

In many ways the elderly are a more heterogeneous group than the young. Because of marked individual variation in aging processes, effective and safe use of drugs in geriatric patients is a matter of careful individualization of the treatment program. Physiological aging does not necessarily parallel chronological aging, but apart from overt disease, which itself often plays a dominant role, it is physiological aging which underlies age differences in the fate and action of drugs.

The purpose of this chapter is to acquaint the clinician with selected aspects of the epidemiology of drug use in the elderly, the influence of aging on patient compliance, the effects of old age on clinical pharmacokinetics and pharmacodynamics, and the general principles of drug therapy in geriatric patients. A clinician who is familiar with the differences in physiology and pharmacology associated with aging will be prepared to individualize treatment and critically evaluate the responses to drugs in elderly patients. Limitations of space preclude an exhaustive discussion of geriatric clinical pharmacology. The interested reader may wish to consult several comprehensive reviews listed at the end of the chapter. Practical therapeutics is discussed by other contributors to this book in relation to specific clinical problems commonly found in geriatric patients.

EPIDEMIOLOGY

DEMOGRAPHIC TRENDS

Although 12 percent of the American population is over age 65, this older age group spends about $3 billion per year for prescription and nonprescription drugs, which

This work has been supported in part by a grant (AG2901) from the National Institutes of Health and by the Veterans Administration.

represents 20 to 25 percent of the total national expenditure. It is projected that by the year 2030 more than 64 million people will be in this age group and that it will constitute at least 21 percent of the population. We may predict, therefore, that expenditures for drugs by the elderly in the United States may eventually constitute 35 to 45 percent of the national total. Unquestionably, the needs of geriatric patients will constitute an increasingly important aspect of medical care in the future.

PATTERNS OF DRUG USE AND DRUG PRESCRIBING

Geriatric patients take more medications than younger patients because they frequently have more diseases than younger and middle-aged patients; indeed, multiple diseases are the rule rather than the exception in the elderly. Surveys of ambulatory populations indicate that up to 90 percent of elderly people are taking at least one medication and most of these individuals are taking two or more.[1] The most commonly used drugs are cardiovascular agents and antihypertensives, analgesics and antiarthritic preparations, sedatives and tranquilizers, and gastrointestinal preparations such as laxatives and antacids. Over-the-counter drugs account for about 40 percent of the medications. In the hospital the number of drugs prescribed increases almost linearly with age and length of stay.[1] In long-term-care facilities multiple drug therapy is commonplace, with two-thirds or more of the patients receiving three or more drugs on a regular basis. Psychotropics are received by up to 75 percent of the patients (compared with 35 percent or less in ambulatory patients), followed in frequency by cardiovascular agents including diuretics and antihypertensives, antibiotics, and others. It has been suggested that the frequently prescribed antipsychotic drugs, such as thioridazine, chlorpromazine, and haloperidol, are used to mold patients into the institutional routine.[2] Hip fracture and cognitive impairment are recognized complications of pyschotropic drug use in the elderly.[3,4] A large number of drugs, mainly sedatives, hypnotics, analgesics, and laxatives, are prescribed on an "as needed" basis. In effect the physician is giving the nurse the responsibility to diagnose and to treat.[1]

ADVERSE DRUG REACTIONS

The extensive use of drugs by geriatric patients obligates the physician to consider reactions to medications in virtually every differential diagnosis. However, adverse reactions to drugs may mimic other disease states, and the problem of determining whether clinical signs and symptoms are, in fact, drug-induced is not always easily resolved. In the complex clinical situation it is often difficult, if not impossible, to distinguish between an untoward event due to a drug and the exacerbation or progression of existing disease.

Although the statistics vary considerably, some studies seem to indicate that adverse drug reactions are a common problem among the elderly. In various patient populations the incidence of adverse drug reactions ranges from about 2 to 10 percent in young patients (age ≤ 30 years) and from as low as 6 to nearly 40 percent in older patients (age ≥ 60 years),[5] but not all studies demonstrate a relationship between age and the incidence of adverse drug reactions.[6] Studies of hospital admissions caused by adverse drug reactions in relation to age reveal similar inconsistencies.[6] Nevertheless, it is generally acknowledged that predisposing factors to adverse drug reactions include advanced age, as well as female sex, small body size, hepatic or renal insufficiency, multiple-drug therapy, and previous drug reactions.[5]

Although the epidemiological data certainly raise concern about the vulnerability of the elderly to adverse drug reactions, the magnitude of the problem is difficult to evaluate because many of the studies either have methodological weaknesses or are prone to misinterpretation.[5–7] The major difficulty is that control for disease severity has not been considered in the analysis. Thus, a relationship between age and adverse drug reactions independent of disease severity remains to be established. It should also be recognized that the true population at risk is not the total number of patients admitted to the hospital but the total number of persons in the immediate community taking drugs.[7] Studies which control for disease severity, prevalence of drug use, and type of drug consumed as well as age are needed to properly evaluate the relationship between age and adverse drug reactions.

PATIENT COMPLIANCE

Compliance with therapeutic regimens is often a critical factor in the successful management of acute and chronic illness. Between 25 and 50 percent of all outpatients fail to take medications as prescribed. Medication errors are prevalent among elderly patients.[8,9] The complexity of the regimen is a factor. A Swedish study has shown that in patients over age 65 the rate of noncompliance doubles (32 versus 69 percent) when more than three drugs are prescribed, whereas in patients less than 65, the rates are similar (28 versus 33 percent).[10] Often, the patient's noncomprehension or lack of a clear understanding of the drug regimen is a greater problem than noncompliance or failure to follow instructions.[9]

Studies using objective measures of compliance, however, indicate that geriatric patients are not necessarily more prone to noncompliance than younger patients. When studies of compliance are performed in larger heterogeneous groups, the rates for different age groups are almost always similar, and in several studies the highest compliance rate was in patients over age 70.[11] A study of antacid therapy revealed that 62 percent of patients over age 60 were adherent to the prescribed regimen compared with only 34 percent of patients less than age 45. The adherence rate was 54 percent in the middle-age group. Of the patients 60 years of age or older, 70 percent were compliant with digoxin therapy and had a mean serum level of 1.1 ng/ml. Similar results were found in younger patients.

Noncompliance or nonadherence to drug therapy does not always result in adverse consequences. The concept of intelligent noncompliance has been proposed to account for the fact that some patients alter prescribed therapy, usually by decreasing the prescribed dose or by not taking their medication at all, in order to minimize adverse effects.[12] Studies in Finland and the United States have found that many elderly patients adjust their medications according to their symptoms. In the digoxin study about 10 percent of patients were judged to be intelligently noncompliant.[11]

Regardless of whether geriatric patients are more or less compliant or engage in intelligent noncompliance to a greater or lesser degree than younger patients, interventions aimed at reducing medication errors are recommended, particularly since this group uses medications extensively and may be at increased risk for adverse effects from drugs. Although some studies have found no beneficial effect from patient instruction and drug labeling, others have shown definite improvement in medication errors and compliance in elderly patients who received counseling by pharmacists and a tear-off calendar or a tablet identification card as a memory aid prior to discharge.[13,14] For some patients it may be appropriate to begin self-administration of medications 1 or 2 weeks prior to discharge from a hospital or extended-care facility while supervision of a nurse is readily available, rather than to confront them suddenly with the responsibility for a complex drug regimen. This approach is both safe and effective.[15] Other methods to enhance compliance are discussed in the last section of this chapter.

PHARMACOKINETICS

Pharmacokinetics may be defined as the study of the time course of absorption, distribution, metabolism, and excretion of drugs and their metabolites from the body and the relationship of drug disposition to the intensity and duration of therapeutic effects. Important and sometimes subtle physiological changes occur with "normal" aging; these changes are independent of the more overt and multiple disease states so prevalent in the geriatric patient. By influencing pharmacokinetics, these age-related changes might be expected to alter drug response. Although this does not seem to be true for all drugs, it is generally acknowledged that older patients are more susceptible to both the therapeutic and toxic

effects of many drugs. Except for drugs predominantly excreted by the kidney, it is not easy to generalize on the type or magnitude of the age differences in pharmacokinetics which have been reported. Some studies of the same drug have produced conflicting results, perhaps due to differences in the criteria for selection of subjects or in the protocol design. It is also quite clear that apparent age differences in drug disposition are multifactorial and influenced by environmental and genetic as well as physiological and pathological factors. Some of these factors are summarized in Table 21-1 and are discussed in greater detail in the sections which follow. It should be emphasized also that all currently available studies are cross-sectional rather than longitudinal in design and can provide information only about age *differences* in pharmacokinetics rather than *changes* with aging.

DRUG ABSORPTION

A number of age-related alterations in the physiology of the gastrointestinal system might be expected to produce alterations in drug absorption. Elevated gastric pH could alter the ionization and solubility of some drugs, and the reduction in splanchnic blood flow might reduce

TABLE 21-1
Summary of Factors Affecting Drug Disposition in the Geriatric Patient

Pharmacokinetic Parameter	Age-Related Physiological Changes	Disease Conditions	Environmental Factors
Absorption	Increased gastric pH Decreased absorptive surface Decreased splanchnic blood flow Decreased gastrointestinal motility	Achlorhydria Diarrhea Gastrectomy Malabsorption syndromes Pancreatitis	Antacids Anticholinergics Cholestyramine Drug interactions Food or meals
Distribution	Decreased cardiac output Decreased total body water Decreased lean body mass Decreased serum albumin Increased α_1-acid glycoprotein Increased body fat	Congestive heart failure Dehydration Edema or ascites Hepatic failure Malnutrition Renal failure	Drug interactions Protein-binding displacement
Metabolism	Decreased hepatic mass Decreased enzyme activity Decreased hepatic blood flow	Congestive heart failure Fever Hepatic insufficiency Malignancy Malnutrition Thyroid disease Viral infection or immunization	Dietary composition Drug interactions Induction of metabolism Inhibition of metabolism Insecticides Tobacco (smoking)
Excretion	Decreased renal blood flow Decreased glomerular filtration rate Decreased tubular secretion	Hypovolemia Renal insufficiency	Drug interactions

the rate and extent of drug absorption. Fewer absorbing cells, delayed gastric emptying, and decreased gastrointestinal motility are other alterations which might affect the absorption of drugs. Although an effect of age on active transport systems has been reported, in general, drugs are absorbed by passive diffusion and would not be influenced by such changes. Most studies show no change with age in either the rate or extent of absorption or in bioavailability, which is the relative amount of drug reaching the systemic circulation after absorption. An increased rate of absorption has been reported for chlordiazepoxide, chlormethiazole, and metoprolol. The rate of digoxin absorption decreases with age. Due to decreased presystemic extraction by the liver, modest increases in the bioavailability of labetolol, lidocaine, and propranolol have been found. The bioavailability of prazosin decreases with age. The clinical importance of these findings is small.

In contrast, pathological or surgical alterations in gastrointestinal function and drugs may decrease substantially the extent of drug absorption.[16] These conditions include gastrectomy, pyloric stenosis, acute and chronic pancreatitis, regional enteritis (Crohn's disease), and malabsorption syndromes, such as adult celiac disease. Concurrent administration of other drugs or food may cause impaired drug absorption. For example, cholestyramine will bind acidic drugs such as aspirin, acetaminophen, phenylbutazone, and penicillin. Antacids may reduce the absorption or bioavailability of a number of drugs including tetracycline, ciprofloxacin, and other systemic quinolone antibiotics, isoniazid, phenothiazines, cimetidine, ranitidine, indomethacin, penicillamine, and iron. Drugs with anticholinergic effects, such as antidepressants, reduce the rate of gastric emptying and result in delayed or incomplete absorption of phenylbutazone, bishydroxycoumarin, lithium, tetracycline, and other drugs. Food may delay entry of a drug into the intestine and decrease tablet dissolution. Cations in food chelate tetracycline. Thus, pathological conditions, concurrent drug therapy, and meals are probably more important factors affecting drug absorption than age alone.

DRUG DISTRIBUTION

Increasing age is associated with several changes which can affect the distribution of drugs in the body. In many patients there is a decline in cardiac output and an increase in peripheral vascular resistance, with a proportionate decrease in hepatic and renal blood flow. A greater fraction of the cardiac output is distributed to the brain, heart, and skeletal muscle.

Body composition is an important determinant of drug disposition, and differs with age. Total body water

is reduced by 10 to 15 percent between the ages of 20 and 80 years with somewhat smaller changes in plasma volume and extracellular fluid. Lean body mass declines with a proportionate increase in body fat (about 18 percent in men and 12 percent in women). These body composition changes will affect the volume of distribution for drugs which distribute mainly into lean body mass including total body water or body fat. With regard to water-soluble drugs, such as cimetidine, digoxin, ethanol, and antipyrine, the volume of distribution declines with age. Exceptions include pancuronium and tobramycin. Several studies indicate that the volume of distribution for some of the lipophilic drugs, such as diazepam, chlordiazepoxide, chlormethiazole, and thiopental, is larger. For other lipophilic drugs, such as amobarbital and lorazepam, the volume of distribution does not differ with age.

Since free-drug concentration is an important determinant of drug distribution and elimination, alterations in the binding of drugs to plasma proteins, red blood cells, and other body tissues can alter pharmacokinetics in aged patients. Serum albumin concentration may be reduced as much as 15 to 20 percent with a concomitant increase in the globulin fraction, such that total serum protein is unchanged. The fractional rate of albumin synthesis is reduced in the elderly and is controlled at a lower set point, which prevents its response to higher protein intakes in that group.[17] In contrast to albumin, the concentration of α_1-acid glycoprotein (AGP) tends to increase with age.

Weakly acidic drugs, such as phenytoin and warfarin, are bound to plasma albumin. Weak bases, such as lidocaine and propranolol, are bound primarily to AGP. In old age the decline in albumin and the increase in AGP concentrations may be associated with reduced and increased protein binding of drugs, respectively.[18] Age differences in protein binding with resultant shifts in free-drug concentration may be important, particularly when highly protein-bound drugs are prescribed. For example, lidocaine shows higher protein binding and smaller volume of distribution in the elderly. Total plasma clearance of phenytoin after single-dose administration has been shown to increase with age as a result of decreased plasma binding and an increase in the availability of free drug for metabolism.[19] With chronic dosing, free-drug concentrations tend to "renormalize," and the importance of age differences in protein binding is diminished. The effect of displacement from binding sites can be predicted using the same principles. Because of reduced albumin levels, the elderly may be more susceptible to the acute effects of multiple-drug therapy on drug binding, especially when highly protein-bound drugs such as salicylates, anticoagulants, and oral hypoglycemics are involved.

HEPATIC DRUG METABOLISM

Studies in experimental animals have demonstrated both reduced activity of the microsomal mixed-function oxidizing system and alterations in microsomal enzyme induction by compounds such as phenobarbital and 3-methylcholanthrene. Apparent age-related changes may not be universal since species, strain, and sex differences must be considered.[20] The available data from microsomal preparations of human liver do not show significant age differences.[21] However, some clinical studies suggest that drug metabolism by the liver is altered in old age.

Hepatic mass bears a relatively constant relationship to body weight (2.5 percent) until middle age, after which it declines by about 0.2 percent of body weight per decade. Regional blood flow to the liver also decreases with advancing age. Estimates of the decline range from 0.3 to 1.5 percent per year and roughly parallel the decline in liver mass. Thus, in a person aged 65 the hepatic blood flow is reduced by 40 to 45 percent compared with a person aged 25.[22] These age-related changes influence hepatic drug metabolism.

Antipyrine is a useful model compound for the study of factors influencing drug metabolism because it is extensively metabolized by oxidation in the liver prior to excretion of its metabolites. Most studies with antipyrine have consistently reported a prolonged half-life and reduced total plasma clearance in older subjects.[23,24] Data also suggest that reduced antipyrine metabolism correlates with reduction in liver volume.[25,26] Interindividual variation (sixfold) greatly exceeds the effect of age such that only 3 percent of the variance in metabolic clearance is explained by age alone.[24] Most of this large interindividual variation is undoubtedly due to a variety of genetic and environmental factors.[27] Thus, age per se probably has only a minor influence on rates of antipyrine metabolism in adult humans.

The benzodiazepine class of sedative-hypnotic and anxiolytic agents has been extensively investigated with the finding that several of these compounds are influenced by age and gender. For example, although conflicting data have been reported,[28] the plasma clearance of free (unbound) drug is somewhat reduced in elderly women and greatly reduced in older men.[29] The clearance of chlordiazepoxide and free desmethyldiazepam is reduced in older men.[30,31] Higher steady-state levels and a longer mean half-life of desalkylflurazepam have been found in elderly compared with young men, but no age-related differences were found in women.[32] It should be recognized that, like flurazepam which is metabolized to desalkylflurazepam, many of the benzodiazepines are converted to active metabolites with half-lives substantially longer than the parent compounds.

Thus, chlordiazepoxide, diazepam, chlorazepate, and prazepam are all converted to desmethyldiazepam which has an elimination half-life as long as 220 hours in the elderly. Because of the tendency for accumulation and excessive sedation, doses should be reduced in older patients. With their relatively short plasma half-lives, absence of active metabolites, and absence of clinically important age-related pharmacokinetic changes, oxazepam, temazepam, and triazolam may be the safest benzodiazepines for the elderly.

Other drugs have been less extensively studied, but in many cases alterations in half-life and plasma clearance can be explained by age differences in volumes of distribution and protein binding. In addition, rates of elimination of drugs metabolized by nonmicrosomal enzymes, including those which catalyze conjugation reactions, in general do not show an age dependence. Such drugs include acetaminophen, carbenoxolone, isoniazid, ethanol, oxazepam, lorazepam, and temazepam.

RENAL EXCRETION

Unlike hepatic drug metabolism for which the effects of aging are less certain and probably less important than the large interindividual variation, diminished renal function (both glomerular and tubular) is common, and its measurement is relatively easy. The extent of impairment may vary from individual to individual, but a clinical test of renal function, such as creatinine clearance, can be used along with plasma-level determinations in adjusting doses and dosage schedules of drugs which are primarily excreted by the kidney. In healthy individuals the average decline in glomerular filtration rate between the ages of 20 and 90 years is about 35 percent.[33] Both urine concentrating ability during water deprivation and renal sodium conservation decline with age, and there is an increased sensitivity to hyperosmolarity.[34]

Daily endogenous creatinine production declines with age owing to the decline in lean body mass. In addition, creatinine clearance falls to a greater extent in the elderly than in the young before the serum creatinine increases. Thus, serum creatinine may be apparently normal despite substantial reduction in glomerular filtration rate. In the absence of direct measurement of creatinine clearance, estimates may be obtained from the following formula[35]:

$$CL_{creatinine} = \frac{(140 - age) \times body\ weight\ (kg)}{72 \times serum\ creatinine}$$

For women the result should be multiplied by 0.85. While this formula does not allow for age differences in lean body weight, a nomogram is available which does attempt to deal with this variable and has been used quite successfully in predicting creatinine clearance.[36]

These methods provide only estimates of renal function. Therefore, it is always important to measure plasma levels of potentially toxic drugs such as digoxin and the aminoglycoside antibiotics. Other drugs whose main route of elimination is via the kidney include cimetidine, pancuronium, penicillin, sulfamethiazole, and tetracycline. The excretion of these has been shown to be reduced in old age.

DIET, SMOKING, AND DRUG INTERACTIONS

Although there is ample evidence to indicate the importance of dietary composition as an environmental determinant of drug metabolism and toxicity in experimental animals and in humans, studies evaluating age and drug metabolism in relation to dietary composition are almost nonexistent. Nutritional deficiencies in the elderly might result from a general decline in health, difficulty in obtaining and preparing food, restricted economic circumstances resulting from retirement, loneliness and social isolation, depression following loss of spouse and friends, and ignorance of good nutrition. Studies have identified protein and vitamin deficiencies in the housebound elderly compared with more active people of equivalent age. It is possible that nutritional deficiencies in the elderly contribute to age differences in drug metabolism. In geriatric patients with ascorbic acid deficiency, supplementation resulted in a decrease in antipyrine half-life and increase in plasma clearance.[37]

Cigarette smoking, which is thought to stimulate drug metabolism through an enzyme-inducing effect of polycyclic hydrocarbons produced by combustion of tobacco, may have a different effect in the elderly compared with the young. In contrast to young smokers, elderly smokers do not show increased clearance of antipyrine or propranolol[38]; however, both young and elderly smokers metabolize theophylline more rapidly than nonsmokers.[39,40]

Several pharmacokinetic drug interactions have been studied in the elderly. The evidence regarding the effect of age on enzyme induction by therapeutic agents is conflicting. Dichloralphenazone[41] and rifampin[42] failed to increase the elimination of antipyrine or quinine. In contrast, induction of theophylline metabolism by phenytoin[40] is similar in healthy young and elderly subjects. Glutethimide has been shown to increase the clearance of antipyrine in elderly patients.[43] Inhibition of drug metabolism may have greater clinical importance than induction when the elimination of a potentially toxic drug is impaired. Available data indicate that geriatric patients are as sensitive as young patients. Cimetidine inhibits the oxidative metabolism of antipyrine,[44,45] desmethyldiazepam,[45] and theophylline[39] to a similar extent in young and elderly subjects.

PHARMACODYNAMICS IN THE ELDERLY

An awareness of the effects of age on pharmacokinetics may not only improve the clinical use of drugs but may also provide insight into the mechanisms of altered pharmacodynamics in geriatric patients. Pharmacodynamics refers to the physiological or psychological response to a drug or combination of drugs. Largely because the studies are difficult to perform, information on drug effects in old age is less available than information on drug kinetics.

In general, old people are more sensitive to the effects of potent analgesics[46,47] and sedatives such as the benzodiazepines than are young people.[48,49] In contrast, studies with isoproterenol,[50,51] propranolol,[50] and verapamil[52] indicate that the elderly are less sensitive to some of the cardiovascular effects of these drugs. The chronotropic and vasorelaxant effects of isoproterenol, beta-adrenergic blockade by propranolol, and PR prolongation by verapamil are reduced. Although beta-receptor density and affinity for antagonist on human lymphocytes are not altered in old age,[53] lower levels of cyclic AMP and adenylate cyclase activity after beta-adrenergic stimulation have been found in lymphocyte preparations from elderly subjects compared with young subjects.[54] Receptor affinity for agonists is reduced in association with reduction in the ability to form the high affinity state for agonists.[55] This suggests an age-related alteration in the interaction between the beta-adrenergic receptor and the guanine nucleotide regulatory protein. Most clinical studies indicate that alpha-receptor function is preserved in old age. Age differences in drug response have been reported for several other drugs, including heparin, methyldopa, tolbutamide, and warfarin, but some studies have produced conflicting results.

GENERAL PRINCIPLES OF GERIATRIC PRESCRIBING

With a few minor modifications, the principles of prescribing medications for the geriatric patient (Table 21-2) are essentially the same as would be applied to any patient, young or old. However, because of multiple disease states and extensive drug use in the elderly, together with the potential for altered drug response and higher incidence of adverse effects compared with the younger patient, it is important to review them.

1. *Evaluate the need for drug therapy.* It should be remembered that not all the diseases which afflict the elderly require drug treatment because they do the pa-

TABLE 21-2
Principles of Geriatric Prescribing

1. Evaluate the need for drug therapy.
   a. Not all diseases afflicting the elderly require drug treatment.
   b. Avoid drugs if possible, but do not withhold on account of age drugs which might enhance the quality of life.
   c. Strive for a diagnosis prior to treatment.
2. Take a careful history of habits and drug use.
   a. Patients often seek advice and receive prescriptions from several physicians.
   b. Knowledge of existing therapy, both prescribed and nonprescribed, helps anticipate potential drug interaction.
   c. Smoking, alcohol, and caffeine may affect drug response.
3. Know the pharmacology of drug prescribed.
   a. Use of few drugs well, rather than many drugs poorly.
   b. Awareness of age-related alterations in drug disposition and drug response is helpful.
4. In general, prescribe smaller doses for the elderly.
   a. Often the standard dose will be too large for the elderly patient.
   b. While the effect of age on hepatic drug metabolism is less predictable, renal excretion of drugs and their active metabolites tends to decline.
5. Titrate drug dosage on the basis of the patient's response.
   a. Establish reasonable therapeutic endpoints.
   b. Adjust dosage until endpoints are reached or unwanted side effects prevent further increases.
   c. Use an adequate dose for the patient. This is particularly important in the treatment of pain associated with malignancy.
   d. Sometimes combination therapy is appropriate and effective.
6. Simplify the therapeutic regimen and encourage compliance.
   a. Try to avoid intermittent schedules. Once- or twice-daily dosage is ideal.
   b. Select a dosage form appropriate for the patient.
   c. Label drug containers clearly. When appropriate, specify standard containers.
   d. Give careful instructions to both patient and a relative or friend. Explain why the drug(s) is(are) being prescribed.
   e. Suggest the use of a medication calendar or diary.
   f. Encourage the return or destruction of old medications.
   g. Recommend the supervision of drug therapy when necessary by a neighbor, relative, or friend, or visiting nurse.
7. Review the treatment plan regularly, and discontinue drugs no longer needed.
8. Remember that drugs may cause illness.

tient no immediate harm. Indeed, the elderly are often better off without some drugs. However, while it is wise to avoid drugs if possible, appropriate drug therapy should not be withheld on account of age if the clinician feels that the patient's symptoms and quality of life would be improved by treatment. For some patients, symptomatic therapy may be all that can be offered, but whenever possible the physician should strive to achieve an accurate diagnosis and institute specific therapy. If the patient's symptoms are due to malnutrition, ill-fitting dentures, social deprivation, inability to pay for previously ordered medication, or abuse or misuse of medications, additional drug therapy is not likely to be helpful and may only complicate the situation.

2. *Take a careful history of habits and drug use.* This is important in all good medical practice, but it is especially important in dealing with the elderly patient who usually has multiple problems and is taking multiple medications. Patients often seek medical care and may receive drugs or prescriptions from several sources (physicians, nurses, pharmacists, and friends or relatives). Knowledge of existing therapy, both prescribed and nonprescribed, helps the clinician avoid duplications and anticipate potential drug interactions and adverse effects.

It is not unusual for a patient to be taking two or more drugs of the same type or with similar side effects. For example, antidepressants, antipsychotic agents, antihistamines, nonprescription "cold" remedies, and sedative preparations all have anticholinergic properties. Individually they may be well-tolerated, but in combination their effects may be additive to produce unwanted toxicity, such as dry mouth, blurred vision, constipation, urinary retention, and a variety of central nervous system side effects.

Since cigarette smoking, alcohol, or caffeine use may modify the response to many drugs, it is important to ask a patient specifically about these habits. The possible use of aspirin, sleeping aids, laxatives, unusual quantities of vitamins, or other nonprescription medications should also be considered. In some cases it may be necessary to recommend that a patient modify the use of such compounds in order to make drug therapy safe or effective. In some instances the patient's habits may actually be a contraindication to the contemplated drug therapy. Unless the patient agrees to change what may have been a long-standing pattern, alternative therapy or no therapy may be the only solution. One example is a clinical indication for chronic anticoagulation in the setting of heavy alcohol use or abuse.

3. *Know the pharmacology of drugs prescribed.* It is preferable to be familiar with a relatively small group of drugs and use them well than to use many drugs poorly. One's ability to use a drug rationally will be enhanced by an awareness of its route of elimination, half-life, duration of action, protein-binding properties, and propensity for interactions with other drugs, along with a knowledge of its major pharmacological actions, side effects, or toxicity. With this knowledge the clinician is usually able to make appropriate adjustments in drug dosage when confronted with complex medical problems, some of which may influence drug disposition. It is also useful to be acquainted with age-related alterations in drug disposition and drug response. The margin between therapeutic effect and toxicity is so small in some cases that a drug which is appropriate for a young patient may be unsuitable for a geriatric patient with the same condition. For example, barbiturates are usually well-tolerated in the young, but they sometimes cause paradoxical reactions in the elderly. They have also been associated with a high incidence of falls and hip fractures and should be avoided. Other types of hypnotics are more appropriate for this age group. The clinician should have a knowledge of the pharmacology of the drugs prescribed; this knowledge will provide an important defense against serious drug reactions, namely the ability to anticipate and recognize early signs of drug toxicity.

4. *In general, prescribe smaller doses for the elderly.* Usually it is better to give a small dose to the older patient than to risk giving too much (Table 21-3). Often the standard dose will be too large for the geriatric patient. The elderly are particularly sensitive to drugs affecting the central nervous system. While the effect of age on hepatic drug metabolism seems to be less predictable, the elimination of drugs (or their active metabolites) which are primarily excreted by the kidney declines with advancing age. This means that smaller maintenance doses may be adequate. However, whether dose adjustments are made depends on the drug. Obviously, penicillin has much wider dosage limits than digoxin or the aminoglycoside antibiotics. Monitoring plasma levels is often useful in adjusting dosage. Dosage, route, and frequency of drug therapy will be determined clinically on the basis of the urgency of the patient's condition, body size and weight, and the therapeutic index and pharmacological properties of the drug. However, as a general rule, caution is a virtue in geriatric drug therapy.

5. *Titrate drug dosage with the patient's response.* The clinician should try to identify signs or symptoms that can be assessed serially for effectiveness of drug therapy. Drug dosage can be increased gradually until the desired therapeutic endpoint is reached or if unwanted toxicity is present or anticipated. It is important to prescribe an adequate dose for the patient. This is particularly important in the management of pain associated with malignancy. For the treatment of hypertension, the control of blood pressure is the obvious therapeutic endpoint, and postural hypotension is an indication of excessive therapy. The side effects of drug toxicity may require that dosage be limited and an additional drug added in order to achieve satisfactory blood pressure control. This is one example where polypharmacy may be desirable and effective. In the treatment of depression and many other disorders, it may be more difficult to be certain of adequate therapy, but careful attention to the patient's symptoms is the best approach. Whenever possible, severity of symptoms should be quantified in a scalelike fashion (e.g., 4+ on a scale of 0 to 5), and the response to therapy monitored and recorded. The patient should also be questioned for the presence of unwanted side effects, particularly during the initial phases of treatment and when changes in treatment or disease status occur. Obviously, if a drug causes more symptoms than it alleviates, it should be discontinued or its dosage reduced.

6. *Simplify the therapeutic regimen and encourage compliance.* Complex drug regimens may be easily mismanaged by the elderly patient with a deteriorating

TABLE 21-3
Examples of Drugs Usually Given in Reduced Dosage in the Elderly*

Drug or Drug Class	Possible Consequences of Standard Dosage Regimen
Aminoglycosides	Ototoxicity and nephrotoxicity
Benzodiazepines	Unwanted CNS depression—more common with larger doses
Carbamazepine	Drowsiness or ataxia may develop
Chlormethiazole	Confusion can occur with large doses
Digoxin	Digitalis toxicity
Haloperidol	Extrapyramidal reactions
Levodopa	Hypotension common
Meperidine	Respiratory depression
Metoclopramide	Confusion common
Thioridazine	Confusion common
Thyroxine	Myocardial infarction
Vitamin D	Renal toxicity

*The drugs listed are examples only; this is not intended to be an exhaustive listing.
SOURCE: World Health Organization.[56]

memory or impaired vision. In order to promote comprehension the following steps are suggested (Table 21-3):

a. Try to avoid intermittent dosage schedules. Once- or twice-daily dosage is ideal whenever feasible. Alternate-day therapy or 5 days a week will be confusing to many patients and will not be followed with accuracy. A reduced dose given daily is more preferable.

b. Select a dosage form appropriate for the patient. In addition to the total number of drugs prescribed, the dosage form, the size, shape, and color of tablets or capsules, and their similarity to one another influence the patient's ability to accurately follow a prescribed treatment plan. Unfortunately, many tablets and capsules with markedly different pharmacological actions are of similar size, shape, and color. This can be confusing to geriatric patients, particularly when vision is impaired and it is difficult for them to determine which preparation they are taking. Since touch and color vision are usually well-preserved, an effort should be made to ensure that preparations to be used together are not of the same shape and color. Many older people have difficulty swallowing. For such patients an elixir, effervescent, or chewable tablets may be more suitable than large tablets or capsules. Occasionally, suppositories may be the dosage form of choice, particularly with renewed interest in developing formulations with improved and more reliable bioavailability.

c. Label drug containers clearly in large print, and, when appropriate, specify standard containers. The patient disabled by arthritis will have difficulty opening safety caps. From the label, patients should be able to identify the names of drugs they are taking and the disease or symptom for which they are being prescribed.

d. Give careful instructions to both the patient and a relative or friend. Explain why the drugs are being prescribed. Concise written directions may be helpful. In a few institutions this is accomplished by a brief discharge summary, which is given to the patient; it lists the major medical problems, treatment plan and medications, and follow-up arrangements. Insofar as possible, patients should be taught to understand their medications, especially the relative importance to their well-being and correct usage and administration. Important potential side effects should be mentioned, and the patient urged to report these if they seem to occur. The involvement of a nurse or pharmacist in this process is often useful.

e. Suggest the use of a medication calendar or diary to record daily drug administration. They may help forgetful patients remember whether they have taken their medications. A variety of medication containers are available which assist in accurate self-administra-

tion of drugs for a period of up to 1 week and can then be restocked by the patient or a visiting nurse or other attendant.

f. Encourage the return or destruction of old, unused medications. The accumulation of old medications from prior treatment programs will serve only to confuse patients. Elderly patients may inadvertently mix new medications with old or take drugs at higher or lower dosages than newly prescribed.

g. Recommend the supervision of drug therapy by a neighbor, relative, friend, or visiting nurse if necessary. In some cases this may permit the geriatric patient to continue to live in the familiar surroundings of home rather than be placed in a shelter care or extended-care facility.

7. *Review the treatment plan regularly, and discontinue drugs no longer needed.* The patient's treatment plan should be reviewed at each clinic visit, or at least every 3 to 6 months. Unless this is done regularly, medications given for specific indications may be continued long after the problem has been resolved. This is particularly true when patients are seen by several clinicians over a period of time.

8. *Remember that drugs may cause illness.* The incidence of adverse drug reactions is correlated with the number of medications prescribed. A drug may be a possible explanation for unusual symptoms which may disappear when the suspected offender is removed from the treatment program.

CONCLUSION

Experienced clinicians know that the prescribing of medications is never a good substitute for taking an adequate medical and social history. Often the relationship of the patient with the physician is more important than the drugs that are prescribed. Favorable morale can be promoted by emphasizing even a small clinical improvement or minor success in therapy. The patient needs to be a partner in the treatment program for the disease or disability. Geriatric patients, like most other patients, greatly appreciate a clinician who is sincerely interested in their emotional and social, as well as their medical and pharmacological, well-being.

REFERENCES

1. Nolan L, O'Malley K: Prescribing for the elderly, part II. Prescribing patterns: Differences due to age. *J Am Geriatr Soc* 36:245, 1988.
2. Ray WA et al: A study of antipsychotic drug use in nursing homes: Epidemiologic evidence suggesting misuse. *Am J Public Health* 70:485, 1980.

3. Ray WA et al: Psychotropic drug use and the risk of hip fracture. *N Engl J Med* 316:363, 1987.

4. Larson EB et al: Adverse drug reactions associated with global cognitive impairment in elderly persons. *Ann Intern Med* 107:169, 1987.

5. Jue SG, Vestal RE: Adverse drug reactions in the elderly: A critical review, in O'Malley K (ed): *Medicine in Old Age—Clinical Pharmacology and Drug Therapy.* Edinburgh, Churchill Livingstone, 1984, p 52.

6. Nolan L, O'Malley K: Prescribing for the elderly, part I. Sensitivity of the elderly to adverse drug reactions. *J Am Geriatr Soc* 36:136, 1988.

7. Klein LE et al: Adverse drug reactions among the elderly: A reassessment. *J Am Geriatr Soc* 29:525, 1981.

8. Schwartz D et al: Medication errors made by elderly, chronically ill patients. *Am J Public Health* 52:2108, 1962.

9. Parkin DM et al: Deviation from prescribed drug treatment after discharge from hospital. *Br Med J* 2:686, 1976.

10. Bergman U, Wilholm B-E: Patient medication on admission to a medical clinic. *Eur J Clin Pharmacol* 20:185, 1981.

11. Weintraub M: Intelligent noncompliance with special emphasis on the elderly. *Contemp Pharm Prac* 4:8, 1981.

12. Weintraub M: Intelligent and capricious noncompliance, in Lasagna L (ed): *Compliance.* Mt. Kisco, NY, Futura, 1976, p 39.

13. Wandless I, Davie JW: Can drug compliance in the elderly be improved? *Br Med J* 2:359, 1977.

14. MacDonald ET et al: Improving drug compliance after hospital discharge. *Br Med J* 2:618, 1977.

15. Libow LS, Mehl B: Self-administration of medications by patients in hospitals or extended care facilities. *J Am Geriatr Soc* 18:81, 1970.

16. Parsons RL: Drug absorption in gastrointestinal disease with particular reference to malabsorption syndromes. *Clin Pharmacokinet* 2:45, 1977.

17. Gersovitz M et al: Albumin synthesis in young and elderly subjects using a new stable isotope methodology: Response to level of protein intake. *Metabolism* 29:1075, 1980.

18. Wallace SM, Verbeeck RK: Plasma protein binding of drugs in the elderly. *Clin Pharmacokinet* 12:41, 1987.

19. Hayes MJ et al: Changes in drug metabolism with increasing age: 2. Phenytoin clearance and protein binding. *Br J Clin Pharmacol* 2:73, 1975.

20. Schmucker DL, Wang RK: Effects of aging on the properties of rhesus monkey liver microsomal NADPH-cytochrome c (P-450) reductase. *Drug Metab Dispos* 15:225, 1987.

21. Woodhouse KW et al: The effect of age on pathways of drug metabolism in human liver. *Age Ageing* 13:328, 1984.

22. Geokas MC, Haverback BJ: The aging gastrointestinal tract. *Am J Surg* 117:881, 1969.

23. O'Malley K et al: Effect of age and sex on human drug metabolism. *Br Med J* 3: 607, 1971.

24. Vestal RE et al: Antipyrine metabolism in man: Influence of age, alcohol, caffeine and smoking. *Clin Pharmacol Ther* 18:425, 1975.

25. Swift CG et al: Antipyrine disposition and liver size in the elderly. *Eur J Clin Pharmacol* 14:149, 1978.

26. Bach B et al: Disposition of antipyrine and phenytoin correlated with age and liver volume in man. *Clin Pharmacokinet* 6:389, 1981.

27. Vesell ES: Genetic and environmental factors affecting drug disposition in man. *Clin Pharmacol Ther* 22:659, 1977.

28. Klotz et al: The effects of age and liver disease on the disposition and elimination of diazepam in adult men. *J Clin Invest* 55:347, 1975.

29. Greenblatt DJ et al: Diazepam disposition determinants. *Clin Pharmacol Ther* 27:301, 1980.

30. Roberts RK et al: The effects of age and parenchymal liver disease on the disposition and elimination of chlordiazepoxide (Librium). *Gastroenterology* 75:479, 1978.

31. Shader RI et al: Absorption and disposition of chlordiazepoxide in young and elderly male volunteers. *J Clin Pharmacol* 17:709, 1977.

32. Greenblatt DJ et al: Desalkylflurazepam kinetics in the elderly following single and multiple doses of flurazepam. *Clin Pharmacol Ther* 29:249, 1981.

33. Rowe JW et al: The effect of age on creatinine clearance in man: A cross-section and longitudinal study. *J Gerontol* 3:155, 1976.

34. Helderman JH et al: The response of arginine vasopressin to intravenous ethanol and hypertonic saline in man: The impact of aging. *J Gerontol* 33:39, 1978.

35. Crockroft DW, Gault MH: Prediction of creatinine clearance from serum creatinine. *Nephron* 16:31, 1976.

36. Siersbaek-Nielsen K et al: Rapid evaluation of creatinine clearance. *Lancet* 1:1133, 1971.

37. Smithard DJ, Langman MJS: The effect of vitamin supplementation upon antipyrine metabolism in the elderly. *Br J Clin Pharmacol* 5:181, 1978.

38. Vestal RE, Wood AJJ: Influence of age and smoking on drug kinetics in man: Studies using model compounds. *Clin Pharmacokinet* 5:309, 1980.

39. Vestal RE et al: Aging and drug interactions. I. Effect of cimetidine and smoking on the oxidation of theophylline and cortisol in healthy men. *J Pharmacol Exp Ther* 241:488, 1987.

40. Crowley JJ et al: Aging and drug interactions. II. Effect of phenytoin and smoking on the oxidation of theophylline and cortisol in healthy men. *J Pharmacol Exp Ther* 245:513, 1988.

41. Salem SAM et al: Reduced induction of drug metabolism in the elderly. *Age Ageing* 7:68, 1978.

42. Twum-Barima Y et al: Impaired enzyme induction by rifampicin in the elderly. *Br J Clin Pharmacol* 17:595, 1984.

43. Pearson MW, Roberts CJC: Drug induction of hepatic enzymes in the elderly. *Age Ageing* 13:313, 1984.

44. Feely J et al: Factors affecting the response to inhibition of drug metabolism by cimetidine—Dose response and sensitivity of elderly and induced subjects. *Br J Clin Pharmacol* 17:77, 1984.

45. Divoll M et al: Cimetidine impairs clearance of antipyrine and desmethyldiazepam in the elderly. *J Am Geriatr Soc* 30:684, 1982.

46. Bellville JW et al: Influence of age on pain relief from analgesics. A study of postoperative patients. *JAMA* 17:1835, 1971.

47. Kaiko RF: Age and morphine analgesia in cancer patients

with postoperative pain. *Clin Pharmacol Ther* 28:823, 1980.

48. Greenblatt DJ et al: Toxicity of high-dose flurazepam in the elderly. *Clin Pharmacol Ther* 21:355, 1977.

49. Reidenberg MM et al: The relationship between diazepam dose, plasma level, age and central nervous system depression in adults. *Clin Pharmacol Ther* 23:371, 1978.

50. Vestal RE et al: Reduced β-adrenoceptor sensitivity in the elderly. *Clin Pharmacol Ther* 26:181, 1979.

51. Van Brummelen P et al: Age-related decrease in cardiac and peripheral vascular responsiveness to isoprenaline: Studies in normal subjects. *Clin Sci* 60:571, 1981.

52. Abernethy DR et al: Verapamil pharmacodynamics and disposition in young and elderly hypertensive patients. *Ann Intern Med* 105:329, 1986.

53. Abrass IB, Scarpace PJ: Human lymphocyte beta-adrenergic receptors are unaltered with age. *J Gerontol* 36:298, 1981.

54. Scarpace PJ: Decreased β-adrenergic responsiveness during senescence. *Fed Proc* 45:51, 1986.

55. Feldman RD et al: Alterations in leukocyte β-receptor affinity with aging. *N Engl J Med* 310:815, 1984.

56. World Health Organization: Health care in the elderly: Report of the technical group on use of medicaments by the elderly. *Drugs* 22:279, 1981.

GENERAL READING

Cusack BJ, Vestal RE: Clinical pharmacology: Special considerations in the elderly, in Calkins E, Davis PJ, Ford AB (eds): *Practice of Geriatric Medicine*. Philadelphia, Saunders, 1986, p 115.

Greenblatt DJ, Sellers EM, Shader RI: Drug disposition in old age. *N Engl J Med* 306:1081, 1982.

Schmucker DL: Aging and drug disposition: An update. *Pharmacol Rev* 37:133, 1985.

Swift CG (ed): *Clinical Pharmacology in the Elderly*. New York, Marcel Dekker, 1987.

Vestal RE (ed): *Drug Treatment in the Elderly*. Sydney, ADIS Health Science Press, 1984.

Vestal RE, Dawson GW: Pharmacology and aging, in Finch CE, Schneider EL (eds): *Handbook of the Biology of Aging*, 2d ed. New York, Van Nostrand Reinhold, 1985, p 744.

Chapter 22

DIFFERENCE IN THE PRESENTATION OF DISEASE

George Rosenthal and Knight Steel

PROBLEMS IN MAKING DIAGNOSES

One of the hallmarks of geriatric medicine is the dictum that disease may present atypically in the elderly. Although the dictum is supported by a large amount of clinical experience, often it is difficult to determine which aspects of disease presentation are due to age and which are simply age-related. Nonetheless, it is important for a physician caring for the elderly to keep in mind that many of the clues he or she learned to look for when making a certain diagnosis may be missing, and therefore it is essential to use a sophisticated diagnostic approach to ensure that many treatable diseases will not be overlooked.

It is considered a truism that data obtained from the patient history are the most important elements in the making of any diagnosis. However, there may be many barriers to eliciting a history from the elderly. First, it should be apparent that because of cultural differences, older people in the United States may well be less likely to report symptoms to physicians than are younger people. Older persons may be reticent to seek medical attention because of concerns about expenses, or they may be cautious about engaging the health care system either because of a failure to understand the technological aspects of medicine or because of a prior bad experience. Another obstacle may be either the elderly person's fear of being taken from home and sent to a chronic facility or feeling that a hospital is a place to die (the elderly patient

We would like to thank Dr. Joseph Stokes from the preventive medicine section at B.U.M.C. for reviewing this chapter.

may note that many peers fail to return to the community once admitted to a hospital).

Other barriers may be language (the elderly being more likely to have a foreign primary language), previous educational and life experiences which result in different perceptions of what is normal, and subtle mental status abnormalities. Any degree of confusion or delirium may be enhanced in the presence of an acute illness or during an exacerbation of a chronic disease. An unfamiliar environment (such as a doctor's office or hospital) or a certain time of day ("sundowning") can be an additional factor. Drugs, both prescription and over-the-counter, are used extensively in older patients and may have an effect on their mental status. Also, drugs used for one condition may blunt the severity of symptoms of a second illness.

The communication of a history also depends on the acuity of hearing and vision, both of which are decreased in many elderly patients. As the years accumulate there is a hearing loss in the high-frequency range. This impairment may be compounded by the background noise that frequently exists in hospitals and clinics or even by earwax. Aging changes and an increased prevalence of diseases (which may be hard to differentiate between) both affect vision. The increased rigidity of the lens and impaired accommodation, coupled with the rising prevalence of glaucoma and cataracts with age, could make reading a questionnaire or the examiner's lips difficult. Also, the aging process is accompanied by changes in various neurotransmitter systems that may account for the high prevalence of depression in the elderly; depression may mask the symptoms of other diseases.

Elderly people afflicted with multiple diseases may

find it difficult to distinguish a new symptom from an ongoing group of somatic concerns. Any symptom which is directly correlated with exertion may be less likely to occur in those suffering from one or more illnesses limiting ambulation. Sometimes the patient feels that a particular symptom comes with growing old and for that reason does not report it, believing that nothing can be done about it. Thus, ageism may afflict the elderly themselves.

Ageism may also be reflected in the attitudes of the caregivers and health care providers. The latter group may thus not look for reversible causes (such as medications) or may not treat as aggressively (as in young patients) those conditions uncovered. When a patient is unable to give a good history, a relative or caregiver is sought for the information. Besides the obvious limitation that a third person is seldom able to provide all the details about a patient, there may be other drawbacks. For example, others who provide the history may have hidden agendas, and they may overplay symptoms so as to have the patient hospitalized or sent to a nursing home or underplay symptoms because they do not want the person to leave home.

Many diseases can present with the same symptom, such as fatigue or decreased appetite. The symptom can even be related to an organ system other than the one with the pathology. An example of this is a change in mental status, decreased functional status, or incontinence in a person with pneumonia or a urinary tract infection. Also, one disease can interface with another, e.g., hyperthyroidism may present as a worsening of congestive heart failure.

Obtaining data from the physical examination may also contain pitfalls. The physical examination may be difficult to perform. Severe arthritic or functional disabilities may prevent older persons from achieving certain positions to allow the examination to be carried out. There are normal physiological changes with aging that may alter the presentation of certain diseases. Fifteen to 30 percent of "normal" elderly have been noted to have an asymptomatic orthostatic drop in blood pressure. Often this is exaggerated in the period immediately following meals. This somewhat common condition may lead to an erroneous diagnosis of a drug side effect or dehydration. The decreased tendency to sweat and the reduced likelihood of an increase in heart rate with stress could lead to a difficulty in making the diagnosis of hypoglycemia. The decreased elasticity of arteries which causes them to be more rigid, can alter the *tardus et brevis* sign as a clue to aortic stenosis. The baseline crackles in the lungs secondary to increased airway closure even at normal tidal volume may suggest to the novice observer the presence of pneumonia or congestive heart failure.

Gathering laboratory data may also be burdensome

and the results may be confusing to the physician. It may be difficult to obtain a computed tomography (CT) scan because the person has severe kyphosis secondary to osteoporosis and cannot lie flat. Other laboratory data, such as the rise in glucose intolerance with aging,[1] which may be due to peripheral resistance to insulin, may be dependent on the amount of physical activity the individual normally undertakes.

Articles discussing differences in the presentation of disease in an older population as compared to the presentation in younger people may have real or potential biases because of all the above reasons. Health care professionals may also add to this bias because of their failure to spend sufficient time to elicit the information required to make the correct diagnosis in the elderly patient (with age there could also be a decrease in the speed of response) or because of inadequate knowledge about the prevalence of a condition in this population. Additionally, if there are delays in making a diagnosis, comparisons of the presentation of disease between young and old populations may reflect differences in the stage of the disease under study. Similarly, there may be tendency to treat or manage diseases differently in one age group as compared to the other, and thus the natural history of an illness may appear to be quite different in the two age groups. The varying age-related symptoms may therefore mirror both symptom management and therapeutic efforts, rather than true differences in the host–illness relationship.

ACUTE CORONARY ARTERY DISEASE

Any study comparing the presentation of disease between a younger and an older population must decide upon a "gold standard," i.e., a definition of the condition under study. Thus if the symptoms of acute coronary artery disease are being investigated, for example, the study may be biased if a coronary angiogram is required to confirm the presence of the disease. The decision of a physician concerning the need or appropriateness for such an invasive test may well be different for the two age groups. If electrocardiogram (ECG) changes are used to ascertain the presence of an acute myocardial infarction, it is necessary to know that previous ECG changes do not preclude the recognition of definitive criteria.

Any comparison in the presentation of disease between age groups should also be interpreted with caution if a single symptom that is traditionally ascribed to the disease when it appears in a younger person is used as the criterion for the condition. Thus, if chest pain is likely to be absent in diabetes and if the older group has a higher prevalence of diabetes mellitus, only the subgroup, older diabetics, may present differently than the young. But if chest pain and shortness of breath are studied as a pair of symptoms of myocardial infarction, then the physician's ability to recognize the disease may be the same for both age groups. Furthermore the reports of "symptomless" acute myocardial infarction may really reflect a failure to ask the right question or the attribution of symptoms to other organs such as the gallbladder. The criteria for defining the disease in question will influence the outcome of the comparison.

Given all of these caveats, considerable data in the literature, including data from the Framingham Heart Study,[2-5] which has followed 5209 individuals for 40 years, suggest that an acute myocardial infarction is more likely to present without chest pain in an older population than it is in a younger one. If chest pain and shortness of breath are used as a pair of symptoms, the incidence of silent myocardial infarction may well not be different between the two generations. The recognition that the symptom *complex* may differ with age enforces the need to be tireless in pursuing historical data. Although these longitudinal studies from Framingham report that 32 percent of ECG-diagnosed myocardial infarctions noted during one or more follow-up examinations had no associated symptoms apparent upon first questioning, in about half of these individuals it was possible to elicit some details of the history that might have been related to the disease (Dr. J. Stokes, personal communication). Thus, although the incidence of a "silent" myocardial infarction, defined by a new Q wave noted between biannual examinations, did in fact increase progressively with age past 65 years, an increase in the incidence of glucose intolerance and a number of the biases mentioned previously make the distinction between the disease presentation in older and younger age groups difficult to interpret.

On the other hand, asymptomatic myocardial ischemia recognized on ambulatory ECG monitoring more frequently occurs in elderly rather than in young individuals. This observation lends credence to the belief that the presentation of coronary artery disease does differ between the ages. This incidence may also be underestimated, as Q waves may revert to a nondiagnostic pattern within 2 years of an acute myocardial infarction.

Other studies of the presentation of acute coronary artery disease suggest that conduction defects, with or without heart block, atrial flutter, and atrial fibrillation, are almost twice as common in the elderly as they are in the young. There are reports that pulmonary edema, congestive heart failure, cardiac rupture, and shock are more common presenting complaints in the elderly. Symptoms suggesting hypoperfusion of the central nervous system are also more common in an older population.

In large studies looking at coronary disease (the

CASS studies),[6] older patients with angina were seen to be sicker than their younger counterparts, with an increased incidence of intermittent medical disease, unstable angina, and heart failure. Additionally, by simple tests of comparison the incidence of anterior myocardial infarction was found to be more common in the elderly group. It should be stressed that comparisons between age groups are difficult to interpret because of the multiple difficulties in making the diagnosis of myocardial infarction in an elderly population. Stress testing is more difficult to carry out in the elderly because of impaired ambulation and an inability to achieve adequate stress during the workout. Echo studies may also be a problem because of chest-wall abnormalities.

In summary, then, it appears that comparative studies between the young and the old with respect to differences in the presentation of coronary artery disease are difficult to make. Nonetheless, in those with coronary artery disease, as an example, it does appear that older individuals are more likely than younger persons to present with dyspnea and without chest pain, and, because of the presence of multiple diseases such as hypertension and diabetes, it is especially important to try to elicit data, especially historical information, which reflect disease presentation in the elderly.

THYROID DISEASE

Thyroid disease provides what is perhaps the most prototypical example of altered disease presentation in the elderly. Both underactivity and overactivity of the gland can create a problem for the diagnostician (see also Chap. 70). Hypothyroidism can manifest the same symptoms and signs that appear in a euthyroid aged individual. Examples of findings common to both are dry skin, alopecia, a decline in the basal metabolic rate, cold intolerance, a decrease in maximal heart rate, and a slower response in some neuromuscular functions. Although with advancing age there is an increasing heterogeneity in thyroid pathology, there are some changes common to both the aged and the myxedematous thyroid gland. These include an increase in interfollicular connective tissue and fibrosis and a decrease in follicular size and stored colloid with atrophy of the glandular epithelium. The prevalence of hypothyroidism rises with age, as do both antithyroglobulin and antimicrosomal titers.[7] Nearly 25 percent of older persons have elevations of one or both by the eighth decade of life, regardless of thyroid status.

Hypothyroidism can also exhibit findings that, though not necessarily a result of aging, appear commonly in the elderly without thyroid disease. A list of these findings includes congestive heart failure, hypertension, alveolar hypoventilation, elevated lipids, vague arthritic complaints, constipation and fecal impaction, altered mental status, and depression. Regrettably this nonspecificity has resulted in many older patients failing to be evaluated for hypothyroidism because the symptom or finding was attributed to another cause or to general old age. Articles from Framingham[8] have shown that there was a lack of sensitivity to this potential disorder in routine examination by a physician, even when the patient's background contained a clue to a possible thyroid problem.

On the other hand, with overactivity of this endocrine gland in the elderly many of the classic findings may be missing. Instead of the usual symptoms that are secondary to increased levels of thyroid hormone, such as tachycardia, tremor, and anxiety, hyperthyroidism in the elderly usually imitates disease from nonendocrine organs, especially the heart, intestine, brain, or muscle.

The physical appearance of the hyperthyroid elderly person will usually be different from that of the nonelderly individual. Graves' disease is the leading cause of thyrotoxicosis in younger patients, whereas toxic multinodular goiter occurs more frequently in the elderly. Seventy-five percent of those over 65 years of age were found to have nodular rather than diffuse goiter. For this reason there might not be the prominence in the neck region that is usually associated with young females with Graves' disease. In a series reported from Australia,[9] 18 percent of thyrotoxic patients had no palpable gland. Davis and Davis[10] reported that only 37 percent of thyrotoxic patients over age 60 had thyroid enlargement detectable on physical examination. The gland may also not be reachable by the examining fingers when the thyroid recedes with the trachea into the thoracic cavity as kyphosis develops. The duration of symptoms is also related to the histology. Forty-nine percent of those with nodular disease had persistent complaints of more than a year as compared with only 22 percent of those with Graves' disease. This might mean a less dramatic presentation in the older individual. With the slower progression of hyperthyroidism in multinodular goiter, the longer duration may put greater stress on the heart, accounting for the predominance of cardiac signs in the elderly. Classic eye findings are also less common in the elderly, found in 28 percent of an older group as compared to 71 percent of a younger group in one study. Palpitations and tremor have been reported in almost 100 percent of young patients as compared to about two-thirds of elderly patients. Sweating has also been noted to be significantly decreased in the elderly. However, an increased prevalence of associated weight loss and arrhythmias (atrial fibrillation and ventricular premature contractions) is noted in the old. The weight loss in the elderly is usually associated with anorexia instead of the hyperphagia seen in younger individuals. About 40 percent of the elderly have been noted to have heart rates of less than 100 beats/min, even when atrial fibrillation is present, and in perhaps 1 in 10 older hyperthyroid persons with atrial fibrillation the rate is under 80 beats/min. This may be due to the relatively high prevalence of atrioventricular (AV) block. Also, in an older population, as compared to a younger population, the male-to-female ratio is more equal, without the female predominance seen in 30- to 50-year-olds.

In one series of 25 thyrotoxic persons over age 75, the average number of symptoms was only two, and two of the patients were asymptomatic, in contrast to the usual occurrence of multiple symptoms in young hyperthyroid persons. Although there may be no difference with age in the level of catecholamines (thought to be a cause of many symptoms of hyperthyroidism), it may be that there is a different presentation in the old due to reduced end-organ responsiveness. There was no correlation among signs and symptoms and hormone levels in the elderly in the series of Tibaldi et al.[11]

The difficulty of making the diagnosis of hyperthyroidism in the elderly is noted by Levine and Sturgis, who proposed the term "masked hyperthyroidism" to describe the situation in which cardiac findings of atrial dysrhythmias, angina pectoris, and cardiac failure are present without the underlying thyrotoxicosis being recognized. Nowadays some cardiac drugs frequently taken by the elderly, such as beta-blockers, may hide the features of hyperthyroidism. Lahey[12] coined the term "apathetic hyperthyroidism" to describe the condition wherein the usual hyperkinetic state is replaced by a depressed, withdrawn, and unanimated appearance. He also noted that agitated excitation and delirium may be part of the presentation of hyperthyroidism. Thus thyroid disease should be considered when investigating any recent or apparently abrupt change in mental status, which is so commonly a matter of concern to the geriatrician. Diarrhea, a concomitant of hyperthyroidism in the young, is usually not present in the elderly, but there may be a decrease in constipation. With a change in bowel habits, weight loss, weakness, and anorexia, an extensive workup for cancer may be undertaken and the diagnosis of hyperthyroidism therefore delayed. The results of thyroid function tests, though not within the scope of this chapter, may also confuse the clinical picture, as there may be an alteration of binding globulins or a change in serum T_3 levels secondary to another systemic illness.[13,14]

INFECTION

Infection is another area in which a diagnosis may be inaccurate or delayed because of an atypical presentation. Autopsy data have confirmed that pneumonia may be the most frequently missed disease in the elderly.

The only clue to the physician may be a history of a fall, a decrease in function, confusion, incontinence, or tachypnea (an especially telling sign). If there is a delay in the diagnosis, pneumonia may be discovered only after the disease has advanced to bacteremia or meningitis. Neck stiffness may be an unreliable sign of meningitis because of associated cervical arthritis or Parkinson's disease.

The characteristic sign of infection is fever, which may be blunted or absent in a small but significant number of the elderly with pneumonia.[15] Glickman and Hibert[16] reported on 25 patients with a mean age of 81 with minimal or absent fever with documented bacteremia. Twenty percent of elderly persons admitted to a hospital with community-acquired pneumonia were afebrile. Older patients with pneumococcal bacteremia had a lower mean temperature response, a lower peak fever, and a higher incidence of an afebrile response than younger patients with the same etiological agent. Keating et al.[17] also found that if fever was present in the elderly it was less likely due to a "benign" viral infection (only 17 percent).

The presence or absence of fever has also been correlated with mortality. In a study of 500 cases, survival increased with a rising febrile response. The highest mortality occurred in those who were afebrile or even hypothermic. Bryant et al.[18] studied 218 patients with gram-negative bacteremia and found that mortality was 71 percent when patient temperature was 35 to 38.2°C and only 27 percent with fevers higher than 39.4°C. The concomitant use of medicines, frequently seen in the elderly, can affect patient temperature. These medicines include nonsteroidals, over-the-counter preparations with antipyretic properties, and steroids. Chronic diseases such as renal failure may also be a factor in blunting the febrile response.

An elevated white blood cell (WBC) count is another finding that may be seen more often in a younger person with infection than in an older one, though different studies have reported disparate results. In the 25 individuals with bacteremia referred to previously,[15] 8 had no leukocytosis, though 4 demonstrated a left shift. However, Finklestein et al.[19] found a similarity of the admission WBC count and heart rate between the older and younger groups. Marrie et al.[20] noticed that 70 percent of patients with community-acquired pneumonia had a WBC count greater than or equal to 10,000 per cubic milliliter when admitted and that this was more frequent in the elderly group (81.5 percent vs. 52.6 percent). Most studies have found that more than 10,000 WBCs is the rule in bacterial pneumonia in the elderly, and even with normal counts early forms (left shift) are present.[21]

The physician's ability to make a diagnosis may also be hampered in the elderly because of the difficulty in obtaining sputum because of an ineffective cough, a decrease in ciliary transport, and the frequent accompaniment of other problems, such as dehydration, congestive heart failure, and chronic pulmonary disease. Patients from long-term care facilities may have colonization of the oropharynx with gram-negative organisms even without pneumonia. The chest x ray may show various patterns of incomplete consolidation as opposed to the typical lobar pattern, which may make it difficult to differentiate infection from congestive heart failure or malignancy.

Tuberculosis is now a disease of the geriatric population.[22,23] There have been recent epidemics reported in nursing homes. A large percentage of elderly people admitted to nursing homes (85 to 90 percent in one Arkansas study) do not react to tuberculin skin testing and are at risk of developing a primary infection (see Chap. 51). Also, there may be reactivation with advancement of chronic disease or malnutrition. The diagnosis is frequently difficult because the clinical aspects are usually more subtle, insidious, and nonspecific than in other forms of pneumonia. In a study of clinical features of pulmonary tuberculosis in young and old veterans, the latter were significantly less likely to demonstrate cavitary lesions on admission radiographs or present with hemoptysis, but they were more likely to present with a right lower lobe infiltrate and complaints of dyspnea. However, symptoms prior to admission, such as fever, anorexia, weight loss, and cough, were equal in the two groups.[24] Skin testing was underutilized, and, although treatment was delayed in the elderly, there was no age-related difference in mortality. In another series the elderly had a decreased incidence of fever, weight loss, night sweats, sputum production, and hemoptysis, although mortality was increased. Fourteen percent of older individuals had a normal chest x ray, as compared to 8 percent of younger individuals.[22]

GASTROINTESTINAL DISEASES

The acute abdomen is another disorder for which diagnosis may be delayed in the elderly because of atypical findings, with a resultant increased mortality, especially if surgery is needed. The reluctance of a physician to send an aged patient to surgery may also be a factor. Also, the elderly population is more likely to have other diseases affecting organs outside of the abdomen, such as cardiac, aortic, or genitourinary illnesses, that can present with abdominal findings.

Acute appendicitis,[25] characteristically a disease of the young, is often not thought of when an older person presents in the emergency room. Although only 5 percent of all cases of appendicitis are seen in the elderly, such cases constitute the majority of fatalities. Perforation of the bowel and gangrene are frequently found at surgery. The symptoms usually include abdominal pain, although it might be mild in severity. Also, the pain may be generalized and the abdomen rigid in an older patient, whereas the pain is likely to localize to the right lower quadrant in a young one.

Abdominal pain may also be diminished or absent in elderly persons with peptic ulcer disease.[26,27] Cinch et al.,[28] reporting on 108 old patients, found that 35 percent had no pain, compared to 5 percent without pain in a younger population. The classic evidence of perforation as sudden pain and rigidity may not occur. Watson et al.[29] found that the most common mode of presentation was bleeding with perforation, a presenting feature in 30 percent of elderly patients. Crohn's disease, although much less likely to be seen in an elderly population than a young one, is reported to present in the elderly with less pain, a decreased prevalence of a palpable abdominal mass, less small-bowel disease, and no family history of inflammatory bowel disease.[30] In one retrospective study of 39 elderly patients with acute cholecystitis, tenderness and peritoneal inflammation were lacking in over 50 percent, although all had some abdominal pain. One-third had a temperature less than 100°F, and 65 percent had a WBC count of less than 10,000. Gangrene and perforation noted at the time of surgery were common.[31]

Thus the geriatrician must always be diligent in seeking out treatable disease by searching among an often confusing array of nonspecific symptoms and undramatic signs. This is true regardless of whether or not any specific symptom or sign has a different prevalence in the older population than it has in younger populations.

REFERENCES

1. DeFronzo RA: Glucose intolerance and aging. *Diabetes Care* 4(4):493, 1981.
2. Kannel WB, Dannenberg AL, Abbott RD: Unrecognized myocardial infarction and hypertension: The Framingham Study. *Am Heart J* 109(3):581, 1985.
3. Stokes J III, Dawber TR: The "silent coronary": The frequency and clinical characteristics of unrecognized myocardial infarction in the Framingham Study. *Ann Intern Med* 50:1359, 1959.
4. MacDonald JB: Presentation of acute myocardial infarction in the elderly—A Review. *Age Ageing* 13:196, 1984.
5. Coodley EL: Clinical spectrum and diagnostic techniques of coronary heart disease in the elderly. *J Am Geriatr Soc* 36:447, 1988.
6. Gersh BJ et al: Comparison of coronary artery bypass surgery and medical therapy in patients 65 years of age or older. *N Engl J Med* 313:217, 1985.
7. Hawkins BR et al: Diagnostic significance of thyroid microsomal antibodies in randomly selected population. *Lancet* 2:1057, 1980.
8. Sawin CT et al: The aging thyroid: Thyroid deficiency in the Framingham Study. *Arch Intern Med* 145:1386, 1985.
9. Stiel JN et al: Thyrotoxicosis in an elderly population. *Med J Aust* 2:986, 1972.
10. Davis PJ, Davis FB: Hyperthyroidism in patients over the age of 60 years. *Medicine* 53:161, 1974.
11. Tibaldi JM et al: Thyrotoxicosis in the very old. *Am J Med* 81:619, 1986.
12. Lahey FH: Apathetic thyroidism. *Ann Surg* 95:1026, 1931.
13. Bartels EC: Hyperthyroidism in patients over 65. *Geriatrics* 20:459, 1965.
14. Nordyke RA et al: Graves disease: Influence of age on clinical findings. *Arch Intern Med* 148:626, 1988.
15. Norman DC et al: Fever and aging. *J Am Geriatr Soc* 33:859, 1985.
16. Glickman R, Hibert D: Afebrile bacteremia, a phenonemon in geriatric patients. *JAMA* 248:1478, 1982.
17. Keating HJ et al: Effect of aging on the clinical significance of fever in ambulatory adult patients. *J Am Geriatr Soc* 32:282, 1984.
18. Bryant RE et al: Factors affecting mortality of gram-negative rod bacteremia. *Arch Intern Med* 127:120, 1971.
19. Finklestein MS et al: Pneumococcal bacteremia in adults: Age dependent differences in presentation and in outcome. *J Am Geriatr Soc* 31:19, 1983.
20. Marrie TJ et al: Community-acquired pneumonia requiring hospitalization: Is it different in the elderly? *J Am Geriatr Soc* 33:671, 1985.
21. Bentley DW: Bacterial pneumonia in the elderly: Clinical features, diagnosis, etiology and treatment. *Gerontology* 30:297, 1984.
22. Alvarez S et al: Pulmonary tuberculosis in elderly men. *Am J Med* 82:602, 1987.
23. Stead WW: Tuberculosis among elderly persons: An outbreak in a nursing home. *Ann Intern Med* 94:606, 1984.
24. Katz PR et al: Clinical features of pulmonary tuberculosis in young and old veterans. *J Am Geriatr Soc* 35:512, 1987.
25. Yusuf M, Dunn E: Appendicitis in the elderly: Learn to discern its untypical picture. *Geriatrics* 34:73, 1979.
26. Coleman JA, Denham MJ: Perforation of peptic ulceration in the elderly. *Aging* 9:257, 1980.
27. Oliver N: Abdominal pain in the elderly. *Aust Fam Physician* 13:402, 1984.
28. Cinch D et al: Absence of abdominal pain in elderly patients with peptic ulcer. *Age Ageing* 13:120, 1984.
29. Watson RJ et al: Duodenal ulcer disease in the elderly: A retrospective study. *Age Ageing* 14:225, 1985.
30. Harper PC et al: Crohn's disease in the elderly. *Arch Intern Med* 146:753, 1986.
31. Morrow DJ et al: Acute cholecystitis in the elderly: A surgical emergency. *Arch Surg* 113:1149, 1978.

Chapter 23

COMPREHENSIVE FUNCTIONAL ASSESSMENT (CFA) IN EVERYDAY PRACTICE

Marsha Duke Fretwell

Assessing the patient is a first and critical step in excellent medical care of both young and old patients. In the elderly this level of care especially emphasizes the functional approach.[1,2] In the biomedical model of care, the elements of assessment traditionally include the chief complaint, the history of present illness, the past medical history, the review of systems, social history, physical examination, and preliminary laboratory evaluation. Attempts to apply this biomedical model of assessment effectively in the frail older patient are frustrated by the nonspecific presentations of illness, extensive and interacting past medical illnesses, an often-positive review of systems, and multiple abnormalities on physical and laboratory evaluation. Cognitive impairments and difficulties with communication may further limit the collection of accurate information. Additionally, issues outside of the biomedical realm, i.e., social, emotional, and economic losses, are known to influence health outcomes significantly. All these issues complicate our ability to assess our older patients efficiently. Without an accurate data base, the potential for missed diagnosis, inappropriate medications, and adverse effects from treatment is greatly enhanced.

ASSESSMENT OF THE PATIENT: THE BIOPSYCHOSOCIAL MODEL

George Engel has proposed,[3] in response to the perceived inadequacies of the biomedical model, that we broaden our traditional data base to include elements from the social and psychological domains. Crucial to frail and dependent members of our society (i.e., infants, children, and frail older persons), this *biopsychosocial model* is especially important for any patient whose acute illness (the mainstay of the biomedical model) occurs in the context of chronic disease. In such individuals, regardless of age and the particular nature of the chronic disease, an effective assessment must include, in addition to the strictly medical problems or diagnoses, information about economic status and emotional, cognitive, social, and physical function. As our health care system shifts from treating primarily acute illness to managing chronic illness, many subtle (or not so subtle) and interactive characteristics of the patient become vital in determining the outcomes of any particular episode of acute illness or trial of medication. While it is appropriately comprehensive and complex as an approach to an individual, the biopsychosocial model appears difficult to apply in the everyday reality of medical practice. In the context of our technologically and quantitatively oriented medical practice, this model seems diffuse, time-consuming, and difficult to relate to everyday medical decision making. Yet, in older and particularly frail patients, the failure to acknowledge the mental and physical complexity of each person often leads to iatrogenesis for the patient and a sense of impotence and frustration for the practitioner.

ASSESSMENT OF THE PATIENT: THE FUNCTIONAL MODEL

A gradual (yet highly variable) decline in functional capacity is a normal phenomenon associated with age.

Superimposed on this gradual decline in function is the combined impact of acute diseases such as myocardial infarctions and cerebrovascular accidents and certain elements of life style such as diet, exercise, and stress. One role of the physician in current practice is to minimize the impact of these exogenous factors and thereby optimize, at any point in time, mental and physical function in aging individuals. This may be done by prevention of disease whenever possible, treatment of disease when necessary, and careful avoidance of iatrogenic illness in older individuals. Finally, this inevitable functional decline can be minimized by careful restoration of the older patient to his or her maximal level of function following each episode of acute illness.

DEFINITION OF FUNCTION

The word *function* is defined by Webster's as follows: "To carry out one's activity or processes." In humans, the word can be used to describe activity at multiple levels, i.e., at the cellular level the membrane's function is to pump sodium out; *or* at a more complex tissue and organ level, the cardiac output is one measure of the heart's function; *or* at the even more complex level of the organism, the ability of an individual to file an income tax return appropriately is a measure which integrates cognitive, physical, social, and economic function.

In the clinical care of older patients, we are interested not only in the function of the patient's heart and lungs, but also in higher-level functions such as the ability to remember to take drugs appropriately, to toilet oneself, to ambulate, to eat, to socialize, or to transport oneself out of the home. These areas of function are the focus of the *functional model*, elaborated by Katz and others[4] in response to the increasing burden of chronic illness and physical disability in our aging population. Because acutely ill older patients usually experience a simultaneous decline in function in several organs which, in turn, may lead to decline in several of the more complex areas of physical, mental, and social functions, an accurate assessment of a patient demands a comprehensive (biopsychosocial) information base. This broad information base is most usefully summarized by using functional measures such as Katz's *activity of daily living*[4] and Lawton's *instrumental activity of daily living.*[5]

THE USEFULNESS OF FUNCTIONAL SUMMARY MEASURES IN EVERYDAY PRACTICE

DIAGNOSIS *Change in functional ability is the most sensitive indicator for identifying new disease.* Although decline in functional reserve is widespread in all older patients, it is frequently not manifest until the person is stressed in some way, either emotionally or physically. Most older patients have "a most vulnerable function."

Usually, it is memory loss, but it may also be the ability to remain appropriately continent or to walk independently. Because of this "most vulnerable" phenomenon in certain older patients, pneumonia, hypothyroidism, urinary tract infection, a myocardial infarction, or simple congestive heart failure may all present initially as confusion, falling, or incontinence. Knowledge of a person's mental or physical function at baseline allows early discrimination of a change in function which in turn promotes earlier detection of disease. Likewise, improvement in a function, such as memory or the ability to feed oneself, becomes a sensitive indication of recovery.

TREATMENT *Measures of functional status that examine the ability of the individual to function independently in a variety of areas are more useful than a list of medical diagnoses in planning appropriate medical treatment or social services.* A diagnosis alone cannot tell you how sick an individual is or how much care he or she needs. For example, the diagnosis of diabetes mellitus carries a broad range of medical and functional implications, from an individual who is diet-controlled and completely functional to one who is hospitalized and requires intensive care for hyperosmolar coma. The medical diagnosis *and* the description of a patient's function give us the most accurate picture of the patient and thereby facilitate the safest and most appropriate use of technology and resources.

PREDICTION OF OUTCOMES *Rates and direction of change in measurement of an individual's mental, physical, and social functions are the most important means of predicting outcomes from illness in older patients.* In acutely ill individuals, the overall prognosis of the individual gives us important information about how aggressively we should use the advanced technology of our medical system. The overall prognosis is best-estimated not only by considering the patient's age and severity of illness, but also by understanding the premorbid level of function and the rate of change that has occurred in function with this particular acute illness. The higher the level of preillness function and the steeper the downward curve, the better the prognosis for recovery. Certain catastrophic and irreversible illnesses like a massive cerebrovascular accident, of course, may override these predictors of outcome.

As the burden of chronic disease increases, there is an increasing risk of functional decline that is not reversible. It is important in any assessment of patient function to evaluate the *cause* and the *potential for reversing* any given episode of functional decline. This process of isolating the cause and differentiating each episode of functional decline into reversible or irreversible improves the accuracy of our predictions of outcome. Assuming that all functional decline in older patients is irreversible is a serious form of ageism which produces unnecessary pessimism for both the doctor and the patient.

In summary then, the *functional model* refers to the use of an individual's past and current state of function in order to

1. Improve diagnostic accuracy
2. Plan medical treatment and social services
3. Monitor the impact of medical treatments and social services
4. Improve the accuracy in prediction of patient outcomes

This model has demonstrable usefulness in the care of older and chronically ill patients. Yet, like the biopsychosocial model, it has not been adopted by the majority of medical practitioners. The *biomedical model* remains the predominant model underlying everyday practice in clinical decision making and care of patients.

COMPREHENSIVE FUNCTIONAL ASSESSMENT: A SYNTHESIS OF THE BIOPSYCHOSOCIAL AND FUNCTIONAL MODELS

A mainstay of geriatric practice in Great Britian, geriatric assessments units (GAUs) have now been identified as the "New Technology of Geriatrics" in the United States. In this country, the concept of the *unit-based* assessment has been expanded to include *consultation* models of assessment and has been applied in acute-care hospitals, in ambulatory care, nursing homes, and rehabilitation programs for geriatric patients. The central feature of the GAU is captured in the words *comprehensive . . . assessment* as reflected by the title of the recent National Institute of Health Consensus Development Conference: *"Comprehensive Geriatric Assessment."* In this context, *comprehensive* refers to the centrality of the multidisciplinary evaluation of the patient in this model. In the GAU or in the comprehensive geriatric assessment, several domains of the patient—physical, mental, social, economic, and functional—are routinely reviewed and integrated into a coordinated plan of care focusing medical treatments and social service interventions on the patient's impairments, disabilities, and dependencies. Over the past 10 years, application of the GAU or of the comprehensive geriatric assessment has routinely involved clinicians from several health care professions: medical, psychiatric, and physical medicine physicians; dentists; nurses; social workers; dietitians; pharmacists; psychologists; and occupational and physical therapists. The effectiveness of these approaches in improving the outcome of patients has been demonstrated in several studies and reflects their routine and explicit use of the functional model[6,7] in making accurate diagnoses, planning treatments, and utilizing rehabilitative services before long-term-care placement. Both the

GAU and comprehensive geriatric assessment approaches also routinely use the biopsychosocial model, but in a more implicit fashion. By including professionals from nursing, social work, psychiatry, and psychology, the information base used to create the coordinated, functionally oriented plan of care is broadened beyond the traditional biomedical model. It contains many different descriptive variables about the patient and acknowledges the interaction among them.

The model of CFA described in this chapter is based on the interdisciplinary team assessment used in the GAU or in comprehensive geriatric assessment and is modified for application by an individual practitioner. Our information base contains the three traditional domains of the biopsychosocial model (Table 23-1) and the two functional scales (top of Table 23-2) of basic and instrumental *activities of daily living* (ADLs). The biomedical, psychological, and social domains provide discrete units of functionally oriented information, while the ADLs provide summaries of the interactive impact of these variables on the patient's everyday life. In each of the major domains, there are subsets of data that are particularly relevant to health outcomes in older patients. For instance, renal function, cardiovascular function, cognitive function, social function, coping function, the patient's values and attitudes toward personal

TABLE 23-1
Comprehensive Functional Assessment

Domains

I. *Biomedical*
  a. *Medical diagnosis* (functional impact 0–5; irreversibility 0–5)
  b. *Medications* (duration, adverse drug reactions, functional impact 0–5; irreversibility 0–5; creatinine clearance
  c. *Nutritional status* (albumin, weight changes, appetite)
  d. *Perceptual function* (hearing, speech, vision)
II. *Psychological*
  a. *Cognitive function:* "mini-mental state"
  b. *Emotional function:* depression, personality type, coping style
  c. *Specific dysfunction:* hostility, anxiety, depression, hallucinations, paranoia
  d. *Values* regarding use of extraordinary therapies, feeding tubes, nursing home placement
III. *Social*
  a. *Individual social skills:* marital history, acceptance of help, presence of confidant
  b. *Support system:* quantity and quality of the system, use of formal support
  c. *Financial resources*

TABLE 23-2

Summary Scales

---

1. *Basic ADLs:* feeding, bathing, dressing, use of toilet, transfer mobility, continence
2. *Instrumental ADLs:* use of transport, shopping, finance, telephone, medications, housework

Individualized Care Plan

Areas of Concern	Recommendations
1. Accurate diagnosis	1.
2. Optimal use of medication	2.
3. Nutrition	3.
4. Cognitive function	4.
5. Emotional function	5.
6. Social support system	6.
7. Mobility	7.
8. Continence	8.
9. Patient values	9.

---

health, and the use of extraordinary means and institutional placement are routinely addressed. From each of the domains, patients' strengths are also identified (such as no cognitive impairment, strong family support, previously independent) and used as positive resources in developing the *individualized care plan* (see Table 23-2). This activity acknowledges that the health outcomes of any patient are the result of a balance between the strengths and weaknesses of the patient and the patient's family as they face the emotional and physical stress of acute and chronic diseases.

The *ADLs* are a means of focusing the entirety of this biopsychosocial model down to a series of functional issues relevant to both the physician and the patient. For the physician, changes in function of the patient are the most important method of achieving accurate diagnosis, prognosis, and appropriate treatment for older patients. For the patient, maintaining physical and mental function is critical for personal independence and dignity. Therefore, in the preparation of each patient's care plan, we not only focus on the acute medical illness at hand, but we routinely evaluate all areas of function that are critical for optimizing the patient's health status and independence.[6]

These eight *areas of concern* (accurate diagnosis, optimal use of medications, nutrition, cognitive function, emotional function, social support system, mobility, continence, and appropriate use of resources) serve as a framework to cue routine review of these areas, known to be important in achieving good health outcomes.

CLINICAL APPLICATIONS OF CFA

The measures of I. Physiology and biomedical markers, II. Medications, and III. Functional status(A) and mental status[8] (B) (see Table 23-3) may be used to describe succinctly the patient's status at several points in time: prior to illness, at beginning of treatment, and following therapeutic interventions. Connecting these information points, we can trace a trajectory of the physiology and function of the patient which allows us to close the information feedback loop and promotes increased understanding of the individual patient and our interventions on her or his behalf. Thus, trials of adding or reducing medications can be evaluated for their effectiveness by comparing pretreatment with posttreatment measures of physiology and function. It is important to define *before initiating therapies* what improvement in a patient's function is desired and what loss of function you risk incurring. As the practitioner develops skills in CFA and applies them to every patient, the multiple and complex variables of the biopsychosocial view become predictable patterns, rather than isolated events. By focusing the *individualized care plan* on both the medical diagnosis and the patient's everyday function *and* by routinely setting the therapeutic goal of improving the mental and physical function of the patient, greater patient-doctor satisfaction with care is achieved. This type of patient outcome management information system also allows one to observe more readily changes in function of the patient over time or in response to a particular intervention. Again, the educational benefit of receiving structured feedback is emphasized.

COST EFFECTIVENESS OF COMPREHENSIVE FUNCTIONAL ASSESSMENT

As outlined above, this combination of the biopsychosocial and functional models of care is the theoretical and practical basis of team function within the geriatric assessment unit (GAU). In the setting of a GAU, this approach has demonstrated utility and proven benefits to health care outcomes. Among these benefits are better diagnostic accuracy and treatment planning, more appropriate placement decisions with fewer referrals to nursing homes, improved functional and mental status of the patient, prolonged survival of the patient, and lower overall use of costly institutional care services.

It will not be possible for every older patient to have the benefit of a formal GAU evaluation. A more cost-effective approach to improved medical care of these complex patients is the incorporation of the biopsychosocial functional model into each physician's patient assessment process. Rather than rely on formal instruments for functional assessment, we suggest approaching each

TABLE 23-3
Data Collection Form for Ongoing Care

I. *Physiology:*
   Weight:
   Blood pressure/Sitting:
                Standing:
   Pulse/Sitting:
          Standing:
   Biomedical markers:
   Fasting blood sugar, albumin, BUN, etc., as required

II. Medications	Date started	Dosage
1.		
2.		
3.		
4.		
5.		
6.		
7.		
8.		
9.		
10.		

IIIA. *Functional status and instrumental activities of daily activities*

Key: No Assistance—NA; With Assistance—WA; Total Care—TC

	NA	WA	TC
1. Walks	—	—	—
2. Transfers in/out of bed/chair/toilet	—	—	—
3. Bathes or showers	—	—	—
4. Dresses (gets clothes on self)	—	—	—
5. Uses toilet (cleans self)	—	—	—
6. Feeds oneself (eats)	—	—	—
7. Continence, bladder	—	—	—
8. Continence, bowel ("Were you able to")	—	—	—
9. Prepares a light meal	—	—	—
10. Does light housework	—	—	—
11. Does laundry	—	—	—
12. Shops for groceries	—	—	—
13. Manages finances	—	—	—
14. Uses telephone	—	—	—
15. Takes medications	—	—	—

patient with the broad domains of biological, psychological, and social functions as a framework. Formal evaluation of cognitive function (Folstein's mini-mental status), ADL, and IADL should be routinely collected (see Table 23-3). The individualized care plan (i.e., problem list) always includes functional problems as well as biomedical ones. Each physician may modify the particular way a question is asked, similar to the approach of taking a history in the traditional biomedical model. In the end, the practicing physician is able to fit such a comprehensive functional assessment into an initial visit of 45 to 60 minutes. Follow-up visits require rechecking only those variables (I. Physiology and biomedical markers, II. Medications, and III. Functional status and mental status) that change over time or in response to treatment.

SUMMARY

We have described the practical application of the biopsychosocial and functional models of assessment in the routine care of older patients. This approach focuses one's efforts on those issues most important to patients. Because of the quantitative capacities of the functional measures used, this approach allows us to select variables from the multiple domains of biomedical, psychological, and social functions, relate them to functional changes, and thereby improve our skills in the prediction, diagnosis, and treatment of medical illnesses. This combination of biopsychosocial systems model with functional model balances the former's comprehensive and integrative vision with a practical and quantitative means of application to the everyday care of older patients.

Table 23-3 (continued)

IIIB. *Mini-mental state*
Objective: To measure decline in brain function.

Maximum Score	Patient Score	
		Orientation
5	_____	What is the (year) (season) (date) (day) (month)?
5	_____	Where are we: (state) (country) (town) (hospital) (floor)?
		Registration/Learning
3	_____	Name three objects: 1 second to say each, then ask the patient all three after you have said them. Give 1 point for each correct answer. Then repeat them until he learns all three. Count trials and record.
		Trials _____
		Attention and Calculation—Sustained Activity
5	_____	Serial 3's: 1 point for each correct. Stop after five answers. *Alternate:* Spell "earth" backward.
		Recall—Short-Term
3	_____	Ask for the three objects repeated above. Give 1 point for each correct.
		Language Comprehension
9	_____	1. Name a pencil and watch (2 points).
		2. Repeat the following: "No ifs, ands, or buts." (1 point).
		3. Follow a three-stage command: "Take a paper in your right hand, fold it in half, and put it on the floor." (3 points).
		4. Each one of the following is 1 point for a total of 3 points:
		a. Ask patient to read and obey: "Close your eyes."
		b. After patient has closed eyes and reopened eyes, ask patient to write a sentence.
		c. Ask patient to copy the design.

Close Your Eyes.
Write a sentence.
Copy the design.

TOTAL SCORE_____30 max.

REFERENCES

1. Becker PM, Cohen HJ: The functional approach to the care of the elderly. *J Am Geriatr Soc* 32:12:923, 19.
2. Besdine RW: The educational utility of comprehensive functional assessment in the elderly. *J Am Geriatr Soc* 31:651, 1983.
3. Engel GL: The clinical application of the biopsychosocial model. *Am J Psychiatry* 137:535, 1980.
4. Katz S: Assessing self-maintenance activities of daily living, mobility and instrumental activities of daily living. *J Am Geriatr Soc* 31:721, 1983.
5. Lawton MP, Moss M, Fulcomer M, Lenban MH: Research and service oriented multilevel assessment instrument. *J Gerontol* 37(1):91, 1982.
6. Rubenstein L: The clinical effectiveness of multidimensional geriatric assessment. *J Am Geriatr Soc* 31:758, 1983.
7. Fretwell MD, Katz S: Functional assessment: Its use in the teaching nursing home, in Schneider EL, Wendland CJ, Zimmer AW, List N, Ory M, (eds): *A New Approach to Geriatric Research, Education and Clinical Care.* New York, Raven Press, 1985, p 129.
8. Folstein MF, Folstein SE. McHugh SR: "Mini-mental state," 1. Practical method for grading the cognitive state of patients for the clinician. *J Psych Res* 12:189, 1975.

GENERAL READING

Kane RA, Kane RL: *Assessment of the Elderly: A Practical Guide to Measurement.* Lexington, MA, Lexington Books, 1981.

Chapter 24

NEUROPSYCHIATRIC ASSESSMENT

Lissy F. Jarvik and John P. Blass

This chapter focuses on the assessment of the elderly patient with neuropsychiatric disabilities. The reader is referred to other chapters for extensive discussions of age changes and specific disorders, including differential diagnosis and the important ethical issues in geriatrics.

PURPOSE OF NEUROPSYCHIATRIC ASSESSMENT

The neuropsychiatric assessment of the geriatric patient serves two major purposes. *First*, it is designed to identify and describe abnormalities in behavior, including impairment of higher mental functions (such as cognition and judgment) as well as motivation, emotion, personality, impulse control, and vegetative functions (such as sleep and appetite). The behavioral abnormalities provide clues to underlying pathology. *Second*, the neuropsychiatric assessment furnishes baseline data for comparison with future behavior. For example, a low score on a verbal learning test calls for interpretation in light of prior performance; such a score may indicate progressive damage if significantly lower than the baseline score, or it may suggest improvement if significantly higher.

The physician who sees geriatric patients must be familiar with the neuropsychiatric assessment and its ramifications to decide whether a patient's deviant behavior at a particular point in time falls within or outside the range of normal variation for that particular patient. Behavioral deviations typically involve a mixture of organic factors, situational influences, personality attributes, and learned maladaptive behaviors. In the geriatric patient, a change in behavior may be the earliest or

This work was supported in part by the Veterans Administration. The opinions expressed are those of the authors and not necessarily those of the Veterans Administration.

only clue to physical illness (e.g., myocardial infarction), adverse drug reaction, drug–drug interaction, or affective disorder.

GENERAL PRINCIPLES GUIDING NEUROPSYCHIATRIC ASSESSMENT IN THE ELDERLY

CENTRAL NERVOUS SYSTEM: AGE CHANGES

Advancing age is frequently associated with an increased sensitivity of the brain to physical insults and their functional expression. Mental symptoms commonly accompany physical illness (sometimes unsuspected) in the elderly, such as thyroid and other endocrine abnormalities, uremia, diabetes, gout, pulmonary disorders, hepatic failure, and nutritional deficiencies. Cardiac insufficiency or emphysema can lead to cerebral anoxia and anoxic confusion, as can myocardial infarction, occlusion or stenosis of the carotid arteries, gastrointestinal bleeding, or surgery. Changes in the brain can accompany atherosclerosis, hypertension, or other vascular disease.[1] According to one report, in as many as 40 percent of elderly patients with myocardial infarction, a cardinal sign is the rapid onset of confusion.[2]

A decline in the number of neurons in certain areas of the brain (but not others[3]) has been observed with increasing age in both healthy individuals[4-6] and those with Parkinsonism[4] or Alzheimer-type dementia.[7-9] These observations gave rise to the conventional theory that as neurons are lost with age, the brain loses redundancy and, therefore, its ability to adapt to its environment. In part because of neuron loss in both the brain and the spinal cord, physical signs are accepted as within normal limits in elderly patients which would be considered abnormal in younger patients, including some postural and gait changes; irregular pupillary outline; loss of tone in the facial, neck, and spinal musculature; loss of ankle jerks; loss of appreciation of tuning fork vibrations at the ankle; some loss of position sense in the toes; and a general decrease in both muscle fiber diameter and muscle bulk, especially in the small muscles of the hands.[10,11] Physiological age changes include decreased frequency of the alpha rhythm on EEG, delayed somatosensory and visually evoked potentials, changes in sleep patterns, reductions in both REM and stage IV sleep, decreased energy, and slower reaction time (see Chap. 88).

MENTAL DISORDERS: AGE DIFFERENCES

Whether age-associated physiologic and psychological changes are inevitable consequences of increasing years or reflect instead prevalent lifestyles, chronic diseases, nutritional patterns, and other exogenous or endogenous factors rather than age per se remains to be determined.

Data on the development of psychiatric conditions during the latter half of the life span pertain largely to age differences rather than age changes, and there are three general but important observations.[12] *First*, the distribution of different mental disorders varies throughout adult and late life; Alzheimer's disease and paraphrenia, for example, are most commonly seen in the elderly, while schizophrenia and mania rarely begin in old age.[13] *Second*, the performance of older people on psychodiagnostic instruments (including measures of personality, mood, and cognition) differs from that of younger adults (see Chaps. 9 and 89). This variation in performance has given rise to suspicion of diagnostic inaccuracy and numerous attempts to "recalibrate" existing instruments for assessment of older people. The importance of age norms is most apparent when diagnosing disorders of mild severity, and their lack may be partly responsible for the fact that distinctions between early forms of dementia and mental changes occurring naturally in old age (sometimes termed benign senescent forgetfulness or age-associated memory impairment) remain elusive. *Third*, there are age differences in risk factors associated with mental illness. Sensory deficits, physical illness, poverty, bereavement, and social or geographic isolation are more common and often occur concomitantly in the elderly. These differences between older and younger patients must be taken into account in the neuropsychiatric assessment.

SYMPTOM PRESENTATION

Older patients tend to emphasize different symptoms than do younger patients; for example, depressed elderly patients are less apt to identify feelings of guilt[14]

and more apt to report cognitive complaints.[15] One of the "aging issues" vis-à-vis diagnosis of depression centers on the concern that older persons without mental disorder who exhibit somatic symptoms or cognitive complaints—because of physical illness or normal aging changes—are misdiagnosed as depressed and receive inappropriate treatment (e.g., antidepressant drugs) with ensuing complications. Alternatively, "true" depression may remain unnoticed and undiagnosed when clinicians assume that fatigue, sleep problems, or memory complaints are natural consequences of aging. Reference has repeatedly been made in the literature to "masked depression,"[16] where dysphoric affect is minimal or denied entirely and somatic complaints predominate; masked depression may be more common among the aged than in other populations.[17]

PHARMACOKINETICS AND POLYPHARMACY

Pharmacokinetics are altered in older patients, and there is an increase in the incidence of drug–drug and drug–disease interactions.[18] These risks apply not only to psychoactive drugs but to drugs in general; they are augmented by a high frequency of drug use[18] and an increased susceptibility of higher mental functions to medication effects independent of patterns of drug use or pharmacokinetics. These factors, singly and in combination, contribute to the high frequency in the elderly of neuropsychiatric illness due to prescription or over-the-counter medications. Although the actual rate is unknown, it is high enough to warrant the inclusion of drugs as a primary cause of secondary dementias.

As Paracelsus, the Swiss physician (Theophrastus Bombastus von Hohenheim, 1493–1541) said some 400 years ago (1538): "What is it that is not poison? Everything is poison, and nothing is without poison. It is only the dose that makes some things not poisonous."[19] Cognitive or behavioral impairment can potentially be caused by any drug but is most frequently seen with some specific classes of medications.[20] The long-acting diazepines, for example, tend to accumulate in older patients, with increasing blood levels over several weeks, exacerbating the potential for dementia, delirium, sedation, ataxia, and falling episodes. Use of any analgesic in an elderly patient with coexisting physical disease or marginal mental reserve may produce idiosyncratic cognitive impairment. Digitalis, even when used at a stable maintenance dose, may cause cognitive change when there is an age-related reduction in renal clearance. Indeed, dementia can be produced by a number of drugs commonly used to treat the elderly, including antihypertensive and antiarrhythmic agents and cimetidine. When drugs with a high rate of anticholinergic activity (such as some antidepressants, antiparkinsonian agents, antihistamines, and nonprescription sedative/hypnotics) are used to treat the elderly, dementia or delirium may be produced without the typical signs of anticholinergic psychosis, i.e., tachycardia, pupillary dilation, and facial flushing. The tricyclic antidepressants should be avoided for patients with narrow-angle glaucoma. Some of the antidepressants can produce serious cardiovascular side effects, especially in patients with preexisting cardiac illness. Special caution should be exercised when using a neuroleptic to treat the elderly patient, since this age group is at increased risk for developing tardive dyskinesia.[21] A high index of suspicion should be maintained when there is a possibility of an iatrogenic, medication-related illness—a much greater problem for most old people than, for example, alcoholism.[12] In any geriatric patient, the presence of syncope, confusion, postural hypotension, hypovolemia, hypokalemia, fatigue, falls, depression, or a new onset of incontinence should signal the possibility of a drug-related cause, and special care should be taken when changing medications to watch for neuroleptic malignant syndrome or toxic confusional state, which can be caused by a single drug or drug combinations.

The ability of rauwolfia derivatives to induce depression is well recognized, but frank depression can also be a side effect of ganglionic blockers and beta blockers. Antidepressant medications can precipitate confusion (e.g., due to the anticholinergic effects of tricyclic antidepressants). Over-the-counter antihistaminic preparations make many younger people sleepy and can induce frank confusion in older individuals; some have well-documented anticholinergic side effects. In general, any medication should be suspect of having direct or indirect side effects on the nervous system.

When a specific drug is suspected of contributing to neuropsychiatric symptoms in an older patient, elimination of the drug from the patient's regimen and close observation for up to several weeks (depending upon the half-life of the drug) is recommended. When discontinuing the drug is contraindicated, however, there are other approaches, including the use of short-acting narcotic antagonists to assess the contribution of narcotic analgesics to cognitive impairment, or physostigmine (a short-acting cholinergic agonist) to evaluate the effect of anticholinergic medications. Other fundamental methods for assessing the role of drugs in the production of neuropsychiatric symptoms include determining blood levels of digitalis, antiarrhythmics, or other such medications, and substitution, when possible, of an equally effective drug with a different mechanism of action.

Assessing the efficacy of psychoactive drugs in the elderly also poses special problems, and some guidelines, as well as a few instruments developed especially for this age group, are available.[22]

COEXISTING PHYSICAL ILLNESS

It is rare to find an older patient without a chronic health problem or a major sensory deficit. The usual figure cited for chronic illness in older persons is about 80 percent.[23] According to a study carried out in an ambulatory health screening program,[24] all but 2 percent of 3067 people over 65 had at least one of 34 common diseases such as heart failure, cataracts, parkinsonism, hypertension, and thyroid dysfunction.

The presence of sensory disorders particularly complicates the neuropsychiatric assessment. For example, are instructions misunderstood and questions answered inappropriately because of hearing impairment or cognitive deficit? Are errors in reproducing designs due to defective vision or defective information processing? To what extent do sensory deficits compound cognitive impairment, mood disorder, paranoid thought disturbances, and other forms of psychopathology?

Similarly, arthritis, cardiovascular disease, diabetes, thyroid disorders, and numerous other comorbid conditions may aggravate psychiatric symptoms. For example, the protean manifestations of depression are difficult to disentangle from symptoms due to other disorders. Poor physical health has been reported to be one of the two most important prognostic indicators for elderly patients with primary depression; the other was severity of initial depressive illness.[25] Late-life depression may be associated with increased mortality.

Physicians' behaviors during medical consultations can contribute to the suppression by the patient of verbal and other cues pointing to psychiatric illness.[26] Changes in the interview technique (such as increasing eye contact, clarifying the patient's complaint, and asking more open-ended questions about physical symptoms) may help clinicians to detect more accurately the presence of physical symptoms as well as psychopathology.

BASIC ELEMENTS OF THE NEUROPSYCHIATRIC ASSESSMENT

HISTORY

The dictum that the most important part of a diagnostic assessment is the history holds true also for the evaluation of behavioral abnormalities in the elderly. A thorough evaluation is time consuming, but nothing else can replace it.

A behavioral abnormality by its nature makes suspect the history obtained from the patient; the index of suspicion is increased when the abnormality is characterized by language deficits and memory loss. If such symptoms are mild, a great deal of information can usually be obtained from the patient; nevertheless, it is essential to use other informants whenever possible (such as family members and others who know the patient well) even though doing so requires taking the history more than once and comparing the different versions. In order to allow frank description of the patient's disabilities, interviews may be conducted in private (i.e., when the patient is not present). Some patients have no collateral informant; in such cases, when medical and other documentation is also lacking, the diagnosis can be exceedingly difficult. Objective information can sometimes be obtained from social workers, nurses, or other community health workers, and every effort should be made to examine previous medical records.

The history should address the nature of the disability, carefully cataloguing the symptoms and the precise details concerning its onset. A medical history should include specific diseases, traumata, surgery, psychiatric disorders, nutrition, alcohol and substance use, and exposure to environmental toxins. Special attention should be given to obtaining complete information on the use of medications, both prescribed and nonprescribed, including vitamins, laxatives, antacids, and nutritional supplements. Patients who are trying to diet or stop smoking may be using pills or a nicotine chewing gum that they neglect to mention because they do not think of these products as drugs.

The importance of an accurate and complete drug history cannot be overemphasized. Even the most benign pharmaceutical preparation can precipitate a behavioral problem if used in combination with other drugs, in the presence of various neurochemical abnormalities due to intercurrent disease, or in dosages too high for an elderly patient to metabolize. It is useful to supplement the history by asking that drugs be brought in for inspection.

All major areas of the life history (childhood, stress, family background, health, marriage, and work) should be covered. An adequate history also includes a thorough and exact family history, which is essential to detect genetic abnormalities, as well as to assess social, cultural, and ethnic variables. A good family history takes time, many probing questions, and much attention to detail. The older the patient, the longer the history, the poorer the memories, and the fewer the informants who are still alive. A history of bipolar disease in the family should raise suspicion of late-onset mania, a history of prior depressive episodes needs to be given weight when evaluating subjective complaints of memory loss, and a history of paranoid personality disorder may be an important clue in the differential diagnosis of suspicious, accusatory behavior.

Information about the patient's educational level should be included; it may be critical, for example, to interpreting neuropsychological test scores.

Diagnostic clues are often presented while taking the history. In the neuropsychiatric assessment it must be kept in mind that psychiatric symptoms need not always be stated directly; they may be signaled by the patient's behavior or described only by another informant. For example, early in the course of Alzheimer's disease, most patients are acutely aware of and deeply concerned about their memory problems; their concern need not signal the presence of another disorder, but it is consonant with another disorder (e.g., anxiety or depression).

The *onset of the disability* can also provide important diagnostic clues. A relatively acute onset suggests an event. This may be an internal event, such as a cerebrovascular accident or the onset of a specific illness, or an external event, such as taking a new medication, using alcohol or drugs of abuse, or making a change in life situation. A series of acute exacerbations with relative plateaus or even improvements between them suggests a series of events. Age is an important risk factor not only for Alzheimer's disease, Pick's disease, and other dementias, but also for strokes (see Chap. 91). An episodic history of behavioral abnormalities in an elderly patient raises the possibility of cardiovascular disease even in the absence of frank strokes. Multi-infarct dementia, seizure disorders, and other rarer syndromes must also be considered. Paranoid ideation and depressive symptoms may have precisely delineated onset. By contrast, the onset of an Alzheimer-type dementia is characteristically vague; if the onset of the dementing process can be dated precisely, another diagnosis should be considered.

The *progression of the illness* provides another important diagnostic clue. Alzheimer's disease, for example, generally progresses relentlessly, although there are patients who have shown no decline over the course of a year or two.[27] The family or other caregiver may report a period of improvement, but a careful history of the events connected with the change is likely to reveal, for example, the removal of intercurrent stressors. If there is true fluctuation in the course, it argues for a more episodic disorder. Agitated depression, mania, and organic delusional syndromes tend to have a more variable course and challenge the skills of the physician conducting the neuropsychiatric assessment.

NEUROPSYCHIATRIC SCREENING

The neuropsychiatric screening evaluation consists primarily of mental status and neurologic examinations; some brief self-rating scales may also be given if indicated. The purpose of the neuropsychiatric screen is to assist in making the diagnosis, or, in the absence of sufficient information for a diagnosis, to determine what specialized evaluations are needed (see "Specialized Evaluations").

The *Mental Status Examination* is particularly important in evaluating behavioral abnormalities, and it is carried out routinely by both neurologists and psychiatrists. It classically evaluates psychomotor activity, gait, speech, attitude, mood, feelings, affect, perception, thought processes, sensorium and cognition (including consciousness, orientation, concentration, memory, information, and intelligence), judgment, insight, and reliability of the patient's reporting abilities. The elderly patient with a neuropsychiatric disorder often presents with somatic complaints, which may be due to physical illness or psychophysiologic disorder, or both. Careful attention should be paid to mood and affect and to the patient's description of the problem. Several short, standardized bedside screening tests of mental status have been developed (see Chaps. 89 and 112). These formal instruments are quantitative, structured tools and are primarily useful for following patients over time. They also depend on the use of language, which is not always available. Nonverbal skills are required for mental status testing in the aphasic patient, and an important observation concerns the patient's ability to participate in nonverbal activities, including self-care. Confusing aphasia (e.g., due to a dominant-sided stroke) with dementia can be a major diagnostic error.

It is important to note that mental status questionnaires, rating scales, and other instruments are not substitutes for neuropsychiatric assessment. Such instruments quantify impressions, but they are not tools to supply diagnoses. No single test or battery of tests replaces the time-consuming, intellectually challenging process of neuropsychodiagnostic assessment now carried out by the physician.

PHYSICAL EXAMINATION

Geriatric patients being evaluated for neuropsychiatric complaints deserve a careful, thorough medical examination, preferably performed by a geriatrician. As mentioned earlier, almost any physical illness and nearly every pharmaceutical substance, as well as a nutritional or other disturbance, can produce psychiatric symptoms in the elderly patient.

LABORATORY TESTS

The extent of clinical laboratory evaluation depends upon how well the patient is known to the practitioner doing the evaluation.[28] For a patient who has been closely followed by a physician, many laboratory investigations may be unnecessary. For a patient with confusion or other neuropsychiatric problems in whom a reliable history is not obtainable (e.g., a confused patient delivered to the emergency room without a reliable informant), a much more extensive evaluation is needed. The selection of laboratory tests should be based on the findings of the physical and mental status examinations and the history. Overtesting may expose the patient to discomfort, inconvenience, excess costs, and the likelihood of false-positive tests that may lead to unnecessary further testing. Undertesting also presents hazards; for example, elderly patients may have unsuspected illness or other conditions with nonspecific presentations hard to distinguish from primary degenerative dementia.

With modifications to be made according to individual circumstances, we recommend complete blood count, electrolyte panel, screening metabolic panel, urinalysis, and electrocardiogram (ECG). Most readily reversible metabolic, endocrine, deficiency, and infectious states, whether causative or complicating, will be revealed by these basic laboratory tests when results are combined with history and physical examination.

Computed tomography (CT) of the brain is indicated when neither the geriatrician's examination nor neurologic and psychiatric consultations have revealed the diagnosis, when a lesion needs to be documented objectively, and sometimes because of medicolegal considerations. Magnetic resonance imaging (MRI) is more sensitive for detection of small infarcts, mass lesions, atrophy of the brainstem, and other subcortical structures, but it is also more expensive. There is controversy about the clinical relevance of a number of findings, especially periventricular lucencies and "unidentified bright objects." Those lesions are common in the cognitively intact elderly, although not as common as in those with dementia. MRI does not depend upon radiation and is said to be safe, but long-term data have yet to be gathered.

Neuroimaging procedures such as CT or MRI scans tend to confirm the results of careful neuropsychiatric assessment. They can show tumors, infarcts, subdural hematomas, and other specific lesions. In Alzheimer's patients, CT scans typically show cortical atrophy with enlargement of the ventricles and sulci. Similar findings in cognitively intact elderly controls, however, makes atrophy on a single study a weak finding, although progressive atrophy on serial studies does correlate with the clinical diagnosis of Alzheimer's disease.[29]

Other laboratory studies that may be appropriate depending upon the history and preliminary diagnosis are chest x ray; tests for syphilis, human immunodeficiency antibodies, or other sexually transmitted diseases; neuroendocrine tests (thyroid function, dexamethasone suppression, catecholamines, renal function, hepatic function); vitamin B and folate levels (for dementia patients); plasma levels of psychotropic drugs (benzodiazepines, antipsychotics, cyclic antidepressants, lithium, carbamazepine); polysomnography (battery including

EEG, ECG, and EMG); carotid ultrasound (in the search for the cause of infarcts); radioisotope cisternography; and lumbar puncture (when other clinical findings suggest an active infection or vasculitis).

SPECIALIZED EVALUATIONS

If the screening assessment described above fails to suggest definitive diagnoses or points to diagnoses requiring further information, specialized evaluations are indicated.

PSYCHIATRIC

Many psychiatric problems are handled routinely by geriatricians who may refer patients to a psychiatrist only when management becomes difficult, when the patient does not respond to treatment (e.g., refractory depression), or when the diagnosis is uncertain (e.g., memory loss or language problems). The following describes some conditions which commonly call for psychiatric referral. The geriatric patient with new onset of a paranoid disorder (as opposed to the schizophrenic patient who has grown old with the disease) should be referred, preferably to a geriatric psychiatrist, for the differential diagnosis between organic and functional mental disorder (and within each category) and for a suggested treatment plan. Such referral is also indicated for the agitated, hyperactive, aggressive, assaultive, anxious, withdrawn, or retarded patient when the diagnosis provides no adequate explanation for the behavior. These behaviors are not part of the normal aging process, nor are poor judgment, hypochondriasis, or sleep disturbances. As mentioned earlier, it is often difficult to determine whether a complaint that would be considered symptomatic in a younger adult (such as insomnia or constipation) is due in the elderly patient to psychopathology (e.g., depression) or to normal aging.

The classic psychiatric examination after preliminary identification (e.g., demographics, living arrangements) consists of recording the chief complaint, history of present illness (including relevant personal history) and prior illness (mental, emotional, and physical), developmental history (from prenatal through adult), family history, and current life situation. If the information is provided, supplemented, or contradicted by someone other than the patient, an adequate description of the additional informants must be included. There is considerable overlap with the history taken by the geriatrician.

The Mental Status Examination covers the patient's appearance, attitude toward the physician, behavior, psychomotor activity, mood, affect (and its appropriateness), perception, stream of thought, thought content, sensorium, cognition, judgment, and insight. Finally, it includes the psychiatrist's impression of the patient's reliability and that of other informants. Details concerning the psychiatric examination are given in standard psychiatric texts.

Some neuropsychiatric diagnostic dilemmas particularly common in the elderly were discussed above, but another deserves special mention, namely, the "pseudodementia" syndrome which can accompany depression.[30] The disorder is more aptly termed the "dementia syndrome of depression," since the dementia-like symptoms it produces are real, not "fake." Major depressive illness, especially in the elderly, can produce a picture of intellectual, memory, and behavior impairment that may be indistinguishable from a dementia due to degenerative brain disease except that it reverts to normal with successful treatment of the depression. (Note that all depressions do not respond to treatment even when there is no doubt of the diagnosis.[31])

In order to have a baseline for recording quantitative changes, psychiatrists employ a number of standardized rating scales.[32,33]

NEUROLOGIC

The divisions between the neurologic, the psychiatric, and the geriatric examination are necessarily blurred. The classic neurologic examination emphasizes signs of motor abnormalities, such as weakness, incoordination, and gait and reflex abnormalities. Sensory signs can be less reliable to the extent that eliciting them requires active patient cooperation; nevertheless, these parts of the examination need to be performed in the evaluation of a patient with a behavioral abnormality, since such abnormalities can give the clue to a specific underlying organic process. For instance, even metastatic cancer to the brain can present clinically as depression.[34] Examination of cranial nerve functions, also part of the classical neurologic examination, can provide information on disabilities which relate in particular ways to behavioral abnormalities; thus, deafness is common in patients with paranoid disorders.[35] The neurologic examination, including techniques for the examination of uncooperative, obtunded, or comatose patients, is described in standard texts.

NEUROPSYCHOLOGICAL

The neuropsychological examination of the elderly patient requires the services of a neuropsychologist specializing in work with older adults. As mentioned previously, the performance of individuals in this age group differs from that of younger adults (see Chap. 89). The neuropsychological evaluation is particularly useful in helping to distinguish dementia from delirium, depression, and other forms of psychopathology; in judging the efficacy of interventions by comparing performance before and after treatment; and in obtaining an inventory of functions preserved in the patient upon which a treatment plan can be built. Following focal or multifocal brain injury, the neuropsychological evaluation can provide additional information about the extent and nature of impairment. When interpreting scores on measures of cognitive function, it is important to have information about the patient's educational and premorbid intellectual level.

To avoid fatiguing the elderly patient, it is best to administer the neuropsychological test battery over several days, not exceeding 1 hour per day, and keeping the time of day constant (whenever possible) to minimize the effects of diurnal variation.

FUNCTIONAL STATUS AND SOCIAL SUPPORT NETWORK

Assessment of functional status or social support network is addressed in other chapters (see also Refs. 11 and 25); they are mentioned here to stress the necessity for their inclusion in the neuropsychiatric assessment. A new suggestion for constructing a support tree can aid understanding of the relationships as well as the resources available to the patient.[36]

ADDITIONAL EVALUATIONS

Isolated laboratory findings which are inconsistent with other clinical information should not be overinterpreted.

Electrophysiology

This examination is usually ordered by a neurologist or psychiatrist. Electroencephalography (EEG) is appropriate for patients with dementia of uncertain etiology or unusual presentation, as well as those who have altered or fluctuating consciousness or suspected seizures. Topographic mapping of the resting state EEG may be useful in identifying focal functional lesions in dementia patients. At this time, the usefulness of other electrophysiologic techniques, such as event-related potentials, is still being defined.

Imaging

CT and MRI scans have been discussed above. Techniques to measure cerebral blood flow and metabolism (PET, SPECT, rCBF) remain, at present, research techniques that have no established *routine* clinical value.

Speech and Language Assessment

The usual mental status examinations rely heavily on speech and language. In patients with language dis-

orders, speech and language analysis can be helpful. Complex language disorders can simulate dementia in some patients; for others, communication between the patient and family can be improved with help from a skillful speech pathologist.

FOLLOW-UP ASSESSMENT

Given the complex nature of the neuropsychiatric disorders prevalent among elderly patients, follow-up assessment assumes vital importance. It enables the physician to check diagnostic accuracy, to monitor treatment, to gain a picture of the course of illness, and to evaluate the changing needs of the patient and the family. For elderly patients with dementia, neuropathologic confirmation of the clinical diagnosis is important for the family members as well as society-at-large.

FAMILY MEMBERS AND CAREGIVERS

Caregivers suffer enormous hardships.[37] Behavioral disorders in the elderly, such as dementia and depression, are *family diseases* in the sense that they affect the family as a whole. It is incumbent upon the clinician caring for these patients to evaluate the health and well-being of members of the support system, particularly the primary caregiver, and offer help determined by the type and severity of the illness. There are numerous publications available, including *The 36-Hour Day*,[38] *Parentcare*,[39] *Understanding Alzheimer's Disease*,[40] and *Treatments for the Alzheimer Patient—The Long Haul*.[41] When appropriate, referrals should be made to specialists or community agencies. Dr. Carl Eisdorfer (see Chap. 106) has put forward the following rule: "When the prime caregiver collapses, the care system collapses."

CONCLUSION

The neuropsychiatric assessment is a pivotal point in the overall evaluation of the elderly patient who is at serious risk for neuropsychiatric disease. It is an essential part of patient assessment and reassessment.

REFERENCES

1. Meyers JS et al: Progressive cerebral ischemia antedates cerebrovascular symptoms by two years. *Ann Neurol* 16:314, 1984.
2. Pathy MS: Clinical presentation of myocardial infarction in the elderly. *Br Heart J* 29:190, 1967.
3. Brody H: An examination of cerebral cortex and brainstem aging, in Terry RD, Gershon S. (eds): *Aging*, vol 3: *Neurobiology of Aging*. New York, Raven Press, 1976.

4. McGeer PL et al: Aging and extrapyramidal function. *Arch Neurol* 34:33, 1977.

5. Mann DMA, Yates PO: The effects of aging on the pigmented nerve cells of the human locus coerulaeus and substantia nigra. *Acta Neuropathol (Berl)* 47:93, 1979.

6. Vijayashankar N, Brody H: A quantitative study of pigmented neurons in the nuclei locus coeruleus and subcoeruleus in man as related to aging. *J Neuropathol Exp Neurol* 38:490, 1979.

7. McGeer PL et al: Aging, Alzheimer's disease, and the cholinergic system of the basal forebrain. *Neurology* 34:741, 1984.

8. Bondareff W et al: Loss of neurons of origin of the adrenergic projection to cerebral cortex (nucleus locus ceruleus) in senile dementia. *Neurology* 32:164, 1981.

9. Corsellis JAN: Aging and dementias, in Blackwood W, Corsellis JAN (eds): *Greenfield's Neuropathology*. London, Arnold, 1976.

10. Carter AB: The neurologic aspects of aging, in Rossman I (ed): *Clinical Geriatrics*, 3d ed. Philadelphia, Lippincott, 1986.

11. Calne DB: Normal aging of the nervous system, in Andres R et al (eds): *Principles of Geriatric Medicine*. New York McGraw-Hill, 1985.

12. LaRue A et al: Aging and mental disorders, in Birren JE, Schaie KW (eds): *Handbook of the Psychology of Aging*, 2d ed. New York, Van Nostrand Reinhold, 1985.

13. Post F: Diagnosis of depression in geriatric patients and treatment modalities appropriate for the population, in Gallant DM, Simpson GM (eds): *Depression: Behavioral, Biochemical, Diagnostic, and Treatment Concepts*. New York, Spectrum, 1976.

14. Small GW et al: The influence of age on guilt expression in major depression. *Int J Geriatr Psychiatry* 1:121, 1986.

15. Raskin A, Rae DS: Psychiatric symptoms in the elderly. *Psychopharmacol Bull* 17:96, 1981.

16. Lopez-Ibor JJ: Masked depressions. *Br J Psychiatry* 120:245, 1972.

17. Lehmann HE: Affective disorders in the aged. *Psychiat Clin North Am* 5:27, 1982.

18. Blaschke TF et al: Drug–drug interactions and aging, in Jarvik LF et al (eds): *Clinical Pharmacology and the Aged Patient*. New York, Raven Press, 1981.

19. Paracelsus: *Epistola dedicatora St. Veit/Karnten: Sieben Defensionen oder Sieben Schutz-, Schirm- und Trutzreden*. Dritte defension, August 24, 1538.

20. Levenson AJ (ed): *Neuropsychiatric Side Effects of Drugs in the Elderly*. New York, Raven Press, 1979.

21. Smith JM, Bladessarini RJ: Changes in prevalence, severity, and recovery in tardive dyskinesia with age. *Arch Gen Psychiatry* 37:1368, 1980.

22. Crook T et al: *Assessment in Geriatric Psychopharmacology*. New Canaan CT, Mark Powley Associates, 1983.

23. Macdonald DI: Physical/mental disorder in old age [from the Alcohol, Drug Abuse, and Mental Health Administration]. *JAMA* 258:1440, 1987.

24. Hale WE et al: Symptom prevalence in the elderly: An evaluation of age, sex, disease, and medication use. *J Am Geriatr Soc* 34:333–340, 1986.

25. Murphy E: The prognosis of depression in old age. *Br J Psychiatry* 142:111, 1983.

26. Davenport S et al: How psychiatric disorders are missed during medical consultations. *Lancet* ii:439, 1987.

27. Katzman R et al: Clinical, pathological, and neurochemical changes in dementia: A subgroup with preserved mental status and numerous neocortical plaques. *Ann Neurol* 23:138, 1988.

28. Larson EB et al: Diagnostic tests in the evaluation of dementia: A prospective study of 200 elderly outpatients. *Arch Intern Med* 146:1917, 1986.

29. Luxenberg JS et al: Rate of ventricular enlargement in dementia of the Alzheimer type correlates with rate of neuropsychological deterioration. *Neurology* 37:1135, 1987.

30. Kiloh LG: Pseudo-dementia. *Acta Psychiat Scand* 37:336, 1961.

31. Gerson SC et al: Antidepressant drug studies, 1964–1986: Empirical evidence for aging patients. *J Clin Psychopharmacol* 8:311, 1988.

32. Wang WS: Neuropsychiatric procedures in the assessment of Alzheimer's disease, senile dementia, and related disorders, in Miller NE, Cohen GD (eds): *Clinical Aspects of Alzheimer's Disease and Senile Dementia*. New York, Raven Press, 1981.

33. Crook T et al (eds): *Assessment in Geriatric Psychopharmacology*. New Canaan CT, Mark Powley Associates, 1983.

34. Barclay LL et al: Cerebral metastases mimicking depression in a "forgetful" attorney. *J Am Geriatr Soc* 32:866, 1984.

35. Cooper AF et al: A comparison of deaf and non-deaf patients with paranoid and affective psychoses. *Br J Psychiatry* 129:532, 1976.

36. Winograd CH: The physician and the Alzheimer patient, in Jarvik LF, Winograd CH (eds): *Treatments for the Alzheimer Patient—The Long Haul*. New York, Springer, 1988.

37. Brody EM: The long haul—a family odyssey, in Jarvik LF, Winograd CH (eds): *Treatments for the Alzheimer Patient—The Long Haul*. New York, Springer, 1988.

38. Mace NL, Rabins PV: *The 36-Hour Day*. Baltimore, Johns Hopkins University Press, 1981.

39. Jarvik LF, Small GW: *Parentcare: A Commonsense Guide for Adult Children*. New York, Crown, 1988.

40. Aronson M (ed): *Understanding Alzheimer's Disease*. New York, Scribner, 1988.

41. Jarvik LF, Winograd CH (eds): *Treatments for the Alzheimer Patient—The Long Haul*. New York, Springer, 1988.

Chapter 25

SOCIAL FACTORS IN CARE: THE ELDERLY PATIENT'S FAMILY

Elaine M. Brody

Among the most consistent findings in gerontological research are those which identify the major effects of social factors on the mental and physical health of older people and, reciprocally, the major consequences of health to their social functioning. In a host of studies physical health is strongly related to all types of well-being, with an extremely regular correlation between health and morale, health and social behavior, and health and leisure time activity.[1] Repeated themes in the literature are the associations between health and life satisfaction[2]; the high correlation between mental and physical illness[3,4] and the strength of their interactions[5]; the role of emotional factors and stress in precipitating physical illness; and the psychological consequences of illness.

The health of older people, then, affects every aspect of their lives: self-esteem, status, capacity for work, income, recreational activities, range of social contacts, living arrangements, and overall lifestyle. It also has a direct impact on the family: the nature of its relationships and the number of contacts with the older family member; its living arrangements; its economic, social, and instrumental activities—even the health of family members.

On the societal level, the health needs of older people affect the economy, social policy, and the social and health care systems. In turn, health is conditioned by social and environmental factors such as standard of living, education, and advances in public health. Although illness may be an impediment to social functioning, the degree of incapacity depends not on the actual impairment alone but on individual and family resources, on the physical environment, and on the availability and utilization of social and medical supports.

These close interrelationships among health factors and social factors make evaluation of the family and social setting of the elderly patient a practical necessity as an essential component of good medical care. Moreover, ignoring salient social-psychological considerations risks both under- and overcare.[6]

The family is generally described as the "informal" support system of the disabled elderly as distinguished from the "formal" support system of government and agency services. Since the family is the major source of health services to the aged, physicians who care for elderly people need information about the roles family members play in providing those services and the effects they experience as a result of their caregiving efforts. This chapter, therefore, will summarize information about the family and other social factors that is relevant to the physician's evaluation of the elderly patient and to the formulation and monitoring of the treatment plan.

THE ROLE OF THE FAMILY

The contemporary physician sees larger numbers of elderly patients and more of their family members than ever before in history. The physician's relationships with the families of the elderly are different from those with the families of younger patients and they often are more complex and time-consuming.

The importance of family members to the health of older people derives in part from the disabilities—that is, the losses in functional capacities—which accompany many of the chronic conditions characteristic of older people and lead to dependence on others for help on a day-to-day basis.

To put the matter in perspective, it is emphasized that most of the elderly function independently despite the fact that most have at least one chronic ailment. Chronic ailments, of course, do not invariably lead to disability and dependency. Nevertheless, a significant proportion of the elderly suffer from disabilities that require the assistance of others to help them function in their daily lives. The 1982 Long-Term Care Survey sponsored by the U.S. Department of Health and Human Services found that approximately 4.6 million noninstitutionalized people 65 years of age, or 18 percent of the total elderly population, have limitations in activities of daily living (ADL) or instrumental activities of daily living (IADL).[7] An additional 5 percent of older people who are also functionally limited reside in nursing homes or other institutions. The ADL indicators used in the survey were bathing, dressing, eating, getting out of bed, getting around indoors, and toileting. The IADL indicators were managing money, moving about outdoors, shopping, doing heavy housework, meal preparation, making phone calls, and taking medications. The major source of help with those functional disabilities proved to be the informal support system; only 15 percent of all "helper days of care" to those needing help with ADL (an extreme form of caregiving) are provided by the formal or nonfamily system.[8] Families often provide this long-term care for many years.

Even when older people do not need day-to-day help, they have higher rates and longer periods of hospitalizations than younger populations (see Chap. 16). An episode of acute illness holds the threat of a decreased level of functional capacity after recovery. As a result, family members of the old are more involved and more visible in the doctor's office, in the home, and at the hospital bedside. They are prominent in every aspect of the patient's medical care: the provision of a medical history and presentation of symptoms, diagnostic and treatment procedures, and implementation of treatment recommendations.

In addition to their major roles in long-term and acute care, family members are the ones who provide the elderly with the emotional support they need—the sense that someone cares and that there is someone on whom to rely at times of need. This is the most universal form of help families provide and the one most wanted by older people.

Family members also are the first-line recipients of information about the health complaints of older people. The vast majority of the elderly consult a relative in a health crisis, and many report their day-to-day chronic symptoms to family members. Those relatives frequently perform a triage function, participating in or making decisions about referrals to health professionals.[9]

The health management problems the older patient presents to family caregivers are qualitatively different from those of other life stages. Apart from the multiplicity and chronicity of the ailments themselves and the dependencies they induce, the symptoms of those ailments can be extraordinarily disturbing. The need for heavy physical care; behavioral manifestations such as forgetfulness, confusion, emotional lability, and incontinence; and an inability to communicate are high on the list of distressing symptoms that may lead to disruptions in the lifestyle of family members and to anxiety about their own future and their own aging processes.

The anxious family may express its problems in behavior that is especially difficult for the physician—multiple repetitive phone calls (sometimes from several family members), over detailed questioning about the patient's condition and prognosis, inappropriate requests for specialty consultations, "shopping" among many doctors, or pleas for medical "cures" that are nonexistent. Though such behavior by some families represents their usual pattern, it may be exaggerated at this time; for most, it relates more directly to their current situations. The family members who are affected by the older person's condition and who affect her care must therefore be understood in the context of their own roles and their own life situations.

Throughout the family life cycle, interdependence of family members is a constant, but the nature and number of each individual's dependencies shift over time. The routine involvement of young parents in the medical care of infants and children is expected and accepted. During young adulthood and the middle years, the main pattern is for doctors and patient to relate directly to each other, with the family participating primarily at time of acute, time-limited illnesses.

During the later stages of life, the family may again assume a major caregiving role. By contrast with the dependencies of the child, however, the older patient's dependencies are chronic rather than temporary or transitional; they foreshadow increasing dependency rather than growing independence and appear with greater variability and irregularity and in different sequential patterns. Moreover, the physical care of an impaired older person requires strength, stamina, and nursing in a different and more difficult way than the care of a young child.

Aged patients also vary with respect to the number and kind of relatives who are involved or available. Younger patients are generally members of a nuclear family and caregiving patterns are relatively clear-cut: parents care for children and for each other. The principal caregiving relative(s) of the older person may be a spouse, an adult child, an elderly sibling, or even a niece, nephew, or grandchild.

CAREGIVING SPOUSES

When the older patient is married, the spouse is the principal provider of care. Elderly men are much more likely than elderly women to have a spouse on whom to rely at times of illness owing to the differences between the sexes in life expectancy and the tendency of men to marry women younger than they are. Most elderly widows are women (there are almost 10 million widowed older people): at age 65 and over, most older women (52 percent) are widowed and most older men (77 percent) are married. Rates of widowhood rise sharply with advancing age. For all people aged 65 and over, the imbalance in the proportions of women to men is 131:100. Between the ages of 75 and 84, the ratio rises to 166; at age 85 and over, there are 224 women to every 100 men.[10]

Whether they are husbands or wives, older people exert extreme efforts in caring for an ill spouse, but their capacities are constrained by their own ages, reduced energy and strength, and age-related ailments. They are the most vulnerable group of caregivers, often experiencing severe strains such as low morale, isolation, loneliness, economic hardship, and "role overload" due to multiple responsibilities.[11]

Elderly caregiving spouses therefore require attention to their own needs for respite, concrete helping services, and emotional support. The physical strain may be accompanied by tremendous anxiety and by fear of losing one's partner in a marriage that may have endured half a century or more.

ADULT CHILDREN AS CAREGIVERS

When an elderly couple has children, they assist the "well" spouse in caring for the patient; when the patient is widowed, the bulk of care is given by adult children,[12] primarily by daughters.[13]

Despite widespread myths to the contrary, research findings have systematically disproved the notion that contemporary adult children are alienated from the aged and do not take care of them as used to be the case in the "good old days." The accumulated evidence documents the strength of intergenerational ties and responsible filial behavior, the frequency of contacts between generations, the predominance of families rather than professionals in the provision of health and social services, the strenuous efforts of family members to avoid institutional placement of the old, and the central role they play in caring for the noninstitutionalized impaired elderly.[14]

Most older people realize their preference to live near, but not with their children. Counting shared households, about 84 percent of those with children live less than an hour away from one of them. Contrary to popular notions about the past, the prevalence of shared households was low in the late nineteenth century as it is now when about 17 percent of the elderly live with an adult child.[15] This happens primarily when the parent is in advanced old age and disability precludes continued independent living. Thus, 36 percent of extremely disabled old people (in need of ADL help) live with an adult child, most of them with a daughter.[16] The proportion of older people living in three-generation households is very small, being about 4 percent at any given time. Because information about two- and three-generation households is cross-sectional, however, it obscures the fact that a much larger proportion of the aged live in an adult child's household at some time during their lives.

The 5 percent of those 65 and over who are in institutions at any one time are outnumbered two to one by equally disabled noninstitutionalized old people who are cared for by their families,[17,18] a proportion that did not change between 1962 and 1975.[12] The role of families is highlighted by the fact that the vast majority (88 percent) of the institutionalized aged are not married (being widowed, divorced, or never married), an even higher percentage of them are childless, and those who have children have fewer children than the noninstitutionalized.[19]

TRENDS AFFECTING CAREGIVING BY ADULT CHILDREN

The well-documented responsible filial behavior has persisted despite two broad influential trends that affect the capacity of adult children to provide care.

DEMOGRAPHIC DEVELOPMENTS

The first trend to cite would be the radical demographic developments that have led to a vast increase in the demands for parent care. During the same time span in which the number and proportion of older people in the population increased dramatically, the birth rate fell sharply. People who are now old therefore have fewer children to share caregiving responsibilities than used to be the case. In addition, since parents and children age together, the adult children of the greatly increased number and proportion of people in advanced old age most often are in middle age, and some are in their sixties or seventies. At present, about 40 percent of people in their late fifties have a surviving parent (some have both parents) as do about 20 percent of those in their early 60s and 10 percent of those in their late 60s.[20]

Many adult children are grandparents; the four generation-family has become commonplace, with almost half of older people with children being at the pinnacle of a four-generation family tree.[21]

Demands for parent care, then, occur at a time of life when the adult children on whom the old depend themselves may be experiencing age-related interpersonal losses, the onset of chronic ailments, lower energy levels, and even retirement. As women advance from 40 years of age to their early 60s, those who have a surviving parent(s) are more and more likely to have that parent be dependent on them, to spend more and more time caring for the parent, to do more difficult caregiving tasks, and to have the parent in their own household.[22] Filial caregivers, however, can be at various ages and stages of life; about one-third are either under 40 or over 60.

WOMEN IN THE LABOR FORCE

The second broad trend—the rapid entry of middle-aged women into the work force—places an additional burden on family caregivers. In addition to confirming the responsible behavior of families, research has identified daughters (and to some extent daughters-in-law) as the particular family members who are the principal caregivers.[12] Daughters provide more than one-third of all long-term-care services for elderly parents, and more than half of all long-term-care services for parents who are the most severely disabled.[16]

The responsibilities of middle-generation women are much greater nowadays than used to be the case. Their traditional roles as wives, homemakers, parents, and grandparents have been augmented to an extent greater than ever before by the role of caregiver to an elderly person. Many women now have an additional role as paid worker in the labor force (some because of career commitment, but most because the money is needed). Sixty percent of women between the ages of 45 and 54 work, and even more surprising, 42 percent of women between the ages of 55 and 64 are in the work force.[23]

EFFECTS OF CAREGIVING ON THE FAMILY

The physical, emotional, and economic effects of caregiving on family members qualify the way in which they can care for the elderly parents. The doctor's expectation of them therefore requires a perspective that includes their own situations and problems. Essential aspects of the physician's evaluation of the patient are a good picture of each unique family constellation and an awareness of family members' symptoms of stress. Though different families react differently to the demands of parent care, genuine concern and affection for the older person are generally at work. At the same time, however, there is concern about themselves, other family members, and the duration and intensity of the caregiving efforts they will need to exert.

The most pervasive and severe effects of caregiving are in the realm of mental and emotional health. Research has found consistently that at least half of family caregivers experience moderate to severe stress in the form of anxiety, depression, lowered morale, sleeplessness, frustration, and emotional exhaustion.[24,25] The lifestyle of the caregiver and her family are affected by loss of privacy, opportunities for socialization, and changes in future plans. Smaller, but significant proportions of caregivers experience negative effects on their physical health (20 to 25 percent) or economic strain (20 percent).

Among the factors that have been identified as predictors of the strains which caregivers experience are an older person's severe disability requiring "heavy" care and the sharing of the caregiver's household that becomes necessary. Also implicated as stressors are characteristics of the older person such as incontinence or the disordered behavior typical of Alzheimer's victims.

Information has been emerging recently about the effects of caregiving on people's work lives. A significant minority of caregivers (13.5 percent of wives, 11.4 percent of husbands, 11.6 percent of daughters, and 5 percent of sons) were found to have left the labor force to provide care for the elderly.[26,16] About one-quarter of working caregivers rearrange their work schedules, reduce the number of their working hours, or experience problems on the job.

Depending on their own personalities as well as on actual demands, family members may feel guilty about not doing enough for the older person. Some are angry (though they may not be aware of their anger or able to express it) at finding themselves in the predicament of needing to do more than they feel able. Unresolved relationship problems (and most families have at least some vestiges of such problems) may be reactivated so that the older person becomes the focus of exacerbated latent and overt problems—between elderly spouses, among the adult children and their spouses, and across several generations.[24,27,28] In some families, bitter conflicts erupt about such issues as how to divide caregiving responsibilities among family members, with whom the older person should live, or who should help with money.

Adult daughters are often under considerable stress from their multiple competing responsibilities, a situation that had led to their characterization as "women-in-the-middle."[19] Those pressures, compounded by emotional conflicts related to the need to set priorities, may place them at high risk of mental and physical breakdown. Many who seek health care for themselves may be doing so in the context of such "role strains." Since what affects them inevitably affects their husbands, children, and other family members, the ripple effect operates to involve the total family. While adult sons are not remiss in affection for their parents or in a sense of responsibility, our culture has designated parent care as well as child care to women as gender-appropriate. When sons become principal caregivers (usually when a daughter is not available), they do less, receive more help from their spouses (the daughters-in-law), and experience less stress.[13]

THE DOCTOR'S RELATIONSHIP WITH THE FAMILY

The information presented above suggests that the physician should view family members of the elderly from two perspectives. First, families are the doctor's reliable partners in providing sustained health and mental health care to aged patients over long periods of time. Second, family caregivers are actual or potential patients themselves since they are at risk for mental or physical problems if their caring roles become unduly stressful. Health professionals should therefore be alert to the signs and symptoms of such stress effects in their aged patients' caregivers.

Balancing his relationships with the patient and with family members who are his partners in the patient's health care makes special demands on the doctor. While family members need to feel that their feelings and practical efforts are appreciated, it is important to preserve the patient's right to be independent to the fullest possible extent. An implication that control has been transferred to others can be detrimental, intensifying feelings of helplessness, hopelessness, and negative self-image, all of which are stimulated by the realities of eroding functions. Doctor and family should be collaborators in fostering the patient's autonomy, inviting participation in treatment planning and decision making, and encouraging the follow-up of rehabilitative regimens that can improve functioning and independence. When family members tend to "take over" too much, the doctor's attitude toward the patient can communicate the respect due to the patient.

It has been pointed out that doctor, patient, and adult child constitute a *triad* (a small group consisting of three people), and that triads always have potential for becoming coalitions of two against one.[29] Patient and child may unite against the doctor, for example, in expecting—even demanding—that he perform magic to cure the patient. The patient may feel left out if the doctor and adult child talk together about the patient—as though the patient were not there. A child wanting to control the situation may subtly enlist the doctor in supporting his or her own position. Or, the doctor and patient may be allies in defending the patient against an adult child's power and control. These tendencies can be minimized by the physician, who is in the best position to maintain objectivity.

Another aspect of the doctor's evaluation concerns the extent to which family members understand the nature of the elderly person's illnesses. Apart from their need for accurate information in order to carry out the treatment prescription, misinformation can increase a family's distress; communication of factual information can enhance care and stem a flow of anxious phone calls. Families also need a straightforward explanation of the possible course of the older person's illness and a realistic discussion of what they can do.

THE ELDERLY WITHOUT CLOSE FAMILY

A significant minority of older people do not have a close family member on whom to rely. The proportion who are deprived in that respect rises with advancing age. At age 75 and over, for example, 68 percent of women and 24 percent of men are widowed and an additional 9 percent of women and 7 percent of men are divorced or have never married. About 20 percent of people who are now 65 and over have never had a child, and an undetermined number are childless because they have outlived their children. For some who have children, geographic distance precludes the availability of a child for supportive health care; for a minority, little or no help can be expected owing to long-standing alienation.

While spouse and children are the first to be relied on, other family members (primarily siblings), neighbors, and friends also play an important role in helping older people. The health-related help they give, however, does not approach in level or duration the help given by family.[30] The assistance friends and neighbors provide to those without close kin is particularly important to them. Nevertheless, the elderly individual without family or whose family is not close at hand and whose illness or disability is severe or likely to be prolonged is at high risk.

THE DOCTOR'S ROLE IN PLANNING

The role of the physician is often expanded beyond that of providing medical care to the point where the physician becomes the focal point of decision making and planning. The doctor is looked to as the objective and understanding professional person who is not caught in the emotional upset of patient and family and who can offer help and guidance. This is an exceptionally demanding situation for the doctor. There are no simple rules for guidance, since each elderly individual and family presents a unique set of personal and social circumstances as well as varying illnesses, ages, personalities, and backgrounds.

THE GOAL

Having an overall goal constitutes a helpful framework within which options can be explored. A noted British geriatrician states the goal as "to enable old people suffering from physical and mental disability to live where they would wish to live if they were not disabled."[31] Most of the elderly, of course, prefer to remain living in their own homes as long as possible. Achievement of that goal depends on factors in both the informal (family) and formal (government and agencies) support systems. Family supports to be evaluated include the nature of the living arrangements of patient and family; the number, ages, health status, proximity, and availability of family members; the historical quality of family relationships; the emotional support given to the caregivers by other members of the family; the changing nature of the older person's condition; and the effects on family members of the effort involved.

There are many formal services, programs, and entitlements that can supplement the family's services, though many are in short supply and the availability of these services varies from community to community. A federally financed system of long-term care is badly needed[32,33] and should include family-focused services such as respite care, in-home services, and day care. Existing and needed services and entitlements that would comprise a long-term-care system are dealt with in Chap. 36.

When continuation of the past living arrangement is not possible, decision making may focus on whether the patient should move to, for example, specialized housing, a senior citizens' apartment building, a retirement community, or a nursing home or other type of institution.

REFERRALS FOR FORMAL SERVICES

Physicians cannot be expected to give in-depth counseling for emotional or relationship problems, to explore the family's specific service needs in great detail, to provide comprehensive information about the availability of each service and the criteria for eligibility, to make referrals to the various service sources, or to monitor the services over time. They are in an excellent position, however, to act as gatekeepers to introduce the patient and family to the complex and confusing array of programs that constitute the "formal" support system. To do so, physicians can refer their patients to the agencies in the community which provide counseling and whose job it is to be informed about the complete range of available services and facilities, to connect older people and their families with those services, and to help mobilize these services. Examples of such organizations are Area Agencies on Aging, family counseling agencies, information and referral services, and (when the patient is hospitalized) hospital social service departments.

WHEN THE PATIENT IS HOSPITALIZED

Hospitalization of the elderly patient may be the point at which a change in living arrangement is signaled. For example, 32 percent of admissions to nursing homes are from hospitals, 13 percent are from another nursing home, 14 percent from other types of facilities, and 41 percent from the older person's own home.[34] When such a profound change in the life of patient and family is a possibility, an interdisciplinary evaluation is a critical necessity, though it rarely occurs.

An orderly decision-making process and social evaluation takes time. Time constraints are severe if discharge planning is initiated at the eleventh hour when hospital care is no longer needed or when there is pressure from a hospital utilization review committee. It is far better to enlist the help of the hospital's department of social services when the patient is first admitted in order to allow time for evaluation of the family's caregiving capacities and of the home environment, to permit selection of an appropriate nursing home if placement is indicated, and to prepare the patient and family for that change.

INSTITUTIONALIZATION

When the possibility of institutionalization of the patient arises, the decision-making process is one of the most delicate situations in which the doctor is involved. In many cases, such involvement is mandatory, since the doctor must certify the medical need for nursing home care if the patient is to be a recipient of Medicaid. More than a million older people are in institutions at any one time (and this number will increase in the future as the number of very old, disabled people increases). One of every four people 65 or over will spend time in a nursing home during their lives.

Older people and their families suffer intensely when institutionalization is being considered or becomes necessary. The older person experiences anxiety, fear, and feelings of rejection and abandonment; family members have painful emotions such as guilt, conflict, sadness, and even shame. Anxieties about separations—including death—are stimulated. Well-meaning, but anxious, families may deny the patient the opportunity to participate in this decision to the fullest extent possible. At the very least, the patient should be fully informed about the options and carefully prepared for any change contemplated.

Unquestionably, much improvement is needed in many institutional facilities to make them decent living situations for the very old, very impaired, socially deprived residents.[19] Many aspects of those environments that are known to have deleterious effects are amenable to modification. Among the detrimental factors identified by research, for example, are lack of preparation for admission or involuntary admissions; negative staff attitudes (belittling or infantilizing); the discouraging of autonomy and independent decision making; and lack of privacy, warmth, and opportunities for social interaction.

More and more physicians treat patients in nursing homes; their participation in the care of the older people who live in those facilities can exert an immeasurable influence on the overall quality of care. The physician is therefore in a pivotal position to improve and maintain the physical and mental health of the elderly residents.

Families of the Institutionalized Elderly

Since the behavior of families of the institutionalized elderly is widely misunderstood, a special word is in order. Not only have the vast majority of families exerted every effort to avoid such placement, but research has shown that, once placement is made, they continue to visit and to sustain their interest and concern. There is also firm evidence that continued relationships with family members are central to the well-being of institutionalized older people.[35] Moreover, families of nursing home residents suffer negative emotional effects from having an institutionalized elderly relative.[36,37] Personnel of institutional facilities, however, often regard family members as complaining or as "interfering" in the patient's care if they ask questions or visit often. The physician's behavior can serve as a model for other staff. Recognition of the legitimacy of the family's interest and willingness to talk with them when the patient lives in a nursing home, just as before when the patient was at home, demonstrates appropriate attitudes and alleviates the family's frustration and anger.

THE LARGER SOCIAL ENVIRONMENT

While the broad social and physical environment is influential to health at any age, older people are more vulnerable to environmental pressures than other age groups.[38] Moreover, the aging phase of life brings into sharp focus the interlocking of health (physical and mental) with aspects of the broader social environment, such as income, the physical environment, the availability of health and social services, facilities and programs, and opportunities for social participation. Thus, for example, illness could be reduced or alleviated by income sufficient to purchase an adequate diet and medications. Similarly, dangerous neighborhoods foster isolation and anxiety, and meaningful social roles could reduce depression. The classic example of such interrelationships poses the question: Does the poor, depressed elderly person with severe cardiovascular disease and arthritis who lives in a third floor walk-up apartment have a health problem, a mental health problem, an economic problem, or a housing problem?

The availability, accessibility, and appropriateness of the physical and mental health systems are important aspects of the older person's social environment. These topics will not be elaborated here since they are discussed in Chap. 36 of this volume.

Briefly, however, it is emphasized that the basic conditions of older people's lives require evaluation by the physician as part of the context of medical care. Though the income level of older people has improved due to social security (SS), supplemental security income (SSI), pensions, and higher life-time earnings, a significant minority still live in poverty. Older women and members of minority groups are overrepresented among the elderly poor. It is obvious that economic circumstances have a direct effect on the older person's ability to purchase health services, medications, housing, nutritious food, and other needs.

The physical environment in which older people live directly affects their health and functioning.[39] Among the environmental factors to be evaluated are: physical barriers in the home (such as steps, poor lighting, and slippery floor surfaces); condition of the dwelling (e.g., in need of repair); neighborhood safety; and proximity to family and friends and to needed health, recreational, shopping, and occupational facilities. The availability of appropriate transportation has emerged as a major issue, since it relates directly to the ability to participate in everyday activities and to obtain access to needed services (including health care); lack of appropriate transportation can result in isolation.

Housing is a problem for many older people. By comparison with younger people, they spend a larger portion of their incomes on their housing and live in older housing. (Maintenance difficulties can be severe for those who are handicapped or frail.) The elderly are often fearful of crime in the neighborhoods in which they live and have a diminished capacity to recover from victimization. Though about 9 percent of older people now live in age-segregated buildings, there is a need for more low-cost housing, particularly housing with built-in supportive services such as health care and meals.[40]

The aging process is accompanied by losses of major social roles such as those of worker, parent of dependent children, spouse, sibling, and friend. The continuity of some roles (such as church or political party membership) and the development of some new ones (such as grandparenting) do not compensate for the loss of the major roles. The older person's physical and mental health is affected by the resultant losses of status and self-esteem and the changes in lifestyle.

CONCLUSION

The overwhelming weight of evidence indicates that the immediate context of family and friends and the larger societal setting contribute significantly to the older person's health and well-being. The physician's evaluation of the social environment therefore is an integral part of patient care.

The diversity of the elderly population in their health status extends to their other characteristics as well. Older people include the young old and the old old, the well-to-do and the poor, the urban and the rural, and those with rich family networks and those without family. Their needs, preferences, and values will vary in accordance with such other factors as ethnicity, level of education, and personality. Furthermore, the aged now include at least two generations of older people who have lived through different periods of history and who have very different backgrounds. The elderly population experiences a one-third turnover each year as some die and new cohorts enter the aging phase of life.

The heterogeneity of older people is reflected in the way individuals react to and comply with medical regimens and procedures. The diversity in their social situations—in the quality and quantity of "informal" resources and in the availability of "formal" supports—also determines the nature of the health program physicians can prescribe. In considering each individual's unique set of social circumstances, doctors are as challenged by the evaluation of the elderly patient's social resources as they are by the evaluation of the medical condition because both factors are intimately related.

All available data indicate that the family has been steadfast and reliable in helping the disabled and sick elderly. It is also well established that the social cost is high, since family efforts are stretched to the point at which caregivers often experience severe stress. While community services cannot do it all in relieving the pressures, a long-term-care system can make a significant contribution toward ameliorating the situation. Public long-term-care insurance is feasible if our values permit its development.[32,33]

REFERENCES

1. Lawton MP, Cohen J: The generality of housing impact on the well-being of older people. *J Gerontol* 29: 194, 1974.
2. Snider EL: Explaining life satisfaction: It's the elderly's attitudes that count. *Soc Sci Q* 61: 253, 1980.
3. Goldfarb AI: Prevalence of psychiatric disorders in metropolitan old age and nursing homes. *J Am Geriatr Soc* 10: 77, 1962.
4. Lowenthal MF: *Lives in Distress.* New York, Basic Books, 1964.
5. Schuckit MA: "Unrecognized Psychiatric Illness in Elderly Medical-Surgical Patients." Paper presented at 27th annual meeting of the Gerontological Society of America, Portland, OR 1974.
6. Snider EL: The elderly and their doctors. *Soc Sci Med* 14A: 527, 1980.
7. Liu K, Manton KG, Liu BM: Home care expenses for the disabled elderly. *Health Care Financ Rev* 7:51, 1985.
8. Doty P, Liu K, Wiener J: An overview of long-term care. *Health Care Financ Rev* 6:69, 1985.
9. Brody EM, Kleban, MH: Physical/mental health symptoms of older people: Whom do they tell? *J Am Geriatr Soc* 29:442, 1981.
10. Allan C, Brotman H: *Chartbook on Aging in America,* Compiled for the 1981 White House Conference on Aging, Washington, Government Printing Office.
11. Fengler AP, Goodrich N: Wives of elderly disabled men: The hidden patients. *Gerontologist* 19:175, 1979.
12. Shanas E: Social myth as hypothesis: The case of the family relations of old people. *Gerontologist* 19:3, 1979.
13. Horowitz A: Sons and daughters as caregivers to older parents: Differences in role performance and consequences. *Gerontologist* 25:612, 1985.
14. Brody EM: The aging of the family. *Ann Am Acad Pol Soc Sci* 438:13, 1978.
15. Mindel CH: Multigenerational family households: Recent trends and implications for the future. *Gerontologist* 19:456, 1979.
16. Stone R, Cafferata GL, Sangl J: Caregivers of the frail elderly: A national profile. *Gerontologist* 27:616, 1987.
17. Brody SJ, Poulshock SW, Masciocchi CF: The family caring unit: A major consideration in the long-term support system. *Gerontologist* 18:556, 1978.
18. General Accounting Office: *The Well-Being of Older People in Cleveland, Ohio: Report to the Congress by the Comptroller General of the United States.* 1977.
19. Brody EM: "Women in the middle" and family help to older people. *Gerontologist* 21:471, 1981.
20. NRTA-AARP: National survey of older Americans, July 1981.
21. Shanas E: Older people and their families: The new pioneers. *J Marriage Fam* 42:9, 1980.
22. Lang A, Brody EM: Characteristics of middle-aged daughters and help to their elderly mothers. *J Marriage Fam* 45:193, 1983.
23. US Department of Labor, Bureau of Labor Statistics: Labor force by sex, age and race. *Earn Employ* 28:167, 1981.
24. Brody EM: Parent care as a normative family stress. *Gerontologist* 25:19, 1985.
25. Horowitz A: Family caregiving to the frail elderly, in Eis-

dorfer C, Lawton MP, Maddox GL (eds): *Annual Review of Gerontology and Geriatrics.* New York, Springer, vol 5, 1985, p. 194.

26. Brody EM, Kleban MH, Johnsen PT, Hoffman C, Schoonover CB: Work status and parent care: A comparison of four groups of women. *Gerontologist* 27:201, 1987.

27. Brody EM, Hoffman C, Kleban MH, Schoonover CB: Parent care and sibling relationships: Perceptions of caregiving daughters and their local siblings. *Gerontologist*, submitted for publication (1988).

28. Schoonover CB, Brody EM, Hoffman C, Kleban MH: "Parent Care and Geographically Distant Children." Paper presented at 40th annual meeting of the Gerontological Society of America, 1987.

29. Rosow I: Coalitions in geriatric medicine, in Haug MR (ed): *Elderly Patients and Their Doctors.* New York, Springer, 1981, p. 137.

30. Cantor M: Neighbors and friends: An overlooked resource in the informal support system. Paper presented at 30th annual meeting of the Gerontological Society of America, San Francisco, 1977.

31. Evans JG: Care of the aging in Great Britain: An overview, in *The Aging: Medical and Social Supports in the Decade of the 80's.* New York, Center on Gerontology, Fordham University, 1981, p. 13.

32. Brody SJ: Strategic planning: The catastrophic approach.

The Donald P Kent Memorial Lecture. *Gerontologist* 27:131, 1987.

33. Rivlin AM, Wiener JM: *Caring for the Disabled Elderly: Who Will Pay?* Washington, Brookings Institution, 1988.

34. *Advance Data, A Comparison of Nursing Home Residents and Discharges from the 1977 National Nursing Home Survey: United States.* National Center for Health Statistics, DHEW (PHS)29, 1978.

35. Brody EM: The role of the family in nursing homes: Implications for research and public policy, in Harper, MS, Lebowitz B (eds): *Mental Illness in Nursing Homes: Agenda for Research.* Washington, Government Printing Office.

36. George LK: *The Dynamics of Caregiver Burden.* Final report submitted to the AARP Andrus Foundation, 1984.

37. Pruchno R, Brody EM: Institutionalization of a parent: Mental health effects, Preliminary results. (In process of development.)

38. Lawton MP, Simon B: The ecology of social interaction in housing for the elderly. *Gerontologist* 8:108, 1968.

39. Lawton MP: Environment and other determinants of well-being in older people. The Robert W. Kleemeier Memorial Lecture. *Gerontologist* 23:349, 1983.

40. Lawton MP: Housing for the elderly in the mid-1980s, in Lesnoff-Caravaglia (ed): *Handbook of Applied Gerontology.* New York, Human Sciences Press, 1987.

Chapter 26

ALTERATIONS OF LABORATORY FINDINGS

H. Malcolm Hodkinson

Adequate investigation of the conditions of elderly patients is an essential prelude to their effective treatment. However, in order to make proper diagnostic use of biochemical, hematological, or other laboratory tests, we need to know the distribution of test results in disease-free individuals who are in other ways comparable (the so-called normal range for the test) and also have estimates of the prior likelihood of disease and of the distribution of test results in those with disease.[1,2] In this chapter we will be concerning ourselves exclusively with this first consideration and looking at changes in normal ranges for laboratory tests in old age.

REFERENCE RANGES

The term *normal range* is not a totally satisfactory one because the word *normal* has several meanings which can confuse us: normal in the sense of Gaussian, normal in the sense of usual, and normal in the sense of nonpathological. We can avoid this confusion by using the term *reference range* so that it is clear that we are speaking of the 95 percent distribution of test results in the reference population, a population of comparable subjects who are of appropriate race, sex, and age and have a defined health status. The health status we define will depend on the use we have in mind for the reference range, and we can perfectly well determine a reference range in a given disease or in patients without a disease as well as in healthy subjects.

RANGES IN OLD AGE

Until about 15 years ago there were very few laboratory reference ranges of any kind which had been determined for elderly subjects. There were a number of valuable studies of changes of reference ranges with age[3-5] which were based on samples from healthy blood donors; however, donors are not permitted to continue beyond the age of 65, and the data stopped at this age. Such studies did show that there were many significant changes in reference ranges with increasing age within the middle period of life and pointed to the need for detailed study of the healthy elderly. Following pioneering work from Glasgow[6] there have been many relevant studies undertaken (see Refs. 2 and 7 for reviews of these). However, a problem throughout such studies is that of defining a truly healthy elderly population; indeed, this may be an intellectual abstraction, and most studies have had to content themselves with apparently well elderly subjects living at home or sometimes, less appropriately perhaps, with those resident in institutions. Insufficient attention has been paid to the effects on laboratory measurements of concurrent medication; most recent surveys have reported that a majority of apparently well old people living at home are on one or more drugs.

MECHANISMS OF ALTERATIONS IN REFERENCE RANGES

Many different mechanisms may underlie the observed changes in laboratory test reference ranges with age. We do not fully understand them all, but many can be rationally explained and will be considered below.

LIMITED EXCRETORY CAPACITY

Limited excretory capacity is clearly of relevance, and an obvious example is the decrease in renal function with age. This decrease is now very well documented (see review by Rowe[8]); the falling glomerular filtration rate

241

readily explains the steady rise in blood urea throughout middle life,[5] which continues into old age.[6] Similar changes are seen for serum creatinine,[5,6] though in this case the rise is less striking because of the tendency for muscle mass to fall with age, thereby reducing the endogenous production of creatinine from breakdown of muscle cells. A similar antagonism of effects may account for the relative stability of reference ranges for serum uric acid through middle life[5] followed by an increase in old age.[9,10] Bilirubin is another common laboratory measurement whose value depends on efficiency of excretion, in this instance biliary excretion, but its reference range does not appear to rise significantly with age.[9]

HORMONAL EFFECTS

There are many hormonal changes through middle life, those of the menopause in females being the most marked, and changes continue into old age. Hormonal changes may have a great many effects on other laboratory parameters as well as altering reference ranges for the hormones themselves. Such effects are most obviously revealed when there is an abrupt change in reference ranges at the time of the menopause. Thus, for example, serum phosphate rises sharply in females after the menopause, in contrast to a steady age-related fall in men.[5] These differences continue into old age, when women have an appreciably higher reference range for phosphate in comparison with men[11]; these differences are thought to be mediated by the relative lack of antagonism of parathormone by sex steroids in the elderly female. Very similar changes that occur in respect to serum calcium are thought to have the same basis, although these changes are of lesser magnitude. A rise in the reference range for serum alkaline phosphatase following the menopause[5] may also reflect this removal of sex hormone inhibition of parathormone. This loss of inhibition could lead to an increase in osteoclastic action on bone, with a consequent rise in osteoblast activity and, hence, a greater production of bone alkaline phosphatase.

SERUM PROTEIN CHANGES

Changes in serum protein have many important effects. There is general agreement that serum albumin shows a steady decline with age throughout adult life.[3-5,9] The reasons for this decline are not fully understood because the relative importance of changes in anabolism and catabolism with age has not been adequately evaluated. The consequence of this fall in serum albumin is that the reference ranges of substances which are substantially bound to albumin may be altered, even though the unbound fraction remains unchanged. For example, total

serum calcium shows a steady fall with age (except for the discontinuous postmenopausal rise in females) that can be attributed to the corresponding fall in albumin to which it is substantially bound, but ionized calcium could remain constant under these same conditions. There are age changes in other carrier proteins which can similarly affect other ranges, such as the range of serum iron[5,12]; however, these age-related physiological falls in carrier proteins are overshadowed by the magnitude of the falls which result nonspecifically from illness.[1,2] It is these major falls which make it necessary to correct, for example, calcium or thyroid hormone levels for protein changes if the results are to be interpreted correctly in the ill elderly patient.

HOMEOSTASIS

With advancing age, homeostasis may deteriorate, and this would be expected to give rise to wider ranges for any metabolite which is less well controlled. This effect is certainly true for blood glucose; all studies show a steady rise in both the mean and the spread of values with increasing age. The breakdown of glucose homeostasis appears to be a complex phenomenon of a multifactorial nature. It is still imperfectly understood despite extensive study.[13] The rises of creatinine and urea with age can be regarded as special cases of homeostatic breakdown related to declining renal function. In general, however, ranges in old age do not show a wider spread, even though there may be changes in mean values. Sodium, an example of a blood constituent subject to close homeostatic control, has a range which is unchanged with age. Similarly, many other reference ranges remain constant with aging. However, even though there is no evidence from reference ranges in the well elderly for any general breakdown of metabolic homeostasis in old age, the elderly do seem to be far more liable to homeostatic disturbances when they become ill. Though serum sodium concentration is maintained in the well elderly, illness can frequently lead to the development of hyponatremia, giving a substantially reduced range for serum sodium in elderly patients.[1,2]

SELECTIVE EFFECTS OF MORTALITY

Selective effects of mortality are thought to have relevance to lipid reference ranges in old age. For example, the reference ranges for cholesterol rise progressively with age in both sexes to peak at around 65 but then fall again in old age.[9,12] This appears to be a complex phenomenon. First, as high cholesterol is a recognized risk factor for coronary heart disease, it is postulated that the reference ranges are lower in old age at least in part because of the earlier death of individuals with high values from coronary heart disease in late middle life. As a corollary, it is also possible that familial longevity may be associated directly with a tendency for lower cholesterol levels.[14] Finally, however, cholesterol levels tend to decline beyond age 60 even in healthy participants in longitudinal studies, notably the Baltimore Longitudinal Study of Aging.[15]

INTAKE OF NUTRIENTS

The main determinant of some blood constituents is the intake of nutrients. For example, the dietary intakes of vitamins and iron are decreased in old age,[16] and serum reference ranges are correspondingly low. Such lower ranges have been variously interpreted; in particular, there has been an unfortunate tendency to take them to represent evidence of deficiency. Deficiency cannot be assumed, however, and can only be substantiated if the lower values can be shown to be associated with impaired health status and their elevation by dietary supplements shown to result in a subsequent improvement in health. Equally, the lower ranges cannot be regarded as aging changes but merely as indicators of lower, though not necessarily inadequate, nutritional intakes of substances which are subject to little, if any, homeostatic control.

The situation with regard to serum 25-hydroxy-vitamin D (25-OHD) can be taken as an illustration of these points, though in this case parent vitamin D is derived rather more from sunlight-dependent synthesis in the skin than from the diet.[17] Both 25-OHD and vitamin D are decreased in the elderly, so a very much lower reference range for 25-OHD is found for the elderly than for younger adults. Study of biochemical parameters of metabolic bone disease and of bone histology findings in elderly subjects demonstrates, however, that very low levels of serum 25-OHD are compatible with health, as evidenced by the absence of any indicators of metabolic bone disease.[18]

Many nutrients—for example, vitamins and iron—are bound to specific carrier proteins, and so protein alterations may also have effects on range. The dietary intake of protein and calories may affect these serum protein levels. Certainly, severe protein-calorie malnutrition is associated with low levels of prealbumin and albumin as well as low levels of more specific carrier proteins such as retinol-binding protein.[19] However, surveys of the diets of old people have not found protein-calorie malnutrition to be a problem in the well elderly, although ill old people are at risk.[16] Reference ranges in health thus relate to intake of a specific nutrient and not to protein and calorie intakes, although in ill old people the latter may also be relevant.

OCCULT DISEASE

Alteration of reference ranges in old age may be caused by occult disease, rather than by any true age change. For example, serum alkaline phosphatase activities show considerable changes with age. Activity levels are very high in childhood and adolescence and fall in early adult life. Thereafter, they rise progressively, particularly in old age.[9,12] The elevation in youth is explained by the far greater osteoblastic activity associated with growth and remodeling of the skeleton. The rise in serum alkaline phosphatase activity levels in older age groups might be a genuine aging effect, though the absence of significant changes in reference ranges of other serum enzymes, for example, aspartate aminotransferase or alanine aminotransferase,[9] is perhaps evidence against this idea. However, there is a real possibility that occult disease might be responsible. Paget's disease can be excluded only by full skeletal survey, which is not often undertaken although this disease is a relatively common condition in old age with reported prevalence of around 5 percent. The inclusion of unrecognized cases of Paget's disease could well explain the higher reference ranges found in the elderly, and occult osteomalacia has also been suggested as another possibility. The erythrocyte sedimentation rate is another example. Sharland[20] followed a group of well old people over a period of several years, during which they remained in good health. He found that the reference range of the sedimentation rate in this study population was far, far higher (3 to 69 mm/h) than the range in younger subjects. It is impossible to know whether to regard this considerable elevation of range as an aging effect or to ascribe it to occult disease which is clinically insignificant. The erythrocyte sedimentation rate is perhaps now becoming something of an anachronism. It represents a complex of changes in fibrinogen, globulins, and albumin, and it is also influenced by the hematocrit. The higher reference range for erythrocyte sedimentation rate in old age can partly be explained by the higher range for fibrinogen[21] and lower range for albumin, both of which will have the effect of elevating the rate. However, the reference range for globulins is also higher in the elderly[9]; this, too, will give higher values for the sedimentation rate and, in particular, is the likely explanation of persistently raised values. The sedimentation rate has been used as an indicator of acute-phase protein changes, but we now have far more specific tests, such as serum C-reactive protein, to replace it.[22,23]

Elevation of globulins in old age may represent occult disease, at least in part. A great variety of individual globulin changes may occur, and these have been reviewed recently.[7] Of particular interest are elevations of gamma globulins. Some of these gammopathies can be attributed to definite disease (for example, multiple myeloma), but others may persist for long periods without any deterioration in the individual's state of health (the so-called benign gammopathies).

It is a moot point as to whether certain individuals' values should be excluded when reference ranges are being established. The practice of authors varies considerably, and published work often fails to clarify the policies that have been adopted in dealing with such outliers in publishing reference ranges for laboratory tests which we use clinically.

INFLUENCE OF MEDICATION ON REFERENCE RANGES

Many elderly people who live at home in a good state of health are nonetheless on long-term medication. Most reference populations on which published ranges have been based have not excluded all subjects on medications or have excluded only those on drugs which the investigator considered likely to affect the test result. This is an important practical point, for there are very large numbers of known drug effects on tests[24] and probably many more which are as yet unrecognized. The difficulties are far greater in the elderly, who are quite often on multiple medications. One geriatric study showed that the range for free-thyroxine-index values in euthyroid patients was appreciably higher than in well elderly subjects in the local community, and the elevated values appeared to be related both to recognized drug effects, such as that of L-dopa, and to other unreported drug effects.[25]

Drugs may affect tests in a variety of ways. They may have a direct influence on the laboratory analysis, or they may have physiological effects so as to genuinely alter the test value. Laboratory effects include such phenomena as underestimation of values due to inhibitory effects of the drug on enzyme actions or overestimations because of cross-reactivity or other technical effects such as fluorescence quenching or competitive binding. In vivo effects may be an expression of the desired effects or the side effects of the drug; for example, electrolyte changes are expected with diuretic therapy, while hyperglycemia or hyperuricemia with thiazide diuretics is a well-known side effect. There are many other, more subtle mechanisms, however. Liver toxicity may lead to elevation of bilirubin or enzyme changes. Similarly, nephrotoxicity may lead to elevation of metabolites excreted by the kidney. These effects may reflect competition for excretory mechanisms as is seen in the elevation of bilirubin after use of radiological contrast media. Alternatively, enhancement of excretion may occur with uricosuric drugs. A variety of effects may occur also by endocrine mechanisms, such as the elevation of thyroid hormones by L-dopa, already cited, which is mediated by pituitary effects. Carrier protein levels may be altered; for example, thyroxine-binding globulin levels may be elevated by estrogens or lowered by androgens or anabolic steroids.

APPROPRIATE REFERENCE RANGES IN GERIATRIC PRACTICE

If our purpose in defining reference ranges is to study age effects on laboratory measurements, then clearly we would wish to choose populations of subjects judged to be healthy. Our difficulties are then purely those of the definition of health, particularly in the older age groups in which the accumulation of nonlethal conditions makes this a rather arbitrary matter; for it would almost certainly not be possible to find an older person who has no demonstrable pathology whatsoever. Though we might have this gerontological interest in ranges, more often our wish to define reference ranges has a practical clinical basis. We need a reference range so that we can compare the result from our patient with it and make some clinical inference. The nature of the reference range needed will now depend on our exact purpose. If, for example, we want to assess an individual's renal function using serum creatinine or blood urea as tests, then the appropriate reference ranges would be from well subjects of similar age, sex, and ethnic origin on similar diet (for urea) and of similar muscle mass (for creatinine) as the individual. Reference ranges of this kind present no great difficulties. However, the situation is a very different one if, for example, we wish to decide whether an ill woman of 80 years old, whom we know to have diseases A, B, and C, might also have disease D for which Test E is the appropriate laboratory test. Test E might be one of many which are affected in a nonspecific way by illness itself. Furthermore, the woman may be on drugs which could affect the test. Ideally, our reference range should be based on a population of patients of similar age, sex, and race who also have diseases A, B, and C and are on the same drugs but differ only in that we know them not to have disease D. In practice, a situation such as this is clearly an ideal we can never hope to attain. We need to recognize the difficulty in interpretation which we face if we use a reference range from a well population, however. There may be an advantage to using a reference range based on patients without disease D rather than on well individuals because the patient population will be far more comparable with our individual patient. However, this approach does not absolve us from the need to understand the effects of illness, other diseases, and therapy on the tests we wish to use.

TABLE 26-1
Reference Ranges which Are Appreciably Different in Old Age*

	Range for Adults		Range for Elderly	
Albumin	37–51 g/liter	(10)	33–49 g/liter	(6)
Globulin	19–33 g/liter	(3)	20–41 g/liter	(6)
Potassium	3.6–4.7 mmol/liter	(3)	3.6–5.2 mmol/liter	(6)
Urea	3.2–7.2 mmol/liter	(3)	3.9–9.9 mmol/liter	(6)
Creatinine	62–123 μmol/liter	(3)	52–159 μmol/liter	(6)
	(0.7–1.4 mg/100 ml)		(0.6–1.8 mg/100 m/liter)	
Uric acid (men)	4.0–7.6 mg/100 ml	(3)	3.1–7.8 mg/dl	(6)
Uric acid (women)	2.6–6.2 mg/100 ml	(3)	2.1–7.7 mg/dl	(6)
Calcium (men)	2.25–2.60 mmol/liter	(3)	2.19–2.59 mmol/liter	(6)
Calcium (women)	2.18–2.55 mmol/liter	(3)	2.18–2.68 mmol/liter	(6)
Alkaline phosphatase (men)	19–75 IU/liter	(4)	22–81 IU/liter	(4)
Alkaline phosphatase (women)	14–67 IU/liter	(4)	22–83 IU/liter	(4)
Phosphate (men)	0.79–1.40 mmol/liter	(4)	0.66–1.27 mmol/liter	(4)
Phosphate (women)	0.82–1.37 mmol/liter	(4)	0.94–1.56 mmol/liter	(4)
T4 (men)	57–143 nmol/liter	(26)	65–151 nmol/liter	(26)
T4 (women)	61–155 nmol/liter	(26)	72–157 nmol/liter	(26)
T3 (men)	0.91–2.83 nmol/liter	(26)	0.20–2.86 nmol/liter	(26)
T3 (women)	0.44–2.80 nmol/liter	(26)	0.60–2.60 nmol/liter	(26)
Erythrocyte sedimentation				
rate (women)	0–7 mm/h	(27)	6–69 mm/h	(20)
Leucocyte count	4000–11,000/mm^3	(27)	3100–8900/mm^3	(28)

*Ranges given are those derived from the sources referenced and are likely to vary slightly from those of many American laboratories, which often do not adjust ranges for gender or age.

LABORATORY VALUES OF CLINICAL SIGNIFICANCE: THE EFFECTS OF AGE

Table 26-1 lists reference ranges for commonly ordered tests which are appropriately different in old age. Tests which are *not* affected by age to any practical extent include

> sodium
> aspartate aminotransferase
> magnesium
> hemoglobin and red cell indices
> chloride
> alanine aminotransferase
> bicarbonate
> bilirubin
> lactate dehydrogenase
> coagulation tests

REFERENCES

1. Hodkinson HM: *Biochemical Diagnosis of the Elderly.* London, Chapman & Hall, 1977.
2. Hodkinson HM: *Clinical Biochemistry of the Elderly.* Edinburgh, Churchill Livingstone, 1984.
3. Roberts LB: The normal ranges, with statistical analysis for seventeen blood constituents. *Clin Chim Acta* 16:69, 1967.
4. Keating FR et al: The relation of age and sex to distribution of values in healthy adults of serum calcium, inorganic phosphorus, magnesium, alkaline phosphatase, total proteins, albumin and blood urea. *J Lab Clin Med* 73:825, 1969.
5. McPherson K et al: The effect of age, sex and other factors on blood chemistry in health. *Clin Chim Acta* 84:373, 1978.
6. Leask RGS et al: Normal values of sixteen blood constituents in the elderly. *Age Ageing* 2:14, 1973.
7. Rochman H: *Clinical Pathology in the Elderly.* Basel, Karger, 1988.
8. Rowe JW: Aging and renal function, in Eisdorfer C (ed): *Annual Review of Gerontology and Geriatrics,* vol 1. New York, Springer, 1980, p 161.
9. Gillibrand D et al: Chemistry reference values as a function of age and sex, including paediatric and geriatric subjects, in Dietz AA (ed): *Aging—Its Chemistry,* vol 1. New York, Springer, 1980, p 161.
10. Reed AH et al: Estimation of normal ranges from a controlled sample population. *Clin Chem* 18:57, 1972.
11. Hodkinson HM: Serum inorganic phosphate in a geriatric inpatient population. *Gerontol Clin* 15:45, 1973.
12. Wilding P et al: Patterns of change for various biochemical constituents detected in well population screening. *Clin Chim Acta* 41:375, 1972.
13. Davidson MB: The effect of aging on carbohydrate metabolism. *Metabolism* 28:688, 1979.

14. Nicholson J et al: Lipid and lipoprotein distributions in octa- and nonagenarians. *Metabolism* 28:51, 1979.

15. Herschkopf RJ, Elahi D, Andres R, Baldwin HL, Raizes GS, Shocken DD, Tobin JD: Longitudinal changes in serum cholesterol in man: An epidemiologic search for an etiology. *J Chron Dis* 35:101, 1982.

16. "A Nutrition Survey of the Elderly," Department of Health & Social Security Reports on Health and Social Subjects, No. 3. London, HMSO, 1972.

17. Hodkinson HM et al: Sex, sunlight, season, diet and the vitamin D status of elderly patients. *J Clin Exp Gerontol* 1:13, 1979.

18. Hodkinson HM, Hodkinson I: Range for 25-hydroxy vitamin D in elderly subjects in whom osteomalacia has been excluded on histological and biochemical criteria. *J Clin Exp Gerontol* 2:133, 1980.

19. Smith FR et al: Serum vitamin A, retinol-binding protein, and prealbumin concentrations in protein-calorie malnutrition: I. A functional defect in hepatic retinol release. *Am J Clin Nutr* 26:973, 1973.

20. Sharland DE: Erythrocyte sedimentation rate: The normal range in the elderly. *J Am Geriatr Soc* 28:346, 1980.

21. Hamilton PJ et al: The effect of age on the fibrinolytic enzyme system. *J Clin Pathol* 27:326, 1974.

22. Kenny RA et al: A comparison of the erythrocyte sedimentation rate and serum C-reactive protein concentration in elderly patients. *Age Ageing* 14:15, 1985.

23. Cox ML et al: Real-time measurement of serum C-reactive protein in the management of infections in the elderly. *Age Ageing* 15:257, 1986.

24. Young DS et al: Effects of drugs on clinical laboratory tests. *Clin Chem* 21:ID, 1975.

25. Baruch ALH et al: Causes of high free-thyroxine-index values in sick euthyroid elderly patients. *Age Ageing* 5:116, 1976.

26. Evered DC et al: Thyroid hormone concentrations in a large-scale community survey; Effect of age, sex, illness and medication. *Clin Chim Acta* 83:223, 1978.

27. Dacie JV, Lewis SM: *Practical Haematology*, 5th ed. Edinburgh, Churchill Livingstone, 1975.

28. Caird FI et al: The leucocyte count in old age. *Age Ageing* 1:239, 1973.

Chapter 27

ACUTE HOSPITAL CARE FOR FRAIL OLDER PATIENTS

Marsha Duke Fretwell

Older patients enter acute care hospitals more frequently, stay longer, and experience more adverse consequences than younger patients. Subsequently, they are discharged more frequently to another health care facility.[1]

This chapter will focus on the experience of frail older patients in the acute care hospital. Interindividual variation among older patients prevents us from using any single marker, such as age, diagnosis, or functional disability, as an accurate predictor of biologic or physiologic frailty.[2] For this discussion, *frailty* in an individual will be defined as an inherent vulnerability to challenge from the environment. It would most likely be seen in our oldest patients or in those "younger" old patients who have a combination of diseases or functional impairments that reduce their capacity to adapt to the stress of acute illness and its treatment in the hospital. Following a review of the factors in the patient and in the hospital environment that appear to influence the outcomes of acute medical care, a description of the results of this interaction between frail older patients and the environment is presented. The chapter concludes with a discussion of a prospective approach to acute hospital care that promotes optimal management of serious illness in frail older patients without increasing the cost of care.

DESCRIPTION OF THE FRAIL PATIENT

The most important demographic change that will influence the frequency of utilization and risk associated with acute hospital care is the rapidly increasing proportion of the older population that is very old, i.e., over the age of

85.[3] This group, on average, has a larger burden of chronic illness and functional disability. It is important to note, however, that even though a portion of these patients may not have any clinical or subclinical organ disease or any abnormalities in physiologic parameters under resting circumstances, these very old individuals may nevertheless deteriorate under circumstances of stress.[4] The stress of illness usually manifests itself first, and most prominently, in the organ with the least functional reserve—often, the brain. Thus, the very old patient who has been functioning well in the community may come into the hospital with pneumonia and suddenly appear extremely agitated and confused.

The additive effect of extreme age and such age-associated conditions as dementia, hip fracture, cerebrovascular accidents, arthritis, and visual disorders on a person's overall ability to withstand environmental challenge has not been clarified, but is probably significant. Additionally, a larger proportion of this group's burden of disease and functional impairment may be irreversible or only very slowly reversible by current therapy. Interindividual variation creates uncertainty in decision making. Generalizations about treatment are unproductive, and may even be counterproductive, as in the case where the presence of one condition greatly influences treatment of another. If we are to understand and achieve optimal outcomes in these frail individuals, we must identify the entire spectrum of their multiple organ diseases. If we do not do so, any subsequent diagnostic or therapeutic maneuver may very likely bring with it unexpected adverse effects.

This shift in focus from attempting to pinpoint a single disease underlying the acute illness to a study of the interaction between the acute illness and the individual's entire burden of disease and disability is one of the major changes that our aging population has brought to the clinical and research agenda of medicine. We now see that the outcome of any acute illness is more dependent upon various attributes of the host, positive or negative, than the absolute virulence of the infecting organism or the progressive nature of the acute disease. Added to this complexity is the fact that in older patients acute illnesses may first present in a vague and nonspecific manner, perhaps only by a functional decline in an unrelated organ system.[5] This may lead, especially in cognitively impaired patients, to a missed or late diagnosis, delayed referral for treatment, and subsequent higher than average severity of illness on presentation to the acute care hospital[6] (see Chap. 22).

DESCRIPTION OF THE TREATMENT AND ENVIRONMENT

Hospital care, with its increased use of medications, invasive catheters and lines, diagnostic tests, and nosocomial infections may be best thought of as a significant source of physiologic stress for the older patient. In fact, all studies examining the complications of the medical and surgical treatments in the acute hospital have shown older patients to be at increased risk for clinical iatrogenesis (Table 27-1).[7–9] One study compared patients who were over 65 years of age with those who were not yet 65 on both medical and surgical wards of a VA hospital.[7] The complication rate for the older group was 45 percent versus 29 percent for the younger group. The most common cause of complications was drugs, but compared with younger patients, older patients also had more infections and trauma in addition to more adverse drug reactions. The rate of procedure-related complications was the same in both old and young. Psychiatric decompensation occurred in nearly 20 percent of the older and in none of the younger patients, suggesting that changes in the location of care and in the providers of that care as well as changes in routine and loss of familiar daily schedules all add up to a major source of psychological stress for older patients in the acute hospital. An earlier study on the medical service of a teaching hospital documented a clinical iatrogenesis rate of 36 percent and noted the associated factors to be increased age, poor condition, increased numbers of drugs, admission from an institution, and increased length of stay.[9]

Another study of general medical patients for evidence of complications that may be considered a side effect of hospitalization itself (i.e., separate from side effects of diagnosis or treatment) suggests that as many as 40.5 percent of persons over the age of 70 years experience loss of mental and physical function unrelated to

TABLE 27-1
Acute Hospital Care for Frail Older Patients: Issues of Physiologic and Functional Iatrogenesis

1. Description of the patient (increased number of individuals over the age of 85 years)
   a. Enhanced vulnerability to stress; reduced ability to adapt to environmental challenge
   b. Increasing burden of diseases and functional dependencies (especially cognitive)
   c. Diseases and functional dependencies more likely to be irreversible, introducing concept of appropriateness of treatments, etc.
   d. Reversible problems require longer period of time for recovery
   e. Enhanced individual variation
   f. Outcomes more dependent on characteristics of the patient, requiring large complex data base for accurate assessment of need and prediction of effects of treatments
2. Description of the treatment and environment of care
   a. Physiologic iatrogenesis
   b. Functional iatrogenesis
   c. Effects of the environment
3. Results of the interaction of frail person and stressful environment; cascade of illness and functional decline
   a. Accelerated functional decline
   b. Excess physiologic morbidity and mortality
   c. Excessive lengths of stay
   d. Unnecessary or premature placement in long-term care
4. Prevention of physiologic and functional iatrogenesis; improved quality of care without increasing lengths of stay and costs of care
   a. Prospective approach: screens for high-risk patients at admission; discuss pivotal role of cognitive function in overall problem of functional decline
   b. Comprehensive assessment
   c. Individualized standards of care and outcome measurements
   d. Attention to patient's prior or current directives for extent of therapy
   e. Definition of quality contains three dimensions
      (1) Physiologic outcomes: optimal treatment of medical, psychiatric, and surgical illnesses
      (2) Functional outcomes: maintenance or improvement of physical or cognitive function depending on diagnosis from (1).
      (3) Fiscal outcomes: optimal physiologic and functional outcomes at the least cost of care

their admitting diagnosis.[10] This is in contrast to 8.5 percent of patients under 70 years. The current disease-oriented model of acute medical care promotes a sequential approach to diagnosis and treatment and generally ignores the practices of restorative care until after the patient is discharged from the hospital. This approach, in combination with the high rate of delirium and psychological decompensation, promotes excessive bed rest, with accompanying loss of mobility, tendency to fall, and increased confusion, incontinence, and aphagia.[10,11]

As a result, additional medical interventions are then focused upon these symptoms. These interventions include restraints, psychotrophic medications, nasogastric tube or hand feedings, and Foley catheters. Finally, complications of these interventions may lead to delirium, agitation, constipation, nosocomial urinary tract infection, aspiration pneumonia, bacteremia, and pressure sores. Figure 27-1 from that study shows the hypothesized pathway of development of these functional complications of hospitalization.

Not discussed in the above study, but a reality in the management of acutely ill older patients, are the impacts or complications of depressionlike syndromes that come *after* the illness. Several studies evaluating older patients entering medical rehabilitation units have documented that 50 to 80 percent of patients suffer from such depression.[12,13] These older patients share several characteristics: severe illnesses, illnesses of long duration with poor prognosis, chronic pain, and prolonged bed rest. All had also experienced a loss of their functional independence. In these studies, all patients whose mood improved also improved in physical and mental function, whereas 75 percent of those whose mood did not improve failed to make any headway in regaining function.

Thus, the common experience of frail older patients in the acute care hospital has several dimensions, each of which may have an adverse impact on the overall outcome of the illness. The very old patient may arrive at the hospital at a later and more severe stage of the illness, may have other chronic conditions that complicate diagnosis and treatment of the presenting illness, may be unable to adapt to a new environment, and may experience additional new problems in that setting which are related to the treatment of the original or presenting illness. The combination of frail patient and unpredictable physiologic and psychosocial stressors over which the individual has little or no control may provide the substrata for the frequently seen emotional and cognitive decompensations that further impair recovery from acute illness. The emerging literature on the direct effect of psychosocial factors on physiologic processes in humans provides further support for this conceptual framework, especially in relation to issues of immunologic function, resistance to infection, and disease outcome.[14]

THE CASCADE OF ILLNESS AND FUNCTIONAL DECLINE: THE INTERACTION OF THE FRAIL OLDER PERSON AND THE STRESS OF ACUTE HOSPITAL CARE

The experience of some frail older patients in the acute care hospital might best be thought of as a "cascade," a word used to describe a process that, once started, proceeds stepwise to its full, seemingly inevitable, conclusion. Often, despite effective treatment of their acute medical illnesses, these individuals decline in functional

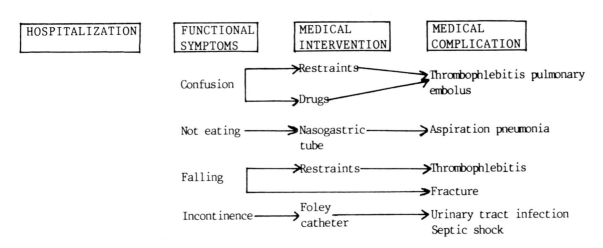

FIGURE 27-1
Hypothesized pathway of development of complications of hospitalization. *(From Gillick, Mureil: Soc Sci Med 16:1033, 1982. Printed in Great Britain. All rights reserved. Reprinted by permission of the author.)*

abilities, developing problems associated with confusion, immobility, incontinence, and malnutrition. Figure 27-2 shows the hypothetical hospital course of the frail older patient. Entitled "Cascade of Illness and Functional Decline," it shows how medications that have the capacity to impair mental function can interact with the patient's anxiety at having been relocated in a strange, new, and admittedly bewildering environment and can set off a complex series of events leading to acute loss of mental and physical function.[15] Additional medical and nursing interventions (Foley catheters, physical restraints, feeding tubes, broad-spectrum antibiotics, anticoagulants, and antipsychotic drugs) are required, adding to the numbers of medications and to the potential for clinical and functional iatrogenesis. It is important to note in this diagram that we have not included the impact of any specific diagnostic tests or therapies that would be utilized for management of the initial illness. Nor have we addressed the influence of the physician's anxiety, which, as it interacts with the concerns of the patient or the family, may be an important catalyst for continuing the cascade of diagnosis, treatment, and functional decline.[16] In this model, an elderly person, perhaps with a mild cognitive deficit can become confused, immobile, and incontinent within a few days after admission. As this process continues, it becomes increasingly difficult to determine cause and effect and to intervene appropriately. Each of these succeeding complications i.e., delirium, urinary tract infection, constipation, aspiration pneumonia, and malnutrition carries with it additional physiologic and psychological stress. Never recovering completely from one complication, the likelihood of recovering from successive complications is diminished. A frequent outcome of this cascade, even if the patient becomes physiologically stable, is a complex of symptoms including anorexia, lack of motivation, difficulty sleeping, and a feeling of depletion and hopelessness. Although this is often referred to as a "depression" because of this cluster of somatic or vegetative symptoms, diagnosis and treatment may be missed because the patient denies any feelings of depression or because the patient's behavior is felt to be an appropriate response to the situation of the illness.[17] Specific diagnostic tests, such as the dexamethasone suppression test, are routinely positive in this mixture of acute illness, stress, and depressionlike symptoms and are therefore not helpful.[18] However, several studies have demonstrated that, if the patient is physiologically stable, response to low-dose tricyclic antidepressants can be good, with improvement in sleep, appetite, and motivation in several days and eventual return to baseline mental and physical function.[12] Interestingly, mood disorders, if they are also present, often require at least 3 weeks of therapy, a response time frame well documented in the psychiatric literature.[19] It may be appropriate to think of these vegetative symptoms and the affective symptoms

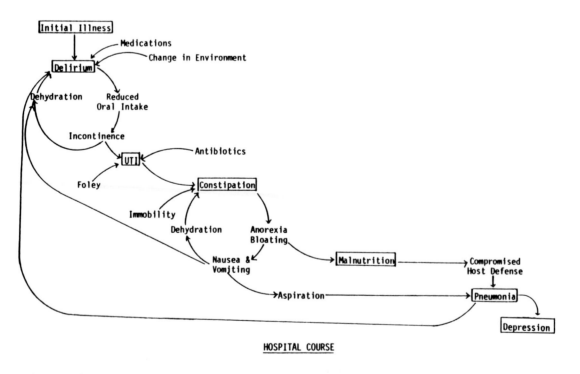

HOSPITAL COURSE

FIGURE 27-2
Cascade of illness and functional decline.

as separate phenomena. In the cascade of illness and functional decline, isolated vegetative symptoms at the end of acute hospitalization may best be understood as both a causal factor, accelerating the decline of function, and, if not treated, a final outcome of the hospitalization. In other words, the functional decline is the result of this vegetative state; it is the stress response of a physiologically frail individual to the recurrent and unpredictable stress of treatment.[15]

PREVENTION OF CLINICAL AND FUNCTIONAL IATROGENESIS: IMPROVED QUALITY OF ACUTE HOSPITAL CARE

If the physiologic characteristics of the aging individual include a reduced capacity to respond to environmental challenge and increased interindividual variation, then the central themes of managing acute illness in frail older patients should highlight individualized treatment plans that reduce the incidence of clinical and functional iatrogenesis and thereby involve the least amount of unnecessary stress. There is evidence from controlled trials of the effectiveness of geriatric assessment units in the care of selected groups of patients at the end of acute hospitalization that demonstrates the ability to create individualized treatment plans that not only improve functional outcomes but also reduce placement in nursing homes, improve patient survival, and reduce overall costs of care.[20] Additionally, one study comparing lengths of stay in a group of hospitalized frail older patients who were cared for by either general internists or a group of geriatricians showed a statistically significant reduction of hospital days in the group cared for by the latter group of doctors.[21] Despite an older age in this group managed by the geriatricians, there was no increase in readmission rates or in mortality after the hospital stay. Presumably an understanding of the principles of geriatric care may therefore allow physicians to provide care for a select group of older patients that involves lower costs without a reduction in the quality of patient outcomes.

Given the current environment of cost containment, it is unlikely that every frail older patient who might benefit from the specialized care of a fellowship-trained geriatrician or a rehabilitation unit that follows up after discharge will receive these services. A more pragmatic method for ensuring the optimal acute care management of frail older patients at the lowest cost in this setting is to modify the hospital care environment in a way that reduces the incidence of clinical and functional iatrogenesis that currently accompanies our best acute medical care. If prospective identification and

tracking of the most frail or vulnerable individuals into a less stressful structure of care is combined with more systematic care after discharge, it is possible that we could achieve better outcomes at no added cost.[22]

PROSPECTIVE IDENTIFICATION OF THE FRAIL OLDER PATIENT

Comprehensive functional assessment (CFA) (see Chap. 23) is the cornerstone of medical management of frail older patients, whether they are stable in the community or in a nursing home or unstable in the emergency room of the acute care hospital. The ideal management of an acutely ill older patient takes place when the attending physician has performed an initial or baseline CFA prior to hospitalization while the patient is at a stable and optimal level of health and function. This CFA provides the physician will full knowledge of coexisting medical problems and their severity, nutritional status, cognitive and emotional function, mobility and continence problems, medication lists, and psychosocial strengths and vulnerabilities. This baseline information of the mental and physical function (and dysfunction) then becomes critical for the accurate identification of a frail older patient. It provides the physician with the opportunity to discuss the use of extraordinary means before the acute illnesses occur and to educate the patient and family in the early recognition of acute illness (rapid declines in physical and mental function, such as anorexia, falling, incontinence, and confusion). Such an assessment process appears to promote the prevention or early detection of acute illness and psychosocial crisis, thereby reducing the eventual utilization of acute hospital care.[23]

The usefulness of a CFA applied before or at admission to the hospital is supported also by cohort studies that have both admission and outcome information about the patients. These show that the patient's functional status at admission, the burden of comorbid conditions, and the estimate of the severity of the presenting illness most accurately predict the outcome from a particular episode of illness.[24–26] Subgroup analysis of those over 70 years with cognitive impairment in this cohort demonstrated that they were older, sicker, and less physiologically stable than the cognitively "intact." These individuals experienced approximately three times the hospital morbidity and mortality of those who were cognitively intact.[6] Another study showed that approximately 70 percent of those over 75 years were cognitively impaired at admission, suggesting that this variable alone may select the most vulnerable individuals.[27] Finally, it appears that entering the hospital from a nursing home is, in most cases, associated with many of the attributes predicting a poor outcome in the acute care hospital.[26] The appropriate CFA of these individuals may most likely take place at the nursing home and may have focused on earlier on-site detection and management of acute decompensations in their chronic illnesses.

INTEGRATING COMPREHENSIVE FUNCTIONAL ASSESSMENT INTO ACUTE HOSPITAL CARE

Selected items of information about the patient, routinely collected in the process of CFA, can form the elements of an admission screen for the frail patient. This screen can be used to identify those patients most likely to experience poor outcomes from acute hospital care. Further assessment can identify those frail patients with and without reversible illnesses or impairments and can help design interventions appropriate to their needs.

The feasibility of integrating comprehensive functional assessment (in this instance, an interdisciplinary team assessment and care process) into the acute care hospital has been examined in a randomized controlled trial.[27] In this study, acutely ill patients over 75 years of age were randomized at admission either to experimental care in a consultative or unit model of geriatric assessment or to standard medical care. Both groups were identical in baseline characteristics, and in both groups the attending physician retained control of the care. There were no statistical differences in the mean lengths of stay and resulting hospital charges. There were actually fewer of the experimental group in the diagnosis-related group (DRG) listing of "outliers," (i.e., those who stayed longer than 2 standard deviations beyond the "length of stay" assigned by the DRG). Thus, if the team is formed from existing hospital staff and integrated into ongoing medical and nursing care, this comprehensive functional assessment and care process can be introduced without any additional expense to the hospital.

QUALITY OF CARE FOR HOSPITALIZED FRAIL OLDER PATIENTS

This chapter outlines an approach to the hospital care of frail older patients that focuses on the maintenance and restoration of the individual's mental and physical function as one of the critical measures of the overall quality of the care received. By describing and analyzing the interrelationships between the patients physiologic and functional status at admission, events in the hospital, and the discharge functional outcomes and cost, the argument is made that additional attention should and can be directed toward identifying and reducing the recurrent and unpredictable challenges of the environment and modalities of treatment for each of these frail individuals in the acute care hospital. In this way, the quality of the experience and the outcomes of the illnesses can be improved without increasing the cost of care.

REFERENCES

1. Garnick DW, Short T: Utilization of hospital inpatient services by elderly Americans, in *Hospital Studies Program.* DHHS (PHS)85-3351, June 1985, p 3.
2. Costa PT, McCrae RR: Concepts of functional or biological age: A critical review, in Andres R, Bierman EL, Hazzard WR (eds): *Principles of Geriatric Medicine.* New York, McGraw-Hill, 1985, pp 30–37.
3. Davis K: Aging and the health care system: Economics and structural issues in the aging society. *J Am Acad Sci* 229, 1986.
4. Williams TF: The future of aging. John Stanley Soulter Lecture. *Arch Phys Med Rehabil* 68:335, June 1987.
5. Gilcrist BA, Rowe JW: The biology of aging, in Rowe JW, Besdine RW (eds): *Health and Disease in Old Age.* Boston, Little Brown, 1982, p 15.
6. Fields SD, MacKenzie CR, Charlson ME, Sax FL: Cognitive impairment: Can it predict the course of hospitalized patients? *J Am Geriatr Soc* 34:579, 1986.
7. Jahnigen D, Hannon C, Laxson L, LaForce FM: Iatrogenic disease in hospitalized elderly veterans. *J Am Geriatr Soc* 30(6):387, 1982.
8. Barry PP: Iatrogenic disorders in the elderly: Preventive techniques. *Geriatrics* 41(9):42, 1986.
9. Steele K: Iatrogenic disease on a medical service. *J Am Geriatr Soc* 32(6):445; 1984.
10. Gillick MR, Serrell NA, Gillick LS: Adverse consequences of hospitalization in the elderly. *Soc Sci Med* 16:1033, 1982.
11. Miller MB: Iatrogenic and nurisgenic effects of prolonged immobilization of the ill aged. *J Am Geriatr Soc* 23:360, 1975.
12. Lakshmanan M, Mion LC, Frengley JD: Effective low dose tricyclic antidepressant treatment for depressed geriatric rehabilitation patients: A double-blind study. *J Am Geriatr Soc* 34:421, 1986.
13. Harris RE, Mion LC, Patterson MB, Frengley JD: Severe illness in older patients: The association between depressive disorders and functional dependency during the recovery phase. *J Am Geriatr Soc* 36(10):890, 1988.
14. Rowe JW, Kahn RL: Human aging: Usual and successful. *Science* 237:143, July 10, 1987. Copyright 1987 by AAAS.
15. Fretwell MD: Management in the acute care setting, in Kelley WN (ed): *Textbook of Internal Medicine.* Philadelphia, Lippincott, 1988, pp 2619–2622.
16. Mold JW, Stein HF: Sounding board: The cascade effect in the clinical care of patients. *N Engl J Med* February 20, p 512, 1986.
17. Fogel B, Fretwell MD: Reclassification of depression in the elderly. *J Am Geriatr Soc* 33(6):446, 1985.
18. Hirshfeld RMA, Koslow SH, Kupfer DJ: The clinical utility of the dexamethasone suppression test in psychiatry. *JAMA* 250:2172, 1983.
19. Amsterdam J, Brunswick D, Mendels J: The clinical ap-

plication of tricyclic antidepressant pharmacokinetics and plasma levels. *Am J Psychiatry* 137(6):654, 1980.

20. Rubenstein L: Effectiveness of a geriatric evaluation unit. *N Engl J Med* 311:26, 1984.

21. Pawlson LG: Hospital length of stay of frail elderly patients. *J Am Geriatr Soc* 36:202, 1988.

22. Fretwell MD: Management alternatives for the geriatric population. *MATRIX* 1(3), 1988.

23. Williams ME, Williams TF, Zimmer JG et al: How does the team approach to out-patient geriatric evaluation compare with traditional care: A report of a randomized controlled trial. *J Am Geriatr Soc* 35(12):1071, 1987.

24. Charlson ME, Sax FL, Mackenzie CR et al: Morbidity during hospitalization: Can we predict it? *J Chron Dis* 40(7):705, 1987.

25. Pompei P, Charlson ME, Douglas RG Jr: Clinical assessments as predictors of one year survival after hospitalization: Implications for prognostic stratification. *J Clin Epidemiol* 41(3):275, 1988.

26. Narain P, Rubenstein LZ, Wieland GD et al: Predictors of immediate and 6-month outcomes in hospitalized elderly patients: The importance of functional status. *J Am Geriatr Soc* 36:775, 1988.

27. Fretwell MD, Raymond PM, McGarvey S et al: The Senior Care Study: A controlled trial of a consultation/unit-based geriatric assessment program in acute care. *J Am Geriatr Soc*, in press, 1989.

Chapter 28

SURGERY
IN THE ELDERLY

Ronnie Ann Rosenthal and Dana K. Andersen

SURGICAL RISKS

GENERAL CONSIDERATIONS

There are several concerns that should influence the decision to proceed with surgery in elderly patients: the clarity of the surgical indication, including the likelihood of progression of disease; the degree of expected improvement after surgery; the hazards of the operative procedure; the likelihood of a serious postoperative complication; the practical limitations imposed on the patient by the disease process; and the needs of the patient to maintain a maximum level of activity or productivity. Nevertheless, patients and physicians frequently think of "surgical risk" as a number indicating the likelihood of operative mortality or morbidity, rather than as the balance between the results of surgical therapy and the consequences of nonoperative management. Therefore, the decision to proceed with surgery in an elderly patient is, in some terms, easier to make in the emergent situation than in the elective one, but it is more likely to have a regrettable outcome.

For example, an active 70-year-old man with occasional right upper-quadrant pain due to cholelithiasis may have elective cholecystectomy withheld because of "age," only to return later with acute suppurative cholecystitis requiring emergency operation. The reluctance to proceed with elective surgery in a mildly symptomatic patient such as this may be based on the fear that the improvement after surgery will be minimal and therefore not justify the risk of operation. However, nonoperative therapy may contribute to the progression of the disease process and result in emergency surgery. The operative mortality rate for this patient is thereby increased from less than 2 percent in the elective setting to over 10 percent under emergent circumstances.

OPERATIVE MORBIDITY AND MORTALITY

Many studies have attempted to quantitate operative morbidity and mortality in the elderly. Linn et al. reviewed 108 such studies published over the past 40 years and found enormous variations in data and conclusions.[1] Findings were difficult to evaluate because many studies failed to separate major procedures from minor procedures, or elective operations from emergent operations. In addition, most studies lacked appropriate control groups. There was general agreement among these studies, however, that operative risk in the elderly is roughly three times greater in the emergency setting than in the elective one (Table 28-1). A review of the studies by decade revealed a progressive decrease in the emergency

TABLE 28-1
Comparison of Mortality Rates by Years Published, Lower Age Included, for General Surgery

Variables	Mortality Rates		
	Overall	Elective	Emergency
Years			
1931–40	10.3	11.0	31.0
1941–50	10.8	5.0	32.1
1951–60	11.1	7.3	21.3
1961–70	14.7	9.2	29.3
1971–80	12.4	9.5	25.1
Lower age			
Under 60	8.4	1.3	—
60–69	11.3	7.5	25.7
70–79	11.4	8.2	26.7
80–89	15.1	11.3	26.6
90 and over	22.1	—	28.0
Number of studies reviewed	66	31	41

SOURCE: From Linn et al.

TABLE 28-2
Percent Mortality by Age and Operative Site

Age (years)	Elective				Emergency		
	Total	Gastro-esophageal	Colon	Biliary	Total	Gastro-esophageal	Colon
Under 40	0	0	0	0	4.5	10.1	—
40–50	0.2	0	0	4.7	6.4	0	16.9
50–60	1.0	4.4	1.9	3.1	7.9	11.6	0
60–70	1.1	2.6	2.7	5.0	14.3	27.2	12.5
70–80	1.9	3.3	8.1	5.7	6.0	0	6.3
80 +	2.3	3.0	5.9	11.8	14.8	18.3	23.3

SOURCE: From Greenburg et al.

operative risk since 1941, together with a surprising increase in elective mortality rates over the same period. Possible reasons cited for this trend included the increased numbers of "higher risk" patients undergoing elective surgery in recent years and the more extensive procedures performed on elderly patients during this period.

More recently, Greenburg et al.[2] reviewed 4900 major surgical procedures and reported mortality rates by age and site under elective versus emergent conditions (Table 28-2). This study and other newer studies confirm that there is a small but significantly increased risk of surgical morbidity and mortality associated with aging and that emergent operations carry at least a threefold greater mortality risk in all age groups, with an even greater risk of death in the elderly.

The data indicate, however, that it is not age alone, but rather the increased prevalence of additional pathology in the aged that is responsible for this increased mortality rate. For example, in a study of 357 patients over 50 years old who underwent colonic resection,[3] the preoperative incidence of associated pathologic conditions rose steadily with age such that, by age 80, only 5 percent of patients had no pathologic process other than the primary surgical illness (Tables 28-3 and 28-4). The mortality rate rose from 0 percent in patients less than 70 years old with fewer than two associated abnormalities to over 16 percent in patients over 70 with two or more abnormalities (Table 28-5). As an isolated factor, age was seen to have no effect on the mortality rate following colon resection.

Accompanying this increased incidence of additional pathologic conditions in the elderly is the normal decline in physiological function associated with the aging process. This decline limits the reserves that the elderly patient can call upon in the face of stress. While routine surgery may be well handled, the additional functional demands of a single postoperative complication are well-recognized to have a significantly negative effect on survival. Wilder and Fishbein[4] reported a 10

TABLE 28-3
Incidence of Preoperative Pathologic Conditions (Percent)

Condition	Age (years)			
	50–59	60–69	70–79	Over 80
Cardiovascular	36	52	57	85
Pulmonary	8	17	20	17
Renal	5	8	24	15
Hepatic	7	10	16	20
Nutritional	2	7	10	22
Other	13	18	21	20

SOURCE: From Boyd et al.

TABLE 28-4
Percent of Patients with Additional Preoperative Pathologic Conditions

Number of Additional Pathologic Conditions	Age (years)			
	50–59	60–69	70–79	Over 80
0	46	33	21	5
1	37	34	28	37
2	13	27	23	41
3 or more	3	8	22	15

SOURCE: From Boyd et al.

TABLE 28-5
Mortality Rates of Young and Elderly Patients Related to Number of Associated Preoperative Pathologic Conditions

	Age Less Than 70		Age Greater Than 70	
	Patients	Percent Mortality	Patients	Percent Mortality
Zero or one condition	0/160	0	1/66	1.5
Two or more conditions	5/58	8.6	11/68	16.2

SOURCE: From Boyd et al.

percent overall mortality for patients over the age of 80 if the postoperative course following a major surgical procedure was uncomplicated. The death rate jumped to 61 percent if there were any postoperative complications, illustrating the limited tolerance of these patients for metabolic demands beyond the surgical procedure itself.

ASSESSMENT OF OPERATIVE RISK

The assessment of operative risk in the elderly must be based upon a precise definition of any physiological declines in function of the individual, as well as the identification of associated pathologic conditions. With these principles in mind, several authors have attempted to establish methods that might appropriately predict surgical risk in the elderly. Djokovic and Hedley-Whyte[5] used the American Society of Anesthesiologists (ASA) Class 1 to 5 preoperative evaluation scale to evaluate 500 consecutive operative patients over 80 years of age. Mortality rates (within 1 month of surgery) rose with increasing class of risk, as expected, from less than 1 percent in Class 2 ("mild to moderate systemic disturbance and/or neonatal or octagenarian category") to 25 percent in Class 4 ("severe systemic life-threatening disorder").

While the ASA evaluation scale is more qualitative than quantitative, in experienced hands it has proved to be accurate in the prediction of operative mortality. A major advance, however, has been the introduction by Del Guercio and Cohn of an objective, preoperative evaluation technique that not only predicts operative risk but also encourages therapeutic intervention designed to reduce risk. Patients are classified into four stages based on functional cardiorespiratory status, as determined by a series of measured and derived physiological parameters obtained by peripheral arterial and central Swan-Ganz catheterization. Stage I patients are those who appear to have no functional deficit and should therefore respond to surgery much as younger patients do. In a study of 148 patients over age 65, no postoperative mortality was seen in Stage I patients.[6] Stage II patients have mild deficits that require no change in operative plan. They do, however, benefit from cardiovascular monitoring intra- and postoperatively. Stage III patients have more significant cardiorespiratory abnormalities that require a delay in surgery while therapeutic measures are taken to ameliorate these abnormalities. Stage III patients who respond to therapy are reclassified as Stage II patients, while those who fail to respond to treatment move on to Stage IV. The postoperative mortality for all patients ultimately classified as Stage II was 8.5 percent. Of those patients who were classified as Stage IV, most were treated with lesser surgical procedures or medical therapy. Of the remaining Stage IV patients who underwent surgery as originally planned, the mortality rate was 100 percent. This method of assessment has become an extremely useful therapeutic as well as predictive modality.

The risk of surgery is therefore an appropriate concern in the elderly. As the incidence of associated dysfunction and disease increases with age, so does surgical morbidity and mortality. It is inappropriate, however, for this general concern to cause surgical therapy to be withheld from those elderly patients who could benefit from it. It is more logical to direct preoperative, intraoperative, and postoperative therapy toward the amelioration of coexisting disabilities and the prevention of predictable complications.

In the sections which follow, attention is focused on the physiological limitations imposed by aging which characteristically influence the surgical patient. In addition, the specific modalities which have been shown to identify and improve these disabilities are reviewed. Special consideration is also given to disease processes which are commonly manifest or are atypical in their presentation in elderly surgical patients.

ASSESSMENT AND TREATMENT OF FUNCTIONAL ABNORMALITIES

Correct management of elderly surgical patients requires an understanding of the normal decline in physiological reserves and the common pathologic conditions associated with aging. Therapy can then be directed toward the attainment of optimal functional status of each organ system in the preoperative, intraoperative, and postoperative periods.

CARDIOVASCULAR FUNCTION

Many studies have shown that cardiovascular disease is the most common abnormality found in aged surgical patients. Forty percent of all patients over age 65 die of cardiovascular disease,[7] and approximately 50 percent of all postoperative mortality in this group can be attributed to abnormalities of the cardiovascular system.[8]

Pathophysiology

There are many age-related morphological changes found in the myocardium, conducting pathways, and valves, but the functional significance of these changes varies considerably.[7] Sclerosis and calcification are common at the aortic valve but are usually not associated with significant functional deficits. Calcification and fibrosis of the mitral valve, however, may impede propagation of depolarization down adjacent Purkinje bundles and result in conduction disturbances. These changes represent potential functional impairments which, in the resting state, are usually of no actual consequence. When the heart is stressed, however, as it is by hemorrhage, hypoxia, volume overload, or myocardial depression caused by sepsis or anesthesia, these age-related myocardial changes become quite significant. The heart maybe unable to respond to the demand for increased cardiac output with appropriate increases in rate and contractility, and circulatory failure may result.

A significant yet frequently overlooked physiological change that accompanies aging and results in perioperative cardiac arrhythmias and conduction abnormalities is the markedly decreased ability of the elderly patient to regulate body temperature.[9] The three determinants of body temperature are ambient temperature, external insulation, and the hypothalamic thermoregulatory mechanisms, which control the ability of the body to generate and conserve heat. In aging, there is a decrease in metabolic rate and a decrease in muscle activity, both of which result in decreased heat production. This decrease is compounded by disease states such as hypothyroidism, hypoadrenalism, cerebrovascular insults, and circulatory failure. In all age groups, anesthesia and surgery often cause lowering of body temperature. Anesthesia causes depression of the central nervous system (including hypothalamic regulatory centers), muscle relaxation (with decreased tone and decreased heat production), and vasodilation (which promotes evaporative heat loss). Surgery further promotes heat loss by the infusion of cool solutions, exposure of peritoneal or pleural surfaces to ambient temperatures, and increased heat losses from contact of skin with wet,

cool drapes. While these changes may be tolerated in young adults, it is well known that they are poorly tolerated in infants, and it is equally true that these changes are not well tolerated in the elderly. As the body temperature approaches 32°C in the awake patient, cerebration is impaired, respiration slows, and hypoxemia develops. Sinus bradycardia and prolonged PR, QRS, and QT intervals appear on the electrocardiogram and are soon followed by ventricular irritability and fibrillation. These arrhythmias are often difficult to correct, and, therefore, the best "treatment" is the careful avoidance of hypothermia.

Evaluation and Management

Many attempts have been made to determine cardiac-related risk in the elderly surgical patient. In a study of 1001 patients, Goldman el al.[10] assigned points to several clinical factors and laboratory findings (Table 28-6) and tabulated a score which in turn correlated with postoperative cardiovascular morbidity and mortality (Table 28-7). A history of previous myocardial infarction within 6 months of operation, which was the most significant factor, was associated with a 37 percent rate of serious postoperative cardiac complication and a 23 percent rate of cardiac death. The presence of congestive heart failure or any rhythm disturbance, but especially premature ventricular contractions (PVCs), significantly increased the risk of cardiac complications as well.

Symptoms referable to arrhythmias require preoperative control, either by medication or through the in-

TABLE 28-6
Assessment of Clinical Significance of Cardiac Risk Factors

	Criteria (Risk Factors)	% Cardiac Complications	% Cardiac Deaths	"Points"
History	Age > 70 years	11	5	5
	MI < 6 months before	37	23	10
Physical exam	S_3 Gallop or JVD*	34	20	11
	Important VAS†	17	13	3
Electrocardiogram	Rhythm other than sinus or PACs	19	9	7
	>5 PVCs/min	30	14	7
General status	Po_2 < 60 or Pco_2 > 50 mmHg; K < 3.0 or HCO_3 < 20 meq/liter; BUN > 50 or Creat. > 3 mg/dl; Abnormal SGOT; Chronic liver disease; Bedridden	11	4	3
Operation	Intraperitoneal, intrathoracic, or aortic	9.5	2.5	4
	Emergency	13	5	4

*JVD, jugular venous distention
†VAS, valvular aortic stenosis
SOURCE: From Goldman et al.

TABLE 28-7
Cardiac Risk Index

Class	Point Total	No or Only Minor Complications (n = 943)	Life-Threatening Complications* (n = 58)	Cardiac Deaths (n = 19)
I (n = 537)	0–5	532 (99)†	5 (0.9)	1 (0.2)
II (n = 316)	6–12	295 (93)	21 (7)	5 (2)
III (n = 130)	13–25	112 (86)	18 (14)	3 (2)
IV (n = 18)	26 +	4 (27)	14 (78)	10 (56)

*Documented intraoperative or postoperative myocardial infarction, pulmonary edema, or ventricular tachycardia.
†Figures in parentheses denote percentages.
SOURCE: From Goldman et al.

sertion of a pacemaker. Right bundle-branch block is a common finding and usually requires no therapy. However, when bifascicular block, second-degree block, complete heart block, or sick sinus syndrome are present, preoperative pacemaker insertion is usually indicated. The evaluation of elderly patients for previous myocardial infarction requires special scrutiny since at least 25 percent of previous infarcts are "silent."

Recent studies indicate that cardiovascular evaluation of elderly surgical patients beyond an assessment of historical, physical, and resting electrocardiographic findings may be especially valuable in the identification of patients at risk for cardiac morbidity and mortality. In a series of over 800 patients evaluated for vascular reconstructive operations, routine electrocardiogram-monitored treadmill tests detected myocardial ischemia in 27 percent of patients with no symptoms of coronary artery disease.[11] This noninvasive technique corroborated the findings of Hertzer et al., who demonstrated angiographically significant coronary artery disease in 25 percent of 1000 patients awaiting surgery for peripheral vascular disease, including 15 percent of patients who had no clinical risk factors for coronary artery disease.[12] Treadmill testing has limited usefulness in the elderly and often debilitated patient, however, and further studies have sought to establish noninvasive, non–exercise-requiring methods for the identification of high cardiac risk.

Radionuclide resting gated pool studies have been useful to stratify risk of coronary ischemia based on cardiac ejection fraction. Pasternack et al. studied 100 patients awaiting vascular reconstructive procedures and found no perioperative infarctions in patients with ejection fractions ranging from 56 to 83 percent, a 19 percent infarct rate in patients with ejection fractions ranging from 36 to 55 percent, and a 75 percent infarction rate in patients with ejection fractions ranging from 26 to 35 percent.[13] Most patients with poor cardiac ejection have clinical signs or symptoms of cardiac disease which

would lead to detailed cardiac evaluation. To identify patients at risk for cardiac ischemia who otherwise demonstrate few or no risk factors, other noninvasive studies have been employed to quantitate myocardial vascularity. Cardiac thallium scanning demonstrates myocardial perfusion; when coupled to physical stress, or pharmacologic vasodilatation, areas of impaired blood flow can be identified and further investigated with angiographic methods. The observation of impaired perfusion following administration of dipyridamole has proved to be useful in the detection of subclinical or occult coronary disease. In a series of over 100 patients being evaluated for vascular reconstructive procedures, the absence of thallium redistribution in 69 patients was associated with only two perioperative ischemic events, while the presence of a reversible defect in 42 patients was accompanied by 16 ischemic events.[14] This form of noninvasive assessment of myocardial vascular reactivity enables the identification of patients with occult disease who may be at high risk for cardiac morbidity in the perioperative period.

In the more invasive evaluation method developed by Del Guercio and Cohn, each patient underwent central venous catheterization with a Swan-Ganz flow-directed catheter, and serial pressures were measured in the right atrium, right ventricle, pulmonary artery, and the wedged pulmonary capillary. Arterial and mixed venous blood gases and cardiac output were determined, and the measured and derived hemodynamic data were tabulated as an "Automated Physiological Profile"[15] (Fig. 28-1). A Sarnoff-type ventricular function curve, demonstrating left-ventricular stroke work as a function of mean pulmonary capillary wedge pressure, was also plotted. It is of interest that only 24 percent of patients over age 65 had normal myocardial contractility as plotted on the Sarnoff curve, and approximately one-third had abnormally high arteriovenous oxygen (AVO_2) differences. The patients with high AVO_2 differences were placed in higher risk categories due to concern that even a modest

FIGURE 28-1
Automated physiological profile. (*Courtesy of LRM Del Guercio and JD Cohn.*)

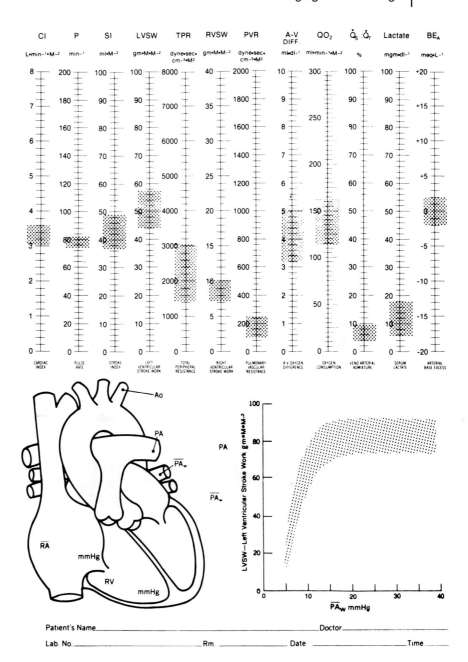

decrease in blood flow intraoperatively might result in serious hypoxia at the tissue level.

Preoperative treatment of patients with abnormal parameters was directed toward improvement of cardiac contractility, as well as volume expansion or depletion, to achieve optimal cardiac output. Pulmonary therapy was begun to improve oxygenation, and in some cases a period of parenteral nutrition was used to improve cardiac and pulmonary function. The use of Swan-Ganz catheterization preoperatively in elderly patients has now received wide acceptance and should be employed routinely.

PULMONARY FUNCTION

Pulmonary disease is the second most common disorder found in elderly surgical patients. Postoperative pulmonary complications are a major cause of mortality and morbidity, occurring in as many as 40 percent of elderly patients undergoing major surgical procedures.

Pathophysiology

The normal decline in respiratory function seen with aging is caused by changes in the chest wall and in the lung.[7] Lung volume and function change with age as the lung loses its reserve capacity. The total lung capacity remains unchanged, but vital capacity falls and residual volume increases by up to 100 percent. There is no specific oxygen transport defect that can be attributed solely to aging, and the oxyhemoglobin dissociation curve remains unchanged.[16] It is important, therefore, to include pulmonary function tests as well as standard blood gas analysis when evaluating the pulmonary status in elderly patients.

Pathologic processes prevalent in the elderly can result in special pulmonary problems which are of particular concern to surgeons. Elderly patients are predisposed to aspiration due to changes in mentation and loss of gag reflex. In the postoperative period, central nervous system depression associated with anesthesia or analgesics, combined with prolonged periods of bed rest, compounds these changes with the all-too-frequent result of aspiration pneumonia. Prolonged inactivity in elderly surgical patients may also promote venous stasis and subsequent pulmonary embolism.

Evaluation and Management

As in the case of cardiovascular disease, attention should be directed toward the identification of those patients with impaired pulmonary function. The patient's history is a significant part of the preoperative evaluation, as there is at least a twofold greater risk of pulmonary complications in patients with positive histories of smoking or preexisting pulmonary disease.[17]

Hodgkin et al.[18] have devised a method for the identification of those patients who are at risk for postoperative ventilatory failure based on their preoperative pulmonary function tests (Fig. 28-2). Those patients falling below the marginal reserve line are likely to have pulmonary problems including ventilatory failure postoperatively. Once high-risk patients are identified, preoperative efforts should be directed toward maximum improvement of pulmonary function. Abstention from smoking is essential, and preoperative breathing exercises are helpful to prevent postoperative atelectasis and the accumulation of secretions. Preoperative sputum cultures are useful in elderly patients with pulmonary abnormalities, and patients with positive cultures should be treated with appropriate antibiotics.

Low serum levels of albumin and transferrin reflect poor nutritional status, which has been shown to correlate strongly with the incidence of pneumonia postoperatively. Poor nutrition is accompanied by weakness of muscles of respiration, impairment of normal immune responses, and low plasma oncotic pressure with subsequent accumulation of interstitial fluid. Therefore, a period of preoperative nutritional supplementation may be indicated. The enteral route is preferred for nutritional

support, but if the underlying surgical condition precludes use of the intestinal tract, parenteral hyperalimentation with high-calorie, high–amino acid solutions may be necessary for the restoration of an adequate nutritional state.

Several studies have sought to determine whether routine prolonged postoperative ventilatory support is helpful in the elderly or high-risk patient. There is no evidence, however, that a mandatory period of mechanical ventilation decreases morbidity or mortality.[19] Elderly patients should therefore be extubated when standard criteria are met. Once extubated, aggressive physiotherapy which emphasizes sustained inspiratory effort using incentive spirometry is most effective in the prevention of complications. Small doses of narcotics sufficient to decrease incisional pain without causing obtundation are useful in the achievement of an effective cough. Humidification of inspired air and frequent nasotracheal suctioning should be used in those patients with feeble cough effort.

The simplest and most effective method to decrease postoperative atelectasis and venous stasis is early mobilization and ambulation. Patients over age 60 have a 25 percent incidence of pulmonary embolus as the primary cause of death, compared to a 3 percent incidence for patients under age 50.[20] Anticoagulants, including small doses of heparin, antiplatelet agents such as dipyridamole and aspirin, and antithrombotic agents, including dextran, have all been studied as prophylactic agents, and each is associated with significant complications and side effects. External compression devices, passive ma-

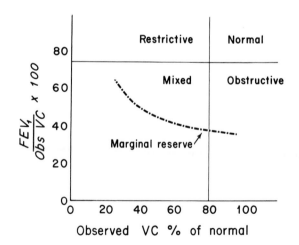

FIGURE 28-2

Modification of Miller's quadrant system for defining predictability of ventilatory insufficiency in the postoperative period. Dotted curve indicates that level below which ventilatory failure may be anticipated. FEV_1, one-second forced expiratory volume; Obs VC, observed vital capacity.

(*From Hodgkin et al.*)

nipulation, and other mechanical methods have been described to promote normal venous flow and to prevent venous thrombosis. In patients who are forced to remain at bed rest, one or more of these treatments may be necessary.[21] In the majority of patients, however, early ambulation achieves all of the benefits and obviates the expense and complications of other methods.

RENAL FUNCTION

Renal failure in the postoperative period often carries a poor prognosis and may be associated with a mortality rate as high as 56 percent.[22] The causes of renal failure in the elderly differ in some respects from those in the young, as does the management.

Pathophysiology

Between the ages of 25 and 85 there is a progressive loss of up to 40 percent of the functional nephrons in the kidney. There is scarring and sclerosis of the glomeruli and atrophy of afferent arterioles. Glomerular filtration rate falls by about 45 percent, and renal plasma flow falls approximately 50 percent by age 85.[7] There is also an abrupt rise in the incidence of urinary tract infections in patients over age 65. This is due, in part, to anatomical changes in the bladder or prostate that promote retention and stasis. The tolerance for nephrotoxic agents, as well as the excretion and metabolism of drugs, also decreases.

Evaluation and Management

With the normal age-related decrease in lean body mass, there is a concomitant decrease in creatinine production. Therefore, calculated creatinine clearance should be assessed using an age-adjusted nomogram.

Renal function may be unintentionally compromised in preoperative patients by the use of highly osmotic radiographic contrast media or as a result of keeping the patient NPO (*nil per os*, nothing by mouth) for a prolonged period of time. Ideal pre- and intraoperative maintenance of adequate blood pressure and urine flow is more easily achieved through use of Swan-Ganz catheterization for monitoring of pulmonary capillary wedge pressure.

If care is taken to maintain appropriate hydration, to avoid nephrotoxic agents, and to prevent hypotension, the incidence of postoperative renal failure can be greatly reduced. Should acute tubular necrosis occur in the postoperative period, the early use of peritoneal dialysis or hemodialysis, combined with early institution of parenteral nutritional support in a limited volume, have been shown to significantly improve survival.[23]

WOUND HEALING, IMMUNE FUNCTION, AND NUTRITION

The ability to resist and overcome infection and the ability to heal wounds are physiological functions of particular interest to surgeons. Infection is a common indication for operation, and it is a frequent surgical complication as well. Inadequate wound healing may be either a cause or an effect of infection. Since aging is accompanied by a decline in host-defense mechanisms and tissue reparative processes, any further impairment of immune responsiveness or wound healing due to nutritional deficiencies is of great significance in elderly patients.

Parameters of immune function, such as delayed cutaneous hypersensitivity, have been useful in the assessment of nutritional status in the young. Unfortunately, age-related changes in immune function have limited the usefulness of these tests in the elderly population. The biochemical indices of nutritional status do not vary significantly with age, however, and levels of serum albumin, transferrin, and retinol-binding protein have proved to be accurate indicators of nutritional status. It has been demonstrated that some immune deficiencies can be reversed and major septic complications can be significantly decreased by appropriate nutritional replacement therapy.[24]

Wound healing begins with a stimulus, to which the response is inflammation (Fig. 28-3). Initially, activation of tissue complement and the elements and products of coagulation cause changes in capillary permeability, accumulation of white blood cells and macrophages, and increased local production of proteins and enzymes. Neutrophils and lymphocytes function to control infection while activated macrophages release angiogenic factors, fibroblast growth factors, and other proteins which are thought to participate in the stimulation of epithelialization. The result of this inflammatory response is the presence at the wound site of the elements necessary for repair, i.e., fibroblasts, neovascular structures, and hypertrophic epithelial cells. The epithelial cells than migrate to cover the wound; proteoglycans, fibronectin, and intracellular connective tissue martix are produced, and fibroblasts commence collagen synthesis.

Pathophysiology

The effects of improper nutrition can be related to wound repair at several points in the wound-repair sequence. The early effects of malnutrition alter the inflammatory response and are therefore related to the nutritional effects on immune function. In the wounds of animals on protein-free diets, the cellular composition of early inflammatory exudates differs from that of control animals. It is theorized that depressed levels of certain components of complement and fibronectin, which are

FIGURE 28-3
Flow diagram of normal wound repair. (*From Hunt TK: World J Surg 4:271, 1980.*)

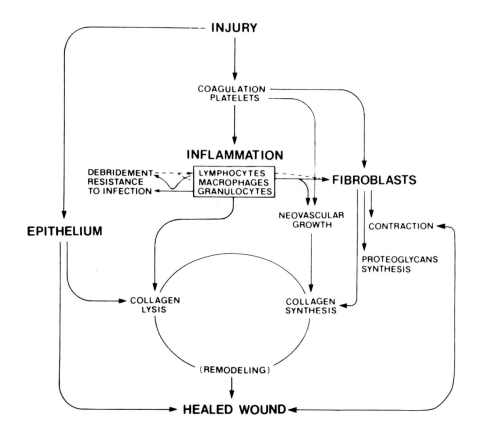

known to exert a chemotactic influence on fibroblasts and macrophages, may be partially responsible for this effect. In children with the protein malnutrition of kwashiorkor, for example, several immune cellular functions have been shown to be defective. Polymorphonuclear leukocytes show impaired in vitro bacteriocidal and fungicidal activity, and monocyte migration is slowed.

Later effects of improper nutrition on wound healing are manifest by disorders in fibroblast proliferation, collagen synthesis, and neovascularization. Protein deficiency or depletion has been shown to cause impaired fibroplasia in rats and dogs. Replacement of specific animo acids, such as methionine and cystine, in protein-depleted rats has been shown to reverse much of the impaired fibroblast proliferation and to increase collagen synthesis. Other specific amino acids, such as lysine and arginine, have also been shown to be particularly influential in rates of wound healing.[25] The deficiency of vitamin C results in impaired collagen synthesis at the level of hydroxylation of lysine and proline, while the deficiency of vitamin A retards epithelialization and decreases rates of collagen synthesis and cross-linking. Trace elements such as zinc, iron, and copper, which serve as cofactors for many enzymes, are also necessary for proper healing.

Although it is a common clinical observation that the wounds of the elderly heal more slowly and are sub-

ject to more complications than the wounds of younger people, the cellular basis for these observations has not yet been clarified. While it is often difficult to separate age-related from disease-related events, animal studies suggest that fibroblast function decreases with age, as does the tissue concentration of enzymes necessary for mucopolysaccharide synthesis. Rates of collagen formation and reorganization decline with age, and the rate of restitution of the microvascular system is slowed. In wound healing, the single most important "nutrient" is oxygen. Low tissue oxygen tension, which accompanies poor perfusion secondary to atherosclerosis or chronic congestive heart failure, impedes normal wound healing,[26] and impaired tissue perfusion is probably the most common cause of wound-healing failure. When improper nutrition and declining immune competence supervene, it is not surprising that the wounds of the elderly appear to heal more slowly and become infected more often.

Evaluation and Management

Serum total protein levels of less than 5.5 g/dl or serum albumin levels of less than 3.0 g/dl indicate poor protein intake. Adequacy of supplementation is best determined by serum assays for transferrin, retinol-binding protein, and prealbumin, which have short half-lives and therefore accurately reflect depletion and repletion.

The loss of cell-mediated immunity may be suspected in patients with total lymphocyte counts less than one-third of normal and confirmed by the absence of delayed cutaneous hypersensitivity reactions to common antigens such as *Candida* and mumps. While some elderly patients may be anergic in the face of normal nutritional parameters, this is not always the case, and a course of nutritional replacement may result in an improvement in immune function and a decrease in major septic complications and mortality.[24]

If nutritional support is necessary, it is best supplied through the enteral route, either by oral supplements or by tube feedings. If the enteral route is not available, intravenous hyperalimentation via centrally positioned catheters has become a commonly used and efficient method of reversing nutritional deficits. More specific information about the content of nutritional support solutions, both enteral and parenteral, can be found elsewhere.[27] Care must be taken not to overlook the need for good tissue oxygenation and perfusion, and measures to improve cardiac and pulmonary function should be considered part of routine preoperative nutritional planning.

SPECIFIC SURGICAL PROBLEMS

GASTROINTESTINAL DISORDERS

Although alterations occur throughout the gastrointestinal tract with aging, certain changes present primarily as surgical problems. Detailed descriptions of many disease entities can be found elsewhere in this text. The following section reviews a number of the more common surgical diseases, as well as some less common diseases which are noteworthy because of their atypical presentation.

Biliary Tract Disease

Biliary tract disease accounts for 26 to 40 percent of acute abdominal disease in the elderly and is the most common indication for abdominal surgery in this age group.[28] Autopsy studies demonstrate an increased incidence of gallstones with advancing age; 50 percent of patients over age 70 are found to have cholelithiasis. The incidence of common bile duct stones also increases with age and approaches twice the overall incidence by age 60. The complications of calculous disease likewise increase with age, such that 24 to 40 percent of elderly patients with biliary stones present with acute cholecystitis versus 7 percent of younger patients.[29]

In a recent, frequently quoted study by Morrow et al.,[30] a strong argument is advanced for early recognition and prompt surgical treatment of biliary tract disease in patients over age 60. In this series, 40 percent of patients over age 60 treated surgically for biliary tract disease presented with acute cholecystitis. Of these, 21 percent had acute suppurative cholecystitis, 18 percent had gangrenous cholecystitis, and 15 percent had a subphrenic or intrahepatic abscess. Among those patients with acute disease, the perioperative mortality was 10 percent and the complication rate was 44 percent. Those treated electively had a mortality of 2 percent and a complication rate of 22 percent.

The high mortality rate for acute disease in the elderly in the Morrow study is consistent with the 9.5 to 16.7 percent mortality rate seen in other series and reflects in part the presence of coexisting disease. Of particular significance, however, was the advanced degree of sepsis present when these patients came to operation. As is true with many other acute abdominal diseases in the elderly, atypical presenting signs and symptoms masked the true extent of the inflammatory process. Nearly one-fourth of the patients with suppurative cholecystitis had no abdominal tenderness, one-third had no temperature elevation, one-third had no elevation in white blood cell counts, and over one-half had no signs of peritonitis in the right upper quadrant. This "benign" response to severe intraabdominal sepsis led to a delay in treatment for over 24 hours in 33 percent of these patients.

It has been a common approach to manage the acute attack of cholecystitis nonoperatively with subsequent elective cholecystectomy planned following the patient's recovery. In Morrow's series of elderly patients, as well as in others, medical management failed in nearly all cases. Medical management in young patients is based on a plan which consists of close observation and repeated abdominal examinations with operative intervention indicated if abdominal signs persist or progress. Since the elderly frequently fail to show diagnostic abdominal signs even with frank pus in the peritoneal cavity, this method of management is unacceptable. There is little question now that acute cholecystitis is a surgical emergency.

Some controversy does still exist, however, about the treatment of symptomatic and asymptomatic gallstones in the elderly. Symptomatic stones are viewed by most authors to be a strong indication for elective operation as soon as the diagnosis is made. Time is allowed preoperatively for correction or treatment of coexisting disease. In patients with asymptomatic stones, elective operation is also frequently recommended; elective operation has an expected mortality of less than 1 percent unless associated diseases are so severe as to make any surgical intervention hazardous.

In light of the prevalence of biliary tract disease, the incidence of acute pathology, the insidious nature of presentation of septic complications, and the significantly increased mortality and morbidity associated with acute disease, elective cholecystectomy in the elderly can be viewed as the conservative rather than the radical approach.

Appendicitis

Appendicitis occurs far less commonly in the elderly than in the young, but it deserves special attention because of the disproportionately high mortality of 6 to 10 percent associated with its occurrence in geriatric patients. As with acute cholecystitis, this is due in part to coexisting disease, but, more significantly, it is also due to the atypical presentation of signs and symptoms. The classical sequence of periumbilical pain followed by anorexia, nausea, vomiting, and localization of pain to the right lower quadrant at or near McBurney's point is uncommon in the elderly. Instead, there is a prolonged period of vague abdominal discomfort. Nausea and anorexia are common, but vomiting is infrequent. As the inflammatory process progresses and localized peritonitis develops, pain may appear in the right lower quadrant. However, in spite of peritonitis, rebound tenderness and abdominal guarding, so common in the young, are absent in 50 percent or more of the elderly. Because of the benign nature of the initial symptoms in the elderly, there is usually a 40- to 60-hour delay before patients seek medical attention. In several published series, this delay has been shown to be compounded by a delay in diagnosis in the hospital, and as many as 40 percent of patients are *not* operated on within 48 hours of admission.[31]

Pathophysiologic changes of aging in the appendix add to the severity of the disease in the elderly. Early perforation has been attributed to narrowing or obliteration of the lumen, fibrosis, and fatty infiltration of the muscle walls, as well as to atherosclerotic changes in the artery to the appendix which result in a blood supply so marginal that minimal obstruction leads to significant edema, vascular thrombosis, necrosis, and perforation. Approximately 70 percent of appendicitis in the elderly is accompanied by perforation at the time of surgery, compared to approximately 20 percent in young adults.

Elderly patients who do well postoperatively are usually those in whom the duration of symptoms has been short, while nearly all the deaths and most of the complications are associated with longer duration of symptoms and the presence of perforation at operation. A high index of suspicion and an awareness of the insidious nature of presentation of acute abdominal pathology is mandatory in caring for the elderly patient. A decrease in the mortality and morbidity of acute appendicitis in elderly patients can be accomplished only by early hospitalization, rapid diagnosis, and expeditious surgery.

Gastric Disorders

Gastric disorders associated with aging include atrophy of the gastric mucosa, decreased acid secretion, an increased incidence of gastric ulceration, and an increased incidence of gastric cancer. Perhaps the most noteworthy consideration, however, is the management of upper gastrointestinal bleeding, which, although not more common in the elderly, is usually more severe and certainly less well tolerated. Excluding esophageal variceal hemorrhage, which is associated with significant mortality in all age groups, upper gastrointestinal hemorrhage is associated with a relatively low mortality of 3 to 5 percent in patients under the age of 60, while in patients over age 60 this mortality increases to 10 to 25 percent.[32]

As the pattern of ulcer disease changes, so does the pattern of bleeding. Gastric ulcer is a disease of the elderly that has a peak incidence in the sixth and seventh decade. Bleeding from gastric ulcers is less amenable to conservative management in general, and recurrence is not uncommon. The presence of diffuse atherosclerosis in the bleeding vessels of the elderly limits the ability of these vessels to constrict and stop bleeding either spontaneously or in response to the administration of vasoconstrictive agents.

Of primary importance in the management of upper gastrointestinal bleeding in the elderly, however, is an awareness of the decreased tolerance of the aged cardiovascular system for the severe stress of hemorrhage and subsequent hypovolemia. Himal et al.[33] analyzed a large group of patients who required surgical therapy of upper gastrointestinal bleeding. Correlates of poor prognosis were age over 60, low admission hemoglobin, greater than 6 units of preoperative transfusion, and lack of diagnosis prior to operation. The best survival was seen in patients in whom diagnosis was made early and operation was performed before transfusion of 6 units of blood was necessary. This was especially true for patients with chronic gastric ulcer, in whom recurrent bleeding is frequent and early operative therapy is accompanied by low mortality. The worst results were seen in patients who came to surgery as failures of prolonged medical therapy.

Management of the elderly patient should therefore be aggressive. Diagnostic studies should be started as soon as bleeding is recognized. Arteriography should be employed early in the course of bleeding, when it can still be used effectively as a therapeutic tool as well as a diagnostic tool. As with all other surgery in elderly patients, an elective setting is better than an emergent one. Therefore if arteriography is performed early and a bleeding site identified, a trial of arterial embolization or intraarterial vasopressin (Pitressin) may be helpful in controlling the bleeding until the patient is prepared for surgery using physiological monitoring techniques described previously.

However, Pitressin is a potent vasoconstrictor not devoid of cardiovascular effects that may limit its usefulness. Recent studies suggest that intraarterial infusion of an alternative agent, such as prostaglandin $F_{2\alpha}$, may demonstrate beneficial vasoconstrictor effects without significant cardiac side effects. The use of alternative agents is still experimental, however, and clinical trials are in progress to assess their usefulness.

If bleeding is massive or long-standing, and the diagnosis has been made by endoscopy or other means, operation should not be delayed. Arteriography as a late attempt at nonoperative management often fails, and it is in this group of failures of medical management that mortality rates are highest.

Colonic Disorders

Colon disorders related to aging are numerous and often of surgical interest. There is an increased incidence of cancer, polyps, and diverticuli. The sigmoid colon may become redundant and twist on its elongated mesentery (volvulus). Vascular degeneration may become manifest as arteriovenous malformations or venous ectasia in the cecum and ascending colon, and vascular occlusion secondary to atherosclerosis may lead to intestinal ischemia or frank necrosis. The complications of these conditions, such as bleeding, infection, and obstruction, are primarily surgical problems.

Cancer of the colon is the second leading cause of cancer deaths. Seventy percent of colon resections in elderly patients are performed for carcinoma, with a mortality rate for elective procedures of about 3 percent. When perforation or obstruction are the presenting signs, both operative and long-term survival decrease markedly. It is therefore essential to make the diagnosis early. Because chronic constipation is a common complaint in the elderly, changes in bowel habits may easily be dismissed as functional. A high index of suspicion, routine stool guaiac determinations, and yearly physical examinations can decrease the incidence of advanced disease.

In addition, however, a policy of aggressive colonoscopic evaluation of patients at increased risk for colon cancer is justified by higher discovery rates of early malignancies; when endoscopic studies are liberally employed, the percent of Dukes' A and B lesions discovered rises nearly fourfold.[34] Of greatest concern, perhaps, is the observation that the occult fecal blood test is *negative* in nearly two-thirds of patients with Dukes' A and B lesions (Fig. 28-4). The routine use of colonoscopy in elderly patients with abdominal or colonic symptoms is therefore appropriate.

Diverticuli are present in at least 40 percent of patients over age 70. Hemorrhage and infection are the most common manifestations, although obstruction also occurs. Diverticulitis presents a significant problem. Surgery is less well tolerated for diverticulitis than for other colon pathology because it is frequently performed in an emergent situation. Conservative management with antibiotics, intravenous hydration, and observation is fraught with the danger inherent in the diagnosis and treatment of acute abdominal pathology in the elderly, that is, the lack of appropriate responses to peritoneal irritation. The majority of patients do respond to conservative therapy, however, and attempts should be made to identify and treat coexisting conditions at the same time in case operation becomes necessary. Diverticuli are also the major cause of massive bleeding per rectum. However, the presence of diverticuli in an elderly patient does not necessarily mean that the source of bleeding has been found. With normal aging, there is vascular

FIGURE 28-4
Percent of patients with negative occult fecal blood tests grouped by stage of colorectal cancer. Tumors ($n = 58$) were identified by liberal use of colonoscopic evaluation in 874 patients, regardless of fecal blood status. (*From Longo et al.*)

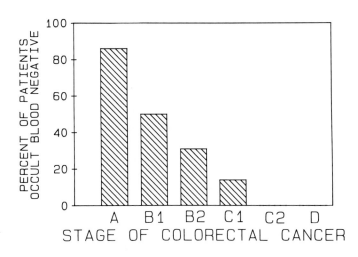

degeneration in the cecum and ascending colon, resulting in arteriovenous malformations and venous ectasias. These changes may exist without consequence, or they may be a source of massive lower gastrointestinal bleeding. Unless the diagnosis is made preoperatively and the bleeding site localized, subtotal colectomy may be necessary as the identification of the bleeding site at operation is usually impossible. Therefore, the *early* use of arteriography and ^{99m}Tc-sulfur colloid scanning to localize the bleeding site is essential in the elderly. Massive bleeding from diverticuli usually stops spontaneously. A judicious trial of nonoperative management with careful replacement of blood losses is therefore justified. Once the diagnosis is established, and if bleeding persists and surgery is required, resection is limited to the region of extravasation identified by angiography or scan.

Volvulus occurs when a redundant portion of colon twists on its elongated, narrow mesentry, forming a closed-loop type of large-bowel obstruction. Volvulus can occur at the cecum, but this is far less common than its occurrence in the sigmoid colon. Sigmoid volvulus accounts for only 5 percent of large-bowel obstruction, but the peculiarities of presentation and treatment require special consideration.

Patients with sigmoid volvulus are usually patients with severe cardiac, pulmonary, neurological, or psychiatric disorders which are accompanied by inactivity. A history of chronic constipation is nearly always present, and the colon has usually become distended and elongated over a prolonged period of time. Patients usually present with obstipation, mild crampy abdominal pain, and occasional nausea and vomiting. There is usually a history of similar episodes in the past which have resolved spontaneously with passage of large amounts of liquid stool and gas. The most striking finding is massive abdominal distension with a disproportionately mild degree of discomfort. More severe constant pain and shock occur late in the course of the disorder as the bowel becomes ischemic due to increasing intestinal-wall tension. Abdominal x rays show the loop of dilated sigmoid that has the appearance of an enormous coffee bean, and barium enema shows the typical "bird's beak" tapering of the distal bowel at the point of torsion.

Unlike other forms of large-bowel obstruction, which usually require immediate surgical decompression, 90 percent of the cases of sigmoid volvulus can be initially managed nonoperatively. Sigmoidoscopy, with passage of a rectal tube through the point of torsion, is usually met with dramatic detorsion and decompression. When this approach fails, colonoscopy may be used effectively. Because of the high incidence of recurrence, the patient is frequently considered for elective sigmoid resection. If signs of strangulation are present at initial examination or at sigmoidoscopy, or if nonoperative de-compression fails, then immediate surgical intervention is indicated. The mortality risk for nonoperative treatment and subsequent elective resection is about 8 percent, while emergency operation for strangulation has an operative mortality rate of nearly 50 percent.[35]

Acute mesenteric ischemia remains a particularly lethal form of acute abdominal pathology in the elderly, with an overall mortality of 70 percent. The ischemia can be occlusive, either from emboli or from thrombosis of vessels narrowed by artherosclerosis, or nonocclusive. The entity of nonocclusive mesenteric ischemia is now reported in 75 percent of cases, with a mortality of 90 percent. It is found in conditions that predispose to low tissue–blood flow, such as shock, myocardial infarction, congestive heart failure, cardiac arrhythmias, and liver disease, or after cardiac or major abdominal surgery. Nonocclusive mesenteric ischemia is thought to be due to splanchnic vasoconstriction secondary to a fall in cardiac output, hypotension due to hypovolemia, or to the use of vasopressor agents.

The high mortality associated with intestinal ischemia is frequently due to the severity of the diseases that predispose to nonocclusive ischemia, as well as to the delay in diagnosis which results from the benign nature of physical signs of acute abdominal catastrophies so typical in the elderly. Boley et al. advocated an aggressive approach for the diagnosis and treatment of acute intestinal ischemia in an attempt to decrease the mortality from this process.[36] They identified the characteristics of patients at risk for the development of mesenteric ischemia to be age greater than 50 years old, with (1) valvular or atherosclerotic cardiovascular disease, (2) long-standing and intractable congestive heart failure, (3) arrhythmias, (4) hypovolemia and hypotension of any etiology, and (5) recent myocardial infarction. If a patient at high risk developed sudden-onset abdominal pain of 2 to 3 hours duration, the patient was begun on a protocol of arteriography, followed by intraarterial papaverine infusion and/or surgery. Survival in this study was a comparatively favorable 54 percent overall. Ten of eleven patients who did not have peritoneal signs indicating advanced ischemia at the time of evaluation survived. Although this aggressive approach is not standard management, it does merit serious consideration for those dealing with large elderly populations.

CARDIOVASCULAR DISORDERS

In recent years, the surgical treatment of peripheral vascular and cardiac disease has been offered to patients almost regardless of age, provided that the general condition of the patient and the nature of the disease process warrant such intervention.

Peripheral Vascular Disease

Atherosclerosis is a diffuse process that is rarely limited to one area only. It is not unusual to find clinically significant cerebrovascular or coronary artery disease in patients whose chief complaints refer to the peripheral vascular system. Unless the peripheral vascular disease requires emergent treatment, as with acute arterial occlusion or impending rupture of an aortic aneurysm, treatment of peripheral disorders should be delayed until the appropriate evaluation of the cardiac and cerebrovascular status is complete. Cerebrovascular or coronary vascular disease should be corrected first if amenable to surgical therapy.

The natural history of the presenting problem is of importance in choosing the proper therapy of vascular disease. Aortic aneurysm presents as a rather urgent problem, as the natural history of an abdominal aortic aneurysm is that of expansion and rupture. Overall operative mortality for abdominal aortic aneurysmectomy is 4 to 5 percent. This mortality doubles in patients over age 75 and rises to over 50 percent if rupture has occurred. In the now classic study of abdominal aortic aneurysm, Szilagyi et al. compared 5-year survival with and without operation.[37] Fifty-three percent of operative cases survived 5 years, while only 19 percent of those managed nonoperatively survived. Thirty-five percent of deaths in the nonoperative group were from rupture. The incidence of rupture in this group was related to the size of the aneurysm. The incidence of rupture for aneurysms smaller than 6 cm was 20 percent, while aneurysms larger than 6 cm had a rupture rate of 43 percent. Size also influenced operative mortality; aneurysms 6 cm or less in diameter were associated with a 2.7 percent death rate, while those of 10 cm or greater were associated with a 22.7 percent death rate. Abdominal aortic aneurysms should therefore be treated early when both operative mortality and risk from rupture are small. In general, aneurysmectomy should be offered to patients with (1) an aneurysm 4 to 6 cm in size if the life expectancy is 10 years or greater, (2) an aneurysm of more than 6 cm in size, or (3) a symptomatic or rapidly expanding aneurysm of any size. Since most abdominal aortic aneurysms occur in patients aged 60 to 69, little controversy exists over the indication for surgery in most patients. However, in spite of the fact that the number of octogenarians with abdominal aortic aneurysm is increasing, some physicians are reluctant to refer patients over age 80 for surgical therapy. With an average life expectancy of 8.2 years for an 80-year-old patient, however, the likelihood of death from rupture of the aneurysm is greater than the risk of death from other causes and is significant enough to warrant the vascular repair.[38] Operation should be withheld only in those patients with severe physiological abnormalities or with small (less than 5 cm), nonexpanding, and asymptomatic aneurysms.

Occlusive peripheral vascular disease can be approached somewhat more conservatively. Only 6 percent of patients with lower-limb claudication alone will require amputation in 2.5 years,[39] and the amputation rate rises to only 12 percent within 10 years.[40] These patients can usually be treated initially with an exercise program to stimulate the development of collateral arterial flow. When rest pain or impending gangrene is present, treatment becomes urgent. Elderly patients usually tolerate prostheses poorly, and attempted rehabilitation after amputation is often disappointing. Surgical attempts at limb salvage are therefore worthwhile. In the past, arteriography with the attendant risk of arterial injection was required to accurately define the location and extent of arterial lesions. Doppler ultrasound, real-time ultrasonic imaging, and ocular and peripheral plethysmography now provide safe, noninvasive modalities for screening patients suspected of having vascular disease. If the presence of vascular disease is confirmed, the lesion can be visualized by digital subtraction angiography. By using venous contrast injection and computerized arterial imaging, this technique provides good definition of arterial lesions without the need for arterial injection and thus provides an alternative to routine arteriography. Once the level of disease has been determined, surgical or angiological procedures can be designed for the individual patient.

For the operative treatment of aortoiliac occlusive disease in elderly patients, the standard transabdominal surgical approach and its attendant risks of prolonged postoperative ileus and pulmonary complications may be avoided by the use of other methods. If the lesion is short and confined to one area, nonoperative balloon angioplasty may successfully relieve the obstruction and allow the patient to avoid operation completely. If the lesion is not amenable to balloon dilatation, the aorta and iliac arteries can be approached through the retroperitoneum anterolaterally. This operative approach results in far fewer gastrointestinal and respiratory complications than other approaches do. Finally, an extra-anatomical bypass, either in the form of an axillo–femoral or femoral–femoral bypass, may be performed under light general anesthesia without muscle relaxants. These bypass grafting procedures can even be performed under local anesthesia if necessary. Patency rates for these grafts, however, are not as good as for anatomically placed grafts, and they should therefore be reserved for patients with significant coexisting physiological impairment.

For arterial occlusive disease below the inguinal ligament, the availability of polytetrafluoroethylene (PTFE), a synthetic graft material, has made above-the-knee femoral–popliteal bypass grafting a simpler, shorter procedure, with long-term patency rates approaching those seen with the use of autologous saphenous vein. These procedures require only light general or spinal anesthesia and can be performed within a short operative time and with a mortality rate of 2 to 3 percent. They are, therefore, good alternatives to amputation, even in the compromised elderly patient.

Cardiac Disease

Cardiac disease remains one of the most prevalent diseases in elderly patients, and it is now well-established that age alone is not a contraindication to cardiac surgery. Coronary artery disease, valvular dysfunction, and hypertrophic myopathy all respond well to surgical treatment, with operative mortality rates comparable to or only slightly higher than those seen in younger patients and with excellent functional results.

Most studies emphasize that selection of patients is important. Good results are seen in patients who are active and have few, if any, associated diseases. Some authors emphasize mental competence, good motivation, and the ability to cooperate in the pre- and postoperative period as the most essential factors for good surgical results. Senile dementia is frequently regarded as an absolute contraindication to cardiac surgical procedures. DeBono et al.[41] studied valve replacement in the elderly and reported an operative mortality of 4.3 percent for patients over age 65, compared to 3.8 percent mortality for younger patients. This low mortality was accompanied by excellent functional results (Table 28-8).

Meyer et al.[42] reviewed the Texas Heart Institute experience with coronary artery bypass grafting in patients over age 70 and reported a progressive improvement in survival, with only one perioperative death in the last 21 patients studied. Other more recent studies confirm that mortality rates for coronary bypass in elderly patients range from 3 to 6 percent.[43] The indications for cardiac surgery in the elderly are basically the

same as those for younger patients, and operation should not be denied merely on the basis of age.

Noncardiac thoracic surgical procedures have become more common as the incidence of lung cancer has risen. Since the 1-year survival for unresected carcinoma of the lung has been reported to be as low as 7 percent, operation can only be beneficial. A recent study of 200 thoracotomies performed in patients over age 70 showed an operative mortality of only 4 percent. Overall 5-year survival was 27 percent, compared to an overall survival for all ages of 30 to 40 percent. When possible, patients were treated with lung-sparing procedures, and these patients had the lowest incidence of postoperative complications. In patients whose lesions were amenable to segmental resection, i.e., those with Stage I disease, the 5-year survival in patients over age 70 was 42 percent, compared to 53 percent for all ages.[44] In this surgical category as well, age is not a contraindication to indicated operative procedures.

REFERENCES

1. Linn BS et al: Evaluation of results of surgical procedures in the elderly. *Ann Surg* 195:90, 1982.
2. Greenburg AG et al: Operative mortality in general surgery. *Am J Surg* 144:22, 1982.
3. Boyd BJ et al: Operative risk factors of colon resection in the elderly. *Ann Surg* 192:743, 1980.
4. Wilder RJ, Fishbein RH: Operative experience with patients over 80 years of age. *Surg Gynecol Obstet* 113:205, 1961.
5. Djokovic JL, Hedley-Whyte J: Prediction of outcome of surgery and anesthesia in patients over 80. *JAMA* 242:2301, 1979.
6. Del Guercio LRM, Cohn JD: Monitoring operative risk in the elderly. *JAMA* 234:1350, 1980.
7. Goldman R: Decline in organ function with aging, in Rossman I (ed): *Clinical Geriatrics*, 2d ed. Philadelphia, Lippincott, 1979, p 23.
8. Cole WH: Prediction of operative reserve in the elderly patient. *Ann Surg* 168:310, 1968.
9. Heyman AD: The effect of incidental hypothermia on the elderly surgical patient. *J Gerontol* 32:46, 1977.
10. Goldman L et al: Multifactorial index of cardiac risk in non-cardiac surgical patients. *N Engl J Med* 297:845, 1977.
11. Arous EJ, Baum PL, Cutler BS: The exercise test in patients with peripheral vascular disease. *Arch Surg* 119:780, 1984.
12. Hertzer NR, Beven EG, Young JR et al: Coronary artery disease in peripheral vascular patients: A classification of 100 coronary angiograms and results of surgical management. *Ann Surg* 199:223, 1984.
13. Pasternack PF, Imperato AM, Riles TS et al: The values of the radionuclide angiogram in the prediction of perioperative myocardial infarction in patients undergoing lower extremity revascularization procedures. *Circulation* 72:1113, 1985.

TABLE 28-8
Functional Class Before and After Operation in 68 Patients Over Age 65

Class	Aortic Valve Replacement (AVR)		Mitral Valve Replacement (MVR)	
	Before	After	Before	After
I	1	32		22*
II	6	3	2	4
III	17	2	4	2
IV	14		24†	

*Two patients underwent both AVR and MVR.
†Three patients underwent both AVR and MVR.
SOURCE: DeBono et al.

14. Eagle KA, Singer DE, Brewster DC et al: Dipyridamole—Thallium scanning in patients undergoing vascular surgery: Optimizing preoperative evaluation of cardiac risk. *JAMA* 257:2185, 1987.

15. Cohn JD et al: The automated physiologic profile. *Crit Care Med* 3:51, 1975.

16. McConn R: Oxygen transport in the elderly and high risk surgical patient, a practical and theoretical approach, in Siegel JH, Chodoff P (eds): *The Aged and High Risk Surgical Patient: Medical, Surgical and Anesthetic Management.* New York, Grune and Stratton, 1976, p 121.

17. Garibaldi RA et al: Risk factors for post-operative pneumonia. *Am J Med* 70:677, 1981.

18. Hodgkin JE et al: Pre-operative evaluation of patients with pulmonary disease. *Mayo Clin Proc* 48:114, 1973.

19. Shackford SR et al: Early extubation versus prophylactic ventilation in the high risk patient: A comparison of post-operative management in prevention of respiratory complication. *Anesth Analg* 60:76, 1981.

20. Morrell MT, Nunhill MS: The post-mortem incidence of pulmonary embolism in a hospitalized population. *Br J Surg* 55:347, 1968.

21. Lee BY et al: Non-invasive detection and prevention of deep-vein thrombosis in geriatric patients. *J Am Geriatr Soc* 28:171, 1980.

22. Fischer JE: Renal failure, in Ballinger WF et al (eds): *Manual of Surgical Nutrition.* New York, Saunders, 1975, p 413.

23. Abel RM: Improved survival from acute renal failure after treatment with intravenous essential amino acids and glucose: Results of a prospective double blind study. *N Engl J Med* 288:695, 1973.

24. Mullen JL et al: Reduction in operative morbidity and mortality by combined pre-operative and post-operative nutritional support. *Ann Surg* 192:604, 1980.

25. Levenson SM, Seifter E: Dysnutrition, wound healing and resistance to infection. *Clin Plast Surg* 4:375, 1977.

26. Nunikosk J: Oxygen and wound healing. *Clin Plast Surg* 4:361, 1977.

27. Randall HT: Enteric Feeding, in Ballinger WF et al (eds): *Manual of Surgical Nutrition.* New York, Saunders, 1975, p 267.

28. Fenyo G: Acute abdominal disease in the elderly. *Am J Surg* 143:757, 1982.

29. Sullivan DM et al: Biliary tract disease in the elderly. *Am J Surg* 143:218, 1982.

30. Morrow DJ et al: Acute cholecystitis in the elderly. *Arch Surg* 113:1149, 1978.

31. Owens BJ, Hamit HF: Appendicitis in the elderly. *Ann Surg* 187:392, 1978.

32. Katz LA: Management of acid peptic disease in the elderly acutely ill, in Siegel JH, Chodoff P (eds): *The Aged and High Risk Surgical Patient: Medical, Surgical and Anesthetic Management.* New York, Grune and Stratton, 1976, p 278.

33. Himal HS et al: The management of upper gastrointestinal hemorrhage—A multi-parametric computer analysis. *Ann Surg* 179:489, 1974.

34. Longo WE, Ballantyne GH, Modlin IM: Colonoscopic detection of early colorectal cancers: Impact of a surgical endoscopy service. *Ann Surg* 207:174, 1988.

35. Storer EH et al: Colon, rectum and anus, in Schwartz SI et al (eds): *Principles of Surgery,* 3d ed. New York, McGraw-Hill, 1979, p 1191.

36. Boley SJ et al: Initial results from an aggressive roentgenological and surgical approach to acute mesenteric ischemia. *Surgery* 82:848, 1972.

37. Szilagyi DE et al: Contribution of abdominal aortic aneurysmectomy to prolongation of life. *Ann Surg* 164:678, 1966.

38. Treiman RL et al: Aneurysmectomy in the octogenarian: A study of morbidity and quality of survival. *Am J Surg* 144:194, 1982.

39. Imperato MD et al: Intermittent claudication: Its natural course. *Surgery* 78:795, 1975.

40. Boyd AM: Obstruction of the lower limb arteries. *Proc R Soc Med J* 55:519, 1962.

41. DeBono AB et al: Heart valve replacement in the elderly. *Br Med J* 2:917, 1978.

42. Meyer J et al: Coronary bypass in patients over 70 years of age: Indications and results. *Am J Cardiol* 36:342, 1975.

43. Richardson JV, Cyrus RJ: Elective coronary artery bypass in the elderly: Experience in a community hospital. *South Med J* 77:30, 1984.

44. Breyer RH et al: Thoracotomy in patients over age seventy years. *Thorac Cardiovasc Surg* 18:187, 1981.

GENERAL READING

Cohen JR, Johnson H, Eaton S et al: Surgical procedures in patients during the tenth decade of life. *Surgery* 104:646, 1988.

Del Guercio LRM, JD Cohn: Monitoring: Methods and significance. *Surg Clin North Am* 56:977, 1976.

Goldman L: Cardiac risks and complications of noncardiac surgery. *Ann Surg* 198:780, 1983.

Greenfield LJ (ed): *Surgery in the Aged.* Philadelphia, Saunders, 1975.

Johnson JC: The medical evaluation and management of the elderly surgical patient. *J Am Geriatr Soc* 31:621, 1983.

Siegel JH, Chodoff P (eds): *The Aged and High Risk Surgical Patient: Medical, Surgical and Anesthetic Management.* New York, Grune and Stratton, 1976.

Chapter 29

ANESTHESIA FOR THE ELDERLY PATIENT

Raymond C. Roy

We will search in vain for scientific evidence demonstrating that this or that convention will indeed improve the lot of our average patient. Nevertheless, such conventions prepared by recognized experts, published by widely respected groups and obviously with the best of intentions of improving the safety of anesthesia will assume a life of their own.

J.S. Gravenstein

Although operative risk is frequently equated to surgical risk, it is really a combination of surgical and anesthetic risks. The prospective evaluation of the effect of anesthetic management on outcome has only recently become the focus of research.[1,2] The pessimist would say that the conclusions to date can be summarized by the introductory quote.[3] The optimist would say that the appropriate questions are finally being addressed with sufficient rigor. The purpose of this chapter will be to present some of this new information in such a way as to help the internist understand how the anesthesiologist approaches the geriatric patient.

OPERATIVE RISK IN PERSPECTIVE

The overall mortality and morbidity of any operative procedure depends on four major risk factors: chronological age, coexisting disease, the surgery, and perioperative care which includes management of anesthesia. Chronological age is not considered a major risk factor until the patient enters his ninth decade.[4] A more important risk factor is the presence and severity of coexisting disease. In a study of 2391 deaths associated with 108,878 anesthetics, the mortality rate for elective operations increased 25-fold in the presence of congestive heart failure, 15-fold with chronic renal failure, 12-fold with ischemic heart disease, and 8-fold with chronic obstructive pulmonary disease.[5] Then, of course, not all operations are associated with the same risks. Mortality

statistics for 301 procedures performed in patients 90 years of age or older are presented in Table 29-1.[6]

Perioperative care can be subdivided into preoperative preparation, premedication, anesthetic management, postoperative analgesia, and postoperative management. In a review of all deaths within 24 hours of surgery, in New South Wales, Australia, between the years 1970 and 1985, poor preoperative preparation was implicated in 40 percent of the cases in which surgery and anesthesia contributed to death.[7] Similarly, in the Confidential Enquiry into Perioperative Death (CEPOD) from the United Kingdom, poor preoperative preparation was implicated in one-third of deaths.[8] The most important aspect of preoperative preparation is the restoration of a normal intravascular volume in patients who are hypovolemic because of dehydration, bowel disorders, sepsis, or blood loss or who are hypervolemic because of congestive heart failure.

The importance of postoperative management is obvious from the differences between the 2- and 30-day mortality rates (Table 29-1). It is particularly important

TABLE 29-1

Percent of Perioperative Mortality in Patients ≥90 Years of Age (n = 301)

Type of Surgery	Mortality After 2 Days, %	Mortality After 30 Days, %
Major vascular	20.0	20.0
Thoracotomy	12.5	37.5
Biliary, liver	6.7	26.7
Bowel, rectal, anal	3.8	23.8
Hip	2.7	8.2
Transurethral prostatic resection, eye	0.0	0.0

SOURCE: From Warner et al.[6]

to recognize that the postoperative patient is different physiologically from the preoperative patient. For example, abdominal surgery significantly reduces vital capacity, functional residual capacity, and arterial oxygen saturation for several days.[9,10] Postoperative complications are more likely to occur in patients with preexisting disease. Not surprisingly, these complications tend to occur in the same organ system affected by the preexisting disease.[11] Postoperative complications are also more likely to occur in patients who have intraoperative problems such as hypertension, hypotension, myocardial ischemia, and dysrhythmias.[11] Prolongation of intense intraoperative monitoring well into the postoperative period may permit recognition of premorbid or morbid events in time for them to be treated and prevent progression to major sequelae. Support for this management philosophy appeared in a study of patients presenting for surgery within 3 months of a myocardial infarction.[12]

If you were to list three of the major risk factors according to their relative contribution to perioperative morbidity, the severity of a coexisting disease would rank first, the surgical procedure would be next, and chronological age would be last. Where does anesthesia—the other risk factor—fit into all of this?

ANESTHETIC RISK

Anesthetic risk can be subdivided into two categories: obvious and subtle. Examples of obvious anesthetic risk are those delineated in the anesthesia consent form written for the layperson (Fig. 29-1).

OBVIOUS ANESTHETIC RISK

In three recent well-conducted prospective studies, the incidence of serious obvious anesthetic complications was low compared to the overall mortality and morbidity rate.[13–15] For example, only 83 episodes of aspiration were observed during 185,358 anesthetic procedures

FIGURE 29-1
Anesthesia consent form.

I understand that in addition to the risks of surgery, anesthesia carries its own risks, but I request the use of anesthetics for my own protection and pain relief. I realize that the type and form of anesthesia may have to be changed before or during the surgery, possibly without explanation to me. Such changes would be made for my own protection and benefit.

A doctor from the anesthesia department has explained to me that there may be complications resulting from the use of *any* anesthetic, and I understand that these complications may include AMONG OTHERS the following:

1. Nausea and vomiting
2. Headache
3. Back pain
4. Damage to blood vessels
5. Dental damage
6. Damage to eyes, nose, or skin
7. Sore throat
8. Vocal cord injury
9. Windpipe injury
10. Respiratory problems
11. Drug reactions
12. Infection
13. Nerve injury
14. Paralysis
15. Brain damage
16. Heart injury
17. Death
18. Damage to baby if you are pregnant now

I understand that medical care is not an exact science and that no guarantee is made as to the outcome of the administration of anesthesia. I have been given an explanation of the proposed plan of anesthesia and have been given the opportunity to ask questions about it as well as alternative forms of anesthesia. I have been given an explanation of the procedures and techniques to be used, as well as the risks and hazards involved, and I believe that I have sufficient information to give this informed consent.

I certify that this form has been fully explained to me, that I have read it or have had it read to me, and that I understand its contents.

_____
Patient or person authorized
to consent for patient

_____
Date and time

I have discussed the contents of this form with the patient, as well as the risks, hazards, and potential complications of anesthesia, in addition to the alternatives to anesthesia.

_____
Physician Signature

_____
Date and time

(0.04 percent), and only 4 of these resulted in death (0.002 percent).[13] The incidence of intraoperative cardiac arrest was 79 occurrences in 112,721 anesthetic procedures (0.07 percent).[14] The incidence of major complications partially or totally related to anesthesia, including aspiration, postoperative respiratory depression, complications of intubation, anaphylactoid shock, severe arrhythmias, myocardial infarction, cardiac arrest, pulmonary edema, coma, and death was 268 complications during 198,103 anesthetic procedures (0.14 percent).[15] The relative risk of complications increased from 1 in the age group 1 to 14 years (0.4 complications per 1000) to 4.7 for ages 55 to 64, to 8.0 for ages 65 to 74, to 13 for those 75 or older (5.2 major complications per 1000).

But, equating increased risk with advanced age is misleading. In healthy patients, the major anesthetic complication rate increases very little as the population ages so that it remains less than 0.2 percent (Fig. 29-2). As the number and severity of coexisting diseases increase, as it does with advancing age, the likelihood of an obvious major anesthetic complication increases to around 1 percent. Thus, a 5- to 6-fold increase in the complication rate is seen with the acquisition of chronic disease as compared to a 1.5-fold increase associated with aging in the absence of disease.[15]

The above studies define a basal anesthetic risk which is significantly lower than overall operative risk. This good news creates a problem for the anesthesia community. To define a complication as clearly anesthesia-related is to imply fault. In a recent closed claims study of deaths during spinal anesthesia, a "new" or "unappreciated" mechanism was proposed.[16] An editorial applauded this concept that not all events leading to bad outcomes are fully understood.[17] Letters appeared disagreeing and supporting the view that these were entirely avoidable errors in management.[18] In England and Australia where it is more readily accepted that disease affects outcome, the obvious contribution of anesthetics to

mortality is 10 percent, surgery 20 percent, and the disease 70 percent.[7,8]

SUBTLE ANESTHETIC RISK

Subtle anesthetic risk is the choice of a technique which increases the likelihood of a premorbid or morbid event occurring over another technique, even though either technique is considered acceptable. Unfortunately, in this area there are more preconceptions than solid information. If a reduction in morbidity could be demonstrated, some of the above 70 percent could be reassigned to the anesthesia category.

If one wanted to randomize patients presenting for surgery associated with a mortality rate of 1 percent to a variation in anesthetic technique that reduced mortality from 1 percent to 0.5 percent, approximately 7400 patients would have to be studied.[1] Thus, studies of subtle anesthetic risk fall into two categories: larger studies using death or major anesthetic morbidity as markers and smaller studies using premorbid events as markers. For example, rather than choose an infrequent outcome such as death or myocardial infarction to monitor, a more frequent outcome such as the number and duration of ischemic episodes is followed. The assumption is then made that a reduction in the frequency of ischemic episodes reduces the incidence of infarction or death.

In summary, the elderly comprise a more heterogeneous population than patients between the ages of 20 and 40.[19] Certain clinical conditions that are present preoperatively are associated with greater postoperative morbidity. Some operations are associated with greater risk than others. Thus, we should draw conclusions regarding the relative superiority of a particular anesthetic technique only from prospective randomized studies, which compare two anesthetic techniques for one specific operation in an elderly population made more homogeneous by selecting only those with similar ages and

FIGURE 29-2
The anesthetic complication rate increases very little with advancing age in the absence of coexisting disease. It increases markedly as the number and severity of coexisting diseases increase. (*Constructed from data presented by Tiret.*[15])

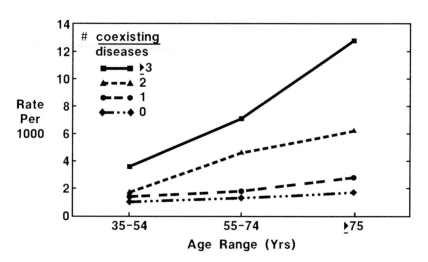

preoperative clinical states. Superiority of a technique is defined as reduced mortality, morbidity, or cost. Premedication[20] and postoperative analgesia[21] must also be controlled as they significantly impact on anesthetic problems and outcome.

REGIONAL VERSUS GENERAL ANESTHESIA

Theoretical Benefits

There is a strongly held clinical impression that regional anesthesia is intrinsically safer than general anesthesia in the elderly when either would be a reasonable choice for a particular operation. Most anesthesiologists themselves would prefer to receive a regional anesthetic when possible if they required surgery.[22] This preference is based on the perception that regional anesthesia is associated with minimal physiologic trespass, less invasive monitoring, fewer complications, and better postoperative analgesia. It is worthwhile discussing attempts to demonstrate these theoretical benefits clinically.

Hemodynamic Changes

Significant cardiovascular changes do occur during spinal and epidural anesthesia. Both involve a major redistribution of blood volume. The denervated lower extremities gain 500 ml in blood, 250 ml from both the intrathoracic and splanchnic vasculature. Note that splanchnic venoconstriction occurs even though this vascular bed is below the level of the block. Profound hypotension occurs in those patients in whom splanchnic venoconstriction does not occur[23] or in whom the splanchnic bed is empty. Patients who are hypovolemic, elderly,[24] or hypertensive[25] are particularly vulnerable.

The definition of, and the response to, this hypotension has come under scrutiny recently. In 65-year-old patients with coronary artery disease without hypertension or heart failure, epidural anesthesia reduced mean arterial pressure (MAP) from 102 to 79 mmHg, increased ejection fraction, and improved left ventricular wall motion. When 500 ml of fluid was infused to restore the MAP, the ejection fraction decreased and the wall motion deteriorated.[26] In patients with poor left ventricular function, epidural anesthesia improved left ventricular ejection fraction from 32 to 41 percent as the MAP decreased from 95 to 79 mmHg. When ephedrine was administered to restore the MAP, the ejection fraction fell.[27] Thus, the commonly held view to keep the blood pressure intraoperatively the same as when the patient was not complaining of angina preoperatively clearly needs to be reevaluated.

The reflex tachycardia which usually occurs with hypotension and hypovolemia is absent during spinal and epidural anesthesia. Lower heart rates are observed at any given blood pressure intraoperatively relative to preoperative controls. Volume administration, or a shift of intravascular volume into the thorax with venoconstrictors, not only returns baroreceptor control to its normal setting,[28] but also undoes the beneficial effects of the regional anesthetic.[26,27] Head-up tilt in 72-year-olds during epidural anesthesia decreases blood pressure and heart rate.[29] Hypotension with bradycardia which does not respond to a head-down tilt requires epinephrine to avoid a cardiac arrest. Atropine takes too long to act in the elderly, especially in this setting of lower cardiac output, and produces an unreliable response. Volume may be required, but it also may take too long to administer to prevent a cardiac arrest.[16]

Thus, significant cardiovascular changes do occur during spinal and epidural anesthesia. The response to deviations from what are perceived to be appropriate hemodynamics is not clear. Occasionally, it may be necessary to place arterial, central venous pressure, or even pulmonary artery catheters to help make these decisions. Generally, this author prefers less volume loading in the elderly prior to spinal or epidural anesthesia than is customary with younger patients, acceptance of lower mean blood pressures (e.g., 75 to 80 mmHg), dopamine or ephedrine for hypotension in patients with congestive heart failure or during epidural anesthesia, and phenylephrine infusions to improve perfusion pressure in patients with left ventricular hypertrophy, tight coronary artery stenosis, or extracranial cerebrovascular disease.

Mortality Studies

A widely quoted prospective study in 1978 suggested that the mortality rate after general anesthesia was four times that after spinal anesthesia in elderly patients presenting for hip surgery. Although these statistics were confirmed in a follow-up study from the same institution,[30] the mortality rate for general anesthesia was much higher than that being reported from other centers.[31] Multiple prospective studies subsequently found no difference in the mortality rates between the two techniques (Table 29-2).[32,33] Thus, the reason to choose a spinal or epidural over general anesthesia must be based on differences in morbidity, cost, or ease of administration.

Deep Venous Thrombosis and Pulmonary Embolism

After hip surgery the incidence of deep vein thrombosis and pulmonary embolism is the same after regional anesthesia in patients who do not receive heparin prophylaxis as it is after general anesthesia in patients who do receive

TABLE 29-2
Prospective, Randomized Studies of Regional versus General Anesthesia for Hip Surgery

			Mortality After 28 Days, %	
Source	*n*	*Age*	*Regional*	*General*
McLaren[30]	116	76	7	28
McKenzie[32]	100	75	10	16
White[32]	40	80	0	0
Davis[32]	132	80	5	13
Wickstrom[32]	169	81	6	6
Valentin[32]	578	79	6	8
Davis[33]	538	80	7	6

prophylaxis.[34-36] If a patient is receiving heparin preoperatively for prophylaxis, regional anesthesia is relatively contraindicated. Regional techniques are not contraindicated in patients taking aspirin if their bleeding times are normal.[37] Also, continuous epidural anesthesia is safe in patients who are to be systemically heparinized for vascular procedures as long as the epidural catheter is placed in advance of the heparin administration.[38,39]

Blood Loss

A significant advantage of regional anesthesia is that it is consistently associated with less blood loss than general anesthesia in patients presenting for hip surgery,[40] transurethral resection of the prostate,[41] and large bowel anastomosis.[42]

Acute Postoperative Somnolence

Prolonged emergence from anesthesia and associated airway management difficulties in the recovery room are common in the elderly after general anesthesia and will be discussed in a later section of this chapter. There is no question that regional anesthesia administered without premedication and intraoperative sedation is associated with less postoperative somnolence than general anesthesia. However, the more sedation that is given, the less this advantage of regional anesthesia manifests itself.[43,44]

Prolonged Postoperative Somnolence or Confusion

Another widely publicized benefit of regional anesthesia is that it is less likely than general anesthesia to be associated with central nervous system changes which persist for several days postoperatively.[45] However, if premedication with anticholinergics which cross the blood-brain barrier, such as atropine and scopolamine, is omitted, and if glycopyrrolate, an anticholinergic agent which does not cross the blood-brain barrier, is substituted for atropine intraoperatively, there is an equal degree of postoperative impairment of mental performance after epidural and general anesthesia in 70-year-olds.[46,47]

Cardiac Complications

The incidence of new T-wave inversions not associated with other signs or symptoms of myocardial ischemia is 18 percent after regional and general anesthesia.[48] The incidence of ischemia has been reported to be greater after regional for lower extremity vascular surgery,[49] but the incidence of congestive heart failure was greater after general anesthesia for abdominal surgery in high-risk patients.[50] Spinal anesthesia has been associated with the relief of myocardial ischemia.[51]

Pulmonary Complications

Pulmonary complications after surgery in comparable groups of patients are primarily dependent on the type of surgery, not on the anesthetic technique. Upper abdominal surgery and intrathoracic surgery carry the highest morbidity. When respiratory function is compared after lower extremity surgery in 65-year-old patients who receive spinal or general anesthesia, there are no significant differences.[52] There was no difference in the incidence of postoperative pneumonia in 65-year-olds who underwent abdominal surgery during general anesthesia followed by systemic analgesia or during combined general-epidural anesthesia and epidural analgesia postoperatively.[53]

Wound Complications

A retrospective study from the 1970s suggested that there was a greater incidence of dehiscence of large bowel anastomoses after general anesthesia than after a combination of epidural and general anesthesia. However, a recent prospective study from the same group found no difference.[42] The incidence of wound infection was higher in high-risk patients after general anesthesia combined with parenteral narcotic analgesia than after combined epidural-general anesthesia with postoperative epidural analgesia.[50]

Anesthetic Failure

There are three components to regional anesthesia failures: (1) inability to deposit local anesthetic in the proper location, (2) incomplete or absent block despite apparent correct deposition of local anesthetic, and (3) duration or extent of surgery exceeding the duration or level of the block. A 10 percent failure rate is reasonable.[24,32,33]

Summary

Most of the theoretical benefits of regional anesthesia have yet to be clinically demonstrated. Certainly they must hold true when comparing general anesthesia to local anesthetic infiltration for excision of a skin lesion. However, they have been seriously challenged when comparing spinal or epidural with general anesthesia. It is the continuing bias of this author that, though the benefits are frequently overstated, regional anesthesia, when possible, is associated with lower morbidity in the elderly. Large prospective studies, however, have yet to demonstrate this superiority. Therefore, if an anesthesiologist prefers general anesthesia in a situation where the internist or the surgeon suggests spinal or epidural, there may be sound reasons for doing so.

WHICH GENERAL ANESTHETIC AGENT?

General anesthesia is a term encompassing a wide variety of anesthetic agents, combinations of agents, and techniques. There are no outcome studies definitively establishing the superiority of the general anesthetic technique considered best by one anesthesiologist over a different one considered best by another for the same operation in the same type patient. There is a trend in the elderly, however, to use shorter-acting agents to off-set the age-related increase in intensity and duration of effect.

POSTOPERATIVE SOMNOLENCE OR CONFUSION

Premedication

Premedication with scopolamine and atropine has already been introduced as a contributor to postoperative somnolence. Moreover, because of their anticholinergic properties, these drugs are given to animals to produce models of Alzheimer's disease. Fortunately, there exists both a substitute, glycopyrrolate, and a reversal agent, physostigmine. The intravenous administration of 1 to 2 mg of physostigmine to an elderly postoperative patient can reverse the sedative effects of anticholinergic agents, benzodiazepines, and residual concentrations of inhalational agents.[54,55] Such patients should be hemodynamically stable and adequately oxygenated and ventilated before physostigmine is given. However, it is still better to omit or to reduce the dose of anesthetic agents rather than to add routinely one more drug to the pharmacologic milieu of the elderly patient.

Relative Overdose

Most prolonged emergence from anesthesia in the elderly is a problem which develops intraoperatively with the administration of a dose of an anesthetic agent appropriate for younger patients. Compared to younger patients, the elderly require lower levels of inhalational anesthesia,[56] lower doses of both narcotics[57] and intravenous agents[58,59] to reach the same electroencephalographic endpoints, and the same initial dose of muscle relaxants.[60] Although pharmacodynamics and pharmacokinetics have been discussed elsewhere (see Chap. 21), at present the general rule seems to be that those agents with specific receptors need lower steady state concentrations in the elderly to produce the same effects as in the young (pharmacodynamic explanation). Those without specific sites of action have a pharmacokinetic explanation, e.g., a reduced volume of distribution so that a given dose yields a higher plasma concentration.

PERIOPERATIVE HYPERTENSION

An example of the hemodynamic problems with which the elderly confront the anesthesiologist is depicted in Fig. 29-3: greater hypotension with the induction of anesthesia and greater hypertension with surgical incision despite a deep level of anesthesia.[61] The swings in blood pressure are intensified in the untreated hypertensive patient. It is very important that a patient's regular antihypertensive medication be considered part of the anesthetic premedication. In addition, supplemental doses of beta blockers or clonidine are advocated to attenuate intraoperative hypertension and its consequence—myocardial ischemia.[62,63] Interestingly, chronic treatment with calcium channel blockers does not reduce the inci-

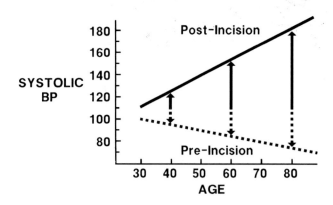

FIGURE 29-3
At equivalent depths of anesthesia, elderly patients, when compared with younger ones, show greater falls in blood pressure in the absence of surgical stimulation and greater increases in blood pressure in response to surgical incision. (*Constructed from data presented by Roizen.*[61])

dence of perioperative ischemia.[64] The major reason to use arterial lines rather than automated blood pressure cuffs is to permit tighter control of intraoperative blood pressure fluctuations with phenylephrine and nitroglycerin infusions.

POSTOPERATIVE HYPOTHERMIA

Anesthetized patients suffer a fall in temperature for four reasons: (1) decreased heat production; (2) heat loss to warm and humidify dry anesthetic gases; (3) heat loss to the environment, especially from viscera exposed to the ambient temperature of the operating room or cool irrigation fluids, e.g., during transurethral resection of the prostate; and (4) interference with the thermoregulatory process.[65,66] Elderly patients tend to cool more rapidly and rewarm more slowly than younger patients.[67]

Shivering, either as an active mechanism to rewarm or as a phenomenon associated with emergence from anesthesia,[68] is very expensive metabolically. Its effects persist for days into the postoperative period. Elderly patients who were allowed to cool to 33.6°C while undergoing bowel surgery showed greater urinary excretion of the amino acid 3-methylhistidine, an indicator of muscle protein breakdown, on postoperative day 2 and greater urinary nitrogen loss on postoperative days 2 and 4 than those whose temperature were kept above 35°C.[69] Acute shivering is associated with increased production of carbon dioxide, which, for example, may lead to respiratory acidosis in the elderly patient splinting from surgical incision and whose ventilatory response is inhibited by narcotics and residual anesthesia. Acute shivering can also be associated with decreased mixed venous oxygen saturation and hypoxia and subsequent myocardial or cerebral ischemia.[70,71] The best way to avoid these problems is to aggressively maintain normothermia intraoperatively. When cooling does occur, suppression of shivering with meperidine or muscle relaxants[72,73] and rewarming with radiant heat is recommended.[74]

POSTOPERATIVE ANALGESIA

An exciting new area of interest to anesthesiologists is postoperative pain relief,[75] formerly the domain of the surgeons. Acute postoperative pain management services now offer patient-controlled analgesia (PCA), intermittent or continuous regional infusions of local anesthetics, and continuous infusion of epidural narcotics in place of conventional intramuscular narcotics. These techniques do more than just provide superior analgesia. Intercostal nerve blocks after cholecystectomy and epidural analgesia after total hip replacement markedly re-

duced the high incidence of postoperative arterial desaturation in elderly patients.[21] Thoracic epidural analgesia also improved diaphragmatic function after upper abdominal surgery.[76] Substitution of narcotics for local anesthetics in the epidural space maintains analgesia, eliminates the sympathectomy, and enables the patient to become more mobile.

The common side effects of epidural narcotics—pruritus, urinary retention, nausea, and vomiting—are all manageable. But there is also a risk of respiratory depression, especially if conventional narcotics and sedatives are administered concurrently. Respiratory monitoring is required. A bag-valve-mask system for ventilation and naloxone must be kept at the bedside. Narcotic and sedative orders should be cleared with the acute postoperative pain management service. With these precautions, thoracic epidurals for thoracotomies and upper abdominal surgery and lumbar epidurals for lower abdominal surgery, suprapubic prostatectomies, and total hip and knee replacements are remarkably safe and effective.[75]

HYPOTENSION AND POSTOPERATIVE RENAL FAILURE

Deliberate or controlled hypotension is an accepted anesthetic technique to reduce intraoperative blood loss. Sustained mean arterial blood pressures of 50 mmHg during anesthesia for total hip arthroplasty were not associated with postoperative renal insufficiency in 60-year-old patients.[77] Unlike inadvertent or uncontrolled hypotension from hemorrhage, dehydration, or cardiac dysfunction, deliberate hypotension is a low-vascular-resistance, normal cardiac output state made possible by a normal blood volume. Hydration minimizes the effects of anesthesia on renal hemodynamics (Table 29-3) and avoids acute oliguria.[78] Moderate hypotension during anesthesia should not be viewed as a causative factor for renal insufficiency, unless it occurs concurrently with other conditions which reduce renal blood flow, such as renal artery stenosis, volume depletion, low cardiac out-

TABLE 29-3
Effect of Hydration on Renal Hemodynamics during Halothane Anesthesia[78]

	Percent of Control		
	*RBF**	*GFR†*	*FF‡*
Dehydrated	39	52	134
Hydrated	88	92	104

*RBF: renal blood flow
†GFR: glomerular filtration rate
‡FF: filtration fraction

put, aortic cross-clamping, or sepsis. Even when 2114 consecutive general medical and noncardiac surgical admissions were screened prospectively for the development or worsening of renal insufficiency, hypotension below 90/60 mmHg was a poor predictor of postoperative renal insufficiency.[79]

BLOOD REPLACEMENT

Although the absolute minimum hemoglobin is now proposed to be 8.0 g/dl,[80] acute normovolemic hemodilution to 9.0 g/dl is not tolerated as well in older patients as it is in younger ones.[81] There is also evidence that oxygen transport across stenotic lesions is better at normal hemoglobin levels than at lower levels between 8 and 10.[82] Therefore, the recommendation is to keep the minimum acceptable hemoglobin reading at 10 g/dl in the elderly surgical patient.

MONITORING

Electrocardiography

Postoperative myocardial infarction appears to be related to perioperative ischemia,[64] but most of these ischemic episodes occur in the absence of hemodynamic abnormalities.[64,83] If a reduction in the number and duration of these episodes does lead to fewer infarctions, then intraoperative monitoring of ischemia becomes essential. The unipolar or modified (bipolar) V_5 lead—the current anesthetic standard of monitoring ischemia—detects 75 percent of the episodes. Lead II, the first choice for atrial dysrhythmia detection, detects only 33 percent. The standard clinical combination of lead II and V_5 is 80 percent sensitive; the combination of V_4 and V_5 is 90 percent effective.[84]

Pulse Oximetry

All anesthesia machines now measure inspired (and frequently exhaled) oxygen tension and are equipped with low oxygen alarms. Many do not allow the administration of less than 30 percent oxygen. The major new addition to oxygen monitoring has been the pulse oximeter. With this device it has been shown that elderly patients frequently need oxygen or airway support after sedative and narcotic medications,[85] during regional anesthesia, during transport from the operating room to the recovery area, and while receiving postoperative analgesia.[21] Fingernail polishes interfere with pulse oximetry by producing an artifactual desaturation.[86] Now anesthesia personnel can suggest to their medical and surgical colleagues that they avoid hypoxia because pulse oximetry

shows patients to have low oxygen saturations preoperatively, during cardiac catheterization and other diagnostic procedures, and in the convalescent period.

Other Monitors

Arterial, central venous pressure, pulmonary artery, and indwelling Foley catheters are inserted in higher-risk elderly patients to help control the hemodynamic changes produced by anesthesia, surgery, and convalescence. The importance of temperature monitoring must be reemphasized. Improvements in less invasive monitors could decrease the use of more invasive ones which are associated with a small, but significant complication rate. For example, the combination of an automated blood pressure cuff, capnograph, and pulse oximeter may eventually reduce the number of arterial blood gases drawn and arterial lines inserted.

INFORMED CONSENT

More and more departments of anesthesia require informed consent for anesthesia separate from that for surgery.[87] A copy of the anesthesia consent form used at North Carolina Baptist Hospital is presented in Fig. 29-1. However, the ability of many elderly patients to comprehend the consent information is reduced compared to younger patients.[88] Furthermore, physical disorders in the elderly are frequently manifested by signs of an acute confusional state.[89] A signature may be obtained, but truly informed consent cannot. In these situations, it is prudent for the anesthesiologist to include family members in the consent process.

Informed consent for anesthesia cannot be obtained by nonanesthesia personnel. Further, informed consent cannot be obtained prior to a patient's preoperative evaluation by his anesthesiologist. Consultation with internists and surgeons may be necessary before the anesthesiologist can devise an anesthetic which will minimize the likelihood of untoward events. Discussion of plans to confront risk are essential in transforming the anesthesia consent form from a list of horrors to a list of precautions.

GOOD CONSULTANT

"Cleared for surgery" is a bad answer to a poorly asked question. It does not provide useful information to help manage the patient. An anesthesiologist who requests a consultation wants advice and specific recommendations. For example, in this patient do T-wave changes indicate myocardial ischemia? If so, is a cardiac work-up indicated? If not, what are they due to? Does this patient require a monitored bed postoperatively? If direct questions are not asked, the consultant should confront the anesthesiologist to find out what specifically is worrying him, i.e., make him ask those direct questions.[90]

SUMMARY

A successful surgical outcome is expected if the patient's reserve organ function is sufficient to restore homeostasis distorted by the surgery. The anesthesiologist views the elderly patient as one who has less reserve than a younger patient. Reserve is maximized with good preoperative preparation of the patient. Surgical stress is minimized with anesthesia and postoperative analgesia. Anesthesia either prevents the activation of the stress response or attenuates the manifestations of the already activated stress response. Because outcome studies have not shown any anesthetic technique to be clearly better than another in every circumstance, several reasonable approaches are always available. Regardless of the choice, the obvious anesthetic risk is almost always low enough that the elderly patient should not be denied surgery because of a fear that he would not tolerate the anesthesia.

REFERENCES

1. Brown DL (ed): *Risk and Outcome in Anesthesia*. Philadelphia, Lippincott, 1988.
2. Roizen MF: But what does it do to outcome? *Anesth Analg* 63:789, 1984 (editorial).
3. Gravenstein JS: Is there minimal essential monitoring? *Anesthesia Patient Safety Foundation Newsletter* 1:2, 1986.
4. Katz S et al: Active life expectancy. *N Engl J Med* 309:1218, 1983.
5. Fowkes FGR et al: Epidemiology in anaesthesia III: Mortality risk in patients with coexisting disease. *Br J Anaesth* 54:819, 1982.
6. Warner MA et al: Surgical procedures among those >90 years of age. *Ann Surg* 207:380, 1988.
7. Holland R: Anaesthetic mortality in New South Wales. *Br J Anaesth* 59:834, 1987.
8. Spence AA: The lessons of CEPOD. *Br J Anaesth* 60:753, 1988 (editorial).
9. Craig DB: Postoperative recovery of pulmonary function. *Anesth Analg* 60:46, 1981.
10. Dureuil B et al: Effects of upper or lower abdominal surgery on diaphragmatic function. *Br J Anaesth* 59:1230, 1987.
11. Duncan PG, Cohen MM: Postoperative complications: Factors of significance to anaesthetic practice. *Can J Anaesth* 34:2, 1987.
12. Rao TLK et al: Reinfarction following anesthesia in patients with myocardial infarction. *Anesthesiology* 59:499, 1983.

13. Olsson GL et al: Aspiration during anesthesia: A computer-aided study of 185,358 anaesthetics. *Acta Anaesthesiol Scand* 30:84, 1986.
14. Cohen MM et al: A survey of 112,000 anaesthetics at one teaching hospital (1975–83). *Can Anaesth Soc J* 33:22, 1986.
15. Tiret L et al: Complications associated with anaesthesia—A prospective survey in France. *Can Anaesth Soc J* 33:336, 1986.
16. Caplan RA et al: Unexpected cardiac arrest during spinal anesthesia: A closed claims analysis of predisposing factors. *Anesthesiology* 68:5, 1988.
17. Keats AS: Anesthesia mortality—A new mechanism. *Anesthesiology* 68:2, 1988 (editorial).
18. Abramowitz J et al: Cardiac arrest during spinal anesthesia. *Anesthesiology* 68:970, 1988 (letters).
19. Zimmer AW et al: Conducting clinical research in geriatric populations. *Ann Intern Med* 103:276, 1985.
20. Thomson IR et al: Premedication and high-dose fentanyl anesthesia for myocardial revascularization: A comparison of lorazepam versus morphine-scopolamine. *Anesthesiology* 68:194, 1988.
21. Catley DM et al: Pronounced, episodic oxygen desaturation in the postoperative period: Its association with ventilatory pattern and analgesic regimen. *Anesthesiology* 63:20, 1985.
22. Broadman LM et al: Regional vs. general anesthesia: A survey of anesthesiologists' personal preference. *Anesth Analg* 66:S20, 1987 (abstract).
23. Arndt JO et al: Peridural anesthesia and the distribution of blood flow in supine humans. *Anesthesiology* 63:616, 1985.
24. Nightingale PJ, Marstrand KT: Subarachnoid anaesthesia with bupivacaine for orthopaedic procedures in the elderly. *Br J Anaesth* 53:369, 1981.
25. Dagnino J, Prys-Roberts C: Anesthesia in the aged hypertensive patient, in Stephen CR, Assaf RAE (eds): *Geriatric Anesthesia*. Boston, Butterworths, 1986.
26. Baron J-F et al: Left ventricular global and regional function during lumbar epidural anesthesia in patients with and without angina pectoris. Influence of volume loading. *Anesthesiology* 66:621, 1987.
27. Coriat P et al: Lumbar epidural anesthesia improves ejection fraction in patients with poor left ventricular function. *Anesthesiology* 67:A259, 1987 (abstract).
28. Baron J-F et al: Influence of venous return on baroreflex control of heart rate during lumbar epidural anesthesia in humans. *Anesthesiology* 64:188, 1986.
29. Ecoffey C et al: Effects of epidural anesthesia on catecholamines, renin activity, and vasopressin changes induced by tilt in elderly men. *Anesthesiology* 62:294, 1985.
30. McLaren AD: Mortality studies. *Regional Anesth* 7:S172, 1982.
31. Coleman SA et al: Outcome after general anaesthesia for repair of fractured neck of femur. *Br J Anaesth* 60:43, 1988.
32. Valentin N et al: Spinal or general anaesthesia for surgery of the fractured hip. *Br J Anaesth* 58:284, 1986.
33. Davis FM et al: Prospective, multi-centre trial of mortality following general or spinal anaesthesia for hip fracture in the elderly. *Br J Anaesth* 59:1080, 1987.

34. Modig J et al: Thromboembolism following total hip replacement. *Regional Anesth* 11:72, 1986.

35. Turpie AGG et al: A randomized controlled trial of a low-molecular-weight heparin (enoxaparin) to prevent deep-vein thrombosis in patients undergoing elective hip surgery. *N Engl J Med* 315:925, 1986.

36. Davis FM et al: Influence of spinal and general anaesthesia on haemostasis during total hip arthroplasty. *Br J Anaesth* 59:561, 1987.

37. Benzon HT et al: Bleeding time and nerve blocks after aspirin. *Reg Anesth* 9:86, 1983.

38. Rao TLK, El-Etr AA: Anticoagulation following placement of epidural and subarachnoid catheters. *Anesthesiology* 55:618, 1981.

39. Odoom JA, Sih IL: Epidural analgesia and anticoagulant therapy. *Anaesthesia* 38:254, 1983.

40. McKenzie PJ, Loach AB: Local anaesthesia for orthopaedic surgery. *Br J Anaesth* 58:779, 1986.

41. Abrams PH et al: Blood loss during transurethral resection of the prostate. *Anaesthesia* 37:71, 1982.

42. Worsley MH et al: High spinal nerve block for large bowel anastomosis. *Br J Anaesth* 60:836, 1988.

43. Philip BK: Supplemental medication for ambulatory procedures under regional anesthesia. *Anesth Analg* 64:1117, 1985.

44. Ricou B et al: Clinical evaluation of a specific benzodiazepine antagonist (RO 15-1788). *Br J Anaesth* 58:1005, 1986.

45. Hole A et al: Epidural versus general anaesthesia for total hip arthroplasty in elderly patients. *Acta Anaesthesiol Scand* 24:279, 1980.

46. Riis J et al: Immediate and long-term mental recovery from general versus epidural anesthesia in elderly patients. *Acta Anaesthesiol Scand* 27:44, 1983.

47. Berggren D et al: Postoperative confusion after anesthesia in elderly patients with femoral neck fractures. *Anesth Analg* 66:497, 1987.

48. Breslow MJ et al: Changes in T-wave morphology following anesthesia and surgery: A common recovery-room phenomenon. *Anesthesiology* 64:398, 1986.

49. Beattie C et al: Myocardial ischemia may be more common with regional than with general anesthesia in high risk patient. *Anesthesiology* 65:A518, 1986 (abstract).

50. Yeager MP et al: Epidural anesthesia and analgesia in high-risk surgical patients. *Anesthesiology* 66:729, 1987.

51. Urmey WF, Lambert DH: Spinal anesthesia associated with reversal of myocardial ischemia. *Anesth Analg* 65:908, 1986.

52. Hedenstierna G, Lofstrom J: Effect of anaesthesia on respiratory function after major lower extremity surgery. *Acta Anaesthesiol Scand* 29:55, 1985.

53. Hjortso NC et al: A controlled study on the effect of epidural analgesia with local anesthetics and morphine on morbidity after abdominal surgery. *Acta Anaesthesiol Scand* 29:790, 1985.

54. Maister AH: Atrial fibrillation following physostigmine. *Can Anaesth Soc J* 30:419, 1983.

55. Roy RC, Stullken EH: Electroencephalographic evidence of arousal in dogs from halothane after doxapram, physostigmine, or naloxone. *Anesthesiology* 55:392, 1981.

56. Munson ES et al: Use of cyclopropane to test generality of anesthetic requirement in the elderly. *Anesth Analg* 63:998, 1984.

57. Scott JC, Stanski DR: Decreased fentanyl/alfentanil requirements with increasing age: A pharmacodynamic basis. *Anesthesiology* 63:A374, 1985 (abstract).

58. Homer TD, Stanski DR: The effect of increasing age on thiopental disposition and anesthetic requirement. *Anesthesiology* 62:714, 1985.

59. Arden JR et al: Increased sensitivity to etomidate in the elderly: Initial distribution versus altered brain response. *Anesthesiology* 65:19, 1986.

60. Rupp SM et al: Pancuronium and vecuronium pharmacokinetics and pharmacodynamics in younger and elderly adults. *Anesthesiology* 67:45, 1987.

61. Roizen MF et al: Aging increases hemodynamic responses to induction and incision. *Anesth Analg* 64:275, 1984 (abstract).

62. Stone JG et al: Myocardial ischemia in untreated hypertensive patients: Effect of a single small oral dose of a beta-adrenergic blocking agent. *Anesthesiology* 68:495, 1988.

63. Ghignone M et al: Anesthesia and ophthalmic surgery in the elderly: The effects of clonidine on intraocular pressure, perioperative hemodynamics, and anesthetic requirement. *Anesthesiology* 68:707, 1988.

64. Slogoff S, Keats AS: Does chronic treatment with calcium entry blocking agents reduce perioperative myocardial ischemia? *Anesthesiology* 68:676, 1988.

65. Flacke JW, Flacke WE: Inadvertent hypothermia: Frequent, insidious, and often serious. *Semin Anesth* 2:183, 1983.

66. Sessler DI et al: Core temperature changes during N20 fentanyl and halothane/02 anesthesia. *Anesthesiology* 67:137, 1987.

67. Vaughan MS et al: Postoperative hypothermia in adults: Relationship of age, anesthesia, and shivering to rewarming. *Anesth Analg* 60:746, 1981.

68. Hammel HT: Anesthetics and body temperature regulation. *Anesthesiology* 68:833, 1988 (editorial).

69. Carli F, Itiaba K: Effect of heat conservation during and after major abdominal surgery on muscle protein breakdown in elderly patients. *Br J Anaesth* 58:502, 1986.

70. Ralley FE et al: The effects of shivering on oxygen consumption and carbon dioxide production in patients rewarming from hypothermic cardiopulmonary bypass. *Can J Anaesth* 35:332, 1988.

71. Zwischenberger JB et al: Suppression of shivering decreases oxygen consumption and improves hemodynamic stability during postoperative rewarming. *Ann Thorac Surg* 43:428, 1987.

72. Pauca AL et al: Effect of pethidine (meperidine), fentanyl and morphine on post-operative shivering in man. *Acta Anaesthesiol Scand* 28:138, 1984.

73. Guffin A et al: Shivering following cardiac surgery: Hemodynamic changes and reversal. *J Cardiothorac Anesth* 1:24, 1987.

74. Sharkey A et al: Inhibition of postanesthetic shivering with radiant heat. *Anesthesiology* 66:249, 1987.

75. Ready LB et al: Development of an anesthesiology-based postoperative pain management service. *Anesthesiology* 68:100, 1988.

76. Mankikian B, Cantineau JP, Bertrand M et al: Improve-

ment of diaphragmatic function by a thoracic epidural block after upper abdominal surgery. *Anesthesiology* 68:379, 1988.

77. Thompson GE et al: Hypotensive anesthesia for total hip arthroplasty. *Anesthesiology* 48:91, 1978.

78. Barry KG et al: Prevention of surgical oliguria and renal-hemodynamic suppression by sustained hydration. *N Engl J Med* 270:1371, 1963.

79. Hou SH et al: Hospital-acquired renal insufficiency: A prospective study. *Am J Med* 74:243, 1983.

80. Carson JL et al: Severity of anaemia and operative mortality and morbidity. *Lancet* i:727, 1988.

81. Rosberg B, Wulff K: Hemodynamics following normovolemic hemodilution in elderly patients. *Acta Anaesth Scand* 25:402, 1981.

82. Crystal GJ, Salem MR: Myocardial oxygenation in selective hemodilution in dogs: Effect of coronary insufficiency. *Anesth Analg* 66:S34, 1987 (abstract).

83. Knight AA et al: Perioperative myocardial ischemia: Importance of the preoperative ischemic pattern. *Anesthesiology* 68:681, 1988.

84. London MJ et al: Intraoperative myocardial ischemia: Localization by continuous 12-lead electrocardiography. *Anesthesiology* 69:232, 1988.

85. Hensley FA et al: Oxygen saturation during preinduction placement of monitoring catheters in the cardiac surgical patient. *Anesthesiology* 66:834, 1987.

86. Cote CJ et al: The effect of nail polish on pulse oximetry. *Anesth Analg* 67:683, 1988.

87. Norton ML, Norton EV: Legal aspects of anesthesia practice, in Miller RD (ed): *Anesthesia*. New York, Churchill Livingstone, 1986, p. 29.

88. Stanley B et al: The elderly patient and informed consent. *JAMA* 252:1302, 1984.

89. LaRue A, Schaeffer J: Psychologic reactions of elderly patients to illness and surgery. *Semin Anesth* 5:36, 1986.

90. Goldman L et al: Ten commandments for effective consultations. *Arch Intern Med* 143:1753, 1983.

Chapter 30

PAIN MANAGEMENT IN THE ELDERLY

Kathleen M. Foley

Effective management of pain in the elderly patient presents a difficult clinical problem for physicians. Treatment of the cause of the pain should always be the initial approach, but syndromes which commonly occur in this population are not always amenable to therapy that successfully removes the cause. Further complicating the formulation of a treatment strategy is that drug therapy, which is the mainstay of treatment, has both desirable and undesirable side effects. The goals of effective pain management should be (1) to provide the patient with adequate relief of pain to undergo the necessary diagnostic and therapeutic procedures to define their pain symptoms and (2) to allow patients to function as they choose and (for the seriously ill patient) to die relatively pain-free.

Critical to developing a pain treatment approach for this group of patients is an understanding of the types of pain (somatic, visceral, deafferentation), the temporal aspects (acute or chronic), the types of patients with pain, and the common pain sites and syndromes. The general principles of pain assessment can be used as an approach to categorize patients. Before considering this approach, however, the chapter will provide a brief summary of the epidemiologic aspects of pain in the elderly.

EPIDEMIOLOGY OF PAIN

There are limited data to assess the prevalence of pain in the elderly population, and there are no extant data on the incidence of acute pain. A large population-based survey noted an age-related reduction in the prevalence of pain in all sites other than joints.[1] For acute postoperative pain, survey data suggest that elderly patients are prescribed fewer and consume fewer analgesic medications than younger patients receive, but their satisfaction with pain relief provided by a postoperative analgesic is greater.[2] Analgesic use, both opioid and non-opioid, falls with age,[3] and the elderly represent the smallest proportion of patients admitted to a pain clinic.[4] There is a difference in the type of chronic pain in the elderly, as compared to a younger population, with a shift in prevalence to particular diagnoses with osteoarthritis, the most prevalent painful condition.[1] Certain neuropathic pain syndromes occur in increasing frequency with age. These include post-herpetic neuralgia, trigeminal neuralgia, and peripheral neuropathy.[5–7] The fact that cancer is the leading cause of death in the elderly population and that one-third of cancer patients with active disease and two-thirds with advanced disease have significant pain suggests cancer pain as an important problem for elderly patients.[8,9]

Survey data, as well as studies of experimental pain, have yielded conflicting data about the pain thresholds in the elderly population,[10] but there is substantial evidence to suggest that in the clinical setting elderly patients report less pain than do younger patients.[11] For example, older patients complain of less pain after myocardial infarction.[12] There are several hypotheses concerning this observation. One hypothesis is that aging patients may actually experience less pain after a nociceptive stimulus; however, pain thresholds do not appear to change with age. The second hypothesis is that pain may be better controlled in the elderly because of enhanced efficacy of the analgesic drugs.[13,14] This aspect will be discussed in the following section on drug therapy. A third hypothesis is that elderly patients may simply report less pain and that this may be related to a combination of increased stoicism, slowness to respond to painful stimuli, and/or a mild cognitive deficit. To what extent each of these factors contributes to the perception of pain and its meaning in the elderly patient remains poorly defined. However, this dearth of data clearly indicates the need for careful expert pain assessment in this patient population.

TEMPORAL ASPECTS OF PAIN

Recent advances in the neuroanatomy, neurophysiology, and neuropharmacology of pain have provided a greater understanding of the peripheral and central nervous system mechanisms of pain.[15,16] The elderly patient will typically have pain of one or more of three types: somatic, visceral, and deafferentation.

Somatic, or nociceptive pain, occurs as a result of activation of peripheral nociceptors in cutaneous and deep tissues. The pain is typically well-localized and is frequently described as aching or gnawing. Examples of somatic pain include joint pain, myofascial and musculoskeletal pain, and, in the cancer patient, bone metastases.

Visceral pain results from infiltration, compression, distension, or stretching of thoracic or abdominal viscera and activation of nociceptors. It may be the result of a primary or metastatic tumor, or it may result from stones in the gallbladder or kidney; it may also occur with gastrointestinal ulceration. Visceral pain, which is often described as deep, squeezing, and pressure-like, is poorly localized and is typically associated with nausea, vomiting, and diaphoresis, particularly when acute. Visceral pain is often referred to cutaneous sites that may be remote from the lesion, as occurs in shoulder pain with diaphragmatic irritation in the patient with liver capsule pain. The pain may also be associated with tenderness in the referred cutaneous site.

Deafferentation pain, the third major type of pain, results from injury to the peripheral and/or central nervous system as a consequence of compression, infiltration, or degeneration of the peripheral nerve or the spinal cord which has occurred as a result of trauma, chemical injury, or toxic metabolic effect. Examples of deafferentation pain include post-herpetic neuralgia, postsurgical pain syndromes, diabetic peripheral neuropathy, and tumor infiltration of the brachial and lumbosacral plexus. Pain resulting from nerve injury is often severe and is different in quality than somatic or visceral pain. It is typically described as a constant, dull ache, often with pressure or a vicelike quality. Superimposed paroxysms of burning or electric shock sensations are common. These paroxysms of pain may be associated with spontaneous ectopic activity in either the peripheral nervous system or the central nervous system.

The pathophysiology of these three types of pain is complex and poorly understood,[15] and although these pain types frequently coexist in patients, their recognition often has direct diagnostic and therapeutic implications. For example, both somatic and visceral pains respond to a wide variety of analgesic agents and anesthetic approaches. In contrast, deafferentation pain is not well-controlled by opioid analgesics and is only partially ameliorated by the use of anesthetic blocks and/or neurosurgical procedures. Somatic and visceral pain are the most common causes of pain in the elderly population, and deafferentation pain is the most difficult and frustrating to treat in this population because of its lack of response to common analgesic approaches. It is commonly believed that the sympathetic nervous system may be involved in all three of these pain states but that it is most consistently involved in acute visceral and deafferentation pain.

Identifying the temporal qualities of pain is useful. The classification of pain into acute pain versus chronic pain is based again on an increased understanding of pain mechanisms and the recognition that the central modulation for these types of pain states may be different. In the clinical setting, awareness of these two types of pain is particularly important in the management of patients as response to treatment is often quite different for these two pain groups. Acute pain is relatively easy to recognize, is amenable to many of the therapeutic approaches, and usually follows a self-limited course in which treatment of the cause is an effective treatment for the pain.

The point at which acute pain becomes chronic is not known, but pain lasting for longer than 3 months is usually considered to be chronic pain.[17] With patients in chronic pain, the persistent pain has usually failed to respond to those modalities directed at the cause of the pain. In these patients, the pain has led to significant changes in personality, lifestyle, and functional ability. Such patients need a management approach which encompasses not only the treatment of the cause of the pain, but also treatment of the complications which have ensued in their functional status, their social lives, and their personality.[18] Post-herpetic neuralgia is a good example of this type of chronic pain syndrome in which a persistent pain has led to a demoralization of the patient and marked limitation in physical activity.[5]

TYPES OF PATIENTS WITH PAIN

Another aspect that can further help to categorize the elderly patient with pain is the consideration of the types of patients with pain. These are listed in Table 30-1.

The first group includes patients with acute or chronic pain associated with a medical illness, e.g., cancer or diabetes. In this group of patients, pain may be the overriding symptom of the medical illness, and its management should be an integral part of the primary treatment approach. Pain management should facilitate the necessary diagnostic and therapeutic interventions.

TABLE 30-1
Types of Patients with Pain

Patients with chronic pain associated with a medical illness (e.g., cancer or diabetes)
Patients with chronic nonmalignant pain and a specific pain syndrome (e.g., lumbar osteoarthritis or lumbar stenosis)
Patients with chronic nonmalignant pain associated with a neuropsychiatric disorder (e.g., depression or dementia)

The second group consists of patients with chronic nonmalignant pain and a specific pain syndrome, e.g., patients with cervical or lumbar osteoarthritis or patients with lumbar stenosis. For this group of patients, management approaches are directed at the cause of the pain, but therapeutic approaches such as surgery or drug therapy may not give the patient complete relief. Providing patients with psychological support, encouraging them to remain as functional as possible, and using analgesic drug therapy appropriately are the major approaches to treatment of this group of patients. Although psychological factors play a role in this group, they usually do not present a significant management issue. What is problematic is that these patients often have reduced vision or hearing, gait instability, or other symptoms which limit their ability to be distracted from their pain.

The third category of patients includes those patients with chronic nonmalignant pain associated with a neuropsychiatric diagnosis, e.g., patients with dementia or patients with depression who complain of pain as an overriding symptom. In this group, patients may present with complaints of a "burning mouth" or "burning vagina." Their pain complaints may also be diffuse, and a

TABLE 30-2
Common Sites of Nonmalignant Pain in the Elderly

Site of Pain	Common Pain Syndromes
Head and Neck	Trigeminal neuralgia, cluster headache, temporal arteritis, cervical osteoarthritis
Joints	Shoulder and hip osteoarthritis, rheumatoid arthritis
Lower back	Lumbar disc disease, lumbar stenosis, lumbar osteoarthritis, osteoporosis, vertebral body collapse
Extremities	Peripheral neuropathy, peripheral vascular disease, reflex sympathetic dystrophy
Cardiac	Angina
Trunk	Postsurgical intercostal neuralgia, diabetic radiculopathy, post-herpetic neuralgia
Gastrointestinal	Hiatus hernia, acute cholecystitis, irritable bowel syndrome, chronic constipation

TABLE 30-3
The Clinical Assessment of the Elderly Patient with Pain

Believe the patient's pain complaint.
Take a careful history of the pain complaint.
Assess the psychosocial status of the patient.
Perform a careful medical and neurologic examination.
Order and personally review the appropriate diagnostic procedures.
Evaluate the extent of disease in the patient with cancer.
Treat the pain to facilitate the diagnostic study.
Consider alternative methods of pain control during the initial evaluation.
Reassess the pain complaint during the prescribed therapy.
Individualize therapy.

careful workup does not reveal the etiology. In such patients, careful assessment of an early dementia and careful assessment of a masked depression are critical in order to formulate an approach directed toward the psychological factors, rather than one directed toward specific treatment for an elusive pain syndrome. Table 30-2 lists the common sites of pain in the elderly patient and some of the common pain syndromes that are seen in this group of patients. A discussion of each of these common pain syndromes is beyond the scope of this chapter. However, what is critical as part of the pain assessment in this group of patients is to define carefully the nature of the pain syndrome, distinguishing nonmalignant from malignant syndromes and ascertaining the degree of psychological component in the pain complaint. Table 30-3 presents a useful approach to the assessment of the elderly patient with pain.

CLINICAL ASSESSMENT OF PAIN

BELIEVE THE PATIENT'S PAIN COMPLAINT

In assessing the patient who complains of pain, it is of utmost importance to respect the complaint. The complaint may represent a pathologic process or may be a somatic delusion or a masked depression. Each of these possible causes must be considered and excluded. The diagnosis of the cause of the pain is not always made on the initial evaluation, and in some instances it may take several months to define the nature of the pain. Therefore, the physician should not draw conclusions too soon or label the patient with a psychiatric diagnosis. Similarly, to misdiagnose a masked depression or to fail to attend to the psychological variables associated with the pain complaint is an equally serious mistake. There is good evidence to suggest that in the majority of elderly patients organic pathology is the most common cause of pain, with psychological/psychiatric disturbances being a less prominent etiologic agent.[19]

TAKE A CAREFUL HISTORY OF THE PAIN COMPLAINT

There is no substitute for a complete history in helping to define the nature of the pain complaint. History taking should begin with the patient's description of the site of pain, its quality, the exacerbating or relieving factors, its exact onset, and associated circumstances. All of these factors can help to clarify whether the pain results from an acute or chronic process and help to categorize the specific pain syndrome.

In the patient with multiple pain complaints, each complaint should be identified and considered systematically. Defining how the pain interferes with the patient's activities of daily living, work, and social life can help place the pain complaint in the setting of the patient's illness. In our experience, the majority of pain syndromes in this population of patients can be defined from a careful history, with the medical and neurologic examination confirming the probable diagnosis. The history helps direct the medical and neurologic examination. Awareness of the referral patterns of pain is also of particular importance. Referred pain in the arm or the leg is often the first presentation of tumor infiltration of the brachial lumbar plexus. Commonly, referred pain sites are tender to palpation, and pain is often misdiagnosed as suggesting local pathology.[20]

It is also critical to verify the history with a family member, particularly in the patient who is unable or unwilling to provide sufficient information. Similarly, in the patient who is a poor historian, the family member may be able to provide essential information that alters the diagnostic approach. For the patient who does not share a common language with the physician, an interpreter should be used. In short, all attempts should be made to obtain a careful history.

ASSESS THE PSYCHOSOCIAL STATUS OF THE PATIENT

As an adjunct to a careful history of the chief complaint, the physician must assess multiple factors, including the age, sex, cultural, environmental, and psychological factors, in directing appropriate diagnostic and therapeutic approaches. From our experience in the elderly patient, the complaint of pain can rarely be assigned to psychological influences alone. In a structured interview, information gathered on the patient's prior medical and psychiatric illnesses, the current level of anxiety and depression, suicidal ideation, and the degree of functional incapacity can provide the data required to detect those patients at high risk for decompensating psychologically in the setting of a painful illness.

PERFORM A CAREFUL MEDICAL AND NEUROLOGIC EXAMINATION

A careful physical and neurologic examination will help provide the necessary data to substantiate the clinical diagnosis. However, if the physical and neurologic examinations are negative, further assessment of the patient should be directed by the clinical history alone. In this particular instance, knowledge of the types of pain syndromes which occur in the elderly population can suggest possible causes of pain and direct early diagnostic intervention. Careful examination of the site of pain may provide sufficient information to make a clinical diagnosis without detailed radiologic examination.

ORDER AND PERSONALLY REVIEW THE DIAGNOSTIC PROCEDURES

The purpose of diagnostic studies is to confirm the clinical diagnosis and to define the area and extent of pathology. The use of computerized axial tomography and magnetic resonance imaging have markedly facilitated the diagnostic workup of the elderly patient. The usefulness of specific procedures must be recognized by the physician ordering such tests.

EVALUATE THE EXTENT OF DISEASE IN THE PATIENT WITH CANCER

The onset of pain in the elderly patient with the diagnosis of cancer does not necessarily imply recurrence of disease. An evaluation of the extent of metastatic disease may help to discern the nature of the cancer pain syndrome. For example, in the patient with carcinoma of the lung who develops post-thoracotomy pain immediately following a thoracotomy for tumor resection, the presence of recurrent disease may be closely associated with the appearance of this post-thoracotomy pain syndrome. In contrast, the post-mastectomy pain syndrome, which occurs secondary to interruption of the intercostobrachial nerve, is never associated with recurrent disease in a causal manner. In the patient with previously resected carcinoma of the colon and perineal pain, an abnormal scan or a rising carcinogenic embryonic antigen (CEA) may help to confirm the fact that the lumbosacral pain represents local nerve infiltration by tumor, even in the absence of radiologic changes.

TREAT THE PAIN TO FACILITATE THE DIAGNOSTIC STUDIES

The persistence of pain debilitates the patient physically and psychologically. Early treatment with analgesics while investigating the source of pain will markedly improve the patient's ability to participate in the necessary diagnostic procedures. No patient should be inadequately evaluated because of his pain. There is no evidence to support the practice of withholding analgesics while the nature of the pain is being established. Adequate pain control will not obscure the diagnosis.

CONSIDER ALTERNATIVE METHODS OF PAIN CONTROL DURING THE INITIAL EVALUATION

A detailed description of the wide variety of methods of pain control is beyond the scope of this chapter, but those approaches commonly used are detailed in Table 30-4. The choice of the method depends on a careful assessment of the pain. Although medical therapy, specifically drug therapy, represents the mainstay of treatment, alternative methods are essential in managing some of the pain problems which occur. These methods should be considered concurrent with the use of analgesics in the management of pain, and the appropriate selection of these approaches depends on the patient's specific pain complaint. For example, in the patient with traumatic injury to a peripheral nerve, the use of autonomic nerve blocks, such as stellate ganglion blocks, can be particularly effective. In the patient with cancer of the colon and unilateral pain in the leg from tumor infiltration of the lumbosacral plexus, cordotomy should be considered as an effective procedure. In the patient with severe osteoarthritis of the hip, surgical replacement of the hip should be considered as the procedure of choice.

REASSESS THE PAIN COMPLAINT DURING THE PRESCRIBED THERAPY

Continual reassessment of the response of the patient's pain complaint to the prescribed therapy provides a useful method of validating the accuracy of the original diagnosis. In patients in whom the response to therapy is less than predicted or in whom exacerbation of the pain occurs, reassessment of the approach to treatment or a search for a new cause of pain should be considered. For example, in the patient with osteoporosis and collapse of a vertebral body, lack of rapid improvement with bedrest and bracing and the development of radicular symptoms and/or signs of myelopathy should make the physician reconsider the diagnosis and reassess the patient with the concern that the collapse may represent tumor infiltration of the vertebral body which was not apparent on the initial studies.

These general principles of pain assessment encompass the clinically relevant facts that the physician needs in order to clarify the cause of pain. Strict attention to

TABLE 30-4
Medical, Anesthetic, Surgical, and Behavioral Approaches to Pain

Type of Approach	Indications
Drug Therapy	
Non-opioid analgesics	Mild-to-moderate somatic and visceral pain
Opioid analgesics	Moderate-to-severe somatic and visceral pain
Adjuvant analgesics	Moderate-to-severe deafferentation pain
Anesthetic Approaches with Local Anesthetics	
Trigger-point injections	Local myofascial pain
Joint capsule injections	Local inflammatory joint pain
Nerve blocks:	
Peripheral	Intercostal neuralgia, acute herpes zoster
Epidural	Perioperative and postoperative pain control or peripheral vascular disease
Intrathecal	Perioperative pain control
Autonomic blocks:	
Stellate ganglion	Reflex sympathetic dystrophy with arm pain, V_1 herpes zoster
Lumbar sympathetic	Reflex sympathetic dystrophy, peripheral vascular disease, lumbosacral plexopathy
Celiac plexus block	Abdominal pain from carcinoma of the pancreas
Neurosurgical Approaches	
Neuroablative	
Dorsal root entry zone lesions (DREZ)	Deafferentation pain in nerve root distribution
Trigeminal radio-frequency lesions	Trigeminal neuralgia
Cordotomy	Unilateral malignant pain below the T1 area
Neurostimulatory	
Dorsal column stimulation	Deafferentation pain of spinal cord or peripheral nerve origin
Thalamic stimulation	Unilateral focal deafferentation pain
Neuropharmacologic	
Epidural and intrathecal opioids	Chronic midline cancer pain and for patients who cannot tolerate systemic opioids

TABLE 30-4
Medical, Anesthetic, Surgical, and Behavioral Approaches
to Pain (*Continued*)

Type of Approach	Indications
Physical Therapy Approaches	
Bracing, splinting, and mechanical devices	Arm, leg, or joint support to minimize pain and facilitate activity
Transcutaneous nerve stimulation	Manage mild peripheral nerve point pain
Full ROM* and ADL† programs	Reduce limitations at joints secondary to extremity pain
Behavioral Approaches (Cognitive-Behavioral)	
Relaxation Biofeedback Hypnosis	Comprehensive approach to manage the psychologic consequences of pain, the meaning of pain, and pain's impact on mood

*ROM, range of motion
†ADL, activities of daily living

these principles provides the physician with an approach that ensures a careful, respectful assessment of the pain complaint for both the patient and physician.

MANAGEMENT OF PAIN—DRUG THERAPY

Drug therapy with non-opioid, opioid, and adjuvant drugs is the mainstay of treatment and should be within the armamentarium of the general physician.[21,22] Other approaches, which usually involve referral to appropriate experts, will not be covered in this chapter. Such approaches include the use of anesthetic, surgical, and behavioral treatment (see Table 30-4).

CLINICAL PHARMACOLOGIC CONSIDERATIONS

In the development of specific guidelines for the use of analgesics in elderly patients, the effect of age on pharmacokinetic and pharmacodynamic responses to analgesic medications must be considered.[13,14] It is probable that all phases of drug pharmacology—absorption, distribution, metabolism, and excretion—are affected by the aging process.[23,24] Absorption may be influenced by age-related decreases in gastric acid production, intestinal blood flow, mucosal cell mass, and gastrointestinal motility.[25,26] The use of concurrent medications and the presence of other medical disease may also diminish absorption.[27] Change in drug distribution can result from

reductions in total body water, lean body mass, and serum protein, and from an increase in body fat.[25] The effect of these changes on drug distribution depends on the lipid solubility of the specific drug and its degree of protein binding. Metabolism can be affected by diminution in hepatic mass and blood flow, as well as by a reduction in enzymatic activity.[28] These changes are most apparent with medication largely metabolized in the liver, including the opioids. Drug excretion can be influenced by an age-related impairment of renal function. This process, which is often subclinical, slows the clearance of drugs in elderly patients and may result in higher plasma drug concentrations.[13,27]

Pharmacodynamic factors also affect elderly patients. Increased receptor sensitivity and concurrent alterations in mental status may account in part for the increased response of elderly patients to non-opioid and opioid drugs. The existing data demonstrate that elderly patients have a diminished ability to bind nonsteroidal anti-inflammatory drugs (NSAIDs), which are highly protein-bound, resulting in rapidly increasing free-drug concentrations after dosing has begun. Increased free-drug concentration adds to the risk of adverse effects. Eliminations of NSAIDs may also be prolonged in the elderly.[22]

The effect of age on the clinical pharmacology of patients taking opioids has been well studied. Belleville reported greater analgesia in elderly patients, as compared to younger patients, after 10-mg and 20-mg doses of morphine.[29] After single-dose morphine studies, Kaiko et al. reported higher plasma levels and slower rates of decline of drug level, suggesting a decrease in morphine clearance.[14,30] Other studies have observed a reduced volume of distribution in elderly patients, and comparable studies have reported similar changes in drug clearance and distribution with other opioids, including meperidine[31] and alfentanil.[32] In summary, alterations in drug metabolism can augment the elderly patient's sensitivity to analgesic drugs.

The guidelines for the rational use of analgesics in this population are listed in Table 30-5. Before these guidelines are discussed, certain caveats must be emphasized. Excessive use of medication should be discouraged, and each drug should have a specific rationale.[33,34] Short-acting medications are preferable to reduce side effects associated with drug accumulation. Detailed instructions to the patient with appropriate pill boxes and calendars can facilitate proper dispensing of drugs. Lastly, effective pain control requires continuous reassessment of drug effects and side effects with titration that provides analgesia that is acceptable to the patient. Of major importance is the recognition that the individualization of therapy must be the overriding consideration in the management of pain.

TABLE 30-5
Guidelines for the Rational Use of Analgesics

1. Choose a specific drug based on the type of pain, its intensity, patient's age, and prior opioid exposure
2. Know the clinical pharmacology of the drug prescribed:
   Duration of analgesic effect
   Pharmacokinetic properties of the drug
   Equianalgesic doses for the route of administration
3. Administer the analgesic on a regular basis after initial titration
4. Use drug combinations that:
   Provide either additive analgesia or reduce side effects (opioid–non-opioid, opioid + hydroxyzine, opioid + amitriptyline)
   Have special analgesic effects in certain conditions (amitriptyline, carbamazepine)
5. Avoid drug combinations that increase sedation without enhancing analgesia
6. Adjust the route of administration to the type of pain, patient status, and possible routes
7. Watch and treat the side effects appropriately:
   Respiratory depression
   Sedation
   Nausea and vomiting
   Constipation
   Multifocal myoclonus & seizures
8. Know the differences between tolerance, physical dependence, and psychological dependence
9. Manage tolerance:
   Switch to an alternative opioid analgesic
   Start with one-half the equianalgesic dose and titrate to pain relief
10. Prevent acute withdrawal:
    Taper drugs slowly
    Use diluted doses of naloxone (0.4 mg in 10 ml of saline) to reverse respiratory depression in the physically dependent patient and administer cautiously
11. Do not use placebos to assess the nature of the pain

GUIDELINES FOR THE USE OF NON-OPIOID AND OPIOID ANALGESICS

Analgesic drugs can be classified in a variety of ways as defined by their chemical receptor and pharmacologic properties, their sites and mechanisms of analgesia, and the intensity of pain for which they are generally used. Based on this concept, analgesic drug therapy can be separated into three broadly defined groups: (1) the mild analgesics, including the non-opioid analgesics and certain weak opioid analgesics (e.g., codeine, oxycodone, and propoxyphene); (2) the strong opioid analgesics, including morphine and related opioids; and (3) the adjuvant analgesic drugs, including those drugs that enhance the analgesic effects of the opioids and those which have intrinsic analgesic activity in certain situations (e.g., amitriptyline).

The mild analgesics include both the non-opioids and the weak opioid analgesics. This group, which represents a first-line approach in the management of patients with mild-to-moderate pain, includes acetaminophen, aspirin, and the NSAIDs (see Table 30-6). These drugs are commonly used orally, and tolerance and physical dependence does not occur with repeated administration. However, their analgesic effectiveness is limited by ceiling effects, i.e., escalation of the dose beyond a certain level (e.g., aspirin at 900 to 1300 mg per dose) does not produce additive analgesia. The NSAIDs have analgesic, antipyretic, and anti-inflammatory actions. Acetaminophen is as potent as aspirin as an analgesic and an antipyretic, but is less effective than aspirin in inflammatory conditions. Both aspirin and acetaminophen are the drugs of first choice because of their proven efficacy for mild-to-moderate pain at a relatively low cost. Patients allergic to aspirin do not exhibit cross-sensitivity to acetaminophen, and acetaminophen does not have the gastrointestinal, hematopoietic, and renal side effects that occur with aspirin. As a group, the NSAIDs have analgesic effectiveness equal to or greater than that of aspirin and share with aspirin the adverse effects. To date, several NSAIDs have been approved by the Food and Drug Administration for use as analgesics for mild-to-moderate pain. The NSAIDs differ among themselves in their pharmacokinetic profiles and duration of analgesic action, e.g., ibuprofen and fenoprofen. The short half-life NSAIDs have the same duration of action as aspirin. Diflunisal and naproxen have longer half-lives and are longer acting. Agents such as choline magnesium trisalicylate have anti-inflammatory properties without the impact on platelets associated with aspirin.[35]

In the elderly patient whose major pain symptoms are related to inflammatory joint disease, the use of NSAIDs for both their analgesic and anti-inflammatory properties is a common approach. It is recommended that each patient be given an adequate trial of one drug on a regular basis before switching the patient to another drug. If the analgesia is not adequate, a trial of other NSAIDs, one at a time, is appropriate. The concurrent use of two different NSAIDs is discouraged because of the available in vitro data suggesting that such combinations compete with each other for protein binding and therefore have diminished analgesic effectiveness.

A stepwise approach to the use of these drugs in patients, balancing the desirable effects of analgesia with the undesirable effects of gastrointestinal or hematopoietic risks, must be achieved. In the patient who has had an adequate trial of these drugs without achieving adequate analgesia, or in whom the non-opioid analgesic is ineffective or poorly tolerated, an opioid analgesic is considered as an alternative drug to manage such mild-

TABLE 30-6
Analgesics Commonly Used Orally for Mild-to-Moderate Pain

Drug	Equianalgesic Dose (mg)*	Starting Oral Dose Range (mg)†	Comments
Nonnarcotics			
Aspirin	650	650	Often used in combination with opioid-type analgesics
Acetaminophen	650	650	Minimal anti-inflammatory properties
Ibuprofen (Motrin)	ND‡	200–400	Higher analgesic potential than aspirin
Fenoprofen (Nalfon)	ND	200–400	Like ibuprofen
Diflunisal (Dolobid)	ND	500–1000	Longer duration of action than ibuprofen; higher analgesic potential than aspirin
Naproxen (Naprosyn)	ND	250–500	Like diflunisal
Morphine-like Agonists			
Codeine	32–65	32–65	"Weak" morphine; often used in combination with non-opioid analgesics; biotransformed, in part to morphine
Oxycodone	5	5–10	Shorter acting; also in combination with non-opioid analgesics (Percodan, Percocet), which limits dose escalation
Meperidine (Demerol)	50	50–100	Shorter acting; biotransformed to nor-meperidine, a toxic metabolite
Propoxyphene HCl (Darvon) Propoxyphene napsylate (Darvon-N)	65–130	65–130	"Weak" narcotic; often used in combination with non-opioid analgesics; long half-life biotransformed to potentially toxic metabolite (norpropoxyphene)
Mixed Agonist–Antagonist			
Pentazocine (Talwin)	50	50–100	In combination with non-opioid; in combination with naloxone to discourage parenteral abuse; causes psychotomimetic effects

*For these equianalgesic doses (see Comments) the time of peak analgesia ranges from 1.5 to 2 hours and the duration from 4 to 6 hours. Oxycodone and meperidine are shorter-acting (3 to 5 hours), and diflunisal and naproxen are longer-acting (8 to 12 hours).
†These are the recommended starting doses from which the optimal dose for each patient is determined by titration and the maximal dose limited by adverse effects.
‡ND, not determined

to-moderate pain. In this instance, codeine, oxycodone, and propoxyphene are classified as the mild opioid analgesics, and they all share the same spectrum of pharmacologic action of morphine. They are most often used in a fixed oral dose mixture with a non-opioid analgesic. They clearly have a higher analgesic potential than the non-opioid drugs, and they serve as a second-line approach in the management of pain. The major advantage of using the combination of a weak opioid with an non-opioid is that there is enhanced additive analgesia.

In order to provide patients with individualized dosing schedules, it is often better to use the components of these mixed combinations separately, e.g., titrating the dose of codeine, without increasing the amount of acetaminophen or aspirin the patient is receiving. This is a useful approach to consider in patients taking a mixture of weak opioids and non-opioids because it avoids the problem of escalation of a fixed dose combination where the additional NSAID may become excessive. The use of these drugs is particularly tailored to the presence of mild-to-moderate pain. In patients with moderate-to-severe pain, it probably is most useful to start with a weak opioid–non-opioid combination and titrate the patient to a strong opioid if inadequate pain relief is obtained. The opioid analgesics that are commonly used for moderate-to-severe pain are listed in Table 30-7. As a group, these drugs are capable of producing analgesia over a wide range of doses. There appears to be no ceiling effect to their analgesia, i.e., as the dose is increased on a logarithmic scale, the increment in analgesia appears to be virtually linear to the point of loss of consciousness.

Choose a Specific Drug for a Specific Type of Pain

All of the opioid analgesics work by binding to opiate receptors in the peripheral and central nervous system. As a group, the opioid drugs can be classified into opioid agonist drugs, which bind to the receptor and produce analgesia, and opioid antagonist drugs, which bind to the receptor and can, in some instances, reverse the effect of morphine at the receptor (e.g., the drug naloxone) or can block the effect of morphine at the receptor but can also produce some degree of analgesia. The commonly available agonist, mixed agonist–antagonist, and partial agonist drugs, as well as the plasma half-life, relative potency, usual starting dose and pertinent pharmacologic facts, are listed in Table 30-7. At times it is not clear to the physician when to consider the choice of an appropriate opioid analgesic. The first and most important rule is that *the choice of the drug should be dependent on the type of pain and its intensity.* For example, in those patients with mild-to-moderate pain who have not responded or could not tolerate a non-opioid analgesic, an

oral opioid analgesic such as codeine or oxycodone is an appropriate choice. Each drug should be given an adequate trial on a regular basis before it is considered to be ineffective.

The next step is to consider the use of one of a series of strong opioid drugs such as morphine, hydromorphone, methadone, or levorphanol. The choice of one strong opioid over another can be based on a series of pharmacologic and pharmacokinetic factors, as well as the experience of the treating physician in the use of these drugs. The exact choice of the opioid analgesic will depend upon the patient's prior opioid exposure, as well as his or her physical and neurologic status. The effective dose to control pain must be determined for each individual patient, and this is, in fact, one of the most difficult aspects in the management of pain with pharmacologic approaches.

The role of opioid antagonist drugs such as pentazocine, nalbuphine, and butorphanol are limited in the management of patients with chronic pain in whom oral drugs are considered as the major approach. These drugs do have a role to play in the acute postoperative management, but their chronic use is not recommended.

Only one drug, buprenorphine, which is a partial agonist–antagonist, is available in an oral form, specifically as a sublingual preparation. It, like the other opioid antagonist drugs, may also precipitate opioid withdrawal in patients receiving opioid analgesics for prolonged periods of time. At the current time, it is available only in Europe, but it has been demonstrated to be effective in both postoperative management and as a first-line agent in the management of patients with mild-to-moderate cancer pain.

Know the Pharmacology of the Drug Prescribed

The next important principle is to know the pharmacology of the drug prescribed. This includes an understanding of the duration of the analgesic effect, which is a result of many factors, including the dose, the intensity of pain, the criteria for analgesia, individual pharmacokinetic variation, and the patient's prior opioid experience. Table 30-7 lists the relative duration for each analgesic at the dose which produced the peak equivalent to that of morphine. It is well-recognized that drugs administered by mouth have a slower onset of action and a longer duration of effect. Drugs given parenterally similarly have a rapid onset of action and a shorter duration of effect. The pharmacokinetics of the drug can vary widely and do not necessarily correlate directly with the analgesic time course. For example, drugs like methadone and levorphanol produce analgesia for 4 to 6 hours, but these drugs accumulate with repetitive dosing, and such accumulation accounts for the untoward effects of sedation and respiratory depression. The plasma half-life

TABLE 30-7
Oral and Parenteral Opioid Analgesics for Moderate-to-Severe Pain

	Equianalgesic Dose (mg)*	Duration (h)†	Plasma Half-Life (h)	Comments
Narcotic Agonists				
Morphine	10 IM	4–6	2–3.5	Standard for comparison; also available in slow-release tablets. Reduce dose in elderly and in renal failure.
	60 PO	4–7		
Codeine	130 IM	4–6	3	Biotransformed to morphine; useful as initial opioid analgesic.
	200‡PO	4–6		
Oxycodone	15 IM	?	?	Short-acting; available alone or as 5-mg dose in combination with aspirin and acetaminophen.
	30 PO	3–5	?	
Levorphanol (Levo-Dromoran)	2 IM	4–6	12–16	Good oral potency; requires careful titration in initial dosing because drug accumulation. Use cautiously in elderly.
	4 PO	4–7	12–16	
Hydromorphone (Dilaudid)	1.5 IM	4–5	2–3	Available in high-potency injectable form (10 mg/ml) for cachectic patients and as rectal suppositories; more soluble than morphine.
	7.5 PO	4–6	2–3	
Oxymorphone (Numorphan)	1 IM	4–6	2–3	Available in parenteral and rectal-suppository forms only.
	10 PR	4–6	2–3	
Meperidine	75 IM	3–4	3–4	Contraindicated in patients with renal disease; accumulation of active toxic metabolite normeperidine produces central nervous system excitation.
	300‡ PO	4–6	12–16	
Methadone (Dolophine)	10 IM	?	15–30	Good oral potency; requires careful titration of the initial dose; drug accumulation occurs.
	20 PO	?	?	
Mixed Agonist–Antagonist Drugs				
Pentazocine (Talwin)	60 IM	4–6	2–3	Limited use for chronic pain; psychotomimetic effects with dose escalation; available only in combination with naloxone, aspirin, or acetaminophen; may precipitate withdrawal in physically dependent patients.
	180‡ PO	4–7	2–3	
Nalbuphine (Nubain)	10 IM	4–6	5	Not available orally; less severe psychotomimetic effects than pentazocine; may precipitate withdrawal in physically dependent patients.
	? PO	?	?	
Butorphanol (Stadol)	2 IM	4–6	2.5–3.5	Not available orally; produces psychotomimetic effects; may precipitate withdrawal in physically dependent patients.
	- PO	?	?	
Partial agonists				
Buprenorphine (Temgesic)	0.4 IM	4–6	?	Not available in United States in SL forms; no psychotomimetic effects; may precipitate withdrawal in tolerant patients.
	0.8 SL	5–6	?	

*IM, intramuscular; PO, oral; PR, rectal; SL, sublingual
†Based on single-dose studies in which an intramuscular dose of each drug listed was compared with morphine to establish the relative potency. Oral doses are those recommended when changing from a parenteral to an oral route. For patients without prior narcotic exposure, the recommended oral starting dose is 30 mg for morphine, 5 mg for methadone, 2 mg for levorphanol, and 4 mg for hydromorphone.
‡The recommended starting doses for these drugs are listed in Table 30-6.

for methadone is approximately 14 to 24 hours and for levorphanol is 12 to 16 hours. Adjustment of dose and dosing interval based upon the plasma half-life may be necessary during the introduction of the drug. As well, plasma half-life can be altered by compromised hepatic and renal function, and dose adjustments and dosing intervals must be individualized. In the elderly patient, one-half of the recommended dose should be given initially because of the effect of age on drug clearance.[30]

Know the Equianalgesic Dose and Route of Administration

Knowledge of the equianalgesic doses can also ensure more appropriate drug use, particularly when switching from one opioid analgesic and from one route of administration to another. Based on clinical experience, patients who have been receiving one opioid analgesic for a long period and then are switched to another opioid to provide better analgesia should be given half the equianalgesic dose of the new drug as the initial starting dose. This is based on the concept that cross-tolerance is incomplete and that relative potency of some of the opioid analgesics may change with repetitive doses.

Administer Analgesics Regularly

Another important consideration is to administer analgesics regularly, which at times may include awakening the patient from sleep. The purpose of this approach is to maintain the patient's pain at a tolerable level. The development of a steady state level may allow reduction in the total amount of drug taken in a 24-hour period. Patients receiving methadone, for example, require a smaller amount of drug than that initially prescribed to control pain once they reach a steady state level. The pharmacologic rationale for this approach is to maintain the plasma level of the drug above the minimal effective concentration for pain relief. Before a physician accepts the fact that an opioid analgesic is ineffective in a particular patient, the drug should be given on a regular basis with the interval between the doses based on the duration of effect of the drug. The time required to reach steady state depends on the half-life of the drug; for example, with morphine, steady state levels can be reached within five to six doses within a 24-hour period, whereas it may take 5 to 7 days to reach steady state with methadone. Full assessment of the analgesic efficacy of a drug therefore cannot be completed often on the first or second day. In the elderly patient, it is wise to use drugs with short half-lives in order to achieve steady state within a 24-hour period and assess the full efficacy of the drug's analgesic action.

Use a Combination of Drugs

Another important consideration is to use a combination of drugs. These are drugs that can either provide additive analgesia, reduce side effects, or reduce the rate of dose escalation of the opioid portion of the combination. Combinations that are known to produce additive analgesic effects include an opioid plus a non-opioid such as aspirin, acetaminophen, or ibuprofen[36,37]; opioid plus an antihistamine, specifically hydroxyzine 100 mg[38]; an opioid plus an amphetamine such as intramuscular dextro-

amphetamine sulfate (Dexedrine) 10 mg.[39] Studies have demonstrated the efficacy of these combinations in single-dose studies using larger doses of hydroxyzine than is often clinically used. In practice, oral hydroxyzine in 25-mg doses has been used on a regular basis with anecdotal observations of its effectiveness. Similarly, dextroamphetamine sulfate in 2.5- to 5-mg oral doses given twice a day and methylphenidate in 5- to 10-mg doses twice a day has been reported anecdotally to reduce the sedative effects of opioids in patients receiving adequate analgesia but with excessive accompanying sedation.[40] These approaches have been used predominantly in the cancer patient who is chronically receiving an opioid and achieving effective analgesia but with excessive sedation.

Several other adjuvant drugs that appear to have analgesic properties of their own include the anticonvulsants that have specific analgesic effects in certain pain syndromes.[41] These drugs are most useful in the management of patients with pain of neuropathic origin such as occurs with brachial and lumbosacral plexopathy in cancer, post-herpetic neuralgia, diabetic peripheral neuropathy, and postsurgical neuropathic pain syndromes. The mechanism of action for these drugs is suppression of spontaneous neuronal firing which occurs following nerve injury. The minimal effective dose for analgesia has not been determined; phenytoin and carbamazepine are the drugs most commonly used. The dose of carbamazepine is usually begun at 100 mg/day and very slowly titrated to analgesia to a dose of no more than 800 mg/day over a 7- to 10-day period. Elderly patients are very sensitive to this drug, and titration at 100-mg doses should be done cautiously, warning the patient about excessive potential side effects including sedation, ataxia, dizziness, and nausea and vomiting. However, this is the drug of choice for the management of patients with, for example, trigeminal neuralgia or for patients with tic-like pain associated with post-herpetic neuralgia. In chronic use with carbamazepine, blood counts should be taken before drug therapy is started, 2 weeks after initiation of therapy, and at regular intervals afterward to assess the degree, if any, of neutropenia. This effect is idiosyncratic but should be watched for when the drug is used on a chronic basis.

Another group of adjuvant drugs includes the tricyclic antidepressants. These are drugs that have analgesic properties in specific pain conditions characterized by neuropathic pain.[42] The mechanism of their analgesic efficacy is thought to be mediated by increasing levels of serotonin in the central nervous system and in part by their effect on norepinephrine modulation of pain. Amitriptyline has been the most widely studied and has been demonstrated to be effective in controlling neuropathic pain in both post-herpetic neuralgia and diabetic neuropathy.[43] The dose of amitriptyline as an analgesic varies from 10 to 75 mg. The starting dose is 10 to 25 mg for the elderly patient, with slow titration of the dose to 75 to 100 mg daily, eventually using a single bedtime dose. Of note, these drugs have significant anticholinergic effects and can precipitate acute glaucoma and also produce urinary retention. They should be used with care in the elderly population, but they do have an important role to play.

Adjust the Route of Administration to the Needs of the Patient

Another important principle of drug therapy is to gear the route of administration to the needs of the patient. The oral route of administration is the most practical, but in patients who require immediate pain relief, parenteral administration, either intramuscular or intravenous, is the route of choice. The rectal route of administration should be considered for patients who cannot take oral drugs or for whom parenteral administration is contraindicated. Several of the more novel routes of drug administration include sublingual administration,[44] continuous subcutaneous infusions,[45] continuous intravenous infusions,[46] and continuous epidural and intrathecal infusions.[47] Each of these approaches can provide the patient with a continuous dosing regimen that can be maintained both in the hospital and at home. Continuous infusions allow for delivery of the minimal effective concentration of drug and facilitate appropriate care at home, particularly in chronic use and particularly in the terminally ill cancer patient. Detailed discussions of these are beyond the scope of this chapter and appropriate references are given.

Treat the Side Effects Appropriately

The use of opioid analgesics can, depending upon the circumstances, have both desirable and undesirable effects. It is the adverse effects that markedly limit the use of the drugs. The most common side effects include respiratory depression, sedation, nausea and vomiting, constipation, urinary retention, and multifocal myoclonus. A host of other side effects, including confusion, hallucinations, nightmares, dizziness, and dysphoria, have been reported by patients acutely and chronically receiving these drugs but are not discussed here in detail.

RESPIRATORY DEPRESSION Respiratory depression is potentially the most serious adverse side effect of opioid analgesics. Therapeutic doses of morphine may depress all phases of respiratory activity (rate, minute volume, and tidal exchange). However, as carbon dioxide accumulates, it stimulates the respiratory center, resulting in a compensatory increase in respiratory rate

that masks the degree of respiratory depression. At equianalgesic doses, the morphine-like agonist drugs produce an equivalent degree of respiratory depression. For these reasons, individuals with impaired respiratory function or bronchial asthma are at greater risk of experiencing clinically significant respiratory depression in response to usual doses of these drugs. When respiratory depression occurs it is usually in the opioid-naive patient following acute administration of an opioid and is associated with other signs of central nervous system depression, including sedation and mental clouding. Tolerance to this effect develops rapidly with repeated drug administration allowing opioid analgesics to be used in the management of chronic cancer pain without significant risk of such depression. When respiratory depression occurs, it can be reversed by the administration of the specific opioid antagonist naloxone. In patients chronically receiving opioids who develop respiratory depression, naloxone, diluted 1 part to 10, should be titrated carefully to prevent the precipitation of severe withdrawal symptoms while reversing the respiratory depression. An endotracheal tube should be placed in the comatose patient before administration of naloxone to prevent aspiration-associated respiratory compromise with excessive salivation and bronchial spasm.

SEDATION AND DROWSINESS Sedation and drowsiness are also common side effects of the opioid analgesics. These effects will vary with the drug and dose and may occur after both single or repetitive administration of opioid drugs. Although these effects may be useful in certain clinical situations, they usually are not desirable components of analgesia, particularly in the ambulatory patient. The effects are mediated through activation of opiate receptors in the reticular formation and diffusely throughout the cortex. Management of these effects includes reducing the individual drug dose and prescribing drug more frequently or switching to an analgesic with a shorter plasma half-life. Amphetamines and methylphenidate in combination with an opioid can be used to counteract these sedative effects. It is critical to discontinue all other drug therapy that might exacerbate the sedative effect of the opioid, including cimetidine, barbiturates, and other anxiolytic medications. In the management of the patient with acute postoperative pain, the use of epidural and intrathecal opioids has been advocated because it leads to the reduction of the sedative effects of the opioids in those particular circumstances.[47]

NAUSEA AND VOMITING The opioid analgesics produce nausea and vomiting by an action limited to the medullary chemoreceptor trigger zone. The incidence of nausea and vomiting is markedly increased in ambulatory patients. Tolerance develops to these side effects with repeated administration of the drug. Nausea caused by one drug does not mean that all drugs will produce similar symptoms. To obviate this effect, the patient should be switched to an alternative opioid analgesic or prescribed an antiemetic, e.g., prochlorperazine or metoclopromide, in combination with the opioid.

CONSTIPATION This side effect occurs because of the action of these drugs at multiple sites in the gastrointestinal tract and in the spinal cord to produce a decrease in intestinal secretion and peristalsis resulting in a dry stool and constipation. When opioid analgesics are started in the elderly patient, provisions for a regular bowel regimen including cathartics and stool-softeners should be instituted.[48] Several bowel regimens have been suggested because of their specific ability to counteract the effect of the opioid drug, but none of these has been studied in a controlled way. Anecdotal survey data suggest that doses far above those for routine bowel management are necessary and that careful attention to dietary factors, combined with the use of a bowel regimen, can reduce patient complaints dramatically. Again, tolerance develops to this effect over time but at a relatively slow rate. This is a critical problem in elderly patients who will often refuse to take pain medications because of concern about developing constipation. Again, aggressive bowel regimens to minimize this side effect can facilitate the patient's ability to obtain analgesia and to prevent the development of severe constipation.

URINARY RETENTION Urinary retention occurs with all of the opioids and appears to be a dose-related effect. It is most common in the elderly male patient with already-compromised bladder function. It is readily reversible with reduction in drug dose and the use of bethanechol chloride (Urecholine).

MULTIFOCAL MYOCLONUS AND SEIZURES Another side effect that has been clearly described with the use of opioid drugs is multifocal myoclonus and seizures. This side effect has been reported in patients receiving multiple doses of meperidine, although signs and symptoms of central nervous system hyperirritability may occur with toxic doses of all the opioid analgesics. In a series of cancer patients receiving meperidine, accumulation of the active metabolite normeperidine is associated with these neurologic signs and symptoms. Management of this hyperirritability includes discontinuing

the meperidine, using intravenous diazepam (Valium) if seizures occur, and substituting morphine to control the persistent pain.[49]

Watch for the Development of Tolerance

Tolerance develops to each of the effects of the opioids at different rates, and it occurs in all patients receiving opioids chronically. The hallmark of tolerance is the patient's complaint of a decrease in the duration of the effective analgesia. Increasing the frequency of or the dose of the opioid is required to provide continued pain relief. Since the analgesic effect is a logarithmic function of the dose of the opioid, a doubling of the dose may be required to restore full analgesia. There is no limit to tolerance, and with appropriate adjustment of dose, patients can continue to obtain pain relief. Of note, cross-tolerance is not complete, and switching to an alternative opioid can often provide effective pain relief. Starting with one-half the equianalgesic dose of the alternative drug, the dose should be titrated for the individual patient. Numerous approaches to slow the development of tolerance include the use of oral drugs, particularly combinations of non-opioids and opioids; the use of local anesthetics to manage a focal area of pain; and the use of neurosurgical procedures, e.g., cordotomy, in the cancer patient with unilateral pain below the waist. Physicians should not be concerned with the dose of drug required to manage the patient; rather, the degree of effective analgesia is the most important fact.

The abrupt discontinuation of opioid analgesics in a patient with significant prior opioid experience will result in signs and symptoms of opioid withdrawal. *Physical dependence* is the name for the condition that includes this appearance of withdrawal signs when an opioid is abruptly stopped. The time course of the withdrawal syndrome is a function of the elimination half-life of the opioid used. To prevent this syndrome from appearing, patients should be slowly weaned from the opioid drugs. Experience indicates that the usual daily dose required to prevent withdrawal is equal to one-fourth of the previously daily dose. Physical dependence must be distinguished from psychological dependence, which is a behavioral pattern of drug use characterized by a continued craving for an opioid manifest as compulsive drug-seeking behavior leading to an overwhelming involvement with the use and procurement of the drug. It is this fear of the patient's becoming addicted that limits both physician prescribing patterns and patient use of opioids. Some patients are reluctant to take any small dose because of this concern. Recent surveys in hospitalized medical patients[50] and analysis of patterns of drug use in a series of cancer patients receiving chronic narcotics[51] suggest that medical use of opioids rarely if ever leads to drug abuse or iatrogenic addiction. In the elderly patient, the chance of addiction is negligible.

Do Not Use Placebos to Assess the Nature of the Pain

The positive response to a placebo for pain is a normal response. The majority of patients participating in analgesic studies respond to placebos at various times during their treatment program. A placebo response does not reveal anything about the underlying nature of the pain and does not help to distinguish somatic pain from a somatic delusion. Placebos should not be used unless the patient has been informed of their use.

CONCLUSION

In summary, drug therapy is the mainstay of treatment for the majority of elderly patients with a wide variety of pain syndromes. However, pain management often may require a multidisciplinary approach, and the numerous approaches are listed in Table 30-4. Each of the approaches requires expertise in the specific area and triaging of care from the primary physician. For example, in the patient with trigeminal neuralgia who fails drug therapy, referral to a neurosurgeon is the next reasonable approach. Similarly, in the patient with reflex sympathetic dystrophy, referral to an anesthesiologist for sympathetic blockade is the first step to consider. Triggerpoint injections and various physical therapy approaches can readily be implemented by the primary physician. It is the careful definition of the pain complaint and diagnosis that is the first and most important step. Drug therapy transcends all levels of the diagnostic and therapeutic approach and should be within the armamentarium of the treating physician.

REFERENCES

1. Sternbach RA: Survey of pain in the United States: The Nuprin Pain Report. *J Clin Pain* 2:49, 1986.
2. Faherty BS, Grier MR: Analgesic medication for elderly people post-surgery. *Nurs Res* 33:369, 1984.
3. Portenoy RK, Kanner RM: Patterns of analgesic prescription and consumption in a university-affiliated community hospital. *Arch Intern Med* 145:439, 1985.
4. Harkins SW, Kwentus J, Price DD: Pain and the elderly, in Benedetti C, Chapman CR, Moricca G (eds): *Advances in Pain Research and Therapy*, vol 7. New York, Raven Press, 1984, pp 103–121.
5. Portenoy RK, Duma C, Foley KM: Acute herpetic and postherpetic neuralgia: Clinical review and current management. *Ann Neurol* 20:651, 1987.
6. Sweet WS: Trigeminal neuralgia, in Foley KM, Payne R (eds): *Current Therapy in Pain*. Philadelphia, Decker, 1989, pp 116–125.
7. Asbury AK, Fields HL: Pain due to peripheral nerve damage, a hypothesis. *Neurology* 34:1587, 1984.
8. Foley KM: Pain syndromes in patients with cancer, in Foley KM, Payne R (eds): *Medical Clinics of North America*, vol 71, no 2. Philadelphia, Saunders, 1987, pp 169–184.
9. Daut RL, Cleeland CS: The prevalence and severity of pain in cancer. *Cancer* 50:1913, 1982.
10. Cauna N: The effect of aging on the receptor organs of the human dermis, in Montagna W (ed): *Advances in Biology of the Skin*. New York, Pergamon Press, 1965, pp 63–96.
11. Crook J, Rideout E, Browne G: The prevalence of pain complaints in a general population. *Pain* 18:299, 1984.
12. McDonald JB: Coronary care in the elderly. *Age Ageing* 12:17, 1983.
13. Reidenberg MM: Drugs in the elderly, in *Medical Clinics of North America*, vol 66. Philadelphia, Saunders, 1982, pp 1073–78.
14. Kaiko RF, Wallenstein SL, Rogers AG, Grabinski PY, Houde RW: Narcotics in the elderly, in *Medical Clinics of North America*, vol 66. Philadelphia, Saunders, 1982, pp 1079–89.
15. Wall PD, Melzack R (eds): *Textbook of Pain*. London, Churchill Livingstone, 1984.
16. Pasternak G: Multiple morphine and enkephalin receptors and the relief of pain. *JAMA* 259:1362, 1988.
17. IASP Subcommittee on Taxonomy Pain Terms: A list with definitions and notes on usage. *Pain* 6:249, 1979.
18. Hendler N, Talo S: Role of the pain clinic, in Payne R, Foley KM (eds): *Medical Clinics of North America*, vol 71, no 2. Philadelphia, Saunders, 1987, pp 23–32.
19. Portenoy RK, Farkash A: Optimal control of non-malignant pain in the elderly. *Geriatrics* 43:29, 1988.
20. Kellgren JG: On the distribution of pain arising from deep somatic structures with charts of segmental pain areas. *Clin Sci* 435:303, 1939.
21. Foley KM, Inturrisi CE: Analgesic drug therapy in cancer pain: Principles and practice, in Payne R, Foley KM (eds): *Medical Clinics of North America*, vol 71, no 2. Philadelphia, Saunders, 1987, pp 207–33.
22. Schlegel SE, Paulus H: Non-steroidal and analgesic therapy in the elderly. *Clin Rheum Dis* 12:245, 1986.
23. Cohen JL: Pharmacokinetic changes in aging. *Am J Med* 80 (suppl 5A):31, 1986.
24. Morgan J, Furst DE: Implications of drug therapy in the elderly. *Clin Rheum Dis* 12:227, 1986.
25. Bender AD: The effect of increased age on the distribution of peripheral blood flow in man. *J Am Geriatr Soc* 13:192, 1965.
26. Geokas, MC, Haverbck BJ: The aging gastrointestinal tract. *Am J Surg* 117:881, 1969.
27. Goldberg PB, Roberts J: Pharmacologic basis for developing rational drug regimens for elderly patients. *Med Clin North Am* 67:315, 1983.
28. Rafksy HA, Newman B: Liver function tests in the aged. (The serum cholesterol partition, bromsulphalein, cephalinflocculation and oral and intravenous hippuric acid test). *Am J Dig Dis*, 10:66, 1965.

29. Belleville JW, Forrest WH, Miller E, Brown BW: Influence of age on pain relief from analgesics. *JAMA* 217:1835, 1971.

30. Kaiko RF: Age and morphine analgesia in cancer patients with postoperative pain. *Clin Pharmacol Ther* 28:823, 1980.

31. Chan K, Kendall MJ, Mitchard M et al: The effect of aging on plasma pethidine concentration. *Br J Pharmacol* 1:297, 1975.

32. Helmers H, Noorduin H, Leeuwen LV: Alfentanil use in the aged: A clinical comparison with its use in young patients. *Eur J Anaesthesiol* 2:347, 1985.

33. Weinberg AD: The etiology, evaluation and treatment of head and facial pain in the elderly. *J Pain Symptom Manage* 3:29, 1988.

34. Thienhaus OJ: Pain in the elderly, in Foley KM, Payne R (eds): *Current Therapy in Pain.* Philadelphia, Decker, 1989, pp 82–9.

35. Cohen FL: Postsurgical pain relief: Patients' status and nurses' medication choices. *Pain* 9:265, 1980.

36. Houde RW, Wallenstein SL, Beaver WT: Evaluation of analgesics in patients with cancer pain, in Lasagna L (ed): *International Encyclopedia of Pharmacology and Therapeutics,* sect 6, *Clinical Pharmacology,* vol 1. New York, Pergamon Press, 1966, pp 59–97.

37. Ferrer-Brechner T, Ganza P: Combination therapy with ibuprofen and methadone for chronic cancer pain. *Am J Med* 77:78, 1984.

38. Beaver WT, Feise G: Comparison of analgesic effects of morphine sulfate, hydroxyzine and their combination in patients with postoperative pain, in Bonica JJ, Albe-Fessard D (eds): *Advances in Pain Research and Therapy,* vol 1. New York, Raven Press, 1976, pp 553–57.

39. Forrest WH, Brown BW, Brown CR et al: Dextroamphetamine with morphine for the treatment of postoperative pain. *N Engl J Med* 296:712, 1977.

40. Bruera E, Chadwick S, Brenneis C, Hanson J, MacDonald RN: Methylphenidate associated with narcotics for the treatment of cancer pain. *Cancer Treat Rep* 71:67, 1987.

41. Swerdlow M: Anticonvulsant drugs and chronic pain. *Clin Neuropharmacol* 7:51, 1984.

42. Walsh TD: Antidepressants and chronic pain. *Clin Neuropharmacol* 6:271, 1983.

43. Watson CRN, Evans RJ, Reed K et al: Amitriptyline vs placebo in postherpetic neuralgia. *Neurology* 32:671, 1982.

44. Weinberg DS, Inturrisi CE, Reidenberg B, Moulin DE, Nip TJ, Wallenstein S, Houde RW, Foley KM: Sublingual absorption of selected opioid analgesics. *Clin Pharmacol Ther* 44:335, 1988.

45. Coyle N, Mauskop A, Maggard J et al: Continuous subcutaneous infusions of opiates in cancer patients with pain. *Oncol Nurs Forum* 13:53, 1986.

46. Portenoy RK, Moulin DE, Rogers AG et al: Intravenous infusions of opioids in cancer pain: Clinical review and guidelines for use. *Cancer Treat Rep* 70:575, 1986.

47. Cousins MJ, Mather LE: Intrathecal and epidural administration of opioids. *Anesthesiology* 61:276, 1984.

48. Portenoy RK: Constipation in the cancer patient: Causes and management. *Med Clin North Am* 71:303, 1987.

49. Kaiko RF, Foley KM, Grabinski PY et al: Central nervous system excitatory effects of meperidine in cancer patients. *Ann Neurol* 13:180, 1983.

50. Porter J, Jick H: Addiction rare in patients treated with narcotics. *N Engl J Med* 302:123, 1980.

51. Kanner RM, Foley KM: Patterns of narcotic drug use in a cancer pain clinic, in *Research Developments in Drug and Alcohol Use. Ann NY Acad Sci* 362:161, 1981.

Chapter 31

ENTERAL/PARENTERAL ALIMENTATION

Edward W. Lipkin

Nutritional support for the elderly is becoming more widespread. Although there is no universally accepted definition of "the elderly,"[1] for the purposes of this chapter the elderly will be considered those over age 65. The recommended dietary allowances (RDAs) for vitamins look upon adults as being divided into two age categories: those aged 23 to 50 years old and those older than 51.[2] The National Health and Nutrition Examination Surveys (NHANES I and II) recognize a distinct category of the elderly ages 65 to 74.[3,4] The physiological processes of aging do not show a distinct bimodal distribution, and thus these data are a poor means of distinguishing between adult and "elderly."

The high prevalence of malnutrition in hospitalized patients and the increasing use of hospital facilities by the elderly suggest the need for adequate programs to support their nutritional requirements. The attempt to design an adequate program of nutritional support for the elderly is complicated by several factors. First is the lack of information about their nutrition requirements. Second is the failure to distinguish between the healthy elderly and those with chronic disease. Third is the lack of "normal" standards for nutritional assessment. And fourth is the physiological limitation to refeeding imposed by the aging process.

NUTRITIONAL NEEDS OF THE ELDERLY

Is there anything unique about the nutritional needs of the elderly? Some commonly accepted myths about good nutrition for the elderly are that (1) caloric requirements per unit of body mass decrease with age in older people; (2) protein requirements per unit of body mass increase with age; and (3) vitamin and micronutrient de-

ficiencies are common in the elderly. The RDAs for vitamins recognize an age of 51 + for the elderly. Based on these recommendations, a significant portion of the elderly fail to consume the RDA for several vitamins.[5,6] Elderly populations, furthermore, often show a significant increment in physiological measures of vitamin sufficiency on supplementation.[7] This information is difficult to interpret in light of the low incidence of clinically apparent vitamin deficiencies in this population and the large incidence of routine vitamin use.[8]

There is no universal agreement about the impact of age on basal metabolic rate (BMR) per unit of body mass. The classic studies of Harris and Benedict[9] and Fleisch[10] both determined that the BMR declines with age. The Harris and Benedict study, however, examined the BMR only in ages 21 to 70, whereas the Fleisch work summarized the data in subjects ages 1 to 80. In the Baltimore Longitudinal Study a significant decline in BMR of 3 to 4 percent per decade and a decline of 5 to 6 percent per decade in total energy expenditure was observed for men ages 20 to 99.[11,12] These data, however, are cross-sectional, and some were not normalized for changes in body mass with age. When examined prospectively over 22 years, Keys et al.[13] observed a 3 percent decline in BMR per kilogram body mass per decade in younger men (mean age 21.9 years at start) but a nonsignificant 1 to 2 percent decline in elderly men (mean age 49.4 years at start). Recent studies of resting energy expenditure (REE) in both women[14,15] and men[16] have suggested a trivial contribution of age to the REE and that differences in REE can be accounted for solely by changes in weight or fat-free mass. The RDA for calories[2] in the elderly is summarized in Table 31-1 and was calculated by assuming that the BMR declines 2 percent per decade over age 50 and that there is a 200 kcal/day reduction in activity up to age 75. Over age 75 the de-

TABLE 31-1
Recommended Energy Intake for the Elderly

Sex	Age	Energy Needs, kcal (with Range)
Males	51–75	2400 (2000–2800)
	76 +	2050 (1650–2450)
Females	51–75	1800 (1400–2200)
	76 +	1600 (1200–2000)

crease in activity-related energy expenditure was assumed to be 500 kcal/day in men and 400 kcal/day in women.

There is no universal agreement about the protein requirements to maintain nitrogen balance in the healthy elderly and no data about protein requirements in illness.[17] The protein requirements for the healthy elderly, however, are thought to be about 0.8 to 1.0 g/kg.[18]

NUTRITIONAL ASSESSMENT: DIFFERENCES AMONG THE ELDERLY

The decision to initiate nutritional support is dependent on the ability to assess nutritional status (Chap. 5). The mainstays of nutritional assessment consist of (1) direct measures of body composition; (2) anthropometric measures; (3) measures of immune response; (4) measures of visceral proteins; and (5) measurements of selected vitamins and micronutrients.

Direct measures of body composition by neutron activation, underwater weighing, or bioelectrical impedance are still largely confined to the research setting. Normative data on body composition of the elderly, furthermore, are not available. Anthropometric measures such as weight, weight for height, skin-fold thickness, and arm muscle circumference are utilized for nutritional assessment on the assumption that they indirectly reflect body composition. The distribution of values for ideal or usual weight for height have an inherently large biological variation as do published measurements of skin-fold thickness and arm muscle circumference.[19,20] The ponderal or body mass index (weight in kilograms divided by height in square meters) has been suggested for nutritional assessment in the elderly.[21] Other standards have been advocated that do not rely on measurements of height but rely on estimates of height based on regressions utilizing knee height[22] or forearm length.[23] These estimates have the advantage of eliminating the variable of loss in height with aging. From the clinical point of view, a more useful measure of change in relative body composition with prognostic significance is the

present body weight as a percentage of the usual body weight. Measures of immune response such as reaction to skin-test antigens and absolute lymphocyte count have a poorly defined applicability to nutritional assessment in the elderly.[24] The effects of age per se on the immune system in the healthy elderly not taking medication is poorly defined, and studies have suggested either improvement[25] or no change[26] in immunological status with refeeding in the malnourished elderly.

Although it has not been extensively studied, it does not appear that the capacity for visceral protein synthesis is impaired in the healthy elderly.[27] Thus, measurements of serum albumin, transferrin, and thyroxine-binding prealbumin have the same prognostic significance in the elderly as in other patient populations. Other visceral proteins such as α_2-macroglobulin, fibronectin, and complement still require validation of their prognostic significance in nutritional assessment.

Serum measures of vitamins and selected micronutrients in the healthy elderly are rarely lower than younger populations.[3,4,7] For routine nutritional assessment in the elderly, therefore, these measures are rarely helpful. Various functional assays of vitamin status such as transketolase activity (thiamine) and erythrocyte glutamate:oxaloacetate transaminase activity (pyridoxine) are impaired in elderly populations and respond to supplementation.[7] These measures of nutritional status may have applicability to nutritional assessment in the elderly, but their general applicability remains to be established.

To summarize (see Table 31-2), nutritional status in the elderly can adequately be assessed in the clinical setting by a combination of data obtained by history, physical examination, and selected serum measures. A detailed weight history including an appreciation of the person's present body weight as a percentage of usual body weight is essential. Measurements of height and forearm length can be utilized for calculation of body

TABLE 31-2
Summary of Selected Laboratory and Historical Data Useful in Nutritional Assessment

Degree of Malnutrition	Weight Loss (Percent of Usual Body Weight)	Serum Albumin, g/dl	Serum Transferrin, mg/dl	Lymphocyte Count, cells per mm³
None	0	3.5–4.5	220–350	>2000
Mild	5–10	2.8–3.4	150–200	1200–2000
Moderate	5–10	2.1–2.7	100–150	800–1200
Severe	>10	<2.1	<100	<800

SOURCE: Abstracted and reproduced from Blackburn GL, Bistrian BR, Maini BS, Schlamm ST, Smith MF: Nutritional and metabolic assessment of the hospitalized patient. *J Parent Ent Nutr* 1:11, 1977.

mass index and weight for forearm length. Notation of drugs that induce protein catabolism including steroids and quantification of excessive losses such as diarrhea leading to protein-calorie deficits are useful. A dietary history and physical examination may suggest vitamin or micronutrient deficiencies. Selected measures of visceral protein status including albumin and transferrin or thyroxine-binding prealbumin quantify the net protein-calorie balance.

INTERVENTION

If specific deficits have been identified, nutritional support merits consideration. A decision must be made regarding enteral versus parenteral supplementation and realistic goals established. In all instances wherein the gastrointestinal tract is accessible and usable, the enteral route is preferred. Short-term access to the gastrointestinal tract is established utilizing small-bore nasoenteral tubes. Nasogastric tubes suitable for suction are inappropriate for enteral feeding because their large size and rigidity predispose the patient to the dangers of aspiration and erosion. Optimal placement of a nasoenteral tube to minimize aspiration is in the distal duodenum. Gastric placement of feeding tubes is less optimal but can be utilized for feeding purposes. Ileus is no absolute contraindication to enteral feeding, provided close attention is paid to residuals and periodic aspiration of gastric contents. Aspiration of greater than 50 ml should initiate discontinuation of enteral feeding and instillation of the equivalent amount of fresh feeding formula at frequent intervals (every 30 minutes if possible) until absorption resumes. The position of all tubes should be verified prior to use by fluoroscopy or x ray. Directed placement has been accomplished utilizing endoscopy[28] for verification of position. The only absolute contraindication to enteral support is a distal obstruction. More proximal obstruction may necessitate surgical jejunostomy placement. Malabsorption, fistulae, or a short gut are also not absolute contraindications to enteral support. Increased losses and failure to stabilize weight within 3 to 5 days of enteral feeding, however, should suggest consideration of supplemental parenteral feeding. Initial selection of enteral supplements (see Table 31-3) should emphasize lactose-free products in light of the high incidence of lactose intolerance in the elderly. For chronic nutritional support, however, milk-based or lactose-containing enteral products are often well tolerated and are a good source of essential fatty acids. Furthermore, although relative lactase deficiency is common, it is often of minimal clinical significance.

Enteral products can be chosen which are either iso- or hyperosmolar. Hyperosmolar tube feedings contain large amounts of osmotically active nutrients such as carbohydrates and amino acids or peptides. Fat does not contribute substantially to the osmolarity of tube feedings. As long as hyperosmolar solutions are delivered into the stomach and there is no increased gastrointestinal transit, these solutions are well tolerated without excessive diarrhea. Hyperosmolar nutrients are not well tolerated, however, if introduced directly into the jejunum. Various sources of carbohydrate, nitrogen, and fat are used to constitute the remainder of the enteral formula (see Table 31-3). Polymeric carbohydrates do not contribute as much to osmolarity as their mono- or disaccharide components. Some experimental evidence supports an increased absorption of di- and tripeptides compared to crystalline amino acids, and intact or partially hydrolyzed protein is much less of an osmolar load than crystalline amino acids. The commonly utilized fat sources (corn, soybean, or safflower oil) all provide sufficient essential fatty acid intake. Medium- and short-chain triglycerides do not require hydrolysis for absorption and are adequately absorbed even in the presence of severe pancreatic insufficiency. However, medium- and short-chain triglycerides are not capable of meeting essential fatty acid requirements. Specialty enteral for-

TABLE 31-3
Basic Formulary Choices in Enteral Feedings

I. Options in enteral feeds
  Whole food
  Defined formula
  Elemental
II. Basic enteral formulas
  Isoosmolar
  Hyperosmolar
  Lactose-free
  Lactose-containing
III. Nutrient density in enteral formulas
  1.0–2.0 kcal/ml
  115–366 g carbohydrate per liter
  9.5–111 g protein per liter
  1.0–91 g fat per liter
IV. Carbohydrate sources in commercial formulas
  Starch
  Glucose polymers
  Disaccharides
  Monosaccharides
V. Protein sources in commercial formulas
  Intact protein
  Hydrolyzed protein
  Crystalline amino acids
VI. Fat sources in commercial formulas
  Corn oil
  Soybean oil
  Safflower oil
  Medium- and short-chain triglycerides
VII. Specialty enteral formulas
  Liver failure
  Renal failure
  Respiratory failure

mulas rely on an enriched branched-chain amino acid content (liver failure), essential amino acids only (renal failure), or increased fat content (respiratory failure). Free water and vitamin supplementation are necessary if this total volume of tube feeding is less than 1800 ml/day, and it is now generally recognized that standard tube feedings are deficient in selenium.[29] Other micronutrient requirements, including iron and zinc, may need to be adjusted upward. There are very little data to support the use of hypoosmotic enteral solutions.

Given the prolonged convalescence required for recovery from chronic illness in the elderly, early attention should be paid to the possible requirements for long-term enteral or venous access. Thus gastrostomy, jejunostomy, or permanent venous-access placement are often the preferred options for nutritional support access in chronic illness. Gastrostomy placement has been facilitated by the use of percutaneous endoscopic procedures,[30,31] thus obviating the need for general anesthesia. However, endoscopic gastrostomy has not been without its own unique lethal complications including necrotizing fasciitis.[32] Feeding tubes should not be sutured in place to avoid potential self-mutilation in disoriented or combative patients. Permanent venous access is limited to indwelling, small-bore Silastic catheters, which either exit percutaneously or are attached to subcutaneous reservoirs. Permanent venous-access catheters require close monitoring by an appropriately educated and oriented patient, family member, or primary caregiver. Periodic nursing follow-up is considered crucial by most care providers. The disoriented or combative patient is at extreme risk from an indwelling catheter for a potentially fatal air embolus, exsanguination, or infection.

The primary goals of nutritional support in the elderly consist of arresting the depletion of cellular mass associated with starvation, injury, and illness. Goals such as reduction of mortality, morbidity, length of hospital stay, preoperative management, or adjuvant treatment for chemo- or radiation therapy and bone marrow transplantation are all secondary goals. A unique consideration in the elderly population with malnutrition is the relatively large proportion of individuals with dementia of the Alzheimer's type.

Alzheimer's disease has been estimated to be the cause of up to 75 percent of all dementias and to have a prevalence of up to 50 percent in all patients admitted to nursing homes[33] (Chap. 92). These patients are at risk for the development of malnutrition and are difficult to feed for a variety of neuropsychiatric and physical reasons. In the early stages of the disease, anxiety, depression, and combative behavior secondary to delusions and hallucinations may result in poor oral intake. Subsequently, aphasia and apraxia may impair the ability for expression of needs, and as a result oral needs may not be met. Agnosia (loss of smell) may depress appetite.

Late in the disease, seizures, decortication, and contractures may not only make voluntary oral intake impossible, but also contribute substantially to morbidity from tube feedings secondary to aspiration. There are also significant moral and ethical issues involved in the initiation and withdrawal of life support for such patients, and these issues are not easily resolved.

If nutritional support is undertaken in the elderly, how is it most optimally monitored? The problems inherent in performing nitrogen balance studies under steady state conditions and the interpretation of "positive nitrogen balance" render data obtained from such studies difficult to interpret under routine hospital conditions. If weight loss has been characteristic of the patient's medical condition or can be expected from an inability to sustain adequate intake for needs, arresting the inexorable weight loss is a realistic goal. On the other hand, attempting to promote weight gain or expecting an increase in lean body mass is not a realistic goal for the acutely ill patient who is not fully mobile. Under almost all circumstances such short-term weight gain reflects accumulation of fluid and not lean body mass.

A change in visceral protein concentration often does not reflect the adequacy of nutritional support. The long half-life of serum albumin (21 days) and its susceptibility to third spacing limit its usefulness as a marker of nutrient repletion. Other serum proteins such as thyroxine-binding prealbumin and somatomedin-C (IGF-1) reflect more adequately net protein-calorie balance. Serial measurements provide a reasonable assessment of the adequacy of nutrient intake complicated only by the sufficiency of liver function. Other visceral proteins have been advocated as serum markers of nutrient repletion including retinol-binding protein and transferrin. Interpretation of retinol-binding protein levels, however, is confounded by vitamin A status and transferrin by iron status and inflammation.

In prescription writing for nutritional support, attention must be paid to requirements for total calories, protein, essential fatty acids, micronutrients, and trace elements. Total caloric requirements can be reasonably estimated in the clinical setting on a per-kilogram dry weight basis,[34] as suggested by Jeejeebhoy (Table 31-4),

TABLE 31-4

Estimates of Energy Needs Applicable to the Elderly Based on Ideal Body Weight (IBW)

Clinical Status	kcal/kg IBW
Basal state	25–30
Maintenance (ambulatory)	30–35
Mild stress and malnutrition	40
Severe injuries and sepsis	50–70
Extensive burns	80

SOURCE: Summarized from Ref. 34 with permission of the author and publisher.

or as an adjustment of the resting energy expenditure measured directly or estimated from the Harris-Benedict equation[35] and as proposed by Long et al. (Table 31-5). The RDAs serve as the standard for provision of other nutrient requirements in the elderly. Furthermore, since the only trace element for which there is an RDA is zinc, the recommendations for trace elements in the adult set by the AMA's Expert Panel (Table 31-6) also suffice for the elderly[36] and may require supplementation of standard tube feeding formulas.

In summary, intervention to supply adequate nutrition to the elderly can be accomplished utilizing a variety of guidelines developed to support the unique nutritional needs of the elderly.

METABOLIC COMPLICATIONS OF NUTRITIONAL SUPPORT IN THE ELDERLY

The physiological changes that occur with aging impose some unique restraints on nutritional support in this age population. The decrease of respiratory, cardiac, and renal function as well as impaired glucose tolerance observed with aging require a conservative and more gradual approach to nutritional repletion than might safely be applied to the younger. Decreased vital capacity may impair gas exchange and promote CO_2 retention with large calorie intakes. Decreased cardiac output and glomerular filtration may promote fluid, sodium, and nitrogen retention leading to the development of edema, azotemia, and congestive heart failure. Impaired renal function including impaired free water excretion, mineral excretion, increased or decreased sodium and potassium excretion all may precipitate more frequent episodes of hypo- or hypernatremia, hypo- or hyperkalemia, hypermagnesemia, and hyperphosphatemia. Acidosis may be more common because of the diminished capacity for renal acidification and impaired respiratory compensation. Impaired glucose tolerance may precipitate hyperosmolarity and difficulties with fluid balance because of the ensuing osmolar diuresis. Hypokalemia may result from excessive urine losses.

Three specific complications of nutritional support of the elderly deserve additional comment. Glucose intolerance, hyponatremia, and diarrhea are common in the tube-fed elderly. Glucose intolerance, however, should always precipitate a search for underlying infection and a reassessment of caloric requirements. Treatment with insulin for glucose intolerance should be reserved to blood glucose levels consistently over 200 mg/dl in the absence of infection or overfeeding. Oral hypoglycemic agents have no place in the management of glucose intolerance in the tube-fed individual.

Hyponatremia in the tube-fed elderly is common and usually results from inappropriate antidiuretic hormone regulation[37–39] or intravascular volume depletion (diuretics, cardiac or liver disease). Treatment usually consists of withdrawing offending drugs, intravascular volume repletion, and limiting free water intake. Serum sodium concentrations greater than 125 mmol/liter, if chronic, are well tolerated and rarely require treatment.

The development of loose and poorly formed stools on tube feeding is common, but should not be equated with diarrhea (greater than 500 g stool output per day). Loose stools are cosmetically unpleasant, but of little physiological consequence; whereas diarrhea may signify malabsorption, enteric pathogens, or small-bowel and/or pancreatic disease and should initiate a search for these entities. The addition of "fiber" to tube feedings has not been shown to consistently improve stool consistency or quantity. On the other hand, maintaining strict aseptic technique in preparation of solutions, discontinuation of offending antibiotics, and slowing the infusion rate as

TABLE 31-5
Estimates of Energy Expenditure in the Elderly Based on Adjustments to the Harris-Benedict Equation

Clinical Condition	Adjustment*
Confined to bed	1.2
Out of bed	1.3
Minor operation	1.2
Skeletal trauma	1.35
Major sepsis	1.60
Severe thermal burn	2.10

*Estimated energy expenditure as a multiple of the basal metabolic rate (BMR) calculated from the Harris-Benedict equations: BMR (men) = 66.47 + 13.75(W) + 5.0(H) − 6.76(A) and BMR (women) = 655.10 + 9.56(W) + 1.85(H) − 4.68(A), where W = weight in kilograms, H = height in centimeters, and A = age in years.
SOURCE: Summarized from Ref. 35 with permission of the author and publisher.

TABLE 31-6
AMA Recommendations for Trace Element Intake Applicable to the Elderly

Trace Element	Dietary Requirement Estimated from Balance Studies, mg/day	Estimated Intravenous Requirements
Zinc	10.1–11.5	2.5–. . . *
Copper	1.21–1.28	0.5–1.5
Chromium	0.29	0.010–0.015†
Manganese	0.7–2.5	0.15–0.8

*In a catabolic adult, 2.0 mg should be added to this estimate. In the presence of jejunostomy, ileostomy, or diarrheal losses, up to 17 mg/kg output may have to be added to this estimate.
†With increased stool losses, this estimate may have to be increased to 0.020 to maintain balance.
SOURCE: Abstracted and summarized from Ref. 27 with permission of the publisher. Copyright 1979, American Medical Association.

well as the addition of antimotility drugs in the management of selected patients to slow transit time will significantly improve tolerance to tube feedings in many individuals.

All these factors suggest that nutritional repletion in the elderly must be approached conservatively with close attention to estimated needs and periodic readjustment of intakes depending on clinical response.

CASE STUDIES AND REVIEW OF BASIC CONCEPTS

CASE NO. 1

An unconscious 80-year-old man is found lying on the floor of his apartment by a neighbor. The emergency medical team arrives on the scene and documents a regular heart rhythm and a blood pressure of 60/0. The patient appears grossly dehydrated. An intravenous infusion of normal saline is started, and the patient transported immediately to the nearest emergency room. In the emergency room the patient is lethargic but arousable. He appears disheveled and has no known relatives. He is given 100 mg thiamine IV. On examination he has a right hemiparesis and expressive aphasia. His weight is 55 kg and, according to his driver's license, he is 6 feet tall (183 cm). A previous medical record is located which confirms that he lives alone and has a long-standing history of hypertension. His last documented weight was 64 kg on a routine outpatient visit 6 months prior to the current incident.

The patient is admitted to the hospital, and a CT scan confirms a left parietal infarct of indeterminate age. A serum albumin level obtained the next day is 2.8 g/dl. The patient, although alert, is incapable of feeding himself, and on the following day a nasoduodenal tube is passed for initiation of enteral feeding. A dietitian assesses the patient as "moderately malnourished" and estimates his dietary needs as 1600 to 2000 kcal and 50 to 60 g protein. Feeding is initiated with an isoosmolar solution at one-half the estimated final rate by a continuous drip. The rate is advanced over the next 2 days to the estimated full rate. Three days after admission the patient develops a pneumonia, and the dietitian recommends increasing the rate of supplementation to 2300 to 2600 kcal/day. Following resolution of the pneumonia, the rate of infusion is again decreased. The patient gradually improves neurologically and is gaining approximately 0.5 kg/week in body weight. After regaining use of the dominant hand and resuming some voluntary oral intake, tube feedings are decreased to nightly infusions only and then discontinued altogether. After a period of rehabilitation, the patient is discharged to a minimal-care nursing home at his usual body weight with a serum albumin of 3.5 g/dl.

COMMENTS This case illustrates the optimal nutritional management of a patient who is moderately malnourished at presentation with a reversible neurological deficit making voluntary oral intake impossible for an indefinite period of time. The patient was given thiamine in the emergency room appropriately on the possibility of long-standing alcohol abuse and to prevent the development of encephalopathy. A diagnosis of "moderate malnutrition" was made based on several criteria: The patient presented at 86 percent of his usual body weight, which represented a weight loss of 9 kg over 6 months. His present body weight represented 73 percent of "ideal" according to age-adjusted "normals" of medium frame derived from the NHANES I and II surveys,[20] and his body mass index had decreased from 19.1 kg/m^2 to 16.4 kg/m^2. His albumin after hydration was decreased, and although not commented on, it would not be surprising to find other obvious physical signs of malnutrition including decreased muscle bulk and depleted subcutaneous fat stores. The prognosis was indeterminate, but it was obvious that voluntary oral intake would be impossible for an indefinite period of time in a patient who was already malnourished. An appropriate decision was made for early initiation of enteral feedings via a nasoduodenal tube. The estimated needs of such a patient are arrived at by a variety of approaches. The estimated resting energy expenditure (REE) from the Harris-Benedict equation is 1200 kcal/day. The RDA is 1650 to 2450 kcal/day. Since the patient was not infected and was immobile, but was moderately malnourished, a reasonable estimate of caloric needs was 25 to 30 kcal/kg ideal body weight (IBW). For this patient of IBW = 67.1 kg, this amounted to 1880 to 2260 kcal, or 1.6 to 1.9 times the estimated REE. Protein needs were calculated as 0.8 to 1.0 g/kg body weight. A standard lactose-free isoosmolar tube feeding was started and rapidly advanced to fulfill estimated requirements. This avoided one of the major pitfalls of tube feedings—the failure to meet estimated needs in a reasonable interval of time. With the development of pneumonia, the patient's requirements were estimated to have increased to 30 to 35 kcal/kg IBW, or 2.2 to 2.5 times the estimated REE. If the same tube feeding is used, this will increase his protein intake to 78 to 88 g/day, or 1.4 to 1.6 g/kg IBW. In this particular case the early institution of tube feeding arrested the patient's malnutrition, which would have worsened with no intake, and resulted in a reasonable weight gain through a period of rehabilitation with normalization of his visceral proteins.

CASE NO. 2

A 60-year-old woman presents to the emergency room complaining of palpitations and abdominal pain. The patient is afebrile, but atrial fibrillation is documented as well as guaiac-positive stool. Abdominal exam is unremarkable except for diffuse pain to deep palpation. An elevated white cell count is noted, and the patient is admitted to the hospital for observation. The patient's heart converts to normal sinus rhythm with treatment, but that night she develops acute abdominal pain and is taken to the operating room for an exploratory laparotomy. During surgery a cyanotic proximal small bowel is noted and apparent occlusion of the superior mesenteric artery. The majority of the small bowel distal to the ligament of Trietz is resected and the duodenum anastomosed to 60 cm of the remaining jejunum. It is possible to revascularize the ileum and colon. A Hickman catheter is inserted in the brachiocephalic vein, advanced to the juncture of the superior vena cava and right atrium, and exteriorized retrograde through the chest wall at the time of surgery. Immediately after the operation, the patient is begun on intravenous alimentation.

The patient's weight is 59.1 kg, and she is 165 cm tall. Her ideal body weight is 68.2 kg, her body mass index is 21.7 kg/m^2, and her estimated resting energy expenditure from the Harris-Benedict equation is 1200 kcal/day. A dietary consult recommends an alimentation solution consisting of 20% dextrose and 4.25% amino acids to be delivered continuously at a target rate of 80 ml/h. Administration of two 500-ml bottles of 10% lipid emulsion weekly is also suggested to prevent essential fatty acid deficiency, and vitamins, electrolytes, minerals, and trace elements are added to the basic solution. Additional fluid is given to maintain adequate hydration. The patient has an uneventful postoperative recovery and resumes oral intake 7 days postoperatively with small amounts of low-fat solid foods. Diarrhea results, but is improved by antimotility agents. The rate of infusion is advanced until all the patient's nutrients are delivered overnight. The patient is encouraged to experiment with her oral intake to develop an awareness of which foods aggravate and which alleviate the diarrhea. She is discharged 3 weeks postoperatively on home parenteral nutrition.

Over the next 2 years the patient's diet is advanced as tolerated and intravenous feedings are decreased. The patient is able to come off intravenous feeding completely, and the Hickman catheter is removed. During this time her family presents her with two additional grandchildren, and she is able to see several of her grandchildren graduate from college. She dies at age 85 of a cerebrovascular accident totally unrelated to her underlying disease.

COMMENTS This case illustrates the optimal nutritional management of an elderly patient with a massive small-bowel resection. Permanent venous access was established at the time of operation with consideration of the long period of convalescence required for recovery

from short-bowel syndrome. Intravenous nutrition was started immediately since the lack of small-bowel absorptive surface and anticipated diarrhea compromise the patient's ability to be sustained on oral intake alone. Oral intake was encouraged to promote residual small-bowel adaptation. Whole food is well tolerated in the form of multiple small feedings, provided that rapid gastrointestinal transit can be controlled and pancreatic exocrine function is intact. The findings at laparotomy suggested a good prognosis. It was possible to preserve the ileum, a significant portion of the jejunum, and the ileocecal valve and large intestine. The presence of an ileum and intact ileocecal valve made massive fat or bile salt malabsorption unlikely, provided that transit time could be controlled.

The initial TPN prescription was written to supply 1857 kcal/day or 1.5 times the estimated REE based on the Harris-Benedict equation. On a per-weight basis, the prescription provided 31 kcal/kg body weight, or 27 kcal/kg ideal body weight. These are reasonable estimates of energy expenditure for a postoperative patient with extensive abdominal surgery who is not infected and is not mobile. The RDA is 1400 to 2200 kcal/day. The patient was also given 1.4 g/kg body weight of crystalline amino acids to meet her protein requirements and 3 percent of her total caloric intake as fat emulsion to meet her requirements for essential fatty acids. The infusion rate was rapidly advanced to convert to cyclic overnight therapy. This allowed the patient greater mobility during the daytime and some time to experiment with oral intake. Home therapy was a reasonable treatment option given the expected long period of bowel adaptation. Despite catastrophic illness, this patient was rehabilitated and able to lead a fully functional existence for the duration of her natural life span. This patient benefited from medical management that focused on her long-term prognosis and not on her chronological age.

REFERENCES

1. Butler RN, McGuire EAH: Foreward. *Am J Clin Nutr* 36:977, 1982.
2. *Recommended Dietary Allowances.* Committee on Dietary Allowances, Food and Nutrition Board, Commission on Life Sciences, National Research Council, 9th ed. Washington: National Academy Press, 1980.
3. *Plan and Operation of the National Health and Nutrition Examination Survey, 1971–1973.* Vital and health statistics, ser I. "Programs and Collection Procedures," no 10. Washington: Government Printing Office, DHEW (HSM) 73-1310, 1975.
4. *Plan and Operation of the Second National Health and Nutrition Examination Survey, 1976–1980.* Vital and health statistics, ser 1, no 232. Washington: Government Printing Office, DHHS (PHS) 81-1317, 1982.

5. Young EA: Evidence relating selected vitamins and minerals to health and disease in the elderly population in the United States: Introduction. *Am J Clin Nutr* 36:979, 1982.

6. U.S. Department of Health and Human Services and U.S. Department of Agriculture: Nutrition Monitoring in the United States—A Report from the Joint Nutrition Monitoring Evaluation Committee. DHHS (PHS) 86-1255. Washington: Government Printing Office, July 1986.

7. Suter PM, Russell RM: Vitamin requirements of the elderly. *Am J Clin Nutr* 45:501, 1987.

8. Garry PJ, Goodwin JS, Hunt WC, Hooper EM, Leonard AG: Nutritional status in a healthy elderly population: Dietary and supplemental intakes. *Am J Clin Nutr* 36:319, 1982.

9. Harris JA, Benedict FG: *Biometric Studies of Basal Metabolism in Man.* Carnegie Institute of Washington Publication 279, 1919.

10. Fleisch PA: Le metabolisme basal standard et sa determination au moyen du "metabocalculator." *Helv Med Acta* 18:23, 1986.

11. McGandy RB, Barrows CH, Spanias A, Meredith A, Stone JL, Norris AH: Nutrient intakes and energy expenditure in men of different ages. *J Gerontol* 21:581, 1966.

12. Munro HN: Nutrient needs and nutritional status in relation to aging. *Drug Nutr Interact* 4:55, 1985.

13. Keys A, Taylor HL, Grande F: Basal metabolism and age of adult man. *Metabolism* 22:579, 1973.

14. Owen OE, Kavle E, Owen RS, Polansky M, Caprio S, Mozzoli MA, Kendrick ZV, Bushman MC, Boden G: A reappraisal of caloric requirements in healthy women. *Am J Clin Nutr* 44:1, 1986.

15. Boer JO, van Es AJH, van Raaij, JMA, Hautvast JGAJ: Energy requirements and energy expenditure of lean and overweight women, measured by indirect calorimetry. *Am J Clin Nutr* 46:13, 1987.

16. Owen OE, Holup JL, D'Alessio DA, Craig ES, Polansky M, Smalley KJ, Kavle EC, Bushman MC, Owen LR, Mozzoli MA, Kendrick ZV, and Boden GH: A reappraisal of the caloric requirements of men. *Am J Clin Nutr* 46:875, 1987.

17. Munro HN, McGandy RB, Hartz SC, Russell RM, Jacob RA, Otradovec CL: Protein nutriture of a group of free-living elderly. *Am J Clin Nutr* 46:586, 1987.

18. Munro HN: Protein nutriture and requirement in elderly people, in Comogyi JC, Fioanza F (eds): *Bibl Nutr Dieta,* no 33, Basel, Karger, 1983, p 61.

19. Master AM, Lasser RP: Tables of average weight and height of Americans aged 65 to 94 years—Relationship of weight and height to survival. *JAMA* 117:658, 1960.

20. Frisancho AR: New standards of weight and body composition by frame size and height for assessment of nutritional status of adults and the elderly. *Am J Clin Nutr* 40:808, 1984.

21. Kergoat M-J, Leclerc BS, PetitClerc C, Imbach A: Discriminant biochemical markers for evaluating the nutritional status of elderly patients in long-term care. *Am J Clin Nutr* 46:849, 1987.

22. Chumlea WC, Roche AF, Steinbaugh ML: Estimating stature from knee height for persons 60 to 90 years of age. *J Am Geriatr Soc* 33:116, 1985.

23. Mitchell CO, Lipschitz DA: Arm length measurement as an alternative to height in nutritional assessment of the elderly. *JPEN* 6:226, 1982.

24. Talbott MC, Miller LT, Kerkvliet NI: Pyridoxine supplementation: Effect on lymphocyte responses in elderly persons. *Am J Clin Nutr* 46:659, 1987.

25. Lipshitz DA, Mitchell CO: The correctability of the nutritional, immune, and hematopoietic manifestations of protein calorie malnutrition in the elderly. *J Am Coll Nutr* 1:17, 1982.

26. Lipschitz DA, Mitchell CO, Steele RW, Milton KY: Nutritional evaluation and supplementation of elderly subjects participating in a "Meals on Wheels" program. *JPEN* 9:343, 1985.

27. Morley JE: Nutritional status of the elderly. *Am J Med* 81:679, 1986.

28. Gallo S, Ramirez A, Elizondo J, Molina G, Ramirez-Acosta J: Endoscopic placement of feeding tubes. *JPEN* 9:747, 1985.

29. Macburney MM, Young L: Formulas, in Rombeau JL, Caldwell MD (eds): *Clinical Nutrition,* vol I, *Enteral and Tube Feeding.* Philadelphia, Saunders, 1984, p 171.

30. Miller RE, Kummer BA, Tiszenkel HI, Kotler DP: Percutaneous endoscopic gastrostomy; Procedure of choice. *Ann Surg* 204:543, 1986.

31. Kirby DF, Craig RM, Tsang T-K, Plotnick BH: Percutaneous endoscopic gastrostomies: A prospective evaluation and review of the literature. *JPEN* 10:155, 1986.

32. Martindale R, Witte M, Hodges G, Kelley J, Harris S, Andersen C: Necrotizing fasciitis as a complication of percutaneous endoscopic gastrostomy. *JPEN* 11:583, 1987.

33. Pepys MB: Amyloidosis, in Weatherall DJ, Ledingham LCG, Warrell DA (eds): *The Oxford Textbook of Medicine,* 2d ed. Oxford, Oxford University Press, 1987, vol 1, p 9.149.

34. Jeejeebhoy KN: Total parenteral nutrition. *Ann R Coll Phys Surg Can* 9:287, 1976.

35. Long CL, Schaffel N, Geiger JW, Schiller WR, Blakemore WS: Metabolic response to injury and illness: Estimation of energy and protein needs from indirect calorimetry and nitrogen balance. *JPEN* 3:452, 1979.

36. AMA Department of Foods and Nutrition: Guidelines for essential trace element preparations for parenteral use. Statement by an expert panel. *JAMA* 241:2051, 1979.

37. Helderman JH, Vestal RE, Rowe JW, Tobin JD, Andres R, Robertson GL: The response of arginine vasopressin to intravenous ethanol and hypertonic saline in man: The impact of aging. *J Gerontol* 33:39, 1978.

38. Anderson RJ, Chung H-M, Kluge R, Shrier RW: Hyponatremia: A prospective analysis of its epidemiology and the pathogenic role of vasopressin. *Ann Intern Med* 102:104, 1985.

39. Gross PA, Pehrisch H, Rascher W, Schomig A, Hackenthal E, Ritz E: Pathogenesis of clinical hyponatremia: Observations of vasopressin and fluid intake in 100 hyponatremic medical patients. *Eur J Clin Invest* 17:123, 1987.

Chapter 32

GERONTOLOGICAL NURSING

Evelynn Clark Gioiella

Gerontological nursing is a specialized area of nursing practice. It involves promoting, maintaining, and restoring the health of elderly clients and their families. It may be practiced in institutions, in the home, or in any setting in which the client is found, even the street. Gerontological nursing focuses on maximizing functional abilities, preventing and minimizing the effects of acute and chronic disabilities, and enhancing the quality of life through the client's final years.

HISTORY

Recognition that nursing practice with the elderly was a specialized area of nursing practice began to develop in the 1950s. The first textbook devoted to care of the aged and the first research on nursing care of the elderly appeared at that time. In 1966, the American Nurses' Association (ANA) established a Division of Geriatric Nursing Practice. This was an important step in the evolution of gerontological nursing from a low-prestige area of practice, having little or no differentiated base of knowledge and confined largely to homes for the elderly, to an accepted specialty in the profession.

Ten years later, in 1976, the ANA changed the name to the Division on Gerontological Nursing reflecting the growing awareness that understanding the aging process and care of the well elderly were as important as care of the ill elderly. In 1984, the division became the Council on Gerontological Nursing which is composed of nurses active in care of the aged as clinicians, educators, administrators, researchers, or policymakers.[1]

EDUCATION OF THE GERONTOLOGICAL NURSE

GENERALIST

Education for gerontological nursing practice is at two levels: generalist and specialist. Generalist education is offered at the baccalaureate degree level and to an increasing degree at the associate level. Recognition that there is a body of knowledge encompassing concepts, theories, and facts from gerontology, geriatrics, and nursing science needed by all nurses practicing with the elderly has led to concerted efforts to integrate this information into basic curricula. Since registered nurses are largely prepared in both associate degree and baccalaureate nursing programs, attempts to integrate have occurred at both levels.

National League for Nursing Accreditation Criteria for Programs in Nursing have been amended to require inclusion of gerontological nursing content and clinical practice. A wide range of texts and mediated instruction materials have been and are being developed to assist this effort.

Education for licensed practical nursing is also examining ways of including limited amounts of knowledge relevant to care of the aged. Recent regulations promulgated in many states require in-service education for aides and others working in nursing homes that includes gerontological nursing knowledge. Thus, knowledge pertinent to care of the elderly is included in all programs that prepare nurses on their assistants, although, the quantity and sophistication of this material varies widely from level to level and from program to program in each level.

Nursing educators have been working to identify

the scope and depth of knowledge needed by the generalist at each level. Articles, monographs, and textbooks have been published as guides for faculty in forwarding this effort.[2]

SPECIALIST

Education for advanced or specialist practice in nursing is at the master's level. The gerontological nurse specialist acquires an in-depth understanding of the interaction of normal aging and pathological processes common to older adults that results in altered health states. The nurse specialist develops the ability to plan and manage the complex nursing care required when clients present with multiple nursing diagnoses requiring an array of appropriate interventions to maintain function.

Specialist education in nursing also focuses on the application of research findings to practice, incorporating knowledge from related disciplines, honing clinical judgment skills, and expanding expertise in working with families and groups. Nurses prepared at this level develop skills as consultants, advocates, educators, managers, and expert practitioners.

A master's degree in gerontological nursing can have one of several role preparation outcomes. The student may elect to concentrate on the clinical specialist role, the nurse practitioner role, the educator role, or the managerial role. The quantity and sophistication of content in gerontological nursing taught with each role will vary, the consensus being that nurses preparing for middle management, as an example, may need less preparation in gerontological nursing diagnosis and prescription than those preparing to be clinical specialists. Preparation for the nurse practitioner role requires additional knowledge and practice expertise in primary care.

CREDENTIALING

There are three systems of credentialing used by the nursing profession: licensure, certification, and accreditation. All three systems impact on education for nursing. Licensure is governed by states or jurisdictions through boards of nursing. Not all states have the same requirements for licensure, either as a practical nurse or as a registered nurse. All jurisdictions, however, do use the same licensing examinations, a different one for each license. These examinations are designed to ensure the basic safety and minimal competency of the practitioner. Individuals educated outside of the United States and its territories must also qualify for and pass these examinations to practice as nurses in the United States.[3] Knowledge related to gerontological nursing is tested in these

examinations but, to date, only at a very minimal level of sophistication.

Certification in gerontological nursing is offered by the American Nurses' Association. It is voluntary and requires advanced nursing education as a gerontological nurse practitioner or practice experience in the field. In 1986, there were 753 nurses certified in advanced gerontological nursing as gerontological nurse practitioners and 4571 nurses certified as generalists in gerontological nursing practice.[3]

Accreditation of nursing education programs is carried out by the National League for Nursing and, in the case of continuing education, by the ANA. Accreditation criteria allows for a variety of approaches to teaching gerontological nursing. No amount of content in any area of nursing is specified. This limits the effectiveness of the accreditation process in ensuring adequate attention to gerontological nursing in the curriculum.

ROLE OF THE GERONTOLOGICAL NURSE

ACUTE CARE

In most practice settings the nurse spends more time with the client than any other member of the health care team. This is especially true in the acute-care setting where the nurse has 24-hour responsibility for coordination and delivery of care to the patient. Virtually all services needed by the patients reach them directly or indirectly through nursing. Nursing strives to provide continuity of total patient care to every client.

Since the majority of patients in medical and surgical acute-care units today are over 65, the nurse on these units needs to have an understanding of gerontological nursing concepts to give appropriate care. To assist the generalist nurse in providing care to the elderly, a gerontological clinical nurse specialist is of increasing importance in most institutions.

The clinical nurse specialist (CNS) serves as a consultant to the service, bringing clinical expertise in gerontological nursing to the patients, staff, and administrators. The CNS prepares for gerontological nursing with a master's degree or doctorate and recognizes that even in the acute-care setting the elderly patient's health care problems are largely chronic in nature and require approaches designed to facilitate long-term management of these problems. Maintenance of functional status and fostering self-care capacity are crucial to care of the aged. This specialist assists the generalist nurse in assessing the impact of normal aging changes on the client, in adjusting nursing care to meet the specific needs of the older adult by preventing the hazards of immobility and further functional decline, in modifying schedules and protocols to elderly sleep patterns when possible, in promoting independence, in providing for repetition and individualized teaching of medications and treatments needed after discharge, and in working with the families and support systems of the patient to facilitate the patient's return to baseline or optimal functional status.

The clinical specialist can provide educational programs for staff designed to provide the latest information on such issues as safety, skin care, nutrition, mobility, and incontinence, which contribute to the quality of care delivered. Programs that address stereotyping, myths, and negative attitudes toward the elderly can also be conducted by the CNS.

Some acute-care institutions have recognized the special needs of their elderly patients by establishing separate geriatric units. At least one study has reported a decreased length of stay for patients in such a setting.[4] A geriatric unit should have a gerontological clinical nurse specialist on staff. The unit environment should be modified to include handrails, accessible bathrooms, reclining chairs in patient rooms, color coding of landmarks, large clocks and calendars, bulletin boards in each room, night lights, and extra-long call bell cords. The opportunity for interdisciplinary team work that focuses on the complex care needs of the frail and often precarious elderly clients admitted to acute-care settings should be enhanced on this specialized unit.

LONG-TERM CARE

The role of the nurse in long-term care has changed since the institution of diagnosis-related group perspective payment methods. Long-term care is growing, acuity of care is increasing, more patients are being discharged to their homes, and fewer patients are terminally ill. This change in patient demographics has increased the need for registered nurses in long-term-care settings. Unfortunately, registered nurses are in short supply, and thus, licensed practical nurses and nursing assistants must fill the patient care gap.

The gerontological nurse in this setting is badly needed but infrequently present. Few nurses in long-term-care settings have any specialized education in gerontological nursing concepts. Those who do are most likely doing nursing administration in the setting. The contribution that a gerontological nurse clinical specialist could make in the long-term-care area has been demonstrated in several model settings including the teaching nursing homes established by the Robert Wood Johnson Project.

The gerontological nursing specialist recognizes that geriatric patients have different needs than younger patients in the same setting. Attention to quality-of-life issues is most important for the elderly in nursing homes. Maintenance of independence, freedom of choice, comfortable environment, safety, and friendship are all as important as basic nursing care. As the number of younger and more acutely ill patients increases in these settings even less attention may be paid to the chronically ill elderly. The gerontological nurse will be even more important for educating the staff to focus on the needs of the elderly who may become second class citizens vis-à-vis, the more acutely ill or younger patients.

A subspecialty that is rapidly developing, especially in long-term-care agencies, is psychogeriatric nursing. Nurses who combined advanced education in gerontological and psychiatric nursing are in demand as therapists and consultants. The increase in Alzheimer's disease and other psychiatric illnesses in the aged population has placed additional burdens on long-term-care facilities in caring for these patients. A psychogeriatric nursing specialist can assist staff to manage patients with disruptive behavior. They can assess and plan for a balance between solitude and social interaction and between patient safety and staff security in caring for the mentally ill elderly.

PRIMARY CARE

During the 1960s the concept of health care as a right for every citizen emerged in the United States. Neighborhood health centers were funded to increase access to primary care for all. *Primary care* was defined as first contact in any episode of illness and responsibility for continuum of care including management of symptoms and appropriate referral.[5] To meet the demands for primary care, nonphysician providers were introduced. The nurse practitioner became one of these providers. The nurse practitioner now plays a major role in providing primary health care, especially to underserved populations.

Numerous studies of the nurse practitioner have been done to assess quality of care, cost effectiveness, acceptability, autonomy, and barriers to practice. A recent review article cites over 240 studies of performance and effectiveness in the literature.[6] In general, the nurse practitioner has been found to provide safe, effective ambulatory care similar in quality to the physician. In the chronic-care area, the nurse practitioner frequently has better outcomes than other providers.[7,8]

Nurse practitioners are more than physician substitutes. Because the nurse combines nursing's focus on family, mutual participation of nurse and client in decision making, psychosocial needs, teaching, counseling, and self-care with primary care skills of diagnosis and management of common acute and chronic illnesses, the nurse provides care that may have an emphasis that is different from that of the physician or physician's assistant. Nurse practitioners have higher success rates with patient compliance in such areas as weight loss, hypertension control, maintenance of medication regimen, and the keeping of appointments than other providers.[9] Research is needed to determine why this is so. Since primary care overlaps medicine and nursing, the nurse practitioner can be both substitutive and complementary to physician providers.

Gerontological nurse practitioners (GNP) are registered nurses with specialized education that prepares them to assume responsibility for delivery of primary health care services to older adults and their families. All GNP programs require an intensive didactic educational experience and mentored practice. The gerontological nurse practitioner manages episodic illness, monitors chronic illnesses, performs histories and physicals including functional assessments, orders tests, refers as appropriate, diagnoses, treats within protocols, and performs nursing interventions. The GNP is concerned with health promotion, identifying risk factors, early detection of illness or functional change due to age, and surveillance and maintenance of health status.

The gerontological nurse practitioner works in many settings including ambulatory care, home care, and long-term care. GNPs express a high level of job satisfaction which is related to autonomy, responsibility, and challenge.[9] The GNP has been particularly effective in managing the care of patients in nursing homes. The primary health care needs of the chronically ill elderly, for the most part, fall within the scope of practice of a gerontological nurse practitioner thus, increasing access to care of this frequently underserved population.

One barrier to the use of the GNPs in this setting is the lack of direct reimbursement by Medicare to the nurse practitioner for services provided. Until the regulations that require a physician to be on site for Medicare Part B reimbursement are changed, use of GNPs in nursing homes, shelters, day care centers, hospices, and other underserved settings will be limited.

HOME CARE

The majority of elderly clients needing nursing services reside at home. The nurse working in home care encounters elderly patients in her caseload regularly. Just as in the acute-care setting, staff nurses in home care need gerontological nursing preparation to work effectively with this population. The gerontological nurse specialist works in the home care arena in the same manner as in the acute-care or long-term-care settings, as a consultant, as staff educator, and as clinician for patients presenting with highly complex maintenance problems.

The nurse visiting the home setting often uncovers problems related to social, family, environment, or care-giver circumstances that are not evident in office or clinic contacts. The elderly client's capacity to manage money, cook, shop, clean, dress, and bathe are routinely assessed by the home care nurse in a situation where direct observation can verify behavior. The nurse can involve caregivers, often spending time teaching and counseling them. The need for respite for the caregiver can also be addressed, if it develops.

The home care nurse is skilled in adapting treatment methods to the home settings, improvising equipment as necessary. Medication management and safety issues are two primary areas of concern for the nurse working with the elderly at home. The nurse also focuses on coordinating the medical and social services required by patients at home, avoiding duplication, confusion, and contradicting prescriptions.

Nurses who work in home care settings through official or voluntary agencies are usually educated in baccalaureate nursing programs. They have specialized knowledge in community health nursing in their curriculum. These nurses are able to assess the community in which they practice to determine what services are available and how accessible and acceptable these services are to clients. The nurse will be able to identify senior citizen centers, day care opportunities, Meals on Wheels, the area agency for aging, telephone reassurance services, and many other services of potential value to the client. The nurse may also be able to assist in developing new services where needed. This type of community nursing is important in any community. However, such service is time-consuming, and there is no remuneration involved. The pressures on agencies providing home care services to maintain profitability may limit the community-focused activities long associated with public health nursing.

SUPPLY AND DEMAND

In 1985 there were an estimated 1.9 million registered nurses in the United States. Of this total, 1.5 million were employed.[3] Today, it is estimated that the employment rate is even higher. Those not employed include a very large percentage over the age of 55. Thus, the number of practicing registered nurses is the largest it has ever been in our history. Yet, in spite of these favorable statistics, we are experiencing an acute shortage of nurses in most areas of the United States. The reasons for the shortage relate to at least two phenomena, an unprecedented increase in demand and a significant number of nurses who work only part-time. Both phenomena will need to be addressed if the shortage is to be solved.

Producing more nurses is not a potential solution at this point in time. Graduations from all types of nursing education programs are falling. Admissions have also decreased significantly.[3] Women, who make up the vast majority of the nursing occupation, no longer choose nursing as a career in large numbers. Other career options offer better salaries, better working conditions, more prestige, more respect, and more autonomy. Women are no longer willing to be undervalued in the workplace. Long-term, this situation must be addressed or the current shortage will increase further. Short-term, the two phenomena cited earlier can be addressed to ease the present crisis.

Demand for nursing services can be better met by careful and judicious use of support personnel and computerization of many time-consuming activities now done by nurses. This will free nurses to do the care that requires the knowledge and skill only the nurse possesses. Demand will also be better met as institutions use nursing staff more appropriately. Nurses prepared in licensed practical nurse, associate degree, and baccalaureate degree programs have different levels of skill in diagnosing, managing, and implementing care in different settings. Work is now going on in several parts of the country to differentiate the competencies and roles of these practitioners.[10] Implementation of differentiated roles will better utilize the skills of the available personnel.

To convert part-time nurses to full-time employees will require improved salaries, child care availability, flexible hours, and the elimination of mandatory overtime. Nurses who are also caring for children or elderly relatives must balance work and family responsibilities. Full-time work is possible only if family responsibilities can also be met.

Data are not available to document how many registered nurses are gerontological nursing specialists. Approximately 115,000 registered nurses work in nursing homes.[3] However, most of these nurses are administrators and do not have specialized education in gerontological nursing. Gerontological nursing practice has never attracted a sufficient number of nurses. Nurses who select this area of practice tend to be older; they appear to be seeking less hectic working environments or are interested in the more autonomous role of the practitioner, clinical specialist, or administrator. Basic preparation of all nurses in gerontological nursing would decrease the need for a very large number of specialists in the field.

The national nursing associations; federal, state, and local governments; other health disciplines; the hospital organizations; foundations; the business community; and consumer groups are all studying the shortage of nursing personnel. Multiple strategies are being proposed to alleviate the problem. Recent articles have delineated the causes, including those mentioned in this section.[11–13]

CONCEPTS BASIC TO NURSING CARE OF THE ELDERLY

THE NURSING PROCESS

The nursing process is central to all nursing practice. It is an organized, systematic, and deliberate series of actions which can be described in phases. These phases include assessment, planning, intervention, and evaluation.

The assessment phase involves taking a nursing history, doing a health assessment, and making a nursing diagnosis. The assessment of elderly clients includes determining functional status and relies on the nurse recognizing changes common to the aging process, as well as deviations related to disease.

The nursing diagnosis is a conclusion reached by the nurse based on the assessment data. The nursing diagnosis is an expression of the status of the client and forms the basis for setting goals and planning interventions. The diagnosis describes the health problem, cause of the problem, and its signs and symptoms. Elderly patients typically present with multiple nursing diagnoses including impaired physical mobility, sleep pattern disturbances, nutritional deficits, alteration in bowel function, sensory perceptual alteration, alteration in thought processes, and chronic fatigue.

The planning phase of the nursing process begins with goal setting and prioritizing goals based on the nursing diagnosis. A plan of care is then developed, outlining the nursing actions appropriate to the situation. The nursing actions selected may be standard interventions known to be effective for the diagnoses being treated, or they may be actions specifically tailored for a constellation of diagnoses being presented. In either instance, the plan of care is developed with the patient and family and is individualized to the patient.

The intervention phase involves implementing the plan to accomplish the goals. A variety of personnel may be involved in carrying out the nursing interventions; however, the registered nurse is accountable for the nursing actions taken by assistants and licensed practical nurses. When caring for aged patients the implementation phase, like the preceding assessment phase, must move slowly. A judicious balance between encouraging self-care to foster independence and assisting the patient to minimize client fatigue and nursing time is required.

The final phase of the nursing process is evaluation. Assessing the effectiveness of interventions is the essence of quality assurance. If goals are not achieved, different strategies may be needed. Barriers not recognized initially may be detected, original goals may not have been realistic, health status may have deteriorated. Ongoing evaluation of process and outcomes is inherent in good nursing practice. Terminal evaluation, after discharge, through a nursing audit is also an important part of the evaluation phase and quality assurance program.

STANDARDS OF CARE

Standards of care and scope of nursing practice are defined by the American Nurses' Association. The scope of gerontological nursing practice has been delineated at both the generalist and advanced practice level.[14] Standards serve as a model for practice, apply in all settings, and can be used to evaluate care. The 11 standards of gerontological practice are as follows:

1. All gerontological nursing services are planned, organized, and directed by a nurse executive. The nurse executive has baccalaureate or master's preparation and has experience in gerontological nursing and administration of long-term-care or acute-care services for older clients.
2. The nurse participates in the generation and testing of theory as a basis for clinical decisions. The nurse uses theoretical concepts to guide the effective practice of gerontological nursing.
3. The health status of the older person is regularly assessed in a comprehensive, accurate, and systematic manner. The information obtained during the health assessment is accessible to and shared with appropriate members of the interdisciplinary health care team, including the older person and the family.
4. The nurse uses health assessment data to determine nursing diagnoses.
5. The nurse develops the plan of care in conjunction with the older person and appropriate others. Mutual goals, priorities, nursing approaches, and measures in the care plan address the therapeutic, preventive, restorative, and rehabilitative needs of the older person. The care plan helps the older person attain and maintain the highest level of health, well-being, and quality of life achievable, as well as a peaceful death. The plan of care facilitates continuity of care over time as the client moves to various care settings and is revised as necessary.
6. The nurse, guided by the plan of care, intervenes to provide care to restore the older person's functional capabilities and to prevent complications and excessive disability. Nursing interventions are derived from nursing diagnoses and are based on gerontology nursing theory.
7. The nurse continually evaluates the client's and family's responses to interventions in order to determine progress toward the attainment of goals and to revise the data base, nursing diagnoses, and plan of care.
8. The nurse collaborates with other members of the health care team in the various settings in which care is given to the older person. The team meets regularly to evaluate the effectiveness of the care plan for the client and family and to adjust the plan of care to accommodate changing needs.
9. The nurse participates in research designed to generate an organized body of gerontological nursing knowledge, disseminates research findings, and uses these findings in practice.
10. The nurse uses the code for nurses established by the American Nurses' Association as a guide for ethical decision making in practice.
11. The nurse assumes responsibility for professional development and contributes to the professional growth of interdisciplinary team members. The nurse participates in peer review and other means of evaluation to ensure the quality of nursing practice.

USE OF ANCILLARY PERSONNEL

Home care and long-term care is provided, in large measure, by aides and assistants trained on the job. As the nursing shortage increases, this pattern of care will become more prevalent in acute-care settings also. Training of nursing assistants is an important activity of gerontological nurse specialists. It is essential that ancillary personnel learn safe practice procedures and gerontological concepts basic to the care of the elderly. A fundamental understanding of changes associated with normal aging and the impact of these changes on behavior is needed by all those involved in caring for this population.

Regulation of the use of ancillary personnel is primary to ensuring high-quality care. Adequate supervision by registered nurses is required to maintain a safe practice environment. This implies that a sufficient number of registered nurses must be employed and that some of these nurses must have specialized education in gerontological nursing. It is very important that regulating bodies recognize that licensed practical nurses do not have the educational background necessary for supervisory, teaching, or many complex caregiving functions and cannot safely perform these usual activities of the registered nurse.

The scarcity of registered nurses in long-term-care and home care settings raises many problems in delivering nursing care. Nurse–patient encounters are by necessity brief, assessment and communication are limited, continuity of care is hard to maintain, and care frequently becomes task-oriented. These problems can result in low morale of patients and staff and poor-quality nursing care. In short, quality control is the major issue in providing care for the elderly in home care and long-term-care settings. Regulation, accreditation, consumer education, and patient advocacy by the health care professions are required to address this concern.

INTERDISCIPLINARY COLLABORATION

The population explosion in the over-65 age group has stimulated the various health professions to examine their educational programs for relevancy to care of the elderly. It is now commonly agreed that all health professions students should have education about the aging process and about the strengths and problems of the aging. It is also becoming recognized that care of the elderly, especially the frail, precarious patient, requires multidisciplinary teamwork. To facilitate interdisciplinary health care delivery, educators and clinicians in nursing, medicine, social work, nutrition, physical therapy, and other disciplines are working together in new ways.

Interdisciplinary collaboration is not easily achieved (see Chap. 19). Tensions related to disagreements regarding the boundaries of the various disciplines, competition for resources, disparity of income levels, differences in educational levels, sexism, stereotyping, and historical practice mitigate against the entire staff working together. Collaboration implies colleagueship which in turn implies equality and mutual respect. Interdisciplinary education and research can contribute to the development of colleagueship. The shared goal of quality health care for the aged can also bring the various disciplines closer together. This includes focus upon issues that are of paramount importance to all members of the team caring for the individual elderly patient (Chap. 19), emphasizing avoidance of iatrogenesis, legal and ethical concerns, patient advocacy, attitudes of ageism among staff and students, and maintaining patient independence and self-esteem.

REFERENCES

1. American Nurses' Association: *Standards and Scope of Gerontological Nursing Practice.* Kansas City, ANA, 1987.
2. Gioiella EG (ed): *Gerontology in the Professional Nursing Curriculum.* New York, National League for Nursing, 1986.
3. American Nurses' Association: *Facts about Nursing 86–87.* Kansas City, ANA, 1987.
4. El-Sherif C: A unit for the acutely ill. *Geriatr Nurs* 7:130, 1986.
5. Diers D, Molde S: Nurses in primary care: The new gatekeepers? *Am J Nurs* 83:742, 1983.
6. Feldman MJ, Ventra M, Crosby F: Studies of nurse practitioner effectiveness. *Nurs Res* 36:303, 1987.
7. Ostwald SK, Abanobi OC: Nurse practitioners in a crowded marketplace. *J Community Health Nurs* 3:145, 1986.
8. Rogers T, Metzgar L, Bauman L: Geriatric nurse practitioners: How are they doing? *Geriatr Nurs* 5:51, 1984.
9. Molde S, Diers D: Nurse practitioner research: Selected literature review and research agenda. *Nurs Res* 34:362, 1985.
10. Primm PL: Differentiated practice for ADN and BSN prepared nurses. *J Prof Nurs* 3:218, 1987.
11. Aiken LH, Mullinex CF: The nurse shortage: Myth or reality? *N Engl J Med* 317:641, 1987.
12. Iglehart JK: Problems facing the nursing profession. *N Engl J Med* 317:646, 1987.
13. American Nurses' Association: "The Nursing Shortage: A Briefing Paper." Unpublished document, Kansas City, 1988.
14. American Nurses' Association: *Standards and Scope of Gerontological Nursing Practice.* Kansas City, ANA, 1987.

GENERAL READING

Bandman E, Bandman B: *Nursing Ethics in the Life Span.* Norwalk, CT, Appleton-Century-Crofts, 1985.

Bernier SL, Small NR: Disruptive behaviors. *J Gerontol Nurs* 14:8, 1988.

Braunstein C, Schlenker R: The impact of change in medicare payment for acute care. *Geriatr Nurs* 6:266, 1985.

Faulkner AO: Interdisciplinary health care teams: An educational approach to improvement of health care for the aged. *Gerontol Geriatr Educ* 5:29, 1985.

Friedman E (ed): *Making Choices: Ethics Issues for Health Care Professionals.* Chicago, American Hospital Association, 1986.

Gallagher AP: A model for change in long-term care. *J Gerontol Nurs* 12:19, 1986.

Geolet DH: The relationship between certification and practice. *Nurse Pract* 11:55, 1986.

Gioiella E, Bevil C: *Nursing Care of the Aging Patient.* Norwalk, CT, Appleton-Century-Crofts, 1985.

Henry OM: How many nurse practitioners are enough? *Am J Public Health* 76:493, 1986.

Mass M, Hardy M: A challenge for the future. *J Gerontol Nurs* 14:8, 1988.

Mezey M, McGivern D (eds): *Nurses, Nurse Practitioners.* Boston, Little, Brown, 1986.

Morishita L, Hansen JC: GNP and long-term care team. *J Gerontol Nurs* 12:15, 1986.

Paremski A et al: A conceptual model for CNS practice. *J Gerontol Nurs* 14:14, 1988.

Schmidt MD: Meet the health care needs of older adults by

using a chronic care model. *J Gerontol Nurs* 11:30, 1985.

Smith DL, Molzahn-Scott AE: A comparison of nursing care requirements in long-term geriatric and acute care nursing units. *J Adv Nurs* 11:315, 1986.

Smith G: Resistance to change in geriatric care. *Int J Nurs Stud* 23:61, 1986.

————: Symposium on the geriatric medical education imperative. *Bull N Y Acad Med* 61:469, 1985.

Whall AL: Geropsychiatry: Therapeutic use of self. *J Gerontol Nurs* 14:38, 1988.

Yura H, Walsh M: *The Nursing Process*, 4th ed. Norwalk, CT, Appleton-Century-Crofts, 1983.

Chapter 33

TRANSITIONAL REHABILITATION: AN APPROACH TO THE PATIENT WITH A NEW DISABILITY

Leo M. Cooney, Jr.

Decisions must be made whenever an elderly person suffers a new disability. Should the elderly patient be placed in a rehabilitation program? Where should this program be accomplished? In the hospital? In a rehabilitation hospital or skilled nursing facility? Or should the patient be returned home? If nursing home placement is being considered, will this placement be temporary or permanent? These decisions have long-term consequences, and they must be made under the pressure of increasingly shorter acute lengths of stay in the hospital coupled with the emotional distress of the new illness and disability on the patient.

The role of the geriatric physician is clear: to assist the patient and the family in making sound decisions, with full knowledge of the expected consequences of these decisions. Knowledge of these expected consequences requires an understanding of how a patient's own physical, mental, and emotional status will affect outcome, how the specific manifestations of the disease will predict outcome, and how the type and site of rehabilitation might affect the end results of this process.

Thoughtful and wise decisions, therefore, require a full assessment of each patient, with particular attention to those aspects of the patient and the patient's condition that will predict outcome. This assessment must then produce a set of realistic goals of the rehabilitative process, with an expectation of the amount of care that the

patient might need once these goals are attained. The patient and the family can then determine where and how these care needs can be met.

PATIENTS WITH STROKES

The approach to a patient with a new stroke exemplifies the process which can lead to knowledgeable and reasonable rehabilitative decisions. This approach must include an understanding of the clinical features of the stroke which predict outcome, a thorough assessment of the patient which includes all these features, and a final determination of the expected goals of the rehabilitative process.

PREDICTIVE FEATURES IN PATIENTS WITH STROKES

A number of recent studies have given physicians information about those factors which can predict the outcome of patients with strokes. Several studies have compared features at presentation of the stroke with the outcome of rehabilitation.

Fullerton[1] reviewed 206 patients who presented to five general hospitals in northern Ireland with strokes. The patients were reviewed within 48 hours of admission and compared with outcome at 6 months. The authors found that leg function, level of consciousness, arm function, weighted mental score, ECG changes, and a test of perceptual dysfunction were significantly and independently related to outcome.

In a similar study, Kotila et al.[2] reviewed all stroke patients hospitalized in two Finnish towns and determined that the following factors at time of presentation of the stroke were associated with a poor prognosis: age over 65, hemiparesis at onset, lower level of consciousness at onset, impairment of memory and intelligence, visual field defects, perceptual deficits, and depression. The clinical severity of the stroke at presentation, defined primarily by altered mental status and the presence of aphasia, along with any extension of the stroke, correlated with a poor outcome in the study from a VA hospital stroke unit.[3]

Prescott[4] reviewed 149 patients admitted to a stroke unit, excluding those patients unconscious at the onset of stroke or previously dependent in daily activities. Subsequent independence could be accurately estimated from an evaluation of upper-limb motor function, postural function, and proprioception.

A number of studies have evaluated predictive factors of patients at time of admission to a rehabilitation unit. These studies evaluated patients 2 to 4 weeks after the onset of their stroke, and excluded patients who were either poor candidates for rehabilitation or who did not require extensive inpatient rehabilitation.

Feigenson's[5] review of patients admitted to such a rehabilitation program determined that the best correlates of a poor outcome were severe weakness on admission, perceptual or cognitive dysfunction, poor motivation, homonymous hemianopsia, and multiple neurologic deficits. Increased age, the presence of hemianopsia or visual inattention, urinary incontinence, motor deficit in the affected arm, and deficits in the patient's sitting balance all correlated inversely with the patient's functional ability at 6 months in Wade's analysis.[6]

Kinsella and Ford[7] found that spatial neglect, seen most frequently in right hemispheric lesions, predicted a poor functional recovery.

Henley[9] found that older age adversely affected survival and outcome from the stroke. The most important predictors of early death were prolonged coma, confusion, perseveration, conjugate gaze deviation, fecal incontinence, and hypotonicity in the lower limbs. The following factors, measured 2 weeks after the onset of the stroke, correlated with a good functional outcome and return of the patient home: high level of consciousness, absence of visual field neglect, positive mood, normal speech, visuospatial ability, stereognosis, presence of isolated limb movement, and the ability to perform the activities of daily living. Of the 172 patients in the study 59 underwent a CT scan of the brain. The side, region, size, and presence or absence of enhancement with contrast did not correlate significantly with outcome.

Several other studies have attempted to correlate CT scan results with outcome in patients with strokes. These studies had been limited, in that all of them have limited patients to those who were selected for a rehabilitation program. Miller and Miyamoto[10] found that their patients with deep lesions (involving the basal ganglia, internal capsule, and thalamus) had worse functional outcomes than those patients with superficial lesions (involving the cerebral hemispheres up to and including the external capsule). The size of the superficial lesion did not affect prognosis.

Lundgren et al.[11] determined that those patients with deep lesions have a significantly higher degree of motor impairment than those with "neocortical" lesions, while the size of the lesion did not influence the motor outcome. A negative CT scan produced a better outcome, while increasing lesion size and depth of lesion predicted a poorer outcome, in a study by Hertanu et al.[12] These authors, however, found that the Barthel Index of functional ability on admission to a rehabilitation unit was a more reliable predictor of outcome than CT scan results.

EVALUATION OF A PATIENT WITH A STROKE

When a physician evaluates a patient with a new stroke, therefore, the presence of altered level of consciousness, incontinence, aphasia, visual field deficits, and a deep lesion seen on CT scan all indicate a poor prognosis. After a period of 7 to 10 days of observation, continued dense hemiparesis, one-sided neglect, perceptual and cognitive deficits, and abnormal proprioception and positional sense must make the rehabilitative team aim a bit lower in their rehabilitative goals.

The physician must use the above information to determine the goals of the rehabilitative process, the most appropriate site of rehabilitation, and the amount of care that the patient may need after inpatient rehabilitation is completed. This determination requires a complete assessment of the patient's ability to respond to rehabilitation.

The rehabilitative assessment must include: (1) the patient's premorbid level of function; (2) the extent of the present disability and prognosis for recovery; (3) the mental acuity of the patient, especially the ability to follow a therapist's instructions and retain these instructions from one session to the next; (4) the physical ability of the patient to endure an intense rehabilitative program; and (5) the patient's motivation and effort in rehabilitation. The physician must also determine the presence and extent of associated diseases, including such conditions as prior strokes, Parkinson's disease, and arthritis, which may affect the progress and success of rehabilitation. He must also determine how the patient's cardiac, pulmonary, and general medical condition will affect the patient's ability to undergo an intensive period of rehabilitation, which may include 3 h/day of physical and occupational therapy.

The physician's evaluation should include not only a complete general and neurologic examination but also a manual muscle examination and evaluation of gait. The manual muscle exam will assess the presence and degree of muscle weakness and associated function, neurologic disease and associated function, and the patient's functional ability. The physician should carefully evaluate the patient's ability to transfer from bed or chair to a standing position as well as the patient's gait and balance. When a patient rises from a chair, attention should be paid to the amount of upper-extremity muscle strength required, strength and stability of wrists, ability to extend the knees and fully straighten the body, and amount of positional change required to go from the sitting to the standing position. The patient should be observed walking if possible. The amount of assistance (minimal, moderate, or maximum), the number of people required for assistance, and the ability of the patient to truly propel the body forward should be noted. The presence of a limp, wide-based gait, flapping gait, or balance disorder must be recorded.

A complete prognostic assessment should also include an evaluation by a physical therapist, occupational therapist, and social worker or discharge planner. The physical therapist will assess a patient's present functional status, ability to follow simple and complex commands, physical status and endurance, ability to use the involved and uninvolved limbs, and need for further rehabilitation.

An evaluation by an occupational therapist prior to setting goals for rehabilitation is essential. The above studies have pointed out the importance of visual field deficits, cognitive and perceptual deficits, neglect, abnormal proprioception, and presence of isolated limb movement in the prognosis of patients with strokes. Occupational therapists, who test for cognitive and perceptual deficits, evaluate and treat upper-extremity dysfunction, and assist the patient to adapt to the complex daily tasks of dressing, feeding, and bathing, have an essential role in the rehabilitative evaluation and process.

The patient's nurse must be questioned about such problems as incontinence, nighttime confusion, and the patient's level of effort in rehabilitation. While patients might perform reasonably well during one or two physical therapy sessions per day, the ultimate success of the rehabilitative process will depend on the full effort that the patient makes throughout the entire day, which is best determined by the patient's nurse.

The social worker or discharge planner must assess the family's commitment and ability to care for the patient after discharge. This commitment is best measured once the family understands the expected goals of inpatient rehabilitation.

GOALS

The most essential step in the rehabilitative planning process is the setting of goals prior to the initiation of therapy. Once the physician, therapist, and nurses have made a complete assessment of the extent of the patient's disability, prognostic factors for recovery, general medical status, mental status, response to initial rehabilitation efforts, and motivation, they should be able to predict the recovery expected from a period of inpatient rehabilitation. This recovery can vary. One patient might be expected only to move independently in bed and to transfer from bed to chair only with the assistance of a family member, while another patient might be expected to achieve complete independence with transfers, walking, stair climbing, and many daily living functions. The patient and the patient's family must understand the practical goals of inpatient rehabilitation so that they can begin to plan for the care needs of the patient prior to the time of discharge from the inpatient rehabilitation setting.

SITE OF REHABILITATION

A number of rehabilitation options are open to elderly patients. While many patients and their families will request the most elaborate and sophisticated program, the intensity of these programs may not be appropriate for each patient. If placed in too intense a program, the patient may require several transfers from institution to institution, and as a result may experience a sense of failure in rehabilitation efforts. An early matching of patient needs to appropriate resources can preclude the failure of expectations, noncoverage of care, and unnecessary transfers.

Patients with new disabilities such as fractured hips, amputations, and strokes or other CNS events can undergo rehabilitation in an acute hospital, in a rehabilitation unit of an acute hospital, in a rehabilitation hospital, in a skilled nursing facility (one type of nursing home), at home, or in a comprehensive outpatient rehabilitation facility.

Rehabilitation hospitals provide a multidisciplinary

approach including a rehabilitation physician, rehabilitation nurses, physical therapists, occupational therapists, speech therapists, social workers, and, usually, the consultative assistance of neuropsychologists, rehabilitation and vocational counselors, and experts in prosthetic and orthotic devices. Rehabilitation units of acute hospitals supply many of these resources but may be limited by the relatively small size of the unit. Patients in such units or hospitals benefit from the close cooperative multidisciplinary approach between the various personnel caring for the patient as well as from the services provided by each discipline. Comprehensive outpatient rehabilitation facilities provide the same type and extent of care provided in rehabilitation hospitals, but in an outpatient setting.

Skilled nursing facilities provide primarily nursing care and physical therapy. While occupational therapy may be available, it is usually on an intermittent basis by contract. In most skilled nursing facilities, it is difficult to achieve close coordination between physician, nursing staff, and physical and occupational therapists.

Most home health care agencies can provide physical therapy, occupational therapy, speech therapy, social work, and skilled nursing care in the home setting. To be eligible for this care in the home, the patient must be homebound. A practical limitation of rehabilitation in this mode is the limited opportunity for multidisciplinary planning, communication, and collaboration in most such programs.

One cannot practically consider the rehabilitation of an elderly person in the United States without taking into account coverage guidelines for Medicare and other insurers. Medicare has very stringent criteria for inpatient hospital stays for rehabilitative care. These guidelines cover both free-standing rehabilitation hospitals and "diagnosis-related-group (DRG) exempt" rehabilitation units of acute hospitals. The *DRG exempt classification* means that when a patient with a problem such as a stroke is transferred from an acute floor to a rehabilitation unit, the hospital can collect per diem charges for the duration of the stay on such a unit in addition to the DRG payment for acute stroke care.

Medicare regulations state that "rehabilitative care in a hospital, rather than in a skilled nursing facility or on an outpatient basis, is reasonable and necessary for a patient who requires a more coordinated, intense program of multiple services than is generally found out of a hospital." To be eligible for reimbursement of such in-hospital care, a patient must fulfill all of the following criteria:

1. Require close medical supervision by a physician trained or experienced in rehabilitation
2. Require 24 h/day rehabilitation nursing
3. Require at least 3 h/day of physical therapy and oc-

cupational therapy, in addition to any other required services
4. Require a multidisciplinary team approach to the delivery of the program
5. Require a coordinated program of care
6. Have a good prospect of significant functional improvement
7. Possess clearly articulated, realistic goals of therapy

In addition, 75 percent of the patients discharged from the rehabilitation hospital or unit must carry one of the following principal diagnoses: stroke, spinal cord injury, congenital deformity, amputation, major multiple trauma, fracture of the femur, brain injury, polyarthritis, neurologic disorders, or burns.

Medicare guidelines for reimbursement of skilled nursing facility rehabilitation care do not require occupational therapy, 3 hours of daily specific rehabilitative care, the care of a rehabilitation physician, or a multidisciplinary approach. Medicare does require 5 days/week of physical therapy, a need for skilled restorative care, and continued significant functional progress.

As a practical matter, most patients transferred to a rehabilitation unit or hospital must be in one of the ten diagnostic categories above, must be able to tolerate at least 3 h/day of therapy, must need occupational therapy in addition to physical therapy, and must require close medical supervision by a rehabilitation physician. To qualify for Medicare coverage in a skilled nursing facility, one must go to that facility for the same reason that one was hospitalized, must require daily physical therapy which could not be given in the home, must have significant functional deficits at the time of transfer, and must show continued significant progress toward a higher level of care.

REHABILITATION OF A PATIENT WITH A FRACTURED HIP

There has been much recent concern about the appropriate site of rehabilitation of elderly patients with hip fractures. Fitzgerald et al.[13] reported on the changing patterns of hip fracture care before and after implementation of the prospective payment system (DRGs). These authors demonstrated that, in one university-affiliated municipal teaching hospital, the mean length of hospitalization fell from 16.6 to 10.3 days after implementation of the prospective payment system. The proportion of patients discharged to a nursing home increased from 21 to 48 percent, and, most importantly, the proportion of patients remaining in nursing homes at 6 months after discharge increased from 13 to 39 percent. Fitzgerald has confirmed his earlier findings with a second study from a large (1120 bed) community hospital with a decrease in mean length of hospitalization from 20.9 to 12.6

days after prospective payment, increase in patients discharged to nursing homes from 38 to 60 percent, and increase in proportion of patients receiving nursing home care 1 year later from 9 to 33 percent.[14]

These studies raise troubling concerns about the wisdom of present choices in caring for patients with hip fractures. There are some clear data in the literature regarding the prognostic indicators for recovery for patients with hip fractures. Miller[15] found that factors that increase the probability of death and nonambulation included advanced age and cerebral dysfunction. Forty-seven percent of patients with cerebral dysfunction died within the first year after injury with only an 18 percent mortality in those patients who were mentally alert and oriented. There was no significant relationship between duration of anesthesia, blood loss, or choice of fixation device and the outcome at 1 year.

Jensen[16] found that mortality in 508 patients with hip fractures was clearly related to the prefracture "social function" of patients, which measured the amount of care they were receiving prior to their fracture. While the mortality rate increased with age, there was a similar increase within each age group based on the social dependence of the patient before fracture. While age and social dependence before fracture were statistically related to mortality, there were no significant associations between mortality and method of treatment, type of fracture, and placement after discharge. Baker[17] confirmed the overwhelming importance of mental status on the prognosis of patients with hip fractures. In this study, 17 of 24 patients with fair to poor mental status had died by 6 months, while only 5 of 26 with good mental status had expired by that time.

Cobey et al.[18] reviewed 108 "healthy" patients with hip fractures who were alert and oriented, independent prior to their injury, and free from "significant systemic illness." These authors found that physical therapists were better predictors of outcome than were nurses or physicians. The therapists found that a patient's motivation, postoperative mental clarity, balance, motor coordination, and stamina were related to independence with ambulation and activities of daily living at 6 months. In addition, there was a good correlation between outcome and the frequency of the patient getting out of the home prior to fracture.

Ceder[19,20] confirmed the importance of social factors in predicting recovery for patients with hip fractures, in that patients who did their own shopping and had frequent social contacts outside their home had a better outcome following hip fracture. These studies confirm the opinions of many that those patients who had a lifelong pattern of independence have a good chance of regaining this independence after a disabling event, while dependent individuals usually require institutional care.

To summarize, the best predictors for a return to good function following a hip fracture are good mental status, good prefracture functional and social status, alertness in the postoperative phase of rehabilitation, good motivation, and high level of independence prior to the fracture.

Two recent presentations at the 1988 American Geriatrics Society meetings have given physicians more information about the appropriate rehabilitation of hip fracture patients. Zuckerman et al.[21] described a multidisciplinary rehabilitation process occurring during an acute hospital stay, which allowed 80 percent of patients to return home. While the results of this program greatly improved the ambulatory status (83 percent independent with walking versus 62 percent of controls) and discharge status (80 percent home versus 49 percent of controls), the length of stay in the hospital was approximately twice the national average for hip fracture patients.

Both the Zuckerman and Fitzgerald studies raise some major public policy issues regarding patients with hip fractures. The present prospective payment system encourages acute hospitals to discharge hip fracture patients as soon as possible. This is probably detrimental to the overall care of these patients, as planned temporary stays in nursing homes too frequently become permanent.

Tinetti and Bonar[22] performed a multiple logistic regression on formerly independent hip fracture patients who were transferred to skilled nursing facilities with the expectation that they could return home. Only 95 of 137 patients (69 percent) were discharged home from these nursing homes in 6 months. The final multiple logistic regressional model identified mental status, social support, ability to bathe independently, and motivation for therapy as factors which contributed independently to discharge home.

The good results obtained in specialized rehabilitation units for patients with fractured hips, compared to the relatively high number of patients permanently placed in nursing homes in Fitzgerald's and Tinetti's studies, raise further questions about the efficacy of fractured hip rehabilitation in skilled nursing facilities. While there are few published studies on rehabilitation in this setting, there are some guidelines to follow in arranging rehabilitation in skilled nursing facilities:

1. At least 20 percent of the facility's beds should be directed to short-term rehabilitation.
2. Therapists should be on the staff of the facility, not on contract.
3. There must be coordination of the nursing and therapist rehabilitation efforts.
4. The facility's staff must have the appropriate re-

sources, skills, and experience for comprehensive discharge planning.

5. A physician with expertise in rehabilitation should be available to the facility on at least a weekly basis.

The frequent presence of a physician with experience in rehabilitation and familiarity with the facility's nursing and rehabilitation staff can be essential to the success of rehabilitation in a skilled nursing facility. This physician can evaluate the patient at the bedside, communicate knowledgeably with the referring orthopedic surgeon, and ensure that rehabilitation proceeds at a pace which will fit the needs of each patient.

The approach to a patient with a hip fracture typifies some of the difficult decisions that face the elderly patient with rehabilitative needs. The hip fracture patient's potential for returning to an independent existence depends on that patient's prior level of function and independence, mental status, balance, stamina, motivation, and capacity for responding to rehabilitation. The patient's physical therapist is the individual best-suited to predict outcome. Those patients with good mental status, rapid return to ambulation in the hospitalized setting, and limited complications can best be managed by completion of inpatient rehabilitation in the acute-care hospital and through direct discharge to the home. Patients whose rehabilitation is complicated by fluctuating mental status, slow return of function, medical problems, or associated physical problems such as prior strokes, Parkinson's disease, and other neurologic abnormalities will have the best chance of return to independence and home if placed in a specialized rehabilitation hospital or unit.

Those patients who have good mental status, good motivation, and a supportive family but whose return toward independence is slowed by limited weight-bearing status, frailty of the patient, and other medical or physical factors may benefit from rehabilitation in a skilled nursing facility. Tight coordination between the staff of the acute hospital and the skilled nursing facility, excellent discharge planning at the skilled nursing facility, and participation by physicians with experience in rehabilitation will enhance the nursing facility's ability to return patients with fractured hips to their own homes.

CARE NEEDS

Families must be given guidance about the amount and type of care that a patient will need after hospital discharge. Once the goals of inpatient rehabilitation have been set, one may translate these goals into how much care the patient will need at home. Families cannot be expected to make realistic decisions about their ability to care for patients at home until they know how much care

will be expected. The patient's ability to perform the activities of daily living correlates well with the amount of care needed at home. These functions of bathing, dressing, eating, toileting, transferring, ambulating, and maintaining continence of bladder and bowel are measured in such scales as the Katz Index of ADL and the Barthel Index.

Few studies have used these indexes in a practical way to assist planning for the care of an elderly patient at home. There are, however, several basic principles which may be helpful in planning care needs. The physical task which is most important for the patient is the ability to transfer in and out of a bed or chair. A patient who cannot transfer from bed to chair or from chair to toilet independently cannot be left alone for substantial periods of time, because of the need to have assistance with toileting. The ability to walk is less important for independence, as patients who are wheelchair-independent yet able to transfer can often function quite independently. Confusion and lack of safety awareness are major problems for frail elderly patients. Patients who know and understand their own limitations can function much more independently than patients who consistently attempt tasks beyond their level of competence.

The following guide, although not confirmed by timed studies, has been helpful in predicting the amount of care that patients will need in the home environment.

1. 24 h/day supervision
   • Patient cannot independently get from bed to chair or chair to toilet
   • Patient unsafe with transfers and walking
   • Patient incontinent
2. 8 h/day
   Patient cannot eat independently
3. 2 to 4 h/day
   • Patient cannot dress independently
   • Patient cannot prepare own meals—can manage with Meals-on-Wheels
4. Daily supervision
   • Help with medications
   • Administering insulin, etc.
5. 3 times per week help
   • Patient cannot bathe independently

PHYSICIAN'S ROLE IN REHABILITATION DECISIONS

Families need as much hard information as possible when faced with difficult decisions after a patient has suffered a new disability. They need to know: How much recovery can be expected from this disability? How long might this recovery take? Where would recovery best proceed? How much of the rehabilitation process will be covered by insurance? How much will the patient be able to do after completion of rehabilitation? What will the patient's care needs be then? How much care will be needed to take the patient home?

While the answers to these questions must be limited to general predictions, there are now enough data in the literature to give a good estimate of the amount of recovery expected, the most appropriate site of rehabilitation, the expected goals of rehabilitation, and the amount of care needed after these goals are met.

A complete assessment of the extent of the patient's disabilities, including perceptual problems, mental status, prior level of function, motivation, and response to rehabilitation must be made based on an understanding of those performance and disease factors which predict outcome. The patient and the patient's family, given reasonable expectations for the results of the rehabilitative process, can then make thoughtful and reasonable decisions about the patient's short-term and long-term care.

REFERENCES

1. Fullerton KJ et al: Prognostic indices in stroke. *Q J Med* 250: 147, 1988.
2. Kotila M et al: The profile of recovery from stroke and factors influencing outcome. *Stroke* 15:1039, 1984.
3. Dove HG et al: Evaluating and predicting outcome of acute cerebral vascular accident. *Stroke* 15:858, 1984.
4. Prescott RJ et al: Predicting functional outcome following acute stroke using a standard clinical examination. *Stroke* 13:641, 1982.
5. Feigenson JS: Factors influencing outcome and length of stay in a stroke rehabilitation unit. *Stroke* 8:651, 1977.
6. Wade FT et al: Predicting Barthel ADL score at 6 months after an acute stroke. *Arch Phys Med Rehabil* 64:24, 1983.
7. Kinsella G, Ford B: Acute recovery patterns in stroke patients. *Med J Aust* 2:663, 1980.
8. Baker RN et al: Survivers of ischemic stroke. *Neurology* 18:933, 1968.
9. Henley S: Who goes home? Predictive factors in stroke recovery. *J Neurol Neurosurg Psychiatry* 48:1, 1985.
10. Miller LS, Miyamoto AT: Computed tomography: Its potential as a predictor of functional recovery following stroke. *Arch Phys Med Rehabil* 60:108, 1979.
11. Lundgren J et al: Site of brain lesion and functional capacity in rehabilitated hemiplegics. *Scand J Rehabil Med* 14:141, 1982.
12. Hertanu JS et al: Stroke rehabilitation: Correlation and prognostic value of computerized tomography and sequential functional assessments. *Arch Phys Med Rehabil* 65:505, 1984.
13. Fitzgerald JF et al: Changing patterns of hip fracture care before and after implementation of the prospective payment system. *JAMA* 258:218, 1987.
14. Fitzgerald JF et al: The care of elderly patients with hip fracture: Changes since implementation of the prospective payment system. *N Engl J Med* 319:1392, 1988.
15. Miller CW: Survival and ambulation following hip fracture. *J Bone Joint Surg* 60-A:930, 1978.
16. Jensen JS: Determining factors for the mortality following hip fractures. *Injury* 15:411, 1984.
17. Baker BR et al: Mental state and other prognostic factors in femoral fractures of the elderly. *J R Coll Gen Pract* 28:557, 1978.
18. Cobey JC et al: Indicators of recovery from fractures of the hip. *Clin Orthop* 117:258, 1976.
19. Ceder L et al: Prognostic indicators and early home rehabilitation in elderly patients with hip fractures. *Clin Orthop* 152:173, 1980.
20. Ceder L et al: Statistical prediction of rehabilitation in elderly patients with hip fractures. *Clin Orthop* 152:185, 1980.
21. Zuckerman et al: Interdisciplinary care of geriatric hip fracture patients. American Geriatrics Society Annual Meeting, A12, 1988.
22. Tinetti M, Bonar S: Predictors of success/failure of SNF rehabilitation for hip fracture patients. American Geriatrics Society Annual Meeting A13, 1988.

Chapter 34

REHABILITATION OF THE GERIATRIC PATIENT

Kenneth Brummel-Smith

Although it is not normal to become disabled as one ages, it is extremely common. Almost all conditions that cause disability are more frequently seen in the older population. Because clinical geriatrics promotes the "functional approach" in the care of the patient, it can be argued that rehabilitation is part of the foundation of geriatric care. Hence, it is incumbent upon the geriatrician to provide a rehabilitation focus for all aspects of the care of the patient.

Rehabilitation is the process of assisting disabled patients in recovering lost physical, psychological, or social skills so that they may be more independent and so that they may live in personally satisfying environments and maintain meaningful social interactions. It can be provided in all types of health care settings, including the home, office, acute or rehabilitation hospital, or long-term-care setting. It requires an interdisciplinary team approach due to the complex nature of the various interventions. Education of the patient plays a central role in the process of rehabilitation. Finally, rehabilitation is a philosophical approach to the patient which recognizes that diagnoses are poor predictors of functional abilities,[1] that interventions directed to enhancing function should be adequately reimbursed by third-party payers, and the patient and the family should always be seen as a key member of the "team."

DEFINITIONS OF DISABILITY

When discussing rehabilitation, it is important to have in mind certain definitions. *Impairment* refers to aberrations at the organ level. Older persons have many impairments. Physiologic decline in organ function is seen in almost all systems. However, in many cases these declinations do not affect the person's ability to carry on daily activities. When the impairment is so severe as to effect an alteration in the person's daily functioning, the person has a *disability*. When the person with a disability has received the proper rehabilitation training to cope with the change in functional status, the person can be, in most cases, fully independent. However, if subjected to ageist policies that limit rehabilitation interventions or if confronted with public buildings that restrict access to those who are able-bodied, the person becomes *handicapped*. Therefore, there are no "handicapped persons," there are only handicapping societies. This chapter will be primarily devoted to persons with a disability. However, the sociopolitical implications of rehabilitation must not be forgotten:

Impairment—organ level
Disability—person level
Handicap—societal level

DEMOGRAPHICS OF DISABILITY

A large portion of persons with a disability are geriatric. While 60 percent of disabled persons are over age 65, 63 percent of disabled elderly are over age 75.[2] Most disabling conditions that require rehabilitation efforts disproportionately affect the elderly. Three-fourths of all strokes occur after age 65.[3] Most amputations occur in elderly people.[4] The average age of hip fractures ranges from 70 to 78 years.[5] Eighty-six percent of those over 65 have at least one chronic condition, and 52 percent of those over age 75 have some limitations in their daily activities.[6]

Certain disabilities, such as decreased ability to walk, feed, or toilet more strongly predict dependency and increase the burden on caregivers.[7] Institutionalization of disabled elders by exhausted family caregivers is very much related to the level of disability in that a greater burden of illness creates greater caregiving needs. Interventions designed to enhance functional abilities have been shown to be cost-effective, leading to fewer hospitalizations later, greater levels of independence, and lower mortality.[8,9]

PRINCIPLES OF REHABILITATION

COMPONENTS OF REHABILITATION

Rehabilitation entails a number of components of care. These components are summarized below.

> Stabilize the primary problem(s)
> Prevent secondary complications
> Restore lost functional abilities
> Promote adaptation of the person to the environment
> Adapt the environment to the person
> Promote family adaptation

Each of these components will require special attention when applied to the geriatric patient. For instance, it may not always be possible to completely stabilize the primary problem in that there may be more than one "primary problem." A 79-year-old with a recent hip fracture may have underlying cardiac disease, hypertension, and mild renal failure necessitating the close supervision of the geriatrician during an inpatient rehabilitation stay. Preventing secondary complications is crucial in geriatric populations because of the relative ease with which such complications develop and the great risk involved in their presence. The types of secondary complications that are frequently seen in older patients are summarized below.

> Anorexia
> Confusion
> Contractures
> Deconditioning
> Depression
> Incontinence
> Pneumonia
> Pressure sores
> Psychological dependency
> Venous thrombosis

Most of these complications are more frequently seen in the elderly patient. Older persons with decreased subcutaneous fat, poor capillary function, and low blood volumes are particularly prone to develop pressure sores. A sacral pressure sore, besides adding great costs to the care of the patient, may necessitate a period of cessation of wheelchair training in the patient who has suffered a stroke, thereby increasing the risk of the development of other secondary complications such as deconditioning or psychological dependence. The all-too-common "cascade of disasters" seen in older hospitalized patients is usually related to the development of a number of secondary complications. Contractures, the shortening of muscles about the joints causing a decrease in the functional range in motion, begin to develop within 24 hours of the cessation of activity.[10] Depending on the length of time the contracture has been present and the degree of limitation, recovery of lost motion may take weeks or may even be impossible. Strength begins to ebb rapidly when a person is immobilized or when there is even a mere decrease in activity. Younger persons have been shown to lose muscle strength at the rate of 5 percent per day when immobilized. The most rapid rate of recovery of lost strength was only 2 percent per day. Studies evaluating older persons' loss of strength have not been done, but it is likely that the rate of loss would at least equal that of younger persons and that recovery would likely be slower. Finally, it appears that the quality of help given may affect the development of secondary complications. Those patients encouraged to maintain the activities of daily living may lose abilities less rapidly than those for whom all activities are assisted.[11] Therefore, a concerted effort by all members of the team, including the patient, to prevent the development of secondary disabilities is required.

Restoration of lost functional abilities is the crux of rehabilitation interventions. Through the use of directed exercises, usually carried out by physical, occupational, and often communication therapists, the patient can relearn how to carry out daily activities. Relearning may range from adopting a novel way of dressing to using specialized assistive aids.

Adaptation of the person to the environment, or of the environment to the person, is especially important in geriatrics. The older person with fewer reserves may be less able to continue an activity that is extremely demanding physiologically. For instance, younger paraplegics can usually learn ambulation techniques using canes and braces. The older person with diminished cardiac reserve will most often need to learn wheelchair mobility skills. The assessment of the home environment also plays a larger role in geriatrics. Opportunities for obtaining new housing may be restricted by financial concerns and personal preferences.

Lastly, training and assisting the family must be provided. Eighty-five percent of all care given to dependent elders is provided by the family.[12] Many of the family caregivers are elderly themselves (spouses and older children). Family caregivers should be approached like any other student. Their knowledge and skills regarding the disabilities and caregiving needs must be assessed and enhanced, and their attitudes toward caregiving should be elicited.

In summary, attention to the various components of rehabilitation will ensure that the greatest level of functional independence can be achieved. The process of providing attention to these components is usually accomplished by a team of clinicians.

REHABILITATION TEAMS

Rehabilitation teams are usually referred to as either multidisciplinary or interdisciplinary. While many geriatricians and physiatrists (specialists in physical medicine and rehabilitation) are involved in interdisciplinary teams, most physicians function in a multidisciplinary setting. Multidisciplinary teams work in consulting relationships, usually seeing the patient individually and communicating with other team members by written notes or telephone contact. The involvement of the individual team members is usually decided by the physician. Interdisciplinary teams meet periodically to discuss the patient's problems and progress. While each team member has a specific area of expertise, there is often considerable overlap in roles. Interdisciplinary teams are usually required for more complex efforts such as inpatient or long-term-care rehabilitation. Reimbursement guidelines may also require the use of the interdisciplinary format.

Team members are usually required to meet periodically to discuss their assessments, establish goals, provide updates on progress toward those goals, and estimate the length of the program needed to meet the patient's goals. Whenever possible, the patient should attend these meetings, or at least the patient's input and response to the team treatment plan should be elicited. A written summary of the meeting is then placed in the patient's record and a copy given to the patient and the family after obtaining the patient's permission.

SPECIAL ASPECTS OF REHABILITATION AND THE OLDER PATIENT

A common feature in all aspects of geriatric care is that treatment of the older person differs in many fundamental ways from treatment of younger persons. So, too, is it

with rehabilitation. Recognition of these differences is vital in order to provide the most effective and appropriate care. The differences can be divided into certain categories. These categories include those that are patient-specific, provider-specific, environment-specific, and, lastly, goal-specific. Each of these categories will be explained in detail.

PATIENT-SPECIFIC DIFFERENCES

Patient-specific differences can be further divided into those that are age-related and those that are disease-related. Finally, using the functional approach, these areas have at their roots biological, psychological, and social components.

Age-Related Changes—Biological

Although there is some controversy over the degree of physiologic change that is expressly age-related, most investigators agree that certain changes in muscle strength and in cardiac and pulmonary function are inevitable. In that rehabilitation often involves intense exercise programs, these changes are likely to affect the older person more directly. Aerobic capacity, Vo_{2max}, declines with advancing age.[13] Declinations in aerobic capacity may even be greater in the "typical" patient who may be deconditioned or who had poor exercise habits prior to developing a disability. Decreases in vital capacity and minute volume may affect exercise further.[14] Lean muscle mass decreases with age, as does muscle strength.[15] Orthostatic changes are frequently seen, particularly in those recently bed-bound. Finally, peripheral vascular resistance rises with age, increasing the risk of hypertensive episodes with new exercise programs.

Age-Related Changes—Psychological

Although it is not normal to have functionally significant changes in cognitive function, certain normal changes may nonetheless affect the older person's participation in a rehabilitation program. Older adults tend to have a slower learning pace and require more repetitions to "engram" physical activities.[16] Patients may have rather fixed ideas regarding the role of exercise in their lives. Personality has been shown to remain rather stable throughout age,[17] and if the person's viewpoint is that one cannot recover from major losses it may impede the learning process. For instance, older persons are less likely to have hopes that they will be able to recover from a disabling condition and more frequently feel that they do not have enough time left to adjust.[18]

Age-Related Changes—Social

Perhaps the greatest age-related change in the social realm is the existence of ageism. As Abdellah notes, "Chronological age in and of itself can be a factor that causes a person not to meet criteria of eligibility for rehabilitation services."[19] A health care professional sometimes may not refer older patients for rehabilitation services owing to fears of their failing or being harmed. Fewer than 5 percent of the caseloads of departments of rehabilitation are persons over the age of 65.[20] These ageist views can even be held by the older person. He or she may feel unworthy of rehabilitation services because of a conviction that the money should be spent on younger persons.

Disease-Related Changes—Biological

Older persons are much more likely to have multiple diseases than their younger counterparts. In a study of community-dwelling elderly Hispanics, 40 percent had greater than four medical problems.[21] Candidates for inpatient rehabilitation programs often come from acute hospitals where they may have been bed-bound for many days, becoming severely deconditioned and losing much strength. A 20° knee flexion contracture increases the energy costs of walking by 35 percent.[22] This increased demand may be just enough to tax the reserve of a person with subclinical coronary insufficiency. Oxygen consumption increases with the use of upper-extremity walking aids or even with the use of a wheelchair, thereby stressing the person with underlying pulmonary insufficiency. A patient who has had a stroke will expend approximately twice the normal amount of energy—even with training—when walking with a hemiparetic gait.[22] Premorbid upper-extremity osteoarthritis will affect the use of a walker when rehabilitating after a hip fracture. Hence, it is a rare patient in geriatric rehabilitation who has only the disabling disease with which to contend.

Disease-Related Changes—Psychological

Underlying psychological problems—both cognitive and affective—often go undetected in both medical and rehabilitation settings.[23,24] Patients, particularly those undergoing stroke rehabilitation, may have low levels of dementia. In the acute hospital their cognitive deficits may go unnoticed because they are not taxed intellectually in that setting. Similarly, depression is frequently encountered in those patients being evaluated or provided with rehabilitation services. These patients may state that they don't "want" to be bothered, or they may present more subtly with decreased energy, lack of interest in activities, or decreased participation in therapeutic exercises. Depression after a stroke is particularly common with as many as 50 percent of patients experiencing it.[25] In another study 28 percent of all rehabilitation patients were clinically depressed and half of these had depressive histories which antedated their disability.[26] Because of these findings it is appropriate to assess each geriatric patient for underlying cognitive or affective disorders.

A problem frequently encountered in rehabilitation settings is the person with "low motivation." Motivation can be evaluated in a comprehensive fashion by looking at the components of decision making that influence a person's choices.[18] These components can be illustrated by this equation.

$$Motivation = \frac{W \times E \times R}{C}$$

In order to understand a person's motivation, one must know what the individual wants (W), what the individual expects (E) will occur after accomplishing the plan, and what reinforcements or rewards (R) are likely to be encountered. These factors are in turn affected by the costs (C), physically, economically, emotionally, or socially. Thus, motivation is highest when the person strongly desires the intervention, expects that it will benefit them, receives a modicum of positive rewards (the sooner, the better), and incurs relatively few costs. When necessary, an investigation to determine the person's component reasons for having low motivation can then be assessed.

There are some changes in motivation that may be age-induced. Older persons tend to make choices toward the status quo, take fewer risks in new situations, require more time in making decisions, and avoid the cost of failure.[18] These changes may make the older person appear less motivated. By providing adequate explanations as to the reasons for a particular activity, projecting a nonjudgmental attitude, and allowing sufficient time to practice, the demands posed by these changes can be minimized.

Disease-Related Changes—Social

As defined earlier, a society handicaps the disabled person when it does not allow the person to function at the highest possible level. The major impact of a disability is social.[27] The social realm is also the area requiring the greatest degree of adaptation. Much of the physical and psychological adaptation to a disability is accomplished during the first 2 years after the disabling problem begins. But social adaptation will continue throughout a person's lifetime. Legislative oversight that does not allow access to public facilities and reimbursement guidelines that limit availability of rehabilitation interventions on account of a person's age or residency (e.g., a nursing home) have the effect of erecting a handicapping barrier that prevents achievement of the person's full potential.

PROVIDER-SPECIFIC DIFFERENCES

There are other differences encountered in geriatric rehabilitation that relate to the providers themselves. These differences are the overlap of roles, the importance of not missing opportunities to intervene on the patient's behalf, and the unfortunate presence of ageist attitudes in some providers.

The roles of each provider often overlap in geriatric settings. The most obvious is the overlap of the role of the geriatrician with that of the physiatrist. Geriatricians are often called upon to coordinate rehabilitation interventions in outpatient settings or in areas where there are no physiatrists. Even when physiatrists are available, the geriatrician may have to advocate for the patient to receive services. One model is seen when the geriatrician helps manage the complex, multiple medical problems, while the physiatrist coordinates the efforts of the rehabilitation team.

Other roles may overlap as well. Nurses may provide counseling services, psychologists may make recommendations regarding psychotropic medication, and occupational or speech therapists may participate in cognitive evaluations. The most effective rehabilitation team is the one that promotes the expression of the full potential of individual team members. It is crucial that this type of interchange occur in geriatric rehabilitation where the patients have multiple problems and psychosocial issues predominate.

One must be careful not to miss opportunities to enable the patient to make even small gains. The adjustment process following a disability is made more difficult with the addition of advanced age, loss of family members, or preexisting medical problems. Simple but enjoyable physical activities done in a group setting may accomplish more in regaining range of motion or strength than a rigorous training program. Recreational therapy can sometimes enable a patient to remove the attention from personal "performance" and still accomplish worthwhile goals. For those patients who are being treated for depression, a therapeutic pass may offer the chance to feel independent and begin to see the value of hospital-based therapies. A prosthetic limb for cosmetic purposes may allow the amputee to engage in community activities, promoting a sense of self-respect.

Finally, it is important to watch that potentially ageist attitudes do not influence decisions regarding rehabilitation. Arguments in favor of rehabilitation for the elderly include the facts that (1) age has not been shown to be determinantal in stroke rehabilitation,[28] (2) even those over age 85 apparently benefit,[29] and (3) such rehabilitation is cost-effective.[30] Unfortunately, however, a number of studies have shown that even those who work in the field of rehabilitation have rather negative attitudes toward elderly persons.[31,32] Therefore the team leader must assess all decisions regarding cessation (or refusal) of therapy as to the possibility that "therapeutic hopelessness" is occurring.

ENVIRONMENT-SPECIFIC DIFFERENCES

As persons age, their interaction with the environment becomes potentially more precarious. These interactions relate to underlying physical status, living surroundings, and social systems. Of course, all persons relate to the environment. However, as one ages, the physiological reserves, underlying medical problems, affective states, and a host of other factors complicate the interaction between the person and the environment.

Often the response of rehabilitation is to change the environment—to make it "safer." This change can occur by providing assistive aids or by modifying the home. But these interventions are also subject to differences when dealing with aging persons. Assistive aids are often unattractive and difficult to use. Unlike eyeglasses, where the "disabled" person can choose a pair that looks attractive, walkers or chrome-plated "grab bars" project an image of illness. Older persons may not have any family members or friends who can install home modifications. Some Retired Senior Volunteer Programs (RSVP) have carpenters available for this purpose, but many communities don't have such support services.

The reimbursement "environment" also affects the provision of rehabilitation to older persons. Currently, Medicare reimbursement guidelines stipulate that those undergoing acute rehabilitation receive 3 hours per day, 6 days a week, of combined physical, occupational, or speech therapies. Some geriatric patients are physically incapable of participating in such an aggressive program yet could benefit from a less intensive schedule. Furthermore, there is evidence that persons receiving the 3-hour intervention don't improve significantly over those receiving less therapy and costs are higher![33] Hospitals that provide patients with a 2-week trial of rehabilitation are often not reimbursed if the patient is discharged to a nursing home in spite of the fact that the patient's functional status has improved. Funds to equip a geriatric patient's car with hand controls are more difficult to obtain than for younger patients. All these problems may lead to the decision to provide rehabilitation services not on the basis of the likelihood of improvement but rather on the likelihood of being reimbursed.

GOAL-SPECIFIC DIFFERENCES

Finally, there are differences seen in the goals of rehabilitation when working with geriatric patients. For instance, physical therapists are often concerned with the patient's gait in terms of safety. Yet it is often better to walk "incorrectly" than to not walk at all. Such decisions are heavily value-laden. Older persons may feel that they would rather take the risk of a fall than be placed in a nursing home. Many older persons fear the loss of independence more than they fear death. The geriatrician may have to advocate for the patient with a fractured hip to receive a more aggressive surgical intervention that will promote independence than one associated with prolonged immobility or non-weight-bearing. The ultimate goal is to promote "independence," as defined by the patient.

REHABILITATION AS THE FOCUS OF GERIATRIC MEDICINE

REHABILITATION IN DIFFERENT CARE SITES

Rehabilitation interventions can be provided across the spectrum of continuing care sites. Medicare coverage for these services is expanding. One must check reimbursement policies in individual states regarding allowances for patients on Medicaid.

The patient's home is an ideal site for providing rehabilitation. Transportation problems are nonexistent, and services can be rendered at lower costs than in hospitals.[34] Medicare does not reimburse for in-home services provided for some nursing, as well as physical and occupational therapies. The home is the best place to assess the patient's ability to function with available equipment, the environment is usually supportive, and carryover of techniques taught during therapy can be accurately assessed. In a study by Liang, patients treated in a home program obtained the greatest degree of functional improvement from home modifications, the next best improvement from instruction in the proper use of assistive aids, and the least from exercises.[35] The ideal home care patient is one who is judged to be able to benefit from rehabilitation in an outpatient setting but who is unable to attend clinics due to transportation difficulties, limited endurance, psychological reasons, or patient choice.

Many patients receive rehabilitation services in outpatient centers. These centers take a variety of forms: physician's offices, private physical (and occupational) therapy practices, Certified Outpatient Rehabilitation Facilities (CORF), day health centers, and hospital-affiliated facilities. These centers offer certain real advantages: access to a wider variety of practitioners and technology, the stimulation of being around other people (a disadvantage to some patients), and the advantage of having more patients served by fewer practitioners. The disadvantage of needing to provide transportation to the clinic often is a major problem with the very old.

It is in the acute hospital where perhaps the greatest unmet need for rehabilitation-oriented interventions is felt. The potential negative effects of acute hospitalization are well known.[36] Functional disability often goes undetected in acute hospitals.[37] Over 50 percent of patients in the acute hospital setting have difficulties with ADLs, and the hospital environment may interfere with functional recovery. With prospective payment it is important to obtain early allied health consultation as well as discharge planning so that the patient in need of rehabilitation may receive preventive interventions while awaiting more intensive interventions. Except when absolutely necessary, patients should be kept out of their beds, walked to the bathroom or diagnostic studies, and encouraged to dress and feed themselves.

The rehabilitation hospital is the classic site for providing such services. This type of hospital may be free-standing, or it may be affiliated with an acute hospital. The "team," as described above, is composed of the full complement of rehabilitation specialists. A physiatrist, or in the case of geriatric rehabilitation units a geriatrician, is usually the team leader. Patients must undergo 3 hours per day of physical, occupational, or speech therapy in order to receive Medicare reimbursement. As of 1988, if the center has an average length of stay greater than 27 days it is not subject to the diagnosis-related group (DRG) prospective payment system. In order to receive reimbursement, patients must make regular progress toward specific goals. Such progress must be documented in regular team meeting notes. Specialization in rehabilitation centers is occurring with the creation of geriatric units, geriatric-ortho units,[38] stroke units,[39] and assessment units.[40] Numerous reports have been made regarding the effectiveness of geriatric rehabilitation [41-43] as well as the fact that age need not be a deterrent to providing rehabilitation.[28,29]

Finally, the nursing home is a site for rehabilitation that is receiving greater attention. Medicare funding can be obtained for those patients requiring physical or occupational therapy. The costs are lower than acute care or intensive rehabilitation, and the results are encouraging.[44] In a study by Reed 17 percent of patients were able to return home.[45] The nursing home offers the opportunity to serve as a referral site for community-based patients to receive rehabilitation as well. Adelman reported that 57 percent of the patients that came from their homes to the nursing home for rehabilitation were able to return home.[46] Therefore, rehabilitation is a process that can be utilized in all medical care settings for the benefit of enhancing the patient's functional capabilities.

ASSESSMENT FOR REHABILITATION POTENTIAL

The greatest potential for rehabilitation is the geriatrician's awareness that rehabilitation interventions may be of benefit. Beyond that awareness, certain features must be assessed. However, no single factor, (or, in some cases, no specific multiple factors) should automatically exclude a person from a trial of rehabilitation interventions. Instead the patient must be assessed in a multidisciplinary fashion to make a final determination.

Assessment should determine what demands patients will encounter in their expected living environment and whether they, at the time of the assessment, have the reserves to meet those demands. Therefore, the assessment will entail evaluations of the physical status and impairments, cognitive and psychological functioning, social and support environment, and economic resources.[47] Specific information regarding assessment instruments is discussed in Chap. 23, and only those features that may affect the outcome of rehabilitation are emphasized here. Each of these features should be considered in light of its present status as well as in view of its premorbid state.

Physical Health and Impairments

Cardiopulmonary—response to exercise, presence of ischemia or COPD

Musculoskeletal—limitations of functional range of motion, deformities, foot problems

Neurologic—sensory deficits, presence of neglect, apraxia, agnosia, perseveration

Functional status—ADLs, continence, nutritional needs

Mobility—gait, balance, prior history of using aids

Skin integrity

Cognitive and Psychological Functioning

Mental status

Affective state

Motivation and desire to participate in program

Goals and wishes for the future

Social and Support Environment

Family—both related and "created" (neighbors, friends, church associates, etc.)

Home environment—accessibility, safety, modifications needed, desire to move

Prior experiences in "learning situations"—education, hobbies, work

Economic Resources

Health insurance and coverage for rehabilitation

Disposable income

Assets

Support from family

Personal values regarding expending resources

There are also specific factors that pertain to individual problems, such as stroke, that may affect decisions regarding prognosis for rehabilitation. These will be discussed below. A decision must be made as to the optimum site for providing rehabilitation. In some cases, especially when physiatrists or other members of the consulting team have limited experience in geriatrics, the geriatrician may be called upon to advocate on the patient's behalf for more intensive interventions.

REHABILITATION OF COMMON GERIATRIC CONDITIONS

STROKE

Rehabilitation plays a significant role in the recovery from stroke. Information regarding risks, prevention, and early treatment of stroke is covered in Chap. 91. The rehabilitation interventions must start in the first 24 hours after a stroke. Pressure sores in the immobilized patient can develop in 2 hours, while contractures can occur within 24 hours.

Although the degree of functional return is largely dependent on chance, the role of rehabilitation is manifold: (1) to prevent the development of secondary disabilities, (2) to train the patient in functional activities, (3) to promote adaptation to persistent deficits, and (4) to help the patient and family adapt.

In those patients who are to regain lost function, most return will be seen in the first month. Some neurologic return of motor function may be seen as late as 6 months after the stroke. In the case of sensory deficits or swallowing problems, some return may be seen up to 2 years following the stroke. Rehabilitation efforts following stroke have been shown to be cost-effective and to help the patient achieve higher functional levels than those not receiving these interventions.[8] Age does not appear to affect rehabilitation outcome.[28] Family members and the patient need accurate prognostic information in order to make informed decisions about care. In general, among survivors of stroke about 10 percent of patients will completely recover, 40 percent will have minimal degrees of disability, 40 percent will have significant levels of dysfunction, and 10 percent will be completely incapacitated. Hence, rehabilitation can potentially benefit 90 percent of stroke survivors.

The Acute Phase

Prevention of secondary disabilities must begin at the time of admission. Regular turning to prevent the development of pressure sores, daily ranging of the extremities, promotion of bowel and bladder control, and exercise of the uninvolved limbs to prevent deconditioning should be provided. The new stroke patient usually has flail limbs. Subluxation of the shoulder needs to be aggressively prevented so that when motor function returns the arm will be more functional. Pain and the development of the hand-shoulder syndrome (reflex sympathetic dystrophy) are also prevented by regular ranging and close attention to proper bed positioning as well as protecting the shoulder when moving the patient.[48] Nerve palsies are also prevented by close attention to body positioning. The use of a footboard is controversial and should not be used to take the place of active ranging. Temporary urinary incontinence is common though other causes (e.g., infections) should be evaluated. Similarly, the patient's cognitive state is usually clear with a single stroke, and the presence of confusion should lead to investigation. Of course, the cornerstone in the management during the acute phase is medical stabilization: controlling blood pressure and other confounding medical problems.

Factors associated with a poor prognosis are[49]:

Flaccid hemiplegia, greater than 2 months duration
Dementia
Persistent bowel/bladder incontinence
Severe neglect or sensory deficits
Global aphasia

Patients without these factors, and in some cases those with one or two of them, should be evaluated for intensive rehabilitation.

The Rehabilitation Phase

Intensive rehabilitation begins once the patient is reasonably stable. In the older person total stability is elusive, and risks of an intervention must be weighed against risks of prolonged bed rest. There is a fairly predictable pattern of motor return. The initially flaccid limb with hyperactive reflexes will next develop a mass flexor synergism, i.e., the limb will flex at multiple joints when movement is attempted. Later a mass extensor synergism will develop. At this point, even with poor control the lower limb may support walking with a brace and adequate physical training. Selective flexion of individual joints usually follows, and, finally, selective extension with decreased flexor tone returns. Much less predictable is the return of sensory function. Whereas motor return is more important to "overall" rehabilita-

tion potential (for instance, independence in ambulation), sensory return is crucial to functional use of the upper extremity.

Physical therapists usually begin with general strengthening, evaluation of transfer abilities, balance (sitting, then standing), and endurance training. Strength should be tested while the patient is standing because he or she may appear weaker if tested supine. Once the patient has good strength (4/5) in the lower extremities and can balance on the uninvolved side, gait training is begun. If the patient has problems with limb advancement, a brace may be needed and also a cane. The most common braces employed with the elderly are ankle-foot-orthoses (AFO). Two types are often used: the double adjustable upright (used to stabilize the position of the ankle and provide some proprioceptive feedback to the knee) and the posterior plastic splint that prevents footdrop but may not significantly lend to stability at the ankle. Functional electrical stimulation (FES) may be used to supplement the patient's muscular activity as well as provide reeducation to paralyzed muscles.

Training in daily self-care activities continues under the auspices of the occupational therapist. The patient's ability to organize and perform motor acts in sequence will often uncover perceptual deficits. Spasticity can sometimes be controlled by weighted utensils. Special utensils such as rocker knives, plate guards, and reachers enable persons with hemiplegia to function more independently. Speech therapists, and in some institutions occupational therapists, contribute to a cognitive retraining program. Accurate early assessment for the presence of aphasia is critical to providing the team with recommendations regarding communication needs.

Two common, and often related, problems deserve special attention. Depression is frequently seen after a stroke.[25] Early treatment of depression enhances the gains made in rehabilitation. A combination of psychotherapy with judicious use of antidepressant medication is needed. Malnutrition is seen all too commonly in rehabilitation settings. A swallowing evaluation, dietary consultation, and, in some cases, short-term use of enteral feedings (Chap. 31) are usually required.

As with all geriatric patients, attention to premorbid problems must be vigilant. Having access to one's dentures, eyeglasses, and clothing enhance the patient's self-esteem and the ability to participate in the rehabilitation program. The patient's family must be actively incorporated into the treatment. Bedside charts that illustrate gains made by the patient and specify goals to be achieved are also helpful.

The Chronic Phase

Once discharged, the patient must learn to cope with society as a disabled person. Frequently the home will need modifications, especially the bathroom. Raised toilet seats with arm frames, grab bars, and a bathtub bench with a hand-held shower hose are usually needed if the patient is not fully independent. The kitchen may also need modifications. The home should be assessed prior to discharge for door width, presence of stairs, adequacy of lighting, safety features, and need for modifications.

Psychologically the patient will need ongoing support as the adjustment process to a major disability may take up to 2 years. Access to therapy, day health centers, or stroke recovery groups should be considered. Patients should be given frank information regarding the extremely low risk of sexual activities causing another stroke.

Social activities should be encouraged. The return of the patient to work or employment can be assessed by a vocational rehabilitation counselor if desired. Transportation needs are particularly important as many geriatric patients who have suffered a stroke will cease driving. Those with right hemisphere lesions often have neglect and should not drive unless the perceptual deficit remits.

HIP FRACTURES

Hip fractures are one of the most common problems treated in geriatrics. Many patients can benefit from rehabilitative intervention. The geriatrician plays an important role in recommending to the orthopedic surgeon the procedure that will allow for maximum independence and early ambulation. In general, those procedures which allow the greatest amount of weight bearing the sooner after the surgery are preferred. Older persons have great difficulty using crutches or "toe-touch" weight-bearing techniques because of general deconditioning and weak upper extremities.

There are two major types of hip fractures: subcapital and trochanteric. The important differentiating feature between these two types is the high rate of avascular necrosis of the femoral head seen in the subcapital type. Currently most subcapital fractures are treated with installation of an Austin-Moore type of prosthesis. This procedure allows weight bearing to tolerance by the second or third day, an important feature considering the negative consequences of immobilization. Trochanteric fractures should be treated aggressively with internal fixation using a compression screw. The patient can usually bear weight to tolerance of pain by the second day.[5] A prosthesis may also be indicated in the patient with a trochanteric fracture who has preexisting joint disease.[50]

In the past, surgeons have recommended non-weight-bearing status for up to 8 weeks in those patients treated with pins or nails. This duration of relative inactivity is much too long for the geriatric patient. Weight bearing in as little as 1 week after such procedures appears to be safe and well tolerated by most patients. Only those patients who are unable to tolerate a surgical procedure or who were bed-bound before the fracture should be treated conservatively with closed reduction.

Rehabilitation begins when the patient is admitted to the hospital. Though controversial, it appears that stabilization of life-threatening medical problems should occur before surgical repair. Patient education, upper-extremity strengthening, preoperative evaluation by physical and occupational therapy, and training in the exercises to be used while in bed can begin immediately. The day of the operation the patient can begin quadriceps contractions and on the first postoperative day the patient can sit up, conduct isometric exercises and gentle flexion/extension at the hip. The patient should be trained to avoid adduction, excessive flexion, and to a lesser degree abduction at the hip.

By the second or third postoperative day the patient can begin supervised ambulation with parallel bars and advance to the use of a walker or cane. A properly fitted cane should have a 1-inch rubber tip, should be long enough to allow 20 to 30° flexion at the elbow when held at the side, and should support no more than 20 to 25 percent of the body weight. It should be used in the hand opposite the injured hip. By the end of the first week the patient should also start proning exercises to strengthen the hip extensors. During the second week stair training can begin. Patients need to be taught to climb stairs with the uninvolved leg first and come down the stairs with the involved leg first ("up with the good, down with the bad").

When training in the use of a walker, patients need to practice advancing the walker about 8 to 12 inches, then the poor leg, and then the good leg. Some older persons may find it easier to advance the good leg first, however. Special walkers are needed for going up stairs, and it is very difficult to carry any object when using a walker.

The site for rehabilitation of patients with hip fractures depends on the preexisting health and social support status of the patient. The most important factor affecting recovery is the patient's general medical condition.[51] Neurologic disease, especially dementia, is the greatest threat. Patients who could be considered for early discharge and home rehabilitation are those with (1) good health (absence of significant medical problems), (2) strong social supports, i.e., the person lives with someone who can help, and (3) adequate ambulation and ADLs within 2 weeks of surgery. All others may require more intensive therapy than can be provided in the home.

AMPUTATION

Amputations are primarily a geriatric phenomenon. Seventy-five percent of amputations occur in people 65 and older. Most of these are below-the-knee (BK). Peripheral vascular disease is the predominant cause. The elderly person has particular problems in rehabilitating after an amputation. Weak upper extremities, underlying cardiovascular problems, skin that is prone to breakdown, and balance problems all contribute to the complexity involved in their care. A large number of older persons have subsequent amputations of the contralateral side.[52] The geriatrician plays a crucial role in managing these problems as well as in deciding on the most appropriate surgical intervention.

BK amputations are much preferred to above-the-knee (AK) procedures. Postoperative mortality is lower, the energy cost of using a prosthesis is much lower, and the chance of walking without the use of assistive aids is greater with a BK amputation. In fact, the energy cost of having two BK amputations is lower than having a single AK amputation.[4] Such energy costs may be insignificant to a younger person but may easily precipitate angina in the predisposed geriatric patient. The use of a BK prosthesis may also be limited in patients with poor cognition, preexisting joint disease of the affected knee, and contralateral sensory deficits. Contralateral vascular disease is a relative contraindication to use of a prosthesis.

Even those patients who are not to receive a prosthesis can benefit from rehabilitation. These patients must be trained in the use of a special amputation-style wheelchair. Bed, chair, and toilet transfers must also be learned. Modifications will need to be made before the patient returns home. Patients with COPD and cardiovascular insufficiency will need to be stabilized because the energy costs of using a wheelchair are higher than that of walking.

If there are no contraindications, all geriatric patients should be considered for the fitting of a prosthesis. Age is not a determinant factor in this consideration. Rehabilitation should begin before the surgical procedure. Exercise training—including upper body, quadriceps, and hip extensor strengthening—and practicing lying prone can begin before a final decision regarding surgery is made. Contractures, the most common complication of amputations, must be prevented daily by active and passive ranging. Proper bed positioning and not allowing pillows to be placed under the knees are also important.

The patient must be trained in care of the stump including massage techniques, wrapping with an Ace bandage or stump shrinker, inspection for skin integrity and hygiene. Transfers with and without the prosthesis can begin immediately postoperatively. Because many geriatric patients will use a wheelchair for long distances

they must also receive training in its use. Training in sitting and single limb balance is also important.

Most patients have a prosthesis fitted 6 to 8 weeks postoperatively to allow for stump shrinkage and healing. A temporary pylon prosthesis is usually employed in the meantime. Some programs have used casts placed at the time of the operation to promote early ambulation. Results in older persons with such programs is limited. A prosthesis is usually prescribed by a physiatrist or orthotist. Most elderly can be fitted with a patello-tendon-supracondylar (PTS) socket with a solid ankle/cushioned heel (SACH) foot. This type is relatively easy to use and lightweight.

About 75 percent of elderly unilateral BK amputees will achieve independent ambulation while only 50 percent of bilateral BK amputees and less than 50 percent of unilateral AK amputees will walk with a prosthesis. One third will have phantom limb sensation but, fortunately, less than 5 percent have severe pain. These symptoms are best treated by massage and physical therapy. Other problems include a change in the socket size with large weight changes (weight loss affects size more than weight gain), neuroma formation, and local skin problems.

PARKINSON'S DISEASE

Parkinson's disease begins in the early geriatric ages. While drug treatment has led to significant improvements in the care of patients with Parkinson's many are never referred for specific physical interventions. The physical treatment of Parkinson's is an example of "preventive" geriatric rehabilitation.

Rehabilitation efforts are aimed at educating the patient in techniques used to counter the effects of the underlying disease, strengthening and endurance training and proper use of assistive equipment. This training can usually be provided as an outpatient and is best provided early in the course of the illness. The maintenance of the learned skills may be enhanced by involvement in a support group.

Gait and balance training are very important. The patient should be taught to look up, consciously counter the flexed posture and lift the toes when stepping through the swing phase. Lengthening the steps and widening the base may also help. A home program of regular exercises to maintain or improve strength ROM and flexibility should be prescribed. Speech therapy for articulation and breathing exercises should be provided. Some patients find singing to be helpful.

When assistive aids become necessary one should avoid the use of canes. The shoulder protraction and internal rotation of the Parkinson's posture may place the tip of the cane between the legs causing a fall. If a walker is prescribed it should have front wheels as pickup walkers may induce a backward fall. Home modifications such as removing shag or throw rugs and placing rails on all steps and bathroom equipment are often necessary.

DECONDITIONING/IMMOBILITY

One of the most common causes of deconditioning is unnecessary prolonged bed rest during hospitalization. Simply sitting in a chair will maintain a modicum of conditioning reflexes. Patients may not be able to return home due to the declines they have suffered in the hospital in spite of having their admitting diagnosis "successfully" treated. The mainstay of treatment is in prevention. Acute hospital patients should have orders for regular out-of-bed activities, be encouraged to walk to diagnostic studies, and be taught bed and chair exercises. Group exercise programs may be especially beneficial.

The presence of deconditioning may go unnoticed if patients do not stress their cardiopulmonary or muscular systems. In deconditioned patients, an exaggerated heart rate or blood pressure response to exercise, decreased muscle power, and decreased endurance are usually found. It is important to measure the patients' capabilities based upon their expected demand in the anticipated living environment. For instance, if the person needs to be ambulatory in the community it has been determined that he or she would need to be able to walk 332 meters at at least 50 percent normal velocity and negotiate 3 steps, a 3 percent ramp, and a curb.[53] Significantly, one does not need to achieve cardiovascular fitness to make gains in independent living. Velocity and safety determine how the person uses the community.

Interventions are directed to enhancing strength, gait stability and velocity, and in building endurance. If the patient is severely deconditioned, the time required to recover lost strength can be estimated to be three times the length of time he or she was immobilized. Some patients with premorbid cardiac or pulmonary disease may need inpatient treatment.

OTHER CONDITIONS

A wide variety of other conditions are amenable to rehabilitation interventions. Only a minority of spinal cord injuries affect older persons, yet over 73 percent of those who were injured after the age of 60 were able to return home with rehabilitation.[54] Arthritic conditions are the most common chronic illness in the geriatric age group. Rehabilitation techniques are extremely important to maintain function of arthritic joints, mobility, and prevent deterioration. Such interventions are particularly important after joint replacement surgery. The use of adaptive equipment and training in joint protection and energy conservation techniques are cornerstones in the rehabilitative approach to the elderly arthritic patient. Rehabilitation has even been used in Alzheimer's disease.[55] Measures to promote the maintenance of ADLs and provide the caregivers with realistic techniques to promote activities are beneficial.[56] Rehabilitation interventions should be considered in the care of all geriatric patients with functional losses.

REFERENCES

1. Williams TF: Keynote speech. Aging and Rehabilitation Conference, Philadelphia, December 2, 1984.
2. Wedgewood J: The place of rehabilitation in geriatric medicine: An overview. *Int Rehabil Med* 7:107, 1985.
3. *National Survey of Stroke.* Bethesda, MD, U.S. Department of Health, Education, and Welfare, NIH 80-2064, 1980, p 6.
4. Clark GS, Blue B, Bearer JB: Rehabilitation of the elderly amputee. *J Am Geriatr Soc* 31:439, 1983.
5. Kumar VN, Redford JB: Rehabilitation of hip fractures in the elderly, *Am Fam Phys* 29:173, 1984.
6. *A Chartbook of the Federal Council on Aging.* Washington, DHHS (OHDS) 81-20704, 1981, p 29.
7. Enright RB, Friss L: Employed care-givers of brain-damaged adults: An assessment of the dual role. Unpublished study, 1987.
8. Lehman JF et al: Stroke: Does rehabilitation affect outcome? *Arch Phys Med Rehabil* 56:375, 1975.
9. Rubenstein LZ, Josephson KR et al: Effectiveness of a geriatric evaluation unit: A randomized trial. *N Engl J Med* 311:1664, 1984.
10. Sharpless JW: *Mossman's a Problem Oriented Approach to Stroke Rehabilitation.* Springfield, IL, Charles C Thomas, 1982.
11. Avorn J, Langer E: Induced disability in nursing home patients. *J Am Geriatr Soc* 30:397, 1982.
12. Brody E: Informal support systems in the rehabilitation of the disabled elderly, in Brody SJ, Ruff GE (eds): *Aging & Rehabilitation.* New York, Springer, 1986.
13. Shepard RJ: World standards of cardiorespiratory performance. *Arch Environ Health* 13:664, 1966.
14. Kohn R: *Principles of Mammalian Aging.* Englewood Cliffs, NJ, Prentice Hall, 1978, p 169.
15. Shock NW, Norris AH: Neuromuscular coordination as a factor in age changes in muscular exercise, in Brunner D, Jokl E (eds): *Physical Activity and Aging.* Basel, Karger, 1970.
16. Huyck MH, Hoyer WJ: Memory, in *Adult Development & Aging.* Belmont, CA, Wadsworth, 1982, chap 5.
17. Costa PT, McCrae RR: Concurrent validation after 20 years: The implications of personality stability for its assessment. *Adv Personality Assess* 4:2, 1984.
18. Kemp B: Psychosocial and mental health issues in rehabilitation of older persons, in Brody S, Ruff G (eds): *Aging and Rehabilitation.* New York, Springer, 1986.
19. Abdellah FG: Public health aspects of rehabilitation of the aged, in Brody S, Ruff G (eds): *Aging and Rehabilitation.* New York, Springer, 1986.

20. Benedict RC, Ganikos ML: Coming to terms with ageism in rehabilitation. *J Rehabil* 47:19, 1981.
21. Lopez-Aqueres W, Kemp B, Plopper M, Staples F, Brummel-Smith K: Health needs of hispanic elderly. *J Am Geriatr Soc* 32:191, 1984.
22. Lehmann JF: Gait analysis: Diagnosis and management, in Kotke FJ (ed): *Krusen's Handbook of Physical Medicine and Rehabilitation.* Philadelphia, Saunders, 1971.
23. Garcia CA, Tweedy JR, Blass JP: Underdiagnosis of cognitive impairment in a rehabilitation setting. *J Am Geriatr Soc* 32:339, 1984.
24. McCartney JR, Palmateer LM: Assessment of cognitive deficit in geriatric patients. *J Am Geriatr Soc* 33:467, 1985.
25. Collin SJ, Lincoln NB: Depression after stroke. *Clin Rehabil* 1:27, 1987.
26. Gans JS: Depression diagnosis in a rehabilitation hospital. *Arch Phys Med Rehabil* 62:386, 1981.
27. Gill C: "Social Aspects of Disability." Geriatric Rehabilitation grand rounds presentation, Rancho Los Amigos Medical Center, 1985.
28. Adler MK, Brown CC, Acton P: Stroke rehabilitation—Is age a determinant? *J Am Geriatr Soc* 28:499, 1980.
29. Parry F: Physical rehabilitation of the old, old patient. *J Am Geriatr Soc* 31:482, 1983.
30. Bennett AE: Cost-effectiveness of rehabilitation for the elderly: Preliminary results from the community hospital research program. *Gerontologist* 20:284, 1980.
31. Burdman GDM: Student and trainee attitudes on aging. *Gerontologist* 14:65, 1974.
32. Rasch JD, Crystal RM, Thomas KR: The perception of the older adult: A study of trainee attitudes. *J Appl Rehabil Counsel* 8:121, 1977.
33. Johnston MV, Miller LS: Cost-effectiveness of the Medicare three-hour regulation. *Arch Phys Med Rehabil* 67:581, 1986.
34. Jarnlo GB, Ceder L, Thorngren KG: Early rehabilitation at home of elderly patients with hip fractures and consumption of resources in primary care. *Scand J Prim Health Care* 2:105, 1984.
35. Liang MH et al: Evaluation of comprehensive rehabilitation services for elderly homebound patients with arthritis and orthopedic disability. *Arthritis Rheum* 27:258, 1984.
36. Steel K et al: Iatrogenic illness on a general medical service at a university hospital. *N Engl J Med* 304:638, 1981.
37. Warshaw G et al: Functional disability in the hospitalized elderly. *JAMA* 248:847, 1982.
38. Sainsbury R et al: An orthopedic geriatric rehabilitation unit: The first two years experience. *N Z Med J* 99:583, 1986.
39. Feigenson JS, Gitlow HS, Greenberg SD: The disability oriented rehabilitation unit—A major factor influencing stroke outcome. *Stroke* 10:5, 1979.
40. Applegate WB et al: A geriatric rehabilitation and assessment unit in a community hospital. *J Am Geriatr Soc* 31:206, 1983.
41. Strax TE, Ledebur J: Rehabilitating the geriatric patient: Potential and limitations. *Geriatrics,* September, 1979, p 99.
42. Keith RA, Breckenridge K, O'Neil WA: Rehabilitation hospital patient characteristics from the hospital utilization project system. *Arch Phys Med Rehabil* 58:260, 1977.
43. Liem PH, Chernoff R, Carter WJ: Geriatric rehabilitation unit: A 3-year outcome. *J Gerontol* 41:44, 1986.
44. Sutton MA: "Homeward bound": A minimal care rehabilitation unit. *Br Med J* 293:319, 1986.
45. Reed JW, Gessner JE: Rehabilitation in the extended care facility. *J Am Geriatr Soc* 27:325, 1979.
46. Adelman RD et al: A community-oriented geriatric rehabilitation unit in a nursing home. *Gerontologist* 27:143, 1987.
47. Klingbeil G: The assessment of rehabilitation potential in the elderly. *Wis Med J* 81:25, 1982.
48. Kozin F et al: The reflex sympathetic dystrophy syndrome. *Am J Med* 60:321, 332, 1976.
49. McDowell FH: Rehabilitating patients with stroke. *Postgrad Med* 59:145, 1976.
50. Sim FH, Sigmond ER: Acute fractures of the femoral neck managed by total hip replacement. *Orthopedics* 9:35, 1986.
51. Ceder LF, Thorgren KG, Wallden B: Prognostic indicators and early home rehabilitation in elderly patients with hip fractures. *Clin Orthop* 152:173, 1980.
52. Mazet R: The geriatric amputee. *Artif Limbs* 11:33, 1967.
53. Cohen JJ, Sven JD, Walker JM, Brummel-Smith K: Establishing criteria for community ambulation. *Topics Geriatr Rehabil* 3:71, 1987.
54. Watson N: Pattern of spinal cord injury in the elderly. *Paraplegia* 14:36, 1976.
55. Reifler BV, Teri L: Rehabilitation and Alzheimer's disease, in Brody S, Ruff G (eds): *Aging and Rehabilitation.* New York, Springer, 1986.
56. Levy LL: A practical guide to the care of the Alzheimer's disease victim: The cognitive disability perspective. *Topics Geriatr Rehabil* 1:16, 1986.

Chapter 35

NURSING HOME CARE

Joseph G. Ouslander

Nursing homes are an integral component of a broad array of long-term care services for elderly and chronically ill, functionally disabled Americans. Other components of the long-term care system are discussed throughout this text (see Chaps. 25, 33, 36, and 37). Despite the desire of most elderly people to remain in their own homes, and the further development of community long-term care services and innovative specialized geriatric units that can prevent or delay nursing home (NH) admission,[1,2] the need and demand for NH care is likely to increase over the next several decades.

Currently over 1.5 million Americans awaken every day in one of over 18,000 nursing homes.[3] While some NHs provide high-quality care, the poor quality of care in many has been repeatedly documented in the medical literature, congressional testimony, and lay press over the last two decades.[3–8] Some of the most poignant descriptions have come from the perspective of NH residents themselves.[9] Despite this widespread documentation, little has been done to improve the process, quality, and outcomes of NH care. The medical profession must accept much of the responsibility for the poor quality of care in NHs. Most physicians do not care for NH residents, and many of those who do provide substandard care. The visits of physicians are usually brief and superficial, documentation in medical records is scanty, treatable conditions are underdiagnosed or misdiagnosed, and psychotropic drugs are overused and misused. Misuse of psychotropic drugs is also due in part to the absence of mental health interventions by appropriately trained professionals.[10,11] Only recently has interest developed in the education of physicians, nurses, and other health professionals in long-term care and in basic biomedical, clinical, and health services research focusing on NHs and NH residents.[12–18]

Despite the logistical, economic, and attitudinal barriers that can foster inadequate medical care in the NH, there are many relatively straightforward principles and strategies that can lead to improvements in the quality of medical care provided to NH residents. Fundamental to achieving these improvements is a clear perspective on the goals of NH care, which are in many respects quite different from the goals of medical care in other settings and patient populations.

The objectives of this chapter are to briefly review some demographic aspects of NH care and then to focus in particular on the clinical care of NH residents and the appropriate strategies to improve the care currently provided. While the focus of the chapter is on medical care, this by no means implies that other aspects of the care residents of NHs receive (such as nursing, psychosocial, rehabilitative) are not just as important, if not more important.

NURSING HOMES AND NURSING HOME RESIDENTS

The increasing number of people age 85 and older with functional disabilities, the potential decrease in availability of family caregivers who currently provide most noninstitutional long-term-care services (due to smaller, more geographically dispersed families and an increase in the number of working women), and continued restrictive eligibility and reimbursement policies for community long-term-care services will all contribute to an increasing demand for NH care over the next several decades (Fig. 35-1).

Close to two-thirds of NHs are under 100 beds in size, and most are run for profit (Table 35-1).[19] Many nonprofit, often religiously affiliated institutions provide several different levels of care at the same site. These range from board and care through intermediate and skilled nursing care. Intermediate care facilities (ICFs) and skilled nursing facilities (SNFs) are both referred to as NHs in this chapter. A recent Institute of Medicine report recommended eliminating the distinction between these two levels of care.[4] A still small but increasing number of NHs are developing affiliations with medical and nursing schools.[12,14,15–18] Many are becoming

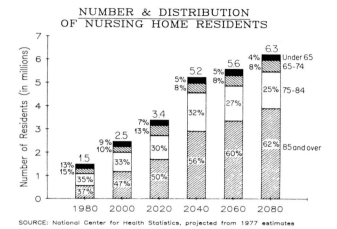

NUMBER & DISTRIBUTION
OF NURSING HOME RESIDENTS

SOURCE: National Center for Health Statistics, projected from 1977 estimates

FIGURE 35-1
Demographics of the nursing home population. (*Reprinted with permission from Ouslander JG, Martin SE, Ref. 27.*)

"vertically integrated" with other geriatric health and social services through affiliations with acute hospitals, health maintenance organizations, and life care communities.

Close to 90 percent of NH employees are nursing staff, predominantly nursing assistants, who provide over 90 percent of hands-on patient care. These individuals are often unlicensed, and their educational background is limited. They frequently do not speak English. The turnover rate for these nursing assistants exceeds 50

percent per year.[20] Less than 20 percent of physicians attend patients at NHs, and when they do, their visits are frequently very brief.[8,21] Most NHs have only part-time social workers and part-time contract physical, occupational, and recreational therapists.

The dynamics of NH populations have been the subject of several recent studies.[22–26] At admission, NH residents appear equally distributed between short stayers (1 to 6 months) and long stayers (who may stay several years). At any one time, however, a cross section of NH residents will reveal a much higher proportion of long stayers. While most NH discharges occur within the first 3 to 6 months after admission, recent studies of NH admissions revealed that only 28 percent were discharged to their own homes and 33 percent were discharged dead. Moreover, 75 percent had died within 2 years.[23,24] Whichever subpopulation is examined, the typical NH resident is an elderly, white, widowed, functionally disabled female. Close to two-thirds of NH patients are women. One-third are 85 or older, one-half have significant degrees of dementia, frequently with associated behavioral disorders, and one-half are incontinent. The majority are nonambulatory and require help in most basic activities of daily living.[19]

For the purpose of discussing clinical care in the NH, it is helpful to subdivide NH residents as depicted in Fig. 35-2.[27] The two basic types of NH residents, short stayers and long stayers, can be further subdivided. Short stayers include (1) patients recovering from

TABLE 35-1
Selected Characteristics of Nursing Homes (1985 data)

Facility Characteristics	Nursing Homes		NH Beds Distribution, %
	Number	Distribution, %	
Total	19,000	100	100
Ownership			
Proprietary	14,300	75	69
Voluntary nonprofit	3,800	20	23
Government	1,000	5	8
Certification			
Certified (total)	14,400	76	89
SNF* Only	3,500	18	19
SNF/ICF†	5,700	30	45
ICF Only	5,300	28	25
Not certified	4,700	24	11
Bed size‡			
Fewer than 50 beds	6,300	33	9
50–99 beds	6,200	33	27
100–199 beds	5,400	28	43
200 beds or more	1,200	6	20

*SNF: Skilled nursing facility.
†ICF: Intermediate care facility.
‡Average bed size is 85 beds.
SOURCE: Adapted from Kane RA, Kane RL, Ref. 19.

FIGURE 35-2
Basic types of nursing home patients. (*Reprinted with permission from Ouslander JG, Martin SE, Ref. 27.*)

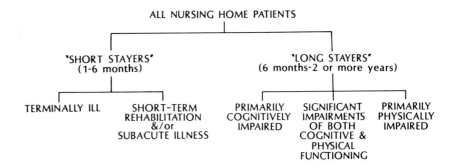

medical and functional problems after an acute illness who have a reasonable expectation of discharge to a lower level of care (e.g., patients recovering from hip fracture, stroke, pneumonia, or decompensated congestive heart failure with prolonged bed rest) and (2) patients who have end-stage or terminal disease (e.g., cancer, severe brain injury, chronic lung disease, or heart failure) and are expected to die in days to weeks. Long stayers are composed of patients with chronic disabilities involving impaired cognitive function (e.g., dementia) or impaired physical function (e.g., stroke, arthritis, multiple sclerosis), or both. The approaches to assessment, the goals for care, and the treatment process differ substantially among these different types of NH residents. The relative proportion of residents of each type can have important programatic and financial implications for individual NHs as well as for NH chains.

THE GOALS OF NURSING HOME CARE

Fundamental to improving the care of NH residents is a clear conception of the goals of care. The key goals of NH care are listed in Table 35-2.[28] While the prevention, identification, and treatment of chronic, subacute, and

TABLE 35-2
Key Goals of Nursing Home Care

Provide a safe and supportive environment for chronically ill and dependent people

Restore and maintain the highest possible level of functional independence

Preserve individual autonomy

Maximize quality of life, perceived well-being, and life satisfaction

Provide comfort and dignity for terminally ill patients and their loved ones

Stabilize and delay progression, whenever possible, of chronic medical conditions

Prevent acute medical and iatrogenic illnesses and identify and treat them rapidly when they do occur

SOURCE: From Kane RL, Ouslander JG, Abrass IB, Ref. 28, with permission.

acute medical conditions are important, most of these goals focus on the functional independence, autonomy, quality of life, comfort, and dignity of the residents. Physicians who care for NH residents must keep these goals in perspective while at the same time addressing the more traditional goals of medical care.

The heterogeneity of the NH population must also be recognized in order to focus and individualize the goals of care. Nursing home residents can be subgrouped into five basic types, as depicted in Fig. 35-2. The focus and goals of care for these five subgroups of NH residents are obviously very different.

Many NHs attempt to isolate these different types of residents geographically. This strategy has several advantages, including the specialized training of staff to care for residents with specific types of problems (e.g., rehabilitation, terminal illness) and the separation of residents with severe dementia and behavioral disturbances from cognitively intact residents. The latter often find interactions with severely demented residents very distressing.

Although it is not always possible to isolate these different types of residents geographically and residents often overlap or change between the types described, subgrouping NH residents in this manner can help the physician and interdisciplinary team focus the care planning process on the most critical and realistic goals for individual residents.

CLINICAL ASPECTS OF CARE FOR NURSING HOME RESIDENTS

In addition to the different goals for care in the NH, several factors make the assessment and treatment of NH residents different from that in other settings (Table 35-3). Many of these factors relate to the process of care, and are discussed in the following section. A fundamental difference in the NH is that medical evaluation and treatment must be complemented by an assessment and care planning process involving staff from multiple disciplines. Data on medical conditions and their treatment are integrated with assessments of the functional, mental, and behavioral status of the resident in order to de-

TABLE 35-3
Factors That Make Assessment and Treatment in the Nursing Home Different from Other Settings

The goals of care are often different (see Table 35-2).

Specific clinical disorders are prevalent among nursing home residents (see Table 35-4).

The approach to health maintenance and prevention differs (see Table 35-6).

Mental and functional status are just as important as, if not more important than, medical diagnoses.

Assessment must be interdisciplinary, including
    Nursing
    Psychosocial
    Rehabilitation
    Nutritional
    Other (e.g., dental, pharmacy, podiatry, audiology, ophthalmology)

Sources of information are variable:
    Patients often cannot give a precise history.
    Family members and nurses' aides with limited assessment skills may provide the most important information.
    Information is often obtained over the telephone.

Administrative procedures for record keeping in both nursing homes and acute hospitals can result in inadequate and disjointed information.

Clinical decision making is complicated for several reasons:
    Many diagnostic and therapeutic procedures are expensive, unavailable, or difficult to obtain and involve higher risks of iatrogenic illness and discomfort than are warranted by the potential outcome.
    The potential long-term benefits of "tight" control of certain chronic illnesses (e.g., diabetes mellitus, congestive heart failure, hypertension) may be outweighed by the risks of iatrogenic illnesses in many very old and functionally disabled residents.
    Many residents are not capable (or questionably capable) of participating in medical decision making, and their personal preferences based on previous decisions are often unknown (see Table 35-8).

The appropriate site for treatment and the level of intensity of such treatment are often difficult decisions that involve medical, emotional, ethical, and legal considerations that may be in conflict with each other in the NH setting.

Logistic considerations, resource constraints, and restrictive reimbursement policies may limit the ability of and incentives for physicians to carry out optimal medical care of nursing home residents.

SOURCE: From Kane Rh, Ouslander JG, Abrass IB, Ref. 28, with permission.

velop a comprehensive data base and individualized plan of care.

Medical evaluation and clinical decision making for NH residents is complicated for several reasons. Unless the physician has cared for a resident before NH admission, it may be difficult to obtain a comprehensive medical data base. Residents may be unable to accurately re-late their medical history or describe their symptoms, and medical records are frequently unavailable or incomplete—especially for residents who have been transferred between NHs and acute hospitals. When acute changes in status occur, initial assessments are often performed by NH staff with limited skills and are transmitted to physicians by telephone. Even when the diagnoses are known or strongly suspected, many diagnostic and therapeutic procedures have an unacceptably high risk-to-benefit ratio among NH residents. For example, a barium enema may cause dehydration or severe fecal impaction; nitrates and other cardiovascular drugs may precipitate syncope or disabling falls in frail ambulatory residents with baseline postural hypotension; and adequate control of blood sugar may be extremely difficult to achieve without a high risk for hypoglycemia among diabetic residents with marginal or fluctuating nutritional intake who may not recognize or complain of hypoglycemic symptoms.

Further compounding these difficulties is the inability of many NH residents to effectively participate in important decisions regarding their medical care. Their prior expressed wishes are often not known, and an appropriate or legal surrogate decision maker has often not been appointed. Several strategies described later in this chapter may help to overcome many of these difficulties.

Table 35-4 lists the most commonly encountered clinical disorders in the NH population. They represent a broad spectrum of chronic medical illnesses; neurologic, psychiatric, and behavioral disorders; and problems which are especially prevalent in the frail elderly—such as incontinence, falls, nutritional disorders, and chronic pain syndromes. Although the incidence of iatrogenic illnesses has not been systematically studied in NHs, it is likely to be as high if not higher than in acute hospitals. The management of many of the conditions listed in Table 35-4 is discussed in some detail in other chapters of this text (see Table of Contents and Index regarding specific conditions). Clinicians caring for NH residents should be especially well versed in the unique medical aspects of managing these conditions in the frail dependent elderly.

In addition to the numerous factors already mentioned that make the medical assessment and treatment of these conditions different, the process of care in NHs also differs substantially from that in acute hospitals, clinics, and home care settings.

PROCESS OF CARE IN THE NURSING HOME

The process of care in NHs is strongly influenced by numerous state and federal regulations, the highly interdisciplinary nature of NH residents' problems, and the

TABLE 35-4
Common Clinical Disorders in the Nursing Home Population

Medical conditions
    Chronic medical illnesses
    Congestive heart failure
    Degenerative joint disease
    Diabetes mellitus
    Obstructive lung disease
    Renal failure
    Infections
        Lower respiratory tract
        Urinary tract
        Skin (pressure sores, vascular ulcers)
        Conjunctivitis
        Gastroenteritis
        Tuberculosis
    Gastrointestinal disorders
        Ulcers
        Reflux esophagitis
        Constipation
        Diarrhea
    Malignancies
Neuropsychiatric conditions
    Dementia
    Behavioral disorders associated with dementia
        Wandering
        Agitation
        Aggression
    Depression
    Neurologic disorders other than dementia
        Stroke
        Parkinsonism
        Multiple sclerosis
        Brain/spinal cord injury
Functional disabilities requiring rehabilitation
    Stroke
    Hip fracture
    Joint replacement
    Amputation
Geriatric problems
    Delirium
    Incontinence
    Gait disturbances, instability, falls
    Malnutrition, feeding difficulties, dehydration
    Pressure sores
    Insomnia
    Chronic pain: musculoskeletal conditions, neuropathies, malignancy
    Iatrogenic disorders
        Adverse drug reactions
        Falls
        Nosocomial infections
        Induced disabilities—restraints and immobility, catheters, unnecessary help with basic activities of daily living
    Death and dying

SOURCE: From Kane RL, Ouslander JG, Abrass IB, Ref. 28, with permission.

training and skills of the staff that delivers most of the hands-on care.

The involvement of the physician in NH care and the nature of medical assessment and treatment offered to NH residents are often limited by logistical and economic factors. Few physicians have offices based either inside the NH or in close proximity to the facility. Many physicians who do visit NHs care for relatively small numbers of residents, often in several different facilities. Most NHs therefore have numerous physicians who make rounds once or twice per month. Although these physicians are not generally present to evaluate acute changes in the status of a resident, they nevertheless often attempt to assess these changes over the telephone. Many NHs do not have the ready availability of laboratory, radiologic, and pharmaceutical services with the capability of rapid response, which further compounds the logistics of evaluating and treating acute changes in medical status. Thus, NH residents are often sent to hospital emergency rooms where they are evaluated by personnel who are generally not familiar with their baseline status and who frequently lack training and interest in the care of frail and dependent elderly patients.

Restrictive Medicare and Medicaid reimbursement policies may also dictate certain patterns of NH care. While physicians are required to visit NH residents only every 30 to 60 days, many residents require more frequent assessment and monitoring of treatment, especially those patients who have the shorter acute hospital stays brought about by the prospective payment system (diagnosis-related groups). Yet, Medicare will generally only reimburse a physician for one routine visit per month, and perhaps one additional visit for an acute problem. Reimbursement for the routine visit is hardly adequate for the time that is required to provide good medical care in the NH, including travel to and from the facility, assessment and treatment planning for residents with multiple problems, communication with members of the interdisciplinary team and the resident's family, and proper documentation in the medical record. Activities which are often essential to good care in the NH, such as attendance at interdisciplinary conferences, family meetings, complex assessments of decision-making capacity, and counseling residents and surrogate decision makers on treatment plans in the event of terminal illness, are generally not reimbursable at all. Medicare intermediaries often restrict reimbursement for rehabilitative services in what seems to be a variable and inequitable manner, thus limiting the treatment options for many residents.[29] Although Medicaid programs vary considerably, most provide minimal coverage for ancillary services that are critical for optimum medical care, and many restrict reimbursement for several types of drugs which may be especially helpful for NH residents.

Amidst these logistic and economic constraints,

TABLE 35-5

Important Aspects of Various Types of Assessments in the Nursing Home (NH)

Types of Assessments	Timing	Major Objectives	Important Aspects
Medical Initial	Within 48 hours of admission	Verify medical diagnoses Document baseline physical findings, mental and functional status, vital signs, and skin condition Attempt to identify potentially remediable, previously unrecognized medical conditions Get to know the resident and family (if this is a new resident) Establish goals for the admission and a medical treatment plan	A thorough review of medical records and physical examination are necessary Relevant medical diagnoses and baseline findings should be clearly and concisely documented in the patient's record Medication lists should be carefully reviewed and only essential medications continued Requests for specific types of assessments and inputs from other disciplines should be made An initial medical problem list should be established
Periodic	Usually monthly	Monitor progress of active medical conditions Update medical orders Communicate with patient and NH staff	Progress notes should include clinical data relevant to active medical conditions and focus on changes in status Unnecessary medications, orders for care, and laboratory tests should be discontinued Mental, functional, and psychosocial status should be reviewed with NH staff, and changes from baseline noted The medical problem list should be updated
As needed	When acute changes in status occur	Identify and treat causes of acute changes	On-site clinical assessment by the physician (or nurse practitioner/physician assistant), as opposed to telephone consultation, will result in more accurate diagnoses, more appropriate treatment, and fewer unnecessary emergency room visits and hospitalization Vital signs, food and fluid intake, and mental status often provide essential information Infection, dehydration, and adverse drug effects should be at the top of the differential diagnosis for acute changes in status

TABLE 35-5 (*CONTINUED*)

Types of Assessments	Timing	Major Objectives	Important Aspects
Major reassessment	Annual	Identify and document any significant changes in status and new potentially remediable conditions	Targeted physical examination and assessment of mental, functional, and psychosocial status and selected laboratory tests should be done (see Table 35-7)
Nursing	Within hours of admission, and then routinely with monitoring of daily and weekly progress	Identify biopsychosocial and functional status strengths and weaknesses Develop an individualized care plan Document baseline data for ongoing assessments	Particular attention should be given to emotional state, personal preferences, and sensory function Careful observation during the first few days of admission is important to detect effects of relocation Potential problems related to other disciplines should be recorded and communicated to appropriate members of the interdisciplinary care team
Psychosocial	Within 1–2 weeks of admissions and as needed thereafter	Identify any potentially serious psychological signs or symptoms and refer to mental health professional, if appropriate Determine past social history, family relationships, and social resources Become familiar with personal preferences regarding living arrangement	Getting to know family members and their preferences and concerns are critical to good NH care Relevant psychosocial data should be communicated to the interdisciplinary team
Rehabilitation (physical and occupational therapy)	Within days of admission and daily or weekly thereafter (depending on the rehabilitation program)	Determine functional status as it relates to basic activities of daily living Identify specific goals and time frame for improving specific areas of function Monitor progress toward goals Assess progress in relation to potential for discharge	Small gains in functional status can improve chances for discharges as well as quality of life Not all residents have areas in which they can reasonably be expected to improve; strategies to maintain function should be developed for these residents Assessment of and recommendations for modifying the environment can be critically important for improving function and discharge planning
Nutritional	Within days of admission and then periodically thereafter	Determine nutritional status and needs Identify dietary preferences Plan an appropriate diet	Restrictive diets may not be medically necessary, and can be unappetizing Weight loss should be identified and reported to nursing and medical staff

(Continued)

337

TABLE 35-5 *(CONTINUED)*
Important Aspects of Various Types of Assessments in the Nursing Home (NH)

Types of Assessments	Timing	Major Objectives	Important Aspects
Interdisciplinary care plan	Within 1–2 weeks of admission and every 3–4 months thereafter	Identify interdisciplinary problems Establish goals and treatment plans Determine when maximum progress toward goals has been reached	Each discipline should prepare specific plans for communication to other team members based on their own assessment
Capacity for medical decision making*	Within days of admission and then whenever changes in status occur	Determine which types of medical decisions the resident is capable of participating in If resident still is capable, encourage him or her to identify a surrogate decision maker in the event he or she becomes incapable of participation in medical decision making If the resident lacks capacity for many or all decisions, appropriate surrogate decision makers should be identified (if not already done)	Residents with varying degrees of dementia may still be capable of participating in many decisions regarding their medical care Attention should be given to potentially reversible factors that can interfere with decision-making capacity (e.g., depression, fear, delirium, metabolic, and drug effects) Family and health professional concerns should be considered, but the resident's desires should be paramount The resident's capacity may fluctuate over time because of physical and emotional conditions
Preferences regarding treatment intensity* and NH routines	Within days of admission and periodically thereafter	Determine resident's wishes as to the intensity of treatment he or she would want in the event of acute or chronic progressive illness	Specificity is important (i.e., "No heroic measures" is ambiguous) Attempt to identify specific procedures the resident would or would not want This assessment is often made by ascertaining the resident's prior expressed wishes (if known), or through surrogate decision-makers (legal guardian, durable power of attorney for health care, family)

*See Table 35-8; these issues are also discussed in more detail in Chap. 39.
SOURCE: From Kane RL, Ouslander JG, Abrass IB, Ref. 28, with permission.

expectations for the care of NH residents are high. Table 35-5 outlines the various types of assessments that are generally recommended for the optimal care of NH residents. Physicians are responsible for completing an initial assessment within 48 hours of admission and for monthly or bimonthly visits thereafter. Licensed nurses assess new residents as soon as they are admitted, on a daily basis, and generally summarize the status of each resident weekly. The extent of involvement of other disciplines in the assessment and care planning process varies depending on the residents' problems, the availability of various professionals, and state regulations. Most states require some type of involvement by the disciplines listed in Tables 35-3 and 35-5.

Representatives from nursing, social service, die- tary, recreational activities, and rehabilitation therapy (physical and/or occupational) participate in an interdis- ciplinary care planning meeting. Residents are generally discussed at this meeting within 2 weeks of admission and quarterly thereafter. The product of these meetings is an interdisciplinary care plan, which separately lists interdisciplinary problems (such as restricted mobility, incontinence, wandering, diminished food intake, poor social interaction, etc.), goals for the resident related to the problem, approaches to achieving these goals, target dates for achieving the goals, and assignment of respon- sibilities for working toward the goals among the various disciplines. These care plans are frequently the subject of careful scrutiny by state and federal auditors. The in- terdisciplinary care planning process serves as a corner- stone for resident management in many facilities, but it is a difficult and time-consuming process which requires leadership and tremendous interdisciplinary (and inter- personal) cooperation.[30] Staffing limitations in relation to the amount of time and effort required makes intensive interdisciplinary care planning and teamwork unrealistic in many nursing homes. Although physicians are usually not directly involved in the care planning meetings in most facilities, they are generally required to review and sign the care plan and may find the team's perspective very valuable in planning subsequent medical care.

STRATEGIES TO IMPROVE MEDICAL CARE IN NURSING HOMES

Several strategies might improve the process of medical care delivered to NH residents. Three such strategies will be described briefly: the use of a comprehensive face sheet and documentation standards, the use of nurse practitioners or physicians' assistants, and a sys- tematic approach to screening, health maintenance, and preventive practices for the elderly dependent NH pop- ulation. In addition to these strategies, strong leadership of a medical director who is appropriately trained and dedicated to improving the facility's quality of medical care is essential in order to develop, implement, and monitor policies and procedures for medical services. The role of the medical director in the NH is discussed in detail elsewhere.[31] He or she should set standards for medical care and serve as an example to the medical staff by caring for some of the residents in the facility. The medical director should also be involved in various com- mittees (representing the pharmacy, infection control, quality assurance) and should involve interested medical staff in these committees as well as educational efforts through formal in-service presentations, teaching rounds, and appropriate documentation procedures.

One of the fundamental problems with the medical care delivered to NH residents is in fact documentation. As already mentioned, NH residents often have multiple coexisting medical problems and long past medical histo- ries. Residents often cannot relate their medical history, and their previous medical records are frequently un- available or incomplete. Thus, it is difficult, and some- times impossible, to obtain a comprehensive medical data base. The effort should, however, be invested and not wasted. Critical aspects of the medical data base should be recorded on one page or face sheet of the medical record. An example of a format for a face sheet is shown in Figure 35-3. The face sheet should also contain some information on the resident's neuropsychiatric and usual mental status, social information such as individu- als to contact at critical times, and information about the resident's treatment status in the event of acute illness. These are data essential to the care of the resident, and should be readily available in one place in the record so that when emergencies arise, when medical consultants see the resident, or when members of the interdiscipli- nary team need an overall perspective, they are easy to locate. The face sheet should be copied and sent to the hospital or other health care facilities to which the resi- dent might be transferred. Time and effort will be re- quired in order to keep the face sheet updated. For facil- ities with access to computers and/or word processing, incorporating the face sheet into a data base should be relatively easy and will facilitate its rapid completion and periodic updating.

Medical documentation in progress notes for rou- tine visits and assessments of acute changes is frequently scanty and/or illegible. "Stable" or "No change" are too frequently the only documentation for routine visits. Even though time constraints may preclude extensive notes, certain standard information should be docu- mented. The SOAP (Subjective, Objective, Assessment, Plan) format for charting routine notes is especially ap- propriate for NH residents (Table 35-6). In facilities in which microcomputers are available, simple data bases with word-processing capabilities can be used to enable physicians to efficiently produce legible, concise, yet comprehensive progress notes.

Another area in which medical documentation is often inadequate relates to the residents' decision- making capacity and treatment preferences. These is- sues are discussed briefly at the end of this chapter as well as in Chap. 39. In addition to placing critical infor- mation on the face sheet and other areas (e.g., identify- ing residents on "No CPR Status" on the front and/or spine of the medical record), it is essential that physi- cians thoroughly and legibly document all discussions they have had with the resident, family, legal guardians, and/or durable power of attorney for health care about these issues. Failure to do so not only may result in poor

IDENTIFYING DATA

Name_____   Age_____

Record No._____

Date of original admission to facility_____/___/___ Most recent readmission____/___/___

Primary physician_____   *(if applicable)*

ACTIVE MEDICAL PROBLEMS

1._____
2._____
3._____
4._____
5._____
6._____
7._____
8._____

NEUROPSYCHIATRIC STATUS

A. Dementia
   ____Absent   ____Present
   If present:
   ____Alzheimer's type
   ____Multi–infarct
   ____Mixed
   ____Other (_____)
   ____Uncertain

B. Psychiatric/behavioral disorders
   1._____
   2._____

C. Usual Mental Status
   _____Alert, oriented, follows direction
   _____Alert, disoriented, but follows
         directions
   _____Alert, disoriented, cannot follow
   _____Not alert (lethargic, comatose)

TREATMENT STATUS   (See note dated___/___/___)

____Full code   ____DNR, do not hospitalize, treat
                              infections, etc. in facility
____DNR, but hospitalize ____Supportive care
                              ____ including enteral feeding
                              ____ no enteral feeding

Signature _____ Date: _____/___/___

PAST HISTORY

A. Acute hospitalizations (since original
      admission to facility)
      Diagnoses   Date (mos/yr)
   1._____   _____
   2._____   _____
   3._____   _____

B. Major Surgical Procedures
      Procedure   Date (yr)
   1._____   _____
   2._____   _____
   3._____   _____

C. Allergies
   1._____
   2._____

SOCIAL INFORMATION

   Name   Phone No.

_____   _____
Closest relative (relationship)

_____   _____
Other relative or friend

_____
Legal guardian

_____
Durable Power for Health Care

Religious Preference:_____

FIGURE 35-3
Example of a face sheet for a nursing home medical record. *(Reprinted with permission from Kane RL, Ouslander JG, Abrass IB, Ref. 28.)*

communication and inappropriate treatment, but in substantial legal liability. Notes about these issues should not be thinned from the medical record and are probably best kept on a separate page behind the face sheet.

A second approach to improving medical care in NHs is the development and implementation of selected screening, health maintenance, and preventive practices. Table 35-7 lists examples of such practices. With few exceptions, the efficacy of these practices has not been well-studied in the NH setting. In addition, not all the practices listed in Table 35-7 are relevant for every NH resident. For example, some of the annual screening examinations are not appropriate for short stayers, or for many long staying residents with end-stage dementia (Fig. 35-2). Thus, the practices outlined in Table 35-6 must be tailored to the specific NH population as well as to the individual resident and must be creatively incorporated into routine care procedures as much as possible in order to be time-efficient, cost-effective, and reimbursable by Medicare.

All long staying residents should have some type of comprehensive, multidisciplinary reevaluation yearly. The efficacy of a routine standard annual history and physical examination and large panels of laboratory tests has been questioned.[32–36] A targeted physical examination and functional assessment and selected laboratory tests are probably beneficial.[36] Because reactivated tuberculosis is relatively common among the chronically ill elderly, all NH residents should have a skin test (with controls) on admission and yearly (unless they have a known prior positive test).[37] Recently, testing for the "booster phenomenon" has been recommended 10 to 14 days after an initial negative test, because there is some incidence (probably in the range of 5 to 15 percent) of conversion to a positive response during this time period which could be falsely interpreted as conversion upon subsequent annual testing. Many NH residents are anergic, which can create difficulty in detecting active cases. Details about recommendations for tuberculosis screening in NHs can be found elsewhere.[37–40]

Because most NH residents have chronic medical conditions which are being actively treated, monitoring of these conditions and their treatment becomes an important aspect of medical care. Several examples of such monitoring are presented in Table 35-7. Vital signs and weight are extremely important to assess accurately on a routine basis, so that when acute or subacute changes occur, they can be compared to the resident's baseline.

Despite the old age and prevalence of chronic medical conditions and functional disabilities among the NH population, several preventive health practices may be effective. Most of these are related to infectious diseases (Table 35-7). One important exception relates to body positioning and range of motion for immobile residents, with the hope of preventing pressure sores, contractures, and aspiration pneumonia. In addition to preventive practices for NH residents, prevention is also rele-

TABLE 35-6
SOAP Format for Medical Progress Notes on NH Residents

Subjective	New complaints
	Symptoms related to active medical conditions
	Reports from nursing staff
	Progress in rehabilitative therapy
	Reports of other interdisciplinary team members
Objective	General appearance
	Weight
	Vital signs
	Physical findings relevant to new complaints and active medical conditions
	Laboratory data
	Consultant reports
Assessment	Presumptive diagnosis(es) for new complaints or changes in status
	Stability of active medical conditions
Plans	Changes in medications or diet
	Nursing interventions (e.g., monitoring or vital signs, skin care, etc.)
	Assessments by other disciplines
	Consultants
	Laboratory studies
	Discharge planning (if relevant)

SOURCE: From Kane RL, Oulsander JG, Abrass IB, Ref. 28, with permission.

TABLE 35-7
Screening, Health Maintenance, and Preventive Practices in the Nursing Home (NH)

Practice	Minimum Recommended Frequency*	Commments
Screening		
History and physical examination	Yearly	Generally required, but yield of routine annual history and physical is debated
		Focused exam probably beneficial, including rectal, breast, and in some women pelvic exam
Weight	Monthly	Generally required
		Persistent weight loss should prompt a search for treatable medical, psychiatric, and functional conditions
Functional status assessment, including gait and mental status testing	Yearly	Functional status usually assessed periodically by nursing staff
		Systematic global functional assessment should be done at least yearly in order to detect potentially treatable conditions or prevent complications such as early dementia, gait disturbances, urinary incontinence

(Continued)

TABLE 35-7 (*CONTINUED*)
Screening, Health Maintenance, and Preventive Practices in the Nursing Home (NH)

Practice	Minimum Recommended Frequency*	Commments
Visual screening	Yearly	Assess acuity, intraocular pressure, identify correctable problems
Auditory	Yearly	Identify correctable problems
Dental	Yearly	Assess status of any remaining teeth, fit of dentures, and identify any pathology
Podiatry	Yearly	More frequently in diabetics and residents with peripheral vascular disease Identify correctable problems and ensure appropriateness of shoes
Tuberculosis	On admission and yearly	All residents and staff should be tested Control skin tests and booster testing is generally recommended for NH residents (see text)

Laboratory tests
  Stool for occult blood
  Complete blood count
  Fasting glucose
  Electrolytes
  Renal function tests
  Albumin, calcium,
    phosphorus
  Thyroid function tests
    (including thyroid-
    stimulating hormone
    (TSH) level)
	Yearly	These tests appear to have reasonable yield in the NH population (see Ref. 36)

Monitoring in selected residents		

All residents
  Vital signs, including
    weight
Diabetics
  Fasting and postprandial glucose, glycosylated hemoglobin
	Monthly	More often if unstable or subacutely ill Fingerstick tests may also be useful if staff can perform reliably

Residents on diuretics or with renal insufficiency (Residents with creatinine level >2, or BUN >35): electrolytes, BUN, creatinine	Every 2–3 months	NH residents are more prone to dehydration, azotemia, hyponatremia, and hypokalemia
Anemic residents who are on iron replacement or who have hemoglobin lower than 10: hemoglobin/hematocrit	Monthly until stable, then every 2–3 months	Iron replacement should be discontinued once hemoglobin value stabilizes
Blood level of drug for residents on specific drugs, e.g., digoxin, phenytoin,	Every 3–6 months	More frequently if drug treatment has just been initiated

TABLE 35-7 *(CONTINUED)*

Practice	Minimum Recommended Frequency*	Commments
quinidine, procainamide, theophylline, nortriptyline		
Prevention		
Influenza		
Vaccine	Yearly	All residents and staff with close resident contact should be vaccinated
Amantadine	Within 24–48 hours of outbreak of suspected influenza type A	Dose should be reduced to 100 mg/day in elderly; further reduction if renal failure present
		Unvaccinated residents and staff should be treated throughout outbreak; those vaccinated can be treated until their symptoms resolve
Pneumococcal/pneumonia bacteremia Pneumococcal vaccine	Once	Efficacy in NH residents is debated
Tetanus Booster	Every 10 years; every 5 years with tetanus-prone wounds	Many elderly people have not received primary vaccinations; they require tetanus toxoid, 250–500 U of tetanus immunoglobulin, and completion of the immunization series with toxoid injection 4–6 weeks later and then 6–12 months after the second injection
Tuberculosis Isoniazid 300 mg/day for 1 year	Skin test conversion in selected residents	Residents with abnormal chest x ray (more than granuloma), diabetes, end-stage renal disease, hematalogic malignancies, steroid or immunosuppressive therapy, malnutrition should be treated
Infections Antimicrobial prophy- laxis for residents at risk†	Generally recommended for dental procedures, genitourinary procedures, and most operative procedures	Chronically catheterized residents should not be treated with continuous prophylaxis (see Chap. 115)
Immobility Body positioning and range of motion for immobile residents	Ongoing	Frequent turning of very immobile residents is necessary to prevent pressure sores
		Semiupright position is necessary for residents with swallowing disorders or enteral feeding to help prevent aspiration
		Range of motion to immobile limbs and joints is

(Continued)

TABLE 35-7 *(CONTINUED)*
Screening, Health Maintenance, and Preventive Practices in the Nursing Home (NH)

Practice	Minimum Recommended Frequency*	Commments
		necessary to prevent contractures
Infection control procedures and surveillance	Ongoing	Policies and protocols should be in effect in all NHs
		Surveillance of all infections should be continuous to identify outbreaks and resistance patterns
Environmental safety	Ongoing	Appropriate lighting and colors, and the removal of hazards for falling are essential in order to prevent accidents
		Routine monitoring of potential safety hazards and accidents may lead to alterations which may prevent further accidents

*Frequency may vary depending on resident's condition.
†See Yoshikowa TT, Norman DC, Ref. 45, for detailed recommendations.
SOURCE: From Kane RL, Ouslander JG, Abrass IB, Ref. 28, with permission.

vant for the entire NH staff. All NH staff who have close contact with residents should be vaccinated against influenza annually.[41] The NH staff must also be intensively educated about infection control procedures such as hand washing, wound care, and catheter care.[42-45]

The facility should have sound policies and procedures for infection control and should monitor patterns of infection and antimicrobial susceptibility carefully. Because of the prevalent and often inappropriate use of antimicrobials, resistant organisms and *Clostridia difficile* diarrhea have become important problems in NHs.[46] Another example of facility-wide prevention relates to environmental safety. Recommendations for assessing and altering the home environment in order to prevent falls are also relevant to NHs. Facilities should monitor falls and other accidents and make routine "environmental rounds" in order to identify potential hazards.

The third strategy that may help improve medical care in NHs is the use of nurse practitioners and physicians' assistants. Although the cost effectiveness of this approach has not been well documented, these health professionals may be especially helpful in carrying out specific functions in the NH setting. Recent legislation has enabled physicians' assistants to bill for certain services under Medicare. Nurse practitioners cannot bill Medicare directly; however several states will reimburse their care, and individual facilities and/or physician's groups will hire them on a salaried basis. Although there is substantial overlap in training and skills, nurse practi-

tioners may have a especially helpful perspective in interacting with nursing staff about the nonmedical aspects of NH resident care. On the other hand, physicians' assistants may be especially helpful in facilities where there is a high concentration of subacutely ill patients who require frequent medical assessment and intervention. Both can be very helpful in implementing some of the screening, monitoring, and preventive practices outlined in Table 35-7, and in communicating with interdisciplinary staff, families, and residents at times when the physician is not in the facility. One of the most appropriate roles for nurse practitioners and physicians' assistants is in the initial assessment of acute or subacute changes in the status of the resident. They can perform a focused history and physical examination and can order appropriate diagnostic studies. Several algorithms have been developed for this purpose,[47] one of which is shown in Fig. 35-4. This strategy enables the on-site assessment of acute change, the detection and treatment of new problems early in their course, more appropriate utilization of acute-hospital emergency rooms, and the rapid identification of residents who need to be hospitalized.

THE NURSING HOME—ACUTE-CARE HOSPITAL INTERFACE

NH residents are frequently transferred back and forth between the NH and one or more acute hospitals. The major reasons for transfer include infection and the need

FIGURE 35-4
Example of an algorithm protocol for the management of acute abdominal pain in the nursing home by a nurse practitioner or physician's assistant. (*Reprinted with permission from Kane RL, Ouslander JG, Abrass IB, Ref. 28.*)

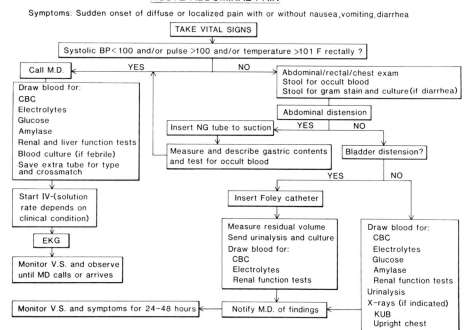

ACUTE ABDOMINAL PAIN

Symptoms: Sudden onset of diffuse or localized pain with or without nausea, vomiting, diarrhea

for parenteral antimicrobials and hydration, as well as certain acute cardiovascular conditions and hip fractures. Transfer to an acute hospital is often a very disruptive process for a chronically ill NH resident. In addition to the effects of the acute illness, NH residents are subject to acute changes in mental status and a myriad of potential iatrogenic problems. Probably the most prevalent of these iatrogenic problems are related to immobility, including deconditioning and difficulty regaining ambulation and/or transfer capabilities, and the development of pressure sores.

Because of the risks of acute hospitalization, the decision to hospitalize a NH resident must carefully weigh a number of factors. A variety of medical, administrative, logistic, economic, and ethical issues can influence decisions to hospitalize NH residents. (It is beyond the scope of this chapter to discuss these issues in detail; they are reviewed at length elsewhere.[48–50]) Very often when NH residents become acutely ill, they simply need a few days of close observation with intravenous antimicrobials and hydration, such as for a lower respiratory or urinary tract infection. Decisions about hospitalization in these situations boil down to the capabilities of the physician and NH staff in providing these services in the NH, the preferences of the resident and the family, and the logistic and administrative arrangements for acute-hospital care. If for example, the NH staff has been trained and has the personnel to institute intravenous therapy without detracting from the care of the other residents, and there is a nurse practitioner or physicians' assistant to perform follow-up assessments, the resident

with an acute infection who is otherwise medically stable may best be managed in the NH. Many facilities, however, have limited nurse staffing; they do not run continuous intravenous infusions, and they do not have nurse practitioners or physicians' assistants and will therefore not be capable of managing these situations adequately.

One of the biggest difficulties arising from the frequent transfer of NH residents to acute hospitals is the disruption in the continuity of medical records at a time when major changes in the residents' status are occurring. Hospitals often receive inadequate information from the NH records upon transfer, and vice versa when the resident is transferred back to the NH. Most NHs begin an entirely new medical record after a resident has been readmitted from an acute hospital stay of longer than 7 to 14 days, which further compounds the difficulty in obtaining an adequate medical data base. Utilizing a face sheet similar to the one depicted in Fig. 35-3 will help provide hospital personnel and physicians (who may be covering the primary physician) with critical data and will help update these data when the face sheet is completed at the NH on readmission. The physician's hospital discharge summaries are rarely available within 24 to 48 hours of the resident's NH admission, and standard intrafacility transfer forms often contain incomplete or ambiguous information. The development of a standard discharge summary form with data tailored to the needs of the NH will greatly improve transfer of information and the assessment process.

These are just a few of many potential strategies for improving care in NHs. In addition to the need for improved medical care, there is a great unmet need for mental health services.[10] Given the prevalence of dementia, depression, and related behavioral disorders in NHs, it is critical that the availability and quality of mental health services for NH residents be improved as quickly as possible.

ETHICAL ISSUES IN NURSING HOME CARE

Ethical issues arise as much, if not more often, in the day-to-day care of NH residents than in the care of patients in any other setting. Since these issues are discussed at length in Chap. 39, they will only be briefly mentioned here. Several of the most common ethical dilemmas that occur in the NH are outlined in Table 35-8. NHs care for an extraordinarily high concentration of individuals who are unable or questionably capable of participating in decisions about their current and future health care. It is among these same individuals that severe functional disabilities and terminal illness are very prevalent. Thus, questions about individual autonomy, decision-making capacity, surrogate decision makers, and the intensity of treatment that should be given at the end of life arise on a daily basis. These questions are both troublesome and complex,[51] but must be dealt with in a straightforward and systematic manner in order to provide optimal medical care to NH residents within the context of ethical principles and state and federal laws. Ethics committees have been established in some NHs, and all NHs should be encouraged to either establish such a committee or to become affiliated with an institution that has one that can serve the NH. In addition to Chap. 39, several recent articles have been written which discuss the issues listed in Table 35-8 in considerable detail.[52–63]

REFERENCES

1. Rubenstein LZ, Josephson KR, Weiland D et al: Effectiveness of a geriatric evaluation unit: A randomized clinical trial. *N Engl J Med* 311:1664, 1984.
2. Rubenstein LZ, Campbell LJ, Kane RL (eds): Geriatric assessment. *Clin Geriatr Med* 3 (No. 1): 1987.
3. Vladek B: *Unloving Care: The Nursing Home Tragedy.* New York, Basic Books, 1980.
4. Institute of Medicine: *Improving the Quality of Care in Nursing Homes.* Washington, DC, National Academy Press, 1986.
5. Moss FE, Halamandaris VJ: *Too Old, Too Sick, Too Bad: Nursing Homes in America.* Germantown, PA, Aspen Systems, 1977.
6. Rango N: Nursing home care in the United States: Prevailing conditions and policy implications. *N Engl J Med* 307:883, 1982.
7. Somers AR: Long-term care for the elderly and disabled: A new health priority. *N Engl J Med* 307:221, 1982.
8. Rabin DL: Physician care in nursing homes. *Ann Intern Med* 94:126, 1981.
9. Anonymous: Is anybody listening? Letter to the Los Angeles Times, September 23, 1979.
10. Ray WA, Federspeil CF, Schaffner W: A study of antipsychotic drug use in nursing homes: Epidemiologic evidence suggesting misuse. *Am J Pub Health* 70(5):485, 1980.
11. Borson S, Liptzin B, Nininger J, Rabins P: Psychiatry in the nursing home. *Am J Psychiat* 144:1412, 1987.

TABLE 35-8
Common Ethical Issues in the Nursing Home (NH)

Ethical Issues*	Examples
Preservation of autonomy	Choices in many areas are limited in most NH (e.g., meal times, sleeping hours)
	Families, physicians and NH staff tend to become paternalistic
Decision-making capacity	Many NH residents are incapable, or questionably capable, of participating in decisions about their care
	There are no standard methods of assessing decision-making capacity in this population
Surrogate decision making	Many NH residents have not clearly stated their preferences or appointed a surrogate before becoming unable to decide for themselves
	Family members may be in conflict, have hidden agendas, or be incapable of making decisions or unwilling to make them
Quality of life	This concept is often entered into decision making, but it is difficult to measure—especially among those with dementia
	Ageist biases can influence perceptions of NH residents' quality of life
Intensity of treatment	A range of options must be considered, including cardiopulmonary resuscitation and mechanical ventilation, hospitalization, treatment of specific conditions (e.g., infection) in the NH without hospitalization, enteral feeding, comfort, or supportive care only

*Approaches to these ethical issues are discussed further in Table 35-5 and Chap. 39.

12. Aiken LH, Mezey MD, Lynaugh JE, et al: Teaching nursing homes: Prospects for improving long-term care. *J Am Geriatr Soc* 33:196, 1985.

13. Health and Public Policy Committee, American College of Physicians: Long-term care of the elderly. *Ann Intern Med* 100:760, 1984.

14. Jahnigen DW, Dramer AM, Robbins LJ, et al: Academic affiliation with a nursing home: Impact on patient outcome. *J Am Geriatr Soc* 33:472, 1985.

15. Libow LS: The teaching nursing home: Past, present and future. *J Am Geriatr Soc* 32:598, 1984.

16. Schneider EL (ed): *The Teaching Nursing Home: A New Approach to Geriatric Research, Education and Clinical Care.* New York, Raven Press, 1985.

17. Williams C: Teaching nursing homes: Their impact on public policy, patient care and medical education. *J Am Geriatr Soc* 33:189, 1985.

18. Wieland GD, Rubenstein LZ, Ouslander JG et al: Organizing an Academic nursing home: Impacts of institutionalized elderly. *JAMA* 255:2622, 1986.

19. Kane RA, Kane RL: *Long Term Care: Principles, Programs and Policies.* New York, Springer, 1987.

20. Waxman HM, Carner EA, Berkenstock G: Job turnover and job satisfaction among nursing home aides. *Gerontologist* 24:503, 1984.

21. Schwartz TB: How to install a first-rate doctor in a third-rate nursing home. *N Engl J Med* 306:743, 1982.

22. Keeler EB, Kane RL, Solomon DH: Short and long-term residents of nursing homes. *Med Care* 19:363, 1981.

23. Lewis MA, Kane RL, Cretin S et al: The immediate and subsequent outcomes of nursing home care. *Am J Public Health* 75:758, 1985.

24. Lewis MA, Cretin S, Kane RL: The natural history of nursing home patients. *Gerontologist* 25:382, 1985.

25. Liu K, Manton KG: The characteristics and utilization pattern of an admission cohort of nursing home patients. *Gerontologist* 22:92, 1983.

26. Liu K, Manton KG: The characteristics and utilization pattern of an admission cohort of nursing homes patients: II. *Gerontologist* 24:70, 1984.

27. Ouslander JG, Martin SE: Assessment in the nursing home. *Clin Geriatr Med* 3:155, February 1987.

28. Kane RL, Ouslander JG, Abrass IB: *Essentials of Clinical Geriatrics*, 2d ed. New York, McGraw-Hill, 1988.

29. Smits HL, Feder J, Scanlon W: Medicare's nursing-home benefit: Variations in interpretation. *N Engl J Med* 307 (6):353, 1981.

30. Baldwin D, Tuskuda R: Interdisciplinary teams, in Cassel C, Walsh J (eds): *Geriatric Medicine.* New York, Springer-Verlag, vol 2, 1985.

31. Levensen, S (ed): *Medical Direction in Long Term Care.* Owings Mills, MD, National Health Publishing, 1988.

32. Gambert SR, Duthie EH, Wiltzius F: The value of the yearly medical evaluation in a nursing home. *J Chron Dis* 35:65, 1982.

33. Irvine PW, Carlson K, Adcock M et al: The value of annual medical examinations in the nursing home. *J Am Geriatr Soc* 32:540, 1984.

34. Domoto K, Ben R, Wei JY et al: Yield of routine annual laboratory screening in the institutionalized elderly. *Am J Public Health* 75:243, 1985.

35. Wolf-Klein GP, Holt T, Silverstone FA et al: Efficacy of routine annual studies in the care of elderly patients. *J*

36. Levenstein MR, Ouslander JG, Rubenstein LZ, Forsythe SB: Yield of routine annual laboratory tests in a skilled nursing home population. *JAMA* 258(14):1909, 1987.

37. Stead WW, Lofgren JP, Warren E, Thomas C: Tuberculosis as an endemic and nosocomial infection among the elderly in nursing homes. *N Engl J Med* 312:1383, 1985.

38. Cooper JK: Decision analysis for tuberculosis prevention treatment in nursing homes. *J Am Geriatr Soc* 34:814, 1986.

39. Stead WW, To T: The significance of the tuberculin skin test in elderly persons. *Ann Intern Med* 107:837, 1987.

40. Stead WW, To T, Harrison RW, Abraham JH: Benefit-risk considerations in preventive treatment of tuberculosis in elderly persons. *Ann Intern Med* 107:843, 1987.

41. Patriarca PA, Arden NH, Koplan JP, Goodman RA: Prevention and control of type A influenza infections in nursing homes: Benefits and costs of four approaches using vaccination and amantadine. *Ann Intern Med* 107:732, 1987.

42. Garibaldi RA, Brodine RN et al: Infections among patients in nursing homes. *N Engl J Med* 305:731, 1981.

43. Crossley KB, Irvine, P, Kaszar DJ, Loewenson RB: Infection control practices in Minnesota Nursing Homes. *JAMA* 254:2918, 1985.

44. Warren JW: Catheters and catheter care. *Clin Geriatr Medi* 2:857, 1986.

45. Yoshikowa TT, Norman DC: *Aging and Clinical Practice: Infectious Diseases.* New York, Igaku Shoin, 1987.

46. Zimmer, JG, Bentley DW, Valenti WM, Watson NM: Systemic antibiotic use in nursing homes: A quality assessment. *J Am Geriatr Soc* 34(10):703, 1986.

47. Martin SE, Turner CL, Mendelsohn S, Ouslander JG: Assessment and initial management of acute medical problems in a nursing home, in Basku G (ed): *Principles and Practice of Acute Geriatric Medicine.* St. Louis, Mosby, 1988.

48. Zimmer JG, Eggert GM, Treat A, Brodows B: Nursing homes as acute care providers: A pilot study of incentives to reduce hospitalizations. *J Am Geriatr Soc* 36:124, 1988.

49. Rubenstein LZ, Ouslander JG, Wieland D: Dynamics and clinical implications of the nursing home–hospital interface. *Clin Geriatr Med* November 4:471, 1988.

50. Ouslander JG: Reducing the hospitalization of nursing home residents. *J Am Geriatr Soc* 36:171, 1988.

51. Glasser, G, Zweibel NR, Cassel CK: The ethnics committee in the nursing home: Results of a national survey. *J Am Geriatr Soc* 36:150, 1988.

52. Brown NK, Thompson DJ: Nontreatment of fever in extended-care facilities. *N Engl J Med* 300:1246, 1979.

53. Besdine RW: Decisions to withhold treatment from nursing home residents. *J Am Geriatr Soc* 30:602, 1983.

54. Hilfiker D: Allowing the debilitated to die. *N Engl J Med* 308:716, 1983.

55. Lo B, Dornbrand L: Guiding the hand that feeds: Caring for the demented elderly. *N Engl J Med* 311(6):402, 1984.

56. Lo B, Dornbrand L: The case of Claire Conroy: Will administrative review safeguard incompetent patients? *Ann Intern* 104:869, 1986.

57. Nevins MA: Analysis of the Supreme Court of New Jersey's decision in the Claire Conroy case. *J Am Geriatr Soc* 34:140, 1986.

58. Volicer L, Rheaume Y, Brown J, Fabiszewski K, Brady R: Hospice approach to the treatment of patients with advanced dementia of the Alzheimer's type. *JAMA* 256(16):2210, 1986.

59. Lynn J: Dying and Dementia. *JAMA* 156(16):2244, 1986.

60. Lynn J (ed): *By No Extraordinary Means—The choice to Forgo Life-sustaining Food and Water.* Bloomington, Indiana University Press, 1986

61. Uhlman RF, Clark H, Pearlman RA, Downs JCM, Addison JH, Haining RG: Medical management decisions in nursing home patients: Principles and policy recommendations. *Ann Intern Med* 106:879, 1987.

62. Steinbrook R, Lo B: Artificial feeding—Solid ground, not a slippery slope. *N Engl J Med* 318:286, 1988.

63. Mott PD, Barker WH: Hospital and medical care use by nursing home patients: The effect of patient care plans. *J Am Geriatr Soc* 36:47, 1988.

Chapter 36

COMMUNITY-BASED LONG-TERM CARE: THE DILEMMA OF QUALITY AND COST

Thomas E. Finucane and John R. Burton

Experienced clinicians will recognize the critical importance of providing a highly integrated continuum of care for the frail elderly—those who are dependent and who are especially vulnerable to uncoordinated care. This continuum must link care provided in an acute hospital with care in a nursing home, rehabilitation program, office practice, day-care center, respite program, and, especially, with other community-based programs and family.

Much national attention in recent decades has been directed at hospital care and in more recent years at nursing home care. Yet millions of elderly Americans require help to continue living at home. Most of this help is provided by unpaid family and friends, usually adult daughters (29 percent) and wives (23 percent). Only 10 percent of caregivers use any formal services.[1] At the same time, a U.S. Senate report noted that in 1984 roughly 80 federal programs were involved directly or indirectly in long-term care.[2] The cost of community-based long-term care services is rising rapidly,[3] yet reliable data about the benefits of the services are quite limited. Developing better evidence will require formidable research efforts.

If concrete evidence of efficacy were to become available, however, difficult policy questions would remain. In the wealthiest country in the world, illiteracy, lack of medical insurance, and homelessness affect millions of people. What should the government's responsibility be to the country's elderly? Is there a minimum level of nutrition, cleanliness, and shelter that should be guaranteed? If so, how can such a guarantee be balanced against other competitors for government dollars?

This chapter begins with background information regarding community-based long-term care programs, the prevalence of disability in community-dwelling elderly, current major federal programs as they apply to home care, and some important policy choices about long-term care. The results of several studies on the efficacy of home care are presented, both in terms of cost and quality of life. The experiences of several community-based long-term care programs are reviewed. Finally, day care and respite care are discussed.

A note of caution about nomenclature: "home care" is often used to refer to work done by a home health agency/visiting-nurse association. In this chapter, the term *home care* is used in its more literal sense to include all programs, particularly multidisciplinary teams and physician house-call programs, through which health care is delivered in the home. Similarly, "long-term care" has often been used to mean "nursing home care." *Long-term care*, too, is used herein in its literal sense, that is, "care delivered over the long term," without regard to the site.

FRAIL ELDERLY LIVING AT HOME

In 1979 an estimated 2 million adults over age 65 and living at home needed help with one or more basic activities of daily living (ADLs).[4] These activities include walking, bathing, dressing, eating, toileting, and transferring from bed or chair. The rate of adults needing help with one or more ADL rises with age: 53 per 1000 for people 65 to 74 years old, 114 per 1000 for those 75 to

84, and 348 per 1000 for those 85 and over. For older adults needing help with instrumental activities of daily living (such as using the telephone, shopping, handling money, preparing meals, etc. [see Chapter 23]), each of the corresponding figures is considerably higher. Finally, surveys have shown that 11 per 1000 adults age 65 to 74 stay in bed most or all of the time. At age 85 and above the rate is 51 per 1000. In all, 2.8 million older adults need the help of another person to remain at home. The rate dependency increases steeply among the "old-old."

Low-income elderly people are more likely to have chronic diseases and are more likely to be functionally dependent than are higher-income elderly people. Among the near-poor elderly, one-third are reduced to poverty by their out-of-pocket medical expenses.[5]

PUBLIC PROGRAMS

The four major public programs paying for long-term care are Medicare, Medicaid, Title XX Social Service Block Grants, and the Older Americans Act. There is forceful budgetary pressure to limit the cost of these programs, presumably by restricting both eligibility and services.[6,7]

Medicare (Title XVIII of the Social Security Act) was initially intended as an insurance program for the acute health problems of the elderly and for the presumably limited period of recovery. As a result, in 1980, only 3 percent of the Medicare budget went for home care funding. Medicare covers 80 percent of government-financed home health services, but coverage is intended only for management of acute illness or short-term recovery. Coverage applies only when there is a skilled nursing need. Similar criteria apply for Medicare coverage of nursing home stays. The interpretation of these criteria is variable; reviewers have considerable latitude in deciding whether to approve particular cases. The program is administered at the state level.[8] In general, Medicare coverage for long-term care either at home or in an institution is limited to a few months. When patients are no longer improving as a result of services, they are no longer eligible for benefits.

In contrast to Medicare, *Medicaid* (Title XIX of the Social Security Act) is intended as a welfare program for poor people regardless of age. Because of stringent eligibility requirements (e.g., a monthly income of less than $334 and liquid assets less than $2500 for a single person in Maryland in 1988) and Byzantine enrollment procedures, many needy people are not covered by Medicaid. About 50 percent of the Medicaid budget is spent on long-term care services, but most of this goes for nursing home care. (Personal care providers are covered by Medicaid.) Other, less "medical" services, such as personal care, homemaker, and chore services can be cov-

ered by Medicaid through Waiver Programs. (In these programs, states may offer community-based services that could lead to reduced institutionalization.) Many elderly must "spend down" to Medicaid eligibility levels in order to become poor enough to receive coverage. (Married couples face particular risk as a result of this policy. If one person requires nursing home placement, his or her spouse is necessarily impoverished simultaneously during "spend down." Legislation, effective in 1989, substantially increases the assets and income that a person may maintain when a spouse is institutionalized with Medicaid funds.)

Social Service Block Grants (Title XX of the Older Americans Act) reimburse states for a variety of social services, such as adult daycare, personal care, protective services, and others. The mix of services and eligibility requirements are defined at the state level. Programs are targeted largely toward low-income people. Little money is appropriated for these services, and Title XX provides only about 5 percent of public funds for long-term care.

Programs of the *Older Americans Act* also receive limited funding. Components include information and referral services, congregate and home-delivered meals, and supportive services similar to those under Title XX.

In summary, a variety of programs provide a variety of services with significant overlap. Nursing home expenditures consume by far the greatest share of total spending. Because of severe budget constraints and difficulty with coordination of services, both eligibility and services are limited.

POLICY QUESTIONS

As mentioned above, society must answer very difficult questions in defining a minimum acceptable level of care. Is it unfair that a person dies for want of a liver transplant, or is it only unfortunate? At the other end of the spectrum, do we wish to guarantee one good meal per day to all of our people, or one bath per week? (Society has agreed, for example, to pay for the care of a pressure sore that involves the subcutaneous fat, but not necessarily to help a bed-bound patient transfer to a chair.) These questions are being considered at a time when their cost implications are perhaps their most salient feature.

The proper reimbursement structure for community-based long-term care is uncertain. The expenses of nursing home placement are, through Medicaid, the most well reimbursed. Incentive is thus created to move people into these institutions. On the other hand, community-based programs would most likely flourish with better reimbursement. Data suggest that, for most recipients, these services would be additional benefits, rather than alternatives to nursing home placements.

Although many of these people have genuine unmet needs, few would actually end up in a nursing home. This effect makes demonstration of costs/savings difficult.

Should society decide to provide in-home services more widely, defining eligibility still would be difficult. Disability in an ADL is defined simply by whether a person does or does not, for example, bathe himself. Whether a person is unable or simply unwilling to perform such activities is not considered. Many of the services under consideration are intrinsically attractive, for example, homemaker and chore services, and inappropriately high utilization is at least a theoretical possibility.[9]

EVIDENCE REGARDING COMMUNITY-BASED LONG-TERM CARE

Presented below is the evidence from several studies that have evaluated community-based programs in terms of cost and quality of life. In a randomized clinical trial, precise definition of the patient groups at entry, the nature of the experimental intervention, and the outcomes to be measured are central to the research design. All three areas have been problematic for studies that have tried to evaluate the efficacy of community-based long-term care. Inconsistencies in design among studies have limited the comparability of results.

Randomization of frail elderly persons was not a feature of early reports. Even when a control group has been included it has been difficult to show comparability among groups. Likelihood of nursing home admission, for example, is a very important variable, and over a dozen papers have tried to define relevant risk factors, with variable results.[6,10,11] Social, medical, functional, financial, and cognitive factors have all been identified in some of the studies, but there is no certain consensus. Nevertheless, increased age, dementia, dependency in ADLs, lack of spouse or child, female sex, and poverty are associated with high risk in most of the studies.

The intervention, noninstitutional care, has varied widely in different studies. Some have focused on personal care and homemaker services, many on skilled nursing care, and many on combinations, including these services as well as the services of physicians, social workers, therapists, and others. Measured outcomes have included mortality, cost, physical function, nursing home placement, and patient and caregiver contentment, among many others. Two reviews of the evidence about the effectiveness of community-based long-term care provide extensive references,[6,12] and one is a meta-analysis of the data.[13] There is general, but not unanimous, agreement about the following conclusions.

Community-based long-term care programs do not appear to affect mortality, likelihood of nursing home admission, or level of physical function. They appear to increase utilization of inpatient and ambulatory medical services, and they probably increase cost. Contentment and overall quality of life, notoriously difficult to measure and susceptible to bias, are probably increased.

Failure to demonstrate "cost-effectiveness" has been explained in several ways. Most people entered in these studies are not likely to enter a nursing home. For those who do, nursing home stays are usually short, and thus not expensive enough to balance program costs. For some very sick patients, nursing home placement may be cheaper than intensive in-home services.[14]

Functioning outside the context of health services research, several community-based programs provide important anecdotal information.

Community-based long-term care services at the Francis Scott Key Medical Center of the Johns Hopkins Health System in Baltimore began in 1979 when a group of physicians began making home visits to an increasingly frail group of elderly out-patients. The program has evolved to care for 150 extremely frail homebound elderly. An attending physician and a patient advocate coordinate a geriatric fellow and eight internal medicine residents who provide the physician home visits. A home health agency under contract provides most of the nursing and personal care services to those patients that are eligible. Nurses, social workers, therapists, fellow, advocate, and attending physician meet weekly to discuss active patients. The program relies on hospital support in addition to fee-for-service billing.

The Home Medical Service at Boston University Hospital began in 1875 at the Homeopathic Medical Dispensary. In the 1930s "obstetrical care and home delivery were commonplace," and in 1950 most of the patients were children. In 1987 the mean age was 80. About 900 patients were divided into 3 teams, each with a nurse coordinator, a social worker, and other support staff. The program was funded through a state demonstration as a capitated Medicaid HMO by the Robert Wood Johnson Foundation and by fee-for-service.[15]

Both of these programs have emphasized the important service provided to patients as well as the education value of such programs, emphasizing as they do so the humanistic values of medical care and the importance of the team and of comprehensive care.[15,16]

In contrast to the programs described above, On Lok Senior Health Services in San Francisco began in 1971 without direct physician involvement. Initially a network of community services were developed for the frail elderly. In 1973 a "day health center" was opened. From 1971 through 1978 the program was supported through federal and state grants. In 1979 outpatient medical services were added. The program is funded now primarily through a Medicare- and Medicaid-waivered, capitated, risk-based Community Care Organization for Dependent Adults. All long-term care services except housing are provided.[17]

Two excellent reviews of several other programs are available; these are resource texts covering all aspects of home care.[6,18]

DAY AND RESPITE CARE

Day-care and respite care programs are examples of efforts initiated in recent years to help frail elderly patients and their caretakers living in the community. Day-care centers are proliferating rapidly. There are two major types: social and medical. Social day-care centers are largely for the more functional elderly. They provide socialization, educational programs, and activities. Some do have a primary medical care and/or a preventive medical care component. These programs are generally available at no or low cost to a participant and are sponsored by government, church, or community agencies. Medical day-care centers, in contrast, provide services to a more frail and dependent group of elders and usually operate on a fee-for-service basis. Here the goal is to relieve the caregiver during some days of the week. Services provided in a medical day-care center may include a meal; nursing services, such as the administration of medications; personal care services, such as bathing and transportation; and some therapies, as well as socialization and recreational activities. Medical day-care centers usually operate 6 to 8 hours per day on a fee-for-service basis. Of the entitlement programs, only Medicaid provides coverage for these services. Average per-day cost is about half that of a nursing home, and this relatively large cost has limited utilization when it represents an out-of-pocket expense to patients and families. Medical day-care centers may be associated with nursing homes, life care communities, or churches, or they may be community-based. While there is a paucity of controlled studies on the efficacy of medical day-care centers, anecdotal evidence suggests that these programs provide significant relief for care givers and may delay or eliminate nursing home placement for some frail elders. Information regarding the availability of day-care centers, their services, and accessibility for any specific community is generally available from state or area offices on aging.

Respite care is short-term nursing home care that provides caregivers with short-term relief from the burden of caring for an elder. Rarely available only a few years ago, respite care is now a service offered by many nursing homes. Stays of 1 to 30 days are available. Except for in the case of a Medicaid recipient, expenses must be borne by the patient or the family. The rate for respite care is that of a typical nursing home $60 to $100 per day. The availability of respite care beds may be limited in some regions and considerable foresight may be necessary to reserve a bed for an anticipated need. State and area offices on aging usually have information regarding respite care beds in a specific locale.

CONCLUSION

The principal way in which home care may reduce total health costs is in reducing the total number of patient-days in nursing homes for certain patients. Several demonstration projects have shown that very careful targeting might make this possible if patients (1) are very disabled yet do not require 24-hour personal supportive care; (2) have less informal support; (3) are in a nursing home but may be capable of discharge with additional support; or (4) have a high probability of nursing home placement. Beyond a certain level of disability and of probability of nursing home admission, however, patients appear to be too frail to be supported in the home.[12]

Brickner et al. pointed out a fundamental limitation of cost savings as a means of judging home care. Describing the program at St. Vincent's in New York City in 1975, they note that "[t]his point is difficult to prove because . . . 22 of the 200 patients would in all likelihood have died at home alone, without being found, at great financial savings to the community."[19]

If saving money is the primary goal of the community-based long-term care, programs must be very accurately targeted to have even a chance of success. If controlling cost is not to be the primary criterion, society must form a consensus about what the goals are to be. The way in which long-term care is financed will naturally shape the services then available.[20] In addition to policy questions, several research questions remain. An assessment tool allowing reliable, reproducible stratification of patients at entry is needed. Conditions of eligibility should be pegged to the evaluation instrument. At some point a patient can no longer reasonably be cared for in the home. Identifying that point is both a policy, a scientific, and a personal issue. Most current home care programs rely on a patchwork of funding sources: public programs, often through waivers of existing programs; grants; fee-for-service; and hospital support. This situation reflects society's ambivalence about funding these efforts, presumably because of fear of the costs. Yet health care workers involved in community-based long-term care are often convinced that they are providing an exceptionally valuable service to extremely frail and vulnerable elderly, as well as providing a very important learning opportunity for physicians-in-training when such programs are integrated into geriatric medical education programs.

REFERENCES

1. National Center for Health Services Research. Research Activities. Who takes care of the disabled elderly? 87:1, 1986.
2. U.S. Senate, Special Committee on Aging. Develop-

ments in Aging: 1984. Vol 1. Washington, Government Printing Office, 191, 1985.

3. Koren MJ: Home care—who cares. *N Engl J Med* 314:917, 1986.

4. Feller BA: Americans needing help to function at home. *Advancedata* (National Center for Health Statistics) 92:1, 1983.

5. Commonwealth Fund Commission on Elderly People Living Alone. Medicare's poor. Baltimore, 1987.

6. Kane RA, Kane RL: *Long-Term Care*. New York, Springer, 1987.

7. Ruchlin HS, Braham RL: Long-term care: A review for the general internist. *J Gen Intern Med* 2:428, 1987.

8. Smits HL, Feder J, Scanlon W: Medicare's nursing home benefit: Variations in interpretation. *N Engl J Med* 307:855, 1982.

9. Kavesh WN: Home care: Process, outcome, cost. *Ann Rev Gerontol Geriatr* 6:135, 1986.

10. Cohen MA, Tell EJ, Wallack SS: The risk factors of nursing home entry among residents of six continuing care retirement communities. *J Gerontol* 43:515, 1988.

11. Greenberg JN, Ginn A: A multivariate analysis of long-term care placement. *Home Health Care Serv Q* 1:75, 1979.

12. Kemper P, Applebaum R, Harrigan M: Community care demonstrations: What have we learned? *Health Care Finance Rev* 8:87, 1987.

13. Hedrick SC, Inui T: The effectiveness and cost of home-care: An information synthesis. *Health Serv Res* 20:851, 1986.

14. Weissert WG: The cost-effectiveness trap. *Generations* 1985, p 47.

15. Steel K: Physician-directed long-term home health care for the elderly—A century-long experience. *J Am Geriatr Soc* 35:264, 1987.

16. Burton J: The house call: An important service for the frail elderly. *J Am Geriatr Soc* 33:291, 1985.

17. Eng C: Multidisciplinary approach to medical care: The On Lok model. *Clin Rep Aging* 1:5, 1987.

18. Spiegel AD: *Home Health Care*, 2d ed. Owings Mills, MD, National Health Publishing, 1987.

19. Brickner PW, Dugue T, Kaufman A et al: The homebound aged: A medically unreached group. *Ann Intern Med* 82:1, 1975.

20. American College of Physicians: Financing long-term care. *Ann Intern Med* 108:279, 1988.

Chapter 37

THE CARE
OF THE DYING PATIENT

Elizabeth Cobbs and Joanne Lynn

All of us are dying. To provide the care that ensures that the end of life is meaningful and comfortable is a privilege. Success requires compassion, technical expertise, and good teamwork. Medical decision making must seek to craft the best life that is possible for patients burdened by progressive chronic disease that is expected to be fatal. In evaluating the merits of potential alternative futures, the patient's symptoms near death and the approximate timing of the dying are essential considerations. Although predicting how long a dying patient will live is unavoidably uncertain, [1-3] estimating prognosis is essential for planning care.

Sometimes appropriate care for dying patients is called *hospice care*. Though relatively few facilities exist, inpatient hospice is a cherished resource for patients with poorly controlled symptoms, inadequate social resources, or temporarily exhausted family caregivers. Outpatient hospice provides coordinated services for dying patients who are at home or in long-term care facilities. Some formal hospice services are reimbursable under Medicare and commercial insurance, though with onerous caps and limits. "Hospice care" also signifies a *concept* of care for dying patients that is designed to relieve suffering and alleviate unwanted symptoms.

APPROACH TO THE PATIENT

IDENTIFYING THE DYING PATIENT

Identifying a patient as dying is unproblemmatic when the patient has an aggressive malignancy which has failed every possible treatment. However, many elderly patients who are dying are not so easily labeled. Because of the difficulty of precisely predicting the remaining time for such patients, few such patients are referred to hospice programs, though they certainly are appropriate recipients of "hospice-type" care.

DOCTOR-PATIENT RELATIONSHIP

Humankind is unique in knowing that each person will die. Yet denial mechanisms effectively push back concerns about mortality, even among caregivers. Confronting mortality in patients can cause anxiety and precipitate dysfunctional defenses. Only when the physician and other key caregivers learn to confront their own fears can management of the patient be effective and appropriately patient-centered. [4]

The patient needs a doctor whose concern for the patient will be lifelong, even in the absence of curative treatments. The effective physician allows time to listen to the patient, as well as time to explain and discuss.

MEDICAL ASSESSMENT

Thorough history taking, including review of old medical records, ordinarily is essential for understanding the story of the patient's past and future course of illness. The physical examination is helpful and, if done well, can help avoid unnecessary and burdensome diagnostic interventions. At times, further medical investigations may be indicated even when cure is impossible. For example, a new symptom may be due to another disease process altogether, and perhaps one that is treatable. On the other hand, the symptom may represent a treatable complication of the underlying disease. Documenting the rate of disease progression might help choose interventions for optimal effect. Knowing that time is short, for example, a patient may be willing to spend funds on round-the-clock nursing care.

PSYCHOSOCIAL ASPECTS OF ASSESSMENT

Strengths or weaknesses in the psychological or social realms of function may be critical contributors to a patient's general well-being. Patients have vastly differing concerns regarding the process of dying: What has been the patient's previous experience of death? What were the experiences of loved ones the patient has seen die? What are this person's fears about dying? Pain? Isolation? Disfigurement? Helplessness? How has the patient coped with difficult situations in the past? The clinician should know about the immediate family and friends and should make efforts to be communicative with them. Often, financial concerns are inextricably bound up with the care of the dying patient. A patient may refuse a costly treatment for fear of bankrupting a spouse or might interfere with needed care by refusing to divulge financial information.

Anticipating the likelihood that the patient will eventually lose the capacity to contribute to decision making, the physician should attempt to make important decisions about future care with the patient and should identify a person who can make decisions as the patient's "surrogate." Commonly, this surrogate will be a close family member, but it may also be a good friend or a professional advisor. The clinician is obliged to be knowledgeable about local legal issues surrounding incompetence and dying in order to counsel patients about durable powers of attorney, living wills, and wills. Durable powers of attorney are especially powerful and flexible and should be used more widely.

THE IMPORTANCE OF TEAMWORK

Optimally, the dying patient is cared for by an interdisciplinary team of professionals and concerned others. The physician often coordinates and leads this team which includes nurses, social workers, clergy, volunteers (as patient advocates and friends), rehabilitation therapists, dietitians, and others.

The quality of interaction among the team members will be reflected in the ability of that team to provide smooth, well-coordinated services to the patient. Patient care is optimal when there exists mutual respect among team members and a fair amount of cross-training. Shared information and expertise enables the team to accomplish more than the individuals could acting independently.

Caring for dying people is stressful for all involved. Even the best solutions and remedies to illness and suffering are far from perfect. Despite the most valiant efforts, mistakes are made, shortcomings are perceived. In addition to providing more holistic and better coordinated patient care, the team approach permits mutual support among team members.

DECISION MAKING

When caring for elderly dying patients, questions without clear answers appear often, "How long do I have?" "What will dying be like?" "What has my life amounted to?" and "Why me?" Compassion, honesty, and spiritual counseling may help. However, the question, "What should be done now?" has to have an answer, and finding it requires attention to ethical and social issues as well as medical possibilities.

A GENERAL FRAMEWORK

Ill elderly individuals rarely have one diagnosis that suffices to explain the entire clinical picture. More frequently there will be a multiplicity of chronic and acute problems, historical elements and physiologic characteristics unique to each patient. When making a decision about care, all must be part of the assessment. The choice of treatment will depend on the patient's overall situation and the goals and desires of that patient. For each patient, there are likely to be several possible "futures" that would constitute reasonable choices. The longest future (i.e., that which puts off death as long as possible) will usually not be the most desirable. The practitioner must avoid basing choices on prejudices about how people should value life with various characteristics.[5]

The physician must also recognize which options are not available. A practitioner is ethically and legally barred from administering a lethal poison to a patient.[6] Certain other options may not be open to the patient because of financial constraints, travel distance, or scarce resources.[7]

RESUSCITATION Treatments should always be judged by what good they can do the patient. In the case of cardiopulmonary resuscitation for dying elderly patients, the chances of bringing prolongation of meaningful life to that patient are extremely slim. Foregoing resuscitation may become a matter of dismissing treatment that is doomed to fail and that might only prolong suffering.

One must always differentiate a "Do Not Resuscitate" (DNR) order from a "Do Nothing" order. The DNR order does not decide other vigorous interventions such as artificial feeding, intravenous antibiotics, or even surgery. Each of these other decisions must be taken up in its own right and in the context in which it arises, keeping in mind the overall goals of treatment.

ARTIFICIAL FEEDING Issues of artificial feeding in dying patients come up frequently. Reasonable people differ as to the desirability of feeding dying patients by artificial means, but the following generally are accepted:

First, that food and water should be provided freely as long as the patient is able to swallow reasonably safely.

Second, artificial methods of providing nourishment to patients who can no longer swallow food and water are sometimes useful or desirable, or both.

Third, patients who are dying do not ordinarily experience discomfort from dehydration and insufficient nutrition. Maintaining "normal" levels of hydration in a dying patient might well actually increase the likelihood of pulmonary edema and distressing respiratory secretions.[8,9]

Fourth, court cases have not required caregivers forcibly to administer artificial feedings to a seriously ill person who objects to such feedings or who would be, on balance, harmed.[10–15]

Each decision should be tailored to the patient and the special circumstances. The patient may have a special event to live for, such as a graduation or the birth of a grandchild. Then, the patient may be motivated to endure the discomfort and added medical monitoring of intravenous hydration in order to survive for that event. In a different patient with a decreasing ability to take oral sustenance, the dying process may be so far progressed that the patient no longer has an interest in pursuing any avenue of aggressive nutritional intervention. The patient or the patient's surrogate may then communicate with the physician that the patient's desire is to forego artificial feeding and let nature take its course. Like all other treatments, artificial feedings have some associated discomforts and risks.

DESIGNING CARE FOR COMFORT

Each clinician develops a repertoire of techniques for managing unwanted symptoms and maximizing function and comfort. The goal is to design a comprehensive approach for care, utilizing medications, interpersonal interactions, optimum nursing technique, and other resources as appropriate.

GENERAL PRINCIPLES

ROUTES OF MEDICATIONS Medications should ordinarily be delivered by the oral route, since that is usually more convenient and the pharmacodynamics are smoother. Parenteral administration usually results in a

faster onset but a shorter duration of action. Once a patient is unable to tolerate oral medications, rectal, subcutaneous, intramuscular, or intravenous routes may be used. Constant infusion (intravenous, subcutaneous, or intrathecal) pumps for opioid analgesics have proved to be useful.

TIMING Most dying patients who are experiencing pain or other troubling symptoms will be more comfortable on a regular, round-the-clock dosing schedule of medication rather than treatment only after the symptoms become apparent. The goal of treatment is to suppress the symptoms and prevent their reemergence between doses. For example, round-the-clock dosing eliminates the "pain behavior" cycle, in which the pain returns in force as the analgesic wears off and the patient must wait until the caregiver can respond and until the medication takes effect. The delay heightens anxiety and exacerbates pain. Pain behavior occurs frequently in the hospital setting where short-staffed nurses may not be able to respond quickly, resulting in an anxious, frightened, dependent, and hurting patient.

BOOSTERS When a symptom occasionally becomes poorly controlled, parenteral boosters between regular doses of oral palliative medications can help restore control of a symptom quickly and can also predict how much more medication might be needed regularly.

SYMPTOM COMPLEXES AND TREATMENTS

PAIN

Pain is a frequent and complex symptom of dying patients.[16,17] The clinician should be alert to the multiple guises of pain. A patient in chronic pain may present as a demanding, hostile, irritable individual who denies "pain." With appropriate treatment an affable, tolerant, and relaxed personality may be restored. A diagnosis of etiology may guide treatment. The sensation of pain is comprised both by the nociception (the perception of the painful stimulus) and by the emotional reaction to it.[18] Both may be treated. Understanding the half-life, pharmacokinetics, relative potencies, and mechanisms of action is extremely important to using analgesics correctly. The most commonly used narcotic analgesics are compared in Table 37-1.

NONNARCOTIC ANALGESICS Mild pain may be treated with aspirin (if tolerated) or acetaminophen on a round-the-clock schedule of 650 mg four times daily. If this is insufficient, other nonsteroidal anti-inflammatory drugs (NSAIDs) may be tried, especially for musculo-

TABLE 37-1
Comparison of Selected Narcotic Analgesics

		Starting Range (mg)	Usual Duration (h)	Approximate Equivalent Dose (mg)
Morphine	*Oral immediate release* Tablets 15, 30 mg Solution 10 or 20 mg/5 ml Concentrated solution 100 mg/5 ml	5–15	3–5	40
	Oral sustained release Tablets 30, 60 mg	*	8–12	
	SQ or IM†	2.5–5.0	3–5	10
Hydromorphone	*Oral* Tablets 1, 2, 3, 4 mg	1–2	4–5	7.5
	Rectal Suppository 3 mg	3	6–8	Highly variable
	SQ or IM	0.5–1.5	4–5	1.5
Levorphanol	*Oral* Tablets 2 mg	1–2	4–6	4.0
Methadone	*Oral* Tablets 5, 10, 40 mg Solution 5 or 10 mg/5 ml	2.5–10.0	3–5	20
Codeine	*Oral*	30–60	4–6	200

*Ordinarily convert to sustained release after stabilization on immediate release preparation.
†SQ, subcutaneous; IM, intramuscular.

skeletal pain such as bone metastases or disuse contractures. If narcotic analgesics are needed, continuing NSAIDs can reduce the amount required.

NARCOTICS If NSAIDs and plain acetaminophen have failed, the fixed combination of codeine and acetaminophen is useful, especially in outpatients, in the dose of 1 to 2 tablets every 3 to 4 hours. The most common side effect is constipation. Oral morphine is the gold standard of narcotic analgesia. The initial dose in a frail elderly person can be as low as 2.5 mg every 4 to 6 hours. The dose and interval can be titrated quickly. Oral morphine comes in tablets, solution, and slow-release tablets. Short-acting preparations are best until pain is under control, and then a regular schedule, using the equivalent dose of longer-acting medications, can be set.

Strong opioids commonly cause drowsiness, constipation, and nausea. Patients usually develop a tolerance to the drowsiness within a few days. The constipation should be aggressively treated with laxatives. The nausea may be suppressed with a nonsedative antiemetic such as haloperidol 0.5 mg every 8 hours. In an agitated patient, a mildly sedating antiemetic such as prochlorperazine (Compazine) may be used.

Physical dependence is a comcomitant of regular use of narcotics. If discontinuation becomes possible, tapering over 5 to 10 days will prevent withdrawal symptoms.

Tolerance to narcotics also occurs, but increased doses of the narcotic continue to achieve pain relief. If need be, switching to a different narcotic and using nonnarcotic agents, anesthetic and neurosurgical interventions, or hypnosis and imaging usually allow effective pain control despite tolerance. Hydromorphone HCl (Dilaudid) can be prepared for parenteral use at 100 mg/ml—a dosage which is concentrated enough for virtually any need.

ADJUVANT ANALGESIC DRUGS Some drugs that are marketed for other purposes have been shown to relieve pain. Hydroxyzine (Atarax, Vistaril) appears to produce an analgesic effect that reduces morphine doses by about one-quarter. Serotonergic antidepressants (amitriptyline, doxepin) potentiate the analgesic effect of narcotics but may also hasten the onset of narcotic tolerance. The sedating side effects can be useful when given at bedtime. Steroids may reduce edema and thereby treat pain in situations such as nerve compression, elevated intracranial pressure, lumen obstruction, bone pain, and possibly lymphedema. Dexamethasone, 4 mg every 6 hours for several days, should provide an adequate trial.

PHYSICAL MEASURES For pain in the distribution of a peripheral nerve, afferent input can be interrupted by nerve blocking procedures or transcutaneous nerve stimulation. If the pain source is intraspinal, the patient may benefit from a neurosurgical procedure ablating the affected spinal roots or a part of the spinal cord. An implanted spinal epidural morphine pump for metastatic cancer can deliver the narcotic directly to the nervous system, thereby greatly reducing total doses and possibly reducing side effects. The implantation can be done under epidural anesthesia and requires placement of a subcutaneous abdominal automatic pump that can be refilled percutaneously every few weeks in the outpatient setting. An implanted spinal electrical stimulator can be used for control of pain in the lower trunk and lower extremities.[19]

PULMONARY SYMPTOMS

RESPIRATORY DISTRESS   Next to pain, dyspnea is a symptom most feared both by patients and caregivers alike. Determining the exact etiology may lead to treatment for dyspnea caused by hypoxemia, poor handling of secretions, anxiety, bronchospasm, or musculoskeletal pain.

Supplemental oxygen, anxiolytics, bronchodilators, analgesics, and drying agents such as atropine may suffice to suppress dyspnea. Morphine and other narcotics dull the sensation of dyspnea from all causes. Control over dyspnea can almost always be achieved through the use of these medications, especially with increasing doses of narcotics. Of course, large doses of sedating drugs may precipitate hypercarbia and respiratory arrest, and so their use is warranted only when these risks are reasonable in light of the patient's other alternatives.

AIRWAY SECRETIONS   The most common cause of troubling bronchial secretions in dying patients is intravenous overhydration. If cardiotonic and diuretic drugs are ineffective or if an untreatable cause is suspected, severe respiratory congestion and distress may be treated with morphine sulfate.

COUGH   Guaifenesin syrup is often adequate. If unrelieved, hydrocodeine syrup may suffice. If sedation is undesirable and the cough is dry, Tessalon can be dramatically effective. The patient should not chew or hold Tessalon in the mouth because it is a powerful local anesthetic.

RESPIRATORY DEPRESSION FROM NARCOTICS
Transient oversedation is not uncommon in dying patients treated with narcotics, but most patients have little ill effect. Unexpected respiratory depression in the setting of stable analgesic doses is more likely to result from another cause, such as metabolic derangement or central nervous system disturbance. In any case, moder-

ate overnarcotization rarely needs treatment, other than precautions regarding aspiration and the monitoring of vital signs and neurologic status. Reversal of the effect of narcotics with naloxone (Narcan) usually causes unpleasant withdrawal symptoms, but may be used if needed.

GASTROINTESTINAL PROBLEMS

ANOREXIA   Anorexia coincides with the last days of many disease processes. Patients often lose interest in food at the same time that they lose the will to live. However, anorexia also may result from local mouth pain or dysphagia from a treatable cause. Attention to food preferences, aesthetics of surroundings, and the presentation of the food are simple but effective measures. Pharmacologic stimulation of appetite is not usually successful, though some claim that an alcoholic cocktail prior to meals may be useful. Some patients respond to steroids with improved appetite.[20]

NAUSEA AND VOMITING   Nausea may be caused by local factors (gastritis, obstruction, etc.) or central factors (tumor, raised intracranial pressure, etc). Antacids and H_2 blockers are commonly used to reduce symptoms. Prochlorperazine (Compazine) or small doses of haloperidol (Haldol) are often effective. Gastric paresis or mild functional ileus may respond to the addition of metaclopramide (Reglan) 10 mg orally before meals.

INTESTINAL OBSTRUCTION   Although most physicians are accustomed to giving aggressive treatments to relieve intestinal obstruction, palliative management may sometimes be better. The spasmodic pain can be relieved by diphenoxylate hydrochloride 2.5 mg with atropine sulfate 0.025 mg (Lomotil) or loperamide hydrochloride 2 mg (Imodium), or narcotics. Many patients prefer occasional emesis to nasogastric suction and may actually absorb enough to live comfortably or even unexpectedly reopen the intestines without surgery.

CONSTIPATION   Constipation is a common complaint of dying patients. In patients who require large amounts of narcotics and whose activity and diet are restricted, constipation may be a constant concern. Often recognition of the problem is delayed even when the patient is in a hospital and receiving careful medical supervision. Through careful monitoring, trouble can be anticipated or caught early.

Adding water and fiber to the diet to create bulky, hydrated stools would be ideal, but these measures may be impractical for dying elderly patients, especially those with chronic constipation, and this is a situation where stool softeners (docusate, psyllium hydrophilic mucilloid) and aggressive treatment with oral cathartics should be tried. If these fail, then manual disimpaction, suppositories, and enemas are in order. Vigilance and persistance are required for prevention and treatment.

DRY MOUTH Anticholinergic medication effects frequently cause a dry and sore mouth. Radiation therapy may also contribute to this painful condition. Gentle and thorough mouth care can alleviate the discomfort to a great degree despite the continuation of the causative medications and poor hydration. Glycerine and citric acid mouth washes are soothing comfort. Viscous xylocaine 1 to 2% or artificial saliva (Salivart) may help.

ORAL THRUSH Oral candidiasis can be extremely debilitating and may prevent adequate oral intake. Symptoms involving the esophagus are not uncommon. A formula entitled "Magic Mouthwash" is very helpful and consists of 1 ounce each of diphenhydramine liquid, Mintox, nystatin, and viscous xylocaine 2%, 5 cc swish and swallow, qid. Nystatin (Mycostatin) oral suspension or troche, Clotrimazole (Mycelex) troches or ketoconazole (Nizoral) may be needed for refractory cases and should be continued for 2 to 4 weeks after all clinical signs are gone.

MENTAL STATUS CHANGES

ANXIETY The dying patient who is uncomfortably anxious needs assessment for potentially treatable causes (such as hypoxemia, pain, or fear). Often, a stable and available professional staff will itself greatly relieve anxiety.

The long-acting benzodiazepines (flurazepam, diazepam) are best avoided. Their effects may be paradoxical and their prolonged half-lives prevent rapid adjustment if the patient is intolerant of their effect. Lorazepam (Ativan) or alprazolam (Xanax) are quite short-acting and would be preferred.

Other useful drugs for anxiety include diphenhydramine (Benadryl) and hydroxyzine (Atarax, Vistaril), which are ordinarily well tolerated and effective for 4 to 6 hours.

HALLUCINATIONS If a patient is hallucinating, antipsychotics such as haloperidol (Haldol), chlorpromazine (Thorazine), and thioridazine (Mellaril) may be useful in minimizing hallucinatory input to the patient's thought processes and provide sedation as well. It is prudent to begin with very low doses (such as haloperidol 0.5 mg) and gradually increase the dose. Some patients may require very little to achieve the desired effect.

DEPRESSION Methylphenidate (Ritalin) may be useful and efficacy can be seen almost immediately. Tricyclic antidepressants are also helpful, with nocturnal sedation often being a welcome side effect. The antidepressant benefits of treatment require at least a few days.

SKIN

SKIN BREAKDOWN Skin breakdown is the scourge of all bedridden patients. Dying people are at special risk since they may encounter all the circumstances that cause skin breakdown: poor nutrition, incontinence of bowel and bladder, decreased mobility, and poor hygiene. Decubitus ulcers are painful and may provide an entry point for deep infection. Thus, they may contribute to further morbidity and early mortality in dying patients.

The patient should be turned at least every 2 hours. Minimizing shearing forces on the skin is crucial; a patient should not be pulled across the sheets. A soft bed covering (such as an eggcrate foam mattress) will also help spread pressure and reduce shear forces. Pressure-reducing mattresses are so expensive that most patients cannot afford them. However, some less expensive products are being developed and may be of some benefit.

FUNGATING TUMORS Large tumor masses on the surface sometimes develop areas of necrosis and infection, with painful, malodorous lesions. Local radiation therapy may be effective for temporary control of the lesion. If persistent capillary bleeding is a problem, pads soaked in epinephrine 1:1000 may help. Moderate persistent bleeding may respond to radiotherapy. Persistent foul odor may be controlled with topical tetracycline.

PRURITIS Medications to suppress itching include diphenhydramine (Benadryl), hydroxyzine (Atarax), or topical mycolog or steroid cream. Skin hydration is helpful and may be achieved with increased fluid intake, lotions, baths, and room humidifiers.

SEIZURES

Patients dying from central nervous system tumors or with profound metabolic changes may develop seizure activity. Generally, the antiseizure regimen is much the same as in other seizure patients. Phenytoin (Dilantin), phenobarbital, carbamazepine (Tegretol), and primidone (Mysoline) are commonly used.

For status epilepticus, IV diazepam (Valium) is preferred. Intramuscular (IM) Valium is erratically absorbed. If there is no IV access, IM lorazepam (Ativan) is preferable, as it is reliably absorbed. It may be given in 2-mg increments until the seizures subside. Lorazepam requires refrigerated storage.

Seizures may come from elevated intracranial pressure, which can sometimes be reduced by steroids. Decadron, 4 mg every 4 hours for 2 to 3 days, provides a reasonable trial of treatment.

GENITOURINARY TRACT

URINARY TRACT INFECTION A patient bothered by urinary tract symptoms such as dysuria or frequency may have an acute urinary tract infection. In light of the bothersome symptoms, it usually is best to treat with the appropriate antibiotics and phenazopyridine (Pyridium).

URINARY INCONTINENCE Incontinence of urine is a common problem in ill elderly patients. The general disapproving attitude toward chronic indwelling (Foley) catheters for geriatric patients may be safely suspended in dying patients. If pain and dysmobility are prominent problems, the indwelling catheter may permit considerable increase in comfort and prevent skin breakdown.

MANAGING DEATH

BEREAVEMENT

The team caring for the patient is in a position to provide much comfort and reassurance to the family and close friends.[21] If there is no ongoing team that ensures bereavement follow-up, the physician should do so.

The family or close friends ordinarily face certain "tasks" during mourning. These tasks need not be performed in any particular order, and there may be significant heterogeneity in the ways different people approach them. The tasks of mourning include

1. Accepting the reality of the loss
2. Experiencing the pain of the loss
3. Adjusting to an environment where the deceased is missing
4. Withdrawing emotional energy from the deceased and reinvesting that energy in other relationships and activities.

The team can facilitate successful mourning in several ways. Before death, they can encourage anticipatory grieving and encourage communication between the patient and the family. The family should be allowed to stay with the body after death, an experience that is immensely helpful toward accepting the reality of the death and reducing fears of unstated feelings. After the death, the family and friends should be encouraged to talk about the deceased. This is especially effective when done a few days following the death with all members of the immediate family present, along with a member of

the clergy. A wide range of emotions is normal. Profoundly dysfunctional or prolonged grieving should be directed to professional counseling.

AESTHETIC CONCERNS

In general, the team strives to care for the patient in a way that is as pleasing as possible to the patient and to the family. Even in an unresponsive patient, for example, great care should be taken to maintain cleanliness and orderliness of appearance. These measures exhibit a lasting respect for the patient that persists despite the progression of the dying process.

DEATH AT HOME

With the help of family, friends, and caregivers, patients may live out their final days at home. So that societal needs are met and families are not overburdened by "procedural tasks" at the time of death, coordination and planning is required. Funeral arrangements should be made in advance. The physician and home care nurse should be available at all times. At the hour of death, the caregiver should notify the physician or nurse so that arrangements can be made for pronouncement of death, notification of the medical examiner (if that is necessary), consideration of autopsy (if not decided in advance), and removal of the body.

REFERENCES

1. Forster L, Lynn J: Predicting life span for applicants to inpatient hospice. *Arch Intern Med* 148:2540, 1988.
2. Parkes CM: Accuracy of predictions of survival in later stages of cancer. *Br Med J* 2:29, 1972.
3. Evans C, McCarthy M: Prognostic uncertainty in terminal care: Can the Karnofsky Index help? *Lancet* 1:204, 1985.
4. Artiss KL, Levine AS: Doctor-patient relation in severe illness. *N Engl J Med* 288:1210, 1974.
5. Pearlman R, Speer J: Quality of life considerations in geriatric care. *J Am Geriatr Soc* 31:113, 1983.
6. The President's Commission for the Study of Ethical Problems in Medicine and Biomedical and Behavioral Research: *Deciding to Forego Life-Sustaining Treatment.* Washington, Government Printing Office, 1983.
7. Lynn J: Legal and ethical issues in palliative health care. *Semin Oncol* 12:476, 1985.
8. Lynn J, Childress JF: Must patients always be given food and water? *Hastings Center Rep* 17:13, 1983.
9. Schmitz P, O'Brien M: Observations on nutrition and hydration in dying cancer patients, in (Lynn J ed): *By No Extraordinary Means: The Choice to Forego Life-Sustaining Food and Water.* Bloomington, Indiana University Press, 1986.
10. Glover J, Lynn J: Update since *Conroy:* 1985–1988, in

By No Extraordinary Means: The Choice to Forego Life-Sustaining Food and Water, 2nd ed. Bloomington, Indiana University Press, 1989.

11. *In re Conroy*, 98 New Jersey, 321, 486, A.2d 1209 (1985).
12. *Bouvia v. County of Riverside*, No., 159780 (California Supreme Court, Riverside County, December 16, 1983).
13. *In re Jobes*, 180 New Jersey, 394, 529 A.2d 434 (1987).
14. *In re Requena*, 213 New Jersey Superior Court 475, 517 A.2d 886 (Superior Court Ch. Division) aff'd 213 N.J. Superior Court 443, 517 A.2d 869 (Superior Court Appelate Division, 1986) (per curiam).
15. *In re Rodas*, No. 86 PR 139 (Colorado District Court Mesa County, January 22, 1987)
16. Foley KM: The treatment of cancer pain. *N Engl J Med* 313:84, 1985.
17. Levy MH: Pain management in advanced cancer. *Semin Oncol* 12:394, 1985.
18. Hillier R: Terminally ill patient: Medical and nursing care, in Aaronson NK, Beckman J (eds): *The Quality of Life of Cancer Patients*. New York, Raven Press, 1987, p. 239.
19. Black P: Neurosurgical management of cancer pain. *Semin Oncol* 12:438, 1985.
20. Levy MH, Catalano RB: Control of common physical symptoms other than pain in patients with terminal disease. *Semin Oncol* 12:411, 1985.
21. Worden JW: Bereavement. *Semin Oncol* 12:472, 1985.

Chapter 38

THE LEGAL ASPECTS OF GERIATRIC MEDICINE: PLANNING AND PROTECTION

J. Dinsmore Adams, Jr., and Constance P. Carden

Practitioners and patients alike complain that our legal system has been unable to keep up with the avalanche of medical technology and the administrative growth it has induced. The patient is upset by loss of control and capacity in a nursing home or other long-term care facility. The family's confidence in its ability to support a loved one is assaulted from both the medical and administrative sides. Physicians fear skyrocketing malpractice premiums and the blizzard of paperwork from government and reimbursement sources. They feel that their professional independence is threatened by a legislature or regulator telling them how to administer a procedure, such as DNR order, and to what length hospitalization is appropriate for a particular illness.

In this context, it is small wonder that it is counterinstinctual for the patient, family member, or physician to add to the cast by calling a lawyer. Nonetheless, since the passage of time will likely lessen the competence and capacity of the patient, thereby reducing the possible courses of action for the patient and family, it is important for the physician to advise the patient and family to consult a lawyer as early as possible, and in many instances, for the physician to do so also. As physicians train themselves to respond to the first instinct in ordering a culture or a spinal tap, so should they seek legal advice for themselves, or encourage the patient or family to seek it when the first inkling of a potential legal problem comes to mind. Just as with a medical problem, the earlier a legal problem is recognized, the better the prognosis for successful resolution. Further, failure to recognize or acknowledge a problem, legal or medical,

increases the physician's potential liabilities. This chapter will outline the legal implications of patients' rights, competence, surrogate decision making, refusal of treatment, and reimbursement and financial management.

THE PROBLEMS: INFORMED CONSENTS AND AUTHORITY TO TREAT

The common goal of medicine and law in the geriatric context is to protect and conserve a patient's health, civil rights, and property as well as possible, and at the same time respect the physician's professional responsibilities and provide protection from liability. All American jurisdictions recognize the common law right to bodily self-determination, and many states have a statutory patient's bill of rights derived from constitutional and common law rights to bodily self-determination and privacy. Accordingly, treating a patient without consent or after consent has been withdrawn may subject the doctor and hospital to civil or even criminal liability.

The paramount legal issue for all parties concerned, then, is authority to treat and the derivative concepts of patients' competence and surrogate decision making. In a time of crisis doctors, families, or patients may lose sight of the fact that all are greatly threatened by any authority to treat problems. Such problems can occur with geriatric patients if proper authority is not documented upon admission because of failure to obtain valid authority from a family surrogate.

INFORMED CONSENT

The law assumes that every adult is competent until a judge signs a court order or judgment ruling that this is no longer so. However, in the health care context, there is often a question whether a legally competent patient can be made sufficiently aware of the consequences of a proposed procedure or treatment to give, withdraw, or modify an informed consent. If the patient cannot be made aware, most caregivers look to a patient's spouse, children, or other family, who, in the absence of a durable power of attorney or court-granted authority, have no actual legal authority whatsoever to give a proxy consent or to make a substituted judgment for the patient. Several situations are discussed below describing how questions of competence and capacity may be met and how a lawyer can help the patient and the doctor.

The most common place to address questions of competence is at admission, preadmission physical exam, or office visit, at which either the patient or a representative generally signs documents, including a consent form authorizing treatment, and a contract evidencing the financial arrangement for payment for medical services. Legal competence does not require that the patient be able to understand a complicated document or medical procedure. However, if the admitting physician or staff believes that the incoming patient may lack sufficient capacity to understand the consequences of the admission or procedure, either the patient or the family should be questioned on the issue of consent and authority.

SURROGATE AUTHORITY

If the consent or contract is to be signed by someone other than the patient, the power of attorney or other source of surrogate authority should be made part of the admission record. If none exists, the physician may need to bring in a social worker, hospital administrator, or lawyer to advise the hospital or family about the necessary documentation. The diplomacy of this inquiry may be difficult, but it will only get more difficult as time passes, and treating a patient without proper authority is dangerous for everyone—including the doctor. Admission is also the appropriate time for inquiry to be made as to who will be the surrogate decision maker if the then-competent patient becomes incompetent or if the patient's elderly spouse becomes incapacitated and unable to act as attorney-in-fact. Part of the dialogue should include a discussion of the patient's wishes regarding the use of life support systems should they become an issue. If the patient and spouse have not considered the problem, they should be encouraged to do so forthwith, in order to avoid the dilemma where the physician or hospital either lacks reliable authority to treat or doesn't

know the patient's wishes. Moreover, such a conversation gives the physician a good indication of whether the entire family is aligned with the patient or treatment policy.

IMPLIED CONSENT

If the admission is made on an emergency basis, relying on implied consent, then the issue of authority to treat should be addressed as soon as is practicable thereafter. The doctor cannot afford to continue to rely on the implied consent to treat after the crisis is passed. Here, again, the lawyer representing either the hospital or the family can be extremely helpful in clarifying authority to treat or the delegation of authority to a surrogate.

WITHDRAWAL OR CHANGES OF CONSENT

Other situations in which consulting a lawyer may help occur at the onset of an acute situation in ongoing or long-term care: A patient may refuse compliance with a doctor's orders or may demand to be discharged against such orders; a patient may complain that relatives are not acting in concert with his or her expressed wishes respecting treatment or the handling of financial matters; or the patient may be facing a major surgical procedure, may have suffered an arrest or stroke, or may suddenly be faced with the diagnosis of a terminal condition or illness. In such situations an attorney is often viewed by the patient or family as an ally independent of the medical establishment, whose assistance in delivering and dealing with unwelcome news may be very helpful to doctor and patient alike. The lawyer can also help connect the medical and outside worlds and allay the patient's or family's fears about financial planning and decision making. The lawyer may assist in the practicalities of discharge and transfer, if the patient refuses to be treated or demands to be discharged. In the latter situation, having both the family lawyer and the hospital lawyer to consult minimizes the unpleasantness for the family and medical staff and reduces possible risks of liability for the physician and the facility. Ensuring that necessary entries are made on charts and, if appropriate, proper documentation of discharge against doctor's orders is important, and at times consulting the hospital lawyer should be considered unless the physician is absolutely sure that all the legal requirements are complied with.

REFUSAL OR WITHDRAWAL OF TREATMENT

After decades of not being talked about, the dying process is now talked about by patients and families. It, too, is an aspect of geriatric practice where legal advice may be necessary. Two issues of special sensitivity are withdrawal and refusal of treatment, especially where such refusal is outside the bounds of acceptable medical treatment. Even more difficult is the attempted enforcement of patients' wishes regarding refusal or withdrawal of treatment by a surrogate, whether spouse, close friend, children, or attorney-in-fact. Here again a physician must make the initial determination of competence. However, the enforceability of a living will or the validity of a durable power of attorney are questions for lawyers as well as doctors. If the presiding physician or the hospital ethics committee has any question about the patient's wishes or competence, or about the authority of a surrogate decision maker, the expert advice of a lawyer should be obtained. Here again, if the patient, family, and physician have talked the problem through ahead of time, the risks and concerns of all involved will be minimized. But physicians have the responsibility of making these inquiries early, so that they may deliver the best care possible. Postponement of addressing the issues can only leave the physician in the painful position of trying to care for the dying patient not knowing what the limits of authority to treat are or what the patient wanted.

INSURANCE, MEDICARE, AND MEDICAID

The final issue which should be addressed earlier rather than later is the question of insurance and Medicare/Medicaid eligibility. Private insurance coverage is a function of the contract with the carrier, and there is no substitute for reading the contract provisions. States may, by complicated regulatory schemes, require policies to contain certain coverage or limit what coverage insurance companies may offer, and they usually cover reimbursement to the hospital, as opposed to reimbursement to the doctor. The intricate and complex rules governing the federal and state Medicare and Medicaid programs, which fill hundreds of pages of federal regulations, require consultation with a specialist. However, it may be useful to highlight a few aspects of eligibility and coverage which can affect choices in treatment.

Medicare is the federal health insurance program for the elderly and disabled; to be eligible, a patient must be at least 65 years old or must have received social security disability benefits for at least 2 years. SSD recipients with end-stage renal disease need not wait 2 years to have Medicare cover their dialysis.

Medicaid is the federal health insurance program for the poor administered by state social service departments. Eligibility is based on financial need, and the eligibility limits on income and savings are extremely low, although the eligibility standards are less stringent

for the spouse of a patient placed in long-term institutional care. Recent changes in federal law now allow patients to qualify for Medicaid by impoverishing themselves through transfers of their assets to others, but if they do so, their Medicaid coverage will not include nursing home care for a variable period, depending on the amount transferred. The maximum length of this period is 30 months. This option will make it possible for more elderly patients than heretofore to qualify for Medicaid.

Medicare gives patients various procedural rights, including the right to appeal from a determination by the hospital that they are medically ready for discharge. The appeal is decided by a Peer Review Organization from outside the hospital which makes an independent evaluation based on the medical record. The purpose of the review is quality control and protection of patients.

Important differences in coverage between Medicare and Medicaid include:

1. Medicaid often covers prescription drugs without any copayment by the patient, whereas Medicare will not begin covering most prescription drugs until 1991 and will require substantial copayments. In some states Medicaid covers only those drugs which are listed on a state-approved prescription drug list.
2. Medicaid covers "custodial" care (e.g., assistance with turning, transferring, toileting, walking, and feeding) in nursing homes and, in some states, at home, whereas Medicare does not. To receive Medicare coverage in a nursing home or at home, the patient must require daily skilled care (e.g., rehabilitation therapy, dressing changes, suctioning, tube feeding, or skilled management of overall treatment), and the need for this care must be certified by the treating physician. Medicare coverage of nursing home care is limited to 150 days. A physician's certification of a patient's need for skilled care in a nursing home will also prevent termination of Medicare coverage for a hospital patient who no longer needs acute care but is waiting for placement.
3. Medicaid in many states covers routine physical exams (checkups), routine foot care, dental care, hearing exams and hearing aids, and eyeglasses, whereas Medicare does not.

Both Medicare and Medicaid use a standard of "medical necessity" in determining whether to pay for specific services. Physicians can assist patients in obtaining coverage for medically necessary treatment by saying plainly in diagnoses and treatment records that the services or equipment are medically necessary, not merely beneficial to the patient.

LEGAL TOOLS AND PROCEDURES

The following is a checklist of possible legal tools and procedures which experience has shown to be effective ways of dealing with proxy or substituted decision making, refusal of treatment, and financial management. The laws of the different states vary, and a local attorney should be consulted to confirm the general principles outlined here.

1. *Power of attorney.* By this simple document, which must be acknowledged before a notary public, one person—the patient (or principal)—empowers another person (agent) to act in the patient's stead. The power of attorney may be specific or limited as to the power or property it covers, such as over a bank account or sale of a house, or general, which permits the agent to do most things affecting property the principal could do personally, except make gifts, act as a fiduciary or sign a will. Powers of attorney can be given to one or more persons, are revocable, and terminate when the principal dies or becomes legally incompetent.

2. *Durable power of attorney.* A durable power, executed while the principal is competent, can also be limited or general, but remains in force after the incompetence of the principal, because it contains the language "this power shall not be affected by my subsequent illness or disability," or similar. The durable power is available in most states and is regarded by many as the best simple mechanism to enable an agent to act for an impaired or disabled person without the expense, delay, and clumsiness of a conservatorship or guardianship proceeding (described below).

Warning: Although they are very useful, powers of attorney, especially general powers, are like signing a blank check and are, therefore, dangerous documents. In the hands of an irresponsible agent or self-dealing relative, they are subject to great abuse and can cause serious problems, especially if the principal has become incompetent and incapable of revoking the power.

Many older people are willing to sign a durable power of attorney, but unwilling to deliver it to the attorney-in-fact, until the need for its use arises. In a few states this problem has been solved by statutes permitting "springing powers" which come into effect only when the principal becomes incompetent, but determination of incompetence is difficult. Another solution to this practical problem is for a third party, such as the lawyer for the principal or some other relative, to hold the power of attorney and release it to the agent only according to oral or written instructions. The principal may or may not wish to disclose even its existence to the agent until needed. If not, the third party's responsibility in holding the power is greatly increased. In general, physicians should refuse to be named as attorneys-in-fact for their patients. Many state statutes forbid a doctor's acting as attorney-in-fact for health care purposes.

3. *Durable power of attorney for health care.* A standard general durable power of attorney, by its terms, appears to and may in fact empower an attorney-in-fact to make health care decisions on behalf of the principal. Nonetheless, questions have been raised about whether a durable power can be so used, especially respecting the refusal of treatment in life-threatening situations and other critical discretionary medical decisions. Some legislatures have responded by passage of durable powers of attorney especially designed for health care. Such documents differ from a regular power, only in that the principal expressly authorizes the agent to make health care decisions in the event of incapacity. These powers may also stipulate a process for decision making and enumerate requests for refusals of certain procedures, such as ventilators or nasogastric feeding. In states which have not passed such laws, but where questions about general durable powers have been passed, it is often advisable to add health care decisions as an enumerated power in a regular durable power.

4. *Inter vivos* or *living trusts.* A *living trust* is a contract between a person (patient) and a person or trust company (trustee) by which the patient transfers legal title to some or all personal property to the trustee to be administered according to the terms of the contract. It may run for the patient's life and then provide a "dispositive" plan for the property (as a will substitute), or it may terminate at death and "pour over" into the estate. The trustee may be given useful special powers, such as authority to pay living and medical expenses, etc. Such trusts have the advantage of being nonpublic documents, which can be tailored to meet many different situations, and they can combine current financial operation with the management and conservation of property and estate planning. Many older people want such a vehicle to relieve them of the day-to-day responsibilities of their business affairs. Since the terms of a trust may affect reimbursement rights, especially Medicaid, an attorney competent in estate planning and knowledgeable about reimbursement eligibility should be consulted.

5. *Living wills.* A *living will* is a document by which a patient indicates the wish that if terminally ill, life-sustaining treatments either should not be initiated or should be discontinued under certain circumstances. Approximately 40 states have passed legislation specifically authorizing living wills, but such wills are enforceable in all states.

It is extremely important that the patient and family discuss with the physician the patient's wishes respecting withdrawal or withholding of treatment. The nursing staff should be included in the discussions, since they are often the first decision makers in a crisis. A living will is very often the best evidence of a patient's wishes, but care must be taken to make sure that it is added to the patient's record and that the presiding physician is aware of it. Living wills often contain or are combined with durable powers of attorney or health care durable powers. Once again, it is in the physician's best interest, as well as the patient's, to have timely legal advice to help the parties achieve the best care and to minimize surprises, stalemates, and liabilities.

6. *Joint accounts.* Joint accounts are often created by elderly spouses to avoid legal costs and achieve simplicity. They are useful tools if the amounts involved are small. But creation of joint interests in valuable assets, such as securities accounts or real estate, may entail serious risk and complications and have adverse estate planning and tax consequences. They can also adversely affect Medicaid eligibility.

7. *Guardianships.* For centuries the court appointment of a guardian of the person and/or property of an incompetent has been the classic legal mechanism by which people with severely impaired capacity were cared for. These proceedings involve a petition filed in court by the patient personally or by a relative or friend alleging that the person is impaired or incompetent, followed by an evidentiary hearing, usually requiring the patient's presence or appointment of a guardian *ad litem* and the presentation of psychiatric or other expert medical testimony. Such a proceeding results in a judicial finding of incompetence, coupled with the appointment of a guardian or committee of the person and/or the property. Even if uncontested, a guardianship proceeding can be unpleasant, expensive, and often protracted. If contested, it can become a traumatic experience for patient and family. If the court declares the patient incompetent, it also results in the loss of the patient's civil rights, such as the rights to vote, to get married, or to make a will or contract. Wherever possible, for emotional as well as financial reasons, guardianship proceedings should be avoided. Sometimes there is no alternative: If, for instance, no close relative exists to act as attorney-in-fact, or the patient resists the needed delegation to a surrogate, then a court proceeding may have to be initiated.

8. *Conservatorships.* Conservatorships, now available in most states, are procedurally similar to guardianships, but do not result in loss of civil rights. Instead, they result in a court-ordered and supervised management of the patient's property and affairs by the appointed conservator. In most cases, a durable power of attorney or trust can achieve most, if not all, of the same results, without the expense and delay of a court proceeding. However, as discussed above, there are situations in which a conservatorship is the least objectionable course, especially if the patient will not acquiesce to the need for delegation of authority or if no appropriate friend or relative will serve. Conservatorships are often used as a last resort when a patient has lost the capacity to manage affairs without having delegated power to anyone else.

9. *Guardian ad litem.* A *guardian ad litem* is a person appointed by a court to represent the interests of an incapacitated person in a legal proceeding. The guardian's role is to report to the court on the best interests of the patient. Such appointments are usually made if there is an apparent conflict of interest between patient and family or if an incompetent person is attempting to forego life-sustaining treatment through a surrogate.

CONCLUSION

In the delivery of geriatric health care services, the patient, physician, and family will likely encounter a series of difficult problems as time or disease diminish the patient's capacity. The physicians and lawyers cannot solve all the problems. Nonetheless, although the interests of the patient and of the physician may not be identical, they largely overlap. Including the lawyer early in the dialogue with the patient, the family, and the physician can greatly facilitate communication on problems of patients' rights, authority to treat, and financial management. As with the delivery of the best care itself, early disclosure and continuing communication are the best prescription.

Chapter 39

ETHICAL ISSUES
IN GERIATRIC CARE

Robert A. Pearlman

The roles and practices of medical providers have evolved throughout history within a context of philosophical and ethical principles. These principles elucidate values and normative standards that define the relationship of medicine to society, the scope of its authority and the extent of its obligations. Although many of the ethical issues implicit in the relationship between a health care provider and patient are timeless, others, reflecting the capabilities and costs created by recent advances in medical technologies, uniquely challenge the consciences of medical providers. When taken together with profound changes in family structure and in social and economic provisions for health care, these challenges generate unprecedented ethical concerns.

Medical literature over the past decade reflects a heightened awareness of the moral dimensions of medical practice. Controversy and research have been stimulated by questions of what medicine should be doing, for whom, and at what cost. Three recent examples are representative of the issues under debate: Should octogenarians receive open-heart surgery?[1] Should expensive medical care be withheld from those in the last year of life?[2] Should transplantations be restricted so that other health services can be provided?[3] Monographs and journal articles now offer useful insights to the problems faced by practitioners, advice on practical skills for dealing with them, and structured approaches to clinical decision making.[4] Ethical issues are being recognized as crucial in their bearing on the formulation of medical protocols and national policies, particularly as they concern the care of the geriatric patient.

Many of the specific circumstances and characteristics of an aging population are perceived as medical problems. This perception is revealed in commentaries and studies on issues such as quality of life, informed consent, mental incapacitation, rationing of scarce medical resources, and loss of independence and autonomy for the elderly nursing home resident. Biomedical ethics is not only germane to these issues, but it is also involved in judgments concerning life-sustaining therapies such as "Do-Not-Resuscitate" (DNR) orders, cardiopulmonary resuscitation (CPR) decisions, and artificial nutrition and hydration. Moreover, many of these issues are being paraphrased into legal and political questions about the adequacy, fairness, and costs of health care for the elderly, who need and use health care the most.

THE TEXTURE OF ETHICAL PROBLEMS IN GERIATRICS

The current increase of attention directed toward ethics in the practice of geriatric medicine is explained by several predisposing factors. Within medical practice itself, innovative technological advances have blurred the distinction between life and death. The process of dying has shifted perceptually and in reality from a matter of mystery to one of conscious human management. With the knowledge and capabilities for doing more than they are certain they should, physicians grapple with the moral implications of death defined as a fitting goal of case strategy rather than as a strategy to be avoided at all cost.[5] Respirators, pacemakers, dialysis, and feeding tubes enable some dying or comatose patients to continue living, yet the benefits often do not obviously outweigh the burdens of added suffering and loss of human dignity. Another aspect of geriatric medicine that generates ethical concern pertains to quality of care. The provision of excellent care to older patients often requires a

This article was supported by the Northwest Health Services Research and Development Field Program and the Geriatric Research, Education and Clinical Center, Seattle Veterans Administration Medical Center.

comprehensive, longitudinal, and interdisciplinary approach (see Chaps. 18 and 19). Yet, health care delivery in the United States does not provide any incentives to encourage or support these characteristics; acute care receives a higher priority than long-term care.

A second set of factors derives from the societal milieu. Cost-containment strategies, competitive interests, and consumerist behaviors imported from the marketplace are being thrust upon providers and patients alike before policies can be formulated that foster a just, explicit rationing of resources.[6] These pressures conflict with many of the central tenets of geriatric care: continuity, comprehensiveness, promotion of maximal independence, and treatment of acute and chronic illnesses. Furthermore, increases in health insurance costs, coinsurance percentages, and deductible payments limit access to health care. This financial limitation conflicts with the attitudes of a majority of Americans, who feel that access to needed health care should not be dependent on ability to pay.[7]

The values and practices of medical practitioners themselves provide a third impetus generating ethical issues. Conflicts between paternalism and the autonomy of the patient are complicated issues of control. Questions over authority and treatment plans are made even more difficult in the face of technological advances which introduce medical as well as moral uncertainty. The physician faces one dilemma if a successful treatment plan inadvertently violates a patient's civil rights and quite another when the success of actions aimed at prolonging life are seen, on balance, to have done more harm than good. What is more, judgments about tests and procedures in individual cases may be affected by generalized concerns over the social costs of medicine. Such accountings are often made in reference to the criteria of patient age, cognitive functioning, quality of life, or expected length of survival. These are external measures of social worth, for which grave concerns have been expressed.[8–10] Furthermore, when physicians give greater importance to societal cost containment than to individual patient benefit without the patient's awareness, they undermine their traditional advocacy role for the patient's well-being and, as a consequence, threaten patient trust in the profession.

Finally, changes in the values, expectations, and capabilities of aging patients are also predisposing factors for many ethical issues in geriatric care. Elderly patients may defer more readily to a physician's authority than younger ones, but still they often desire more information and involvement than physicians provide. As public awareness of technological advances in medicine expands, patients or their families may insist on requesting procedures the physician considers to be not in the best interest of the patient, beyond established medical standards, or simply useless. Moreover, the elderly often have serious limitations in their functional activities and present with cognitive dysfunctions, two predisposing factors for dependence and vulnerability. These circumstances may be compounded by additional factors such as sensory impairment, reduced reaction time, slower speech, and diminished function in response to stress. Care for the elderly can, therefore, impose upon the physician unusual demands and high moral obligation. In the provision of care to the elderly, physicians need to recognize threats to patient autonomy, independence, and individuality, and to avoid these threats if possible. This approach to care should reduce unnecessary patient humiliation and help patients retain their dignity.

REASONING ABOUT DILEMMAS

In a dynamic pluralistic society, issues of good versus bad, right versus wrong, and just versus unjust are rarely capable of resolution by reference to a single, simple, authoritative standard. Although the specific application of absolute standards for human conduct can seem clear and compelling, centuries of careful reasoning in the Western tradition have proven that such instances are exceedingly rare. Total relativity is not less problematic, even though individual cases differ and circumstances vary tremendously. Our cultural experience in ethical reasoning has shown that neither rigid absolutism nor wide-open situational relativity provides workable, satisfying solutions. The important concerns in medical practice, touching on issues such as human dignity, freedom of choice, and life and death, present moral dilemmas in which no single thing done or left undone can serve all wants or needs and for which there is no unblemished, unambiguous sense of the "best thing to do." A careful process of reasoning can be the most effective means of resolving such cases and ascertaining the "best thing to do."

Moral dilemmas in a medical context commonly involve conflicts either between justifiable principles or between principles and consequences. Under most circumstances, physicians and patients alike consider the outcomes, or consequences, of medical care, and in the majority of situations this approach seems obvious and appropriate to both those giving and receiving care; questions of treatment are answered by what works best or produces the desired results. In morally problematic cases, however, the facts may be unclear or contradictory, or the affected parties may have fundamentally different views on what constitutes the best outcome. Consider two examples: Should a demented patient's refusal of treatment be accepted when his family considers the treatment to be in his best interest? Should a patient who has shown a repeated inability to care for himself be allowed to refuse nursing home placement?

When consequences alone are taken as the measure of best response to dilemmas, three critical limitations occur. First and most obviously, the future is uncertain and unpredictable. Second, it is usually impossible to gauge how far and in what way the consequences of a medical decision may reverberate for the patient. For the practitioner, endpoints for such calculations are usually within the time frame of the present treatment regimen or hospitalization. For the patient, however, the measures keep running. Months or years may pass before the final outcomes are established. Third, the physician and patient may hold different values and opinions about what constitutes a good outcome. Physicians may value a normal range of laboratory and physical measures for disease conditions such as blood sugar for diabetes mellitus, blood pressure for hypertension, and serum levels for many prescribed medications. In contrast, patients often may value their independence, lifestyle, and family interactions to a greater degree than their health. As a result, patients often seem noncompliant with physician recommendations. For example, they take prescribed medications only when it is convenient and often engage in unhealthy activities, such as smoking cigarettes and driving automobiles without seat belts. Consideration of consequences alone, therefore, rarely provides an adequate basis for response to a moral dilemma. Principles must also be weighed.

Resolving moral issues by examining them in terms of important and basic principles, sometimes called deontological, can be a helpful guide for patient management. One significant principle in Western societies is that of autonomy, or self-determination. This principle derives from a fundamental right of privacy under which adults of sound mind are considered to be in control of their own bodies and, by extension, their own fate. Many legal cases have articulated this principle; two deserve special note. In *Schloendorff v. Society of New York Hospital* in 1914, Judge Cordoza stated that "every human being of adult years and sound mind has a right to determine what shall be done with his own body."[11] In 1965, the Supreme Court of the United States supported the rights of a Connecticut married couple to procure a contraceptive device, referring to a right of privacy based on the penumbrae of the First, Third, Fourth, Fifth, and Ninth Amendments.[12] A second guiding set of principles is beneficence and nonmaleficence; that is, the doing of good and the avoiding of harm. In *Epidemics*, Hippocrates first stated the maxim: *primum non nocere*.[13] Both of these principles are reiterated in medical codes from antiquity to the present. Justice and a commitment to fairness define another important guiding set of principles. These principles play a role in resource allocation determinations and informed consent, but also apply broadly to discrimination issues in which social worth characteristics of the patient are considered.

These principles are important points of reference in the physician's process of ethical reasoning. Yet a course of action deemed moral by the standard of one principle could be clearly wrong and inappropriate in terms of another. Ethical choice involves more than just the outcome of a decision or course of action. To the physician responding to a moral dilemma, "ethical" should be descriptive of a *process* of reasoning and careful consideration. Careful attention should be directed beyond medical indications to individual preferences, patient-determined quality of life, and external factors such as insurance and organizational policies.[8] The role of process in responding to ethical issues in geriatric care is especially prominent.

General issues of informed consent, rationing of medical resources, quality of life, and withholding tests or treatments suggest the diversity, frequency, and seriousness of moral questions involving elderly patients. Reasoning about these dilemmas is presented in the section that follows.

INFORMED CONSENT

Although the foundations of informed consent derive from both legal and ethical traditions, the purpose of informed consent also supports the goals of medical care. Properly understood and utilized, informed consent can become a useful means for improving communication between patients and health care providers, educating patients, increasing their responsible investment in their own care, and identifying appropriate goals for medical treatments.

For consent to be meaningful, the individual giving consent must be competent, informed, and free of coercion.[14] Relevant information must be communicated and understood, the responsibility for which falls to the physician.[14,15] The patient then has, within very broad parameters, the freedom to accept or reject a proposed treatment or diagnostic test. Paraphrased as a question, the patient asks and then decides, "What course of treatment, if any, offers me the chances of achieving the benefit I wish at risks I am willing to take?" Obviously, the question is highly personal and subjective; the answer may have little connection to what, from a strictly medical viewpoint, would be the best thing to do or even to what might seem rational or reasonable. The idea that the patient's response is free of coercion means that a patient should be able to choose any option without feeling intimidated.

The basic elements of informed consent presume the information needs of a reasoning individual.[15] These needs include a clear rationale for the recommended test or procedure, comprising a statement of the underlying problem as well as a statement of the expected benefits and the likelihood of their achievement with each option. The information provided must also include a clear description of the likelihood of any untoward events associated with each option identified as high risk/low probability or low risk/high probability and with the alternatives, including no treatment.

Many studies describe the problems inherent in achieving true informed consent.[16–20] Patients often sign consent forms not knowing or unable to recall the basic medical information. They are uncomfortable assuming responsibility for their course of treatment and may be afraid to ask questions necessary to be enlightened "shoppers." In the elderly patient, comprehension difficulties may be further compounded by specific characteristics such as diminished visual and/or auditory acuity and cognitive dysfunction.

Attitudes and practices of health care professionals may also interfere with effective consent. Time constraints, lack of understanding of culturally relevant risks to the patient, or minimizing alternatives less acceptable from a medical perspective result in a loss of positive opportunities for creative, effective consent techniques. Documentation by cursory procedures may signify a misunderstanding that consent has low value or is optional. Physicians may brush over risks and alternatives. Furthermore, the consent process may be considered appropriate only for procedures that are risky from a litigation standpoint.

A recent study documented one major barrier to informed consent: communication.[21] Incomplete communication between health care providers and patients concerning procedures done to patients corresponded with incomplete patient comprehension. Rationale and potential benefits were communicated/comprehended about half of the time, which was more often than the occurrence of communication/comprehension about risks and options, which took place less than one-quarter of the time. Furthermore, communication/comprehension increased selectively with very invasive procedures, but not with clinically important or risky procedures.

Recommendations for improving consent practices have dealt mainly with the improvement of procedures and forms through simplified language, clearer descriptions, mutual consents between patients and physicians, and two-stage procedures in which confirmation of understanding is obtained before proceeding. A recently proposed recommendation suggests that informed consent become an ongoing process rather than a one-time, event-oriented activity.[22] This recommended reorientation highlights the belief that patients have a unique knowledge of their own history and facts, a unique ability to evaluate their own symptoms, and a responsibility for approving their own health care. A patient who assumes a more active role in the prescribed course of therapy will generally be better prepared to accept the outcome and less likely to blame the physician for any unsatisfactory results. Such improvements of form, matched with improvements of attitude and understanding, encourage prospects for the enhanced protection of the rights and interests of elderly patients.

EQUITABLE DISTRIBUTION OF MEDICAL RESOURCES

A majority of the population maintain that the quality and quantity of health care should be available to everyone and not be provided on the basis of ability to pay,[7] yet attitudes have been fostered which seem to support the conflicting goals of rationing. This conundrum reflects the high overall costs of care, the increasing use of expensive technologies, questions about benefits of expenditures made in a patient's last year of life, pressures from large corporate consumers of health care to lower premiums, and pressure by hospitals to minimize unprofitable practices. Furthermore, for physicians the dilemma is heightened because there is no corresponding guarantee that cost containment or selective allocation will lead to a greater good or the promotion of just societal outcomes.

The American Geriatric Society's policy on the allocation of scarce medical resources makes several important points.[23] According to that policy, careful, reasoned, *public* debate, based on an adequate knowledge base, is necessary before any policy decisions can be made to ration health care. Efforts to allocate resources should focus on unnecessary spending and waste in all areas of medical care and must not target a specific area or population, such as the elderly. In this regard, a person's chronological age, per se, should not be used as a criterion for exclusion from a given therapy. The findings of the Society were that disproportionately greater per capita expenditures for the elderly were appropriate, given the greater need for medical care in that age group. Most importantly for the practitioner, considerations of resource distribution should not outweigh efforts to maximize an individual patient's welfare.

The physician as a trusted, loyal caregiver has a multifaceted role in assuring fair rationing of medical resources. Identifying those patients who would not benefit from treatment, practicing medicine that is cost-effective, planning treatment on the basis of patient goals and health care aspirations, and avoiding wasteful practices are some straightforward measures to implement. The physician may also need to employ decision-analysis methods in order to better understand the diagnostic value of tests in relation to the desired outcomes of patients.

The role of the physician is more complicated when dealing with institutions, but the responsibility remains to encourage development of explicit, understandable, defensible, and fair policies that are open to review, criticism, and revision within the institutional setting. Physicians need to avoid pressures such as premature hospital discharge based on diagnosis-related groups (DRGs) when such pressures conflict with the patient's best interests.[24] The proper place for societal gatekeeping is at the front door of policies throughout the system, not at the bedside of a vulnerable patient.[25] Moreover, physicians need to remember that DRG cutoffs represent mean values. Thus, for a specific medical problem, some patients require more hospital days and some fewer.

A good patient–caregiver relationship can be maintained with consideration given to rationing of resources if such policies are openly discussed with patients. In this way, the trust factor will continue to be a primary consideration.

Two recent books discuss rationing of medical resources with the explicit consideration of limiting care to the elderly. Both books are intended to promote public debate. In *Setting Limits*, Daniel Callahan argues that the goal of health care should be to promote quality of life, function, and independence and to reduce suffering, premature deaths, and morbidity during a "full, natural life span."[26] However, because (1) the elderly can often be sustained beyond a natural life span, (2) individualistic needs and preferences for health care may lead to limitless provision of such services, and (3) younger and future generations are consequently at risk for being deprived of goods or services, he recommends restricting health care to the elderly who have lived a full, natural life. He recommends all the same that age, per se, be rejected as a criterion for rationing, that any restriction of medical treatment should accompany an increase in other forms of care to the targeted elderly population, and that the ethics of intergenerational responsibilities should replace the individualistic orientation among the elderly.

In contrast to Callahan's arguments based on natural life span, intergenerational responsibilities, and a proposed societal allocation scheme, in *Just Health Care* Norman Daniels argues for a philosophy of health care that provides differential amounts of opportunity for health care at different stages of an individual's life.[27] Rather than consider interpersonal rationing, he suggests intrapersonal rationing across different stages of life. Therefore, throughout a life span all individuals would be treated equally. This idea obviates the problems of justly distributing resources between age groups. However, like Callahan's ideas, they should serve as initial points of discussion as our society tries to tackle limiting health care fairly.

PHYSICIAN VALUES: OLD AGE AND QUALITY OF LIFE

Age discrimination in the delivery of health care is generally unacceptable. Despite this, physicians often treat older persons differently, even when controlling for stage of disease and comorbidity. Studies have shown that physicians are both less aggressive and comprehensive with older patients.[27a,27b] Although advanced age may increase risks from a treatment and reduce the duration of benefit because of limited life expectancy, these are only two factors that influence whether a treatment's benefits outweigh its risks. Chronological age should not be used as a proxy for a negative characteristic such as poor quality of life, nor should it justify withholding efficacious treatment.

Patient quality of life is discussed frequently as a factor affecting life-sustaining medical decisions for chronically ill patients.[2,8,28–36] This factor is particularly relevant in decision making for mentally incapacitated patients without advance care directives. In these circumstances physicians often try to consider patient quality of life in order to justify the decisions they must make without knowing a patient's wishes.

Many factors make determinations of quality of life difficult to predict. The term *quality of life* has no obvious meaning; it is not clear to which empirical states the term refers, nor is it manifest how any particular person will evaluate those states. In addition, the traditional pressures in acute care facilities for aggressive treatment and the uncertainties of diagnosis and prognosis make predictions of patient quality of life difficult. Other complicating issues include the physician's subjective values relative to the patient's characteristics, inadequate communication between physicians and patients, and basic problems with the measurement of quality of life.[29,31,37,38] In situations in which quality of life connotes a vague set of attributes and conditions, the variability of perceptions of a patient's quality of life may be great.

Recent studies highlight the inherent ambiguity of the concept of quality of life. In one study, 205 physicians evaluated the same patient management problem and frequently justified their treatment decisions based on perceived quality of life of the patient.[29] Some of the physicians chose to treat because of good quality of life, while others withheld treatment because of poor quality of life. In other studies physicians systematically underrated patient quality of life as compared to the patient's self-rating.[32,38,39] Physicians appear to overemphasize the contribution of health to overall quality of life and underestimate the importance of finances, relationships, and housing.[32]

The ambiguous concept of quality of life can be used

responsibly when clinicians attune their interactions with patients to the values and goals of the patient. In these contexts, a patient's own evaluation of the quality of his or her life may determine the choice of a therapeutic intervention and what is beneficial or in his or her best interest. An example is when a clinician recommends a walker rather than a nursing home for a patient with irreversible gait instability, in order to comply with the patient's desire to remain independent. A less common example is when a clinician accepts a competent elderly patient's refusal of treatment because from the patient's perspective the proposed intervention will only improve the patient's health, and not the overall quality of life. When consideration of a patient's quality of life is grounded in the patient's self-evaluation, ethical concerns are rarely raised.

Using quality of life as a factor in decisions involving life-sustaining procedures, however, can represent a crucial ethical concern in patient care.[30,35] With an informed, competent patient who is able to communicate his or her feelings, respect for patient autonomy should foster respect for the patient's attitudes about the use of life-sustaining procedures. The underlying rationale is that this type of patient is able to determine what is beneficial for himself or herself on the basis of his or her perceived current or future quality of life. This situation requires that a clinician's subjective evaluation of the patient's quality of life generally be secondary to the patient's opinions.[14] Ethical problems appear only when a patient's competency is in doubt or an incompetent patient's family or health care provider proposes that the patient's quality of life does not justify a medical intervention. When a patient is unable to communicate his or her feelings about life-sustaining procedures, quality of life may be considered a decisive factor only if the patient's quality of life falls below a minimum standard and intervention would only preserve this condition or maintain organic life.[8] One definition for minimal threshold of life quality is extreme physical debilitation and a complete loss of sensory and intellectual activity.[8,40] Only when the qualities common to human interaction (i.e., ability to reason, experience emotions, and enter into relationships) have been irreversibly lost should the clinician's assessment of the patient's quality of life determine withholding of life-supporting therapy. The epidemiological concept of specificity is particularly relevant in these situations.

Physicians need to be aware of and avoid subjective judgments of poor quality of life based on socioeconomic or other value-laden attributes. This minimum standard reflects respect for personal function, cerebration, the essential qualities of being human, and the sanctity of human life. These guidelines attempt to protect patient autonomy, to ensure justice by preventing capricious decision making based on personal preferences, and to promote beneficial results for patients.

WITHDRAWING AND WITHHOLDING LIFE-SUSTAINING PROCEDURES

Withholding or withdrawing life-sustaining therapies is one of the most troublesome ethical issues in geriatric care and is relevant to concerns about rationing of medical resources and quality of life decisions. These judgments frequently occur under circumstances of clinical futility: it becomes apparent to the physician and/or the patient that treatment is not benefiting the patient. Research data are inconclusive on the epidemiology and nature of decision making as it concerns tests and procedures. Often, orders are written within 24 hours prior to the patient's death and are associated with patient characteristics, such as being elderly, nonambulatory, incontinent, and demented and having resided in a nursing home.[41-44] Physicians may believe they understand the wishes of their patients, but they may inadvertently override them. Research data in fact suggest inadequate physician–patient communication and errors in both excessive overtreatment and undertreatment.[32,45,46] Unfortunately, physician inaccuracy does not appear to improve with either longer patient–physician relationships nor comparable ages between patient and physician.[47]

There is great ambiguity with the terminology used to describe the withdrawing or withholding of life-sustaining procedures. For example, the word *euthanasia*, Greek for "good death," has come to describe many different things. Active euthanasia, the affirmative and intentional doing of something to cause the death of an individual, is prohibited by law and condemned by professional standards. When passive, however, euthanasia is described approvingly as simply allowing a patient to die and considered permissible under certain specified circumstances. Both forms of euthanasia refer, at least ideally, to instances in which the patient voluntarily desires death. Interestingly, both also may share the same intentions, justification, motives, methods, and outcomes.[48] "Extraordinary," "heroics," and "imminent" are confusing terms, meaningless outside a narrow and quite selectively biased context, that are used to justify passive, voluntary euthanasia. The American Medical Association's policy statement on euthanasia demonstrates the aforementioned ambiguity: "the cessation of extraordinary or heroic measures to prolong life is permissible when there is irrefutable evidence that biological death is imminent."[49]

American courts have contributed important insights about professional roles and standards and patients' rights to determine medical care for themselves, including the issues of voluntary, passive euthanasia and withholding therapies.[50] Developing patterns of case law reflect society's stresses in coming to grips with the issues of man's increasing ability to "manage" death. Legal decisions resulting from public debate on these topics can provide useful guidance for the making of ethical decisions. The President's Commission for the Study of Ethical Problems in Medicine and Biomedical and Behavioral Research in 1983 also made a number of helpful and influential observations.[9] Some suggestions to keep in mind from these sources are discussed below.

GENERAL RECOMMENDATIONS

It is essential that the voluntary choice of a competent and informed patient be allowed to determine whether or not life-sustaining therapy will be undertaken. This respects the principle of autonomy. The right of choice extends to patients incapable of making decisions for whatever reason, including chronic cognitive dysfunction or coma. In these instances, previous expressions of the patient's preferences, even unwritten, can be considered valid signposts and accepted as authentic expressions. Appropriate surrogates for incompetent adults, generally family members, should attempt to replicate decisions the patient would have made. If lack of evidence exists as to wishes, surrogates should seek to protect the patient's best interests. The courts, in their role as protectors of the rights of the individual, should promote surrogate decision making with substituted judgments reflecting the expressed wishes of the patient, and then, if necessary, with determinations of the patient's best interests inferred from patient goals and values. In this regard, while recognizing that patients have rights to reject or accept recommended treatment, and respecting the principle of beneficence, it will be assumed the interests of most patients will best be served by presuming in favor of sustaining life. As matters both of legal and medical professional responsibility, the primary obligation for ensuring morally justified processes of decision making lies with the physician.

The physician's reasoning about whether a choice that leads to a premature death is acceptable or not should be directed by the degree to which a patient is benefited or burdened by a treatment. Proportionate benefit/burden assessments fall within guidelines of the principles of doing good and avoiding harm and are reasonable approaches to decision making as long as they are patient-centered. It is the responsibility of the physician to assist the patient or surrogate in decisions by providing complete and realistic information regarding prognosis and the potential benefits and risks with various therapeutic options, especially those involving withholding or withdrawing therapy.[51]

In nonemergency cases, patient autonomy or self-determination may be overridden selectively, but only under highly unusual circumstances. One situation is when major depression directly interferes with the ability to make an informed, reasoned decision. Another situation occurs when a state's rights outweigh those of the individual. Both cases would involve judicial review. In theory, an infringement on the patient's autonomy is expected to result in long-term enhancement of the patient's (or his family's) self-determination and well-being.

CPR AND DNR ORDERS

Several approaches have been suggested recently to promote patient autonomy and maximize the useful applications of the benefit/burden rationale.[9,36,52] An outline of the Commission's approach to decision making is presented in Table 39-1. More recently, however, physicians have suggested that life-sustaining procedures should not have to be offered if they represent futile or meaningless therapy.[34,53] A rational alternative approach to decision making regarding CPR or any other life-sustaining treatment that considers medical futility and patient-derived quality of life is offered by Tomlinson and Brody (see Table 39-2).[35]

Physician communication with the patient should seek to identify patient values where possible, so that when crisis situations occur, the patient's views and

TABLE 39-1
Resuscitation (CPR) of Competent Patients—Physician's Assessment in Relation to Patient's Preference

Physician's Assessment	Patient Favors CPR*	No Preference	Patient Opposes CPR*
CPR would benefit patient	Try CPR	Try CPR	Do not try CPR; review decision†
Benefit of CPR unclear	Try CPR	Try CPR	Do not try CPR
CPR would not benefit patient	Try CPR; review decision†	Do not try CPR	Do not try CPR

*Based on an adequate understanding of the relevant information.
†Such a conflict calls for careful reexamination by both patient and physician. If neither the physician's assessment nor the patient's preference changes, then the competent patient's decision should be honored.
SOURCE: From President's Commission for the Study of Ethical Problems in Medicine and Biomedical and Behavioral Research. Decision to forego life-sustaining treatment. Washington, Government Printing Office, 1983, p 244.

TABLE 39-2
Contrasts among Rationales for DNR Orders

Rationale	Patient's Values Relevant?	Implications for Other Treatments?
No medical benefit	No	No
Poor quality of life after CPR	Yes	No
Poor quality of life before CPR	Yes	Yes

SOURCE: From Tomlinson T, Brody H: Ethics and communication in Do-Not-Resuscitate orders. *N Engl J Med* 318:44, 1988.

preferences can be controlling of outcomes.[34] Discussions regarding CPR should focus on whether it serves the patient's goals, and such discussions should be repeated at various stages of health because patient values may change.[54] Partial codes are appropriate only when they reflect the wishes of the patient or surrogate.[34] Slow codes are not ethically justifiable.

Informed choices about cardiopulmonary resuscitation, as with other interventions, require clear and candid information about benefits (likelihood of in-hospital survival), risks (likelihood of complications such as anoxic encephalopathy, fractured ribs, and death), and alternatives (death, if cardiopulmonary arrest occurs).

Current practice for Do-Not-Resuscitate orders requires that there be written and signed consent forms by either the patient or surrogate decision maker. Although this may appear cumbersome and different from traditional indications for written consent, it helps prevent covert decision making without patient (or surrogate) participation. Advance care directives such as Natural Death Acts, living wills, and durable powers of attorney for health care decisions can allow competent patients to express their values for potential future use under conditions of mental incapacitation. Natural Death Acts are legislatively approved living wills that allow competent patients to direct their physicians to withhold or withdraw life-sustaining procedures under specified conditions. Durable powers of attorney for health care decisions are persons that competent patients empower to make health care decisions on their behalf if they ever become mentally incapacitated.

Because many elderly patients reside in nursing homes prior to their deaths, admission to the nursing homes is the ideal time for implementing an advance care directive.[55] A proposed nursing home advance care policy that provides background information about cardiopulmonary resuscitation, and thus fosters more informed decision making, is presented in Table 39-3.

Unfortunately, most policies and recommendations which have been developed thus far pertain only to terminally ill, imminently dying patients. Table 39-4 presents an approach unique in that it extends the logic

and rights regarding care for the dying to other patients. It is oriented to and based upon ethical principles rather than legal considerations and should therefore be discussed with a legal counselor to ascertain the context of legal review in a particular jurisdiction. For example, in several states withholding artificial hydration and nutrition is prohibited from being part of an advance care directive.[56]

Recently, evidence has been presented that suggests that preferences regarding life-sustaining procedures are not well understood by a patient's physician, nurse, or spouse.[47,57] Furthermore, although a patient's preferences may remain stable over time, they change across both different baseline states of health (e.g., hypothetical stroke, hypothetical dementia) and life-sustaining procedures (CPR, CPR requiring mechanical ventilation, artificial hydration, and nutrition).[54,58] Therefore, new attempts at obtaining advance care directives or eliciting patient values should inquire about multiple life-sustaining procedures under several health scenarios. The health scenarios can include the actual present situation as well as conditions that would interfere with the patient's ability to express his or her preferences, such as coma, severe stroke, and dementia. Appropriate inquiries into treatment preferences should include CPR, CPR requiring ventilation, artificial hydration and nutrition, antibiotics for infection, hospitalization for care, hospitalization as a place to die, surgery, dialysis, chemotherapy, cardiovascular drugs, blood, and intensive care unit services. Additional useful information might include the desired duration of mechanical ventilation and artificial hydration and nutrition to sustain life in coma or dementia conditions. An alternative approach to eliciting patient values would inquire about circumstances considered to be worse than death.

Another part of an advance care directive should designate a proxy decision maker (surrogate). Without this designation, a common hierarchy to identify a surrogate decision maker will often be imposed. The hierarchy is usually the spouse first and then consensus by all adult children, parents, and siblings. This ordering might not be appropriate for an elderly patient without a traditional family structure. The surrogate decision maker should be the individual who knows the patient's values the best and can speak on his or her behalf.

ARTIFICIAL HYDRATION AND NUTRITION

One of the most difficult and controversial issues for withholding care has centered upon artificial means for providing nutrition and hydration. These problems are somewhat different from the life-sustaining treatments discussed above, for while nutrition and hydration qualify as life-sustaining procedures, the giving of food and water is often considered a general moral duty, has tre-

TABLE 39-3

Nursing Home Patient Directives for Management of General Medical Problems and Cardiac Arrest

Patient Directives to Physicians and Caregivers

Below you are given the opportunity to indicate your health care preferences should you become unable to communicate them in the future. You are asked to indicate your preferences for two situations, serious medical problems, and "cardiac arrest." *These decisions may be changed at any time.*

1. Approach to Medical Problems

In most instances when medical problems arise, patients discuss the situation with their physicians and make decisions about a preferred course of action. Sometimes the need for decisions arises when patients are unable to communicate their wishes. To ensure that your wishes are followed as closely as possible under such circumstances your guidance in the approach to serious medical problems is requested.

Please indicate your choice below:

_____ All possible measures should be taken including hospitalization, consultations, surgery, and life-support systems. (If no choice is indicated this option will initially be followed. If you remain unable to communicate your preferences, your physician and closest relative or guardian will decide what would be in your best interest regarding further treatment.)

_____ All measures considered appropriate by the individual designated below should be taken. My condition and the probable outcome of these measures should be taken into consideration.

Designated individual:

Name of designee: _____

Relationship: _____

Alternate designee: _____

Relationship: _____

_____ Measures that can return me to my usual state should be taken, but measures considered principally life-prolonging should be avoided.

_____ Treat only to improve comfort and dignity.

Additional instructions: (If you wish to provide additional instructions regarding your medical care, please list them here.)

_____

_____

_____

2. In Case of Cardiac Arrest

Virtually all medical decisions that arise will be made with your physician, or, if you become unable to communicate the decisions will be covered in the medical measures you specified in the "Approach to Medical Problems." A separate decision needs to be made, however, regarding treatment should you experience "cardiac arrest" (heart stoppage). Cardiac arrest results in death unless promptly treated. Should cardiac arrest occur, a technique for revival called cardiopulmonary resuscitation (CPR) is available. This technique involves artificial ventilation (breathing), chest compressions and often drugs and electric shocks, as well. If cardiac arrest occurs CPR must be started immediately to optimize changes for survival. There is no time for consultation; therefore, a decision regarding CPR needs to be made in advance.

Washington State law requires that attempts at revival must be made unless there has been a specific request not to use such efforts.

The following general information about cardiac arrest may be helpful in your decision making:

1. Most deaths in a nursing home follow a long-term decline in the person's health. Approximately 5% to 20% of ill elderly persons who have cardiac arrest survive if they receive CPR. Survival is much less likely if resuscitation is initiated 5 or more minutes after cardiac arrest occurs. Approximately 60% of patients who survive cardiac arrest have permanent brain damage such as memory loss, coma, or paralysis.
2. Sudden death is thought to be painless.
3. Successful resuscitation is followed by transfer to a hospital for other measures.

Do you wish to receive CPR (cardiopulmonary resuscitation) if you should have cardiac arrest, or would you prefer to accept this event as the end of your natural life? Please indicate your choice:

_____ All efforts should be made at revival in the event of cardiac arrest.

_____ No efforts at revival should be made, and I will accept cardiac arrest as the end of my natural life.

Additional instructions (if any): _____

_____

_____

_____

Patient's name _____

Patient's signature _____ Date _____

Witness: _____ Relationship _____

Witness: _____ Relationship _____

SOURCE: From Uhlmann RF et al: Medical management decisions in nursing home patients: Principles and policy recommendations. *Ann Intern Med* 106:883, 1987.

mendous symbolic value as a caring gesture, and is sometimes considered basic nursing care. Since all people require food and water, the provision of food and water is considered by some to represent supportive care. Withholding food and water also leads to starvation and dehydration, and subsequently to death. As a result, it has been considered by some to be the proximate cause of death.[59,60] The role of health care providers is to sometimes cure, occasionally relieve, and always comfort.[59] Consequently, many physicians support artificial hydration and nutrition because they view it as a comforting gesture.[59,61] Other reservations about withholding the provision of food and water include the appearance of abandonment, the suffering associated with

TABLE 39-4
Approach to Patients or Their Surrogates Requesting the Witholding or Withdrawing of Life-Sustaining Procedures

	Health Status	
	Terminally Ill or Irreversible Coma	*Not Terminally Ill*
Capable of making a carefully considered specific decision	1. Per patient's wishes. 2. If M.D.-patient disagree, discuss. 3. If irreconcilable disagreement, either defer to patient's wishes or transfer care to another physician.	1. Per patient's wishes. 2. If M.D.-patient disagree, discuss. 3. If irreconcilable disagreement, either transfer care to another physician or evaluate for capacity to make informed choice.
Mentally incapacitated with wishes known	1. Per surrogate's expression of patient's wishes. 2. If M.D.-surrogate disagree, discuss. 3. If irreconcilable disagreement, either defer to surrogate's wishes or transfer care to another physician.	1. Per surrogate's expression of patient's wishes. 2. If M.D.-surrogate disagree, discuss. 3. If irreconcilable disagreement, either defer to surrogate's wishes or transfer care to another physician.
Mentally incapacitated without known wishes	1. Per surrogate's expression of patient's best interests. 2. If M.D.-surrogate disagree, discuss. 3. If irreconcilable disagreement, either defer to surrogate's wishes, transfer care to another physician, or seek guardianship review. 4. If a surrogate does not exist, life-sustaining procedures may be withdrawn or withheld if they are merely futile (i.e., prolong the dying process without any apparent benefit).	1. Seek guardianship review to confirm best interests.

SOURCE: From Pearlman RA, Speer JB: Philosophical and ethical issues, in Kelley WN (ed): *Textbook of Internal Medicine*. Philadelphia, Lippincott, 1988, p 2618.

starvation and dehydration, its use as a cost-containment strategy, its capricious use on patients with impaired quality of life, and the fear of a "slippery slope" that undermines the value of life.[59,62,63]

Although several cases reviewed by courts have had conflicting results, the prevailing opinion considers that the use of tubes or intravenous lines (i.e., artificial means) makes the procedures medical care and not routine nursing care.[50,56,64] Therefore, withholding or withdrawing of these procedures should follow the general guidelines discussed in the previous section. Unless a patient explicitly requests not to receive artificial hydration and nutrition, the burdens of providing this care must outweigh the benefits if its withholding or withdrawing is to be considered justifiable. In cases where doubt exists as to the benefits of treatment, trials of support with hydration and nutrition often clarify the burden/benefit balance.[60] Interestingly, medical consensus is developing that dehydration and malnutrition lead to sedation, diminished awareness, and increased pain threshold, which may all reduce suffering prior to death.[65] The only discomfort can be ameliorated with nursing attention to a patient's dry lips and mouth.

MENTAL INCAPACITATION

Persons are presumed to be mentally competent. Mental incompetency is a legal determination which indicates that a patient is incapable of understanding the implications of his or her decisions and choices. Mental incompetence in the law is thus a sliding scale assessment that requires compelling proof and depends greatly on the issues at stake. In many cases, for example, it is easier to prove incompetence to handle financial affairs than it is to reach this finding when what is at stake is the patient's best interest in terms of health and well-being. The best example of this difference is the frequent use of durable power of attorney for VA finances among elderly veterans who have difficulty managing their VA pensions; these durable powers of attorney are rarely also empowered to manage a patient's health care decisions.

A physician may question the competence of patients under many situations, including acute stress, treatment refusal, and coma. Unfortunately, the issue of incompetence or mental incapacitation has been associated frequently with paternalistic actions to override the patient's autonomy. Use of surrogate decision makers is often considered more acceptable with invasive or risky procedures. However, if our society's commitment to personal self-determination is fundamental, then when the stakes regarding the outcome of a patient's decisions get higher, reliance on the surrogate should be more constrained.

The use of durable powers of attorney for health or advance care directives is perhaps the most far-reaching recommendation to facilitate decision making for seemingly incompetent patients. In these situations, respectively, either another individual is empowered to make health care decisions or the patient expresses his or her values and preferences at an earlier point in time. Both of these approaches for enhancing patient self-control have application in many states, and they are especially useful for patients who develop severe dementia or an acute altered mental state and require immediate treatment decisions. It should be noted, however, that the diagnosis of dementia does not necessarily make a patient mentally incapacitated. The judgment should be based on a documented inability to make an informed decision. Furthermore, the elderly are at increased risk of transient episodes of incapacity to make decisions for a variety of reasons (e.g., disease exacerbation, medication side effects, and change in the environment). The potential reversibility of these conditions requires that the physician pursue the cause of altered mental status. For these reasons, and on account of complexities in the family's role as surrogate helpers with decisions, physicians should not automatically seek out a surrogate decision maker for patients who appear to be incapable of making informed choices.

CHALLENGES OF THE INSTITUTIONAL SETTING

Ethical issues are pervasive in this nation's arrangements for long-term care. The physician should be sensitive to issues arising out of the voluntariness of nursing home placement and exercise a careful monitoring role over the patient's transfers from acute to long-term settings. Within these institutions are implicit threats to human dignity and individuality, such as shared rooms and bathrooms, fixed eating times, and scheduled activities that reflect staffing patterns. The physician should be aware of concerns about personal freedom and mobility and about limitations on personal expressions. For example, the use of restraints, both physical and chemical, should not be employed if a less restrictive option is available. Physicians should know whether the nursing home they recommend has a policy that allows wandering in a protected area or has sufficient volunteers and staff so that physical constraints are used sparingly.

SUGGESTIONS

In this chapter, respect for patient self-determination and the balance between benefits and burdens have been stressed. In addition, the primacy of the physician's responsibility to the patient as a medical care advocate has been emphasized. Care of the elderly is complicated by multiple problems interwoven with physiological, social, functional, and economic complexities. Technology offers blessings and curses, giving the physician the opportunity to ask, "Will this serve my patient's best interests?" Cost concerns have affected medical care and health systems so that the physician also has to ask, "Am I still serving my patient's interests? If not, does the patient know it so that he or she can purchase another package?" If the quality of chronic long-term care is not at the same level as other aspects of care in our health care systems, the physician also ought to ask, "What can I do as an individual? What can my professional organization do? If society knew about the problems that exist, would it approve or would it consider my profession to have been in a conspiracy of silence?"

In conclusion, there are several suggestions that are offered to help avoid and resolve ethical dilemmas. First, physicians should identify the difference between medical and nonmedical problems. Just because ethical or social issues arise in the medical context does not mean that physicians have the knowledge to "treat" them or the social warrant to apply the force of medical expertise. Second, physicians should be aware of personal values that may influence their thoughts about treatment. Age, quality of life, pain, select diagnoses such as cancer or incontinence, and other attributes have been shown to bias physicians' judgment so that they inadvertently act in a discriminatory fashion. Third, dilemmas often seem to exist because no one has talked to the patient. It is only through communication that physicians ascertain patient values, interests, and perceived benefits. An important topic for communication is the patient's preferences regarding the future use of life-sustaining procedures. Fourth, patients usually know their own values, interests, and benefits better than anyone else. Fifth, patient stress, a treatment refusal, or even a diagnosis of dementia are not invariant grounds for mental incapacitation. For example, treatment refusal may merely reflect a difference in the relative value of health as defined by the physician to other values of importance to the patient. Sixth, trained ethics consultants and ethics committees may help health care providers decipher the conflicting issues in a case and promote clearer thinking and ethically reasoned actions. And last, the elderly are at risk for ethical dilemmas arising in the health "care" system. The vulnerability that accrues with their physical disabilities and socioeconomic limitations warrants special attention to prevent any unfair practices.

REFERENCES

1. Edmonds LH et al: Open-heart surgery in octogenarians. *N Engl J Med* 319:131, 1988.
2. Avorn J: Benefit and cost analysis in geriatric care: Turning age discrimination into health policy. *N Engl J Med* 310:1294, 1984.
3. Welch HG, Larson EB: Dealing with limited resources. The Oregon decision to curtail funding for organ transplantation. *N Engl J Med* 319:171, 1988.
4. Jonsen AR et al: The ethics of medicine: An annotated bibliography of recent literature. *Ann Intern Med* 92:136, 1980.
5. Hilfiker D: Allowing the debilitated to die: Facing our ethical choices. *N Engl J Med* 308:716, 1983.
6. Miller FH, Miller GAH: Why saying no to patients in the United States is so hard. Cost containment, justice, and provider autonomy. *N Engl J Med* 314:1380, 1986.
7. Cambridge Reports, Inc. HMQ Survey: A mandate for high quality health care. *Health Manage Q* 4:3, 1986.
8. Jonsen AR et al: *Clinical Ethics: A Practical Approach to Ethical Decisions in Clinical Medicine*, 2d ed. New York, Macmillan, 1986.
9. President's Commission for the Study of Ethical Problems in Medicine and Biomedical and Behavioral Research. Decision to forego life-sustaining treatment. Washington, Government Printing Office, 1983.
10. Fox RC, Swazey JP: *The Courage of Fact*. Chicago, University of Chicago, 1978.
11. *Schloendorff v. Society of New York Hospital* 211 N.Y. 125, 1914.
12. *Griswold v. Connecticut* 381 U.S. 479, 1965.
13. Sandulescu C: *Primum non nocere*: Philosophical commentaries on a medical aphorism. *Acta Antiqua* (Academiae Scientiarium Hungaricae) 13:359, 1965.
14. President's Commission for the Study of Ethical Problems in Medicine and Biomedical and Behavioral Research. Making health care decisions: The ethical and legal implications of informed consent in the patient-practitioner relationship. Washington, Government Printing Office, 1982, p 38.
15. *Canterburg v. Spence* U.S. Court of Appeals, District of Columbia Grant, 464 F. 2d 772, 1972.
16. Meisel A, Roth LH: What we do and do not know about informed consent. *JAMA* 246:2473, 1981.
17. Lidz CW et al: Barriers to informed consent. *Ann Intern Med* 99:539, 1983.
18. Stanley B et al: The elderly patient and informed consent. *JAMA* 252:1302, 1984.
19. Cross AW, Churchill LR: Ethical and cultural dimensions of informed consent: A case study and analysis. *Ann Intern Med* 96:110, 1982.
20. Cassileth BR et al: Informed consent: Why are its goals imperfectly realized? *N Engl J Med* 302:896, 1980.
21. Wu WC, Pearlman RA: Consent in medical decision making: The role of communication. *J Gen Intern Med* 3:9, 1988.
22. Lidz CW et al: Two models of implementing informed consent. *Arch Intern Med* 148:1385, 1988.
23. American Geriatrics Society: Allocation of medical resources. *Am Geriatr Soc Newsletter* 15:5, 1986.
24. Relman AS: Practicing medicine in the new business climate. *N Engl J Med* 316:1150, 1987.
25. Reagan MD: Physicians as gatekeepers: A complex challenge. *N Engl J Med* 317: 1731, 1987.
26. Callahan D: *Setting Limits: Medical Goals in an Aging Society*. New York, Simon and Schuster, 1987.
27. Daniels N: *Just Health Care*. New York, Cambridge University Press, 1985.
27a. Sudnow D: *Passing On*. Englewood Cliffs, NJ, Prentice-Hall, 1967.
27b. Wetle T: Age as a risk factor for inadequate treatment. *JAMA* 258:516, 1987.
28. Crane D: *The Sancity of Social Life: Physician's Treatment of Critically Ill Patients*. New York, Russel Sage, 1975.
29. Pearlman RA et al: Variability in physician bioethical decision-making: A case study of euthanasia. *Ann Intern Med* 97:420, 1982.
30. Pearlman RA, Jonsen A: The use of quality of life considerations in medical decision making. *J Am Geriatr Soc* 33:344, 1985.
31. Lo B, Jonsen AR: Clinical decisions to limit treatment. *Ann Intern Med* 93:764, 1980.
32. Starr TJ et al: Quality of life and resuscitation decisions in elderly patients. *J Gen Intern Med* 1:373, 1986.
33. Frampton MW, Mayewski RJ: Physicians' and nurses' attitudes toward withholding treatment in a community hospital. *J Gen Intern Med* 2:394, 1987.
34. Perkins HS: Ethics at the end of life: Practical principles for making resuscitation decisions. *J Gen Intern Med* 1:170, 1986.
35. Tomlinson T, Brody H: Ethics and communication in Do-Not-Resuscitate orders. *N Engl J Med* 318:43, 1988.
36. Miles SH et al: The do-not-resuscitate order in a teaching hospital: Considerations and a suggested policy. *Ann Intern Med* 96:660, 1982.
37. Spitzer WO et al: Measuring the quality of life of cancer patients: A concise QL-index for use by physicians. *J Chronic Dis* 34:585, 1981.
38. Flanagan JC: Measurement of quality of life: Current state of the art. *Arch Phys Med Rehabil* 63:56, 1982.
39. Pearlman RA, Uhlmann RF: Quality of life in chronic diseases: Perceptions of elderly patients. *J Gerontol* 43:M25, 1988.
40. Fletcher J: Four indicators of humanhood: The enquiry matures. *Hastings Cent Rep* 4:4, 1974.
41. Uhlmann RF et al: Epidemiology of no-code orders in an academic hospital. *West J Med* 140:114, 1984.
42. Charlson ME et al: Resuscitation: How do we decide? *JAMA* 255:1316, 1986.
43. Brown NK, Thompson DJ: Nontreatment of fever in extended care facilities. *N Engl J Med* 300:1246, 1979.
44. Farber NJ et al: Cardiopulmonary resuscitation (CPR): Patient factors and decision making. *Arch Intern Med* 144:2229, 1984.
45. Bedell SE, Delbanco TL: Choices about cardiopulmonary resuscitation in the hospital—when do physicians talk with patients? *N Engl J Med* 310:1089, 1984.
46. Shmerling RH et al: Discussing cardiopulmonary resuscitation: A study of elderly outpatients. *J Gen Intern Med* 3:317, 1988.
47. Uhlmann RF et al: Ability of physicians and spouses to predict resuscitation preferences of elderly patients. *J Gerontol* 43:M115, 1988.
48. Rachels J: Active and passive euthanasia. *N Engl J Med* 292:78, 1975.

49. American Medical Association: Current opinions of the council on ethical and judical affairs of the American Medical Association. Chicago, American Medical Association, 1986, p 12.

50. Emanuel EJ: A review of the ethical and legal aspects of terminating medical care. *Am J Med* 84:291, 1988.

51. Wanzer SH et al: The physician's responsibility toward helplessly ill patients. *N Engl J Med* 310(15):955, 1984.

52. Brett AS, McCollough LB: When patients request specific interventions: Defining the limits of the physicians obligation. *N Engl J Med* 315:1347, 1986.

53. Blackhall LJ: Must we always use CPR? *N Engl J Med* 317:1281, 1987.

54. Pearlman RA, Uhlmann RF: Resuscitation preferences: Are they generalizeable? *Gerontologist* 28:105A, 1988.

55. Uhlmann RF et al: Medical management decisions in nursing homes patients: Principles and policy recommendations. *Ann Intern Med* 106:879, 1987.

56. Steinbrook R, Lo B: Artificial feeding—solid ground, not a slippery slope. *N Engl J Med* 318:286, 1988.

57. Uhlmann RF et al: Understanding of elderly patients' resuscitation preferences by physicians and nurses. *West J Med* (in press).

58. Everhart MA, Pearlman RA: Stability of patient preferences regarding life sustaining treatments: *Clin Res* 36:711A, 1988.

59. Siegler M, Weisbard AJ: Against the emerging stream: Should fluids and nutritional support be discontinued? *Arch Intern Med* 145:129, 1985.

60. Meilaender G: On removing food and water: Against the stream. *Hastings Cent Rep* 14:11, 1984.

61. Micetich KC et al: Are intravenous fluids morally required for a dying patient? *Arch Intern Med* 143:975, 1983.

62. Smith DG, Wigton RS: Modeling decisions to use tube feeding in seriously ill patients. *Arch Intern Med* 147:1242, 1987.

63. Siegler M, Shiedermayer DL: Should fluid and nutritional support be withheld from terminally ill patients? Tube feeding in hospice settings. *Am J Hospice Care* March/April:32, 1987.

64. Lynn J, Childress JF: Must patients always be given food and water? *Hastings Cent Rep* 13:17, 1983.

65. Abrams FR: Withholding treatment when death is not imminent. *Geriatrics* 42:77, 1987.

Part Three

DISEASES
OF THE ORGAN
SYSTEMS

Chapter 40

AGING OF HUMAN SKIN

Arthur K. Balin

The expression and treatment of cutaneous disease in the elderly differs from that in younger adults. Anatomic changes in aging skin result in altered physiologic behavior and susceptibility to disease. Decreased epidermal renewal and decreased tissue repair accompanies the aging process. The rate of hair and nail growth declines, as well as the quantity of eccrine, apocrine, and sebum secretion. There are alterations in immune surveillance and antigen presentation with aging. The cutaneous vascular supply is decreased, leading to decreases in inflammatory response, absorption, and cutaneous clearance. Impaired thermal regulation, tactile sensitivity, and pain perception occur as an individual ages. This chapter summarizes the major changes that occur during the intrinsic aging process of the skin to help facilitate recognition and treatment of skin disease in the older patient. Because of space limitations, the reader is referred to the recently published text *Aging and the Skin*[1] for a more comprehensive discussion of cutaneous changes that occur with aging.

The skin is one of the most complex body organs. It is not only stratified horizontally into three compartments, the epidermis, dermis, and subcutis, but it is also perforated vertically by a variety of appendages which produce different products: sebum, hair, eccrine sweat, and apocrine sweat. The epidermis alone is a mixture of five cell types, of which three are of major importance: the keratinocyte, which creates the keratinized horny layer; the melanocyte, which makes melanin; and the Langerhans' cell, which performs peripheral immune surveillance as part of the macrophage system.

CHANGES IN HUMAN SKIN WITH AGE

STRATUM CORNEUM

During the aging process there is little change in the number of layers of cells that compose the stratum cor-

neum. Both the thickness of the stratum corneum and its diffusional resistance to water vapor are similar in young and old people. Thus, the essential barrier function of the stratum corneum is preserved during aging. However, the moisture content of the stratum corneum in the aged has been observed to be lower than that in younger adults.[2] As a consequence, the stratum corneum of aged skin is somewhat more brittle. In addition, the corneocytes of aging skin have been found to become larger and less cohesive (Table 40-1).

Turnover of the stratum corneum reflects the renewal time of the epidermis and has been found to take longer in the aged individual. For example, studies using fluorescent marker techniques have shown the average stratum corneum replacement time of volar skin to be 20.4 ± 3.1 days in women aged 87.6 ± 4 years and 13.5 ± 2 days in younger women between 21 and 40 years of age.[3,4]

Consequences of changes in the stratum corneum during aging include dry skin and roughness with aberrant light scattering. The longer renewal time means that irritant and sensitizing substances that contact the skin will remain longer and that substances that are placed on the skin, including medications, take longer to be shed. The treatment time needed to clear superficial fungal infections is increased because of the slower stratum corneum renewal.

VIABLE EPIDERMIS

Keratinocytes

The thickness of the epidermis between the rete ridges remains constant or decreases only slightly during intrinsic aging[5] (Table 40-2). There is, however, a pronounced effacement of the rete ridges during aging. The basal keratinocytes with the highest degree of proliferative capacity and proliferative reserve are located at the bottom of the epidermal rete ridges, and the effacement of these structures reflects the decreased proliferative

383

TABLE 40-1
Anatomic Changes in the Stratum Corneum with Age

Thickness remains intact
Number of cell layers is unchanged (14–17)
Barrier function to water is maintained
Moisture content decreases
Cellular cohesion decreases
Turnover time increases
Cell size increases

TABLE 40-2
Anatomic Changes in the Epidermis with Age

Little to no decrease in epidermal thickness
Pronounced effacement of the rete ridges
Decreased area of contact between dermis and epidermis
Basal cells
    Fewer per unit area
    Greater variability in size and shape
    Loss of microvilli
Cytoheterogeneity of the individual keratinocyte nuclei
Decreased number of Langerhans' cells
Decreased number of melanocytes

reserve of the aged epidermis. Fewer basal cells per unit area leads to a decrease in the reproductive compartment and decreased epidermal turnover. Basal cells of elderly donors from skin regions that are exposed to light show greater variability in size, shape, and electron density than similar regions from young donors.[6] Basal cells from aged individuals have a paucity of microvilli. Other investigators have found that basal cells are larger and cells in the spinous layer are smaller in elderly individuals.[7] Certain epidermal functions, such as vitamin D production, are decreased in aged epidermis.

The decrease in the epidermal rete ridges also results in a decreased area of contact between the dermis and epidermis. The mean area of the dermal-epidermal junction per square millimeter of body surface area decreases from 2.67 ± 0.68 mm at 21 to 40 years of age to 1.90 ± 0.41 mm at 61 to 80 years of age.[8] This decreased area of contact results in an epidermis that separates from the underlying dermis much more easily in the elderly than in the younger individual. Simple trauma, such as the application and removal of a Band-Aid or the wearing of a tightly fitting shoe, can readily peel off the epidermis in the elderly. It has been possible to quantitate the age-related differences in dermal-epidermal adherence by inducing a suction blister under controlled conditions and observing the time it takes for blistering to occur.

Since, in steady state conditions, the renewal of the stratum corneum proceeds at the same rate as the renewal of the epidermis, the figures quoted above for the time it takes to replace the stratum corneum also apply to epidermal renewal. Grove[9] has shown that epidermal renewal does not decline linearly with age; he found similar rates in people ages 20 to 25 and 40 to 45 but slower rates in people ages 60 to 65. These changes cause epidermal wound healing to take longer in the elderly. As with the stratum corneum, substances that come in contact with the epidermis remain for a longer time before they are shed. Cytoheterogeneity of the individual keratinocyte nuclei is observed in aged skin, which may reflect some disordered regulation of proliferation and could contribute to the excess cutaneous growths such as seborrheic keratosis and skin tags that are nearly universal in the elderly.[10]

The epidermal changes which occur in response to photodamage differ from those seen in intrinsic aging. The initial response to ultraviolet light is a hyperproliferative response to injury and a thickening of the epidermis. Late effects of severe ultraviolet irradiation injury result in marked epidermal atrophy. Further discussion of differences between "photoaging" and intrinsic aging is presented elsewhere in this chapter.

Langerhans' Cells

The number of Langerhans' cells is decreased even in sun-protected aged skin; the number decreases even more in sun-damaged skin. Gilchrest et al.[11] showed that sun-protected skin from young adults had 10 ± 0.8 epidermal Langerhans' cells per 1-micron section and from older adults (with a mean age of 69) had 5.8 ± 1.1 cells per 1-micron section. The decreased number of Langerhans' cells leads to a decreased ability to sensitize with contact allergens. In addition, in experimental animals the ultraviolet light–induced decrease in Langerhans' cells leads to improper antigen presentation resulting in the production of suppressor T cells that impair tumor rejection.

Melanocytes

Most of the studies that have measured the number of melanocytes as a function of age have employed only a small number of subjects and have not adequately controlled for the amount of light exposure the subject received before measurement. In aggregate, it does appear that there is some decline in the number of melanocytes with age,[12,13] but the frequently quoted statistic of a 10 percent decline per decade is based on limited observations. Probably more important, however, are the observations that the function of the remaining melanocytes is abnormal. One consequence of these changes is that ultraviolet exposure produces less effective pigment protection in the elderly.

Graying of hair is a manifestation of loss of melanocyte function and is one of the earliest changes we associate with aging. In an Australian study of 6000 males, some gray hair was found in 22 percent of men ages 25 to 34, 61 percent of men ages 35 to 44, 89 percent of men ages 45 to 54, and 94 percent of men older than age 55. The observation that scattered individual hairs go gray independently of their neighbors illustrates the heterogeneity that is characteristic of aging.

DERMIS

Structural Elements

The dermis becomes thinner with age. In addition, it becomes more acellular and avascular (Table 40-3). Black,[14] using a radiographic technique to measure the thickness of skin in vivo, showed that the thickness of forearm skin in men declines from 1.3 mm at age 30 to 0.9 mm at age 80. Measurements of the total amount of dermal collagen reveal a decrease of about 1 percent per year. The remaining collagen fibers thicken, become less soluble, have less capacity to swell, and become more resistant to digestion by collagenase.[15] Histologically, the collagen fibers appear to be deposited haphazardly in coarse ropelike bundles, rather than in an orderly fashion as in younger skin.

Men have a thicker dermis than women. For example, the dermal thickness of forearm skin in men is 1.3 mm as compared to 1.1 mm in women. This difference may explain why female skin seems to deteriorate more readily with aging. Thinner skin is more susceptible to actinic damage and trauma.

Elastic Tissue

Photoaging and intrinsic aging show different changes in elastic tissue. In intrinsic aging the fine subepidermal oxytalan fibers are lost, eventually contributing to superficial laxity, loss of resiliency, and the finely wrinkled appearance of the skin (Table 40-4). These intrinsic de-

TABLE 40-3
Anatomic Changes in the Dermis with Age

Decreased thickness of dermis
Decreased area of contact and adherence of dermis to epidermis
Decreased number of fibroblasts, macrophages, and mast cells
Decreased collagen
Alteration and loss of elastic tissue
Diminished vasculature
Decreased glycosaminoglycans
Decreased number of pacinian and Meissner's corpuscles

TABLE 40-4
Changes in Elastic Fibers with Intrinsic Aging

30–50 years old
Disappearance of the subepidermal oxytalan fibers
Abnormalities (thicker or thinner) in the elaunin and elastic fibers
50–70 years old
Papillary dermis devoid of oxytalan fibers
Progressive abnormality in elaunin and elastic fibers
Beginning of cystic spaces within elastin matrix
Collagen bundles less dense
>70 years old
Larger cystic spaces in elastin matrix with lacunae separating microfibrils
Elastin core thinner
Dense microfibrillar areas more numerous, in clumps
No inflammatory infiltrate; quiescent fibroblasts

generative changes in the elastic tissue begin at about age 30. As they progress, cystic spaces are seen under the electron microscope as the elastin matrix degenerates. The regression of the subepidermal elastic network permits old skin to be stretched over a large distance at low loads.

The changes of *photoaging* include a great increase in the elastotic material in the dermis (Table 40-5). These changes are superimposed upon and eventually mask the intrinsic changes of aging. The elastotic material seen in actinically damaged skin is composed of clumps of 8- to 11-nm microfibrils.[16,17] The desmosine content of this material is increased compared to nonphotoaged (normal) skin,[18] indicating that elastotic material derives from degenerated elastin rather than from collagen. As the photodamage progresses, the elastic fibers become thicker, more numerous, and tightly coiled.[19] Histologic sections of these tightly coiled elastic fibers appear as fragmented elastic fibers.

TABLE 40-5
Changes in Elastic Fibers with Photoaging*

Early changes
Hyperplasia and degeneration of fibers in the reticular dermis
Separation from the epidermis by a narrow band of normal dermis
Fibers focally thicker or thinner and coiled
Later changes
Thicker, more tangled fibers
Increase in size of microfibrillar masses
Appearance of diffuse clumps of amorphous, granular elastotic material
Absence of inflammation; quiescent fibroblasts

*Superimposed upon, and eventually masking, intrinsic changes of aging.

Cells in the Dermis

The number of cells in the dermis decreases with age. Studies of surgically excised abdominal skin showed a decline of approximately 50 percent in the number of cell nuclei from infancy to age 61 years in Caucasian males. There is about a 20 percent decline in the number of cells in the dermis by age 30.[20] The numbers of fibroblasts, macrophages, and mast cells decrease with age. The fibroblast becomes a shrunken, narrower fibrocyte that contains decreased cytoplasm, and there is a decrease in the turnover of the dermal matrix components.

Mast Cells

The number of mast cells found in the dermis decreases with age. The decrease in mast cells helps to explain the observation that it is harder to raise wheals in the elderly by histamine-releasing drugs and also the observation that urticaria is uncommon in the elderly. Also, heparin, found in mast cells, stimulates capillary endothelial cell migration in vitro, and its relative absence may help contribute to the paucity of vasculature in the elderly dermis.[21]

Microcirculation

Regression and disorganization of small vessels is a prominent feature of aged skin. As the rete ridges flatten, the capillary loops that were present in the dermal papilla disappear. In addition, the small vessels about the cutaneous appendages decrease. This is especially prominent in actinic damage. Braverman et al.[22,23] have demonstrated that vessels in intrinsically aged sun-protected skin become thinner and have a decrease (or absence) in the number of surrounding veil cells. The changes in the microvasculature of photodamaged skin differ from those found in intrinsically aged skin in that photodamaged skin manifests a marked thickening of the postcapillary venular walls.

The minimization of the cutaneous vasculature during aging has profound clinical consequences (Table 40-6). These include a decreased inflammatory response,

TABLE 40-6
Physiologic Changes in the Vasculature with Aging

Decreased inflammatory response
Decreased absorption
Decreased urticarial reactions
Decreased thermal regulation
Decreased sweating
Delayed wound healing
Ecchymoses and delayed resolution
Muted clinical presentation of cutaneous disease

decreased absorption, decreased clearance, decreased urticarial reactions, decreased sweating, delayed wound healing, impaired thermal regulation, easy bruisability, and a muted clinical presentation of many cutaneous diseases.

The decreased vasculature can be observed in the pallor of aged skin. The superficial blood supply is particularly important for thermal regulation. The temperature drop between the groin and the feet is greater in the aged. The aged quickly experience coldness when the temperature falls, and the aged are predisposed to hypothermia and hyperthermia (see below and Chap. 111). Even brief exposure to cold may lead to hypothermia. Hypothermia is due both to the inability to divert blood efficiently and to a loss of insulating subcutaneous tissue. The young have greater vasoconstriction; they also shiver more and generate more metabolic heat. In addition, the old may fail to take corrective action when it is cold because of decreased pain perception. A comfortable temperature for the aged is 75 to 80°F, far above the recommended level for public institutions.

Because of the decreased microvasculature in elderly skin, it takes longer to absorb substances applied to the skin and longer to clear substances injected into the skin. For example, Kligman has shown that it took twice as long for 65-year-olds to absorb radioactive testosterone rubbed on the skin or to resolve an intradermally injected saline wheal as it did for 30-year-olds.[24]

Clinically, this decreased clearance can prolong cases of contact dermatitis. Probably more important, however, is that many skin diseases are distinctive because of their pattern or degree of inflammation. We can be seriously hampered in the ability to diagnose disease in the aged unless we recognize that some of the cardinal signs of inflammation, including redness, heat, and swelling, may be absent in the aged patient. Cellulitis, for example, can be much more difficult to recognize without these signs.

The decreased blood supply may also necessitate some modification in therapy. Fewer applications of a topical medication may be appropriate because of the decrease in clearance. These observations must be taken into consideration in the development and dosage of transdermal therapy.

Cutaneous Nerves

Cutaneous free nerve endings are little affected anatomically during aging, although tactile sensitivity is decreased. The number of pacinian corpuscles decreases by about two-thirds between the ages of 20 and 90. Meissner's corpuscles also decrease in number to a similar extent.

Physiologic tests reveal less acuity in pain perception, and the pain reaction threshold is decreased. The aged are thus less capable of sensing danger and reacting appropriately. One consequence is that burns tend to be more serious and widespread in the elderly. Overall, the dermal changes discussed have a number of disparate physiologic consequences, which are summarized in Table 40-7.

SUBCUTANEOUS TISSUE

The subcutaneous tissue serves as a shock absorber and a calorie storage depot. The subcutaneous tissue also modulates conductive heat loss. Generally, the proportion of body that is fat increases until age 70, but there are great regional differences in the distribution of this fat. For example, the amount of subcutaneous fat is decreased on the face and dorsum of hands, but it is increased around the abdomen and thighs.[25] As the subcutaneous tissue resorbs, the risk of hypothermia and injury increases. The subcutaneous tissue protects organisms from blunt and pressure-related trauma and serves as an insulator against heat loss. The loss of this protective padding results in an increase in problems of weight-bearing and pressure-prone surfaces.

ECCRINE SWEAT

There is a reduction in the overall number of sweat glands in aged skin, along with a decrease in the functional capacity of the remaining glands. With age, recruitment of sweat by thermal stimuli takes longer, and the density of actively secreting glands decreases. Impairment of evaporative heat loss due to attenuated dermal vasculature and decreased sweating leads to an increased risk of heatstroke during hot weather. As compared to the young, in the aged there is a decrease in sweating response to dry heat and to experimentally injected intradermal acetylcholine.

APOCRINE SWEAT

There is a decrease in apocrine secretion with age that appears to be primarily due to the age-associated decrease in testosterone levels. The decreased apocrine secretion results in a decrease in body odor. Therefore, the need for antiperspirants and deodorants in the elderly is decreased.

SEBACEOUS GLANDS

Sebaceous glands are also androgen-dependent. The size of the sebaceous glands increases in the elderly, while the transit time of the individual maturing sebaceous cells is 4 to 6 days longer in the aged person. Plewig and

TABLE 40-7
Physiologic Changes in the Dermis with Aging

Skin more easily damaged
Delayed wound healing
Decreased inflammatory response
Decreased protection from ultraviolet light
Decreased urticarial reaction
Wrinkling, sagging skin
Skin easily stretched under low loads
Loss of resiliency
Diminished absorption
Altered thermal regulation
Decreased sensitivity to pain and pressure

Kligman[26] showed that the average sebaceous gland size increased from 0.23 mm^2 in young adults to 0.40 mm^2 in the elderly. The sebaceous pore also gets larger with age. However, despite the increased size of the sebaceous glands, there is a decrease in sebum output by 40 to 50 percent with age. These data are corroborated by other investigators[27] who found a similar increase in sebaceous gland size with advancing age. Additionally, there is a decrease in the size of the individual sebocyte, smaller cytoplasmic oil droplets within the sebocytes, decreased free cholesterol in sebum, and an increase in the squalene fraction of sebum. The proliferative activity of the sebaceous gland decreases with age. These changes lead to solar sebaceous hyperplasia, which are huge sebaceous follicles. The decrease in sebum secretion with age may contribute to dry skin.

Sebaceous gland size increases with age in non-sun-exposed sebaceous glands, such as the Fordyce spots within the mouth. However, sebaceous gland hyperplasia is worsened by chronic sun damage.

HAIR

For scalp hair, the rate of hair growth declines and the diameter of the individual terminal hair decreases with age. There is an increased percentage of hairs in the telogen or resting stages of the cycle. Graying of hairs occurs because of a progressive loss of functional melanocytes from the hair follicle bulb. Hair growth, however, presents a paradox. Not all hair shows a decrease in growth with age. In women older than 65 years there is an increase in hair on the lip and chin, although the same women have a decrease in hair on the head, axillae, and pubis. Men lose scalp and beard hair but have an increase in the growth of hair over their ears, eyebrows, and nostrils. Understanding the mechanisms that are responsible for the androgen-dependent conversion of vellus hair to terminal hair and vice versa in different body regions at the same time may provide important insights into the processes of differentiation and aging.

NAIL GROWTH

Nail growth declines with age. The overall mean growth rate of thumbnails declines from approximately 0.75 mm/week at 20 to 29 years of age to 0.5 mm/week at 80 to 89 years of age.[28,29] Because of this decrease in nail growth rate, treatment for fungal diseases of the nail should be prolonged in the elderly. Nails become brittle and lusterless with aging, and longitudinal striations with ridging and beading form on the nail plate.

ALTERATIONS IN CUTANEOUS PHYSIOLOGIC FUNCTION WITH AGE

The section above has highlighted the major physiologic consequences of the anatomic changes that occur due to the intrinsic aging process. Table 40-8 summarizes the alterations in cutaneous physiologic functions that are caused by intrinsic aging. These changes result in altered expression of cutaneous disease and indicate a need for specific modifications in treatment and prevention of cutaneous disease in the elderly.

DERMAL-EPIDERMAL COHESION

The aged epidermis loses its rete ridges and the dermal papillae retract. The result is a flat dermal-epidermal junction instead of the normal undulations. The microvilli of basal cells also disappear. These changes inevitably lessen the adhesion of the epidermis to the dermis. This explains why the epidermis of quite old persons is so easily peeled off by shearing stresses.

Cohesion may be quantified by applying negative

TABLE 40-8
Alterations in Cutaneous Physiologic Functions Caused by Intrinsic Aging

Decreased
 Epidermal renewal
 Wound healing, tissue repair
 Hair growth
 Nail growth
 Eccrine and apocrine gland secretion
 Sebum secretion
 Immune surveillance
 Antigen presentation
 Inflammatory response
 Vascular supply
 Absorption
 Response to heat and cold
 Tactile sensitivity
 Pain perception
 Vitamin D synthesis
 Photoprotection

pressure to a small circle of skin and determining the time required to raise a blister. The separation is clean, just above the basal lamina. Kiistala[30] is the inventor and master of the suction blister technique. He found that blistering time diminished continuously and linearly with aging. With 200 mm of suction, the mean in the 20- to 24-year-old group was 116 ± 27 minutes, in contrast to 36 ± 12 minutes in individuals over age 90. One must be wary of simplistic interpretations. To be sure, the dermal-epidermal junction becomes flat, but other changes also occur; that is, the subepidermal fine elastic fibers disappear while the deeper ones become coarse, tangled, and abnormal. The tissue is more easily stretched and deformed. This alone could shear off the epidermis more quickly. Suction blisters are also temperature-dependent. Blistering occurs more rapidly at higher temperatures, being twice as fast at 40°C as it is at 30°C.

PERMEABILITY

There is a widespread belief that elderly skin is more permeable than younger skin. This seems fitting in view of the thin, dry skin associated with the aged; however, there are little data to support the idea. The sparse data which exist were obtained by methods that would not be acceptable today.

The stratum corneum is the rate-limiting barrier to the diffusion of substances across the skin. Its diffusional resistance is directly proportional to its thickness. Despite regressive alterations in the epidermis, the stratum corneum is extraordinarily well preserved, even in badly sun-damaged skin. Years ago, Christophers and Kligman[31] found that the number of cell layers in cantharidin blister roofs of the back were the same for old as for young subjects, about 15. In studies of ammonium hydroxide blistering times, there was no age-related difference in the number of horny cell layers at two protected sites, the mean being about 16.[32]

A convenient and reliable way to assess barrier function is to determine transepidermal water loss, which is entirely controlled by the stratum corneum. In vitro, measurements of diffusional water loss through isolated sheets of horny layer did not show an increase in the aged group.[33] If anything, Tagami's in vivo finding that it took at least 50 percent longer for the fluorescent dye tetrachlorosalicylanilide to penetrate the full thickness of the horny layer of the forearms of subjects over age 65 would point to increased diffusional resistance.[34] Thus, the stratum corneum of the aged is not thinner and its barrier function is not impaired, even though exfoliated horny cells show cytologic irregularities and great variability.[35]

The term *percutaneous absorption* is often used to describe permeability behavior. It must be understood that this involves more than simple penetration or flux, which is the amount diffusing across the horny layer in a given time. Percutaneous absorption literally refers to the amount absorbed into the circulation, of which flux is only one factor.

Depending on blood flow, substances that diffuse at the same rate might not be equivalently absorbed. An attenuated microvasculature in the aged would result in decreased dermal clearance, allowing higher levels to build up and diminishing the concentration gradient. Fick's law dictates that this would retard penetration. Thus, it is not paradoxical that Malkinson,[36] monitoring the surface disappearance of ^{14}C-testosterone, found the absorption in men over age 75 to be less than one-third that in young males.

Unless one takes into account the deletion of the small vessels, misinterpretations are bound to arise. After applying a potent vasodilator (trafuryl), Tagami[37] found that 17 of 20 young men showed erythema within 10 minutes while only 9 of 20 older men did so. This finding cannot be used to support the conclusion that aged skin is less permeable. With far fewer vessels, one would expect less redness. One could similarly misinterpret the finding that it takes much longer to evoke a full ammonium hydroxide blister in the aged. This does not imply a better barrier, although in the young, the blistering time is proportional to the number of cell layers.[38] Fluid to fill the blisters has to originate from the microcirculation, which is much reduced in the elderly. In fact, in a few very old persons, the blister may never fill with fluid no matter how long the exposure.[39]

More work is needed, but it seems safe to conclude that the aged do not absorb topical substances more rapidly than the young do and probably absorb substances less rapidly. This does not put them out of danger of systemic toxicity from external toxins. A case in point is the elderly woman who extensively applied calamine lotion containing only 1% phenol to her entire body twice daily. She suffered convulsions in 10 days, reproduced by reexposure.[40] The combination of a large area of application with decreased dermal (and probably renal) clearance led to elevated blood vessels.

WOUND HEALING

Dermatologic surgeons sometimes prefer aged patients, who, in contrast to younger subjects, have more lax skin, less tendency to form hypertrophic scars or keloids, and lower cosmetic expectations. Investigators studying age-related alterations in physiologic function, however, have observed a decreased rate of healing and a decreased final wound strength in older mammals. Hard experimental data in humans are limited but do support the contention that wound healing is slower in older persons.

When trying to understand the importance of alterations in wound healing with age, we have the obligation to quantify the loss in ability to repair and to estimate the approximate age at which the impairment becomes clinically significant. The studies of DuNuoy,[41] a surgeon in World War I, represent one of the first attempts to quantitate wound healing as a function of age. DuNuoy derived a cicatrization index which was devised to describe the rate of healing of war wounds.[42] It was found that 30-year-old men healed more slowly than 20-year-olds; the same decrement was noted in the comparison between 40- and 30-year-old individuals. It is difficult, however, to put much stock in this work in view of the fact that no two wounds could have been alike under the conditions of warfare in the preantibiotic era. The variability in depth and size of wounds, degree of contamination, source of injury, and available general medical care must have been very great from one case to the next.

Nothing that we have been able to measure so far has enabled us to distinguish physiologic differences between 20- and 30-year-olds, nor, for that matter, differences between the two-decade span between ages 20 and 40. Orentreich and Selmanowitz[43] tried to confirm DuNuoy's work in experimental animals. They made wounds in dogs of different ages and calculated the slopes of the healing curves. They found that older animals healed more slowly than younger animals. In rodents and canines, younger animals heal more quickly, as a number of controlled studies have shown. The question is whether this decline starts shortly after maturation, continuing steadily downward, or whether there is a plateau till much later in life with an appreciable decline thereafter.

Surgical experience clearly demonstrates that even the very old can effectively repair extensive wounds. Most surgeons are not the least bit daunted in performing major operations on the elderly, including head and neck dissections, cardiac surgery, and abdominal aneurysmectomy.[44] The predictably high success rate has tended to obscure substantial differences in wound repair.[45] In dermatology, Mohs chemosurgery is regularly performed on elderly subjects with extensive or recurrent squamous cell or basal cell cancers of the face, often involving massive tissue removal down to the bony understructures.

Nonetheless, clinicians do know that age is of consequence and should not be blithely dismissed. For example, most dehiscences of abdominal surgical wounds occur in older subjects.[46] In a cooperative study of 19 Veterans Administration hospitals, wound dehiscence after surgery for duodenal ulcer increased from 1 percent in patients ages 30 to 39 to 5 percent in those over age 70[47] (Table 40-9). The time required for postsurgical care is also increased in old age.

TABLE 40-9
Incidence of Wound Dehiscence with Age

Age	Patients	Disrupted Wound	%
20–29	98	0	0
30–39	589	5	0.9
40–49	991	13	1.3
50–59	523	13	2.5
60–69	495	22	4.4
70–79	274	13	4.7
80+	18	1	5.5
Total	2988	67	2.3

SOURCE: Data from Veterans Administration Cooperative Study of Surgery for duodenal ulcer (Mendoza, Postlethwaite, and Johnson, Ref. 47). See text for explanation.

Sandblum, Peterson, and Muren[48] measured the force required to disrupt incisions in humans, finding that the tensile strength of 5-day wounds was considerably lower in the elderly. Likewise, in implanted sponges left in human incisions, Vilijanto[49] found that the amount of collagen deposited in 7 days decreased with increasing age of the patients.

Considering more superficial wounds, Orentreich has done more than 12,000 dermabrasions on the face using a rotating wire brush on frozen skin. He estimates that reepithelialization takes about 10 days for 25-year-olds; 15 days for 50-year-olds; and 21 days for patients over 75 years old.[50] Grove[51] has conducted a rigorous study on the healing of superficial wounds in humans. He raised up ammonium hydroxide blisters and determined the time for the surface markings to be completely restored in two age cohorts, ages 18 to 25 years and 65 to 75 years. After unroofing the blisters of two protected sites on the arm and forearm, Grove found that the elderly cohort lagged behind the young cohort at every stage of repair. Restoration times were more variable in the elderly, emphasizing the universality of the principle of enhanced variance in the aged. Importantly, persons who looked the oldest healed the slowest, a conclusion previously reached in the Baltimore Longitudinal Study of Aging correlating aged appearance with objective measurements of aging.

The upshot of these diverse investigations is that the healing powers of the skin are stoutly preserved in the aged and are not a limiting factor in survival. However, it should never be forgotten that medical complications after surgery are more numerous and hazardous in the elderly.[52]

INFLAMMATORY RESPONSES

The literature is contradictory regarding whether aged persons have altered inflammatory responses to chemical and physical stimuli. The practical question for cutaneous gerontologists is: Are the elderly at increased risk of being injured by the numerous chemicals in the environment? Without belaboring the issue, it can be stated categorically that acute inflammatory reactions of all kinds are muted and reduced in the aged. The attenuated microvasculature, discussed elsewhere, furnishes an adequate explanation for the inability of the elderly to mount an inflammatory reaction as speedily and as intensely as the young. Systemic studies by Kligman and colleagues, using a brigade of diverse toxic substances, have supported this reduced capability to react. Across the board, the elderly respond far less sharply to croton oil, cationic and anionic surfactants, weak acids, and solvents (dimethylsulfoxide, kerosene). Regularly, higher concentrations produce weaker reactions, whether the end-points are wheals, bullae, vesicles, pustules, dermatitis, redness, etc.[53]

Some earlier investigators have appreciated this weakening of the inflammatory response in the aged. After age 55, the pustular response to topical potassium iodide diminishes markedly. Bettley and Donaghue[54] found that patch test reactions to toilet soaps were diminished in older persons. Carlizza and Bologna[55] found fewer inflammatory cells in cantharidin blisters from older subjects, a finding we would have predicted. Reduced responses are not limited to chemical irritants. Gilchrest and her associates irradiated buttock skin with 3 MEDs (minimal erythema dose) from a mercury vapor lamp.[56] In comparison to young subjects, individuals between 62 and 81 years of age showed diminished erythema, edema, microscopic sunburn cells, and histamine levels. Thus, the total response was attenuated and evolved more slowly. This pattern is characteristic of the aged and is partly explained by fewer mast cells and a greater resistance to degranulation.

The failure to react promptly to a toxic stimulus carries with it the danger of continued exposure to noxious agents. The elderly have no early warning detection system. Redness appearing shortly after exposure warns a young person to desist. In the aged, because of a long latency period, applications may continue until suddenly the tissue collapses, sometimes with ulceration. It is only in this sense that the elderly may be characterized as reacting more vigorously to toxic agents. The elderly should be cautioned regarding self-treatment with home remedies so abundantly at hand.

VITAMIN D SYNTHESIS

MacLaughlin and Holick measured the relation between aging and the ability of human skin to synthesize vitamin D_3. There is a twofold decrease in the concentration of 7-dehydrocholesterol in epidermis from adult to old age. The ability of aging skin to convert previtamin D_3 to provitamin D_3 under the influence of ultraviolet light was also examined; postirradiation levels of previtamin D_3 in 82-year-old skin was 40 percent that of 8-year-old skin. These results are important, because vitamin D deficiency can contribute to osteomalacia and osteoporosis, conditions commonly seen in the elderly. Since skin is the major site for the synthesis of vitamin D precursors, it has long been held that vitamin D deficiency in the elderly is due to decreased sun exposure. Thus, elderly skin is actually less responsive to the effect of ultraviolet irradiation in converting provitamin D_3 to previtamin D_3,[57] a fact that may contribute to vitamin D deficiency in the elderly.

CLINICAL CONDITIONS IN THE ELDERLY

PREVALENCE OF VARIOUS SKIN CONDITIONS

The appearance of aging skin is one of the most obvious visual clues to the age of an individual. Substantial experimental data demonstrate that there is a progressive alteration in the physiologic function of the skin with age, which in turn leads to a progressive reduction in the individual's ability to adapt to environmental change and predisposes the individual to skin diseases that frequently accompany the aging process. Several investigators have examined the skin of healthy elderly individuals to determine the prevalence of skin disease in the elderly.

As regards the magnitude of skin disorders among the elderly in the United States, the most complete data are derived from a Health and Nutritional Survey by the U.S. Public Health Service between 1971 and 1974. More than 20,000 noninstitutionalized persons, 1 to 74 years of age, selected by the U.S. Census Bureau as representative of the population, were examined by dermatologists.[58] A skin condition was judged to be significant if it was serious enough to require treatment by a doctor. The staggering burden of skin conditions in persons over 70 years of age is reflected in a prevalence rate of 66 percent (Table 40-10). About a third of these affected persons had more than one skin problem; multiple skin conditions were a characteristic of the very old, and these conditions were in different categories than conditions in the young.

It should not be supposed that we have a clear picture of the skin afflictions of the elderly. Of the few surveys available in different parts of the world, the samples are small and nonrepresentative. The data in any given study are strongly influenced by such factors as race, socioeconomic status, ethnicity, climate, availability of medical care, etc.[59,60] The skin records life's hardships in strong surface etchings.[61]

TABLE 40-10

Prevalence Rate (per 1000 People) for Significant Skin Conditions among Individuals Ages 1–74 in the United States

Age	All Significant Skin Conditions	Diseases of Sebaceous Glands	Dermatophyte	Tumors	Seborrheic Dermatitis
5	180	8	4	20	8
10	260	71	16	20	10
15	480	240	32	32	16
20	490	210	54	37	32
30	450	96	88	38	38
40	480	42	125	42	42
50	530	21	154	85	31
60	560	33	146	133	29
70	660	38	125	183	25

SOURCE: Johnson and Roberts, Ref. 58. See text for explanation.

From our own experience, we know with certainty that the skin problems encountered in public institutions for elderly indigent are more numerous, more serious, and otherwise different than those encountered in healthy residents of retirement complexes. The medically unhealthy have more skin problems, and these problems are more distressing. Also, those elderly persons institutionalized the longest have the greatest problems with their skin. We have also observed that cardiovascular and psychotropic drugs markedly influence the expression of skin diseases, often provoking or intensifying such conditions as seborrheic dermatitis and stasis dermatitis. Prevalence rates may reflect patterns of drug taking. Drug use is heavy in the aged; often two to four different drugs are being consumed daily. The variables are so numerous that no two populations studied to date are even remotely alike. Because of this variability, every statement about age-associated skin conditions must be extremely guarded.

Tindall and Smith[62] examined 163 community volunteers over 64 years of age in North Carolina. They found that loss of skin elasticity occurred in 94 percent of persons over the age of 64; seborrheic keratoses occurred in 80 percent, comedones in 81 percent, xerosis in 77 percent, and cherry angiomata in 75 percent of the individuals studied (Table 40-11). Although not included in the list of medical problems requiring professional medical attention, these conditions are almost universal and are important because they are the most frequent changes in aging skin. Benign tumors, angiomas, skin tags, nevi, lentigines, and seborrheic keratoses were exceedingly common. Almost 4 of 5 people examined had ringworm of the feet, and a similar percentage had dry skin. Almost a third had a premalignant lesion (actinic keratosis). There were 16 separate conditions which occurred in at least 10 percent of this sample. Most had

TABLE 40-11

Frequency of Skin Abnormalities in Individuals over 64 Years Old*

Rank	Percent
Lax skin	94
Seborrheic keratoses	88
Comedones	81
Dermatophytosis	79
Xerosis	77
Cherry angioma	75
Nevi	63
Skin tags	56
Lentigo	51
Varicosities	48
Seborrheic dermatitis	31
Schamberg's disease	31
Spider angiomas	29
Actinic keratoses	28
Neurogenic excoriations	12
Rosacea	12

*The study examined 163 individuals 64 years old or older. The population was composed of 52 white males, 52 white females, 28 black males, and 31 black females.
SOURCE: From Tindall and Smith, Ref. 62.

TABLE 40-13

Frequency of Skin Lesions in 222 Residents of the Orthodox Jewish Home for the Aged*

	Males		Females	
Diagnosis	N	%	N	%
Senile angioma	70	71.4	109	87.9
Nevus	41	41.8	66	53.2
Lentigo	35	35.8	67	54.
Comedones	44	44.8	35	28.1
Seborrheic keratosis	29	29.3	47	37.9
Tinea pedis	22	22.4	42	33.8
Fordyce's disease	9	9.1	15	12.1
Hallux valgus	1	1	22	17.7
Intertrigo	1	1	18	14.5
Tinea cruris	13	13.2	0	0
Seborrheic dermatitis	11	11.2	7	5.6
Shamberg's disease	10	10.2	8	6.4

*The study examined 222 residents of the Orthodox Jewish Home for the Aged. The group was composed of 98 males and 124 females and had the following age distribution: 60–70 years, 12; 71–80 years, 98; 81–90 years, 84; 91 years and older, 28.
SOURCE: From Zakon, Goldberg, and Forman, Ref. 63.

more than one skin problem, including varicosities. The absolute frequency of the lesions varies with race (Table 40-12) and population studied (Table 40-13),[63] but the general trends are similar.

Other surveys in private practices and in various institutions bear out the high incidence of skin abnormalities in the elderly. High concordance is found for such common, age-associated lesions as xerosis, angiomas, lax skin, seborrheic keratoses, and others. The prevalence of less common diseases differs appreciably. For example, Tindall and Smith[64] observed seborrheic dermatitis in a third and rosacea in 12 percent. On the other hand, a Danish group found seborrheic dermatitis in only 7 percent and rosacea in 0.2 percent among 587 subjects in a municipal home for the elderly.[65] Eczematous conditions were not frequent in Tindall and Smith's

series but were noted in 25 percent in Droller's[66] study of the elderly living at home. In the course of one year in a chronic care facility in New York, Young[67] found that over 65 percent of patients developed a skin disorder and 50 percent had two disorders.

Where sunlight is abundant the elderly will, of course, have more solar lentigines, actinic keratoses, solar comedones, etc., which reflect cumulative exposure to radiation.[68] Then, too, the data must be analyzed in regard to sex. Seborrheic dermatitis is considerably more common in males, while skin tags, so frequent in females, are actually rare in males. Some lesions are practically universal in all old persons, especially vascular abnormalities such as cherry angiomas. Likewise, virtually all aged individuals have trichostasis spinulosa and pigmented macules of one kind or another.[69,70]

The common denominator in all studies is the fre-

TABLE 40-12

Distribution of Some Common Lesions by Race in Individuals over 64 Years of Age

Lesions	White		Black	
	Female (N = 52), %	Male (N = 52), %	Female (N = 31), %	Male (N = 28), %
Seborrheic keratoses (10 or more)	38	54	61	61
Nevi (5 or more)	23	37	27	46
Cherry angiomas (5 or more)	77	77	45	11
Varicosities	58	56	39	29

SOURCE: From Tindall and Smith, Ref. 62.

quency and multiplicity of skin abnormalities in the aged. While some lesions like seborrheic keratoses and lentigos are of purely cosmetic interest, others certainly are not, including the practically universal pruritic, rough, dry, scaling skin (xerosis).

Treatable skin conditions are worsened in the presence of the following: poor general health, emotional deterioration (chronic brain damage), and inactivity. These factors spell inability to provide proper daily skin care, including cleaning and grooming. In the aged, skin health is a function of skin care.

It is a cliché these days to talk about the graying of America, meaning that the aged are the fastest growing segment of the population. Of course, graying is the best known stigma of aging, as surveys show. In a particular population, over 60 percent of persons between the ages of 35 and 45 showed some scalp graying; this figure reached 95 percent in those over age 55.[71] Hair melanocytes are called upon to produce great quantities of melanin to supply cortical cells. Is this why they "wear out" so much earlier than skin melanocytes?

THE EXPRESSION OF SKIN DISEASES IN THE ELDERLY

The most distinguished textbook of dermatology in the English language has this to say: "The features and course of many lesions are not significantly altered by age."[72] This statement is inaccurate. The fact is that common skin disorders are frequently so muted, blurred, and morphologically transformed in the aged that diagnosis is delayed or missed altogether. Dermatologists can usually recognize psoriasis and lichen planus in young persons at glance, without a thorough search of the whole body and without histology. The same diseases in the elderly may leave the expert diagnostician bewildered. Especially in the very old (over age 85), it is likely that the cause of a specific skin abnormality remains unrecognized. Dermatology is a different specialty for those who work among the aged. Care and treatment are generally substandard, except for the manual removal of various neoplasms.

Dermatitis, whatever its origin—irritation, allergy, stasis, microbial infection, drugs, and others—tends to behave differently in the elderly than in the young. Unless quickly cleared, the dermatitis tends to become chronic, to spread widely (a process known as autoeczematization), and to respond sluggishly to treatment.[73] Healing is slow and unpredictable.[74] Thus, speedy diagnosis and treatment are exceedingly important to prevent chronicity, extension, and refractoriness.

Some chronic diseases tend to regress in the elderly. Atopic dermatitis is rare. Plaque-type psoriasis, if not converted to a pustular eruption by overtreatment, usually declines. One might anticipate that hy-

perproliferative dermatoses would tend to fade as a result of age-dependent declines in mitotic activity. Dandruff, a result of increased production of horny cells, disappears.[75]

This regression of some diseases is counterbalanced to some extent by the emergence in the elderly of disorders which may achieve prevalence rates considerably higher than in earlier adult life. Seborrheic dermatitis (Fig. 40-1) of the scalp and face, in males particularly, is a striking example. Confinement to bed by severe illness (coronary infarction, for example) greatly aggravates seborrheic dermatitis, and it may generalize[76] (Fig. 40-2). Immobilization generally worsens chronic skin diseases. Rosacea (Fig. 40-3A and B) which starts in young adulthood may become severe, culminating in such extreme exhibitions as rhinophyma (Fig. 40-4).

Chronic photosensitivity reactions, especially those of allergic origin, reach their highest prevalence in older persons. There are virtually disabling, maddeningly pruritic diseases which mainly localize on the face of older men. The two best known examples are allergic contact dermatitis due to airborne pollen (ragweed) and photocontact allergy due to halogenated salicylanilides (optical bacteriostats) (Fig. 40-5). These may result in a severe photodermatitis which grotesquely thickens the skin. Such individuals are called persistent light-reactors, and they are exquisitely sensitive to the entire ultraviolet spectrum; the allergen cannot always be identified. Actinically damaged skin, with its attenuated blood supply, is the substrate in which these photodermatoses de-

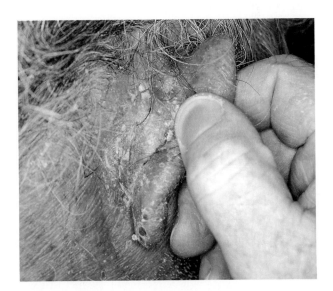

FIGURE 40-1

This patient has severe seborrheic dermatitis characterized by yellow greasy scales with erythema of the involved skin. The posterior auricular area is a common location for this disorder. In this figure, and the remainder of the figures in this chapter, the black and white photographs do not fully convey the color and texture of the morphology.

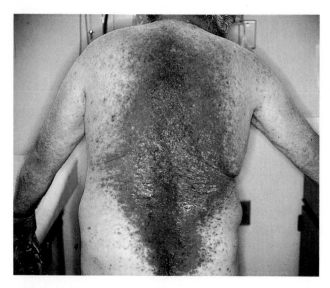

FIGURE 40-2
Exacerbation and generalization of seborrheic dermatitis to involve most of this man's back occurred during prolonged confinement to bed while hospitalized. Greasy, yellowish scaling is present in the middle of the back, with bright erythema extending over most of the remainder of the back. The differential diagnoses would include psoriasis and candidiasis.

velop. Sunlight worsens a number of skin disorders. Rosacea is a case in point. Because the elderly like to retire to sunny places, the aggravating effect of sunlight should be kept in mind.

Interdigital athlete's foot (Fig. 40-6A) is common in old age and often extends beyond the confines of the fifth interspace; it is invariably accompanied by onychomyco-

sis (Fig. 40-6B). Slower turnover of the horny layer, a depressed inflammatory response, and decreased cellular immunity contribute to chronicity.

The integument of the elderly is at especially high risk of injury from burns, chemical irritation, and trauma, owing to decreased sensory perception and slower reaction times. Particularly telling examples of chemical toxicity derive from the diminished capacity to mount an inflammatory response promptly. For example, a keratolytic solution of salicylic acid and propylene glycol, often used for dry skin, will, if applied b.i.d. to the face of a young person, incite scaling and redness in a few days. In the elderly, skin so treated may remain silent for 2 to 3 weeks before suddenly exploding into a severe dermatitis from toxic overload. Household cleaning and disinfectant solutions are often used by the elderly to stop itching and are a genuine hazard. The sensible, safe management of pruritus in the elderly requires knowledge and experience.[77]

It is important to recognize that primary pyodermas due to *Staphylococcus aureus* and beta-hemolytic streptococci may not call forth the customary signs of pain, heat, and redness. A furuncle may present as a cold abscess, and cellulitis may show only an indolent swelling. An infection serious enough to provoke fever and leukocytes in the young may be silent in the old. Bacterial pneumonia, a prototypical "silent" disease in the elderly, comes on quietly and without altering signs (such as fever), sometimes resulting in delayed treatment and sometimes resulting in a quiet death.

A high order of suspicion is indicated for every widespread eruption that cannot be readily identified. It

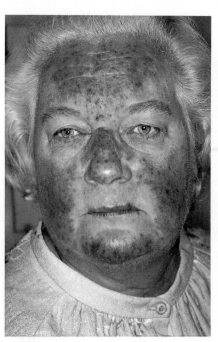

A

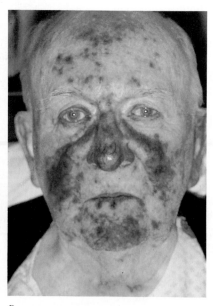

B

FIGURE 40-3A AND B
Rosacea, formerly called acne rosacea, is characterized by erythematous papules, telangiectasia, and pustules on the central face. The condition can also involve the forehead and sides of the face. In part *B*, the patient has erythematous lesions extending to the vermillion border of the lower lip, a feature which is usually absent in perioral dermatitis.

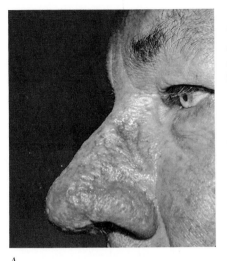
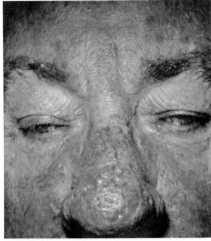

A   *B*

FIGURE 40-4*A* AND *B*
One form of rosacea can progress to cause enlargement of the nose, called rhinophyma. Present are enlarged sebaceous glands, telangiectasia, irregular thickening of the skin, and mild background erythema.

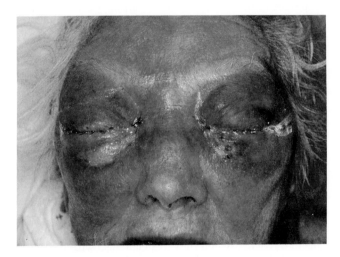

FIGURE 40-5
This patient has a severe contact dermatitis with erythema, edema, vesiculation, and a secondary bacterial infection involving the skin around the eyes. The secondary bacterial infection is characterized by a golden yellow crusting of the nasal bridge and along the inner portion of the upper eyelids.

is surprising how easy it is to miss a diagnosis of scabies which has only maddening pruritus as the signal feature, the lesions being otherwise unrecognizable. These cryptic cases can be the unsuspected source of major epidemics in institutions.[78] Also, the expression of skin disease is modified by nutritional deficiencies. Scurvy is more frequent than realized. Many old-old persons, particularly those living alone or those with various disabilities, do not have an adequate diet. Patients with zinc deficiencies suffer exotic rashes which cannot be recognized clinically and which adversely affect cell-mediated immunity.[79]

The expression of a vitamin or mineral deficiency is very easily overlooked because it is regarded as part of the diverse cutaneous alterations which inevitably come with age.[80] Thus, markedly xerotic skin due to iron deficiency with anemia may arouse no interest, since almost all elderly people suffer from dry skin. Likewise, purpura is so familiar that the diagnostic follicular hemorrhages of scurvy are not even seen. Perlèche from a lack

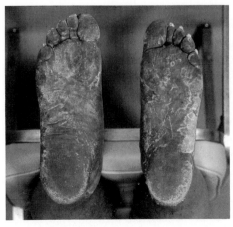
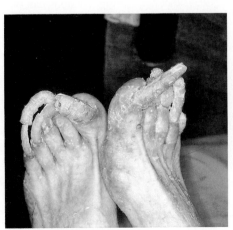

A   *B*

FIGURE 40-6
A. Tinea pedis, caused by dermatophytes, produces erythema, scaling, and fissuring in the skin of the feet. Sometimes, just a dry scale may be apparent, particularly in older individuals. *B.* The infection can spread to involve the toenails. Tinea pedis often involves the nails (onychomycosis) and is manifested by subungual hyperkeratosis and a yellowish discoloration of the nail plate. In addition, this patient has severe onychogryphosis, which is thickening and curvature of the nails due to chronic neglect.

of vitamin B will likely be put down to drooling at the corners of the mouth or will be diagnosed as moniliasis. Finally, when infections are recognized, clinicians should be on the lookout for exotic organisms, such as yeastlike fungi, unusual gram-negatives, and unfamiliar anaerobes. These should not be dismissed as contaminants.

SKIN AGING AND INTERNAL DISORDERS

Dermatologists are fond of pointing out that the skin often provides important clues to the diagnosis of systemic diseases. Skin involvement may be part of the generalized disease, or the skin may in various ways reflect deeper happenings in the body. Whole books have been written dealing with the external expressions of internal disease.[81] Since aging is accompanied by an increased risk of internal diseases which are life-threatening and disabling, the skin's role as a diagnostic window becomes even more worthy of attention.

What are the integumental alterations in older individuals which might betray a serious internal disorder? First of all, a cautionary note must be introduced regarding purely statistical associations. Correlations will be found among all conditions for which prevalence increases with age. The unsuspecting clinician can fall into naïve errors. For example, trichostasis spinulosa, in which many vellus hairs are retained in dilated follicles of facial skin, increases steadily with advancing age. This condition has been spuriously linked to nephropathy. Similarly, a high-sounding syndrome (Favre-Racouchot, Fig. 40-7), which is nothing more than the presence of huge comedones in severely sun-damaged skin, has

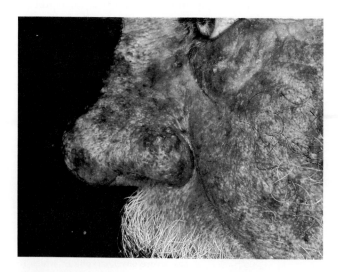

FIGURE 40-7
Nodular elastosis with cysts and comedones (Favre-Racouchot syndrome) due to sun damage in this patient has produced yellow plaques of skin with dilated pores and enlarged plugged follicles (blackheads) on the nose and lateral to the cheeks. This patient also has erythema and telangiectasia caused by chronic sun damage.

been speciously linked to kidney disease. It has also been claimed, falsely, that premature graying of the hair indicates predisposition to atherosclerosis and hypertension.[82] Persons with early graying, a heredity attribute, are not known to be at any greater risk for any disease.

On the other hand, the association between transparent skin and osteoporosis and rheumatoid arthritis is doubtlessly valid.[83] Transparent skin is not simply thin skin. Thin skin, which is very common in aged women, is still opaque, and its collagen content is fairly normal. In contrast, McConkey and coworkers[84] described the features of transparent skin as follows: collagen was not organized in bundles but was loosely arranged as fine fibrils separated by an increased quantity of ground substance as shown by stains for mucopolysaccharides. The water content in transparent skin was generally over 95 percent, in contrast to the normal value of about 75 percent. Thus, transparent skin is qualitatively very different from thin skin. The importance of these observations is that the same mechanisms which underlie osteoporosis and rheumatoid arthritis may be operative in producing transparent skin.

The limited mobility of elderly persons with osteoporosis and arthritis may contribute to "disuse" thinning of the dermis. Dermal thickness may now be swiftly determined by pulsed ultrasound and may offer a new way to forecast or monitor osteoporosis, a disorder of epidemic proportions in elderly women. Despite its potential importance, nothing is known regarding the influence of exercise on dermal metabolism and structure.

Horan, Poxty, and Fox[85] have described the "white nails of old age," which they associate also with osteoporosis and thin skin in the institutionalized elderly. They, too, suspect a collagen disorder.

Dermopathy, which takes the form of shallow, pigmented, pretibial atrophic patches, unquestionably develops earlier and becomes more extensive and severe in older, insulin-dependent diabetics. Though similar lesions can occur in nondiabetics to a much lesser degree, the term "diabetic dermopathy" is appropriate.[86] The condition has been experimentally induced in diabetics (but not in normal control individuals) by brief heating, 60°C for 5 seconds, or by dry ice freezing.[87] Dermopathy, really an angiopathy related to necrobiosis lipoidica diabeticorum, may be viewed as a characteristic outcome of the microvascular defect in diabetics.[88] Skin lesions may be an important prognosticator of early diabetes. Experimental provocation of lesions by simple cutaneous insults is a promising, practically untapped area in clinical research.

Likewise, the sign of Leser-Trélat, a sudden outcropping of numerous, rapidly growing seborrheic keratoses, is unequivocally associated with internal malignancy, although a tumor is not found in every case.[89] The keratoses seem to have a growth dependency on the tumor, for they sometimes regress after surgical removal of the tumor.

Some other associations are intriguing but provoke skepticism. Skin tags around the neck and shoulders are common in older women, but are rather rare in men. According to Margolis,[90] their presence in males raises up a suspicion of diabetes. He examined 500 admissions to a Veterans Administration hospital in Texas of whom only 20 were female. Of 47 males with skin tags, 34 had chemical diabetes. He also observed 62 diabetics who did not have skin tags.

It is also difficult to give credence to a diagonal earlobe crease as a risk factor in coronary artery disease. Lichstein et al.,[91] however, believe that this easily noticed sign may be a significant indicator. They examined 53 patients with coronary artery disease and found ear creases in 47 percent. The incidence in the control group was only 30 percent. Later, they conducted consecutive autopsies on 113 older patients and were able to establish a relation between the degree of sclerosis of the coronary arteries and the extent of the creases. Coronary artery sclerosis was most prominent in those with bilateral creases.[92] These creases evidently begin to appear in middle age, but their development is a mystery. Wyre[93] presented additional evidence of a strong association between bilateral creases and coronary artery disease in older patients.

Phlebectasias are very common in the aged. In males past age 50, more than 50 percent were noted by Bean[94] to have caviar spots of the tongue, while about 15 percent of males had angiokeratomas of the scrotum (Fig. 40-8). Venous lakes of the lips are also part of the spectrum of markedly dilated venules, presumably a consequence of decreasing support of the surrounding

connective tissue. For the most part these are harmless lesions without import. Kocsard, Ofner, and D'Absera[95] found that angiokeratomas (caviar tongue, venous lakes, and cherry angiomas; Fig. 40-9) were common among 350 males. However, the angiokeratomas occurred independently of each other and did not aggregate in statistically significant clusters (i.e., their coexistence was accidental). On the other hand, caviar spots and scrotal phlebectasias in males are occasionally associated with multiple hemangiomas of the gut, giving rise to repeated episodes of gastrointestinal bleeding.[96] Perhaps the report of Givs[97] should be taken more seriously. It reported vascular lesions of the lip in about 25 percent of patients with peptic ulcers. Kocsard et al. speculate that caviar tongue, which they found in 50 percent of persons past 50, showed histologic changes resembling solar elastosis.[98] They ascribe this to hot food, which is an interesting idea, since heat can produce elastosis in the skin.

Finally, while it has not been unequivocally established that drug reactions (Fig. 40-10) are more common in the elderly as compared to younger subjects taking the same multiple drugs, gerontologists generally believe that the reactions in the elderly are more serious. For example, in rheumatoid arthritis patients taking penicillamine, skin rashes severe enough to cause discontinuation were far more common in elderly patients than in younger patients, and toxicity was greater.[99] It is easy to overlook the role of drugs when, as in the case of penicillamine, they induce pruritus, dryness, and xerosis, which are already common in the aged.[100] In the elderly, drugs are probably more likely to precipitate autoimmune disorders, such as pemphigus and bullous pemphigoid (Fig. 40-11, Fig. 40-12A and B).

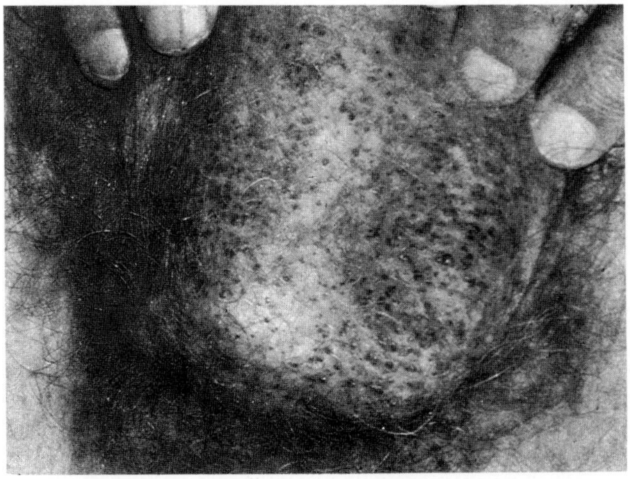

FIGURE 40-8
Angiokeratomas of Fordyce are a localized form of angiokeratomas occurring on the scrotum in middle-aged and elderly men. They are vascular papules 2–4 mm in diameter which histologically show dilated capillaries in the upper dermis. These lesions are purple vascular papules.

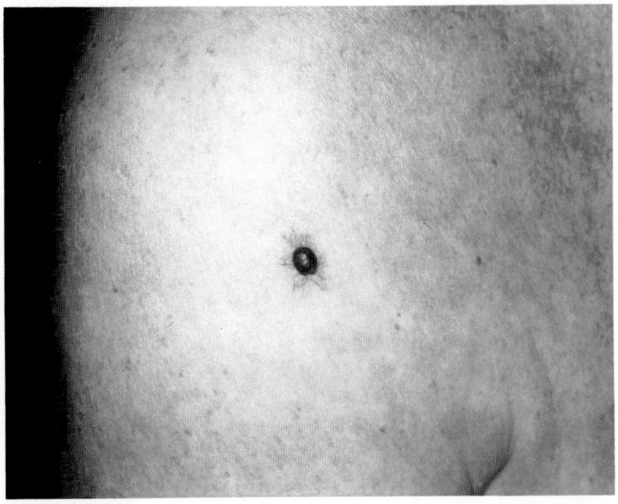

FIGURE 40-9
Cherry angiomas are bright red-domed shaped papules which commonly occur on the trunk beginning in early adulthood. They can progressively enlarge and the number of lesions tends to increase with age.

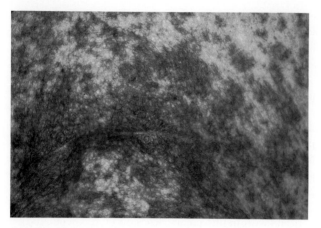

FIGURE 40-10
Drug eruption with typical morbilliform (measles-like) appearance, showing erythematous macules and papules, many of which are coalescent.

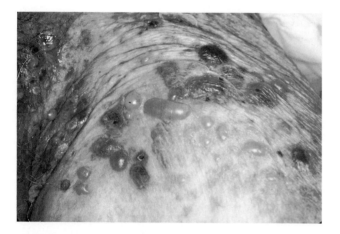

FIGURE 40-11
Bullous pemphigoid, an autoimmune blistering disease in which IgG is deposited along the basement membrane zone of the skin and sometimes mucosa, occurs most commonly in elderly persons and may result in death in severely debilitated individuals. Intact, tense blisters occur on normal and erythematous skin. Crusting may develop after the blisters break.

SPECIFIC CLINICAL CONDITIONS PREVALENT IN THE ELDERLY

It is beyond the scope of this chapter to detail all skin conditions found in the elderly. The reader is referred to one of the excellent and comprehensive textbooks of dermatology for a discussion of specific dermatologic conditions. Our primary focus has been to review the anatomic and physiologic changes in the skin that occur with age and to describe how these changes affect the presentation of clinical skin disease in the elderly. Some skin diseases are more prevalent in older individuals than in their younger counterparts, while other skin diseases run a more severe or protracted course in the elderly. Certain common cutaneous symptoms are nearly universal in older persons and are a major source of chronic discomfort. Therapeutic measures that are effective for a given disease in the young might be inappropriate in older persons because of unacceptable side effects.[101] Thus differences exist in the practice of cutaneous medicine with younger patients as compared with older patients. Several representative conditions of particular importance to the elderly will be discussed.

SEBORRHEIC KERATOSES

A number of cutaneous tumors of epidermal keratinocytes are prevalent in the elderly. Seborrheic keratoses are common, benign epithelial neoplasms. They occur more frequently as individuals advance in age. They have been found in up to 88 percent of persons over the age of 65; about 50 percent of those persons with seborrheic keratosis had 10 or more lesions.[102] Seborrheic keratoses appear to be dominantly inherited, but they seldom appear before middle age. They are found on the skin in those areas of the body that are rich in sebaceous glands, such as the trunk, face, and extremities. Seborrheic keratoses are brown, sharply demarcated, and

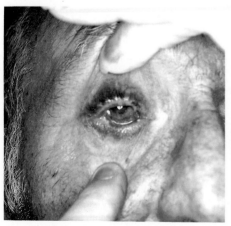

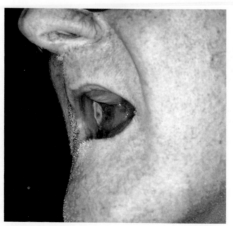

FIGURE 40-12
Cicatricial pemphigoid can produce scarring of mucosal surfaces such as the conjuctiva *(A)* and oral mucosa *(B)*. In part *B*, there is erythematous ulceration of the buccal mucosa, with overlying whitish pseudomembrane, composed of a proteinaceous exudate.

A

B

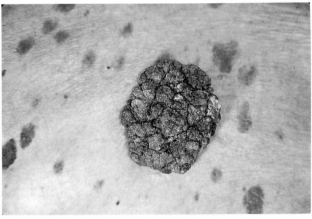

A

B

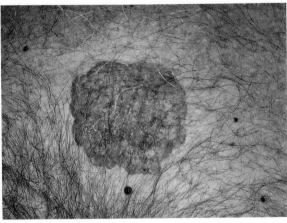

C

FIGURE 40-13

Seborrheic keratoses can vary in color from dark black to tan or flesh colored depending on the amount of melanin present. They are sharply demarcated, raised, and have a waxy, stuck-on appearance. *A.* This deeply pigmented seborrheic keratosis is surrounded by smaller seborrheic keratoses and lentigines. Occasionally, dark black lesions are mistaken for melanoma. *B.* Note the waxy verrucous surface. *C.* This tan and brown lesion shows the typical stuck-on waxy appearance. A few incidental cherry angiomata are scattered around this lesion on the skin.

slightly raised. They look as if they have been stuck on the skin surface. Most have a verrucous surface with a soft, friable consistency (Fig. 40-13*A*, *B*, *C*).

Histologically there is an accumulation of immature keratinocytes between the basal layer and the keratinizing surface of the epidermis.[103] Pseudohorn cysts and true horn pearls made of laminated keratin are common in seborrheic keratoses. The amount of melanin in a seborrheic keratosis is variable, and inexperienced observers have been known to mistake a seborrheic keratosis for a melanoma (Fig. 40-13*A*). Occasionally a seborrheic keratosis can become twisted and inflamed or infarcted. When a seborrheic keratosis becomes inflamed, the histologic picture changes. Some of the basaloid cells differentiate into squamous cells, showing mitotic figures. Numerous whorls or eddies of cells appear that resemble poorly differentiated horn pearls. The appearance of these features resembles that of squamous cell carcinoma.[104] This phenomenon can be reproduced experimentally by applying croton oil to a seborrheic keratosis. The keratosis becomes irritated and inflamed, and histologically the basaloid cells differentiate into squamous cells with whorls and eddies. These observations support

the view that keratinocytes in a seborrheic keratosis are not permanently deranged but rather are delayed in their maturation. Surprisingly little is known about the biology of these lesions when one considers that they are one of the most common growths on the skin.

The sign of Leser-Trélat is the sudden appearance and rapid increase in size and number of seborrheic keratoses on skin that was previously blemish-free. This condition is associated with the development of an internal malignancy which is usually an adenocarcinoma.[105–108]

ACTINIC KERATOSES

Several neoplastic conditions that are common in the elderly are associated with environmental damage to the skin. These conditions include actinic keratoses, Bowen's disease, squamous cell carcinoma, and basal cell carcinoma. The changes that most persons equate with aging of the skin are due to chronic solar damage. Prolonged exposure to ultraviolet irradiation leads to cutaneous atrophy, alterations in pigmentation, wrinkling, dryness, telangiectasia, and solar elastosis. UVB, at wavelengths between 290 and 310 nm, describes the spectral range that produces sunburn, and it is also thought to be the irradiation mainly responsible for actinic damage to the skin.[109] Some of the strongest evidence that implicates ultraviolet light as being important in the etiology of epidermal tumors comes from epidemiologic data correlating the incidence of tumors with degree of pigmentary protection. The individual principally at risk is light-skinned and easily sunburned, and he or she does not tan. Other strong epidemiologic data correlate an increased incidence of skin tumors with decreasing latitude and increasing sun exposure.

Actinic keratoses, or solar keratoses, are composed of clones of anaplastic keratinocytes confined to the epidermis and occur commonly on sun-damaged skin of elderly individuals (Fig. 40-14). If left untreated, they may progress and invade through the basement membrane of the epidermal-dermal junction, thereby becoming invasive squamous cell carcinomas.

Actinic keratoses are extremely common in elderly individuals who have had extensive sun exposure. The National Health and Nutrition Examination investigators found that the prevalence of actinic keratoses in the white population increased with age, irrespective of gender or degree of sun exposure. Male sex and sun exposure, however, predisposed an individual to a larger number of actinic keratoses. This census study found a high prevalence of actinic keratoses in the elderly population of the United States. For example, in the 65- to 74-year age range, 55 percent of the males and 37 percent of the females with high sun exposure had actinic keratoses as compared with 19 percent of the males and 12 percent of the females with low sun exposure.[110] Although this study excluded individuals over the age of 75, other surveys indicate that the prevalence of actinic keratoses continues to increase beyond age 75.[111] Caucasian populations that are subject to greater amounts of sun exposure than the average American population have an even higher prevalence of actinic keratoses. In

some Australian cities, up to 80 percent of the elderly women and 95 percent of the elderly men have actinic keratoses.[112] Actinic keratoses usually occur on skin damaged from sun exposure, such as the bald scalp, the face, and the forearms. They are more common in fair-skinned individuals and are almost never seen in blacks. These observations strongly suggest that chronic exposure to sunlight is an important etiologic factor (Fig. 40-15).

The carcinogenic property of sunlight resides mainly in the UVB range. Experimental evidence indicates that exposure to ultraviolet light causes damage to cellular DNA by formation of thymidine dimers. If not properly repaired, these dimers may give rise to mutations and transformed cells which then become cancerous. Skin cancers are particularly common in patients with xeroderma pigmentosum, an inherited condition characterized by defective repair of DNA damage induced by ultraviolet light. Several studies have shown that lymphocytes and skin fibroblasts obtained from people with multiple actinic keratoses have an impaired ability to repair their DNA after an ultraviolet light exposure as compared to those obtained from age-matched controls without actinic keratoses. The etiologic significance of this finding remains uncertain.[113–115]

Actinic keratoses occur as well-demarcated, scaly, rough papules on sun-exposed skin surfaces. Color varies from tan to red, but sometimes they are the same color as the surrounding skin. As a result, some lesions are more easily palpated than seen. In some lesions, known as pigmented actinic keratoses, an increased amount of pigmentation renders the lesions a striking brown color. Actinic keratoses are usually small, measuring from a few millimeters to 1 or 2 cm in size. Depending on degree of

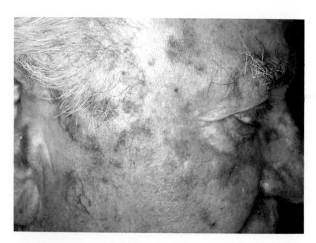

FIGURE 40-14
Actinic keratoses on cheek and forehead. Each lesion occurs as a rough, discrete, erythematous scaly papule with a varying degree of induration. Each actinic keratosis has a 1 in 1000 chance per year of progressing to invasive squamous cell carcinoma.

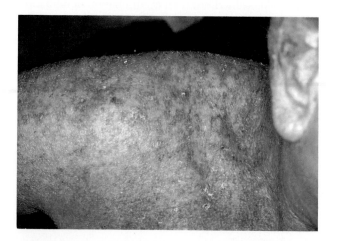

FIGURE 40-15
Actinic keratoses can occur on any part of the skin which has been chronically exposed to sunlight. This individual has multiple actinic keratoses on the shoulder and chest, each of which is an erythematous, rough, scaly papule.

prior sun exposure, a given patient may have one lesion, a few lesions, or hundreds of lesions. There are often other signs of actinic damage in the surrounding skin, including wrinkling, dryness, and yellow discoloration from solar elastosis. Actinic keratoses can occur at the base of cutaneous horns (Fig. 40-16). Solar keratoses have been reported to occur on the conjunctiva.[116]

Spreading pigmented actinic keratosis is an unusual variant of actinic keratosis. Clinically, the lesions in this condition are characterized by large size (over 1 cm), brown pigmentation, and a tendency for centrifugal spread.[117,118] These lesions can mimic lentigo maligna in clinical appearance.

Histologically, actinic keratoses are well-demarcated islands of abnormal keratinocytes with overlying parakeratosis. Cells of the entire stratum malpighii show a loss of polarity. The nuclei of the cells are large, irregular, and hyperchromatic, giving rise to a pleomorphic or atypical appearance. These cells produce a nucleated stratum corneum without the formation of a normal intact granular layer. Cells of the hair follicles and sweat gland ducts appear normal and keratinize normally. Changes of solar elastosis are invariably present in the underlying dermis.

Progression from Carcinoma In Situ to Invasive Squamous Cell Carcinoma

Progression of actinic keratosis to invasive squamous cell carcinoma occurs when buds of atypical keratinocytes extend deep into the dermis, leading to detached nests of abnormal cells capable of autonomous growth. Clinically, the lesion may become thicker, more indurated,

and enlarged (Fig. 40-17). Such signs, however, are not always present and are not substitutes for histologic confirmation of dermal invasion.

Marks et al. examined 1040 people over the age of 40 and found that 616 (59 percent) had a total of 4746 actinic keratoses. One year later, they reexamined the affected individuals and found that while some of the actinic keratoses had spontaneously resolved clinically, overall there was a 22 percent increase in the total number of actinic keratoses. Most importantly, the study found that the incidence of progression to invasive squamous cell carcinoma was 0.24 percent per actinic keratosis per year.[119] Subsequently, Marks et al. have enlarged upon this study by following 21,905 actinic keratoses for a 1-year period and determining a yearly incidence of progression to invasion of about 0.1 percent per actinic keratosis. Marks et al. found, on the average, 7.7 actinic keratoses per person.[120] These figures would indicate that, on the average, an individual with actinic keratoses would have a likelihood of 1 to 2 percent per year or 10 to 20 percent in 10 years of developing an invasive squamous cell carcinoma (Fig. 40-18). This estimate agrees reasonably well with data obtained from a number of pathologic series. Montgomery estimated that in 20 to 25 percent of patients with actinic keratoses, squamous cell carcinoma would develop in one more of the lesions.[121] Graham and Helwig have reported results from several series of patients, including 750 patients with actinic keratoses in Philadelphia and over 5000 patients with lesions of actinic keratoses accessioned at the Armed Forces Institute of Pathology. The investigators have consistently found that 12 to 13 percent of the patients experience progression of at least

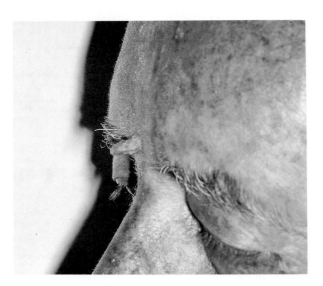

FIGURE 40-16
A cutaneous horn protrudes from the glabellar region. Actinic keratoses or squamous cell carcinomas can often be found at the base of these lesions.

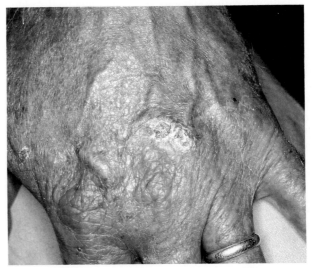

FIGURE 40-17
This thick crusted lesion on the hand began as an actinic keratosis and developed into an invasive squamous cell carcinoma. It is a nodular lesion with indurated borders and central crusting.

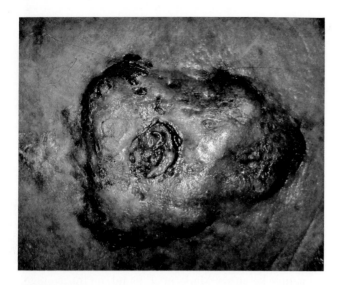

FIGURE 40-18
This lesion on the forehead shows the result of neglect of actinic damage resulting in invasive squamous cell carcinoma. It is an erythematous nodule with crusting and ulceration. Approximately 2 percent of invasive squamous cell carcinomas that arise in actinic keratoses metastasize to distant sites.

one actinic keratosis to invasive squamous cell carcinoma.[122]

In contrast to squamous cell carcinoma arising from burn scars, osteomyelitis sinuses, and chronic wounds, squamous cell carcinomas that originate from actinic keratoses metastasize infrequently. The rate of metastases of squamous cell carcinomas arising in actinic keratoses ranges between 0.5 percent and 3 percent, depending on the series consulted.[123–125] Moller et al. followed 211 patients with invasive squamous cell carcinomas for 16 to 26 years and found a 3 percent incidence of metastasis in 153 patients with squamous cell carcinoma of the skin; 11 percent of 55 patients with mucous membrane squamous cell carcinoma had metastases.[126]

Treatment

A variety of therapeutic methods are available for the patient with actinic keratoses.[127] Optimal choice depends on the number of lesions, the extent of involvement, and the patient's general state of health.

For the patient with a few lesions and little evidence of actinic damage, destructive techniques such as cryotherapy, curettage, electrodessication, chemical cauterization with phenol or trichloroacetic acid, or excisional surgery can be successfully employed. A cream or solution of 1 to 5% 5-fluorouracil (5-FU) can be effectively employed topically to treat people with actinic keratoses. This treatment is particularly useful for patients with moderate actinic damage because it can uncover and treat subclinical lesions. Preparations containing 5-FU can be used successfully to treat patients with

widespread extensive actinic damage, although adequate treatment is usually a prolonged, uncomfortable, and unsightly endeavor for the patient (Fig. 40-19). In selected patients with extensive involvement and numerous actinic keratoses, dermabrasion may be the treatment of choice. Dermabrasion is extremely effective in eradicating large numbers of actinic keratoses, particularly on the face and scalp. Generally the period of cosmetic incapacitation is longer with 5-FU than with dermabrasion, particularly if the 5-FU is administered with the regional section technique. Additionally, the final cosmetic result with dermabrasion is usually superior to that with 5-FU because dermabrasion destroys the skin uniformly, which then heals uniformly, while 5-FU destroys individual lesions but not the surrounding aged skin. A number of experienced dermatologists believe that "5-FU is not as efficacious as dermabrasion in long-term prevention of recurrent dyskeratotic and malignant cutaneous disease."[128–131]

Preliminary evidence indicates that topical tretinoin may be helpful in clearing actinic keratoses.[132] In particular, it was found to be useful as an adjunct to 5-FU. In order to further define the usefulness of topical tretinoin in treatment of facial actinic keratoses, Balin et al. treated 30 patients with multiple actinic keratoses for 15 months. They found that after 15 months of therapy (consisting of an average of 500 applications of tretinoin, 0.05% or 0.1% as tolerated by the patient), the average number of actinic keratoses decreased to 40 percent of the pretreatment number, and the average lesion size and area decreased to 25 percent of the pretreatment value. They found that improvement was more marked in patients with early actinic keratoses. Advanced lesions responded poorly, and a few progressed to invasive squamous cell carcinoma. Side effects were minor, and

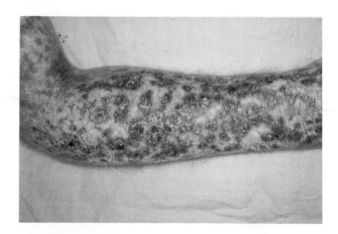

FIGURE 40-19
This patient's arm was treated with topical 5% 5-fluorouracil and Retin-A. Many subclinical actinic keratoses are uncovered by this treatment. The lesions become erythematous and then ulcerate forming scabs and crusts.

the treatment was generally well tolerated. Their data suggest that topical tretinoin may be employed as an adjunctive treatment in the therapy of early actinic keratoses.[133] Further studies are needed to ascertain whether actinic keratoses that clinically improve with tretinoin therapy recur after treatment is discontinued.

BOWEN'S DISEASE

Bowen's disease is another form of squamous cell carcinoma in situ (Fig. 40-20). It may occur anywhere on the skin but is more common on covered surfaces. Three factors have been implicated in the etiology of Bowen's disease: exposure to ultraviolet irradiation, arsenic, and papovaviruses and oncornaviruses.[134]

Clinically, Bowen's disease appears as a slowly enlarging erythematous patch of sharp but irregular outline showing little or no infiltration. Within the patch there are areas of crusting. Fifty-five percent of patients have more than one lesion. Lesions of Bowen's disease can occur on the glans penis, the vulva, and the oral mucosa; in these locations the lesions are called erythroplasia of Queyrat.

Many cases of Bowen's disease develop in persons who ingested inorganic arsenic many years prior to disease presentation. Some persons report that they received Fowler's solution, which was commonly used to treat asthma and various other medical problems and which contained 1% potassium arsenite.[135] In other persons the source of arsenic is thought to have been well water or insecticides. Arsenical keratoses of the palms and soles are verrucous, pale papules without surrounding inflammation (Fig. 40-21). They occur in 40 percent

FIGURE 40-21
These keratotic papules on the sole are arsenical keratoses which occur in 40 percent of patients exposed to arsenic. Multiple keratin-filled pits and papules are observed.

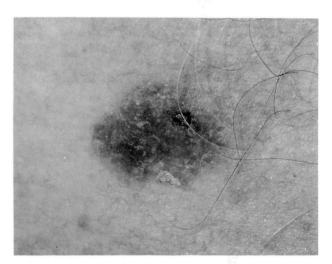

FIGURE 40-22
Bowen's disease arising in an area of arsenical keratosis. There is erythema, scaling, and crusting. These lesions usually are not indurated, in contrast to invasive squamous cell carcinoma.

of patients who receive arsenic and histologically are analogous to Bowen's disease (Fig. 40-22). Fifteen to 30 percent of patients with Bowen's disease on a non-sun-exposed site develop internal malignancies, and presumably this is due to exposure to arsenic.[136–140]

The histologic pattern seen in Bowen's disease is full-thickness epidermal dysplasia. Dysplastic cells often fill the acral portions of the appendages. The dysplastic cells are swollen and clumped and contain markedly atypical mitotic figures. The epidermis shows acanthosis with elongation and thickening of the rete ridges. The thickened horny layer consists largely of parakeratotic

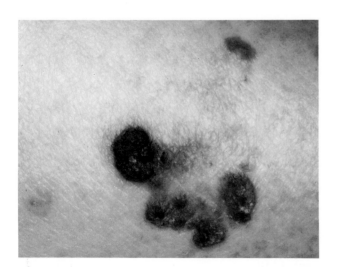

FIGURE 40-20
Bowen's disease occurs more commonly on non-sun-exposed areas but may occur anywhere on the skin. These are bright red papules and plaques with mild scaling.

cells. Cells throughout the epidermis lie in complete disorder.[141]

SQUAMOUS CELL CARCINOMA

In addition to actinic keratoses and Bowen's disease, conditions predisposing to squamous cell carcinoma include arsenic exposure, radiation exposure, scarring from a previous injury such as a burn or chronic leg ulcer, and exposure to heat. Squamous cell carcinoma may occur anywhere on the skin or mucous membranes, but it rarely arises from normal-appearing skin. Clinically, there is commonly a shallow ulcer surrounded by a wide, elevated, and indurated border. Often the ulcer is covered by a crust that conceals a red, granular base. Occasionally raised verrucoid lesions without ulceration occur.[142]

Squamous cell carcinoma is a malignant, invasive carcinoma (Fig. 40-18). Histologically, there are irregular masses of epidermal cells proliferating downward and invading the dermis. The invading tumor masses are composed of varying proportions of normal squamous cells and of atypical cells. These atypical cells demonstrate variations in the size and shape of the cells, hyperchromasia and hyperplasia of the nuclei, absence of intracellular bridges, keratinization of individual cells, and the presence of atypical mitotic figures. In squamous cell carcinoma, differentiation is in the direction of keratinization. Horn pearls are concentric layers of squamous cells with gradually increasing keratinization toward the center. The dermis often shows marked inflammatory reaction. Histologic grading of squamous cell carcinoma depends on the percentage of keratinizing cells, percentage of atypical cells, number of mitotic figures, and depth of invasion. The incidence of metastasis varies from 0.5 to 3 percent in squamous cell carcinomas arising in an actinic keratosis to 25 to 30 percent in those arising in a chronic osteomyelitic sinus or in radiodermatitis.

BASAL CELL CARCINOMA

The most common skin cancer, and hence the most common cancer in the United States, is the basal cell carcinoma (Figs. 40-23, 40-24, 40-25, and 40-26). This type of lesion is found most commonly on the head and neck of men, especially those who sunburn easily and have had chronic sun exposure. These lesions are uncommon in darkly pigmented races. The distribution of lesions on the face, however, does not correlate well with the area of maximal exposure to light. These lesions are common on the eyelids, on the inner canthus of the eye, and behind the ear, and are not so common on the back of the hand or the forearm. Actinic keratoses develop into squamous cell carcinomas but not into basal cell tumors.

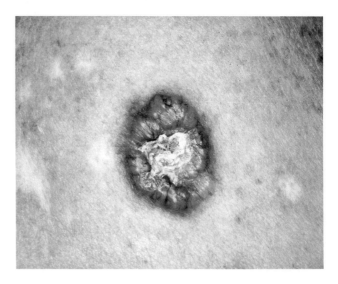

FIGURE 40-23
Typical appearing basal cell carcinoma with pearly, translucent erythematous raised border with telangiectasia and central ulceration and crusting. Morphology has been formerly described as "rodent ulcer."

Basal cell epitheliomas generally occur on hair-bearing skin in adults, usually as single lesions. Predisposing features include chronic sun exposure, exposure to X-irradiation, burn scars, and xeroderma pigmentosum.

Basal cell epitheliomas rarely metastasize but can be locally quite destructive. There are several different clinical types of basal cell epithelioma. Most common is the noduloulcerative basal cell epithelioma, which begins as a small, waxy nodule with small telangiectatic vessels on the surface and a translucent, rolled border. The nodule increases in size and undergoes central ul-

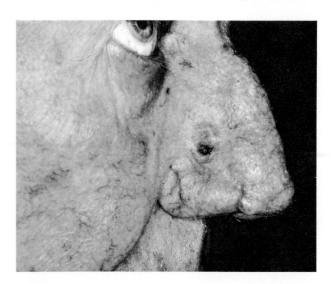

FIGURE 40-24
On the side of the nose, there is a typical appearing basal cell carcinoma with a pearly, translucent raised border, telangiectasia, and central erosion and crusting. In this lesion, the border is not erythematous.

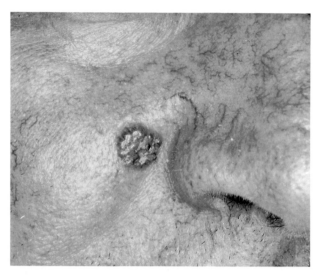

FIGURE 40-25
Pigmented basal cell carcinoma. This is a nodule with irregular surface whose color ranges from light to dark brown. Telangiectasia is present at the border.

ceration. The typical lesion consists of a slowly enlarging ulcer surrounded by a pearly, rolled border. This represents the so-called rodent ulcer. Basal cell carcinomas can contain melanin pigment. The morpheaform, or fibrosing, basal cell epithelioma appears as an indurated, yellowish plaque with an ill-defined border. The overlying skin remains intact for a long time before ulceration develops.

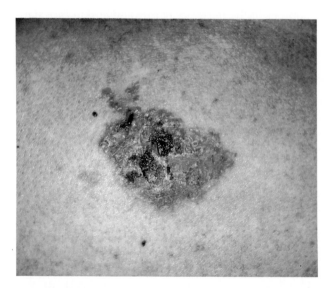

FIGURE 40-26
Superficial basal cell carcinoma is characterized by superficial, horizontal spreading rather than by deep invasion. Usually, it is faintly erythematous. This lesion demonstrates ulceration with crusting. The borders show the typical features of basal cell carcinoma such as translucence, pearly color, and telangiectasia.

Superficial, multifocal basal cell epitheliomas consist of one or several erythematous, scaling, only slightly infiltrated patches that slowly increase in size by peripheral extension. The patches are surrounded by a fine, threadlike, pearly border and usually show small areas of superficial ulceration and crusting. The center may show smooth, atrophic scarring. Superficial basal cell epitheliomas occur predominantly on the trunk.

Histologically, the tumor cells have a large oval or elongated nucleus and relatively little cytoplasm. The nuclei are uniform, compact, and dark-staining. They do not show variation in size or in staining, nor are there abnormal mitoses. The basal cells at the periphery of the tumor appear to line up, a phenomenon known as peripheral palisading. A connective tissue stroma is always present with the epithelial tumor masses, indicating that a mutual relationship exists between the tumor and its mesodermal stroma. Most basal cell tumors provoke a round-cell, lymphohistiocytic inflammatory reaction.

Basal cell tumors are thought to originate from immature pluripotential cells of the epidermis. They can mature and differentiate in a pattern resembling any of the epithelial structures. Their behavior is governed (as is that of normal immature cells) by the connective tissue in their proximity. Experimental production of basal cell epitheliomas has been accomplished in rats with chemical carcinogens. Reproduction with exposure to ultraviolet light has not been accomplished.

Several investigators have shown that exposure to ultraviolet light alters the immune system in experimental animals, facilitating the development of fatal skin tumors.[143,144] This ultraviolet-induced immunologic tolerance of ultraviolet-induced tumors is quite specific, because the animals will continue to reject transplanted tumors caused by oncogenic viruses or chemical carcinogens. It has also been shown that exposure to ultraviolet irradiation causes the development of hapten-specific suppressor T cells. The ultraviolet-induced, abnormal antigen-presenting cell is thought to be the epidermal Langerhans' cell. The full relevance of these studies to the human system remains incompletely known. Alterations in immune function with age and by chronic sun exposure are almost certain to contribute to the development of tumors in exposed skin that are so prevalent in the elderly.

IATROGENIC TUMORS

Dermatologists are quite familiar with the large numbers of premalignant tumors (solar keratoses, for example) which can suddenly spring up in an immunosuppressed patient.[145] Moreover, these behave more aggressively and tend to transform into invasive, rapidly growing tumors. Frequent clinical surveillance of the integument is essential in patients who are receiving chemotherapy for cancer or other serious diseases.

It is impossible to exaggerate the contributions of experimental tumor biology to the understanding of human malignancy. Nowhere are these contributions more dramatic than in tumors of the skin. Penn[146] has brought together a vast amount of information relating to the development of skin cancers in immunosuppressed patients. Transplant centers throughout the world are the main source of this important knowledge. Immunosuppressive agents are used, of course, to prevent rejection of the homografts. Almost half of the malignancies which arise in patients with impaired immune surveillance occur in the skin. The great majority of these are squamous cell cancers. In Australia, which has the highest incidence of skin cancers, the incidence of these malignancies is increased about 20 times. In New South Wales, a fivefold increase in malignant melanoma has been recorded. The impact of immunosuppression is made clear by the fact that these tumors arise in patients who are much younger than expected for these conditions (about a 30-year difference).

The great majority of these iatrogenic tumors occurred in sun-exposed areas, and almost half of the patients had multiple tumors. Some hapless individuals had 30 to 40 carcinomas. Almost 10 percent of skin cancers were associated with internal malignancy.

The tumors are also far more aggressive, tending to metastasize much more rapidly than tumors which arise spontaneously on sun-damaged skin. Thus, a new threat has been added, the high killing capacity of these tumors in immunocompromised subjects. It must be noted, of course, that immunosuppressive agents may be carcinogenic in their own right. Animal studies demonstrate that these drugs greatly potentiate ultraviolet-induced tumors. They can incite new tumors even while curing the original malignancy.[147]

PREVENTION STRATEGIES

There are many fruits to be harvested by a deeper knowledge of skin aging. More than with lesions and disorders of any other organ, a considerable number of skin lesions afflicting the elderly are preventable or treatable. They are not the result of the passage of time but rather the consequences of cumulative environmental insults. Chemical, physical, and mechanical trauma impinge continuously on the skin. Unless protective steps are taken, these insults will prematurely damage the fabric. Sunlight, owing mainly to its ultraviolet component (abetted by infrared radiation received concomitantly), is a notorious enemy of good skin.[148] Moreover, the damage is hidden from the surface view for more than a decade, delaying defensive behavior. Practically all of the dreary stigmata registered on the "old" face are

sunshine-induced, viz, precancers (actinic keratoses), cancers (basal and squamous), lentigo maligna (which may become invasive and lethal), a half-dozen benign growths (senile lentigos, freckles, etc.), and saggy, stretchable, redundant, inelastic, coarse, wrinkled, and yellowed skin.

The ruined landscape of the skin is the consequence of poor hygiene, not the wretched work of father time. While avoidance of midday sunlight would largely prevent these debasements, the routine use of sunscreens with a high sun protective factor (SPF 15) would be almost as effective. Studies in albino hairless mice, which lack the adaptive response of tanning, show that even SPF-2 sunscreens can decrease ultraviolet-induced tumors.[149] Those who think it futile to warn against the ravages of sunlight in a sun-worshiping culture should take note that the sunscreen business has exploded in the past decade, largely owing to raised consciousness. Indeed, it is mainly because of studies by dermatologists that the current sunscreens are so many times more effective than the feeble ones available several decades ago.[150]

Despite this shining example of what can be accomplished once scientific information is transmitted via the educational or even promotional process, the enormous potential for retarding age-dependent skin changes has scarcely been tapped. Exposed skin is also susceptible to damage by wind, cold, and low-humidity environments. Add to this the abrasions of daily life, the innumerable chemical insults in the household and the workplace, plus new recreational risks in a more prosperous, exercise-conscious, mobile population, and one then begins to appreciate the necessity of preventive skin care starting at an early age.

HERPES ZOSTER

Herpes zoster is a localized, painful, neurocutaneous eruption caused by reactivation of a latent neurotropic virus—the varicella-zoster virus. This condition is discussed in detail in Chap. 121.

BULLOUS PEMPHIGOID

Bullous pemphigoid (Fig. 40-11) is a chronic, self-limited disease of the elderly characterized by subepidermal blisters on the skin and, occasionally, on mucous membranes.[151–153] Circulating basement membrane zone antibodies can be detected in the serum of patients, and deposits of immunoglobulin and complement can be identified in skin samples beneath the basal cells.

It is not agreed whether bullous pemphigoid occurs more frequently in association with other autoimmune diseases; in pemphigus, such an association is agreed to exist. Despite many reports in previous literature, there is not an increased association of malignant neoplasms with bullous pemphigoid over that which would be expected in any elderly population group. Systemic steroid therapy is beneficial in bullous pemphigoid, especially when combined with other immunosuppressive drugs such as azathioprine or methotrexate. Complications of high-dose, prolonged steroid therapy in elderly persons, however, must be carefully considered and vigorously guarded against when treating bullous pemphigoid.

The cause of bullous pemphigoid is unknown. The component parts of the immunologic reaction participating in the pathophysiology of bullous pemphigoid are gradually being identified, but agreement has not been reached as to what initiates the reaction. Exacerbations of bullous pemphigoid, as well as acute onset of the condition, have been reported to follow drug reactions, phototherapy, or other cutaneous injury. Such observations, plus the predilection of the disease for older persons, suggest that bullous pemphigoid appears in the skin when there is a change in the homeostatic relationship between the host and the environment. Modifications in immunologic reactivity are likely to be involved.

STASIS DERMATITIS AND STASIS ULCERS

Venous insufficiency is responsible for another common cutaneous affliction of older persons—stasis dermatitis and stasis ulcers (Figs. 40-27 and 40-28). The chronicity and refractory nature of this problem are well known. Stasis ulcers account for discouraging immobility and prolonged hospitalization of many otherwise healthy el-

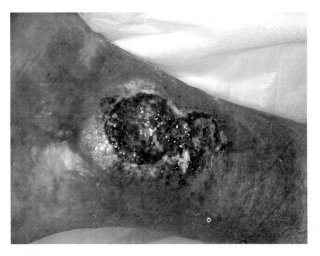

FIGURE 40-28
Stasis ulcer caused by venous insufficiency. An ulcer can be seen filled with purulent exudate and granulation tissue surrounded by erythema and hyperpigmentation, changes due to stasis dermatitis.

derly people. Treatment is unsatisfactory. Most successful programs are conservative and require the patient to soak the ulcers, debride necrotic tissue, treat bacterial infections, manage the dermatitis with topical steroids and lubricants, and wait for the ulceration to reepithelialize. Grafting of the ulcers is sometimes required. Various alternatives to grafting have been alleged to speed the healing process, including application of amniotic membranes, gold foil, benzoyl peroxide, and sugar. Most of these modalities have been short-lived, with no controlled studies to demonstrate their efficacy. Cultivation of epidermal cells and full-thickness skin equivalents, as well as topical application of various cell-derived growth factors, represent new and intriguing therapies.

Another interesting development has been the discovery that patients with stasis dermatitis are more susceptible to allergic contact hypersensitivity to a variety of agents than are persons with other chronic dermatoses. Dermatitis and leg ulcers do not develop in all persons with varicose veins. Underlying immunologic factors may be responsible for chronic stasis dermatitis and may have profound implications for new therapeutic approaches.

PRURITUS

Pruritus, or itching, is the most common dermatologic complaint of older people.[154] "Dry skin" is often credited with causing this incapacitating affliction, and it is true that xerosis is commonly observed. Seborrheic dermatitis is also prevalent in the elderly, however, and there are numerous other specific conditions that can account for the itching symptoms. Thus, it is inappropri-

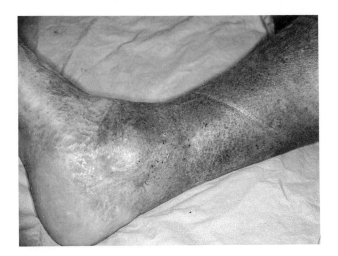

FIGURE 40-27
Stasis dermatitis, which is secondary to venous insufficiency. A scar, representing a healed ulcer, is present above the medial malleolus. There is extensive brownish hyperpigmentation which is a consequence of chronic stasis dermatitis.

ate to dismiss pruritus as banal; quite often it can be an important symptom of other disease.

The sensation of itching is picked up by various types of nerve endings and transmitted by way of the sensory nerves, located below the dermal-epidermal junction, to the posterior nerve roots and the spinal cord.[155] The bright and well-localized sensation of spontaneous itch is transmitted by delta fibers of the A class of myelinated nerves, which are 10 micrometers in diameter and conduct at about 10 meters per second. The unpleasant and poorly localized itch sensation is transmitted by C fibers of unmyelinated nerves, which are 5.5 micrometers in diameter and conduct at about 1 meter per second. Itch and pain are transmitted similarly, but not identically, by C fibers. Heat, for example, blocks itch but spares the sensation of pain. Pain can decrease itch perception. A great deal is unknown about the neurophysiology of itching. An ideal antipruritic agent—antihistamine, narcoleptic, or anti-inflammatory—has not been identified.[156] One problem is the lack of a good model system in which to study in human beings the induction of pruritus and its control. Histamine, proteases, and other agents have been used to induce itching.[157]

SEBORRHEIC DERMATITIS

Itching in older people may also be caused by inflammatory dermatoses. Seborrheic dermatitis is very common in elderly people, but its cause is unknown (Fig. 40-1). The prevalence of seborrheic dermatitis in parkinsonism and at times of stress and fatigue implicates neurologic factors. Etiologic roles for sebum and yeast have been proposed for seborrheic dermatitis. The condition does not develop unless the sebaceous glands are active, which probably accounts for its prevalence during infancy and in postpubertal individuals. The standard treatments for seborrheic dermatitis involve the use of tar shampoos and topical hydrocortisone. Recently, the use of topical ketoconazole has been shown to be an effective therapy for seborrheic dermatitis.

XEROSIS

There is much to be learned about xerosis, which is another cause of itching. Xerosis is due in part to decreased eccrine sweating, decreased sebum production, decreased water content of the stratum corneum, and decreased cohesion of corneocytes. Changes in production of sebum may contribute to the development of senile xerosis if the water-retaining property of the stratum corneum in old age is reduced when the amount of

sebum is reduced.[158,159] The role played by the keratinization process in determining xerosis is also unclear. Keratinization is partially controlled by age-related processes.

CONCLUSION: PHYSICAL APPEARANCE OF AGED SKIN

Although the appearance of aged skin is not normally thought of as having medical significance, it is of great concern to the aging members of our population. There is increasing evidence that an individual's appearance is an important factor contributing to an individual's self-concept. Recent psychological studies have found that the physically attractive aged are more optimistic and more social, have better personalities, and enjoy feelings of better health, than their nonattractive peers.[160,161] Additionally, data have become available to support the common contention that the overall visual assessment of an individual represents one of the best ways to estimate a person's biologic age. The Baltimore Longitudinal Study of Aging has been underway at the Gerontology Research Center of the National Institute of Aging since 1958 and has involved the serial measurement of 24 tests of physiologic age in over 1000 males. Borkan and Norris compared the men who were judged to look the oldest for their stated ages with those who appeared the youngest for their stated ages. These groups were compared with respect to each of the biologic measurements. On 19 of 24 tests, the subgroup of men who looked the oldest for their stated ages were biologically older as well. Further, the subjects who died since the start of the study were biologically older in 19 of 24 variables.[162] Tables 40-14, 40-15, and 40-16 review anatomic factors and environmental factors that contribute to the physical appearance of aged skin.

TABLE 40-14
Environmental Factors Contributing to Wrinkling of the Skin

Photodamage
Wind and cold exposure (decreased humidity)
Repeated facial movements
    Facial expressions
    Smoking
    Sleep pattern
    Squinting from sunlight
Gravity
Gain or loss of weight

TABLE 40-15
Anatomic Factors Contributing to Wrinkling of the Skin

Loss of dermal substance
  Decreased fibroblasts
  Decreased collagen
  Decreased glycosaminoglycans
Changes in elastic fibers
  Papillary dermis: regression of oxytalan fiber network
  Reticular dermis: thickened, branched, and coiled fibers
Decreased stratum corneum moisture content
Loss of subcutaneous tissue
Resorption of underlying bony structure

TABLE 40-16
Anatomic Factors Contributing to Physical Characteristics of Aged Skin

Pallor
  Decreased vascularity
  Loss of papillary dermal capillary loops
  Decreased melanocytes and pigment production
Xerosis (dry skin)
  Decreased eccrine sweating
  Decreased sebum production
  Decreased water content of stratum corneum
  Decreased cohesion of corneocytes
Purpura (bruising)
  Thinning of vascular walls
  Diminished dermal protection of blood vessels
  Thinning of dermis
  Decreased subcutaneous fat cushioning

REFERENCES

1. Balin AK, Kligman AL (eds): *Aging and the Skin.* New York, Raven Press, 1989.
2. Potts RO, Buras EM, Chrisman DA: Changes with age in the moisture content of human skin. *J Invest Dermatol* 82:97, 1984.
3. Baker H, Blair C: Cell replacement in the human stratum corneum in old age. *Br J Dermatol* 80:367, 1968.
4. Baker H, Kligman AM: Technique for estimating turnover time of human stratum corneum. *Arch Dermatol* 95:408, 1967.
5. Whitton J, Everall JD: The thickness of the epidermis. *Br J Dermatol* 98:467, 1973.
6. Kligman AM: Perspectives and problems in cutaneous gerontology. *J Invest Dermatol* 73:39, 1979.
7. Tosti A, Fazzini ML, Villardita S: Quantitative changes in epidermis of aged humans. *G Ital Chir Dermatol Oncol* 2(3):180, 1987.
8. Katzberg A: The area of the dermal-epidermal junction in human skin. *Anat Rec* 131:717, 1958.
9. Grove G: Age-associated changes in human epidermal cell renewal and repair, in Balin AK, Kligman AM (eds): *Aging and the Skin.* New York, Raven Press, 1989, pp 193–204.
10. Tindall JP, Smith JG: Skin lesions of the aged and their association with internal changes. *JAMA* 186:1039, 1963.
11. Gilchrest BA, Murphy G, Soter NA: Effect of chronologic aging and ultraviolet irradiation on Langerhans' cells in human epidermis. *J Invest Dermatol* 79:85, 1982.
12. Snell RS, Bischitz PG: The melanocytes and melanin in human abdominal wall skin: A survey made at different ages in both sexes and during pregnancy. *J Anat* 97:361, 1963.
13. Staricco RJ, Pinkus J: Quantitative and qualitative data on the pigment cells of adult human epidermis. *J Invest Dermatol* 28:33, 1957.
14. Black M: A modified radiographic method for measuring skin thickness. *Br J Dermatol* 81:661, 1969.
15. Shuster S, Black MM: The influence of age and sex on skin thickness, skin collagen and density. *Br J Dermatol* 93:639, 1975.
16. Lavker R: Structural alterations in exposed and unexposed aged skin. *J Invest Dermatol* 73:59, 1979.
17. Lavker R, Zheng P, Dong G: Aged skin: A study by light, transmission electron, and scanning electron microscopy. *J Invest Dermatol* 88:44S, 1987.
18. King GS, Mohan VS, Starcher BS: Radioimmunoassay for desmosine. *Connect Tissue Res* 7:263, 1980.
19. Montagna W, Carlisle K: Structural changes in aging human skin. *J Invest Dermatol* 73:47, 1979.
20. Andrew W, Behnke R, Sato T: Changes with advancing age in the cell population of human dermis. *Gerontologia* 10:1, 1964.
21. Aizkham RG et al: *J Exp Med* 152:931, 1980.
22. Braverman IM, Fonferko E: Studies in cutaneous aging. II. The microvasculature. *J Invest Dermatol* 78:444, 1982.
23. Braverman IM, Sibley J, Keh-Yen A: A study of the veil cells around normal, diabetic and aged cutaneous microvessels. *J Invest Dermatol* 86:57, 1986.
24. Kligman AM: Perspectives and problems in cutaneous gerontology. *J Invest Dermatol* 73:39, 1979.
25. Kligman AM, Grove GL, Balin AK: Aging of human skin, in Finch CE, Schneider EL (eds): *Handbook of the Biology of Aging.* New York, Van Nostrand Reinhold, 1985, pp 820–841.
26. Plewig G, Kligman AM: Proliferative activity of the sebaceous glands of the aged. *J Invest Dermatol* 70:314, 1978.
27. Luderschmidt C, Kindermann D: Sebostasis of the aged. *G Ital Chir Dermatol Oncol* 2:192, 1987.
28. Hamilton JB, Terada H, Mestler GE: Studies of growth throughout the life span in Japanese: Growth and size of nails and their relationship to age, sex, heredity, and other factors. *J Gerontol* 10:400, 1955.
29. Orentreich N, Sharp N: Keratin replacement as an aging parameter. *J Soc Cosmetic Chem* 18:537, 1967.
30. Kiistala U: Dermo-epidermal separation: The influence of age, sex and body region on suction blister formations. *Ann Clin Res* 4:10, 1972.
31. Christophers E, Kligman AM: Percutaneous absorption in aged skin. in Montagna W (ed): *Advances in Biology*

of the Skin, vol 6. Oxford, Pergamon Press, 1965, pp 163–175.

32. Grove GL, Duncan S, Kligman AM: Effect of aging on the blistering of human skin with ammonium hydroxide. *Br J Dermatol* 107:393, 1982.

33. Christophers E, Kligman AM: Percutaneous absorption in aged skin, in Montagna W (ed): *Advances in Biology of the Skin*, vol 6. Oxford, Pergamon Press, 1965, pp 163–175.

34. Tagami H: Functional characteristics of aged skin. *Acta Dermatol* Kyoto, 66:19, 1972.

35. Grove GL: Exfoliative cytological procedures as a nonintrusive method for dermatogerontological studies. *J Invest Dermatol* 73:67, 1979.

36. Malkinson FD: Studies on the percutaneous absorption of ^{14}C-labelled steroid by use of the gas flow cell. *J Invest Dermatol* 31:19, 1958.

37. Tagami H: Functional characteristics of aged skin. *Acta Dermatol* Kyoto, 66:19, 1972.

38. Frosch PJ, Kligman AM: Rapid blister formation with ammonium hydroxide. *Br J Dermatol* 96:461, 1977.

39. Grove GL, Duncan S, Kligman AM: Effect of aging on the blistering of human skin with ammonium hydroxide. *Br J Dermatol* 107:393, 1982.

40. Light SE: Convulsive seizures following the application of phenol to the skin. *Northeast Med* 30:232, 1935.

41. DuNuoy P: *Biological Time*. New York, Macmillan, 1936.

42. Carrel A, DuNuoy P: Cicatrization of wounds. *J Exp Med* 34:339, 1921.

43. Orentreich N, Selmanowitz VJ: Levels of biological functions with aging. *Trans Acad Sci*, Series B 31:992, 1969.

44. Yung CW, Goodson WA, Hunt TK: Wound healing and aging. *J Invest Dermatol* 73:88, 1979.

45. Claus G, Gotham B: Results of geriatric surgery. *Acta Chir Scand* 357:85, 1966.

46. Halasz NA: Dehiscence of laparotomy wounds. *Am J Surg* 116:210, 1968.

47. Mendoza CB, Postlethwaite RW, Johnson WD: Incidence of wound disruption following operation. *Arch Surg* 101:396, 1970.

48. Sandblum PH, Peterson P, Muren A: Determination of the tensile strength of healing wounds as a clinical test. *Acta Chir Scand* 105:252, 1953.

49. Vilijanto JA: A sponge implant method for testing connective tissue regeneration in surgical patients. *Acta Chir Scand* 135:297, 1969.

50. Orentreich N, Selmanowitz VJ: Levels of biological functions with aging. *Trans Acad Sci*, Series B, 31:992, 1969.

51. Grove GL: Age-related differences in healing of superficial skin wounds in humans. *Arch Dermatol Res* 272:381, 1982.

52. McGuirt WF, Loery S, McCabe BF, Kruse CJ: The risks of major head and neck surgery in the aged population. *Laryngoscope* 87:1378, 1977.

53. Grove GL, Lavker RM, Holze E, Kligman AM: Use of nonintrusive tests to monitor age-associated changes in human skin. *J Soc Cosmetic Chem* 32:15, 1981.

54. Bettley FR, Donaghue E: The irritant effect of soap upon the normal skin. *Br J Dermatol* 72:67, 1960.

55. Carlizzi L, Bologna E: Variazioni della reattivatá cutanea in rapporto con l'eta. *Bull Soc Ital Biol Sper* 41:344, 1965.

56. Gilchrest BA, Stoff JS, Soter NA: Chronologic aging alters the response to UV-induced inflammation in human skin. *J Invest Dermatol* 79:11, 1982.

57. MacLaughlin J, Holick MF: Aging decreases the capacity of human skin to produce vitamin D_3. *J Clin Invest* 76:1536, 1985.

58. Johnson MLT, Roberts J: Prevalence of dermatologic disease among persons 1–74 years of age. *Advance Data*, no 4, U.S. Dept. of Health, Education and Welfare, 1977.

59. Droller H: Dermatologic findings in a random sample of old persons. *Geriatrics* 10:421, 1953.

60. Waisman M: A clinical look of the aging skin. *Postgrad Med* 66:87, 1979.

61. Verbov J: Skin problems in the older patient. *Practitioner* 215:612, 1975.

62. Tindall JP, Smith JG: Skin lesions of the aged and their association with internal changes. *JAMA* 186:1039, 1963.

63. Zakon S, Goldberg A, Forman I: Geriatric dermatoses: A survey of the skin of the aged. *IMJ* 101:37, 1952.

64. Tindall JP, Smith JG: Skin lesions of the aged and their association with internal changes. *JAMA* 186:1039, 1963.

65. Weismann K, Krakaver R, Wancher B: Prevalence of skin diseases in old age. *Acta Derm Venereol* 66:352, 1981.

66. Droller H: Dermatologic findings in a random sample of old persons. *Geriatrics* 10:421, 1953.

67. Young AW: Dermatogeriatric problems in the chronic disease hospital. *NY State J Med* 63:1748, 1965.

68. Johnson SAM: Skin changes of the sunset years. *Cutis* 18:351, 1976.

69. Goldschmidt H, Hojyp-Tomoka M, Kligman AM: Trichostasis spinulosa. *Hautarzt* 26:299, 1975.

70. Hodgson C: Senile lentigo. *Arch Dermatol* 87:197, 1963.

71. Keogh EV, Walsh RJ: Rate of graying human hair. *Nature* 207:877, 1965.

72. Rook AR, Wilkinson DS, Ebling FJG: *Textbook of Dermatology*, 3d ed. London, Blackwell Scientific Publications, 1979.

73. Tindall JP: Geriatric dermatology, in *Normal Aging II*. Durham, NC, Duke University Press, 1974, pp 3–26.

74. Epstein J: Dermatitis in the aged. *Geriatrics* 1:369, 1946.

75. Leyden JJ, McGinley KJ, Grove GL, Kligman AM: Age-related differences in the rate of desquamation of the skin surface cells, in Cristofalo VJ, Adelman RD, Roberts J (eds): *Pharmacologic Intervention of the Aging Process*. New York, Plenum Press, 1979, pp 297–298.

76. Tager A, Berlin C, Schen RJ: Seborrheic dermatitis in acute cardiac disease. *Br J Dermatol* 76:367, 1964.

77. Thorne EG: Coping with pruritus, a common geriatric complaint. *Geriatrics* 33:47, 1978.

78. Tschin EH: What treatment for skin infestations in the elderly? *Geriatrics* 37:38, 1982.

79. Sandstead HH, Henriksen LK, Greger JL: Zinc nutriture in the elderly in relation to taste acuity, immune response, and wound healing. *Am J Clin Nutr* 36:1046, 1982.

80. Bienia R, Ratcliff S, Barbour GL, Kummer M: Malnutrition in the hospitalized geriatric patient. *J Am Geriatr Soc* 30:433, 1982.

81. Braverman IM: *Skin Signs of Systemic Disease*, 2d ed. Philadelphia, Saunders, 1981.

82. Stoughton RB: Physiological changes from maturity through senescence. *JAMA* 179:636, 1962.

83. McConkey B, Fraser GM, Bligh AS, Whitely H: Transparent skin and osteoporosis. *Lancet* 1:693, 1963.

84. McConkey B, Walton KW, Carney SA, Lawrence JC, Ricketts CR: Significance of the occurrence of transparent skin. *Ann Rheum Dis* 26:210, 1967.

85. Horan MA, Poxty JA, Fox RA: The white nails of old age. *J Am Geriatr Soc* 30:734, 1982.

86. Melen H: An atrophic circumscribed skin lesion in the lower extremities of diabetics. *Acta Med Scand* 4:423, 1964.

87. Lithner F: Cutaneous reactions of the extremities of diabetics to local thermal trauma. *Acta Med Scand* 198:319, 1975.

88. Bauer M, Levan NE: Diabetic dermangiopathy. *Br J Dermatol* 83:528, 1970.

89. Bravin TB: The Leser-Trélat sign. *Br Med J* 2:437, 1966.

90. Margolis J: Skin tags—a frequent sign of diabetes mellitus. *N Engl J Med* 294:1184, 1976.

91. Lichstein E, Chadda KD, Naik D, Gupta PK: Diagonal ear lobe crease prevalence and implications as a coronary risk factor. *N Engl J Med* 290:615, 1974.

92. Lichstein E, Chadda KD, Gupta PK: Diagonal ear lobe crease and coronary artery disease. *Ann Intern Med* 85:337, 1967.

93. Wyre HW: The diagonal ear lobe crease—a cutaneous manifestation of coronary artery diseases. *Cutis* 23:327, 1979.

94. Bean WB: *Vascular Spiders and Related Lesions of the Skin*. Springfield, IL, Charles C Thomas, 1958.

95. Kocsard E, Ofner F, D'Absera V: The phlebectasias of old age: Incidence and diagnostic importance. *J Am Geriatr Soc* 18:31, 1970.

96. Miller D, Akers W: Multiple phlebectasias of the jejunum. *Arch Intern Med* 121:180, 1968.

97. Givs JA: Vascular formation of the lip and peptic ulcer. *JAMA* 183:725, 1963.

98. Kocsard E, Ofner F, D'Absera V: The histopathology of caviar tongue. *Dermatologica* 140:318, 1970.

99. Kean WF, Dwosh IL, Ford PM, Kelly WG, Dok CM: Efficacy and toxicity of D-penicillamine for rheumatoid disease in the elderly. *J Am Geriatr Soc* 30:94, 1982.

100. Yung CW, Hambrick G: D-penicillamine-induced pemphigus syndrome. *J Am Acad Dermatol* 6:317, 1982.

101. Gilchrest BA: Some gerontologic considerations in the practice of dermatology. *Arch Dermatol* 115:1343, 1979.

102. Tindall JP, Smith JG Jr: Skin lesions of the aged. *JAMA* 186:1039, 1963.

103. Pinkus H, Merigan A: *A Guide to Dermatohistopathology*, 3d ed. New York, Appleton-Century-Crofts, 1981.

104. Mevorah D, Mishima Y: Cellular response of seborrheic keratosis following croton oil irritation and surgical trauma. *Dermatologica* 131:452, 1965.

105. Curry SS, King LE: The sign of Leser-Trélat. *Arch Dermatol* 116:1059, 1980.

106. Dantzig PI: Sign of Leser-Trélat. *Arch Dermatol* 108:700, 1973.

107. Liddell K, White JE, Caldwell IW: Seborrheic keratosis and carcinoma of large bowel. *Br J Dermatol* 92:449, 1975.

108. Ronchese F: Keratoses, cancer and the sign of Leser-Trélat. *Cancer* 18:1003, 1965.

109. Parish J, White H, Pathak M: Photomedicine, in Fitzpatrick T et al (eds): *Dermatology in General Medicine*, 2d ed. New York, McGraw-Hill, 1979, pp 942–944.

110. Engel A, Johnson ML, Haynes SG: Health effects of sunlight exposure in the United States: Results from the first National Health and Nutrition Examination Survey, 1971–1974. *Arch Dermatol* 124:72, 1988.

111. Zagula-Mally ZW, Rosenberg EW, Kashgarian M: Frequency of skin cancer and solar keratoses in a rural southern county as determined by population sampling. *Cancer* 34:345, 1974.

112. Marks R, Selwood TS: Solar keratoses: The association with erythemal ultraviolet radiation in Australia. *Cancer* 56:2332, 1985.

113. Abo-Darub JM, MacKie R, Pitts JD: DNA repair in cells from patients with actinic keratoses. *J Invest Dermatol* 80:241, 1983.

114. Lambert B, Ringborg U, Swanbeck G: Ultraviolet-induced DNA repair synthesis in lymphocytes from patients with actinic keratoses. *J Invest Dermatol* 67:594, 1976.

115. Sbano E, Andreassi L, Fimiami M, Valentino A, Baiocchi R: DNA repair after UV irradiation in skin fibroblasts from patients with actinic keratosis. *Arch Dermatol Res* 262:55, 1978.

116. Clear AS, Chirambo MC, Hutt SR: Solar keratosis, pterygium, and squamous cell carcinoma of the conjunctiva in Malawi. *Br J Ophthalmol* 63:102, 1979.

117. James MP, Wells GC, Whimster IW: Spreading pigmented actinic keratoses. *Br J Dermatol* 98:373, 1978.

118. Subrt P, Jorizzo JL, Apisarnthanarax P: Spreading pigmented actinic keratosis. *J Am Acad Dermatol* 8:63, 1983.

119. Marks R, Foley P, Goodman G, Hage B, Selwood TS: Spontaneous remission of solar keratoses: The case for conservative management. *Br J Dermatol* 115:649, 1986.

120. Marks R, Rennie G, Selwood TS: Malignant transformation of solar keratoses to squamous cell carcinoma. *Lancet* I:795, 1988.

121. Montgomery H: Keratosis senilis, in Ormsby OS, Montgomery H (eds): *Diseases of the Skin*, 8th ed. Philadelphia, Lea & Febiger, 1955, pp 846–849.

122. Graham JH, Helwig EB: Cutaneous premalignant lesions, in Montagna W, Dobson RL (eds): *Advances in Biology of the Skin: Carcinogenesis*. Oxford, Pergamon, 1966, pp 277–327.

123. Lund HZ: How often does squamous cell carcinoma of the skin metastasize? *Arch Dermatol* 92:635, 1965.

124. Marks R: Nonmelanotic skin cancer and solar keratoses: The quiet 20th century epidemic *Int J Dermatol* 26:201, 1987.

125. Morgan RJ: Metastases from squamous cell epitheliomas of the skin, in Epstein E (ed): *Controversies in Dermatology*. Philadelphia, Saunders, 1984, pp 134–139.

126. Moller R, Reymann F, Hou-Jensen K: Metastases in dermatological patients with squamous cell carcinoma. *Arch Dermatol* 115:703, 1979.

127. Balin AK, Lin AN, Pratt L: Actinic keratoses. *J Cutan Aging Cosmet Dermatol* 1:77, 1988.

128. Epstein E Sr: Dermabrasion, in Epstein E, Epstein E Jr (eds): *Skin Surgery*, 5th ed. Springfield, IL, Charles C Thomas, 1982, pp 593–610.

129. Burks JW, Marascalco J, Clark WH: Half-face planing of precancerous skin after five years. *Arch Dermatol* 88:572, 1963.

130. Field LM: On the value of dermabrasion in the management of actinic keratoses, in Epstein E (ed): *Controversies in Dermatology*. Philadelphia, Saunders, 1984, pp 96–102.

131. Winton GB, Salasche SJ: Dermabrasion of the scalp as a treatment for actinic damage. *J Am Acad Dermatol* 14:661, 1986.

132. Peck GL: Topical tretinoin in actinic keratosis and basal cell carcinoma. *J Am Acad Dermatol* 15:829, 1986.

133. Balin AK, Lin AN, Pratt L: Actinic keratoses. *J Cutan Aging Cosmet Dermatol* 1:77, 1988.

134. Braverman I: *Skin Signs of Systemic Disease*, 2d ed. Philadelphia, Saunders, 1981, pp 67–89.

135. Braverman I: *Skin Signs of Systemic Disease*, 2d ed. Philadelphia, Saunders, 1981, pp 67–89.

136. Andersen S, La C, Nielsen A, Reymann F: Relationship between Bowen's disease and internal malignant tumors. *Arch Dermatol* 108:367, 1973.

137. Epstein E: Association of Bowen's disease with visceral cancer. *Arch Dermatol* 82:349, 1960.

138. Graham JH, Helwig EB: Bowen's disease and its relationship to systemic cancer. *Arch Dermatol* 83:738, 1961.

139. Hugo NE, Conway H: Bowen's disease: Its malignant potential and relationship to systemic cancer. *Plast Reconstr Surg* 39:109, 1967.

140. Peterka ES, Lynch FW, Goltz RW: An association between Bowen's disease and internal cancer. *Arch Dermatol* 84:623, 1961.

141. Pinkus H, Merigan A: *A Guide to Dermatohistopathology*, 3d ed. New York, Appleton-Century-Crofts, 1981.

142. Lever W: *Histopathology of the Skin*, 5th ed. Philadelphia, Lippincott, 1975, pp 467–483.

143. Greene MI, Sy M, Kripke M, Benacerraf B: Impairment of antigen presenting cell function by ultraviolet radiation. *Proc Natl Acad Sci USA* 76:6591, 1979.

144. Kripke M: Immunologic mechanisms in UV radiation carcinogenesis. *Adv Cancer Res* 34:69, 1981.

145. Harville D, Aaron J: Cutaneous oncogenesis and immunosuppression. *Cutis* 11:188, 1973.

146. Penn I: Immunosuppression and skin cancer. *Clin Plas Surg* 7:361, 1980.

147. Koranda FC, Loeffler RT, Koranda DM: Accelerated induction of skin cancers by ultraviolet radiation in hairless mice treated with immunosuppressive agents. *Surg Forum* 26:145, 1935.

148. Kligman AM: Early destructive effect of sunlight in human skin. *JAMA* 210:2377, 1969.

149. Kligman LH, Aiken FJ, Kligman AM: Prevention of ultraviolet damage to the dermis of hairless mice by sunscreens. *J Invest Dermatol* 78:181, 1982.

150. Kaidbey KH, Kligman AM: An appraisal of the efficacy and substantivity of the new hi-potency sunscreens. *J Am Acad Dermatol* 4:566, 1981.

151. Burton JL, Harman RRM, Peachey RDG et al: Azathioprine plus prednisone in treatment of pemphigoid. *Br Med J* 2:1190, 1978.

152. Callen JP: Internal disorders associated with bullous disease of the skin. *J Am Acad Dermatol* 3:107, 1980.

153. Lever WJ: Pemphigus and pemphigoid. *J Am Acad Dermatol* 1:2, 1979.

154. Kligman AM: Perspectives and problems in cutaneous gerontology. *J Invest Dermatol* 73:39, 1979.

155. Loring AL: Pathophysiology of pruritus, in Fitzpatrick TB et al (eds): *Dermatology in General Medicine*, 2d ed. New York, McGraw-Hill, 1979, pp 221–224.

156. Arnold AJ, Simpson JG, Jones HE, Ahmed AR: Suppression of histamine-induced pruritus by hydroxyzine and various neuroleptics. *J Am Acad Dermatol* 1:509, 1979.

157. Hagermark O, Hokfelt T, Pernow B: Flare and itch induced by substance P in human skin. *J Invest Dermatol* 71:233, 1978.

158. Plewig G, Kligman AM: Proliferative activity of the sebaceous glands of the aged. *J Invest Dermatol* 70:314, 1978.

159. Pochi PE, Strauss JS, Downing DT: Age-related changes in sebaceous gland activity. *J Invest Dermatol* 73:108, 1979.

160. Graham JA: The psychotherapeutic value of cosmetics. *Cosmet Technol* 5(1):15, 1983.

161. Kligman AM, Graham JA: The psychology of cutaneous aging, in Balin AK, Kligman AM (eds): *Aging and the Skin*. New York, Raven Press, 1989, pp 347–359.

162. Borkan GA, Norris AH: Assessment of biological age using a profile of physical parameters. *J Gerontol* 35:177, 1980.

Chapter 41

THE ORAL CAVITY

Bruce J. Baum and Jonathan A. Ship

Studies on the status of the oral cavity in the elderly have been infrequent and often limited in scope. In particular, there is a notable deficiency in the amount of epidemiologic data available to describe oral tissues, both in health and disease, across the human life span. While information is available from national surveys on dental and periodontal status, it must be stressed that this information is derived from cross-sectional, not longitudinal, studies. Furthermore, almost no broad descriptive population data exist on salivary gland function, oral mucosal status, oral chemosensory performance (taste, smell), and oral motor function. This is unfortunate since many of the common stereotypes about aging and oral health status reflect on these functions. Most of these generalizations are unsubstantiated,[1] a situation which can cause considerable confusion for both the patient and clinician.

The oral cavity serves two essential functions in human physiology: the production of speech and the initiation of alimentation. Discussion of the status of the oral cavity during aging must consider the impact of any disturbance of these functions on the elderly individual's life.

To enable humans to speak and to process food, many specialized tissues have evolved in the mouth. The teeth, the periodontium, and the muscles of mastication exist to prepare food for deglutition. The tongue, besides having a central role in communication, also is a key participant in food bolus preparation and translocation. Salivary glands provide a secretion with multiple functions. Saliva, in addition to lubricating all oral mucosal tissues (keeping them intact and pliable), also moistens the developing food bolus, permitting it to be fashioned into a swallow-acceptable form. All of these tissue activities are finely coordinated, and a disturbance in any one tissue function can significantly compromise speech and/ or alimentation and diminish the quality of a patient's life.

In addition, it is necessary to remember that the oral cavity is exposed to the external world and is potentially vulnerable to a limitless number of environmental insults. Exquisite mechanisms have evolved to protect the mouth and permit normal oral function. The oral cavity is richly endowed with sensory systems which contribute to our enjoyment of food and alert us to potential problems. These include mechanisms for taste (and its inextricable relationship with smell), thermal, textural, tactile, and pain discrimination. Also, saliva has an important protective role and contains a broad spectrum of antimicrobial proteins which modulate oral bacterial and fungal colonization. Other proteins maintain the functional integrity of the teeth by keeping saliva supersaturated with calcium and phosphate salts and in effect repairing incipient caries (tooth decay) by a remineralization process.

This chapter will focus on specific oral tissues and their functions. It will present both what a clinician can reasonably expect to encounter as "normal" oral physiological status in the older adult and the way common systemic disease and its treatment may affect the oral tissues during aging.

THE DENTITION AND PERIODONTIUM

The loss of teeth has long been associated with aging. As noted in Table 41-1, recent national health surveys demonstrate that approximately 40 percent of Americans over the age of 65 are edentulous.[2] Although the prevalence of edentulous adults has dramatically decreased since the first National Health Survey in 1957–1958, an adult in the senior population (older than age 65) has an average of 11 missing teeth. Advances in dental treatment, disease prevention, increased availability of dental care, and improved awareness of dental needs recently have resulted in significant gains in dental health.

Tooth loss is attributed to two major etiologic processes: dental caries and periodontal disease. Caries affects the exposed dental surfaces, and periodontal disease is confined to the supporting bony and ligamentous dental structures. With current trends of increasing

TABLE 41-1
Demographic Findings on the Dental Status of Adults in the United States

A. Percent of Edentulous Adults

Ages	1957–1958	1960–1962	1971–1974	1985–1986
45–54	22.4	20.0	16.0	9.0
55–64	38.1	36.3	33.2	15.6
65–74	55.4	49.4	45.5	36.9

B. Percent of Adults with 1 or More Dental Visits Within a Year of Interview

Sample	1963–1964	1969	1978–1979	1985–1986	% Change*
Total U.S.	42.0	45.0	50.0	58.5	+39.3
65+	20.8	23.2	32.5	37.5	+80.3

C. Percent of Adults with No Dental Visits Within 5 Years of Interview

Sample	1963–1964	1969	1978–1979	1985–1986
Total U.S.	14.0	13.2	13.6	8.3
65+	51.7	46.9	44.0	26.5

D. Utilization of Dental Services by Dentate and Edentulous Adults, Aged 65+[†]

	Dentate Adults	Edentulous Adults
Adults with 1 or more dental visits within a year of interview	54.5%	13.0%
Adults with no dental visits within 5 years of interview	10.9%	49.1%

*Based on changes from 1963–1964 to 1985–1986.
[†]Based on the NIDR Survey (1985–1986).
SOURCE: Derived from National Health Surveys (year indicated) and the National Institute of Dental Research (NIDR) Survey of Oral Health in U.S. Adults (1985–1986).

tooth retention in the elderly, there is a correspondingly greater risk for their development of both of these disease entities.

A tooth consists of several mineralized and nonmineralized components supported by the periodontal ligament and alveolar bone. The outer dental structure is enamel, and it is the hardest, most mineralized component, consisting of about 90 percent hydroxyapatite. Enamel, which covers the coronal aspect of the tooth, is the first hard tissue exposed to caries-causing bacteria. Dentin constitutes the main portion of the tooth structure, extending almost the entire length of the tooth. It is covered by enamel on the crown and by cementum on the root. Cementum covers the root of the tooth and is the least mineralized of the three components (approximately 50 percent), making it the most susceptible to caries-causing bacteria. The central, nonmineralized portion is the dental pulp, which houses the vascular, lymphatic, and neuronal supply to the tooth.

The periodontium consists of those tissues which invest and support the tooth. It is divided into the gingival unit (gums) and the attachment apparatus (cementum, periodontal ligament, and alveolar bony process). Gingivitis occurs when the gingival unit is inflamed. Periodontitis (or periodontal disease) exists when there is an inflammation and appreciable loss of the attachment apparatus due to the presence of pathogenic microorganisms.

Tooth loss in children and young adults is predominantly caused by dental caries. In middle-aged and older adults, the loss of the dentition primarily results from periodontal disease.

There are two classifications of dental caries, coronal caries and root surface caries, named according to which surface of the tooth has been affected. Coronal caries, the most common caries in young adults and children, occurs when the enamel and dentin of the coronal portion of the tooth is affected. In older adults, if gingival recession or periodontal disease causes the root surfaces of the tooth to become exposed to the oral environment, it is common for root surface or cervical caries to occur.

The principal (though by no means exclusive) coronal caries–causing microorganism in humans is *Streptococcus mutans*.[3] It is believed that predominantly different bacterial species initiate caries on the root surfaces, but this has not yet been proved convincingly.[4] While *Streptococcus mutans* and *Lactobacillus* strains more often are associated with coronal caries, other streptococci, actinomycetes, and enterococci are identified with cervical caries. The caries-causing bacteria reside on the tooth surface in what is commonly called dental plaque. This is a soft, firmly adherent mass, containing, in addition to bacteria, food debris, desquamated cells, and bacterial products. Acid production by bacteria in plaque dissolves the mineral contents of the enamel, dentin, or cementum. The exposed protein constituents are destroyed by hydrolytic enzymes, and caries results.[5] Dental plaque is considered to be a primary etiologic factor in dental caries, as well as a principal source of pathogenic organisms in periodontal disease. Microbial populations of plaque have been found to be qualitatively different in young and elderly subjects.[6]

A variety of oral microorganisms, through direct bacterial toxicity or via indirect mechanisms, result in the inflammatory responses and tissue destruction seen with periodontal disease.[7] The microbial species cross the gingival epithelium and enter subepithelial tissues where they activate specific host-defense mechanisms. Eventually this causes tissue destruction, including bone loss and tooth morbidity.

As the dentulous individual ages, the susceptibility to coronal caries diminishes and the prevalence of root surface caries increases. There is an 18-fold increase in the average number of tooth surfaces with root caries between persons age 20 and those age 64.[8] In addition, older persons frequently suffer from recurrent or secondary coronal caries (decay around existing restored surfaces).

Studies in the United States reveal an increase in the mean number of decayed and filled teeth among dentulous adults in the older age cohorts over the last 30 years.[9] These trends are likely a reflection of the increased retention of the natural dentition and a greater utilization of dental services by older adults, rather than a true increase in dental caries activity[10] (see Table 41-1). However, epidemiologic projections suggest that significant increases in the prevalence of root surface caries will be occurring in aging populations.[10]

Demographic studies have identified certain periodontal changes which occur in aging individuals. For example, older adults show an increase in dental plaque and calculus (calcified dental plaque), as well as an increase in the frequency of bleeding gingival tissues. Also, recession of the gingiva and loss of periodontal attachment are observed more often among older persons. As noted earlier, older adults have a greater probability of developing periodontal disease.[11] Currently it is believed that periodontal disease proceeds through a series of episodic attacks rather than occurring as a slowly progressing, continuous process.[12] It is not known whether older individuals are more susceptible to periodontal destruction than younger individuals. However, many systemic diseases and therapeutic regimens common to older individuals may adversely affect periodontal health.

For the older person with teeth, caries and periodontal disease are significant concerns and may be a source of pain and discomfort. The systemic health of an already compromised individual may be further threatened by bleeding and suppurating gingiva and coronal and cervical caries. With the loss of teeth, mastication, phonation, and deglutition may be perturbed. Also, social contact and nutritional status may be affected in the substantially edentulous aging individual.

Caries and periodontal disease require dental treatment. Regular dental care, including preventive dental procedures such as prophylaxis and fluoride applications, can help prevent tooth loss in the older individual.

Although evidence exists that older age groups in the United States have dramatically increased their utilization of dental services in the past 25 years (Table 41-1), more than 25 percent of individuals older than 65 have not seen a dental professional in the past 5 years.[2] It is likely that dental caries and periodontal disease will remain a substantial oral health concern for older individuals. Adequate oral health care for the elderly should include preventive dental treatment and increased availability and utilization of dental health services. In addition, elderly persons with teeth are four times more likely to visit a dentist than are those wearing complete dentures.[2] Persons with oral prostheses often experience multiple problems related to those appliances. They should be encouraged to have routine oral examinations and treatment necessary to maintain the prosthesis.

SALIVARY GLANDS

There are three major pairs of salivary glands (parotid, submandibular, sublingual) and several minor glands (e.g., labial, palatal, buccal) whose principal function is the exocrine production of saliva. Each gland type makes a unique secretion derived from either mucous or serous cell types, forming the fluid in the mouth termed *whole saliva*. Saliva includes many constituents which are critical to the maintenance of oral health (see Table 41-2). Saliva's most important functions are lubrication of the oral mucosa, promotion of remineralization of teeth, and protection against microbial infections. Although the role of saliva in digestion is limited, saliva helps prepare the food bolus for deglutition and is responsible for dissolving tastants and delivering them to taste buds.

TABLE 41-2
Major Roles of Saliva in the Maintenance of Oral Health

Lubrication of oral mucosa
Buffering acids produced by oral bacteria
Antibacterial and antifungal activities
Mechanical cleansing
Mediation of taste acuity
Remineralization of teeth

Until recently it was believed that a diminution of saliva production occurred with aging. However, recent studies have revealed that in healthy older adults there is no diminution in the volume of saliva produced.[13] Unstimulated and stimulated parotid fluid outputs among nonmedicated healthy adults of different ages are not different.[13] Similar investigations have been performed examining the fluid output from the submandibular and sublingual glands, but a consensus has not been reached. One report[14] suggested diminished submandibular/sublingual saliva production in older persons, while a more recent study[15] reported no age-related changes in this secretion among healthy nonmedicated adults. In the absence of complicating factors such as certain systemic diseases and medication use, it can be assumed that there is no generalized age-related perturbation in salivary fluid production. In addition, there appear to be no significant alterations in the composition of saliva in older persons.[16]

These physiological findings contrast with the morphological changes seen in aging salivary glands. Human parotid and submandibular glands lose approximately 20–30 percent of their parenchymal tissue over the adult life span.[17] The loss is primarily of acinar components, while proportional increases are seen in ductal cells and in fat, vascular, and connective tissues. Although it is known that acinar components are primarily responsible for the secretion of saliva,[18] it is not known why, in the presence of a significant reduction in the gland acinar volume, total fluid production does not diminish with increasing age. It has been suggested that salivary glands possess a functional reserve capacity,[15,19] enabling the glands to maintain fluid output throughout the human adult life span.

The clinician must recognize that generalized significant changes in salivary gland physiology do not occur normally with aging. Thus, one should not expect patient complaints, inferential of altered salivary gland function, to be a "normal" sequela of aging. Such complaints are indicative of disease or its treatment. Xerostomia, the subjective complaint of oral dryness, is a common condition linked with altered salivary gland performance. The most frequent cause of salivary gland dysfunction is iatrogenic. Many medications taken by older persons reduce or alter salivary gland performance.[20] These include anticholinergic, antihypertensive, antidepressant, diuretic, and antihistaminic preparations. Additionally, common forms of oncologic therapy, such as cytotoxic chemotherapy and radiation for head and neck neoplasms, can have direct and dramatic deleterious effects on salivary glands.

The single most common disease affecting salivary glands is Sjögren's syndrome, an autoimmune exocrinopathy predominantly occurring in postmenopausal women. In addition, although not frequently seen, many inflammatory and obstructive salivary gland disorders (e.g., bacterial infections, sialoliths, trauma, neoplasms) result in reduced gland function.

It is likely that a clinician often will encounter older patients with oral complaints related to salivary gland dysfunction. Regardless of the cause, any of the major oral physiological roles influenced by saliva (Table 41-2) may be adversely affected. With gland dysfunction, increased dental caries will ensue rapidly, accelerating the possibility of tooth loss. The oral mucosa can become dessicated and cracked, leaving the host more susceptible to microbial infection. Further, salivary gland dysfunction can lead to difficulty in swallowing or speaking at length, pain (which may arise from either the teeth or the oral soft tissues), and diminished food enjoyment.

SENSORY FUNCTION

There are many reports which suggest that food enjoyment, recognition, and taste decline as a function of age.[21,22] Similarly, a number of studies imply that elderly individuals manifest significant nutritional deficits.[23] Recently it has been suggested that there is a true anorexia (loss of appetite) associated with aging.[24] It is likely that this anorexia results from both behavioral and physiological factors.[25] Perturbations in taste and smell, or in other oral sensory modalities, may occur with age and reduce the rewards of eating,[25] thus contributing to a diminished interest in food in the elderly.

Taste receptors of the human gustatory system are distributed throughout the oropharynx and are innervated by three cranial nerves, VII, IX, and X.[26] Early reports indicated that the number of lingual taste buds declined with age, but recent studies, both in humans[27,28] and rodents,[29] do not support such a conclusion. The registration of a taste phenomenon is complicated, since, besides gustatory receptors, the olfactory apparatus and central integrative functions are involved. Clinically, the ability to taste is most often evaluated at two levels: (1) *threshold*, the most common measure, a "molecular level" event which reflects the lowest concentration of a tastant which an individual can recognize as being different than water; and (2) *suprathreshold*, a measure which is reflective of the ability to taste the intensity of substances at daily life, functional concentrations. Furthermore, other than detection, recognition, and intensity, the normal sensation of taste involves a hedonic component, i.e., the degree of pleasantness.

Many earlier reports on the higher frequency of taste complaints among older persons studied institutionalized persons rather than examining the healthy elderly.[1] Recent studies evaluating subjective reports of taste function among generally healthy community-dwelling persons showed only modest changes to occur with increased age (in approximately 10 percent of those studied). However, among elderly persons taking prescription medications, there was a significant increase (threefold) in the frequency of subjective complaints of taste dysfunction.[30]

Several recent, carefully controlled studies have objectively evaluated gustatory function in different aged, generally healthy persons. Most efforts have been directed at threshold measures,[31–33] including all four taste qualities (sweet, sour, salty, and bitter). In general, the decremental changes detected were modest and taste-quality specific. For example, the ability of older persons to detect salt decreased slightly with age, while no change in the detection threshold for sucrose (sweet) was noted. The importance of medication usage and place of residence in the evaluation of taste dysfunction was confirmed recently in threshold studies of institutionalized and noninstitutionalized elderly men by Spitzer.[33] Institutionalized men and men using more prescription mediations had significantly elevated taste thresholds.

However, threshold measures do not directly address the function of the gustatory apparatus in "normal" living (e.g., the level of sugar needed in a cup of coffee). Recently, several studies of suprathreshold gustatory function have been reported[23,34,35] which include evaluations of either the four basic taste qualities or a mixed protein hydrolysate. In general, the same conclusions drawn from threshold studies can be made: changes are specific to taste quality, with no general age-related deterioration in taste function. Other studies have evaluated the more complicated problems of flavor perception,[36] food recognition,[22] and preference.[37] Although results are not uniform, older individuals do relatively less well when performance is assessed in these tasks.[30] Murphy[38] has provided data to suggest that it is diminished olfactory performance which handicaps the assessment of complex stimuli (food analogues) by older individuals. There is considerable support for alterations in olfactory function becoming more prevalent with old age (see below).

A patient's oral hygiene and dental health may considerably influence taste judgments.[39] For example, inadequate removal of food particles could allow their breakdown or metabolic conversion by oral microorganisms to noxious, unpleasant substances. This may be exaggerated in patients with dental prostheses. Also, periodontal diseases can result in accumulations of putrified acidic materials which may leak into the oral cavity and alter taste sensation. Similarly, periapical dental infections, with subsequent fistula formation, may contribute continuous, low levels of purulent matter to the mouth.

Olfactory receptor neurons are quite different than taste receptors. There is little study of olfactory innervation with increased age in humans. Rodent studies suggest that olfactory receptor number increases approximately threefold from 2 to 18 months, remains constant until about 29 months, and thereafter decreases precipitously (approximately 50 percent) by 33 months.[40] The biological significance of such change has not been determined.[26]

A number of objective studies have examined olfactory function with increased age. These include studies of thresholds, suprathreshold intensity judgments, and odor recognition. In aggregate, the available data suggest that olfactory performance declines with increased age. For example, Murphy[37] studied the threshold, intensity, and pleasantness of menthol in a healthy, ambulatory group of young adult and elderly persons. She observed that for elderly persons the average threshold was higher, the ability to perceive suprathreshold intensity was blunted, and the judgment of pleasantness reduced when compared to younger subjects. Several studies have examined the effects of age on odor recognition, and all are in general agreement that elderly individuals show reduced ability to successfully accomplish these tasks (e.g., see Doty et al.[41]). Most older individuals showed a significant loss in ability to correctly identify the presented odors.

However, in the real world we typically do not taste a single tastant in aqueous form, nor do we consume foods which solely contain olfactory cues. While it is convenient and objective to use simple stimuli to assess chemosensory performance, foods are chemosensory mixtures, and the most relevant (yet most difficult to obtain) measures of gustatory and olfactory function will come from using complex food analogs. As noted earlier, several such studies have demonstrated the presence of age-related reductions in chemosensory performance.[22,36,38] In one study,[38] younger subjects were significantly better than older subjects at recognizing stimuli in blended food. However, when younger persons repeated the test with their airways occluded, their performances dropped to the level seen with elderly individuals. An obvious interpretation from this study is that the daily life chemosensory functions of older individuals are handicapped because of diminished olfactory performance. It has been suggested, in fact, by Schiffman and Warwick,[42] that the "anorexia of aging" for many persons can be reduced or reversed when flavor enhancers are added to foods.

Many other sensory cues (temperature, texture, etc.) participate in the experience of food enjoyment. However, there is little study of these oral sensory functions and their status with respect to age.

ORAL MUCOSA

The soft tissue lining of the mouth, the oral mucosa, may be characterized by three general tissue types: (1) well-keratinized tissue, with a dense connective tissue layer firmly attached to underlying bone (e.g., marginal gingiva, palatal mucosa); (2) slightly keratinized and freely moveable tissue (e.g., labial and buccal mucosa, floor of the mouth); and (3) specialized mucosa (e.g., dorsum of the tongue). The primary function of the oral mucosa is to act as a barrier to protect the underlying structures from desiccation, noxious chemicals, trauma, thermal stress, and infection. The oral mucosa plays a key role in the defense of the oral cavity. At present there are no commonly accepted, useful clinical tools for measuring the functional status of this mucosal barrier. Consequently, most available information is limited and is in the form of histologic evaluations without any direct functional correlates.

Aging has been frequently associated with changes in the oral mucosa that are similar to changes in the skin, with the epithelium becoming thinner and less hydrated and thus supposedly more susceptible to injury.[43] The reasons for such changes (if they are normally a sequela of aging) could be complex and may include alterations in protein synthesis, responsiveness to growth factors, and other regulatory mediators. Grossly, changes in the vascularity of oral mucosa (due to atherosclerosis) most likely contribute to an alteration in mucosal integrity because of reductions in cellular nutrient access and oxygenation. Mucosal, alveolar, and gingival arteries show the effects of arteriosclerosis, and clinically varicosities on the floor of the mouth and lateral and ventral surfaces of the tongue (comparable to varicosities on the lower extremities) are apparent in elderly patients.

The maintenance of mucosal integrity depends on the ability of the oral epithelium to respond to insult. Insults can be in the nature of physical compromise or chemical or microbiological threat. Many studies have documented that the immune system undergoes a marked decline with age, and it is likely that this decline extends to mucosal immunity.[44] Therefore, the oral mucosa may be more susceptible to the transmission of infectious diseases, as well as to delayed wound healing. Skin wounds in young and old subjects gain strength at a parallel rate, but in older individuals wounds cease to gain strength significantly earlier than in younger persons.[45] Similar findings have been reported in the healing of gingival tissues.[46] In particular, it is believed that cell renewal (i.e., mitotic rates) and the synthesis of proteins associated with keratinization of the mucosa occur at a slower rate in aging individuals, but normal tissue architecture and patterns of histodifferentiation, which are probably dependent upon complex interactions with the underlying connective tissue, do not display any changes with age.[47] It must be stressed that an adequate characterization of the status of the oral mucosa, particularly as regards cell proliferation and tissue renewal, does not exist.[48]

Alterations in the oral mucosa of edentulous older persons are likely elicited and/or exacerbated by the presence of removable dental prostheses. The denture-bearing mucosa of aged maxillary and mandibular ridges show significant morphological changes.[49,50] Ill-fitting dentures can produce mechanical trauma to the oral tissues, as well as cause mucosal hyperplasia. Oral candidiasis frequently is found on denture-bearing areas in the edentulous individual, often occurring with angular cheilitis (deep fissuring and ulceration of the epithelium at the commissures of the mouth).

Oral mucosal alterations in the older person are often a result of both local factors (dental state, condition of dentures, consumption of tobacco, secretion of saliva) and systemic disease.[51] Long-term utilization of antibiotics will frequently result in oral candidal infections, while drugs with xerostomic side effects (see above) will likewise increase the potential for mucosal injury. Most concerns about oral mucosal disease in older persons are similar to those for younger adults, and the reader is referred to a comprehensive text dealing with these problems.[52]

Oral cancers comprise approximately 5 percent of all malignancies, and about 95 percent of all oral cancers occur in persons over 40 years of age. The average age at the time of diagnosis is about 60. Males are more than twice as likely to develop oral cancer than females.[53] Neoplasms may arise in all oral soft and hard tissues, oropharyngeal, and salivary gland regions. The clinical appearance of an oral carcinoma is quite diverse (ulcerative, erythematous, leukoplakic, papillary) and may be innocuous as well as asymptomatic.[54] If a patient presents with an unusual and suspicious lesion with no readily apparent cause (such as with a denture sore), the patient should be referred to a specialist more familiar with the appearance of the oral mucosa. Carcinoma should be considered as part of a differential diagnosis with any oral lesion.

MOTOR FUNCTION

The oral motor apparatus is involved in several routine yet intricate functions (speech, posture, mastication, and swallowing). Regulation of these activities may occur at three levels: the local neuromuscular unit, central neuronal pathways, and systemic influences. In general, aging is associated with changes in neuromuscular systems.[55,56] Recent animal studies by McCarter and McGee[57] strongly suggest it is unlikely that age-associated deficiencies in motor function are related to the composition and contractile function of skeletal muscles (the lateral omohyoid and soleus were studied). Rather, such changes are probably related to other factors, e.g., neuromuscular transmission or propagation of nerve impulses.

Studies of oral motor function have shown that some alterations in performance (mastication, swallowing, oral muscular posture, and tone) can be expected with increased age.[58-60] The changes appear to be more common among predominantly edentulous persons than among those with a natural dentition. The most frequently reported oral motor disturbance in the elderly is related to altered mastication.[58] Utilizing an objective method of measuring food particle size, Feldman and colleagues have demonstrated that even fully dentate older persons are less able to adequately prepare food for swallowing than are younger individuals.[58] Similar findings are suggested by the work of Heath.[61] Feldman et al.[58] also reported that older persons tend to swallow larger-sized food particles than do younger adults. This suggests that there is a diminution in masticatory efficiency, which can be further exacerbated among individuals with a compromised dentition.

Following mastication, a food bolus is translocated to the pharynx. This phase of swallowing (the oral phase) requires well-coordinated neuromuscular processing, an intact mucosal barrier, and adequate saliva production. Alterations in any of these components can disturb the oral phase.[62,63] Ultrasonic imaging provides a convenient way to visualize this swallowing phase. In healthy young adults the oral phase takes about 1.5–2.0 seconds with only the endogenous salivary secretions in the mouth (so-called dry swallow). When a 5-ml water bolus is present (i.e., wet swallow), the total time for the oral phase is reduced to about 1.0–1.5 seconds. In older persons, the duration of the oral phase of both dry and wet swallows is significantly increased (taking 50 to 100 percent longer).[60] While these changes are statistically significant, patients with frank neuropathy may display oral swallow times that are 4 to 6 times longer and may not even be able to produce the recognizable characteristics of an oral swallow. It seems, then, that during normal aging, subclinical oral neuromotor changes occur in the swallowing mechanism. By themselves these changes may not be of biological significance; however, when viewed in the context of the findings of Feldman et al.,[58] under unusual or stressful conditions these perturbations may place the older person (especially the person with dentures) at some risk to choking or aspiration. Individuals with a suggestive history of these possible problems should be counseled by the clinician or referred for rehabilitative therapy.

The temporomandibular joint (TMJ) is located between the glenoid fossa and the condylar process of the mandible. The TMJ exhibits a functionally unique gliding and hinge-like movement. It is of particular interest to clinicians, for it is the focus of a variety of craniofacial pain disorders. Using radiographic and postmortem evaluations, several investigators have reported that various components of this joint undergo degenerative alterations with increased age.[64] Recent work, however, does not confirm TMJ functional impairment as a normal age-associated event.[65] In general, two types of pathology are associated with the TMJ: *articular* (related to the joint itself) and *nonarticular* (pathology occurring in structures unrelated to the joint but causing similar or referred symptomatology).[66] Many types of articular abnormalities common to all joints affect the TMJ, including trauma, ankylosis, dislocation, and arthritis. Nonarticular disorders may result from a variety of clinical entities, including trigeminal neuralgia, dental pulpitis, and otitis. The most common nonarticular disorder is the myofascial pain dysfunction (MPD) syndrome. Generally, most MPD cases are felt to be psychophysiological and are associated with jaw-clenching or tooth-grinding habits related to stress. Such actions can result in muscle fatigue and subsequent spasm.

Several studies have evaluated aspects of speech production in the elderly and reported characteristic changes that increase with age.[67,68] These include statistically significant alterations in such activities as tongue shape and function during specific phoneme production[67] and frequency variability.[68] However, among healthy older persons these changes do not compromise or alter speech in any perceptible way.[67] There are also age-associated alterations in intraoral and maxillofacial posture. Drooping of the lower face and lips in the elderly results not only from the loss of supporting hard tissues but also from a diminished tone of the circumoral muscles.[59] These latter changes may elicit aesthetic concerns and can often lead to embarrassment from drooling or food spills due to the inability of the older individual to competently close the lips while eating or speaking. Often, the drooling caused by reduced circumoral muscle tone can result in complaints of excess salivation by an elderly person.

In addition, it should be recognized that significant oral motor disorders may result from a number of therapeutic drug regimens, e.g., there is a frequent association of tardive dyskinesias with phenothiazine therapy. Such dyskinesias may include diminished performance and speech pathoses, as well as frank alteration in movement (chorea, athetosis).

REFERENCES

1. Baum BJ: Research on aging and oral health: An assessment of current status and future needs. *Spec Care Dent* 1:156, 1981.
2. Miller et al: The National Survey of Oral Health in U.S. Adults: 1985–1986. Washington, Government Printing Office, DHHS (NIH) 87-2868, 1987.
3. Shaw JH: Causes and control of dental caries. *N Engl J Med* 317:996, 1987.
4. Seichter U: Root surface caries: A critical literature review. *J Am Dent Assoc* 115:305, 1987.
5. Menaker L: *The Biological Basis of Dental Caries.* Hagerstown, MD, Harper & Row, 1980.

6. Holm-Pedersen P et al: Composition and metabolic activity of dental plaque from healthy young and elderly individuals. *J Dent Res* 59:77, 1980.

7. Listgarten M: Nature of periodontal diseases: Pathogenic mechanisms. *J Periodont Res* 22:172, 1987.

8. Katz RV et al: Prevalence and intraoral distribution of root caries in an adult population. *Caries Res* 16:265, 1982.

9. Ship JA, Ship II: Trends in oral health in the aging population. *Dent Clin North Am* 33:33, 1989.

10. Banting DW: Dental caries in the elderly. *Gerodontology* 3:55, 1984.

11. Douglass C et al: The potential for increase in the periodontal diseases of the aged populations. *J Periodontal* 54:721, 1983.

12. Haffajee AD, Socransky SS: Attachment level changes in destructive periodontal diseases. *J Clin Periodontal* 13:461, 1986.

13. Baum BJ: Salivary gland function during aging. *Gerodontics* 2:61,1986.

14. Pedersen W et al: Age-dependent decreases in human submandibular gland flow rates as measured under resting and poststimulation conditions. *J Dent Res* 64:822, 1985.

15. Tylenda CA et al: Evaluation of submandibular salivary flow rate in different age groups. *J Dent Res* 67:1225, 1988.

16. Baum BJ: Saliva secretion and composition, in Ferguson DB (ed): *The Aging Mouth.* Basel, Karger, 1987, p 126.

17. Scott J: Structural age changes in salivary glands, in Ferguson DB (ed): *The Aging Mouth.* Basel, Karger, 1987, p 40.

18. Young JA, van Lennep EW: Transport in salivary and salt glands, in Giebisch G et al (eds): *Membrane Transport in Biology.* Berlin, Springer-Verlag, 1979, p 563.

19. Scott J: Structure and function in aging human salivary glands. *Gerodontology* 5:149, 1986.

20. Sreebny LM, Schwartz SS: A reference guide to drugs and dry mouth. *Gerodontology* 5:75, 1986.

21. Cohen T, Gitman L: Oral complaints and taste perception in the aged. *J Gerontol* 14:294, 1959.

22. Schiffman SS: Food recognition in the elderly. *J Gerontol* 32:586, 1977.

23. Murphy C, Withee J: Age and biochemical status predict preference for casein hydrolysate. *J Gerontol* 42:73, 1987.

24. Morley JE, Silver AJ: Anorexia in the elderly. *Neurobiol Aging* 9:9, 1988.

25. Shock NW: Commentary on anorexia in the elderly. *Neurobiol Aging* 9:17, 1988.

26. Mistretta CM: Aging effects on anatomy and neurophysiology of taste and smell. *Gerodontology* 3:131, 1984.

27. Arvidson K: Human taste: Response and taste bud number in fungiform papillae. *Science* 209:807, 1980.

28. Miller IJ Jr: Human taste bud density across adult age groups. *J Gerontol* 43:B26, 1988.

29. Mistretta CM, Baum BJ: Quantitative study of taste buds in fungiform and circumvallate papillae of young and aged rats. *J Anat* 138:323, 1984.

30. Weiffenbach JW: Taste and smell perception. *Gerodontology* 3:137, 1984.

31. Grzegorcyk PB et al: Age-related differences in salt taste acuity. *J Gerontol* 34:834, 1979.

32. Weiffenbach JM et al: Taste thresholds: Quality specific variation with human aging. *J Gerontol* 37:372, 1982.

33. Spitzer ME: Taste acuity in institutionalized and noninstitutionalized elderly men. *J Gerontol* 43:P71, 1988.

34. Bartoshuk LM et al: Taste and aging. *J Gerontol* 41:51, 1986.

35. Weiffenbach JM et al: Taste intensity perception in aging. *J Gerontol* 41:460, 1986.

36. Steven DA, Lawless HT: Age-related changes in flavor perception. *Appetite* 2:127, 1981.

37. Murphy C: Age-related effects on the threshold, psychophysical function and pleasantness of menthol. *J Gerontol* 38:217, 1983.

38. Murphy C: Taste and smell in the elderly, in Meiselman HL, Rivlin RS (eds): *Clinical Measurements of Taste and Smell.* New York, Macmillan, 1986, p 343.

39. Langan MJ, Yearick ES: The effects of improved oral hygiene on taste perception and nutrition of the elderly. *J Gerontol* 31:413, 1976.

40. Hinds JW, McNelly NA: Aging in the rat olfactory system: Correlation of changes in the olfactory epithelium and olfactory bulb. *J Comp Neurol* 203:441, 1981.

41. Doty RL et al: Development of the University of Pennsylvania Smell Identification Test: A standardized microencapsulated test of olfactory function. *Physiol Behav* 32:489, 1984.

42. Schiffman SS, Warwick ZS: Flavor enhancement of foods for the elderly can reverse anorexia. *Neurobiol Aging* 9:24, 1988.

43. Miles AEW: Sans teeth: Changes in oral tissues with advancing age. *Proc R Soc Med* 65:801, 1972.

44. Schmucker DL, Daniels CK: Aging, gastrointestinal infections, and mucosal immunity. *J Am Geriatr Soc* 34:377, 1986.

45. Goodson WH, Hunt TK: Wound healing and aging. *J Invest Dermatol* 73:88, 1979.

46. Holm-Pedersen P, Loe H: Wound healing in the gingiva of young and old individuals. *Scand J Dent Res* 79:40, 1971.

47. Mackenzie IC, Hill MW: Connective tissue influences on patterns of epithelial architecture and keratinization in skin and oral mucosa of mouse. *Cell Tissue Res* 235:551, 1984.

48. Hill MW: The influence of aging on skin and oral mucosa. *Gerodontology* 3:35, 1984.

49. Nedelman CI, Bernick S: The significance of age changes in human alveolar mucosa and bone. *J Prosthet Dent* 39:495, 1978.

50. Watson IB, MacDonald DG: Oral mucosa and complete dentures. *J Prosthet Dent* 47:133, 1982.

51. Osterberg T et al: The condition of the oral mucosa at age 70: A population study. *Gerodontology* 4:71, 1985.

52. McCarthy PL, Shklar G: *Diseases of the Oral Mucosa.* Philadelphia, Lea and Febiger, 1980.

53. National Cancer Institute Monograph 57: Surveillance, epidemiology, and end results: Incidence and mortality data, 1973–1977. Washington, Government Printing Office, DHEW (NIH) 81-2330, 1981.

54. Silverman S: *Oral Cancer.* New York, American Cancer Society, 1985.

55. McCarter R: Effects of age on the contraction of mammalian skeletal muscle, in Kaldor G, DiBattista WJ (eds): *Aging in Muscles.* New York, Raven Press, 1978, p 1.

56. Pradhan SN: Central neurotransmitters and aging. *Life Sci* 26:1643, 1980.

57. McCarter R, McGee J: Influence of nutrition and aging

on the composition and function of rat skeletal muscle. *J Gerontol* 42:432, 1987.

58. Feldman RS et al: Aging and mastication: Changes in performance and in the swallowing threshold with natural dentition. *J Am Geriatr Soc* 28:97, 1980.

59. Baum BJ, Bodner L: Aging and oral motor function: Evidence for altered performance among older persons. *J Dent Res* 62:2, 1983.

60. Sonies BC et al: Durational aspects of the oral-pharyngeal phase of swallow in normal adults. *Dysphagia* 3:1, 1988.

61. Heath MR: The effect of maximum biting force and bone loss upon masticatory function and dietary selection of the elderly. *Int Dent J* 32:345, 1982.

62. Sonies BC et al: Speech and swallowing in the elderly. *Gerodontology* 3:115, 1984.

63. Hughes CV et al: Oral-pharyngeal dysphagia: A common sequela of salivary gland dysfunction. *Dysphagia* 1:173, 1987.

64. Tonna EA: Aging of skeletal-dental systems and supporting tissues, in Finch CE, Hayflick L (eds): *Handbook of the Biology of Aging*. New York, Van Nostrand Reinhold, 1977, p 470.

65. Heft MW: Prevalence of TMJ signs and symptoms in the elderly. *Gerodontology* 3:125, 1984.

66. Laskin DM: Dental and oral disorders, in Berkow R (ed): *The Merck Manual*. Rahway, NJ, Merck, 1977, p 1654.

67. Sonies BC et al: Tongue motion in elderly adults: Initial in situ observations. *J Gerontol* 39:279, 1984.

68. Benjamin BJ: Frequency variability in the aged voice. *J Gerontol* 36:722, 1981.

Chapter 42

THE EYE

Einar Stefánsson

Good eyesight is important to the quality of life at any age. Eye disease and blindness are more frequent with advancing age. Many eye diseases have no early symptoms. For example a patient with glaucoma may be unaware of the disease and of the gradual loss of vision. Regular eye examinations by an ophthalmologist are an essential part of the health care of any elderly individual.

ROUTINE EYE EXAMINATION

A routine ophthalmologic examination consists of the patient's history, an assessment of visual function, and physical examination of the eye and adnexa.

HISTORY

Important symptoms of eye disease include: Change in visual acuity or visual fields, distortion of images; pain in or around the eye or sensitivity to light; an abnormal appearance of the eye or eyelids; increased or decreased tear flow; and double vision (diplopia).

Sudden loss of vision is generally associated with acute and sometimes emergent eye diseases, such as a rhegmatogenous retinal detachment or ischemic optic neuropathy, and requires immediate attention. On the other hand a gradual decline in vision over several months or years is more likely to be due to a slowly progressive disorder such as a cataract. Distortion (metamorphopsia) in the central visual field is a common first symptom of age-related macular degeneration. Elderly patients who make this complaint need immediate attention for the suspected disease process. Transient visual loss (amaurosis fugax) results from a temporary occlusion of the central retinal artery usually by embolism. Visual field defects can be caused by a variety of eye and central nervous system diseases. Floaters (spots) before the eyes are usually caused by benign vitreous opacities or by the blood corpuscles in the retinal capil-

laries (entoptic phenomenon). A sudden increase in floaters or a shower of floaters, especially if associated with the perception of light flashes (photopsia), may accompany a posterior vitreous detachment, and the patient should be examined to rule out retinal breaks.

Patients frequently associate headaches with their eyes, but eye diseases are infrequently the cause of headaches. Severe eye pain can accompany acute closed-angle glaucoma. Eye pain and photophobia (sensitivity to light) are symptoms of intraocular inflammation, for example, iritis. Headache and loss of vision can be caused by temporal arteritis. Foreign body sensation in the eye is usually caused by corneal disorders such as corneal abrasions, foreign bodies, and keratitis. Dry eyes are a common cause of burning and itching as is conjunctivitis and other infections of the eye surface and lids.

True diplopia (double vision) disappears if one eye is covered. It results from misalignment of the eyes, commonly caused by disorders affecting the cranial nerves or the central nervous system.

EYE EXAMINATION BY THE GENERAL PHYSICIAN

Eye examination begins with the visual acuity determination which can be done with a Snellen chart at 20 feet and with a near reading chart. Each eye is tested separately with and without the patient's glasses. If the patient cannot see the Snellen chart at 20 feet, she or he is moved closer to the chart. If the letters cannot be seen at all, the ability to count fingers or to see hand movement or light is tested. The peripheral visual field can be estimated by having the patient fixate on the examiner's nose and asking the patient to count fingers in each quadrant of the visual field. The Amsler grid tests the central visual field especially for distortion and field defects and is especially useful in age-related macular degeneration.

The physical examination of the eye should be done

in good light and is aided by a hand light. The eyelids, conjunctiva, and cornea are examined for foreign bodies, inflammation, and defects. However, the eye can be fully examined only with the aid of the slit-lamp microscope. The pupil should be inspected for size and shape, color, and reaction to light. Normal pupils are round and dark; they react equally to light. Unequal pupils can be a normal variant (essential anisocoria) or caused by a variety of diseases in the eye and central nervous system as well as drugs.

Measurement of intraocular tension is commonly performed by applanation tonometry or pneumotonometry by the ophthalmologist but is most easily performed with Shiotz indentation tonometry by the general practitioner. The cornea is numbed with a drop of anesthetic (for example, proparacaine 0.5%), and the tonometer is placed vertically on the cornea of the supine patient. The reading on the tonometer scale is converted into millimeters of mercury (mmHg) with a conversion table.

Direct ophthalmoscopy is an essential part of any general physical examination. The physician examines the optic nerve, retinal vessels, macula, and the posterior part of the eye for signs of ocular or systemic disease.

ANATOMY AND PHYSIOLOGY OF THE EYE

The eye is a roughly spherical organ, about an inch in diameter, surrounded by fat and connective tissue in the orbit. Four recti and two oblique muscles are attached to the eye, and these are innervated by the oculomotor, trochlear, and abducens nerves (cranial nerves III, IV, and VI). The ophthalmic branch of the trigeminal nerve (cranial nerve V) supplies the sensory innervation for the eye. The optic nerve (cranial nerve II) carries the ganglion cell axons from the retina to the rest of the brain. The eye wall consists of the sclera and cornea on the outside followed by the uvea (iris, ciliary body, and choroid) with the retina forming the innermost layer in the posterior segment of the eye. The inside of the eye consists of transparent avascular tissues. The anterior and posterior chambers of the eye are filled with the aqeous humor which is formed in the ciliary processes and flows through the posterior chamber and the pupil into the anterior chamber and out through the angle of Schlemm. The crystalline lens separates the posterior chamber from the vitreous humor which fills the vitreous cavity in the back of the eye. The retina contains the rod and cone photoreceptors and bipolar, amacrine, horizontal, glial, and ganglion cells, whose axons form the optic nerve. The retina receives nutrition from the retinal circulation supplied by the central retinal artery and vein and from the underlying choroidal circulation.

EYE DISEASES IN THE ELDERLY

EYELIDS

Eyelid disease ranges from abnormal position and movement to infection and tumors.

In entropion the eyelid margin is turned inward, and the eyelashes can irritate the cornea and conjunctiva causing irritation, epithelial defects, and secondary infection (Fig. 42-1). The cornea must be protected from constant irritation by the eyelashes, and frequently a surgical procedure is necessary to rotate the eyelid margin outward. Pulling the skin of the lower lid down with an adhesive tape strip may give temporary relief.

In ectropion the eyelid is turned away from the eye, resulting in exposure of the conjunctiva and cornea with damage to the corneal epithelium due to excessive drying (Fig. 42-2). Atonic ectropion is seen following facial nerve paralysis. Cicatricial ectropion occurs with contraction of the skin following injury and usually requires surgical correction.

Blepharoptosis can result from disorders involving the levator palpebrae, including myasthenia gravis. Acquired blepharoptosis in elderly people frequently results from dehiscence in the aponeurosis of the levator palpebrae superior muscle (Fig. 42-3). If the eyelid is covering the visual axis or is cosmetically unacceptable to the patient, the condition can be corrected surgically.

Lagophthalmos is the condition in which the patient is unable to close the eyelids, and exposure of the cornea and conjunctiva results. This can result from facial nerve paralysis, proptosis, and other disorders. Damage from exposure of the cornea must be prevented with lubrication and/or surgery.

Blepharospasm is an involuntary tonic and, usually, bilateral contraction of the orbicularis oculi muscle that

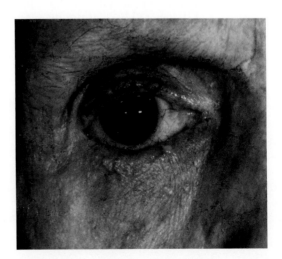

FIGURE 42-1
Spastic entropion. The lower eyelid margin is turned inward, and the eyelashes rub against the eye. (*Courtesy of J. Dutton, M.D.*)

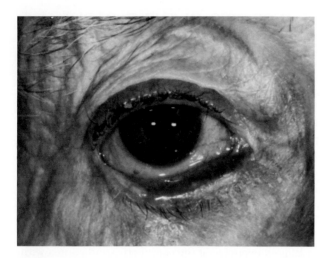

FIGURE 42-2
Ectropion. The lower lid is turned away from the eye. The conjunctiva and cornea are exposed. (*Courtesy of J. Dutton, M.D.*)

can last for seconds to several minutes and can be disabling to the patient. It may involve other muscles of the face.

In blepharochalasis, atrophy and loss of elasticity in the skin of the eyelid causes wrinkles and skin folds; this is a cosmetic problem that is only rarely functional in nature.

In trichiasis the eyelashes are directed toward the globe and irritate the cornea and conjunctiva, causing epithelial erosions and secondary infections. Treatment is surgical and includes removal of eyelashes.

Blepharitis is a chronic inflammation in the eyelid margins. It frequently has a chronic recurrent course with occasional episodes of blepharoconjunctivitis, sometimes complicated by chalazia. The treatment consists of cleaning the eyelid margins with warm water, sometimes with mild baby shampoo. Antibiotics are reserved for treatment of the acute phase of the disease.

A chalazion is a chronic inflammatory lipogranuloma of a meibomian gland. It is usually a painless lump in the eyelid (Fig. 42-4). It often disappears spontaneously but sometimes has to be treated surgically. A meibomian gland carcinoma can be mistaken for a chalazion and should be considered if a chalazion recurs.

Hordeolum (stye) is an acute suppurative inflammation in an eyelash follicle or gland. They tend to be red, painful, and swollen. Hot compresses and topical antibiotics are used to treat hordeola.

Basal cell carcinoma is the most common malignant neoplastic tumor of the skin of the eyelids. It tends to have a nodular appearance sometimes with ulceration centrally (Fig. 42-5). Basal cell carcinomas usually grow slowly. Skin lesions suspected of being basal cell carcinomas should be biopsied or preferably excised for histological examination. Large tumors may need extensive oculoplastic surgery for removal and reconstruction.

Squamous cell carcinoma is less common than basal cell carcinoma but may have a similar appearance (Fig. 42-6). Biopsy and excision are indicated when squamous cell carcinoma is suspected.

THE CONJUNCTIVA

The conjunctiva is a thin mucous membrane that covers the posterior surface of the eyelids and the white part of the eye. Common diseases of the conjunctiva include infections from bacteria, viruses, and chlamydia as well as allergic conjunctivitis. Benign growth of fibrovascular tissue is common, and malignant tumors are less common.

Conjunctivitis can be caused by a variety of infectious and noninfectious agents such as bacteria, viruses, fungi, toxins, and irritating chemicals. The patient presents with red eyes, irritation, and tearing or exudation that may be purulent. Vision is usually not impaired. Infectious and allergic conjunctivitis tends to be bilateral. The diagnosis is based on history and clinical examination, with attention to the conjunctival inflammation and exudation, as well as to the eyelids and lacrimal sys-

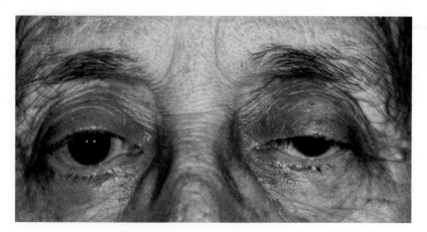

FIGURE 42-3
Blepharoptosis resulting from levator palpebrae aponeurosis dehiscence. (*Courtesy of J. Dutton, M.D.*)

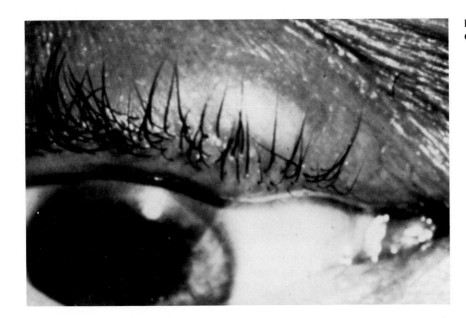

FIGURE 42-4
Chalazion. (*Courtesy of J. Dutton, M.D.*)

tem. Gram's stain and culture of conjunctival exudate can help identify the cause.

Bacterial conjunctivitis is frequently caused by staphylococci, streptococci, or gram-negative bacteria. The patient may complain of difficulty in opening the eyelids in the morning because of dried pus on the eyelashes. While most forms of bacterial conjunctivitis are self-limited, topical antibiotics are helpful. Conjunctivitis caused by *Neisseria gonorrhoeae* produces a copious purulent exudate. This acute conjunctivitis is diagnosed by Gram's stain and culture and is treated with systemic as well as topical antibiotics.

Trachoma and inclusion conjunctivitis is caused by the *Chlamydia trachomatis*. Chlamydia eye infection in adults is frequently associated with a chlamydial genital infection. Trachoma is a chronic bilateral cicatricial conjunctivitis, which is a very common cause of blindness in the world, especially in developing countries. Chlamydia can be treated with sulfonamides, tetracycline or erythromycin administered systemically.

Viral conjunctivitis is sometimes associated with other viral infections such as pharyngitis. Some viruses cause infection of the cornea and the conjunctiva simultaneously. The viral forms of conjunctivitis are usually bilateral with red eyes, but with less exudation than the bacterial conjunctividities. Most are self-limiting.

Allergic conjunctivitis can arise from a multitude of

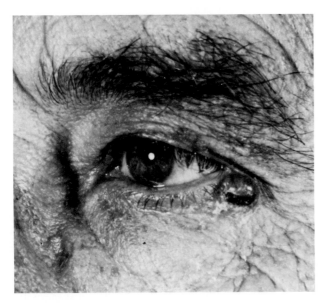

FIGURE 42-5
Basal cell carcinoma of the lower eyelid.

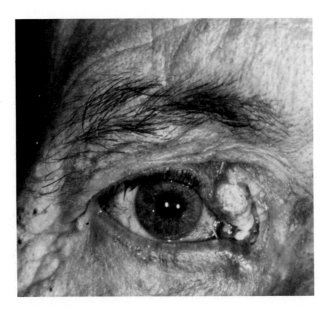

FIGURE 42-6
Squamous cell carcinoma involving the inner canthus and upper eyelid. (*Courtesy of J. Dutton, M.D.*)

allergens and is frequently accompanied by hay fever or other allergic disorders. The symptoms include itching with swollen conjunctiva and clear secretions.

Pterygium is a wing-shaped benign fibrovascular tissue that grows onto the cornea, usually from the nasal conjunctiva. If it covers the visual axle, it may be removed surgically. Carcinoma of the conjunctiva is less common and includes squamous cell carcinoma and melanoma.

THE CORNEA

The cornea is an avascular, transparent tissue consisting of an epithelium which is lubricated by the tears, stroma, and endothelium. Since light must pass through the transparent cornea, diseases that reduce the corneal transparency will reduce visual acuity. The cornea is very sensitive to defects and foreign bodies in the epithelium, which produce a foreign-body sensation or severe pain with lacrimation. While the cornea can only be fully examined with the slit-lamp microscope, a penlight and magnifying lens can be used as well. Fluorescein sodium can be used to ease the diagnoses of epithelial defects.

Corneal ulcers can be caused by bacteria and fungi. Whitish infiltration of the epithelium and stroma is usually accompanied by foreign-body sensation and an inflamed red eye. Early diagnosis with Gram's stain and culture of scrapings from the corneal ulcer is essential, and the patient suspected of having a corneal ulcer should be referred immediately to an ophthalmologist. Common pathogens include staphylococci, streptococci, pseudomonas, and other gram-negative bacteria. Fungal corneal ulcers are less common. Treatment is initiated after diagnostic tests have been initiated and include topical, subconjunctival, and sometimes systemic antibiotics.

Herpes keratitis is usually unilateral and may be recurrent. The patient complains of foreign-body sensation, lacrimation, and reduced visual acuity if the central cornea is involved. Examination reveals a dendritic lesion in the epithelium endothelium, which is best seen with fluorescein staining and a blue light. Treatment is usually with topical antiviral agents (idoxuridine, vidarabine, acyclovir, or trifluorothymidine). Corticosteroids can exacerbate herpes keratitis, and indiscriminatory use of corticosteroids containing eye drops should be avoided.

Corneal abrasions are often caused by an accidental scratch of the eye. The epithelial defect stains with fluorescein sodium and is best seen in blue light. Treatment is with an antibiotic ointment and a tight eye patch. The patient should be observed until the epithelium heals.

Corneal edema is sometimes caused by an endothelial dystrophy or by loss of endothelium following cataract surgery. Corneal edema reduces visual acuity and may necessitate a penetrating keratoplasty for visual rehabilitation.

THE LACRIMAL APPARATUS

Dry eyes and decreased tear secretion is common in the elderly. The patient may complain of irritated, burning eyes sometimes with foreign-body sensation. Examination may reveal punctate epithelial erosions of the conjunctiva and cornea that may stain with fluorescein or with rose bengal stain. Tear secretion is reduced and may be measured with a filter paper (Schirmer). Treatment of dry eyes is primarily with artificial tear drops and ointments, which may be used as frequently as needed to provide relief.

Acute dacryocystitis is an infection of the lacrimal sac which presents with redness, tenderness, and swelling adjacent to the inner canthus of the eye. Treatment is by systemic antibiotics.

The lacrimal gland may harbor benign as well as malignant tumors. Benign mixed tumor and benign lymphoid hyperplasia are the most common benign tumors, whereas adenoid cystic carcinoma is the most common malignant tumor. A lacrimal gland tumor may cause a fullness of the outer portion of the upper eyelid or may displace the eye downward. Treatment is by surgical excision.

CATARACT

A cataract is an opacity in the crystalline lens. Cataracts are very common in elderly people. In one population study, 15 percent of people, 52 to 85 years of age had cataracts resulting in visual acuity of 20/30 or less. Cataracts cause a gradual decrease in vision which is not accompanied by pain or inflammation. Glare, for example from car headlights, is a common complaint of cataract patients. Nuclear cataracts can induce myopia that sometimes allows elderly people to once again read without their reading glasses. Examination of the lens is best done with the slit-lamp microscope and dilated pupil. It is difficult to see mild cataracts with a penlight illumination, but moderate or severe cataracts may show as yellow, brown, or whitish opacities in the lens.

If the cataract causes significant visual impairment, the lens can be surgically removed and, in some cases, replaced with a plastic lens implant. In most cases cataract surgery is elective and should only be performed if the patient's visual handicap justifies surgery. Cataract extraction is a very common intraocular surgical procedure and has a high rate of success. In most cases the optical effect of the crystalline lens is replaced with a plastic lens implant which is permanently placed inside the eye. The optical power of the crystalline lens can also be replaced with a contact lens, glasses, or keratorefractive surgery.

GLAUCOMA

Glaucoma involves increased intraocular pressure, optic nerve atrophy with cupping of the optic disk (Fig. 42-7), and characteristic visual field defects (Fig. 42-8). Primary open-angle glaucoma is by far the most common type of glaucoma. Other types include primary angle-closure glaucoma, a variety of secondary glaucomas resulting from inflammation, trauma, corticosteroids, or iris neovascularization, and congenital glaucomas.

Open-angle glaucoma is usually asymptomatic in the beginning. The patient is unaware of the elevated intraocular pressure, gradual loss of visual field, and optic nerve cupping. Measurement of intraocular pressure and ophthalmoscopic examination of the optic nerve head should be done regularly in elderly individuals. While most ophthalmologists use applanation tonometry to measure the intraocular pressure, the Schiotz indentation tonometer is less expensive and easier to use for the general practitioner. A drop of anesthetic (proparacaine 0.5%) is placed in the eye of the supine patient and the tonometer placed vertically on the cornea. Pressure above 21 mmHg is considered abnormally high.

The optic disk should be examined with the ophthalmoscope, paying attention to the size of the optic cup and the shape of the optic nerve rim. A difference in the optic disk cup between fellow eyes may suggest early

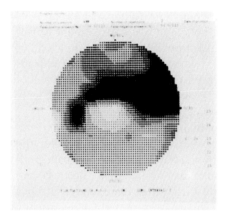

FIGURE 42-8
Arcuate visual field defect in glaucoma. (*Courtesy of M.B. Shields, M.D.*)

glaucomatous change. Visual field defects in glaucoma are subtle in the beginning, and careful visual field testing is needed to diagnose any change. Confrontation visual fields testing is unreliable for early glaucoma.

Chronic open-angle glaucoma is usually treated medically with eye drops such as pilocarpine, beta blockers (timolol), epinephrine, and related drugs (dipivefrin). Carbonic anhydrase inhibitors (acetazolamide) may be administered systemically. If medical treatment fails to control the glaucoma, laser trabeculoplasty or surgical filtering procedures may be needed. Chronic open-angle glaucoma is usually diagnosed in the latter part of life and usually must be treated for life.

In primary angle-closure glaucoma, the iris and lens move forward to close the angle of Schlemm and trabecular meshwork. This results in an acute rise in intraocular pressure with severe pain, a semidilated pupil, steamy cornea, and markedly reduced vision. Angle-closure glaucoma is a sight-threatening emergency. Treatment includes laser iridotomy as well as medication to lower intraocular pressure. Angle closure can also be secondary to a variety of eye diseases. Neovascular glaucoma may occur following central retinal vein occlusion or diabetic retinopathy, or may occur in a patient with carotid artery stenosis.

THE UVEA

The uvea consists of the iris, ciliary body, and the choroid. Uveal diseases include inflammatory and neoplastic disorders.

Acute anterior uveitis (iritis) is associated with severe pain and sensitivity to light, reduced vision, deposits on the endothelial surface of the cornea, and inflammatory cells in the aqueous humor. Iris nodules may be seen as well. Anterior uveitis is frequently idiopathic, but can also be related to other inflammatory diseases

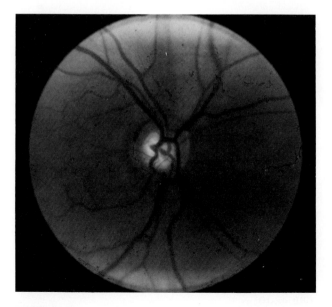

FIGURE 42-7
Optic nerve head with a moderate cup resulting from glaucomatous optic nerve atrophy. (*Courtesy of M.B. Shields, M.D.*)

such as ankylosing spondylitis, Reiter's syndrome, regional enteritis, and Behçet's disease. Treatment is usually with topical corticosteroid drops (subconjunctival or systemic steroids in severe cases) and mydriatric drops (atropine sulfate 1%). Posterior uveitis affecting the choroid and retina may result in decreased vision with little or no pain.

Bacterial endophthalmitis may occur after penetrating ocular trauma or eye surgery, if bacteria enter the eye. This condition is associated with intense pain, redness of the eye, and reduction in vision. Bacterial endopthalmitis is a sight-threatening emergency. Vitreous and aqueous humor should be aspirated for microscopy examination and culture, and treatment is initiated as soon as possible with intraocular, topical, and systemic antibiotics.

Malignant melanoma is the most common primary intraocular tumor (Fig. 42-9). It usually involves the choroid and may also involve the ciliary body or iris. The first symptoms may be metamorphopsia resulting from the serous retinal detachment over the tumor. Ophthalmoscopy reveals a grayish-brown mass elevating the retina. Frequently, a serous detachment of the retina is seen surrounding the tumor. Ultrasound examination may aid in the diagnosis. Treatment is enucleation, radiation, or in some cases photocoagulation. Metastatic carcinoma is another common cause of choroidal tumors.

THE RETINA

The retina lines the inside of the eye posteriorly. The rod and cone photoreceptors form the outer border of the retina adjacent to the retinal pigment epithelium and choroid. The photoreceptors connect to the bipolar cells and ganglion cells in the inner retina, and the axons of the ganglion cells form the optic nerve. The inner retina receives nutrients from the retinal circulation by way of the retinal artery and vein. The outer retina is nourished from the choroidal circulation.

The main symptom of retinal diseases is reduction or disturbance in vision without pain. Disease involving the macula may reduce the central vision or cause distortion of images. Diseases involving the peripheral retina may cause peripheral field defects and night blindness. Traction on the retina may cause photopsia (the perception of light flashes).

Occlusion of the central retinal artery causes sudden painless loss of vision in one eye. The cause of occlusion is usually embolism resulting from atherosclerosis (Fig. 42-10). Following retinal artery occlusion, the retina develops whitish-gray edema with a cherry-red spot in the fovea centralis. Treatment includes trying to dislodge the embolus with ocular massage, reduction of intraocular pressure with medication, and in some cases an anterior chamber paracentesis. Breathing oxygen or 95% oxygen with 5% carbon dioxide may lengthen the survival time of the retina. Vision may be restored if the occlusion is relieved within 2 hours, but after that, progressive permanent damage occurs.

Central retinal vein occlusion causes a rapid painless reduction in vision. Ophthalmoscopic examination shows dilated and tortuous retinal veins with intraretinal hemorrhages (Fig. 42-11). Central retinal vein occlusion sometimes leads to iris neovascularization and neovascular glaucoma. The likelihood of this complication is reduced with panretinal laser photocoagulation. Branch retinal vein occlusion may lead to neovascularization of the retina and hemorrhage into the vitreous cavity. Reti-

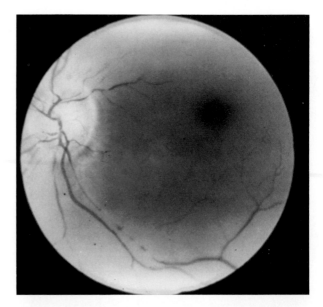

FIGURE 42-10
Central retinal artery occlusion. The blood column is interrupted in the retinal arterioles. Ischemic grayish-white edema involves the inner retina except in the fovea, where a cherry-red spot remains.

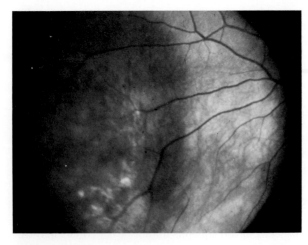

FIGURE 42-9
Malignant melanoma of the choroid.

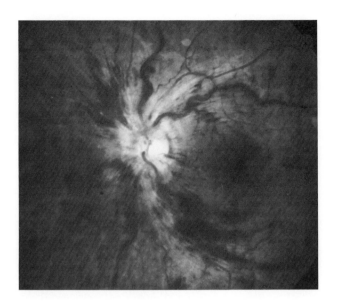

FIGURE 42-11
Central retinal vein occlusion.

nal edema can also result from branch retinal vein occlusion. Laser photocoagulation is helpful in treating these complications.

Cystoid macular edema may occur following cataract extraction and may also be seen in a variety of retinal vascular diseases. The retina is thickened with an accumulation of fluid in the outer plexiform layer. Visual acuity is decreased to the 20/200 range.

Retinitis can be caused by a variety of infectious agents. Cytomegalovirus retinitis is frequently seen in immunocompromised patients including those with acquired immune deficiency syndrome. (Fig. 42-12).

AGE-RELATED MACULAR DEGENERATION

Age-related macular degeneration (AMD) was previously known as senile macular degeneration and is a major cause of legal blindness in patients over 65 years of age in the United States. The clinical features of age-related macular degeneration include drusen, degenerative changes in the pigment epithelium and in Bruch's membrane, and subretinal neovascular membranes sometimes with hemorrhage (Fig. 42-13). Drusen appears ophthalmoscopically as multiple pale-yellow spots. They are hyaline nodules in Bruch's membrane. The development of a subretinal neovascular membrane may be associated with distortion in the central visual field and decreased visual acuity. The distortion is frequently the first symptom and is highly suggestive of age-related macular degeneration in the elderly patient. A patient suspected of having age-related macular degeneration with a subretinal neovascular membrane needs immediate referral to an ophthalmologist where a fluorescein angiography may determine the presence of a neovascular membrane. Laser treatment of neovascular membranes is helpful in some cases.

RETINAL DETACHMENT

A retinal detachment may be caused by a break in the retina (rhegmatogenous retinal detachment), by traction from fibrous membranes on the surface of the retina, or by exudation into the subretinal space. Rhegmatogenous retinal detachments result from vitreous traction tearing the retina, allowing fluid to accumulate between the ret-

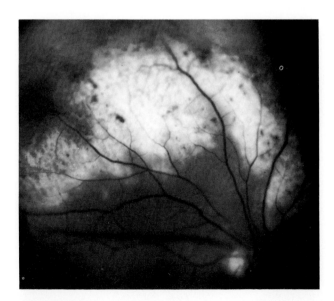

FIGURE 42-12
Cytomegalovirus retinitis in a patient with acquired immune deficiency syndrome.

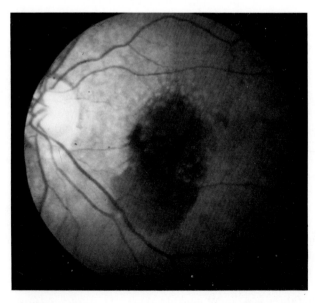

FIGURE 42-13
Age-related macular degeneration with a subretinal hemorrhage. Drusen is seen as yellow-white spots at the level of Bruch's membrane.

ina and the retinal pigment epithelium. The retina is detached from the retinal pigment epithelium and choroid, which normally provide nutrition to the outer retina. If untreated, a rhegmatogenous retinal detachment will usually spread to involve the entire retina.

The first symptoms may be the sensation of light flashes (photopsia) sometimes accompanied by a shower of floaters. The patient may then become aware of a shadow in the periphery of the visual field. This scotoma may spread rapidly to involve the entire visual field in a matter of days. When the retinal detachment involves the macula, visual acuity is severely reduced. A retinal detachment is best diagnosed by indirect ophthalmoscopy.

The treatment of rhegmatogenous retinal detachment is surgical. A silicone sponge or band is placed on the outside of the eye to buckle the wall of the eye inward in the area of the retinal break. In some cases the subretinal fluid is drained and freezing treatment is applied to the area of the retinal break to induce a chorioretinal scar in this area.

Traction retinal detachments are seen in diabetic eye disease as well as following trauma and other diseases. The treatment is by vitreous surgery. Serous or exudative retinal detachment are seen with malignant melanoma of the choroid and with inflammatory diseases. The treatment depends on the cause of the exudation.

DIABETIC EYE DISEASE

Diabetic eye disease is a major cause of blindness (Fig. 42-14). The prevalence of severe diabetic eye disease increases with the length of time the patient has had diabetes mellitus. The prevalence of diabetic retinopathy is 7 percent in patients who have had diabetes for less than 10 years, 26 percent in patients with diabetes for 10 to 14 years, and 63 percent in patients who have had diabetes for more than 15 years. Diabetic retinopathy is divided into background, or nonproliferative, retinopathy and the more severe proliferative retinopathy. Background diabetic retinopathy is characterized by microaneurysms which appear as little red dots in the retina, whitish hard and soft exudates, and dot hemorrhages. Visual acuity may be normal, unless diabetic macular edema is present. Diabetic macular edema is a common cause of reduced vision in diabetics. This is characterized by thickened retina and hard exudates in the macular area. Diabetic macular edema may be treated with laser photocoagulation.

Proliferative diabetic retinopathy is characterized by the formation of new blood vessels growing from the optic nerve head or other retinal areas into the vitreous gel (Fig. 42-15). These vessels may bleed into the vitreous gel causing a vitreous hemorrhage and reduced vision. The fibrovascular proliferation can also cause trac-

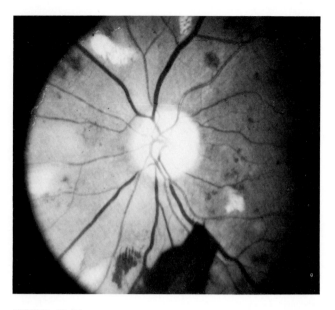

FIGURE 42-14
Diabetic retinopathy. Intraretinal point hemorrhages and flame-shaped nerve fiber layer hemorrhages are seen. A large subhyaloid hemorrhage originates from a retinal venule. White cotton-wool spots (soft exudates) are seen in all quadrants.

tion retinal detachments. Treatment of proliferative diabetic retinopathy is by laser photocoagulation. The late complications of vitreous hemorrhage and traction retinal detachment require vitreous surgery.

Significant diabetic retinopathy including retinal neovascularization may develop without symptoms. Regular eye examinations by an ophthalmologist are essential to allow early diagnosis and treatment of diabetic eye disease.

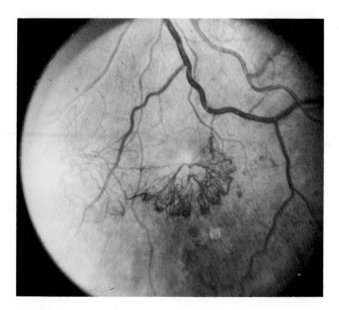

FIGURE 42-15
Retinal neovascularization in a patient with proliferative diabetic retinopathy.

OPTICAL DEFECTS OF THE EYE

Emmetropia is the ideal optical condition in which light rays parallel to the visual axis focus on the fovea. Ametropia is the absence of emmetropia and is divided into hyperopia (farsighted), myopia (nearsighted), and astigmatism. In hyperopia, parallel rays are brought into focus behind the eye. This condition can be corrected with a condensing (+) spectacle or contact lens. In myopia, parallel rays are brought into focus in front of the retina, either because the refractive power of the anterior segment of the eye is too great or because the eye is too long. This condition can be corrected with a diverging (−) spectacle or contact lens. Recently, a surgical treatment, radial keratotomy, has been advocated for surgical correction of myopia. In astigmatism, the refractive error of the eye is different in one meridian from another. Astigmatism may be corrected with glasses or contact lenses.

Presbyopia results from loss of the ability to accommodate or change the shape of the crystalline lens to focus on objects near at hand. The loss of accommodation is gradual over the first half of life and presbyopia starts in people between 40 and 50 years of age. The main symptom of presbyopia is inability to see near objects. Presbyopia is treated with convex lenses (reading glasses) or bifocal glasses.

THE ORBIT

Diseases of the orbit may manifest themselves as displacement of the globe (proptosis or exophthalmos) as well as pain, redness, and swelling. Proptosis of the eye may result from Graves disease, idiopathic orbital inflammation (pseudotumor), bacterial or fungal infection, as well as from neoplastic tumors, including hemangioma and lymphomatous disease.

Temporal arteritis may cause anterior ischemic optic neuropathy in the elderly patient. The patient suffers from malaise, temporal headache, arthralgias, low-grade fever, anemia, and weight loss. Typically the erythrocyte sedimentation rate is increased. Temporal artery biopsy shows giant cell arteritis. If the arteritis involves the ophthalmic artery, blindness may result. If left untreated, the arteritis may involve the other eye as well. Treatment is by systemic corticosteroids.

Chapter 43

AUDITORY AND VESTIBULAR DYSFUNCTION IN AGING

Thomas S. Rees and Larry G. Duckert

AUDITORY DYSFUNCTION AND AGING

Previous chapters have reported the number of elderly persons in the United States and future projections for that number. Of all the chronic conditions affecting the noninstitutionalized elderly, hearing loss is the third most prevalent condition, exceeded only by arthritis and hypertensive disease.[1] It is certainly intuitive that the elderly are much more likely to have hearing impairment than younger persons. While only slightly more than 1 percent of people under the age of 17 have hearing loss, the prevalence rises to 12 percent between the ages of 45 and 64, to 24 percent between the ages of 65 and 74, and up to 39 percent for ages over 75.[2] This last statistic is especially pertinent since the over-75 population, which has the highest prevalence of hearing loss, is growing at a faster rate than the elderly population as a whole. In the Framingham Heart Study Cohort (ages 57 to 89), the prevalence of hearing loss for the most important frequencies was 36 percent.[3] While about 7 million persons over the age of 65 now have significant hearing loss, continuation of the current trends suggests that this figure will rise to more than 11 million by the year 2000.

When one considers certain special populations of the aged, the prevalence of hearing loss is found to be even greater. People in nursing homes have as high as 70 percent hearing loss prevalence.[4] There is also an inverse relationship between income and hearing loss, as elderly people of low economic status have poorer hearing than elderly people with higher incomes.[5] Hearing loss in the elderly is the most common auditory disorder in the entire population.

GENERAL CONSIDERATIONS

The effect of the aging process on the human auditory system is manifested by deterioration in each of the two critical dimensions of hearing; namely, reduction in threshold sensitivity and reduction in the ability to understand speech. As early as 1899, Zwaardemaker reported that the high-frequency ranges were the first ranges affected by advancing age.[6] Since then, numerous studies have documented a characteristic pure tone finding associated with aging involving a symmetric bilateral high-frequency hearing loss.[7-9] Loss of high-frequency sensitivity due to biologic aging in the auditory system may, in fact, begin very early, as even infants lose hair cells in the basal end of the cochlea.[10, 11]

The loss in threshold sensitivity is insidious in onset, involving the highest frequencies initially and slowly progressing to become clinically manifest in the fifth to sixth decades. Since most audiometers include only the frequency range up to 8000 Hz, threshold elevations that occur in the range of 8000 to 20,000 Hz are not detected in routine testing; therefore, hearing loss due to aging or other factors is not documented clinically until it reaches frequencies at or below 8000 Hz. Tinnitus is often an associated symptom of deteriorating hearing sensitivity, and its onset may even precede subjective recognition of a hearing loss. Males usually have poorer hearing than females at every age.[12]

Most often, the presbycusic patient does not complain of difficulty in hearing per se but is more likely to report difficulties in understanding speech. The common complaint of "I hear you, but I can't understand you" reflects not only the problem in hearing high-frequency consonant sounds due to the high-frequency threshold loss, but also can reflect the effects of central nervous system (CNS) auditory deterioration. As early as 1948, Gaeth observed that elderly patients have more difficulty with word-intelligibility tests than would be expected from younger patients with comparable sensitivity loss.[13] This observation was subsequently substantiated by Jerger, who investigated speech-understanding performance by age decade with the amount of pure tone sensitivity loss held constant.[14] At any level of sensitivity loss, systematic decrement of speech intelligibility was demonstrated with increasing age.

Whenever the speech message is degraded, the elderly listener's difficulties increase dramatically more than do the difficulties of younger listeners. That is, elderly persons have considerably greater problems than younger persons in understanding rapid speech, foreign accents, and speech transmitted via poor transmitting equipment or under unfavorable acoustic conditions.[15–17] These difficulties are accentuated when background noise or competing speech are present, as in group situations. Welsh and associates have suggested that these decrements are due to a central integrative and synthesizing hearing disability which reflects a progressive deterioration of the CNS; they have called this phenomenon "central presbycusis."[18] Such problems in the auditory processing of degraded speech by the aged have been shown to occur even when peripheral auditory function is clinically normal.

PSYCHOSOCIAL IMPLICATIONS OF HEARING LOSS

Although hearing impairment is most often not life-threatening and does not directly restrict physical activity, it is disabling since it interferes with quality of life. The psychosocial impact of a hearing loss is poorly understood and poorly appreciated. Indeed, even people who live with a hearing-impaired person rarely fully grasp the all-pervasive effects of hearing impairment on daily living. The many ways in which we depend upon our hearing are simply not recognized until hearing loss is experienced directly or unless a very close acquaintance has impaired hearing. Few aspects of daily living are not impacted by hearing loss in some way.

The primary impact of hearing loss is on communication, most notably free and easy communication. Due to the interference with communication caused by hearing loss, a sense of isolation is imposed on the hearing impaired which can hinder opportunities for education, work, recreation, worship, entertainment, and so forth. A further sense of isolation can result from the inability to relate to the variety of sounds which keep us in contact with our environment, such as the sounds of nature (e.g., animals, wind, and rain), the sounds of civilization (e.g., people, traffic, and telephones), the sounds of warning or danger (e.g., sirens, alarms, and smoke detectors), as well as the many sounds which provide important everyday information (e.g., running water, microwave buzzers, and boiling water).

Misunderstanding, mistrust, and lack of sympathy for the hearing impaired seem to be built into our cultural heritage. These attitudes are certainly quite different from our perceptions and treatment of blindness. Often the symptoms of hearing loss (for example, not answering when spoken to, answering inappropriately, or requiring repetition) encourage other people to talk to and treat the hearing impaired as if their cognitive abilities were also diminished. This treatment seems to be applied especially often to the elderly hearing impaired, since associations with senility are also construed.

The two most commonly reported consequences of hearing loss in the elderly are depression[19–21] and social isolation.[22,23] In addition, significant hearing loss can impact the elderly by producing or aggravating embarrassment, fatigue, increased irritability and tension, avoidance and negativism.[24] Herbst has reported the association of age-related hearing loss with poor general health, reduction in interpersonal interplay, and reduced enjoyment of life.[25] The relationship of hearing loss in the elderly with the symptoms of paranoia has been reviewed by Zimbardo et al.[26] Since hearing loss is typically very gradual in onset and progression, the impaired individual and the individual's acquaintances may not be aware of the deficit. Not being able to hear may create frustration, anger, and suspiciousness that others are whispering and perhaps talking about the hearing-impaired person. Over time, social relationships may deteriorate, leaving the individual in isolation and with diminished quality of life. At the least, the psychosocial ramifications of hearing loss indicate the need for early identification and rehabilitation of the hearing-impaired elderly.

ANATOMIC AND PHYSIOLOGIC CORRELATES OF HEARING LOSS

External Ear

Aging affects the external ear and canal primarily by altering the nature of the skin and the cerumen glands contained therein. Cerumen glands are modified sweat glands and are found in addition to apocrine glands and sebaceous glands in the ear canal. The secretions from these glands, in addition to desquamated skin, combine to form cerumen. The aging process causes a reduction in the activity of the apocrine sweat glands and a decrease in the number of modified apocrine or cerumen glands. While there is no correlation between age and the amount of cerumen that is produced, the reduced activity and the number of cerumen glands does correlate with the tendency for the cerumen of older individuals to become dryer. This may, in part, explain why cerumen impactions tend to be more common in the ear canals of older patients.

Atrophy of the epithelial sebaceous glands causes a decrease in the epithelial oiliness and skin hydration. Dryness of the skin contributes to pruritus in the external auditory canal and is a common complaint in older patients. The skin itself is often atrophic and is easily injured by the insertion of cotton tip applicators provoked by the pruritus. This irritation leads to further itching and the scratch-itch cycle may provoke trauma and infection. Despite this, there does not appear to be a higher incidence of external ear infections in the older age group. It is important, however, that patients be discouraged from traumatizing the canal or further drying the skin with water or alcohol. In the absence of obvious infection or dermatitis, pruritus may be controlled by regular use of small amounts of baby oil.

Middle Ear

The effectiveness of the middle ear sound conduction mechanism depends on the integrity of the ossicular chain and the dexterity of its joints. The aging process causes degenerative changes in the articular surfaces throughout the body, and, not surprisingly, those of the middle ear are not excluded. The incudomalleal and the incudostapedial joints are synovial in nature and, as such, are lined by articular cartilages and surrounded by an elastic tissue capsule. Histological studies have demonstrated degenerative changes within these joints which increase with age.[27] Calcification and even obliteration of portions of the joint space may occur. Despite these observations, the significance of the arthritic changes as they relate to sound transmission appears to be negligible. It would appear that the aging effects on the ossicular chain have a minimal effect on middle ear function and are not clinically significant. Presbycusis is, therefore, exclusively a manifestation of inner ear degeneration.

Inner Ear

As with so many other organ systems in the body, the auditory system functions with decreasing efficiency after the fourth and fifth decades of life. Cells of the auditory pathways are unique, and because of their highly specialized function they cannot reproduce. In addition, they have very limited regenerative ability; therefore, the length of their cell life is determined by environmental influences and their ability to adjust and adapt.

Numerous variables contribute to the degeneration of the sensory and neural elements. These may include diet and nutrition, cholesterol metabolism, arteriosclerosis, and the organism's response to physical stress. It is likely that certain individuals are prone to the development of presbycusis at an earlier age due to hereditary factors which may make their auditory system less durable and more exposed to both internal and external insult.

A variety of studies have been undertaken to assess the effects of environmental noise and serum cholesterol on the onset of presbycusis. While it appears that individuals with lower serum cholesterol and lower rates of coronary heart disease have better high-frequency hearing than age-matched controls, it is impossible to eliminate the multitude of other factors which may effect the onset of presbycusis. In general, it is impossible to define precisely the contributions of environmental and genetic factors to age-dependent hearing loss.

The clinical manifestations of presbycusis have been observed and categorized into four different types. Early efforts by Crowe et al.[28] and Saxon[29] described two types, one involving the organ of Corti and the other involving the cochlear neurons. These types have subsequently been termed *sensory presbycusis* and *neural presbycusis*, respectively, by Schuknecht, who has also described two additional types, *strial presbycusis* and *cochlear conductive presbycusis*.[30] The four types of presbycusis identified by Schuknecht represent a more precise definition of the degenerative process based on clinical manifestations and their histopathological correlates.

1. *Sensory presbycusis.* Sensory presbycusis is characterized by a predominantly high-frequency, sensorineural hearing loss. The deterioration usually begins at middle age and is slowly progressive. The histological correlate is degeneration of the organ of Corti at the basal end of the cochlea. Early in the course of the process, the organ of Corti may appear flattened and distorted. These changes are followed by degeneration of the supporting cells, as well as the sensory cells, and eventual dedifferentiation of the organ of Corti into an epithelial mound on the basilar membrane. That these changes are restricted to a few millimeters of the basilar turn explains the abrupt high-tone loss. Ganglion cell loss parallels in distribution and magnitude the degeneration of the organ of Corti.

2. *Neural presbycusis.* Neural presbycusis is characterized by a sensorineural hearing loss, and while the audiogram of the condition typically has a downward curve, the high-frequency deficit is less abrupt as compared to sensory presbycusis. More importantly, the hearing loss is characterized by loss of speech discrimination which is in excess of what would be predicted for the amount of pure tone loss. The reduced discrimination scores are a reflection of the reduction in population of cochlear neurons in the presence of a functional organ of Corti. Often there is an associated loss of neurons in the higher auditory pathways, and patients with progressive neural presbycusis may demonstrate other degenerative changes in the CNS manifested by incoordination, loss of memory, and central auditory processing disorders. Apparently the neuronal degeneration may occur at any age, but it does not become clinically manifest until the neuronal population falls below a critical level and interferes with transmission and processing.

3. *Strial (metabolic) presbycusis.* The stria vascularis is located on the lateral wall of the cochlear duct and

is instrumental in maintaining the biochemical balance of the inner ear fluids and, therefore, the endolymphatic potential. The stria vascularis is also believed to be the source of endolymphatic fluid formation. Large amounts of oxidative enzymes necessary for glucose metabolism are also found within the stria. It is no wonder, then, that atrophy of the stria should result in a significant hearing loss. Degeneration of this tissue results in a progressive hearing loss which begins in the middle to older age groups. The audiometric pattern is usually flat, and speech discrimination is preserved. There may be patchy atrophy of the stria in the middle and apical turns of the cochlea, but more severe degeneration may occur. In general, the neuronal population is preserved, accounting for the excellent speech discrimination scores which may remain normal until the threshold elevation exceeds 50 decibels (dB).

4. *Cochlear conductive presbycusis.* This type of presbycusis is characterized by a straight-line descending audiometric pattern. Speech discrimination scores are reduced in proportion to the degree of pure tone loss. A definite histopathological correlate to cochlear conductive presbycusis has yet to be described. Whether or not this type of presbycusis actually exists is controversial; however, a number of degenerative patterns have been identified and offered as an explanation for the clinical condition. One such theory suggests as an explanation the stiffening of the basilar membrane, which interferes in cochlear motion mechanics. Another theory attributes the condition to hyalinization and deposition of calcium salts within the basilar membrane. Atrophic changes begin during childhood in the spiral ligament and progress through adulthood. The atrophy is distributed preferentially in the apical turns and is less severe in the basal turn. These atrophic changes may alter the configuration of the cochlear duct or may actually cause separation of the basilar membrane from the lateral wall.

It is unlikely that any one given individual with presbycusic hearing loss will fit exactly one of the four pure forms of presbycusis described. Certain aspects of the hearing loss may more closely approximate one of the four types described and implicate a specific histopathological process which will help explain the audiometric pattern. In addition to changes in the pure tone thresholds and discrimination scores which may be explained on the basis of reduced ganglion cell populations, further disability may result from degeneration within more centrally located auditory pathways.

CLINICAL EVALUATION OF HEARING LOSS

The identification and evaluation of hearing disorders should be an integral component of geriatric medicine, although the subject is largely neglected by many primary care providers. Despite the high prevalence of hearing loss in the elderly, primary care physicians often fail to recognize the presence of hearing loss; even when hearing loss is suspected or reported to the physician, more than one-half of such cases are not referred for further evaluation or treatment.[24] Bess has further suggested that often primary care physicians look upon hearing loss in the elderly in the same way that our society at large does; namely, that hearing loss is a common by-product of aging and there is little value in providing rehabilitation for these patients. This suggestion is consistent with a 1980 Gallup Survey which reported that only 18 percent of those persons with hearing loss wear hearing aids.

Identification of Hearing Loss

Physical diagnosis textbooks are confusing and contradictory in their recommended approaches to auditory evaluation. A survey of recent editions of nine physical examination textbooks showed that only two of the nine recommended audiograms. The number of textbooks in which specific auditory screening tests were recommended were as follows: whispered voice, seven; tuning forks, six; spoken voice, five; watch tick, four; and finger friction, one. In addition, the methods of test administration and interpretation varied considerably.[31]

Even though the elderly do not generally appear with medically manageable hearing loss, physical examination of the ears is necessary and important, so as to rule out potentially treatable conductive hearing deficits. At times, cerumen impactions are noted; however, while the removal of occluding cerumen can indeed result in hearing improvement in some, all too often the hearing loss is in the sensorineural system. Attention should also be directed to the status and mobility of the tympanic membrane, as past ear disease or perforations can cause conductive hearing loss.

Typically, most hearing-impaired persons will seem to hear quite well in the confines of an office examination room and when asked about the presence of hearing loss will inevitably report that you can be heard quite well. One must be aware, however, that the office environment is generally quiet, without distracting background noises, and the patient is being afforded visual cues. Even persons with severe hearing loss can do rather well in understanding in such acoustically and visually ideal situations. Thus, communication with the physician is certainly quite different from communication in the patient's everyday world.

It is important for the physician to ask the aged patient carefully directed questions regarding specific hearing difficulties, such as problems hearing in groups, hearing soft voices, hearing voices at a distance, hearing on the telephone, and so forth. Not surprisingly, direct questions will often identify hearing loss undetected by the physical exam.

The most sensitive screening tool available in an office is a screening audiometer. Tuning forks are notoriously ineffective in hearing loss identification, since low-frequency tuning fork results usually do not indicate hearing difficulties because age-related hearing loss is predominantly high frequency. Screening audiometers are simple and low-cost tools, easily utilized by office personnel and relatively easy to interpret.

An Audioscope, which is a portable screening audiometer housed within an otoscope, is available for use by primary care providers (Fig. 43-1). It includes four frequencies and three intensity levels. Studies of the Audioscope's validity show that it can accurately differentiate among hearing-impaired and unimpaired adults.[32,33] Snyder has provided a review of the technique and interpretation of office screening audiometry.[34]

In order to evaluate hearing handicap, a number of self-assessment inventories have been developed.[35–37] These tests quantify hearing handicap by including questions about the situational and psychosocial aspects of decreased hearing. One of these tests, the Hearing Handicap Inventory for the Elderly (HHIE), is specifically designed for use with noninstitutionalized elderly.[38] This 25-item questionnaire assesses the effects of hearing loss on emotional and social adjustment. A shortened version of only 10 items is also available.[39] Information gained from such self-assessment tests helps provide insight as to the extent of the handicap caused by hearing loss.

Audiologic Evaluation of Hearing Loss

The clinical assessment of hearing loss includes the completion of an audiogram (Fig. 43-2). The frequency scale along the abscissa is measured for the octave frequencies of 250 Hz through 8000 Hz. The most critical frequencies for speech reception and understanding are 500, 1000, 2000, and 3000 Hz; these frequencies are used in the AMA computation of hearing loss percentage.[40]

The intensity scale on the ordinate of the audiogram is measured in decibels ranging from a very faint −10 dB Hearing Level (HL) up to a very loud 110 dB HL. The 0 dB HL represents the average hearing sensitivity threshold for young adults. Sensitivity thresholds are obtained for each frequency for each ear separately using earphones. Since air conduction testing measures the responsiveness of the entire auditory system, from the ear canal through the middle ear to the cochlea and associated neural pathways to the brain, any loss by air conduction may be due to a disorder anywhere in the entire auditory system.

The use of pure tone bone conduction audiometry defines the general anatomic location of the hearing disorder, since sound transmission by bone conduction bypasses the outer and middle ear. An oscillator is placed behind the ear to be tested and sensitivity thresholds are obtained for the frequencies from 250 to 4000 Hz.

In addition to establishing pure tone thresholds, the measurement of sensitivity for speech and the assessment of speech discrimination (intelligibility) is important. The Speech Reception Threshold (SRT) involves

FIGURE 43-1
The Audioscope: A screening audiometer housed within an otoscope. Has four frequencies (500, 1000, 2000, and 4000 Hz) and three intensity levels (20, 25, and 40 dB HL). *(Photograph courtesy of Welch-Allyn, Inc., Skaneateles Falls, N.Y.)*

FIGURE 43-2

The Audiogram: Frequency in Hz is plotted on the abscissa and intensity in dB is plotted on the ordinate. This audiogram shows normal auditory sensitivity and 100 percent speech discrimination.

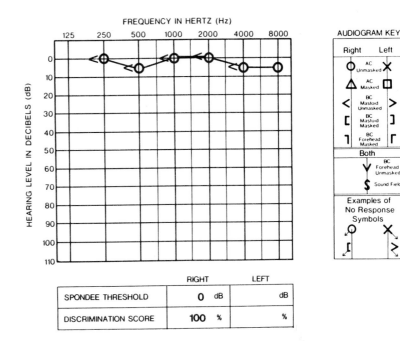

	RIGHT	LEFT
SPONDEE THRESHOLD	0 dB	dB
DISCRIMINATION SCORE	100 %	%

presenting two-syllable words through each earphone separately and finding the softest level at which 50 percent of the words can be identified. This level should agree within ±10 dB of the pure tone average (PTA) thresholds of 500, 1000, and 2000 Hz; it serves as a reliability check on the pure tone threshold levels.

Since age-related hearing loss is often manifested not only by sensitivity loss but also by a reduction in speech understanding, the assessment of speech intelligibility (clarity of speech) is an integral component of the audiologic assessment. The speech discrimination evaluation involves presentation of 25 to 50 monosyllabic words to each ear at comfortably loud levels. The percentage of correct responses is the speech discrimination score. This test is not a sensitivity test, as is the SRT or pure tone test, because the words are presented at levels well above the sensitivity threshold. Speech discrimination results provide information as to the extent of the communication handicap caused by the hearing loss.

Audiologic Test Interpretation

DEGREE OF HEARING LOSS The results obtained from the air conduction evaluation provide quantitative information as to the *amount* of hearing loss. While classification systems have been developed that relate the amount of air conduction hearing loss to the expected degree of handicap imposed by the hearing loss, they are of questionable validity since they do not consider the effects of speech discrimination difficulties, etiologic factors, age, demands upon hearing, or hearing loss configuration. For example, a 70-year-old in an institutionalized setting may not be "handicapped" by a 40-dB HL

hearing loss; however, a 70-year-old active adult may feel withdrawn and depressed due to a similar amount of hearing loss.

LOCATION OF AUDITORY IMPAIRMENT The general anatomic area of a particular case of hearing loss can be determined by comparing the air conduction and bone conduction thresholds. A conductive hearing loss is present when air conduction results demonstrate a hearing loss but bone conduction results are within the normal range (Fig. 43-3). The difference between the air and bone conduction thresholds reflects the amount of conductive hearing impairment and is termed the *air-bone gap*. The etiology of the conductive loss cannot be determined by the audiogram alone, as any obstruction in the sound-conducting mechanism of the ear, from the external canal (e.g., cerumen impaction or foreign body) through the middle ear (e.g., middle ear effusion, otosclerosis, or ossicular disarticulation) may be the cause of the conductive hearing loss. Patients with pure conductive hearing loss have normal speech discrimination abilities (92 to 100 percent), since the sensorineural system is not impaired. Speech needs only to be presented at louder levels than normal to compensate for the conductive deficit.

When a hearing loss is present by air conduction *and* by bone conduction, a sensorineural hearing loss is present (Fig. 43-4). The origin could be in the cochlea, in the associated neural pathways, or in both the sensory and neural auditory system.

Speech discrimination test results in cases of sensorineural hearing loss often provide important diagnostic and rehabilitative signs. In general, pure cochlear le-

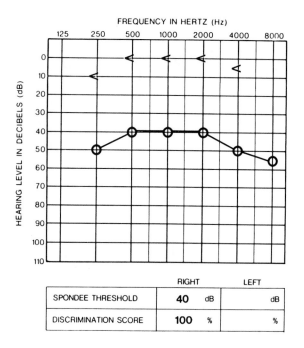

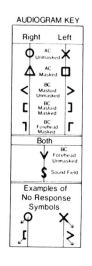

FIGURE 43-3
Conductive hearing loss: A hearing loss is present for air conduction but with normal hearing for bone conduction. Speech discrimination is normal since no sensorineural involvement is present.

	RIGHT		LEFT	
SPONDEE THRESHOLD	**40**	dB		dB
DISCRIMINATION SCORE	**100**	%		%

sions show speech discrimination scores which are compatible with the amount of hearing loss. On the other hand, retrocochlear disorders often demonstrate speech-discrimination scores disproportionately poorer than would be expected from the pure tone audiometric results. For example, a sensorineural loss of 40 dB HL with a 72 percent speech discrimination score would be consistent with cochlear involvement, whereas a similar amount of hearing loss with only 10 percent speech discrimination would suggest the possibility of neural involvement. In addition, the better the speech discrimination results, the better the prognosis for hearing aid success due to less distortion in the auditory system.

A loss in hearing sensitivity for bone conduction with a greater loss for air conduction represents a mixed hearing loss (Fig. 43-5). Speech discrimination performance reflects the amount and etiology of the sensorineural impairment. Correction of the conductive component by medical or surgical treatment should leave a sensorineural loss only, as reflected by the bone conduction thresholds.

REHABILITATION OF HEARING LOSS

Hearing Aid Amplification

It has been reported that of all persons with hearing loss, only 5 percent can be helped medically.[5] This percentage would undoubtedly be even lower in the elderly

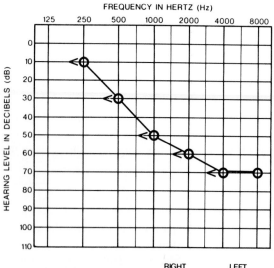

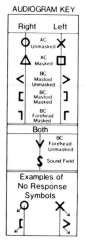

FIGURE 43-4
Sensorineural hearing loss: A similar amount of hearing loss is present for both air and bone conduction. This configuration is often found in age-related hearing loss, as hearing is normal for the low frequencies but shows impairment in the higher frequencies. Speech discrimination is relatively good (82 percent) but is reduced from normal.

	RIGHT		LEFT	
SPONDEE THRESHOLD	**50**	dB		dB
DISCRIMINATION SCORE	**82**	%		%

FIGURE 43-5

Mixed hearing loss: A hearing loss is present for bone conduction but has greater loss for air conduction. Speech discrimination is reduced (70 percent), reflecting the sensorineural component of the hearing loss.

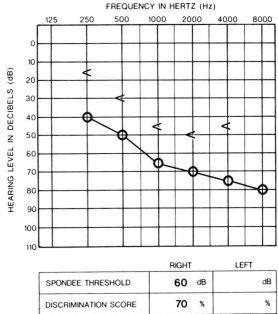

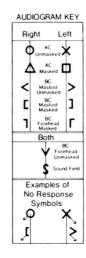

	RIGHT	LEFT
SPONDEE THRESHOLD	**60** dB	dB
DISCRIMINATION SCORE	**70** %	%

population due to the higher incidence of sensorineural impairment found in the elderly. Consequently, the most important rehabilitative approach for hearing-impaired elderly is the hearing aid.

A hearing aid is simply a miniature, personal loudspeaker system designed to increase the intensity of sound and to deliver it to the ear with as little distortion as possible. While their physical appearance may vary considerably, all hearing aids have the following basic components and functions: (1) input microphone, which converts sound to electrical energy; (2) amplifier, which increases the strength of the electrical signal; (3) output receiver, which converts the amplified signal back into acoustic energy; (4) battery, which provides the power for the hearing aid; and (5) volume control, which permits the user to adjust the loudness of the amplified sound.

As shown in Fig. 43-6, there are several basic types of hearing aids which are available for the hearing impaired:

1. *Behind-the-ear (BTE).* The components of the BTE aid fit into a curved case behind the ear, and sound is conducted via a tube to an earmold in the ear canal. While there are many BTE aids available, each model can provide varying amplification as required by the hearing loss.

2. *Eyeglass hearing aid.* The components of this aid fit within the temple piece of an eyeglass frame and are connected via a tube to an earmold. Eyeglass hearing aids are quite uncommon since persons needing both eyeglasses and hearing aids find the combined use of both quite restricting.

3. *In-the-ear (ITE).* The ITE aid is a self-contained

FIGURE 43-6

Hearing aid types (clockwise from left): Body aid, behind-the-ear aid, in-the-ear aid, and in-the-canal aid.

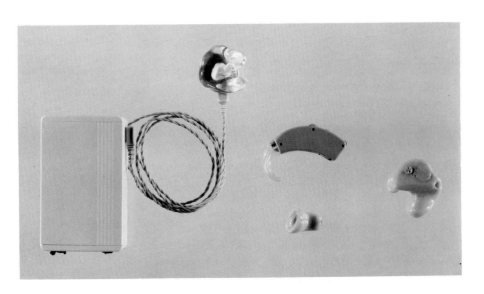

unit which fits into the bowl of the external ear. ITE aids in the past provided poor quality performance; however, technological developments have markedly improved these aids, making them the preferred aids for many elderly patients. They also have the advantages of cosmetic appeal and ease of insertion and adjustment. They are custom fit to meet the anatomic and acoustical requirements of each patient.

4. *In-the-canal (ITC).* The ITC aid fits entirely within the external ear canal and thus possesses very desired cosmetic appeal. Their amplification is similar to most BTE and ITE aids. Their major drawback relates to fitting those persons with dexterity problems, who have difficulty in inserting and adjusting these very small aids.

5. *Body hearing aids.* The body or pocket hearing aid is the largest and most cumbersome of all hearing aids. These aids comprise less than 2 percent of hearing aids, as they are needed only by those with severe-profound hearing loss and those who are unable to manipulate the other types of hearing aids.

HEARING AID CANDIDACY Several misconceptions exist as to who should be considered as candidates for hearing aid use. While it was once popular to specify the amount of hearing loss necessary for hearing aid candidacy, such criteria do not hold merit. The most important criteria relate to the patient's communicative difficulties, acceptance of the hearing loss, and motivation to try amplification. Whether regulated by state laws or local dispensing practices, most hearing aid dispensers offer at least a 30-day trial period prior to purchase. With this in mind, the hearing-impaired senior should be encouraged to pursue the use of amplification.

It is a disservice to the patient to discourage a hearing aid trial due to the outdated notion that a hearing aid does not help "nerve deafness." Whereas hearing aids were not very helpful for sensorineural deficits many years ago, this is simply not the case today due to the substantial improvements in hearing aid technology. Also, some physicians merely tell their patients that they can probably "get by" without a hearing aid and should wait until the hearing loss progresses in future years. Discouraging a hearing aid trial for an individual with communicative difficulties and a potentially remediable hearing loss serves only to invite isolation and frustration. Unless assurance and support is provided, hearing-impaired elderly patients may unfortunately postpone and avoid the use of amplification.

Once a hearing loss has been identified and medical or surgical treatment is not indicated, referral to a certified clinical audiologist should be made. The clinical audiologist is a university-trained professional in the nonmedical management of hearing loss, whether with hearing aid amplification, rehabilitation therapies, assistive listening devices, or a combination of rehabilitative approaches. While some hearing aid dealers are relatively skilled in the evaluation of hearing impairment and the fitting of hearing aids, others possess only minimal training and are more oriented to sales. Many states, in fact, require that a hearing aid dealer only meet the minimal requirements of being 18 years old and passing a state licensing examination; educational criteria are typically not required. The clinical audiologist, on the other hand, holds at least a master's degree in the evaluation and rehabilitation of hearing loss.

After the necessary interview and evaluation, an audiologist/dispenser will recommend a type of hearing aid or aids, the acoustical requirements of the aids, and training in the use of amplification. The potential advantages and limitations of hearing aids are reviewed, and follow-up is provided during the initial trial, as well as post-purchase period.

HEARING AID PROGNOSTIC FACTORS Adaptation to hearing aid use is at times difficult, and successful adjustment is dependent to a large degree on the personality dynamics of the individual. Often the senior adult is resistant to amplification because of the social stigma associated with hearing loss. Since our culture unfortunately views hearing loss as a consequence of aging, resistance to a hearing aid is inevitable. Kapteyn reported that the variables most important to hearing aid satisfaction were psychosocial, rather than auditory.[41] Factors of motivation, personal adjustment, and family support were more related to hearing aid satisfaction than the adequacy of the hearing aid fit or auditory discrimination ability.

Rupp et al. have summarized the important factors for successful hearing aid use in the elderly by offering "The Feasibility Scale for Predicting Hearing Aid Use."[42] Included in this scale are the following items for evaluation in determining potential hearing aid success:

1. Motivation and mode of referral (self vs. family)
2. Self-assessment of listening difficulties (realistic vs. denial)
3. Verbalization as to "fault" of communicative difficulties (self-caused vs. projection on others)
4. Magnitude of hearing loss and understanding difficulties (before and after amplification)
5. Informal verbalizations during initial hearing aid trial (positive vs. negative)
6. Flexibility and adaptability of patient
7. Age (65 years vs. 90+ years)
8. Hand and finger dexterity and general mobility (good vs. limited)
9. Visual ability (adequate vs. limited)
10. Financial resources (adequate vs. very limited)

11. Significant other person for assistance and support (available vs. none)

After the hearing-impaired senior is assessed on each of the above factors, a score is obtained as to the anticipated prognosis for hearing aid acceptance and use. While the scale has not been without criticism, it does incorporate those factors of importance in hearing aid success. Not infrequently, however, there are some hearing-impaired seniors who, although scoring poorly on the scale, do accept and utilize amplification effectively.

Aural Rehabilitation: Speech Reading/Auditory Training

Speech reading is the use of visual cues to aid in speech understanding. The term *speech reading* is more accepted than the older term *lip reading*, for it encompasses not only the recognition of lip movements, but also the interpretation of facial expressions, body movements, and gestures. All people, whether hearing-impaired or not, use speech reading to some extent, although perhaps they are not conscious of the importance of visual input in enhancing understanding. It is not surprising that many hearing-impaired persons, particularly those with a slowly progressive hearing loss, develop these skills through necessity and without formal training.

While of considerable help, the use of speech reading alone cannot provide complete understanding of speech. Only about one-third of English speech sounds are clearly visible. While certain sounds are relatively easy to see on the lips ("f" and "th"), others are not visible ("k" and "g"), and some are indistinguishable from each other ("b" and "p").

Speech reading is usually taught in conjunction with auditory training and hearing aid orientation. Auditory training teaches the listener to make the most effective use of the minimal auditory cues imposed by the hearing loss. The combination of visual input coupled with auditory input is superior to either one alone for the understanding of speech. Hearing aid orientation is often helpful for the senior hearing-impaired person, as it includes training in the effective use of amplification, including such basic skills as insertion and adjustment of the hearing aid, battery replacement, and manipulation of the hearing aid and the environment. Such programs are often held at senior citizen centers, community speech and hearing centers, and university audiology clinics. Aural rehabilitation strategies also try to teach the patient to be a more assertive listener. Those persons who quietly accept not understanding merely invite continued social isolation. Self-help groups are available; most notable is the Self Help for Hard of Hearing People (SHHH) organization, which offers local groups as well as an active national organization and a journal. The hearing-impaired listener should also inform others as to the most effective means of communication. Table 43-1 lists several considerations which are of importance to the listener and should be used by those who interact with hearing-impaired persons.

Assistive Listening Devices (ALDs)

Although substantial improvements have been achieved in hearing aid design and application, few hearing impaired, if any, can ever come close to achieving normal auditory functioning with hearing aid use alone. The inherent physiologic restrictions imposed by age-related hearing loss, coupled with the electronic limitations of hearing aids, render normal hearing impossible, especially considering the levels of noise and background interference found in most public places. The amplification of unwanted sounds (e.g., other talkers in a crowd, background noise, or ventilation) by a hearing aid often causes the desired message to be rendered unintelligible.

Assistive listening devices (ALDs) comprise a growing number of situation-specific amplification systems designed for use in difficult listening situations. ALDs generally use a microphone placed close to the desired sound source (e.g., a television, theater stage, or speaker's podium), and sound is directly transmitted to the listener; transmission methods include infrared, audio loop, FM radio, or direct audio input. Such direct transmission of sound to the listener improves the signal-to-noise ratio. That is, the desired message is enhanced, while competing extraneous noises are decreased, thus permitting improved comprehension. ALDs are becoming more available in churches, theaters, and classrooms, and hearing-impaired seniors are able to avoid the isolation imposed by not hearing a sermon, a play, or a public address.

TABLE 43-1
Guidelines for Communicating with the Hearing Impaired

- Get listener's attention before speaking.
- Face listener directly to afford visual cues (do not cover mouth while talking or turn face away).
- Try to reduce background noise (turn down TV, radio, etc.).
- Use facial expressions and gestures.
- Speak slowly and clearly with more pauses than usual.
- Speak only slightly louder than normal; do not shout.
- Rephrase message if listener does not understand, rather than repeating it word for word.
- Alert listener to changes in topic before proceeding.
- Do not turn and walk away while talking.

Amplified telephones, low-frequency doorbells and telephone ringers, and closed-captioned TV decoders are just a few examples of a number of devices currently available for the hearing impaired for everyday use. Flashing alarm clocks, alarm bed vibrators, and flashing smoke detectors provide valuable help for severely hearing-impaired individuals. Telephone communication is now possible for severely hearing-impaired people with the use of telephone devices for the deaf (TDDs). These instruments use a typed message for transmission of a written message to an LED display and/or printer.

VESTIBULAR DYSFUNCTION AND AGING

GENERAL CONSIDERATIONS

Vestibular dysfunction associated with aging may be manifested by a sensation of unsteadiness, disequilibrium, or true vertigo. Complaints of these sensations are very common in the older age group; the sensations are experienced by at least 50 percent of those living alone after age 60.[43]

Maintenance of balance is a complex function which depends not only upon the integrity of the vestibular system but also on visual cues and proprioceptive input. It is necessary, of course, that the more central pathways also be intact to integrate the signals from the periphery. As it does with other parts of the body, aging affects the visual and proprioceptive systems, as well as central processing, all of which contribute to the patient's disequilibrium. Clearly, imbalance in the aged individual is not solely a result of vestibular degeneration, but is instead multifactorial. As is true of the cochlea, the peripheral vestibular sensory cells have little or no capacity for regeneration. The peripheral and the more central portions of the vestibular system are also subject to the effects of vascular insufficiency, which may compound the problem.

CLINICAL EVALUATION OF VESTIBULAR PROBLEMS

The geriatric patient may describe dizziness in a variety of ways, including light-headedness, imbalance, or true spinning vertigo. It is important that the clinician attempt to differentiate between the central, peripheral, and systemic causes of dizziness based on the patient's subjective description. Vestibular vertigo is more often severe, disabling, and associated with other systemic effects. Central vertigo is less intense and nausea is less common. The nystagmus may be vertical. Systemic causes of vertigo may be associated with visual or neurological deficits, medications, or cardiovascular disorders.

The patient evaluation must consider the diagnostic multiplicity. A complete blood count, electrolyte and metabolic profile, sedimentation rate, electrocardiogram, and computerized tomography of the brain, with contrast enhancement with attention to the posterior fossa, are also useful.

Audiometry and electronystagmography (ENG) are obtained to evaluate the peripheral vestibular system. With respect to ENG, it is intuitive that the degenerative changes in the sensory and neural epithelium on the vestibular labyrinth would result in measurable reduction in vestibular function. Responses to caloric irrigations, however, have produced a spectrum of activity ranging from reduced, to normal, to increased nystagmus.

Efforts to evaluate equilibrium must measure factors other than vestibular degeneration and consider the multitude of factors responsible for maintaining balance. Tests of equilibrium demonstrate a significant reduction in performance with increasing age. This reduction in function begins at middle age, coincidental with the observed histological changes in the vestibular portion of the inner ear.

ANATOMIC AND PHYSIOLOGIC CORRELATES OF VESTIBULAR DYSFUNCTION

It is very likely that the vestibular labyrinth undergoes the same type of age-dependent degenerative changes as the cochlea. Sensory cell and ganglion cell degeneration occurs and remaining cells have been shown to accumulate the lipoprotein lipofuscin. The distribution of this pigment within the sensory epithelium of the vestibular labyrinth carries the same implication as does its distribution in the cochlea. The presence of these granules probably indicates reduced protein synthesis as a consequence of aging.[44]

Sensory Degeneration

Sensory epithelium age-related degeneration may result in a substantial reduction in the number of sensory cells in the cristae of the semicircular canals as well as in the maculae of both the saccule and utricle.[45] Cystic degeneration of the epithelium of the sensory epithelium has also been observed in these structures.[46] Vesiculation within the supporting cells and other degenerative changes of undetermined significance have also been observed.

The otoconia of the maculae are not spared by the aging process. Whereas in younger individuals the otoconia form a continuous layer over the new epithelium, large defects in this layer are apparent in older individuals.[47] Degeneration of the otoconia is a very slow and progressive process. Changes in the surface of the otoconia betray a slow process of dissolution, resulting in absorption of the crystal.

Neuronal Degeneration

Neuronal degeneration parallels the loss of sensory epithelium within the labyrinth. People over the age of 70 may demonstrate a loss of 40 to 50 percent of the number of myelinated nerve fibers present in a normal 30-year-old; this reduction begins slowly, shortly after the age of 40.[48] The myelinated fibers of the cristae appear to be more sensitive to the degenerative aging process and suffer the greatest loss. In addition to the loss of neural fibers, there is also a reduction in the number of Scarpa's ganglion cells after the age of 50.

Histological Correlates

It is difficult to classify the vestibulopathies of aging for most of which there are no pathological and histopathological correlates. Based on the clinical manifestations observed in patients with disequilibrium of aging, Schuknecht has described four types, one of which, cupulolithiasis of aging, is supported by pathological documentation.[30]

CUPULOLITHIASIS OF AGING Cupulolithiasis of aging is defined by vertiginous attacks precipitated by head position. The onset is usually insidious in the older individual and chronic. The attacks may occur quite abruptly and cause the patient to fall to the ground. In most cases, because the vertigo is precipitated by head position, patients learn to avoid the precipitating head positions and live with their disability. Histological studies have revealed deposits of debris on the cupula of the posterior semicircular canal in patients with this disorder. It is believed that this debris is generated by breakdown and atrophy of the utricle and semicircular canals which then settles in the more dependent part of the vestibular labyrinth and becomes fixed to the cupula of the posterior semicircular canal. These deposits then effect cupular deflections influenced by head position.

AMPULLARY DISEQUILIBRIUM OF AGING Patients with ampullary disequilibrium of aging describe vertigo which is precipitated by rotational head movement. A sense of rotation may persist after completion of the movement. Patients may complain of persistent disequilibrium after movements which repeatedly exercise the ampullary mechanism of the semicircular canals. This being the case, it is most likely that degenerative changes within the ampullated ends of the semicircular canals are responsible for the disequilibrium. A reduction in the response to caloric stimulation would support this diagnosis in the aging patient.

MACULAR DISEQUILIBRIUM OF AGING Changes in head position may also be responsible for evoking macular disequilibrium of aging. In contrast to ampullary disequilibrium in which inciting movement was rotatory, changes in position relative to the direction of gravity appear to be responsible in this condition. After the head has been held in a position for a length of time, patients may be disturbed by disequilibrium which appears to be provoked by linear, as opposed to angular, movement. Sitting up in bed is a common provocative movement and may be confused with orthostatic hypotension. There may be no other evidence of vascular insufficiency, however, and the caloric response, in contrast to the condition of ampullary disequilibrium, will be normal.

VESTIBULAR ATAXIA OF AGING Vestibular ataxia of aging is characterized by a constant sensation of disequilibrium and unsteadiness when walking. The patient's gait is broad-based, and there is a tendency to weave in an effort to maintain the center of gravity. If the patient remains stationary there is no disequilibrium. Histological documentation of this condition is lacking; however, it is Schuknecht's belief that more central lesions involving the vestibular nerve nuclei and the vestibular tracts may be responsible. This condition may be the vestibular counterpart of neural presbycusis.

The subjective sensation of dizziness is generally more difficult for an elderly patient to define than is an age-related hearing loss. Patients describe the sensation of dizziness in a variety of ways, according to their perceptions of the balance distortion. It is the responsibility of the clinician, therefore, to differentiate those conditions which produce nonvestibular dizziness from true vestibular dysfunction. In the elderly individual, conditions which produce true vestibular dysfunction are multiple and include central neurologic causes and metabolic imbalance, vascular insufficiency, and drug effects, among others.

REFERENCES

1. Feller BA: Prevalence of selected impairments, U.S. 1977. *Vital Health Stat* ser 10:134, DHHS 81-1562. Washington, US Govt Printing Office, 1981.
2. US Dept of Health and Human Services, National Center for Health Statistics. Unpublished data. Health Interview Survey, 1981.
3. Moscicki EK et al: Hearing loss in the elderly: An epidemiologic study of the Framingham Heart Study Cohort. *Ear Hear* 6:184, 1985.
4. Schow R, Nerbonne M: Hearing level in nursing home residents. *J Speech Hear Disord* 45:124, 1980.

5. Maurer JF, Rupp RR: *Hearing and Aging: Tactics for Intervention.* New York, Grune and Stratton, 1979.

6. Zwaardemaker H: Der verlust an hohen tonen mit zunehmendem alter, ein neues gesetz. *Arch Ohr Nas Kehlklteilk* 47, 1899.

7. Glorig A, Roberts J: Hearing levels of adults by age and sex, U.S. 1960–1962. *Vital Health Stat* ser 11: 11, Washington, US Dept of Health, Education and Welfare, 1965.

8. Spoor A, Passchier-Vermeer W: Spread in hearing levels of non-noise exposed people at various ages. *Int Audiol* 8:328, 1969.

9. Rowland M: Basic data on hearing levels of adults 25–74 years, U.S. 1970–75. Washington, US Pub Health Service, US Dept of Health, Education and Welfare 11:215, 1980.

10. Johnsson LG, Hawkins JE: Sensory and neural degeneration with aging, as seen in microdissections of the human inner ear. *Ann Otol Rhinol Laryngol* 81:179, 1972.

11. Johnsson LG, Hawkins JE: Vascular changes in the human inner ear associated with aging. *Ann Otol Rhinol Laryngol* 81:364, 1972.

12. Arnst DJ: Presbycusis, in Katz J (ed): *Handbook of Clinical Audiology.* Baltimore, Williams and Wilkins, 1985, p 707.

13. Gaeth J: A study of phonemic regression in relation to hearing loss. Unpublished doctoral dissertation. Northwestern University, Evanston, IL, 1948.

14. Jerger J: Audiological findings in aging. *Adv Otorhinolaryngol* 20:115, 1973.

15. Bergman M: Central disorders of hearing in the elderly, in Hinchcliffe R (ed): *Hearing and Balance in the Elderly.* New York, Churchill-Livingstone, 1983, p 145.

16. Rousch J: Aging and binaural auditory processing. *Semin Hear* G:135, 1985.

17. Marshall L: Auditory processing in aging listeners. *J Speech Hear Disord* 46:226, 1981.

18. Welsh LW et al: Central presbycusis. *Laryngoscope* 95:128, 1985.

19. Ventry IM: Hearing and hearing impairment in the elderly, in Wilder CH, Weinstein BE (eds): *Aging and Communication Problems in Management.* New York, Haworth Press, 1984, p 7.

20. Herbst KG, Humphrey C: Hearing impairment and mental state in the elderly living at home. *Br Med J* 281:903, 1980.

21. Jones DA et al: Hearing difficulty and its psychological implications for the elderly. *J Epidemiol Community Health.* 38:75, 1984.

22. Weinstein BE, Ventry IM: Hearing impairment and social isolation in the elderly. *J Speech Hear Res* 25:593, 1982.

23. Norris ML, Cunningham DR: Social impact of hearing loss in the aged. *J Gerontol* 36:727, 1981.

24. Bess F: Changing hearing aid rehabilitation for the growing elderly (CHARGE), in Robinette MS, Bauch CD (eds): *Proceedings of a Symposium in Audiology.* Rochester, Mayo Clinic-Mayo Foundation, 1987.

25. Herbst KG: Psycho-social consequences of disorders of hearing in the elderly, in Hinchcliffe R (ed): *Hearing and Balance in the Elderly.* New York, Churchill-Livingstone, 1983, p 174.

26. Zimbardo PG et al: Induced hearing deficit generates experimental paranoia. *Science* 212:1529, 1981.

27. Ethalm B, Belal A: Senile changes in the middle ear joints. *Ann Otol Rhinol Laryngol* 83:49, 1974.

28. Crowe SJ et al: Observations in the pathology of hightone deafness. *Johns Hopkins Hosp Bull* 54:315, 1934.

29. Saxon A: Pathologic und klinde der altersschwerhaerigkeit. *Acta Otolaryngol* [Suppl 23], 1937.

30. Schuknecht AF: *Pathology of the Ear.* Cambridge: Harvard University Press, 1974.

31. Uhlmann RF et al: Accuracy of auditory screening tests in demented and non-demented elderly. *J Gen Intern Med* (still in press).

32. Bienvenue GR et al: The Audioscope: A clinical tool for otoscopic and audiometric examination. *Ear Hear* 6:251, 1985.

33. Frank T, Petersen DR: Accuracy of a 40 dB HL Audioscope and audiometer screening for adults. *Ear Hear* 8:180, 1987.

34. Snyder JM: Office audiometry. *J Fam Pract* 19:535, 1984.

35. High W et al: Scale for self-assessment of handicap. *J Speech Hear Disord* 29:215, 1984.

36. Noble WG, Atherly GRC: The Hearing Measurement Scale: A questionnaire for the assessment of auditory disability. *J Aud Res* 10:229, 1970.

37. Giolas TG et al: Hearing performance inventory. *J Speech Hear Disord* 44:169, 1979.

38. Ventry IM, Weinstein BE: The Hearing Handicap Inventory for the Elderly: A new tool. *Ear Hear* 3:128, 1982.

39. Ventry I, Weinstein B: Identification of elderly people with hearing problems. ASHA 25:37, 1983.

40. American Academy of Otolaryngology: Committee on Hearing and Equilibrium and the American Council of Otolaryngology Committee on the Medical Aspects of Noise: Guide for the evaluation of hearing handicap. *JAMA* 241:2055, 1979.

41. Kapteyn T: Satisfaction with fitted hearing aids. II. An investigation into the influence of psychosocial factors. *Scand Audiol* 6:171, 1977.

42. Rupp R et al: A feasibility scale for predicting hearing aid use (FSPHAU) with older individuals. *J Acad Rehab Aud* 10:81, 1977.

43. Droller H, Pembarton J: Vertigo in a random sample of elderly people living in their homes. *J Laryngol Otol* 67:689, 1953.

44. Mann DMA et al: The relationship between lipofuscin pigment and aging in the human nervous system. *J Neurol Sci* 37:83, 1978.

45. Engstrom H: Structural changes in the vestibular epithelia in elderly monkeys and humans. *Adv Otorhinolaryngol* 22:93, 1977.

46. Rosenthal U: Epithelial cysts in the human vestibular apparatus. *J Laryngol Otol* 88:105, 1974.

47. Ross MD: Observations in normal and degenerating human otoconia. *Ann Otol Rhinol Laryngol* 85:310, 1976.

48. Bergstrom B: Morphology of the vestibular nerve. II. The number of myelinated vestibular nerve fibers in man at various stages. *Acta Otolaryngol* 76:173, 1973.

The Cardiovascular System

Chapter 44

ALTERATIONS IN CIRCULATORY FUNCTION

Edward G. Lakatta and Gary Gerstenblith

A review of the literature describing measured functional decline in various organ systems indicates that the rate of decline varies dramatically among organs within an individual subject and that within a given organ system there is substantial variation among subjects. This implies that some other factors may be potent modulators of a "biological clock" or of genetic mechanisms that determine how we age.

One factor that modulates the "aging process" is the occurrence of specific processes that we have traditionally referred to as "disease." Quantitative information as to age-associated alterations in cardiovascular function is essential in attempting to differentiate the cardiovascular limitations of an elderly individual which are disease-related from those which may fall within expected normal limits. Much of cardiovascular disease identification and evaluation is made by the physician through assessment of the functional capacity of the heart as it pumps in relationship to the hemodynamic load placed upon it. For example, severity of cardiac disease is most frequently graded in terms of left-ventricular hemodynamic measurements of pressure and/or volumes at rest or during exercise. Such values must be compared with those of normal individuals in the same age group.

Occult disease can be easily overlooked and can cause marked functional impairments. This consideration is especially pertinent to investigation of the effect of age on cardiovascular function in humans because coronary atherosclerosis, which increases exponentially with age, is present in an occult form in at least as great a number of elderly persons as the overt form of this disease.[1,2]

In addition to an increased prevalence of disease, changes in lifestyle occur concomitantly with advancing age. These include changes in habits of physical activity, eating, drinking, smoking, personality characteristics, etc. The impact of lifestyle variables on an aging process is presently not well defined. However, data are emerging to indicate that different nutritional habits may result in changes in arterial structure and function. It has been well established in unselected populations that the average daily physical activity level declines progressively with age.[3] Chronic exercise changes not only the function of the heart but also the heart size. Because the magnitude of the physical-conditioning effect can be so great, studies which attempt to investigate to what extent a disease or an aging process alters cardiovascular function (particularly reserve function) must be controlled for the physical activity status or at least consider it in the interpretation of the results.[4-6]

In summary, interactions among lifestyle, disease, and aging (Fig. 44-1) can have a substantial impact on cardiovascular function, and such interactions can alter the manifestations of "pure" aging effects on the cardiovascular system. Thus, elucidation of the presence and nature of an aging process, manifest as changes in cardiovascular structure and function, is a formidable task. Given the difficulty in quantifying and controlling lifestyle variables and occult disease, it is not surprising that the literature contains widely differing perspectives of how cardiovascular function changes with age.

This chapter presents the current perspectives concerning age-associated alterations in cardiovascular function of the normal human and, where appropriate, of animal models. The interaction of disease with these age-associated alterations of function and the clinical assessment of the cardiovascular system in the aged individual is discussed in Chap. 46.

CARDIOVASCULAR STRUCTURE AND FUNCTION AT REST

The overall control of cardiovascular function results from a complex interaction of modulating influences (Fig. 44-2). In some instances the changes in some of these variables that result from aging or disease are compensatory and enhance overall cardiovascular function,

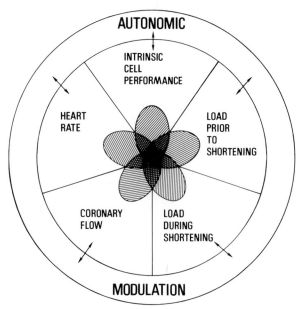

DETERMINANTS OF CARDIAC OUTPUT

FIGURE 44-2
Factors that regulate cardiovascular performance. The ovals have been drawn to overlap each other in order to indicate the interaction among these parameters. The bidirectional arrows also indicate that each factor is not only modulated by, but also in part determines, the autonomic tone. (*From EG Lakatta, J Chronic Dis 36:15, 1983.*)

whereas in other instances the changes may compromise function. In assessing the capacity of the intact cardiovascular system, it is often difficult to quantify the contribution of each factor in Fig. 44-2. However, in attempting to define the mechanisms that are operative during failure of the system, each of these regulatory factors must be studied, to the extent feasible, in isolation. "Failure" of the cardiovascular system is a relative concept; a limitation may be manifest at rest or may be detected only in response to graded stress. Therefore, studies conducted over a range of stressful conditions must be employed to detect and define evidence of any age-associated compromise in cardiovascular function.

Figure 44-3 summarizes the results of some studies that have measured cardiac output across a broad age range. The cardiac output (or cardiac index) at rest, as measured in different individuals of varying age (i.e., cross-sectional studies), has been found to remain unchanged, to decrease substantially, or even to increase slightly with age. The variability likely stems from heterogeneity of selection criteria among the various studies.

HEART RATE

Resting heart rate is not markedly affected by age. Variation in sinus rate with respiration is diminished with advancing age.[7,8] The spontaneous variation in heart rate

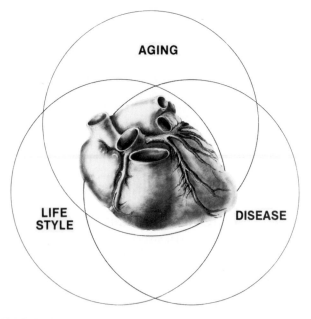

FIGURE 44-1
Diseases and changes in lifestyle occur with advancing age. Interactions among these and an "aging process" make it difficult to identify or characterize the effect of age on the heart. (*From Lakatta, Ref. 1.*)

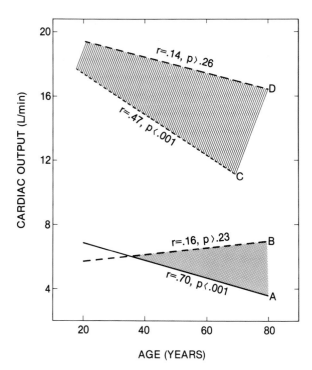

FIGURE 44-3
Cardiac output measured at rest and during exercise at exhaustion in the upright position vs. age. (*Line A [least squares linear regression] from M Branfronbrener, Circulation 12:557, 1955; lines B and D from Rodeheffer et al., Ref. 13; line C from Julius et al., Ref. 63.*)

monitored over a 24-hour period in men free from coronary artery disease also decreases with age.[9] The intrinsic sinus rate, i.e., that measured in the presence of both sympathetic and parasympathetic blockade, is significantly diminished with age: at age 20 the average intrinsic heart rate is 104 beats per minute as compared with 92 beats per minute in a 45- to 55-year age group.[10]

PRELOAD OR FILLING

Left ventricular pump function is dependent on preload, measured as the end-diastolic volume, the afterload or impedance to the ejection of the blood from the ventricle, and the inotropic or contractile state of the ventricular muscle (Fig. 44-2). Resting left-ventricular end-diastolic dimension,[11] area,[12] and volume,[13] as estimated by M-mode echocardiography, two-diminsional echocardiography, and gated blood pool scans, respectively, do not change significantly or may increase slightly with age in healthy adults. The chest x ray evaluated in longitudinal studies indicates that an increase in the cardiothoracic ratio from 0.405 to 0.427 occurs over a mean period of 12 years.[14,15] This is due to a slightly increased cardiac and decreased thoracic diameter; the latter may be due to decreased rib cage mobility.

Although the left-ventricular volume at end-diastole is not diminished in healthy elderly individuals, many studies have observed that the rate at which the left ventricle fills with blood during early diastole is markedly reduced (by about 50 percent) with aging between the ages of 20 and 80 (Fig. 44-4). This may be due to age-associated alterations in passive left-ventricular stiffness, but it is also likely that it refects in part the age-associated prolonged relaxation phase of cardiac muscle contraction.[16–18] This reduction in filling rate is not of sufficient magnitude, however, to lead to a reduction in end-diastolic filling volume at rest. Enhanced ventricular filling later in diastole in elderly subjects is an adaptive mechanism to maintain an adequate filling volume. This results largely from an enhanced atrial contribution to ventricular filling (Fig. 44-4).

AFTERLOAD AND IMPEDANCE TO EJECTION

Cardiac afterload or impedance to ejection becomes modestly increased at rest with aging in humans. In part this is due to an increase in arterial pressure. Most studies have shown that systolic pressure rises within the normal range with advancing age in men and women.[19,20] In some studies, diastolic pressure was found to increase, but the extent to which this occurs is

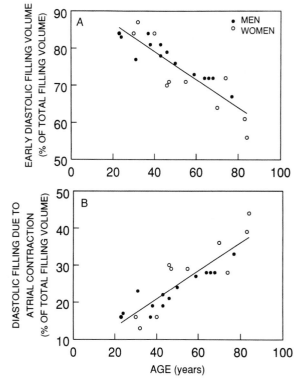

FIGURE 44-4
Comparison between the early diastolic (*top*) and atrial (*bottom*) contributions to left-ventricular filling assessed by echo Doppler technique in healthy men and women of a broad age range. (*From CJ Swinne et al., J Am Coll Cardiol 13:56A, 1989.*)

very small compared with the change in systolic pressure.

Many studies have focused on the effect of age on physical characteristics of the arteries. Both in vitro and in vivo studies have indicated that arterial stiffness increases with age. Pulse wave velocity also has been shown to increase in humans with age in elderly individuals,[21] and the reflected pulse waves from the periphery return back to the base of the aorta during the ejection period.[22] It should be emphasized that the age changes in elastic moduli, pulse wave velocity, and arterial rigidity are attributable to a diffuse process that occurs in the vessel wall and cannot be explained on the basis of atherosclerosis. Although the stress-strain curves of aged vessels suggest that there is a loss of elastin and an increase in collagen, an absolute change in the amount of these substances need not be present to explain a change in physical properties. Age changes may involve a decrease in the coiling and twisting of molecular collagen chains and reduction in effective chain length.

An increase in aortic volume which occurs with age in normal humans may tend to compensate for this loss of elasticity, since a larger aorta accommodates a given volume injected into it with less change in radius. However, increased stiffness results in less diastolic recoil and, therefore, a decreased aortic contribution to forward flow, and the larger blood-filled aorta at end-diastolic increases impedance by requiring the heart to accelerate the blood against larger inertial forces when systole begins. Even if the aortic pressure–volume relationship were partially offset by this increase in aortic volume, however, the increased aortic stiffness and early reflected pulse waves and the larger blood volume of the aorta with age cause the aortic input impedance to increase with age.[23]

Moderate myocardial hypertrophy (Fig. 44-5), which is a successful adaptation to maintain a normal heart volume and pump function in the presence of modestly increased systolic arterial pressure, has been demonstrated to occur with aging in several studies, regardless of how subjects were chosen.[24] This cardiac hypertrophy is due largely to an increase in myocyte size and may reflect an age-associated cardiac adaptation to changes in the arterial system. But is this increase in vascular stiffness a manifestation of "normal" aging? Such a conclusion can be seriously challenged by cross-cultural studies such as the one in Fig. 44-6, which shows that an urban population that consumes two times more sodium chloride than a rural population exhibits a marked acceleration of the increase in arterial stiffness with age.

CONTRACTILE BEHAVIOR OF THE HEART

The contractile state or level of excitation-contraction coupling present in the myocardium itself is difficult to

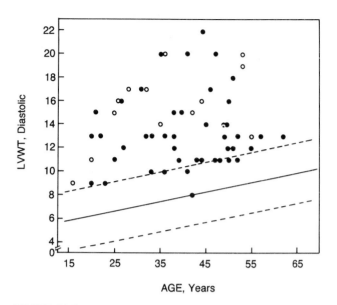

FIGURE 44-5

Least squares linear regression of left-ventricular end-diastolic wall thickness (LVWT) on age in healthy men and women as measured by echocardiography (solid line, mean; dotted lines, ±2s D of the mean). Circles indicate the LVWT in patients with severe hypertension or aortic valve disease. (*From AL Sjogren, Ann Clin Res 4:310, 1972.*)

ascertain in the intact circulatory system given the interaction of the multiple modulators of cardiac function (Fig. 44-2). Thus, our understanding of the effect of age on intrinsic cardiac muscle performance has come from studies in isolated hearts or cardiac muscle isolated from the hearts of animals. While numerous studies have documented that properties of muscle isolated from human hearts are very much like those of muscle isolated from hearts of most other mammals, it remains to be documented that the effect of age is similar in all species. Thus, some caution is advisable when extrapolating data from animal models. In some cases, however, similar age-related phenomena have been observed across a wide range of species, including humans, and in these instances some degree of extrapolation to the human aging model may be justified.

Several studies in isolated cardiac muscle have indicated that the capacity to develop force is not compromised in the senescent myocardium. With advancing age, i.e., the onset of senescence, characteristic changes in many aspects of cardiac muscle excitation-contraction coupling mechanisms have been noted to occur (see Lakatta[25] for review). Specifically, in an isometric contraction, i.e., one in which the ends of the muscle are fixed, the transmembrane action potential (Fig. 44-7A), the myoplasmic $[Ca^{2+}]$ (Ca_i) transient that initiates contraction (aequorin light, Fig. 44-7C), and the resultant contraction (Fig. 44-7B) are longer in duration in senescent versus younger adult rats. It is noteworthy that contraction time in humans determined noninvasively from measurement of time intervals of the cardiac cycle is also

FIGURE 44-6
The mean aortic pressure and aortic pulse wave velocity as a function of age in two Chinese populations. (*Redrawn from AP Avolio et al., Circulation 71:202, 1985.*)

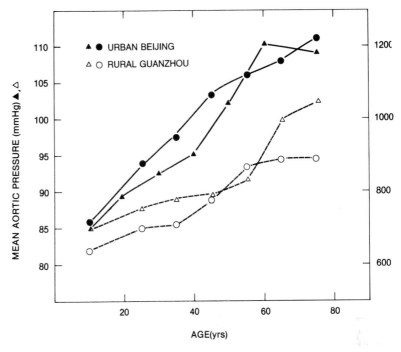

prolonged.[18] Prolonged systolic contractile activation may be a cause of the decrease in the observed early diastolic filling rate (Fig. 44-4). The rate at which the sarcoplasmic reticulum pumps Ca^{2+} decreases with aging (Fig. 44-7D). In isotonic contractions, i.e., those in which one of the muscle ends is not fixed and in which macroscopic muscle shortening is permitted to occur, the speed and extent of shortening are less in cardiac muscle from senescent rats than they are in muscle from younger adult rats. The myosin isozyme composition shifts from predominantly V_1 (rapid ATP hydrolytic isozyme) to predominantly V_3 (slower hydrolytic isozyme)

FIGURE 44-7
Representative data depicting differences in various aspects of excitation-contraction coupling mechanisms measured between young adult (6- to 9-month-old) and senescent (24- to 26-month-old) rat hearts. *A.* Transmembrane action potential. (*From JY Wei et al., Am J Physiol 246:H784, 1984.*) *B.* Isometric contraction. (*From JY Wei et al., Am J Physiol 246:H784, 1984.*) *C.* Ca_i transient. *Inset* shows relationship of Ca^{2+} transient (1) to contraction (2). (*From CH Orchard and EG Lakatta, J Gen Physiol 86:637, 1985.*) *D.* Sarcoplasmic reticulum Ca^{2+} uptake rate. (*From JP Froehlich et al., J Mol Cell Cardiol 10:427, 1978.*) *E.* Ca^{2+} stimulated ATPase activity; myosin isozyme composition (50 percent) of the heterodimer (V_2) is included in the total percentage of V_1. (*From Ref. 26.*) *F.* Dynamic stiffness, derived from the relationship of stiffness to force measurements made during the twitch. (*From HA Spurgeon et al., Am J Physiol 232(4):H373, 1977.*) *Inset* shows how dynamic stiffness measurements are made. Resting force or twitch force in two sequential contractions in the presence (*upper*) and absence (*lower*) of 17-Hz sinusoidal length perturbations (<1 percent of muscle length) is measured. When the unperturbed signals are subtracted from the perturbed one, an approximation of force development owing only to the length perturbation at rest or throughout the time course of the muscle contraction is derived. Stiffness is the change in force per change in length. Dynamic stiffness in resting muscle measured across a range of resting muscle lengths (not shown) is not age-related. Active dynamic stiffness (i.e., that measured during the contraction) is a linear function of force. An age difference is noted in the slope coefficient (0.41 ± 0.14 in the adult muscle, *n* = 8, versus 0.76 ± 0.06 in the senescent muscles, *n* = 17, *p* < .03), while the intercept is not age-related (12.9 ± 0.14 in the adult muscle versus 12.7 ± 1.3 in the senescent muscles). (*Montage from ML Weisfeldt et al., in Braunwald E (ed): Heart Disease: A Textbook of Cardiovascular Medicine 3d ed, New York, Raven Press, 1988.*)

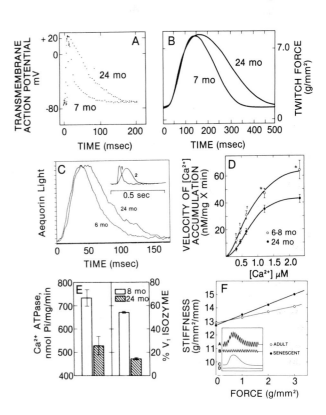

with senescence (Fig. 44-7E). The time required for restitution of the excitation-contraction coupling cycle is prolonged in senescent muscle, as evidenced by the muscle's relative inability to produce a contraction in response to premature stimuli.

Whether the prolonged action potential with aging results from increased net inward or decreased net outward current has not yet been determined. A prolonged Ca_i transient can also cause a prolonged action potential, since Ca^{2+} modulation of the Na/Ca exchanger or the nonspecific cation conductance (sometimes referred to as the transient inward current) produces a depolarization.[26] The prolonged time course of the Ca_i transient may also affect other aspects of the cardiac contraction that depend on Ca^{2+} myofilament interactions, including the time to peak force, the relaxation time, and the ability of the myofilaments to shorten and stiffen at differing times following excitation. Muscle stiffness is measured as the ratio of the change in force in response to a change in muscle length. "Active dynamic" stiffness is measured as the response to small sinusoidal changes in muscle length made during the contraction (Fig. 44-7F, inset). It has been experimentally determined that as force increases with time during a contraction, so too does the active dynamic stiffness, and this stiffness is a linear function of the force (Fig. 44-7F). The slope coefficient of the active stiffness force relationship increases in senescence, but the intercept of the relationship does not. The time to peak stiffness and to half-relaxation of peak stiffness are also prolonged in senescent versus younger adult cardiac muscle. A possible explanation for the prolonged time course of active stiffness during contraction is as follows: at times during the contraction, when force is still increasing, Ca_i is decreasing (Fig. 44-7C, inset), but Ca_i remains higher in senescent than in younger adult muscles. This results in a relative increase in Ca^{2+} myofilament interaction in senescent muscles at these later times. In the intact heart, prolonged myocardial stiffness enables the continual ejection of blood during late systole, an adaptation that is required in the face of enhanced vascular stiffness and early reflected pulse waves. Thus, while each of the alterations in excitation-contraction coupling in Fig. 44-7 may individually be construed as a functional decline, consideration of the entire *pattern* of changes that occurs with aging permits a hypothesis that these changes may indeed be adaptive rather than decremental in nature.

Additional evidence supporting the notion that the age-associated changes depicted in Fig. 44-7 are adaptive in nature stems from the observation that these changes do not occur independently of each other. Specifically, the *pattern* of changes in excitation-contraction coupling mechanisms that occurs with aging can be mimicked in younger animals by chronic experimental hypertension in younger animals.[24] At least one of these

changes in Fig. 44-7, i.e., the shift in the myosin isoform, is a change in genetic expression of protein synthesis (a pretranscriptional change). It is currently unknown whether the changes in the various cell membrane functions depicted in Fig. 44-7 are due to changes in the expression of proteins that determine or modulate ion channel or ionic carrier activities at the sarcolemma (prolonged action potential) or the sarcoplasmic reticulum pump (prolonged Ca^{2+} transient; decreases in sarcoplasmic reticulum Ca^{2+} transport rate). However, it is tempting to speculate that since these changes do not occur in isolation from one another, they are all directed from within the genome. This would require a "logic" within the genome that controls the simultaneous expression of multiple genes in order for cellular adaptation to occur. In the case of aging and experimental hypertension, altered myocardial cell loading would be the macroscopic stimulus that signals this genetic logic to alter protein expression. The microscopic signal that transduces the signal is presently unknown, but it could be something like stretch or a change in ion gradients (Ca^{2+}, H^+) resulting from altered mechanical loading of cardiac cells.

Thyroxine administration produces a *pattern* of change in these variables in the opposite direction of aging and experimental hypertension, and it can partially reverse age-associated changes in contraction duration and myosin isozyme expression.[27]

CORONARY FLOW

There are no data in normal humans regarding the effect of age on coronary flow. In the nonworking isolated rat heart, coronary flow per gram heart under normoxic conditions is not altered with advanced age.[28] Earlier studies have documented a decrease in the number of capillaries in the 26- and 27-month-old rat heart versus the 4-month-old rat heart.[29] However, it is difficult to interpret this as indicating that the senescent heart may be chronically ischemic because it has been demonstrated that the capillary density is not fixed but can increase appropriately with the stimulation of chronic physical conditioning.[30]

SUMMARY

In summary, resting heart rate is not age-related. There is little, if any, alteration in ventricular preload (diastolic volume), although the clearly rapid rate of filling may be slowed. There is an increase in afterload to left-ventricular ejection, which is due to arterial stiffening and is reflected in the age-associated increase in systolic blood pressure, but this is a modest age-associated change in normal subjects and is compensated for in healthy individuals, in large part by the age-associated left-ventricular hypertrophy. The net result of the age-associated changes in heart architecture and contractile properties, in spite of changes in aortic distensibility, permits the aged heart to function normally at rest. Thus, the fraction of end-diastolic volume ejected with each beat (ejection fraction) does not decline with age.[11,13] The velocity of circumferential shortening is also not age-related at rest.[11]

CARDIOVASCULAR RESPONSE TO STRESS

The cardiovascular response to stress (e.g., to increases in arterial pressure or to physical exercise) in older individuals is of considerable interest in clinical medicine. First, as physicians we are called upon to provide advice and information concerning the broad aspects of cardiovascular potential of the elderly, e.g., the effect or importance of conditioning on the maintenance of activity. Second, the cardiovascular response to stress is of importance in assessing the ability of older individuals to respond to disease states. Third, the cardiovascular response to stress has considerable value in terms of the diagnosis and management of patients with primary cardiovascular disease. Since the prevalence of cardiovascular disease is so high and progressive with age in the American population, it is of considerable importance to understand what the disease-free capabilities of the cardiovascular system are in response to exercise. Diagnostic tests which are designed to identify either the presence or severity of cardiovascular disease frequently utilize exercise testing to enhance the ability of the testing procedure to either detect or quantitate the severity of cardiovascular disease. It is very clear that the value of such diagnostic tests and the validity of their interpretation are dependent upon rather precise information as to the normal limits of such stress-testing procedures relative to age.

POSTURAL STRESS

The hemodynamic response to a postural stress is also mediated by a change in end-diastolic volume. While it was suggested in some older studies that aging alters the hemodynamic response to a postural change,[31–33] measurements of the effect of posture on absolute left-ventricular volumes were not made in these studies. In a recent study, cardiac volumes were measured by equilibrium gated cardiac blood pool scans and heart rate in the supine and sitting positions in 64 male volunteer subjects (ages 25 to 80) who had been rigorously

screened to exclude cardiovascular disease.[34] After the upright position was assumed, the average cardiac output of all subjects was unchanged, but heart rate increased and stroke volume decreased due to a decrease in end-diastolic volume. Neither the supine or sitting cardiac output nor the average postural change in cardiac output, cardiac volumes, or heart rate was age-related. While the average cardiac output among the subjects was unaltered with a change in posture, in some individuals it increased slightly, while in others it decreased. The postural change in cardiac output among the individuals correlated (by linear regression analysis) with (1) a change in heart rate in younger subjects only and (2) a change in stroke volume in all age groups; the slope of this relationship was greater in older than in younger subjects. The postural change in stroke volume was strongly correlated with a change in end-diastolic volume, and this relationship did not vary with age. Thus, although the average postural change in cardiac output among healthy subjects is not age-related, a given change in cardiac output with posture in an older individual depends more on a change in end-diastolic and stroke volume and less on a heart rate change than it does in younger individuals. This result, like the response to vigorous upright exercise (see below), indicates in the elderly a greater reliance on the Frank-Starling mechanism than on heart rate for a given change in cardiac output in response to perturbations from the basal supine state.

PRESSOR STRESS

Left-ventricular contractile function in response to pressor stress has been studied via ultrasound techniques in a small, selected cross-sectional population of normal human subjects.[35] Those features of the echocardiogram relating to left-ventricular function (i.e., end-diastolic and systolic dimensions, ejection fraction, and the velocity of circumferential fiber shortening) did not differ with age prior to or during a 30-mmHg increase in systolic pressure induced by phenylephrine. In the presence of beta-blockade (propranolol) during a pressor stress with phenylephrine, end-diastolic dimension increased in the elderly subjects but did not change in the young subjects. The ejection parameters of ventricular function, though, were unchanged. This study appears to show that the heart of the older individual evidences a small decrease in contractility in normal subjects that is evident only after blockade of the sympathetic nervous system and in the face of a significant pressure stress. Under these conditions the heart of an older individual dilates more, thus utilizing the Frank-Starling mechanism. This mechanism is an intrinsic property of cardiac muscle whereby performance is augmented as the muscle length or left-ventricular size is increased.

DYNAMIC EXERCISE STRESS

During exercise, changes in the mechanisms (Fig. 44-2) responsible for the augmentation of cardiac output during exercise are reasonably well understood from studies in experimental animals and in humans. As exercise begins, vagal tone decreases, cardiac output is initially augmented by an increase in venous return resulting from an increase in heart rate and sympathetic constriction of venous capacitance beds. Concomitantly, an increased work load is placed on the heart during the ejection of blood, reflected, in part, by an increase in systolic blood pressure. Nevertheless, the amount of blood ejected from the left ventricle with each beat (i.e., the difference between end-systolic and end-diastolic volume, or the stroke volume) increases, reflecting the fact that an increase in myocardial performance outweighs the increase in left-ventricular systolic load. These cardiac adaptations to exercise continue as moderately severe levels of exercise are encountered; the heart rate and performance of left-ventricular myocardium continue to increase as cardiac output and left-ventricular load are augmented as exercise proceeds. An additional factor, the Frank-Starling mechanism, also comes into play. Thus, during exercise there can be an increase in end-diastolic volume, and this can promote a larger stroke volume with each heart beat.

It might be expected that age-related changes in the cardiovascular system might be initially manifest or most pronounced during exercise when cardiovascular function must increase (up to as much as four- to fivefold) above the basal level. While the increase in heart rate during exhaustive exercise is less in many elderly subjects than it is in younger subjects, some elderly subjects can increase stroke volume to compensate for the heart-

rate deficit (Fig. 44-8). Thus, the hearts of these elderly subjects exhibit Starling's law of the heart as an adaptive mechanism to preserve cardiac output during exercise in the presence of a reduced heart rate. Elderly individuals who do not exhibit this mechanism to increase stroke volume and who also have a reduced heart rate compared to younger individuals do not increase cardiac output during severe exercise to the extent that younger individuals do (see line C in Fig. 44-3). However, whether the reduced physical work capacity of these individuals is exclusively limited by limitations of cardiac function is uncertain (see below).

The change in ejection fraction between rest and exercise is used clinically as a diagnostic test for the detection and quantification of the severity of cardiac disease, particularly ischemic heart disease. Ejection fraction is thus of considerable clinical interest. As noted, there is no age-associated alteration in ejection fraction at rest, and at low levels of exercise ejection fraction is unchanged with age. At higher levels of exercise and at exhaustion, an age-associated decrease in the change in ejection fraction (Fig. 44-9) is accompanied by less of a reduction in end-systolic volume in older individuals than in younger individuals (Fig. 44-8), reflecting an age-associated decrease in augmentation of myocardial factors or an increase in vascular loading. Even so, in most healthy subjects rigorously screened to exclude the presence of coronary artery disease, ejection fraction increases with exercise, although this increase is smaller in magnitude in older individuals than it is in younger ones (Fig. 44-9B). When a study population contains many elderly individuals who have coronary artery disease, the ejection fraction during exercise does not increase, or it *decreases* to a fraction below that at rest

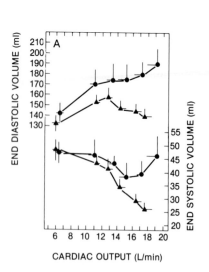

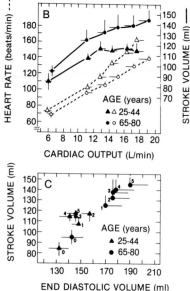

FIGURE 44-8

The relationship of end-diastolic volume and end-systolic volume (A) and stroke volume and heart rate (B) to a given cardiac output at rest and during graded upright bicycle exercise in rigorously screened older volunteer subjects. During vigorous exercise these older subjects have a diminution in heart rate but an increase in stroke volume as compared to the younger subjects; this is not accomplished by a greater reduction in end-systolic volume but rather by an increase (as much as 30 percent) in end-diastolic volume. This hemodynamic profile, redrawn in C, is an example of Starling's law of the heart and resembles that observed during beta-adrenergic blockade. The numbers 0–5 indicate progressive exercise work loads from rest (work load 0). (*Redrawn from Rodeheffer et al., Ref. 13.*)

FIGURE 44-9

(*A*) Effect of age on the change in left-ventricular ejection fraction from the resting level to that at maximum voluntary exercise in apparently healthy subjects. However, during exercise a large number of these elderly volunteers exhibited left-ventricular wall motion abnormalities, possibly due to coronary artery disease and coronary insufficiency during the exercise stress. (*Redrawn from Port E et al., N Engl J Med 303:1133, 1980.*) (*B*) Effect of age on change in left-ventricular ejection fraction from resting level to that at maximum voluntary exercise in subjects from the Baltimore Longitudinal Study of Aging. M, males; F, females. (*Redrawn from Rodeheffer et al., Ref. 13.*)

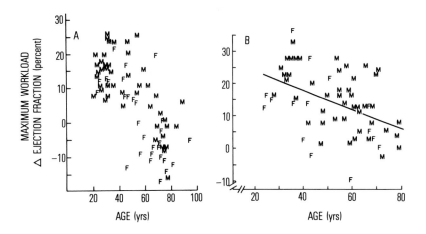

(Fig. 44-9A). This result is a manifestation of the interaction of coronary artery disease and aging (Fig. 44-1) and must not be confused with an *age-related* change in cardiac pump function.

BETA-ADRENERGIC STIMULATION

The hemodynamic profile of elderly individuals in Fig. 44-8 is strikingly similar to that of younger subjects who exercise in the presence of beta-adrenergic blockade.[36] These observations have led to the hypothesis that perhaps the most marked changes in cardiovascular response to stress that occur with aging in healthy subjects vigorously screened to exclude occult disease and highly motivated to perform exercise are due to a reduction in the efficacy of the beta-adrenergic modulation of cardiovascular function.[36,37]

Catecholamines have a major modulatory influence on cardiovascular performance during acute stressful situations. Clinical evidence of an enhanced elaboration of catecholamines is found in the measurement of an increase in their levels within the plasma. The average basal level of norepinephrine has been found to increase with advancing age in many studies (but not all). Virtually all studies have found that in response to stress the average level of norepinephrine increases to a greater extent in elderly than in younger individuals (Fig. 44-10).[8,38–44] It is noteworthy, however, that while the average plasma epinephrine and norepinephrine levels during perturbations from the basal state in elderly subjects are greater than in younger ones, there is substantial heterogeneity among elderly individuals.

Beta-adrenergic stimulation modulates the heart rate, arterial tone, and myocardial contractility. Both the beta-adrenergic relaxation of arterial smooth muscle and the enhancement of myocardial performance (see below) facilitate ejection of blood from the heart. Deficits in either with aging may be implicated in the alterations in the ventricular ejection pattern in some elderly individuals, as shown in Figs. 44-8 and 44-9.

There is abundant evidence to indicate that both arterial and venous dilitation[45–51] responses to beta-adrenergic stimulation decline with age. Direct evidence for a reduction in the ability of beta-adrenergic stimulation to relax vascular muscle comes from studies in isolated aortic muscle from young adult and senescent animals[46,48,50] which demonstrate a diminution in relaxation in response to beta-adrenergic agonists but not in response to nonadrenergic relaxants. A deficiency in arterial dilatation during exercise, in addition to structural changes that may occur within the large vessels with age, may contribute to an increase in vascular impedance during exercise[52] over and above that increase which may already be present at rest. Some studies have indicated that alpha-adrenergic modulation of vascular function is not age-related.[45,53]

While studies in animal models provide little support for the notion that the intrinsic contractile reserve of cardiac muscle (measured as peak force or pressure) or peak rates of force or pressure development decrease with aging, even in senescent myocardium,[25] the beta-adrenergic modulation of these mechanisms that governs the effectiveness of myocardial excitation-contraction coupling decreases in advanced age. A deficiency in myocardial reserve could be explained, in part, on this basis.[36,54,55]

The beta-adrenergic modulation of pacemaker cells accounts, in part, for the increase in heart rate during exercise. The effect of bolus infusions of beta-adrenergic agonists to increase heart rate (Fig. 44-11) diminishes with advancing age.[43,56–60] The *maximum* heart-rate response to isoproterenol infusion is also diminished in senescent versus younger adult beagles[61] and remains diminished even in the presence of full vagal blockade with atropine. In contrast, the maximum heart rate that can be elicited by external electrical pacing, which was far in excess of that elicited by isoproterenol infusion, is not age-related. Isoproterenol infusions in intact rats have also produced a diminished increase in heart rate with age.[62]

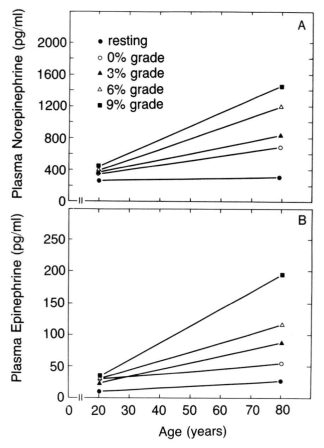

FIGURE 44-10

Panels *A* and *B* depict norepinephrine (NE) and epinephrine (E) levels versus age at rest (●) and at common external submaximal treadmill work loads of 0% (○), 3% (▲), 6% (△), and 9% (■) grades. The 9% grade represents maximal effort for three subjects, ages 54, 68, and 72, respectively. NE is unrelated to age at rest but increases with age at each work load. The slope of the NE-age regression increases progressively from 5.36 pg/yr, $r = .44$, at 0% grade to 17.92 pg/yr, $r = .64$, at 9% grade. E increases with age both at rest and at each common external work load. As with NE, the slope of the plasma E–age regression increases, from 0.67 pg/yr, $r = .42$, at 0% grade to 2.82 pg/yr, $r = .65$, at 9% grade. Both NE and E were also greater in elderly than in younger subjects at maximum exercise (not shown). All subjects were participants of the Baltimore Longitudinal Study of Aging (BLSA) who were judged to be free from occult coronary artery disease by a thorough examination that included prior stress testing with electrocardiographic monitoring. (*From Fleg et al., Ref. 39.*)

PHYSICAL WORK CAPACITY AND AGING

The maximum oxygen consumption rate (Vo_{2max}) achieved during stress can increase to greater than ninefold over the basal level. There has been a persistent debate among exercise physiologists as to which factors limit Vo_{2max} in individuals of a given age. Similarly, whether the same factors are limiting in subjects of different ages is not known with certainty.[4] A ninefold increase in Vo_2 during exercise cannot be achieved by a four- to fivefold increase in cardiac output. Thus, in ad-

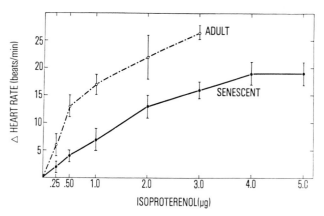

FIGURE 44-11

The effect of age on the increase in heart rate in response to varying concentrations of isoproterenol in BLSA participants. Points indicate mean $C = SEM$. At all concentrations above 0.5 μg, the effect of age is significant at $p < .005$. Adult age = 18–34 years, $n = 16$; senescent age = 62–80 years, $n = 20$. (*From Lakatta, Ref. 54, as redrawn from Yin et al., Ref. 60.*)

dition to an increase in cardiac output, O_2 extraction by working tissues increases and causes the arteriovenous O_2 difference to increase (up to twofold during strenuous exercise). This results in part from an increase (up to 15-fold) in the relative proportion of cardiac output delivered to working muscles.[5]

The evidence to suggest that the central circulatory function limits the peak Vo_2 achieved during exercise in elderly individuals is indirect and unconvincing. Studies to date have failed to demonstrate a plateau in cardiac output across the two highest external work loads achieved. In fact, such studies have been interpreted to indicate that the cardiac response for the work performed (Vo_2 achieved) in elderly subjects during exercise is as adequate as that in younger subjects.[6,63] As there was no evidence that elderly subjects stop exercising because of insufficiency of the central circulation, these studies cannot be interpreted with certainty to indicate that the adequacy of central circulatory function declines with age. Rather, the lower peak cardiac output measured at exhaustion in elderly versus younger individuals could be the *result* of a lesser amount of work performed by elderly subjects (rather than the *cause* of a diminished work capacity). Limitation of work capacity could be due to noncardiac factors. Although present evidence has failed to directly substantiate the notion that a limitation of cardiac output exclusively limits peak Vo_2 or work capacity in elderly subjects, this notion continues to be popularized, based on estimates of cardiac output from measurements of Vo_2 and heart rate at maximum exercise and extrapolated estimates of stroke volume and arteriovenous O_2.[64] This approach ignores age-related changes that have been noted to occur in muscle mass,[65,66] in the peak arteriovenous O_2 difference[63] and variation that can occur with aging in the pattern of the stroke volume increase during exercise (e.g., that depicted in Fig. 44-8).

The extent of the decline in the maximum work capacity and Vo_{2max} and maximum cardiac output with advancing adult age varies with lifestyle (e.g., with physical-conditioning status) and with presence of disease (occult or clinical). As noted, an increasing prevalence of occult coronary artery disease and generalized atherosclerotic vascular changes occur with advancing age. Additionally, changes in lifestyle occur such that elderly subjects become less physically conditioned than their younger adult counterparts. The motivation to continue to exercise may decrease in sedentary elderly subjects. Orthopedic function may limit maximum work capacity in some subjects. A decline in peak Vo_2 with age cannot be considered to be due to an age-related decline in central circulatory performance if an age difference in muscle mass or in the ability to shunt blood to exercising muscles cannot be excluded with certainty. This is not a trivial issue, given that a greater than tenfold increase in blood flow and oxygen utilization by muscle occurs during exercise.[5] The impact of normalization of peak Vo_2 for an index of muscle mass, i.e., the creatinine excretion, has recently been demonstrated.[67] Given these formidable obstacles to the interpretation of measurements of aerobic capacity in elderly subjects, the extent to which it declines due to age per se and the mechanisms of this decline need to be reassessed.

SUMMARY

One of the major age-associated alterations in the cardiovascular response to exercise is a striking age-associated decrease in heart-rate response. Despite this decrease in heart-rate response, overall cardiac output at any given work load level can be maintained in some healthy older individuals as a result of an augmentation of stroke volume in the older subject above that seen in the young as exercise progresses. The major mechanism available to augment stroke volume in the older subject is the Frank-Starling mechanism. End-diastolic volume increases with exercise to a greater extent in some older subjects than in younger ones, leading to an increase in the volume of blood ejected from the left ventricle. The reduction in end-systolic volume and the increase in ejection fraction at peak exercise decrease with age and likely result from deficient myocardial performance or augmented afterload. This could be due to a deficiency in the beta-adrenergic stimulation which enhances myocardial contractility or to enhanced aortic impedance. Although in older subjects there is a decrease in the maximum physical work capacity, even among the healthy older subjects, it has become more clear that this limitation in exercise is not solely due to limitations in the central circulation. Rather, the limitations of exercise

ability in the aged subject may well be related to peripheral factors. It is most remarkable that, in fact, cardiac output can be maintained at high levels at rest and during exercise in the community-dwelling, highly motivated aged individual. Alterations in cardiac function which exceed the identified limits for aging changes for healthy elderly individuals discussed herein are most likely a manifestation of the interaction of physical deconditioning on cardiovascular disease, both of which are, unfortunately, so prevalent within our population.

REFERENCES

1. Lakatta EG: Health, disease, and cardiovascular aging, in Institute of Medicine and National Research Council, Committee on an Aging Society (eds): *Health in an Older Society.* Washington, National Academy Press, 1985, p 73.

2. Elveback L, Lie JT: Combined high incidence of coronary artery disease at autopsy in Olmstead County, Minnesota, 1950–1979. *Circulation* 70:345, 1984.

3. McGandy RB et al: Nutrient intakes and energy expenditure in men of different ages. *J Gerontol* 21:581, 1966.

4. Raven PB, Mitchell J: The effect of aging on the cardiovascular response to dynamic and static exercise. *Aging* 12:269, 1980.

5. Clausen JP: Effects of physical conditioning: A hypothesis concerning circulatory adjustment to exercise. *Scand J Clin Lab Invest* 24:305, 1969.

6. Strandell T: Circulatory studies on healthy old men, with special reference to the limitation of the maximal physical working capacity. *Acta Med Scand* 175 (suppl 414):2, 1964.

7. Davies HEF: Respiratory change in heart rate, sinus arrhythmia in the elderly. *Gerontol Clin* 17:96, 1975.

8. Pfeifer MA et al: Differential changes of autonomic nervous system function with age in man. *Am J Med* 75:249, 1983.

9. Kostis JB et al: The effect of age on heart rate in subjects free of heart disease. *Circulation* 65:141, 1982.

10. Jose AD: Effect on combined sympathetic and parasympathetic blockade on heart rate and cardiac function in man. *Am J Cardiol* 18:476, 1966.

11. Gerstenblith G et al: Echocardiographic assessment of a normal adult aging population. *Circulation* 56:273, 1977.

12. VanTosh A et al: Ventricular dimensional changes during submaximal exercise: Effect of aging in normal man. *Circulation* 62:III–129, 1980.

13. Rodeheffer RJ et al: Exercise cardiac output is maintained with advancing age in healthy human subjects: Cardiac dilation and increased stroke volume compensate for diminished heart rate. *Circulation* 69:203, 1984.

14. Potter JF et al: The effect of age on the cardiothoracic ratio of men. *J Am Geriatr Soc* 30:404, 1982.

15. Ensor RE et al: Longitudinal chest x-ray changes in normal man. *J Gerontol* 38:307, 1983.

16. Lakatta EG et al: Prolonged contraction duration in aged myocardium. *J Clin Invest* 55:61, 1975.

17. Lakatta EG, Yin FCP: Myocardial aging: Functional al-

terations and related cellular mechanisms. *Am J Physiol* 242(Heart Circ Physiol 11):H927, 1982.

18. Harrison TR et al: The relationship of age to the duration of contraction, ejection, and relaxation of the normal human heart. *Am Heart J* 67:189, 1964.

19. Kannel WB: Blood pressure and the development of cardiovascular disease in the aged, in Caird FI, Dall JLC, Kennedy RD (eds): *Cardiology in Old Age*. New York, Plenum, 1976, p 143.

20. Page LB, Sid JJ: Medical management of primary hypertension. *N Engl J Med* 287:960, 1972.

21. Landowne M: The relation between intra-arterial pressure and impact pulse wave velocity with regard to age and arteriosclerosis. *J Gerontol* 13:153, 1958.

22. O'Rourke MF: *Arterial Function in Health and Disease*. New York, Churchill Livingstone, 1982.

23. Nichols WW et al: Effects of age on ventricular coupling. *Am J Cardiol* 55:1179, 1985.

24. Lakatta EG: Do hypertension and aging have a similar effect on the myocardium? *Circulation* 75(suppl I):I–69, 1987.

25. Lakatta EG: Cardiac muscle changes in senescence. *Annu Rev Physiol* 49:519, 1987.

26. Noble D: The surprising heart: A review of recent progress in cardiac electrophysiology. *J Physiol* 353:1, 1984.

27. Effron MB et al: Changes in myosin isoenzymes, ATPase activity, and contraction duration in rat cardiac muscle with aging can be modulated by thyroxine. *Circ Res* 60:238, 1987.

28. Weisfeldt ML et al: Coronary flow and oxygen extraction in the perfused heart of senescent male rats. *J Appl Physiol* 30:44, 1971.

29. Rukusan K, Poupa O: Capillaries and muscle fibres in the heart of old rats. *Gerontologia* 9:107, 1964.

30. Tomanek RJ: Effect of age and exercise on the extent of the myocardial capillary bed. *Anat Rec* 167:55, 1970.

31. Granath A et al: Studies on the central circulation at rest and during exercise in the supine and sitting position. *Acta Med Scand* 169:125, 1961.

32. Granath A et al: Circulation in healthy old men studied by right heart catheterization at rest and during exercise in supine and sitting position. *Acta Med Scand* 176:425, 1964.

33. Nixon JV et al: Ventricular performance in human hearts aged 61 to 73 years. *Am J Cardiol* 56:932, 1985.

34. Rodeheffer RJ: Postural changes in cardiac volumes in men in relation to adult age. *Exp Gerontol* 21:367, 1986.

35. Yin FCP et al: Age-associated decrease in ventricular response to hemodynamic stress during beta-adrenergic blockade. *Br Heart J* 40:1349, 1978.

36. Lakatta EG: Altered autonomic modulation of cardiovascular function with adult aging: Perspectives from studies ranging from man to cell, in Stone HL, Weglicki WB (eds): *Pathobiology of Cardiovascular Injury*. Boston, Martinus Nijhoff, 1985, p 441.

37. Filburn CR, Lakatta EG: Aging alterations in beta-adrenergic modulation of cardiac cell function, in Johnson J Jr (ed): *Aging and Cell Function*, vol 2. New York, Plenum, 1984, p 211.

38. Bertel OO et al: Decreased beta-adrenoreceptor responsiveness as related to age, blood pressure, and plasma catecholamines in patients with essential hypertension. *Hypertension* 2:130, 1980.

39. Fleg JL et al: Age-related augmentation of plasma catecholamines during dynamic exercise in healthy males. *J Appl Physiol* 59:1033, 1985.

40. Palmer GJ et al: Response of norepinephrine and blood pressure to stress increases with age. *J Gerontol* 33:482, 1978.

41. Rowe JW, Troen BR: Sympathetic nervous system and aging in man. *Endocr Rev* 1:167, 1980.

42. Sowers JR et al: Plasma norephinephrine responses to posture and isometric exercise increase with age in the absence of obesity. *J Gerontol* 38:315, 1983.

43. Young JB et al: Enhanced plasma norepinephrine response to upright posture and oral glucose administration in elderly human subjects. *Metabolism* 29:532, 1980.

44. Ziegler MG et al: Plasma noradrenaline increases with age. *Nature* 261:333, 1976.

45. Pan HY et al: Decline in beta adrenergic receptor-mediated vascular relaxation with aging in man. *J Pharmacol Exp Ther* 239:802, 1986.

46. Fleisch JH: Age-related decrease in beta adrenoceptor activity of the cardiovascular system. *Trends Pharmacol Sci* 2:337, 1981.

47. Fleisch JH, Hooker CS: The relationship between age and relaxation of vascular smooth muscle in the rabbit and rat. *Circ Res* 38:243, 1976.

48. Godfraind T: Alternative mechanisms for the potentiation of the relaxation evoked by isoprenaline in aortae from young and aged rats. *Eur J Pharmacol* 53:273, 1979.

49. O'Donnell SR, Wanstall JC: Beta-1 and beta-2 adrenoceptor-mediated responses in preparations of pulmonary artery and aorta from young and aged rats. *J Pharmacol Exp Ther* 228:733, 1984.

50. Tsujimoto G et al: Age-related decrease in beta adrenergic receptor-mediated vascular smooth muscle relaxation. *J Pharmacol Exp Ther* 239:411, 1986.

51. Van Brummelin P et al: Age-related decrease in cardiac and peripheral vascular responsiveness to isoprenaline: Studies in normal subjects. *Clin Sci* 60:571, 1981.

52. Yin FCP et al: Role of aortic input impedance in the decreased cardiovascular response to exercise with aging in dogs. *J Clin Invest* 68:28, 1981.

53. Duckles SP et al: Vascular adrenergic neuroeffector function does not decline in aged rats. *Circ Res* 56:109, 1985.

54. Lakatta EG: Age-related alterations in the cardiovascular response to adrenergic mediated stress. *Fed Proc* 39:3173, 1980.

55. Lakatta EG: Diminished beta-adrenergic modulation of cardiovascular function in advanced age. *Geriatr Cardiol* 4:185, 1986.

56. Kuramoto K et al: Electrocardiographic and hemodynamic evaluations of isoproterenol test in elderly ischemic heart disease. *Jpn Circ J* 42:955, 1978.

57. Lakatta EG: Alterations in the cardiovascular system that occur in advanced age. *Fed Proc* 38:163, 1979.

58. London GM et al: Isoproterenol sensitivity and total body clearance of propranolol in hypertensive patients. *J Clin Pharmacol* 16:174, 1976.

59. Vestal RE et al: Reduced beta-adrenoreceptor sensitivity in the elderly. *Clin Pharmacol Ther* 26:181, 1979.

60. Yin FCP et al: Age-associated decrease in chronotropic response to isoproterenol. *Circulation* 54:II–167, 1976.

61. Yin FCP et al: Age-associated decrease in heart rate response to isoproterenol in dogs. *Mech Ageing Dev* 10:17, 1979.

62. O'Connor SW et al: Age-associated decrease of adenylate cyclase activity in rat myocardium. *Mech Ageing Dev* 16:91, 1981.

63. Julius S et al: Influence of age on the hemodynamic response to exercise. *Circulation* 36:222, 1967.

64. Bruce RA: Functional aerobic capacity, exercise, and aging, in Andres R, Bierman EL, Hazzard WR (eds): *Principles of Geriatric Medicine.* New York, McGraw-Hill, 1985, p 87.

65. Borkan GA et al: Age changes in body composition revealed by computed tomography. *J Gerontol* 38:673, 1983.

66. Tzankoff SP, Norris HA: Effect of muscle mass decrease on age-related BMR changes. *J Appl Physiol* 43(6):1001, 1977.

67. Fleg JL, Lakatta EG: Role of muscle loss in the age-associated reduction in Vo_{2max}. *J Appl Physiol* 65(3):1147, 1988.

Chapter 45

AGING AND ATHEROSCLEROSIS

Edwin L. Bierman

Atherosclerosis, a distinctly age-related disorder, is responsible for the majority of deaths in most westernized societies and is by far the leading cause of death in the United States above age 65.[1] It is the most common disorder included under the rubric of arteriosclerosis, a generic term for thickening and hardening of the arterial wall. Atherosclerosis is a disorder of the larger arteries that underlies most coronary artery disease and peripheral arterial disease of the lower extremities and also plays a major role in cerebrovascular disease. Nonatheromatous forms of arteriosclerosis include focal calcific arteriosclerosis (Mönckeberg's sclerosis) and arteriolosclerosis.

NATURAL HISTORY

Atherosclerosis in humans appears to begin very early in life and develops progressively over the years, resulting in an exponential increase in the incidence of clinical atherosclerotic events (myocardial infarction, angina pectoris, cerebrovascular accidents, gangrene) with age (Fig. 45-1). A high prevalence of atherosclerotic changes in the arteries of American males as early as the second and third decades of life has been documented from autopsies of casualties of war in Korea and Vietnam. Despite differences in prevalence rates of atherosclerosis among various countries, there is a progressively increasing mortality with age from atherosclerosis-related diseases.[2] In the United States, more than 80 percent of cases of atherosclerotic cardiovascular disease are found in individuals over age 65.

Thus, atherosclerosis is almost a universal age-related phenomenon in human populations and is therefore closely linked to aging. It is also apparent that atherosclerosis is a multifactorial disease. The hypothesis presented in this chapter and earlier reviews[3,4] is that both intrinsic aging processes and environmental factors (such as diet) operate over many years and are superimposed on unknown genetic factors to produce the disorder. Clearly, atherosclerosis is not simply the result of unmodified intrinsic biological aging processes, since most mammalian species age without spontaneously developing atherosclerosis. Furthermore, there are populations in the world that age to the life span appropriate to the human species without developing clinical evidence of atherosclerosis. Therefore, although there may be almost universal prevalence of atherosclerosis, there is considerable difference in the prevalence rate in various parts of the world, probably related to factors other than age per se.[1] The dramatic increased prevalence of atherosclerosis during the last century, albeit partly related to improved diagnosis, presumably largely reflects the marked increase in human life span.

NONATHEROMATOUS ARTERIOSCLEROSIS

Focal calcific arteriosclerosis (Mönckeberg's sclerosis), a disorder of the medial layer of medium-sized muscular arteries, is also related to aging. It is rare in individuals below age 50 and affects both sexes indiscriminately. The process involves degeneration of medial smooth muscle cells followed by calcium deposition, which gives a characteristic radiological appearance consisting of regular concentric calcifications in cross section and a railroad track in longitudinal section, most often seen in arteries in the pelvis, legs, and feet. These changes are common in the elderly but alone do not narrow the arterial lumen, have little effect on the circulation, and may have little functional significance. However, in the lower extremities, medial sclerosis is often associated with atherosclerosis, contributing to arterial occlusion. In individuals with diabetes mellitus, or who are receiving

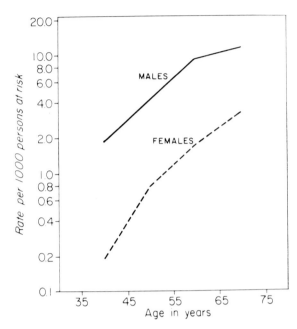

FIGURE 45-1
Average annual incidence rate of the first myocardial infarction in the Framingham population during a 16-year follow-up.

TABLE 45-1
Risk Factors for Atherosclerosis

Not Reversible

Aging
Male sex
Genetic traits—positive family history of premature athero-
    sclerosis

Reversible

Cigarette smoking
Hypertension
Obesity

Potentially or Partially Reversible

Hyperlipidemia-hypercholesterolemia and/or hypertriglyceri-
    demia
Hyperglycemia and diabetes mellitus
Low levels of high-density lipoprotein (HDL)

Other Possible Factors

Physical inactivity
Emotional stress and/or personality type

long-term corticosteroid drugs, focal calcification may be accelerated and severe. Focal calcification also is responsible for the arteriosclerotic aortic valve in the elderly which may progress to the severe calcific aortic stenosis of the aged.

Since little is known of the pathogenesis of either focal calcification or arteriolosclerosis (a degenerative disorder of arterioles in visceral organs related to hypertension) in relation to aging or otherwise, the remainder of the chapter will be devoted to a discussion of atherosclerosis, one of the scourges of modern industrialized civilizations.

RISK FACTORS FOR ATHEROSCLEROSIS IN RELATION TO AGING

A number of conditions and habits are present more frequently in individuals who develop atherosclerosis than in the general population ("risk factors"). Most people below age 65 with atherosclerosis have one or more identifiable risk factors other than aging per se (Table 45-1). The presence of multiple risk factors makes a person more likely to develop a clinical atherosclerotic event and to do so earlier than a person with no risk factors. Thus there is a lower prevalence of the major risk factors among the elderly afflicted with their first clinical manifestation.

Among the risk factors, age, male sex, and genetic factors are currently considered to be nonreversible, whereas there is continually emerging evidence that

elimination of cigarette smoking, treatment of hypertension, and reduction of marked obesity reverse the high risk for atherosclerosis attributable to those factors.[1] Potentially reversible factors currently under study include hyperglycemia and the various forms of hyperlipidemia.

These factors are not mutually exclusive since they clearly interact. For example, obesity appears to be causally associated with hypertension, hyperglycemia, hypercholesterolemia, hypertriglyceridemia, and low high-density lipoprotein (HDL) cholesterol. Genetic factors may play a role by exerting direct effects on arterial wall structure and metabolism, or they may act indirectly via such factors as hypertension, hyperlipidemia, diabetes, and obesity. Aging appears to be one of the more complex factors associated with the development of atherosclerosis, since many of the risk factors in themselves are related to aging, e.g., elevated blood pressure, hyperglycemia, and hyperlipidemia. Thus in addition to possible involvement of intrinsic aging in atherogenesis (perhaps through effects on arterial wall metabolism), a variety of associated metabolic factors are also age-dependent.

OBESITY

There is both an inexorable and a preventable increase in adiposity with aging. Even if body weight remains constant throughout life, there are changes in body composition with a decline in lean body mass (muscle and bone) and a reciprocal increase in the proportion of fat tissue, resulting in an increase in relative adiposity and a decrease in caloric requirements with age. Actually, in most westernized populations, body weight does not remain constant with age, perhaps because caloric intake is not decreased in harmony with reduced requirements, resulting in an absolute increase in adiposity as well.[5] Obesity, defined as more than 30 percent above average weight, appears to be important in atherogenesis since, in general, morbidity and mortality from atherosclerotic heart disease are higher in direct relation to the degree of overweight, particularly apparent before age 50.[6] Recent studies have shown a close relationship between the regional distribution of obesity (i.e., abdominal) and coronary atherosclerosis.[7]

HYPERTENSION

Blood pressure levels also appear to increase inexorably with age, and the risk of atherosclerosis appears to increase progressively with increasing blood pressure (and can be diminished by therapeutic reduction of blood pressure).[8] The nature of this age relation, however, varies among populations, since there are remote populations that appear to age without any changes in blood pressure levels, perhaps in relation to physical activity or salt intake. In contrast to other age-related risk factors, hypertension appears to increase the development of atherosclerosis throughout the age span[9] (see Chap. 48, "Hypertension"). It is an especially strong risk factor for cerebrovascular lesions resulting in stroke.

HYPERGLYCEMIA

Blood glucose levels increase progressively with age in most population studies,[10] and hyperglycemia in turn appears to play a significant role in the development of atherosclerosis.[11] A high prevalence of diabetes and hyperglycemia is associated with clinically evident atherosclerosis. Increasing abdominal adiposity and decreasing physical activity probably play some role in the progressive increase in circulating glucose levels with age,[12] since there are primitive populations who remain active and thin and show minimal age-related changes. This suggests that intrinsic aging effects on glucose metabolism and glucoregulatory hormone homeostasis are present and contributory, but superimposed environmental factors, such as caloric excess, amplify the age-related effect. In known Type II diabetics, there is at least a two-fold increase in incidence of myocardial infarction compared with the incidence in nondiabetics.

HYPERLIPIDEMIA

Both hypercholesterolemia and hypertriglyceridemia appear to be important age-related risk factors for the

development of atherosclerosis. While genetic factors are important for emergence of premature atherosclerosis in affected individuals from families with one of the familial hyperlipidemias,[13] triglyceride and cholesterol levels in whole populations are also important, since they appear to increase with age.[14] Adiposity may play a critical role in the age-associated increase in triglyceride and cholesterol levels since curves for the increase in plasma triglyceride with age and comparable curves for plasma cholesterol with age are superimposable on the obesity-age curve in populations.[3] Again, in primitive people who remain thin throughout adulthood, serum lipids do not increase with age. Metabolic mechanisms have been postulated whereby abdominal obesity, which is associated with insulin resistance and compensatory hyperinsulinemia, promotes enhanced production of triglyceride- and cholesterol-rich lipoproteins from the liver. Studies in humans have shown that overweight individuals have higher production rates of both triglyceride and cholesterol. Current concepts of plasma lipoprotein transport suggest that accumulation of cholesterol in the circulation may in part be secondary to excessive production of triglyceride-rich lipoproteins.[15] Furthermore, progressive accumulation of cholesterol in the bulk tissues of humans occurs during the lifetime, particularly in connective and adipose tissues. Thus, aging is associated with an expansion of both circulating and tissue pools of cholesterol.

The importance of hyperlipidemia as a risk factor for atherosclerosis varies in relation to age. Serum cholesterol levels appear to relate to the development of coronary heart disease in males, predominantly below the age of 40, but much less so in older individuals.[8] In a study in Seattle of the role of genetic forms of hyperlipidemia in clinical atherosclerosis in which 500 consecutive survivors of myocardial infarction were tested, hyperlipidemia was present in about one-third of the group. Approximately one-half of the males and two-thirds of the females below age 50 had either hypertriglyceridemia, hypercholesterolemia, or both. In contrast, in individuals over age 70, the prevalence of atherosclerotic coronary disease was very high, yet very few males had hyperlipidemia and only about one-fourth of the females had elevated lipid levels. Thus in both sexes there appeared to be a progressive decline with age in association of hyperlipidemia with this disorder.[16]

More than half of the hyperlipidemic-atherosclerotic survivors appeared to have simple, monogenic, familial disorders inherited as an autosomal dominant trait (familial combined hyperlipidemia, familial hypertriglyceridemia, and familial hypercholesterolemia, in descending order of frequency). These simply inherited hyperlipidemias (particularly familial hypercholesterolemia) were more frequent in myocardial infarction survivors below age 60 than in those who were older. In contrast, nonmonogenic forms of hyperlipidemia occurred with equal frequency above and below age 60.[4] Thus, it appears that genes associated with the simply inherited hyperlipidemias accelerate changes seen with age leading to atherosclerosis prematurely. There is no agreement as to whether blood lipid levels continue to predict atherosclerosis in the elderly.

Several lipoprotein fractions transport cholesterol (see Chap. 73). Low-density lipoproteins (LDLs) carry most of the plasma cholesterol, and LDL cholesterol levels thus usually parallel plasma cholesterol concentrations and are directly related to the risk of atherosclerosis. In contrast, HDLs, which carry about 20 percent of the plasma cholesterol, are inversely related to the risk of atherosclerosis.[17] Thus, high HDL cholesterol levels are considered to be protective. HDL cholesterol levels do not appear to change with age after puberty, but other age-related factors, such as obesity and hypertriglyceridemia, are associated with low HDL cholesterol levels. Low HDL levels do appear to continue to predict the emergence of coronary heart disease over age 65.[19]

PATHOGENESIS OF ATHEROSCLEROSIS IN RELATION TO AGING

CELL BIOLOGY OF ARTERIAL WALL AND THEORIES OF ATHEROGENESIS

One generally accepted theory for the pathogenesis of atherosclerosis consistent with a variety of experimental evidence is the *reaction to injury* hypothesis.[18] According to this theory, the endothelial cells lining the intima are exposed to repeated or continuing insults to their integrity. The injury to the endothelium may be subtle or gross, resulting in a loss of the ability of the cells to function as a complete barrier. Examples of types of injury to the endothelium include chemical injury, as in chronic hypercholesterolemia, mechanical stress associated with hypertension, and immunological injury, as may be seen after cardiac or renal transplantation. Loss of endothelial cells at susceptible sites in the arterial tree would lead to exposure of the subendothelial tissue to increased concentrations of plasma constituents, and a sequence of events including monocyte and platelet adherence, migration of monocytes into the arterial wall to become macrophages, platelet aggregation and formation of microthrombi, and release of platelet granular components, including a potent mitogenic factor. This "platelet-derived growth factor," in conjunction with other plasma constituents, including lipoproteins and hormones such as insulin, could stimulate both the migration of medial smooth muscle cells into the intima and their proliferation at these sites of injury. These prolifer-

ating smooth muscle cells would deposit a connective tissue matrix and accumulate lipid, a process that would be particularly enhanced with hyperlipidemia. Macrophages derived from circulating blood monocytes also accumulate lipid. Thus repeated or chronic injury could lead to a slowly progressing lesion involving a gradual increase in smooth muscle cells, macrophages, connective tissue, and lipid. Areas where the shearing stress on endothelial cells is increased, such as branch points or bifurcation of vessels, would be at greater risk. As the lesions progress and the intima becomes thicker, blood flow over the sites will be altered and potentially place the lining endothelial cells at even greater risk for further injury, leading to an inexorable cycle of events culminating in the complicated lesion. However, a single or a few injurious episodes may lead to a proliferative response that could regress, in contrast to continued or chronic injury. This reaction-to-injury hypothesis thus is consistent with the known intimal thickening observed during normal aging, would explain how many of the etiological factors implicated in atherogenesis might enhance lesion formation, might explain how inhibitors of platelet aggression could interfere with lesion formation, and fosters some optimism regarding the possibility of interrupting progression of or even producing regression of these lesions.

POTENTIAL ROLE OF AGING PROCESSES IN ATHEROGENESIS

Other theories of atherogenesis are not mutually exclusive and relate to aging processes as well. The *monoclonal hypothesis* suggests, on the basis of single isoenzyme types found in lesions,[20] that the intimal proliferative lesions result from the multiplication of single individual smooth muscle cells, as do benign tumors. In this manner, mitogenic, and possibly mutagenic, factors that might stimulate smooth muscle cell proliferation would act on single cells. Focal *clonal senescence* may explain how intrinsic aging processes contribute to atherosclerosis. According to this theory,[21] the intimal smooth muscle cells that proliferate to form an atheroma are normally under feedback control by diffusible agents (mitosis inhibitors) formed by the smooth muscle cells in the contiguous media, and this feedback control system tends to fail with age as these controlling cells die and are not adequately replaced. This is consistent with the recent observation that cultured human arterial smooth muscle cells, like fibroblasts, show a decline in their ability to replicate as a function of donor age.[22] If this loss of replicative potential applies to a controlling population of smooth muscle cells, then cells that are usually suppressed would be able to proliferate.

Intrinsic aging and loss of replicative potential, if it occurs in endothelial cells, could be critical, since it would lead to loss of integrity of the endothelial lining of the artery wall, the initial step leading to the progression of events in the reaction to injury hypothesis.

The *lysosomal theory* suggests that altered lysosomal function might contribute to atherogenesis. Since lysosomal enzymes can accomplish the generalized degradation of cellular components required for continuing renewal, this system has been implicated in cellular aging and the accumulation of lipofuscin, or "age pigment." It has been suggested that increased deposition of lipids in arterial smooth muscle cells may be related in part to a relative deficiency in the activity of lysosomal cholesterol ester hydrolase.[23] This would result in increased accumulation of cholesterol esters within the cells, perhaps accentuated by lipid overloading of lysosomes, eventually leading to cell death and extracellular lipid deposition. Consonant with this idea, impaired degradation of LDL by human arterial smooth muscle cells cultured from older donors has been observed.[24] Since LDL binding to the specific high-affinity receptors on arterial smooth muscle cells does not appear to decrease with donor age, smooth muscle cells are not protected from the increasing LDL concentrations associated with aging. These observations may be relevant to the enhanced accumulation of cellular cholesterol and LDL observed in atherosclerotic lesions in vivo.

AGE-ASSOCIATED RISK FACTORS AND THE PATHOBIOLOGY OF ATHEROSCLEROSIS

OBESITY

Adiposity produces insulin resistance in peripheral tissues (mainly muscle and adipose), which leads to compensatory hyperinsulinemia. The liver is not resistant to some effects of insulin, and enhanced production of triglyceride-rich lipoproteins results, leading to elevated plasma triglyceride and cholesterol levels. Thus it has been demonstrated that body weight is related not only to triglyceride levels but also to cholesterol levels. Concomitantly, obesity is associated with increased total body cholesterol synthesis. Obesity, particularly the abdominal type, produces higher circulating levels of insulin, both in the basal state and after stimulation with glucose or other secretagogues. Since obesity is related to atherosclerosis—both directly and via hypertension, hypertriglyceridemia, hypercholesterolemia, and hyperglycemia—it is not surprising that many studies show a relationship between serum insulin levels, particularly after oral glucose intake, and atherosclerotic disease of the coronary and peripheral arteries.[11] A few studies, however, suggest that this association between insulin and atherosclerosis occurs independently of obesity. It

has been postulated that insulin may directly affect arterial wall metabolism, leading to increased endogenous lipid synthesis and thus predisposing to atherosclerosis. Insulin has been shown in physiological concentrations to stimulate proliferation of arterial smooth muscle cells and enhance binding of LDL and very low density lipoproteins (VLDL) to fibroblasts; it therefore may be one of the plasma factors gaining increased access to the intima and media after endothelial injury and thus may be an additional factor in atheroma formation.

HYPERTENSION

High mean arterial pressures may enhance atherogenesis by directly producing injury via mechanical stress on endothelial cells at specific high pressure sites in the arterial tree. This would allow the sequence of events in the chronic injury hypothesis of atherogenesis to take place. In addition, hypertension might allow more lipoproteins to be transported through intact endothelial lining cells by altering permeability. Hypertension markedly increases lysosomal enzyme activity, presumably owing to stimulation of the cellular disposal system by the internalization of increased amounts of plasma substances. This might lead to increased cell degeneration and release of the highly destructive enzymes (within the lysosomes) into the arterial wall. Experimental hypertension also increases the thickness of the intimal smooth muscle layer in the arterial wall and increases connective tissue elements. It is possible that continued high pressure within the artery in vivo produces changes in the ability of smooth muscle cells or stem cells to proliferate. Studies using human aortic coarctation as a model have shown that smooth muscle cells cultured from tissue proximal to the site of coarctation had fewer population doublings and a slower replication rate than cells grown from a distal site.[25] Since the proximal cells presumably had been stimulated to divide excessively in vivo by chronic exposure to elevated intra-arterial pressure, these results suggest that the number of prior smooth muscle cell divisions limits their further replicative potential. Thus characteristics of accelerated aging can be induced by chronic exposure to hypertension, which may be relevant to atherogenesis.

DIABETES AND HYPERGLYCEMIA

Diabetes could provide a unique contribution to atherogenesis. Although the fundamental genetic abnormalities in the varieties of human diabetes mellitus remain unknown, it has been suggested that one type of genetic diabetes in humans is associated with a primary cellular abnormality intrinsic to all cells, resulting in a decreased life span of individual cells, which in turn results in increased cell turnover in tissues. If arterial endothelial and smooth muscle cells are intrinsically defective in diabetes, accelerated atherogenesis can be readily postulated on the basis of any one of the current theories of pathogenesis. Platelet dysfunction in diabetes might also play a role.

The role of glucose in atheroma formation, if any, is poorly understood. Hyperglycemia is known to affect aortic wall metabolism. Sorbitol, a product of the insulin-independent aldose reductase pathway of glucose metabolism (the polyol pathway), accumulates in the arterial wall in the presence of high glucose concentrations, resulting in osmotic effects including increased cell water content and decreased oxygenation. Increased glucose also appears to stimulate proliferation of cultured arterial smooth muscle cells. Glycosylation of key arterial wall proteins impairing their function might also play a role. For example, glycosylated collagen has a great avidity for binding and trapping LDL. Further, glycosylated LDL may more readily deliver cholesterol to arterial cells.

HYPERLIPIDEMIA

The development of atherosclerosis accelerates in approximate quantitative relation to the degree of hyperlipidemia.[8] A long-established theory suggests that the higher the circulating levels of lipoprotein, the more likely they are to gain entry into the arterial wall. By an acceleration of the usual transendothelial transport, large concentrations of cholesterol-rich lipoproteins within the arterial wall could overwhelm the ability of smooth muscle cells and macrophages to metabolize them. Low-density lipoproteins have been immunologically identified in atheroma, and in humans there is a direct relationship between plasma cholesterol and arterial lipoprotein cholesterol concentration. High-density lipoproteins may be protective by virtue of their ability to promote cholesterol removal from artery wall cells. Chemically modified lipoproteins, possibly produced in hyperlipidemic disorders, could gain access to the scavenger arterial wall macrophages leading to formation of foam cells, as in xanthomas. The lipid that accumulates in the arterial wall with increasing age possibly results from infiltration of plasma cholesterol-rich lipoproteins. However, atheromatous lesions are associated with a more marked increase in arterial wall lipids than that associated with increasing age, which may result in part from injury to the endothelium, possibly produced by chronic hyperlipidemia, as demonstrated in cholesterol-fed monkeys. A further possible mechanism for accelerated atherogenesis in hyperlipidemia is related to the ability of LDL to stimulate proliferation of arterial smooth muscle cells.

Although not directly age-related, cigarette smoking is too powerful a risk factor to be overlooked. The effect of chronic smoke inhalation from cigarettes could result in repetitive injury to endothelial cells, thereby accelerating atherogenesis. Hypoxia stimulates proliferation of cultured human arterial smooth muscle cells; thus, since cigarette smoking is associated with high levels of carboxyhemoglobin and low oxygen delivery to tissues, another mechanism for atherogenesis is suggested. Hypoxia could produce diminished lysosomal enzyme degradative ability, as evidenced by impaired degradation of LDL by smooth muscle cells,[26] causing LDL to accumulate in the cells. Consistent with this suggestion is the fact that aortic lesions resembling atheroma have been produced in experimental animals by systemic hypoxia, and lipid accumulation in the arterial wall of cholesterol-fed rabbits and monkeys appears to be increased by hypoxia.

REVERSIBILITY AND REGRESSION IN RELATION TO AGING

ANIMAL MODELS

In 1933, Anitschkow observed that lesions induced in cholesterol-fed rabbits appear to regress when the animals are placed on a normal diet. More recent extension of this type of study to cholesterol-fed nonhuman primates[27] has provided firm evidence for reversibility and regression. The usual protocol has been to induce lesions of varying severity, by feeding the atherogenic diet to young monkeys for several years, and then to switch diets to a chow or low-fat diet, sacrificing the animals at intervals. Aortic and coronary lesions have been shown to decrease in size and in content of lipid, cells, and connective tissue. The relevance of these studies lasting a few years to the human lesions evolving over decades is open to some question, however. The mechanisms of regression are under study. In general, it appears that lower circulating levels of cholesterol and LDL lead to a healing endothelium, decreased ingress of LDL into the artery wall, less cell proliferation and collagen synthesis, and more egress of cholesterol from cells and wall. These studies have not yet approached the question of repeated insults (or repeated induction and regression cycles) which may be more relevant to the question of aging and atherosclerosis in humans.

HUMANS

Both retrospective and prospective human epidemiological studies support the concepts of reversibility and regression. Clinical and autopsy studies during the world wars showed less severe atherosclerosis in malnourished subjects, providing circumstantial evidence. Recent studies of plaque regression in living human subjects are providing some evidence of regression of advanced atherosclerosis based on functional effects and on evaluation of plaque size by sequential arteriographs taken before and after a period of treatment. Treatments now under study include ileal bypass operations, drug-treated hyperlipidemias, and combinations of diet, exercise, and drug therapy. Advanced atherosclerotic lesions appear to respond more favorably when serum cholesterol levels are reduced to the low levels that prevail in animals or humans consuming a low-fat, low-cholesterol diet. The effect of age has not been studied directly since most of the subjects have been hyperlipidemic and relatively young.

PREVENTION

The steps taken to delay or prevent atheroma formation ("primary prevention") must begin early in life, long before there is a suspicion of the existence of clinical disease. Steps taken to prevent recurrence of disease ("secondary prevention") later in life will not necessarily be the same. Although an effective program has not been defined with certainty, enough is known to guide in both identification of those individuals with a higher risk and in development of measures that probably will reduce that risk. Thus prevention currently is equated with risk-factor reduction.

Whole communities can be influenced to reduce smoking, change diet, and lower blood pressure levels by mass-media educational efforts.[28] There has been a trend toward lower consumption of cholesterol and saturated fat in the United States, coupled with increasing attention to reducing overweight and the use of exercise programs. Concomitantly, and perhaps causally, there has been a decline in mortality from atherosclerotic disease almost uniquely in the United States during the past 20 years.[1] Treatment of hyperlipidemia in some instances has been shown to reduce atherosclerotic involvement of peripheral and coronary arteries by both invasive and noninvasive measurement. Therefore, efforts to prevent atherogenesis and to interrupt progression by risk factor reduction seem warranted.

The National Cholesterol Education Program has recommended screening, classification, and treatment of adults with "high risk" cholesterol levels.[29] However, no specific recommendations were made for individuals over 65, since the data to support interventions directed at lowering cholesterol levels in the elderly are sparse.

CONCLUSION

Atherosclerosis, the most prevalent form of arteriosclerosis, occurs so commonly with aging in industrialized populations that the disorder can be mistaken for a natural consequence of intrinsic aging rather than a superimposed disease. In this multifactorial disorder, environmental factors (such as diet) appear to operate over many years (age-related) in concert with intrinsic cellular aging processes and genetic determinants to generate the disease.

Since alteration of intrinsic aging processes and genetic manipulation remain only theoretical possibilities, efforts should be directed at understanding and reversing the age-related environmental factors that act over time and accelerate atherogenesis throughout the life span.

REFERENCES

1. U.S. Department of Health and Human Services: "Arteriosclerosis 1981," *Report of the Working Group on Arteriosclerosis of the NHLBI.* PHS NIH 81-2034, 1981.
2. Eggen DA, Solberg LA: Variation of atherosclerosis with age. *Lab Invest* 18:571, 1968.
3. Bierman EL: Ageing and atherosclerosis, in Stout R. (ed): *Arterial Disease in the Elderly.* Churchill Livingstone, New York, 1984, p 17.
4. Bierman EL: Arteriosclerosis and aging, in Finch CE, Schneider EL (eds): *Handbook of the Biology of Aging.* Van Nostrand Reinhold, New York, 1985, p 842.
5. Montoye HJ, Epstein FH, Kjelsberg MO: The measurement of body fatness: A study in a total community. *Am J Clin Nutr* 16:417, 1965.
6. Hubert HB et al: Obesity as an independent risk factor for cardiovascular disease: A 26-year follow-up of participants in the Framingham Heart Study. *Circulation* 67:968, 1983.
7. Stern MP, Haffner SM: Body fat distribution and hyperinsulinemia as risk factors for diabetes and cardiovascular disease. *Arteriosclerosis* 6:123, 1986.
8. Dawber TR: Risk factors for atherosclerotic disease, in *Current Concepts.* Kalamazoo, MI, Upjohn, 1975.
9. Kannel WB: Role of blood pressure in cardiovascular morbidity and mortality. *Prog Cardiovasc Dis* 17:5, 1974.
10. Hayner NS et al: Carbohydrate tolerance and diabetes in a total community, Tecumseh, Michigan. *Diabetes* 14:413, 1965.
11. Stout RW: Blood glucose and atherosclerosis. *Arteriosclerosis* 1:227, 1981.
12. DeFronzo RA: Glucose intolerance and aging. *Diabetes Care* 4:493, 1981.
13. Motulsky AG: The genetic hyperlipidemias. *N Engl J Med* 294:823, 1976.
14. U.S. Department of Health and Human Services: *The Lipid Research Clinics Population Studies Data Book,* vol I, *The Prevalence Study.* PHS NIH 80-1527, 1980.
15. Bierman EL, Glomset JA: Disorders of lipid metabolism, in Wilson JD, Foster DW (eds): *Williams Textbook of Endocrinology,* 7th ed. Philadelphia, Saunders, 1985, p 1108.
16. Goldstein JL et al: Hyperlipidemia in coronary heart disease. *J Clin Invest* 52:1533, 1973.
17. Tyroler HA (ed): Epidemiology of plasma HDL choles-

terol levels: The lipid research clinics program prevalence study. *Circulation* 62 (suppl IV), 1980.

18. Ross R: The pathogenesis of atherosclerosis of blood—an update. *N Engl J Med* 314:488, 1986.
19. Gordon T et al: High density lipoprotein as a protective factor against coronary heart disease. The Framingham Study. *Am J Med* 62:707, 1977.
20. Benditt EP, Benditt JM: Evidence for a monoclonal origin of human atherosclerotic plaques. *Proc Natl Acad Sci USA* 70:1753, 1973.
21. Martin G, Ogburn C, Sprague C: Senescence and vascular disease, in Cristofalo VJ, Roberts J, Adelmann RC (eds): *Explorations in Aging.* New York, Plenum, 1975, p 163.
22. Bierman EL: The effect of donor age on the *in vitro* lifespan of cultured human arterial smooth muscle cells. *In Vitro* 14:951, 1978.
23. Wolinsky H: The role of lysosomes in vascular disease: A unifying theme. *Ann NY Acad Sci* 275:238, 1976.
24. Bierman EL, Albers JJ, Chait A: Effect of donor age on the binding and degradation of low density lipoproteins by cultured human arterial smooth muscle cells. *J Gerontol* 34:483, 1979.
25. Bierman EL, Brewer C, Baum D: Hypertension decreases replication potential of arterial smooth muscle cells: Aortic coarctation in humans as a model. *Proc Soc Exp Biol Med* 166:335, 1981.
26. Albers JJ, Bierman EL: The effect of hypoxia on uptake and degradation of low density lipoproteins by cultured human arterial smooth muscle cells. *Biochim Biophys Acta* 424:422, 1976.
27. Wissler RW: Current status of regression studies, in Paoletti R, Gotto AM Jr (eds): *Atherosclerosis Reviews.* New York, Raven, 1978, vol 3, p 213.
28. Farquhar JW et al: Community education for cardiovascular health. *Lancet* 1:1192, 1977.
29. National Cholesterol Education Program: Report of the National Cholesterol Education Program Expert Panel on Detection. Evaluation and Treatment of High Blood Cholesterol in Adults. *Arch Intern Med* 148:36, 1988.

Chapter 46

DISORDERS
OF THE HEART

Gary Gerstenblith and Edward G. Lakatta

The proportion and number of our population which is 65 years of age or older are growing rapidly. In this age group, heart disease is the most frequent reason for hospitalization and death. The detection of disorders of the heart in elderly individuals depends in part on an understanding of how aging alone affects the routine clinically obtained parameters which are used to measure cardiac structure and function. The certainty of the answer depends on the subjects studied and the techniques used. It is important that the subjects examined be free of cardiovascular disease and that the methods used not be influenced by age-associated changes in noncardiovascular organ systems. The physiological changes described in Chap. 44 provide an altered substrate upon which specific pathologic conditions are imposed. The diagnosis and management of heart disease, as well as the response to therapy, are affected by these physiological changes.

ISCHEMIC HEART DISEASE

The major cause of death in elderly persons, as in middle-aged persons, is atherosclerotic disease.[1] It has been estimated that 55 percent of all deaths are due to either coronary or cerebral ischemia or infarction. That subclinical manifestations of coronary disease are present at a relatively young age is illustrated in Fig. 46-1A. Postmortem studies (Fig. 46-1B) also indicate that there is a dramatic age-related increase in the prevalence of significant disease, reaching a level as high as 50 to 60 percent in men at age 60 years before peaking.[2–4] A recent autopsy study indicates that the prevalence of significant stenoses in individuals dying over the age of 60 has actually increased over the past 20 years.[5] It is unclear whether this increase is due to aging per se or to

the additional accumulation of other risk factors over time. Since age itself is the greatest risk factor for the development of coronary artery disease,[4] the complex interaction of other risk factors with age has to be understood before the true contribution of these other risk factors can be quantified.

The prevalence of symptomatic coronary disease is only 10 to 50 percent of the true prevalence of all coronary disease.[4] If one adds resting electrocardiographic abnormalities to the presence or history of angina or infarction, the identification rate is only slightly improved. Stress testing, however, can significantly improve the sensitivity of identification of the population with disease (Fig. 46-1B). The sensitivity of exercise testing for the detection of coronary disease is increased with age, although the specificity declines somewhat (see Table 46-1).[6] The predictive accuracy of a negative test also decreases in older populations with a high prevalence of disease. Both sensitivity and specificity are improved by the addition of radionuclide stress testing, and with the use of both stress and resting criteria true prevalence figures (Fig. 46-1B) are approached.[7,8] The presence of both electrocardiographic and thallium scintigraphy evidence of ischemia in asymptomatic individuals is associated, independent of conventional risk factors, with a 3.8-fold increase in relative risk of subsequent coronary events.[9]

Standard symptoms of ischemic heart disease do not differ significantly in the elderly, with the exception that dyspnea may be as common a presenting symptom as chest pain.[10] If an older person's activities are limited by musculoskeletal, respiratory, or other problems, he or she may not be able to exercise sufficiently to be aware of anginal symptoms. Ischemic-induced diminished left-ventricular compliance may result in more symptoms in an older individual because of preexisting age-related changes in myocardial and pericardial compliance and

466

FIGURE 46-1

A. The effect of age on the prevalence of fibrous plaques, calcified lesions, and fixed stenosis >50 percent of vessel area in any major coronary artery in hearts from subjects who died of all causes. Number of hearts examined is given by the number in parentheses adjacent to each symbol. (*Reconstructed from Tejada et al.[3]*) B. The effect of age on coronary artery stenosis in hearts from white males who died from all causes in Rochester, Minnesota, and in New Orleans and the prevalence of coronary artery disease in living Baltimore Longitudinal Study of Aging participants by resting criteria alone (history of angina or myocardial infarction; abnormal resting ECG, i.e., Minnesota codes 4:1, 25:1, or 26:1) and by resting plus stress[2] criteria (ECG positive for ischemia during maximum exercise treadmill test, i.e., Minnesota code 11:1 or 18:1 or an abnormal thallium scan during maximum exercise but not at rest). The number of hearts in the Rochester study is given in parentheses. Note the marked increase in the ability to detect the presence of coronary disease in living persons when stress criteria are employed in older participants in addition to the usual clinical epidemiologic criteria. (*Reconstructed from Refs. 2, 3, and 5.*)

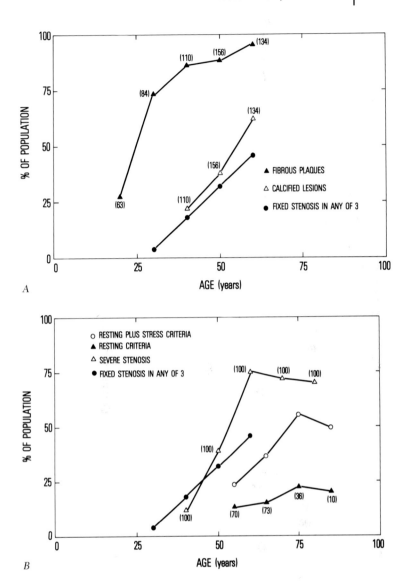

diastolic relaxation[11–13] and thus may lead to more frequent and/or more rapidly appearing symptoms of heart failure, such as dyspnea.

ANGINA PECTORIS

Treatment of angina in the elderly often begins by detecting reversible precipitating factors commonly found in this age group, including anemia, congestive heart failure, "masked" hyperthyroidism, and hypertension. Treatment of these may relieve angina. It should also be remembered that atherosclerosis is a progressive disease and that, although it has sometimes been asserted that risk factor reduction is less important in the older patient, recent evidence suggests that successful treatment of hypertension[14,15] and smoking cessation[16] decrease cardiovascular mortality in the elderly.

Pharmacologic Therapy

Nitrates, beta-blockers, and calcium antagonists are used to treat symptomatic ischemia. The hypotensive effects of nitrates may be potentiated by altered cardiovascular reflexes, diminished plasma volume, incompetent venous valves, and other factors often present in the

TABLE 46-1
Effects of Age on Sensitivity and Specificity of Treadmill Exercise Test

Age (Years)	Sensitivity (%)	Specificity (%)
<40	56	84
40–49	65	85
50–59	74	88
>60	84	70

SOURCE: Reprinted from Ref. 6.

elderly. Although altered pharmacokinetics of propranolol in the elderly[17,18] may increase plasma levels of the drug, the physiological response has been reported to be diminished.[19] The choice of whether to use a beta-one selective or nonselective or a hydrophilic or lipophilic beta-blocker should be guided by associated medical conditions, particularly pulmonary, renal, or hepatic disease. It should be noted that the ability of timolol and propranolol to decrease recurrent infarction and death in the postinfarction setting is at least as significant in older individuals as it is in the rest of the patient population.[20,21] Calcium channel antagonists have proved useful in the treatment of a broad spectrum of patients who have rest angina.[22,23] These agents vasodilate coronary and peripheral vessels and thus can potentially increase myocardial oxygen supply and decrease oxygen demand.

Coronary Angioplasty

Although the National Heart, Lung and Blood Institute PTCA Registry initially reported increased in-hospital mortality associated with angioplasty and a lower success rate in patients over 65 years of age,[24] more recent reports indicate a low mortality (0.8 percent) which does not differ from that in younger patients.[25] Angioplasty is now listed as an "evolving indication" for angina in patients over 75 years of age.[26] Angioplasty is particularly useful in the older patient with significant symptoms despite medical therapy who is at increased risk of surgery because of other associated medical conditions, including pulmonary disease, diabetes, and left-ventricular dysfunction.

MYOCARDIAL INFARCTION

The mortality caused by myocardial infarction in individuals over 70 years of age is reported to be twice that in younger individuals.[27] This may not be due to an independent effect of age, but rather to a greater severity and duration of disease; when individuals of different ages are matched for clinical status and other variables which influence prognosis in patients with coronary artery disease, the age difference in mortality is either lessened or obliterated.[28,29] The increased likelihood with age of heart failure, pulmonary edema, and cardiogenic shock[29,30] is probably due to prior myocardial damage, larger infarctions, and/or poorer reserve in the remaining noninfarcted regions. The latter could be related to changes in both intrinsic contractility and a diminished response to beta-adrenergic stimulation (see Chap. 44). It has not been determined with certainty whether age-related changes in the conduction system increase the likelihood of the development of second-degree or complete heart block following acute infarction. Although it has been suggested that such conduction disturbances

are twice as common in those over age 70 as they are in younger individuals, another report disclosed no age trend.[28-30] The incidence of serious ventricular arrhythmias in the acute infarct setting is not age-related. Cardiac rupture is more common in older than in younger patients.[31,32] This could be related to the increased prevalence of hypertension in the elderly, a difference in the size of the infarcted region, or an age-related change in the inflammatory response to infarction.

Thrombolytic Therapy

Catheterization studies reported in 1980 indicated a high prevalence of coronary thrombosis in patients presenting within the first 6 hours of transmural infarction.[33] Several randomized studies have subsequently been conducted assessing the effectiveness of early thrombolysis on survival and left-ventricular function in patients with known and suspected infarction and have shown, overall, that early thrombolysis decreases mortality and improves ventricular function.[34-38] Some of these studies have reported analyses of patient subsets of different ages (see Table 46-2).[34,36-38] It is interesting to note that these recent studies also indicate a striking several-fold mortality increase in the older patient subsets in the placebo groups. The benefit of thrombolysis appears to increase with age up to 75 years, probably because of the age-related increase in mortality in the control groups. Beyond age 75, the benefit is decreased and the risk of cerebral hemorrhage is increased.[39] It should also be noted that older individuals have an increased prevalence of severe hypertension and history of cerebrovascular accidents, which are both contraindications for

TABLE 46-2

Mortality (Percent) in Age Subsets Following Thrombolytic Therapy for Acute Myocardial Infarction

Age (Years)	Treatment	Placebo	Age (Years)	Treatment	Placebo
*GISSI**			*ISIS-2‡*		
≤65	5.7	7.7	<60	4.2	5.8
65–74	16.6	18.1	60–69	10.0	14.4
>75	28.9	33.1	>70	18.2	21.0
ASSET†			*AIMS§*		
≤55	3.8	4.4	<65	5.2	8.5
56–65	6.5	7.9	65–70	12.2	30.2
66–75	10.8	16.4			

*GISSI: Thrombolytic agent, streptokinase. Mortality assessed at 21 days.[34]
†ASSET: Thrombolytic agent, tPA. Mortality assessed at 1 month.[36]
‡ISIS-2: Thrombolytic agent, streptokinase. Mortality assessed at 5 weeks.[38]
§AIMS: Thrombolytic agent, APSAC. Mortality assessed at 1 month.[37]

thrombolysis. For those without these associated conditions, age greater than 75 years is only a relative contraindication to thrombolytic therapy. In assessing the benefit/risk ratio in making the decision to use thrombolytic therapy in these patients, therefore, it should be remembered that the benefit will vary with the size and site of the infarct (i.e., older patients with large anterior infarcts will probably receive the most benefit). Otherwise, there are no specific changes in the choice of medical therapy for infarction that depend on the age of the patient, although the dose of some drugs may have to be decreased if renal or hepatic clearance is diminished.

Coronary Bypass Surgery

Elderly patients undergoing bypass surgery experience an early mortality of 5 to 6 percent.[40] This is somewhat higher than the rate for younger patients (2 to 3 percent), but it is still very low and may be due in part to an increase in associated risk factors such as abnormal left-ventricular function, other associated medical conditions such as diabetes, and more severe coronary artery disease. Independent predictors of perioperative and 5-year survival in patients age 65 or older from the CASS Registry are presented in Table 46-3. Age alone should not be considered a contraindication for otherwise needed cardiac surgery.

CONGESTIVE HEART FAILURE

PATHOPHYSIOLOGY

The prevalence and incidence of heart failure increase so markedly with age (Fig. 46-2) that approximately 75 percent of all ambulatory patients with heart failure are 60 years of age or older.[41,42] Some investigators have sug-

TABLE 46-3
Predictors of Survival in Patients Undergoing Coronary Bypass Surgery

Perioperative Survival

1. Left main coronary stenosis ≥70% in association with left dominant circulation
2. Left-ventricular end-diastolic pressure
3. Current cigarette smoking
4. Pulmonary rales on auscultation
5. Number of associated medical diseases

Five-Year Survival (in Perioperative Survivors)

1. Number of associated medical diseases
2. Functional impairment due to congestive heart failure
3. Severity of abnormal left-ventricular wall motion (determined angiographically)
4. Left-ventricular end-diastolic pressure

gested that a cardiomyopathy due to aging alone might cause congestive heart failure.[43] However, the results of studies discussed in Chap. 44 suggest that this view is no longer tenable and that aging changes in the heart or vasculature alone do not result in failure symptoms at rest. There are age-related adaptations in the cardiovascular response to stress, however, which may modify the clinical manifestations of those cardiac diseases which result in congestive failure symptoms.

Postmortem studies of elderly patients with heart failure reveal that the underlying pathologies are similar to those found in middle-aged individuals.[44] These pathologies are ischemic, hypertensive, and calcific degenerative valvular disease. In the absence of pathology such as one of these valvular diseases, it is unlikely that aging changes alone can cause failure. It has been suggested that the presence of several coexisting pathological processes, each of which in itself would not otherwise cause failure, could be responsible for heart failure in the elderly.[44] Although amyloid deposition is frequently found in the senescent heart, it occurs primarily in the atria and in the vast majority of cases is not significant enough to contribute to heart failure. An interesting group of elderly patients with hypertensive hypertrophic cardiomyopathy has been described.[45] Females made up more than three-quarters of the reported group, and symptoms consisted primarily of dyspnea and chest pain. The diagnosis is made by echocardiography, which

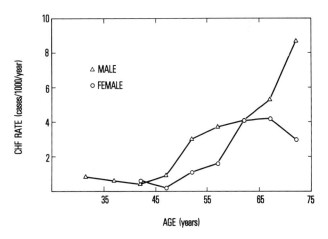

FIGURE 46-2
Average annual incidence of congestive heart failure (CHF) according to age and sex based on 16-year follow-up results of the Framingham Heart Study. A minimum of two major criteria and one minor criterion occurring concurrently were required for a diagnosis of CHF. Major criteria used were paroxysmal nocturnal dyspnea or orthopnea, neck vein distention, rales, cardiomegaly, acute pulmonary edema, S₃ gallop, increased venous pressure ≥16 cm of water, circulation time ≥25 s, positive hepatojugular reflux. Minor criteria used were ankle edema, night cough, dyspnea or exertion, hepatomegaly, pleural effusion, vital capacity one-third from maximum, tachycardia (rate of ≥120 beats/min). A major or minor criterion was a weight loss of ≥4.5 kg within 5 days of treatment. (*Reconstructed from McKee et al.*[42])

shows exaggerated contractile function, small systolic and diastolic cavity dimensions, and prolonged and reduced early diastolic filling. Gated blood pool and echocardiographic studies in a broad spectrum of healthy participants of the Baltimore Longitudinal Study of Aging indicate that this does not characterize elderly women in general. Rather, small, thick, and hyperfunctional left ventricles are features of small hypertensive individuals of any age or sex.[46]

Some of the traditional symptoms used to diagnose heart failure may be obscured in the elderly. Rales may more commonly be due to pulmonary disease in an older patient and ankle edema may be related to poor venous drainage rather than to right heart failure.[47] Alternatively, elderly persons with cardiac pathology and physical limitations due to other diseases may not be able to stress themselves sufficiently to induce failure symptoms which are not present at rest.

TREATMENT

Although the incidence and prevalence of congestive heart failure increase exponentially with age, the risk and benefit of several therapeutic modalities have not been thoroughly examined in the elderly. Probably the most commonly used medication is digitalis. The pharmacokinetics of digoxin would be altered by the reduced volume of distribution and decline in creatinine clearance associated with age.[48] It is important to remember that because muscle mass decreases with advanced age, creatinine clearance may be markedly diminished even though serum creatinine levels remain in the normal range. After oral or intravenous administration of the drug, the half-life is longer and serum levels higher in older individuals.[49,50] Although the influence of age alone on the inotropic response to digitalis glycosides in humans has not been examined, the inotropic effect is diminished in senescence in both isolated rat myocardium and in intact dogs.[51,52] This is apparently not due to an age difference in relative Na-K ATPase inhibition. The serum level required to initiate toxic arrhythmias, specifically ventricular arrhythmias in the beagle model, is also not age-related.[52] Also of interest are clinical reports that the drug can be withdrawn without clinical deterioration in some patients in sinus rhythm with chronic congestive heart failure, many of whom are elderly.[53–55] The magnitude of the response to digitalis is likely related to the cause of heart failure, its chronicity, and its severity, as well as to the patient's age. In view of the high incidence of toxicity associated with digitalis use in the elderly population,[56,57] it may be prudent to initiate therapy with vasodilators and/or diuretics in those elderly patients who are in sinus rhythm. It should be noted that in elderly individuals with hypertensive hypertrophic cardiomyopathy, treatment with vasodilators

is associated with clinical deterioration, whereas patients treated with beta-blockers or calcium antagonists, which, respectively, extend the time course and enhance diastolic relaxation, were markedly improved.[45]

Several age-associated changes in renal function may alter the older person's response to volume loads and diuretics. The first of these is a decline in the glomerular filtration rate of approximately 40 to 50 percent by the age of 80 in normal individuals without renal disease.[58] Another important age-associated change is a decrease in basal renin activity of 30 to 50 percent in the elderly.[59,60] This age difference becomes more pronounced during diuretic administration, which normally increases renin levels. Decreased renin results in a reduction in serum aldosterone[61] which, when associated with the diminished glomerular filtration rate, tends to increase the risk of hyperkalemia resulting from the administration of potassium supplements or diuretics such as spironolactone or triamterene which interfere with the renal excretion of potassium. Another age-associated change which may render the older individual more susceptible to the complications of diuretic therapy is oversecretion of antidiuretic hormone (ADH). ADH levels are elevated in the elderly when such patients are subject to stress[62] and do not respond normally to the administration of pharmacological agents[63] which normally inhibit ADH secretion. Thus, hyponatremia may be more frequent and marked in the elderly during a cardiovascular stress or during administration of diuretics. However, as with the cardiac measurements discussed earlier in this chapter, there is considerable heterogeneity in the elderly, and this characterization of the elderly is useful only for setting general guidelines for precautions to be considered. The specific therapeutic maneuvers must be tailored to each patient's individual characteristics.

ELECTROPHYSIOLOGY

Age-associated histological changes occur throughout most of the cardiac impulse and conduction system.[64] Most hearts from elderly individuals show a decrease in the number of pacemaker cells in the sinus node. This decrease begins at 60 years of age and then becomes more pronounced; at age 75, fewer than 20 percent of the cells normally present in the young adult are found. Although pronounced changes in the atrioventricular node have not been described, there are several age-related changes present in the bundle of His. These include a loss of muscle cells and an increase in fibrous and adipose tissue, as well as amyloid infiltration. There is also a decrease in the number of cells in the fascicle which connects the main bundle of His to the left bundle. Severe bundle-branch fibrosis and degenerative calcification are rarely seen. Idiopathic bundle-branch fibrosis is the most common cause of chronic atrioventricular block in patients over 65 years of age. This entity was originally described by Aschoff and Moncheberg. Lev has described a type of fibrosis which occurs predominately in the proximal portions of the bundles,[65] while Lenegre has emphasized a diffuse process involving the entire bundle branches.[66] Degenerative calcification extending from the aortic and mitral valve rings is also found, though less frequently. Other causes of heart block include ischemic disease and diffuse fibrosis, as well as degeneration involving both the muscles and conducting system.

The intrinsic sinus node rate, in the presence of parasympathetic and sympathetic blockade, decreases with age,[67] as does the respiratory variation in sinus rate.[68] Although sinus bradycardia in the elderly is frequently present, the heart rate of the elderly can increase in response to exercise or pharmacological interventions. The maximum heart rate achieved, however, decreases with age.[69,70] In both nonselected populations and in those free of cardiovascular disease,[71-74] the prevalence of ectopic activity increases with age. In 98 elderly disease-free participants of the Baltimore Longitudinal Study of Aging, 24-hour electrocardiographic recordings disclosed frequent supraventricular and ventricular premature beats (i.e., more than 100 during the monitoring period) in 25 to 17 percent, respectively, of the population (see Table 46-4). Thirty-five percent of the subjects exhibited multiform ventricular ectopic

TABLE 46-4
Ventricular Arrhythmias in 98 Healthy Subjects Age 60–85

Arrhythmias	No. Subjects	Percentage of Total
Ventricular		
Any	78	80
≥ 5 in any hour	76	78
≥ 30 in any hour	37	38
≥ 60 in any hour	12	12
≥ 100 in 24 hours	17	17
Multiform	34	35
Ventricular couplets	11	11
Ventricular tachycardia	4	4
R on T phenomena	1	1
Accelerated idio- ventricular rhythm	1	1
Supraventricular		
Any	86	88
Isolated ectopic beats	86	88
≥ 30 in any hour	22	22
≥ 100 in 24 hours	25	26
Benign slow atrial tachycardia	27	28
Paroxysmal atrial tachycardia	13	13
Atrial flutter	1	1
Accelerated junctional rhythm	1	1

beats. The incidence of ventricular tachycardia was 4 percent, and couplets were present in an additional 11 percent. The incidence of exercise-induced ventricular ectopy increases with age in otherwise healthy individuals as well, although short-term follow-up has not shown any subsequent increase in cardiac events.[75,76]

Prolongation of the PR interval to 220 or 240 ms, which occurs frequently with advanced age, is due primarily to an increase in the A-H rather than the H-V interval and is not considered to be pathologic.[77] The prevalence of complete heart block is less than 1 percent in both unselected and clinical populations. A leftward shift in the QRS axis occurs with aging and may be related (1) to the described fibrotic changes occurring in the anterior superior division of the left bundle or in the myocardium, (2) to mild left-ventricular hypertrophy, or (3) to a change in the spatial orientation of the heart in the chest.

DIAGNOSIS

The diagnosis of supraventricular and ventricular arrhythmias does not differ markedly in the elderly from diagnosis in younger individuals. It should be remembered that significant carotid stenoses and sensitivity to carotid sinus massage increase with age[78] and that increased atrial size and fibrosis may render the atria more prone to fibrillation. Previous studies have indicated that "lone" atrial fibrillation is associated with an increase in both stroke and cardiovascular mortality.[79] Elderly patients with supraventricular arrhythmias should be evaluated for hyperthyroidism since cardiac signs and symptoms may be the presenting and major manifestations of this disorder in the elderly.

ANTIARRHYTHMIC THERAPY

The effect of aging on the pharmacokinetics of digitalis, lidocaine, and quinidine, drugs commonly used for antiarrhythmic therapy, has been investigated. As mentioned above, the steady state plasma concentration of digoxin for any given dose regimen is increased in the elderly because of the reduced volume of distribution and decline in creatinine clearance. It is therefore recommended that, in general, the maintenance dose be reduced to 0.125 mg daily or less in the elderly. During the stress of an infarction, cardiac output and therefore hepatic blood flow may be decreased more in the elderly, and if so this would require a reduction in the dose of any lidocaine administered.[80] Mental confusion in the intensive care unit setting should not be automatically attributed to senile changes, since age-related differences in cardiac performance and blood flow are frequently exaggerated during stress.

The volume of distribution and serum levels of

quinidine after acute intravenous injection are not age-related.[81] However, quinidine clearance is diminished, averaging 2.64 ml/min/kg in a group aged 60 to 69 years and 4.04 ml/min/kg in a younger group aged 23 to 29 years. The elimination of the drug in the same study was prolonged to 9.7 hours in the older group, compared with 7.3 hours in the younger one. This may predispose to quinidine toxicity in the elderly.

The experience with pacemaker therapy has been good in the elderly, and long-term survival in elderly patients with pacemakers is identical to that of an age-matched population without pacemakers (Fig. 46-3).[82] The new models which synchronize atrial and ventricular contractions may be especially useful in this age group, as diastolic filling and cardiac output may be more dependent on a properly timed atrial systole in an older, stiffer left ventricle.

VALVULAR HEART DISEASE

MITRAL VALVE

The most common cause of mitral disease in the elderly is believed to be rheumatic.[83] Of patients with mitral disease of rheumatic cause, approximately two-thirds are said to have predominant incompetence and one-half to have aortic valvular disease as well.[84] However, there is a major shift with increasing age in the underlying condi-

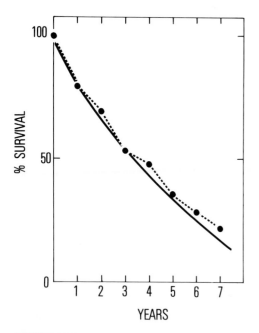

FIGURE 46-3
Survival of patients over 80 years of age treated with a permanent pacemaker for complete heart block (dotted line) and that in an age-matched group (solid line). (*Redrawn from Siddons.*[82])

tion responsible for mitral regurgitation, from rheumatic to ischemic heart disease resulting in papillary muscle dysfunction.

The physical signs of mitral stenosis are often obscured, and at times mitral stenosis is a surprise diagnosis in elderly females with chronic "pulmonary" disease. There are no unusual findings on auscultation, but, as in younger patients, the diastolic rumble and accentuated S_1 may be less intense when cardiac output is diminished. Thus to the extent that associated disease may reduce cardiac output, these signs may be obscured. The systolic murmur of mitral regurgitation is also present in the elderly patient but may be assigned less significance than a similar murmur found in a younger individual because of the increased prevalence of systolic murmurs, in general, in the elderly. The elderly patient's chest x ray and echocardiogram findings are similar to those of younger patients except for the small increase in cardiothoracic ratio and left-ventricular wall thickness noted in Chap. 44. The most important determinants of prognosis are the presence of failure and the atrial rhythm. Perhaps because of the stiffer left ventricle, which would increase dependence on atrial systole, the development of atrial fibrillation is an important unfavorable prognostic sign.

Mitral valve prolapse is often due to mucoid changes in the valve[85] and usually results in minimal mitral insufficiency. Severe mitral regurgitation is occasionally present and is often associated with ruptured chordae tendineae and/or bacterial endocarditis. The hallmarks of mitral prolapse are ejection clicks, late systolic murmurs, and specific echocardiographic features. Calcification of the mitral annulus[86,87] is also usually asymptomatic and is most frequently diagnosed by the inverted C shape of calcium present on chest x-ray or by heavy calcification seen in the mitral area on echocardiography. The usual murmur is related to mitral insufficiency, but stenosis may also occur. Complications include endocarditis and extension of the calcification into the His bundle and peripheral bundle branches, resulting in conduction disturbances.

AORTIC VALVE

Systolic murmurs resembling aortic stenosis are frequent in patients over 70 years of age. The murmur is usually due to sclerosis of the aortic cusps and is clinically unimportant. Significant aortic stenosis, however, is not infrequent in the elderly. This disease is often rapidly progressive. The etiology relates to the age of the patient.[85] Rheumatic fever is most common in individuals under 55 years of age, and calcification of a congenital bicuspid valve is most common in those 55 to 70 years of age. Degenerative calcification is most frequent in those older than age 75. Most of the clinical signs of significant stenosis in older patients are similar to those found in young patients. The most important indications of pathology are the extension of the murmur into late systole, a low pulse pressure, and a slowly rising carotid pulse. These signs may not be present, however, even in the setting of severe stenosis, because of the age-associated increased stiffness of the central arteries. An S_4 gallop and reversed splitting of the second heart sound may be present more often in healthy older individuals than in younger individuals. Electrocardiographic evidence of left-ventricular hypertrophy is helpful. Although echocardiographically determined left-ventricular wall thickness increases with age, the change is minimal when compared with pathologic states. Heavy calcification of the aortic valve on the echocardiogram does suggest significant obstruction. The main differentials are idiopathic hypertrophic subaortic stenosis, which can be diagnosed with echocardiography, and valvular sclerosis, which can be distinguished by the cardiac examination and is the most common cause of systolic murmurs in the aortic area in the elderly. Doppler echocardiography may also be particularly useful in establishing the severity of valvular stenosis.

It should be noted that infectious endocarditis is a frequent cause of serious valvular pathology in elderly patients without prior known valvular disease. This is probably related to the increasing number of older patients who undergo diagnostic and therapeutic bowel, urinary, biliary, and pulmonary procedures, which can result in bacteremia.[88,89] Dental disease is also more prevalent.

The medical treatment of valvular disease in the elderly is similar to that in younger patients, though the comments above regarding the use of digitalis and diuretics should be kept in mind. The mortality of those aged 65 years or greater undergoing aortic and mitral valve replacement is generally low.[90–93] Because of poor long-term results with aortic valvuloplasty,[94] this should be considered as only palliative therapy in patients with definite contraindications to surgery, which is the preferred therapy.

ATRIAL SEPTAL DEFECT

One of the more common congenital abnormalities, which may become manifest in the older age groups, is an atrial septal defect. Altered left-ventricular diastolic compliance in older individuals due to ischemia, hypertension, or aging itself may increase left-to-right shunting at the atrial level and cause right heart failure. Atrial fibrillation is often associated with increasing failure and may be the presenting rhythm in such a patient. The prognosis is better with surgical than with medical treatment in this group of patients.[95]

REFERENCES

1. World Health Organization: The ten leading causes of death for selected countries in North America, Europe and Oceania, 1969, 1970 and 1971. *World Health Stat Rep* 27:563, 1974.
2. White NK et al: The relationship of the degree of coronary atherosclerosis with age in men. *Circulation* 1:645, 1950.
3. Tejada C et al: Distribution of coronary and aortic atherosclerosis by geographic location, race, and sex. *Lab Invest* 18:49, 1968.
4. Lakatta EG, Gerstenblith G: Cardiovascular system, in Rowe JW, Besdine RW (eds): *Health and Disease in Old Age*. Boston, Little, Brown, 1982, p 195.
5. Elveback L, Lie JT: Continued high incidence of coronary artery disease at autopsy in Olmstead County, Minnesota, 1950–1979. *Circulation* 70:345, 1984.
6. Hlatky MA, Pryor DB, Harrell FE, Califf RM, Mark DB, Rosati RA: Factors affecting sensitivity and specificity of exercise electrocardiography: Multivariate analysis. *Am J Med* 77:64, 1984.
7. Gerstenblith G et al: Stress testing redefines the prevalence of coronary artery disease in epidemiologic studies. *Circulation* 62(suppl III):308, 1980.
8. Melin JA et al: Diagnostic value of exercise electrocardiography and thallium myocardial scintigraphy in patients without previous myocardial infarction: A Bayesean approach. *Circulation* 63:1019, 1981.
9. Fleg JL, Gerstenblith G, Zonderman AB et al: Long-term significance of exercise-induced silent ischemia detected by ECG and thallium scintigraphy in asymptomatic volunteers. *Circulation* 76(suppl IV):395, 1987.
10. Pathy MS: Clinical features of ischemic heart disease, in Caird FI, Dall JLC, Kennedy RD (eds): *Cardiology in Old Age*. New York, Plenum, 1976, p 143.
11. Templeton GH et al: Contraction duration and diastolic stiffness in aged canine left ventricle, in Kobayashi T, Sano T, Dhalla NS (eds): *Recent Advances in Studies on Cardiac Structure and Metabolism*, vol II, *Heart Function and Metabolism*. Baltimore, University Park Press, 1978, p 169.
12. Spurgeon HA et al: Increased dynamic stiffness of trabeculae carneae from senescent rats. *Am J Physiol* 232:H373, 1977.
13. Weisfeldt ML et al: Resting and active mechanical properties of carneae from aged male rats. *Am J Physiol* 220:1921, 1977.
14. Hypertension Detection and Follow-up Program Cooperative Group: Five-year findings of the Hypertension Detection and Follow-up Program: Mortality by race, sex, and age. *JAMA* 242:2572, 1979.
15. European Working Party on High Blood Pressure in the Elderly: Mortality and morbidity results from the European Working Party on High Blood Pressure in the Elderly Trial. *Lancet* 1:1249, 1985.
16. Jajich CL, Ostfeldt AM, Freeman DH: Smoking and coronary heart disease mortality in the elderly. *JAMA* 252:2831, 1984.
17. Castleden CM et al: The effect of age on plasma levels of propranolol and practolol in man. *Br J Clin Pharmacol* 2:303, 1975.

18. Bukler FR et al: Antihypertensive beta blocking action as related to renin and age: A pharmacologic tool to identify pathogenetic mechanisms in essential hypertension. *Am J Cardiol* 36:653, 1975.

19. Vestal RE et al: Reduced beta-adrenoreceptor sensitivity in the elderly. *Clin Pharmacol Ther* 26:181, 1979.

20. The Norwegian Multicenter Study Group: Timolol-induced reduction in mortality and reinfarction in patients surviving acute myocardial infarction. *N Engl J Med* 304:801, 1981.

21. Beta Blocker Heart Attack Study Group: The Beta-Blocker Heart Attack Trial. *JAMA* 246:2073, 1981.

22. Antman E et al: Nifedipine therapy for coronary artery spasm: Experience in 127 patients. *N Engl J Med* 302:1269, 1980.

23. Gerstenblith G, Ouyang P, Achuff SC et al: Nifedipine in unstable angina: Double-blind randomized trial. *N Engl J Med* 306:885, 1982.

24. Mock MB, Holmes DR, Vlietstra RE et al: Percutaneous transluminal coronary angioplasty (PTCA) in the elderly patient: Experience in the National Heart, Lung and Blood Institute PTCA Registry. *Am J Cardiol* 53:89C, 1984.

25. Raizner AE, Hurst RG, Lewis JM et al: Transluminal coronary angioplasty in the elderly. *Am J Cardiol* 57:29, 1986.

26. Bourassa MG, Alderman EL, Bertrand M, de la Fuente L, Gratsianski A, Kaltenbach M, King SB, Nobuyoshi M, Romaniuk P, Ryan RJ, Serruys PW, Smith HC, Sousa JE, Bothig S, Rapaport E: Report of the Joint ISFC/WHO Task Force on Coronary Angioplasty. *Circulation* 78:780, 1988.

27. Kincaid DT, Botti RE: Acute myocardial infarction in the elderly. *Chest* 64:170, 1973.

28. Honey GE, Truelove SC: Prognostic factors in myocardial infarction. *Lancet* 1:1155 1957.

29. Schnur S: Mortality rates in acute myocardial infarction: III. The relation of patient's age to prognosis. *Ann Intern Med* 44:294, 1954.

30. Williams BO et al: The elderly in a coronary care unit. *Br Med J* 2:451, 1960.

31. Zerman FD, Rodstein M: Cardiac rupture complicating myocardial infarction in the aged. *Ann Intern Med* 105:431, 1960.

32. Biorck G et al: Studies on myocardial infarction in Malmo 1935–1954: III. Follow-up studies from hospital material. *Acta Med Scand* 162:81, 1958.

33. DeWood MA, Spores J, Notske R, Mouser LT, Burroughs R, Golden MS, Lang HT: Prevalence of total coronary occlusion during the early hours of transmural myocardial infarction. *N Engl J Med* 303:897, 1980.

34. Gruppo Italiano per lo studio della streptochinasi nell'infarto miocardico (GISSI): Effectiveness of intravenous thrombolytic therapy in acute myocardial infarction. *Lancet* i:397, 1986.

35. Guerci AD, Gerstenblith G, Brinker JA et al: A randomized trial of intravenous tissue plasminogen activator for acute myocardial infarction with subsequent randomization to elective coronary angioplasty. *N Engl J Med* 317:1613, 1987.

36. Wilcox RG, Olsson CG, Skene AM, von der Lippe G, Jensen G, Hampton JR: Trial of tissue plasminogen activator for mortality reduction in acute myocardial infarction. *Lancet* ii:525, 1988.

37. AIMS Trial Study Group: Effect of intravenous APSAC on mortality after acute myocardial infarction: Preliminary report of a placebo-controlled clinical trial. *Lancet* i:545, 1988.

38. ISIS-2 (Second International Study of Infarct Survival Collaborative Group): Randomized trial of intravenous streptokinase, oral aspirin, both, or neither among 17,187 cases of suspected acute myocardial infarction: ISIS-2. *Lancet* 2:349, 1988.

39. Lew AS, Hod H, Cercek B, Shah PK, Ganz W: Mortality and morbidity rates of patients older and younger than 75 years with acute myocardial infarction treated with intravenous streptokinase. *Am J Cardiol* 59:1, 1987.

40. Gersh BJ et al: Coronary arteriography and coronary artery bypass surgery: Morbidity and mortality in patients ages 65 years or older. *Circulation* 67:483, 1983.

41. Klainer LM et al: The epidemiology of cardiac failure. *J Chronic Dis* 18:797, 1965.

42. McKee PA et al: The natural history of congestive heart failure: The Framingham Study. *N Engl J Med* 285:1441, 1971.

43. Dock W: Cardiomyopathies of the senescent and senile. *Cardiovasc Clin* 4:362, 1972.

44. Pomerance A: Pathology of the heart with and without cardiac failure in the aged. *Br Heart J* 27:697, 1965.

45. Topol EJ, Traill TA, Fortuin NJ: Hypertensive hypertrophic cardiomyopathy of the elderly. *N Engl J Med* 312:277, 1985.

46. Lima JA, Fleg JL, Waclawiw M, Lima SD, Gerstenblith G: Cardiac structure and function in elderly women: Is there a distinctive profile? *Circulation* 78(suppl II):63, 1988.

47. Caird FI: Clinical examination and investigation of the heart, in Caird FI, Dall JLC, Kennedy RD (eds): *Cardiology in Old Age*. New York, Plenum, 1976, p 128.

48. Rowe JW: Fluid and electrolyte disturbances in the elderly, in Harris R (ed): *Geriatric Medicine*. New York, Physician Program, 1979, unit 1, lesson 4.

49. Triggs EJ, Nation RL: Pharmacokinetics in the aged: A review. *J Pharmacokinet Biopharm* 3:387, 1975.

50. Ewy GA et al: Digoxin metabolism in the elderly. *Circulation* 39:449, 1969.

51. Gerstenblith G, Spurgeon HA, Frohlich JP, Weisfeldt ML, Lakatta EG: Diminished inotropic responsiveness to ouabain in aged rat myocardium. *Circ Res* 44:517, 1979.

52. Guarnieri T et al: Diminished inotropic response but unaltered toxicity to acetystrophanthidin in the senescent beagle. *Circulation* 60:1548, 1979.

53. Fleg JL et al: Is digoxin really important in treatment of compensated heart failure? *Am J Med* 73:244, 1982.

54. Gheorghiade M, Beller GA: Effects of discontinuing maintenance digoxin therapy in patients with ischemic heart disease and congestive heart failure in sinus rhythm. *Am J Cardiol* 51:1243, 1983.

55. Lee DCS et al: Heart failure in outpatients: A randomized trial of digoxin versus placebo. *N Engl J Med* 306:699, 1982.

56. Shapiro S et al: The epidemiology of digoxin: A study in three Boston hospitals. *J Chronic Dis* 22:361, 1969.

57. Beller GA et al: Digitalis intoxication: A prospective clini-

cal study with serum level correlations. *N Engl J Med* 284:989, 1971.

58. Rowe J et al: The effect of age on creatine clearance in men: Cross-sectional and longitudinal study. *J Gerontol* 31:155, 1976.

59. Epstein M, Hollenberg NK: Age as a determinant of renal sodium conservation in normal men. *J Lab Clin Med* 87:411, 1976.

60. Weidmann P et al: Effect of aging on plasma renin and aldosterone in normal man. *Kidney Int* 8:325, 1975.

61. Flood C et al: The metabolism and secretion of aldosterone in elderly subjects. *J Clin Invest* 46:960, 1967.

62. Deutch S et al: Postoperative hyponatremia with the inappropriate release of antidiuretic hormone. *Anesthesiology* 27:250, 1966.

63. Weissinan PN et al: Chlorpropamide hyponatermia. *N Engl J Med* 284:65, 1971.

64. Davies MJ: Pathology of the conduction system, in Caird FI, Dall JLC, Kennedy RD (eds): *Cardiology in Old Age*. New York, Plenum, 1976, p 57.

65. Lev M: The pathology of complete atrioventricular block. *Prog Cardiovasc Dis* 6:317, 1964.

66. Lenegre J: Etiology and pathology of bilateral bundle branch block in relation to complete heart block. *Prog Cardiovasc Dis* 6:409, 1964.

67. Jose AD: Effect of combined sympathetic and parasympathetic blockade on heart rate and cardiac function in man. *Am J Cardiol* 18:476, 1966.

68. Davies HEF: Respiratory change in heart rate, sinus arrhythmia in the elderly. *Gerontol Clin* 17:96, 1975.

69. Julius S et al: Influence of age on the hemodynamic response to exercise. *Circulation* 36:222, 1967.

70. Rodeheffer RJ et al: Exercise cardiac output is maintained with advancing age in healthy human subjects: Cardiac dilatation and increased stroke volume compensate for a diminished heart rate. *Circulation* 69:203, 1984.

71. Chiang BN et al: Relationship of premature systoles to coronary heart disease and sudden death in the Tecumseh epidemiologic study. *Ann Intern Med* 70:1159, 1969.

72. Raftery EB, Cashman PM: Long-term recording of the electrocardiogram in a normal population. *Postgrad Med J* 52(suppl 7):32, 1976.

73. Simonson E: Differentiation between normal and abnormal, in *Electrocardiography*. St. Louis, Mosby, 1961.

74. Fleg JL, Kennedy HL: Cardiac arrhythmias in a healthy elderly population: Detection by 24-hour ambulatory electrocardiography. *Chest* 81:302, 1982.

75. Fleg JF, Lakatta EG: Prevalence and prognosis of exercise-induced nonsustained ventricular tachycardia in apparently healthy volunteers. *Am J Cardiol* 54:762, 1984.

76. Busby MJ, Fleg JL, Lakatta EG: Significance of exercise-induced frequent or repetitive ventricular ectopic beats in apparently healthy volunteers. *J Am Coll Cardiol* 8:55A, 1987 (abstract).

77. Das DN, Fleg JL, Lakatta EG: Effects of age on the components of atrioventricular conduction in normal man. *Am J Cardiol* 49:II-1031, 1982.

78. Mankikar GD, Clark ANG: Cardiac effects of carotid sinus massage in old age. *Age Ageing* 4:86, 1975.

79. Brand FFN, Abbott RD, Kannel WB, Wolf PA: Characteristics and prognosis of lone atrial fibrillation: Thirty year followup in the Framingham Study. *JAMA* 254:3449, 1985.

80. Harrison DC: Should lidocaine be administered routinely to all patients after acute myocardial infarction? *Circulation* 58:581, 1978.

81. Ochs HR et al: Reduced quinidine clearance in elderly persons. *Am J Cardiol* 42:481, 1978.

82. Siddons H: Death in long-term paced patients. *Br Heart J* 36:1201, 1974.

83. Caird FI: Valvular heart disease, in Caird FI, Dall JLC, Kennedy RD (eds): *Cardiology in Old Age*. New York, Plenum, 1976, p 231.

84. Bedford PD, Caird FI: *Valvular Disease of the Heart in Old Age*. London, Churchill, 1960.

85. Pomerance A: Pathology of the myocardium and valves, in Caird FI, Dall JLC, Kennedy RD (eds): *Cardiology in Old Age*. New York, Plenum, 1976.

86. Fulkerson PK: Calcification of the mitral annulus: Implications for the geriatric patient. *Geriatr Med Today* 1:51, 1982.

87. Korn D et al: Massive calcification of the mitral annulus. *N Engl J Med* 267:900, 1962.

88. Ries K: Endocarditis in the elderly, in Kaye D (ed): *Infective Endocarditis*. Baltimore, University Park Press, 1976.

89. Glecker J: Diagnostic aspects of subacute bacterial endocarditis in the elderly. *Arch Intern Med* 102:761, 1958.

90. Hochberg MS, Morrow AG, Michaelis LL, McIntosh CI, Redwood DR, Epstein SE: Aortic valve replacement in the elderly: Encouraging postoperative clinical and hemodynamic results. *Arch Surg* 112:1475, 1977.

91. Kaplan O, Yakirevich V, Vidne BA: Aortic valve replacement in septuagenarians. *Texas Heart Inst J* 12:295, 1985.

92. Hochberg MS, Derkae WM, Conkle DM, McIntosh CL, Epstein SE, Morrow AG: Mitral valve replacement in elderly patients: Encouraging postoperative clinical and hemodynamic results. *J Cardiovasc Thorac Surg* 77:422, 1979.

93. Jamieson WRE, Dooner J, Munro AI et al: Cardiac valve replacement in the elderly: A review of 320 cases. *Circulation* 64:II-177, 1981.

94. Litvack F, Jakubowski AT, Buchbinder NA, Eigler N: Lack of sustained clinical improvement in an elderly population after percutaneous aortic valvuloplasty. *Am J Cardiol* 62:270, 1988.

95. St. John Sutton et al: Atrial septal defect in patients ages 60 years or older: Operative results and long-term postoperative follow-up. *Circulation* 64:402, 1981.

Chapter 47

PERIPHERAL VASCULAR DISEASE

Brian L. Thiele and D. Eugene Strandness, Jr.

Atherosclerosis is the most common condition affecting the arterial system in the elderly. Attempts to identify a single causative factor responsible for the development of atherosclerosis have so far been unsuccessful, but a number of predisposing factors, when present in isolation or in combination, are known to increase the risk of development of this disease. Foremost among these appear to be cigarette smoking, hypertension, lipoprotein abnormalities, the presence of diabetes mellitus, and a positive family history. While symptoms related to this disease most commonly appear in the fifth and sixth decades, a significant number of complications continue to occur with increasing age.

ARTERIOSCLEROSIS OBLITERANS

PATHOGENESIS AND DISEASE PATTERNS

Current evidence suggests that the development of atherosclerosis is a continued response of the arterial wall to various types of endothelial injury.[1] Mechanical, chemical, and physical factors have been implicated in the initial damage to the lining of the arterial system and probably play a significant role in the continuing development of these lesions. There is also evidence to suggest that the arterial wall response to injury tends to vary and depends in part on the anatomic location of the vessel. Thus, it appears that arteries in different locations are either more susceptible to injury or respond to this insult in different ways.[2]

The early lesions of atherosclerosis commonly develop at the orifices of the intercostal and lumbar arteries, the distal portion of the superficial femoral artery, and the common iliac artery. Conduit arteries or those with no major branches throughout their course also appear to be susceptible to the early development of the atherosclerotic lesion. For as yet unknown reasons, diabetics have a peculiar predilection to the development of the disease at an early stage in the tibioperoneal arteries of the leg.[3]

The early plaques are usually flat with an intact or minimally denuded endothelial covering. Over time, the plaque undergoes significant changes: development of calcification, increase in size to encroach upon the lumen, hemorrhage within the plaque, and subsequent loss of surface covering with ulceration. It is the development of the complicated plaque that is usually associated with the development of symptoms.[4]

The majority of the clinical problems associated with atherosclerosis are the result of three phenomena: interference with the blood supply by the narrowing of the lumen, the sudden interruption of blood flow by thrombosis on a plaque, and the release of microemboli from ulcerated lesions.

PATHOPHYSIOLOGY OF ARTERIAL OBSTRUCTION

The major causes of acute arterial occlusion include embolism, thrombosis, and trauma. The most common source for emboli is from the heart, with the second being from an ulcerated atherosclerotic plaque at some point in the arterial system. Thrombosis does not occur in the normal arterial system. It develops when there has been some disruption of the endothelium exposing the subendothelial collagen to the flowing elements in blood.

Under resting flow conditions, the cross-sectional area of the artery in the region of the atherosclerotic plaque must be reduced by 80 percent before there is a decrease in pressure and flow.[5] Thus, flow is maintained at normal levels until the disease has reached a far-advanced stage. It is now known that resting levels of blood flow can be maintained at normal levels even with total occlusion because of the development of collateral circulation. Most commonly, symptoms occur when the arterial system cannot meet the metabolic demands of the limb during exercise. Under these circumstances, the collateral arteries are unable to accommodate the increase in blood flow needed to maintain perfusion.

As noted earlier, embolization from atherosclerotic plaques may also be responsible for the development of symptoms.[6] The most common site for this to occur is the carotid bifurcation, but it can also occur at the limbs. These emboli may arise from any point in the artery where plaques occur. These emboli are usually small and result in the occlusion of small vessels, such as the digital arteries in the toes.[7] It is rare for emboli arising from atherosclerosis plaques to be large enough to occlude major vessels such as the superficial femoral artery. When embolic occlusion of large arteries occurs, it is usually secondary to mural thrombi in the cardiac chambers.[8]

While it is now well-appreciated that thrombosis at the site of high-grade stenosis is often the terminal event leading to profound myocardial ischemia, it is not commonly recognized that this also occurs in the lower limb arteries and the carotid bifurcation. In the limbs, the event is usually not catastrophic because of the excellent collateral circulation and the relatively low metabolic requirements. Nonetheless, this condition is common and may be the cause of sudden worsening in a patient who is known to have chronic lower limb ischemia.

CLINICAL FEATURES

Lower Limb Ischemia

The clinical manifestations with an acute occlusion depend entirely upon the size of the thrombus or embolus and the immediate availability of the collateral circulation. When the ischemia is serious enough to threaten the viability of the limb, time is of the essence since irreversible tissue changes begin within 4 to 6 hours after the event. Recognition of the ischemia and its extent is best considered in terms of the six *P*'s, which include pain, pallor, paresthesia, pulselessness, and paralysis. The sixth *P*, which is the most important, is the physician, who must appreciate the importance of these symptoms and signs and seek immediate help from a vascular surgeon. Failure to do so will result in the needless loss of many limbs.

The most common presenting complaint in patients with chronic arterial occlusion of the lower limb arteries is intermittent claudication. This symptom is usually described as a dull ache that appears usually in the calf, is precipitated by exercise, and relieved by rest. The most constant clinical feature of claudication is the walk-pain-rest cycle that is very consistent from day to day and is always aggravated by an increase in the exercise load, such as walking up an incline. This symptom never occurs in the absence of exercise and is not related to changes in posture.

The level of arterial occlusion may be surmised from a consideration of the muscle groups in which the symptoms appear. Obstruction of the superficial femoral artery results in calf claudication. When the iliac arteries are involved, the blood supply to both the calf and thigh muscles is impaired, and both muscle groups may be the site of symptoms. More proximal obstruction of the common iliac artery or the abdominal aorta will interfere with the blood supply of the musculature in the buttocks, thighs, and calves, all of which may be the site of pain. Obstruction at this level may also be responsible for the development of impotence in the male.

When more than one named artery of the arterial system is occluded or diffusely affected by atherosclerosis, the symptoms are usually more severe, with claudication developing even with minimal exercise. It is also under these circumstances that blood flow may be unable to meet resting requirements and lead to the development of rest pain. The rest pain is a severe, aching pain, usually located in the forefoot and digits, which is always aggravated by elevation and partially or totally relieved when the limb is dependent. Characteristically, patients first become aware of this symptom at night, with partial or complete relief obtained by suspending the leg over the side of the bed.

When blood flow to the foot is marginal, minor trauma frequently results in the development of a non-healing ischemic ulceration. If something is not done to improve blood flow, tissue necrosis or gangrene may then develop. The severe ischemia seen in these circumstances also interferes with the ability of the tissues to resist or combat infection, which may also be responsible for rapid and marked additional tissue loss.

As noted earlier, atherosclerotic or thrombotic material from ulcerated plaques may embolize into the distal circulation and produce occlusion of the small arteries. This condition most commonly involves the plantar and digital arteries and is recognized clinically as the "blue-toes syndrome."[6–8]

Aneurysms

In some patients, atherosclerotic disease is not attended by a decrease in the cross-sectional area of the lumen of an artery but leads rather to weakening of the wall and local dilatation with the development of an aneurysm. This complication is predominantly a disease of males, with the peak incidence occurring in the sixth decade, or slightly later than that for the complications of arteriosclerosis obliterans. The most common sites for the development of atherosclerotic aneurysms are the abdominal aorta below the renal arteries, the popliteal artery, the iliac arteries, and the femoral arteries. Aneurysms of the abdominal aorta usually occur in isolation but in a small proportion of patients may be associated with aneurysms at one or more of these other sites.[9] When peripheral aneurysms are present, however, they are frequently bilateral and coexist at multiple sites.

Because of the weakening of the arterial wall in the region of the aneurysm, the most frequent complication is rupture. Factors that appear to predispose to this complication are the coexistence of hypertension and aneurysms of the abdominal aorta that are in excess of 6 cm in largest diameter.[10] While abdominal aneurysms are lined with a compacted layer of platelet-fibrin-thrombus, it is rare for emboli to occur from this site. By way of contrast, embolization and/or thrombosis of the aneurysms is the most common complication of popliteal aneurysms.[11] Because these aneurysms are in close proximity to major veins and nerves, the enlarging sac may compromise these structures, leading to symptoms that mimic deep vein thrombosis or peripheral neuropathy. Thrombosis of these aneurysms is attended with a high incidence of subsequent amputation because of severe ischemia.[12-14]

CLINICAL FEATURES OF ANEURYSMS

Most arterial aneurysms, regardless of their location, enlarge slowly and will usually not produce symptoms until a relatively large size is obtained. When a patient develops symptoms in the presence of an abdominal aortic aneurysm, this is usually an ominous sign and should alert the physician that a true emergency exists. The classic triad of ruptured abdominal aneurysms is pain, the presence of a pulsatile mass, and hypotension. The pain associated with rupture of aneurysms is often severe and unremitting. Because of the urgency involved in the successful management of ruptured abdominal aortic aneurysms, any patient over 50 years old who presents with abdominal pain should be carefully evaluated for the presence of this lesion.

Iliac aneurysms are extremely difficult to diagnose, largely because of the difficulty of palpating them deep in the pelvis. In addition, rupture of these aneurysms is frequently associated with unusual pain syndromes, some of which may direct the physician's attention to the lower urinary tract, while others, caused by irritation of the femoral or obturator nerves, will result in hip, thigh, or knee pain as the primary presenting complaint.

Although the complication of rupture of abdominal aneurysms is largely size-related, the relationship between size and complications of peripheral arterial aneurysm is not as common. The classic presentation of popliteal aneurysms is thrombosis and/or distal embolization with acute ischemia of the leg and foot. Once this complication has occurred, the likelihood of amputation varies from 15 to 50 percent.[14] This high incidence of limb loss is the reason for the aggressive surgical approach to these lesions when diagnosed, even if they are asymptomatic.

CLINICAL EVALUATION

Intermittent claudication, while easily recognized when it occurs in its classic form, is frequently confused with leg pain during ambulation that is secondary to neurospinal causes, called pseudoclaudication. The two can usually be distinguished on the basis of the history. In true claudication, the walk-pain-rest cycle is constant from day to day; with pseudoclaudication, the patient has both good and bad days. In addition, neurospinal disorders frequently require the patient either to sit down or lie down for relief of pain.

The type 2 diabetic poses special problems because of several features that are distinct to diabetes.[3] The major differences between vascular disease in diabetics and in nondiabetics is with regard to the following: (1) the more extensive involvement with atherosclerosis, particularly below the knee; (2) the frequent occurrence of a peripheral neuropathy (approximately 30 percent), which complicates healing; and (3) the lowered resistance to infection. All of these factors complicate the management of the patient's condition.

The presence of significant arterial disease can usually be suspected on the basis of the history. As noted previously, intermittent claudication is rarely confused with other problems as long as the history of walk-pain-rest cycle is consistent from day to day and pain is not present during periods of rest. Similar considerations apply in the evaluation of pain which occurs at rest. It cannot be stressed too much that a thorough history with attention to the details of the symptomatology as outlined above is necessary because, although atherosclerotic occlusive disease is frequently present in the elderly population, it may not be responsible for the patient's symptoms.

The important physical findings to be elicited include the presence of bruits at specific locations; namely, over the aorta, iliac vessels, and distal superficial femoral artery. In addition to auscultation for such bruits, the volume of pulses at the foot, popliteal, and femoral level should also be assessed. Pulses are absent distal to the site or sites of occlusion and constitute the major physical findings. In addition to the evaluation for the presence or absence of pulses, the aorta, iliac, femoral, and popliteal should be specifically examined for undue prominence that may alert the examining physician to the fact that aneurysmal disease is present. In chronic ischemia, there may be loss of hair and an atrophy of the skin that produces the characteristic thin, shiny appearance. These changes are seen predominantly in the distal leg and foot. Nail growth is also disturbed in severe cases, with the resulting development of bizarre-shaped, hypertrophic nails. In severe cases, ulceration may be present, usually occurring over sites of frequent trauma and often precipitated by ill-fitting shoes.

In the diabetic patient, it is also important to evaluate the status of the peripheral nervous system to determine whether a peripheral neuropathy coexists with the arterial disease. Clinically, evaluation of all patients with vascular disease should include not only a detailed examination of the area in which symptoms are present, but also a thorough examination of the whole of the vascular system, including that of the head and neck, the upper limbs, and the cardiac system. Bilateral arm pressures should be recorded, with a significant finding being a differential of 15 mmHg or greater between the two brachial pressures. The supraclavicular and neck areas should be auscultated for the presence of bruits.

At the conclusion of the history and physical examination, the examining physician should have decided whether the patient does have chronic occlusive vascular disease in the extremities, the site at which the occlusions or disease are present, and, finally, whether the symptomatology is consistent with the findings.

ANCILLARY DIAGNOSTIC AIDS Since arterial occlusion always produces a pressure drop across the involved segment, its presence can be confirmed by measuring the systolic pressure at the ankle using an ultrasonic velocity detector. This measurement is usually expressed as the ankle/arm index and normally should be greater than or equal to 1. When only one arterial segment is occluded, the index is usually greater than 0.5. When multiple levels of obstruction are present, it is often less than 0.5.[15] The absolute pressure level recorded is also of importance. If greater than 40 to 50 mmHg, the perfusion at rest is usually adequate to maintain tissue requirements. Pressures below this level are often associated with ischemic rest pain, and ulcers, when present, will usually not heal unless arterial inflow is improved.

While the diagnosis of intermittent claudication is usually not difficult to make, it is useful to establish the degree of walking disability and the physiological response to exercise. This is best done by a vascular laboratory and with a test that consists of walking on a treadmill at 2 mph on a 12 percent grade for 5 minutes, or until forced to stop by symptoms. Normally, in an individual without obstruction, the ankle systolic pressure after exercise will increase or remain unchanged. With arterial obstruction and claudication, the ankle pressure will fall to low levels and recover very slowly to the preexercise level.[16] If the pressure at the ankle falls to below 80 percent of the baseline and requires greater

than 3 minutes to recover, the condition is considered abnormal.

Whenever an arterial aneurysm is suspected at any level of the limb or the abdominal aorta, an ultrasonic B-mode examination should be ordered, which provides an accurate estimation of arterial size, both in the longitudinal and transverse dimensions of the vessel.[17] This simple test has largely replaced conventional x rays of the abdomen for both establishing the diagnosis and estimating size. It also provides an excellent method of following the progress of the aneurysm with regard to changes in size.

TREATMENT

Chronic Ischemia

Most patients with arterial occlusive disease and intermittent claudication are treated conservatively and will never require operative correction.[18] It is important to attempt to control the associated risk factors, particularly cigarette smoking. Patients should be informed that if they continue to smoke, their arterial disease will continue to progress, and they may be placed in jeopardy for possible limb loss. In addition to discontinuing smoking, patients should optimize their weight and embark on a regular exercise program. Significant improvement can occur, particularly in patients with a recent history of the onset of claudication.

The only medication that has proved to be of any benefit for patients with claudication is pentoxifylline, which is an agent that lowers blood viscosity by making red blood cells more deformable. Patients who take this drug may in some instances obtain some mild improvement in their symptoms.[19]

If a patient is severely disabled and cannot work or carry out daily activities, then surgical correction may be considered. It is important at this stage to consult with an experienced vascular surgeon to assess the location of the problems and the feasibility of a surgical procedure. Arteriography to delineate the location and extent of involvement should be undertaken only if surgery is seriously contemplated. A variety of surgical options are available that can, in most instances, be tailored to the disease location and the patient's general physical condition.[20,21]

In selected cases, it may be feasible to dilate focal areas of stenosis with a balloon catheter. This method has the best chance of success in the common and external iliac artery segments. While the long-term results have not been documented as yet, the initial results for the proximal lesions are very good. The success rates are not as good for femoropopliteal stenoses or occlusions.[22] These procedures must always be performed as a joint venture between the vascular surgeon and the radiologist.

When the patient showers microemboli to one or both feet, we have been quite conservative, treating the patient with aspirin. While the dose is controversial, we have tended to give a total of 650 mg daily. If the microemboli are not controlled by this management, it may be necessary to perform arteriography to find the source and carry out direct arterial surgery.

The patient with ischemic rest pain and ulceration is an entirely different problem. In general, unless blood flow can be improved to the limb, tissue loss is inevitable, usually at the below-knee level. It is important to be aggressive at this stage before tissue damage becomes irreversible and the patient is committed to an amputation.

In the context of arterial disease, the patient with diabetes mellitus presents special problems and requires more attention.[3,23] It is now well-established that patients with diabetes have more extensive arterial involvement of the tibial and peroneal arteries, the same degree of disease in the superficial femoral artery, and less in the aortoiliac segment. The propensity to develop occlusive disease in the medium-sized arteries below the knee has a more profound effect on perfusion of the foot and also makes a surgical procedure less likely to succeed.

The other major factor that leads to the higher incidence of tissue necrosis in diabetics is the high incidence of neuropathy; up to 30 percent of diabetics will have this problem.[3] The inability to appreciate deep pain sensation often leads to the development of calluses and nonhealing ulcers over points of pressure or irritation such as might occur with a poorly fitting shoe. It must be emphasized that ulceration and secondary infection can occur with a neuropathy alone, independent of any arterial involvement. When the two problems coexist, the situation is often irretrievable. Thus, even improving the blood supply to a neuropathic foot will not ensure healing to the same degree it does in a nondiabetic with arterial disease. Since no effective method of treating the neuropathy is available, therapeutic measures require considerable patience and time.

If an ulcer develops secondary to a neuropathy alone, it is important to treat the lesion with limited surgical débridement and aggressive therapy of any secondary infection. When osteomyelitis or joint space involvement occurs, then amputation, which must be tailored to the location of the problem, becomes mandatory. If there is coexisting arterial disease that can be successfully bypassed, this should be done, provided there is some assurance that a limited foot amputation may be feasible.

Aneurysms

The patients with aortic aneurysms pose particularly difficult problems. If rupture occurs, operation is, of course, mandatory, but the mortality rate will be very high, ranging from 15 to 80 percent.[24] Because of the very high mortality associated with rupture, elective resection is recommended, for which the mortality rate will be much lower—in the 2 to 5 percent range. The difficult decision rests in selecting those patients who should be operated on when they are asymptomatic.

The best data available suggest that if an aneurysm is greater than 6 cm in diameter, the likelihood of rupture is at least 50 percent over the next 2 years.[10,24,25] In the elderly population, the decision to be aggressive is most dependent upon the degree of involvement in other major organ systems such as the heart, lung, and kidneys, because it is usually failure of one or more of these systems in the postoperative period that results in patient mortality. With improvements in surgical technique, anesthetic management, and postoperative care, it is possible to perform aneurysm resection in those considered at risk (defined as an aneurysm greater than 6 cm) with an acceptable mortality rate of 2 percent or less.

For patients in their late seventies and eighties in whom an aneurysm is relatively small (less than 6 cm), control of hypertension and regular follow-up at 3- to 6-month intervals with repeat B-mode scans are recommended. If the aneurysms show signs of enlarging, then the physician is justified in pursuing a more aggressive approach of surgical resection.

Peripheral aneurysms, particularly in the popliteal segment, should be removed or bypassed unless there is a medical contraindication.[11] Thrombosis of a popliteal aneurysm is associated with a high incidence of limb loss. Also, the removal of a popliteal aneurysm is not associated with the same operative risk as a resection of an abdominal aneurysm with all its potential for cardiopulmonary complications.

Results of Therapy

In approaching the treatment of any patient with peripheral arterial disease, it is important to remember that the chance of limb loss, even if untreated, is relatively low. In the nondiabetic, the chance of limb loss is approximately 1 percent per year. However, when it is associated with diabetes, this figure will rise to about 5 percent per year, emphasizing the problems associated with this disease, as mentioned earlier.[23]

Surgical therapy for the treatment of intermittent claudication secondary to aortoiliac disease will give satisfactory results. Patency of the reconstructed segment will be maintained in 80 percent of the patients up to 5 years.[20] It must be remembered, however, that the operative mortality even in highly selected cases will approach 2 percent; thus, surgical therapy should not be undertaken lightly.

The operative management for the treatment of ischemia at rest and gangrene limited to the digits requires a great deal of judgment and evaluation to assess which form of therapy is most apt to give the best results. There is accumulating evidence that the appropriate use of long bypass grafts, even to the level of the ankle, is often able to provide both good early and long-term results. With better follow-up and attention devoted to the monitoring of the bypass vein grafts, long-term patency rates of 80 percent at 5 years are now feasible.

The results of aortic aneurysm resection in the long term are good. If the patient survives the operative procedure, the subsequent complications relate to the progression of occlusive disease if present, which is variable and unpredictable, and those complications that occur secondary to the prosthesis used to replace the aneurysms. The most feared complications are graft infection and aortoenteric fistulas. Fortunately, these occur in 1 percent or fewer of patients undergoing the procedures. Unfortunately, when they do occur, these complications are often lethal and tax the judgment and ingenuity of even the best vascular surgeons.

POSTTHROMBOTIC SYNDROME

When acute venous thrombosis develops, the involved vein is usually totally occluded, forcing the blood to follow alternative collateral pathways to the heart. The subsequent course of events depends upon several factors that include the extent of the residual occlusion and the development of valvular incompetence.[26] When the occlusion involves the iliofemoral segment, the major complaints include edema, heaviness, and thigh pain with exercise (venous claudication). This pain will only occur with vigorous exercise, so it is rarely a problem in the elderly, who usually can not exercise enough to produce this complaint.

A more common problem comes with the development of valvular incompetence in the veins below the knee. When this occurs, there is reflux of blood with calf contraction, edema, pain, and the development of pigmentation along the medial side of the lower leg. If the reflux and edema is allowed to persist, the patient may develop an ulceration in the pigmented area that is difficult to heal. The most appropriate therapy is to apply a semirigid dressing from the base of the toes to below the knee; the dressing should be changed weekly. This therapy permits the patient to remain ambulatory and is successful in promoting healing in at least 90 percent of cases. After healing is accomplished, it is critical that the patient be fitted with a short leg-compression hose to prevent swelling and recurrent ulceration. If this regimen does not work, it may be necessary to apply a skin graft, but this step is not usually required.

EXTRACRANIAL ARTERIAL DISEASE

Stroke is the third most common cause of death caused by arterial disease in the United States. While there is no doubt that it may be due to intracranial involvement, atherosclerosis of the extracranial arteries is now known to be a common and important factor in the pathogenesis of transient ischemic attacks and strokes.[27,28] Recognition of this fact is important because there is increasing evidence that disease in this area can, in selected patients, be treated successfully with surgery or antiplatelet agents.

PATHOGENESIS OF TRANSIENT CEREBRAL ISCHEMIC ATTACKS AND STROKES

For reasons poorly understood, atherosclerosis of the extracranial arteries tends to occur at branch points and bifurcations, sparing those arteries without branches and whose course is relatively straight. The most important site of involvement is the carotid bifurcation, where the atherosclerotic plaque will remain confined and be the source of problems.[27,29,30] Disease in this location produces problems by either a reduction in hemispheric blood flow or emboli to the brain.

The clinical outcome in any patient depends upon factors that are impossible to predict. In theory, at least, the brain would appear to be ideally protected against a total occlusion of one or more of its vessels of supply because of the Circle of Willis. That the brain can in effect function well in the presence of significant disease is evidenced by patients who can survive unilateral or even bilateral occlusion of the internal carotid arteries. However, it is now well-known that the Circle of Willis is often incomplete and in some patients cannot function to preserve hemispheric or regional blood flow even if the occlusion occurs gradually.[30]

The realization that the surface of a plaque at the carotid bifurcation can ulcerate and be the source of microemboli to the brain represented a major advance in our understanding of the etiology of transient ischemic attacks and stroke.[27] Thus, it is currently accepted that up to 70 percent of patients in this category will have emboli as the basis for their cerebral ischemia and not a total reduction in hemispheric blood flow caused by a high-grade stenosis or a total occlusion of the internal carotid artery.

CLINICAL PRESENTATION

For clinical purposes, it is convenient to subdivide patients into the following categories: (1) those with asymptomatic bruit; (2) those with focal symptoms; and (3) those with nonfocal symptoms.

The patient with a bruit in mid and high position of the neck must be considered as suspect for harboring a carotid bifurcation plaque. However, it is a nonspecific finding and does lead to a dilemma that will be addressed in the following sections.

Patients with focal symptoms are generally subdivided into the following categories: (1) those suffering transient ischemic attacks (TIAs), (2) those with reversible ischemic neurological deficit (RIND), and (3) those with a completed stroke. This classification is generally used to refer to problems that occur in the distribution of the internal carotid artery, and the symptoms produced are related to neurological dysfunction in the area of the brain supplied by that vessel. The most classic are disturbances of motor and sensory function and monocular visual disturbances.

The transient ischemic attacks are abrupt in onset and will resolve within a matter of minutes. For example, in the case of the eye, fleeting blindness (amaurosis fugax) may occur, which is described as a window shade being pulled across the field of vision. The duration of the deficit that one is willing to accept as signifying an ischemic event is somewhat variable, but if it persists in excess of 1 hour and then clears completely, it is probably more appropriately classified as a reversible ischemic neurological deficit. The important fact to keep in mind is that the patient is neurologically normal after the attack has subsided.

Those with a completed stroke develop a deficit that remains fixed or at best shows improvement over days or weeks, but continued neurological impairment of some degree usually persists. The therapeutic implications in this group of patients are obviously different from those with reversible deficits.

Those patients with nonfocal and nonhemispheric symptoms are the most confusing and difficult to evaluate clinically. The potpourri of symptoms includes vertigo, ataxia, diplopia, drop attacks, dysarthria, syncope, dizziness, decreased mentation, and seizures. When these symptoms develop and are not related to some other definable etiology, the patients are often evaluated for the presence of vascular disease, particularly if they are elderly or have evidence of arterial disease in the neck or other locations. It should be stressed that a thorough neurological evaluation should be performed in these circumstances to exclude other causes before one is satisfied that the symptoms are related to extracranial vascular disease.

DIAGNOSIS

The keystone of establishing a diagnosis is to discover a lesion or set of lesions that appear to be appropriate for the clinical picture. This may be relatively simple or complex, depending upon the presenting complaints.

The patient with an asymptomatic bruit presents a dilemma more with regard to management than workup.

As already indicated, the bruit itself is nonspecific and does not predict with a high degree of accuracy the state of the carotid bifurcation. It has been shown that approximately one-third of the patients with such a finding will have a high-grade stenosis (50 to 99 percent diameter reduction), about 6 percent will be normal, and about 6 percent will have a total occlusion of the internal carotid artery. The remainder will have disease of a lesser degree, narrowing the carotid artery by 10 to 49 percent.[29]

Of great importance is the relationship between the degree of narrowing and the occurrence of TIAs, strokes, and total occlusions of the internal carotid artery. It has been shown that patients with a greater than 80 percent diameter reducing lesion of the internal carotid artery have a very high incidence of ischemic events within the first 6 to 9 months after discovery of the lesion.[29,30] The lesion is usually discovered by ultrasonic duplex scanning in asymptomatic patients who are found to have a cervical bruit. It should be noted that such high-grade or preocclusive lesions are found in about 6 percent of all asymptomatic patients with bruits.

With the availability of ultrasonic duplex scanning in most hospitals, it is not necessary to resort to arteriography to establish the presence and degree of carotid bifurcation involvement. The test is so accurate that it can be used for screening purposes and is an ideal method for following the natural history of the disease, regardless of how it is treated.[31]

Patients with focal TIAs or a completed stroke are in general considered candidates for arteriography, which will more clearly define the location and extent of the involvement. Screening with noninvasive tests is often considered unnecessary; such tests may be useful, however, particularly if an operation is to be carried out and postoperative studies are to be performed to follow the progress of the operated segment and the contralateral carotid artery, which is so often a site of disease involvement.

Patients with nonhemispheric symptoms and/or signs present great difficulties in evaluation. It is generally assumed that if the nonspecific symptoms are due to vascular disease involving the extracranial arterial circulation, it must be on the basis of flow-reducing lesions, i.e., high-grade stenoses or total occlusions. If high-grade stenoses or occlusions are not found by noninvasive testing, it is very unlikely that the symptoms are due to extracranial arterial disease.

There are specific situations in which a good cause-and-effect relationship exists between nonspecific symptoms and vascular disease, such as the subclavian steal syndrome wherein blood may be siphoned away from the posterior circulation via the vertebral artery.[32] This syndrome occurs when there is a proximal stenosis or occlusion of the subclavian artery and can easily be detected by measuring the blood pressure in both arms. There should not be a differential of greater than 15 mmHg between the two arms.

It cannot be emphasized too strongly that the workup in all categories of patients with symptoms may have to include a computerized tomography (CT) scan, electroencephalogram (EEG), and a complete neurological evaluation to avoid missing intracranial lesions such as tumors, which may be responsible for a patient's complaints.

THERAPY

There are few areas in the field of vascular disease where there is more controversy. With regard to the entire cohort of patients with vascular disease, the annual rate of events—TIAs and strokes—is quite low, about 4 percent each year. On the other hand, if one examines the event rate as a function of the degree of narrowing, the results are striking for the very tight stenoses (greater than 80 percent diameter reduction). The event rate here is on the order of 50 percent, with most occurring in the first 6 months after discovery. At the present time, carotid endarterectomy can be considered for the patients with the high-grade lesions. It is safe to follow the other patients and possibly treat them with aspirin.[29,30,33]

For the patient with focal symptoms secondary to carotid bifurcation disease, opinion is also divided. However, if a good surgical team is available that has a combined morbidity and mortality rate below 5 percent, it is justified to consider carotid endarterectomy. It must be remembered that this operation is designed to prevent the occurrence of cerebral ischemic events and will have little effect on mortality. The most common cause of death in this group of patients is myocardial infarction.

Those patients with nonfocal symptoms pose the greatest problems in management. If they can be associated with a lesion such as occlusion of the subclavian artery with reversal of flow in the vertebral artery, it may be justified to consider operation. However, the symptoms must be disabling before surgical therapy is contemplated. These patients often will improve without any definitive therapy.

RESULTS

The only medical therapy currently available to treat symptomatic patients with ischemic symptoms secondary to extracranial arterial disease is aspirin. In the controlled studies that have been done, this therapy appears to be effective in reducing the occurrence of transient ischemic events, stroke, and myocardial infarction, when taken together as endpoints.[33] The dose of aspirin used is controversial and is still under investigation.

Since the randomized trials used full dose—325 mg three times a day—that is what we currently recommend.

Carotid endarterectomy appears to be a durable operation with a very low incidence of postoperative occlusions and recurrent ischemic events.[30] Controlled clinical trials are under way to investigate this option further, but the data will not be available for several years.

REFERENCES

1. Ross T, Glomset JA: Pathogenesis of atherosclerosis. *N Engl J Med* 295:369, 1976.
2. Haimovici H, Maier N, Strauss L: Fate of aortic homografts in experimental canine atherosclerosis: 1. Study of fresh thoracic implants into abdominal aorta. *Arch Surg* 76:282, 1958.
3. Strandness DE Jr, Priest RE, Gibbons GE: Combined clinical and pathologic study of diabetic and non-diabetic peripheral arterial disease. *Diabetes* 13:366, 1964.
4. Haimovici H (ed): *Vascular Surgery: Principles and Techniques.* New York, McGraw-Hill, 1976, chap 15.
5. May AG, DeWeese JA, Rob CG: Hemodynamic effects of arterial stenosis. *Surgery* 53:513, 1964.
6. Wagner RB, Marin AS: Peripheral atheroembolism: Confirmation of a clinical concept with case report and review of the literature. *Surgery* 73:353, 1973.
7. Crane C: Atherothrombotic embolism to lower extremities in arteriosclerosis. *Arch Surg* 94:96, 1967.
8. Hight DW, Tilney NI, Cough NP: Changing clinical trends in patients with peripheral arterial emboli. *Surgery* 79:172, 1976.
9. Hirsch HJ et al: Aortic and lower extremity arterial aneurysms. *J Clin Ultrasound* 9:29, 1981.
10. Estes JE Jr: Abdominal aortic aneurysms: Study of 102 cases. *Circulation* 2:258, 1950.
11. Crawford ES, DeBakey ME: Popliteal artery arteriosclerotic aneurysms. *Circulation* 32:515, 1965.
12. Edmunds LH, Darling RC, Linton RR: Surgical management of popliteal aneurysms. *Circulation* 32:517, 1965.
13. Bouhoutsos J, Martin P: Popliteal aneurysms: A review of 116 cases. *Br J Surg* 61:469, 1974.
14. Gifford RW, Hines EA Jr, James JM: An analysis and follow-up study of 100 popliteal aneurysms. *Surgery* 33:284, 1953.
15. Carter SA: Clinical measurement of systolic pressures in limbs with arterial occlusive disease. *JAMA* 207:1869, 1969.
16. Carter SA: Response of ankle systolic pressure to leg exercise in mild or questionable arterial disease. *N Engl J Med* 287:578, 1972.
17. Leopold G, Goldberger L, Bernstein E: Ultrasonic detection and evaluation of abdominal aortic aneurysms. *Surgery* 72:939, 1972.
18. Boyd AM: The natural cause of arteriosclerosis of the lower extremities. *Angiology* 61:10, 1960.
19. Porter JM, Cutler BS, Lee B et al: Pentoxifylline efficacy in the treatment of intermittent claudication: Multicenter controlled double-blind trial with objective assessment of

chronic occlusive arterial disease patients. *Am Heart J* 2:66, 1982.

20. Nevelsteen AR et al: Aortofemoral grafting: Factors influencing late results. *Surgery* 88:642, 1980.

21. Sumner DS, Strandness DE Jr: Hemodynamic studies before and after extended bypass graft to the tibial and peroneal arteries. *Surgery* 86:442, 1979.

22. Rutherford RB, Patt A, Kumpe DA: The current role of percutaneous transluminal angioplasty, in Greenhalgh RM, Jamieson CW, Nicolaides AN (eds): *Vascular Surgery: Issues in Current Practice*. New York, Grune & Stratton, 1986, chap 17.

23. Silbert S, Zazeela H: Prognosis in arteriosclerotic peripheral vascular disease. *JAMA* 166:1816, 1958.

24. Gore I, Hirst AE Jr: Arteriosclerotic aneurysms of the abdominal aorta: A review. *Prog Cardiovasc Dis* 16:113, 1973.

25. Bergan JJ, Yao JST, Flinn WR, McCarthy WJ: New findings in aortic aneurysm surgery, in Bergan JJ, Yao JST (eds): *Arterial Surgery*. New York, Grune and Stratton, 1988, pp 287–298.

26. Strandness DE Jr, Thiele BL: *Selected Topics in Venous Disorders*. Mt. Kisco, NY, Futura Publishing Co, 1981, chap 5.

27. Imparato AM, Riles TS, Gorstein F: The carotid bifurcation plaque: Pathological findings associated with cerebral ischemia. *Stroke* 10:238, 1979.

28. Thompson JE, Talkington CM: Carotid endarterectomy. *Ann Surg* 184:1, 1976.

29. Roederer GO, Langlois YE, Jager KA et al: The natural history of carotid arterial disease in asymptomatic patients with cervical bruits. *Stroke* 15:605, 1984.

30. Moneta GL, Taylor DC, Nicholls SC et al: Operative versus nonoperative management of asymptomatic high-grade internal carotid artery stenosis: Improved results with endarterectomy. *Stroke* 18:1005, 1987.

31. Langlois YE, Roederer GO, Strandness DE Jr: Ultrasonic evaluation of the carotid bifurcation. *Echocardiography* 4:99, 1987.

32. Santschi DR et al: The subclavian steal syndrome: Clinical and angiographic considerations in 74 cases in adults. *J Thorac Cardiovasc Surg* 51:103, 1966.

33. The Canadian Cooperative Study Group: A randomized trial of aspirin and sulfinpyrazone in threatened stroke. *N Engl J Med* 299:53, 1978.

Chapter 48

HYPERTENSION

William B. Applegate

In the last few years there has been an explosion of new knowledge on the epidemiology, pathophysiology, and treatment of hypertension in the elderly. Estimates of the prevalence of hypertension in the elderly vary greatly depending on the age and race of the population, the blood pressure cut points used for the definition of hypertension, and the numbers of measurements made.[1-3] Although hypertension is very prevalent in the elderly, most current prevalence figures are overestimates. The combination of data from clinical trials lending support to the notion that at least some forms of hypertension in the elderly should be treated[4] and the proliferation of new pharmacologic agents has stimulated the growing tendency to treat as many as 40 percent of elderly persons with some form of antihypertensive medication.[5]

Since the risk of future cardiovascular morbid and mortal events rises in a continuous fashion as either systolic blood pressure (SBP) or diastolic blood pressure (DBP) rises, there is really no threshold of either SBP or DBP which can definitively be described as "hypertensive."[6] Nonetheless, for the purposes of clarity, this chapter will use the following definitions based on clinical convention and on recommendations from a National Heart, Lung, and Blood Institute advisory committee:[2]

> *Isolated Systolic Hypertension* (ISH) = SBP greater than or equal to 160 mmHg and DBP less than 90 mmHg
>
> *Systolic-Diastolic Hypertension* (SDH) = SBP greater than 140–160 mmHg and DBP greater than or equal to 90 mmHg

PHYSIOLOGY

The exact *causal* mechanisms for hypertension in the elderly and whether they are that different from the mechanisms involved in hypertension in younger persons remain to be fully elucidated. As will be pointed out below, much of the supposed rise in prevalence in hypertension in persons over age 65 is actually attributable to a rise in ISH rather than a rise in SDH. It has been presumed that structural changes in the large vessels play a predominant role in the rise in SBP levels with age. However, the degree to which vascular structural changes versus functional changes contribute to hypertension in the elderly is still not completely clear. Both a decrease in connective tissue elasticity and an increase in the prevalence of atherosclerosis result in an increase in peripheral vascular resistance and aortic impedance with age.[7-10] Vascular morphologic changes which occur in hypertension include hypertrophy and hyperplasia of the smooth muscle cells,[11,12] changes in collagen and elastin in the vessel wall,[13] and possible hyperplasia of the cells in the vascular endothelium.[13,14] The structural changes that occur with aging are qualitatively similar to, but not as extreme as, the changes observed with hypertension.[15] A recent study in laboratory rats indicates that blood pressure lowering in both normotensive and hypertensive rats could prevent the development of age-related changes in the vascular wall.[16] Simon et al. have found a strong negative correlation between large-vessel compliance and systolic pressure in older patients.[17] It has been shown that a decrease in aortic compliance results in greater resistance to systolic ejection and frequently results in disproportionate elevations of SBP.[10]

In addition to undergoing structural changes, the vascular system also undergoes functional changes associated with hypertension and aging. Studies of age-related changes in alpha-adrenergic responsiveness of vascular smooth muscle have produced somewhat conflicting results.[18-22] However, the bulk of the evidence seems to indicate that alpha-adrenergic responsiveness of the vascular smooth muscle is not greatly changed with age.[23] It is more clear that the beta-adrenergic responsiveness of vascular smooth muscle declines with age,[24,25] with a consequent decrease in the relaxation of vascular smooth muscle.[26] This decrease may be specific to the beta-adrenergic system, since aging vessels continue to respond to other vasodilators, such as nitroglycerin.[15,25] Abrass has postulated that the increase in peripheral resistance in elderly hypertensives may in part be due to diminished beta-adrenergic-mediated vasodilation while alpha-adrenergic-mediated vasoconstriction continues unabated.[23]

It is possible that age-related vascular changes in responsiveness to vasoactive agents could be related to alterations in the handling of the calcium cation. Carrier et al. reported that in aged rats alterations in calcium concentration did not affect vascular smooth muscle responsiveness to norepinephrine.[18] On the other hand, Cohen and Berkowitz found aortas from old rats were quite dependent on extracellular calcium for the extent of norepinephrine-induced contraction.[19] Although the role of calcium in hypertension in the elderly has not been well defined, it should be noted that hypertension in the elderly responds well to treatment with calcium antagonists.[27] Recently, Lindner and colleagues have reported that, in young and middle-aged patients, plasma from patients with essential diastolic hypertension increased the intracellular calcium in platelets taken from normal subjects, suggesting that certain factors in the plasma of patients with essential hypertension may increase calcium content within vascular smooth muscle cells[28] and play a role in increasing peripheral vascular resistance.

Whether or not the renin-angiotensin system or the renal management of electrolytes and water plays a central role in the pathogenesis of hypertension in the elderly is uncertain. It appears likely that both systems are involved to some extent, but probably have a secondary role. It is clear that, on average, plasma renin levels decline with age.[29] Both basal plasma renin levels and the renin response to sodium depletion,[30,31] diuretic administration,[32] and upright posture decline with age.[33,34] However, neither the concentration of plasma renin substrate[30,31] nor levels of inactive renin decline in the elderly.[35] It is possible that the mechanisms responsible for converting inactive renin to active renin are primarily affected by age, but the exact reason for the decline in plasma renin levels with age is unknown.[33] Some studies of elderly hypertensive patients estimate that approximately 20 percent of elderly patients have relatively high renin values,[36] while other studies indicate that the proportion with high renin values is considerably lower than that.[37] Even though the prevalence of high renin levels may be low in elderly hypertensives, the renin-angiotensin system must play some role in the pathogenesis or maintenance of hypertension in a majority of elderly hypertensives, since most will experience significant blood pressure lowering when given an angiotensin converting enzyme inhibitor.[38] There is also a reduction in plasma aldosterone levels with age, but this decline is not as great as the decrease in renin levels.[33]

The role of the kidney in hypertension in the elderly is not well defined. Longitudinal studies indicate that there is a decline in glomerular filtration rate and creatinine clearance with age, even in the absence of renal or vascular disease.[39] Elderly persons are less able both to maximally retain and to excrete sodium. Studies indicate that it takes elderly subjects longer to excrete a given saline load, but the sodium is eventually excreted rather than retained.[32] Also, the ability of the kidney to respond maximally to antidiuretic hormone declines with age.[40] To date it does not appear that renal and adrenal mechanisms play a predominant role in the pathogenesis of hypertension in the elderly.

Studies of cardiovascular hemodynamics in elderly hypertensives have indicated that elderly patients with either ISH or SDH have increased peripheral vascular resistance.[37,41] Messerli and colleagues found that elderly patients with SDH had lower resting cardiac output, heart rate, stroke volume, intravascular volume, renal blood flow, and plasma renin activity when compared to younger patients with SDH.[37] Vardan and colleagues reported that elderly patients with ISH had variable cardiac output and stroke volume.[41,42] Unfortunately, studies of cardiovascular hemodynamics in elderly hypertensives have been limited to date by small and possibly nonrepresentative samples. Few of the subjects have been over age 70, and the studies do not separate out the effects of aging versus increased blood pressure over time. It would be hazardous to make sweeping treatment recommendations based on such a limited data base. However, the most consistent cardiovascular physiologic change in elderly patients with either SDH or ISH is increased peripheral vascular resistance. The presumed pathophysiology of hypertension in the elderly is summarized in Table 48-1.

PREVALENCE AND RISK

As mentioned above, several epidemiologic studies have indicated that average SBP increases throughout the life span in most countries, while average DBP rises until age 55 to 60.[43] This increase in blood pressure occurs both in persons who have previously been classified as hypertensive plus those who have been normotensive. However, data from Framingham and other studies indicate that not all individuals experience this aging-related increase in blood pressure.[43] In addition, population studies from primitive societies indicate that average blood pressure does not tend to rise with age.[44] Such populations tend not to have the age-related weight gain usually seen in industrialized societies, have higher levels of habitual physical exercise, and consume diets low in sodium and rich in potassium.[44]

Unfortunately, the prevalence of SDH and ISH is

TABLE 48-1
Physiology of Hypertension in the Elderly

Vascular systems
    Decreased distensibility
    Increased atherosclerosis
    Normal alpha-adrenergic function
    Decreased beta-adrenergic function
Renin-angiotensin system
    Decreased renin levels
    Probable secondary role
Cardiovascular hemodynamics
    Increased peripheral resistance
    Decreased cardiac output
    Decreased renal blood flow
    Decreased plasma volume

considerable in the elderly. Since average DBP tends to level off around age 55, the prevalence of SDH tends to level off in persons over age 55 to 60.[43,45] Therefore, although some authors speak in general terms of the rise in the prevalence of hypertension with age, the prevalence of SDH rises little if at all with advanced age.[46,47] Actually, it is the rise in ISH which accounts for most of the overall increase in the prevalence of "hypertension" with advancing age.[45] Prevalence estimates of either SDH or ISH depend on the number of measurements taken (prevalence decreases to an extent with increasing numbers of measurement), the level of DBP or SBP used in the definition, and the population studied. When prevalence estimates for SDH and ISH are based on studies like the Hypertension Detection and Follow-up Program (HDFP) and the Systolic Hypertension in the Elderly Program (SHEP), which utilize measurements on more than one occasion, it appears that the prevalence of SDH in the elderly is about 15 percent in whites and 25 percent in blacks, while the prevalence of ISH varies with age from 10 to 20 percent.[46,47] Therefore, the total prevalence of hypertension in the elderly is not quite as high as the figure of 50 to 60 percent which is frequently reported.[1]

Although the clinical treatment of hypertension has classically focused on DBP levels, epidemiologic data indicate that for middle-aged and older adults, SBP is more predictive of future cardiovascular morbidity and mortality than is DBP.[48,49] For instance, analysis of the Framingham data indicates that DBP is somewhat more predictive of the development of coronary heart disease (CHD) in persons under age 45, but, as age continues to increase above 45 years, DBP declines somewhat in its ability to predict future CHD while SBP increases in its ability to predict CHD.[49] Above age 60, SBP is more predictive of CHD; in fact, in the elderly, SBP alone is as predictive as the combination of SBP and DBP. Both SBP and DBP are highly predictive of future cerebrovas-

cular events. Analysis of Framingham data indicates that 42 percent of strokes in elderly men and 70 percent of strokes in elderly women are directly attributable to hypertension.[49] Again, SBP appears to be slightly more predictive than DBP, and the risk gradients for SBP do not wane with advancing age. Elevations of SBP are in part related to decreased arterial distensibility and increased rigidity of the major blood vessels, as measured by the depth of the dicrotic notch in pulse-wave recordings, which flattens with age.[8,50] However, when changes in the pulse wave are held constant, increased SBP is still predictive of future cardiovascular events.[8]

When all cardiovascular risk factors are taken into account in the elderly, it is clear that an increased level of SBP is the single greatest risk factor (other than age itself) for increased cardiovascular disease in this population.[43] It is also clear that increased blood pressure does interact with some of the other traditional cardiovascular risk factors to compound the risk.[43] For instance, although total serum cholesterol declines somewhat in predictive power as a cardiovascular risk factor in the elderly, it still confers some element of risk (especially when fractionated into the high-density lipoprotein/low-density lipoprotein [HDL/LDL] ratio) and compounds the risk for hypertensives.[43] Also, it has been known for some years that the development of left ventricular hypertrophy (LVH) is itself an independent cardiovascular risk factor.[51] Recent reports from the Framingham study indicate that LVH is more prevalent in the elderly and is highly correlated with increased SBP.[52] It is also becoming more clear that LVH in hypertensives confers increased risk of ventricular arrythmias.[53]

RISK/BENEFIT RATIO OF THERAPY

Whether and how to treat hypertension in the elderly depends on a consideration of the risk/benefit ratio specific to old age.[3] Because treatment in the elderly has historically been cautious because of the concern about adverse side effects, these will be considered first. Although SDH and ISH have been shown to be associated with increased epidemiologic risk of subsequent cardiovascular disease, concerns about the toxicity from antihypertensive therapy in the elderly have led many authors to advise restraint or even therapeutic nihilism with regard to the treatment of hypertension in the elderly.[54] Theoretically, there are reasons why the risk/benefit ratio for the treatment of hypertension might increase with age. It is thought that the elderly are particularly susceptible to many of the side effects of antihypertensive medication.[55] For instance, it has been shown that elderly patients are more likely than younger patients to develop hyponatremia and hypokalemia when treated with standard doses of diuretics.[55,56] It is also thought that older patients are more likely to develop side effects such as depression and confusion when treated with antihypertensive medications that affect the central nervous system (medications such as beta-blockers or drugs that affect the alpha-adrenergic nervous system).[57] As mentioned previously, there is good evidence that the baroreceptor reflex becomes less sensitive with age.[58,59] As a result, the elderly could be more sensitive to the postural hypotensive effects of antihypertensive medications, with a consequent propensity for falls and fractures.[60]

Although some investigators have argued that elderly persons with hypertension actually need the higher blood pressure to adequately perfuse vital organs such as the brain and kidney,[61] most studies have not shown that judicious use of antihypertensive medications in the elderly has a significant adverse effect on either renal or cerebral perfusion.[62–64] It is clear from the work of Strandgaard et al. that in middle-aged patients with chronic essential hypertension the pressure–flow curve for cerebral autoregulation is reset to the right so that the chronic hypertensive would be more susceptible to cerebral hypoperfusion if the mean arterial pressure were lowered substantially and acutely.[65] It is quite possible that a similar situation might exist in an elderly patient who has been hypertensive for a number of years. Further work has indicated that cautious, slow lowering of blood pressure to normal levels in the chronic hypertensive with continued control results in a resetting of the cerebral pressure–flow autoregulation curve[64,66] to the left, i.e., toward a more normal configuration. A few studies in middle-aged hypertensives suggest that acute initiation of antihypertensive drugs can lower cerebral perfusion modestly,[64,67,68] but chronic administration of appropriate doses of antihypertensive medications does not adversely affect cerebral blood flow.[62,64,66,69,70]

Actually there are surprisingly few data from large-scale clinical trials to definitively address the issue of the toxicity of antihypertensive medication in the elderly. A group of investigators from the Hypertension Detection and Follow-Up Program (HDFP) has reported that the total rate of adverse effects in this trial of the treatment of mild-to-moderate SDH was less for the subgroup aged 60 to 69 years at entry than for those under age 50.[71] While these data are helpful, it should be remembered that persons in the age range 60 to 69 would really be classified as "young old" and may not be as susceptible to side effects as the "old old" (aged 75 years and up). In addition, such trials tend to select the most "well" subjects and are not necessarily representative of elderly patients who have one or more serious comorbid diseases. The largest set of data available on the toxicity of antihypertensive therapy in the elderly comes from the European Working Party on Hypertension in the Elderly (EWPHE) randomized study of the efficacy of the treatment of SDH in a cohort of patients with a mean age at entry of 72 years.[4] Early reports from this trial indicate that treatment with a thiazide-triamterene combination (followed by alphamethyldopa as a second-step agent when needed) resulted in mild increases in glucose intolerance, serum creatinine, and uric acid and a mild decrease in serum potassium in the treatment group.[72] Treatment does not appear to have had a significant long-term effect on serum cholesterol levels.[73] To date only limited data on side effects have been reported. There was no significant difference between the treatment and control group in the rate at which patients were dropped from the study because of presumed drug-related side effects. The biochemical side effects listed above were not thought to outweigh the benefits of treatment (described later).

Questions still remain about the possible degree of negative impact antihypertensive therapy may have on the quality of life for elderly patients. Only a few trials of antihypertensive drug therapy have ever been reported in any population (young or old) which have adequately quantitated the impact of the reported adverse effects on the subjects' quality of life.[74,75] Most trials have simply counted the total number of adverse effects reported, without attempting to qualitatively or quantitatively describe the degree of impact on physical, emotional, or cognitive function or overall perceptions of quality of life.[75] Quality-of-life issues which are important to the elderly and which may be influenced by antihypertensive therapy (but which have not been well-studied to date) include emotional state (depression, life satisfaction, anxiety), cognitive or intellectual processing (memory, psychomotor speed, problem solving), physical function (ability to perform self-care tasks, upper- and lower-extremity speed, gait and balance), and social interaction (social activities, contacts).[76] The adage "In the elderly it is as important to add life to years as years to life" is appropriate here.

EVIDENCE FOR EFFICACY OF ANTIHYPERTENSIVE THERAPY

Despite continued concern about the potential toxicity of antihypertensive therapy in the elderly, evidence already exists that the benefits of treating SDH, at least for relatively healthy elderly persons under age 80 years, outweigh the potential adverse effects.[3] For ISH, there are currently not enough data available from which to make a definitive statement. However, ongoing studies in both the United States and Britain should shed considerable light in the next few years on the benefits of treating ISH. The current evidence that the treatment of SDH and ISH are beneficial is described below.

SYSTOLIC-DIASTOLIC HYPERTENSION

Since the Veterans Administration (VA) Cooperative Studies reported in 1967, 1970, and 1972, it has been generally accepted that treating adults under age 69 with a DBP greater than 104 mmHg would reduce subsequent morbidity and mortality from hypertension.[77] The results of the VA trial were indeterminant for adults with a DBP between 90 and 104 mmHg. As with most large trials of the efficacy of the drug treatment of SDH, the oldest persons enrolled in this trial were aged 69 years on entry. The VA study collaborators did analyze their results for the cohort aged 60 to 69 years. There was a 32 percent lower rate of morbid events in this subgroup, but the numbers of subjects were small and the differences did not reach statistical significance.

Subsequent hypertension trials have tended to focus on the benefit of drug treatment of mild–moderate SDH (DBP 90 to 115 mmHg). In the HDFP multicenter trial, in randomized patients with SDH the 5-year total mortality was 17 percent lower for the special care (SC) than for the referred care (RC) group, and cardiovascular mortality was 19 percent lower.[78] The HDFP included 2376 participants aged 60 to 69 years, and the SC group showed a significant 16.4 percent reduction in total mortality for this age cohort. A recent report from the HDFP study group reported on additional follow-up for over 8 years for most of the study cohort.[111] As shown in Table 48-2, after 8 years the oldest subgroup still showed mortality trends in favor of the SC group, although the magnitude of the differences had declined somewhat in the oldest cohort. The Australian Trial in Mild Hypertension

randomized participants aged 40 to 69 years with a mean baseline DBP of 95 to 109 mmHg to medication treatment or placebo.[79] Although there was no significant difference between the two groups in total mortality, the treatment group did show a two-thirds reduction in cardiovascular deaths. Analyses of the frequency of total trial endpoints (both fatal and nonfatal) seemed to show a reduction in both cardiovascular and cerebrovascular events. For the subgroup aged 60 to 69 years at entry, there was a 39 percent reduction in trial endpoints in the treatment group.[80] Although the differences on the intention-to-treat analysis for the 60- to 69-year-old subgroup did not reach statistical significance, the magnitude of the apparent relative benefit in the older treatment subgroup was as great as that for the overall study cohort.

Since most major hypertension trials have only studied selected groups of "young-old" persons, the EWPHE study was designed to investigate whether medication treatment of SDH in a wider age range of elderly subjects was effective. This trial enrolled persons over age 60 (mean age 72) to treatment or placebo.[4] After an 8-year follow-up period, analyses revealed no effect on all-cause mortality but a significant 27 percent reduction in the cardiovascular mortality rate. There was a statistically significant 38 percent reduction in cardiac mortality, as well as a 32 percent reduction in cerebrovascular mortality which did not reach statistical significance. Further analysis of the EWPHE data indicates that the beneficial effects of treatment on cardiovascular mortality seemed to be limited to participants who were under age 80 at entry.[81] Treatment appeared to be effective for participants at all levels of entry SBP from 160 to 239 mmHg, but treatment did not appear to have an impact on participants with entry DBP in the range of 90 to 95 mmHg. The investigators in this study have concluded that treatment resulted in 29 fewer cardiovascular events and 14 fewer cardiovascular deaths per 1000 patient-years of treatment. In sum, it appears that the treatment of SDH in the elderly is beneficial (at least in persons under age 80 with a DBP greater than 95 mmHg).

Table 48-3 illustrates the percent reduction and the absolute reduction in cardiovascular morbidity or mortality for the treatment group versus the placebo group for the studies described above. In general, treated patients over age 60 had relative reductions in morbidity or mortality similar to those seen for patients under age 50. However, when the data from these studies are analyzed by the absolute number of events prevented per 1000 person-years of drug treatment, it is also clear from these studies that more total events are prevented in participants over age 60. Because elderly people have higher cardiovascular event rates, if they experience the same percentage benefit from drug treatment of diastolic hy-

TABLE 48-2
Hypertension Detection and Follow-Up Program (Five-Year and Eight-Year Mortality by Age)

| | Life-Table Death Rates per 1000 Participants | | |
Life-Table Follow-Up Period	SC	RC	(RC-SC)/RC (%)
30 to 49 years old			
5.0-year trial	33.4	34.7	3.7
8.3-year trial/post-trial follow-up	63.3	76.2	16.9
50 to 59 years old			
5.0-year trial	62.5	83.8	25.4
8.3-year trial/post-trial follow-up	122.3	151.3	24.2
60 to 69 years old			
5.0-year trial	127.3	152.8	16.7
8.3-year trial/post-trial follow-up	258.7	273.0	5.2

SOURCE: *JAMA*, 259:2119, 1988.

TABLE 48-3
Impact of Antihypertensive Therapy on Cardiovascular Morbidity and Mortality by Age Group

Study	Relative Reduction* (Percent)		Absolute Reduction† (per 1000 Person-Years)	
	<50 Years	>60 Years	<50 Years	>60 Years
VA Cooperative (morbidity)	55	59	21	100
HDFP (mortality)	6	16	2	25
Australian (cardiovascular trial end-points)	20	26	5	10

*Relative reduction is the percentage decline in the event rate in the intervention group as compared to the rate in the placebo group.
†Absolute reduction is the total number of events prevented in the treatment group versus the comparison group, per 1000 person-years of treatment.

pertension, then the total number of events reduced is greater in the elderly. It should also be noted from Table 48-3 that the estimated absolute benefit from the drug treatment of diastolic hypertension in persons over age 60 varied from 10 events prevented per 1000 person-years up to 100 events per 1000 person-years, depending on whether the initial level of diastolic hypertension was mild-to-moderate or severe. This level of benefit is significant and would account for the reduction of many thousands of morbid and mortal events if the entire population of elderly hypertensives in this country were treated. Nevertheless, the lower levels of absolute benefit for the treatment of mild SDH may or may not be sufficient for certain elderly *individuals* to want to undertake therapy, particularly if treatment has a substantial adverse effect on an individual's quality of life.

ISOLATED SYSTOLIC HYPERTENSION

To date there are limited data available on the potential benefits of treatment of ISH. One early descriptive study of a large group of elderly black patients with SDH treated over an extensive period of time indicated that even when DBP was well-controlled, continued elevation of SBP was associated with greater subsequent cardiovascular morbidity and mortality.[82] In this study, 503 elderly (over age 60) black hypertensives were followed for up to 9 years in a community public health chronic disease clinic system. Only those patients whose DBP was always under 90 mmHg were studied. The study cohort was divided into the following subgroups: those

whose SBP was >160 mmHg at each visit (mean SBP = 184 mmHg, mean DBP = 87.6 mmHg); those whose SBP was at times >160 mmHg (mean SBP = 151 mmHg, mean DBP = 84 mmHg); and those whose SBP was <160 mmHg at every visit (mean SBP = 137 mmHg, mean DBP = 78 mmHg). Although cardiovascular morbidity and mortality rates were highest in the first group, cardiovascular morbidity and mortality rates were 50 percent higher in the group with the greatest control (lowest levels) of SBP and DBP as compared to the intermediate group. Therefore, this study raised a question as to whether too aggressive a treatment of hypertension could be harmful.

In the pilot study for the SHEP trial, 551 elderly subjects with ISH (SBP >160 mmHg and DBP <90 mmHg) were randomized to treatment with chlorthalidone and a step-two drug if needed, versus placebo.[83] Seventy-five percent of patients in the treatment group had their SBP lowered to the goal with the diuretic alone. Mean blood pressure declined by 30/7 mmHg in the treatment group and 11/4 mmHg in the control group. Therefore, adequate lowering of SBP occurred primarily through the use of the diuretic and was relatively easy to accomplish without an undue decline in DBP. This pilot study was not designed with a sufficient sample size to provide the definitive answer on the impact of treatment on cardiovascular morbidity and mortality. Although the treatment group showed a trend toward the lowering of the stroke rate, none of the differences between the two groups reached statistical significance. Therefore, definitive recommendations on the treatment of ISH will have to await the outcome of the ongoing multicenter main SHEP trial.

CORONARY HEART DISEASE

Clinical trials on the treatment of SDH have shown that treatment lowers the rate of strokes and heart failure but has little effect on rates of CHD.[3,84] Several theories have been raised to explain this. It is possible that too vigorous a lowering of DBP may actually result in impaired coronary artery blood flow, particularly to the subendocardial layer during diastole.[85] Three recent descriptive studies have shown that there may be a J-shaped relationship between treated DBP and mortality from myocardial infarction.[82,85,86] Two studies of middle-aged treated diastolic hypertensives[85,86] and one of elderly treated diastolic hypertensives[82] have shown that those individuals with the very lowest treated levels of DBP had higher rates of myocardial infarction. Some light has been shed on this issue by the studies of Coope and Warrender,[87,88] who performed a single-blind, randomized, placebo-controlled study of the treatment of SDH in elderly patients. Treatment apparently lowered the subsequent rate of strokes but not the rate of myocardial infarction. Further analysis of these data revealed a J-shaped relationship between entry DBP and subsequent rates of fatal and nonfatal myocardial infarction, but this relationship was true for both the treatment and the placebo groups. Therefore, a likely explanation for these findings is that the subjects with the lowest levels of DBP may have had a higher prevalence of prior cardiovascular disease with a reduction in the heart's ability to generate a higher DBP. Nonetheless, prudence would dictate that it is best not to treat SDH in elderly patients in an overly aggressive manner.

It also possible that the diuretics used in many hypertension clinical trials partially offset the beneficial impact of blood pressure lowering by adversely affecting other risk factors, particularly lipid and glucose homeostasis. At present it is not possible to make a definitive statement about this issue. A recent prospective descriptive study by Samuelsson et al. has shown in middle-aged subjects that a reduction in SBP or DBP which is not accompanied by a reduction in cholesterol (if elevated) has less impact unless both risk factors are improved.[86] However, results from the EWPHE study and the recent SHEP pilot study trial indicate that diuretic treatment has only a transient adverse effect on serum lipids.[73,83] This lack of effect on lipids in the elderly may be due to metabolic differences which occur with age or to the fact that these two trials used lower doses of diuretics. On balance, there are not enough negative data to proscribe use of diuretics in the elderly, but individual patients treated with diuretics who develop significant alterations of lipid or glucose levels should be placed on other agents.

DIAGNOSTIC APPROACH

The basic approach to the evaluation of the elderly hypertensive patient involves accurately determining the baseline blood pressure, assessing any possible end-organ damage, and (in certain cases) ruling out any underlying conditions which might have caused the blood pressure to rise.[3] Since blood pressure is highly variable, it is important that the average of three readings on two or three occasions of measurement be used to define the baseline blood pressure.[1,89] High blood pressure readings show regression to the mean, so high initial blood pressure readings often are lower on the second and third follow-up visits. Evidence indicates that 40 percent of the elderly are being treated for hypertension at any point in time, many of whom may have been classified as normotensive if an adequate number of initial measurements had been taken.[5] Therefore, inadequate numbers of occasions of measurement of blood pressure have led to falsely high prevalence estimates in the literature and to overtreatment in practice. It should be noted that el-

derly hypertensive patients should have baseline (and periodic) evaluation of both supine and standing blood pressure, since the prevalence of postural hypotension increases with age and can be seriously aggravated by treatment with antihypertensive medications.[60,90]

Recently, several authors have written that pseudohypertension may be a fairly common problem in the elderly, frequently causing overestimation of the real blood pressure.[91–93] Pseudohypertension occurs in elderly patients with thickened or calcified arteries that are not easily compressed by the standard blood pressure cuff. If the arterial wall itself is hardened or calcified, there is a tendency for indirect measurement of the blood pressure with a standard sphygmomanometer to overestimate the pressure as compared to the "true" pressure obtained through direct intraarterial measurement.

Most experts in the field believe that pseudohypertension is not a highly prevalent condition. In fact, taking too few blood pressure measurements is probably a greater source of overestimation of blood pressure in the elderly than is pseudohypertension. All experts agree that an occasional elderly patient will be seen with very rigid or calcified vessels in whom the indirect method of blood pressure measurement may substantially overestimate the actual blood pressure. Elderly patients with substantial elevations of SBP or DBP who have no evidence of hypertension-related end-organ damage are one group of patients in whom this entity should be considered. Also, treated elderly hypertensives who have symptoms of chronic low blood pressure (extreme fatigue or faintness) in the face of normal cuff pressures should be considered. The Osler Maneuver can aid the clinician in determining if pseudohypertension might be a problem.[92] In the Osler Maneuver, the blood pressure cuff is inflated above systolic pressure, and the brachial and radial arteries are palpated to determine if the artery is still palpable. If the artery is still palpable, the patient has rigid arteries and could have pseudohypertension; otherwise, it is unlikely that pseudohypertension is present. Therefore, only those elderly patients clinically suspected of having pseudohypertension need be checked for this disorder.

The assessment for end-organ damage should include examination of the retina for hypertensive changes, examination of the peripheral pulses, and examination of the chest x ray and the electrocardiogram (ECG) for signs of LVH. Recent studies indicate that LVH heightens the risk for cardiovascular morbidity and mortality.[51] In addition, it appears that adequate treatment of hypertension may result in regression of LVH.[94] The presence of signs of end-organ damage should sway the clinician toward treatment in cases where the elevation of the blood pressure is borderline.

Most elderly patients with SDH or ISH have no

underlying reversible disorder that, if treated, will result in reversal of their hypertension.[1] The diagnostic evaluation of the elderly hypertensive should include the same baseline tests recommended for evaluation of younger hypertensives: thorough history and physical examination, hematocrit, serum potassium and creatinine, urinalysis for protein, chest x ray, and ECG. Further evaluation for possible underlying causes of secondary hypertension should be undertaken in the elderly only if (1) there is a sudden onset of increased DBP greater than or equal to 105 mmHg in a person over the age of 55, (2) the DBP continues to average above 100 mmHg despite rational triple-drug therapy, (3) the elderly patient develops accelerated hypertension, or (4) the patient demonstrates spontaneous hypokalemia (not related to drug therapy) or symptoms highly suggestive of pheochromocytoma.[1] The presence of an abdominal bruit, especially if epigastric and radiating into the flank, is also an important physical sign suggesting the need for further evaluation.

TREATMENT

Once an elderly patient has been classified as having either SDH or ISH, there are basically two major types of therapy available. Nonpharmacologic therapy, including weight loss, sodium restriction, moderate consistent aerobic exercise, and relaxation therapy, may be helpful in some individual patients, particularly those with borderline elevations of blood pressure.[95,96] Unfortunately, the only studies of the efficacy of these measures currently available have been conducted on young-to-middle-aged patients.[97,98] Data currently available indicate that moderate weight loss (if a patient is overweight) is the most effective nonpharmacologic treatment of hypertension.[97] The only question regarding the efficacy of weight loss concerns the high rate of regaining the lost weight over an extended period of time. Studies of sodium restriction indicate that approximately one-third of hypertensive patients will respond to sodium restriction, especially if sodium intake can be decreased below 80 meq/day.[98] Many elderly persons tend to purchase substantial quantities of prepackaged or canned foods, which are high in sodium, and clinicians frequently find that their elderly patients would rather take a diuretic than severely restrict their salt. The limited data currently available on the impact of exercise and relaxation therapy on hypertension indicate that either intervention can have modest short-term beneficial effects on blood pressure.[96]

If nonpharmacologic therapy fails or is not appropriate, the clinician is left with pharmacologic therapy. The pathophysiology of hypertension in the elderly (as described earlier) may include high peripheral resistance,

low renin levels, and a tendency to lower cardiac output.[37] In addition, it is known that as the cardiovascular system ages it becomes less sensitive to both beta-adrenergic stimulation and beta blockade.[99] Based on these physiologic patterns, some experts have predicted that medications which work directly on peripheral resistance, such as diuretics, vasodilators, or calcium channel blockers, will prove to be the most effective antihypertensive agents in the elderly. However, treatment decisions based solely on pathophysiologic considerations have not always proved the most clinically useful in the field of hypertension. Elderly hypertensives are probably physiologically more heterogeneous than has been realized to date, and theoretically less favored drugs, such as beta-blockers and angiotensin converting enzyme inhibitors, do effectively lower blood pressure in the elderly.[100] There is currently only a modest amount of adequate clinical data available comparing the efficacy of various antihypertensive regimens in the elderly. Most of the large clinical trials which have shown some benefit of treating SDH in the elderly have used a diuretic as the first-step drug. Most studies which purport to compare different antihypertensive regimens in the elderly do not have adequate sample sizes to make a definitive statement. The clinician should be aware that many of the newer antihypertensive agents are frequently 10 to 30 times more expensive than a generically prescribed diuretic. Although these differences in cost may not be meaningful to some individuals, the aggregate impact of more expensive treatment strategies, if used in most elderly patients, may well be to add $500 million to $1 billion in charges to the nation's health care costs. For this reason, a few comments about specific classes of therapeutic agents is appropriate.[3]

DIURETICS

There are ample data available that thiazide diuretics and their equivalents are effective in lowering both systolic and diastolic pressure in the elderly. As a class, diuretics tend to lower peripheral vascular resistance and have minimal effect on cardiac output, but they may have adverse effects on serum lipids, potassium, and creatinine.[72,94] Both the EWPHE trial and the SHEP pilot study reported that diuretics are very effective in controlling SDH and ISH, while causing a minimum of side effects. Both studies do confirm that diuretics tend to lower serum potassium and raise serum creatinine and glucose slightly.

Most of the controversy surrounding diuretics has resulted from some controversial findings from the Multiple Risk Factor Intervention Trial (MRFIT).[101] In this study, hypertensive males who had ECG abnormalities at baseline and were treated with a diuretic had a higher CHD death rate than did the comparable placebo group.[101] Certainly diuretics can induce hypokalemia, which can in turn lead to cardiac arrythmias.[102] However, analysis of the MRFIT data shows no relationship between either the participant's most recent potassium level or the presence of ventricular premature beats and CHD mortality.[103] Also, it is curious that the increased mortality attributed to diuretic treatment occurred only in the subset of participants treated with hydrochlorothiazide rather than with chlorthalidone.[104] Further doubts about the significance of the MRFIT findings stem from the fact that they arose from a post hoc analysis and could well be due to chance alone.

Nonetheless, the issue of treatment-related CHD is still not easily dismissed. The HDFP group reanalyzed its data and concluded that there was no evidence that the treatment of hypertensives with baseline ECG abnormalities with a diuretic caused an adverse CHD death rate.[105] This conclusion is indeed warranted for the entire HDFP cohort, which included blacks and whites and males and females. When the recent HDFP data are closely scrutinized, however, it is clear that white males in HDFP who were hypertensive and had resting ECG abnormalities *did* have higher CHD death rates for the special care group. Also, follow-up analysis of the Oslo trial on the treatment of mild hypertension (a study of middle-aged white males) indicated that participants with baseline ECG abnormalities had somewhat higher total CHD event rates.[106] Therefore, it is possible that, for some reason, white males are particularly likely to have an adverse effect of diuretic treatment of hypertension *if* they have baseline ECG abnormalities. Whether this concern can be extrapolated to elderly males is totally unknown; however, it may be prudent to recommend that elderly hypertensive males with baseline ECG abnormalities, particularly LVH, not receive diuretic therapy.

BETA-BLOCKERS

Because of the concern regarding the adverse effects of diuretics, many experts have recommended a beta-blocker as the drug of first choice in the treatment of the elderly. As discussed previously, there are a number of theoretical reasons why beta-blockers might not be as effective in lowering blood pressure in the elderly as they are in younger patients. However, two large randomized trials comparing a beta-blocker with a diuretic as initial therapy of hypertension in the elderly have shown that the beta-blocker and the diuretic were equivalent in efficacy and in side effect rates.[107,108] While the beta-blockers may not be physiologically ideal antihypertensives in the elderly, clinical trial data support the fact that they are generally safe and effective. If a beta-blocker is used it is probably best to use a less lipid-soluble one, such as atenolol, because central ner-

vous system side effects, such as depression and lethargy, have been reported with many of the beta-blockers that penetrate the central nervous system.[57]

CALCIUM CHANNEL BLOCKERS

There are no good data available from randomized trials comparing the efficacy of the currently available calcium channel blockers with other commonly used antihypertensive agents in the elderly. Since calcium channel blockers decrease vascular resistance and have no significant effects on serum lipids or the central nervous system, they are theoretically ideal antihypertensive agents in the elderly.[94] Pool and colleagues conducted a randomized, placebo-controlled trial of the efficacy of diltiazem as monotherapy for diastolic hypertension (DBP 95 to 110 mmHg).[27] There were 77 participants entered into the study (average age 58). The participants over age 60 had a significantly greater reduction in SBP and in standing blood pressure than did the subjects under age 60. There was no increase in orthostatic blood pressure drop in the diltiazem-treated group and no change in resting heart rate.

ANGIOTENSIN CONVERTING ENZYME (ACE) INHIBITORS

For theoretical reasons, ACE inhibitors should be less effective in elderly hypertensives than in younger hypertensives. ACE inhibitors do lower peripheral resistance while having no adverse effects on serum lipids or cardiac output; however, the risk of inducing hyperkalemia must be kept in mind. As described earlier, most elderly hypertensives do not have elevated renin levels, so inhibition of the renin-angiotensin axis might have less effect. On the other hand, although the acute blood pressure response to ACE inhibitors is correlated with plasma renin levels, the chronic blood pressure response is not as highly correlated.[94] Moreover, ACE inhibitors also decrease kinin (vasodilators) clearance and may alter renal prostaglandin synthesis. Therefore, the ACE inhibitors are capable of lowering blood pressure in hypertensives who do not have high renin levels. Jenkins has reported on a large surveillance study of captopril use with 975 patients over age 65.[38] Overall, captopril appeared to be effective in lowering blood pressure in the elderly, but the authors report that only 15 percent of patients were treated with captopril alone, while 42 percent were treated with captopril plus a diuretic, 7 percent with captopril plus one other drug, and 36 percent with captopril plus two other drugs. These figures cast a question on the efficacy of the ACE inhibitors as monotherapy for hypertension in the elderly.

OTHER ANTIHYPERTENSIVE AGENTS

Insufficient data exist to support definitive statements about many other antihypertensive agents in the elderly. However, one recent study did indicate that reserpine in low doses was as at least as effective as alphamethyldopa as a step-two agent for hypertension in the elderly.[109] Several experts have suggested that various vasodilators may also be effective in the treatment of hypertension in the elderly. Although definitive comparative data are lacking, it does appear that hydralizine is effective in the elderly, with less accompanying reflex tachycardia than is seen in younger patients.[110] Also, both the alpha-beta-blocker labetolol and the alpha-blocker prazosin are probably effective, with a decreased risk of central nervous system side effects, but they can at times cause significant postural hypotension in the elderly.

In summary, the underlying pathophysiology and hemodynamics of hypertension in the elderly does cause the clinician to conceptually favor drugs which primarily lower peripheral vascular resistance and have relatively lower central nervous system side effects. However, ample studies are available that indicate that some drugs which make less conceptual sense are also generally effective and well tolerated. As a second point, although the benefit of treatment of ISH has not been proved, the magnitude of benefit from drug treatment of SDH has been well documented. The magnitude of benefit is substantial from a public health perspective, but some individual patients may refuse therapy for this level of predicted benefit, particularly if medication-related side effects which substantially impair quality of life cannot be avoided. Finally, data from the EWPHE study do indicate that the benefit from treating SDH may disappear for patients of advanced age (above 80 years old). This does not mean that a biologically (rather than *chronologically*) young 80-year-old with SDH should not be treated.

RECOMMENDATIONS

Since diuretics need to be given only once a day, are relatively inexpensive, and have a large amount of data supporting their efficacy in lowering both blood pressure and subsequent morbidity and mortality, they are still considered the drugs of first choice for most elderly patients.[3] Diuretics should only be used in low doses, at the equivalent of 25 mg of hydrochlorothiazide or less per day. However, white males with underlying serious ECG abnormalities or persons with lipid abnormalities (or who develop lipid abnormalities on treatment) may be candidates for alternative therapy. Beta-blockers, calcium channel blockers, and mild doses of vasodilators (in the absence of significant postural hypotension) are all

TABLE 48-4
Treatment Guidelines for Hypertension in the Elderly

1. SDH (DBP >100 mmHg*): Treat with medications.
2. Mild SDH (DBP 90–100 mmHg): Use nonpharmacologic therapy. If average DBP remains >95 mmHg, add medication.
3. ISH (SBP 160 mmHg, DBP <90 mmHg): Decision to treat is left to individual clinician and patient.
4. If pharmacologic therapy is initiated, the initial dose for any medication should be one-half the standard dose in younger patients. Furthermore, the interval between dosage adjustments should be greater than it is for younger patients. All in all, more visits and a longer time may be required to reach a stable therapeutic regimen in older patients.
5. Modest goals for blood pressure lowering should be set, and therapy should not be so aggressive as to cause side effects which seriously impair quality of life.

*Blood pressure levels assume average of three occasions of measurement.

acceptable alternatives, but these are usually more expensive than diuretics. The choice of a second-step antihypertensive agent if the blood pressure is not controlled with a first-step agent depends mostly on individual patient differences since there are no data available on the relative benefits of various second-step regimens in the elderly. Finally, the concept of step care is currently under reconsideration, and alternative monotherapy may prove to be more appropriate than use of an additional drug, especially in elderly patients in whom simplification of drug regimens is an enduring principle of care. See Table 48-4 for a summary of recommendations.

REFERENCES

1. Statement on hypertension in the elderly; Report of the Working Group on Hypertension in the Elderly. *JAMA* 256:70, 1986.
2. The Final Report of the Sub-Committee on Hypertension Definition and Prevalence of the 1984 Joint National Committee. Hypertension Prevalence and Status of Awareness, Treatment and Control in the United States. *Hypertension* 7:457, 1985.
3. Applegate WB: Hypertension in elderly patients. *Ann Intern Med* 110:901, 1989.
4. Amery A, Birkenhager W, Brixko P, Bulpitt C: Mortality and morbidity results from the European Working Party on High Blood Pressure in the Elderly Trial. *Lancet* 2:1349, 1985.
5. Furberg CD, and Black DM for the SHEP Research Group: The Systolic Hypertension in the Elderly Pilot Program: Methodological issues. *Eur Heart J* 9:223, 1988.

6. Kannel WB: Some lessons in cardiovascular epidemiology from Framingham. *Am J Cardiol* 37:269, 1976.

7. Hallock P, Benson IC: Studies of the elastic properties of human isolated aorta. *J Clin Invest* 16:595, 1937.

8. Kannel WB, Wolf PA, McGee DL, Dawber TR, McNamara P, Castelli WP: Systolic blood pressure, arterior rigidity, and risks of stroke. *JAMA* 245:1225, 1981.

9. Chobanian AV: Pathophysiologic considerations in the treatment of the elderly hypertension patients. *Am J Cardiol* 52:49D, 1983.

10. Tarazi RC, Martini F, Dustan HP: The role of aortic distensibility in hypertension, in Milliez P, Sasar M (eds): *International Symposium on Hypertension.* Monaco, Boehringer Ingleheim, 1975, pp 143–145.

11. Rorive GL, Carlier PJ, Foindant JM: Hyperplasia of smooth muscle cells associated with the development and reversal of renal hypertension. *Clin Sci* 59:335S, 1980.

12. Kanbe P, Nara Y, Tagami M, Yamori Y: Studies of hypertension induced vascular high cultured smooth muscle cells from spontaneously hypertensive rats. *Hypertension* 5:887, 1983.

13. Wolinsky HA: Response of the rat aortic wall to hypertension: Morphological and chemical studies. *Circ Res* 26:507, 1970.

14. Haudenschild CC, Prescott MF, Chobanian AV: Endothelial and subendothelial cells in experimental hypertension and aging. *Hypertension* 3(suppl 1):148, 1981.

15. Soltis EE, Webb RC, Bohr DF: The vasculature in hypertension and aging, in Horan MJ, Steinberg GM, Dunbar JB, Hadley EC (eds): *Blood Pressure Regulation and Aging.* Biomedical Information Corp, New York, 1986.

16. Haudenschild CC, Chobanian AV: Blood pressure lowering age-related changes in the rat aortic intima. *Hypertension* 6:562, 1984.

17. Simon AC, Safar MA, Levenson JA, Kheder AM, Levy BI: Systolic hypertension: Hemodynamic mechanism and choice of antihypertensive treatment. *Am J Cardiol* 44:505, 1979.

18. Carrier GO, Jackson CV, Owen MP: Influence of age on norepinephrine-induced vascular contractions as a function of extracellular calcium. *Res Commun Chem Pathol Pharmacol* 26:433, 1979.

19. Cohen ML, Berkowitz BA: Vascular contraction: Effective age and extracellular calcium. *Blood Vessels* 13:139, 1976.

20. Brink C, Duncan PG, Douglas JS: Decreased vascular sensitivity to histamine during aging. *Agents Actions* 14:8, 1984.

21. Elliott HL, Sumner BJ, McLein K et al: Effective age on vascular alpha adrenoreceptor responsiveness in man. *Clin Sci* 63:305S, 1982.

22. Scott PJ, Reid JL: The effect of age on the responses of human isolated arteries to noradrenalin. *Br J Clin Pharmacol* 13:237, 1982.

23. Abrass IB: Catecholamine levels and vascular responsiveness in aging, in Horan MJ, Steinberg GM, Dunbar JB, Hadley EC (eds): *Blood Pressure Regulation and Aging.* Biomedical Information Corp, New York, 1986.

24. Fleich JH, Malin HM, Brodie BB: Beta-receptor activity in the aorta: Variations with age and species. *Circ Res* 26:151, 1970.

25. Fleich JH, Hooker CS: The relationship between age and relaxation of vascular smooth muscle in the rabbit and rat. *Circ Res* 38:243, 1976.

26. Van Brummelen P, Buhler FR, Kiowski W, Amann FW: Age-related increase in cardiac and peripheral vascular responses to isoproterenol, studies in normal subjects. *Clin Sci* 60:571, 1981.

27. Pool PE, Massie BM, Venkataram AN et al: Diltiazem as a model therapy for systemic hypertension. *Am J Cardiol* 57:212, 1986.

28. Lindner A, Kenny MN, Meacham AJ: Effects of a circulating factor in patients with essential hypertension on intracellular-free calcium in normal platelets. *N Engl J Med* 316:509, 1987.

29. Scott P, Giese J: Age and the renin-angiotensin system. *Acta Med Scand* 676(suppl):45, 1983.

30. Crane MG, Harris JJ: Effect of aging on renin activity and aldosterone excretion. *J Lab Clin Med* 87:947, 1976.

31. Noth RH, Lasman MN, Tan SY et al: Age and the renin-aldosterone system. *Arch Intern Med* 137:1414, 1977.

32. Luft FC, Grim CE, Fineberg N, Weinberger MC: Effects of volume expansion and contraction in normotensive whites, blacks, and subjects of different ages. *Circulation* 59:643, 1979.

33. Krakof LR: Renal and adrenal mechanisms pertinent to hypertension in an aging population, in Horan MJ, Steinberg GM, Dunbar JAB, Hadley EC (eds): *Blood Pressure Regulation and Aging.* Biomedical Information Corp, New York, 1986.

34. Weidmann P, Beretta-Piccoli C, Ziegler WH et al: Age versus urinary sodium for judging renin, aldosterone, and catecholamine levels. *Kidney Int* 14:619, 1978.

35. Nakamaru M, Ogihara T, Hata T et al: The effect of age on active and cryoactive plasma renin in normal subjects and patients with essential hypertension. *Jpn Circ J* 45:1231, 1981.

36. Niarchos AP, Laragh JH: Renin dependency in isolated systolic hypertension. *Am J Med* 77:407, 1984.

37. Messerli FH, Sundgaard-Riise K, Ventura HO, Dunn FG, Glade LB, Frolich ED: Essential hypertension in the elderly: Hemodynamics, intravascular volume, plasma renin activity, and circulating catecholamine levels. *Lancet* 2:983, 1983.

38. Jenkins AC, Knill JR, Dreslinski GR: Captopril in the treatment of elderly hypertensive patients. *Arch Intern Med* 145:2029, 1985.

39. Rowe JW, Andres R, Tobin JAD et al: The effect of age on creatinine clearance in men: A cross-sectional and longitudinal study. *J Gerontol* 31:155, 1976.

40. Rowe JW, Shock NW, DeFronzo RA: The influence of age on the renal response to water deprivation in man. *Nephron* 17:270, 1976.

41. Vardan S, Mookherjee S, Warner R, Smulyan H: Systolic hypertension in the elderly: Hemodynamic response to long term thiazide therapy. *JAMA* 250:2807, 1983.

42. Vardan S, Dunsky MH, Hill E et al: Systemic systolic hypertension in the elderly: Correlation of hemodynamics, plasma volume, renin, aldosterone, urinary metanephrines, and response to thiazide therapy. *Am J Cardiol* 58:1030, 1986.

43. Kannel WB, Gordon T: Evaluation of cardiovascular risk in the elderly: The Framingham Study. *Bull NY Acad Med* 54:573, 1978.

44. Page LB, Friedlander J: Blood pressure, age, and cultural change, in Horan MJ, Steinberg GM, Dunbar JB, Hadley EC, (eds): *Blood Pressure Regulation and Aging, Proceedings from an NIH Symposium*. Biomedical Information Corp, New York, 1986.

45. Drizd T, Dannenberg A, Engel A: Blood pressure levels in persons 18–74 years of age in 1976–1980 and trends in blood pressure from 1960–1980 in the United States. Vital Health Statistics, no. 11. Washington, Government Printing Office, DHHS (PHS) 86-1684, 1986.

46. Hypertension Detection and Follow-up Program Cooperative Group: Blood pressure studies in 14 communities. *JAMA* 237:2385, 1977.

47. Vogt TM, Ireland CC, Black D, Camel G, Hughes G: Recruitment of elderly volunteers for multi-center clinical trial; The SHEP pilot study. *Controlled Clin Trials* 7:118, 1986.

48. Build and Blood Pressure Study. Chicago, Society of Actuaries, 1959.

49. Kannel WB, Gordon T, Schwartz MJ: Systolic vs. diastolic blood pressure and risk of coronary heart disease. *Am J Cardiol* 27:335, 1971.

50. Hickler RB: Aging and hypertension: Hemodynamic implications of systolic pressure trends. *J Am Geriatr Soc* 31:421, 1983.

51. Kannel WB, Gordon T, Castelli WB, Margolis JR: Electro-cardiographic left ventricular hypertrophy and risk of coronary heart disease. *Ann Intern Med* 72:813, 1970.

52. Savage DD, Garrison RJ, Kannel WB, Levy D, Anderson SJ, Stokes J, Feinleib M, Castelli WP: The spectrum of left ventricular hypertrophy in a general population sample: The Framingham Study. *Circulation* 75(suppl 1):126, 1987.

53. McLenachan JM, Henderson E, Morris KI, Dargie HJ: Ventricular arrhythmia in patients with hypertensive left ventricular hypertrophy. *N Engl J Med* 317:787, 1987.

54. Williamson, J, Chopin JM: Adverse reactions to prescribed drugs in the elderly: A multicenter investigation. *Aging* 1980;9:73-80.

55. Jackson G, Piersoianouski TA, Mohon W et al: Inappropriate antihypertensive therapy in the elderly. *Lancet* 2:1317, 1976.

56. Flanenbaun W: Diuretic use in the elderly; Potential for diuretic-induced hypokalemia. *Am J Cardiol* 57:38A, 1986.

57. Avorn J, Everitt DE, Weiss S: Increased antidepressant use in patients prescribed beta-blockers. *JAMA* 255:357, 1986.

58. Gribbin B, Pickering TG, Sleigh P, Peto R: Effect of age and high blood pressure on baroreflex sensitivity in man. *Cardiovasc Res* 29:424, 1971.

59. Lipsitz LA: Abnormalities in blood pressure hemostasis associated with aging and hypertension, in Horan MJ, Steinberg M, Dunbar JB, Hadley EC (eds): *Blood Pressure Regulation and Aging, Proceedings from an NIH Symposium*. Biomedical Information Corp, New York, 1986.

60. Caird FL, Andrews GR, Kennedy RD: Effect of posture on blood pressure in the elderly. *Br Heart J* 35:527, 1973.

61. Jones JV, Graham DI: Hypertension and the cerebral circulation—its relevance to the elderly. *Am Heart J* 96:270, 1978.

62. Strandgaard S: Cerebral blood flow and antihypertensive drugs in the elderly. *Acta Med Scand* 676(suppl):103, 1983.

63. Ram CBS, Meese R, Kaplan NM, Debous MD, Bonte FJ, Forland SC, Cutler RE: Antihypertensive therapy of the elderly: Effects on blood pressure and cerebral blood flow. *Am J Med* 82(suppl 1A):53, 1987.

64. Bertel O, Marx BE: Effects of antihypertensive treatment on cerebral perfusion. *Am J Med* 82(suppl 3B):29, 1987.

65. Strandgaard S, Olesen J, Skinhoj E, Lassen NA: Auto-regulation of brain circulation and severe arterial hypertension. *Br Med J* 3:507, 1973.

66. Strangaard S: Auto-regulation of cerebral blood flow in hypertensive patients. *Circulation* 53:720, 1976.

67. Meyer JS, Okamoto S, Sari A, Koto A et al: Effects of beta-adrenergic blockade on cerebral auto-regulation and chemical vasomotor control in patients with stroke. *Stroke* 5:167, 1974.

68. Aquayagi M, Deshmukh VD, Meyer JS et al: Effect of beta-adrenergic blockade with propranolol on cerebral blood flow, auto-regulation, and CO_2 responsiveness. *Stroke* 7:219, 1976.

69. Griffith DNW, James IM, Newbura PA, Wollard ML: The effect of beta adrenergic receptor blocking drugs on cerebral blood flow. *Br J Clin Pharmacol* 7:491, 1979.

70. Barry I, Sevendson UG, Vorsurp S et al: The effect of chronic hypertension and antihypertensive drugs on the cerebral circulation space. *Acta Med Scand* 678(suppl):37, 1982.

71. Curb JD, Borhani NO, Blaszkowski TP et al: Long-term surveillance for adverse effects of antihypertensive drugs. *JAMA* 253:3263, 1985.

72. Amery A, Berthauz P, Birkenhager W et al: Antihypertensive therapy in patients above 60: Third interim report of the European Working Party on High Blood Pressure in the Elderly. *Acta Cardiol* 33:113, 1978.

73. Amery A, Birkenhager W, Bulpitt C: Influence of antihypertensive therapy on serum cholesterol in elderly hypertensive patients. *Acta Cardiol* 37:235, 1982.

74. Crogg SH, Levin S, Testa MA et al: The effects of antihypertensive therapy on the quality of life. *N Engl J Med* 314:1657, 1986.

75. Toth PJ, Horwitz RI: Conflicting clinical trials and the uncertainty of treating mild hypertension. *Am J Med* 75:482, 1983.

76. Wenger NK, Matteson ME, Furberg CD, Elinson J: *Assessment of Quality of Life in Clinical Trials and Cardiovascular Therapies*. LeJacq Publishing, 1984.

77. Veterans Administration Cooperative Study Group: Effects of treatment in hypertension: Results in patients with diastolic blood pressure 90/114. *JAMA* 1213:1143, 1970.

78. Hypertension Detection Follow-up Cooperative Group: 5 Year Findings of the Hypertension Detection Follow-up Program. *JAMA* 242:2562, 1979.

79. Management Committee of the Australian National Blood Pressure Study: Prognostic factors in the treatment of mild hypertension. *Circulation* 69:668, 1984.

80. National Heart Foundation of Australia: Treatment of

mild hypertension in the elderly. *Med J Aust* 247:633, 1981.

81. Amery A, Birkenhager W, Brixko R, Bulpitt C et al: Efficacy of antihypertensive drug treatment according to age, sex, blood pressure, and previous cardiovascular disease in patients over the age of 60. *Lancet* 1:589, 1986.

82. Applegate WB, Vander Zwaag R, Dismike SE et al: Control systolic blood pressure in elderly black patients. *J Am Geriatr Soc* 30:391, 1982.

83. Hulley SB, Furberg CD, Gurland B, McDonald R, Perry HM, Schnaper HW, Schoenberger JA, Smith WM, Vogt TM: Systolic hypertension in the elderly program: Antihypertensive efficacy of chlorthalidone. *Am J Cardiol* 56:913, 1985.

84. Culter JA, Furberg CD: Drug treatment trials in hypertension: A review. *Prev Med* 14:499, 1985.

85. Cruickshank JM, Thorp JM, Zacharias FJ: Benefits and potential harm of lowering high blood pressure. *Lancet* 1:581, 1987.

86. Samuelsson O, Wilhelmsen L, Anderson OK, Pennert K, Berglund G: Cardiovascular morbidity in relation to change in blood pressure and serum cholesterol levels and treated hypertension. *JAMA* 258:1768, 1987.

87. Coope J, Warrender TS: Randomized trial of treatment of hypertension in elderly patients in primary care. *Br Med J* 293:1145, 1986.

88. Coope J, Warrender TS: Lowering blood pressure. *Lancet* 1:1380, 1987.

89. Joint National Committee in Detection: Treatment and Evaluation of High Blood Pressure, 1984 Report. NIH, Bethesda, MD, 84-1088, 1984.

90. Mader SL, Josephson KR, Rubenstein LZ: Low prevalence of postural hypotension among community dwelling elderly. *JAMA* 258:1511, 1987.

91. Spence JD, Sibbald WJ, Cape RD: Pseudohypertension in the elderly. *Clin Sci Mol Med* 55:399, 1978.

92. Messerli FH, Ventura HO, Amodeo C: Osler's maneuver and pseudohypertension. *N Engl J Med* 312:1548, 1985.

93. Vardan S, Mookherjee S, Warner R, Smulyan H: Systolic hypertension: Direct and indirect blood pressure measurements. *Arch Intern Med* 143:935, 1983.

94. Dzau BJ: Evolution of the clinical management of hypertension. *Am J Med* 82:36, 1987.

95. Kaplan NM: Non-drug treatment of hypertension. *Ann Intern Med* 102:359, 1985.

96. Final Report of the Subcommittee on Nonpharmacological Therapy of the 1984 Joint National Committee on Detection, Evaluation, and Treatment of High Blood Pressure: Nonpharmacological approaches to the control of high blood pressure. *Hypertension* 8:444, 1986.

97. Langford HG, Blanfox D, Oberman A et al: Dietary therapy slows the return of hypertension after stopping prolonged medication. *JAMA* 253:657, 1987.

98. Stamler R, Stamler J, Grimm R et al: Nutritional therapy for high blood pressure. *JAMA* 257:1484, 1987.

99. Vestal RE, Wood AZ, Schand DG: Reduced beta-adrenoceptor sensitivity in the elderly. *Clin Pharmacol Ther* 26:181, 1979.

100. Freis ED for the VA Cooperative Study Group: Age and antihypertensive drugs hydrochlorothiazide, bendroflumethiazide, nadolol and captopril. *Am J Cardiol* 61:17, 1988.

101. Multiple Risk Factor Intervention Trial Research Group: Multiple Risk Factor Intervention Trial. *JAMA* 248:1465, 1982.

102. Whelton PK, Watson AJ: Diuretic-induced hypokalemia and cardiac arrhythmias. *Am J Cardiol* 58:5A, 1986.

103. Kuller LH, Hulley SB, Cohen JD, Neaton J: Unexpected effects of treating hypertension in men with electrocardiographic abnormalities: A critical analysis. *Circulation* 73:114, 1987.

104. Moser M: Implications of the clinical trials on the management of hypertension. *Hypertension* 9(suppl III):80, 1987.

105. Hypertension Detection and Follow-up Program Cooperative Research Group: The effect of antihypertensive drug treatment on mortality in the presence of resting electrocardiographic abnormalities at baseline. *Circulation* 70:996, 1984.

106. Holme I, Helgeland A, Hjermannl I, Leren P, Lund-Larsen PG: Treatment of mild hypertension with diuretics: The importance of ECG abnormalities in the Oslo Studies and in MRFIT. *JAMA* 251:1298, 1984.

107. Andersen GS: Atenolol vs bendroflumethiazide in middle aged and elderly hypertensives. *Acta Med Scand* 218:165, 1985.

108. Wikstrand J, Westergren G, Berglund G et al: Antihypertensive treatment with metoprolol or hydrochlorothiazide in patients aged 60–75 years. *JAMA* 255:1304, 1986.

109. Applegate WB, Carper ER, Kahn SE et al: Comparisons of the use of reserpine vs alphamethyldopa for the second step treatment of hypertension in the elderly. *J Am Geriatr Soc* 33:109, 1985.

110. Veterans Administration Cooperative Study Group on Antihypertensive Agents: Efficacy of nadolol alone and combined with bendroflumethiazide and hydralazine for systemic hypertension. *Am J Cardiol* 52:1230, 1983.

111. Hypertension Detection and Follow-up Program Cooperative Group: Persistence of reduction in blood pressure and mortality participants in the Hypertension Dectection and Follow-up Program. *JAMA* 259:2113, 1988.

SECTION B

The Respiratory System

Chapter 49

AGING OF THE RESPIRATORY SYSTEM

Melvyn S. Tockman

PATHOPHYSIOLOGY OF THE AGING LUNG

Common pulmonary problems are found with increased frequency in the elderly. The altered pulmonary physiology associated with aging impairs the ability of the lung to clear infectious and environmental insults once handled easily by the more youthful lung. In addition to diminished lung function, the geriatric patient loses important nonpulmonary defense mechanisms. Neurological disorders and sedation lead to an increased tendency for aspiration through altered swallowing and impaired cough. Diminished activity of effector T cells, perhaps due to enhancement of suppressor cells or reduced capacity for functional differentiation, reduces the likelihood of containing a pulmonary insult.

The changes in pulmonary function with age are of fundamental importance, since impaired function (airways obstruction) is associated with increased rates of death from all causes (primarily cardiovascular disease and chronic obstructive pulmonary disease, COPD).[1,2] Further, ventilatory obstruction is associated with risk of subsequent lung cancer mortality.[3] *Thus, impaired pulmonary function on spirometric testing can identify increased risk for three of the five leading causes of death*

in men and for three of the seven leading causes of death in women.[4] These observations, made after adjustment for other risk factors including cigarette smoking, provide compelling reasons to assess pulmonary function even in "normal" elderly individuals.

Following the end of adolescent growth and development, the age-related increase in lung volumes slows (after age 17 in females, after age 19 in males); forced expiratory airflows reach a maximum between 20 and 24 years of age in both sexes.[5] Further aging leads to a progressive decline in lung function, although until 40 years of age, the age-related decrease in forced vital capacity (FVC) and maximal expiratory flow rate are thought to be due to changes in body weight and strength rather than to attrition of tissues.[6]

This subsequent loss of lung function accelerates slightly as age increases[7] but is remarkably consistent across populations,[8] averaging for nonsmoking males 14 to 30 cc/year of FVC and 23 to 32 cc/year of one-second forced expiratory volume (FEV_1). Nonsmoking females show slightly lesser rates of decline (FVC, 15 to 24 cc/year; FEV_1, 19 to 26 cc/year) (see Tables 49-1 and 49-2). The relatively constant rate of decline of lung function associated with aging suggests that (in the absence of additional respiratory insult) the most important factor

TABLE 49-1
Predicted Changes in Normal Pulmonary Function for Males (as Determined by the Age Coefficient Term from Male Reference Value Prediction Equations)

Pulmonary Function	Equation	95% Confidence Interval	Loss of Function per Year of Age	Reference
TLC	$0.0795*H + 0.0032*Age - 7.333$	1.61	(increase) 3 ml	Morris et al.[26]
FRC	$0.0472*H + 0.0090*Age - 5.290$	1.46	(increase) 9 ml	Morris et al.[26]
RV	$0.0216*H + 0.0207*Age - 2.840$	0.76	(increase) 20 ml	Morris et al.[26]
FVC	$0.0600*H - 0.0214*Age - 4.650$	1.115	21 ml	Crapo et al.[8]
FEV$_1$	$0.0414*H - 0.0244*Age - 2.190$	0.842	24 ml	Crapo et al.[8]
FEV$_1$/FVC	$-0.1300*H - 0.152*Age + 110.49$	8.28	0.15%	Crapo et al.[8]
Pa$_{O_2}$	$-0.323*Age - 100.10$		0.32 torr	Sorbini et al.[18]
N$_2$P$_{111}$	$+0.010*Age + 0.710$	0.84	(increase) 0.01% N$_2$/liter	Buist and Ross[15]
DLco$-$sb	$0.4160*H - 0.219*Age - 26.34$	8.20	0.2 ml CO/min/mmHg	Crapo and Morris[16]
Hgb corr. (Cotes)	$0.4100*H - 0.210*Age - 26.31$	8.20	0.2 ml CO/min/mmHg	Crapo and Morris[16]
Vo$_2$ max	$-0.032*Age + 4.2$ (SD $\pm$ 0.4)		32 ml O$_2$/min	Jones et al.[23]
Expressed per kg	$-0.550*Age - 60$ (SD $\pm$ 7.5)		0.55 ml/kg/min	Jones et al.[23]

*Note lower boundary of normal determined by calculating predicted value from equation, then subtracting the 95% confidence interval.

determining whether individuals fall below the threshold of pulmonary impairment with advancing age is the level of forced expiration they reach at the completion of their growth.[9]

EFFECT OF AGING ON THE INTERACTION BETWEEN LUNG AND CHEST WALL

The volume of the resting lung (functional residual capacity, FRC) is determined by the equilibrium between the inward elastic tissue forces of the lung and the outward forces of the ribs and muscles of respiration. The loss of inward elastic recoil seen with increased age (especially after age 55) is usually evenly matched by a re-

duction of respiratory muscle strength and increased rib stiffness.[6,10] This balance is shown by the lack of change in total lung capacity (TLC) and the minimal increase of the FRC with increasing age (see Table 49-1 and Fig. 49-1).

During forced expiration, increasing contraction of chest wall voluntary muscles increases intrathoracic pressure and expiratory airflow until dynamic compression of the airways limits further expiratory flow (after approximately 25 percent) of the vital capacity has been exhaled. Collapse of the airways (at the equal pressure point) is prevented only by intraalveolar (upstream) pressure, generated by elastic recoil within the lung.[11] The inward elastic recoil of the lung results from the

TABLE 49-2
Predicted Changes in Normal Pulmonary Function for Females (as Determined by the Age Coefficient Term from Female Reference Value Prediction Equations)

Pulmonary Function	Equation	95% Confidence Interval	Loss of Function per Year of Age	Reference
TLC	$0.0590*H + 0.0000*Age - 4.537$	1.08	(increase) 00 ml	Morris et al.[26]
FRC	$0.0360*H + 0.0031*Age - 3.182$	1.06	(increase) 3 ml	Morris et al.[26]
RV	$0.0197*H + 0.0201*Age - 2.421$	0.78	(increase) 3 ml	Morris et al.[26]
FVC	$0.0491*H - 0.0216*Age - 3.590$	0.676	22 ml	Crapo et al.[8]
FEV$_1$	$0.0342*H - 0.0255*Age - 1.578$	0.561	26 ml	Crapo et al.[8]
FEV$_1$/FVC	$-0.2020*H - 0.252*Age + 126.58$	9.06	0.25%	Crapo et al.[8]
Pa$_{O_2}$	$-0.323*Age - 100.10$		0.32 torr	Sorbini et al.[18]
N$_2$P$_{111}$ (< 60 yr old)	$+0.009*Age + 1.036$	1.12	(increase) 0.01% N$_2$/liter	Buist and Ross[15]
N$_2$P$_{111}$ (≥ 60 yr old)	$+0.058*Age + 1.777$	2.55	(increase) 0.06% N$_2$/liter	Buist and Ross[15]
DLco$-$sb	$0.256*H - 0.144*Age - 8.36$	6.0	0.1 ml CO/min/mmHg	Crapo and Morris[16]
Hgb corr. (Cotes)	$0.282*H - 0.157*Age - 10.89$	6.1	0.1 ml CO/min/mmHg	Crapo and Morris[16]
Vo$_2$ max	$-0.014*Age + 2.6$ (SD $\pm$ 0.4)		14 ml O$_2$/min	Jones et al.[23]
Expressed per kg	$-0.370*Age - 48$ (SD $\pm$ 7.0)		0.37 ml/kg/min	Jones et al.[23]

*Note lower boundary of normal determined by calculating predicted value from equation, then subtracting the 95% confidence interval.

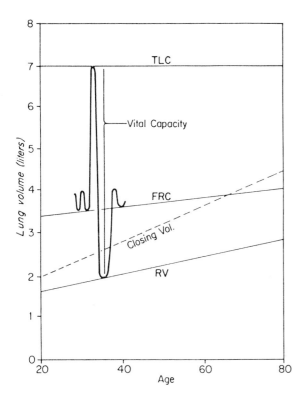

FIGURE 49-1
The effect of age on subdivisions of lung volume: TLC = total lung capacity, FRC = functional residual capacity, RV = residual volume. Values shown are for men of average height; the changes with age are similar for women.

combination of parenchymal elastic fibers and the surface forces generated at the air–fluid interface of the terminal respiratory units. The elastic fibers within alveolar walls are tethered to the respiratory and terminal bronchioles, helping to maintain the patency of these small conducting airways at low lung volumes. There is no evidence for an aging change in the length or diameter of these fibers,[12] but rather for an age-associated disruption of elastic fiber attachments.[13] The loss of these elastic attachments leads to increased compliance of affected alveoli, collapse of the small conducting airways, nonuniformity of alveolar ventilation, and air trapping. There is no evidence for an aging effect on either the inward directed air–fluid surface forces or on the effectiveness of surfactant which mitigates these forces.[14]

The residual volume (RV) is the amount of air which remains in the lungs after a maximal exhalation. During younger years while peripheral airways are patent, the RV is determined by the minimum size reached by the bony thorax and the maximum ascent of the diaphragm. External compression of the young chest can, in fact, expel additional air from the lungs. The RV increases with age (Fig. 49-1), reflecting air trapped in peripheral airways following loss of the elastic fiber attachments described above. As the TLC remains constant with increasing age, the increase in RV comes at the expense of

the vital capacity (VC), reducing the amount of air that can be blown from the lungs after a maximal inhalation (Fig. 49-1).

DISTRIBUTION OF VENTILATION

The distending force of the thoracic wall is modified by gravity. The erect individual has a declining gradient of distending (pleural) pressure from the apex to the base of the lung. As a result of this distending pressure gradient, airways at the apex of the lung are more widely patent than those at the base. As the lung empties from maximum to minimum distension during a normal expiration, the narrower airways at the base of the lung close first, and closure progresses from base to apex. The single-breath nitrogen (SBN$_2$) washout technique has been used to determine the uniformity of alveolar ventilation and the lung volume at which small conducting airways collapse (the closing volume, CV; see Fig. 49-1).[15] Nonuniformity of ventilation is shown by an increased slope of the SBN$_2$ phase III (alveolar plateau), while the volume at which the terminal respiratory units begin to close is demonstrated by elevations of the SBN$_2$ phase IV (closing volume). With advancing age, the slope of the N$_2$P$_{III}$ increases (see Tables 49-1 and 49-2) and the closing capacity (closing volume plus residual volume) may exceed the FRC, indicating that closure of terminal respiratory units occurs before the end of a normal tidal breath. Closing capacity begins to exceed the supine FRC at about 44 years of age and the sitting FRC at approximately 65 years of age.

DIFFUSING CAPACITY

Diffusion of gas from the alveoli into the blood depends upon two factors: the total area and thickness of the alveolar-capillary membrane, and the ability of the blood elements to absorb the gas. Progressive age-related decreases in total pulmonary diffusing capacity are usually due to both morphologic changes (loss of surface area of the alveolar-capillary membrane) and increasing inhomogeneities in ventilation and/or blood flow.[6]

The single-breath carbon monoxide diffusing capacity (DL$_{CO}$) increases to a maximum in the early twenties and thereafter undergoes a gradual decline with age. This reduction has been estimated to be approximately 0.5 percent (0.2 ml CO/min/mmHg)/year (see Tables 49-1 and 49-2). The age-related decline in DL$_{CO}$ is not linear, although linear prediction regressions are used.[16] Women are found to have 10 percent lower diffusion capacity values than men for the same age and height.[17]

ARTERIAL O$_2$ TENSION

Although at rest, airways and alveoli at the base are more nearly closed than are apical structures, at maximum inspiration all alveolar units distend to approximately equal size. Thus, a greater proportion of the inhaled breath must go to the basal airways. In a fortunate arrangement, the greater proportion of blood circulates also to the bases of the lung providing, in the normal individual, a ventilation–perfusion ratio of near unity. This matching of ventilation and perfusion leads to optimal gas exchange.

Inflammatory destruction or aging of alveolar structures leads to deterioration of the match of ventilation with perfusion. While collapse of peripheral airways decreases ventilation to alveoli, perfusion remains unaffected. These changes are accentuated by factors that reduce the FRC (e.g., the supine posture, obesity, small airway closure from inflammation/edema). A ventilation–perfusion imbalance results in regional shunting of blood, impaired oxygen uptake, and arterial oxygen desaturation. Arterial O_2 tension follows a linear deterioration with age of approximately 0.3 percent Pa_{O_2} per year (see Tables 49-1 and 49-2).[18] Transfer of the more rapidly diffusable carbon dioxide is limited only by the rate of alveolar ventilation.

For the elderly individual, the consequences of a ventilation–perfusion mismatch are particularly harsh. The Pa_{O_2} (and thus O_2 delivery) may be further compromised by age-associated reductions in cardiac output.[19] When ventilation and perfusion are evenly matched, changing cardiac output has no effect on Pa_{O_2}. However, as ventilation–perfusion inequalities worsen, the Pa_{O_2} at any given cardiac output decreases; the further loss of cardiac output magnifies the reduction of O_2 delivery. It is possible, therefore, that the association (described above) between airways obstruction and mortality may be mediated partly by mechanical limitations of ventilation and a lowered arterial O_2 tension.

CONTROL OF BREATHING

Otherwise healthy older persons may be more vulnerable to transient reductions in levels of arterial oxygen tension (e.g., during pneumonia, exacerbation of COPD) due to age-related diminished responsiveness to hypoxia and hypercapnia.[20] The ventilatory response to hypoxia is reduced by half in healthy older men (64 to 73 years of age) compared with young healthy men (22 to 30 years of age), while the ventilatory response to CO_2 is reduced by approximately 40 percent. Although the reasons for this suppression of breathing are still under study, it appears that age attenuates chemoreceptor function, either at peripheral chemoreceptors or in the integrating central nervous system pathway.

The reduced ventilatory responses to hypoxia and hypercapnia observed in the elderly are independent of the aging mechanical properties of the lung.[21] The decreased inspiratory occlusion pressure (a measure of the total neuromuscular drive to breath), which accompanies the decreased drives of hypoxia and hypercapnia, is unaffected by the compliance of the respiratory system. Thus, the elderly, who are the most likely to be afflicted with chronic pulmonary diseases, are least able to defend against acute hypoxia or hypercapnia because of reductions in both their mechanical ability to ventilate and their neural drive to breathe.

EXERCISE CAPACITY

Physical work capacity (fitness) is generally assessed by measurement of the ability to deliver O_2 to the tissues (maximal O_2 consumption, or $V_{O_2 max}$).[22] Three systems must interact to transport O_2 from the outside air to the working muscles: pulmonary ventilation, blood circulation, and muscle tissue. At any age the $V_{O_2 max}$ is related to the physical dimensions of these three components: pulmonary (vital capacity, diffusing capacity), cardiovascular (heart volume, blood volume, red blood cell mass), and skeletal muscle mass. The importance of body size to the measurement of $V_{O_2 max}$ is reflected by the inclusion of weight in the measurement (expressed as maximal O_2 uptake per kilogram of body weight, or $V_{O_2 max}/kg$). Cardiorespiratory performance is even more closely related to lean body mass than to weight (especially in obese subjects). Lean body mass may be obtained from body weight by correcting for body fat, as estimated from skinfold measurements or underwater weighing.

The increase in work capacity ($V_{O_2 max}$) observed during childhood and adolescence is due to the growth of lungs, heart, and muscle. Following a plateau in the mid-twenties, the $V_{O_2 max}$ gradually declines due to reductions in two of these three components (cardiac output and muscle mass) seen with advancing years.[23] The gradual linear decline of O_2 delivery (32 ml/min/year in men and 14 ml/min/year in women) can be described by a prediction equation (see Tables 49-1 and 49-2) dependent only upon body size and age (which correlates with cardiac output and muscle mass).

Although ventilatory function also declines with age, reduced ventilation seldom limits exercise in healthy subjects. However, in patients with a ventilatory capacity reduced sufficiently to limit exercise performance, the FEV_1 is a reasonably accurate indicator of maximal ventilation in exercise. More typically, the reduced $V_{O_2 max}$ seen in elderly individuals with mild to moderate airways obstruction is due to cardiovascular deconditioning associated with lowered levels of habitual physical activity.

The differences in exercise performance between similarly aged men and women largely disappear when factors such as size (lean body mass), hemoglobin level, and levels of training are taken into account. Regular training can substantially slow the decline in maximal oxygen delivery due to age-related cardiovascular deconditioning.[6] Commenting on the results of a period of exercise training of sedentary subjects, a recent study concluded "the increase in $\dot{V}E/\dot{V}O_2$ (ventilatory response for a given oxygen uptake) during submaximal exercise observed with aging can be reversed by endurance training, and that after training, previously sedentary older individuals breathe at the same percentage of MVV during maximal exercise as highly trained (master) athletes of similar age."[24]

DEFENSE MECHANISMS

Clearance

An intact cough reflex is a necessary defense under conditions of dysphagia and impaired esophageal motility, which are more frequently encountered in old age. While cough is not essential for normal clearance of the respiratory tract, it is a powerful adjunct when normal mucociliary clearance is overloaded by foreign materials or secretions. Loss of an effective cough reflex (and subsequent aspiration) also contributes to an increased susceptibility to pneumonia in the elderly. While there seems to be an inverse relationship between age and the rate of mucociliary transport, the importance of mucous transport as a pulmonary defense mechanism has not yet been demonstrated experimentally.[25] Nevertheless, clinical observations of patients with primary ciliary immotility of Kartagener's syndrome (situs inversus, chronic sinusitis, and bronchiectasis) demonstrate recurrent respiratory tract infections, chronic bronchitis, and bronchiectasis.[25]

Humoral Immunity

Humoral immune competence is only roughly predicted by immunoglobulin levels in the bloodstream. Despite the lack of age-related change in IgA and IgG concentrations, the antibody response to extrinsic antigens, such as pneumococcal and influenza vaccines, is reduced considerably in old age. It is possible that this diminished antibody response reflects age-related reductions in T-cell helper activity, increases in T-cell supressor activity, or the reduced ability of B cells to produce normal high-affinity antibodies in response to antigen (all of which have been observed). The increased circulating immunoglobulin seen in older individuals may reflect increased production of antibody to various intrinsic antigens (i.e., autoantibodies), which replaces production of specific antibodies.[6]

Cellular Immunity

An age-related decline in functional ability has most clearly been seen in cell-mediated immunity. There is a reduced blastogenic response (to plant mitogens phytohemagglutinin and pokeweed mitogen) of lymphocytes from elderly adults (75 to 90 years old) compared with younger adults (25 to 50 years old). As measured by delayed hypersensitivity (the number of positive skin test reactions to five common antigens), reduced cellular immunity among individuals over 60 years of age has been correlated with increased mortality over the subsequent 2 years. Finally, the decline of cell-mediated immunity with increasing age correlates with an increasing frequency of reactivation tuberculosis.

USE OF TESTS OF PULMONARY FUNCTION

INITIAL ASSESSMENT OF NORMALITY

A test such as spirometry should be obtained at baseline for every patient and at 5-year intervals thereafter (in the absence of occupational or environmental exposure) or more frequently if the patient is potentially exposed to inhaled toxins. A young normal lung should be able to expel 80 percent of its vital capacity in the first second (a FEV_1/FVC ratio of 80 percent). Normalizing to the VC is an excellent way to standardize ventilatory function in healthy individuals. However, with the onset of pulmonary impairment, not only the one-second forced expiratory volume, but also the forced vital capacity, are both likely to deteriorate. In the absence of a constant VC, investigators have standardized their patients' results to spirometry from cross-sectional surveys of "normal" ("healthy," nonsmoking) individuals. These "normal" results are expressed as linear regression functions of age and height, separately for males and for females (see Tables 49-1 and 49-2).

There are a variety of prediction equations in the literature, and, until recently, their selection has been somewhat arbitrary. The research populations studied to develop these prediction equations are often quite different from the populations encountered in a chest clinic. The 1988 Snowbird conference now recommends that directors of pulmonary function laboratories select the equation which best predicts as normal a sample of the clinically normal individuals tested in their laboratories. Since few of these prediction equations have included sufficient numbers of normal elderly individuals, it is advisable to inquire regarding the origin of the prediction equation used by the lab.

The prediction equation estimates the average function for individuals of similar sex, age, height, and race. The variation in normal pulmonary function is relatively constant across the range of adult ages and heights so that the normal 95 percent of the population will fall within a fixed interval of the predicted range. The lower limit of normal can be calculated by subtracting a constant quantity from the predicted value for each test. Prediction equations and the appropriate subtraction constants for white males and females are given in Tables 49-1 and 49-2.

This method for determining the lower limit of normal replaces the commonly used 80 percent of predicted. If 80 percent of predicted were taken as the lower limit of normal, then as the predicted value got smaller with increasing age, the range of normal would become spuriously narrower. Several examples should clarify the point. From the FEV_1 prediction equation (Table 49-1), a 25-year-old man of 170 cm would be expected to have an FEV_1 of 4.2 liters. A male of similar age and height would still be considered to have a normal FEV_1 if he exhaled 4.2 − 0.842 liters (95 percent confidence interval constant determined from table) or 3.4 liters. For a young man, this lower limit is 80 percent of the predicted value. Similarly, a 60-year-old man of 165 cm would be expected to have an FEV_1 of 3.2 liters. The lower limit of normal for this predicted value is 2.3 liters (3.2 − 0.842 liters) or 74 percent of predicted. These considerations are particularly important for the elderly, where progressively smaller normal values would increase the likelihood of misclassification.

Blacks have a similar pulmonary geometry to whites, and their lungs have similar mechanical emptying characteristics. For any given standing height, however, blacks have a smaller trunk (smaller trunk/height ratio). A reduction of 12 percent from the white predicted value accommodates the racial difference in pulmonary function somewhat better than a regression based upon "sitting height."

ASSESSMENT OF RISK FOR MORBIDITY AND MORTALITY

The risks for heart disease, chronic obstructive lung disease, and lung cancer are not limited to the small proportion of the population with "abnormal" pulmonary function. Rather, there is a continuous increase in risk associated with progressively lower (although still normal) levels of ventilatory function. It is therefore of great importance to assess not only the initial pulmonary function, but the trend of pulmonary function with advancing

age. Considerable pulmonary function may be lost before an individual crosses into the clinically abnormal range.

At the end of pulmonary growth and development the ranking (percentile) of an individual's pulmonary function within the population might be ascertained in the same way that pediatric growth curves plot the percentile of height and weight for age.[27] Thereafter, at subsequent evaluations, it can be determined whether an individual's lung function is maintaining its expected ("normal") rate of decline or describes a more rapid rate of decline by crossing percentiles. Examples of these pulmonary function percentile curves (for FEV_1 and FVC for males and females) are provided in Figs. 49-2 and 49-3. Elderly individuals with a more rapid rate of decline in pulmonary function may be correctly perceived to be at risk for mortality from several causes well in advance of developing "abnormal" pulmonary function.

ASSESSMENT OF THE TYPE AND EXTENT OF PULMONARY DISORDER

Finally, the common respiratory diseases—restrictive pattern, asthma, chronic bronchitis, and emphysema—can be distinguished by simple pulmonary function tests. Once a pulmonary function is recognized as abnormal (Tables 49-1 and 49-2), the abnormality may be quantified by the guidelines in Table 49-3.

The inability to inhale a normal volume of air is recognized as a "restrictive pattern" on the spirogram by the presence of a normal FEV_1/FVC and a reduced FVC. Restriction may be due to a scarring of the lung, to weakness or loss of neural stimuli to chest wall muscles, or to changes in the shape of the bony thorax. Substantial obstruction with air trapping may produce a "mixed" pattern, but the underlying obstruction is often obvious if the forced expiration is carried out for at least 10 seconds. If the appearance of restriction persists, lung volume measurement is appropriate.

The obstructive diseases—asthma, chronic bronchitis, and emphysema—all demonstrate a reduction of the FEV_1/FVC on spirometry. Reversible obstruction is the hallmark of asthma (conventionally defined as an in-

TABLE 49-3
Quantitation of Impaired Pulmonary Function*

	FVC	FEV₁/FVC	TLC or RV	DLco
Normal	Within 1 CI	Within 1 CI	Within 1 CI	Within 1 CI
Slight (minimal)	1–1.75	1–2	±1–1.5	1–1.75
Moderate	>1.75–2.5	2–4	±>1.5–2.0	>1.75–2.5
Severe	>2.5	>4	±>2.0	>2.5

*Expressed as numbers of confidence intervals (CI) to be subtracted from predicted value.

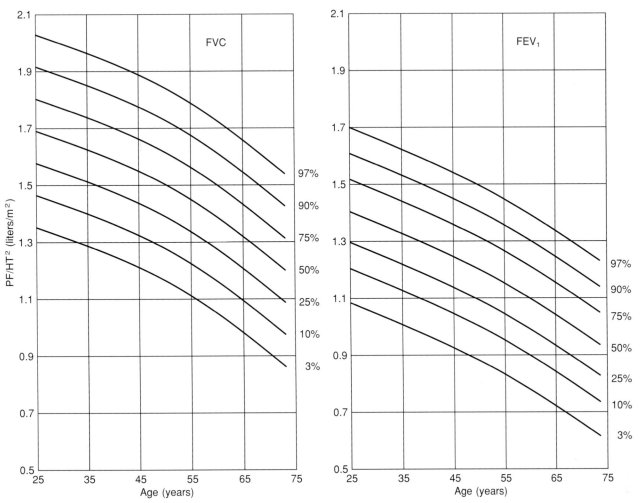

FIGURE 49-2
Percentile charts for height standardized pulmonary function of men. The "percentiles" of pulmonary function (liters) divided by height (meters) squared (PF/HT²) presented here and in Figure 49-3 are based upon measurements of white, nonsmokers who reported no respiratory symptoms, and who were drawn from a random sample of adults in six U.S. cities. *(Redrawn from Dockery DW et al: Distribution of forced expiratory volume in one second and forced vital capacity in healthy, white, adult never-smokers in six U.S. cities. Am Rev Respir Dis 131:511, 1985.)*

crease in FEV_1 equal to or greater than 15 percent of baseline). Bronchodilator reversibility may be absent when the pulmonary function is normal or severely abnormal. Incomplete reversibility suggests a component of "asthmatic bronchitis." The chronic (nonreversible) obstructive pulmonary diseases (chronic bronchitis and emphysema) both manifest a low FEV_1, but the destruction of the alveolar-capillary membrane associated with emphysema produces a lowered DLCO in that condition.

APPROACH TO THE GERIATRIC PATIENT WITH DISORDERS OF THE RESPIRATORY SYSTEM

Lung disease in the elderly has certain unique features. First, some importance must be attached to the setting in which the elderly patient is seen. As will be discussed in later chapters, pneumonia is 50 times more frequent among residents of chronic care facilities than expected in the population at large. In contrast, elderly individuals residing in the community seem not to have an increased prevalence of pneumonia but do more poorly than younger individuals when pulmonary infections develop. Even with appropriate antibiotic therapy, elderly patients with pneumonia sustain a 15 to 20 percent mortality. Advanced age also modifies the organisms likely to be responsible for a pneumonic infiltrate.

Obviously, such factors as depressed level of consciousness and reduced level of self-care, which have been shown to contribute to the risk of pneumonia, also enhance the likelihood that such individuals will be institutionalized. Thus, the increased risk of pneumonia observed in institutionalized patients is certainly due in some part to the underlying reasons for which the individual remains in the institution. Yet, the institutional

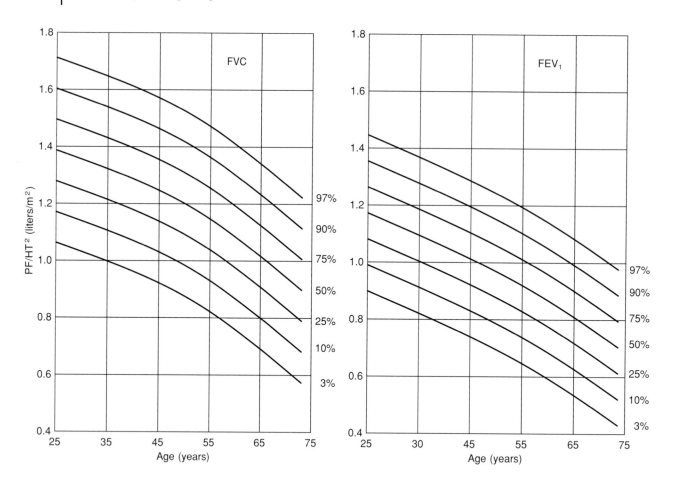

FIGURE 49-3
Percentile charts for height standardized pulmonary function of women. *(Redrawn from Dockery DW et al: Distribution of forced expiratory volume in one second and forced vital capacity in healthy, white, adult never-smokers in six U.S. cities. Am Rev Respir Dis 131:511, 1985.)*

setting itself adds to the risk of pulmonary infection in the elderly patient. In the closed populations of chronic care facilities, the attack rates among nonvaccinated or immune-depressed elderly for both influenza and tuberculosis are striking.

It must be appreciated that the clinical presentation of elderly individuals may be different from that of younger adults. The blunted inflammatory response in the presence of infection is often a source of missed diagnoses in the aged patient. The presentations of pneumococcal pneumonia as a bronchopneumonia (instead of lobar consolidation) or tuberculosis as a military disease (instead of an apical infiltrate) are both more common in the elderly patient.

In contrast, the obstructive airways diseases have been so closely associated with advanced age that their presence often evokes little interest by the physician. Nevertheless, since 1968 there has been a progressive increase in the age-adjusted death rate from chronic obstructive pulmonary disease (COPD). In the United States, more than 4 million persons are estimated to have COPD, and in 1979 $5 billion was spent for direct

and indirect costs arising from COPD. The ease with which this condition can be detected by spirometry and the observation of slowing of ventilatory deterioration following smoking cessation strongly support the clinical recommendation that older smokers be routinely evaluated with this test.

Other conditions which might be responsible for dyspnea in the elderly patient, such as congestive heart failure, interstitial lung disease, or pulmonary emboli, should be routinely included in the differential diagnosis. However, diminished reserve in the elderly patient limits the vigor with which diagnosis and therapy can be pursued. The use of exercise to evaluate dyspnea must be limited to those elderly in otherwise good clinical condition. Agents affecting both the sympathetic and parasympathetic nervous systems used in the diagnosis and treatment of lung disorders may affect the aging heart. Antibiotics required for pulmonary infection may lead to further compromise through nephrotoxicity of elderly kidneys with diminished reserve. Steroid and anticoagulation therapy may lead to a myriad of complications. Perhaps more than at any other time of adulthood, the geriatric pulmonary patient must be evaluated and treated in the context of *primum non nocere.*

One of the great challenges facing the physician responsible for the care of the elderly is ensuring that comprehensive medical care does not begin and end at the hospital door. This is especially true for chronic respiratory disease. The fluctuating respiratory impairment associated with seasonal change, episodic upper respiratory tract infections, and other intercurrent illness will require a variety of medical and nonmedical responses to maintain the health of the elderly respiratory patient. The physican must both recognize the need for respiratory outpatient support services and appreciate that other professionals, including a respiratory nurse, a res-

TABLE 49-4
Services Needed for Comprehensive Respiratory Outpatient Care

1. Comprehensive evaluation
   a. Complete medical evaluation
   b. Evaluation of patient and family financial and emotional support
2. Interval medical attention
3. Pulmonary function studies
4. Chest radiography
5. General laboratory services
   a. Bacteriology
   b. Hematology
   c. Chemistry
   d. Cytology
6. Electrocardiography
7. Immunization services
8. Drugs, medical supplies, and equipment
9. Routine transportation and communication
10. Emergency services (mobile unit with expertise) to bring patient from remote area to intensive care facility
11. Bronchial hygiene
12. Breathing instruction
13. Physical conditioning
14. Nutrition
    a. Counseling
    b. Provision of adequate nourishment
15. Homemaker and housekeeping services
16. Personal hygiene services (bathing, shampooing, etc.)
17. Psychosocial counseling
18. Financial support and planning
19. Vocational counseling
    a. For patient, family, or both
    b. Job training and placement
20. Environmental control
    a. Occupational exposures
    b. Household exposures
21. Education
    a. Patient
    b. Family
    c. Professional
22. Patient interaction groups

piratory therapist, and a social worker, will often be required to provide them. There should be someone in the physician's office whom the patient can call regarding access to support services. A list of outpatient services, which have been required by outpatients with chronic obstructive lung diseases, is shown in Table 49-4. It is important that the physician's representative not only be knowledgeable about obtaining such services, but also be able to recognize when such services are needed and make recommendations to both physician and patient. Unfortunately, delivery of adequate outpatient care to the aged respiratory patient has not kept pace with the improvements in diagnosis and therapy. The recognition of geriatric pulmonary disease and its appropriate treatment in the context of the diminished physiological, emotional, and social reserves of the elderly make the practice of geriatric pulmonary medicine particularly challenging.

REFERENCES

1. Beaty TH, Newill CA, Cohen BH, Tockman MS, Bryant SH, Spurgeon HA: Effects of pulmonary function on mortality. *J Chronic Dis* 38:703, 1985.
2. Tockman MS, Comstock GW: Respiratory risk factors and mortality: Longitudinal studies in Washington Country, Maryland. *Am Rev Respir Dis* (Suppl) 139, 1989.
3. Tockman MS, Anthonisen NR, Wright EC, Donithan MG: Airways obstruction and the risk for lung cancer. *Ann Intern Med* 106:512, 1987.
4. Silverberg E, Lubera J: Cancer statistics, 1986. *CA* 36:9, 1986.
5. Schwartz JD, Katz SA, Fegley RW, Tockman MS: Analysis of spirometric data from a national sample of healthy 6- to 24-year-olds (NHANES II). *Am Rev Respir Dis* 138:1405, 1988.
6. Murray JF: Aging, in *The Normal Lung*, 2d ed. Philadelphia, Saunders, 1986, pp 339–360.
7. Fletcher CM, Peto R, Tinker C, Speizer FE: *The Natural History of Chronic Bronchitis and Emphysema. An eight-year study of early chronic obstructive lung disease in working men in London.* New York, Oxford University Press, 1976.
8. Crapo RO, Morris AH, Gardner RM: Reference spirometric values using techniques and equipment that meet ATS recommendations. *Am Rev Respir Dis* 123:659, 1981.
9. Dockery DW, Speizer FE, Ferris BG Jr, Ware JH, Louis TA, Spiro A: Cumulative and reversible effects of lifetime smoking on simple tests of lung function in adults. *Am Rev Respir Dis* 137:286, 1988.
10. Turner JM, Mead J, Wohl ME: Elasticity of human lungs in relation to age. *J Appl Physiol* 25:664, 1968.
11. Mead J, Turner JM, Macklem PT, Little JB: Significance of the relationship between lung recoil and maximum expiratory flow. *J Appl Physiol* 22:95, 1967.
12. Niewoehner DE, Kleinerman J: Morphometric study of elastic fibers in normal and emphysematous human lungs. *Am Rev Respir Dis* 115:15, 1977.

13. Petty TL, Silvers GW, Stanford RE: Mild emphysema is associated with reduced elastic recoil and increased lung size but not with air-flow limitation. *Am Rev Respir Dis* 136:867, 1987.

14. Rooney SA: State of art. The surfactant system and lung phospholipid biochemistry. *Am Rev Respir Dis* 131:439, 1985.

15. Buist AS, Ross BB: Quantitative analysis of the alveolar plateau in the diagnosis of early airway obstruction. *Am Rev Respir Dis* 108:1078, 1973.

16. Crapo RO, Morris AH: Standardized single breath normal values for carbon monoxide diffusing capacity. *Am Rev Respir Dis* 123:185, 1981.

17. Forster RE, Dubois AB, Briscoe WA, Fisher AB: *The Lung*, 3d ed. Chicago, Year Book Medical Publishers, 1986, p 213.

18. Sorbini CA, Brassi V, Solinas E, Muiesan G: Arterial oxygen tension in relation to age in healthy subjects. *Respiration* 25:3, 1968.

19. West JB, Wagner PD: Pulmonary gas exchange, in West JB, Wagner PD (eds): *Bioengineering Aspects of the Lung*. New York, Marcel Dekker, 1977, pp 361–457.

20. Kronenberg RS, Drage CW: Attenuation of the ventilatory and heart rate responses to hypoxia and hypercapnia with aging in normal men. *J Clin Invest* 52:1812, 1973.

21. Peterson DD, Pack AI, Silage DA, Fishman AP: Effects of aging on ventilatory and occlusion pressure responses to hypoxia and hypercapnea. *Am Rev Respir Dis* 124:387, 1981.

22. Davies CTM: The oxygen-transporting system in relation to age. *Clin Sci* 42:1, 1972.

23. Jones NL, Moran Campbell EJ, Edwards RHT, Robertson DG: *Clinical Exercise Testing*. Philadelphia, Saunders, 1975.

24. Yerg JE, Seals DR, Hagberg JM, Holloszy JO: Effect of endurance exercise training on ventilatory function in older individuals. *J Appl Physiol* 58:791, 1985.

25. Wanner A: Pulmonary defense mechanisms: Mucociliary clearance, in Simmons DH (ed): *Current Pulmonology*, vol 2. Boston, Houghton Mifflin, 1980, pp 325–356.

26. Morris AM et al: *Clinical Pulmonary Function Testing: A Manual of Uniform Laboratory Procedures*, 2d ed. Salt Lake City, Intermountain Thoracic Society, 1984.

27. Dockery DW, Ware JH, Ferris BG Jr, Glicksberg DS, Fay ME, Spiro A, Speizer FE: Distribution of forced expiratory volume in one second and forced vital capacity in healthy, white, adult never-smokers in six U.S. cities. *Am Rev Respir Dis* 131:511, 1985.

28. Miller A (ed): *Pulmonary Function Tests in Clinical and Occupational Lung Disease*. New York, Grune and Stratton, 1986.

Chapter 50

PNEUMONIA

John G. Bartlett

Pneumonia has long been recognized as a special problem for the elderly. Hourmann and Dechambre published a series of papers entitled "Pneumonia in the Aged" in 1835, less than 20 years following Laennec's classic description of the disease.[1] Osler referred to pneumonia as the "special enemy of old age" in the first edition of his textbook and as "the friend of the aged" in the third edition; he eventually succumbed to pneumonia.

There has obviously been a significant improvement in the prognosis for pneumonia since these early descriptions, especially since antibiotics have become available. Nevertheless, infection of the lower respiratory tract remains the fifth leading category of disease responsible for death in the United States, and it is the most common lethal infection. Available data show that elderly patients continue to be at particular risk in terms of incidence, morbidity, and mortality. The major recognized predisposing factors include immunosenescence, a multiplicity of associated diseases, high rates of pharyngeal colonization with gram-negative bacilli, and the institutional setting. The predominant pathogens in these patients are pneumococci, gram-negative bacilli, anaerobic bacteria, *Haemophilus influenzae*, *Legionella*, and influenza. Recommendations for management should account for somewhat different bacteriologic patterns as compared to patterns in younger patients, a definite age-related mortality, and special considerations regarding therapeutic intervention.

INCIDENCE AND PROGNOSIS

A review of 44,684 cases of pneumonia in Massachusetts from 1921 to 1930 showed that the per capita incidence of pneumonia increased approximately fivefold for persons in the eighth decade of life as compared to those in the second decade of life.[2] Far more striking, however, was a nearly 100-fold increase in the mortality rate ascribed to pneumonia, an incidence which increased by approximately 10 percent for each decade of life beyond the age of 20. These studies in the preantibiotic era demonstrated an age-related susceptibility which is independent of modern chemotherapy. The availability of modern chemotherapy has modified these statistics considerably. A more recent population-based survey in Houston showed the annual rate of hospitalization for pneumonia (per 10,000 persons) was 30 to 60 cases during 3 years for persons over 65 years old compared to a rate of about 5 to 15 cases during 3 years for all other age categories (by decade) for adults.[3] Lower respiratory tract infections are found in 25 to 60 percent of elderly patients at autopsy, and this kind of infection represents the most common cause of death in centenarians.

Nosocomial pneumonia is a well-recognized problem in acute care facilities, where it accounts for approximately 15 percent of all hospital-acquired infections and is the most frequent lethal nosocomial infection. Less readily apparent, however, is the comparable risk noted in chronic care facilities.[4–6] To put these observations in an appropriate perspective, it should be noted that the total number of beds in nursing homes actually exceeds the total number of hospital beds in the United States; 20 percent of persons over the age of 65 spend some time in a nursing home facility, and approximately 5 percent of persons over the age of 65 are nursing home residents at any point in time.[5] Surveys of residents in nursing homes and chronic care facilities show that the prevalence of pneumonia is similar to that noted in acute care hospitals, an incidence of approximately 100 cases per 1000 patient-years.[7] A review of 750 psychiatric patients over age 60 who were institutionalized showed that age-specific death rates were increased approximately sixfold over the anticipated rate during the first year following institutionalization and that pneumonia was the major cause of death in these patients.[8] The risk of fatal pneumonia was, in fact, approximately 50 times the rate noted for age-matched controls who were not institutionalized. The magnitude of this difference exceeded that for all other disease categories. These data account for the current concern regarding pneumonia in the elderly with special attention to older individuals in acute or chronic care facilities.

PREDISPOSING FACTORS

There are numerous factors which contribute to the increased incidence and exaggerated mortality of pneumonia in the elderly. The most important has clearly been identified as influenza, based on a wealth of data showing that the rates for hospitalization and mortality ascribed to lower respiratory tract infections show a direct correlation with the seasonal and annual incidence of influenza.[3] Hospitalization or death is infrequently ascribed to influenza per se; instead, it is usually the result of a superimposed complication. Changes in pulmonary function which are part of the aging process that are believed to account for enhanced susceptibility are decreased effectiveness of cough, increased residual volume, increased compliance, increased closing volume, decreased diffusing capacity, and reduced oxygen saturation.[9] There is little evidence that these alterations in lung physiology associated with aging confer a substantial risk for pneumonia.[10–12] However, the compromise in pulmonary function appears to markedly increase susceptibility to morbid consequences with any further insult. A similar conclusion applies to chronic obstructive lung disease and chronic bronchitis, which are especially common in older individuals. A population-based study to assess risk factors associated with hospitalization for pneumonia showed that the highest risk rate was for persons over age 65 with chronic pulmonary conditions.[3] Thus, these patients may not have a striking increase in prevalence rates of pneumonia, but they seem to do poorly when pulmonary infections develop. Some conditions encountered in the elderly are associated with increased incidence and increased morbidity for bacterial pneumonia according to experimental animal studies. As noted, the most important is influenza; additional factors include severe hypoxia, pulmonary edema, acidosis, alcohol intoxication, other forms of viral pneumonia, and azotemia.

Lung defenses against invading microorganisms involve complex interrelated factors, including the mucociliary elevator, the alveolar macrophage, polymorphonuclear leukocytes, humoral defenses, and the cell-mediated immune system. Studies in healthy, aged volunteers show that the functional capacity for most of these factors remains intact with age or is only mildly reduced. For example, humoral defenses as measured by serum antibody response to vaccination with tetanus or pneumococcal vaccine show a somewhat blunted response which is, nevertheless, generally adequate to

provide "protective" levels in the elderly.[12] The functional capacity of leukocytes also appears to be maintained with advancing age. The most clearly defined and pronounced defect which occurs as a consequence of aging concerns T-lymphocyte function. This includes an intrinsic defect in effector T lymphocytes, enhanced activity of suppressor T lymphocytes, and an increase in committed precursors with reduced capacity for functional diversity.[10] The result of these deficiencies is readily demonstrable by the increased rate of anergy noted with common skin test antigens, which presumably accounts for the increased incidence of tuberculosis or possibly other opportunistic pathogens; however, it does not readily explain the enhanced risk for the most common pathogens, such as pneumococci, gram-negative bacilli, or anaerobes.

One of the major contributing factors to increased susceptibility to pneumonia concerns the multiplicity of conditions which predispose to aspiration. These include sedative use, neurologic diseases, and other conditions associated with reduced consciousness or dysphagia. Compounding the problem is the loss of an effective cough reflex which commonly accompanies reduced consciousness. The result is a reduction in the usual clearance mechanisms which protect the lower airways from abnormal entry of secretions originating in the oral cavity or stomach. These factors have been invoked to explain excessive rates of pneumonia among elderly psychiatric patients, patients with senile dementia, and patients with chronic organic brain syndrome.

Another predisposing factor of recent interest has been the recognition that colonization of the oropharynx with gram-negative bacilli predisposes to gram-negative bacillary pneumonia. Early studies suggested that this mechanism was a major factor in the increased risk for pneumonia among hospitalized patients. Rates of colonization, as well as the incidence of pneumonia, correlated directly with the severity of the associated diseases. The relevance of this work to pneumonia in the elderly concerns the excessive colonization rate noted in patients of advanced age.[13] The prevalence of positive throat cultures for gram-negative bacilli appears to be directly related to the level of care required, suggesting that the patient's functional capacity for self-care is a critical factor.

ETIOLOGIC AGENTS

Available data suggest that the most important microbial pathogens in sporadic cases of pneumonia in the elderly are bacteria. However, information concerning the distribution of specific pathogens in these patients is sharply limited. The problem is that examination of expectorated sputum, the most frequently utilized specimen source for microbiological studies, is fraught with problems in interpretation due to contamination of the specimen which occurs during passage through the upper airways. Most studies of pneumonia show that no likely pathogen is recovered in 30 to 50 percent of cases, and many of the organisms implicated in the remaining cases are largely the matter of arbitrary judgment. Studies utilizing more readily acceptable diagnostic sources, such as cultures of transtracheal aspirates, blood cultures, and serologic studies, show that the following organisms account for most cases of pneumonia in the elderly: *Streptococcus pneumoniae*, gram-negative bacilli, anaerobic bacteria, *Legionella pneumophila*, and influenza virus.

STREPTOCOCCUS PNEUMONIAE

S. pneumoniae is generally regarded as the major bacterial cause of community-acquired pneumonia in elderly patients, as well as in younger individuals. The recovery rate of this organism in expectorated sputa ranges from 15 to 70 percent. Roentgenographic changes with pneumococcal pneumonia are somewhat different in elderly patients in that a bronchopneumonia pattern is far more common than lobar consolidation. The clinical presentation tends to be more subtle in that elderly patients often have minimal complaints and are frequently afebrile.[11] The outcome with pneumococcal pneumonia is also decidedly different in this group. Studies in the preantibiotic era showed a mortality rate of about 70 percent for those in the seventh decade compared to 10 percent among patients 10 to 12 years old.[2] Even with appropriate antibiotic therapy, the mortality rate is 15 to 20 percent for all elderly patients, and it is about 50 percent for those with pneumococcal bacteremia.[2,7,11,12] These data concerning pneumococcal pneumonia show somewhat different patterns in chest x rays in the elderly (as compared to patterns in younger patients) and mortality rates which are clearly age-related, both with and without antibiotic treatment.

GRAM-NEGATIVE BACILLI

Gram-negative bacilli play a relatively minor role in most cases of community-acquired pneumonia, even in elderly patients. This infection is far more common in patients who either are hospitalized or are residents of chronic care facilities. In such settings, coliforms and pseudomonads account for approximately 40 to 60 percent of all pneumonia cases.[13,14] The presumed source of the bacteria is the colonic flora, with subsequent oropharynx colonization in patients rendered susceptible by serious associated diseases or reduced capacity for self-care as discussed above. An alternative source is gastric contents. Colonization of the stomach with large num-

bers of bacteria occurs with gastric achlorhydria, which is most common in elderly patients and those receiving antacids or H_2-receptor antagonists. With the source of organisms in either the stomach or oropharyngeal secretions, the presumed mechanism of entry into the lower airways is by aspiration or "microaspiration" in reference to occult aspiration of small volumes, as distinguished from large-volume aspiration, which is traditionally referred to as "aspiration pneumonia." Another mechanism of acquisition is by dissemination as small-particle aerosols from reservoir nebulizers employed with ventilation equipment or introduced with instrumentation of the lower airways. The usual pathogens transferred in this fashion are bacteria which survive well in water, such as *Pseudomonas aeruginosa*, other pseudomonads, *Serratia marcescens*, *Achromobacter*, *Flavobacterium*, and *Acinetobacter*.

The predominant gram-negative bacillus causing pneumonia is usually *Klebsiella pneumoniae*,[15] although different hospitals may show distinctive epidemiologic patterns, and there are often distinctive patterns within hospitals as well. The classic description of *Klebsiella* pneumonia (Friedländer's pneumonia) includes a precipitous onset, severe prostration, rigors, spiking fever, pleuritic chest pain, a productive cough, sputum which appears like currant jelly, x-ray evidence of consolidation with a predilection for the right upper lobe, and a propensity for tissue necrosis with abscess formation. The disease, as originally described by Friedländer, usually occurred in debilitated hosts and was especially common in alcoholics. More recent studies suggest that *Klebsiella* pneumonia is most common in the institutional setting and that the clinical presentation shows few features which will distinguish this type of pneumonia from other bacterial infections of the lower airways.[15] This may reflect involvement of different serotypes of *Klebsiella* compared to those noted in earlier studies. Other gram-negative bacteria which are commonly encountered in pneumonia acquired in the institutional setting include *Enterobacter*, *Pseudomonas* sp., *Proteus*, *Escherichia coli*, and *S. marcescens*. Clinical features with these gram-negative bacillary pneumonias also show no unique features, particularly in clinical or radiographic presentation.[16] However, one disturbing factor is the high mortality rate which is generally reported at 25 to 50 percent.[15,16]

ANAEROBIC BACTERIA

The role of anaerobic bacteria as pulmonary pathogens was well established at the turn of the century, but these organisms continue to represent elusive pathogens that are often unrecognized and seldom confirmed. The most likely explanation is that expectorated sputum is not valid for meaningful anaerobic culture. Thus, invasive diagnostic tests such as transtracheal aspiration must be performed in order to establish the etiologic diagnosis. An additional problem is the relatively fastidious nature of these organisms which makes identification require specialized microbiological techniques that have not been available in most laboratories until recent years.

Most patients with anaerobic pulmonary infections have aspiration pneumonia or its sequelae, including empyema, or lung abscess.[17] The usual criteria for the diagnosis of aspiration pneumonia are clinical symptoms of a lower respiratory tract infection, roentgenographic evidence for pneumonia involving a dependent pulmonary segment, and an associated condition which predisposes to aspiration. The most common predisposing conditions are compromised consciousness due to alcoholism, general anesthesia, seizure disorder, sedative use, neurologic disorders, and other illnesses associated with altered consciousness. Dysphagia due to esophageal disease or neurologic disorder (such as Parkinson's disease) also predispose to aspiration. The usual source of the inoculum in these cases is secretions from the upper airway which contain large concentrations of anaerobic bacteria. The major source for anaerobes involved in pulmonary infections is the gingival crevice; hence, periodontal disease may represent an additional associated risk factor. Patients who are edentulous have a reduced incidence of anaerobic pulmonary infections, although such an infection may occasionally occur, most commonly in the presence of a bronchogenic neoplasm.

The clinical presentation of anaerobic pulmonary infections shows considerable variation.[17,18] Some patients have acute symptoms which may resemble pulmonary infections due to other bacterial pathogens such as pneumococci. Other patients have a much more indolent, chronically evolving course with few symptoms other than low-grade fever and cough, which may persist for weeks or months prior to the patient's seeking medical attention. A particularly common sequela is necrosis of tissue resulting in a lung abscess or a bronchopleural fistula with empyema. It is in this advanced stage of the infection that sputum often has a putrid odor that is considered diagnostic of anaerobic infections. There are many patients, especially elderly individuals, who present with relatively subtle symptoms and a smoldering course, which may be referred to as "hypostatic pneumonia," "nursing home pneumonia," or "walking pneumonia," depending on the clinical setting. The etiologic agent for these infections is usually not discerned, but it is likely that anaerobic bacteria are involved in a major portion.

The mortality rate for anaerobic pulmonary infections is generally low if appropriate antimicrobial agents are used. Penicillin has traditionally been regarded as the preferred agent. Clindamycin is equally effective and may be preferred for patients with serious infections, patients who have contraindications to penicillin, or patients who fail to respond to a penicillin trial.[19]

STAPHYLOCOCCUS AUREUS

S. *aureus* is an important pulmonary pathogen in 10 to 30 percent of nosocomial pneumonias, including infections acquired in the nursing home setting.[15] It is also relatively common in bacterial infections superimposed on influenza. Clinical features of staphylococcal pneumonia include x-ray evidence of a bronchopneumonia (consolidation is rare) and a variable course which may be acute and fulminant or relatively chronic and indolent. Tissue necrosis with abscess formation is well-documented in some cases, but it is far less common than is generally appreciated. Most strains produce β-lactamase and require drugs such as nafcillin or cephalosporins. A disturbing finding in recent years is the increased prevalence of methicillin-resistant strains of S. *aureus*.[20] These strains are most frequently encountered as nosocomial pathogens in large, university-affiliated medical centers, and vancomycin is the preferred drug.

HAEMOPHILUS INFLUENZAE

H. *influenzae* is second only to pneumococcus as a potential pathogen recovered in expectorated sputum samples from elderly patients with community-acquired pneumonia. This organism also frequently colonizes the upper airways, making it difficult to interpret the significance of isolation in expectorated samples. Despite this confusion, H. *influenzae* pneumonia is a well-documented entity which appears to be especially common in elderly patients with chronic pulmonary disease. This organism and the pneumococcus are also the two most frequent organisms implicated in exacerbations of chronic bronchitis. When H. *influenzae* causes pneumonia, there are no distinctive clinical features that set it apart from pneumonia caused by other common bacterial pathogens.

LEGIONELLA PNEUMOPHILA

Legionnaires' disease, caused by L. *pneumophila*, became the focus of national interest in 1976 with the epidemic in Philadelphia. A review of 182 cases at that convention showed that 75 percent of the patients were over the age of 40 and the risk of infection among those over age 60 was approximately twice the risk for younger individuals. Subsequent studies of this disease have continued to show a direct correlation between the attack rate and age.[21]

Legionnaires' disease may occur sporadically or in epidemics; the epidemics have most frequently occurred in buildings such as hotels or hospitals. The natural habitat of the putative agent is water, and the major source of the organism in outbreaks, when one has been detected, is either the condensate of air conditioning cooling towers or potable water (resulting in contaminated showerheads). In either event, the organism is presumably inhaled following aerosolization. Common symptoms include high fever, cough which is usually nonproductive, pulmonary infiltrates, and certain extrapulmonary symptoms which are present with variable frequency. Another form of legionellosis is Pontiac fever, a flulike illness characterized by chills, fever, myalgias, and headache but showing no clinical or radiographic evidence for pneumonia. This form of the disease is associated with a favorable prognosis even in the absence of antibiotic treatment.

The organisms responsible for legionellosis include multiple species in the genus *Legionella*, but the most frequent pathogen is *L. pneumophila*. Methods to detect legionellosis include cultivation of the organism from respiratory specimens such as expectorated sputum, direct fluorescent (DFA) staining of specimens, or serology.[22] The most expedient method is the DFA stain, which is highly specific but has a sensitivity of only 50 to 70 percent using expectorated sputum. The preferred treatment is erythromycin, with dose recommendations of 4 g/day given intravenously for seriously ill individuals. The prognosis is relatively good for the patient with legionnaires' disease who is properly treated and does not have compromised immunologic defenses. As might be expected, advanced age is associated with a somewhat higher mortality rate. For example, in the original Philadelphia epidemic, it was noted that the mortality rate for victims over age 55 was 30 percent, approximately twice the rate noted for younger individuals.[23]

INFLUENZA

Viruses that play relatively important roles in lower respiratory tract infections among elderly patients are influenza, parainfluenza, and respiratory synctial viruses.[24,25] The most important in terms of incidence and morbidity is clearly influenza.[24–29] Attack rates for influenza are highly variable, depending on antigenic patterns, strain virulence, and immunization status of the population. Attack rates are also age-related, so that persons over 70 years of age have an incidence of approximately four times that of persons under age 40. More impressive, however, is the increased morbidity and mortality associated with influenza in patients of advanced age or with debilitating associated diseases. One of the major complications is primary influenza pneumonia, which may follow a rapidly lethal course. Alternatively, influenza may be complicated by a bacterial superinfection which often occurs 7 to 10 days after the onset of symptoms at a time when there is a relatively small viral load but an apparent paralysis of alveolar macrophage activity as a sequela to the prior infection. The most frequently implicated bacterial agents responsible for superinfections in this setting are *S. pneumoniae* and *S. aureus*. Amantadine has established efficacy for the treatment of infections involving influenza A virus when given within 48 hours of the inception of symptoms. This drug is also advocated for prevention, particularly in closed populations such as nursing homes, where many in the residents have not received appropriate vaccines.[30]

MANAGEMENT

Recommendations for the diagnostic evaluation and therapy of pneumonia in the elderly utilize the basic principles which apply to pneumonia in general. The diagnosis is based on the usual clinical parameters such as fever, leukocytosis, and, most importantly, the demonstration of an infiltrate on chest x ray. It should be noted that the differential diagnosis in patients with these findings may include multiple noninfectious diseases such as atelectasis, pulmonary embolism with infarction, and congestive heart failure. The demonstration of a pulmonary infiltrate on chest x ray is a necessary requirement for the diagnosis of pneumonia. On rare occasions, this finding will not be demonstrable in the early phases of acute infections, but it is usually present when the patient is initially seen, and it is invariably seen within 24 hours after the onset of symptoms.

Many elderly patients present with rather subtle clinical findings and roentgenographic evidence of a pulmonary infiltrate in one or both lower lobes; as mentioned earlier, such cases are often referred to as "hypostatic pneumonia," "nursing home pneumonia," or "walking pneumonia."[11,31] These cases are usually due to bacterial infections and usually respond to antibiotic therapy directed against anaerobic bacteria or pneumococci. It should also be emphasized that some of the common associated findings in patients with acute pulmonary infections are less readily apparent in the elderly population. Elderly individuals are less likely to develop high fevers and, on some occasions, will have no demonstrable fever.[11] Similarly, elderly individuals are less likely to mount a vigorous leukocytic response, hence the peripheral white blood count, while elevated, does not usually reach levels comparable to those seen in acute bacterial pulmonary infections in younger patients. These factors may make the diagnosis less readily apparent in the elderly patient.

A major goal in management is identification of the etiologic agent so as to provide a guideline for the selection of antimicrobial agents. Most infections in elderly patients are due to the bacterial pathogens noted above, and the time-honored specimen for diagnostic evaluation is expectorated sputum. Unfortunately, this specimen source is fraught with a considerable diagnostic inaccuracy due to contamination by the normal flora during passage through the upper airways. Nearly all studies of pneumonia which utilize expectorated sputa show that no clear etiologic agent can be identified in 30 to 40 percent of cases and that even those which do yield potential pulmonary pathogens must be interpreted with caution since these organisms may simply reflect oropharyngeal colonization. This especially applies to gram-negative bacilli, which, as noted above, are frequently present in the upper airways of elderly individuals. A commonly advocated method for improving the quality of expectorated sputum bacteriology is the use of cytologic screening with cultures restricted to specimens showing large numbers of polymorphonuclear leukocytes on microscopic examination. Gram stains of specimens may actually provide more useful information than a culture would. An additional advantage is that the results are immediately available and may be used at the time that therapeutic decisions are required. A particularly common mistake is to overdiagnose pneumococcal pneumonia because of the prevalence of gram-positive cocci in chains, which are almost universally present in saliva. Transtracheal aspiration is a more accurate specimen source since this procedure bypasses the contaminating bacteria from the upper airways. Nevertheless, it is an invasive diagnostic technique which is occasionally associated with serious complications and should be reserved for patients with serious infections, particularly those with nondiagnostic expectorated samples.

The emphasis here regarding specimen sources concerns the usual bacterial causes of pneumonia. Different principles apply to the detection of other etiologic agents such as influenza, mycobacteria, pathogenic fungi, *Legionella,* and most opportunistic pathogens. Numerous studies have shown that elderly individuals have compromised T-lymphocyte function with suppressed cell-mediated immunity and age-related anergy to skin test antigens. Despite this defect, age per se does not appear to confer a major risk for the usual opportunistic pathogens which are encountered in other patients with similar defects, such as *Pneumocystis carinii, Aspergillus, Mucor,* herpes simplex, toxoplasmosis, *Strongyloides,* and *Nocardia.* Thus, these organisms should not be highly suspect in patients of advanced age unless there are other associated risk factors, such as corticosteroid administration, lymphoproliferative disorders, cancer chemotherapy, or HIV infection.

The use of specific therapeutic agents in elderly individuals does not differ from use recommendations for younger individuals, with a few exceptions. Antimicrobial agents with potential nephrotoxicity must be used with particular caution in the elderly, including careful monitoring of serum levels and measurements of renal function. Elderly patients with even normal renal function by the usual laboratory standards have a considerable reduction in nephric reserve and are far more likely to develop nephrotoxicity than are their younger counterparts. Intravenous administration of fluids, electrolytes, and other forms of osmotic loading must often be done carefully as well, due to reduced cardiac reserve. Hypersensitivity reactions do not occur more frequently in elderly patients, although there is an age-associated risk for antibiotic-associated colitis. There are also multiple potential drug interactions between antibiotics and therapeutic agents commonly utilized by elderly patients, particularly sodium warfarin (Coumadin). These data suggest that the usual antibiotic options for the treatment of pneumonia apply to patients of advanced age, although therapeutic monitoring must often be done with greater care.

Recommendations for specific types of pneumonia are provided in Table 50-1. For seriously ill patients with community-acquired pneumonia and no defined etiologic agent, we recommend the combination of erythromycin and cefuroxime (or cefamandole) or erythromycin and trimethoprim-sulfamethoxazole. For empiric treatment of nosocomial pneumonia the concern is relatively resistant gram-negative bacilli, and common recommendations include an aminoglycoside plus an antipseudomonad penicillin, a cephalosporin, or imipenem.

The anticipated response of bacterial pneumonias to antibiotic therapy is variable, but a general rule is that changes in x ray are delayed and often progress in the initial phases of appropriate treatment so that other clinical parameters are more valuable for therapeutic monitoring early in the course. Considerations for patients with inadequate response include (1) wrong diagnosis; (2) inappropriate antibiotic; (3) inadequate drug dose (which is most common with aminoglycosides); (4) adverse drug reaction, usually in the form of drug fever; (5) superinfection; and (6) inadequate host. One of the more common explanations in elderly patients concerns inadequate response due to far-advanced disease in a host who simply cannot respond. Continued and sometimes aggressive evaluation for alternative diagnoses is appropriate for such individuals. This may include bronchoscopy, attempts to detect alternative etiologic agents, and studies for noninfectious or concurrent diseases. However, the common practice of repeated cultures of expectorated sputum samples with changes in the chemotherapeutic regimen on the basis of each new resistant isolate

TABLE 50-1
Recommendations for Treatment of Specific Types of Pneumonia

Organism	Agent*	Alternative (Comments)
Bacteria		
S. pneumoniae	Penicillin	Cephalosporins, chloramphenicol, tetracycline, erythromycin, clindamycin
S. aureus Methicillin-sensitive	Penicillinase-resistant penicillin*	Cephalosporins (1st or 2d gen.), clindamycin, vancomycin
Methicillin-resistant	Vancomcyin	Sulfa-trimethoprim
Klebsiella†	Aminoglycoside + cephalosporin	Cephalosporin (alone) Aminoglycoside + piperacillin Imipenem
Pseudomonas†	Aminoglycoside + antipseudomonad penicillin*	Aminoglycoside + imipenem, ceftazidime, cefoperazone, or ciprofloxacin
Gram-negative bacilli (other)†	Aminoglycoside + cephalosporin, ampicillin, or carbenicillin	
H. influenzae†	Ampicillin or cefamandole (cefuroxime)	Tetracycline, chloramphenicol, sulfa-trimethoprim
Anaerobes	Penicillin or clindamycin	Tetracycline, cephalosporin, chloramphenicol, imipenem, metronidazole + penicillin
Nocardia	Sulfonamides	Sulfa-trimethoprim, minocycline, doxycycline
Legionella	Erythromycin	Erythromycin + rifampin, sulfa-trimethoprim + rifampin
Mycoplasma	Erythromycin or tetracycline	
TWAR	Tetracycline	Erythromycin
Fungi		
Histoplasma, blastomycosis, coccidioidomycosis	Ketoconazole	Amphotericin B (Histoplasmosis and coccidioidmycosis confined to the lung is usually not treated)
Candida, Aspergillus	Amphotericin B ± 5 fluorocytosine	
Phycomycetes (Mucor)	Amphotericin B	
Viruses		
Herpes simplex	Acyclovir	
Varicella-zoster	Acyclovir	
Influenza A	Amatadine	
P. carinii	Sulfa-trimethoprim	Pentamidine

*Antipseudomonad penicillins: Ticarcillin, piperacillin, mezlocillin, and azlocillin are usually considered equally effective; in vitro testing facilitates choice.
Penicillinase-resistant penicillins: Nafcillin, oxacillin, and methicillin.
Cephalosporins: In vitro testing determines choice.
Aminoglycosides: In vitro testing facilitates choice between tobramycin, gentamicin, and amikacin.
†GNB: In vitro testing required.

which is recovered cannot be justified. These specimens are expected to yield resistant organisms during the course of therapy, and a careful distinction must be made between superinfected sputum and superinfected patient. Follow-up x rays after apparent recovery are necessary to ensure that pulmonary infiltrates have cleared to exclude predisposing pulmonary lesions such as bronchogenic neoplasms.

PREVENTION

Nosocomial infections play a well-established role in acute care hospitals, and elderly patients are especially vulnerable in this setting. Less well-recognized and controlled is the analogous problem in nursing homes, where several surveys have shown that the risk of nosocomial infection is about the same as it is for acute care hospitals, i.e., about 5 to 10 percent per year. The most celebrated pulmonary infections noted in this setting are influenza and tuberculosis and, to a lesser extent, gram-negative bacillary pneumonias, respiratory syncytial virus, and parainfluenza viruses. These experiences illustrate the need for standard infection control procedures, which often are not established or are not enforced.[4,5,32] Immunization against influenza and pneumococci is commonly advocated for elderly patients as a potentially effective means of preventive care which is easily accomplished at little risk. The anticipated protection rate with influenza against strains included in the vaccine is approximately 70 percent for the general population when the epidemic and vaccine strains are identical, but the rate appears to be lower for elderly persons.[28–30] Nevertheless, this vaccine is recommended for all persons over age 65, as well as other high-risk patients and health care personnel, especially residents of nursing homes.[30] Amantidine may be used to prevent or to treat influenza, although caution is advised in elderly patients with respect to possible central nervous system toxicity.

Pneumococcal vaccine is more controversial. Studies of serologic response show that elderly patients generally develop "protective" titers following immunization with the polyvalent vaccine which is commercially available. Unfortunately, clinical trials in outpatients over the age of 45 and residents of chronic care facilities have shown minimal reduction in the overall incidence of pneumonia or pneumococcal pneumonia.[7,12,33,34] This vaccine may be advocated for elderly persons in view of theoretical advantages and paucity of side effects, but it cannot be endorsed with enthusiasm on the basis of clinical trials, which have failed to demonstrate benefit in terms of reducing either the incidence or severity of pneumococcal infections in the elderly.[7,12,32,33]

Prophylactic use of antibiotics in the susceptible host may be theoretically attractive, especially in the patient who is prone to aspiration. However, utilization of this approach has not successfully reduced the incidence of pulmonary infections and, in fact, appears to enhance the risk of infection involving resistant strains.

Epidemics of pneumonia are likely to occur in institutions such as hospitals or nursing homes and may have devastating consequences. These epidemics are usually due to viral infections, particularly influenza, but also may be due to respiratory syncytial virus and parainfluenza.[24] Unlike bacterial infections, these epidemics tend to involve all exposed persons, rather than just the debilitated hosts. Acquisition is from an exogenous source rather than endogenous source, and the organisms responsible are usually implicated concurrently in community outbreaks. Attack rates in nursing homes are often 25 to 65 percent, with case-fatality rates averaging 10 percent. Preventive measures include restriction of visi-

tors and elective admissions, restriction of afflicted personnel, and respiratory isolation for patients with documented infections. These outbreaks may be blunted or prevented by immunization with influenza vaccine. Although the vaccine is not as effective in the elderly, the Advisory Committee on Immunization Practices has designated nursing home residents as the highest priority for influenza vaccination.[30] The vaccine is considered safe, is inexpensive ($2 to $3 per dose), and is reported to be both effective and cost-effective in this setting. Vaccine efficacy when the epidemic strain and the vaccine strain are identical varies between 40 and 95 percent for morbidity and mortality.[29] In several studies the vaccine proved to be not especially effective in preventing illness, but it showed a more impressive record for preventing severe disease resulting in hospitalization, pneumonia, or death.[29] As expected, efficacy for disease prevention and morbidity is less when the epidemic strain has drifted from the vaccine strain.

Amantadine also may be used for prevention of, as well as treatment of, influenza A. Again, the Advisory Committee on Immunization Practices has given the highest priority to amantadine for the control of presumed influenza A outbreaks in institutions with high-risk patients.[30] In these cases, the drug should be given to all residents, regardless of vaccine status, as soon as possible after the outbreak is recognized and as long as there is influenza activity in the community. The recommended dose for prophylaxis for all adults and for treatment of patients over 65 years old is 100 mg/day; reduced doses are indicated in the presence of renal failure.

REFERENCES

1. Hourmann and Dechambre: Recherches pour servir à l'histoire des maladies des vieillards, faites à la salpetrière. Maladies des organes de la respiration. *Arch Gen Med (Paris)* 8:405, 1835.

2. Heffron R: *Pneumonia.* Cambridge, MA, Harvard University Press, 1939, pp 304–308, 707–710.

3. Glezen WP, Decker M, Perrotta DM: Survey of underlying conditions of persons hospitalized with acute respiratory disease during influenza epidemics in Houston, 1978–1981. *Am Rev Respir Dis* 136:550, 1987.

4. Haley RW, Culver DH, White JW et al: The nationwide nosocomial infection rate: A need for vital statistics. *Am J Epidemiol* 121:159, 1985.

5. Garibaldi RA, Brodine S, Matsumiya S: Infections among patients in nursing homes: Policies, prevalence and problems. *N Engl J Med* 305:731, 1981.

6. Setia U, Serventi I, Lorenz P: Nosocomial infections among patients in a long term care facility: Spectrum, prevalence and risk factors. *Am J Infect Control* 13:57, 1985.

7. Bentley DW: Pneumococcal vaccine in the institutional-

ized elderly: Review of past and recent studies. *Rev Resp Dis* 3:561, 1981.

8. Craig TJ, Lin SP: Mortality among elderly psychiatric patients: Basis for preventive intervention. *J Am Geriatr Soc* 29:181, 1981.

9. Dhar S, Subramaniam SR, Leonora RAK: Aging and the respiratory system. *Med Clin North Am* 60:1121, 1976.

10. Weksler ME: The senescence of the immune system. *Hosp Pract* 16:53, 1981.

11. Esposito AL: Community-acquired bacteremic pneumococcal pneumonia: Effect of age on manifestations and outcome. *Arch Intern Med* 144:945, 1984.

12. Forrester HL, Jahnigen DW, LaForce FM: Inefficacy of pneumococcal vaccine in a high-risk population. *Am J Med* 83:425, 1987.

13. Valenti WM, Trudell RG, Bentley DW: Factors predisposing to oropharyngeal colonization with gram-negative bacilli in the aged. *N Engl J Med* 298:1108, 1978.

14. Garb JL, Brown RB, Garb JR et al: Differences in etiology of pneumonias in nursing home and community patients. *JAMA* 240:2169, 1978.

15. Bartlett JG, O'Keefe P, Tally FP, Louie TJ, Gorbach SL: The bacteriology of hospital-acquired pneumonia. *Arch Intern Med* 146:868, 1986.

16. LaForce FM: Hospital-acquired gram-negative rod pneumonias: An overview. *Am J Med* 70:644, 1981.

17. Bartlett JG: Anaerobic bacterial infections of the lung. *Chest* 91:901, 1987.

18. Bartlett JG, Finegold SM: Anaerobic infections of the lung and pleural space. *Am Rev Resp Dis* 110:56, 1974.

19. Levison ME, Mangura CT, Lorber B, Abrutyn E, Pesanti EL, Levy RS et al: Clindamycin compared with penicillin for the treatment of anaerobic lung abscess. *Ann Intern Med* 98:466, 1983.

20. Peacock JE, Moorman DR, Wenzel RP, Mandell GL: Methicillin-resistant *Staphylococcus aureus:* Microbiologic characteristics, antimicrobial susceptibilities, and assessment of virulence of an epidemic strain. *J Infect Dis* 144:575, 1981.

21. Tsai TF, Finn DR, Pilkaytis BD, Tsai TF, Storch C, Broome CV: Sporadic legionellosis in the United States: The first thousand cases. *Ann Intern Med* 31:219, 1980.

22. Edelstein PH, Meyer RD: Legionnaires' disease: A review. *Chest* 85:114, 1984.

23. Fraser DW, Tsai TR, Orenstein W, Parkin WE et al: Legionnaires' disease: Description of an epidemic of pneumonia. *N Engl J Med* 297:1189, 1977.

24. Gross PA, Rodstein M, LaMontane RJ, Kaslow RA et al: Epidemiology of acute respiratory illness during an influenza outbreak in a nursing home. *Arch Intern Med* 148:559, 1988.

25. Hall WN, Goodman RA, Noble GR, Kendal AP, Steece RS: An outbreak of influenza B in an elderly population. *J Infect Dis* 144:297, 1981.

26. Mathur U, Bentley DW, Hall CB: Concurrent respiratory syncytial virus and influenza A infections in the institutionalized elderly and chronically ill. *Ann Intern Med* 3:49, 1980.

27. Centers for Disease Control: Outbreaks of influenza among nursing home residents. *MMWR* 34:478, 1985.

28. Patriarca PA, Weber JA, Parker RA, Hall WN et al: Efficacy of influenza vaccine in nursing homes. *JAMA* 253:1136, 1985.

29. Gross PA, Quinnan GV, Rodstein M, LaMontagne JR et al: Association of influenza immunization with reduction in mortality in an elderly population. *Arch Intern Med* 148:562, 1988.

30. Centers for Disease Control: Prevention and control of influenza. *Ann Intern Med* 107:521, 1987.

31. Verghese A, Berk SL: Bacterial pneumonia in the elderly. *Medicine* 62:271, 1983.

32. Crossley KB, Irvine P, Kaszar DJ et al: Infection control precautions in Minnesota nursing homes. *JAMA* 254:2918, 1985.

33. Broome CV: Efficacy of pneumococcal polysaccharide vaccines. *Rev Infect Dis* 3:582, 1981.

34. Simberkoff MS, Cross AP, Al-Ibrahim M et al: Efficacy of pneumococcal vaccine in high-risk patients: Results of a Veterans Administration Cooperative Study. *N Engl J Med* 315:1318, 1986.

Chapter 51

TUBERCULOSIS: A SPECIAL PROBLEM IN THE ELDERLY

William W. Stead and Asim K. Dutt

The term *tuberculosis* means disease caused by *Mycobacterium tuberculosis*, although other mycobacteria can produce similar pathology in humans. The most common tuberculosis presentation is chronic fibrotic or cavitary disease of the lung, although extrapulmonary sites, such as kidney, bones, and the meninges may be either the principal or the secondary site. The clinical course is most commonly a slowly progressive process marked by cough, low-grade fever, weakness, and loss of weight. However, the presentation may be much more acute, actually simulating bacterial pneumonia. Both courses occur in the elderly and may afford a great diagnostic challenge. Tuberculosis always warrants consideration in respiratory infections in older persons because of its frequency, its tendency to appear in persons not previously suspected of the infection, and its communicability and because it is the most easily treated serious infectious disease that is likely to occur in this age group.

ETIOLOGY, TRANSMISSION, AND PATHOGENESIS

Mycobacterium tuberculosis is a nonmotile slender rod, 2 to 4 μm in length and 0.4 to 0.8 μm in width, which grows so slowly on culture medium that 3 to 6 weeks are required for sufficient growth to permit identification. The bacillus is aerobic, but the presence of CO_2 in low concentration accelerates its growth. Owing to the waxy nature of the cell wall, most stains will not adhere to it.

Transmission of tuberculosis occurs almost exclusively as droplet nuclei. Rarely, transmission may occur from direct contact with infectious materials, e.g., in pathologists and laboratory workers. Tiny droplets of respiratory secretions are aerosolized by coughing, singing, sneezing, and even talking. The droplets rapidly evaporate, leaving a droplet nucleus of 1 to 5 μm in size, which may contain several viable bacilli. When inhaled, droplet nuclei of such size may reach and be deposited on alveolar surfaces. There, in the tuberculin-negative (nonimmune) person, they begin to multiply unimpeded, reaching the regional lymph nodes and even the bloodstream before being limited by sensitized T lymphocytes and responsive macrophages. Bacilli deposited in small numbers in organs with low oxygen tension (liver, spleen, bone marrow), where multiplication is not favored, are generally eliminated readily. Those which are deposited in organs with a high oxygen tension, e.g., at the apices of the lungs, kidney, and brain, may multiply fairly rapidly. Within a few weeks, specific immunity mediated by T lymphocytes develops and is usually effective in controlling the infection at both the primary and metastatic sites. However, in 5 percent of newly infected persons, the replication of the bacilli continues and may produce clinical tuberculosis within 3 to 12 months. Even in those in whom the infection is controlled, the bacilli may recrudesce years or decades later and produce disease. The determining factors for the recrudescence of ancient infection are not well understood, but nutrition and competence of T-cell function are almost surely involved. Immunosuppression, human immunodeficiency virus (HIV) infection, poor nutrition, and complicating diseases—e.g., silicosis, lymphoreticular diseases, and prior gastrectomy—all appear to reduce resistance and make it more likely for a dormant tuberculosis infection to reactivate and produce disease.

The dominant cause of tuberculosis in elderly persons is recrudescence of an old infection acquired many years earlier.

Transmission is best checked by early detection and effective chemotherapy of each infectious person. Most infection in contacts is implanted before the discovery of the disease and initiation of chemotherapy in the index case. Cough and the number of bacilli in the sputum are both rapidly reduced by effective chemotherapy. The infectiousness of the patient drops rapidly within a week or two, even though the sputum may contain bacilli in the smear and/or culture. Patients are generally considered noninfectious after 10 to 14 days of effective chemotherapy.

Decontamination of the hospital environment of a patient with infectious tuberculosis is possible by ventilation with fresh air and beaming ultraviolet light across the top of the room. Tubercle bacilli in droplet nuclei which reach the upper air of the room are quickly killed, and this largely decontaminates the room. Thus, patients may safely be admitted to a general hospital when necessary. Many patients can even be treated as outpatients from the start.

CLINICAL TUBERCULOSIS

Although adult tuberculosis may develop in any organ, it usually develops in the apex of one or both lungs as a fibrocaseous infiltrate. Hematogenous dissemination may occur at any state of disease and produce miliary tuberculosis or meningitis. Infected persons generally develop a strong immunity. Reinfection with tubercle bacilli is a problem in the United States principally among elderly persons whose infection is so remote and completely healed that the immune memory of the T cells has been lost (see below).

PRIMARY INFECTION

Primary infection usually produces only a mild, febrile illness with malaise which subsides without therapy. However, in a previously tuberculin-negative resident of a nursing home, a primary infection may progress to produce chronic cavitary tuberculosis or even death (often ascribed to antibiotic-unresponsive pneumonia). The correct diagnosis of tuberculosis is rarely made unless the patient happens to be part of an outbreak of the disease, because determination of the cause of pneumonia in the elderly is not often pursued. There may be a tuberculous pleural effusion, but this is often mistakenly ascribed to congestive heart failure. The occurrence of progressive primary tuberculosis has been reported among very elderly tuberculin-negative persons after exposure in a nursing home.

CHRONIC PULMONARY TUBERCULOSIS

Tubercle bacilli which have lain dormant for years or decades in healed lesions may reactivate at any time. This is most common in the healed lesions at the apex of the lung, nodules often referred to as Simon foci. The characteristic of this form of disease is chronicity, cavitation, and production of a fibrous reaction (caseation). The bacilli are abundant in the caseum which facilitates airborne transmission by droplet nuclei. The earliest complaints are malaise, weight loss, fatigue, depression, and cough. Sputum is usually yellow or green and may be blood-streaked. Dull chest ache or pleuritic pain may be present. Shortness of breath may occur with pleural effusion or from extensive damage of the lung due to a rapidly developing tuberculous pneumonia. Adult respiratory distress syndrome may develop if miliary spread occurs. A manifestation that is seen more commonly among the elderly than others is tuberculous bronchitis which leads to segmental atelectasis, most commonly in the anterior segment of an upper lobe or in the lingula or middle lobe. It is often assumed to be caused by a tumor unless bronchoscopy is performed with appropriate biopsy and bronchial washing for acid-fast bacillus (AFB) cultures.

PLEURAL DISEASE

Involvement of the pleura can occur either soon after initial infection or as a result of later reactivation of infection. In either case, the cause is usually rupture of a small peripheral lesion. The effusion is evoked by the T-cell response to the antigen released into the pleural space.

DIAGNOSIS

Physical signs are of little help in detecting the presence of pulmonary tuberculosis in the great majority of cases. The chest roentgenogram is essential in recognizing the infiltrative process. Comparison of the present film with one taken 6 months to several years earlier further enhances its value, because minor changes in old fibrotic areas can be appreciated only by this means. Reticulonodular infiltration in the apicoposterior segments of one or both upper lobes, with or without cavitation, is the most common abnormality seen in reactivation tuberculosis. Bilateral distribution of a nodular infiltration in the upper zones of the lungs is highly suggestive of tuberculosis. Extensive consolidation of a lobe of the lung may occur due to tuberculous pneumonia. The lower lobe and opposite lung may become involved through bronchial spread. In progressive primary infection in elderly nursing home residents (see below) the infiltration most commonly involves the mid- and lower lung fields rather than the apical zones. Thus, almost any distribution of infiltration is compatible with tuberculosis. Miliary tuberculosis is more common in elderly persons today than in any other age group. It may be a result of either recent or recrudescent infection. In either case it is usually due to rupture of a caseous focus into the bloodstream.

Skin testing with tuberculin is important among the elderly in two circumstances: (1) whenever a diagnosis of tuberculosis is suspected and (2) where patients have had close contact with a recently discovered case of tuberculosis. The intermediate strength of tuberculin (5 tuberculin units) should be used and injected intradermally. If initially negative, the test should be repeated in 1 to 3 weeks to see if a positive reaction can be elicited by recall of T-cell response. Contrary to common dogma, most elderly persons are tuberculin-negative, despite the fact that the majority had at one time been infected and were tuberculin-positive. Studies have shown that in only about 10 percent of instances is the failure to react actually due to anergy. Thus, the tuberculin test does have significance in the elderly when tuberculosis is suspected. If negative, the patient should be tested for anergy with other common delayed-hypersensitivity allergins, e.g., mumps, *Candida*, *Trichophyton*, or streptokinase, because this would invalidate the negative tuberculin test. Conversion from negative tuberculin status (especially if negative on two occasions) to a positive reaction (especially if large, i.e., equal to or greater than 15 mm) signifies a new tuberculosis infection.

A stained smear of the sputum, body fluid, or tissue is helpful in identifying tubercle bacilli if present in large numbers. Early morning expectoration specimens, at least three in number, should be submitted for smear and culture. When sputum cannot be produced spontaneously, nebulized water or saline may be inhaled to stimulate the bronchial secretion. While low-power screening of a smear stained with auromine rhodomine stain is rapid, all suspicious slides must be confirmed by overstaining with the Ziehl-Neelsen or Kenyoun method. Aspiration of gastric content for bacteriological examination has largely been superseded by flexible fiberoptic bronchoscopy for bronchial washing, bronchial brushing, and transbronchial biopsy. This modality has greatly facilitated early diagnosis.

The final proof of tuberculosis can only be the isolation of *M. tuberculosis* from the body secretion, bronchial washing, or tissue. While cultural growth may be apparent within 3 or 4 weeks, cultures should be held for at least 6 to 8 weeks, because small inocula may take this long to produce visible growth. Laboratory methods can distinguish *M. tuberculosis* from other mycobacteria

which may occasionally cause disease. The production of niacin by *M. tuberculosis* permits identification of this species. There are times when all efforts at finding tubercle bacilli fail, probably because the number of bacilli is small (as in progressive primary infection) or because the right material was not examined. The association of a positive tuberculin skin test, compatible clinical picture, and roentgenographic abnormalities/or a granulomatous tissue reaction is sufficient evidence on which to start antituberculosis chemotherapy, pending culture results, even if the organisms cannot be found by microscopy.

In patients with pleural effusion, careful study of the pleural fluid and pleural biopsy is necessary. Tuberculous pleural fluid is an exudate. Cells are predominantly monocytic, and the pH moderately reduced, i.e., 7.00 to 7.25. Bacilli are seldom seen in smear examinations of the fluid, and even the culture is positive in only about 20 percent of those who appear to have tuberculous effusion. Pleural tissue obtained by needle biopsy should be examined histologically by special stain for the bacilli and also cultured in liquid medium. This enhances the chance of positive bacteriology over the culture of pleural effusion alone. A presumptive diagnosis of tuberculous pleurisy is made from the finding of granuloma in the tissue associated with a positive reaction to purified protein derivative (PPD), even though culture of the fluid fails to grow the bacilli. This is also applicable to pericardial disease.

In tuberculous meningitis, lumbar puncture usually reveals elevated pressure, clear fluid with increased protein content, reduced glucose, and increased white blood cell count with predominance of lymphocytes. The fluid must be cultured, but therapy should be initiated on the basis of a clinical diagnosis without waiting for the culture report, because delay may lead to brain damage.

For early diagnosis of disseminated tuberculosis, biopsies of bone marrow, liver, and lymph nodes are helpful in the search for caseating granuloma containing acid-fast bacilli. Biopsy is also necessary for the diagnosis of bone and joint disease. Early morning specimens of urine should be examined for smear and culture in the diagnosis of genitourinary tuberculosis. Similarly peritoneal fluid and tissue may aid in the diagnosis of abdominal tuberculosis.

In patients with lung infiltration, negative studies for fungal diseases, and positive PPD skin test in whom bacteriological confirmation cannot be obtained, it is acceptable to begin treatment for tuberculosis empirically to observe its effect on the illness. Such patients must be evaluated 10 to 12 weeks after initiation of therapy to establish whether therapy has been beneficial. If the disease has not shown response clinically and radiographically, aggressive diagnostic measures including an open-lung biopsy should be considered without delay.

TREATMENT

The treatment of tuberculosis is based on intensive and prolonged exposure of the organisms to bactericidal drugs. The overwhelming factor in recovery, irrespective of the site of involvement, is regular ingestion of adequate drugs for the necessary duration of therapy. Theoretically, the treatment should be effective in every case. However, in practice, occasional failures occur due to (1) failure of the physician to prescribe the proper drugs, (2) failure of the drugs, or (3) failure of the patient to take them properly. Commonly used antituberculosis drugs, their dosages, side effects, and mode of action are shown in Table 51-1.

Former Therapy

For over 25 years, the chemotherapy of tuberculosis has depended upon the use of one bactericidal drug, isoniazid (INH), and one bacteriostatic drug, either *para*-aminosalicylic acid (PAS) or ethambutol (EMB), with an initial supplement of streptomycin (SM) for 2 to 3 months in cavitary smear-positive cases. This treatment is highly effective, provided two drugs are taken for a prolonged period, i.e., 18 to 24 months. The long duration of treatment necessary to prevent relapse has been the major disadvantage of this regimen. The EMB or PAS contribute only for 8 to 12 months to prevent growth of INH-resistant mutants. Final elimination of organisms is completely dependent upon prolonged administration of INH.

Current Therapy

In recent years, with the addition of other potent bactericidal drugs—rifampin (RIF) and pyrazinamide (PZA)—it has become possible to treat even advanced cases of tuberculosis in half or one-third the time formerly required and with even greater effectiveness.

It is important to realize that bacilli are susceptible to the action of drugs *only* during replication. Tubercle bacilli exist in three different populations in the tuberculous host. The large population, about 1×10^7 to 1×10^9 in cavitary areas, is extracellular and replicates rapidly owing to presence of high oxygen tension and a neutral or slightly alkaline medium. It is thus most rapidly eliminated by bactericidal therapy. The second population is small, about 1×10^4 to 1×10^5, and is located in the acid environment inside macrophages. These organisms divide infrequently owing to low oxygen tension inside the cells. PZA is highly effective in this environment. The third population is also small and is located in the neutral medium in small, closed caseous nodules; it divides infrequently. Elimination of slowly dividing organ-

isms requires prolonged therapy. RIF is an effective drug for this.

Tubercle bacilli mutate naturally at known frequencies (about once in 100,000 divisions) to produce mutants resistant to any effective drug, even when no drug is present. Resistance of the population develops through elimination of sensitive bacilli and multiplication of the resistant mutants. Mutants resistant to each drug occur independently. Thus, mutants resistant to two bactericidal drugs occur extremely rarely.

The principle of modern chemotherapy is shown diagrammatically in Fig. 51-1. A combination of two bactericidal drugs, INH and RIF, is bactericidal for actively multiplying bacilli and also for organisms which are slowly or intermittently dividing in the lesion. Rapid eradication of actively multiplying large populations usually renders the sputum culture negative within 2 to 3 months. Prolonged use of the drugs is required to kill the slowly or intermittently multiplying organisms and to effectively sterilize the lesion, so that relapses will not occur after the chemotherapy is stopped.

Thus, in newly diagnosed patients, the suggested regimen is INH 300 mg and RIF 600 mg daily for 9 months. However, after an initial therapy for 1 month with daily INH and RIF, the drugs can be given twice weekly in doses of INH 900 mg and RIF 600 mg for another 8 months. The latter regimen has proved highly successful in over 95 percent of patients in Arkansas. The advantages of such a regimen are reduced cost of medications and the ease of administering supervised medication in noncompliant or forgetful patients. Some authorities consider adding EMB (25 mg/kg body weight) daily or SM 0.5 to 1 g daily 5 days a week for 2 or 3 months initially, with the combination of INH and RIF. However, these drugs have not been shown to add anything to the bactericidal activity except to ensure against the presence of primary INH resistance. In the United States, where the incidence of INH resistance is generally less than 2 percent, the addition of a third drug is not often necessary in elderly persons whose disease is caused by organisms acquired long before the advent of chemotherapy.

Recent observations indicate that if four bactericidal drugs, i.e., RIF, INH, PZA, and SM, are given daily for 2 months and then followed by INH and RIF for another 4 months, fully effective therapy can be completed in 6 months. In one of the studies, EMB (25 mg/kg body weight) replaced SM in the regimen with equal effectiveness to make the regimen an oral one throughout. Initial intensive treatment with four drugs also ensures against the presence of initial INH resistance. A current multicenter trial by the Centers for Disease Control indicates that INH, RIF, and PZA for 2 months initially, followed by INH and RIF for another 4 months may be

TABLE 51-1
Antituberculosis Drugs: Mode of Action, Dosage, and Side Effects

Drug	Dosage Daily	Dosage Twice Weekly	Side Effects	Mode of Action
Bactericidal Drugs:				
Streptomycin	10–15 mg/kg (usually 0.5–1.0 g) 5 days/week IM*	20–25 mg/kg (usually 1.0–1.5 g) IM	Vestibular, or auditory, nerve (cranial nerve VIII) damage, dizziness, vertigo ataxia, nephrotoxicity, allergic fever, rash	Active against rapidly multiplying bacilli in neutral or slightly alkaline extracellular medium
Capreomycin	Same as above	Same as above	Same as above	Same as above
Isoniazid (INH)	5 mg/kg (usually 300 mg) PO† or IM	15 mg/kg (usually 900 mg) PO	Peripheral neuritis, hepatotoxicity, allergic fever and rash, lupus erythematosus phenomenon	Acts strongly on rapidly dividing extracellular and acts weakly on slowly multiplying intracellular bacilli
Rifampin (RIF)	10 mg/kg (usually 450–600 mg) PO	10 mg/kg (usually 450–600 mg) PO	Hepatotoxicity, nausea and vomiting, allergic fever and rash, flulike syndrome, petechiae with thrombocytopenia or acute renal failure during intermittent therapy	Acts on both rapidly and slowly multiplying bacilli either extracellular or intracellular, particularly on slowly multiplying "persisters"
LM427 (Ansamycin)	150–300 mg PO		Same as above	Same as above
Pyrazinamide (PZA)	30–35 mg/kg (usually 2.5 g) PO	45–50 mg/kg (usually 3.0–3.5 mg) PO	Hyperuricemia, hepatotoxicity, allergic fever and rash	Active in acid pH medium on intracellular bacilli
Bacteriostatic Drugs: Ethambutol (EMB)	15–25 mg/kg (usually 800–1600 mg) PO	50 mg/kg PO	Optic neuritis, skin rash	Weekly active against both extracellular and intracellular bacilli to inhibit the development of resistant bacilli
Ethionamide	10–15 mg/kg (usually 500–750 mg) in divided doses PO		Same as above	Nausea, vomiting, anorexia, allergic fever and rash
Cycloserine	15–20 mg/kg (usually 0.75–1.0 g) in divided doses with 100 mg of pyridoxine PO		Same as above	Personality changes, psychosis, convulsions, rash
Para-aminosalicylic acid (PAS)	150 mg/kg (usually 12 g) in divided doses PO		Nausea, vomiting, diarrhea, hepatotoxicity, allergic rash and fever	Weak action on extracellular bacilli; inhibits development of drug-resistant organisms
Thiacetazone (not available in the United States)	150 mg daily PO		Allergic rash and fever, Stevens-Johnson syndrome, blood disorders, nausea and vomiting	Same as above
Clofazimine (antileprosy)	100 mg tid, PO		Pigmentation of skin, abdominal pain	Against *Mycobacterium intracellulare*

*IM = intramuscular.
†PO = oral.

FIGURE 51-1
Schematic of effects of drugs on tuberculosis in achieving a lasting cure of the disease and avoiding later relapse. Failure to eliminate large populations of organisms in the cavitary area results in drug resistance, while late relapse is due to regrowth of persisters which are still totally sensitive to the medications.

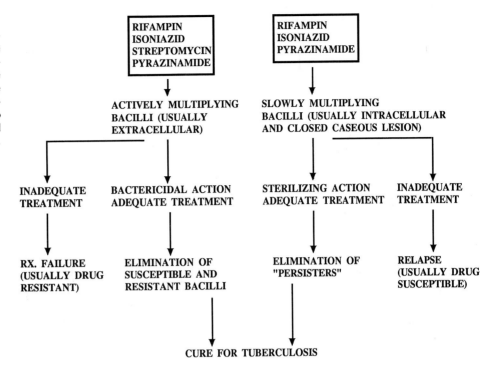

adequate for treatment. Streptomycin or EMB may not be necessary during the first 2 months. Morever, INH and RIF may be given twice weekly during the last 4 months of therapy. The benefit of more rapid therapy of elderly persons must be balanced against greater potential toxicity from additional drugs.

Bactericidal therapy with INH and RIF as well as initial therapy with four bactericidal drugs are well tolerated by most patients, even when elderly. The hepatic toxicity ranges from 3 to 4 percent, and even alcoholics tolerated the regimen well. Intermittent administration of a large dose of RIF may give rise to an occasional hypersensitivity reaction manifest by a flulike syndrome and thrombocytopenia with or without purpura. In the dose of 600 mg RIF twice weekly, however, the incidence of these allergic side effects is less than 1 percent. Other minor side effects, e.g., gastrointestinal intolerance, rash, and fever, are encountered in less than 5 percent of patients.

Treatment of Tuberculosis Due to INH-Resistant Bacilli

The use of only two drugs does involve a risk if the organisms happen to be resistant to one of the drugs. This would be equivalent to therapy with a single drug to which the organisms will soon become resistant. Drug resistance should be suspected in patients who are failures or who relapse from former chemotherapy, who have acquired disease in countries with high prevalence of drug-resistant organisms, who had received INH preventive treatment in the past, or who are suspected to have acquired the disease from a patient with drug-resistant organisms. In such persons, therapy should be started with SM, 1 g daily 5 days/week (reduce by 50 percent if over age 60 or if renal function is impaired), INH 300 mg, RIF 600 mg, and PZA 30 mg/kg body weight daily for 8 weeks until the susceptibility test results are known. If the organisms show sensitivity to INH and RIF, therapy may then be completed with INH and RIF daily or twice weekly for a total period of 6 months. If the organisms prove to be resistant to INH, therapy is completed with SM 2 days/week and RIF 600 mg and PZA 45 to 50 mg/kg body weight 2 days/week for a total of 9 months. INH may be included in the regimen for its possible action in the persistently sensitive bacilli in the smaller populations. EMB 25 mg/kg may replace SM in any of the above regimens. The regimen is well tolerated with little increase in side effects over the standard two-drug regimen.

Noncompliance in taking oral medications may run as high as 25 percent, particularly among alcoholics, among forgetful, often elderly patients, and among patients with psychiatric problems. In such patients supervised short-course chemotherapy is recommended. Twice-weekly administration of the drugs facilitates direct supervision of ingestion of the drugs. Streptomycin, RIF, PZA, INH, and EMB are the drugs which can be used in twice-per-week therapy, while other remaining antituberculosis drugs are used on a daily basis.

EXTRAPULMONARY TUBERCULOSIS

The treatment of extrapulmonary tuberculosis is the same as described above for pulmonary tuberculosis. Theoretically, the bacterial populations in extrapulmonary tuberculosis lesions are smaller than in cavitary pulmonary lesions. Thus, they do not require more prolonged chemotherapy or additional drugs. The surgical principle of draining an accumulation of pus must be observed, however.

OTHER CONSIDERATIONS

The treatment of tuberculosis coexisting with diabetes, malignancy, or corticosteroid therapy for a disease such as arthritis requires no additional drugs or prolongation of therapy beyond the usual 9 months. Treatment of tuberculosis in patients with concomitant (HIV) infection is the same, but it is prudent to prolong the duration of therapy for 4 months.

Surgical intervention is rarely necessary in any form of tuberculosis, provided proper chemotherapy is administered. Rarely, lobectomy may be necessary in patients with massive hemoptysis. Empyema and bronchopleural fistula usually need proper surgical intervention for drainage and obliteration of the space.

Corticosteroid therapy is seldom indicated in tuberculosis. However, hydrocortisone or equivalent steroids may produce dramatic improvement in patients who are very ill with high fever and/or hypoxemia. The steroids should be tapered off gradually over a period of 2 to 4 weeks to avoid the "rebound" phenomenon.

Surveillance of the patient for toxicity and bacteriological response is essential. Sputum specimens should be submitted at least twice a month initially until the cultures are negative. This is the best way to follow the effect of therapy. Thereafter, the examination should be carried out every 2 months during chemotherapy and for 6 months after completion of therapy. Surveillance should be maintained monthly for side effects of the drugs or noncompliance by patients throughout the chemotherapy period. The patient should be told to watch for symptoms of toxicity, e.g., nausea, vomiting, anorexia, and jaundice. If toxicity is suspected, drugs should be stopped immediately and blood drawn for serum glutamic oxaloacetic transaminase (SGOT) estimation. If the SGOT rises three to five times above the baseline, hepatic toxicity from INH is present. Unless the reaction is quite severe, the offending drug should be determined with sequential challenge with a half dose of each drug separately after the patient has recovered from the reaction and the SGOT has returned to normal. Often the reaction does not recur, and therapy may be completed as planned. If RIF is implicated, EMB may be substituted and treatment continued for 18 months. However, if INH cannot be resumed, SM and PZA or EMB and PZA should be substituted.

PROGNOSIS

With effective and adequate chemotherapy, 95 percent of patients who tolerate drugs are cured and may be expected to remain free from clinical tuberculosis. The risk of relapse in these patients is very small, and their follow-up need not be prolonged. Initial factors such as extent of disease, cavitation, age, sex, and surgical therapy are of no significance for the relapse of the disease.

SPECIAL PROBLEM OF TUBERCULOSIS IN THE ELDERLY

While it is true that a large proportion of elderly persons represent the survivors of heavy exposure and infection in early life, it is not true that most of them are tuberculin-positive today. It has always been accepted as conventional wisdom that "once tuberculin-positive, always so." From studies of the distribution of tuberculin reactions by age, it is known that in the 1930s and 1940s, when the present cohort of people in their eighties were in their thirties and forties, these people were about 80 to 90 percent tuberculin-positive. By 1961, when the people of this cohort were in their sixties, they were about 40 percent positive. When recently retested in Arkansas, they were found consistently to be about 20 to 30 percent positive. This is higher than the proportion of younger persons who are positive today but amazingly low by comparison with the same cohort in earlier years.

Over 50 percent of the new cases of tuberculosis in Arkansas occur in persons who are 65 years of age or older, with men predominating 2 to 1. This shift to old age for the tuberculosis cases is out of all proportion to the number of elderly persons in the population. This has led us to realize that elderly persons who still react to tuberculin are at a greater risk of developing tuberculosis than younger reactors are. Indeed, the rate is four times as great for persons age 65 or older than for persons of 40 to 60 years of age. When one relates the risk of developing tuberculosis per 100,000 *tuberculin reactors*, it approaches 1 percent annually which is about the same risk that tuberculin reactors have when there is radiographic evidence of healed scars of pulmonary tuberculosis. The practical implication of this fact is that tuberculosis must always be considered a possibility in any elderly person with a pulmonary infection and especially if the individual is known already to be tuberculin-positive.

Another problem derives from this same set of facts:

When elderly persons live in the close quarters of a nursing home, any reactor who develops active tuberculosis may endanger close associates who are nonreactors. It is in this way that an outbreak of tuberculosis may be set off in a nursing home, and most of the other cases are of the primary (or new infection) type. Persons who have lost their ability to react to tuberculin are again easy prey for the bacillus.

While the problem of anergy cannot be dismissed, it appears unlikely as the explanation of most of the reversion of reactors to negative even in old age. When newly infected, most older persons show a vigorous reaction to 5 TU of PPD (equal to or greater than 15 mm). Thus, it appears that their reactivity had simply waned with time after complete and natural eradication of the organisms from the earlier infection with a gradual loss of the memory of the T cells for the antigen.

PREVENTION OF TUBERCULOSIS IN THE ELDERLY

The guidelines for preventive therapy of tuberculin reactors published by the American Thoracic Society and the Centers for Disease Control recommend preventive therapy for reactors beyond the age of 35 only (1) if they are *converters*, close or household contacts of an active case; (2) if they are shown to have scars of postprimary tuberculosis; (3) if they are silicotic or diabetic; (4) if they have had a gastrectomy, or (5) if they are to be on prolonged corticosteroid therapy. Our experience in nursing homes has shown us that the indication of tuberculin conversion is paramount. Not to treat demonstrable tuberculin converters is to invite development of clinical tuberculosis in 7 to 11 percent of instances, resulting in additional cases and further spread of the infection. Therefore, it is essential to establish the tuberculin status of elderly patients in nursing homes or other long-term care facilities. To prevent spread of infection, we require that the tuberculin status of each new resident admitted to a nursing home in Arkansas be determined (with two tests if the first is negative) and a record kept of the result. Positive reactions are noted on the front of the chart as a reminder to both physician and nurse to submit sputum for smear and culture for tuberculosis with any lower respiratory infection. If an active case is discovered, it is a simple matter to retest the previous nonreactors to determine which residents should be given preventive therapy with INH. By this means spread of tuberculosis among the residents and to visitors and employees can be eliminated.

Monitoring for toxic side effects of INH is largely clinical (observing for anorexia, nausea, or vomiting). After that, it should be determined whether hepatitis is present by appropriate tests of hepatic cell dysfunction. About 90 percent of elderly persons tolerate INH without difficulty, which is enough to curtail an incipient epidemic. Those who cannot tolerate the medication can be monitored clinically and radiographically for evidence of incipient disease.

GENERAL READING

Comstock GW: Epidemiology of tuberculosis. *Am Rev Respir Dis* 125 (suppl): 8–15, 1982.

Dutt AK, Moers D, Stead WW: Short course chemotherapy for tuberculosis with mainly twice weekly isoniazid and rifampin: Community physicians seven years experience with mainly outpatients: *Am J Med* 77:233, 1984.

Dutt AK, Moers D, Stead WW: Nine month largely twice weekly INH and rifampin therapy for extrapulmonary tuberculosis: *Ann Intern Med* 104:7, 1986.

Fox W: Whither short course chemotherapy? *Br J Dis Chest* 75:331, 1981.

Grosset J: The sterilizing value of rifampicin and pyrazinamide in experimental short course chemotherapy. *Tubercle* 53:5, 1978.

Grosset J: Bacteriological basis of short course chemotherapy for tuberculosis. *Clin Chest Med* 1:231, 1980.

Houk UN et al: The epidemiology of tuberculosis infection in a close environment. *Arch Environ Health* 16:26, 1968.

Riley RL, O'Grady F: *Airborne Infection: Transmission and Control.* New York, Macmillan, 1961, p 26.

Stead WW: Pathogenesis of a first episode of chronic pulmonary tuberculosis in man: Recrudescence of residual of the primary infection or exotenous re-infection? *Am Rev Respir Dis* 95:729, 1967.

Stead WW, Lofgren, JP: Tuberculosis as an endemic and nosocomial infection in nursing homes. *N Engl J Med* 312:1483, 1985.

Stead WW, To T: The significance of the tuberculin skin test in elderly persons. *Ann Intern Med* 107:837, 1987.

Stead WW: Undetected tuberculosis in prison. Source of infection of community at large. *JAMA* 260:2544, 1978.

Stead WW: Tuberculosis among elderly persons: An outbreak in nursing home. *Ann Intern Med* 94:666, 1981.

Stead WW, Dutt AK: What's new in tuberculosis? *Am J Med* 71:1, 1981.

Stead WW, Dutt AK: Changing chemotherapy of tuberculosis, in Isselbacher KJ et al (eds): *Harrison's Principles of Internal Medicine Update III.* New York, McGraw-Hill, 1982.

Stead WW, Lofgren JP: Does the risk of tuberculosis increase in old age? *J Infect Dis,* 147:951, 1983.

Stead WW, To T, Harrison RW, Abraham JH: Benefit-risk consideration in preventive treatment for tuberculosis in elderly persons. *Ann Intern Med* 107:843, 1987.

Chapter 52

CHRONIC AIRWAYS OBSTRUCTION AND RESPIRATORY FAILURE

Peter B. Terry

The chronic obstructive pulmonary diseases include asthma, chronic bronchitis, and emphysema. Traditionally when speaking of chronic obstructive pulmonary disease (COPD) physicians mean chronic bronchitis and emphysema. This latter definition will be used throughout this chapter, and asthma will be discussed as a separate topic.

ASTHMA

The recognition of asthma depends upon the demonstration of increased responsiveness of the airways to a variety of stimuli and the reversibility of the airways obstruction either spontaneously or with therapy. Reversible airways obstruction may follow exposure to bronchial irritants, cholinergic stimuli, cold air, or exercise. Airway caliber is primarily determined by bronchiolar smooth muscle tone. Irritant receptors located between bronchial epithelial cells transmit efferent impulses to ganglia within the bronchial wall. Cholinergic postganglionic fibers innervate both bronchial smooth muscle and mucous glands. Contraction of the smooth muscle fibers may result from either stimulation of the irritant receptors or direct stimulation of smooth muscle by mast cell mediators released in response to IgE and antigen. A later, more slowly reversible phase of asthma results from an inflammatory response, including edema of airway walls and intraluminal secretions.

PREVALENCE AND ETIOLOGY

Inconsistent definitions of asthma and the lack of documentation of the natural history of this condition make it difficult to determine the incidence of asthma or to determine whether asthma contributes to chronic airways obstruction. Studies have shown a familial predisposition to asthma; however, this feature alone is not sufficiently predictive to be of clinical value. Certain extrinsic factors may initiate or provoke a predisposed individual into an attack of asthma, although the mechanism of this association is not often clear. Extrinsic agents which frequently provoke attacks of asthma are listed in Table 52-1.

The age of onset of asthma seems to manifest a bimodal and possibly a trimodal distribution.[1] A very high incidence of asthma is found during childhood, followed by a marked decline in new cases through adolescence. In a second peak during young adulthood, most newly diagnosed cases of asthma occur in atopic individuals (especially women) who demonstrate skin-test reactivity. Only 3 percent and 1 percent of asthmatics have their onset of disease after the ages of 60 and 70, respectively.[2] After the age of 40, there seems to be no relation between skin-test reactivity and the development of asthma, and the sex ratio is equalized. Only a minority of older asthmatics can be demonstrated to be allergic (atopic) by the presence of increased IgE levels.[3]

CLINICAL PRESENTATION

Although wheezing and dyspnea are the usual presenting symptoms, the older asthma patient may instead

TABLE 52-1
Exogenous Stimuli Which Provoke Asthma

Viral Respiratory Infection

These are perhaps the most common provocation in established asthma. They are suspected as an asthma-initiating event in previously unaffected individuals.

Irritants

Both specific (antigenic, see below) and nonspecific irritants can produce bronchospasm. Common irritants include tobacco smoke, perfumes, and air pollutants.

Allergens

These are specific antigens which affect only susceptible patients. These specific irritants are of greatest importance for early-age-onset asthma and are of considerably less importance for adult-onset disease.

Aspirin and Other Prostaglandin Inhibitors

The role of aspirin in inhibiting the arachidonic acid pathway of prostaglandin synthesis also seems to be responsible for stimulation of bronchiolar smooth muscle.

Exercise and Cold Air

Lowered airway temperature produced by ambient climate or high airflow during exercise results in increased bronchiolar smooth muscle tone.

Emotional Factors

The mechanisms by which emotional factors lead to bronchospasm and the reasons for the wide variety of individual responsiveness to these factors are unknown.

present with paroxysmal nocturnal dyspnea or episodic cough. The physical examination may demonstrate wheezing and hyperinflation. The narrowed airway caliber leads to closure of the bronchioles which results in air trapping (hyperinflation) and breathing at higher lung volumes. Hyperinflation results in an increased work of respiration and also the use of extrathoracic muscles. The increasingly negative intrapleural pressures needed to inspire at high lung volumes also result in pulsus paradoxus. It is sometimes difficult to distinguish whether the hyperinflation observed in the elderly patient is due to an acute attack of asthma or whether it results instead from age-related changes and other chronic obstructive airways diseases.[4]

LABORATORY STUDIES

The diagnosis of asthma depends upon documentation of reversible airways obstruction. This may be accomplished by spirometry, peak flow meter, or flow-volume loop. Skin testing, eosinophilia of sputum and blood, and evidence of hyperinflation on the chest roentgenogram are all supportive findings, but they cannot establish the diagnosis of reversible obstruction. Occasionally chronic airways obstruction may masquerade as asthma. Measurement of the single breath diffusing capacity (surface area of gas transfer) may distinguish asthma (normal diffusing capacity) from emphysema (lowered diffusing capacity) in such cases.

TREATMENT

When specific extrinsic stimuli can be demonstrated to be responsible for asthma, the removal of the patient from exposure to those stimuli is the simplest, most effective therapy. However, the majority of older asthmatics do not have a specific extrinsic stimulus responsible for their disease, and the physician must then rely upon drug treatment. Theophylline preparations and β-agonists are the mainstays of drug treatment.[5]

Adrenergic agents may act by increasing intracellular levels of cyclic AMP. The ideal adrenergic agent dilates constricted airways without affecting the cardiovascular system. Beta$_2$- (β_2-) adrenergic receptors are found predominantly in the lungs. β_2-Sympathomimetic agents (terbutaline, metaproterenol, albuterol) have been developed and allow more liberal use of adrenergic agents in asthma. However, even these "specific" β-agonists may affect the cardiovascular system at higher doses. In the older asthmatic, β_2 agents are particularly efficacious when heart disease is present. Inhalation of these drugs is the preferred route of delivery because it is associated with acceptably low blood levels (minimal side effects) at a time of maximal bronchodilation. Conversely, the injudicious use of β-blockade drugs in the elderly with heart disease (propranolol) or with eye disease (timolol) may lead to exacerbations of asthma.

Theophylline, the most commonly used form of xanthine, may act by inhibiting phosphodiesterase, leading to a delay in the destruction of cyclic AMP. The greatest degree of bronchodilation is achieved with the least risk of side effects when the serum levels are between 10 and 20 μg/ml. There is wide variation in individual rates of breakdown and excretion, so dose schedules must be tailored to the patient by monitoring blood levels. Predetermined dosage schedules cannot be assumed to be maximally efficacious in the absence of blood level measurement. Reduced xanthine doses are needed in the elderly, in individuals with heart failure or liver disease, and in those taking cimetidine.[6] Cigarette smoking and phenytoin may accelerate xanthine destruction.

Steroids have a definite role in asthma management, although their mechanism is not well defined.[7] Steroids are generally added during the acute attack when initial therapy with xanthines and β-agonists fails to control symptoms. Early use of steroids is encouraged because the onset of steroid action may not occur for 6 hours or more. After control of the acute attack, however, the chronic use of systemic steroids is to be avoided in the elderly. Complications of chronic steroid use in this population include accelerated osteoporosis, cataract formation, diabetes, and congestive heart failure. Acceptable control of chronic asthma can be achieved by inhaled steroid preparations (e.g., beclomethasone), which perform effectively at much lower systemic blood levels and thus with a lower incidence of side effects than is seen with systemic steroids.

Atropine and other anticholinergic agents have been used in asthma management because of their ability to produce bronchodilation. Doses of the anticholinergics may need to be limited in the elderly owing to the side effects of tachycardia and urinary retention. Inhaled atropine derivatives which minimize these side effects are now available.

Aerosol bronchodilator medication may be delivered by a nebulizer. Effective delivery of bronchodilator has not been shown to be enhanced by the use of intermittent positive pressure ventilators. Furthermore, intermittent positive pressure breathing (IPPB) delivery systems have been incriminated in the development of pneumothoraces in asthma.

Expectorants and mucolytic agents have not been satisfactorily demonstrated to be of clear benefit in patients with asthma. Adequate hydration appears to be as important and effective in allowing asthmatic patients to rid themselves of secretion. Sedation should be avoided in asthmatics. The reassurance of a physician or nurse is often as helpful as tranquilizers or sedatives and avoids the medication side effects.

PROGNOSIS

Longitudinal studies have not been conducted in asthma in the elderly. However, available evidence suggests that spontaneous remissions occur in about 20 percent of cases, but death rates due to asthma appear to be higher in the elderly than in the younger asthmatic.

CHRONIC OBSTRUCTIVE PULMONARY DISEASE

By convention, chronic bronchitis is defined by a history of chronic cough with sputum production on most days of the week for 3 months of the year for 2 consecutive years. Thus it is a historical diagnosis. Emphysema is defined by the demonstration of abnormal dilation and destruction of lung acinar units distal to the terminal bronchioles. Because the lung is seldom biopsied in clinical practice, however, emphysema is defined clinically by a constellation of historical and physical findings, radiographs, and pulmonary function tests. While considered separate diseases, emphysema and bronchitis often coexist in the same patient because cigarette smoking is the most common cause of both diseases.

COPD is a slowly progressive disabling condition which limits the quantity and quality of life. Because the deleterious effects of cigarette smoking on the respiratory system require prolonged exposure, COPD usually presents in late middle age or old age.

EPIDEMIOLOGY

COPD affects approximately 10 percent of the population in the United States. Respiratory failure due principally to complication of COPD is the fifth leading cause of death in this country and continues to increase in fatality rate (in contrast to the decreasing trend in heart disease). Males continue to be affected more than females, but the discrepancy between the sexes is narrowing because of the increased incidence of cigarette smoking among women over the past 40 years.

Chronic bronchitis, more prevalent and less disabling than emphysema, nevertheless has a significant economic impact in this country and other industrialized countries because of the number of workdays lost due to exacerbations caused by infections. In contrast, emphysema, which is much less prevalent, is a leading cause of chronic disability and a major contributor to the health care costs in this country.

ETIOLOGY

Epidemiologic studies have clearly shown the overwhelming importance of cigarette smoking in the development of COPD.[8] In chronic bronchitis the frequency of chronic cough and sputum production seems to relate to current exposure to airway irritants. In population studies, up to 90 percent of heavy smokers report a chronic productive cough. The frequency of this symptom increases with increasing amounts smoked and disappears in most with smoking cessation. However, not all patients with chronic bronchitis develop chronic airways obstruction. It is clear that almost all of those who develop irreversible airways obstruction have been cigarette smokers. In particular, susceptible heavy cigarette smokers have been observed to have a more rapid decline in their forced expired volume in the first second of their spirogram than light smokers and nonsmokers. In nonsmokers, an average loss of 25 to 30 cc per year of the forced expired volume in the first second is observed. In cigarette smokers, the loss may be 2 to 3 times this amount per year. Most importantly, discontinuation of smoking has been associated with return to a rate of decline in pulmonary function that is similar to the rate for nonsmokers.

Emphysematous changes have been found in about one-half of the autopsies done in patients over the age of 60; however, symptomatic emphysema occurs in only a small fraction of the population. Cigarette smoking is the major cause of emphysema, with age, sex, genetics, pollution, socioeconomic status, infections, and occupational exposure being cofactors.

PATHOPHYSIOLOGY AND CLINICAL CORRELATES

Uncomplicated chronic bronchitis may be manifest only by chronic productive cough, with little evidence of airways obstruction and few findings (perhaps rhonchi) on clinical examination. Transient exacerbations of a productive cough often follow acute respiratory infections and episodes of air pollution. Nevertheless, longitudinal studies have failed to demonstrate that chronic productive cough alone is a risk factor for either obstructive lung disease or mortality.

When airways obstruction is present in chronic bronchitis, the symptoms found include wheezing, dyspnea, and recurrent acute chest illnesses. Longitudinal follow-up of individuals with dyspnea has shown an increased mortality among this group; however, much of this mortality is cardiovascular, suggesting that at least some of the reported dyspnea may be due to heart disease.

In chronic bronchitis, airway narrowing due to hypertrophy of smooth muscle and hyperplasia of mucus-producing glands may lead to an uneven distribution of ventilation within the lungs. This imbalance of ventilation and perfusion may be aggravated by airway closure due to disease and the effect of aging on elastic recoil of the lung when the patient lays supine. Hypoventilation associated with airway narrowing may be further aggravated by the blunting of the hypoxic and hypercarbic responses observed with aging. In such cases, wheezing, severe hypoxemia, secondary polycythemia, and cor pulmonale may result. These symptoms and signs may be confused with heart failure in the elderly patient.

The earliest pathological changes of emphysema are suggested by studies in young smokers showing an inflammatory reaction surrounding the terminal bronchioles. This is associated with an asymptomatic state, but careful testing shows subtle abnormalities of small airways function. With time and the cumulative effects of inhalation of irritants, the alveolar septa distal to these terminal bronchioles are destroyed, leading to a loss of elastic support and premature closure of small airways. The loss of recoil leads to hyperinflation (barrel chest) of the chest with a decreasing mechanical advantage of the muscles of respiration. This results in an inappropriate

work load for a given level of ventilation, which may partially explain the dyspnea in these patients. Because this destruction proceeds slowly but relentlessly, the onset of symptoms is gradual, with most patients presenting between the ages of 55 and 65 when their forced expired volume in the first second reaches approximately 1.5 liters.

Patients presenting with an underlying history of slowly progressive dyspnea interspersed with periods of moderate or severe dyspnea often have a bronchospastic component to their disease. As the disease progresses, many patients become malnourished as evidenced by their asthenic habitus and abnormal parameters of muscle mass and fat deposition. This malnourishment is attributed to inadequate caloric intake coupled with an increased work of breathing.

DIAGNOSIS

Since the diagnosis of chronic bronchitis is a historical one, no further testing is necessary to confirm its presence. To determine whether obstructive bronchitis is present, spirometry is performed; if the FEV_1 is less than 70 percent of the forced vital capacity, then significant obstruction is considered to be present. Hypoxemia and cor pulmonale may be suspected from a history of cyanosis, edema, and progressive dyspnea; these diagnoses are confirmed by arterial blood gases, by echocardiography of the right heart, and, less commonly, by electrocardiogram.

The diagnosis of emphysema is suspected when a cigarette smoker describes slowly progressive dyspnea and the physical examination reveals an increased anteroposterior (AP) diameter of the chest coupled with distant breath sounds and flattened and relatively immobile diaphragms. The diagnosis of emphysema is confirmed when a patient presents with the symptoms and signs noted above coupled with the specific pulmonary function changes noted below.

LABORATORY STUDIES

Significant emphysema may be present without radiographic evidence of disease, indicating that the x-ray criteria of hyperinflation are relatively insensitive. In these cases, pulmonary function tests are most helpful in confirming the clinical suspicion. Airways obstruction is always present on spirometry. The increased lung compliance in emphysema is reflected in an increase in the functional residual capacity (FRC) and residual volume (RV). Both FRC and RV may be increased with aging but generally not to the extent found with emphysema. The loss of surface area of gas transfer in emphysema is reflected in the diffusing capacity, which is always reduced. Arterial blood gases may or may not show hypoxemia and/or hypercarbia. An elevated hematocrit and elevated serum bicarbonate reflect the chronicity of the hypoxemia and hypercarbia, respectively.

TREATMENT

Strategies are directed toward relieving the sensation of dyspnea, preventing further destruction of lung tissue, and preventing secondary cardiovascular changes. The initial evaluation usually determines the long-term strategy. A patient presenting with dyspnea, modest obstruction with a reversible component, hypoxemia, and evidence of persistent exposure to inhale irritants may benefit greatly from an aggressive interventional program. Alternatively, it is important to recognize the elderly patient with minimal exercise capacity, unresponsive airways, and end-stage parenchymal destruction. In these patients the focus of treatment should be on psychological support and on changing the patient's environment to allow him or her to carry out daily functions with a minimum of effort.

It is especially important in the elderly COPD patient to give written treatment instructions because instructions concerning medications, exercises, and preventive measures can be lengthy, and hypoxemia may promote loss of short-term memory.

The treatment for chronic bronchitis and emphysema due to inhaled substances (cigarettes, industrial inhalants) is to remove the person from contact with the agent(s). This may rid the person of the symptoms of cough and sputum production; however, dyspnea, airways obstruction, and hypoxemia may persist.

The component of dyspnea is due to the increased work of breathing, coupled with respiratory muscle fatigue and hypoxemia in some instances. The work of breathing is principally due to increased airways resistance, inefficient gas exchange, and mechanically disadvantaged respiratory muscles. Reversible airways obstruction (15 percent or greater increase in FEV_1 postbronchodilator) may be treated with sympathomimetics, theophylline preparations, and/or steroids.

Aerosolized sympathomimetic bronchodilators are commonly used in the elderly patient because of their minimal cardiovascular side effects. Unfortunately, many elderly patients may not be able to coordinate inhalation with use of the hand-held nebulizers. This problem can be circumvented either by using a "spacer" attached to the nebulizer or by using an electrically powered compressor nebulizer. Treatment should be initiated with one of the most β_2-selective agents (metaproterenol, terbutaline, albuterol) in lowest recommended daily dosage (1 or 2 puffs four times per day). Diseases of the aged which are adversely affected by sympathomimetics include tremors, diabetes, glaucoma, and headaches.[9]

While the effects of atropine in asthma have been known for years, it has only recently been appreciated that atropine-like compounds may be helpful in COPD patients. Recent studies have shown a significant increase in airflow rates after use of inhaled atropine analogues. It is thought that these substances may act on large airways. Care must be taken in their use in the elderly because excessive doses may lead to urinary retention or may have an adverse effect in some patients with glaucoma.

Theophylline preparations, more popular in this country in recent years, are increasingly being recognized to have variable rates of metabolism, especially in the elderly. Furthermore, the commonly accepted therapeutic window of 5 to 20 mg/ml is more frequently recognized to be associated with significant side effects in select patients. Diseases and drugs associated with aging, including hepatic congestion, obesity, heart failure, hypoxemia, fever, erythromycin, and cimetidine, can delay the metabolism of theophylline. As a general rule, lower doses of theophylline are recommended for each decade after the age of 50.

Steroids have played an increasing role in the management of elderly COPD patients with reversible airways obstruction already on a combination of sympathomimetics and theophylline preparations. They appear to shorten the length of in-hospital stay in COPD patients with acute respiratory failure and may further reduce airways obstruction in otherwise stable patients. A dosage of 0.5 mg per kg of methylprednisolone every 6 hours for 3 days has been shown to be effective in the treatment of respiratory failure in COPD patients. Unfortunately, long-term steroid therapy in the elderly may accentuate existing problems, including osteoporosis, cataracts, glaucoma, psychosis, diabetes, and hypertension. Calcium supplementation (1 to 2 g/day) and vitamin D (50,000 units) once weekly, coupled with physical exercise, may retard the bone changes frequently seen in the elderly. Topical steroids are less likely to be associated with side effects but also may be less effective in the elderly.

Hypoxemia, if present, should be treated with the lowest concentration of oxygen which raises the arterial oxygen to approximately 65 mmHg. In highly selected patients with high oxygen requirements, transtracheal oxygen may be of more benefit than traditional nasal prongs. Exercise in the form of walking should be encouraged. Direct training of the diaphragm using diaphragmatic exercises may be effective in reducing the sensation of dyspnea.

Agents purported to loosen secretions and promote mucus clearance have not been proved to be more efficacious than adequate hydration. In fact, hot drinks and chicken soup may be more effective in the expectoration of secretions.

Emphysema patients lose lung function at an accelerated rate compared with persons without emphysema, and therefore every effort should be made to minimize inhaled irritants and infectious agents which accelerate destruction. Influenza and antipneumococcal vaccination should be considered in the fall. Patients should be reminded to avoid large crowds in poorly ventilated areas during the flu season. Amantadine taken prophylactically appears to prevent or modify influenza A[10] infections. Symptoms of respiratory infections should be aggressively evaluated and treated. Prolonged hypoxemia leading to polycythemia, pulmonary hypertension, and right-ventricular decompensation is now effectively treated with supplemental oxygen and the judicious use of diuretics. Therapies of equivocal or no benefit include intermittent positive pressure ventilation and the use of digitalis preparation in patients with exclusive right-ventricular failure. Narcoleptics and tranquilizers should be avoided, especially in patients who demonstrate CO_2 retention.

RESPIRATORY FAILURE

Respiratory failure represents the fifth leading cause of death in the United States. Over 70 percent of deaths in patients with pneumonia are attributed to respiratory failure. Thus, if one considers the total number of deaths attributed to respiratory causes including the influenza-pneumonia complex, the number approaches 100,000 per year, which is similar to that produced by accidents, the fourth leading cause of death in the United States. COPD with death from respiratory failure is the only chronic disease which continues to show a yearly increase in mortality.[11]

Acute respiratory failure (ARF) is usually defined as a condition in which the respiratory apparatus is unable to supply adequate oxygen (O_2) to or eliminate sufficient carbon dioxide (CO_2) from vital organs and tissues. It implies an unstable physiological state in which deterioration in gas exchange is more likely than improvement. Respiratory failure can occur at any age, but it is more prevalent in the elderly because COPD usually does not become symptomatic until after age 55 and because pneumonia, sepsis, or pulmonary edema are more likely to overload the aged respiratory system, owing to malnutrition, muscle fatigue, or change in level of consciousness.

When dealing with acute respiratory failure, the effect of aging on the lung is usually clinically insignificant. However, many other supporting organs may have reduced reserve, and extreme care must be employed in administering fluids, using drugs, and anticipating nonrespiratory organ failure. It is important to emphasize that the statistical survival picture in the critical care unit

does not take into account the duration or quality of life thereafter. Although patients with COPD often have repeat episodes of respiratory failure, some individuals may retain a sufficiently satisfactory quality of life, even after six episodes, to live "happily" at home.

Respiratory failure may be divided into two main categories—that which is manifest by both hypercapnea and hypoxemia and that which is manifest predominantly (or entirely) by hypoxemia.

HYPERCAPNIC RESPIRATORY FAILURE

Acute hypercapnic respiratory failure is not a "disease" but rather a physiological derangement that results from one or more pathological events (see Table 52-2). This form of ARF may occur either in previously healthy individuals without specific lung injury or in persons with underlying pulmonary disease. When severe underlying chronic pulmonary disease is present, a minor precipitating event may produce severe acute respiratory decompensation. Knowledge of the pathogenesis and physiological alterations responsible for ARF is critical in determining a specific diagnosis and establishing appropriate therapy.

Hypercapnic respiratory failure implies inadequate ventilation of the lungs, with or without intrinsic lung disease. An example of respiratory failure due to failure of the respiratory apparatus without intrinsic lung dis-

TABLE 52-2
Common Causes of Hypercapnic Respiratory Failure

1. Factors affecting respiratory control
   a. Primary intracranial disease (tumor, vascular)
   b. Trauma and raised intracranial pressure
   c. Drugs, poisons, and toxins
   d. Central hypoventilation
   e. Excess oxygen administration in hypercapnic patient
2. Neurological and neuromuscular diseases
   a. Spinal cord lesions (trauma, degenerative, vascular)
   b. Acute polyneuritis
   c. Myasthenia gravis
   d. Polymyositis
3. Metabolic derangements
   a. Severe acidosis
   b. Severe alkalosis
   c. Hypokalemia
   d. Hypophosphatemia
   e. Hypomagnesemia
4. Lungs and airway disease
   a. Upper-airway disease (fixed, variable, or sleep-dependent)
   b. Lower-airway disease (COPD, asthma)
5. Musculoskeletal abnormalities
   a. Kyphoscoliosis
   b. Ankylosing spondylitis (rare)
6. Obesity-hypoventilation syndrome

ease is myasthenia gravis. An example of respiratory failure due to combined lung disease and respiratory muscle failure is found in the patient with bronchitis and emphysema who develops bronchopneumonia. Hypoxemia in varying degrees always accompanies hypercapnic respiratory failure, but it is minimized when there is no intrinsic lung disease or the patient is breathing supplemental oxygen. In a previously healthy individual, a Pa_{CO_2} greater than 45 mmHg constitutes ARF. Pa_{CO_2} values greater than 55 mmHg usually indicate ARF in patients with known COPD and previously normal CO_2 levels. As the CO_2 accumulates, the fractional concentration of O_2 in the alveolus decreases and hypoxemia results. Depending on the underlying physiological condition of the lungs, hypoxemia may be substantially greater than that explained on the basis of CO_2 accumulation alone. In ARF associated with COPD, severe hypoxemia due to perfusion of poorly ventilated lung areas is also present.

Hypercapnea may result from increased CO_2 production, decreased alveolar ventilation, or both. An increase in CO_2 production rarely results in increased Pa_{CO_2} except with malignant hyperthermia or grand mal seizures. Decreased alveolar ventilation is the major cause of an elevated Pa_{CO_2}. Alveolar ventilation may be reduced by an absolute decrease in minute ventilation which usually results from alterations in the control mechanism of respiration or inadequate force to drive the respiratory apparatus (Table 52-2). When an imbalance in ventilation and perfusion causes a large percentage of dead space or wasted ventilation, as in COPD, adequate removal of CO_2 may be insufficient despite increased minute ventilation.

Hypoxemia may result from pure alveolar hypoventilation, with the severity of the hypoxemia determined by the degree of hypoventilation, as defined by the alveolar air equation

$$PA_{O_2} = FI_{O_2} - \frac{Pa_{CO_2}}{0.8}$$

or, at sea level,

$$PA_{O_2} = 150 - (Pa_{CO_2} \times 1.2)$$

A relatively normal alveolar-arterial O_2 gradient (<15 mmHg) is often a clue to reduced minute ventilation as the cause of hypercapnic respiratory failure.

Hypoxemia also results from perfusion of poorly ventilated lung units. This always occurs with lower airway disease, such as asthma and COPD, and may be present with the obesity-hypoventilation syndrome and kyphoscoliotic cardiopulmonary disease. Hypoxemia secondary to ventilation-perfusion abnormalities is variable in other causes of combined ARF and depends on the degree of underlying pulmonary disease.

The presentation of hypercapnic respiratory failure can be divided into those conditions in which the hypercapnea is due to decreased minute ventilation (Table 52-2, categories 1 to 3 and 4a) and those conditions in which the respiratory failure results from severe ventilation-perfusion mismatch (Table 52-2, category 4b). Conditions in categories 5 and 6 in Table 52-2 are usually due to varying degrees of decreased minute ventilation and increased wasted ventilation. Their presentation is similar to that of the conditions in category 4b. More than one-half of the clinical cases of hypercapnic-hypoxic respiratory failure come from category 4b. The frequency of presentation of the other multiple causes of respiratory failure depends on a particular hospital's referral base.

HYPERCAPNIC RESPIRATORY FAILURE SECONDARY TO DECREASED MINUTE VENTILATION

The presentation of patients with hypercapnic failure secondary to decreased minute ventilation varies from a sudden onset, as seen in high cervical cord trauma or tetanus, to the slower time course seen in polyneuritis or myasthenia gravis. An even slower onset is observed in hypothyroidism and muscular dystrophy. In a number of chronic neuromuscular conditions seen in the elderly, a minor acute respiratory insult may precipitate sudden respiratory failure by worsening the underlying neuromuscular condition (myasthenia gravis) or abruptly reducing pulmonary function (aspiration pneumonia in parkinsonism).

The degree of respiratory failure usually correlates with the loss of vital capacity in neuromuscular and metabolic conditions. The diagnosis can be determined only by evaluation of arterial blood gases. Patients with a vital capacity around 1 liter and arterial Pa_{CO_2} approaching 45 mmHg should be closely monitored in a respiratory intensive care unit. Early intubation is indicated when a Pa_{CO_2} of greater than 45 mmHg is observed in a patient with reversible disease who is demonstrating obvious respiratory distress.

HYPERCAPNIC RESPIRATORY FAILURE SECONDARY TO MISMATCH OF VENTILATION AND PERFUSION

Asthma and COPD are the major causes of respiratory failure due to mismatch of ventilation and perfusion coupled with respiratory muscle fatigue.[12] The diagnosis, detection of potentially severe attacks, and treatment of asthma have been previously discussed. The majority of patients with ARF secondary to COPD have a long history of chronic cough, sputum production, prolonged heavy cigarette consumption, wheezing, and shortness of breath. Many of these patients have been diagnosed as having "asthma,"emphysema, or chronic bronchitis or have experienced multiple episodes of respiratory infection. A significant percentage have experienced episodes of respiratory failure.

The onset of respiratory failure in a patient with COPD is characterized by gradually progressive dyspnea often associated with an increase or change in chronic cough or sputum. A recent minor respiratory infection often precedes the increasing dyspnea or cough. Dyspnea eventually becomes severe, prompting medical attention. Occasionally, patients present with obtundation, twitching, asterixis, cyanosis, and coma. Sudden onset of dyspnea or chest pain occurs in the minority of patients with ARF due to COPD.

Physical examination usually reveals an anxious individual with severe respiratory distress. Breathing is often labored with some increase in respiratory rate. Accessory muscles of respiration are active. However, in the presence of severe respiratory failure or following the use of respiratory-depressant drugs (often given for agitation or insomnia), respiratory rate and depth may not appear abnormal, and the patient's level of consciousness may be grossly altered. This particular clinical presentation is characteristic of patients who have received high oxygen concentrations en route to the hospital.

Examination of the chest in patients with ARF secondary to COPD usually reveals hyperresonance, decreased breath sounds, and prolonged expiration. Wheezing or rales may or may not be present. Tachycardia is frequent, and a variety of cardiac arrhythmias, usually supraventricular, is common. The blood pressure may be moderately elevated. Signs of pulmonary hypertension or right-ventricular failure are often present.[13] Cyanosis may be obvious, but its clinical absence does not rule out significant hypoxemia. Papilledema is most often observed in comatose patients but may occasionally be the only impressive finding in respiratory failure.

Abnormalities in arterial blood gases are the only definitive means of diagnosing hypercapnic respiratory failure. In the presence of an acute symptomatic respiratory, circulatory, or central nervous system alterations, a presumptive diagnosis of ARF should be made if the Pa_{CO_2} is greater than 55 mmHg and the pH is markedly low. There is little margin for error under these circumstances, and it is better to follow therapeutic maneuvers with frequent measurements of blood gases.

A chest film may reveal the presence of hyperinflation, obvious chronic underlying lung disease, pneumothorax, or acute pulmonary infiltrates, but in a number of patients with severe respiratory failure, the chest roentgenogram is not helpful. The electrocardiogram (ECG) may show evidence of cor pulmonale. The hematocrit may be elevated in patients with chronic hypoxemia and hypercarbia. There may be concomitant peptic ulcer disease, which may be associated with low-grade intestinal blood loss. Leukocytosis suggests infection, but leukoerythroblastic responses may follow the stress of severe hypoxemia.

MANAGEMENT OF HYPERCAPNIC RESPIRATORY FAILURE SECONDARY TO CHRONIC OBSTRUCTIVE LUNG DISEASE

Few rules are universally applicable to the treatment of ARF, even when the discussion is limited to only one of the responsible diseases. However, this chapter will offer some guidelines to management, stressing principles of patient care which apply to the majority of affected older individuals. These principles include (1) application of immediate lifesaving measures, (2) determination of the precipitating factors, (3) treatment of the underlying condition, and (4) repeat assessment of the patient's condition.

Appropriate lifesaving measures for ARF revolve around immediately correcting hypoxemia, determining the need for emergency intubation or assisted ventilation, and providing adequate circulatory support. Frequent monitoring is required of arterial blood gases, systemic arterial pressure, spirometry, urinary output, and the concentration of hemoglobin and electrolytes.

Most patients who develop ARF have a reversible precipitating factor that has resulted in decreased alveolar ventilation. On many occasions the precipitating event is increased bronchospasm associated with a change in weather, minor infection, or failure to take medication. Infection may also increase bronchial secretions, reduce functional pulmonary parenchyma, or increase CO_2 production, overwhelming an already limited respiratory system. Occasionally, inadvertent sedative administration or more obvious factors, such as pneumothorax, cardiac arrhythmias, left-ventricular failure, or dehydration, may have developed.

Oxygen

If, as in the majority of cases, the patient is alert or only minimally confused and has a stable cardiovascular status, low-flow controlled O_2 should be instituted ($F_{I_{O_2}}$ = 0.24 via a Venturi mask).[14] Adequate oxygenation is nearly always achieved without difficulty; however, this may take serial increases in respiratory $F_{I_{O_2}}$ to as high as 0.5. The patient should be transferred to an intensive care unit or other appropriate setting for monitoring immediately after supplemental O_2 is begun.

Bronchodilators

Specific measures to improve airway resistance usually include nebulized β_2-sympathomimetics and intravenously administered aminophylline. An increased incidence of tachycardia and other supraventricular and ventricular arrhythmias, including complex types, has been reported in older patients receiving combination therapy. Therapy is best monitored in cooperative patients by serial spirograms and serum theophylline levels. Failure to improve airflow limitation makes questionable the continued use of potentially dangerous bronchodilators. However, many experts administer low dosages of bronchodilators even without objective airway response in the hope that unmeasurable improvements in small airways may occur or that mucociliary transport, right-ventricular function, respiratory drive, or diaphragmatic fatigue will be improved.[15] The older and more critically ill patient should receive the lowest suggested doses of bronchodilators unless some evidence of improvement is associated with these drugs. Nebulization of β_2-selective agonists results in the fewest cardiac or neuromuscular side effects. Older patients with baseline senile tremor can be expected to have the most obvious tremor during aggressive therapy, but this may not be related to other systemic toxicity. Maintenance theophylline by continuous intravenous infusion must be substantially reduced in patients over 50 years of age or with congestive heart failure, cor pulmonale, and liver failure. Concomitant use of cimetidine and erythromycin can elevate the serum levels by 50 percent and 25 percent, respectively. It is not uncommon for the arterial O_2 tension to fall slightly during the administration of nebulized or intravenous bronchodilators.

Tracheobronchial Secretions

Thick mucoid secretions may worsen airway obstruction. Adequate hydration is the best known expectorant since it enhances mucus flow. In the presence of purulent bronchial secretions, acute febrile bronchitis, or overt pneumonia, appropriate antibiotic therapy should be administered. *Streptococcus pneumoniae* and *Haemophilus influenzae* are the more common pathogens seen in this setting. Broad-spectrum coverage (ampicillin, tetracycline, or erythromycin) has been most successful in the absence of identification of a specific pathogen.

Pulmonary physical therapy with vibration, percussion, and postural drainage may aid expectoration in patients with copious secretions. Tracheal suctioning can help with removal of tenacious secretions but may result in increased hypoxia, reflux bronchospasm, and cardiac arrhythmias; the procedure should therefore be performed with great caution.

Fluids and Electrolytes

Adequate hydration is needed to maintain appropriate venous return and cardiac output. Increased filling of the right ventricle is required in the presence of pulmonary hypertension. Therefore, an increased peripheral blood volume is needed to maintain adequate venous return. Cardiac glycosides are of questionable value in ARF.

In patients with cor pulmonale, diuretics are often associated with an increased incidence of arrhythmias. The use of diuretics is indicated in patients with severe hepatic and pulmonary congestion and marked peripheral edema. If diuretics are used, supplemental KCl should be given. Hypochloremic hypokalemic metabolic alkalosis often occurs following forced diuresis. A significant metabolic alkalosis may precipitate arrhythmias and decrease respiratory drive with further elevation in Pa_{CO_2}. Hypophosphatemia should be corrected as it may contribute to respiratory failure.

Assisted Ventilation

Most COPD patients hospitalized with hypercapnea and ARF improve following conservative therapy without the need for ventilatory support. Mortality has decreased significantly as more conservative therapy has replaced early use of artificial ventilation. If a patient continues to deteriorate despite controlled supplemental O_2, bronchodilators, antibiotics, and correction of fluid and electrolyte problems, assisted ventilation may be indicated. There is no specific level of Pa_{CO_2} which precludes continuation of conservative therapy. Progressive deterioration of mental status, marked acidemia, and respiratory distress are the major indicators for ventilatory support.

If inadequate alveolar ventilation is to be effectively increased by a mechanical ventilator, an endotracheal tube must be inserted. Intubation results in laryngeal and tracheal irritation and loss of effective cough, and it increases the risk of sinus and respiratory infections. It is also a source of discomfort in the conscious and alert patient. For these reasons, the decision to utilize artificial ventilation in a patient with acute respiratory failure should not be undertaken lightly.

Long-term intubation requires the use of nasotracheal or orotracheal tubes with a high-compliance cuff to lessen pressure damage to the tracheal mucosa. These cuffs should be inflated to less than 25 cm of H_2O pressure, or just enough to permit a small leak to occur during peak inflation. They do not have to be deflated periodically. With careful handling, endotracheal tubes may be kept in place for as long as 2 to 3 weeks. When artificial ventilation for a period longer than 3 weeks is required, a tracheostomy usually is performed. The most important indication for early tracheostomy is the presence of copious, tenacious secretions which cannot be adequately removed through the endotracheal tube. Tracheostomy is a surgical procedure which carries some risk of bleeding, pneumothorax, infection, and injury to the recurrent laryngeal nerve. In addition, there is an increased incidence of aspiration in the presence of a tracheostomy tube. Frequent complications of assisted ventilation include the induction of hypotension and post-hypercapnic metabolic alkalosis.

It is difficult to generalize about indications for extubation. If a patient is able to maintain for several hours a spontaneous unassisted minute ventilation similar to that produced by the ventilator and a stable Pa_{CO_2}, weaning is usually successful. Patients with the combination of an inspiratory force greater than -20 cmH_2O and forced vital capacity greater than 15 cc/kg can usually be weaned from the ventilator.

Recovery from respiratory failure in hypercapnic patients with decreased minute ventilation depends on the nature of the underlying condition and other supportive care. Some patients with neuromuscular disease may require months of, or even permanent, assisted ventilation. Electrical pacing of the phrenic nerve may be helpful in some central hypoventilation syndromes. A long-term commitment to respiratory support with an artificial ventilator should be avoided in patients with progressive neuromuscular disease who are not suffering from an acute reversible cause of respiratory failure.

The mortality from all causes of hypercapnic ARF approximates 20 percent; however, the cause of respiratory failure, age of patient, and previous state of health markedly alter survivorship. Mortality is less than 5 percent following a drug overdose, while in patients with acute exacerbations of COPD, mortality is reported to be over 30 percent. Survival in this latter group is markedly influenced by the previous functional status, activities of daily living prior to decompensation, body weight, and associated medical problems, and not by the level of arterial blood gases or age at the time of diagnosis.

HYPOXIC RESPIRATORY FAILURE

Hypoxic respiratory failure may be defined as any condition producing severe arterial hypoxemia (Pa_{O_2} less than 50 mmHg) which cannot be corrected by increasing the inspired O_2 concentration to 50 percent ($FI_{O_2} = 0.5$). Although both a Pa_{O_2} less than 50 mmHg and an FI_{O_2} greater than 50 percent are arbitrary levels, they represent critical physiological landmarks. At a Pa_{O_2} of 50 mmHg, hemoglobin is approximately 80 percent saturated, and further small reductions in Pa_{O_2} produce very significant reductions in arterial O_2 content. There is little reserve under this circumstance. Although healthy individuals may tolerate reductions of arterial O_2 tensions to this level, patients appear to be severely symptomatic. The symptoms, therefore, are related to both the hypoxemia and the lung disease causing the hypoxemia. An FI_{O_2} of 0.5 is probably the highest level which

can be safely given to a patient without concern for the development of oxygen toxicity. In addition, an FI_{O_2} of 0.5 usually corrects the hypoxemia associated with hypercapnic respiratory failure and the vast majority of conditions in which gas exchange is not the dominant clinical problem. If hypoxemia is corrected by an FI_{O_2} of 0.5, the management of the patient is markedly simplified.

Diseases which produce hypoxic respiratory failure are characterized by right-to-left intrapulmonary shunting of blood which is not corrected by high levels of supplemental O_2. Both lungs are usually extensively involved, although the pathology may be limited to large focal areas of disease, as seen in lobar pneumonia. Total ventilation is almost always increased, and alveolar ventilation is only rarely reduced. The differentiation between hypercapnic and hypoxic respiratory failure, although somewhat artificial, is convenient because it allows the grouping of conditions that often have a similar pathophysiological origin or require similar therapeutic interventions.

Acute hypoxic respiratory failure includes a variety of acute, nonspecific pulmonary injuries (Table 52-3)

TABLE 52-3
Disorders Associated with Adult Respiratory Distress Syndrome (ARDS)

Aspiration
    Gastric contents (acid or particulate)
    Fresh or salt water
Central nervous system
    Trauma
    Anoxia
    Seizures
Drug overdose
    Acetylsalicylic acid
    Heroin
    Methadone
    Hydrochlorothiazide
Hematological alterations
    Disseminated intravascular coagulation
    Massive blood transfusion
Infection
    Peritonitis
    Sepsis (gram-positive or gram-negative)
    Viral pneumonia
Inhalation of toxins
    Oxygen (high concentrations, greater than 60 percent)
    Smoke
    Corrosive chemicals (NO_2, HCl)
Metabolic disorders
    Pancreatitis
    Uremia
Shock (any etiology, although rare in cardiogenic shock)
Trauma
    Fat emboli
    Lung contusion (after cardiopulmonary resuscitation)

which result in severe hypoxemia and normal Pa_{CO_2}. These injuries present a common clinical appearance, the adult respiratory distress syndrome (ARDS). The most important differential is to distinguish ARDS from acute pulmonary edema secondary to congestive heart failure. The diagnosis of cardiogenic pulmonary edema is usually made easily by a history of heart disease and orthopnea and the presence of a gallop rhythm, cardiomegaly, abnormal electrocardiogram, or elevated venous pressure.

PATHOGENESIS

An increase in the permeability of the vascular endothelium is central to the pathogenesis of the pulmonary changes in ARDS.[16] Table 52-4 lists some of the postulated mechanisms for endothelial injury resulting in increased capillary leakage and accumulation of pulmonary extravascular fluid.[17] The diagnosis of ARDS depends on recognition of a symptom complex combined with characteristic physiological alterations. Most patients have experienced no previous respiratory problem. With the onset of the events listed in Table 52-4, there may be a period of mild-to-moderate respiratory embarrassment, often completely overshadowed by a variety of complex nonrespiratory problems. However, in several hours to a few days the patient begins to experience marked respiratory distress associated with tachypnea. Sputum that is pink and frothy to burgundy red may be expectorated. Homogeneous patchy infiltrates on the chest film quickly become diffuse, and air bronchograms are often present. Asymmetrical or inhomogeneous infiltrates, a perihilar distribution of the infiltrate, air-fluid levels, lobar atelectasis, or unexplained pleural effusions suggest etiologies other than ARDS.

The goals of therapy are to treat the underlying causes, maintain oxygen delivery, reduce pulmonary edema, and avoid complications.[18] Treatment of the precipitating condition has often been satisfactorily begun prior to clinical detection of lung injury. Initial therapy directed at improving O_2 delivery requires attempts at elevating arterial O_2 content and optimizing cardiac output. O_2 content may be improved by increasing O_2 saturation and hemoglobin concentration. High concentrations of O_2 (100 percent) are relatively ineffective in improving O_2 delivery, and their use for prolonged periods produces oxidant injury to the lung. The exact level or duration of high $F_{I_{O_2}}$ exposure necessary to produce pulmonary injury is unknown. Most authorities feel that breathing greater than 60 percent O_2 for more than 24 hours should be avoided.

The most effective means of reducing right-to-left interpulmonary shunting and improving arterial O_2 tension in ARDS is to increase lung volume by increasing transpulmonary pressure at end-expiration, i.e., positive end-expiratory pressure (PEEP).[19]

TABLE 52-4
Suggested Mechanisms for Endothelial Injury and Pulmonary Edema in Adult Respiratory Distress Syndrome

1. Corrosive effects of gastric contents in aspiration
2. Direct effect by drugs such as acetylsalicylic acid
3. Activation of alternative pathways of the complement cascade resulting in pulmonary vascular leukostasis and release of lysozymic enzymes and superoxide radicals in hemorrhagic, septic, and non-specific shock
4. Inflammatory destruction in viral infection
5. Excessive production of oxidants (H_2O_2, O_2) with inhalation of chemicals or O_2
6. Pulmonary venous hypertension following central nervous system injury or anoxia producing an unexplained persistent endothelial leak

In practice, this is accomplished by the use of continuous positive pressure ventilation (CPPV).[20] Continuous positive airway pressure (CPAP) using a tight-fitting mask is usually beneficial in young, strong, fully alert individuals whose respiratory failure is likely to persist for only a brief period of time. CPAP is usually not appropriate for chronically ill, debilitated, or elderly patients. Regardless of the method of delivery, the level of PEEP required to improve the hypoxemia varies inversely with the pulmonary compliance. Stiffer lungs require greater transpulmonary pressures for expansion. Only enough PEEP should be given to allow an adequate arterial O_2 tension ($Pa_{O_2} = 60$ mmHg, equivalent to an arterial saturation of approximately 90 percent) at an $F_{I_{O_2}}$ of 60 percent or less.

Meticulous attention to details often determines success in the management of affected patients. Intravenous lines should be replaced at 3- to 4-day intervals using sterile techniques. A Foley catheter should be used only when a condom catheter is inadequate. Attempts should be made to turn the patient frequently and to look for impending skin breakdown. Nutrition must be adequate and appropriate to failed organ systems. Attempts should be made to use enteral feeding if possible.

The patient's psychological stresses must be dealt with by giving complete and honest explanations for diagnostic procedures and therapeutic trials. Comfort, reassurance, and family support are critical elements in the successful treatment of the elderly patient with respiratory failure.

Since hypoxic respiratory failure occurs in a heterogeneous population and no definition is, as yet, uniformly accepted, the prognosis is not known. The overall mortality has been estimated to be around 50 percent. If ARF is the only problem, mortality may be somewhat lower. However, if the failure of other systems also occurs (renal, cardiac), the mortality is closer to 80 percent.

REFERENCES

1. Derrick EH: The significance of the age of onset of asthma. *Med J Aust* 1:1317, 1971.
2. Braman SS, Davis SM: Wheezing in the elderly. *Geriatr Clin North Am* 2(2):269, 1986.
3. Ford RM: Etiology of asthma: A review of 11,551 cases. *Med J Aust* 1:628, 1969.
4. Campbell EJ, Lefrak SS: How aging affects the structure and function of the respiratory system. *Geriatrics* 68:74, 1978.
5. Rossing TH, Fanta CH, McFadden ER Jr: A controlled trial of the use of single versus combined-drug therapy in the treatment of acute episodes of asthma. *Am Rev Respir Dis* 123(2):190, 1981.
6. Koenig HG, Blake RL: Rational theophylline use in older asthmatics. *Geriatrics* 41(8):49, 1986.
7. Fish JE, Summer WR: Acute lower airway obstruction: Asthma, in *Respiratory Emergencies*, 2d ed. St. Louis, Mosby, 1982, pp 144–165.
8. Speizer FE, Tager IB: Epidemiology of chronic mucus hypersecretion and obstructive airways disease. *Epidemiol Rev* 1:124, 1979.
9. Zimet I: Management of respiratory problems in the aged. *J Am Geriatr Soc* 30(11):S36, 1982.
10. Dolin R et al: A controlled trial of amantadine and rimantadine in the prophylaxis of influenzae A infection. *N Engl J Med* 37:580, 1982.
11. Mahler DA, Barlow PB, Matthay RA: Chronic obstructive pulmonary disease. *Clin Geriatr Med* 2(2):285, 1986.
12. Koerner SK, Malovany RJ: Acute respiratory insufficiency and cor pulmonale: Pathophysiology, clinical features and management. *Am Heart J* 88:115, 1974.
13. Robotham JL: Cardiovascular disturbances in chronic respiratory insufficiency. *Am J Cardiol* 47(4):941, 1981.
14. Nocturnal Oxygen Therapy Trial Group: Continuous or nocturnal oxygen therapy in hypoxemic chronic obstructive lung disease. *Ann Intern Med* 93:391, 1980.
15. Cubier M et al: Aminophylline improves diaphragmatic contractiltity. *N Engl J Med* 305:249, 1981.
16. Lamy M et al: Pathologic features and mechanisms of hypoxemia in adult respiratory distress syndrome. *Am Rev Respir Dis* 114(2):267, 1976.
17. Rinaldo JE, Rogers RM: Adult respiratory-distress syndrome: Changing concepts of lung injury and repair. *N Engl J Med* 306:900, 1982.
18. Wood LDH, Prewitt RM: Cardiovascular management in acute hypoxemic respiratory failure. *Am J Cardiol* 47(4):963, 1981.
19. Suter PM, Fairley HB, Isenberg MD: Optimum end-expiratory airway pressure in patients with acute pulmonary failure. *N Engl J Med* 292(6):284, 1975.
20. Tyler DC: Positive end-expiratory pressure: A review *Crit Care Med* 11:300, 1983.

Chapter 53

INTERSTITIAL LUNG DISEASE, HYPERSENSITIVITY PNEUMONITIS, AND PULMONARY VASCULAR DISEASE IN THE ELDERLY

Brian P. Zehr and Gary W. Hunninghake

INTERSTITIAL LUNG DISEASE

The interstitial lung diseases are a heterogeneous group of disorders characterized by inflammation (alveolitis) and destruction of the gas-exchange units (alveoli, capillaries, and small airways) and by interstitial fibrosis. Over 100 different disorders have been described. In some of these disorders, e.g., silicosis and asbestosis, the inciting agent which triggers the disease process is known; in others, such as idiopathic pulmonary fibrosis and sarcoidosis, the cause is unknown. Regardless of the etiology, each of these disorders can progress to end-stage lung disease and death of a patient if sufficient numbers of gas-exchange units are destroyed by the disease process.

Although there are no interstitial lung diseases which affect only the elderly, this age group is susceptible to virtually all lung diseases, including the interstitial disorders. These diseases may be of recent onset, or they may be long-standing disorders which began at a much younger age. In this discussion, no attempt will be made to evaluate all of the interstitial lung disorders nor will

the etiology and/or the mechanisms of lung parenchymal injury in these diseases be delineated, except where this information is relevant to therapy; this information is readily available, however, in recent reviews. Instead, this chapter will focus on the clinical evaluation and care of elderly patients with interstitial lung disease.

CLINICAL MANIFESTATIONS

The earliest symptoms of interstitial disease are usually nonspecific: fatigue, shortness of breath on exertion, vague loss of a sense of well-being, and often a chronic, nonproductive cough. These symptoms are sometimes first noted after a flulike illness. On physical examination, sharp, crackling rales may be heard throughout the chest, and clubbing of the fingers and toes may be present. As the disease progresses, the shortness of breath increases and becomes even more severe with minimal exertion. If the disorder evolves into an end-stage lung disease, there is a distressing dyspnea, even at rest, and, finally, death of the patient. Although patients may die in respiratory failure, the terminal event frequently is pneumonia, myocardial infarction, stroke, pulmonary embolus, arrhythmia, or acute right- or left-ventricular failure.

PULMONARY FUNCTIONS

When the patient is first seen, it is very important to obtain complete pulmonary function studies. Optimally, these studies should include measurement of spirometry, lung volumes, diffusing capacity, and arterial blood gases. The results of these studies will confirm the presence and determine the severity of the lung disease. In addition, these studies are extremely useful as baseline studies to determine whether there is a subsequent progression of the disorder.

In patients with interstitial lung disease, the pulmonary functions are characterized by: (1) decreased lung volumes such as the TLC, VC, RV, and FRC (see Table 53-1); (2) decreased DL_{CO}; and (3) decreased Pa_{O_2}, with an increased alveolar-arterial oxygen gradient. Both of the latter two abnormalities are magnified with exercise. In some patients, an obstruction to airflow may also be present. Although some of these alterations in pulmonary functions may occur as a result of aging, it is usually not difficult to distinguish aging-associated alterations in lung function from those which occur as a result of the presence of an interstitial lung disease (Table 53-1). In this regard, the measurements of the TLC, RV, and FRC by body box plethysmography are especially useful since these lung volumes do not normally decrease with aging alone. In addition, the Pa_{O_2} and the alveolar-arterial oxygen gradient do not worsen with exercise in older individuals unless and underlying interstitial disorder is present. Finally, an abnormal chest film often identifies interstitial lung disease as the cause of the altered pulmonary functions.

Exercise studies may be associated with a higher risk of morbidity and/or mortality in the elderly and are therefore reserved for patients in relatively good clinical condition. The following examples demonstrate instances in which exercise studies may be useful in the evaluation of the elderly: (1) since the Pa_{O_2} decreases and the alveolar-arterial oxygen gradient widens with exercise in the presence of even mild interstitial lung disease, exercise studies may be useful to detect or to essentially rule out the presence of an underlying interstitial disorder in patients with relatively normal chest films and pulmonary functions; (2) since the Pa_{O_2} of these patients decreases with exercise, these studies may be useful for monitoring the patients' need for oxygen therapy; (3) in patients with other causes for dyspnea, such as cardiovascular disease or poor muscle tone, exercise studies may be useful in determining the relative contribution of the lung disease versus the extrapulmonary disorders to the patients' shortness of breath.

TABLE 53-1

Effect of Interstitial Lung Diseases and Aging on Pulmonary Functions

Pulmonary Function*	Interstitial Lung Disease[†]	Aging
Lung Volumes		
TLC	↓	N
VC	↓	↓
FRC	↓	↑
RV	↓	↑
Spirometry		
FEV_1	↓	↓
FVC	↓	↓
FEF_{25-75}	↓	↓
Diffusing Capacity	↓	↓
Pa_{O_2}	↓	↓

*TLC, total lung capacity; VC, vital capacity; FRC, functional residual capacity; RV, residual volume; FEV_1, forced expiratory volume in 1 s; FVC, forced vital capacity; FEF_{25-75}, forced expiratory flow between 25 and 75 percent of vital capacity; Pa_{O_2}, partial pressure of oxygen in arterial blood.
[†]N = normal; ↓ = decreased; ↑ = increased. Data from normal populations allow an age adjustment on the predicted values for individual patients.

RADIOGRAPHY

In interstitial lung disease, the radiograph usually shows a diffuse infiltrate which may be reticular, nodular, or reticulonodular in character (Fig. 53-1). In some disorders, such as idiopathic pulmonary fibrosis, the radiographic findings are nonspecific and may be mimicked by a number of other interstitial disorders. In others, like silicosis, the massive fibrotic lesions in the upper lung zones, together with enlarged hilar lymph nodes surrounded by eggshell calcifications, strongly suggest the correct diagnosis. The reader is referred to standard textbooks of pulmonary medicine for a complete discussion of the typical radiographic features of all the interstitial lung disorders.

While the chest radiograph is very useful in establishing the presence of an interstitial lung disorder, the radiographic findings usually correlate poorly with the results of pulmonary function tests and with the patient's dyspnea. Serial radiographs are obtained periodically to evaluate the patient for the presence of congestive heart failure, pleural effusion, or new parenchymal infiltrates, which may or may not be related to the underlying interstitial disease.

BLOOD TESTS

Analysis of blood tests provides only a limited amount of information regarding either the diagnosis or progres-

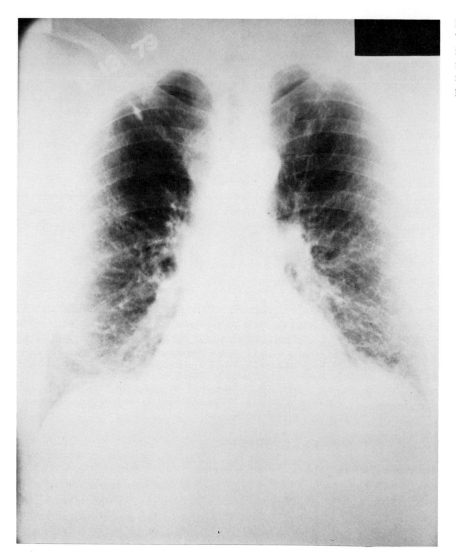

FIGURE 53-1
The chest x ray is of a 65-year-old male with interstitial lung disease associated with rheumatoid arthritis. The x ray shows a diffuse reticulonodular infiltrate which is more prominent in the lower lung zones.

sion of various interstitial lung diseases. For example, an elevated erythrocyte sedimentation rate does not necessarily indicate that the lung disease is active and, therefore, should be treated, nor does a normal erythrocyte sedimentation rate preclude progression of the disorder. In addition, increased titers of autoantibodies, such as antinuclear antibody and rheumatoid factor, are frequently present in interstitial lung disease; therefore, the presence of these autoantibodies may suggest, but does not establish, the presence of an interstitial lung disease associated with the collagen vascular disorders. Furthermore, the titers of these autoantibodies do not correlate with the progression of the lung disease in patients with collagen vascular diseases. Other tests which may suggest a specific diagnosis are precipitating antibodies to inhaled organic antigens in hypersensitivity pneumonitis and increased titers of angiotensin converting enzyme in sarcoidosis. Neither of these tests, however, can be used to determine the need for and/or adequacy of therapy in these disorders.

BRONCHOALVEOLAR LAVAGE AND GALLIUM 67 LUNG SCANS

As noted above, the interstitial lung diseases are characterized by alveolitis, destruction of gas-exchange units, and interstitial fibrosis. Two tests which proved specific information regarding the intensity of the alveolitis and, therefore, the need for therapy are bronchoalveolar lavage and gallium 67 lung scans. The greatest amount of information is provided when the tests are used together. For example, patients with a negative gallium scan have a relatively good prognosis and are not usually benefited by specific therapy. On the other hand, patients with positive scans may also have a good prognosis if their lavage is relatively normal. Patients who require therapy usually have both an abnormal lavage and a positive gallium scan. Since the technique of bronchoalveolar lavage is not available in most institutions at the present time, its use will not be discussed further. Gallium 67 lung scans are readily available and may be a useful way to follow patients with interstitial lung diseases.

GENERAL APPROACH TO ELDERLY PATIENTS WITH INTERSTITIAL LUNG DISEASE

The presence of an interstitial lung disease is usually established with both a chest film and pulmonary function studies. The pulmonary function studies should include, if possible, spirometry, lung volumes, diffusing capacity, and a resting Pa_{O_2}. These studies are not only useful as diagnostic tools, but they are also crucial for monitoring the subsequent course and response to therapy of the lung disease. For these reasons, it is mandatory that complete physiological studies be performed prior to the initiation of therapy.

If the cause of an interstitial disorder is not known, it is imperative to reevaluate the patient with a thorough history and physical examination. Although over 100 different types of interstitial lung disease have been described, the most common disorders in the elderly are idiopathic pulmonary fibrosis, interstitial lung disease associated with the collagen vascular diseases, sarcoidosis, occupational lung diseases, hypersensitivity pneumonitis, and interstitial lung disease caused by drugs and irradiation.

A complete occupational history is especially important in the elderly because exposure at a much younger age to various inorganic dusts, such as silica or asbestos, may not result in a symptomatic lung disease until much later in life. Although a lung biopsy is sometimes required, the diagnosis of occupational lung disease can usually be established with a thorough history, pulmonary function studies, and compatible chest radiograph. There is no evidence that the natural history of these disorders is altered with the use of corticosteroid and/or cytotoxic therapy. Recurrent infections, especially episodes of bronchitis with production of purulent sputum, are very common in these patients and usually require antibiotic therapy. In addition, patients with silicosis have a high incidence of tuberculous infections, which must be treated since these infections appear to accelerate the progression of the underlying interstitial disease. (Hypersensitivity pneumonitis in the elderly, resulting from organic dust inhalation, will be discussed in detail in the next section.)

Interstitial lung disease caused by drugs and irradiation may also be identified by a careful history. For example, interstitial lung disease may be caused by a variety of drugs which are administered to treat various malignancies. The antitumor agents associated with the highest incidence of interstitial lung disease are busulfan and bleomycin. Examples of other types of drugs which may cause interstitial lung disease include various antibiotics (especially nitrofurantoin), propranolol, gold salts, phenytoin, and methysergide. For a complete list, the reader is referred to recent review articles. Therapy of these disorders includes discontinuation of the offending drug and, frequently, a short course of corticosteroids. Local lung irradiation administered to treat various tumors is also routinely associated with the development of interstitial fibrosis.

The diagnosis of the interstitial lung diseases associated with the collagen vascular disorders must be based upon evidence of a multisystem disease. Serologic abnormalities, such as elevated titers of rheumatoid factor or antinuclear antibody, are not sufficient to make the diagnosis of a collagen vascular disease in the absence of compatible systemic manifestations. In this context, elevated titers of rheumatoid factor and/or antinuclear antibody are also frequently found in the occupational lung diseases and idiopathic pulmonary fibrosis. Although all the collagen vascular diseases may be associated with the development of interstitial lung disorders, the disease which is most often associated with this lung disorder in the elderly is rheumatoid arthritis. In fact, this may be the most common interstitial lung disease in this age group. The interstitial lung disease associated with rheumatoid arthritis is frequently mild in the elderly and in some patients may require no specific therapy. In other patients, however, the untreated disorder may follow a malignant course and require aggressive therapy with corticosteroids and/or cytotoxic agents. The following general guidelines can be utilized to treat the interstitial lung diseases associated with the other collagen vascular disorders:

1. Disorders such as scleroderma and ankylosing spondylitis should not be treated, even in the presence of severe lung disease, since they do not routinely respond to therapy.
2. Disorders such as Wegener's granulomatosis and the polyarteritis nodosa group of vasculitides which are associated with vasculitis of large or medium-size vessels should be treated with cyclophosphamide. Corticosteroids may also be necessary in these disorders for a short period of time until the disease stabilizes.
3. Corticosteroids are the initial therapy of choice in the other disorders; if the lung disease remains active and progresses in spite of corticosteroid therapy, the patient is then switched to cyclophosphamide.

Idiopathic pulmonary fibrosis is a chronic disorder of unknown etiology which frequently occurs in older individuals. The disorder is limited to the lung, and the diagnosis can be established only after all other causes of interstitial lung disease have been excluded. In most cases, this requires an open-lung biopsy. Corticosteroids are the drugs of choice in this disorder; cyclophosphamide may be used in cases in which the disease progresses while the patient is taking adequate amounts of corticosteroids.

Pulmonary sarcoidosis usually comes to clinical attention in younger patients. However, this is a common disorder, and it is not unusual for it to be detected in older individuals. In contrast to the disease in younger patients, the disease in the elderly is more frequently inactive or end-stage. For this reason, many elderly patients with sarcoidosis are not benefited by corticosteroid therapy. The diagnosis is usually established by transbronchial biopsy which shows typical noncaseating granulomata. Other granulomatous lung disease (such as tuberculosis) must be excluded before the diagnosis of sarcoidosis can be firmly established.

GENERAL APPROACH TO THERAPY

The therapy of elderly patients with interstitial lung disease is complicated by the fact that these patients may be very fragile, may have other illnesses, and may be subject to a higher incidence of side effects from corticosteroid and/or cytotoxic therapy. Thus, it is important that therapy results in an improvement in the overall condition of the patient rather than just improvement in the interstitial lung disease. After the diagnosis is established and baseline pulmonary functions and chest radiographs are obtained, it is important to answer the following question: (1) Is the patient's particular interstitial lung disease likely to respond to therapy? (2) Does the patient have a coexisting extrapulmonary disease which may be significantly aggravated by corticosteroid and/or cytotoxic therapy? (3) Would the patient's overall prognosis or sense of well-being improve were the lung disease to respond to therapy? (4) Is the lung disease sufficiently active to warrant therapy?

The purpose of the first question is to prevent exposure of the patient to corticosteroid and/or cytotoxic therapy for a lung disorder which is unlikely to respond to these agents. For example, the occupational lung diseases resulting from exposure to inorganic particulates and the lung diseases associated with scleroderma and ankylosing spondylitis rarely respond to immunosuppressive therapy, and frequently the overall clinical status of such patients is worsened by these agents.

The second relates to the fact that there is a high incidence of cardiovascular disease, systemic hypertension, diabetes mellitus, joint disease, and other disorders in elderly patients. Corticosteroids administered as therapy for an interstitial lung disease may significantly aggravate or accelerate these disease processes. For this reason, the physician might choose not to treat a mild interstitial lung disease with corticosteroids in a patient with an extrapulmonary disorder which might be significantly worsened by these agents. In patients who require therapy for their lung disease, these considerations are only relative contraindications against therapy,

since these complications can usually be managed with other medical therapies.

The third question is related to the prognosis of the patient, independent of the interstitial lung disease. For example, in some elderly patients, an extrapulmonary disorder may be present which will result in their demise in the near future; it would not be prudent to treat with immunosuppressive agents an interstitial lung disorder which will not cause a patient significant problems during his or her life span. In contrast, the patient's quality of life or the severity of the extrapulmonary disorders may be significantly improved by therapy of the lung disease. These are judgments which must be made on an individual basis.

The fourth question is pertinent to the therapy of interstitial lung disease in any patient population and is related to the likelihood that the disease will improve with therapy or progress without therapy. This information is not readily obtained from a single chest radiograph or set of pulmonary functions since abnormalities detected by these tests may be due either to active and therefore potentially treatable disease (caused by ongoing inflammation in the lung) or to "burnt out" and therefore untreatable disease (due to the presence of end-stage fibrosis only). Those tests which may give information relevant to the activity of the lung disease are limited to bronchoalveolar lavage and gallium 67 lung scans. As noted above, since bronchoalveolar lavage may not be readily available, the test most frequently utilized is the gallium 67 lung scan. If the lung scan is negative, probably the best course is to withhold therapy and follow the patient with serial pulmonary function tests. If the pulmonary function tests remain stable over a period of time, it may not be necessary to treat the patient. If the pulmonary functions deteriorate, a trial of immunosuppressive therapy may be indicated. If the lung scan is positive, a trial of therapy may be indicated after the initial evaluation of the patient.

It should be kept in mind that dyspnea in elderly patients with interstitial lung disease may also be due to extrapulmonary disorders such as congestive heart failure or pulmonary infections. The sense of well-being of these patients is usually markedly improved by therapy of these associated conditions. In addition, dyspnea or fatigue with exertion commonly occurs in patients with interstitial lung disease because they have a relatively fixed cardiac output and the Pa_{O_2} drops with exercise. This may be ameliorated with supplemental oxygen therapy.

HYPERSENSITIVITY PNEUMONITIS

Hypersensitivity pneumonitis is characterized by an inflammation of the lung parenchyma following inhalation of an organic antigen. The response is limited to the alveoli and terminal airways. A variety of organic antigens have been implicated including bacteria, saprophytic fungi, and animal danders and proteins (Table 53-2).

Although most elderly patients will no longer be employed in occupations that would likely expose them to organic antigens found in the workplace, hypersensitivity pneumonitis is still a diagnosis that should be considered among elderly patients with respiratory disease. In addition to occupational sources, sensitizing antigens may be present in heating, air conditioning, or humidifying equipment that has been contaminated with microorganisms. Also, the excreta and proteinaceous material from pigeons, parakeets, parrots, and other domesticated birds can be a source of sensitizing antigen. Finally, elderly patients may suffer from chronic pulmonary symptoms resulting from occupational exposures which occurred many years earlier.

The offending antigens are small (1 to 3 μm) and, therefore, are deposited in the alveoli and terminal airways. Once sensitization has occurred, the stage is set for the development of a hypersensitivity response on subsequent exposure. This most likely occurs as a result of a type IV cell-mediated hypersensitivity reaction. The presence of a precipitating antibody directed against the offending agent serves as a marker of exposure but does not differentiate between those exposed individuals who do not have the disease and those who do. In fact, normal individuals without obvious exposure histories may have precipitating antibodies.

CLINICAL FEATURES

In the acute form of the disease, respiratory and systemic symptoms develop within 4 to 6 hours of exposure and consist of dyspnea, cough, fevers, chills, malaise, and myalgias. The patient usually appears to be acutely ill, and the pulmonary exam reveals inspiratory crackles, predominantly in the lower lung fields. A chest x ray taken during the acute phase may show a finely nodular, bilateral alveolar filling pattern. Routine laboratory data are nonspecific, although the white blood count may exceed 25,000 with a left shift. Eosinophilia is not usually seen. If measured at the time of the acute illness, pulmonary function studies will show a decreased FVC and FEV_1, reduced lung volumes, a decreased diffusing capacity, and hypoxemia. These acute episodes will be followed by resolution of symptoms and normalization of chest x ray, pulmonary function tests, and laboratory abnormalities within 18 to 24 hours of removal from the offending agent. This classic acute form of the disease is rarely seen in elderly patients.

Most often, elderly patients present with the chronic form of hypersensitivity pneumonitis. This form of the disease is not characterized by acute exacerbations of symptoms with reexposure. Instead, these patients present with signs and symptoms similar to those seen in other interstitial lung diseases, including progressive shortness of breath, sputum production, chronic cough, weight loss, and malaise. Pulmonary function studies will show persistent restrictive physiology, and the chest x ray will be consistent with a diffuse interstitial process. Without a careful history and a high index of suspicion, chronic hypersensitivity pneumonitis may be difficult to distinguish from other interstitial lung disorders, especially idiopathic pulmonary fibrosis.

TABLE 53-2
Examples of Hypersensitivity Pneumonitis

Disease	Source of Antigen	Antigen
Farmer's lung	Contaminated hay, grain, silage	Thermophilic actinomyces*
Bird-fancier's or pigeon-breeder's lung	Avian excreta	Parrot, pigeon, parakeet, chicken, dove proteins
Bagassosis	Contaminated bagasse (sugar cane)	Thermophilic actinomyces
Mushroom-worker's lung	Mushroom compost	Thermophilic actinomyces, other
Humidifier or air conditioner lung	Contaminated water from humidifiers and air conditioners	Thermophilic antinomyces, *Aureobasidium pullulans*, amoeba, others
Woodworker's lung	Pine and spruce pulp; oak, cedar, mahogany dusts	Wood dust, alternaria
Sauna-taker's lung	Contaminated sauna steam	*A. pullulans*, other
Malt-worker's lung	Moldy barley	*Aspergillus fumigatus, Aspergillus clavatus*
Sequoiosis	Redwood sawdust	*Aureobasidium, Graphium*
Maple bark–stripper's disease	Maple bark	*Cryptostroma corticale*
Miller's lung	Infested wheat flour	*Sitophilas granarius* (wheat weevil)
Coffee worker's lung	Coffee beans	Coffee bean dust

*Thermophilic actinomyces include *Thermoactinomyces vulgaris, T. saccharri, T. viridis, T. candidus,* and *Micropolyspora faeni.*

DIAGNOSIS

Greater that 90 percent of patients with hypersensitivity pneumonitis will have precipitating antibodies directed against the offending agent. Serologic studies, however, have a low degree of specificity for disease. Up to 30 to 40 percent of exposed but asymptomatic individuals will also demonstrate precipitating antibodies. Therefore, a positive serologic study may raise the suspicion of hypersensitivity pneumonitis, but it does not confirm the diagnosis.

During episodes of acute disease, leukocytosis without eosinophilia is frequently seen. Serum immunoglobulins may be mildly increased, and sometimes the rheumatoid factor may become transiently positive. Erythrocyte sedimentation rate may be normal or slightly increased. Studies of bronchoalveolar lavage fluid from patients with chronic hypersensitivity pneumonitis reveal an increase in total cell numbers and a significant elevation in the percentage of suppressor (OKT-8$^+$) T lymphocytes.

Unfortunately, no single laboratory test or combination of tests is specific for the diagnosis of hypersensitivity pneumonitis. However, the diagnosis of hypersensitivity pneumonitis can usually be made with relative certainty when an appropriate history is confirmed by positive serology and characteristic chest x ray and pulmonary function abnormalities. If other diagnoses are strongly suspected, an open-lung biopsy may be necessary. This typically demonstrates an interstitial pneumonitis consisting primarily of lymphocytes and plasma cells that infiltrate alveolar walls. Interstitial fibrosis, granulomata, and bronchiolitis obliterans can also be seen.

THERAPY AND PROGNOSIS

No specific therapy is required for mild forms of acute hypersensitivity pneumonitis. Avoidance of the offending antigen will usually result in resolution of symptoms within 24 hours. More severe attacks, however, may require prednisone as well as routine supportive care. The therapy of chronic hypersensitivity pneumonitis includes both avoidance of antigen and, in most instances, a trial of corticosteroids. Therapy of the chronic form of the disease usually improves symptoms and pulmonary functions. Lung function may not return to normal, however, because of the pulmonary fibrosis which is frequently associated with this disorder.

PULMONARY VASCULAR DISEASE

A detailed review of the entire range of pulmonary vascular disease is beyond the scope of this chapter; therefore, the focus will be on two disorders which are commonly seen in the geriatric population, pulmonary embolism and pulmonary hypertension. These disorders are interrelated in that pulmonary embolism can cause both acute and chronic pulmonary hypertension, and pulmonary hypertension and its sequela, right heart failure, can predispose to recurrent thromboembolism.

PULMONARY HYPERTENSION

The pressure in the pulmonary circulation is a result of both blood flow and vascular resistance. Blood flow through the lungs is almost identical to the output of the left ventricle of the heart; yet the mean pulmonary arterial pressure is only about one-seventh of the mean systemic arterial pressure. This implies that resistance in the pulmonary circulation is low in healthy individuals. In addition, when flow increases (as with exercise), pulmonary resistance may decrease further through vasodilatation, as well as through recruitment of previously unperfused pulmonary vessels. In spite of this impressive ability to maintain a low pressure in the face of widely varying flow rates, the pressure in the pulmonary circulation can become abnormally elevated in a number of pathologic states. Pulmonary pressures are considered to be abnormally elevated when the pulmonary artery systolic pressure exceeds 30 mmHg and the mean pulmonary artery pressure exceeds 20 mmHg.

ETIOLOGY

A number of cardiac abnormalities, such as atrial septal defect and ventricular septal defect, will result in pulmonary hypertension through an increase in pulmonary blood flow. These disorders usually become clinically manifest before old age and, therefore, are uncommon causes of newly diagnosed pulmonary hypertension in the geriatric population.

Disorders which result in a passive increase in pulmonary resistance by impeding pulmonary venous drainage also cause pulmonary hypertension. These include disorders such as mitral stenosis and left-ventricular failure. Mitral stenosis has become an uncommon cause of pulmonary hypertension as a result of valvular surgery and a decreased incidence of rheumatic fever. For this reason, the most common cause of "passive" pulmonary hypertension in elderly patients is left-ventricular failure, most commonly due to ischemic or hypertensive cardiomyopathy.

There are a number of other disorders which cause pulmonary hypertension by obstructing or obliterating the pulmonary vasculature. Pulmonary thromboembolism can result in both acute and chronic pulmonary hypertension. This will not occur, however, until 50 to 60 percent of the cross-sectional area of the circulation is obstructed in a previously normal lung. Obliterative vascular changes can occur in a number of other disorders associated with pulmonary vasculitis, interstitial lung disease, or emphysema.

Increased pulmonary resistance can also result from pulmonary vasoconstriction. Clearly, the most important pulmonary artery vasoconstrictor is alveolar hypoxemia. This response accounts for the majority, if not all, of the pulmonary hypertension seen with disorders such as sleep apnea syndrome and the obesity hypoventilation (pickwickian) syndrome. A number of disorders cause pulmonary hypertension through more than one mechanism. In diseases such as emphysema and pulmonary fibrosis, both hypoxemic vasoconstriction and destruction of the pulmonary vasculature may occur.

CLINICAL FINDINGS

Dyspnea, especially with exertion, is usually the earliest symptom noted by patients with pulmonary hypertension. This dyspnea is often attributable to the underlying disorder which caused the pulmonary hypertension (e.g., emphysema, congestive heart failure, or interstitial lung disease). However, pulmonary hypertension per se can also cause dyspnea, although the exact mechanism for this is not known. Fatigue is also frequently present and probably is a consequence of the impaired cardiac output. Angina-like chest pain is sometimes noted and may occur as a result of right-ventricular ischemia. Due to the high intercapillary pressures, microvascular aneurysms can form which protrude into the alveolar lumen. Rupture of these vessels can cause hemoptysis and/or pulmonary infiltrates. Finally, hoarseness is associated with severe, long-standing pulmonary hypertension. This is probably due to pressure on the left recurrent laryngeal nerve as it passes between the aorta and a dilated pulmonary artery.

The chronic load imposed on the right ventricle by prolonged pulmonary hypertension can lead to right-ventricular hypertrophy and dilatation. Right-ventricular failure may ensue if the degree of pulmonary hypertension is severe. Unfortunately, the findings of chronic pulmonary hypertension frequently are detected late in the course of the disease, after cardiac dysfunction has occurred. If right-ventricular failure develops, there is usually evidence of tricuspid insufficiency, peripheral edema, and/or hepatic enlargement.

There are a number of tests which can support a clinical impression of pulmonary hypertension. An electrocardiogram may reveal changes consistent with right-ventricular strain and/or hypertrophy. Right-ventricular dilatation and an increased width of the descending branch of the right pulmonary artery may also be noted on chest x ray. The chest x ray may also reveal changes in the lung parenchyma which suggest a cause of the pulmonary hypertension (e.g., emphysema, interstitial lung disease, or congestive heart failure). There are no commonly used noninvasive tests, however, that allow for accurate quantitation of the degree of pulmonary hypertension. This requires right heart catheterization and direct measurement of pulmonary artery pressures.

THERAPY

In all cases of pulmonary hypertension, the major therapeutic effort should be directed toward treating an underlying disease which contributes to the elevated pulmonary pressures. For example, recurrent pulmonary emboli should be treated with anticoagulation and/or vena caval interruption, if indicated; patients with left-ventricular dysfunction should receive appropriate therapy of their congestive heart failure; the pulmonary vasculitides usually improve with immunosuppressive therapy; mitral valve surgery may be indicated for those with mitral stenosis; morbidly obese patients often are helped by procedures designed for weight reduction; and patients with hypoxemia should receive supplemental oxygen.

Of the currently available pulmonary vasodilators, oxygen is clearly the most efficacious. Not only can it decrease pulmonary vascular resistance through vasodilation, but it can also decrease blood viscosity when the viscosity is caused by secondary polycythemia. Oxygen therapy has also been shown to improve neuropsychiatric symptoms and improve long-term survival. Therefore, it is essential that all hypoxemic patients receive adequate oxygen therapy. Although there have been many studies which have examined other potential pulmonary vasodilators, no agent has yet been shown to be consistently effective. In part this may be due to the fact that subsets of patients likely to benefit from vasodilator therapy have not been clearly identified. Although a trial of vasodilators may be warranted in selected individuals, these drugs are not without significant risks, and, initially, they require careful invasive monitoring to document both safety and efficacy.

PULMONARY EMBOLISM

Pulmonary embolism is a major cause of morbidity and mortality in elderly patients. This high rate of morbidity and mortality is not primarily due to a lack of effective treatment but, in large part, is caused by failure to consider the diagnosis and institute early therapy. In this regard, if a patient survives the first hour of a pulmonary embolism and appropriate therapy is instituted, the mortality rate is about 8 percent. Unfortunately, pulmonary embolism is not diagnosed in many patients, and in this undiagnosed group the mortality rate may be as high as 30 percent. An even more profound impact on morbidity and mortality would be realized if patients at risk for the development of pulmonary embolism were identified and prophylactic therapy instituted before the development of venous thrombosis.

Greater than 90 percent of pulmonary emboli originate from the deep venous system of the pelvis and thighs. Rarely, if ever, do venous thrombi of the superficial venous system embolize. Calf vein thrombi, however, can propagate to the deep veins of the thigh in 5 to 20 percent of cases and may result in embolic disease of the lung. Three abnormalities commonly predispose patients to develop venous thrombosis: venous stasis, injury to vascular endothelium, and alterations in coagulability. Of these, venous stasis is, in most patients, the most important. As a group, elderly patients have a greater incidence of pulmonary emboli as compared to younger patients. Many predisposing factors frequently are present in the elderly, including congestive heart failure, chronic venous insufficiency, and immobility associated with various underlying disease states. Therefore, prophylaxis to prevent the development of venous thrombosis is especially important in the geriatric population.

CLINICAL FEATURES

The classic presentation of pulmonary embolism includes the sudden onset of shortness of breath, apprehension, pleuritic chest pain, hemoptysis, and a pleural friction rub, occurring in the setting of thrombophlebitis. With massive pulmonary emboli, signs of acute cor pulmonale may also be seen. More often, however, pulmonary embolism occurs with minimal signs and symptoms. The classic presentation of pulmonary embolism occurs in less than 20 percent of patients. Additionally, symptoms are usually nonspecific and can be confused with other disorders such as congestive heart failure, acute myocardial infarction, pneumonia, or atelectasis. One of the most common presentations is unexplained tachypnea and/or shortness of breath. Other findings which may be present are fever and bronchospasm.

DIAGNOSIS

Pulmonary embolism can be difficult to diagnose with certainty. As noted, the signs and symptoms and physical findings may be nonspecific and frequently minimal. Although nonspecific, the following studies are frequently obtained as part of the evaluation for pulmonary embolism. The white blood cell count may be mildly elevated but rarely exceeds 15,000 per cubic millimeter. Characteristically there is a decrease in Pa_{O_2}, although 10 to 15 percent of patients will have a normal Pa_{O_2}. Not infrequently, the Pa_{CO_2} will be decreased due to hyperventilation.

The chest x ray may reveal abnormalities; however, these are often subtle and nonspecific. They include platelike atelectases, an elevated diaphragm, pleural effusion, decreased vascular markings on the affected side (Westermark's sign), and infiltrates such as the classic Hampton's Hump (a homogeneous, wedge-shaped, pleural-based density which extends toward the hilum and results from pulmonary infarction).

Nonspecific changes are usually present on the electrocardiogram, which may be abnormal, at least transiently, in most patients with acute pulmonary embolism. In the appropriate clinical setting, findings compatible with acute right-ventricular strain are strongly suggestive of the presence of pulmonary emboli.

A more useful test is the perfusion lung scan. When multiple views of the lung are used, a negative perfusion scan virtually eliminates the diagnosis of pulmonary embolism. Frequently, however, some abnormality in perfusion exists in the elderly, and therefore this study must be supplemented with a ventilation scan. A high-probability ventilation/perfusion scan is said to occur when at least a segmental or larger perfusion defect occurs in an area of normal ventilation (a V/Q mismatch). A high-probability V/Q scan correctly diagnoses the presence of pulmonary embolism in greater than 85 percent of patients with angiographically proven pulmonary emboli. In combination with a good clinical history for pulmonary embolus, a high-probability V/Q scan is frequently sufficient evidence upon which to base treatment. The role of a low-probability scan in establishing a diagnosis is less clear. If the clinical suspicion of pulmonary embolus is low, a low-probability scan may be sufficient to exclude pulmonary emboli. If the clinical suspicion is high, however, further diagnostic studies are needed to exclude or establish the diagnosis. These studies could include contrast venography or impedance plethysmography of the lower extremities. If these tests are abnormal, anticoagulation may be warranted.

Pulmonary angiography remains the gold standard for the diagnosis of pulmonary emboli. The serious nature of undiagnosed and untreated pulmonary emboli, as well as the risks of therapy, justify its use in many circumstances. These include the following situations: (1) when the clinical impression is consistent with pulmonary embolism but the V/Q scan is of low or indeterminate probability; (2) when there is a probable pulmonary embolism based on V/Q scan and clinical history but either the risk of anticoagulation is great or vena caval interruption is being considered; (3) in the case of probable massive pulmonary embolism when surgical embolectomy or thrombolytic therapy is being considered; and (4) when there is a previous, unconfirmed diagnosis of "recurrent pulmonary emboli" and the V/Q scan is of a low or indeterminate probability.

TREATMENT

Once the diagnosis of pulmonary embolism is confirmed, the treatment is usually intravenous heparin followed by a course of oral anticoagulation. Heparin therapy is continued for 7 to 10 days, and the rate of infusion is adjusted to maintain an activated partial thromboplastin time at a value of 1½ to 2 times the normal laboratory control range. Oral anticoagulation is started 1 to 2 days after the initiation of heparin therapy. Recent studies have shown that when oral anticoagulation therapy is monitored with a prothrombin time that uses rabbit brain thromboplastin (as is the case with most labs in the United States), adequate anticoagulation with fewer bleeding complications can be obtained when the prothrombin time is maintained between 1¼ and 1½ of control values as compared to more intensive therapy. If the underlying problem which led to the initial venous thrombosis is corrected, then 6 weeks of oral anticoagulation is probably sufficient; otherwise, at least 3 months of oral anticoagulation should be used. Exceptions are those individuals who have ongoing risk factors such as antithrombin III deficiency, protein C deficiency, underlying adenocarcinoma, or a history of two or more episodes of venous thrombosis and/or pulmonary embolism. Anticoagulation may need to be continued for an indefinite period of time in these individuals.

Other methods of therapy are used in certain instances. For the patient with massive pulmonary embolism that results in hemodynamic deterioration, thrombolytic agents such as streptokinase or urokinase may be warranted if there is no contraindication to their use. The role of the newer fibrin-specific agents, such as tissue plasminogen activator, is still being defined. Alternatively, pulmonary embolectomy may be considered in patients with massive pulmonary emboli which have caused a marked decrease in cardiac output and right heart failure. Additionally, vena caval devices, such as a Greenfield filter, are used in settings of recurrent pulmonary emboli while the patient is receiving adequate anticoagulation; pulmonary embolism or active iliofemoral thrombosis in a patient with a contraindication to anticoagulation; development of bleeding or other complications referable to anticoagulation therapy; or following surgical pulmonary thrombectomy. The greatest impact on morbidity and mortality in elderly patients, however, could be achieved with the institution of timely prophylactic therapy to prevent venous thrombosis.

GENERAL READING

Interstitial Lung Disease

Becklake MR: Asbestos-related diseases of the lung and other organs: Their epidemiology and implications for clinical practice. *Am Rev Respir Dis* 114:187, 1976.

Carrington CB, Gaensler EA: Clinical-pathologic approach to diffuse infiltrative lung disease, in Thurlbeck WM, Abell MR (eds): *The Lung: Structure, Function and Disease.* Baltimore, Williams & Wilkins, 1978, pp 58–87.

Carrington CB, Gaensler EA, Coutu RE, Fitzgerald MX, Gupta

RG: Natural history and treated course of usual and desquamative interstitial pneumonia. *N Engl J Med* 298:801, 1978.

Crystal RG, Fulmer JD, Roberts WC, Moss ML, Line BR, Reynolds HY: Idiopathic pulmonary fibrosis: Clinical, histologic, radiographic, physiologic, scintigraphic, cytologic, and biochemical aspects. *Ann Intern Med* 85:769, 1976.

Crystal RG, Gadek JE, Ferrans VJ, Fulmer JD, Line BR, Hunninghake GW: Interstitial lung disease: Current concepts of pathogenesis, staging, and therapy. *Am J Med* 70:542, 1981.

Fishman AP: *Pulmonary Diseases and Disorders*, 2d ed. New York, McGraw-Hill, 1988.

Fraser RG, Pare JAP: *Diagnosis of Diseases of the Chest*, 2d ed, vol 3. Philadelphia, Saunders, 1979.

Hunninghake GW, Fauci AS: State of the art—pulmonary disorders associated with the collagen vascular diseases. *Am Rev Respir Dis* 119:471, 1979.

Hunninghake GW, Gadek JE, Kawanami O, Ferrans VJ, Crystal RG: Inflammatory and immune processes in the human lung in health and disease: Evaluation by bronchoalveolar lavage. *Am J Pathol* 97:149, 1979.

Braunwald E et al (eds): *Harrison's Principles of Internal Medicine*, 11th ed. New York, McGraw-Hill, 1987.

Morgan WKC, Lapp NL: Respiratory disease in coal miners. *Am Rev Respir Dis* 113:531, 1976.

Spencer H: *Pathology of the Lung*, vols 1 and 2. Philadelphia, Saunders, 1977.

Wyngaarden JB, Smith LH (eds): *Textbook of Medicine*, vols 1 and 2. Philadelphia, Saunders, 1982.

Hypersensitivity Pneumonitis

Braun SR, do Pico GA, Tsiatis A, Horvath E, Dickie AA, Rankin J: Farmer's lung disease: Long-term clinical and physiologic outcome. *Am Rev Resp Dis* df119:185, 1979.

Emanuel DA, Kryda MJ: Farmer's lung disease. *Clin Rev Allergy* 1:509, 1983.

Richerson HB: Hypersensitivity pneumonitis—pathology and pathogenesis. *Clin Rev Allergy* 1:469, 1983.

Stankus RP, Salvaggio JE: Hypersensitivity pneumonitis. *Clin Chest Med* 4:55, 1983.

Pulmonary Vascular Disease

Dalen JE, Hirsh J et al: ACCP-NHLBI National Conference on Antithrombotic Therapy. *Chest* 89(suppl):1S, 1986.

Hirsh J et al: Venous thromboembolism: Prevention, diagnosis and treatment. *Chest* 89(suppl):369S, 1986.

Keller CA, Shepard JW, Chun DS, Vasquez P, Dolon GF: Pulmonary hypertension in chronic obstructive pulmonary disease: Multivariate analysis. *Chest* 90:185, 1986.

Matthay RA, Bergen HJ: Cardiovascular performance in chronic obstructive pulmonary disease. *Med Clin North Am* 65:489, 1981.

Nocturnal Oxygen Therapy Trial Group: Continuous nocturnal oxygen therapy in hypoxemic chronic obstructive lung disease. *Ann Intern Med* 93:391, 1980.

Rosenow EC, Osmundson PJ, Brown ML: Pulmonary embolism. *Mayo Clin Proc* 56:161, 1981.

Rounds S, Hill NS: Pulmonary hypertensive disease. *Chest* 85:397, 1984.

Sharma GVRK, Sasalova AA: Diagnosis and treatment of pulmonary embolism. *Med Clin North Am* 63(1):239, 1979.

Chapter 54

LUNG CANCER

Melvyn S. Tockman and Wilmot C. Ball, Jr.

EPIDEMIOLOGY

Lung cancer is the most frequently occurring cancer in the United States. Approximately 150,000 new lung cancer cases and 136,000 lung cancer deaths were expected in 1987 alone. Lung cancer primarily is a disease of older individuals who have smoked cigarettes. When lung cancer mortality rates are examined by age, there is a continuous increase in mortality for the older age groups for both males and females. This increase may reflect both the high risk found in elderly persons who have used nonfiltered, high tar and nicotine cigarettes for most of their lives and the longer smoking duration of these individuals. Although lung cancer is more often a disease of older males, recent increases in death rates among females have reduced the male-to-female ratio of lung cancer deaths to 2:1. By 1984, female lung cancer deaths had exceeded those from breast cancer, making lung cancer the most common cancer in the elderly of both sexes.

Cigarettes are responsible for 85 percent of lung cancer in the United States. Nine major prospective studies have shown that cigarette smokers on average are 10 times as likely to develop lung cancer as are nonsmokers. An individual who smokes one pack of cigarettes per day has one chance in eight of dying from lung cancer. The risk of developing lung cancer increases further with the intensity of cigarette smoking, the duration of the smoking habit, the depth of inhalation, and the tar and nicotine content of the cigarette. Conversely, the risk of lung cancer falls with smoking cessation. The risk of dying of lung cancer among former smokers who have abstained for 10 to 15 years is only slightly greater than the risk of lung cancer death in nonsmokers. Risk for lung cancer increases further among smokers in proportion to their degree of airways obstruction. Recent studies have shown that smokers with ventilatory obstruction have a fivefold greater risk for lung cancer (after adjustment for age and level of smoking) than do smokers without obstruction.

After cigarette smoking, asbestos is the next most common exposure which leads to lung cancer. A history of asbestos exposure among insulation workers increased the risk of cancer of the lung approximately fivefold. The combination of both cigarette smoking (10-fold risk) and asbestos exposure (5-fold risk) increased the risk to more than 50-fold for the cigarette-smoking asbestos worker over the nonexposed nonsmoker. Clearly, elderly smokers with a history of asbestos exposure must be urged to stop smoking. Other occupational exposures including radiation, aromatic hydrocarbons, arsenic, chromium, coal products, iron oxide, mustard gas, nickel, and chlormethyl ether have been associated with an increased risk of lung cancer, although synergy with cigarette smoking has been demonstrated only with asbestos and radiation exposure. In addition to exposure risk factors, those individuals with a familial history of lung cancer have also been found to be at greater risk of death from this cause.

Clinical trials of mass lung cancer screening by periodic chest x ray and examination of sputum cell morphology did not demonstrate enhanced early-stage lung cancer detection and cure. Recently, murine monoclonal antibodies to a glycolipid antigen of small-cell lung cancer (SCLC) and a protein antigen of non-small-cell (NSC) lung cancer have been applied to the sputum specimens preserved from one of the lung cancer screening trials. This study demonstrated recognition of neoplastic antigen expression 2 years in advance of clinical cancer with a 91 percent sensitivity and an 88 percent specificity. While these techniques have the potential to reduce lung cancer mortality, studies to test this hypothesis are just emerging. Therefore, until screening can be widely advocated, detection of localized lung cancer must depend upon careful clinical attention to those individuals at highest risk for lung cancer (obstructed, elderly cigarette smokers).

Non-small-cell lung cancer (NSCLC) may be divided into three histological groupings: epidermoid or squamous carcinoma, adenocarcinoma, and large-cell carcinoma. The NSCLCs are considered together because therapy and prognosis are more closely related to cancer stage and patient activity status than to cell type. In general, the three NSC lung cancers commonly show a poor response to conventional chemotherapy but share a potential for cure with surgical resection in some patients.

Prognostic estimates for NSCLC are based on clinical stage for operable NSCLC and performance stage for metastatic disease. A TNM system has been developed (and has been recently revised) in which T describes the extent of the tumor, N the regional nodal involvement, and M the presence or absence of metastases. The TNM categories are then grouped into stages in order of probable survival to select patients for either surgical or nonsurgical therapy (see Table 54-1 for a description of stages I, II, III, and IV). Lung cancers through stage IIIa, but not stage IIIb, may be amenable to curative surgical resection.

DIAGNOSIS

The symptoms of bronchogenic cancer can be considered in two categories, those due to intrathoracic spread and those due to extrathoracic spread. Most patients come to medical attention because of symptoms related to the chest. The change in a chronic cough, occurrence of hemoptysis, onset (or progression) of dyspnea, and chest pain have classically been recognized in association with lung cancer. SCLC and rapidly progressive NSCLC, however, may first be recognized by the onset of symptoms of distant metastases. The common sites of extrathoracic metastases include brain, bone, and liver. Headache, focal weakness, and seizures may herald intracranial metastases. Persistent pain of spine and ribs are frequent signs of bony metastases. Hepatic metastases may be recognized by a dull aching in the right upper quadrant. Often, nonspecific fatigue, anorexia, or paraneoplastic syndromes may lead to physician recognition of the presence of cancer. Paraneoplastic syndromes may simulate a peripheral neuropathy, a lower motor neuron syndrome, or a cerebellar disorder. Pulmonary osteoarthropathy and endocrine syndromes such as the inappropriate secretion of antidiuretic hormone (ADH) or adrenocorticotropic hormone (ACTH) are also seen. Yet, while symptoms may lead a patient to medical attention, it is unusual for symptomatic cancer to be amenable to cure by current modes of therapy. Unfortunately, asymptomatic lung cancer is not necessarily "early" either. The lung cancer screening studies have shown that approximately one-half of the asymptomatic lung cancer cases were already advanced (stages III–IV) at the time of detection.

Any patient in whom the possibility of lung cancer is entertained should undergo evaluation to answer three

TABLE 54-1
Survival with Lung Cancer Depends Upon Activity Level and Stage of the Disease

Activity Level

I. Fully independent
Able to continue usual life pattern with no restriction
II. Minimally limited activity
Although able to do productive work, has begun to modify life pattern and has difficulty keeping up with peers
III. Moderately limited activity
Although not able to do productive work, is capable of self-care and is not homebound
IV. Markedly limited activity
Homebound but capable of self-care
V. Bedridden
Incapable of self-care

Stage

Occult Stage
Malignant cells in bronchopulmonary secretions, but not visualized radiographically or bronchoscopically

Stage 0
Carcinoma in situ

Stage I
Tumor of any size not involving structures outside the lung and with no lymph node metastases

Stage II
Same as stage I except with metastases to ipsilateral peribronchial or hilar lymph nodes

Stage IIIa
Tumor extending into chest wall or involving a main bronchus within 2 cm of the carina, OR metastases to ipsilateral mediastinal or subcarinal lymph nodes

Stage IIIb
Tumor extending into major mediastinal structures or causing malignant pleural effusion, OR metastases to scalene or supraclavicular lymph nodes or to contralateral mediastinal or hilar lymph nodes

Stage IV
Tumor with distant metastases

questions. First, does the patient have a primary lung cancer? Second, if a primary lung cancer is present, is it localized? Third, if it is localized, can the patient tolerate resection? The sequence in Table 54-2 is suggested for the conduct of the clinical evaluation of lung cancer.

The initial evaluation for lung cancer begins with

TABLE 54-2

Suggested Sequence for the Diagnostic Evaluation of an Elderly Patient with Suspected Lung Cancer

Initial Evaluation

Chest x ray
  Should be read by the clinician as well as the radiologist
  Should be compared with previous chest x rays
Sputum cytology
  Induction with nebulized hypertonic saline increases yield
  Positive cytology may also result from an upper airway
    cancer
Urine and stool for occult blood, serum chemistries, and
    complete blood count
  Minimizes the possibility of an extrathoracic primary
  Evaluates paraneoplastic syndromes
  Evaluates ability to tolerate chemotherapy
Spirometry and arterial blood gases
  Low value removes surgery as a therapeutic option (may
    alter aggressiveness of remaining workup)

Further Evaluation

Computed tomography of the chest
  Permits radiographic staging of the tumor
  Guides prethoracotomy mediastinoscopy, transbronchial,
    or needle biopsy
Computed tomography of brain and abdomen
Radionuclide scanning of bones
  Permits noninvasive staging of distant metastases
Prethoracotomy biopsy
  Pathology review required prior to definitive therapy to
    distinguish small-cell from non-small-cell cancer

the chest x ray. It is most important that the clinician read the chest x ray personally. This independent second reading will lower the chance of missing lung lesions that later prove to be lung cancer. Films should not be read in isolation, and old films should be obtained for comparison whenever possible. The pattern of change demonstrated by serial radiographs is crucial. The absence of radiographic change for a period of 2 years is strong presumptive evidence of benignity. Except for such radiographic stability or the presence of central, homogeneous, or popcorn calcifications, all of which indicate benignity, no radiographic criteria can reliably distinguish benign from malignant lesions.

At the present time, computed tomography (CT) is the best method for the radiographic TNM staging of lung cancer. The excellent contrast of the cross-sectional CT often resolves complicated anatomic presentations seen on chest radiographs (e.g., opaque hemithorax or pleural effusion). In evaluating tumor involvement of the mediastinum, however, the CT scan can only determine lymph node size, not tumor involvement. Normal-sized nodes (smaller than 1 cm) may harbor metastases, and nodes larger than 1 cm are often benign. Furthermore,

N_1 disease (hilum involvement) does not eliminate the need for a pneumonectomy in an otherwise operable patient. Magnetic resonance imaging (MRI) may help to evaluate mediastinal lymph nodes (see below). Generally, however, surgical sampling of lymph nodes is required to stage the mediastinum.

At some stage in the clinical course the sputum cytology has been found to be positive in more than 90 percent of lung cancers. While the frequency of positive cytologies in preclinical lung cancer is considerably lower (approximately 25 percent), the cytological examination of an induced sputum specimen is noninvasive and relatively inexpensive and should be undertaken in any subject in whom lung cancer is suspected. The induction procedure is thought to be important. In one study, only 20 percent of the cytologically detected cancers were identified without induction. Two cautions should be noted. First, the absence of a positive sputum cytology does not mean that cancer is not present. Second, the presence of a positive cytology and a positive chest x ray does not mean that the positive cytology has necessarily originated from the region of the chest x ray abnormality. Lung cancer may be a multifocal disease in the bronchial epithelium, and not all sites may be radiographically apparent. In addition, a positive sputum cytology often results from an upper airway cancer, which is not surprising given the association of both upper and lower airway cancers with cigarette smoking.

Urine and stool specimens should be tested for occult blood on three occasions to minimize the possibility that an occult extrathoracic primary lesion is responsible for a chest x-ray nodule. In an asymptomatic individual with three normal urine and stool examinations and a normal alkaline phosphatase, the likelihood of missing an extrathoracic primary is less than 2.5 percent.

Spirometry and measurement of arterial blood gases are performed as part of the preoperative evaluation because elimination of surgery as a therapeutic option for lung cancer may alter the aggressiveness of the remainder of the workup. Although the elderly male cigarette smokers at high risk for lung cancer are also at high risk for chronic obstructive pulmonary disease, few of these individuals will have an FEV_1 less than 1 liter, demonstrate alveolar hypoventilation (retain CO_2), or have pulmonary hypertension, all contraindications to pulmonary resection. Nevertheless, patients with impaired pulmonary function may be considered for segmental or wedge resection of the primary tumor, or for "curative" radiotherapy.

A rule-of-thumb evaluation of adequate respiratory reserve might consist of the following: If, after climbing three flights of stairs with the physician, the patient is able to hold a conversation without pausing for breath, his or her respiratory reserve is probably adequate to undergo thoracotomy with lobectomy. A somewhat more quantitative estimate would suggest that after re-section, the patient should be left with at least 1.0 liter of FEV_1 to avoid crippling postoperative dyspnea. An esti-mate of the effect of resection can be obtained by a quan-titative partition of a ventilation scan. For example, if 45 percent of the ventilation goes to the left lung during a scan, it can be estimated that 45 percent of the ventila-tory function would be lost if a left pneumonectomy were performed. If this percentage is then subtracted from the preoperative FEV_1, an estimate of postopera-tive ventilatory function results. Studies have shown that this estimation technique is quite good for pneumonec-tomies but considerably less accurate for lobectomies, tending to overestimate the loss in these cases.

Serum chemistries and complete blood counts are obtained to evaluate the more common sites of extra-thoracic metastases, to look for common paraneoplastic syndromes (inappropriate ADH, increased ACTH pro-duction, leukemoid reaction, myelophthisic anemia), and to evaluate the patient's ability to tolerate chemo-therapy. CT of the brain and abdomen has replaced brain and liver/spleen scanning for the evaluation of metastatic spread of lung cancer to these organs. A nor-mal radionuclide bone scan should eliminate the need for a radiographic skeletal survey, unless there is an indi-cation for obtaining a specific image (for example, bone pain at a specific site). Although the bone scan is more sensitive in detecting metastases than is the radiograph (which only becomes abnormal when sufficient bone destruction has occurred), the radiograph may demon-strate nonmalignant (e.g., degenerative) causes for in-creased activity on a bone scan. In individuals for whom curative surgery is not contemplated, the least invasive route is then chosen to obtain a tissue diagnosis. Bron-choscopy, transthoracic needle biopsy, and supraclavic-ular node biopsy are useful, minimally invasive tech-niques.

For those individuals in whom activity status and stage suggest the possibility of curative intervention, further evaluation is warranted to minimize the possibil-ity of occult metastases. The nature of this extended workup depends upon the findings on the chest x ray. Three patterns deserve particular attention: the negative chest x ray, the solitary pulmonary nodule, and the chest x-ray evidence of intrathoracic metastases.

NEGATIVE CHEST X RAY

If, on initial evaluation, a positive cytology was found in a patient with a negative chest x ray, fiberoptic bron-choscopy should be preceded by an otolaryngologist's evaluation of the upper airway. During the broncho-scopic examination of the cytology-positive, x ray–negative patient, brushings from each segment should be collected separately. This facilitates tumor localiza-tion when subtle mucosal changes escape visual recogni-tion. If the cytological specimens fail to show at least moderate atypia after a comprehensive brushing, then it is unlikely that bronchial neoplasia is responsible for the abnormal sputum cytology, and the upper airway should be examined further with direct laryngoscopy.

THE SOLITARY PULMONARY NODULE

If the initial chest x ray shows a parenchymal mass sur-rounded by air-containing lung and there is no evidence of an extrathoracic primary, one must try to obtain previ-ous chest x rays. If these films show that the lesion was present and unchanged for 2 or more years, no further action is indicated. An annual follow-up chest x ray is reasonable, but there is no proven benefit to this proce-dure.

If old films are not available, or if old films show a change in lesion size, then CT scanning is done to look for calcification. If homogeneous, popcorn, or central calcification is present, no further action is necessary at that time. Other calcification patterns or absence of cal-cification calls for further workup.

At this point the age of the patient becomes impor-tant. A noncalcified pulmonary nodule in an individual over age 40 is likely to be malignant. Thoracotomy and resection is indicated unless (1) the lesion is shown radi-ographically to have doubled its volume within 1 month (in which case it is probably inflammatory) or (2) medical evidence accumulated during the initial evaluation indi-cates that the patient cannot tolerate these procedures. In both situations, fiberoptic bronchoscopy with a trans-bronchial biopsy or a percutaneous needle biopsy should be undertaken and the results used as a guide to ther-apy. The purpose of the biopsy is to bring back a definite tissue diagnosis in an individual with a low risk of malig-nancy and spare the patient an unnecessary thoracot-omy. Individuals over 40 years of age who have a newly developing, noncalcified lesion have a high risk of malig-nancy. These individuals, too, should be biopsied to es-tablish the cell type (SCLC or NSCLC) prior to thoracot-omy. Fiberoptic bronchoscopy should be undertaken preoperatively in all cases to evaluate margins prior to resection. Lesions less than 2 cm from the carina may not be resectable (stage IIIa). Mediastinoscopy or trans-bronchial needle biopsy of the carina may be useful for staging such cases.

CHEST X RAY EVIDENCE OF INTRATHORACIC METASTASES

If hilar or mediastinal adenopathy is present, additional studies are needed. Fluoroscopy may delineate loss of diaphragmatic movement, but radiographic contrast studies of the mediastinum have largely been supplanted by CT scanning. Distinction of hilar and mediastinal nodes from vascular structures may be assisted by MRI. The high-contrast MRI images are produced without ionizing radiation or contrast media. In addition to heightened contrast, MRI can produce sagittal and coronal projections to clarify anatomic relationships. However, MRI cannot detect calcification (especially in pulmonary nodules) and appears to be inferior to CT in spatial resolution, limiting the usefulness of MRI for evaluating parenchymal structures.

The discovery of hilar or mediastinal adenopathy raises the likelihood that resection will not be curative. Transtracheal needle biopsy, mediastinoscopy, or parasternal exploration should be undertaken prior to thoracotomy to minimize the morbidity in potentially unresectable patients. If mediastinoscopy is negative, one may proceed directly to a thoracotomy. A positive mediastinoscopy terminates surgical therapy in many institutions. A needle biopsy is generally employed to confirm a diagnosis of cancer in potentially unresectable individuals for whom mediastinoscopy is not appropriate.

THERAPY

Thoracotomy and resection achieve the greatest likelihood of long-term cure of lung cancer. In younger patients, a decision to recommend resection is strongly influenced by the poor prognosis in patients who do not have surgery, since most eventually die from their disease. Lung cancer discovered before the onset of symptoms in some patients may allow survival of 2 to 5 years or more. There is evidence that these relatively slower-growing lung cancers are more common in the elderly. Surgery therefore deserves serious consideration even in patients over age 70; however, resection will be advisable in only a minority of such patients, since with increasing age operative morbidity and mortality increase while the benefits of successful resection are reduced.

Features predictive of a surgical cure include peripheral tumor location and documented slow growth on serial films with a well-differentiated histological appearance. The risk of death from thoracotomy is increased by the presence of coexisting medical illness, particularly obstructive lung disease and coronary artery disease, both of which are common in the elderly patient who has been a smoker. Resection for cancer is hardly ever justified after age 70 if an estimate of postoperative pulmonary function predicts that the remaining FEV_1 will be less than 1.0 liter or if any degree of CO_2 retention is present. The presence of angina, heart failure, poorly controlled arrhythmia, or recent myocardial infarction is also usually regarded as a contraindication to surgery.

Even in the very fit older patient, there is an increased operative risk which must be weighed against potential benefits of resection. By selection of patients and extent of resection, perioperative mortality rates have varied from 2 to 20 percent in patients over age 70 undergoing resection for lung cancer. The incidence of major complications and death was significantly greater among patients undergoing pneumonectomy than among patients undergoing subsegmental or segmental resections. The high complication rate for extensive resection in this age group must be compared with actuarial survival. Five-year survival rates of 13 percent have been reported for patients undergoing pneumonectomy, 21 percent after lobectomy, and 42 percent after segmental resection. Therefore, at the present state of the art, the risk associated with pneumonectomy may outweigh its potential benefit for the 70-year-old patient with lung cancer.

Some patients who survive "curative resection" experience a prolonged and difficult convalescence because of postoperative pain, exertional dyspnea, and problems with nutrition and stamina. It is not uncommon to see an elderly patient who never regains his or her former feeling of well-being after surgery. This fact is especially important in deciding whether to attempt resection in the asymptomatic patient. It is well to bear in mind that older patients often place a high value on comfortable short-term survival, and, if they understand clearly the risks and benefits, they may be disinclined to gamble in order to be eligible for long-term survival.

Although surgery remains the therapy of choice for potentially curable lesions (localized cancer, good activity status), for the majority of elderly patients, therapy must be designed to relieve discomfort (palliation) and control complications. Radiotherapy is the primary mode of palliative treatment. Yet it must also be realized that, like surgery, radiotherapy is only locally effective. The focal effects of the primary tumor or its metastases frequently respond well to this treatment. However, neither adjuvant radiotherapy (pre- or postoperative) nor chemotherapy has been shown to improve survival, while both of these treatments result in side effects. The general approach to NSCLC therapy, therefore, has been to withhold intervention until symptoms appear.

Local complications of the tumor mass which frequently cause symptoms are due to tumor obstruction of hollow structures. Perhaps the most common of these are atelectasis and pneumonia from bronchial obstruction, dysphagia from esophageal obstruction, and superior vascular congestion from superior vena caval obstruction. Palliative radiotherapy in doses of 2000 rads over 1 week is frequently successful in relieving such obstruction. The symptoms produced by extrapulmonary metastases depend upon the site affected. Bone metastases to spine and rib are frequently quite painful and may further result in neural compression. Bone metastases often respond dramatically to low-dose palliative radiation. Similarly, focal brain metastases often respond to a combination of Decadron (to reduce local inflammation) and radiotherapy. The use of radiotherapy to treat intracranial metastases without prior protection with steroids or mannitol may lead to further complications as the brain swells from irradiation. Due to the high rates of brain metastases in adenocarcinoma and large-cell carcinoma, some physicians administer prophylactic cranial irradiation to patients with these types of cancer.

Inoperable patients with stage I or stage II disease (with sufficient pulmonary reserve) may be considered for radiation therapy with curative intent. Among those with excellent performance status, up to a 20 percent 3-year survival rate may be expected if a course of irradiation with curative intent can be completed. Patients who are inoperable due to locally or regionally advanced tumors are treated with radiation therapy, surgery, or a combination of the two. Although the majority of these patients do not achieve complete response to radiation, there is a reproducible long-term survival benefit in 5 to 10 percent of patients treated with this modality, and significant palliation often results.

At the present time, the proven role of chemotherapy in the treatment of non-small-cell bronchogenic carcinoma is limited to the use of alkylating agents in the pleural space to control recurrent pleural effusion. Systemic chemotherapy does have a role in the treatment of SCLC. The disseminated presentation of this cell type has meant that local therapies are useful only for diagnosis (surgery) or palliation (radiotherapy). Systemic combination chemotherapy has been able to induce a short-term response in more than two-thirds of cases of SCLC. Combination chemotherapy has increased the median survival of this cancer from 4 months (untreated) to approximately 1 year. Although prolonged survivals are uncommon, 5 to 10 percent of SCLC patients remain free of disease for more than 2 years from the start of therapy. Many of these 2-year survivors may be cured of their SCLC. Yet the overall, unsatisfactory long-term response of SCLC to current therapy means that all patients with this type of cancer should be considered for inclusion in investigational treatment protocols at the time of diagnosis. The National Cancer Institute maintains a listing of currently active treatment protocols on their Physicians Data Query (PDQ) data base.

PROGNOSIS

General prognostic statements may be based upon cell type. The best survivals have been observed with epidermoid and adenocarcinomas, and the poorest with the anaplastic tumors (large-cell and small-cell undifferentiated). Within each cell type, the degree of differentiation has prognostic significance. Patients with well-differentiated cancers have a better survival rate. However, the histological distinctions between cell types are not always well-defined. As a result, it is unwise to base therapeutic plans upon cell type alone, except to distinguish small-cell from non-small-cell cancer. Small-cell cancer of the lung is characterized by a rapid growth rate and early dissemination. Accounting for about 25 percent of clinical lung cancer, small-cell usually presents with signs of extrathoracic spread to bone, brain, or liver. Approximately one-third of patients with small-cell carcinoma will have limited stage disease (tumor confined to one hemithorax, the mediastinum, and the supraclavicular lymph nodes) at the time of diagnosis. Most 2-year disease-free survivors come from this group, and a median survival of 10 to 16 months can be expected with current therapy. However, the majority of patients with SCLC have extensive stage disease at the time of diagnosis (tumor spread beyond the supraclavicular areas, commonly to brain and marrow) and may expect a median survival of 6 to 12 months.

Survival in non-small-cell cancer has been shown to be related more closely to activity level and stage than to either cell type or subsequent therapy. Patients may be divided into three prognostic groups of roughly equivalent size. Patients in the first group (stages I and II) have surgically resectable tumors. This group has the best prognosis (30 to 80 percent 5-year survival). Elderly patients in this group who have medical contraindications to curative surgery can be considered for curative radiation therapy with an expected cure rate at 5 years of approximately 20 percent. The second group includes those patients with either local or regional lymph node metastases limited to the hemithorax with tumor (stage IIIa). Patients in this group, treated with radiation therapy alone or in combination with surgery, have an overall 5-year survival of 10 percent or less, and the median survival is less than a year. The group with the poorest prognosis includes patients found with distant metastases at the time of diagnosis (stage IV). Patients in this group are treated for palliation of symptoms and may expect a median survival of less than 6 months. Five-year survival of patients with distant metastases is rare. Patients with good performance status and limited number of sites of distant metastases have received a 2- to 3-month benefit from clinical trials of combined chemotherapy.

GENERAL READING

Ali MK, Mountain CF, Ewer MS et al: Predicting loss of pulmonary function after pulmonary resection for bronchogenic carcinoma. *Chest* 77:337, 1980.

American Joint Committee on Cancer: Staging of cancer at specific anatomic sites: Lung, in *Manual for Staging of Cancer*, 2d ed. Philadelphia, Lippincott, 1983, pp 99–105.

American Thoracic Society: Clinical staging of primary lung cancer. *Am Rev Respir Dis* 127:659, 1983.

Baker RR, Lillemoe KD, Tockman MS: The indications for transcervical mediastinoscopy in patients with stage I bronchogenic carcinoma. *Surg Gynecol Obstet* 148:860, 1979.

Breyer RH et al: Thoracotomy in patients over age seventy years. *J Thorac Cardiovasc Surg* 81:187, 1981.

Chasen MH: Imaging primary lung cancers, pleural cancers, and metastatic disease. *CA* 37(4):194, 1987.

Gail MH, Eagan RT, Feld R et al: Prognostic factors in patients with resected stage I non-small cell lung cancer: A report from the Lung Cancer Study Group. *Cancer* 54(9):1802, 1984.

Ginsberg RJ, Hill LD, Eagan RT et al: Modern thirty-day operative mortality for surgical resections in lung cancer. *J Thorac Cardiovasc Surg* 86(5):654, 1983.

Hoffmann TH, Ransdell HT: Comparison of lobectomy and wedge resection for carcinoma of the lung. *J Thorac Cardiovasc Surg* 79(2):211, 1980.

Hubbard SM, Henney JE, DeVita VT Jr: A computer data base for information on cancer treatment. *N Engl J Med* 316:315, 1987.

Libshitz HI, McKenna RJ: Mediastinal lymph node size in lung cancer. *AJR* 143:715, 1984.

Martini N, Beattie EJ: Results of surgical treatment in Stage I lung cancer. *J Thorac Cardiovasc Surg* 74(4):499, 1977.

Mountain CF: A new international staging system for lung cancer. *Chest* 89(suppl 4):225, 1986.

Nagasaki F, Flehinger BJ, Martini N: Complications of surgery in the treatment of carcinoma of the lung. *Chest* 82:25, 1982.

Osterlind K, Hansen HH, Hansen M et al: Mortality and morbidity in long-term surviving patients treated with chemotherapy with or without irradiation for small-cell lung cancer. *J Clin Oncol* 4(7):1044, 1986.

Perry MC, Eaton WL, Propert KJ et al: Chemotherapy with or without radiation therapy in limited small-cell carcinoma of the lung. *N Engl J Med* 316(15):912, 1987.

Ross WM: How to deal with bronchogenic carcinoma in the elderly. *Geriatrics* 31(6):107, 1976.

Selikoff IJ, Hammond EC, Churg J: Asbestos exposure, smoking and neoplasia. *JAMA* 204:106, 1968.

Silverberg E, Lubera J: Cancer statistics, 1987. *CA* 37(1):2, 1987.

Tockman MS, Gupta PK, Meyers JD et al: Sensitive and specific monoclonal antibody recognition of human lung cancer antigen on preserved sputum cells: A new approach to early lung cancer detection. *J Clin Oncol* 6:1685, 1988.

Tockman MS, Anthonisen NR, Wright EC, Donithan MG: Airways obstruction and the risk for lung cancer. *Ann Intern Med* 106:512, 1987.

U.S. Department of Health, Education, and Welfare: Smoking and Health: A Report of the Surgeon General. Washington, Government Printing Office, (PHS) 79-50066, 1979.

SECTION C

The Renal System
and
Urinary Tract

Chapter 55

AGING CHANGES
IN RENAL FUNCTION

Laurence H. Beck and John M. Burkart

The kidneys of elderly individuals are smaller than those of younger individuals, and have lower blood flow and a lower filtration rate. In addition, many of the homeostatic functions of the kidney are less robust in the elderly, leading to a greater likelihood of failure under stress. A healthy controversy continues about the genesis of these changes, i.e., whether the changes are age-associated or disease-associated. For the most part, data currently available have been derived from numerous cross-sectional studies, usually of apparently healthy aged individuals. Nevertheless, the relatively fewer longitudinal studies carried out on "clinically clean" aging cohorts have, in general, confirmed the conclusions of the cross-sectional studies, indicating aging per se as a major contributor to renal changes.

Despite the anatomic, histologic, and functional changes to be described herein, the aging kidney remains capable of maintaining body fluid and solute homeostasis remarkably well, even into the ninth and tenth decades of life, unless concurrent disease or severe stresses are imposed. In most elderly individuals, the loss of function is accompanied by no clinical signs or symptoms, and the internal environment is adequately maintained.

ANATOMIC CHANGES

The normal adult kidney weighs 150 to 200 g at age 30. There is a gradual decrease in mass with aging, so that by age 90 the average weight is 20 to 30 percent less, or 110 to 150 g.[1] Concomitantly, the renal size decreases. McLachlan and Wasserman studied the length, area, and distensibility of kidneys from patients having intravenous urograms. They found that kidney length decreased by about 0.5 cm per decade after age 50; furthermore, they estimated that renal volume decreased 40 percent by age 90.[2]

Most of the tissue lost with aging is from the renal cortex[3] and represents parallel glomerular and tubular loss.[4] The total number of glomeruli falls by 30 to 40 percent by age 80,[5] and the glomerular surface area decreases progressively after age 40.[6] Equally important is the increasing number of totally sclerotic (and presumably nonfunctioning) glomeruli. Although fewer than 1 percent of glomeruli are sclerotic in the young adult, this percentage rises to 10 to 30 percent by age 80.[7,8] Within surviving glomeruli, numerous changes have been noted, including decreased size and number of glomerular tufts, increased basement membrane thickness, and expanded mesangium.[4,6,9]

Several vascular changes have been described in the aging kidney.[4,10,11] In the cortex, both the afferent and efferent arterioles tend to atrophy in a parallel manner, resulting in a bloodless glomerulus. In the juxtamedullary region, the atrophy is asymmetric, so that afferent-efferent arteriolar fistulas (so-called continuous units) are formed. The result is that while cortical blood flow is reduced, juxtamedullary flow may be paradoxically increased (relative to overall renal blood flow). This increase probably contributes to the urinary concentrating deficit in the elderly patient by interfering with the countercurrent system balance of flows.[12]

The tubules also undergo changes. The number and length of proximal tubules decrease,[4] whereas tubular diverticula become common in the distal nephron.[6] Baert and Steg have suggested that these diverticula may be the progenitors of the common simple cysts seen in the aged kidney.[13]

The vascular and tubular changes in the aging kidney are often accompanied by mild interstitial fibrosis. Taken in concert, these vascular, tubular, and interstitial changes resemble those seen in several mild chronic interstitial diseases. From a functional standpoint, therefore, it is useful to consider these changes as the "tubulointerstitial nephropathy of the elderly."

RENAL BLOOD FLOW

Numerous cross-sectional studies have documented a fall in total renal blood flow of about 10 percent per decade after age 20, so that renal blood flow (RBF) in the octogenarian averages only 300 ml/min, compared to 600 ml/min in the young adult.[14,15,16] Probably as a result of the anatomic changes described above, the major decrement in RBF is from the cortex. Hollenberg and colleagues, using the xenon washout technique in healthy potential kidney donors, demonstrated that in the cortex there is a progressive decrease in RBF per renal mass with age, suggesting that the decreased RBF is not secondary to tissue loss but is probably primary in *causing* the parenchymal atrophy.[16] Furthermore, they demonstrated less responsiveness of RBF to physiologic and pharmacologic maneuvers (saline infusion, acetylcholine) in older individuals than in younger individuals. The decrease in RBF probably results from the combina-

tion of decreased cardiac output and age-related changes in the larger hilar, arcuate, and interlobar arteries.

GLOMERULAR FILTRATION RATE

Given the fall in total RBF and the decrease in size and number of glomeruli, it is not surprising that the glomerular filtration rate (GFR) progressively decreases with age. Cross-sectional and longitudinal studies, using a variety of methodologies, have shown that GFR remains stable after adolescence, through age 30 to 35, and then falls at the rate of about 8 to 10 ml/min/1.73 m^2/decade. In a large cross-sectional study of 548 normal men at the Gerontology Research Center of the National Institute of Aging, Rowe and colleagues noted a mean creatinine clearance of 140 ml/min/1.73 m^2 at age 30, with a progressive fall thereafter to 97 ml/min/1.73 m^2 at age 80.[17]

More recently, Lindeman and coworkers reported the results of creatinine clearance measurements in a large number of normal volunteers followed for up to 23 years in the Baltimore Longitudinal Study of Aging.[18] These men were carefully studied every 12 to 18 months; those with a minimum of five studies were reported. Of 446 normal volunteers who entered the study, a group of 254 was selected on the basis of absence of hypertension, urinary tract disease, or diuretic use. The mean decrease in creatinine clearance for this group was 0.75 ml/min/year. There was a normal distribution of values around the mean, including about 30 percent of subjects who showed no significant decrease in creatinine clearance over time.

The mechanism for the declining GFR over time is unknown. A number of theories have evolved which parallel the theories of aging per se. Recently, Anderson and Brenner, drawing upon aging animal models, have suggested that the decrease in glomerular filtration rate that accompanies aging is a consequence of persistent glomerular hyperfiltration resulting from the usual high-protein diet of modern humans.[19] Animal models have demonstrated that protein restriction can virtually eliminate the sclerotic glomerular changes that occur in normally aging rats fed an ad libitum diet. Although there is little direct support for this theory in humans, it has attracted widespread support.

The fall in creatinine clearance with age is not accompanied by a rise in serum creatinine concentration, which remains essentially unchanged over the duration of adult life. Therefore, it follows that daily creatinine production (and urinary excretion of creatinine) must fall in parallel with the decrease in creatinine clearance. Such a decline was documented by Rowe and colleagues[17] and reflects the decreasing muscle mass with aging which parallels the fall in GFR. The important clinical consequences of these observations are that a normal serum creatinine concentration of 0.8 mg/dl in an 80-year-old man reflects a GFR which is 40 to 50 percent less than the GFR of a 30-year-old of the same size with creatinine concentration of 0.8 mg/dl.

Several authors have sought to develop formulas or nomograms to predict the creatinine clearance in individuals from the steady-state serum creatinine concentration, taking into account the fall in GFR with age. The most widely used is that of Cockcroft and Gault[20]:

$$\text{Creatinine clearance} = \frac{(140 - \text{age, yr}) \ (\text{weight, kg})}{72 \times \left(\begin{array}{c} \text{serum creatinine} \\ \text{concentration, mg/dl} \end{array}\right)}$$

Because of the time and logistical difficulties in collecting complete 24-hour urine specimens to calculate creatinine clearance, this formula is employed frequently, particularly for elderly individuals and for drug-dosing nomograms (see Chap. 21). Although such a formula is preferable to using the serum creatinine concentration alone, it must be recognized that the variability that characterizes the physiology of elderly individuals makes this and other formulas imprecise. Particularly when renally cleared toxic drug dosages are being calculated, measurement of creatinine clearance and/or appropriate serum drug levels is strongly recommended.

TUBULAR FUNCTIONS

With the exception of urinary concentration and dilution, tubular functions in the aged have not been well characterized nor extensively studied. The available data do suggest, however, that, as with other renal functional parameters, the homeostatic limits are narrowed in the aging kidney for glucose transport, acid excretion, and sodium transport.

A series of studies carried out by Dontas and co-workers[21] and by Shock and his colleagues[22,23] addressed proximal tubular reabsorption and secretory capacity by measuring tubular transport of glucose, para-amino hippurate (PAH), and iodopyracet (Diodrast). Effective renal plasma flow (measured as PAH clearance) falls linearly from the fourth through the ninth decade. The filtration fraction remains constant throughout most of adult life, then shows a modest increase during the seventh, eighth, and ninth decades. Tubular transport maximums for PAH and Diodrast fall progressively with age, but do so in a way parallel to the fall in GFR. These findings have been interpreted to indicate support for the intact nephron hypothesis, i.e., the hypothesis that there is not a specific age-associated defect in transport of these substances, but as nephrons atrophy with age the total transport capacity decreases.

Glucose transport by the kidney was evaluated by Miller, McDonald, and Shock[23] in individuals ranging in age from 20 to 90 years old. Maximum transport capacity for glucose (T_mG) was measured by standard clearance methods. The authors reported a fall in T_mG from 359 mg/min/liter/1.73 m² at age 30 to 219 mg/min/liter/1.73 m² at age 85. This decrease in T_mG closely paralleled the observed fall in GFR, so that the GFR:T_mG ratio remained constant across the decades. These findings also support the intact nephron hypothesis, suggesting that there is no specific defect in glucose transport per se, but the total capacity falls as the number of nephrons decreases with age.

In contrast to the diminished T_mG, the renal glucose threshold is increased with age.[24] This discrepancy has not been well explained but may be due to selective loss of nephrons with low individual thresholds, resulting in less splay in the titration curve.

Although acid-base parameters are normal under basal conditions, the ability to respond to an acid load is impaired in the elderly. Adler and colleagues administered 0.1 g/kg ammonium chloride (NH_4Cl) to 26 normal volunteers, including nine aged 72 to 93.[25] All men demonstrated a rapid increase in renal acid excretion, and minimum urinary pH was similar in young and old; however, the older men excreted only 19 percent of the acid load over 8 hours, compared to 35 percent excreted by the younger men. The decrease in net acid excretion was due to a decrease of both urinary NH_4 and phosphorus. Because the inulin clearance of the older men was markedly lower than that of the younger men, the authors concluded that the decrease in acid excretory capacity was proportional to the decrease in GFR and was the result of decreased nephron mass.

Recently, Agarwal and Cabebe[26] used ammonium chloride loading to assess acid excretion in 16 healthy male volunteers aged 29 to 86. Baseline net acid excretions were similar between young and old, as were ammonia excretion and titratable acid excretion when factored for GFR. After the short NH_4Cl load, despite an equivalent fall in plasma bicarbonate concentration, the older individuals showed significantly decreased net acid excretion in 6 hours as compared to that of the younger men. This defect was characterized by a slight difference in minimal urinary pH and a large decrease in NH_4 excretion, both absolute and when factored for GFR.

SODIUM HANDLING

The limits of sodium excretion and sodium conservation have not been systematically addressed in the elderly, although it is probable that homeostatic flexibility is reduced, as with other solutes. It is usually stated that the aging kidney is sodium-wasting and that older individuals are more likely to become salt-depleted during periods of sodium deprivation. These presumptions are only weakly corroborated by experimental data. Epstein and Hollenberg compared the time required to achieve sodium balance when healthy young (under 30) and older (over 60) adults were placed on a very low (10 meq) sodium diet.[27] The half-time necessary for sodium balance was 17.6 hours in the younger individuals, compared to 31 hours in the elderly individuals. Although this difference was statistically significant, the clinical implication is uncertain. On the other hand, Weidmann and coworkers found similar weight reduction (about 2.5 percent of body weight) in young (ages 20 to 30) versus older (ages 60 to 70) adults after 6 days of a 10 meq sodium diet, suggesting no serious impairment of sodium conservation in younger elderly individuals.[28]

If sodium conservation is limited, it may be due to defects in the renin-aldosterone axis that have been repeatedly demonstrated in older subjects. Tsunoda and colleagues, for example, found that although total renin concentration remains stable with age, there is an age-dependent decline in *active* renin concentration, as well as in plasma aldosterone concentration.[29] Similarly, basal and stimulated plasma aldosterone concentration has been shown to decrease with age.[30] Weidmann and colleagues evaluated the effect of sodium intake and posture on two groups of healthy volunteers of both sexes: twelve aged 20 to 30 and seven aged 62 to 70. Renin concentration, plasma renin activity (PRA), and serum aldosterone concentrations were measured on a low (10 meq/day) and high (120 meq/day) sodium diet, and in the supine and upright positions. Despite comparable sodium and fluid balance between young and old, all measurements were lower in the older age group, and these changes were most pronounced in patients measured in the upright position while on the low sodium intake. Interestingly, the aldosterone response to adrenocorticotropic hormone (ACTH) was similar between the two groups, suggesting that the diminished postural and volume-mediated aldosterone concentrations were due principally to the blunted renin response and not to any defect in the adrenal cortex.[28]

It is widely held that the elderly have diminished capacity to handle acute sodium loads. Although the decrease in GFR with age might well limit the rate of an acute response to volume expansion, systematic evaluation of the response to sodium loads has not been reported in older individuals. Of interest are recent studies[31–34] reporting that circulating levels of atrial natriuretic peptide (ANP) are higher in elderly individuals than in younger persons on the same sodium intake. Metabolic clearance of ANP is prolonged in elderly,[33] and it has been suggested that there may be a diminished cellular response[31] to the peptide. It is uncertain whether these differences have physiologic importance in the maintenance of sodium homeostasis.

POTASSIUM HOMEOSTASIS

It is commonly believed that potassium homeostasis is impaired in old people and that they are more prone to hyperkalemia and hypokalemia, when stressed, than are their younger counterparts.[35] However, there are few systematic studies of the effect of age on potassium homeostasis. In one study,[36] the body compositions of 40 healthy elderly men and women (mean age 79) from a retirement community were compared with the body compositions of 20 healthy young medical students. Exchangeable potassium was 10 to 25 percent lower in the older subjects; this was correlated with, but out of proportion to, the lower lean body mass. Serum potassium concentration was not different between the two groups. These data suggest that potassium homeostasis is normal on standard dietary intakes.

Although several factors (decreased GFR, blunted renin-aldosterone axis, decreased tubular mass) predict that defense against hyperkalemia in the face of increased potassium loads may be impaired, such potassium-loading studies have not been reported. Similarly, the capacity for potassium conservation in the face of decreased intake or of nonrenal potassium loss has not been studied.

WATER HOMEOSTASIS

Age-associated changes in water metabolism are the best characterized of all the renal functional changes, in part because the clinical consequences can be so dramatic in the elderly.

Total body water, in both absolute and relative terms, decreases with age.[36] The proportion of body mass represented by water falls progressively with aging from about 55 to 60 percent at age 20 to 45 to 55 percent at age 80. This decrease is much more pronounced in women than in men, principally due to their proportionately decreased lean body mass and hence increased proportion of body fat. Because of the decrease in starting body water volume, losses and gains of water in women will be reflected in more pronounced changes in body fluid osmolality.

In order to excrete a concentrated urine in the setting of fluid deprivation or hypertonicity of body fluids, a person needs an intact posterior pituitary capable of secreting vasopressin (antidiuretic hormone [ADH]), intact renal circulation and medullary solute gradient, and renal tubules that are responsive to ADH. Each of these components of the system has been evaluated in elderly subjects in an attempt to explain the well-described decrease in maximal urinary concentration.[37,38]

The pituitary response to osmotic and nonosmotic stimuli has been reported by several investigators. Although it has been suggested by some[12] that central ADH release is impaired, it is clear that this is not the case, and that, in fact, elderly subjects have normal to *supra*normal responses to a variety of stimuli.

Helderman and colleagues[39] evaluated the pituitary ADH responses to ethanol and to hypertonic saline infusions in healthy elderly (aged 34 to 92, recruited from the Baltimore Longitudinal Study of Aging cohort) and compared them to those in younger individuals (aged 21 to 49). Baseline serum osmolality, plasma sodium concentration, and plasma immunoreactive arginine vasopressin (AVP) concentrations were similar. Both young and old demonstrated a prompt fall in AVP after an infusion of ethanol, a known inhibitor of pituitary vasopressin secretion. The suppression was much briefer in the older subjects, however, despite similar blood alcohol levels in the two groups. When hypertonic saline was infused to raise plasma osmolality, there was an increase in AVP in both groups, but the concentrations in the older subjects were almost double those in the younger subjects. For any given plasma osmolality, this increase in AVP levels can be considered the sensitivity of the hypothalamic-pituitary osmoreceptors; the sensitivity is clearly exaggerated in elderly subjects. Other investigators have found elevated *basal* AVP levels in healthy elderly as compared to levels in younger individuals.[40]

Despite the unimpaired AVP secretory capacity in elderly individuals, maximal urinary concentration after water deprivation is impaired. Over 50 years ago, Lewis and Alving evaluated "normal men," aged 40 to 101, for their capacity to concentrate the urine after 24 hours of a "dry diet" (total fluid deprivation). Twenty men were studied in each age decade up to age 90. There was a progressive decrease in maximal specific gravity by decade after age 40, so that the average specific gravity at age 40 was 1.030, but by age 90 it had fallen to 1.023.[37]

More recently, Rowe and coworkers studied 98 active community-dwelling men from the Baltimore Longitudinal Study of Aging after 12 hours of water deprivation.[38] Mean urine osmolality was reported for men in age groups representing 20-year intervals. There was a fall in maximal osmolality from 1109 mosm/kg for ages 20 to 39, to 1051 mosm/kg for ages 40 to 59, to 882 mosm/kg for ages 60 to 79. Analysis of individual data indicated that the decrease in urinary osmolality was not correlated with the level of creatinine clearance (which also fell with increasing age).

Several investigators have evaluated the responsiveness of the kidney to vasopressin. Lindeman and colleagues measured the response of normal men, aged 17 to 88 years, to submaximal vasopressin infusion (8 mU per hour) administered during a water diuresis.[41] Although their subjects had demonstrated an age-related decrease in maximal urinary osmolality (U_{max}) after 20 hours of water deprivation, the antidiuretic response to submaximal vasopressin during water diuresis was not different between younger and older men.

On the other hand, Miller and Shock, using a similar protocol, gave large doses of vasopressin (0.5 mU/kg body weight) to healthy adult males ages 26 to 86 during a sustained water diuresis.[42] Urine/plasma inulin ratios (U/P_{inulin}) was used as a measure of concentrating ability. Mean U/P_{inulin} was progressively lower with increasing age; mean value was 115 for the young men (mean age 35), 75 for the middle-aged men (mean age 55), and only 40 for the older men (mean age 73).

For humans, it is not known whether the age-related decrease in responsiveness to vasopressin is due to defective medullary circulation, altered medullary solute gradient, or a defect in the tubular cellular response to hormone. The relative increase in medullary blood flow and an increasing solute load to the intact remaining nephrons of the aging kidney could combine to decrease the medullary gradient.[43] On the other hand, studies in the aging rat, attempting to ascertain the mechanism of the age-related concentrating defect, have suggested that there is a decrease in water permeability along the collecting duct.[44]

The decreasing maximal urinary concentrating ability with age, while real, should not be clinically significant unless water loss is severe or thirst, the other arm of the homeostatic system, is not intact. Unfortunately, for most elderly individuals thirst appears to be blunted. In an elegantly simple study, Phillips and colleagues recently evaluated the pituitary and renal response, as well as thirst response, to 24 hours of water deprivation in two groups of healthy men, aged 20 to 31 and aged 67 to 75.[45] Corroborating other studies, this study demonstrated increased plasma AVP levels and decreased urine osmolality in the older group after dehydration. Thirst, measured by a previously validated visual-analogue rating scale, revealed marked differences between young and old. Thirst ratings in younger individuals rose rapidly during deprivation and were significantly higher than during baseline. In contrast, the older subjects' ratings did not differ significantly before and after 24 hours of water deprivation. Even more striking was the spontaneous water intake after the end of the deprivation, when both groups were given free access to water. The younger men drank more water than the elderly men and quickly restored plasma osmolality to normal; the elderly had not corrected themselves after 2 hours, despite equal access to water. Other investigators have demonstrated this striking thirst deficit in healthy older subjects,[46] as well as in healthy-appearing elderly individuals with a prior history of a cerebrovascular accident.[47]

In summary, the water conservation defect and tendency to dehydration in the elderly is multifactorial in origin. Total body water is diminished as a proportion of weight. Despite normal to supranormal vasopressin release in the face of hyperosmolality, the elderly person's renal response to vasopressin is blunted, compared to the response of younger individuals, resulting in diminished urinary concentration. Superimposed upon these changes, the thirst response to dehydration is blunted or absent in normal aged persons.

The ability of elderly individuals' kidneys to dilute the urine and to excrete a water load have not been extensively evaluated. Healthy young adults excrete 80 percent or more of a standard oral water load (20 ml/kg) within 5 hours after ingestion, and they achieve a minimum urine osmolality of less than 100 mosm/kg. Lindeman and colleagues reported the minimal urine osmolality after such a load to be 52 mosm/kg in a group of young men (mean age 31), 74 mosm/kg in a group of middle-aged men (mean age 60), and 92 mosm/kg in a group of older men (mean age 84).[41] Free water clearance (C_{H_2O}), similarly, was lower in the older group, although when factored for GFR the values were not different, suggesting that the difference in minimal urinary osmolality was due to the increased solute load per nephron in the elderly.[40]

Recently, Crowe and colleagues[46] carried out similar studies in a small number of healthy men (mean age 72) and came to a similar conclusion: there is a decrease in diluting capacity with age that is explained by the fall in GFR. Plasma AVP levels were measured and were found to be equally depressed after the water load in young and old groups, indicating that the decreased water excretion was not due to continuing inappropriate ADH secretion.

CLINICAL CONSEQUENCES OF PHYSIOLOGIC CHANGES

The functional changes of the aging kidney do not, of themselves, lead to clinical disease or disability. On the other hand, they leave the elderly individual much more vulnerable to a variety of environmental, disease-related, and drug-induced stresses. For example, the depressed GFR of the octogenarian, while not in a range to cause symptomatic retention of nitrogenous wastes, is much closer to the "uremic threshold" than the GFR of a younger person. Renal or nonrenal illnesses resulting in further depression of the GFR may lead to symptomatic renal failure with surprising rapidity in the elderly patient. Similarly, because the clearance of many potentially toxic drugs is primarily through glomerular filtra-

tion, the risk of such toxicity is markedly increased in normal elderly patients unless judicious dosage reduction is applied. The principles of appropriate drug dose modification are found in Chap. 21.

Illness (and the management thereof) is a common setting for the occurrence of fluid and electrolyte disorders in elderly persons. Disorders of water metabolism in particular (hyponatremia and hypernatremia) are prevalent among elderly inpatients.[48,49,50] In the following sections, the common disorders of salt, water, and potassium homeostasis will be reviewed.

DISORDERS OF SALT (SODIUM) METABOLISM

The total body content of sodium is the principal determinant of extracellular and intravascular fluid volume. Deficiency of sodium results in hypovolemia with its attendant clinical signs: tachycardia, hypotension, oliguria, and azotemia. Excess total body sodium results in edema with or without circulatory congestion.

Volume depletion is a common result of gastrointestinal disorders in the elderly. Primary salt losses occur through vomiting or diarrhea; anorexia often prevents oral replenishment. Although younger individuals would rapidly reduce urinary excretion of sodium to zero in such situations, the older patient, because of the sluggish renin-angiotensin and aldosterone response described previously, continues to excrete sodium inappropriately, contributing to further volume depletion. Since organ hypoperfusion is particularly dangerous to the elderly patient, it is imperative for the clinician to anticipate this tendency toward hypovolemia and take steps to counteract it, administering salt by the most appropriate route, both prophylactically and therapeutically. For patients with frank hypotension, the salt repletion should be rapid and parenteral, and it should always consist of physiologic ("normal") saline solution or colloid-containing fluid (plasma or blood). Only after circulatory stability has been achieved should the patient be switched to a nonisotonic solution.

When dealing with salt loads, the low GFR of the elderly does not ordinarily prevent prompt sodium excretion unless large quantities are administered acutely. However, the frequent concurrence of heart disease may prevent the requisite increase in cardiac output and renal blood flow necessary to deliver that load to the nephron for excretion. Elderly patients are therefore more susceptible to pulmonary edema under conditions of such salt loads.

DISORDERS OF WATER METABOLISM

The serum sodium concentration is usually the best index of total body water balance: hyponatremia occurs whenever there is a relative excess of water (relative to sodium content) and almost always indicates a defect in, or limitation upon, water excretion. Hypernatremia, on the other hand, is virtually always the consequence of relative water lack.

Hyponatremia

The prevalence of hyponatremia increases with age, particularly in hospitalized patients.[48,51] In one study carried out in a geriatric inpatient unit, 11.3 percent of all patients had a serum sodium concentration less than 130 mmol/liter, and 4.5 percent were below 125 mmol/liter.[51] The prevalence of hyponatremia has been reported to be somewhat lower, but still common (8 percent), in geriatric outpatients[52] and even higher (22 percent) in a chronic disease facility.[53] A recent study of prognosis in patients found to be hyponatremic on hospital admission indicated that this is a marker for serious illness: the likelihood of death in the hospital for someone with hyponatremia on admission was seven times the rate in nonhyponatremic-matched controls (8.7 percent vs. 1.1 percent).[54]

Patients with hyponatremia are usually classified clinically into one of three general pathophysiologic groups: (1) patients who are truly volume-depleted, as those with chronic diarrhea or diuretic-induced hypovolemia; (2) patients with edema states and excess total body sodium; (3) patients who are normovolemic, most of whom fit the definition of the syndrome of inappropriate antidiuretic hormone secretion (SIADH). Treatment of patients in the first category is straightforward: repletion of intravascular and extracellular fluid volume with colloid or normal saline usually allows rapid excretion of the excess water and correction of the hyponatremia. Patients in the second group require management of the underlying edema-forming state (e.g., congestive heart failure or cirrhosis), as well as judicious free water restriction.

Patients who fit into the third category are common among hyponatremic elderly because the diseases associated with SIADH are particularly prevalent (e.g., cancers, respiratory disorders, hypothyroidism, and central nervous system disease). In addition, a number of drugs used in the elderly can cause a drug-induced SIADH. Some of these drugs, such as chlorpropamide and indomethacin appear to enhance the renal tubular action of ADH, while others, such as carbamazepine, narcotics, and tricyclic antidepressants, increase central ADH release. It has been suggested that normal aging itself can be a "cause" of SIADH.[55]

Diuretic-induced hyponatremia appears to be particularly common in elderly patients.[56] Although some of these patients, particularly those with marked potassium losses, are normovolemic and mimic idiopathic SIADH,[57] most cases are probably due to salt and volume depletion with volume-stimulated ADH secretion.[58] Correction is usually easily accomplished by discontinuation of diuretics and cautious salt administration.

Mild hyponatremia usually results in no appreciable clinical symptoms. However, hyponatremia that is severe (below 125 mmol/liter) or that develops rapidly is often accompanied by central nervous system symptoms, including lethargy, somnolence, seizures, and coma. These symptoms are all thought to be due to neuronal cell swelling in the brain leading to increased intracranial pressure.

For mild hyponatremia unaccompanied by neurologic symptoms, management is simply to restrict free water intake. It must be remembered, however, that a patient with a persistently concentrated urine due to SIADH is dependent upon insensible loss for water excretion. Since, in the absence of fever, these losses rarely exceed 1000 ml per day, the restriction of intake must be below that level.

For more severe or symptomatic hyponatremia, more rapid correction is warranted. Although hypertonic (3%) sodium chloride solution can be used, the resultant volume expansion may overwhelm the circulatory system of an elderly patient and lead to pulmonary edema. Therefore, the well-described and effective technique of using a potent loop diuretic such as furosemide in combination with normal or hypertonic saline in an isovolemic "exchange" is safer.[59] There is controversy over the proper rate of correction of hyponatremia. A number of cases of a serious and potentially fatal central nervous system disorder, central pontine myelinolyis (CPM), have been described in patients who were severely hyponatremic and corrected rapidly. This disorder has not occurred in patients who were corrected rapidly but to less-than-normal values of serum sodium. Because the consequences of sustained severe hyponatremia are so dire, it is recommended that correction be made at the rate of about 2 mmol/liter until a concentration of about 124 to 130 mmol/liter is reached; then the correction should be slowed. Regardless of the speed of correction, neurologic symptoms often require days following full correction for recovery in the elderly. Persistence of somnolence or other signs should not prompt an invasive neurologic workup unless additional suggestive signs are present.

Hypernatremia

The multiple defects in water conservation described previously make dehydration and hypernatremia an ever-present threat in sick or disabled elderly persons. Illness-induced water loss, lack of thirst, and lack of access to water (due to immobility or neurologic depression) combine to make hypernatremic dehydration the most common fluid-electrolyte disorder in older individuals. Hypernatremia has been used as a marker for a poor prognosis in hospitalized patients[60] and for neglect in nursing home populations.[61]

Hypernatremia occurs frequently in sick elderly patients. Snyder and colleagues reviewed records at a general community teaching hospital over 2 years; of all hospital admissions for patients over the age of 60, 1.1 percent had confirmed hypernatremia (plasma sodium concentration greater than 148 mmol/liter).[49] Half of the cases of hypernatremia were present on admission; the others developed during hospitalization. Whereas overall mortality of the elderly patients was 6 percent, mortality in the hypernatremic group was 42 percent! Mortality of hypernatremic patients was similarly high (48 percent) in another hospital series report by Mahowald and Himmelstein.[60]

The symptoms of hypernatremia are similar to those of hyponatremia; neurologic signs predominate, with obtundation, lethargy, and coma being the most common. These signs are thought to result from neuronal cell dehydration and brain shrinkage.

Management of hypernatremic dehydration consists of correcting intravascular hypovolemia first (with normal saline) and then correcting the hypertonicity by administering hypotonic fluids. Since many elderly patients with hypernatremia have suffered combined salt and water losses, this second phase of correction should be with hypotonic saline ($\frac{1}{2}$ or $\frac{1}{4}$ normal). However, if the hypernatremia is the result of pure water loss (as may occur in unattended coma), then repletion can be with water alone (enteral water or intravenous dextrose and water).

The volume of free water required to restore body fluid tonicity to normal can be roughly estimated by the equation

$$\text{Water deficit} = [60\% \times \text{current body weight (kg)}] \times [(PNa/140) - 1]$$

where PNa = current plasma sodium concentration (mmol/liter). In severe dehydration, one-half of the estimated deficit should be corrected over the first 24 hours, with the remaining correction occurring over the ensuing 48 to 72 hours. There is a danger in correcting the plasma sodium concentration to normal too rapidly—the paradoxical development of cerebral edema with worsening neurologic signs. This condition is thought to occur as the result of the production of "idiogenic osmols" in the brain during the period of dehydration. Because these osmotic particles cannot be rapidly inactivated, administered water is osmotically drawn into the intracellular space, resulting in cell swelling if the administration is too rapid. As in the case with the correc-

tion of hypotonicity, neurologic recovery may lag behind metabolic correction by several days.

DISORDERS OF POTASSIUM METABOLISM

Hyperkalemia

The combination of decreased GFR and sluggish renin-aldosterone system means that elderly persons are frequently operating near the upper limit of tolerance for potassium excretion even on a normal diet. Therefore, any large increase in load or further impairment in excretion can lead to serious hyperkalemia. Many acute illnesses are associated with rapid tissue catabolism, leading to release of potassium from lean body mass into the circulation. The same is true of internal bleeding, into the gastrointestinal tract or into soft tissues, since red blood cells are a source of large quantities of potassium. Also, one must be aware that many older patients with hypertension or congestive heart failure who are placed on a low-sodium diet are unknowingly consuming a diet high in potassium, particularly if placed on a sodium-free salt substitute.

Probably the most common cause of hyperkalemia in elderly patients is the use of drugs that interfere with potassium excretion. Potassium-sparing diuretics (e.g., spironolactone, triamterene, and amiloride) are thought to be the major culprits.[48] These drugs, by interfering with distal renal tubular potassium secretion (the principal source of potassium excretion), can result in serious hyperkalemia by decreasing potassium clearance by the kidneys. Bender and colleagues reported that 12 percent of a large group of elderly hypertensive individuals given a diuretic combination including triamterene became hyperkalemic.[62] More recently, nonsteroidal anti-inflammatory drugs (NSAIDs) may be becoming the major source of drug-induced hyperkalemia in elderly patients[63] since these drugs combine to block renin secretion and to depress GFR. Because of the known physiologic effects of angiotensin converting enzyme (ACE) inhibitors, it is likely that these drugs also may predispose to hyperkalemia in the elderly. For these reasons, monitoring serum potassium levels in elderly patients on potassium-sparing diuretics is important, especially if renal dysfunction exaggerating the propensity for hyperkalemia coexists.

The principles underlying the treatment of hyperkalemia are no different for older patients than for younger patients. Protocols can be found in standard textbooks.

Hypokalemia

Hypokalemia is also common in elderly patients,[48] and its clinical consequences can be serious. Although weakness and apathy may be the most common clinical manifestations of hypokalemia, gastrointestinal effects, including constipation, impaction, and ileus, are causes of morbidity. The most serious side effect of hypokalemia is its predisposition to tachyarrhythmia, particularly in individuals taking digitalis glycosides.

The causes of hypokalemia in elderly patients are similar to causes in younger patients, the most prevalent being gastrointestinal loss or diuretic-induced renal loss. In addition, the average daily intake of dietary potassium is probably lower in the majority of older individuals than it was when they were younger.

In recent surveys, diuretics are among the most commonly used drugs in the elderly.[63] Reviews of the incidence of hypokalemia in this population are sparse, but they range between 0 percent and 60 percent; this may be particularly common with longer-acting diuretics such as chlorthalidone.[64]

The management of hypokalemia in the elderly should follow the same management principles employed for younger patients. One of the most important tasks of the primary physician is to assess whether the risks of hypokalemia outweigh the risk of treatment.[65] Because of the tendency toward hyperkalemia in elderly individuals, described above, the physician must be very cautious in prescribing potassium supplements or potassium-sparing diuretics on a chronic basis without close follow-up.

REFERENCES

1. McLachlan M: Anatomic structural and vascular changes in the aging kidney, in Nunez JFM, Cameron JS (eds): *Renal Function and Disease in the Elderly*. London, Butterworths, 1987, pp 3–26.
2. McLachlan M, Wasserman P: Changes in size and distensibility of the aging kidney. *Br J Radiol* 54:488, 1981.
3. Dunnill MS, Halley W: Some observations on the quantitative anatomy of the kidney. *J Pathol* 110:113, 1973.
4. Goyal VK: Changes with age in the human kidney. *Exp Gerontol* 17:321, 1982.
5. McLachlan MSF et al: Vascular and glomerular changes in the ageing kidney. *J Pathol* 121:65, 1977.
6. Darmady EM: The parameters of the ageing kidney. *J Pathol* 109:195, 1973.
7. Kaplan C et al: Age-related incidence of sclerotic glomeruli in human kidneys. *Am J Pathol* 80:227, 1975.
8. Kappel B, Olsen S: Cortical interstitial tissue and sclerosed glomeruli in the normal human kidney, related to age and sex. *Virchows Arch* [A] 387:271, 1980.
9. Steffes MW et al: Quantitative glomerular morphology of the normal human kidney. *Lab Invest* 49:82, 1983.
10. Ljungqvist A, Lagergran C: Normal intrarenal arterial pattern in adult and ageing human kidney. *J Anat* 96:285, 1962.
11. Takazakura E et al: Intrarenal vascular changes with age and disease. *Kidney Int* 2:224, 1972.
12. Brown W et al: Aging and the kidney. *Arch Intern Med* 146:1790, 1986.
13. Baert L, Steg A: Is the diverticulum of the distal and collecting tubules a preliminary stage of the simple cyst in the adult? *J Urol* 118:707, 1977.
14. Davies DF, Shock NW: Age changes in glomerular filtration rate, effective renal plasma flow, and tubular excretory capacity in adult males. *J Clin Invest* 29:496, 1950.
15. Papper S: The effects of age in reducing renal function. *Geriatrics* 28:83, 1973.
16. Hollenberg NK et al: Senescence and the renal vasculature in normal man. *Circ Res* 34:309, 1974.
17. Rowe JW et al: The effect of age on creatinine clearance in man: A cross-sectional and longitudinal study. *J Gerontol* 31:155, 1976.
18. Lindeman RD et al: Longitudinal studies on the rate of decline in renal function with age. *J Am Geriatr Soc* 33:278, 1985.
19. Anderson S, Brenner BM: Effects of aging on the renal glomerulus. *Am J Med* 80:435, 1986.
20. Cockcroft DW, Gault MH: Prediction of creatinine clearance from serum creatinine. *Nephron* 16:31, 1976.
21. Dontas AS et al: Mechanisms of renal tubular defects in old age. *Postgrad Med J* 48:295, 1972.
22. Watkins DM, Shock NW: Agewise standard value for C_{In}, C_{PAH}, and T^m_{PAH} in adult males. *J Clin Invest* 34:969, 1955.
23. Miller JH et al: Age changes in the maximal rate of renal tubular reabsorption of glucose. *J Gerontol* 7:196, 1952.
24. Butterfield WJH et al: Renal glucose threshold variations with age. *Br Med J* 4:505, 1967.
25. Adler S et al: Effect of acute acid loading on urinary acid excretion by the aging human kidney. *J Lab Clin Med* 72:78, 1968.
26. Agarwal BN, Cabebe FG: Renal acidification in elderly subjects. *Nephron* 26:291, 1980.
27. Epstein M, Hollenberg NK: Age as a determinant of renal sodium conservation in normal man. *J Lab Clin Med* 82:411, 1979.
28. Weidmann P et al: Effect of aging on plasma renin and aldosterone in normal man. *Kidney Int* 8:325, 1975.
29. Tsunoda K et al: Effect of aging on the renin-angiotensin-aldosterone system in normal subjects: Simultaneous measurement of active and inactive renin, renin substrate, and aldosterone in plasma. *J Clin Endocrinol Metab* 62:384, 1986.
30. Hegstad R et al: Aging and aldosterone. *Am J Med* 74:442, 1983.
31. Ohashi M et al: High plasma concentrations of human atrial natriuretic polypeptide in aged man. *J Clin Endocrinol Metab* 64:81, 1987.
32. Haller BG et al: Effects of posture and ageing on circulating atrial natriuretic peptide levels in man. *J Hypertens* 5:551, 1987.
33. Ohashi M et al: Pharmacokinetics of synthetic alpha-human atrial natriuretic polypeptide in normal men; Effect of aging. *Regul Pept* 19:265, 1987.
34. Hartter E et al: Circadian variation and age dependence of human atrial natriuretic peptide levels in hospitalized patients. *Horm Metab Res* 19:490, 1987.

35. Stern N, Tuck ML: Homeostatic fragility in the elderly. *Cardiol Clin* 4:201, 1986.

36. Fulop T et al: Body composition in elderly people. *Gerontology* 31:6, 1985.

37. Lewis WH, Alving AS: Changes with age in renal function in adult men. *Am J Physiol* 123:500, 1938.

38. Rowe JW et al: The influence of age on urinary concentrating ability in man. *Nephron* 17:270, 1976.

39. Helderman JH et al: The response of arginine vasopressin to intravenous ethanol and hypertonic saline in man: The impact of aging. *J Gerontol* 33:39, 1978.

40. Davis PJ, Davis FB: Water excretion in the elderly. *Endocrinol Metabol Clin* 16:867, 1987.

41. Lindeman RD et al: Influence of age, renal disease, hypertension, diuretics, and calcium on the antidiuretic responses to suboptimal infusions of vasopressin. *J Lab Clin Med* 68:206, 1966.

42. Miller JH, Shock NW: Age differences in the renal tubular response to antidiuretic hormone. *J Gerontol* 8:446, 1953.

43. Bichet DG, Schrier RW: Renal function and diseases in the aged, in Schrier RW (ed): *Clinical Internal Medicine in the Aged.* Philadelphia, Saunders, 1982, pp 211–221.

44. Bengele HH et al: Urinary concentrating defect in the aging rat. *Am J Physiol* 240:F147, 1981.

45. Phillips RA et al: Reduced thirst after water deprivation in healthy elderly men. *N Engl J Med* 311:753, 1984.

46. Crowe MJ et al: Altered water excretion in healthy elderly men. *Age Aging* 16:285, 1987.

47. Miller PD et al: Hypodipsia in geriatric patients. *Am J Med* 73:354, 1982.

48. Lye M: Electrolyte disorders in the elderly. *Clin Endocrin Metab* 13:377, 1984.

49. Snyder NA et al: Hypernatremia in elderly patients. *Ann Intern Med* 107:309, 1987.

50. Beck LH, Lavizzo-Mourey RJ: Geriatric hypernatremia. *Ann Intern Med* 107:768, 1987.

51. Sunderam SG, Mankikar GD: Hyponatraemia in the elderly. *Age Ageing* 12:77, 1983.

52. Miller M: Fluid and electrolyte balance in the elderly. *Geriatrics* 42:65, 1987.

53. Kleinfeld M et al: Hyponatremia as observed in a chronic disease facility. *J Am Geriatr Soc* 27:156, 1979.

54. Tierney WM et al: The prognosis of hyponatremia at hospital admission. *J Gen Intern Med* 1:380, 1986.

55. Goldstein CS et al: Idiopathic syndrome of inappropriate antidiuretic hormone secretion possibly related to advanced age. *Ann Intern Med* 99:185, 1983.

56. Ashouri OS: Severe diuretic-induced hyponatremia: A series of eight patients. *Arch Intern Med* 146:1295, 1986.

57. Fichman MP et al: Diuretic-induced hyponatremia. *Ann Intern Med* 75:853, 1971.

58. Ghose RR: Plasma arginine vasopressin in hyponatraemic patients receiving diuretics. *Postgrad Med J* 61:1043, 1985.

59. Hantman D et al: Rapid correction of hyponatremia in the syndrome of inappropriate secretion of antidiuretic hormone. *Ann Intern Med* 78:870, 1973.

60. Mahowald JM, Himmelstein DU: Hypernatremia in the elderly: Relation to infection and mortality. *J Am Geriatr Soc* 24:177, 1981.

61. Himmelstein DU et al: Hypernatremic dehydration in nursing home patients: An indicator of neglect. *J Am Geriatr Soc* 31:466, 1983.

62. Bender AD et al: Use of a diuretic combination of triamterene and hydrochlorothiazide in elderly patients. *J Am Geriatr Soc* 15:166, 1967.

63. Lamy PP: Renal effects of nonsteroidal antiinflammatory drugs; Heightened risk to the elderly? *J Am Geriatr Soc* 34:361, 1986.

64. Flamenbaum W: Diuretic use in the elderly: Potential for diuretic-induced hypokalemia. *Am J Cardiol* 57:38A, 1986.

65. Harrington JT et al: Our national obsession with potassium. *Am J Med* 73:155, 1982.

Chapter 56

RENAL DISEASES
IN THE ELDERLY

John M. Burkart and Laurence H. Beck

Virtually every disease or condition that affects the kidneys of children or young adults can occur as well in patients above the age of 65. In general, the presentation and manifestations in the elderly are similar to those in younger patients, although the underlying intrinsic age-related changes in renal function described in Chap. 55 may alter the expression or course of the disease. In addition, some kidney diseases become increasingly prevalent with age, while others are found exclusively in elderly individuals.

The presence of concurrent disease is more often the rule than the exception in the very old. Chronic conditions involving the cardiopulmonary, skeletal, and gastrointestinal systems may modify the presentation or expression of renal disease, giving support to the familiar observation that common diseases may present uncommonly in the elderly. An example is the onset of acute glomerulonephritis in the older patient: hypertension and congestive heart failure may dominate the clinical picture, whereas oliguria and smoky urine is the more classic presentation in the younger patient.

The diagnostic approach needs to be modified in evaluating an elderly person with suspected or manifest kidney disease. Reference has already been made in Chap. 55 about the need to recognize the lower rate of creatinine production in the elderly and the effect of this change in serum creatinine concentration and estimated creatinine clearance. In addition, the increased susceptibility to acute renal failure demands particular caution in the use of radioiodinated contrast agents. For many evaluations, if not most, the information obtained from a renal sonogram and/or nuclear scan will be adequate and will avoid the risk of dye-induced nephrotoxicity. Similarly, underlying vascular disease and decreased renal size makes renal biopsy a higher risk procedure in the very old patient than it is in the younger patient. The

clinician must carefully weigh the diagnostic benefit against this increased risk of complication.

The following chapter reviews the major clinical renal syndromes: vascular disease, vasculitis, glomerular disease, tubulointerstitial disease, acute renal failure, chronic renal failure, and end-stage renal disease (ESRD). The discussion will highlight prevalence patterns, when available, and the characteristics of the syndromes which require particular attention in the elderly patient.

VASCULAR DISEASES OF THE KIDNEY

RENOVASCULAR DISEASE

Renovascular disease, by definition an anatomical narrowing of the renal artery usually due to atherosclerotic disease, is particularly common among the elderly population, which is predisposed to atherosclerosis. Holley et al. found that 40 percent of normotensives and 77 percent of hypertensives had some degree of renal artery stenosis at autopsy.[1] Despite its high prevalence, the presence of renovascular disease itself does not necessarily result in a complicating disease state such as hypertension, chronic renal insufficiency, acute arterial occlusion, or artheroembolism. However, in selected patients with a critical degree of narrowing, disease may occur. An elderly patient who suddenly develops hypertension, a patient whose blood pressure has been chronically well controlled but suddenly develops accelerating hypertension, a patient who develops acute renal failure when treated with an angiotensin converting enzyme inhibitor, or a patient with known atherosclerotic disease and chronic renal insufficiency of uncertain etiology should have renovascular disease included in his or her differential diagnosis. Renovascular disease is an important disease state to consider because of the potential for treatment, and even for "cure."

An arteriogram remains the gold standard for the diagnosis of renovascular disease. Digital subtraction arteriography has come into vogue as a useful screening test and is relatively noninvasive for the patient. However, if surgery is contemplated, an arteriogram will eventually be needed. Both tests can be done with minimal risk in an elderly patient (the patient should always be hydrated prior to the procedure). A renogram also has some usefulness as a screening test but is not as sensitive or specific as arteriography. It is most helpful when used as a noninvasive way to follow progression of the disease.

The natural history of untreated atherosclerotic renal artery disease is one of slow progression which could result in worsening blood pressure, chronic renal insufficiency, and even ESRD.[2] Both angioplasty[3] and surgery[4] have been reported to result in improvement or cure of renovascular hypertension. In certain patients with chronic renal insufficiency thought to be ischemic in nature, surgery has proven to be of long-term benefit. Chronic medical therapy with antihypertensive agents may result in blood pressure control but seldom causes improvement of renal function or prevention of further renal parenchymal loss.[4] Consequently, if the patient is at minimal risk for surgical correction or angioplasty, these options should be considered. For a further discussion of renovascular disease and hypertension, see Chap. 48.

THROMBOEMBOLIC DISORDERS

Thromboembolic disease of the renal artery is unusual. A large autopsy series collected over a 20-year interval revealed an incidence of 1.4 percent (205 of 14,411). Of these, only 2 cases were diagnosed ante mortem.[5] Embolism is by far the most common cause of occlusion. The heart is the usual site of origin, resulting from conditions such as mural thrombus, prosthetic valves, vegetations, congestive heart failure, left atrial disease, or arrhythmias. Formation of a thrombus in situ (renal artery thrombus) is also common; it is usually the result of blunt abdominal trauma, surgery, angiographic catheters, or a hypercoagulable state.

The clinical manifestations of renal artery thrombosis are extremely variable. Patients may present dramatically with fever, flank pain, nausea, and vomiting associated with a rapidly rising blood urea nitrogen (BUN), or they may be completely asymptomatic. Bilateral thrombosis results in acute oliguric renal failure, whereas thrombosis of a segment of a renal artery may go undiagnosed because of the development of collateral circulation. The pathologic result of prolonged renal artery oc-

clusion is infarction, with resultant loss of renal parenchymal mass. Leukocyturia, albuminuria, and microscopic hematuria or proteinuria are common but are not always present.[6] Serum glutamic-oxaloacetic transaminase (SGOT) and lactate dehydrogenase (LDH) usually rise within 1 to 2 days postinfarction, and the LDH may remain elevated for up to 2 weeks. Radiologic evidence of infarction can be demonstrated with an intravenous pyelogram, radionucleotide scanning, computerized tomography, or selective renal arteriograms.

If indicated, the goal of early management is blood pressure control and an attempt to restore renal blood flow. Recovery of renal function is frequently demonstrated if surgical intervention occurs within 1 week postinfarction.[7] Late management is usually concerned with the treatment of any resulting hypertension or chronic renal insufficiency.

ATHEROEMBOLIC DISEASES

Atheroembolic disease (cholesterol emboli) was first described by Panum in 1862. Autopsy incidence of renal atheroembolic disease in patients greater than 80 years old is reported at nearly 12 percent[8]; however, this diagnosis is seldom made ante mortem due to the multiple clinical presentations of the disease, the low index of clinical suspicion, and the fact that atheroemboli are not always clinically significant.

Potential risk factors include intraarterial cannulation, surgical manipulation of large arteries, anticoagulation,[9] and those risk factors associated with diffuse atherosclerotic disease. Emboli may even occur spontaneously or in association with lifting, coughing, or straining.[10] A retrospective study of 71 autopsy patients who had undergone diagnostic arteriography showed an overall incidence of atheroembolism of approximately 27 percent.[11]

Atheroemboli affect primarily those organs perfused by the aorta. Of these, the kidney is affected most often. Presentation may be localized to one organ system, or it may be systemic and be misdiagnosed as polyarteritis nodosa, polymyositis, subacute bacterial endocarditis, or cryoglobulinemia. Fever is commonly present, as is fluctuating, difficult-to-control hypertension. Malignant hypertension has occasionally been reported[12] and is thought to be due to increased renin release from the ischemic renal parenchyma. Transient eosinophilia and decreased complement levels have been described but are not found consistently.[13] There may be associated increases in SGOT and LDH. Nonspecific leukocyturia, proteinuria, and/or hematuria may be seen. Livedo reticularis of the skin, or other organ system damage, may be noted. Diagnosis is made on the basis of clinical suspicion and skin, muscle, or renal biopsy findings.

Treatment for the disease is mainly supportive, and renal function may return in some patients who require dialysis acutely. End-stage renal failure is, unfortunately, a frequent complication, especially in those with chronic embolization.[13]

SYSTEMIC NECROTIZING VASCULITIS

The systemic vasculitides are a heterogeneous group of disorders characterized by inflammation and necrosis of blood vessels. The clinical manifestations are myriad and include vague constitutional symptoms, fever, purpura, arthritis, mononeuritis multiplex, central nervous system dysfunction, and infarction of various organs. Depending on the criteria used, some degree of renal involvement occurs in 70 to 90 percent of patients.[14]

The necrotizing vasculitides are probably immunopathogenic in nature. The prevailing theory is that injury occurs from the deposition of immune complexes in blood vessel walls,[15] although cell-mediated mechanisms may also be involved.[16] Because of the broad spectrum of diseases involved, it is difficult to succinctly classify these diseases into various groups. The diagnosis is often evasive because of the nonspecific clinical features at presentation and an occasional paucity of pathologic findings. To be sure, there is no pathognomonic glomerular lesion of vasculitis. However, renal biopsy is useful, as the presence of a focal segmental necrotizing glomerulonephritis with minimal endocapillary proliferation or basement membrane abnormalities is presumptive evidence for a systemic vasculitis.[17]

Early diagnosis and treatment of systemic vasculitis is important to prevent complications and end-organ damage. A recent view by Weiss and Crissman[18] showed that 57 to 78 percent of patients with various types of necrotizing vasculitis involving the kidney progressed to ESRD. The development of ESRD appeared to be related to both the timing of the diagnosis and the promptness with which therapy was initiated.

POLYARTERITIS NODOSA

The vasculitic syndrome of polyarteritis nodosa consists of a variable mix of fevers, weight loss, anemia, arthritis, dermatitis, myopathy, neuropathy, hypertension, and gastrointestinal and renal diseases. Mononeuritis multiplex is a typical feature of peripheral nerve involvement, and testicular pain is fairly common. The peak incidence occurs in the sixth decade of life, and males are affected twice as often as females. The urinary sediment typically is very active, and protein, red blood cells, white blood cells, and red blood cell casts are usually seen. Nephrotic syndrome is unusual, and progressive renal failure is usually a late manifestation of the disease.[14] Diagnosis is based on biopsy findings of an involved organ or

arteriographic evidence of multiple aneurysm formation.[19] The classic form of polyarteritis nodosa involves segmental inflammation of small and medium-sized muscular arteries. "Microscopic polyarteritis nodosa" is an overlap syndrome caused by disease involving the small arterioles and capillaries of major visceral organs.

The typical course of polyarteritis nodosa is highly variable, but 50 percent of patients follow a low-grade remitting course. Deaths related directly to the vasculitis itself occur early in the disease course, whereas later deaths are due to organ failure from vascular compromise or from a complication of treatment.[20] Although the treatment of polyarteritis nodosa is controversial, a consensus exists about the use of corticosteroids. The controversy exists when reviewing various reports on the efficacy of cytotoxic drugs. Major reviews by Balow[17] and Fauci[16] favor the use of cyclophosphamine in conjunction with maintenance steroids.

OTHER FORMS OF SYSTEMIC VASCULITIS

The other forms of systemic necrotizing vasculitis also occur in elderly populations, but with much less frequency. Examples include cutaneous hypersensitivity vasculitis, Wegener's granulomatosis, and the vasculitides associated with systemic disease processes such as systemic lupus erythematosus. In recent years the prognosis for all of these conditions has shown improvement that is coincidental with more aggressive therapy with cyclophosphamine and prednisone. Treatments for these specific disorders are outlined in recent publications.[18,21]

GLOMERULAR DISEASES

In the elderly population, the renal glomerulus is subject to a variety of insults which may result in clinical disease. The resulting glomerular lesions are associated with a high degree of morbidity and mortality. Increasing numbers of elderly patients are now being accepted into ESRD programs, often because of an undiagnosed glomerulonephritis. Recent reports have shown that efficacious treatments exist for some glomerular diseases, and therefore any elderly patient with presumptive evidence for a glomerular lesion should be evaluated appropriately to rule out a reversible lesion or a preventable disease state.

PREVALANCE

The actual incidence and prevalence rates of glomerular diseases in the elderly are unknown for several reasons. Glomerular diseases often mimic other more common medical diseases of the elderly, making the diagnosis difficult. Most nephrologists can recall diagnosing nephrotic syndrome in a patient first treated for heart failure or finding a pulmonary renal syndrome in a patient initially treated for pneumonia. This difficulty of diagnosis is supported by a recent literature review of 46 patients over 50 years of age who presented with classic signs and symptoms of acute glomerulonephritis, of whom only five were initially diagnosed correctly.[22]

Older literature would suggest that glomerulonephritis in the elderly is rare.[23,24] In one review of 173 cases of glomerulonephritis, none of the patients was over the age of 60.[23] Perhaps consequently, there appears to be a low index of clinical suspicion for glomerular disease in the elderly patient, and the disease often goes undiagnosed ante mortem.[25] However, recent literature dealing specifically with either acute glomerulonephritis[26] or nephrotic syndrome[27] in the elderly concludes that these diseases are more prevalent than initially believed. Newer data like these should help physicians become more aware of these disease possibilities in the elderly patient.

CLINICAL PRESENTATION

There are three major clinical syndromes associated with glomerular disease in the elderly: (1) persistent asymptomatic urinary abnormalities, (2) the nephritic syndrome, and (3) the nephrotic syndrome. Although each of these presentations can mimic other common medical illnesses, these presentations should certainly make the physician consider the presence of underlying glomerular pathology. Certain types of glomerular lesions tend to present in specific ways, but these syndromes are not mutually exclusive. The physician can seldom predict the actual renal pathology from clinical signs and symptoms alone, although an important diagnostic clue is the rate of reduction, if any, of glomerular filtration rate (GFR). Patients can present with (1) normal GFR, (2) chronic renal insufficiency, (3) an acute reduction in GFR, (4) rapid progression to renal failure, or (5) ESRD. Occasionally the clinical manifestations of the disease are obvious enough to lead to a specific diagnosis such as Type I crescentic glomerulonephritis, as in a patient with pulmonary hemorrhage, oligoanuria, a nephritic sediment, and a positive circulating antiglomerular basement membrane antibody (Goodpasture's disease). However, in other patients who only have asymptomatic urinary abnormalities, a high index of suspicion and consideration of a renal biopsy may be needed to correctly diagnose an underlying glomerular disease.

ACUTE GLOMERULONEPHRITIS

Acute glomerulonephritis is a syndrome characterized by the abrupt onset of hematuria and proteinuria, often accompanied by edema, hypertension, and a reduction

in GFR. With few exceptions, the underlying disease process is immunologic in nature and can be subdivided into the following classifications: (1) diseases mediated by antibodies directed at specific antigens native to the glomerulus itself; (2) damage from immune complex deposition (circulating immune complexes or those formed in situ); or (3) damage due to cell-mediated effects. Organ involvement may be systemic or localized to the kidney. Although all types of glomerulonephritis have been reported in the elderly (Table 56-1), most are infrequent except for rapidly progressive glomerulonephritis with crescent formation without immunoglobulin deposition.[28] Some of these disease states are potentially treatable, and therefore recognition is important in order to prevent progression to ESRD.

Clinical Manifestations

In most cases the clinical manifestations of acute glomerulonephritis are fairly fulminant and consist of hematuria, proteinuria, red blood cell casts, edema, hypertension, oligoanuria, and a decline in GFR. Not all patients have all manifestations, and some may only have asymptomatic urinary abnormalities. It is important to realize that asymptomatic hematuria or proteinuria are not normal changes associated with aging of the kidney

TABLE 56-1
Comparative Prevalence of the Different Glomerular Diseases Found on Renal Biopsy in Elderly Patients and in Younger Patients

Diagnosis	Elderly Adults > 60 Years Old %	Other Patients < 60 Years Old, %
Primary glomerular disease	69.0	56.0
Idiopathic crescentic nephritis	11.0	4.0
Membranous nephropathy	15.0	6.0
Minimal-change disease	4.0	7.0
Focal proliferative mesangial glomerulonephritis	13.0	10.0
Diffuse proliferative glomerulonephritis	3.5	2.0
Chronic glomerulonephritis	5.0	7.0
Membranoproliferative glomerulonephritis	1.0	9.0
Glomerulosclerosis	10.0	8.0
Focal sclerosis	1.0	3.0
Secondary renal disease	23.0	29.0
Vasculitis	6.0	3.0
Amyloidosis	9.0	1.0
Other systemic disease	8.5	25.0
Miscellaneous	8.0	15.0

and that these are signs of pathology involving the kidney, ureter, or bladder.

Rapidly progressive glomerulonephritis with crescent formation is the most common discrete glomerular disease found in elderly populations. Most of these cases have negative immunofluorescent microscopy findings, suggesting that the process is not immunoglobulin-mediated. The exact pathogenic mechanisms are unknown, but they are thought to be cell-mediated.[28] This is of interest because of the well-described decline in cell-mediated immunity associated with aging.[29] At the present time there is no explanation for this apparent paradox. Along with the above-mentioned clinical signs and symptoms, constitutional symptoms and other findings of systemic disease involvement are also occasionally found, suggesting that this form of acute glomerulonephritis may be a type of vasculitis.[30] The historical prognosis is poor, but recent data suggest that "pulse" methylprednisolone may be helpful in preventing progression to ESRD.[31]

Pathologic Findings

Light-microscopic examination of renal biopsy or autopsy material from an elderly patient with acute glomerulonephritis most often shows changes produced by a crescentic glomerulonephritis (40 to 66 percent) or, less commonly, a postinfective glomerulonephritis (16 to 20 percent).[32,33] Other types of glomerular pathology are also seen, especially those associated with a systemic vasculitis or collagen vascular disease, but with much less frequency.

Prognosis

Acute glomerulonephritis in the elderly has a poor prognosis when compared to its prognosis in younger age groups.[33] The reasons for this are multifactorial but are mostly due to the patient's older age, other associated illnesses, a higher incidence of oligoanuria necessitating dialysis, and the underlying systemic diseases that cause the glomerulonephritis itself.

Diagnosis

Clinical signs and symptoms are usually present that allow the physician to make the diagnosis. However, the cardiovascular manifestations of the disease usually are predominant, and therefore cardiac disease is more often considered than renal disease.[34] ASO titers should be obtained, but in elderly patients they occasionally do not rise, necessitating other serologic tests, such as anti-DNAase B or antihyaluronidase levels.[35] Other tests should include rheumatologic studies such as an antinuclear antibodies (ANA) and rheumatoid factor, complement levels,[36] blood cultures, cryoglobulin level, hepa-

titis B surface antigen, blood cultures to rule out endocarditis, and a protein immunoelectrophoresis. Renal biopsy should be considered despite its increased risk in an elderly patient.

Treatment

The treatment of acute glomerulonephritis in the elderly is based not only on the underlying disease state and renal biopsy findings but also on the patient's other associated underlying diseases, his or her physical condition, and the likelihood of response to treatment. Most therapeutic interventions would include corticosteroids, cytotoxic drugs such as cyclophosphamide or azathioprine, or both. Because of the potential for side effects, the patient's overall medical history needs to be considered very closely. If the acute glomerulonephritis is associated with a systemic disease, the treatment for the glomerular lesion usually involves treatment of the systemic disease process. Specific treatments exist for some of the idiopathic types of glomerulonephritis found in the elderly patient and are guided by renal biopsy findings.[35] At least 50 percent of patients with rapidly progressive forms of glomerulonephritis stabilize or improve after treatment with high-dose oral prednisolone or "pulse" methylprednisolone.[31]

NEPHROTIC SYNDROME

The nephrotic syndrome consists of urinary protein losses in excess of 3.5 g/1.73 m^2 body surface area per day, in association with hypoalbuminemia, hyperlipidemia, a hypercoagulable state, and peripheral edema. The onset is usually insidious, and, because the major clinical manifestation of the disease is generalized edema, elderly patients are frequently thought to have congestive heart failure. The etiologies of nephrotic syndrome are diverse and include such disease states as primary glomerular diseases, glomerular disease secondary to drugs, neoplasia, chronic infections, and other systemic diseases.

Incidence in the Elderly

About one in four cases of nephrotic syndrome in adults occurs in patients over the age of 60.[37] However, the exact incidence and prevalence rates for nephrotic syndrome in the elderly are unknown because of the frequency of its misdiagnosis.

Clinical Manifestations

Patients usually present with generalized edema, hypertension (33 percent), and renal failure (30 percent).[38] If a systemic disease is the cause of the nephrotic syndrome, there may be associated extrarenal manifestations of that disease. The urine contains protein and oval fat bodies and may occasionally have some nephritic elements.

Pathologic Findings

In a recent review of five published series of nephrotic syndrome in patients over 60 years of age, the most common light-microscopic finding was membranous nephropathy.[22] Minimal-change disease and amyloidosis were the next most common findings. Other primary glomerular diseases are occassionally seen in association with nephrotic syndrome in the elderly, as are lesions associated with systemic disease processes such as diabetes.

Prognosis

Membranous glomerulonephritis is thought to have a favorable prognosis. Johnson and Couser have reported that 50 percent of patients progress to ESRD, while 25 percent of patients have stable renal function but persistent urinary abnormalities, and the remaining 25 percent of patients have a spontaneous remission.[39] For those patients with membranous glomerulonephritis who seem to have progressive disease, there is some evidence that medical intervention is helpful. The Collaborative Study of the Adult Idiopathic Nephrotic Syndrome showed increased remissions and decreased progression to ESRD independent of age with the use of short-term alternate-day prednisone.[40] Other treatment modalities using chlorambucil and prednisone may also be efficacious.[41] Membranous glomerulonephritis has been associated with cancer in approximately 7 percent of cases.[42] In these patients the prognosis is usually dependent on that of the associated neoplasm. Therefore, adults with a renal biopsy diagnosis of membranous glomerulonephritis should always have a complete physical, and other appropriate laboratory studies done to detect a treatable cancer, not only at the time of presentation, but also during subsequent years of follow-up.

Minimal-change glomerulonephritis is felt to be a treatable disease as well, with a very good prognosis in adults, including the elderly population. In review of 50 patients, 80 percent responded to glucocorticoid treatment,[22] and progression to ESRD was unusual.

Amyloidosis causes 9 to 20 percent of cases of nephrotic syndrome in elderly patients (see Chap. 87). Primary amyloidosis is characterized by heavy proteinuria, a serum monoclonal gamma globulin spike, and, usually, progressive renal insufficiency. Unfortunately, there is no known effective treatment for primary amyloidosis, although melphalan and prednisone have been used with some success.[43] Most patients die within 14 months of this diagnosis.

Diagnosis

Nephrotic syndrome is often masked by other concomitant medical diseases so a high index of clinical suspicion must be maintained. Evaluation should include serologic studies such as an ANA, rheumatoid factor, complement studies, hepatitis B antigen studies, blood cultures, serum and urine protein immunoelectrophoresis, and an initial search for neoplasia. Histologic definition of the glomerular disease is important from a diagnostic, treatment, and prognostic standpoint, and therefore renal biopsy should be considered.

Treatment

The treatment of nephrotic syndrome should first be directed toward patient symptomatology and should include sodium restriction and judicious use of diuretics. Any underlying systemic disease that may be causing the glomerular lesion should then be treated. Treatment of the idiopathic forms of glomerulonephritis, such as membranous and minimal-change glomerulonephritis, usually consists of corticosteroids and/or cytotoxic drugs as previously described.[35,40,41] Because of the potential side effects of these treatments, the physician must always consider the patient's overall condition, the natural history of the disease, and the risk/benefit ratio of using these drugs in the individual patient. Concomitant tuberculosis or other chronic infections should always be excluded.

TUBULOINTERSTITIAL NEPHRITIS

Tubulointerstitial nephritis and *interstitial nephritis* are terms used interchangably to describe processes that principally damage the renal interstitium. The etiologies of these diseases are diverse and include infectious, physical, chemical, immunologic, hereditary, drug, and unknown causes. As a group, tubulointestinal nephritides are important disease states because they are common, and some are amenable to prevention and treatment. The elderly are especially predisposed to develop these diseases because older people are more prone to infection, may have other acute or chronic medical illnesses, and are frequently on medication that may damage the renal insterstitium.

Aging itself is associated with a progressive decrease in the kidneys' ability to defend the internal environment (see Chap. 55). These changes are associated with the presence of histologic changes in the interstitium and therefore can be considered the tubulointerstitial nephropathy of the elderly. However, interstitial disease in the geriatric patient is not limited to the aging process per se. As mentioned, there are systemic diseases to which the elderly are also predisposed that can cause interstitial damage. Therefore, careful consideration of these diagnoses must be given before ascribing the chronic renal insufficiency and urinary findings to aging alone.

FUNCTIONAL DEFECTS

Despite the heterogeneous group of etiologies causing tubulointerstitial nephritis, the functional abnormalities induced are similar. These include (1) impaired ability to concentrate the urine, (2) impaired ability to excrete an acid load, (3) impaired ability to conserve salt, and (4) impaired ability to excrete potassium. Clinically these abnormalities are manifested by polyuria, nocturia, metabolic acidosis, salt wasting, and hyperkalemia out of proportion to the patient's impairment in GFR. While these abnormalities can occur with any type of renal disease when near end-stage, in tubulointerstitial nephritis these occur early in the disease course.

In addition to functional abnormalities a number of other clinical features are suggestive of tubulointerstitial nephritis. In contrast to patients with glomerular disease, patients with tubulointerstitial nephritis usually present with less than 2 g of proteinuria per 24 hours. The urinary sediment is characterized by the presence of white blood cells and occasionally white blood cell casts. Red blood cells are less frequent, and oval fat bodies and red blood cell casts are distinctly unusual. Eosinophiluria, best demonstrated by Wright's stain, may be seen in the setting of drug-induced tubulointerstitial nephritis. Clinically, and to some degree pathologically, these diseases can be divided into acute and chronic forms.

ACUTE TUBULOINTERSTITIAL NEPHRITIS

The two most common and well-recognized forms of acute tubulointerstitial nephritis are acute bacterial pyelonephritis and acute drug-induced hypersensitivity reactions.

Acute Bacterial Pyelonephritis

Acute bacterial pyelonephritis is a disabling infection in the elderly that is usually due to gram-negative infections. It occurs in both sexes and is the most common form of renal disease in the aged. One autopsy series of patients aged 50 to 101 reported a 20 percent prevalence rate of pyelonephritis.[44] As with other renal diseases of the elderly, the disease is often a diagnostic challenge, for affected patients do not always present with the classic findings found in a younger population. Costovertebral angle tenderness, irritative voiding symptoms, and leukocytosis are unusual, whereas bacteremia, central nervous system changes, tachypnea, and hypotension

are common.[45] The diagnostic evaluation should include urinalysis and urine and blood cultures. Blood cultures are positive in greater than 50 percent of elderly patients with pyelonephritis,[46] so that despite absence of clinical symptoms, a positive blood culture in a septic elderly patient with an organism identical to one recovered from the urine provides strong presumptive evidence for pyelonephritis.

Therapy is aimed at treating any systemic manifestations of the disease and at eradication of the infection. Septic shock may necessitate central venous pressure monitoring to guide fluid replacement, especially in patients with heart failure. Other medical complications, such as disseminated intravascular coagulation and adult respiratory distress syndrome, may occur and require respiratory support and further supportive care.

Initial treatment in a septic patient should include an aminoglycoside antibiotic. Once the etiologic agent has been identified amd susceptibility tests completed, a more specific agent that is less nephrotoxic can be substituted. Appropriate agents would include drugs such as third-generation cephalosporins and the newer penicillins. Patients with uncomplicated pyelonephritis should show improvement within 48 to 72 hours after initiation of antibiotics. If the expected improvement has not occurred, the physician should obtain an ultrasound examination of the collecting system and kidneys to rule out an impediment to urinary flow such as a renal calculus, a sloughed renal papilla, or any other anatomical form of obstruction (such as prostatic disease). Finally, perinephric abscess must also be excluded, for its treatment would most often include aggressive surgical intervention. A patient who does not appear septic at the time of presentation could initially be treated with an intravenous cephalosporin, ampicillin, or one of the newer penicillins. In uncomplicated cases, the usual duration of treatment is 10 days to avoid side effects from the antibiotic, such as pseudomembranous colitis.[47] Patients with complicated conditions may require longer therapy. Patients with anatomical abnormalities require urologic evaluation.

Drug-Induced Hypersensitivity

Acute interstitial nephritis due to hypersensitivity to drugs is a well-recognized and increasingly common cause of acute renal failure.[48] Most reported cases have been due to methicillin or other beta lactam derivatives[49]; however, this reaction has been reported in association with over 40 drugs[50] and therefore must always be considered in a patient on medications who develops acute renal failure.

The clinical presentation is variable and seldom classic in an elderly patient. Fever is present in 81 to 100 percent of patients, with microscopic hematuria in about

90 percent. Eighty percent develop eosinophilia, but this is usually transient, lasting 1 or 2 days. A maculopapular rash is seen in less than half of the patients.[51] Sterile pyuria, eosinophiluria, and proteinuria may also be seen. The classical clinical triad of rash, fever, and eosinophilia is only seen in one-third of cases, so a high index of suspicion of the syndrome is imperative.[50]

The mainstay of therapy for acute allergic interstitial nephritis is to discontinue the offending agent. Supportive care and dialysis, if needed, are also indicated. Further therapy is controversial, and there are no good prospective randomized studies in the literature to support the use of corticosteroids in the treatment of all patients with allergic interstitial nephritis; however, this approach has been suggested by some authors[52-54] for selected patients. Galpin et al.[52] compared outcomes in treated and untreated adults. The numbers in the two groups were small, but the serum creatinine returned to baseline more often and faster in the treated versus the untreated group. Certainly, once an individual has developed known allergic interstitial nephritis in response to a certain drug, this class of drug should be avoided in the future.

Other Forms of Acute Interstitial Nephritis

Acute interstitial nephritis occasionally occurs in other settings. It rarely occurs in association with nephrotic syndrome in patients using nonsteroidal anti-inflammatory durgs (NSAIDs). Cimetidine has been reported to cause allergic interstitial nephritis due to an alteration in cell-mediated immunity. Through unknown mechanisms it has occasionally developed in association with systemic infection. An idiopathic form of allergic interstitial nephritis also exists. Discussion and treatment of these diseases can be found in most textbooks of nephrology.

CHRONIC INTERSTITIAL NEPHRITIS

The interstitium of the kidney is especially susceptible to toxic injury for a multitude of reasons. Normal physiologic processes that metabolize drugs can cause toxic metabolic products to concentrate in the medulla, predisposing it to injury. Systemic diseases may also cause chronic injury to the interstitium. Immunologic mechanisms can cause chronic damage to the interstitium and renal tubules. Finally, subtle, chronic damage to the renal microcirculation can cause ischemic injury. The end result of these types of chronic injury is renal insufficiency which may ultimately progress to ESRD.

Analgesic Nephropathy

Chronic consumption of compound analgesics can cause chronic renal insufficiency[55] which may lead to ESRD.[56]

Renal tubular acidosis, nephrocalcinosis, and chronic renal insufficiency are also common. Although most patients present in their forties, older patients can also present with the disease. The classic patient is female and has a history of peptic ulcer disease, headache, anemia, and sterile pyuria. The patients tyically have ingested large quantities of analgesic mixtures.[57] The cause of the renal damage is unknown, and early literature seemed to implicate phenacetin. Removal of phenacetin from compound analgesics in Canada has resulted in significant reduction in new cases of analgesic nephropathy,[58] although the Australian experience has not been as rewarding. Discontinuation of analgesic consumption usually results in a stabilization or slight improvement of renal dysfunction, although in some patients continued deterioration occurs. An increased risk for the development of uroepithelial carcinomas has also been reported.[59] Induction time for development of these carcinomas in a Swedish series was 22 years, with a range of 9 to 42 years. Therefore, even though analgesic consumption may have halted, complications of the disease may occur in older patients.

Hypercalcemic Nephropathy

Chronic hypercalcemia, whether it occurs in primary hyperparathyroidism, multiple myeloma, sarcoidosis, or vitamin D intoxication, or from metastatic bone disease, can produce both functional and structural damage to the renal interstitium. The most common functional deficiency is a concentrating defect associated with hypercalcemia. Renal tubular acidosis, salt-losing nephropathy, and chronic renal insufficiency are also seen. Clinically, hypercalcemia is initially characterized by an acute reversible prerenal type of actue renal failure. This is primarily due to marked polyuria and solute loss as well as to vasoconstriction of efferent arterioles. Hypercalcemia can also cause slow, progressive damage which may lead to chronic renal insufficiency. Treatment is directed at normalizing the hypercalcemia, replacing volume deficits, and correcting any underlying systemic disease processes.

NEOPLASTIC DISEASES ASSOCIATED WITH INTERSTITIAL NEPHRITIS

Neoplastic diseases may damage the renal interstitium in a multitude of ways. Direct renal invasion of the kidneys may occur with leukemia or lymphoma, or by metastatic spread from other organ primaries. As mentioned, hypercalcemia due to cancer can cause interstitial disease as can hyperuricemia, amyloidosis, or excessive radiation therapy.

Multiple myeloma is associated with multiple types of renal dysfunction. These include proteinuria, acute renal failure, progressive renal insufficiency, isolated renal tubular defects, amyloidosis, and pyelonephritis. By far the most important pathogenic factor in the development of the chronic renal insufficiency of multiple myeloma is light-chain proteinuria, which may precipitate within the tubules and cause intrarenal obstruction or direct toxic damage.[60] Multiple myeloma is predominantly a disease of the elderly (median age at diagnosis is 60) and therefore needs to be considered in all elderly patients with proteinuria. Proteinuria is present in virtually all patients, and acute renal failure is common. Factors which can precipitate acute renal failure are hypercalcemia, dehydration, and certain nephrotoxic drugs. These factors seem to facilitate intrarenal precipitation of proteinaceous casts in these patients.[61] Progressive renal insufficiency in patients with multiple myeloma is far more common than acute renal failure and is most common in patients with immunoglobulin D myeloma or those with kappa light chains in their urine. In patients presenting with acute or chronic renal failure, survival is on the average less than 2 years.[62]

To make the diagnosis the physician should obtain a protein immunoelectrophoresis on both the serum and urine, along with obtaining urine for Bence Jones proteins. Other studies include a bone marrow aspirate and appropriate radiologic exams.

The main principle in the management of renal complications of myeloma is prevention. It is important to maintain adequate hydration, avoid use of nephrotoxic drugs, minimize use of intravenous contrast usage, and vigorously treat hypercalcemia and hyperuricemia.[63] Treatment of the myeloma itself usually involves prednisone and other cytotoxic drugs.

AGE-ASSOCIATED INTERSTITIAL DISEASE

Aging itself is associated with a progressive decrease in the ability of the kidney to withstand major challenges to the patient's overall fluid and electrolyte balance. This decreased ability is due primarily to age-related renal tubular dysfunction which is termed *tubulointerstitial nephropathy of the elderly*. Although there are also age-related decreases in GFR, as mentioned in Chap. 55, these do not account for all the observed changes in renal function. There are histologic changes in the renal interstitium associated with aging,[64] and hence the term *tubulointerstitial nephropathy of the elderly* is warranted. The major clinical manifestations of this syndrome are the same as those seen with any type of interstitial damage. For the most part these defects are primarily renal in origin, but they can certainly be exacerbated by the known age-related decrease in aldosterone production[65] and renin[66] secretion. Pyuria (present in up to one-third of patients over age 70), crystaluria, and minor increases in protein excretion are the typical urinary findings of tubulointerstitial nephropathy in the elderly.

ACUTE RENAL FAILURE

Acute renal failure is an abrupt decrease in renal function sufficient to cause an increase in serum BUN and creatinine concentrations. The etiologies of acute renal failure in the elderly are myriad and, as in younger age groups, can be divided into one of six major syndromes: prerenal azotemia, acute intrinsic renal failure (acute tubular necrosis), acute glomerulonephritis or vasculitis, acute interstitial nephritis, acute renovascular disease, and obstructive uropathy. The elderly population is especially prone to developing acute renal failure, which accounts for a significant amount of morbidity in these patients. A recent study found that 20 percent of all patients admitted to a geriatric unit had significant renal impairment[67]; therefore, anyone taking care of elderly patients must be acquainted with the differential diagnosis and evaluation of acute renal failure.

PRERENAL AZOTEMIA

Prerenal azotemia due to dehydration is especially common in elderly patients because of both the age-related decrease in renal function and the inability of the geriatric kidney to defend maximally against changes in the internal environment (see Chap. 55). Causes of prerenal azotemia include volume depletion from both extrarenal and renal losses (vomiting, nasogastric suction, diarrhea, mineralocorticoid deficiency, osmotic diuresis such as with hyperglycemia, and congestive heart failure). The treatment of these conditions is first to replace any volume losses and then to treat the underlying disease leading to the decreased perfusion of the kidney.

ACUTE TUBULAR NECROSIS

Decreases in GFR resulting from prolonged renal ischemia or from a nephrotoxin that are not immediately reversed upon discontinuation of the insult are classified as causing acute tubular necrosis (ATN). Pathologically the kidneys do not always demonstrate specific changes, and there does not appear to be an absolute structural/functional correlation. Physiologically there is a prolonged cellular insult, which then results in sustained vasoconstriction, tubular obstruction, and decreased glomerular permeability. Clinically one finds azotemia, and examination of the urinary sediment reveals granular casts, occasional white blood cells, and renal tubular cells. The patients may or may not be oliguric.

The causes of ATN are multifactorial and can be divided into two general etiological groups: ischemic and nephrotoxic. Renal hypoperfusion is the most frequently recognized single insult leading to ATN.[68] Renal hypoperfusion can occur in the setting of intravascular volume depletion, decreased cardiac output, increased renovascular resistance, or renovascular obstruction; it can also occur postsurgically for unknown causes or by interference in renal autoregulation. Major surgery is implicated in 30 percent of cases. Interestingly, systemic hypotension does not need to occur. Hypotension was only documented in 50 percent of cases of postsurgical acute renal failure in a recent review by Hou and colleagues.[69] The most critical factor in the development of ATN is an actual decrease in renal blood flow with a subsequent decrease in GFR. This decrease in renal blood flow can then cause graded renal parenchymal damage, manifested clinically by (1) mild reduction in GFR (prerenal azotemia), (2) frank ischemic damage (acute tubular necrosis), or (3) bilateral renal cortical necrosis. Elderly populations are likely to have multiple predisposing factors for the development of renal hypoperfusion, partially explaining the high incidence of ATN in these groups.

Antibiotics, particularly aminoglycosides,[70] are among the most common causes of nephrotoxic ATN. Inappropriate use and overdosage of aminoglycosides are important risk factors. Many physicians erroneously estimate a normal GFR in an elderly patient based on the serum creatinine concentration and fail to recognize that this serum creatinine concentration is "normal" only because of a decrease in muscle mass associated with aging. The GFR may actually be lower than expected despite the normal serum creatinine (see Chaps. 21 and 55). A creatinine clearance should always be estimated when ordering dosages of an aminoglycoside and the total dose reduced by either increasing the interval between doses or decreasing the amount of drug given per dose. Other common causes of nephrotoxic ATN include the use of radioiodinated contrast agents, pigment nephropathy (myoglobin), amphotericin B, and some chemotherapeutic agents (e.g., *cis*-platinum).

Treatment is directed toward discontinuation of the offending agent (if possible) and general supportive care. Supportive care should include a close determination of volume status and treatment of any volume deficiencies, if present, watching for signs or symptoms of electrolyte imbalance, monitoring patients' acid-base status, and prescribing dialysis (if indicated). In most cases the renal dysfunction is reversible, but not always back to baseline levels. Anuria and a prolonged course are poor prognostic signs.

INTERFERENCE WITH RENAL AUTOREGULATION

The increased use of two new classes of drugs, angiotension-I converting enzyme inhibitors and prostaglandin synthetase inhibitors, has resulted in increasing reports of acute renal failure associated with their use. In general, the acute renal failure occurs under conditions in which renal autoregulation of the afferent and efferent arteriolar tone is important for maintenance of GFRs.

NSAIDs such as propionic acid derivatives (ibuprofen, naproxen, and fenoprofen) and indolacetic acid derivatives (tolmetin sodium [Tolectin] and indomethacin) have been reported to cause acute renal failure in selected patients. These patients have tended to have a reduction in the actual, or "effective," renal perfusion associated with states such as congestive heart failure, cirrhosis, nephrotic syndrome, sepsis, and preexisting renal disease.[71] In these disease states, the renin-angiotensin cascade is activated. This angiotensin II–induced vasoconstriction of afferent and efferent arterioles could further decrease renal perfusion and GFRs. Normally renal prostaglandins are also produced in this circumstance, inducing an important compensatory vasodilatation to counterbalance the vasoconstriction and thereby maintaining the GFR through intrinsic renal autoregulation. However, since NSAIDs decrease prostaglandin synthesis, this can leave the angiotensin II–induced vasoconstriction unopposed, causing acute renal failure.[72] Discontinuation of the drug usually results in improvement of the condition of renal dysfunction.

Angiotensin converting enzyme (ACE) inhibitors (captopril, enalapril, and lisinopril) have been reported to produce a severe deterioration in renal function in patients with renal artery disease.[73] In patients with a critical degree of renal artery stenosis a low perfusion pressure exists, so maintenance of the GFR depends on the crucial balance of afferent and efferent arteriolar resistance. These resistant arterioles are regulated primarily by the renin-angiotensin system.[74] Inhibition of angiotensin II production by use of an ACE inhibitor then blocks this renal autoregulation, resulting in a decreasing GFR and subsequent acute renal failure. As in NSAID-induced disease, the renal dysfunction usually reverses with discontinuation of the drug; this reversal reaction is the mainstay of treatment. In patients in whom this dysfunction has been demonstrated, the physician must consider that the patient may have underlying atherosclerotic renovascular disease.

OBSTRUCTIVE UROPATHY

Obstruction to urinary flow can cause acute or chronic renal failure. Urinary flow obstruction can be due to extra- or intraureteral problems, bladder outlet obstruction, or urethral obstruction. Elderly patients are predisposed to prostatic, pelvic, or other abdominal cancers, such as lymphoma, all of which may obstruct urinary flow; therefore, it is of utmost importance that a renal ultrasound or other radiologic study be obtained to rule out obstruction in all causes of acute renal failure in an elderly patient. Many of the causes of obstruction are amenable to medical treatment or surgical therapy, with resulting reversal of renal dysfunction.

CHRONIC RENAL FAILURE

Chronic renal failure and the signs and symptoms thereof are the net result of irreversible damage to renal parenchymal mass. The clinical manifestations are similar no matter what disease process caused the initial damage. Chronic glomerular, interstitial, renovascular, metabolic, immunologic, or obstructive disease states can all cause chronic renal failure and may progress to ESRD.

A brief overview of treatable causes of ESRD was recently published.[75] Of utmost importance in any patient with newly diagnosed renal failure is an attempt to find a reversible cause for the disease and remedy it. If no specific treatment exists, an attempt to prevent progression should be initiated which includes controlling any coexisting diabetes, hypertension,[76] and perhaps excessive protein intake. Recent work by Meyer and his colleagues[77] has suggested that excessive protein intake in the setting of chronic renal insufficiency may hasten the progression to end-stage disease by causing progressive glomerular sclerosis or capillary hypertension and glomerular hyperfiltration.

It has also been demonstrated that in individual patients, renal disease tends to progress at a constant rate. A graphic plot of 1/serum creatinine versus time for each patient tends to form a linear rate of progression.[78] Chronic follow-up of these patients should show the expected rate of decline of renal function. Although an accelerating decline may be part of the natural history of the disease, if the rate of decline is found to be faster than expected, the physician must suspect development of another intercurrent medical illness. Such compounding problems may include urinary tract infection, uncontrolled hypertension, renal artery disease, de novo glomerulonephritis, de novo interstitial nephritis, drug-induced renal dysfunction, or anatomical obstruction to urinary outflow. Treatment is then aimed at attempting to reverse the acute renal failure resulting from the superimposed illness.

SODIUM AND WATER

As the GFR declines, the remaining nephrons must be able to excrete an ever-increasing percentage of the filtered load of sodium. In some patients the sodium intake overwhelms the remaining kidney's ability to excrete the daily ingested load. These patients may need sodium restriction to prevent volume overload. An occasional elderly patient will be misdiagnosed as developing heart failure and unnecessarily placed on digoxin when the actual problem is excessive sodium intake (more appropriate treatment would be salt restriction and diuretics). When diuretics are needed to maintain volume status in a patient with chronic renal insufficiency, loop diuretics, such as furosemide or ethacrynic acid, are preferable. To determine the amount of sodium intake needed per day, a 24-hour urine collection for sodium excretion should be obtained. In most patients, a 2- to 4-g sodium-restricted diet is sufficient to maintain sodium balance. However, sodium conservation is impaired in a few patients, such as those with adult polycystic kidney disease, chronic interstitial nephritis, or medullary cystic disease; it is also impaired in some patients just as a result of aging. In these patients with impaired conservation, 24-hour urine sodium losses may be as much as 10 to 20 g per day.[79] These patients would then need sodium supplementation rather than restriction to maintain a normal extracellular fluid volume.

Patients with chronic renal failure also have a decreased ability to excrete a water load. For these patients the amount of daily water intake can be estimated by measuring daily urine output and adding about 500 ml for insensible losses to that total.

POTASSIUM HOMEOSTASIS

Potassium is freely filtered by the glomerulus, reabsorbed proximally and secreted distally. Most of the potassium excreted in the urine comes from distal secretion. This distal secretion is facilitated by aldosterone. Unless hyporeninemia or hypoaldosteronism is present, it is very unusual for a patient with chronic renal insufficiency to become hyperkalemic unless the GFR is less than 10 ml/min. Selective hypoaldosteronism is common in elderly patients, especially those with diabetes. In that circumstance, an elderly patient may become hyperkalemic sooner than expected as evidenced by measured creatinine clearance alone.[80] Potassium loss also occurs via colonic excretion and is increased in patients with chronic renal insufficiency. Presumably this is aldosterone-dependent. Constipation is a common problem for the elderly, and treatment of hyperphosphatemia in patients with chronic renal failure with aluminum-containing phosphate binders can aggravate both constipation and tendency toward hyperkalemia.

Treatment of hyperkalemia is tailored toward the severity of its elevation. In mild cases, prevention is the goal, which is achieved by restricting dietary potassium intake or by facilitating potassium exchange by the distal renal tubule. Dietary intake should be restricted to 2 g per day. The use of oral sodium bicarbonate and/or mineralocorticoids can facilitate potassium secretion distally. If medical therapy is attempted, the physician must watch for salt and water overload from the increased sodium intake. Symptomatic hyperkalemia requires acute intervention. Intravenous glucose, insulin, sodium bicarbonate, and/or calcium chloride may temporarily reverse the cardiac manifestations of hyperkalemia by facilitating movement into the cells.[81] However, these therapies do not reduce the total body stores of potassium and so must be followed by oral or rectal administration of sodium polystyrene sulfonate (Kayexalate), forced renal losses through diuresis, or dialysis.

ACID-BASE STATUS

Patients with chronic renal failure tend to develop a metabolic acidosis due to the kidneys' decreased ability to excrete the normal daily acid production. Respiratory compensation is usually adequate to maintain a nearly normal systemic pH. However, it may be necessary to treat the acidosis when the serum bicarbonate level falls to less than 18 meq/liter. This is especially true for an elderly patient who may have concomitant respiratory disease and not be able to compensate adequately for the acidosis, or for those patients with ischemic cardiac disease in which systemic acidosis may predispose to arrhythmias. Appropriate treatment involves the use of oral sodium bicarbonate or calcium carbonate to buffer the acid load. Calcium carbonate may be preferable, in that it reduces the sodium load and may also help prevent development of renal osteodystrophy by binding dietary phosphorus.

CALCIUM AND PHOSPHORUS METABOLISM

Progressive renal insufficiency results in major alterations in calcium and phosphorus metabolism. These alterations are due to the combined effects of phosphate retention, decreased production of 1,25-dihydroxy vitamin D, and increased parathyroid hormone levels. The decreased availability of 1,25-dihydroxy vitamin D causes decreased intestinal absorption of calcium and also decreases the effectiveness of the action of parathyroid hormone on bone. These decreases, along with the phosphorus retention, tend to cause a decrease in the serum ionized calcium which leads to a secondary increase in parathyroid hormone levels. Consequently, early in chronic renal insufficiency, normocalcemia is maintained at the expense of an ever-increasing level of parathyroid hormone.[82] This secondary hyperparathyroidism can lead to renal osteodystrophy, bone pain, development of proximal muscle weakness, and occasionally hypercalcemia. Hypercalcemia in the face of hyperphosphatemia can result in metastatic calcification of arteries, bones, and heart, as well as deposition of calcium phosphate in the skin, which may cause pruritis.

Initial treatment is aimed at preventing progressive hyperparathyroidism. Of primary importance is the restriction of dietary phosphorus intake. Unfortunately, this usually results in a concomitant restriction of calcium intake, so supplemental calcium must also be provided. If the hyperphosphatemia persists despite dietary restriction, then phosphate binders should be added. Aluminum hydroxide or calcium carbonate is given with meals to bind phosphorus in the gut and prevent its absorption. Aluminum hydroxide–containing binders have been associated with the development of a disabling form of osteomalacia in patients with chronic renal insufficiency and ESRD[83]; consequently, excessive doses should be avoided. Calcium carbonate has the added advantages not only of binding phosphate and providing calcium supplementation but also of avoiding possible aluminum accumulation (a suspected cause of dementia in certain patients on long-term aluminum hydroxide therapy). Supplemental vitamin D should be considered when hypocalcemia persists despite normal phosphate levels or when there is a progressive rise in serum alkaline phosphatase. Serum alkaline phosphatase levels can be used as a marker for prevailing parathyroid hormone activity. A slowly increasing level suggests that the present serum calcium level is being maintained at the expense of calcium loss from bone. The various forms of vitamin D should facilitate calcium absorption from the gut, raising the serum calcium and tending to decrease parathyroid hormone levels. Dosage adjustment is often needed to avoid hypercalcemia, for hypercalcemia has been reported to accelerate the progression to ESRD.[84]

DIETARY PROTEIN INTAKE

Nitrogen balance is important in patients with chronic renal insufficiency. Excessive protein intake by patients with chronic renal insufficiency may both hasten onset of uremic symptoms and accelerate the progression to ESRD.[77] Conversely, symptoms of uremia may be decreased and, in some cases, dialysis avoided by restricting protein intake. Of therapeutic importance are preliminary studies which suggest that protein restriction may slow or prevent the progression to ESRD.[85] A multicenter trial investigating the role of modification of diet in the progression of renal disease is presently in progress. To achieve optimal nitrogen balance, patients with chronic renal failure should ingest between 0.5 to 1.0 g protein/kg body weight per day, predominantly high biological value protein.

DIET AND VITAMINS

Patients with chronic renal failure may develop folate, vitamin C, and pyridoxine deficiencies. Therefore, a multivitamin supplying these vitamins is usually prescribed. Vitamin D deficiency due to loss of renal parenchymal mass has already been discussed. Vitamins A and E should be avoided, for their stores normally increase in association with chronic renal failure.

SYSTEMIC COMPLICATIONS OF CHRONIC RENAL FAILURE

Anemia is associated with chronic renal failure and is due to multiple factors: erythropoietin levels are decreased as renal parenchymal mass falls, vitamin deficiencies may predispose to anemia, red blood cell life is shortened in uremic plasma, repeated phlebotomies may tend to deplete iron stores, there may be associated gastrointestinal blood loss, and drugs such as nonsteroidal anti-inflammatory agents and beta-blockers may decrease the effect of circulating levels of erythropoietin on the uremic bone marrow. Normally transfusion is not indicated for hemoglobin levels in the range of 7 g/100 ml or above unless the patient is symptomatic. For older patients with underlying atherosclerotic heart disease, maintenance of a hemoglobin level of 10 g/100 ml or greater would be a reasonable goal of therapy to prevent congestive heart failure or angina.

DRUG DOSAGES

Many drugs are metabolized and/or excreted by the kidney. As GFRs drop, lower doses of these drugs are needed. One important example of this principle is insulin, which is usually filtered and then metabolized by the proximal tubules. It is common for a diabetic patient with chronic renal insufficiency to need less insulin as the disease progresses. Many elderly patients develop concomitant heart disease such as congestive heart failure. It is important to remember to reduce the dose of digoxin in these patients, with a recommended starting dose of 0.125 mg every other day. Serum levels should be monitored. Potentially nephrotoxic drugs, such as aminoglycosides, are clearly more risky in patients with impaired renal function. Drugs that are nontoxic in patients with normal renal function may become hazardous and actually further suppress already impaired renal function.

As mentioned previously, the physiologic decline in GFR seen in the elderly is not accompanied by a parallel rise in serum creatinine. Hence actual creatinine clearance, rather than serum creatinine concentrations, should be used to guide drug dosages for renally excreted drugs. Twenty-four-hour urine collection is the best way to determine creatinine clearance and therefore estimate GFR. Nomograms and formulas may also be used to estimate creatinine clearance, but may overpredict actual clearances in the geriatric population.

Drugs must always be considered as a cause of renal dysfunction. Of particular relevance to geriatrics is the occurrence of drug-induced renal dysfunction in patients using NSAIDs, in whom NSAIDs can variously cause nephrotic syndrome (usually with a minimal-change lesion), renal papillary necrosis, hypernatremia, hyperkalemia, water intoxication, or "resistant hypertension."

INDICATIONS FOR DIALYSIS

There is no absolute level of BUN or creatinine above which dialysis is always indicated. A creatinine of 4 in a 90-year-old female may reflect a worse creatinine clearance than a creatinine of 8 in a 20-year-old male. In general, the patient should begin chronic dialysis once the first symptoms of uremia occur. These include protean symptoms such as anorexia, weight loss, or a decrease in the patients' overall exercise tolerance. Absolute indications for dialysis include severe acid-base disturbances, intractable hyperkalemia, volume overload unresponsive to medical therapy, encephalopathy, pericarditis, and progressive peripheral neuropathy. The patient's overall functional status, other personal preferences, and the appropriateness of instituting such life-supportive therapy should be addressed before either acute or chronic dialysis therapy is begun.

END-STAGE RENAL DISEASE

Since dialysis as a form of renal replacement therapy was begun in the early 1960s, the end-stage renal disease (ESRD) population in the United States has grown to over 60,000.[86] Along with this growth there has been a marked increase in the incidence of ESRD in patients age 55 and older. This increase is not due as much to a change in various disease spectrums as it is to the extension of medical coverage to most patients with ESRD and to older patients, including those with illnesses such as diabetes (Social Security Amendment of 1972—Public Law #92-603, Section 2991). In Michigan, for example, the yearly number of patients aged 0 to 54 who entered ESRD programs changed very little from 1974 to 1983, whereas there was a marked increase in the number of patients entering the program over this time span who were aged 55 and older.[87] In Europe 8 percent of all patients with ESRD were greater than 65 years of age at the start of their therapy.[88] Recent Department of Health and Human Services data, reporting on total case loads for ESRD patients, showed that 15 percent of all patients seen were over the age of 70.[89] Consequently, in some ESRD networks the mean age of a dialysis population has increased to 55.7 years old.[87]

The elderly patients with ESRD typically present a number of problems. Not only do they have ESRD, but they are also likely to have other complicating medical illnesses. They also have to adjust to the aging of their peers, families, and, in some, the progressive loss of their support systems. Equally important is the fact that the cost of ESRD can be a considerable financial burden for many patients. Close attention needs to be paid to their special needs by counseling, discussing the various therapeutic modalities available to them, and, importantly, explaining the expected benefits and possible ramifications of treatment on the individual patient's quality of life. This kind of discussion certainly should be undertaken before initiating long-term maintenance dialysis therapy.

Because of older age and the likelihood of other concomitant medical problems, the older dialysis patient's life expectancy is less than that of younger patients. According to data from the End-Stage Renal Disease Medical Information System (ESRD MIS), published annually by Medicare,[86] between 1974 and 1979 the overall 1-year survival rate of all Medicare-covered ESRD patients was approximately 81 percent. Yearly survival rates were similar. For patients older than 75, the 1-year survival rate was 52 percent in 1974 and 65 percent in 1979. Despite this lower life expectancy, most nephrologists are not averse to offering maintenance dialysis therapy to elderly patients.

One reason for offering this therapy is based on the quality-of-life issues. A patient's personal quality of life is best judged by the individual patient and family, not by those providing care. Studies by Westlie et al.[90] and Chester et al.[91] suggest that the majority of older patients in their dialysis populations did not consider themselves worse off than their peers. Bailey et al.[92] looked at rehabilitation in old and young dialysis patients and concluded that elderly patients had comparable levels of rehabilitation when compared to younger patients. These reports strongly support providing ESRD therapy to all patients without age restriction but do not eliminate the need for assessing each individual's potential benefits from dialysis and approaching the patient with a multidisciplinary effort when explaining dialysis options.

Elderly patients with ESRD, like younger patients, have multiple therapeutic options available for them. These options include hemodialysis, chronic ambulatory peritoneal dialysis, renal transplantation, conservative medical therapy, or acceptance of death from uremia.

HEMODIALYSIS

Hemodialysis represents a common therapeutic approach to ESRD in the elderly. Chester et al.[91] analyzed data from their hemodialysis patients aged 80 or greater and found that hemodialysis provided them with an average of 22 months of additional life expectancy versus patients in the comparison group (mean age 42), who had an average survival of 39 months. Taken in this context, although survival for elderly hemodialysis patients is statistically less than that of younger patients, quality of life in older patients was equal to or better than that found in younger age groups.

The increased mortality rate in the elderly group is due to multiple associated risk factors. Among these are age, which in itself increases the risk of dying by 1.2 for each added decade of life,[93] and any concomitant medical diseases. The increased prevalence of coronary artery

disease in elderly patients increases the risk for dialysis-induced angina, arrhythmias, hypotension, and cerebrovascular accidents. The presence of coronary artery disease and its associated conditions does not preclude treatment of ESRD, but it does make the patient's individual treatment somewhat more difficult. Maintenance of a high hemoglobin, which may somewhat alleviate these problems, currently requires close attention to blood loss and frequent transfusions; however, with the advent of synthetic erythropoietin[94] easier maintenance of a normal hemoglobin is on the horizon. Cardiovascular drugs used to treat underlying arrhythmias, angina, or hypertension require close attention to dosing. Mental status changes are common and may be due to concurrent drug use, underlying central nervous system pathology, or complications of uremia and dialysis itself. "Dialysis dementia,"[95] which may be due to the accumulation of aluminum, must always be considered in elderly patients with faltering mental status or syndromes of failure to thrive.

Special care must be taken when considering hemodialysis access creation. Some data suggest that construction of autogenous arteriovenous fistulas in elderly patients is less feasible than in the general population[96] and should only be considered in selected patients. Prognostic factors which collectively militate against autogenous reconstruction are diabetes, prolonged incidence of secondary hyperparathyroidism, diffuse atherosclerotic disease, previous stroke with paresis or paralysis of the extremity, repeated venepunctures or history of intravenous cannulation of the vein. If autogenous construction is not possible, taper Gore-tex grafts seem to produce better survival rates with fewer complications.[96]

PERITONEAL DIALYSIS

Continuous ambulatory peritoneal dialysis (CAPD) was first described in 1976[97] but was not widely used until 1978. CAPD uses a sterile, closed system composed primarily of the peritoneal cavity, a chronic indwelling catheter, connecting tubing, and a collapsible plastic dialysate bag. Peritoneal fluid dwells in the peritoneal cavity for 4- to 8-hour periods during which "dialysis" occurs. After each such period, the dialysate is drained, a new bag connected, and dialysate refilled by gravity. Various forms of continuous cyclic peritoneal dialysis and intermittent peritoneal dialysis (IPD) are offshoots of CAPD. These techniques involve 4 to 12 rapid exchanges of dialysate, usually during the night, with the help of an automated cycling machine.

By 1983 15.3 percent of the total dialysis population was dialyzing at home, of which 62.5 percent was using CAPD.[86] Along with the increase in number of patients using CAPD, the percentage of these patients over the age of 60 has increased from an estimated 31 percent in

1981 to 1983[98] to 48 percent by 1986.[99] Elderly patients therefore presently account for at least one-third of CAPD populations, and as CAPD becomes a more accepted technique, the absolute number of elderly patients on this form of ESRD therapy is expected to grow.

Reasons for choosing CAPD include the convenience of dialyzing at home, the stability of serum chemistries, the reduction of stress placed on the cardiovascular system, patient preference, and physician selection bias. Because of the smaller numbers of users and problems with selection bias, there are few data that compare relative survival rates on CAPD versus hemodialysis specifically in elderly patients. It is estimated that in comparison to mortality for younger populations (aged 20 to 59) there is an approximate twofold increase in mortality for the elderly patients at 6, 12, and 19 months after starting peritoneal dialysis.[98] This increase probably represents the expected age-specific mortality because at present other non-age-specific risk factors have not been identified.

Morbidity associated with CAPD includes peritonitis, catheter tunnel and exit site infections, pancreatitis, and failure of the technique. Catheter function and longevity are actually the same or better in older versus younger populations,[100] while overall morbidity, technique survival, and biochemical control are similar between groups of young versus old CAPD populations.

TRANSPLANTATION

It has generally been thought that older patients were considered to be at high mortality risk after undergoing renal transplantation. However, recent studies have suggested that since 1980 there is no statistically significant difference in survival rates over a 4-year period of follow-up for transplant recipients less than 40, 40 to 50, and greater than 50 years old[101] (few of such recipients were truly elderly, however). As with all groups, the greatest attrition rates for the elderly recipients occurred during the first year after transplantation. While recipient survival rates have improved over those from the 1960s, the main causes of death and their rank order have remained fairly constant. Infections, cardiovascular diseases, and stroke continue to be the principal causes of death in older transplant populations.

One-year graft survival was no different (or possibly even better) in older patients versus younger patients.[102] The use of newer, more specific immunosuppressive drugs, such as cyclosporin A, and the generalized decline in T-cell function associated with aging[29] may facilitate graft survival in elderly patients. The adverse side of this phenomenon would be an increased predisposition to infectious complications, which in fact has been reported for transplant patients over the age of 50.[103] Despite the increased risk associated with infections and the potential cardiovascular risks associated with surgery and immunosuppressive drugs, reported 1- and 3-year survival rates for transplant patients age 50 or greater was 84 percent. This is in contrast to reported 1- and 3-year survival rates for almost 36,000 dialysis patients over the age of 50 of 77 percent and 48 percent, respectively.[104] While this difference may be due in part to the rigorous patient selection for transplantation, it suggests that transplantation is a viable mode of therapy for selected older patients with ESRD.

REFERENCES

1. Holley KE et al: Renal artery stenosis. A clinico-pathologic study in normotensive and hypertensive patients. *Am J Med* 37:14, 1964

2. Schrieber MJ et al: The natural history of atherosclerotic and fibrous renal artery disease. *Urol Clin North Am* 11:383, 1984.

3. Sos TA et al: Percutaneous transluminal renal angioplasty in renovascular hypertension due to atheroma or fibromuscular dysplasia. *N Engl J Med* 309:274, 1983.

4. Dean RH: Comparison of medical and surgical treatment of renovascular hypertension. *Nephron* 44:101, 1986.

5. Humphreys MH, Alfrey AC: Vascular diseases of the kidney, in Brenner BM, Rector FC (eds): *The Kidney*. Philadelphia, Saunders, 1981, p 1175.

6. Peterson NE, McDonald DF: Renal embolization. *J Urol* 100:140, 1968.

7. Loomis L et al: Dynamic treatment of renal artery embolism: A case report and review of the literature. *J Urol* 96:131, 1966.

8. Sieniewicz DJ et al: Atheromatous emboli to the kidneys. *Radiology* 92:1231, 1969.

9. Oster P et al: Blood clotting and cholesterol embolization. *JAMA* 242:2070, 1979.

10. Eliot RS et al: Atheromatous embolism. *Circulation* 30:611, 1964.

11. Ramierez G et al: Cholesterol embolization: A complication of angiography. *Arch Intern Med* 138:1430, 1978.

12. Dalakos TG et al: "Malignant" hypertension resulting from atheromatous embolization predominantly of the kidney. *Am J Med* 57:135, 1974.

13. Meyrier A et al: Atheromatous renal disease. *Am J Med* 85:139, 1988.

14. Davson J et al: The kidney in periarteritis nodosa. *Am J Med* 17:175, 1948.

15. Cochrane CG, Dixon FJ: Antigen-antibody complex induced disease, in Meischer PA, Muller-Eberhard HJ (eds): *Textbook of Immunopathology*, 2d ed, vol 1. New York, Grune & Stratton, 1976, p 137.

16. Fauci AS et al: The spectrum of vasculitis. Clinical, pathologic, immunologic, and therapeutic considerations. *Ann Intern Med* 89:660, 1978.

17. Balow JE: Renal vasculitis. *Kidney Int* 27:954, 1985.

18. Weiss MA, Crissman JD: Segmental necrotizing glomerulonephritis: Diagnostic, prognostic, and therapeutic significance. *Am J Kidney Dis* 6:199, 1985.

19. Travers RL et al: Polyarteritis nodosa: A clinical and angiographic analysis of 17 cases. *Semin Arthritis Rheum* 8:184, 1979.

20. Cupps TR, Fauci AS: *The Vasculitides.* Philadelphia, Saunders, 1981.
21. Balow JE, Austin HA: Vasculitic diseases of the kidney, in Suki WN, Massry SG (eds): *Therapy of Renal Diseases and Related Disorders.* Boston, Martinus Nijhoff, 1984, p 273.
22. Brown WN: Glomerulonephritis in the elderly, in Michelis MF et al (eds): *Geriatric Nephrology.* New York, Field, Rich and Associates, 1986, p 90.
23. Ellis A, Toronto MD: Natural history of Bright's disease. Clinical, histological and experimental observations. *Lancet* 1:1, 1942.
24. Fishberg AM: *Hypertension and Nephritis,* 5th ed. Philadelphia, Lea & Febiger, 1954, p 529.
25. Nesson HR, Robbins SL: Glomerulonephritis in older age groups. *Arch Intern Med* 105:23, 1960.
26. Montoliu J et al: Acute and rapidly progressive forms of glomerulonephritis in the elderly. *J Am Geriatr Soc* 29:108, 1981.
27. Zech P et al: The nephrotic syndrome in adults aged over 60: Etiology, evaluation and treatment of 76 cases. *Clin Nephrol* 18:232, 1982.
28. Abrass CK: Glomerulonephritis in the elderly. *Am J Nephrol* 5:409, 1985.
29. Roberts-Thompson IC et al: Aging, immune response and mortality. *Lancet* 2:368, 1974.
30. Stilmant MM et al: Crescentic glomerulonephritis without immune deposits: Clinicopathologic features. *Kidney Int* 15:184, 1979.
31. Bolton WK: Crescentic glomerulonephritis, in Glassock RJ (ed): *Current Therapy in Nephrology and Hypertension.* Philadelphia, BC Decker Inc, 1984, p 213.
32. Arieff AI et al: Acute glomerulonephritis in the elderly. *Geriatrics* 26:74, 1971.
33. Potviliege PR et al: Necropsy study on glomerulonephritis in the elderly. *J Clin Pathol* 28:891, 1975.
34. Samiy AH et al: Acute glomerulonephritis in elderly patients: Report of seven cases over sixty years of age. *Ann Intern Med* 54:603, 1961.
35. Glassock RJ et al: Primary glomerular disease, in Brenner BM, Rector FC (eds): *The Kidney.* Philadelphia, Saunders, 1981, p 929.
36. Madaio MP, Harrington JT: The diagnosis of acute glomerulonephritis. *N Engl J Med* 309:1299, 1983.
37. Fawcett LW et al: Nephrotic syndrome in the elderly. *Br Med J* 2:387, 1971.
38. Lustig S et al: Nephrotic syndrome in the elderly. *Isr J Med Sci* 18:1010, 1982.
39. Johnson RJ, Couser WG: Membranous nephropathy, in Glassock RJ (ed): *Current Therapy in Nephrology and Hypertension.* Philadelphia, BC Decker Inc, 1984, p 207.
40. Collaborative Study of the Adult Idiopathic Nephrotic Syndrome: A controlled study of short-term prednisone treatment in adults with membranous nephropathy. *N Engl J Med* 301:1301, 1979.
41. Ponticelli C et al: Controlled trial of methylprednisolone and chlorambucil in idiopathic membranous nephropathy. *N Engl J Med* 310:946, 1984.
42. Donadio JV et al: Idiopathic membranous nephropathy: The natural history of untreated patients. *Kidney Int* 33:708, 1988.
43. Kyle RA et al: Primary systemic amyloidosis. Resolution of the nephrotic syndrome with melphalan and prednisone. *Arch Intern Med* 142:1445, 1982.
44. Brocklehurst JC: *Textbook of Geriatric Medicine and Gerontology.* Edinburgh, Churchill Livingstone, 1973, p 296.
45. Gleckman R et al: Acute pyelonephritis in the elderly. *South Med J* 75:551, 1982.
46. Gleckman RA et al: Urosepsis: A phenomenon unique to elderly women. *J Urol* 133:176, 1985.
47. Gleckman RA: Infectious problems in the geriatric nephrology patient, in Michelis MF et al (eds): *Geriatric Nephrology.* New York, Field, Rich and Associates, 1986, p 58.
48. Kleinknecht D et al: Acute interstitial nephritis due to drug hypersensitivity. An up-to-date review with a report of 19 cases. *Adv Nephrol* 13:271, 1983.
49. Appel GB, Neu HG: Acute interstitial nephritis induced by B Lactam antibiotics, in Fillastre JH et al (eds): *Antibiotic Nephrotoxicity.* Paris, INSERM, 1984.
50. Appel GB, Kunis CL: Acute tubulointerstitial nephritis, in Cotran RS (ed): *Tubulointerstitial Nephropathies. Contemporary Issues in Nephrology,* vol 10. New York, Churchill Livingstone, 1982, p 151.
51. Cotran RS et al: Tubulointerstitial diseases, in Brenner BM, Rector FC (eds): *The Kidney.* Philadelphia, Saunders, 1986, p 1143.
52. Galpin JE et al: Acute interstitial nephritis due to methicillin. *Am J Med* 65:756, 1978.
53. Linton AL: Acute interstitial nephritis due to drugs. *Ann Intern Med* 93:735, 1980.
54. Laberke HG, Bohle A: Acute interstitial nephritis: Correlations between clinical and morphological findings. *Clin Nephrol* 14:263, 1980.
55. Dawborn JK et al: The association of peptic ulceration, chronic renal disease and analgesic abuse. *Q J Med* 35:69, 1966.
56. Buckalew VM Jr, Schey HM: Analgesic nephropathy: A significant cause of morbidity in the United States. *Am J Kidney Dis* 2:164, 1986.
57. Murray TG, Goldberg M: Analgesic-associated nephropathy in the U.S.A.: Epidemiologic, clinical and pathogenetic features. *Kidney Int* 13:64, 1978.
58. Wilson DR, Gault MM: Declining incidence of analgesic nephropathy in Canada. *Can Med Assoc J* 127:500, 1982.
59. Gonwa TA et al: Analgesic associated nephropathy and transitional cell carcinoma of the urinary tract. *Kidney Int* 93:249, 1980.
60. Hill GS et al: Renal lesions in multiple myeloma: Their relationship to associated protein abnormalities. *Am J Kidney Dis* 2:423, 1983.
61. Hoyer JR, Seiler MW: Pathophysiology of Tamm-Horsfall protein. *Kidney Int* 16:999, 1979.
62. Alexanian R et al: Prognostic factors in multiple myeloma. *Cancer* 36:1192, 1975.
63. Cohen HJ, Rundles W: Managing the complications of multiple myeloma. *Arch Intern Med* 135:177, 1975.
64. Anderson S, Brenner BM: The aging kidney: Structure, function, mechanisms, and therapeutic implications. *J Am Geriatr Soc* 35:590, 1987.
65. DeFronzo RA: Hyperkalemia and hyporeninemic hypoaldosteronism. *Kidney Int* 17:118, 1980.

66. Noth RH et al: Age and the renin-aldosterone system. *Arch Intern Med* 137:1414, 1977.

67. Kafetz K, Hodkinson H: Uraemia in the elderly. *J Clin Exp Geriatr* 4:63, 1982.

68. Rasmussen HH, Ibels LS: Acute renal failure. Multivariate analysis of causes and risk factors. *Am J Med* 73:211, 1982.

69. Hou SH et al: Hospital-acquired renal insufficiency: A prospective study. *Am J Med* 74:243, 1983.

70. Humes DH: Aminoglycoside nephrotoxicity. *Kidney Int* 33:900, 1988.

71. Henrich WL, Blachley JD: Acute renal failure with prostaglandin inhibitors. *Semin Nephrol* 1:57, 1981.

72. Carmichael J, Shankel SW: Effects of nonsteroidal anti-inflammatory drugs on prostaglandins and renal function. *Am J Med* 78:992, 1985.

73. Hricik DE et al: Captopril-induced functional renal insufficiency in patients with bilateral renal artery stenosis or renal artery stenosis *N Engl J Med* 308:373, 1983.

74. Blythe WB: Captopril and renal autoregulation. *N Engl J Med* 308:390, 1983.

75. Burkart JM et al: Prevention of renal failure, in Maher JR (ed): *Replacement of Renal Function by Dialysis*, 3d ed. Boston, Martinus Nijhoff, 1988.

76. Baldwin DS, Neugarten J: Blood pressure control and progression of renal insufficiency, in Mitch WE et al (eds): *The Progressive Nature of Renal Disease*. New York, Churchill Livingstone, 1986, p 81.

77. Meyer TW et al: Dietary protein intake and progressive glomerular sclerosis: The role of capillary hypertension and hyperperfusion in the progression of renal disease. *Ann Intern Med* 98:832, 1983.

78. Mitch WE: A simple method of estimating progression of chronic renal failure. *Lancet* 2:1326, 1976.

79. Stanbury SW, Mahler RF: Salt-wasting renal disease: Metabolic observations on a patient with "salt-losing nephritis." *Q J Med* 28:425, 1959.

80. Michelis MF, Murdaugh HV: Selective hypoaldosteronism. *Am J Med* 59:1, 1975.

81. Tannen RL: The patient with hypokalemia or hyperkalemia, in Schrier RW (ed): *Manual of Nephrology. Diagnosis and Therapy*, 2d ed. Boston, Little, Brown and Company, 1985, p 31.

82. Slatopolsky ER et al: On the pathogenesis of hyperparathyroidism in chronic experimental renal insufficiency in the dog. *J Clin Invest* 50:492, 1971.

83. Benno I et al: Aluminum associated bone disease: Clinico-pathologic correlation. *Am J Kidney Dis* 2:255, 1982.

84. Johnson WJ: Use of vitamin D analogs in renal osteodystrophy. *Semin Nephrol* 6:31, 1986.

85. Maschio G et al: Effects of dietary protein and phosphorus restriction on the progression of early renal failure. *Kidney Int* 22:371, 1982.

86. Rosansky SJ, Eggers PW: Trends in the US end-stage renal disease population: 1973–1983. *Am J Kidney Dis* 9:91, 1987.

87. Port FK et al: Outcome of treatment modalities for geriatric end-stage renal disease: The Michigan kidney registry, in Michelis MF et al (eds): *Geriatric Nephrology*. New York, Field, Rich and Associates, 1986, p 149.

88. Wing AJ et al: Peritoneal dialysis results in the EDTA Registry, in Nolph KD (ed): *Peritoneal Dialysis*. Boston, Martinus Nijholl, 1985, p 637.

89. End-Stage Renal Disease Program Medical Information System: Facility Survey Tables, 1982. Health Care Financing Administration, Bureau of Support Services, 1982.

90. Westlie L et al: Mortality, morbidity, and life satisfaction in the very old dialysis patient. *Trans Am Soc Artificial Intern Organs* 30:21, 1984.

91. Chester AC et al: Hemodialysis in the eighth and ninth decades of life *Arch Intern Med* 139:1001, 1979.

92. Bailey GL et al: Hemodialysis and renal transplantation in patients of the 50–80 age group. *J Am Geriatr Soc* 20:421, 1972.

93. Capelli JP et al: Comparative analysis of survival on home hemodialysis, in-center hemodialysis, and chronic peritoneal dialysis (CAPD-IPD) therapies. *Dial Transplant* 14:38, 1977.

94. Eschback JW et al: Correction of the anemia of end-stage renal disease with recombinant human erythropoietin. *N Engl J Med* 316:73, 1987.

95. Alfrey AC: Dialysis encephalopathy. *Kidney Int* 29:S53, 1986.

96. Hinsdale JG et al: Vascular access for hemodialysis in the elderly: Results and perspectives in a geriatric population. *Dial Transplant* 14:560, 1985.

97. Popovich RP et al: The definition of a novel portable/wearable equilibrium peritoneal dialysis technique. *Trans Am Soc Artificial Intern Organs* 5:64, 1976

98. Steinberg SM et al: A comprehensive report on the experience of patients on continuous ambulatory peritoneal dialysis for the treatment of end-stage renal disease. *Am J Kidney Dis* 4:233, 1984.

99. Nolph KD et al: Special studies from the NIH Registry. *Peritoneal Dialysis Bull* 6:28, 1986.

100. Nissenen AR et al: CAPD in the elderly—regional experience, in Maher JF, Einchester JF (eds): *International Peritoneal Congress Proceedings*. New York, Field, Rich and Associates, 1985, p 312.

101. Riggio RR et al: Transplantation in the elderly, in Michelis MF et al (eds): *Geriatric Nephrology*. New York, Field, Rich and Associates, 1986, p 141.

102. Lee PG, Terasaki PI: Effect of age on kidney transplants, in Terasaki PI (ed). Los Angeles, UCLA Tissue Typing Laboratory, 1985, p 123.

103. Sommer BG et al: Renal transplantation in patients over 50 years of age. *Trans Proc* 13:33, 1981.

104. Krakauer H et al: The recent U.S. experience in the treatment of end stage renal disease by dialysis and transplantation. *N Engl J Med* 308:1558, 1983.

Chapter 57

DISORDERS
OF THE PROSTATE

Charles B. Brendler

This chapter discusses two common disorders of the prostate: benign prostatic hyperplasia (BPH) and adenocarcinoma of the prostate. Prior to discussing these diseases, a brief review of the normal anatomy, physiology, and biochemistry of the prostate is provided.

THE NORMAL PROSTATE

ANATOMY

The normal adult prostate is a firm, elastic organ weighing about 20 grams. It is located caudad to the base of the bladder and is traversed by the first portion of the urethra. It is bordered anteriorly by the symphysis pubis and posteriorly by the rectum. The paired seminal vesicles are attached to the prostate and are located posterior to the bladder (Fig. 57-1).

A cross section of the human prostate reveals two concentric anatomic regions: the inner periurethral zone composed of short glands and the outer peripheral zone composed of longer, branched glands.[1] These regions are separated by a thin layer of fibroelastic tissue, the so-called surgical capsule (Fig. 57-2). BPH arises within the inner periurethral zone in a specific region near the verumontanum called the transition zone.[2] In contrast, prostatic carcinoma usually arises in the outer peripheral zone.[3]

PHYSIOLOGY

Although it seems probable that the secretions of the prostate and other sex accessory organs protect or enhance the functional properties of the spermatozoa, the exact function of the prostate is unknown. Of the total average human ejaculate volume of 3.5 ml, the prostate

secretes 0.5 ml, and the seminal vesicles secrete 2.0 to 2.5 ml.[4,5]

Two specific components of prostatic secretion, zinc and acid phosphatase, have aroused interest because of their high concentrations in seminal fluid. The concentration of zinc is higher in the prostate than in any other organ in the body.[6] Its function is unknown, but an anti-inflammatory role has been suggested since the concentration of zinc in the prostatic secretions of men with bacterial prostatitis has been reported to be lower than in control patients.[7]

The biological function of acid phosphatase is also unknown. Prostate cancer cells often continue to secrete acid phosphatase after they have metastasized, and the

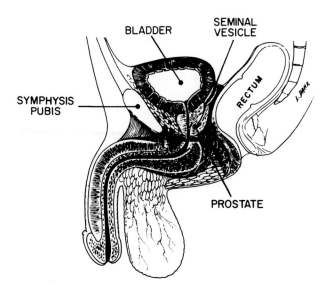

FIGURE 57-1
The anatomic relationship of the prostate to adjacent structures. *(After Brendler H, in Glenn JF (ed): Urologic Surgery, 3d ed. Philadelphia, Lippincott, 1983.)*

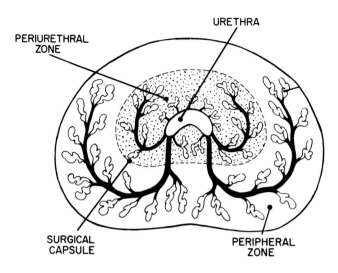

FIGURE 57-2
A coronal section through the prostate demonstrating the anatomic relationships between the urethra, periurethral tissue, surgical capsule, and the peripheral tissue. *(After Brendler H, in Glenn JF (ed): Urologic Surgery, 3d ed. Philadelphia, Lippincott, 1983.)*

measurement of prostatic acid phosphatase in the serum is used both as a screening test for prostatic carcinoma and as a means of following the response to therapy in patients with metastatic disease.[8,9]

BIOCHEMISTRY

The growth and secretory functions of the prostate are dependent on functioning testes; prostatic maturation will not occur in a male castrated before puberty. Testosterone, the major circulating androgen, diffuses passively through the cell membrane of the prostatic epithelial cell. Testosterone is then converted to dihydrotestosterone (DHT) by the enzyme 5α-reductase.[10] DHT is the major active androgenic metabolite within the prostate; once formed, it is bound to a cytoplasmic receptor and transported to the nucleus. The DHT-receptor complex binds to the nuclear chromatin and initiates RNA synthesis, protein synthesis, and cell replication (Fig. 57-3.)[11-13]

Estrogens inhibit prostatic growth and exert their major effect by blocking the release of luteinizing hormone from the pituitary, thus inhibiting testicular synthesis of testosterone. If castrated animals are given both estrogens and androgens, normal prostate growth occurs, indicating that estrogens do not block androgen-induced growth in the prostate itself.[14]

BENIGN PROSTATIC HYPERPLASIA

INCIDENCE

BPH is a disease of advancing age. Histologically, BPH is rarely identified before age 40[15]; subsequently, how-

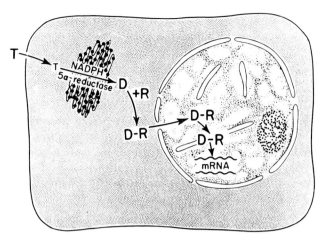

FIGURE 57-3
Concepts of androgen action in the prostate. T, testosterone; D, dihydrotestosterone; R, androgen-receptor protein; mRNA, messenger RNA. *(From Wilson JD, Am J Med 68:745, 1980.)*

ever, the incidence progressively increases to about 90 percent by age 80.[16] Clinically, BPH begins to produce symptoms of urethral obstruction at about age 50. Thereafter, the incidence and severity of symptoms increases with age as both the incidence of BPH and the average prostate weight simultaneously increase (Fig. 57-4).[16] In 1968, Lytton and associates estimated that the probability of a 40-year-old man requiring an operation for BPH was 10 percent.[17] In 1983, Birkhoff concluded that the rate of prostatectomy had doubled, and estimated that the probability of a 50-year-old man requiring prostatectomy was 20 to 25 percent.[18]

ETIOLOGY

Although the exact etiology of BPH is unknown, it is closely related to both aging and age-associated changes in circulating hormones. As stated above, BPH seldom presents clinically before age 50, and, thereafter, the incidence of the disease increases with age. Circulating androgens also play a role; BPH does not develop in men who are castrated or lose testicular function before puberty.[19] In the dog, the only other species known to develop the disease, castration causes marked regression of established BPH.[20] In the human, castration causes atrophy of prostatic epithelium.[21]

With aging, serum testosterone levels decline while serum estrogen levels increase, resulting in an increase in the ratio of plasma estrogens to plasma testosterone.[22] It is unclear, however, whether these shifts in circulating hormone levels are directly involved in the pathogenesis of BPH. There is evidence, however, that androgens and estrogens act synergistically in the development of BPH in the dog.[23] Furthermore, administration of estrogens in the dog results in a twofold increase in prostatic androgen receptor.[24]

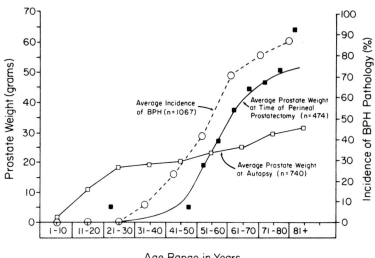

FIGURE 57-4
Age-related alterations in human prostatic pathology: incidence of BPH at autopsy in 1067 men based on histologic criteria (open circles); average prostatic weight at autopsy in 740 men (open boxes); average prostatic weight at time of simple perineal prostatectomy for BPH in 474 men (closed boxes). *(From Berry SJ et al, J Urol 132:474, 1984. © by Williams & Wilkins, 1984.)*

Further evidence that hormones are involved in the etiology of BPH is provided by the fact that, in both dog and man, the development of BPH is associated with an enzymatic shift within the prostate that favors the accumulation of DHT.[25,26] It is somewhat paradoxical that actual levels of DHT are not elevated in BPH tissue,[27] but there is, nevertheless, a definite alteration in steroid metabolism within the hyperplastic gland.

PATHOGENESIS

As the hyperplastic prostate enlarges it compresses the urethra, producing symptoms of urinary obstruction that ultimately may progress to urinary retention. Urethral obstruction may cause incomplete emptying of the bladder, giving rise to urinary stasis, urinary tract infection, and bladder calculi. Furthermore, hypertrophy of the bladder muscle may cause hydronephrosis and bladder diverticula. Bladder neoplasms are more likely to arise in bladder diverticula, especially if the diverticula drain poorly and are chronically infected.[28]

SYMPTOMS

Symptoms due to BPH can be categorized as either obstructive or irritative. Obstructive symptoms include hesitancy to initiate voiding, straining to void, decreased force and caliber of the urinary stream, prolonged dribbling after micturition, a sensation of incomplete bladder emptying, and urinary retention. These symptoms result directly from narrowing of the bladder neck and prostatic urethra by the hyperplastic prostate.

Irritative symptoms include urinary frequency, nocturia, dysuria, urgency, and urge incontinence. These symptoms may result from incomplete emptying of the bladder with voiding or may be due to urinary tract infection secondary to prostatic obstruction. More commonly, irritative symptoms result from reduced bladder compliance as a result of prostatic obstruction.[29]

It is important to recognize and distinguish patients who present mainly with irritative symptoms, since these symptoms may be caused by other conditions unrelated to prostatic obstruction, such as bladder carcinoma, neurogenic bladder, and urinary tract infection. All too frequently, patients with irritative urinary tract symptoms are presumed to have prostatic obstruction without receiving an adequate diagnostic evaluation, resulting in delayed and sometimes inappropriate therapy.

PHYSICAL EXAMINATION

Other than a distended bladder, the usual physical findings in BPH are confined to the prostate. Examination of the prostate should be performed with the patient either in the knee-chest position or bent over the bed with his chest touching his elbows. The examining glove should be well-lubricated, and the index finger should be inserted slowly into the rectum to allow the anal sphincter time to relax. A helpful maneuver is for the physician to place his or her other hand against the patient's lower abdomen, which helps steady the patient and allows gentle counterpressure as the examining finger is advanced into the rectum.

The normal prostate is the size of a walnut and has the consistency of a pencil eraser. The hyperplastic prostate is variably enlarged, usually no more than two or three times normal size, but occasionally exceeding the size of a lemon. The consistency remains rubbery but is somewhat more fleshy than normal, particularly in the larger glands. It should be noted that rectal examination affords only a rough estimate of prostatic size and should never be relied upon to rule out prostatic obstruction. A much more accurate appraisal of prostatic size can be obtained with ultrasonography and cystourethroscopy.

The rectal examination is, however, the single most valuable screening test for prostatic carcinoma. The entire posterior surface of the gland should be examined for areas of induration suggestive of malignancy. After examination of the prostate, the full length of the index finger should be advanced into the rectum and a careful circumferential examination performed to rule out carcinoma of the rectum. A stool guaiac also should be obtained.

DIAGNOSTIC TESTS

The most valuable test for documenting urinary obstruction is measurement of the urinary flow rate.[30] Inexpensive flowmeters are available that allow an accurate determination of the patient's voided volume and peak urinary flow rate. These values are plotted along with the patient's age on a nomogram. It must be emphasized that a decreased flow rate per se is never an indication for prostatectomy, but uroflometry, when used and interpreted correctly, is an excellent physiologic test for prostatic obstruction.

An abdominal ultrasound examination is useful to rule out pathology of the upper urinary tract, such as hydronephrosis, stones, or renal masses. Furthermore, ultrasound measurement of postvoid residual urine volume and prostatic size is extremely accurate.

Cystourethroscopy often is employed as a screening test for prostatic obstruction, but its value in this regard is limited because the anatomic appearance of the bladder neck and prostatic urethra during cystourethroscopy may be misleading. An anatomically small prostate may produce significant obstruction during voiding, while an anatomically large prostate may produce little or no obstruction at all.[31] The place for cystourethroscopy is in the operating room after the decision to perform a prostatectomy has been made. With the patient under anesthesia, a full evaluation of the prostatic urethra can be made, and also a decision as to whether the prostate is small enough to be resected transurethrally, or whether it is sufficiently large to require open surgical removal. Before proceeding to prostatectomy, a careful inspection of the bladder is made to rule out bladder diverticula, stones, and, most importantly, tumors.

Other tests that may be helpful in evaluating patients with symptoms of BPH include a retrograde urethrogram when a urethral stricture is suspected, and formal urodynamic testing including a cystometrogram in patients with complex voiding symptomatology or a suspected neurogenic bladder.

TREATMENT

The usual treatment for BPH is surgical removal of the obstructing hyperplastic periurethral prostatic tissue. The indications for prostatectomy are (1) voiding symptoms that are troublesome to the patient, (2) urinary retention, (3) recurrent urinary tract infections caused by postvoid residual urine, (4) compromised renal function due to hydronephrosis from prostatic obstruction, (5) recurrent gross hematuria with no other explanation, and (6) urge incontinence due to prostatic obstruction.

The surgical objective of a partial prostatectomy done for BPH is to reestablish a wide open bladder neck and prostatic urethra by removing all the hyperplastic prostatic tissue. Surgical removal of this tissue is facilitated by the presence of the surgical capsule, a layer of fibroelastic tissue separating the periurethral adenoma from the peripheral prostate.

Prostatectomy for benign hyperplasia can be accomplished either by transurethral resection or by open surgical enucleation of the adenoma. The decision as to whether a transurethral or an open prostatectomy is done is usually based on the size of the gland. Since transurethral prostatectomy carries a lower morbidity than open prostatectomy,[32] adenomas of less than 70 grams are usually approached transurethrally. Regardless of the surgical approach employed, the surgical objective is the same, i.e., to remove all the hyperplastic tissue down to the surgical capsule, leaving the peripheral prostate intact.

Although prostatectomy is usually performed with low morbidity and excellent results, some patients are not candidates for surgical procedures because of uncorrectable bleeding diatheses or high anesthetic risk. For these patients, pharmacological manipulation of the prostate has been attempted. Clinical studies using alpha-blocking agents,[33] antiandrogens,[34] and antihypercholesterolemic agents[35] have been reported to favorably affect voiding function in some patients with BPH.

Recently there has been interest in the use of luteinizing hormone releasing hormone (LHRH) agonists to treat BPH. Chronic administration of LHRH agonists reduces serum testosterone to castrate levels, resulting in atrophy of the prostatic epithelium. Peters and Walsh[36] reported on nine patients who were surgical candidates for prostatectomy but were treated with an LHRH agonist for 6 months instead of undergoing surgery. Three of nine patients had significant improvement in peak urinary flow rates, and improvement in flow rate correlated with regression in prostatic size. Morphological analysis of prostatic biopsy specimens showed regression of glandular epithelium for all patients during treatment. However, a wide variation in the effect of LHRH agonists has been reported, and this is likely due to the inhomogeneity in both histologic appearance and clinical presentation of patients with BPH.[37] Schlegel and Brendler recently reported on the successful management of a hemophiliac with urinary retention due to BPH, using an LHRH agonist.[38]

CARCINOMA OF THE PROSTATE

INCIDENCE

Carcinoma of the prostate is rare before age 50, but the incidence subsequently increases steadily with age. Overall, it is the second most common malignancy in American men and the third most common cause of cancer deaths in men over age 55 (behind lung cancer and colorectal cancer). Carcinoma of the prostate is more common among black Americans (22 deaths per 100,000 men) than white Americans (14 deaths per 100,000 men).[39]

ETIOLOGY

The etiology of prostatic carcinoma is unknown. Although the disease does not occur in men castrated before puberty and regresses following castration or estrogen therapy, a precise hormonal etiology has not been established. BPH does not appear to be causally related.[40] Environmental factors may be involved since men migrating from areas where prostatic cancer is uncommon to areas where it is more common develop the disease with increased frequency.[41] Oncogenic viruses have been detected within prostatic cancer cells, but a direct etiologic relationship has not been established.[42]

PATHOGENESIS

Ninety-five percent of prostatic cancers are adenocarcinomas, with the remainder being transitional cell carcinomas, squamous cell carcinomas, and sarcomas. Adenocarcinoma of the prostate usually arises in the peripheral region of the prostate, although it commonly invades the periurethral tissue where BPH originates, subsequently producing urethral obstruction. Prostate cancer may produce ureteral obstruction either by direct extension into the bladder or by spreading behind the bladder through the seminal vesicles.[43] Distant spread occurs through lymphatic and hematogenous routes. The pelvic lymph nodes and skeleton are the most frequent sites of metastatic disease, and the pelvis and lumbar spine are the bones most commonly involved. Visceral metastases occur later and less commonly; the lungs, liver, and adrenals are the organs most frequently involved.[43]

The natural history of prostatic cancer is unpredictable and seems to vary considerably among individual patients. In some men the disease progresses very slowly, and patients may do well for many years without treatment. However, in other patients the disease pursues an extremely fulminant course with rapid metastatic spread and early death. In general, we lack the ability to predict which patients can be followed conservatively and which patients deserve prompt treatment. Until we develop this prognostic ability, we are obliged to treat patients with prostatic cancer aggressively, to the extent that an individual's age and general health permit.[44]

SYMPTOMS

Early carcinoma of the prostate is asymptomatic. As the disease spreads into the urethra, it may cause symptoms of urinary obstruction indistinguishable from those produced by BPH. If the tumor has progressed to obstruct the ureters, the patient may present with uremia. Skeletal pain and pathological fractures caused by metastatic disease may be the initial symptoms of advanced disease.

PHYSICAL EXAMINATION

The patient may present with lymphadenopathy, signs of uremia and congestive heart failure, or urinary retention with a distended bladder. More commonly, the pathological physical findings are confined to the prostate. On rectal examination the prostate feels harder than the normal or hyperplastic prostate, and the normal boundaries of the gland may be obscured. Approximately 50 percent of localized indurated areas within the prostate will prove to be malignant, with the remainder being due to prostatic calculi, inflammation, prostatic infarction, or postsurgical change in a patient having previously undergone a partial prostatectomy for BPH.[45] If induration is detected that is suggestive of carcinoma, the examiner should determine whether it is focal or diffuse in nature and whether it seems to extend beyond the border of the prostate.

DIAGNOSIS

In the past the diagnosis of prostatic cancer was made by performing an open surgical biopsy of the prostate through the perineum. Open biopsy is seldom performed today and has been replaced by the techniques of core-needle biopsy and fine-needle aspiration of the prostate, which have significantly less morbidity than an open biopsy.

Core-needle biopsy is usually done with a Tru-Cut needle that is introduced either through the perineum or through the rectum. Both transrectal and transperineal techniques are accurate with reported false-negative rates of about 10 percent.[46] Transrectal biopsy is somewhat easier to master since the needle is advanced over a finger within the rectum directly into the prostate, and therefore may be more accurate for those inexperienced with the transperineal technique. However, because the needle is advanced through the rectal wall, transrectal biopsy is associated with a significant risk of sepsis, and blood cultures are subsequently positive in up to 85 percent of patients.[47] Although the risk of sepsis can be reduced significantly by administering a preoperative cleansing enema and parenteral antibiotics,[48] it is advisable to hospitalize patients overnight for observation and continued antibiotic treatment following a transrectal biopsy.

Transperineal biopsy, while more difficult to master, is nearly as accurate and much safer than the transrectal approach since rectal contamination is avoided. Perioperative antibiotics are not required in a patient undergoing a transperineal biopsy unless the rectal wall is violated, and hospital admission usually is unnecessary.[49]

Fine-needle aspiration of the prostate was introduced in Scandinavia several years ago and is gaining increasing acceptance elsewhere.[50] This technique is performed using a 22-gauge needle that is advanced through the rectum into the prostate. The needle is moved to and fro within the prostate, and suction is applied; the aspirated cells are then smeared on a microscopic slide, fixed with either air or alcohol, and stained for subsequent cytologic examination. Fine-needle aspiration in experienced hands is very accurate, with false-positive and false-negative rates reported to be about 10 percent.[51] The accuracy of fine-needle aspiration may be increased with transrectal ultrasonic guidance of the needle into the suspicious lesion. Fine-needle aspiration has very little morbidity and will probably replace core-needle biopsy techniques as further experience is gained.

STAGING CLASSIFICATION

The treatment of prostatic carcinoma depends primarily on the stage of the disease. In the United States the most widely used staging system is that proposed by Whitmore, which includes four staging categories: A, B, C, and D.[52] Alternative staging systems include the use of the Roman numerals I, II, III, and IV instead of letters and the TNM (tumor, nodes, metastases) system devised by the International Union Against Cancer (UICC).[53] The Whitmore staging system will be used in the following discussion and is summarized in Fig. 57-5.

Stage A prostatic carcinoma refers to tumors that are discovered incidentally on histological examination of prostatic tissue that has been removed for presumed BPH. Stage A tumors are subdivided into stage A-1 lesions, which are well-differentiated or moderately well-differentiated tumors involving less than 5 percent of the removed tissue, and stage A-2 lesions, which are either poorly differentiated or involve more than 5 percent of the removed tissue.

Stage B refers to tumors that are palpable on rectal examination and that are confined within the boundaries of the prostate. Stage B-1 includes tumors involving less

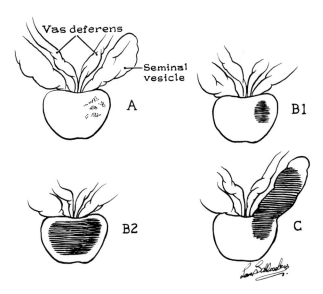

FIGURE 57-5
Whitmore staging classification of prostatic carcinoma. A, microscopic disease in a clinically benign gland; B-1, nodule involving less than one posterior lobe; B-2, nodule involving one entire lobe or both posterior lobes; C, extension beyond the peripheral capsule of the prostate; stage D (not pictured), metastatic disease.

than one posterior lobe, and stage B-2 includes tumors that involve one whole or both posterior lobes.

Stage C includes tumors that extend beyond the boundaries of the prostate but are confined within the pelvis. These tumors have penetrated the peripheral capsule of the prostate and may extend cephalad into the seminal vesicles or laterally toward the bony pelvic sidewalls.

Stage D includes metastatic tumors. Stage D-1 includes tumors which have spread to the pelvic lymph nodes, while stage D-2 implies distant metastatic disease.

STAGING EVALUATION

Since the treatment of prostatic carcinoma is predicated largely on the stage of the tumor, accurate staging is essential in order to properly manage this disease. While the digital rectal examination remains the standard technique to assess the local extent of tumor, there has been considerable interest in recent years in the alternative staging techniques of transrectal ultrasound, pelvic computerized tomography (CT) scan, and magnetic resonance imaging (MRI) analysis. Pelvic CT scan has not proved reliable in the staging of prostatic carcinoma,[54] and experience with MRI is limited.

There has been considerable experience with transrectal ultrasound in both the diagnosis and staging of prostatic cancer, but the value of this technique remains controversial. Although early reports suggested that transrectal ultrasound was more sensitive than digital rectal examination in detecting prostate cancer,[55,56] more recent studies have shown unexceptably low specificity with this technique, due to a high rate of false-positives.[57] The ultrasonographic appearance of prostate cancer is extremely variable and may include hypoechoic, hyperechoic, and mixed lesions. Therefore, at the present time, transrectal ultrasound does not appear to be reliable in screening men for prostate cancer. Similarly, transrectal ultrasound appears to have low sensitivity in the staging of prostatic cancer due to the inability of the technique to detect microscopic capsular penetration and seminal vesicle involvement.[58] Thus, at the present time, digital rectal examination remains the gold standard for both the diagnosis and localized staging of prostatic carcinoma.

Determination of serum acid phosphatase remains the basic screening test for metastatic prostatic cancer. The best assay for acid phosphatase is a colorimetric enzymatic assay using thymolphthalein monophosphate as the substrate.[59] Using this technique, an abnormally elevated value is about 70 percent sensitive and virtually 100 percent specific for metastatic disease. Although radioimmunoassay of acid phosphatase is more sensitive,[60] it is far less specific for metastatic disease, a factor which has limited its application in the evaluation of patients with prostatic carcinoma.[61]

Prostate-specific antigen (PSA) is a newly discovered protein that is produced exclusively in the epithelial cells of prostatic ducts.[62] PSA is a glycoprotein that is immunologically and biochemically distinct from prostatic acid phosphatase.[63] Both monoclonal[64] and polyclonal antisera[65] have been developed for the detection of PSA in the serum as well as in the seminal fluid of patients with prostatic disease. PSA does not appear valuable in the diagnosis or staging of prostatic cancer, because patients with stages A to C of the disease have serum PSA levels that are not statistically different from patients with BPH.[66] However, since PSA is produced exclusively by the prostate, serum levels should decline to essentially zero in patients who have been cured of their disease. Detectable serum levels of PSA following radical prostatectomy therefore are highly suggestive of residual carcinoma.[67]

Besides serum prostatic acid phosphatase, the other test that is obtained routinely to detect metastatic disease is a radionuclide bone scan. The bone scan is highly accurate and much more sensitive than conventional skeletal radiography.[68] The combination of serum acid phosphatase determination and radionuclide bone scanning will accurately detect most patients with distant metastatic disease.

In patients with a normal serum prostatic acid phosphatase and radionuclide bone scan, it is often desirable to assess the pelvic lymph nodes for metastatic disease. Unfortunately, radiologic assessment of the pelvic lymph nodes has proved difficult. Pedal lymphangiography has proved unreliable, mainly because this technique does not consistently demonstrate the primary sites of lymphatic drainage from the prostate which are the obturator and hypogastric lymphatic chains. Pelvic CT scan has proved similarly unreliable. Therefore, in patients with otherwise localized disease, a staging pelvic lymphadenectomy usually is done prior to performing a radical prostatectomy. Pelvic lymphadenectomy usually is performed in conjunction with radical prostatectomy relying on a frozen-section evaluation of the lymph nodes.[69] Pelvic lymphadenectomy has a low morbidity and seems justified as a staging procedure to spare those patients with positive lymph nodes a radical prostatectomy.[70]

TREATMENT

Patients with stage A-1 disease traditionally have been treated conservatively since the disease was thought to be latent and of no clinical significance. Recent data, however, have shown that 16 percent of untreated patients with A-1 disease will develop metastatic carcinoma of the prostate within 10 years.[71] Thus, it may be advisable to treat aggressively healthy men under age 65 who have stage A-1 disease.

Patients with stages A-2 and B disease require further therapy since, untreated, many will progress to develop metastatic disease.[72,73] The treatment options for these clinical stages include radical prostatectomy and radiation therapy. Radical prostatectomy involves the surgical removal of the entire prostate and seminal vesicles and is accomplished either through a perineal or retropubic approach (Fig. 57-6). The cure rate for patients undergoing radical prostatectomy for localized dis-

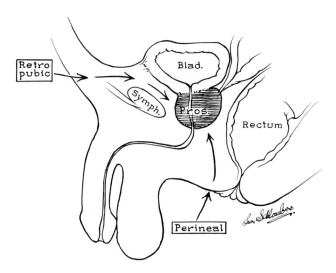

FIGURE 57-6
Anatomic drawing depicting the retropubic and perineal approaches to the prostate.

ease is excellent, with the 15-year survival rate for patients with pathologically confined disease equaling that of age-matched men without prostatic cancer.[74]

The major complications of radical prostatectomy include urinary incontinence and impotence. However, with recent advances in surgical technique, the risk of significant urinary incontinence currently is less than 1 percent.[75] Furthermore, recent understanding of pelvic anatomy has allowed identification and preservation of the nerves to the corpora cavernosa of the penis, allowing preservation of potency in over 70 percent of patients.[76,77]

Radiation therapy is administered either via external beam or via interstitial radioactive seeds that are implanted surgically into the prostate. Although in some series the success rates with radiation therapy approach those achieved with radical prostatectomy,[78,79] in other series the results are not nearly as favorable.[80,81] Although the issue remains controversial, radiation therapy seems most appropriate in patients with localized disease who either are unwilling to undergo radical prostatectomy or are not surgical candidates for reasons of age and health. Radiation therapy also is the treatment of choice for patients with clinical stage C disease that has extended beyond the borders of the prostate and is therefore not curable surgically.

Hormonal therapy remains the mainstay of treatment for patients with stage D disease. The objective of endocrine therapy is to deprive prostatic tumors of circulating androgens and thereby produce regression of both primary and metastatic lesions. Hormonal ablation can be achieved either by castration or by administration of exogenous estrogens. Diethylstilbestrol (DES) administered at a dose of 3 mg per day lowers plasma testosterone to castrate levels.[82] Lower doses of DES may produce incomplete suppression of testosterone, while doses higher than 3 mg produce no further suppression and are associated with an increased incidence of cardiovascular complications.[83]

Recently there has been interest in alternative methods of androgen ablation using LH-RH analogs either alone or in combination with antiandrogens.[84] Although equally effective to conventional hormonal therapy, these new agents have not been shown to provide any additional therapeutic benefit.[85] This is because prostatic cancer is composed of a heterogeneous cell population, some cells being hormone-sensitive and others hormone-resistant. Relapse following hormonal therapy is due to continued growth of hormone-resistant cells,[86] and further attempts to lower serum testosterone provide no additional palliation.[87]

Patient response to hormonal therapy varies considerably: 10 percent of patients live less than 6 months, 50 percent survive less than 3 years, and only 10 percent live longer than 10 years.[88] The timing of endocrine therapy also appears to make little difference clinically in the course of the disease.[89] Initiation of treatment at the time of diagnosis may provide a longer symptom-free interval but little in the way of effective palliation once relapse has occurred. For this reason, in the hope of providing increased long-term palliation it may be preferable to delay hormonal therapy until the patient has become symptomatic.

Unfortunately, effective chemotherapy for relapsing hormone-resistant carcinoma of the prostate is at present unavailable, and clinical trials to date of nonhormonal cytotoxic agents have yielded discouraging results.[90,91] A major goal for the future is to develop new forms of therapy that will be effective against the hormone-resistant cell population. The discovery of such agents will represent a major advance in the treatment of this disease.

REFERENCES

1. Franks LM: Benign nodular hyperplasia of the prostate: A review. *Annu Rev Coll Surg Engl* 14:92, 1954.
2. McNeal JE: Origin and evolution of benign prostatic enlargement. *Invest Urol* 15:340, 1978.
3. McNeal JE: Origin and development of carcinoma in the prostate. *Cancer* 23:24, 1969.
4. Lundquist, F et al: Purification and properties of some enzymes in human seminal plasma. *Biochem J* 56:69, 1955.
5. Zaneveld LJD: The human ejaculate and its potential for fertility control, in Sciarra JJ (ed): *Control of Male Fertility*. New York, Harper & Row, 1975.
6. Mackenzie AR et al: Zinc content of expressed human prostatic fluid. *Nature* 193:72, 1962.
7. Fair WR, Wehner N: The prostatic antibacterial factor: Identity and significance, in Marberger H et al (eds): *Prostatic Disease*, vol 6. New York, Liss, 1976.
8. Gutman AB, Gutman EB: An acid phosphatase occurring in serum of patients with metastasizing carcinoma of the prostate gland. *J Clin Invest* 17:473, 1938.
9. Huggins C, Hodges CV: Studies on prostate cancer: I. The effect of castration, of estrogen and of androgen injection on serum phosphatases in metastatic carcinoma of the prostate. *Cancer Res* 1:293, 1941.
10. Bruchovsky N, Wilson JD: The conversion of testosterone to 5α-androstan-17β-ol-3-one by rat prostate in vivo and in vitro. *J Biol Chem* 243:2012, 1968a.
11. Liao S et al: Biochemical aspects of androgen receptors and cell stimulation of the prostate, in Grayhack JT et al (eds): *Benign Prostatic Hyperplasia*. Proceedings of a workshop sponsored by the Kidney Disease and Urology Program of the NIAMDD, Feb. 20–21, 1975, Washington, Government Printing Office, 1976, p 33.
12. Mainwaring WIP, Milroy EJG: Metabolism and binding of androgens in the human prostate, in Grayhack JT et al (eds): *Benign Prostatic Hyperplasia*. Proceedings of a workshop sponsored by the Kidney Disease and Urology Program of the NIAMDD, Feb. 20–21, 1975, Washington, Government Printing Office, 1976.

13. Moore RJ, Wilson JD: Androgen transport and metabolism in the prostate, in Grayhack JT et al (eds): *Benign Prostatic Hyperplasia*. Proceedings of a workshop sponsored by the Kidney Disease and Urology Program of the NIAMDD, Feb, 20–21, 1975, Washington, Government Printing Office, 1976, p 21.

14. Walsh PC: Physiologic basis for hormonal therapy in carcinoma of the prostate. *Urol Clin North Am* 2:125, 1975.

15. Harbitz TB, Haugen OA: Histology of the prostate in elderly men. *Acta Pathol Microbiol Immunol Scand [A]* 80:756, 1972.

16. Berry SJ: The development of human benign prostatic hyperplasia with age. *J Urol* 132:474, 1984.

17. Lytton B et al: The incidence of benign prostatic hyperplasia. *J Urol* 99:639, 1968.

18. Birkhoff JD: Natural history of benign prostatic hypertrophy, in Hinman F (ed): *Benign Prostatic Hypertrophy*. New York, Springer-Verlag, 1983, p 5.

19. Wilson JD: The pathogenesis of benign prostatic hyperplasia. *Am J Med* 68:745, 1980.

20. Huggins C, Clark PJ: Quantitative studies of prostatic secretion: II. The effect of castration and of estrogen injection on the normal and on the hyperplastic prostate glands of dogs. *J Exp Med* 72:747, 1940.

21. Wendel EF et al: The effect of orchiectomy and estrogens on benign prostatic hyperplasia. *J Urol* 108:116, 1972.

22. Vermeulen A: Testicular hormonal secretion and aging in males, in Grayhack JT et al (eds): *Benign Prostatic Hyperplasia*. Washington, Department of Health, Education, and Welfare, 1975, 1977.

23. Walsh PC, Wilson JD: The induction of prostatic hypertrophy in the dog with androstanediol. *J Clin Invest* 57:1093, 1976.

24. Moore RJ et al: Regulation of cytoplasmic dihydrotestosterone binding in dog prostate by 17β-estradiol. *J Clin Invest* 63:351, 1979.

25. Isaacs, JT, Coffey DS: Changes in dihydrotestosterone metabolism associated with the development of canine benign prostatic hyperplasia. *Endocrinology* 108:445, 1981.

26. Isaacs JT et al: Changes in the metabolism of dihydrotestosterone in the hyperplastic human prostate. *J Clin Endocrinol Metab* 56:139, 1983.

27. Walsh PE et al: The tissue content of dihydrotestosterone in human prostatic hyperplasia is not supranormal. *J Clin Invest* 72:1772, 1983.

28. Piconi JR et al: Rapid development of carcinoma in diverticulum of bladder: A pitfall in conservative management. *Urology* 2:676, 1973.

29. Turner-Warwick R: Observations on the function and dysfunction of the sphincter and detrusor mechanisms. *Urol Clin North Am* 6:11, 1979.

30. Abrams P, Torrens M: Urine flow studies. *Urol Clin North Am* 6:71, 1979.

31. Turner-Warwick RT: A urodynamic review of bladder outlet obstruction in the male and its clinical implications. *Urol Clin North Am* 6:171, 1979.

32. Perrin P et al: Forty years of transurethral prostatic resection. *J Urol* 116:757, 1976.

33. Caine M: The place of pharmacologic treatment in benign prostatic hyperplasia. *Semin Urol* 4:311, 1985.

34. Caine M et al: The treatment of benign prostatic hypertrophy with flutamide (SCH 13521): A placebo-controlled study. *J Urol* 114:564, 1975.

35. Resnick MI et al: Assessment of the antihypercholesterolemic drug, probucol, in benign prostatic hyperplasia. *J Urol* 129:206, 1983.

36. Peters CA, Walsh PC: The effect of nafarelin acetate, a luteinizing-hormone-releasing hormone agonist, on benign prostatic hyperplasia. *N Engl J Med* 317:599, 1987.

37. Schroeder FH et al: Benign prostatic hyperplasia treated by castration or the LH-RH analogue Buserelin: A report on 6 cases. *Eur Urol* 12:318, 1986.

38. Schlegel PN, and Brendler CB: Successful management of a hemophiliac with urinary retention due to benign prostatic hyperplasia using a luteinizing hormone-releasing hormone agonist. *J Urol* (in press).

39. Silverberg E, Holleb AI: Major trends in cancer: 25 year survey. *Cancer* 25:2, 1975.

40. Armenian HK et al: Relation between benign prostatic hyperplasia and cancer of the prostate: A prospective and retrospective study. *Lancet* 2:115, 1974.

41. Gyorkey F: Some aspects of cancer of the prostate gland, in Busch H (ed): *Methods in Cancer Research*, vol 7. New York, Academic, 1973, p 279.

42. Tannenbaum M, Lattimer JK: Similar virus-like particles found in cancers of the prostate and breast. *J Urol* 103:471, 1970.

43. Catalona WF, Scott WW: Carcinoma of the prostate, in Walsh PC et al (eds): *Campbell's Urology*, 5th ed. Philadelphia, Saunders, 1986, p 1463.

44. Jewett HJ: The present status of radical prostatectomy for stages A and B prostatic cancer. *Urol Clin North Am* 2:105, 1975.

45. Jewett HJ: Significance of the palpable prostatic nodule. *JAMA* 160:838, 1956.

46. Zincke H et al: Confidence in the negative transrectal biopsy. *Surg Gynecol Obstet* 126:78, 1973.

47. Eaton AC: The safety of transrectal biopsy of the prostate as an outpatient investigation. *Br J Urol* 53:144, 1981.

48. Rees M et al: Povidone-iodine antisepsis for transrectal prostatic biopsy. *Br Med J* 281:650, 1980.

49. Packer MG et al: Prophylactic antibiotics and foley catheter usage in transperineal needle biopsy of the prostate. *J Urol* 131:687, 1984.

50. Kaufman JJ et al: Aspiration biopsy of prostate. *Urology* 19:587, 1982.

51. Melograna F et al: Prospective controlled assessment of fine-needle prostatic aspiration. *Urology* 19:47, 1982.

52. Whitmore WF Jr: Symposium on hormones and cancer therapy. Hormone therapy in prostatic cancer. *Am J Med* 21:697, 1956.

53. *UICC TNM Klassifikation der malignen Tumoren*, ed 3. Berlin, Springer-Verlag, 1979, p 114.

54. Salo JO et al: Computerized tomography and transrectal ultrasound in the assessment of local extension of prostatic cancer before radical retropubic prostatectomy. *J Urol* 137:435, 1987.

55. Watanabe H et al: Mass screening program for prostatic diseases with transrectal ultrasonotomography. *J Urol* 117:746, 1977.

56. Brooman PJC et al: A comparison between digital examination and perrectal ultrasound in the evaluation of the prostate. *Br J Urol* 53:617, 1981.

57. Chodak GW et al: Comparison of digital examination and transrectal ultrasonography for the diagnosis of prostatic cancer. *J Urol* 135:951, 1986.

58. Pontes JE et al: Preoperative evaluation of localized prostatic carcinoma by transrectal ultrasonography. *J Urol* 134:289, 1985.

59. Roy AV et al: Sodium thymolphthalein monophosphate: A new acid phosphatase substrate with greater specificity for the prostatic enzyme in serum. *Clin Chem* 17:1093, 1971.

60. Foti AG et al: Detection of prostatic cancer by solid-phase radioimmunoassay of serum prostatic acid phosphatase. *N Engl J Med* 297:1357, 1977.

61. Bruce AW et al: An objective look at acid phosphatase determinations: A comparison of biochemical and immunochemical methods. *Br J Urol* 51:21113, 1979.

62. Papsidero LD et al: Prostate antigen: A marker for human prostatic epithelial cells. *J Natl Cancer Inst* 66:37, 1981.

63. Wang MC et al: Prostatic antigen: A new potential marker for prostatic cancer. *Prostate* 2:89, 1981.

64. Papsidero LD et al: Monoclonal antibody (F5) to human prostate antigen. *Hybridoma* 2:139, 1983.

65. Nadji M et al: Prostatic-specific antigen: An immunohistologic marker for prostatic neoplasms. *Cancer* 48:1129, 1981.

66. Ercole CJ et al: Prostatic specific antigen and prostatic acid phosphatase in the monitoring and staging of patients with prostatic cancer. *J Urol* 138:1181, 1987.

67. Oesterling JE et al: Prostatic specific antigen in the pre- and postoperative evaluation of localized prostatic cancer treated with radical prostatectomy. *J Urol* 139:766, 1988.

68. Lentle B et al: Technetium-99m polyphosphate bone scanning in carcinoma of the prostate. *Br J Urol* 46:543, 1974.

69. Epstein JI et al: Frozen section detection of lymph node metastases in prostatic carcinoma: Accuracy in grossly uninvolved pelvic lymphadenectomy specimens. *J Urol* 136:1234, 1986.

70. Brendler CB et al: Staging pelvic lymphadenectomy for carcinoma of the prostate: Risk versus benefit. *J Urol* 124:849, 1980.

71. Epstein JI et al: Prognosis of untreated stage A1 prostatic carcinoma: A study of 94 cases with extended followup. *J Urol* 136:837, 1986.

72. Hanash KA et al: Carcinoma of the prostate: A 15-year followup. *J Urol* 107:450, 1972.

73. Cantrell BB et al: Pathological factors that influence prognosis in stage A prostatic cancer: The influence of extent versus grade. *J Urol* 125:516, 1981.

74. Gibbons RP et al: Total prostatectomy for localized prostatic cancer. *J Urol* 131:73, 1984.

75. Frohmuller HGW: Radical prostatectomy in Europe: Trends and future prospectives, in Jacobi GH, Hohenfellner R (eds): *Prostate Cancer*. Baltimore, Williams & Wilkins, 1982, p 165.

76. Walsh PC, Donker PJ: Impotence following radical prostatectomy: Insight into etiology and prevention. *J Urol* 128:492, 1982.

77. Walsh PC et al: Radical prostatectomy with preservation of sexual function: Anatomical and pathological considerations. *Prostate* 4:473, 1983.

78. Bagshaw MA et al: External beam radiation therapy of carcinoma of the prostate. *Cancer* 36:723, 1975.

79. Van der Werf-Messing B: Radiation therapy of carcinoma of the prostate, in Jacobi GH, Hohenfellner R (eds): *Prostate Cancer*. Baltimore, Williams & Wilkins, 1982, p 195.

80. Kiesling VJ et al: External beam radiotherapy for adenocarcinoma of the prostate: A clinical follow-up. *J Urol* 124:851, 1980.

81. Paulson DF et al: Radical surgery versus radiotherapy for adenocarcinoma of the prostate. *J Urol* 128:502, 1982b.

82. Shearer RJ et al: Plasma testosterone: An accurate monitor of hormone treatment in prostatic cancer. *Br J Urol* 45:668, 1973.

83. Glashan RW, Robinson MRG: Cardiovascular complications in the treatment of prostatic cancer. *Br J Urol* 53:624, 1981.

84. Labrie F et al: New hormonal therapy in prostatic cancer: Combined treatment with an LHRH agonist and an antiandrogen. *Clin Invest Med* 5:267, 1982.

85. The Leuprolide Study Group: Leuprolide versus DES in the initial therapy of advanced prostatic cancer: A randomized prospective trial. *N Engl J Med* 311:1281, 1984.

86. Isaacs JT, Kyprianou N: Development of androgen-independent tumor cells and their implications for the treatment of prostatic cancer. *Urol Res* 15:133, 1987.

87. Schulze H et al: Inability of complete androgen blockade to increase survival of patients with advanced prostatic cancer as compared to standard hormonal therapy. *J Urol* 137:909, 1987.

88. Blackard CE et al: Orchiectomy for advanced prostatic carcinoma. A reevaluation. *Urology* 1:553, 1973.

89. Veterans Administration Cooperative Urological Research Group: Treatment and survival of patients with cancer of the prostate. *Surg Gynecol Obstet* 124:1011, 1967.

90. Muss HB et al: Cyclophosphamide versus cyclophosphamide, methotrexate, and 5-fluorouracil in advanced prostatic cancer: A randomized trial. *Cancer* 47:1949, 1981.

91. Straus MJ et al: Treatment of advanced prostate cancer with cyclophosphamide, doxorubicin, and methotrexate. *Cancer Treat Rep* 66:1797, 1982.

SECTION D

The Gastrointestinal System

Chapter 58

AGING OF THE GASTROINTESTINAL SYSTEM

James B. Nelson and Donald O. Castell

The gastrointestinal tract, on the whole, retains normal physiologic function during the aging process, in large part due to the inherent redundancy incorporated into this multi-organ system. Still, definable changes in both animal and human digestive systems with increasing age have been reported, and may lead to alterations in function, especially during times of stress. On the other hand, some of these age-associated changes may be adaptive, helping to maintain homeostasis over time. Moreover, difficulties are encountered when interpreting aging studies which relate to individual species variation.

It is the purpose of this chapter to review alterations in the structure and function of the gastrointestinal tract with increasing age, relating this information to possible pathologic consequences which might develop. More detailed information regarding specific disease states associated with aging in the gastrointestinal tract will be discussed in the chapters which follow. Table 58-1 summarizes the changes in digestive function that develop with age.

AGING AND PHARYNGOESOPHAGEAL FUNCTION

The act of swallowing can be subdivided into three distinct stages: the voluntary or oral stage, the involuntary or pharyngeal phase, and the esophageal stage.[1] The oral and pharyngeal stages are regulated by cortical and medullary swallowing centers with output directed at skeletal muscle groups. The proximal esophagus also contains skeletal muscle; however, the distal portion contains smooth muscle regulated by its own intrinsic nervous system.

Analogous to the dysfunction in mastication which can develop due to a reduction in lean muscle mass over age, the skeletal muscle involved in the oral and pharyngeal phase of swallowing can also become altered. In a study evaluating skeletal muscle fiber changes from the pharyngeal constrictor from 50 necropsies (subject ages 1 to 93), there was an age-associated decrease in the smaller fraction of type I fibers. In addition, the standard

593

TABLE 58-1
Age-Related Changes in Digestive Function

Oral cavity		Colon	
Mastication	↓	Mucosa	↓
Mandibular bone	↓	Musculature	↓
Salivary flow	↓ (−)	Transit	↓
Taste sensation	↓	Diverticular disease	↑
Pharynx/esophagus		Anus/rectum	
Pharyngeal muscles	↓	Muscle wall elasticity	↓
Esophageal motility	?	Continence	↓
Gastroesophageal reflux	(−)	Innervation	↓ ?
Stomach		Pancreas	
Gastric emptying	?	Weight/size	(−)
Acid production	↓	Ductal size	↑
Pepsin production	?	Acinar glands	↓
Gastrin production	↑	Secretion	(−)?
Gastric mucosa	↓ (−)	Bile ducts/gallbladder	
Small intestine		Bile duct size	↑
Transit time	(−)	Gallbladder emptying	(−)
Motility/smooth muscle	↑	Gallstones	↑
Innervation	↓	Liver	
Mucosa	?	Size	↓
Absorption/enzyme activity		Blood flow	↓
Water/electrolytes	↓	Hepatocyte number	↓
Disaccharidases (lactase)	↓ (−)	Metabolic functions	
Fat	(−)	Bromsulphalein (BSP) clearance	↓
Fat-soluble vitamins	↑	Microsomal oxidation (antipyrine)	↓
Water-soluble vitamins	(−)	Nonmicrosomal oxidation (alcohol)	(−)
Vitamin D	↓	Demethylation (benzodiazapines)	↓
Folate/vitamin B_{12}	(−)	Conjugation (INH)	(−)
Protein	(−)	Superoxide dismutase/catalase	↓
Calcium	↓	Protein synthesis (vitamin K)	
Iron	↓	Albumin synthesis	? ↓

Key: ↓, Impaired or altered structure/function; ↑, increased or improved structure/ function; (−), no change; ?, uncertain.

deviation of fiber diameters was significantly larger in the older group (over age 50) along with a general trend towards hypertrophy of individual muscle fibers and decreased fiber density.[2] These findings may translate into actual functional changes during the oropharyngeal phase of swallowing. One study of 100 asymptomatic individuals over age 65 found 22 subjects who had pharyngeal muscle weakness and abnormal cricopharyngeal relaxation with puddling of barium in the valleculae and pyriform sinuses. A few also demonstrated tracheal aspiration of barium, possibly due to cricopharyngeal muscle weakness.[3]

Morphological changes during the aging process can also be demonstrated in the smooth muscle of the esophagus. In elderly individuals, as compared with a group of younger individuals, a decrease in the number of myenteric ganglion cells per unit area along with thickening of the smooth muscle layer has been described.[4,5] Like the pharynx and skeletal muscle portion of the esophagus,

the standard deviation of smooth muscle fiber diameters was greater in the aged group, with hypertrophy outweighing atrophy. An overall decrease in slow-acting, type I fibers also develops in the aging distal esophagus along with a corresponding decrease in the density of fibers per unit area.[2]

Controversy remains about whether aging itself leads to disordered esophageal function. An early study by Soergel et al. evaluated esophageal function in a group of 15 nonagenarians by means of intraluminal manometry and barium radiography.[6] The only exclusion criteria were the presence of gastric disease, esophageal disease, or central nervous system disease other than senile dementia. Cineradiographic findings included frequent nonpropulsive, tertiary contractions coupled with delayed esophageal emptying and moderate uniform dilatation, which corresponded to a high incidence of nonpropulsive contractions after swallows, decreased lower esophageal sphincter (LES) relaxations, and a greater incidence of intrathoracic sphincters. Secondary peristalsis initiated by intraluminal balloon distension was less often impaired. The conclusion was that a "presbyesophagus" developed in older individuals with a motility pattern that resembled diffuse esophageal spasm.

Ten years later a similar study was conducted by Hollis and Castell, who compared esophageal motility using intraluminal pressure transducers in a group of elderly men (70 to 87 years old) and a young adult control group (19 to 27 years old).[7] In this study, however, none of the elderly men had a history of diabetes or neuropathy, which had not been excluded in the earlier study. In contrast to the previous report, there was no increase in abnormal motility in the group of elderly men as manifested by the normal frequency of peristaltic contractions and LES relaxations occurring after a swallow. The number of spontaneous contractions did not differ either between the two groups. An age-related reduction in amplitude of esophageal contractions was seen, however, in a subgroup of 80-year-olds, implying an intact neural system with a weakening of the smooth muscle.[8]

In a group of healthy individuals over age 60, Khan et al. found an increased frequency of abnormal LES responses to deglutition, including a reduced amplitude of the after-contraction, as compared to that of a group under age 40. The older group also showed a reduced amplitude of peristaltic contraction in the upper and lower esophagus, reduced peristaltic velocity, and an increased frequency of simultaneous contractions.[9] Basal LES pressures were comparable between the two groups. In contrast, Csendes et al. found no differences in amplitude or duration of waves in the distal esophagus, but resting LES pressure did tend to decrease after the age of 65.[10] A decrease in the percentage of peristaltic waves was also observed.

Finally, a recent study using well-accepted modern manometric techniques found an increase in distal esophageal amplitude and duration with age, peaking in the fifth decade, with individuals over the age of 60 showing decreased values.[11] In this study, age had no effect on peristaltic velocity, basal LES pressures, or frequency of "abnormal" double- and triple-peaked wave forms.

One can conclude, therefore, that in normal healthy individuals, the physiologic function of the esophagus is well-preserved with increasing age, save for, perhaps, in very old age. Further support for this conclusion includes a study in which the frequency of spontaneous gastroesophageal reflux, as measured by an ambulatory pH system, was no different between a group of normal volunteers with a mean age of 49 years and a group with a mean age of 22 years.[12] Whether the same finding holds at the further age extreme has yet to be determined. Age-associated changes of the esophageal mucosa have not been extensively studied.

AGING AND GASTRIC FUNCTION

Because of its accessibility, gastric function, both secretory and motor activities, has been well studied. Conflicting reports, however, have emerged regarding the effect of age on gastric emptying, in part due to the various modalities used to study emptying.

Gastric emptying involves a complex interaction of physiologic events influenced by dietary composition, physical activity, and central nervous system (CNS) input.[13,14] Gastric motility varies in fasting and fed states, fasting activity being manifested by cyclic contractile activity determined by the interdigestive migrating motor complex (MMC), which is the primary means of emptying nondigestible solids. During the fed state, "receptive relaxation" occurs in the fundus to accommodate the food bolus, mediated by noncholinergic, nonadrenergic inhibition. Associated with the reservoir function of the fundus is an increase in antral peristalsis effectively grinding solids against a closed pylorus into liquified chyme. Finally, metered emptying of food into the duodenum occurs via complex neurohumoral regulatory mechanisms, permitting more rapid emptying of liquids or suspended particles less than 2 mm in size.

It is not surprising that aging may adversely affect these precise gastric regulatory mechanisms. Conflicting data, however, have been reported. Some early fluoroscopic studies of hunger-associated gastric activity in dogs found that older animals had a longer fasting pattern and shorter hunger-associated activity than their younger counterparts.[15] Early human investigations utilizing gross fluoroscopic techniques found no difference in gastric emptying between a group of elderly men and a group of young adults.[16] Unfortunately, interpretation of these early studies was hampered by the use of nonphysiologic ingestants like barium or micropaque.[17] A more recent study, using radiolabeled orange juice, found that gastric emptying half-times were significantly prolonged in a group of 11 older individuals (ages 72 to 86) compared with those of 7 healthy young volunteers (ages 22 to 31). More definite conclusions cannot be extrapolated from these data due to the limited sample size and the fact that the elderly group also suffered from systemic diseases.[18] Using a dual-isotope technique, Moore et al. studied gastric emptying of solid and liquid meals in young males, mean age 31, and an older group of men with a mean age of 76.[19] Both groups were comparable in that no participant had a history of diabetes or gastrointestinal diseases. This study, too, found a delay in liquid emptying in the aged group while solid food emptying appeared to be unaffected by age. A loss in the differential emptying of liquids and solids was also observed (Figs. 58-1 and 58-2).

Stability of solid-food emptying has been demonstrated in other studies in both man and rat.[19–22] The mechanism behind the loss of differential emptying of solids and liquids across age remains unclear; however, diminished fundal contractility possibly due to abnormalities in the oblique muscle layer is one possible explanation.[19] There are animal data which indicate that aging may result in a decrease in cholinergic gastric smooth muscle receptors.[23] Alternatively, there may be an impairment in adaptive relaxation in the elderly.[24] Further complicating the picture is a study showing that in patients with gastric achlorhydria, gastric emptying of solids is delayed but can be improved with intragastric instillation of acid or treatment with the dopamine-receptor antagonist, metoclopramide.[25]

How these observed changes in gastric emptying clinically affect elderly patients remains an open question, since most patients are asymptomatic. Theoretically, factors leading to an increased variance in drug pharmacokinetics in the elderly may be, in part, due to changes in gastric emptying.[26]

There is little controversy that aging does result in an overall decline in gastric acid output, probably due to a reduction in parietal cell mass. One of the earliest studies found a significant decline with age in both basal and histamine-augmented acid secretion in humans, especially in women.[27] In fact, it was estimated that in women, peak acid output declines by approximately 5 meq/h per decade over the age of 30. This original report studied a relatively small number of individuals, especially few over the age of 60. A larger study conducted by Grossman et al., however, confirmed the findings.[28] Using betazole (Histalog), basal and stimu-

lated acid output decreased after the age of 50 with a greater decline in males. Histalog-fast achlorhydria was present in 21 percent of the men versus 10 percent of the women.

In a later study, Andrews et al. were able to correlate peak, histamine-stimulated, gastric acid secretion with gastric mucosal atrophy and decreases in the number of parietal cells.[29] Another recent study, however, failed to demonstrate a significant decrease in peak acid output using pentagastrin, despite declines in parietal cell mass.[30] Since parietal cells are stimulated by histamine, gastrin, and acetylcholine via three separate receptor systems, accommodations may be made when dysfunction develops in one agonist-receptor system. More definite declines in acid output tend to be associated with increases in the severity of atrophic mucosal changes.[31]

The development of relative achlorhydria over age may theoretically decrease absorption of weakly acidic drugs since formation of less lipophilic, and, therefore, less permeable compounds occurs at higher pH. To date there have been no studies which have documented this phenomenon. One study found no difference in absorption of the antibiotic tetracycline between achlorhydric elderly and young, normal subjects.[32]

There are inconsistencies in the literature with regard to pepsin secretion over age. In one study using pepsinogen as an indicator of pepsin secretion, age appeared to have no significant effect on pepsin secretion.[33] A more recent report utilizing a radioimmunoassay (RIA) for serum pepsinogen I found 40 percent of tested individuals over age 70 had values less than 50 ng/dl compared to only 5 percent of subjects below 40 with values in that range.[34]

Serum gastrin levels, determined by RIA in hu-

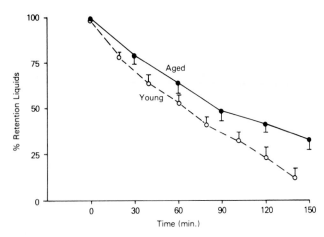

FIGURE 58-1

Percent liquid tracer retention in young (○————○) and aged (●————●) study groups. Each counting interval represents a mean of the normalized counts ± SEM (brackets). *(From Moore JG et al, Dig Dis Sci 28:340, 1983.)*

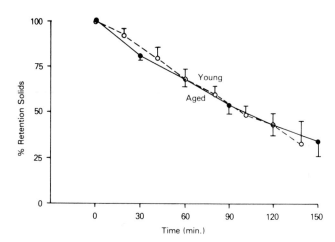

FIGURE 58-2

Percent solid tracer retention in young (○————○) and aged (●————●) study groups. Each counting interval represents a mean of the normalized counts ± SEM (brackets). *(From Moore JG et al, Dig Dis Sci 28:340, 1983.)*

mans, have been more clearly shown to increase over age, an effect believed to be secondary to achlorhydria due to long-standing type A gastritis which spares the antrum.[35] In the absence of inhibition by acid, the increase in functional G (gastrin) cell mass is reflected by age-related increases in basal- and protein-stimulated gastrin secretion.[36]

Gastric mucosal changes represent a balance between cellular death and cellular renewal, with mucosal atrophy developing due to accelerated cellular death or decreased renewal. Several studies have reported atrophy of the gastric mucosa occurring with increasing age. However, the reported incidence of age-related gastric mucosal changes varies widely depending on whether histologic or biochemical data were evaluated and on the methodologies employed. An early study of vacuum-tube gastric mucosal biopsies from 30 subjects over age 60 found no evidence of mucosal atrophy.[37] Supporting this finding, in part, is a recent report which found an actual increase in the total number of gastric cells per milligram tissue weight with no change in the number of parietal cells per milligram mucosa with age.[38] However, the number of nonparietal cells was increased, indicating a change in mucosal composition, in part due to atrophy. In fact, the weight of evidence favors an increased incidence of gastric mucosal atrophy with age. Andrews et al. found some degree of atrophic gastritis in 23 of 24 asymptomatic subjects over 60.[29] In a larger study, Kekki et al. found a concomitant increase in the incidence and severity of atrophic changes in the body mucosa which correlated with a reduction of acid output with increasing age.[31] However, the finding by Bird et al. of near-normal histology in up to one-third of achlorhydric patients over 80, as well as the lack of correlation between age and the degree of atrophic changes, underlines the fact that age is not the sole determinant of gastric atrophy.[39] Recent data suggest an increased frequency of antibodies to *Campylobacter pyloris* over age, a potential pathogen causing gastritis.[40]

Additional factors complicating interpretation of gastric mucosal changes with age include studies showing a greater progression of atrophic gastritis proximally along the lesser curvature[41]; progression of atrophic and metaplastic changes in the antrum as compared to the fundus[42]; and actual improvement in superficial body gastritis in 18 percent of patients followed over 20 years.[43]

Aside from affecting secretory function, an important feature associated with atrophic gastritis is the development of intestinal metaplasia, a possible precursor for gastric carcinoma. A study from Japan showed an increase in diffuse-type metaplasia with age which correlated with the degree of atrophic changes.[44] What mechanism underlies these mucosal changes remains unclear; however, recent data suggest a role for sulfated glycos-

aminoglycans, which may vary in composition and amount with age.[45]

AGING AND SMALL-INTESTINAL FUNCTION

Age-related alterations in small-intestinal motility have been evaluated in animals and humans, with studies of both in vivo transit and in vitro smooth-muscle activity. In a study using [85]Sr-labeled microspheres as a nonabsorbable marker of small intestinal transit in Wistar rats, total transit time did not vary across the life span.[21] This finding is supported by another animal study using the well-accepted aging model, the Fischer 344 rat. Here, too, small-intestinal transit did not change between a group of young, postpubertal animals (5 to 12 months old) and a senescent group (26 to 28 months old) using ^{51}Cr-marker and geometric-mean analysis.[46] Lin and Hayton, however, found that the transit rates in 31-month-old senescent rats were higher in the proximal small intestine, but significantly lower in the distal small intestine as compared to the rates in a group of mature, 16-month-old animals.[47]

Human studies have also corroborated relative stability of small-intestinal transit over age. Early studies using liquid barium movement during small-bowel studies to estimate transit time have shown no change in transit time over several age groups.[48] Even a more recent report utilizing breath-hydrogen measurements to estimate small-bowel transit found no differences in transit times between younger and elderly groups of individuals.[24] Anuras and Sutherland examined small-intestinal motility using jejunal manometry in a group of 10 healthy older subjects, mean age 72, and 10 younger adults, mean age 25. While the motility pattern during the fasting period was no different between the two groups, the motility index during the fed state was significantly reduced in elderly subjects, suggesting age-related alterations in the neurohumoral response to food.[49]

In contrast to the relatively stable pattern of small-intestinal motility in vivo, a variety of in vitro studies have demonstrated dynamic changes with age. In a recent report by Kobashi et al., a decrease in sensitivity to the smooth-muscle agonist acetylcholine (ACh) was observed at mid-age in Wistar rat jejunal muscle strips, followed by an increase during senescence. This decrease corresponded to increases in acetylcholinesterase activity in the mid-age and aged groups, suggesting a form of adaptive supersensitivity developing in senescence.[50] A form of supersensitivity was also observed by Bortoff et al., who found that both maximal tension and sensitivity of cat jejunal circular smooth-muscle strips to ACh was higher in older animals than in younger ones.[51]

Work completed in our laboratory has also demonstrated increases in sensitivity of Fischer 344 rat ileal circular smooth muscle with age in depolarizing concentrations of potassium chloride, possibly due to changes in calcium utilization and/or the contractile mechanism.[52] Therefore, the reported stability of small-intestinal motility over age may, in part, be due to ongoing changes at the neuromuscular level.

There is a paucity of information regarding the morphometric changes in the enteric nerves and muscularis externa of the small intestine with age. What little information is available suggests a drop-off in neuron number along with an increase in thickness and cross-sectional area of the muscle coat with age.[53,54] Possible age-related changes in specific receptors and neurotransmitters await further investigation.

Much more detailed information is available on age-associated changes in small-intestinal size, weight, and villus morphology. Moog reported an age-related increase in the absolute and relative weights of mice small intestine from 6 to 24 months of age, especially in the terminal ileal region where amyloid-like material accumulated in the lamina propria.[55] Penzes, on the other hand, found no significant age differences in small-intestinal total carbon and nitrogen content per fat-free dry weight of the female rat.[56] Small-intestinal length has been shown to increase with age in male Wistar rats but stay the same with age in the female Wistar rats.[21,57] Comparable human data are, however, lacking.

Studies also differ regarding aging effects on mucosal architecture. An age-associated increase in jejunal villus height, as well as villus atrophy and irregular architecture, have been reported in rats.[58,59] Regional differences seem to exist, since the changes appear to be confined primarily to the proximal and distal small intestine.[59,60] Animal studies have also indicated stability in the number of villi over age, although in the proximal rat small intestine, fusion of villi becomes more frequent with age.[61] Ultrastructural changes with age have also been noted in the microvilli, which shorten and become more disoriented.[62] Although one might anticipate a concomitant reduction in mucosal absorptive area, such a reduction has not been borne out by additional animal studies.[63]

Complicating interpretation of animal data is the lack of consistency in nutrition and the presence or absence of infections, all of which can influence mucosal architecture. In a recent study using the Fischer 344 rat, a barrier-reared animal kept on a constant nutritional regimen, aged animals demonstrated no change in villus crypt length or villus height in the proximal small intestine and showed an actual increase in ileal villus height.[64]

More limited data are available on the aging human small intestine. Warren et al. analyzed peroral jejunal biopsies from 10 young individuals and 10 older individuals ages 60 to 73.[65] The average villus height and height of the individual enterocyte did not vary between the two groups. Mucosal surface area was reduced over age using a template method. However, when postmortem specimens from younger adults are compared with biopsy specimens from older individuals, a mean reduction in villus height is found.[66] Proximal jejunal villi are also found to be shorter and broader in young adults than they are in children, as seen using scanning electron microscopy analysis.[67] It is obvious that species differences exist which make definite conclusions difficult. It is also difficult to equate structure with function as studies have demonstrated age-related alterations in epithelial enzyme expression despite an unchanged villus structure.[68]

Finally, are there detectable age-related differences in mucosal cellular kinetics? The answers, again, are inconsistent. Being a highly prolific tissue, the small-intestinal mucosa renews itself continuously by migration of crypt cells to the villus tip, where they are sloughed. In the classic studies of Lesher, a prolonged crypt-to-villus transit time was observed in the upper intestine of aging mice with the villus becoming populated with more mature cells.[69] A compensatory increase in crypt-to-villus ratio has also been reported, balancing the reduction in proliferation.[70] Once again, regional differences exist with no changes in proliferative rates in the ileum.[71] A recent report, using the more standardized Fischer rat model, however, found no differences in crypt-cell migration between young and old animals. Further clouding the picture is evidence suggesting only modest changes in protein synthesis in the mouse small intestine, with ribosomal synthetic capacity increasing despite decreased ribosomal activity.[72]

It is readily apparent that the absorptive capacity of the small intestine is influenced by a host of factors, including the number and integrity of absorbing cells, the mucosal surface, the ingested material, intestinal motility and blood flow, gastric emptying, and the status of the unstirred water layer.[8] Interestingly, the absorption of compounds with a high lipid-solubility, specifically vitamin A, is faster in elderly subjects, reflecting a possible change in the composition of the unstirred layer.[73] In addition, mechanisms of water and electrolyte transport may vary with age, decreasing particularly in the jejunum and ileum of rats.[74]

Brush-border enzyme activity has been evaluated primarily in animal models. Levels of the marker enzymes alkaline phosphatase and acid phosphatase are decreased in old rats, possibly due to a reduction in the number of enterocytes.[61] Human jejunal alkaline phosphatase activity is also decreased in older individuals, although the mechanism is unclear.[75] The disaccharidases, maltase, sucrase, and lactase, also demonstrate reduced activity in aged rats.[76] Holt has recently found a similar decrease in the specific activities of sucrase, maltase, lactase, and adenosine deaminase in the upper intestines of old Fischer 344 rats, in part due to a delay in enzyme differentiation resulting in an increase in the proportion of undifferentiated villus epithelial cells.[77] Human jejunal lactase activity also decreases with age, with the other disaccharidases remaining relatively stable until the seventh decade and then declining.[75]

How do these morphological and biochemical changes in the small intestine translate into functional changes in absorption? With regard to carbohydrates, D-xylose is the best-studied. This pentose is passively absorbed by the small bowel and therefore has been used to assess the integrity of the small intestine. Early investigations indicated an age-related decline in xylose absorption. More recently, however, Kendall used both oral and intravenous administration to show that the supposed decline in absorption was, in fact, reduced excretion secondary to renal impairment developing with age.[78] A subsequent study found a 26 percent prevalence of impaired D-xylose absorption in a group of subjects over age 63, though only urinary measurements were performed.[79] Indeed, when corrected serum levels are evaluated, D-xylose malabsorption does not appear to develop with age except perhaps beyond 80 years.[80] A more recent report, using a pharmacokinetic approach, did demonstrate declines in the absorption rate constant for D-xylose, indicating some, albeit minor, reductions in absorption with advancing age.[81] Similarly, the affinity constant for D-glucose absorption increases with age in rats, indicating a decline in carrier affinity.[82] This effect, however, may be counterbalanced by resistance changes in the unstirred water layer such that glucose uptake remains stable.[83]

Human data on the subject of carbohydrate absorption are scant; however, one study measuring postprandial breath-hydrogen appearance from meals containing varying amounts of carbohydrates found excess breath-hydrogen excretion in one-third of subjects over age 65.[84] It is likely, however, that significant carbohydrate malabsorption reflects a combination of factors, including changes in gastric emptying, intestinal transit, and the bacterial flora.

Studies on fat malabsorption are fraught with technical problems which vary with the methodology used. Using micronephelometry to assess the light-scattering index in the plasma of individuals who consumed a 100-g fat meal, fat absorption was impaired in a group of elderly subjects and could be partially corrected with pancreatic supplement.[85] Animal (rat) data also suggest an impairment over age in fat absorption when assessed using labeled triolein.[86] However, human studies using [^{14}C] triolein found no significant differences in fat absorption between healthy young and old subjects.[87]

More interesting are the studies suggesting a differential pattern of fat absorption across age. While triglyceride absorption may be reduced, cholesterol absorption may in fact increase with age.[88,89] Thus, while fat absorption may be altered with age, other changes, including pancreatic function and gastric emptying, may have a greater impact than the mucosal integrity. In addition, the clinical importance may only become apparent with consumption of a high-fat diet.[90]

The absorption of fat-soluble vitamins, notably vitamins A and K, is increased in the elderly.[73,91] Data derived from rats, on the other hand, suggest a mucosal defect in vitamin D absorption with age as measured by [^{14}C] vitamin D_3 uptake perfused intraduodenally.[86] In elderly humans, impaired intestinal absorption of ^{3}H-cholecalciferol has also been described in addition to lower serum levels of the active metabolite 1,25-dihydroxyvitamin D_3.[92,93] The overall importance of age-related changes in vitamin D absorption remains unclear; however, one cannot exclude vitamin D malabsorption as a contributing factor in the development of osteoporosis.

With some exceptions, increasing malabsorption of water-soluble vitamins with age does not appear to develop. Vitamin B_1 (thiamine) absorption, when assessed by measurement of urinary thiamine excretion, decreased in senescent rats.[94] However, Thompson found no significant differences in thiamine excretion between a group of young human subjects and a group of 80-year-old human subjects.[95] Low plasma levels of vitamin C (ascorbic acid), present in many elderly individuals, are likely due to reduced intake, rather than malabsorption.[96] Reduced levels of erythrocyte folate in many older individuals was, in one study, felt to be due to impaired absorption of dietary folate.[97] However, this theory was refuted in another report which showed no differences in folate absorption as estimated by measurement of urinary ^{3}H-folate up to the age of 70.[98]

Malabsorptive states can also result from vitamin B_{12} (cyanocobalamin) deficiency; however, age itself does not appear to affect ileal absorption of the vitamin.[99] Fleming and Barrows observed no difference in radiolabeled-B_{12} absorption in three age groups of rats.[100] McEvoy, studying whole-body retention of ^{58}Co-B_{12} in 51 healthy adults, found no correlation between B_{12} absorption and age.[101] Other conditions, including gastric achlorhydria, pernicious anemia, pancreatic insufficiency, and ileal disease, have a greater impact on B_{12} absorption than age alone.

In general, the process of protein digestion and assimilation remains intact throughout the life span. One animal study indicated that neutral amino acids were absorbed with a lower affinity than basic amino acids at old age; however, human studies are lacking.[82]

Finally, with regard to mineral absorption, much

information has been gathered indicating that calcium absorption declines with age.[102–107] It has not been settled as to whether the age-associated defect in calcium absorption is due to associated vitamin D deficiency or a decline in the content or responsiveness of calcium-binding proteins in the intestinal mucosa.

Serum levels of both iron and transferrin have been reported to fall with advanced age; however, iron absorption appears to remain intact. Marx compared iron absorption in 40 active elderly individuals over age 65 with iron absorption in 25 young, healthy subjects using a double-isotope technique.[108] While mucosal iron uptake or transfer did not show decreased levels in the aged group, red-cell iron uptake did, suggesting ineffective erythropoiesis. Still, some degree of food-iron malabsorption may occur in the elderly, due primarily to the prevalence of gastric achlorhydria reducing the absorption of nonheme iron.[109]

AGING AND COLONIC FUNCTION

The colon executes a variety of functions, including absorption, secretion, and motility, as well as functioning as a storage organ. Data are scant regarding the structural alterations in the colon as a function of age. Yamajata compared biopsy specimens from healthy subjects with autopsy specimens.[110] Age-related changes included mucosal atrophy, abnormalities of the mucosal glands, cellular infiltration of the mucosa and lamina propria, hypertrophy of the muscularis mucosa, and arteriolar sclerosis. In contrast to the unatrophied condition of small intestinal smooth muscle, atrophy of the muscularis externa develops, along with an increase in the connective tissue component. Evaluation of colonic epithelial cells using an electron microscope has shown vacuolization and nuclear abnormalities, along with an increase in electron density within the cytoplasm and nucleus.[8]

Information regarding age-associated changes in colonic transit comes largely from animal studies. Varga, using [85]Sr-labeled microspheres to measure intestinal transit in rats, found an age-related delay in transit through the cecum and large intestine.[21] A more recent study by McDougal et al. confirmed this finding.[96] Using the Fischer 344 rat model, and calculating the geometric mean of a radioactive tracer, the study found colonic transit to be significantly slower in senescent animals as compared with postpubertal animals. This slowing correlated with an increase in diameter of the senescent colons along with decreases in maximum response in vitro to both electrical and cholinergic stimulation. No age-related differences in the water content of the feces were found. The overall conclusion was that decreased colonic transit was due to decreased responsiveness to

neurotransmitters, along with a deficit in innervation. Decreased transit has also been observed in aged humans; however, constipation has been related to a decrease in fecal water content, which contrasts with the animal data.[111,112]

Preliminary data suggest additional mechanisms underlying derangements in colonic activity with aging. An age-associated decline in the amplitude of inhibitory junctional potentials corresponds to a decrease in either the release of inhibitory neurotransmitters or the number of binding sites.[113] This decrease may result in a form of functional obstruction as segmentation predominates over mass movement. There may also be increases in opioid receptor subtypes, possibly resulting in a greater sensitivity to the inhibitory effects of endogenous opioids over age.[114]

It has long been known that diverticular disease increases in incidence with age, affecting up to 30 percent of individuals over age 60, and perhaps 60 percent of people over age 80.[115] Speculation as to the genesis of diverticula includes age-associated alterations in connective tissue elements and/or changes in colonic pressures. In fact, as previously noted, there is an increase with age in the amount of fibrosis and elastin in both muscle layers in the normal sigmoid colon, but no such changes in elastin content develop in the muscular layer with diverticular disease. What is found is an increase in the number of fine and coarse elastin fibers in the taeniae coli, with an increase in thickness of taenia and circular smooth muscle. One theory, therefore, would be that an age-associated shortening of the colon, secondary to changes in the taenia, creates higher intraluminal pressures.[116] Indeed, others have shown that the colon in diverticular disease does become more distensible.[117] Age alone, however, cannot be the only factor influencing the development of diverticular disease since repeat barium enema examinations have demonstrated stabilized disease in 70 percent of patients after 5 years.[118] Environmental factors, especially dietary fiber, must play an equally important role.[119]

AGING AND ANORECTAL FUNCTION

Normal defecation and continence are the result of programmed activation or inhibition of pelvic and anorectal muscles. Several studies have now established that aging is associated with alterations in anorectal activity. In a study comparing healthy elderly subjects with younger subjects using anorectal manometry, loss of muscle elasticity with aging was suggested since the elderly group experienced lower maximum tolerance and higher pressures at similar volumes.[120] The rectal distending balloon also elicited internal sphincter relaxation at smaller volumes, but, interestingly, the subjective perception of rectal distension was unchanged with age.

Additional studies have come to somewhat different conclusions, depending on the sex distribution, the health of the subjects, and the methodology employed. A recent report evaluated anorectal function with intra-luminal transducers in 18 healthy elderly subjects (mean age 72) and 18 healthy young volunteers (mean age 29). Age did not significantly affect anal length, highest anal resting zone, pull-through pressures at rest and during voluntary squeeze, threshold or amplitude of the rectosphincteric reflex, threshold of sensation, critical volume, or rectal wall elasticity.[121] When these data were analyzed by gender, females had a significantly lower maximum anal resting zone, lower anal pull-through pressures during rest and voluntary squeeze, and a lower threshold of rectal sensation than the corresponding group of males. This observation emphasizes the need for adequate sex matching when assessing the results of such studies. In a larger study of 88 continent subjects separated by sex into three age groups (younger than 40, 40 to 60, and over 60), aging was associated with decreased anal pressure at rest, along with reduced maximum anal squeeze pressure and pressure in the rectal ampulla, especially after the age of 60 in both sexes.[122]

Lastly, Bannister et al. compared anorectal function in a group of 37 elderly subjects, all with concomitant medical illnesses and on various medications, with anorectal function in a group of 48 young, healthy volunteers.[123] The older group had significantly lower mean basal and squeeze anal pressures, the differences being greater in the female part of the group. Higher rectal pressures in response to distension, along with reduced maximum-tolerated volumes and slower stimulated defecation, also were seen in the elderly group. More importantly, elderly females also required less rectal distension to produce a sustained relaxation of the anal sphincter, produced a less obtuse anorectal angle when straining, and had greater perineal descent than their younger counterparts. Hence, the risk of fecal incontinence is accentuated in the elderly and especially in elderly females, owing to intrinsic musculature weakness compounded by birth trauma and postmenopausal changes in connective tissue elasticity.

While no systematic study of age-related alterations in myoneural elements involved in anorectal function has been performed, electrophysiologic studies of the external anal sphincter in patients with and without fecal incontinence indicate that aging is associated with an increase in motor-unit fiber density. The studies were performed using single-fiber electromyography (Fig. 58-3). The associated increase suggests that denervation, followed by renervation of muscle fibers from undamaged axons, develops with age.[124] When denervation is more severe, as has been demonstrated histologically,

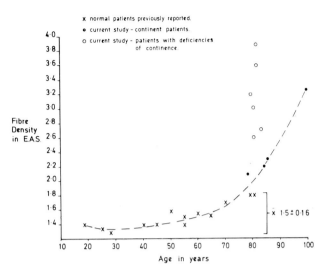

FIGURE 58-3
The relation between fiber density in the external anal sphincter and age in 23 patients. The data from 13 normal patients previously reported have also been recorded. The fiber densities in the 6 patients with varying degrees of incontinence segregate above the projected curve of fiber densities in normal subjects (EAS = external anal sphincter). *(From Percy JP et al, Age Aging 11:175, 1982.)*

higher motor-unit fiber densities develop with resulting fecal incontinence.[125] The correlation between denervation and incontinence is, however, not that close, so that other factors, such as looseness of the stool and diminished cerebral function, must coexist before incontinence develops.

AGING AND PANCREATIC FUNCTION

As an organ of secretion, the pancreas has many functions, which include secreting proteolytic and lipolytic enzymes, neutralizing gastric acid secretion, and maintaining glucose homeostasis. Roughly 20 percent of the dry weight of the pancreas is enzyme protein.[8] Perhaps one of the pancreas's most striking characteristics is its large functional reserve capacity, requiring 90 percent loss of function before signs of insufficiency, such as steatorrhea, develop.

Based on autopsy series, there is little change in the weight of the pancreas with age expressed as either absolute average weight or percent of total body weight.[126] Also, Zimmerman et al. found no change in the overall size of the gland in people 15 to 90 years old.[127] Postmortem studies, however, have shown an age-associated dilatation of the main pancreatic ducts and ectasia of branched ducts.[128] Sahel evaluated endoscopic retrograde cholangiopancreatography (ERCP) studies in 125 subjects over age 70 and found an age-associated increase in the caliber of the main pancreatic duct.[129] In addition, 5.8 percent of subjects demonstrated incomplete stenosis of the pancreatic ducts without other pathologic changes.

Morphometric and ultrastructural studies of the exocrine pancreas have shown an increased amount of intralobular fibrous material along with some focal fatty deposition in the normal pancreas over the age of 70.[127] Acinar atrophy due to shrinkage of individual acini, acinar cell vacuolization, absence of zymogen granules, and dilatation of ductal structures containing inspissated PAS-positive material are additional age-related phenomena that develop in both humans and rats.[130–132] Squamous metaplasia of intralobular and interlobular ducts, proliferation of ductal cells, and alterations in the amount of nuclear material have also been demonstrated. Slavin has shown a large quantity of perivascular lipofuscin-containing cells and an increase in the amount of lysosomes in acinar cells of aging rats.[133]

Age-related vascular lesions include fibrotic thickening of the walls of small and medium-sized arteries, necrosis of the intima, and infiltration by mononuclear cells and eosinophils in rats.[132] In a human series of 423 autopsies of individuals aged 0 to 92 years, minor focal changes of arterioslcerosis were detected.[134]

As one might anticipate in an organ with such a large reserve capacity, the aforementioned changes in structure do not necessarily correlate with physiologic changes in secretion. Part of the difficulty in interpreting the data again lies in the variety of methodologies used to assess pancreatic secretory function. In favor of the stability of pancreatic function over the age span is a study by Rosenberg et al., who assessed pancreatic fluid and bicarbonate output in response to intravenous secretin and found no differences in 59 subjects above and 44 below the age of 50.[135] Supporting this study are the studies of Gullo et al., who initially evaluated pancreatic bicarbonate secretion and output of trypsin, chymotrypsin, and lipase in response to continuous IV infusion of secretin and cerulein in 25 elderly and 30 young subjects.[136] Only mild decreases in enzyme output were observed in 3 of the elderly subjects, with no age-associated changes in the volume of the duodenal aspirate or bicarbonate output. A more recent study by the same group using the fluorescein dilaurate test found no differences in pancreatic function between the patients under 80 years and those over 80.[137]

In contrast, three other studies indicate an age-related decline in pancreatic function. Fikry performed the secretin test in 23 subjects aged 60 to 72 and found a decrease in the volume of the duodenal aspirate, with a selective reduction in amylase and trypsin levels and no change in lipase output.[138] Bartos and Groh found decreases in bicarbonate and amylase output only after repeated injections of secretin and cholecystokinin (CCK) in 10 subjects between ages 61 and 73, suggesting

a decline in reserve capacity.[139] Both studies have been criticized because of methodological problems, including the use of one stimulant and possible incomplete recovery of the duodenal juice. However, a recent study by Laugier, who performed duodenal aspirates across a wide age range (15 to 75 years), found pancreatic volume and bicarbonate concentration peaking in the fourth decade, then declining. By contrast, outputs of lipase, phospholipase, and trypsin declined linearly with age.[140] In addition, decreased outputs of volume and protein (or lipase) in response to secretin or CCK were observed, especially after age 65.

Assessment of serum levels of pancreatic enzymes has also yielded conflicting information. Both unchanged and increased serum immunoreactive trypsin levels have been noted over age, the latter attributed to impaired renal function.[141,142] Carrere et al. also observed no difference in serum trypsin 1 levels or serum lipase levels and activity between 35 elderly and 51 young subjects.[143] By contrast, Mohiuddin et al. reported significant increases in serum trypsin and lipase levels over age; the increase was attributed to an age-associated "leakage" of enzymes out of acinar cells.[144]

AGING AND HEPATOBILIARY FUNCTION

The common bile duct undergoes changes with age similar to those that occur in the main pancreatic duct. In a study of IV cholangiography on 84 healthy Japanese individuals, the common bile duct progressively dilated with age.[145] The mean diameter at age 20 was 6.8 mm, while at age 70 it was 9.2 mm. Distally, however, the preampullary portion progressively narrows with age.[146] How these changes are related to the increasing incidence of cholelithiasis and choledocholithiasis with age remains unclear.[147,148]

The gallbladder serves several functions, including concentration and delivery of bile to the small intestine. The effect of age on the concentrating ability of the gallbladder has not been investigated. Cholecystographic examinations have demonstrated stability of gallbladder emptying with increasing age.[149] Part of the pathogenesis of gallstones relates to the lithogenicity of bile. A numerical value, the lithogenic index, has been developed to describe the relative solubility of cholesterol in bile, with higher values reflecting more saturated bile. Valdivieso et al. addressed the effect of age on bile saturation by comparing biliary lipid composition in a group of Chilean women under 25 to that of an older group over 50.[150] The proportions of phospholipids and cholesterol increased significantly in the older group, which corresponded to an increased lithogenic index. Supersaturated bile was found in only 8.3 percent of the young women whereas it was found in 41.7 percent of the older women (Fig. 58-4). Since there was no change in total bile acid and cholic acid pools, it was speculated that aging resulted in an increase in canalicular lipid secretion, resembling that which is seen in obesity. Trash et al. also found the lithogenic index to rise with age.[151] It therefore seems likely that gallstone occurrence in the aged is related to alterations in biliary lipid composition.

A variety of morphological and functional changes have been demonstrated in the aging liver. Liver size gradually decreases with increasing age, accounting for 2.5 percent of total body weight before age 50 but only 1.6 percent at age 90.[126] In addition, the liver gradually conforms with age to the shape of adjoining structures. One study showed that the livers of Japanese women were markedly domed, probably due to tight belts worn as part of traditional dress.[152]

Liver blood flow also appears to decrease with age. Estimated declines of 0.3 to 1.5 percent per year have been reported.[153–155] The potential clinical importance of the change in hepatic blood flow with advancing age is obvious when one realizes the importance of the liver in drug metabolism.

Microscopically, the liver undergoes numerous alterations with age. An early study listed the following as the most common histologic alterations in biopsies of normal subjects over age 70: mild ductular proliferation,

especially around portal tracts; mixed periportal inflammatory infiltrate; single or small areas of liver cell necrosis; and increased amounts of lipofuscin pigment in Kupffer's cells in over one-third of the subjects.[156] More recent work by Watanabe and Tanaka defines additional changes in hepatocyte morphology, including a decrease in the number of hepatocytes accompanied by increases in mean cell volume and variance in cell size, variation in nuclear size and volume of nuclear DNA, and an increase in aneuploidy and binucleate cells. These findings, along with the finding of a decreased number but increased volume of mitochondria and lysosomes, seem to indicate that the remaining hepatocytes are hyperfunctioning, possibly to compensate for their reduced numbers.[157] Supporting this indication is the study of Schmucker, who found a decrease in the surface area of the Golgi apparatus but an increase in the amount of rough and smooth endoplasmic reticulum.[158]

Functional changes in the liver with age have been defined in a variety of ways. Standard liver function tests, including serum concentrations of bilirubin, aminotransaminases, and alkaline phosphatase, do not vary significantly with age.[159] Albumin and transferrin levels have been reported to either decrease or remain stable.[155,160] Unfortunately, these standard liver function tests do not measure dynamic functions.

The clearance of anionic dyes such as sulfobromophthalein (Bromsulphalein, or BSP) by the liver is one such dynamic test. After IV administration, sulfobromophthalein is extracted from blood, stored in hepatocytes, and finally excreted unchanged in bile. An early report, using constant IV infusion of BSP, demonstrated that while the storage capacity declined with age, the secretory transport maximum did not.[161] Using simultaneous cytofluorometric measurements of BSP retention and nuclear DNA in rat hepatocytes, Nakanishi further defined the nature of the storage defect by showing a selective decrease in the storage capacity of polyploid cells which increase in number with age.[162]

Microsomal oxidation and hydroxylation has been evaluated using clearance of the drug antipyrine, but the results have been controversial. In a study of 307 healthy males, ages 18 to 92, a decline of 18.5 percent in antipyrine clearance was seen in the older subjects.[163] However, when looked at using multiple regression analysis, other environmental factors, specifically caffeine and cigarette use, were highly correlated with enhanced antipyrine metabolism and were considerably lower in prevalence in the older males. In fact, smoking alone accounted for 12 percent of the changes in metabolism, with age accounting for only 3 percent. Nonetheless, Swift found lower antipyrine clearances in a group of elderly, otherwise healthy nonsmokers (ages 75 to 86) as compared to the clearances of a younger group (ages 20 to 29).[164] Greenblatt et al., who studied antipyrine

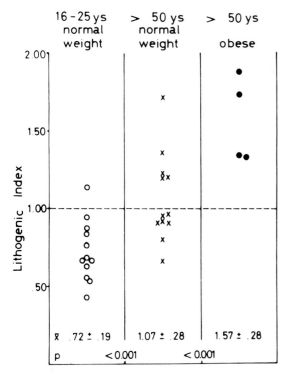

FIGURE 58-4
Lithogenic indexes of fasting gallbladder bile in young normal, older normal, and older obese Chilean women. *(From Valdivieso V et al, Gastroenterology 74:871, 1978.)*

kinetics in 51 smoking and nonsmoking adults, also concluded that age was the most significant variable affecting clearance rates.[165] In addition, Salem et al. reported that liver enzymes of older individuals are less "inducible," which may compound the effects of age on mixed oxidase function.[166]

The nutritional status of an older patient has also been shown to impact on microsomal oxidative metabolism. Reduced antipyrine clearance was observed in a group of elderly patients found to be ascorbic-acid deficient. Following correction of the deficiency with a 2-week course of multivitamins, antipyrine metabolism normalized.[167]

Acetanilid is an alternative drug used to assess hepatic microsomal oxidation. Impaired oxidation was suggested in a group of 23 subjects over 65 as the half-life of acetanilid was increased in this group.[26] Nonmicrosomal oxidation via alcohol dehydrogenase appears to be unaffected by age, as the rate of elimination of ethanol administered intravenously was constant in 50 healthy subjects ages 21 to 81.[168]

Demethylation is another means of drug metabolism by the liver. Specifically, the benzodiazepines, chlordiazepine and diazepam, are eliminated by this process, as is the drug aminopyrine. Jori found the half-life of aminopyrine was increased to 8.1 hours in 40 elderly subjects (over age 65), compared to 3.3 hours in 25- to 30-year-olds.[169] Likewise, plasma clearance of chlordiazepoxide and diazepam is reduced with increasing age, necessitating dosing adjustments in older patients[170,171] (Chap. 21).

While a number of animal studies have shown an absolute reduction with age in microsomal enzyme activity, such as that of NADH-cytochrome C reductase and cytochrome P-450, human studies have not.[172] James et al. found no age-related changes in the activities of the microsomal enzymes aldrin epoxidase and 7-ethoxycoumarin-0-diethylase in humans, and no alterations in microsomal protein content per unit wet weight of liver.[173] The nonmicrosomal system, utilizing glutathione, which assists in metabolizing such drugs as acetaminophen, was also not reduced over age in noncirrhotic patients.

Hepatic conjugation reactions, such as acetylation in the case of isoniazid or glucuronidation, the primary mode of metabolism of oxazepam or lorazepam, are not altered by age.[174,175] Drugs which undergo high hepatic first-pass metabolism by extraction from the blood may have altered clearance with age due to the age-related reductions in hepatic blood flow previously mentioned. This effect was demonstrated with propranolol.[176]

Total body-protein synthesis as measured by ^{15}N-glycine was lower by 37 percent in a group of 69- to 91-year-olds than the total for a group of subjects in their early twenties.[177] This finding was attributed to impaired hepatic production. Indeed, while the metabolism of warfarin is unaffected by age, the amount of the drug necessary to achieve therapeutic anticoagulation is decreased in older individuals presumably due to decreased synthesis of vitamin K–dependent factors.[178]

Data regarding the synthesis and breakdown of albumin in humans have been conflicting, despite evidence suggesting a reduction in serum levels with increasing age.[179] One study showed that while a decreased plasma-albumin concentration developed in a group of older subjects (64 to 78 years old) on a low-protein diet, the rate of albumin synthesis was comparable to that of a group of younger subjects (19 to 24 years old), suggesting that albumin synthesis is controlled at a lower set point in the elderly.[180] In addition, a number of drugs highly bound to albumin, including diazepam and phenytoin, have reduced binding with age, permitting more free drug in the serum.[172,181]

A final point should be made regarding the activity of "protective" hepatic enzymes, such as superoxide dismutase (SOD) and catalase, which, respectively, protect against oxygen free radicals and prevent peroxidation. Studies have demonstrated a 50 percent reduction in the specific activity of these enzymes in aged animals.[182] The importance of protecting the organism from environmental toxins is obvious; however, the relevance of this finding as it applies to aging humans remains uncertain.

In summary, the liver undergoes several changes with advancing age including a decrease in size, a decrease in blood flow, alterations in hepatocyte size and ultrastructural features including increased aneuploidy, ductular proliferation and liver cell necrosis, reduced protein synthesis, and a reduction in metabolism of a number of drugs, possibly contributing to the increased frequency of adverse drug reactions found in the elderly.

REFERENCES

1. Nelson JB, Castell DO: Esophageal motility disorders. *Dis Mon* 34:299, 1988.
2. Leese G, Hopwood D: Muscle fibre typing in the human pharyngeal constrictors and oesophagus: The effect of aging. *Acta Anat* 127:77, 1986.
3. Piaget F, Fouillet J: Le pharynx et l'oesuphage seniles: Etude clinique radiologique et radiocinematographique. *J Med Lyon* 40:951, 1959.
4. Almy TP: Factors leading to digestive disorders in the elderly. *Bull NY Acad Med* 57:709, 1981.
5. Eckhardt VF, Le Compte PM: Esophageal ganglia and smooth muscle in the elderly. *Dig Dis* 23:443, 1978.
6. Soergel KH, Zboralske FF, Amberg JR: Presbyesophagus: Esophageal motility in nonagenerians. *J Clin Invest* 43:1472, 1964.
7. Hollis JB, Castell DO: Esophageal function in elderly men. A new look at "presbyesophagus." *Ann Intern Med* 80:371, 1974.

8. Geokas MC, Conteas CN, Majumdar APN: The aging gastrointestinal tract, liver, and pancreas. *Clin Geriatr Med* 1:177, 1985.

9. Khan TA et al: Esophageal motility in the elderly. *Dig Dis Sci* 22:1049, 1977.

10. Csendes A et al: Relation of gastroesophageal sphincter pressure and esophageal contractile waves to age in man. *Scand J Gastroenterol* 13:443, 1978.

11. Richter JE et al: Esophageal manometry in 95 healthy adult volunteers. Variability of pressures with age and frequency of "abnormal" contractions. *Dig Dis Sci* 32:583, 1987.

12. Spence RAJ et al: Does age influence normal gastro-oesophageal reflux? *Gut* 26:794, 1985.

13. Castell DO, Dubois A: *Esophageal and Gastric Emptying*. Boca Raton, CRC Press, 1984.

14. Minami H: The physiology and pathophysiology of gastric emptying in humans. *Gastroenterology* 86:1592, 1984.

15. Carlson AJ: *The Control of Hunger in Health and Disease*. Chicago, University of Chicago Press, 1916, pp 56, 119.

16. Van Liere EJ, Northup DW: The emptying time of the stomach of old people. *Am J Physiol* 134:719, 1941.

17. Webster SGP, Leeming JT: Assessment of small bowel function in the elderly using a modified xylose tolerance test. *Gut* 16:109, 1975.

18. Evans MA et al: Gastric emptying rate in the elderly: Implications for drug therapy. *J Am Geriatr Soc* 29:201, 1981.

19. Moore JG et al: Effect of age on gastric emptying of liquid-solid meals in man. *Dig Dis Sci* 28:340, 1983.

20. Davies WT et al: Gastric emptying in atrophic gastritis and carcinoma of the stomach. *Scand J Gastroenterol* 6:297, 1971.

21. Varga F: Transit time changes with age in the gastrointestinal tract of the rat. *Digestion* 14:319, 1976.

22. McDougal JW et al: Intestinal transit and gastric emptying in young and senescent rats. *Dig Dis Sci* 25:A-15, 1980.

23. Goldberg PB, Roberts J: Effect of age on rat smooth muscle cholinergic receptors. *Gerontologist* 20:111, 1980.

24. Kupfer RM et al: Gastric emptying and small bowel transit rate in the elderly. *J Am Geriatr Soc* 33:340, 1985.

25. Frank EB et al: Abnormal gastric emptying in patients with atrophic gastritis with or without pernicious anemia. *Gastroenterology* 80:1151, 1981.

26. James OFW: Gastrointestinal and liver function in old age. *Clin Gastroenterol* 12:671, 1983.

27. Baron JH: Studies of basal and peak acid output with an augmented histamine test. *Gut* 4:136, 1963.

28. Grossman MI et al: Basal and histolog-stimulated gastric secretion in control subjects and in patients with peptic ulcer or gastric ulcer. *Gastroenterology* 45:14, 1963.

29. Andrews GR et al: Atrophic gastritis in the aged. *Aust Ann Med* 16:230, 1967.

30. Gialosa A, Cheli R: Correlations anatomosecretoires gastriques en fonction de l'age chez des sujets ayant une muguegues fundique normale. *Gastroenterol Clin* 3:647, 1979.

31. Kekki M et al: Age- and sex-related behavior of gastric acid secretion at the population level. *Scand J Gastroenterol* 17:737, 1982.

32. Kramer PA et al: Tetracycline absorption in elderly patients with achlorhydria. *Clin Pharmacol Ther* 23:467, 1978.

33. Bock OAA et al: The serum pepsinogen level with special reference to the histology of the gastric mucosa. *Gut* 4:106, 1963.

34. Samloff JM et al: Serum group I pepsinogens by radioimmunoassay in control subjects and patients with peptic ulcer. *Gastroenterology* 69:83, 1975.

35. McGuigan JE, Trudeau WL: Serum gastrin concentrations in pernicious anemia. *N Engl J Med* 282:358, 1970.

36. Korman MG et al: Progressive increase in the functional G cell mass with age in atrophic gastritis. *Gut* 14:549, 1973.

37. Palmer ED: The stage of the gastric mucosa of elderly persons without upper gastrointestinal symptoms. *J Am Geriatr Soc* 2:171, 1954.

38. Ruoff HJ et al: Morphologically different biopsy specimens of the human gastric mucosa. I. The use of enzymatic cell isolation for quantitative determination of parietal cells. *Pharmacology* 33:121, 1986.

39. Bird T et al: Gastric histology and its relation to anemia in the elderly. *Gerontology* 23:309, 1977.

40. Perez-Perez GJ et al: Campylobacter pylori antibodies in humans. *Ann Intern Med* 109:11, 1988.

41. Kimura K: Chronological transition of the fundipyloric border determined by stepwise biopsy of the lesser and greater curvatures of the stomach. *Gastroenterology* 63:584, 1972.

42. Ormiston MC et al: Five year follow-up study of gastritis. *J Clin Pathol* 35:757, 1982.

43. Ihamäki T et al: Long-term observation of subjects with normal mucosa and with superficial gastritis: Results of 23–27 years' follow-up examinations. *Scand J Gastroenterol* 13:771, 1978.

44. Nakano G, Nakamura T: Histopathological study of intestinal metaplasia of postmortem stomachs in the aged Japanese. *Cancer Detect Prev* 4:361, 1981.

45. Geocze S et al: Sulfated glycosaminoglycan composition of human gastric mucosa: Effect of aging, chronic superficial gastritis and adenocarcinoma. *Braz J Med Biol Res* 18:487, 1985.

46. McDougal JN et al: Age-related changes in colonic function in rats. *Am J Physiol* 247:G542, 1984.

47. Lin CF, Hayton WL: GI motility and subepithelial blood flow in mature and senescent rats. *Age Ageing* 6:46, 1983.

48. Kim SK: Small intestine transit time in the normal small bowel study. *Am J Roentgen* 104:522, 1968.

49. Anuras S, Sutherland J: Small intestinal manometry in healthy elderly subjects. *J Am Geriatr Soc* 32:581, 1984.

50. Kobashi YL et al: Age-related changes in the reactivity of the rat jejunum to cholinoceptor agonists. *Eur J Pharmacol* 115:133, 1985.

51. Bortoff A et al: Age-related changes in mechanical properties of cat circular intestinal muscle, in Christensen J (ed): *Gastrointestinal Motility*. New York, Raven Press, 1980, p 161.

52. Nelson JB et al: Evaluating age-related changes in rat

ileal smooth muscle activity using KCl and chemical skinning. *Gastroenterology* 92:1551, 1987.

53. Nelson JB et al: Histologic changes associated with aging in rat ileal smooth muscle: Correlation with physiologic data. *Gastroenterology* 92:1551, 1987.
54. Gabella G: Unpublished data, 1988.
55. Moog F: The small intestine in old mice: Growth, alkaline phosphatase, and disaccharidase activities, and deposition of amyloid. *Exp Gerontol* 12:223, 1977.
56. Penzes L: Data on the chemical composition of the aging intestine. *Digestion* 3:174, 1970.
57. Penzes L: Letter to the editor. *Exp Gerontol* 17:243, 1982.
58. Ecknauer R et al: Intestinal morphology and cell production rate in aging rats. *J Gerontol* 37:151, 1982.
59. Hohn P et al: Differentiation and aging of the rat intestinal mucosa. II. Morphological, enzyme, histochemical and disc electrophoretic aspects of the aging of the small intestine mucosa. *Mech Ageing Dev* 7:217, 1978.
60. Jakab L, Penzes L: Relationship between glucose absorption and villus height in aging. *Experientia* 37:740, 1981.
61. Penzes L: Intestinal response in aging: Changes in reserve capacity. *Acta Med Hung* 41:263, 1984.
62. Rowlatt C: Cell aging in the intestinal tract, in Cristofalo V, Holeckova E (eds): *Cell Impairment in Aging and Development*, vol 53, *Advances in Experimental Medicine and Biology*. New York, Plenum Press, 1975, p 215.
63. Meshkinpour H et al: Influence of aging on the surface area of the small intestine in the rat. *Exp Gerontol* 16:399, 1981.
64. Holt PR et al: Effect of aging upon small intestinal structure in the Fischer rat. *J Gerontol* 39:642, 1984.
65. Warren PM et al: Age changes in small intestinal mucosa. *Lancet* 2:849, 1978.
66. Webster SGP, Leeming JT: The appearance of the small bowel mucosa in old age. *Age Ageing* 4:168, 1975.
67. Stenling R et al: Surface ultrastructure of the small intestine mucosa in healthy children and adults: A scanning electron microscopic study with some methodological aspects. *Ultrastruct Pathol* 6:131, 1984.
68. Holt PR: Effects of aging upon intestinal absorption, in Moment G (ed): *Nutritional Approaches to Aging*, Research Uniscience Series, Methods in Aging Research. Boca Raton, CRC Press, 1982, p 157.
69. Lesher S et al: Influence of age on transit time of cells of mouse intestinal epithelium. I. Duodenum. *J Lab Invest* 10:291, 1962.
70. Clarke WJL, Anderson JW: The effects of age on mucosal morphology and epithelial cell production in rat small intestine. *J Anat* 123:805, 1977.
71. Fry RJM et al: Influence of age on transit time of cells of mouse intestinal epithelium. III. Ileum. *J Lab Invest* 11:289, 1962.
72. Goldspink DF et al: Protein synthesis during the developmental growth of the small and large intestine of the rat. *Biochem J* 217:527, 1984.
73. Krazinski SD et al: Aging changes vitamin A absorption characteristics. *Gastroenterology* 88:1715, 1985.
74. Esposito G et al: Age-related changes in rat intestinal transport of D-glucose, sodium, and water. *Am J Physiol* 249:G328, 1985.
75. Welsh JD et al: Intestinal disaccharidase activities in relation to age, race, and mucosal damage. *Gastroenterology* 75:847, 1978.
76. Rommel K, Böhmer R: Beziehungen znishchen lebensalter, intestinal en disaccharidasen und monosaccharidabsorption der ratte. *Ärztl Forschg* 26:453, 1972.
77. Holt PR et al: Delayed enzyme expression: A defect of aging rat gut. *Gastroenterology* 89:1026, 1985.
78. Kendall MJ: The influence of age on the xylose absorption test. *Gut* 11:498, 1970.
79. Webster SGP, Leeming JT: Assessment of small bowel function using a modified xylose absorption test. *Gut* 16:109, 1975.
80. Montgomery RD et al: The aging gut: A study of intestinal absorption in relation to nutrition in the elderly. *Q J Med* 47:197, 1978.
81. Laue R et al: Age-dependent alterations of intestinal absorption. I. Theoretical aspects. *Arch Gerontol Geriatr* 3:87, 1984.
82. Penzes L: Intestinal absorption in the aged. *Acta Med Acad Sci Hung* 37:203, 1980.
83. Thomson ABR: Unstirred water layer and age-dependent changes in rabbit jejunal D-glucose transport. *Am J Physiol* 236:E685, 1979.
84. Feibusch J, Holt PR: Impaired absorption capacity for carbohydrates in the elderly. *Am J Clin Nutr* 32:942, 1979.
85. Webster SGP et al: A comparison of fat absorption in young and old subjects. *Age Ageing* 6:113, 1977.
86. Holt PR, Dominguez AA: Intestinal absorption of triglyceride and vitamin D_3 in aged and young rats. *Dig Dis Sci* 26:1109, 1981.
87. McEvoy A: Investigation of intestinal malabsorption in the elderly, in Evans JG, Laird FI (eds): *Advanced Geriatric Medicine*. London: Pitman, 1982, p 100.
88. Becker GH et al: Fat absorption in young and old age. *Gastroenterology* 14:80, 1950.
89. Hollander D et al: Does essential fatty acid absorption change with age? *J Lipid Res* 25:129, 1984.
90. Werner I, Hambraeus L: The digestive capacity of elderly people, in Carlson LA (ed): *Nutrition in Old Age*. Uppsala, Sweden, Almquist and Wiksell, 1978, p 55.
91. Hollander D, Morgan D: Aging: Its influence on vitamin A intestinal absorption in vivo by the rat. *Exp Gerontol* 14:301, 1979.
92. Barragry JM et al: Intestinal cholecalciferol absorption in the elderly and in younger adults. *Clin Sci Mol Med* 55:213, 1978.
93. Gallagher JC et al: Intestinal calcium absorption and serum vitamin D metabolites in normal subjects and osteoporotic patients. *J Clin Invest* 64:729, 1979.
94. Rafsky HA, Newman B: Vitamin B_1 excretion in the aged. *Gastroenterology* 1:737, 1943.
95. Thomson AD: Thiamine absorption in old age. *Gerontol Clin* 8:354, 1966.
96. Booth JB, Todd GB: Subclinical scurvy-hypovitaminosis C. *Geriatrics* 27:130, 1972.
97. Baker H et al: Severe impairment of dietary folate utilization in the elderly. *J Am Geriatr Soc* 26:218, 1978.
98. Elsborg L: Reversible malabsorption of folic acid in the elderly with nutritional folate deficiency. *Acta Haematol* 55:140, 1976.

99. Hyams DE: The absorption of vitamin B$_{12}$ in the elderly. *Gerontol Clin* 6:193, 1964.

100. Fleming BB, Barrows CH: The influence of aging on intestinal absorption of vitamin B$_{12}$ and niacin in rats. *Exp Gerontol* 17:121, 1982.

101. McEvoy AW et al: Vitamin B$_{12}$ absorption from the gut does not decline with age in normal elderly humans. *Age Ageing* 11:180, 1982.

102. Schachter D et al: Accumulation of ^{45}Ca by slices of the small intestine. *Am J Physiol* 198:275, 1960.

103. Ambrecht HJ et al: Effect of age on intestinal calcium absorption and adaptation to dietary calcium. *Am J Physiol* 236:E769, 1979.

104. Avioli LV et al: The influence of age on the absorption of ^{47}Ca in women and its relation to ^{47}Ca absorption in post-menopausal osteoporosis. *J Clin Invest* 44:1960, 1965.

105. Bullamore MR et al: Effect of age on calcium absorption. *Lancet* 2:535, 1970.

106. Ireland P, Fordtran JS: Effect of dietary calcium and age on jejunal calcium absorption in humans studied by intestinal perfusion. *J Clin Invest* 52:2672, 1973.

107. Nordin BEC et al: Calcium absorption in the elderly. *Cell Tissue Res* 21:442, 1976.

108. Marx JJM: Normal iron absorption and decreased red cell iron uptake in the aged. *Blood* 53:204, 1979.

109. Jacobs P et al: Role of hydrochloric acid in iron absorption. *J Appl Physiol* 19:187, 1964.

110. Yamajata A: Histopathological studies of the colon due to age. *Jpn J Gastroenterol* 62:224, 1965.

111. Broclehurst JC, Kahn MY: Study of fecal stasis in old age and in the use of "Dorbanex" in its prevention. *Gerontol Clin* 11:293, 1969.

112. Burkitt DP et al: Dietary fiber and disease. *JAMA* 229:1068, 1974.

113. Koch TR et al: Changes in some electrophysiological properties of circular muscle from normal sigmoid colon of aging patient. *Gastroenterology* 90:1497, 1986.

114. Culpepper-Morgan J et al: Increased mu and kappa opiate receptors in guinea pig colon. *Gastroenterology* 94:A82, 1988.

115. Whiteway J, Morson BC: Pathology of ageing-diverticular disease. *Clin Gastroenterol* 14:829, 1985.

116. Parks TG: Natural history of diverticular disease of the colon. *Clin Gastroenterol* 4:53, 1975.

117. Smith AN, Shepherd J: The strength of the colon wall in diverticular disease. *Br J Surg* 63:666A, 1976.

118. Homer JL: Natural history of diverticulosis of the colon. *Am J Dig Dis* 3:343, 1958.

119. Painter NS, Burkitt DP: Diverticular disease of the sigmoid colon, a 20th century problem. *Clin Gastroenterol* 4:3, 1975.

120. Ihre T: Studies on anal function in continent and incontinent patients. *Scand J Gastroenterol* 9(suppl):1, 1974.

121. Leoning-Baucke V, Anuras S: Effects of age and sex on anorectal manometry. *Am J Gastroenterol* 80:50, 1985.

122. Poos RJ et al: Influence of age and sex on anal sphincters: manometric evaluation of anorectal continence. *Eur Surg Res* 18:343, 1986.

123. Bannister JJ et al: Effect of ageing on anorectal function. *Gut* 28:353, 1987.

124. Percy JP et al: A neurogenic factor in fecal incontinence in the elderly. *Age Ageing* 11:175, 1982.

125. Parks AG et al: Sphincter denervation in anorectal incontinence and rectal prolapse. *Gut* 18:656, 1977.

126. Calloway NC et al: Uncertainties in geriatric data. II: Organ size. *J Am Geriatr Soc* 13:20, 1965.

127. Zimmerman W et al: Das normale pankreas darstellung im sonogramm in Abhängigkent zum lebenstalter. *Fortschr Med* 99:1178, 1981.

128. Kreel L, Sandin B: Changes in pancreatic morphology in association with aging. *Gut* 14:962, 1973.

129. Sahel J et al: Morphometrique de la pancreatographie endoscopique normale du sujet age. *Gastroenterol Hepatol* 15:574, 1979.

130. Andrew W: Senile changes in the pancreas of Wistar Institute rats and of man with special regard to the similarity of locule and cavity formation. *Am J Anat* 74:97, 1944.

131. Martin ED: Different pathomorphological aspects of pancreatic fibrosis, correlated with etiology: Anatomical study of 300 cases, in Gyr KE (ed): *Pancreatitis: Concepts and Classification*. New York, Elsevier, 1984, p 77.

132. Kendrey G, Roe FJC: Histopathological changes in the pancreas of laboratory rats. *Lab Anim* 3:207, 1969.

133. Slavin BG et al: Morphological changes in the ageing mammalian pancreas, in John JE Jr (ed): *Ageing Cell Structure*, vol 2. New York, Plenum Press, 1984.

134. Aoyama S et al: Histopathological study on aging of the pancreas from 423 autopsy cases. *Jpn J Geriatr* 16:574, 1979.

135. Rosenberg IR et al: The effect of age and sex upon human pancreatic secretion of fluid and bicarbonate. *Gastroenterology* 50:191, 1966.

136. Gullo L et al: Exocrine pancreatic function in the elderly. *Gerontology* 29:407, 1983.

137. Gullo L et al: Aging and exocrine pancreatic function. *J Am Geriatr Soc* 134:790, 1986.

138. Fikry ME: Exocrine pancreatic functions in the aged. *J Am Geriatr Soc* 16:463, 1968.

139. Bartos V, Groh J: The effect of repeated stimulation of the pancreas on the pancreatic secretion in young and aged men. *Gerontol Clin* 11:56, 1969.

140. Laugier R, Sarles H: The pancreas. *Clin Gastroenterol* 14:749, 1985.

141. Ventrucci M et al: Comparative study of serum pancreatic isoamylase, lipase, and trypsin-like immunoreactivity in pancreatic disease. *Digestion* 28:114, 1983.

142. Koehn HD, Mostbeck A: Age-dependence of immunoreactive trypsin concentrations in serum. *Clin Chem* 27:502, 1981.

143. Carrere J et al: Human serum pancreatic lipase and trypsin 1 in aging: Enzymatic and immunoenzymatic assays. *J Gerontol* 42:315, 1987.

144. Mohiuddin J et al: Serum pancreatic enzymes in the elderly. *Ann Clin Biochem* 21:102, 1984.

145. Nagase M et al: Surgical significance of dilation of the common bile duct with special reference to choledocholithiasis. *Jpn J Surg* 10:296, 1980.

146. Nakadi I: Changes in morphology of the distal common bile duct associated with aging. *Gastroenterol Jpn* 16:54, 1981.

147. Bateson MC: Gallbladder disease and cholecystectomy rates are independently variable. *Lancet* 2:621, 1984.

148. Glenn F, McSherry CK: Calculous biliary tract disease, in *Current Problems in Surgery.* Chicago, Yearbook Med Publ, June 1975, p 1.

149. Boyden EA, Grantham SA Jr: Evacuation of the gallbladder in old age. *Surg Gynecol Obstet* 62:34, 1936.

150. Valdivieso V et al: Effect of aging on biliary lipid composition and bile acid metabolism in normal Chilean women. *Gastroenterology* 74:871, 1978.

151. Trash DB et al: The influence of age on cholesterol saturation of bile. *Gut* 17:394, 1976.

152. Okuda K et al: Ageing and gross anatomical alterations of the liver, in Kitani K (ed): *Liver and Ageing.* Amsterdam, Elsevier, 1978, p 159.

153. Sherlock S et al: Splanchnic blood flow in man by the bromsulphthalein method. *J Lab Clin Med* 35:823, 1950.

154. Koff RS et al: Absence of an age effect of sulfobromophthalein retention in healthy men. *Gastroenterology* 65:300, 1973.

155. Mooney H et al: Alterations in the liver with ageing. *Clin Gastroenterol* 14:757, 1985.

156. Schaffner F, Popper H: Nonspecific reactive hepatitis in aged and infirm people. *Am J Dig Dis* 4:389, 1959.

157. Watanabe T, Tanaka Y: Age-related alterations in the size of human hepatocytes. *Virchows Arch* 39:9, 1982.

158. Schmucker DL: Age-related changes in hepatic fine structure: A quantitative analysis. *J Gerontol* 31:135, 1976.

159. Kampmann JP et al: Effect of age on liver function. *Geriatrics* 30:91, 1975.

160. McEvoy AW, James OFW: Anthropometric indices in normal elderly subjects. *Age Ageing* 11:97, 1982.

161. Thompson EN, Williams R: Effect of age on liver function with particular reference to bromsulphthalein excretion. *Gut* 6:26, 1965.

162. Nakanishi K et al: Decline of bromosulfophthalein storage capacity in polyploid hepatocytes demonstrated by cytofluorometry. *J Exp Gerontol* 15:103, 1980.

163. Vestal RE et al: Antipyrine metabolism in man: Influence of age, alcohol, caffeine, and smoking. *Clin Pharmacol Ther* 18:425, 1975.

164. Swift CG et al: Antipyrine disposition and liver size in the elderly. *Eur J Clin Pharmacol* 14:149, 1978.

165. Greenblatt DJ et al: Antipyrine kinetics in the elderly: Prediction of age-related changes in benzodiazepine oxidizing capacity. *J Pharmacol Exp Ther* 20:120, 1982.

166. Salem SAM et al: Reduced induction of drug metabolism in the elderly. *Age Ageing* 7:68, 1978.

167. Smithard DJ, Langman MJS: The effect of vitamin supplementation upon antipyrine metabolism in the elderly. *Br J Clin Pharmacol* 5:181, 1978.

168. Vestal RE et al: Ageing and ethanol metabolism. *Clin Pharmacol Ther* 21:343, 1977.

169. Jori A et al: Rate of aminopyrine disappearance in young and aged humans. *Pharmacology* 8:273, 1972.

170. Roberts RK et al: Effect of age and parenchymal liver disease on the disposition and elimination of chlordiazepoxide. *Gastroenterology* 75:479, 1978.

171. Macklon AF et al: The effect of age on the pharmacokinetics of diazepam. *Clin Sci* 59:479, 1980.

172. Kato R: Hepatic microsomal drug metabolising enzymes in aged rats—history and future problems, in Kitani K (ed): *Liver and Ageing.* Amsterdam, Elsevier, 1978, p 287.

173. James OFW et al: Lack of ageing effect on human microsomal mono-oxygenase enzyme activities, in Kitani K (ed): *Liver and Ageing.* Amsterdam, Elsevier, 1982, p 395.

174. Farah F et al: Hepatic drug acetylation and oxidation—effects in man. *Br Med J* 2:155, 1977.

175. Wilkinson CR: The effects of liver disease and ageing on the disposition of diazepam, chlorodiazepoxide, oxazepam, and lorazepam in man. *Acta Psychiatr Scand* 274(suppl):56, 1978.

176. Castleden CM, George C: The effect of ageing on hepatic clearance of propranolol. *Br J Clin Pharmacol* 7:49, 1979.

177. Young VR et al: Total human body protein synthesis in relation to protein requirements at various ages. *Nature* 253:192, 1975.

178. Shepherd AMM et al: Age as a determinant of sensitivity to warfarin. *Br J Clin Pharmacol* 4:315, 1977.

179. Greenblatt DJ: Reduced serum albumin concentration in the elderly: A report from the Boston Collaborative Drug Surveillance Program. *J Am Geriatr Soc* 27:20, 1979.

180. Gersovitz M et al: Albumin synthesis in young and elderly subjects using a new stable isotope methodology: Responses to level of protein intake. *Metabolism* 29:1075, 1980.

181. Hayes MJ et al: Changes in drug metabolism with increasing age. *Br J Clin Pharmacol* 2:73, 1975.

182. Gershon H, Gershon D: Inactive enzyme molecules in aging mice. *Proc Nat Acad Sci USA* 70:909, 1973.

Chapter 59

DISORDERS OF THE ESOPHAGUS

Wallace C. Wu and Joel E. Richter

Esophageal symptoms in the elderly are more similar than dissimilar to those in younger adults. However, the disease pattern may be somewhat different. Congenital lesions are rare, while some diseases such as motor disorders, esophageal strictures of various causes, and pill-induced esophagitis may be more common in the elderly population. These and other esophageal lesions will be discussed in this chapter. Dysphagia from lesions proximal to the esophagus is called *oropharyngeal dysphagia*. This can be caused by local lesions of the mouth, tongue, and pharynx and also by a variety of neuromuscular disorders. Oropharyngeal dysphagia is covered in Chap. 118 and will not be discussed here.

GASTROESOPHAGEAL REFLUX DISEASE

Gastroesophageal reflux is an extremely common problem in our population. A recent Gallup survey found 20 percent of the American population suffered from heartburn more than three times a month and an additional 25 percent had experienced monthly heartburn. heartburn is the major indication for antacid consumption in the United States.[1] Several studies have shown that the prevalence of heartburn as well as endoscopic esophagitis increases after age 50 years.[2,3]

PATHOPHYSIOLOGY

Prolonged pH recordings have shown that many healthy subjects have daily episodes of acid reflux without symptoms—"physiologic reflux." These episodes occur after meals and are short-lived; they almost never occur at night.[4] The gradation from "physiologic" to "pathologic" reflux is a multifactorial process. The major antireflux

barrier is the lower esophageal sphincter. However, other contributing factors include esophageal acid clearance, irritating effects of the gastric contents, delayed gastric emptying, and the intrinsic resistance of the esophageal mucosa.

SYMPTOMS

The classic symptoms of gastroesophageal reflux disease include heartburn, acid regurgitation, water brash, and dysphagia. *Heartburn* (pyrosis) is a substernal burning sensation with a typical upward moving character. When the refluxed material flows into the mouth, it is called *regurgitation*. Both heartburn and regurgitation occur particularly after meals and with postural changes such as lying down or stooping over. *Water brash* is the sudden appearance of a slightly sour salty fluid in the mouth. Dysphagia is a frequent complaint of reflux patients. Persistent or slowly progressive dysphagia for solids is often due to fibrosis and stricture formation. It can be caused by inflammation alone or by concomitant motility disturbances. However, severe esophagitis and its complications in the elderly can be entirely asymptomatic.

Gastroesophageal reflux disease may also present with symptoms not immediately referable to the gastrointestinal tract. The development of chest pain in an adult patient raises the possibility of ischemic heart disease. However, 10 to 30 percent of patients undergoing coronary angiography have normal studies. Recent investigations suggest that acid reflux is the cause of noncardiac chest pain in 20 to 46 percent of these patients.[5] Aspiration into the airways of reflux material may lead to laryngeal and bronchopulmonary symptoms. Persistent hoarseness, laryngeal granulomas, and subglottic stenosis may result from intermittent acid reflux. Chronic persistent cough and recurring aspiration pneumonitis may be due to gastroesophageal reflux disease. There is also mounting evidence of an association between reflux disease and asthma. Acid reflux may induce asthma either by microaspiration of acid or via vagally mediated bronchospasm triggered by intraesophageal acid exposure.[6]

DIAGNOSIS

Tests for gastroesophageal reflux disease evaluate different variables in the disease spectrum.[7] Unfortunately no single test has been accepted as the "gold standard" for diagnosis. In addition, the ease of administration, the need for technical training, special equipment, expense, and discomfort to the patient are important factors in determining the priority with which diagnostic tests are administered and the decision to have the tests done by generalists or by specialists. Based on these variables, the following diagnostic and therapeutic approaches to the patient with gastroesophageal reflux disease are suggested (Fig. 59-1).

Barium Esophagram

Multiphasic views of the esophagus permit good visualization of mucosal detail and excellent definition of hiatal

hernia, ulcers, rings, and strictures. Although insensitive to mild inflammatory changes, radiologic sensitivity and specificity approaches 100 percent in more severe grades of esophagitis.[8] Radiographic evidence of reflux may be demonstrated in up to 40 percent of symptomatic patients, but this is a nonspecific finding as it can also be induced in approximately 25 percent of asymptomatic individuals. Hiatal hernias are more commonly observed in reflux patients and may impair esophageal acid clearance. The barium swallow with upper GI series is used primarily as a screening test to exclude other diagnoses (peptic ulcer disease) and to identify possible reflux complications.

Acid Perfusion (Bernstein) Test

This is a simple test whose reported sensitivity and specificity approaches 80 percent.[7] It demonstrates sensitivity of the distal esophagus to acid. If the patient's symptoms (heartburn or chest pain) can be reproduced by acid instillation, a working diagnosis of reflux disease is confirmed and the patient treated appropriately. The test can be performed in the office, as it requires only a nasogastric tube and bottles of saline and 0.1N HC1.

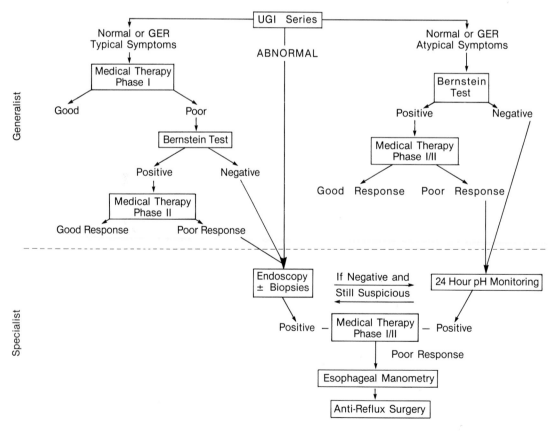

FIGURE 59-1
Symptoms suggestive of gastroesophageal reflux.

Endoscopy with Biopsies

Endoscopic findings of esophagitis provide the most definitive diagnosis of gastroesophageal reflux disease, but these may be absent in up to 50 percent of symptomatic patients.[7] The presence of erosions, friability, exudate, ulcers, or strictures allows a more definitive diagnosis of reflux injury (specificity 95 percent).[7] Mucosal biopsies may improve the diagnostic yield but are unnecessary with clear-cut changes of esophagitis. One exception would be patients with suspected Barrett's esophagus, where a mucosal biopsy is important to identify the abnormal columnar epithelium.

Esophageal Manometry

Although lower esophageal sphincter pressure is a major determinant of gastroesophageal reflux, an *isolated* measurement is not an important diagnostic discriminator. Therefore, manometry should be reserved for patients in whom another diagnosis is suspected (esophageal motility disorder) or prior to antireflux surgery. For patients with severe reflux disease having either weak peristaltic pressures or severely disordered peristalsis, fundoplication may result in severe postoperative dysphagia due to poor esophageal clearance. If this abnormality is noted before surgery, it may provide a warning to the surgeon to do a "loose" plication.

24-Hour pH Monitoring

A pH probe placed 5 cm above the lower esophageal sphincter permits monitoring of esophageal acid exposure through time. It provides the most physiologic measurements of acid reflux incorporating information obtained over an extended time period.[9] A 24-hour ambulatory pH monitoring is now done with the patient in the work or home environment.[10] It is difficult to assess the sensitivity of this test since it is generally accepted as the standard to which other diagnostic tests are compared. Although ambulatory pH systems are readily available, the expense and discomfort of such monitoring makes it appropriate only for the more difficult cases. It may be most helpful in patients with atypical symptoms or those who have clear-cut reflux symptoms in whom other tests have been negative and it may also provide a correlation between pulmonary, ear, nose, and throat, or chest pain symptoms, and reflux episodes.

TREATMENT

Patients with symptomatic gastroesophageal reflux disease should be approached from the point of view that this is usually a long-standing, chronic disease. An overall medical and surgical approach may be structured by dividing current therapies into three phases (Table 59-1).[17]

Lifestyle Modifications

An underemphasized aspect of medical therapy is lifestyle modifications. Elevation of the head of the bed on six-inch blocks significantly decreases nocturnal esophageal acid exposure. Recent studies suggest that this maneuver alone is nearly as effective as an H_2 blocker without head elevation.[12] There are at least two potential benefits of diet modification. Certain foods, including fats, chocolates, excessive alcohol, and carminatives, impair lower esophageal sphincter function, while other foods, including citrus juices, tomato products, and coffee, are direct irritants.[13] In addition, many patients have more symptoms after large meals, particularly if such meals are taken less than 3 hours prior to retiring. Cigarette smoking produces a marked reduction in lower esophageal sphincter pressure and should be avoided. Weight reduction is a traditional component of the treatment of obese patients. Loss of a few critical pounds may be sufficient to control symptoms. Finally, drugs that lower sphincter pressure or interfere with esophageal or gastric emptying may facilitate gastroesophageal reflux. This category includes the anticholinergics, calcium channel blockers, theophylline, diazepam, and beta-adrenergic agonists. If possible, these drugs should be avoided in patients with gastroesophageal reflux disease.

Antacids and Alginic Acid

Antacids are widely used for their acid neutralizing effect and also because they increase lower esophageal sphincter pressure. In uncontrolled studies, antacids seem to be effective in controlling symptoms in 60 to 70 percent

TABLE 59-1
Treatment of Gastroesophageal Reflux Disease

I. Phase I therapy
  A. Lifestyle modification
    1. Elevation of head of bed (6 inches)
    2. Dietary modification
    3. Weight loss
    4. Decrease or stop smoking
    5. Avoid potentially harmful medications
  B. Antacids or alginic acid
II. Phase II therapy
  A. Inhibit gastric acid output: cimetidine, ranitidine, famotidine, nizatidine
  B. Promotility agents—usually used with H_2 blockers
  C. Cytoprotective agents—sucralfate?
III. Phase III therapy
  Antireflux surgery

of patients. However, a recent study suggests antacids may be no more effective than placebo therapy.[14] Nevertheless, in clinical practice, antacids (one dose 30 minutes after meals and at bedtime) and lifestyle modifications appear to be effective in the control of intermittent mild-to-moderate symptoms of reflux disease. Alginic acid combined with antacids (Gaviscon) form a viscous foam which floats on the surface of gastric contents, acting as a mechanical barrier. The usual dose is two tablets chewed 30 minutes after meals and at bedtime. Clinical studies suggest that Gaviscon may be effective in the relief of reflux symptoms, but it is probably no better than antacid therapy.

Histamine—H₂ Blockers

These markedly decrease acid production and are the most potent single agents available for the treatment of gastroesophageal reflux disease. Cimetidine (300 mg with meals and at bedtime) and ranitidine (150 mg bid) have consistently been shown to relieve reflux symptoms and decrease the use of antacids compared to placebo. Both drugs also allow endoscopic and histologic healing of esophagitis, though the data are more convincing for ranitidine.[11] Famotidine and nizatidine appear to be similar in effectiveness to ranitidine, but clinical studies of these agents in reflux disease are still pending. The H₂ blockers should be initial therapy for patients with severe reflux symptoms or endoscopic esophagitis. Unlike their application in treating ulcer disease, H₂ blockers should be administered in divided dosages. Over 50 percent of patients with reflux esophagitis will relapse when medical therapy is discontinued.[15] Therefore, maintenance H₂ blocker therapy may be indicated in these patients. Preliminary studies suggest that divided dosages also will be required for prevention of relapses.

Promotility Drugs

Bethanechol is a cholinergic agent that increases lower esophageal sphincter pressure and improves esophageal acid clearance. Metoclopramide, a dopamine antagonist, increases lower esophageal sphincter pressure and improves gastric emptying. Both drugs decrease reflux symptoms and antacid use, but only bethanechol has been convincingly shown to heal the esophagitis. Promotility drugs may be effective alone, but they are more commonly used in conjunction with H₂ blockers in patients with more recalcitrant reflux symptoms. The development of newer promotility drugs such as domperidone and cisapride may produce more effective agents with fewer side effects.

Sucralfate

Sucralfate binds to ulcerated mucosa, protecting it from acid, pepsin, and bile, thus providing an alternative approach to acid-peptic disease. European studies found sucralfate as effective as antacids, Gaviscon, or H₂ blockers in the treatment of reflux esophagitis. However, preliminary studies from the United States suggest that it may not be as effective. Sucralfate is given in a dose of 1 g 30 minutes before meals and bedtime. In the elderly patient, the large tablet may produce some difficulty with swallowing. This can be avoided by dissolving the tablet in water for 1 or 2 minutes.

Surgery

An estimated 10 percent of reflux patients require surgery because of intractable reflux symptoms or complications. Except for patients with Barrett's esophagus, surgical interventions are seldom necessary in the elderly. The antireflux procedures improve lower esophageal sphincter pressure and decrease reflux episodes. Surgery initially improves symptoms in over 90 percent of patients, but the competency of the surgical repair appears to deteriorate with time.[16]

COMPLICATIONS

Complications of reflux disease generally result from long-standing chronic acid exposure of the distal esophagus.

Peptic Strictures

Strictures result from fibrous scarring of the distal esophagus. Patients with such strictures usually complain of solid-food dysphagia but may or may not have heartburn. Strictures can usually be managed by medical therapy combined with intermittent bougie dilatations as needed to maintain an adequate degree of swallowing.[17] The procedure of dilatation is well tolerated even in the elderly and has a low complication rate.

Barrett's Esophagus

In some patients with long-standing reflux esophagitis, the normal squamous epithelium undergoes metaplastic changes to specialized columnar epithelium, i.e., Barrett's esophagus. The prevalence of this lesion varies. Barrett's esophagus is reported in 11 to 36 percent of patients with endoscopic esophagitis and 44 percent of patients with chronic peptic esophageal strictures.[18] It is usually diagnosed in middle or late life. There is a strong male predominance (65 to 80 percent) of cases, and the disease is rare in blacks. Of great concern, up to one-third of patients presenting with adenocarcinoma associated with Barrett's epithelium describe no prior symptoms of gastroesophageal reflux disease. The prevalence of adenocarcinoma in Barrett's esophagus is about 10 percent. Subsequent development of malignancy in a previously defined Barrett's esophagus, however, is much less frequent (1 in 81 to 1 in 441 cases person/ years). The presence of specialized columnar epithelium, or a long segment of Barrett's esophagus, increases the likelihood of developing an adenocarcinoma. Effective long-term prevention of gastroesophageal reflux is required, but whether this can best be achieved with combination medical therapy or surgery needs to be established. The increased incidence of adenocarcinoma suggests that these patients should be placed in an endoscopic surveillance program, though the rate and frequency of its development is uncertain at this time.

ESOPHAGEAL MOTOR DISORDERS

Recent advances in investigative methods have enabled the classification of esophageal motor disorders in a more logical manner based on manometric and radiologic studies (Table 59-2). These are the only methods that actually assess abnormalities in esophageal peristalsis. Endoscopy contributes little in the evaluation of these diseases since its main role is to rule out mucosal lesions. It has been thought that aging may cause abnormalities in primary peristalsis (presbyesophagus). However, the initial study describing this phenomenon[19] included subjects with a variety of medical disorders such as peripheral neuropathies and diabetes mellitus. When a group of healthy elderly subjects was studied,[20] no defects in peristalsis were seen, although contraction amplitudes were diminished in the very elderly. At present the definition of presbyesophagus thus remains unclear.

ACHALASIA

Achalasia is the best recognized of all the esophageal motor disorders. It is characterized by the absence of normal peristalsis in the smooth muscle portion of the esophagus. Lower esophageal sphincter pressure is generally elevated, and the sphincter does not relax completely on deglutition.[21] These abnormalities are secondary to the absence of ganglion cells in Auerbach's plexuses, resulting in a functional obstruction at the level of the lower esophageal sphincter.

Achalasia is not uncommon in the elderly. Patients usually present with either esophageal or respiratory symptoms. Dysphagia for both solids and liquids is the main esophageal symptom. Postural maneuvers resulting in increase in intrathoracic pressure may facilitate passage of the bolus. Odynophagia is uncommon, but chest pain, presumably secondary to esophageal dysmotility, is not. Heartburn can be present, owing to esophageal stasis rather than reflux. Regurgitation of retained material resulting in aspiration may occur. Weight loss and malnutrition may also be significant.

TABLE 59-2
Esophageal Motor Disorders

Primary esophageal motor disorders
1. Achalasia: Aperistalsis in esophageal body, high lower esophageal sphincter (LES) pressure with incomplete relaxation
2. Diffuse esophageal spasm: Nonperistaltic contractions with intermittent normal peristalsis
3. Nutcracker esophagus: Normal peristalsis with high peristaltic amplitude
4. Hypertensive LES: Mean LES pressure > 50 mmHg with normal relaxation and normal peristalsis
5. Nonspecific esophageal motor disorders

Secondary esophageal motor disorders:
1. Collagen-vascular diseases: progressive systemic sclerosis, systemic lupus erythematosus, etc.
2. Endocrine and metabolic disorders: diabetes mellitus, hyper- and hypothyroidism, amyloidosis
3. Neuromuscular diseases: myotonic dystrophy, myasthenia gravis, multiple sclerosis, Parkinson's disease, cerebrovascular diseases, amyotrophic lateral sclerosis
4. Chronic idiopathic intestinal pseudoobstruction
5. Chagas' disease
6. ? Aging (presbyesophagus)

Diagnosis is confirmed by radiology and esophageal manometry. Occasionally the diagnosis may be made by a chest film showing a markedly dilated and tortuous esophagus with retained food and fluid. Esophagram will show the absence of normal peristaltic activity with or without esophageal dilatation, and the hypertensive lower esophageal sphincter will fail to relax, giving a characteristic "beak" appearance. However, these abnormalities may be missed on routine esophagraphy. Esophageal manometry, therefore, is the diagnostic procedure of choice. Radionuclide testing with both solids and liquids will also demonstrate esophageal retention. Endoscopy is not necessary in establishing the diagnosis of achalasia. However, it is extremely useful in differentiating achalasia from peptic strictures or from a carcinoma at the gastroesophageal junction. Hence, it should be performed in all cases.

The major differential diagnoses are peptic stricture caused by gastroesophageal reflux disease or infiltrating carcinoma arising from the gastroesophageal junction[22] and other types of motor disorders. Esophagram, endoscopy, and manometry would permit the differentiation. Patients with a markedly dilated esophagus from long-standing achalasia also are at an increased risk of developing squamous cell carcinoma of the esophagus.

Pharmacologic therapy with nitrates and calcium channel blockers[23,24] may be tried. By relaxing the smooth muscle, they decrease the lower esophageal sphincter pressure and improve esophageal emptying. Short-term studies suggest that some patients may benefit from these two medications, but long-term drug efficacy data are not available. Mechanical disruption of the lower esophageal sphincter with a balloon dilator (pneumatic dilatation)[25] or surgery[26,27] are the two therapeutic options. The former is performed by placing a specially constructed balloon across the gastroesophageal junction. The balloon is then inflated to mechanically disrupt the lower esophageal sphincter. The major complication is esophageal perforation, which occurs approximately 5 percent of the time. Esophageal myotomy is a surgical procedure in which the muscle at the gastroesophageal junction is cut (Heller myotomy). Its major complication can be severe gastroesophageal reflux disease. Controversy surrounds the initial choice of therapy for patients with achalasia. We recommend performing a pneumatic dilatation first and, if unsuccessful, repeating it once, after which surgery should be performed.

DIFFUSE ESOPHAGEAL SPASM

Diffuse esophageal spasm is characterized by dysphagia and chest pain.[21,28] Esophageal manometry shows normal peristalsis interrupted by simultaneous (nonperistaltic) contractions. As shown in Table 59-2, other abnormalities may also coexist. The pathogenesis is uncertain. Thickening of the esophageal muscular wall has been reported, but ganglion cell loss has not been observed.

Clinically, patients can have chest pain, which may be indistinguishable from cardiac pain. Intermittent and nonprogressive dysphagia for solids and liquids may also occur. Diagnosis is made by esophagram and manometry. Esophagram reveals nonperistaltic contractions with to-and-fro movement and segmentation. Therapy has thus far been disappointing. Short- and long-acting nitrates, anticholinergics or calcium channel blockers can be tried. Pneumatic dilatations may be performed in patients with documented lower esophageal sphincter dysfunction. In patients with intractable symptoms a long myotomy may provide some relief.[29]

OTHER ESOPHAGEAL MOTOR DISORDERS

"Nutcracker esophagus" is characterized by the presence of high-amplitude peristaltic contractions in the distal esophagus with or without increased peristaltic duration. Found in a large number of patients who present initially with noncardiac chest pain, it is thought that the increased peristaltic pressure may be the source of the pain. However, evidence suggests that many patients may have underlying psychological disorders, and the elevated pressure may be just a footprint of these emotional disturbances.[30] Therapeutic trials with calcium channel blockers and antidepressants have shown some promise in treating this ailment.

A variety of other abnormalities also seen on manometry cannot be categorized as achalasia, diffuse esophageal spasm, or nutcracker esophagus. They are collectively known as *nonspecific esophageal motor disorders*. Patients may or may not be symptomatic, and quite often the motor disorder may be secondary to a variety of medical illnesses (Table 59-2). In general, no therapy is needed.

NONCARDIAC CHEST PAIN

At least 20 percent of patients with chest pain undergoing coronary arteriogram will be found to have normal or insignificant coronary artery disease. In at least half of these patients the esophagus may be the potential cause of their discomfort.[31] Nutcracker esophagus is the most common manometric finding. Provocative tests using acid infusion, endrophonium, and balloon distension also may indict the esophagus as the primary cause of chest pain. At this time therapy for many of these disorders remains difficult. Gastroesophageal reflux disease must be ruled out, since it is eminently treatable.

ESOPHAGEAL RINGS AND WEBS

Esophageal rings and webs are thin diaphragmlike membranes interrupting the lumen of the esophagus. They are called *rings* if situated at the squamocolumnar junction, and *webs* if they are located anywhere else along the body of the esophagus.[32] They are common and are often incidental findings at esophagram and endoscopy. The two most common varieties are the cervical esophageal web and the lower esophageal (Schatzki) ring.

CERVICAL ESOPHAGEAL WEBS

A cervical esophageal web is located in the immediate postcricoid area. Women are predominantly affected and may have iron deficiency anemia. This is called the *Patterson-Kelly*, or *Plummer-Vision*, *syndrome*. Cervical web may be an incidental finding, but 15 percent of such patients complain of dysphagia. The pathogenesis of this entity is unknown. The diagnosis is made by cineradiography. Endoscopy may miss this lesion unless the instrument is passed under direct vision. The major differential diagnosis includes inflammatory stricture, postcricoid impression due to venous plexus distension and, most importantly, postcricoid carcinoma. Treatment consists of rupturing the web either with the endoscope or with esophageal bougies.

LOWER ESOPHAGEAL, OR SCHATZKI, RING

Lower esophageal (Schatzki) rings are extremely common, being found with a frequency of 6 to 14 percent in routine barium examinations of the esophagus. Symptomatic rings, however, are far less common, occurring in approximately 0.5 percent of such examinations.[32,33] Lower esophageal rings are found to lie at the squamocolumnar junction. The pathogenesis of the lower esophageal ring is unknown. Although the association is widely cited, there is no definite evidence that the lower esophageal ring is related to gastroesophageal reflux disease.

The lower esophageal ring is probably the most common cause of intermittent solid-food dysphagia. The patient may also present with acute obstruction. The caliber of the ring is the main factor in determining symptoms. In general, rings less than 13 mm in diameter are always symptomatic, whereas rings larger than 20 mm rarely produce symptoms.[34] The absence of an effective propulsive force, i.e., abnormal peristalsis, may also contribute to symptoms in some patients.

Rings are best demonstrated by esophagram. However, the lower esophagus must be adequately distended for the ring to be visualized. A marshmallow or barium tablet may help distend the lower esophagus and confirm the diagnosis. Upper GI endoscopy may miss these rings if the lower esophagus has not been fully distended. Treatment[32,33] consists of esophageal dilatation with a single large-size bougie (i.e., 50 French). Patients not responding may need pneumatic dilatation.

ESOPHAGEAL DIVERTICULA

Esophageal diverticula are divided into three categories: Zenker's diverticulum, arising just above the upper esophageal sphincter; traction or midthoracic diverticulum; and epiphrenic diverticulum, if it arises just above the lower esophageal sphincter. Zenker's and epiphrenic diverticula are thought to result from discoordinated motility, at the cricopharyngeus and lower esophagus, respectively.[35,36] Traction diverticulum was initially thought to be due to scarring and traction on the esophagus by external inflammatory processes in the mediastinum. Recently it has been shown that up to half of these patients have associated esophageal motor disorders.[37]

Patients may complain of dysphagia. This may result from either the associated motor disturbances or because the diverticula become filled with food. In the case of Zenker's, the sac may become noticeable in the neck. These patients may also complain of gurgling, regurgitation of ingested food. These diverticula can become so large that they distort the normal anatomy of the esophagus.

Radiology is the diagnostic approach of choice, since endoscopy may be difficult and even dangerous. Manometry may be helpful in ruling out associated motor disorders. The treatment is surgical. Diverticulectomy is usually done together with therapy directed at the un-

derlying motor disorder. This may include a cervical myotomy in patients with Zenker's and cricopharyngeal discoordination or esophageal myotomy for patients with associated diffuse esophageal spasm or achalasia.[36,38]

MALLORY-WEISS SYNDROME

Mallory-Weiss syndrome proceeds from longitudinal mucosal tears 1 to 5 cm in length along the lower esophagus or gastric fundus. Such tears often straddle the gastroesophageal junction. This is one of the most common causes of upper gastrointestinal bleeding.[39] Two associated clinical events frequently occur. Almost half the patients give a history of excessive alcohol intake. Many will also have retching and vomiting prior to hematemesis. Such tears may also be iatrogenic, having been reported after endoscopy and placement of nasogastric tubes. The tear presumably occurs because of sudden changes in intraabdominal pressure due to retching or vomiting. Whether this lesion is related to hiatal hernia remains to be proved. Bleeding is usually mild but may be of significant volume to produce shock. Diagnosis is made by endoscopy. Upper GI series, in general, is not helpful.

Management is supportive, as most Mallory-Weiss tears will stop bleeding spontaneously. Healing is nearly complete in 3 days. However, up to one-third of patients have continued hemorrhage requiring intervention. Results of nonsurgical intervention, including balloon tamponade, vasopressin infusion, selective embolization and various endoscopic methods, have been inconsistent at best. Surgical intervention may be required.

INFECTIONS OF THE ESOPHAGUS

Infections of the esophagus were once thought to be rare. However, the advent of the barium esophagram and endoscopy with biopsy and cytology have increased the diagnostic yield, particularly in susceptible patients.[40] Esophageal infections occur primarily in patients with underlying disorders such as malignancy (especially leukemia and lymphoma), diabetes mellitus and other endocrine disorders (hypothyroidism, hypoparathyroidism, and hypoadrenalism), a history of using antibiotics, cytotoxic agents, immunosuppressives and corticosteroids, and in those who are immunodeficient or malnourished. However, these infections can also occur in healthy individuals. The two most frequent infections of the esophagus are caused by *Candida albicans* and herpes simplex virus. Symptoms usually consist of dysphagia, odynophagia, substernal burning, and awareness of the food bolus passing down the esophagus, but patients may be asymptomatic. Examination of the oral cavity for lesions can be helpful when present. Absence of oral herpetic or monilial lesions does not rule out esophageal involvement.

CANDIDIASIS

Candida albicans may account for up to 75 percent of esophageal infections. Many of these patients may have no predisposing diseases. The presence of swallowing difficulties in patients with predisposing factors should alert the clinicians to the diagnosis of esophageal candidiasis.[41,42] The diagnosis can be suggested by barium esophagram. However, definitive diagnosis requires endoscopy, biopsy, and cytology. The major differential diagnoses are other infectious causes of esophagitis, and severe gastroesophageal reflux disease. Treatment consists of correcting the underlying predisposing factors together with the institution of nystatin, ketoconazole, or amphotericin B.[43]

HERPES SIMPLEX

Herpes simplex infection of the esophagus is less common than candidiasis. Clinical presentation is similar in both diseases. Radiographically and endoscopically, herpes is characterized by clean, punched-out ulcerations which are quite distinct from candidiasis.[44] However, the two diseases can coexist, particularly in severely immunosuppressed patients. Endoscopy, biopsies with cultures, and cytology are, in general, diagnostic. Intravenous and oral acyclovir is now the treatment of choice.

MEDICATION-INDUCED ESOPHAGEAL INJURY

Esophageal injury as a result of oral medications was first reported in 1970. Since then many cases have been reported.[45] It is now clear that medication-induced esophageal injury may be a commonly overlooked cause of esophageal disease, particularly in the elderly.[46] Doxycycline and other tetracycline preparations are the most common culprits reported in this country. Other potential offending medications included potassium chloride, quinidine, clindamycin, lincomycin, ferrous sulfate, alprenolol, ascorbic acid, phenobarbital, theophyline, cromolyn, aspirin, and a variety of nonsteroidal anti-inflammatory agents.

Esophageal damage is caused by direct injury to the mucosa from prolonged contact with the causative agent. This usually results in a localized inflammatory reaction, culminating in an ulceration and, rarely, in stricture formation.[47] The most common sites of injury are near the level of the aortic arch and the distal esophagus. The former site may be predisposed to injury because of im-

pingement of the great vessels or because of the transition from skeletal to smooth muscle, and also in patients with low peristaltic amplitude. Pills and capsules have been shown to remain in the esophagus of supine healthy subjects, particularly the elderly, for a significant period of time.[46]

Most patients give a characteristic history of dysphagia for the particular offending medications taken at bedtime, followed by the acute onset of odynophagia. A barium examination and/or endoscopy will show the discrete esophageal ulceration, usually in the proximal two-thirds of the esophagus. Treatment consists of withdrawing the offending medication if possible. Viscous lidocaine may be helpful, and it seems reasonable to institute antireflux therapy to minimize further injury. Patients should be instructed to take their medications in the upright position with an ample quantity of liquids and to avoid immediately returning to bed.

TUMORS OF THE ESOPHAGUS

Benign neoplasms of the esophagus such as leiomyoma, lipoma, squamous papilloma and inflammatory polyps are quite rare. They are usually discovered incidentally during radiologic or endoscopic examination performed for nonesophageal complaints. However, they can be symptomatic, requiring surgical or endoscopic removal.

SQUAMOUS CARCINOMA

In the United States black males tend to have the highest risk to develop squamous cell carcinoma of the esophagus. Their incidence is four times that of the white male (15.6 per 100,000 versus 4 per 100,000). The two major identifiable environmental factors that predispose to squamous carcinoma of the esophagus are alcohol and smoking. Other predisposing factors include a history of lye stricture and chronic stasis as a result of untreatable achalasia.

Progressive dysphagia first for solids and then for liquids is the cardinal symptom. This may be accompanied by pain. Anorexia and significant weight loss are also usually present. The occasional patient may present with complications such as aspiration pneumonia or fistula formation. Diagnosis is made by esophagram and endoscopy. Direct biopsies plus cytology will provide histologic confirmation in almost all cases. Benign stricture, particularly as a result of gastroesophageal reflux disease, is the major item in the differential diagnosis. The extent of tumor involvement outside of the esophageal lumen can be assessed by computerized tomography of the chest. Recently endoscopic ultrasonography has been shown to be of some value in staging the disease.

The esophagus is in direct contact with most mediastinal structures. This together with the absence of a serosa leads to early spread of esophageal cancer. Hence, the results of therapy are rather dismal. There is still no general agreement on the best therapy for patients with squamous cell carcinoma of the esophagus.[48,49,51] In Western countries the 5-year survival is less than 10 percent. However, in the Orient, survival rates of about 25 percent have been achieved by performing aggressive surgery[50] and early screening with brush cytology. At this time most patients with localized disease should have surgery as primary therapy. The presence of metastasis will make the patient a candidate for radiation therapy.[51] All squamous cell carcinomas are initially radiosensitive. Most tumors will shrink, and some patients may even achieve a cure.

Since results of treatment are so poor, many palliative methods have been devised. The aim is to alleviate dysphagia so the patient can avoid aspiration and maintain nutrition. This can be achieved by several methods, including periodic esophageal bougie dilatation, placement of an esophageal stent to maintain luminal patency, or application of laser on electrocautery to temporarily relieve the obstruction.[52,53] Tracheoesophageal fistulas can also be temporarily occluded by placement of a stent.

ADENOCARCINOMA

Adenocarcinoma comprises 3 to 7 percent of the malignant carcinomas of the esophagus. It most commonly arises in Barrett's epithelium of the esophagus but occasionally develops from mucous glands deep in the esophagus. The major differentiation is an adenocarcinoma of the gastric fundus with extension into the esophagus. The clinical presentation is similar to squamous carcinoma. Diagnosis is confirmed by endoscopy with biopsies and cytology. Unlike squamous cell carcinoma this lesion is not radiosensitive. Therefore, primary therapy is surgical removal. Unfortunately, because of early metastasis, results are poor and 5-year survival is less than 10 percent.

OTHER DISEASES

The esophagus may be involved in a variety of systemic ailments. Progressive systemic sclerosis is classically associated with esophageal aperistalsis and decreased lower esophageal sphincter pressure. This combination may result in troubling gastroesophageal reflux.[54] Patients with diabetes mellitus and neuropathy can also have esophageal motor disturbance. Fortunately, these patients are usually asymptomatic. Chronic alcoholism together with peripheral neuropathy may also be associated with the loss of primary and secondary peristalsis. Pemphigoid and epidermolysis bullosa can affect the esophagus just as they affect the skin, in the form of bullous lesions. The esophagus can also be affected with deep ulcerations in Behçet's disease. In patients with bone marrow transplant, the esophagus may be involved in graft-versus-host disease. This is characterized by severe inflammation with mucosal fibrosis. Endoscopy and x ray may reveal esophageal webs, strictures, and aperistalsis.

Since many elderly patients are edentulous, with associated esophageal diseases, food impaction is relatively common. Most of these patients can be treated expectantly. However, if the bolus has been impacted in the esophagus for a significant period of time, endoscopic removal may be required.[55] It is imperative that these patients should have an esophageal workup to rule out an underlying esophageal ailment.

REFERENCES

1. Graham DY, Smith JL et al: Why do apparently healthy people use antacid tablets? *Am J Gastroenterol* 78:257, 1983.
2. Thompson WG, Keaton KW: Heartburn and globus in apparently healthy people. *Can Med Assoc J* 126:46, 1982.
3. Brunner PL, Karmody AM et al: Severe peptic esophagitis. *Gut* 10:831, 1969.
4. DeMeester TR, Johnson LF et al: Patterns of gastroesophageal reflux in health and disease. *Ann Surg* 184:459, 1976.
5. DeMeester TR, O'Sullivan GC et al: Esophageal function in patients with angina-type chest pain and normal coronary angiogram. *Ann Surg* 196:488, 1982.
6. Barish CF, Wu WC et al: Respiratory complications of gastroesophageal reflux. *Arch Intern Med* 145:1882, 1985.
7. Richter JE, Castell DO: Gastroesophageal reflux: Pathogenesis, diagnosis and therapy. *Ann Intern Med* 97:93, 1982.
8. Ott DJ, Wu WC et al: Reflux esophagitis revisited. *Gastrointest Radiol* 6:1, 1981.
9. Johnson LF, DeMeester TR: Twenty-four hour pH monitoring of the distal esophagus. A quantitative measure of esophageal reflux. *Am J Gastroenterol* 62:325, 1974.
10. Ward BW, Wu WC et al: Ambulatory 24 hour esophageal pH monitoring: Technology searching for a clinical application. *J Clin Gastroenterol* 8(suppl):59, 1986.
11. Richter JE: A critical review of current medical therapy for gastroesophageal reflux disease. *J Clin Gastroenterol* 8(suppl 1):72, 1986.
12. Harvey RF, Hadley N et al: Effects of sleeping with the bed head raised and of ranitidine in patients with severe peptic oesophagitis. *Lancet* 2:1200, 1987.
13. Richter JE, Castell DO: Drugs, foods and other substances in the cause and treatment of reflux esophagitis. *Med Clin North Am* 65:1223, 1981.

14. Graham DL, Patterson DJ: Double-blind comparison of liquid antacid and placebo in the treatment of symptomatic reflux esophagitis. *Dig Dis Sci* 559, 1983.

15. Liberman DA: Medical therapy for chronic reflux esophagitis. Long-term follow-up. *Arch Intern Med* 147:1717, 1987.

16. Brand DL, Eastwood IR et al: Esophageal symptoms, manometry and histology before and after anti-reflux surgery. *Gastroenterology* 76:1393, 1979.

17. Patterson DJ, Graham DY et al: Natural history of benign esophageal stricture treated by dilatation. *Gastroenterology* 85:346, 1983.

18. Spechler SJ, Goyal RK: Barrett's esophagus. *N Engl J Med* 315:362, 1986.

19. Soergel KH, Zboralski F et al: Presbyesophagus: Esophageal motility in nonagenarians. *J Clin Invest* 43:1472, 1964.

20. Hollis JB, Castell DO: Esophageal function in elderly men: A new look at presbyesophagus. *Ann Intern Med* 80:371, 1974.

21. Castell DO: Achalasia and diffuse esophageal spasm. *Arch Intern Med* 136:571, 1976.

22. Tucker HJ, Snape WJ et al: Achalasia secondary to carcinoma: Manometric and clinical features. *Ann Intern Med* 89:315, 1978.

23. Gelfond M, Rozen P et al: Effect of nitrates on LOS pressure in achalasia: A potential therapeutic aid. *Gut* 22:312, 1981.

24. Bokrtolotti M, Labo G: Clinical and manometric effects of nifedipine in patients with esophageal achalasia. *Gastroenterology* 80:39, 1981.

25. Vantrappen G, Hellemans J: Treatment of achalasia and related motor disorders. *Gastroenterology* 79:144, 1980.

26. Okike N, Payne WS et al: Esophagomyotomy versus forceful dilatation for achalasia of the esophagus: Results in 899 patients. *Ann Thorac Surg* 28:119, 1979.

27. Csendes A, Velsco N et al: A prospective randomized study comparing forceful dilatation and esophagomyotomy in patients with achalasia of the esophagus. *Gastroenterology* 80:789, 1981.

28. Richter JE, Castell DO: Diffuse esophageal spasm. A reappraisal. *Ann Intern Med* 100:242, 1984.

29. Ellis FH, Olsen AM et al: Surgical treatment of esophageal hypermotility disturbances. *JAMA* 188:862, 1964.

30. Richter JE, Obrecht WF et al: Psychological similarities between patients with the nutcracker esophagus and the irritable bowel syndrome. *Dig Dis Sci* 31:131, 1986.

31. Katz PO, Dalton CB et al: Esophageal testing of patients with noncardiac chest pain or dysphagia. *Ann Intern Med* 106:593, 1987.

32. Wu WC: Esophageal rings and webs, in Castell DO, Johnson LF (eds): *Esophageal Function in Health and Disease.* New York, Elsevier, 1983, p 73.

33. Goyal RK, Bauer JL et al: The nature and location of lower esophageal ring. *N Engl J Med* 284:1775, 1971.

34. Schatzki R: The lower esophageal ring: Long-term follow-up of symptomatic and asymptomatic rings. *Am J Roentgenol* 90:805, 1963.

35. Debas HT, Payne WS et al: Physiopathology of lower esophageal diverticulum and its implications for treatment. *Surg Gynecol Obstet* 151:593, 1980.

36. Borrie J, Wilson RL: Esophageal diverticula: Principles of management and appraisal of classification. *Thorax* 35:759, 1980.

37. Kaye MD: Oesophageal motor dysfunction in patients with diverticula of the mid-thoracic oesophagus. *Thorax* 29:666, 1974.

38. Ellis FH, Schlegel JF et al: Cricopharyngeal myotomy for pharyngo-esophageal diverticulum. *Ann Surg* 170:340, 1969.

39. Graham Dy, Schwartz SJ: The spectrum of the Mallory-Weiss tear. *Medicine* 57:307, 1978.

40. Wheeler RR, Peacock JE et al: Esophagitis in the immunocomprised host: Role of esophagoscopy in diagnosis. *Rev Infect Dis* 9:88, 1987.

41. Kodsi BE, Wickremesinghe PC et al: Candida esophagitis: A prospective study of 27 cases. *Gastroenterology* 71:715, 1976.

42. Scott BB, Jenkins D: Gastro-oesophageal candidiasis. *Gut* 23:137, 1982.

43. Horsburgh CR, Kirkplatrick CM: Long-term therapy of chronic mucocutaneous candidiasis with ketoconazole. Experience with 21 patients. *Am J Med* 74(suppl 10):23, 1983.

44. Howiler W, Goldberg HI: Oesophageal involvement in herpes simplex. *Gastroenterology* 70:775, 1976.

45. Kikendall JW, Friedman AC et al: Pill-induced esophageal injury. Case reports and review of the medical literature. *Dig Dis Sci* 28:174, 1983.

46. Eypasch EP, Bailey RT et al: Age influences capsule entrapment in the esophagus. *Gastroenterology* 94:A120, 1988.

47. Bonavina L, DeMeester TR et al: Drug-induced esophageal strictures. *Ann Surg* 206:173, 1987.

48. Parker EF, Moertel CG: Carcinoma of the esophagus: Is there a role for surgery? *Dig Dis Sci* 23:730, 1978.

49. Earlam R, Cunha-Melo JR: Oesophageal squamous cell carcinoma: I. A critical review of surgery. *Br J Surg* 67:31, 1980.

50. Wong J: Esophageal resection for cancer: The rationale of current practice. *Am J Surg* 153:18, 1987.

51. Earlam R, Cunha-Melo JR: Oesopohageal squamous carcinoma: II. A critical review of radiotherapy. *Br J Surg* 67:457, 1980.

52. Peura D, Heit H et al: Esophageal prosthesis in cancer. *Am J Dig Dis* 23:796, 1978.

53. Fleischer D, Kessler F: Endoscopic Nd:Yad laser therapy for carcinoma of the esophagus: A new form of palliative treatment. *Gastroenterology* 85:600, 1983.

54. Turner R, Lipshutz W et al: Esophageal dysfunction in collagen disease. *Am J Med Sci* 265:191, 1973.

55. Webb WA: Management of foreign bodies of the upper gastrointestinal tract. *Gastroenterology* 94:204, 1988.

Chapter 60

DISORDERS OF THE STOMACH AND DUODENUM

Robert M. Kerr

The stomach of the elderly person reflects changes wrought by long years of use (physiological aging) and sometimes abuse (pathological aging). It is well established that most tissues are constantly being destroyed and replaced by a regenerative process at a rate more or less sufficient to maintain the status quo. If regeneration is not quite perfect, over many years, gradual changes can be expected, culminating in obvious histological and physiological modifications. As these alterations are slow to occur and physiological reserves are substantial, it is likely that fairly gross deviations from the original condition are necessary before an individual is aware that something is amiss. Moreover, as organ systems become less efficient, medications are used to bolster their lagging function. However, a chemical that improves one organ system may injure another system directly or adversely affect its physiological function (as is the case with nonsteroidal anti-inflammatory drugs [NSAIDs]). The following topics relating to the stomach and duodenum have been selected for discussion because of their importance and common occurrence in the elderly population: gastritis, peptic ulcer disease, motility disorders, bleeding, and neoplasia.

GASTRITIS

The diagnosis of "gastritis" implies that there is either active inflammation of the gastric mucosa or changes suggestive of prior inflammation. Although gastritis has been a recognized entity for over 100 years, it is only recently that modern endoscopic and biopsy techniques have allowed convenient study. Recent observations coupling histochemical, immunological, and cell kinetic studies suggest the following classification:

Acute gastritis
Chronic atrophic gastritis[1]
   Type A: Fundal changes with a normal antrum
      Superficial
      Chronic
      Atrophic
   Type B: Antral and fundal changes
Hypertrophic gastritis

ACUTE GASTRITIS

Acute gastritis (mucosal damage) can be seen after ingestion of any number of locally toxic substances.[2] The elderly may be more prone to such occurrences. Not only are their normal defenses commonly diminished by aging, but they also take more medications as they age, some of which directly injure the mucosa. In other words, insults that a younger stomach might absorb with impunity are more likely to result in more profound symptoms and signs in the elderly. Alcohol and NSAIDs are the primary agents that cause acute injury. There is also much current interest in the role of *Campylobacter pylori* in this process.[3] Other bacterial infections, as well as viral and fungal agents, are also causal possibilities. An aging stomach often produces less of the acid[4,5] that ordinarily kills most ingested organisms; hence, gastric infections are more prevalent in the elderly. One proposed consequence of this change is an increased risk to bacterial aspiration pneumonia in elderly persons with gastroesophageal reflux (including that secondary to indwelling nasogastric tubes). Mucosal biopsy of the stomach reveals variable superficial inflammatory changes, depending on the cause.

Symptoms are nonspecific. Some patients have none, while others develop vague, ill-defined upper gastrointestinal (GI) complaints such as anorexia, bloating, and intermittent nausea. Weight loss may be a problem with protracted symptoms. Routine tests are unremarkable. The diagnosis is usually made by history and endoscopic findings. Generally, the disease is relatively short-lived and heals spontaneously; therefore, treatment is supportive. The physician should discontinue NSAIDs when possible and add antinauseants if necessary. If *Campylobacter pylori* is identified, a trial of one of the antibiotics known to affect this organism followed by bismuth is worth consideration, but there are scant data to support such treatment to date.

CHRONIC GASTRITIS

Chronic gastritis is common in the general population. Random biopsy samples reveal an increase with age and a slight male preponderance.[4,6] Chronic gastritis can predominantly involve either the fundus (type A) or the antrum (type B).

Fundal Gastritis (Type A)

The antrum is usually normal in a patient with fundal gastritis. Histological changes in the fundus have one of three possible appearances: (1) superficial gastritis, (2) chronic gastritis, and (3) gastric atrophy. With superficial gastritis, an uncommon condition, an infiltrate of lymphocytes and plasma cells is limited to the outer one-third of the mucosa, and the fundal glands appear normal. This picture contrasts with that of atrophic gastritis, in which the full thickness of the mucosa is involved. In this circumstance gland tubules show varying degrees of atrophy and some appear to be absent. Chief and parietal cells are decreased. Spaces left by disappearing structures are replaced by mucus-secreting glands, and scattered goblet cells are seen. Gastric atrophy is distinguished by the *absence* of fundal glands. Epithelium and crypts have been replaced by goblet cells. Inflammatory changes are minimal or entirely absent. These changes are considered "intestinal metaplasia" because the tissue takes on the appearance of intestinal epithelium; absorptive function and histochemical changes compatible with intestinal epithelium have also been described. There are two types of intestinalization. One has the appearance of the small bowel, with Paneth's and endocrine cells; the other, with increased goblet cells and no Paneth's cells, is more reminiscent of the colon.[7]

The loss of parietal cells is associated with reduced or absent acid production. Because the antrum is normal in cases of fundal gastritis, serum gastrin levels can be remarkably elevated.[8,9] Antibodies to the parietal cell, as well as binding and blocking antibodies to intrinsic factor, are often detected, and when these antibodies are present, vitamin B_{12} malabsorption is common. Thyroid antibodies are present in greater than 50 percent of patients with pernicious anemia, while parietal cell antibodies are more commonly identified with Hashimoto's thyroiditis, thyrotoxicosis, and hypothyroidism. Whether the presence of various antibodies is the cause or the result of histological changes remains controversial.[10]

Antral Gastritis (Type B)

The antrum is primarily involved in antral gastritis, with variable changes in the fundus. Antral histology is hard to evaluate because the mucosa is thick and normally has some cellular infiltrate. The degree of infiltration, whether the pyloric glands are obliterated, and the extent of intestinal metaplasia are subjective attributes used to grade antral gastritis. Serum gastrin is often reduced. Parietal cell antibodies are usually absent, and impairment of acid secretion is generally mild. Associated lesions include gastric ulcer and gastric cancer. The genesis of type B gastritis is thought to involve some "environmental" factors, such as the chronic ingestion of nitrates or other irritants. In a comprehensive review of *Campylobacter pylori*, the concept that this organism is responsible for type B gastritis is persuasively presented.[11]

Clinical Concerns

Clinical manifestations of chornic gastritis are nonspecific and include early satiety, weight loss, and bloating after meals. Some patients with antral gastritis paradoxically complain of heartburn (rarely with nocturnal awakening). As many as 60 percent of patients have no complaints. The diagnosis may be suggested radiographically by loss of normal gastric fold pattern. However, endoscopy with biopsy is considered the diagnostic procedure of choice. Currently, gastric secretory testing is not routinely practiced. Measurement of serum pepsinogen I may be of some interest, as it is elevated in superficial gastritis[12] and decreased in severe atrophic gastritis.[13]

Treatment

In the treatment of chronic gastritis, dyspeptic symptoms of some patients with achlorhydria will (paradoxically) respond to antacids. Likewise, the empirical use of 2 teaspoons of a mixture of equal parts of elixir Benadryl (diphenhydramine hydrochloride), liquid Donnatal, and a liquid antacid taken half an hour before meals may also relieve symptoms in some patients. This prescription seems particularly useful for patients with type A gastritis. Many patients with chronic gastritis are afraid that they have cancer. Once the nature of the problem is correctly identified, reassurance goes a long way toward relieving or at least making the complaints tolerable. With severe type B gastritis, if *Campylobacter pylori* is identified, a trial of treatment is reasonable. Anemia can occur with either variety of gastritis. It is important to correctly classify and treat the underlying cause.

Complications

The complications of chronic gastritis include an increased likelihood of gastric carcinoid. Many atrophic patients have a markedly elevated serum gastrin. Gastrin is known to be trophic for the enterochromaffin-like cells. Perhaps, this explains why there is an increased prevalence of carcinoid in the stomachs of patients with gastric atrophy. A small proportion of such patients (20 percent) will have metastases when the carcinoid is first identified, confirming the malignant potential.[14] Adenocarcinoma of the stomach is also increased in patients with atrophic gastritis. Some studies suggest that antral gastritis has the closer association. Fortunately, malignancies are slow to develop and seem related to the duration of the condition. The progression from superficial to atrophic gastritis may take up to 20 years.[15] Among those with chronic gastritis, some will develop cancer in the evolution of these changes, but it is not possible to identify who is especially at risk. Of 116 patients with atrophic gastritis followed for 22 to 26 years, approximately 10 percent developed cancer.[6] Other studies have shown a similar incidence, but these studies were of shorter duration (6 to 20 years), and it was not clear how long the gastritis had actually been present before the diagnosis was made.[16] On the negative side, one recent study failed to document an increased cancer risk for patients with pernicious anemia.[17]

How should the clinician manage this group of patients who may have an increased chance for developing cancer? On the one hand, it intuitively seems that the early detection of gastric cancer should be lifesaving. Moreover, if the technology is available to provide screening, it should be used regardless of cost. On the other hand, to endorse such an approach would expose the majority of these patients to the expense and hazard of endoscopy and biopsy with little chance of finding a significant lesion. Furthermore, there is little to indicate that early diagnosis of these cancers makes the patient more comfortable or prolongs life. Thus a reasonable approach is to offer a screening examination every 5 years or as needed, should there be a change in symptoms. Obviously, other health factors will weigh heavily as to when and whether screening should be undertaken.

HYPERTROPHIC GASTRITIS

Ménétrier described diffuse thickening of the gastric wall by excessive proliferation of the mucosa about 100 years ago. In this circumstance the weight of the stomach is increased and the folds are often greater than 1 cm wide and 3 cm high. Increased polymorphonuclear leukocytes are present in dilated crypts, while increased lymphocytes occur in the muscularis mucosa and lamina propria. Symptoms are nonspecific and include anorexia, nausea, occasionally vomiting, postprandial aching epigastric pain, and, in some cases, profound weight loss. Protein loss may occur through the enlarged gastric folds, causing hypoproteinemia with its associated symptoms. The major difference between patients with and patients without protein loss is that the former have a greater incidence of weight loss, edema, diarrhea, and skin rash. The differential diagnosis of hyperrugosity of the stomach includes the Zollinger-Ellison syndrome, lymphoma, histoplasmosis, and even secondary syphilis. Endoscopic snare biopsy is most useful in establishing the diagnosis. The use of H_2 blockers is the initial treatment of choice, although improvement is often transient with their use. There have been anecdotal reports of therapeutic success with corticosteroids, anticholinergics, and tranexamic acid. Surgery may be necessary for unremitting pain that does not yield to other treatment attempts.[18]

PEPTIC ULCER

A number of ingredients, whether acting alone, or in various combinations, are thought to be responsible for the genesis of gastric and duodenal ulcers. The gastrointestinal mucosa is constantly bombarded by substances capable of causing injury (acid, pepsin, and various ingested substances), but the potential for significant damage is normally nicely balanced by a remarkable defensive armament (mucous, mucosal blood flow, epithelial cell proliferation, and so on). Thus, minor insults are steadily delivered to the mucosa, but ordinarily the extent of injury is limited, and repair is prompt. An extraordinary insult in the face of a normal defense mechanism or else a routine attack against decreased defenses can upset this process and cause more extensive mucosal injury. Ordinarily, it is neither purely one circumstance or another but rather some combination of circumstances that results in ulceration. When the results of an attack are sufficiently gross, the patient is aware of symptoms and the clinician is likely to observe inflammation and/or ulceration in the mucosa on radiologic or endoscopic examination.

The fundamental ability to produce acid and pepsin, as well as the characteristics that offer mucosal protection, is genetically determined. With advancing age, all these factors are altered, but not always simultaneously nor to the same degree. Moreover, the less robust mucosa of the elderly person may also be exposed to various toxic insults (e.g., tobacco, ethanol, or NSAIDs) which tilt the delicate balance of damage and repair toward destruction. That ulcers occur in small areas illustrates the importance of local factors; if local factors did not matter, the entire mucosal surface would tend to slough. As is the case with type B gastritis, there is much current interest in the role of *Campylobacter pylori* in the pathogenesis and persistence of ulcers, but whether these organisms are found in the presence of injured mucosa, or injure the mucosa by their presence, remains controversial. Thus, there are remarkable similarities in the pathogenesis of gastric and duodenal ulcers; that different portions of the upper gut are affected reflects discrepancies in the way the stomach and duodenum defend themselves against acid, pepsin, and other insults.

GASTRIC ULCER

The incidence of gastric ulcer rises with age.[19] Gastric ulcers are generally located on the lesser curvature on the border between antral and acid-secreting mucosa. The migration of this junction toward the gastric fundus with advancing age explains why gastric ulcers in the stomach of the elderly patient are often located high on the lesser curvature.[4] Gastric ulcers account for nearly one-half the peptic ulcers in patients over age 60 and for most of the ulcers requiring surgery.[20] With increasing patient age, the frequency of complications also rises. About one-half of patients over age 70 with ulcers can be expected to suffer significant complications.[5] Bleeding is the major problem and often occurs without prior symptoms. Recurrent hemorrhage within a week of the initial episode of bleeding has been reported in as many as 30 percent of patients with bleeding ulcers.[21] Perforation, the other major complication, is often accompanied by an excess risk of mortality[22] because collapse of other organ systems may so dominate the clinical picture that abdominal pain is subdued and poorly localized, and the diagnosis may thereby be delayed by as much as 24 hours.

Obstruction from gastric ulcers is rare. Cancer of the stomach is not a true complication of gastric ulcers. Chronic irritation caused by the ulcer does not lead to a malignant change; rather, malignancies ulcerate and then masquerade as benign ulcers. As many as 5 percent of all gastric ulcers may be malignant at diagnoses.[23,24] Giant ulcers (3 cm in diameter or more) are also more

common in the elderly. The symptoms of giant ulcers are atypical and often of short duration; about one-half of patients with giant ulcers will experience a major hemorrhage, while perforation is surprisingly infrequent. The majority of giant gastric ulcers are benign.[25,26]

DUODENAL ULCER

The majority of patients with duodenal ulcers do not have excessive acid output. Moreover, there is a gradual decrease in gastric acid production with advancing age. For these reasons, a less robust defense against acid and pepsin is thought to be central in the genesis of ulcers in the elderly and would account for the fact that there is no reduction in the incidence of duodenal ulcers with advancing age.[27,28] The complications of duodenal ulcer are similar to those of gastric ulcer, though outlet obstruction is much more common with duodenal ulcer. With advancing age, the frequency of complications increases in a fashion similar to that noted for gastric ulcer, with hemorrhage and perforation as the dominant problems. Duodenal ulcers are seldom confused with malignancy because cancer of the duodenum is extremely rare. Giant duodenal ulcers are uncommon but are important to diagnose.[29,30] These are ulcers that are greater than 2 cm in diameter, involve a substantial portion of the duodenal bulb, are more common in males (generally in their seventies), and often appear without antecedent symptoms. The pain of giant duodenal ulcer may mimic pancreatic or biliary disease. Weight loss is common because food ingestion aggravates the pain. The most frequent complication is bleeding (often massive), while perforation occasionally occurs. Duodenal obstruction can be present, but it usually develops late in the evolution of giant duodenal ulcers. Low albumin levels have been reported and reflect poor nutrition, as well as protein loss through the large ulcer bed.

CLINICAL MANIFESTATIONS

Symptoms accompanying either gastric ulcer or duodenal ulcer are variable. Gnawing epigastric discomfort that occurs an hour or so after meals and is relieved by food is common to both ailments. Pain immediately increased by eating is more usual with gastric ulcer. Nocturnal wakening with either ulcer suggests a more aggressive process. Back pain, more common with duodenal ulcer, can be the patient's presenting symptom and clouds the issue by suggesting an orthopedic or pancreatic problem. Many patients complain of anorexia, bloating, and a change in bowel habits. Both gastric and duodenal ulcers may be accompanied by chronic blood loss to the extent that cardiac and/or nervous system may overshadow symptoms of the gut. Acute hemorrhage can be the presenting manifestation of either type of ulcer.

Patients who bleed are generally older (over age 65), have a prior history of complications, and often have been taking NSAIDs.[31]

DIAGNOSIS

The possibility of an ulcer is suggested by history and by physical examination. With a history of duodenal ulcer spanning many years, the development of nausea and vomiting may suggest scarring of the duodenum and gastric outlet obstruction. Observing undigested food in the vomitus or eliciting a succussion splash are important diagnostic clues. Positive identification of an ulcer requires visualization of the stomach and duodenum. Endoscopy is more accurate than x ray and for this reason is preferred. Although either method is ordinarily satisfactory, a confusing radiographic appearance may require endoscopic clarification. The major endoscopic hazard is respiratory depression from overzealous premedication. Most elderly patients require very little sedative, and the endoscopic procedure is generally well tolerated.

TREATMENT

The dictum of "no acid, no ulcer" remains true for both benign gastric and duodenal ulcers. Accordingly, treatment for either variety consists of modifying acid production and bolstering mucosal defenses. Dietary manipulation is useful only insofar as it may alleviate symptoms. The patient is advised to eat at least three small, nutritious meals per day, avoid foods known to aggravate symptoms, and discontinue use of any exogenous ulcer-promoting substances such as NSAIDs, ethanol, and tobacco. Once these issues are addressed, other options which may accelerate ulcer healing include (1) neutralizing acid after its production, (2) interfering with acid production, and (3) protecting the damaged mucosa. In prospective controlled studies, there is no significant difference among these options regarding the results of short-term treatment. The choice among these options depends primarily on the clinical situation, but it is also influenced to some extent by patient/physician preference and economics.

A small, uncomplicated ulcer causing only daytime symptoms is best treated with antacids. (Be aware that antacids vary considerably in their sodium content.) With nocturnal awakening, a potent H_2 blocker taken at bedtime for 6 to 8 weeks is advisable. Ranitidine and famotidine seemingly have fewer adverse central nervous system effects than cimetidine, but cimetidine is equally good if the patient is known to tolerate this medication. Nizatidine is too new to permit comments as to its relative utility. Vigorous acid suppression at night is sensible, because this is the time when intragastric pH is normally low and there is no convenient way of dealing with this phenomenon. It is acceptable to add daytime antacids if necessary. If an ulcer is due to NSAIDs, recurrence is uncommon if the NSAIDs are stopped. Gastric and duodenal ulcers not attributable to NSAIDs are prone to recur, but the average time before recurrence is approximately 4 months.[32] For this reason, it is acceptable to discontinue treatment after an initial response and reinstitute it as needed.

Sucralfate, while it does not affect hydrogen ion secretion or neutralize acid, offers the same increase in the rate of healing as that produced by H_2 blockers. This effect is apparently a reflection of several of sucralfate's properties.[33] One is that the disassociated sucralfate molecule adheres to the base of the ulcer and protects it from the action of acid-activated pepsin. This protective effect allows maximum epithelial growth from the ulcer margin. Also, sucralfate apparently stimulates endogenous prostaglandin formation, enhances mucosal bicarbonate production, and binds to pepsin and bile. An alternative medication, tripotassium dicitrato bismuthate (TDB), a colloidal bismuth preparation, has been extensively studied over a number of years outside the United States. While its mode of action is generally similar to that of sucralfate, it has been found to inhibit *Campylobacter pylori* growth. TDB is not available in this country, but bismuth sodium tartrate (Pepto-Bismol) apparently has a similar effect. Although the role of *Campylobacter pylori* has stirred much investigative activity, identification and eradication of this organism remains controversial, as does its relationship to ulcer cause and treatment.[34]

If a patient has had a giant ulcer healed medically or suffered a serious complication (bleed or perforation), then long-term H_2 blocker use is recommended. This usage should be continued for at least 1 year; indefinite treatment is recommended for the very old and/or infirm who have had major hemorrhage not related to NSAID use. In the case of a "silent bleed" there are no specific guidelines, but it would seem appropriate to continue use of H_2 blockers longer and make sure that other factors promoting ulcers have been eliminated. As for pyloric and duodenal obstruction, balloon dilatation may be considered depending on the clinical situation.

Where treatment of duodenal and gastric ulcers differs is in relation to follow-up. Usually duodenal ulcers, once diagnosed, can be treated with confidence as long as the patient feels better. Subsequent assessment of healing is not necessary. In contrast, because a small percentage of gastric ulcers are actually malignancies, following the patient with gastric ulcer to the point of documented healing is prudent. If the ulcer was initially well-seen radiographically, follow-up x rays should suffice. However, if the ulcer was missed outright, or the roentgen signs are equivocal, or the ulcer fails to heal in a reasonable period of time, endoscopic follow-up is required. A persistently nonhealing ulcer always raises the question of patient compliance versus malignancy. Considering the cost of some medications, patient compliance may be a significant problem. Surgery is generally reserved for treatment of complications and nonhealing gastric ulcers.

GASTRIC EMPTYING DISORDERS

During and after a meal, the fundus of the stomach functions as a reservoir while the antrum is a grinding, mixing, and pumping station. It is well known that fluids empty from the stomach more rapidly than solids and that solids will not empty until their size is reduced to less than 2 mm in diameter. How the stomach distinguishes between fluid and solid is unknown. Between meals, vigorous contractile activity begins in the stomach, sweeps down the antrum and across the pylorus, and proceeds down the small bowel to the colon. These contractions are so vigorous that the stomach is purged of any debris retained due to insufficient size reduction. The mechanisms controlling these complex processes have not been thoroughly explained, but they involve a delicate coordination of neural and hormonal events. It is probable that a single lapse in any one or a combination of these processes will result in a gastric emptying disorder. It seems likely that the aging process exacts a toll in this regard, but it is uncertain to what degree. Crucial factors include a patient's medical condition and medication requirements. In any event, it is well known that many puzzling symptoms can be explained by defects in the gastric motility process. Several recent reviews discuss various aspects of gastric motility and its disorders.[35–38]

CLINICAL CONCERNS

Rapid gastric emptying is usually a result of gastric surgery. Postgastrectomy symptoms include gastrointestinal symptoms (nausea, vomiting, pain, and diarrhea) and vasomotor symptoms (sweating, tachycardia, flushing, etc.). This is not a special problem of aging and will not be discussed further. In contrast, impaired gastric emptying, while it can be found at any age, is perhaps more common in the elderly. Many possible causes can contribute to poor emptying of the stomach, and they can be easily confused with other medical problems. Conditions resulting in slowed gastric emptying are termed *gastric stasis syndromes*, while the result is identified as *gastroparesis*.

Historical features are often vague. Frequent complaints include early satiety, bloating, chronic nausea, and weight loss. Vomiting, if present, often occurs late in the day, and the vomitus may contain food eaten a num-

ber of hours before the occurrence. A succussion splash observed 4 hours after a patient's last ingestion of food or fluid is a characteristic physical finding. Because the symptoms are vague, the first test performed is often an upper GI x ray. This x ray will not yield useful information unless food in a large atonic stomach is observed when the patient is known to have fasted for many hours prior to the examination. To eliminate the possibility of a remediable mechanical outlet obstruction, endoscopy is advisable. Although there are numerous marker techniques and considerable day-to-day variation within single subjects,[39] the best diagnostic method to confirm the clinical impression is that of a solid-phase gastric emptying study. This study need not be performed on every patient, but it is helpful for a patient who has bothersome symptoms that are unexplained by other tests.

The most common cause for impaired gastric emptying is anatomic obstruction. Such an obstruction is usually the result of duodenal or pyloric scarring from chronic peptic ulcer, but antral carcinoma must be considered, especially in the elderly. In the absence of outlet obstruction, there are a number of potential causes for gastroparesis, including disorders of the central nervous system (CNS), drugs (particularly those with anticholinergic properties and pain medications), diabetes (autonomic dysfunction), muscular disorders (myopathies, scleroderma), and a small number of causes that remain "idiopathic" for lack of some other clinical association. The condition may be transient (as is medication-induced gastroparesis) or permanent.

TREATMENT

Therapy is not always satisfactory. First the physician must identify and eliminate causes such as drugs that impair gastric emptying, diabetes, or remedial CNS problems. Those patients who do not respond to simple remedial measures may benefit from dietary modification because the stomach handles liquids differently than solids. Small, frequent feedings of a liquid or blenderized diet is sometimes useful. The patient who is still symptomatic may benefit from the addition of pharmacological agents. The available options are bethanechol, metoclopramide, domperidone, and Cisapride. Bethanechol, a cholinergic agent, can be tried in doses of 10 to 20 mg before meals, although response to treatment is inconsistent.[40] Side effects are generally infrequent and mild; if there is no response at these levels, it is unlikely that larger doses will improve results. Metoclopramide acts both centrally and peripherally. The central effect is to suppress the chemoreceptor trigger zone (CTZ), while the peripheral effect may be related to local release of acetylcholine, sensitization of muscarinic receptors, or inhibition of dopamine.[41] At a dose of 10 mg, taken before meals, a significant number of patients will experience symptoms of irritability and excitation; dystonic reactions can also occur. Because the drug elevates prolactin levels, galactorrhea, breast enlargement, and menstrual disorders have been reported in nonelderly individuals. Patients experiencing side effects can sometimes tolerate a small dose of metoclopramide in combination with bethanechol. Domperidone blocks dopaminergic receptors peripherally and has very few (if any) CNS effects because it does not cross the blood-brain barrier and has no cholinergic activity.[42] Domperidone is available in this country on a compassionate use basis, and it may be worth trying in patients with serious problems who may benefit from metoclopramide but cannot tolerate the side effects. Cisapride (Janssen Pharmaceutica, Inc.) is a recent addition to the list of gastrointestinal "prokinetic" agents. In contrast to metoclopramide and domperidone, Cisapride has no antidopaminergic properties[43] but acts mainly to release acetylcholine from myenteric nerves.[44] Cisapride increases gastric emptying in normal subjects,[45] dyspeptic subjects with delayed gastric emptying,[46] and subjects with progressive systemic sclerosis.[47] Like domperidone, it may be available on a compassionate-use basis for selected patients.

GI BLEEDING

Upper GI bleeding is a major problem in the elderly that is associated with a high mortality (10 to 25 percent).[48,49] This rate may increase to 50 percent if massive bleeding alone (loss of 25 percent or more, of blood volume) is considered.[48] Azotemia, peripheral vascular failure, and dehydration can develop quickly. These complications are challenging to manage in a fragile patient who may have marginal cardiac reserve. Thus, an important objective in dealing with bleeding patients is to recognize early those who have massive hemorrhage which is unlikely to respond to medical management or who are likely to have recurrent bleeding episodes. In this special group, avoiding needless delay in surgical intervention should minimize complications and improve overall survival. Important causes of bleeding from the stomach and duodenum in the elderly are (1) Mallory-Weiss tear, (2) gastric or duodenal ulcer, (3) malignancy, (4) Dieulafoy lesion,[50] (5) bleeding from hiatal hernia,[51] (6) gastritis, and (7) vascular malformations.[52]

Vomiting of blood leaves no doubt that a patient's hemorrhage is from the upper gut. Occasionally a patient with upper GI bleeding will not vomit blood but will instead produce maroon-colored stools. Marooncolored stools indicate that the blood was not greatly altered by passing through the intestine. One possibility is that bleeding was low in the gut and, due to the proximity of the rectum, was retained long enough to cause

minor changes in appearance. Alternatively, an upper GI source may produce a similar result; however, this takes a massive hemorrhage, and it is likely the patient will have a history of syncope and/or shock. A more leisurely bleeding episode is usually accompanied by shortness of breath, weakness, melena, and sometimes syncope. If there is some doubt that the bleeding is of upper gut origin, then an abruptly rising blood urea nitrogen (BUN) may provide a useful clue, as this is not expected if bleeding comes from the lower gut.

During the history and physical examination, venous access with one or more large-bore IVs should be established and blood components administered as required. It is important to avoid fluid overload in an elderly patient with a marginal cardiorespiratory reserve; thus, it is prudent to have some means of monitoring central venous pressure. If the bleeding is massive and the patient has taken aspirin within 5 to 6 days, or other NSAIDs within 2 to 3 days, then the possible need for platelets should be considered. Despite the lack of convincing data to support the use of H_2 blockers in the actively bleeding patient[53] (a view not universally shared[54]), most centers continue to use acid-reducing and/or acid-neutralizing therapy. Continuous infusion of H_2 blockers would seem to be the most logical approach,[55] although the risk of delirium and other effects (especially with cimetidine) requires careful consideration and surveillance. At least initially, a nasogastric (NG) tube is useful until a better grasp of the source and extent of bleeding is established. Gross blood from an NG tube guarantees an active upper GI source; however, bleeding can be intermittent, so a negative aspirate does not rule out an upper GI source. In the presence of *active* bleeding, almost all clinicians would agree that maintaining an NG tube in place is appropriate, as this may give an early clue to accelerating blood loss. Moreover, the tube will be necessary should surgery be required. Water or saline lavage may be helpful in evaluating the extent of the bleeding. In the elderly it is better to use water so as to avoid an inadvertent salt load. Whether the water should be iced or at room temperature is debatable; room temperature water interferes less with blood coagulation.[56] The question of whether *all* upper GI bleeders should have an NG tube also remains controversial. For example, in a patient who has stopped bleeding, an NG tube may give an early warning of recurrent bleeding before a change in the central venous pressure is observed, but in some cases the presence of the tube may actually promote recurrent bleeding. Finally, if an upper GI source has been identified from which there is neither active bleeding nor a significant risk for rebleeding, then it is best to leave the NG tube out.

While some studies suggest that mortality and transfusion requirements are not significantly altered by early endoscopy, most accept the notion that it is more comfortable to manage bleeding when its source and nature are known. Elderly patients tolerate endoscopy with little discomfort and no appreciable risk of increased morbidity.[57] Moreover, with endoscopy the severity of the bleeding can be assessed and certain patients suitable for early surgery singled out. About 85 percent of all upper GI bleeding episodes can be expected to stop spontaneously. Can patients who are going to continue bleeding be identified early? Endoscopic as well as clinical clues may help in this regard. The majority of cases in which there is an active spurting of blood on initial endoscopy will require surgery; it is best not to delay. In the case of oozing, probably half will need urgent surgery. In this case, if the patient is stable and has tolerated the bleeding well, it is reasonable to closely monitor the evolution of the bleeding episode but to be poised to proceed directly to surgery should the need arise. If the bleeding has stopped, and there is an adherent clot (either fresh or old) or visible vessel, there is a significant chance for rebleeding, although the incidence will vary. If one opts for medical management, careful monitoring is mandatory. In general, gastric ulcers are more likely to rebleed than duodenal ulcers, but the presence of an ooze or clot in conjunction with either variety may have mortal consequences.[58] Specific lesions prone to rebleeding include giant ulcers, Dieulafoy lesions, malignancies, and vascular ectasias. Clean gastric and duodenal ulcers, Mallory-Weiss tears, and gastritis are less likely to bleed again, and conservative management can be continued with reasonable confidence.

Clinical presentation is also extremely useful in predicting outcome. For example, a patient who presents with a sudden hemorrhage culminating in shock is obviously bleeding from a large vessel. Clearly, fibrin plugs in a large vascular defect are likely to be unstable, and recurrent bleeding will be common. The severity of the bleed is also reflected in the transfusion requirements. At the time of admission, approximately one-third of patients will not require transfusion, approximately one-third will require less than 4 units of blood, and the remaining one-third will have bleeding that is heavy and recurrent. The majority needing surgery are from this last group (requiring greater than 6 units of blood[59]). If there is a reasonable indication for surgery and a major medical complication does not coexist, elderly patients will tolerate the surgery surprisingly well. An occasional severe bleeder will have such an overwhelming surgical risk that laser, heater probe, bipolar electrocautery, or even radiological intervention are considered.[60] Generally, patients in such desperate straits have a dismal outcome regardless of treatment efforts, and they are probably best served by offering meticulous supportive care. Clearly, medical/surgical management of the fragile,

unstable, elderly bleeding patient with multiple medical problems remains a major challenge.

GASTRIC NEOPLASMS

ADENOCARCINOMA

Gastric cancer has for unknown reasons been decreasing in prevalence in this country. Several decades ago it was the most common type of cancer in the United States, but it now ranks third in frequency among GI neoplasms. In this country, the incidence remains in the range of 25,000 new cases per year, the majority of which occur in the over-60 population.[61] A 2 to 1 male preponderance persists. Dietary factors traditionally have been suspected to play an important role. Much effort has been devoted to the identification of carcinogens that might be responsible. Some of these are food contaminates (polycyclic hydrocarbons) while others (nitrosamines) may be produced in the stomach in vivo. Genetics may play a role, but this has been hard to prove. Preexisting conditions that may be considered premalignant include atrophic gastritis, subtotal gastrectomy, and polyps.

Gastric neoplasms vary widely in appearance. The possibilities range from polypoid lesions growing into the lumen of the stomach to diffuse infiltrating neoplasms that can come to involve the entire stomach wall (either of which may be ulcerated), or any variation between these extremes. Early gastric cancer, first reported by the Japanese in the early 1960s, was originally thought to be confined to Japan. In recent years it has been identified in most other areas of the world, albeit less commonly. By definition, early gastric cancer neoplasms are superficial and, at the time of detection, show no evidence of spread; thus, early recognition is important to ensure a favorable outcome. Screening for early gastric cancer is routinely practiced in Japan, where 90 percent 5-year survival rates are reported. In the United States the tumor is relatively unusual (4 to 13 percent of all gastric cancers[62,63]) making routine evaluation of asymptomatic patients impractical. The majority of gastric neoplasms that are ulcerated begin in the antrum and metastasize early, while the polypoid tumors are more likely to be in the proximal stomach. Direct invasion of adjacent organs, as well as blood and lymphatic metastases, are common.

Most gastric cancer in the United States is detected at a time when it has already spread. Partially contributing to this feature is an average delay of 6 to 12 months between onset of symptoms and establishment of diagnosis. Loss of taste for meats, as well as early satiety and nausea, is probably responsible for the weight loss noted in 70 to 80 percent of patients with gastric cancer. The decreased food intake contributes to the common complaint of constipation. Pain is reported in about 70 percent of patients, but there is nothing characteristic in its description, and the location varies widely. Some patients may experience a fullness relieved with belching, while others will have nonspecific dyspeptic complaints simulating peptic ulcer disease. Chronic blood loss is common but hematemesis is unusual. The location of the tumor may dictate the presenting complaint. For example, tumors involving the fundus often cause dysphagia, while antral tumors may give gastric outlet obstruction. Metastases cause symptoms based on the location and may contribute to the development of ascites, jaundice, and neurological symptoms. When the initial presenting symptoms of patients with "early gastric cancer" are compared with those of patients harboring advanced disease, it turns out that most individuals in both groups were studied because of "indigestion." Thus, the hope of identifying gastric cancer at an early stage by history is remote; by the time symptoms occur, the disease is usually well-established. The physical examination is equally unrewarding other than that the patient looks poorly, has evidence of weight loss, and may demonstrate evidence of complications due to metastatic disease.

Routine laboratory examinations are appropriate in patients with gastric cancer. However, sophisticated tests such as pepsinogen I, carcinoembryonic antigen (CEA), gastrins, and gastric analysis, while of some academic interest, have little practical value in clearly establishing the diagnosis. Upper GI x rays when properly performed are reasonably accurate in identifying the nature of the problem, but endoscopy with biopsy and cytology is more sensitive and yields a tissue diagnosis. The differentiation of a benign gastric ulcer from a malignant lesion is important. For this reason, following an ulcer to complete healing (by either endoscopy or x ray) is important and will identify the majority of patients harboring a malignancy. To delay with diagnosis of gastric cancer by 8 weeks or so will have no effect on treatment or outcome.

Treatment by chemotherapy, radiation, and immunotherapy is not satisfactory. The best hope for a modest improvement in survival is surgery. Roughly 80 percent of all patients with gastric cancer are considered suitable candidates for laparotomy. Of this group, less than half are found at the time of surgery to be candidates for curative resection.[64] Despite these "encouraging" statistics, only 15 to 25 percent of patients who undergo "curative resection" will survive for 5 years.[65] However, compared with doing no surgery (1-year survival 5 percent), surgery for those who can tolerate it has a somewhat better outlook. But a heavy penalty is paid for this modest improvement in survival. In some instances patients are subjected to a procedure with high morbidity

without achieving any improvement, while in other instances demise is hastened. Age should not be a criterion for determining whether to operate or not; more important factors include a patient's general medical status and whether (and what) other medical conditions coexist. There are no absolute right answers, but careful thought and considerable judgment are required to advise for or against surgery. Patients not suitable for surgical treatment may be considered for palliation with radiation, chemotherapy, or various local modalities applied via endoscope. The expected benefits in the elderly are minimal at best.

BENIGN TUMORS

A number of benign tumors occur in the stomach and are found more frequently in the elderly population. A general idea of the relative frequency of the most common tumors is as follows: (1) hyperplastic polyps, 38 percent; (2) adenomatous polys, 10 percent; and (3) leiomyoma, 24 percent. The remainder are obscure tumors such as fibromas, lipomas, leiomyoblastomas, and ectopic pancreas, each of which can account for up to 5 percent of the total.[66]

Hyperplastic polyps range in size from 0.5 to 3 cm but generally are less than 1 cm in diameter. They frequently are multiple and occur predominantly in the antrum. Although true malignant degeneration of hyperplastic polyps is rare, there is an increase in malignancy elsewhere in the stomach. When multiple polyps are present in the stomach, both hyperplastic and adenomatous polyps can coexist. As with adenomas in the colon, gastric adenomas can be papillary (villous) or tubular (adenomatous). The incidence of carcinomatous degeneration of such adenomas has been reported to be as high as 70 percent.[67] Moreover, patients with gastric adenomas have a higher incidence of associated gastric cancer elsewhere in the stomach than do patients with hyperplastic polyps. Leiomyomas are the most common smooth muscle tumor. Other mesenchymal tumors such as fibromas and neural tumors are occasionally encountered.

Over one-half of all gastric tumors are found incidentally during the course of an investigation taking place for some other reason. Most hyperplastic polyps are asymptomatic. Occult bleeding may occur with any polyp type, while massive GI hemorrhage is usually associated with leiomyomas. Diagnosis is radiographic and endoscopic. Treatment remains controversial. Large hyperplastic polyps that are bleeding or causing obstructive symptoms by prolapsing through the pylorus should be removed endoscopically. Other polyps 1 cm or greater are generally removed if there is doubt as to their nature. There are a significant number of patients who bleed after polypectomy. It is important that aspirin and other NSAIDs be stopped a week or so before any such procedure. In the case of a bleeding leiomyoma, surgical removal is the only practical therapy.

LYMPHOMAS

Lymphoma is much less common than adenocarcinoma. Of the extra nodal lymphomas, gastric lymphoma is the most common. Symptoms and roentgenographic signs are very similar to adenocarcinoma in as many as 60 percent of patients. The presence of large, irregular gastric folds, large ulcerated masses, and antral narrowing are more in keeping with lymphoma than with adenocarcinoma.[68,69] Endoscopic biopsy is important, as treatments of lymphoma and adenocarcinoma are markedly different. However, definite endoscopic diagnosis can be elusive and may require repeat examination and mucosal snare biopsy.[70] Treatment of lymphomas can be quite complex. Generally, patients with early gastric lymphoma who undergo surgery may expect a 5-year survival of 80 percent.[71] However, it is not possible to extrapolate such aggressive treatment to the elderly population because other afflictions often alter the long-term outlook. The sagacious physician understands that most elderly patients are best served by avoiding surgery and proceeding directly with radiation and/or chemotherapy. Overall, the expected 5-year survival rate is approximately 50 percent.

Other, rare malignancies include gastric myosarcomas and carcinoid tumors. With regard to the carcinoid, it is of interest that gastrin is known to be trophic for enterochromaffin-like cells and that there is an increased number of gastric carcinoids in achlorhydric patients with elevated serum gastrin levels. What effect long-term treatment with H_2 blockers or potassium/hydrogen ATPase inhibitors may have on this phenomenon remains to be seen.

REFERENCES

1. Correa P: The epidemiology and pathogenesis of gastritis. Three etiologic entities, in Van den Ren L (ed): *Frontiers of Gastrointestinal Research*. Basel, S Karger, 1980, p 98.
2. Rotterdam H, Sommers SC: *Biopsy Diagnosis of the Digestive Tract*. New York, Raven Press, 1981, p 59.
3. Blaser MJ: Gastric Campylobacter-like organisms, gastritis, and peptic ulcers. *Gastroenterology* 93:371, 1987.
4. Kratz K, Jablonowski H: Functional and histological gastric changes with age, in Hellmans J, Vantrappen G (eds): *Gastrointestinal Tract Disorders in the Elderly*. Edinburgh, Churchill Livingstone, 1984 p 62.
5. Steinheber FU: Ageing and the stomach. *Clin Gastroenterol* 14:657, 1985.
6. Sirula M, Varis K: Gastritis, in Sircus W, Smith AN (eds): *Scientific Foundations of Gastroenterology*. Philadelphia, Saunders, 1980, p 357.
7. Barwick KW: Chronic gastritis: The pathologist's role. *Pathol Annu* 22:223, 1987.
8. Stockbrugger R et al: Serum gastrin and atrophic gastritis in achlorhydric patients with and without pernicious anemia. *Scand J Gastroenterol* 11:713, 1976.
9. Stockbrugger R et al: Antral gastritis cells and serum gastrin in achlorhydria. *Scand J Gastroenterol* 12:209, 1977.
10. Maclaurin BP: The stomach—pernicious anemia and gastritis, in Asquith P (ed): *Immunology of the Gastrointestinal Tract*. Edinburgh, Churchill Livingston, 1979, p 55.
11. Wyatt J, Dixon MR: Chronic gastritis—a pathogenetic approach. *J Pathol* 54:113, 1988.
12. Spiro HM, Schwartz RDL: Superficial gastritis: A cause of temporary achlorhydria and hyperpepsinemia. *N Engl J Med* 259:682, 1958.
13. Samloff IM et al: Relationships among serum pepsinogen I, serum pepsinogen II and gastric mucosal histology: A study in relatives of patients with pernicious anemia. *Gastroenterology* 83:204, 1982.
14. Broch K et al: Endocrine cell proliferation and carcinoid development: A review of new aspects of hypergastrinemic atrophic gastritis. *Digestion* 35(suppl I):106, 1986.
15. Siurala M et al: Prevalence of gastritis in the rural population. *Scand J Gastroenterol* 3:211, 1968.
16. Svendsen JH et al: Gastric cancer risk in achlorhydric patients: A long-term follow-up study. *Scand J Gastroenterol* 21:16, 1986.
17. Schafer LW et al: Risk of development of gastric carcinoma in patients with pernicious anemia: A population based study in Rochester, Minnesota. *Mayo Clin Proc* 60:444, 1985.
18. Cooper BT: Menetrier's disease. *Dig Dis Sci* 5:33, 1987.
19. Mowat NAD et al: The natural history of gastric ulcer in a community: A 4 year study. *Q J Med* 44:45, 1975.
20. Leverat M et al: Peptic ulcer in patients over 60: Experience in 287 cases. *Am J Dig Dis* 11:279, 1966.
21. Northfield TC: Factors predisposing to recurrent hemorrhage after acute gastrointestinal bleeding. *Br Med J* 1:26, 1971.
22. Stafford CE et al: Complications of peptic ulcer in the aged. *California Med* 84:92, 1956.
23. Malmaeus J, Nilsson F: Endoscopy in the management of gastric ulcer disease. *Acta Chir Scand* 147:55, 1981.
24. Tragardh B, Haglund U: Endoscopic diagnosis of gastric ulcer: Evaluation of benefits of endoscopic follow-up observation for malignancy. *Acta Chir Scand* 151:37, 1985.
25. Strange SL: Giant innocent gastric ulcer in the elderly. *Gerontol Clin* 5:171, 1963.
26. Cohen I, Sartin J: Giant gastric ulcer. *Ann Surg* 147:749, 1958.
27. Elashoff JD, Grossman MI: Trends in hospital admissions and death rate for peptic ulcer in the United States from 1970–1978. *Gastroenterology* 78:280, 1980.
28. Permutt RP, Cello JP: Duodenal ulcer disease in the hospitalized elderly patient. *Dig Dis Sci* 27:1, 1982.
29. Mistilis SP et al: Giant duodenal ulcer. *Ann Intern Med* 59:155, 1963.
30. Klamer TW, Mahr MM: Giant duodenal ulcer: A dangerous variant of a common illness. *Am J Surg* 135:760, 1978.
31. Mathewson K et al: Which peptic ulcer patients bleed? *Gut* 29:70, 1988.

32. Dawson J et al: Effect of Ranitidine on gastric ulcer healing and recurrence. *Scand J Gastroenterol* 19:665, 1984.

33. Colin-Jones DG: There is more to healing ulcers than suppressing acid. *Gut* 27:475, 1986.

34. Blaser MJ: Gastric Campylobacter-like organisms, gastritis, and peptic ulcer disease. *Gastroenterology* 93:371, 1987.

35. Vantrappen G et al: Gastrointestinal motility disorders. *Dig Dis Sci* 31(suppl):55, 1986.

36. Kim CH, Malagelada J-R: Electrical activity of the stomach: Clinical implications. *Mayo Clin Proc* 61:205, 1986.

37. Funch-Jensen P: Basal upper gastrointestinal motility in healthy people. *Scand J Gastroenterol* 128(suppl):52, 1987.

38. Minami H, McCallum RW: The physiology and pathophysiology of gastric emptying in humans. *Gastroenterology* 86:1592, 1984.

39. Brophy CM et al: Variability of gastric emptying measurements in man employing standardized radiolabeled meals. *Dig Dis Sci* 31:799, 1986.

40. Sheiner HJ, Catchpole BN: Drug therapy for post gastrectomy gastric stasis. *Br J Surg* 69:608, 1976.

41. Albibi R, McCallum RW: Metoclopramide: Pharmacology and clinical applications. *Ann Intern Med* 98:86, 1984.

42. Brugmans J: Domperidone (R33,812): An appraisal of the literature, in Poster DS, Penta JS, Bruno S (eds): *Treatment of Cancer Chemotherapy-Induced Nausea and Vomiting.* New York, Masson, 1981, p 177.

43. Van Nueten JM et al: Gastrointestinal motility-stimulating properties of Cisapride, a non-antidopaminergic non-cholinergic compound, in Roman C (ed): *Gastrointestinal Motility.* Lancaster, MTP Press, 1983, p 513.

44. Schuurkes JAJ et al: Stimulating effects of Cisapride on autoduodenal motility in conscious dogs, in Roman C (ed): *Gastrointestinal Motility.* Lancaster, MTP Press, 1983, p 95.

45. Bateman DN: The action of Cisapride on gastric emptying and the pharmacokinetics of oral diazepam. *Eur J Clin Pharmacol* 30:205, 1986.

46. Jian R et al: Measurement of gastric emptying in dyspeptic patients: Effective new gastrokinetic agent (Cisapride). *Gut* 26:352, 1985.

47. Horowitz M et al: Effects of Cisapride on gastric and esophageal emptying in progressive systemic sclerosis. *Gastroenterology* 93:311, 1987.

48. Schiller FR et al: Hematemesis and melena, with reference to factors influencing the outcome. *Br Med J* 2:714, 1970.

49. Schaffner JA: Acute gastrointestinal bleeding. *J Intensive Care Med* 1:289, 1986.

50. Veldhugzen Van Zanten SJO et al: Recurrent massive hematemesis from Dieulafoy vascular malformations—A review of 101 cases. *Gut* 27:213, 1986.

51. Cameron AJ, Higgins JA: Linear gastric erosion: A lesion associated with large diaphragmatic hernia and chronic blood loss. *Gastroenterology* 91:338, 1986.

52. Quintero E et al: Upper gastrointestinal bleeding caused by gastroduodenal vascular malformations: Incidence, diagnosis and treatment. *Dig Dis Sci* 31:897, 1986.

53. Pingelton SK: Recognition and management of upper gastrointestinal hemorrhage. *Am J Med* 83(suppl 6a):41, 1987.

54. Collins R, Langman M: Treatment with histamine H_2 antagonists in acute upper gastrointestinal hemorrhage. *N Engl J Med* 313:660, 1985.

55. Siepler JK: A dosage alternative for H_2 receptor antagonists, constant infusion. *Clin Ther* 8(suppl A):24, 1986.

56. Ponsky JL et al: Saline irrigation in gastric hemorrhage: Effect of temperature. *J Surg Res* 28:204, 1980.

57. Brussaard CC, Vandewoude MFJ: A prospective analysis of elective upper gastrointestinal endoscopy in the elderly. *Gastrointest Endosc* 34:1118, 1988.

58. Chang-Chien C-S et al: Different implications of stigmata of recent hemorrhage in gastric and duodenal ulcer. *Dig Dis Sci* 33:400, 1988.

59. Peterson WL et al: Routine early endoscopy in upper gastrointestinal bleeding: A randomized controlled trial. *N Engl J Med* 304:925, 1981.

60. Kovacs TUG, Jensen DM: Endoscopic control of gastrointestinal hemorrhage. *Annu Rev Med* 38:267, 1987.

61. Keppen M: Upper gastrointestinal malignancies in the elderly. *Clin Geriatr Med* 3:637, 1987.

62. Bringaze WL et al: Early gastric cancer: 21 year experience. *Ann Surg* 204:103, 1986.

63. Green PHR et al: Early gastric cancer. *Gastroenterology* 81:247, 1981.

64. Dupont BJ et al: Adenocarcinoma of the stomach: Review of 1,497 cases. *Cancer* 41:941, 1978.

65. Myers WC et al: Adenocarcinoma of the stomach: Changing pattern over the last four decades. *Ann Surg* 205:1, 1987.

66. Nelson RS, Lanza FL: Benign and malignant tumors of the stomach (other than carcinoma), in Berk JE et al (eds): *Bockus Gastroenterology,* vol II, *Esophagus, Stomach and Duodenum.* Philadelphia, Saunders, 1985, p 1255.

67. Tomasolo J: Gastric polyps: Histologic types and their relationship to gastric carcinoma. *Cancer* 27:1346, 1971.

68. Loehr WJ et al: Primary lymphoma of the gastrointestinal tract: A review of 100 cases. *Ann Surg* 170:232, 1969.

69. Lewin KJ et al: Lymphoma of the gastrointestinal tract: The study of 117 cases presenting with gastrointestinal disease. *Cancer* 42:693, 1978.

70. Spinelli P et al: Endoscopic diagnosis of gastric lymphoma. *Endoscopy* 12:211, 1980.

71. Weingrad DN et al: Primary gastrointestinal lymphoma: A 30 year review. *Cancer* 49:1258, 1982.

Chapter 61

HEPATOBILIARY DISORDERS

John H. Gilliam III

THE EFFECT OF AGING ON THE LIVER

Morphologic derangements in the liver with aging are comparatively slight. With age, there is a decline in weight of the entire liver and of each of its respective lobules. Grossly, the liver is characterized by brown atrophy. The color change is due to accumulation of lipofuscin granules in lysosomes, possibly due to food contaminants that the hepatocytes cannot clear. Similar changes occur in younger patients with severe malnutrition; therefore, brown atrophy is not specific to aging. However, hepatocytes are decreased in number and larger in aging, while in malnutrition they are smaller but of normal number. Intake of higher dietary protein may accelerate aging changes seen at autopsy.[1,2] The ability of the aged liver to regenerate after injury or partial resection is slightly delayed. Protein synthesis remains intact, but catabolism of synthesized proteins may be impaired. There is an increase in extrahepatocytic space and in intralobular collagen with aging, but collagen synthesis is reduced and no functional impairment results.[1]

Functional derangements in livers of aged persons in good health are also slight. Liver blood chemistries remain normal in the elderly; when they are abnormal, liver disease is indicated. Data on changes in specific biochemical function in aged hepatocytes are very conflicting but suggest no consistent alterations. There is reduced mitochondrial mass which, coupled with the reduced liver mass and mild alterations in hepatic blood flow, may result in altered drug metabolism.[1,3]

JAUNDICE IN THE ELDERLY

The majority of elderly patients with jaundice have biliary tract obstruction; malignant obstruction is more common than choledocholithiasis. Hepatitis is less common in the elderly and is more likely to be drug-induced[4–6] when present.

Obstructive jaundice is to be suspected when there is a history of biliary colic, pruritis, and acholic stools, or if there is recurrent fluctuation in severity, stable deep jaundice, or progressive jaundice.[4] Helpful findings are a palpable gallbladder and a cholestatic liver blood test pattern. Absence of malaise and anorexia, and the history of epigastric and back pain exacerbated by eating, might lead the physician to suspect pancreatic cancer. It should be noted that marked elevation in aminotransferases is not specific for hepatocellular disease and may occur with extrahepatic biliary tract obstruction.[7,8] An unusual manifestation of severe obstructive jaundice is sinus node dysfunction. If significant sinus bradycardia develops in a patient with obstructive jaundice, electrocardiographic monitoring is necessary.[9]

Should the spleen be enlarged, an underlying myeloproliferative disorder, cirrhosis, hemolysis, or splenic vein thrombosis (from pancreatic cancer or pancreatitis) should be suspected. A spongy feel to an enlarged liver may indicate congestive heart failure. A pulsatile liver is indicative of tricuspid insufficiency. The presence of unconjugated hyperbilirubinemia is seen when pulmonary infarction is superimposed on congestive heart failure. Other causes of jaundice include hemolytic anemias, septicemia, lymphoreticular malignancies, transfusions, and hypotension.

Evaluation of the elderly jaundiced patient should include an imaging study to exclude extrahepatic biliary obstruction. The most convenient and cost-effective approach is ultrasonic evaluation of the gallbladder, biliary tree, liver, and pancreas.[10] Ultrasonic evaluation is the best initial evaluation in the author's opinion, but computed tomography is also an excellent diagnostic test. Endoscopic retrograde cholangiopancreatography

(ERCP) or percutaneous cholangiography may be necessary. The reader is referred to several excellent reviews on the diagnostic approach in obstructive jaundice.[11–14] (It is important to remember that imaging studies do not resolve all cases of cholestasis correctly, since obstructive jaundice can present with normal-size ducts.) If cholestasis is present but there is no evidence of dilated bile ducts, a good medication history should be obtained and intrahepatic cholestasis considered. A liver biopsy is then warranted.

DRUG-INDUCED LIVER INJURY

Since elderly patients have many medical diseases and drugs are frequently prescribed for them, it is surprising that adverse reactions to drugs do not occur more frequently than they do in the elderly. Still, adverse reactions of all types occur in approximately 15 percent of elderly patients over age 60, 20 percent over age 70,[15] and 24 percent over age 80.[16] Up to 20 percent of jaundice in elderly patients may be drug-induced.[17] It remains unclear whether liver aging alone explains this finding, since the elderly are prescribed drugs more frequently than are younger patients and possess altered pharmacokinetics in extrahepatic drug metabolism as well.[18,19]

As classified by Zimmerman, drug reactions fall into three general types: hepatocellular, mixed hepatocellular, and cholestatic. Hepatotoxicity occurs through varied mechanisms. Toxins which are cytotoxic are "direct," and those which cause subcellular organelle injury are "indirect." Some agents affect only certain hosts and are idiosyncratic, acting by allergic mechanisms or by formation of toxic metabolites. The reader is referred to Zimmerman's comprehensive textbook for a thorough review of this subject; consult this reference when confronted with a patient with hepatotoxic injury.[20]

Whatever the drug responsible, it appears to be well-documented that liver toxicity becomes more severe with advancing age. In one large series[21], halothane hepatotoxicity was fatal in 3 of 14 patients (21 percent) under age 30 and in 27 of 37 (73 percent) over age 70. It is considered rare to recover from fulminant hepatic failure from any cause after age 50, although the mortality below this age also remains distressingly high. Susceptibility to isoniazid hepatitis increases from 0.3 percent under age 34 to 2.3 percent at age 50 or older.[22]

Many commonly used drugs cause liver toxicity: antihypertensives (alphamethyldopa), antibiotics (nitrofurantoin, sulfonamides, ketoconazole, penicillin, erythromycin, and tetracycline), anticonvulsants (diphenylhydantoin), psychotropic drugs (chlorpromazine and imipramine), hormones (estrogens and anabolic steroids), oral hypoglycemics, nonsteroidal anti-inflammatory drugs, antineoplastic drugs, and anesthetic agents.

The list of drugs causing liver toxicity is extensive and has been recently tabulated.[23]

In most cases, drug toxicity stops upon recognition and withdrawal of the offending agent. Drug hepatotoxicity is not often severe, and survival depends primarily on the nature and severity of the underlying lesion at the time the drug is stopped. Cholestasis can persist for months after cessation of phenothiazines[24] and imipramine,[25] however. Several drugs can cause chronic hepatitis and should be considered in the differential diagnosis of chronic hepatitis in the elderly.[26]

ALCOHOL-INDUCED LIVER INJURY

Alcoholic hepatitis is an uncommon disease in the elderly, but it does occur in occasional patients over age 60. The symptoms of anorexia, nausea, abdominal pain, and weight loss are similar to those of viral hepatitis. Physical findings of hepatomegaly, depleted nutritional stores, jaundice, and ascites are common.[27] The level of alanine aminotransferase (abbreviated ALT or SGPT) in alcoholic hepatitis is one-half or less of the level of aspartate aminotransferase (abbreviated AST or SGOT), in contrast to the levels of these substances in viral hepatitis. In severe cases, fever and leukocytosis are more common. Specific markers associated with a poor survival include encephalopathy, azotemia, prolongation of prothrombin time, and leukocytosis.[28] Alcoholic hepatitis can occur with or without cirrhosis. Liver biopsy is diagnostic but is not necessary for diagnosis when the illness is severe. Abstinence and attention to caloric intake are recommended for treatment.[29]

Particular mention should be made about acetaminophen use in alcoholic patients. Acetaminophen-induced hepatotoxicity can occur without overdose at therapeutic levels in alcoholic patients. At initial patient evaluation, a careful history should be obtained that includes any use of over-the-counter products that contain acetaminophen. A STAT acetaminophen blood level should be obtained and therapy initiated with acetylcysteine as indicated by the blood level and history. Later, the hepatic enzyme pattern will discriminate acetaminophen-induced hepatitis from alcoholic hepatitis since the SGOT and lactate dehydrogenase (LDH) will be markedly elevated in the former. Noting this pattern of hepatic enzymes will not be useful in preventing liver necrosis, however, since acetylcysteine is not helpful after 12 hours.[30,31]

VIRAL HEPATITIS

In the older literature, several series emphasized that viral hepatitis is increasingly common with age; in one series, acute fulminant hepatitis was more prevalent in an elderly population than in a younger population.[32]

These series preceded the current improvements in serodiagnostic testing, however. A recent report of 159 patients with acute viral hepatitis found 74 (47 percent) to be type B and 85 (53 percent) to be non-B, many of whom had hepatitis A. Of interest, only 4 (2.5 percent) were age 65 or older.[33] This report suggests that viral hepatitis is infrequent in the elderly.

Hepatitis B can cause severe acute hepatitis, particularly if delta agent hepatitis is superimposed. Elderly patients are more likely to have an acute fulminant course and to be sicker if chronic hepatitis B ensues.[34]

Non-A, non-B (NANB) hepatitis is most frequently transfusion- or hospital-acquired in the elderly. There is also a sporadic form. NANB hepatitis is caused by at least two separate viruses. Approximately 20 percent of cases are anicteric, and 30 to 50 percent of cases will develop chronic hepatitis after initial infection. Typically the viruses have low virulence, though acute fulminant hepatitis can occur. Most cases of NANB hepatitis are mildly symptomatic and are discovered by blood chemistry screening. Non-A, non-B hepatitis can progress to cirrhosis and, as with hepatitis B, can cause hepatocellular carcinoma.[34]

CHRONIC HEPATITIS

As in younger patients, in older patients autoimmune chronic active hepatitis (CAH) must be distinguished from chronic viral hepatitis (B or NANB), chronic drug-induced hepatitis, and other chronic liver diseases. Primary biliary cirrhosis and choledocholithiasis must be excluded. Serologic testing is useful. Characteristic findings in autoimmune CAH are elevated globulins (polyclonal on protein electrophoresis and type IgG on immunoglobulin quantitation), positive anti–smooth-muscle antibody (anti-actin antibody), and positive antinuclear antibody.[35] Antimitochondrial antibody may be positive, but it is typically in lower titer than anti–smooth-muscle antibody. Also typical is elevation of transaminase to 5 to 15 times normal, and rouleaux may be found on peripheral blood smear. Liver biopsy is diagnostic, revealing a lymphoplasmocytic portal infiltrate with piecemeal or bridging necrosis. Cirrhosis may be present. The intralobular bile ductules are normal.

Some patients present with an acute course; in these cases a 6-month history is not necessary for the diagnosis. Up to 20 percent of autoimmune CAH may present after age 60, and treatment may be more difficult in the elderly. Prednisone (or prednisolone) with or without azathioprine is considered standard therapy.[36]

CIRRHOSIS

Cirrhosis, a prevalent disease in the elderly, is the fifth leading cause of death in older men and the sixth in older women (aged 55 to 74).[28] It is not unusual for patients in this age group to present with complications of cirrhosis such as variceal bleeding, ascites, or encephalopathy. An evaluation to determine the cause of cirrhosis is indicated, and laboratory evaluation coupled with liver biopsy can be diagnostic. A few pertinent causes are discussed below.

Hemochromatosis becomes symptomatic in the fifth decade for men and often the sixth decade for women. Patients present with lassitude, a metallic gray skin color, cirrhosis, diabetes, arthritis, loss of libido, and congestive heart failure. Serum ferritin is markedly elevated, and transferrin saturation is high. Liver biopsy for routine stains and iron quantitation is diagnostic. Aggressive phlebotomies yield dramatic therapeutic results, markedly improving survival and quality of life.[37] If the diagnosis can be established and treatment begun before cirrhosis develops, survival is normal. If cirrhosis is present at diagnosis, survival on treatment is diminished and there is a late risk of developing hepatocellular carcinoma.[38]

Primary biliary cirrhosis (PBC) has 6–10:1 female preponderance and a mean age of onset of 50 to 55. Usually the onset is insidious. The most common symptom is pruritus, followed by fatigability, jaundice, osteoporosis with vertebral fractures, xanthomas, and other features of advanced cirrhosis. Up to 50 percent with PBC are asymptomatic, but the development of jaundice is an ominous sign.[39] Antimitochondrial antibody is present in about 95 percent of patients during the course of the disease. IgM and IgG immunoglobulins are elevated. Plasmacytic portal infiltration and destruction of intralobular ductules are found. Cirrhosis may be absent or present in PBC, and granulomas may imply a more benign prognosis. Other autoimmune diseases may be associated with PBC, including Sjögren's syndrome, thyroiditis, rheumatoid arthritis, and lupus. Treatment is supportive with supplemental calcium and vitamins A, D, E, and K. Cholestyramine may help the pruritus.[40] D-penicillamine is now known not to be helpful,[41] but early reports show an effect from colchicine.[42]

Deficiency of α-1-antitrypsin may present late in life and is a cause of "cryptogenic" cirrhosis. Diagnosis is by confirmation of reduced blood levels of α-1-antitrypsin or by blood Pi typing with para-aminosalicylic acid (PAS) positive-diastase resistant intracytoplasmic globules being seen in periportal hepatocytes on biopsy.[43] No specific treatment is available.

THE LIVER IN CIRCULATORY FAILURE

When the body is in shock from any cause, ischemic liver injury can result because of circulatory failure. Injury may be mild, with marked transaminase and LDH elevation, or may be severe, with frank liver infarction, centrizonal necrosis, and subsequent death.[44] As in any organ system, the severity of the injury depends on the duration and degree of hypotension.

Postoperative jaundice may have many causes and is a true diagnostic challenge.[45] There is a very high incidence of jaundice (23 percent) after open heart surgery; the incidence of jaundice classified as moderate or severe in this case is 7 percent according to one recent prospective report from Taiwan.[46]

Chronic congestive heart failure is well known to cause mild jaundice frequently, the level of bilirubin being greater than 2 mg% in one-third of cases. Jaundice may be severe in heart failure with development of cardiac cirrhosis.[47,48] Occasionally, ischemic hepatitis may develop from left heart failure alone that mimics viral hepatitis in its biochemical manifestations.[49] Treatment is directed at the underlying heart disease.

PYOGENIC LIVER ABSCESS AND SEPSIS

Most commonly, pyogenic liver abscess develops from biliary tract disease with ascending cholangitis.[50] In these cases, treatment is directed at relief of the biliary tract obstruction and coverage with parenteral broad-spectrum antibiotics. Solitary pyogenic abscesses develop from septicemia or intraabdominal infections. Treatment is by surgical or percutaneous drainage combined with appropriate antibiotic coverage.[51] With either type of pyogenic abscess, patients present with right upper-quadrant pain, fever, and jaundice. The diagnosis can be made with any imaging study and should be investigated aggressively when these symptoms are present.

Jaundice due to septicemia without liver abscess is not common in the elderly. Hepatomegaly may be present. When liver biopsy is done, cholestasis is seen. Successful treatment of the underlying septicemia will correct the hepatic functional abnormalities.[52]

THE EFFECT OF AGING ON THE GALLBLADDER AND THE BILIARY TRACT

There are minimal effects of aging on the anatomy of the biliary tract. The common bile duct enlarges slightly in association with narrowing of the sphincter of Oddi. There is little effect of aging on gallbladder size or contractility. However, gallstone disease is far more common in elderly patients than it is in younger patients. Surgery has always been the mainstay of treatment and remains so for gallbladder disease. However, many advances in endoscopic therapy, percutaneous therapy, lithotripsy, and dissolution therapy have begun to revolutionize current management of biliary tract stones.

Further, benign and malignant strictures often can be managed without surgery. These newer techniques are appealing for older patients and will be discussed briefly below.

CHOLELITHIASIS

The most common abdominal operation performed in the elderly population is cholecystectomy, and the total number of cholecystectomies performed annually in the United States has been estimated at 500,000. Most gallbladder diseases are due to gallstones. Gallstones are composed of cholesterol, calcium bile salts, and protein, in various proportions. By gross appearance, gallstones are commonly classified as cholesterol, black pigment, or brown pigment in type. The principal component of gallbladder stones is cholesterol, which is insoluble in water. Cholesterol is solubilized in bile as micelles, which are formed by phospholipids (mainly lecithin) and primary bile salts. It is believed that cholesterol gallstones form after bile becomes supersaturated with cholesterol. Nucleation factors lead to coalescence of cholesterol crystals, followed by gallstone growth. When the gallbladder is healthy, it acidifies and concentrates gallbladder bile, and it contracts vigorously in response to meals. In the presence of gallbladder disease, these functions are impaired. Cholesterol gallstones are generally radiolucent, and pigment stones are calcified and radiopaque. Mixed stones are not unusual.[53]

Diagnosis of cholethiasis is by oral cholecystogram or abdominal ultrasound. Oral cholecystography is a superior way to evaluate stone size and number, determine whether the stones float, and evaluate gallbladder function (cystic duct patency and contractility of the gallbladder fundus). Abdominal ultrasound is better when patients are acutely ill, and it may detect gallstones in some patients in whom stones were missed on visualizing oral cholecystograms. One comparative study estimates the sensitivity of ultrasound at 93 percent and of oral cholecystogram at 65 percent in detecting gallstones in patients coming to elective cholecystectomy. However, when adenomyosis and cholesterolosis are considered, oral cholecystogram correctly diagnosed 87 percent of patients with gallbladder disease.[54]

SILENT GALLSTONES

Many patients have gallstones without abdominal pain. Gracie and Ransohoff studied a healthy population made up predominantly of men and found the cumulative probability of developing biliary colic to be 10 percent by 5 years, 15 percent by 10 years, and 18 percent by 15 and 20 years.[55] There were no deaths from biliary tract disease. They later used decision analysis to argue against prophylactic cholecystectomy,[56] but their study has been criticized because it examines the course in a predominantly male, nondiabetic population. Management of silent gallstones remains controversial, but prophylactic cholecystectomy in the elderly is riskier than in a younger population. Careful observation is acceptable practice in elderly patients with symptomatic gallstones.

Nonsurgical treatment of gallbladder stones in elderly patients with symptomatic gallbladder stones is a new alternative, but experience is still limited. In patients with functioning gallbladders and solitary stones, extracorporeal shock wave lithotripsy (ESWL) fragmentation combined with low-dose oral dissolution therapy has promise.[57] Its major limitations are its lack of efficacy in patients with multiple gallstones and its cost. Immediate chemical dissolution with methyl tert-butyl ether (MTBE) is another advance. This technique is applicable to patients with multiple cholesterol gallstones without cystic duct obstruction. A catheter is placed percutaneously and transhepatically into the gallbladder. After stabilization overnight, MTBE is lavaged and aspirated over several hours. The disadvantages of MTBE include the risks of capsular and gallbladder puncture, its applicability only to pure-cholesterol gallstones, and the difficulty of administering the treatment.[58] MTBE will play a minor role in gallstone disease because of these limitations.

Dissolution of gallstones by administration of oral bile acids has been investigated thoroughly. After initial enthusiasm, the final report on chenodeoxycholic acid (Chenodiol) therapy from the National Cooperative Gallstone Study was disappointing. Complete dissolution occurred in only 13.5 percent of patients given "high-dose" chenodeoxycholic acid (750 mg/day) at 2 years. In addition to costliness, chenodeoxycholic acid has the disadvantages of causing diarrhea in about 30 percent of patients and causing some patients to develop lithocholate-induced hepatotoxicity.[59] After several years of relative disinterest, however, enthusiasm is rising again for oral bile acid therapy for a variety of reasons. First, it is now known that bedtime dosing is more effective than dosing with meals.[60] Second, a higher dose of chenodiol is more effective.[61] Third and most important, a different oral bile acid, ursodeoxycholic acid, is now available in the United States. Ursodeoxycholic acid does not cause diarrhea or lithocholate-induced hepatotoxicity. Its maximum effectiveness is at a dose 7 to 8 mg/kg, instead of the 13 to 15 mg/kg dose used for chenodiol.[62] The two drugs may be used in low-dose combination.[63] However, the maximum complete stone dissolution from oral bile acid therapy likely will not exceed 29 percent in one year.[62] Oral bile acid therapy will thus have an adjunctive role with ESWL.

In summary, these recent developments in nonsurgical management of occasionally symptomatic gallstones are encouraging. However, cholecystectomy still remains the most effective treatment.

ACUTE CHOLECYSTITIS

In contrast to silent gallstones, acute cholecystitis is a serious and often subtle disease in the elderly. The mechanism in acute calculous cholecystitis is obstruction of the cystic duct by calculi. Following this, lipids permeate the gallbladder wall, the gallbladder dilates, mucosal blood flow decreases as pressure increases, and infection develops. It has been emphasized that the physical findings are subtle. Peritoneal signs are seen in less than one-half of cases, the fever is frequently low-grade, and some patients have no abdominal tenderness. It is not uncommon for patients to present with a toxic appearance and disorientation, but without abdominal signs.[64] Leukocytosis was seen in only about two-thirds of patients in this category. About 40 percent of patients identified as being acutely ill with cholecystitis had empyema, gangrene, or perforation, and 15 percent had subphrenic, subhepatic, or liver abscesses.[64] Although *Escherichia coli* and *Klebsiella* are the most common infecting organisms, anaerobic infection is not uncommon, and cephalosporins alone will provide inadequate coverage.

The mortality from surgery for acute cholecystitis in the elderly is high. One large series reported a mortality rate of 9.8 percent in patients age 65 or older.[65] Obviously, this high mortality reflects the severity of the disease and the associated diseases of this age group. There is no effective therapy other than surgery. Successful medical therapy is not possible in acutely ill patients. Stabilization of medical diseases should be as expedient as possible, and surgery should not be delayed. The diagnosis will be relatively easy if acute emphysematous cholecystitis is present[66] or if classic abdominal findings are present. If these conditions are not present, abdominal ultrasound and radionuclide scanning are the procedures of choice.

Acalculous cholecystitis is similar to acute calculous cholecystitis in clinical presentation and is most prevalent after surgery, trauma, or repeated transfusions. It may also occur in patients with burns (or with prolonged reliance on total parenteral nutrition) or in patients with cancer. Gangrenous gallbladders are found in 40 percent of patients with acalculous cholecystitis, and perforation is common.[67,68] The diagnosis may be difficult but should be suspected in the appropriate setting.

CHOLEDOCHOLITHIASIS

Typically, choledocholithiasis presents with obstructive jaundice as its principal manifestation. In elderly patients with intact gallbladders, one series found presenting symptoms to be pain and jaundice in 75.5 percent, pain alone in 18 percent, and jaundice alone in 6.5 percent. Of the patients in this series, 27 percent had acute cholangitis and 18 percent had acute pancreatitis (at presentation).[69] In patients with acute cholecystitis, 10 to 30 percent of patients may have choledocholithiasis. In one large endoscopic series, 53 percent of patients with choledocholithiasis had intact gallbladders.[70] Surgical series have a greater proportion of patients with intact gallbladders, as would be expected.

Most common duct stones in patients with in situ gallbladders are cholesterol stones, but ductular pigment stones are quite common. In the elderly, the presence of periampullary duodenal diverticula is thought to be of pathogenic importance in development of biliary calculi. Once patients have had cholecystectomy, the incidence of recurrent choledocholithiasis is reduced. However, if symptoms of pancreatobiliary disease later develop, calculi will be found in 87.5 percent of patients with periampullary diverticula but in only 39 percent of patients without periampullary diverticula.[71] It is also known that bile cultures for *E. coli* are more likely to be positive if duodenal diverticula are located closer to the ampulla than if they are remotely located. It is speculated there may be excessive β-glucuronidase in the bile of these patients, allowing easier formation of pigment stones.[72] The incidence of duodenal diverticula increases with age, but it has not been possible to attribute specific manometric abnormalities of the sphincter of Oddi to the presence of diverticula.

The preferred treatment of choledocholithiasis in patients age 70 or older, or in patients of any age who are unfit for surgery, is endoscopic sphincterotomy (ES). Extensive worldwide experience with ES has changed management for many patients who previously required surgery. ES with complete clearance of all ductular stones by Dormia basket or balloon catheters can be achieved in at least 74 percent of all cases attempted. ES alone can be achieved in almost all cases.[69,72] Complications occur in 10 to 20 percent of cases, manifesting most frequently as cholangitis; bleeding, pancreatitis, and perforation occur considerably less frequently. Numerous series have shown mortality from ES to be less than 1.5 percent.[70,73–75] In the setting of acute suppurative cholangitis, the mortality is higher, but the mortality from ES remains significantly lower than from surgery.[72] For patients with in situ gallbladders, the likelihood of subsequent need for cholecystectomy in long-term follow-up is in the order of 5 percent. There is an early risk of causing acute cholecystitis or empyema of the gallbladder, particularly if clinically evident cholangitis is present at the time of ES.[69,70] If ductular clearance is not achievable, placement of biliary prostheses or nasobiliary drains is useful. Intraductal infusion of mono-actanoin is sometimes effective but is useless for pigment stones.[76]

If ES and clearance of ductular stones fails, reappraisal of fitness for surgery is indicated. Surgery is certainly warranted if acute cholecystitis is present. Mortality rates from operative common duct exploration vary, but for patients over age 60 the rates generally approach 6 to 12 percent. Mortality is higher in emergency surgery.[77–80] Most operative deaths are cardiovascular in origin and reflect the significant associated diseases in the elderly population with biliary tract stones. Postoperative morbidity is higher in all surgical series than that reported with successful endoscopic management. However, some elderly patients with unextractable ductular stones are quite fit and tolerate surgery well. Obviously, clinical judgment is extremely important in these decisions and surgical consultation may be required.

Newer modalities are developing for those who cannot tolerate surgery. Percutaneous radiographic assistance for endoscopic procedures is a major advance. Extracorporeal shock wave lithotripsy and direct laser or electrohydraulic lithotripsy by choledochoscopy are exciting advances. It is becoming unusual in specialized centers to fail in endoscopic or nonsurgical ductular stone clearance in poor operative candidates. Experience is still limited to a few centers, however, and these specialized treatments are not available widely.

ADENOCARCINOMA OF THE GALLBLADDER

Although the incidence is low, adenocarcinoma of the gallbladder is seen in about 1 percent of cholecystectomy specimens and is more common in autopsy series. It is rare in patients under age 50, and the peak incidence is in women in the sixth and seventh decades. The majority of cases (60 to 90 percent) are associated with gallstones, but a causal relationship has not been established. The tumor usually is not detected by imaging techniques and is diagnosed surgically. Western countries have reduced the mortality significantly, owing to widespread cholecystectomy in older patients. Since the tumor invades early, it is often diagnosed after obstructive jaundice develops from metastases to the porta hepatis.[81] The best management of gallbladder cancer is surgical.

Endoscopic or transhepatic palliation can be beneficial. Endoscopic stent placement can palliate the jaundice, reduce the frequency of cholangitis, and prolong survival.[82] If endoscopic stent placement cannot be achieved or if the intrahepatic biliary tree is incompletely decompressed after endoscopic therapy, percutaneous drain placement is necessary to prevent cholangitis. Percutaneous drains can be converted to internal-external drains or used to assist endoscopic stent placement. Regardless of the techniques used, palliative drainage is worthwhile and prolongs survival. Adenocarcinomas are not radiosensitive and respond poorly to chemotherapy. The overall 5-year survival rate for carcinoma of the gallbladder is 1 to 3 percent, but it is 10.6 percent if all disease is resectable.[83]

ADENOCARCINOMA OF THE BILE DUCTS

Malignant tumors of the bile ducts usually are adenocarcinomas. They occur with a peak incidence in patients in their early seventh decade (more commonly in men) and are less frequent than gallbladder carcinoma. These tumors are more commonly scirrhous in type, less commonly bulky, and may be multicentric in origin. Bile duct carcinomas are known to be associated with parasitic bile duct infestation in the Orient, thorotrast contrast infusion, sclerosing cholangitis, and choledochal cysts. In the West, bile duct carcinomas generally occur without a known predisposing cause. Biliary lithiasis is associated with this tumor, but a causal relationship has not been established.

The prognosis is poor. The best treatment is surgical resection, and this approach is optional when the tumor involves the extrahepatic biliary tree and is resectable. Some tumors can be resected at the bifurcation, and stents can be placed surgically to decompress the intrahepatic biliary tree.[84] Palliation usually requires generous excision of the extrahepatic biliary tree and a choledochoenteric or hepaticodochoenteric anastomosis. Distal cholangiolar carcinomas can be managed by a pylorus-sparing Whipple procedure.

Secondary problems with bile duct obstruction and cholangitis are substantial and contribute to the morbidity and mortality from bile duct carcinomas. These tumors respond poorly to radiation therapy or chemotherapy. Unresectable bile duct carcinomas are treated by placement of endoscopic or percutaneous stents.[82,85]

REFERENCES

1. Popper H: Aging and the liver, in Popper H, Schaffner F (eds): *Progress in Liver Diseases*, vol 8. New York, Grune & Stratton, 1986, pp 659–683.
2. Tauchi H, Sato T: Hepatic cells of the aged, in Kitani K (ed): *Liver and Aging*. Amsterdam, Elsevier/North Holland, 1978, pp 3–19.
3. Greenblatt DJ, Seller EM, Shader RI: Drug disposition in old age. *N Engl J Med* 306:1081, 1982.
4. O'Brien GF, Tan CV: Jaundice in the geriatric patient. *Geriatrics* 25:114, 1970.
5. Huete-Armijo A, Exton-Smith AN: Causes and diagnosis of jaundice in the elderly. *Br Med J* 1:1113, 1962.
6. Naso F, Thompson CM: Hyperbilirubinemia in the patient past 50. *Geriatrics* 22:206, 1967.
7. Patwardhan RV, Smith OJ, Farmelant MH: Serum transaminase levels and cholescintigraphic abnormalities in acute biliary tract obstruction. *Arch Intern Med* 147:1249, 1987.
8. Ginsberg AL: Very high levels of SGOT and LDL in patients with extrahepatic biliary tract obstruction. *Dig Dis* 15:803, 1970.
9. Bashour TT, Antonini C, Fisher J: Severe sinus node dysfunction in obstructive jaundice. *Ann Intern Med* 103:384, 1985.
10. Tandon BN, Rana S, Acharya SK: Bedside ultrasonography: A low-cost definitive diagnostic procedure in obstructive jaundice. *J Clin Gastroenterol* 9:353, 1987.
11. O'Connor KW, Snodgrass PJ, Swonder JE et al: A blinded prospective study comparing four current noninvasive approaches in the differential diagnosis of medical versus surgical jaundice. *Gastroenterology* 94:1498, 1983.
12. Vennes JA, Bond JH: Approach to the jaundiced patient. *Gastroenterology* 84:1615, 1983.
13. Richter JM, Silverstein MD, Schapiro R: Suspected obstructive jaundice: A decision analysis of diagnostic strategies. *Ann Intern Med* 99:46, 1983.
14. Scharschmidt BF, Goldberg HI, Schmid R: Current concepts in diagnosis: Approach to the patient with cholestatic jaundice. *N Engl J Med* 308:1515, 1983.
15. Hurwitz N: Predisposing factors in adverse reactions to drugs. *Br Med J* 1:536, 1969.
16. Seidl LG, Thornton GF, Smith JW, Cluff LE: Studies on the epidemiology of adverse drug reactions. III. Reactions in patients on a general medical service. *Bull Johns Hopkins Hosp* 119:299, 1966.
17. Eastwood HDH: Causes of jaundice in the elderly. *Gerontol Clin* 13: 69, 1971.
18. Roberts J, Turner N: Pharmacodynamic basis for altered drug action in the elderly. *Clin Geriatr Med* 4(1):127, 1988.
19. Vestal RE: Drug use in the elderly: A review of problems and special considerations. *Drugs* 16:358, 1978.
20. Zimmerman HJ: *Hepatotoxicity: The Adverse Effects of Drugs and Other Chemicals on the Liver*. New York, Appleton-Century-Crofts, 1978.
21. Inman WHW, Mushin WW: Jaundice after repeated exposure to halothane. *Br Med J* ii:1455, 1978.
22. Mitchell JR, Zimmerman HJ, Ishak KG et al: Isoniazid liver injury: Clinical spectrum, pathology, and probable pathogenesis. *Ann Intern Med* 84:181, 1976.
23. Ludwig J, Axelsen R: Drug effects on the liver: An updated tabular compilation of drugs and drug-related hepatic diseases. *Dig Dis Sci* 28:651, 1983.
24. Ishak KG, Irey NS: Hepatic injury associated with phenothiazines: Clinicopathologic and follow-up study of 36 patients. *Arch Pathol* 93:283, 1972.
25. Horst DA, Grace ND, LeCompte PM: Prolonged cholestasis and progressive hepatic fibrosis following imipramine therapy. *Gastroenterology* 79:550, 1980.
26. Maddrey WC, Boitnott JK: Drug-induced chronic liver disease. *Gastroenterology* 72:1348, 1977.
27. Lischner MW, Alexander JF, Galambos JT: Natural history of alcoholic hepatitis. I. The acute disease. *Am J Dig Dis* 16:481, 1971.
28. Galambos JT: *Cirrhosis*, vol 17, *Major Problems in Internal Medicine*. Philadelphia, Saunders, 1979.
29. Saunders JB: Alcoholic liver disease in the 1980's. *Br Med J* 287:1819, 1983.
30. Kaysen GA, Pond SM, Roper MH et al: Combined hepatic and renal injury in alcoholics during therapeutic use of acetaminophen. *Arch Intern Med* 145:2019, 1985.

31. Hall AH, Rumack BH: The treatment of acute acetaminophen poisoning. *J Intensive Care Med* 1:29, 1986.

32. Fenster LF: Viral hepatitis in the elderly: An analysis of 23 patients over 65 years of age. *Gastroenterology* 78:535, 1965.

33. Osmon DR, Melton J III, Keys TF et al: Viral hepatitis: A population-based study in Rochester, Minn, 1971–1980. *Arch Intern Med* 147:1235, 1987.

34. Koff RS, Galambos JT: Viral hepatitis, in Schiff L, Shiff ER (eds): *Diseases of the Liver*, 6th ed. Philadelphia, Lippincott, 1987, pp 457–581.

35. Maddrey WC: Subdivisions of idiopathic autoimmune chronic active hepatitis. *Hepatology* 7:1372, 1987.

36. Sherlock S: *Diseases of the Liver and Biliary System*, 7th ed. Boston, Blackwell, 1985.

37. Williams R, Smith PM, Spicer EJF et al: Venesection therapy in idiopathic hemochromatosis. *Q J Med* 38:1, 1969.

38. Niederan C, Fischer R, Sonnenberg A et al: Survival and causes of death in cirrhotic and noncirrhotic patients with primary hemochromatosis. *N Engl J Med* 313:1256, 1985.

39. Kapelman B, Schaffner F: The natural history of primary biliary cirrhosis. *Semin Liver Dis* 1:273, 1981.

40. Kaplan MM: Primary biliary cirrhosis. *N Engl J Med* 316:521, 1987.

41. Dickson ER, Fleming TR, Wiesner RH et al: Trial of penicillamine in advanced primary biliary cirrhosis. *N Engl J Med* 312:1011, 1985.

42. Kaplan MM, Alling DW, Zimmerman HJ et al: A prospective trial of colchicine for primary biliary cirrhosis. *N Engl J Med* 315:1448, 1986.

43. Rakela J, Goldschmiedt M, Ludwig J: Late manifestation of chronic liver disease in adults with alpha-1-antitrypsin deficiency. *Dis Dig Sci* 32:1358, 1987.

44. De la Monte SM, Arcidi JM, Moore GW, Hutchins GM: Midzonal necrosis as a pattern of hepatocellular injury after shock. *Gastroenterology* 86:627, 1984.

45. Lamont JT, Isselbacher KJ: Current concepts: Postoperative jaundice. *N Engl J Med* 288:305, 1973.

46. Chu C-M, Chang C-H, Liaw Y-F, Hsieh M-J: Jaundice after open heart surgery: A prospective study. *Thorax* 39:52, 1984.

47. Sherlock S: The liver in heart failure: Relation of anatomical, functional and circulatory changes. *Br Heart J* 13:273, 1951.

48. Sherlock S: The liver in circulatory failure, in Schiff L, Schiff ER (eds): *Diseases of the Liver*, 6th ed. Philadelphia, Lippincott, 1987, pp 1051–1057.

49. Cohen JA, Kaplan MM: Left-sided heart failure presenting as hepatitis. *Gastroenterology* 74:583, 1978.

50. Rubin RH, Swartz MN, Malt R: Hepatic abscess: Changes in clinical, bacteriologic and therapeutic aspects. *Am J Med* 57:601, 1974.

51. McDonald MI, Corey GR, Gallis HA, Durack DT: Single and multiple pyogenic liver abscesses: Natural history, diagnosis and treatment with emphasis on percutaneous drainage. *Medicine* 63:291, 1984.

52. Zimmerman HJ, Fang M, Utili R et al: Jaundice due to bacterial infection. *Gastroenterology* 77:362, 1979.

53. Schoenfield LJ, Marks JW: Formation and treatment of gallstones, in Schiff L, Schiff ER (eds): *Diseases of the Liver*, 6th ed. Philadelphia, Lippincott, 1987, pp 1267–1288.

54. Gelfand DW, Wolfman NT, Ott DJ, Watson NE Jr, Chen YM, Dale WJ: Oral cholecystography vs. gallbladder sonography: A prospective, blinded reappraisal. *AJR* 151:69, 1988.

55. Gracie WA, Ransohoff DF: The natural history of silent gallstones: The innocent gallstone is not a myth. *N Engl J Med* 307:798, 1982.

56. Ransohoff DF, Gracie WA, Wolfenson LB, Newhauser D: Prophylactic cholecystectomy or expectant management for silent gallstones: A decision analysis to assess survival. *Ann Intern Med* 99:199, 1983.

57. Sauerbruch T, Delius M, Paumgartner G, Hall J, Wess O, Weber W: Fragmentation of gallstones by extracorporeal shock waves. *N Engl J Med* 314:818, 1986.

58. Allen MJ, Borody TJ, Bugliosi TF, May GR, LaRusso NF, Thistle JL: Rapid dissolution of gallstones by methyl tert-butyl ether: Preliminary observations. *N Engl J Med* 312:217, 1985.

59. Schoenfield LJ, Lachin JM et al: Chenodiol (chenodeoxycholic acid) for dissolution of gallstones: The National Cooperative Gallstone Study. A controlled trial of efficacy and safety. *Ann Intern Med* 95:257, 1981.

60. Kupfer RM, Maudgal DP, Northfield TC: Gallstone dissolution rate during chenic acid therapy: Effect of bedtime administration plus low cholesterol diet. *Dig Dis Sci* 27:1025, 1982.

61. Tangedahl T, Carey WD, Ferguson DR et al: Drug and treatment efficacy of chenodeoxycholic acid in 97 patients with cholelithiasis and increased surgical risk. *Dig Dis Sci* 28:545, 1983.

62. Erlinger S, Go AL, Husson J-M, Fevery J: Franco-Belgian cooperative study of ursodeoxycholic acid in the medical dissolution of gallstones: A double-blind, randomized, dose-response study, and comparison with chenodeoxycholic acid. *Hepatology* 4:308, 1984.

63. Podda M, Zuin M, Dioguardi ML, Festorazzi S, Dioguardi N: A combination of chenodeoxycholic acid and ursodeoxycholic acid is more effective than either alone in reducing biliary cholesterol saturation. *Hepatology* 2:334, 1982.

64. Morrow DJ, Thompson J, Wilson SE: Acute cholecystitis in the elderly: A surgical emergency. *Arch Surg* 113:1149, 1978.

65. Glenn F: Surgical management of acute cholecystitis in patients 65 years of age or older. *Ann Surg* 193:56, 1981.

66. May RE, Strong R: Acute emphysematous cholecystitis. *Br J Surg* 58:453, 1971.

67. Glenn F, Becker CG: Acute acalculous cholecystitis: An increasing entity. *Ann Surg* 195:131, 1982.

68. Howard RJ: Acute acalculous cholecystitis. *Am J Surg* 141:194, 1981.

69. Davidson BR, Neoptolemos JP, Carr-Locke DL: Endoscopic sphincterotomy for common bile duct calculi in patients with gallbladder in situ considered unfit for surgery. *Gut* 29:114, 1988.

70. Escourrou J, Cordova JA, Lazorthes F, Frexinos J, Ribet A: Early and late complications after endoscopic spincterotomy for biliary lithiasis with and without the gallbladder "in situ." *Gut* 25:598, 1984.

71. Lotveit T, Osnes M, Larsen S: Recurrent biliary calculi: Duodenal diverticula as a predisposing factor. *Ann Surg* 196:30, 1982.

72. Wurbs DFW: Calculus disease of the bile ducts, in Sivak

MV Jr (ed): *Gastroenterologic Endoscopy.* Philadelphia, Saunders, 1987, pp 652–672.

73. Safrany L: Duodenoscopic sphincterotomy and gallstone removal. *Gastroenterology* 72:338, 1977.

74. Siegel JH: Endoscopic papillotomy in the treatment of biliary tract disease: 258 procedures and results. *Dig Dis Sci* 26:1057, 1981.

75. Wurbs D: Endoscopic papillotomy. *Scand J Gastroenterol* 17(suppl 77):107, 1982.

76. Palmer KR, Hofmann AF: Intraductal mono-octanoin for the direct dissolution of bile duct stones: Experience in 343 patients. *Gut* 27:196, 1986.

77. Cotton PB: Endoscopic management of bile duct stones; (apples and oranges). *Gut* 25:587, 1984.

78. Sheridan WG, Williams HOL, Lewis MH: Morbidity and mortality of common bile duct exploration. *Br J Surg* 74:1095, 1987.

79. McSherry CK, Glenn F: The incidence and causes of death following surgery for nonmalignant biliary tract disease. *Ann Surg* 191:271, 1980.

80. Pitt HA, Cameron JL, Postier RG, Gadacz TR: Factors affecting mortality in biliary tract surgery. *Am J Surg* 141:66, 1981.

81. Warren KW, Williams CI, Tan EGC: Diseases of the gallbladder and bile ducts, in Schiff L, Schiff ER (eds): *Diseases of the Liver*, 6th ed. Philadelphia, Lippincott, 1987, pp 1289–1335.

82. Deviere J, Baize M, deToeuf J, Cremer M: Long-term follow-up of patients with hilar malignant stricture treated by endoscopic internal biliary drainage. *Gastrointest Endosc* 34:95, 1988.

83. Appleman RM, Morlock CG, Dahlin DC, Adson MA: Long-term survival in carcinoma of the gallbladder. *Surg Gynecol Obstet* 117:459, 1963.

84. Cameron JL, Broe P, Zuidema GD: Proximal bile duct tumors: Surgical management with silastic transhepatic biliary stents. *Ann Surg* 196:412, 1982.

85. Huibregtse K, Tytgat GN: Palliative treatment of obstructive jaundice by transpapillary introduction of large bore bile duct endoprosthesis: Experience in 45 patients. *Gut* 23:371, 1982.

GENERAL READING

Brandt LJ: Pancreas, liver, and gallbladder, in Rossman I (ed): *Clinical Geriatrics.* Philadelphia, Lippincott, 1986, pp 302–325.

Chapter 62

PANCREATIC DISORDERS

John H. Gilliam III

AGING AND THE PANCREAS

Healthy, elderly patients without pancreatic disease have normal pancreatic exocrine function. Gullo and coworkers found 60 nonhospitalized elderly persons (mean age 78) who had normal pancreatic exocrine function, as measured by the flourescein dilaurate (pancreolauryl) test; there was no difference in the pancreatic function of these healthy elderly persons as compared to the pancreatic function of a healthy control population (mean age 36). The study population was nutritionally normal, had no recognizable digestive diseases, and had no history of diabetes or alcoholism.[1] Secretin testing has previously shown no change in bicarbonate output with age, although males under age 50 have a higher peak volume output than males over age 50.[2] A further study, using continuous IV infusion of secretin and cerulein, found elderly subjects to secrete normal volumes of pancreatic juice containing normal amounts of bicarbonate, trypsin, and chymotrypsin.[3] Although the literature is limited on this subject, these studies confirm the clinical impression that age does not affect pancreatic function.

However, there are some impressive morphologic alterations that occur with aging. Of patients over age 50, 79 percent were found at autopsy to have "adipose tissue invasion."[4] The degree of adipose tissue present correlated with obesity but not with sex. Atherosclerosis affecting the pancreas is common, though pancreatic infarction is quite rare.[5] Dilation of acini and ductules is common in the elderly and may be focal or quite diffuse.[4,6] In some elderly patients, ductular ectasia becomes cystic. Associated with these findings, periductular, intralobular, and perilobular fibrosis frequently occurs.[7] The width of the main pancreatic duct on necropsy ductograms increased about 8 percent per decade in one study,[6] but other studies have had difficulty confirming this finding. There is a tendency with advanced age for the pancreas to lie in a lower craniocaudal position. Calcifications in surrounding arteries are common.

The era of endoscopic retrograde cholangiopancreatography (ERCP) has produced extensive worldwide experience with pancreatic ductograms. It is clear that there is a wide range of normality in the size of the main pancreatic duct. There is also variation in the degree of opacification of branches, the ease of acinar filling, and the course of the ducts. By use of the ERCP technique it has been shown that the length of the pancreatic duct does not change with age.[8] This variability of the normal pancreatic ductogram has led to difficulties for endoscopists in avoiding false-positive diagnoses. Cotton found no correlation between duct width and age,[9] and he considered the cystic changes described by Kreel and Sandin[6] to be rare. More recently, the difficulties of interpreting pancreatic ductograms in elderly patients were reevaluated in an autopsy series. Six endoscopists were asked independently to grade ductograms obtained at autopsy without knowledge of the histologic findings. Of 69 ductograms of different human pancreata without pancreatitis, 81 percent were interpreted as showing chronic pancreatitis (37 percent minimal, 33 percent moderate, 11 percent severe).[7] Upon correlation of the ductograms with histology and gross inspection, it became clear that the ductular changes seen were due to perilobular fibrosis. It was speculated that this developed because of intraductal epithelial hyperplasia. In summary, the morphologic changes in the pancreas from aging may be striking and are far greater, it would seem, than alterations of functional significance. Experienced endoscopists will be aware of the difficulties involved in interpreting ERCP findings and will be cautious in diagnosing chronic pancreatitis in elderly patients.

ACUTE PANCREATITIS

Acute pancreatitis in the elderly is an uncommon de novo condition. As in younger patients, it presents with abdominal pain or tenderness, hyperamylasemia, and nausea with or without vomiting. The pain is steady, lasts for hours, and often bores through to the back. Flexing the back in various positions may ease the pain somewhat. Acute pancreatitis may manifest as a very mild illness, with pain as the predominant symptom and few abdominal signs. However, it also can present as a fulminant illness, with symptoms of shock, respiratory distress, renal failure, pericarditis, myoclonus or coma, hypocalcemia, leukocytosis, and fever. The symptoms of most patients with acute pancreatitis will fall between these two extremes.[10]

The diagnosis often is difficult. While hyperamylasemia is the rule, it is well known that hyperamylasemia is not specific for pancreatitis and may be present in burns, diabetic ketoacidosis, small-bowel ischemia or obstruction, ovarian carcinomas, tubal pregnancy, macroamylasemia, and severe renal failure. Distinguishing acute pancreatitis from macroamylasemia is not problematic, since urine excretion of amylase is marked in acute pancreatitis and minimal in macroamylasemia. However, several of the other conditions listed above can cause an elevated amylase/creatinine clearance ratio. The early enthusiasm for the amylase/creatinine clearance ratio[11] as a specific diagnostic test has waned after extensive experience has shown that the specificity is low.[12]

Much attention has been given to development of other serodiagnostic tests which might be more specific than the serum amylase. Serum lipase is more specific than amylase and is a useful, rapidly obtainable ancillary test. Pancreatic isoamylase and trypsinogen assays have been employed, but they are not available in most STAT labs. Pancreatic isoamylase can be valuable in subacute situations because salivary amylase elevation can be excluded.[13] All these blood tests have been studied critically by Steinberg and coworkers. With confirmation by ultrasound, computerized tomography, and/or laparotomy as the "gold standard," the following data were obtained from a series of 39 patients. In diagnosing pancreatitis, sensitivities were as follows: amylase (Beckman) 94.9 percent, amylase (Phadebas) 94.9 percent, trypsinogen RIA 97.4 percent, lipase 86.5 percent, and pancreatic isoamylase 92.3 percent. Specificities were as follows: amylase (Beckman) 88.9 percent, amylase (Phadebas) 86.0 percent, trypsinogen RIA 82.8 percent, lipase 99.0 percent, and pancreatic isoamylase 85.1 percent.[14]

Imaging studies are important ancillary tests. Abdominal ultrasound can be very helpful and diagnostic; however, its usefulness can be impaired by ileus or obesity. Computerized tomography is an excellent diagnostic test which does not have these problems. However, critically ill patients may not be able to withstand the procedure. An imaging study is indicated in acute pancreatitis to look for pseudocyst. Available imaging techniques may underestimate or overestimate the diagnosis, and there exists no perfect test[15] to define pancreatic pseudocysts.

Criteria for evaluating the severity of acute pancreatitis have been established in several reports.[16–20] Age over 55 years is an independent variable associated with a higher mortality. Although there is no study of pancreatitis restricted to a geriatric population, it seems likely that alcoholic pancreatitis occurs less frequently in this age group than in a younger population. Gallstones are found in 60 percent of patients with pancreatitis who are not alcoholic[20] and are a major cause of pancreatitis in the elderly. Other important causes are drugs, hyperlipidemia, trauma, and pancreatic cancer.

GALLSTONE PANCREATITIS

Gallstone passage into the common bile duct commonly causes temporary obstruction of the papilla of Vater. When pancreatic secretions are blocked, pancreatitis results. Patients may present with mild or fulminant pancreatitis. Debate has been active regarding the appropriate timing of surgery for biliary pancreatitis.[21] Kelly has recommended surgery within 72 hours if the pancreatitis worsens, but he found the best outcome to occur when surgery was delayed 5 to 7 days from onset.[22] There has been a shift to endoscopic sphincterotomy as recommended treatment, if available, after several centers have shown that ERCP does not exacerbate pancreatitis. Duodenoscopy often confirms stone impaction at the ampulla. The first large series of patients treated by endoscopic sphincterotomy was that studied by Classen et al.[23] A later series by Safrany and Cotton confirmed the safety of endoscopic sphincterotomy in acute stone impaction with severe pancreatitis and found that the improvement after successful treatment was often dramatic.[24] Endoscopic treatment of gallstone pancreatitis has not replaced surgery, but it has some definite advantages in very ill elderly patients. The risk of subsequent pancreatitis is diminished after endoscopic sphincterotomy. All experts in this area recommend definitive treatment because recurrent pancreatitis will occur in over 30 percent of patients if surgery or adequate endoscopic sphinctertomy is not done.[21]

HYPERLIPIDEMIA AND PANCREATITIS

There is well-recognized association in patients between the condition of chylomicronemia, and recurrent acute pancreatitis. A low-fat diet can prevent further attacks of pancreatitis in patients in this group.[25] More commonly, moderate hypertriglyceridemia (type IV hyperlipoproteinemia) is seen transiently with attacks of acute pancreatitis, typically in alcoholic patients.[26] If serum is not obtained at admission, chylomicronemia can be missed, and patients may be misclassified.[27] It is best to restudy lipid profiles after resolution of symptoms, if hyperlipoproteinema is found. Since chylomicronemia appears to decline in incidence with age, severe hypertriglyceridemia as a cause of pancreatitis is uncommon in the elderly and is distinctly rare except in poorly controlled diabetics in this age group. Hypertriglyceridemia aggravated by estrogen or alcohol abuse would be even less common in elderly subjects.

DRUGS AND PANCREATITIS

Pancreatitis appears to be associated with use of azathioprine, thiazides, sulfonamides, furosemide, estrogens, and tetracycline.[28] A probable association exists with corticosteroid use. Other possible associations exist but are largely based on case reports. The physician is advised to consider drugs as a source of pancreatitis in the elderly, but the incidence is low. This subject has been well reviewed.[28,29]

GENERAL CONSIDERATIONS IN ACUTE PANCREATITIS

The differential diagnosis of acute pancreatitis in the elderly certainly includes pancreatic carcinoma, which may present as pancreatitis. This is discussed subsequently.

Management of the acute attack is well standardized, regardless of age or cause. Patients are given IV fluids aggressively and are kept NPO or begun on nasogastric suction if the illness is severe. Attention to the balance of serum electrolytes, calcium, and magnesium is mandatory. Pulmonary, renal, and central nervous system complications require additional attention. Antibiotics, aprotonin, and somatostatin are not helpful. Surgery is to be avoided, except in gallstone pancreatitis.[10,30,31]

CHRONIC PANCREATITIS

Chronic pancreatitis is usually due to alcoholism. Therefore, the incidence of chronic pancreatitis in the elderly is low, since most alcoholic patients with this complication will not live to reach old age. However, enough alcoholics with pancreatic insufficiency secondary to chronic alcoholic pancreatitis survive to make this the second most common cause of steatorrhea (after celiac disease) beyond age 65.[32] Gallstone pancreatitis does not cause chronic pancreatitis; however, chronic pancreatitis can result from traumatic, idiopathic, or familial pancreatitis.

Steatorrhea is a hallmark symptom, but this does not occur unless pancreatic lipase excretion is 10 percent or less of normal output.[33] Steatorrhea *can* develop acutely, along with pain, from pancreatic cancer. Therefore, one should use caution in ascribing steatorrhea to chronic pancreatitis in the elderly when the diagnosis is not long-standing or clear. Pain is a typical symptom of chronic pancreatitis, particularly in alcoholic patients, but it is certainly not required for the diagnosis. Diabetes mellitus is also typical. Diabetes due to chronic pancreatitis is often brittle because there is a failure also of glucagon secretion, thus rendering patients more susceptible to recurrent hypoglycemic attacks when treated with insulin. Still, insulin is the preferred treatment for diabetes due to chronic pancreatitis. Oral hypoglycemics are generally ineffective.

Pancreatic exocrine function can be evaluated by several methods. The standard test is the 72-hour stool fat collection, which should be obtained on an outpatient basis with the patient eating standardized meals. While not tremendously popular, this remains the best method for defining steatorrhea. Considerable effort has been made to find other, more acceptable tests. Promising results are reported from measurement of serum trypsin-like immunoreactivity[34] and the bentiromide test.[35]

Pancreatic enzyme replacement is the treatment for steatorrhea due to pancreatic insufficiency. Several preparations are available, and the most potent ones are the more effective. The effectiveness of this therapy can be enhanced by simultaneous administration of sodium bicarbonate or cimetidine, since lipase can be permanently inactivated below a pH of 4. There are variations in patient tolerance, and the best preparation to use is the one each individual patient will tolerate.[10,36]

PANCREATIC CANCER

Pancreatic cancer is common, and the incidence is increasing. In men, it is the fourth most common cause of cancer deaths; in women, it is the fifth most common. Three percent of cancers and 5 percent of deaths from cancer in the United States are due to this malignancy.[37] Most patients die within six months of the diagnosis of pancreatic cancer, and the 5-year survival is less than 1 percent.[38]

Despite intense interest in aggressive therapies, the course of this disease has been altered very little in the last several decades. One problem is the failure to diagnose the disease at an early, resectable stage. Although two-thirds of pancreatic malignancies are located in the head of the pancreas, obstructive jaundice develops when the disease is already incurable. There are no early symptoms. Another problem is that aggressive use of abdominal ultrasound and computerized tomography has not led to earlier diagnosis.

Frequently, patients still present with painless obstructive jaundice, often with a palpable gallbladder. It is also not uncommon for patients to present with constant, boring, epigastric pain, exacerbated by meals, which may radiate straight through to the back. Anorexia, weight loss, and depression are also common presenting symptoms. Depression is such a well-known presenting finding that unexplained depression in an elderly male without an antecedent history mandates a search for pancreatic cancer. A previously stable diabetic whose diabetes becomes brittle may have developed pancreatic cancer.

There are numerous ways to diagnose pancreatic cancer. Perhaps the best initial diagnostic study is computerized axial tomography, which has a sensitivity of 94 percent but a specificity of only 60 percent.[39] Other useful modalities include celiac angiography, ERCP, ultrasound, and exploratory laparotomy.[39,40] A major advance in diagnosis is the development of Chiba needle aspiration biopsy, guided by ultrasound or computerized axial tomography, which has improved the specificity of imaging techniques. Additionally, there is preliminary evidence that a reliable blood test may now be available, namely, CA 19-9, which appears to have very good sensitivity and specificity for the diagnosis of pancreatic cancer.[41]

Therapy of pancreatic cancer remains problematic and ineffective. Surgery does not prolong survival, but it is considerably more effective if the disease is ampullary carcinoma and not pancreatic carcinoma. Surgery may be indicated to perform palliative choledochoenterostomy, gastroenterostomy, and occasionally a diverting pancreaticojejunostomy. Surgery is currently needed only occasionally to establish the diagnosis. It is increasingly possible to place endoscopic or percutaneous stents to alleviate obstructive jaundice. As a palliative goal, bypassing malignant biliary obstruction is reasonable therapy for pruritis. However, cholangitis may be induced, especially if biliary drainage is not optimized. Chemotherapy and radiotherapy have been disappointing in this disease.

SUMMARY

Aging does not appear to alter pancreatic efficiency to a degree that is functionally important independent of well-characterized diseases, though changes in the anat-omy of the acini and ducts can be demonstrated. Acute pancreatitis is less prevalent with advancing age, which is attributable to a declining incidence of alcoholism and hypertrigliceridemia with age. Biliary tract disease and drugs are relatively more common as causes of acute pancreatitis in the elderly. Management of acute pancreatitis in elderly patients does not differ from management in younger patients, though concomitant disease and limited physiological reserves may pose special problems. Chronic pancreatic insufficiency often reflects antecedent alcoholic pancreatitis. Pancreatic carcinoma remains a devastating disease that accounts for an increasing percentage of carcinoma deaths, especially in the elderly.

REFERENCES

1. Gullo L et al: Aging and exocrine pancreatic function. *J Am Geriatr Soc* 34:790, 1986.
2. Rosenberg IR et al: The effect of age and sex upon human pancreatic secretion of fluid and bicarbonate. *Gastroenterology* 50:191,1966.
3. Gullo L et al: Exocrine pancreatic function in the elderly. *Gerontology* 29:407, 1983.
4. Wallace SA, Ashworth CT: Early degenerative lesions of the pancreas. *Texas State J Med* 37:584, 1942.
5. McKay JW et al: Infarcts of the pancreas. *Gastroenterology* 35:256, 1958.
6. Kreel L, Sandin B: Changes in pancreatic morphology associated with aging. *Gut* 14:962, 1973.
7. Schmitz-Moormann P et al: Comparative radiological and morphological study of human pancreas: Pancreatitis-like changes in post-mortem ductograms and their morphological pattern. Possible implication for ERCP. *Gut* 26:406, 1985.
8. Kasugai T et al: Endoscopic pancreatography. I. The normal endoscopic pancreatocholangiogram. *Gastroenterology* 63:217, 1972.
9. Cotton PB: The normal endoscopic pancreatogram. *Endoscopy* 6:65, 1974.
10. Banks PA: *Pancreatitis*. New York, Plenum, 1979.
11. Warshaw AI, Fuller AF: Specificity of increased renal clearance of amylase in diagnosis of acute pancreatitis. *N Engl J Med* 292:325, 1975.
12. Levitt MD, Johnson SG: Is the C_{am}/C_{cr} ratio of value for the diagnosis of pancreatitis? *Gastroenterology* 75:118, 1978.
13. Moossa AR: Diagnostic tests and procedures in acute pancreatitis. *N Engl J Med* 311:639, 1984.
14. Steinberg WM et al: Diagnostic assays in acute pancreatitis: A study of sensitivity and specificity. *Ann Intern Med* 102:576, 1985.
15. Spechler SJ: How much can we know about acute pancreatitis? *Ann Intern Med* 102:704, 1985.
16. Ranson JHC et al: Prognostic signs and the role of operative management in acute pancreatitis. *Surg Gynecol Obstet* 139:69, 1974.
17. Blamey SL et al: Prognostic factors in acute pancreatitis. *Gut* 25:1340, 1984.

18. Williamson RCN: Early assessment of severity in acute pancreatitis. *Gut* 25:1331, 1984.

19. Corfield AP et al: Prediction of severity in acute pancreatitis: Prospective comparison of three prognostic indices. *Lancet* 2:403, 1985.

20. Ranson JHC: Etiological and prognostic factors in human acute pancreatitis: A review. *Am J Gastroenterol* 77:633, 1982.

21. Ranson JHC: The timing of biliary surgery in acute pancreatitis. *Ann Surg* 189:654, 1979.

22. Kelly TR: Gallstone pancreatitis: The timing of surgery. *Surgery* 88:345, 1980.

23. Classen M: Pancreatitis—an indication for endoscopic papillotomy? *Endoscopy* 10:223, 1978.

24. Safrany L, Cotton PB: A preliminary report: Urgent duodenoscopic sphincterotomy for acute gallstone pancreatitis. *Surgery* 89:424, 1981.

25. Farmer RG et al: Hyperlipoproteinemia and pancreatitis. *Am J Med* 54:161, 1973.

26. Buck A et al: Hyperlipidemia and pancreatitis. *World J Surg* 4:307, 1980.

27. Cameron JL, Margolis S: Invited commentary. *World J Surg* 4:312, 1980.

28. Mallory A, Kern F Jr: Drug-induced pancreatitis: A critical review. *Gastroenterology* 78:813, 1980.

29. Nakashima Y, Howard JM: Drug-induced acute pancreatitis. *Surg Gynecol Obstet* 145:105, 1977.

30. Geokas MC et al: Acute pancreatitis. *Ann Intern Med* 103:86, 1985.

31. Soergel KH: Medical treatment of acute pancreatitis: What is the evidence? *Gastroenterology* 74:620, 1978.

32. Price HL et al: Steatorrhea in the elderly. *Br Med J* 1:1582, 1977.

33. DiMagno EP, Go VLW, Summerskill WJH: Relations between pancreatic enzyme outputs and malabsorption in severe pancreatic insufficiency. *N Engl J Med* 288:813, 1973.

34. Jacobsen DG et al: Trypsin-like immunoreactivity as a test for pancreatic insufficiency. *N Engl J Med* 310:1307, 1984.

35. Toskes PP: Bentiromide as a test of exocrine pancreatic function in adult patients with pancreatic exocrine insufficiency: Determination of appropriate dose and urinary collection interval. *Gastroenterology* 85:565, 1983.

36. Regan PT et al: Comparative effects of antacids, cimetidine and enteric coating on the therapeutic response to oral enzymes in severe pancreatic insufficiency. *N Engl J Med* 297:854, 1977

37. Hermann RE, Cooperman AM: Current concepts in cancer: Cancer of the pancreas. *N Engl J Med* 301:482, 1979.

38. Aoki K, Ogawa H: Cancer of the pancreas: International mortality trends. World Health Stat Rep 31:2, 1978.

39. Fitzgerald PJ et al. The value of diagnostic aids in detecting pancreas cancer. *Cancer* 41:868, 1978.

40. DiMagno EP, Malagelada J-R, Taylor WF, Go VLW: A prospective comparison of current diagnostic tests for pancreatic cancer. *N Engl J Med* 297:737, 1977.

41. Steinberg WM, Gelfand R, Anderson KK: Comparison of the sensitivity and specificity of the CA 19-9 and carcinoembryonic antigen assays in detecting cancer of the pancreas. *Gastroenterology* 90:343, 1986.

Chapter 63

COLONIC DISORDERS

Lawrence J. Cheskin and Marvin M. Schuster

A number of colonic disorders are of particular importance in the elderly patient, because of both marked age-associated increases in prevalence and differences in presentation and prognosis between young and old patients with the same disease. Some of these disorders are discussed elsewhere, i.e., fecal incontinence (Chap. 116), constipation (Chap. 119), and diarrhea and inflammatory bowel disease (Chap. 120).

This chapter will focus on two diseases of major importance in developed countries: diverticular disease and carcinoma of the colorectum. While these are obviously quite different disorders which happen to affect the same organ, they are epidemiologically linked. In addition, both diseases show an age-associated increase in prevalence, most strikingly for diverticular disease. Both are more common in westernized countries, and there is some evidence that this is because of dietary differences, in particular intake of dietary fiber, which is low in areas with a high incidence of these diseases.

DIVERTICULAR DISEASE

The terminology used for related conditions is widely misunderstood. *Diverticular disease* refers to the entire spectrum of manifestations described in this condition. *Diverticulosis* refers simply to the anatomic presence of colonic diverticula, without presuming that there are any symptoms associated with this finding. *Diverticulitis* refers to an inflammatory condition which involves one or more colonic diverticula and is almost always symptomatic. *Painful diverticular disease* refers to symptomatic diverticulosis in the absence of evidence of diverticular inflammation.

EPIDEMIOLOGY AND PATHOGENESIS

The prevalence of colonic diverticula is strongly correlated with advancing age. Diverticula are uncommon before the age of 40 (less than 5 to 10 percent preva-

lence) and increase to over 50 percent prevalence after the age of 70.[1] It has also been found that the number of diverticula per patient is greater in older patients.[2]

As noted, diverticular disease is seen almost exclusively in westernized countries. It has been postulated that differences in diet, in particular intake of dietary fiber, contribute to these differences in prevalence.[3,4] Evidence in support of this hypothesis includes the following:

1. Diverticular disease was virtually unknown before 1900, coincident with the start of milling, which removes two-thirds of the fiber content of flour.
2. Vegetarians have a much lower prevalence of diverticular disease than nonvegetarians.
3. Dietary fiber is lower among both vegetarians and nonvegetarians who have diverticular disease than those who do not have diverticular disease.[5]
4. Animal studies show that a life-long low fiber diet, but not a high fiber diet, is associated with the formation of diverticula.[6]

While the association of low dietary fiber and diverticular disease is well established, the mechanism is less clear. It is known that there are higher levels of motility and intraluminal pressure in colonic segments which bear diverticula than in normal segments, particularly in response to meals or cholinergic stimuli.[7] These areas of high pressure are associated with hypertrophy of circular muscle (myochosis) and possibly the formation of diverticula, since biophysical law dictates that narrowing of the lumen of a closed tube will result in an inversely proportional increase in intraluminal pressure. It is not known why abnormalities in colonic motility and muscle hypertrophy exist in diverticular disease, or why there is such a striking correlation with increasing age. The increase in collagen seen in the aging colon may play a role here, leading to shortening and narrowing of the colon and higher intraluminal pressures.

Diverticular disease usually is seen with multiple rather than single diverticula. In fact, the lesions are technically not diverticula at all but herniations of the mucosa through gaps in the muscular layers, often at points of entry of blood vessels. Two areas are most susceptible to herniation. The first area is between the taenia coli, longitudinal gatherings of muscle which are present throughout the colon but not in the rectum or appendix (locations which almost never develop diverticula). The second area of susceptibility is in the narrow bands of connective tissue between rings of circular muscle. The segment of colon which accounts for 75 percent of all diverticula is the sigmoid colon. It is thought that the narrow caliber of the sigmoid results in higher intraluminal pressure and hence a greater risk of herniation. Diverticula occur in decreasing frequency as one moves proximally in the colon.

CLINICAL FEATURES

As noted, there is a wide range of clinical presentation. Perhaps 80 to 85 percent of diverticulosis never presents clinically, either because it is entirely asymptomatic or because the symptoms are mild and infrequent and insufficient to cause the patient to seek medical attention. Symptomatic disease presents either as painful diverticular disease (75 percent) or as diverticulitis or hemorrhage (25 percent). In most cases which become symptomatic, the anatomic abnormality of diverticulosis is present several years before the onset of symptoms. There are some cases, however, in which characteristic symptoms (left lower quadrant pain, often after constipation) precede anatomic disease.[8] In these cases barium enema examination will often reveal saw-toothed spasm and thickening of the muscular wall of the colon, called myochosis. This is considered a prediverticular condition.

Diverticular Disease

Painful diverticular disease presents as attacks of colicky or steady left lower quadrant abdominal pain, usually exacerbated after meals and improved by bowel movement or passage of flatus. Alteration in bowel habit, more often constipation than diarrhea or alternating constipation and diarrhea, is seen in 46 to 63 percent of cases.[2,9] Physical examination of the abdomen may reveal a tender loop of sigmoid colon in the left lower quadrant, but the exam is often unremarkable. The presence of a fever or elevated blood leukocyte count or signs of peritonitis point toward an attack not of painful diverticular disease but to the more serious inflammatory condition, diverticulitis.

Diverticulitis

Diverticulitis, inflammation of one or more diverticula and pericolic tissues, is thought to develop when perfo-

ration of one or more diverticula occurs. These perforations may be microscopic or macroscopic. The perforation may be the result of persistent high pressures intraluminally or may be preceded by an inflammatory process of any etiology which weakens the wall of the diverticula. Diverticulitis increases in incidence with age and the duration of the prerequisite diverticulosis. This complication of diverticulosis is also more common in those individuals with the highest number of diverticula. The inflamed diverticula are almost always located in the sigmoid colon. When macroscopic perforations occur, abscesses form between the colon and neighboring tissues, with accompanying scarring and granulation tissue as healing occurs. Thus, fistulas may form to the bladder, vagina (especially posthysterectomy), small bowel, or skin. Rarely, free perforation into the peritoneal cavity occurs, and the patient presents with a surgical abdomen.[9] Diverticular abscesses have a variable natural history: they may resolve spontaneously, either by draining back into the colonic lumen or by becoming walled off and healing, or may enlarge.

Classically, the pain of acute diverticulitis is severe, persistent and abrupt in onset, increases in severity with time with localization to the left lower quadrant, and is accompanied by a variable amount of anorexia, nausea, and/or vomiting. Altered bowel function is common, more often constipation than diarrhea, and sometimes alternating constipation and diarrhea. Urinary frequency, dysuria, or abdominal pain aggravated by micturition may indicate involvement of the bladder in the inflammatory process or simply diverticulitis contiguous to the urinary tract. This may lead to the development of a colovesical fistula, often marked by symptoms of pneumaturia or fecaluria. Fever with or without chills is usually present and is sometimes the presenting complaint.

On physical examination, localized tenderness is usually present in the left lower quadrant, although occasionally suprapubic or right lower quadrant signs predominate and may be mistaken for acute appendicitis. The abdomen is often distended, tympanitic to percussion, with the bowel sounds diminished. A localized tender mass may be felt at the site of inflammation. Signs of generalized peritonitis are rare unless free perforation has occurred, though the psoas and/or obturator signs may be positive and there may be some rebound tenderness locally. About a quarter of patients with diverticulitis will have rectal bleeding, usually occult. Thus carcinoma of the rectum or colon should be ruled out as well as inflammatory or ischemic bowel disease. A leukocytosis is almost invariably present, frequently with a shift to earlier forms. The urine sediment may reveal white or red blood cells when the bladder or ureter is involved in the inflammatory process.

One must be aware that the classical presentation of acute diverticulitis described above may be altered in the elderly patient. In particular, the symptoms and signs are often less striking. For example, fever may be absent, the abdominal examination may not show impressive tenderness, there may be no mass felt, and the pain may not be very severe. None of these negative findings should lead one to strike diverticulitis from the differential diagnosis of the elderly patient with an acute abdominal or pelvic complaint, especially when colonic diverticula are known to be present. Even when the presentation is more typical of acute diverticulitis, the severity of the attack should not be underestimated when the symptoms are mild or the leukocytosis unimpressive. In older patients, the total picture may be muted even when the disease is quite severe. It is prudent to examine such patients carefully over a period of days so that a sudden worsening of the patient's condition is detected early.

The diagnosis is made largely on clinical grounds, but some auxiliary testing is helpful. Flat and upright (or lateral decubitus) abdominal radiographs may show evidence of adynamic ileus or, less commonly, mechanical obstruction. The location and extent of the inflammatory mass may be revealed. Occasionally, air in the bladder or free in the abdomen will point to colovesical fistula or free perforation, respectively. Because diverticulitis is usually a clinical diagnosis and shares presenting features with several other diseases of the colorectum, notably carcinoma, inflammatory bowel disease, and ischemic colitis, most authorities recommend that a sigmoidoscopy, either rigid or fiberoptic, be performed early. A flexible sigmoidoscopy performed without vigorous bowel preparation will help rule out these other diseases, as well as show whether there are diverticula present in the sigmoid. Air insufflation during the procedure is kept to a minimum to avoid worsening or causing perforation. It is probably best not to advance the instrument into diverticula-containing areas until the patient's condition has improved and several weeks have passed to allow for healing of the acute inflammation. At that point, either a barium enema or a full colonoscopy should be performed to examine the remainder of the colon, in particular to rule out carcinoma proximal to the rectosigmoid region. Radiographic findings in diverticulitis, besides diverticula, may include confined extravasation of contrast material outside of the bowel through a perforated diverticulum, intraluminal abscess cavities, fistulae, or a mass effect on the outline of the bowel from an inflammatory focus. Local colonic spasm or thickening of the wall may be seen but, as an isolated finding, is not evidence for diverticulitis.

Treatment in most cases of suspected acute diverticulitis requires hospitalization, especially in the elderly patient who has multiple medical problems or is debilitated. Conservative therapy should be tried first. The bowel and the patient should be put to rest, with intravenous hydration, analgesics, and broad spectrum anti-biotics to cover gram-positive cocci and both aerobic and anaerobic gram-negative gut flora. A common antibiotic regimen is ampicillin and metronidazole or gentamicin. In selected mild cases, outpatient treatment with an oral agent like tetracycline can be tried if there is minimal or no fever or leukocytosis. Although at least three-quarters of patients will respond to conservative medical management, it is prudent to obtain a surgical consultation on admission to the hospital so that, should it become necessary, surgery can be performed expeditiously. The patient should be followed closely, and signs of worsening inflammation or lack of response to treatment should be considered as indications for excision of the inflamed segment of the colon. Clinical improvement is usually seen in 3 to 10 days if the patient is going to respond to medical treatment. If the response is favorable, the diet can be advanced over a few days to a normal diet. In fact, it is probably safe to allow a clear liquid diet from the start of treatment if there are no signs of obstruction such as abdominal distension or nausea. For those patients who respond to medical treatment, a recurrence rate of 25 percent can be expected, most of which will occur in the first 5 years.[10] A fiber supplement and/or a high fiber diet is usually recommended for patients who have recovered from an attack of acute diverticulitis. For those patients who do not respond to medical treatment, especially with spreading peritonitis, urgent resection is indicated. In younger patients in whom peritoneal contamination is slight or contained in a small abscess, resection with primary anastomosis is feasible. For most elderly patients, however, a two-stage procedure is necessary: the first a resection with diverting colostomy proximal to the resection; the second a takedown of the colostomy with reestablishment of intestinal continuity.

Bleeding

Bleeding from diverticula is the most common cause of major lower gastrointestinal tract hemorrhage in the elderly,[11] followed by bleeding from angiodysplasias. Some 10 to 25 percent of patients with diverticular disease will at some point have bleeding through the rectum, of which 3 to 5 percent will be severe hemorrhage rather than occult bleeding. It must be borne in mind that rectal bleeding in a patient with known diverticular disease is not necessarily related to the diverticula. Such patients may be bleeding from angiodysplastic or neoplastic lesions, hemorrhoids, or inflammatory or ischemic bowel disease rather than a diverticulum. In one study, colonoscopy performed right after hemorrhage in patients with diverticular disease revealed a 30 percent prevalence of second lesions which might cause the hemorrhage.[12] Diverticular bleeding, in contrast to diverticulitis, involves the right rather than the left colon in two-thirds of cases. A single diverticulum is usually the source of bleeding and results when the medium of one of the small arteries which penetrates the muscular wall next to a diverticulum becomes thinned and ruptures. The cause of this thinning is not clear, but it does not appear to be related to an inflammatory process.

Classically, diverticular hemorrhage occurs in an elderly patient with previously undiagnosed, or at least previously asymptomatic, diverticular disease. The patient presents suddenly with mild lower abdominal discomfort, urgency, and subsequently passes a large dark red, maroon, or melenic stool. More bloody bowel movements often occur over the next few days, but some 80 percent of patients stop bleeding spontaneously with conservative treatment. The recurrence rate is 20 to 25 percent and increases with each subsequent episode of bleeding.

The diagnostic certainty can be increased in a patient presenting with classical features by a series of studies. First, a nasogastric tube should be passed and gastric or duodenal fluid aspirated and checked for blood. If blood is absent, this will essentially rule out a rapid upper gastrointestinal tract bleeding site. Next, proctoscopy can be performed to rule out a diffuse inflammatory process and hemorrhoidal bleeding. If the rate of bleeding appears to be high and continuing, selective mesenteric arteriography may be performed to localize a site of extravasation and often will distinguish a diverticulum from an angiodysplasia or a tumor. If the rate of bleeding is felt to be less than 1 ml/min, arteriography is unlikely to demonstrate extravasation, though it may still identify possible bleeding sites, especially an anatomic vascular anomaly. For slower rates of bleeding, a ^{99m}Tc-tagged red blood cell scan is much more sensitive than arteriography, but it can only define the approximate site of bleeding, not determine the type of lesion responsible for the bleeding. Nonetheless, this anatomic information can be very useful, especially if surgical resection is ultimately required. Colonoscopy is difficult to perform when massive bleeding is occurring but is very useful in defining possible bleeding sites when bleeding has slowed or ceased.

Treatment of diverticular bleeding, like diverticulitis, should be conservative, with hospitalization, bed rest, bowel rest, blood transfusions, and correction of any coagulopathy. When active bleeding continues and has been identified by selective mesenteric arteriography as being diverticular (or angiodysplastic) in origin, vasoconstriction with intraarterial vasopressin or local embolization can be attempted. Though these procedures entail a risk of precipitating bowel wall infarction, they are worth trying, particularly in elderly patients who are poor surgical risks. Massive or persistent hemorrhage which does not respond to conservative treatment or interventional radiologic procedures is a surgical emergency. Surgical resection should also be considered on an elective basis after recurrent hemorrhages if the risk of

recurrence appears to outweigh the risk of surgery. The choice of operation is controversial and beyond the scope of this discussion; but, in general, partial colectomy is recommended when the site of bleeding has been well established, while subtotal colectomy is necessary when the patient is exsanguinating and the site is uncertain.

COLORECTAL CANCER

EPIDEMIOLOGY AND PATHOGENESIS

In the United States, cancers of the colon and rectum account for 14 and 16 percent of all cancers in men and women, respectively, and, after lung and breast cancers, are the third leading cause of cancer deaths overall, the second leading cause in men, and the first in women over age 75.[13] Men have about a 6 percent lifetime chance of developing a colorectal cancer; women have about the same. The incidence is 4 to 5 times higher in people 65 and older than in the 45- to 64-year-old age group.[14] For women, this ratio is higher for colorectal cancers than it is for cancer in general. The incidence of colorectal cancer continues to rise throughout life, approximately doubling with each decade over age 50, to age 75 and older. More than two-thirds of colorectal cancers occur in people 65 or older. The death rate from colorectal cancer has not changed significantly in the past 50 years. Overall 5-year survival is less than 50 percent and is somewhat worse in geriatric groups, even after adjusting for increases in other causes of death in the elderly.

It is now well established that there is a gradual continuum of changes in the colonic epithelium which lead to an invasive cancer. The earliest macroscopically identifiable of these precursor lesions is the adenomatous polyp. Hyperplastic polyps, which are similar in gross appearance to adenomatous polyps, are thought to have no malignant potential, but adenomatous polyps do. It is not clear exactly what proportion of these premalignant lesions will progress to frank carcinoma (certainly less than 10 percent),[15] but it is clear that virtually all cancers of the colorectum arise from these precursors.[16] The chance of an individual polyp containing invasive cancer rises with its size (>2 cm $= 40$ percent), degree of cellular atypia, and histologic type. A minimum of approximately 5 years is needed for an early polyp to become an invasive cancer. This is reflected in the fact that the incidence curve for adenomatous polyps parallels that for colorectal cancer, shifted to the left by 5 to 10 years.[17]

The stage at which a cancer of the colorectum is detected has a marked effect on the patient's outcome. Cancers confined to the mucosal layers (Dukes' stage A) result in about an 80 to 90 percent 5-year survival, compared to about 1 to 2 percent for metastatic cancers

(Dukes' stage D).[18,19] Currently, only about 20 percent of colorectal cancers are diagnosed at these local stages (Dukes' A or B), and it has been estimated that it takes 4 years on average for tumors to progress from Dukes' A to Dukes' D.[20] Over 85 percent of tumors detected while asymptomatic are still at Dukes' stages A or B. Thus, early detection of tumors can have a potentially major impact on the death rate from this important form of cancer. Fortunately, colorectal polyps are directly accessible to the physician via fiberoptic endoscopy and can be safely removed with a wire snare and electrocautery, avoiding surgery in most cases. The most complete and most accurate form of screening for colorectal lesions involves examining the entire organ with a colonoscope. Since this procedure is costly, requires extensive bowel preparation, and is technically fairly difficult, lack of unlimited resources dictates that full colonoscopy be reserved for those patients with known disease or symptoms and those at higher than average risk for colorectal cancer. Although some shift to the proximal colon has occurred in the past decade, the distribution of colorectal cancer is still weighted to the distal portion of the colon and the rectum. About 60 percent of cancers and 70 percent of polyps are in the left colon, within reach of a 60-centimeter flexible sigmoidoscope. Thus, screening of people at average risk can be accomplished fairly effectively with a far lesser degree of resource utilization. Flexible sigmoidoscopy technique can be learned by nonspecialists in a short time, takes an average of 10 minutes to complete,[21] and has a very low incidence of complications when performed in the elderly for screening purposes.[22] Who should be screened and by which methods are critical and still controversial questions. Although much is known about certain high-risk groups, such as patients with long-standing ulcerative colitis or the autosomal dominant familial polyposis syndrome, there is much less known about screening in the far larger population at average or moderately increased risk of colorectal polyps and carcinomas. Besides familial polyposis, there are several other syndromes with strong genetic components, including Gardner's syndrome, site-specific colorectal cancer, and cancer family syndrome. These patients may develop early-onset and often multiple cancers with a proximal colon site predominance.[23–25]

Factors which cause more modest increases in the risk of colorectal cancer include personal or family history of colorectal, breast, or endometrial carcinoma, age, and the presence of adenomatous polyps. The degree of cancer risk rises with the number of adenomas present. Diet, in particular one low in fiber and high in fat, probably is a risk factor as well.[26,27]

Primary prevention is an attractive method of reducing the mortality from colorectal cancer, although the etiology and risk factors are not as clear-cut as in lung cancer, for example. Epidemiologic studies reveal that there is a broad range of colorectal cancer incidence across geographic boundaries around the world. In general, third-world countries have far lower age-adjusted incidences than industrialized areas, although there are notable differences even among industrialized nations (for example, Japan is low, whereas the United States is high). These epidemiologic studies have correlated the incidence of large bowel cancer with various dietary constituents, notably fats, meats, sugar, and total caloric intake.[28–30] At least 14 case-control studies have also been done, with conflicting results. Conflicting findings in part arise from methodologic differences, but it seems also true that the specific factors which influence the risk of large bowel cancer depend on the general dietary pattern in the population under study.[31]

One popular hypothesis relates increased risk of colorectal cancer to a high-fat, low-fiber diet.[32,33] The rate of degradation of cholesterol and primary bile acids to secondary bile acids by bacterial 7-α-dehydroxylases is increased in populations at high risk for,[34] and patients with, colorectal cancer.[35] Some of these bacterially degraded bile acid products are known carcinogens,[36] and are cocarcinogens[37–40] and comutagens[41] in animal models.

Bacterial 7-α-dehydroxylation is inhibited at a pH of less than 6.5.[42,43] Acidification of the stool results from increasing the fiber content of the diet,[44] probably because of degradation of fiber constituents to short-chain fatty acids by colonic anaerobes.[45,46] Indeed, bran consumption results in a reduced proportion of degraded bile acids in bile.[47,48] The ingestion of the nonabsorbed sugar lactulose, or ingestion of milk in lactose-intolerant individuals, would also be expected to acidify the stool[49] and thus inhibit 7-α-dehydroxylation of bile acids. Increased consumption of fats did not alter fecal pH in one study[44] but does raise fecal bile acid excretion,[50] since 7-α-dehydroxylases are inducible[42] with increased substrate. This induction would only occur if the pH were conducive, however, raising the possibility that an acidified colonic environment would negate the effect of a high-fat, low-fiber diet on fecal bile acid metabolism.[51]

There is evidence in the rat dimethylhydrazine colon carcinogenesis model that acidification of stool reduces the risk of this experimental cancer.[52] In humans, fecal pH correlated with the population risk of colon cancer in one study,[53] although fecal pH could not be correlated with fiber intake. This may be because fecal pH does not accurately reflect intracolonic pH.[54]

Thus, there is considerable experimental evidence to suggest that a complex interaction between dietary substrate, bacterial metabolism, and colonic pH influences the production of potentially carcinogenic substances. This, coupled with mechanical factors such as intestinal motility (duration of exposure to carcinogenic conditions) and genetic factors, may determine the individual's risk of developing colorectal polyps and cancer.

CLINICAL FEATURES

Although the prognosis becomes significantly worse in symptomatic patients, many patients do not seek medical care until worrisome symptoms occur. The most common presenting symptoms of colorectal cancer are bleeding through the rectum and changes in bowel habit. The site of the lesion influences which presenting features are most common. Left-sided colonic lesions tend to cause narrowing of the colonic lumen as they grow so that obstructive symptoms may occur. A change in bowel habits is reported, usually constipation, sometimes with pencil-thin stools and occasionally diarrhea. Bleeding from rectal and left-sided lesions is commonly visible in the stool. Right-sided colonic tumors grow in a wider-bore environment and one in which the stool traffic is liquid rather than semisolid as in the left colon. Thus, right-sided tumors rarely present with obstructive symptoms. Instead they cause bleeding which is usually slow and not visible in the stool; so the patient is more likely to present with symptoms of anemia than hematochezia. Occasionally, right-sided tumors cause abdominal discomfort in the right lower quadrant. Premalignant adenomatous lesions are usually asymptomatic, though they often bleed, usually in an intermittent fashion which is detectable upon testing the stool for occult blood. A specific pathologic type of polyp, the villous adenoma, can present with profuse watery diarrhea. Villous adenomas are particularly likely to progress to or already contain a malignancy.

The physical examination of the patient with a noncancerous polyp or an early-stage carcinoma is usually unrevealing, unless the lesion happens to be within reach of the examining finger in the rectum or there are signs of anemia. With a larger but potentially still resectable tumor, a mass may be felt in the abdomen. Patients with more advanced lesions may show signs of weight loss, liver enlargement or ascites from metastases, or a Virchow's node. The examination of an elderly patient should include a digital rectal examination and testing of the stool that adheres to the glove for occult blood. If the specimen is negative for blood, three additional specimens should be obtained on consecutive days.

In older patients with suggestive symptoms or blood in the stools, the diagnosis of colorectal adenoma or carcinoma is best made by colonoscopic biopsy or excision. Many clinicians begin with a rigid or flexible sigmoidoscopy. If this reveals a polyp or tumor, biopsy specimens are taken and the rest of the colon examined with a colonoscope to rule out synchronous lesions. If sigmoidoscopy has been negative, the remainder of the colon can be examined by air-contrast barium enema. The barium enema is more likely than colonoscopy to miss small lesions, and it must be followed by a colonoscopy to obtain biopsy specimens if an abnormality is found. It is, however, less costly than colonoscopy. The alternative is to proceed directly from symptoms or rectal bleeding to full colonoscopy. It should be emphasized that discovery of hemorrhoids on rectal examination or sigmoidoscopy is not adequate assurance that the source of bleeding through the rectum or cause of a change in bowel habits has been discovered. This is especially true in elderly patients because of the rising incidence of adenomas and carcinomas of the colorectum with advancing age.

TREATMENT

When polyps have been found, all should be removed during colonoscopy by electrocautery unless they are too large to remove safely. Biopsy specimens can be obtained of large lesions to confirm that they are cancerous, and they can then be removed surgically. Pathologic examination of polyps excised during colonoscopy will define the type of polyp, whether there is evidence of a malignant focus, and whether there are malignant cells invading the submucosa or stalk of the polyp. Hyperplastic-type polyps, unlike tubular or villous adenomas, are generally believed to have no malignant potential and do not place the patient in a high-risk category for screening purposes.

Initial laboratory tests which may be helpful on the workup of patients with colorectal adenoma or carcinoma are a complete blood count with red cell indices, serum transaminases, γ-glutamyltranspeptidase, bilirubin, and alkaline phosphatase.

Further treatment is required for frank carcinomas of the colorectum or polyps, which, upon colonoscopic excision, prove to have a focus of malignancy which invades the submucosa or involves only the mucosa but is not excised in its entirety. Surgical excision, the extent of which is determined by the depth of invasion of the tumor and other findings at laparotomy, is the only potentially curative treatment available. In advanced lesions involving lymph nodes but without distant metastases, adjuvant chemotherapy or radiotherapy may have a slight benefit, but there is no accepted standard of treatment of such lesions. The 5-year survival ranges from 13 to 40 percent. Patients with metastatic lesions noted at the time of diagnosis or at laparotomy have a dismal prognosis. Palliative treatment is then indicated. Removal of the tumor mass is not recommended routinely but only when a specific indication exists, such as bleeding or obstruction by the mass.

In patients who will have potentially curative surgery, the level of serum carcinoembryonic antigen (CEA) may be useful in postoperative follow-up. Often, this antigen will be elevated preoperatively, return to normal postoperatively, and give early warning of tumor recurrence if a rise in level is noted at a later time. Its sensitivity, however, ranges from only 30 percent in Dukes' A to 83 percent in Dukes' stage D tumors.[55,56] Smokers[57] and patients with liver disease, peptic ulcer, pancreatitis, diverticulitis, and inflammatory bowel disease have a higher false-positive rate than other controls.[58] Older patients also have slightly higher levels of CEA on average than younger persons, more than can be accounted for by a greater prevalence of the benign conditions associated with elevated CEA levels in the elderly.[59] As a result of these limitations, CEA has come to be viewed as a more effective tool for assessing patients with known colorectal tumors for recurrence and response to treatment than as a screening tool for the presence of tumor. The risk of recurrence is high following curative resection. Over half of recurrences are local.[60] Follow-up of patients with resected colorectal carcinoma should include periodic history and physical examinations, including stools for occult blood, a CEA level every 3 months for at least 5 years, and colonoscopy every 6 months for 3 years, then annually thereafter.

Because of the high incidence of colorectal cancer in the United States and the real potential for decreasing mortality and morbidity by secondary prevention (i.e., removing precancerous adenomas), the American Cancer Society has made recommendations for screening the population at large over the age of 50. The recommendations include periodic stool testing for occult blood, digital rectal examinations, and sigmoidoscopy.

Occult blood testing is based on a chemical reaction usually involving a guaiac-hemoglobin-peroxidase reaction. Stools are collected on 3 different days and, depending on the specific commercial product, may be tested by the patient or returned to the laboratory. Since colonic lesions often bleed only intermittently, sensitivity is improved the more specimens are taken. It is also improved by rehydration of the stool smear before testing, but specificity then falls.[61] True false-positive tests may result from taking iron supplements, ascorbic acid, cimetidine, iodine or large portions of rare red meat, raw broccoli, turnips, radishes, parsnips, or cauliflower.[62] Other false-positives are indeed from internal bleeding, such as peptic ulcers, erosions from nonsteroidal anti-inflammatory compounds, menses, or hemorrhoids, but not from cancer or polyps.

Mass screening programs have yielded a rate of positive tests from 1 to 8 percent.[63–66] Of these positives, 8 to 15 percent prove to have cancer and 9 to 36 percent adenomas.[67] The rest have no lesion that is found.

One reasonable approach to screening average-risk elderly patients for colorectal adenomas and carcinoma is to perform a rectal examination and test stools for occult blood at least yearly and preferably more frequently if the patient is being seen anyway for other reasons. A flexible sigmoidoscopy should be done even if the history and rectal exam is normal and the stools show no occult blood. If the sigmoidoscopy is normal, it should be repeated once more in a year, then once every 5 years unless symptoms develop or a stool specimen shows occult blood. If any sigmoidoscopy reveals an adenomatous polyp, a full colonoscopy should be performed since the presence of an adenoma in the rectosigmoid is associated with a 25 to 34 percent prevalence of more proximal colonic adenomas.[68] Also, if the stools are ever found to contain occult blood, a full colonoscopy (or a barium enema plus proctoscopy) is the minimum advisable workup.

Once a polyp with malignant potential has been discovered, the patient is considered at high risk for recurrence for the indefinite future and should be screened with semiannual tests for stools for occult blood and annual to biannual colonoscopy. If two annual colonoscopes reveal no further adenomas, it is reasonable to begin stretching out the time between screenings to as long as every 3 to 5 years.

REFERENCES

1. Whiteway J, Morson BC: Pathology of ageing: Diverticular disease. *Clin Gastroenterol* 14:829, 1985.
2. Parks TG: Natural history of diverticular disease of the colon. *Br Med J* 4:639, 1969.
3. Painter NS, Burkitt DP: Diverticular disease of the colon: A deficiency disease of western civilization. *Br Med J* 2:440, 1971.
4. Burkitt DP et al: Effect of dietary fiber on stools and the transit time and its role in the causation of disease. *Lancet* 2:1408, 1972.
5. Gear JSS et al: Symptomless diverticular disease and intake of dietary fiber. *Lancet* 1:511, 1979.
6. Hodgson WJB: An interim report on the production of colonic diverticulosis in the rabbit. *Gut* 13:802, 1972.
7. Painter NS, Truelove SC: The intraluminal pressure patterns in diverticulosis of the colon. *Gut* 5:201, 365, 1964.
8. Havia T: Diverticulosis of the colon: A clinical and histologic study. *Acta Chir Scand* 137:415S, 1971.
9. Parks TG: Natural history of diverticular disease of the colon. *Clin Gastroenterol* 4:53, 1975.
10. Larson DM, Masters SS et al: Medical and surgical therapy in diverticular disease. *Gastroenterology* 71:734, 1976.
11. Boley SJ et al: Lower intestinal bleeding in the elderly. *Am J Surg* 137:57, 1979.
12. Tedesco F et al: Colonoscopic evaluation of rectal bleeding: A study of 304 patients. *Ann Intern Med* 89:907, 1978.
13. Cancer Statistics, 1988. *CA* 38(1):9, 1988.
14. Baranovsky A, Myers MH: Cancer incidence and survival in patients 65 years of age and older. *CA* 36(1):26, 1986.
15. Winawer SJ, Stewart E, Gottlieb L et al: National polyp study, abstract. *Gastroenterology* 80:1316, 1981.
16. Morson BC: Genesis of colorectal cancer. *Clin Gastroenterol* 5:505, 1976.
17. Bernstein MA, Feczko PJ, Halpert RD, Simms SM, Ackerman LV: Distribution of colonic polyps: Increased inci-

dence of proximal lesions in older patients. *Radiology* 155:35, 1985.

18. Turvnen MJ, Peltokallio P: Surgical results in 657 patients with colorectal cancer. *Dis Colon Rectum* 26:606, 1983.

19. Jarvinsen HJ, Turvnen MJ: Colorectal carcinoma before 40 years of age: Prognosis and predisposing conditions. *Scand J Gastroenterol* 104:99, 1984.

20. Eddy DM, Nugent FW, Eddy JF et al: Screening for colorectal cancer in a high-risk population: Results of a mathematical model. *Gastroenterology* 92:682, 1987.

21. Winawer SJ, Leidner SD, Boyle C, Kurtz RC: Comparison of flexible sigmoidoscopy with other diagnostic techniques in the diagnosis of rectocolon neoplasia. *Dig Dis Sci* 24:277, 1979.

22. Helzberg JH, McCallum RW: Flexible sigmoidoscopy-safety and usefulness in the geriatric patient. *Geriatrics* 40(5):105, 1985.

23. Love RR, Morrissey JF: Colonoscopy in asymptomatic individuals with a family history of colorectal cancer. *Arch Intern Med* 144:2209, 1984.

24. Mecklin JP, Jarvinen HJ: Clinical features of colorectal carcinoma in cancer family syndrome. *Dis Colon Rectum* 29:160, 1986.

25. Lynch HT, Kimberling W, Albano WA et al: Hereditary nonpolyposis colorectal cancer (Lynch syndromes I and II). *Cancer* 56:934, 1985.

26. Kritchevsky D: Diet, nutrition and cancer: The role of fiber. *Cancer* 58:1830, 1986.

27. McKeown-Eyssenge GE: Fiber intake in different populations and colon cancer risk. *Prev Med* 16:532, 1987.

28. Wynder EL: The epidemiology of large bowel cancer. *Cancer Res* 35:3388, 1975.

29. Drasar BS, Irving D: Environmental factors and cancer of the colon and breast. *Br J Cancer* 27:167, 1973.

30. Armstrong B, Doll R: Environmental factors and cancer incidence and mortality in different countries with special reference to dietary practices. *Int J Cancer* 15:617, 1975.

31. Macquart-Moulin G et al: Case-control study on colorectal cancer and diet in Marseilles. *Int J Cancer* 38:183, 1986.

32. Haenszel W et al: Large bowel cancer in Hawaiian Japanese. *J Natl Cancer Inst* 51:1765, 1973.

33. Wynder EL, Reddy BS: Diet and cancer of the colon. *Curr Concepts Nutr* 6:55, 1977.

34. Hill MJ et al: Bacteria and aetiology of cancer of large bowel. *Lancet* 1:95, 1971.

35. Mastromarino AJ et al: Fecal profiles of anaerobic microflora of large bowel cancer patients and patients with nonhereditary large bowel polyps. *Cancer Res* 38:4458, 1978.

36. Hill MJ: Bacteria and the etiology of colonic cancer. *Cancer* 34:815, 1974.

37. Narisawa T et al: Promoting effect of bile acids on colon carcinogenesis after intrarectal instillation of N-methyl-N-nitrosoguanidine in rats. *J Natl Cancer Inst* 53:1093, 1974.

38. Reddy BS et al: Promoting effect of bile acids on colon carcinogenesis in germ-free and conventional F344 rats. *Cancer Res* 32:3238, 1977.

39. Cohen BI et al: Effect of cholic acid feeding on N-methyl-N-nitrosourea induced colon tumours and cell kinetics in rats. *J Natl Cancer Inst* 64:573, 1980.

40. Martin MS et al: Effect of dietary chenodeoxycholic acid on intestinal carcinogenesis induced by 1,2-dimethylhydrazine in mice. *Br J Cancer* 43:884, 1981.

41. Wilpart M et al: Mutagenicity of 1,2-dimethyl hydrazine towards *Salmonella typhimurium;* co-mutagenic effect of secondary bile acids. *Carcinogenesis* 4:45, 1983.

42. Aries V, Hill MJ: Degradation of steroids by intestinal bacteria II. *Biochim Biophys Acta* 202:535, 1970.

43. Thornton JR, Heaton KW: Do colonic bacteria contribute to cholesterol gallstone formation? Effects of lactulose on bile. *Br Med J* 1:1018, 1981.

44. Walker ARP et al: Fecal pH value and its modification by dietary means in South African black and white school children. *S Afr Med J* 33:495, 1979.

45. Cummings JH et al: Changes in fecal composition and colonic function due to cereal fiber. *Am J Clin Nutr* 28:1468, 1976.

46. Hellendoorn EW: Fermentation as the principal cause of the physiologic activity of indigestible food residue, in Spiller GA, Amen RJ (eds): *Topics in Dietary Fiber Research.* New York, Plenum Press, 1978.

47. Pomare EW et al: The effect of wheat bran upon bile salt metabolism and lipid composition of bile in gallstone patients. *Am J Dig Dis* 21:521, 1976.

48. McDougall RM et al: Effect of wheat bran on serum lipoproteins and biliary lipids. *Can J Surg* 21:433, 1978.

49. Bowen RL et al: Effects of lactulose and other laxatives on ileal and colonic pH as measured by a radiotelemetry device. *Gut* 15:999, 1974.

50. Cummings JH et al: Influence of diets high and low in animal fat on bowel habit, gastrointestinal transit, fecal microflora, bile acid and fat excretion. *J Clin Invest* 61:953, 1978.

51. Thornton JR: High colonic pH promotes colorectal cancer. *Lancet* 1:1081, 1981.

52. Samuelson SL et al: Protective role of faecal pH in experimental colon carcinogenesis. *J R Soc Med* 78:230, 1985.

53. Walker ARP et al: Faecal pH, dietary fiber intake, and proneness to colon cancer in four South African populations. *Br J Cancer* 53:4898, 1986.

54. Lupton JR et al: Influence of luminal pH on rat large bowel epithelial cell cycle. *Am J Physiol* 249:G382, 1985.

55. Wanebo HJ et al: Pre-operative CEA as a prognostic indicator in colorectal cancer. *N Engl J Med* 299:448, 1978.

56. Herbeth B, Bagrel A: A study of factors influencing plasma CEA levels in an unselected population. *Oncodeo Biol Med* 1:191, 1980.

57. Clarke C et al: CEA and smoking. *J R Coll Physicians Lond* 14:227, 1980.

58. Fletcher RH: Carcinoembryonic antigen. *Ann Intern Med* 104:66, 1986.

59. Toniton Y et al: Cumulative effects of age and pathology on plasma CEA in an unselected elderly population. *Eur J Cancer Clin Oncol* 20:369, 1984.

60. Rao AR et al: Patterns of recurrence following curative resection alone for adenocarcinoma of the rectum and sigmoid colon. *Cancer* 48:1492, 1981.

61. Simon JB: The pros and cons of fecal occult blood testing for colorectal neoplasms. *Cancer Metastasis Rev* 6:397, 1987.

62. Norfleet RG: Effect of diet on fecal occult blood testing in

patients with colorectal polyps. *Dig Dis Sci* 31:498–501, 1986.

63. Johnson MG, Jolly PC: Analysis of a mass colorectal cancer screening program for cost-effectiveness. *Am J Surg* 154(3):261, 1987.

64. Kronborg O et al: Initial mass screening for colorectal cancer with fecal occult blood test. A prospective randomized study at Funen in Denmark. *Scand J Gastroenterol* 22(6):677, 1987.

65. Hardcastle JD et al: Fecal occult blood screening for colorectal cancer in the general population. Results of a controlled trial. *Cancer* 58(2):397, 1986.

66. Norfleet RG et al: Hemoccult screening for colorectal neoplasms. Report of a mail-out project without dietary restriction in a prepaid health plan. *Wis Med J* 82(4):23, 1983.

67. Winawer SJ et al: Screening for colorectal cancer. *Bull WHO* 65(1):105, 1987.

68. Warden MG et al: The role of colonoscopy and flexible sigmoidoscopy in screening for colorectal carcinoma. *Dis Colon Rectum* 30:52, 1987.

SECTION E

The Hematologic System

Chapter 64

AGING OF THE HEMATOPOIETIC SYSTEM

David A. Lipschitz

NORMAL BONE MARROW FUNCTION

Hematopoiesis is regulated by a complex series of interactions between hematopoietic cells, their stromal microenvironment, and diffusable regulatory molecules that affect cellular proliferation. The orderly development of the hematopoietic system in vivo and the maintenance of homeostasis requires that a strict balance be maintained between self-renewal, differentiation, maturation, and cell loss. Within the hematopoietic system, populations of terminally differentiated cells are continually entering the peripheral blood to be replaced by cells from a transit or amplification compartment. The earliest morphologically recognizable (differentiated) cells of the myeloid and erythroid series are the myeloblasts and proerythroblasts (Fig. 64-1). These cells are derived from the morphologically unrecognizable progenitor, or stem, cells that can be identified only by appropriate in vitro culture techniques. There are two forms of erythroid stem cells. A more primitive precursor, which forms large colonies in cultures containing high concentrations of erythropoietin, is referred to as a *burst-forming unit erythroid (BFU-E)*. This precursor is thought to give rise to a more mature stem cell which

develops colonies in culture at shorter intervals and requires lower erythropoietin concentrations. It is the immediate precursor of the proerythroblast and is referred to as the *colony-forming unit erythroid (CFU-E)*. A committed myeloid stem cell, or colony-forming unit culture (CFU-C), which is known as colony-forming unit granulocyte/macrophage (CFU-GM), is the immediate precursor of the myeloblast. The committed progenitor cell compartments are supplied in turn by a common pluripotent stem cell, which is derived from totipotential stem cells that have the capacity to differentiate into either hematopoietic or lymphoid cells.[1] The hierarchy of cellular proliferation and differentiation through this pathway is shown in Fig. 64-1. The pluripotent hematopoietic stem cell is termed *colony-forming unit spleen (CFU-S)* by virtue of its ability to produce colonies in spleens of lethally irradiated mice. CFU-S is also capable of repopulating the marrow of irradiated recipients and preventing marrow failure.[2] A unique feature of the CFU-S compartment is the ability to divide and give rise to an identical multipotential daughter cell and a progenitor cell that is committed to specific hematopoietic development. It is the self-renewal capacity that allows a small CFU-S compartment to amplify into large numbers of differentiated hematopoietic cells. The CFU-S is

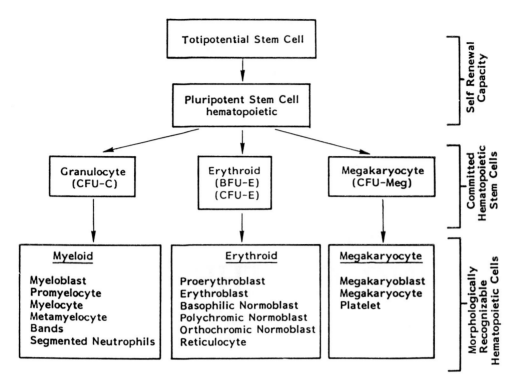

FIGURE 64-1
The hierarchy and production of hematopoietic precursors from primitive pluripotent stem cells.

the earliest hematopoietic cell that can be satisfactorily assayed and constitutes a powerful research tool for studying differentiation and growth control.[2] There is very little information on factors regulating these cells. There is evidence that the number of CFU-S in cell cycle is minimal but that cycling can be greatly increased if demands for regeneration are increased.[3] Most evidence suggests that regulation of proliferative control is local and is presumably mediated by the environmental milieu.[4] Furthermore, studies have shown that the cellular milieu can also influence cell production and differentiation.[5] If commitment is defined as a loss of pluripotentiality, there is some evidence that committed cells, restricted to one or two of the hematopoietic cell lines, can undergo extensive (but not indefinite) self-renewal in vivo.[6]

EFFECT OF AGE ON CFU-S

One of the major questions with regard to the aging hematopoietic system is whether the pluripotent hematopoietic stem cell has a finite replicative capacity. There is evidence that CFU-S has a heterogeneous self-renewal capacity and an age structure in which young CFU-S with high self-renewal capacity produce older CFU-S with decreasing self-renewal capacity and increasing differentiation potential.[7,8] This hypothesis has been strengthened by studies of long-term bone marrow

culture, which have shown that CFU-S with a high replicative history are likely to be recruited into committed progenitor cells more readily than those which have divided a fewer number of times.[9] It has been shown that maintenance of hematopoiesis in long-term bone marrow culture varies inversely with the age of the donor from which the culture was initiated.[10] Additional evidence for a finite replicative capacity for stem cells has been obtained in a series of elegant studies in which stem cell kinetics and myeloid cell production was examined in long-term bone marrow cultures subjected to varying doses of irradiation.[11–13]

Studies using serial transplantation to assess finite replicative capacity have yielded conflicting results. Among studies suggesting the important effect of age have been those demonstrating that when cells are subjected to in vivo serial transfer by repeated injection into lethally irradiated recipients, they gradually lose their ability to self-replicate.[8,14] There is also evidence that CFU-S from young donors are better able to repopulate the marrow of irradiated mice than stem cells obtained from old donors. The growth capacity of old stem cells remains characteristically "old," even after prolonged self-replication in the bone marrow of young recipients. This fact suggests an intrinsic characteristic of the CFU-S which cannot readily be altered. However, the spleen-colonizing growth capacity of young stem cells can be reduced by allowing them to self-replicate in old recipients. Thus the characteristics of the environment (notably the age of the recipient) may also influence replicative capacity. Other host factors affect the rate of colonization. An inadequate architectural milieu in the old spleen may retard the seeding of transplanted stem cells.[5]

Against these studies are those reporting that CFU-S decline minimally, or not at all, with age.[15] Ogden and Micklem[16] have simultaneously transplanted two bone marrow cell populations with different chromosome markers into lethally irradiated syngeneic recipients. One marrow population was obtained from young and one from old donors. No consistent difference in the rates of spleen colonization was noted. More recent evidence suggests that results of earlier serial transplant studies were related to methodological artifact.[17,18] However, even if its life span is finite, it is clear that the CFU-S cell has a reserve capacity to produce adequate numbers of hematopoietic cells for periods that far exceed the maximum life expectancy of the animal.[19]

EFFECT OF AGE ON NORMAL BONE MARROW FUNCTION IN MICE

As in many aspects of hematology, studies of the effect of aging on hematopoiesis have been dominated by investigations in mice, research in humans being far less definitive. Recent studies have examined the effect of age on the number of committed hematopoietic stem cells and on the number of differentiated hematopoietic bone marrow cells.[20] In mice no age-related reduction in the number of erythroid (BFU-E, CFU-E) or myeloid/macrophage (CFU-C) progenitor cells occurs. In addition, the number of differentiated erythroid and myeloid precursors in the bone marrow is unaffected by age in normal animals. Erythrokinetic studies show that red blood cell survival is unchanged with aging, that the plasma iron turnover and erythron iron turnover are unchanged, and that red blood cell mass is normal. The apparent anemia frequently observed in aged mice thus appears to be due to an expansion of plasma volume.

These findings and those of others[21,22] indicate that no change in basal hematopoiesis occurs with aging. The aging process is typically characterized by a reduction in reserve capacity. Thus, although basal function may be normal, the ability to respond to increased demands is frequently compromised. There is evidence that this principle applies to the aged hematopoietic system as well. For example, older mice recover their hemoglobin values more slowly after phlebotomy than do young mice.[23,24] Furthermore, when aged animals are placed in a high-altitude chamber, the expected increase in hemoglobin level is more variable and tends to be lower in older as compared with younger animals.[25] Interpretation of data after phlebotomy or exposure to high altitude is difficult because many other physiologic variables determine the measured hematopoietic response. For example, alterations in cardiorespiratory or renal function may compromise the ability of the bone marrow from old animals to respond to increased stimulation.

To overcome these criticisms, in vivo and in vitro models have been developed that allow the study of hematopoiesis while minimizing other variables.[25] This can be achieved by creating polycythemia in mice by the injection of homologous red cells. This results in a predictable suppression of erythropoiesis that is characterized by marked decreases in bone marrow differentiated erythroid cell and CFU-E number. When erythropoietin is injected into these animals, a predictable and measurable wave of erythropoiesis occurs. Twenty-four hours after injection, bone marrow CFU-E and proerythroblasts are significantly increased. After 48 hours polychromic and orthochromic normoblasts are elevated. Between 48 and 72 hours these cells leave the bone marrow and appear in the blood as reticulocytes. These studies demonstrate that old polycythemic mice develop a smaller wave of erythropoiesis after erythropoietin injection than do young animals. The number of new red blood cells appearing in the circulation after injection of erythropoietin is significantly lower in the aged. The decrease in response does not, however, universally affect all erythroid precursors. Thus, the increase in proerythroblast and normoblast (differentiated cell) number after the injection of erythropoietin is significantly less in old as compared with young animals. In contrast, the increase in the committed erythroid progenitor cell number (CFU-E) after erythropoietin injection was identical in both young and old animals, suggesting that a uniform defect in the proliferative response of all cells does not occur with aging. The mechanism for the reduced responsiveness of differentiated cells in the aged remains to be determined.

Erythropoietin is the most important stimulator of erythropoiesis. In vitro culture methods are available that allow the examination of the responsiveness to erythropoietin of the erythroid stem cells (BFU-E and CFU-E) and of differentiated erythroid cells that have the capacity to divide. The number of colonies that develop from erythroid stem cells increases in direct proportion to the concentration of erythropoietin in the cultures. In addition, the level of differentiated erythroid cell proliferation varies in direct proportion to the erythropoietin concentration. These methods are ideally suited for the study of the effect of age on erythropoiesis.[26] Results found when young and old bone marrow is studied using this in vitro approach confirm the in vivo findings described. Thus, when differentiated cells from aged animals are cultured in the presence of erythropoietin, the proliferative response to the increased stimulation is significantly lower than when bone marrow from young animals is studied. Proliferation is, however, identical when the effect of increasing concentrations of erythropoietin on CFU-E and BFU-E cultures from the marrow of old or young mice is examined.

The fragility of the aged hematopoietic system is further highlighted by studies on mice approaching their maximal life expectancy.[20] The median life span of C57BL/6 mice is 24 months, but the maximum reported life expectancy is 48 months. Provided 48-month-old mice are housed in individual cages (one animal per cage), no change in hematopoiesis is seen. If, however, they are housed in groups of five animals per cage, a significant alteration in bone marrow function occurs. The animals become more anemic, and the number of stem cells in their bone marrow decreases. Significant decreases also occur in the morphologically recognizable erythroid precursors. These findings are identical to hematopoietic changes described with overcrowding. The effects of overcrowding, however, are only seen when young, or even 24-month-old animals, are housed in groups of 10 mice per cage. This finding indicates that a minor stress like overcrowding, which does not affect hematopoiesis in young animals, causes significant abnormalities in aged animals.

EFFECT OF AGE ON HEMATOPOIESIS IN HUMANS

The evaluation of hematopoiesis in older humans is made virtually impossible by the complex interaction of environmental variable with the host over extended periods of time. This particularly applies to hematopoiesis which is very sensitive to a large series of extraneous variables. For example, Fig. 64-2 illustrates the large number of factors which may modulate erythropoietic function in elderly subjects. Controlling for these external variables is extremely difficult and makes difficult the determination of whether any decrements occur in hematopoietic function as a consequence of age alone. An extensive study has been performed on a group of carefully selected, healthy young and elderly subjects who were clearly hematologically normal (Table 64-1).[27] When hematopoiesis was evaluated in these individuals, no significant differences in peripheral blood or ferrokinetic data could be demonstrated. Furthermore quantitation of bone marrow hematopoietic stem cells and differentiated precursors demonstrated no significant differences between the young and the elderly group. Recently a series of longitudinal studies of hematologic parameters on a group of affluent subjects examined in New Mexico demonstrated no obvious hematologic problem and no abnormalities developed during a 3-year follow-up.[28] Based upon these observations and

TABLE 64-1
Hematologic Profile in Young and Elderly Hematologically Normal Subjects

	Young	*Elderly*
Age (years)	34.0 ± 2.0*	78.0 ± 2.0
Hemoglobin (g/dl)	15.4 ± 0.3	15.0 ± 0.2
Mean corpuscular volume (fl)	89.0 ± 0.9	90.7 ± 1.8
Serum iron (μg/dl)	107.0 ± 8.1	93.0 ± 5.0
TIBC (μg/dl)	297.0 ± 10.0	307.0 ± 13.0
Saturation (%)	36.0 ± 3.0	30.1 ± 2.2
Serum ferritin (ng/ml)	126.0 ± 17.0	219.0 ± 26.0
Proto:heme (μmol/mol)	24.4 ± 1.4	22.0 ± 1.8
Vitamin B_{12} (μg/ml)	476.0 ± 34.0	451.0 ± 34.0
Serum folate (ng/ml)	5.6 ± 0.8	4.8 ± 0.5
Retic index	1.1 ± 0.3	1.0 ± 0.2
Leukocyte ($\times 10^3/\mu$l)	8.8 ± 0.4	7.6 ± 0.5
Neutrophils ($\times 10^3/\mu$l)	5.9 ± 0.3	4.5 ± 0.6
Lymphocyte ($\times 10^3/\mu$l)	1.9 ± 0.8	1.9 ± 0.3
Platelet ($\times 10^3/\mu$l)	361.0 ± 38.0	277.0 ± 2.1
EIT†	0.5 ± 0.1	0.5 ± 0.1
Total myeloid precursors ($\times 10^9$ cells/kg)	38.0 ± 16.0	40.0 ± 15.0
CFU-C (-10^6/kg)	0.9 ± 0.3	0.7 ± 0.2

* Mean ± SE.
† Erythron iron turnover (mg/dl whole blood per day).

the animal studies described above, it is highly likely that no age-related change in basal hematopoiesis occurs with aging. However, it also seems likely that elderly humans have a compromised reserve capacity that will result in a diminished ability of an elderly subject's marrow to compensate for a given degree of acute or chronic disease than will a young subject, making the elderly more prone to the development of disease-induced hematologic abnormalities. As discussed in Chap. 65, anemia that is not due to the commonly recognized causes is prevalent in apparently healthy elderly subjects.[29] This anemia appears not to be a consequence of normal aging but rather a response to a stress that would be unlikely to cause a hematologic problem in younger individuals.

EFFECT OF AGE ON NEUTROPHIL FUNCTION IN HUMANS

The most critical function of neutrophils appears to be phagocytosis and killing of bacteria. For this to occur, the neutrophil must be able to adhere to endothelial surfaces, migrate to the site of inflammation (and undergo chemotaxis), and engulf and then kill the ingested bacteria. Killing is achieved by the generation of a series of toxic radicles and microbicidal halogens and by the release of a series of enzymes located in neutrophil granules. The process of bacterial killing is associated with a

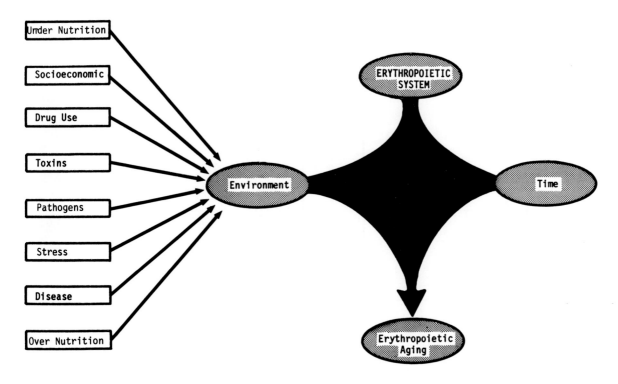

FIGURE 64-2
External variables likely to modify age-related decrements in erythropoiesis.

hundredfold increase in neutrophil metabolism and oxygen uptake. This reaction is referred to as the *respiratory burst*.[30,31] The neutrophil also plays an important role in the inflammatory response.

Neutrophil function can be assessed by measuring the ability of the neutrophils to phagocytose and kill bacteria. Alternatively, neutrophils can be exposed to a series of chemotactic peptides or other reagents which stimulate the respiratory burst and cause the secretion of enzymes from neutrophil granules. The burst can be evaluated by assessing oxygen metabolism in the cells. Alternatively the end products of the burst, namely the generation of superoxide which is the first step in the generation of toxic radicles, can be measured.

Utilizing these approaches, a series of studies has examined the effects of aging on neutrophil function. In response to a wide variety of stimuli, the respiratory burst activity of neutrophils from elderly individuals is decreased and the level of various neutrophil enzymes secreted during degranulation is reduced.[32–35] A typical response of a neutrophil from the elderly is shown in Fig. 64-3. In this study, secretion of the enzyme lysozyme was determined in the basal state and following the challenge of the cell by the chemotactic peptide formyl-methyl-leucine-phenylalanine (FMLP). In neutrophils from the young and the old, secretion in the basal state is very similar. Following stimulation, however, the rate and total amount of enzyme released is clearly reduced in the old. This response in a single cell bears remarka-

ble similarity to the effects of age on the decrements in response of many organ systems. Because function can be measured in the basal state and following stimulation, in which metabolic function is markedly amplified, the neutrophil offers a unique opportunity to examine the effects of aging on cellular function.

Utilizing the neutrophil, studies have examined the effects of age on signal transduction.[35] It is generally recognized that cytosolic calcium plays a central role in the response of cells to stimulation. Age-related abnormalities in cellular calcium kinetics have been suggested in a number of other organ and cellular systems and are regarded as an important mechanism accounting for the age-related decline in a wide variety of cellular metabolic events.[36] Utilizing the fluorescent probe Quin-2, basal cytosolic calcium concentration has been shown to be significantly reduced in neutrophils obtained from old volunteers as compared to those from young. Furthermore, following stimulation by FMLP, mobilization of calcium to the cytosol, which triggers many metabolic events, is significantly lower in old as compared to young neutrophils.[35] Additional studies have shown that the flux of extracellular calcium across the cell membrane to the cytosol is also compromised in the aged neutrophil. Finally calcium ATPase concentration and efflux of calcium from the cell following activation is also diminished. Of particular interest is the fact that pharmacologic elevation of cytosolic calcium in old neutrophils can effectively correct the age-related decline in neutrophil

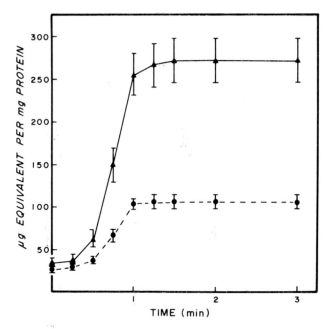

FIGURE 64-3
Secretion of the enzyme lysozyme in the basal state and at various times following activation of the neutrophil by FMLP. The mean ± SEM is shown for neutrophils obtained from six young volunteers (▲———▲) and six elderly volunteers (●———●).

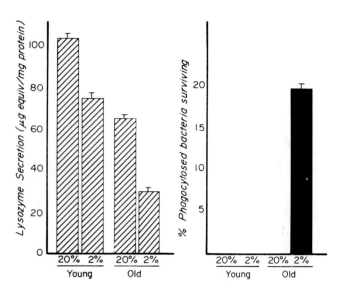

FIGURE 64-4
Secretion of the enzyme lysozyme (left-hand panel) following activation of neutrophils from young (6-month-old) or old (24-month-old) mice fed a 20 percent (normal) or 2 percent protein diet for 3 weeks prior to sacrifice. The right-hand panel shows the percentage of phagocytosed bacteria not killed by neutrophils from young and old mice fed a 2 percent or 20 percent protein diet. The results clearly demonstrate that neutrophils obtained from old mice fed a 2 percent protein diet are unable to kill all phagocytosed bacteria.

function. Finally there is good evidence that the decrement in neutrophil function occurring as a consequence of aging reflects a yet-to-be-identified potentially reversible abnormality of the cell membrane.[37]

The above studies are important because they provide useful insights into the fundamental mechanism that accounts for the diminished ability of aged cells to respond to stimulation. An important question, however, is whether the decline in neutrophil function, described as a consequence of aging, has any clinical relevance. Although neutrophil function is diminished with aging, the defect is not large enough to interfere with the ability of neutrophils from the elderly to phagocytose or to kill bacteria. However, the diminished neutrophil reserve capacity does have relevance. It has recently been shown that when mice are made protein-deficient, a modest reduction occurs in neutrophil function which is very similar to that seen with aging.[38] In old mice the effect of protein deficiency and aging are additive, so that in this circumstance neutrophil function decreases to a level where the ability of the cell to undertake its critically important roles of phagocytosis and bacterial killing is severely compromised (Fig. 64-4). This finding is of particular importance as it may help explain the high prevalence of serious bacterial infection in hospitalized and older individuals, who are frequently malnourished. It also demonstrates the relevance of diminished reserve capacity resulting in increased susceptibility to disease.

SUMMARY

Based principally on studies of mice, close evaluation of the effect of age on hematopoiesis at the organ or cellular level demonstrates evidence of diminished reserve capacity. Abnormalities in function, not evident in the basal state, become apparent when function is amplified by appropriate stimulation. In addition to being reduced, the response of the aged tends to be more variable. Given comparable stress, hematologic abnormalities are likely to occur earlier and to be of greater severity in the old as compared to the young.

REFERENCES

1. Schofield R: The pluripotent stem cell. *Clin Haematol* 8:221, 1979.
2. Till JE, McCulloch EA: A direct measurement of the radiation sensitivity of normal mouse bone marrow cells. *Rad Res* 14:213, 1961.
3. Becker AJ, McCulloch EA, Siminovitch L et al: The effect of differing demands for blood cell production on DNA synthesis by hemopoietic colony-forming cells of mice. *Blood* 26:296, 1965.
4. Gidali J, Lajtha LG: Regulation of haemopoietic stem cell turnover in partially irradiated mice. *Cell Tissue Kinet* 5:147, 1972.
5. Wolf NS: The haemopoietic microenvironment. *Clin Haematol* 8:469, 1979.

6. Phillips RA: Stem cell heterogeneity: Pluripotent and committed stem cells of the myeloid and lymphoid lineages, in Clarkson B et al (eds): *Differentiation of Normal and Neoplastic Hematopoietic Cells.* Cold Spring Harbor, NY, Cold Spring Harbor Conference on Cell Proliferation, 1978, pp 109–120.

7. Schofield R, Lajtha LG: Effect of isopropyl methane sulphonate (MS) on haemopoietic colony-forming cells. *Br J Haematol* 25:195, 1974.

8. Schofield R, Lord BI, Kyffin S et al: Self maintenance capacity of CFU-S. *J Cell Physiol* 103:355, 1980.

9. Mauch P, Greenberger JS, Botnick L et al: Evidence of structured variation in self-renewal capacity within long-term bone marrow cultures. *Proc Natl Acad Sci USA* 77:2927, 1980.

10. Lipschitz DA, MicGinnis SK, Udupa BK: The use of long-term marrow culture as a model for the aging process. *Age* 6:122, 1983.

11. Hellman S, Botnick L, Hannon EC et al: Proliferative capacity of murine hematopoietic stem cells. *Proc Natl Acad Sci USA* 75:490, 1978.

12. Reincke U, Hannon EC, Rosenbalt M et al: Proliferative capacity of murine hematopoietic stem cells in vitro. *Science* 215:1619, 1982.

13. Mauch P, Botnick LE, Hannon EC et al: Decline in bone marrow proliferative capacity as a function of age. *Blood* 60:245, 1982.

14. Albright JA, Makinodan T: Decline in the growth potential of spleen-colonizing bone marrow stem cells of long lived aging mice. *J Exp Med* 144:1204, 1976.

15. Chen MG: Age related changes in hematopoietic stem cell population of a long lived hybrid mouse. *J Cell Physiol* 78:225, 1971.

16. Ogden DA, Micklem HS: The fate of serially transplanted bone marrow cell populations from young and old donors. *Transplantation* 22:287, 1976.

17. Harrison DE, Astle CM, Delaittre JA: Loss of proliferative capacity in immunohemopoietic stem cells caused by serial transplantation rather than aging. *J Exp Med* 147:1526, 1978.

18. Ross EAM, Anderson N, Micklem HS: Serial depletion and regeneration of the murine hematopoietic system. Implication for hematopoietic organization and the study of cellular aging. *J Exp Med* 155:432, 1982.

19. Harrison DE: Normal production of erythrocytes by mouse bone marrow continuous for 73 months. *Proc Natl Acad Sci USA* 70:3184, 1972.

20. Williams LH, Udupa KB, Lipschitz DA: An evaluation of the effect of age on hematopoiesis in C57BL/6 mouse. *Exp Hematol* 14:827, 1986.

21. Everitt AV, Webb C: The blood picture of the aging male rat. *J Gerontol* 13:255, 1958.

22. Coggle JE, Proukakis C: The effect of age on the bone marrow cellularity of the mouse. *Gerontologia* 16:25, 1970.

23. Boggs DR, Patrene KD: Hematopoiesis and aging III: Anemia and a blunted erythropoietic response to hemorrhage in aged mice. *Am J Hematol* 19:327, 1985.

24. Tyan ML: Old mice: Marrow response to bleeding and endotoxin. *Proc Soc Exp Biol Med* 169:295, 1982.

25. Udupa KB, Lipschitz DA: Erythropoiesis in the aged mouse I. Response to stimulation in vivo. *J Lab Clin Med* 103:574, 1984.

26. Udupa KB, Lipschitz DA: Erythropoiesis in the aged mouse II. Response to stimulation in vitro. *J Lab Clin Med* 103:581, 1984.

27. Lipschitz DA, Udupa KB, Milton KY et al: Effect of age on hematopoiesis in man. *Blood* 63:502, 1984.

28. Garry PJ, Goodwin JS, Hunt WC: Iron status and anemia in the elderly. *J Am Geriatr Soc* 31:389, 1983.

29. Lipschitz DA, Mitchell CO, Thompson C: The anemia of senescence. *Am J Hematol* 11:47, 1981.

30. Babior BM, Cohen HJ: Measurement of neutrophil function: Phagocytosis, degranulation, the respiratory burst and bacterial killing, in Cline MJ (ed): *Leukocyte Function.* New York, Churchill Livingstone, 1981.

31. Babior BM, Kipnes RS, Curnutte JT: Biological defense mechanisms. The production by leukocytes of superoxide, a potential bactericidal agent. *J Clin Invest* 52:741, 1973.

32. McLaughlin B, O'Malley K, Cotten TG: Age-related differences in granulocyte chemotaxis and degranulation. *Clin Sci* 70:59, 1986.

33. Nagel JE, Pyle RS, Chrest FJ, Adler WH: Oxidative metabolism and bactericidal capacity of polymorphonuclear leukocyte from young and aged adults. *J Gerontol* 37:529, 1982.

34. Suzuki K, Swenson C, Sasagawa S et al: Age-related decline in lysosomal enzyme release from polymorphonuclear leukocytes after N-formyl-methionylleucyl-phenylalanine stimulation. *Exp Hematol* 11:1005, 1982.

35. Lipschitz DA, Udupa KB, Boxer LA: The role of calcium in the age-related decline of neutrophil function. *Blood* 71:659, 1988.

36. Gee MV, Shikawa UI, Baum BJ, Roth GS: Impaired adrenergic stimulation of rat parotid cell glucose oxidation during aging: The role of calcium. *J Gerontol* 41:331, 1986.

37. Lipschitz DA, Udupa KB, Boxer LA: Evidence that microenvironmental factors account for the age-related decline in neutrophil function. *Blood* 70:1131, 1987.

38. Lipschitz DA, Udupa KB: Influence of aging and protein deficiency on neutrophil function. *J Gerontol* 41:690, 1986.

Chapter 65

ANEMIA
IN THE ELDERLY

David A. Lipschitz

Anemia is a common clinical problem among all age groups including the elderly. A high prevalence has been documented in hospitalized older subjects, in those attending geriatric clinics, and in institutionalized older individuals.[1-5] Recent evidence suggests that, provided stringent criteria are employed for the selection of apparently normal subjects, the elderly should have minimal, if any, decline in hemoglobin values. This chapter will review the causes of anemia and will present evidence to show that declines in hemoglobin levels with advancing age are not a consequence of the normal aging process. A rational approach to the clinical evaluation of subjects with anemia will be presented.

PREVALENCE OF ANEMIA

Epidemiologic studies from the United States, Canada, and Europe[1-5] demonstrate a high prevalence of anemia in the elderly. Studies from Great Britain, in particular, have determined the incidence of anemia in large numbers of subjects older than 60 years. In both men and women, the prevalence of anemia increased significantly with each successive decade. A recent analysis of the second National Health and Nutrition Education Survey (HANES 2) demonstrated a significant reduction in hemoglobin levels with advancing age in apparently healthy males and a minimal, although significant, decrease in elderly females.[6] Based as it was upon a lower normal limit of 14 g/dl, a very large percentage of elderly males would be found to be anemic. This study proposed that the reduction for males was a consequence of aging and suggested that age-specific reference standards for hemoglobin concentration for the elderly be adopted.

The cause of mild anemia in apparently healthy elderly subjects is often obscure.[7] A careful assessment of

hematopoiesis in these individuals may reveal mild marrow failure as evidenced by reductions in bone marrow differentiated and stem cell number and modest decreases in peripheral leukocyte counts.[8]

A major unanswered question is whether this decline in hemoglobin with advancing age is a consequence of the normal aging process. Of particular importance in this regard is the recent finding that anemia is rare in an affluent, healthy elderly population examined in New Mexico.[9] None of the elderly males and females in this group was anemic. Furthermore, longitudinal monitoring of these subjects over a 5-year period failed to demonstrate an increased prevalence of anemia. Based upon this observation it is highly likely that the decrease in hemoglobin seen commonly with advancing age is not a consequence of the normal aging process but that it is related to extrinsic variables.

Recent studies have implicated inflammation or chronic disease as the likely cause of the anemia.[10] Clearly the high prevalence of such diseases, especially in the sick elderly, is germane to the high prevalence of anemia in such persons. A second possibility is that the anemia has a nutritional basis. This is suggested by a closer examination of data obtained in epidemiologic surveys in which anemia has been shown to be most prevalent in low socioeconomic populations. Such populations also have a high prevalence of nutritional deficiencies. Relevant to this hypothesis, in a comprehensive nutritional and hematologic evaluation of a group of 73 elderly veterans living in a domiciliary facility, a high prevalence of anemia was present. Evaluation demonstrated that iron deficiency, folate deficiency, or other usually described causes of anemia were rare. A multivariate analysis of the data using age and hematopoietic and nutritional factors as covariants demonstrated that while age appeared to be the major variable accounting for the decline in immunologic measurements observed in this elderly population, age did not appear to be important in the prevalence of anemia. In contrast, serum albumin, transferrin, and prealbumin, markers of nutritional status, appeared to be strong correlates of anemia. Further evidence consistent with the theory that a nutritional cause contributes to the anemia comes from the marked similarity between the alterations in immunologic and hematopoietic function that occur with aging and those that occur with protein deprivation (Table 65-1). This raises the possibility that protein deprivation in some form may contribute to the hematopoietic changes normally ascribed to aging. Furthermore, there is evidence that correction of protein-energy malnutrition in the hospitalized elderly can markedly improve hematopoietic function.[11] In these subjects, interpretation of improvements in hematologic status is extremely difficult; however, any hospitalized elderly individual has coexisting diseases that affect hematopoietic function. Thus the overall improvement seen with nutritional rehabilitation may reflect an improvement in the medical

TABLE 65-1
Similarities between Changes in Immune and Hematopoietic Function Caused by Aging or Protein-Energy Malnutrition

	Aging	Protein-Energy Malnutrition
Cell-mediated immunity		
Delayed cutaneous hypersensitivity	Decreased	Decreased
T-cell number	Decreased	Decreased
Percent of T suppressor cells	Increased	Increased
Blastogenic response to mitogen	Decreased	Decreased
Humoral immunity		
B-cell number	Unchanged	Unchanged
Antibody production	Moderately decreased	Moderately decreased
Erythropoiesis		
Hemoglobin	Decreased	Decreased
Marrow erythroid cells	Decreased	Decreased
CFU-E number*	Decreased	Decreased
BFU-E number†	Normal	Normal
Myelopoiesis		
Granulocyte number	Reduced	Reduced
Granulocytosis after endotoxin administration	Decreased	Decreased
CFU-C number‡	Decreased	Decreased

*Colony-forming unit erythroid.
†Burst-forming unit erythroid.
‡Colony-forming unit culture.

status of the patient. In a more recent study the effect of increased feeding on hematopoietic status was examined in relatively healthy elderly individuals who lived at home and were ambulatory, but who were also underweight and had marginal evidence of protein-energy deprivation. By providing polymeric dietary supplements to these subjects between meals, it was possible to correct nutritional deficiencies and obtain weight gain. Despite a positive impact on nutritional status, however, the anemia, invariably present in this population, did not improve.[12]

Some conclusions can be drawn from these observations. It is clear that significant nutritional deficiencies aggravate or unmask hematologic abnormalities in the elderly. Even in apparently healthy older individuals, it is possible that nutritional factors contribute to hematopoietic changes, but alternative mechanisms other than simple nutritional deficiency must be considered. One possibility is that marginal reductions of one nutrient acting alone or of most nutrients acting in combination, over a prolonged period of time, may modulate hematopoietic change usually ascribed to aging. Alternatively, nutrient delivery to the target organ may be altered with aging, or changes in nutrient-target interaction may occur. These possibilities could account for the higher prevalence of anemia reported in epidemiologic studies. They remain, however, no more than potential hypotheses that require further research.

EVALUATION OF ANEMIA IN THE ELDERLY

For practical purposes 12 g/dl is recommended as a lower limit of normal for hemoglobin for both elderly men and elderly women. Attempting to define the cause of anemia when the hemoglobin concentration is between 12 and 14 g/dl in elderly men rarely yields a specific cause. Even at a level of 12 g/dl, a decision as to how aggressively to evaluate a patient must rest on clinical judgment. The complex nature of the problems that older individuals present together with the high probability of multiple abnormalities occurring simultaneously makes this much judgment critical. On the other hand, once a decision has been made to investigate a low hemoglobin reading in an older person, the principles involved in assessment and evaluation are very similar to those which would be used in subjects of any age group. The causes of the various anemias seen in the elderly are summarized in Table 65-2.

The initial approach to the patient with anemia must include a complete history and physical examination, as well as a complete blood count (CBC) to allow an evaluation of red blood cell size. *Microcytosis*, defined as a mean corpuscular volume (MCV) of less than 84 fl

TABLE 65-2
Physiologic Classification of Anemia

Hypoproliferative	Ineffective	Hemolytic
1. Iron-deficient erythropoiesis	1. Megaloblastic	1. Immunologic
a. Iron deficiency	*a.* Vitamin B_{12}	*a.* Idiopathic
b. Chronic disease	*b.* Folate	*b.* Secondary to drug,
c. Inflammation	*c.* Refractory	tumor, or disease
2. Erythropoietin lack	2. Microcytic	2. Intrinsic
a. Renal	*a.* Thalassemia	*a.* Metabolic
b. Nutritional	*b.* Sideroblastic	*b.* Abnormal hemoglobin
c. Endocrine		
3. Stem cell dysfunction	3. Normocytic	3. Extrinsic
a. Aplastic anemia	*a.* Stromal disease	*a.* Mechanical
b. Red blood cell aplasia	*b.* Dimorphic	*b.* Lytic substance

(Coulter counter), indicates an impairment of hemoglobin synthesis. Macrocytosis, defined as an MCV of over 100 fl, may be caused by increased reticulocytes, or, more frequently, by an abnormality in nuclear maturation.

Red cell production is estimated from the reticulocyte production index. Hemolytic anemia usually has a reticulocyte index greater than 3, whereas a failure of production is indicated by a reticulocyte index of less than 2. Decreased production is present in the hypoproliferative anemias or by ineffective erythropoiesis. The latter is characterized by significant increases in erythroid cell proliferation. Due to maturation abnormalities, these cells are unable to exit the bone marrow and are destroyed by marrow reticuloendothelial cells in the process of intramedullary hemolysis. This disorder may be associated with either macrocytosis or microcytosis. An elevated LDH and indirect hyperbilirubinemia result from the increased destruction of red cell precursors in the marrow and may be used to distinguish ineffective erythropoiesis from hypoproliferative anemia. After excluding hemolytic anemia because of the absence of a high reticulocyte index, the further approach required in defining the cause of the anemia is outlined in Fig. 65-1. Observation may be reasonable for those older individuals who have a mild decrease in hemoglobin (10.5 to 12 g/dl), a normal reticulocyte index, normochromic, normocytic indices, no leukocyte or platelet abnormalities, and no occult blood in the stool. The importance of serial evaluation of the stool for occult blood in such circumstances cannot be overemphasized. Further investigation is indicated if the anemia worsens or if a change in the peripheral blood pattern occurs. For individuals who have mild anemia and hypochromic, microcytic indices or for those who have more severe anemia with normochromic, normocytic indices, a more extensive workup is required. The presence of macrocytosis also warrants additional investigation.

THE HYPOPROLIFERATIVE ANEMIAS

The majority of anemias in the elderly will be of the hypoproliferative type, most commonly associated with inadequate iron supply for erythropoiesis. This is diagnosed by the presence of a decreased serum iron and a reduced transferrin saturation. Absolute iron deficiency (blood loss) is the most common cause of iron-deficient erythropoiesis in younger subjects. In the elderly the cause is more likely to be the "anemia of chronic disease" or anemia associated with inflammation. Iron-deficient erythropoiesis in these disorders results from a defective ability of the reticuloendothelial system to reutilize iron derived from senescent red cells. Thus tissue iron stores are normal or increased, resulting in a serum ferritin concentration above 50 ng/ml and a reduction in the total iron-binding capacity (TIBC). This contrasts with a low serum ferritin and high TIBC which reflect absent iron stores in blood loss anemia.

Blood loss, the anemia of inflammation and chronic disease, and anemia associated with protein-energy malnutrition are the most prevalent anemias in elderly populations. In younger individuals iron deficiency anemia is usually due to either blood loss or, rarely, nutritional iron deficiency. In both men and women a progressive increase in iron stores occurs with advancing age. In older men tissue iron stores average 1200 mg, and in women iron stores increase from a mean of 300 mg to approximately 800 mg over the decade following menopause. Thus nutritional iron deficiency is very rare in the elderly despite the prominence of other nutritional problems. When unexplained iron deficiency does occur, it is almost exclusively due to blood loss from the intestinal tract even if bleeding is not detected by repeated stool guaiac determinations. Other routes of bleeding may occur but are usually easily recognizable (epistaxis, abnormal bleeding from the uterus, hema-

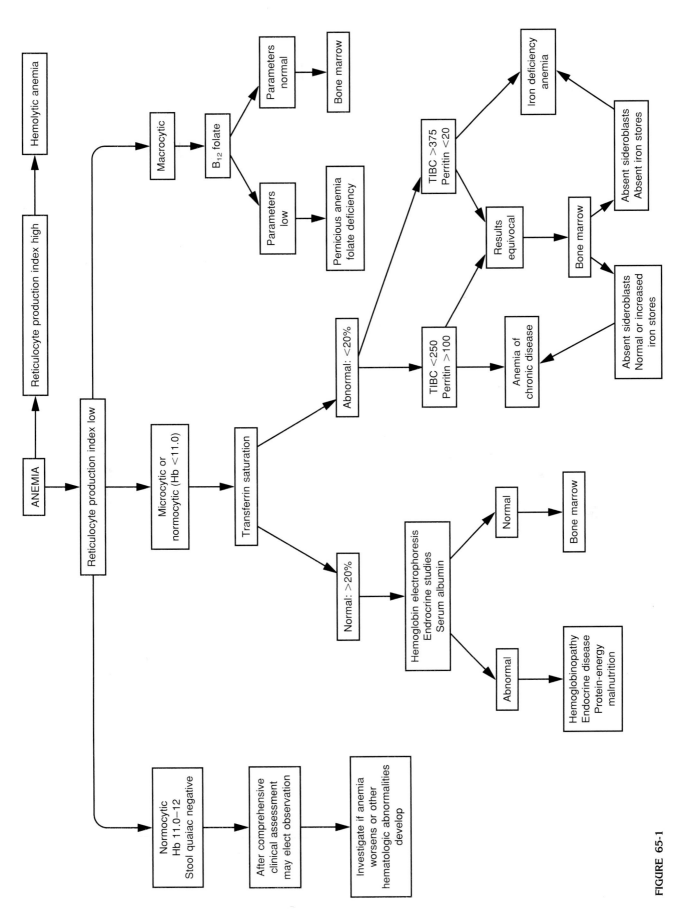

FIGURE 65-1

turia). The causes of gastrointestinal blood loss in the elderly include drugs (notably aspirin and NSAID) and bleeding due to a neoplasm. Angiodysplasia of the large bowel and diverticular disease are also frequent causes but should be considered only after neoplasm has been excluded. Rarely, iron deficiency can result from malabsorption or urinary losses of iron which occur in the face of intravascular hemolysis.

Inflammation is a second important cause of hypoproliferature anemia in the elderly. Inflammation may be the result of bacterial infection, an immune reaction, tissue necrosis, or neoplasm. Usually the decrease in hemoglobin is moderate. Hematologic findings differ from iron deficiency in that the iron block is less severe and microcytosis is usually minimal. The term *anemia of chronic disease* is often used to explain an anemia associated with some other major disease process (e.g., cancer) but in which evidence of inflammation may be lacking (indeed, the mechanisms involved with or without demonstrable inflammation may prove to be the same). Occasionally, the anemia may be the initial manifestation of an occult disease. It is critical for the clinician to be aware of this possibility and to ensure a rational and appropriate workup. Inadequate food intake and increased tissue breakdown may contribute to the severity of the anemia. Treatment is aimed at the underlying disease. Only rarely is anemia severe enough to require transfusion. Iron therapy is usually ineffective owing to the limited absorption of iron in the presence of inflammation and the trapping of parenteral iron in the macrophage.

A multifactorial etiology of anemia is more likely in frail older subjects with multiple medical problems. A classic example is a patient with active rheumatoid disease who has lost blood as a result of aspirin ingestion. Similarly, protein-energy malnutrition or blood loss will markedly aggravate the anemia associated with neoplasia. The possibility of a multifactorial etiology, including blood loss, malnutrition, folate deficiency, or hemolytic disease, should be considered when the anemia of chronic disease or inflammation is associated with a hemoglobin reading below 10 g/dl. In this circumstance laboratory investigations frequently give equivocal results and hence a bone marrow examination may be helpful to identify treatable causes of the anemias.

Marrow failure due to interference with proliferation of hematopoietic cells commonly occurs in the elderly. These disorders are generally associated with suppression of all marrow elements and are suggested by the presence of peripheral pancytopenia. Common causes include drugs, immune damage to the stem cell population, intrinsic marrow lesions, and marrow replacement by malignant cells or fibrous tissue. The latter is usually associated with a myelophthisic blood picture (nucleated red cells, giant platelets, and metamyelocytes

on smear) as a reflection of the disruption of marrow stromal architecture. The presence of pancytopenia in the absence of iron deficiency as a cause for abnormal erythropoiesis is an indication for bone marrow aspiration ad biopsy. Occasionally there occurs isolated suppression of erythropoiesis, referred to as pure red cell aplasia. This disorder may be drug-related or may be caused by benign or malignant abnormalities of lymphocytes including thymoma. Subjects with this disorder present with isolated anemia, an elevated serum iron, and absent erythroid precursors on bone marrow examination.

INEFFECTIVE ERYTHROPOIESIS

Macrocytic anemias in the elderly may result from either vitamin B_{12} or folate deficiency. The prevalence of pernicious anemia increases progressively with advancing age. Pernicious anemia occurs most frequently in subjects over the age of 60 and is more common in women. This disorder results from malabsorption of vitamin B_{12} as a consequence of antibodies acting against gastric parietal cells and intrinsic factor. Atrophic gastritis and decreased secretion of intrinsic factor occur, resulting in failure of vitamin B_{12} absorption. The anemia may be very severe, presenting with weakness and a lemon-yellow skin discoloration. Neurologic abnormalities, including peripheral neuropathy, ataxia, loss of position sense, and upper motor neuron signs, are frequent. Behavioral abnormalities and dementia are well described. Occasionally there is evidence of a more generalized autoimmune disorder, manifesting with myxedema, hypoadrenalism, and vitiligo. The presence of pancytopenia, macrocytosis, hypersegmented polymorphonuclear leukocytes in the peripheral smear, a decreased reticulocyte index, and an increased LDH and indirect hyperbilirubinemia suggest a diagnosis of megaloblastic anemia. The bone marrow classically shows giant metamyelocytes, hypersegmented polymorphonuclear leukocytes, and enlarged erythroid precursors with more hemoglobin than would be expected from the immaturity of their nuclei (nuclear cytoplasmic dissociation). The diagnosis vitamin B_{12} deficiency is made by demonstrating serum vitamin B_{12} concentration of less than 100 pg/ml. Vitamin B_{12} deficiency may also be caused by diseases of the ileum. The Schilling test is able to distinguish a deficiency of intrinsic factor (malabsorption correction by ingested vitamin B_{12} and intrinsic factor) from an abnormality in the ability of the ileum to absorb the vitamin B_{12}-intrinsic factor complex (absorption still impaired with intrinsic factor plus vitamin B_{12}). Treatment consists of weekly or biweekly injection of 100 μg of vitamin B_{12} until stores are replenished. A maintenance dose of 100 μg at monthly intervals is then adequate to prevent recurrence of the anemia.

Epidemiologic studies have generally shown an adequate folate intake in the healthier elderly. Folate deficiency of sufficient severity to cause anemia in the elderly is most frequently found in association with protein-energy malnutrition and/or excessive alcohol consumption. Alcohol and various other drugs are also known to interfere with folate absorption and internal metabolism. Vulnerability to deficiency is significantly greater when folate requirements are increased as a result of inflammation, neoplastic disease, or hemolytic anemia. The hematologic profile is identical to that described for vitamin B_{12} deficiency. The diagnosis is made by the demonstration of significant reductions in the serum (greater than 2 ng/ml) or, better, red cell (greater than 100 ng/ml) folate concentration. Prior to commencement of therapy with folate, it is important to exclude vitamin B_{12} deficiency, as treatment with folate can aggravate or unmask the neurologic abnormalities in the latter disorder.

The major causes of microcytosis and ineffective erythropoiesis are thalassemia and the sideroblastic anemias. Although thalassemia is generally diagnosed at an earlier age, there are reports of its initial detection in older people (generally of the "minor" variety). On the other hand, acquired sideroblastic anemia is primarily a disease of the elderly. This anemia is actually a heterogenous group of disorders characterized by the presence of iron deposits in the mitochondria of normoblasts. These deposits are a consequence of impaired heme synthesis. Their presence usually reflects an intrinsic marrow lesion (idiopathic), but may also be secondary to inflammation, neoplasia, or drug ingestion. The common finding is the presence of a dimorphic red cell population, one of which is markedly hypochromic while the other is well-filled with hemoglobin. The diagnosis is made by the demonstration of ringed sideroblasts in the bone marrow as well as the presence of maturation abnormalities of myeloid and erythroid precursors. A fraction of elderly patients with sideroblastic anemia show some response to pharmacologic doses of pyridoxine (200 mg three times daily). This dose should be given to all patients until it becomes apparent that a rise in hemoglobin concentration will not occur. For those patients unresponsive to pyridoxine, the anemia must be treated symptomatically.

Di Guglielmo's syndrome is more common in older than in younger people presenting with megaloblastic erythroid precursors. Frequently, abnormal sideroblasts will also be seen. The peripheral smear usually demonstrates pancytopenia with occasional nucleated red cells or immature myeloid and megakaryocytic precursors. The bone marrow is markedly hyperplastic. It is essential to exclude the presence of vitamin B_{12} and folate

deficiency, and a trial of pyridoxine may be indicated. Treatment is usually supportive. There is some evidence that Di Guglielmo's syndrome is *premalignant*, evolving rarely into a subacute or acute myelogenous leukemia.

HEMOLYTIC ANEMIAS

The causes of hemolytic anemia in the elderly are somewhat different from those found in younger subjects. Although most patients with congenital disorders will have previously been identified, an occasional patient with congenital hemolytic anemia may present for the first time with symptoms related to cholelithiasis. Autoimmune hemolytic anemia is by far the commonest cause in the elderly. The diagnosis is made by the presence of a positive Coombs test. In younger subjects an etiology of the autoimmune hemolysis is only rarely identified. In the elderly, on the other hand, the anemia is more likely to be associated with a lymphoproliferative disorder (non-Hodgkin's lymphoma or chronic lymphocytic leukemia), collagen vascular disease, or drug ingestion. Steroids and splenectomy are usually effective in patients with red cell antibodies of the IgG type. Patients with red cell antibodies of the IgM variety are more likely to be refractory to such treatment.

A disorder of some importance in the aged is microangiopathic hemolytic anemia. This is usually associated with severe infections, disseminated neoplasm, or cardiac valvular disease and presents with not only hemolytic anemia but also with a consumptive coagulopathy. The presence of red cell fragmentation, thrombocytopenia, a prolonged partial thromboplastin time and hemosiderinuria should suggest this diagnosis.

SUMMARY

Anemia is a common problem in the elderly. Aging per se may be associated with a slight reduction in hemoglobin levels, especially in urea, but hemoglobin levels of less than 12 g/dl suggest significant disease and should be investigated. Commonly, coexisting chronic disease, with or without overt inflammation, is thought to account for hemoglobin levels of as low as 10.5 g/dl, attributable to mild bone marrow suppression. Subclinical or overt malnutrition may also contribute to such hypoproliferative anemia. More specific causes of anemia include blood loss iron deficiency, necessitating assiduous examination for occult gastrointestinal disease. Ineffective erythropoiesis is an important alternative cause of anemia. This requires consideration of vitamin B_{12} deficiency, pernicious anemia, and folate deficiency, especially prevalent in the elderly. Hemolytic processes are also important causes of anemia in the elderly, especially those attributable to drug reactions.

REFERENCES

1. Hill RD: The prevalence of anemia in the over-65s in a rural practice. *Practitioner* 217:963, 1967.
2. McLennan WJ, Andrews GR, Macleod C, Caird FI: Anaemia in the elderly. *Q J Med* 52:1, 1973.
3. Myers MA, Saunders CRG, Chalmers DG: The hemoglobin level of fit elderly people. *Lancet* 2:261, 1968.
4. Nutrition Canada: National Survey. Ottawa, Canada, Information Canada, 1973.
5. Parson PL, Whithey JL, Kilpatrick GS: The prevalence of anemia in the elderly. *Practitioner* 195:656, 1965.
6. Yip R, Johnson C, Dallman PR: Age-related changes in laboratory values used in the diagnosis of anemia and iron deficiency. *Am J Clin Nutr* 39:427, 1984.
7. Lipschitz DA, Mitchell CO, Thompson C: The anemia of senescence. *Am J Hematol* 11:47, 1981.
8. Lipschitz DA, Udupa KB, Milton KY, Thompson C: Effect of age on hematopoiesis in man. *Blood* 63:502, 1984.
9. Garry PJ, Goodwin JS, Hunt WC: Iron status and anemia in the elderly. *J Am Geriatr Soc* 31:389, 1983.
10. Dallman PR, Yip R, Johnson C: Prevalence and causes of anemia in the United States, 1976 to 1980. *Am J Clin Nutr* 39:437, 1984.
11. Lipschitz DA, Mitchell CO: The correctability of the nutritional, immune and hematopoietic manifestations of protein calorie malnutrition in the elderly. *J Am Coll Nutr* 1:17, 1982.
12. Lipschitz DA, Mitchell CO, Steel RW, Milton KY: Nutritional evaluation and supplementation of elderly subjects participating in a "meals on wheels" program. *JPEN* 9:343, 1984.

Chapter 66

WHITE CELL DISORDERS

Robert L. Capizzi, Bayard L. Powell, and Julia M. Cruz

White blood cells (WBC) provide major host defense mechanisms against invading pathogens through phagocytosis and the immune response. In addition, lymphocytes provide immune surveillance against the development of cancer. The clinical manifestations of disease are the result of over- or underproduction of one or more of the WBC series which include the granulocytes— neutrophils, basophils, and eosinophils—and/or the lymphocytes and monocytes. The acuteness of the process is related to the number of the cells, their degree of maturity, and their functional capacity. Thus, initial manifestations of diseases of WBC include signs and symptoms of infectious and neoplastic diseases.

In many instances the disorders of WBC, be they benign or malignant, also involve abnormalities of the red blood cells and platelets. In these situations, the signs and symptoms of disease at presentation may include those secondary to anemia, i.e., weakness and easy fatigability, and/or thrombocytopenia, i.e., easy bruisability, gingival bleeding, and hematuria. A careful history and physical examination, with examination of the peripheral blood and bone marrow, will establish a diagnosis in almost all cases. Age in adulthood has no effect on the range of normal of the peripheral blood count and differential. Thus, any departure from the norm is consistent with a disease process. The most common WBC disorders in the elderly are neoplastic diseases.

Table 66-1 categories the spectrum of WBC disorders as encountered in clinical practice. All the major headings are more common in older patients. Full details of these processes can be found in textbooks on hematology and oncology. The present discussion will highlight these conditions in the perspective of geriatric medicine.

LACK OF PRODUCTION

DRUG/TOXIN EFFECTS

Geriatric patients may commonly take a number of proprietary and prescribed drugs, many of which may have a greater or lesser propensity for isolated neutropenia or pancytopenia.

Given that the bone marrow is one of the more rapidly proliferating organs of the body, exposure to noxious agents may temporarily or permanently inhibit production of one or more of the formed elements of the blood. The list of possible offenders is legion. Table 66-2 lists some of the more common offenders. In a situation of isolated neutropenia or pancytopenia, the physician should immediately ask what medications the patient is taking and how long the patient has been taking them. Short duration should not remove the possibility of drug-induced (pan- or) neutrocytopenia; it could be an idiosyncratic reaction.[1]

Drug effects on the bone marrow range from mild neutropenias (more common) to frank agranulocytosis. In this latter situation, the RBC and platelets may be unaffected. Drug-induced reduction of the granulocytic series may be a direct toxic effect as with many cancer chemotherapeutic drugs or may be the result of an immunologic phenomenon wherein a drug-antibody complex reacts with mature neutrophils and their precursors in the bone marrow. Upon withdrawal of the offending agent, there may be a relatively brisk marrow recovery within 14 to 21 days. A bone marrow examination during this recovery period may reveal a large number of immature elements which may be confused with an acute leukemia. If this is a possibility, a test of time (an additional 2 to 3 weeks) will provide the answer: The recov-

TABLE 66-1
Disorders of White Blood Cells

I. Lack of production
  A. Drug or toxin suppression which may be temporary or permanent
  B. Ineffective myelopoiesis secondary to B_{12} or folate deficiency
II. Increased destruction
  Immune neutropenia 2° to rheumatologic disorders, Felty's syndrome, and lymphoproliferative malignancies
III. Increased splenic sequestration
  Congestive splenomegaly with cirrhosis; Gaucher's disease, etc.
IV. Neoplastic diseases
  A. Primary hematologic
    1. Myelodysplastic syndromes (MDS)
    2. Acute leukemias
      a. Acute myelogenous leukemia (AML)
      b. Acute lymphocytic leukemia (ALL)
    3. Chronic leukemias
      a. Chronic lymphocytic leukemia (CLL)
      b. Chronic granulocytic leukemia (CGL)
  B. Cancers metastatic to bone marrow
    Most commonly breast, lung, prostate, and lymphomas
V. Normal count with impaired function
  A. Diabetes mellitus: Impaired PMN function
  B. Chronic renal failure: Impaired PMN and lymphocyte function

ering marrow will go on to differentiate and the leukemic marrow will either stay the same or will worsen. Other marrow toxins include a variety of household and industrial chemicals—especially organic solvents, naphthalenes, insecticides, and herbicides. Chemical exposure from hobbies or occupations must therefore be part of history taking. While the hematologic effects of drug and chemical exposure are frequently reversible, some may result in myelodysplastic syndromes or aplastic anemia which, in turn, may eventuate into frank acute myelogenous leukemia.[2]

NUTRITIONAL DEFICIENCY

Mild neutropenia may be associated with nutritional anemias secondary to folate or B_{12} deficiency. Older individuals living alone may not be attentive to their diet for various socioeconomic or medical reasons. The main source of folates are in fresh green vegetables, many fruits, and beans. Cooking and canning destroys folates. The body's folate stores can be depleted within 4 to 5 months of poor dietary intake. Thus, a dietary history may provide an important clue to the diagnosis of the hematologic problem. Dietary folate deficiency may be aggravated by alcoholism and chronic hemolysis.[3]

In contrast, body stores of vitamin B_{12} are not readily depleted by poor dietary habits, even steady "tea-and-toast" diets. It takes 3 to 5 years to deplete the body stores of vitamin B_{12}. However, gastric atrophy is more common with increasing age, and this may lead to failure of gastric secretion of intrinsic factor, which binds to dietary cobalamin—a step necessary in the absorption of this vitamin by the ileal mucosa. Other conditions causing a B_{12} deficiency include a history of gastrectomy or subtotal small-bowel (ileal) resection. It should be noted that neurologic signs and symptoms of B_{12} deficiency may be confused with other neurologic problems in the elderly. These include peripheral paresthesias (peripheral neuritis), loss of balance (posterior column damage), spasticity (lateral column damage), and impaired cerebration. Any of these neurologic signs and symptoms may be readily attributed to "old age." The physician should be alert to the potential for their ready correction with vitamin B_{12}.[4]

INCREASED DESTRUCTION

Immune neutropenia may be associated with various rheumatologic conditions, e.g., systemic lupus erythematosus, rheumatoid arthritis, polyserositis, and lymphoproliferative malignancies. In these situations, the

TABLE 66-2
Agranulocytosis/Neutropenia Caused by Drugs

1. Cancer chemotherapeutic agents
2. Drugs for ulcer disease: cimetidine
3. Thiazide diuretics
4. Oral hypoglycemic drugs
5. Anti-inflammatory/antiarthritic drugs:
   Phenylbutazone and related drugs
   Indomethacin
   Penicillamine
   Gold salts
   Colchicine
6. Cardiovascular drugs:
   Procainamide
   Hydralazine
   Quinidine
   Captopril
   Methyldopa
7. Antibiotics:
   Semisynthetic penicillins
   Cephalosporins
   Sulfa drugs
   Vancomycin
8. Phenothiazines
9. Thyroid suppressants
10. Antiepileptic drugs:
    Phenytoin and derivatives
    Carbamazepine

neutropenia is due to the elimination of immunoglobulin-coated granulocytes by the reticuloendothelial system.[5] The neutropenia of Felty's syndrome (rheumatoid arthritis, splenomegaly, and neutropenia) has a complex etiology which includes immune destruction and suppression as well as splenic sequestration.[6]

SPLENIC SEQUESTRATION

Any condition causing splenomegaly may lead to sequestration of sufficient neutrophils to cause mild to moderate neutropenia as a component of the pancytopenia of hypersplenism.

NEOPLASTIC DISEASES OF THE HEMATOPOIETIC SYSTEM

Leukemia is the neoplastic disease of the white blood cells. While the overall incidence rates have remained relatively stable over the past five decades, overall mortality from leukemia has been reduced substantially as a result of the excellent cure rates for acute lymphoblastic leukemia in childhood.[7] Cure of hematologic neoplasms in elderly patients has lagged behind for two major reasons: (1) the predominance of chronic leukemias in the elderly, which to date are incurable, and (2) inability of the elderly to tolerate potentially curative approaches to acute leukemia, which include aggressive chemotherapy and bone marrow transplantation. The relative incidence rates of the leukemias as a function of age are noted in Fig. 66-1.[8] The following discussion will present highlights of these neoplastic processes.

MYELODYSPLASTIC (PRELEUKEMIC) SYNDROMES

The *myelodysplastic syndromes* (MDS), frequently referred to as *preleukemia*, encompass a group of hematopoietic disorders characterized by ineffective hematopoiesis with peripheral blood cytopenias and hypercellularity of the bone marrow. All the myelodysplastic syndromes are associated with some degree of predisposition to develop acute myelogenous leukemia (AML); however, diseases such as chronic myelogenous leukemia, the other myeloproliferative disorders, and Fanconi's anemia that are also associated with an increased risk of AML are not classified as MDS.

The true incidence of myelodysplastic syndromes is not known. About two-thirds of patients with MDS are elderly males. Median age at diagnosis is 65 to 70 years.[9–11] The nomenclature associated with myelodysplastic syndromes is confusing. Terms found in the literature include odoleukemia (threshold of leukemia),

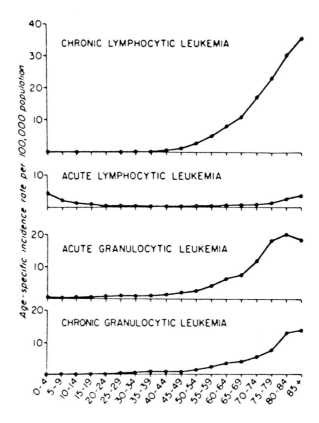

FIGURE 66-1
Age-specific incidence of hematopoietic malignancies in the United States, 1973–1977. *(From Young JL, Percy CL, Asire SJ (eds): Cancer Institute and Mortality in the United States, 1973–77, Natl Cancer Inst Monogr 57:73, June 1981.)*

subacute myeloid leukemia, smoldering leukemia, dysmyelopoietic syndrome, and preleukemia.

In 1982, the French-American-British (FAB) Cooperative Group established a classification system with five diagnostic categories based on peripheral blood and bone marrow characteristics.[12] These include refractory anemia (RA), RA with ring sideroblasts (RARS), RA with excess blasts (RAEB), RAEB in transformation (RAEBT), and chronic myelomonocytic leukemia (CMML) (Table 66-3). Patients with refractory anemia (RA) or refractory anemia with ring sideroblasts (RARS) have < 1 percent of such blasts in the peripheral blood and < 5 percent of blasts in the bone marrow; reticulocytopenia and dyserythropoiesis are the predominant features for these disorders. RARS is distinguished from RA by the presence of ringed sideroblasts in the bone marrow. The granulocytic and megakaryocytic series are usually relatively normal. Patients with refractory anemia with excess blasts (RAEB), and RAEB in transformation (RAEBT) are distinguished by the percentage of blasts in the peripheral blood and bone marrow. These patients usually have hypercellular marrows with prominent dysgranulopoiesis in addition to abnormalities in the erythrocytic and megakaryocytic series. Patients with RAEB have < 5 percent blasts in the peripheral blood, and their bone marrow has 5 to 20 percent blasts. Patients with RAEBT have (1) ≥ 5 percent blasts in the peripheral blood, or (2) 21 to 30 percent blasts in the bone marrow, or (3) presence of Auer bodies (rods) in granulocyte precursors. Patients with chronic myelomonocytic leukemia (CMML) have an absolute monocytosis (≥ 1000 per mm^3) with < 5 percent blasts in the peripheral blood; the bone marrow has ≤ 20 percent blasts, often with an increased number of monocytic precursors. A common additional finding in patients with MDS is the presence of one or more cytogenetic abnormalities in approximately 40 to 60 percent of patients, most frequently involving chromosomes 5, 7, 8, or 20.

The natural history of patients with MDS syndromes is quite variable. Estimates of risk of progression to acute leukemia and median survival for the subgroups are outlined in Table 66-3.[10] Prognostic factors, in addition to FAB subgroup, include the presence of cytogenetic abnormalities or secondary or mutagen-induced MDS, which are associated with a poor prognosis.

The clinical course of patients with RAEB, RAEBT, and CMML is frequently complicated by serious, and sometimes fatal, infection and hemorrhage related to pancytopenia. Patients who develop AML after MDS have a lower frequency and duration of response to standard therapy than patients with de novo AML.[13]

There are no proven effective therapies for MDS. Recent reviews of therapeutic trials with corticosteroids, androgens, possible cyto-differentiating agents (low-dose cytosine arabinoside, 13-*cis*-retinoic acid, vitamin D analogues), cytotoxic chemotherapy, and bone marrow transplantation have detailed disappointing results. Supportive care with red cell and platelet transfusion, and antibiotics for infection is still standard therapy for most patients with MDS.[10,14,15] Studies are under way to assess the utility of recombinant hematopoietic growth factors as stimulants of normal bone marrow function in patients with MDS; initial results are promising.[16]

ACUTE MYELOGENOUS LEUKEMIA (AML)

The average annual age-adjusted incidence of acute myelogenous leukemia in the United States is 2.8 per 100,000 with a mortality rate of 2.3 per 100,000 population. The incidence increases with age in adults over age 35 to rates of 6.9 per 100,000 in persons ages 60 to 64, 8.2 per 100,000 in ages 65 to 69, 12.6 per 100,000 in ages 70 to 74, and > 20 per 100,000 persons ≥ age 75. The incidence of AML is higher in white males living in industrialized areas in developed countries, suggesting environmental exposure as a possible cause. The potential roles of genetic and environmental factors in the development of AML have been recently reviewed.[17–19]

Patients with AML usually present with evidence of bone marrow failure—anemia, bleeding due to thrombocytopenia, and/or infection secondary to granulocytopenia. An international classification system (FAB) details subtypes of AML (M1 through M7). This distinction is based on morphology, histochemical characteristics, and immunologic phenotyping.[20,21] A special feature of acute promyelocytic leukemia (FAB-M3) is a high incidence of disseminated intravascular coagulation (DIC).

If untreated or unresponsive to chemotherapy, AML may be rapidly fatal (median survival < 2 months). The major causes of death are overwhelming infection and hemorrhage related to the disease-associated cytopenias.

Standard induction therapy for AML is combination chemotherapy which includes cytosine arabinoside (ara-C) and daunorubicin. These drugs yield complete remissions in 30 to 80 percent of patients, depending

TABLE 66-3
Characteristics and Prognosis of Myelodysplastic Syndromes (MDS)

| Subgroup | Percent of Blasts | | Progression to AML, % | Median Survival, months |
	In Peripheral Blood	In Bone Marrow		
Refractory anemia (RA)	<1	<5	10	70
Refractory anemia with ring sideroblasts (RARS)	<1	<5	15	65
Chronic myelomonocytic leukemia (CMML)	<5	≤20	30	10
Refractory anemia with excess blasts (RAEB)	<5	5–20	40	10
Refractory anemia with excess blasts in transformation (RAEBT)	≥5	21–30	60	5

upon various prognostic factors. Increased age is an important negative prognostic factor.[22-25] The poorer prognosis associated with increased age is related to a higher frequency of fatal infections and hemorrhage during the period of disease- and treatment-related marrow hypoplasia (induction deaths), not due to chemotherapy failure (residual or resistant leukemia). While complete remission (CR) rates have usually been 60 to 80 percent in younger patients with AML, the CR rate in patients ≥ age 60 has generally been < 50 percent (frequently with induction death rates approximating 50 percent).[22-25] Attempts to improve response rates in older patients with AML have included attenuated doses of standard therapy[26] and treatment with low-dose cytosine arabinoside[27]; these treatments have resulted in decreased induction death rates but without improved CR rates. The role of more aggressive therapies, including bone marrow transplantation, has been very limited in elderly patients because of the high rates of complications and prohibitive toxicity.

The median duration of complete remission is approximately 1 year and a small percentage (≤ 15 percent) will be cured of their leukemia. Patients who achieve complete remissions should be considered for therapy after remission in an attempt to prevent relapse. However, the exact role and optimal type of such therapy remains controversial.[28,29]

The roles of other prognostic factors (other than age) within the elderly population are not well defined, but lower performance status and the presence of a preceding myelodysplastic syndrome are generally considered indicators of a poorer outcome.

ACUTE LYMPHOBLASTIC LEUKEMIA (ALL)

ALL is primarily a disease of children (Fig. 66-1). With available therapy today, this childhood neoplasm is curable in the majority of patients. The statistics on curability are a function of cellular phenotype and other prognostic factors and can range from < 10 percent to as high as 70 or 80 percent.[7,30-32]

ALL in adults is not the same as the childhood disease. Firstly, the frequency of complete response is lower: 70 to 75 percent in adults[33] as opposed to 90 to 98 percent[7] in children. Secondly, the remission duration and curability using the same therapy as in the children's protocols is considerably less.[34,35] Important prognostic features for outcome in the treatment of ALL include age,[34,36-38] cytogenetics,[39-47] and surface phenotype. Poor prognosis is especially associated with the presence of chromosomal translocations such as Philadelphia chromosome (Ph[1]) $t(9;22)$, $t(4;11)$, $t(8;14)$, $t(8;2)$, or $t(8;22)$,[40-47] and with surface phenotype indicating B-cell[33] or mixed lymphoid-myeloid surface markers (also called *biphenotypic leukemia*).[48]

To date, treatment of the adult patient with ALL has been based on the experience with the disease in children. The initial goal of therapy is to correct problems secondary to bone marrow failure, that is, to treat anemia with blood transfusions, treat documented or suspected infection, and control bleeding. Specific anti-leukemia treatment is then directed toward the achievement of a complete remission. Induction chemotherapy therapy for ALL, very different from that for AML, usually includes the use of prednisone, vincristine, daunorubicin, and asparaginase. While these drugs are well tolerated in children, increasing age is associated with poorer drug tolerance. Mortality, usually from infection and/or bleeding during the induction process, may occur in 10 to 20 percent of elderly patients.

In contrast to the treatment of AML, it is widely accepted that patients with ALL require therapy after remission. This phase of treatment—once the patient is in complete remission—has been referred to as *maintenance therapy*. When such therapy is more vigorous, it has also been called *intensification*. The optimal therapy after remission and the duration of such therapy remains to be defined and is the subject of intensive investigation at present. Most programs utilize multiple drugs administered in a cyclic fashion over a 2- to 3-year period.

Deliberate treatment to the craniospinal axis (CNS prophylaxis) is standard practice in the treatment of childhood ALL. While the incidence of CNS leukemia is lower in adults compared to children, treatment to the CNS is also part of ALL therapy in adults. This usually consists of intrathecal methotrexate and/or cranial radiation.

With the above intensive treatment plan, the median duration of remission is approximately 2 years with 35 to 45 percent of patients disease-free at 5 years.[33] One contributing feature to this poorer response duration in adults as opposed to children is the inability to deliver optimal chemotherapy at maximal doses due to comorbid diseases.[33]

CHRONIC LYMPHOCYTIC LEUKEMIA (CLL)

The chronic lymphocytic leukemias (CLL) are disorders of clonal proliferation of mature lymphoid cells in the peripheral blood, bone marrow, and lymphoid organs of the body. CLL is seen only in older adults with mean age at diagnosis of 60 years. The reported incidence of 3 per 100,000 in Western countries may be a significant underestimate since many patients are asymptomatic for years. There is no racial difference in the United States between blacks and whites, but there are very few cases in the Far East and among patients of Oriental descent. Initially CLL was thought to be a homogenous condition with variable disease activity. The identification of cell surface markers for lymphocytes and development of special stains have led to the recognition of four major subtypes: B cell, T cell, prolymphocytic, and hairy cell.[49,50]

B-Cell CLL

B-cell CLL accounts for over 95 percent of all patients. Twenty percent of patients are identified with asymptomatic lymphocytosis during evaluation for other medical problems.[49] In most patients, the disease has a gradual progression spanning several years, and the extent of the lymphoid burden at diagnosis correlates well with length of preexisting disease. In some patients the disease has a more aggressive course, and progression to advanced clinical stages occurs within a few months of diagnosis.[51,52]

Three criteria are required to make the diagnosis; peripheral blood lymphocytosis > 15,000 lymphocytes per μl, bone marrow aspirate with > 30 percent lymphocytes in the presence of normal or increased cellularity, and cell surface markers showing a clonal proliferation of lymphocytes.[49,53] The original classification by Rai implies an orderly progression from lymphocytosis alone to the successive development of adenopathy, organomegaly, and eventually anemia with thrombocytopenia.[53] The importance of these variables has been confirmed, and modifications have been suggested by Mandelli to allow for variability in clinical presentation. Pattern of bone marrow infiltration and sex are also prognostic factors (Table 66-4).[54,55]

Therapy for B-cell CLL is palliative and therefore should be reserved for patients who are symptomatic or who have signs of progressive disease by clinical or laboratory criteria. The mainstay of therapy has been oral alkylating agents (chlorambucil or cyclophosphamide) for control of lymphoid proliferation and steroids for autoimmune complications. Leukocytosis alone (stage 0) does not require therapy since the prognosis of these patients is excellent in the absence of the other poor prognostic factors. The rate of increase of leukocytosis is a better indicator of disease activity than the absolute count. Leukostasis associated with high circulating blast counts does not generally occur in this condition since most of the lymphocytes are mature, small cells. Rare reports of hyperleukocytosis with symptoms have been reported when the WBC exceeds 900,000 per mm^3, and most clinicians institute therapy when the WBC is about 200,000 per mm^3.[49,56]

Treatment with chemotherapy or local radiation can be used to control symptoms in patients with stage I or II disease; however, symptomatic improvement does not change survival.[49,56] In contrast, when treated with combination chemotherapy, half the patients with stage III or IV are reported to have an improved median survival ranging from 1.5 years to more than 4 years.[57-60]

Autoimmune manifestations of CLL are common and include development of antibodies to platelets and red cells (IgG and C3 on direct antiglobulin test) and to erythroid precursors, resulting in red cell aplasia. All these complications are indications for therapy with steroids or intravenous gamma globulin for refractory cases of red cell aplasia.[49,56,61]

Recurrent infections are the most common complications leading to death in CLL. Patients with stage 0 have no increased risk of infection. In anticipation of gradual deterioration in immune response, pneumococcal vaccine and boosters should be administered while the potential for response is still intact. All other patients

TABLE 66-4
Chronic Lymphocytic Leukemia (CLL)

| Stage | Parameter | RAI Classification | | | | | Immunologic Parameters | | | | Survival in Years |
| | | | | | | | T-Cell Defect | B-Cell Defect Immunoglobulin Levels | | | |
		Lymphocytosis >15,000/mm³	Lymph-adenopathy	Organ-omegaly	Anemia <11 g/dl	Thrombo-cytopenia <100,000	Anergy	M	G	A	
0	Lymphocytosis	+	−	−	−	−	0%	NL	NL	NL	≥12
I	Low-risk (patients with any* one variable)	+	*	*	*	*	0%	↓	NL	NL	7.0–10.0
II	Intermediate-risk (patients with any* two variables)	+	*	*	*	*	30%	↓	↓	NL	4.0–9.0
III	High-risk (patients with any* three variables)	+	*	*	*	*	70%	↓	↓	↓	1.6–2.0
IV	High-risk (patients with any* four variables)	+	+	+	+	+	70%	↓	↓	↓	1.6–2.0

have higher risks for infection. As the disease advances clinically, the immune function becomes increasingly compromised (Table 66-4) with susceptibility to viral, bacterial, and fungal infections.[53,62,63]

Patients should avoid direct contact with the body fluids of children who have received live-virus vaccines (oral polio, measles-mumps-rubella) for the duration of viral shedding. Quantitative immunoglobulins should be monitored for prognostic and potentially therapeutic purposes. A preliminary study has shown encouraging results with monthly administration of gamma globulin for patients with low IgG levels.[62–64]

T-Cell CLL

T-cell CLL is a rare subtype of CLL that accounts for less than 3 percent of all CLL cases. The term encompasses many diverse T-cell clonal proliferations ranging from a relatively indolent form to the aggressive peripheral T-cell lymphoma leukemia associated with the virus of the same name. The clinical manifestations of these diseases include hyperleukocytosis, skin infiltration, massive splenomegaly, and relatively mild lymphadenopathy and bone marrow involvement. Cell surface markers in the peripheral blood show a clonal proliferation of the malignant T cell. CLL involving all the T-cell subtypes (helper, suppressor, and killer cells) have been described.[65,66]

Prolymphocytic Leukemia

This subtype is characterized by marked lymphocytosis (> 100,000 lymphocytes per mm³), extensive bone marrow infiltration, massive splenomegaly, and minimal adenopathy. The cell has been named *prolymphocyte*, but it is not an intermediate form between a lymphoblast and a mature lymphocyte. The prolymphocyte is larger than a lymphocyte with a characteristic dense border outlining a prominent nucleolus. The cells can be either B or T cell in origin.[67–69]

Most patients have advanced clinical disease at presentation, and their prognosis parallels that of patients with stage III and IV B-cell CLL. Therapy for these patients requires multiagent chemotherapy to control the splenomegaly and leukocytosis.[70,71] Radiation therapy to palliate splenic engorgement may be helpful in older patients. Patients become increasingly refractory to therapy, with an expected survival of 1.5 years and death due to uncontrolled disease.[49,68]

Hairy Cell Leukemia

Hairy cell leukemia is a rare subtype of CLL almost exclusively seen in men over the age of 60. The clinical features include massive splenomegaly, absence of ade-

nopathy, and peripheral pancytopenia. The diagnosis is made by the morphological characteristics of the circulating lymphocytes, which are small and have cytoplasmic projections ("hairs"). Definitive diagnosis is made histochemically with the TRAP (tartrate-resistant acid phosphatase) stain. Cell surface markers show B cell and monocytic origins for these cells.[72,73] Bone marrow aspiration usually yields little material (dry tap), and bone marrow biopsy shows increased cellularity with diffuse infiltration by the hairy cells. The spleen is infiltrated with the same clone of cells. Infections with gram-negative and staphylococcal species are the predominant complication.

Splenectomy was the treatment of choice in the past with improvement of neutropenia in about 50 percent of patients for 8 to 10 years. Most recently α-interferon (α-IFN) has been shown to produce partial and complete remissions in over 50 percent of patients. This has become the treatment of choice, sparing many patients a surgical procedure and the devastating effects of the splenectomy on the immune system.[74,75]

CHRONIC GRANULOCYTIC LEUKEMIA (CGL)

Chronic granulocytic leukemia (CGL) is a disorder of excess production of mature granulocytes which eventually transforms to a clinical picture similar to acute leukemia with an overgrowth of immature cells (blast crisis). It is the least common general type of leukemia, accounting for 15 percent of all leukemias with an age-adjusted incidence rate of 1 per 100,000 without geographic, sex, or racial differences.[76,77]

Diagnosis is made by the demonstration of granulocytosis in the peripheral blood with a predominance of segmented neutrophils and myelocytes, increased basophils and eosinophils, increased bone marrow cellularity, a low leukocyte alkaline phosphatase (LAP) score, and the presence of the Philadelphia chromosome (Ph¹) t(9;22).[77,78] In the past the disease has been divided into Ph¹+ and Ph¹−; however, it is now felt that the diagnosis of CGL should be reserved for those with Ph¹ chromosome.[79]

The disease characteristically proceeds through three phases: chronic, accelerated, and terminal (blastic) phase. The length of the chronic phase is highly variable—from 1.5 years to 14 years (median duration of 3 years). In the chronic phase, the disease is easily controlled without aggressive therapy. The accelerated phase begins with gradual increases in white cells, platelets, and spleen size. Initially good maturation persists, but eventually more blasts are seen in the peripheral blood, and higher doses of medication are required to maintain control. This phase generally lasts a few months but may extend over 1 year. The terminal phase of the disease is indistinguishable from acute leukemia. The blasts have myeloid surface markers in 85 percent of the patients and lymphoid markers in the remaining 15 percent.[80-83]

Patients in the chronic phase with WBC in the range of 50,000 to 100,000 per mm^3 and platelet counts ≤ 500,000 per mm^3 may require no therapy. The goal of therapy is to palliate symptoms and complications relative to splenomegaly and thrombocytosis. Effective agents for CGL in the chronic phase include hydroxyurea, busulfan, and, most recently, α-IFN. To date, none of these agents has changed the natural history of disease, but α-IFN has shown some promise in decreasing the percentage of cells exhibiting the Ph^1 chromosome. Allogeneic bone marrow transplantation in the chronic phase appears promising, with better than 30 percent long-term disease-free survival. The severe morbidity of this treatment limits this option to younger patients.[84,85]

Treatment of the accelerated phase centers on palliative control of symptoms, the blood count, and organomegaly. Treatment of the blast transformation depends on the cell origin of the blasts. Myeloid blastic states respond poorly to therapy, and no standard therapy is available. Lymphoid blastic states can be controlled for 6 to 12 months, with standard combination regimens as used for de novo ALL.[83]

CANCERS METASTATIC TO BONE MARROW

Many of the common malignancies (see Chap. 7) have a propensity for metastasis to the bone and bone marrow. These include carcinomas of the breast, lung, prostate, and the lymphomas. Space-occupying lesions in the bone marrow which crowd out normal hematopoietic elements are termed *myelophthisis*. Manifestations of myelophthisis in the peripheral blood include pancytopenia and leukoerythroblastosis. Pancytopenias may be aggravated by nutritional deficiencies, especially folate deficiency.

QUALITATIVE WHITE BLOOD CELL DEFECTS

Patients with severe diabetes mellitus and chronic renal failure may have impaired polymorphonuclear neutrophil and lymphocyte function. Consequently, they are prone to serious infections.

REFERENCES

1. Young GAR, Vincent PC: Drug-induced agranulocytosis. *Clin Haematol* 9:483, 1980.
2. Camitta BM et al: Aplastic anemia. Pathogenesis, diagnoses, treatment and prognosis. *N Engl J Med* 306:645; 712, 1982.
3. Eichner ER: The hematological disorders of alcoholism. *Am J Med* 54:621, 1973.
4. Reynolds EH: Neurological aspects of folate and vitamin B$_{12}$ metabolism. *Clin Haematol* 5:661, 1976.
5. Boxer LA et al: Autoimmune neutropenia. *N Engl J Med* 293:748, 1975.
6. Blumfelder TM et al: Felty's syndrome: Effects of splenectomy upon granulocyte count and granulocyte-associated IgG. *Ann Intern Med* 94:623, 1981.
7. Riehm H et al: Acute lymphoblastic leukemia, in Voute PA et al (eds): *Cancer in Children: Clinical Management.* Heidelberg, Springer-Verlag, 1986, p 99.
8. Young JL et al (eds): Cancer Incidence and Mortality in the United States 1973–77, *Natl Cancer Inst Monogr* 57:73, 1981.
9. Saarni MI, Linman JW: Preleukemia: The hematologic syndrome preceding acute leukemia. *Am J Med* 55:38, 1973.
10. Koeffler HP: Myelodysplastic syndromes (preleukemia). *Semin Hematol* 23:284, 1986.
11. Bagby GC Jr: The concept of preleukemia: Clinical and laboratory studies. *CRC Crit Rev Oncol/Hematol* 4:203, 1986.
12. Bennett JM et al: The French-American-British (FAB) Co-operative Group. Proposals for the classifications of the myelodysplastic syndromes. *Br J Haematol* 51:189, 1982.
13. Estey EH et al: Causes of initial remission induction failure in acute myelogenous leukemia. *Blood* 50:309, 1982.
14. Buzaid AC et al: Management of myelodysplastic syndrome. *Am J Med* 80:1149, 1986.
15. Tricot GJ et al: Management of the myelodysplastic syndromes. *Semin Oncol* 14:444, 1987.
16. Vadhan-Raj S et al: Effects of recombinant human granulocyte-macrophage colony stimulating factor in patients with myelodysplastic syndromes. *N Engl J Med* 317:1545, 1987.
17. Young JL Jr et al (eds): *Surveillance, Epidemiology, and End Results: Incidence and Mortality Data, 1973–77,* National Cancer Institute Monograph 57. Washington, Government Printing Office, 1981.
18. Cutler SJ, Young JL (eds): *Third National Cancer Survey: Incidence Data,* National Cancer Institute Monograph 41. Washington, Government Printing Office, 1975.
19. Sandler DP: Epidemiology of acute myelogenous leukemia. *Semin Oncol* 14:359, 1987.
20. Bennett JM et al: Proposed revised criteria for the classification of acute myeloid leukemia: A report of the French-American-British Cooperative Group. *Ann Intern Med* 103:626, 1985.
21. Bennett JM et al: Criteria for the diagnosis of acute leukemia of megakaryocyte lineage (M7): A report of the French-American-British Cooperative Group. *Ann Intern Med* 103:460, 1985.
22. Rai KR et al: Treatment of acute myelocytic leukemia: A study by Cancer and Leukemia Group B. *Blood* 58:1203, 1981.
23. Yates J et al: Cytosine arabinoside with daunorubicin or adriamycin for therapy of acute myelocytic leukemia: A CALGB study. *Blood* 60:464, 1982.
24. Estey EH et al: Causes of initial remission induction failure in acute myelogenous leukemia. *Blood* 60:309, 1982.

25. Keating MJ et al: Treatment of patients over 50 years of age with acute myelogenous leukemia with a combination of rubidazone and cytosine arabinoside, vincristine, and prednisone (ROAP). *Blood* 58:584, 1981.

26. Kahn SB et al: Full dose versus attenuated dose daunorubicin, cytosine, arabinoside, and 6-thioguanine in the treatment of acute nonlymphocytic leukemia in the elderly. *J Clin Oncol* 2:865, 1984.

27. Cheson BD et al: A critical appraisal of low-dose cytosine arabinoside in patients with acute non-lymphocytic leukemia and myelodysplastic syndromes. *J Clin Oncol* 4:1854, 1986.

28. Gale RP, Foon KA: Therapy of acute myelogenous leukemia. *Semin Hematol* 24:40, 1987.

29. Mayer RJ: Current chemotherapeutic treatment approaches to the management of previously untreated adults with de novo acute myelogenous leukemia. *Semin Oncol* 14:384, 1987.

30. Crist WM et al: Immunologic markers in childhood acute lymphocytic leukemia. *Semin Oncol* 17:105, 1985.

31. Williams DL et al: Prognostic importance of chromosome number in 136 untreated children with acute lymphoblastic leukemia. *Blood* 60:864, 1982.

32. Niemeyer CM et al: Comparative analysis of treatment programs for childhood acute lymphoblastic leukemia. *Semin Oncol* 12:122, 1985.

33. Hoelzer D, Gale RP: Acute lymphoblastic leukemia in adults: Recent progress, future direction. *Semin Hematol* 24:27, 1987.

34. Gee TS et al: Acute lymphoblastic leukemia in adults and children: Difference in response with similar therapeutic regimens. *Cancer* 37:1256, 1976.

35. Sackmann-Muriel SF et al: Evaluation of induction of remission, intensification and central nervous system prophylactic treatment in acute lymphoblastic leukemia. *Cancer* 34:418, 1974.

36. Baccarani M et al: Adolescent and adult acute lymphoblastic leukemia: Prognostic features and outcome of therapy: A study of 293 patients. *Blood* 60:677, 1982.

37. Zippin C et al: Variations in survival among patients with acute lymphocytic leukemia. *Blood* 37:52, 1971.

38. Jacquillat C et al: Prognosis and treatment of acute lymphoblastic leukemia: Study of 650 patients. *Cancer Chemother Pharmacol* 1:113, 1978.

39. Third International Workshop on Chromosomes in Leukemia. Chromosomal abnormalities and their clinical significance in acute lymphoblastic leukemia. *Cancer Res* 43:868, 1983.

40. Catvosky D: Ph[1]-positive acute leukaemia and chronic granulocytic leukaemia: One or two diseases? *Br J Haematol* 42:493, 1979.

41. Ben-Bassat I, Gale RP: Hybrid acute leukemia. *Leuk Res* 8:929, 1984.

42. Arthur DC et al: Translocation 4;11 in acute lymphoblastic leukemia: Clinical characteristics and prognostic significance. *Blood* 59:96, 1982.

43. Parkin JL et al: Acute leukemia associated with the t(4;11) chromosome rearrangement: Ultrastructural and immunologic characteristics. *Blood* 60:1321, 1982.

44. Manolov G, Manolova Y: Marker band in one chromosome 14 from Burkitt lymphomas. *Nature* 237:33, 1972.

45. Zech L et al: Characteristic chromosomal abnormalities in biopsies and lymphoid-cell lines from patients with Burkitt and non-Burkitt lymphomas. *Int J Cancer* 17:47, 1976.

46. Van den Berghe H et al: Variant translocation in Burkitt lymphoma. *Cancer Genet Cytogenet* 1:9, 1979.

47. Berger R et al: A new translocation in Burkitt's tumor cells. *Hum Genet* 53:111, 1979.

48. Sobol RE et al: Adult acute lymphoblastic leukemia phenotypes defined by monoclonal antibodies. *Blood* 65:730, 1985.

49. Rai KR et al: Chronic lymphocytic leukemia. *Med Clin North Am* 68(3):697, 1984.

50. Boggs DR: Factors influencing the duration of survival of patients with chronic lymphocytic leukemia. *Am J Med* 40:243, 1966.

51. Gale RP, Foon FA: Biology of chronic lymphocytic leukemia. *Semin Hematol* 24(4):209, 1987.

52. Freedman AS, Nadler LM: B cell development in chronic lymphocytic leukemia. *Semin Hematol* 24(4):230, 1987.

53. Rai KR et al: Clinical staging of chronic lymphocytic leukemia. *Blood* 46:219, 1975.

54. Mandelli F et al: Prognosis in chronic lymphocytic leukemia: A Retrospective Multicenter Study from the GIMEMA Group I. *Clin Oncol* 5:398, 1987.

55. Monserrat E, Rozman C: Bone marrow biopsy in chronic lymphocytic leukemia: A review of its prognostic importance. *Blood Cells* 12(2):315, 1987.

56. Foon KA, Gale RP: Staging and therapy of chronic lymphocytic leukemia. *Semin Hematol* 24(4):264, 1987.

57. Paule B et al: The possible role of radiotherapy in chronic lymphocytic leukemia: A critical review. *Radiother Oncol* 4(1):45, 1985.

58. Kempin S et al: Combination chemotherapy of advanced chronic lymphocytic leukemia: The M-2 protocol. *Blood* 60:1110, 1982.

59. Sawitsky A et al: Comparison of daily versus intermittent chlorambucil and prednisone therapy in the treatment of patients with chronic lymphocytic leukemia. *Blood* 50:1049, 1977.

60. Travade P et al: New trends in CLL treatment. *Blood Cells* 12(2):485, 1987.

61. Abe T et al: Clinical effect of intravenous immunoglobulin on chronic idiopathic thrombocytopenia purpura. *Blut* 47:69, 1984.

62. Rai KR: A review of the prognostic role of cytogenetic, phenotypic, morphologic and immune function characteristics in chronic lymphocytic leukemia. *Blood Cells* 12(2):327, 1987.

63. Wilson W et al: Pulmonary disease in the immunocompromised host. *Mayo Clin Proc* 60:610, 1985.

64. Rai KR et al: Studies in clinical staging, lymphocyte function and markers as an approach to the treatment of chronic lymphocytic leukemia, in Silker AS, Bue JL (eds). New York, Plenum, 1981.

65. Pandalfi F: T-CLL and allied diseases: New insights into classification and pathogenesis. *Diagn Immunol* 14(2):61, 1986.

66. Phyliky RL: T cell chronic lymphocytic leukemia with morphologic and immunologic characteristics of cytotoxic/suppression phenotype. *Mayo Clin Proc* 58:709, 1983.

67. Cohen HJ et al: Hairy cell leukemia. Cellular characteristics including surface immunoglobulin dynamics and biosynthesis. *Blood* 53:764, 1979.

68. Galton DA et al: Prolymphocytic leukaemia. *Br J Haematol* 27:7, 1974.

69. Bearman RM et al: Prolymphocytic leukemia: Clinical, histopathological, and cytochemical observations. *Cancer* 42:2360, 1978.

70. Sibbald R et al: Complete remission in prolymphocytic leukemia with the combination of chemotherapy—CHOP. *Br J Haematol* 42:488, 1979.

71. Taylor HG et al: Prolymphocytic leukemia: Treatment with combination chemotherapy to include doxorubicin. *Cancer* 49:1524, 1982.

72. Utsinger P et al: Hairy cell leukemia: B lymphocyte and phagocytic properties. *Blood* 49:19, 1977.

73. Steis RG, Longo DL: Update on the treatment of hairy cell leukemia, in Devita VT, Hellman S, Rosenberg SA (eds): *Important Advances in Oncology*. Philadelphia, Lippincott, 1988.

74. Qruesada JR et al: Alpha interferon for induction of remission in hairy cell leukemia. *N Engl J Med* 310:15, 1984.

75. Golomb HM et al: Hairy cell leukemia: A 5 year update on 71 patients. *Ann Intern Med* 29:245, 1984.

76. Spiers AS: The clinical features of chronic granulocytic leukemia. *Clin Haematol* 6:77, 1977.

77. Spiers ASD: Chronic granulocytic leukemia. *Med Clin North Am* 68:713, 1984.

78. Spiers AS et al: The peripheral blood in chronic granulocytic leukaemia. *Scand J Haematol* 18:25, 1977.

79. Baikie AG: Chronic granulocytic leukemia: The metamorphosis of a conditional neoplasm to an autonomous one. Proceedings of 4th Congress of the Asian and Pacific Society of Hematology, 1969.

80. Rosenthal S et al: Blast crisis of chronic granulocytic leukemia. Morphologic variants and therapeutic implications. *Am J Med* 63:547, 1977.

81. Koeffler HP, Golde DW: Chronic myelogenous leukemia—New concepts. *N Engl J Med* 304:1201, 1981.

82. Cervantes F, Rosman C: A multivariate analysis of prognostic factors in chronic myelocytic leukemia. *Blood* 50:1298, 1982.

83. Marks SM et al: Terminal transferase as a predictor of initial responsiveness to vincristine and prednisone in blastic chronic myelogenous. *N Engl J Med* 298:812, 1978.

84. Thomas ED, Fefer A: Marrow transplantation in the treatment of leukemia, in Gunz FW, Henderson ES (eds): *Leukemia*. New York, Grune & Stratton, 1983.

85. Schwartz JH, Cannelo GP: Hydroxyurea in the management of hematologic complications of chronic granulocytic leukemia. *Blood* 46:11, 1975.

Chapter 67

PLATELETS AND ARTERIAL THROMBOSIS

Laurence A. Harker

Platelets are essential for normal hemostasis; they perform four distinct functions: (1) continual maintenance of vascular integrity by sealing over deficiencies of the endothelium, (2) initial arrest of bleeding through the formation of provisional platelet plugs, (3) stabilization with fibrin to form a permanent hemostatic plug by assembly of factor X and prothrombin-activating complexes to form thrombin on the platelet surface, and (4) promotion of vascular healing through endothelial cell migration, together with intimal smooth muscle cell migration and proliferation, by release of chemotactic factors, adhesion molecules, and mitogens (Figs. 67-1 to 67-3). Additionally, platelet responses are centrally involved in arterial thrombogenesis. Rational management approaches are dependent upon an understanding of the pathobiology of these processes. With aging there is an increasing frequency of both quantitative and qualitative acquired disorders of platelets in addition to escalating thrombotic consequences of arterial vascular disease.

PLATELET HEMOSTATIC PLUG FORMATION

Endothelial disruption leads rapidly to platelet adhesion, degranulation, and recruitment,[1-4] thereby forming an enlarging hemostatic mass (Fig. 67-1).

The process of platelet adhesion involves transport of platelets to the surface and the interaction of platelet surface glycoproteins with connective tissue elements of the subendothelium. The platelet surface glycoproteins (GP) involved in platelet adhesion include GPIb/IX complex, GPIIb/IIIa complex, and possibly GPIa and GPIV. GPIb serves as the principal surface receptor that attaches platelets to exposed subendothelium, and in the platelet membrane GPIX is noncovalently bound to GPIb to form a GPIb/IX complex. This pathway of platelet adhesion is mediated by von Willebrand factor (vWF) adsorbed to collagen or other connective tissue components of subendothelium. When bound to the vessel wall, vWF acquires a conformational change that permits vWF-platelet interactions to occur. GPIb mediates attachment of platelets to vWF predominantly at high shear rates, implying that this mechanism is especially important in small blood vessels. GPIa has a role in platelet adhesion, either as a platelet receptor for collagen, or in the interaction of platelets with an essential cofactor of platelet adhesion to collagen. Collagen also binds to other adhesive proteins such as vWF, fibronectin, vitronectin, and thrombospondin which in turn bind to platelets. vWF, fibronectin, and vitronectin bind to platelet GP IIb/IIIa complexes; thrombospondin forms complexes with platelet-GPIV. Subendothelial structural components that are exposed to varying degrees at or near the surface of denuded vessels and that are most reactive to platelets include amorphous basement membranelike material, defined basement membranelike material, and collagen fibrils.[5] These reactive components induce the sequence of adhesion, spreading, and release of platelet storage granules.

Platelet adhesion initiates a series of complex, interactive platelet recruitment reactions (Fig. 67-1) including release of dense granule adenosine diphosphate (ADP) from adherent platelets, release of α-granule constituents, and activation of platelet membrane phospholipase complex leading to the generation of thromboxane A_2 (TxA_2). The recruitment of platelets into forming thrombi requires that the platelet-membrane GPIIb/

This research was supported in part by research grants HL31950, HL41357, and HL41619 from the National Institutes of Health, US Public Health Service.

679

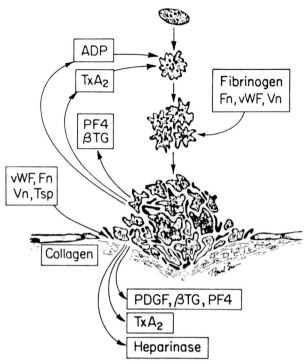

FIGURE 67-1

Platelet adhesion and recruitment. Platelets adhere to subendothelial connective tissue elements at sites of endothelial disruption, primarily through vWF ligand formation between platelet receptor GPIb and subendothelial collagen. The adhesive proteins, fibronectin, vitronectin, and thrombospondin, may also participate in adhesion to subendothelium through platelet receptors GPIIb/IIIa and GPIV. Platelet adhesion initiates a series of complex interactive platelet recruitment reactions comprising: (1) release of dense granule ADP; (2) release of platelet membrane phospholipase complex to form TxA$_2$; and (3) release of α granule–binding proteins (including fibrinogen, vWF, fibronectin, vitronectin, and thrombospondin). Platelet recruitment requires expression of GPIIb/IIIa as a ligand receptor. Generally, platelet-platelet binding occurs through calcium-dependent bridging with fibrinogen. (Reproduced by permission from Williams WJ et al: Hematology, 4th ed, New York, McGraw-Hill, 1990, Chapter 161.)

GPIIIa heterodimer complex undergoes a rapid conformational change to become expressed as a ligand receptor. Generally, platelet-platelet interactions are formed through calcium-dependent interplatelet bridging with divalent fibrinogen as ligand. The expression of fibrinogen-binding determinants on GPIIb/IIIa is known to be under intracellular control, being inhibited by agents that increase the cytoplasmic concentration of cyclic AMP or depress arachidonic acid metabolism. ADP promotes platelet aggregation by binding to specific platelet receptors and inducing platelet shape change and a decrease in cAMP activity. Irreversible platelet recruitment is mediated through, and dependent on, the release of endogenous ADP from dense granules and the synthesis of thromboxane A$_2$.

Thrombin plays a pivotal role in the formation of hemostatic plug formation (Fig. 67-2). The platelet surface promotes the molecular assembly of the prothrom-

binase complex for thrombin generation through extrinsic and intrinsic pathways of coagulation.[6] Injured vascular cells express tissue factor which activates factor VII. Factor Xa, produced by proteolytic activation of the factor X zymogen by activated factor VII complexed with tissue factor, forms a complex with factor Va on the membrane surface and in the presence of calcium ions, which converts prothrombin to thrombin. The formation of both the factor VIIIa–containing and factor Va–containing catalytic complexes on the same surface facilitates the overall localization and rate enhancement of the reaction since newly formed factor Xa on the membrane surface interacts with a waiting factor Va. Indeed, the rate at which thrombin is generated is increased more than 300,000-fold by this sterically optimal association of the factors bound to platelets. Thus, the generation of small amounts of thrombin initiates potent positive feedback mechanisms on the platelet surface for explosive local conversion of prothrombin to thrombin.

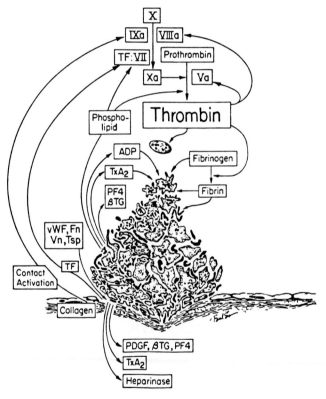

FIGURE 67-2

Central role of thrombin in platelet recruitment. Thrombin is the most important pathophysiologic initiator of platelet recruitment. Whereas thrombin activates platelets independently at concentrations less than those required to convert fibrinogen to fibrin, it also enhances platelet aggregation through ADP- and TxA$_2$-mediated pathways. Thrombin forms on the platelet surface at a 300,000-fold increased rate through either intrinsic factor VIIIa–dependent or extrinsic factor Va–mediated pathways. Fibrin serves to consolidate the enlarging thrombotic mass. (Reproduced by permission from Williams WJ et al: Hematology, 4th ed, New York, McGraw-Hill, 1990, Chapter 161.)

REGULATION OF HEMOSTATIC PLUG FORMATION

The extension of hemostatic plug formation is effectively limited to the site of vascular injury by a number of important protective mechanisms[7-9] (Fig. 67-3). For example, intact endothelial cells adjacent to the site of injury reduce platelet reactivity by degrading proaggregatory ADP released by platelets to inactive adenosine monophosphate (AMP) and inhibitory adenosine by a membrane-associated adenosine diphosphatase (ADPase) and rapid removal of proaggregatory vasoactive amines. Also, flowing blood removes activated coagulation factors that are subsequently cleared from the blood during passage through the liver.

The most important mechanisms for limiting thrombus extension are related to effects on thrombin activity or its production and involve (1) inhibition of thrombin action, (2) a reduction in thrombin production, and (3) thrombin-stimulated production of antithrombotic factors.[5-9] There are at least six known thrombin-related mechanisms acting locally to limit thrombus extension.

First, circulating thrombin is directly inactivated by plasma protease inhibitors. Antithrombin III inhibits thrombin and the coagulation factors IXa, Xa, and XIa. Antithrombin neutralizes thrombin by forming a complex, albeit at a relatively slow rate. However, heparin increases the rate of this complex formation 1000-fold.

A second reaction prevents the escape of thrombin into the circulation through enhancement of thrombin–antithrombin III complex formation on the endothelial surface. Endothelial cells produce a variety of glycosaminoglycans, particularly heparan sulfate. These heparin-like molecules exist within the vasculature and express their anticoagulant activities via interactions with antithrombin III.

The third process is a thrombin-mediated, endothelial cell-dependent activation of protein C. In this reaction thrombin avidly binds to thrombomodulin on the endothelium. Protein C also binds to thrombomodulin

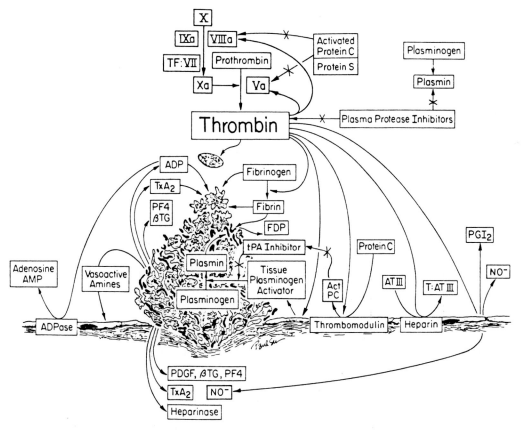

FIGURE 67-3

Regulatory mechanisms limiting the extension of thrombus formation. Intravascular extension of thrombus is limited by multiple protective mechanisms. The most important of these mechanisms are related to the presence of thrombin and/or intact endothelium and include (1) inactivation by complex formation with plasma antithrombin III; (2) facilitation by endothelial heparan sulfate of the inactive thrombin:antithrombin III complex formation; (3) down-regulation of thrombin formation through destruction of surface-bound factor VIIIa and factor Va by activated protein C formed by thrombomodulin-dependent thrombin cleavage, and thrombin-mediated release from endothelium of (4) tissue plasminogen activator, (5) PGI$_2$, and (6) nitric oxide. Additionally, intact endothelium adjacent to forming thrombus inactivates ADP and vasoactive amines released from activated platelets. *(Reproduced by permission from Williams WJ et al: Hematology, 4th ed, New York, McGraw-Hill, 1990, Chapter 161.)*

forming a trimolecular complex analogous to the pro-thrombinase complex on platelets. When thrombin is bound to thrombomodulin, it is not capable of activating factor V, cleaving fibrinogen, or activating platelets. Activated protein C inhibits coagulation by destroying platelet-bound factors Va and VIIIa activities. Protein S is an important cofactor for activated protein C and is produced by both the platelets and endothelium. Thus, association of thrombin with intact adjacent endothelium initiates negative feedback mechanisms that down-regulate its own production.

Fourth, the thrombotic mass is decreased by thrombin-enhanced release of tissue plasminogen activator from endothelial cells. Fifth, thrombin stimulates endothelial cells to produce increased amounts of prostaglandin I_2 (PGI_2), a potent platelet antiaggregant and vasodilator. Finally, thrombin increases production of nitric oxide (endothelial-derived relaxing factor), which induces vasodilation locally and inhibits platelet function directly and synergistically with PGI_2.

Under some circumstances endothelium may promote thrombin formation by presenting the receptor apparatus for the conversion of prothrombin to thrombin. Moreover, endothelial cells produce factor V, provide phospholipid, and express tissue factor. With inflammation endothelial cells participate in cell surface activation of the coagulation cascade. Experimentally, exposure of endothelial cells to endotoxin, interleukin-1 (IL-1), or tumor necrosis factor induces tissue factor production and expression, and activation of coagulation via factor VII. Additionally, IL-1, endotoxin, or tumor necrosis factor seem to down-regulate the activation of protein C.

PATHOGENESIS OF ARTERIAL THROMBUS FORMATION

Thrombus forms in vivo from blood constituents on altered endovascular surfaces or cardiovascular devices as a pathologic consequence of activating hemostatic mechanisms under variable flow conditions. The thrombotic process in arteries involves a complex-integrated interaction among (1) abnormal surface, (2) platelets, and (3) activated coagulation factors to form a localized stable mechanical mass that subsequently undergoes slow dissolution by (4) fibrinolysis. In arteries, occluding thrombus interrupts blood flow to dependent tissues, causing ischemia or infarction. Arterial thrombus may also embolize downstream to occlude blood vessels distally. Thrombotic and thromboembolic vascular occlusion play important roles in the pathogenesis of heart attacks and strokes. These events rise exponentially with age and are, therefore, important causes of morbidity and mortality in the elderly.

Whereas normal vascular endothelium is nonreac-tive with constituents of circulating blood, altered endothelium and denuded vascular or prosthetic surfaces activate platelets and proteins in the coagulation cascade that are central to thrombus formation (Figs. 67-1 and 67-2). Three major factors determine the site, composition, and size of a thrombus: (1) mechanical effects in which blood flow is predominant; (2) abnormalities of the vessel wall; and (3) alterations in the constituents of the blood (Virchow's triad). Thrombus that forms in the arterial circulation where flow is relatively undisturbed will consist primarily of platelets and some stabilizing fibrin ("white thrombus"). Important distinctions between arterial and venous thrombogenesis are illustrated by kinetic studies using labeled platelets and fibrinogen. In patients with ongoing arterial thromboembolism, the important role of platelets in the thrombotic process is evidenced as selective platelet consumption, i.e., shortened platelet survival and increased platelet turnover without increased turnover of circulating fibrinogen. On the other hand, ongoing venous thrombosis is manifest kinetically as increased turnover of both platelets and fibrinogen at equivalent rates; venous thrombogenesis reflects thrombus formation under static or low-shear flow conditions. Thus, the nature of the thrombus has therapeutic implications; i.e., fibrin formation in venous thrombosis is effectively inhibited by anticoagulants such as heparin or warfarin, whereas arterial thrombi may be prevented by agents that block platelet activation.

Patients may be predisposed to clinical arterial thrombosis because they have (1) detectable ongoing but asymptomatic thrombus formation that may evolve into symptomatic thrombi, (2) a genetic abnormality of the thrombotic process and its regulation, or (3) a clinical condition that statistically correlates with the development of arterial thrombotic events.

Biochemically specific markers have been developed for detecting fibrin formation, fibrinolysis, and platelet release and for proteins that modulate the coagulation and fibrinolytic processes.[1,2,8–12] Two platelet-specific proteins have been studied as markers of platelet activation: βTG and PF4. These proteins are localized in the α granules of resting platelets, and approximately 70 percent are released during the platelet-release reaction. Sensitive radioimmunoassays for both of these platelet-specific proteins are commercially available. Care must be taken in drawing blood and in preparing blood for assay to prevent artifactual release of these proteins during blood collection and processing. Failure to comply with these rigorous conditions produces falsely high and variable plasma levels. Increased levels of fibrinopeptide A (FPA) occur in patients with venous thrombosis and pulmonary embolism. This test is sensitive to intravascular thrombin but is not entirely specific for intravascular thrombosis. Prothrombin activation fragment F1.2 circulates in humans under normal conditions and is detectably elevated in various thrombotic syndromes. Assays for the detection of plasmin:antiplasmin complex and D-dimer in plasma have also been developed and show promise in clinical testing. At present, these blood tests of ongoing thrombus formation are primarily useful for monitoring the effects of therapy, without documented usefulness for identifying individual patients at risk.

Risk factors for arterial disease include hypertension, cigarette smoking, hyperlipidemia, diabetes, and occasionally, essential thrombocytosis (Table 67-1). Of these, high blood pressure causes a greater risk for cerebral arteries, whereas smoking and diabetes pose the greatest danger for peripheral arteries. Although experimentally there is a consistent relationship between the circulating platelet count and the amount of thrombus formed, the clinical association is much less well established. The frequency of arterial thrombosis in nephrotic syndrome is also increased, and this has been attributed to hyperresponsive platelets.

ANTITHROMBOTIC THERAPY FOR ARTERIAL THROMBOSIS

Currently available drugs that affect platelet function have a number of well-established clinical indications at present.[12] Pharmacologic modification of platelet behavior reduces the thromboembolic complications in a number of arterial vascular disorders and in patients with prosthetic cardiovascular devices. These high-flow, platelet-dependent thrombotic processes are resistant to conventional heparin or warfarin anticoagulant therapy.

TABLE 67-1
Clinical Risk Factors Predisposing to Arterial Thrombosis

Abnormal vascular surface
  Atherosclerosis
  Hyperlipidemia
  Diabetes
  Homocystinemia
  Hypertension
  Cigarette smoking
  Estrogen therapy
  Prosthetic cardiovascular device
Vascular occlusion and hyperviscosity
  Sickle cell disease
  Polycythemia
  Plasma cell dyscrasias
    (macroglobulinemia)
Increased platelet reactivity
  Thrombocytosis
  ?Nephrotic syndrome
Others
  ?Lack of physical exercise

There is now unequivocal evidence that aspirin and ticlopidine are effective antiplatelet agents in subgroups of patients with ischemic heart disease and cerebrovascular disease. Dipyridamole reduces thromboembolic complications of mitral valve prostheses when used in combination with oral anticoagulation.

Aspirin

Aspirin irreversibly inactivates the enzyme cyclooxygenase,[13] which, in the platelet, is responsible for the conversion of arachidonic acid to thromboxane A_2, and in vascular wall cells is responsible for the conversion of arachidonic acid to PGI_2. Thromboxane A_2 induces platelet aggregation and vasoconstriction; PGI_2 inhibits platelet recruitment and induces vasodilation.

Aspirin is rapidly absorbed in the stomach and upper intestine with peak plasma levels occurring at 15 to 20 minutes; platelet function is inhibited by 1 hour. Although the plasma concentration of aspirin decays with a half-life of 15 to 20 minutes, the platelet-inhibitory effect lasts for the life span of the platelets (9 or 10 days) because of irreversible acetylation. Aspirin also acetylates cyclooxygenase in preformed platelets in megakaryocytes. Since the side effects of aspirin are dose-dependent and many of the clinical conditions in which aspirin is effective require that the drug be used long-term, the lowest effective dose should be administered.

A differential effect on inhibition of thromboxane A_2 and PGI_2 biosynthesis has been reported with low-dose aspirin when these eicosanoids are measured as urinary metabolites, but this differential effect is absent when the assays of TxA_2 and PGI_2 are performed on vascular wall biopsy tissue or when the assays are performed on blood sampled from standardized skin incisions. This apparent discrepancy may be caused by the short-lived effects of aspirin on PGI_2 formation that is not reflected in the overall measurement of PGI_2 metabolites in the urine formed over 24 hours. There is increasing evidence that the clinical relevance of inhibiting PGI_2 production has been exaggerated in the past and that it is, at most, of limited importance. Aspirin does not cause a generalized bleeding abnormality unless it is given to patients with an underlying hemorrhagic defect (e.g., hemophilia or uremia) or unless it is combined with anticoagulants. However, there is now good evidence that aspirin increases operative blood loss in heparinized patients undergoing open-heart surgery.[14] There is also evidence that when combined with oral anticoagulants, aspirin produces a significant increase in gastrointestinal blood loss.

Antithrombotic effects of aspirin have been reported with doses that have varied between 100 mg/day to over 1.5 g/day.[12–18] Low doses of aspirin (100 mg/day) have been reported to be effective in preventing aortocoronary bypass shunt thrombosis and thrombosis of arterial venous shunts in patients undergoing long-term hemodialysis (160 mg/day). There is also now evidence that aspirin is effective in cerebral ischemia in a dose of 300 mg/day. However, there is no evidence that low doses are either more effective or less effective than high doses.

Two recent clinical trials of aspirin for primary prevention of myocardial infarction (MI) give conflicting results. Whereas a dose of 325 mg aspirin every other day has been reported to reduce the incidence of fatal and nonfatal MI significantly,[17] no apparent additional effect was found for a dose of 500 mg/day.[18] It is not clear that this discrepancy in results is the consequence of the difference in dose, particularly since the study reporting benefit with the smaller dose of aspirin included many more patients and, therefore, has a greater chance (because of increased power) of demonstrating a true benefit. Although this preliminary report of a study evaluating the effectiveness of aspirin (325 mg every second day) in the primary prevention of vascular disease suggests a beneficial effect of aspirin, it would be prudent at this stage to recommend prophylactic aspirin only in individuals who are at high risk for vascular disease.

Acute coronary occlusion and restenosis following angioplasty are not prevented by aspirin or the combination of aspirin and dipyridamole.[19]

Dipyridamole

Dipyridamole, a coronary vasodilator with weak inhibitor effects on phosphodiesterase activity, appears to increase inhibitory cAMP levels in platelets by elevating blood adenosine levels through the blockade of adenosine uptake by red cells and vascular wall cells. Aspirin potentiates the antithrombotic effects of dipyridamole in the baboon by mechanisms independent of inactivation of platelet cyclooxygenase.[12]

Dipyridamole decreases thromboembolism in patients with artificial heart valves (in combination with anticoagulants).[20] Dipyridamole (75 mg, 3 times daily) in association with aspirin (325 mg 3 times daily) has been reported by one group of investigators to be more effective than aspirin alone in reducing the progression of peripheral vascular disease.[21] However, this finding requires independent confirmation before this therapy can be recommended. Also, in patients with membranoproliferative glomerulonephritis, treatment with dipyridamole (75 mg 3 times daily) in combination with aspirin (325 mg 3 times daily) slowed the deterioration of renal function and the development of end-stage renal disease; the relative importance of the drug combination compared with the drugs used singly or at different dosage remains to be determined. In five clinical trials of antithrombotic therapy in cerebrovascular and coronary

heart disease, the combination of aspirin and dipyridamole was no more effective than aspirin alone.[15] Moreover, in a meta analysis of all relevant trials, no significant difference between aspirin and aspirin plus dipyridamole is evident for those clinical disorders.

Ticlopidine

Of the antiplatelet drugs currently available for clinical investigation, ticlopidine is one of the most potent and has several important theoretical advantages over existing drugs.[22,23] Ticlopidine is chemically unrelated to other antiplatelet drugs and appears to have a unique, albeit unknown, mechanism of action. It is neither a prostaglandin synthesis inhibitor nor a cAMP-phosphodiesterase inhibitor. Several days of oral dosing are required to achieve maximal antiplatelet activity, and the inhibition of platelet function disappears gradually over several days after the drug has been discontinued. There are several reports indicating that ticlopidine may act on the platelet membrane, perhaps during megakaryocytopoiesis, to alter its reactivity. The global antiplatelet activity of ticlopidine, its prolonged duration of suppressed platelet function, and its apparently novel mechanism of action set the drug apart from currently available antiplatelet agents. However, it has gastrointestinal side effects and produces (reversible) neutropenia in occasional patients by some unknown, idiosyncratic mechanism.

In patients with transient ischemic attacks ticlopidine (250 mg twice daily) is superior to aspirin (650 mg twice daily) in reducing stroke and death.[24] In the ticlopidine-aspirin study (TAS) involving 55 centers in North America, 3069 patients with either transient focal ischemia of the brain or eye or minor stroke within 3 months of treatment were randomized in a blinded manner to one of the two treatments. Primary outcomes were death and nonfatal stroke. Secondary outcomes were nonfatal acute myocardial infarction and other vascular events. The minimum follow-up period was one and a half years. Ticlopidine decreased primary outcome events by one-third compared with aspirin therapy.

Ticlopidine is the only therapy to date that has been shown to be efficacious in the secondary prevention of stroke.[25] The Canadian American Ticlopidine Study (CATS), a randomized, placebo-controlled, double-blind multicenter study, assessed the efficacy and safety of ticlopidine in patients who had suffered a thromboembolic stroke no less than 1 week or more than 4 months prior to entry to the study. The primary assessment of efficacy was based on a cluster of outcome events including recurrence of stroke, the occurrence of myocardial infarction, or cardiovascular death. Twenty-four clinical centers entered a total of 1072 patients, each randomly allocated to receive either ticlopidine (250 mg) or the placebo twice daily for the duration of the study. Patients were followed for an average of 25 months. Primary outcomes were reduced by one-third in the treated versus the placebo groups.

Ticlopidine is currently under study regarding its effects on ischemic heart disease and peripheral vascular disease.

Dietary Omega-3 Fatty Acids

It has been proposed that ingestion of omega-3 fatty acids as a dietary supplement will prevent or delay atherosclerosis and thrombosis.[15] Initial studies of plasma lipids and hemostatic function in Eskimos revealed somewhat lower cholesterol and triglyceride levels and a mild but definite prolongation of the bleeding time, incorporation of omega-3 fatty acids into platelets, decreased platelet aggregation responses, and a decrease in the platelet count. It has been suggested that omega-3 fatty acids alter prostanoid generation by platelets and vessel walls, producing a shift in the TxA_2/PGI_2 balance, i.e., platelets produce relatively inactive TxA_3 and formation of thromboxane A_2 is reduced, while vessels form biologically active prostaglandins I_3 and I_2.

A series of epidemiologic studies shows that increased fish content in the diet correlates with reduced cardiovascular morbidity and mortality. Furthermore, when fish oils are fed to humans, substantial amounts of the omega-3 polyunsaturated fatty acids accumulate in platelet membrane phospholipids and produce modest prolongation of the bleeding time, a mild inhibition of platelet aggregation, decreased capacity of platelets to produce thromboxane A_2, and reduced urinary excretion of endogenously produced thromboxane B_2 metabolites with only small amounts of TxB_3 metabolites.

The possibility that dietary fish oil may have a salutary effect on platelet-vessel interactions in atherosclerotic vascular disease has also been examined. Intimal proliferation is reduced in saphenous veins interposed in the arterial circulation of dogs fed a hypercholesterolemic diet supplemented with fish oil. Additionally, fish oil fed to swine undergoing carotid angioplasty reduces the amount of vasoconstriction and deposition of radiolabeled platelets at the injury site. The development of atherosclerosis in swine, rhesus monkeys, and cynomolgus monkeys is also reduced by omega-3 fatty acid supplementation. The mechanism(s) by which omega-3 fatty acids might impede atherogenesis remain(s) to be clarified.

Although dietary fish oil or purified preparations of omega-3 fatty acids appear promising as antithrombotic or antiatherosclerotic agents, there are no prospective controlled clinical trials in humans in which fish oil has been adequately tested as an antithrombotic or antiatherosclerotic agent. Until the results of such trials are available, the use of fish oil or purified omega-3 fatty acids cannot be recommended for prophylaxis or therapy of vascular disease or thrombosis in humans. More evidence needs to be generated on the potential for bleeding, the possible increase in hemorrhagic or thrombotic stroke, and potential carcinogenicity or immunosuppressive properties of fish oil before embarking on expensive controlled clinical trials.

QUANTITATIVE DISORDERS OF PLATELETS

Alterations in the platelet concentrations of circulating blood greatly affect the hemostatic, thrombotic, and repair functions of the platelet.[26] Under physiologic circumstances in humans, platelets circulate as flat disks at a concentration of $250 \pm 40 \times 10^9$/liter with a mean volume of 9.5 ± 1.2 femtoliter and survival time of 9 or 10 days. The splenic pool comprises about one-fourth of the blood platelets and is in dynamic equilibrium with the general circulation. The marrow megakaryocytes provide the substrate cytoplasm that becomes fragmented and released into the circulation following a 7- to 9-day period of maturation. There are about 15×10^6 megakaryocytes/kg body weight, averaging 15×10^3 femtoliter and giving rise to about 1000 to 1500 platelets each. Platelet production in the marrow is regulated to meet the requirements for circulating platelets by altering: (1) the rate of megakaryocyte formation from precursor cells, (2) endoreduplication and thus the amount of platelet-producing cytoplasm per megakaryocyte, and (3) the rate of cytoplasmic maturation and release. The regulation of platelet production appears to be dependent on the circulating mass of platelets rather than the circulating count.

Megakaryocyte numbers and size (ploidy) appear to be independently regulated. The bulk of megakaryocytic cytoplasm is effectively delivered to the circulation as platelets (effective platelet production) when measured as platelet turnover (platelet count divided by platelet survival time and corrected for splenic pooling). Impairment in the formation of viable platelets despite adequate marrow megakaryocytic cytoplasm is referred to as *ineffective platelet production*.

Based on platelet kinetic studies in patients, the mechanisms underlying thrombocytopenia include disorders of production, distribution or dilution, destruction, or some combination of abnormalities.[26] Disorders of platelet production include decreased megakaryocytopoiesis and ineffective platelet production (Table 67-2).

Platelet destruction may be selective, or may occur in concert with localized or systemic activation of the coagulation cascade (Table 67-3). An acute shortening of platelet survival time produces a proportional decrease

TABLE 67-2
Disorders of Platelet Production

A. Decreased megakaryocytopoiesis
   1. Congenital disorders (Fanconi's anemia, TAR syndrome, intrauterine infection or drugs, etc.)
   2. Acquired hypoplasia (drugs, chemicals, radiation, infection, alcohol, insecticides, thymoma, lupus erythematosus, idiopathic, etc.)
   3. Marrow replacement (metastatic carcinoma, myeloma, leukemia, lymphoma, myelofibrosis, etc.)
   4. Other disorders
B. Ineffective platelet production
   1. Hereditary thrombocytopenia (autosomal dominant, May-Hegglin anomaly, Wiskott-Aldrich syndrome, etc.)
   2. B_{12} or folate deficiency
   3. Other (di Guglielmo's syndrome, paroxysmal nocturnal hemoglobinuria, preleukemia, etc.)

in the platelet count. Within a few days of continuing thrombocytopenia, increases of 2 to 8 times the normal platelet production may occur, but thrombocytopenia persists if the production rate cannot compensate for the rate of destruction.

Immune platelet destruction may be mediated by autoantibody against a platelet autoantigen, antibody against a platelet alloantigen due to transfusion or pregnancy, antibody against an autologous or heterologous antigen absorbed to the platelet surface, or the attachment of immune complexes to the platelet surface. Platelet destruction results from phagocytosis of the sensitized platelets or from complement-induced lysis. The thrombocytopenia may be an isolated primary disease or may be associated with other diseases or with the administration of drugs. When the platelet count is less than 30×10^9/liter, the megakaryocyte mass is generally increased due to greater number and size of the megakaryocytes. However, megakaryocytopoiesis may not be detectably increased when the platelet count is only modestly reduced. The most common types of immune thrombocytopenia are shown in Table 67-3.

Some drugs, such as those used in the chemotherapy of malignant disease, cause predictable marrow damage and thrombocytopenia. Busulfan and melphalan, for example, have potent effects on megakaryocytopoiesis that may be long-lasting. Generally, agents that affect the cell cycle suppress the erythroid and myeloid series to a greater extent than megakaryocytes. Other drugs cause marrow damage less predictably and infrequently. Chloramphenicol is the most common drug associated with the development of aplasia, occurring in one-quarter of all cases implicating drugs. Other drugs are listed in Table 67-4.

Thrombocytopenia due to drugs may be caused by either suppression of platelet production or by intravascular destruction. Intravascular destruction may result from a toxic effect (e.g., ristocetin) or an immune event causing platelet destruction. The role of the immune

TABLE 67-3
Disorders of Platelet Destruction

A. Combined consumption
   1. Snake venoms
   2. Tissue injury (surgical, trauma, anoxia, toxic necrosis, etc.)
   3. Obstetric complications (abruptio placentae, retained dead fetus, amniotic fluid embolism, toxemia, etc.)
   4. Neoplasms (promyelocytic leukemia, carcinoma, hemangioma, etc.)
   5. Infection (bacterial, viral, rickettsial, etc.)
   6. Intravascular hemolysis
B. Isolated platelet consumption
   1. Thrombotic thrombocytopenic purpura
   2. Hemolytic-uremic syndrome
   3. Vasculitis (disseminated lupus erythematosus, other collagen vascular disease, infection, toxemia of pregnancy, etc.)
   4. Cardiopulmonary devices
   5. von Willebrand's disease
C. Immune destruction
   1. Idiopathic (acute, chronic, transplacental, etc.)
   2. Alloantibodies (after transfusion, neonatal, etc.)
   3. Drug-induced antibodies (gold, quinine, quinidine, sulphonamide derivatives, etc.)
   4. Secondary to another disease (collagen-vascular disorders, lymphoproliferative disorders, solid tumors, infections, etc.)

TABLE 67-4
Drug-induced Thrombocytopenia

A. Agents affecting production
   1. Cytoxic drugs (alkylators, antimetabolites, etc.)
   2. Alcohol
   3. Estrogens
   4. Thiazides
   5. Agents associated with marrow aplasia (benzene, chloramphenicol, phenylbutazone, etc.)
B. Agents implicated in immune thrombocytopenia
   1. Antibiotics (penicillins, cephalosporins, sulphonamides, isoniazid, rifampin)
   2. Antihypertensives and diuretics (α-methyldopa, furosemide, thiazides)
   3. Anti-inflammatory drugs (aspirin, acetaminophen, gold salts, chloroquine, phenylbutazone)
   4. Cardiac medications (quinidine, digitoxin, nitroglycerine)
   5. Neuropsychiatric drugs (diphenylhydantoin, carbamazepine, despiramine, phenothiazines)
   6. Oral hypoglycemic agents (tolbutamide, chlorpropamide)
   7. Miscellaneous (heparin, quinine, propylthiouracil)

system in some drug-associated thrombocytopenias, such as that associated with heparin, is still unclear. While a large number of drugs reportedly cause immune thrombocytopenia, the great majority of instances are due to only a few agents, i.e., quinidine, quinine, gold salts, sulphonamides, sulphonamide derivatives, chlorthiazide, chloroquine, and rifampin.

In kinetic terms, a platelet count greater than normal can result only from increased production since survival does not become prolonged beyond normal values. In the majority of cases, production is effective. About one-quarter of the patients with thrombocytosis occurring in the myeloproliferative diseases may have a component of ineffective production. The increased production of platelets is either autonomous or reactive. There is no evidence at present that thrombocytosis occurs as a compensatory response to impaired platelet function. This suggests that the normal regulatory processes of platelet production are keyed to circulating concentration or mass rather than to some aspect of hemostatic function, at least as currently evaluated.

QUALITATIVE DISORDERS OF PLATELETS

The congenital disorders of platelet function have been studied extensively and have provided important insights into platelet physiology and pathophysiology[4,27]; however, these defects are uncommon in clinical medicine. On the other hand, acquired syndromes of platelet dysfunction[28,29] are more complex, less well studied, and more difficult to classify, but occur frequently in a wide variety of clinical settings. A wide spectrum of acquired abnormalities of the platelet function have been identified and, on the whole, result in mild bleeding disorders (Table 67-5).

The screening laboratory evaluation of platelet function begins with a platelet count and a template bleeding time (Fig. 67-4). The bleeding time is a simple, reproducible test of overall platelet function and has a normal range of 5.5 ± 1.5 minutes.[22] The bleeding time is significantly but variably prolonged in patients with a serious platelet functional defect (obtained with adequate platelet count). A qualitative abnormality superimposed on thrombocytopenia manifests as an inappropriately prolonged bleeding time for the degree of thrombocytopenia (Fig. 67-4).

Light microscopic examination of a stained blood film may also be useful. In most situations of suspected platelet dysfunction, a screening evaluation of the coagulant activity is required including measurements of vWF. Platelet aggregation is now widely available for the evaluation of platelet function and may provide useful diagnostic information. It is particularly important to

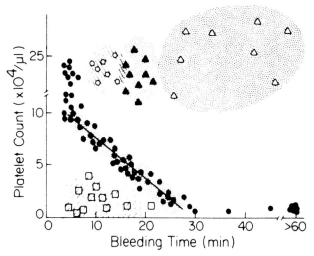

FIGURE 67-4

Relationship of bleeding time to circulating platelet count in normal subjects and in patients with thrombocytopenia resulting from increased production of platelets (solid circles). Platelet functional defects are also represented in subjects taking aspirin (open circles), in those with uremia (solid triangles), and in those with inherited von Willebrand's disease (open triangles). *(Reproduced by permission from Thompson AR and Harker LA: Manual of Hemostasis and Thrombosis, 3d ed, Philadelphia, Davis, 1983, p 61.)*

assess the response to dilute collagen if storage-pool disease is suspected. However, high-performance liquid chromatographic measurements of dense granule ADP and ATP are required to differentiate storage-pool deficiency from aspirinlike defects. Platelet α-granule contents may be evaluated by measuring releasable pools of PF4 and β thromboglobulin (β-TG) using commercially available radioimmunoassay. Platelet arachidonic acid metabolism may be evaluated by measuring its stable end product, thromboxane B_2, using radioimmunoassay or by noting an absence of in vitro platelet aggregation to added arachidonic acid. In some patients, a diagnosis of rare disorders may be feasible only through a platelet research facility.

von Willebrand Disease

Von Willebrand disease (vWD) is a heterogeneous bleeding disorder characterized by a prolonged bleeding time, quantitative or qualitative abnormalities of vWF, and usually low factor VIII activity. The activity of vWF is decreased in patients with vWD. Although most cases of vWD are inherited, a number of patients have been described in whom this disease has produced bleeding manifestations later in life, without previous abnormal hemostasis. Most of these patients have had associated collagen vascular diseases, lymphoproliferative disorders, including monoclonal gammopathy of unknown significance, angiodysplasia, or Wilms' tumor. Laboratory findings in these cases have included prolonged bleeding time and decreased plasma levels of vWF and

TABLE 67-5
Disorders of Platelet Function

	Hereditary	Acquired
Disorders of adhesion	Collagen receptor deficiency Bernard-Soulier syndrome von Willebrand disease	Acquired von Willebrand disease Uremia Drugs (e.g., dipyridamole)
Disorders of platelet aggregation	Thrombasthenia Afibrinogenemia	Myeloproliferative syndromes Fibrin(ogen) degradation products (e.g., consumptive coagulopathy), liver disease, fibrinolytic therapy Macromolecules (e.g., paraproteins and dextran) Drugs (e.g., semisynthetic penicillins)

Disorders of release
  Storage granule deficiency
    α Granule deficiency
 	
    δ Granule deficiency
	
	Gray platelet syndrome
	Autosomal recessive disorders
	Albinism
	
	Familial deficiencies
		
		Myelodysplasia
		Cardiopulmonary bypass surgery
		Immune-mediated release (e.g., idiopathic thrombocytopenic purpura, collagen vascular diseases)
		Drugs (e.g., reserpine, methysergide, tricyclics, phenothiazines)

Defective release mechanisms	Cyclooxygenase deficiency Thromboxane synthetase deficiency	Platelet dyspoiesis (e.g., myelodysplastic syndromes) Drugs (e.g., aspirin and other nonsteroidal anti-inflammatory drugs, furosemide, nitrofurantoin) Ethanol Diet
Altered nucleotide metabolism	Glycogen storage disease Fructose-1,6-diphosphate deficiency	Drugs (e.g., phosphodiesterase inhibitors), stimulators of adenyl cyclase (e.g., PGE_1, PGI_2, PGD_2)*
Disorders of thrombin formation	Platelet factor 3 deficiency Factor V receptor deficiency	Drugs (e.g., heparin, hirudin, antithrombins)

*PGE_1 = prostaglandin E_1; PGI_2 = prostaglandin I_2; PGD_2 = prostaglandin D_2.

factor VIII. In some cases an inhibitor against factor vWF has been demonstrated. In patients with lymphoproliferative disorders, the abnormal lymphocytes may have contributed to an accelerated clearance of vWF from the circulation because abnormal lymphoid cells bound vWF and factor VIII. In patients with acquired vWD, spontaneous remissions and remissions following therapy with steroids and radiation have been reported. It has been proposed that in clinically severe forms of acquired vWD, a trial of glucocorticoids may be warranted in addition to appropriate management of the underlying disorder.

Uremia

Patients with acute or chronic renal failure develop bleeding manifestations predominantly in the mucocutaneous areas, including ecchymoses, purpura, epistaxis, and bleeding from the gastrointestinal tract. In addition, hemorrhagic pericardial effusions and intracranial hemorrhage may occur. Most evidence to date suggests that the bleeding complications in uremia result from impairment in the platelet interaction with subendothelium. Although platelet counts may be somewhat decreased in some patients, thrombocytopenia is not the principal problem in these patients. A number of defects in platelet function testing have been reported in patients with uremia, i.e., retention of platelets in glass bead columns, platelet aggregation responses to agents such as ADP, epinephrine, and collagen, and platelet factor 3 availability. These impairments in platelet responses correlate with a prolonged bleeding time that appears to predict clinical bleeding. There is no convincing correlation between bleeding time or platelet retention and the serum levels of creatinine, urea, potassium, or uric acid.

A number of studies have revealed that the prolongation in bleeding time and some of the impairments in platelet function are fully corrected by peritoneal dialysis and at least partially by hemodialysis. This has led to the hypothesis that accumulation of some as yet unidentified metabolite in plasma may be the underlying cause of the platelet dysfunction. Among the substances implicated in uremic platelet dysfunction, guanidinosuccinic acid has been reported to be present in significant quantities in blood from uremic patients and, at the levels found in uremic serum, has been reported to cause mild changes in platelet structure and to inhibit in vitro platelet factor 3 activation and platelet aggregation induced by ADP, epinephrine, and collagen. Other substances implicated in a similar role include phenolic acids. In vitro addition of creatinine, phosphate, potassium, and mannitol or changes in pH within the range encountered in severely uremic patients appear not to reproduce the qualitative platelet defects in aggregation, platelet factor 3 availability, and clot retraction.

Transient correction of the bleeding tendency can be produced in patients with uremia by cryoprecipitate or desmopressin. These therapies may be useful in patients who have acute bleeding or require urgent surgery.

Fibrin(ogen)olytic Degradation Products

The bleeding time in patients with consumptive coagulopathy is often prolonged, and bleeding complications occur even when the platelet count is only mildly depressed or normal, evidencing defects in platelet function. The clinical importance of platelet dysfunction in these patients is not always obvious since other defects in the hemostatic apparatus may also be present.

Plasmin degrades both fibrinogen and fibrin to fragments X, Y, D, and E, which inhibit polymerization of fibrin monomer to fibrin and which also inhibit platelet aggregation. Polymerizing fibrin can interact with platelets to promote aggregation and secretion, and plasma proteolytic degradation products of fibrin(ogen) may block sites on polymerizing fibrin that interact with platelets. Therapy primarily involves platelet transfusions and that of the underlying cause of the consumptive coagulopathy.

Macromolecules

Bleeding manifestations are not uncommon in patients with dysproteinemias, particularly Waldenström's macroglobulinemia and IgA myeloma. A number of abnormalities have been described in the hemostatic system of these patients. Qualitative defects of platelets, evidenced by prolonged bleeding times, impaired platelet retention in glass bead filters, platelet factor 3 availability, and platelet aggregation, have been reported. The mechanism by which the paraproteins influence platelet function has been attributed to coating of the platelet membrane by paraproteins with interference of receptor function.

An improvement is usually seen when therapy of the underlying plasma cell dyscrasia successfully lowers the immunoprotein level. Indeed, in some patients with high levels of monoclonal protein, therapy with platelet concentrates may be ineffective, and plasmapheresis may be required to lower the paraprotein level and acutely ameliorate the bleeding tendency.

Liver Disease

Defects in bleeding time and platelet aggregation responses associated with hemorrhagic complications occur in patients with severe hepatic dysfunction. The relative importance of defective platelet function in the pathogenesis of hemorrhage is variable in view of the multiple and complex abnormalities of coagulation frequently found in these patients. It has been suggested that elevations in fibrin(ogen) degradation products (FDP) impair platelet aggregation in these patients, although the impairment of aggregation responses have been shown not to correlate with plasma FDP levels. Alternately, the dysfibrinogenemia found in patients with cirrhosis may contribute to platelet dysfunction.

Myelodysplasia

The documented qualitative platelet functional defects associated with bleeding complications have occurred in patients with acute granulocytic leukemia, hairy cell leukemia, lymphocytic leukemia, preleukemia, and myelomonocytic leukemia. A variety of morphological abnormalities have been described, including abnormally shaped giant platelets with decreased microtubules and abnormal cytoplasmic granules. Functional abnormalities have been described in these patients, including defects in platelet coagulant activity, aggregation, and secretion. The secretory defect has been attributed to a variety of abnormalities, including storage-pool deficiency, a primary secretory defect, and defective thromboxane synthesis. Abnormal platelet aggregation responses to thrombin and collagen in acute granulocytic leukemia have been associated with a decrease in the number of platelet membrane binding sites for thrombin.

The degree of platelet dysfunction, as measured by the prolongation in bleeding time, has been directly correlated with the dense granule ADP content. Moreover, the reduction in dense granule ADP content may be caused by a progressive loss of dense granule contents in vivo during the time the platelets remain in circulation. Presumably, this abnormality represents a defect in the dense granule storage apparatus.

Drugs

A common cause of acquired defects of platelet function is the administration of drugs since many pharmacologic agents affect platelet function.

AGENTS THAT INFLUENCE PROSTANOID SYNTHE-SES (ANTI-INFLAMMATORY AGENTS) Aspirin prolongs the bleeding time in many normal individuals at doses generally used clinically and has long been known to inhibit the second phase of platelet aggregation and secretion. The mechanism by which this inhibition of platelet function occurs involves the irreversible acetylation of the cyclooxygenase in platelets that converts arachidonic acid to prostaglandin endoperoxides and thromboxanes that play a role in platelet activation. Nonsteroidal anti-inflammatory agents other than aspirin also inhibit thromboxane synthesis. However, their effects are generally due to reversible and competitive inhibition of cyclooxygenase with blocking of secretion, as contrasted with the irreversible effects of aspirin. Included among these drugs are indomethacin, phenylbutazone, ibuprofen, and sulphinpyrazone.

ADENYLATE CYCLASE ACTIVATORS AND PHOS-PHODIESTERASE INHIBITORS Platelet responses to a variety of agonists can be inhibited when cyclic AMP (cAMP) levels are elevated either by agents that activate the adenylate cyclase that converts ATP to cAMP or by agents that inhibit the cyclic nucleotide phosphodiesterase that converts cAMP to AMP. Included in the former category are inhibitory prostanoids such as PGI_2, PGE_1 and PGD_2, whereas the latter group includes the pyrimidopyrimidine drugs such as dipyridamole, a coronary vasodilator that inhibits platelet aggregation in vitro and prolongs platelet survival in vivo. Thus, agents that activate adenylate cyclase potentiate the action of those that inhibit phosphodiesterase. Although other phosphodiesterase inhibitors—including the methylxanthines such as caffeine, theophylline, aminophylline, and papaverine—can inhibit platelet aggregation in vitro, the blood levels achieved in vivo are insufficient to affect platelets. Dipyridamole and aspirin act synergistically through pharmacokinetic interactions in vivo.

ANTIMICROBIAL AGENTS Purpura, prolonged bleeding time, and platelet aggregation defects are found in patients given high doses of carbenicillin or some other antibiotics including penicillin G, ticarcillin, ampicillin, and cephalothin. These drugs inhibit platelet aggregation and secretion as well as platelet adherence to subendothelial structures and collagen-coated surfaces. Both penicillin G and carbenicillin have been shown to inhibit the binding of various agonists, including epinephrine, ADP, and the von Willebrand factor, to their specific platelet membrane receptors.

HEPARIN Although bleeding complications in patients treated with heparin for thromboembolic disorders are generally due to inhibition of blood coagulation, heparin has also been found to inhibit platelet aggregation and secretion. It has been proposed that platelet aggregation, especially by high-molecular-weight heparin fractions with little anticoagulant activity, might interfere with platelet function by inducing a refractory state in platelets. These effects of heparin on platelets should be distinguished from the severe, delayed immune-mediated thrombocytopenia.

DEXTRANS These polysaccharides of various molecular weights prolong the bleeding time and inhibit a variety of platelet responses, including retention in glass bead columns, aggregation, secretion, and platelet coagulant activity. The mechanism may be related to coating the platelet surface, or inhibition of fibrin binding on fibrin polymerization.

ETHANOL Patients with liver disease often have complex hemostatic abnormalities, including evidence of platelet dysfunction. An important consideration in alcoholics with liver disease is the effect of ethanol on platelet function as well as platelet counts. Ethanol may affect arachidonate metabolism in platelets or, alternately, may be related to platelet membrane stabilization or alteration of storage-pool nucleotides or cyclic AMP levels by ethanol.

MISCELLANEOUS DRUGS Many other drugs may cause abnormalities of platelet behavior, although their effects are not generally manifest clinically by abnormal bleeding or by prolongation of the bleeding time.

REFERENCES

1. Turitto VT, Baumgartner HR: Platelet-surface interactions, in Colman RW, Hirsh J, Marder VJ, Salzman EW (eds): *Hemostasis and Thrombosis: Basic Principles and Clinical Practice*, 2d ed. Philadelphia, Lippincott, 1987, p 555.
2. Crawford N, Scrutton MC: Biochemistry of the blood platelet, in Bloom AL, Thomas DP (eds): *Hemostasis and Thrombosis*, 2d ed. New York, Churchill Livingstone, 1987, p 47.
3. Sixma JJ: Role of blood platelets, plasma proteins and the vessel wall in haemostasis, in Bloom AL, Thomas DP (eds): *Hemostasis and Thrombosis*, 2d ed. New York, Churchill Livingstone, 1987, p 47.
4. George JN, Nurden AT, Phillips DR: Molecular defects in interactions of platelets with the vessel wall. *N Engl J Med* 311:1084, 1984.
5. Baumgartner HR, Muggli R: Adhesion and aggregation: Morphological demonstration and quantitation in vivo and in vitro, in Gordon JL (ed): *Platelets in Biology and Pathology*. Amsterdam, Elsevier Biomedical Press, 1976, p 23.
6. Mann KG, Tracy PB, Krishnaswamy S et al: Platelets and coagulation, in Verstraete M, Vermylen J, Lijnen R, Ar-

nout J (eds): *Thrombosis and Haemostasis 1987*. Leuven, Leuven University Press, 1987, p 505.

7. Harker LA: Pathogenesis of thrombosis, in Williams WJ, Beutler E, Erslev AJ, Lichtman MA (eds): *Hematology*, 4th ed. New York, McGraw-Hill, 1990.

8. Rosenberg RD: Regulation of the hemostatic mechanism, in Stamatoyannopoulos G, Nienhuis AW, Leder P, Majerus PW (eds): *The Molecular Basis of Blood Diseases*. Philadelphia, Saunders, 1987, p 534.

9. Hemker HC: The mode of action of heparin in plasma, in Verstraete M, Vermylen J, Lijnen R, Arnout J (eds): *Thrombosis and Haemostasis*. Leuven, Leuven University Press, 1987.

10. Files JC, Malpass TW, Yee EK et al: Studies of human platelet alpha granule release in vivo. *Blood* 58:607, 1981.

11. Nossel HL, Ti M, Kaplan KL et al: The generation of fibrinopeptide A in clinical blood samples. *J Clin Invest* 58:1136, 1976.

12. Harker LA, Gent M: The use of agents that modify platelet function in the management of thrombotic disorders, in Colman RW, Hirsh J, Marder VJ, Salzman EW (eds): *Hemostasis and Thrombosis: Basic Principles and Clinical Practice*, 2d ed. Philadelphia, Lippincott, 1987, p 1438.

13. Majerus PW: Arachidonate metabolism in vascular disorders. *J Clin Invest* 72:1521, 1983.

14. Goldman S, Copeland J, Moritz T et al: Improvement in early saphenous vein graft patency after coronary artery bypass surgery with antiplatelet therapy: Results of a Veterans Administration cooperative study. *Circulation* 77:1324, 1988.

15. Harker LA: Antithrombotic therapy, in Williams WJ, Beutler E, Erslev AJ, Lichtman MA (eds): *Hematology*, 4th ed. New York, McGraw-Hill, 1990.

16. UK-TIA Study Group: The UK-TIA aspirin trial: Interim results. *Br Med J* 296:316, 1987.

17. The Steering Committee of The Physicians Health Study Research Group: Special Report: Preliminary report: Findings from the aspirin component of the ongoing physicians' health study. *N Engl J Med* 318:262, 1988.

18. Peto R, Gray R, Collins R et al: Randomized trial of prophylactic daily aspirin in British male doctors. *Br Med J* 296:313, 1987.

19. Schwartz L, Bourassa MG, Lesperance J et al: Aspirin and dipyridamole in the prevention of restenosis after percutaneous transluminal coronary angioplasty. *N Engl J Med* 318:1714, 1988.

20. Sullivan JM, Harken DE, Gorlin R: Pharmacologic control of thromboembolic complications of cardiac-valve replacement. *N Engl J Med* 284:1392, 1971.

21. Hess H, Mietaschk A, Deichsel G: Drug-induced inhibition of platelet function delays progression of peripheral occlusive arterial disease. A prospective double-blind arteriographically controlled trial. *Lancet* 1:415, 1985.

22. O'Brien JR: Ticlopidine. *Haemostasis* 13(suppl 2):1, 1983.

23. Gordon JL: Ticlopidine: Quo Vadis? *Agents Actions* 15(suppl):1, 1984.

24. Gent M: The Canadian American Ticlopidine Study (CATS) in thromboembolic stroke (Abstract), in *XXII Congress of the International Society of Hematology, Milan, August 28–September 2, 1988. Book of Abstracts: Symposia, Oral and Poster Presentations*, p 75.

25. Hass WK: The Ticlopidine-Aspirin Study (TASS): Review and results (Abstract), in *XXII Congress of the International Society of Hematology, Milan, August 28–September 2, 1988. Book of Abstracts: Symposia, Oral and Poster Presentations*, p 75.

26. Burstein SA, McMillan RM, Harker LA: Quantitative platelet disorders, in Bloom AL, Thomas DP (eds): *Haemostasis and Thrombosis*, 2d ed. New York, Churchill Livingstone, 1987, p 333.

27. Weiss HJ: Inherited disorders of platelet secretion, in Colman RW, Hirsh J, Marder VJ, Salzman EW (eds): *Hemostasis and Thrombosis: Basic Principles and Clinical Practice*, 2d ed. Philadelphia, Lippincott, 1987, p 741.

28. Rao AK, Walsh PN: Acquired qualitative platelet disorders. *Clin Haemotol* 12:201, 1983.

29. Lusher JM, Mammen EF, McCoy LE, Walz DA (eds): Factor VIII/vWF and platelet formation and function in health and disease. *Ann NY Acad Sci* 509:188, 1981.

Chapter 68

COAGULATION DISORDERS, VENOUS THROMBOSIS, AND ANTITHROMBOTIC THERAPY

Arthur R. Thompson

BLEEDING DISORDERS DUE TO COAGULATION FACTOR DEFECTS

A ruptured aortic aneurysm is the most dramatic illustration of age-related damage to a vessel wall. The attendant shock, hypotension, and massive transfusion contribute to further hemorrhage by producing dilutional and consumptive thrombocytopenias. Generalized oozing from disseminated intravascular coagulation (DIC) may occur. Milder hemostatic disorders of the blood vessels, platelets, or coagulation factors are more subtle defects frequently encountered in the elderly. In the face of any bleeding episode, be it spontaneous or associated with vascular damage such as trauma, surgery, or occult gastrointestinal lesions, even mild defects should be considered since they will increase the amount of bleeding.

It is well appreciated that older patients tolerate acute blood loss poorly. The sympathetic vasoconstrictive response may be dulled, and organs with previously compromised circulation are at great risk of ischemia or frank infarction. Consequently, preoperative patients must be screened carefully. Any clue from the history, including previous responses to surgery and trauma, or from even mildly abnormal screening test results, requires an explanation. This may guide one to specific therapy to minimize bleeding.

For longstanding disorders, the patient's history or, occasionally, their physical examination suggests the presence of a bleeding disorder. The laboratory screening results define the nature of the defect. At times, either the clinical assessment or the laboratory results may

be misleading. Consequently, the clinician needs to appreciate the limitations of information gained from a patient's clinical presentation and integrate screening test results with the clinical presentation.

HEREDITARY COAGULATION DISORDERS

Congenital coagulation factor deficiencies have a frequency of about 1 in 10,000 in all populations. Three disorders, hemophilias A and B and von Willebrand's disease (vWD), account for most of the patients. Milder forms are twice as prevalent as severe deficiencies. Therefore a significant percentage of these patients will not encounter prolonged bleeding or poor wound healing until they are older. Indeed, the major risk to patients with milder disorders is unanticipated bleeding following trauma, surgery, or dental extractions, even if the diagnosis is known. An "interaction effect" of vascular lesions with mild factor deficiencies may occur. An example is in elderly patients with intractable gastrointestinal blood loss from angiodysplasia with the mild hemostatic defect as a contributing factor.

Recognition and Diagnosis of Congenital Bleeding Disorders

The most sensitive screening test for a mild congenital coagulation defect is a careful personal and family history. In particular, evidence of delayed, intermittent, or prolonged microvascular oozing should be sought. Delayed bleeding and poor wound healing are the hallmarks of these disorders.

In screening for congenital factor defects, a sensitive partial thromboplastin time (PTT) is usually prolonged. If the screening tests are equivocal, or if they are normal but the clinical suspicion is strong, specific factor assays may reveal a mild factor defect. Patients with factor assay results above 30 percent usually have hemostatic levels, except for some variants of vWD. In vWD, a template bleeding time should be prolonged. Milder cases of hemophilia generally have factor VIII or IX clotting activities between 6 and 30 percent of the normal pool. Patients with the common, mild, autosomal dominant form of von Willebrand's disease usually have factor VIII activities between 15 and 45 percent of normal and comparable levels of von Willebrand factor (vWF). vWF is measured as the ability to "aggregate" fixed platelets in the presence of ristocetin (ristocetin-induced platelet aggregation, or RIPA) or as a vWF antigen level. An accurate laboratory diagnosis is necessary before proper treatment can be selected since therapy for these disorders is different.

Management of Congenital Bleeding Disorders

The mainstay of treatment has been the use of blood component therapy to provide concentrated amounts of the defective or deficient factor. It is important to recognize, however, that there are alternatives for some of the patients with mild hemophilia A and von Willebrand's disease.[1]

For factor VIII preparations, concentrated forms occur either as cryoprecipitate, which is usually frozen and then reconstituted in saline and pooled prior to use, or as lyophilized materials. Lyophilized clinical concentrates come either from volunteer systems such as the American Red Cross, or from paid donors for commercial plasma fractionation companies. Cryoprecipitate contains vWF, in addition to factor VIII and fibrinogen in concentrated amounts and is thus the treatment of choice for vWD. It is also less expensive, when available, and it exposes recipients to a smaller donor pool than the lyophilized concentrates. Commercial factor VIII concentrates are usually ineffective in vWD and more expensive for replacement therapy in hemophilia. Heat treatment largely inactivates human immunodeficiency virus (HIV) but not hepatitis viruses. A solvent-detergent method, introduced by the New York Blood Center, may inactivate the latter. Recently, two factor VIII preparations have been produced utilizing monoclonal antibody purifications. They may be safe products for patients whose exposure to transfusion-transmitted viral viruses has been limited. The first clinical trial with recombinant factor VIII, which should be totally viral-free, began in 1987; large-scale production appears a few years off.

Upon infusion with a synthetic analog of vasopressin, DDAVP (desmopressin), factor VIII, and vWF levels essentially double. In patients with the mildest forms of hemophilia A or with vWD, this is often equivalent to a dose of cryoprecipitate or concentrate to achieve initial hemostasis. The mechanism appears to be release of bound and/or stored factor VIII–vWF complex on the endothelial cells; new synthesis is therefore required as patients are usually refractory to a second dose for 48 hours or more. Occasional flushing and exacerbations of migraines are noted in some subjects due to vasoactive properties of this synthetic hormone; infusion is contraindicated in patients with coronary artery disease.

For hemophilia B, plasma should be considered for routine treatment of most patients with milder defects, because of the hazards associated with commercial concentrates. However, the volume required for plasma infusion is large and volume overload may occur. Lyophilized concentrates are derived from large pools of volunteer or paid donors, and viral risks also apply. An additional risk in the crude concentrates containing factor IX is of thrombosis or disseminated intravascular coagulation. Postoperatively minimal hemostatic levels must be exceeded for 10 to 14 days until wound healing has occurred.

ACQUIRED AND COMPLEX HEMOSTATIC DISORDERS

Acquired coagulation factor defects can occur throughout life, and are frequently associated with specific clinical settings.[2] They may be mild and may present simply as enhanced operative bleeding. If the individual's hemostatic response has not been previously challenged, they must be distinguished from congenital disorders. They can also present as acute generalized bleeding, and are often associated with abnormalities of more than one screening test. In the latter setting, the results of late-stage screening tests should be evaluated first, as a low fibrinogen level can prolong other kinetic screening tests, and trace heparin contamination may be apparent from a long thrombin time.

Circulating Anticoagulants

Pathologic circulating anticoagulants present as acquired hemostatic defects. Inhibitors are usually immunoglobulins, and can be recognized in screening tests such as the PTT, where prolongation is *not* corrected by a 1:1 mix of the patient's plasma with a normal plasma pool. The pathologic inhibitors may either be directed against a specific clotting factor or may have a more general mechanism, as seen with lupuslike inhibitors. Therapeutic anticoagulants as additional forms of inhibition will be discussed under antithrombotic therapy below.

SPECIFIC FACTOR INHIBITORS These anticoagulants are most commonly antibodies against factor VIII. Specific factor inhibitors may occur spontaneously, particularly in elderly individuals, or they may occur as one of the postpartum autoimmune phenomena or in association with chronic inflammatory conditions such as rheumatoid arthritis. They may be seen with lymphoproliferative malignancies including myeloma. They also occur in 10 percent of patients with severe hemophilia A as alloantibodies after exposure to transfused factor VIII. Antibodies against the von Willebrand portion of the factor VIII–vWF complex which may not inhibit the procoagulant activity have been described and lead to an acquired bleeding tendency. In these patients, the bleeding time should be prolonged and a low level of ristocetin cofactor (functional vWF activity) observed, even if the PTT is normal. Less commonly, specific inhibitors of factors V, VII, IX, XI, or XIII are found as autoantibodies. Anti-factor V inhibitors usually occur following surgery, antibiotic therapy, or transfusions and prolong both the prothrombin time (PT) and PTT. The level measured in vitro may have no bearing upon the clinical severity since it does not assess the degree of inhibition of platelet factor V.

Treatment of patients with nonhemophilic acquired inhibitors using high-dose steroids is frequently successful, and titers often decrease in several days and may disappear within a few weeks. Acutely, massive doses of factor VIII may achieve hemostasis in bleeding patients with specific factor VIII inhibitors, particularly if the titer is relatively low. Unlike hemophilic inhibitors, these transfusions are not associated with a delayed "boost response" of the titer. Many anti-factor VIII antibodies have little cross-reactivity with porcine factor VIII, and a more purified preparation is now available. Intravenous gamma globulin or cytotoxic immunosuppressive therapy have been helpful in some cases. Plasmapheresis may be added in life-threatening, uncontrollable hemorrhage. For factor V inhibitors associated with bleeding, platelet concentrates can provide factor V.

LUPUSLIKE INHIBITORS In systemic lupus erythematosus, patients with active disease frequently demonstrate prolongation of both PT and, to a greater extent, PTT. Although not corrected by the 1:1 mixture, specific interactions with any clotting factors cannot be identified. This is due to a specificity for the test reagent phospholipid which provides the surfaces for factor X and prothrombin activations. The inhibitors do *not* neutralize platelet phospholipid and do not function, in vivo, as anticoagulants. Prothrombin activation may also be impaired; in other cases, contact activation is primarily interfered with. Thus, there may be more than one antibody or site of action of these inhibitors. In clotting factor assays, these inhibitors behave differently from specific factor VIII inhibitors, although the latter are occasionally found concurrently in patients with lupus. The classic lupuslike inhibitor has been seen as the presenting symptom of lupus and has also been found in the drug-related lupus syndromes. It can occur in patients with AIDS or transiently after a viral illness, and it is often not associated with lupus. It is even found in a small percentage of normal subjects, and so it is best to refer to it as a "lupuslike" inhibitor.

The antibody specificity of the lupuslike inhibitor is of interest. Even human monoclonal antibodies isolated from splenic lymphocytes have shown reactivity with both DNA and negatively charged phospholipids used in the PTT. Antibodies to cardiolipin can often be demonstrated when the inhibitor is present, but either may occur independently.[3] When prolonged bleeding is encountered in patients with lupus, it is likely to be due to a concomitant platelet disorder or an antiprothrombin or factor VIII autoantibody. Ironically, there is actually an increased association of the inhibitors with thrombosis. For example, the incidence of venous thromboembolic events is doubled when a patient with the full lupus syndrome also has demonstrable antiphospholipid antibodies. The risk of thrombosis is relative, and events are frequently the net effect of several conditions, both acquired and congenital.

Vitamin K Disorders

Vitamin K is a fat-soluble vitamin. The mechanisms of its action has been elucidated in studies of prothrombin and factors VII, IX, and X following coumarin antagonists (Fig. 68-1). Two other γ-carboxyglutamyl or Gla-containing plasma proteins, protein C and protein S, are a proenzyme and cofactor which become an anticoagulant complex when activated. Gla residues have also been found in proteins in bone matrix, in the lens of the eye, and even in atherosclerotic plaques. Interference with a bone protein is presumably the mechanism of the abnormalities found in the specific embryopathy associated with coumarin ingestion during the first trimester of pregnancy.

Vitamin K deficiency may occur as an acquired defect in association with generalized fat malabsorption of the intestine in which vitamins D, A, and E are also poorly absorbed. Many plants provide dietary vitamin K. It is also synthesized by gastrointestinal flora and absorbed. Thus, in the absence of malabsorption, vitamin K deficiency usually occurs with inadequate oral intake in the presence of broad-spectrum antibiotics. This is most frequently encountered after these conditions are met for approximately 2 weeks, during which stores of the vitamin are depleted. When vitamin K has not been added to hyperalimentation fluids in acutely ill patients on antibiotics, they frequently present with oozing, or at

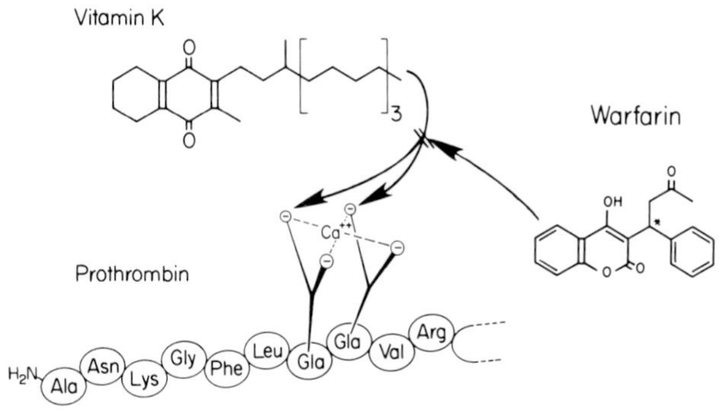

FIGURE 68-1

Carboxylation of vitamin K–dependent clotting factors. Vitamin K functions as a cofactor in a hepatocellular carboxylase reaction which introduces carboxyl groups to glutamyl residues. The dicarboxylic amino acids are referred to as "Glas." They allow these trace plasma proteins to form a specific calcium-dependent conformation that interacts with phospholipid surfaces. The factors are thus able to achieve a sufficient local concentration to be activated and, in turn, interact with their cofactors and substrates on platelet surfaces. In vitamin K deficiency or antagonism, as by warfarin, this posttranslational carboxylation is incomplete, and abnormal proteins circulate with impaired clotting activity.

least prolonged intrinsic and extrinsic screening tests, some 10 to 15 days into their course.

Less commonly, an occasional patient on high doses of aspirin, usually 16 or more tablets per day (as in severe rheumatoid arthritis), will show a vitamin K–deficient defect. This may relate to hereditary resistance to warfarin therapy in persons with markedly increased requirements for vitamin K, although such individuals usually have normal levels of the vitamin K–dependent factors when not on an antagonist. Occasionally, and usually in an elderly patient, vitamin K deficiency occurs despite an adequate diet and in the absence of antibiotics. Overdosage of coumarin anticoagulants, whether accidental in children, an error in therapeutic regulation, or even surreptitious ingestion, can lead to bleeding within several hours. Certain third-generation cephalosporins with a *N*-methyl thiotetrazol ring (e.g., cefoperazone) compete with vitamin K, especially in sensitive, ill, and elderly patients, producing the typical bleeding tendency.

In considering management of vitamin K deficiency, one must first assess for bleeding or immediate risk of bleeding (as with emergency surgery) to determine if rapid reversal of the deficiency is indicated. The rates of synthesis of the vitamin K–dependent factors are the inverse of the disappearance half-lives, determined after institution of antagonists or by levels of factors following their infusion. Therefore, with major bleeding episodes, or with the need for surgery, rapid correction of the defect with plasma or whole blood transfusion is necessary. The volume load of replacement becomes critical, as sufficient factors must be infused to raise lev-

els to 30 to 50 percent of normal as minimum levels. In an adult this usually means 4 to 6 units (U) of plasma or whole blood. Parenteral vitamin K should, of course, also be administered immediately. Vitamin K cannot be relied upon to provide hemostatic levels of the clotting factors for 1 to 2 days, and more plasma may be needed first. Lyophilized concentrates of the vitamin K–dependent factors are to be avoided because of their high risk of viral exposure (especially non-A, non-B hepatitis) and of thrombosis. Factor VII levels are quite low in some preparations as well.

Liver Disease

Abnormalities of hepatocellular protein synthesis are best correlated with the PT. In severe liver disease, the PT and the PTT remain prolonged despite parenteral therapy with water-soluble vitamin K. These screening tests largely reflect the depression of factors II, VII, IX, and X, and when levels of circulating protein are assessed antigenically, for example, they are usually low (i.e., an absolute production defect). Earlier in the course of liver disease, the screening tests may partially correct a few days following vitamin K therapy, suggesting that the carboxylase system (see vitamin K deficiency above) can be enhanced with excess vitamin cofactor. In early liver failure, it is possible to depress levels of factor VII out of proportion to other vitamin K–dependent factors. In this case, the PT is disproportionately prolonged when compared to the PTT. A sensitive early marker for hepatocyte disease is the demonstration of traces of immunoreactive prothrombin which is not fully carboxylated.

Several hemostatic defects occur in patients with liver disease.[4] These include the accumulation of higher-than-normal levels of nonclottable fibrinogen-fibrin species in the plasma, largely related to decreased clearance. Although they test positively in a common latex screen for degradation products, they seldom reflect actual plasmin cleavage. These or other catabolic products lead to some platelet and fibrinogen dysfunction, prolonging the bleeding time and thrombin time to up to twice normal. Another mechanism which produces fibrinogen dysfunction involves production of fibrinogen with increased carbohydrate content (sialic acid), which then behaves in vitro as a defective fibrinogen molecule similar to fetal fibrinogen. Finally, decreased platelet production, ineffective (folate-deficient) production, increased splenic pooling, and a direct toxic effect of alcohol may all contribute to moderately severe thrombocytopenia in patients with alcoholic liver disease.

Management of bleeding in patients with liver disease can be extremely difficult. For upper gastrointestinal hemorrhage, iced saline lavage, balloon compression, or local arterial infusions of angiotensin may be lifesaving maneuvers. It is essential to consider in all such patients, however, that the amount of bleeding is being enhanced by one or more of the above hemostatic defects. In severe liver disease the defects are frequently multiple, and attempts to treat with concentrates of the vitamin K–dependent clotting factors, for example, have corrected the prolonged PT and PTT, while failing to promote hemostasis. For thrombocytopenic patients, platelet concentrates are indicated, although the recovery in vivo may be decreased by splenomegaly or consumptive processes, or both. Clotting factors are best replaced by transfusion of whole blood (or packed cells with plasma), which contains hemostatic levels of all the clotting factors lowered in this state.

Disseminated Intravascular Coagulation

DIC is a frequently encountered entity in which platelets and fibrinogen are consumed. It is important to consider it in terms of its severity because it is often subclinical. With severe defects, abnormal or generalized bleeding may occur. DIC is more common with advancing age, largely due to the frequency of associated conditions.

PATHOGENESIS OF DIC Activation of the coagulation system, thrombin generation, and platelet interaction result in the consumption of platelets and fibrinogen. As a secondary phenomenon, fibrin polymers, smaller fibrin strands, and even fibrinogen are degraded by the lytic mechanism. The stimulus, or "trigger," for clotting can occur either by direct enzymatic activation of a clotting factor or by the release of an activator-procoagulant such as tissue factor. Tissue factor release occurs in vitro with stimulated monocytes. It appears that in different clinical settings, specific trigger reactions vary.

The sequence of events in DIC and its relationship to thrombosis are best illustrated by studies of women undergoing intrauterine infusion of hypertonic saline for abortion (see Ref. 5). Within minutes after infusion, free fibrinopeptide A can be detected, signaling that thrombin has been produced; about the same time, levels of β-thromboglobulin and platelet factor 4 rise as thrombin stimulates platelets to undergo the release of their α granules. Once fibrinogen has had its A peptides removed, it can form small polymers. A B-β peptide (residues 1-42), which contains three times as many amino acids as the B fibrinopeptide, is released by plasmin action (Fig. 68-2). The peak time of the thrombin-mediated reactions occurs 1 to 2 hours after administration of the saline, whereas the B-β peptide peaks at 4 hours, paralleling the formation of other fibrin degradation products (FDPs). Plasmin action is thus secondary. Fortunately, DIC in this setting is almost always subclinical.

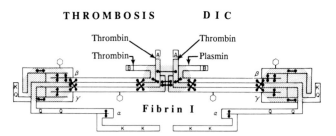

FIGURE 68-2
Proteolysis of fibrinogen: DIC versus thrombosis. Fibrinogen is shown with its three pairs of chains, A-α, B-β, and γ. The trinodular structure consists of a central disulfide-bonded amino-terminal domain which is flanked by the two carboxy-terminal (or D) domains of the β and γ chains. Disulfides are connected dots; major carbohydrates, hexagons; K and Q, cross-linking site residues. Thrombin interacts with fibrinogen to first remove the short, amino-terminal A peptides from the α chains. The resulting product, fibrin I, is capable of polymerizing. When there is sufficient thrombin generated for a thrombotic response, the amino-terminal B peptides are subsequently removed from the β chains as formation of a clot ensues (left). Under situations with more minimal or diffuse thrombin generation, plasmin is also formed and cleaves a longer fragment from the amino terminus of the B-β chain (right). Radioimmunoassays specific for the fibrinopeptide A are available but are not specific for distinguishing between the two pathways. Immunoreactive B-β 1-42 peptide results from plasmin cleavage (see Ref. 5). *(Adapted from Thompson AR and Harker LA, Manual of Hemostasis and Thrombosis, 3d ed, Philadelphia, Davis, 1983.)*

LABORATORY DIAGNOSIS OF DIC The demonstration of increased utilization of platelets and fibrinogen is reflected in the research setting by a shortened survival of ^{51}Cr-platelets and ^{125}I-fibrinogen. With these techniques, it has been possible to demonstrate increased consumption in patients undergoing elective surgery, for example, where the degree of consumption is at least semiquantitatively related to the degree of surgical injury. With normal liver and bone marrow function, however, increased production readily compensates for mildly increased destruction, so that levels of fibrinogen and platelet counts are usually not altered in these situations. When synthetic capacities are exceeded, however, platelet count and fibrinogen levels fall; these tend to decrease in concert. In the acute, severe forms of this syndrome, thrombocytopenia to well below 100,000 platelets per μl and hypofibrinogenemia to below 100 mg/dl will occur. With the accumulation of FDPs, as evidence of secondary fibrinolysis, inhibition of platelet function further limits hemostasis. At levels of fibrinogen below 80 to 100 mg/dl, these degradation products can also significantly interfere with the routine kinetic screening test for fibrinogen, resulting in a falsely low level when compared with the total clottable protein method for fibrinogen. The thrombin time is also prolonged by the antithrombin effect of FDPs.

Many routine tests for FDPs are semiquantitative and not necessarily specific. If one regards any normal individual as 1+, most patients with liver disease have 2+ reactions, and in DIC, 3+ reactions may be encountered in the commonly used agglutination assay. With further degradation of fibrin-fibrinogen molecules, however, smaller fragments are produced and rapidly cleared; thus, DIC may exist in the absence of a positive test. On the other hand, certain individuals with elevated γ globulins, as in chronic inflammatory conditions, may give false-positive FDP results. Increased levels in liver disease are usually not due to specific plasmin-digested fragments. The problems of specificity can be circumvented by more specific immunologic assays, and such tests are becoming available in clinical laboratories. Antibodies to DD dimer pairs are more specific in detecting plasmin cleavage, for example.

The presence of fragmented red cells on blood smears (microangiopathy) may be seen in vasculitis or in diseases of primary platelet consumption, as well as in individuals with hypertension. Their presence is thus not specific for DIC; conversely, these cells are frequently absent in patients with documented consumption. Thus, the best laboratory diagnostic indicators for clinically significant DIC are a decreased platelet count and decreased fibrinogen level. Provided that the synthetic capacities of the marrow and liver are not impaired, the degree of depression is similar. Recovery of the fibrinogen level occurs more rapidly than new platelet production.

ASSOCIATED DISEASES DIC can complicate a vast array of underlying disorders. Awareness of these disorders is important to avoid delay in recognizing the complication. Not infrequently, a fall in both platelet count and fibrinogen level may herald the onset of the condition itself, as is frequently seen in bacterial sepsis. The problem for the clinician, once DIC has been recognized, is to identify possible trigger mechanisms. For mechanisms which are treatable, the underlying condition should be treated rapidly while providing supportive measures as discussed below.

It is useful to view conditions in terms of their possible mechanisms of triggering DIC. Although uncommon clinically, a direct procoagulant effect is best represented by the occasional occurrence in acute hemorrhagic pancreatitis, in which trypsinlike enzymes overwhelm the naturally occurring plasma inhibitors and activate clotting. Intravascular activation may also account for the DIC occasionally seen after infusion of crude, commercial concentrates of vitamin K–dependent clotting factors. Disruption of cells with release of neutral proteases occurs in tissue injury or intravascular cell lysis, and may also lead to DIC. The malignancy most frequently complicated by severe DIC is acute promyelocytic leukemia. This appears to be related to intravascular release of neutral proteases from the non-

specific granules. Other forms of acute leukemia may have significant DIC. It is frequently clinically significant as an added hemostatic defect, in addition to the underlying compromise in platelet production. Metastatic prostatic carcinoma is often associated with more chronic consumption that can be moderately severe.

The vasculature is an especially important area for potential mechanisms, as shock, hypotension, and acidosis lead to increased venous stasis and thus promote coagulation. Endothelial cell injury occurs in patients with burns, and injury of these cells is at least theoretically one mechanism by which endotoxin can induce DIC in gram-negative sepsis. The mechanisms of inducing DIC by different infectious agents are frequently complex and varied. In bacterial sepsis, falling platelet counts and fibrinogen levels may be the early signs of an acute onset with or without an endotoxin-producing organism. This is encountered frequently in patients with bone marrow granulocyte suppression due to leukemia or to cancer chemotherapy, or both. It should be emphasized, moreover, that the most common treatable conditions causing overt DIC are hypotension and sepsis, even in patients with malignancies.

MANAGEMENT OF DIC In severe DIC, attention to the underlying condition is essential as an immediate step. Blood volume may require expansion to elevate blood pressure. If sepsis is a strong possibility, antibacterial therapy should be initiated immediately, prior to confirmatory culture results. Beyond these and other immediate supportive measures, however, the clinical severity of DIC as related to the clinical condition of the patient must be assessed. If the patient is not bleeding actively, either in a generalized fashion or from a localized lesion, no further hemostatic therapy may be indicated. However, as the major complication of DIC is bleeding, blood component replacement becomes the next line of defense. Transfusion with whole blood (or red cells and plasma) for blood loss is generally sufficient to maintain hemostatic levels of clotting factors in moderately severe DIC. When the fibrinogen level is extremely low, additional hemostatic benefit can be achieved by a concentrated form of fibrinogen, cryoprecipitate. Platelet concentrates are frequently the major replaceable hemostatic component that controls bleeding. Although platelet dysfunction induced by fibrinogen-fibrin degradation products would also apply to transfused platelets, this should only lead to their use at somewhat higher counts than if an individual had normally functioning platelets. At least one autopsy series has shown that treating with blood components does not simply add "fuel to the fire" or enhance the process of microvascular damage,[6] as occurs in the rabbit. Indeed, in situations in which hemorrhagic shock may be triggering DIC, it is of the utmost importance to attempt to achieve a normal hemostatic mechanism as quickly as possible.

Attempts to inhibit clotting or fibrinolysis were formerly common approaches in DIC. Heparin therapy, especially by continuous intravenous infusion, has been used to disrupt the effect of an ongoing stimulus for consumption of coagulation factors. Levels of fibrinogen and factors V and VIII improve rapidly after institution of this anticoagulant, but its use in the management of DIC is hazardous. In effect, one substitutes one severe hemostatic defect, that of heparinization, for that accompanying DIC. When DIC is severe enough to produce bleeding, the results of the additional defect can be catastrophic. In patients in whom bleeding is not a prominent clinical feature, there is seldom need to intervene, except for measures directed at the underlying associated disease. Furthermore, the underlying clinical stimulus may have diminished by the time the clinical syndrome is recognized, so that any intervention directed toward the clotting factor or toward fibrinolytic mechanisms may be too late. Clinically, significant bleeding, as the major complication of DIC, is best managed by blood component replacement.

Other Degradative or Consumptive States

There is no evidence that normal catabolism of clotting factors occurs by in vivo clot formation, but in some clinical situations, rather selective consumption of fibrinogen has been observed. Although fibrinolysis in DIC is a secondary event, on rare occasions fibrinogen can be degraded out of proportion to platelet consumption. This is seen after massive brain or tissue trauma where, in effect, a bolus of tissue factor is delivered to the circulation. It can also occur after envenomation with fibrinogen-cleaving enzymes, such as following crotalus (rattlesnake) bites. A second consumptive situation is the alteration of contact activation and factor XII seen in some patients with the nephrotic syndrome. It is unclear whether this represents a pathogenic effect or a secondary phenomenon. Increased turnover of contact factors has also been observed in some patients with DIC. A final mechanism leading to specific deficiency has been reported in a few patients with amyloidosis leading to acquired factor X deficiency. This seems to reflect the capacity of some amyloid substances to bind this factor.

Massive Transfusion

Transfusion of large quantities of blood into an actively bleeding patient can lead to alterations of the clotting factor screening tests, despite the fact that hemostatic levels of the factors themselves are usually well preserved.[7] Local lesions, such as trauma or rupture of an abdominal aortic aneurysm, are often responsible for the

blood loss, but after 10 to 20 U of whole blood or its equivalent have been transfused, most patients will become thrombocytopenic. Platelet dysfunction is a frequent concomitant disorder. Thus, the major hemostatic defect involves platelets, and initial therapy should be directed at monitoring and maintaining a count near 100,000 per μl.

Low levels of clotting factors are uncommon without underlying defects, unless the predominant transfusion products are packed red cells and saline or albumin. This is seen increasingly with the use of intraoperative cell-saving devices. Whole blood stored at 4°C for 3 to 5 weeks maintains normal levels of all clotting factors except factors V and VIII. Factor V remains at levels above its minimum for hemostasis (which is around 15 percent), whereas factor VIII falls to around 20 percent in a few days. Excessive blood replacement per se seldom leads to circulating factor VIII levels below 30 to 50 percent. When it does, cryoprecipitate is the safest blood product to transfuse. It also provides a concentrated form of fibrinogen, which is usually needed at this point because of the additional effects from DIC.

The screening tests affected include the bleeding and thrombin times, reflecting some degree of DIC usually associated with hypotension; fibrinogen degradation products may also be elevated. Particularly in an emergent setting, one must anticipate errors in sample collection or inadvertent heparin contamination, so that results must always be compared to the clinical severity of bleeding. On the whole, however, fibrinogen levels—and certainly those of the vitamin K–dependent factors—usually remain above the minimum for hemostasis despite rapid infusion of large quantities of whole blood or of red cells and plasma.

There are local, nonsurgical measures to promote hemostasis, as with upper gastrointestinal bleeding. On the other hand, continued rapid blood loss leads to hypotension, DIC, and more massive transfusion requirements that might be minimized by an early operative procedure. In either event, screening for mild hemostatic defects is imperative, as specific blood components may be indicated to decrease the amount of blood loss from the vascular lesions. As with DIC, the first line of defense beyond the replacement of whole blood or its equivalent is to ensure an adequate platelet count for primary hemostasis.

VENOUS THROMBOTIC DISORDERS

Thrombosis with or without embolism is a major cause of morbidity and mortality in western culture. Venous thromboembolic diseases have a marked age-related incidence that has been shown to be independent of other risk factors. They are relatively uncommon in patients under age 40 but are encountered frequently in those over 70. These rates are graphically displayed in Fig. 68-3, where two-thirds of hospitalized patients between the ages of 70 and 80 years developed calf-vein thrombosis as demonstrated by radiolabeled fibrinogen deposition.

The geriatric patient is in double jeopardy when confronted with venous thromboembolism. On the one hand, usual difficulties of recognition and diagnosis are confounded by underlying or previous lung or venous diseases. On the other hand, there is a heightened tendency of bleeding when anticoagulant therapy is administered due to age-related changes in the vessel walls. Therefore, in the older patient, it is even more compelling to attend to preventive measures and to establish the diagnosis with certainty prior to treatment.

In this section, hereditary and acquired risk factors for venous thrombotic disorders are reviewed. Specific anticoagulant and fibrinolytic agents are discussed followed by comments on the clinical management of deep venous thrombosis and pulmonary embolism.

RISK FACTORS FOR VENOUS THROMBOTIC DISORDERS

A major dilemma facing clinicians and clinical investigators is to recognize and assign relative significance to

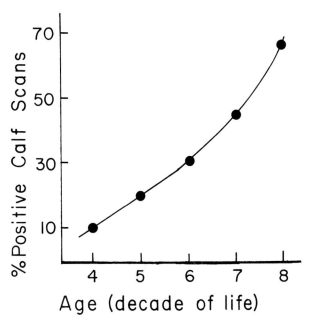

FIGURE 68-3

Age and venous thrombi. The incidence of positive calf scans in hospitalized patients is plotted against age in decade of life. Patients with acute myocardial infarction, surgery, or stroke were scanned serially after ^{125}I-fibrinogen administration to define significant accumulations in the deep veins of their calves. (*Adapted from Hirsh J et al, Venous Thromboembolism, New York, Grune & Stratton, 1981, p 22, with permission.*)

specific predisposing risk factors for thrombosis. Within the venous system, increased stasis accompanies immobilization, obesity, congestive heart failure, or pregnancy. Other important risk factors include recent surgery, neoplastic diseases, and myeloproliferative diseases in which there may be some stimulus for increased activation of coagulation factors. In patients with the nephrotic syndrome, an acquired deficiency of antithrombin III appears to relate best to the risk of venous thrombosis. Hereditary low levels of antithrombin III, protein C, protein S, or heparin cofactor II can also be associated with increased risk of venous thrombosis beginning at a younger age.[8] These patients have impaired control mechanisms that normally limit the growth of thrombus formation as diagrammed in Fig. 68-4. Consequently, thrombi extend beyond that required to achieve hemostasis. With either acquired or congenital predispositions, thrombi often occur in a clinical setting where several risk factors are combined. This would account for the increased incidence with age. A final mechanism leading to increased risk of thrombosis is inadequate fibrinolysis. This can either be on a congenital or acquired basis and may relate to defective tissue plasminogen activator (tPA) or an impairment of its release from endothelial cells. Excessive levels of plasminogen activator inhibitor(s) may also impede normal clot lysis as do some congenitally dysfunctional plasminogens or fibrinogens.

Current clinical laboratory tests are of limited use in detecting the increased risk of venous thromboembolic disorders. In polycythemia vera, elevated whole blood viscosity contributes to the increased risk, particularly if the hematocrit reading is greater than 60 percent. In dysproteinemias, hyperviscosity may be suggested by the level and type of immunoglobulin present. In the past, elevated levels of specific clotting factors were thought to indicate a hypercoagulable state. However, they simply reflect inflammatory responses which in and of themselves do not represent specific venous thrombotic risks.

Experimentally, more direct evidence for coagulation factor activation in vitro can be obtained from highly sensitive immunoassays.[5] When prothrombin is activated, the amino-terminal portion, fragment 1 + 2, or F_{1+2} (Fig. 68-4), is formed and can be detected in blood samples. The effects of thrombin on fibrinogen can also be measured by immunoassays specific for free fibrinopeptide A or FPA. When thrombin interacts with an endothelial cell surface protein, thrombomodulin, its specificity is redirected to become a potent activator of protein C. Accordingly, immunoassays specific for the activated form of protein C or for its activation peptide PCP (which remains soluble when plasma proteins are precipitated) can also indicate that thrombin has been formed. Specific assays for enzyme-inhibitor complexes,

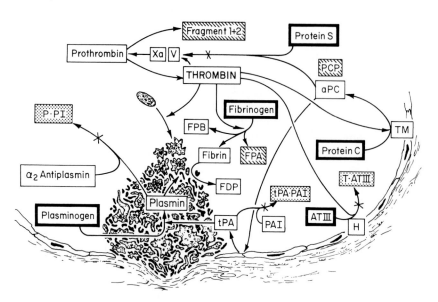

FIGURE 68-4

Detection of ongoing venous thrombotic tendencies. Thrombin generation is central to the hemostatic responses involving clotting factors, platelets, the endothelium, and finally, the fibrinolytic mechanism. Trace amounts of thrombin activate platelets and markedly enhance the cofactor activities of factors V and VIII. In interacting with the endothelium, thrombin activates protein C (to aPC) which with a cofactor, protein S, "down-regulates" clotting; aPC also promotes clot lysis. The generation of thrombin can be monitored (hatched boxes) by circulating levels of the amino-terminal prothrombin fragment 1 + 2. Proteolytic effects of thrombin are detected by assays specific for fibrinopeptide A (FPA), activated protein C (aPC) or protein C activation peptide (PCP). X marks indicate inhibitory pathways with enzyme-inhibitor complexes stippled. Hereditary tendencies for venous thrombotic disorders at earlier ages (heavy boxes) include heterozygous states for antithrombin III, protein C, or protein S deficiencies, and some patients with abnormal fibrinogens or plasminogens. Other abbreviations: ATIII, antithrombin III; FDP, fibrin(ogen) degradation products; FPB, fibrinopeptide B; H, heparinlike proteoglycans on the endothelial surface; PAI, plasminogen activator inhibitor(s); tPA, tissue plasminogen activator; TM, thrombomodulin, a transmembrane protein on the surface of endothelial cells. *(Adapted from Thompson AR and Harker LA, Manual of Hemostasis and Thrombosis, 3d ed, Philadelphia, Davis, 1983.)*

including thrombin-antithrombin III, plasmin–α-antiplasmin, and tissue plasminogen activator–plasminogen activator inhibitor have been developed and might become useful clinically. In patients with congenital thrombotic tendencies, FPA results showed only a higher trend, whereas F_{1+2} and PCP results were significantly higher and correlated with each other when compared to normal age-matched subjects. Values of the latter two markers were considerably lower in patients on chronic warfarin, even at low doses, when compared to prethrombotic or even normal subjects. F_{1+2} and PCP were significantly higher in normative subjects of increasing age.[9] It is hoped that clinical immunoassays will emerge from these and similar studies to better assess the risk of thrombosis and/or the adequacy of antithrombotic therapy in individual patients.

ANTITHROMBOTIC AGENTS

Anticoagulants

Inhibition of coagulation remains the primary mode of treatment for dissolving blood clots while preventing re-

currences, particularly within the venous system. They include the immediately active, potent, parenteral agent, heparin, and the less potent oral agents which are coumarin derivatives.[10]

HEPARIN This sulfonated mucopolysaccharide acts by binding through a specific sequence of sugar residues to the normally circulating plasma protease inhibitor antithrombin III. The heparin–antithrombin III complex becomes an immediate inhibitor of activated coagulation proteases. Preparations are standardized for their in vitro anticoagulant effect but vary in their content of inactive polysaccharide. The effect of heparin is gauged by the results of tests of intrinsic clotting (e.g., the PTT) which are doubled when heparin is in the therapeutic range.

There is considerable variability in doses of heparin required among patients, and even within the same patient at different times in the course of a disease. An average adult is given an intravenous bolus of 75 U/kg body weight to institute heparin therapy followed by infusion from 15 to 20 U/(kg)(h). Patients with acute pulmonary emboli frequently require the higher dosage levels. The half-life is around an hour and a half. Therefore, after instituting or adjusting therapy, the PTT should be checked about 4 hours later. Thereafter, daily monitoring is helpful, particularly when administration is by continuous intravenous infusion, to minimize the risks of either thrombotic recurrence or bleeding.

The major complication of anticoagulant therapy is bleeding, and this complication is more frequently encountered on intermittent bolus as opposed to continuous infusion administration. About 2 to 3 percent of patients receiving heparin develop thrombocytopenia, and if it is their first exposure to the drug, this often occurs around the fifth day of therapy. In some patients this may be immune-mediated, but it may also reflect platelet-aggregating effects of nonactive fractions within the heparin preparation. It can occur with low-dose subcutaneous administration and even from the trace amounts in heparin-lock intravenous systems or the heparin used to flush venous access or arterial lines. In some but not all patients, platelet counts may stabilize despite continued therapy. Occasionally, preparations from a different animal source or low-molecular-weight heparins have been substituted with success. When heparin is administered over several months, osteopenia and, occasionally, alopecia can be encountered. Heparin is indicated in deep venous thrombosis and pulmonary embolism and is also used in patients during hemodialysis and cardiopulmonary bypass operations. Its effects can be immediately reversed by tight ionic binding to the basic histone, protamine, where 1 mg neutralizes approximately 100 U of heparin.

WARFARIN As a vitamin K antagonist, warfarin is chemically similar to the naphthoquinone derivative vitamin K; it contains a coumarin nucleus (see Fig. 68-1). Orally ingested anticoagulants function as antagonists to the vitamin K–dependent carboxylations of factors II, VII, IX, and X. This is due to inhibition of epoxide reductase in the hepatocyte, an enzyme which regenerates active vitamin K for the carboxylase system. Their effect is monitored by the prolongation of the PT. Early in the course of administering the drug, the PT predominantly reflects depletion of factor VII, which has the shortest half-life. The PT does not correlate with a clinically effective anticoagulant level until equilibration has been achieved with a net effect on all four factor levels, which takes about 5 days. Therefore, a "loading dose" of more than 10 mg is not helpful. There is a wide range of sensitivities to warfarin which encompasses nearly a 10-fold difference (from 2 to 18 mg/day) in maintenance dosages in different individuals. It is helpful to recall that the monitoring PT reflects a dose given 36 to 48 hours previously. Although the major risk of anticoagulant therapy is bleeding, this is minimized by achieving only a partial

hemostatic defect which is clinically similar to mild hemophilia.

For the last several years, reagents for PTs in North America have been less sensitive than they previously were and less sensitive than are tests commonly available throughout Europe. It is now appreciated that former recommendations for "doubling" of the PT represent overanticoagulation and lead to an increased risk of bleeding. For secondary prophylaxis of venous thromboembolism, for example, prolongation of the PT to one and a half times normal should represent adequate protection against recurrence with a lower risk of bleeding. Attempts have been made to normalize the less sensitive PTs, which generally use rabbit brain thromboplastins, to more sensitive tests employing human brain reagents by an "international normalized ratio," or INR. Although this allows one to correlate the risk of bleeding to the more sensitive tests that are therapeutic with PTs about twice prolonged and standardizes tests in different laboratories or with different reagents, it fails to obviate the basic shortcomings of using an insensitive test. Problems using an INR are particularly apparent in the first several days of warfarin therapy. Immunoassays have been developed which are much more predictive of risks. For example, the bleeding risk appears highest when the levels of fully carboxylated prothrombin are quite low.[11] On the other hand, evidence of thrombin generation indicates the degree to which the underlying thrombotic tendency has been inhibited.[5] It is hoped that these or similar assays will soon become available in clinical laboratories.

Numerous drug interactions occur with warfarin, and they can reflect either potentiation or antagonism of the drug's effect. This is particularly relevant to elderly patients who are more likely to be receiving multiple drugs in their therapeutic regimen. In addition, any drug independently interfering with hemostasis will increase the risk of bleeding. Within large, carefully monitored series, the risk of a major bleeding episode is around 2 to 4 percent per year of treatment, and about 10 percent of those complications are fatal. Major episodes of bleeding in 10 percent of patients at 3 months and 40 percent of patients followed for 5 years have been seen in other series.[12] Any new or painful symptom in a patient on anticoagulants should be considered as a bleeding complication until proved otherwise. Warfarin is associated with a fetal bony embryopathy when administered to women during their first trimester of pregnancy, although no bony complications have been reported in adults on long-term treatment. Warfarin-induced necrotic skin lesions are a rare, but striking, complication. In some cases they are associated with larger loading doses and in others, with heterozygous protein C deficiency.

Oral anticoagulant therapy is indicated to prevent

recurrence of venous thromboembolism for an intermediate period of time after full-dose heparinization and to prevent arterial thromboemboli from the heart. Warfarin is antagonized by vitamin K, but immediate reversal of warfarin is indicated only with massive or life-threatening bleeding or emergent need of surgery. In these situations, in addition to vitamin K, plasma should be given to acutely raise the vitamin K–dependent factors to levels above 30 to 40 percent. This may require 1 to 1.5 liters of plasma (4 to 6 U). For relatively minor bleeding in a patient with an ongoing high risk of thrombosis or an abnormally prolonged PT alone, it is advisable to reduce or withhold a warfarin dose (or that of potentiating drug) and follow the PT until it returns to the therapeutic range. When vitamin K is used, it can be extremely difficult to reequilibrate the anticoagulant effect when continued therapy is truly indicated.

Fibrinolytic Agents

Thrombi are normally dissolved by the patient's fibrinolytic system, which can be activated therapeutically by streptokinase, urokinase, or tissue plasminogen activator (tPA). These plasminogen activators differ in their mechanisms of action but produce the same effect.[13] Streptokinase is a bacterial protein which forms a one-to-one complex with plasminogen, enabling it to generate plasmin from other plasminogen molecules. Urokinase is a protease from human urine, which enzymatically cleaves plasminogen to form the active fibrinolytic enzyme. The third activator, derived from tissues and available as a recombinant product, differs primarily in that its action is partially dependent upon binding to fibrin. In this situation, systemic fibrinogenolytic effects are minimized. Fibrinolytic therapy is most effective when begun acutely after thrombus formation. There are numerous contraindications to its use, of which active bleeding or a recent stroke are considered absolute. Use within 2 weeks of major trauma, surgery, or biopsy procedures is hazardous because fibrin clots in a healing wound may also be dissolved.

To achieve a therapeutic effect, enough streptokinase or urokinase has to be infused to overcome the body's inhibitory systems. Recommended doses include: for streptokinase 250,000 U given over 30 minutes initially, followed by 100,000 U/h by continuous infusions; for urokinase, the loading dose is 4400 U/kg body weight over 10 minutes followed by 4400 U/(kg)(h). Infusions are maintained for 24 hours for pulmonary embolism and for 24 to 72 hours for deep venous thrombosis. It is sufficient in monitoring systemic fibrinolytic therapy to demonstrate that the thrombin time is at least doubled, being the net effect of hypofibrinogenemia and increased degradation products. The excess or free plasmin produced by these agents not only digests fibrin in the thrombi but also destroys much of the circulating fibrinogen and factors V and VIII. This produces a potentially serious hemostatic defect. Although extensively studied in coronary artery thrombosis, any distinct benefit of tPA in venous thrombotic disorders remains to be established.

Currently, fibrinolytic therapy is indicated in the occasional patient with acute massive pulmonary embolism, or submassive embolism with shock. It has been suggested that it preserves normal pulmonary function better than heparin alone in all patients with pulmonary emboli, but long-term results need to accrue. Streptokinase has also been approved for the treatment of deep venous thrombosis, where it may decrease the "ill-defined" incidence of the postphlebitic syndrome. Pending the results of future studies and/or safer agents, however, routine use in deep venous thrombosis currently poses an undue hemorrhagic risk. Other uses include arterial thromboemboli where surgery is contraindicated, and recently occluded cannulae. It should be noted that the retail cost of urokinase is more than sixfold higher than streptokinase, although, being of human origin, reactions and resistance are much less common. Recombinant tPA is considerably more expensive.

Upon discontinuation of fibrinolytic therapy, the effect is rapidly dissipated since the half-lives of the therapeutic agents are on the order of 15 minutes. Full-dose heparinization is then begun about 1 hour thereafter. When major bleeding occurs during the course of fibrinolytic therapy, the agent should be discontinued and the acute effect will normalize in about an hour. Bleeding may well be correlated with low fibrinogen levels, so cryoprecipitate, which is a concentrate of fibrinogen as well as factor VIII and von Willebrand factor, may be indicated. When immediate reversal of active plasmin is required, a competitive inhibitor, epsilon-aminocaproic acid (5 g intravenously every 30 minutes), is an effective antagonist.

ANTITHROMBOTIC THERAPY
Management of Venous Thrombotic Disorders

Antithrombotic therapy should be instituted once the diagnosis of deep venous thrombosis or pulmonary embolism has been established.[14] The majority of patients should be given full doses of heparin. Occasionally, as for patients with massive pulmonary embolism or submassive embolism with shock, fibrinolytic agents will be given before anticoagulants to more rapidly dissolve the emboli. The standard approach to anticoagulation involves an intravenous bolus of heparin followed by continuous infusion and daily monitoring. Infusion is maintained for 7 to 10 days, but at least 3 to 5 days before heparin is discontinued warfarin is begun with doses adjusted according to the results of the PT after the first two doses. It is not known precisely how long to maintain patients on oral anticoagulants, but the risk of recurrence, even in uncomplicated cases, may remain high for several weeks. For a distal thrombus in the deep calf veins, 6 weeks of therapy is usually sufficient, whereas 3 to 6 months is generally recommended for more proximal disease or for pulmonary embolism. Patients with a greater risk of recurrence require longer periods of treatment which can be achieved by either long-term oral anticoagulants or full doses of subcutaneous heparin (e.g., 12,000 U every 12 hours) with at least weekly monitoring and appropriate dosage adjustments. Low-dose heparin should never be used to manage established venous thromboembolic disease.

Surgical thrombectomies are rarely indicated. In patients with active bleeding or in whom anticoagulants are otherwise contraindicated, an umbrella filter in the vena cava is sometimes useful to temporarily prevent lower extremity or pelvic vein emboli.

Prevention of Venous Thrombosis

Prophylaxis of venous thromboembolism has received considerable attention with the primary experimental tool being calf scanning for radiolabeled fibrinogen deposition. For operative and immediately postoperative periods, low-dose subcutaneous heparin (5000 U every 8 to 12 hours) reduces the incidence of labeled fibrinogen deposition from around 25 to 5 percent, except in patients undergoing hip surgery, where it remains high. In a large cooperative study of surgical patients over 40 years of age, autopsy-proven deaths from pulmonary emboli were reduced by low-dose heparin, but it is not clear to what extent these results can be generalized to medical patients or even to surgical patients in North America today.

Whereas low-dose heparin is generally safe and is advocated in patients with a moderate risk of venous thromboembolic disease, intermittent calf compression during the procedure is equally effective in surgical patients. Attention to physical exercise of the lower ex-

tremities may be at least as important as heparin in the prevention of venous thromboembolism. Pulmonary emboli following myocardial infarction, for example, are impressively less frequent than they were two decades ago; earlier ambulation can be credited with the major portion of this change. For patients at high risk of venous thrombotic disorders, full-dose anticoagulation is required; alternatively, dextran, as used intraoperatively, may be effective.

REFERENCES

1. Kasper CK, Dietrich SL: Comprehensive management of hemophilia. *Clin Haematol* 14:489, 1985.
2. Prentice CRM: Acquired coagulation disorders. *Clin Haematol* 14:413, 1985.
3. Harris EN et al: Antiphospholipid antibodies—Autoantibodies with a difference. *Ann Rev Med* 39:261, 1988.
4. Kelly DA, Tuddenham EG: Hemostatic problems in liver-disease. *Gut* 27:339, 1986.
5. Bauer KA, Rosenberg RD: The pathophysiology of the prethrombotic state in humans: Insights gained from studies using markers of hemostatic system activation. *Blood* 70:343, 1987.
6. Mant MJ et al: Severe, acute disseminated intravascular coagulation. *Am J Med* 67:557, 1979.
7. Bennett B, Towler HMA: Hemostatic response to trauma. *Br Med Bull* 41:274, 1985.
8. Comp PC: Hereditary disorders predisposing to thrombosis. *Prog Hemost Thromb* 8:71, 1986.
9. Bauer KA et al: Aging-associated changes in indices of thrombin generation and protein C activation in humans. Normative aging study. *J Clin Invest* 80:1527, 1987.
10. Wessler S, Gitel SN: Pharmacology of heparin and warfarin. *J Am Coll Cardiol* 8:10B, 1986.
11. Furie B et al: Comparison of the native prothrombin antigen and the prothrombin time for monitoring oral anticoagulant therapy. *Blood* 64:445, 1984.
12. Petitti DB et al: Duration of warfarin anticoagulant therapy and the probabilities of recurrent thromboembolism and hemorrhage. *Am J Med* 81:255, 1986.
13. Collen D, Stump DC, Gold HK: Thrombolytic therapy. *Ann Rev Med* 39:405, 1988.
14. Hirsh J: Treatment of pulmonary embolism. *Ann Rev Med* 39:91, 1987.

SECTION F

The Endocrine and Metabolic Systems

Chapter 69

AGING OF THE ENDOCRINE SYSTEM

L. Cass Terry and Jeffrey B. Halter

Central nervous system (CNS) control of anterior pituitary hormone secretion is mediated by episodic release of neuropeptides (releasing or release-inhibiting hormones) and neurotransmitters (biogenic amines) into the hypothalamic-adenohypophyseal (hypophyseal) portal circulation from hypothalamic tuberoinfundibular neurons and neurosecretory axons from other brain regions (Fig. 69-1). On a higher order, the activity of these tuberoinfundibular neurons is influenced by a complex neural network of biogenic aminergic and peptidergic neurons from the brainstem, limbic system, diencephalon, and neocortex. These systems are autoregulated by inhibitory feedback mechanisms at several levels, including hypothalamic (ultrashort), pituitary (short), and end organ (long) loops and multiple metabolic factors (i.e., blood glucose, thyroid hormone) that act on brain and pituitary. These intricate and sensitive neuroendocrine systems are influenced by internal oscillators or biologic clocks, as well as several higher cortical functions such as sleep, stress, exercise, and depression.

The aging process can alter neuroendocrine function at multiple levels (i.e., through its effects on biogenic aminergic and peptidergic neurons, anterior pituitary cells, and end organs) (Fig. 69-1). In this chapter we will describe age-related disturbances in growth hormone (GH), adrenocorticotropin (ACTH), and male gon-

adotropin (LH/FSH) secretion and review clinical disorders of the neuroendocrine system relevant to the elderly.

NEUROTRANSMITTER REGULATION

There is abundant evidence that biogenic aminergic and peptidergic neurons strongly influence the secretion of hypothalamic hormones.[1,2] Those most studied are the "classic" neurotransmitters dopamine, norepinephrine, epinephrine, and serotonin and the opioids. Other bioamines and peptides have been studied less extensively, and the data are somewhat confounding and inconclusive.[2]

DOPAMINE

The predominant dopaminergic innervation of the hypothalamus is by the tuberoinfundibular, tuberohypophyseal, and incertohypothalamic systems.[1,3] Most information on aging attends to the tuberoinfundibular system. Although histochemical studies have shown the number of dopamine cell bodies do not change with age in rats, there is a marked decrease in the steady state concentration of dopamine and its rate-limiting biosynthetic enzyme tyrosine hydroxylase and a decline in dopamine

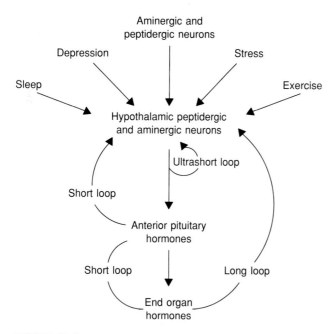

FIGURE 69-1
The hypothalamic-pituitary unit and factors that affect its activity, including inputs from other brain regions and feedback regulatory systems at several levels.

turnover, a more reliable index of dopaminergic activity, in the hypothalamus.[1] Also, the processing of dopamine by the anterior pituitary decreases in aged animals, and these changes are not observed in longer living strains of animals.[1] Thus, with aging the amount of dopamine delivered to the pituitary is decreased. Since dopamine exerts a tonic inhibitory action on prolactin, this may explain the association of high plasma prolactin levels in aged animals.[2,3]

NOREPINEPHRINE

The hypothalamus is innervated by the dorsal and ventral noradrenergic bundles that originate from brainstem nuclei and send axons to several hypothalamic regions. Numerous studies have shown that norepinephrine levels and turnover and its biosynthetic enzyme (dopamine-β-hydroxylase) decline with age in rodents and other animal species.[1,3] Also, in aged female rats there is a decreased ability of noradrenergic neurons to respond to ovarian signals.[1,3] The noradrenergic system exerts a stimulatory influence on secretion of several pituitary hormones (i.e., growth hormone, luteinizing hormone, and thyrotropin),[2] and its age-associated decline may be directly related to hyposecretion of these hormones.

SEROTONIN

The indoleamine serotonin has a purported role in neuroendocrine regulation.[1,2] Serotoninergic neurons in the ventral and dorsal raphe nuclei of the brainstem project

axons to hypothalamic structures.[1,2] Although tyrosine hydroxylase, the rate-limiting enzyme for serotonin synthesis, declines with age, the data on brain serotonin levels are conflicting.[1,3] Thus, to date, there is no consistent age-related effect on serotonin.

OPIOIDS

There is evidence that the steady state levels of proopiomelanocortin-derived peptides (ACTH, β-endorphin, β-lipotropin, and a 16 kDa fragment) decline with age.[1,2,4] Also, the posttranslational processing of β-endorphin is decreased in old rats.[1] Because decreased brain concentrations could reflect diminished synthesis or enhanced release, Simpkins and Millard[1] have hypothesized that old rats may be "hypo- or hyperopioid." It remains to be determined which, if either, condition occurs with aging. Both states could provide an explanation for some of the neuroendocrine manifestations of aging, including disruption of autonomic nervous system function.[1–3]

THE HYPOTHALAMIC-PITUITARY-ADRENAL AXIS

The hypothalamic-pituitary-adrenal (HPA) system (Fig. 69-2) consists of three elements: (1) corticotropin-releasing hormone (CRH or CRF), which is synthesized by hypothalamic neurons and released from their nerve terminals into capillaries of the hypophyseal portal system; (2) corticotropin (ACTH, adrenocorticotropic hormone) secreted by anterior pituitary corticotropes into the circulation; and (3) adrenal hormones, primarily glucocorticoids, from the adrenal cortex.

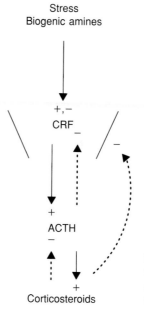

FIGURE 69-2
The hypothalamic-pituitary-adrenal axis. Inhibitory feedback pathways are represented by broken lines.

The HPA is considered by many[2] to be the "quintessential" neuroendocrine system because it most clearly portrays complex interactions between the brain and the endocrine system to (1) maintain homeostasis and control the response to exogenous and endogenous stimuli (i.e., stress response) and (2) generate hormonal secretory rhythms.

CORTICOTROPIN-RELEASING HORMONE

Characterization and Actions

The isolation and synthesis of human CRH in 1981 was the culmination of 26 years of intensive research by several investigators.[2] It contains 41 amino acids, and it is identical in humans and rats. CRH stimulates ACTH secretion which, in turn, acts on the zona reticularis of the adrenal cortex to release glucocorticoids, predominantly cortisol in humans and corticosterone in rats. There is evidence that CRH facilitates ACTH secretion by stimulation of 3'5'-cyclic-AMP after binding to specific receptors on pituitary cell membranes.[2] Its action is calcium dependent, and it enhances phospholipid methylation.

The plasma half-life of CRH is 12 and 73 minutes for the fast and slow components respectively.[2] Thus, ACTH and cortisol remain elevated for 2 to 3 hours after an intravenous CRH bolus. CRH has been measured in pituitary portal blood of rats and cerebrospinal fluid of humans.[2] Immunoneutralization of circulating CRH in laboratory animals causes a marked decrease in basal and stress-induced plasma ACTH levels.[2] Although CRH stimulates β-endorphin and other proopiomelanocortin-derived peptides, it has little, if any, physiologic action on other pituitary hormones.

The neurohypophyseal hormone vasopressin also has an effect on corticotropic cells to cause ACTH release, although vasopressin is on the order of 1000 times less potent than CRH.[2] However, vasopressin, as well as epinephrine and norepinephrine, have marked synergistic actions with CRH to facilitate pituitary ACTH secretion.[2]

In addition to its pituitary effects, CRH stimulates the sympathetic nervous system to cause release of adrenal epinephrine and norepinephrine and increase blood pressure and heart rate.[2] These actions are accompanied by behavioral changes manifested primarily by increased locomotor activity and arousal, signs indicative of the stress response. These effects may be mediated by CRH systems outside the hypothalamus.

ACTH

Characterization and Actions

Human ACTH is a peptide that contains 39 amino acids of which the first 19 are essential for its action on the adrenal cortex.[2] Adrenocorticotropic hormone is derived from the prohormone proopiomelanocortin (POMC). The peptides derived from processing of POMC include ACTH, β-lipotropin, β-endorphin, and a 16 kDa fragment. In addition to the anterior pituitary, discrete brain regions are known to synthesize and secrete POMC-derived ACTH and β-endorphin, and the POMC gene has been found in the neurohypophysis, gastrointestinal tract, and a variety of endocrine neoplasms.[2] These regions react differently to CRH and feedback inhibition by glucocorticoids.

ACTH acts on the adrenal cortex to stimulate glucocorticoid and androcorticoid (sex hormone) secretion by binding to specific receptors and activation of a "second messenger system." Its effect on mineralocorticoids (i.e., aldosterone) is relatively minor compared to that of the renin-angiotensin system.

Physiologic Secretion

ACTH is secreted episodically with an underlying diurnal pattern. The highest plasma levels are seen in the morning (4 to 9 A.M.), and the lowest occur around midnight.[2] This rhythm is generated by the hypothalamus and its connections through the release of CRH. In fact, steady state levels of hypothalamic CRH vary diurnally in rats, and lesions of the hypothalamus attenuate or abolish diurnal cortisol secretion.[2]

There is evidence to indicate that extrahypothalamic brain regions have differential effects on hypothalamic CRH neurons.[2] For example, within the limbic system the amygdala appears to facilitate and the hippocampus attenuate ACTH secretion, whereas midbrain structures have both effects on the pituitary-adrenal axis.

Neurotransmitter Control

The effects of pharmacologic agents on ACTH are believed to be mediated by their actions on CRH. The literature is confusing because of the variability of responses of different laboratory animals to different aminergic agonists and antagonists. In humans, α-adrenergic activation and β-adrenergic blockade facilitate the ACTH response to insulin-induced hypoglycemic stress.[2] Also, there is evidence that serotonin and acetylcholine enhance ACTH and GABA is inhibitory.[2]

The opioids β-endorphin and met-enkephalin decrease plasma ACTH levels, and the opiate receptor blocker naloxone has the opposite effect.[2] It is not clear whether opioids directly inhibit CRH release or activate an aminergic pathway, which, in turn, inhibits CRH. Because CRH stimulates β-endorphin, opioid suppression of ACTH secretion may represent a feedback inhibitory mechanism.

Feedback Inhibition

Glucocorticoids are thought to be primary regulators of CRH and ACTH section. Receptors for glucocorticoids have been demonstrated in the pituitary and several brain regions, including hypothalamic nuclei that contain CRH.[2] Adrenalectomy increases steady state levels of hypothalamic CRH, and cortisol administration has the opposite effect. Also, glucocorticoid administration blunts the pituitary response to CRH, reduces CRH receptors, decreases pituitary ACTH levels, inhibits 3'5'-cyclic-AMP, and suppresses the synthesis of mRNA that codes for POMC.[2]

The hippocampus contains the highest density of neurons with glucocorticoid receptors,[2] and, as mentioned previously, stimulation of this region inhibits ACTH secretion. It has been hypothesized that a decrease in hippocampal glucocorticoid receptors may explain the impaired ability of older animals to terminate the adrenocortical response to stress[2] (see below). Although a short loop feedback pathway for ACTH has been proposed,[2] the data are contradictory and inconclusive. To date, an ultrashort loop feedback pathway for CRH has not been demonstrated.

ADRENAL HORMONES

Cortisol is the principal glucocorticoid secreted in humans. ACTH has a direct effect on glucocorticoid-containing cells to cause immediate release of cortisol. The half-life of cortisol in plasma is 60 to 90 minutes, and approximately 10 percent circulates in the free form, which is available to cells.[2] Cortisol has effects on cell membranes and the genes that code for regulatory enzymes that regulate lipid, carbohydrate, and protein metabolism and stimulate cell differentiation.[2] ACTH also stimulates androcorticoids (dehydroepiandrosterone) and the mineralocorticoid aldosterone. Adrenal androgens are converted to testosterone in peripheral tissues, and aldosterone is primarily under control by the renin-angiotensin system.

EFFECTS OF AGING ON THE HPA

ACTH and Glucocorticoid Secretion

At this writing there are no reports on age-related alterations in steady state concentrations or release of CRH from brain tissue. Thus, it is possible only to make inferences about CRH secretion from analysis of plasma ACTH and glucocorticoid levels. Age-related changes in basal ACTH and cortisol secretion are subtle, and clear-cut abnormalities occur rarely.[1,5] Sonntag et al.[6] described decreased peak plasma ACTH levels during the diurnal surge, but they found no change in diurnal corticosterone concentrations in male Fischer rats. Others have found no change in the circadian rhythm of either ACTH or corticosterone in male rats and a slight decrease in corticosterone release in females.[1] Halbreich et al.[7] reported a decrease in the mean 24-hour plasma cortisol levels of aged individuals. In an elegant chronobiologic study, Sherman et al.[8] demonstrated a significant age-related phase advance of the cortisol rhythm, similar to that found in depressed patients.

Pituitary and Adrenal Involvement

In aged female rats, Barnea et al.[9] demonstrated that tissue concentrations of POMC-derived peptides in the basal hypothalamus were decreased up to 50 percent compared to young rats. However, no release or turnover studies have been performed to determine if this effect is due to decreased synthesis or increased release or degradation.

Adrenal cortical cells show ultrastructural changes in mitochondria with age,[10] and biochemical alterations have been reported.[5] Popplewell et al.[11,12] have shown that aging is associated with a decreased ability of adrenals to acquire, synthesize, and process cholesterol needed for steroidogenesis. However, the importance of these activity changes in steroidogenic enzymes on corticosterone production capacity is unknown.

Although there is a suggestion that the adrenal responsiveness to ACTH may be decreased in aged rats and humans,[5,13] both species maintain this capability to a high degree. In fact, Sonntag et al.[6] found that aged male rats showed an increased adrenal sensitivity to ACTH, and they suggested that this is responsible for maintenance of the corticosterone rhythm in the presence of decreased plasma ACTH levels in older rats.

Stress Activation and Feedback Inhibition

The age-related disruption of the HPA most consistently demonstrated is the response to and recovery from situations that increase plasma levels of ACTH and glucocorticoids (i.e., stress). Following HPA activation, elderly people excrete larger amounts of cortisol[14] and both hormones remain elevated for a much longer period of time compared to younger adults.[1,2,5] Also, dexamethasone causes less suppression of cortisol in older patients,[15,16] a factor to consider when performing dexamethasone suppression tests for depression in elderly patients. This appears to be due to a defect in feedback inhibition by glucocorticoids, and it may represent a diminution in hippocampal glucocorticoid receptors, the activation of which is believed to inhibit CRH release.[17]

CRH in Alzheimer's Disease

Numerous investigations provide evidence that brain CRH systems are affected by Alzheimer's disease. It has been demonstrated that CRH levels in brain regions and cerebrospinal fluid are decreased in this disorder.[18,19] This diminution in CRH correlates with a reduction in choline acetyl transferase,[20] the enzyme responsible for acetylcholine biosynthesis. There is a decrease in CRH receptor binding in brain and blood lymphocytes,[21,22] which may be accompanied by an "upregulation" of cerebral cortical CRH receptors.[21] Also, the increase in plasma cortisol normally observed after opiate receptor blockade with naltrexone is not seen in patients with Alzheimer's disease.[16,23] The clinical significance of these findings remains to be determined.

CONCLUSIONS

The bulk of evidence indicates that of the alterations in the HPA that develop with aging, the one most clearly demonstrable is a diminution in feedback inhibition of ACTH and/or CRH systems by glucocorticoids. Thus, there appears to be a prolonged response to HPA activation by stressful stimuli, suggesting an imbalance in the recovery phase of HPA-mediated homeostasis. The significance of decreased brain CRH levels in the pathogenesis and treatment of Alzheimer's disease is currently under investigation.

GROWTH HORMONE

CHARACTERIZATION AND ACTIONS

Two forms of human growth hormone (GH) (Fig. 69-3) are synthesized by anterior pituitary somatotropes. Approximately 85 percent of pituitary GH is a polypeptide with a molecular weight of 21,500, and the remaining 15 percent is a smaller molecule which has a deletion of 15 amino acids from residues 32 to 46.[2] Both molecules possess "growth-promoting" activity, and the larger one has "insulin-like" activity and a diabetogenic action with "anti-insulin" effects,[2] all of which are probably region-specific on the molecule.

Circulating human GH is unbound, has an estimated half-life between 17 to 45 minutes, and is believed to act at several sites rather than a specific target organ.[2] The actions attributed to GH include stimulation of skeletal and muscle growth, enhancement of amino acid uptake, and regulation of lipolysis. Although GH can act directly on chondrocytes, most of its actions are believed to be mediated by its ability to stimulate synthesis and/or release of somatomedin C and IGF I and II in hepatic, and possibly renal, cells.[2]

PHYSIOLOGIC SECRETION

Although secretory patterns vary with species, GH is released episodically in several experimental animals and humans.[2] The control and generation of this endog-

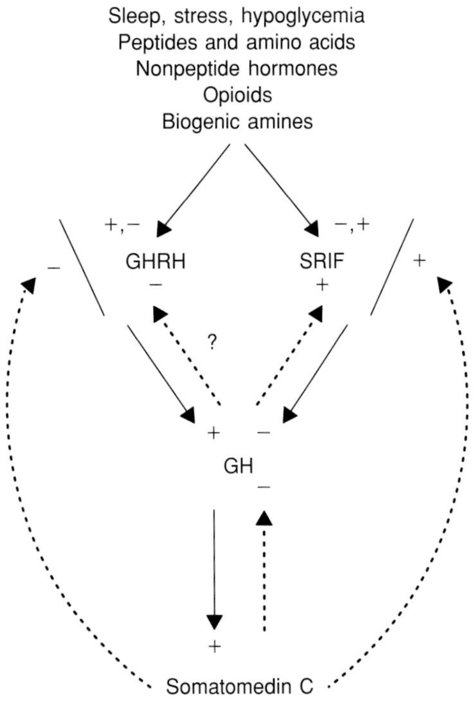

FIGURE 69-3
The hypothalamic-pituitary-somatomedin axis. Multiple factors affect hypothalamic release of growth hormone-releasing hormone (**GHRH**) and the GH-inhibiting hormone somatostatin (**SRIF**). Inhibitory feedback pathways are represented by broken lines.

enous rhythm is mediated by the episodic release of GH-releasing hormone (GHRH) and somatostatin (GH-release-inhibiting hormone) from hypothalamic tuberoinfundibular neurons into the hypophyseal portal circulation.[2] The disconnected hypothalamus can maintain pulsatile GH in rats, but the rhythm and plasma concentrations are altered, suggesting that hypothalamic afferent connections influence the timing and generation of GH release through their effects on GHRH and somatostatin neurons.

Several physiologic and pathologic conditions stimulate GH. These effects are believed to be mediated by activation of brain regions that project to the hypothalamus, and there is evidence that many are mediated by specific neurotransmitter systems.[2] For instance, α-adrenergic blockade inhibits GH release induced by exercise and hypoglycemia in humans, and there is evidence in experimental animals that GH released by activation of "extrahypothalamic" regions or opiate receptors is mediated by catecholamines.[2] Also, sleep-associated GH secretion may involve both serotoninergic and cholinergic neurotransmission.

NEUROTRANSMITTER CONTROL

Neuropharmacologic studies have focused on four biogenic amines: dopamine, norepinephrine, epinephrine, and serotonin. There is general agreement that human GH secretion is modulated by these agents, but it is not clear as to whether they act by excitation of GHRH or inhibition of somatostatin systems. Evidence is sufficient to conclude that α-adrenergic and dopaminergic receptor activation facilitates GH secretion, and β-adrenergic receptor stimulation inhibits it.[2] The roles of serotonin and other amines, amino acids, and other small peptides in GH control are not well established.

Morphine and endogenous opioids and their analogs increase plasma GH concentrations in humans and animals.[1,2] Although GH release induced by severe physical exercise is blocked by opiate receptor blockade with naloxone, this agent has little effect, if any, on stress-induced or basal GH secretion.[1,2] Thus, except for drastic stress, there in no indication that endogenous opioids are involved in GH release.

FEEDBACK INHIBITION

Growth hormone can inhibit its own secretion in animals by several demonstrated feedback control mechanisms, but more investigation is needed to show GH feedback in humans. Both GH and somatomedin C stimulate somatostatin release from the rat hypothalamus. Also, somatomedin C acts directly on the pituitary to inhibit the action of GHRH.[2] It remains to be determined as to whether somatomedin C or GH have direct hypothalamic actions to inhibit GHRH release.

EFFECTS OF AGING

Physiologic Secretion

Amplitude and frequency of GH secretory episodes in humans are determined by age.[1,2,24] For humans entering puberty there is a marked increase in the magnitude and frequency of GH bursts. Those bursts that occur early in sleep are the highest. As early adulthood is approached, the amount of GH secreted declines, especially during sleep. Several recent experiments in humans and animals clearly demonstrate that GH secretion declines progressively in aging males.[1,2,25] This decline is also most evident during sleep.[26]

The rat is the most frequently studied laboratory animal, and, therefore, most attempts to ascertain the mechanism of the age-related diminution in GH derive from this species. In the adult male rat, plasma GH rises abruptly in a rhythmic pattern every 3 hours from low or unmeasurable levels to a zenith greater than 1000 ng/ml. These secretory episodes last for approximately 1 hour, followed by a return of plasma GH to low nadir levels.[2] Female rats have a more variable secretory profile in that the GH bursts occur more frequently, the peak amplitudes are lower, the nadir levels are higher, and there is variation with the estrous cycle.[1,2,27] These oscillating secretory rhythms can be analyzed in terms of

peak and trough amplitude, pulse frequency, and total amount of GH secreted over a time period.

In the aged male rat there is a marked decrease in the total amount of GH secreted.[1,24] Analysis of their secretory profiles indicates a marked decline in the GH secretory peaks, whereas the frequency and nadir levels are relatively unaffected.[1,25] Aged females exhibit lower peak amplitudes and higher interpeak basal GH levels.[1] Similar findings have been observed in monkeys, baboons, and sheep.[1] This age-related impairment in GH secretion is accompanied by diminution of plasma somatomedin C levels.[1,28]

Sites of Involvement

There are several sites at which the hypothalamic-pituitary axis could be affected by the aging process. Because catecholaminergic neurotransmission declines with aging, the amount of dopamine, norepinephrine, and epinephrine delivered to GHRH and somatostatin nerve terminals may be reduced, resulting in either decreased GHRH or increased somatostatin release. Sonntag et al.[24] have shown that L-dopa restores GH pulse amplitudes to levels found in young adult rats, and clonidine-induced GH release is diminished in old male rats. Also, there is a diminution of catecholamine-dependent morphine-induced GH in aged male rodents.[1] Thus, the age-associated decline in catecholaminergic, specifically noradrenergic, tone may contribute to hyposomatotropinism in senescent animals and humans.

HYPOTHALAMUS: GROWTH HORMONE-RELEASING HORMONE (GHRH) Immunoneutralization of circulating GHRH with specific antisera abolishes or reduces episodic GH release,[2] indicating that this peptide is essential to generate pulsatile GH secretion. Morimoto et al.[29] have demonstrated a decrease in median eminence GHRH terminals of aged male rats, but there was no change in the number of GHRH cell bodies. Crew et al.[30] observed a decrease in GH and prolactin mRNA in old mice. In contrast, Cocchi et al.[31] found no change in immunoassayable hypothalamic GHRH concentrations in old male and female rats. To date, there have been no studies on GHRH release from hypothalamic tissue. Although the data are somewhat confounding, a decrease in GHRH terminals, synthesis, or release could account for the decline in the GH pulse amplitude with aging.

HYPOTHALAMUS: SOMATOSTATIN In contrast to GHRH, there is a large body of evidence to support the theory that somatostatin secretion increases with age in male rats. Using immunocytochemical and radioimmunoassay techniques, investigators have demonstrated a decreased hypothalamic somatostatin concentration and

a reduced density of somatostatin nerve terminals in the median eminence of male rats.[1] In contrast, Morimoto et al.,[29] using the PAP immunocytochemical procedure, found no difference between young and old in the density of somatostatin positive terminals in the median eminence. However, in vivo and in vitro experiments in aged male rats have shown that (1) immunoneutralization of circulating somatostatin increases plasma GH levels and the pituitary response to GHRH when compared to young adults,[1] and (2) potassium-induced somatostatin release from hypothalami is enhanced along with an increase in the proportion of somatostatin-28 compared to somatostatin-14.[1] Somatostatin-28 is more potent in its ability to inhibit GH secretion, and it has a longer half-life than the 14 amino acid molecule.[2] Data regarding somatostatin activity in female rats[1] is conflicting and inconclusive at present.

Further support for the hypothesis of age-induced facilitation of somatostatin release derives from studies on stress-related GH changes in the rat and human. In the rat, stress causes suppression of pulsatile secretion, a phenomenon that is believed to be mediated by somatostatin.[2] It has been shown that stress-induced GH inhibition is greater in mature versus postnatal female rats.[32] In humans, hypoglycemic stress induced by insulin facilitates GH release.[2] Wakabayashi et al.[33] observed that hypoglycemia-induced GH release is greater than GHRH-induced GH release in older males, whereas, in children, both provocative stimuli release equal amounts of GH, suggesting that basal somatostatin release is greater in older men. Thus, evidence is convincing that aging is associated with enhanced somatostatin secretion.

PITUITARY RESPONSIVENESS TO GHRH   In addition to age-related alterations in aminergic and peptidergic factors that regulate GH secretion, there is increasing evidence of changes in pituitary somatotrope responsiveness to GHRH and somatostatin. While there is general agreement from in vivo studies that GHRH-stimulated GH release declines in aged rats and humans,[1,25,34–37] the effect is more difficult to detect in males. In vitro studies on the isolated pituitary are in conflict. Ceda et al.[34] found the GH releasing ability of GHRH was partially impaired in cultured pituitary cells from old male rats, whereas basal GH release was unaffected. On the other hand, Sonntag and Gough[25] observed similar GHRH-induced GH release from pituitary slices of old, middle-aged, and young rats, but basal release was reduced by 50 percent in old compared to young rats. These variations may be due to different methodologies (i.e., tissue preparations) and age and strain differences. They demonstrate that the variability in experimental results increases significantly in aged animals.

Pituitary studies on the age-related cAMP response to GHRH demonstrate less variability than the GH response to this peptide. Two laboratories have shown that GHRH-facilitated cAMP accumulation is decreased in the pituitaries of aged animals.[34,38] Also, Robberecht et al.[39] have shown that the efficacy of GHRH to stimulate adenylate cyclase activity was decreased by approximately 50 percent, with no change in the potency of GHRH, in old and senescent rats. Their data suggest that "neither the coupling between receptors, the stimulatory guanyl nucleotide regulatory binding site and the catalytic unit nor the efficacy of the catalytic unit" are affected in aged animals, and they concluded that aging induced a selective loss of functional GHRH receptors.[39] These results must be interpreted with the caveat that the diminished GH response to GHRH in the aged may be due to a concomitant decrease in pituitary GH content.[1]

PITUITARY RESPONSIVENESS TO SOMATOSTATIN
Developmental studies on pituitary sensitivity to somatostatin clearly show an age-related effect. Khorram et al.[40] observed that early postnatal pituitary cells are relatively resistant to GH inhibition by somatostatin. These results were confirmed by Cutler et al.[41] when they demonstrated that the inhibitory effect of somatostatin on basal, GHRH-, and cAMP-stimulated GH from pituitary cell cultures is age-dependent. Thus, it appears that pituitary somatotropes become more sensitive to somatostatin inhibition with age.

Feedback Inhibition and Peripheral Effects

Data are scant in regard to age-related disturbances in the feedback regulation and peripheral effects of GH. It is possible that the ultrashort loop feedback inhibition of somatostatin upon itself is defective. Also, there may be altered responsiveness of the hypothalamic-pituitary axis to gonadal and adrenal steroids.[2,42–44] Low plasma somatomedin concentrations probably result from decreased circulating GH, and this condition would not be expected to inhibit GH secretion. Increased clearance or decreased responsiveness to GH at the peripheral level is not likely because (1) the plasma half-life of circulating GH is not changed with age,[45] (2) old rats respond to GH administration by an increase in growth[46] and regeneration of thymic tissue,[47] which is normally lost with aging, and (3) there is no change in the diabetogenic action of GH with age.[48]

CONCLUSIONS

Investigations of the age-related decline in episodic GH secretion point to several sites in the hypothalamic-pituitary axis where there may be disruption of regulatory mechanisms. At the extrahypothalamic level, there is evidence for diminished catecholamine neurotransmission that could cause decreased stimulation of GHRH or enhanced suppression of somatostatin release. At the hypothalamic level, a large number of studies provides convincing evidence that somatostatin release is increased in aged animals, and the proportion of the more potent and longer lasting form, somatostatin-28, increases with age. It is not clear if the synthesis and/or release of GHRH declines with age. At the pituitary level, some studies suggest that the pituitary responsiveness to GHRH is decreased, possibly due to a loss of functional GHRH receptors. However, this may be due to the age-associated decline in pituitary GH content. Evidence from developmental studies indicates that the inhibitory influence of somatostatin on pituitary somatotropes is facilitated during the aging process. Finally, there is no evidence to indicate that feedback inhibition, plasma clearance, or the peripheral actions of GH are significantly altered in aged animals.

THE HYPOTHALAMIC-PITUITARY-TESTICULAR AXIS

The hypothalamic-pituitary-ovarian axis is the subject of another chapter (Chap. 74), and the actions and characterizations of gonadotropin-releasing hormone (GnRH) and the gonadotropins, luteinizing hormone (LH) and follicle-stimulating hormone (FSH), are described therein. This section will focus on the hypothalamic-pituitary-testicular axis (HPT) (Fig. 69-4) and the effects of aging upon it.

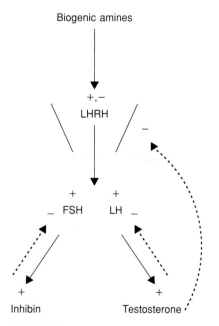

FIGURE 69-4
The hypothalamic-pituitary-testicular axis. Luteinizing hormone-releasing hormone (LHRH or GnRH) stimulates release of LH and FSH. Inhibitory feedback pathways are represented by dotted lines.

GONADOTROPIN-RELEASING HORMONE

The hypothalamus controls LH and FSH secretion by the episodic release of GnRH into the capillaries of the hypophyseal portal system (Fig. 69-4). The effects of GnRH on the gonadotropins are highly specific, and immunoneutralization of circulating GnRH inhibits episodic LH and FSH secretion.[2] GnRH is secreted in bursts approximately every 60 to 90 minutes. This secretory pattern is suppressed if GnRH is infused continuously; it must be administered episodically at a similar frequency to sustain high levels of FSH and LH.[2] Also, evidence indicates that the frequency of GnRH pulses determines the ratio of FSH/LH secreted (e.g., infrequent pulses increase this ratio).[2] Hypothalamic GnRH neurons in males control the onset of puberty, generation of basal episodic secretion, and the integration of sexual behavior and performance.[2,49]

GONADOTROPINS AND GONADAL HORMONES

Luteinizing hormone stimulates the secretion of testosterone from testicular interstitial Leydig cells. Follicle-stimulating hormone facilitates the secretion of the peptide inhibin by the testicular Sertoli cells. Inhibin feeds back to regulate FSH secretion. FSH also stimulates the secretion of androgen-binding protein by the Sertoli cells.[2] Testosterone is the cardinal androgenic steroid in humans. It is synthesized from cholesterol in the mitochondria and cytosol of the Leydig cells of the testis. A similar biosynthesis occurs at a much lower level in the adrenal cortex.[2] Testosterone is reduced by target tissues to its active form, 5-α-dihydrotestosterone, which binds to cytoplasmic androgen receptors.[49] Because approximately 80 percent of circulating 5-α-dihydrotestosterone derives from these tissues, levels of this steroid are thought to be a reliable index of the amount of available testosterone.[49]

NEUROTRANSMITTER CONTROL

Numerous experiments have been performed to determine which neurotransmitters have a function as regulators of the HPT.[1,2] The bulk of evidence indicates that norepinephrine stimulates LH release, and activation of opioid receptors is inhibitory. Also, α-melanocyte-stimulating hormone and substance P facilitate and CRH and neuropeptide Y inhibit LH secretion.[2] Literature concerning other aminergic and peptidergic transmitters is extensive and inconclusive.

FEEDBACK INHIBITION

Pathways involved in feedback regulation of gonadotropin and androgen secretion are illustrated in Fig.

69-4. Abnormally low plasma levels of testosterone cause an increase in FSH and LH release, and high androgen concentrations inhibit gonadotropin secretion. Also, testosterone administration causes suppression of FSH and LH by actions believed to occur at a hypothalamic site.[2] Finally, there is evidence to indicate that inhibin suppresses FSH, whereas testosterone has a greater feedback inhibitory effect on LH.[2]

EFFECTS OF AGING ON THE HPT
Testicular Function

There is considerable evidence from both human and animal studies suggesting that primary testicular failure is a manifestation of aging. While aging related declines of testicular function may be accentuated by primary testicular disease or other systemic factors including acute and chronic illness, alterations of testicular function can be demonstrated even in otherwise healthy individuals. There is a decrease in testicular size in men,[50] which is associated with a decrease in the number of both the Leydig cells which make testosterone[51] and the Sertoli cells which produce sperm.[51] The decline in Sertoli cell number is functionally significant, as it is associated with decreased sperm production. There is also recent evidence for a decrease in production of inhibin in human aging.[52] Similarly, the decline of Leydig cell number is associated with a decrease in serum testosterone levels as well as bioavailable testosterone (testosterone not bound to sex hormone binding globulin). While the age-related decline of testosterone levels is modest in magnitude and somewhat variable, it has been documented in multiple studies.[1,53,54] The age-related increase of FSH and LH, which has also been observed in multiple studies, suggests that the age-related decline of testicular function is primarily due to a testicular problem.

Pituitary and Feedback Regulation

FSH and LH levels increase with age in response to the age-related decline of testosterone and inhibin. However, there is evidence suggesting that these increases may not represent a fully normal pituitary response. The LH secretory response to LHRH stimulation appears to decline somewhat with age.[55] In addition, there is recent evidence that some elderly individuals secrete relatively less bioactive LH, particularly in response to LHRH stimulation.[56] However, this alteration may be subtle and there is not uniform agreement.[54] Because testosterone and inhibin levels are critical to interpretation of pituitary responses, subtle defects may be missed when comparisons are made between groups of individuals with differing testosterone or inhibin levels.

Hypothalamic Factors: GnRH

There is general agreement that hypothalamic GnRH declines with age in male rats.[1] In addition, the LH response to clomiphene (a substance that blocks hypothalamic estrogen receptors and therefore feedback inhibition) is decreased, suggesting either a decrease in GnRH release or in pituitary responsiveness. In humans the characteristics of LH pulse frequency and amplitude have been used as indirect markers of GnRH secretion. No age effects on LH pulse patterns have been observed.[54,56] Similar FSH and LH responses to clomiphene have been reported in young and elderly humans.[52,54] However, a diminished LH response to another antiestrogen, tamoxifen, has also been reported.[56] Again, differences in testosterone and inhibin levels between young and old may interfere with the ability to pick up subtle defects in hypothalamic regulation.

Hypothalamic Factors: Opioids

The role of opioids in age-related changes in the HPT axis is unclear. The opioid β-endorphin inhibits GnRH release.[57] Thus increased opioid activity could contribute to diminished GnRH release with age. However, this seems unlikely since treatment of aged males with naloxone has little effect on plasma LH, whereas in young males there is a significant LH response.[1]

Hypothalamic Factors: Prolactin

There is evidence of a minor age-related increase in the basal prolactin level and a modest increase of the prolactin response to thyrotropin-releasing hormone.[58] However, it is unlikely that these small changes with age contribute much to the age effect on the HPT axis.

CONCLUSION

There is considerable evidence that normal aging is accompanied by primary testicular failure that is modest in degree in most individuals. This age-related testicular failure results in diminished availability of testosterone and inhibin as well as a decrease in sperm production. While there is a gonadotropin response to this testicular failure, there is growing evidence for subtle defects in hypothalamic-pituitary regulation that may contribute to the age-related decline in testicular function. Because of the role that the central neurotransmitter norepinephrine and opioids play in regulation of the hypothalamic pituitary axis, alterations in these central neurotransmitters with aging may contribute to the hypothalamic-pituitary alterations observed.

DISORDERS OF THE NEUROENDOCRINE SYSTEM

Disorders of the neuroendocrine system have clinical features related to hormone excess, hormone deficiency, or local physical effects from endocrine tumors. Particularly in the area of hormone deficiency states, there may be some challenge to clinical recognition in an elderly patient population. Symptoms of adrenal, testicular, or pituitary insufficiency tend to be nonspecific and include weight loss, fatigue, loss of appetite, muscle wasting, and impaired sexual function. As any of these findings may be manifestations of chronic illness in an older person, it is understandable that an endocrine cause for such symptoms, which would be relatively rare, can be overlooked. The diagnostic challenge is further compounded by age-related changes in neuroendocrine function, as detailed previously, since decreased growth hormone and testosterone production occur with age in the absence of neuroendocrine disease.

HYPOTHALAMIC-PITUITARY DISORDERS

Hypopituitarism

Pituitary failure is a relatively rare condition, but it can clearly occur in older people. Major causes include autoimmune destruction, infarction, infection (particularly tuberculosis), metastatic tumor, and infiltrating diseases such as amyloidosis or hemochromatosis. Hypopituitarism can also result from the presence of a large pituitary tumor secreting growth hormone, ACTH, or prolactin. Although symptoms may be nonspecific, a diagnosis of hypopituitarism should be considered seriously in any male with a decline in sexual function and other evidence of hypogonadism. The finding of testosterone levels lower than what would be expected for age, associated with a lack of increase of gonadotropins, provides the basis for further investigation. Such further investigation should include provocative testing of the HPA axis, thyroid function tests, and imaging studies of the sella turcica. The lack of elevation of gonadotropins in a postmenopausal woman is also suggestive of pituitary failure. Since the pituitary-gonadal axis is particularly sensitive to interruption by pituitary disease, it is unusual to find significant pituitary dysfunction in the absence of abnormalities of the pituitary-gonadal system. As hormone replacement therapy can completely reverse the widespread functional deterioration that usually accompanies pituitary failure, it is a diagnosis worthy of consideration even though it is relatively uncommon.

Acromegaly

The clinical syndrome of acromegaly is due to chronic excessive secretion of growth hormone as a result of a growth hormone secreting tumor. The clinical syndrome is recognized by thickening of the skin and soft tissues, which is the predominant cause of the characteristic enlargement of extremities and coarsening of facial features. An increase in the diameter of bones and excessive growth of the mandible leading to protrusion of the jaw are also characteristic. Mass effects of the pituitary tumor can also be present and include headaches and visual field defects. However, these findings are relatively uncommon. The diagnosis of acromegaly can generally be confirmed quite easily with measurement of circulating growth hormone, although the levels may be highly variable and in some patients difficult to differentiate from the normal range. Serum levels of somatomedin are elevated in acromegaly and can confirm the diagnosis. Acromegaly can contribute to age-related conditions including hypertension, heart disease, diabetes mellitus, and osteoarthritis. For these reasons, treatment should be seriously considered, while recognizing that reversal of bony enlargement or joint disease may not be feasible. Pituitary surgery via the transsphenoidal route or external radiation may be helpful to control the disease, but they are not often curative. More recently, use of a long-acting analog of somatostatin has shown promise as an approach to long-term management of this problem.[59,60]

Hyperprolactinemia

Elevated production of prolactin resulting in hyperprolactinemia is a relatively common endocrine problem which can result in hypogonadism and contribute to age-related changes in sexual function. Thus measurement of serum prolactin is an important part of the workup of any man with sexual dysfunction. There is also evidence that the hypogonadism associated with elevated prolactin levels can result in accentuation of age-related bone loss in men and may contribute to the development of osteoporosis.[61] Thus prolactin measurement should also be part of the workup for osteoporosis in a male.

Elevated prolactin levels may result from disease of the hypothalamus interfering with inhibitory dopaminergic pathways that regulate prolactin production or can result from a prolactin-secreting tumor of the pituitary (prolactinoma). Drugs that inhibit the dopamine system, such as phenothiazines, cimetidine, and others, can also cause elevations of serum prolactin. Hypothyroidism also generally results in an increased prolactin level because TRH is a stimulus for prolactin secretion. Since hypothalamic disorders generally cause alterations of multiple hormone systems, it is usually not difficult to differentiate between hypothalamic versus pituitary causes of elevated prolactin levels. Once interfering drugs are eliminated as a cause of elevated prolactin, the focus for further workup should be on the pituitary. Modern computed tomographic scans can allow demonstration of both large pituitary tumors as well as very small ones (microadenomas) which can be the source of increased prolactin production.

When considering treatment for hyperprolactinemia, there are many options available. These include surgery, radiotherapy, drugs, and no intervention. As the natural history of microadenomas is not established, particularly among the elderly, simple observation may be the most appropriate course to take. However, given the potential adverse effects of elevated prolactin production on gonadal function in men and on bone metabolism it may make sense to be more aggressive with intervention. Large tumors may require intervention because of mass effect and generally can be approached surgically by the transsphenoidal route. Dopaminergic agonists are available and can be used effectively to lower prolactin levels and also to reduce tumor size during long-term treatment.[62]

Gynecomastia

Enlargement of breast gland tissue in males is a common finding that may be due to multiple alterations in the hormone milieu. The prevalence of gynecomastia appears to increase with age.[63] Asymptomatic gynecomastia of modest size and not associated with other evidence of endocrine disease is generally not clinically significant. In contrast, the presence of tenderness on physical examination and/or a history of recent breast tenderness associated with the finding of gynecomastia requires further workup. Important factors to consider in the differential diagnosis of gynecomastia include states of increased estrogen production, such as chronic liver disease and during the early recovery phase of malnutrition (refeeding gynecomastia); states associated with elevated gonadotropins, including primary hypogonadism and ectopic gonadotropin production by tumors; and multiple drugs that can influence breast gland tissue. These include estrogens, digitalis, cimetidine, spironolactone, and a host of others. Drugs and the combination of drugs and other illness were the causes of nearly two-thirds of all cases of symptomatic gynecomastia in a male veteran population.[63] It should be kept in mind that carcinoma of the breast can occur in male patients and should receive appropriate workup if suspicious signs are present. Gynecomastia can be quite uncomfortable and may require treatment. Surgical removal is one consideration, but antiestrogens such as tamoxifen may be preferable for short-term management. Identification of contributing medications and their removal is the preferred treatment when possible.

TESTICULAR DISORDERS

As indicated previously, normal aging is accompanied by a somewhat variable decline in testicular function which appears to be due to primary changes in the testis. The question that has been difficult to answer is when does this age-related decline in testicular function reach the point at which a clinically important androgen deficiency exists. As discussed in more detail in Chap. 10, there is a concomitant decline in sexual function with age in men. However, it is clear that this decline in sexual function and the increased rate of impotence in men with age has a complex origin, one component of which may be the age-related decline in gonadal function. Similarly, declines in muscle strength, muscle mass, and bone mass with aging in males may be the result of multiple factors including chronic illness, disability, nutritional problems, and others. The role of the age-related decline in androgen levels as a contributing factor to these problems has not been defined.

On the other hand, there is no doubt that overt gonadal failure with clinical androgen deficiency can occur in elderly men. Surveys of populations of elderly men with sexual dysfunction suggest that a small percentage of such individuals have clearly subnormal testosterone levels, even compared to age-matched controls. While the prevalence of overt hypogonadism is probably less than 10 percent of elderly males with sexual dysfunction,[64] such individuals are candidates for testosterone replacement therapy. Clearcut guidelines for determining which patients are candidates for hormone replacement therapy have not been established. However, it seems reasonable to consider treating patients with a serum testosterone level below 300 ng/dl (usual lower limit of normal is 400 ng/dl).

In general, patients with long-standing gonadal failure do not complain of sexual dysfunction or provide a history of poor sexual function in the past unless questioned specifically about this topic. The diagnosis is often made at the time of physical examination when very small testes are observed, often accompanied by significant gynecomastia. Laboratory findings will confirm a very low testosterone level associated with elevated gonadotropins when there is primary testicular failure. The finding of low or normal range gonadotropin levels in this setting should focus attention on the pituitary for further workup. Because such patients may be unconcerned about their lack of sexual function and interest, it could be argued that hormone replacement therapy is not appropriate for some individuals. However, the important anabolic effects of androgens on muscle and bone provide a rationale for treatment even if sexual function is not an important issue.

In trying to determine whether hormone replacement is indicated for a given patient, it is important to consider also the possibility that prostatic growth will accompany hormone replacement and lead to urinary tract symptoms. In addition family counseling is necessary to some degree because interest in sexual activity will likely increase with hormone replacement and may disrupt long patterns of sexual inactivity. A reasonable approach is to initiate therapy with testosterone for a few months and then reevaluate the overall situation to determine whether hormone replacement should be maintained in the long term. In the authors' experience, it is distinctly unusual for males with even long-standing hypogonadism to request discontinuation of testosterone after it has been initiated.

Although oral androgens are widely available, most carry a risk of hepatic toxicity. Thus intramuscular injection of testosterone remains the treatment of choice. Patients can either be taught to self-administer the testosterone or other arrangements can often be made for injections at home. Long-acting preparations are available which require an injection once every 2 to 4 weeks. A more short-acting preparation should be used to initiate therapy, although injections every other day will be required. This approach allows rapid discontinuation if adverse effects appear. It should be remembered that testosterone can be metabolized to estrogen. Thus during the initial phases of treatment, gynecomastia may actually worsen. However, with longer term treatment gonadotropin levels will be suppressed and gynecomastia generally resolves.

DISORDERS OF THE ADRENAL GLAND

Clinical problems of the adrenal gland that may occur in elderly patients result from overproduction of adrenal steroids, underproduction of adrenal steroids, or adrenal neoplasms. There is no evidence that older people are particularly prone to the development of these relatively rare adrenal problems. However, many of the clinical problems seen in elderly people could be manifestations of adrenal disease. These range from hypertension and diabetes mellitus associated with overproduction of glucocorticoids or mineralocorticoids to weight loss, fatigue, and hypotension that are manifestations of adrenal insufficiency. Thus, it is important to keep adrenal disorders in mind when evaluating elderly patients who present with these problems. This by no means implies that all elderly patients with hypertension, diabetes, or weight loss should be worked up extensively for adrenal disease. This is a situation in which the physical examination and routine laboratory assessment are particularly important means for screening. Benign adrenal neoplasia is increasingly recognized in older individuals who are subjected to abdominal imaging procedures for workup of a variety of clinical findings. Because benign adrenal neoplasms are common, incidental findings on abdominal imaging studies do not merit extensive further workup unless there is a specific clinical indication.

Glucocorticoid Excess

Cushing's syndrome due to excessive secretion of cortisol can result from primary disease of the adrenal gland (either a benign or malignant neoplasm), from overproduction of ACTH by the pituitary (a condition usually referred to as Cushing's disease), or from ectopic secretion of ACTH or CRF from a malignant tumor. All of these are rare conditions that are recognized clinically by the classic features of Cushing's syndrome in the absence of an exogenous source of steroids. The workup involves documentation of excessive production of cortisol. This is usually done by showing failure of normal suppression after overnight treatment with dexamethasone and/or by measuring urinary excretion of free cortisol. Once excessive cortisol production is documented, the patient should be referred to an endocrinologist for further workup to establish the primary cause of the syndrome. Treatment is then targeted at the primary cause.

Mineralocorticoid Excess

Overproduction of mineralocorticoid by the adrenal gland (Conn's syndrome) is an uncommon cause of hypertension due to an adrenal tumor or hyperplasia. Workup for this syndrome is indicated in patients with hypertension who have hypokalemia in the absence of diuretic therapy. Although suppressed plasma renin is a characteristic of this syndrome, the age-related decline in renin levels interferes with the use of renin measurement to help in screening. The key is to document elevated aldosterone levels. Because the conditions for making such measurements are critical and the results can help to distinguish between an adrenal adenoma and hyperplasia, this workup should be carried out by an endocrinologist.

Adrenal Insufficiency

Bilateral adrenal cortical failure (Addison's disease) is a dramatic clinical syndrome that is life threatening. Weakness, fatigue, and weight loss are virtually pathognomonic findings. They are associated with hyperpigmentation of the skin due to increased ACTH, hypotension, and electrolyte abnormalities including hyponatremia and hyperkalemia. Adrenal insufficiency can be due to autoimmune destruction, infection (such as tuberculosis), hemorrhage from anticoagulant therapy, adrenal infiltration as in amyloidosis, or metastatic tumor. The diagnosis can be established by a simple ACTH stimulation test documenting low cortisol levels and failure of those levels to increase after injection. Treatment is straightforward and life saving. It involves replacement doses of a glucocorticoid with appropriate increases of the dose during times of stressful illness. Patients with primary adrenal failure often can be managed with cortisone alone, although a mineralocorticoid may also be necessary in some patients.

REFERENCES

1. Simpkins JW, Millard WJ: Influence of age on neurotransmitter function. *Endocrinol Metab Clin North Am* 16:893, 1987.

2. Martin JB, Reichlin S: *Clinical Neuroendocrinology,* 2d ed. Philadelphia, Davis, 1987.

3. Meites J (ed): *Neuroendocrinology of Aging.* New York, Plenum, 1983.

4. Forman LJ et al: Immunoreactive β-endorphin in the plasma, pituitary and hypothalamus of young and old male rats. *Neurobiol Aging* 2:281, 1981.

5. Riegle GD: Changes in hypothalamic control of ACTH and adrenal cortical functions during aging, in Meites J (ed): *Neuroendocrinology of Aging.* New York, Plenum, 1983, p 309.

6. Sonntag WE et al: Diminished diurnal secretion of adrenocorticotropin (ACTH), but not corticosterone, in old male rats: Possible relation to increased adrenal sensitivity to ACTH in vivo. *Endocrinology* 120:2308, 1987.

7. Halbreich U et al: Effect of age and sex on cortisol secretion in depressives and normals. *Psychiatry Res* 13:221, 1984.

8. Sherman B et al: Age-related changes in the circadian rhythm of plasma cortisol in man. *J Clin Endocrinol Metab* 61:439, 1985.

9. Barnea A et al: A reduction in the concentration of immunoreactive corticotropin, melanotropin and lipotropin in the brain of the aging rat. *Brain Res* 232:345, 1982.

10. Murakoshi M et al: Mitochondrial alterations in aged rat adrenal cortical cells. *Tokai J Exp Clin Med* 10:531, 1985.

11. Popplewell PY, Azhar S: Effects of aging on cholesterol content and cholesterol-metabolizing enzymes in the rat adrenal gland. *Endocrinology* 121:64, 1987.

12. Popplewell PY et al: The influence of age on steroidogenic enzyme activities of the rat adrenal gland: Enhanced expression of cholesterol side-chain cleavage activity. *Endocrinology* 120:2521, 1987.

13. Potter CL et al: Aldosterone production and hormone responsiveness in adrenal glomerulosa cells from cows of different ages. *Gerontology* 33:77, 1987.

14. Jacobs S et al: Urinary-free cortisol excretion in relation to age in acutely stressed persons with depressive symptoms. *Psychosom Med* 46:213, 1984.

15. Stuck AE et al: Kinetics of prednisolone and endogenous cortisol suppression in the elderly. *Clin Pharmacol Ther* 43:354, 1988.

16. Weiner MF et al: Influence of age and relative weight on cortisol suppression in normal subjects. *Am J Psychiatry* 144:646, 1987.

17. Sapolsy R et al: The neuroendocrinology of stress and aging: The glucocorticoid cascade hypothesis. *Endocrine Rev* 7:284, 1986.

18. Mouradian MM et al: Spinal fluid CRF reduction in Alzheimer's disease. *Neuropeptides* 8:393, 1986.

19. Bissette G et al: Corticotropin-releasing factor-like immunoreactivity in senile dementia of the Alzheimer type. Reduced cortical and striatal concentrations. *JAMA* 254:3067, 1985.

20. Whitehouse PJ et al: Reductions in corticotropin releasing factor-like immunoreactivity in cerebral cortex in Alzheimer's disease, Parkinson's disease, and progressive supranuclear palsy. *Neurology* 37:905, 1987.

21. de Souza EB et al: CRH defects in Alzheimer's and other neurologic diseases. *Hosp Pract [Off]* 23:59, 1988.

22. Singh VK et al: Binding of [125I] corticotropin releasing factor to blood immunocytes and its reduction in Alzheimer's disease. *Immunol Lett* 18:5, 1988.

23. Pomara N et al: Loss of the cortisol response to naltrexone in Alzheimer's disease. *Biol Psychiatry* 23:726, 1988.

24. Sonntag WE et al: Changes in growth hormone secretion in aging rats and man, and possible relation to diminished physiological functions, in Mietes J (ed): *Neuroendocrinology of Aging.* New York, Plenum, 1983, p 275.

25. Sonntag WE, Gough MA: Growth hormone releasing hormone induced release of growth hormone in aging male rats: Dependence on pharmacological manipulation and endogenous somatostatin release. *Neuroendocrinology* 47:482, 1988.

26. Terry LC et al: Physiologic secretion of growth hormone and prolactin in male and female rats. *Clin Endocrinol* 6:19S, 1977.

27. Prinz P et al: Plasma growth hormone during sleep in young and aged men. *J. Gerontol* 38:519, 1983.

28. Rudman D et al: Hyposomatomedinemia in the men of a Veterans Administration nursing home: Prevalence and correlates. *Gerontology* 33:307, 1987.

29. Morimoto N et al: Age-related changes in growth hormone releasing factor and somatostatin in the rat hypothalamus. *Neuroendocrinology* 47:459, 1988.

30. Crew MD et al: Age-related decreases of growth hormone and prolactin gene expression in the mouse pituitary. *Endocrinology* 121:1251, 1987.

31. Cocchi D et al: Defective growth hormone response to growth hormone-releasing factor (GRF) in aged rats, in Biggio G, Spano PF, Toffano G, Gessa GL (eds): *Modulation of Central and Peripheral Transmitter Function.* Berlin, Springer, 1986, p 331.

32. Strbak V et al: Maturation of the inhibitory response of growth hormone secretion to ether stress in postnatal rat. *Neuroendocrinology* 40:377, 1985.

33. Wakabayashi I et al: A divergence of plasma growth hormone response between growth hormone-releasing factor and insulin-induced hypoglycaemia among middle-aged healthy male subjects. *Clin Endocrinol (Oxf)* 24:279, 1986.

34. Ceda GP et al: Diminished pituitary responsiveness to growth hormone-releasing factor in aging male rats. *Endocrinology* 118:2109, 1986.

35. Shibasaki T et al: Age-related changes in plasma growth hormone response to growth hormone-releasing factor in man. *J Clin Endocrinol Metab* 58:212, 1984.

36. Lang I et al: Effects of sex and age on growth hormone response to growth hormone-releasing hormone in healthy individuals. *J Clin Endocrinol Metab* 65:535, 1987.

37. Pavlov E et al: Responses of growth hormone (GH) and somatomedin-C to GH-releasing hormone in healthy aging men. *J Clin Endocrinol Metab* 62:595, 1986.

38. Parenti M et al: Different regulation of growth hormone-releasing factor-sensitive adenylate cyclase in the anterior pituitary of young and aged rats. *Endocrinology* 121:1649, 1987.

39. Robberecht P et al: Decreased stimulation of adenylate cyclase by growth hormone-releasing factor in the anterior pituitary of old rats. *Neuroendocrinology* 44:429, 1986.

40. Khorram O et al: Development of hypothalamic control of growth hormone secretion in the rat. *Endocrinology* 113:720, 1983.

41. Cutler L et al: The effect of age on somatostatin suppression of basal, growth hormone (GH)-releasing factor-

stimulated, and dibutyryl adenosine 3',5'-monophosphate-stimulated GH release from rat pituitary cells in monolayer culture. *Endocrinology* 119:152, 1986.

42. Ho KY et al: Effects of sex and age on the 24-hour profile of growth hormone secretion in man: Importance of endogenous estradiol concentrations. *J Clin Endocrinol Metab* 64:51, 1987.

43. Mobbs CV et al: Age-correlated and ovary-dependent changes in relationships between plasma estradiol and luteinizing hormone, prolactin, and growth hormone in female C57BL/6J mice. *Endocrinology* 116:813, 1985.

44. Jansson JO et al: Influence of gonadal steroids on age- and sex-related secretory patterns of growth hormone in the rat. *Endocrinology* 114:1287, 1984.

45. Goya RG et al: Half-life of plasma growth hormone in young and old conscious female rats. *Exp Gerontol* 22:27, 1987.

46. Turner JD et al: Interaction between hypersomatotropism and age in the Wistar-Furth rat. *Growth* 50:402, 1986.

47. Kelley KW et al: GH3 pituitary adenoma cells can reverse thymic aging in rats. *Proc Natl Acad Sci USA* 83:5663, 1986.

48. Sonntag WE et al: Increased secretion of somatostatin-28 from hypothalamic neurons of aged rats in vitro. *Brain Res* 380:229, 1986.

49. Harman SM: Relation of the neuroendocrine system to reproductive decline in men, in Meites J (ed): *Neuroendocrinology of Aging.* New York, Plenum, 1983, p 203.

50. Stearns EL et al: Declining testicular function with age. *Am J Med* 57:761, 1974.

51. Neaves W et al: Leydig cell numbers, daily sperm production, and serum gonadotropin levels in aging men. *J Clin Endocrinol Metab* 59:756, 1984.

52. Tenover J et al: Decreased serum inhibin levels in normal elderly men: Evidence for a decline in Sertoli cell function with aging. *J Clin Endocrinol Metab* 67:455, 1988.

53. Davidson J et al: Hormonal changes and sexual function in aging men. *J Clin Endocrinol Metab* 57:71, 1983.

54. Tenover J et al: The effects of aging in normal men on bioavailable testosterone and luteinizing hormone secretion: Response to clomiphene citrate. *J Clin Endocrinol Metab* 65:1118, 1987.

55. Harman SM et al: Reproductive hormones in aging men. II. Basal pituitary gonadotropins and gonadotropin responses to luteinizing hormone-releasing hormone. *J Clin Endocrinol Metab* 54:547, 1982.

56. Urban R et al: Attenuated release of biologically active luteinizing hormone in healthy aging men. *J Clin Invest* 81:1020, 1988.

57. Morley J: Neuropeptides, behavior, and aging. *J Am Geriatr Soc* 34:52, 1986.

58. Blackman MR et al: Basal serum prolactin levels and prolactin responses to constant infusions of thyrotropin releasing hormone in healthy aging men. *J Gerontol* 41:699, 1986.

59. Steven WJ et al: Long-term treatment of acromegaly with the somatostatin analogue. *N Engl J Med* 313:1576, 1985.

60. Barnard L et al: Treatment of resistant acromegaly with a long-acting somatostatin analogue. *Ann Intern Med* 105:856, 1986.

61. Greenspan S et al: Osteoporosis in men with hyperprolactinemic hypogonadism. *Ann Intern Med* 104:777, 1986.

62. Liuzzi A et al: Low doses of dopamine agonists in the long-term treatment of macroprolactinomas. *N Engl J Med* 313:656, 1985.

63. Carlson H: Gynecomastia. *N Engl J Med* 303:795, 1980.

64. Kaiser F et al: Impotence and aging: Clinical and hormonal factors. *J Am Geriatr Soc* 36:511, 1988.

Chapter 70

THYROID DISEASES

Robert I. Gregerman

HYPERTHYROIDISM

For several reasons, the diagnosis of hyperthyroidism in the elderly is more difficult than in the young. A number of features considered in the young to be "typical" of hyperthyroidism are encountered less often or are less apparent at advanced age. Hence, the patient presents fewer diagnostic cues to the physician. Another factor contributing to difficulty of diagnosis is the frequent co-existence or suspected presence in the elderly of other diseases, to which symptoms and findings may be erroneously ascribed. Young patients are less likely to carry such diagnostic diversions. The remaining difficulty is that the ordinary laboratory tests for hyperthyroidism can fail to be diagnostic in some elderly hyperthyroid individuals. A special consideration is so-called apathetic hyperthyroidism, a clinical state which occurs mainly in the elderly, although it may on rare occasions be encountered in young persons.

Comparisons of the features of hyperthyroidism in the young versus the old can also be difficult. Although a number of studies of hyperthyroidism in the elderly are available, most do not provide comparative data for young patients. The definition of "elderly" or "old" also varies considerably among studies, although most define the elderly as individuals over 60 or 65 years. Clinical findings also undoubtedly vary for genetic or other reasons in different populations in various parts of the world. Nonetheless, it is clear that many aspects of hyperthyroidism are strongly age-dependent.

INCIDENCE OF HYPERTHYROIDISM IN THE ELDERLY

Many clinicians are under the mistaken impression that hyperthyroidism is more common in the young than in the old, or are simply less likely to consider the possibility of hyperthyroidism in the elderly because of an erroneous belief that hyperthyroidism is uncommon in this age group. In fact, studies of the occurrence of the dis-ease in persons over age 60 show a sevenfold greater prevalence than in persons below this age. This statistical fact has led to the rather startling conclusion that hyperthyroidism should be considered a disease of old age.[1]

SYMPTOMS AND SIGNS OF HYPERTHYROIDISM IN THE ELDERLY

Constitutional

Systemic or constitutional symptoms include lack of energy, easy fatigability, and lassitude. Often the patient is merely aware of feeling unwell and—unless prompted—is unable to articulate the complaints. About 50 percent of young patients have these symptoms; fewer than 25 percent of the elderly admit to such problems.[2,3]

Weight loss, nearly as frequent a symptom in hyperthyroidism as is "nervousness," is seen in 60 to 70 percent of hyperthyroid patients of all ages. Those elderly patients who experience marked weight loss often become severely debilitated or develop apathetic hyperthyroidism (see below).

Heat intolerance, a classic symptom of hyperthyroidism, is certainly seen in the elderly but may be seen less frequently, since in some series this complaint can be elicited in only 25 percent of the elderly compared with 50 percent of young patients. However, in other studies, 60 to 70 percent of the elderly admitted to heat intolerance.

Neuromuscular

The dominant presence in hyperthyroidism of central nervous system symptoms is not generally appreciated as such, but all physicians recognize that many patients with hyperthyroidism are "nervous." This vague term includes such symptoms as restlessness (hyperkinesis), irritability, and tremor. The complaint of nervousness is the most common manifestation of hyperthyroidism and is seen in most young patients but in less than 50 percent of the elderly. Tremor—present in 50 percent of the elderly—may be erroneously ascribed to "aging." Other central nervous system symptoms such as depression and withdrawal are seen occasionally.[2,3] Autonomic nervous system symptoms referable to the heart and gastrointestinal tract are discussed below. A variety of less common neurological manifestations of thyroid disease have been recently reviewed.[4]

Muscle weakness, contrary to expectation, is seen in only about 5 percent of elderly patients. While few young individuals complain of this problem spontaneously, some 20 percent will admit to this symptom on specific questioning or can be shown to have weakness on testing. Classically, severe muscle weakness affects the proximal musculature predominantly. Rheumatic complaints, although quite common in elderly patients, do not appear to be increased in hyperthyroidism.

Gastrointestinal

In young patients, a classic symptom of hyperthyroidism is increased appetite, while anorexia is only occasionally encountered. In elderly patients, increased appetite is seen in only about 10 percent while in some 30 percent of cases anorexia is a major feature. When anorexia occurs, weight loss may be striking. Such "unexplained" weight loss in the elderly may trigger a search for a "hidden malignancy."

Not generally appreciated is the occurrence in some elderly patients not only of anorexia but of nausea, vomiting, abdominal pain, and diarrhea. Clinical focus on the gastrointestinal tract in such cases is not surprising. Less common features are dry mouth and dysphagia. Occasionally, constipation rather than increased frequency of stools or diarrhea may occur, but these variations are not unique for the elderly. As many as 15 percent of elderly patients with hyperthyroidism show a combination of anorexia, constipation, and weight loss, a triad strongly suggestive of gastrointestinal tract carcinoma.

Cardiac

Palpitations—awareness of forceful, rapid, or irregular heart action—are very common in young patients, being seen in 75 percent or more of cases. Such cardiac symptoms are also seen in at least 50 percent of the elderly. On the other hand, tachycardia—generally thought to be an almost invariable finding in hyperthyroidism—is seen in no more that 50 percent of cases, whether young or old. Atrial fibrillation is a classic cardiac manifestation of hyperthyroidism, but it is less well known that this problem—when it develops—does so almost exclusively in older patients.

Congestive heart failure occurs in more than 50 percent of elderly patients with hyperthyroidism. A significant number of patients present initially in acute pulmonary edema. While congestive failure due to hyperthyroidism can occur in young persons, it does so infrequently and only in patients with severe, longstanding disease.

Angina in the elderly may be precipitated by hyperthyroidism, or preexistent angina may be exacerbated. Perhaps surprisingly, no obvious tendency to myocardial infarction is noted. It is not generally appreciated that in occasional young persons hyperthyroidism may produce angina pectoris and even myocardial infarction in the absence of angiographic evidence of ischemic heart disease.[5] The possible contribution of this phenomenon to symptoms of angina in the elderly is unknown.

Eye

An important difference between the hyperthyroidism of the young and the elderly is the striking lack of eye findings in old persons, due in large measure to the fact that at least 50 percent of elderly patients have nodular goiter rather than Graves' disease as the cause of their hyperthyroidism. Although hyperthyroidism of any cause can produce minor eye findings, such as lid retraction, lid lag, or stare, only Graves' disease produces major eye problems such as proptosis and exophthalmos. Severe exophthalmos is relatively rare in the young, but it seems to be even less common for elderly persons with Graves' disease to develop severe eye involvement.

Thyroid Enlargement

Almost all young persons with hyperthyroidism have a visibly or palpably enlarged thyroid, while in the elderly about 30 percent do not have even a palpably enlarged gland. In 10 to 15 percent of the elderly no thyroid enlargement can be discerned even by scanning or sonography. The important clinical point is that lack of thyroid enlargement in the elderly by no means excludes a diagnosis of hyperthyroidism.

LABORATORY TESTS IN THE DIAGNOSIS OF THYROID DISEASE IN THE ELDERLY
General

The effect of age on thyroid function tests has been extensively studied. Age, per se, has little effect on the usual parameters of thyroid function. On the other hand, the effects of nonthyroidal illness—which occurs so frequently in the elderly—can have marked effects on these measurements and can obscure correct diagnosis. Furthermore, some of the tests are of little use in the elderly or can actually be dangerous.

Detailed descriptions of thyroid function tests are given elsewhere.[6-8] Below is a brief review of the essentials of such tests followed by a discussion of their results and interpretation in elderly patients.

Standard Tests of Thyroid Function

The standard tests of thyroid function are serum thyroxine (T_4), triiodothyronine (T_3), and triiodothyronine resin uptake (T_3RU). The measurement of serum thyrotropin (TSH) is also invaluable in some situations. Nomenclature for these and related tests can be confusing. The reader may wish to refer to a more comprehensive set of definitions than can be summarized here.[6,7]

The T_3RU test is an indirect measure of thyroxine-binding globulin (TBG), the major protein carrier for T_4 in plasma. The T_3RU is usually reported as the percentage of T_3 absorbed or taken up by a nonspecific absorbent (resin), but it is preferably expressed as a ratio of the patient's test sample to a standard reference serum example (T_3U ratio). A new name for such tests—Thyroid Hormone-Binding Ratio—has been recommended.[7] Recently, some laboratories have started to use direct measurements of TBG as an alternative to the less precise but generally available T_3U ratio. No clear clinical advantage of direct measurement of TBG is yet apparent.

The T_4 is currently measured by radioimmunoassay or displacement analysis. These methods are not directly subject to interference by iodine contamination, although some iodine-containing compounds have effects on thyroxine metabolism and may thereby affect T_4 levels (see "Iodide-Induced Thyrotoxicosis in the Elderly" below).

The T_4 is always assessed in conjunction with T_3U ratio. A high (or low) T_4 can be interpreted as reflecting T_4 secretion only if the plasma binding of T_4 is normal, i.e., only if the TBG (T_3U ratio) is normal. For convenience, the T_4 and T_3U ratio are often combined to give a so-called free-T_4 index (FT$_4$I) by simply multiplying one number times the other ($T_4 \times T_3U$ ratio). This procedure "compensates" for the high or low T_4 which results from abnormality of TBG concentration. The FT$_4$I is also reported by some laboratories as the "T_7" or "T_{12}."

Another test related to the T_4 is the "free T_4 (FT$_4$)," the small fraction of the T_4 that is not bound to protein. In most cases the FT$_4$I parallels the free T_4. The free T_4 is estimated by determining both the T_4 and the non-protein-bound T_4, using equilibrium dialysis (dialyzable fraction), ultrafiltration, or some other technique; the product of T_4 times the dialyzable or ultrafiltrable fraction is the free T_4. Although the free T_4 has long been touted as the most sensitive indicator of hyperthyroidism, problems of interpretation arise in many seriously ill patients, since a variety of nonthyroidal diseases ranging from acute infections to liver disease can result in elevation of the free T_4. The probable explanation for

this phenomenon is the appearance in the plasma during nonthyroidal illness of an inhibitor of protein binding. In this situation the T_4 is normal or low; the free T_4 is elevated only because the dialyzable fraction is increased. Thus, an elevated free T_4 is *not* a specific finding related solely to thyroid status. This latter consideration is important, since many elderly patients suspected of having hyperthyroidism will, in fact, have other nonthyroidal illness that may elevate the free T_4. The diagnosis of hyperthyroidism should be made with great caution if only the free T_4 is elevated.

The T_3 in serum is measured by radioimmunoassay. Like T_4, T_3 measurement is not directly affected by iodide-containing compounds, but its level may be influenced—invariably in a downward direction—by many factors other than thyroid function.

The serum T_3 in young persons is almost always elevated in hyperthyroidism, and the T_3 has been said to be the single most sensitive indicator of hyperthyroidism. A small but diagnostically important proportion of hyperthyroid patients of any age and due to any cause show elevation *only* of the T_3 ("T_3 toxicosis").

Only a small proportion of very elderly patients normally have a minimally low T_3 due to age, per se. However, many nonspecific illnesses, drugs, and even decreased food intake depress the T_3 in the elderly and young alike. Such mechanisms presumably contribute to the finding that the T_3 may not be increased during hyperthyroidism in the elderly (see below).

TSH and the TRH Test

Determination of the serum thyrotropin (TSH) is useful in the diagnosis of hypothyroidism but until recently has not been helpful in hyperthyroidism. Newly available assays are sensitive enough to discern the suppression of TSH that occurs in the presence of even a slightly excessive serum concentration of T_4 or T_3. Thus, the serum TSH in patients with hyperthyroidism is depressed, although it was reported as being within the normal range in older assays. At present the literature does not contain sufficient information concerning the reliability of these new "ultrasensitive" assays in varied clinical situations or in the elderly. At this time a diagnosis of hyperthyroidism in an elderly patient should not be based on suppression of TSH or excluded because the TSH is not suppressed.

Determination of serum TSH after intravenous administration of thyrotropin-releasing hormone (TRH) is useful in diagnosing suspected cases of hyperthyroidism in young persons (TRH test). The normal increase of TSH that follows TRH administration is blunted or abolished by the excessive amounts of thyroid hormones that are produced in hyperthyroidism. The test is used when the diagnosis is suspected but blood hormone levels (T_4,

T_3) are only borderline. In its simplest form, the test is performed by obtaining a baseline serum TSH, administering an intravenous bolus injection of 500 μg TRH, and obtaining another TSH after 20 and 30 minutes, at which time TSH is maximally increased. In the elderly, an additional sample should be obtained at 60 minutes, since the response may occasionally be delayed, especially in the elderly sick.

A *reproducible* increase of serum TSH greater than 2 to 3 μU/ml above the baseline value is a normal response which effectively excludes the diagnosis of hyperthyroidism in patients of any age. However, failure of an elderly person to respond to TRH should not be unequivocally interpreted to indicate the presence of hyperthyroidism, since at advanced age decreased or absent response to TRH is common and can be a normal finding.[9] The response to TRH at any age is also blunted or absent in many patients with severe nonthyroidal illness and in individuals given such agents as glucocorticoids and dopamine. Euthyroid patients with multinodular goiter may also fail to respond to TRH.[10]

Thyroidal Radioiodide Uptake (RaIU) Tests

RaIU tests are now much less often used—or needed—than in the past. These tests are far more expensive and time-consuming than measurements of blood hormones. Test values may be depressed by contamination from iodide-containing compounds, especially in hospitalized patients. Moreover, in recent studies of the utility of RaIU tests in the elderly, it has been clear that RaIU tests have lost much of their earlier diagnostic value. In a review that covered the period 1957–70, the RaIU was diagnostic in over 90 percent of cases.[3] Since then normal values for RaIU have fallen in both euthyroid and hyperthyroid patients—presumably a result of increased dietary iodide—and the tests have become much less helpful. In young persons the RaIU is still diagnostic in nearly 90 percent, but in the elderly only 50 percent have diagnostic values. In elderly hyperthyroid patients with multinodular goiter, diagnostic values are seen in only 30 percent, despite adjustment of the normal range downward in recent years.[11] Thus, the RaIU is not likely to be diagnostically helpful and should certainly not be used early in an evaluation, while a normal or even a low uptake is not evidence against a diagnosis of hyperthyroidism. The decreased uptake of radioiodide of recent years has also had the consequence that the dose of RaI used therapeutically must be considerably increased [see "RaI Therapy of Hyperthyroidism due to Toxic Adenoma ("Toxic Nodule")" below].

Special situations in which measurement of RaIU remains helpful are hyperthyroidism due to iodides and lymphocytic ("silent") thyroiditis; in both situations the RaIU is characteristically low (<5 percent) (see below).

Occasionally, measurement of RaIU is made as a "by-product" of radionuclide scanning of the thyroid. The use of RaIU for suppression testing to determine autonomous thyroid function in suspected hyperthyroidism is now rarely performed. Suppression tests involve administration of T_3 or T_4 and should be undertaken with caution—if at all—in the elderly. The preferred alternative to suppression testing is the TRH test. Both suppression tests and the TRH test may be abnormal in nontoxic nodular goiter.[10] Details of suppression testing are given elsewhere.[8]

RESULTS OF LABORATORY TESTS IN HYPERTHYROID ELDERLY PATIENTS

T_4 and T_3 in Blood

Only a few surveys of hyperthyroidism in the elderly present their clinical findings in correlation with thyroid hormone measurements using currently employed thyroid function tests. Studies using the older protein-bound iodine (PBI) but with no measurements of TBG (T_3RU, FT_4I) reported up to 20 percent of elderly clinically hyperthyroid patients to have normal values, while fewer than 10 percent of young patients had determinations that were within the normal range.[3] Some of these patients with normal PBI must have had abnormal TBG and would not have shown a normal FT_4I had these measurements been made. However, even recent studies show that about 10 percent of both elderly and young patients with hyperthyroidism can have a normal T_4 *and* FT_4I. Some of these patients have hyperthyroidism due to elevated serum T_3 (T_3 toxicosis).

The serum T_3 is considered by some—at least in young patients—to be the single most sensitive indicator of hyperthyroidism. Elevation of T_3 is virtually diagnostic of hyperthyroidism and a finding of special importance, since an elevated T_3 excludes the possibility of misdiagnosis based on only an elevation of T_4 (and FT_4I) due to nonthyroidal illness in the elderly (see below). However, although the T_3 is elevated in more than 90 percent of young patients, it has been reported normal in up to 30 to 40 percent of elderly hyperthyroid patients.[11]

The explanation for the failure of T_3 to be elevated in some elderly patients with hyperthyroidism is not entirely clear. However, this phenomenon undoubtedly relates in part to the dual origin of T_3. Normally, most of the T_3 in serum arises from deiodination of T_4; only a small amount arises by direct secretion from the thyroid. In hyperthyroidism an increased but variable amount of T_3 is directly secreted by the thyroid. Several factors, including nonthyroidal illness, drugs, and even decreased food intake, all of which are present with increased frequency in the elderly, can depress the serum T_3 by interfering with the extrathyroidal conversion of T_4

to T_3. The expected result in the hyperthyroid patient would be a lowering of T_3—which would otherwise be elevated—into the normal range. One would not, however, expect a markedly low T_3 in a hyperthyroid elderly person.

Other factors may operate to lower the T_3 in the elderly hyperthyroid patient. The thyroidal secretion ratio of T_3/T_4 is in part determined by the plasma iodide level, a low T_3/T_4 secretion ratio being favored by a high level of plasma iodide. Since the plasma iodide level is positively correlated with age,[9] the result may be reduced thyroidal secretion of T_3 in the elderly hyperthyroid patient.

Despite the apparently normal T_3 in a significant proportion of elderly hyperthyroid patients, hyperthyroidism due only to excess levels of T_3 with normal T_4 and FT_4I (T_3 toxicosis) does occasionally occur in elderly patients. The estimated number of such cases varies but probably does not exceed 5 percent of hyperthyroid patients at any age.

The reduced frequency of elevation of T_3 in elderly hyperthyroid patients should not be misconstrued or used as an argument against T_3 testing in the elderly. Testing of T_3 as part of the *initial* evaluation process is still useful when expeditious evaluation is essential or T_3 toxicosis must be excluded. An elevated T_3 helps to differentiate true hyperthyroidism from elevation of T_4 (and FT_4I) due to nonspecific illness (see below). It should also be noted that high-dose radiocontrast agents can elevate the T_4 (and FT_4I) and decrease the T_3 for up to 3 weeks following cholecystography.[12] When considerations of cost are important or screening is the goal, measurement of the T_3 test may be deferred until the serum T_4 (and FT_4I) are known.

Nonhyperthyroid Elevation of T_4 (and FT_4I) in the Elderly: Hyperthyroxinemia of Nonspecific Illness

It is now generally appreciated that severe nonthyroidal illness can depress the T_4 (and FT_4I). This phenomenon has been termed the *euthyroid sick syndrome* and is discussed elsewhere (see "Hypothyroidism" below). Not generally appreciated, however, is the realization that nonthyroidal illness can produce a different type of euthyroid sick syndrome in which the T_4 is elevated rather than reduced. The term *euthyroid hyperthyroxinemia* has been used for such cases. The problem is not unique in the elderly, because it can be encountered in young persons, especially those newly admitted to a hospital with an acute psychiatric diagnosis.[13] However, in the latter cases the elevation of T_4 (and also of FT_4I and even T_3) subsides within a week or two. The situation in the elderly is usually more difficult to resolve. Given a severely ill elderly person with a constellation of nonspecific findings, the issue of hyperthyroidism may properly

be raised. Elevation of T_4 (and FT_4I) is by no means rare in such persons, and some of these patients may be inappropriately diagnosed as having hyperthyroidism.[1,3] Useful tests in this situation are the determination of T_3, since elevation of the T_3 unequivocally confirms a diagnosis of hyperthyroidism and the TRH test which—if the test is normal—excludes the diagnosis. However, it must be reiterated that the T_3 may not be elevated in hyperthyroidism in the elderly, while age and illness often impair the normal response to TRH. When patients with T_4 elevation due to nonthyroidal illness are followed—without intervention, if the clinical situation permits—the hyperthyroxinemia subsides and the clinical course eventually reveals the euthyroid state of the patient.[13]

SPECIAL VARIANTS OF HYPERTHYROIDISM IN THE ELDERLY: MASKED AND APATHETIC HYPERTHYROIDISM

These terms have been used to describe clinical types of hyperthyroidism which are seen mainly in the elderly.[14] The term *masked* was used to denote patients who presented with thyrotoxic cardiac disease where focus on this single system involvement masked the underlying problem. Hyperthyroidism in the elderly is so frequently masked and this situation is so common that the term has probably outlived its usefulness. If the term is retained, one should note that the system responsible for the masking can be digestive or central nervous as well as cardiac; the remainder of the clinical picture is that of hyperthyroidism in the elderly.

The term *apathetic hyperthyroidism*—originally used a half-century ago—described a form of thyrotoxicosis in which the usual hyperkinesis of the typical young hyperthyroid patient was replaced by "nonactivation." The latter term, originally applied to the entire patient, has proved to be remarkably accurate and predictive, since we now clearly appreciate the frequent failure of thyroid hormone excess to activate or enhance activity of the central and autonomic nervous systems of the elderly. The patients were originally described as quiet and disinterested or apathetic. We are now more inclined to use the term *depressed*, at least until the diagnosis of hyperthyroidism is appreciated. Another originally described feature—now rarely if ever seen—was pigmented, cool, dry skin which was often wrinkled and gave the patient an appearance of being older than his or her chronological age. Additional features were smaller than expected thyroid, absence of usual eye signs but with occasional blepharoptosis, and absence of tachycardia. These negative features are now regularly associated with hyperthyroidism in the elderly; rarely a similar picture may be seen in a young person. When a group of apathetic patients was defined using the term to include

(1) blunted affect and/or depression, (2) absence of hyperkinetic motor activity, and (3) slowed mentation (retarded response to questioning, slow speech, and short attention span), all the remaining features—including those of the laboratory—were those that we can now identify as characteristic of hyperthyroidism in the elderly.[2] Thus, the term *apathetic hyperthyroidism* is probably best used to describe cases which show "nonactivation" and its attendant psychological and psychiatric features rather than a distinctive clinical and laboratory entity, as it has been considered by some.[14]

Iodide-Induced Thyrotoxicosis (IIT) in the Elderly

Iodide, iodine-containing x-ray contrast agents, and iodine-containing drugs can induce hyperthyroidism in patients without previous thyroid disease, as well as in individuals with previous hyperthyroidism or Graves' disease, and in those with preexisting nodular or nonnodular goiter. In regions where goiter is still endemic or iodide intake is very low because iodization of salt was never introduced (e.g., Germany), the occurrence of this phenomenon seems to be much higher than in the United States.[15]

A number of reports suggest that the risk of IIT is greatest in the elderly. Subjects with nodular goiters of long standing seem to be at greatest risk. In cases of nonendemic goiter, women are more often affected by IIT than are men. In the absence of preexisting thyroid disease, men more often develop IIT. Evidence of Graves' disease is absent. The thyroid may not be enlarged and is nontender. When enlargement is present, it may resolve with resolution of the disease. The RaIU is low. Characteristically, the disease is self-limited (1 to 6 months).

The elderly are more likely than the young to undergo radiographic examinations that employ iodine-containing contrast media (gallbladder examinations, pyelograms, angiograms, computed tomography using "enhancement"), and these may contribute to increased risk of developing IIT. The physician should be especially alert to the subsequent development of IIT in elderly patients who have undergone radiographic examinations 6 months to several years earlier. Another issue is that of iodide-containing drugs. Such agents are rarely used in the United States, but one, amiodarone, is widely used in Europe for treatment of angina pectoris and arrhythmias and was recently introduced here. About 2 percent of patients receiving this drug have developed IIT. This agent, like some compounds used to visualize the gallbladder, can inhibit the conversion of T_4 to T_3 and produce mild increase of the T_4 *and* TSH. Elevation of T_4 alone should not be taken as evidence for hyperthyroidism in the situation.[15]

The therapy of IIT is symptomatic and similar to that of hyperthyroidism due to painless thyroiditis (see below).

Hyperthyroidism due to Lymphocytic "Silent" (or "Painless") Thyroiditis

In the past few years a variant of thyroiditis has been found to be responsible for an increasing number of cases of hyperthyroidism. The syndrome is associated with lymphocytic infiltration of the thyroid, minimal-to-modest painless and nontender thyroid enlargement, depression of RaIU, a relatively mild degree of hyperthyroidism, and a self-limited course of several months. Blood levels of both T_4 and T_3 are elevated.[16] Most cases have been described in young women, often in the postpartum state, but cases in the elderly have been recognized.[17] The disease can be suspected if the RaIU—often the only clue to diagnosis—is obtained and found to be very low (less than 5 percent). Definitive diagnosis can, of course, be made only by needle biopsy of the thyroid. Symptomatic therapy with propranolol is appropriate. RaI therapy is neither appropriate nor possible in view of the low RaIU, and there is no clear rationale for the use of antithyroid drugs.

A recent epidemic of thyrotoxicosis was traced to the widespread use of ground beef that inadvertently contained thyroid glands.[18] The possibility has been raised that some of the cases of thyrotoxicosis originally described as "silent thyroiditis" with transient hyperthyroidism may in fact have been due to this source of exogenous thyroid hormone.[19] However, while silent thyroiditis may be a heterogeneous syndrome, it cannot be so easily explained away. Follow-up of the original cases has shown that nearly 50 percent of cases had persistent thyroid disease of some sort, while a significant number developed hypothyroidism. These issues have no special relevance to geriatric medicine, except that elderly patients have been involved and the topic has received much attention in the recent past.

THERAPY OF HYPERTHYROIDISM IN THE ELDERLY

For most elderly patients with hyperthyroidism, whether due to Graves' disease or nodular goiter, radioactive iodide (^{131}I, RaI) is the therapy of choice. Surgery is rarely—if ever—indicated for hyperthyroidism in the elderly. Moreover, the conventional approach used for young persons—in which a low initial RaI dose is used in an attempt to avoid hypothyroidism—should be modified for the elderly. The conventional approach for the young often requires multiple doses of RaI, thus delaying and prolonging the time required for restoration of the euthyroid state. For a variety of obvious medical reasons, such delay is not acceptable in the elderly. If serious consequences of hyperthyroidism are not already present, they may develop before therapy is completed; some therapeutic urgency is thus always present in older patients. Therefore, relatively large doses of RaI should be used in treatment of the elderly. The use of such doses of RaI—which raises concerns about possible long-term adverse effects of radiation in young patients—is not a concern in the older age-group.

The large doses of RaI used to eliminate the hyperthyroid state rapidly are also more likely to produce hypothyroidism. Such therapy has been termed *deliberate thyroid ablation.* It is the author's preferred method of administering RaI to elderly patients. In most cases, hyperthyroidism is eliminated within 4 to 6 weeks; complications are not seen. Even when ablative doses of RaI are used, a second dose may occasionally be necessary. Concern over exacerbation of the hyperthyroidism by RaI is essentially anecdotal and based on isolated reports from the early days of RaI therapy. These exacerbations were attributed to increased circulating thyroid hormone caused by destruction of the thyroid, but the observations were based on measurements of PBI, which included nonhormonal iodine, and not on measurements of the specific thyroid hormones, T_4 and T_3. Serial observations of the latter following ablative RaI therapy have given no evidence for even transiently increased hormone levels; rather, T_4 and T_3 fall progressively, beginning almost immediately following the RaI. Ablative doses of RaI are in the range of 12 to 15 mCi for small to moderately enlarged thyroid glands; doses of up to 30 mCi may be used for large glands or multinodular goiters. Determination of RaIU is helpful to the therapist in selection of the dose.

Use of Thioamide Antithyroid Drugs

There remains a place for the use of propylthouracil or methimazole in the elderly. In order to assure that the time needed to reach the euthyroid state will be as short as possible, an antithyroid drug may be administered following the RaI. If the physician is concerned—despite the assurances offered above—about the possibility of exacerbation of the hyperthyroidism, the patient may be made euthyroid with an antithyroid drug prior to definitive treatment with RaI, the therapeutic dose given, and the drug possibly readministered afterward. Details of antithyroid drug dosage, monitoring of the patient following RaI, etc., are given in standard texts on the subject.[8]

It is important to recall that in the elderly—as in the young—the use of a prolonged course of antithyroid drugs in an attempt to allow a remission in Graves' disease is attended by less than a 50 percent chance of success. Furthermore, a remission following drug therapy can never be expected in hyperthyroidism due to nodular goiter. Since at least one-half of cases of hyperthyroidism in the elderly are due to nodular goiter, and no more than one-half of those due to Graves' disease can expect remission, RaI becomes the definitive therapy for 75 percent or more of all cases of hyperthyroidism in the elderly.

Adjunctive Therapy with β-Blockers and Iodide

Propranolol is useful for symptomatic relief of tachycardia, restlessness, and tremor. Large doses of propranolol may be necessary in hyperthyroidism (up to 640 mg/day). Theoretically, at least, the use of such large doses in elderly individuals may precipitate or worsen heart failure by depressing already compromised myocardial contractility. However, if rapid heart rate contributes to the failure, propranolol should be tried judiciously. Several reports suggest that guanethidine may be a useful adjunct to therapy of severe hyperthyroidism with congestive heart failure, at least in younger patients. While experience is limited, this drug should be kept in mind as an alternative to propranolol. Dosage in hyperthyroidism—like that of propranolol—greatly exceeds that for treatment of hypertension. Postural hypotension due to guanethidine is not a problem while the patient is hyperthyroid but develops as the hyperthyroidism is controlled by RaIU or antithyroid drugs. The newer β-blockers such as atenolol and timolol have had limited use in the treatment of hyperthyroidism. While undoubtedly effective, their advantages over propranolol remain to be proved. Some of these agents may be less likely than propranolol to produce bronchospasm or to depress myocardial contractility. The propranolol-like drug practolol, withdrawn from use in Europe because of noncardiac toxicity and never available in the United States, was successfully used in the treatment of cardiac failure associated with hyperthyroidism. Pindolol, a blocker with intrinsic sympathomimetic activity, is not only less effective than propranolol in reducing heart rate in hypothyroid patients but also may accelerate tachycardia, although other manifestations of hyperthyroidism may be ameliorated.

Iodide therapy should be used in patients with severe disease and those in need of rapid control. Iodide should not be given immediately prior to therapy with RaI but may follow, either alone or in combination with an antithyroid drug. The dose is 1 drop (50 mg) of a saturated solution of potassium iodide (KI) given twice daily. Larger doses are unnecessary and may lead to iodide toxicity.[15] As soon as the T_4 has returned to the normal range, iodide can be discontinued.

RaI Therapy of Hyperthyroidism due to Toxic Adenoma ("Toxic Nodule")

Although RaI is effective therapy for hyperthyroidism due to toxic adenoma, relatively large doses may be necessary. When treating younger patients, some authorities are reluctant to treat with RaI because of the large doses required, but in the elderly RaI remains the therapy of choice. A large, ablative dose of 30 to 50 mCi of ^{131}I (delivering 10 to 15 mCi to the adenoma) should be used. If the surrounding normal tissue—which is suppressed—survives the therapy, the patient may become euthyroid; hypothyroidism, if it ensues, should be treated in the usual way. Surgery may occasionally have a place in the treatment of an elderly patient with a toxic adenoma. The procedure may be performed as a simple nodulectomy under regional-block anesthesia.[20]

Follow-up Post-RaI and Treatment of Ablation-Related Hypothyroidism

If RaI is the sole therapy and an antithyroid drug is not used, the T_4 monitors thyroid function quite well. The T_4 should fall significantly within a few weeks. If the T_4 fails to reach normal levels within 8 weeks, additional RaI should be given. As soon as the T_4 falls below the normal range, or the patient develops symptoms of hypothyroidism, thyroxine can be added to avoid the development of severe hypothyroidism. If the patient is very old or has had major complications, especially ischemic or dysrhythmic cardiac disease, the dose of thyroxine can be 0.025 mg daily by mouth; otherwise 0.075 mg can be given from the onset (see "Therapy of Hypothyroidism in the Elderly" below). Further adjustment of dosage upward or downward at several monthly intervals can then be made as necessary, based on the T_4. It is not necessary to raise the T_4 to a level which returns the elevated TSH entirely to normal, although a normal TSH is a precise physiological endpoint.

HYPOTHYROIDISM

The problem of hypothyroidism in the elderly deserves special attention for several reasons. Not only is hypothyroidism commonly encountered at advanced age, but in the elderly the diagnosis becomes more difficult and can be easily overlooked. The cause of the diagnostic difficulty in the elderly has long been recognized.[21]

> It is precisely at this time of life that gradual degenerative processes are usually expected and are tolerated—if reluctantly. All well and good—unless the true diagnosis is myxedema. How easy it is to attribute to age rather than to myxedema such conditions as mental slowing, lack of energy, neurotic or psychotic behavior, loss of . . . hearing, odd paresthesias, gain in weight, musculoskeletal discomfort, unsteady gait, change in facial appearance, and dry skin. The changes are often so subtle and gradual that the patient, his family, and his physician have almost continuously observed them and are thrown off guard . . . .

The most difficult step in diagnosis is the simple clinical appreciation of the possibility that the patient may be hypothyroid. Once the thought occurs to the physician, aspects of the history and physical examination will fall into place and the laboratory findings will easily confirm the diagnosis.

Even when patients have been successfully treated for hypothyroidism—either idiopathic or iatrogenic following radioiodide therapy of hyperthyroidism—problems can arise.[21]

> When they are young and alert enough to have relatives or physicians who are sufficiently interested in them to supervise their medical care, the treatment of myxedema is remarkably simple. It is precisely when such patients are older, when their judgment is perhaps less good, and when they are without this close surveillance that they become most vulnerable not only to the common habit of stopping the use of thyroid substance but also to the effects of lack of thyroid hormone to the point of irreversible pathophysiologic changes.

Several studies of large populations have shown that about 2 percent of apparently healthy adults are clinically hypothyroid; most of these individuals are in the later decades. With laboratory screening procedures an even larger percentage of the elderly—perhaps 4 percent of those over 60—can be shown to have previously unrecognized hypothyroidism at the time of admission to a hospital. In a recent study of patients over age 60 who were screened for thyroid disease on admission to a hospital, a startling 12 percent had hypothyroidism.[22]

CAUSES OF HYPOTHYROIDISM IN THE ELDERLY

While the same causes can produce hypothyroidism in the elderly as in young persons, most cases in the elderly are nongoitrous, idiopathic, and autoimmune; i.e., the vast majority show elevations of thyroid autoantibodies in the plasma. An ever-increasing number of cases are iatrogenic, i.e., the result of previous therapy of hyperthyroidism with radioiodide or by surgery.

As populations grow older, an increasing proportion of persons have elevations of serum thyrotropin (TSH) while their serum thyroxine (T_4) is still quite normal. These individuals are felt to have autoimmune thyroiditis which has produced hypothyroidism of a degree that provokes increased secretion of TSH and elevation of blood TSH—a sensitive indicator of hypothyroidism—but has not yet produced clinically obvious manifestations. They represent a subset of the elderly who are victims of an age-related autoimmune disease process, but they do not represent the fate of all persons as they age.

Much was written in the past of the notion that aging is due to hypothyroidism or of age-related alteration of thyroid hormone action on peripheral tissues. Although aging is accompanied by decreased metabolic rate and decreased rate of thyroid hormone secretion, these changes find their causes in changes of body composition with age and in the mechanisms for metabolic disposal of thyroid hormones. No evidence exists in the human for any gross alteration of thyroid hormone action during aging. These concepts are discussed in detail elsewhere.[9]

CLINICAL PRESENTATION OF HYPOTHYROIDISM IN THE ELDERLY

There has long been a tendency to describe the symptoms of hypothyroidism as either "classic" or, conversely, uncommon or unusual. The latter symptoms are in fact not nearly as unusual as once believed and are now being more widely recognized.[21,23] Relative frequencies of occurrence of various signs and symptoms vary widely in different reports.

The so-called classic symptoms and signs of hypothyroidism are slowness of speech, thought, and movement; hoarse voice; cold intolerance; facial puffiness (myxedema); thickening and scaling of skin with an acquired yellowish tint (carotenemia); dryness and coarseness of hair; nonpitting peripheral edema; bradycardia; slowed gastrointestinal function with constipation; and delay of relaxation phase of deep tendon reflexes. These and other less common findings are described in more detail below. However, from the point of view of clinical recognition of hypothyroidism in the elderly, an important fact has been appreciated only recently. In contrast to the currently and widely held notion that classic symptoms dominate the clinical presentation of most elderly patients making recognition of the disease readily apparent, the fact is that only about one-third of all cases present with such findings; two-thirds present with nothing more than debilitation and apathy. Thus, the clinical recognition of hypothyroidism in the elderly can be very difficult. A strong argument for screening by laboratory means has been made.[24,25] The validity of this view should become apparent from the information presented below.

Hypothyroidism Versus Myxedema

The deposition of mucopolysaccharides in subcutaneous and other tissues and the development of fluid accumulations in body cavities and joints constitute the clinical state known as *myxedema*. Not generally appreciated is the very important fact that symptomatic hypothyroidism may occur in the absence of overt myxedema. Thus, the terms *hypothyroidism* and *myxedema* are not truly interchangeable and should not be used as such. Hypothyroidism in the elderly—because it is more likely to remain unappreciated for a long period and because even severe cases may escape diagnosis—is more likely to be associated with true myxedema than is hypothyroidism in young persons.

CLINICAL FEATURES CONTRASTED IN YOUNG VERSUS ELDERLY INDIVIDUALS

Psychological and Psychiatric Manifestations

Lethargy and increased sleep requirement are common with hypothyroidism at all ages but may be erroneously attributed to aging when encountered in the elderly. Hypothyroid patients are classically placid and torporous, showing sluggish mental function with exceedingly slow patterns of thought and speech. It has been believed that in the elderly hypothyroidism may cause a reversible type of dementia characterized by confusion and disorientation. Other commonly encountered mental changes include impaired cognitive function, decreased level of awareness, irritability, and paranoia. Occasionally psychosis—colorfully described as myxedema madness—may occur. An important study of newly diagnosed cases of hypothyroidism in elderly patients presents a different concept.[24] About one-quarter of the patients were found to have a depressive illness and a much smaller number paranoia or delirium. The number of depressed patients was several times greater than in a control group, suggesting that hypothyroidism in the elderly predisposes to the development of these psychiatric disturbances. In contrast, no excess number of cases of dementia was seen. Response to thyroxine therapy of the depressed and paranoid patients was excellent while the demented patients did not respond. These results notwithstanding, it is certainly true that occasional hypothyroid patients with dementia do recover with thyroxine therapy; unfortunately, they appear to be disappointingly exceptional. The earlier literature on this subject and other neurological aspects of hypothyroidism have been well reviewed.[4]

Dementia in Hypothyroidism

It is true that senile dementia is not infrequently accompanied by hypothyroidism. However, coincidental association would not be unexpected in view of the frequency of both diseases. While many have held the view that dementia may be *caused* by hypothyroidism (myxedema), this conclusion is not statistically established.[24] Furthermore, only rarely will a truly demented hypothyroid individual return to normal psychiatric function following restoration of the euthyroid state (see above). A somewhat more optimistic viewpoint may be held by those who fail to differentiate between dementia and the slowed but appropriate mentation of the severely hypothyroid person. It is probably the reversibility of this slowed mentation that has given rise to the notion that hypothyroidism may produce an easily treatable form of dementia.

Central Nervous System

Cold intolerance due to temperature malregulation is a common phenomenon in the very old, resulting in hypothermia on minimal exposure to modest reductions of environmental temperature. These phenomena are exaggerated in hypothyroidism in which frank hypothermia may occasionally become the presenting manifestation. A clue in the differential diagnosis is the occasional occurrence of pink to red skin color resulting from peripheral vasodilation in nonhypothyroid elderly patients who are hypothermic. One does not encounter such skin changes in hypothyroidism.

Impairment of VIIIth nerve function seems to be a special feature of the hypothyroid state. Both auditory and vestibular branches can be affected, although the auditory manifestations are more common and more generally recognized. Decreased auditory acuity is, of course, an invariable accompaniment of aging (presbycusis), but hypothyroidism can also produce hearing loss and tinnitus. Again, these problems—when they develop—are often attributed to aging. Fluid accumulations in middle ear and/or endolymph have been blamed for the hearing loss of hypothyroidism. The deafness associated with hypothyroidism is frequently reversible with treatment. Ataxia and vertigo may also be seen, presumably related to a similar mechanism. Improvement is said to occur when the hypothyroid state is treated.

Cerebellar Function

Cerebellar function—like cerebral function—may also be affected in hypothyroidism. When this uncommon event occurs, it is always in the elderly. Ataxia is common and is often mistakenly attributed to aging. Patients may offer as their presenting complaints unsteadiness, loss of equilibrium, poor balance, and even incoordination of their extremities. However, nystagmus and intention tremor are rare. Reversibility with therapy is usual, but coexistence of hypothyroidism with other neurological problems is not uncommon in the elderly. When neurological deficits disappointingly remain after therapy of the hypothyroidism, it is often not possible to determine whether the effects of hypothyroidism were irreversible or whether the hypothyroidism did, in fact, occur concomitantly with some other neuropathic process.

Other Neuromuscular Problems

Complex disturbances of respiratory function can occur in severe hypothyroidism. These include impaired chest wall mechanics and complicated disturbances of upper airway function. Recently, an increased prevalence of hypothyroidism has been noted in patients with the sleep apnea syndrome. Such problems may contribute to the pathophysiology of myxedema coma, but—aside from the likelihood that this dreaded complication is more likely to occur in old persons—no special relationship to aging is clear.

Peripheral Nervous System

Many elderly patients with hypothyroidism complain of paresthesias in their extremities. The most common of such problems in hypothyroid patients of all ages is a nerve entrapment syndrome in which the median nerve is compressed in the carpal tunnel. However, this change is also seen in association with many other clinical states and does not seem to be especially associated with advanced age.

Skin

Classic changes of skin in hypothyroidism include dryness, scaling, and subcutaneous thickening ("doughy" consistency), the latter due to mucopolysaccharide deposition. In the elderly, in whom epidermal atrophy is common, the superimposition of the changes of hypothyroidism may produce a combination of changes which result in a stiff, translucent appearance described as "parchment-like." These changes are especially easy to appreciate over the backs of the hands and the forearms. While many hypothyroid persons develop puffiness or fullness around the eyes, elderly persons are especially prone to develop fluid- (lymph) filled sacs ("bags of water") beneath the lower eyelids. This sign is not pathognomonic, but its presence should be a strong clue to the possible presence of hypothyroidism in the elderly. The mechanism of edema formation in myxedema has been studied.[26]

Diffuse loss of scalp hair is common in the elderly hypothyroid patient. Clinical anecdote has it that the loss of the outer third of eyebrows—well-described in younger patients—occurs infrequently in the elderly.

Musculoskeletal and Rheumatic Disorders

One of the most common accompaniments of aging is the development of musculoskeletal disease, especially osteoarthritis. Furthermore, arthritis-like symptoms are very common in hypothyroid patients. Osteoarthritis, however, should be diagnosed on the basis of objective findings in the elderly—as in all patients.

The problem of diagnosis may be compounded by the development in hypothyroidism of joint swelling with synovial effusions containing calcium pyrophosphate crystals, but signs of active joint inflammation will be lacking. These findings can easily and erroneously be attributed to minor degrees of osteoarthritis shown on x ray. Other possible misdiagnoses include seronegative rheumatoid arthritis and fibrositis.

Although painful extremities, back pain, stiffness, cramps, and other symptoms are all too readily ascribed to "arthritis," careful history-taking can provide the first clue to the nonarthritic nature of these symptoms in hypothyroidism which are, in fact, due to myopathy rather than skeletal changes. Patients usually complain of muscle weakness or easy fatigability and have difficulty with repetitive movements. The myopathy is accompanied by elevated concentrations of muscle enzymes in the plasma. Creatine phosphokinase (CPK) is especially likely to be increased, but serum glutamic oxaloacetic transaminase (SGOT), aldolase, and lactic dehydrogenase are also increased in up to 80 percent of hypothyroid patients and in all with significant muscular symptoms. Response to therapy is gratifying, but worsening of symptoms may occur during the first few weeks following institution of therapy. Hypertrophy of muscle and pseudomyotonia are rare in hypothyroidism and are not age-related.

Gastrointestinal Disorders

Constipation is such a common complaint in the elderly that it is not likely to alert the physician to the possibility of this frequent accompaniment of hypothyroidism. A diagnosis of hypothyroidism may be suggested by the radiologist who discovers megacolon during barium examination of the colon.

Cardiovascular

Whether hypothyroidism in the human is associated with accelerated atherosclerosis has been debated for many years. Recent evidence suggests that women with Hashimoto's thyroiditis have an increased frequency of ischemic heart disease. Certainly hypercholesterolemia and hyperlipidemia are accompaniments of the hypothyroid state. The experimental induction of hypothyroidism has been a common device to ensure the development of diet-induced atherosclerosis in experimental animals. Thus, experimental evidence suggests that severe hypothyroidism may predispose to atherosclerotic disease.

Hypothyroidism appears to impair cardiac function and can result in cardiomegaly. In addition, pericardial effusion is not infrequent and may produce the appearance of cardiomegaly, sometimes in association with pleural effusions. Whether overt congestive heart failure can occur as a result of hypothyroid cardiomyopathy is not clear. Occasionally ascites may be a presenting feature of hypothyroidism. Usually, but not always, other manifestations of the disease are readily apparent by this point of severity. In the elderly the presence of ascites is not infrequently attributed to heart failure, especially if cardiomegaly (unrecognized pericardial effusion) is simultaneously present and there is peripheral swelling, albeit nonpitting edema. These diagnostic errors are not uncommon in the elderly. However, given these cir-

cumstances, it is not surprising that congestive heart failure may be diagnosed in elderly patients and a digitalis glycoside administered. Clinical digitalis toxicity may then result from increased sensitivity to digitalis and decreased metabolic clearance that are both present in hypothyroidism.

Hypertension, like hypothyroidism, is positively correlated with age, and their coexistence is not remarkable. However, hypothyroidism appears to predispose to the development of hypertension. Perhaps related is the documented increase of plasma norepinephrine which increases with aging but in a striking fashion only in hypothyroid persons. In any event, some 30 to 50 percent of hypothyroid hypertensive patients can be expected to become normotensive when treated with thyroid hormone. A short duration of hypothyroidism seems to be associated with reversibility of the hypertensive state.

Renal and Electrolyte

Abnormalities of water metabolism occur in many hypothyroid patients, although it is only a minority who show hyponatremia, the ultimate expression of an inability to excrete water normally. Underlying these abnormalities are several factors, including altered renal hemodynamics and excessive secretion of ADH. Overtly hyponatremic patients with hypothyroidism are nearly always elderly. Whether this in some way relates to the known effect of age on water metabolism and the enhanced secretion of ADH[27] or is merely a reflection of the association of hypothyroidism with advanced age is not clear. Nonetheless, hypothyroidism must be included in the differential diagnosis of the syndrome of inappropriate secretion of antidiuretic hormone (SIADH) and chronic hyponatremia in the elderly.

Hematological

Elderly individuals who develop a macrocytic anemia come under investigation for deficiency of vitamin B_{12} (pernicious anemia) or folate deficiency (dietary); another possibility is hypothyroidism. Clues to the differential diagnosis can be found in the morphology of the polymorphonuclear leukocytes (multilobed) and platelets (enlarged) in vitamin B_{12} or folate deficiency; these changes do not occur in hypothyroidism in which only the red blood cells are affected. Macrocytosis in a hypothyroid patient may occasionally be due to true vitamin B_{12} deficiency which coexists because of the 20-fold increased incidence of pernicious anemia in patients with autoimmune thyroid disease. Rarely, in an old person with hypothyroidism and macrocytosis, the red cell abnormality may not disappear with replacement hormone therapy, since the very elderly may have a mild macrocytosis (mean corpuscular volume ± 100 μm^3) which is apparently related to aging per se.

Drug Effects

Elderly patients are often more sensitive to the pharmacological toxic effects of drugs than the young. Similar drug effects are seen in hypothyroid patients. When hypothyroidism occurs in the elderly, the effect appears to be additive. The usual doses of sedative drugs may produce somnolence or coma, while ordinary anesthesia may result in paralysis of the respiratory center. Prolonged periods may be required to recover from ordinary general anesthesia. These phenomena constitute a cogent argument against elective surgery for elderly patients known to have hypothyroidism.

Coma as a Complication in the Elderly

Myxedema coma only rarely occurs in young individuals and seems to be mainly a complication of the hypothyroid state in the elderly.

Severe headaches may precede the onset of coma. Coma can be precipitated by such factors as hypothermia on exposure to cold (even that which can be encountered in a home that is not well heated), trauma, infectious illness (e.g., pneumonia), drugs (hypnotics, sedatives, analgesics, anesthetics, or the psychotropic agents so commonly used in the elderly), and nonspecific stress (trauma). Some have suggested that coma results from "immediate" causes such as electrolyte disturbances (hyponatremia, hypokalemia), hypoglycemia, and respiratory failure with hypoxia and hypercapnia. In most patients some of these features are present but not to a degree that would ordinarily be expected to result in coma. Not well appreciated is the prodrome of severe frontal or occipital headache and new onset of grand mal seizures ending in coma.[28] In some of these patients the use of anticonvulsants in conventional dosage may contribute to prolongation of the duration of the coma.

Contrary to general belief, patients with coma due to hypothyroidism may regain consciousness without having received specific therapy with thyroxine. The physician should not be dissuaded from the diagnosis nor from institution of thyroid hormone therapy by apparently spontaneous recovery from coma. There is agreement among most experts that thyroid hormone therapy should be promptly and vigorously instituted as soon as the diagnosis of coma due to hypothyroidism is made or seriously considered. Differentiation of myxedema coma from the "euthyroid sick syndrome" is discussed below.

LABORATORY DIAGNOSIS

The usual indices of thyroid function (T_4, T_4 index, and T_3) sometimes need special consideration in diagnosis of hypothyroidism in the elderly. Moreover, the interpretation of the serum thyrotropin (TSH) level may not be readily made in some cases (see below).

Ordinarily, in the ambulatory patient the diagnosis of hypothyroidism will be confirmed by the combination of a low T_4 (and T_4 index) and a high TSH. Provided the elderly individual under consideration is not acutely or seriously chronically ill with another illness, this combination of test results is diagnostic of at least biochemical hypothyroidism. If the laboratory findings surface during a screening process, determining whether the patient is hypothyroid clinically may initially be impossible. In some of these cases, identification of the signs and symptoms attributable to hypothyroidism can only be made retrospectively following several months of treatment.

Determinations of plasma T_3 are not useful in the diagnosis of hypothyroidism in the elderly. The T_3 is minimally—if at all—reduced in *normal* elderly persons but is nonspecifically depressed by all manner of pathophysiological states, including such common situations as reduced intake of food.

Interpretation of Elevation of TSH in the Elderly

An increased TSH is considered the most sensitive indicator of hypothyroidism in patients of all ages. Increased frequency of TSH elevation in association with increasing age has been reported and is considered to reflect an increasing frequency of early thyroid gland failure due to autoimmune thyroiditis.[29,30]

A frequently encountered clinical situation is that in which an apparently euthyroid patient is found to have a T_4 within the normal range and a TSH that is modestly elevated above the upper limits of normal but is below 15-20 $\mu U/ml$. Depending on the cut-off point for the elevation of TSH, some 15 percent of patients over 60 show such findings. Women are several-fold more likely than men to show such elevations. The significance of this situation is not completely clear, but a recent study has clarified several issues.[31] Serial determinations of T_4 over a period of 4 years in elderly patients with elevated TSH values have shown that overt thyroid failure with T_4 falling below the normal range occurs in one-third. All those with initial TSH levels above 20 $\mu U/ml$ and 80 percent of those with high titers of thyroid antimicrosomal antibodies became hypothyroid. Conversely, none of the patients with low titers of thyroid autoantibodies developed thyroid gland failure. The levels of TSH elevation and the presence of thyroid autoantibodies are therefore prognostically important and help identify those patients who should receive prophylactic therapy with thyroxine.

The status of those patients who have minimal elevations of TSH and no demonstrable thyroid autoantibodies is less clear. However, several recent studies question the heretofore accepted absolute specificity of clinical TSH measurements made by radioimmunoassay. The serum of some individuals has been shown to contain heterotypic antibodies (cross-reacting antibodies to one of the anti-TSH antibodies used in radioimmunoassay). These antibodies produce spurious elevations of TSH in standard radioimmunoassays and can be expected to produce falsely low values in the newly introduced immunoradiometric assays (IRMA). One would expect—although it has not been proved—that the frequency of encounters with such spurious elevations of heterotypic antibodies would increase with increasing age and be more common in women, as is the case for increased frequency to TSH elevations.

Clearly not all of the observed elevations of TSH in the elderly are artifactual. A simultaneous reduction of T_4 and elevation of TSH is good evidence for hypothyroidism. Nonetheless, yet another—albeit speculative—explanation for the frequent occurrence in the elderly of elevation of TSH in the presence of normal T_4 is that the TSH secreted by some elderly persons may not contain full biological activity. In two other clinical situations, evidence for abnormal glycosylation of TSH has been obtained; first, in some persons with the low T_4 state of severe nonthyroidal illness, and, second, in hypothyroidism due to pituitary or hypothalamic disease. Until the issue of TSH assay specificity is settled, an elevation of TSH in an elderly person with serum T_4 still well within the normal range should be interpreted cautiously, since a diagnosis of hypothyroidism may not always be justified. The issue is also relevant to the use of TSH in monitoring replacement therapy (see below). High titers of thyroid autoantibodies (antithyroglobulin, antimicrosomal) in association with elevated TSH favors both diagnoses, autoimmune thyroiditis and hypothyroidism.

LOW T_4 STATE OF SEVERE NONTHYROIDAL ILLNESS (EUTHYROID SICK SYNDROME) VERSUS HYPOTHYROIDISM

Quite frequently the diagnosis of hypothyroidism is considered in severely ill elderly patients such as those encountered in a hospital's intensive care unit. The possibility of hypothyroidism is usually raised by some aspect of the gross appearance of the patient or a finding such as hypothermia, often in association with sepsis. The plasma T_4, free-T_4 index, and T_3 may be well into the hypothyroid range. However, a diagnosis of hypothyroidism cannot be made on the basis of these results alone. The free T_4—as opposed to the free-T_4 index—may be elevated, normal, or low; if low, the value will often not be reduced in proportion to the T_4 and free-T_4 index. In most such cases the TSH—rather than being

elevated as it is in hypothyroidism—is "normal," a finding which rules out primary hypothyroidism but does not exclude the rare possibility of secondary (pituitary) hypothyroidism. The TRH test is normal or—in the most severely ill—blunted.[32] In those cases in which the TRH test is normal, secondary hypothyroidism can be excluded. In the others, secondary hypothyroidism remains a possibility, although a remote one, given the rarity of pituitary-hypothalamic disease. The mortality rate associated with this phenomenon is very high. However, if clinical recovery ensues, the T_4 returns to normal. The TSH may actually be somewhat increased during the recovery phase, so that both the T_4 and TSH lie within the hypothyroid range at this point in time.[33] When this is the case, only serial measurements will distinguish the situation from that of hypothyroidism. Prudence dictates that if the clinical findings are suggestive of hypothyroidism, treatment with thyroid hormone be instituted. In the absence of pressing clinical findings, serial measurements may be in order and hormone therapy can be deferred.

To date this euthyroid sick syndrome has been recognized predominantly in severely ill patients, but it also occurs in chronically ill, nonhospitalized individuals. This phenomenon must be considered to avoid an incorrect diagnosis of hypothyroidism in these elderly patients. The entire concept is under active study. Recent evidence indicates that TSH secretion is suppressed and that serum TSH is actually greatly reduced during this syndrome, but this is demonstrable only with an ultrasensitive radioimmunoassay for TSH[34]; ordinary assays reveal "normal" values for TSH. Thus, it is possible that the syndrome is in fact a form of secondary hypothyroidism. At the present time, the limited information available concerning the possible efficacy of replacement therapy with thyroid hormone (T_4 and/or T_3) under these circumstances does not show any benefit. Some have ascribed a homeostatic, protective effect to the low T_3 state. This complex syndrome has been recently reviewed and discussed elsewhere.[34,35]

THERAPY OF HYPOTHYROIDISM IN THE ELDERLY

Several principles should be observed. First, the maintenance dose of thyroxine is less in the elderly than in young patients. Second, therapy should be instituted slowly and cautiously in the old. Third, adequate therapy should not be unduly delayed or denied because of medical considerations which may seem reasonable but are in fact inappropriate. Lastly, therapy of hypothyroidism, at any age but especially in the elderly, should be with thyroxine, administered as a preparation which can be relied upon to be accurate in dosage and of predictable bioavailability (see below).

Direct demonstration of a decreased thyroid hormone secretion rate with increasing age suggested some years ago that the clinically suspected decreased thyroid hormone requirement of elderly patients was in fact correct. However, only recently have studies of the replacement dose of thyroxine in the elderly used restoration of a normal serum TSH as the endpoint. These studies indicate a considerable reduction from the usual dose in the young.[36–38] Whereas most young persons need from 0.1 to 0.125 mg of thyroxine daily, some old persons need as little as 0.05 mg. The variability is very great, however, and so a maintenance level must be found for each individual and may have to be reduced as the years pass.

In young adults without known preexistent cardiac disease, replacement therapy can be safely initiated with the maintenance dose of 0.1 to 0.125 mg of thyroxine given daily. In the elderly, the major reason for initiating replacement therapy at a low dose is concern for the possibility of inducing cardiac events such as myocardial infarction or arrhythmias. These concerns are in turn based on anecdotal experience but seem to be valid. Accordingly, therapy can be initiated at a dose of thyroxine of 0.025 or 0.05 mg with—in the absence of untoward clinical consequences—incremental increases of 0.025 mg at 2- to 4-week intervals until the full maintenance dose is reached. Complications with such a conservative approach seem to be rare, but several months may be required to produce a significant clinical response. The physician should offer strong reassurance and encouragement during this time.

When an elderly patient has known cardiac disease, especially preexistent angina, therapy must be initiated even more cautiously. Physicians are often reluctant to initiate therapy at all in such patients, since usual clinical teaching states that thyroxine therapy will exacerbate angina. Such is not always the case. Cautious initiation of therapy should be attempted using 0.025 mg of thyroxine—or even less—with increments as tolerated at 4-week intervals. Restoration of euthyroid state—or at least relief of myxedema—may actually be accompanied by improvement in anginal symptoms. Furthermore, it is important to realize that in such circumstances the patient may be much improved even by a dose of thyroxine that is less than optimal. For example, some tolerable degree of angina may develop at a dose of thyroxine that is sufficient to eliminate grossly symptomatic myxedema even while some clinical or laboratory evidence of hypothyroidism persists. In such a situation the patient will undoubtedly have been markedly improved from an overall symptomatic standpoint. Some of these patients will be responsive to intensive therapy of angina by the usual means. The precise indications for the use of antianginal drugs (β-blockers, calcium-channel blockers) in such patients is not clear, but they should proba-

bly be judiciously employed with special attention to dosage, since it might possibly be affected by the hypothyroid state. To discontinue or deny hormone therapy out of fear of dire consequences is, however, not an uncommon mistake. Therapy should also not be withheld on the assumption that other coexistent disease, e.g., chronic lung disease, contraindicates initiation of thyroxine therapy. The issues of thyroid status, replacement therapy, angina, and the problems related to coronary angiography and coronary bypass surgery continue to receive attention.[39]

The objective of replacement therapy with thyroxine in the elderly is to restore the euthyroid state, if possible, or at least to eliminate the gross manifestations of hypothyroidism. Monitoring of thyroxine therapy in the elderly is first and foremost clinical; the laboratory is important *but* adjunctive. In young patients, thyroxine is given until the T_4 is within the normal range. The plasma thyrotropin (TSH) may then be determined and the dose of thyroxine further increased until the elevated TSH is returned to normal. This approach should be modified in the elderly to the extent that a return of the T_4 to the normal range may be sufficient. No compelling need exists to restore the TSH to normal, since this may occur at a level of T_4 that is unacceptably high from the point of view of clinical symptoms, e.g., angina pectoris. Moreover, the possibility of artifactual elevation of TSH should be borne in mind (see "Interpretation of Elevation of TSH in the Elderly," above). Obviously, if both T_4 and TSH can be normalized, so much the better. In monitoring the response of the serum T_4, attention should be given to the timing of the replacement dose of thyroxine. Administration of thyroxine by mouth is followed by an increase of serum T_4 lasting for at least 6 hours; thus, the blood sample should be obtained prior to the daily dose, rather than soon afterward.

Much has been written over the past few years concerning the variability of potency of thyroxine preparations.[40–42] In the elderly, especially, in whom inappropriate dosage of hormone during replacement therapy may have adverse effects, this issue is of special concern. By the time that reformulation of a widely used brand of thyroxine occurred in 1982, it was realized that earlier preparations had contained less hormone and/or bioavailability than they had been thought to contain. These circumstances resulted in the use of significantly higher stated doses of thyroxine than are now considered appropriate. Moreover, at least one-half of the generic brands examined were found to contain considerably less than the stated amount of hormone.[40] The two major brand names of thyroxine in current use in the United States are Synthroid (Flint) and Levothyroid (Rorer); both products appear to be reliable and predictable. Generic preparations may be equally efficacious but remain suspect despite reassurances from the U.S. Food and Drug

Administration. For most patients, considerations of a relatively small difference of cost will not be important enough for the physician to risk introducing a possible element of error into replacement therapy with thyroxine.

GOITER

Goiter—an enlarged thyroid gland—is the most common thyroid abnormality at any age. The term implies nothing about the thyroid's functional state, although thyroid enlargement may be the first clue to detection of abnormal thyroid function. The presence of a goiter demands careful clinical and laboratory evaluation, especially in the elderly in whom the assessment of clinical thyroid status may be especially difficult.

Diffuse goiter, also termed *simple goiter*, denotes a thyroid which is uniformly and more or less symmetrically enlarged without apparent palpable irregularity. (Some use the term simple goiter to denote any nontoxic or nonhyperfunctioning gland, regardless of its anatomy.) Diffuse goiter is uncommon in elderly patients. Its presence in this age group should suggest Graves' disease, thyroiditis, drug effect, or such rarities as lymphoma or amyloid infiltration of the thyroid.

Sporadic goiter occurs in a small percentage of the population and increases in frequency with age. Goiter in the elderly is most often multinodular. This type of thyroid enlargement is sporadic and of unknown cause. The thyroid—if examined pathologically—typically shows multiple nodules of varying size, areas of fibrosis, cyst formation, and degenerative changes. Although such glands were in past years due to iodine deficiency, the widespread use of iodized salt has essentially eliminated this cause in the United States. However, some elderly patients may have been iodine-deficient during youth, especially if they lived in the Appalachian region, the midwest, and some other inland localities. Although natural goitrogens are known to occur in cabbage and related vegetables and in the water supplies of certain localities, the cause of multinodular goiter can generally not be ascertained for a particular patient.

RECOGNITION OF GOITER

A visible mass may be noted by the patient or physician or is detected by palpation during routine physical examination. In the elderly, an enlarged thyroid is often neither visible nor readily palpable but is an incidental finding when x-ray examination of the chest or esophagus is performed. In these cases, a mass in the superior mediastinum or retrosternal space is noted by the radiologist, who may suggest the diagnosis. Asymptomatic displacement (deviation) of the trachea or esophagus is common in such cases. Confirmation of the nature of the mass can be obtained by radionuclide scanning, while computed tomography can help delineate its location. Valsalva maneuver may bring the gland into the neck where it becomes visible or palpable.

Obstruction of the trachea or esophagus can be produced by a large goiter, but dysphagia should not be readily attributed to a minor degree of thyroid enlargement. Hoarseness may occur owing to involvement of the recurrent laryngeal nerve, but such a complication is rare in benign enlargement. The development of hoarseness suggests thyroid neoplasm.

Goiters large enough to compress—as opposed to merely displace—the trachea are uncommon. However, the possibility of tracheal narrowing should be considered in any elderly patient with a goiter or tracheal deviation who has symptoms of respiratory distress. Sudden development or worsening of this symptom suggests rapid enlargement of the goiter, usually due to hemorrhage in an area of cystic degeneration. Tracheal narrowing can be evaluated by plain films, CT scan, or ventilation flow-loop study, the latter being the most sensitive, since the compressed trachea may collapse during exhalation.

DIFFERENTIAL DIAGNOSIS

Clinical and laboratory assessment of thyroid function, plus testing for thyroid autoantibodies, should be made in all cases of goiter. The clinician must recognize that the functional state of a goiter may change with time, sometimes rather rapidly, and hence the precise diagnosis may not be possible on a single examination. Elderly patients may be found to have normal thyroid function by clinical and laboratory examinations, only to develop hyperthyroidism over the subsequent year or more. An argument can be made for periodic reevaluation of such individuals by routine laboratory testing at intervals of 1 to 2 years.

Goiter in association with hyperthyroidism suggests Graves' disease, toxic nodular goiter, or a hyperfunctioning ("hot") nodule. Hypofunction in association with goiter is likely to represent Hashimoto's thyroiditis (see "Hypothyroidism" above), but other possibilities such as drug ingestion may have to be excluded. Thyroid autoantibodies are elevated to diagnostic levels in 90 percent of cases of Hashimoto's thyroiditis. Determination of such antibodies (antithyroglobulin and antimicrosomal) is now routine in the evaluation of goiter.

If the clinical and laboratory assessments indicate normal thyroid function, the diagnosis of nontoxic or euthyroid goiter is made. Multinodular enlargement almost always indicates a process of many years standing. Differentiation of diffuse enlargement from nodular enlargement may require scintiscanning or sonography, since small nodules may be missed on physical examination. When only small, nonpalpable nodules are present, an optimally performed scan may show irregular ("patchy") uptake of tracer, but even the best scintiscanning techniques can delineate nodules of only about 1 cm in size. A goiter composed of many such small nodules may appear to represent a nonnodular thyroid on both physical examination and scan. High-resolution sonography is a useful complement or alternative to scintiscanning. Micronodules as small as 0.5 cm can be delineated and precise assessment of overall size and nodularity of the gland can be made. A proper history will point to the possibility that the goiter may be drug-induced. Rapidity of enlargement may help differentiate benign from malignant lesions, while the presence or absence of pain will help in identifying inflammatory thyroiditis.

TREATMENT OF GOITER

In patients up to about age 40 to 50, suppression therapy of goiter is often properly undertaken for cosmetic reasons. Suppression therapy is also clearly indicated for these relatively young individuals with many years of life expectancy during which time mechanical problems can be anticipated if further thyroid enlargement occurs.

In many elderly patients, the duration of the goiter will not be known to the physician at the time of discovery, but the goiter can generally be presumed to have been present for many years. Such goiters—if they have not already produced the mechanical problems of tracheal narrowing or interference with esophageal function—are not likely to do so in the future. Accordingly, suppression therapy is not recommended for such patients, although such therapy can be expected to result in prevention of further thyroid enlargement. If undertaken in the elderly, the dose of thyroid hormone should be reduced. Some 20 to 50 percent of nontoxic nodular goiters are nonsuppressible.[10] Suppression in such patients can, if not carefully monitored, lead to iatrogenic hyperthyroidism. Obviously, if nonsuppressibility is demonstrated, the therapy should be terminated. Details of monitoring of suppression therapy are given elsewhere (Ref. 8 and see below).

Goiter so large as to produce not merely a deviation but significant tracheal compression, as assessed above, or to interfere with swallowing has become a rarity. Dysphagia attributable to goiter does occur, but unless the symptom is severe, surgery should be undertaken with reluctance. Surgical removal of a goiter producing significant airway obstruction, although attended by significant morbidity, may have to be considered in the elderly, since suppression therapy is unlikely to be effective in reducing the size of large, long-standing, invariably multinodular goiters. If surgery is to be undertaken, the fact must be borne in mind that the proce-

dure may be technically difficult and should be performed only by an experienced thoracic surgeon. Radioiodide can be considered for such cases, especially in the elderly with other serious medical problems that add to surgical morbidity or mortality. While the response is slow and multiple doses may be required, a useful reduction in size of the goiter may be achieved. Concern may be expressed that, in any patient with a severely compromised airway, the transient swelling that sometimes occurs following radioiodide treatment could further narrow the trachea and is at least a theoretical hazard of this form of therapy. A recent series of such cases was, however, successfully treated in this fashion.[43]

ISSUE OF CARCINOMA IN MULTINODULAR GOITER

The occurrence of carcinoma in multinodular goiter has been debated for years. Although a significant proportion of thyroids from older persons harbor microscopic carcinomas, these are of no clinical significance. In the elderly, multinodular goiter should be considered to be a benign disease; surgical excision is rarely—if ever—warranted out of concern for carcinoma. Rapid enlargement of a dominant nodule in an elderly patient with multinodular goiter prompts concern over the possibility of development of an anaplastic carcinoma but is almost always due to hemorrhage or cyst formation.

SUBACUTE THYROIDITIS

Classic subacute thyroiditis, also known as granulomatous or de Quervain's thyroiditis, is fairly common in young persons but rare in elderly patients. Painful thyroid enlargement in the elderly should suggest hemorrhage into a cyst or nodule or anaplastic carcinoma. If, on clinical grounds, these diagnoses are unlikely, subacute thyroiditis can be considered. The term *subacute* is often deceiving and sometimes inappropriate. Although the onset may be insidious, it is perhaps just as often acute over several days. Many patients give a history of recent antecedent upper respiratory tract infection.

The earliest symptom may be referred pain, usually to the ear, but pain can appear to originate in the jaw or occiput. The phase may last a few hours or days before tenderness and discomfort in the thyroid area becomes apparent. Initially, pain and swelling of the thyroid are often unilateral, but the process usually does not remain localized to only one lobe for more than a few days. Systemic symptoms include fever, especially in acute cases, intense fatigue, and malaise. The course may be protracted with symptoms persisting for months, although usually they subside within a week or two.

Erythrocyte sedimentation rate is elevated. Early in the disease, the thyroidal radioioidide uptake is often depressed, while plasma T_4 may be elevated. Mild cases show no such laboratory changes or only borderline abnormalities. Significant titers of thyroid autoantibodies are not common but can be seen.

Clinical hyperthyroidism occasionally accompanies subacute thyroiditis (see above). Rarely hypothyroidism develops and lasts several months. Permanent hypothyroidism is very unusual.

THERAPY

Therapy for subacute thyroiditis is symptomatic. The patient should be strongly reassured concerning the benign, self-limited character of the disorder. Thyroid tenderness often responds within several days to aspirin in doses sufficient to maintain therapeutic (anti-inflammatory) blood levels. Codeine can be added if neck discomfort is severe, but its use in the elderly may precipitate fecal impaction. In less than 10 percent of cases the process may be severe enough to require glucocorticoid therapy (30 to 60 mg of prednisone daily or equivalent). Glucocorticoids produce prompt relief of pain and tenderness but, if the disease is severe enough to require their use, will usually then be necessary for weeks to several months. Relapse is common when therapy is discontinued, and retreatment may be needed.

THYROID NEOPLASMS

THYROID NODULES

As shown in the Framingham study, thyroid nodules are common and were found in 3 percent of adults between the ages of 30 and 60. New nodules appeared at the rate of 1 case per 1000 people per year. Other studies suggest that about 5 percent of all women over age 50 have a thyroid nodule. These nodules—regardless of their histopathology—are almost all clinically nonaggressive. In the Framingham study, follow-up of up to 15 years showed not one nodule behaving in a clinically aggressive manner; i.e., not a single *clinical* case of thyroid cancer was seen to develop. This study has never been challenged, but on the other hand corroboration has not been forthcoming, a fact that no doubt reflects the difficulties of longitudinal studies of this type. In another study in which all patients with nodules were treated with thyroid hormone suppression, no cancers developed in follow-ups of 5 to 15 years while two-thirds of the nodules regressed or disappeared.

The frequency of new nodule appearance after age 50 falls off rapidly, so that by age 80 very few new nodules will be encountered. Consideration of such nodules in the elderly is given below.

Clinical Approach to the Elderly Patient with a Solitary Thyroid Nodule

In encountering an apparently solitary thyroid nodule in an elderly person, several issues must be considered. Is the nodule new? Is it solitary, or is it part of a nodular goiter? If it is truly solitary, what is its functional status? What should be done about it?

In establishing whether the patient has only a single nodule, palpation by an experienced examiner is essential. Frequently the "solitary" nodule, especially in the elderly patient, turns out to be one of several in a nodular goiter. An apparently single nodule in a clearly enlarged thyroid is probably one of several, since an enlarged gland is likely to be harboring many small, nondiscrete nodules. Sonography (ultrasound echogram) is very useful in delineating the anatomy of the nodule and, importantly, whether the remainder of the thyroid is enlarged and/or nodular. This noninvasive procedure also usually provides an objective determination of nodule size as a basis for follow-up. Cysts, uncommon in the elderly, are benign lesions which can be readily identified by ultrasound.

The functional state of the solitary nodule can be surmised from the results of the T_4 (FT_4I) and T_3. Elevated values many be associated with hyperthyroidism, the presence of which may not have been previously appreciated. The nodule may be hyperfunctioning relative to the remainder of the gland ("hot" nodule), even though it may not produce amounts of thyroid hormone sufficient to elevate the T_4 or T_3 above the normal range. If the nodule is clearly hyperfunctioning as shown by the serum T_4 or T_3, a radionuclide scan should be performed to confirm that it is hot, followed by RaI therapy (or surgical removal), as discussed under "Hyperthyroidism" above. Only about 5 percent of hyperthyroidism is due to hot nodules. These lesions are always benign. Clinical hyperthyroidism, if it is to develop from a hot nodule, will do so over 3 to 4 years with lesions that are at least 3 to 4 cm in diameter. About 30 percent of hot nodules go on to produce hyperthyroidism; the remainder remain functionally stable or eventually involute. All hot nodules should be followed up by means of laboratory testing every 2 years.

Most nodules are "cold," i.e., functionally hypoactive relative to the remainder of the gland. The diagnostic workup and therapeutic approach to these lesions will be determined by a number of clinical considerations which are related to age of the patient and the biological potential of the nodule. In the elderly, even more than in the young, a conservative approach is necessary.

The major concern with most nodules is, of course, malignancy. How much of a risk does this hold for the patient over age 50 or 60? In general, the older the patient, the less likely the nodule is to be cancerous. The incidence of cancerous nodules peaks at age 50 and falls off rapidly thereafter. Most nodules represent benign lesions; 75 to 90 percent are adenomas or cysts. Thus, the overall risk is small if nothing further is done. The risk is smaller still when one recalls that the remaining percent of lesions—if they were excised—would prove to be clinically—if not pathologically—relatively benign papillary or follicular carcinomas. These lesions are almost always nonlethal and slow-growing, so that a conservative course is always feasible. This view is taken despite the recent realization that papillary or follicular carcinomas occurring in women over age 50 or men over age 40 are those most likely to be associated with a poor prognosis.[44-46] However, it should still be recalled that the vast majority of carcinomas, even in these older groups, follow a clinically benign course. Anaplastic carcinoma is a malignancy found only in the elderly, but it is not likely to present as a single, small nodule of a few centimeters' size (see below).

Given this sanguine set of considerations of the likelihood of carcinoma in nodules and the behavior of those lesions that are carcinomas, should one then pursue the diagnostic workup at all? In the author's opinion, observation alone or suppression therapy with follow-up by clinical examination (preferably with sonogram) at 3 to 6 months is a safe approach especially applicable in the elderly. However, until recently many physicians proceeded to immediate surgical excision of all nodules. Currently, many medical experts recommend needle biopsy using fine-needle aspiration for cytological examination, or aspiration with small bore needle for histological examination. These procedures are safe, direct, and useful, but their limitations are several and go beyond the ability of operator (endocrinologist or surgeon) to obtain a satisfactory specimen. Although it is probably possible to make an accurate diagnosis in about 90 percent of cases biopsied, it must be strongly stressed that the most important consideration in the use of needle biopsy is the expertise of the pathologist examining the biopsy material. If a specially trained pathologist is not available, or if the patient is reluctant to have an invasive procedure, needle biopsy should be avoided and a conservative course adopted (below). It is important to realize that the clinical outcome will be unaffected by the choice of any of these available approaches: immediate excision; biopsy followed by excision; or treatment by suppression of TSH. Suppression therapy must not be equated with procrastination or no therapy.[47]

Suppression Therapy of the Cold Nodule

In considering suppression therapy for the cold nodule, it is reassuring to recall that 75 to 90 percent are benign lesions. Of the 10 percent that are papillary or follicular carcinomas, those with the most favorable prognosis

(least likely to follow an aggressive course) are in younger patients (men below age 40, women below age 50[44]). It is questionable, however, whether one should consider these latter statistics in view of the relative rarity and benignity of thyroid carcinoma versus the increased risk of surgery and reduced life expectancy of individuals of advanced age. A conservative approach will usually be advisable.

A conservative treatment program involves suppression of thyrotropin (TSH) with thyroxine (Synthroid) or triiodothyronine (Cytomel). This can be safely undertaken if the dose of thyroxine or triiodothyronine is low—as appropriate for age—and periodic clinical observation and attention to the serum T_4 (at 3 months and later at 6- to 12-month intervals) are undertaken. Enough thyroxine (0.075 to 0.125 mg) should be given to maintain the T_4 at the upper limits of normal. Triiodothyronine can also be used for suppression therapy, but it is not recommended since the dose is more difficult to monitor. If triiodothyronine is used, a dose of 15 to 25 μg daily is sufficient, provided that the T_4 drops to less that 5 μg/100 ml after several months; otherwise the dose is raised every 2 to 3 months up to 30 to 35 μg, as necessary. A dose of 50 μg is still used by some physicians but is almost always supraphysiologic even in young patients. Recent availability of sensitive assays that can measure TSH below the lower limits of normal should prove to be useful in the monitoring of suppression, but experience to date is limited. If a nodule progresses in size despite suppression (clinically or preferably sonographically determined at 6-month intervals), surgical removal will be indicated. Clearly, closer observation is necessary for the first few months in an elderly person in whom anaplastic carcinoma is a significant consideration.

THYROID CARCINOMAS

In the United States only about 1200 persons die of thyroid carcinoma each year. More than one-half of these deaths are due to anaplastic carcinoma. The remainder are due to aggressive or metastatic follicular carcinoma or, rarely, papillary carcinoma. Anaplastic carcinoma is almost unknown below age 35, but by age 50 about 10 percent, and by age 80 nearly half, *of the small number of cases of thyroid carcinoma encountered at these ages* are of the anaplastic type. These lesions appear to arise in preexistent nodular goiters.

The clinical presentation of anaplastic carcinoma is likely to be as a new, rapidly enlarging mass. Symptoms develop early and are likely to involve pain, hoarseness, dysphagia, or hemoptysis. Presentation as a small, discrete nodule is uncommon. Clinical reexamination at monthly intervals for several months will delineate the situation. No evidence exists to suggest that early extirpation is more likely to result in a cure. Needle biopsy—

if available—may be useful in selecting patients for early surgery. If an anaplastic lesion is found, surgery should be attempted, since resectable disease without evidence of metastases can be associated with long-term survival in 20 to 30 percent of cases, even when extension outside the thyroid capsule has occurred. Anaplastic carcinomas of the small-cell type may be confused—even by expert pathologists—with the rare case of lymphoma arising in the thyroid. Lymphoma, unlike anaplastic carcinoma, is radiosensitive and amenable to radiotherapy and/or chemotherapy. Medullary carcinoma, accounting for no more than 1 to 2 percent of thyroid cancer, is not likely to be encountered in elderly patients.

Surgical Removal versus Suppression Therapy of Cold Nodules

In the elderly all thyroid carcinomas diagnosed by needle biopsy need not be surgically removed. Conservative therapy alone (TSH suppression as described above) may well be indicated for the very elderly with an established diagnosis of papillary or even follicular thyroid carcinoma. Having excluded anaplastic carcinoma, one must consider the indolent, clinically benign course of most thyroid cancers against the expected longevity of the elderly person. The use of needle biopsy was introduced to reduce the frequency of unnecessary surgical procedures in an area of the United States where common practice dictated that all nodules should promptly be surgically excised. It would be unfortunate if the introduction of the needle biopsy resulted in an increased number of operations for suspected or real thyroid carcinoma in the elderly.

Radiation-Associated Thyroid Carcinoma

Low-dose irradiation of the thyroid is a stimulus to thyroid carcinogenesis, with a latency period of one to several decades. In recent years thyroid carcinomas have been reported to occur with increased incidence in patients who received radiation therapy some years earlier for enlarged tonsils, adenoids, or thymus; acne; cervical lymphadenopathy; etc. A distinction must be made between treatment with penetrating external radiation and local irradiation with point sources (radium rod and plaque treatment). Thyroid carcinoma has not been related to such limited exposure.

In the reports purporting to show a relationship between external radiation and the development of thyroid carcinoma, as many as one-third of irradiated individuals have been found to develop thyroid carcinoma. Papillary and follicular carcinomas have been seen in about the same ratio as in nonirradiated patients. A relationship between exposure to radiation and development of medullary and anaplastic carcinoma has not

been observed. The biological behavior of radiation-induced carcinomas appears to be similar to the behavior of those that appear spontaneously. Almost as rapidly as the association between radiation therapy to the head and neck and thyroid carcinoma was noted, reports refuting such association have appeared.

If no thyroid abnormality is palpable in an elderly patient with a past history of radiation exposure, reexamination of the patient by palpation at 2-year intervals should suffice. Routine scanning procedures for patients with nonpalpable lesions are not indicated.

REFERENCES

1. Rønnov V, Kirkegaard C: Hyperthyroidism—A disease of old age? *Br Med J* 1:41, 1973.
2. Stiel JN, Hales IB, Reeve TS: Thyrotoxicosis in an elderly population. *Med J Aust* 2:986, 1972.
3. Davis PJ, Davis FB: Hyperthyroidism in patients over the age of 60 years. *Medicine* 53:161, 1974.
4. Swanson JW, Kelly JJ, McConahey WM: Neurologic aspects of thyroid dysfunction. *Mayo Clinic Proc* 56:504, 1981.
5. Resnekov L, Falicov RE: Thyrotoxicosis and lactate-producing angina pectoris with normal coronary arteries. *Br Heart J* 39:1051, 1977.
6. Larsen PR: Thyroid hormone concentrations, in Ingbar SH, Braverman LE (eds): *Werner's The Thyroid*, 5th ed. Philadelphia, Lippincott, pp 479–501.
7. Larsen PR et al: Revised nomenclature for tests of thyroid hormone and thyroid-related proteins in serum. *J Clin Endocrinol Metab* 64:1089, 1987.
8. Gregerman RI: Thyroid disorders, in Barker LR, Burton JR, Zieve PD (eds): *Principles of Ambulatory Medicine*. Baltimore, Williams & Wilkins, 1986, pp 987–1012.
9. Gregerman RI: Intrinsic physiologic variables, in Ingbar SH, Braverman LE (eds): *Werner's The Thyroid*, 5th ed. Philadelphia, Lippincott, 1986, pp 361–381.
10. Smeulers J et al: Response to thyrotropin-releasing hormone and triiodothyronine suppressibility in euthyroid multinodular goiter. *Clin Endocrinol* 7:389, 1977.
11. Caplan RH et al: Thyroid function tests in elderly hyperthyroid patients. *J Am Geriatr Soc* 26:116, 1978.
12. Reiner RG et al: Thyroid, renal and hepatic function tests following cholecystography with high-dose contrast agents. *Dig Dis Sci* 25:379, 1980.
13. Borst GC et al: Euthyroid hyperthyroxinemia. *Ann Intern Med* 98:366, 1983.
14. Thomas FB, Mazzaferri EL, Skillman TG: Apathetic thyrotoxicosis: A distinctive clinical and laboratory entity. *Ann Intern Med* 72:679, 1970.
15. Fradkin JE, Wolff J: Iodide-induced thyrotoxicosis. *Medicine* 62:1, 1983.
16. Nicolai TF et al: Lymphocytic thyroiditis with spontaneously resolving hyperthyroidism and subacute thyroiditis: Long-term follow-up. *Arch Intern Med* 141:1455, 1981.
17. Gordon M, Gryfe CI: Hyperthyroidism with painless subacute thyroiditis in the elderly. *JAMA* 246:2354, 1981.
18. Hedberg CW et al: An outbreak of thyrotoxicosis caused

by the consumption of bovine thyroid gland in ground beef. *N Engl J Med* 316:993, 1987.

19. McMillin JM: Hamburger thyrotoxicosis: The endocrinologist as sleuth. *Thyroid Today* 11(2):1, 1988.

20. Hamburger J: The autonomously functioning thyroid adenoma (editorial). *N Engl J Med* 309:1512, 1983.

21. Zellmann HE: Unusual aspects of myxedema. *Geriatrics* 23:140, 1968.

22. Livingston EH et al: Prevalence of thyroid disease and abnormal thyroid tests in older hospitalized and ambulatory persons. *J Am Geriatr Soc* 35:109, 1987.

23. Klein I, Levey GS: Unusual manifestations of hypothyroidism. *Arch Int Med* 144:123, 1984.

24. Bahemuka M, Hodkinson HM: Screening for hypothyroidism in elderly inpatients. *Br Med J* 2:601, 1975.

25. Atkinson RL et al: Occult thyroid disease in an elderly hospitalized population. *J Gerontol* 33:372, 1978.

26. Parving H-H et al: Mechanisms of edema formation in myxedema—Increased protein extravasation and relatively slow lymphatic drainage. *N Engl J Med* 301:406, 1979.

27. Gregerman RI, Bierman EL: Aging and hormones, in Williams RH (ed): *Textbook of Endocrinology.* Philadelphia, Saunders, 1981, pp 1192–1212.

28. Impallomeni MG: Unusual presentation of myxoedema coma in the elderly. *Age Aging* 6:71, 1977.

29. Tunbridge WMG et al: The spectrum of thyroid disease in a community: The Wickham survey. *Clin Endocrinol* 7:481, 1977.

30. Sawin CT et al: The aging thyroid. Increased prevalence of elevated serum thyrotropin levels in the elderly. *JAMA* 242:247, 1979.

31. Rosenthal MJ et al: Thyroid failure in the elderly. Microsomal antibodies as discriminant for therapy. *JAMA* 258:209, 1987.

32. Vierhapper H et al: Impaired secretion of TSH in critically ill patients with "low T$_4$ syndrome." *Acta Endocrinol* 101:542, 1982.

33. Bacci V, Schussler GC, Kaplan TB: The relationship between serum triiodothyronine and thyrotropin during systemic illness. *J Clin Endocrinol Metab* 54:1229, 1982.

34. Wehmann RE et al: Suppression of thyrotropin in the low thyroxine state of severe nonthyroidal illness. *N Engl J Med* 312:546, 1985.

35. Wartofsky L, Burman KD: Alterations in thyroid function in patients with systemic illness: The euthyroid sick syndrome. *Endocrine Rev* 3:164, 1982.

36. Rosenbaum RL, Barzel US: Levothyroxine replacement dose for primary hypothyroidism decreases with age. *Ann Intern Med* 96:53, 1982.

37. Sawin CT et al: Aging and the thyroid. *Am J Med* 75:206, 1983.

38. Davis FB et al: Estimation of physiologic thyroxine replacement dose in hypothyroid patients. *Arch Intern Med* 144:1752, 1984.

39. Klein I, Levey GS: Thyroxine therapy, hypothyroid patients, and coronary revascularization. *Ann Intern Med* 96:250, 1982.

40. Dong BJ, Young VR, Rapoport B et al: The non-equivalence of levothyroxine products. *Drug Intell Clin Pharm* 20:77, 1986.

41. Bantle JP: Replacement therapy with levothyroxine: Evolving concepts. *Thyroid Today* 10:1, 1987.

42. Fish LH et al: Replacement dose, metabolism and bioavailability of levothyroxine in the treatment of hypothyroidism: Role of triiodothyronine in pituitary feedback in humans. *N Engl J Med* 316:764, 1987.

43. Kay TWH et al: Treatment of non-toxic multinodular goiter with radioactive iodine. *Am J Med* 84:19, 1988.

44. Cady B et al: Changing clinical, pathologic, therapeutic and survival patterns in differentiated thyroid carcinoma. *Ann Surg* 184:541, 1976.

45. Samaan NA et al: Impact of therapy for differentiated carcinoma of the thyroid: An analysis of 706 cases. *J Clin Endocrinol Metab* 56:1131, 1983.

46. Høie J et al: Distant metastases in papillary thyroid cancer: A review of 91 patients. *Cancer* 61:1, 1988.

47. Molitch ME et al: The cold thyroid nodule: An analysis of diagnostic and therapeutic options. *Endocr Rev* 5:185, 1984.

Chapter 71

DIABETES MELLITUS IN THE ELDERLY

Andrew P. Goldberg, Reubin Andres, and Edwin L. Bierman

Diabetes mellitus is a disease that has been recognized for centuries by the presence of high blood glucose levels. However, it is a more complex condition than simply an abnormality in glucose regulation due to an inadequate amount of insulin, and should be viewed as a syndrome characterized by generalized metabolic dysfunction and a variety of clinical disorders. Diabetes mellitus is primarily characterized by abnormal glucose metabolism, but is also associated with abnormal regulation of lipid and protein metabolism and with the development of vascular and nervous system disease.

The elderly are more susceptible to abnormalities in glucoregulation than younger people; however, it is not usually hyperglycemia that leads to the diagnosis of diabetes in older people. Rather, the most common presenting signs of diabetes in older people are the degenerative changes in blood vessels and nerves of the body leading to atherosclerotic complications, neuropathy, renal failure, and retinopathy. While the Diabetes Control and Complications Trial seeks to determine the relationship of control of hyperglycemia to the development of vascular complications in younger patients with insulin-dependent diabetes mellitus (IDDM), the duration of undiagnosed, poorly controlled, non-insulin-dependent diabetes mellitus (NIDDM) is of greatest significance in the pathogenesis of complications from diabetes in older people. The effects of treating hyperglycemia or other major risk factors for atherosclerosis on the incidence of complications in older people with diabetes mellitus are unknown because older patients are usually excluded from participation in intervention trials due to their high incidence of comorbidity.

Many of the clinical manifestations and consequences of diabetes mellitus in older people often re-

The authors are indebted to Mrs. Beverly Eldrett and Mrs. Gloria Kruba for typing this manuscript.

semble age-related pathophysiologic changes. Declines in organ function commonly associated with aging occur more frequently and at an accelerated rate in diabetics. It is most often the development of cataracts, the onset of symptoms and signs of atherosclerotic vascular disease, the decline in peripheral sensory and motor neural function, or the deterioration in renal function which heralds the onset of diabetes in older people. Rarely are presenting symptoms acute, as in insulin-dependent ketosis-prone diabetes mellitus (IDDM); rather, the slow, gradual onset and progression of complications of diabetes of the non-insulin-dependent ketosis-resistant type (NIDDM) characterizes the disease in the elderly. This chapter focuses on the pathophysiology, diagnosis, clinical management, and complications of type II or non-insulin-dependent diabetes, the most common disorder of impaired glucoregulation in older people.

GLUCOSE INTOLERANCE IN OLDER PEOPLE

A decline in glucose tolerance with aging has been observed in the majority of human studies. The underlying mechanisms for hyperglycemia and glucose intolerance with aging suggest that there are differences in the pathophysiology and clinical presentation of glucose intolerance with aging compared to those seen in NIDDM. Major abnormalities in glucose homeostasis occur most often in the elderly in the absence of the characteristic clinical complications of diabetes mellitus. Glucose intolerance in older people is most often associated with a variety of conditions which commonly occur in older people, that is, the purported "secondary aging phenomena" of obesity, physical deconditioning due to inactivity, reduced muscle mass and improper diet, as well as the development of coexistent diseases which require

739

older people to take multiple medications that may affect glucose tolerance and insulin action. There may not even be a primary defect in insulin action or pancreatic beta cell function, and rarely are there changes in capillary basement membrane structure or the vessel wall in older people with glucose intolerance. Whether or not this is a disease, and whether the older patient with glucose intolerance alone is at heightened risk for the development of complications, excessive morbidity, and rapid progression to mortality if untreated is not known. A rational approach to this conundrum is central to understanding the pathophysiology and to formulating the appropriate treatment for the older diabetic patient.

There is an age-related increase in the prevalence of diabetes mellitus, undiagnosed diabetes, and impaired glucose tolerance (Table 71-1). The ability to dispose of an oral glucose load is reduced in more than 40 percent of individuals older than 60 years of age.[1,2] If the usual "normal" criteria of the National Diabetes Data Group (NDDG) for the diagnosis of diabetes mellitus are applied to older populations, nearly 50 percent of individuals over 60 would have an abnormal glucose tolerance test without overt symptoms or disease and would be considered diabetic by NDDG standards.[2] Such a decline in glucose tolerance in the absence of systemic disease could well be considered a physiologic sequela of the aging process, not a disease per se.

PATHOPHYSIOLOGY OF GLUCOSE INTOLERANCE IN THE ELDERLY

Numerous studies indicate a very slight 1 mg/dl per decade age-related increase after maturity in fasting plasma glucose levels in healthy, older individuals. This small age-related increase in fasting glucose levels is accompanied, however, by a striking 9 to 10 mg/dl per decade increase in plasma glucose levels 2 hours after an oral glucose challenge.[3,4] These higher postprandial glucose levels may cause slight increases in hemoglobin A_{1c} levels with age.[5] However, despite these age-related increases in fasting and 2-hour glucose levels during oral glucose tolerance testing, glucose tolerance usually remains within the normal range without evidence of clinical diabetes in most older subjects.

The primary metabolic defect in diabetes mellitus is a disturbance in glucose homeostasis. This disturbance may be the result of one or more functional abnormalities in three major organ systems: muscle, the major tissue utilizing glucose in the body; the endocrine pancreas, which secretes the insulin and glucagon necessary for glucose utilization by tissues and the regulation of hepatic glucose production; and the liver, which as the sole producer of glucose in the fasted state is critical for glucoregulation. In diabetes of the non-insulin-dependent type, there may be impaired insulin secretion by the pancreatic beta cell, ineffective insulin action at tissues and cells, overproduction of glucose by the liver, or the combined effects of all these processes limiting the ability to maintain glucose homeostasis.[6-9]

The oral glucose tolerance test is not ideal for determining the mechanism for the deterioration in glucose tolerance with aging because plasma glucose levels are not maintained constant during the test due to variable gastrointestinal absorption. This causes a different glycemic stimulus to the pancreatic beta cell during the test, making comparisons of plasma insulin levels and the extrapolation to secretion among individuals impossible. Furthermore, gut hormones, glucagon, somatostatin, growth hormone, and sympathoadrenal responses will affect the insulin response to glucose, and the effects of aging on the responses of these hormones to glucose are uncertain.

The problems inherent to the oral glucose tolerance test are obviated by the glucose clamp technique, where the glucose or insulin stimulus can be controlled to permit the measurement of endogenous insulin secretion and action at an elevated plasma glucose level (hyperglycemic clamp) or glucose utilization in response to the infusion during euglycemia (euglycemic hyperinsulinemic clamp).[10] When insulin is infused at varying rates and the plasma glucose maintained constant by simultaneous glucose infusion, whole body insulin sensitivity can be determined and insulin-glucose dose response curves constructed (Fig. 71-1). Several studies report an impaired effect of insulin on glucose utilization in healthy nondiabetic older people compared to younger controls.[11-14] The dose-response curves of older persons with normal glucose tolerance tend to be

TABLE 71-1
Oral Glucose Tolerance Test Results in the National Health and Nutrition Examination Survey II (1976–1980)

	Age in Years			
	20–44	*45–54*	*55–64*	*65–74*
1. Diabetes known prior to testing	1.1%	4.3%	6.6%	9.3%
2. Diabetes revealed through testing	1.0%	4.4%	6.5%	8.6%
Total prevalence of diabetes	2.1%	8.7%	13.1%	17.9%
3. Impaired glucose tolerance	6.5%	14.9%	15.2%	22.9%
Total diabetes and impaired glucose tolerance	8.6%	23.6%	28.3%	40.8%

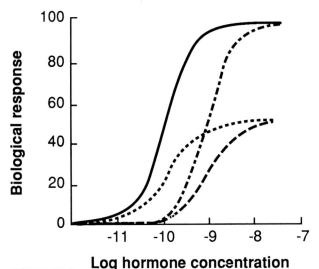

FIGURE 71-1

Insulin resistance involves three forms of altered biological response to insulin compared to normal (———): decreased sensitivity (— — — —); decreased responsiveness (- - - -); and decreased sensitivity and responsiveness (— — —).

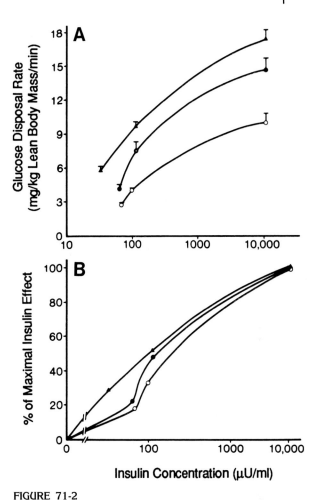

FIGURE 71-2

A. Mean dose-response glucose utilization curves in response to different insulin doses for nonelderly (▲), elderly with normal glucose tolerance tests (●), and elderly with nondiagnostic glucose tolerance tests (○). *B.* Mean dose-response curves for the three groups in Fig. *A* plotted as the percentage of maximal glucose utilization at each insulin concentration infused.

shifted to the right (Fig. 71-2), but maximal glucose utilization in response to very high doses of insulin is normal.[12,13] The mild reduction in the ability of insulin to suppress hepatic glucose production in older individuals confirms the presence of insulin resistance in older people.[12,15] This defect in insulin action has been attributed to a receptor defect in some studies[16,17] and to an abnormality distal to the receptor by investigators who found normal receptor binding in the presence of impaired glucose utilization.[12,13,18,19] This is supported by the finding of additional defects in intracellular enzyme adaptation and activity in animals with aging.[20] Although there have been isolated reports of impaired insulin secretion accompanying impaired glucose utilization in older subjects,[14] the results of most in vivo and in vitro studies support the hypothesis that a postreceptor defect in insulin action is responsible for the decline in glucose tolerance and insulin sensitivity with aging.

Despite the prevalence of these defects in insulin action with aging, many older individuals exhibit insulin sensitivity and glucose tolerance comparable to that seen in younger normal individuals.[21] In selected healthy older men, screened for disease and matched as closely as possible to younger men for percent body fat, maximal aerobic capacity and regional distribution of body fat, measurement of insulin sensitivity during euglycemic clamps (mg glucose utilized/kg fat-free mass/min/μU/ml insulin) was comparable to younger controls and directly related to maximal aerobic capacity.[22] The improved glucose tolerance seen in older people after 3 days of high-carbohydrate feeding suggests that dietary factors also play a significant role in the metabolic responses to oral glucose in the elderly.[23] Thus, in the selection of older and younger subjects for study, not only should subjects be matched for obesity, maximal

aerobic capacity, body fat distribution, and health, but pretest diets and activity also should be controlled prior to the performance of tests to evaluate glucose metabolism.

The disease NIDDM in older individuals is characterized by fasting and postprandial hyperglycemia, glucosuria, and other clinical manifestations of diabetes mellitus (Table 71-2). Diabetes coexists with obesity in most older people, and is for the most part ketosis-resistant. However, under stressful conditions such as infection or surgery, insulin resistance may exceed endogenous insulin secretory capacity and frank hypoinsulinemia may ensue, necessitating insulin therapy to avoid ketoacidosis. Although over 90 percent of patients with NIDDM have a positive family history of diabetes, the linkage between genetic mechanisms and disease is not as evident as with insulin-dependent diabetes. However, the high concordance rate for NIDDM in monozygotic twins after age 40 and the chlorpropamide-associated flushing with alcohol observed in fami-

TABLE 71-2
Clinical Symptoms and Signs of Diabetes Mellitus in the Elderly

1. Unexplained weight loss, fatigue, and cataracts are often the presenting symptom.
2. Classical polyuria, polydipsia, and polyphagia occur rarely.
3. Cataracts, microaneurysms, and retinal detachment are common findings.
4. Recurrent bacterial or fungal infections of skin (pruritus vulvae in females), intertriginous ureas, and urinary tract tend to heal slowly. Dermatologists and urologists often make the diagnosis.
5. Neurologic dysfunction, including paresthesias, dysesthesias, and hypesthesias, muscle weakness and pain (amyotrophy), cranial nerve palsies (mononeuropathy), and autonomic dysfunction of the gastrointestinal tract (diarrhea), cardiovascular system (postural hypotension), reproductive system (impotence), and bladder (atony, overflow incontinence) are seen more often than in younger patients.
6. Arterial disease (macroangiopathy) involving the cardiovascular system (silent ischemia, angina, and myocardial infarction), cerebral vasculature (transient ischemia, and stroke), or peripheral vasculature (diabetic foot, gangrene) is a common presentation.
7. Small-vessel disease (microangiopathy) involving the eyes (macular disease, hemorrhages, exudates) and kidneys (proteinuria, glomerulopathy, uremia) occurs often, and may be the presenting symptom.
8. Associated endocrine-metabolic abnormalities, including obesity, hyperlipidemia, and osteoporosis occur commonly with the disease.
9. A family history of NIDDM or IDDM and a history of gestational diabetes or large babies may be common.
10. Lesions of the skin such as diabetic dermopathy, Dupuytren's contractures, and facial rubeosis occur less often.

lies where NIDDM is present without vascular complications suggest that genetic factors are operative in the disease process.[24,25]

Thus, independent processes influence the decline in glucose intolerance associated with aging. In the first, the so-called lifestyle habits of overeating, consumption of a low-carbohydrate high-fat diet, and physical inactivity have profound effects on glucose tolerance; modification of diet,[23] body weight, and exercise capacity[26–28] improves glucose tolerance. A large population study showed that less than 10 percent of the variance in the total plasma glucose response could be attributed to differences in age.[29] Results of other investigations suggest that when the variables of body composition (percent body fat and waist-to-hip ratio) and physical conditioning status (indexed as $Vo_{2,max}$) are taken into account, the decline in glucose tolerance and insulin sensitivity with aging is reduced.[22,30]

Although glucose intolerance and insulin resistance frequently occur with aging, further deterioration might be avoided in older patients who remain healthy, lean, and physically active. Older individuals with impaired glucose tolerance and no other symptoms or signs of NIDDM should be counseled to change their poor lifestyle habits of overeating the wrong foods and physical inactivity to attempt to reduce risk of progression to disease, since at all ages, morbidity and mortality increases dramatically in individuals with diabetes mellitus. In those older people where abnormal glucose tolerance and hyperglycemia progress to non-insulin-dependent diabetes, macrovascular disease develops at an accelerated rate causing atherosclerosis of the coronary, cerebral, and peripheral vessels while microvascular angiopathy progresses in the kidney, retina, and nervous system. The macroangiopathic complications cause the major morbidity and mortality in older diabetics; hence, vigorous treatment seems prudent to prevent macroangiopathy.[31–33] However, the effects of vigorous therapy to control hyperglycemia and reduce other risk factors for atherosclerosis, such as hyperlipidemia, cigarette smoking, and hypertension, on the progression of macro- and microangiopathic vascular complications in older diabetics are not known.

PREVALENCE OF DIABETES IN OLDER POPULATIONS

Non-insulin-dependent diabetes mellitus is the more prevalent form of diabetes in older populations, and in Western societies it affects approximately one out of every ten whites over 65 years of age and one out of every four people who are over 85 years of age.[34,35] A few studies have examined racial differences in glucose tolerance among blacks and whites living in the same environment. In Evans County, Georgia, the prevalence of diabetes among individuals in the fifth decade of life was twofold higher in black females than among either white females, white males, or black males.[36] A National Health Survey found a 60 percent higher age-adjusted prevalence of diabetes in blacks than whites between the ages 18 and 79 years, and a greater proportion of blacks than whites with plasma glucose levels exceeding 200 mg/dl 1 hour after the ingestion of 50 g glucose.[37]

The incidence rate of NIDDM in older individuals increases from 5 to 6 per 1000 persons per year to as high as 8 to 10 per 1000 persons in surveys of individuals ages 70 to 79. However, extremely high rates are observed in populations where there is a heightened prevalence of obesity, specifically the Nauruans and Pima Indians. Among these people the incidence of diabetes in men age 50 to 59 years is 40 to 50 per 1000 people per year.[38–40] Perhaps the best up-to-date estimates of the prevalence of diagnosed and undiagnosed diabetes in the

United States are available from the 1976 Health Interview Survey and the National Health and Nutrition Examination Survey II.[1] Using the glucose tolerance test criteria proposed by the National Diabetes Data Group,[2] the results of these surveys indicate that the total prevalence of NIDDM increases from 2.6 percent in the age group 20 to 44 years to 17.9 percent among 65 to 74-year-olds (Table 71-1). The prevalence of undiagnosed diabetes in the older group equals the estimate of diagnosed NIDDM, and an additional 23 percent of the older individuals were found to have impaired glucose tolerance. These data probably underestimate the prevalence of diabetes among older populations, since nearly 15 percent of institutionalized nursing home patients have the disease[41] and are usually excluded from "free living" representative statistics.

While differences in dietary practice and physical activity have been considered possible explanations for the divergent incidence of diabetes among older and younger people as well as among blacks and whites, the prevalence of obesity, reduced muscle mass, and socioeconomic and environmental factors must be considered when age, race, and gender differences in glucose tolerance occur among ethnic groups in Western societies. Accurate age-, gender-, and race-adjusted guidelines for the diagnosis of diabetes are needed to decide whether treatment will prevent complications of the disease or result in iatrogenic complications such as hypoglycemia. For example, should the criteria for diagnosis and treatment of a hyperglycemic 35-year-old be the same as for a hyperglycemic 85-year-old? Will the outcomes be the same? Are the risks of aggressive therapy comparable? In the absence of specific markers for NIDDM and its evolution, it is impossible to determine who is at risk for complications and whether the risk factors for complications are similar or different among younger and older patients. Moreover, it is not known whether the development of NIDDM in older persons can be substantially modified by interventions other than drug therapy. The physician's ability to treat diabetes optimally will require resolution of these issues and the accurate quantification of the prevalence and consequences of diabetes in older populations. This will depend on the quality of the techniques used to determine that diabetes is present, the criteria for diagnosis, the accurate assessment of the natural history and evolution of complications in diabetes, and the determination of the effects of different modes of treatment on the outcomes for the patient.

DIAGNOSTIC CRITERIA FOR DIABETES MELLITUS

The results of glucose tolerance testing in older individuals and the expression of age-specific criteria for diagnosis of diabetes are based on studies which are poorly standardized with respect to the administered dose of glucose, the uniformity of the pretest diet, the activity of the subjects during testing, the timing and method of blood sampling, and the techniques used to measure plasma glucose levels. Predisposing factors such as obesity, physical inactivity, drugs, and other diseases may contribute to the development of hyperglycemia in older individuals, and this condition probably represents a different disorder than NIDDM. While syndromes of hyperglycemia share the characteristic glucose intolerance, the pathophysiology of the hyperglycemia is often different, and the complications will differ based on the cause of the hyperglycemic state. These pathophysiologic aspects of hyperglycemia and glucose intolerance need to be considered before vigorous treatment with drugs is considered in the older individual with asymptomatic hyperglycemia.

In older individuals the clinical signs and symptoms of diabetes may be subtle, and some individuals may require glucose tolerance testing when there is a strong clinical suspicion of the disease, even in the presence of a normal fasting plasma glucose level (Table 71-2). If the decision to test a patient for diabetes is based upon a wide variety of symptoms and historical information, then the full oral glucose tolerance test should be performed since abnormal results may be obtained no matter what the fasting glucose level. Furthermore, a corroborating test should be done if an abnormal response is obtained. In the older patient with hyperglycemia and clinical symptoms and signs of diabetes (Table 71-2), the diagnosis can be made easily and treatment initiated without fear of a false-positive diagnosis. Although undiagnosed diabetes exists in about 3 percent of the American population, the prevalence of undiagnosed and diagnosed diabetes increases with aging.[1]

The currently recommended diagnostic tests for diabetes are neither 100 percent specific nor 100 percent sensitive. Rather, there is considerable overlap between test results in normals and individuals with diabetes because the sensitivity and specificity of diagnostic testing frequently vary inversely. Highly sensitive tests would detect all individuals with diabetes (there are no false negatives) but misdiagnose some normals, whereas highly specific tests will correctly identify all normals (no false positives occur) and miss some individuals with diabetes by classifying them as being normal. Considering these facts, it is our belief that the risk to the patient of inappropriate diagnosis of NIDDM outweighs the benefits gained by the indiscriminate screening for diabetes in older individuals. Yet, testing for diabetes is somewhat analogous to screening for high cholesterol and hypertension, since hyperglycemia, hypertension, and hypercholesterolemia are all major risk factors for atherosclerotic disease and warrant medical evaluation and treatment.

When should the physician be concerned about making a diagnosis of diabetes mellitus in an older individual? Should all older individuals be screened for diabetes mellitus, or should evaluation be limited to those with a high risk in whom the disease is present or likely to develop? In the absence of a definitive marker for diabetes independent of the fasting plasma glucose concentration, the physician must balance finding asymptomatic diabetes versus the potential dangers of making a diagnosis of diabetes in a person who does not have the disease and is not likely to develop it. The social, medical, and economic implications of a false-positive diagnosis must be carefully weighed against the dangers inherent in making a false-negative diagnosis of normality (Table 71-3). We recommend testing for diabetes as part of the routine annual physical examination of all older patients; when the fasting plasma glucose is normal, the course is obvious, but when fasting hyperglycemia occurs unexpectedly, the diagnostic evaluation becomes more complex, especially in the asymptomatic older patient.

The National Diabetes Data Group (NDDG) standards for the diagnosis of diabetes are conservative for older people and extremely liberal for younger adults since the cutoff points for the diagnosis of diabetes mellitus are probably high for younger individuals. The standards emphasize the importance of measuring the fasting plasma glucose concentration rather than performing a full oral glucose tolerance test. However, although the NDDG standards for the glucose tolerance

test[2] are not age-adjusted, they are endorsed because they err on the side of specificity rather than sensitivity and avoid a false-positive diagnosis of diabetes. The NDDG report is comprehensive in its description of the exact techniques for the performance of the oral glucose tolerance test for diabetes in adults and in its definition of diagnostic standards and specific criteria for interpreting the test and diagnosing the disease. There is a detailed scheme for the clinical classification of diabetes as well as other diseases associated with hyperglycemia which are not regarded as diabetes in themselves. We are confident that with new epidemiologic and experimental evidence, especially in the elderly, the standards of the NDDG will be modified in the future.

Measurement of Fasting Plasma Glucose

Measuring the fasting plasma glucose concentration is advantageous because of the relative consistency and reproducibility day to day of the concentration in people whose readings lie either in the normal or abnormal range (>140 mg/dl). An individual is rarely diabetic at one time and normal at another, and the fasting plasma glucose is relatively unaltered by age. The plasma glucose measurement is easy to standardize since an overnight fast can commonly be achieved with little excess burden to physician or patient. Furthermore, the measurement is performed rapidly, cheaply, and conveniently, and it is rarely (and, if so, minimally) affected by the caloric intake, the composition of the diet, or physical activity prior to the test.[42]

The cut point for fasting plasma glucose recommended by NDDG for a firm diagnosis of diabetes is set at 140 mg/dl, even though some investigators propose that the upper limit of normal be 115 mg/dl. The higher value maximizes test specificity, since oral glucose tolerance tests show a diabetic response in all individuals with fasting plasma glucose levels ≥140 mg/dl. The NDDG report states that people with fasting plasma glucose concentrations between 120 and 139 mg/dl probably will have abnormal glucose tolerance tests, and even levels between 115 and 124 mg/dl must be viewed with suspicion. This borderline zone might even extend down a bit further, but age-adjusted standards and epidemiologic information are needed to relate them to the development of diabetes. If a fasting glucose value above 140 mg/dl is confirmed by a second test, it is indicative of diabetes, and glucose tolerance testing is not required. However, below the level of 140 mg/dl, glucose tolerance should be considered if the clinical suspicion for diabetes is high.

The Oral Glucose Tolerance Test

Prior to making a decision to perform a glucose tolerance test, it is important to consider the consequences of a

TABLE 71-3
Risks of Misdiagnosing Diabetes in Older People

False-Positive Diagnosis	*False-Negative Diagnosis*
1. Treatment with hypoglycemic medicines (insulin or oral agents) and the potential for side effects	1. Inadequate preparation (treatment) at time of stressful events such as surgery, infection, trauma, burns, heart attack, athletics
2. Change in lifestyle with unnecessary alteration in social behavior, including food choices, alcohol consumption, fasting, prolonged exercise, and stressful situations	2. Lack of knowledge of importance to lose weight, change diet, and exercise—especially for obese patients
3. Increased cost of medical insurance and requirements for treatment and follow-up care	3. Lack of knowledge of increased risk to family
4. Inappropriate labeling of family members as being at risk	4. Failure to institute health care habits to aggressively prevent and treat the complications characteristic of the disease
5. Bias in employment	

false-positive as well as a false-negative diagnosis of diabetes (Table 71-3). For the false-positive test, these consequences include the possibility of inappropriate treatment with hypoglycemic drugs and the potential risk for life-threatening hypoglycemia, unnecessary lifestyle changes affecting social behavior, increased medical and insurance costs related to the "diabetic label," and potential bias in employment. On the other hand, failure to diagnose diabetes may lead to inadequate awareness of the need for appropriate health care habits to prevent the chronic vascular and neuropathic complications of the disease and the failure to inform family members at high risk. This may be of particular concern at times of stress, especially if the diabetic is inadquately prepared or is treated inappropriately for a condition and develops the complications of severe ketoacidosis (due to insulin deficiency) or hyperosmolar nonketotic coma due to severe dehydration or coexistent sepsis. The risk-to-benefit ratio clearly weighs in the favor of making an accurate diagnosis of diabetes mellitus in older individuals at high risk for stress and comorbidity which further increases their risk of complications from borderline or asymptomatic NIDDM.

Symptoms and signs of diabetes may persist in the presence of a normal fasting plasma glucose concentration in some older people. Under these conditions, the measurement of the plasma glucose response to an oral glucose load represents the most sensitive way to detect the diabetic state. The oral glucose tolerance test (OGTT) should always be made in the morning after an overnight 10- to 16-hour fast under resting conditions without cigarette smoking. After a fasting blood sample is drawn, sampling should be made at 30-minute intervals for 2 hours after oral administration of a 75-g or body-size-adjusted dose (1 g/kg body weight or 40 g/m^2 body surface area). Measurement of glucose should be done on venous plasma by a glucose oxidase method. The interpretation of the results depends first upon the fasting plasma glucose level, second on the glucose value at 2 hours, and third upon the highest glucose level of the three intermediate time points, 30, 60, and 90 minutes. There is one cut point for intermediate time points and two cut points for the 2-hour value, at 140 and 200 mg/dl (Fig. 71-3A). Thus, there are six test possibilities (Fig. 71-3B). The terminology for these test results include: diabetic (glucose ≥ 200 mg at both intermediate and 2-hour time points), normal (glucose below 200 and below 140 mg/dl at these two time points), impaired glucose tolerance (glucose ≥ 200 and between 140 and 199 mg at the intermediate time points), and nondiagnostic for the other three categories of results. Criteria for an abnormal 2-hour glucose value prior to report of the NDDG was set at 140 mg/dl. Hence moving the 2-hour criteria from 140 to 200 has, in effect, greatly reduced the percentage of test results in a diabetic range, especially in middle-aged and older individuals.

There are a relatively high percentage of older individuals classified as impaired, and some unreported fraction of older people must be in the nondiagnostic range. According to these criteria, perhaps only about half of all people 70 years or older might receive a completely normal label after oral glucose tolerance testing.

Other Diagnostic Tests for Diabetes in Older Individuals

Measurement of glycosylated hemoglobin (HbA$_{1c}$) is a possible test which might offer advantages over the fasting plasma glucose level and oral glucose tolerance test in making a diagnosis of diabetes in older individuals. This is because its measurement theoretically reflects the time integrated blood glucose level over the 120-day life span of the erythrocyte. The positive relationship between age and hemoglobin A$_{1c}$, and the finding of a large number of false-positive results in normal people limits the usefulness of the glycosylated hemoglobin level as a single diagnostic test for diabetes mellitus.[5]

The intravenous glucose tolerance test (IVGTT) has been used most frequently, especially in research studies, to diagnose diabetes. The decline in glucose disappearance rate with aging is approximately 0.2 percent/minute per decade. Whereas values above 1.0 percent per minute are considered normal, a decrease in glucose disappearance with aging has been reported. While the impact of age on glucose metabolism is demonstrated by the IVGTT, recommendations for establishing criteria for the test are limited by the relatively few studies which have utilized this technique to diagnose diabetes mellitus. The cortisone oral glucose tolerance test and the intravenous tolbutamide response test serve primarily as research tools, but also have demonstrated an age-related decline in glucose tolerance. Thus, except for the oral glucose tolerance test, there are limited reference data for other diagnostic tests for diabetes.

CLASSIFICATION OF DIABETES MELLITUS

There are four mutually exclusive clinically relevant subclasses of diabetes mellitus:

1. *Type I, or insulin-dependent diabetes mellitus (IDDM)*, is caused by an autoimmune destructive process in the beta cells of pancreatic islets. It accounts for 10 to 20 percent of known cases of diabetes occurring primarily in patients under 45 years of age in the general population; but a very small percentage of older diabetics have IDDM. Patients with IDDM present with an accelerating history of glucosuria, weight loss, and anorexia, often for less than 2 months. They are thin and usually symptomatic with ketoacidosis, the primary mode of presentation. Although greater than 90 percent of older diabetics are ketosis-resistant and have type II

diabetes mellitus, or NIDDM, under stressful acute medical conditions such as surgery, infections, or acute myocardial infarction, the older patient with NIDDM may become ketosis-prone and require insulin therapy. With resolution of the acute medical condition these patients usually return to their normal non-insulin-dependent state.

2. *Idiopathic type II diabetes mellitus (NIDDM)* defines a group of patients over the age of 50 years who are either obese at presentation or who have been obese in the past. Among older people, it is the most common form of diabetes. There is usually significant glucose intolerance for a number of years before the detection of the syndrome. Rarely is there an acute precipitating event in NIDDM; these patients are usually first seen for complications of the disease, either in a coronary care unit or by an ophthalmologist, neurologist, nephrologist, or gynecologist. Genetic factors seem to be operative in NIDDM since up to 25 percent of parents and 40 percent of siblings of these patients have impaired or diabetic glucose tolerance tests. To date, no specific HLA serotypes have been identified as in IDDM. Typically 80 percent of patients with NIDDM are or have been obese and 20 percent are of normal weight; however, obesity itself is not a primary cause of this disease. Studies among the Pima Indians support the likelihood that the presence of obesity may be one factor which hastens the transition from impaired glucose tolerance to the actual development of NIDDM.[40] The coexistence of obesity with NIDDM worsens the degree of hyperglycemia and the severity of the syndrome; dietary adherence and

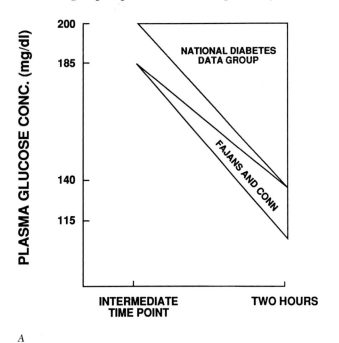

A

FIGURE 71-3

A. The National Diabetes Data Group standards for interpreting the oral glucose tolerance test are depicted in comparison with the old Fajans and Conn criteria. The shift upward toward higher glucose levels in the new versus the old criteria is apparent at both the intermediate and 2-h time points. *B.* These are the diagnostic categories for results of the oral glucose tolerance test according to the National Diabetes Data Group criteria. These have been related to the actual cutoff points defining the diagnostic triangle in Fig. *A.*

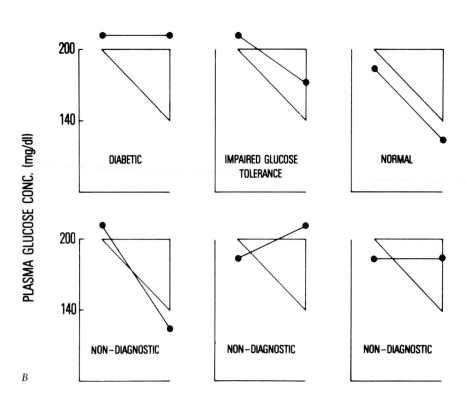

B

weight reduction improve glucose tolerance and reduce symptoms and complications in many obese patients with NIDDM.[26,31]

In some patients with NIDDM, especially those that are at ideal body weight, increasing hyperglycemia may require treatment with insulin despite therapy with a proper diet and exercise regimen. Some of these patients may develop progressive hypoinsulinemia as the disease progresses, while others may develop another disease that worsens glucose metabolism. In most cases, however, worsening of hyperglycemia in older patients with NIDDM suggests that there is an acute underlying infection or stress. Treatment of the acute condition usually returns glucose regulation to baseline and allows insulin to be discontinued.

3. A history of *gestational diabetes* is of particular importance in older women. Of the 2 percent of pregnant women who exhibit glucose intolerance of sufficient magnitude to qualify for the diagnosis of gestational diabetes. half may be expected to become diabetic within 15 to 20 years. This disorder most resembles NIDDM, and although clinically mild, it is worsened by increased body weight, especially in an upper body distribution. These women often develop hypertension, which increases morbidity and mortality.[43] The treatment of hypertension in these women with thiazide diuretics or beta blockers and the administration of estrogen containing compounds to relieve menopausal symptoms may worsen the diabetic state.[44] Therefore, older women with a history of gestational diabetes or large babies should be monitored periodically for the emergence of NIDDM.

4. Diabetes mellitus can be *secondary to other diseases or drugs* that promote the development of insulin resistance and hyperglycemia in older individuals in a manner similar to that seen in NIDDM. Older people often are treated with various drugs to control hypertension, arthritis, seizures, depression, or postmenopausal symptoms which also will worsen glucose tolerance (Table 71-4). Progressive pancreatic disease due to chronic pancreatitis, alcoholism, or carcinoma may lead to pancreatectomy and the need for insulin replacement. Other diseases such as Cushing's syndrome, glucagonoma, acromegaly, hemochromatosis, pheochromocytoma, and primary aldosteronism should be considered as possible, but rare, causes of hyperglycemia in the elderly.

IMPLICATIONS OF DIABETES IN OLDER POPULATIONS

What are the implications of a positive glucose tolerance test in older individuals? For normal and diabetic categories of glucose tolerance, the clinical implications are clear. Age-specific mortality rates are consistently higher in overt diabetes from complications of atherosclerosis, especially myocardial infarction and stroke.[45,46] The clinical outcomes of people in the impaired and nondiagnostic categories and their incidence of diabetic vascular complications, coronary heart disease, stroke, and overall mortality rate is important but unknown information. Longitudinal studies are needed to determine the clinical significance of these diagnostic categories.

In addition to the uncertainty of the clinical outcome of the various diagnostic categories of glucose tolerance, a major problem with the interpretation of the oral glucose tolerance test is its lack of reproducibility. Glucose tolerance differing by greater than 50 mg/dl has been demonstrated on retesting. A large number of acute and chronic medical conditions, the administration of certain drugs (Table 71-4), physical inactivity, dietary intake of carbohydrate and caloric amount prior to testing and age affect the oral glucose tolerance test. Even when these factors are controlled, there is a significant degree of test/retest variability in the results of the oral glucose tolerance test. Because of this, an absolutely cer-

TABLE 71-4
Commonly Used Drugs Affecting Glucose Tolerance in Older Persons

Worsen Hyperglycemia	*Potentiate Hypoglycemia*
1. Diuretics (thiazide, chlorthalidone, furosemide)	1. Alcohol
2. Glucocorticoids	2. Beta blockers (propranolol)
3. Estrogens (birth control pills)	3. Bishydroxycoumarin
4. Nicotinic acid	4. Monamine oxidase inhibitors
5. Phenothiazines	5. Phenylbutazone
6. Phenytoins	6. Salicylates (large doses)
7. Sympathomimetic agents	7. Sulfonamides, sulfonylureas
8. Lithium	8. Cimetidine
9. Sugar-containing medications	9. Anabolic steroids
	10. Insulin

tain diagnosis of diabetes mellitus should not be made solely on the basis of one oral glucose tolerance test unless it is demonstrated that the test is abnormal on two occasions and conditions known to affect the validity of the glucose tolerance test are absent or strictly controlled.

Age, the level of hyperglycemia, and the severity and duration of obesity are major predictors of the natural history of diabetes in most people with borderline glucose tolerance; however, morbidity and mortality from cardiovascular causes in borderline diabetics is significantly affected by the coexistence of other coronary risk factors, especially systolic hypertension, hyperlipidemia, cigarette smoking, and male gender.[31-33] That NIDDM is as potent a risk factor for cardiovascular disease in women as it is in men indicates that other factors, such as sex steroid hormone metabolism, the regional distribution of body fat, physical conditioning status, and insulin resistance require consideration.[43,47-50]

Whether one is dealing with the disease NIDDM or with a natural sequela of the aging process in the older patient, hyperglycemia creates a therapeutic dilemma for the geriatrician. In the absence of atherosclerotic vascular complications, neuropathy, renal disease, cataracts, or retinopathy in the hyperglycemic older patient at the time of initial evaluation, other disorders or drugs should be considered initially as the cause of hyperglycemia. The most prominent one is obesity, but obese and mildly overweight individuals are often sedentary, and physical inactivity may be equally important in understanding the pathogenesis of hyperglycemia in older people. Obese older sedentary individuals often have hypertension requiring treatment with diuretics which may worsen glucose homeostasis and reduce renal perfusion. As renal blood flow declines, renin and angiotensin levels increase, leading to renal hypertension and ultimately a deterioration in renal function. These individuals present with diabetes and nephropathy, yet the natural history of the disease is not due solely to diabetes. Although NIDDM usually does not present in a standard fashion in older patients (Table 71-2), the presence of subtle signs of diabetes such as weight loss or fatigue, impaired vision, nocturia, urinary incontinence, nonspecific dysaesthesias and paresthesias, diarrhea, postural hypotension, a recurrent poorly healing peripheral vascular foot lesion, and increased susceptibility to infection usually confirm the diagnosis in the older individual with suspected diabetes. However, this clinical pattern does not occur in all older individuals with hyperglycemia.

If the progressive deterioration in glucose tolerance that accompanies aging represents a stage in the evolution of the diabetic syndrome and the potential for subsequent deleterious complications, then treatment is indicated. Although it is not yet known whether the microvascular complications of neuropathy and retinopathy

can be prevented with vigorous treatment of hyperglycemia, the macrovascular complications of NIDDM are multifactorial in origin and tend to progress unless (1) preventive measures are instituted to normalize blood pressure, lipids, and body weight, (2) cigarettes are eliminated, and (3) hyperglycemia is properly controlled. If the natural history of the diabetic syndrome in older individuals were known (i.e., whether or not the decline in glucose tolerance with advancing age was a disease or a physiologic benign consequence of the aging process), properly designed therapeutic interventions could be initiated to reduce risk for the development of complications from the disease. When the inappropriate diagnosis is made and therapy initiated, however, the risk of complications, such as hypoglycemia, increases dramatically in older people.

COMPLICATIONS OF DIABETES IN OLDER PEOPLE

The results of longitudinal studies examining the clinical course of older people with borderline diabetes or impaired glucose tolerance are inconsistent, but the prevalence of diabetes increases with advancing age, and death from cardiovascular complications is increased in older diabetics as well as in borderline diabetics when compared to normal older people.[31-33,45,46] There are three major clinical complications of diabetes: The first involves accelerated atherosclerosis of large vessels; the second, microvascular disease of capillary basement membranes in the kidney and retina; and the third, neuropathy, causing peripheral sensorimotor defects and autonomic nervous system dysfunction. These clinical disorders are present in many diabetic patients and cause most of the disability and death related to the disease.

The economic burden of diabetes in the United States is estimated at between 25 and 30 million hospital days costing \$8 to \$10 billion a year for direct medical costs and nearly the same amount for disability and premature death related to the vascular complications of the disease. In the older patient, diabetes increases the incidence of age-related complications as follows: Renal disease and blindness are increased approximately 25-fold; vascular insufficiency and gangrene are increased 20-fold; hypertension is increased threefold; myocardial infarction is increased 2.5-fold; and stroke is increased twofold.[51-57]

The pathogenesis of the complications of diabetes is multifactorial, and they occur more often in older patients. In addition to the long-term detrimental effects of hyperglycemia and hyperinsulinemia on blood vessels, medical complications in diabetes are related to the coexistence of risk factors for accelerated atherosclerosis, especially hyperlipidemia, hypertension, obesity, and cigarette smoking. The macrovascular complications of diabetes primarily affect mortality,[33,51–53] while the microvascular complications are responsible for chronic morbidity associated with retinopathy, nephropathy, and neuropathy.[54–57] The high incidence of atherosclerosis and vascular compromise which occurs with advancing age in Western societies makes diabetes the prototypic disease for studying accelerated atherosclerosis in aging humans. Obesity and hypertension, common in older diabetics, worsen hyperlipidemia and cardiovascular and renal function, increasing the severity of atherosclerotic vascular disease and raising morbidity and mortality from macro- and microvascular complications.[32,33,45]

Data from the Framingham Study suggest that, with increasing age and duration of diabetes, both the hypertensive and/or hyperlipidemic diabetic is at heightened risk for vascular complications and early mortality from myocardial infarction and stroke.[33] Every manifestation of coronary artery disease occurs with increased frequency and severity in the diabetic. Non-insulin-dependent diabetics commonly have high plasma triglyceride, cholesterol, and apoprotein B and reduced high-density lipoprotein cholesterol (HDL-C) and apoprotein A-I levels.[58] The heightened prevalence of these lipid abnormalities, coupled with hyperglycemia and hyperinsulinemia, promotes the formation of atheroma (see also Chap. 45).[58–60] Risk for coronary disease is more pronounced in women with NIDDM than in men; hence, diabetes seems to eliminate the protective advantage afforded females over aging males from complications of coronary artery disease. This may be related to the upper body fat distribution characteristic of older women with NIDDM.[47]

The syndromes of silent ischemia and silent myocardial infarction are also more common in diabetics than in nondiabetics, and their complications are greater.[52] This is because of the nature of the neuropathic disease associated with diabetes. Pain perception is reduced in NIDDM, and functional abnormalities in contractile properties of the myocardium lead to the development of microaneurysms, interstitial fibrosis, and myocardial degeneration. This results in myopathy, and causes diabetics to have more congestive heart failure, arrhythmias, and conduction defects during ischemic episodes and to have more myocardial infarctions than nondiabetic patients. All these factors increase mortality during infarction twofold in the diabetic male and 4.5-fold in the diabetic female when compared to nondiabetic controls.

The development of arteriosclerotic complications in NIDDM is probably also related to genetic factors. The insoluble collagen fraction and matrix in diabetics becomes resistant to digestion by collagenase and enriched in glycosaminoglycan complexes and glycosylated

protein products.[59] One mechanism by which this process is initiated is by nonenzymatic glycosylation of proteins to advanced glycosylation end products which form within arterial walls and interact synergistically with platelets, macrophages, and cholesterol esters to form atheroma.[59] The proliferation of arterial smooth muscle cells are enhanced in NIDDM due to the increased secretion of intrinsic growth factors from cells (platelet-derived growth factor and macrophage-derived growth factor), which in turn enhances platelet aggregation, smooth muscle cell proliferation, and connective tissue synthesis, thus promoting atherogenesis (see also Chap. 45).[60–62] Coexistent hyperinsulinemia and hyperlipidemia in this atherogenic environment promotes atherosclerosis, narrows blood vessels and leads to cardiovascular, cerebrovascular, and peripheral vascular disease with the resultant complications of heart attack, stroke, ulcers, and gangrene. Whether or not the heightened incidence of vascular complications in older diabetic patients can be prevented or delayed by early detection of diabetes and by aggressive medical and/or surgical intervention in patients with atherosclerotic vascular disease to ultimately reduce morbidity and prolong survival has not been determined.

MANAGEMENT OF THE OLDER DIABETIC

The goals of treatment of older patients with NIDDM are to achieve good control of hyperglycemia in the hope of minimizing long-term organ complications while simultaneously providing good medical care to avoid the risks of vigorous treatment—the most serious of which is hypoglycemia. It is estimated that treatment with insulin or oral sulfonylureas is needed for only one-half of older diabetics; hence, it is incumbent on the physician to select carefully those diabetic patients for whom drug therapy is required. Many elderly patients already have macrovascular and microvascular complications at the time diabetes is discovered, and it is important to prevent these conditions from worsening.

The NIH Consensus Conference on Diet and Exercise in Non-insulin Dependent Diabetes Mellitus[26] concluded that achievement and maintenance of normal weight is the cornerstone of therapy for NIDDM. Oral agents should be added only as necessary to maintain blood glucose near normal. Exercise training, on the other hand, in the obese patient with NIDDM (80 percent of NIDDM patients are obese) has variable effects on metabolic control, and in some patients these may be small in magnitude. Despite the minimal impact of physical exercise alone in the treatment of the obese patient with NIDDM, regular aerobic exercise was recommended as a useful adjunct to dietary therapy in some patients. The efficacy of smoking cessation, dietary changes, physical conditioning, aggressive treatment of hypertension and hyperlipidemia, or combinations thereof in preventing the macrovascular and microvascular complications of diabetes are unfortunately unknown, especially in the elderly where the socioeconomic costs and morbidity and mortality from atherosclerotic complications related to NIDDM are highest. Diagnostic criteria and specific therapeutic guidelines for the management of hyperglycemia and other metabolic consequences of diabetes are needed if the conundrum, whether or not to treat NIDDM in the asymptomatic older individual, is to be resolved and the heightened prevalence of vascular complications and increased morbidity and mortality from diabetes mellitus in older people is to be reduced.

Older diabetic patients frequently have other diseases which require additional therapy, and there are often special conditions associated with the aging process that may affect the treatment of diabetes (Table 71-5). These special conditions should be understood so that optimal therapy can be provided. First, a complete as-

TABLE 71-5
Special Issues in Care of Older Diabetics

Activity level: Gait, coordination, flexibility, strength, agility
Special senses: Vision, taste, smell, hearing, position, hunger, thirst
Diet: Appetite, food preferences, dentition and salivation, ability to prepare food, feed self and eat (tremor, arthritis), body weight
Drugs: Other medications and their potential for adverse interactions (toxicity), drug excretion and dose adjustment, alcohol, caffeine, allergy
Social factors: Living alone, poverty, hygiene, resistance to change in habits, education
Other diseases (by system):
  Cardiovascular: Hypertension, postural hypotension, ischemia (silent), previous infarction, arrhythmias, peripheral vascular insufficiency, cardiomyopathy
  Pulmonary: Smoking, bronchitis, hypoxia, asthma, chronic obstructive lung disease
  Central nervous: Mental status, memory, sensory perception, motor and autonomic function, tremor, stroke
  Renal: Uremia, nephrotic syndrome, papillitis, pyelonephritis
  Gastrointestinal: Motility, constipation, diarrhea, nutrient absorption, blood loss
  Hepatobiliary: Obstruction, inflammation, gallstones
  Hematologic: Anemia, bleeding, bruisability
  Musculoskeletal: Arthritis, deformity, weakness, wasting
  Integumentary: Infections, rashes, poor healing
  Neuropsychiatric: Cognitive and affective disorders, need for supervision, dementia, sleep behavior
  Infections: Pruritus, urinary tract, otitis, foot ulcers, cholecystitis, fasciitis
  General (chronic): Weight loss, fever, neoplasia, abscess, tuberculosis

sessment of the patient with a full history physical examination and laboratory evaluation is necessary. Attention should focus on: general (chronic) conditions such as dietary habits, weight loss, chills, fever, inactivity, gastrointestinal function, and special senses; coexistent disease of the cardiovascular, pulmonary, renal, hepatobiliary, and central nervous systems; the use of other drugs; the integrity of the musculoskeletal and integumentary systems, especially the feet; mental status and cognitive function; and the social situation. The laboratory evaluation should include an electrocardiogram, measurement of the functional status of the major organ systems and plasma lipids, urinalysis, and a 24-hour urine collection for measurement of glucose, protein, and creatinine clearance.

Treatment goals should focus initially on the presence of coexistent medical and social factors, other than diabetes itself, which may affect metabolic control. Coexistent diseases should be treated with medications which do not alter glucose homeostasis (Table 71-4). Drug interactions are a major concern, especially with respect to toxicity and risk for hypoglycemia or paradoxical hyperglycemia. First-generation oral sulfonylureas are bound to albumin for transport, and their effectiveness is reduced in hypoalbuminemic states (nephrosis) or when other drugs are taken which are ionically bound to albumin (bishydroxycoumarin, phenylbutazone, salicylates, and others). Declining renal function or hepatic dysfunction delays sulfonylurea and insulin clearance, potentiating hypoglycemia. Concurrent infections, often obscure, may worsen glycemic control and suddenly cause a previously diet-controlled patient to require insulin therapy. Impaired food absorption, delayed gastric emptying, or dumping syndrome can further enhance metabolic instability in the diabetic.

The next treatment goals involve counseling in diet and physical activity habits. It is often essential to involve family and other professionals (dietitian, nurse, and exercise physiologist) in this aspect of care, so that the patient can readily agree to the dietary and activity changes built around already established patterns of life. This is of particular importance in the older patient with central nervous system dysfunction, limitations in activity, or impairments in special senses.

DIETARY GUIDELINES FOR OLDER DIABETICS

The diet program should address factors such as dentition, salivation, and altered taste which may affect food preference in older patients. The diet should fulfill the principles of the American Diabetes Association Diet[63] for proper nutrition. These principles include—in addition to the restriction of calories in overweight patients to promote weight loss of $\frac{1}{2}$ to 1 lb per week—a diet whose composition is enriched in complex carbohydrates and fiber to 55 to 60 percent of daily caloric intake. For most patients the diet should contain <30 percent of calories as fat (<10 percent as saturated fat) and not more than 300 mg/day cholesterol; but the diet may need adjustment to treat hyperlipidemia according to the guidelines of the American Heart Association.[64]

Weight reduction and its maintenance are the cornerstone of therapy for the obese, older patient with NIDDM.[26] In addition to improving glucose tolerance and insulin sensitivity, weight loss also lowers blood pressure as well as plasma cholesterol and triglyceride, and raises high-density lipoprotein cholesterol (HDL-C) in most obese diabetic patients. Once sufficient weight is lost, a weight-maintaining diet should be determined. The diet plan should be written out for the patient and for those who prepare the food. Regular follow-up sessions with the patient and caretaker are recommended for continuing education and to monitor body weight and compliance.[65]

EXERCISE FOR OLDER DIABETICS

In view of the reported increase in insulin sensitivity, improvement in glucose tolerance, reduction in body weight, and improvement in plasma lipids and blood pressure achieved by exercise training in some diabetics, regular physical exercise is advocated as an adjunct to diet in the treatment of NIDDM.[26] In the treated patient with NIDDM, exercise training often results in the reduction in dosage or discontinuation of oral sulfonylurea agents. However, most of the benefits of exercise training are based on results from high-intensity training programs in young and middle-aged individuals and cannot be readily extrapolated to diabetic patients over 65 years of age. Since atherosclerotic complications, renal disease, retinopathy, musculoskeletal and neurologic dysfunction are common in older diabetics, involvement in programs of physical activity should be preceded by a thorough physical examination with special attention to the vascular system, extremities, and eyes. Functional capacity should be determined during a physician-administered exercise treadmill stress test with electrocardiographic, blood pressure, and symptom monitoring to identify patients with silent ischemia, exercise-induced arrhythmias, hypertension, or autonomic dysfunction causing vascular and central nervous system instability during exercise. All risks for adverse physiologic (cardiovascular, pulmonary, metabolic-hypoglycemic, musculoskeletal) responses during exercise are best determined during this test. Patients with abnormal exercise stress tests should be referred for further evaluation by a specialist in the area of dysfunction.

The exercise prescription should be based on the patient's functional capacity, as determined by physical examination and the results of an exercise stress test. If oxygen consumption can be measured during the stress test, functional capacity can be expressed in ml/(kg)(min) oxygen consumed and related to heart rate. The intensity of activity can then be defined, with the peak and average intensity of exercise estimated by determining 60 and 85 percent of the functional capacity. This can be easily related to heart rate, and the target heart rate during exercise calculated as the training intensity or percentage of functional capacity × (maximal exercise heart rate − resting heart rate) + the resting heart rate. The energy expenditure for most physical activities is calculated in METS [1 MET − resting oxygen consumption = 3.5 ml/(kg)(min), or 1 kcal/(kg)(h)] and can be extrapolated to a safe range of exercise intensity (4 to 8 METS) for most older individuals who display no cardiovascular limitations during maximal exercise stress testing. Target heart rate is then monitored during exercise sessions as an index of training intensity. It is also worthwhile to monitor perceived exertion during exercise stress testing in older individuals using a visual analog scale, where 6 is the least and 20 the most intense, to monitor subjective responses during training. In individuals over 65 years of age, as well as in those with NIDDM, the stress test should be reviewed by a cardiologist, and advice should be sought from an exercise physiologist in designing the prescription for physical activity.

Initial physical activity should be supervised and undertaken in a slow, sequential manner to ensure that the patient's capabilities are not exceeded, that injury is prevented, and that cardiovascular (blood pressure, pulse) responses are safe and appropriate. Aerobic conditioning (walking, swimming, stationary bicycling, and jogging) involving movement of major muscle groups is the preferred type of exercise because energy expenditure (METS) is usually known, and these activities tend to enhance glucose utilization to the greatest extent. Exercise associated with straining and breath holding, such as low repetition weight lifting and nautilus isometric exercises are high tension and may raise blood pressure and increase risk of retinal detachment, vitreous hemorrhage, stroke, and albuminuria. The duration, frequency, and progression of exercise should be slow, with frequent monitoring and reassessment of exercise capacity on the treadmill with electrocardiographic monitoring if hemodynamic instability develops. Attention also should be given to proper foot care and avoidance of injury during exercise.

COMPLIANCE TO DIET AND EXERCISE

Compliance is the major problem in maintaining diet and the optimal body weight to control hyperglycemia in NIDDM.[65] Recidivism is high, and few obese patients successfully maintain good eating habits and weight loss after completion of participation in the structured program. Physical activity may be an effective adjunct to diet therapy because it enhances weight loss by increasing utilization of ingested calories and may improve psychosocial state and sense of well-being even during periods of caloric restriction. The increased energy expended during exercise training (100 kcal/mile walking or running) may permit fewer dietary restrictions during weight loss and enhance compliance during weight loss and its maintenance phase. Research is needed to determine guidelines for the design of the most effective treatment and maintenance programs for obese patients with NIDDM.

Older people fear injury during exercise, and caution is recommended to avoid this complication by prescribing a slow progression of exercise intensity, frequency, and duration. Rarely does an older person return to a program following an injury precipitated during exercise. The use of behavior modification techniques in conjunction with the exercise program may improve the treatment outcome, but prolonged maintenance varies directly with the success of the follow-up program. Peer pressure, frequent telephone contact by the therapist and frequent maintenance meetings seem to produce the best success. When the patient is unable to comply and hyperglycemia persists, drug therapy is indicated to improve metabolic control and avoid complications.

DRUG THERAPY IN THE MANAGEMENT OF OLDER DIABETICS

In addition to treating hyperglycemia in the older patient with NIDDM, other measures of management include treatment of systolic and diastolic hypertension and hyperlipidemia, and the cessation of cigarette smoking. These are major risk factors for atherosclerosis in nondiabetics, and they accelerate the progression of atherosclerosis in diabetics. Their successful management is of utmost importance because of the impact of these conditions on the progression of atherosclerosis in diabetes and the possibility that their control will reduce the incidence of coronary artery disease and other vascular complications in diabetic patients.

Treatment with oral sulfonylureas or insulin should be considered in the older diabetic patient with persistent symptomatic hyperglycemia (polyuria, polyphagia, polydipsia) causing weight loss, fatigue, weakness, and recurrent infection. This type of patient usually responds to therapy with oral sulfonylureas provided that there is concurrent adherence to diet and exercise regimens. Twenty percent of older diabetics are lean and do not respond to oral sulfonylureas because they are insulinopenic. These patients may present with ketoacidosis or develop it during stressful events, such as surgery, infection, or myocardial infarction. Older diabetic patients with multiple risk factors for metabolic and vascular complications which are worsened by persistent hyperglycemia require aggressive treatment. These patients are prone to infections and have deteriorating renal function and retinopathy; they often develop hypertriglyceridemia and recurrent pancreatitis due to chylomicronemia,[66] and they are at risk for life-threatening acidosis[67] or hyperosmolarity[68] during stress. In general, these patients tend to do poorly owing to the coexistence of multiple vascular complications from NIDDM, but better control of hyperglycemia and risk factors for atherosclerosis may be achieved in some patients with strict adherence to diet, combined insulin and sulfonylurea therapy, and the addition of a lipid-lowering drug.

Several sulfonylurea drugs of varying potency and duration of action are available for use as oral hypoglycemic agents (Table 71-6). The use of these drugs to control hyperglycemia, prevent neurologic, renal and ophthalmologic complications, and retard the progression of coronary artery disease in patients of any age with NIDDM remains uncertain as a result of the controversial findings of the University Group Diabetes Program (UGDP) study. The metabolic advantages of oral sulfonylureas over adequate doses of insulin are not clear,[69] even though their mode of action affects the major underlying metabolic abnormalities in NIDDM, i.e., peripheral insulin resistance, increased hepatic glucose production, and impaired insulin secretion.[70,71] Benefits of oral sulfonylurea therapy in older patients, other than

TABLE 71-6
Oral Sulfonylurea Drugs

Sulfonylurea	Dosage (day^{-1}), mg	Onset of Action, h	Duration of Action, h	Route of Excretion	Activity of Metabolite
1. First-generation					
Tolbutamide	500–3000	0.5–1.0	6–12	Urine/inactive	
Tolazamide	100–1000	4–6	12–24	Urine/inactive	
Chlorpropamide	100–750	1–2	24–90	Urine/inactive	
2. Second-generation					
Glipizide	5–40	1–3	12–18	Urine/inactive	
Glyburide	2.5–20	0.5–1	16–24	50% urine/active 50% bile/active	

convenience of oral medication, include reduction in risk of hyperosmolar coma and ketoacidosis, high degree of efficacy, and relative ease of acceptance without need of the major behavioral changes required by insulin therapy. However, these drugs have no place in the management of insulin-dependent diabetes, ketoacidosis, or hyperglycemic hyperosmolar nonketotic coma.

There are several problems associated with the use of sulfonylureas to control hyperglycemia, and these seem to occur more often and are more severe in the elderly. The most serious is prolonged hypoglycemia, probably related to irregular and reduced caloric intake and declines in drug metabolism common in the elderly. Older people receiving these agents must eat regularly, as they may be less likely to recognize hypoglycemic symptoms or mount an adequate counterregulatory hormone response (catecholamines, glucagon, and growth hormone) to maintain glucose homeostasis.

Treatment with oral sulfonylureas should begin at a low dose in older patients because they may be exquisitely sensitive to these drugs. We advise the use of second-generation sulfonylureas because the risk for hypoglycemia is lower than with the longer-acting first-generation oral sulfonylureas. Second-generation oral sulfonylureas bind nonionically to albumin and have a lower risk for displacement by anionic drugs, as was seen with the first-generation oral agent, chlorpropamide. There is virtually no evidence of an antidiuretic effect with the second-generation drugs, although rare cases have occurred in patients with renal disease on diuretic therapy. Both glyburide and glipizide are administered once a day and are of comparable efficacy in lowering glucose in older patients with NIDDM. Although the half-life of glyburide is slightly longer than glipizide and its metabolites are active, an advantage of glyburide over glipizide is its dual clearance by the liver and kidney, which may reduce risk for hypoglycemia in patients with impaired renal or hepatic function.

There are three types of secondary failure with oral sulfonylurea agents, all of which occur more often in older people. The first is where there is progression of disease and glycemic control is inadequate despite maximal doses of oral sulfonylureas and adherence to diet and exercise. This type of failure occurs most often in lean older people, where combined therapy with oral agents and insulin may be successful. This should be used only in patients capable of home blood glucose monitoring, as the risk of nocturnal hypoglycemia is high in older patients, and evening insulin should be administered with extreme caution. Results of combined therapy are highly variable, and controlled studies are needed to determine the characteristics of patients most likely to respond favorably. The second type of therapeutic failure with the oral sulfonylurea drugs is the temporary or reversible deterioration in glycemic control during periods of illness, infection, or stress. Insulin treatment is needed at

these times, and oral therapy usually can be reinstated when the acute problem resolves. The third and most common failure associated with oral sulfonylurea therapy is dietary noncompliance, and this occurs often, even in younger patients. In such cases insulin therapy transiently improves hyperglycemia, but wide fluctuations in glucose levels and the metabolic effects of increasing doses of insulin promote overeating and weight gain. Intensive dietary counseling, behavioral therapy, and caretaker education often work, but in the more obese noncompliant patient, hospitalization for very low calorie feeding may be the only alternative.[72]

Regimens for insulin administration in older diabetics do not differ from those routinely used for younger diabetics, but the goals of management should be modified. Attempts to "normalize" blood glucose completely by intensive insulinization carry the risk of hypoglycemia and precipitation of vascular accidents in an already compromised vascular system, and should therefore be avoided. It is almost always possible to reduce plasma glucose levels to the desired level with insulin, but in the older patient the physician should aim to lower hyperglycemia to an asymptomatic state (i.e., no polyuria, polydipsia, weight loss, fatigue, or polyphagia) and maintain an optimal level of social function and well-being. Urine glucose testing is an inadequate way to monitor therapeutic response, not only because of the usual poor correlation of glucosuria with blood glucose levels, but also because of the elevated and variable renal threshold for glucose excretion with aging. Home blood glucose monitoring in the initial stages of insulin therapy, with measurement of glycosylated hemoglobin levels for assessment of control in the more stable patient, are useful approaches to long-term management. Impairment of vision may require the use of premixed insulin in a supply of disposable syringes or devices that permit the accurate withdrawal of insulin from the vial. Such patients may also be candidates for therapy with oral agents.

In summary, most obese older NIDDM patients do not need insulin; compliance to diet and increased physical activity usually improves insulin sensitivity and lowers blood glucose. Patients with persistent symptomatic hyperglycemia (despite adherence to diet and exercise) manifested by weight loss, polyuria, fatigue, and recurrent infections should be treated initially with an oral sulfonylurea until sufficient weight is lost and symptoms abate. The use of second-generation agents, glipizide or glyburide, is recommended over the first-generation agents chlorpropamide, tolazamide, or tolbutamide, because of their more rapid absorption and metabolism, lower risk of drug interactions due to nonionic binding to albumin, and lower risk for hyponatremia and hypoglycemia. Nevertheless, the risks of treatment with either oral sulfonylurea or insulin, particularly hypoglycemia are increased in the older diabetic. In the absence of evidence that tight control of glycemia in the normal range reduces risk for diabetic complications in older individuals, it seems prudent to manage the older diabetic conservatively by limiting the risk of hypoglycemia and balancing the control of hyperglycemia, hyperlipidemia, and hypertension at levels to prevent the progression of vascular disease and maintain an optimal lifestyle.

ACUTE EMERGENCIES IN OLDER DIABETICS

DIABETIC KETOACIDOSIS

Worsening of hyperglycemia, despite adherence to diet and activity regimes may occur due to an increase in the severity of diabetes, causing insulinopenia and the development of ketoacidosis. Older patients who are prone to ketoacidosis often have coexistent disease and are lean or cachectic. These patients not only require insulin to prevent serious ketoacidosis, coma, and death, but also need aggressive treatment for any coexistent diseases.

The incidence of diabetic ketoacidosis in older diabetics is lower than in younger diabetics, but the fatality rate is much higher. The heightened mortality reflects the serious nature of the underlying diseases that may precipitate ketoacidosis in older diabetics (e.g., sepsis, surgical emergency, and acute vascular occlusion) and the possibility that ketoacidosis may present in atypical fashion with stroke or confusion, causing a delay in diagnosis and the institution of therapy.

Diabetic ketoacidosis in older patients must be distinguished from septic shock, since hyperventilation, hypotension, oliguria, peripheral vascular collapse, central nervous system disturbances, and low plasma bicarbonate are common to both conditions. Infection is a leading cause of diabetic ketoacidosis in older patients,[73] and may be present in as many as 40 percent of patients with ketoacidosis, with septicemia present in about 6 percent. Infections are more common in diabetics, and most infections, when established, run a more florid course. Diabetics are particularly susceptible to urinary tract infections, candidiasis, cholecystitis, pneumoccal pneumonia, influenza, and staphylococcal skin infections. Pseudomonas infection may cause malignant otitis externa or necrotizing fasciitis in older diabetics. Mortality from diabetic ketoacidosis is much higher when associated with infection than with other precipitating causes. It is imperative that a thorough search for the site of infection be instituted and appropriate therapy started promptly if infection is suspected in older diabetics presenting with ketoacidosis.

Aside from infection, other major factors responsible for death in ketoacidosis are arterial thrombosis and shock.[74] Older diabetics are more likely to have preexisting atherosclerosis resulting in compromised circulatory dynamics, aggravated by reduced cardiac output and autonomic neuropathy. Aggressive insulin therapy during ketoacidosis often transiently lowers intravascular volume by reducing the glucose-associated osmotic effect; thus, fluids must be aggressively replaced during treatment. Oxygen delivery to tissues may also be worsened during the early stages of correction of ketoacidosis. The patient may continue to be at risk for the development of arterial occlusions for several days following successful treatment of ketoacidosis.

Hypovolemic shock is also responsible for a large proportion of fatalities from ketoacidosis in the elderly. The severity of initial intravascular volume depletion appears to be a major prognostic index for a subsequent unfavorable therapeutic outcome. Commonly, patients may have lost 10 percent of their body weight as fluid. Replacement with half-normal saline is less effective than with isotonic saline, which should be administered as rapidly as required to restore intravascular volume promptly and to prevent shock and oliguria.

In the treatment of ketoacidosis, normal circulating effective insulin levels can be achieved by low-dose insulin treatment regimens. Intramuscular (IM) or intravenous (IV) administration of regular insulin [e.g., 5 to 10 U IM every hour or 0.15 U/kg normal body weight as a bolus IV, followed by a continuous IV infusion of 0.15 U/(kg/(h)] is simple, rapid, and usually effective. These routes minimize the development of late-onset hypoglycemia. Frequent monitoring of physiologic responses is required (glucose, potassium, bicarbonate, urine output) and increases in insulin dosage, fluids, and electrolytes must be considered when the glucose-lowering response and correction of acidosis is inadequate. In conditions where blood volume is reduced, transfusion may be necessary to adequately restore tissue perfusion and oxygen transport.

HYPEROSMOLAR NONKETOTIC COMA

Hyperosmolar nonketotic coma, which affects older patients more frequently than ketoacidosis, is characterized by an insidious onset of drowsiness ultimately resulting in frank coma.[68,75] The average age of patients with this syndrome is 65 years; the condition is associated with a 40 to 70 percent mortality rate.

Hyperosmolar nonketotic coma may develop insidiously over a period of days in patients without previously diagnosed diabetes. A very high index of suspicion is essential, since early diagnosis and aggressive therapy reduces mortality. Unfortunately, misdiagnosis is common. The typical patient gradually becomes sleepy, confused, or semicomatose; appears dehydrated; and may have localizing neurologic signs that can be mistaken for a stroke. There may be a family history of diabetes, and about half the patients are known to have mild non-insulin-dependent diabetes. In most cases there is a history of several days of increasing polyuria and thirst, acute or chronic treatment with certain precipitating drugs, or a history of a recent medical procedure known to be associated with hyperosmolar nonketotic coma (Table 71-7).

A critical feature of hyperosmolar nonketotic coma is that thirst becomes impaired (possibly due to effects of severe hyperosmolarity, hyperglycemia, or concomitant drug therapy on the hypothalamic thirst center), resulting in a cycle of progressive dehydration, volume depletion, and hyperosmolarity. Reduced renal function and inability to respond to hyperglycemic hyperosmolarity may predispose patients to progress to a hyperosmolar state. The absence of ketosis in the presence of severe hyperglycemia occurs due to adequate circulating insulin levels for suppression of fatty acid mobilization from adipose tissue and consequent ketogenesis. However, insulin levels are inadequate to normalize glucose metabolism in the presence of osmotic diuresis and dehydration.

Clinical features of hyperosmolar nonketotic coma include severe hyperglycemia (plasma glucose usually greater than 600 mg/dl) in the absence of ketoacidosis, profound dehydration, and variable neurologic signs ranging from confusion to coma. The severity of the depressed sensorium is directly related to the degree of hyperosmolarity and is mediated via intracellular dehydration of the brain. Serum osmolarity often exceeds 350 mosmol/kg water, and hemoconcentration may be followed by both arterial and venous thrombosis, which are frequent complications of this disorder. A massive osmotic diuresis due to prolonged, severe hyperglycemia results in a greater loss of water than electrolytes. Serum sodium and potassium concentrations are usually high, but may be normal or low depending on the balance between the intravascular and extravascular volume and a history of previous diuretic therapy.

TABLE 71-7
Drugs and Procedures Associated with Hyperglycemic Hyperosmolar Nonketotic Coma

Drugs	*Procedures*
Diuretics (thiazides, furosemide, diazoxide, chlorthalidone, ethacrynic acid)	Hemodialysis and peritoneal dialysis
Immunosuppressive agents (glucocorticoids)	Intravenous hyperalimentation
Propranolol	Intravenous dye injection (pyelogram, cardiac catheterization, etc.)
Phenytoin	
Cimetidine	
CNS-active drugs (chlorpromazine)	

The goal of therapy is to correct the severe volume depletion (up to one-fourth of body water may be lost) and the hyperosmolar state. As in diabetic ketoacidosis, a careful search should be made for correctable underlying precipitating factors (infections, vascular accidents, and diuretics). Fluid replacement is the cornerstone of treatment, and insulin administration is needed to reduce the osmotic diuresis caused by hyperglycemia. Several liters of half-normal saline with added potassium should be administered rapidly, while central venous pressure and urine output are monitored to avoid congestive heart failure. A total of 6 to 18 liters of fluid in 24 to 36 hours may be necessary, with 8 to 10 liters being the average. If hypotension is present, isotonic saline should be infused initially and 5 percent glucose in water added when the plasma glucose falls below 300 mg/dl. Urine output, electrolytes, the electrocardiogram, and central venous pressure require constant monitoring. Regular insulin should be given IM or IV with 25 U recommended as an initial dose to be repeated every 2 hours if blood glucose does not fall more than 100 mg/ml. Often no additional insulin is required after the initial dose. Following recovery from this metabolic disorder, the patient rarely needs insulin to manage what is usually a mild diabetic state.

Regardless of the therapy required to control hyperglycemia in the older diabetic or to treat acute complications of ketoacidosis or nonketotic hyperglycemic hyperosmolar coma, caution must be exercised because older patients are extremely sensitive to glucose-lowering drugs. Whatever the medical condition requiring drug therapy, the incidence of adverse side effects and drug interactions is increased in the elderly. Often in the older diabetic, the side effect may be more serious than the symptoms and consequences of diabetes itself. The older diabetic patient is at particular risk for drug toxicity because of diabetes-related complications affecting hepatic and renal drug metabolism, reducing blood flow to organs and altering gastrointestinal absorption to change drug pharmacokinetics. It is recommended that drug dosing be conservative in older diabetic patients: Start low, and gradually increase while monitoring for organ toxicity and titrating symptoms and biochemical parameters for optimal therapeutic efficacy.

CONCLUDING REMARKS

Aging and diabetes express their morbidity through common mechanisms leading to the development of micro- and macrovascular complications involving the heart, eyes, kidneys, and nervous system. Macrovascular disease (atherosclerosis) is the most common feature of diabetes in the elderly, the age group most susceptible to the clinical consequences of atherosclerosis. Diabetes accelerates the atherosclerotic process, primarily through direct effects on the vascular wall, but also due to coexistent hyperlipidemia, hyperinsulinemia, hypertension, and abnormal cellular function common to the disease.

Interactions among the social (lifestyle) and biological changes that accompany aging can lead to a pathophysiologic condition resembling diabetes, but the clinical presentation is often subtle and rarely is there severe fasting hyperglycemia with massive glucosuria or clinical complications of the disease. This condition often improves after loss of weight, modification of the diet, and an increase in physical activity, suggesting that lifestyle habits are important risk factors for glucose intolerance and hyperglycemia in some older individuals. Similar lifestyle changes will benefit the health of older people with NIDDM and its clinical complications, yet often drug therapy is needed to control hyperglycemia and reduce risk for vascular complications in these patients.

Despite its prevalence, there is a paucity of knowledge of the natural history of diabetes in the elderly and the long-term effects of treatment on complications, quality of life, and survival. In general, conservative management of hyperglycemia is prudent for older patients because of the increased hazards of overtreatment. Whether the decline in glucose tolerance with aging is a natural physiologic consequence of the aging process that requires no treatment or whether it presages an accelerated phase of aging, progressive atherosclerosis, and death is not known. Understanding the consequences of hyperglycemia and diabetes in older individuals and the effects of therapy on morbidity, mortality, and long-term survival in the elderly will enhance our understanding of the physiology of aging and its interaction with lifestyle and disease.

REFERENCES

1. Harris M: The prevalence of diabetes, undiagnosed diabetes and impaired glucose tolerance in the United States, Melish JS, Hanna J, Baba S (eds): *Genetic Environmental Interaction in Diabetes Mellitus*. Amsterdam, Excerpta Medica, 1982, p 70.
2. National Diabetes Data Group: Classification and diagnosis of diabetes mellitus and other categories of glucose intolerance. *Diabetes* 28:1039, 1979.
3. Andres, R: Aging and diabetes. *Med Clin North Am* 55:835, 1971.
4. Davidson MB: The effect of aging on carbohydrate metabolism: A review of the English literature and a practical approach to the diagnosis of diabetes mellitus in the elderly. *Metabolism* 28:688, 1978.
5. Graf RJ et al: Glucosylated hemoglobin in normal subjects and subjects with maturity onset diabetes: Evidence for a saturable system in man. *Diabetes* 27:834, 1978.
6. Kahn CR: Insulin resistance, insulin insensitivity, insulin unresponsiveness: A necessary distinction. *Metabolism* 27:1893, 1978.
7. Olefsky JO, Kolterman OG: Mechanisms of insulin resistance in obesity and noninsulin dependent (type II) diabetes. *Am J Med* 70:151, 1981.
8. Kolterman OG et al: Receptor and postreceptor defects contribute to insulin resistance in noninsulin dependent diabetes mellitus. *J Clin Invest* 68:957, 1981.
9. Ward WK et al: Pathophysiology of insulin secretion in noninsulin dependent diabetes mellitus. *Diabetes Care* 7:491, 1984.
10. DeFronzo RA et al: Glucose clamp technique: A method for quantifying insulin secretion and resistance. *Am J Physiol* 237:E214, 1979.
11. DeFronzo RA: Glucose intolerance and aging: Evidence for tissue insensitivity to insulin. *Diabetes* 28:1095, 1979.
12. Fink RI et al: Mechanism of insulin resistance in aging. *J Clin Invest* 71:1523, 1983.
13. Rowe JW et al: Characterization of the insulin resistance of aging. *J Clin Invest* 71:1581, 1983.
14. Chen M et al: Pathogenesis of age-related glucose intolerance in man: Insulin resistance and decreased beta-cell function. *J Clin Endocrinol Metab* 60:13, 1985.
15. Jackson RA et al: Influence of aging on hepatic and peripheral glucose metabolism in humans. *Diabetes* 37:119, 1988.
16. Pagano G et al: Insulin resistance in the aged: The role of peripheral insulin receptors. *Metabolism* 30:46, 1981.
17. Lonnroth P, Smith U: Aging enhances the insulin resistance in obesity through both receptor and postreceptor alterations. *J Clin Endocrinol Metab* 62:433, 1986.
18. Fink RI et al: The role of the glucose transport system in the postreceptor defect in insulin action associated with human aging. *J Clin Endocrinol Metab* 58:721, 1984.
19. Fink RI et al: The effects of aging on glucose mediated glucose disposal and glucose transport. *J Clin Invest* 77:2034, 1986.
20. Kaiser FE et al: Comparison of age-related decreases in the basal and carbohydrate inducible levels of lipogenic enzymes in adipose tissue and liver. *Metabolism* 32:838, 1983.
21. Seals D et al: Glucose tolerance in young and older athletes and sedentary men. *J Appl Physiol* 56:1521, 1984.
22. Coon P et al: Increased physical fitness attenuates the age-related decline in insulin sensitivity. *Gerontologist* 28:233A, 1988.
23. Chen M et al: The role of dietary carbohydrate in the decreased glucose tolerance of the elderly. *J Am Geriatr Soc* 35:417, 1987.
24. Tattersall RB, Pyke DA: Diabetes in identical twins. *Lancet* 2:1120, 1972.
25. Albin J, Rifkin H: Etiologies of diabetes mellitus. *Med Clin North Am* 66:1209, 1982.
26. National Institutes of Health: Consensus development conference on diet and exercise in non-insulin dependent diabetes mellitus. *Diabetes Care* 10:639, 1987.
27. Schneider SH et al: Studies on the mechanisms of improved glucose control during regular exercise in type 2 (non-insulin dependent) diabetes. *Diabetologia* 26:355, 1984.
28. Goldberg AP: Health promotion and aging: "physical exercise," in *Surgeon General's Workshop, Health Promotion and Aging*. Washington, 1988, pp C1.

29. Zavaroni I et al: Effect of age and environmental factors on glucose tolerance and insulin secretion in a worker population. *J Am Geriatr Soc* 34:271, 1986.

30. Shimokata H et al: Is age a primary determinant of glucose tolerance? *Gerontologist* 28:232A, 1988.

31. Bierman EL, Brunzell JD: Interrelation of atherosclerosis, abnormal lipid metabolism and diabetes mellitus, in Katzen HM, Mahler RJ (eds): *Diabetes, Obesity and Vascular Disease: Metabolic and Molecular Inter-relationships.* Part I. New York, Wiley, 1978, pp 187.

32. Nathan DM et al: Non-insulin dependent diabetes in older patients: Complications and risk factors. *Am J Med* 81:837, 1986.

33. Kannel WB: Lipids and diabetes in coronary heart disease: Insights from the Framingham study. *Am Heart J* 110:1100, 1985.

34. Wilson PNF et al: Epidemiology of diabetes in the elderly: The Framingham study. *Am J Med* 80 (suppl 5A):3, 1982.

35. Bennett PH: Diabetes in the elderly: Diagnosis and epidemiology. *Geriatrics* 39:37, 1984.

36. Deubner DC et al: Logistic model estimation of death attributable to risk factors for cardiovascular disease in Evans County, Georgia. *Am J Epidemiol* 112:135, 1980.

37. National Center for Health Statistics: Glucose levels in adults: United States 1960–1962. *Vital Health Stat* ser 11, no 18. Washington, Government Printing Office, 1966.

38. Zimmet P et al: The high incidence of diabetes mellitus in the Micronesian population of Nauru. *Acta Diabetol Lat* 19:75, 1982.

39. Knowler WC et al: Diabetes incidence and prevalence in Pima Indians. A 19-fold-greater incidence than in Rochester, Minnesota. *Am J Epidemiol* 108:497, 1978.

40. Knowler WC et al: Diabetes incidence in Pima Indians: Contributions of obesity and parental diabetes. *Am J Epidemiol* 113:144, 1981.

41. Mooradian AD et al: Diabetes in elderly nursing home patients. A survey of clinical characteristics and management. *J Am Geriatr Soc* 36:391, 1988.

42. West KM: Screening detection and diagnosis, in *Epidemiology of Diabetes and Its Vascular Lesions.* New York, Elsevier, 1978.

43. Lapidus L et al: Distribution of adipose tissue and risk of cardiovascular disease and death: A 12 year follow-up of participants in the population study of women in Gothenburg, Sweden. *Brit Med J* 289:1257, 1984.

44. Houston MC: The effects of antihypertensive drugs on glucose intolerance in hypertensive nondiabetics and diabetics. *Am Heart J* 115:640, 1988.

45. Pyorala K et al: Diabetes and atherosclerosis: An epidemiological view. *Diabetes/Metab Rev* 3(2):463, 1987.

46. Jarett RJ et al: The Bedford survey: 10 year mortality rates in newly diagnosed diabetics, borderline diabetics, and normal glycemic controls, and risk indices for coronary artery disease in borderline diabetics. *Diabetologia* 22:79, 1983.

47. Hartz AJ et al: The association of girth measurements with disease in 32,856 women. *Am J Epidemiol* 119:71, 1984.

48. Stern MP, Haffner SM: Body fat distribution and hyperinsulinemia as risk factors for diabetes and cardiovascular disease. *Arteriosclerosis* 6:123, 1986.

49. Larsson B et al: Abdominal adipose tissue distribution, obesity and risk of cardiovascular disease and death: 13 year follow-up of participants in the study of men born in 1913. *Brit Med J* 288:1401, 1984.

50. Vague J: The degree of masculine differentiation of obesity, a factor determining predisposition to diabetes, atherosclerosis, gout and uric calculus disease. *Am J Clin Nutr* 4:20, 1956.

51. Barrett-Conner E, Orchard T: Diabetes and heart disease, in *Diabetes in America.* Bethesda, MD, National Diabetes Data Group, DHHS(NIH)85-1468, 1985.

52. Nesto RW, Phillips, RT: Asymptomatic myocardial ischemia in diabetic patients. *Am J Med* 80 (suppl C):40, 1986.

53. Palumbo PJ, Melton LJ III: Peripheral vascular disease and diabetes, in *Diabetes in America.* Bethesda, MD, National Diabetes Data Group, DHHS(NIH)85-1468, 1985.

54. Brunzell JD: Obesity and risk for cardiovascular disease. *Contemp Issues Clin Nutr* 4:3, 1983.

55. Green DR: Acute and chronic complications of diabetes mellitus in older patients. *Am J Med* 80 (suppl C):39, 1986.

56. Ewing W, Clarke BF: Diabetic autonomic neuropathy: Present insight in future prospects. *Diabetes Care* 9:648, 1986.

57. Rosenstalk J, Raskin T: Early diabetic nephropathy assessment and potential therapeutic interventions. *Diabetes Care* 9:529, 1986.

58. Schonfeld G: Diabetes, lipoproteins, and atherosclerosis. *Metabolism* 34 (suppl 1):45, 1985.

59. Cerami A et al: Protein glycosylation and the pathogenesis of atherosclerosis. *Metabolism* 34 (suppl 1):37, 1985.

60. Stolar MN: Atherosclerosis in diabetes: The role of hyperinsulinemia. *Metabolism* 37:1, 1988.

61. King GL: Cell biology as an approach to the study of vascular complications of diabetes. *Metabolism* 34 (suppl 1):17, 1985.

62. Stout RW: Insulin and atheroma—An update. *Lancet* 1:1077, 1987.

63. Special report: Principles of nutrition and dietary recommendations for individuals with diabetes mellitus. *Diabetes* 20:633, 1971; *Diabetes* 28:1027, 1979.

64. AHA Nutrition Committee and Council on Arteriosclerosis: Joint Statement. Recommendations for the Treatment of Hyperlipidemia in Adults. *Arteriosclerosis* 4:445A, 1984.

65. Wing RR et al: Behavioral change, weight loss, and physiological improvements in type II diabetic patients. *J Consult Clin Psychol* 53:111, 1985.

66. Brunzell JD, Bierman, EL: Chylomicronemia syndrome: interaction of genetic and acquired hypertriglyceridemia. *Med Clin North Am* 66:455, 1982.

67. Watkins PJ: ABC of diabetes: Diabetic emergencies. *Br Med J* 285:360, 1982.

68. Podolsky S: Hyperosmolar nonketotic coma in the elderly diabetic. *Med Clin North Am* 62:815, 1978.

69. Nathan DM et al: Glyburide or insulin for metabolic control in non-insulin-dependent diabetes mellitus. *Ann Intern Med* 109:334, 1988.

70. Jaspan JB: Monitoring and controlling the patient with noninsulin dependent diabetes mellitus. *Metabolism* 36:22, 1987.

71. Gerich JE: Sulfonylureas in the treatment of diabetes mellitus—1985. *Mayo Clin Proc* 60:439, 1985.

72. Davidson JK et al: The Memphis and Atlanta continuing care program for diabetes: II. Comparative analysis of demographic characteristics, treatment, method and outcomes over a 9 to 10 year follow-up period. *Diabetes Care* 7:25, 1984.

73. Smith IM: Common infections in the elderly diabetic. *Geriatrics* 35:55, 1980.

74. Clements RS, Vourganti B: Fatal diabetic ketoacidosis: Major causes and approaches to their prevention. *Diabetes Care* 1:314, 1978.

75. Wachtel TJ et al: Prognostic factors in the diabetic hyperosmolar state. *J Am Geriatr Soc* 35:737, 1987.

Chapter 72

MORTALITY AND OBESITY: THE RATIONALE FOR AGE-SPECIFIC HEIGHT-WEIGHT TABLES

Reubin Andres

It is generally recognized that both extremely high and extremely low degrees of fat accumulation have serious health consequences. In economically advanced societies a large fraction of the adult population is frequently within the dangerously overweight range, while a smaller fraction is in the seriously underweight range. To quantify those fractions accurately requires the definition of the "normal" weight range. This effort has, especially in recent years, become very controversial.

STANDARDS OF NORMAL WEIGHT

Attempts at defining normal weight have sometimes been based upon statistical analysis of height and weight distributions in populations, but the selections of the weight range judged to be abnormal have been entirely arbitrary. The notion that the average weight of 20- to 25-year-old subjects is ideal for all subsequent ages has been widely accepted, but this seemingly reasonable assumption is, as will be shown, incorrect.

The setting of normal weight standards is more properly accomplished by analyzing the association of weight with other risk factors present in those subjects or, better, by long-term follow-up studies of populations in which the independent variable is an index of obesity and the dependent variables are such outcomes as specific diseases (heart disease, diabetes, cancer, stroke) or, indeed, mortality itself. In fact with a variable such as adiposity, a multidimensional interplay of beneficial and harmful effects would be anticipated. Harm might be

expected to exceed benefit at both extremes of the adiposity distribution curves within populations.

It is remarkable that, until the 1960s, a variable as easily measured as weight-for-height was examined as a risk factor for mortality only by the pioneering efforts of the life insurance industry. Periodic analyses of their conclusions have been presented for the past 70 years—in 1913, 1932, 1942–1943, 1959, and most recently in 1983. The last three sets of height-weight tables have had identical formats: separate tables for men and women, heights in inches, and three overlapping ranges of weight for each of three body frame categories (small, medium, and large). These sets of tables were devised by actuaries of the Metropolitan Life Insurance Company. Weight ranges in the 1942–1943 tables were identified as "ideal," the 1959 weights were downgraded to "desirable," and the 1983 tables are identified simply as "1983 height-weight tables."[1]

The insurance industry studies that provide the primary data from which these tables were constructed have been criticized on a number of grounds: (1) Subjects seeking insurance do not represent a random sample of the general population; (2) those who are granted policies represent a further selection of elite subjects (from a health standpoint); (3) some subjects are represented more than once since individual policies (rather than subjects) are tabulated; (4) heights and weights have not been invariably measured (some are simply statements made by the subjects); furthermore, (5) height and weight measurements alone are poor estimates of body fatness; (6) no anthropometric measurements of body frame were made; and (7) the possible confound of cigarette smoking with body weight and with mortality was not considered.

Data are, however, now available from a large number of other populations which provide estimates of obesity and its relationship to mortality. These populations are all selective in one respect or another, but, as in all epidemiological studies of this sort, the search for patterns of consistency may provide cumulative evidence of some biological principles which are generalizable to all human beings or at least to the ones living in developed societies. (There are no data from economically underdeveloped areas of the world.) The basic design of each consisted of an assessment of height and weight (and, rarely, of other anthropometric indices of obesity) of each member of a selected population at one moment in the life span. From these measurements an index of obesity was assigned to each subject. Generally, one or another of the available weight tables was selected as the reference standard; the 1959 Desirable Weight Table has been most commonly chosen, although recently even the 1913 version was used. When the 1959 table has been used, the middle of the weight range for the medium frame was selected as the single weight goal. A *relative weight* (RW) or *obesity index* was then computed for each subject by dividing the subject's actual weight by the weight goal for his or her height. Thus a man 69 inches tall whose actual weight was 149 pounds and whose weight goal was also 149 pounds would have an RW of 1.00; another of the same height whose actual weight was 179 pounds would have an RW of 1.20 and would generally be described as 20 percent overweight. The actual RW value obtained by such calculations obviously depends upon the particular reference base selected. Consequently subjects described as being 20 percent overweight in two studies may indeed not be comparably obese if different reference bases were used to classify them.

COMPUTATION OF BODY MASS INDEX

To avoid the problem of different reference bases the computation of a *body mass index* or *Quetelet index* has been gaining favor as a technique for combining height and weight into a single index of relative obesity. In most populations weight increases directly with the height squared. Thus weight divided by height squared (wt/ht^2) may be used to "correct" for height, and this quotient defines the body mass index. It is important to realize that the midweights for the medium frame in the 1959 Desirable Weight Table divided by their respective heights squared give values for the body mass index which average 21.6 for men and to 21.2 for women, pro-

vided the weight and heights squared are expressed in metric units (kilograms per square meter) and that suitable corrections are made for clothing weight and shoe height. (It has been recommended that for men and for women, respectively, 7 and 5 pounds should be subtracted for weight of clothes and that 1 and 2 inches should be subtracted for height of shoes from the values given in the Metropolitan tables.) In other words, body mass indices of 21.6 and 21.2 in the 1959 tables are equivalent to an RW of 1.00 for men and women. This equivalency conversion is a useful aid in the interpretation of the body mass index for those unfamiliar with its use as an index of relative obesity. In the 1983 tables the recommended adjustments for the weight of clothing are 5 and 3 pounds for men and women, respectively, and 1 inch for both for the height of shoes.

The use of height and weight as the sole measurements upon which to assess obesity is subject to overt error in some individuals. The weight standards used in the selection of recruits during World War I seemed reasonable until it became obvious that young men who were burly and muscular (but not fat) were being excluded from service. A number of techniques are available for estimating body fatness,[2] but these have generally not been applied to population studies, since their complexity precludes their use for measuring large numbers of individuals. Despite this limitation, in population groups it is the "overweight" who tend overwhelmingly to be the "over-fat"; conclusions based upon analyses in which height and weight have been measured agree remarkably well with analyses based, for example, upon skinfold thickness measurements, a more direct index of true fatness.[3]

If relative obesity is defined as the percentage of total body weight composed of fat, then young adults and elderly subjects of the same height and weight are not comparably obese. There is an inexorable loss of lean body mass (or cellular mass) with advancing age. This loss is primarily skeletal muscle. Thus, if body weight is maintained without change during aging, this can be accomplished only by replacing skeletal muscle to some extent by connective tissue but predominantly by fat. This biological fact would not, in itself, introduce an error into recommendations which might be made concerning body weight, provided the studies upon which the recommendations are based have taken age into account.

EFFECT OF BODY WEIGHT ON MORTALITY

In this chapter consideration will be given mainly to the effect of body weight on total mortality in different age segments of populations. In one sense this is a very limited approach, since other deleterious effects of obesity could also be considered. Mortality is, however, the quintessential "endpoint," and it is mortality which has been used in the construction of the height-weight tables. It is conceivable, indeed nearly certain, that recommended weights based upon mortality will be higher than those which, for example, would be associated with the lowest prevalence of diabetes mellitus, hypertension, and hyperlipidemia. Weight tables based upon the mortality of healthy populations are applicable only to individuals of comparable health status, not to persons who are hypertensive, hyperlipidemic, or diabetic. This fact is rarely appreciated.

There are now some 50 other populations which have undergone study in a manner comparable with that performed by the insurance industry. The technical quality of these studies varies greatly, and comparisons among them are difficult for a number of reasons: (1) No standardized techniques for assessing the independent variable (obesity) have been proposed or followed; (2) the techniques used for selecting and sampling the population vary (some samples represent "captive" populations such as employees, others are recruited as community volunteers and the response rates vary, others are self-selected, etc.); (3) follow-up periods sometimes cover only a small fraction of the human life span; (4) eligibility for inclusion in the original sample differs widely since some studies apply no exclusionary health criteria, while in others initial health examinations may be very thorough; (5) variables which interact with obesity and which also influence mortality (cigarette smoking is the prime example) have rarely been analyzed and reported; and (6) sample sizes vary from several dozen to several million subjects. The wide diversity in the types of populations selected for study is, of course, an advantage even if differences in results among them can rarely be explained adequately.

Results from a number of these studies have been summarized recently.[4,5] Several of the more important ones will be summarized here. Ancel Keys[3] reported 10-year follow-up studies in some 12,000 men from seven countries (the United States, Japan, Yugoslavia, Italy, Greece, the Netherlands, and Finland) aged 40 to 59 years at entry. Relative weight was determined from height and weight, and in six of the countries an index of obesity also was derived from skinfold measurements. Croatians and Serbians in Yugoslavia were analyzed separately; thus eight populations were reported. Mortality data were presented for deciles of relative weight in each population, but the number of deaths in some groups was so small that I have collapsed the data into quintiles. In seven of the eight populations the highest mortality occurred in the leanest quintile. Lowest mortality was in the heaviest quintile in three populations, in next to the

heaviest in two, in the middle quintile in two, and in the lightest quintile in one population. Furthermore in the seven populations which had skinfold measurements, the highest mortality occurred in either the leanest or next to the leanest quintile in five groups, and the lowest mortality occurred either in the middle quintile or the most obese quintile in six of the seven groups.

The American Cancer Society[6] enrolled about 750,000 apparently healthy men and women from 26 states and followed them for 12 years. Heights and weights were obtained by a questionnaire. Subjects were assigned relative weights based upon age-sex group averages from this population. However, the men aged 30 to 70 years in this study were on average 14 to 16 percent heavier than the mid-weights for the medium frame from the 1959 Desirable Weight Table, while women in the study averaged 8 to 18 percent above their "desirable" weights. The lowest mortality occurred in men of average weight, i.e., distinctly above desirable, and in women generally in the 80 to 89 relative weight category, i.e., essentially at their desirable weight. However, the 80- to 89-year-old men and women with lowest mortality were distinctly on the overweight side at enrollment, albeit there was little weight effect on mortality across the entire weight spectrum.

A report from the Framingham Heart Study[7] analyzed the mortality experience of nonsmoking male and female survivors after they reached age 65. The follow-up period averaged 9.5 years. Subjects were divided into four unequal sized body mass index (BMI) groups and the relative risk of dying was computed for each group. In men lowest mortality occurred in the 23.0 to 25.2 BMI group and in women in the 24.1 to 26.1 group. Mortality in the next higher BMI group (up to about 28.5 in men and women) was higher, but the increase was not statistically significant. These values may be compared to the Metropolitan 1959 recommendations (about 19.7 to 24.7 in men and 18.8 to 24.2 in women) and to the Metropolitan 1983 Tables (about 20.5 to 25.8 in men and 19.6 to 26.1 in women). The Gerontology Research Center (GRC) table recommends values for 65-year-old men and women ranging from 23.9 to 29.7. Thus, the lowest mortality in Framingham older men and women falls within the upper one-third or so of the Metropolitan 1983 weights and within the lower one-third or so of the GRC weights.

An impressive, comprehensively analyzed study has been reported by Waaler.[8] All persons over age 15 in Norway (but excluding Oslo) were invited to participate. In all, over 1.7 million persons were enrolled and followed for 16 years. The report is a model of clarity of analysis and presentation. It clearly demonstrates U-shaped BMI:mortality curves from ages 20 to 24 years into the very oldest age groups, but with a progressive flattening of the curves. BMI becomes less and less associated with mortality as aging progresses. In general, minimal mortality occurred at BMIs of about 25 in the later years in both men and women.

Several arguments have been raised in criticism of studies relating body weight to mortality.[9] These include (1) failure to take cigarette smoking into account; (2) failure to exclude subjects at entry into the study who were already ill, had been losing weight, and were destined to die early; (3) inappropriate multiple regression analyses; and (4) relatively short follow-up periods. The theoretical basis of the smoking argument is that in most populations smokers weigh less than nonsmokers and certainly have higher mortality rates. Thus curves relating body weight to mortality will be distorted because of "contamination" of the true weight effect by the associated smoking effect. This confound can be tested by examining the weight–mortality association separately in smokers and in nonsmokers. When this has been done, the BMI:mortality U-shaped curves have been found to be very similar in shape. Minimal mortality occurs at about the same body weights in smokers as in nonsmokers, and the nadirs for both groups are about the same as that for all subjects. For example, in an analysis not yet published of the National Health and Nutrition Survey I Follow-up Study (NHFUS) of 15 years duration (Zonderman, Costa, and Andres), minimal mortality in 55- to 74-year-old white men occurred at BMIs of 27.7 in smokers, 26.7 in nonsmokers, and 27.4 in the combined group—values all far in excess of the Metropolitan 1959 and 1983 standards but quite in agreement with the GRC table. A review of other studies shows similar results, for example, the 30-year Framingham report by Feinleib.[10]

The objection that weight-losing ill patients might have been included in some studies has been met in various ways by different investigators: (1) Clinical evaluation at the time of recruitment allows the identification (and subsequent exclusion) of subjects with significant illnesses; (2) subjects who die in the earlier years of the study have been excluded; and (3) subjects who report significant unexplained weight loss in the preenrollment period have been excluded. There are no convincing data, however, that failure to "clean-up" the population makes a significant impact on the shape of the weight:mortality curve. In the NHFUS referred to above, the BMI of 55 to 74-year-old white men was 27.9 in the total population and 27.4 after 28 percent of the total enrollees were excluded either because of the presence of identifiable diseases or because they died within the first 2 years of follow-up. In white women comparable values were 27.5 and 27.2 (22 percent excluded).

Relatively short follow-up periods probably distort results primarily in studies with relatively small initial enrollment and therefore with relatively few deaths.

This problem is obviously more serious in studies of younger populations who manifest low mortality rates to begin with. Waaler,[11] in a summary of the remarkable study of 1.7 million Norwegians, noted that " . . . in studies with few observations there might be difficulties in demonstrating any correlation at all between BMI and mortality. As the size of the material is increasing, the first observation will be some linear positive correlation. This will be partly obscured by the U-shape, which will be visible only in rather big study populations . . . " In his study Waaler showed that the excess mortality of very lean and very obese individuals can be seen clearly at 1 or 2 years of follow-up and at all annual analyses up to the end of his study at 16 years. In the NHFUS analysis, the 15-year follow-up of individuals enrolled for study at ages 55 to 75 years results in the deaths of one-third of the women and one-half of the men by the time their status is determined at ages 70 to 90 years. Thus 15 years is, in fact, a long follow-up period for older individuals provided a sample of at least several hundred men and an equal or greater number of women have been initially enrolled.

AN ANALYSIS OF ACTUARIAL DATA

The weight standards for Americans in this century have clearly been those produced by actuaries of the Metropolitan Life Insurance Company. A National Institutes of Health Consensus Development Conference on Health Implications of Obesity[12] did not show preference for either the 1983 version of the tables [1] or the 1959 version,[13] but it clearly did favor their use. The tables were recognized as being deficient in that age was not included as a variable, but no age recommendations were offered. The 1983 version provided some liberalization of the weight ranges previously recommended. Because of this, criticism has been raised by those who believe that the public should be advised to remain distinctly lean. Since actuarilly derived tables have become the generally accepted weight standards since the 1942–1943 version was published, it is surprising that updated tables based upon the most recent experience of the insurance industry should be criticized and that the 1959 version based, in essence, on data collected from 1935 to 1953 should be supported. Therefore, it is necessary to consider the source of the data from which the height-weight tables are derived. The mortality experience of 25 companies was pooled and has been reported in great detail in book form as the *Build Study 1979*.[14] Mortality data were presented on nearly 4,200,000 policies taken out between 1954 and 1972 on men and women 15 to 69 years of age. Data on ages 15 to 19 are sparse and will not be considered further. The total experience includes some 106,000 deaths, an unparalleled number. The mortality ratio (actual/expected number of deaths) was presented separately for each age decade from 20 to 29 through 60 to 69 years for men and for women. Subjects were divided into one of five height groups, from very short to very tall; for each height group subjects were placed into one of eighteen weight groups from very light to very heavy. Theoretically, there could be as many as 90 height-weight groups for each age decade for each sex. Actually, data were not available on some of the more extreme groups, for example, very short subjects of the highest weight.

We have taken advantage of this comprehensive compilation of data to carry out an independent analysis of the insurance experience. The data from the large number of height-weight groups can be combined and analyzed for each sex-age group by computing the mean body mass index for each category. An example of such data demonstrates that the mortality ratios follow a U-shaped distribution (Fig. 72-1) with high mortality at both the very low and very high body mass indices (BMIs) and with lowest mortality at an intermediate zone. A quadratic equation defines a curve which fits the actual data points very well:

Mortality ratio
$$= a + b \text{ (body mass index)} + c \text{ (body mass index)}^2$$

From the equations derived for each of the five age decades for both men and women, the nadir of each curve can be computed. The nadir represents that body mass index associated with the lowest mortality. The plot of these nadirs (Fig. 72-2) shows that there is a progressive increase in the "best" BMI with age in both sexes and that there is no consistent difference across the age span of five decades between men and women.

Since a useful table of recommended weights must provide a *range* of weights rather than a single point, we made an empirical decision based on the fact that the quadratic curve intersects the 100 percent mortality line at two points (Fig. 72-1). The BMI values at those two points represent the upper and lower BMI limits for mortality ratios which are less than the average. Since these BMI limits are very similar in men and women, the weight goals do not need to be adjusted for gender. Women, who are, on average, fatter than men across the age spectrum, evidently benefit from this adiposity.

A recommended height-weight table has been constructed (Table 72-1), which presents the computed weight ranges for each age decade 20 to 29 through 60 to 69 years. For comparison, the corresponding weight ranges from the 1983 Metropolitan Life Insurance Company tables are also shown. Since no anthropometric data were available on the insured subjects other than height and weight, the individual weight ranges for each of the three body frames represent only a conjecture of the weight adjustment that should be permitted for

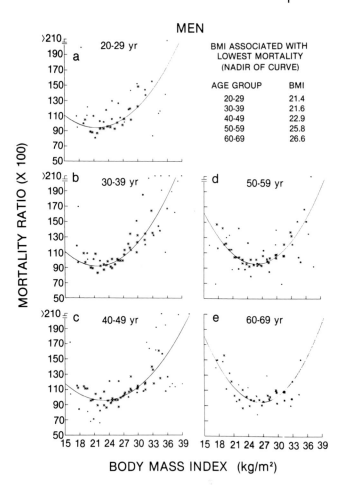

FIGURE 72-1
The U-shaped relationships between body mass index (BMI) and mortality ratio. Data are derived from the *Build Study 1979*.[14] The curves were constructed from the quadratic relationship between the two variables. A mortality ratio of 100 represents the average or expected mortality for the specific age-sex group. The nadirs of the curves represent that BMI associated with minimal mortality. The two points at which the curves intersect the 100 mortality ratio line represent those BMIs associated with mortality ratios less than the average; those BMIs can, therefore, be used to define a recommended weight range.

frame size. It would seem preferable to provide an age-adjusted table (for which data are available) and to avoid a frame-adjusted table (for which data are not available).

Over the major portion of the height spectrum, the 1983 Metropolitan Life Insurance Company weight range for men and women[1] falls near the weights in the age-adjusted table for individuals in their thirties or forties. Thus the 1983 Metropolitan Life Insurance Company tables provide weights that are higher than the primary insurance data would justify for young adults and lower than the insurance data would dictate for older adults. The increase weight allowance in our age-specific table is close to 10 pounds per decade of life or 1 pound

TABLE 72-1

Comparison of the Weight-for-Height Tables from Actuarial Data: Non-Age-Corrected Metropolitan Life Insurance Company and Age-Specific Gerontology Research Center Recommendations

| Height (ft and in) | Metropolitan 1983 Weights* (25–59 yr) | | Gerontology Research Center* (Age-specific Weight Range for Men and Women) | | | | |
	Men	Women	20–29 yr	30–39 yr	40–49 yr	50–59 yr	60–69 yr
4 10		100–131	84–111	92–119	99–127	107–135	115–142
4 11		101–134	87–115	95–123	103–131	111–139	119–147
5 0		103–137	90–119	98–127	106–135	114–143	123–152
5 1	123–145	105–140	93–123	101–131	110–140	118–148	127–157
5 2	125–148	108–144	96–127	105–136	113–144	122–153	131–163
5 3	127–151	111–148	99–131	108–140	117–149	126–158	135–168
5 4	129–155	114–152	102–135	112–145	121–154	130–163	140–173
5 5	131–159	117–156	106–140	115–149	125–159	134–168	144–179
5 6	133–163	120–160	109–144	119–154	129–164	138–174	148–184
5 7	135–167	123–164	112–148	122–159	133–169	143–179	153–190
5 8	137–171	126–167	116–153	126–163	137–174	147–184	158–196
5 9	139–175	129–170	119–157	130–168	141–179	151–190	162–201
5 10	141–179	132–173	122–162	134–173	145–184	156–195	167–207
5 11	144–183	135–176	126–167	137–178	149–190	160–201	172–213
6 0	147–187		129–171	141–183	153–195	165–207	177–219
6 1	150–192		133–176	145–188	157–200	169–213	182–225
6 2	153–197		137–181	149–194	162–206	174–219	187–232
6 3	157–202		141–186	153–199	166–212	179–225	192–238
6 4			144–191	157–205	171–218	184–231	197–244

*Values in this table are for height without shoes and weight without clothes. The Metropolitan Life Insurance Company[1] presented a table for nude heights and weights (Table 4) as well as a table for heights and weights clothed (Table 1).

per year, somewhat in excess of the actual mean weight increase that occurs in American men and women across the adult age span.

It must be stressed that tables of recommended weight are applicable only to subjects who do not have medical conditions which, in themselves, are affected by or which affect body weight. Furthermore, it is difficult to recommend weights for individuals over the age of 70. Data from the American Cancer Society Study[6] for men and women in their seventies and eighties suggest that the weight gain permitted with increasing age should be maintained into very old age. A number of other studies of elderly populations also suggest that the weights associated with lowest mortality remain on the relatively high side.

IMPORTANCE OF DISTRIBUTION OF BODY FAT

There are several recent studies which may cause a total reconsideration of recommendations for body weight.[15,16] These concern not only weight itself, but also the epidemiological implications of the distribution of body fat—"where fat?" in addition to "how fat?", as it were. The suggestions have been made that when fat is distributed primarily in the lower part of the body (hips, buttocks, and thighs), the obesity is relatively benign;

associated abnormalities of blood pressure, glucose tolerance, and serum lipid levels may not occur. In con-

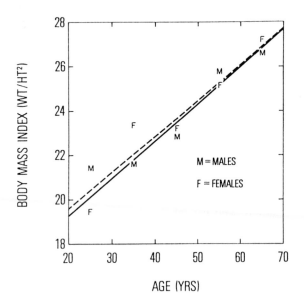

FIGURE 72-2

The effect of age on the BMI associated with lowest mortality. Minimal mortality points were computed for each age-sex group as indicated in Figure 72-1. The regression lines were computed separately for men (———) and for women (– – –). Note that there is a strong effect of age on the BMI associated with lowest mortality and that the regression lines for men and women are nearly identical. (Based upon data reported in *Build Study 1979*.[13])

trast, when the fat is distributed intraabdominally or in the neck, shoulder, and arm areas, the obesity takes on a more "malignant" metabolic prognosis. A simple measure of fat distribution may be the ratio of waist circumference to hip circumference. These few studies are intriguing and of potentially great importance. It is an area which should develop rapidly in the next few years.

In summary, it would appear that for healthy individuals the weights associated with minimal mortality increase with age and that the old saw that one's best weight is that achieved at age 20 or 25 needs to be discarded. There appears to be a rather broad range of weight associated with low mortality; weights both below and above those limits become increasingly harmful. More refined weight prescriptions modified for body habitus and age will have to await the compilation of evidence that is not available at the present time. Rapid advances in adipocyte physiology, including studies of regional differences in the adipocytes, and carefully designed longitudinal obesity-mortality studies will cause major revisions in our current thoughts concerning age-specific ranges of desirable body weight.

REFERENCES

1. *1983 Metropolitan Height and Weight Tables. Stat Bull Metropol Life Ins Co* 64 (Jan–Jun):2, 1983.
2. Grande F: Assessment of body fat in man, in Bray GA (ed): *Obesity in Perspective*. U.S. Department of Health, Education, and Welfare Publication (NIH) 75-708, 1975, p 189.
3. Keys A: *Seven Countries: A Multivariate Analysis of Death and Coronary Heart Disease*. Cambridge, Harvard, 1980.
4. Andres R: Effect of obesity on total mortality. *Int J Obes* 4:381, 1980.
5. Andres R: Aging, diabetes, and obesity: Standards of normality. *Mt Sinai J Med (NY)* 48:489, 1981.
6. Lew EA, Garfinkel L: Variations in mortality by weight among 750,000 men and women. *J Chronic Dis* 32:563, 1979.
7. Harris T et al: Body mass index and mortality among nonsmoking older persons: The Framingham Heart Study. *JAMA* 259:1520, 1988.
8. Waaler HT: Height, weight and mortality. The Norwegian experience. *Acta Med Scand* 215(Suppl 679):1, 1984.
9. Manson J et al: Body weight and longevity: A reassessment. *JAMA* 257:353, 1987.
10. Feinleib J: Epidemiology of obesity in relation to health hazards. *Ann Intern Med* 103:1019, 1985.
11. Waaler HT: Hazard of obesity—the Norwegian experience. *Acta Med Scand [Suppl]* 223(Suppl 723):17, 1988.
12. Foster WR, Burton BT (eds): Health implications of obesity. *Ann Intern Med* 103 (Number 6, Part 2):979, 1985.
13. New weight standards for men and women. *Stat Bull* 40 (Nov–Dec):1, 1959.
14. *Build Study 1979*. Chicago, Society of Actuaries and Association of Life Insurance Medical Directors of America, 1980.
15. Björntorp P, Smith U, Lönnroth P (eds): Health implications of obesity. *Acta Med Scand* 223 (Suppl 723):1, 1988.
16. Shimokata H et al: Studies in the distribution of body fat: I. Effects of age, sex, and obesity. *J Gerontol* 44:M66, 1989.

Chapter 73

AGING AND PLASMA LIPOPROTEINS

Norman E. Miller

During the past decade there have been numerous major advances in lipid research. Prominent among these advances are the identification of several lipoprotein receptors, the emergence of the plasma high-density lipoprotein (HDL) cholesterol concentration as a major risk factor for coronary heart disease (CHD), and the completion of several clinical trials that have provided unequivocal evidence that reduction of the plasma low-density lipoprotein (LDL) concentration is effective in reducing atherogenesis and incidence of CHD in middle-aged men. Now that the importance of lipoprotein metabolism in relation to atherogenesis has been established, attention is being directed toward related areas of lipid research. Notable among these is the interaction between lipoprotein metabolism and the aging process. This chapter summarizes our current knowledge in this important area.

HUMAN LIPOPROTEIN METABOLISM

Plasma lipoprotein metabolism can be regarded as being composed of four processes: the transport of exogenous lipids from the ileum to hepatic and extrahepatic tissues; the transport of endogenously synthesized triglyceride from the liver to peripheral cells; the transport of cholesterol to peripheral tissues; and the movement of cholesterol from peripheral tissues to the liver for elimination (reverse cholesterol transport). Although this division into four processes is convenient for descriptive purposes, it is artificial, as will become apparent, because the different components of lipoprotein metabolism interact with each other.

Exogenous lipids enter the circulation via thoracic duct lymph in chylomicrons. Circulating chylomicrons have three major protein components: apoprotein (apo) B48 (the structural protein, synthesized in the ileum); apo E; and apos CI, CII, and CIII (synthesized in the liver and acquired by transfer from circulating HDL). Hydrolysis of the glyceride in the core of the particles is catalyzed by lipoprotein lipase (LPL), an enzyme which is bound to the capillary endothelium in several peripheral tissues (e.g., myocardium, skeletal muscle, and adipose tissue) and is activated by apo CII. The free fatty acids that are released are oxidized or utilized for glyceride synthesis in the tissues. As the chylomicrons diminish in size, redundant surface material (unesterified cholesterol, phospholipid, and apos CI to CIII) is released and interacts with HDL. The loss of C apoproteins enables the remnant particle to interact with receptors in the plasma membranes of hepatocytes (apo E or remnant receptors), resulting in their endocytosis and catabolism. In this way the majority of the cholesterol originally incorporated into nascent chylomicrons (together with additional cholesteryl esters originating in HDL, discussed later) is transferred to the liver.

Cholesterol and glyceride synthesized in hepatocytes are incorporated into very low density lipoproteins (VLDL). These lipoproteins are similar to chylomicrons but are smaller and more dense; also, they contain apo B100, not apo B48, as the structural protein. VLDL glyceride is hydrolyzed by LPL in peripheral tissues, and the resulting core remnants are known as intermediate-density lipoproteins (IDL). These lipoproteins are partially cleared by hepatocytes, via receptors (called apo B100/E or LDL receptors) that recognize both apo B100 and apo E. Other IDL particles are removed by peripheral cells or converted to LDL particles, which are cholesteryl ester-rich particles whose sole apoprotein is apo B100. These LDL particles are removed from the circulation mostly via the apo B100/E receptors in hepatocytes and peripheral cells.

The delivery of cholesterol to cells occurs predominantly via the receptor-mediated uptake of LDL. Endocytosis of LDL particles results in their hydrolysis in lysosomes. The cholesterol so released exerts three effects on cellular metabolism: inhibition of LDL-receptor synthesis; suppression of the rate-limiting enzyme in cholesterol synthesis, HMG CoA reductase; and stimulation of intracellular cholesterol esterification by an increase in the activity of acyl-CoA: cholesterol acyltransferase. Cholesterol acquired by cells in this way is utilized for membrane synthesis. In the adrenal cortex and gonads, LDL uptake also provides the principal source of cholesterol for steroid hormone synthesis.

Reverse transport of cholesterol from peripheral tissues to the liver, for elimination in the bile and conversion to bile acids, is mediated by HDL. Small, phospholipid-rich, apo A1-containing particles are thought to be the primary acceptors of cholesterol in the interstitium of tissues and the precursors of circulating HDL. Following entry into the circulation, the cholesterol of these particles is esterified by plasma lecithin: cholesterol acyltransferase. A proportion of the cholesteryl esters so formed enters the cores of the HDL particles, increasing the size of the particles and decreasing their density. The majority, however, is transferred to triglyceride-rich lipoproteins via a transfer protein. The delivery of cholesteryl esters to the liver probably occurs by several processes: uptake of IDL and LDL via the apo B100/E receptors; uptake of mature HDL particles via the apo E receptors, and possibly also via receptors for apo AI; and transfer of cholesteryl ester from HDL particles to hepatocytes. Nascent HDL particles, which cannot normally be identified in plasma, are probably synthesized in the liver and ileum and also derived from the surface material released from lipolyzed chylomicrons and VLDL. For detailed reviews of lipoprotein metabolism, see Shepherd[1] and Mayes.[2]

In normal fasted subjects, chylomicrons are absent from plasma, and the majority of plasma triglyceride and cholesterol resides in VLDL and LDL respectively. In most middle-aged and elderly North Americans, 60 to 80 percent of plasma cholesterol is in LDL and 15 to 30 percent is in HDL.

LIPOPROTEINS AS RISK FACTORS FOR CORONARY DISEASE

The well-recognized positive association between plasma total cholesterol concentration (reflecting LDL cholesterol) and CHD incidence has been demonstrated in numerous industrialized communities and also exists between populations. The relationship is continuous, graded, and independent of other CHD risk factors such as blood pressure and cigarette smoking. Reduction of plasma LDL concentration has been shown to reduce the progression of atherosclerosis and incidence of CHD in middle-aged men. This is thought to reflect a direct effect of LDL, or, more likely, a modified form of the lipoprotein, on the deposition of cholesterol in the developing atherosclerotic plaque. It is probable that other cholesterol-rich lipoproteins (i.e., chylomicron remnants and IDL) are also atherogenic, although unequivocal evidence for this theory is not available. The relationship of mortality to serum cholesterol concentration in middle-aged North American men is shown in Fig. 73-1.[3]

Independent of its association with LDL concentration, CHD risk is also inversely related to the concentration of HDL cholesterol. This relationship probably reflects the function of HDL in the reverse transport of cholesterol from the arterial wall. Although the effectiveness of HDL-raising therapy in the prevention of CHD has not yet been formally tested, incidental evidence that increasing HDL cholesterol pharmacologically can be associated with a reduction of CHD incidence or atherogenesis has emerged from several clinical trials of cholesterol-lowering therapy.

The combined effect of the associations of CHD incidence with both LDL and HDL cholesterol is to generate a strong positive correlation between CHD risk and the LDL cholesterol/HDL cholesterol ratio. In the United States this ratio provides the most powerful lipid risk factor for CHD in both men and women. For more detailed reviews of these subjects see Lee[4] and Miller.[5]

AGE-RELATED CHANGES IN LIPOPROTEINS

CHANGES IN LIPOPROTEINS DURING AGING IN INDUSTRIALIZED COMMUNITIES

Plasma Total and LDL Cholesterol

Uniformly low plasma cholesterol concentrations have been demonstrated at birth in many diverse populations. Typical reported mean values are 60 to 70 mg/dl, about half of this being in LDL. During the first week of life, rapid increases in plasma total and LDL cholesterol concentrations occur. Thereafter, they rise more slowly for 4 to 6 years before reaching a period of relative stability during ages 6 to 12. Further major increases occur during adolescence and adulthood in both sexes. In the Lipid Research Clinics (LRC) study, for example, mean LDL cholesterol in white North American males increased by about 35 percent between ages 20 to 24 and 45 to 49, after which it remained constant until about age 70, when it declined.[6] The LDL cholesterol level in white females ages 20 to 24 was similar to that in males of the same age. However, the rate of rise during aging in

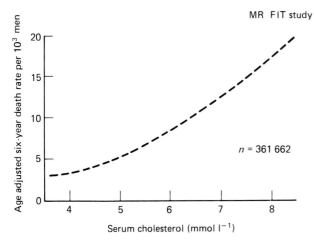

FIGURE 73-1
Six-year mortality in 361,662 men aged 35 to 57 in relation to serum cholesterol in the Multiple Risk Factor Intervention Trial.[3] *(Reproduced from Shepherd,[1] with permission.)*

women was lower than it was during aging in men, such that the mean concentration in females at ages 45 to 49 was about 10 percent lower than in males. While no further increase occurred in men after age 49, a continued rise was recorded in women up to ages 65 to 69, after which there was a fall. These data are summarized in Fig. 73-2. Similar results have been reported from other

cross-sectional studies in the United States, Britain, and Europe.[7] That these data reflect genuine age-related changes, and not selective mortality, has been confirmed by longitudinal surveillance of cohorts.[8–10]

High-Density Lipoprotein

During childhood no consistent difference in HDL cholesterol has been observed between the sexes, in both of which the concentration remains stable until puberty. At this time HDL cholesterol declines in boys, whereas no change occurs in girls, resulting in a difference between the sexes that is maintained throughout adult life. Between ages 20 and 55, HDL cholesterol is stable in males, after which there is a small rise. In females it tends to increase slowly until ages 55 to 60, after which there is a decline (see Fig. 73-2).

Plasma Triglyceride

Plasma triglyceride concentration is low at birth and increases progressively in both sexes throughout childhood, adolescence, and adulthood, reflecting a rise in VLDL concentration. As with LDL, the rate of rise of VLDL is greater in males than in females, so that by ages 40 to 44 plasma triglyceride averages are about 45 percent higher in men than in women. The triglyceride increase in men continues until about age 55, when a gradual decline begins. In contrast, triglyceride levels in women continue to rise up to the age of 70. Data from the LRC study appear in Fig. 73-3.

CHANGES IN LIPOPROTEINS DURING AGING IN NONINDUSTRIALIZED COMMUNITIES

In most nonindustrialized communities that have been studied, little or no age-associated increase in plasma total or LDL cholesterol concentration has been observed. Communities studied include the highlanders of New Guinea[11] (Fig. 73-4), the Tarahumara Indians of Mexico,[12] Melanesians,[13] certain nomads of Kenya,[14] rural blacks in South Africa,[15] Kalahari bushmen,[16] and rural Guatemalan Indians.[17] Although these are cross-sectional observations only, they are important because they suggest that a rise in LDL concentration is not an inevitable consequence of aging in humans, but probably a consequence of an element of the Western lifestyle. Examination of the diets and habits of such groups may lead to the identification of the underlying causal factors in Westernized societies.

CLINICAL SIGNIFICANCE OF AGE-RELATED CHANGES IN LIPOPROTEINS

From the standpoint of CHD incidence in Western communities, the most significant changes that occur in lipo-

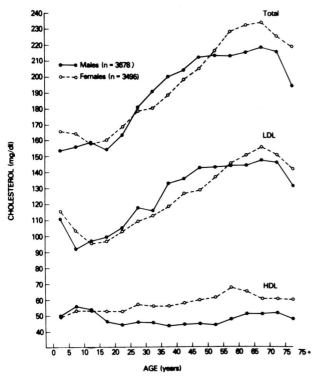

FIGURE 73-2
Changes in plasma total cholesterol, LDL cholesterol, and HDL cholesterol during aging in males and females in the Lipid Research Clinics study. *(Reproduced from Rifkind et al.[6] with permission.)*

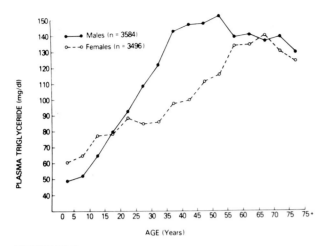

FIGURE 73-3
Changes in plasma triglyceride concentration during aging in males and females in the Lipid Research Clinics study. *(Reproduced from Rifkind et al.[6] with permission.)*

proteins during aging are the rise in LDL cholesterol during adolescence and adulthood in both sexes and the decrease in HDL cholesterol in males during puberty.

In the epidemiologic sense, the sex difference in HDL cholesterol explains a proportion of the higher incidence of CHD suffered by men, as compared to women of childbearing age. Population comparisons have suggested that the sex difference in HDL is smaller in nonindustrialized communities with a low incidence of CHD than in industrialized communities. The reason for this is not known.[18]

The decline in HDL cholesterol concentration that

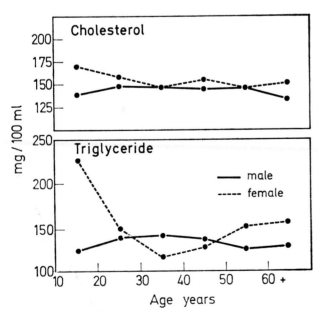

FIGURE 73-4
Plasma cholesterol and triglyceride concentrations in 777 New Guinea natives. *(Reproduced from Goldrick et al.[11] with permission.)*

occurs late in life in women is of uncertain significance. Although it seems likely to be related to declining ovarian function, clear evidence for this is not available. Nor is it certain that the natural menopause is causally associated with an acceleration of atherogenesis in women.[18]

On the basis of the known relationship of CHD incidence to LDL concentration in adults, the rise in LDL cholesterol that occurs during aging must make a very substantial contribution to morbidity and mortality from CHD in middle-aged and elderly North American men and women. There can be no doubt that the incidence of CHD in such individuals would be very much lower if their LDL concentrations remained unchanged after adolescence. Although it is difficult to estimate the true magnitude of the impact of LDL cholesterol concentrations, consideration of the rise in mean LDL cholesterol that was observed in men between the ages of 20 and 50 in the LRC study, together with the known relationship of CHD to plasma cholesterol in North American men,[3] suggests that the effect might be to increase mortality by more than twofold in middle age.

It has already been noted that an age-related rise in LDL does not occur in many nonindustrialized communities and may therefore be avoidable in industrialized ones. Also important is the fact that once a rise in LDL has occurred, it cannot readily be reversed. Although LDL can be reduced in middle age by diet, the magnitude of the reduction that can be maintained is usually much less than the rise in concentration that has occurred since adolescence. Thus, whereas in LRC males LDL cholesterol averaged about 30 percent lower at 20 years old than at 50 years old,[6] long-term trials of CHD prevention by diet in middle-aged men have generally achieved mean reductions of only 7 to 15 percent.[19]

Another point worth emphasizing is that the increase in mean LDL concentration in Westernized communities reflects a general trend that occurs in most members of society (albeit to differing degrees) and not the presence of a subpopulation of "responders" who are uniquely predisposed to an effect of aging on LDL for genetic or environmental reasons. There are two lines of evidence for this. First, comparison of the frequency distributions of plasma cholesterol in young and older adults has provided no evidence for the emergence of bimodality. Second, and more importantly, follow-up of cohorts of individuals for several years has demonstrated significant "tracking" of plasma cholesterol concentration with time.[8–10]

In summary, therefore, the age-related rise in LDL concentration (1) constitutes a major cause of CHD in Western communities, (2) occurs in the majority of subjects, (3) is avoidable, and (4) is largely irreversible. These features highlight the importance of understanding the underlying metabolic mechanisms.

AGING AND LIPOPROTEIN METABOLISM

HIGH-DENSITY LIPOPROTEIN

The metabolic factors which underlie the changes in plasma lipoproteins that occur during aging are not clear. Most attention has been directed toward the decrease in HDL cholesterol that occurs in boys at puberty. That this decrease is related to an effect of gonadal steroids seems likely, as the administration of sex hormones and related synthetic steroids have been found to produce changes in HDL in the anticipated directions. Furthermore, it has been shown by longitudinal observation of boys that the magnitude of the decrease in HDL cholesterol during sexual maturation is correlated with the changes in plasma testosterone and estradiol. On the other hand, the epidemiologic associations between HDL and circulating sex hormones within the sexes have been inconsistent. Also, the effects on lipids of hormones administered systemically have been less striking than those of hormones administered orally, suggesting that the oral route may have a first-pass effect on the liver that is unphysiologic.

Most metabolic studies have focused on the activity of hepatic lipase (which may be involved in HDL catabolism), the activity of LPL (which influences HDL cholesterol indirectly via the catabolism of triglyceride-rich lipoproteins), and the synthesis of apo AI, the major protein of HDL. Since women of childbearing age have lower hepatic lipase activities, greater rates of apo AI synthesis, and possibly higher LPL activities than men, changes in one or more of these may account for the effect of puberty on HDL. The effects of administered steroids on apo AI synthesis and hepatic lipase activity have been compatible with this concept. However, as no longitudinal measurements of these or any other parameters of lipoprotein metabolism have been made in males during sexual maturation, no certain conclusions can be drawn about the changes in HDL metabolism which occur at this time. The published literature in this area has recently been extensively reviewed.[18]

PLASMA VLDL AND TRIGLYCERIDE

The progressive increase in VLDL concentration that occurs up to ages 50 to 55 in men and ages 65 to 70 in women may be a consequence of different metabolic factors operating at different times.[7] No data on VLDL metabolism as a function of age in humans are available. A potential explanation for the rise in VLDL that occurs after age 20 has been provided by evidence that postheparin plasma LPL activity diminishes in both men and women during this time.[20] The extent to which this decrease may be secondary to an age-related increase in

body fat or an alteration in body fat distribution has not been investigated. Under other circumstances, a decrease in LPL activity would be expected also to lower HDL cholesterol. As a progressive fall in HDL does not occur during adulthood in either sex, another factor must be operating to increase HDL production and/or to diminish its clearance. This factor does not seem to be related to a decrease in hepatic lipase activity.[20]

LOW-DENSITY LIPOPROTEIN

The rise in the concentration of LDL during early and middle adulthood could be a consequence of an increase in LDL production rate and/or a decrease in its fractional catabolic rate (FCR). Evidence supporting the second possibility was presented by Miller,[21] who pooled data on LDL apo B FCR culled from the literature. A decline in FCR with age was found in four groups of subjects: normal men, normal women, heterozygous familial hypercholesterolemic (FH) men, and FH women (Fig. 73-5). In contrast, no change in LDL production rate was apparent. Three studies have since confirmed that the FCR of LDL apo B declines during aging in healthy men.[22-24] In two of these studies no change in LDL production rate was reported.[22,23] In the third study production rate also increased with age,[24] and it has been argued that the decline in the FCR in these subjects could have been secondary to saturation of LDL receptors.[25]

It has already been mentioned that the principal regulatable route of LDL catabolism is via hepatic LDL receptors. In middle-aged and elderly subjects, LDL concentration is a negative function of hepatic LDL receptor activity.[26] However, no data are available on the changes in receptor activity that occur in vivo during aging. Although a decline in LDL receptor synthesis has been observed on repeated subculture of human fibroblasts,[27] the rate at which derepressed cultured human cells endocytose and degrade radiolabeled LDL has not been found to be correlated negatively with the age of the donor (reviewed by Miller[21]). On the contrary, in a recent study a positive correlation was observed in fibroblasts cultured from 27 subjects aged 5 to 64.[28] In the same study, derepressed fibroblasts from 48 subjects aged 84 to 95 had a range of receptor activities which was similar to that of the fibroblasts from the younger subjects.

As each of these studies was carried out using cells that had been preincubated in lipoprotein-deficient medium (so as to maximally stimulate LDL-receptor synthesis), their results indicate that the machinery for synthesizing receptors in the cell types studied (vascular smooth muscle, fibroblasts, lymphocytes) remains intact during aging. The receptor activities of derepressed cells may not reflect their activities in vivo, however, when

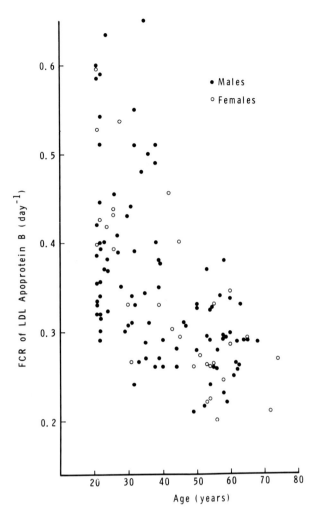

FIGURE 73-5
Relationship of the fractional catabolic rate of LDL apo B to age in 94 men and 32 women. *(Reproduced from Miller[21] with permission.)*

receptor synthesis is influenced by multiple genetic, hormonal, and intracellular factors. For example, as estradiol and triiodothyronine have each been shown to stimulate receptor synthesis in tissue culture and animals, decreases in the circulating concentration of these hormones during aging might lead to decreased receptor synthesis in vivo which would not be detected in cultured cells. Alternatively, or additionally, receptor synthesis could be suppressed by any accumulation of unesterified cholesterol that might occur in cells during aging. Good evidence that such an accumulation does occur in members of industrialized communities has been provided by multicompartmental analysis of plasma-cholesterol-specific radioactivity:time curves and by chemical measurement of cholesterol in tissue biopsies (reviewed in Miller[29]). In contrast, in the Japanese, in whom plasma LDL concentrations were much lower than in Western societies, no age-related increase in tissue cholesterol content was detected.[30] Froberg noted that the rate of increase in skeletal muscle cholesterol was greater in CHD victims than in healthy subjects.[31]

DIET AND OBESITY

The possibility that environmental factors may underlie the increase in plasma cholesterol concentration during adolescence and adulthood is suggested by the absence of any similar change in certain nonindustrialized communities. Of particular significance in this context is the observation that South African blacks develop an age-related rise in plasma cholesterol when they move from a rural to an urban lifestyle.[15] Such data clearly indicate that an environmental factor is operative. To date, two potential factors have been investigated: the rise in adiposity that accompanies aging in most members of Western societies and the possibility of a slow, cumulative effect of a component of the Western diet.

There is good evidence that obesity affects lipoprotein metabolism: overweight individuals tend to have higher VLDL and LDL levels and lower HDL cholesterol levels than lean subjects of similar age. However, the effect of overweight on plasma total and LDL cholesterol is smaller than its effect on VLDL and HDL.[32] It is not surprising, therefore, that an age-related rise in relative body weight has been found not to provide a complete explanation for the rise in LDL cholesterol. Although the increase may be greater in individuals who gain weight,[33] a significant increase also occurs in subjects who maintain constant weight throughout their adult lives.[33,34] Nevertheless, as aging tends to be associated with an increase in body fat and a decrease in lean body mass, the possibility cannot be excluded that, even in those whose weights remain constant, the rise in VLDL and LDL may be related, at least in part, to altered body composition.

Communities in which no age-related rise in plasma cholesterol occurs generally consume diets low in saturated fat and cholesterol. Experimental evidence that dietary fat may be important has been provided by the demonstration that an age-related rise in plasma cholesterol occurred in hamsters only when saturated glycerides were added to their diet.[35] However, a specific dietary factor has not yet been clearly implicated in human studies. In a recent study of British men and women, age-related increases in plasma cholesterol were recorded in vegetarians, vegans, fish-eaters, and meat-eaters,[36] suggesting that dietary fatty acids may not be very important. A rise in plasma cholesterol was also observed in Greenlandic Eskimos, who consume a diet rich in long-chain polyunsaturated fatty acids. However, this rise reflected increases in both LDL and HDL (with no increase in VLDL), and the increment in LDL was much less than that seen in Danish controls.[37] Aging does not appear to be accompanied by a major increase in the short-term sensitivity of plasma cholesterol concentration to dietary cholesterol.[38,39] There is no information on the extent to which the age-related rise in LDL in humans is influenced by the amounts of cholesterol or fiber that are regularly consumed. The implications of these observations are that, while it may be possible to reduce the magnitude of the age-related rise in LDL by maintaining ideal body weight, avoidance of any rise at all will probably require other modifications of the Western diet or lifestyle; the nature of the modifications remains to be identified.

LONGEVITY SYNDROMES

Two disorders of lipoprotein metabolism which aggregate in families and are associated with a rarity of CHD and longevity have been described. These disorders have been termed *longevity syndromes*.[40] They are familial hypobetalipoproteinemia (characterized by very low concentrations of VLDL and LDL) and familial hyperalphalipoproteinemia (characterized by very high HDL levels). The molecular bases of these disorders have not yet been defined, although both are almost certainly biochemically heterogeneous. Because of its favorable prognostic significance, familial hypobetalipoproteinemia must be distinguished from secondary hypobetalipoproteinemia resulting from malnutrition, liver disease, or gammopathy, all of which are increased in the elderly. Hyperalphalipoproteinemia may also be secondary to alcoholism, insulin-replacement therapy in diabetes mellitus, and treatment with enzyme-inducing agents such as phenytoin, phenobarbital, and carbamazepine.

HYPERLIPIDEMIA IN THE ELDERLY

DIAGNOSIS OF HYPERCHOLESTEROLEMIA

For clinical purposes the term *elderly* will be applied to all persons age 65 or older. The frequency with which hypercholesterolemia is diagnosed in this section of the community will be influenced greatly by our attitude toward the age-related rise in plasma cholesterol concentration. If it is regarded as a normal component of the aging process, it would be reasonable to use as an arbitrary diagnostic cut-off point the same centile of age-specific plasma cholesterol concentration as is used in young adults. With this approach the prevalence of hypercholesterolemia will be the same irrespective of age (as it is defined by the centile selected), but the concentration at which hypercholesterolemia is diagnosed will progressively change throughout adult life. On the other hand, if the age-related rise is a pathologic response to one or more components of the Western lifestyle, the concentration used as the cut-off point in the elderly should be the same as that used in young individuals. This approach will produce a very much higher prevalence of the diagnosis of hypercholesterolemia in older

than in younger subjects (though since cholesterol levels in both sexes tend to level off or even decline beyond age 65, this prevalence will either stabilize or diminish progressively in old age as defined herein).

In previous sections a strong case has been made for regarding the rise in plasma cholesterol with age as unphysiologic. If this is true, it follows that a substantial proportion of elderly subjects in industrialized societies are hypercholesterolemic. On the other hand, we need to be aware that widespread advocation of aggressive lipid-lowering diets for the elderly might aggravate nutritional problems that are already prevalent in this section of the community. The generally prescribed lipid-lowering diets incorporate calorie restriction (if the individual is considered to be overweight) and restriction of eggs, meat, and dairy products. While such a diet is now considered beneficial in young and middle-aged adults with adequate nutrient intakes, strict adherence to the limitations imposed could prove hazardous to some elderly patients, for whom provision of adequate calories, protein, and calcium may be more important than the consequences of a moderate degree of hypercholesterolemia.

The National Cholesterol Education Program (NCEP)[41] has recently recommended that plasma cholesterol concentrations below 200 mg/dl be considered desirable for adults aged 20 or older. By advocating that the same cut-off concentration be used in adults of all ages, the NCEP acknowledges that the age-related rise in cholesterol represents an abnormal state. But is it realistic to apply the same cut-off levels in the elderly as in young and middle-aged adults? A plasma cholesterol of 200 mg/dl corresponds to about the 75th centile in white American males aged 25 to 29, but to about the 40th centile in males aged 65 to 69 (Table 73-1).[42] Thus, the application of the NCEP recommendation to the elderly would create an unmanageable number of patients being investigated and treated for hypercholesterolemia (60 percent of the population). Taking also into account the evidence that plasma cholesterol appears to be a less reliable CHD risk factor in elderly than in middle-aged North Americans,[43] this author recommends that concentrations below 260 mg/dl in men and 280 mg/dl in women (corresponding to about the 90th centile for elderly white North Americans—see Table 73-1) be considered desirable after age 65.

MANAGEMENT OF HYPERCHOLESTEROLEMIA

When considering the management of an elderly patient diagnosed as having hypercholesterolemia, the physician needs to consider a number of points. First, as raised cholesterol levels are more likely to reflect a high HDL level in elderly patients than in younger subjects (because of the higher prevalence of familial hyperal-

TABLE 73-1
Plasma Total and LDL Cholesterol Concentrations (mg/dl) in Elderly White Men and Women
(Not Taking Hormones) in North America

Sex	Age (yr)	Centiles of Total Cholesterol				Centiles of LDL Cholesterol			
		50	75	90	95	50	75	90	95
Males	65–69	210	233	258	274	146	170	199	210
	70+	205	229	252	270	142	164	182	186
Females	65–69	229	256	280	303	156	189	208	223
	70+	226	253	278	289	146	170	189	207

SOURCE: From the Lipid Research Clinics Prevalence Study.[42]

phalipoproteinemia), quantification of HDL cholesterol is particularly important in this group. Second, because of the increased prevalence of disease in the elderly, the presence of hyperlipidemia in them is more likely to be secondary to antihypertensive medication, non-insulin-dependent diabetes, monoclonal gammopathy, renal disease, and other disorder-related factors that are not as common in young adults. Third, as epidemiologic data suggest that LDL cholesterol is a weaker predictor of CHD incidence in the elderly than it is in middle-aged subjects,[43] and as there have been no clinical trials of CHD prevention in the elderly, aggressive lipid-lowering drug therapy is more difficult to justify in this age group. Fourth, care should be taken to ensure that those patients who are prescribed lipid-lowering diets have adequate nutritional intake in other respects, as already discussed. Finally, as low plasma cholesterol concentrations have been shown to be associated with increased mortality in hospitalized patients,[44] it might be considered prudent to terminate or reduce any lipid-lowering diet or medication in such elderly patients until the mechanism of this epidemiologic association is understood.

If lipid-lowering drug therapy is prescribed in an elderly patient, particular care needs to be taken with a number of the drugs that are currently available. The use of *d*-thyroxine has been precluded by the demonstration that it produces arrhythmias and increased mortality in patients with established atherosclerosis.[45] Care needs to be taken with the bile-acid-sequestering resins (cholestyramine and colestipol), as they produce constipation in some individuals. Nicotinic acid has been found to increase the incidence of arrhythmias in middle-aged men with atherosclerosis, although the group of subjects that included those men benefited from a significant reduction in nonfatal myocardial infarction.[46] It should also be remembered that drug-related disease is generally more common in the elderly than in younger adults and that drug elimination via the kidneys and/or liver may be impaired in the elderly. Hence, only rarely is lipid-lowering drug therapy justified in elderly hyperlipidemic patients.

The NCEP provides detailed guidelines for the management of hypercholesterolemia.[41] For the elderly these guidelines can be simplified in a way that takes into account the aforementioned considerations. The following scheme is recommended for all elderly subjects who are found to have a plasma cholesterol level >260 mg/dl (men) or >280 mg/dl (women). First, the measurement should be repeated (not necessarily under fasting conditions). If the mean of the two results is not raised, the patient should be reassured and seen again in one year. If the mean value is raised, another sample should be collected in the fasted state for measurement of cholesterol, triglyceride, and HDL cholesterol, and for estimation of LDL cholesterol as: cholesterol minus (triglyceride/5) minus HDL. If LDL cholesterol is < 200 mg/dl in men or < 210 mg/dl in women (sex-specific 90th centiles), the patient should be reassured and seen in one year. If LDL cholesterol is raised, it is important to screen for diseases known to cause secondary hyperlipidemia and to treat any such condition if present. If no cause is found, the next decision should be based on the HDL cholesterol level. If this exceeds the 90th centile (75 mg/dl in elderly men, and 80 mg/dl in elderly women; see Table 73-2), the patient should be reassured and seen again one year later. Patients with lower HDL cholesterol levels should be treated by Phase I dietary fat modification according to the NCEP guidelines.[41] If after 6 weeks this diet has reduced LDL to a "normal" value, as described previously, it should be continued and the patient seen every 6 months. If LDL is not reduced sufficiently by the Phase I diet, the Phase II diet of the NCEP should be prescribed (which dictates greater restriction of saturated fat and cholesterol) and the patient given another 6-week follow-up appointment. Patients whose LDL concentrations remain high should be considered for drug therapy, but only if: (1) there is clinical evidence of CHD or peripheral vascular disease, or the patient has already had coronary artery surgery; and/or (2) there are two or more coexistent CHD risk factors; and/or (3) the LDL cholesterol level is grossly elevated (>300 mg/dl). If any evidence of renal or hepatic dysfunction is found on biochemical screening, a modest dose of a nonabsorbable bile acid–binding resin should be prescribed (i.e., cho-

TABLE 73-2
Plasma Triglyceride and HDL Cholesterol Concentrations (mg/dl) in Elderly White Men and Women (Not Taking Hormones) in North America

Sex	Age (yr)	Centiles of Triglyceride			Centiles of HDL Cholesterol				
		90	*95*	*10*	*25*	*50*	*75*	*90*
Males	65–69	208	267	33	39	49	62	74
	70+	212	258	33	40	48	56	70
Females	65–69	204	243	38	46	60	71	79
	70+	204	237	37	48	60	69	82

SOURCE: From the Lipid Research Clinics Prevalence Study.[42]

lestyramine or colestipol, 5 or 6 g three times daily). If hepatic and renal functions are normal, gemfibrozil (600 mg twice daily) or lovastatin (40 mg daily) should be prescribed. If the patient has a history of gallbladder disease, lovastatin is preferred to gemfibrozil. If the patient has an HDL cholesterol below the 50th centile (50 mg/dl in men and 60 mg/dl in women; see Table 73-2), gemfibrozil is preferred, as in younger adults gemfibrozil has been shown to reduce CHD risk in part via its HDL-raising activity, particularly in individuals with initially low HDL concentrations.[47] With prescription of either drug the patient should be seen initially at 2-week intervals for 8 weeks to check for clinical side effects and for increases in liver enzymes. Patients taking lovastatin should be examined for lens opacities by slit lamp before treatment and annually thereafter. Lovastatin and gemfibrozil should not be given together, as the combination may produce a high incidence of myositis.

HYPERTRIGLYCERIDEMIA

As hypertriglyceridemia per se does not appear to be an independent risk factor for CHD, a raised level of triglycerides need not be treated in the elderly, unless the increase is severe and associated with pancreatitis. As in younger patients, such severe hypertriglyceridemia usually proceeds from the combination of an otherwise benign familial form of hypertriglyceridemia and a secondary cause, most commonly poorly controlled diabetes, alcoholism, or estrogen therapy. In such instances the initial approach to management is by control of the secondary cause. If additional treatment is required, gemfibrozil is the drug of choice, with nicotinic acid as an alternative. Descriptions of the properties and uses of lipid-lowering drugs can be obtained from readily available sources.[1,48,49]

REFERENCES

1. Shepherd J (ed): *Bailliere's Clinical Endocrinology and Metabolism*, vol 1, no 3: *Lipoprotein Metabolism*. London, Bailliere Tindall, 1987.

2. Mayes PA: Metabolism of lipids, in Martin DW, Mayes PA, Rodwell VW (eds): *Harper's Review of Biochemistry*, 19th ed. Los Altos, CA, Lange Medical Publications, 1983, pp 224–264.

3. Martin MJ, Hulley SB, Browner WS, Kuller LH, Wentworth D: Serum cholesterol, blood pressure and mortality: Implications from a cohort of 361,662 men. *Lancet* 2:933, 1986.

4. Lee KT (ed): *Atherosclerosis*, vol 454. *Ann NY Acad Sci* 1985.

5. Miller GJ: The epidemiology of plasma lipoproteins and atherosclerotic disease, in Miller NE, Lewis B (eds): *Lipoproteins, Atherosclerosis and Coronary Heart Disease*. Amsterdam, Elsevier, 1981, pp 59–71.

6. Rifkind B, Tamir I, Heiss G: Preliminary high density lipoprotein findings. The Lipid Research Clinic Program, in Gotto AM, Miller NE, Oliver MF (eds): *High Density Lipoproteins and Atherosclerosis*. Amsterdam, Elsevier, 1978, pp 109–119.

7. Miller NE, Miller GJ: Lipids and lipoproteins throughout the human lifespan in relation to ageing and atherosclerosis, in Stout RW (ed): *Arterial Disease in the Elderly*. Edinburgh, Churchill Livingstone, 1984, pp 32–56.

8. Gordon T, Shurtleff D: The Framingham Study, Section 29. Means at each examination and inter-examination variation of specified characteristics. DHEW (NIH) 74–478, Washington, Government Printing Office, 1974.

9. Clarke DA, Allen MF, Wilson FH: Longitudinal study of serum lipids. 12-year report. *Am J Clin Nutr* 20:743, 1967.

10. Barzilay J, Froom P, Forecast D et al: The predictive value of cholesterol in young men for an elevated cholesterol ten to twelve years later. *Public Health* 100:223, 1986.

11. Goldrick RB, Sinnett PF, Whyte HM: An assessment of coronary heart disease and coronary risk factors in a New Guinea highland population, in Jones RJ (ed): *Atherosclerosis*. Berlin, Springer-Verlag, 1970, pp 366–368.

12. Connor WE, Cerqueira MT, Connor RW et al: The plasma lipids, lipoproteins and diet of the Tarahumara Indians of Mexico. *Am J Clin Nutr* 31:1131, 1978.

13. Page LB, Damon A, Moellering RC: Antecedents of cardiovascular disease in six Solomon Islands societies. *Circulation* 44:1132, 1974.

14. Shaper AG, Jones KW: Serum cholesterol in camel-herding nomads. *Lancet* 2:1305, 1962.

15. Rossouw JE, Van Stadeu VA, Benade AJS et al: Is it normal for serum cholesterol to rise with age? in Fidge NH,

Nestel PJ (eds): *Atherosclerosis VII.* Amsterdam, Elsevier, 1986, pp 37–40.

16. Truswell AS, Hansen JDL: Serum-lipids in bushmen. *Lancet* 2:684, 1968.

17. Mendez J, Tejada C, Flores M: Serum lipids levels among rural Guatemalan Indians. *Am J Clin Nutr* 10:403, 1962.

18. Godsland IF, Wynn V, Crook D, Miller NE: Sex, plasma lipoproteins and atherosclerosis: Prevailing assumptions and outstanding questions. *Am Heart J* 114:1467, 1987.

19. Mann JI, Marr JW: Trials of diets to control hyperlipidaemia, in Miller NE, Lewis B (eds): *Lipoproteins, Atherosclerosis and Coronary Heart Disease.* Amsterdam, Elsevier, 1981, pp 197–210.

20. Huttunen JK, Ehnholm C, Kekki M, Nikkila EA: Postheparin plasma lipoprotein lipase and hepatic lipase in normal subjects and in patients with hypertriglyceridemia: Correlation to sex, age and various parameters of triglyceride metabolism. *Clin Sci Mol Med* 50:249, 1976.

21. Miller NE: Why does plasma low density lipoprotein concentration in adults increase with age? *Lancet* 1:263, 1984.

22. Ericsson S, Eriksson M, Berglund L, Einarsson K, Angelin B: Reduction of fractional catabolic rate of low density lipoproteins with increasing age. *Eur J Clin Invest* 16(part II):A54, 1986.

23. Kesaniemi YA, Farkkila M, Kervinen K et al: Regulation of low-density lipoprotein apolipoprotein B levels. *Am Heart J* 113(2):508, 1987.

24. Grundy SM, Vega GL, Bilheimer D: Kinetic mechanisms determining variability in low density lipoprotein levels and rise with age. *Arteriosclerosis* 5:623, 1985.

25. Meddings JB, Dietschy JM: Regulation of plasma levels of low-density lipoprotein cholesterol: Interpretation of data on low-density lipoprotein turnover in man. *Circulation* 74:805, 1986.

26. Nanjee MN, Miller NE: Relationships of hepatic low density lipoprotein (LDL) receptor activity to plasma LDL cholesterol, apoprotein B and free tri-iodothyronine concentration in humans. *Clin Res* 36:304A, 1988.

27. Lee H-C, Paz MA, Gallop PM: Low density lipoprotein receptor binding in aging human diploid fibroblasts in culture. *J Biol Chem* 257:8912, 1982.

28. Leren TP, Maartmann-Moe K, Berg K: Low density lipoprotein receptor activity in cultured skin fibroblasts from octa- and nonagenarians. *Clin Genet* 27:433, 1985.

29. Miller NE: On the associations of body cholesterol pool size with age, HDL cholesterol and plasma total cholesterol concentration in humans. *Atherosclerosis* 67:163, 1987.

30. Insull WM, Hsi B, Yoshimura S: Comparison of tissue cholesterols in Japanese and American men. *J Lab Clin Med* 72:885, 1968.

31. Froberg SO: Concentration of cholesterol and triglycerides in skeletal muscle of healthy men and myocardial infarction patients. *Acta Med Scand* 194:553, 1973.

32. Kannel WB, Gordon T, Castelli WP: Obesity, lipids and glucose intolerance. The Framingham Study. *Am J Clin Nutr* 32:1238, 1979.

33. Montoye HJ, Epstein FH, Kjelsberg MO: Relationship between serum cholesterol and body fatness. An epidemiologic study. *Am J Clin Nutr* 18:397, 1966.

34. Nanas S, Pan W-H, Stamler J et al: The role of relative weight in the positive association between age and serum cholesterol in men and women. *J Chronic Dis* 40:887, 1987.

35. Spady DK, Dietschy JM: Aging does not alter receptor-dependent or -independent LDL transport in the hamster. *Arteriosclerosis* 7:497a, 1987.

36. Thorogood M, Carter R, Benfield L, McPherson K, Mann JI: Plasma lipids and lipoprotein cholesterol concentrations in people with different diets in Britain. *Br Med J* 295:351, 1987.

37. Bang HO, Dyerberg J, Nielsen AB: Plasma lipid and lipoprotein pattern in Greenlandic west-coast Eskimos. *Lancet* 1:1143, 1971.

38. Bronsgeest-Schoute DC, Hermus RJJ, Dallinga-Thie GM, Hautvast JGAJ: Dependence of the effects of dietary cholesterol and experimental conditions on serum lipids in man. III. The effect on serum cholesterol of removal of eggs from the diet of free-living habitually egg-eating people. *Am J Clin Nutr* 32:2193, 1979.

39. Beynen AC, Katan MB: Reproducibility of the variations between humans in the response of serum cholesterol to cessation of egg consumption. *Atherosclerosis* 57:19, 1985.

40. Glueck CJ, Fallat RW, Millet F et al: Familial hyperalphalipoproteinemia: Studies in 18 kindreds. *Metabolism* 24:1243, 1975.

41. Report of the National Cholesterol Education Program Expert Panel on Detection, Evaluation and Treatment of High Blood Cholesterol in Adults. *Arch Intern Med* 148:36, 1988.

42. The Lipid Research Clinics Population Studies Data Book. Vol I. The Prevalence Study. Washington, Government Printing Office, DHHS (NIH) 80–1527, 1980.

43. Gordon T, Castelli WP, Hjortland MC, Kannel WB, Dawber TR: High density lipoprotein as a protective factor against coronary heart disease. The Framingham Study. *Am J Med* 62:707, 1977.

44. Oster P, Muchowski H, Hueck CC, Schlierf G: The prognostic significance of hypocholesterolemia in hospitalized patients. *Klin Wochenschr* 59:857, 1981.

45. Coronary Drug Project Research Group. Findings leading to further modifications of its protocol with respect to dextrothyroxine. *JAMA* 220:996, 1972.

46. Coronary Drug Project Research Group. Clofibrate and niacin in coronary heart disease. *JAMA*, 231:360, 1975.

47. Frick MH, Elo O, Haapa K et al: Helsinki Heart Study: Primary prevention trial with gemfibrozil in middle-aged men with dyslipidemia. *N Engl J Med* 317:1237, 1987.

48. Thompson GR: Dietary and pharmacological control of lipoprotein metabolism, in Miller NE, Lewis B (eds): *Lipoproteins, Atherosclerosis and Coronary Heart Disease.* Amsterdam, Elsevier, 1981, pp 129–143.

49. Assmann G: *Lipid Metabolism and Atherosclerosis.* Stuttgart, Schattauer Verlag, 1982.

Chapter 74

THE MENOPAUSE AND ESTROGEN REPLACEMENT THERAPY

Mikal Janelle Odom, Bruce R. Carr, and Paul C. MacDonald

The term *menopause* refers to the cessation of menses, although it commonly is used to refer to the *climacteric*, the transitional period in a woman's life in which there is progressive loss of ovarian function. During this time, a woman usually experiences various endocrine, somatic, and psychological changes.

The median age of menopause in the United States is 50 to 51 years.[1] The average age of menopause has remained constant and does not appear to be related to the age of onset of menarche, socioeconomic conditions, race, parity, height, or weight. The age of menopause, however, may be affected by smoking; the findings of recent studies are suggestive that cigarette smokers experience an earlier spontaneous menopause than do nonsmokers.[2,3] In light of the fact that U.S. women have an average life expectancy of 79 years (Table 74-1), approximately one-third of a woman's life is spent after the menopause. Thus, a goodly proportion of primary-care physicians' time is spent in the medical management of postmenopausal women. It is estimated that by the year 2000, the life expectancy of women will extend more than 30 years after the menopause.[1] With an increase in the total number of women living to the age of menopause and beyond, it is important that the physiological changes of the female climacteric be understood and that the health problems of women during this period be addressed. In this chapter, we will review the changes associated with the female climacteric as well as present our current understanding of the benefits and risks of estrogen replacement therapy during the postmenopausal years.

ENDOCRINE CHANGES DURING THE FEMALE CLIMACTERIC

The principal endocrine changes that are characteristic of the female climacteric are caused primarily by decreased ovarian estrogen secretion. This cessation of ovarian estrogen secretion is caused, in turn, by a loss of ova and associated follicles, mainly by atresia, a process that begins before birth (at 20 weeks of gestation) and continues until menopause. The ovary contains a maximum number of follicles during fetal life at midgestation (approximately 7 million); thereafter the number decreases, and by the time of birth, approximately only 1 million remain (Fig. 74-1). At menarche, the number of ova has decreased to 400,000, and by the time of menopause only a few follicles can be demonstrated.[4] Relatively few ova are lost by ovulation, however—on average, fewer than 500.

There is evidence in support of the view that the ovary becomes less responsive to gonadotropins a few years prior to the time of menopause. First, in women over 45 the length of the ovarian cycle often is shortened, primarily because of a decrease in the length of the follicular phase; after ovulation the length of the luteal phase remains unaffected. Second, associated with a shortened follicular phase, the plasma levels of 17β-estradiol are lower during the follicular and luteal phases of the cycle.[5] The decreased levels of 17β-estradiol probably are caused by a diminished capacity for (or resistance of) the remaining follicles to secrete estrogen, because the metabolic clearance rate of 17β-estradiol is not

TABLE 74-1
Life Expectancy at Birth (years) in Selected Countries in 1965 and in 1983

Country	Men 1965	Men 1983	Women 1965	Women 1983
Angola	34	42	37	44
Argentina	63	66	69	73
Bangladesh	45	49	44	50
Brazil	55	61	59	66
China	55	65	59	69
Cuba	65	73	69	77
India	46	56	44	54
Indonesia	43	52	45	55
Japan	68	74	73	79
Jordan	49	63	51	65
Korea, Rep. of	55	64	58	71
Mexico	58	64	61	68
Nigeria	40	47	43	50
Pakistan	46	51	44	49
Sudan	39	47	41	49
Sweden	72	75	76	80
USA	67	72	74	79
USSR	65	65	74	74

SOURCE: Adapted from *World Development Report 1985*, London, Oxford University Press, 1985. Reproduced with permission from Mishell DR: *Menopause—Physiology and Pharmacology*, Chicago, Year Book Medical Publishers, 1987, p 8.

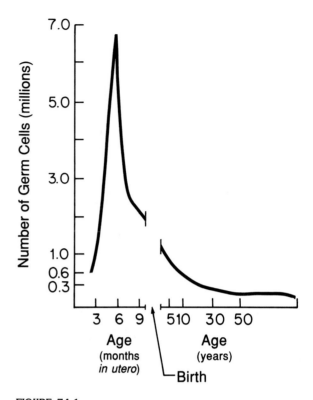

FIGURE 74-1
Changes in germ cell number in the human ovary with increasing age. *(Adapted from Baker TG: Oogenesis and ovulation, in Austin CR, Short RV (eds): Reproduction in Mammals. I. Germ Cells and Fertilization. London: Cambridge Univ. Press, 1972, p 14. Used with permission from Rebar RW: Premature Menopause, Seminars in Reproductive Endocrinology, New York, Thieme-Stratton, 1983, vol 1, No. 2, 1970.)*

increased in postmenopausal women.[6] Presumably in response to decreasing levels of 17β-estradiol and a resulting decrease in negative feedback to the hypothalamopituitary axis, follicle-stimulating hormone (FSH) levels are greater in perimenopausal women during the ovarian cycle. Later, there is a more variable increase in blood luteinizing hormone (LH) levels. Later still, as the time of menopause nears, the interval between menses lengthens, anovulatory cycles are common, and finally menstruation ceases as the capacity of the few remaining ovarian follicles to respond to gonadotropins diminishes to zero.

After menopause, the levels of plasma gonadotropins and the concentrations of the major circulating C_{19} steroids and estrogens are altered compared with values found in premenopausal women during the early follicular phase of the cycle. The cessation of follicular development that leads to a decline in the production of 17β-estradiol and other hormones causes further loss of negative feedback to the hypothalamopituitary centers (Fig. 74-2). In turn, the levels of gonadotropins increase, with levels of FSH rising to a greater extent than those of LH. The higher concentration of FSH than of LH in postmenopausal women is believed to be due to a loss of suppression of FSH by follicular inhibin or due to the fact that FSH is cleared less rapidly than LH because of

the higher sialic acid content of FSH. Gonadotropin-releasing hormone (GnRH), administered to postmenopausal women, causes a pronounced increase in the secretion of both LH and FSH, similar to the enhanced hypothalamopituitary secretion of GnRH that occurs in other forms of ovarian failure.[7] Some investigators find that the concentrations of both gonadotropins remain fairly constant after the age of 60,[7] but others report a downward trend during later decades of life.[8]

Estrogen and C_{19}-steroid levels in postmenopausal women are reduced significantly compared with those in women during reproductive life. Estrogen production in postmenopausal women is diminished, but not totally absent. Estrogen secretion by the postmenopausal ovary is minimal, however, and oophorectomy does not cause any further decline in estrogen levels.[9] Plasma levels of 17β-estradiol, the principal estrogen secreted during reproductive life, are lower than levels of estrone in postmenopausal women. Furthermore, the adrenal cortex does not secrete significant quantities of estrogen in pre- or postmenopausal women.[9] As neither the ovary nor the adrenal of postmenopausal women secretes significant quantities of estrogens, what then is the source

FIGURE 74-2

Levels of pituitary and steroid hormones in premenopausal women compared to postmenopausal women during days 2 to 4 of the menstrual cycle. *(Reproduced with permission from Yen SSC: J Reprod Med 18:287, 1977. In Yen SSC, Jaffe RB: Reproductive Endocrinology, Philadelphia, W.B. Saunders, 1986, p 408.)*

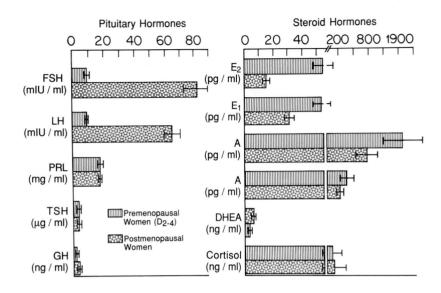

of the estrogen produced in such women? In ovulatory women, circulating estrogens are derived from 2 sources: (1) direct secretion by the ovary and (2) extraglandular conversion of a circulating prehormone to estrogen. Sixty percent of estrogen formation during the ovarian cycle, on average, is in the form of 17β-estradiol secreted into the plasma directly by the ovaries, and the remainder of the estrogen produced consists of estrone formed primarily in extraglandular tissues from plasma androstenedione, which serves as a circulating prehormone for estrone synthesis.[10] After menopause, extraglandular formation of estrone becomes the dominant (indeed, almost exclusive) pathway for estrogen synthesis. The principal sites of extraglandular aromatization of androstenedione are adipose tissue, bone, muscle, skin, and brain. Because a major site of extraglandular estrogen synthesis is adipose tissue, the rate of conversion or extent of aromatization increases with obesity (Fig. 74-3) as well as with age, liver disease, and hyperthyroidism.[10] Thus, total estrogen production may be considerable in obese postmenopausal women and may be as great or greater than in premenopausal women, recognizing that the principal estrogen produced has shifted from the more potent 17β-estradiol to the biologically weaker estrone. Estrone production also may increase when there is an increase in circulating substrate (androstenedione), such as can occur with ovarian tumors.[10]

Prior to menopause, plasma androstenedione is derived almost equally from the adrenal and the ovary; but after menopause, the ovarian secretion of androstenedione is minimal and the plasma levels of androstenedione fall by 50 percent (Table 74-2). The menopausal ovary does continue to secrete very small amounts of testosterone, which is believed to be formed in the stromal cells, the principal structural component of the ovary of postmenopausal women.[9]

STRUCTURAL AND PHYSIOLOGICAL CHANGES ASSOCIATED WITH THE MENOPAUSE

The ovary of the postmenopausal woman is reduced in size, weighing less than 2.5 g, and is wrinkled or prunelike in appearance. The cortical area is reduced in size because of loss of ova and follicular cells, and thus the stromal cells predominate. As a result of decreased 17β-estradiol secretion in postmenopausal women, there is a progressive decrease in weight and size of the organs of the female genitourinary tract and the breasts. The endometrium becomes thin and atrophic in most postmenopausal women, although cystic hyperplasia may be present in up to 20 percent of such women. As a consequence of estrogen deficiency, the vaginal mucosa and

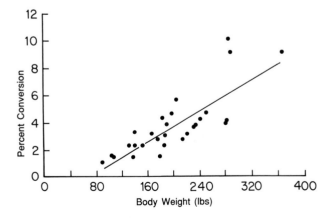

FIGURE 74-3

Correlation of extent of conversion of androstenedione to estrone $[\rho]_{BU}^{AEI}$ with increasing body weight due principally to increased body fat accumulation in postmenopausal women. Correlation coefficient = 0.74. *(Reproduced with permission from Paul C. MacDonald.[10])*

TABLE 74-2
Comparison of Plasma Sex Hormone Concentrations in Pre- and Postmenopausal Women

Hormone Concentration	Premenopausal		Postmenopausal
	Min	Max	
Estradiol, pg/ml	50–60	300–500	5–25
Estrone, pg/ml	30–40	150–300	20–60
Progesterone, ng/ml	0.5–1.0	10–20	0.5
Androstenedione, ng/ml		1.0–2.0	0.3–1.0
Testosterone, ng/ml		0.3–0.8	0.1–0.5

SOURCE: From Mishell DR: *Menopause—Physiology and Pharmacology*, Chicago, Year Book Medical Publishers, 1987, p 48. Reproduced with permission.

the urethra also become thin and atrophic. The mild degrees of hirsutism noted by many postmenopausal women may be due to diminished estrogen production and unopposed testosterone action at the hair follicle unit. There is a general decrease in scalp, pubic, and axillary hair and a decrease in skinfold thickness with a thinning of the epidermis in particular.

It should be mentioned that cancer of the female reproductive tract prior to the menopause is relatively rare except for that involving the uterine cervix; but afterward, the incidence of vulvar, vaginal, uterine, and ovarian cancer increases, which may be a result of metabolic events associated with the aging process per se or the hormonal milieu of the postmenopause. Certain symptoms or disorders believed to be characteristic of the postmenopausal woman are caused primarily by the decrease in ovarian secretion of estrogen, and some of these disorders are of such magnitude as to cause significant physical, emotional, and economic hardships.

The term *menopausal syndrome* is used to describe a spectrum of symptoms that may occur at or about the time of the menopause. These symptoms include the hot flush (vasomotor instability), dryness and atrophy of the urogenital epithelium and vagina, and probably other related disorders that include osteoporosis and psychological symptoms including insomnia, mood changes, irritability, and nervousness. The vasomotor symptoms and urogenital atrophy are related more clearly to the estrogen deficiency of the menopause.

The pathogenesis of the hot flush is unclear. The findings of recent studies are suggestive of a close relationship between the hot flush and pulses of LH secretion.[11,12] Hot flushes do occur in some women after hypophysectomy, however, and also in women treated with GnRH analogs, suggesting that the menopausal syndrome is not due solely to increased levels or pulses of gonadotropin.[13] Also, estrogen replacement (to be discussed later), which alleviates these symptoms, does not fully suppress gonadotropin levels. Thus, it appears that higher central nervous symptom centers, such as the

hypothalamus, are more likely to be the site of the development of vasomotor symptoms. There is evidence that alterations in catecholamine or prostaglandin metabolism in conjunction with low estrogen production may play a role in the pathogenesis of these symptoms.[14,15]

VASOMOTOR SYMPTOMS AND GENITOURINARY CHANGES

The most clear-cut benefits of estrogen therapy in menopausal women as well as the primary indications for estrogen use are in the relief of vasomotor instability and atrophy of the urogenital epithelium. Approximately 30 to 80 percent of menopausal women experience hot flushes. Of these, 80 percent will have them for more than 1 year.[16] Rarely, though, do hot flushes continue more than 5 years after menopause.

In a very detailed description of the hot flush, Hannan noted that the first symptom was a pressure sensation in the head that progressed in intensity until the flush occurred.[17] Occasionally, heart palpitations were experienced. The hot flush itself, which had the sensation of heat or burning, began in the head and neck and spread over the entire body. After this, the women experienced total body sweating, especially in the head, upper chest, back, and neck. The entire episode lasted from seconds to as long as 30 minutes. A change in skin conductance, as measured by perspiration, is the first quantifiable sign of a hot flush.[18] This is followed by a change in skin temperature, indicating cutaneous dilation and subsequently a drop in core temperature an average of 0.2°C. Subjective sensations of the hot flush are usually gone when physiological changes can still be detected. Vasomotor instability occurs only in women in whom there is a fairly sudden loss of ovarian estrogen secretion (either by surgical or natural processes) or sudden discontinuation of estrogen therapy.[19,20] Women with Turner's syndrome, who have low levels of estrogen, experience hot flushes only if they are first treated with estrogens, followed by discontinuation of estrogen therapy.[21] Circulating estrogen levels have not been found to change before or after a hot flush, though adrenal steroids (cortisol, androstenedione, and dehydroepiandrosterone) are noted to be significantly increased[20] (Fig. 74-4). LH release does appear to increase, coincident with the onset of the hot flush (Fig. 74-5), although studies of FSH release during the flush are contradictory.[11,12] The exact mechanisms for the generation of a hot flush are unknown although it does appear to involve altered central thermoregulatory function.

Although estrogen treatment of hot flushes usually is effective and relief is prompt, not all women are relieved of these symptoms by estrogen. Furthermore, in

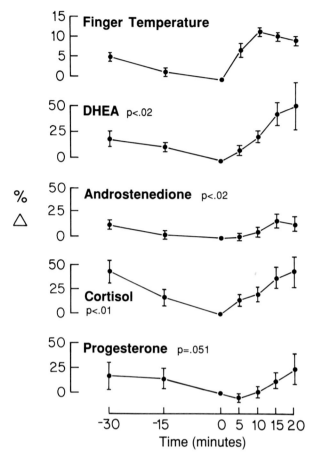

FIGURE 74-4
Increased levels of serum DHEA, androstenedione, and cortisol at the time of the hot flush as measured by a change in finger temperature in menopausal women. *(Reproduced with permission from Meldrum DR et al: J Clin Endo Metab 50:685, 1980. In Mishell DR: Menopause—Physiology and Pharmacology, Chicago, Year Book Medical Publishers, 1987, p 63.)*

all investigations in which the effectiveness of estrogen to relieve vasomotor symptoms was evaluated, a high degree (25 percent) of relief of symptoms also was found with placebo therapy. Thus, some of these symptoms may not be due singularly to estrogen deficiency. Diminished estrogen production also leads to atrophy of the vagina and symptoms of atrophic vaginitis. Atrophic vaginitis is characterized by itching, discomfort, burning, dyspareunia, and sometimes vaginal bleeding as the epithelium thins. Estrogen deficiency also can lead to loss of uterine support with subsequent uterine descensus. Other symptoms of estrogen deficiency include urinary urgency and stress incontinence, dysuria, and urinary frequency. Estrogen treatment is effective in relieving the symptoms of atrophic vaginitis and other symptoms of estrogen deficiency of the lower urinary tract. There is no direct evidence in support of the notion that estrogen maintains or restores the youthful appearance of skin, subcutaneous tissue, or hair in postmenopausal women. It has been found that skin collagen

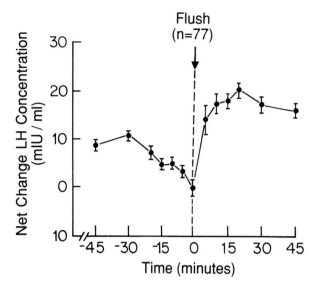

FIGURE 74-5
Increase in mean serum LH concentration (±SEM) coinciding with the onset of a hot flush. *(Reproduced with permission from Yen SSC, Jaffee RB, in Reproductive Endocrinology: Physiology, Pathophysiology and Clinical Management, Philadelphia, W.B. Saunders, 1986, p 411.)*

content after the menopause decreases in an exponential fashion and correlates significantly with the number of years after the menopause.[22] Estrogen therapy, however, has been reported to increase skin collagen in postmenopausal women.[23]

OTHER SYMPTOMS

After the menopause, symptoms such as depression, anxiety, fatigue, and irritability appear to increase. Campbell and Whitehead found that estrogen treatment of women with severe hot flushes was associated with a significant reduction in the symptoms of anxiety, irritability, and insomnia and with improvement in memory when compared to control subjects. These authors suggest that reduction of hot flushes during sleep results in an improvement in sleep quality and thus prevents symptoms of chronic sleep disturbances.[24] Other investigators have observed a decrease in sleep latency and an increase in rapid-eye-movement sleep with estrogen therapy.[25]

ESTROGEN THERAPY AND OSTEOPOROSIS

Osteoporosis (see Chap. 77) is defined as the loss of structural support in trabecular bone, predominantly of the axial skeleton. Bone loss after the menopause appears to proceed at a rate of 1 to 2 percent per year.[26] By the age of 80, there is an estimated loss of 50 percent of bone mass in white women. Thus, if left untreated, osteoporosis is one of the most devastating diseases of aged women. It has been estimated that 25 percent of all women over the age of 60 have radiological evidence of vertebral crush fractures.[27] Such fractures in the elderly (and the complications thereof) are a major cause of death as well as disability and morbidity (Fig. 74-6).

Estrogen deficiency is believed to be a major cause for bone loss in women. Estrogen treatment attenuates height loss, improves calcium balance and bone density, and reduces the number of vertebral, wrist, and hip fractures in young castrate and postmenopausal women.[28,29] Many earlier clinical studies focused on measurements of the peripheral skeleton and not the axial skeleton. These techniques included radiogrammetry (measuring cortical thickness and its area in the metacarpals) and

single photon absorptiometry (measuring the amount of cortical bone in the distal radius).[30,31] Unfortunately, these did not address the axial skeleton where the effects of osteoporosis on trabecular bone are most severe. Dual-photon absorptiometry and computerized tomography (CT) techniques are used most commonly to evaluate vertebral bone mass.[32,33]

The major risk factors known to increase the risk of osteoporosis include white or Asian heritage; low body weight; hypoestrogenism; early menopause; positive family history for osteoporosis; diet low in calcium and vitamin D; diet high in caffeine, phosphate, alcohol, and protein; cigarette smoking; and a sedentary lifestyle (Table 74-3).[34] Maximum skeletal mass is achieved in the first three decades of life, but white women attain the least; black men attain the greatest amount; and white men and black women attain intermediate amounts. Persons who are immobilized for long times lose bone mass, and bone fragility develops, i.e., increased bone resorption with normal rates of bone formation.[35] Postmenopausal women require a daily intake of 1500 mg elemental calcium to keep up with bone losses. This requirement is not met in the average U.S. diet. It has been demonstrated that reduced amounts of endogenous estrogen levels are correlated with increased urinary calcium excretion[36] (Fig. 74-7). Estrogen is believed to increase bone turnover via an indirect mechanism because estrogen receptors have not definitively been found in bone,[37,38] (though recent studies have been highly suggestive of the presence of such receptors). Estrogen deficiency may lead to an increased sensitivity to PTH in bone, whereas the sensitivity in other organs such as the kidney and intestine remains the same. The end result would be increased bone resorption and mobilization of calcium without increased urinary or intestinal conservation of calcium. A second theory involves the decreased secretion of calcitonin, which is secreted by the thyroid and opposes PTH action. Lobo and colleagues found no difference in calcitonin levels in pre- and postmenopausal women before or after oral estrogen therapy.[39]

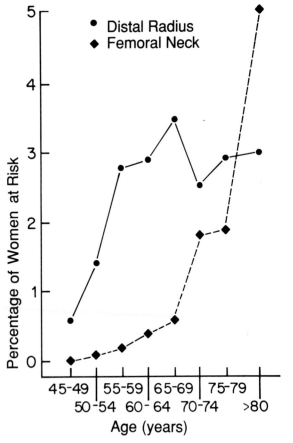

FIGURE 74-6
Relationship of the incidence of fractures of the distal radius and femoral neck with the age of women. *(Reproduced with permission from Aitken JM: Bone metabolism in postmenopausal women. In Beard RJ (ed): The Menopause: A Guide to Current Research and Practice, Lancaster, England, MTP Press, 1976, p 99.)*

TABLE 74-3
Major Risk Factors for Osteoporosis

Hypoestrogenism
Low body weight
White or oriental race
Early menopause
Positive family history for osteoporosis
Diet low in calcium and vitamin D
Diet high in caffeine, phosphate, and protein
Alcoholism
Cigarette smoking
Sedentary lifestyle

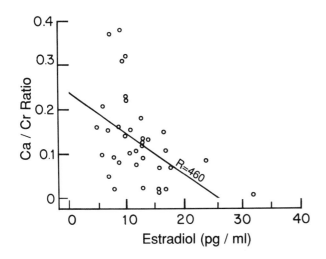

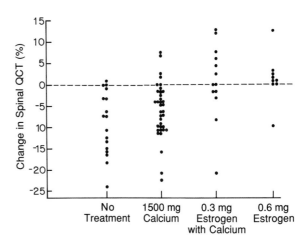

FIGURE 74-8
Change in spinal quantitative computed axial tomography after 1 year in untreated menopausal women compared to menopausal women treated with 1500 mg calcium, 0.3 mg conjugated estrogen plus calcium, or 0.6 mg conjugated estrogen daily. *(Reproduced with permission from Genast HK et al: Quantitative computed tomography for spinal mineral assessment in osteoporosis.* **Proceedings of the Copenhagen International Symposium on Osteoporosis, 1984, p 69.)***

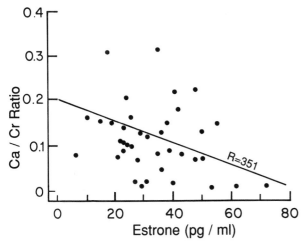

FIGURE 74-7
Correlation of Ca:Cr ratio with levels of circulating estradiol (*p* < .005) and estrone (*p* < .05). *(Reproduced with permission from Frumar AM et al: Relationship of fasting urinary calcium to circulating estrogen and body weight in postmenopausal women.* **J Clin Endo Metab 50:70, 1980.)***

The findings of recent studies are indicative that early and long-term estrogen replacement in women undergoing early menopause (due to surgical or natural causes) is beneficial. Bone loss, as measured by bone biopsy and indirect techniques, was prevented by a delay in bone resorption, and an actual decrease in the rate of development of fractures was reported in women who ingested estrogens.[40–42] In addition, in a recent study, women receiving 1500 mg calcium each day in combination with 0.3 mg of conjugated estrogen were found to have minimal evidence of bone loss or decreased bone mass (0.6 percent)—by lumbar trabecular bone CT scan—in comparison with subjects who were untreated or treated with calcium alone and who lost 8.5 and 6.2 percent, respectively[43] (Fig. 74-8). Estrogen treatment also appears to produce a short-term positive effect on calcium balance. Thus, it appears that if estro-

gen replacement is to be of optimum benefit, replacement should be initiated before serious loss of bone density has occurred.

EFFECTS OF ESTROGEN ON OTHER POSTMENOPAUSAL CONDITIONS

CARDIOVASCULAR EFFECTS

Although oral contraceptive use is known to increase blood pressure in some women (5 percent), this has not been observed with estrogen replacement therapy.[44,45] One study by Wren and Routledge of women using piperazine estrone sulfate showed a decrease in both systolic and diastolic blood pressure in women with or without antihypertensive therapy[46] (Table 74-4). In contrast to combination oral contraceptive use, there does not appear to be an increased incidence of thromboembolism or stroke in women on estrogen replacement therapy as compared with controls.

Estrogen replacement therapy is known to change the lipid profiles of older women (Table 74-5). Serum cholesterol was decreased 4 percent in women on estrogen and median serum triglycerides increased 26 percent. Median high-density lipoproteins (HDL) cholesterol levels rose 10 percent and median low-density lipoprotein (LDL) cholesterol was reduced 11 percent.[47] Both increased levels of LDL and decreased levels of HDL correlate positively with risk for coronary heart disease, the opposite of what is seen in estrogen users.

TABLE 74-4
Piperazine Estrone Sulfate: On and Not on Antihypertensives

	Mean	SD	t	P	N
On antihypertensives (N = 34)					
Systolic visit 1	151.26	22.65	—	—	34
Systolic visit 2	143.03	16.45	—	—	34
Mean change	−8.23	17.21	2.79	<0.01	
Diastolic visit 1	91.82	9.69	—		34
Diastolic visit 2	86.53	10.72	—		34
Mean change	−5.29	9.29	3.32	<0.01	34
Not on antihypertensives (N = 150)					
Systolic visit 1	134.77	16.35	—	—	150
Systolic visit 2	130.41	15.42	—	—	150
Mean change	−4.36	15.35	3.48	<0.001	150
Diastolic visit 1	84.37	9.83	—	—	150
Diastolic visit 2	81.08	9.32	—	—	150
Mean change	−3.29	9.49	4.25	<0.001	150

SOURCE: Reproduced with permission from Wren BC, Routledge AD. From Droegemueller W et al: *Comprehensive Gynecology*, St. Louis, C.V. Mosby Company, 1987, p 1098.

Other studies have shown even greater decreases in LDL cholesterol and greater increases in HDL.

The effect of postmenopausal estrogen therapy on coronary heart disease (CHD) is controversial. The incidence rate of CHD in women on noncontraceptive estrogen therapy, however, appears to be less than that of nonestrogen-treated controls. In a few studies, however, a beneficial effect was not demonstrated (Table 74-6).[48]

GALLBLADDER DISEASE

The investigators of the Boston Collaborative Drug Surveillance Study reported a significant increase in the development of gallbladder disease in postmenopausal women taking conjugated estrogens,[49] presumably because estrogen therapy causes an increase in biliary cholesterol concentration.

TABLE 74-5
Concentrations of Lipids and Lipoproteins in Users and Nonusers of Estrogen

	Mean ± SD (Median)	
Lipid Profile	**Nonuser**	**Equine Estrogen**
Cholesterol	230 ± 44.3 (226)	219 ± 33.9 (218)*
Triglyceride	174 ± 66.9 (100)	141 ± 71.5 (126)*
HDL cholesterol	61 ± 15.6 (61)	69 ± 17.7 (67)*
LDL cholesterol	154 ± 43.8 (147)	133 ± 33.9 (131)*
VLDL cholesterol	16 ± 13.8 (13)	18 ± 12.5 (16)

*$p < 0.05$.
SOURCE: Reproduced with permission from Wahl P et al: Effect of estrogen/progestin potency on lipid/lipoprotein cholesterol. *N Engl J Med* 308:802, 1983. From Droegemueller W et al: *Comprehensive Gynecology*, St. Louis, C.V. Mosby Company, 1987, p 1100.

BREAST DISEASE

The breast is a target organ of estrogen, and some breast tumors are found to be estrogen-responsive. For these and other reasons, there has been great concern that estrogen treatment of postmenopausal women might contribute to the development of benign and malignant breast disease. In studies of the relationship between breast cancer and estrogen use, there are reports both for and against a relationship between dose and duration of estrogen therapy and the development of breast cancer.[50-56] Based on currently available data, it appears that long-term use of estrogen in small doses does not substantially increase the risk of breast cancer. Even though such therapy does not increase the incidence or severity of breast cancer, estrogen therapy should not be instituted if preexisting breast disease exists and should be discontinued if benign or malignant breast disease develops.

TABLE 74-6
Risk of Coronary Heart Disease in Prospective Studies of Hormone Replacement Therapy

Investigator	N	Endpoint	Relative Risk
Burch et al., 1974	737	CHD	0.4
Hammond et al., 1974	610	CHD	0.3
Petitti et al., 1979	1,675	MI	1.2
Petitti et al., 1986	1,675	MI	0.5*
Wilson et al., 1985	1,234	CHD	1.9
Stampfer et al., 1985	32,317	CHD	0.5
Bush et al., 1987	2,270	Fatal CHD	0.37

*Study addressed total mortality.

ENDOMETRIAL CANCER

Evidence exists that estrogen treatment and increased amounts of endogenously produced estrogen in postmenopausal women are associated with an increased incidence of endometrial adenocarcinoma.[57,58] It is now known that those postmenopausal women with the features commonly associated with endometrial cancer, namely, aging and obesity, are those women who produce the most estrogen in extraglandular sites. Increased endogenous estrogen formation occurs in these women because the extent of conversion of plasma androstenedione to estrone in extraglandular sites increases with aging, obesity, and liver disease.[10,30]

Despite such physiological evidence, it was not until 1975 that an increased frequency of endometrial carcinoma in association with estrogen treatment of postmenopausal women was established in the United States.[57,58] Moreover, the areas of the United States with higher incidence of endometrial cancer also were those geographical areas in which the sales of conjugated estrogen were greatest.[59] Between the years 1970 and 1975, the incidence of endometrial carcinoma rose from 70 to 124 cases per 100,000 women each year, but this dropped to 102 per 100,000 women by 1977. The rise and fall of reported cases of endometrial cancer were closely parallel to the sales of conjugated estrogen in the United States.[60]

From the findings of numerous studies, the relative risk of developing endometrial cancer in postmenopausal estrogen users is between 6- and 8-fold, and the risk increases both with duration of treatment and as a function of the dose of estrogen. But despite the large body of evidence linking the association of endometrial carcinoma and estrogen use, two types of doubt concerning the clinical significance of the association have been raised. First, in spite of an increased incidence of endometrial carcinoma in the United States, there is no evidence of increased mortality from endometrial cancer.[61] This probably reflects the fact that the increased incidence of endometrial cancer in estrogen users involves low-grade malignancy and possibly also the inherent difficulty in separating low-grade endometrial adenocarcinoma from various forms of endometrial hyperplasia. Secondly, other epidemiologists have argued that the increased risk associated with estrogen usage has been exaggerated because of problems inherent in obtaining adequate controls for retrospective analysis.[62] In spite of these arguments, it is likely that a small but significant risk of development of endometrial adenocarcinoma among postmenopausal women on unopposed estrogen replacement (i.e., without cyclic progestational therapy) occurs, but the risk usually is for low-grade malignancy, and the effect on life expectancy in most women is minimal.

OTHER GENITAL NEOPLASIAS

There appears to be no increased risk of developing cancer of the ovary, cervix, fallopian tubes, vagina, or vulva in women taking long-term postmenopausal estrogen replacement.

THERAPEUTIC RECOMMENDATIONS

The use of various estrogens for menopausal symptoms does not take into account the importance of cyclic 17β-estradiol secretion or the role of progesterone in modifying the effects of estrogen on target tissues. Thus, estrogen replacement therapy does not mimic the natural or physiological hormone production that occurs during reproductive life which is, in fact, treatment rather than replacement therapy. But, this surely is of no clinical relevance because clearly the cyclic changes in hormone formation in young women are directed singularly to optimizing the likelihood of successful pregnancy. Furthermore, there is no one agreed-upon clinical or laboratory value to assess adequately the dose of estrogen to be given other than the amelioration of hot flushes. In most studies where attempts were made to investigate optimum dosage, it was common that various therapeutic agents with diverse dosages and treatment periods were used. Therefore, it has been difficult to interpret the clinical and laboratory effects of the various estrogens used. Furthermore, even in those studies in which various doses of conjugated estrogens were found to suppress gonadotropin levels (but not to normal), varying effects on vaginal cytology, urinary calcium excretion, and stimulation of liver protein synthesis [renin substrate and sex hormone–binding globulin (SHBG)] were observed.[63]

Estrogens act on target tissues after the free hormone enters the cell by simple diffusion and thence becomes bound to a specific receptor in the nucleus.[64] Thereafter, the estrogen-receptor complex reacts with the nuclear chromatin and directs messenger RNA synthesis and eventually protein synthesis. The metabolic fate of the various estrogens is variable: e.g., 17β-estradiol in micronized form is converted largely to estrone before reaching the target tissues. But, the primary hormone that ultimately is associated with the estrogen receptor is a potent hormone, e.g., 17β-estradiol, ethinyl estradiol.

The estrogen preparations available for oral use are synthetic estrogens with a 17α-ethinyl group (ethinyl estradiol, mestranol, quinestrol), nonsteroidal estrogens (diethylstilbestrol), and natural estrogens, e.g., conjugated estrogens prepared from pregnant mares' urine, and micronized 17β-estradiol.

A variety of other medications are somewhat effective in relieving vasomotor symptoms but do not correct urogenital tract atrophy or osteoporosis. Among these agents are progestins (medroxyprogesterone acetate, 20 mg/day orally or 150 mg IM monthly, and megestrol 40 mg daily); somewhat less effective results have been obtained with clonidine, propranolol, naloxone, and sedatives in some women in whom estrogens are contraindicated.

Currently, estrogen therapy is recommended in all estrogen-deficient women in whom there is no contraindication. The most commonly used treatment regimen in the United States is 0.625 mg conjugated equine estrogen or estrone sulfate for the first 25 days of each month. Another popular route of administration is transdermal delivery of estradiol (E_2). A 4-cm patch (containing 0.05 mg) can produce constant levels of E_2 of approximately 72 pg/ml and levels of E_1 of 37 pg/ml.[65] With this route of administration, hepatic effects are limited, but the patch must be replaced every 3 or 4 days. Subcutaneous implants of hormone, while effective, do not provide for easy discontinuance of treatment if complications develop. Various estrogen-containing vaginal creams offer an effective alternative to oral replacement therapy.

Because unopposed estrogen use in postmenopausal women has clearly been associated with an increased incidence of endometrial hyperplasia and endometrial cancer, many investigators and physicians have advocated that women in whom the uterus is present also receive 10 to 13 days of progestogen to oppose the effect of estrogen on the uterus. The addition of progestogens to both continuous and cyclic estrogen treatment regimens is associated with a decreased incidence of endometrial hyperplasia and endometrial cancer.[66–69] Of at least theoretical concern, progestogen treatment also may lead to increased LDL and decreased HDL, risk indices for coronary heart disease.[70] However, this effect appears to be dependent upon the potency, dose, and length of therapy of the progestin. Addition of oral micronized natural progesterone at 200 mg/day for 10 days of each treatment cycle, did not appear to influence HDL cholesterol or its subfractions. Micronized progesterone may thus be an alternative to the synthetic progestins used currently. Continuous daily treatment with both an estrogen and progestogen has also been advocated by some, although the alterations in lipids need to be addressed more closely. In women without a uterus, estrogens used alone are sufficient and progestogens are not recommended.

CONCLUSION

After the menopause, the rate of estrogen production decreases, but the postmenopausal state is not one of absolute estrogen deprivation. There is a transfer from 17β-estradiol predominance to one of estrone dominance; most if not all estrone is formed in extraglandular sites. Low-dose estrogen is effective for treatment of vasomotor symptoms and urogenital atrophy. Estrogen is beneficial in preventing symptoms of osteoporosis in young castrate women and is effective in preventing fractures in older women when treatment is started early. The only established risks for estrogen treatment of the postmenopausal women are in the incidence of endometrial cancer in those women with a uterus and the development of gallbladder disease. All women who are treated with estrogen must be evaluated carefully at semiannual visits for blood pressure elevation, breast masses, and the development of endometrial hyperplasia. Most gynecologists recommend endometrial biopsy prior to treatment and yearly thereafter for women on replacement estrogen treatment alone, and less frequently when combined with a progestogen.

In the future, considerable research effort must be directed to define the pathophysiology of vasomotor symptoms, alternatives to steroid hormone replacement for the treatment of such symptoms, the mechanism of development and prevention of osteoporosis, the lipid changes associated with various treatment modalities, and the role of estrogens in the pathogenesis of endometrial carcinoma. As the number of women who live beyond the menopause increases, evaluation and treatment of menopausal disorders will continue to be of monumental importance in the health care of women.

REFERENCES

1. Bureau of the Census: *A Statistical Portrait of Women in the U.S.*, Publication 58, Current Population Report, Special Studies Series. Washington, Dept. of Commerce, p 23, 1976.
2. Utian WH: *Menopause in Modern Perspective*. New York, Appleton-Century-Crofts, 1980.
3. Linquist O, Bengtsson C: Menopausal age in relation to smoking. *Acta Med Scand* 205:73, 1979.
4. Baker TG: A quantitative and cytological study of sperm cells in human ovaries. *Proc R Soc (Biol)* 158:417, 1963.
5. Sherman BM, Korenman SG: Hormonal characteristics of the human menstrual cycle throughout reproductive life. *J Clin Invest* 55:699, 1975.
6. Longcope C: Metabolic clearance and blood production rates of estrogens in postmenopausal women. *Am J Obstet Gynecol* 111:778, 1971.
7. Scaglin HM et al: Pituitary LH and FSH secretion and responsiveness in women of old age. *Acta Endocrinol (Kbh)* 81:673, 1976.
8. Chakravarti S et al: Hormonal profiles after the menopause. *Br Med J* 2:784, 1976.
9. Judd HL: Hormonal dynamics associated with the menopause. *Clin Obstet Gynecol* 19:775, 1976.
10. Siiteri PK, MacDonald PC: Role of extraglandular estrogen in human endocrinology, in Greep RO, Astwood E

(eds): *Handbook of Physiology: Endocrinology*. Washington, American Physiological Society, vol 2, pt 1, 1973, p 615.

11. Tataryn IV et al: LH, FSH and skin temperature during the menopausal hot flash. *J Clin Endocrinol Metab* 49:152, 1979.

12. Casper RF et al: Menopausal flushes: A neuroendocrine link with pulsatile luteinizing hormone secretion. *Science* 205:823, 1979.

13. Mulley G et al: Hot flushes after hypophysectomy. *Br Med J* 2:1062, 1977.

14. Axelrod J: Relationship between catecholamines and other hormones. *Recent Prog Horm Res* 31:1, 1975.

15. Brody MJ, Kadowitz PJ: Prostaglandins as modulators of the autonomic nervous system. *Fed Proc* 33:48, 1974.

16. Jaszmann LJB et al: The menopausal symptoms. *Med Gynecol Sociol* 4:268, 1969.

17. Hannan JH: In Bailliere, Tindall and Cox (eds): *The Flushings of the Menopause*. London, 1927, p 1.

18. Tataryn I et al: Postmenopausal hot flushes: A disorder of thermoregulation. *Maturitas* 2:101, 1980.

19. Ausel S et al: Vasomotor symptoms, serum estrogens and gonadotropin levels in surgical menopause. *Am J Obstet Gynecol* 126:165, 1976.

20. Meldrum D et al: Gonadotropins, estrogens, and adrenal steroids during the menopausal hot flush. *J Clin Endocrinol Metab* 50:685, 1980.

21. Yen SSC: The biology of menopause. *J Reprod Med* 18:287, 1977.

22. Brincat M et al: The long term effects of the menopause and of administration of sex hormones on skin collagen and skin thickness. *Br J Obstet Gynaecol* 92:256, 1985.

23. Brincat M et al: Skin collagen changes in postmenopausal women receiving different regimes of estrogen therapy. *Obstet Gynecol* 70:123, 1987.

24. Campbell S, Whitehead M: Oestrogen therapy and the menopause syndrome. *Clin Obstet Gynecol* 4:31, 1977.

25. Schiff I et al: Effects of estrogens on sleep and psychological state of hypogonadal women. *JAMA* 242:2405, 1979.

26. Gordon G et al: Prevention of age related bone loss. *Proc Arnold O. Beckman Conference Clin Chem* 3:1, 1980.

27. Heanly RP: Estrogens and postmenopausal osteoporosis. *Clin Obstet Gynecol* 19:791, 1976.

28. Gordon GS: Postmenopausal osteoporosis: Cause, prevention and treatment. *Clin Obstet Gynecol* 4:169, 1977.

29. Horsman A et al: Prospective trial of oestrogen and calcium on postmenopausal women. *Br Med J* 2:789, 1977.

30. Garn SM: The earlier gain and later loss of cortical bone, in *Nutritional Perspective*. Springfield, Ill, Charles C Thomas, 1970, p 146.

31. Cameron JR et al: Measurement of bone mineral in vivo: An improved method. *Science* 142:230, 1963.

32. Madsen M et al: Vertebral and total body mineral content by dual absorptiometry, in Pors-Nielsen S, Hjorting-Hansen E (eds): *Calcified Tissues*. 1975. Copenhagen, FAPL Publishing, 1976, p 361.

33. Cann CE et al: Spinal mineral loss in oophorectomized women: Determination of quantitative computed tomography. *JAMA* 244:2056, 1980.

34. Shoemaker ES et al: Estrogen treatment of postmenopausal women: Benefits and risks. *JAMA* 238:1524, 1977.

35. Trotter M et al: Densities of bones of white and negro skeletons. *J Bone Joint Surg* 42A:50, 1960.

36. Frumar AM et al: Relationship of fasting urinary calcium to circulating estrogen and body weight in postmenopausal women. *J Clin Endocrinol Metab* 50:70, 1980.

37. Nutik G, Cruess RL: Estrogen receptors in bone. An evaluation of the uptake of estrogen into bone cells. *Proc Exp Biol Med* 146:265, 1974.

38. Chen TL, Feldman D: Distinction between alpha-fetoprotein and intra-cellular estrogen receptors: Evidence against the presence of estradiol receptors in rat bone. *Endocrinology* 102:236, 1978.

39. Lobo RA et al: Estrogen and progestin effects on urinary calcium and calcitrophic hormones in surgically-induced postmenopausal women. *Horm Metab Res* 17:369, 1985.

40. Hutchinson TA et al: Post-menopausal oestrogens protect against fractures of hip and distal radius. A case-control study. *Lancet* 2(8245):705, 1979.

41. Weiss NS et al: Decreased risk of fractures of the hip and lower forearm with postmenopausal use of oestrogen. *N Engl J Med* 303:1195, 1980.

42. Johnson RE et al: The risk of hip fracture in postmenopausal females with and without estrogen drug exposure. *Am J Public Health* 71:138, 1981.

43. Ettinger B et al: Menopausal bone loss: Effects of conjugated oestrogen and/or high calcium diet. *Maturitas* 6(2):108 (39), 1984.

44. Barrett-Conner E et al: Heart disease risk factors and hormone use in postmenopausal women. *JAMA* 241:2167, 1979.

45. Pfeffer RI et al: Estrogen use and blood pressure in later life. *Am J Epidemiol* 110:469, 1979.

46. Wren BG, Routledge AD: The effect of type and dose of oestrogen on the blood pressure of post-menopausal women. *Maturitas* 5:135, 1983.

47. Wallentin L, Larsson-Cohn U: Metabolic and hormonal effects of postmenopausal oestrogen replacement treatment. II. Plasma lipids. *Acta Endocrinol [Copenh]* 86:597, 1977.

48. Ross RK et al: Estrogen use and cardiovascular disease, in Mishell DR (ed): *Menopause: Physiology and Pharmacology*. Chicago, Year Book Medical Publishers, 1987, p 217.

49. Boston Collaborative Drug Surveillance Program: Surgically confirmed gallbladder disease, venous thromboembolism, and breast tumors in relation to postmenopausal estrogen therapy. *N Engl J Med* 290:15, 1974.

50. Ross RK et al: A case-control study of menopausal estrogen therapy and breast cancer. *JAMA* 243:1635, 1980.

51. Jick H et al: Replacement estrogens and breast cancer. *Am J Epidemiol* 112:586, 1980.

52. Brinton LA et al: Menopausal estrogen use and breast cancer. *Cancer* 47:2577, 1981.

53. Hoover R et al: Conjugated estrogens and breast cancer risk. *J Natl Cancer Inst* 67:815, 1981.

54. Hiatt RA et al: Exogenous estrogen and breast cancer after oophorectomy. *Cancer* 54:139, 1984.

55. Kaufman DW et al: Noncontraceptive estrogen use and the risk of breast cancer. *JAMA* 252:63, 1984.

56. Kelsey JL et al: Exogenous estrogens and other factors in the epidemiology of breast cancer. *J Natl Cancer Inst* 67:327, 1981.

57. Smith DC et al: Association of exogenous estrogen and endometrial carcinoma. *N Engl J Med* 293:1167, 1975.

58. Ziel HK, Finkle WD: Increased risk of endometrial carcinoma among users of conjugated estrogens. *N Engl J Med* 293:1167, 1975.

59. Weiss NS et al: Endometrial cancer in relation to patterns of menopausal estrogen use. *JAMA* 242:261, 1979.
60. Walker AM, Jick DH: Declining rates of endometrial cancer. *Obstet Gynecol* 56:733, 1980.
61. Disaia PJ, Creasman WT: Adenocarcinoma of the uterus, in *Clinical Gynecologic Oncology*. St. Louis, Mosby, 1981, p 128.
62. Horwitz RI, Feinstein AR: Alternative analytic methods for case-control studies of estrogens and endometrial carcinoma. *N Engl J Med* 229:1089, 1978.
63. Geola FL et al: Biologic effects of various doses of conjugated estrogens in postmenopausal women. *J Clin Endocrinol Metab* 51:620, 1980.
64. Welshons WV et al: Nuclear localization of unoccupied receptors for glucocorticoids, estrogens, and progesterone in GH_3 cells. *Endocrinology* 117:2140, 1985.
65. Laufer LR et al: Estrogen replacement therapy by transdermal estradiol administratives. *Am J Obstet Gynecol* 146:533, 1983.
66. Hammond CB et al: Effects of long-term estrogen replacement therapy. II. Neoplasia. *Am J Obstet Gynecol* 133:531, 1979.
67. Gambrell RD: The prevention of endometrial carcinoma in postmenopausal women with progestins. *Maturitas* 1:107, 1978.
68. Thom MH et al: Prevention and treatment of endometrial disease in climacteric women receiving oestrogen therapy. *Lancet* 2:455, 1979.
69. Paterson MEL et al: Endometrial disease after treatment with oestrogens and progestogens in the climacteric. *Br Med J* 1:822, 1980.
70. Burkman RT: Lipid and lipoprotein changes in relation to oral contraception and hormonal replacement therapy. *Fertil Steril 49* (suppl) (5):39S, 1988.

Chapter 75

BREAST DISEASES OF ELDERLY WOMEN

Roger E. Moe

In 1984, the number of deaths from cancer in United States women 55 years old and older exceeded the number from each of the other main causes of death except heart disease. Breast cancer led to more deaths than any other cancer in adult women up to the age of 74.[1] Women aged 65 years or more incur about one-third of all breast cancers, judging from a national survey from 742 hospitals with a total of 24,136 cases.[2] When all stages of breast cancer in that survey are combined, 43 percent of patients aged 65 to 74 were alive and free of cancer after 5 years, as were 32 percent of patients aged 75 or more. If there are 41,000 deaths among 130,000 expected new cases of breast cancer in our population currently, one can speculate that about 15,000 of these deaths will be in geriatric patients.

Fortunately, available methods of screening patients for breast cancer are most effective in geriatric patients, potentially reducing the mortality by one-third with proper treatment.

INCIDENCE OF BREAST CANCER

As is well known, the incidence of breast cancer in United States women of different ages rises continuously with increasing age. What is not so well known is that this persistently rising incidence does not seem to be an inevitable correlate of aging. Haagensen shows graphs of age-specific incidence of breast cancer in different countries, and the incidence of breast cancer actually falls after menopause in women in Japan, Poland, and Greece.[3]

Also not so well known is a practical idea of what the incidence figures actually mean. It is easy to glance at a steeply increasing age-incidence curve for breast cancer and come away with an astoundingly exaggerated idea of

what the figures are for elderly patients. The figures are expressed as annual rates per 100,000 women, large numbers which lose meaning because we clinicians do not think in terms of 100,000 women. When we convert incidence figures to the number of cases per 1000 women, we get a better perspective (Table 75-1). Specifically, there are 4 cases per 1000 women in the United States at the high end of an incidence curve, for age 85. The rest of the figures are lower. By comparison, the corresponding figure for women 50 years old is about 2 cases per 1000 women; for women 40 years old, about 1 case per 1000 women.

When one discusses factors of increasing risk for breast cancer, it is important to have some of these baseline figures in mind for proper perspective. Recall that 90 percent of all women will not get breast cancer in their lifetimes.

These statements in no way minimize the challenge to the clinician to ferret out breast cancer as early as possible. Patients who come to a clinic for health care will have a higher discovery rate for breast cancer than incidence figures suggest. Patients who come to a surgeon will have a much higher rate. There is no reason for complacency.

BACKGROUND PHYSIOLOGY

During reproductive years, interior breast tissue consists of fibrous connective tissue and milk gland tissue (fibroglandular tissue). The fibrous tissue provides support for a branching network of tiny thread-sized hollow epithelial tubes—milk glands. Each of these hollow tubes or ducts ends in a small group of blind projections (acini), like fingers on a microscopic-size inflated rubber glove. Each group of acini and connective tissue makes

TABLE 75-1
Age-Specific Incidence Rates of Female Breast Cancer in the 13-County Area of Western Washington Covered by the Cancer Surveillance System

Age, yr	Rate per 100,000 Women	Rate per 1000 Women
50–64	253.8	2–3
65+	314.3	3–4

SOURCE: Thomas DB: Personal communication. University of Washington and the Fred Hutchinson Cancer Research Center, Seattle, 1982.

up a lobule, analogous to a grape on a stem. Wellings et al. look at the lobule and its terminal duct as a unit, the principal histological site where cancer, cysts, and certain other pathology arise.[4]

Unfortunately, epithelial tissue (which is the source of breast cancer) cannot be felt separately by the clinician; a large part of what is felt is the fibrous tissue. Nor is the epithelial tissue discretely identifiable on mammograms, except perhaps right under the nipple in some patients; even there it is difficult to tell what is actually fibrous tissue as distinguished from intraductal epithelial tissue. So the surrounding fibrous tissue (which is not the source of breast cancer) obscures ductal pathology during palpation and in radiographs.

After menopause, glandular tissue atrophies; lobules disappear, and ducts become disrupted and sparse.[5] Gradually the fibroglandular tissue becomes replaced by fat (which is not a source of breast cancer). Islands of fat emerge here and there throughout the fibroglandular tissue (adipose metaplasia), and this may progress until a large part of or nearly all of the internal tissue is fat. If the patient receives estrogens, fibroglandular tissue is

maintained to a considerable degree, although the glandular architecture is not fully normal.[6]

Jensen points out that sometimes a lobule fails to regress and continues to exist in seemingly autonomous fashion.[7] Such a lobule becomes hyperplastic, or, in some instances, atypical, potentially evolving into a cancer. Jensen also points out another finding which is intriguing—that some lobules reappear in breasts of patients in their seventies and eighties. Further comments on this will be made later.

Milk gland epithelial changes already described are reflections of target tissue responses to endocrine changes at menopause. The principal changes which affect breast tissue are cessation of cyclic stimulation by estrogen and progesterone from ovaries. But that is not to say estrogenic stimulation of breast tissue comes to a halt (Figs. 75-1 and 75-2). Persistent estrogenic stimulation (without progesterone) results from extraglandular enzymatic conversion of circulating androgens into estrogens.[8] Such estrogen precursors are, first, androstenedione from the adrenal gland and to a small extent from the postmenopausal ovary, forming estrone in peripheral tissues such as fat, and, second, testosterone from the postmenopausal ovary, converting partly to estradiol, also in peripheral tissues. Plasma estrone concentration in postmenopausal women exceeds plasma estradiol concentration, a ratio which is the reverse of that in premenopausal women.

From the standpoint of potential breast effects, it is worth noting that the rate of conversion of androstenedione into estrone increases with advancing age. One might suspect that this rate would decrease, but the percent conversion may increase nearly four times by age 80 from age 60.[9] According to Nisker and Siiteri, elevated androstenedione conversion may produce estrone

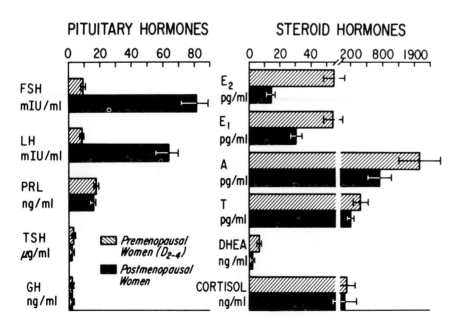

FIGURE 75-1
Circulating levels of hormones in premenopausal and postmenopausal women. E1, estrone; E2, estradiol; A, androstenedione; T, testosterone. (*From Yen SSC, J Reprod Med 18:290, 1977. Journal of Reproductive Medicine, Inc., with permission.*)

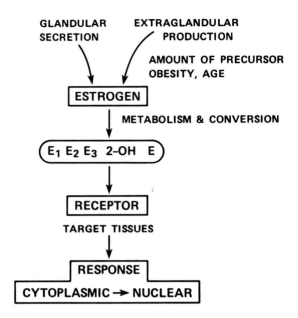

GLANDULAR SECRETION   EXTRAGLANDULAR PRODUCTION

AMOUNT OF PRECURSOR
OBESITY, AGE

ESTROGEN

METABOLISM & CONVERSION

E_1 E_2 E_3 2-OH E

RECEPTOR

TARGET TISSUES

RESPONSE
CYTOPLASMIC → NUCLEAR

1) DELIVERY RATE
2) MODULATING HORMONES
3) SYNERGISTIC FACTORS

FIGURE 75-2
Extraglandular estrogen production in postmenopausal women, with modulating factors. E1, estrone; E2, estradiol; E3, estriol; OH E2, hydroxy estrone. *(From Yen SSC, J Reprod Med 18:291, 1977. Journal of Reproductive Medicine, Inc., with permission.)*

in excess of 100 μg/day, increasing blood levels of both estrone and estradiol with obvious biological effects. Vaginal bleeding can result even with no ovarian function.[10] What is more, the production of estrone from androstenedione is increased by obesity, a frequent condition in geriatric patients.[11,12] Obesity is also associated with decreased blood levels of sex hormone–binding globulin, yielding a higher level of free-acting estrogen because of decreased binding.[10] Moreover, recent work by Jones et al. has demonstrated increased levels of unbound estradiol and lower levels of sex hormone–binding globulin in breast cancer patients as compared to matched controls.[13]

Further relevant information is in a report from Chakravarti et al. about hormone levels in 60 normal postmenopausal women of various ages.[14] Blood estradiol concentrations were found to increase at 20 and 30 years following menopause. Six of their elderly patients had blood levels as high as the lower end of normal for women in reproductive years. Therefore, putting together various kinds of information cited above, some older geriatric patients surprisingly have more estrogenic activity in breast tissue than women two or three decades younger. By the same token, some histological information corresponds with that viewpoint. Kramer and Rush studied mammary duct tissue obtained at au-

topsies of women aged 70 years and older without breast cancer.[15] Intense intraductal epithelial proliferation existed in some patients; this suggested estrogenic stimulation. But the ovaries had atropic cortices, not likely to be a source of estrogen, or the ovaries had been previously removed. These authors considered the adrenal cortex as the most likely source of hormones leading to epithelial proliferation.

Estrogenic effects may be a reason why Jensen sees more lobules in histological sections of breast tissue from women around 80 years old than in tissue from women around 60 years old, as mentioned earlier. Huseby and Thomas, for example, observed that estrogen therapy stimulated lobule formation as well as small-duct proliferation in a normal breast. It seems possible, then, that steady endogenous estrogen effects without cyclic variation and without opposition by progesterone are of more than minor significance.

Laboratory research with in vitro models for human breast cancer now suggests that estradiol may alter gene expression controlling many enzymes involved in cell growth. What is more, multiple growth factors are secreted by human breast cancer cells under estrogenic control.[16]

SPECTRUM OF PATHOLOGY

Although a geriatric patient may have no clinical signs of breast cancer or even benign disease, it is likely that microscopic pathology exists. The kinds of pathology found in the previously cited autopsy series performed by Kramer and Rush are notable because of frequent association of epithelial hyperplasia with breast cancer.[17] Of these women, 62 percent had areas of intraductal hyperplasia, which was severe or atypical in 37 percent of the total cases.[15] Discrete intraductal stalked papillomas were found in 15 cases, associated in two instances with carcinoma in situ. Among the 70 cases, there were four with carcinoma in situ (not invasive) and one case with occult invasive ductal carcinoma. No cases with in situ or invasive lobular carcinoma were found. The authors pointed out that "involved ducts were often few in number, widely scattered and limited to a few slides from a given breast. . . ." Often, other benign changes were seen, too, such as small cysts in 89 percent of cases.

According to such data, breast tissue in elderly women may exhibit extensive atrophy and regression of fibroglandular tissue, while sites of epithelial hyperplasia of a severe degree can exist at the same time, including atypical hyperplasia or in situ carcinoma.

Other relevant data on breast pathology in geriatric patients are gleaned from surgical procedures. Haagensen classified his cases according to dominant surgical pathology, a classification which probably includes judgment of the surgeon about findings during operation as well as judgment by the pathologist.[18] For example, duct ectasia is the most common pathology besides breast cancer encountered in geriatric patients (Table 75-2). Haagensen stated that several dilated ducts are seen beneath the nipple during a dissection. The process of dilatation extends peripherally, and this is a process of epithelial atrophy—not proliferation. This, he says, is a disease of the aging breast. In contrast, he regards fibroadenomas as a disease of youth, cystic disease as a disease of middle life, and fibrous disease and adenosis tumor as disease of premenopausal years. (Adenosis tumor is proliferation of lobular acini to an extent great enough to form a palpable mass.) The dramatic disproportion of cancer cases compared with benign cases in geriatric patients in this series is skewed, presumably because of Haagensen's renown as a breast cancer surgeon.

SCREENING FOR EARLY DETECTION OF BREAST LESIONS

Which geriatric patients are at high risk for breast cancer and need to be in a screening program, and which patients are at low risk and do not need to be in such a program? A long list of risk factors pertains to breast cancer, a topic nicely reviewed by Thomas.[19] These factors will not be discussed in detail here because none of them really changes the screening approach to geriatric patients. No geriatric patients qualify as low-risk patients who do not need screening. Age alone is sufficient basis for risk which warrants screening for breast cancer.

A more practical side of the issue of who should be

TABLE 75-2
Breast Pathology in Geriatric Patients Aged 65 and Older

Pathology	Total Patients	Geriatric Patients	Percent Geriatric Patients
Gross cysts	2017	0	0
Fibrous disease	119	0	0
Adenosis tumor	70	0	0
Fibroadenoma	619	2	0.3
Fat necrosis (traumatic)	44	8	18.2
Cystosarcoma phyllodes	84	7	8.3
Intraductal papilloma	179	21	11.7
Duct ectasia	67	14	20.9
Total	3199	52	1.6
Breast cancer	6000	1352	22.5

SOURCE: Compiled from age-related data on breast pathology, after Haagensen.[18]

screened pertains to family relatives of geriatric patients who already have breast cancer or other cancers. For background, breast cancer in a premenopausal patient signals the possibility of familial disease or increased risk of breast cancer in first-degree relatives.[20] With some patterns of genetic transmission of high risk, premenopausal relatives of breast cancer patients deserve not merely special surveillance but possibly prophylactic removal of breast tissue.[21]

In 1946, Jacobsen published a statistical-genealogical analysis of 299 probands with breast cancer and their families, including 3130 relatives; controls were 200 healthy individuals of the same ages as the probands.[22] Distribution of time of onset of breast cancer in the probands showed two peaks, between ages 45 and 49 and between ages 60 and 64. A similar picture occurred in 1565 women with breast cancer from the Danish Cancer Registry. When the probands were sorted out on the basis of cancer in relatives—one group of 46 probands with no cases of cancer among the relatives and the other group of 154 with relatives who had breast cancer—the relatives with cancer (familial trait) corresponded to the younger probands in the first peak of the distribution curve. Probands who lacked relatives with breast cancer were in the second peak, between ages 60 and 64.

According to Anderson, familial risk of breast cancer is especially significant in patients with early age of onset and bilaterality of breast cancer, but considerably less significant with late ages of onset and unilateral disease, as with elderly patients.[20] There was a risk pattern for unilateral postmenopausal breast cancer when the proband had two sisters with breast cancer and a mother without breast cancer,[19] but this was not a high risk.[23]

Still, a perusal of the pedigrees in Jacobsen's article,[22] Lynch's book,[21] Haagensen's book,[3] and elsewhere clearly shows that some geriatric patients will incur breast cancer as a first instance of what later seems to fit a familial pattern with further cases emerging. And Lynch has shown that other kinds of cancer—not just breast cancer—can be part of the familial risk pattern.[21] Certain families, such as some with cancer of the colon, revealed breast cancer with onset as late as age 84, and some geriatric cancer patients might alert the clinician to familial disease, including breast cancer, even though familial disease is more prevalent in young patients. At least a careful family history of all forms of cancer should be obtained.

Mammography is the most effective screening method, in conjunction with self-examination and medical examination, for detecting breast cancer in geriatric patients at this time. Strax presented controlled data from screening 20,166 patients with mammography and physical examination.[24] Mortality from breast cancer was reduced in that program by about one-third in patients over 50 years of age.[25] More recently, over 280,000 women were screened in the Breast Cancer Detection Demonstration Project (BCDDP).[26] In the BCDDP, the highest breast cancer detection rate in various age brackets was 12.9 per 1000 screenings in 1 year, among 7207 women aged 70 to 74. Moreover, the highest detection rate of all for minimal breast cancers (noninfiltrating and infiltrating less than 1 cm) was 4.3 per 1000 screenings, in that same group of geriatric patients. Such minimal breast cancers in other patients have been reported curable with about 95 percent disease-free status after 10 years.[27]

Still further, Carlile et al. have shown that the ratio of biopsies positive for breast cancer in 10,053 women screened in Seattle is higher for older women than for younger women: 39 percent positive biopsies for persons aged 55 to 75 and over versus 27 percent for persons aged 35 to 54.[28] These authors also found that mammograms in older women are less often dense (less likely to obscure an existing breast cancer) than in younger women, and that older women trained in breast self-examination continue to practice this more frequently than younger women. Overall, geriatric patients compose potentially the most rewarding age group for breast cancer screening with monthly self-examinations and annual medical examination and mammography.

The place of other technology such as ultrasound is not yet settled. A major deficit of ultrasound is the failure to demonstrate calcifications the size of pinheads, present in 40 percent of breast cancers and a prime indicator of highly curable breast cancer too small to be felt. Ultrasound can demonstrate cysts, which are not a large problem in the elderly. Thermography was used early in the Breast Cancer Detection Demonstration Project but was later dropped because of disappointing results. Breast temperature changes in the thermograms seem to be at best an indirect sign of pathology, unlike mammographic changes.

CLINICAL PRESENTATION

With geriatric patients one cannot apply a descriptive cliché like "fibrocystic disease" and then say "follow the patient," a euphemism for doing nothing. Breast cancer is a likely possibility in geriatric patients, with or without symptoms. Among 1443 consecutive patients with breast problems in my personal series, 75 patients (5.2 percent) were aged 65 or older. Of these patients, 28 (37.3 percent) had breast cancer when seen or had had breast cancer previously. Four more patients without breast cancer had cancer of the endometrium. So 32 geriatric patients (42.7 percent) out of 75 have been treated for cancer of endocrine target tissue. Moreover, two of the breast cancer patients (one bilateral) also had ovarian cancer.

Breast cancer in geriatric patients gives clues to its presence no differently than in patients who are not as old. The age range for geriatric patients is an arbitrary choice, of course, and there are numerous cancers in the age decade before age 65 which are similar in clinical characteristics. These cancers in my series were found because of a dominant nontender or tender palpable lump, a mammographic shadow or calcific pattern, local tenderness without a lump, nipple itching, nipple discharge, nipple deviation or skin tethering, and a pulling sensation. Ultrasound failed to detect breast cancer in one patient; only a few patients had this test. To the clinician faced with one patient, a frequency distribution of these findings is of no help. From a practical standpoint, geriatric breasts commonly have an array of large normal fat lumps which confuse some clinicians and make it difficult to palpate cancers; but the same fatty tissue creates a low-density background against which even tiny cancers can be seen in mammograms, making mammograms very useful.

There is another topic of importance regarding geriatric patients, completely overlooked in clean lists of diagnoses, symptoms, and signs. This topic is polypharmacy; geriatric patients frequently are taking an array of medicines. Some of these medicines are actual hormones; some have indirect hormone activity; many others have effects which are uncertain. Of the 75 patients referred to above, 46 (61.3 percent) had been taking one or more medicines potentially related to breast effects, and 26 had been taking estrogens, mainly conjugated estrogens, usually for a period of years (Table 75-3).

Besides the 26 patients treated with estrogens, 11 were treated with thyroid drugs, 12 with cardiac drugs, 10 with antihypertensives, and 6 with tranquilizers. All these kinds of medicine have been implicated, at least by association, with breast disease.

With one-third of the patients having taken estrogens, and with some obese patients who might have elevated plasma estrogens, one would expect estrogen-related breast disease. Breast cancer frequency has not been shown to increase from exogenous estrogens in humans, according to a review by Drill.[29] Even so, in

TABLE 75-3
Estrogen Medication and Symptoms and Signs Often Related to Estrogens in 75 Geriatric Patients

26 patients (34.7%)	
Estrogens only	14 patients
Estrogens plus other medications	12 patients
27 patients (36%) with breast pain and tenderness	
Estrogens only	13 patients
No medication	8 patients
Thyroid medication	4 patients
Multiple drugs	2 patients

the 26 patients included here having taken estrogens, six had breast cancer and four had endometrial cancer. Gross cysts, a common type of pathology in premenopausal patients, usually remit after the menopause unless estrogens are taken. Indeed, gross cysts are rarely found in other reports about elderly patients. Cysts large enough to be palpable were proved by needle aspiration or biopsy in 10 of my patients, and four of these patients were 80 years old or more. Six were taking estrogens; six were taking cardiac glycosides; nine were taking two to four drugs. Five of these patients had breast pain or tenderness.

In this series, 27 patients (36 percent) had breast pain or tenderness when questioned. Not all were taking estrogens (Table 75-3). Because of breast pain suspected to be of estrogenic origin but with lack of estrogen medication, the plasma estrogen levels of eight patients were measured. These tests were not obtained as part of a controlled study; they were obtained to seek evidence of possible estrogen elevation from adrenal hyperplasia or ovarian tumors, since breast pain has been observed with such tumors.[30] A report by Fienberg had described six postmenopausal women with estrogen-producing tumors; two of those women had had breast cancer 2 to 5 years previously, although this may have been incidental.[31] None of my patients had estrogen-producing tumors. But five of the estradiol levels and two of the estrone levels were higher than those reported by Yen for postmenopausal patients. Admittedly, differences in laboratory methodology make such comparisons unreliable. At the same time, further investigation of estrogens is warranted in patients with unexplained breast pain after cancer is ruled out. Two of my geriatric patients with breast pain were treated with estrogen receptor blockade using tamoxifen. Both patients had remission of symptoms.

DIAGNOSIS AND TREATMENT

There is no current technology other than microscopy which can accurately diagnose breast cancer; likewise, except for fluid aspiration, which proves the existence of a cyst, only microscopy can accurately diagnose benign breast disease. An unexplained breast symptom or tissue abnormality requires investigation in geriatric patients. Use of mammography to follow a questionable shadow should not be done. Biopsy is necessary. If a mammographic shadow is not a palpable lesion, radiological localization should be used to guide the surgeon's dissection; the operative specimen should be x-rayed and follow-up mammograms obtained in order to determine that the lesion has in fact been removed. Needle biopsies of palpable lumps are useful only if a positive diagnosis of breast cancer is obtained. A negative diagnosis

for breast cancer should be disregarded and open biopsy undertaken. A portion of every cancer must be assayed for estrogen receptor proteins and also progesterone receptor proteins and flow cytometry if sufficient tissue is available. Hormone receptor information is very important for treating breast cancer in the event that it recurs. Even for primary breast cancer, useful prognostic data come from receptor protein assays.[32]

If breast cancer is found, the principles of treating primary breast cancer in geriatric patients are the same as for treating younger patients. Breast cancer commonly occurs in more than one place in the same breast, and so the whole breast must be treated. And presence or absence of cancer in regional lymph nodes, in conjunction with measured primary tumor size, yields essential prognostic data. Microscopic evaluation of excised lymph nodes is the only way to obtain this information accurately; partial axillary dissection is not as accurate for this purpose as complete axillary dissection.[33,34]

The method of obtaining best possible therapeutic results should not be altered because of age alone, except for possible adjuvant chemotherapy, which will be mentioned later. Stoll reviewed the effect of age on growth pattern of breast cancer.[35] A variety of parameters were considered, and no evidence was found to prove a less malignant or more malignant course of breast cancer in elderly women. Moreover, elderly women have ample life expectancy to experience trouble from inadequate treatment of breast cancer. Herbsman[36] cited national statistics to the effect that "life expectancy of an American female at age 70 in 1975 was 14.4 years, gradually decreased to 8.7 years at age 80 but was still 6.7 years at age 85."

Is the operative mortality too high from surgical treatment of breast cancer in elderly women? I have never seen anyone die of a mastectomy, with or without axillary dissection, young or old. Deaths occurring in 20,000 women within 1 month of operation for invasive breast cancer were studied by Schneiderman and Axtell.[37] For all stages of breast cancer, the highest operative mortality was 0.8 percent, in patients aged 75 and older. For localized disease, operative mortality in that same age group was only 0.45 percent. For regional disease, women aged 75 and older had an operative mortality of 1.56 percent.

If the operative mortality is low among breast cancer patients, what are the results of surgical treatment? In the series described by Herbsman et al.,[36] 138 patients over 70 years of age underwent simple mastectomy, modified radical mastectomy, or radical mastectomy. Absolute survival after localized disease treated only by mastectomy decreased more rapidly in 5 years for elderly patients than for younger patients, except that a younger group of patients under 50 years old had a decreasing survival rate much like the oldest group. Mortality due only to breast cancer within 5 years after operation, however, was low in the elderly group, leaving an absolute survival rate of 86 percent for localized disease and 51 percent for regional disease. There were no postoperative deaths. Turning to crude survival, considering deaths from all causes, this time in 74 women over age 80 who underwent definitive major surgery for breast cancer, 40 percent of patients with stage I disease were alive 5 years later.[38] Also, Goldenberg et al. found that elderly women specifically treated by operation for breast cancer had a fourfold better survival experience than the untreated patient or the patient given only palliative therapy.[39] Thus, the consensus of the authors cited above is that age alone is not a reason to forgo a surgical procedure such as total mastectomy and axillary dissection.

Let us then consider end results of all treatment of breast cancer in geriatric women. Data from the Cancer Surveillance System are provided by Thomas for a 13-county area in western Washington.[40] The total population is about 2.8 million people, and all cases of cancer are accessed. Women 50 years of age and older with breast cancer were divided into two age brackets: ages 50 to 64 years, 3756 cases; and age 65 and older (geriatric patients), 4075 cases. The relative survival for all patients was determined, comparing patients with other women at the same ages not having breast cancer in the general population, including deaths from all causes. Table 75-4 and Fig. 75-3 show no significant difference for relative survival after breast cancer in the two age brackets.

Less than a total mastectomy may be appropriate for patients in poor health with short life expectancy, pro-

TABLE 75-4

Relative Survival Rates for Patients with Breast Cancer by Age and Time from Diagnosis in the Cancer Surveillance System

Year after Diagnosis	50–64 Years Old	65+ Years Old
1	0.96	0.97
2	0.90	0.91
3	0.83	0.86
4	0.78	0.81
5	0.75	0.78
6	0.71	0.74
7	0.67	0.69
8	0.65	0.63

SOURCE: Thomas DB: Personal communication. University of Washington and the Fred Hutchinson Cancer Research Center, Seattle, 1982.

viding the surgeon does not cut across cancer. For that matter, it is not technically difficult to remove all or most of a thin, pendulous breast under local anesthesia if necessary; this can be done in half an hour. Full axillary dissection should not be done if a patient cannot cooperate with a shoulder-motion rehabilitation program or if the contralateral arm or shoulder is lame.

Radiation therapy as principal treatment for curable primary breast cancer may be considered after excision of the tumor with clear margins in selected patients. As far as lumpectomy and primary irradiation are concerned, not all centers accept patients aged 70 years and older for this treatment on a cosmetic basis. Also, most series in different parts of the world do not have much therapeutic data for elderly patients 10 years or more after treatment. This information is still in flux. Further-

FIGURE 75-3
Comparative survival including deaths from all causes in 3756 women aged 50 to 64 and 4075 women aged 65 and over. *(Courtesy of D. B. Thomas, Cancer Surveillance System, University of Washington, and the Fred Hutchinson Cancer Research Center, Seattle, 1982.)*

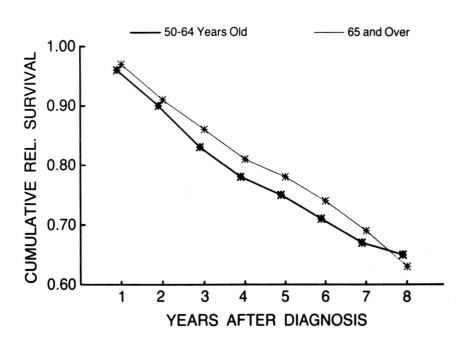

more, logistics of daily transportation for weeks of irradiation can be a problem for some geriatric patients. On the other hand, one should not assume that elderly patients are uninterested in cosmetic choices. If younger patients deserve a discussion of cosmetic choices in treatment, so do older patients.

Appropriate staging procedures are no different for geriatric patients than for younger patients. Those with small cancers and clinically negative lymph nodes warrant mammograms to screen the other breast, chest x rays, liver function tests, and bone scans if musculoskeletal symptoms exist (as with arthritis). These scans, with related x rays, are primarily to provide a current baseline for later comparison, because changes not from cancer but from arthritis could be confusing in judging significance of new symptoms at a later date. Staging for more advanced breast cancer, using computerized tomography, radioisotope scans, or ultrasound scans, would be augmented according to the specific dictates of each case.

When both clinical staging and pathological staging are completed after surgery, adjuvant treatment depends upon the status of excised lymph nodes and status of estrogen and progesterone receptors in the cancer. Fisher's data showed that breast cancer patients with as few as four lymph nodes positive for cancer approach an 85 percent likelihood of more disease somewhere in the body, within 5 years.[41] Likewise, Haagensen's data showed that when 8 to 11 axillary lymph nodes are positive, local recurrence after mastectomy is high—around 30 percent.[42] Patients with positive lymph nodes need multimodal therapy—not just surgery. Postmenopausal individuals are candidates for adjuvant chemotherapy.[43,44] Our medical oncologists do not use a specific age limit, but many geriatric patients over 70 years old might not tolerate the chemotherapeutic regimen. As indicated earlier, many of these individuals are taking cardiac drugs or antihypertensive drugs. One of the more useful agents, doxorubicin, could be hazardous to such patients because of myocardial side effects. When geriatric patients with positive lymph nodes have breast cancers with positive estrogen and/or progesterone receptor assays, adjuvant therapy with tamoxifen, an inhibitor of estrogen binding, is well tolerated and beneficial. Indeed, even patients with negative lymph nodes are now reported to have statistically significant improvement in disease-free survival with adjuvant chemotherapy or tamoxifen.[45]

CONCLUSION

Women aged 65 and over are an unusually interesting group among patients with breast disease. They may have deceptively rising plasma estrogen levels in later years; they are on numerous medications which can affect breast tissue; they may have scattered areas of epithelial hyperplasia to a severe degree; and they frequently have breast cancer, sometimes endometrial cancer.

Geriatric patients also are the age group most apt to have very effective screening mammograms, showing the small cancers which are highly curable.

Breast cancers in geriatric patients are no more or less aggressive than in younger patients. Age alone is no basis for less than optimal surgical treatment, and operative mortality for geriatric patients is very low. These patients have ample life expectancy during which cancer can recur if inadequately treated. Unless modified directly because of ill health, treatment goals for these patients are similar to those for younger patients.

REFERENCES

1. Silverberg ES, Lubera J: Cancer Statistics, 1987. *CA* 37:2, 1987.
2. Vana J et al: "Long-Term Patient Care Evaluation Study for Carcinoma of the Female Breast," Final Report, Commission on Cancer, Am Coll Surg. Chicago, Feb. 21, 1979.
3. Haagensen CD et al: *Breast Cancer, Risk and Detection.* Philadelphia, Saunders, 1981, p 11.
4. Wellings SR et al: An atlas of subgross pathology of the human breast with special reference to possible precancerous lesions. *J Natl Cancer Inst* 55:321, 1975.
5. Hayward JL, Parks AG: Alterations in the microanatomy of the breast as a result of changes in the hormonal environment, in Currie ER (ed): *Endocrine Aspects of Breast Cancer.* Proc Conf University Glasgow, July 8 to 10, 1957. Edinburgh, E and S Livingstone, 1958, p 133.
6. Huseby RA, Thomas LB: Histological and histochemical alterations in the normal breast tissues of patients with advanced breast cancer being treated with estrogenic hormones. *Cancer* 7:54, 1954.
7. Jensen HM: Breast pathology, emphasizing precancerous and cancer-associated lesions. *Comment Res Breast Dis* 2:41, 1981.
8. Yen SSC, Jaffe RB: *Reproductive Endocrinology. Physiology, Pathophysiology and Clinical Management.* Philadelphia, Saunders, 1978, p 261.
9. Mishell DR Jr, Davajan V: *Reproductive Endocrinology, Infertility and Contraception.* Philadelphia, Davis, 1979, p 162.
10. Nisker JA, Siiteri PK: Estrogens and breast cancer. *Clin Obstet Gynecol* 24:301, 1981.
11. Judd HL et al: Serum androgens and estrogens in postmenopausal women with and without endometrial cancer. *Am J Obstet Gynecol* 136:859, 1980.
12. Siiteri PK: Extraglandular oestrogen formation and serum binding of oestradiol: Relationship to cancer. *J Endocrinol* 89:119, 1981.
13. Jones LA et al: Bioavailability of estradiol as a marker for breast cancer risk assessment. *Cancer Res* 47:5224, 1987.

14. Chakravarti S et al: Hormonal profiles after the menopause. *Br Med J* Oct 2:784, 1976.

15. Kramer WM, Rush BF Jr: Mammary duct proliferation in the elderly. A histopathologic study. *Cancer* 31:130, 1973.

16. Lippman ME: Steroid hormone receptors and mechanisms of growth regulation of human breast cancer, in Lippman ME et al (eds): *Diagnosis and Management of Breast Cancer.* Philadelphia, Saunders, 1988, p 326.

17. Gallager HS, Hutter RVP: Pathology and pathogenesis of breast cancer, in Gallager HS et al (eds): *The Breast.* St. Louis, Mosby, 1978, p 49.

18. Haagensen CD: *Diseases of the Breast,* 2d ed. Philadelphia, Saunders, 1971.

19. Thomas DB: Epidemiologic and related studies of breast cancer etiology, in Lillienfeld AM (ed): *Reviews in Cancer Epidemiology,* vol I. New York, Elsevier/North-Holland, 1980, p 153.

20. Anderson DE: A genetic study of human breast cancer. *J Natl Cancer Inst* 48:1029, 1972.

21. Lynch HT et al: Genetic counselling, patient and family management: Familial breast cancer, in Lynch HT (ed): *Genetics and Breast Cancer.* New York, Van Nostrand Reinhold, 1981, p 196.

22. Jacobsen O: *Heredity in Breast Cancer. A Genetic and Clinical Study of Two Hundred Probands.* London, HK Lewis, 1946.

23. Anderson DE: Genetic study of breast cancer: Identification of a high risk group. *Cancer* 34:1090, 1974.

24. Strax P et al: Mammography and clinical examination in mass screening for cancer of the breast. *Cancer* 20:2184, 1967.

25. Shapiro S et al: Changes in 5 year breast cancer mortality in a breast cancer screening program, in Proc Seventh Natl Cancer Conf. Philadelphia, Lippincott, 1973, p 663.

26. Baker LH: Breast cancer detection demonstration project: Five-year summary report. *CA* 32:194, 1982.

27. Wanebo HJ et al: Treatment of minimal breast cancer. *Cancer* 33:349, 1974.

28. Carlile T et al: Breast cancer screening in the elderly. (Unpublished.)

29. Drill VA: An overview of studies on estrogens, oral contraceptives and breast cancer. *Prog Drug Res* 25:159, 1981.

30. Rome RM et al: Functioning ovarian tumors in postmenopausal women. *Obstet Gynecol* 57:705, 1981.

31. Fienberg R: Ovarian estrogenic tumors and diffuse estrogenic thecomatosis in postmenopausal colporrhagia. *Am J Obstet Gynecol* 76:851, 1958.

32. McGuire WL: Hormone receptors: Their role in predicting prognosis and response to endocrine therapy. *Semin Oncol* 5:428, 1978.

33. Davies GC et al: Assessment of axillary lymph node status. *Ann Surg* 192:148, 1980.

34. Smith JA III et al: Carcinoma of the breast. Analysis of total lymph node involvement versus level of metastasis. *Cancer* 39:527, 1977.

35. Stoll BA: Effect of age on growth pattern. *New Aspects Breast Cancer* 2:129, 1976.

36. Herbsman H et al: Survival following breast cancer surgery in the elderly. *Cancer* 47:2358, 1981.

37. Schneiderman MA, Axtell LM: Deaths among female patients with carcinoma of the breast treated by a surgical procedure only. *Surg Gynecol Obstet* 148:193, 1979.

38. Crosby CH et al: Carcinoma of the breast: Surgical management of patients with special conditions. *Cancer* 28:1628, 1971.

39. Goldenberg IS et al: Survival patterns of elderly women with breast cancer. *Arch Surg* 99:649, 1969.

40. Thomas DB: Personal communication, 1982.

41. Fisher B: Surgical adjuvant therapy for breast cancer. *Cancer* 30:1556, 1972.

42. Haagensen CD: *Diseases of the Breast,* 2d ed. Philadelphia, Saunders, 1971, p 708.

43. Bonadonna G, Valagussa P: Dose–response effect of adjuvant chemotherapy in breast cancer. *N Engl J Med* 304:10, 1981.

44. Rivkin S et al: Adjuvant chemotherapy for operable breast cancer with positive axillary nodes: A comparison of CMFVP versus L-PAM, in Salmon SE, Jones SE (eds): *Adjuvant Therapy of Cancer III.* New York, Grune & Stratton, 1981, p 445.

45. Clinical Alert from The National Cancer Institute. May 18, 1988.

Disorders of Bone and Mineral Metabolism

Chapter 76

CALCIUM AND BONE HOMEOSTASIS WITH AGING

Marius E. Kraenzlin, John C. Jennings, and David J. Baylink

This chapter deals with calcium (Ca) metabolism and bone metabolism and the interaction between these two systems, especially during aging. The function of Ca metabolism is to assure a normal serum Ca, whereas the function of bone metabolism is not only to participate in serum Ca regulation but also to provide adequate mechanical support. During aging, serum Ca is maintained within the normal range whereas in both sexes there is a progressive loss of bone. Therefore, the major focus of this chapter is on bone metabolism. Nonetheless, we still comprehensively address Ca metabolism during aging for two reasons: (1) primary abnormalities in bone metabolism (such as immobilization) produce counterregulatory effects on Ca metabolism and (2) age-related abnormalities in Ca metabolism can cause bone loss.

Thus, it is clear that Ca metabolism and bone metabolism are highly integrated. On the other hand, the regulation of serum Ca and the regulation of bone density can be two opposing processes. For example, during Ca deficiency the serum Ca regulation system attempts to remove bone to correct the decrease in serum Ca, whereas the bone density regulatory system (i.e., the coupling of bone formation [BF] to bone resorption [BR]*) attempts to oppose this action and maintain an appropriate bone density for mechanical needs. In such a situation, the serum Ca regulatory system takes precedence, and bone is lost. This situation emphasizes the importance of a normal serum Ca to the organism. Indeed, the reason that abnormalities in serum Ca are not seen with aging is because such abnormalities are detrimental to cell function; the same is not true for abnormalities in bone metabolism. Consequently, in patients with age-related Ca deficiency one may see a normal serum Ca maintained at the expense of the development

---

*Coupling is the process by which BF is quantitatively entrained to prior BR; the process is discussed in detail later in this chapter (see "Regulation of Bone Remodeling and Bone Density").

of osteoporosis (i.e., the osteoporosis is a trade-off for a normal serum Ca). Ca metabolism is an important aspect of bone metabolism; however, as will be discussed, there are many other variables besides Ca metabolism that influence bone density regulation.

The goals of this chapter are to show how Ca metabolism and bone metabolism are regulated and how the regulatory processes of these two systems are integrated; to discuss other variables that influence bone density regulation; and to propose conceptual models on how the effects of aging on Ca metabolism, bone metabolism, and these other variables cause bone loss. This chapter deals with current models and concepts of bone and Ca metabolism, whereas the remainder of the chapters in this section deal with more traditional didactic approaches to the management of disorders of Ca metabolism and bone metabolism.

CALCIUM METABOLISM AND SERUM CALCIUM REGULATION

In normal subjects and during aging, the extracellular fluid concentration of Ca remains in the normal range in spite of extensive exchanges of Ca between extracellular fluid, the intestine, the skeleton, and the kidney. This remarkable regulation of the extracellular concentration of Ca is achieved by the actions and interactions of parathyroid hormone (PTH), vitamin D, and calcitonin on these organs. Figure 76-1 is a schematic overview of the three organs and three hormones involved in normal serum Ca regulation. In this section, we will describe the mechanisms by which each of these organs and hormones regulates Ca and emphasize how specific aspects of this system change with age.

Before discussing the mechanics of how the system works, we wish to briefly describe concepts pertinent to the functional goals of Ca metabolism in the three major organs involved: intestine, kidney, and bone. Ca metabolism by intestine and kidney has only one function, namely to maintain serum Ca, whereas Ca metabolism by bone functions not only to maintain serum Ca but also to maintain an appropriate bone density. Accordingly, Ca metabolism by intestine and kidney is regulated by systemic hormones such as PTH, whereas Ca metabolism by bone is regulated both by systemic hormones which direct bone participation in serum Ca homeostasis and by local mechanisms intrinsic to bone which are involved in adapting bone density to mechanical needs.

ORGANS INVOLVED IN CALCIUM METABOLISM

Small Intestine

The small intestine regulates serum Ca homeostasis through the absorption of dietary Ca. Normal dietary Ca intake is approximately 800 to 1200 mg/day, of which 15 to 40 percent is absorbed in the proximal small intestine by both active transport and passive diffusion. Vitamin D, after conversion to its active metabolite, $1,25(OH)_2$-vitamin D (abbreviated 1,25D), is the major hormone controlling the active component of the intestinal absorption of Ca, such that when the levels of 1,25D rise, intestinal Ca absorption increases, and when levels of 1,25D decrease, intestinal Ca absorption also decreases. Active transport is most important at low concentrations of Ca in the bowel lumen. Ca absorption via passive diffusion is concentration-dependent and is important at high Ca concentrations in the gut lumen.[1,2]

Normally, intestinal Ca absorption is carefully regulated to meet the body's need to regulate serum Ca. Variation in dietary Ca intake is counterbalanced by changes in the efficiency of Ca absorption, i.e., fractional Ca absorption increases with low Ca intake and vice versa. It is significant that this adaptive response is blunted with aging in both men and women. The efficiency of intestinal Ca absorption in the elderly does not increase when dietary Ca intake is decreased to the same extent that it does in young individuals.[3,4] This age-related decline in Ca absorption can be attributed to both decreased concentrations of 1,25D and to primary changes in the ability of the intestine to transport Ca. This decreased Ca absorption may be further aggravated in some elderly subjects by (1) diminished gastric acid production (gastric acid is required for solubilization of the Ca), (2) development of acquired lactase deficiency with aging with consequent avoidance of dairy products,

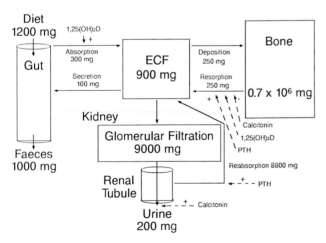

FIGURE 76-1
The principal organs and hormones involved in mass calcium transport and the approximate daily flux rates of calcium between the compartments in young normal females. The sizes of the compartments are given in mg and the daily flux rates are indicated next to the corresponding arrows.

and (3) a lower overall dietary Ca intake compared with that of young individuals.[4-6]

The age-related decrease in Ca absorption (which is clearly the most detrimental change in Ca metabolism during aging) leads to a slight decrease in serum Ca concentrations (within the normal range) which subsequently leads to an increase in PTH secretion (discussed later). This increase in PTH in turn stimulates BR in order to maintain normal serum Ca levels (Fig. 76-2).

Kidney

The second major organ involved in mass Ca transport is the kidney, which both filters and reabsorbs Ca. About 9 g of Ca is filtered per 24 hours by glomeruli, and 90 percent of the filtered Ca is reabsorbed in the proximal tubule. Ca reabsorption in the proximal tubule is not controlled by Ca-regulating hormones but is coupled to sodium reabsorption. About 10 percent of the filtered Ca is delivered to the distal tubules where Ca reabsorption is tightly controlled by PTH which acts to increase Ca reabsorption. This response to PTH occurs within minutes and thus provides a mechanism for acute maintenance of normocalcemia.[1,2] Only about 1 to 2 percent of filtered Ca is excreted in urine (Fig. 76-1).

Although the glomerular filtration rate (GFR) decreases with aging in both men and women, there is no direct evidence for impairment in renal tubular Ca handling with aging. Moreover, urine Ca declines with aging, a change which is opposite to what one would expect if there were an age-related decline in renal tubular function. Nonetheless, it is still possible that the decline in urine Ca is not as great as it should be based on the decline in GFR and on the level of Ca deficiency that attends aging.

Bone

The third organ system involved in serum Ca regulation is bone, which is the major Ca reservoir and serves both as a supply and as a "sink" for serum Ca. In young and aged normal adults BR delivers approximately 200 to 600 mg/day of Ca into the extracellular fluid. In young normal adults, the amount of osteoclastic BR is balanced by an equivalent amount of bone matrix formation and mineralization such that about 200 to 600 mg/day of Ca enters the skeleton.[1,2] In contrast to this broad range of rates of BR and of BF, the overall Ca balance (total loss or gain of Ca) varies from 0 to about 30 mg/day, suggesting that even during aging the rates of BF and BR are coupled fairly closely. In females, given a total peak skeletal Ca of 700 g, 30 mg/day is a small loss rate. However, over a period of 30 years, the accumulated loss would be almost one-half of the total skeletal Ca. Thus, even a modestly impaired coupling of BF to BR can eventually lead to significant bone loss.

HORMONES INVOLVED IN SERUM CALCIUM REGULATION

Parathyroid Hormone

PTH, an 84-amino-acid peptide, plays a predominant role in the maintenance of Ca homeostasis, as evidenced by the life-threatening hypocalcemia that may occur after parathyroidectomy. PTH increases serum Ca levels by the following mechanisms: (1) stimulation of renal tubular Ca reabsorption; (2) stimulation of the 1α-hydroxylase activity, which increases conversion of 25(OH)-vitamin D (25D) to 1,25D; and (3) mobilization of Ca from bone by stimulation of osteoclastic BR[2] (at physiologic concentrations, PTH, without 1,25D, is ineffective in increasing osteoclastic BR).

PTH synthesis and secretion is regulated by the concentration of ionized Ca in extracellular fluids. For example, when serum Ca levels fall, PTH is released, whereas increased serum Ca inhibits PTH secretion. The secreted peptide is metabolized in the serum, liver, and kidney, which results in several circulating fragments.[2] The biologically active aminoterminal fragments and the intact molecule, which represent approximately 5 to 10 percent of the measurable immunoreactive plasma PTH, have a short circulating half-life (minutes). The biologically inactive carboxyterminal (C-terminal) fragments, which represent approximately 80 percent of the measurable serum PTH, have a long circulating half-life (hours). The aminoterminal fragments are taken up by the kidney and bone and, to a lesser extent, filtered and degraded in the kidney. The C-terminal fragments

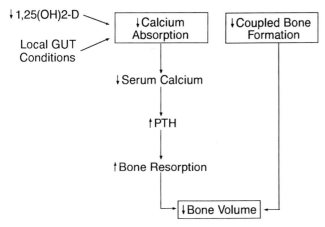

FIGURE 76-2
Model of mechanisms of bone loss in both sexes after about 65 years of age. Variable degrees of calcium malabsorption occur which lead to increased PTH-mediated bone resorption. In addition, there may be an age-related impairment of the coupling of bone formation to bone resorption. These two defects lead to decreased bone density. (See text for details.)

are eliminated by glomerular filtration. The clinical significance of these features of PTH metabolism is that, with the decrease in GFR during aging, there will be an accumulation of inactive C-terminal fragments in serum such that a radioimmunoassay (RIA) based on a C-terminal epitope could lead to overestimation of the PTH status of the individual.[7]

Most studies have shown an increase of circulating PTH levels with age.[8-12] The increase of serum PTH during aging could reflect a reduced glomerular clearance of PTH by the kidney, an increase in PTH secretion, altered peripheral metabolism of PTH, or a combination of these variables. Because there is an age-related increase in nephrogenous adenosine 3':5'-cyclic phosphate (cyclic AMP) and an age-related decrease in tubular maximum phosphate reabsorption (two changes which are suggestive of increased PTH action), it seems likely that there is a true increase in circulating biologically active PTH with aging.[9] This rise of PTH activity with aging is clearly not an indication of primary hyperparathyroidism, since serum Ca tends to decline slightly during aging.* It seems likely that the age-related decline in the efficiency of intestinal Ca absorption coupled with the decrease in dietary Ca intake contributes to this secondary hyperparathyroidism.

Vitamin D

The normal metabolism of vitamin D is schematically represented in Fig. 76-3. The production of vitamin D_3 by photoconversion of 7-dehydrocholesterol to vitamin D_3 in the skin by action of ultraviolet light is one of the two major sources of circulating vitamin D. In the United States, supplementation of the diet with vitamin D_2 (primarily in milk and other processed dairy products) is the other major source of vitamin D.[13,14] Vitamin D_2 and vitamin D_3 are metabolized identically, and their active metabolites are essentially equipotent. Thus, further distinction between D_2 and D_3 will not be made in the following discussion of vitamin D metabolism.

Vitamin D is synthesized in the skin, released into the bloodstream where it binds to a carrier protein, and then transported first to sites of critical metabolism (liver and kidney) and finally to its site of action on distant target organs. Thus, since vitamin D fulfills the criteria of a hormone, skin is analogous to an endocrine organ. The first step in vitamin D metabolism is the hydroxylation of vitamin D to 25D by the hepatic enzyme, vitamin D 25-hydroxylase. This initial hydroxylation of vitamin D is closely dependent upon substrate (vitamin D) concentration (Fig. 76-3) and does not appear to be regulated by hormonal control. The biologically active form

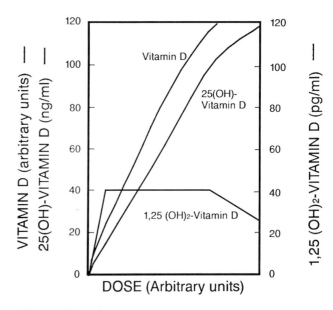

FIGURE 76-3
Schema of the synthesis of 25(OH)-vitamin D (25D) from vitamin D and of 1,25(OH)$_2$-vitamin D (1,25D) from 25D. Production of 25D is clearly dependent on the concentration of vitamin D throughout the entire range of serum concentrations of vitamin D. In contrast, production of 1,25D, the active metabolite, is constant except at extremely high (>100) or at extremely low (<8) concentrations of 25D. Serum 25D begins to drop when serum 25D falls below 8 ng/ml (i.e., when the effect of PTH to increase renal 1α-hydroxylase can no longer compensate for the decreased substrate, 25(OH)-vitamin D). Serum 1,25D begins to fall sometime after serum 25D exceeds 100 ng/ml (i.e., a level which is sufficiently high for 25D to act on the 1,25D nuclear acceptor).

of vitamin D, 1,25D, is produced by a second hydroxylation in the kidney which is mediated by 25D 1α-hydroxylase.[13,14] The activity of the renal 1α-hydroxylase is directly regulated by serum PTH, serum Ca, serum phosphorus concentrations, and possibly by other factors such as estradiol and other steroid hormones.[14] Unlike the hepatic 25D hydroxylation, 1,25D hydroxylation is largely independent of substrate except at very low and very high concentrations of 25D (Fig. 76-3). Vitamin D is the hormone precursor, 25D is the circulating storage form of the hormone (though at supraphysiologic concentrations it has activities identical to 1,25D), and 1,25D is the active hormone which (like 25D) is transported in serum (associated with a carrier protein) to its major target organs, intestine and bone, where it acts in the following ways:

1. *Small intestine.* 1,25D increases the absorption of Ca and stimulates the formation of a specific intracellular Ca-binding protein in the small intestine. This Ca-binding protein is thought to be somehow associated with the epithelial transcellular transport of Ca. 1,25D controls about 60 percent of the active intestinal Ca absorption.[15]

*In females this decline occurs more than 10 years after menopause; shortly after menopause serum Ca increases and serum PTH decreases (see "Regulation of Bone Remodeling and Bone Density").

2. *Bone.* Vitamin D promotes the mineralization of newly formed bone by providing an adequate supply of Ca to maintain serum Ca. Vitamin D also directly promotes BR by acting synergistically with PTH to increase the number and the differentiation of osteoclasts (Oc).[16,17]

With respect to age-related changes in the vitamin D endocrine system, there is a linear decrease of plasma 25D and 1,25D levels between the ages of 65 and 90.[18–20] Serum 25D must decrease to less than 8 ng/ml to alter Ca metabolism. Such levels may occur in elderly subjects by any one or a combination of the causes listed in Table 76-1. Causes 1 to 5 in Table 76-1 lead first to a decrease in serum 25D. Decrements of serum 25D due to inadequate exposure to sunlight may be seen particularly in housebound elderly subjects. Only cause 6 involves a direct impairment of the mechanism whereby 25D is converted to 1,25D. The precise cause of this age-related impairment is unclear. However, the defect involves a diminished ability of the kidney to increase 1α-hydroxylase in response to PTH, as evidenced by the finding that in elderly subjects prolonged infusion of PTH results in a markedly impaired serum 1,25D response compared to that of young normal individuals under the same conditions.[21] This abnormality could place a relatively greater burden on PTH target organs (i.e., bone and kidney) and a relatively lesser burden on gut to maintain serum Ca during aging. Consequently, compared to serum Ca levels in young adults, serum Ca levels in aging adults would be maintained relatively more from bone than gut, a situation which could contribute to age-related bone loss.

Calcitonin

Calcitonin is a 32-amino-acid peptide which is produced by the parafollicular C cells within the thyroid gland. Physiologic doses of calcitonin decrease BR by a direct action on the Oc. Calcitonin is secreted in response to rises in serum Ca and may also be secreted in response to a Ca-containing meal via stimulation of gastrin re-

TABLE 76-1
Causes of Vitamin D Deficiency in the Elderly

1. Deprivation of sunlight
2. Diminished capacity of the skin to convert cholesterol to vitamin D
3. Intestinal malabsorption of the fat-soluble vitamin D
4. Diminished dietary vitamin D intake by avoidance of vitamin D–supplemented dairy products
5. Drug-induced increase in 25(OH)-vitamin D degradation in the liver (e.g., diphenylhydantoin, phenobarbital)
6. Diminished production of 1,25(OH)$_2$-vitamin D by the kidney (selective partial resistance to PTH)

lease. This may serve to prevent the potential rise in serum Ca in the immediate postprandial state and in so doing conserve bone. It seems unlikely, however, that calcitonin plays a significant role in chronic serum Ca regulation in the human since in states of extreme calcitonin excess (e.g., medullary carcinoma of the thyroid) and extreme deficiency (e.g., total thyroidectomy) there do not appear to be major abnormalities in the regulation of serum Ca.[22] Subjects with very high calcitonin concentrations do have reduced bone turnover; BF as well as BR is reduced. The decrease in BF presumably reflects a coupling of BF to the decrease in BR.

With aging there is a decrease in serum total calcitonin concentrations which appears to represent a decrease in the inactive fragments rather than the biologically active intact calcitonin.[23] In conclusion, PTH and 1,25D, but not calcitonin, appear to be involved in age-related bone loss.

BONE METABOLISM AND BONE DENSITY REGULATION WITH AGING

Bone density, which is regulated by local as well as systemic factors, declines with aging. Age-related bone loss is due to several factors, including age-related changes in serum Ca regulation (as already discussed), age-related changes in gonadal hormones, and changes in intrinsic mechanisms of bone density regulation. In this section we will (1) outline the basic principles of bone structure, bone cells, bone remodeling, and bone density regulation; (2) describe the changes in these parameters that occur with aging; and (3) present conceptual models of postmenopausal bone loss and of age-related bone loss.

BONE STRUCTURE

Skeletal tissue consists of cortical and trabecular bone. These two types of bone are sufficiently different in structure so as to behave differently; therefore, they will be considered separately. Cortical bone accounts for three-fourths of the weight of the skeleton. Cortical bone forms the outer wall of all bones but is found primarily in the long bones of the appendicular skeleton. Cortical bone consists of tightly packed osteons or haversian systems. It has a low surface-to-volume ratio (i.e., low porosity) and, since BF and BR occur on surfaces, accounts for only one-third of the total remodeling surface.

Two important structural changes occur in cortical bone with aging: (1) reduction in cortical thickness and (2) an increase in cortical porosity. Progressive cortical thinning occurs mainly by removal of bone from the inner or endosteal surface and results from increased BR which is not entirely compensated by an increase in BF. The increase in the porosity occurs by erosion of the

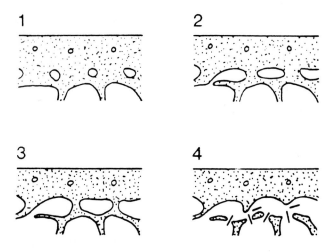

FIGURE 76-4
Microscopic evolution of cortical bone loss. Successive stages in osteoclast-dependent thinning of cortical bone: (1) normal adult cortex; (2) enlargement of the subendosteal spaces and communication of these spaces with the marrow cavity; (3) further enlargement of these spaces and conversion of the inner third of the cortex to a structure that topographically resembles trabecular bone, with an attending expansion of the marrow cavity; (4) perforation and disconnection of the new trabecular structures.[24] (*Adapted with permission from Parfitt AM: Age-related structural changes in trabecular and cortical bone. Calcif Tissue Int 36(suppl):S123, 1984.*)

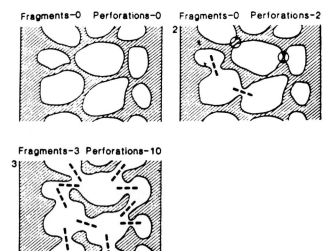

FIGURE 76-5
Microscopic evolution of trabecular bone loss. Successive stages in the conversion of the continuous network of trabeculae present at skeletal maturity to the discontinuous network seen in the elderly. Fragments are isolated trabecular profiles seen in the two-dimensional sections; they are connected in the third dimension rather than lying free in the marrow space. Perforations are the focal breaks in continuity postulated to initiate loss of entire trabeculae.[24] (*Adapted with permission from Parfitt AM: Age-related structural changes in trabecular and cortical bone. Calcif Tissue Int 36(suppl):S123, 1984.*)

haversian systems, a process which is more pronounced near the endosteal surface (Fig. 76-4),[24] perhaps because of the continuity between the endosteum and nearby haversian systems.

Trabecular bone accounts for the remaining 25 percent of the skeletal weight and is found largely in the axial skeleton, the flat bones, and the ends of long bones. Trabecular bone has a high surface-to-volume ratio (i.e., high porosity) due to its three-dimensional branching network, is surrounded by active or fatty hematopoietic tissue, and is contained within a cortical shell. It accounts for three-fourths of the total skeletal remodeling surface. The configuration and orientation of the trabeculae in the three-dimensional network is determined by the mechanical stresses in the corresponding bone structure. This configuration provides maximum tensile and compressive strength with minimum weight.

With aging, trabecular bone loss occurs as a result of thinning of normal trabeculae and of destruction of entire trabeculae.[25,26] This latter mechanism accounts for two-thirds of trabecular bone loss and leads to a change in the network arrangement (Fig. 76-5).[24] Current dogma indicates that these lost trabeculae cannot be replaced. Thus, during aging, some trabeculae are removed and the remaining trabeculae become thinner.[25] The possible mechanisms underlying the loss of trabecular and cortical bone are discussed later in this chapter in the section on bone remodeling and bone density regulation.

BONE CELLS

There are two major types of cells in bone: the osteoblast (Ob) and the osteoclast (Oc). The function of the mature forms of these cell types is relatively clear: the Ob produces bone matrix and the Oc removes (resorbs) bone matrix. The mechanisms by which these differentiated cells arise from their putative stem cell precursors are now being extensively studied and are addressed briefly below.

Osteoblasts

The presumed stem cell for Ob is mesenchymal in origin. Under the influence of growth factors (GF) and perhaps unknown factors, progeny of the Ob stem cell differentiate into "preosteoblasts" and then to mature Ob. Bone substance contains several traditional GF including insulin-like growth factor I (IGF-I), IGF-II, transforming growth factor β (TGF-β), platelet-derived growth factor (PDGF), and basic fibroblast growth factor (FGF).[27–30] The mature Ob probably produces these GF[31] as well as constituents of bone matrix, including type I collagen, proteoglycans, phosphoproteins, and osteocalcin. The mature Ob is identified by a high concentration of alkaline phosphatase in its plasma membrane and by osteocalcin synthesis. There is evidence that Ob function decreases with aging. It is not clear whether this age-related decline in matrix synthesis is due to a decrease in the number of Ob or to a decrease in synthetic activity per Ob or to both.

Osteocytes

Ultimately Ob become entrapped in bone matrix; in this condition they are referred to as osteocytes. The function of osteocytes is controversial. Our hypothesis is that osteocytes sense increases or decreases in mechanical strain relative to the prevailing bone density and then send chemical messages to surface lining cells (i.e., resting Ob) which then elaborate GF (or other chemical messengers) to effect an increase or decrease in bone density through changes in BF and BR, thereby providing a means for bone density to adapt appropriately to changes in mechanical stress. In the same vein, osteocytes could detect microdamage, (originating from excess local bone stress) and subsequently send a chemical message to surface lining cells which could respond by elaborating chemical messages to stimulate proliferation of Oc precursors and, ultimately, BR. The resulting cavity would then be filled in with new bone as described in Fig. 76-6.

This model responds to stress, but not to all stress, in a stereotypical manner. In vivo, different types of mechanical stress lead to different bone cell activities. Compressive forces lead to increased BF, whereas tensional forces lead to increased BR. Thus osteocytes and lining cells must have the ability to send out appropriate signals (to increase or decrease Ob and to increase or decrease Oc), depending on the type of stress manifested.

In interstitial (deep) bone (which in a 65-year-old individual could have a half-life of over 15 years) osteocytes may die. Perilacunar bone density is low relative to interlacunar bone density when osteocytes are functioning normally but increases following osteocyte death.[32] Thus, with increased age-related osteocyte death, interstitial bone becomes hypermineralized and thus brittle. This brittle bone would be more likely to develop microdamage, and the proposed osteocytic signals for repair/remodeling would be reduced (due to the decrease in viable osteocytes). The accumulation of microdamage and reduced signal for repair would then ultimately lead to increased risk for fracture of the corresponding bone.

Osteoclasts

A number of lines of evidence suggest that the Oc stem cell is a mononuclear cell of the hemopoietic lineage. The mononuclear stem cell progeny, under the influence of 1,25D and certain cytokines (discussed later), fuse and form multinucleated Oc which resorb bone. There is currently no evidence that there are deficiencies in Oc function with aging. Indeed, for age-

related bone loss to occur, osteoclastic BR must exceed osteoblastic BF.

Interaction Between Osteoblasts and Osteoclasts

There is considerable evidence that Oc metabolism is controlled in part by Ob. Ob produce factors which increase Oc production (such as 1,25D, interleukin-1 [IL-1], granulocyte/monocyte colony stimulating factor [GM-CSF], and IL-3)[33,34] and at least one, TGF-β, which decreases Oc production (Fig. 76-7).[35,35a] These factors are thought to act in a paracrine manner to regulate Oc precursor proliferation and differentiation. Another finding that implicates Ob in the regulation of BR is that Ob must be present in in vitro systems for PTH to increase BR.[36] Apparently, Ob process the information derived from interaction with molecules such as PTH and then send unknown chemical messages to Oc (and perhaps their precursors) to increase BR (Fig. 76-6A). Thus, Ob play an essential intermediary role in directing Oc functions. Why should Ob regulate BR? One reason could be that Ob (because of their communication with osteocytes) are in a better geographic position than Oc to detect microdamage and variations in bone strain. In our model of these cellular interactions, osteocytes sense when there is excess microdamage and signal the nearby Ob to produce certain cytokines, such as GM-CSF and IL-1, which in turn act on Oc precursors in a paracrine manner to generate an increase in Oc number. The Oc excavate the damaged bone and the cavity is refilled with healthy bone in a manner similar to that illustrated in Fig. 76-6. There is no direct evidence that this repair process is impaired with aging. However, pertinent to this issue is that in general the ability to repair declines with aging.

REGULATION OF BONE REMODELING AND BONE DENSITY

After cessation of growth at skeletal maturity, both trabecular and cortical bone are subject to continuous replacement, a process called remodeling. Remodeling does not occur uniformly throughout the bone surface but rather takes place in microscopically discrete local sites.[24,37] In cortical bone, it has been shown that formation of new bone within the cortex occurs only at sites where bone has been resorbed. In cortical bone, the resorptive phase lasts for 30 days, the bone-forming phase lasts about 130 days, and a further 3 to 6 months may be required for the bone to become fully mineralized.[37] Although the phenomenon of BR preceding BF tends to apply to the skeleton in general, this constraint does not always apply to the periosteum or endosteum of cortical bone, or to trabecular bone. Accordingly, under

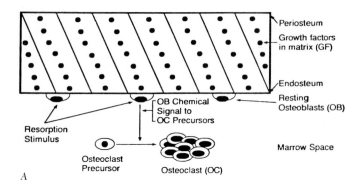

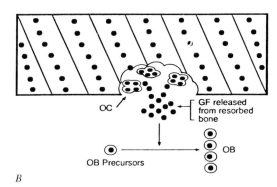

A

B

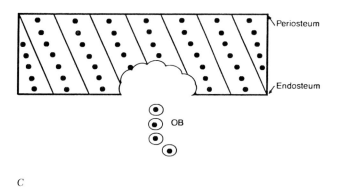

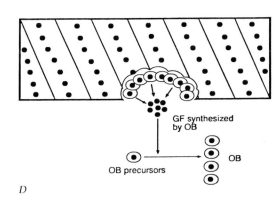

C

D

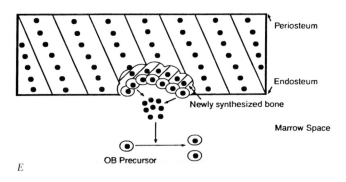

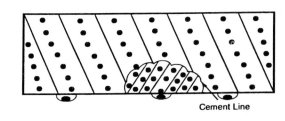

E

F

FIGURE 76-6

Model of successive stages of the coupling of bone formation to bone resorption. *A.* Bone resorption is initiated by a systemic stimulus such as PTH which acts on resting osteoblasts (Ob) to produce a chemical signal which in turn acts on osteoclast (Oc) precursors to produce more Oc and on Oc to increase their resorption activity. *B.* Oc excavate bone and in so doing release growth factors (GF) from bone substance. These GF act on Ob precursors to produce Ob. *C.* Resorptive phase is complete and Oc disappear from the surface of the resorptive cavity. *D.* Mature Ob formed during the resorptive phase now line up on the cavity surface and begin to fill in cavity with new bone. These contemporary Ob produce GF which act on Ob precursors to produce more Ob. *E.* The extent of resorptive cavity fill-in is determined by the amount of GF produced by contemporary Ob. The amount of GF produced is determined by signals acting on Ob. One such signal could be an electrochemical signal (produced by normal mechanical loading) which stimulates GF release by these contemporary Ob. *F.* The amount of new bone formed is equal to the amount of old bone resorbed (i.e., bone formation and bone resorption are coupled).

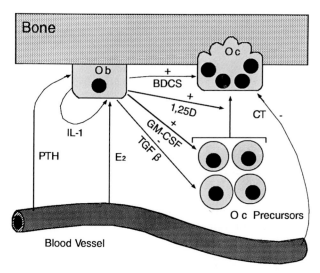

FIGURE 76-7

Model for the regulation of bone resorption (BR) by osteoblasts (Ob). Two major systemic regulators of the Ob are PTH and estrogen (E$_2$). We propose that PTH increases BR through two mechanisms: (1) by increasing the release of osteoblast-derived osteoclast stimulator (BDCS) (a factor which has not yet been isolated and characterized); BDCS acts on mature osteoclasts (Oc) to increase bone resorbing activity; and (2) by increasing the release of GM-CSF. GM-CSF increases the production and maturation of Oc precursors (e.g., increases Oc number). PTH may stimulate BDCS and/or GM-CSF release directly or may stimulate increases in Ob and/or marrow cell production of IL-1, which then stimulates Ob production of BDCS and/or GM-CSF. According to our model, E$_2$ decreases BR by inhibiting Ob and/or marrow cell release of IL-1 and by increasing Ob release of TGF beta. 1,25D, which is produced by Ob but which also may be derived from the serum, promotes differentiation (e.g., fusion) of the Oc precursors. In the absence of 1,25D, PTH can increase Oc activity but not Oc number. Lastly, calcitonin (CT) decreases BR by directly inhibiting Oc activity. This model was developed to provide a conceptual framework for understanding Ob–Oc interactions. As with any model, certain details (e.g., direct vs. indirect actions of PTH) should become more definitive with further investigation.

certain conditions, these sites may exhibit BF without prior resorption.[24]

Regulation of Bone Remodeling

Bone remodeling is the process whereby old bone is replaced by new bone. There are three important quantitative variables characterizing bone remodeling.

1. *The rate of bone remodeling.* This rate is the quantity of bone remodeled (resorbed and formed) per unit of time, expressed as a fraction of the bone volume. The rate of bone remodeling throughout the skeleton seems to be regulated largely by systemic factors, whereas the other two aspects of bone remodeling (site of bone remodeling and balance of bone remodeling) are strongly influenced by local factors. Systemic factors that affect the rate include PTH, calcitonin, 1,25D, thyroid hormone, estrogen, and testosterone. For example, pa-

tients with hyperthyroidism or with primary hyperparathyroidism typically have increased bone remodeling, whereas those with hypoparathyroidism typically have very low levels of bone remodeling.

The significance of the remodeling rate in terms of bone loss (at least in postmenopausal subjects) is that the higher the remodeling rate (or the BR rate) the greater the absolute loss of bone density (Fig. 76-8). Interestingly, the coupling defect (associated with estrogen deficiency) appears to be a fixed percentage of the remodeling rate, so that as the remodeling rate increases the absolute rate of bone loss increases (Fig. 76-8). Conversely, inhibition of BR leads to a decrease in the absolute bone loss rate.

2. *The sites where remodeling occurs.* While we do not have a comprehensive knowledge of the factors which determine where remodeling occurs, we do know that mechanical factors are an important determinant and perhaps *the* most important determinant, of where remodeling occurs. Mechanical factors include microdamage and mechanical strain. A localized increase in strain results in a corresponding local increase in BF. This mechanism could apply to the increase in bone density in the dominant (but not the nondominant) arm of a tennis player. Conversely, the localized decrease in strain that occurs in immobilization or in the weightlessness of space flight is accompanied by decreased BF, and thus leads to bone loss.[38,39]

3. *Coupling: the balance between the amount of bone resorbed and formed at a given site.* This balance is determined by the efficiency of the coupling mechanism (i.e., the coupling or entraining of BF to BR). The exis-

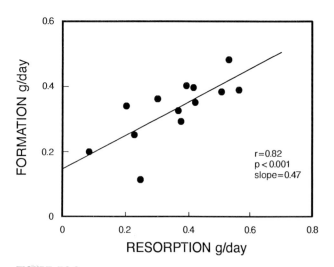

FIGURE 76-8

Relationship between bone formation and bone resorption in postmenopausal osteoporosis. The slope of 0.47 indicates poor coupling. (Appropriate coupling would give a slope of 1.0.) The coupling defect tends to be a fixed percentage of the bone resorption rate such that as the bone resorption rate increases, the amount of absolute bone loss also increases.

tence of such a mechanism has been known for many years,[40,41] but the mechanics of the phenomenon are only now beginning to be unraveled. A key finding regarding the mechanism was the demonstration in vitro that coupling is intrinsic to bone and is not dependent on systemic hormones.[42] Thus coupling is a local phenomenon occurring at discrete sites along the bone surface (Fig. 76-6). Another step toward the clarification of the coupling mechanism was the finding that GF are involved in this process. Accordingly, in vitro studies have disclosed that GF are released from bone substance during BR, and that this GF activity might function to stimulate the proliferation of Ob precursors which would ultimately differentiate and fill in the resorptive cavity.[31] As previously mentioned, the GF found in bone substances include IGF-I, IGF-II, PDGF, FGF, and TGF-β.[27–30] These GF probably account for the remarkable regenerative capacity of bone, as well as the coupling phenomenon.

Regulation of Bone Density

We propose that bone density is regulated by the coupling of BF to BR. Our hypothetical model of coupling is depicted in Fig. 76-6. The GF stored in matrix are released during the initial phase of BR and subsequently stimulate the proliferation and differentiation of nearby Ob precursors. When the osteoclastic resorptive phase is completed, this expanded pool of Ob then attaches to the walls of the resorptive cavity and produces bone to fill in the resorption cavity. The final extent of filling in of the resorption cavity is determined by the number of Ob created. The number of Ob created is determined by the amount of GF released by BR and, subsequently, by the amount of GF released from those contemporary Ob involved in filling in the resorption cavity. For example, exercise-mediated local increases in mechanical strain could enhance GF production by contemporary Ob and result in an actual overfill of the surface cavity. If the strain rates are unchanged, the fill-in would be normal as depicted. In contrast, during glucocorticoid excess the amount of resorption cavity fill-in (as evidenced by mean wall thickness*) is impaired.[43] Thus it is apparent that the final amount of cavity fill-in is dependent upon regulatory cues originating from outside the Ob, some from bone mechanical factors and others from systemic hormones.

There is strong evidence that coupling is impaired with aging, but the exact details of this impairment at the cellular and molecular levels are unknown. For example, the influence of age on the quantity of GF present in matrix and released by Ob has not yet been determined.

*Mean wall thickness is the width of bone formed during the total formation phase.

On the other hand, while there is no direct evidence that Ob synthesis or bone matrix concentration of GF decreases with aging, there is evidence that serum IGF-I (a GF produced by bone as well as other tissues) and growth hormone concentrations decrease with aging.[44,45] This evidence raises the possibility that production of local GF in bone may be decreased during aging, a change which could result in defective coupling of BF to BR and thus produce bone loss with aging.

PHYSIOLOGICALLY APPROPRIATE IMPAIRED COUPLING There are situations in which so-called impaired coupling is physiologically appropriate, namely during Ca or phosphate deficiency. If this were not the case, bone could not serve one of its most important functions, i.e., to provide a reservoir of mineral during times of Ca or phosphate deficiency. Thus, during Ca deficiency there is a deliberate attempt by Ca-regulating hormones to cause impaired coupling and in so doing release Ca from bone stores. Ca deficiency is an example of impaired coupling mediated by systemic factors (i.e., increased PTH and 1,25D, together with a decreased serum Ca). Physiologically appropriate impaired coupling can also originate from bone itself (i.e., the bone loss that occurs with immobilization). This is locally mediated, as evidenced by the fact that only the immobilized limb is affected. In the above three examples of physiologically appropriate impaired coupling, BR increase and BF fails to increase correspondingly. While we do not know the exact mechanism of this inadequate adaptive increase in BF, we do know that one of the most important bone GF, IGF-II, decreases in serum in rats which are immobilized.[46] This decrease would appear to represent a failure of GF production by contemporary Ob (steps C and D in Fig. 76-6), apparently due to inadequate mechanical tonic stimuli. Apart from these three examples, Ca deficiency, phosphate deficiency, and immobilization, all other types of impaired coupling are pathological.

PATHOLOGICAL IMPAIRED COUPLING Pathological impaired coupling causes inappropriate bone loss and ultimately leads to osteoporosis. In both sexes, peak bone density is achieved at 20 to 40 years of age, and, subsequently, bone loss begins to occur at about 40 years of age (Fig. 76-9) and vertebral trabecular bone loss may occur even earlier in normal premenopausal women.[46a] By definition the cause is impaired coupling, but whether the impaired coupling is bone-mediated or systemically mediated is unknown. At present there are no known systemic factors which would account for this defect.

Females In females the primary age-related coupling defect occurs at about 50 years of age (at the menopause)

(Fig. 76-9) and is due to estrogen deficiency. Several hypotheses have been advanced to explain the mechanism whereby estrogen deficiency causes bone loss. We have integrated the pertinent information on estrogen into the model shown in Fig. 76-10. This model incorporates three major mechanisms:

1. *Increased bone resorption.* Recently, estrogen receptors have been found on Ob but not on Oc.[47,48] Thus, estrogen may modulate the action of Ob to regulate BR (by perturbation of the Ob chemical resorptive signals to Oc and their precursors) such that a deficiency of estrogen could impair this regulation and lead to accelerated BR. Regarding potential resorptive signals from Ob, estrogen deficiency could: (1) increase 1,25D, GM-CSF, IL-1, or IL-3, which are produced by Ob and which stimulate proliferation of Oc precursors or (2) decrease TGF-β, which is produced by Ob and which inhibits the proliferation of Oc precursors.[35a] The latter possibility is supported by the finding that estrogen stimulates TGF-β production by Ob.[49]
2. *Impaired coupling of BF to the increased BR.* Estrogens are now known to stimulate GF production by Ob[49] such that a deficiency of estrogen could impair GF production and thereby lead to impaired coupling.
3. *Counterregulatory negative calcium balance.* According to our model, the negative Ca balance is the result, not the cause, of bone loss, i.e., it is the result of serum Ca homeostatic adjustments to unload the Ca released by the increased net BR.

These effects of estrogen deficiency result in a rapid loss of bone throughout the skeleton. This rapid bone loss abates after about 5 to 10 years, at which time bone loss still occurs but less rapidly (Fig. 76-10). Why estrogen deficiency causes this rapid bone loss and why the rate of loss decreases in 5 to 10 years is unknown. Perhaps estrogen controls a specific fraction of the total skeleton, and once that fraction is gone estrogen deficiency is without further effect; or perhaps the mechanical consequences of the rapid bone loss invoke compensatory bone changes which retard further bone loss. In any case, the ability of estrogen therapy to prevent this bone loss emphasizes the fact that these skeletal changes are mediated specifically by estrogen deficiency.

In females, the third phase of bone loss begins at about 65 years of age and occurs at a rate which is slower than that seen during the second or postmenopausal phase. It seems likely that there are several factors contributing to bone loss during this third phase. One important factor is the Ca deficiency which arises as a result of a low Ca intake and decreased efficiency of Ca absorption. In this phase of bone loss the PTH is high, consis-

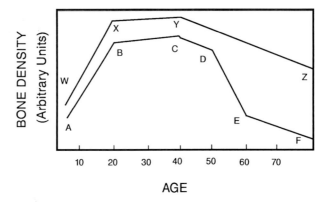

FIGURE 76-9
Schematic representation of the life span changes in bone density in males and females. The graphic demonstrates the following: (1) there is a rapid rise of bone density during puberty in both sexes (A–B in females, W–X in males); (2) males (X and Y) achieve a higher peak bone density than do females (B and C); (3) there is a gradual loss of density in both sexes beginning at 40 years of age (C–D in females); (4) the rate of bone loss increases dramatically at the menopause (D–E); (5) in females at about 60 years of age there is a decline in the rate of bone loss (E–F); and (6) in males there is a relatively constant rate of bone loss from 40 to 65 years of age (Y–Z) with a possible accelerated loss for the years thereafter (see text).

tent with a Ca deficiency state (i.e., secondary hyperparathyroidism, as shown in Fig. 76-2), whereas in estrogen deficiency the serum PTH is low (Fig. 76-10) because the increased BR is non-PTH-mediated.

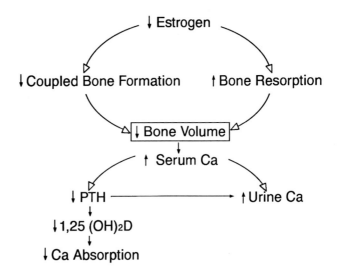

FIGURE 76-10
Model of mechanisms of bone loss and consequent counterregulatory effects in estrogen deficiency. Ob have estrogen receptors, and it is probable that the effects of estrogen deficiency are mediated by the Ob. Ob are known to produce resorptive signals which can act on Oc and Oc precursors. Estrogen deficiency may enhance these signals. Estrogen also stimulates Ob to secrete bone GF such that a deficiency of estrogen could impair coupling. The increase in BR with impaired coupling of BF to BR leads to bone loss, which in turn invokes serum calcium counterregulatory mechanisms to prevent the enhanced calcium release to increase serum calcium. (See text for details.)

Again, the fact that bone loss occurs means that there is impaired coupling. The question is whether the impaired coupling is or is not physiologically appropriate. Ca deficiency does lead to physiologically appropriate impaired coupling, but probably only when the Ca deficiency is moderate to severe. In young adults, mild Ca deficiency probably results in conservation of Ca by gut and kidney such that very little Ca is lost from bone. Additionally in young adults with mild Ca deficiency, serum Ca regulation tends to increase BR, but this increase is successfully opposed by the bone density regulation (i.e., the bone-coupling mechanism), which limits the bone loss from its reservoir. However, during aging there is a defect in the ability of PTH to increase serum 1,25D, a change which during a low Ca stress would limit the participation of gut and enhance the participation of bone in serum Ca regulation. Based on these considerations, the poor coupling seen in the elderly as a result of mild Ca deficiency would appear to be pathological. In addition, during aging there may be several causes of impaired coupling, including a specific age-related defect in the coupling mechanism.

Males In males, bone loss begins at about 40 years of age and continues at the same slow rate until about 65 years of age, at which time it may accelerate somewhat (Fig. 76-9). At the present time there are insufficient longitudinal data to establish such an accelerated bone loss phase. On the other hand, an accelerated bone loss would not be surprising since both testosterone deficiency and Ca deficiency begin to manifest themselves at this time.

Males begin to show a decrease in serum testosterone at about 65 years of age. This gonadal hormone deficiency in males differs in two ways from that seen in females: (1) not all men have a decrease in testosterone and (2) the decrease in testosterone is gradual, extending over a period of years. Accordingly, not all men become testosterone-deficient with age, and those that do express variable degrees of deficiency. Although it is now well established that testosterone deficiency is a risk factor for bone loss, much less is known about the specific pathophysiological effects of testosterone than of estrogen on skeletal tissue.

There is evidence that testosterone deficiency, like estrogen deficiency, is associated with an increase in BR.[50] Moreover, testosterone appears to be more anabolic for bone cells than estrogen; thus, testosterone deficiency would be expected to impair BF.[39] This could explain how testosterone deficiency impairs the coupled increase in BF in response to the attending increase in BR. In summary, testosterone deficiency clearly causes bone loss, and the information available about the actions of testosterone deficiency suggests that these actions are qualitatively similar to those of estrogen.

The other major known risk factor for bone loss with aging in men, particularly those over 70 years old, is Ca deficiency. The causes of Ca deficiency in elderly males have not been as well defined as the causes of Ca deficiency in elderly women; however, it has been established that in males, as in females, the efficacy of Ca absorption decreases with age. In addition, it seems likely that the other factors leading to Ca deficiency in females also apply to males. In any case, serum PTH increases with aging in males, and it seems likely that Ca deficiency strongly contributes to this change.

Genetic Influences on Bone Density

Bone loss by itself has no practical significance. During the aging process the significance of bone loss is that it weakens the skeleton and increases the risk of fractures; therefore, in this chapter we have focused on bone loss and its mechanisms. However, whether bone loss will weaken the skeleton depends on not only the loss rate but also the bone density at the start of the losing process. Thus, as a final point, this section deals briefly with peak bone density.

There is considerable variation in the bone density in elderly individuals. This residual bone density is the result of complex interactions of peak bone density, hormonal status, and lifestyle determinants such as nutrition and exercise, as well as the age-related changes in Ca and bone metabolism. As described above, bone density in a given individual is determined by the peak bone density at skeletal maturity and the subsequent rates of bone loss with aging. Subjects with a lower peak bone density are at risk for fractures at a younger age (Fig. 76-11). Twin studies demonstrate a strong genetic component in juvenile twins indicating that peak bone

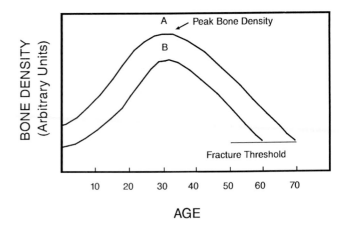

FIGURE 76-11
Effect of peak bone density on the age the patient will become at risk for fracture (i.e., when the fracture threshold will be reached). Individual B, with a lower peak bone density than that of A, but with a rate of bone loss similar to A, would reach the fracture threshold 10 years earlier than A.

density has a hereditary component.[51,52] On the other hand, the genetic influence decreases with aging.[53,54] Thus, genetic factors appear to be more dominant in the development of peak bone density, while environmental and hormonal factors appear to be more dominant in the loss of bone density.

REFERENCES

1. Corvilain J et al: Calcium homeostasis and pathogenesis of hypercalcemia. *Horm Res* 20:8, 1984.
2. Stewart AF: Calcium metabolism without anguish. *Postgrad Med* 77:2831, 1985.
3. Gallagher JC et al: Intestinal calcium absorption and serum vitamin D metabolites in normal subjects and osteoporotic patients. *J Clin Invest* 64:729, 1979.
4. Heaney RP et al: Calcium nutrition and bone health in the elderly. *Am J Clin Nutr* 36:986, 1982.
5. Recker RR: Calcium absorption and achlorhydria. *N Engl J Med* 313:70, 1985.
6. Newcomer AD et al: Lactase deficiency: Prevalence in osteoporosis. *Ann Intern Med* 89:218, 1978.
7. Arnaud CD et al: Influence of immunoheterogeneity of circulating parathyroid hormone results of radioimmunoassays of serum in man. *Am J Med* 56:785, 1974.
8. Gallagher JC et al: The effect of age on serum immunoreactive parathyroid hormone in normal and osteoporotic women. *J Lab Clin Med* 95:373, 1980.
9. Insogna KL et al: Effect of age on serum immunoreactive parathyroid hormone and its biological effects. *J Clin Endocrinol Metab* 53:1072, 1981.
10. Young G et al: Age-related rise in parathyroid hormone in man: The use of intact and midmolecule antisera to distinguish hormone secretion from retention. *J Bone Miner Res* 2:367, 1987.
11. Forero MS et al: Effect of age on circulating immunoreactive and bioactive parathyroid hormone levels in women. *J Bone Miner Res* 2:363, 1987.
12. Epstein S et al: The influence of age on bone mineral regulating hormones. *Bone* 7:421, 1986.
13. DeLuca HF: The vitamin D story: A collaborative effort of basic science and clinical medicine. *FASEB J* 2:224, 1988.
14. Bell NH: Vitamin D-endocrine system. *J Clin Invest* 76:1, 1985.
15. Sheikh MS et al: Role of vitamin D–dependent and vitamin D–independent mechanisms in absorption of food calcium. *J Clin Invest* 81:126, 1988.
16. Baylink DJ et al: Vitamin D and bone formation in mineralization, in Norman AW, Schaefer K, Herrath D, Grigoleit HG (eds): *Chemical, Biochemical, and Clinical Endocrinology of Calcium Metabolism.* Berlin, W. deGruyter, 1982, p. 363.
17. Maierhofer WJ et al: Bone resorption stimulated by elevated serum 1: 25-(OH)$_2$-vitamin D concentrations in healthy men. *Kidney Int* 24:555, 1983.
18. Lamberg-Allardt C: The relationship between serum 25-hydroxyvitamin D levels and other variables related to Ca and phosphorus metabolism in the elderly. *Acta Endocrinol* 105:139, 1984.
19. Fujisawa Y et al: Role of change in vitamin D metabolism with age in calcium and phosphorus metabolism in normal human subjects. *J Clin Endocrinol Metab* 59:719, 1984.
20. Greenspan SL et al: Osteoporosis in men with hyperprolactinemic hypogonadism. *Ann Intern Med* 104:777, 1986.
21. Slovik DM et al: Deficient production of 1,25-dihydroxyvitamin D in elderly osteoporotic patients. *N Engl J Med* 305:372, 1981.
22. Ziegler R et al: Calcitonin in human pathophysiology. *Horm Res* 20:65, 1984.
23. Tiegs RD et al: Calcitonin secretion in postmenopausal osteoporosis. *N Engl J Med* 312:1097, 1985.
24. Parfitt AM: Bone remodeling and bone loss: Understanding the pathophysiology of osteoporosis. *Clin Obstet Gynecol* 30:789, 1987.
25. Weinstein RS, Hutson MS: Decreased trabecular width and increased trabecular spacing contribute to bone loss with age. *Bone* 8:137, 1987.
26. Bergot C et al: Measurement of anisotropic vertebral trabecular bone loss during aging by quantitative image analysis. *Calcif Tissue Int* 43:143, 1988.
27. Hauschka PV et al: Growth factors in bone matrix. *J Biol Chem* 261:12665, 1986.
28. Linkhart TA et al: Characterization of mitogenic activities extracted from bovine bone matrix. *Bone* 7:479, 1986.
29. Mohan S et al: Identification and quantification of four distinct growth factors stored in human bone matrix. *J Bone Miner Res* 2(suppl 1):44(abstract), 1987.
30. Seyedin SM et al: Purification and characterization of two cartilage inducing factors from bovine demineralized bone. *Proc Natl Acad Sci USA* 82:2267, 1985.
31. Farley JR et al: In vitro evidence that bone formation may be coupled to resorption by release of mitogen(s) from resorbing bone. *Metabolism* 36:314, 1987.
32. Frost HM: *Bone Remodelling Dynamics.* Springfield, IL, Charles C. Thomas, 1963.
33. Howard GA et al: Human bone cells in culture metabolize 25(OH)D$_3$ to 1,25(OH)$_2$D$_3$ and 24,25(OH)$_2$D$_3$. *J Biol Chem* 256:7738, 1981.
34. Felix R et al: Production of hemopoietic growth factors by bone tissue and bone cells in culture. *J Bone Miner Res* 3:27, 1988.
35. Pfeilschifter J et al: Transforming growth factor beta inhibits bone resorption in fetal rat long bone cultures. *J Clin Invest* 82:680, 1988.
35a. Chenu C et al: Transforming growth factor beta inhibits formation of osteoclast-like cells in long-term human marrow culture. *Proc Natl Acad Sci USA* 85:5683, 1988.
36. McSheehy PMJ, Chambers TJ: Osteoblast-like cells in the presence of parathyroid hormone release soluble factor that stimulates osteoclastic bone resorption. *Endocrinology* 119:1654, 1986.
37. Eriksen EF: Normal and pathological remodeling of human trabecular bone: Three dimensional reconstruction of remodeling sequence in normals and in metabolic bone disease. *Endocr Rev* 7:379, 1986.
38. Globus, RK et al: The temporal response of bone to unloading. *Endocrinology* 118:733, 1986.
39. Minaire P et al: Quantitative histological data on disuse osteoporosis. *Calcif Tissue Res* 17:57, 1974.

40. Harris WH, Heaney RP: Skeletal renewal and metabolic bone disease. *N Engl J Med* 280:193, 1969.

41. Frost HM: *Bone Biodynamics.* Boston, Little, Brown, 1964.

42. Howard GA et al: Parathyroid hormone stimulates bone formation and resorption in organ culture: Evidence for a coupling mechanism. *Proc Natl Acad Sci USA* 78:3204, 1981.

43. Bressot C et al: Histomorphometric profile, pathophysiology and reversibility of corticosteroid-induced osteoporosis. *Metab Bone Res Rel Res* 1:303, 1979.

44. Bennett AE et al: Insulin-like growth factors I and II: Aging and bone density in women. *J Clin Endocrinol Metab* 59:701, 1984.

45. Hammerman MR: Insulin-like growth factors and aging. *Endocrinol Metab Clin North Am* 16:995, 1987.

46. Sibonga J et al: Impairment of bone formation (BF) in response to skeletal unloading is associated with a skeletal growth factor (SGF) deficit. *J Bone Miner Res* 3(suppl 1):502(abstract), 1988.

46a. Buchanan JR et al: Early vertebral trabecular bone loss in normal premenopausal women. *J Bone Miner Res* 3:583, 1988.

47. Eriksen EF et al: Evidence of estrogen receptors in normal human osteoblast-like cells. *Science* 241:84, 1988.

48. Komm BS et al: Estrogen binding, receptor mRNA, and biologic response in osteoblast-like osteosarcoma cells. *Science* 241:81, 1988.

49. Gray TK et al: Estrogen may mediate its effects on bone cells by signalling the elaboration of growth factors. *J Bone Miner Res* 3(suppl 1):552(abstract), 1988.

50. Foresta C et al: Osteoporosis and decline of gonadal function in the elderly male. *Horm Res* 19:18, 1984.

51. Dequeker J et al: Genetic determinants of bone mineral content at the spine and radius: A twin study. *Bone* 8:207, 1987.

52. Smith DM et al: Genetic factors in determining bone mass. *J Clin Invest* 52:2800, 1973.

53. Moller M et al: Metacarpal morphometry in monozygotic and dizygotic elderly twins. *Calcif Tissue Int* 25:197, 1978.

54. Christian JC et al: Heritability of adult bone density and the loss of bone mass in aging male twins. *J Bone Miner Res* 3(suppl 1):583(abstract), 1988.

Chapter 77

OSTEOPOROSIS

Charles H. Chesnut III

Primary osteoporosis, which is postmenopausal in the female and senile in the male, and secondary osteoporosis, which is associated with other diseases or medications (Cushing's disease, corticosteroids, etc.), are the most common of the metabolic bone diseases in the elderly. A classification of such osteoporoses is noted in Table 77-1.

DEFINITION

Common to all osteoporotic conditions is a reduction of bone mass and bone mass per unit volume to a level leading to fracture, especially of the vertebrae, distal radius, and proximal femur. *Skeletal osteopenia* generally refers to bone mass reduction, while *osteoporosis* usually refers to bone mass reduction to a point of fracture, although it is obvious that the application of the two terms may differ only by a fall or other appropriate trauma. While bone mass is reduced in osteoporosis, current data suggest that the bone composition which is present is essentially normal,[1] although bone architecture may be compromised.[2]

EPIDEMIOLOGY

Osteoporosis is a public health problem of epidemic proportions, particularly for the elderly. An estimated 1.3 million fractures per year are attributable to osteoporosis in the United States alone.[3] In 1985, 247,000 hip fractures occurred in the United States; such fractures carry a 5 to 20 percent excess mortality during the year after the fracture. Eight percent of women currently 35 years old will experience a hip fracture in later life. Economically, the expenses of osteoporotic fractures are overwhelming; direct and indirect costs of osteoporosis (including lost productivity, long-term nursing care, etc.) were estimated to be 7 to 10 billion dollars in 1986. The morbidity of the osteoporotic fracture, particularly of the hip, is considerable for both the elderly individual as well as for society, as the deterioration in the quality of life following fracture may be catastrophic.

PATHOGENESIS

Osteoporosis is a heterogeneous disease of multiple etiologies. In secondary osteoporosis, the pathogenesis of bone mass loss and fractures may be readily apparent (e.g., corticosteroid excess in Cushing's disease); in primary osteoporosis the exact pathogenesis may be more difficult to define. The pathogenesis of primary osteoporosis, however, may be approached from the standpoint of osteopenia and osteoporosis as defined previously. Osteopenia may be due to multiple causes, including inadequate bone mass at skeletal maturity (age 12 to 21 for females), and/or to subsequent age-related and postmenopausal bone loss. Regardless of the pathogenesis of the osteopenia, osteoporosis with fracture is *principally* due to low bone mass; it should, however, be noted that other determinants of fracture include bone quality (trabecular architecture and the ability to heal microfractures) and propensity to fall (see Fig. 77-1). The latter determinant is most important for the elderly, since decreased neuromuscular coordination, as well as such environmental factors as medication-induced confusion/

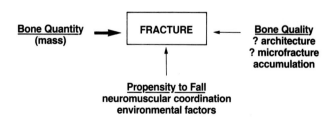

FIGURE 77-1
Determinants of osteoporotic fracture, including bone quality and propensity to fall. *(From Chesnut CH: Osteoporosis, in DeLisa J (ed): Rehabilitation Medicine: Principles and Practice. Philadelphia, Lippincott, 1988, p 866, with permission.)*

TABLE 77-1
Classification of the Osteoporoses

Primary Osteoporosis (basic etiology unknown, no associated disease)
    Postmenopausal osteoporosis (elderly females)
    Senile osteoporosis (elderly males)
Secondary Osteoporosis (secondary to heritable or acquired abnormalities/diseases, or to physiological abnormality)
    Hyperparathyroidism
    Cushing's disease
    Multiple myeloma
    Hyperthyroidism, endogenous and iatrogenic
    Idiopathic hypercalciuria:
        Due to renal calcium leak
        Due to renal phosphate leak
    Malabsorption (including partial gastrectomy)
    25(OH) D deficiency:
        Due to chronic liver disease
        Due to chronic anticonvulsant therapy (diphenylhydantoin, barbiturates)
    1,25(OH)$_2$ D deficiency due to lack of renal synthesis, associated with chronic renal failure
    Adult hypophosphatasia
    Chronic renal failure (renal osteodystrophy)
    Chronic hepatic failure (hepatic osteodystrophy)
    Osteogenesis imperfecta tarda
    Male hypogonadism (Klinefelter's syndrome)
    Female hypogonadism (Turner's syndrome)
    Conditions consistent with hypoestrogenism secondary to anorexia and/or exercise:
        Anorexia nervosa
        Exercise-induced amenorrhea
    Conditions associated with disuse:
        Paraplegia/hemiplegia
        Immobilization
        Prolonged bed rest
    Alcoholism
    Diabetes mellitus (?)
    Rheumatoid arthritis
    Chronic obstructive pulmonary disease
    Systemic mastocytosis
    Associated with the usage of the following medications:
        Corticosteroids
        Heparin
        Anticonvulsants (as noted above)
        Excess thyroid hormone replacement (as noted above)
    Hemochromatosis
    Malignancy

SOURCE: Adapted from Chesnut CH: Osteoporosis, in DeLisa J (ed): *Rehabilitation Medicine: Principles and Practice.* Philadelphia, Lippincott, 1988, pp 865–875.

dizziness and the use of throw rugs, will increase the occurrence of falls. As a fracture determinant, the increased number and traumatic severity of falls in the elderly population may be of equal importance to bone quantity and quality.

The pathogenetic basis of inadequate bone mass, particularly in the elderly, may also be considered from

the standpoint of *tissue, hormonal,* and *cellular abnormalities.* The basic abnormality in all types of osteoporosis is a disturbance of the normal bone remodeling sequences at the *tissue* level. To fully understand the pathogenesis of osteoporosis, therefore, a knowledge of bone remodeling is necessary (Fig. 77-2).

Bone is constantly turning over (remodeling); the skeleton acts as a reservoir for calcium, and the remodeling process provides calcium to the organism without sacrificing the skeleton. As noted in Fig. 77-2*B,* an increase in bone resorption as mediated by the osteoclast (the bone cell primarily responsible for bone resorption) is the initial event in normal bone remodeling. This event is typically followed within 40 to 60 days by an increase in bone formation as mediated by the osteoblast (the bone cell primarily responsible for bone formation). Bone resorption and formation are normally and homeostatically coupled: an increase or decrease in resorption produces a corresponding increase or decrease in formation with no net change in bone mass. However, in postmenopausal and probably senile osteoporosis, as noted in Fig. 77-2*C,* bone resorption is increased over normal resorption levels without a corresponding increase in bone formation, leading to a net loss in bone mass. In other forms of osteoporosis, such as corticosteroid-induced osteoporosis, a primary decrease in bone formation may occur as noted in Fig. 77-2*D,* with a similar result in either situation (Fig. 77-2*C* or 77-2*D*) of a loss of bone mass leading to an increased risk for fracture. Such abnormalities of bone remodeling at the tissue level may therefore contribute to the pathogenesis of the disease.

The etiology of such an increase in bone resorption in osteoporosis is unclear, but it is undoubtedly related to *hormonal* alterations. Changes in a number of hormonal modalities (estrogen, parathyroid hormone, calcitonin, and the D metabolites) affect bone cell function and bone mass. While there are numerous age- and menopause-related alterations in the physiology of such

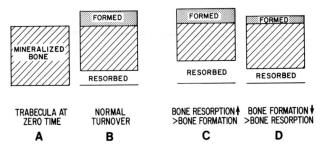

FIGURE 77-2
Pathogenesis of osteoporosis at the tissue level. A disruption of normal bone-remodeling sequences: *A* and *B* denote a bone trabecula at 0 time and with normal bone turnover, respectively; *C* and *D* denote two possible mechanisms of abnormal bone remodeling. *(From Chesnut CH, Kribbs PJ: Osteoporosis: Some aspects of pathophysiology and therapy. J Prosthet Dent 48:407, 1982, with permission.)*

hormones, a pathogenetic hormonal abnormality specific for osteoporosis (excluding the osteopenias associated with hypercorticism) has rarely been defined. Estrogen deficiency is, however, most frequently incriminated in the pathogenesis of postmenopausal osteoporosis; indeed, estrogen deficiency of any etiology, including early oophorectomy,[4] exercise- or anorexia-induced amenorrhea,[5] and the postmenopausal state, is associated with bone mass loss. The specific mechanism of estrogen's effect on bone is unclear, although estrogen receptors have recently been noted in osteoblast-like cells.[6,7] A reasonable hypothesis for estrogen's effect is its apparent ability to decrease bone resorption, possibly by decreasing the responsiveness of the osteoclast to endogenous circulating immunoreactive parathyroid hormone (iPTH).[8] Such a decreased responsiveness of the osteoclast may be mediated through signals from the osteoblast (with its postulated estrogen receptors). Estrogen deficiency from any cause would then result in increased skeletal responsiveness to PTH, increased bone resorption, a subsequent transient increase in serum calcium, and a resultant decrease in iPTH secretion. With such a decrease in iPTH, a reduction in formation of the active form of vitamin D, $1,25(OH)_2$ cholecalciferol would be expected (the renal $1\,\alpha$-hydroxylase enzyme requires PTH for its action), and a consequent decrease in calcium absorption would then occur.[9] A number of such hormonal perturbations are indeed documented in osteoporotic populations; however, all postmenopausal females are relatively estrogen-deficient, but not all develop osteoporosis. Menopause and its subsequent estrogen deficiency is therefore an incomplete pathogenetic explanation for postmenopausal osteoporosis; it also does not explain senile osteoporosis.

In approximately 10 percent of osteoporotic women, iPTH levels are increased, and in these patients PTH may be related causally to bone loss through an increase in bone resorption. In the majority of postmenopausal osteoporotic females, however, PTH levels are normal or low compared to those of normal elderly females; as noted previously, a low serum PTH may have a permissive or sustaining pathogenetic role in maintaining bone mass loss (through decreased $1,25(OH)_2$ D production). However, the overall contribution of PTH to the pathogenesis of osteoporosis is unclear.

A number of abnormalities of two additional calciotrophic hormones, vitamin D and calcitonin, also occur with aging. Decreased serum levels of $1,25(OH)_2$ D and impaired conversion of $25(OH)$ D to $1,25(OH)_2$ D have been noted in the aged; however, a vitamin D abnormality specific for osteoporosis (rather than simply for aging) has not been fully defined. A postulated defect in osteoporosis of the renal $1\,\alpha$-hydroxylation of $25(OH)$ D in response to PTH has been proposed[10] but not conclusively proved.[11] Nevertheless, calcium absorption does decrease with aging and is even

lower in patients with postmenopausal osteoporosis.[12] A deficiency of the hormone calcitonin could also contribute to ongoing bone loss; calcitonin inhibits osteoclast activity and may thus decrease osteoclastic bone resorption. While serum levels of immunoreactive calcitonin are indeed lower in women than in men and decrease with age, a decreased calcitonin secretion in osteoporotic women, as compared to secretion in normal aged women, has not been conclusively proved.[13,14] The pathogenetic roles in osteoporosis of the D metabolites and calcitonin are unclear.

Conclusive evidence of *cellular* abnormalities contributing to the pathogenesis of osteoporosis is also lacking, principally due to an inability to define bone cell (osteoblast, osteoclast, or osteocyte) abnormalities which are specific for osteoporosis and separate from bone cell abnormalities which may occur with aging alone. As noted previously in the discussion of bone remodeling, it may be that failure of the osteoblast, due to either decreased cell number or decreased cell activity, may accompany advancing age, but such failure is not specific for osteoporosis.

In conclusion, the specific pathogenesis of osteoporosis is quite possibly a combination of heretofore undefined cellular, hormonal, and tissue abnormalities; such abnormalities, however, all contribute to a deficiency of bone mass, which, in combination with other previously noted determinants, may result in bone loss and subsequent osteoporotic fractures.

RISK FACTORS

Multiple risk factors (Table 77-2) may act independently or in combination to produce diminished bone mass in an individual patient. Presumably the presence of one or more of these risk factors in the elderly increases the risk of accelerated bone loss and subsequent fracture; the weighting of each of these risk factors in terms of relative etiological importance in osteoporosis is undefined, although presumably in the elderly female estrogen depletion, calcium deficiency (either decreased calcium intake or decreased efficiency of calcium absorption), diminished peak bone mass in adolescence, and diminished physical activity are the most important.

In senile osteoporosis in males, alcoholism and testosterone depletion must be considered as significant risk factors; in the elderly male, however, the specific etiology of osteopenia and osteoporosis may be difficult to define.[15]

CLINICAL PRESENTATION

A fracture of the proximal femur, the distal forearm, the ribs, and especially the vertebrae, associated typically with minimal trauma, is usually the first clinical indica-

TABLE 77-2
**Factors Contributing to the Risk of Osteopenia/
Osteoporosis in the Elderly**

Estrogen depletion (in the female):
  Postmenopausal state (natural or artificial)
  History of athletic amenorrhea, anorexia nervosa, oligo-
    menorrhea, etc.
Calcium deficiency
Diminished peak bone mass at skeletal maturity; varies with
  sex, race, and heredity
Diminished physical activity
Testosterone depletion (in males)
Aging
Leanness (adipose tissue is the major source of postmeno-
  pausal extragonadal estrogen production)
Alcoholism
Smoking
Excessive dietary protein intake (resulting in increased loss
  of calcium in the urine)
Medications (corticosteroids, excessive thyroid hormone,
  prolonged heparin usage)

SOURCE: Adapted from Chesnut CH: Osteoporosis, DeLisa J (ed): *Rehabilitation Medicine: Principles and Practice.* Philadelphia, Lippincott, 1988, pp 865–875.

tion of osteoporosis, both primary and secondary. While hip, rib, and forearm fractures present with obvious pain symptoms, in some patients vertebral fractures may occur asymptomatically. More frequently, however, there will be acute onset of pain in the area of the affected vertebra, with lateral pain radiation, paravertebral muscle spasm, and tenderness to percussion over the vertebra. Such pain may persist for 6 to 8 weeks and then subside until the next fracture occurs. The persistence of pain beyond 6 months at the site of previous vertebral fractures suggests etiologies other than osteoporosis for the pain complex (e.g., psychiatric, medical/legal, or pathological-metastatic etiologies). In some individuals, typically those who are postmenopausal, the disease may relentlessly progress with 4 to 6 spinal fractures occurring; the etiology of this progressive form of osteoporosis is unclear, but it seems to occur in younger women (age 50 to 60) and may be associated with an accelerated trabecular bone loss. It is unlikely that osteoporosis produces pain in the absence of fracture, although it is possible that painful vertebral microfractures may develop; such microfractures may not be seen on x ray but may be detected on radionuclide bone scan.

Kyphosis ("dowager's hump" deformity), loss of height, and chronic back pain (mid-thoracic or lumbosacral) presumably secondary to mechanical deformity and paraspinous muscle spasm, may result from collapsed or severely wedged vertebrae. In addition, with progressive spinal deformity and height loss, abdominal protuberance and gastrointestinal discomfort (constipation) may occur, as well as a degree of pulmonary insuffi-

ciency secondary to thoracic cage deformity. In some severely affected individuals, the spinal deformity is sufficient to produce a painful rubbing of the lower ribs on the iliac crest.

DIAGNOSIS

Osteoporosis is diagnosed absolutely only in the presence of an atraumatic fracture of spine, femur, and/or distal radius. However, it is obviously of value from the standpoint of patient management to evaluate the patient at risk for fracture prior to the fracture occurring, as well as to determine the cause of the fracture in patients in whom a fracture has occurred. Prior to describing such a diagnostic evaluation, a brief outline of techniques available for invasively and noninvasively measuring the quantity and quality of bone mass is indicated, as such techniques are currently an integral part of the diagnostic osteoporosis workup.

PRINCIPLES OF THE MEASUREMENT OF BONE MASS QUANTITY AND QUALITY

As noted previously, bone mass is the primary, although not the sole, determinant of fracture; theoretically, therefore, measurements of bone mass quantity and quality would be of value in patients with bone-wasting diseases such as osteoporosis in predicting the risk of fracture, assessing the severity of bone wasting, and assessing the response of bone to treatment.[16–19] Procedures currently available for quantitation of bone mass include single- and dual-photon absorptiometry (SPA and DPA), x-ray densitometry (XD), computer tomography (CT), and total body calcium by neutron activation analysis (TBC-NAA). Measurement of ultrasound (US) velocity/speed can theoretically both quantitate bone mass and measure its quality.[20] Usage of SPA, DPA, XD, and CT provide quantitations of bone mass at the axial and appendicular sites, which are the principal areas usually involved in osteoporosis (e.g., the spine, wrist, and hip); in addition, it is also possible to quantitate bone mass at the os calcis (using SPA) and throughout the entire skeleton (using TBC-NAA or DPA), and possibly to qualitate and quantitate bone mass at the patella (using US).

The invasive technique of iliac crest bone biopsy (BX) may quantitate bone mass at this site; in addition, some aspects of bone quality can be assessed. It should be kept in mind that x rays of the spine are quite insensitive for quantitating bone mass, since 30 to 35 percent of bone mass must be lost before radiographic demineralization is detected. On the other hand, the x ray is obviously the primary discriminant of the presence of osteoporosis (e.g., presence of a fracture) and in this sense provides the final diagnostic information regarding the presence or absence of osteoporotic disease. Anterior and posterior vertebral height loss are also presumably precursors of an absolute spinal compression fracture, and their presence would indicate some risk for osteoporosis that the practitioner, without access to bone-mass quantitating and qualitating techniques, may use in diagnostic deliberations.

The ideal noninvasive and invasive techniques would be those quantitating and possibly qualitating primarily trabecular bone, which is metabolically more active than cortical bone and may be preferentially altered in osteoporosis and by osteoporosis therapy. The spine and hip would be the sites targeted for measurement, as they are the sites most associated with osteoporosis morbidity, although obviously Colles' fracture of the wrist is a component of the osteoporosis disease spectrum. The ideal technique would also be one capable of discriminating between normal and osteoporotic populations and of identifying individuals at risk for fracture. Acceptable precision and accuracy, low radiation exposure, a reasonable cost, acceptability to patients, and applicability to assessing therapeutic response would be other features of the ideal noninvasive and invasive techniques.

SPECIFIC TECHNIQUES

The techniques described previously satisfy the ideal criteria to varying degrees (see Table 77-3). For instance,

SPA possesses a reasonable cost, precision, and low radiation exposure, but utilizes primarily a quantitation of cortical bone mass at the wrist, which is neither the site nor the type of bone usually involved in osteoporosis. No definitive evidence[21] exists that measurement of wrist bone mass significantly predicts hip or spine bone mass, or bone-mass change.[22] The DPA, XD, and CT techniques are therefore currently the most utilized methodologies, since they quantitate bone mass at the two principal target sites of osteoporosis, the spine and the hip. Measurement of the total skeleton with DPA and XD is available but is used primarily in research studies. The cost of DPA and CT is higher than with SPA; radiation dose is high with CT, although quite acceptable with DPA and XD; and quality control and patient logistics are acceptable with each of these techniques. Precision and accuracy are quite reasonable with DPA and XD, although in both, accuracy may be compromised in the elderly by the presence of extraskeletal calcification, such as osteophytes and aortic calcification. Marrow fat provides a significant accuracy error for single-energy CT; such an error may be corrected with dual-energy CT but with a subsequent decrease in precision and an increased radiation dose.

With DPA, XD, and CT, difficulties may arise in accuracy owing to previously compressed vertebral bodies, kyphosis, and vertebral sclerosis. DPA and XD quantitate both trabecular and cortical bone mass of the entire vertebral body, including the spinous and trans-

TABLE 77-3
Noninvasive and Invasive Techniques for Quantitating/Qualitating Bone Mass

Technique	Site Measured	Cortical/ Trabecular %	Precision/ Accuracy	Discrimination	Response to Therapy	Radiation	Cost	Remarks
SPA	Radius/ulna: (a)distal	80–95/20–25	±2–4%/ ± 3–4%	—	±*	10 mrem	$75–125	*estrogens
	(b)ultradistal	25/75	±2–4%/?	?	?			
	Os calcis	20/80	±2–4%/?	?	?			
DPA-XD	Spine:L1–L4*	35/65	±2–5%@/ ± 2–4%	±&	+&	10 mrem	$150–200#	*total vertebral body including spinous process @ XD 2% & XD? # XD $75
	Femur:neck	75/25	±3–5%/?	—	?	10 mrem	$50–75	
	:trochanter	50/50	±3–5%/?	+	?	10 mrem		
CT	Single-energy spine:T12–L4*	5/95	±3–5%/ ± 6–30%**	±	+	500–750 mrem	$125–175	*area of interest *within* vertebral body**? due to marrow fat
	Dual-energy spine:T12–L4*	5/95	±5–10%/ ± 5%	?	?	750 mrem	?	
TBC-NAA	Total skeleton	80/20	±2%/ ± 5%	±	+	2000 mrem	$750	
US	Patella, os calcis	?5/95	3–5%/?	±	?	—	$25–50	5-minute test
BX	Iliac crest	1° trabecular	15–25%/?	±	±	—	$500–600	invasive

SOURCE: Chesnut CH: Measurement of bone mass. *Triangle, Sandoz J Med Sci* 27:37, 1988. (Copyright Sandoz Ltd., Basle, Switzerland, with permission.)

verse processes, the posterior elements, and also calcification within surrounding tissues. CT measures almost exclusively trabecular bone within the vertebral body; in terms of fracture risk, such a measurement may provide a biologically more important quantitation of bone mass than a measurement of the entire vertebral body. Femoral bone mass may be measured at multiple sites with DPA and XD; precision and radiation exposure are acceptable. However, the contribution of bone-mass quantity to the risk of subsequent hip fracture is unknown.[23] XD provides improved precision, decreased scanning time, improved resolution, and possibly a lower procedure cost; preliminary results with this instrument indicate its definite potential to supplant other techniques for quantitating bone mass at the spine and hip. Although SPA, DPA, XD, and CT lack the ability to definitively discriminate between normal populations and populations with osteoporotic fractures,[24] all can be used to follow the response of bone mass to therapy.

TBC-NAA has been used in the past as a noninvasive research technique for assessing response to osteoporosis treatment. It is a precise and accurate procedure, but its high radiation dosage, cost, limited availability, predominantly cortical bone-mass measurement, and lack of definite discriminatory ability make it less acceptable than the other available techniques for widespread usage.

US provides a measurement of bone quantity and, presumably, bone quality in the patella and os calcis. At both these sites, the bone is primarily trabecular, and precision is acceptable (although accuracy is as yet undefined). In studies to date,[20] the discrimination of US is equivalent to that of SPA, DPA, and CT. An improved scanning time (3 to 5 minutes), a lower cost, and a lack of radiation exposure are US's putative assets.

BX quantitates primarily trabecular bone at the iliac crest. While useful information in terms of bone remodeling may be obtained about the mechanism of drug action on bone mass, BX would obviously not be utilized in the individual patient to follow response to treatment. Its poor precision and its cost, as well as the occasional side effects associated with its invasive nature, would prevent its widespread usage for quantitation of bone mass or for assessing treatment response. Indeed, its primary value in the individual patient is to exclude other diseases of bone wasting, such as osteomalacia, multiple myeloma, and hyperparathyroidism.

INDICATIONS FOR THE NONINVASIVE TECHNIQUES

When used appropriately, the noninvasive techniques (particularly DPA, XD, and CT) are of definite value in the clinical evaluation of the osteopenic or osteoporotic patient. The clinical situations in which they may be used are as follows:

1. In selected perimenopausal and postmenopausal patients in defining their risk for subsequent fracture, when combined with the assessment and presence of historical risk factors (see Table 77-2).
2. In defining the need for prophylactic estrogen therapy.
3. In screening for significant bone loss and conditions in which osteopenia is an accompanying manifestation, such as exercise-induced amenorrhea and steroid-induced osteopenia.
4. In following response to treatment.
5. In research endeavors, such as epidemiologic and clinical therapy studies.

At the present time, there appears to be little justification for the use of noninvasive bone-mass quantitating techniques in mass screening of all perimenopausal women[25–27] or in quantitating the severity and/or progression (exclusive of therapy) of disease in the osteoporotic patient.

DIAGNOSTIC EVALUATION OF THE PATIENT AT RISK FOR OSTEOPOROSIS

The at-risk patient (most frequently the immediately postmenopausal woman) requires a relatively brief evaluation:

1. A brief history to determine the absence of the medical conditions noted in Table 77-1 which result in secondary osteoporoses and to determine the presence of the risk factors noted in Table 77-2.
2. A brief physical examination to exclude the secondary osteoporoses (hyperthyroidism, Cushing's disease, etc.).
3. A minimal laboratory evaluation to include a determination of serum calcium, phosphorus, and alkaline phosphatase levels, as well as a 24-hour urine calcium/creatinine determination; however, the overall cost-benefit ratio of even these minimal procedures is unproven. In primary osteoporosis, laboratory tests typically are normal; such tests are utilized primarily to exclude other diseases (with the exception of urinary calcium, as noted below), and frequently such exclusion can be accomplished by the history and physical examination alone.
4. A measurement, noninvasively, of bone-mass quantity (and in the future, possibly bone-mass quality as well), usually at the spine (using DPA, XD, or CT), in the individual patient with positive risk factors. If such a bone-mass measurement is low, more aggressive prophylactic therapy (e.g., estrogen) may be indicated; if the measurement is normal, activity and increased calcium intake may be sufficient.

DIAGNOSTIC EVALUATION OF THE PATIENT WITH OSTEOPOROSIS (FRACTURES)

The patient with osteoporosis, most frequently a female in her late fifties, sixties, or seventies, may present with 1 to 6 vertebral fractures and requires a more thorough evaluation:

1. A complete history, again to determine the presence of risk factors and, specifically, to exclude medical conditions resulting in the secondary osteoporoses. In this elderly age group, the search for other diseases is most important, since multiple myeloma, hyperparathyroidism, and hyperthyroidism are not uncommon.

2. A more thorough physical examination is performed, but again it is primarily to exclude the secondary osteoporoses. In addition to the physical findings noted in the previous evaluation, alveolar ridge resorption resulting in dental osteopenia with missing teeth and dentures, as well as proximal muscle weakness and discomfort in osteomalacia, should also be kept in mind.

3. A maximal laboratory evaluation in this group may be indicated: serum ionized and total calcium, PTH, phosphorus, protein electrophoresis, complete blood count (CBC), and vitamin D congeners. A 24-hour urine collection for calcium/creatinine remains a mainstay of the evaluation of the osteoporotic patient; assessment of dietary calcium adequacy and dietary calcium gut absorption and the absence of idiopathic hypercalciuria (either due to a renal leak of calcium or to hyperabsorption of calcium at the gut level) can be obtained. If the urinary calcium level is low, either inadequate calcium intake or absorption, or a vitamin D abnormality, must be considered; if the value is high, either dietary calcium excess or idiopathic hypercalciuria is a possibility. A 24-hour urinary hydroxyproline sample and serum GLA protein (gamma-carboxyglutamic acid or osteocalcin, a noncollagenous bone protein measurable in serum) can also be obtained; they can monitor possible states of high bone remodeling, which may respond particularly to antiresorptive therapeutic agents. A low serum GLA protein and a low 24-hour urine hydroxyproline may indicate low remodeling and an inactive and senescent bone. Such a condition may respond more favorably to bone-forming therapies. Lastly, BX may be used primarily to exclude osteomalacia or other metabolic bone disease.

4. A noninvasive measurement of spinal bone mass will be of value as a baseline measurement to monitor response to treatment over time; such a measurement may also quantitate the severity of the disease, but such a quantitation should not be the primary indication for such a procedure.

DIAGNOSTIC EVALUATION OF THE OSTEOPOROTIC PATIENT WITH BACK PAIN

Acute and/or chronic back pain in the osteoporotic patient may be related to recent compression fractures, to mechanical derangement of the spine (such as kyphosis), and/or to paraspinous muscle spasm. As noted previously, the radionuclide bone scan can be used in the evaluation of back pain. Increased radionuclide accretion at the site of a recent fracture (usually a vertebral body, but also the hip) usually indicates ongoing bone formation and bone healing, although a fracture nonunion will also demonstrate increased radionuclide uptake. Normal radionuclide accretion indicates that healing is complete and that the metabolic activity at that site is normal. A positive scan correlates well with the presence of acute pain and indicates the need for continued aggressive therapies such as a back brace, analgesia, etc. A normal scan reflects reasonable healing and a subsequent lesser need for aggressive therapy; a bone scan typically returns to normal within 6 months after fracture. Continued back or hip pain in the presence of a normal bone scan suggests a nonskeletal origin of the pain, such as paraspinous muscle spasm. However, a positive bone scan with a negative x ray of the same spinal site, in the absence of metastatic disease, is a combination which may indicate a microfracture (stress fracture) of a vertebral body or proximal femur; such a microfracture may progress in time to a radiographically demonstrable macrofracture. Aggressive therapy, including short-term immobilization, may prevent completion of such an incipient fracture.

TREATMENT

Osteoporosis therapy may be divided into symptomatic treatment and treatment of the underlying disease (skeletal osteopenia/bone mass loss).

SYMPTOMATIC TREATMENT

Spinal compression fractures, due to either primary or secondary osteoporosis, may result in significant pain necessitating analgesia, limitation of activity, and a back support capable of reducing spinal movement and resultant pain. Such limitation of activity may involve short-term bed rest (3 to 5 days); it is imperative that extensive and prolonged bed rest with associated spinal immobilization (a situation in which bone resorption may exceed bone formation at the tissue level) be avoided so as to prevent increased bone wasting. In addition, should a back support be utilized, a flexible back brace is indicated; a rigid back brace with near-total spinal immobilization, while decreasing pain, may increase bone loss if used over an extensive period of time (months) and thus would be counterproductive.

The acute pain phase of spinal osteoporosis may last for 1 to 2 months; then the pain eventually lessens and the fractured vertebral body heals. In a number of patients, however, the acute pain phase may be replaced within 2 to 4 months following fracture by a particularly debilitating, chronic, and frequently severe lumbosacral discomfort.[28] Such discomfort may be secondary to lumbosacral muscle spasm, in turn produced by an accentuated lumbar lordosis compensating for the thoracic kyphosis resulting from fracture. Such a chronic pain phase may last for months; mild analgesia, muscle relaxants, heat, and rest periods in a reclining position will alleviate muscle spasm. A flexible lumbar back support (and time) will also be of value in managing this condition.

Concomitant with this period of acute and/or chronic back pain, a number of the specific pharmacological therapies noted below may be prescribed; it should be noted that such therapies (with the possible exception of calcitonin) are not expected to alleviate pain symptomatology, but rather to treat the underlying bone loss associated with osteoporosis. However, if such therapy can increase bone mass, or slow bone mass loss, further fracture may not occur; in the absence of fractures, pain symptomatology will usually, but not always, improve.

Symptomatic treatment of hip and wrist fractures is described in standard orthopedic texts.

TREATMENT OF BONE MASS DEFICIENCY (SKELETAL OSTEOPENIA/OSTEOPOROSIS)

Treatment of secondary osteoporoses may be accomplished by treatment of the underlying disease (e.g., alleviation of the hyperthyroid state). However, the ideal goal of treatment in any form of osteoporosis and osteopenia would be either prophylactic or restorative, depending on the patient's bone mass and fracture history. As an inadequate skeletal mass is the primary determinant of fracture risk in the osteopenic or osteoporotic patient, in an aging subject with relatively normal bone mass and no previous fracture, the therapeutic goal involves a slowing of age-related bone loss and maintenance of current bone mass. On the other hand, in subjects with a low bone mass and previous fracture, therapy should involve not only a slowing of age-related bone loss, but also restoration of bone previously lost.

Prevention of bone loss may be accomplished by a decrease in bone resorption if the process of bone formation is maintained at its normal level. A similar bone loss prevention will occur if bone formation decreases to the same degree as bone resorption, as no *net* change in bone mass will result. Restoration of previously lost bone mass, however, ideally requires both an increase in formation and a decrease in resorption, although an in-

crease in resorption with a greater increase in formation or a decrease in resorption with a lesser decrease in formation will also result in the desired *net* positive bone mass change.

As noted in Table 77-4, several therapeutic agents slow the loss of bone mass by decreasing bone resorption ("anti–bone resorbers"). The primary efficacy of such therapeutic modalities may be prophylactic, in that they prevent significant bone loss. Such anti–bone-resorbing agents, such as estrogen, would have their greatest therapeutic rationale in patients in whom bone mass has not decreased below a hypothetical fracture threshold, as is often seen immediately after the menopause (Fig. 77-3). In such a clinical situation, bone mass would be maintained above a fracture threshold and presumably would be sufficient to prevent fractures. On the other hand, the use of anti–bone-resorbing agents as single therapy in patients with osteoporotic fractures (and an associated lower bone mass) is of questionable value; an inadequate bone mass would be maintained, and without a restoration of previously lost bone mass, the patient would remain at risk for further fractures.

As also noted in Table 77-4, a number of therapeutic agents are capable of increasing bone formation ("positive bone formers"); such agents would restore previously lost bone mass and theoretically prevent further fractures. As shown in Fig. 77-3, such positive bone formers would increase bone mass and possibly elevate skeletal mass above the hypothetical fracture threshold, thus again decreasing the occurrence of future fractures. A combination of a positive bone-forming agent with an anti–bone-resorbing agent would be of particular value for the patient with osteoporotic fractures and low bone mass, as, according to this therapeutic rationale, it would both prevent further loss and replace bone previously lost.

TABLE 77-4

Therapeutic Agents for Osteoporosis to Slow Bone Loss and/or to Increase Bone Formation

Decreased Bone Resorption (Anti–bone-resorbers)
Calcium
Estrogen
Calcitonin
Bisphosphonates*
Increased Bone Formation (Positive bone formers)
Sodium fluoride*
Testosterone*
Anabolic steroids*
Exercise

* Experimental
SOURCE: Adapted from Chesnut CH: Osteoporosis, in DeLisa J (ed): *Rehabilitation Medicine: Principles and Practice.* Philadelphia, Lippincott, 1988, pp 865–875.

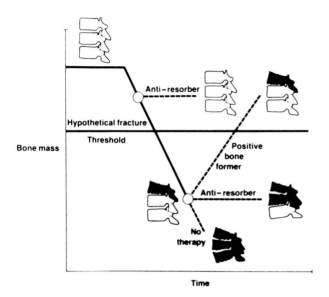

FIGURE 77-3
Therapy of osteoporosis based on bone mass; darker vertebrae represent compression fractures. *(From Chesnut CH: Treatment of postmenopausal osteoporosis. Compr Ther 10:41, 1984, with permission.)*

SPECIFIC THERAPIES (see Tables 77-4 and 77-5)

Calcium

A therapeutic rationale for calcium therapy in osteoporosis exists: calcium, which is a major component of hydroxyapatite crystal, presumably can decrease PTH-mediated bone resorption via a slight and transient elevation in serum calcium and therefore may function as an anti–bone resorber. Calcium absorption is low in osteoporotic women as compared to absorption levels in age-matched normal women; calcium intake is deficient in teenage, perimenopausal, and postmenopausal women in the United States. However, whether calcium is of value in preventing bone loss in all individuals over an extended period of time is unproven. Current data do support a decrease in hip fractures in patients receiving high calcium intakes[29,30] and an improvement in bone density at the iliac crest in patients who were previously calcium-deficient.[31] Other evidence, however, suggests that up to 2000 mg of calcium daily is not effective in preventing either cortical or trabecular bone loss[32] in the immediately menopausal woman.

It does appear that a significant proportion of the population, perhaps those individuals with chronically low calcium intake, responds to increasing calcium intake with bone-mass stabilization for a significant period of time; at the present time, however, it is impossible to identify these patients. It seems reasonable to ensure a calcium intake of a minimum of 1000 to 1500 mg per day in all perimenopausal and postmenopausal women[33]; calcium is generally safe (in the absence of previous neph-

TABLE 77-5
Specific Therapies

Medication	Usual Dosage*	Side Effects
Calcium	1000–1500 mg qd	↑ Urinary calcium
Multivitamin with D_2 or D_3	400 IU qd	None known
Estrogen	.625 mg qd (Premarin or equivalent) cycled 21/30 days with/ without progesterone	Endometrial carcinoma, thrombo-embolic disease
Calcitonin (salmon or synthetic)	50–100 IU units qd/ qod IM/sub Q (Calcimar or equivalent)	Flushing, local skin irritation
Bisphosphonates (EHDP)†	Not yet defined	Mild diar-rhea—mineral-ization defect?
Sodium fluoride†	44–88 mg qd	Gastric upset, tendonitis, arthritis, plantar fasciitis
Anabolic steroids (stanozolol†—Winstrol or equivalent)	2 mg tid cycled 3/4 weeks	↓ HDL, liver toxicity, masculiniz-ation

*Oral unless otherwise specified.
†Experimental therapy; not approved for usage by the FDA.
SOURCE: Adapted from Chesnut CH: Osteoporosis, in DeLisa J (ed): *Rehabilitation Medicine: Principles and Practice.* Philadelphia, Lippincott, 1988, pp 865–875.

rolithiasis or idiopathic hypercalciuria), comparatively inexpensive, and logistically simple to ingest. Milk and dairy products and calcium supplements are reasonable sources of calcium; calcium carbonate is currently perhaps the most efficacious calcium supplement, since 40 percent of this preparation is elemental calcium. Calcium citrate, however, has the postulated advantages of increased solubility in the urine and, possibly, increased bioavailability. The practitioner should remember that excessive calcium intake may result in elevated urinary calcium levels and, rarely, a predisposition to kidney stones and nephrocalcinosis; however, urinary calcium excretions of up to 250 mg per 24 hours are acceptable in persons without a history of nephrolithiasis.

Intermittent intravenous calcium infusion and thiazide diuretics have not proven to be efficacious in improving bone mass status. The putative rationale for thiazide usage would be a reduction in urinary calcium and a subsequent improvement in calcium balance.

Vitamin D

A multivitamin with 400 IU of vitamin D is a logical part of the prophylaxis and therapy of postmenopausal osteoporosis; a mild dietary vitamin D deficiency may exist in the elderly. Vitamin D (D_2 or D_3) dosages greater than 1000 IU/day are contraindicated for the treatment of postmenopausal or senile osteoporosis; PTH-mediated bone resorption may occur due to a permissive effect of vitamin D on PTH action. Unfortunately, current evidence with such active forms of vitamin D as $1,25(OH)_2 D$ does not support its usage in osteoporosis.[34]

Estrogens

The estrogen compounds are primarily anti–bone resorbers and they prevent bone-mass loss by decreasing the responsiveness of bone to PTH; a direct or mediated action on bone cells remains a possibility. Estrogens maintain bone mass, but restoration of bone mass previously lost is minimal. Their use as sole therapeutic modalities in women with low bone mass and spinal compression fractures is therefore questionable (Fig. 77-3); status quo of a compromised bone mass is maintained, but presumably a risk for fracture remains. Therefore, the primary value of estrogens in osteoporosis would appear to be prophylactic or in combination with agents that stimulate bone formation.[35] A daily dosage of 0.625 mg of conjugated equine estrogen (Premarin) or its equivalent is indicated to prevent bone loss; transdermal estrogen remains an experimental preparation for the treatment of osteoporosis.

Side effects of estrogen administration include endometrial carcinoma, thromboembolic disease, and, questionably, an association with gallbladder disease and breast carcinoma (aggravation of breast carcinoma may occur with estrogen therapy). Endometrial cancer can be prevented by cycling estrogen with a progestational agent, but this is done at the expense of recurrent episodes of uterine bleeding after the menopause. In addition, a possibly beneficial effect of estrogens on lipids may be circumvented by its combination with certain progestational agents. In the woman with an intact uterus who does elect to receive "unopposed" estrogen therapy (without progesterone), a pelvic examination and (possibly) endometrial biopsies are indicated at yearly intervals.

As primarily an anti–bone-resorbing agent, estrogen should be given for maximal benefit as soon as possible after the menopause and continued (if there are no contraindications) through perhaps age 60 to 65. Treating osteoporosis with estrogens alone after the age of 65 would appear to be of limited value if an effect on bone mass is the primary indication for estrogen administration.

Calcitonin

Calcitonin is an inhibitor of osteoclast activity and, as such, has a reasonable therapeutic rationale as an anti–bone-resorbing agent. Studies[36] indicate short-term efficacy (26 months) of synthetic salmon calcitonin (Calcimar or its equivalent) in slowing bone loss and in transiently increasing bone mass by an inhibition of bone resorption without a simultaneous inhibition of bone formation mechanisms. Efficacy beyond 26 months is unconfirmed; an apparent "resistance" to drug action (possibly due to a down-regulation of receptor sites) may occur after 16 months of use. Alteration of drug dosage may alleviate this apparent loss of drug effect (e.g., 50 IU of synthetic salmon calcitonin every other day may be superior to 100 IU every day). The expense and route of administration (subcutaneously or intramuscularly) of calcitonin may prevent its extensive use in the osteoporotic patient. Calcitonin is, however, quite safe, and as such it may be a reasonable prophylactic alternative to estrogen therapy if a more suitable route of administration can be found. In this light, preliminary studies with nasal spray calcitonin[37] suggest this formulation to be a suitable prophylactic agent. In the future, calcitonin via nasal spray may be indicated for prophylaxis in patients unable or unwilling to utilize estrogen therapy and via injection either alone or in combination with positive bone formers for patients with osteoporosis. In addition, calcitonin may have an analgesic effect in osteoporotic women; such an effect may be mediated by a stimulation of endorphins or by prostaglandin inhibition. In the pain associated with acute spinal fracture, a dosage of 50 to 100 IU every day or every other day for 1 to 2 weeks may be of value.

Bisphosphonates

The bisphosphonates (originally "diphosphonates") are potentially beneficial anti–bone-resorbers which chemisorb to bone crystal, decreasing bone resorption and overall bone remodeling. These agents are currently experimental and are under evaluation for the treatment of osteoporosis; EHDP [ethane-1-hydroxy-1,1-diphosphonate acid (Didronel)] has proven effectiveness in the treatment of Paget's disease of bone. Whether it will prove effective in the treatment of osteoporosis is unclear; when given in intermittent fashion the medication is quite safe, although the exact dosage has yet to be defined. In addition, it may be used in combination with other therapeutic agents in the so-called ADFR (intermittent cycled therapy consisting of Activation of bone remodeling, Depression of bone resorption, a Free period of no treatment, and Repeat of the cycle) therapeutic program, although its efficacy in such a program is unproven.[38] Such a program utilizes an anti-bone resorbing agent in combination with therapies stimulating bone remodeling and bone formation; therapy is administered in pulsed intermittent fashion.

Sodium Fluoride

Sodium fluoride is a proven positive bone former; with its use an increase in bone mass occurs by stimulation of the osteoblast. With fluoride administration a new bone crystal (fluorapatite) is produced; with formation of such a new bone crystal some concern has arisen regarding structural integrity of bone and a possibly greater fracture potential. Current data,[39] however, do suggest satisfactory skeletal strength in individuals treated with sodium fluoride. The drug would therefore be of value in increasing bone mass (as compared to the previously noted agents, which primarily decrease bone-mass loss) and conceivably in preventing fractures; as noted in Fig. 77-3, sodium fluoride, alone or in combination with anti–bone-resorbing agents, would be of value in patients with compromised bone mass and previous fractures, since presumably sodium fluoride could elevate bone mass above a hypothetical fracture threshold.

Sodium fluoride remains an experimental agent; its therapeutic dosage appears to be 44 to 88 mg per day in divided doses. While theoretically it is best taken on an empty stomach due to its poor gastric absorption, its side effects of nausea, vomiting, and general gastric upset often necessitate its ingestion immediately after meals.

Side effects of sodium fluoride are significant and include gastric symptoms, peptic ulcer disease, tendonitis/fasciitis, and exacerbation of arthritic symptoms. Perhaps 35 percent of patients are unable to tolerate sodium fluoride due to its side effects; in addition, about 25 to 35 percent of osteoporotic patients will show a limited response to such therapy.

Anabolic Steroids

A primary increase in bone formation, probably due to osteoblastic stimulation without a corresponding increase in bone resorption, was noted following treatment of postmenopausal osteoporotic women with the anabolic steroid stanozolol over 2 years.[40] It would therefore appear that this group of agents would be of value in both slowing bone loss and restoring bone previously lost, in a fashion similar to sodium fluoride. Side effects, including elevation of hepatic enzymes, fluid retention, androgenic effects, and high-density lipoprotein (HDL) reduction, prevent these agents' widespread use in osteoporosis, and they are not currently approved for therapy by the Food and Drug Administration. Although such side effects appear to be dose-related, the physician using these agents should be cognizant of their potential

for side effects and should balance the need for an effective treatment against the tendency for less desirous side effects.

Exercise

A reasonable exercise program should be an integral part of any osteoporosis treatment regimen; exercise is presumably of value because it increases bone formation to a greater extent than bone resorption, with a subsequent increase in bone mass. Weight-bearing exercise, such as walking and aerobics, is usually recommended. In general, exercise should be performed up to and possibly slightly beyond the point of bone pain, although it is frequently important to reduce exercise in a patient who suffers an acute spinal fracture. A flexion exercise program may be contraindicated; extension or isometric exercises seem to be more appropriate for patients with postmenopausal osteoporosis.[41]

OSTEOPOROSIS THERAPY: GENERAL RECOMMENDATIONS

In patients with essentially normal bone mass and without fractures (typically patients who are immediately postmenopausal) who are nevertheless at high risk for development of significant osteopenia and bone loss, a therapy of increased calcium intake, a multivitamin with vitamin D, an exercise program, and avoidance of such risk factors as alcoholism and cigarette smoking should be recommended. Estrogen should be strongly considered in the absence of contraindications to this medication. The rationale of this therapeutic regimen is prevention of significant bone loss.

On the other hand, for patients with low bone mass and fractures, a therapy of calcium, vitamin D supplements, exercise, avoidance of risk factors, and a positive bone-former such as sodium fluoride could be prescribed. Estrogens or calcitonin could be added for combination therapy, particularly if a therapeutic response is lacking from initial therapy. The rationale for this therapeutic program is restoration of bone mass previously lost and the prevention of further loss.

THERAPY FOR SECONDARY OSTEOPOROSIS

In secondary osteoporosis, the principle aim may be discontinuation of the osteopenia-producing entities (e.g., corticosteroids, heparin, or thyroid medication) or treatment of the underlying pathological process (e.g., hyperthyroidism or Cushing's disease). Whether the therapies for primary osteoporosis are of equal value in the treatment of secondary osteoporoses is unclear; the treatment of corticosteroid-induced osteopenia and osteoporosis is particularly disappointing. While such therapeutic regimens as calcium, vitamin D replacement (50,000 IU of vitamin D orally weekly for 12 weeks), sodium fluoride, and possibly thiazides may be of value,[42] definitive data establishing efficacy of such therapeutic regimens are lacking in these conditions.

MONITORING RESPONSE TO TREATMENT

Obviously, the ultimate determinant of therapeutic success is the absence of new spine, wrist, and hip fractures; the occurrence of new fractures, particularly at the spine, after 12 months of treatment suggests therapeutic failure and necessitates reevaluation of therapy. Monitoring bone mass at different skeletal sites such as the spine and hip by currently available techniques may be advantageous in defining trends in bone-mass change; presumably, a stabilization of bone mass or an increase in bone mass over time would indicate a beneficial therapeutic response.

CONCLUSIONS

Osteoporosis is a major disease in the elderly population, in terms of both morbidity (and possible mortality) and economics. Definite advances have been possible over the last decade in the diagnosis and treatment of this disease, and, with increasing attention to the health care needs of the elderly, it is likely that such diagnostic and therapeutic advances will continue. It is imperative that the geriatrician be cognizant of these developments.

REFERENCES

1. Burnell JM, Baylink DJ, Chesnut CH et al: Bone matrix and mineral abnormalities in postmenopausal osteoporosis. *Metabolism* 31:1113, 1982.
2. Parfitt AM, Matthews CHE, Villanueva AR et al: Relationships between surface, volume and thickness of iliac trabecular bone in aging and in osteoporosis. *J Clin Invest* 72:1396, 1983.
3. Office of Medical Applications of Research, National Institutes of Health: Osteoporosis. *JAMA* 252:799, 1984.
4. Richelson LS, Wahner HW, Melton LJ, Riggs BL: Relative contributions of aging and estrogen deficiency to postmenopausal bone loss. *N Engl J Med* 311:1273, 1984.
5. Drinkwater BL, Nilson K, Chesnut CH et al: Bone mineral content of amenorrheic and eumenorrheic athletes. *N Engl J Med* 311:277, 1984.
6. Erickson EF, Colvard DS, Berg NS et al: Evidence of estrogen receptors in normal human osteoblast-like cells. *Science* 241:84, 1988.
7. Komm BS, Terpening CM, Benz DJ et al: Estrogen binding, receptor mRNA, and biologic response to osteoblast-like osteosarcoma cells. *Science* 241:81, 1988.
8. Heaney RF: A unified concept of osteoporosis. *Am J Med* 39:377, 1965.
9. Gallagher JC, Riggs BL, DeLuca HF: Effect of estrogen on calcium absorption and vitamin D metabolism in postmenopausal osteoporosis. *J Clin Endocrinol Metab* 51:1359, 1980.
10. Slovik DM, Adams JS, Neer RM et al: Deficient production of 1,25-dihydroxyvitamin D in elderly osteoporotic patients. *N Engl J Med* 305:372, 1981.
11. Riggs BL, Hamstra A, DeLuca HF: Assessment of 25-hydroxy vitamin D 1-α-hydroxylase reserve in postmenopausal osteoporosis by administration of parathyroid extract. *J Clin Endocrinol Metab* 53:833, 1981.
12. Gallagher JC, Riggs BL, Eisman J et al: Intestinal calcium absorption and serum vitamin D metabolites in normal subjects and osteoporotic subjects: Effects of age and dietary calcium. *J Clin Invest* 64:729, 1979.
13. Taggart HM, Chesnut CH, Ivey JL et al: Deficient calcitonin response to calcium stimulation in postmenopausal osteoporosis. *Lancet* 2:475, 1982.
14. Tiegs RD, Body JS, Wahner HW et al: Calcitonin secretion in postmenopausal osteoporosis. *N Engl J Med* 312:1097, 1985.
15. Seeman E, Melton LJ, O'Fallon WM et al: Risk factors for spinal osteoporosis in men. *Am J Med* 75:997, 1983.
16. Chesnut CH: Noninvasive methods of measuring bone mass, in Avioli LV (ed): *The Osteoporotic Syndrome, Detection, Prevention, and Treatment*. Orlando, Grune & Stratton, 1987, p 31.
17. Mazess RB: *Skeletal Research*, vol 2. New York, Academic Press, 1983, p 277.
18. Wahner HW, Dunn WL, Riggs BL: Assessment of bone mineral: Part 1. *J Nucl Med* 25:1134, 1984.
19. Wahner HW, Dunn WL, Riggs BL: Assessment of bone mineral: Part 2. *J Nucl Med* 25:1241, 1984.
20. Heaney RP, Avioli LV, Chesnut CH et al: Osteoporotic bone fragility: Detection by ultrasound transmission velocity. *JAMA*, 1989 (in press).
21. Ott SM, Kilcoyne RF, Chesnut CH: Comparisons among methods of measuring bone mass and relationship to severity of vertebral fracture in osteoporosis. *J Clin Endocrinol Metab* 66:501, 1987.
22. Ott SM, Kilcoyne RF, Chesnut CH: Longitudinal changes in bone mass after one year as measured by different techniques in patients with osteoporosis. *Calcif Tissue Int* 39:139, 1986.
23. Cummings SR: Are patients with hip fractures more osteoporotic? *Am J Med* 78:487, 1985.
24. Ott SM, Kilcoyne RF, Chesnut CH: Ability of four different techniques of measuring bone mass to diagnose vertebral fractures in postmenopausal women. *J Bone Miner Res* 2:201, 1987.
25. Cummings SR, Black D: Should perimenopausal women be screened for osteoporosis? *Ann Intern Med* 104:817, 1986.
26. Ott SM: Should women get screening bone mass measurements? (Editorial). *Ann Intern Med* 104:876, 1986.
27. Hall FM, Davis MA, Baran DT: Bone mineral screening for osteoporosis. (Editorial). *N Engl J Med* 316:212, 1987.

28. Frost HM: Managing the skeletal pain and disability of osteoporosis. *Orthop Clin North Am* 3:561, 1972.

29. Matkovic V, Kostial K, Simonovic I et al: Bone status and fracture rates in two regions of Yugoslavia. *Am J Clin Nutr* 32:540, 1979.

30. Holbrook TL, Barrett-Connor E, Wingard DL: Dietary calcium and risk of hip fracture: 14-year prospective population study. *Lancet* 1046: Nov 5, 1988.

31. Burnell JM, Baylink DJ, Chesnut CH, Teubner EJ: The role of calcium deficiency in postmenopausal osteoporosis. *Calcif Tissue Int* 38:187, 1986.

32. Riis BL, Thomson K, Christiansen C: Does calcium supplementation prevent postmenopausal bone loss? *N Engl J Med* 316:173, 1987.

33. Physicians Resource Manual on Osteoporosis. National Osteoporosis Foundation, 1625 Eye Street NW, Washington, DC 20006, 1987.

34. Ott SM, Chesnut CH: Calcitriol treatment is not effective in postmenopausal osteoporosis. *Ann Intern Med* 110:267, 1989.

35. Chesnut CH: An appraisal of the role of estrogens in the treatment of postmenopausal osteoporosis. *J Am Geriatr Soc* 32:604, 1986.

36. Gruber HE, Ivey JL, Baylink DJ et al: Long-term calcitonin therapy in postmenopausal osteoporosis. *Metabolism* 33:295, 1984.

37. Reginster JY, Denis D, Albert A et al: One year controlled randomized trial of prevention of early postmenopausal bone loss by intranasal calcitonin. *Lancet* 1481: Dec 25, 1987.

38. Pacifici R, McMurty C, Vered I et al: Coherence therapy does not prevent axial bone loss in osteoporotic women: A preliminary comparative study. *J Clin Endocrinol Metab* 66:747, 1988.

39. Riggs BL, Melton LJ: Involutional osteoporosis. *N Engl J Med* 314:1676, 1986.

40. Chesnut CH, Ivey JL, Gruber HE et al: Stanozolol in postmenopausal osteoporosis: Therapeutic efficacy and possible mechanisms of action. *Metabolism* 32:571, 1983.

41. Sinaki M, Mikkelsen BA: Postmenopausal spinal osteoporosis: Flexion versus extension exercises. *Arch Phys Med Rehabil* 65:593, 1984.

42. Baylink DJ: Glucocorticoid-induced osteoporosis. *N Engl J Med* 309:306, 1983.

GENERAL READING

Avioli LV (ed): *The Osteoporotic Syndrome, Detection, Prevention and Treatment.* Orlando, Grune & Stratton, 1987.

Genant HK (ed): *Osteoporosis Update 1987.* San Francisco, Radiology Research & Education Foundation, University of California Printing Series, 1987.

Riggs BL, Melton LJ: Involutional osteoporosis. *N Engl J Med* 314:1676, 1986.

Riggs BL, Melton JL (eds): *Osteoporosis: Etiology, Diagnosis and Management.* New York, Raven Press, 1988.

Physicians Resource Manual on Osteoporosis. National Osteoporosis Foundation, 1625 Eye Street NW, Washington, DC 20006, 1987.

Chapter 78

OSTEOMALACIA

David J. Baylink

GENERAL CONSIDERATIONS

Osteomalacia is a term used to describe a group of diseases characterized by a mineralization defect. Clinically, this leads to plastic deformities (Fig. 78-1) and bone pain as a consequence of fractures. Osteomalacia, however, is an uncommon disease. In patients presenting with spontaneous compression fractures, less than 5 percent will have histological evidence of osteomalacia, the remainder showing osteoporosis. A higher fraction of patients with metabolic bone disease will show osteomalacia in such clinics as gastrointestinal and renal, inasmuch as small bowel diseases and renal disease can result in osteomalacia (Table 78-1). The importance of making the diagnosis of osteomalacia lies in the fact that osteomalacia is, in general, readily cured by treatment. This is the reason that one rarely sees severe osteomalacia with pseudofractures and severe bone pain (i.e., most osteomalacic patients are treated and cured before severe osteomalacia evolves). One exception to this is a form of osteomalacia of renal failure that does not respond to routine treatment, and thus severe osteomalacia may be seen in renal clinics.

The causes of osteomalacia most likely to be seen in the elderly are shown in Table 78-1. Accordingly, in the geriatric population the most common causes of osteomalacia are some form of vitamin D deficiency or phosphate deficiency. In general, bone biopsy is required for a definitive diagnosis of osteomalacia, but it does not usually distinguish the cause of the osteomalacia. Similarly, x-ray and clinical findings are not sufficiently distinctive to separate the different causes of osteomalacia. These different forms of osteomalacia are, however, distinguishable on the basis of serum and urine chemistries.

PATHOGENESIS

In bone biopsies the characteristic feature of osteomalacia is excess osteoid tissue (Fig. 78-2). This excess of osteoid tissue results because, at a given bone-forming sur-

TABLE 78-1
Causes of Osteomalacia in the Elderly

I. Vitamin D deficiency
  A. Insufficient parent compounds
    1. Inadequate sunlight exposure*: vitamin D_3 deficiency
    2. Inadequate gut absorption*: vitamin D_2 deficiency
      a. Dietary deficiency
      b. Small intestinal diseases with malabsorption
      c. Partial gastrectomy
  B. Impaired metabolite conversion
    1. Liver disease: 25-OHD deficiency
    2. Anticonvulsant therapy: 25-OHD deficiency
    3. Chronic renal failure: 1,25-diOHD deficiency
II. Phosphate deficiency
  A. Ingestion of phosphate binders (e.g., aluminum hydroxide)
  B. Renal phosphate leak
    1. Idiopathic
    2. Neoplasms (soft tissue tumors, prostate cancer)
    3. Hereditary
      a. X-linked
      b. Idiopathic hypercalciuria
III. Drug and chemical inhibition of mineralization
  A. Fluoride therapy
  B. Diphosphonate therapy
  C. Aluminum toxicity in renal failure patients

*Both of these factors must be inadequate to cause a deficiency of parent compounds.

face, the rate of osteoid deposition exceeds the rate at which mineral is deposited, resulting in increased osteoid width (Fig. 78-3). Additionally, the amount of surface involved in matrix formation is increased. The increase in osteoid width is not specific evidence of a mineralization defect, since osteoid width tends to normally increase as the linear formation rate (the width of bone matrix added per day) increases. By adjusting for variations in linear formation (as determined by tetracycline labeling), one can calculate a mineralization lag time (the time between the deposition of matrix and the subse-

FIGURE 78-1
X ray showing severely deformed pelvis in an elderly female with vitamin D–deficiency osteomalacia (i.e., plastic deformity of bone).

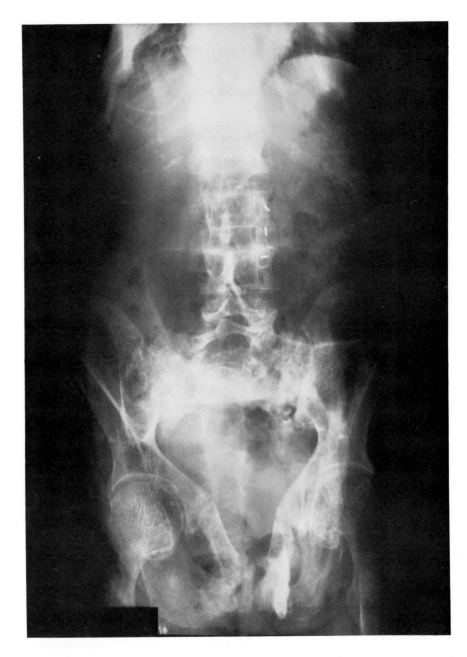

quent initiation of mineralization in this matrix) which is a parameter reflecting only mineralization. A prolonged lag time is definitive evidence for osteomalacia.

The cause of the increase in forming surface in osteomalacia is not established. One explanation is that because the half-life of osteoid is prolonged, there will be an accumulation of osteoid-covered surface. Alternatively, the hormonal changes attending osteomalacia may actually result in stimulation of production of new osteoblasts. Because different types of osteomalacia have different hormonal changes, yet all types have increased forming surface, it follows that of the two, the prolonged half-life of osteoid is the more likely explanation for the accumulation of forming surface.

Osteoid matrix is not deposited in a mature, mineralizable state but must undergo certain chemical changes before mineralization can be initiated. One of the matrix changes which occurs at the mineralizing front immediately before mineral deposition begins is a loss of proteoglycans. In experimental animals with osteomalacia, a loss of proteoglycans is delayed regardless of the cause of the osteomalacia.

This observation has led to the concept that osteomalacia is due to defective osteoblastic removal of proteoglycans, which are known to inhibit calcium salt deposition. Thus, in osteomalacia there may be inadequate preparation of osteoid for mineral deposition. This raises the question as to what regulates osteoid matrix maturation. Although it has been suggested that vitamin D metabolites such as 1,25-dihydroxy vitamin D promote mineralization, this is a controversial issue. On the basis of experimental animal studies it seems unlikely that in

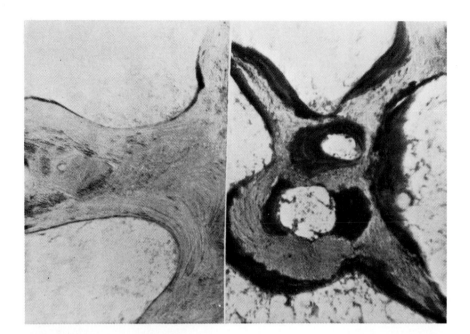

FIGURE 78-2
Goldner's stained mineralized sections of bone from a normal subject (left) and from a patient with severe osteomalacia (right). Osteoid appears black and mineralized bone gray. In the biopsy from the patient with osteomalacia, there is an increased amount of surface covered with osteoid and an increase in osteoid width.

vitamin D–deficiency osteomalacia (in animals or humans), the defective mineralization is caused by the lack of a direct action of 1,25-dihydroxy vitamin D on bone mineralization processes. Accordingly, the mineralization defect in vitamin D–deficient rats is corrected by adjustment of the low serum calcium alone. The implication from this conclusion is that vitamin D metabolites do not have direct action on osteoblasts to promote mineralization.

If osteomalacia is due to inadequate osteoid maturation and if vitamin D metabolites do not directly regulate osteoid maturation, what is the cause of the mineralization defect in osteomalacia? In animals and humans, hypocalcemia, regardless of its cause or of the attending hormonal changes, is associated with osteomalacia. This includes the hypocalcemia of vitamin D deficiency. Similarly, hypophosphatemia, whether associated with a high or low serum 1,25-dihydroxy vitamin D, results in osteomalacia. This emphasizes the importance of serum calcium and phosphate in the regulation of osteoid maturation by osteoblasts.

An additional or alternative explanation for the cause of osteomalacia is that the lowered serum calcium times phosphate product, which is frequently seen in

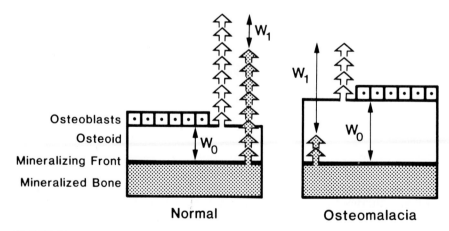

Osteoblasts
Osteoid
Mineralizing Front
Mineralized Bone

Normal   **Osteomalacia**

FIGURE 78-3
Schema of the pathogenesis of osteomalacia. Osteoblasts form osteoid matrix which undergoes a maturation process before mineralization is initiated at the mineralizing front. W_0 = osteoid width at 0 time, W_1 = osteoid width at a later time. The open arrows indicate the linear rate at which the osteoid front advances. (The greater the number of arrows, the greater the rate of advancement.) The speckled arrows indicate linear rate of advancement of the mineralizing front. Under normal conditions, the production of osteoid and the maturation of osteoid are proceeding at identical rates, and therefore advancement of the osteoid front and mineralizing front are traveling at identical rates, such that osteoid width at time W_1 is identical to that seen at time W_0. In osteomalacia, the following three important changes are illustrated: (1) Both of the above rates are depressed. (2) Osteoid width is increased at W_0 because during the development of osteomalacia the rate of advancement of the mineralizing front is less than the rate of advancement of the osteoid front. (3) Osteoid width is greater at W_1 than at W_0 because of this continuing disparity.

osteomalacia, does not allow precipitation of mineral salts at the mineralizing front (Fig. 78-3). However, the serum calcium times phosphate product does not show a constant relationship with bone mineralization parameters. For example, in patients treated with Didronel the serum calcium times phosphate product is normal or increased, yet osteomalacia occurs. Even in vitamin D–deficiency osteomalacia, the serum product is not highly correlated with mineralization parameters. Apparently, mineralization is more regulated by osteoblasts and bone matrix characteristics than by availability of calcium and phosphate for precipitation.

In conclusion, in vitamin D deficiency, the cause of the impairment in osteoid maturation is probably not the depressed calcium times phosphate product, but rather the attending hypocalcemia (and hypophosphatemia) which apparently inhibits the action of osteoblasts to promote osteoid maturation.

DISORDERS OF VITAMIN D METABOLISM

Special emphasis is placed on vitamin D metabolism because vitamin D deficiency is the most common cause of osteomalacia in the elderly (Table 78-1). A schema of normal vitamin D metabolism is shown in Fig. 78-4. Actually, vitamin D is not a vitamin, but a hormone, and the generalities which apply to steroid hormones also apply to vitamin D. Thus, the active metabolite of vitamin D, 1,25-diOHD, is bound to a carrier protein in serum, acts on cells via binding to a nuclear acceptor molecule, has precursors metabolized in different tissues, and has a serum level which is under tight physiological regulation through negative feedback mechanisms.

Because vitamin D is metabolized in several tissues (Fig. 78-4), there are several metabolic sites which may produce vitamin D deficiency. Vitamin D_3 (cholecalciferol) is synthesized in skin from 7-dihydrocholesterol in response to ultraviolet (UV) irradiation (Fig. 78-4). If there is inadequate exposure to sunlight, vitamin D deficiency may result. It will not invariably result because there is another source of vitamin D: milk is supplemented with vitamin D_2 (ergocalciferol) produced by UV irradiation of the plant sterol, ergosterol, Vitamin D_2 and D_3 are chemically distinct but biologically quite similar. Thus, to become vitamin D–deficient because of insufficient parent compounds, one must have inadequate sun exposure and also inadequate absorption of vitamin D_2 from gut. It is noteworthy that subjects over 70 years of age are at risk for this combined deficiency state, apparently because skin production and gut absorption of the vitamin tend to decline with old age.

Vitamin D deficiency can also result from diseases which affect the liver, intestine, and kidney as described

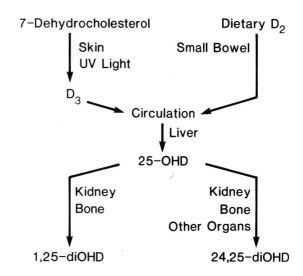

FIGURE 78-4
Schema of normal vitamin D metabolism.

below. Vitamins D_2 and D_3 are converted in the liver to 25-OHD_2 and 25-OHD_3, respectively (Fig. 78-4). In hepatic cellular diseases this conversion can be impaired with a resultant decrease in serum 25-OHD (25-OHD_2 plus 25-OHD_3).* Serum 25-OHD is further metabolized in the kidney to the biologically active metabolite, 1,25-diOHD. A deficiency of 25-OHD results in a compensatory increase in the 1α-hydroxylase activity in kidney, mediated in part by an increase in serum PTH, and as a result a normal serum level of 1,25-diOHD is maintained until a substantial decrease in 25-OHD occurs, at which time serum 1,25-diOHD begins to decline. Certain drugs increase liver activity of drug-metabolizing enzymes which indiscriminately destroy 25-OHD and thereby cause vitamin D deficiency. Disease of the small intestine can cause impairment of fat absorption and thus a dietary deficiency of vitamin D_2 (Fig. 78-4, Table 78-1), but again the patient will not become vitamin D–deficient unless skin production of vitamin D_3 is also diminished. Because optimum fat absorption also requires adequate bile secretion, malabsorption of vitamin D_2 may be seen in biliary diseases. The final organ which, when diseased, may result in vitamin D deficiency is the kidney, which acts to convert 25-OHD to 1,25-diOHD in response to physiological cues (Fig. 78-4).

A deficiency of 1,25-diOHD due to decreased kidney production ultimately leads to osteomalacia. Decreased kidney production of 1,25-diOHD is most commonly seen in renal failure, probably as a result of decreased renal mass. Thus, in renal failure, there is a progressive decline in renal mass, which leads to a de-

---

*A decrease in serum 25-OHD is not invariably associated with osteomalacia; in mild vitamin D deficiency (i.e., without hypocalcemia) osteomalacia does not occur, whereas with vitamin D deficiency sufficient to cause hypocalcemia, osteomalacia uniformly occurs.

crease in 1,25-diOHD production, which in turn leads to hypocalcemia and ultimately to osteomalacia. There are two additional causes of a deficiency of 1,25-diOHD at the kidney level, neither of which is common. First there is idiopathic impairment of 1,25-diOHD production without renal failure, which seems to occur at any age and has been documented to occur after 50 years of age. Second, there is a soft-tissue tumor that is associated with severe hypophosphatemia, decreased serum 1,25-diOHD levels, and resistance to vitamin D. In both of these latter situations one sees osteomalacia. Most, if not all, of these abnormalities of D metabolism leading to osteomalacia can be effectively treated.

The conversion of vitamin D to 25-OHD in liver depends on the serum level of vitamin D, whereas the conversion of 25-OHD to 1,25-diOHD is not influenced by normal variations in serum 25-OHD, but instead is determined by physiological needs. Thus, when serum PTH is increased, for example in response to low dietary calcium, there is increased 1,25-diOHD production as a result of direct action of PTH on kidney cells. This increased 1,25-diOHD acts on target cells to increase calcium absorption and also bone resorption which, in turn, increase serum calcium and thus close the negative feedback loop. Similarly, 1,25-diOHD increases in response to low dietary phosphate by a mechanism which does not involve PTH, and the high serum 1,25-diOHD tends to correct the low serum phosphate by directly stimulating enteral phosphate absorption and also osteoclastic bone resorption. Other physiological conditions requiring increased amounts of calcium or phosphate, such as pregnancy, are also associated with elevated serum 1,25-diOHD.

DISORDERS OF PHOSPHATE METABOLISM

The second most common cause of osteomalacia in the elderly is hypophosphatemia. Mild hypophosphatemia usually results in osteoporosis, whereas moderate to severe cases (i.e., a decrease of about 1 mg/dl or more) produce osteomalacia. A schema of normal phosphate metabolism is shown in Fig. 78-5. Three organs are involved in mass transfer of phosphate: bone, kidney, and gut (Fig. 78-5); however, only abnormal function of the kidney results in decreased serum phosphate in the elderly. Because phosphate is ubiquitous in nature and is so well-absorbed (Fig. 78-5), a selective dietary deficiency of phosphate does not occur naturally. A deficient absorption of phosphate may occur, however, when phosphate binders (antacids) are used to treat gastrointestinal disorders, and ingestion of these antacids may result in hypophosphatemia and osteomalacia. The most common cause of hypophosphatemia is an impaired renal tubular maximum phosphate (TmP) reabsorption. In adults, serum phosphate is largely regulated by TmP.

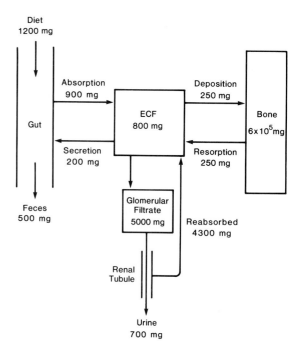

FIGURE 78-5
Schema of normal phosphate metabolism. All values associated with fluxes are in milligrams per day. For example, dietary phosphorus intake is 1200 mg/day. The values for ECF and bone represent phosphate content in milligrams.

A chronically depressed TmP and the corresponding hypophosphatemia can be due to either an acquired or a hereditary abnormality. Patients with severe hereditary hypophosphatemia will exhibit signs of childhood rickets, such as short stature and bone deformities. The causes of acquired forms of impaired TmP are poorly understood, with the exception that there is a soft-tissue tumor which produces severe hypophosphatemia by depression of TmP and which, also produces impaired renal 1α-hydroxylase activity resulting in a concomitant deficiency of 1,25-diOHD. Both metabolic abnormalities are rapidly corrected by removal of the tumor. Severe hypophosphatemia associated with such tumors results in marked muscle weakness, a complication not experienced by hereditary x-linked hypophosphatemic patients.

Because physiological hypophosphatemia is seen after ingestion of glucose or other rapidly metabolizable substrates, a correct diagnosis of hypophosphatemia must be made from analysis of *fasting* serum samples. Hypophosphatemia in the elderly is rare, but since it can be effectively treated, serum phosphate levels should routinely be determined in all patients presenting with metabolic bone disease.

BONE BIOPSY FINDINGS

Each of the three following bone sites has been used to obtain bone for histological evaluations: anterior iliac crest, a transilial site, and posterior iliac crest. Normal values are available for the anterior iliac crest and trans-ilial sites, but not the posterior iliac crest site. The latter site sampled with a Jamshidi needle, however, is the least traumatic. The major disadvantage of the bone biopsy approach to the diagnosis of osteomalacia is the lack of sensitivity of this method—a deficiency which is largely due to the lack of precision of the measurements, which in turn is a result of an inability to reproducibly sample a given bone site. Because of this inherent problem, it is difficult to detect mild degrees of osteomalacia by this method.

The other pitfall of this method results in false-positive conclusions and occurs when excessive osteoid width or osteoid area (both of which can occur with high bone formation rates) are equated with evidence of osteomalacia. This problem is not encountered when the mineralization lag time is used. To measure this parameter, however, there is a requirement for quantitation and also for special methods to process undemineralized bone specimens (Fig. 78-2), which are necessary for visualization of osteoid and also of tetracycline time markers.

Another parameter used to assess mineralization is the percentage of mineralizing front (i.e., the interface between osteoid and mineralized bone) which takes up a tetracycline label in vivo or in vitro. The percentage of mineralizing front, which is tetracycline-labeled, is typically decreased in osteomalacia. Even without tetracycline-labeling information, when osteoid width is increased and extends to a cement line, this is definitive evidence for a mineralization defect.

A bone biopsy can be definitive in making a diagnosis of osteomalacia, but it does not usually provide diagnostic information regarding the cause of the osteomalacia. Although there may be somewhat more evidence of bone resorption and more marrow fibrosis in the phosphate-deficiency osteomalacia as compared with vitamin D–deficiency osteomalacia, such changes are usually not of sufficient magnitude to be discriminatory. In both causes of osteomalacia, osteoblast size tends to be decreased. On the other hand, when osteocyte lacunae are enlarged and osteoid surfaces are irregular, a toxic osteomalacia, for example, due to sodium fluoride, should be considered.

X-RAY FINDINGS

There are three x-ray features specific for osteomalacia, none of which occurs early during the evolution of this disease. First, in trabecular bone regions, such as the vertebral body, the trabecular architecture appears blurred and fuzzy. Second, pseudofractures are characteristic of osteomalacia but, again, are usually seen only with severe disease (Fig. 78-6). These appear as radiolucent bands usually flanked by radiopaque bands, repre-

senting abundant callous formations. Rarely, one sees a pseudofracture in a patient without osteomalacia but with a low bone turnover rate. Pseudofractures due to osteomalacia are frequently bilateral, and commonly affected bones include the ulna (Fig. 78-6), scapula, pelvis, inner aspect of the femur near the femoral neck, metatarsals, and ribs. Inability to repair microdamage (because of the mineralization defect) is thought to be involved in the pathogenesis of pseudofractures. In untreated patients such fractures may be present for years. Third, patients with severe osteomalacia combined with osteoporosis may exhibit plastic deformities (Fig. 78-1). This complication is usually seen in patients who are 70 years of age or older and who have severe vitamin D deficiency.

BONE MASS AND BONE SCAN FINDINGS

The bone density of patients with osteomalacia may vary from high to low and can be measured by several methods. Two techniques used in clinical practice are radiogrametry, a measurement of cortical thickness, and single-photon absorptiometry, which measures the amount of mineral at a standardized site, usually the radius. Neither cortical thickness nor bone density measurements, however, distinguish osteomalacia from osteoporosis. Cortical thickness and bone density (measured by photon absorptiometry) usually change in the same direction. Theoretically, bone density could be low in osteomalacia, even when cortical thickness is not, because the photon absorption technique is sensitive to changes in mineral concentration within bone substance such as the replacement of bone with mineral-free osteoid matrix. In practice, however, bone density and cortical thickness are usually normal in patients with mild to moderate osteomalacia. In severe osteomalacia, bone density is decreased, and in osteomalacia complicated by osteoporosis, both parameters are low. Bone density is increased in certain renal tubular disorders which cause osteomalacia, but such disorders are rare in the elderly. In addition, renal osteodystrophy occasionally exhibits the combination of increased bone density and mild osteomalacia.

A bone scan is one procedure with the potential to discriminate osteomalacia from osteoporosis. A bone scan demonstrates normal generalized skeletal uptake of the bone-seeking radionuclide in osteoporosis, but increased generalized skeletal uptake of the radionuclide in osteomalacia. In osteomalacia the increased radionuclide uptake is due to the increased length of the mineralizing front which contains the reactive bone mineral that fixes the radionuclide. Unfortunately, like many other discriminatory tests, the bone scan is positive for osteomalacia only when the disease is moderate to severe.

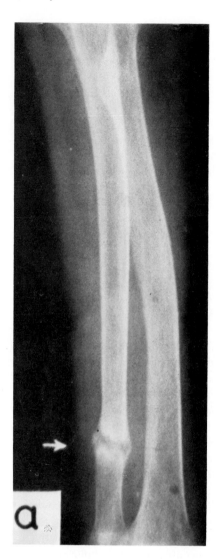
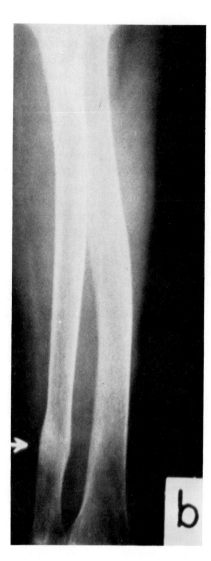

FIGURE 78-6
X rays of pseudofracture of the ulna in the patient with severe osteomalacia, shown in Fig. 78-7. The pseudofracture before treatment is shown in panel a and the pseudofracture after 3 months of vitamin D therapy is shown in panel b.

LABORATORY FINDINGS

One of the regulatory mechanisms for maintenance of serum calcium and phosphate is an inhibition of calcium and phosphate deposition in bone when serum levels of either ion drop below the physiological level. This action is probably a direct ion effect on osteoblasts. Although there are other regulators of bone mineral deposition, it is quite unusual to see osteomalacia, especially in the elderly, without a depressed serum calcium and/or serum phosphate. Hypophosphatasia and fluoride intoxication exhibit normal serum calcium and phosphate and thus are exceptions to this generality. In severe vitamin D deficiency, one sees depressed serum calcium, phosphate, and 25-OHD, increased serum alkaline phosphatase (bone isoenzyme) and PTH, and a decrease in urine calcium excretion, i.e., 50 mg/day or less. With less severe vitamin D deficiency one may see only one or two of the above changes.

There are two syndromes of hypophosphatemia, and while both result in osteomalacia, it is important to distinguish between them because their treatment is different. (1) The patient will manifest hypophosphatemia and a high urine calcium. Hypercalciuria results from an increased calcium absorption which is a consequence of a high serum 1,25-diOHD level, which in turn occurs in response to the hypophosphatemia. (2) The patient will have hypophosphatemia without a high urine calcium. Such patients have a 1α-hydroxylase abnormality as well as a renal tubular phosphate transport abnormality, such that the low serum phosphate cannot increase the 1α-hydroxylase activity. The effect of a low serum phosphate to increase the serum 1,25-diOHD is part of a normal regulatory mechanism whereby 1,25-diOHD acts to increase serum phosphate. 1,25-diOHD increases serum phosphate: (1) by increasing enteral calcium absorption which in turn increases serum phosphate by decreasing serum PTH, (2) by increasing enteral phosphate absorption, and (3) by increasing bone resorption. Because 1,25-diOHD stimulates bone resorption, one might expect a high urine hydroxyproline in patients with a high serum 1,25-diOHD, but not in patients with a normal serum 1,25-diOHD. Unfortunately, hydroxy-proline is not a good discriminator between these two forms of hypophosphatemia, perhaps in part because urine hydroxyproline excretion is a poor measure of bone resorption. Serum alkaline phosphatase is consistently elevated in both forms of hypophosphatemia when osteomalacia is present.

In summary, it is very uncommon to see an elderly patient who has moderate to severe osteomalacia without a decrease in serum calcium or phosphate or an increase in alkaline phosphatase.

CLINICAL FINDINGS

The patient with osteomalacia due to either vitamin D deficiency or phosphate deficiency may complain of diffuse bone pain and tenderness, bony deformities, muscle weakness, increased fatigability, and emotional depression. During the evolution of vitamin D deficiency, muscle weakness, increased fatigability, and depression appear before bone pain and tenderness. Although these earlier symptoms are not specific for vitamin D deficiency, only vitamin D treatment abolishes them. Thus correction of these nonspecific symptoms with this specific treatment can be of diagnostic value.

Regarding skeletal pain, some pseudofractures are painful and some are not, and not all skeletal pain is limited to sites of pseudofractures. Skeletal pain at sites which appear normal by x ray is probably a consequence of microfractures which usually are evident by bone scan. Osteomalacia, like osteoporosis, can weaken the skeleton and thus result in fractures with little trauma. In hypophosphatemia, as in vitamin D deficiency, muscle weakness and general debilitation may be more prominent than skeletal symptoms early in the evaluation of the disease. For both vitamin D deficiency and hypophosphatemia the proximal muscles are predominantly involved. Patients with severe osteomalacia may have a wide-based, cautious shuffle—wide-based because of muscle weakness and a shuffle (i.e., scooting the sole along the ground) because any jarring motion precipitates pain in pseudofractures and other skeletal sites.

ILLUSTRATIVE CASE HISTORY

A 70-year-old female presented with muscular weakness, symptoms of emotional depression, weight loss, and generalized skeletal pains (Fig. 78-7). The patient was experiencing severe skeletal pain and was depressed to the extent that she wished to be left alone to die. On physical examination she was emaciated, had a wide-based, cautious gait, dorsal kyphosis, and weak and flaccid muscles, and complained of tenderness over the

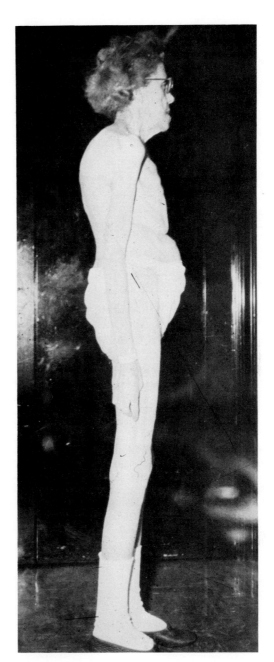

FIGURE 78-7
Photograph of patient with severe osteomalacia as a consequence of malabsorption syndrome. This patient exhibits severe dorsal kyphosis, flaccid abdominal muscles, and emaciation.

right scapula (Fig. 78-7). X rays revealed a total of 23 pseudofractures, one of which was located in the tender site in the right scapula. The most obvious pseudofracture was in the ulna (Fig. 78-6). A bone biopsy revealed severe osteomalacia. A small bowel biopsy showed the typical changes of gluten enteropathy, and the serum changes were consistent with osteomalacia as a consequence of vitamin D deficiency: serum calcium and phosphate and urine calcium were decreased, and serum alkaline phosphatase was elevated (Fig. 78-8). The ma-

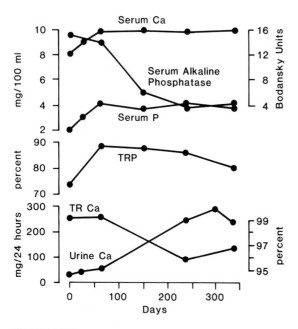

FIGURE 78-8

Serum and urine chemical data, before and during 1 year of vitamin D treatment in the patient with severe osteomalacia shown in Fig. 78-7. At 0 time, therapy with vitamin D, 100,000 IU/day, and oral calcium supplements of 2 g/day was initiated. Because of the urine calcium of approximately 250 mg/24 h at 240 days of treatment, the dose of vitamin D was decreased to 50,000 IU/day. However, the urine calcium continued to rise to the abnormally high value of 300 mg/day, and at this point vitamin D was discontinued. In retrospect, the vitamin D should have been discontinued at 240 days, when the urine calcium was 250 mg/24 h, which is the upper limit of normal for females. Serum calcium, serum phosphate, and tubular reabsorption of phosphate (TRP) were all depressed initially and were all corrected after approximately 2 months of therapy. In contrast, the serum alkaline phosphatase, which may reflect osteoblast number, was not corrected until approximately 240 days of therapy. Before therapy, urine calcium was low at less than 50 mg/24 h, as is typical in vitamin D–deficiency osteomalacia. The percentage of tubular reabsorption of calcium (TR Ca) was high before treatment, contributing to the low urine calcium, and decreased as urine calcium subsequently increased. Presumably, before therapy serum PTH was high and serum 1,25-diOHD was low, and during therapy they both normalized.

jority of her symptoms had been present and progressive over the previous 2 years with the exception of weight loss, which began approximately 5 years before admission.

The mechanisms responsible for the chemical changes shown in Fig. 78-8 were as follows: Fat malabsorption led to a decreased serum vitamin D_2 level which, in turn, resulted in a decreased serum 25-OHD. When the latter became severe, the 1,25-diOHD level dropped, and this resulted in two independent changes: (1) decreased calcium absorption and (2) an impaired ability of PTH to liberate bone mineral, which together acted to increase serum PTH. The secondary hyperparathyroidism increased the tubular reabsorption of calcium in an attempt to rectify the hypocalcemia and also de-

creased the tubular reabsorption of phosphate which contributed to the hypophosphatemia.

The patient was placed on a gluten-free diet and given 100,000 IU of vitamin D_2 and 2 g calcium daily. Within 3 months the pseudofracture of the radius was almost healed (Fig. 78-6), and within 6 to 9 months the patient was completely free of skeletal pain, had gained weight, and was without any symptoms of depression and increased fatigability. After approximately 8 months of therapy, the urine calcium was found to be in excess of 200 mg/day (Fig. 78-8), and, therefore, the vitamin D_2 dose was reduced to 50,000 IU daily. However, on the next examination the urine calcium continued to increase, and vitamin D_2 was thus discontinued. A biopsy at the end of the 1-year treatment period revealed complete healing of the osteomalacia.

DIFFERENTIAL DIAGNOSIS

In a patient presenting with a spontaneous compression fracture, the differential diagnosis is between osteomalacia and osteoporosis. In both disorders, the bone mineral content is decreased, and thus bone mineral content measurements are not discriminatory; neither are skeletal x rays, except when the osteomalacia is moderate to severe. Although the matrix/mineral ratio is clearly higher in osteomalacia than in osteoporosis, there are no noninvasive techniques to measure this parameter. The most unambiguous means to distinguish these two diseases is the bone biopsy. As mentioned earlier, however, the bone biopsy technique lacks statistical sensitivity and thus is definitive in only moderate to severe osteomalacia.

Several kinds of changes not seen in osteoporosis are typical of severe osteomalacia due to vitamin D deficiency: generalized bone pain; muscular weakness and increased fatigability; decreased serum calcium, serum phosphate, urine calcium, and serum 25-OHD; increased serum alkaline phosphatase and serum PTH; increased osteoid width and decreased osteoid maturation by bone biopsy; and pseudofractures by x ray. Patients with osteoporosis have none of these changes, and thus severe osteomalacia is easily distinguished from primary osteoporosis. Of these later changes, the most sensitive are the serum and urine chemical changes. However, these chemical changes are not specific for osteomalacia and thus can, if used inappropriately, give a false-positive diagnosis. For example, a patient with a slight decrease in serum calcium, a marked decrease in urine calcium, and a slight increase in serum alkaline phosphatase may have calcium deficiency osteoporosis rather than osteomalacia.

A serum 25-OHD determination should distinguish between these two diagnoses (being low in vitamin D–

deficiency osteomalacia and normal in calcium-deficiency osteoporosis) with one exception: The test is not yet sufficiently reliable to base therapeutic decisions on small changes. (The same is true of the serum 1,25-diOHD assay.) Thus, a borderline low serum 25-OHD of 8 ng/ml does not exclude vitamin D deficiency. In practice such a diagnostic problem in which the serum and urine changes suggest osteomalacia, but could be due to a secondary type of osteoporosis, is readily resolved by giving a therapeutic trial of vitamin D_2, 50,000 IU/day without additional calcium for 30 to 60 days. This dose of vitamin D_2 for 30 days will not produce vitamin D toxicity (i.e., increased serum or urine calcium above normal) in vitamin D–deficient or vitamin D–replete patients. Those that are vitamin D–deficient usually require more than 30 days of vitamin D treatment to replete their vitamin D stores. Thus, if after 1 month of vitamin D treatment serum calcium is within the normal range and urine calcium does not exceed 150 mg/day, a second month of vitamin D therapy can be safely administered.

The endpoints for distinguishing whether the patient has vitamin D deficiency on the basis of this therapeutic trial are changes in symptoms and, of course, changes in serum and urine parameters. Thus, this amount of vitamin D will correct the serum and urine calcium and the high serum alkaline phosphatase when due to vitamin D deficiency, but not when due to calcium deficiency. Additionally, if after vitamin D treatment, the patient has increased energy and less fatigability, it is reasonably certain that this patient had vitamin D deficiency. On the other hand, as mentioned earlier, mild vitamin D deficiency is not necessarily accompanied by osteomalacia. Thus, this therapeutic trial does not allow the physician to distinguish between the patient with mild vitamin D deficiency and the patient with mild vitamin D deficiency associated with osteomalacia. Instead, this maneuver corrects any vitamin D deficiency or osteomalacia that might have been present. Once this is accomplished, the physician can then proceed to treat any residual bone mass deficit.

TREATMENT

For the treatment of vitamin D deficiency there are several forms of vitamin D which are used: the parent compound vitamin D, 25-OHD, and 1,25-diOHD. One might reason that it would be physiologically most rational to use vitamin D for a nutritional deficiency, 25-OHD therapy for the low serum 25-OHD seen in liver cirrhosis, and 1,25-diOHD therapy for the low serum 1,25-diOHD seen in renal failure. Notwithstanding, there are few clinical situations in which any one of these agents would not produce satisfactory results. For example, if given a high dose of vitamin D (e.g., 10,000

IU/day), patients with liver cirrhosis can produce normal amounts of 25-OHD. In addition, it is important to appreciate that 25-OHD at high concentrations acts in a manner identical to that of 1,25-diOHD. This plus the fact that the amount of 25-OHD produced is proportional to the amount of vitamin D administered means that vitamin D therapy is usually completely adequate in any type of vitamin D–deficiency osteomalacia, including that due to liver or kidney disease. However, the effective dose of vitamin D varies considerably among these different causes of vitamin D deficiency. In nutritional deficiency 1000 U/day is adequate.* In liver disease 5000 to 10,000 IU/day may be required to produce normal levels of 25-OHD. In renal failure the serum 25-OHD levels are not depressed, as is the case for nutritional deficiency and vitamin D deficiencies associated with liver disease. Moreover, in renal failure the objective is to raise serum 25-OHD above the physiological range to where the concentration of 25-OHD is high enough for this metabolite to function as 1,25-diOHD. This occurs when serum 25-OHD levels exceed 150 ng/ml compared with normal levels of 20 ng/ml. Vitamin D at a dose of 50,000 units/day or more on a chronic basis is needed to produce such levels. Alternatively, 25-OHD, 50 μg/day, or 1,25-diOHD at 0.5 μg/day is required for appropriate physiological responses in renal failure.

The advantage of vitamin D over the other two metabolites is that it is less expensive. The advantages of 1,25-diOHD over 25-OHD or vitamin D are that 1,25-diOHD acts more quickly and its action dissipates more quickly. Thus, when hypercalcemia is a complication of treatment, it spontaneously resolves more quickly after 1,25-diOHD than after 25-OHD or vitamin D therapy. Compromising these advantages somewhat is that 1,25-diOHD tends to produce hypercalcemia more frequently than does vitamin D treatment. The reason for the more rapid action of 1,25-diOHD over vitamin D is that 1,25-diOHD is biologically active without further metabolism, whereas under physiological conditions vitamin D must be metabolized to 25-OHD and then to 1,25-diOHD before it is biologically active. The reasons for the differential duration of action of vitamin D and its metabolites are as follows: (1) Because vitamin D is stored in body fat, this storage depot must be depleted before the action of vitamin D dissipates.† (2) 25-OHD, which in high concentrations acts directly on target tissues without further metabolism, has a longer duration of action than does 1,25-diOHD because its affinity for

---

*Total treatment time can be reduced by giving 50,000 IU/day for 2 to 3 months instead of 1000 IU/day for 6 or more months.

†The hypercalcemia produced by Vitamin D is relatively prolonged not only because Vitamin D is stored in fat but also because the active metabolite in this circumstance is 25-OHD, and this metabolite has a serum halflife longer than that of 1,25-diOHD.

vitamin D–binding protein in blood is much greater than that of 1,25-diOHD. Accordingly, the serum half-life of 25-OHD is 10 days and that of 1,25-diOHD less than 1 day.

The objective of therapy with vitamin D or its metabolites is correction of hypocalcemia without overcorrection. In severe osteomalacia the serum calcium will be corrected before the bones are healed (Fig. 78-8; compare serum alkaline phosphatase curve with serum calcium curve). Once the serum calcium is corrected, the bones will eventually heal. When renal failure is not present, 24-h urine calcium can be used as an endpoint to establish proper dose. For example, in nutritional vitamin D deficiency an increase in urine calcium from 50 to 150 mg/day suggests adequate vitamin D therapy. When urine calcium exceeds 200 mg/day, vitamin D therapy should be withdrawn for two reasons: First, a urine calcium of >250 mg/day in females and >300 mg/day in males can result in renal stone formation and, second, hypercalciuria heralds hypercalcemia, which is the most serious complication of vitamin D therapy. Serum and urine calcium should be monitored every 1 to 3 months during vitamin D therapy and every 1 to 4 weeks during 25-OHD or 1,25-diOHD therapy. Monitoring is needed because even before the bones are healed the patient can develop hypercalcemia, and because one needs evidence of an effective dose, which varies considerably from patient to patient.

All patients with vitamin D–deficiency osteomalacia should receive adequate amounts of calcium during vitamin D treatment. The normal recommended allowance in a young adult of either sex is 800 mg of calcium per day, whereas in postmenopausal women the requirement for zero calcium balance increases to 1500 mg/day. Patients with vitamin D–deficiency osteomalacia should receive at least this much calcium, and healing may occur faster if the patient receives an amount in excess of the recommended allowance, such as 2 g daily. The most commonly prescribed forms of calcium are calcium carbonate salts, which are readily absorbed except in patients with achlorhydria.* These include Tums, which contain 200 mg of calcium per tablet, and Os-Cal, which contains 250 mg of calcium per tablet. Calcium phosphate preparations are also available, but the absorption of calcium from these preparations is more uncertain than that of calcium carbonate preparations. Moreover, although phosphate is an important component of bone mineral, phosphate is ubiquitous in dietary constituents and absorbed much more readily than is calcium; there-

fore, oral phosphate supplementation is unnecessary in vitamin D–deficiency osteomalacia.

For treatment of osteomalacia due to phosphate deficiency, one uses neutral phosphate salts. A solution of neutral phosphate salt can be made up at a local pharmacy or is commercially available as Neutrophos, which is a sodium- and potassium-containing neutral phosphate salt, or as Neutrophos K, which contains no sodium. Patients requiring phosphate therapy for osteomalacia usually have a renal phosphate leak, i.e., a depressed tubular maximum for phosphate reabsorption. Thus, after phosphate salt ingestion, the postabsorptive increase in serum phosphorus is only transient. Nevertheless, by administering 500 mg of phosphate, four times a day, it is usually possible to correct the serum phosphate levels for sufficient time to allow normal, or at least improved, bone mineralization.

Some patients may require more than 2 g of phosphate per day for correction of the osteomalacia. However, adults who take more than 2 g/day frequently have an unacceptable amount of diarrhea. Gastrointestinal symptoms are the main complication of neutral phosphate salts taken orally. When phosphates are given intravenously, they can cause soft-tissue calcifications, but this is not a problem when phosphate is given orally in doses of less than 3 to 4 g/day to patients with normal serum levels of calcium and creatinine. The effect of phosphate treatment on bone mineralization can be monitored by serial measurement of serum alkaline phosphatase, which will decrease to normal as the osteomalacia heals, and of radial bone mass by photon absorptiometry, which will show a detectable increase in 1 year if the osteomalacia is severe.

In those patients with osteomalacia due to phosphate deficiency who also have a depressed serum level of 1,25-diOHD, it is important to add vitamin D or a metabolite to the therapeutic program. If this is not done, the serum calcium will tend to fall, which will lead to a rise in the serum PTH, which in turn will further depress the TmP and thereby lead to a drop in the basal serum phosphate level. Thus, by administering vitamin D to maintain a normal or high normal serum calcium, one can maintain, or even increase, the TmP. Because of this indirect effect of vitamin D (via depression of PTH) to increase TmP, it is important to use the highest dose of vitamin D that does not produce hypercalciuria, which is defined as a urine calcium of > 250 mg/day in females and > 300 mg/day in males. The form of vitamin D (vitamin D, 25-OHD, or 1,25-diOHD) is not important; rather, it is the dosage required to increase calcium absorption to the point where serum calcium is borderline high that will determine drug efficacy.

---

*Even with achlorhydria, significant amounts of calcium (i.e., about 70 percent of that absorbed in the presence of normal gastric acidity) are absorbed from calcium carbonate preparations.

Chapter 79

HYPERPARATHYROIDISM IN THE ELDERLY

Kenneth W. Lyles

BACKGROUND

Hyperparathyroidism is a common disorder of calcium, phosphorus, and bone metabolism caused by increased circulating levels of parathyroid hormone (PTH). Over the past three decades the diagnosis of primary hyperparathyroidism has become more common with the introduction of routine multiphasic serum chemistry studies. The disease occurs twice as frequently in women as in men; current incidence rates are 2 cases per 1000 women over 60 years of age and 1 case per 1000 men over 60 years of age.[1] Most of these cases are asymptomatic at presentation. Hyperparathyroidism is a disease of importance to geriatricians because it occurs with increasing frequency in older patients.

In hyperparathyroidism, PTH is inappropriately secreted by single or multiple glands in the presence of increased serum calcium levels. The disease is considered primary when autonomous hypersecretion of PTH is due to a single adenoma, diffuse hyperplasia, multiple adenomas, or, rarely, a parathyroid carcinoma. Secondary hyperparathyroidism occurs when there is a prolonged hypocalcemic stimulus, as in cases of vitamin D deficiency or chronic renal failure. Tertiary hyperparathyroidism occurs in patients with chronic secondary hyperparathyroidism who develop autonomous hypersecretion of PTH and hypercalcemia, e.g., patients who undergo successful kidney transplants. This chapter will focus on primary hyperparathyroidism only.

ETIOLOGY AND PATHOLOGY

The etiology of primary hyperparathyroidism is unknown. When calcium is infused into hypercalcemic hyperparathyroid patients, there is a failure to suppress the PTH levels. Furthermore, when cells from hyper-parathyroid glands are incubated in vitro, higher levels of ionized calcium in the medium are required to suppress PTH release than are required to suppress PTH release from cells from normal glands.[2] These data suggest that in part the abnormality occurring in the parathyroid gland is an elevation of the set point at which ionized calcium levels suppress PTH release.

In most cases of hyperparathyroidism, no etiologic agent can be identified; these represent sporadic cases. Recent work suggests that previous neck exposure to ionizing radiation is associated with an increased incidence of hyperparathyroidism.[3] Lithium, when used for therapy of bipolar disorders, is associated with hypercalcemia and increased PTH levels in up to 10 percent of patients. A few causes of hyperparathyroidism, usually parathyroid hyperplasia, are familial disorders which have an autosomal dominant mode of transmission: (1) familial hyperparathyroidism; (2) multiple endocrine neoplasia type I (Wermer's syndrome: hyperparathyroidism, islet cell tumors, and pituitary tumors); (3) multiple endocrine neoplasia type II (Sipple's syndrome: medullary carcinoma of the thyroid, pheochromocytoma, and hyperparathyroidism).[4,5] Only rarely does hyperparathyroidism occur in multiple endocrine neoplasia type IIB or III (medullary carcinoma of the thyroid, pheochromocytoma, mucosal neuromas, and marfanoid body habitus).[6]

The pathological abnormality in the parathyroid gland(s) may be an adenoma, four-gland hyperplasia, multiple adenomas, or carcinoma. Single adenomas cause 80 percent of cases of hyperparathyroidism. Hyperplasia of all four glands is found in 15 percent of cases; parathyroid carcinomas and multiple adenomas comprise the remainder. Frequently, determining whether a single gland is an adenoma or chief cell hyperplasia is difficult to do by histological features alone. Often it is necessary to consider the gross pathology seen at operation to classify the disease. An adenoma is diagnosed when only one abnormal gland is found (all other glands are normal). Chief cell hyperplasia is diagnosed when more than one abnormal gland is found. Controversy currently exists regarding whether it is possible to have multiple adenomas. In several studies, enlargement of only two glands was documented, with the remaining two being normal.[7] A rarer form of parathyroid hyperplasia is called "water-clear cell" hyperplasia, in which large, membrane-lined vesicles fill the cytoplasm. Finally, parathyroid carcinoma is diagnosed by finding mitotic figures in the gland or finding capsular or vascular invasion in pathological specimens obtained during surgery.

SIGNS AND SYMPTOMS

Patients with primary hyperparathyroidism can present with a varying spectrum of signs and symptoms ranging from a total lack of symptoms to acute hypercalcemic crisis. Currently, diagnosis is usually made by routine calcium measurements with multichannel screening chemistries in a patient with either no symptoms or only weakness or easy fatigability; acute hypercalcemic crisis is now a rare form of presentation.[8] Most of the specific signs and symptoms of hyperparathyroidism involve the skeleton or the kidneys.

The specific bone lesion in hyperparathyroidism is osteitis fibrosa cystica. This lesion can be demonstrated on bone biopsy as a reduction in trabecular bone volume, increased areas of bone resorption (Howship's lacunae) filled with multinucleated osteoclasts, and areas of peritrabecular fibrosis. Hyperparathyroidism can be diagnosed radiographically with magnified fine-grain radiographs of the hands showing subperiosteal resorption and loss of the distal tuft of the phalanges (Fig. 79-1) or the distal end of the clavicles. While all patients with hyperparathyroidism have bone biopsy abnormalities, not all patients have demonstrable radiographic abnormalities. Radiographic evidence of subperiosteal resorption is specific for hyperparathyroidism. Given the current tendency for earlier diagnosis, it is rare to see this lesion in primary hyperparathyroidism; it is more frequently seen in secondary hyperparathyroidism from chronic renal failure.

Other skeletal abnormalities include diffuse osteopenia or osteosclerosis which, when present in the skull gives a mottled "salt and pepper" appearance (Fig. 79-2). In more severe cases, brown tumors or bone cysts made up of collections of osteoclasts and fibrous tissue are found in hands, feet, ribs, long bones, jaws, or pelvic bones. These lesions can produce pain, or they may result in fracture. Patients with radiographic evidence of hyperparathyroidism have elevations of the skeletal isoenzyme alkaline phosphate in serum, and in the urine

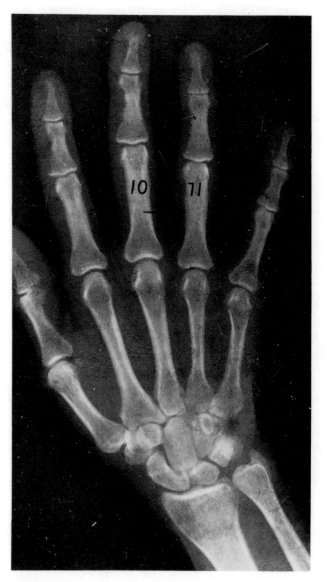

FIGURE 79-1
Hand radiograph from a hyperparathyroid patient showing subperiosteal bone resorption of most prominent on the radial side of the proximal and middle phalanges of the first two fingers. Also note early loss of the distal phalangeal tuft. *(Photo courtesy of Dr. Salutario Martinez, Department of Radiology, Duke University Medical Center.)*

there are increased amounts of hydroxyproline reflecting increased bone resorption.

Recently the effect of hyperparathyroidism on bone mineral density and its role in osteoporosis have been evaluated. With improved techniques to measure bone mineral content, it is possible to measure changes in both trabecular and cortical bone envelopes. Several cross-sectional studies have suggested that hyperparathyroid subjects have decreased amounts of trabecular bone in the vertebrae.[9,10] Longitudinal studies show that bone loss can vary, with some hyperparathyroid patients losing bone and others not doing so.[11] More recently, several groups have suggested that hyperparathyroidism results in cortical bone loss, rather than trabecular bone loss.[12,13] Thus, bone loss with this disease is variable.

Nephrolithiasis occurs in 20 to 25 percent of hyperparathyroid patients, and the stone usually contains calcium oxalate or calcium phosphate. Of patients with kidney stones, approximately 5 percent have hyperparathyroidism. PTH causes a proximal renal tubular acidosis, increasing bicarbonate loss and decreasing hydrogen ion excretion, as well as lowering the phosphate reabsorption threshold. These changes cause a hyperchloremic metabolic acidosis, and up to 50 percent of patients will be hypophosphatemic. Long-standing hyperparathyroidism can cause nephrocalcinosis and a subsequent decline in the glomerular filtration rate. Hypercalcemia can lead to nephrogenic diabetes insipidus when the renal tubule becomes unresponsive to the action of antidiuretic hormone. PTH acts on the renal tubule by stimulating adenylate cyclase with the formation of the intracellular messenger cyclic AMP. Urinary cyclic AMP levels are increased in over 80 percent of patients with this disorder.

Most other signs and symptoms of hyperparathyroidism can be attributed to the resultant hypercalcemia or, more specifically, the elevated ionized calcium level. *Gastrointestinal* disorders include anorexia, nausea, vomiting, and constipation. Peptic ulcer disease occurs with increased frequency, and, rarely, it may be the first clue of a multiple endocrine neoplasia Type I syndrome (gastrinoma). Pancreatitis can also occur or be exacerbated by the hypercalcemia. *Central nervous system* dis-

orders include impaired cognition, recent memory loss, anosmia, depression, lethargy, and coma. Thus, hypercalcemia and hyperparathyroidism are rare but important considerations in the differential diagnosis of depression and dementia in the elderly. *Neuromuscular* disturbances include a proximal weakness, more prominent in lower than in upper extremities, and pruritis caused by metastatic calcification in the skin. *Articular* disturbances include pseudogout from calcium pyrophosphate crystal deposition in articular cartilage, calcific tendonitis, and chondrocalcinosis. The main *cardiovascular* disturbance is an increased frequency of hypertension.

Physical signs are unusual in hyperparathyroidism. Soft tissue calcification can cause pseudogout or cutaneous calcification. When present in the eye, deposits of calcium phosphate crystals can cause conjunctivitis. In the cornea, band keratopathy (a vertical line of calcium phosphate deposition parallel to and within the ocular limbus) is best appreciated with a slit-lamp examination. Enlarged parathyroid glands are difficult to palpate in the neck; generally when a nodule is found in the neck of a suspected hyperparathyroid patient, it represents thyroid rather than parathyroid tissue.

DIAGNOSIS

Primary hyperparathyroidism is diagnosed by elevated serum calcium levels and, frequently, associated hypophosphatemia, without any other apparent disease or drug causing the abnormalities. Over the last 25 years techniques for measuring PTH have improved significantly, making it possible to diagnose hyperparathyroidism directly, rather than by exclusion as had been done previously. Thus, to prove hyperparathyroidism, serum PTH levels should be measured directly. Early assays measured the carboxy-terminal portion of PTH.[14] Since this fragment is cleared by the kidney, the diagnosis of hypercalcemia in patients with renal insufficiency was confounded. With improvement in assay techniques and development of amino-terminal and especially midmolecule and intact assays,[15,16] it is now easier to discriminate between parathyroid and nonparathyroid causes of elevations in serum calcium levels. Most clinical PTH assays have been validated so that the laboratory provides a range reflecting previous experience with the assay and showing where the patient's PTH and serum calcium levels fall in relation to the laboratory's other cases of hyperparathyroidism. In most nonparathyroid causes of hypercalcemia, PTH levels will be suppressed, except in the unusual case of a malignant neoplasm that produces PTH. As will be discussed below, malignancy-associated hypercalcemia is always a concern in the differential diagnosis of hypercalcemia, but neoplasms that are actually proven to produce active PTH

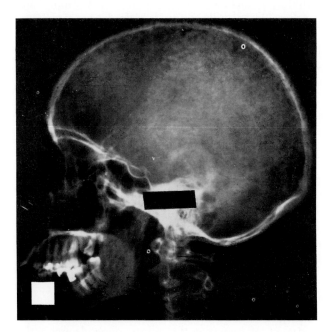

FIGURE 79-2
Skull x ray from a hyperparathyroid patient showing the classic "salt and pepper" appearance. (*Photo courtesy of Dr. Salutario Martinez, Department of Radiology, Duke University Medical Center.*)

are unusual, most such cases being renal, pancreatic, or hepatic carcinomas.[16] In such instances the PTH-related peptide secreted by the tumor does not usually cross-react with PTH of parathyroid origin in the immunoassays employed in most laboratories.

Serum phosphate levels may be low in hyperparathyroidism, but they can be normal, especially if there is renal impairment. Although PTH does cause phosphaturia, other factors such as dietary intake and time of day may affect renal phosphate handling. Furthermore, patients with malignancy-associated hypercalcemia can have a decrease in the renal phosphate reabsorption threshold from hypercalcemia per se or from the tumor-derived peptides which produce the hypercalcemia.[17] Other serum electrolyte abnormalities, such as elevated chloride, low bicarbonate, and low magnesium levels, are not specific enough to be of diagnostic value. Both an elevated serum alkaline phosphatase level and increased urinary hydroxyproline level suggest significant skeletal involvement from hyperparathyroidism; in such cases, fine-grain radiographs of the hands should be obtained in order to search for evidence of subperiosteal resorption.

Patients who are being evaluated for hyperparathyroidism should have a 24-hour urine calcium excretion measured. Twenty-four-hour calcium values above 100 mg in a hypercalcemic patient will exclude the diagnosis of familial hypercalcemic hypocalciuria, a disorder with normal PTH levels which does not require surgery.[18] Determination of nephrogenous cyclic AMP with serum and urine cyclic AMP is utilized less frequently to diagnose primary hyperparathyroidism, since patients with malignancy-associated hypercalcemia also have elevated levels.

Routine use of preoperative localization of abnormal parathyroid tissue in hyperparathyroidism should not be part of the diagnostic evaluation, since noninvasive imaging techniques require further development before being valid for such application. Arteriography and selective venous catheterization looking for "stepped-up" levels is a technically difficult procedure and should be performed by experienced hands only when hyperparathyroidism persists after a failed neck exploration.

DIFFERENTIAL DIAGNOSIS

The differential diagnosis of hyperparathyroidism is that of hypercalcemia, which can be caused by a diverse group of diseases and drugs (Table 79-1). A major concern when hypercalcemia is encountered is whether it is due to a neoplasm. The clinical setting must be considered. Most patients with malignancy-associated hypercalcemia have obvious neoplastic disease on thorough examination and routine diagnostic workup.[19] Thus, a chest x ray, a mammogram, and a serum and urine pro-

TABLE 79-1
Differential Diagnosis of Hypercalcemia

Increased Parathyroid Hormone Levels
  Primary hyperparathyroidism
  Malignancy-associated hypercalcemia (rare)
Normal-to-Low Parathyroid Hormone Levels
  Malignancy-associated hypercalcemia:
    Hematological malignancies
    Nonhematological malignancies
  Calcium supplementation
  Thiazide diuretics
  Familial hypocalciuric hypercalcemia
  Hyperthyroidism
  Vitamin D intoxication
  Chronic granulomatous diseases
  Immobilization
  Retinoic acid derivative usage
  Milk-alkali syndrome

tein electrophoresis should be ordered when evaluating hypercalcemia. Since primary hyperparathyroidism is a common disease in older women, an elderly female with hypercalcemia without obvious evidence of malignant disease will be more likely to have primary hyperparathyroidism than occult malignancy.[19]

Familial hypocalciuria hypercalcemia (FHH) should be considered in an evaluation of hypercalcemia. Although uncommon, FHH can present with hypercalcemia, but there is usually a family history reflecting an autosomal dominant mode of inheritance, and 24-hour urinary calcium excretion is below 100 mg. At present no adverse effects of the hypercalcemia have been reported from affected kindreds under supervision,[20] and parathyroidectomy does not alter the hypercalcemia.

Drugs that cause hypercalcemia, such as thiazide diuretics and calcium supplements, can be excluded by withdrawing them for 4 weeks and making sure that serum calcium levels return to normal. Hypercalcemia caused by vitamin D intoxication can be diagnosed by measuring 25-hydroxyvitamin D levels and finding a level above 120 ng/ml. Hypercalcemia can be found in sarcoidosis, tuberculosis, and chronic fungal infections. The mechanism in all these diseases is believed to be increased production of 1,25-dihydroxyvitamin D by the granulomatous tissue, which causes increased calcium absorption from the gastrointestinal tract. Other diseases causing hypercalcemia, such as hyperthyroidism, adrenal insufficiency, and vitamin D intoxication, should be diagnosed by their historical or clinical features.

THERAPY

Treatment of hyperparathyroidism depends upon the way in which the patient presents to the physician. Since most cases are asymptomatic at presentation, no immediate therapy is usually necessary, and a thorough diagnostic evaluation can be undertaken. When the patient presents with a hypercalcemic crisis (e.g., obtunded with serum calcium levels of greater than 13 mg/dl), management of the hypercalcemia must take precedence over diagnostic studies. Most hypercalcemic patients are dehydrated and may require several liters of parenteral fluids to lower the serum calcium into the 11.0 mg/dl range. Once hydration has been reestablished and the patient is stable, further decisions about therapy can be made.

At this time there is no effective chronic medical therapy for primary hyperparathyroidism. Beta-blockers, estrogen therapy in postmenopausal women, phosphate supplementation with potassium phosphate (Neutra-Phos-K), etidronate disodium (Didronel), or oral cellulose phosphate with dietary calcium restriction may lower serum calcium levels, while other aspects of the disease may progress.[21] Therefore, long-term management of hyperparathyroidism must involve a decision about whether to intervene surgically or to follow the patient until there is an indication for surgery.

Since many cases of hyperparathyroidism are asymptomatic and without any potential complications of the disease at diagnosis, immediate surgery is not necessary, and some patients may never need an operation.[22] Understanding of long-term complications is incomplete, and no study has randomized asymptomatic patients to surgery or medical follow-up. It would appear, however, that patients with serum calcium levels below 11.0 mg/dl and no other evidence of disease can be safely followed. Since many of the patients are postmenopausal women, there is a risk of accelerating bone loss leading to osteoporosis.[23] At present, no markers are available in lieu of direct measurements to suggest who will lose bone, develop nephrolithiasis, or have a decline in glomerular filtration rate. Therefore, patients in whom the diagnosis of "biochemical hyperparathyroidism" is made require close follow-up; in addition, they should be educated about the signs and symptoms of hypercalcemia. These patients should have yearly serum measurements of calcium and creatinine, as well as a yearly KUB x ray searching for nephrolithiasis. Postmenopausal women should have a noninvasive measurement of bone mineral density yearly. Thus, if physician and patient decide not to operate for hyperparathyroidism, education and long-term follow-up are necessary.

For patients who require surgery, the most important aspect is referral to a surgeon who is experienced in neck disections and identification of parathyroid glands. With an experienced surgeon, parathyroidectomy is usually not a major procedure unless the sternum must be split to find a substernal gland. All four glands should be identified and biopsied for histological confirmation. Since 80 percent of the cases of hyperparathyroidism are caused by a single adenoma, removal of the offending gland is curative. When hyperplasia is identified, most surgeons remove three and one-half glands, marking the remaining portion of gland so it can be identified if necessary in the future. Transplantation of parathyroid tissue into the forearm after removal of all of the glands from the neck is used by some surgeons, especially when they anticipate removing more tissue should hyperplasia become a problem at a later time (e.g., with chronic renal failure).

Postoperatively, patients should be watched closely for 72 hours for signs of hypocalcemia. Nervousness, tingling, and a positive Chvostek or Trousseau sign may indicate hypocalcemia, which should be confirmed by total or ionized serum calcium levels. Many patients have transient hypocalcemia, and additional calcium should be given only if the level is below 8.0 mg/dl. Intravenous calcium as the chloride or gluconate salt may be given for several days, but persistent hypocalcemia will require oral calcium in a dose of 1000 to 1200 mg daily. If hypocalcemia is severe, 1,25-dihydroxyvitamin D (calcitriol) can be added at 0.5 to 1.0 μg/day in doses divided every 12 hours. Calcitriol can cause hypercalcemia and hypercalciuria; therefore, serum and urine levels must be monitored. Patients who have developed hypocalcemia from skeletal uptake of calcium and phosphorus with healing of osteitis fibrosa cystica ("hungry bones") have normal or low serum phosphorus levels. This complication is currently rare because of early detection of the disease; treatment with calcium supplements and calcitriol can be necessary for up to 3 months. Permanent hypoparathyroidism is a rare complication of parathyroidectomy (when performed by experienced surgeons), but it can occur. Hypocalcemia with persistent hyperphosphatemia postoperatively suggests hypoparathyroidism. This can occur transiently from bruising of the glands as they are identified and biopsied at surgery, so follow-up is required to determine whether parathyroid function returns over time. Finally, hyperparathyroid patients can have low serum magnesium levels, another cause of hypocalcemia. Thus, the serum magnesium level should be checked if hypocalcemia develops postoperatively. Since serum magnesium levels may not reflect tissue stores, patients should receive parenteral magnesium if a low normal level is found.

REFERENCES

1. Heath H III, Hodgson SF, Kennedy MA: Primary hyperparathyroidism incidence, morbidity, and potential impact in a community. *N Engl J Med* 302:189, 1980.
2. Brown EM, Brennan MF, Hurwitz S et al: Dispersed cells prepared from human parathyroid glands: Distinct calcium sensitivity of adenoma vs primary hyperplasia. *J Clin Endocrinol Metab* 46:267, 1978.

3. Katz A, Braunstein GD: Clinical, biochemical, and pathologic features of radiation-associated hyperparathyroidism. *Arch Intern Med* 143:79, 1983.

4. Wermer P: Genetic aspects of adenomatosis of endocrine glands. *Am J Med* 16:363, 1954.

5. Sipple JH: The association of pheochromocytoma with carcinoma of the thyroid gland. *JAMA* 31:163, 1961.

6. Marx SJ, Powell D, Shimkin PM et al: Familial hyperparathyroidism: Mild hypercalcemia in at least nine members of a kindred. *Ann Intern Med* 78:371, 1973.

7. Verdonk CA, Edis AJ: Parathyroid double adenomas: Fact or fiction? *Surgery* 90:523, 1981.

8. Fitzpatrick LA, Bilezikian JP: Acute primary hyperparathyroidism. *Am J Med* 82:275, 1987.

9. Richardson ML, Pozzi-Mucelli RS, Genant HK: Bone mineral changes in primary hyperparathyroidism. *Skeletal Radiol* 15:85, 1986.

10. Pak CYC, Kaplan R, Browne R: Photon absorptiometric analysis of bone density in primary hyperparathyroidism. *Lancet* 2:7, 1975.

11. Potts JT Jr: Diseases of the parathyroid gland and other hyper- and hypocalcemic disorders, in Braunwald E, Isselbacher KJ, Petersdorf RG, Wilson JD, Martin JB, Fauci AS (eds): *Harrison's Principles of Internal Medicine*, 11th ed. New York, McGraw-Hill, 1987, p 1870.

12. Parfitt AM, Kleerkoper M, Rno D, Stanciu J, Villanueva AR: Cellular mechanisms of cortical thinning in primary hyperparathyroidism (PHPT). *J Bone Miner Res* 2(suppl I):384, 1987 (abstract).

13. Shane E, de la Cruz L, Ott SM: Photon absorptiometry and bone histomorphometry show preferential loss of cortical bone in renal patients. *Clin Res* 36:802, 1988 (abstract).

14. Mallette LE, Tuma SN, Berger RE et al: Radioimmunoassay for the middle region of human parathyroid hormone using an homologous antiserum with a carboxy-terminal fragment of bovine parathyroid hormone as radioligand. *J Clin Endocrinol Metab* 54:1017, 1982.

15. Potts JT Jr, Segre GV, Endres OB: *Current Clinical Concepts: Assessment of Parathyroid Function with an N-Terminal Specific Radioimmunoassay for Intact Parathyroid Hormone*. San Juan Capistrano, CA, Nichols Institute Reference Laboratories, 1987.

16. Kocherberger GG, Lyles KW: Skeletal disorders in malignant disease. *Clin Geriatr Med* 3:561, 1987.

17. Broadus AE, Mangin M, Ikeda K et al: Humoral hypercalcemia of cancer identification of a novel parathyroid hormone-like peptide. *N Engl J Med* 319:556, 1988.

18. Mary SJ, Spiegel AM, Levine MA et al: Familial hypocalciuric hypercalcemia: The relation to primary parathyroid hyperplasia. *N Engl J Med* 307:416, 1982.

19. Mundy GR, Martin TJ: The hypercalcemia of malignancy: Pathogenesis and management. *Metabolism* 31:1247, 1982.

20. Law WM Jr, Heath H III: Familial benign hypercalcemia (hypocalciuric hypercalcemia): Clinical and pathogenetic studies in 21 families. *Ann Intern Med* 102:511, 1985.

21. Bilezikian JP: The medical management of primary hyperparathyroidism. *Ann Intern Med* 96:198, 1982.

22. Bilezikian JP: Surgery or no surgery for primary hyperparathyroidism. *Ann Intern Med* 102:402, 1988.

23. Kochersberger GG, Buckley NJ, Leight GS et al: What is the clinical significance of bone loss in primary hyperparathyroidism? *Arch Intern Med* 147:1951, 1987.

Chapter 80

PAGET'S DISEASE OF BONE

Frederick R. Singer

EPIDEMIOLOGY

Paget's disease of bone is a common disorder of the elderly in England, Australia, New Zealand, North America, and continental Europe. In these areas the disease may affect 3 percent or more of the population over 40 years of age.[1] In contrast, this condition is rarely diagnosed in Scandinavian countries, Japan, China, or India.

In most studies the disease has been reported to affect males slightly more often than females. It is also now more widely appreciated that multiple members of a family may manifest Paget's disease. As many as 25 percent of patients have at least one family member with the disease. In most instances the patterns of familial aggregation suggest an autosomal dominant transmission of the disease. In a number of families genetic susceptibility is also suggested by the finding of linkage between the HLA haplotype and the clinical manifestations of the disease.

PATHOLOGY

The pathogenesis of Paget's disease involves several stages. In the earliest phase a proliferation of osteoclasts produces a localized loss of bone which is followed by an influx of undifferentiated mesenchymal cells into the marrow spaces and by proliferation of blood vessels in marrow spaces filled with fibrous connective tissue.[2] The osteoclasts often are much larger than normal and as many as 100 nuclei may be seen in a cross-section of a single cell.[3] These bone-resorbing cells often contain nuclear and cytoplasmic inclusions which resemble viral nucleocapsids of the Paramyxoviridae family of viruses. These inclusions have not been observed in other bone or bone marrow cells.

In most lesions of Paget's disease osteoclastic activity is accompanied by equally intense osteoblastic activity. Numerous plump osteoblasts overlie previously resorbed bone surfaces and studies utilizing tetracycline labeling of bone indicate that the rate of bone formation is increased.

The bone in Paget's disease is usually lamellar in character and normally mineralized, although in very active lesions woven bone may be present as well as regions of poorly mineralized osteoid. A characteristic mosaic pattern of the bone matrix features irregularly shaped pieces of lamellar bone with an erratic pattern of cement lines, undoubtedly a consequence of disorderly and accelerated bone resorption and formation. Despite the fact that Paget's disease is initiated by a localized increase in bone resorption, most fully developed lesions actually exhibit increased bone mass.

Occasionally the disease may reach a "burned out" stage in which the sclerotic lesion may remain in the absence of excessive bone cell activity. The adjacent marrow usually consists mainly of fat cells with few areas of hematopoietic or fibrovascular elements.

ETIOLOGY

A variety of hypotheses have been proposed to explain the genesis of Paget's disease (Table 80-1). No convincing data have been accumulated indicating that Paget's disease is a disorder of hormonal imbalance, vascular disorder, neoplasm, autoimmune disorder, or inborn error of connective tissue.

A viral cause of Paget's disease appears to be a reasonable possibility at present.[4] Patients with Paget's disease and slow-virus infections of the nervous system such as subacute sclerosing panencephalitis share a

TABLE 80-1
Proposed Causes of Paget's Disease

Hormonal imbalance
    Hyperparathyroidism
    Excess growth hormone secretion
    Adrenal insufficiency
    Calcitonin deficiency
Vascular disorder
Neoplasm
Autoimmune disorder
Inborn error of connective tissue
Slow-virus infection

TABLE 80-2
Clinical Manifestations of Paget's Disease

Musculoskeletal
    Pain (bone or joint)
    Deformity (including skeletal enlargement)
Neurologic
    Hearing loss and, less commonly, other cranial nerve
      deficits
    Pain from spinal stenosis
    Muscle weakness
    Bladder and/or bowel dysfunction
Cardiovascular
    High cardiac output
    Congestive heart failure
    Increased skin temperature over affected extremities
Metabolic
    Symptoms of hypercalcemia in immobilized patients
    Hypercalciuria and renal stones
Angioid streaks of retina

number of clinical and pathologic characteristics. These include a long subclinical course, the absence of fever, localization of the disease to a single organ, the absence of polymorphonuclear leukocytes in pathologic lesions, the presence of characteristic giant cells in these lesions, and the presence of intracellular viral nucleocapsid-like structures in all patients.

There has been partial success in identifying the nuclear and cytoplasmic inclusions found in the osteoclasts of Paget's disease. Immunohistologic studies of bone biopsies or surgical specimens have revealed the antigens of a number of Paramyxoviridae viruses, particularly measles and respiratory syncytial virus, in the osteoclasts of Paget's disease.[5,6] In addition mRNA of the nucleocapsid proteins of measles[7] and respiratory syncytial virus[8] has been identified in pathologic material. However, as yet, an infectious virus has not been isolated from long-term cultures of pagetic bone cells.

CLINICAL MANIFESTATIONS AND COMPLICATIONS

The disease may affect any part of the skeleton and may be unifocal or multifocal.[9] Thus, there is a wide spectrum of clinical presentations which depend on the sites and severity of the lesions. However, it should be emphasized that many individuals with Paget's disease are asymptomatic and may not require treatment.

The symptoms and signs of Paget's disease are outlined in Table 80-2.

Bone pain in Paget's disease is generally mild to moderate. Severe pain usually indicates a neurologic complication or more frequently degenerative arthritis. Paget's disease involving the pelvis, femur, and tibia is not infrequently associated with symptomatic degenerative arthritis of the hip and knee joints, probably due to abnormal biomechanics brought on by alterations in bone structure. Acute pain also develops as a consequence of pathologic fractures of affected vertebral bodies, long bones, and, less commonly, the pelvis.

The most serious complication in patients with Paget's disease is the development of a malignant bone tumor.[10] Osteosarcomas, chondrosarcomas, fibrosarcomas, or tumors of mixed histology may develop, almost always in a preexisting pagetic lesion. Therefore, these tumors are very difficult to detect at an early stage. Rapid worsening of bone pain and/or deformity should indicate the need for radiologic evaluation followed by bone biopsy if suspicion of a tumor remains. Despite recent advances in the therapy of malignant bone tumors, the prognosis remains poor in patients with Paget's disease. Fortunately, these tumors develop in fewer than 1 percent of patients.

Benign bone tumors may also arise in pagetic lesions; giant cell tumors are most common. These tumors are often locally aggressive and tend to recur after surgery.

LABORATORY EVALUATION

RADIOLOGY

The diagnosis of Paget's disease is almost always established by the characteristic roentgenographic appearance of the lesions. As in the case of the pathologic evolution of the disease, there are distinct stages of Paget's disease detected radiologically.[11]

The earliest detectable lesions of Paget's disease are osteolytic and are usually most readily observed in the skull and long bones. In the skull, discrete oval or round areas of osteopenia have been termed *osteoporosis circumscripta* (Fig. 80-1). In lower-extremity long bones the disease usually begins as a localized lesion in the subchondral region of the epiphyses. The lesion usually has a V or arrowhead shape at its advancing edge. These

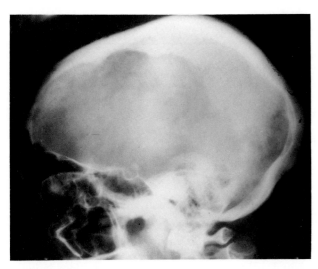

FIGURE 80-1
Extensive osteolytic lesion in the skull of a 62-year-old man with Paget's disease.

lesions have been observed to progress toward the opposite end of the affected long bone at an average rate of approximately 1 cm/year in untreated patients.

As the osteolytic process slowly progresses to involve much of the long bone or skull, the more familiar osteosclerotic (or "osteoblastic") lesions of Paget's disease replace the osteolytic regions. Over a period of many years the bone becomes chaotic in structure and thickened. The overall bone size may increase considerably. In the skull a "cotton-wool" appearance may develop (Fig. 80-2). Bowing of the weight-bearing long bones is common when the disease involves most of the bone. In some cases incomplete small transverse fissures are found in the cortex along the convex side of the bowed long bone. These lesions may precede pathologic fractures.

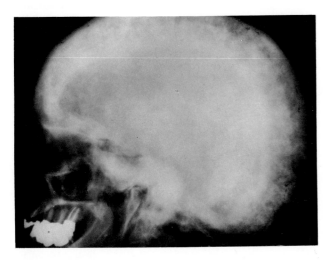

FIGURE 80-2
Skull of a 70-year-old man with Paget's disease exhibiting marked calvarial thickening and generalized patchy sclerosis.

In the final stage of a pagetic lesion involving an entire bone, there is predominance of osteosclerosis, although secondary osteolytic fronts may be present.

The development of a neoplasm in lesions of Paget's disease is particularly difficult to detect in an early stage since the chaotic underlying structure obscures the presence of the neoplastic lesions. In the case of a malignant lesion the suspicion is often raised when the tumor finally erodes through the cortex into the surrounding soft tissue.

Computerized tomography and magnetic resonance imaging are newer modalities of diagnostic imaging whose full role has not been established in the care of patients with Paget's disease. However, in patients with back pain, computerized tomography has been particularly useful in defining whether degenerative arthritis, spinal stenosis, or nerve root impingement are likely to be responsible for the symptoms.

A variety of radioisotopes can be used to assess the metabolic activity of pagetic lesions. Most commonly technetium 99m–labeled bisphosphonates are used.[12] These are bone-seeking agents whose localization in bone appears dependent both upon relative vascularity and on the extent of hydroxyapatite crystal surface available for binding of the bisphosphonate. Bone scans utilizing the radiolabeled bisphosphonates have been extensively demonstrated to be far more sensitive in detecting asymptomatic lesions of Paget's disease than roentgenograms, although "burned-out" sclerotic lesions may be missed. Bone scans should be done when there is a question of the activity of a particular lesion of Paget's disease or when it is desirable to document the full extent of the disease.

Gallium 67 uptake, reflecting cellular activity, can also localize pagetic lesions and is a reasonably sensitive means of following the response to calcitonin therapy.[13]

BIOCHEMISTRY

The measurement of alkaline phosphatase activity in the circulation is the most frequently used test in the biochemical assessment of Paget's disease. The activity of this enzyme, which is located in the plasma membrane of osteoblasts, is believed to reflect the number and functional state of osteoblasts in patients with bone disease who are not pregnant and who have no other disease which might produce a rise in other isoenzymes of alkaline phosphatase. In Paget's disease the level of alkaline phosphatase activity has been found to correlate with the extent of the skeleton affected by the disease as established by roentgenographic survey.[14] In untreated patients serial alkaline phosphatase determinations generally reveal a constant or slowly rising level of activity over a period of years. It should also be appreciated that normal levels of alkaline phosphatase activity in patients with small regions of skeletal involvement do not necessarily indicate burned-out disease since intense activity in these lesions often can be demonstrated by bone scan.

Urinary hydroxyproline excretion is a biochemical index of bone matrix resorption. It is usually measured in a 24-hour urine specimen while the patient is on a low gelatin diet, although a fasting urinary hydroxyproline/creatinine measurement provides equally relevant information. As with serum alkaline phosphatase activity, hydroxyproline excretion correlates well with the extent of Paget's disease.[14] This test should not be considered a routine test in Paget's disease, but it is indicated when a patient has a complicating disorder which produces elevation of extraskeletal alkaline phosphatase activity. As in the case of total serum alkaline phosphatase activity, measurement of urinary hydroxyproline excretion is not specific for metabolic activity of bone. Excretion of this amino acid may be increased in patients with extensive burns or skin diseases such as psoriasis.

TREATMENT

GENERAL CONSIDERATIONS AND INDICATIONS

In evaluating a symptomatic patient with Paget's disease, it is important to consider whether the main complaints are, in fact, due to Paget's disease. In many cases the symptoms that cause the patient to seek care are not a direct consequence of Paget's disease. This is particularly true in patients who have degenerative arthritis.[14] Close attention to the nature of the symptoms, the physical examination, and the roentgenograms should allow the clinician to determine whether treatment of Paget's disease is indicated.

Table 80-3 lists indications for drug therapy of Paget's disease. Since safe and effective drug therapy has been available for less than 20 years, the indications for treatment continue to evolve as experience with the available drugs expands.

DRUG THERAPY

At present, three drugs have been approved for treating Paget's disease in the United States: salmon calcitonin, human calcitonin, and disodium etidronate. The treatment schedules and special characteristics of each agent are indicated in Table 80-4. Biochemical indices are decreased by 50 percent during chronic treatment. The clinical benefits of long-term calcitonin therapy include relief of bone pain, reduction of increased cardiac output, reversal of some neurologic deficits, stabilization of hearing deficit, healing of osteolytic lesions, and reduction in complications of orthopedic surgery.

Side effects (usually minor) occur in about 20 per-

TABLE 80-3
Indications for Drug Therapy of Paget's Disease

Bone pain
Preparation for orthopedic surgery
Prevention or treatment of medical complications such as hypercalcemia and high-output congestive heart failure
Prevention or treatment of neurologic complications including hearing loss and spinal cord or nerve dysfunction
Prevention of fracture or skeletal deformity in patients with rapidly progressive osteolytic lesions or in young patients

cent of patients treated with salmon calcitonin and in a higher percentage treated with human calcitonin. These include nausea, vomiting, facial flushing, perioral paresthesias, metallic taste sensation, chills, and polyuria. Tetany is extremely rare, and allergic reactions induced by salmon calcitonin are also rare.

Resistance to chronic salmon calcitonin therapy develops in more than 20 percent of patients after a successful initial treatment period.[15] This is usually associated with high titers of anti-salmon calcitonin antibodies in the circulation. These patients are responsive to treat-

TABLE 80-4
Drug Therapy of Paget's Disease

Drug	Effective Regimen	Special Characteristics
Salmon calcitonin	50–100 MRC units subcutaneously daily or three times weekly	Anti-salmon calcitonin antibodies develop in 60%; clinical resistance in >20%.
Human calcitonin	0.5 mg subcutaneously daily	Effective in salmon calcitonin resistant patients with high antibody titers. Nausea is common side effect.
Disodium etidronate	5 mg/kg body weight orally for 6 months	Effective orally. Sometimes a remission of years occurs after 6 months therapy. Some patients have transient increased bone pain. Osteolytic lesions do not heal. Osteomalacia occurs at high doses.

ment with human calcitonin. A small number of patients have become resistant to either salmon or human calcitonin in the absence of any circulating antibodies.

Questions about calcitonin therapy which still need to be answered include should the dosage be based on the extent and activity of the patient's disease and how long the hormone should be administered. Patients with rapidly progressive osteolytic disease may require higher doses to produce healing of the lesions. If long-term treatment with calcitonin is discontinued, exacerbation of biochemical abnormalities and symptoms usually occurs within 1 year.

Preliminary studies using a nasal spray form of salmon calcitonin suggest that this mode of administration may replace injections in the future.[16]

The bisphosphonates (formerly diphosphonates) are pyrophosphate (P-O-P) analogues whose pharmacologic effects are to inhibit both bone resorption and formation.[17] They bind to hydroxyapatite crystals and may remain in bone for a prolonged time after treatment is discontinued.

Disodium etidronate is currently the only bisphosphonate approved for use in the United States. The advantage of this agent is that it can be used orally, although absorption is poor and rather variable. After absorption it localizes to bone and to sites of ectopic calcification, or it is excreted unchanged in the urine. A standard recommended dose of disodium etidronate (5 mg/kg body weight daily for 6 months) produces suppression of disease activity and symptoms in a similar manner as calcitonin, with several exceptions. Although bone pain is usually relieved, there is a paradoxical increase in pain in 10 percent of patients. However, pain lessens if the drug is discontinued. Another surprising difference is that the drug seldom heals osteolytic lesions despite improvement of biochemical indices.[11,18] Therefore it is preferable to use calcitonin in patients with osteolytic lesions. Side effects are less common than with calcitonin; loose bowel movements and nausea are uncommon. Hyperphosphatemia commonly occurs, particularly if higher than recommended doses are given. High doses also produce a mineralization defect and may predispose to pathologic fractures.

After the recommended 6-month treatment course, biochemical and symptomatic remissions may persist for months or, occasionally, for years. In most patients biochemical indices return toward pretreatment levels within a year. When symptoms recur, the 6-month treatment can be given again.

Second and third generation bisphosphonates have been developed which do not produce a mineralization defect at the doses used. These are still undergoing experimental testing.

Plicamycin (mithramycin) is a toxic cancer drug which can be used to treat severe Paget's disease but should probably be limited to patients who fail to respond adequately to other drugs.[19] A combination of oral calcium supplementation and chlorthalidone has been reported to reduce bone pain and partially suppress biochemical indexes in patients with Paget's disease.[20] It is the least expensive means of treatment.

SURGERY

Surgical intervention in Paget's disease is most often needed when degenerative arthritis of the hip or knee

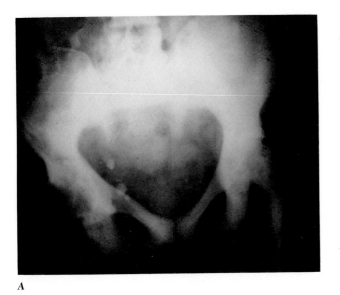
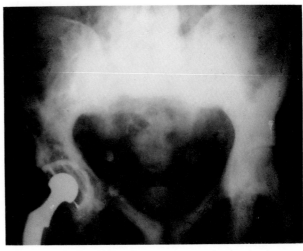

A   B

FIGURE 80-3
A. Pelvis of a 64-year-old woman revealing extensive Paget's disease with loss of the right hip joint space. The patient had marked pain on weight bearing. *B.* After total hip replacement the patient could ambulate without pain.

produces severe pain on weight bearing and impaired mobility. Often anti-inflammatory agents produce little relief of symptoms in such patients. Total hip replacement is highly effective in relieving hip pain and restoring mobility of patients with hip disease[21] (Fig. 80-3A and B), and tibial osteotomy is similarly effective in relieving knee pain in patients with severe tibial bowing.[22] Surgery may also be required in patients with neurologic symptoms related to basilar impression, spinal stenosis, or nerve root compression. Prior to any surgery it is desirable, if possible, to reduce disease activity by drug therapy in order to prevent excessive blood loss during orthopedic procedures. A reduction in serum alkaline phosphatase activity approaching 50 percent of pretreatment levels is probably adequate preoperative control.

REFERENCES

1. Singer FR: Paget's disease of bone, in Martin TJ, Raisz LG (eds): *Clinical Endocrinology of Calcium Metabolism.* New York, Dekker, 1987, p 369.
2. Schmorl G: Uber Ostitis Deformans Paget. *Virchows Arch Path Anat Physiol* 283:694, 1932.
3. Rubinstein MA et al: Osteoblasts and osteoclasts in bone marrow aspiration. *Arch Intern Med* 92:684, 1953.
4. Singer FR, Mills BG: Evidence for a viral etiology of Paget's disease of bone. *Clin Orthop Relat Res* 178:245, 1983.
5. Rebel A et al: Viral antigens in osteoclasts from Paget's disease of bone. *Lancet* 2:344, 1980.
6. Mills BG et al: Evidence for both respiratory syncytial virus and measles virus antigens in the osteoclasts of patients with Paget's disease of bone. *Clin Orthop Relat Res* 183:303, 1984.
7. Basle MF et al: Measles virus RNA detected in Paget's disease bone tissue by in situ hybridization. *J Gen Virol* 67:907, 1986.
8. Mills BG et al: Evidence for nucleocapsid gene of respiratory syncytial virus in Paget bone derived cells. *J Bone Miner Res* 3(suppl 1):S93, 1988.
9. Ziegler R et al: Paget's disease of bone in West Germany. Prevalence and distribution. *Clin Orthop Relat Res* 194:199, 1985.
10. Barry HC: *Paget's Disease of Bone.* Baltimore, Williams & Wilkins, 1969.
11. Maldague B, Malghem J: Dynamic radiologic patterns of Paget's disease of bone. *Clin Orthop Relat Res* 217:126, 1987.
12. Vellenga CJLR et al: Untreated Paget disease of bone studied by scintigraphy. *Radiology* 153:799, 1984.
13. Waxman AD et al: Gallium scanning in Paget's disease of bone. Effect of calcitonin. *Am J Roentgenol* 134:303, 1980.
14. Franck WA et al: Rheumatic manifestations of Paget's disease of bone. *Am J Med* 56:592, 1974.
15. Singer FR et al: Salmon calcitonin therapy for Paget's disease of bone. The problem of acquired clinical resistance. *Arthritis Rheum* 23:1148, 1980.
16. Nagant de Deuxchaisnes C et al: New modes of administration of salmon calcitonin in Paget's disease. *Clin Orthop Rel Res* 217:56, 1987.
17. Fleisch H: Bisphosphonates: Mechanisms of action and clinical applications, in Peck WA (ed): *Bone and Mineral Research Annual 1.* Amsterdam, Excerpta Medica, 1983, p 319.
18. Nagant de Deuxchaisnes C et al: The action of the main therapeutic regimens on Paget's disease of bone, with a note on the effect of vitamin D deficiency. *Arthritis Rheum* 23:1215, 1980.
19. Lebbin D et al: Outpatient treatment of Paget's disease of bone with mithramycin. *JAMA* 213:1153, 1970.
20. Evans RA et al: Long-term experience with a calcium-thiazide treatment for Paget's disease of bone. *Miner Electrolyte Metab* 8:325, 1982.
21. McDonald DJ et al: Total hip arthroplasty in Paget's disease. *J Bone Joint Surg* 69A:766, 1987.
22. Myers M, Singer FR: Osteotomy for tibia vara in Paget's disease under cover of calcitonin. *J Bone Joint Surg* 60A:810, 1978.

The Muscle
and Joint Systems

Chapter 81

AGING AND THE
MUSCULOSKELETAL SYSTEM

David Hamerman

This chapter reviews biochemical aspects of connective tissue components that constitute the musculoskeletal system. The focus is on age-related changes in this system in general, and a more detailed consideration of diarthrodial joints and the evolution of osteoarthritis (OA) in particular. Discussion will focus primarily on human pathophysiology rather than on findings in animals or animal models. Aging changes in bone relate fundamentally to those seen in osteoporosis, a subject reviewed elsewhere in this text and not discussed further in this chapter.

DIARTHRODIAL JOINTS

ARTICULAR CARTILAGE

Overview

The articular surface of diarthrodial joints is composed of hyaline cartilage. Special features of this cartilage must

be considered in relation to the maintenance of its integrity for articulation. The first consideration is that articular cartilage is avascular and must derive nutrients from the synovial fluid and the subchondral spaces to sustain metabolic functions of the chondrocytes.[1] The factors that contribute to the maintenance of the normal avascular state of articular cartilage are not well understood, but may be due in part to the presence of protease inhibitors.[2] Part of the reparative processes in OA involves the invasion of cartilage by vascular and cellular elements from the subchondral marrow, resulting in the formation of new cartilage and bone (osteophyte). Thus, in OA, not only is cartilage lost, but the native state of articular cartilage is violated, and calcification and ossification[3] take place in the remnants of the original hyaline cartilage.

A second consideration relating to articular cartilage is that the chondrocytes are responsible for the production of the extracellular environment. It is on the integrity of the macromolecules of this matrix that maintenance of mechanical properties during articulation depends.[4,5] It is also coming to be understood that matrix in turn plays a key role in modulating the metabolic functions of the chondrocytes.[6] Matrix depletion in OA seems to be a key factor in promoting proliferation of

Original studies described in this chapter were supported in part by a grant from the National Institute on Aging, Teaching Nursing Home Award (AG-03949). Dr. Michael Klagsbrun critically reviewed Table 81-2. Margarita LaSalle provided expert secretarial assistance.

cells which normally have a very low mitotic rate. The proliferating chondrocytes form clones, or clusters, and at least early in the course of OA, synthesize more matrix components and even some molecular species not present normally.[7]

A third aspect of cartilage is "compositional heterogeneity," i.e., changes in the cell appearance and the macromolecular composition of the matrix from the surface to the base.[1,8,9] Cells at the surface are somewhat flattened, while those in the basal parts are oval. The collagen meshwork is more dense at the surface, and the proteoglycans (PG) are of smaller molecular weight and generally not linked with hyaluronate (HA) because of the absence of link protein. Chondrocytes at the surface do not make keratan sulfate (KS) as they do in the more basal parts of the cartilage. These surface and basal characteristics vary somewhat among individuals. Muir has stated that "the quality of human cartilage in a given joint differs from one person to another and might be better suited to withstand mechanical stresses in some joints than in others."[9]

There is thus an extraordinary system of checks and balances which are modified in the aging process and in the evolution of OA. Studies on the biochemical basis for alterations in cartilage utilize essentially three approaches: (1) extraction of matrix components from the cartilage itself; (2) organ cultures, in which plugs or slices of cartilage are maintained in medium in vitro for days or weeks; (3) culture of cells dispersed from cartilage and studied initially or in subsequent passages. Obviously, approaches (2) and (3) are more conducive to manipulation of the experimental conditions. Use has also been made of a variety of isotopes to label newly synthesized macromolecular components. Radiolabeled precursors include leucine for noncollagen proteins, sulfate for PG, glucosamine for PG and HA, and proline for collagen. Labeled components are extracted and subjected to further isolation and purification by density gradient centrifugation or column chromatography to study the molecular species.

While consistency can be a factor in the use of animal models[10] in which, for example, the cruciate ligament or the meniscus can be severed or the joint immobilized under tension, and cartilage lesions resembling OA may be noted, the evolution of OA will ultimately have to be addressed in humans. Here we run into the experimental problem of sampling cartilages whose spectrum of change may vary widely even in the same joint, from visibly unaffected to denuded sites.[11]

Biochemistry

Cartilage is composed of over 70 percent water, as well as chondrocytes and macromolecular components that constitute the matrix. A detailed description of the macromolecular composition of articular cartilage is beyond the scope of this chapter, and several extensive reviews may be consulted.[1,4,5,7,12] The basic concepts are these:

1. Proteoglycans (PG) (Fig. 81-1) are an important part of cartilage. The molecular weight of PG ranges from 1×10^6 to 2×10^6. The PG consist of a protein backbone to which polysaccharide chains called glycosaminoglycans (GAG) are attached. These GAG contain an amino sugar and anionic or negatively charged group. Thus, KS is a dimer of galactose and acetylglucosamine with a sulfate ester. Chondroitin sulfate (CS) is a dimer of acetylgalactosamine with a sulfate ester on the fourth or sixth carbon and glucuronic acid. Towards the N-terminal part of the PG, where the PG is devoid of GAG, there is a region identified as hyaluronate-binding to designate a critical further assembly of macromolecules: the binding of many PG monomers by way of a link protein to a central filament of HA, which creates an enormous proteoglycan aggregate (PGA) (molecular weight $40-100 \times 10^6$). Note that not all PG monomers are "aggregating."

2. The predominant (90 percent) collagen of articular cartilage is type II.[13-15] Three chains designated $[\alpha 1(11)]_3$ constitute a triple helix, with nonhelical ends. Some "minor" collagens exist in cartilage, particularly type IX, to which PG chains are joined and which "is an excellent candidate to be involved in organizing and stabilizing the meshwork of type II collagen fibers in hyaline cartilage."[15]

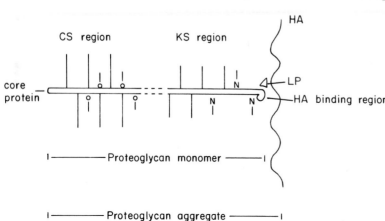

FIGURE 81-1

This is a diagram of the proteoglycan aggregate. The proteoglycan subunit or monomer has a hyaluronic acid–binding (HA-binding) region at the N-terminal part of the core protein, and the linkage to HA is further stabilized by link protein (LP). Attached to the core protein are side chains of glycosaminoglycans with regions enriched in chondroitin sulfate (CS) or keratan sulfate (KS). Short chains of oligosaccharides are also attached to the protein core by N-linkage through asparagine or O-linkage through serine or threonine. (*Adapted from Hunziker and Schenk.*[4])

The interactions between the chondrocyte, pericellular PG, and type II collagen, may be promoted by a recently identified collagen-binding glycoprotein (molecular weight 34,000) called anchorin CII, isolated from chondrocyte membranes.[6] Other components, such as chondronectin, that may mediate adhesion of chondrocytes to collagen, are reviewed by von der Mark et al.[6] These interactions are of the highest significance, because, as we will review below, they are disrupted in OA, and matrix changes in turn alter chondrocyte metabolic responses.

Mechanical Properties

The condition of the matrix is determined by the enormous PGA whose extended negatively charged GAG chains retain water and are constrained from full expansion by a dense collagen network.[7] It is as if there were innumerable coiled springs, first responding to load bearing by being further compressed and extruding water onto the surface of cartilage ("weeping lubrication"[16]), and then by regaining a more extended domain when the compressive force is relaxed, increasing the swelling pressure, and imbibing water from the surface of the cartilage. The integrity of the macromolecules of the matrix is thus the key to the mechanical properties of the intact articular cartilage; to the extent that the matrix molecules are altered in aging and in OA, normal joint function is impaired.

Aging in Cartilage

"Maturation" may be more appropriate than "aging" as a designation of changes that occur in cartilage during aging since it is arbitrary to state when aging ensues. Indeed, aging occurs throughout development.[17] Thus, in fetal cartilage, as compared with aging cartilage, the PG monomers are larger in size, more uniform in length (less polydisperse), and contain virtually no KS. In postfetal maturation, the CS chains decrease both in number and in size, and much of the sulfate in CS changes from position 4 to position 6. In addition, the content of KS increases.[18,19] There are obviously many factors that could explain such changes.[18] One factor is changes in the activity of the various enzymes in the chondrocyte responsible for the synthesis of GAG chains. A second possibility is proteolytic cleavage between the CS and KS portion of the protein core, which would produce shortened protein cores with CS chains and enrichment in both protein and KS in those fragments containing the HA-binding region retained within the tissues.[20] A third possible factor is the presence of altered stresses across the joint that could modify chondrocyte function, leading to enrichment in KS. Increased sulfated GAG synthesis was observed in chondrocyte cultures subjected to intermittent compressive force.[21]

Although diminished PG content itself may not be a factor in age-related decrease in tensile strength of articular cartilage,[22] aging cartilage does have impaired mechanical properties attributable to altered structure of the PG and collagens in the matrix.[23] An age-related factor seems to contribute to "fatigue life" of cartilage: the projections for how long it takes for cartilage to fatigue are much longer for a 50-year-old than for a 60-year-old.[24]

Investigators have been searching for a valid in vitro model of aging. In one study, femoral head cartilage from subjects ranging in age from 4 to 48 years without known articular disease was a source of explants maintained in culture for over 3 weeks.[25] Newly synthesized PG retained their large hydrodynamic size.

Evolution of Osteoarthritis: Cartilage Biochemistry

Epidemiologic studies relate OA to aging; biochemical studies, however, distinguish changes in aging cartilage from those in osteoarthritic cartilage (Table 81-1).[9,26] Yet, as Solursh has pointed out, "from the perspective of the developmental biologist, OA, like aging, can be considered a developmentally related process."[17] In animal models, as well as in human cartilage, the hydration of cartilage appears to be critical because the increased hydration of OA does not seem to reflect a change in the quality of the PG;[27] the increased hydration is, rather, a result of the altered collagen fiber network, which, when it loses its tight weave, may promote water imbibition. This change in collagen, along with dilution of PG, leads to a functional deterioration of the tissue and loss of PG, at least in part, by diffusion out. Pressure loading produces more deformation and less elastic return, with increased contact pressure on subchondral bone.[28] Whatever the "program of the chondrocyte," an altered intercellular environment contributes to conditions less

TABLE 81-1

Comparison of Articular Cartilage Changes in Aging and Osteoarthritis

Criteria	Aging	Osteoarthritis
Water content	Decreased	Increased
GAG		
CS	Normal or slightly less	Decreased
Ratio CS 4/6	Decreased	Increased
KS	Increased	Decreased
HA	Increased	Decreased
PG		
Aggregation	Normal	Diminished
Monomer size	Decreased	Decreased
Link protein	Fragmented	Normal
Proteases	"Normal"	Increased

SOURCE: Based on information from Muir[5,9] and Brandt.[26]

optimal for maintaining normal synthetic patterns and indeed may promote abnormal conditions such as release of hydrolytic enzymes.[29]

Problems in studying the biochemistry of cartilage in OA are, as noted, the profound nonuniformity of the state of the local disease process in the joint, the duration over years, and the mix of degradative and reparative changes.[30] It is agreed that KS is decreased, sulfate in CS on position 4 is increased with respect to position 6, and HA is decreased. Articular cartilage obtained from autopsy specimens shows increased neutral metalloprotease activity accompanying fibrillation primarily in the superficial layer.[29] Caution has been expressed, however, about attributing PG changes to rampant hydrolytic action in the tissues,[31] because many studies show no change in PG monomer size. The ability of PG monomers to aggregate to HA may also be unchanged. Traces of new collagen types, such as type I,[13,32] may occur, as well as alterations that include glycosylated variants of type II.[33] However, in mouse temporomandibular joint, no major shift in collagen types occurred in "aging osteoarthritic cartilages."[34]

EXPLANT CULTURES In other studies, cartilage slices were isolated from femoral heads resected for OA, and "special care was taken to exclude osteophytic or repair cartilage." The lesions were apparently not far advanced. In vitro labeling of these cartilage slices showed enhanced PG synthesis and even more marked increase in HA.[35]

In cartilage explant systems from calves,[36] steers,[37] and pigs,[38] manipulation of the culture conditions may in days produce changes in PG turnover that could shed light in terms of what happens over years in humans. Bear in mind that changes in PG, rather than in collagen, are the hallmark of acute changes in the matrix most frequently studied, because PG are more amenable to dynamic study and turn over at a rate faster than collagen. There are several ways to manipulate the culture environment to affect PG turnover: (1) modify the medium content of nutrients (particularly in regard to serum and/or growth factors), (2) add mediators that affect chondrocyte metabolism, or (3) add components that directly degrade PG molecules in the matrix.

Under short-term in vitro conditions, removal of serum from the culture medium virtually shuts down chondrocyte PG synthesis, and matrix PG content falls.[36,37] Even more intriguing is that the chondrocyte responds further by mediating loss of PG from the matrix. The proof of cell participation in PG loss (i.e., increased turnover) is that this process can be arrested by the use of a metabolic inhibitor of protein synthesis (cycloheximide).[37] This situation cannot be duplicated in vivo, of course. Indeed, in vivo the reverse process may occur: mediators may act on the chondrocyte and not

only inhibit PG synthesis, but also accelerate release of proteases and collagenase which can clip the PG core protein, or collagen, respectively.[39] Perhaps the mediator most intensively studied is interleukin-1 (IL-1), whose history began not in connective tissue research but in immunology, when it was identified as a major immunoregulator of T cell function.[40] Its applicability to connective tissues came from two sources: evidence that blood monocyte/macrophages induced synovial cell cultures to release a factor that appears to be IL-1[41] and the finding that porcine synovia itself produced a component termed catabolin,[42] subsequently shown to be identical to IL-1, that degraded cartilage. Indeed, IL-1 has been isolated directly from human synovial cells,[43,44] and its role in inducing chondrocyte release of hydrolytic and inflammatory components has been extensively studied.[39] Other mediators that activate IL-1 (lipopolysaccharides) or act directly on chondrocytes (retinol, phorbol esters) may depress chondrocyte PG synthesis and enhance hydrolytic enzyme release.[38] Mediator action in the joint highlights the intimate relationship and interactions between the synovial membrane, synovial fluid, cartilage surface, and the chondrocytes within the cartilage itself.[45]

Mediator action in the joint is clearly relevant to OA in several dimensions. First is the ability of mediators to promote cell interactions within the various tissues of the joint, as noted previously. Second is the likelihood that a variety of stimuli in the joint fluid that are derived from degradation products of cartilage could activate release of IL-1 from synovial cells over time.[45] Third is the evidence that IL-1 is present in synovial fluid from osteoarthritic joints.[46] The picture that emerges is a dynamic one of mediator release which may be intermittent over time, modifying chondrocyte metabolic functions, especially the quantity and quality of the PG delivered to the matrix, and selective local release of hydrolases.

Addition of degradative enzymes, such as trypsin or leukocyte elastase, to explant cultures can directly degrade matrix PG, which are then released into the medium. Matrix depletion is usually followed by matrix reformation, but this was not the case following use of elastase.[38]

CHONDROCYTE CULTURES In vitro studies of chondrocytes in culture extend the concept of the dynamic state of cartilage and the remarkable susceptibility of the chondrocyte to environmental conditions. Studies of bovine cartilage show that chondrocyte structure and function vary from the more superficial zones to the more basal, as noted earlier. Slices from bovine cartilage were obtained at different depths, and the chondrocytes dispersed into agarose gels.[47] The most superficial cells from the tangential zone appeared to be somewhat flat; they divided infrequently and failed to deposit a matrix rich in PG. On the other hand, deeper cells showed more typical oval morphology, divided frequently, and formed small clusters of cells within a matrix rich in PG interlaced with fine collagen fibrils. These chondrocytes incorporated more labeled sulfate into the PG, which turned over more slowly than PG produced by the superficial cells.

Whether chondrocytes dispersed from human osteoarthritic cartilage can be used as a model to study the disease in vitro is not entirely clear, but a number of studies along these lines have been done.[48-51] Several populations of PG can be isolated from the culture medium, which may reflect the functional heterogeneity of the cells in cultures.[49] Chondrocytes from osteoarthritic cartilage display in vitro findings often associated with their state in vivo. Thus, chondrocyte cultures from cartilage lesions of moderate grade appeared to synthesize more PG and to produce more proteoglycanases than chondrocytes derived from normal cartilage.[52] The observation that enhanced PG synthesis may be maintained in subculture of the chondrocytes[50,51] raises the possibility of a genetic change, rather than an extrinsic condition carried over from the matrix in the early chondrocyte cultures.

It is difficult to evaluate the potential relevance to aging and OA of chondrocyte behavior in cell culture without considering how culture conditions may induce changes in cell behavior. This discussion goes into some detail because information on the senescence and pathology of connective tissue cells in vivo is often derived from observations on the behavior of such cells in vitro.

Our purpose is to focus primarily on the chondrocyte and to examine the following issues: (1) the relation of chondrocyte longevity in culture to the age of the donor; and (2) the identification of biosynthetic markers of chondrocyte phenotype in vitro, the fidelity of phenotype maintenance during cell passage, and the factors that influence (destabilize or maintain) phenotypic markers in vitro.

CHONDROCYTE LONGEVITY AND DONOR AGE

Chondrocytes follow the principle observed for many cell types derived from donors who do not have syndromes of premature aging[53]: there is an inverse relationship between donor age and the length of time of in vitro proliferation. Articular chondrocytes from young animals underwent more doublings in vitro (i.e., a longer culture life span) than those from older animals.[54,55] However, in late passage cells, morphological alterations occurred whereby cells did not resemble their original morphology. Altered morphology in subsequent passage appeared to relate to the so-called dedifferentiation or modulation of chondrocytes in vitro,[56] rather than to contamination with and emergence of other cell lines.

MARKERS OF CHONDROCYTE PHENOTYPE IN VITRO

A general principle of chondrocyte cultures is that these cells should maintain in vitro the properties relating to macromolecular synthesis that they demonstrate in the intact cartilage. These collective biosynthetic properties relate to the phenotypic expression of the chondrocyte, and have been defined primarily by synthesis of cartilage-specific proteoglycans and type II collagen, as discussed above. When chondrocytes fail to sustain synthesis of cartilage-specific PG and type II collagen, they are said to have "modulated" or "dedifferentiated" (the latter referring to a permanent, nonreversible change). The in vivo environment of chondrocytes is clearly quite different from in vitro conditions.[56] Over 20 years ago, Holtzer[57] and his coworkers first described the phenotypic lability of chondrocytes in culture during repeated passage (subculture), whereby cell shape changed from oval to a more stellate or fibroblastic appearance, and altered PG and collagen components were observed. Benya[14] has pointed out that the products of the generalized modulated phenotype consist of type I collagen and species-dependent variations in type III collagen (present in rabbit cells but not in chick cells). These alterations were said *not* to be related to cell aging because the modulated collagen phenotype could be reversed. Pacifici and coworkers[58] also observed that "aging changes" in PG synthesis by organ cultures of chick cartilages at different ages were different from those expressed by successive generations of chondrocytes in culture.

Thus, phenotypic alterations do not appear to be a reflection of senescence.[56] The actual biochemical basis for phenotypic alteration in vitro is not well understood, but modulation can be induced not only by cell passage but also by drugs (bromodeoxyuridine), embryo extracts, phorbol esters, fibronectin, or vitamin A.[56]

Of great potential importance are factors that tend to *preserve* the phenotypic stability of the chondrocyte—important for the validity of studies conducted on such cells in vitro, but also because of potential applicability to cartilage in vivo. One way to preserve the chondrocyte phenotype in vitro is to maintain its rounded shape.[13,17,56,59] There are a number of ways to achieve this effect, such as by coating the tissue culture dish with methacrylate to prevent cell adhesiveness and flattening[59] or by maintaining the cells in a more viscous medium (collagen gels, agar, or agarose).[13,47] These mechanical aspects of in vitro culture systems have their counterpart in vivo, where the matrix "stabilizes and controls the cellular phenotype."[6] Moreover, rounded cell shape has a fundamental effect on developing cartilage cells, favoring chondrogenic differentiation and chondrogenesis.[17]

Factors that promote cell growth have recently come under investigation in terms of their ability to maintain cell phenotype in vitro. A wide variety of such growth factors are now known[60–62] (Table 81-2). Many of them promote replication and synthesis of macromolecules by connective tissue cells.[63] Chondrocyte replication in vitro can be stimulated by growth factors derived from the pituitary,[64] brain,[65] or cartilage itself.[66] So-called cartilage-derived growth factor isolated by the technique of heparin-affinity chromatography[67] is a cationic polypeptide of about 18,000 daltons that appears identical to basic fibroblast growth factor (bFGF). bFGF has been noted to preserve the chondrocyte phenotype in vitro.[68] bFGF also induces proliferation of rabbit and chick chondrocytes in soft agar where they otherwise proliferate poorly, and a large amount of cartilaginous matrix is produced.

Thus far we have been discussing the fully expressed chondrocyte (the differentiated cell) and the factors that stabilize its phenotypic expression. It must be made clear that loss of phenotype (dedifferentiation) does not refer to the cell that has yet to emerge in terms of its metabolic expression. In order to consider cells that have yet to express their chondrogenic properties we must go "back in developmental time" to the undifferentiated mesenchymal cells in the embryo. It might appear that this is not relevant to a chapter dealing with age-related cell changes, but mesenchymal cells in the

TABLE 81-2
Growth Factors with Relevance to the Musculoskeletal System*

Growth Factor	Structure	Source	Actions
PDGF	PDGF-I 31 kDa PDGF-II 28 kDa Cationic 2 chains linked (S—S bond)	Mononuclear cells Macrophages Platelets	Mitogen for fibroblasts and smooth muscle cells but *not* endothelial cells Promotes collagenase, PGE_2 release Promotes wound healing Competence factor in cell division
EGF	5.8 kDa	Submaxillary glands Biological fluids (urine, milk, saliva)	Promotes skeletal growth
HBGF†	Acidic FGF 18 kDa Basic FGF 18 kDa (53% homology)	Neural tissue Bone Above, and cells of many other tissues	Angiogenesis Mitogen Angiogenesis Mitogen Wound healing
TGF	∝ 7.8 kDa β-1 25 kDa β-2 25 kDa (70% homology)	Transformed cells Platelets Bone Soft tissues Cartilage Kidney	Transforming factor Binds to EGF receptor Angiogenesis Angiogenesis in vivo Growth inhibiting in most cell types in vitro Promotes myo-chondro- genesis Macrophage and fibro- blast chemotaxis Wound healing Bone formation
IGF-I	7.6 kDa	Somatomedins in plasma and	Regulated by growth hormone
IGF-II	7.4 kDa	tissues related to insulin	Cartilage and bone growth

*Growth-promoting substances not included: hematopoietic growth factors (Burgess AW: *Immunology Today* 7:351, 1986), tissue necrosis factor, interferons, and interleukins.[61]
†Refers to heparin-binding growth factors which are characterized by affinity to columns of heparin-Sepharose and elution at about 1.1 *M* NaCl (aFGF) or at about 1.7 *M* NaCl (bFGF).
SOURCE: Based on information from Deuel,[60] Goetzl et al.,[61] Rifkin and Klagsbrun,[62] Canalis et al.,[70] and Folkman and Klagsbrun (*Science* 235:442, 1987).

embryo are in the earliest phase of a process that has yet to evolve, and in this sense their behavior is relevant to aging. However, the intent is not to review chondrogenesis[17] but rather to mention briefly growth factors that influence the expression of mesenchymal cell differentiation. A number of studies have been made of the capacity of bone matrix to promote differentiation of mesenchymal cells to form new cartilage and bone.[69–71] The so-called cartilage-inducing factor A from bovine demineralized bone[72] appears to be identical to transforming growth factor-β (TGF-β), a 25,000-dalton component that interacts with other growth factors to influence cell functions.[61,62]

The extrapolation of in vitro cell culture studies to in vivo application is obviously complex, but the discussion above illustrates the potential for exciting new nonpharmacologic therapeutic approaches in OA.[73] One such approach would be to apply bonding agents to the cartilage matrix as a mechanical means to preserve chondrocyte phenotypic expression.[74] Another approach would be to use specific growth factors in the joint in a form that permitted their slow release into the cartilage to promote cell proliferation and synthesis of matrix components. The further potential for therapeutic application of growth factors in OA derives from their use in animal models to promote wound healing or to repair cartilage defects.[66]

SYNOVIAL MEMBRANE

In the diarthrodial joint, the synovial membrane forms the surface of the capsule enclosing the joint cavity. The structure of the synovial membrane in "normal" (younger) human joints, as revealed by light microscopy, shows a layer of lining cells, capillaries, a fibrous and/or fatty stroma, and virtually no inflammatory cells.[75] Few studies appear to have been done on aged joints, although fibrotic changes in the synovial membrane may occur with aging. The extent and significance of inflammation in OA has been the subject of controversy, but many studies reveal evidence for inflammatory changes, including vascular proliferation and engorgement, lining cell proliferation, and foci of round cell infiltrates.[75]

The lining cells in the synovial membrane can be visualized by cytochemical means that reveal their metabolic activities and cell shape; spindle-shaped cells, or those with extended cytoplasmic processes, were observed in situ,[76] which is of significance in terms of similar-appearing cells in tissue culture (discussed later). Immunofluorescent methods localize hyaluronate-protein and a component immunologically like cartilage proteinpolysaccharide within the lining cells.[75]

On the basis of studies using the electron microscope,[75] the lining cells were classified into type A—macrophage-like—and type B—fibroblast-like. An "intermediate" cell, type C, has been described, and may be more prevalent in rheumatoid arthritis.

Synovial cells can be dispersed from the membrane by enzymatic digestion with hyaluronidase and collagenase, and maintained in culture.[77] A functionally and morphologically heterogeneous cell population is revealed, accounting for the diversity of components synthesized and secreted by the synovial cells into the culture medium (Table 81-3). Whether the same lining cells are responsible for the synthesis of HA and sulfated GAG is not known, nor is it known whether aging or OA affects the synthesis of sulfated PG.

In the past few years several laboratories have attempted to characterize the synovial cells in culture based on morphology, immunologic properties, and secretory functions.[44,78] In general, three types of cells have been identified: a round or rhombic-shaped macrophage-like cell; an elongated, spindle-shaped fibroblast-like cell; and a novel cell with a stellate or dendritic appearance and long cytoplasmic processes. The macrophage-like cell is probably equivalent to the type A cell and is phagocytic in vitro. The fibroblast-like cell is similar in appearance to type B cells and is only slightly phagocytic. The dendritic cells, which are not phagocytic, secrete collagenase, and their cell surface membrane stains for Ia antigen—a marker for tissue macrophages. The Ia-positive cells are in a lineage similar to epidermal Langerhans cells and may be the principal accessory cell for antigen presentation to lymphocytes.[79] Reversion between synovial cell types is possible in vitro, since addition of prostaglandins (PGE$_2$) converts a fibroblast-like cell to a dendritic cell, and removal of PGE$_2$ from the medium reverts the cell back.[44]

The dendritic cells appear to be mainly responsible for IL-1 secretion,[44] but the other cell types can induce it as well, to a lesser extent. The fact that silica particles induce IL-1 secretion to a greater degree than that which occurs in resting cells is strong support for the role of a variety of cartilage-derived particulate stimuli present in the joint fluid, such as collagens and PG, which could be taken up by the lining cells and provoke an on-going secretory response.[45]

TABLE 81-3
Components Secreted by Synovial Cell Cultures In Vitro

Collagen
Collagenase and other proteases
Prostaglandins
Interleukin-1
Plasminogen activator
Component related to cartilage PG
GAG (HA, CS, DS)

SOURCE: From information in Goto et al.[44] and Hamerman et al.[77]

SYNOVIAL FLUID

So-called normal synovial fluid has been obtained from cadaver knees[80] for which joint palpation or inspection suggests absence of joint disease, or obtained from the knees of volunteers.[81] Usually less than 1 ml of highly viscous fluid is obtained, and the components of the fluid can be divided into those derived from the lining cells of the synovial membrane—such as HA and traces of sulfated GAG—and those derived from the plasma circulating in the capillaries—cells, proteins, glucose, and electrolytes. In 1958, lower levels of HA were found in synovial fluid from knee joints of older deceased subjects as compared to HA levels in synovial fluid of younger subjects,[80] but there does not yet seem to be any systematic study of HA levels in synovial fluid from aging joints.

The viscosity of synovial fluid is due to the presence of high molecular weight HA. Whether the lubricating function of the fluid is due to the polymerized HA or to a glycoprotein ("lubricin")[82] is not clear. Lubricating properties of synovial fluid in OA generally do not seem to be impaired.[83] Synovial fluid has been analyzed for markers of inflammation[81] or cartilage breakdown.[84-87] The presence of KS and PG fragments in synovial fluid (or serum) provides an important new area for study in relation to aging changes, the evolution of cartilage damage in OA, and inflammatory joint diseases.[84-87]

MENISCUS

The menisci are fibrocartilages on the opposing surfaces of the femur and tibia in the knee. This brief discussion is drawn largely from the recent comprehensive review by Ghosh and colleagues.[88] The functions of the menisci are to increase joint congruency, stabilize the joint, improve articular cartilage nutrition and lubrication, and facilitate the rotation of opposing articular surfaces of the joint during the "lock home" movement. Collagen types I and II, rather than PG, appear to contribute most significantly to the tensile properties of the menisci. The PG are similar to those in articular cartilage, but with more dermatan sulfate (DS).

Aging appears to be accompanied by a fall in noncollagenous matrix proteins between the ages of 30 to 70, but the significance of this decrease in functional terms is not clear. Studies suggest that, as observed with articular cartilage chondrocytes, the "fibrochondrocytes" of the menisci respond to IL-1 and release collagenase and proteoglycanases. The inner and central regions of the meniscus are most susceptible to horizontal tears, perhaps secondary to degeneration of the meniscus core, with serious consequences for joint function and the potential for evolution of OA.

SKELETAL MUSCLE

Three types of skeletal muscle fibers can be identified in adults: Type I (slow twitch, high oxidative fiber), Type IIA (fast twitch, high oxidative fiber), and Type IIB (fast twitch, slow oxidative fiber).[89] Loss of muscle mass occurs with aging, and a selective decrease in the type II fibers is observed, while there is an increase in the proportion of tension developed by the type I fiber. The decline in fiber number is not uniform in all muscles and may be less in those muscles in constant use (e.g., the diaphragm) than in those whose use is more intermittent (e.g., the lower extremities).

Despite decline in a number of physiologic functions of muscle (e.g., hand grip strength), as well as structural and biochemical changes, aging does not necessarily result in compromised muscle function.[90] Indeed, several persons have succeeded in completing marathons after achieving advanced age.[90] Whether muscle strength in human subjects diminishes with aging is unclear; more recent studies suggest that this presumed event may be diminished or delayed by exercise and, in rats, by life-prolonging food restriction.[89] In a study of muscles of the human ankle joint,[91] a decrease in muscle strength did not begin until the sixth decade, and the decrease was modest even in those reaching age 75 who remained active. By the age of 90, muscle strength was reduced by half; however, there is a physiologic adaptation to training with improvement in performance level at any age. "It is apparent that the human biological system has a substantial reserve capacity that can overcome measured degenerative changes that occur with aging."[90]

Factors extrinsic to muscle may contribute to aging changes. One such factor is "functional denervation caused by deleterious change in the neuromuscular junction such that synaptic contact and neurotrophic influences are reduced."[92] Increased resting acetylcholine released per action potential in aged rats may downregulate receptors and lead to synaptic depression.[93]

Mesenchymal cells in the limb bud evolve as primitive myoblasts or chondroblasts.[94] The view that such primitive cells follow a predestined pattern constitutes the so-called lineage hypothesis of differentiation, in contrast to the view that there exists in the limb bud a population of uncommitted, multipotential cells that under specific environmental conditions can be induced to differentiate into muscle, cartilage, or other connective tissues. Studies with a monoclonal antibody (designated CSAT) support the lineage theory.[94] In cultures of the limb bud, CSAT induced selective detachment of those cells destined to be myogenic and left attached to the plate those cells destined to be chondrocytes.

The fine structure of muscle cells and the biochemical and anatomical basis for contraction have been discussed elsewhere.[95,96] In postnatal life, fiber hypertrophy has been thought to occur rather than new fiber formation, yet there is actually enhanced DNA and protein synthesis in the muscle of the maturing rat from day 20 to 140.[97] The cell type that appears to make the greatest contribution to such synthetic activities in the muscle is the satellite cell. In adult life, satellite cells are inactive and actually decline in number with aging. They can be activated by injury; however, growth factors can modulate the action of satellite cells in vitro.[97] Insulin-like growth factors (IGF) stimulated satellite cell proliferation and differentiation; pituitary- or brain-derived FGF (with insulin) stimulated proliferation but suppressed differentiation of a muscle cell line; TGF-β appeared to inhibit differentiation of myoblasts and satellite cells.

TENDON

Tendon is a dense connective tissue. Polarized light studies revealed rows of cells that transmit forces between muscle and bone.[98] Type I collagen makes up 70 percent of the dry weight of tendon, with other types including III and VI; the PG includes DS and CS. Stiffness of the tendon increases with age, as does nonregainable deformation in cyclic loading.[99] This may increase the tendency for injuries in the event of violent stresses, especially when the tendon or ligament is attached to osteoporotic bone.

Age-related loss in the water content of dense connective tissues may reflect decline in GAG. In tendons of aging male rats, reduction in the galactosamine-containing moiety (i.e., CS or DS) occurred, with unchanged HA.[100] Exercise appeared to retard age-related loss of tendon GAG (galactosamine). Biosynthesis and/or molecular assembly of PG is affected by variations in mechanical stimuli on the tendon.

While the PG enmeshed in type II collagen fibers are the components that provide for the mechanical properties of articular cartilage, the tensile strength that characterizes tendons, ligaments, and the menisci are due to their content of collagen and elastin (fibrous proteins).[101] The particular arrangement of the collagen and elastin chains that has relevance to aging relates to cross-linking based on aldehyde formation from lysine or hydroxylysine side chains.[101] The only enzyme required, lysyl oxidase, serves both collagen and elastin. In elastin, desmosine and isodesmosine are the main cross-linking residues derived from lysine. Inhibited cross-linking is part of the underlying pathology in several inborn diseases of collagen. The relation of cross-linking to aging is not clear, but enhanced cross-linking of the fibrous proteins may contribute to strength of the tendons, while in bone, cross-linkage seems to decrease with age, contributing to mechanical weakness.[102]

INTERVERTEBRAL DISCS

The three major components that constitute the "physical mechanism"[103] of the intervertebral disc are the bony end plates, the gel structure of the nucleus pulposus, and the walls of the annulus fibrosus. The disc components are in the class of fibrocartilage, consisting of a mixture of dense connective tissue (the outer annulus) and a hyaline-like cartilage gel (the inner nucleus). The end plates covering the vertebral bodies are hyaline cartilage attached directly to the disc by way of collagen fibers.

A shock-absorbing function is performed when the end plates take the vertical stresses on the spine and transmit them to the elastic annulus by way of the gelatinous nucleus. As in articular cartilage, chondrocytes in the disc produce a highly hydrated PG gel restrained within a network of collagen fibers. Once again, the mechanical properties of a structure undergoing compressive forces are dependent on the interplay between the PG and the collagen. The disc PG components are, on average, considerably smaller than those from cartilage. The outer annulus contains mostly type I collagen, while mostly type II collagen is present in the inner annulus and in the nucleus.[104]

With aging, the water content of the nucleus drops from over 85 percent to somewhere in the range of 70 to 75 percent; the PG units decrease in size, and fewer aggregate with HA. These changes appear to occur at about age 40 when the nucleus becomes increasingly fibrillar and loses its gel form and its capacity for shock absorbance.[104] These changes in the nucleus place stress on the wall of the annulus. At a weak point, a fissure may occur with extension of semisolid nuclear gel through the annular wall. However, while disc degeneration increases with old age, this is not invariable; in a study of lumbar discs,[105] 72 percent of the discs from elderly subjects did not show "pathologic disc degeneration." Since weight bearing is concentrated on the lower two lumbar disc spaces, disc degeneration and thinning are more prone to occur there.

REFERENCES

1. Poole AR: Physiology of cartilage: Formation, function, and destruction, in Cruess RL (ed): *Musculoskeletal System: Embryology, Biochemistry, and Physiology.* New York, Churchill Livingston, 1982, p 289.
2. Kuettner KE et al: Protease inhibitors in cartilage. *Arthritis Rheum* 20(suppl 6):124S, 1977.
3. Poole AR, Rosenberg LC: Proteoglycans, chondrocalcin, and the calcification of cartilage matrix in endochondral ossification, in Wight TN, Mecham RP (eds): *Biology of the Proteoglycans.* New York, Academic Press, 1987, p 187.

4. Hunziker EB, Schenk RK: Structural organization of proteoglycans in cartilage, in Wight TN, Mechan RP (eds): *Biology of the Proteoglycans.* New York, Academic Press, 1987, p 155.

5. Muir H: Heberden Oration, 1976: Molecular approach to the understanding of osteoarthrosis. *Ann Rheum Dis* 36:199, 1977.

6. Von der Mark K et al: Role of Anchorin CII in the interaction of chondrocytes with extracellular collagen, in Kuettner KE, Schlayerbach R, Hascall VC (eds): *Articular Cartilage Biochemistry.* New York, Raven Press, 1986, p 125.

7. Mankin HJ, Treadwell BV: Osteoarthritis: A 1987 update. *Bull Rheum Dis* 38:1, 1986.

8. Pita JC et al: Studies on the potential reversibility of osteoarthritis in some experimental animal models, in Kuettner KE, Schlayerbach R, Hascall VC (eds): *Articular Cartilage Biochemistry.* New York, Raven Press, 1986, p 349.

9. Muir H: Current and future trends in articular cartilage research and osteoarthritis, in Kuettner KE, Schlayerbach R, Hascall VC (eds): *Articular Cartilage Biochemistry.* New York, Raven Press, 1986, p 423.

10. Schwartz ER: Animal models: A means to study the pathogenesis of osteoarthritis. *J Rheumatol* 14(suppl 14):101, 1987.

11. Weiss C, Mirow S: An ultrastructural study of osteoarthritic changes in the articular cartilage of human knees. *J Bone Joint Surg* 54A:954, 1972.

12. Hardingham TE et al: Cartilage proteoglycans, in Evered D, Whelan J (eds): *Functions of the Proteoglycans.* Chichester, Wiley-Ciba Foundation Symposium 124, p 39.

13. Nimni ME: Collagen: Structure, function, and metabolism in normal and fibrotic tissues. *Semin Arthritis Rheum* 13:1, 1983.

14. Benya PD, Brown PD: Modulation of the chondrocyte phenotype *in vitro*, in Kuettner KE, Schlayerbach R, Hascall VC (eds): *Articular Cartilage Biochemistry.* New York, Raven Press, 1986, p 219.

15. Mayne R, Irwin MH: Collagen types in cartilage, in Kuettner KE, Schlayerbach R, Hascall VC (eds): *Articular Cartilage Biochemistry.* New York, Raven Press, 1986, p 23.

16. McCutchen CW: Lubrication of joints, in Sokoloff L (ed): *The Joints and Synovial Fluid.* New York, Academic Press, 1978, p 437.

17. Solursh M: Environmental regulation of limb chondrogenesis, in Kuettner KE, Schlayerbach R, Hascall VC (eds): *Articular Cartilage Biochemistry.* New York, Raven Press, 1986, p 145.

18. Roughley PJ: Changes in cartilage proteoglycan structure during ageing: Origin and effects—a review. *Agents Actions* Suppl 18:19, 1986.

19. Thonar EJ-MA, Kuettner KE: Biochemical basis of age-related changes in proteoglycans, in Wight TN, Mecham RP (eds): *Biology of Proteoglycans.* New York, Academic Press, 1987, p 211.

20. Rosenberg LC, Buckwalter JA: Cartilage proteoglycans, in Kuettner KE, Schlayerbach R, Hascall VC (eds): *Articular Cartilage Biochemistry.* New York, Raven Press, 1986, p 39.

21. Van Kampen GPJ et al: Cartilage response to mechanical force in high-density chondrocyte cultures. *Arthritis Rheum* 28:419, 1985.

22. Roberts S et al: Mechanical and biochemical properties of human articular cartilage in osteoarthritic femoral heads and in autopsy specimens. *J Bone Joint Surg* 68B:278, 1986.

23. Kempson GE: Relationship between the tensile properties of articular cartilage from the human knee and age. *Ann Rheum Dis* 41:508, 1982.

24. Unsworth A: Some biomechanical factors in osteoarthritis. *Br J Rheumatol* 23:173, 1984.

25. Shuckett R, Malemud CJ: An *in vitro* model of ageing and human articular cartilage sulfated-proteoglycans. *Mech Ageing Dev* 34:73, 1986.

26. Brandt KD: Osteoarthritis. Relation to aging. *Clin Geriatr Med* 4:279, 1988.

27. Maroudas A et al: Physicochemical properties and functional behavior of normal and osteoarthritic human cartilage, in Kuettner KE, Schlayerbach R, Hascall VC (eds): *Articular Cartilage Biochemistry.* New York, Raven Press, 1986, p 311.

28. Radin EL: Mechanical factors in the causation of osteoarthritis. *Rheumatology* 7:46, 1982.

29. Martel-Pelletier J, Pelletier JP: Neutral metalloproteases and age-related changes in human articular cartilage. *Ann Rheum Dis* 46:363, 1987.

30. Bayliss MT: Proteoglycan structure in normal and osteoarthritic human cartilage, in Kuettner KE, Schlayerbach R, Hascall VC (eds): *Articular Cartilage Biochemistry.* New York, Raven Press, 1986, p 295.

31. Hascall VC: Discussion in Kuettner KE, Schlayerbach R, Hascall VC (eds): *Articular Cartilage Biochemistry.* New York, Raven Press, 1985, p 211.

32. Zlabinger GJ et al: Changes in collagen synthesis of human chondrocyte cultures: Development of a human model, demonstration of collagen conversion by immunofluorescence. *Rheumatol Int* 6:63, 1986.

33. Nemeth-Csoka M, Meszaros T: Minor collagens in arthrotic human cartilage. *Acta Orthop Scand* 54:613, 1983.

34. Livne E et al: Morphologic and cytochemical changes in maturing and osteoarthritic articular cartilage in the temporomandibular joint of mice. *Arthritis Rheum* 28:1027, 1985.

35. Ryu J et al: Biochemical and metabolic abnormalities in normal and osteoarthritic human articular cartilage. *Arthritis Rheum* 27:49, 1984.

36. Hascall VC et al: Biosynthesis and turnover of proteoglycans in organ culture of bovine articular cartilage. *J Rheumatol* 10(suppl 11):45, 1983.

37. Handley CJ et al: Steady-state metabolism in cartilage explants, in Kuettner KE, Schlayerbach R, Hascall VC (eds): *Articular Cartilage Biochemistry.* New York, Raven Press, 1986, p 163.

38. Tyler JA: Articular cartilage cultured with catabolin (pig interleukin 1) synthesizes a decreased number of normal proteoglycan molecules. *Biochem J* 227:869, 1985.

39. McGuire-Goldring MB et al: *In vitro* activation of human chondrocytes and synoviocytes by a human interleukin-1-like factor. *Arthritis Rheum* 27:654, 1984.

40. Oppenheim JJ: Lymphokines: Their role in lymphocyte responses: Properties of interleukin-1. *Fed Proc* 41:257, 1982.

41. Krane S: Heberden Oration, 1980: Aspects of the cell biology of the rheumatoid synovial lesion. *Ann Rheum Dis* 40:433, 1981.

42. Dingle JT, Tyler JA: Role of intercellular messengers in the control of cartilage matrix dynamics, in Kuettner KE, Schlayerbach R, Hascall VC (eds): *Articular Cartilage Biochemistry*. New York, Raven Press, 1986, p 181.

43. Wood DD et al: Release of interleukin-1 from human synovial tissue *in vitro*. *Arthritis Rheum* 28:853, 1985.

44. Goto M et al: Spontaneous production of an interleukin-1-like factor by cloned rheumatoid synovial cells in long-term culture. *J Clin Invest* 80:786, 1987.

45. Hamerman D, Klagsbrun M: Osteoarthritis: Emerging evidence for cell interactions in the breakdown and remodelling of cartilage. *Am J Med* 78:495, 1985.

46. Wood DD et al: Isolation of an interleukin-1-like factor from human joint effusions. *Arthritis Rheum* 26:975, 1983.

47. Aydelotte MB et al: Articular chondrocytes cultured in agarose gel for study of chondrocytic chondrolysis, in Kuettner KE, Schlayerbach R, Hascall VC (eds): *Articular Cartilage Biochemistry*. New York, Raven Press, 1986, p 235.

48. Teshima R et al: Comparative rates of proteoglycan synthesis and size of proteoglycans in normal and osteoarthritic chondrocytes. *Arthritis Rheum* 26:1225, 1983.

49. Malemud CJ: Biosynthesis of sulfated proteoglycans *in vitro* by cells derived from human osteochondrophytic spurs of the femoral head. *Connect Tissue Res* 12:319, 1984.

50. Harmond M-F et al: Proteoglycan synthesis in chondrocyte cultures from osteoarthrotic and normal articular cartilage. *Biochim Biophys Acta* 717:190, 1982.

51. Oegema TR Jr, Thompson RC Jr: Metabolism of chondrocytes derived from normal and osteoarthritic human cartilage, in Kuettner KE, Schlayerbach R, Hascall VC (eds): *Articular Cartilage Biochemistry*. New York, Raven Press, 1986, p 257.

52. Nojima T et al: Secretion of higher level of active proteoglycanases from human osteoarthritic chondrocytes. *Arthritis Rheum* 29:292, 1986.

53. Goldstein S et al: Protein synthetic fidelity in aging human fibroblasts in Werner's Syndrome and human aging. *Adv Exp Med Biol* 190:495, 1985.

54. Adolphe M et al: Effects of donor's age on growth kinetics of rabbit articular chondrocytes in culture. *Mech Ageing Dev* 23:191, 1983.

55. Evans CH, Georgescu HI: Observations on the senescence of cells derived from articular cartilage. *Mech Ageing Dev* 22:179, 1983.

56. Von der Mark K: Differentiation, modulation and dedifferentiation of chondrocytes. *Rheumatology* 10:272, 1986.

57. Holtzer H et al: The loss of phenotypic traits by differentiated cells *in vitro*. I. Dedifferentiation of cartilage cells. *Proc Natl Acad Sci USA* 46:1533, 1960.

58. Pacifici M et al: Changes in the sulfated proteoglycans synthesized by "aging" chondrocytes. *J Biol Chem* 256:1029, 1981.

59. Glowacki J et al: Cell shape and phenotypic expression in chondrocytes. *Proc Soc Exp Biol Med* 172:93, 1983.

60. Deuel TF: Polypeptide growth factors: Roles in normal and abnormal cell growth. *Annu Rev Cell Biol* 3:443, 1987.

61. Goetzl EJ, Ullrich A, Williams LT (eds): Molecular bases for the regulation of cellular growth, differentiation, and transformation. *J Cell Physiol* Suppl 5, 1987.

62. Rifkin DB, Klagsbrun M (eds): *Angiogenesis: Mechanisms and Pathobiology*. Cold Spring Harbor, NY, Cold Spring Harbor Laboratory, 1987.

63. Castor CW, Cabral AR: Growth factors in human disease: The realities, pitfalls, and promise. *Semin Arthritis Rheum* 15:33, 1985.

64. Jones KL et al: The growth of cultured rabbit articular chondrocytes is stimulated by pituitary growth factors but not by purified human growth hormone or ovine prolactin. *Endocrinology* 118:2588, 1986.

65. Sachs BL et al: Response of articular chondrocytes to pituitary fibroblast growth factor (FGF). *J Cell Physiol* 112:15, 1982.

66. Hamerman D et al: A cartilage-derived growth factor enhances hyaluronate synthesis and diminishes sulfated glycosaminoglycan synthesis in chondrocytes. *J Cell Physiol* 127:317, 1986.

67. Sullivan R, Klagsbrun M: Purification of cartilage-derived growth factor by heparin affinity chromatography. *J Biol Chem* 260:2399, 1985.

68. Kato Y, Gospodarowicz D: Sulfated proteoglycan synthesis by confluent cultures of rabbit costal chondrocytes grown in the presence of fibroblast growth factors. *J Cell Biol* 100:477, 1985.

69. Urist MR: The origin of cartilage: Investigations in the quest of chondrogenic DNA, in Hall BK (ed): *Cartilage: Development, Differentiation, and Growth*, vol 2. New York, Academic Press, 1983, p 2.

70. Canalis E et al: Growth factors and the regulation of bone remodelling. *J Clin Invest* 81:277, 1988.

71. Reddi AH: Extracellular matrix and development, in Piez K, Reddi AH (eds): *Extracellular Matrix Biochemistry*. New York, Elsevier Press, 1984, p 375.

72. Seydin SM et al: Cartilage-inducing Factor-A. *J Biol Chem* 261:5693, 1986.

73. Hamerman D: Osteoarthritis. *Orthop Rev* 27:353, 1988.

74. Cheung DT, Nimni ME: Mechanisms of cross-linking of proteins by glutaraldehyde: Reactions with model compounds. *Connect Tissue Res* 10:187, 1982.

75. Hamerman D et al: The structure and chemistry of the synovial membrane in health and disease, in Bittar EE, Bittar N (eds): *The Biological Basis of Medicine*, vol 3. New York, Academic Press, 1969, p 269.

76. Hamerman D et al: Comparative histology and metabolism of synovial tissue in normal and arthritic joints, in Mills LC, Mayer JH (eds): *Inflammation and Diseases of Connective Tissue*. Philadelphia, WB Saunders, 1961, p 158.

77. Hamerman D et al: Glycosaminoglycans produced by human synovial cell cultures. *Coll Relat Res* 2:313, 1982.

78. Winchester RJ, Burmester GR: Demonstration of Ia antigens on certain dendritic cells and on a novel elongate cell found in human synovial tissue. *Scand J Immunol* 14:439, 1981.

79. Harding B, Knight SC: The distribution of dendritic cells in the synovial fluids of patients with arthritis. *Clin Exp Immunol* 63:594, 1986.

80. Hamerman D, Schuster H: Hyaluronate in normal human synovial fluid. *J Clin Invest* 37:56, 1958.

81. Fawthrop F et al: A comparison of normal and pathological synovial fluid. *Br J Rheumatol* 24:61, 1985.

82. Swan D et al: The lubricating activity of human synovial fluids. *Arthritis Rheum* 27:552, 1984.

83. Davis WH Jr et al: Boundary lubricating ability of synovial fluid in degenerative joint disease. *Arthritis Rheum* 21:754, 1978.

84. Thonar EJ-MA et al: Quantification of keratan sulfate in blood as a marker of cartilage metabolism. *Arthritis Rheum* 28:1367, 1985.

85. Witter J et al: The immunologic detection and characterization of cartilage proteoglycan degradation products in synovial fluids of patients with arthritis. *Arthritis Rheum* 30:519, 1987.

86. Saxne T et al: Difference in cartilage proteoglycan level in synovial fluid in early rheumatoid arthritis and reactive arthritis. *Lancet* II:127, 1985.

87. Hascall VC, Glant TT: Editorial. Proteoglycan epitopes as potential markers of normal and pathologic cartilage metabolism. *Arthritis Rheum* 30:586, 1987.

88. Ghosh P et al: The knee joint meniscus: A fibrocartilage of some distinction. *Clin Orthop* 224:52, 1987.

89. Kalu DN, Masoro EJ: The biology of aging with particular reference to the musculoskeletal system. *Clin Geriatr Med* 4:257, 1988.

90. Jokl P: The biology of aging muscle—quantitative versus qualitative findings of performance capacity and age, in Nelson CL, Dwyer AP (eds): *The Aging Musculoskeletal System: Physiological and Pathological Problems.* Lexington, MA, Collamore Press, 1984, p 49.

91. Vandervoort AA, McComas AJ: Contractile changes in opposing muscles of the human ankle joint with aging. *J Appl Physiol* 61:361, 1986.

92. Fitts RH et al: The effect of ageing and exercise on skeletal muscle function. *Mech Ageing Dev* 27:161, 1984.

93. Smith DO: Acetylcholine storage, release and leakage at the neuromuscular junction of mature adult and aged rats. *J Phyiol* 347:161, 1984.

94. Sasse J et al: Separation of precursor myogenic and chondrogenic cells in early limb bud mesenchyme by a monoclonal antibody. *J Cell Biol* 99:1856, 1984.

95. Karpate G: Muscle: Structure, organization and healing, in Cruess L (ed): *The Musculoskeletal System: Embryology, Biochemistry, and Physiology.* New York, Churchill Livingston, 1982, p 323.

96. Allen RE et al: Cellular aspects of muscle growth: Myogenic cell proliferation. *J Anim Sci* 49:115, 1979.

97. Allen RE, Boxhorn LK: Inhibition of skeletal muscle satellite cell differentiation by transforming growth factor-beta. *J Cell Physiol* 133:567, 1987.

98. Silver FH: *Biological Materials: Structure, Mechanical Properties, and Modeling of Soft Tissues.* New York, New York University Press, 1987.

99. Vidiik A: Age-related changes in connective tissues, in *Lectures on Gerontology.* London, Academic Press, 1982, p 173.

100. Vailas AC et al: Patella tendon matrix changes associated with aging and voluntary exercise. *J Appl Physiol* 58:1572, 1985.

101. Eyre DR et al: Cross-lining in collagen and elastin. *Annu Rev Biochem* 53:717, 1984.

102. Danielson CC et al: Mechanical properties of collagen from decalcified rat femur in relation to age and *in vitro* maturation. *Calcif Tissue Int* 39:69, 1986.

103. Happey F: Studies on the structure of the human intervertebral disc in relation to its functional and aging processes, in Sokoloff L (ed): *The Joints and Synovial Fluid.* New York, Academic Press, 1980, vol II, p 95.

104. Urban J, Maroudas A: The chemistry of the intervertebral disc in relation to its physiological function and requirements. *Clin Rheum Dis* 6:51, 1980.

105. Twomey LT, Taylor JR: Age changes in lumbar vertebra and intervertebral discs. *Clin Orthop* 224:97, 1987.

Chapter 82

POLYMYALGIA RHEUMATICA AND GIANT CELL ARTERITIS

William J. Arnold

Polymyalgia rheumatica (PMR) and giant cell arteritis (GCA) are separate but closely related clinical entities predominantly occurring in adults over the age of 55. In several reports concerning GCA, PMR has been noted in 40 to 60 percent of patients, while in patients with PMR, GCA has been found in 0 to 80 percent.[1] The rapid and often impressive response of patients to oral glucocorticoids, with reversal of either a debilitating, inflammatory clinical disease (PMR) or a potentially life-threatening form of vasculitis (GCA), requires that the geriatrician have a high index of suspicion for the presence of these two illnesses.

Historically, PMR has been difficult to define[2]; however, recent studies have clearly shown it to be characterized by symmetrical aching, stiffness, and tenderness in the muscle groups in the pectoral and pelvic regions. In the laboratory PMR is characterized by a marked elevation of the erythrocyte sedimentation rate (ESR), usually greater than 50 mm/h by the Westergren technique.[3,4,5] Other associated features, such as depression, weight loss, anorexia, and synovitis, highlight the systemic nature of the inflammatory process in this illness.

GCA is a condition that typically involves medium-size arteries characterized by the presence of an internal elastic lamina; most commonly GCA involves arteries branching off the ascending aorta.[6,7] The classic symptoms of this illness are caused by inflammation of the temporal artery, which produces unilateral headache, local tenderness, and diminution of the temporal artery pulse.[8] Additional local manifestations of vascular insufficiency in cranial vessels include jaw claudication, blindness, and areas of gangrene in the scalp or tongue due to occlusion of arterial supply. However, up to a third of the patients with biopsy-proven temporal arteritis may present only with symptoms of PMR. The major advance

in the treatment of these two diseases has been an increased awareness of the diagnosis and prompt institution of glucocorticoid therapy.

CLINICAL FEATURES

Since neither PMR nor GCA has absolutely diagnostic clinical or laboratory findings, an accurate diagnosis requires assembly of a characteristic constellation of signs and symptoms. The initial manifestations of PMR may be either abrupt or gradual in onset, but typically a patient will go to bed feeling well and wake up the next morning with remarkable stiffness and aching. The stiffness and aching in the pectoral and pelvic girdle may extend up to the neck and into the proximal aspects of the thighs, respectively. Indeed, the abrupt nature of the onset of the symptoms has suggested a possible infectious etiology in some cases.[9] Alternatively, a gradual onset of aching and stiffness in the pectoral and pelvic muscles, associated with depression, lethargy, and weight loss, may be the presenting manifestations. Patients usually report stiffness lasting greater than 30 minutes on arising in the morning, and, while the stiffness is similar in severity and distribution to that seen in rheumatoid arthritis, PMR less frequently affects the smaller joints of the hands and feet.[10] Typical physical findings in patients with PMR include tenderness but not weakness in the proximal muscles such as the deltoid, trapezius, gluteus, and quadriceps muscles. There is evidence for synovitis in up to one-third of PMR patients.[4,11] Usually the synovitis is most prominent in the knees, with presence of effusion, but wrist and shoulder swelling have also been reported.[11]

While the initial clinical manifestations of GCA may be those of PMR in up to one-third of the patients, the next most frequent initial manifestations reflect the presence of inflammation in the temporal artery and include local temporal artery tenderness, swelling, and unilateral headache.[8] The headache pain is usually described as lancinating or throbbing and is usually confined specifically to the area of the inflamed temporal artery. Visual symptoms may be present initially and include scotomata and partial or complete blindness. Thus, the constellation of headache and fever associated with visual symptoms in the patient presenting with the clinical syndrome suggestive of PMR strongly argues for the underlying presence of GCA. Infrequent but more specific signs of the presence of GCA include jaw and tongue claudication. Patients will note the presence of pain in the area of the masseter muscles while chewing meat. Once primary dental problems have been excluded, a high degree of specificity exists for the relationship between jaw claudication and GCA.[8] In addition, a recent study has pointed out that 10 percent of patients with GCA have prominent respiratory tract symptoms, including cough and sore throat.[12] The authors suggested that GCA should be considered in an elderly patient with a new cough or throat pain without obvious cause.

PATHOLOGY AND LABORATORY FEATURES

The characteristic laboratory abnormality for both PMR and GCA is an elevation of the Westergren ESR. Elevations above 50 mm/h and often above 100 mm/h are characteristic of both diseases. It is to be noted, however, that some patients with biopsy-proven GCA have been shown to have a normal ESR.[13] Moreover, some studies have suggested that Westergren ESR values over 20 mm/hr can be seen in normal elderly patients. However, a recent thorough study demonstrates that in the nonanemic, non-hypoalbuminemic elderly patient a Westergren ESR over 20 mm/hr should raise the possibility of an inflammatory disease such as PMR or GCA.[14] Since it is possible to have marked daily variation in the ESR in the presence of an otherwise typical clinical syndrome for PMR and GCA, a test reflecting a normal or only slightly elevated ESR should be repeated before the PMR/GCA diagnosis is discarded. The presence of a positive antinuclear antibody, anti-DNA antibody, or rheumatoid factor test argues strongly against the diagnosis of PMR/GCA.[8] However, with age, elevated levels of antinuclear antibodies and rheumatoid factor may be found in the normal population.[15] Thus, in the elderly, the diagnosis of PMR/GCA should not be discarded too hastily if serologic studies are borderline positive.

Biopsy of the temporal arteries should be performed in all patients in whom clinical features suggest

the presence of GCA. If the biopsy is negative on one side, some authors have suggested repeating the biopsy on the other side.[16] Great care should be used to obtain at least a 2.5 cm segment of temporal artery, and serial horizontal as well as longitudinal sections should be examined microscopically in order to confidently predict the presence or absence of arterial inflammation. Typical pathology of GCA includes destruction of the internal elastic lamina with a mononuclear cell infiltrate and the presence of giant cells in the arterial wall.[8] Occlusion of the lumen of the artery due to edema and thrombosis may occur. Typically these patients have coincidental presence of changes suggestive of atherosclerosis with intima hyperplasia and cholesterol clefts. In fact, these coincidental changes of atherosclerosis make arteriography of limited use in differentiating vasculitic from atherosclerotic regions.[17]

In some patients with PMR, technetium-99m pertechnetate joint scintiscans have been shown to be positive, particularly in the area of the shoulders and axial skeleton.[18] These scans per se are of no diagnostic value, but they do illustrate the frequent occurrence of synovitis in these patients and suggest that the muscle tenderness may be due more to this underlying synovitis than to any primary involvement of the muscle itself. In fact, arthroscopic examination of the shoulder joint with biopsy in 17 patients has demonstrated synovitis which, on occasion, may resemble that found in patients with rheumatoid arthritis.[19]

DIFFERENTIAL DIAGNOSIS

The differential diagnosis of PMR and GCA in an elderly population can be extensive. While psychiatric disturbances, various forms of dementia, and fibrositis can be associated with localized muscle tenderness, fatiguability, weight loss, and general signs of inanition, these illnesses are characterized by a normal Westergren ESR. The presence of fever, aching, stiffness, and anorexia associated with an elevated ESR can suggest the presence of infection which must be excluded specifically, based upon localizing signs or symptoms. Often an infectious process, such as a chronic urinary tract infection, is the cause most difficult to exclude. Occasionally, patients with PMR have been found to have a malignancy. In particular, patients with hypernephroma, multiple myeloma, and disseminated prostate cancer can have evidence for systemic inflammation, aching and stiffness with an axial predominance, and joint and muscle pain that can be confused with PMR.[9] However, these patients typically fail to respond to low doses of glucocorticoids. As mentioned above, the presence of positive serologic studies for rheumatoid factor or antinuclear antibodies must be considered as strong evidence for the presence of rheumatoid arthritis and systemic lupus erythematosus respectively. While histology of Takayasu's arteritis is similar to that of GCA, the remarkably different age and sex of the population affected by Takayasu's suggest that the two are different diseases.[8] Finally, in elderly patients being evaluated for fever of undetermined origin, even blind temporal artery biopsy in the absence of localizing clinical features can be positive.

TREATMENT AND COURSE

The similarity between PMR and GCA extends to the beneficial effect that glucocorticoid therapy has on both of these illnesses. One of the proposed diagnostic criteria for patients with PMR is the prompt and often dramatic response to doses of prednisone less than 20 mg per day that is seen within 4 to 5 days of the institution of therapy.[4,5] The clinical features of the illness, particularly the muscle aching and stiffness, as well as anorexia and fatigability, disappear promptly and rapidly. In patients with GCA, a disappearance of fever, if initially present, also occurs in a similar time course. However, prednisone dosage for patients with GCA is considerably greater than that used for patients with PMR; the dosage for GCA should be in the range of 45 to 60 mg per day. In patients with GCA, if local symptoms of inflammation in the temporal artery, headaches, or other presenting manifestations do not improve, then the dosage should be increased by 25 percent every 24 to 48 hours until symptomatic response is obtained. When a patient is given prompt aggressive treatment for GCA, it is unusual for blindness or other serious manifestations to occur after the institution of glucocorticoid therapy.[8] In fact, in situations in which the diagnosis is highly suspect, prednisone therapy should be begun prior to obtaining a temporal artery biopsy. While committing a patient to long-term, high-dose glucocorticoid therapy is inadvisable in the absence of biopsy evidence for GCA, the possibility that serious consequences will occur prior to the time that the biopsy results are available argues for the prompt institution of glucocorticoid therapy. If the biopsy is negative, the glucocorticoids can be discontinued with little likelihood of significant side effects.

In general, prednisone therapy should be continued at an unchanged dosage for the first month and then tapered only gradually by no more than 5 to 10 percent of the total dose every 2 weeks. The ability to continue to taper prednisone or the need to reinstitute higher doses is judged by the presence of signs or symptoms of reactivation of the disease, as well as by monitoring the ESR on a monthly basis. The total course of therapy in patients with PMR usually is in the range of 1 year, while patients with GCA usually require 2 years of therapy.[4,5,8] While both illnesses had been thought to be

remittent diseases, recent evidence indicates that chronic glucocorticoid therapy may be required in both groups of patients.[4,5]

PATHOGENESIS

Because of the prominence of the symptoms of muscle aching and stiffness, patients with polymyalgia rheumatica have been considered to have a primary muscle abnormality. However, biopsy studies of muscle have failed to reveal any specific abnormalities. In fact, the only abnormality shown has been related to the presence of synovial inflammation. Studies by O'Duffy with joint scintigraphy suggest that PMR may, in fact, be an illness of synovial inflammation of the axial skeleton with involvement of the shoulders and hips.[18] Chou and Schumacher confirmed the presence of synovial inflammation by analyzing synovial biopsy specimens from six patients.[20] Healey reported the occurrence of significant effusions in the knees, wrists, and shoulders in up to one-third of the patients with polymyalgia rheumatica.[11] Synovial fluid aspiration in the majority of these patients revealed inflammatory synovial fluid with from 4100 to 21,000 white cells per cubic millimeter. Thus there is strong evidence for a significant component of synovitis often resembling that seen in rheumatoid arthritis. This observation coincides with the clinical observation that some conditions initially diagnosed as PMR may develop into typical rheumatoid arthritis.[10] However, there has not been a report of erosive destructive articular disease seen in patients with PMR. No significant human leukocyte antigen (HLA) association has been found, but the illness has been described in twins and clearly shows a predilection for the Caucasian population, suggesting a possible genetic predisposition.[8]

In patients with GCA, evidence for the presence of circulating immune complexes or immune complex deposition in the artery has not been consistently found.[8] This suggests that the pathogenesis is most likely related to the mononuclear cell infiltrate and in particular the T lymphocytes, which have been shown to express HLA-DR antigens, indicating that immunologic activation has taken place.[21]

REFERENCES

1. Hunder GG, Allen GL: Giant cell arteritis: A review. *Bull Rheum Dis* 29:980, 1978–79.
2. Bober HS: Myalgic syndrome with constitutional effects: Polymyalgia rheumatica. *Ann Rheum Dis* 16:230, 1957.
3. Healey LA, Parker F, Welski KR: Polymyalgia rheumatica and giant cell arteritis. *Arthritis Rheum* 14:138, 1971.
4. Chuang T-Y, Hunder GG, Ilstrup DM, Kurland LT: Polymyalgia rheumatica—A 10 year epidemiologic and clinical study. *Ann Intern Med* 97:672, 1982.

5. Ayoub WT, Franklin CM, Torritti D: Polymyalgia rheumatica—Duration of therapy and long-term outcome. *Am J Med* 79:309, 1985.

6. Wilkerson IMS, Russell RWR: Arteries of the head and neck in giant cell arteritis: A pathological study to show the pattern of arterial involvement. *Arch Neurol* 27:378, 1972.

7. Klein RG, Hunder GG, Stansar AW, Ships SG: Large artery involvement in giant cell (temporal) arteritis. *Ann Intern Med* 83:806, 1975.

8. Hunder GG, Hazleman BL: Giant cell arteritis and polymyalgia rheumatica, in Kelly NN, Harris ED, Ruddy SR, and Sledge CB (eds): *Textbook of Rheumatology.* Philadelphia, Saunders, 1984, p 1166.

9. Olhagen B: Polmyalgia rheumatica. *Clin Rheum Dis* 12(1):33, 1986.

10. Healey LA: Polymyalgia rheumatica and the ARA criteria for rheumatoid arthritis. *Arthritis Rheum* 26:1417, 1983.

11. Healy LA: Long-term follow-up of polymyalgia rheumatica: Evidence for synovitis. *Semin Arthritis Rheum* 13:322, 1984.

12. Larson TS, Hall S, Hepper NGG, Hunder GG: Respiratory tract symptoms as a clue to giant cell arteritis. *Ann Intern Med* 101:594, 1984.

13. Ellis ME, Ralston S: The ESR in the diagnosis and management of the polymyalgia/giant cell arteritis syndrome. *Ann Rheum Dis* 42:168, 1983.

14. Crawford J, Eye-Boland MK, Cohen HJ: Clinical utility of erythrocyte sedimentation rate and plasma protein analysis in the elderly. *Am J Med* 82:239, 1987.

15. Goodwin JS, Searles RP, Teung KSK: Immunological responses of a healthy elderly population. *Clin Exp Immunol* 48:403, 1982.

16. Hall S, Persellin S, Lie JT, et al: The therapeutic impact of temporal artery biopsy. *Lancet* 2:1217, 1983.

17. Sewel JR, Allison DJ, Tarin D, Hughes GRV: Combined temporal arteriography and selective biopsy in suspected giant cell arteritis. *Ann Rheum Dis* 39:124, 1980.

18. O'Duffy JD, Wahner HW, Hunder GG: Joint imaging in polymyalgia rheumatica. *Mayo Clin Proc* 51:515, 1976.

19. Douglas WAC, Martin BA, Morris JH: Polymyalgia rheumatica: An arthroscopic study of the shoulder joint. *Ann Rheum Dis* 42:311, 1983.

20. Chou C-T, Schumacher HR: Clinical and pathologic studies of synovitis in polymyalgia rheumatica. *Arthritis Rheum* 27:1107, 1984.

21. Andersson R, Jonsson R, Tarkowski A et al: T-cell subsets and expression of immunological activation markers in the arterial walls of patients with giant cell arteritis. *Ann Rheum Dis* 46:915, 1987.

Chapter 83

POLYMYOSITIS AND DERMATOMYOSITIS

William J. Arnold

Adult polymyositis/dermatomyositis (PM/DM) is a systemic rheumatic disease characterized by muscle weakness, proximal weakness being greater than distal. PM/DM is associated to a variable degree with cutaneous abnormalities, vasculitis, malignancies, and other rheumatic diseases (e.g., systemic lupus erythematosus, scleroderma, and Sjögren's syndrome).[1] In the PM/DM patient with the typical history, physical findings, and laboratory abnormalities, the therapy of PM/DM centers around oral glucocorticoids and, in some patients, immunosuppressives.[2] The geriatrician should be particularly attuned to the possibility of this diagnosis since patients with PM/DM over age 50 have an increased incidence of malignancy.

CLASSIFICATION

While various classification schemes have been proposed, the scheme of Bohan and Peter, as modified subsequently by Hochberg et al., has relied upon clinical criteria primarily.[3,4,5] In Table 83-1, the classification draws attention to the presence of isolated PM (type I) and DM (type II), in addition to PM/DM associated with malignancy (type III), while highlighting the fact that PM/DM can also be seen in the presence of other rheumatic diseases (Type IV). While the classification scheme is presently of limited usefulness etiologically, it is likely future investigation will reveal different therapies and prognoses for individuals in these different classifications. For example, it is clear that patients with type IV PM/DM associated with connective tissue illnesses do not have an increased incidence of malignancy. Also, patients with type I, II, and IV respond much better to oral glucocorticoids than do patients with malignancy.[2] While there is no statistically significant difference in

age, sex, or racial background among the four types, other studies have noted an increased incidence of Type III in patients over age 50.[6]

CLINICAL CHARACTERISTICS OF SPECIFIC TYPES OF ADULT PM/DM

Type I PM and Type II DM typically pursue an uncertain clinical course.[7] They most commonly occur in females around the age of 40. The intensity of the dermal and muscular manifestations wax and wane, but usually in coincidence with one another. However, while glucocorticoid and immunosuppressive therapy may alter an exacerbation of the illness, the natural course of the disease is not necessarily affected by therapy. This means that exacerbations can probably not be avoided by "remission-inducing" therapy such as that used for rheumatoid arthritis.

Virtually all patients with Type I or II PM/DM will have muscular weakness.[5] While clinical emphasis is usually placed upon proximal muscle weakness, it should be noted that the distal muscles may also be weak. However, weakness is always greater proximally than distally. This is clearly the reverse of most neuropathies, in which distal weakness is greater than proximal. Weakness can be assessed by formal grading levels such as those in Table 83-2. The formal levels are useful in communicating with other members of the health care team, as well as in longitudinal assessment of therapy. Proximal muscle weakness is most prominent in the pelvic girdle and thighs. This weakness is associated with difficulty getting into and out of a chair and with going up and down stairs. In addition, this weakness can lead to a sensation of clumsiness and a tendency to fall. Most patients will also have proximal muscle weakness in the

TABLE 83-1
Classification and Demographic Features of Myositis by Patient Group

Patient Characteristics	PM (I)	DM (II)	Cancer (III)	Overlap (IV)	Total
Number of patients	31	21	6	18	76
Definite	21 (67.7%)	20 (95.2%)	2 (33.3%)	13 (72.2%)	56 (73.7%)
Mean age	50.0	38.8	57.1	40.9	45.3
Sex (M:F)	11:20	4:17	2:4	2:16	19:57
Race (white:nonwhite)	17:14	14:7	5:1	9:9	45:31

SOURCE: Modified from Hochberg et al.[5]

pectoral girdle and neck, causing difficulty with raising the arms higher than horizontal or holding up the head. Of note is the very infrequent involvement of the ocular muscles, which serves to differentiate PM from myasthenia gravis, another cause of weakness. Of major concern is the presence of dysphagia. This symptom usually represents weakness in the striated muscles of the pharynx and upper esophagus. Dysphagia is most prominent for solid foods but also occurs for liquids and may be associated with nasal regurgitation and spontaneous aspiration.

The rash of Type II DM occurs in about 30 percent of all patients with inflammatory myopathy and usually represents the only difference between Type I PM and Type II DM. The rash usually occurs in conjunction with active muscle disease and appears as a violaceous discoloration with edema of the eyelids (heliotrope) associated with scaly and slightly elevated red skin patches located on the elbows, knuckles, knees, and occasionally on the ankles.[8] A reddish suffusion with slight scaling can also be seen on the face, forehead, and V of the neck. In addition, there may be true vasculitic lesions in the periungual area or on the pulp of the fingertips.

Other prominent clinical features in patients with adult Type I PM or Type II DM include pulmonary and cardiac abnormalities.[9,10] Patients have been reported to most frequently have a diffuse interstitial pulmonary fibrosis similar to that seen in systemic rheumatic diseases. In addition, pleuritis and a transitory pneumonitis are also frequent findings. The most common pulmonary symptoms are dyspnea, cough, and chest pain.

The presence of cardiac involvement is a major de-

TABLE 83-2
Grading Levels of Muscle Function

0   No evidence of muscle contraction
1   Muscle contraction occurs but does not cause joint movement
2   Full range of function without gravity
3   Full range of function with gravity
4   Full range of function against gravity with moderate resistance
5   Full range of function against gravity with full resistance

terminant of survival in PM/DM.[5,10] The most common cardiac involvement, which has been seen in 25 to 49 percent of patients with PM/DM, includes ECG abnormalities usually manifest as ST-T wave changes (with an occasional patient with ventricular arrhythmia). Clinically evident congestive heart failure has also been present in 3 to 25 percent of patients with cardiac abnormalities.

Based on several recent studies, reports of the total frequency of malignancy among adult patients with PM/DM vary from 7 to 24 percent.[6,11] As a group these patients with Type III PM/DM tend to be older, ranging from 55 to 62 years old. While cases of malignancy associated with PM have been reported, a clear relationship is most strongly present for DM and malignancy. In patients with Type III, the malignancy may occur before, coincident with, or at a time after the diagnosis of the myositis. This clear lack of a temporal relationship between the malignancy and the muscle disease, as well as a lack of a specific associated malignancy, has suggested that the relationship between malignancy and myositis may be coincidental. Malignancies most frequently found mirror those of general frequency in the population and include breast, colon, lung, and uterine cancer. Rarely are lymphomas or Hodgkin's disease found in association with myositis.

Patients with myositis associated with other systemic rheumatic diseases (Type IV) may be found to have Sjögren's syndrome, systemic lupus erythematosus, scleroderma, and occasionally rheumatoid arthritis. In this case, serologic studies and other clinical features such as Raynaud's phenomenon or polyarthritis and other features suggestive of the diagnosis are usually a prominent part of the clinical syndrome.[5]

LABORATORY FEATURES

The clinical diagnosis of myositis requires the typical clinical syndrome with history and physical findings of muscle weakness and/or skin manifestations accompanied by an elevation of the serum muscle enzymes, electromyographic features, and muscle biopsy evidence.[3]

While the diagnosis can be made in the absence of any one or two of the above, even with the typical clinical history, the lack of all these laboratory features makes the diagnosis of PM/DM definitely suspect. Creatine kinase (CK) elevation is seen in virtually 100 percent of patients with active muscle inflammation. Serial determination of CK is the best laboratory adjunct in assessing the need for continued glucocorticoid or immunosuppressive therapy.

Electromyographic features of myositis include fibrillations, polyphasic action potentials, and spontaneous depolarizations.[12] None of these features is specific for the diagnosis of myositis and can be associated with degenerating/regenerating skeletal muscle from a nerve injury or trauma.

Muscle biopsies may be taken either with an open or needle technique and show evidence for active muscle inflammation manifest by perivascular or diffuse infiltration of lymphocytes accompanied by evidence for skeletal muscle degeneration and regeneration. The muscle biopsy may be negative in patients with documented myositis.[13] Sampling error is most frequently cited as the reason for a negative muscle biopsy. However, the biopsy may be guided by electromyogram (EMG) findings in the contralateral muscle or possibly in the future by magnetic resonance imaging (MRI).[14]

TREATMENT

Treatment of patients with idiopathic adult PM/DM centers around the use of high-dose glucocorticoid therapy initially, with a gradual tapering combined with a commitment to a long-term course of therapy.[7] Usually the initial dosage given after the diagnosis is made is a minimum of 60 mg/day in divided doses. This dosage is continued until the muscle enzymes have normalized and the patient has regained strength, which usually takes a period of a minimum of 2 weeks and often up to 2 months. Following this initial therapy, the prednisone may be tapered by 5 to 10 percent of the daily dose every 2 weeks while monitoring serial muscle enzymes (usually CK) and muscle strength at monthly intervals. While eventually up to 75 percent of patients can be tapered off prednisone, the remaining patients will require a continuing daily or alternate-day dose to maintain improvement. Treatment with as little as 5 mg of prednisone daily or every other day is not an unusual long-term maintenance dose for these patients between exacerbations.

In patients whose signs and symptoms fail to be adequately controlled after 3 to 6 months or who experience significant side effects due to the high doses of glucocorticoid required for control, immunosuppressive drugs have been successfully employed. Therapy with methotrexate or azathioprine (Imuran) has been reported to benefit patients with steroid-resistant PM/DM. Intravenous use of methotrexate in doses from 0.5 to 0.8 mg/kg, initially given daily, then monthly, has been shown to result in clinical and laboratory improvement.[15] Imuran in the amount of 1.5 to 2.0 mg/kg given orally in divided dose has also been effective.[16]

In addition to medications, a rehabilitation/exercise program should also be employed throughout the course of the disease. The employment of muscle-strengthening and range-of-motion (ROM) exercises should begin with the initial diagnosis; however, in the first 2 months only gentle ROM to prevent joint and tendon contractures is appropriate. Later on a home program with gait training, proper assistive devices, and home modifications to prevent falls, assist in toileting, and aid with other activities of daily living can be very helpful.

PATHOGENESIS

Numerous lines of evidence indicate the role of a viral etiology in some patients with adult PM/DM. During the course of influenza A or B and Coxsackie virus disease (also called epidemic pleurodynia and Bornholm disease), patients may develop typical clinical features of PM with CK values over 15 times normal.[17,18] Also, many reports indicate the presence of myxovirus-like and picornavirus-like particles on electron microscope examination of muscle biopsy specimen from patients with PM.[19,20] Another common observation, most frequently found in children, is vasculitis, which can be suggestive of polyarteritis nodosa. Circulating immune complexes and immune complexes in blood vessel walls have been found in some of these patients.[21,22]

PROGNOSIS

The survival statistics for patients with adult PM/DM have improved dramatically. In the pre-glucocorticoid era a mortality rate of 50 percent was seen for 38 patients at the Mayo Clinic before 1940.[23] However, in a recent series of 74 patients, 83 percent survived at 8 years after entry.[5] In this recent study, age at diagnosis was the most dramatic factor influencing survival. Of 39 patients age 45 years and above, 12 (30.8 percent) died during the follow-up compared with only 1 of 37 patients (2.4 percent) under age 44 ($p < 0.005$).[5] There were no statistically significant differences in the frequency of various clinical features, including malignancy, in the two patient groups. In the same series, cardiac involvement was the most important clinical factor associated with a poor prognosis.[5] Nine of the 28 patients (32.1 percent) with cardiac involvement at entry died during follow-up compared with only 4 (8.3 percent) of the remaining 48 patients ($p < 0.05$). Other studies have also noted that these two factors, age and cardiac involvement, influence prognosis.[24,25]

REFERENCES

1. Isenberg D: Myositis in other connective tissue disorders. *Clin Rheum Dis* 10(1):151, 1984.
2. Ansell BM: Management of polymyositis and dermatomyositis. *Clin Rheum Dis* 10(1):205, 1984.
3. Bohan A, Peter JB: Polymyositis and dermatomyositis. *N Engl J Med* 292:344, 1975.
4. Bohan A, Peter JB, Boman RL, Pearson CM: A computer-assisted analysis of 153 patients with polymyositis and dermatomyositis *Medicine* 56:255, 1977.
5. Hochberg MC, Feldman D, Stevens MB: Adult onset polymyositis/dermatomyositis: An analysis of clinical and laboratory features and survival in 76 patients. *Semin Arthritis Rheum* 15(3):168, 1986.
6. Callen JP: Myositis and malignancy. *Clin Rheum Dis* 10(1):117, 1984.
7. Bradley WG: Inflammatory diseases of muscle, in Kelley WN, Harris ED, Ruddy SR, Sledge CB (eds): *Textbook of Rheumatology*. Philadelphia, Saunders, 1984, p 1223.
8. Keil H: The manifestations in the skin and mucous membranes in dermatomyositis. *Ann Intern Med* 16:828. 1975.
9. Dickey BF, Myers AR: Pulmonary disease in polymyositis/dermatomyositis. *Semin Arthritis Rheum* 14:60, 1984.
10. Askari AD, Heuttner TL: Cardiac abnormalities in polymyositis/dermatomyositis. *Semin Arthritis Rheum* 12:208, 1982.
11. Barnes BE: Dermatomyositis and malignancy: A review of the literature. *Ann Intern Med* 84:68, 1976.
12. Payan J: Electromyography in polymyositis and some related disorders. *Clin Rheum Dis* 10(1):75, 1984.
13. DeVere R, Bradley WG: Polymyositis: Its presentation, morbidity and mortality. *Brain* 98:637, 1975.
14. Kaufman LD, Gruber BL, Gerstman DP, Kaell AT: Preliminary observations on the role of magnetic resonance imaging for polymyositis and dermatomyositis. *Ann Rheum Dis* 46:569, 1987.
15. Metzger AL, Bohan A, Goldberg LS et al: Polymyositis and dermatomyositis: Combined methotrexate and corticosteroid therapy. *Ann Intern Med* 81:182, 1974.
16. Bunch TW: Prednisone and azathioprine for polymyositis: Long-term follow-up. *Arthritis Rheum* 24:45, 1981.
17. Middleton PJ, Alexander RM, Szymanski WT: Severe myositis during recovery from influenza. *Lancet* 2:533, 1970.
18. McKenlay IA, Mitchell I: Transient acute myositis in childhood. *Arch Dis Child* 51:135, 1976.
19. Chou S-M: Myxo-virus like structures in a case of human chronic polymyositis. *Science* 158:1453, 1967.
20. Chou S-M, Gutmann L: Picorna-like crystals in subacute polymyositis. *Neurology* 20:205, 1970.
21. Banker BQ, Victor M: Dermatomyositis (systemic angiopathy) of childhood. *Medicine* 45:261, 1966.
22. Whitaker JN, Engel WK: Vascular deposits of immunoglobulin and complement in idiopathic inflammatory myopathy. *N Engl J Med* 286:333, 1972.
23. Wedgewood JP, Cook CD, Cohen J: Dermatomyositis. *Pediatrics* 12:447, 1953.
24. Benbasset J, Gefel D, Larholt K et al: Prognostic factors in polymyositis/dermatomyositis. *Arthritis Rheum* 28:249, 1985.
25. Henrikkson KG, Sandstedt P: Polymyositis—Treatment and prognosis: A study of 107 patients. *Acta Neurol Scand* 65:280, 1982.

Chapter 84

RHEUMATOID ARTHRITIS

M. E. Csuka and James S. Goodwin

Rheumatoid arthritis (RA) is a systemic disease, the major manifestation of which is a symmetric, inflammatory polyarthritis. RA is relevant to geriatric medicine for several reasons. First, RA is a chronic disease; the great majority of patients survive into old age. Second, RA can initially present in old age. Because the diagnosis of RA is based almost entirely on clinical information, the background of joint symptomatology in elderly patients makes the recognition of RA difficult. Third, there is some indication that RA may present differently in elderly patients than it does in younger patients; physicians caring for the elderly should be aware of these different patterns of disease presentation. Fourth, the extraarticular manifestations of RA typically occur in long-standing disease, which means that elderly patients with RA are more likely to manifest these complications. Finally, while the treatment of RA in the elderly is similar to that in younger patients, more attention has to be paid to issues of patient mobility and independence. Many elderly patients are already close to the edge in terms of maintaining physical independence, and a disease such as RA can push them over.

In this chapter we will outline what is known about the pathophysiology, epidemiology, natural history, diagnosis, treatment, and complications of RA. We will emphasize those issues outlined in the first paragraph; that is, those issues specifically relevant to RA in older populations. Two recurring themes should become apparent in the ensuing discussion. The first is how little we actually know about RA in the elderly. There are surprisingly few studies of any aspects of RA in older patients—disease presentation, epidemiology, response to treatment, and so on—and the information that does exist is sometimes contradictory. The second theme is related to the first and involves the difficulties in studying RA in the elderly. The diagnosis of RA is made primarily on clinical grounds. Lacking the specific etiology or etiologies for RA, we also lack a "gold standard" for diagnosis. In the early decades of this century, many diseases now recognized as separate entities were in-

cluded under the name RA. Ankylosing spondylitis, psoriatic arthritis, Lyme arthritis, Reiter's disease, and the arthritis of inflammatory bowel disease were split off from RA over time as their distinctive clinical presentations and/or laboratory manifestations became apparent. This evolution is continuous; we are, at least in theory, gradually approaching the state where what we call "RA" is indeed a single disease. In this regard, the diagnosis of RA in elderly subjects encompasses a far more heterogeneous set of conditions than it does in younger subjects. This is represented schematically in Fig. 84-1. The message of this figure is that older patients diagnosed with RA actually have a variety of diseases responsible for their clinical conditions. The relative proportions given to examples of those diseases in the figure are entirely arbitrary and most certainly inaccurate. The reasons for this heterogeneous set of diseases resulting in the diagnosis of RA in elderly people, which will become apparent as the chapter progresses, involve such issues as false-positive laboratory tests, a high prevalence of non-RA joint diseases, nonspecificity of symptoms, overlap of clinical presentation among collagen-vascular diseases, and lack of definitive diagnostic tests. The point we wish to emphasize at this juncture is that the diversity of diseases under the rubric of RA in the elderly makes investigation of this disorder very difficult. The large differences among various reports on the clinical presentation or natural history of RA in the elderly become understandable when one appreciates that, in actuality, a *group* of diseases is being studied, and different clinical presentations, natural histories, and responses to treatment will be found for RA in the elderly depending on the relative proportions of these various diseases in the particular group of elderly "RA patients" being studied.

ETIOLOGY AND PATHOGENESIS

Despite decades of intense research, the specific initiating event in RA that triggers an inflammatory response

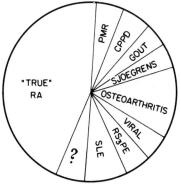

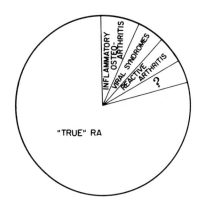

RA IN THE ELDERLY   RA IN YOUNGER PATIENTS

FIGURE 84-1
Schematic representation of diseases resulting in the diagnosis of rheumatoid arthritis in old versus young patients.

and chronic stimulation of the immune system has eluded identification. A genetic predisposition is evidenced by the association of seropositive RA with the HLA-DR4 haplotype.

Bacterial, spirochetal, and viral infections are etiologic in the development of a variety of arthritic syndromes. The difficulty in implicating a specific infectious agent in any arthritic syndrome is illustrated by experimental mycoplasma arthritis. Although a chronic destructive arthropathy develops, the organism is isolated only during the initial inflammatory response.[1] A similar picture is seen with Lyme disease.

In recent years the Epstein-Barr virus (EBV) has received much attention as a possible etiologic agent in RA. EBV binds to a membrane receptor on B lymphocytes and stimulates antibody production without the presence of antigen. Patients with RA have elevated antibodies to rheumatoid arthritis nuclear antigen (RANA), an unusual EBV antigen, and high titers to more common EBV antigens are found in most patients studied. The T cells of RA patients are defective in their ability to regulate EBV stimulation of B cells in vitro. More recently, amino acid homology between determinants on rheumatoid arthritis–linked HLA molecules and a specific glycoprotein, gp110, on EBV has been found, suggesting that a cross-reactive immune response to EBV may be important in the pathogenesis of RA.[2]

A characteristic serologic abnormality found in the majority of patients with RA is the presence of rheumatoid factor. Rheumatoid factors are antibodies reacting with a specific site on the Fc portion of IgG that is expressed when antibody binds to antigen. Although their presence correlates with the development of erosive disease and rheumatoid nodules, they may be found in a variety of other diseases associated with chronic antigenic stimulation (syphilis, tuberculosis, infective endocarditis, lepromatous leprosy, schistosomiasis, etc.), as well as in healthy elderly individuals.

The earliest lesions seen in synovial biopsies of RA patients are proliferation of the synovial lining cells and

perivascular accumulation of lymphocytes. Obliteration by inflammatory cells and thrombi are characteristic microvascular abnormalities. In established disease, the synovial lining cells proliferate and the normally acellular connective tissue is infiltrated with mononuclear cells, which include activated T cells, B cells, and monocytes. Both IgG and IgM are produced, with rheumatoid factor production being disproportionately high compared to that produced by peripheral blood lymphocytes. As local antibody production continues, immune complexes are formed and deposited in the synovial tissue, resulting in complement activation via the classic and alternate pathway (Fig. 84-2).

Polymorphonuclear cells and monocytes phagocytize these complexes, stimulating the release of lysosomal proteinases that can digest collagen, cartilage matrix, and elastic tissue. Oxygen free radicals are formed which cause direct cellular damage. Arachidonic acid is oxi-

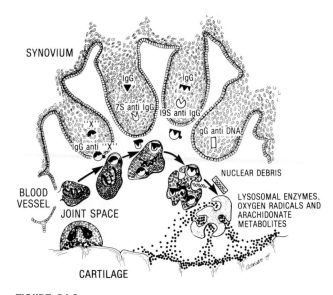

FIGURE 84-2
Schematic illustration of synovial inflammatory response in rheumatoid arthritis.

dized resulting in the production of prostaglandins and leukotrienes. As the inflammatory reaction continues unchecked, the chronic proliferative phase occurs, causing the destruction of articular cartilage, ligaments, tendons, and bone.

EPIDEMIOLOGY

RA has a worldwide distribution. The prevalence in the United States is estimated at 1 to 2 percent. Although it can initially present at both extremes of age, it has a peak incidence in the third and fourth decades. Because RA is a chronic disease, one would expect the prevalence to rise with age. However, for the reasons discussed earlier, it is difficult to accurately determine prevalence rates in elderly populations. In addition, the intensely inflammatory initial phase may subside with time, and the residual joint disease of RA may blend with other age- or time-related rheumatic processes, such as osteoarthritis giving rise to relatively nonspecific joint disease in old age. If one simply uses early American Rheumatology Association (ARA) criteria, some absurdly high prevalence rates are produced. For example, one study reported prevalence rates for RA in 75-year-olds at 23 percent for women and 14 percent for men.[3] A more recent study estimated an overall prevalence at age 79 of 10 percent, but in a subset of this sample subjected to more intensive examination, the true prevalence was found to be only 2 percent.[4]

Overall, women outnumber men by a two- or three-to-one ratio, and the predominance of women is maintained in older-onset disease. However, in studies of classic seropositive disease the ratio is closer to unity. Lower formal educational levels are associated with higher morbidity and mortality.[5] A retrospective population-based study at Vanderbilt University has recently challenged the concept that the diagnosis of RA does not influence life expectancy.[6] Severe dysfunction in RA patients was associated with a 5-year survival of 50 percent or less. Another recent study has supported an overall increased mortality in patients with RA.[7] Thus another factor influencing the prevalence of RA in old age may relate to such premature mortality.

DIAGNOSIS

The lack of an identified etiology or accurate definition for RA has posed limitations on investigators of the disease. The ARA developed a set of diagnostic criteria to assist in defining patients for population studies.[8] While these criteria were developed for use in population studies of disease prevalence, they were quickly incorporated into medical education and clinical practice. Five

or more criteria (indicating definite RA) yielded a sensitivity of 70 percent and a specificity of 91 percent for rheumatologist-diagnosed definite RA. The studies determining sensitivity and specificity were not carried out in elderly patients. To improve the sensitivity of the ARA classification, revised criteria have been proposed (Table 84-1).[9]

CLINICAL FEATURES

RA is a systemic disorder with primary manifestations in the joints. The clinical course is highly variable and may include episodes of acute flares interspersed between relatively quiescent periods. The majority of patients of all ages have an insidious onset with gradual recruitment of joints. Fatigue, myalgias, and malaise may precede the joint symptoms by weeks to months. Occasionally a mono-oligoarthritis is the initial manifestation and will evolve into the more typical symmetric polyarthritis with time. A prominent symptom in almost all patients with RA is morning stiffness, or the so-called gel phenomenon. In untreated patients this typically lasts from 2 hours to all day, and the duration of stiffness can be used to assess response to therapy. Stiffness is often more prominent in the hands but can involve all joints. Presence and duration of morning stiffness is very useful in differentiating RA from osteoarthritis, in which, if stiffness is present, it is almost always of less than 30 minutes duration. On the other hand, morning stiffness does not help differentiate RA from other inflammatory diseases such as polymyalgia rheumatica (PMR), systemic lupus erythematosus, the spondyloarthropathies, or chronic pseudogout.

Swelling, tenderness, and loss of function are found in the proximal interphalangeal joints, metacarpals, wrists, elbows, knees, ankles, and metatarsals. Although not commonly cited as involved, the distal interphalangeal joints can be inflamed in up to 80 percent of patients; however, this is rarely the predominant site of actual joint disease. While the hallmark of RA is its symmetry, one exception to this phenomenon is when the disease develops in a hemiplegic patient, in which case the paralyzed side is often spared.

Over the past three decades there have been a number of reports describing RA presenting in older patients.[10–16] While there are disagreements among the various reports, one can also find messages common to most of them. These are as follows:

1. A substantial number of patients with RA initially diagnosed in old age have a presentation and course indistinguishable from that of younger patients. These individuals are almost always seropositive.
2. As many as one-third of older RA patients have an

TABLE 84-1   1987 Revised Criteria for Classification of Rheumatoid Arthritis*

Criterion	Description
1. Morning stiffness	Morning stiffness in and around the joints, lasting at least 1 hour before maximal improvement.
2. Arthritis of three or more joint areas	At least three joint areas simultaneously have had soft tissue swelling or fluid (not bony overgrowth alone) observed by a physician. The 14 possible areas are right or left PIPs, MCPs, wrist, elbow, knee, and MTP joints.
3. Arthritis of hand joints	At least one area swollen (as defined above) in a wrist, MCP, or PIP joint.
4. Symmetric arthritis	Simultaneous involvement of the same joint areas (as defined in No. 2) on both sides of the body (bilateral involvement of PIPs, MCPs, or MTPs is acceptable without absolute symmetry).
5. Rheumatoid nodules	Subcutaneous nodules, over bony prominences or extensor surfaces, or in juxtaarticular regions, observed by a physician.
6. Serum rheumatoid factor	Demonstration of abnormal amounts of serum rheumatoid factor by any method for which the result has been positive in <5% of normal control subjects.
7. Radiographic changes	Radiographic changes typical of rheumatoid arthritis on posteroanterior hand and wrist radiographs, which must include erosions or unequivocal bone decalcification localized in or most marked adjacent to the involved joints (osteoarthritis changes alone do not qualify).

*For classification purposes, a patient shall be said to have rheumatoid arthritis if he or she has satisfied at least four of these seven criteria. Criteria 1 through 4 must have been present for at least 6 weeks. Patients with two clinical diagnoses are not included. Designation as classic, definite, or probable rheumatoid arthritis is not to be made. PIPs, proximal interphalangeal joints; MCPs, metacarpophalangeal joints; MTPs, metatarsophalangeal joints.
SOURCE: From Arnett FC et al: The 1987 revised American Rheumatism Association criteria for classification of rheumatoid arthritis. *Arthritis Rheum* 31:315, 1988.

acute onset, with prominence of systemic features such as weight loss, fever, myalgias, and morning stiffness. This presentation, which has been termed "Benign Rheumatoid Arthritis of the Aged,"[12] tends to have a good prognosis, often with complete remission of symptoms.

3. Another common presentation is: large-joint involvement, particularly the shoulders, hips, and wrists, with sparing of the hands; high erythrocyte sedimentation rate (ESR); negative rheumatoid factor; and excellent response to low doses of steroids. Healey considers this presentation to be on a continuum with PMR/giant cell arteritis rather than a form of RA.[16,17] Some of the patients in the "acute onset" category also fit into the "PMR-like" category.

Only one study has compared the clinical features of elderly-onset RA to the clinical features of RA in a younger population with similar disease duration (Table 84-2).[14] An abrupt onset, with symptoms peaking in days to weeks, was noted twice as often in the older-onset subgroup. A PMR-like onset, defined as shoulder or hip synovitis, absence of nodules, ESR > 50 mm/h, and a negative rheumatoid factor (RF), was also more common. In the elderly group, subcutaneous nodules and seropositivity were less frequently present at disease onset or at final evaluation than they were in the younger group. Although total joint scores were comparable, the older-onset group tended to have more hip and shoulder involvement, while the younger-onset group had more small-joint inflammation at onset. Overall, the older-onset group had a better outcome with respect to morn-

TABLE 84-2
Comparison of Older-Onset RA (ORA) vs. Younger-Onset RA (YRA) at Presentation*

Presentation Features	ORA – N = 78	YRA – N = 134
Age at onset	67.2 ± 4.7	46.6 ± 10.0
Disease duration at first evaluation	1.1 ± 1.9	1.9 ± 2.5
Positive family history	21%	24%
Abrupt onset	27%	14%
Morning stiffness	85%	90%
PMR symptoms	23%	5%†
Total joint score	4.9 ± 2.6	5.1 ± 3.6
Small-joint disease	24%	46%†
Shoulder synovitis	56%	36%
Rheumatoid nodules	6%	20%
ESR	52 ± 1.6	40.7 ± 23.6
Positive rheumatoid factor	48%	72%†

*Values are mean ± standard deviation unless designated otherwise.
†Statistically significant.
SOURCE: From Deal CL et al: The clinical features of elderly-onset rheumatoid arthritis. *Arthritis Rheum* 28:987, 1985.

ing stiffness, fatigue, total joint scores, ESR, and subjective assessments. Seropositivity was a poor prognostic indicator.

In addition to the three major patterns described above, smaller subsets of RA in the elderly that seem to have a common presentation, response to treatment, and prognosis have been separated out by different investigators. For example, McCarty et al.[18] have recently described a group of elderly patients that present acutely with symmetrical small-joint synovitis accompanied by pitting edema of the hands and feet. They named this syndrome RS$_3$PE. The arthritis is seronegative, nonerosive, and may go into complete remission after hydroxychloroquine therapy. An interesting aspect of this syndrome is that most of the patients are HLA-B7 positive. In addition, Healey has described a group of elderly patients with a mild, nonprogressive arthritis that responds well to medication. These individuals are seropositive and have a high prevalence of Sjögren's syndrome.[17]

COMPLICATIONS OF RA

JOINTS

The late complications of RA are, as would be expected, most common in older people. Chronic inflammation of the small joints of the hands can eventually lead to characteristic deformities. Hyperextension of the proximal interphalangeal (PIP) joint due to contracture of the intrinsic muscle tendons in association with distal interphalangeal (DIP) joint flexion is the swan neck deformity. The boutonniere deformity develops when the central slip of the extensor digitorum tendon ruptures, resulting in fixed flexion of the PIP joint. Chronic swelling of the metacarpophalangeal (MCP) joints stretches the collageral ligaments and extensor tendons. With time the extensor tendons may subluxate to the ulnar side of the joint. Rupture of the flexor tendon at the level of the MCP joint and the extensor digitorum tendons at the wrist are also common. Except in the carpal and tarsal joints, bony ankylosis is rare. Inflammation of the elbow results in flexion contractures.

Metatarsophalangeal (MTP) joints may be the first to demonstrate erosive disease. Patients complain of a sensation of walking on pebbles. The transverse arch collapses, transferring weight bearing to the MTP heads. Inflammation of the ankle and subtalar joints contributes to overall foot disability and leads to eversion of the hindfoot.

Knee involvement is frequent and is often the impetus for medical consultation. Flexion contractures are the rule, with progression to a valgus deformity. Ligamentous laxity and atrophy of the quadriceps muscle contribute to joint instability. Hip involvement is char-

acterized by diffuse joint-space narrowing and central migration on x ray.

Cervical spine involvement most often presents with painful limitation of neck motion. The most serious complication is atlantoaxial subluxation or atlantoaxial imposition toward the foramen magnum. The development of severe neck pain, paresthesias of the hands and feet, urinary retention or incontinence, involuntary leg spasms, and "stone" or "marble" sensation in the limbs or trunk are warning signs requiring immediate investigation.[19] Physical examination will reveal multiple neurologic defects, including long tract signs and lower-extremity hyperreflexia. Position sense and two-point discrimination are lost. If left untreated, quadriplegia and/or respiratory arrest can ensue. Subluxation of the lower cervical vertebrae also occurs, most commonly at C3-C4.

It is not uncommon for RA to appear to have "burned out" in elderly patients with long-standing disease. Typically, these patients will have the stigmata of chronic disease, such as joint instability and deformities, but will have few complaints of pain or stiffness and little evidence of active synovitis on examination. However, these patients reveal continued active inflammation on synovial biopsy. Thus, it is the patients' response to the disease which has burned out, not the chronic inflammatory process itself. This is important to realize, because patients with "burned out" RA are still at risk for developing extraarticular complications (discussed below).

EXTRAARTICULAR MANIFESTATIONS

Students of medicine are often puzzled as to why a chronic joint disease such as RA can also involve many other organ systems in the body. Perhaps a more appropriate question is why a systemic disease such as RA has as its primary manifestation inflammation of the joints. Virtually all patients with RA will have extraarticular involvement if it is searched for assiduously; for example, more than half of RA patients show lymphocytic infiltration of minor salivary glands on lip biopsy.[20] The extraarticular manifestations of RA are more common in the elderly population because they generally relate to duration of disease, and they are most common in seropositive individuals. The major extraarticular manifestations of RA are discussed below.

Sjögren's Syndrome

Sjögren's syndrome (keratoconjunctivitis sicca plus xerostomia) is a frequent complication of long-standing RA. However, the symptoms of dry eyes and dry mouth are also common in the healthy elderly population. Indeed, positive Schirmer's tests have low specificity for Sjögren's syndrome in the elderly. The dry mouth can be bothersome and contributes to dental caries and poorly fitting dentures. Perhaps more serious are the complications of dry eyes, which includes corneal ulcerations and infections. Any individual with RA admitting to eye irritation, photosensitivity, foreign-body sensation, or lack of tears should be presumed to have Sjögren's syndrome and referred for ophthalmological evaluation, including rose bengal staining. It is important to remember that patients with secondary Sjögren's syndrome rarely complain of dry mucous membranes on their own.[21] Artificial saliva and tears are the mainstay of therapy. Anticholinergic drugs should be avoided.

Rheumatoid Nodules

Rheumatoid nodules are frequently associated with other systemic features. Rarely do they appear as the major clinical manifestation of rheumatoid disease. Nodules are less frequently reported in disease with onset in older age, but this may relate more to the shorter duration of observation. Nodules develop subcutaneously in areas subjected to microtrauma such as the olecranon, the occiput, the Achilles tendon, the ischial tuberosity, the bridge of the nose, and other extensor tendons. In the chronically debilitated patient the overlying skin may break down, producing a painful, poorly healing ulcer which is prone to infection. Treatment may require excision and even skin grafting. Lesions that may be mistaken for rheumatoid nodules include gouty tophi, sebaceous cysts, basal cell carcinoma, ganglions, xanthomata, and multicentric reticulohistiocytosis nodules.

Ocular Complications

The most common ocular complications of RA relate to the clinical manifestations of the sicca syndrome in the cornea and conjunctiva. Patients complain of burning, grittiness, and loss of tear production. Episcleritis usually appears suddenly and is recognized as a raised lesion surrounded by intense vascularity over the anterior sclera. Scleritis is a rare but more serious complication. It occasionally presents as an acute, painful inflammatory condition but more commonly is a slowly progressive nodular destructive process of the sclera (scleromalacia perforans). Its occurrence is associated with disease of more than 10 years duration, is more common in women, and is associated with other signs of vasculitis. The complications of scleritis include choroiditis with retinal detachment, sclerosing keratitis, cataracts, secondary glaucoma, and perforation. Treatment of scleritis frequently requires the use of systemic corticosteroids and cytotoxic agents.

Pleuropulmonary Complications

Pleural effusions are the most frequent pleuropulmonary manifestation and are found more commonly in older men. The effusion may antedate the onset of arthritis.

Although the onset may be acute and associated with fever, a gradually developing effusion is more typical. The exudate is characterized by a pH of less than 7.2, elevated protein and lactate dehydrogenase levels, and a low glucose level. None of these findings rules out an infectious cause for the effusion. The presence of rheumatoid factor is helpful but is not necessary for the diagnosis and can be found in other conditions. The presence of cholesterol crystals reflects chronicity. Cytologic examination reveals lymphocytes and occasionally eosinophilia. Pleural biopsy is helpful to confirm other disorders, such as tuberculosis, but is generally nondiagnostic for RA.

Intrapulmonary rheumatoid nodules, as with effusions, are more common in men with subcutaneous nodules and long-standing disease. They are usually multiple and bilateral, though solitary nodules can occur and need to be differentiated from carcinoma. Their course is often unpredictable and bears no relation to the overall activity of the disease. Rupture of nodules in a subpleural location can cause pneumothorax.

Fibrosing alveolitis, associated with high titer rheumatoid factor and subcutaneous nodules, occurs more frequently in men. Obliterative bronchiolitis has been described and is a rare complication of rheumatoid lung. The initial cases reported described a fulminant disorder culminating in death, but milder forms have been recognized. Drugs used in the treatment of RA, including gold salts and methotrexate, are associated with pulmonary hypersensitivity reactions which must be differentiated from primary lung disease.

Cardiac Complications

Clinically significant cardiac manifestations of RA are rare in comparison with autopsy findings of cardiac involvement. Pericardial disease is the rule at postmortem, and subclinical pericarditis is not uncommon in patients undergoing echocardiography. Death due to cardiac causes in patients with RA, however, bears more relation to age-induced atherosclerosis than to RA itself. Rheumatoid granulomas may rarely be responsible for valvular disease and conduction defects.

Neurologic Complications

Neurologic complications occur in about 10 percent of patients with RA. A diffuse distal neuropathy similar to diabetic and alcoholic neuropathies is characterized by numbness of the hands and feet in a stocking-glove distribution. Light touch, pin prick, and vibratory sensation are lost or diminished, though position sense is maintained. The occurrence of mononeuritis multiplex has a poor prognosis and is associated with widespread vasculitis.

Entrapment neuropathies such as carpal and tarsal

tunnel syndromes may complicate RA when inflammation or edema cause pressure on peripheral nerves as they pass near affected joints. Other nerves susceptible to entrapment are the ulnar nerve at the elbow or wrist, the radial or posterior interosseous nerve at the lateral epicondyle, and the anterior tibial nerve in the popliteal space. Symptoms usually respond to control of the inflammatory process with immobilization, local corticosteroid injection, or systemic therapy.

Vasculitis

Inflammatory changes in arterioles and venules are the most common early changes seen in rheumatoid synovitis. With prolonged disease a more widespread arteritis has been described in less than 1 percent of patients who seek medical attention. This arteritis is characterized by polyneuropathy, digital gangrene, skin ulceration, and intestinal infarction. The prognosis is poor. It is more common in men, with an acute onset after years of seropositive, erosive RA associated with rheumatoid nodules. There are some data to suggest that this syndrome may be associated with the initiation or rapid withdrawal of high doses of steroids. The syndrome may evolve over several months and requires aggressive therapy with cytotoxic agents.

Felty's Syndrome

Felty's syndrome occurs in less than 5 percent of RA patients seeking medical attention. It is characterized by splenomegaly, neutropenia, leg ulcers, and generalized lymphadenopathy. Accelerated red cell destruction complicates the usual anemia of chronic disease, and increased platelet destruction may also be seen. Recurrent gram-positive infections are an indication for splenectomy, though neutropenia may remain unaltered. Some authors also recommend cytotoxic drugs for this condition.

Amyloidosis

Secondary amyloidosis is a complication of many chronic inflammatory diseases, including RA. Patients with long-standing RA who develop cardiac, renal, or neuropathic diseases may have secondary amyloidosis, which can be found on rectal biopsy or biopsy of the involved tissue. Amyloidosis is discussed more fully in Chapter 87.

LABORATORY EVALUATION

As stated earlier, the diagnosis of RA is made clinically. The laboratory findings mostly reflect the nonspecific abnormalities of a chronic inflammatory disease, including a normocytic, normochromic anemia, low serum iron and iron-binding capacity, thrombocytosis, occasional leukocytosis and eosinophilia, elevated ESR and C-reactive protein, and hypergammaglobulinemia. Baseline liver-function tests, urinalysis, and serum creatinine are important for monitoring potential drug toxicity. A positive rheumatoid factor, one of the ARA criteria for the diagnosis of RA, is much less helpful in the evaluation of elderly patients because of the high prevalence of false-positive tests. Indeed, the prevalence of positive tests for many autoantibodies rises with age (Table 84-3).[22]

RADIOGRAPHIC EVALUATION

Soft-tissue swelling, periarticular osteoporosis, juxtaarticular erosions, and diffuse joint-space narrowing are the radiologic hallmarks of RA. However, these relatively subtle manifestations become less obvious in an older patient with preexisting degenerative changes. Differentiation from osteoarthritis is made easier when the inflammation involves joints not typical of this disorder, such as the MCPs and wrists. In the knee, tricompartment as opposed to medial joint-space narrowing would be more typical of RA. Degenerative disease of the cervical spine most frequently involves C5-C6, with joint-space narrowing and osteophytes, while RA is recognized as presenting with diffuse intervertebral disc-space narrowing and erosions of the odontoid.

TABLE 84-3
Autoantibodies and Circulating Immune Complexes in Healthy Elderly Subjects

Assay	Older Subjects Positive/Total Tested	Young Controls % Positive	Positive/Total Tested	% Positive
Antinuclear Ab	50/278	18	4/98	4
Rheumatoid factor	38/278	14	4/98	4
Lymphocytotoxic Ab	27/278	10	3/93	3
Circulating immune complexes	43/197	22	5/100	5

SOURCE: From Goodwin JS: Immunologic responses of a healthy elderly population. *Clin Exp Immunol* 48:403, 1982.

DIFFERENTIAL DIAGNOSIS

The importance of accurate differential diagnosis in RA relates to the relatively selective response of some diseases to specific therapies. It does not matter so much whether a patient presenting with predominantly large-joint complaints, systemic symptoms, high ESR, and negative rheumatoid factor is classified as PMR or is called a PMR-like presentation of RA, so long as the clinician understands that such patients tend to respond poorly to nonsteroidal anti-inflammatory drugs (NSAIDs) and do well on low doses of steroids. Similarly, the impetus for identifying patients with chronic pseudogout who might otherwise be diagnosed as having RA comes from the knowledge that these patients may respond well to chronic low-dose colchicine and poorly to gold.

TREATMENT

The treatment of RA is empirical. The natural history of the disease may span decades, with fluctuations in the intensity of inflammation and disability. The foundation of a successful therapeutic regimen is a working partnership between the patient and physician, which is facilitated when both the patient and family have a basic understanding of the disease and realistic expectations about response to therapy and prognosis. The concept of a chronic disease with no known cure is often a cause of much anxiety and depression. Attention to psychosocial issues is as important as drug therapy.[23] The local Arthritis Foundation can be very helpful in providing patient education and support groups. Three realistic goals to be emphasized are the relief of symptoms, preservation of joint function, and the maintenance of a reasonable lifestyle.

Physical rest cannot be overemphasized as a time-honored remedy for the effects of acute inflammation. It is important that the patient and all members of the patient's family understand that daily rest is an integral part of the medical treatment. The degree of rest may vary from an hour of bed rest in the afternoon for mild disease to hospitalization for severe uncontrolled inflammation.[24] A recent study has supported the benefit of short-term hospitalization (1 to 2 weeks) over standard outpatient therapy.[25] Unfortunately, the introduction of diagnosis-related groups (DRGs) has limited the use of hospitalization in the elderly population, as the benefits of noninvasive therapy are difficult to quantitate. Most European countries have a much better appreciation of the very real benefits of physical and mental rest in the treatment of chronic conditions, and several mechanisms have evolved to provide such therapy. Indeed, spa ther-apy is routinely funded by the health insurance systems of many European countries.

MEDICATIONS

The mainstay of drug therapy in RA is the use of NSAIDs. The use of aspirin and other salicylates in elderly individuals is discouraged because many older individuals do not predictably experience tinnitus as the first symptom of salicylate toxicity. Instead, they can slip into stupor, coma, and even death on "therapeutic" levels of aspirin intake. Physicians using salicylates to treat arthritis in elderly patients should be aware that salicylate toxicity is a relatively common and frequently unrecognized cause of subacute or acute confusional states in the older patients and may also be misdiagnosed as sepsis, pulmonary embolus, or other acute problems if it is not considered in the differential diagnosis.[26]

Although the newer nonsteroidals are not more effective than aspirin, they offer a better therapeutic profile, with respect to gastrointestinal and central nervous system (CNS) toxicity, and better compliance with less frequent dosing. In addition to producing gastrointestinal toxicity, these drugs may cause fluid retention, edema, hypertension, and congestive heart failure in patients with borderline cardiovascular function. While interference with renal function is a relatively rare complication of NSAIDs, the risk factors for the occurrence of such a toxicity (preexisting renal disease, decreased intravascular volume, congestive heart failure, diuretic use) are all more common in elderly patients. It is wise to assess a serum creatinine before and several weeks after starting therapy. As a general rule, NSAIDs should be avoided in individuals with serum creatinine above 2.0 mg/dl. Global CNS toxicity manifested by loss of concentration, memory problems, or personality changes can occur after NSAID administration to elderly patients, and all individuals over age 65 receiving these drugs should be warned about this potential complication.[27] Indomethacin is more frequently associated with CNS toxicity than are other NSAIDs.

In the past several years there have been published reports of several large, blinded trials of various NSAIDs in elderly subjects. There do not appear to be any important changes in serum half-life with age for any of the widely used drugs.

SECOND-LINE THERAPY

When NSAIDs are not sufficient to control RA, disease-modifying antirheumatic drugs are introduced. In addition to suppressing inflammation, these drugs may effect a partial or complete remission in the disease process. Another attribute these agents have in common is that their mechanisms of action are entirely unknown.

Parenteral gold salts have been used for more than 60 years. The majority of patients will respond favorably to gold shots within 3 to 6 months. Injections are continued indefinitely as long as there is a therapeutic response without signs of toxicity. Common adverse reactions include dermatitis, mucositis, pruritus, proteinuria, and blood dyscrasias. A complete blood cell count, platelet count, and urinalysis are performed prior to each gold injection, and if there is an adverse effect the drug is discontinued temporarily or permanently, depending on the severity of the effect. Cholestatic hepatitis, enterocolitis, pneumonitis, and peripheral neuropathies are less common reactions. Withdrawal for toxicity occurs in 20 to 40 percent of patients. The efficacy and toxicity of gold therapy would appear to be similar in young and old patients with RA.[28,29,30]

An oral gold preparation (auranofin) has been approved for use in RA. It efficacy is similar to, but perhaps somewhat less than, the parenteral preparation. Diarrhea is the most frequently reported side effect and occurs in as many as one-third of patients. Rashes, blood dyscrasias, and proteinuria are less frequently seen with oral versus parenteral gold, but still require monitoring.

Antimalarial drugs are effective in RA. Hydroxychloroquine is particularly useful when the disease is slowly progressive but not yet erosive. It can induce remissions when used in the therapy of the newly described RS$_3$PE syndrome.[18] Retinotoxicity is the most serious complication of antimalarial therapy. Early lesions are recognized as visual field defects and abnormal macular pigmentation, which are indistinguishable from senile macular degeneration. Baseline and annual ophthalmologic evaluations are recommended. Self-monitoring between formal examinations is easily accomplished with an Amsler grid. Corneal drug deposits and accommodation defects are reversible when the drug is discontinued. Other uncommon side effects include dyspepsia, vomiting, rash, proximal myopathy, psychosis, and blood dyscrasias.

Penicillamine therapy may be useful in patients who are unresponsive to gold or antimalarials. Full therapeutic response may take up to 6 months. Side effects include dysgeusia, rash, proteinuria, drug fever, and bone marrow suppression. Laboratory monitoring is the same as with gold. Rarer complications include the development of polymyositis, Goodpasture's syndrome, myasthenia gravis, systemic lupus erythematosus, and bullous pemphigoid.

IMMUNOSUPPRESSIVES

Immunosuppressive drug therapy is reserved for progressive disease refractory to standard therapy. Azathioprine has received Food and Drug Administration (FDA) approval for the treatment of RA. Toxic reactions include leukopenia, thrombocytopenia, infection, nausea, vomiting, allergic reactions, and hepatotoxicity. Dose-related leukopenia and thrombocytopenia are the most frequent side effects and require routine monitoring. With azathioprine, as with all immunosuppressive drugs, the physician must be aware that the decreased marrow reserves of the elderly patient put him or her at increased risk for serious bone marrow toxicity. While this is an obvious concern, several studies have not supported a link between azathioprine use in RA and an increased risk of subsequent malignancy, with the exception of an increase in non-Hodgkin's lymphoma.[31]

Cyclophosphamide has a limited role in the treatment of RA. Serious side effects include the induction of malignancies (particularly of the bladder), hemorrhagic cystitis, and infection. Frequent monitoring of the white blood cell count is required. Patients are advised to maintain a high fluid intake (2 to 4 liters/day) to reduce the risk of hemorrhage cystitis.

The use of methotrexate on RA dates back to the early 1950s, but it was not until the late 1970s and early 1980s that a renewed interest in the treatment of RA with this agent prompted a reevaluation of it. One advantage over the more traditional remissive agents is that a positive response is seen frequently within the first month. Methotrexate is usually administered one day per week, either in a single dose or divided into two or three doses. Some physicians prefer weekly intramuscular injections to ensure easier monitoring of compliance and toxicity. Discontinuation of methotrexate treatment because of side effects is required in about one-third of patients. Commonly occurring side effects include gastrointestinal problems, mouth ulcers, anemia, decreased white cell and platelet counts, and alopecia. Bone marrow suppression and hypersensitivity pneumonitis occur in less than 1 percent of treated cases. Toxicity is more prominent in patients with reduced kidney function, which is of special concern in the elderly.

From experience with methotrexate use in treating psoriasis, there is known to be a long-term risk for liver cirrhosis in 3 to 5 percent of patients using methotrexate. Liver biopsy is recommended after 2 years on the drug. Alcoholism, diabetes, and obesity have been identified as significant risk factors for this complication. It is not clear whether advanced age increases the risk of hepatic toxicity with methotrexate.

Combination drug therapies have also been tried for severe recalcitrant disease. The choice of such combinations and drug doses has been empirical. A low-dose combination of cyclophosphamide, azathioprine, and hydroxychloroquine was evaluated in one group of patients older than 50 years of age. This combination was effective in suppressing inflammation, although it was associated with significant serious side effects, including deaths from cancer.[32] Less toxic combinations are under evaluation.

CORTICOSTEROIDS

Although corticosteroid therapy can reduce rheumatoid inflammation, the long-term side effects limit their usefulness, except in patients with serious extraarticular manifestations. Low doses (5 mg) of prednisone per day have been advocated for the interim before the beneficial effects of a disease-modifying agent are realized. Once the disease is controlled, the prednisone dose should be gradually tapered to zero. This approach has been particularly popular for the treatment of RA in the elderly.[33] As mentioned previously, the PMR-like presentation of RA responds particularly well to 10 to 15 mg of prednisone daily.

REHABILITATION

The importance of a basic physical therapy program in conjunction with medication must be understood by the patient. The goals are to maintain range of motion, prevent disuse atrophy of muscle, and limit deformity. The development of hand deformities with the loss of manual dexterity is a major risk factor for institutionalization among elderly arthritics. The importance of rest has already been stated. To prevent joint contractures, patients should be instructed in a simple range-of-motion program. Moving all the joints gently through a full range of motion once daily will accomplish this end. Gentle isotonic or isometric exercises are helpful in maintaining muscle strength.

Splints are useful as adjuncts in resting acutely inflamed joints, relieving pain, and minimizing deformity. Volar wrist splints are worn at night, as well as during the day when inflammation is severe. Leg splints of molded plastic may help in the prevention of knee or ankle contractures. Splints should be removed at least once a day to allow performance of range-of-motion exercises. Much benefit can be gained by proper attention to footwear, including the use of orthopedic shoes, medial wedges, and metatarsal bars.

The cervical spine is a frequent source of discomfort. A soft cervical collar may be worn at night and acts as a splint. Specialized pillows which support the neck in a neutral position are also helpful at night, as many patients find the collar to be constricting.

Canes can be quite useful in relieving pain and permitting ambulation, especially for hip arthritis. A cane with a T-bar handle is preferred for the RA patient to minimize stress on the hand. The use of other assistive devices can best be determined by an occupational therapist's in-home evaluation. Bathtub bars, special doorknobs, and raised toilet seats are particularly helpful to an elderly patient living alone. Such simple modifications may be the difference between maintaining or losing functional independence.

SURGERY

The primary indication for surgery is the failure of medical therapy, as evidenced by the persistence of pain, deformity, and restricted motion. The list of surgical procedures employed in arthritis includes synovectomy, tenolysis, fusion, and total joint replacement. Total joint replacement, especially of the hip, is the most successful intervention for restoring function in a previously destroyed, painful joint. Patients with generalized RA are more limited in their activity and therefore have less risk of failure after joint replacement.

The main indication for hand surgery is decreased function of the hand and wrist, rather than pain. Repair of ruptured tendons is a relatively simple procedure. Corrective surgery of an early boutonniere or swan neck deformity may be indicated, but in many elderly patients this deformity is more likely to be long-standing and fixed. Instability of the thumb joint can be corrected by arthrodesis, which restores pincer function. The decision to intervene will depend on the patient's demands and expectations.

Indication for operative correction of cervical spine disease is based on neurologic findings.[34] Pain without neurologic signs is best treated with a well-fitting collar.

Advanced age, alone, is not a contraindication to surgery for arthritis. Evaluation of coexistent medical problems, such as ischemic heart disease, chronic urinary infection, and pulmonary disease, needs to be addressed. Problems of recessed mandibles, cervical spine disease, and rheumatoid lung disease will require special consideration by the anesthesiologist, but they are not contraindications per se. In addition to the expected complications of surgery, RA patients are more susceptible to infection, operative fractures, and blood loss.

SUMMARY

The issues surrounding the diagnosis and treatment of rheumatoid arthritis are typical of the fundamental difficulties in geriatric medicine. The cohort of individuals in their seventies currently diagnosed with RA represent a different spectrum of conditions from the cohort of 40- to 50-year-olds with the same diagnosis (Fig. 84-1). The risks for both overdiagnosis and underdiagnosis of RA are much greater in elderly patients. In addition, the therapeutic goals established for elderly patients with RA must fundamentally address the threat of loss of functional independence, leading to institutionalization. Finally, concern about toxicity from treatment of elderly

RA patients cannot be addressed merely by the expectation that the side effects of drugs seen in young people will be more frequent in the aged. Often, whole new patterns of toxicity emerge in the elderly, and these can go unnoticed if they are not appreciated as a risk a priori.

REFERENCES

1. Decker JL, Barden JA, in Dumonde DC (ed): *Infection and Immunology in the Rheumatic Diseases.* Oxford, Blackwell, 1976.
2. Roudier J et al: Two copies of the HLA Dw4/Dw14/DR1 rheumatoid arthritis (RA) susceptibility determinant QKRAA/QRRAA are present on the Epstein-Barr Virus (EBV) glycoprotein gp110. *Arthritis Rheum* 31:S12, 1988.
3. Engel A et al: Rheumatoid arthritis in adults. *Vital Health Stat* 11:1, 1966.
4. Bergstrom et al: Prevalence of rheumatoid arthritis, osteoarthritis, chondrocalcinosis and gouty arthritis at age 79. *J Rheumatol* 13:527, 1986.
5. Pincus T, Callahan LF: Formal education as a marker for increased mortality and morbidity in rheumatoid arthritis. *J Chronic Dis* 38:973, 1985.
6. Pincus T, Callahan LF: Taking mortality in rheumatoid arthritis seriously: Predictive markers, socioeconomic status and comorbidity. *J Rheumatol* 13:841, 1986.
7. Mitchell DM et al: Survival, prognosis and causes of death in rheumatoid arthritis. *Arthritis Rheum* 29:706, 1986.
8. Ropes MW et al: 1958 revision of diagnostic criteria for rheumatoid arthritis. *Arthritis Rheum* 2:16, 1959.
9. Arnett FC et al: The 1987 revised American Rheumatism Association criteria for classification of rheumatoid arthritis. *Arthritis Rheum* 31:315, 1988.
10. Cecil RS, Krammerer WH: Rheumatoid arthritis in the aged. *Am J Med* 13:439, 1951.
11. Terkeltaub R et al: A clinical study of older age rheumatoid arthritis with comparison to a younger onset group. *J Rheumatol* 10:418, 1983.
12. Corrigan AB et al: Benign rheumatoid arthritis of the aged. *Br Med J* 1:444, 1974.
13. Brown JS, Jones DA: The onset of rheumatoid arthritis in the aged. *J Am Geriatr Soc* 25:873, 1967.
14. Deal CL et al: The clinical features of elderly-onset rheumatoid arthritis. *Arthritis Rheum* 28:987, 1985.
15. Moesmann G: Clinical features in subacute rheumatoid arthritis in old age. *Acta Rheum Scand* 14:285, 1968.
16. Healey LA, Sheets PK: The relation of polymyalgia rheumatica to rheumatoid arthritis. *J Rheumatol* 15:750, 1988.
17. Healey LA: Rheumatoid arthritis in the elderly. *Clin Rheum Dis* 12(1):173, 1986.
18. McCarty DJ et al: Remitting seronegative symmetrical synovitis with pitting edema. (RS$_3$PPE) syndrome. *JAMA* 254:2763, 1985.
19. Meijers KSE et al: Cervical myelopathy in rheumatoid arthritis. *Clin Exp Rheumatol* 2:239, 1984.
20. Williams RC: *Rheumatoid Arthritis as Systemic Disease.* Philadelphia, Saunders, 1974.
21. Andonopoulos AP et al: Secondary Sjögren's syndrome in rheumatoid arthritis. *J Rheumatol* 14:1098, 1987.
22. Goodwin JS et al: Immunological responses of a healthy elderly population. *Clin Exp Immunol* 48:403, 1982.
23. Parker J et al: Pain in rheumatoid arthritis: Relationship to demographic, medical, and psychological factors. *J Rheumatol* 15:433, 1988.
24. Lee P et al: Benefits of hospitalization in rheumatoid arthritis. *Am J Med* 43:205, 1974.
25. Anderson RB et al: Patient outcome following inpatient vs. outpatient treatment of RA. *J Rheumatol* 15:556, 1988.
26. Anderson RJ et al: Unrecognized adult salicylate intoxication. *Ann Intern Med* 85:745, 1976.
27. Goodwin JS, Regan M: Cognitive dysfunction associated with naproxen and ibuprofen in the elderly. *Arthritis Rheum* 25:1013, 1982.
28. Dahl SL et al: Slow acting antirheumatic drugs in the treatment of elderly patients with rheumatoid arthritis. *Arthritis Rheum* 31:S79, 1988.
29. Ehrlich GE et al: Rheumatoid arthritis in the aged. *Geriatrics* 7:103, 1970.
30. Kean WF et al: Gold therapy in the elderly rheumatoid arthritis patient. *Arthritis Rheum* 26:705, 1983.
31. McDuffie FC (ed): Neoplasms in rheumatoid arthritis: Update on clinical and epidemiologic data. *Am J Med* 78(suppl 1A):1, 1985.
32. Csuka ME et al: Treatment of intractable rheumatoid arthritis with combined cyclophosphamide, azathioprine, and hydroxychloroquine: A follow-up study. *JAMA* 255:2315, 1986.
33. Lockie LM, Gomez EM: The benefit of small doses of adrenocorticosteroids in treatment of elderly rheumatoid arthritis. *Arthritis Rheum* 25:S115, 1982.
34. Bentley G, Dowd GSE: Surgical treatment of arthritis in the elderly. *Clin Rheum Dis* 12:291, 1986.

Chapter 85

OSTEOARTHRITIS

Walter H. Ettinger, Jr., and Maradee A. Davis

Osteoarthritis (OA) is the most prevalent arthritic condition that affects human beings; it has been estimated that 50 million people in the United States are afflicted with OA.[1] A majority of affected persons are over the age of 65, and osteoarthritis can lead to considerable pain and disability; thus, OA represents an important health and social concern in the elderly.

OA is a disease localized to diarthrodial joints and characterized by degeneration of hyaline cartilage with secondary changes in the periarticular bone and soft tissues. There is increasing consensus that OA is not a single disorder but rather a heterogeneous group of disorders which most likely results from a complex interplay of several factors all of which ends in a stereotypical final common pathway of joint damage.[2] Thus, OA may be somewhat analogous to congestive heart failure or end-stage renal disease, both of which result from a number of different diseases and/or pathophysiologic processes.[2,3] OA is best described, then, as affecting a specific joint and resulting from a specific etiologic agent and/or risk factor(s). In many instances, however, these features are unknown. OA may be defined generically by an analysis of its clinical, pathologic, and biologic characteristics. Mankin and Treadwell have recently put forth a working definition of OA modified from a definition developed in a multidisciplinary workshop held in 1985 on the etiopathogenesis of OA.[4,5] They define OA as

> a slowly progressive, monarticular (or less common, polyarticular) disorder of unknown cause occurring late in life that principally affects the hands and large weight-bearing joints, and is characterized clinically by pain, deformity, and limitation of motion and pathologically by focal erosive lesions, cartilage destruction, subchondral sclerosis, cyst formation and large osteophytes at the joint motion. The disease appears to originate in the cartilage and the changes in that tissue, virtually pathognomonic, are progressively more severe with advancing disease. Structural aberrations in the underlying bone and when present inflammatory alterations in the synovium, are usually milder and considered secondary. Systemic abnormalities have not been detected.

PREVALENCE

There is a considerable amount of literature on the epidemiology of OA. However, much of what has been written is descriptive and occasionally methodologically flawed. For the most part, epidemiologic studies of OA have relied on the presence of radiographic changes of joints to define the presence or absence of disease. There are several disadvantages to this approach. First, not all investigators use the same radiographic criteria, and there is variation in applying standard criteria which have been developed.[6] Second, the validity, reliability, and scaling properties of the most commonly used radiologic criteria have not been tested. Third, certain radiologic features of OA, such as osteophytes, may not reflect progressive disease. Finally, radiographs are limited because of their inability to detect early changes in cartilage. Newer radiologic imaging techniques such as magnetic resonance imaging (MRI) scanning and ultrasound may be better at detecting OA, but the reliability and validity of these techniques have not yet been tested. Similarly, several biomarkers of OA have been proposed, but they are not yet available for use in large-scale studies.

Several national surveys performed by the National Center for Health Statistics indicate that radiographic evidence of OA is very common.[7-10] The hands (i.e., the distal interphalangeal, proximal interphalangeal, and first carpometacarpal joints) are the most commonly affected sites. The United States Health Examination Survey (HES I) estimated that approximately 30 percent of persons aged 18 to 79 years had OA of the hands ranging from mild to severe. These prevalence figures increase with age: 79 percent of men and 86 percent of women aged 75 to 79 years had radiographic evidence of hand OA.[9] The knee joint is the next most frequently involved joint. Data from National Health and Nutrition Examination Study (NHANES I) indicate that 8 percent of men and 18 percent of women ages 65 to 74 had OA of the knee[11]; the presence of radiographic knee OA in the Framingham cohort of persons ages 63 to 94 was 33 percent.[12] The feet are also commonly affected by OA. In HES I, 30 percent of men and 32 percent of women ages 75 to 79 had OA of the feet.[9] The hip joint is less frequently affected by OA than are the hands, knees, or feet: Kellgren and Lawrence reported a prevalence of 19 percent for men and 12 percent for women 55 to 64 years old,[13] while the NHANES I reported prevalence was 2.6 percent for men and 2.8 percent for women ages 55 to 64.

Use of these prevalence rates may be somewhat misleading, however, as many persons with radiographic OA do not have symptoms referable to the disease. For example, Lawrence et al. found that only 9 percent of men and 25 percent of women with moderate or severe radiographic evidence of OA in the distal interphalangeal joints reported pain in these joints.[14] Data from NHANES I indicate that 43 percent of persons with knee OA report pain, while data from the Framingham cohort indicate that only 40 percent of persons ages 63 to 94 with radiographic evidence of knee OA report symptoms.[12,15] Similarly, only 28 percent of persons with moderate radiographic evidence of hip OA report pain, whereas 57 percent of those with severe hip OA report symptoms.[9]

When symptoms are present, OA can be a major cause of activity limitation, yet there are few studies which have quantified the degree to which OA affects health or functional status in older adults. Using data from the National Health Interview Studies, Fried et al. have concluded that arthritis is the leading cause of disability in the elderly because arthritis is a common disease and persons with arthritis report at least a moderate amount of activity limitation.[16] Other investigators have reported that persons with a diagnosis of OA have a higher prevalence of self-reported inability to carry out instrumental activities of daily living and avocations.[17] However, there is little information regarding disability as it relates to OA of specific joints. In general, OA of weight-bearing joints (hips, knees, spine) is associated with greater disability than OA of the hands. Data from the Baltimore Longitudinal Study of Aging indicate that persons with radiographic OA of the knee who report pain have significantly more limitation of physical activity, mobility, and ability to perform activities of daily living (as measured by the Arthritis Impact Measurement Scales[18]) than do age-matched controls without knee OA (Fig. 85-1). However, persons with radiographic OA of the knee but without knee pain reported no more disability than did controls. This suggests that only painful OA of the knee leads to a limitation of functional activity and that asymptomatic OA may be of little clinical significance. Other factors in addition to the dis-

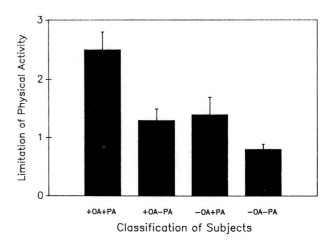

FIGURE 85-1

Limitation of physical activity as measured by the Arthritis Impact Measurement Scales in 511 adult participants of the Baltimore Longitudinal Study of Aging. Subjects were grouped as having radiographic OA of the knee with a report of knee pain (+OA + P), radiographic OA without pain (+OA − P), absence of OA but reporting pain (−OA + P), and neither OA or pain (−OA − P).

ease itself are related to symptoms and health status. The degree of self-reported pain and psychological distress in persons with OA of the knee is related to personality, as people with higher degrees of neuroticism report more pain, anxiety, and depressive symptoms given the same degree of radiographic disease.[19] Additionally, women with OA report more symptoms but less disability than do men with OA.[15]

The studies cited above are cross-sectional and do not give information about the progression of disease. Only a few studies have followed patients with OA longitudinally. Data from the Baltimore Longitudinal Study of Aging suggest that radiographic progression of OA of the interphalangeal joints is slow but inexorable over a 10- to 15-year period. Men followed for fewer than 5 years had little detectable progression of disease on x ray, while a majority of those who were followed for more than 10 years had worsening of the disease process; virtually no one had regression of the osteoarthritic process.[20] In contrast, an older study of hip OA over a 10-year period showed clinical improvement and radiographic recovery of the joint space.[21] This finding suggests at least partial reversal of OA of the hip and raises the question of whether OA follows a natural progression or whether regression is possible.

HISTOLOGY AND BIOCHEMISTRY

Whereas the initiating factor, pathogenesis, and progression of osteoarthritis may vary from joint to joint, certain anatomic and biochemical features are consistently present in intermediate and late-stage human OA.[22] The hyaline cartilage shows one or more of the following features: (1) fibrillation characterized by splitting of the noncalcified cartilage, (2) horizontal splitting of the cartilage which occurs between the uncalcified and calcified zone, (3) thinning of cartilage and erosions which can progress to expose calcified cartilage and, finally, bone. Just below the cartilage, there is osteocyte necrosis in subchondral bone and excessive osteoblastic and osteoclastic activity. Exposed bone is often interspersed with plugs of new fibrous or chondroid tissue that extend to the synovial interface through gaps in the subarticular bone plate. In addition, new bone formation is often seen away from the areas of cartilage destruction. Of note is that cartilage destruction can occur in the absence of any evidence of extensive bone remodeling or osteophytic lipping and that osteophytes may occur in the absence of cartilage destruction, raising the possibility that the two processes may be unrelated.[23] The synovium and joint capsule also show a variety of pathologic changes. Fibrosis occurs, and adherence and entrapment of bony or cartilaginous debris often leads to formation of multinucleate giant cells. Inflammatory changes, such as proliferation of synovial lining cells and mild-to-moderate mononuclear cell infiltrates, are also seen.[24] Biochemical changes in osteoarthritic cartilage include increased water content, change in the collagen weave, and a decreased proteoglycan concentration with shortening of the side chains and diminished aggregation. In advanced disease, proteoglycan subunits become small and fragmented.[5,25,26]

The pathologic and biochemical changes in cartilage appear to be mediated by chondrocytes, the cells which normally maintain hyaline cartilage. In osteoarthritic joints, these cells become metabolically active, and, although the exact mechanism is unknown, these cells respond to cytokines and other inflammatory mediators. A characteristic response of the cells includes (1) increased synthesis of deoxyribonucleic acid; (2) increased synthesis of proteoglycan, hyaluronate, and collagen; and (3) release of degradative enzymes such as neutral proteases, cathepsin, and collagenase.[5] This latter response damages the cartilage matrix components (collagen and proteoglycans). As a result, the cartilage tends to swell and develops altered biomechanical properties which in turn lead to joint dysfunction.

ETIOLOGY AND PATHOGENESIS

Several factors have been identified that are thought to be important in initiating or accelerating the progression of OA. In epidemiologic studies, chronologic age has been the factor most strongly and consistently associated with the development of OA. The influence of age on the incidence of OA varies from joint to joint, but some radiographic evidence of OA is found in a majority of persons over the age of 75. The sharp increase in the prevalence of OA with advancing age is apparently independent of socioeconomic status and has been observed both in the United States and Great Britain. Yet the mechanisms by which age is associated with OA are unclear; biophysical, anatomic, ultrastructural, and biomechanical factors may be involved. However, the biochemical changes that occur in joint cartilage with age are different from those which characterize OA cartilage. The water content of aging cartilage is decreased, as is the ratio of chondroitin-4-sulfate to chondroitin-6-sulfate; this situation is the opposite of that found in OA cartilage. Similarly, the keratin sulfate and hyaluronic acid content of aging cartilage is increased opposite to what is found in osteoarthritic cartilage.[27] Nonetheless, it may be that the age-associated changes increase the susceptibility of the articular cartilage to biomechanical stress or other etiologic factors and thus predispose to OA. A second hypothesis is that age-associated processes, such as glucose intolerance, obesity, osteoporosis, and hormonal changes, affect cartilage metabolism (or other components of the joint) directly or makes the joints more susceptible to the effects of other etiologic agents.

There are prominent gender differences in the prevalence, location, and severity of OA. In general, women have a higher prevalence and severity of OA of the hands, knees, ankles, and feet; men have a higher prevalence of OA of the spine and hips, as well as disc degeneration of the spine.[28,29] It has been suggested that sex differences in OA represent a difference in some systemic, hormonal, or constitutional factors or that factors such as obesity and occupational stress are associated with sex differences in OA. It has also been hypothesized that there is a protective role of estrogens until the time of menopause which may account for some of the sex differences in prevalence.[29]

There are also differences in the distribution and prevalence of OA across races. For example, knee OA is more common in blacks than in whites in the United States, and the prevalence of hip OA has been found to be low in Asian populations, including Indians and Chinese.[11,28,29] Studies of the Blackfoot and Pima Indians in the United States suggest a higher prevalence of OA than that found in the general United States population; Alaskan Eskimos have been found to have a low incidence of hand OA.[1,29]

Numerous types of mechanical stresses have been described in association with OA: single impact stress, gross anatomic damage, subtle mechanical derangement (such as long-standing internal derangement of the knee), joint hypermobility, multiple repeated impacts (such as pneumatic drill operators), and prolonged or repeated heavy overuse.[28] Occupational studies have most frequently focused on industrial workers and athletes, and the results, although suggestive of an association between physical activities and OA, are not clearly consistent. For example, data from HES I indicate that a higher-than-expected prevalence of hand OA was found in craftsmen and a lower-than-expected prevalence of hand OA was found in male clerical workers, private household workers, and service workers.[10] In contrast, there are numerous studies that report no particular association between OA and athletes, runners, or persons who perform heavy labor. Furthermore, it may be that these occupations or activities do not predispose to OA but only increase the number of injuries a person sustains, which appears to be a risk factor for OA. For example, a recent analysis of the NHANES I data revealed that in persons with unilateral OA of the knee, 15 percent of persons with right-knee OA reported previous injury to the right knee, and 27 percent of persons with left-knee OA reported previous knee injury to the left knee.[30]

Several studies now indicate that obesity is a risk factor for osteoarthritis of the knee.[31–33] The mechanisms by which obesity might cause knee OA are not clearly understood. Obesity may be a mechanical stress that results in excessive wear and tear on the joint, or obesity may act indirectly, through associated metabolic abnormalities such as diabetes and hyperuricemia that influence cartilage metabolism. A recent study is supportive of a mechanical but not a metabolic link between obesity and knee OA since controlling for serum cholesterol, serum uric acid, diabetes, body fat distribution, and blood pressure did not reduce the association between obesity and knee OA.[34] Of note, there seems to be no difference in association between obesity and symptomatic versus asymptomatic knee OA, suggesting that obesity is a predictor of pathologic OA but not symptomatic knee OA.

Although most data do not suggest that metabolic factors are important for OA of the knee, this does not preclude the fact that certain systemic factors may influence cartilage metabolism in specific joints. There is some evidence for a link between diabetes and OA, possibly through elevated growth hormone levels, which alter cartilage metabolism and increase bone density.[35] Hyperuricemia has been found more frequently in persons with generalized OA and in younger men with knee OA. Hypertension has been observed to be associated with generalized OA in elderly men, independent of obesity.[31,36]

An inverse relationship has been observed between OA and osteoporosis in some studies.[37] Evidence from animal studies suggests than an increase in bone density in the subchondral region may decrease the shock-absorbing properties of bone and increase the forces on the cartilage, thus predisposing to the development of

OA. Conversely, less dense (osteoporotic) bone may be relatively protective and reduce the risk of cartilage damage. However, while this is an intriguing and potentially clinically important hypothesis, it requires further investigation that will control for confounding factors (such as obesity and total body mass) which may protect against osteoporosis but increase the risk of OA.

There is little information about genetic predisposition to OA. Heberden's nodes have been found to occur twice as often in mothers and three times as often in sisters of women with Heberden's nodes as compared with the incidence in the general population. It has been hypothesized that this genetic mechanism involves a single, sex-influenced autosomal gene. Kellgren and Lawrence have studied genetic factors in relation to generalized OA, and they have suggested that the inheritance pattern of generalized OA is similar to that for Heberden's nodes alone. However, the inheritance pattern for non-nodal generalized OA appears to be polygenic. No correlation has been reported for OA with blood types or any HLA antigens.[1,28,29] It has been hypothesized that a subset of OA may be caused by a general predisposition due to a systemic factor or alteration in cartilage metabolism. However, an alternate explanation is that multiple joint involvement may be simply the result of the increased prevalence of single joints with age. This conundrum remains to be resolved, and at the present time there is no definitive evidence which suggests a generalized form of this disease.

CLINICAL MANAGEMENT

Clinically, OA is characterized by joint pain which is relieved by rest and made worse by movement of the joint. As opposed to the inflammatory arthritides, there is an absence of prolonged (greater than 30 minutes) morning stiffness, joint swelling, or warmth, as well as an absence of systemic symptoms such as fatigue, weight loss, and fever with OA. Usually, OA is a monarticular or oligoarticular disease and has a specific pattern of joint involvement which includes distal interphalangeal joints, proximal interphalangeal joints, first carpometacarpal joint, cervical and lumbar spine, hips, knees, and toes. The metacarpophalangeal joints (with the notable exception of the first joint), wrists, elbows, shoulders, and ankles are spared. In fact, symptoms in these latter joints strongly suggest another diagnosis. Of note, although the typical pathologic features of OA occur in the facet joints of the spine, disc degeneration and syndromes such as diffuse skeletal hyperostosis (DISH) may be very different entities than OA of the diarthrodial joints. From a clinical perspective, however, it is reasonable to include such syndromes in a discussion of OA because at the present time clinical management is similar.

Physical examination of an osteoarthritic joint shows limitation of motion, deformity of the joint and adjacent bone, crepitation, bony hypertrophy, and occasionally an intraarticular effusion and/or synovial hypertrophy.[5] If symptomatic, pain on movement and mild tenderness may also be found. In examining a specific joint, the physician must take care to rule out nonarthritic causes of pain such as bursitis, tendonitis, nerve root compression syndromes, reflex sympathetic dystrophy, and soft-tissue infections.[38] The physical examination of a patient with musculoskeletal pain should include a performance-based examination of the musculoskeletal system.[39] This can be divided into three areas: function of the upper extremities, function of the back, and function of the lower extremities. When examining the upper extremities, the physician should test grip strength, ability to hold objects such as eating utensils or writing instruments, and the ability to raise the arms over the head and to externally rotate and extend the arm (a movement which is usually necessary for independent dressing). In the examination of the back, the ability to bend at the waist should be tested in order to determine whether the patient can tie shoes or pick up an object from the floor. Examination of the lower extremity focuses on mobility. Thus, the examiner should test the patient's ability to rise from a chair, maintain standing balance, initiate and maintain gait, turn, and return to the sitting position.[39] Additionally, the patient's endurance should be tested by asking him or her to walk continuously for up to 5 minutes. Both the total distance and degree of fatigue can be quantified. The importance of a performance examination cannot be overemphasized because it is the consequences of musculoskeletal disease on functional status which is of ultimate importance in the older patient. Finally, the examination of the musculoskeletal system must be put in the context of a more general exam in order to detect conditions which may affect the toxicity or outcome of treatment.

The diagnosis of OA is made using the clinical history, the physical examination, and the presence of osteoarthritic changes on radiograph. Characteristic radiographic features of OA include the presence of osteophytes, subchondral sclerosis and cysts, and asymmetric loss of joint space (implying degradation of cartilage). However, it must be noted that changes of OA (and degenerative disc disease) are commonly found in radiographs of older patients, but many of these patients are asymptomatic. In general, other laboratory data will not be helpful.[5,38] Abnormalities in the erythrocyte sedimentation rate (ESR), white blood cell count, and hemoglobin, and the presence of autoantibodies, are not associated with OA. However, one may be misled if these diagnostic tests are abnormal, as the ESR may be elevated or autoantibodies present in low titre in apparently healthy older persons.[40] If a joint effusion is present,

examination of synovial fluid from affected joints reveals only a mild leukocytosis (less than 2,000 cells) and no other diagnostic features.[41]

TREATMENT

In treating the older patient with OA, it is helpful to separate measures of disease process from the effects of OA on the patient's function. To do this, it is useful to use a conceptual framework such as that outlined in the World Health Organization (WHO) International Classification of Impairments, Disabilities, and Handicaps.[42] The terms of this typology are defined as follows:

1. An *impairment* is any loss or abnormality of psychological, physiologic, or anatomic structure within an organ system of the body (the loss or abnormality can be temporary or permanent). An example relevant to OA is restricted range of motion or pain on motion.
2. A *disability* is an inability to perform an activity in the manner or within the range considered normal for an individual. Thus, a disability is a loss of ability to perform a compound function such as walking.
3. A *handicap* is a limitation of the fulfillments of an individual's role depending on age, sex, and other social and cultural factors. A handicap, therefore, is a social disadvantage from an impairment or disability. Examples would include loss of employment, social interaction, or inability for self-care.

Using this classification, the latter two outcome measures, disability and handicap, focus on consequences that are most important to the patient. Thus, the following three principles should govern treatment of osteoarthritis[43]:

1. Therapy should be aimed at restoration of function and improvement of the patient's quality of life; treatment of a specific impairment that does not improve function or patient satisfaction should be avoided.
2. The patient should be actively involved in the decision-making process, and his or her preferences should guide the specific goals of therapy. The goals of therapy need to be well-defined and realistic. For example, a patient may be physically capable of undertaking a rehabilitation program after total joint replacement, but an underlying dementia and cognitive impairment may keep him or her from learning the principles of such restorative care, thus resulting in treatment failure.
3. A multi-faceted approach to therapy should be used in the patient with OA. This includes treatment of

pain, physical and occupational therapy, education and psychological support, and environmental manipulation (Table 85-1).[43-45]

When deciding on a diagnostic regimen for OA, it must be appreciated that many factors in the older individual with OA may increase morbidity, including physiologic changes associated with aging, other chronic disease, psychological factors, environment, and iatrogenic problems (Table 85-2). Thus, the physician must decide if treatment of OA alone will result in functional improvement or whether treatment of other problems will also need to be undertaken to improve function. Conversely, several of these associated changes may make treatment more toxic and therefore less successful and more difficult.

NONSURGICAL THERAPIES

Since pain is the most common and disabling symptom of OA and that which most frequently leads to disability, pain relief is the cornerstone of therapy. Several non-pharmacologic strategies, including resting of joints when symptoms are at their worst, adjustment of activities to avoid repetitive movements that aggravate symptoms, and weight loss, are important measures.

When medication is needed, the most commonly used drugs are salicylates and nonsteroidal anti-inflammatory agents[46] (Table 85-3). The rationale for the use of these agents is that inhibition of cyclooxygenase and lipogenase results in decreased production of prostaglandins and other products of the arachidonic acid pathway which are important inflammatory mediators. There is no good evidence that one nonsteroidal anti-inflammatory drug is more efficacious than another in treating OA. However, the individual response to these agents varies greatly, and several drugs may be tried on a patient before relief is obtained. Except for the cost of salicylates, which is relatively inexpensive, the cost of any of

TABLE 85-1
Therapy of Osteoarthritis

Patient education and psychological guidance
Physical therapy
  Range-of-motion exercises
  Strengthening exercises
  Endurance (aerobic) exercises
  Weight loss
Pharmacologic therapy for pain relief
  Anti-inflammatory agents
  Intraarticular steroids
Surgery
  Arthroscopy
  Osteotomy
  Arthroplasty

TABLE 85-2
Conditions Which Cause Comorbidity in Osteoarthritis

Physiologic Changes Associated With Aging

Neurologic system
  Motor: loss of muscle mass and strength; diminished balance reflexes
  Sensory: diminished proprioceptive and vibratory input; slowed reaction time
Cardiovascular system
  Blunted baroreceptor reflexes
  Decrease in aerobic capacity

Chronic Diseases

Musculoskeletal
  Fractures
  Primary muscle disease
  Painful conditions of the feet
Neurologic
  Stroke
  Parkinson's disease
  Degenerative dementias
Cardiovascular
  Congestive heart failure
  Atherosclerotic vascular disease
Pulmonary (chronic obstructive pulmonary disease)
Other
  Blindness
  Severe systemic illness

Psychologic Factors

Depression
Fear of injury
Lack of motivation

Environmental and Iatrogenic Factors

Forced immobility
Physical obstructions
Lack of social supports
Medication side effects

these other drugs is approximately equal when a therapeutic dose is prescribed. The dosage schedule varies from 1 to 4 times per day. In general, the pharmacokinetics of these drugs is not altered in the elderly, with the possible exceptions of piroxicam and naproxen, which may have longer half-lives in older persons. Thus, for most of these drugs, the dosage schedule is similar for older and younger patients. The limiting factor in the use of the drugs is their toxicity, and the major side effects of these agents are similar (see Table 85-4).[46-48] Each drug differs, however, in its propensity and frequency in inducing these side effects. Consequently, the choice of drugs should partially rest on the individual's tolerance or potential for serious toxicity. The most common side effect of the nonsteroidal agents is gastrointes-

TABLE 85-3
Nonsteroidal Anti-Inflammatory Drugs

Drug	Dosage
Piroxicam	10–20 mg, once/day
Sulindac	150–200 mg, twice/day
Diflunisal	500 mg, twice/day
Naproxen	250–750 mg, twice/day
Diclofenac	50–75 mg, 2 or 3 times/day
Ibuprofen	400–800 mg, 3 or 4 times/day
Fenoprofen	600–800 mg, 3 or 4 times/day
Tolmetin sodium	300–400 mg, 3 or 4 times/day
Meclofemanate sodium	50–100 mg, 3 or 4 times/day
Indomethacin	25–50 mg, 3 or 4 times/day
Ketoprofen	50–75 mg, 3 or 4 times/day
Aspirin	600–1200 mg, 3 or 4 times/day
Nonacetylated salicylates	3–4 g/day
Magnesium choline salicylate	
Sodium salicylate	
Salicylsalicylic acid	

tinal upset. This side effect occurs in up to 25 percent of patients, and it often occurs without evidence of ulceration or bleeding but may necessitate discontinuation of the drug. Gastrointestinal bleeding and peptic ulcer disease is a serious side effect with all of these nonsteroidal agents. Recent studies have indicated increased morbidity and even death in older patients using these drugs.[47] Unfortunately, there is no correlation between subjective symptoms and ulceration or bleeding, so the latter can occur without any warning. There is considerable

TABLE 85-4
Major Toxicities of Nonsteroidal Anti-Inflammatory Drugs

Gastrointestinal
  Dyspepsia, anorexia
  Mucosal ulceration
  Upper gastrointestinal bleeding
Nephrotoxicity
  Acute renal insufficiency or failure
  Sodium, fluid retention
  Hyperkalemia
  Interstitial nephritis
  Papillary necrosis
Central nervous system
  Headache
  Tinnitus
  Cognitive dysfunction
Anticoagulant effects
  Decreased plate aggregation
  Displacement of warfarin from albumin
Hepatotoxicity
Hypersensitivity
  Hives
  Anaphylaxis

progress in developing pharmacologic agents which protect the gastric mucosa, which, if administered simultaneously with the nonsteroidal anti-inflammatory drugs, would reduce gastric toxicity.

Nonsteroidal anti-inflammatory drugs are a common cause of nephrotoxic acute renal failure.[48] The mechanism by which these drugs cause renal insufficiency is through the inhibition of prostaglandin production. Prostaglandins act as a compensatory mechanism to maintain renal blood flow and glomerular filtration rate (GFR). Thus, since use of these nonsteroidal agents may lead to a decreased GFR, hyperkalemia, fluid retention, and exacerbation of hypertension, they should be used with caution in patients with underlying renal disease, congestive heart failure, volume depletion, and liver disease. Preliminary evidence suggests that sulindac may cause less renal toxicity than the other nonsteroidal anti-inflammatory drugs as its active form is not found in the kidney.[49] Occasionally these drugs, particularly fenoprofen, may cause interstitial nephritis and, if used for prolonged periods of time, papillary necrosis. An important potential toxicity reported in the elderly is cognitive dysfunction and personality changes, although the mechanism of the central nervous system toxicity is unknown.

Other analgesic agents may be used in the treatment of OA. Acetaminophen, when used on a regular dosage schedule, may be effective and should be considered as a first line of therapy or if nonsteroidal anti-inflammatory agents are not tolerated. In general, systemic corticosteroids and narcotic analgesics should be avoided. There is a role for intraarticular steroids, however, and the main indication is presence of a large painful joint or an effusion that is unresponsive to other modalities.

Physical therapy is an important part of the treatment of OA, both in restoration and maintenance of function. Patients with painful OA of the lower extremities tend to be excessively sedentary and are at risk to develop loss of muscle power and cardiovascular conditioning. Exercise is used to maintain or increase range of motion of the joint, prevent contractures, and increase the strength in the periarticular musculature. Both isometric and isotonic exercises are prescribed to increase the strength of hip flexors, hip extenders, hip abductors, and knee extenders (quadriceps). In addition, patients with OA have a low aerobic exercise capacity, and it is likely that at least some of the disability associated with OA is due to this cardiovascular deconditioning. Recent studies have indicated that patients with arthritis may exercise to improve their cardiovascular conditioning and functional status without exacerbating joint symptoms.[50] Thus, it is reasonable to prescribe a component of an aerobic exercise such as walking, bicycling, and/or swimming as part of the patient's therapy. Although there is little disability associated with OA of the hands, the occupational therapist should be consulted in patients with hand dysfunction. The occupational therapist also can be used to assess a patient's home environment and make recommendations for changes that may improve patient functioning in the home.

SURGICAL THERAPIES

Arthroscopic lavage of the knee and osteotomy have been found to reduce symptoms in osteoarthritic knee joints. Remissions of several months or longer have been reported after arthroscopy, but symptoms often recur. Although these treatments are generally well tolerated, the precise indications for these therapies are unknown, and there are few studies which have assessed this form of treatment. A patient's age may affect the usefulness of these therapies, particularly osteotomy.

Total joint replacement is an effective and safe form of treatment in many patients.[51] In choosing patients to undergo knee or hip arthroplasty, several factors must be considered: Is the patient likely to improve his or her functional status after surgery? Is the patient and his or her family (caregiver) well informed of the benefits, risks, and period of recovery after surgery? Does the patient have other conditions which will preclude active participation in the therapy required to promote successful rehabilitation? The primary care provider needs to be actively involved in the decision to use total joint arthroplasty and must help in preparing his or her patient for surgery, as well as participating in the recovery phase.

After total hip replacement, the patient usually requires bed rest for 1 to 4 days, which is followed by a period of gait training and partial progressive weight bearing on the affected hip with crutches for 2 to 3 months. Patients should receive prophylactic antibiotic coverage before surgery, as well as prophylactic anticoagulation. Complications may occur in up to 20 percent of patients undergoing total hip replacement, including fatal conditions such as pulmonary embolism, prosthetic infection, and myocardial infarction. The major long-term complication of total hip replacement is loosening of the prosthetic components within the bone. However, new technology, such as the cementless joint, may reduce this problem.[52] Patients with total knee replacements are allowed to walk on the third or fourth postoperative day using a walker or crutches when weight bearing is tolerated. Range of motion is started almost immediately now that continuous passive motion machines are being used. Complications of total knee replacement include delayed wound healing and wound drainage, perineal nerve palsy, and infection.

REFERENCES

1. Peyron JG: The epidemiology of arthritis, in Moskowitz RW, Howell DS, Goldberg VM et al (eds): *Osteoarthritis: Diagnosis and Management*. Philadelphia, Saunders, 1984, pp 9–27.
2. Dieppe PA: Osteoarthritis: Are we asking the right questions? *Br J Rheumatol* 23:161, 1984.
3. Kellgren JH: Osteoarthrosis. *Arthritis Rheum* 8:568, 1965.
4. Mankin HJ, Brandt KD, Shulman LE: Workshop on Etiopathogenesis of Osteoarthritis: Proceedings and recommendations. *J Rheumatol* 13:1130, 1986.
5. Mankin HJ, Treadwell BV: Osteoarthritis: A 1987 update. *Bull Rheum Dis* 36:1, 1988.
6. Department of Rheumatology and Medical Illustration, University of Manchester and Manchester Royal Infirmary and the Empire Rheumatism Council's Field Unit: *Atlas of Standard Radiographs of Arthritis*, in *The Epidemiology of Chronic Rheumatism*, vol 2. Oxford, Blackwell Scientific, 1963.
7. National Center for Health Statistics: *The HANES Study: Final Report*. Philadelphia, Temple University, Health Services and Mental Health Administration, Institute for Survery Research, (HSM) 110-73-376, 1974.
8. National Center for Health Statistics: *Public Use Data Tape Documentation: Arthritis, Ages 25–74*. Hyattsville, MD, 1981 (National Health and Nutrition Examination Survey, 1971–75, tape 4121).
9. Roberts J, Burch TA: *Prevalence of Osteoarthritis in Adults by Age, Sex, Race and Geographic Area: United States, 1960–62*. Vital and health statistics. Ser II, no 15. Washington, National Center for Health Statistics, (PHS) 1000, 1966.
10. Engel A, Burch TA: *Osteoarthritis in Adults: By Selected Demographic Characteristics: United States 1960–62*. Vital and health statistics. Ser II, no 20. Washington, National Center for Health Statistics, (PHS) 1000, 1966.
11. Maurer K: *Basic Data on Arthritis, Knee, Hip, and Sacroiliac Joints in Adults Ages 25–74 Years: United States, 1971–1975*. (Vital and health statistics. Ser 11, no 213.) Hyattsville, MD, National Center for Health Statistics, DHEW (PHS) 79-1661, 1979.
12. Felson DT, Narmarka A, Anderson J et al: The prevalence of knee osteoarthritis in the elderly: The Framingham Osteoarthritis Study. *Arthritis Rheum* 30:914, 1987.
13. Kellgren JH, Lawrence JS: Osteoarthritis and disc degeneration in an urban population. *Ann Rheum Dis* 17:388, 1958.
14. Lawrence JS, Brenner JM, Bier F: Osteo-arthosis: Prevalence in the population and relationship between symptoms and x-ray changes. *Ann Rheum Dis* 25:1024, 1966.
15. Davis MA: Sex differences in reporting osteoarthritic symptoms: A sociomedical approach. *J Health Soc Behav* 22:298, 1981.
16. Fried L, Bush T: Attributed risk of morbidity: A method for assessing disease impact in the elderly. *Epidemiol Rev* 10:48, 1988.
17. Yelin E, Lubeck P, Holman H et al: The impact of rheumatoid arthritis and osteoarthritis: The activities of patients with rheumatoid arthritis and osteoarthritis compared to controls. *J Rheumatol* 14:710, 1987.

18. Meenam RF, Gertman DM, Mason JH, Dunaub R: The Arthritis Impact Measurement Scales. *Arthritis Rheum* 25:1048, 1982.

19. Ettinger WH, Zonderman AB, Costa PT, Miller DC, Hochberg MC: Influence of disease severity and personality on health status in subjects with osteoarthritis of the knee. *Clin Res* 34:364A, 1986.

20. Busby J, Tobin J, Ettinger W, Plato C: Progression of osteoarthritis (OA): Significance of starting level, age, and length of follow up. *Gerontologist* 26:141, 1986.

21. Perry GH, Smith MJF, Whiteside CG: Spontaneous recovery of the joint space in degenerative hip disease. *Ann Rheum Dis* 31:440, 1972.

22. Meachim G, Brook G: The pathology of osteoarthritis, in Moskowitz RW, Howell DS, Goldberg VM et al (eds): *Osteoarthritis: Diagnosis and Management.* Philadelphia, Saunders, 1984, pp 29–42.

23. Heinborg J, Nilsson BE: The relationship between osteophytes in the knee joint; osteoarthritis and aging. *Acta Orthop Scand* 44:69, 1973.

24. Meachim G, Hardinge K, Williams DR: Methods of correlating pathological and radiologic findings in osteoarthritis of the hip. *J Radiol* 45:670, 1972.

25. Muir H: Current and future trends in articular cartilage research and osteoarthritis, in Kuettner KE, Schleyerback R, Hascall VC (eds): *Articular Cartilage Biochemistry.* New York, Raven Press, 1986, pp 423–40.

26. Mankin HJ, Lippiello L: Biochemical and metabolic abnormalities in articular cartilage from osteoarthritic hips. *J Bone Joint Surg* 52A:424, 1970.

27. Brandt KD: Osteoarthritis. *Clin Geriatr Med* 4:279, 1988.

28. Davis MA: Epidemiology of osteroarthritis. *Clin Geriatr Med* 4:241, 1988.

29. Peyron JG: Epidemiologic and etiologic approach of osteoarthritis. *Semin Arthritis Rheum* 8:288, 1979.

30. Davis MA, Ettinger WH, Neuhaus JM et al: Knee injury and obesity as risk factors for unilateral and bilateral osteoarthritis of the knee (OAK). *Am J Epidemiol*, in press.

31. Anderson J, Felson D: Factors associated with osteoarthritis of the knee in the HANES I Survey: Evidence for an association with overweight, race and physical demands of work. *Am J Epidemiol* 128:179, 1988.

32. Davis MA, Ettinger WH, Neuhaus JM et al: Sex differences in osteoarthritis of the knee: The role of obesity. *Am J Epidemiol* 127:1019, 1988.

33. Felson DT, Anderson JJ, Naimark A et al: Obesity and knee osteoarthritis: The Framingham Study. *Ann Intern Med* 109:18, 1988.

34. Davis MA, Ettinger WH, Neuhaus JM: The role of metabolic factors and blood pressure in the association of obesity with osteoarthritis of the knee. *J Rheumatol* 15:1827, 1989.

35. Denko CW, Boja B, Moskowitz RW: Serum levels of insulin and insulin-like growth factor (IGF-1) in osteoarthritis (OA). *Arthritis Rheum* 30(suppl 4):S132, 1987.

36. Acheson RM, Collart AB: New Haven survey of joint diseases. XVII. Relationship between some systemic characteristics and osteoarthritis in a general population. *Ann Rheum Dis* 1975; 34:379–387.

37. Dequeker J, Goris P, Uytterhoeven R: Osteoarthritis and osteoarthritis (osteoarthrosis). *JAMA* 249:1448, 1983.

38. Ettinger WH: Approach to the diagnosis and management of musculoskeletal disease. *Clin Geriatr Med* 4:269, 1988.

39. Tinetti ME, Ginter SF: Identifying mobility dysfunctions in elderly patients. *JAMA* 259:1190, 1988.

40. Hodkinson HM: Alternations of laboratory finding, in Andres R, Bierman E, Hazzard W (eds): *Principles of Geriatric Medicine.* New York, McGraw-Hill, 1985, pp 387–96.

41. McCarty DJ: Synovial fluid, in McCarty DJ (ed): *Arthritis and Allied Conditions.* Philadelphia, Lea & Febiger, 1985, pp 54–75.

42. World Health Organization: *The International Classification of Impairments, Disabilities and Handicaps.* Geneva, World Health Organization, 1980.

43. Ettinger WH: Immobility, in Kelly W (ed): *Textbook of Internal Medicine.* Philadelphia, Lippincott, 1989, pp 2635–2640.

44. Wigley FM: Osteoarthritis: Practical management in older patients. *Geriatrics* 39:101, 1984.

45. Ettinger WH: An update on the pathogenesis and treatment of osteoarthritis. *Adv Orthop Surg* 19:157, 1984.

46. Schlegel SI, Paulus HE: Update on NSAID use in rheumatic diseases. *Bull Rheum Dis* 36:1, 1986.

47. Griffin MR, Ray WA, Schaffner W: Nonsteroidal anti-inflammatory drug use and death from peptic ulcer in elderly persons. *Ann Intern Med* 109:359, 1988.

48. Garella S, Matarese R: Renal effects of prostaglandins and clinical adverse effects on nonsteroidal anti-inflammatory agents. *Medicine* 63:165, 1984.

49. Ciabattoni G, Anotti GA, Pierucci A et al: Effects of sulindac and ibuprofen in patients with chronic glomerular disease. *N Engl J Med* 310:279, 1984.

50. Harkom TM, Lampman RM, Banwell BF, Castor CW: *Arthritis Rheum* 28:32, 1985.

51. Liang MH, Culler KE, Larson MG et al: Lost effectiveness of total joint replacement in osteoarthritis. *Arthritis Rheum* 29:937, 1986.

52. Morrey BF, Kavanagh BF: Cementless joint replacement: Current status and future. *Bull Rheum Dis* 37:1, 1987.

Chapter 86

GOUT AND CHONDROCALCINOSIS (PSEUDOGOUT)

J. Edwin Seegmiller

Both gout[1] and chondrocalcinosis (pseudogout)[2] are examples of crystal-induced arthritis. They differ, however, in the type of crystal responsible, the mechanism of the crystal formation, the sites of crystal deposition, and, to some degree, the clinical presentation, age profile, and sex of patients affected. They also differ historically. The clinical features of acute gouty arthritis are so distinctive that it was readily recognized and described by Hippocrates in the fourth century B.C. Chondrocalcinosis was first described in Czechoslovakia as a distinctive radiographic pattern of calcium deposition in and about joints, by Zitnan and Sitaj,[3] and the crystals in synovial fluid responsible for the acute inflammatory reaction were first identified by McCarty et al. in 1962.[4] Gouty arthritis is predominantly a disease of young adult males, with presentation usually as a monoarticular involvement of a peripheral joint. Females seldom have gout before the menopause. On the other hand, chondrocalcinosis affects both males and females, in a ratio of 1.5 to 1, and is seldom seen below age 50; the incidence increases remarkably with increasing age beyond the fifth decade. In an over-90 age group admitted to a British nursing home, fully one-half of the individuals showed x-ray evidence of chondrocalcinosis.[5] In both gout and chondrocalcinosis deposits of aggregated crystals can accumulate in and about some joints without necessarily producing an attack of acute arthritis; in both disorders this accumulation is associated with dispersion of crystals in the synovial fluid, where they undergo phagocytosis and elicit an intense inflammatory re-

sponse. Gout is very seldom seen in association with rheumatoid arthritis, while chondrocalcinosis is quite frequently found in association with osteoarthritis. Furthermore, the clinical presentation of chondrocalcinosis can mimic a wide range of rheumatological syndromes, including septic arthritis, gout (whence the term *pseudogout*), osteoarthritis, traumatic arthritis, neuropathic joint disease, and ankylosing spondylitis. In both disorders enzyme abnormalities of purine metabolism have been described in some but not all patients.[1,6]

GOUT

Gouty arthritis results from the deposition of needle-shaped crystals of monosodium urate in and about the joints from supersaturated hyperuricemic extracellular body fluids. Both degree and duration of hyperuricemia appear to be determinants for the chance formation of the first seed crystal, which then leads to further crystal deposition. Once sufficient crystals accumulate in the joint space to pass a critical threshold, the body initiates an attack on the crystals by phagocytic cells, thus treating the crystals as the equivalent of invading microorganisms. The resulting intense inflammatory response, with its sudden onset usually in a single joint of the extremity, produces clinical symptoms of intense pain, exquisite tenderness, redness, swelling, and warmth, which together constitute the clinical presentation of the acute attack of gout. Even if untreated the acute attack will gradually subside over a 1- or 2-week period, and the patient may go many months or even years before experiencing a second acute attack in the same or a different joint. The course with time varies greatly from

Supported in part by Clayton Foundation for Research, California Division, The Greenwall Foundation, and Public Health Service Grants AM13622 and AG00402.

one patient to another. Some patients experience acute attacks only rarely. In others the disease can progress over the years if untreated, with the intervals between attacks becoming shorter and a chronic stage eventually developing with progressive and permanent destruction of joints and subchondral bone; a concurrent progressive renal impairment may accelerate the progress of the disease and can become life-threatening. Precipitating factors for developing the acute attack include environmental events, such as emotional upset, minor trauma, surgery, unusual exertions or exercise, and ingestion of certain drugs, foods, or alcoholic drinks.

HYPERURICEMIA

Hyperuricemia is a condition defined by a serum urate value above 7.0 mg/dl. This value is also approximately the limit of solubility for monosodium urate in plasma.[1] The hyperuricemia responsible for development of gout results from a heterogeneous group of biochemical and physiological abnormalities of function. In approximately 10 percent of patients a genetically determined excessive synthesis of the purine precursors of uric acid is responsible, but in the majority of patients purine synthesis is normal and a diminished renal excretion of uric acid is the cause of the hyperuricemia. In still other patients both mechanisms contribute in varying degrees to the hyperuricemia. Hyperuricemia can also result from the side effects of a number of drugs, such as salicylates at doses less than 3 g/day, pyrazinamide, and several antihypertensive drugs with the notable exception of spironolactones. Hyperuricemia and gout can also result from chronic alcohol ingestion or from toxic effects of low-level lead poisoning.

Initially hyperuricemia is entirely without clinical symptoms and may remain so throughout a person's life, especially in patients who show only a modest degree of hyperuricemia. However, around 15 to 25 percent of hyperuricemic subjects eventually experience the deposition of crystals composed of monosodium urate monohydrate in and about the joint, with the resulting intermittent attacks of acute gouty arthritis. As deposits accumulate they can lead to clinically palpabale nodules called tophi, which, in an advanced state of development, can produce a progressive permanent erosive damage to joint cartilage and bone. When tophaceous deposits are near the surface, the overlying skin shows a light pink coloring; from time to time the tophus may break through the skin and discharge a white, chalky material which, under the microscope, shows myriads of tiny needle-shaped crystals of monosodium urate. Similar deposits in the parenchyma of the kidney can lead to the deterioration of renal function. Kidneys can be further compromised by the frequent development of renal calculi composed of uric acid or calcium oxalate.

ASSOCIATED DISORDERS

Gouty arthritis can be associated with a wide range of other clinical disorders. This possibility of associated disease mandates a complete examination, especially when the patient presents with the first attack. The associated disorders include hemolytic anemia; a wide range of myeloproliferative diseases; psoriasis; endocrine abnormalities, including hypothyroidism, hypoparathyroidism, and hyperparathyroidism; vascular disease, including hypertension and myocardial infarction; renal disease; and glomerulonephritis. In addition, gout can result from a number of hereditary diseases. Among those associated with an excessive rate of purine synthesis are certain X-linked enzyme defects, for which a family history can be of particular value in showing maternal inheritance characteristic of X-linked disorders. Virtually complete deficiency of the enzyme hypoxanthine guanine phosphoribosyltransferase (HPRT) results in Lesch-Nyhan disease,[7] with its choreoathetosis, spasticity, and compulsive self-mutilation, as well as a four- to sixfold increase in uric acid production which leads to early onset of gouty arthritis, uric acid kidney stones, and progressive damage to kidneys.[1,8] Patients with a less severe enzyme deficit show a marked attenuation of the clinical expression of the syndrome, with less severe expression of the neurological symptoms. Other patients with more residual HPRT enzyme activity show no neurological symptoms and show only a two- to threefold increase over normal in uric acid production, but they still have the uric acid kidney stones and gouty arthritis that result from higher-than-normal uric acid levels. The latter two features are also found in another X-linked enzyme abnormality, in which they are caused by a genetically determined increase in activity of the enzyme phosphoribosylpyrophosphate synthetase.[9] In at least three families this enzyme abnormality has been associated with hereditary deafness and other neurological abnormalities.[10] Other hereditary diseases associated with excessive uric acid production and gout include glycogen storage disease (type I)[11] and symmetric adenolipomatosis.[12]

The following hereditary disorders show a normal rate of purine synthesis with a diminished renal clearance of uric acid to account for the hyperuricemia: hereditary nephritis, polycystic kidney disease, Pitressin-resistant nephrogenic diabetes insipidus, and branched-chain ketoaciduria (maple syrup urine disease). In addition, glycogen storage disease type I shows both excessive production and diminished renal excretion.[10]

The following miscellaneous conditions can be associated with development of a hyperuricemia: obesity, starvation, exercise, psoriasis, respiratory acidosis, diabetic ketoacidosis, beryllium disease and lead poisoning, hyperoxaluria, cystinuria, Down's syndrome, idiopathic hypercalciuria, sarcoidosis, Paget's disease of bone, Bartter's syndrome, postadrenalectomy, and alcoholism.

DIAGNOSIS

The clinical features of the acute gouty attack are usually sufficiently characteristic to permit a presumptive diagnosis to be made at the bedside. The acute attack characteristically comes on suddenly and usually involves a single peripheral joint in an otherwise healthy, middle-aged male. However, two or more peripheral joints are involved in approximately 5 percent of patients with gout. Approximately half of the patients show involvement of the first metatarsophalangeal joint in the first attack, and this involvement is seen at some time in the course of the disease in around 90 percent of patients. The pain progresses within a few hours of its onset to an intense severity that is often incapacitating. The affected joint shows marked swelling, exquisite pain, and tenderness, with varying degrees of erythema and warmth. The pain can be either throbbing or constant, but it is often worse at night and is usually so severe that the patient cannot bear any weight on the joint. These symptoms at the peak presentation suggest inflammation from a septic joint or cellulitis with the overlying skin being red, tense and shiny. Furthermore, systemic symptoms of chilliness, fever, and leukocytosis are also commonly found. As a consequence, patients may receive inappropriate and unsuccessful treatment with antibiotics. In general, the swelling involved in a septic process of a joint is associated with a more doughy consistency of the area and a more pronounced pitting edema than is noted with the acute gouty attack. In addition, lymphangitis and lymphadenopathy are present in the nodes draining the septic joint but are seldom seen in the acute gouty process. A very careful examination for skin abrasion or other port of entry for the invading organism in septic arthritis is often helpful in making the correct diagnosis.

With progression of the acute gouty attack, the skin overlying the joint develops a characteristic violaceous hue and reveals dilated veins. During subsidence of the attack the skin often develops a scaling desquamation with a moderate pruritus and appears somewhat wrinkled and thin. For many years a prompt therapeutic response of the pain to the administration of the ancient drug colchicine has been used as a diagnostic test for gout. In the early years of the disease, even an untreated acute attack will regress spontaneously, over a variable period ranging from days to weeks, leaving no residual symptoms whatsoever, although more slowly than when treated. The presence of a family history of gout or renal calculi and a personal history of recurrent monoarticular arthritis are additional clinical features supporting the presumptive diagnosis. An intense search should be made for the presence of tophi, which are found most often around previously affected joints, over tendonous insertions in peripheral joints, or at sites of previous trauma. The presence of tophi on the helix of the ear can be especially helpful in the diagnosis.

It is important, particularly in patients presenting for the first time, to distinguish the acute attack from a septic process. In addition to the clues on physical examination noted above, this is best done by aspirating joint fluid using sterile precautions, then culturing a portion of it, centrifuging the remainder, and preparing a Gram's stain on a portion of the sediment for detection of bacteria. The remainder of the concentrated sediment is transferred into a hemocytometer chamber for microscopic examination for detection of the characteristic needle-shaped crystals of monosodium urate monohydrate. The crystals are most readily seen by examining the fluid under cross-polarizing filters with one polarizing filter placed on the light source of the microscope and the other in the eyepiece. The rotation of polarized light by the crystals allows them to be readily seen as bright needles against a black background. In sediment from fluid aspirated during an acute attack, over 90 percent of the crystals are found to be engulfed in phagocytes. By inserting a first-order red compensator (retardation plate) filter into the optical system, the negatively birefringent crystals of monosodium urate monohydrate can readily be distinguished from the positively birefringent crystals of calcium pyrophosphate dihydrate characteristic of chondrocalcinosis (pseudogout). Under these conditions the crystals of monosodium urate located at right angles to the plane of polarization show a yellow color, whereas crystals of calcium pyrophosphate show a lavender or blue color. (A few patients will show both types of crystals.) This procedure is especially helpful in distinguishing gouty tophi from darwinian tubercles on the ear from subcutaneous lipomatous nodules or the subcutaneous nodules of rheumatoid arthritis. Tophi about the elbow are often difficult to distinguish from rheumatoid nodules. A biopsy of such a nodule with a frozen section or fixation in alcohol with examination of unstained sections using polarizing filters should reveal the presence of urate crystals. While staining procedures usually remove the crystals, the surrounding granulomatous changes characteristic of gouty arthritis are distinctive.

The typical radiologic lesion in gout results from tophus formation and consists of a "punched out" area in the subchondral bone, most frequently in the first metatarsophalangeal joint. In some cases this lesion may appear before any other evidence of tophaceous gout. With progression of the disease, subchondral tophi can enlarge, and they may appear in and about other joints with resulting destruction of the phalangeal joints in more advanced stages of the disease.

TREATMENT

As a result of improvements in therapy over the past four decades, virtually all patients with gouty arthritis can now enjoy a full and productive life without serious disability from their arthritis, provided they are diagnosed early and are maintained under continuous therapy with adequate supervision. As a result the emphasis has shifted from simple treatment of the recurring acute attacks to a preventive program aimed at management of the disease by correcting the underlying chemical disorder of hyperuricemia.

This therapeutic objective can be achieved by relatively simple procedures: (1) termination of the acute attack with one of a variety of anti-inflammatory drugs now available; (2) use of daily colchicine as prophylaxis against recurrence of the acute attack, especially during recovery from an attack and throughout the first few months of therapy with a drug for controlling the hyperuricemia; (3) evaluation of uric acid production in the 24-hour urine after equilibration on a diet virtually free of purines as a guide to selection of the drug most appropriate for maintenance therapy; and (4) initiation of treatment with a drug for lowering the serum urate to the normal range, which must be initiated during a quiescent stage of the disease. Experience shows that institution of such drugs *during* an acute attack delays recovery and exacerbates the attack. The objective of lowering of serum urate to the unsaturated normal range (below 7 mg/dl) is to permit unsaturated body fluids to dissolve away all crystals of monosodium urate, thus removing the cause of the acute attacks and preventing the development of tophaceous gout, with its attendant potential for permanent joint and renal damage.

The severity of pain and disability usually seen in the patient with acute gouty arthritis demands intervention, even though the attacks are self-limited and show spontaneous recovery in 1 to 2 weeks. General measures for control of the acute attack include complete rest of the affected joint, a high fluid intake of 2 to 3 liters per day, a diet low in purines, and avoidance of alcohol. The intense pain frequently requires use of an analgesic or even a narcotic drug such as meperidine (Demerol). Usually 50 to 100 mg is required to control the severe pain. The attack can be readily terminated by the highly specific traditional drug, colchicine, at 0.5 mg given hourly until the relief of pain or the appearance of nausea or diarrhea, at which point the colchicine is stopped. Intravenously administered colchicine, 2 mg in 20 ml saline, produces a more rapid response and usually avoids the gastrointestinal side effects. Colchicine must not be administered by this route to patients with impaired renal function, however, and extravasation must be avoided. The pain also responds readily to indomethacin at a dosage of 50 mg three to four times daily for 2 or 3 days, with tapering of dose and discontinuation in a week; or to use of a wide range of newer anti-inflammatory drugs that have largely replaced colchicine. Although phenylbutazone has been used effectively in the past, a high incidence of serious side effects limits its use at present.

CLASSIFICATION

Since lowering the serum urate to the normal range requires a patient's lifetime commitment to a specific therapy, it is worthwhile to take extra time to obtain the basal daily uric acid production, which is then used to select the drug for lowering serum urate that will meet the patient's specific needs. This is best done as the acute attack is subsiding, while the patient is taking prophylactic daily colchicine (0.5 mg two to three times daily as tolerated) to prevent exacerbation or recurrence. This is a convenient time to evaluate the patient's 24-hour excretion of uric acid and creatinine while compliance in following instructions for this test is likely to be optimal. During this period, alcoholic drinks, as well as drugs such as aspirin, allopurinol, or uricosuric drugs or x-ray contrast drugs which are known to alter uric acid production or excretion, are to be avoided. The patient is usually sufficiently motivated by his or her recent experiences with the acute attack to follow a diet virtually free of purines for a 6-day period. This requires elimination of meat, fish, chicken, beans, peas, fermented beverages, and caffeine-containing drinks from the diet. Although caffeine does not produce uric acid, its end product, methylated uric acid, can register as uric acid in the colorimetric assays in general use. Dairy products are used as the major source of protein during the test period. During the last 3 days of the diet each 24-hour urine sample is collected in a large bottle containing 3 ml of toluene or 0.25 g of thymol crystals as preservative to allow assessment of the degree of uric acid production. The urine should be stored at room temperature to minimize the amount of sediment formed. After completely dissolving any sediment present in each bottle of the urine by warming and agitation, the total volume of each day's urine is measured and an aliquot sent to the laboratory for analysis of uric acid and creatinine, along with a blood sample for analysis of serum urate and creatinine. The upper range of normal excretion for an adult male is 600 mg uric acid/24 hours. A normal serum urate at the end of the collection period is evidence of the magnitude of the contribution of dietary habits, particularly excessive alcohol ingestion, as a major factor in generation of hyperuricemia. In occasional patients mere avoidance of alcohol is sufficient to maintain the serum urate in the normal range. In an obese patient a modest degree of hyperuricemia can be corrected by weight loss, which can be presented as a possible valid alternative to drug treatment if the patient wishes to explore it. However, starvation diets without adequate carbohydrate and protein intake should be avoided, as they exacerbate the hyperuricemia and can induce an attack of gout.

Patients should be warned of the increased risk of developing an acute attack during the first few months after initiation of treatment with any drug given to lower the serum urate concentration to the normal range. This tendency is greatly diminished by prophylactic colchicine, 0.5 mg two or three times daily. The patient should be advised to reduce the dose of colchicine if gastrointestinal symptoms develop and to take an extra dose at the very first sign of an impending attack.

Patients who show no evidence of renal calculi or impaired renal function and who are excreting less than 600 mg of uric acid per day are producing normal amounts of uric acid; their hyperuricemia thus results from a decreased renal efficiency in uric acid excretion. Their primary deficit in renal excretion of uric acid can be corrected by administration of the uricosuric drug probenecid, initially at a dosage of 0.25 g ($\frac{1}{2}$ tablet) daily with a gradual increase over the course of a week to a maintenance dosage of 0.5 g twice daily; additional increases in dosage to as high as 1.0 g three times daily may be used as needed to maintain the serum urate concentration in the normal range (below 7.0 mg/dl). Sulfinpyrazone is an alternative uricosuric drug of greater potency (than probenecid) which may be needed in some patients. It is started at a dosage of 50 mg ($\frac{1}{2}$ tablet) once daily and increased gradually over a 2-day period to 100 mg three or four times daily. If necessary, up to twice this amount can be used, but this further increase is very seldom required. Benzbromarone is an even more potent uricosuric drug that has been in use in Europe for several years. It is administered in a divided dose of up to 300 mg/day.

The increased risk of developing renal calculi in patients with gout provides reason for their developing the habit of drinking 3 liters of fluid (mostly water) per day to counter this tendency; this increased fluid intake can be presented as a very inexpensive and real form of health insurance against the risk of renal caluli development. Since salicylates block the action of uricosuric drugs, they must be avoided and can be replaced by acetaminophen (Tylenol), which does not have the blocking effect and provides comparable analgesia. The most frequent adverse reactions to uricosuric drugs are gastrointestinal symptoms and skin rash; hepatic necrosis or bone marrow depression are rare occurrences.

Patients excreting greater than 600 mg of uric acid per day are producing excessive amounts of uric acid and should be started on allopurinol, 100 mg daily as a single daily dose, after full recovery from the acute attack. The slow excretion of allopurinol makes divided doses unnec-

essary. Allopurinol not only blocks uric acid production by inhibiting the enzyme xanthine oxidase responsible for its synthesis but also diminishes the excessive purine synthesis in most patients, except those with Lesch-Nyhan disease or its variants.[1] Other indications for using allopurinol are intolerance of the uricosuric drug, evidence of impaired renal function, or the presence of uric acid calculi of the urinary tract. The latter will eventually undergo dissolution with continued allopurinol therapy. For each patient, follow-up examinations of serum urate should be done initially at monthly intervals until the proper dose of allopurinol (usually 300 mg daily) is found; then the examinations should be performed at 6-month intervals, along with routine checks on renal and hematological function, to prevent recurrence of the disease. The objective of this approach is to maintain the serum urate in the normal range throughout life. The results are most gratifying to the patient, who thereby can live an essentially normal life without incapacitation from gouty arthritis. If the serum urate is maintained in the normal range, eventually even the most severe deposits of tophaceous gout will be resolved, and most joints, with the exception of those permanently damaged by erosive action of the tophi, will be restored to essentially normal function.

CHONDROCALCINOSIS (PSEUDOGOUT)

Pseudogout was the term first used to describe the clinical syndrome of acute gout-like arthritis associated with the presence of crystals of calcium pyrophosphate dihydrate in synovial fluid.[4] Subsequent studies showed this gout-like presentation to be just one aspect of the far larger range of clinical presentations of patients showing radiologic evidence of a characteristic pattern of calcification within the joints, which is called *chondrocalcinosis*[3] and more precisely designated as *calcium pyrophosphate dihydrate (CPPD) crystal deposition disease.*[2]

CPPD crystal deposition disease shows similarities to gouty arthritis in that it is a crystal-induced arthritis with intermittent acute attacks associated with appearance of crystals within phagocytes in the joint fluid and a consequent acute inflammatory reaction.[2,4] The overall incidence is also comparable with that of gout.

Chondrocalcinosis differs from gouty arthritis in a number of important ways. It shows a far wider range of clinical presentations. Instead of needle-shaped crystals of monosodium urate monohydrate deposited in and about the joint as seen in gouty arthritis, the deposits of crystals in chondrocalcinosis consist of rhombic or broad-shaped crystals of calcium pyrophosphate dihydrate that are typically found as a punctate or lamellar layer in the mid-zone of the cartilage. This is most often seen on x ray of the knee in meniscal fibrocartilage, as well as in the articular cartilage of the knee, in the articular disk of the distal radioulnar joint of the wrist, and, less frequently, in and about other major joints.[13]

The mechanism of formation of the crystals in chondrocalcinosis is entirely different from that responsible for formation of crystals in gout. The plasma and other extracellular body fluids, with the exception of synovial fluid, show no elevation of either pyrophosphate or calcium in most patients with chondrocalcinosis.[2,14] Likewise, the calculated mean concentration of calcium and pyrophosphate in the cytoplasm of cells does not exceed the theoretical solubility product constant for this crystal.[15] This has led to the view that crystals may arise in a matrix vesicle rather than within the intracellular or extracellular space. A possible role for calcium pyrophosphate has been proposed as an intermediate source of the calcium used for the formation of hydroxyapatite in the growth plate of the bone and possibly in bone remodeling. Excised cartilage from affected patients readily releases pyrophosphate into the surrounding medium.[16] Furthermore, chondrocytes cultured from affected patients show a two- to threefold increase over normal in intracellular pyrophosphate content,[17] as do fibroblasts or lymphoblasts cultured from the same patients,[18] thus providing evidence of a generalized metabolic abnormality with clinical pathology limited to the cartilage.[19] Increased activity of the ectoenzyme nucleoside triphosphate pyrophosphohydrolase has been found both in cartilage extracts and in fibroblasts cultured from patients with sporadic but not familial forms of the disease.[19–21]

Several large pedigrees of hereditary chondrocalcinosis have been reported, most of which show evidence of a dominant pattern of inheritance.[18,22–24] The close association of osteoarthritis and chondrocalcinosis[5] has been recently confirmed by autopsy studies showing a frequency of concurrence of these diseases sixfold greater than would be expected from the chance association represented by the respective frequencies of both individual diseases in the population.[5,25] The discovery of modest elevations of pyrophosphate in synovial fluid of patients with more severe osteoarthritis suggests a possible metabolic link between the two diseases.[1] The greater-than-expected association of the pseudogout form of this disease with osteoarthritis in later years of life has suggested that it might result from clefts generated by the cartilage degeneration of osteoarthritis opening up passages by which crystals are more readily deposited into articular space to produce acute or subacute inflammation of one or more joints. Of particular interest is the fact that radiologic evidence of chondrocalcinosis is seldom found below age 50, while in the age group over 90 some 50 percent of patients show such evidence.[5] An exception is the appearance of chondrocalcinosis in ado-

lescents in an inbred population of the Chiloé Island off the coast of southern Peru.[23] In chondrocalcinosis the distribution of affected joints differs from that found in gouty arthritis.[2] The joint most frequently involved with chondrocalcinosis is the knee, followed by the wrist and shoulders. Unlike gouty arthritis, both males and females are affected in the older age group.

ASSOCIATED DISORDERS

A rational basis for the association of chondrocalcinosis with metabolic disorders such as hyperparathyroidism exists in the accompanying increase in the serum calcium concentration; in hereditary hypophosphatemia from a hereditary deficiency of alkaline phosphatase the rational basis for association exists in the elevated concentration of pyrophosphate in serum and urine that occurs in this disorder. Less rational associations have been reported with hemochromatosis, hypophosphaturia, hypothyroidism, ochronotic arthritis, Wilson's disease, and even gout. In fact, some 20 percent of patients with chondrocalcinosis show hyperuricemia. The sporadic form of chondrocalcinosis is the most common form, but in some cases this may in fact represent a late-onset hereditary form.

CLINICAL PRESENTATION

CPPD deposition disease shows a wide range of clinical presentation that can resemble infectious arthritis, gout, rheumatoid arthritis, osteoarthritis, traumatic arthritis, neuropathic joint disease, or ankylosing spondylitis. McCarty has described five clinical patterns based on a clinical analysis of 80 cases.[2]

Pseudogout

In approximately one-third of patients with CPPD deposition disease, presentation consists of acute attacks similar to those of gout, lasting from 1 day to several weeks. These most commonly present in the knees, wrists, and shoulders, with only occasional presentation in the first metatarsophalangeal joint. Fever may be present, especially in older patients, suggesting a septic arthritis. Joint aspiration and crystal identification are necessary for proper diagnosis. The attacks can be precipitated by trauma, severe illness, or initiation of diuretic therapy.

Pseudo–Rheumatoid Arthritis

Multiple joint involvement mimicking rheumatoid arthritis occurs in less than 10 percent of the patients, but unlike patients with rheumatoid arthritis, chondrocalcinosis patients with pseudo–rheumatoid arthritis usually show one to several joints that are more intensely inflamed than others. However, the differential diagnosis can be very difficult since both diseases may coexist in the same individual. Nonspecific symptoms of inflammation, such as morning stiffness and fatigue, are common, as are such signs as synovial thickening, localized pitting edema, and limitation of joint motion. Erythrocyte sedimentation rates may also be elevated. A variant has been described that can cause substantial clinical confusion: the patient, usually elderly, has multiple acutely inflamed joints, marked leukocytosis, fever of 102 to 104°F, and mental confusion or disorientation. A systemic septic process is usually suspected by the physician and antibiotics are prescribed without benefit. The entire clinical picture in such patients responds promptly to anti-inflammatory therapy.

Pseudo-Arthritis

The pseudo-arthritis presentation characterizes approximately one-half of the patients. The preponderance of such cases is in women. They show a progressive degeneration of multiple joints with the knees most commonly affected, followed in decreasing frequency by the wrists, metacarpophalangeal joints, hips, spine, shoulders, elbows, and ankles. Involvement is most often symmetric bilaterally, and flexion contractures of involved joints are common. Pseudo-arthritis frequently involves joints not usually involved in primary osteoarthritis, including the wrists, elbows, shoulders, and metacarpophalangeal joints. Indeed, such aberrant involvement should raise suspicion of this possible variant. Approximately one-half of the patients with this type of presentation also have a history of episodes of superimposed acute attacks. CPPD crystals are often found in synovial fluid, even in joints that show no radiologic evidence typical of this disease.

Lanthanic (Asymptomatic) Chondrocalcinosis

Lanthanic chondrocalcinosis is the most common presentation of all, in which most of the joints showing CPPD deposits are asymptomatic, even in patients with acute or chronic symptoms in other joints. This presentation is most commonly associated with relatively mild wrist complaints and genu varus deformities.

Pseudoneuropathic Chondrocalcinosis

Pseudoneuropathic chondrocalcinosis is the least common form of presentation, in which severe degeneration of the neuropathic type (Charcot-like joint) has been found in the absence of neurological abnormalities. It is also found in patients with Tabes dorsalis.

DIAGNOSIS

The diagnosis is based on one of the above clinical presentations along with x-ray demonstration of chondrocalcinosis, as well as the demonstration in joint fluid of the characteristic weakly positive birefringent rhomboid or rod-like crystals by compensated polarized light microscopy (see description above). Synovial fluid may contain a few leukocytes or as many as $100,000/mm^3$ in the acutely inflamed joints, but the usual range is between 2000 and 20,000 leukocytes/mm^3.

PROGNOSIS AND MANAGEMENT

As in gouty arthritis, acute attacks are usually self-limited and joint function preserved. More severe destructive changes are seen in patients showing the pseudorheumatoid, pseudo-osteoarthritic, and pseudoneuropathic type of presentation associated with loss of joint function. Intravenous colchicine at a dose of 2 mg may be quite effective in the management of some acute attacks. Nonsteroidal anti-inflammatory agents are also useful in the management of either acute or chronic forms of inflammation. Other nonpharmacological modalities of treatment useful in other forms of joint inflammation have a similar role in the treatment of symptomatic chondrocalcinosis. As yet no rational approach is known for correction of the underlying metabolic abnormality responsible for crystal formation and the resulting development of the disease. Patients with this disease should be screened for detection of the associated metabolic diseases mentioned above.

REFERENCES

1. Seegmiller JE: Disease of purine and pyrimidine metabolism, in Bondy PK, Rosenberg LE (eds): *Metabolic Control and Disease*, 8th ed. Philadelphia, Saunders, 1980, p 777.
2. Ryan LM, McCarty DJ: Calcium pyrophosphate crystal deposition disease; pseudogout; articular chondrocalcinosis, in McCarty DJ (ed): *Arthritis and Allied Conditions: A Textbook of Rheumatology*, 10th ed. Philadelphia, Lea & Febiger, 1985, p 1515.
3. Zitnan D, Sitaj D: Chondrocalcinosis polyarticularis (familiaris). *Cesk Radiol* 14:27, 1960.
4. McCarty DJ et al: The significance of calcium phosphate crystals in the synovial fluid of arthritis patients: The "pseudogout syndrome." I. Clinical aspects. *Ann Intern Med* 56:711, 1962.
5. Wilkins E et al: Osteoarthritis and articular chondrocalcinosis in the elderly. *Ann Rheum Dis* 42:280, 1983.
6. Tenenbaum J et al: Comparison of phosphohydrolase activities from articular cartilage in calcium pyrophosphate deposition disease and primary osteoarthritis. *Arthritis Rheum* 24:492, 1981.
7. Seegmiller JE et al: Enzyme defect associated with a sex-

linked human neurological disorder and excessive purine synthesis. *Science* 155:1682, 1967.

8. Lesch M, Nyhan WL: A familial disorder of uric acid metabolism and central nervous system function. *Am J Med* 36:561, 1964.

9. Becker MA et al: Purine overproduction in man associated with increased phosphoribosylpyrophosphate synthetase activity. *Science* 179:1123, 1973.

10. Seegmiller JE: Disorders of purine and pyrimidine metabolism, in Emery A, Rimoin D (eds): *The Principles and Practices of Medical Genetics*, 2d ed. New York, Churchill Livingstone (in press).

11. Alepa FP et al: Relationships between glycogen storage disease and tophaceous gout. *Am J Med* 42:58, 1967.

12. Greene ML et al: Benign symmetric lipomatosis (Launois-Bensaude adenolipomatosis) with gout and hyperlipoproteinemia. *Am J Med* 48:239, 1970.

13. Resnick D: Crystal-induced arthropathy: Gout and pseudogout. *JAMA* 242:2440, 1979.

14. Russell RGG et al: Inorganic pyrophosphate in plasma, urine and synovial fluid of patients with pyrophosphate arthropathy (chondrocalcinosis, or pseudogout). *Lancet* 2:899, 1970.

15. Dieppe P, Watt I: Crystal deposition in osteoarthritis: An opportunistic event? *Clin Rheum Dis* 11:367, 1985.

16. Howell DS et al: Pyrophosphate release by osteoarthritis cartilage incubates. *Arthritis Rheum* 19:488, 1976.

17. Lust G et al: Inorganic pyrophosphate and proteoglycan metabolism in cultured human articular chondrocytes and fibroblasts. *Arthritis Rheum* 19:479, 1976.

18. Lust G et al: Increased pyrophosphate in fibroblasts and lymphoblasts from patients with hereditary diffuse articular chondrocalcinosis. *Science* 214:809, 1981.

19. Ryan LM et al: Elevated intracellular pyrophosphate (PPi) and ecto-nucleoside triphosphate pyrophosphohydrolase activity (NTPPH) in fibroblasts of patients with calcium pyrophosphate dihydrate (CPPD) crystal deposition disease. *Clin Res* 32:792A 1984, (Abstract).

20. Tenenbaum J et al: Comparison of phosphohydrolase activities from articular cartilage in calcium pyrophosphate deposition disease and primary osteoarthritis. *Arthritis Rheum* 24:492, 1981.

21. Ryan LM et al: Pyrophosphohydrolase activity and inorganic pyrophosphate content of cultured human skin fibroblasts: Elevated levels in some patients with calcium pyrophosphate dihydrate deposition disease. *J Clin Invest* 77:1689, 1986.

22. Van der Korst JK, Gerard J: Articular chondrocalcinosis in a Dutch pedigree. *Arthritis Rheum* 19:405, 1976.

23. Reginato AJ: Articular chondrocalcinosis in the Chiloé Islanders. *Arthritis Rheum* 19:395, 1976.

24. McKusick V: *Mendelian Inheritance in Man*, 7th ed. The Johns Hopkins University Press, 1986.

25. Sokoloff L, Varma AA: Chondrocalcinosis in surgically resected joints. *Arthritis Rheum* 31:750, 1988.

Chapter 87

AMYLOID

Evan Calkins and John R. Wright

Amyloidosis is a condition of many faces. For the patient and his or her family, systemic amyloidosis is a frightening and depressing prospect, since, for most patients, effective prevention and treatment are elusive. All too often patients with amyloidosis develop a predictable series of disease manifestations culminating in death, often within a short period of years. For the clinician, amyloidosis presents an array of clinical syndromes manifested frequently by involvement of multiple organs. For the basic scientist, amyloid provides opportunities in molecular biology and a fascinating clue to the nature of Alzheimer's disease. Consequently, in recent years, amyloidosis has assumed a prominent position among the problems of aging.

OVERVIEW

NATURE OF AMYLOID

The term *amyloid* refers to an array of proteins which share common properties relating largely to their secondary chemical structure.[1,2] All forms of amyloid exhibit affinity for the dye Congo red, yielding characteristic green birefringence under polarized light. This affinity is due to a quaternary structure of nonbranching microfibrils, evident on electron microscopy.[3] Although of variable length, each amyloid fibril usually measures 8 to 10 nm in diameter, and in isolated preparations all share a β-pleated sheet as a secondary structure. It is believed that this secondary structure imparts insolubility in mammalian tissue environments and resistance to proteolysis.

A variety of proteins, unrelated except for their ability to form β-pleated sheets either spontaneously or upon degradation, have been implicated as the major constituents of amyloid. Some amyloid deposits localize to specific organs; others are distributed throughout the body and, depending upon location and extent, may result in systemic disease. As each protein is different, so are the circumstances under which deposition occurs. It

is upon this accumulated knowledge base that a working classification of amyloidosis has emerged (Table 87-1).[4]

In addition to showing the amyloid fibril protein itself, electron microscopy of amyloid extracts shows, in nearly all forms of amyloid, a small pentagonal constituent. This so-called p-component has been demonstrated immunohistochemically in most, although not all, types of amyloid.[5] It is a normal component of glomerular basement membrane and of elastic tissue[6] and appears to be related to a family of pentameric proteins which includes C-reactive protein.[7] It also exhibits the property of calcium-dependent binding.[8]

ORIGIN AND DYNAMICS

In most instances, the amyloid fibril is derived from a precursor protein of larger molecular weight. An exception is the type of amyloid accompanying chronic hemodialysis,[9,10] in which the entire circulating precursor, beta$_2$-microglobulin, may be involved. In some animal models, splenic extracts from animals primed to form amyloid will accelerate amyloid formation after a single injection of the extract.[11] The precise nature of this amyloid enhancing factor (AEF) is not known.

Amyloid, once formed, is quite resistant to proteolytic digestion, although in secondary amyloidosis (AA), removal of the underlying inflammatory or immunologic stimulus is occasionally followed by complete resorption. In rabbits, even if one continues an amyloid-induction regimen, splenic amyloid is eventually removed, apparently through a process of macrophagic phagocytosis.[12] Factors controlling amyloid resorption are poorly understood, and the event is clinically unpredictable.

GENETIC ASPECTS

In both humans and experimental animals genetic factors play an important role in the amyloid formation. Several forms of the disease occur in high frequency in certain isolated populations which, for geographic or social reasons, have become inbred.[13,14] For example, in

TABLE 87-1
Chemical Types of Amyloid Fibril Proteins Verified by Amino Acid Sequencing and Their Associations with Different Clinical Categories of Amyloid Disease

Clinical Type	Chemical Type	Amyloid Protein	Related Protein
Idiopathic (primary amyloidosis)			
Systemic	AL	A kappa, A lambda	IgL (V kappa, V lambda)
Localized	AL	A kappa, A lambda	IgL (V kappa, V lambda)
Myeloma-associated amyloidosis	AL	A kappa, A lambda	IgL (V kappa, V lambda)
Reactive (secondary) amyloidosis	AA	AA	SAA
Heredofamilial amyloidosis			
Recessive, autosomal:			
Familial Mediterranean fever (FMF)	AA	AA	SAA
Dominant, autosomal:			
Familial amyloid polyneuropathy (FAP)	AF_p	Prealbumin variant	Prealbumin
Familial amyloid cardiomyopathy (FAC)	AF_c	Prealbumin-like	Prealbumin
Hereditary cerebral hemorrhage with amyloidosis (HCHWA)	AF_b	Gamma-trace-like	Gamma-trace microprotein
Senile cardiac amyloidosis	AS_c	Prealbumin-like	Prealbumin
Alzheimer's disease		Beta-protein	?
Down's syndrome		Beta-protein	?
Endocrine-related amyloidosis:	AE		
Medullary carcinoma of the thyroid	AE_t	(Pro-?) calcitonin	Calcitonin
Amyloidosis in chronic hemodialysis patients	AH	Beta$_2$-microglobulin-like	Beta$_2$-microglobulin
Experimental amyloidosis in various animals	AA	AA	SAA
Senile amyloidosis in mouse (SAM)	AS_{sam}	Apo A-II-like	Apo A-II

SOURCE: From Husby G, Sletten K: Editorial review: Chemical and clinical classification of amyloidosis 1985. *Scand J Immunol* 23:253, 1986.

certain Icelandic families, amyloid is deposited almost exclusively in the cerebral arteries, leading to a high frequency of spontaneous cerebral hemorrhage and early death.[15] Recently, the defect in several of these genetic disorders has been assigned to specific chromosomal abnormalities.[16–20] Amyloid in familial amyloid polyneuropathy (FAP) is associated with amino acid substitutions in transthyretin, formerly known as prealbumin. Similar defects have been observed in other genetic syndromes characterized by cardiomyopathy.[14]

The type of amyloid associated with familial Mediterranean fever[21] is the only major familial amyloid syndrome in which the precursor protein is SAA. This serum component is also the precursor of amyloid fibrils in "secondary" or "reactive" amyloidosis and the type common to experimental animals. The amyloid syndrome associated with familial Mediterranean fever is one of the few types of amyloidosis that can effectively be prevented—with colchicine.[22]

CLASSIFICATION AND CLINICAL CHARACTERISTICS

As implied above, despite rather unique physical characteristics, amyloid fibrils vary in chemical composition according to clinical syndrome and exhibit homology with an appropriate variety of putative precursor proteins.[4,23] In clinical practice in this country three amyloid syndromes predominate. These include so-called secondary or reactive amyloidosis (amyloid AA), usually associated with prolonged inflammatory disease, and amyloid AL, which is associated with overproduction of immunoglobulin light chains, either with or without frank B cell malignancy. Various forms of amyloidosis occurring in advanced age are referred to collectively as senile amyloidosis, but are subclassified according to the site of predominant involvement, for example, senile cardiac amyloidosis (ASc).

Figure 87-1 depicts the age at death of patients with amyloid AA, AL, and ASc from a previously reported series.[24] It can be seen that amyloid AA is, predominantly, a disease of youth or middle age, while most patients with amyloid AL die in the fifth or sixth decade. Amyloid ASc occurs chiefly in patients over age 60 and, although infrequently the actual cause of symptoms or death, appears to be particularly innocuous in patients over 90.[24,25] Amyloidosis as a clinical entity is far from common. Our group, which sees essentially all cases diagnosed clinically or by biopsy in a region with a population of over one million, encounters only about six new patients each year.

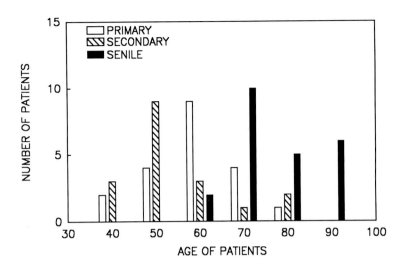

FIGURE 87-1
Age at death, by decade, of 61 patients with either primary (AL), secondary (AA), or senile cardiac (ASc) amyloidosis. (*Adapted from Wright and Calkins.*[24])

AMYLOID AA (SECONDARY OR REACTIVE AMYLOIDOSIS)

The clinical characteristics of amyloid AA consist predominantly of renal involvement, although hepatomegaly, splenomegaly, and gastrointestinal symptoms may also occur. The initial manifestation, proteinuria, is followed by frank nephrotic syndrome and, in time (usually within 3 years), by renal failure with decreasing proteinuria. With chronic dialysis, survival may be extended 6 or 8 more years. While in most such patients amyloid AA deposits are found in the heart at death, cardiac signs and symptoms, during life, are usually due to unrelated conditions.[24]

The amyloid AA fibril bears homology with a normal serum glycoprotein SAA, an "acute phase reactant" synthesized in the liver, which becomes strikingly elevated in patients with inflammatory disease. The mere association of amyloidosis with a chronic inflammatory condition, such as rheumatoid arthritis or ulcerative colitis, does not prove that the amyloid is of the AA type; these chronic conditions may occur coincidentally in patients with other forms of amyloidosis. Apparently, deposition of one form of amyloid neither increases nor decreases the chances of acquiring a second variety.[26,27]

The frequency of AA amyloidosis appears to have declined markedly in this country. Of the 15 patients we have followed recently, all but two have had amyloid AL.

AMYLOID BETA₂-MICROGLOBULIN (DIALYSIS-RELATED AMYLOIDOSIS)

In recent years, some patients undergoing prolonged hemodialysis have accumulated a peculiar form of amyloid in the carpal bones, adjacent to joints, and in synovium.[28] The amyloid fibrils are homologous with beta₂-microglobulin.[9,10,29] This phenomenon appears to be related to the type of dialysis membrane used, a possible explanation for the increased frequency of this syndrome in Europe. Clinical manifestations include carpal tunnel syndrome, severe involvement of the shoulders, hips, and knees, and destructive amyloid accumulations in bone. Like amyloid AA, beta₂-microglobulin amyloid is sensitive to permanganate denaturation.[10,24]

AMYLOID AL (LIGHT CHAIN–RELATED AMYLOIDOSIS)

Amyloid AL is by far the most frequent amyloid syndrome seen in this country. Amyloid AL fibrils bear homology with monoclonal immunoglobulin light chains, which are almost always present in the patient's plasma, urine, or both. Amyloid AL may complicate the clinical course of up to 15 percent of myeloma patients, but more often it occurs in the absence of frank B cell malignancy. The mechanisms controlling light chain transformation are unknown, and many patients with elevated circulating monoclonal light chains never develop amyloidosis.

The clinical manifestations of AL amyloidosis in the elderly do not differ significantly from those in younger individuals. Deposits can be found in virtually any organ, including the heart, kidneys, tongue, gastrointestinal tract, skin, carpal ligaments, voluntary and smooth muscle, liver, and spleen. A variety of clinical syndromes can result; for example, renal involvement is often accompanied by severe postural hypotension. Infiltration of the tongue may be so severe as to interfere with phonation and the ability to masticate or to direct the food toward the esophagus. Involvement of the gastrointestinal tract may be extensive and diffuse, resulting in dysphagia, indigestion, pyloric obstruction, malabsorption, or bleeding from any portion of the alimentary canal. Gastrointestinal manifestations constitute the major clinical problem in one-third of the AL patients in our current series. Skin involvement is usually characterized by irregular blotchy purpura or raised papules, either waxy or hemorrhagic in nature, often clustered in the neck folds, around the eyes, axillae, or inguinal regions. The skin lesions are so characteristic that they provide an important clue to the diagnosis.

All patients with amyloid AL exhibit cardiac amyloid at autopsy.[24] Echocardiography and scintigraphy scans usually reveal thickening of the ventricular wall and interventricular septum and a reduced ejection fraction. Conduction defects are evident in many patients and approximately one-third die suddenly, presumably of arrhythmia. Complete heart block, seen in almost 25 percent of patients, may be unresponsive to pacemaker therapy. Many of these patients exhibit angina pectoris, and, in approximately 25 percent, the electrocardiogram suggests "previous myocardial infarction," due not to ischemic injury but to the amyloid infiltrate itself. In our recent series, the median duration of illness in patients with primary amyloidosis was 2 years, with a range of 4 months to 11 years. Treatment is largely symptomatic, although several studies have indicated slight (statistical) improvement in morbidity, and possibly longevity, with targeted therapy (for example with colchicine, prednisone, and melphalan).[30–32]

AMYLOID IN AGING

The relationship and potential importance of amyloid and aging was slow to gain attention. Widespread amyloid deposition in aging humans was first pointed out by Schwartz, who demonstrated trace amounts of amyloid in a number of organ systems in a significant proportion of elderly patients autopsied at a mental hospital.[33,34] These observations were subsequently confirmed in a general hospital patient population[35]; as illustrated in Fig. 87-2, the majority of persons dying at age 90 or older will exhibit traces of amyloid in one organ or another. Since in most instances these accumulations appear to have no clinical significance, it is difficult to regard the mere presence of amyloid as indicative of disease. Instead, amyloid appears to be part of the normal process of growing old.

Occasionally, however, at autopsy, patients with severe cardiac disease are found to have massive amyloid infiltration of the heart.[24,25,36,37] In one study,[24] each of seven such patients had a history of prolonged intractable cardiac failure, frequently accompanied by atrial fibrillation but without the "ischemic" ECG changes noted in AL patients. In contrast to cardiomyopathy due to amyloid AL, most ASc patients had demonstrable cardiomegaly as revealed by x ray and physical examination; at death, all but one heart weighed in excess of 650 g. Interestingly, six of the seven patients studied were black males, the oldest being 87 years. Review of the total clinical course for these patients disclosed a mean interval of 14 years between initial cardiac manifestations and death. One 66-year-old black man, with congestive failure for 20 years, had been rejected from the army 37 years previously because of cardiomegaly.

In seeking the reason for the divergent clinical manifestations of amyloid heart disease due to AL and ASc, Wright observed that AL amyloid involved both the heart interstitium and the small intramyocardial vessels; indeed, the process appeared to begin in the latter. In contrast, in 21 out of 23 ASc patients, amyloid infiltration was found to be largely confined to the interstitium; intramyocardial vessel involvement predominated in only two.[24] In amyloid AL it would appear that the high frequency of arrhythmia, angina, and "ischemic" ECG changes may be due to amyloid deposition in the small intramyocardial coronary vessels. On the other hand, in

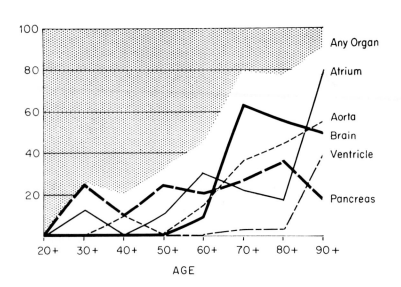

FIGURE 87-2

Frequency of amyloid deposition in different organs with each succeeding decade as determined in a general hospital patient population at autopsy. (*Adapted from Wright et al.*[35])

amyloid ASc the main cardiac manifestation, intractable congestive heart failure, occurs only in patients with striking cardiomegaly, presumably due to years of gradual amyloid accumulation within the cardiac interstitium.

The primary structure of ASc amyloid protein has homology with human prealbumin.[38,39] Yet another form of senile amyloidosis, involving the atria, appears to represent accumulation of a different protein.[40] Aortic amyloid is also a common phenomenon of aging,[41] but neither of the latter appear to have clinical relevance.[36,42]

At present, therapy for patients with ASc amyloidosis is confined to diuretics, vasodilators, and "afterload" reduction therapy. Digitalis should be avoided. Successful cardiac transplantation has been reported in at least one patient with apparently localized cardiac amyloidosis.[43] Since in ASc amyloidosis significant involvement is confined to the heart, a patient with this entity and no other contraindications might be a good candidate for transplantation.

CEREBRAL AMYLOID

The brains of elderly individuals frequently contain lesions exhibiting the histochemical characteristics of amyloid. One such characteristic, the intraneuronal neurofibrillary tangle, is comprised of two 3- to 5-nm-wide filaments twisted around one another to form fibrils with a characteristic periodicity; these structures are commonly referred to as paired helical filaments (PHF). Although the ultrastructure of these fibrils is not typical of what most investigators would regard as amyloid, the fibrils do exhibit classic amyloid staining characteristics.

A second age-related amyloid lesion of the brain is the so-called senile ("neuritic") plaque, consisting of a peripheral zone of degenerating neuronal processes and, often, a cell-free core of amyloid. A third lesion involves the small vessels of the meninges and cerebral cortex. It has been proposed that this so-called congophilic angiopathy may be implicated in the genesis of the senile plaque.[44,45]

RELATIONSHIP OF CEREBRAL AMYLOID AND ALZHEIMER'S DISEASE

Until about 20 years ago, cognitive disease in the elderly, so-called senile brain disease, was attributed primarily to cerebral atherosclerosis. In 1968, Blessed et al.[46] presented a classic paper describing a highly significant correlation (albeit a statistical one) between the extent of cognitive deficit and the number of senile plaques. A few years later, in a somewhat similar study, the same general association was found. However, when subjects were stratified by decade, within a given age cohort, this correlation was no longer statistically valid.[47] Clinical experience confirms the fact that a number of patients with severe cognitive deficits characteristic of Alzheimer's disease may exhibit minimal numbers of senile plaques; conversely, other patients with striking concentrations of senile plaques, as revealed by histologic examination, may have exhibited no cognitive or behavioral abnormalities prior to death.

Although the work of Blessed et al. has not been repeated, the finding of a high concentration of senile plaques in certain target areas of the brain is now recognized as valid grounds for the histologic diagnosis of Alzheimer's disease,[48] and the nature of these amyloid lesions has been the subject of a rapidly expanding body of scientific effort during the past 2 or 3 years. In 1984, Glenner and Wong isolated the amyloid protein from the meningeal vessels of Alzheimer's disease patients, confirmed its β-pleated sheet conformation, established its amino acid composition, and labeled the protein β-peptide, now commonly referred to as β-protein.[49] They subsequently identified the same protein within neuritic plaques and postulated that the amyloid precursor might be transported by means of the small arterioles to the sites of senile plaque formation,[45] thus echoing a proposal made by Scholz nearly 50 years ago.[44] Antibodies to a protein isolated from plaques and designated A4,[50] closely related to but not identical with β-protein, have also been shown to detect neurofibrillary tangles.[51] There is recent evidence that A4 polypeptide is derived from a much larger precursor protein expressing the characteristics of a membrane-spanning glycoprotein.[52]

GENE EXPRESSION IN CEREBRAL AMYLOID AND ALZHEIMER'S DISEASE

A number of observations suggest that genetic factors may play an important role in the pathogenesis of Alzheimer's disease.[53] Approximately 10 percent of Alzheimer's patients have familial Alzheimer's disease (FAD), an autosomal dominant condition associated with the early onset of symptoms. Families of patients with Down's syndrome exhibit an increased frequency of Alzheimer's disease, and nearly all Down's patients who live beyond the age of 40 display the cognitive and neurologic symptoms of Alzheimer's disease. Amyloid fibrils isolated from patients with Alzheimer's disease and those with Down's syndrome have identical amino acid sequences.[54] These factors have raised the possibility that the pathogenesis of Alzheimer's disease may be related to a defect in the long arm of chromosome 21. Utilizing cell lines from four families with FAD and restrictive fragment polymorphism analysis, the FAD gene has been mapped to the long arm of chromosome 21,[55] at a site, however, distinct from the Down's syndrome locus.

In another approach, cDNA probes have been used to localize the β-protein (A4) gene to the proximal end of the long arm of chromosome 21, distant, by a wide margin, from the site involved in Down's syndrome and from the FAD locus described above.[55-59] The gene responsible for the synthesis of A4 protein is not confined to the brain, but can also be found in kidney, thymus, muscle, and heart.[60] Demonstration of the same protein in the brains of a wide variety of animal species[61] not only suggests models for future study but also illustrates the stability of the gene throughout phylogeny and implies some biological importance for the β-protein.

Further evidence against the theory that this β-protein gene is responsible for Alzheimer's disease is the fact that β-protein from patients with Alzheimer's disease appears to be identical to that found in normal individuals.[61,62] The fact that the lesions in Alzheimer's disease and cerebral amyloidosis of the aged are not accompanied by similar deposits in the heart, skin, kidney, gastrointestinal tract, and so on, despite the ubiquitous nature of the β-protein gene, suggests that other factors either repress amyloid formation in these other organs or facilitate its formation in the brain. Pettigrew et al.,[63] utilizing perchloric acid extracts of brains obtained at autopsy and in biopsies of patients with Alzheimer's disease, have shown, by nuclear magnetic resonance analysis, that these brains do exhibit abnormalities in membrane-related compounds. In view of the possible relationship to cell membranes, cited above, amyloid β-protein might be generated by injuries specific to the brain which target cell membranes.

In summary, we now have a growing fund of knowledge concerning the structure and composition of the amyloid associated with Alzheimer's disease and of the genetic loci which appear to be involved. However, we do not yet have conclusive evidence that these amyloid lesions are responsible for the behavioral changes characterizing this condition.

TIME, AGING, AND AMYLOIDOSIS

The various amyloid syndromes present interesting and possibly important models for assessing possible interrelationships between time, aging, and disease. It has been suggested that so-called diseases of aging can be divided into age-related disease and age-dependent disease.[64] The development of AA amyloidosis, although a condition of adolescence to mid-adulthood (and only occasionally old age), clearly requires an appreciable passage of time. Since during this process the patients are growing older, the disorder is age-related, but it is not age-dependent. A similar case might be made for ASc amyloidosis.

In familial amyloid polyneuropathy and amyloid associated with familial Mediterranean fever, both the gene and the precursor protein are identifiable in childhood, yet the disorder does not become evident until after the passage of many years. Clearly a better understanding of the processes controlling the course of these diseases may have important relevance for our understanding of Alzheimer's disease.[60]

Khachaturian[65] has suggested that a potentially useful model for this process may exist in the concept known in digital logic as the "AND gate." For example, in Alzheimer's disease, important predisposing "gates" might be conceptualized as (1) genetic predisposition, (2) cerebral microvascular pathology, (3) aluminum intoxication, (4) changes in oxidative metabolism, (5) other changes in brain chemistry, and (6) reductions in cerebral blood flow. It is uncertain whether aging would also be a predisposing "gate," or whether it becomes relevant only because, as a person ages, opportunities for other gate closures are obviously increased.

REFERENCES

1. Glenner GG: Amyloid deposits and amyloidosis: The beta-fibrilloses. *N Engl J Med* 302:1283, 1980.
2. Cohen HS, Connors LN: The pathogenesis and biochemistry of amyloidosis. *J Pathol* 151:1, 1987.
3. Cohen AS, Calkins E: Electron microscopic observations on a fibrous component in amyloid of diverse origins. *Nature* 183:1202, 1959.
4. Husby G, Sletten K: Editorial review: Chemical and clinical classification of amyloidosis 1985. *Scand J Immunol* 23:253, 1986.
5. Shirahama T et al: Widespread occurrence of AP in amyloidotic tissues: An immunohistochemical observation. *Virchows Arch [B]* 48:197, 1985.
6. Breathreach SM et al: Amyloid P component is located on elastic fibre microfibrils in normal human tissue. *Nature* 293:652, 1981.
7. Osmand AP et al: Characterization of C-reactive protein and the complement subcomponent C1t as homologous proteins displaying cyclic pentameric symmetry (Pentraxins). *Proc Natl Acad Sci USA* 74:739, 1977.
8. Potempa LA et al: Effect of divalent metal ions and pH upon the binding reactivity of human serum amyloid P component, a c-reactive protein homologue, for zymozan. Preferential reactivity in the presence of copper and acidic pH. *J Biol Chem* 260:12142, 1985.
9. Bardin T: Dialysis related amyloidosis: Editorial. *J Rheumatol* 14:647, 1987.
10. Shirahama T et al: Histochemical and immunohistochemical characterization of amyloid associated with chronic hemodialysis as β2-microglobulin. *Lab Invest* 53:705, 1985.
11. Kisilevsky R, Boudreau L: The effects of amyloid-enhancing factor and splenectomy. *Lab Invest* 48:53, 1983.
12. Wright JR et al: Amyloid resorption: Possible role of multinucleated giant cells. The apparent failure of penicillamine treatment. *Johns Hopkins Med J* 130:278, 1972.

13. Benson MD: Medical Genetics XXIV. Hereditary amyloidosis—disease entity and clinical model. *Hosp Pract* March 15, 1988, p 125.

14. Benson MD et al: Hereditary amyloidosis: Description of a new American kindred with late onset cardiomyopathy. *Arthritis Rheum* 30:195, 1987.

15. Jenson O et al: Hereditary cystation C (gamma trace) amyloid angiopathy of the CNS causing cerebral hemorrhage. *Acta Neurol Scand* 76:102, 1987.

16. Whitehead AS et al: Cloning of human prealbumin with DNA: Localization of the gene to chromosome 18 and detection of a variant prealbumin allele in a family with familial amyloid polyneuropathy. *Mol Biol Med* 2:411, 1984.

17. Wallace MR et al: Localization of the human prealbumin gene to chromosome 18. *Biochem Biophys Res Commun* 129:753, 1985.

18. Nakazato M et al: Childhood detection of familial amyloidotic polyneuropathy. *Lancet* 1:99, 1985.

19. Saraiva MTM et al: Biochemical marker in familial amyloidotic polyneuropathy, Portuguese type. Family studies on the transthyretin (prealbumin)–methionine-30 variant. *J Clin Invest* 76:2171, 1985.

20. Mita S et al: Familial amyloidotic polyneuropathy diagnosed by cloned human prealbumin cDNA. *Neurology* 36:298, 1986.

21. Sohar E et al: Familial Mediterranean fever, a survey of 470 cases and review of the literature. *Am J Med* 43:227, 1987.

22. Zemer D et al: Colchicine in the prevention and treatment of the amyloidosis of familial Mediterranean fever. *N Engl J Med* 314:1001, 1986.

23. Castano EM, Frangione B: Biology of disease: Human amyloidosis, Alzheimer disease and related disorders. *Lab Invest* 58:122, 1988.

24. Wright JR, Calkins E: Clinical-pathologic differentiation of common amyloid syndromes. *Medicine* 60:429, 1981.

25. Olson LJ et al: Senile cardiac amyloidosis with myocardial dysfunction diagnosis by endomyocardial biopsy and immunochemistry. *N Engl J Med* 317:738, 1987.

26. Ozdemir AI et al: Influence of rheumatoid arthritis on amyloidosis of aging: Comparison of 47 rheumatoid patients with 47 controls matched for age and sex. *N Engl J Med* 285:534, 1971.

27. Limas C et al: Amyloidosis and multiple myeloma. A reevaluation using an age-matched control population. *Am J Med* 54:166, 1973.

28. Brown EA et al: Dialysis arthropathy: Complication of long term treatment with haemodialysis. *Br Med J* 292:163, 1985.

29. Gorevic PD et al: Beta-2 microglobulin is an amyloidogenic protein in man. *J Clin Invest* 76:2425, 1985.

30. Benson MD: Treatment of AL amyloidosis with melphalan, prednisone and colchicine. *Arthritis Rheum* 29:683, 1986.

31. Kyle RA et al: Primary systemic amyloidosis: Comparison of melphalan, prednisone versus colchicine. *Am J Med* 79:708, 1985.

32. Gertz MA, Kyle RA: Response of primary hepatic amyloidosis to melphalan and prednisone: A case report and review of the literature. *Mayo Clin Proc* 61:218, 1986.

33. Schwartz P: Senile cerebral pancreatic insular and cardiac amyloidosis. *Trans NY Acad Sci* 27:393, 1965.

34. Schwartz P et al: Fluorescence microscopy demonstration of cerebro-vascular and pancreatic insular amyloid in presenile and senile states. *J Am Geriatr Soc* 13:199, 1965.

35. Wright JR et al: Relationship of amyloid to aging. Review of the literature and systematic study of 83 patients derived from a general hospital population. *Medicine* 48:39, 1969.

36. Wright JR, Calkins E: Amyloid in the aged heart: Frequency and clinical significance. *J Am Geriatr Soc* 23:97, 1975.

37. Cornwell GG III et al: Frequency and distribution of senile cardiovascular amyloid: A clinicopathologic correlation. *Am J Med* 75:618, 1983.

38. Sletten K et al: Senile cardiac amyloid related to prealbumin. *Scand J Immunol* 12:503, 1980.

39. Gorevic PG et al: Systemic senile amyloidosis: Identification of a new prealbumin (transthyretin) variant in cardiac tissue: Structural similarity to one form of familial amyloidotic polyneuropathy. *J Clin Invest* 1988 (in press).

40. Westermark P et al: Senile cardiac amyloidosis: Evidence of two different amyloid substances in the aging heart. *Scand J Immunol* 10:303, 1979.

41. Cornwell GG III et al: Senile aortic amyloid: A third distinctive type of age-related cardiovascular amyloid. *Am J Pathol* 108:135, 1982.

42. Wright JR, Calkins E: Relationship of amyloid deposits in the human aorta to aortic atherosclerosis: A postmortem study of 100 individuals over 60 years of age. *Lab Invest* 30:767, 1974.

43. Conner R: Heart transplantation for cardiac amyloidosis. *J Heart Transplant* 7:165, 1988.

44. Scholz W: Studien zur pathologie der hirngefaesse II. Die drusige entartung der hirnarterien und kapillaren (Eine form senile gefaesserkrankung). *Z Ges Neurol Psychiatr* 162:694, 1938.

45. Wong CW et al: Neurologic plaques and cerebrovascular amyloid in Alzheimer Disease are antigenetically related. *Proc Soc Natl Acad Sci* 82:8729, 1985.

46. Blessed G et al: The association between quantitative measures of dementia and of senile change in the cerebral grey matter of elderly subjects. *Br J Psychiatry* 114:797, 1968.

47. Wright JR, Calkins E: Unpublished observations.

48. Khachaturian ZS: Diagnosis of Alzheimer disease. *Arch Neurol* 42:1097, 1985.

49. Glenner GG, Wong CW: Alzheimer's disease: Initial report of the purification and characteristics of a novel cerebrovascular amyloid protein. *Biochem Biophys Res Commun* 120:885, 1984.

50. Masters CL et al: Amyloid plaque core protein in Alzheimer disease and Down syndrome. *Proc Natl Acad Sci USA* 82:4245, 1985.

51. Majocha RE, Marotta CA: Molecular and genetic investigations on Alzheimer brain amyloid. *J Geriatr Psychiatr Neurol* 1:65, 1988.

52. Kang J et al: The precursor of Alzheimer disease amyloid A4 protein resembles a cell-surface precursor. *Nature* 325:733, 1987.

53. Katzman R: Alzheimer's disease: Medical Progress. *N Engl J Med* 314:964, 1986.

54. Glenner GG, Wong CW: Alzheimer's disease and Down's syndrome: Sharing of a unique cerebrovascular amyloid fibril protein. *Biochem Biophys Res Commun* 122:1131, 1984.

55. St. George-Hyslop PH et al: The genetic defect causing familial Alzheimer's disease maps on chromosome 21. *Science* 235:885, 1987.

56. Goldgaber D et al: Characterization and chromosomal localization of a cDNA encoding brain amyloid of Alzheimer's disease. *Science* 235:877, 1987.

57. Tanzi RE et al: Alzheimer β protein gene: cDNA, mRNA distribution, and genetic linkage near the Alzheimer locus. *Science* 235:880, 1987.

58. Robakis NK et al: Molecular cloning and characterization of a cDNA encoding the cerebrovascular and the neuritic plaque amyloid peptides. *Proc Natl Acad Sci USA* 84:4190, 1987.

59. Goldgaber D et al: Isolation, characterization and chromosomal localization of human brain cDNA clones coding for the precursor of the amyloid of brain in Alzheimer's disease, Down's syndrome. *J Neural Transm* 24(suppl):23, 1987.

60. Martin JB: Molecular genetics: Applications to the clinical neurosciences. *Science* 238:765, 1987.

61. Selkoe DJ et al: Conservation of brain amyloid proteins in aged mammals and humans with Alzheimer's disease. *Science* 235:873, 1987.

62. Bahmanyar S et al: Localization of amyloid β protein messenger RNA in brains from patients with Alzheimer's disease. *Science* 237:77, 1987.

63. Pettigrew JW et al: 31 p nuclearmagnetic resonance study of the brain in Alzheimer's disease. *J Neuropathol Exp Neurol* 47:235, 1988.

64. Brody JA, Schneider EL: Diseases and disorders of aging: An hypothesis. *J Chronic Dis* 39:871, 1986.

65. Khachaturian ZA: Aluminum toxicity among other views on the etiology of Alzheimer disease. *Neurobiol Aging* 7:537, 1986.

SECTION I

The Nervous System

Chapter 88

NEUROCHEMISTRY OF THE AGING HUMAN BRAIN

Judes Poirier and Caleb E. Finch

Aging of the human central nervous system has often been associated with an irreversible loss of functions and a decline of its global abilities. This oversimplified picture is far from a true reflection of the plastic nature of the adult brain, which has a remarkable ability to compensate functionally for neuronal loss or atrophy. There is some significant age-related loss of neurons, loss of dendritic arborization, and loss of enzymes and receptors involved in the neurotransmission function of the brain, but, as we discuss later, these losses should not be considered as a *general* or even necessary phenomena. On the contrary, the loss of function is usually associated with *specific* areas of the brain. We also emphasize that the reported changes described in the biochemistry and structure of the aging human brain do not necessarily affect the ordinary activities of living or occupational performance until 75 years of age. Even at later ages, a fortunate subgroup of us will remain remarkably intact.[1]

Studies of age-related diseases like Alzheimer's, Parkinson's, and Huntington's have helped us to understand how the aging brain copes with selective, but se-

Supported by a training grant of Le Fond de la Recherche en Santé du Québec and by the ADRC grant #AG05142 and the John D. and Catherine T. MacArthur Foundation Research Program On Successful Aging.

vere, dysfunctions. For example, in Parkinson's disease the striatum must lose more than 70 percent of its endogenous dopamine content before abnormal motor symptoms appear. This ability of the brain to function despite a severe loss of neurons is only one demonstration of its impressive plastic ability. It is thus important to keep in mind that the different types of loss (or gain) that we will describe later may not necessarily have immediate functional correlates in the view of the brain's plastic ability. Limited space precludes discussion of animal data except nonhuman primates. For more complete reviews, see Rogers and Bloom[2] and Morgan et al.[3]

USUAL AGING IN HUMAN BRAIN

MORPHOLOGICAL CONSIDERATIONS The brain undergoes an early period of growth, remains relatively stable during the adulthood, and then slowly declines during senescence. A major distinction must, however, be drawn between aging in neurons as opposed to aging in other cell types. Peripheral cells in some tissues retain mitogenic capacity throughout the human life span (hematopoiesis), whereas proliferation is lost in others during differentiation (myocardium). In the brain, differentiated neurons cannot go through cell division, whereas glia can. Neurons, therefore, are not replaced when they die, whereas glia may proliferate. However, compensatory dendrite proliferation with age, as observed in several labs, was proposed as a means by which selected neuronal pathways are able to maintain contact with their target despite neuronal losses.[4] The view that human brain usually undergoes general atrophy[5] has been recently challenged by CT scan longitudinal studies showing highly selective atrophy in restricted areas.[6,7] It is accompanied by a net reduction in the blood flow that reaches 10 to 15 percent while the capillary network of the cerebral cortex appears to increase in diameter, volume, and length, explaining why the cerebral blood flow is reduced.[8]

The extent of neuronal loss is presently quite controversial, mostly because of diverse technical considerations. However, most evidence indicates some neuronal loss (10 to 60 percent) with normal aging in the human and primate neocortex, cerebellum, and the hippocampus, whereas cell loss may be less dramatic in subcortical structures (except for the locus coeruleus).[4] Loss of neurons in cortical structures varies greatly between regions. The superior temporal gyrus loses as much as 55 percent of its neuronal content, whereas the inferior temporal gyrus and the tip of the temporal lobe shows only a 10 to 35 percent loss.[4] Readers may note that decrease in cortical volume with age may exaggerate neuronal loss. Current data indicate that the age-related cortical neuronal loss is most prominent in large neurons, whereas in the subcortical pigmented structures like the substantia nigra and the locus coeruleus, cells with most neuromelanin appear to be more vulnerable.[9] The nucleus basalis of Maynert also suffers little or no neuronal loss with aging. These discrepancies might be related to unrecognized senile dementia or other neurological diseases. Small cortical neurons are difficult to evaluate since the loss of large neurons will generally induce glial proliferation whose cells are small like some cortical neurons. Primates also show age-related, region-specific loss of cortical neurons.

On the other hand, there is an increased dendritic growth in some neurons of the cerebral cortex and hippocampus of aging humans and nonhuman primates.[4,10] Thus, it is not surprising to observe some neurochemical compensatory mechanisms in the areas affected by neuronal loss. Before describing in detail the neurochemical alterations of the aging, we will review age changes in the brain bulk constituents.

CHEMICAL CONSTITUENTS OF THE AGING BRAIN

PROTEINS The decrease in weight observed in human brain with aging is associated with a concomitant loss of proteins that appears to be proportional to the gain of water.[11] The average quantity of proteins is reduced with aging but not all proteins are affected. For example, abnormal proteins contained in intraneuronal neurofibrillary tangles and neuritic plaques with extracellular amyloid increase with age and are sometimes referred to as age markers. During Alzheimer's disease, plaques and tangles accumulate in the hippocampus, some cortical regions, and the nucleus basalis of Maynert while other regions remain relatively free of changes, e.g., primary sensory cortex. On the other hand, an impressive list of enzymes not related to neurotransmission showed marked decreases of activity or amount. Among others, these include fructose-6-phosphate dehydrogenase, glucose-6-phosphate dehydrogenase, and glycerol-3-phosphate dehydrogenase which are involved in glucose catabolism. Carbonic anhydrase, a key enzyme in CO_2 detoxification is also reduced. For more complete lists of enzymes and proteins modified by the aging process, see Refs. 2, 12, 13.

NUCLEIC ACIDS Neurons of the central nervous system contain the same amount of DNA as in any other somatic cells, and little or no change of the DNA content is reported in the brain. However, the story is noticeably different with RNA content. Because messenger RNA populations are thought to vary widely between types of neurons due to selective transcription, it is no surprise that RNA changes with age vary between brain regions. In the neurons of the hypoglossal nucleus, the total RNA content increases in the first two decades of life and then decreases through the ninth decades.[14] Similar biphasic changes occur in the motor neurons of the ventrolateral nucleus, with decreases after 50 years.[15] In the hippocampus, the concentration of bulk neuron RNA in nondemented individuals increases by more than 50 percent at advanced ages in the subicular region, whereas neurons in the cortex of the same individuals had less RNA.[16] The relation of changes in RNA to protein synthesis is presently unknown.

LIPIDS Lipids account for more than half of the dry weight of the brain. A loss of total lipid occurs after 50 years of age.[17] However, the total lipid content is effectively increased or is unchanged during the same period because of the global loss of brain weight.[18] Some have proposed that the loss of lipid may be due to age changes in the proportion of gray and white matter. There is also a correlation between the loss of myelin and the brain content of cerebroside and ethanolamine plasmalogen,[17] the latter two major components being constituents of myelin. Other lipids like ganglioside, choline phosphoglyceride, ethanolamine phosphoglyceride, sphingomyelin, and cholesterol are also reduced in the aging human brain.[17,18] Although little is known about the changes of lipid turnover in the human brain, aging rodents show a decreased lipid turnover rate and a decreased lipid concentration that parallels a decrease of lipid catabolism and synthesis.[18]

BIOCHEMICAL ASPECTS OF CONDUCTION AND NEUROTRANSMISSION

PRINCIPLES OF NEUROTRANSMITTER BIOLOGY

The transmission of neuronal information can be subdivided into two distinct mechanisms: An *electrical* counterpart that carries the information from the cell body along the axon to the terminals and a *chemical* counterpart that is activated by the arriving action potential which triggers the release of neurotransmitters at the terminal level. The chemical cascade is initiated by the entry of Ca^{2+} into the terminals which, in turn, promotes the fusion of the neurotransmitter-containing vesicles with the plasma membrane. The transmission between two neurons involves the synthesis, storage, and release of one or more different neurotransmitters in response to nerve-ending depolarization. These neurotransmitters have been classified as inhibitory, excitatory, or modulatory. Modulatory neurotransmitters have certain effects on the other neurotransmitters. Once released, a neurotransmitter diffuses to the postsynaptic membrane, where it binds transiently with highly specific receptor proteins. The complex formed by the transmitter and its receptor then modulates the electrical excitability of the postsynaptic cell and promotes inhibition, stimulation, modulation (or a combination of all three) of an electric impulse through modification of the polarization state of the cell. Once the signal is transmitted, the receptor releases its neurotransmitter into the synaptic cleft where it is deactivated by specific catabolic enzymes or sequestered by presynaptic surfaces.

PRE- AND POSTMORTEM CONSIDERATIONS

Study of the biochemical and neurochemical changes in aging human brain is complicated by the variability of postmortem intervals until the specimen is fixed or frozen. Agonal states strongly influence the structure and the chemistry of the brain and often differ widely among individuals. The handling of postmortem tissues has not yet been set by common conventions, and protocols for freezing tend to vary greatly among institutions. One has also to consider that an underlying disease might be present in some of the so-called control brains. A careful neuropathological investigation is needed for each specimen to minimize confusion with non-age-related changes.

CATECHOLAMINES AND SEROTONIN

The catecholamine neurotransmitter family is composed of three distinct neurotransmitters: dopamine, norepinephrine, and epinephrine. Although dopamine is a precursor of norepinephrine and epinephrine and norepinephrine a precursor of epinephrine, each has a separate brain localization and relative distinct functions. These neurotransmitters are mostly involved in the control and modulation of visceral functions and of emotions and attention. Serotonin, whose amino acid precursor is tryptophan, is known to be involved in many central regulatory processes, including drinking, respiration, heart beat, thermoregulation, sleep, and memory.

During aging in apparently normal individuals, several investigators have showed a significant loss of synthetic capability of certain catecholaminergic and serotonergic neurons. Tyrosine hydroxylase (TH), the enzyme that converts tyrosine into dihydroxyphenylalanine (dopa), becomes somewhat reduced with age in the caudate nucleus, putamen, and the amygdala but not in the hypothalamus.[19,20] However, most of the decline of TH activity occurs before 20 years of age. Under such circumstances, it seems more appropriate to talk of relative changes. The extent of changes in dopa decarboxylase (DCC) which converts dopa into dopamine, varies tremendously between regions, and no conclusion is yet possible.[21] The dopamine content is particularly reduced in the striatum, up to 50 percent by 75 years, as well as in mesencephalic structures. Dopamine β-hydroxylase activity, which converts dopamine to norepinephrine, is not notably affected by aging.[22] The loss of TH, DCC, dopamine, and norepinephrine closely parallel the loss of dopaminergic and noradrenergic neurons described in the substantia nigra and the locus coeruleus. Two enzymes degrade dopamine and noradrenaline: monoamine oxidase (MAO), mainly the MAO-B subtype, and catechol-*o*-methyltransferase (COMT) which appear to be differentially altered with aging. MAO activity is consistently elevated with aging in the frontal cortex, striatum, globus pallidus, and substantia nigra in humans, whereas COMT activity remains unchanged except in the hippocampus where it is increased.[23,24] However, COMT activity in rodent brains changes differentially than in human; it tends to parallel MAO increases with age. The increase in MAO (and perhaps COMT) with age is consistent with the apparent increases of monoamine catabolites observed in the cerebrospinal fluid of elderly patients.[23,25]

At least two types of dopaminergic receptors have been investigated in the human aging striatum, the D1 receptor which is positively linked to adenylate cyclase activity and the D2 receptor which appears to be negatively coupled with adenylate cyclase. The human striatum loses approximately 2 percent of its D2 receptors per decade, whereas little or no change in D1 receptor content has been reported with aging in the striatum.[26,27] These observations strengthen the results obtained by positron emission tomography (PET) scan studies in vivo.[28,29] As for noradrenergic receptors, the beta subtypes appear to decrease in the cerebellum with aging. This is corroborated by rodent studies where most of the brain regions studied (including the cerebellum) present a 20 to 30 percent loss.[30] Finally, serotonin receptors are reduced in the cerebral cortex, but not in the striatum of aging humans.[30,31]

ACETYLCHOLINE

Cholinergic neurons synthesize acetylcholine from choline and acetyl coenzyme A (acetyl-CoA). The enzymes responsible for its degradation and its synthesis are synthesized in the soma and are transported to the terminals. Acetyl-CoA, which comes from pyruvate metabolism, is combined with choline via the activity of choline acetyltransferase (CAT). The choline can be taken up directly through synaptic membranes, or it may be formed from the catabolism of phosphatidylcholine. Once released from its vesicular form, acetylcholine can interact pre- and postsynaptically with two types of receptors, namely the nicotinic and muscarinic receptors. Finally, the neurotransmitter is inactivated by acetylcholinesterase (AChE), while free choline is released from the process. CAT and AChE activity change little with normal aging in human brain. CAT activity appears to be prominently reduced in the cerebral cortex but remains unchanged in the striatum.[19] The loss of CAT activity is accompanied by a significant reduction (20 to 85 percent) of AChE activity, and choline uptake in the human cortex with aging. Studies in rhesus monkeys show a similar loss of AChE after 20 years of age.[32] Loss of cholinergic function with age is, however, still controversial; inclusion of unrecognized Alzheimer's disease specimens might be responsible for the trend. Acetylcholine, as is the case for tryptophan hydroxylase, is too labile to be accurately measured in human postmortem tissues.

Muscarinic receptors are significantly reduced in the cerebral cortex and hippocampus with age, but not in the basal ganglia.[31] Nicotinic receptors, on the other hand, are reduced only in the cortical structures.

GABA AND GLUTAMIC ACID

Gamma aminobutyric acid (GABA) and glutamate are both metabolic intermediates and neurotransmitters. Their respective metabolisms are strongly interrelated. Glutamic acid decarboxylase (GAD) catalyzes the conversion of glutamate into GABA in neurons, whereas the conversion of GABA into glutamine in glial cells is mediated by glutamine synthetase. Subsequently, glutamine

is taken up by the neurons and transformed into glutamate via glutaminase activity. There appears to be no specific storage of glutamate and GABA in the terminals, in contrast to catecholaminergic and acetylcholine neurotransmitters. GABA release is known to have mostly inhibitory actions at the postsynaptic level, whereas glutamate promotes a postsynaptic stimulatory response. Since little is known about the neurobiology of glutamate in the aging human brain, this discussion will focus on GABA metabolism. GAD activity falls (20 to 30 percent) with age in human cortical areas and in the thalamus.[21] GAD activity is also reduced in the basal ganglia.[21] GABA uptake is decreased in the neocortex with age, but the receptor binding of muscimol, a GABA agonist, increases in the temporal lobe with age in humans.[2] Similar changes were observed in the frontal cortex when investigated using a GABA binding assay. The increased sensitivity of elderly patients to benzodiazepines has prompted several investigators to study the interaction of GABA with benzodiazepine binding sites. However, neither benzodiazepine binding nor GABA interaction with benzodiazepine receptors appear affected by the aging process in humans.[2]

Caution is needed in interpreting studies of amino acid neurotransmitter metabolism, since it is difficult for the moment to distinguish the neurotransmitter-related functions from those of intermediary metabolism. Some of the changes might simply reflect altered metabolism and not altered neurotransmission. It should also be noted that GAD is affected by preterminal coma conditions and certain antibiotics.

NEUROPEPTIDES

The synthesis of neuropeptides can occur from two different pathways. For short peptides, like carnosine and glutathione, enzymes called *synthetases* catalyze the synthesis from amino acid components. But for most of the larger peptides found in the central nervous system—like nerve growth factor, ACTH, or the endorphins—a prohormone is synthesized via the usual translation of messenger RNA. The prohormone is processed in the secretory granules during the axonal transport, and the mature peptides are secreted. Fortunately for neurochemists, most neuropeptides are quite stable post mortem. There is no loss of substance P with aging in the frontal cortex, caudate nucleus, globus pallidus, thalamus, or hypothalamus, whereas an important decrease has been observed in the putamen.[33] No changes have been noted in somatostatin level in the striatum, frontal cortex, globus pallidus, or in the substantia nigra in normal human subjects.[33] In contrast, Alzheimer's disease patients show a severe loss of somatostatin (approximately 60 percent) in the hippocampus[34,35] and in cortex.[36]

Neurotensin levels in the human frontal cortex, caudate nucleus, putamen, nucleus accumbens, olfactory tubercles, septum, and globus pallidus remain unchanged during the life span.[33] However, a loss of neurotensin (approximately 40 percent) was found in the substantia nigra with aging in humans, but not in rats. The vasoactive intestinal peptide (VIP) content of the human temporal lobe increases between the sixth and the ninth decades.[37] Little is known about the role of these peptides, their metabolism, or the effects of a loss (or a gain) in the aging human brain.

The dynamics of secretion of pituitary hormones show age-related changes in humans which represent the altered secretion of neuropeptide-releasing hormones by the hypothalamus. Both sexes tend to have fewer nocturnal episodes of growth hormone secretion. The wide differences between individuals may reflect the undefined effects of exercise, diet, or adiposity. The pulsatile secretions of LH also decrease in frequency and amplitude in elderly men, again with wide individual differences. These changes also occur in aging rodents and may be linked in future studies to altered neurotransmitter regulation.[38]

AGE-RELATED DISEASES OF THE AGING BRAIN

Any description of the neurochemical alterations of the brain due to aging requires mention of the most important late-age-onset neurological diseases, namely Parkinson's disease (PD) and Alzheimer's disease (AD). In patients who die in "preclinical" phases of these diseases and who are therefore classified as "neurologically intact controls," changes due to early phases of these diseases may be attributed to "normal" aging. As the average age of the population in industrialized countries has persistently increased over the last decades, more and more individuals have become at risk to develop one of these terrible age-related diseases of the central nervous system. By the end of the century, more than 15 percent of the total population in the United States will be over 65, and at progressively increased risk for AD and PD.

PARKINSON'S DISEASE

The clinical features,[39,40] pathology,[41] and treatment[42] of Parkinson's disease (PD) are discussed in detail in Chap. 94.

BIOCHEMICAL ABNORMALITIES Although the etiology of PD still remains unknown, the 90 percent (or more) loss of dopamine in the substantia nigra–striatum axis is almost certainly responsible for most symptoms. Moreover, PD symptoms can be induced by means of specific dopamine antagonists, by the virus which caused the epidemic of *Encephalitis lethargica* earlier this century, or by chemical compounds such as carbon monoxide, manganese, or n-methyl-4-phenyl-1,2,3,6-tetrahydropyridine (MPTP). The genetic risk factors in PD have not been established. The abnormal neurochemical parameters observed in PD are summarized in Table 88-1.

ALZHEIMER'S DISEASE

The clinical features,[43–47] structural neuropathology,[43,48] and treatment[50] of Alzheimer's disease are discussed in detail in Chap. 92.

BIOCHEMICAL CHARACTERISTICS Four different ascending projection pathways are involved in Alzheimer's disease: (1) the cholinergic system, which arises from the nucleus basalis of Maynert; (2) the noradrenergic system, which arises from the locus coeruleus; (3) the serotoninergic pathway, which arises from the raphe nucleus and the dorsal tegmentum; and (4) the reticular projection, which arises from the paramedian reticular nucleus. There is also recent evidence for a progressive disconnection of the hippocampus from the rest of the brain[49] and a loss of connections between different cortical areas.[48] It is common to compare AD to aging. As is the case with late age, there is a significant loss of neurons in the locus coeruleus and in the nucleus basalis of Maynert in AD. Plaques and tangles which are common markers of aging are more numerous in AD, particularly in early-onset AD (see Chap. 92).

Table 88-2 summarizes the neurotransmitter changes in AD. The loss of cholinergic function is one of the most important neurotransmitter alterations reported in AD. Choline acetyltransferase as well as acetylcholinesterase are severely reduced in the cerebral cortex and hippocampus of Alzheimer patients. The cholinergic loss occurs as early as the first year of the disease, but varies widely among subjects. Muscarinic (postsynaptic) receptors appear unchanged. Somatostatin, a neuropeptide present in medium-size and large neurons, also decreases in the hippocampus and cerebral cortex.

CONCLUSION

It is no longer possible to associate the aging of the brain with loss of function and structure without taking into consideration the plastic nature of the central nervous system. Although there is an age-related loss of neurons, this loss remains restricted to specific areas of the brain and is often associated with compensatory dendritic proliferation. On the other hand, there are still uncertainties concerning which, if any, of the age-related changes

TABLE 88-1
Neurochemical Parameters in Parkinson's Disease

	Areas												
	SNA	CAU	PUT	PAL	FCx	VTA	HIP	HYP	ACC	A25	SIN	LC	OLF
Dopamine	−	−	−		−	−	−	−	−	−			−
D1 Receptor			0										
D2 Receptor		+	+										
Tyrosine hydroxylase	−	−	−	−									
Dopa decarboxylase	−	−	−	−									
Homovanillic acid	−	−	−										
Noradrenalin	−	−	−					−	−			−	
Serotonin	−							−					
Choline acetyl transferase					−						−		
Glutamic acid decarboxylase	0	0	0		0			0	0		0		
Peptides													
Met-enkephalin	−	0	−	−	0	−	0	0					
Leu-enkephalin	0	0	−	−	0	0	0	0					
Substance P	−	0	−	0	0	0	0	0					
CCK-8	−	0	0	0	0	0	0	0					
Somatostatin	0	0	0	0	−*	0	−*	0					
TRH	0	0	0	0	0	0	0	0					
Bombesin	0	−	0	−	0	0	0	0					
Neurotensin	0	0	0	0	0	0		−					

Key: SNA: substantia nigra, CAU: caudate, PUT: putamen, PAL: globus pallidus, FCx: frontal cortex, VTA: ventral tegmental area, HIP: hippocampus, HYP: hypothalamus, ACC: nucleus accumbens, A25: Broca's area 25, SIN: substantia innominata, LC: locus coeruleus, OLF: olfactory tubercules. −: Decreased, 0: not changed, +: increased in Parkinson's disease versus age-matched controls, −*: decrease in demented patients.
SOURCE: Adapted from Barbeau[39] and Jellinger.[41]

are physiological consequences of aging and which might be of unrecognized disease origin. The new techniques of molecular biology have great potential in resolving these unknowns.

REFERENCES

1. Katzman R, Terry R: Normal aging of the nervous system, in Katzman R, Terry R (eds): *The Neurobiology of Aging.* Philadelphia, Davis, 1983, p 15.
2. Rogers J, Bloom FE: Neurotransmitter metabolism and function in the aging central nervous system, in Finch CE, Schneider EL (eds): *Handbook of the Biology of Aging.* New York, Van Nostrand Reinhold, 1985, p 645.
3. Morgan DG et al: Dopamine and serotonin system in human and rodent brain: Effects of age and neurodegenerative disease. *J Am Geriatr Soc* 35:334, 1987.
4. Coleman PD, Flood DG: Neuron numbers and dendritic extent in normal aging and Alzheimer's disease. *Neurobiol Aging* 8:521, 1987.
5. DeKaban AS, Sadowsky BS: Changes in brain weight during the life span of human life: Relation of brain weight to body heights and body weights. *Ann Neurol* 4:345, 1978.
6. Duara R et al: Human brain glucose utilization and cognitive function in relation to age. *Ann Neurol* 16:702, 1984.
7. Stafford JL et al: Age-related differences in CT scan measurements. *Adv Neurol* 45:409, 1988.
8. Meier-Ruge W et al: Effect of age on morphological and biochemical parameters of the human brain, in Stein (ed): *The Psychobiology of Aging.* North Holland, Elsevier, 1980, p 297.
9. Mann DMA, Yates PO: Pathogenesis of Parkinson's disease. *Arch Neurol* 39:545, 1982.
10. Cotman CW, Anderson KJ: Synaptic plasticity and functional stabilization in the hippocampal formation: Possible role in Alzheimer's disease. *Adv Neurol* 47:313, 1988.
11. Davis JM, Himwich WA: Neurochemistry of the developing and aging mammalian brain, in Ordy JM, Brizzee KR (eds): *Neurobiology of Aging.* New York, Plenum, 1975, p 329.
12. Finch CE: Enzyme activities, gene function and ageing in mammals. *Exp Gerontol* 7:53, 1972.
13. Wilson PD: Enzyme levels in animals of various ages, in Florini JR, Adelman RC, Roth GS (eds): *CRC Handbook of Biochemistry in Aging.* Boca Raton, FL, CRC Press, 1981, p 163.
14. Uemura F, Hartmann HA: Age-related changes in RNA content and volume of the human hypoglossal neuron. *Brain Res Bull* 3:207, 1978.
15. Hyden H: Biochemical and molecular aspects of learning and memory, in *Biological and Clinical Aspects of the Central Nervous System.* Basel, Sandoz Symposium, 1967, p 17.
16. Uemura F, Hartmann HA: RNA content and volume of

TABLE 88-2
Neurochemical Parameters in Alzheimer's Disease

	Areas																				
	SNA	CAU	PUT	PAL	LC	PONS	THAL	HYP	MAM	AMYG	CING	HIP	CER	NA	CCNE	MIDB	SIN	TCx	OCx	PCx	FCx
Acetylcholine																					
Choline acetyl transferase (Chat)	−	−				−	−	−	−	−	−	−	−	−	−	−	−	−	−	−	−
Acetylcholinesterase	−	−				−	−	−	−	−	−	−	−	−	−			−		−	−
Muscarinic receptor		0	0		0						0							0		0	0
Gamma aminobutyric acid	0	0	0	0				0/−		−								−	0	0	0
Glutamic acid decarboxylase	0	0			0	0	0	0	0	0	−	0	0	−		−	−	−	−		0
GABA receptor		−	0								0							+/−	0		0
Glutamate receptor	0/+	0			0		0														
Noradrenaline		−	−	−		−					−#	−#						−#			0
Dopamine beta hydroxylase												−						−			
Alpha- and beta adrenergic											0							0	0	0	0
Dopamine receptor		0	0								0										0
Serotonin		−				−					−	−									−
Serotoninergic receptor								−	0	−								−		−	−
Somatostatin											−							−		−	−
Substance P											−	−						−	−		−
Oxytocin	0	0		0	0	0					−							−	0	0	0
Cholecystokinin	0	0	0								0							0	0	0	0
Vasoactive intestinal peptide		0	0								0							0	0	0	0
Corticotropin-releasing Factor	−					0	0			0			0					0	−	0	−

Key: SNA: substantia nigra, CAU: caudate, PUT: putamen, PAL: pallidum, LC: locus coeruleus, THAL: thalamus, HIP: hippocampus, HYP: hypothalamus, MAM: mamillary bodies, AMYG: amygdala, NA: nucleus accumbens, CING: cingulate cortex, CER: cerebellum, MIDB: mid brain, SIN: substantia innominata, TCx: temporal cortex, OCx: occipital cortex, PCx: parietal cortex, FCx: frontal cortex. #: young patients (age < 79), CCNE: calcarine cortex. −: Decreased, 0: not changed, +: increased in Alzheimer's disease versus age-matched controls.
SOURCE: Adapted from Terry and Katzman[45] and Morgan et al.[31]

nerve cell bodies in human brain. *Exp Neurol* 65:107, 1979.

17. Rouser G et al: Lipids in the nervous system of different species as a function of age, in Paoletti R, Kritchevsky K (eds): *Advances in Lipid Research.* New York, Academic, 1972, p 261.

18. Horrock LA et al: Changes in brain during aging, in Ordy JM, Brizzee KR (eds): *Neurobiology of Aging.* New York, Plenum, 1975, p 359.

19. McGeer EG, McGeer PL: Neurotransmitter metabolism and the aging brain, in Terry RD, Gershon S (eds): *Neurobiology of Aging.* New York, Raven, 1976, vol 3, p 389.

20. Pradhan SN: Central neurotransmitters and aging. *Life Sci* 26:1643, 1980.

21. McGeer EG: Aging and the neurotransmitter metabolism in the brain, in Katzman R, Terry RD, Bick KL (eds): *Alzheimer's Disease: Senile Dementia and Related Disorders.* New York, Raven, 1978, p 427.

22. Grote SS et al: Study of selected catecholamine metabolizing enzymes: A comparison of depressive suicides and alcoholic suicides with controls. *J Neurochem* 23:791, 1974.

23. Robinson DS et al: Aging, monoamines and monoamine oxidases. *Lancet* 1:290, 1972.

24. Robinson DS: Changes in monoamines oxidase and monoamines in human development and aging. *Fed Proc* 34:103, 1975.

25. Stahl SM et al: CSF monoamine metabolites in movement disorders and normal aging. *Arch Neurol* 42:166, 1985.

26. Seeman P et al: Human brain dopamine receptors in children and aging adults. *Synapse* 1:399, 1987.

27. Morgan DG et al: Divergent changes in D-1 and D-2 dopamine binding sites in human brain during aging. *Neurobiol Aging* 8:195, 1987.

28. Baron JC et al: Loss of striatal (^{76}Br-) bromospiperone binding sites demonstrated by positron tomography in progressive supranuclear palsy. *J Cereb Blood Flow Metab* 6:131, 1986.

29. Wong et al: Effect of age on dopamine and serotonin receptors measured by positron tomography in the living human brain. *Science* 226:1393, 1984.

30. Hess GD, Roth GS: Receptors and aging, in Johnson JE (ed): *Aging and Cell Function.* New York, Plenum, 1984, p 149.

31. Morgan DG et al: Neurotransmitter receptors in normal human aging and Alzheimer's disease, in Sen AK, Lee TY (eds): *Receptors and Ligands in Neurological Disorders.* London, Cambridge University Press, 1988, p 120.

32. Ordy JM et al: Life-span neurochemical changes in the human and non human primate brain, in Brody H, Harman D, Ordy JM (eds): *Clinical, Morphological and Neurochemical Aspects in the Central Nervous System.* New York, Raven, 1975, p 133.

33. Buck SH et al: Survey of substance P, somatostatin and neurotensin levels in aging in the rat and human central nervous system. *Neurobiol Aging* 2:257, 1981.

34. Davies P et al: Reduced somatostatin-like immunoreactivity in the cerebral cortex form cases from Alzheimer's disease and Alzheimer senile dementia. *Nature* 288:279, 1980.

35. Morrisson JH et al: Somatostatin immunoreactivity in neuritic plaques of Alzheimer's patients. *Nature* 314:90, 1985.

36. Rossor MN et al: Neurochemical characteristics of early and late onset types of Alzheimer's disease. *Br Med J* 288:961, 1984.

37. Perry EK et al: Neurochemical activities in human temporal lobe related to aging and Alzheimer-type changes. *Neurobiol Aging* 2:251, 1981.

38. Finch CE: Neural and endocrine determinants of senescence: Investigation of causality and reversibility by laboratory and clinical interventions, in Warner HR, Butler RN, Sprott RL, Schneider EL (eds): *Modern Biological Theories of Aging.* New York, Raven, 1987, p 261.

39. Barbeau A: Parkinson's disease: Clinical features and etiopathology, in Vinken PJ, Bruyn GW, Klawans HL (eds): *Handbook of Clinical Neurology.* New York, Elsevier, 1986, p 87.

40. Schoenberg BS et al: Prevalence of Parkinson's disease in the biracial population of Copiah county, Mississippi. *Neurology* 35:841, 1985.

41. Jellinger K: Pathology of Parkinson's disease, in Fahn S, Marsden CD, Jenner P, Teychenne P (eds): *Recent Developments in Parkinson's Disease.* New York, Raven, 1986, p 33.

42. Campanella G et al: Drugs affecting movement disorders. *Ann Rev Pharmacol Toxicol* 27:113, 1986.

43. Katzman R: Alzheimer's disease. *N Engl J Med* 314:964, 1986.

44. Eslinger PJ, Damasio AR: Preserved motor learning in Alzheimer's disease: Implications for anatomy and behavior. *J Neurosci* 6:3006, 1986.

45. Terry RD, Katzman R: Senile dementia of Alzheimer type. *Ann Neurol* 14:497, 1983.

46. St George-Hyslop PH et al: The genetic defect causing familial Alzheimer's disease maps on chromosome 21. *Science* 235:887, 1987.

47. Bird TD et al: Familial Alzheimer's disease in American descendants of the Volga germans: Probable genetic founder effect. *Ann Neurol* 23:25, 1988.

48. Morrisson JH et al: Anatomic and molecular characteristics of vulnerable neocortical neurons in Alzheimer's disease, in Finch CE, Davies P (eds): *Branbury Report: Alzheimer's Disease.* Cold Spring Harbor, NY, Cold Spring Harbor Laboratory, 1989 (in press).

49. Hyman BT et al: Alzheimer's disease: Cell-specific pathology isolates the hippocampal formation. *Science* 225:1168, 1984.

50. Summers WK et al: Oral tetrahydroaminoacridine in long-term treatment of senile dementia, Alzheimer's type. *N Engl J Med* 315:1241, 1986.

Chapter 89

COGNITION AND AGING

Marilyn S. Albert

Significant changes in cognitive function develop with age. These changes are evident in several major aspects of mental ability. However, declines do not develop uniformly, either within or across cognitive domains. The nature of the change that occurs, the point at which changes become apparent, and the magnitude and rate of change vary, depending upon the cognitive function in question. This chapter will discuss general methodological issues pertaining to the assessment of cognitive changes with age and review recent findings concerning six major areas of cognitive ability: attention, language, memory, visuospatial ability, conceptualization, and general intelligence.

GENERAL METHODOLOGICAL ISSUES

One of the most important methodological difficulties relevant to the study of cognitive change with age concerns subject sampling and generational change. Most studies of aging have been cross-sectional. That is, groups of subjects of different ages are compared with one another (e.g., people in their thirties are compared with those in their seventies). It is now clear that in comparisons of this nature, one is not only contrasting individuals who differ in age but individuals who differ in a number of other important dimensions as well. Persons who are in their seventies today differ widely in early health care and nutritional experience, educational opportunity, and sociocultural expectations from individuals who are in their thirties today. Older persons tend to have either a poorer-quality education or fewer years of formal schooling, in addition to poorer nutrition and early health care. Older individuals generally feel more intimidated in a testing situation than younger individuals for whom testing has been a more recent and frequent experience. These generational or "cohort" differences appear to maximize the age differences one finds in psychological test performance.

In longitudinal testing, the same individuals are repeatedly evaluated over time. Age changes are therefore determined by comparing subsequent test sessions with the baseline evaluation. Since testing intervals are generally separated by many years (e.g., 5- to 7-year intervals), longitudinal studies have great difficulty in recontacting and retesting subjects. The dropout rates in some otherwise well-conducted longitudinal studies are as high as 50 percent. Factors such as relocation, physical illness, cognitive dysfunction, and death contribute to the loss of subjects over time. It has been shown that the subset of the test population that does not return tends to perform more poorly than those who continue to participate in longitudinal retesting.[1] Thus longitudinal studies probably minimize age differences.

In an attempt to resolve the methodological problems of cross-sectional and longitudinal studies, Schaie and his associates[2] developed a testing procedure called a *cohort-sequential design*. In this paradigm, subjects of different ages are tested longitudinally (e.g., at times 1 and 2). A second set of subjects, with the same age distribution as the first, is then tested longitudinally. The first test session of the second group roughly coincides with the second test session of the first group. Thus subjects of the same age, but different cohorts, are evaluated. Age changes can therefore be studied while time of measurement is controlled.

This approach to the study of age-related change represents an important contribution to the field. However, since the cost of such an undertaking is considerable, most investigators continue to employ cross-sectional study techniques. When reviewing the results of these cross-sectional data, one therefore needs to consider how well cohort differences have been controlled and how much they are likely to have contributed to the study results.

The other general issue that should be pointed out with regard to measures of cognition with age is the increasing variability that is evident among individuals in the older age ranges. This is, in fact, not only true for cognition but is also true for physiologic measurements in the elderly. There is both increasing intraindividual and interindividual variability with age. The intraindividual variability is reflected by the fact that within the same individual some functions change and others do not. An individual whose verbal IQ remains relatively stable into the eighth or ninth decade may still show a significant decline in performance IQ. Similarly, an individual whose nerve conduction velocity undergoes little significant change may well have considerable reductions in cardiac output.

Perhaps more striking is the interindividual variability that one observes among people as they age. While the mean value of a particular variable may decline substantially with age, one can find many elderly subjects whose scores fall within the range of individuals 20 or 30 years younger than themselves. Gerontological research has consistently demonstrated that many older persons show little cognitive, physiologic, or functional loss when compared with their younger counterparts, even though the mean for their age group may have declined. Since they have escaped the "usual" aging pattern, these persons have recently been said to represent "successful aging."[3] Although previous research has focused almost entirely on general trends among elderly subjects, it has been argued that more attention should be focused on these "unusual" individuals.[3] The study of successful aging is not merely the obverse of looking for age-related declines. One must ask not only what is maintained with age and why, but what factors enable some individuals to maintain high function even when the average individual is showing declines. If future studies suggest that the factors that contribute to successful aging are under external control, then there is the possibility that gerontologists can contribute to the expansion of the number of people who age successfully in future generations.

ATTENTION

The concept of attention is presently thought to encompass at least three interrelated aspects: sustained attention, or vigilance; selective attention, or the ability to extract relevant from irrelevant information; and attentional capacity, or the total attentional resources available to an individual (see Refs. 4 and 5 for reviews).

Tests that evaluate sustained attention assess an individual's ability to focus on a simple task and perform it without losing track of the object of the task. Memory demands are minimized in tests of sustained attention by limiting the information that needs to be remembered to material that falls within a person's immediate memory span (i.e., 5 ± 2). Digit span forward is the most commonly used test of attention since it is included on both

the Wechsler Adult Intelligence Scale (WAIS)[6] and the Wechsler Memory Scale (WMS).[7] Visual and auditory continuous performance tasks that require the individual to identify a repeating letter (e.g., "A") or a repeated letter sequence (e.g., "I before X") are another common means of evaluating sustained attention.[8]

Numerous studies have demonstrated that tests of sustained attention are performed extremely well into old age. These studies indicate that there is less than one standard deviation of change between ages 20 and 80.

Selective attention is generally assessed by paradigms that require the subject to ignore irrelevant information. For example, a subject may be asked to detect a target as the number of nontargets increases. Earlier studies indicated that older individuals have difficulty in performing tasks that require them to ignore irrelevant stimuli.[9] However, recent studies have demonstrated that this is not the case.[10–12] It seems likely that previous results were related to the perceptual difficulties of older individuals in discriminating targets, rather than attentional difficulties in ignoring irrelevant information.

A variety of procedures have been used to assess attentional capacity. These have typically employed the dual-task methodology in which two tasks must be performed simultaneously. The best-known of these dual-task procedures is the dichotic listening paradigm of Broadbent.[13] In this task, two short series of digits, letters, or words are presented simultaneously through earphones, one series to each ear. The subject is asked to report both series. Dichotic listening tasks have typically shown large age differences, even among subjects in their early sixties.[14–16] However, it has recently been shown[16] that performance on a dichotic listening paradigm which was impaired with age did not correlate with performance on other dual-task paradigms. These data suggest that all dual-task paradigms need not be impaired with age. It is therefore important to determine why divided attention, as assessed by the dichotic listening task, is altered with age while other dual-task paradigms continue to be performed well. One possibility is that dual-task paradigms that require the individual to deal with novel or complex material show age-related decrements while familiar and well-practiced skills do not.

LANGUAGE

Linguistic ability is thought to encompass at least four domains: phonologic, lexical, syntactic, and semantic. Until recently, it was assumed that all linguistic abilities were preserved into very old age, primarily because performance on the Vocabulary subtest of the Wechsler Adult Intelligence Scale, the best general estimate of verbal intelligence, is well maintained until individuals are in their eighties.[17] However, within the last decade, a number of studies have shown that although most aspects of linguistic ability are preserved in the elderly, at least one aspect, semantic knowledge, declines with age.

Phonologic knowledge refers to the use of the sounds of language and the rules for their combination. Phonologic capabilities are well preserved with age.[18]

Lexical knowledge refers to both the lexical representation of a word (i.e., the name of an item) and its semantic representation (i.e., the meaning of a word). The lexicon of healthy older individuals appears to be intact, as are the semantic relationships of the lexicon.[19–21]

Syntactic knowledge refers to the ability to meaningfully combine words. A large number of studies have shown that age has little effect on syntax.[22–26]

The one area of language function that appears to change significantly with age is *semantic knowledge*. One way of assessing the semantic aspects of word retrieval is by testing naming. The most commonly used naming tests entail showing a person a picture of a common object and asking them to produce the name. Several groups of investigators have reported that scores on naming tests such as these decrease with age.[27–30] However, as shown in Fig. 89-1, declines in naming ability do not become statistically significant until subjects are in their seventies.[30]

Verbal fluency also assesses semantic ability. In a verbal fluency task, a subject is asked to name as many examples of a category (e.g., "animals" or "vegetables") as possible in a specified period of time (e.g., 1 minute) or as many words beginning with a particular letter (e.g., "F") within a specified period of time. Several studies report a decline in verbal fluency with age.[30–32] These changes also occur relatively late in the life span

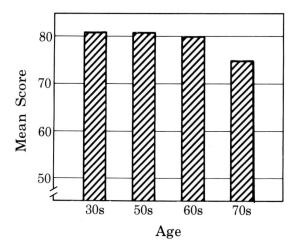

FIGURE 89-1
Performance on the Boston Naming Test by subjects age 30 to 80 years. There is a significant decline in accuracy by subjects in their seventies.

(>70 years). Thus, semantic linguistic ability appears to change with advancing age, while other aspects of linguistic ability are relatively well preserved.

MEMORY

Memory is currently conceptualized as a series of specific yet interactive stores, consisting of sensory memory, primary memory, and secondary memory.[33,34]

Sensory memory represents the earliest stage of information processing. It concerns perceiving and attending to information. It is modality-specific (i.e., visual, auditory, haptic), highly unstable, and characterized by rapid decay (i.e., losses occur after 1/3 second). There is a considerable amount of information to indicate that changes in sensory memory are minimal with age.[35–37] For example, the time necessary to identify a single letter does not change with age.[35]

Primary memory, once called short-term memory, pertains to the ability to retain a small amount of information over a brief period of time. Information must be actively rehearsed to be retained in primary memory. Numerous studies also indicate that primary memory shows few, if any, losses with age. For example, most studies have found no significant age differences in digit span forward,[38,39] no age differences in word span,[40] and moderate differences in letter span.[41]

Secondary, or long-term, memory is viewed as a memory store that can contain an unlimited amount of information for an indefinite period of time (e.g., hours, days, years). In contrast to the minimal age changes in sensory and primary memory, there are substantial changes in secondary memory. The degree of loss is related to the type of material to-be-remembered and the method of assessment. Large age differences are found in free recall.[41–44] When given a large amount of new information to retain over a relatively long delay, individuals show declines in memory at a relatively early age. Figure 89-2 shows the performance of a group of optimally healthy subjects on the delayed recall of two paragraphs from the Wechsler Memory Scale. As can be seen, declines in memory are evident on this task by age 50.[45] Age decrements are, however, greater when subjects are asked to recall information than when they are asked to recognize which of several stimuli they were previously exposed to. This is true whether words,[46] line drawings,[47] or pictures[48] are used.

It should be pointed out that age-related changes in memory also appear to be related to initial intellectual ability, as well as to a person's socioeconomic status and personality characteristics. For example, both Craik et al.[49] and Arbuckle et al.[50] found that the point at which age declines in memory become significant is related to the amount of education and/or verbal intelli-

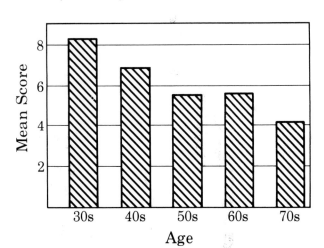

FIGURE 89-2
Delayed recall of paragraphs from the Wechsler Memory Scale by subjects 30 to 80 years old. There is a significant decline in performance by age 50.

gence of the subjects, with the better-educated subjects showing the least amount of change. Arbuckle[50] also found that personality characteristics, such as introversion, were related to performance on memory tests.

VISUOSPATIAL ABILITY

Visuospatial ability, the ability to perceive and function in the spatial domain, is generally assessed by both the production and recognition of figures. Complex visual tasks, such as the ability to identify incomplete figures,[51] the ability to recognize embedded figures,[52] and the ability to arrange blocks into a design,[53,54] show declines in the elderly. Perhaps more importantly, the perception and production of relatively simple three-dimensional drawings is altered with age. For example, Plude et al.[55] asked groups of young and old adults (whose mean ages were 21 and 67, respectively, and who were equated for static visual acuity) to draw a cube to command. The drawings of the young adults were rated as significantly better than those of the elderly. In addition, the older subjects were less accurate than the young in judging the adequacy of drawings of cubes that were distorted to varying degrees. The elderly were also less accurate than the young in discriminating between distorted and undistorted cubes. Thus, both the ability to perceive and reproduce figures in three dimension is apparently altered with age.

CONCEPTUALIZATION

Conceptualization refers to the ability to form concepts, switch from one concept or category to another, generalize from a single instance, and apply rules or principles.

Therefore, tests of conceptualization generally assess abstraction capacities and/or mental flexibility.

A large variety of tests have been developed to examine conceptualization. They include tests of proverb interpretation, reasoning, sorting, and set shifting. Some of these tasks make substantive memory demands and therefore show significant changes with age. However, conceptualization tasks that do not make substantive memory demands also demonstrate age differences. For example, series completion tasks that require the subject to examine a series of letters or numbers and determine the rule that governs the sequencing of the items show significant age-related change.[56–60] Some investigators[60] developed specially constructed series completion problems in order to determine whether declines were related to alterations in the ability to appreciate abstract concepts or to declines in the ability to detect cyclic periodicity. They concluded that age-related alterations on series completion tasks were the result of progressive problems in abstraction and flexibility rather than an inability to detect cyclic periodicity. Consistent with these findings are the results of proverb interpretation tasks, which also show substantial age-related change.[61,62] The greatest age differences appear among subjects in their seventies (see Fig. 89-3).

GENERAL INTELLIGENCE

Intelligence tests examine many of the abilities previously discussed, but they do so in a complex manner. This is because intelligence tests were designed to predict with a reasonable degree of certainty how a person would function in an academic environment. They were not designed as a complete assessment of cognitive func-

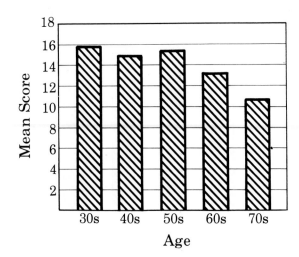

FIGURE 89-3
Performance on Gorham's Proverb Test by subjects 30 to 80 years old. There is a significant decline among subjects in their seventies.

tion. Thus, intelligence tests do not assess all aspects of cognitive ability. For example, the Wechsler Adult Intelligence Scale does not include an evaluation of memory. In addition, IQ tests do not assess cognitive abilities in relative isolation from one another. Many of the tests require a complex interaction of cognitive abilities to be performed well, and they often depend on speed for an adequate level of performance. Nevertheless, intelligence testing has been one of the most widely explored topics in the field of the psychology of aging.

There is widespread agreement that there are changes in intelligence test performance with age. There has, however, been considerable debate concerning both the point at which declines occur and the magnitude of the declines. The age at which decrements are observed appears to be determined by the methodology employed. There is some consensus that relatively little decline in performance occurs until people are about 50.[3,63–66] After this age, results differ depending upon whether cross-sectional or longitudinal methods were employed. The cross-sectional method shows declines of one standard deviation or more beginning about 60.[53,67,68] Over the age of 70, scores drop sharply.[53] The longitudinal method shows declines among subjects beginning in the late sixties. Both methodologies find substantial declines after individuals are in their midseventies. Thus the major difference between the results of cross-sectional and longitudinal investigations is observed between subjects in their early fifties to late sixties. In this age range, the cross-sectional method shows greater age declines than the longitudinal method. Figure 89-4 shows the results of a cohort-sequential study of intelligence conducted by Schaie and his colleagues.[59]

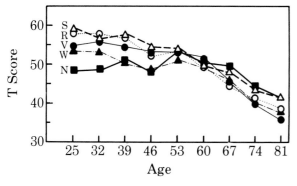

FIGURE 89-4
Factor score changes with age on the Primary Mental Abilities Test derived from a sequential design methodology. The within-subjects analysis showed significant age decrement on all subtests after approximately age 60. The factors on the Primary Mental Abilities Test are: S = space, R = reasoning, V = verbal, W = word fluency, N = number. (From Schaie KW: *The Seattle Longitudinal Study: A 21-year exploration of psychometric intelligence in adulthood,* in Schaie KW (ed): *Longitudinal Studies of Adult Psychological Development.* New York, Guilford, 1983. Copyright 1983 by the Guilford Press. Reprinted with permission.)

SUMMARY

In summary, several aspects of cognitive ability are altered with age. Cross-sectional studies indicate that the earliest change is in secondary memory function: the ability to retain relatively large amounts of information over long periods of time. Subjects in their midfifties are significantly different from younger individuals. Proficiency at constructional tasks, divided-attention capabilities, and general intelligence show alterations in the midsixties. Abstraction and naming ability are significantly different when subjects are in their seventies. Longitudinal findings, where they exist, are comparable, although—as is generally the case with longitudinal studies—declines occur slightly later in the life span.

There is, however, great variability in the degree of cognitive change shown by older individuals. Whereas a sufficient number of older individuals experience change so that the mean of the group is reduced, many older subjects continue to perform as well as subjects many decades younger than themselves. The cause of this variability is unknown. However, it cannot be entirely the result of the presence of clinical disease, since there is an increase in variance with age on the tasks described above, even among optimally healthy older individuals.

There is recent evidence to suggest that at least some of the differences in cognitive function one observes as people get older are related to the structural and functional changes that occur in the brain with age, even among optimally healthy individuals. There are substantial age-related changes in brain structure[69] and brain function[70] among such individuals. Many of these neuroanatomic and neurophysiologic changes are highly correlated with age-related changes in cognition.[45] For example, discriminant scores derived from an analysis of neuropsychological test data in subjects 30 to 80 years of age are highly correlated with discriminant scores derived from measures of fluid volume on computerized tomography (CT) scans in the same individuals ($r = .53$, $p < .0001$). While one cannot conclude on the basis of a correlation that there is a causal relationship between the changes in these measures of brain structure and function with age, these results do indicate that the pattern of change is similar. Subsequent cross-sectional and longitudinal studies should help to further explore the causal relationship associated with these brain-behavior relationships.

REFERENCES

1. Kleemier RW: Intellectual change in the senium. *Proceedings of the Social Statistics Section of the American Statistical Association,* 1962, p 290.
2. Schaie KW, Labouvie GV, Buech BU: Generational and

cohort-specific differences in adult cognitive function: A fourteen-year study of independent samples. *Dev Psychol* 9:151, 1973.

3. Rowe JW, Kahn R: Human aging: Usual versus successful. *Science* 237:143, 1987.

4. Parasuraman R, Davies R: *Varieties of Attention.* New York, Academic, 1984.

5. Hasher L, Zacks RT: Automatic and effortful processes in memory. *J Exp Psychol* 108:356, 1979.

6. Wechsler D: *The Assessment and Appraisal of Adult Intelligence.* Baltimore, Williams & Wilkins, 1958.

7. Wechsler D: A standardized memory scale for clinical use. *J Psychol* 19:87, 1945.

8. Mirsky A: Attention: A neuropsychological perspective, in *Education and the Brain.* Chicago, National Society for the Study of Education, 1978.

9. Rabbitt PMA: An age decrement in the ability to ignore irrelevant information. *J Gerontol* 20:233, 1965.

10. Gilmore GC, Tobias TR, Royer FL: Aging and similarity grouping in visual search. *J Gerontol* 40:586, 1985.

11. Nissen MJ, Corkin S: Effectiveness of attentional cueing in older and younger adults. *J Gerontol* 40:185, 1985.

12. Nebes RD, Madden DJ: The use of focused attention in visual search by young and old adults. *Exp Aging Res* 9:139, 1983.

13. Broadbent DE: *Perception and Communication.* New York, Pergamon, 1958.

14. Clark L, Knowles J: Age differences in dichotic listening performance. *J Gerontol* 28:173, 1973.

15. Braune R, Wickens CD: The functional age profile. An objective decision criterion for the assessment of pilot performance capacities and capabilities. *Human Factors* 27:549, 1985.

16. Wickens CD, Braune R, Stokes A: Age differences in the speed and capacity of information processing: 1. A dual-task approach. *Psychol Aging* 2:70, 1987.

17. Owens NA: Age and mental abilities: A longitudinal study. *Genet Psychol Monog* 48:3, 1953.

18. Bayles KA, Kaszniak AW: Communication and cognition, in *Normal Aging and Dementia.* Boston, Little, Brown, 1987.

19. Howard DV, McAndrews MP, Lasaga MI: Semantic priming of lexical decisions in young and old adults. *J Gerontol* 36:707, 1981.

20. Cerella J, Fozard JL: Lexical access and age. *Dev Psychol* 20:235, 1984.

21. Bowles NL, Poon LW: Aging and retrieval of words in semantic memory. *J Gerontol* 40:71, 1985.

22. Obler LK, Nicholas M, Albert ML, Woodward S: On comprehension across the adult life span. *Cortex* 21:273, 1985.

23. Nebes RD, Andrews-Kulis MS: The effect of age on the speed of sentence formation and incidental learning. *Exp Aging Res* 2:315, 1976.

24. DeRenzi E: A shortened version of the Token Test, in Boller F, Dennis M (eds): *Auditory Comprehension: Clinical and Experimental Studies with the Token Test.* New York, Academic, 1979, p 33.

25. Orgass B, Poeck K: Clinical validation of a new test for aphasia: An experimental study of the Token Test. *Cortex* 2:222, 1966.

26. Noll JD, Randolph SR: Auditory semantic, syntactic, and retention errors made by aphasic subjects on the Token Test. *J Commun Disorders* 11:543, 1978.

27. Borod J, Goodglass H, Kaplan E: Normative data on the Boston Diagnostic Aphasia Examination, parietal lobe battery, and Boston Naming Test. *J Clin Neuropsychol* 2:209, 1980.

28. Goodglass H: Naming disorders in aphasia and aging, in Obler LK, Albert ML (eds): *Language and Communication in the Elderly: Clinical, Therapeutic, and Experimental Issues.* Lexington, MA, Lexington Books, 1980, p 37.

29. LaBarge E, Edwards D, Knesevich JW: Performance of normal elderly on the Boston Naming Test. *Brain Lang* 27:380, 1986.

30. Albert MS, Heller HS, Milberg W: Changes in naming ability with age. *Psychol Aging* 3:173, 1988.

31. Obler LK, Albert ML: Language and aging: A neurobehavioral analysis, in Beasley DS, Davis GA (eds): *Aging: Communication Processes and Disorders.* New York, Grune & Stratton, 1981, p 107.

32. Spreen O, Benton A: *Neurosensory Center Comprehensive Examination for Aphasia.* Victoria, BC, Neuropsychology Laboratory, Department of Psychology, University of Victoria, 1969.

33. Waugh, NC, Norman DA: Primary memory. *Psychol Rev* 72:89, 1965.

34. Tulving E: Episodic and semantic memory, in Tulving E, Donaldson W (eds): *Organization of Memory.* New York, Academic, 1972, p 381.

35. Walsh DA, Till RE, Williams MV: Age differences in peripheral perceptual processing: A monoptic backward masking investigation. *J Exp Psychol (Hum Percept)* 4:232, 1978.

36. Cerella J, Poon LW, Fozard JL: Age and iconic read-out. *J Gerontol* 37:197, 1982.

37. Cerella J, Poon LW: Age and parafoveal sensitivity. *Gerontologist* 76 (Abstract), 1981.

38. Drachman DA, Leavitt J: Memory impairment in the aged: Storage versus retrieval deficit. *J Exp Psychol* 93:302, 1972.

39. Kriauciunas R: The relationship of age and retention interval activity in short term memory. *J Gerontol* 23:169, 1968.

40. Talland GA: Three estimates of the word span and their stability over the adult years. *Q J Exp Psychol* 17:301, 1965.

41. Botwinick J, Storandt M: *Memory, Related Functions and Age.* Springfield, IL, Charles C Thomas, 1974.

42. Kausler DH, Lair CV: Associative strength and paired-associate learning in elderly subjects. *J Gerontol* 21:278, 1966.

43. Gilbert JG, Levee RF: Patterns of declining memory. *J Gerontol* 26:70, 1971.

44. Craik FIM: Age differences in human memory, in Birren JE, Schaie KW (eds): *Handbook of the Psychology of Aging.* New York, Van Nostrand Reinhold, 1977, p 384.

45. Albert MS, Duffy FH, Naeser MA: Nonlinear changes in cognition and their neurophysiologic correlates. *Can J Psychol* 41:141, 1987.

46. Erber JT: Age differences in recognition memory. *J Gerontol* 29:177, 1974.

47. Harwood E, Naylor GFK: Recall and recognition in elderly and young subjects. *Aust J Psychol* 21:251, 1969.

48. Howell SC: Familiarity and complexity in perceptual recognition. *J Gerontol* 27:364, 1972.
49. Craik FIM, Byrd M, Swanson JM: Patterns of memory loss in three elderly samples. *Psychol Aging* 2:79, 1987.
50. Arbuckle TY, Gold D, Andres D: Cognitive functioning of older people in relation to social and personality variables. *Psychol Aging* 1:55, 1986.
51. Danziger WL, Salthouse TA: Age and the perception of incomplete figures. *Exp Aging Res* 4:67, 1978.
52. Axelrod S, Cohen LD: Senescence and embedded-figure performance in vision and touch. *Percept Mot Skills* 12:283, 1961.
53. Doppelt JE, Wallace WL: Standardization of the Wechsler Adult Intelligence Scale for older persons. *J Abnorm Soc Psychol* 51:312, 1955.
54. Klodin VM: "Verbal Facilitation of Perceptual-Integrative Performance in Relation to Age." Doctoral dissertation. St. Louis, Washington University, 1975.
55. Plude DJ, Milberg WP, Cerella J: Age differences in depicting and perceiving tridimensionality in simple line drawings. *Exp Aging Res* 12:221, 1986.
56. Cornelius SW: Classic pattern of intellectual aging: Test familiarity, difficulty and performance. *J Gerontol* 39:201, 1984.
57. Hooper FH, Hooper JO, Colbert KC: *Personality and Memory Correlates of Intellectual Functioning: Young Adulthood to Old Age*. Basel, Karger, 1984.
58. Lachman ME, Jelalian E: Self-efficacy and attributions for intellectual performance in young and elderly adults. *J Gerontol* 39:577, 1984.
59. Schaie KW: The Seattle Longitudinal Study: A 21-year exploration of psychometric intelligence in adulthood, in Schaie K (ed): *Longitudinal Studies of Adult Psychological Development*. New York, Guilford, 1983, p 64.
60. Salthouse TA, Prill K: Inferences about age impairments in inferential reasoning. *Psychol Aging* 2:43, 1987.
61. Bromley D: Effects of age on intellectual output. *J Gerontol* 12:318, 1957.
62. Albert MS: Cognitive function, in Albert MS, Moss MB (eds): *Geriatric Neuropsychology*. New York, Guilford, 1988, p 33.
63. Owens WA: Age and mental abilities: A second adult follow-up. *J Educ Psychol* 57:311, 1966.
64. Riegel KF, Riegel RM, Meyer G: Socio-psychological factors of aging: A cohort-sequential analysis. *Human Dev* 10:27, 1967.
65. Eisdorfer C, Wilkie F: Intellectual changes with advancing age, in Jarvik LF, Eisdorfer C, Blum JE (eds): *Intellectual Functioning in Adults*. New York, Springer, 1973, p 21.
66. Blum JE, Clark ET, Jarvik LF: The New York State Psychiatric Institute study of aging twins, in Jarvik LF, Eisdorfer C, Blum JE (eds): *Intellectual Functioning in Adults*. New York, Springer, 1973, p 13.
67. Green RF: Age-intelligence relationship between ages sixteen and sixty-four: A rising trend. *Dev Psychol* 1:618, 1969.
68. Schaie KW: Rigidity-flexibility and intelligence: A cross-sectional study of the adult life-span from 20 to 70. *Psychol Monogr* 72:462, 1958.
69. Stafford JL, Albert MS, Naeser MH, Sandor T, Garvey AJ: Age-related differences in CT scan measurements. *Arch Neurol* 45:409, 1988.
70. Duffy F, Albert M, McAnulty G, Garvey AJ: Age-related differences in brain electrical activity of healthy subjects. *Ann Neurol* 16:430, 1984.

Chapter 90

DELIRIUM (ACUTE CONFUSIONAL STATES)

Zbigniew J. Lipowski

Delirium, also referred to as "acute confusional states," is one of the most frequently encountered mental disorders in hospitalized elderly patients and, for this and other reasons, holds a "central position in the medicine of old age."[1] Despite its high prevalence and obvious clinical importance, however, this syndrome is often misdiagnosed and has received little attention from investigators.[2,3] The formulation of explicit diagnostic criteria and the introduction of uniform terminology in this area in recent years should help in the diagnosis of this common syndrome and do much to encourage research.[2-4]

DELIRIUM DEFINED

Delirium is an organic mental syndrome featuring global cognitive impairment, disturbances of attention, reduced level of consciousness, increased or reduced psychomotor activity, and disorganized sleep-wake cycle.[2-4] Its onset is acute and the duration brief (usually less than 1 month). The severity of its symptoms tends to fluctuate unpredictably over the course of a day and to be most marked during the night. These features set delirium apart from all mental disorders and reflect widespread cerebral dysfunction. It can occur at any age but is by far most common among the elderly.

FREQUENCY AND IMPORTANCE OF DELIRIUM

Few epidemiological studies of delirium in the elderly have been carried out to date, and the reported incidence and prevalence figures vary widely.[3,5,6] Its re- ported frequency is liable to be different in a geriatric unit as opposed to that in a psychiatric or general medical or surgical ward, for example. A geriatric multicenter British study found that 35 percent of patients aged 65 years and older had delirium at some point during the index hospitalization.[7] About 15 percent of elderly patients admitted to general medical wards are delirious on admission,[3] while 25 to 35 percent of those found to be cognitively intact on initial examination develop delirium during their hospital stay.[3,8] The incidence of the syndrome is positively correlated with advanced age.[9] Nine percent of 2000 patients aged 55 and older admitted to a department of medicine in a university hospital were demented on admission and 41.4 percent of them were also found to be delirious, while 25 percent of all delirious patients were demented.[10] These findings highlight the frequent concurrence of delirium and dementia in the elderly general hospital patients.

Delirium in the elderly is important not only because it is highly prevalent but also because it often constitutes a presenting feature of physical illness or drug intoxication.[1,3,5,6] Should its diagnosis be missed, the patient's underlying medical condition could also remain undiagnosed and untreated, with potentially lethal consequences. In an elderly patient, the syndrome may be the most conspicuous presenting feature of a myocardial infarction, pneumonia, or subacute bacterial endocarditis, for example. The onset of delirium in a demented patient may be mistaken for an exacerbation of the dementia, with consequent failure to diagnose and treat the underlying disease. Delirium has a high mortality, ranging between about 20 and 40 percent, that is, about twice that of comparable nondelirious patients.[3] Agitated, disoriented, or fearful delirious patients are at high risk of sustaining an injury, such as a fracture following a fall, resulting from attempts at escape. They may pull out intravenous catheters or tear off sutures. Moreover, measures commonly undertaken to control their agitation involve parenteral injection of a neuroleptic drug and application of physical restraints. The former may cause serious hypotension, while the latter may result in deep-vein thrombophlebitis and pulmonary embolism.[11] Medicolegal consequences may follow self-injury. Finally, delirious elderly patients are likely to have longer hospitalization, and hence care of these patients is liable to cost more.[8] For all these reasons, prevention of the occurrence of the syndrome, or at least of its more severe forms, should be a primary goal.

CLINICAL FEATURES

The clinical picture of delirium is often protean, and this may result in failure to diagnose it.[2,3,5,6,8,12] As no systematic studies of its clinical features in the elderly have been carried out to date, one has to assume that they do not differ substantially from those displayed by the younger patients; the following account is based on this assumption.

TYPE OF ONSET

Delirium comes on acutely, usually over a period of a few days, and often manifests itself first at night. An elderly patient may develop it more insidiously than a younger one. Prodromal symptoms may herald its onset over the course of several days. They include restlessness, anxiety, difficulty in thinking clearly, insomnia, disturbing dreams, and even fleeting hallucinations.

GLOBAL DISORDER OF COGNITION

This constitutes one of the essential features of delirium. *Global* in this context implies that the main cognitive functions, i.e., thinking, memory, and perception, are all impaired or abnormal to some extent, resulting in what is commonly referred to as "confusion." To put it differently, acquisition, processing, retention, retrieval, and utilization of information for the purpose of learning, problem solving, and goal-directed behavior are all impaired, rendering the person more or less helpless and in need of protective care.[3]

Thinking in delirium is disorganized and incoherent, and the patient has difficulty in directing it at will. In some patients it is dreamlike (oneiric) and rich in imagery and fantasy, while in others it is simply impoverished. The ability to think logically and sequentially, to solve problems, to use abstract concepts, and to plan action is invariably compromised to some extent in these patients. As a result, their grasp of a situation, judgment, and spatiotemporal orientation are impaired. As a rule, they are disoriented as to time—that is, they display an inability to state correctly the date, day of the week, and time of the day. Such temporal disorientation may fluctuate in degree over the course of the day and tends to be most marked at night. It is the first form of disorientation to be exhibited by the patient and the last one to clear up. More severely delirious patients are also disoriented as to place and other persons. Typically, they tend to mistake an unfamiliar place or person for one that is familiar to them. In the most severe cases, they are totally disoriented as to time, unaware of their whereabouts, and unable to recognize their own next of kin.

A form of thought abnormality displayed by some, but not by all, delirious patients is the expression of false beliefs, i.e., delusions. They are most often persecutory, poorly systematized, fleeting, and readily influenced by changing environmental stimuli. The most common type of delusion in delirium is the belief in the veridical nature of one's hallucinations. Confabulations may also be present and are difficult to tell apart from delusions.

Memory in delirium is impaired in all its aspects: registration, retention, and recall. Immediate recall, or short-term memory, is impaired probably as a result of reduced attention span. Both retrograde and anterograde amnesia of some degree are present. Recent memory tends to be more impaired than remote memory, and the patient has diminished capacity to acquire new information. Some degree of amnesia for the experience of delirium after its resolution is the rule.

Perception in delirium is marked by reduced ability to discriminate and integrate percepts. Perceptual disturbances in delirium often include illusions, i.e. mislabeling of sensory stimuli, and hallucinations, i.e., experiences of perceptual vividness that occur in the absence of actual sensory stimuli. About 40 to 70 percent of delirious patients hallucinate[12]; some observers assert that the elderly do so less often than the younger patients.[13] The illusions and hallucinations may involve any sensory modality, but are typically visual or visual and auditory. While common, their presence is not necessary for the diagnosis of delirium. Most patients accept their hallucinations as real, and since such phenomena tend to be vivid and threatening, the patients respond with anger or fear and resulting attempts at fight or flight. Some patients hallucinate only at night and may display difficulty in telling apart their hallucinations from dreams and true perceptions. This form of confusion, if present, is quite typical of delirium. The hallucinations may range in complexity from simple visual and auditory misperceptions to complex scenes, involving animals in motion or human figures.[12]

The above cognitive deficits and abnormalities constitute an essential diagnostic feature of delirium.[4] They tend to fluctuate in severity over the course of a day, being most marked during the night. At any time the patient may be rather lucid for a varying period (lucid interval), only to become severely impaired again at a later time. Such irregular and unpredictable fluctuations of the cognitive impairment in the course of just one day, with nocturnal exacerbation, are strongly suggestive of delirium and are seldom exhibited in any other mental disorder.

GLOBAL DISORDER OF ATTENTION AND CONSCIOUSNESS

Disturbances of the major aspects of attention are invariably present. Alertness (vigilance) or readiness to respond to sensory stimuli as well as the ability to mobilize, shift, sustain, and direct attention at will are always disturbed to some extent. Alertness may be either abnormally increased or decreased, but in either case the selectiveness and directiveness of attention are impaired.[2-4,6,12] Both the predominantly hypoalert and the predominantly hyperalert patient show a reduced attention span, that is, they are distractible. Just as cognitive impairment tends to fluctuate unpredictably over the course of a day, so do the attentional disturbances. Consequently, such patients are more or less accessible and able to respond coherently to attempts to communicate with them. Some writers refer to delirium as "global disorders of attention," implying thereby that attentional deficits and abnormalities are its basic psychopathological feature.[14] Basic or not, these disorders of attention are among the significant diagnostic criteria for delirium and help distinguish it from dementia—another global cognitive disorder.

For about a century, delirium has been regarded as a disorder of consciousness (awareness).[12] The concept of "consciousness," however, has never been defined in a generally accepted manner and its meaning remains ambiguous.[12,15] More specifically, delirium has been considered by many authors to be characterized by, or to be a manifestation of, the so-called clouding of consciousness. This vague and redundant concept implies no more than the presence of global cognitive-attentional deficits[12,15] and has been dropped from the latest edition of the official classification of mental disorders.[4] The classification now speaks instead of a "reduced level of consciousness" as one of the characteristic features of delirium.[4] This concept implies a diminished ability to be aware of one's self and one's environment, to respond to sensory inputs in a selective and sustained manner, and to be able to relate the incoming information to previously acquired knowledge and hence to grasp its meaning.

DISORDERED SLEEP-WAKE CYCLE

Disorganization of the circadian sleep-wake cycle is an essential feature of delirium.[4,12] Wakefulness is either abnormally increased and the patient sleeps little or not at all, or it is reduced during the day but excessive during the night. Typically, but not invariably, the patient suffers from insomnia at night and displays drowsiness and periods of sleep of varying duration during the day. The sleep-wake cycle may be reversed. Night sleep is usually fragmented and reduced, and the patient tends to be restless, agitated, confused, and hallucinating while awake during the night.

DISORDER OF PSYCHOMOTOR BEHAVIOR

A disturbance of both verbal and nonverbal psychomotor activity is the last essential feature of delirium.[4] A delirious patient may be predominantly either hyperactive or hypoactive. Some patients shift unpredictably from abnormally increased psychomotor activity to lethargy or even stupor and vice versa.[3,12,15] This feature of delirium has been described since antiquity[3,12] and has led some more recent writers to propose that two distinct syndromes may be distinguished on the basis of the type of abnormal psychomotor behavior displayed by the patient.[16] According to this viewpoint, alcohol withdrawal delirium (delirium tremens) represents the prototype of delirium generally. By contrast, other writers, including the present one, subscribe to a *unitary* concept of the syndrome and regard both extremes of psychomotor behavior as entirely compatible with its diagnosis.[2,3,12,15,17] Psychomotorically *hyperactive* patients are usually hyperalert, agitated, and hallucinating. By contrast, *hypoactive* patients tend to be hypoalert, drowsy, and less likely to experience hallucinations. The delirium of hypoactive patients is likely to go undiagnosed, as such patients do not disturb the staff. Many elderly patients, especially those suffering from delirium due to a metabolic encephalopathy, are predominantly hypoactive-hypoalert. Some patients display involuntary movements such as a coarse tremor or asterixis.

ASSOCIATED FEATURES

Delirious patients may display a broad gamut of emotions—such as fear, anger, depression, apathy, or euphoria—that make the clinical picture more complex and variable. One of these emotions may predominate or one of them may suddenly be replaced by another in an unpredictable fashion. Sympathetic nervous system hyperarousal, manifested by flushed face, dilated pupils, tachycardia, sweating, and elevated blood pressure, usually accompanies emotional excitement.

COURSE AND OUTCOME

By definition, delirium is a transient disorder, one that seldom lasts more than a month. In an elderly patient it tends to last longer than in a younger one. In the majority of cases the outcome is favorable, and the patient returns to the premorbid level of functioning. In many elderly patients, however, delirium is a sign of terminal illness, one followed by death, and hence an ominous prognostic sign.[3] In an unknown proportion of cases, it is followed by a chronic organic mental syndrome such as dementia.

ETIOLOGY OF DELIRIUM

Delirium is due to one or more organic factors that bring about widespread cerebral dysfunction.[3,4,12] In the elderly, the etiology is often multifactorial.[3] One may distinguish predisposing, facilitating, and precipitating (organic) causal factors.[12] Age over 60 years, brain damage, and chronic cerebral disease with dementia constitute the main predisposing factors.[3,12] Psychological stress, sleep loss, and sensory deprivation and overload may be regarded as factors that facilitate the development of delirium and also help maintain it.[12] The precipitating (organic) causal factors fall into four main classes[2]: (1) primary cerebral diseases; (2) systemic diseases affecting the brain secondarily, notably metabolic encephalopathies, neoplasms, infections, and cardiovascular and collagen diseases; (3) intoxication with exogenous substances, including medical and recreational drugs, and poisons of plant, animal, and industrial origin; and (4) withdrawal from substances of abuse in a person addicted to them, mostly alcohol and sedative-hypnotic drugs. In elderly patients, more than one organic factor is often implicated. Intoxication with medical, especially anticholinergic, drugs is probably the most common cause of delirium in the elderly person. Other common causes include congestive heart failure, pneumonia, urinary tract infection, cancer, uremia, hypokalemia, dehydration and/or sodium depletion, and cerebral infarction involving the right hemisphere.[3,5,6,8,12,14,18–24]

PATHOGENESIS OF DELIRIUM

Three major pathogenetic hypotheses may be distinguished: (1) the neurochemical, (2) the stress hypercortisolemia, and (3) the localizational.[2,3,6,8,12,14,17,18]

General reduction of cerebral oxidative metabolism has been proposed to account for the cognitive-attentional impairment in delirium and for the commonly associated slowing of the EEG background activity.[17] Reduced metabolism results in decreased synthesis of the brain neurotransmitters, notably acetylcholine and adrenaline.[18] Relative deficiency of acetylcholine appears to constitute a major pathogenetic mechanism in delirium, especially in metabolic-toxic encephalopathy.[18]

This neurochemical hypothesis has been supported by experimental studies in which delirium induced by various anticholinergic agents could be reversed by physostigmine salicylate, a cholinesterase inhibitor.[12,25] The central cholinergic system is affected by aging, and even more so by degenerative brain disease, with resulting reduction in acetylcholine synthesis.[26] This factor may partly account for the predisposition of the elderly, especially those demented, to the development of delirium.

Some authors have hypothesized that delirium in the elderly represents a manifestation of acute stress, one induced by a variety of stressors, including the psychosocial ones, and mediated by abnormally elevated plasma levels of cortisol.[27] Hypercortisolemia tends to impair selective attention and information processing.[28] The stress hypothesis needs to be further tested. Finally, some writers postulate that delirium is a global disorder of attention, one caused by acute focal lesions, such as infarction, in the right hemisphere's anatomical substrates of attention.[14,29] Such "narrow localizationism,"[30] however, is unlikely to account for the pathogenesis of delirium, which in the vast majority of cases appears to be mediated by a reduction in brain metabolism as a whole. Such reduction may in some cases result from certain focal cerebral lesions. Future studies using positron emission tomography should help settle this issue.

DIAGNOSIS AND DIFFERENTIAL DIAGNOSIS

The diagnosis of delirium involves two crucial steps: first, its recognition on the basis of history and the essential clinical features and, second, identification of its cause (or causes).[3,12] No specific diagnostic test for the syndrome has yet been devised, and its diagnosis must be made on clinical grounds. Acute onset of global cognitive and attentional deficits and abnormalities, whose severity fluctuates during the day and tends to be highest at night, is practically diagnostic.[2] The cognitive-attentional impairment is elicited and observed at the bedside and may be quantified with the help of one of the commonly used scales such as the Mini-Mental State.[31]

Delirium needs to be distinguished from dementia, a functional psychosis (schizophrenia, mania), and a psychogenic dissociative state.[2,3,12] History of cognitive impairment present for months or years; stable course over the course of a day; relatively normal alertness, attention, and level of consciousness; and lack of concurrent physical illness or drug intoxication all suggest the diagnosis of dementia.[2,3] Delirium lasting longer than a month indicates that the diagnosis should be changed to dementia, fully or partly reversible or not reversible.[32]

An acutely schizophrenic or manic patient may appear to be confused but, on close inquiry, fails to show cognitive deficits, and is more likely to have predominantly auditory hallucinations and systematized delusions.[2] An electroencephalogram (EEG) may help, in that in delirium, in contrast to a functional psychosis or a psychogenic dissociative state, it features diffuse slowing of the background activity.[17] In delirium due to alcohol or sedative hypnotic withdrawal, the EEG usually shows excessive low-amplitude fast activity.[33]

MANAGEMENT OF DELIRIUM

The management of delirium involves two key aspects: first, treatment of the underlying disease condition causing cerebral dysfunction and, second, symptomatic and supportive therapy.[2,3,12] In an elderly patient, all drugs, notably those with anticholinergic action, are suspect; they should be withdrawn or their dosage be reduced. Polypharmacy is contraindicated. The etiology of delirium has to be established by physical, including neurological, examination and selected laboratory tests.[3]

Symptomatic treatment involves treating agitation with haloperidol orally or parenterally, in a dose of 0.5 to 5 mg twice a day.[2,3,12,34] General supportive measures imply ensuring water and electrolyte balance, adequate nutrition, and vitamin supply. The patient needs to be cared for in a quiet, well-lit room. Good nursing care is essential and should feature reorientation, reassurance, and emotional support. Psychiatric consultation is often indicated to help with the diagnosis, management, and medicolegal issues (consent for treatment).[35] Prevention of severe delirium should be the goal in all cases; it has been achieved in many cases of hip fracture, for example, a condition associated with an incidence of delirium as high as 50 percent.[36]

REFERENCES

1. Hodkinson HM: *Common Symptoms of Disease in the Elderly.* Oxford, Blackwell, 1976.
2. Lipowski ZJ: Delirium (acute confusional states). *JAMA* 258:1789, 1987.
3. Lipowski ZJ: Transient cognitive disorders (delirium, acute confusional states) in the elderly. *Am J Psychiatry* 140:1426, 1983.
4. *Diagnostic and Statistical Manual of Mental Disorders,* 3d ed (rev). Washington, American Psychiatric Association, 1987.
5. Beresin EV: Delirium in the elderly. *J Geriatr Psychiatry Neurol* 1:127, 1988.
6. Lipowski ZJ: Acute confusional states (delirium) in the elderly, in Albert ML (ed): *Clinical Neurology of Old Age.* New York, Oxford University Press, 1984, p 277.
7. Hodkinson HM: Mental impairment in the elderly. *J R Coll Physicians Lond* 7:305, 1973.
8. Levkoff SE, Besdine RW, Wetle T: Acute confusional states (delirium) in the hospitalized elderly. *Annu Rev Gerontol Geriatr* 6:1, 1986.
9. Warshaw GA et al: Functional disability in the hospitalized elderly. *JAMA* 248:847, 1982.
10. Erkinjuntti T et al: Dementia among medical inpatients. *Arch Intern Med* 146:1923, 1986.
11. Gillick MR et al: Adverse consequences of hospitalization in the elderly. *Soc Sci Med* 16:1033, 1982.
12. Lipowski ZJ: *Delirium: Acute Brain Failure in Man.* Springfield, IL, Charles C Thomas, 1980.
13. Simon A, Cahan RB: The acute brain syndrome in geriatric patients. *Psychiatr Res Rep* 16:8, 1963.
14. Geschwind N: Disorders of attention. *Philos Trans R Soc Lond [Biol]* 298:173, 1982.
15. Lipowski ZJ: Delirium (acute confusional states) in later life. *N Engl J Med,* 1989 (in press).
16. Adams RD, Victor M: *Principles of Neurology,* 4th ed. New York, McGraw-Hill, 1989.
17. Engel GL, Romano J: Delirium, a syndrome of cerebral insufficiency. *J Chron Dis* 9:260, 1959.
18. Blass JP, Plum F: Metabolic encephalopathies in older adults, in Katzman R, Terry RD (eds): *The Neurology of Aging.* Philadelphia, Davis, 1983, p 189.
19. Flint FJ, Richards SM: Organic basis of confusional states in the elderly. *Br Med J* 2:1537, 1956.
20. Jolley D: Acute confusional states in the elderly, in Coakley D (ed): *Acute Geriatric Medicine.* London, Croon Helm, 1981, p 175.
21. Koponen H et al: Acute confusional states in the elderly: A radiological evaluation. *Acta Psychiatr Scand* 76:726, 1987.
22. Organic mental impairment in the elderly. *J R Coll Physicians* [Lond] 15:141, 1981.
23. Senility reconsidered. *JAMA* 244:259, 1980.
24. Seymour DG et al: Acute confusional states and dementia in the elderly: The role of dehydration/volume depletion, physical illness and age. *Age Ageing* 9:137, 1980.
25. Itil T, Fink M: Anticholinergic drug-induced delirium: Experimental modification, quantitative EEG and behavioral correlations. *J Nerv Ment Dis* 143:492, 1966.
26. Gibson GE et al: Brain acetylcholine synthesis declines with senescence. *Science* 213:674, 1981.
27. Kral VA: Confusional states: Description and management, in Howells JG (ed): *Modern Perspectives in the Psychiatry of Old Age.* New York, Brunner/Mazel, 1975, p 356.
28. Rubinow DR et al: Cortisol hypersecretion and cognitive impairment in depression. *Arch Gen Psychiatry* 41:279, 1984.
29. Mori E, Yamadori A: Acute confusional state and acute agitated delirium. *Arch Neurol* 44:1139, 1987.
30. Miller L: "Narrow localizationism" in psychiatric neuropsychology. *Psychol Med* 16:729, 1986.
31. Anthony JC et al: Limits of the "Mini-Mental State" as a screening test for dementia and delirium among hospital patients. *Psychol Med* 12:397, 1982.
32. Mahler ME et al: Treatable dementias. *West J Med* 146:705, 1987.

33. Brenner RP: The electroencephalogram in altered states of consciousness. *Neurol Clin* 3:615, 1985.

34. Steinhart MJ: The use of haloperidol in geriatric patients with organic mental disorder. *Curr Ther Res* 33:132, 1983.

35. Fogel BS et al: Legal aspects of the treatment of delirium. *Hosp Community Psychiatry* 37:154, 1986.

36. Williams MA et al: Reducing acute confusional states in elderly patients with hip fractures. *Res Nurs Health* 8:329, 1985.

Chapter 91

STROKE
IN THE ELDERLY

Christopher Power and Vladimir Hachinski

This chapter provides a concise review of stroke in the elderly and outlines an approach to understanding and managing stroke.

THE PROBLEM

BACKGROUND

Stroke is a worldwide cause of disability. It is largely a disease of the elderly: 85 percent of the patients suffering from stroke are over 65 years old.[1] It is the third most important cause of death in North America.[2] The financial costs in the United States surpass $7 billion annually,[3] and the human cost is immeasurable.

Clinicians in the past have generally regarded therapy for stroke as a futile gesture. Now, however, scientifically based medical intervention is a reality,[4,5] and extensive epidemiologic studies identifying risk factors have been added to the medical armamentarium in reducing the incidence of stroke.[6,7] On the horizon are some active treatments such as the use of thrombolytic agents in stroke.[8]

The natural history of stroke is, however, not well described, and the actual intravessel changes during stroke in humans are poorly understood. Traditionally, stroke has been thought of in subtypes such as thrombotic, embolic, subarachnoid or intercerebral hemorrhage, and transient ischemic attack (TIA).[9,10] A simpler approach designed to aid in the management of stroke is described in the following discussion (Table 91-1).

Major Stroke

This category includes two major types. Ischemic stroke is caused by either embolism (from the heart or great vessels) or intravessel thrombosis. Stroke due to embo-lism may be associated with secondary hemorrhage. Hemorrhagic stroke is characterized by hemorrhage as the primary event, as in subarachnoid hemorrhage or intracerebral hemorrhage. The approaches to diagnosis and management of cerebral ischemia and of primary hemorrhage are very different.

The Deteriorating Stroke

Worsening of the initial signs and symptoms or the onset of additional signs and symptoms characterize the deteriorating stroke. This condition requires specific attention in diagnosis and management.

TIA and Minor Stroke

TIA or a minor stroke may present a diagnostic problem. The *TIA* is defined as a strokelike syndrome which traditionally resolves completely within 24 hours, although it usually lasts no more than 10 to 15 minutes. In contrast, a minor stroke leaves the patient with minimal residual deficit.

TABLE 91-1
Classification of Stroke

Major stroke
   Ischemia (embolic and thrombotic)
   Primary hemorrhage (intracerebral and subarachnoid)
Deteriorating stroke
   Initial signs and symptoms (exacerbation)
   Additional signs and symptoms
TIA and minor stroke
   Strokelike signs and symptoms which resolve or leave
    minimal deficit
The young stroke (less than 45 years)

The Young Stroke

Stroke before the age of 45 is classed as a *young stroke.* There are special diagnostic considerations which only are relevant to that age group. It is discussed at length elsewhere.

IDENTIFYING THE PROBLEM

The History

As in many neurological conditions, a good history is essential in diagnosing stroke. Specific details of the onset of the stroke and the temporal profile of succeeding events are important in arriving at a diagnosis. Specific features such as unilateral weakness, aphasia, or an accompanying headache are also important. Previous neurological events, such as TIAs, provide useful information in diagnosing stroke as do other details of past medical history, such as hypertension, atrial fibrillation, and ischemic heart disease. Up to 50 percent of stroke patients have suffered from previous TIAs.[10] Anticoagulant use increases suspicion of a hemorrhagic stroke.

The Physical Examination

Physical examination is an important component of the diagnosis of stroke. Auscultation is a useful tool in identifying the site of stenosis in the major arteries. Palpation of blood vessels is not advisable as there is a possibility of dislodging thrombi in major vessels in the neck.

In evaluating the awake patient with stroke, certain features deserve special attention. Hemiparesis may be a key feature in identifying a contralateral cerebral lesion. A thrombotic lesion in the circulation of the anterior cerebral artery will lead to maximal weakness of the leg, while a middle cerebral artery occlusion is more likely to cause a hemiparesis with maximal involvement of the arm. Deep tendon reflexes tend to be increased in the side contralateral to the cerebral lesion, and a positive Babinski reflex is often present. Coordination should be tested with rapid alternating movements. Unilateral incoordination suggests a cerebellar lesion on the ipsilateral side.

In the sensory exam, findings can be subtle. The pattern of sensory loss is useful. For example a unilateral sensory loss which "splits" the trunk is very suggestive of a diencephalic contralateral lesion.

Cranial nerve abnormalities are important in identifying the site of the lesion. In lesions that involve the frontal motor areas, the patient will look to the side of the lesion. In brainstem lesions, the patient tends to look away from the lesion. A pure hemianopsia suggests a lesion in the territory of the posterior cerebral artery (occipital lobe). Facial weakness can occur with a contralatral hemispheric lesion, or an ipsilateral brainstem lesion. Absent or sluggish corneal reflexes may occur

with contralateral hemispheric lesions, or ipsilateral brainstem lesions. Dysarthria usually occurs with brainstem lesions. A brainstem lesion will typically create difficulty swallowing (dysphagia).

A major clue to the site of the lesion will be the presence or absence of aphasia. Most aphasias arise from left hemispheric lesions.[11] There are a number of types of aphasia which are well described elsewhere.[12] In Broca's nonfluent aphasia, the patient's comprehension and ability to repeat are preserved but speech lacks fluency. This form of aphasia arises from damage to the posterior third of the frontal convolution of the left hemisphere. In Wernicke's aphasia, fluency is preserved, but comprehension is poor. This form of aphasia arises from lesions of Wernicke's area in the posterior temporal lobe. A conduction aphasia results from lesions in the arcuate fasciculus (connecting Wernicke's and Broca's areas) and gives rise to profound difficulties in repeating. In transcortical motor aphasia, the ability to comprehend and to repeat are preserved, while fluency is compromised. In transcortical sensory aphasia, repetition and fluency are preserved, but comprehension is limited. In anomic aphasia, the ability to name objects is limited. Anomic aphasia may arise from lesions of the angular gyrus of the left hemisphere.

Lesions in the right hemisphere characteristically produce greater obtundation than corresponding left hemisphere lesions, and often hemi-neglect syndromes. Another cardinal feature of right hemisphere lesions is the lack of emotional modulation in speech, which may be misinterpreted as a form of depression.

The approach to the unconscious patient begins with the assessment of the patient's response to verbal commands. This is followed by evaluating the patient's response to deep pain, both centrally and peripherally. Cranial nerve examination helps identify the site of the lesion. Pontine lesions characteristically give rise to pinpoint pupils, whereas unilateral midbrain lesions give rise to a dilated ipsilateral pupil. The absence of corneal reflex also points to a pontine lesion. Testing for "doll's eyes" or using cold caloric testing may reveal a brainstem lesion. The absence of a gag reflex suggests medullary involvement. Hemispheric lesions can give rise to coma through herniation, with compression of the brainstem due to increased intracranial pressure forcing the entire neuroaxis caudally. Cerebellar lesions can give rise to coma through direct pressure on the brainstem; such lesions also accentuate hydrocephalus. Brainstem lesions usually give rise to coma through direct damage to the reticular activating system.

Laboratory Investigations

Laboratory investigations are important in defining the etiology of a stroke (Table 91-2). The CT scan will deter-

TABLE 91-2
Investigations

I. *Basic*

Complete blood counts—electrolytes, urea, creatinine, prothrombin time, partial thromboplastin time; chest x ray; ECG; CT scan of brain (radioisotope brain scan when CT not available)

II. *Additional* (as indicated clinically)
1. Echocardiogram
2. Holter monitor
3. MRI scan
4. Angiogram

mine if the stroke is hemorrhagic, thus guiding the clinician in choosing the appropriate therapy. CT is also valuable for ruling out other causes of acute neurological deficit, such as subdural hematomas. MRI scan is becoming increasingly available, and may be more sensitive than CT for detecting strokes. Cerebral angiography remains useful when it is necessary to identify the vessels involved. The usual clinical laboratory studies include complete blood count, prothrombin and partial thromboplastin times, electrolytes, urea, creatinine, glucose, ECG, and chest x-ray. Echocardiograms can detect mural thrombi (which are a potential source of emboli) and valvular disease.

Differential Diagnosis

A common misdiagnosis of stroke occurs in patients who have suffered seizures. The seizure may take the form of merely a sensory phenomenon unilaterally. Alternatively, the patient may be left with a hemiparesis following a seizure which is called *Todd's paralysis*. This form of paralysis may last up to 24 hours or more, particularly in elderly patients.[13] Coma may arise not only from stroke, but also from other structural or metabolic causes.[14] Other entities to consider in the differential diagnosis include subdural hematomas due to trauma or an underlying bleeding diathesis. Complicated migraine can give rise to a strokelike picture in which there is hemiparesis. Hypoglycemia should be considered in the differential diagnosis of stroke as it may present with a focal neurological findings. And, finally, trauma should be considered in a patient particularly if little history is available.

MANAGEMENT OF STROKE

GENERAL PRINCIPLES

The management of stroke involves four areas which need to be carefully addressed.[15] The primary area includes general care of the patient to avoid complications and to increase comfort. In this category, specific details

include nasogastric tubes for nutrition, Foley catheters, and frequent turning of the patient to prevent decubitus ulcers (Table 91-3). The second area includes specific treatments, depending on the type of stroke. This includes anticoagulation for a cardiac embolic stroke. The third area is prevention: identifying risk factors for patients who have threatened stroke or who have suffered strokes. The final area in the management of stroke includes rehabilitation (discussed in Chap. 34).

MAJOR STROKE

Ischemia

Blood pressure control is a key feature in the management of stroke. The patient who presents stroke often has hypertension. Immediate control of blood pressure is not necessary as it tends to decrease spontaneously. However, regular monitoring of blood pressure is important. If the blood pressure remains greater than 200 torr systolic or 120 torr diastolic, antihypertensive medications are required.

Hyperglycemia at admission in the stroke patient is also known to be a risk factor, worsening the prognosis.[16] Seizures should be controlled promptly and fluid balance maintained (dehydration avoided).

Osmolar therapy is a well established, albeit short-lived, therapeutic modality in patients with large hemispheric lesions or in patients who are deteriorating acutely due to herniation.[17] Mannitol in a 20% solution is given intravenously usually beginning with 300 ml followed by 150 ml every 6 hours. Since mannitol has a rebound effect, it is usually used as a prelude to surgical decompression.

Anticoagulation has been a controversial therapy in stroke. Initial heparin therapy is felt to be of value in strokes due to underlying embolism secondary to cardiac disease. In our unit, heparin is given as 1000 U/h initially, and the partial thromboplastin time is maintained within the therapeutic range for approximately a week. Patients with suspected mural thrombi due to myocardial infarction are treated preventively with a coumadin

TABLE 91-3
Essential Care of Stroke Patients

1. Regular vital signs with careful monitoring
2. Cardiac monitoring
3. Indwelling catheter*
4. Oxygenation by mask*
5. Intubation*
6. Maintenance of circulation
7. Control of seizures
8. Treatment of infection
9. Maintenance of fluid and nutritional balance
10. Judicious sedation

*As required.

derivative after initial heparin therapy.[18] Patients with atrial fibrillation or severe valvular disease receive anticoagulation treatment throughout their life spans, although there are few clinical trials to support this practice. The risk of intracranial hemorrhage with anticoagulation in cardiac embolism is acceptably small.[19] A recent study suggests that anticoagulants are of little value in managing patients with nonembolic ischemic stroke.[20]

Various new but as yet unproven therapies have emerged recently. These include calcium blockers (nimodipine), which in one study have been shown to improve prognosis in patients with acute strokes when started immediately following stroke.[21] Other, more experimental, therapies include thrombolytic agents such as streptokinase and tissue plasminogen activator. At least two large studies are examining the safety and efficacy of these agents in stroke.[22] Therapies which have not proved to be of value in completed stroke include hemodilution,[23] barbiturates,[24] and steroids.[25]

Hemorrhage

Subarachnoid hemorrhage and intracerebral hemorrhage often progress rapidly and therefore demand immediate diagnosis. A CT scan is the most efficient way to diagnose these conditions. The causes of subarachnoid hemorrhage include berry aneurysm, arterial venous malformation, or a bleeding diathesis. Treatment of the primary hemorrhage involves general measures outlined above in the section on management of ischemia. However, the blood pressure should promptly be controlled. For patients who are severely obtunded and apneic, intubation and care in an ICU setting is appropriate. One should consider mannitol therapy to reduce the risk of increased intracranial pressure and subsequent herniation. Subarachnoid hemorrhage is often a treatable condition particularly in ruptured berry aneurysms. Once the diagnosis is made by CT scan and confirmed, if necessary, by lumbar puncture, an angiogram will permit localization of the aneurysm. Aneurysms may be clipped. The trend is to do so soon after the initial event to prevent rebleeding.[26] In our institution, patients as old as 80 years have been treated surgically for such aneurysms.

The most likely cause of intracerebral hemorrhage in the elderly is no longer believed to be hypertension but congophilic (amyloid) angiopathy.[27] Underlying bleeding diatheses should also be considered, such as DIC, or iatrogenic causes, such as anticoagulants.

If a hemorrhage is small, it often resolves with conservative management. In the case of a large lobar intraparenchymal hematoma, complicated by hydrocephalus or herniation, surgical removal of the clot is appropriate.[28] Craniotomy can be done to remove a clot, or, alternatively, a ventriculostomy may be inserted.

DETERIORATING STROKE

Approximately 30 percent of patients with stroke requiring medical attention improve, 40 percent remain stable, and 30 percent go on to deteriorate following the initial stroke.[29] In the deteriorating stroke patient the presenting signs and symptoms may worsen and additional signs and symptoms may develop.

Patients deteriorate for a number of reasons. Cerebral edema is one.[30] It increases intracranial pressure and can eventually cause herniation. Other causes of progression in a deteriorating stroke include a secondary hemorrhage in an embolic stroke or recurrent bleeding in a hemorrhagic stroke. Hydrocephalus may exacerbate a patient's condition, particularly with a cerebellar or cerebral hemorrhagic stroke.

Systemic causes of deterioration can be important. Cardiac disease can exacerbate a stroke, especially atrial fibrillation with recurrent cerebral emboli, other arrhythmias, and acute myocardial infarction with hypotension.

Other systemic disorders can cause a stroke patient to deteriorate. They include pulmonary embolus, pneumonia (perhaps secondary to aspiration), the syndrome of inappropriate antidiuretic hormone secretion, renal or hepatic failure, and urinary tract infection (Table 91-4).

Patients with strokes are often misinterpreted as having deteriorated after excessive drug therapies. The most notorious agents in the elderly include opiates and benzodiazepines. It is important to use these drugs sparingly in patients with stroke.

The important consideration in a deteriorating stroke is to look for and treat the causes of the deterioration.

TIA AND MINOR STROKE

The signs and symptoms of TIAs are outlined in Table 91-5.[32] The most frequent presentations of a TIA due to carotid artery disease are transient monocular blindness, contralateral weakness and sensory symptoms, and lan-

TABLE 91-4
Systemic Disorders (28 Patients, 25 Percent) Associated with Stroke Deterioration in 112 Patients

Cardiac disorders		15
Serious cardiac arrhythmias	7	
Recurrent cardiac emboli	3	
Acute myocardial infarction	2	
Heart failure	3	
Respiratory disorders		6
Metabolic disorders		3
Other		4

SOURCE: From Hachinski VC, Norris JW: *The Acute Stroke.* Philadelphia, Davis, 1985, p 135.

TABLE 91-5
Diagnostic Guidelines Proposed by the Study Group for TIAs

Carotid TIA

1. Motor dysfunction: weakness, paralysis, clumsiness of one limb or both limbs on the same side
2. Sensory alteration: numbness, loss of sensation, paresthesias involving one or both limbs on the same side
3. Speech or language disturbance: difficulty in speaking or writing; incomprehension of language in reading or in performing calculations
4. Visual disturbances: loss of vision in one eye or part of one eye in a person with previously intact vision; homonymous hemianopia
5. A combination of any of the above

(When sensorimotor manifestations occur, they usually appear all at one time, i.e., without a "spread" or "march" effect.)

Vertebrobasilar TIA

1. Motor dysfunction similar to above but sometimes changing from side to side in different attacks and varying in degree from slight loss of voluntary movement to quadriplegia
2. Sensory alteration: as above but usually involving one or both sides of the face, mouth, or tongue
3. Visual loss: as above but including partial loss of vision in both homonymous fields (bilateral homonymous hemianopia); homonymous hemianopia
4. Disequilibrium of gait or postural disturbance, ataxia, imbalance, or unsteadiness
5. Diplopia, dysphagia, dysarthria, or vertigo: none of these symptoms alone should be considered evidence of a vertebrobasilar TIA
6. Combinations of the above

Symptoms Not Considered TIA

1. Altered consciousness or syncope
2. Dizziness, "wooziness," or giddiness
3. Impaired vision associated with alterations of consciousness
4. Amnesia alone, confusion alone, vertigo alone, diplopia alone, dysphagia alone, or dysarthria alone
5. Tonic-clonic motor activity
6. March of motor or sensory deficits
7. Focal symptoms associated with migraine headache
8. Bowel or bladder incontinence

SOURCE: Adapted from Study Group on TIA Criteria and Detection (Heyman A et al 32).

guage disturbances. The most common symptoms associated with TIA in the vertebrobasilar arteries are bilateral visual blurring, diplopia, ataxia, and dizziness.[31] Uncommon presentations of TIAs include headache, seizures, coma, drop attacks, and transient global amnesia. Transient global amnesia is a syndrome of transient confusion and loss of memory and is thought to involve compromise of the circulation of the posterior cerebral artery.[33]

The differential diagnosis of TIA deserves special attention and includes the following entities. A Todd's paralysis following a seizure will often masquerade as a TIA. Complicated migraine with hemiparesis or aphasia may be misinterpreted as a TIA. In *benign migraine equivalent* in the elderly, symptoms comparable to TIA occur with no clear evidence of any vascular disease. The underlying pathophysiology of this condition is not clear.[34] Tumors and hypoglycemia may also present as a TIA.

The guidelines for investigations of TIA in the elderly are outlined in Table 91-2. Special attention should be paid to cardiac arrhythmias. Holter monitoring should be done. In cases in which diagnosis of TIA is difficult to differentiate from seizure, an EEG may be illuminating. In those patients who are thought to have carotid circulation TIAs and who may be surgical candidates, angiography is essential to establish the degree and site of stenosis in the carotid circulation. At times, in patients with TIAs of the vertebrobasilar circulation, angiography may be useful in ruling out conditions such as basilar tip aneurysms.

Treatment of TIAs is controversial. There are two phases. The immediate phase of treatment of TIA involves patients who are suffering from what are called *crescendo* TIAs. These occur with increasing frequency until a stroke eventually afflicts the patient. Although there are no controlled trials to support anticoagulation of these patients, this is generally thought to be of benefit in preventing a major stroke.

Long-term treatment of TIAs includes the use of aspirin which has been shown repeatedly to be effective in preventing strokes or to reduce the risk of stroke in up to 30 percent of males.[4,5] Recently, ticlopidine has been shown to be more effective than aspirin. The North American Symptomatic Carotid Endarterectomy Trial (NASCET) is examining efficacy of carotid endarterectomy in reducing the risk of stroke in patients with TIAs and stenosis in the carotid circulation,[36] since the benefit of carotid surgery in preventing strokes has not been proved. The results of this trial will not be available for at least another 5 years. Recommendation of a carotid endarterectomy to patients rests largely on the clinician's previous experience as well as on the skills of the surgeon who will be performing the procedure. This is best done in the context of a clinical trial and a program of close control of risk factors and treatment with antiplatelet agents.

CONDITIONS ACCOMPANYING STROKE IN THE ELDERLY— MULTI-INFARCT DEMENTIA

Multi-infarct dementia (MID) has also been called "atherosclerotic dementia," although the term *MID* is preferable because of the low correlation between dementia and diffuse large-vessel atherosclerosis.[37] At the same time it should be noted that patients with large cerebral infarctions frequently are demented.[38] With an increasing number of lacunar strokes associated with hypertension, a steady decline of cognitive function has been observed. The interpretation of white matter changes associated with dementia on CT or MRI scan is an area of intense investigation.[39] A clear understanding of these changes has not yet emerged in part because such changes are common in a significant proportion of "neurologically intact" older people.

The likelihood that dementia is due to a vascular cause may be evaluated by an ischemic score.[40] (See Table 91-6.)

PREVENTION OF STROKE

Major risk factors for stroke include hypertension, heart disease, TIAs and previous strokes, polycythemia, diabetes mellitus, increased fibrinogen, asymptomatic bruits, age, sex, and genetic factors. Less important risk factors include obesity, diet, hypercholesterolemia and hyperlipidemia, smoking, alcohol, and inactivity (Table 91-7). There are no trials that adequately study these risk factors in the elderly.

TABLE 91-6
Ischemic Score*

Feature	Score
Abrupt onset	2
Stepwise deterioration	1
Fluctuating course	2
Nocturnal confusion	1
Relative preservation of personality	1
Depression	1
Somatic complaints	1
Emotional incontinence	1
History of hypertension	1
History of strokes	2
Evidence of associated atherosclerosis	1
Focal neurological symptoms	2
Focal neurological signs	2

*A score of 4 or less suggests Alzheimer's disease, and a score of 7 or more suggests multi-infarct dementia.
SOURCE: From Hachinski VC et al: Cerebral blood flow in dementia. *Arch Neurol* 32:634, 1975.

Over the past 30 years the incidence of stroke has decreased. Controlled studies have correlated the mortality due to stroke with improved control of hypertension.[41–43] These studies are largely based on diastolic blood pressure. There are studies which argue that systolic hypertension is a major risk factor for stroke.[44] It remains to be seen whether therapy for systolic hypertension affects mortality and morbidity related to stroke.

Various cardiac diseases increase the risk of stroke. Both chronic and intermittent atrial fibrillation have been reported to increase the risk of stroke up to fivefold, and atrial fibrillation with valvular disease is thought to increase the risk of stroke by 17-fold.[45] In patients with chronic atrial fibrillation in whom cardiac conversion is not possible, anticoagulation may be appropriate, especially after previous thromboembolic events. Coronary artery disease (myocardial ischemia) and congestive heart failure have also been shown to be risk factors for stroke. Anticoagulation in these conditions is controversial, but prophylactic anticoagulation in acute MI is thought to be of benefit in preventing stroke.[18]

Polycythemia increases the risk of stroke.[7] However, whether lowering the hematocrit reduces the risk remains to be proved. Diabetes has been shown to be an independent risk factor for stroke, but the role of treatment of diabetes in stroke prevention is not established.

One of the most controversial risk factors in stroke is the asymptomatic bruit. From the Framingham Study it has been shown that an asymptomatic bruit is associated

TABLE 91-7
Incidence of Risk Factors in 820 Patients with Completed Stroke Admitted to the Toronto Unit

Risk Factor	Cerebral Infarction (742)	Cerebral Hemorrhage (78)	Matched Controls (98)
Cardiac disease	75%	63%	12%
Hypertension	50%	48%	22%
Diabetes	18%	11%	0%
Peripheral vascular disease	20%	13%	12%
Cervical bruit	22%	9%	2%
TIAs	33%	18%	0%

SOURCE: From Hachinski VC, Norris JW: *The Acute Stroke*. Philadelphia, Davis, 1985, p 260.

with a 2.6-fold increase in the risk of stroke over an 8-year period,[46] and it appears that the degree of stenosis also predicts the risk of stroke.[47] At present, we feel that carotid endarterectomy for the asymptomatic bruit is not appropriate therapy, but this recommendation is subject to the results of ongoing multicenter trials.

TIAs and previous stroke are important risk factors for stroke.[48,49] Antiplatelet agents such as aspirin or ticlopidine reduce the risk of stroke in patients with TIAs.

Elevated fibrinogen is also a risk factor for stroke, but specific therapies directed toward it remain to be evaluated in terms of stroke prevention.[50] Age, sex, and genetic predisposition are also important risk factors (Fig. 91-1). However, there are no specific treatments for these conditions.[49] Studies of risk factors for stroke include both elderly and middle-aged patients. Some of the risk factors may become less important in old age. The most important risk factors warranting special attention in the elderly include hypertension, cardiac disease, and TIAs. These conditions become more frequent with increasing age, and have been shown to be treatable with resultant reduction in the incidence of stroke.

CONCLUSION

Stroke in the elderly is a major medical problem in terms of disability as well as economic factors. Beneficial therapeutic and preventive options are now available. There are few studies on prevention and therapy of stroke focusing specifically on elderly patients. Greater interest in this aspect of geriatric medicine is needed.

REFERENCES

1. Whisnant JP: The decline of stroke. *Stroke* 15(1):160, 1984.
2. Kurtzke JF: Epidemiology of cerebrovascular disease, in Seikert RG (ed): *Cerebrovascular Survey Report, NINCDS*. Bethesda, MD, 1980, p 135.
3. Weinfeld FD (ed): The National Survey of Stroke. *Stroke* 12 (suppl 1):I–71, 1981.
4. The Canadian Cooperative Study: A randomized trial of aspirin and sulphinpyrazone in threatened stroke. *N Engl J Med* 199:53, 1978.
5. A Swedish Cooperative Study: High dose acetylcylic acid after cerebral infarction. *Stroke* 18:325, 1987.

FIGURE 91-1
Risk of stroke, by sex and age. (From National Survey of Stroke. DHEW (NIH) 80-2069, 1980.)

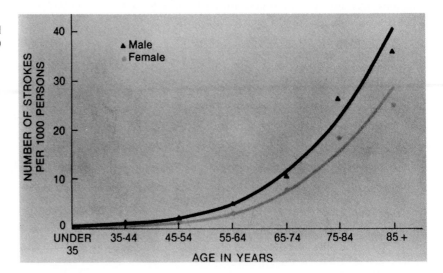

6. Dyken ML et al: Risk factors in stroke. *Stroke* 15:1105, 1984.

7. Kannel WB et al: Hemoglobin and the risk of cerebral infarction. The Framingham Study. *Stroke* 3:409, 1972.

8. Del Zoppo GT et al: Thrombolytic therapy in stroke: Possibilities and hazards. *Stroke* 17:595, 1986.

9. Hachinski VC, Norris JW: *The Acute Stroke*. Philadelphia, Davis, 1985.

10. Mohr JP et al: The Harvard Cooperative Stroke Registry: A prospective registry. *Neurology* 28:754, 1978.

11. Benson DF: *Aphasia, Alexia and Agraphia*. New York, Churchill Livingstone, 1979, p 141.

12. Kertesz A (ed): *Localization in Neuropsychology*. New York, Academic Press, 1983.

13. Adams RD, Victor M: *Principles of Neurology*, 3d ed. New York, McGraw-Hill, 1986, p 231.

14. Plum F, Posner JB: *The Diagnosis of Stupor and Coma*. Philadelphia, Davis, 1982, p 127.

15. Caplan L: A general therapeutic perspective on stroke treatment, in Dunkle RE, Schmidely TW (eds): *Stroke in the Elderly*. New York, Springer, 1987, p 60.

16. Woo E et al: Admission glucose level in relation to mortality and morbidity outcome in 252 stroke patients. *Stroke* 19:185, 1988.

17. Mathew NT et al: Double blind evaluation of glycerol therapy in cerebral infarction. *Lancet* 2:1327, 1972.

18. Ebert RV: Anticoagulants in acute myocardial infarction: Results of a cooperative clinical trial. *JAMA* 225:724, 1973.

19. Furlan AT et al: Hemorrhage and anticoagulation after nonseptic embolic brain infarction. *Neurology* 32:280, 1982.

20. Duke RJ et al: Intravenous heparin for the prevention of stroke progression in acute partial stable stroke: A randomized controlled trial. *Ann Intern Med* 105:825, 1986.

21. Gelmers HJ et al: A controlled trial of nimodipine in acute ischemic stroke. *N Engl J Med* 318:203, 1988.

22. Brott T et al: Very early therapy for cerebral infarction with tissue plasminogen activator (tPA). *Stroke* 19:133, 1988.

23. Matthews WB et al: A double blind trial of Detran 40 in the treatment of ischemic stroke. *Brain* 99:193, 1976.

24. Woodcock B et al: High dose barbiturates in non-traumatic brain swelling: ICP reduction and effect on outcome. *Stroke* 13:785, 1982.

25. Norris JW, Hachinski VC: Megadose steroid therapy in ischemic stroke. *Stroke* 16:18, 1985.

26. Kassel NF et al: The international study on the timing of aneurysm surgery—an update. *Stroke* 15:466, 1984.

27. Gilbert JJ, Vinters HV: Cerebral amyloid angiopathy: Incidence and complications in the aging brain. II. The distribution of amyloid vascular changes. *Stroke* 14:924, 1983.

28. Hewleg-Larsen S et al: Prognosis for patients treated conservatively for spontaneous intracerebral hematomas. *Stroke* 15:1045, 1984.

29. Hachinski VC, Norris JW: The deteriorating stroke, in Meyer JS et al (eds): *Cerebral Vascular Disease*. Amsterdam, Excerpta Medica, 1980, p 315.

30. Bruce DA, Hertig, HI: Incidence, course and significance of cerebral edema associated with cerebral infarction, in Price TR, Nelson E (eds): *Cerebrovascular Diseases*. New York, Raven Press, 1979, p 91.

31. Futty DE et al: Cooperative study of hospital frequency and character of transient attacks vs. symptom analysis. *JAMA* 238:2386, 1977.

32. Study Group on TIA Criteria and Detection (Heyman A et al): xi. Transient focal cerebral ischemia: Epidemiological and clinical aspects. *Stroke* 5:277, 1974.

33. Victor M et al: Memory loss with lesions of the hippocampal formation. *Arch Neurol* 5:244, 1961.

34. Fisher CM: Late life migraine accompaniments as a cause of unexplained transient ischemic attacks. *Can J Neurol Sci* 7:9, 1980.

35. Gent M et al: The Canadian American Ticlopidine Study (CATS) in thromboembolic stroke. *N Engl J Med* (submitted).

36. North American Symptomatic Carotid Endarterectomy Study Group: Carotid endarterectomy: Three critical evaluations (Editorial). *Stroke* 18:987, 1987.

37. Worm-Peterson J, Pakkenburg H: Atherosclerosis of cerebral arteries, pathological and clinical correlations. *J Gerontol* 23:445, 1968.

38. Tomlinson BE et al: Observations on the brains of demented old people. *J Neurol Sci* 11:205, 1970.

39. Hachinski VC et al: Leuko-araiosis. *Arch Neurol* 44:21, 1987.

40. Hachinski VC et al: Cerebral blood flow in dementia. *Arch Neurol* 32:632, 1975.

41. Dyken ML: Symptoms, epidemiology and risk factors, in Dunkle R, Schmidley JW (eds): *Stroke in the Elderly*. New York, Springer, 1987, p 3.

42. Medical Research Council Working Body: MRC trial of treatment of mild hypertension: Principal results. *Br Med J* 291:97, 1985.

43. European Working Party on high blood pressure in the elderly: Mortality and morbidity results. *Lancet* 1:1349, 1985.

44. Kannel WB et al: Systolic blood pressure arterial rigidity and risk of stroke—The Framingham Study. *JAMA* 245:1225, 1981.

45. Wolf PA et al: Epidemiologic assessment of chronic atrial fibrillation and the risk of stroke—The Framingham Study. *Neurology* 28:973, 1978.

46. Wolf PA et al: Asymptomatic carotid bruit and risk of stroke—The Framingham Study. *JAMA* 245:1442, 1981.

47. Chambers BR, Norris JW: Outcome in patients with asymptomatic neck bruits. *N Engl J Med* 315:860, 1986.

48. Wolf PA et al: Current status of risk factors for stroke, in Barnett HJM (ed): *Neurologic Clinics*. Philadelphia, Saunders, 1983, vol 1, p 315.

49. Robins M, Baum HM: The National Survey of Stroke: Incidence. *Stroke* 12 (suppl 1):I-45, 1981.

50. Wilhelmson L et al: Fibrinogen as a risk factor for stroke and myocardial infarction. *N Engl J Med* 311:501, 1984.

Chapter 92

ALZHEIMER'S DISEASE

Richard Mayeux

Alzheimer's disease is the most common cause of dementia in the elderly and is consistently the most frequent postmortem diagnosis for those entering a hospital with dementia.[1] This progressive disabling degenerative process accounted for the majority of those persons found to be demented in a small Midwestern community over a 4-year period.[2]

Alois Alzheimer described this illness as a specific disease over 80 years ago,[3] but many of its pathological features had been recognized before that time. Although the disease was originally considered primarily as a cause of presenile dementia, in 1964 pioneering investigations by Terry and associates[4] indicated that Alzheimer's disease was also the cause of senile dementia. Roth and associates[5,6] observed a relationship between the severity of dementia during life and the quantity of the defining pathological changes at death in elderly psychiatric patients. In 1975, Katzman[7] brought the "malignancy" of the condition to the attention of clinicians, and he and others[8] warned of an impending epidemic in the future. This prediction was based on two parallel observations: Alzheimer's disease rapidly increases in frequency after the age of 60, and in most industrialized countries life expectancy is increasing.

Most clinicians are aware of the devastating effects of Alzheimer's disease. Currently, it has been proposed that life expectancy is halved,[9] that the quality of life is reduced for the patient and family,[10] and that the cost of health care is exorbitantly high.[11] However, basic and clinical research in Alzheimer's disease has increased significantly, resulting in a proliferation of information regarding early manifestations and the natural history of the disorder, improved diagnostic methods and management, as well as insight into the pathogenesis of what Lewis Thomas has referred to as the "disease of the century."

CLINICAL DIAGNOSIS

The most consistent symptom and finding in patients with Alzheimer's disease is memory loss. However, memory loss is seldom the only feature. A gradual decline in intellectual function that is also progressive is the hallmark and an essential component of the criteria for primary degenerative dementia in the revised third edition of the *Diagnostic and Statistical Manual of Mental Disorders* (Table 92-1).[12] Other features include impairment in orientation, judgment and problem solving, language, and perception. A joint work group of the National Institute of Communicative Disorders and Stroke and the Alzheimer's Disease and Related Disorders Association (NINCDS-ADRDA)[13] extended these criteria to enable clinicians to have a range of certainty in the diagnosis of Alzheimer's disease: probable, possible, and definite (Table 92-2). Postmortem studies have validated these criteria.[14]

A diagnosis of probable Alzheimer's disease is suggested for patients between ages 40 and 90 who, in the absence of systemic diseases or other brain disorders which might cause dementia or altered conciousness, are found to have intellectual decline that can be documented by neuropsychological tests. Memory and at least one of the following higher brain functions—judgment, language, perception, or cognition—must be defective. In patients whose laboratory studies are generally normal, lack of the ability to be independent in activities of daily living, and associated symptoms such as depression, hallucinations, and outbursts of irrational verbal or physical behavior, also support the diagnosis. A diagnosis of possible Alzheimer's disease is used when a second condition is present that might contribute to the dementia but is not considered to be a causal factor.[13] A diagnosis of definite Alzheimer's disease is reserved for

TABLE 92-1
Characteristics of Dementia

A. Demonstrable evidence of impairment in short- and long-term memory. Impairment in short-term memory (inability to learn new information) may be indicated by inability to remember three objects after five minutes. Long-term memory impairment (inability to remember information that was known in the past) may be indicated by inability to remember past personal information (e.g., what happened yesterday, birthplace, occupation) or facts of common knowledge (e.g., past Presidents, well-known dates).

B. At least one of the following:

   (1) impairment in abstract thinking, as indicated by inability to find similarities and differences between related words, difficulty in defining words and concepts, and other similar tasks

   (2) impaired judgment, as indicated by inability to make reasonable plans to deal with interpersonal, family, and job-related problems and issues

   (3) other disturbances of higher cortical function, such as aphasia (disorder of language), apraxia (inability to carry out motor activities despite intact comprehension and motor function), agnosia (failure to recognize or identify objects despite intact sensory function), and "constructional difficulty" (e.g., inability to copy three-dimensional figures, assemble blocks, or arrange sticks in specific designs)

   (4) personality change, i.e., alteration or accentuation of premorbid traits

C. The disturbance in A and B significantly interferes with work or usual social activities or relationships with others.

D. Not occurring exclusively during the course of Delirium.

E. Either (1) or (2):

   (1) there is evidence from the history, physical examination, or laboratory tests of a specific organic factor (or factors) judged to be etiologically related to the disturbance

   (2) in the absence of such evidence, an etiologic organic factor can be presumed if the disturbance cannot be accounted for by any nonorganic mental disorder, e.g., Major Depression accounting for cognitive impairment

SOURCE: Reprinted from Ref. 12, with permission.

patients in whom the clinical criteria are met and for whom there is confirmation of the diagnosis by pathological evidence found at autopsy or with brain biopsy.

These clinical criteria and other similar criteria[15] used for research are remarkably accurate during life at predicting those patients who will have the characteristic pathological changes in the brain at death. Because of the ease with which these criteria can be adapted to the examination of patients with dementia, the clinician can develop a routine examination that will assure an accurate diagnosis of Alzheimer's disease in demented patients over 85 percent of the time.

COGNITIVE AND BEHAVIORAL MANIFESTATIONS

Memory loss is the most common presenting feature of Alzheimer's disease, but change in personality or impairment in ability to perform demanding intellectual tasks such as calculations may herald the onset. Nonetheless, memory for recent events and the ability to learn new information are affected and deteriorate over time. Recall of past events and previously acquired information may also be defective. Orientation to time and place may become a problem near or at the time of disease onset. On examination, the patient may have difficulty learning a name and address or a list of words. Recall of memorable events may be spotty and even grossly impaired.

Language impairment is also prevalent among patients with Alzheimer's disease.[16,17] Anomia, or word-finding difficulty, often begins with the onset of dementia. Cummings and associates[16] have reported a progression to a transcortical, sensory-like aphasia in most patients. Severe language disturbance has been associated with a poor prognosis[18] and is often present in familial Alzheimer's disease.[19] Some consider the aphasia of Alzheimer's disease to be rather specific, distinguishing it from dementia associated with stroke or with Parkinson's disease.[20] It is also critical to separate the syndrome of progressive aphasia without dementia[21,22] from aphasia associated with dementia because of its better prognosis. This rare disorder has a pattern of impairment that does not include memory loss; brain imaging and pathology support the focal nature of this disorder.[22]

Patients with Alzheimer's disease manifest a visuospatial disturbance often characterized by difficulty getting around the neighborhood or house. Simple constructional tasks can be disturbed, such as drawing the face of a clock, as illustrated in Fig. 92-1.[23] In fact, a full "parietal lobe syndrome" can be present.[24] "Dressing apraxia," difficulty following directions, and getting lost in a familiar place are each a type of visuospatial disorder that occurs with Alzheimer's disease.

The loss of interest in activities such as personal habits or community affairs parallels the intellectual decline. This may be a result of the dementia, but many patients become apathetic before dementia is severe. When apathy with depression is present, the diagnosis can be confusing because of the resemblance to dementia. However, depression occurs in about one-third of patients with clinically diagnosed Alzheimer's disease.[25]

TABLE 92-2
Criteria for Clinical Diagnosis of Alzheimer's Disease

I. The criteria for the clinical diagnosis of PROBABLE Alzheimer's disease include:

    dementia established by clinical examination and documented by the Mini-Mental Test,[28] Blessed Dementia Scale,[6] or some similar examination, and confirmed by neuropsychological tests;

    deficits in two or more areas of cognition;

    progressive worsening of memory and other cognitive functions;

    no disturbance of consciousness;

    onset between ages 40 and 90, most often after age 65; and

    absence of systemic disorders or other brain diseases that in and of themselves could account for the progressive deficits in memory and cognition.

II. The diagnosis of PROBABLE Alzheimer's disease is supported by:

    progressive deterioration of specific cognitive functions such as language (aphasia), motor skills (apraxia), and perception (agnosia);

    impaired activities of daily living and altered patterns of behavior;

    family history of similar disorders, particularly if confirmed neuropathologically; and

    laboratory results of

        normal lumbar puncture as evaluated by standard techniques,

        normal pattern or nonspecific changes in EEG, such as increased slow-wave activity, and

        evidence of cerebral atrophy on CT with progressive documented by serial observation.

III. Other clinical features consistent with the diagnosis of PROBABLE Alzheimer's disease, after exclusion of causes of dementia other than Alzheimer's disease, include:

    plateaus in the course of progression of the illness;

    associated symptoms of depression, insomnia, incontinence, delusions, illusions, hallucinations, catastrophic verbal, emotional, or physical outbursts, sexual disorders, and weight loss;

    other neurologic abnormalities in some patients, especially with more advanced disease and including motor signs such as increased muscle tone, myoclonus, or gait disorder.

    seizures in advanced disease; and

    CT normal for age.

IV. Features that make the diagnosis of PROBABLE Alzheimer's disease uncertain or unlikely include:

    sudden, apoplectic onset;

    focal neurologic findings such as hemiparesis, sensory loss, visual field deficits, and incoordination early in the course of the illness; and

    seizures or gait disturbances at the onset or very early in the course of the illness.

V. Clinical diagnosis of POSSIBLE Alzheimer's disease:

    may be made on the basis of the dementia syndrome, in the absence of other neurologic, psychiatric, or systemic disorders sufficient to cause dementia, and in the presence of variations in the onset, in the presentation, or in the clinical course;

    may be made in the presence of a second systemic or brain disorder sufficient to produce dementia, which is not considered to be *the* cause of the dementia; and

    should be used in research studies when a single, gradually progressive severe cognitive deficit is identified in the absence of other identifiable cause.

VI. Criteria for diagnosis of DEFINITE Alzheimer's disease are:

    the clinical criteria for probably Alzheimer's disease and

    histopathologic evidence obtained from a biopsy or autopsy.

VII. Classification of Alzheimer's disease for research purposes should specify features that may differentiate subtypes of the disorder, such as:

    familial occurrence;

    onset before age of 65;

    presence of trisomy-21; and

    coexistence of other relevant conditions such as Parkinson's disease.

SOURCE: Reprinted from Ref. 13, with permission.

Delusions and hallucinations are prevalent in patients with Alzheimer's disease and may be associated with a more rapid decline in function.[26] The delusions are usually simple in content and may or may not be of a paranoid type.[27] Abusive or belligerent behavior can accompany delusions, occur independently or in tandem, and pose serious management problems.[27]

Most of these cognitive and behavioral manifestations can be observed during a routine office visit or bedside examination, but the clinical history should be obtained from the patient's spouse, a relative, or a companion. A few brief scales are available and are useful guides for the assessment of cognition, but most do not include the neurological or medical examinations or methods necessary to identify depression and psychosis. Excellent brief cognitive scales include the Mini-Mental State Examination,[28] the Blessed Dementia Rating Scale,[6] and the Orientation-Memory-Concentration

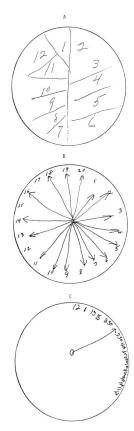

FIGURE 92-1
Examples of clocks drawn by three patients with Alzheimer's disease. There is a general disorganization and tendency to perseverate numbers and "hands." Spatial neglect is suggested in clock C. (*Clock samples provided by Gerald Dal Pan, M.D., Hospital of University of Pennsylvania.*[23])

test.[29] The Alzheimer's Disease Rating Scale[30] has the advantage of including some questions regarding behavior. In general, these scales are quite valid measures and are reliable for clinical use. The Clinical Dementia Rating Scale is also a good measure of severity in patients with Alzheimer's disease.[31]

PHYSICAL MANIFESTATIONS

Most often patients with Alzheimer's disease appear to be in excellent health. However, this appearance can be deceptive because research criteria for diagnosis often exclude other metabolic diseases and disorders that can be associated with dementia. Patients with stroke[32] and those with Parkinson's disease[33] can also develop Alzheimer's disease. In the NINCDS-ADRDA classification,[13] patients with coexisting or possibly contributing disorders are classified as having possible Alzheimer's disease.

The neurological examination changes very little as Alzheimer's disease continues its devastating effect on the intellectual functions of the brain.[34] The cranial nerves, sensation, and gross motor functions remain in-

tact, but primitive reflexes or "frontal release" signs and some higher sensory functions, such as smell, may be impaired. Muscle tone may be increased, resulting in rigidity, a plastic-like resistance to passive movement.[35] This type of rigidity may or may not be accompanied by a stooped posture resembling parkinsonism. This feature occurs in about one-third of patients and may be associated with a greater severity of illness.[36] There are accompanying changes in the substantia nigra in these patients which suggest an overlap between Parkinson's disease and Alzheimer's disease.[37]

Myoclonus (rapid, brief, irregular muscle jerks) occur in 10 to 15 percent of patients, and these movements are also associated with greater severity of disease.[35] Myoclonus can vary from random simple movements of a muscle to gross regular movements of limbs and trunk.[38] Seizures, both myoclonic and generalized, may occur in as many as 20 percent of patients and may coexist in the same person.[39]

Some of the physical signs mentioned above have pathological and biochemical correlates in the brain which will be described later, but, more importantly, may have predictive power with regard to prognosis. Stern and associates[36] and others[37,40] have found that patients diagnosed as having probable Alzheimer's disease who have these signs progress more rapidly in terms of cognitive and functional disability than patients in whom these signs do not appear.

LABORATORY STUDIES

There have been several attempts to identify a consistent peripheral marker for Alzheimer's disease[41–43]; so far, no marker is available. Analysis of blood chemistries and the hematological profile are performed as screens to eliminate metabolic diseases associated with dementia, such as hypothyroidism and combined systems disorder.

The cerebrospinal fluid obtained by lumbar puncture is normal in Alzheimer's disease, and some have advocated eliminating it from the routine clinical assessment of dementia.[44,45] However, this might conceal the condition of the rare patient with cryptococcal or other fungal meningitis or of the patient with an occult malignancy.

Standard brain imaging, such as skull radiographs, computed tomography, or magnetic resonance, offers little specific information in the diagnosis of Alzheimer's disease. However, these studies are part of a standard workup intended to exclude stroke or tumor as a cause of dementia.

Experimental brain imaging techniques, such as positron emission tomography (PET)[46] and single photon emission computed tomography (SPECT),[47] are newer techniques that use labeled compounds such as glucose to determine the metabolic activity in the brains of living patients with Alzheimer's disease. Investigators have identified an area of reduced metabolic activity at the junction of the temporal, parietal, and occipital areas of both cerebral hemispheres.[46,47] The pathogenesis of this metabolic defect is unknown, but it is consistently identified. The expense and technology required to use these instruments may limit their use on a wide scale for diagnosis. In contrast, regional cerebral blood flow, which uses radioactive xenon to measure cortical perfusion, and, indirectly, metabolic activity, is less expensive and requires less technical expertise. The same focal defect described above for PET and SPECT is identifiable in confirmed cases of Alzheimer's disease.[48] More recently, regional cerebral blood flow has been suggested for use in the early stage of the diagnostic process.[49]

The electroencephalogram (EEG) measures cortical function, but its usefulness in the diagnosis and management of dementia is questionable. The EEG changes during the aging process. For example, the mean alpha rhythm for young adults is approximately 10 to 10.5 Hz, but for an older person (70 to 80 years of age) it averages between 8.5 to 9 Hz.[50] Conversely, beta activity, which occurs at a rate of about 18 to 30 Hz in young and elderly subjects, persists with age. Activities normally infrequent in the EEG of the young adult, such as theta and delta rhythm, are commonly reported over temporal regions, particularly on the left, in people over the age of 60.[50] The EEG in Alzheimer's disease shows a reduction in the posterior dominant alpha rhythm in proportion to the severity of dementia and may have some predictive utility.[51] As the severity of dementia increases, mild and intermittent reduction in the posterior rhythm to 7 Hz and then to theta and delta rhythms occurs. Generalized slowing of all cerebral activity occurs with progression. Other neurophysiologic measures, such as contingent negative variation, P-300 waves, evoked potentials, and computerized electroencephalography, may prove to be useful in the diagnosis of dementia, but the application of these techniques in the diagnosis is still under investigation.[52]

EPIDEMIOLOGY

The prevalence of clinically diagnosed Alzheimer's disease has been reviewed by Rocca et al.[53] and is summarized in Table 92-3. For people 65 years of age and older the prevalence ranged from 390/100,000 in Turku, Finland,[54] to 5800/100,000 in Great Britain.[55] This wide variation in rates probably reflects differences in diagnostic criteria and case ascertainment. Nonetheless, the age-specific prevalence of clinically diagnosed Alzheimer's disease increases with each decade. In nearly all the studies mentioned in Table 92-3 the prevalence rate more than doubles between the sixth and eighth decades of life. Because of the increase in the population over 65 years of age, a dramatic increase in the prevalence of Alzheimer's disease is anticipated over the next several years in developed countries. In France, for example, a 9 percent increase in the prevalence is expected by the year 2000, while in Japan a 76.6 percent increase is projected. The United States falls in the middle, at 42 percent.[53]

The incidence of clinically diagnosed Alzheimer's disease also rises acutely with advanced age.[53] Table 92-4 summarizes six major studies of the incidence of Alzheimer's disease. The age-specific incidence rates for all people over 60 again varied but was alarmingly high, ranging from about 69.4 new cases of Alzheimer's disease per 100,000 annually in Finland[54] to 260 cases per 100,000 annually in the United States. The differences in rates have been attributed to the inclusion of other diagnoses, such as senile psychosis and multi-infarct dementia. A more recent investigation used strict diagnostic criteria for dementia and found an incidence rate of 123.2 per 100,000 annually in Rochester, Minnesota, for people over 30 years of age.[2]

There may be cultural or ethnic differences in the prevalence and incidence rates of Alzheimer's disease. Treves et al.[56] found higher rates of Alzheimer's disease occurring before age 60 among European Jews than among the Afro-Asian-born Jews in Israel. In Copiah

TABLE 92-3
Prevalence of Clinically Diagnosed Alzheimer's Disease

Location	Year(s)	Population	Age Range (Years)	Prevalence Rates
Great Britain	1960–4	Urban (rs)*	>65	4200/100,000
Sweden	1964	Rural (cs)	>60	740/100,000
Japan	1965	Urban (rs)	>65	1900/100,000
Great Britain	1970	Urban (rs)	>65	5800/100,000
Finland	1976	Urban (pb)	>45	390/100,000
Finland	1977–80	Population	>30	900/100,000
		representative	>65	3600/100,000
United States	1978	Rural population	>40	500/100,000

*Please note: (rs) means random sample, (cs) means complete survey, and (pb) means population based.
SOURCE: This table was adapted from Rocca et al: Epidemiology of clinically diagnosed Alzheimer's disease. *Ann Neurol* 19:415, 1986.

TABLE 92-4
Incidence Rates of Clinically Diagnosed Alzheimer's Disease

Location	Year(s)	Population	Age Range (Years)	Incidence Rates
Sweden	1964	Rural (cs)*	>60	127/100,000 py
United States	1958–78	Cohort	>60	260/100,000 py†
Finland	1973–6	Urban population	>45	69.4/100,000 py
Israel	1974–8	Hospital population‡	40–60	2.4/100,000 py
United States	1960–4	Urban	>30	123/100,000 py

*Please note: (cs) means complete survey and py means person-years.
†Calculated from Table 8-2 in Ref. 58.
‡Refers to a hospital-based study in Israel using the National Disease Registry.

county, the prevalence of severe dementia was slightly higher for blacks and for women than for whites or men.[57] Neither study has been replicated.

RISK FACTORS

The analytic studies examining risk factors for Alzheimer's disease are complicated by the potential misdiagnosis of patients, as well as the difficulty in obtaining historical information because informants other than the patient need to be interviewed. In spite of these complications, a few putative risk factors have consistently emerged and are listed in Table 92-5. Family history of dementia is an important risk factor, but the relationship between head injury and thyroid disease has not been confirmed.[58,59] There is an increased frequency of Down's syndrome in the families of patients with Alzheimer's disease,[60,61] and the majority of Down's syndrome patients develop clinical and pathological Alzheimer's disease.[62]

An important risk factor is family history of dementia, particularly in a sibling. For many years it was recognized that Alzheimer's disease occurred in an autosomal dominant pattern in some families, but this was considered unusual. In some families with early onset Alzheimer's disease, 50 percent of their relatives are affected in subsequent generations. Breitner and colleagues[63] have suggested that the "morbid risk" (the likelihood of developing Alzheimer's disease) by a given age can be as high

TABLE 92-5
Putative Risk Factors for Alzheimer's Disease

1. Family history of dementia (OR[a] = 2.6 to 11)
2. Down's syndrome (OR = 4)
3. Maternal age (OR = 0.4 to 4.7*)
4. Head injury (OR = 4.5 to 5.3*)
5. Thyroid disease (OR = 2.3 to 3.5*)

[a]Please note: OR indicates the odds ratio or the odds risk ratio. This is the odds of Alzheimer's disease given the risk factor. The * implies that the confidence of this calculation is not always statistically significant.
SOURCE: This table was adapted from Table 4 of Rocca et al.[53]

as 50 percent if all family members are followed long enough, as noted in the graph in Fig. 92-2. Because the cumulative incidence of clinically diagnosed Alzheimer's disease increases to about 50 percent by age 87, even in the more typical late-onset form of the disease, genetic transmission is implied.

The association between Down's syndrome and Alzheimer's disease in both clinical and pathological features indicated the exploration of chromosome 21. Indeed, St. George-Hyslop and associates[64] used genetic-linkage analysis in four large pedigrees with autosomal dominant Alzheimer's disease and discovered polymorphism of an anonymous DNA marker on the long arm of chromosome 21 that segregated with the trait. Genetic heterogeneity has not been definitively established, and the search for other large pedigrees is in progress.

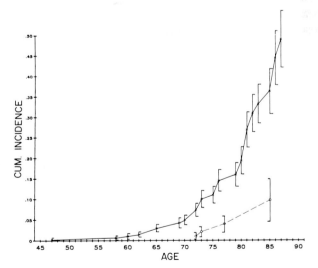

FIGURE 92-2
The cumulative incidence of an Alzheimer-type dementia in first-degree relatives of probands with Alzheimer's disease compared to elderly controls. The authors conclude that there may be a 50 percent morbid risk by age 90 for first-degree relatives. (*Reprinted with permission from Breitner JCS et al: Familial aggregation in Alzheimer's disease: Comparison of risk among relatives of early- and late-onset cases, and among male and female relatives in successive generations. Neurology 38:207, 1988.*)

PATHOLOGY

The histologic criteria for Alzheimer's disease consists primarily of an abundance of senile plaques (neuritic plaques) and neurofibrillary tangles in the neocortex and hippocampus. Specific diagnostic criteria suggested by a work group at the National Institute on Aging include quantities of senile plaques and neurofibrillary tangles for different age groups.[65] These criteria have been validated to some extent in at least one clinicopathological study.[14] Alzheimer's disease is pathologically, qualitatively, and quantitatively distinct from normal aging of the brain. Most patients with Alzheimer's disease have a slight reduction in brain weight, with the majority ranging from 900 to 1100 grams. Mild to moderate cerebral cortical atrophy can be present, although many patients show little or no atrophy. The subcortical areas, including the centrum semiovale (white matter), also diminish in size, which results in the enlargement of the lateral ventricles.

Senile or neuritic plaques, neurofibrillary tangles, amyloid deposition, neuronal loss, granulovacuolar degeneration, and Hirano bodies are the major microscopic elements seen in Alzheimer's disease. Senile plaques are complex structures composed of distended neuritic processes, extracellular amyloid, glial processes, and occasional microglia and astrocytes. These are best demonstrated by silver impregnation; the neuritic plaques generally have a central core of amyloid surrounded by a granular ring of filamentous or rodlike argyrophilic material (Fig. 92-3). Senile plaques are present in large numbers in the amygdala, hippocampus, and cerebral cortex, and rarely in the brain stem and basal ganglia. There is a quantitative relationship between the number of senile plaques and the severity of dementia,[6] as well

as a reduction in choline acetyltransferase activity, a biochemical marker for acetylcholine.[66]

The protein content of the amyloid core has been under investigation in recent years. Selkoe and others[67,68] believe that the amyloid fibers seen in Alzheimer's disease brains consist of low-molecular-weight, hydrophobic protein or proteins that readily aggregate to form polymers which are insoluble by the usual laboratory methods. The amyloid core of the senile plaque, a ubiquitous finding in the brain in Alzheimer's disease, is a peptide termed *A4 peptide*. This peptide, termed β amyloid protein, is a hydrophobic portion of a transmembrane glycoprotein that has three forms due to alternate mRNA splicing within the same gene.[69–71] Aluminum silicate may accumulate in the plaque.[72] The gene for the encoding of this amyloid protein localizes to chromosome 21,[73] but it is not the gene for familial Alzheimer's disease. Moreover, the β protein gene in this chromosome also codes for a β protein gene product that is identical in amounts and characteristics in normal elderly and Alzheimer's disease brain.

Neurofibrillary tangles, initially described by Alois Alzheimer in 1907, are neuronal cytoplasmic collections of tangled filaments present in abundance in the neocortex, hippocampus, amygdala, basal forebrain, substantia nigra, locus ceruleus, and other brain stem nuclei. They are also frequently present in the cortex and, in particular, the hippocampus. Neurofibrillary tangles consist of a neurofilament protein which is normally not found in the neuronal perikaryon.[74] The neurofibrillary tangle consists in large part of paired helical filaments which contain epitopes reacting with antibodies for tau proteins that are abnormally phosphorylated,[75] with microtubule-associated protein,[76] and with neurofilaments and gangliosides.[77,78] The tangle may contain some of the

FIGURE 92-3

A senile plaque with a dense core of amyloid protein. It is surrounded by a ring of filamentous material. These structures are present in the brains of normal elderly but are increased in quantity in patients with Alzheimer's disease. The number of senile plaques also correlates with the severity of dementia. (*Photograph provided by James Goldman, M.D., Ph.D. of Columbia University and the New York State Psychiatric Institute.*)

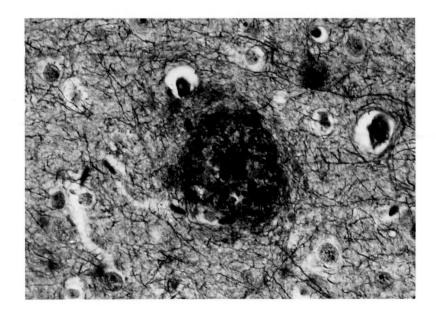

same peptides as the plaque,[79] and the amyloid-core protein contains a 100 kDa protein bearing a sequence homologous to tau.[80] Neurofibrillary tangles are found in Down's syndrome, dementia associated with boxing (dementia pugilistica), and the Parkinson dementia complex of Guam. They are also present in the brains of normal elderly and may represent a nonspecific response to a variety of insults.

Amyloid β protein deposition occurs not only in senile plaques but also in the walls of capillaries, arterioles, and small arteries in the brain in subarachnoid spaces. Almost all patients with Alzheimer's disease have these changes.[81] The protein is very similar to the amyloid proteins previously described for the senile plaque. The marker on chromosome 21 for familial Alzheimer's disease is not linked to the β amyloid protein gene, suggesting that its product is not abnormal.

Neuronal loss is one of the major histologic features of Alzheimer's disease and is greatest in the neocortex, particularly the temporal lobe hippocampus, subiculum, and superior and inferior parietal lobes. To a lesser extent the amygdala shows a reduction of overall volume as well as neuron number. Neuronal loss is a striking feature of the cholinergic basal forebrain nucleus of Meynert[82] and the septal nuclei; both correlate with the changes seen in the cholinergic system.[83] There are substantial losses of neurons from other brain stem nuclear centers, such as the locus ceruleus, substantia nigra, and raphe.[84-87]

Granulovacuolar degeneration consists of cytoplasmic structures composed of a central argyrophilic granule surrounded by a vacuole. These can be multiple and may be found in the pyramidal layer of the hippocampus. They are composed of electron-dense granular filaments surrounded by a membrane-bound clear zone. They contain tubulin-like immunoreactivity and occur in a number of diseases, as well as in normal aging.

The Hirano body is a small filament which is an eosinophilic ovoid or spherical intracytoplasmic inclusion commonly seen in the pyramidal layer of the hippocampus in Alzheimer's disease. It contains actin and is seen in other diseases and in normal aging.

A remarkable overlap between the pathological as well as clinical features of Alzheimer's disease and Parkinson's disease was alluded to earlier. Numerous studies indicate that patients with Parkinson's disease become demented, and, when they do, it is usually the result of coexistent Alzheimer's disease.[33,88-90] Similarly, patients with Alzheimer's disease develop parkinsonian features[35,40] with an associated loss of pigmented neurons in the substantia nigra, primarily from the pars compacta and locus ceruleus.[37] Lewy bodies (round eosinophilic hyalin cytoplasmic inclusions) are present in some remaining neurons in the substantia nigra. Often Lewy bodies are found in the basal forebrain in patients with either disease and in patients with both problems.

BIOCHEMISTRY

Neurotransmitter alterations were recognized approximately 10 years ago in Alzheimer's disease.[91] Most studies have described cortical neurochemical abnormalities such as the loss of presynaptic cholinergic, noradrenergic, and serotonergic markers; these abnormalities are thought to be due to neuronal dysfunction in afferent connections from subcortical neuronal sites.[92] However, the changes in the cholinergic system occur very early in the disease and can be seen in newly diagnosed patients by brain biopsy.[93] Reductions in certain peptides such as somatostatin-like reactivity and corticotropin-releasing factor probably reflect the loss of intrinsic cortical neurons.[94-99] Other neuropeptides have also been implicated, such as vasopressin,[100] substance P, and neuropeptide Y.[101-103] Alterations in gamma aminobutyric acid and its related receptors are also probably due to the loss of intrinsic neurons and afferent projections as well.[104-106]

A relationship between the loss of neurotransmitter markers and neurofibrillary tangles and senile plaques exists.[66,83] The cholinergic markers previously mentioned have the most striking correlation to the presence of senile plaques, as well as neurofibrillary tangles, but somatostatin, glutamine, and other neurotransmitters also relate to these morphologic features.

A consistent abnormality which has opened the way for treatment is the loss of cortical presynaptic cholinergic markers, such as choline acetyltransferase, the rate-limiting enzyme for the production of acetylcholine. Remarkably, muscarinic receptors appear to be normal,[93] but Whitehouse and others[107-109] have described a reduction in nicotinic receptors. More variable losses for noradrenergic and serotonergic markers in the brain stem occur due to loss of cells in both the locus ceruleus and the raphe nuclei.[110] The magnitude of these losses and their behavioral correlations have not been forthcoming but are currently under investigation. Most of these neurochemical abnormalities involve classic neurotransmitters found in subcortical nuclei which project to the cortex.

It is quite unlikely that a single neurotransmitter deficiency can account for the numerous manifestations related to Alzheimer's disease. Numerous transmitters and neuropeptides may be related to the pathogenesis of this disorder. The specific relationships between diseased neuronal populations, chemical losses or changes, and behavior have yet to be determined. In the simplest sequence, the cholinergic system appears to be related to memory, but, as yet, enhancing cholinergic metabolism has not reversed the course of Alzheimer's disease.

The primary cause of cholinergic neuron loss is not established, and there is little evidence that this loss in the basal forebrain is caused by a mechanism distinct from that leading to the loss of other neurotransmitter systems. It can be assumed, however, that the loss of various neurotransmitters is secondary to neuronal loss and cytopathological lesions found in Alzheimer's disease rather than their cause. It is suspected that macromolecular changes that accompany neuronal degeneration occurring with normal brain aging, and in Alzheimer's disease, play a role in progressive cell death, loss or change in neurotransmitter systems, and the subsequent abnormalities of behavior.

MANAGEMENT

EXPERIMENTAL THERAPIES

The "cholinergic hypothesis"[111] provides a rationale for specific treatment strategies in Alzheimer's disease. The data supporting this hypothesis as the pathogenesis of the core manifestation of Alzheimer's disease, memory impairment, are compelling:

1. Scopolamine induces a loss of memory and a decline in cognitive skills in young people that is reversed by physostigmine.[111]
2. Choline acetyltransferase activity, an index of acetylcholine production, is significantly reduced in Alzheimer's disease.[112]
3. The severity of dementia is related to the degree of choline acetyltransferase reduction in Alzheimer's disease.[66]
4. Significant cell loss in the basal forebrain cholinergic complex occurs in Alzheimer's disease.[83]

Although the cholinergic hypothesis is controversial, numerous attempts to correct the cholinergic deficit have been explored. As yet, no attempt has been successful, but a great number of investigators are now focused on correcting the cholinergic deficit presumed to be a mechanism of the major portion of intellectual deterioration in Alzheimer's disease. Some argue that acetylcholine is not the only biochemical deficit and that an effort should be made to examine methods to enhance other neurotransmitters and peptides. While it may be true that other biochemical alterations play a role, the link between memory and normal cholinergic function remains, and the cholinergic hypothesis needs to be further explored by pharmacological means before it is abandoned.

The rationale for precursor loading is based on the observation that acetylcholine production is increased following the administration of choline in animals[113] and lecithin (phosphatidylcholine) in man.[114] Several clinical trials, both open and double-blind crossover studies, were disappointing. There is also no evidence of physiological changes.[115] Little benefit from these agents has been demonstrated, but side effects still occur. The predominant side effects include abdominal bloating, diarrhea, nausea, and, in some instances, weight gain.

Although the precursor approach has generally been disappointing, it may fail because of the lack of acetyl Co-A, the other factor essential to acetylcholine production. Support for this view is provided in studies indicating slight improvement when lecithin or choline is combined with a nootropic, such as piracetam, a drug considered by some to enhance cerebral metabolism.[116–118]

The most widely studied cholinomimetics are anticholinesterase inhibitors, and, in particular, physostigmine. These compounds act by preserving synaptically released acetylcholine. While there are encouraging reports indicating clinical improvement with physostigmine, there are also reports of little to no change. This may reflect inadequate or erratic absorption or failure of physostigmine to enter the central nervous system. In the studies indicating improvement with this agent, entry into the central nervous system has been documented directly or indirectly.[119,120]

Intravenous administration of physostigmine, first in a patient with postencephalitic amnesia[121] and later in patients with Alzheimer's disease,[122] led to many further investigations. Improved recall performance at higher dosages was usually not accompanied by a practical or functional benefit. The complexity of intravenous administration led some investigators to resort to oral administration of physostigmine. Again, good results were minimal, yet still encouraging, particularly in patients who were able to tolerate high doses of the oral agent. Presently, there are numerous studies of oral physostigmine, and some have indicated slight yet significant improvement in recent memory.[119,120,123–126] These reports indicate that short-term memory, long-term memory, and constructional ability[126] may improve and intrusion errors may be reduced.[119,125] Although investigators demonstrate a slight benefit from oral physostigmine, none has reported an improvement in the performance of activities of daily living.

Anticholinesterase inhibition is not without its problems. Both oral and intravenous physostigmine have short half-lives, and both are cleared from the plasma within 2 hours, requiring frequent administration. Nausea, vomiting, postural hypotension, diaphoresis, stomach cramps, and fecal and urinary incontinence are side effects that predictably occur within the first 30 minutes of oral administration.[119,125] Myoclonus has been observed in two patients following oral administration for longer periods of time.[127]

Summers et al.[128] recently reported beneficial effects with another anticholinesterase inhibitor, tetrahydroaminoacridine. Their first study,[129] in 1981, was an open trial in which 6 of 12 patients improved. In a more recent study,[128] 14 of 17 different patients improved in tasks of orientation and recent memory. Additionally, global severity measures were said to have improved in 12 of the 14 subjects after 1 year. The benefit was also observed in practical terms, such that families reported remarkable change in function. Side effects were minimal, seen in only about one-half of the subjects, and included nausea, belching, vomiting, diarrhea, excessive micturition, and diaphoresis. All were considered mild or negligible. These results have been viewed skeptically by many because of the unconventional measures used to indicate change and because other investigators have not appreciated such a significant improvement.[130] Davis and Mohs, in an accompanying editorial,[131] praised the work because of the rational path followed to extend the cholinergic hypothesis. Subsequently a national study was temporarily halted because of liver toxicity with similar doses of the medication.

Anticholinesterase inhibitors may represent the best available choice at the present time, though the pharmacokinetics of these agents do pose problems for investigators and clinicians. Absorption is incredibly variable, and this may be a crucial point because improvement seems to rely on high concentrations of the drug. However, side effects, and the inverted "U" function, preclude higher doses.[132] Davis and Mohs also caution that any strategy that relies on the integrity of the remaining cholinergic neurons for its efficacy in a degenerative process like Alzheimer's disease is "ultimately flawed."[131] On the other hand, others have found long-term benefits following the oral administration of physostigmine for as long as 6 months to 1 year.[132]

Muscarinic cholinergic agonists, which mimic the effects of acetylcholine, have also been administered with some success to patients with Alzheimer's disease. In fact, Christie and associates[133] reported no difference in the response of 11 patients to intravenous physostigmine as compared to arecoline. The improvement was minimal, but the study was conducted in a single-blind, crossover fashion and indicated improved recall in subjects regardless of the compound administered. Other cholinergic agonists produce slight yet significant improvement in cognitive function, mood, social behavior, and psychomotor speed.[134,135]

Subcutaneous administration of bethanechol, a potent cholinergic agonist, has been reported to improve attention, but has little effect on memory and other cognitive function.[136] Intrathecal administration of bethanechol was praised at one point on national television as a "cure" for Alzheimer's disease[137]; another investigation found improved mood and behavior without change in mental function.[138]

Side effects with direct agonists are similar to those of other cholinomimetics. Intrathecal administration, however, has its unique problems of sterile encephalitis and parkinsonism.[137]

Other agents employed in the treatment of Alzheimer's disease have focused on peptide-related or sus-pected abnormalities[139–143]; none has consistently improved cognition. The only medication approved for the treatment of Alzheimer's disease, dihydroergotamine, has had extensive investigation without much demonstration of improvement.[144]

PRACTICAL MANAGEMENT

Psychiatric manifestations listed as "other clinical features" consistent with the diagnosis of probable Alzheimer's disease by the NINCDS-ADRDA criteria[13] include: depression, insomnia; incontinence; delusions; hallucinations; illusions; and catastrophic verbal, emotional, or physical outbursts; sexual disorders; and weight loss. Numerous studies suggest that antipsychotics used for hallucinations are effective and can also be used to control paranoid or disturbing behaviors.[27]

Controlled studies of neuroleptics have been equivocal. There is limited evidence to suggest that neuroleptics may be effective in relatively low doses in some patients. Because no neuroleptic has been shown to be consistently better than any other, it may be best to withdraw them periodically to reaffirm the need for their use. Most studies have focused on inpatients rather than outpatients, and it is unclear how effective these medications would be in an outpatient setting. In a recent study by Devenand et al.,[145] low dose haloperidol was effective in reducing delusions, but side effects occurred, including parkinsonism and worsening of intellectual function.

Several studies have compared haloperidol, a high-potency drug with low anticholinergic properties, to thioridazine, a low-potency drug with high anticholinergic effects. No difference has been observed, and, if anything, a marginal advantage for thioridazine was noted. It would be expected that a medication with high anticholinergic properties would increase the chances of adverse effects, but this was not observed.[146–149]

Some clinicians consider benzodiazepines to be better than thioridazine in the management of symptoms such as anxiety, insomnia, and agitation in patients without hallucinations or delusions. However, in a double-blind study in which thioridazine was compared to diazepam on measures of anxiety and global psychopathology, thioridazine was better.[146] In fact, in most controlled studies, thioridazine apparently had a greater number of responders with a reduction in behavioral problems than did any other medication. In nursing home studies examining issues such as anxiety and functional disability, thioridazine appears to be the drug of choice.[147–149]

Side effects are certainly to be expected with neuroleptics and include sedation, extrapyramidal syndrome, orthostatic hypotension, and anticholinergic effects including dry mouth, blurred vision, and urinary retention. For this reason, neuroleptics should be started at extremely low doses and raised gradually while monitoring closely for adverse effects. Orthostatic hypotension has profound implications in the elderly, but appears to be relatively uncommon if low dosages of neuroleptics are maintained. It is best to use a noctural dosing schedule so that hypotension is not a problem. Psychomotor retardation and extrapyramidal side effects are much more common in medications such as haloperidol and increase the disability associated with dementia. There is some evidence to suggest that elderly demented patients may be at increased risk for developing tardive dyskinesia with consequent severe movement and feeding difficulties.

CONCLUSIONS

Fortunately, interest in Alzheimer's disease and related disorders has increased at a time when answers are sorely needed. The establishment of Alzheimer's Disease Research Centers on a state and federal level signifies the extent to which the public is willing to support research efforts concerned with this disease. Because of the growing numbers of individuals reaching the age of greatest risk, this effort will have to be sustained until the etiology, the pathogenesis, and a treatment of Alzheimer's disease are found.

REFERENCES

1. Wells CE: Diagnostic evaluation and treatment in dementia, in Wells CE (ed): *Dementia*, 2d ed. Philadelphia, Davis, 1977, pp 247–276.
2. Schoenberg BS, Kokmen E, Okazaki H: Alzheimer's disease and other dementing illnesses in a defined United States population: Incidence rates and clinical features. *Ann Neurol* 22:724, 1987.
3. Alzheimer A: Uber eine eigenartige Erkangkung der Hirnrinde. *All Z Psychiatr* 64:146, 1907.
4. Terry RD, Gonatas NK, Weiss M: Ultrastructural studies in Alzheimer's presenile dementia. *Am J Pathol* 44:269, 1964.
5. Roth M: The natural history of mental disorder in old age. *J Ment Sci* 101:281, 1955.
6. Blessed G, Tomlinson BE, Roth M: The association between quantitative measures of dementia and of senile change in the cerebral gray matter of elderly subjects. *Br J Psychiatry* 114:797, 1968.
7. Katzman R: The prevalence and malignancy of Alzheimer disease: A major killer. *Arch Neurol* 33:217, 1976.
8. Plum F: Dementia: An approaching epidemic. *Nature* 279:372, 1979.
9. Neilsen J, Homma A, Bjorn-Henriksen T: Follow-up 15 years after a geronto-psychiatric prevalence study. Conditions concerning death, cause of death, and life expectancy in relation to psychiatric diagnosis. *J Gerontol* 32:554, 1977.
10. Pfeffer RI, Afifi AA, Chance JM: Prevalence of Alzheimer's disease in a retirement community. *Am J Epidemiol* 125:420, 1987.
11. Kay DWK, Bergmann K, McKechnie AA: Mental illness and hospital usage in the elderly: A random sample follow-up. *Compr Psychiatry* 11:26, 1970.
12. American Psychiatric Association: *Diagnostic and Statistical Manual of Mental Disorders*, 3d ed. Washington, D.C., 1987.
13. McKhann G, Drachman D, Folstein M et al: Clinical diagnosis of Alzheimer's disease: Report of the NINCDS-ADRDA work group under the auspices of the Department of Health and Human Services Task Force on Alzheimer's Disease. *Neurology* 34:939, 1984.
14. Tierney MC, Fisher RH, Lewis AJ, Zorzitto ML, Snow WG, Reid DW, Nieuwstraten P: The NINCDS-ADRDA Work Group criteria for the clinical diagnosis of probable Alzheimer's disease: A clinico-pathologic study of 57 cases. *Neurology* 38:359, 1988.
15. Morris JC, McKeel DW, Fulling K, Torack RM, Berg L: Validation of clinical diagnostic criteria for Alzheimer's disease. *Ann Neurol* 24:17, 1988.
16. Cummings JL, Benson DF, Hill MA, Read S: Aphasia in dementia of the Alzheimer type. *Neurology* 35:394, 1985.
17. Kirshner HS, Webb WG, Kelly MP, Wells CE: Language disturbance: An initial symptom of cortical degenerations and dementia. *Arch Neurol* 41:491, 1984.
18. Kaszniak AW, Fox J, Gandell DL: Predictors of mortality in presenile and senile dementia. *Ann Neurol* 3:246, 1978.
19. Folstein MF, Breitner JCS: Language disorder predicts familial Alzheimer's disease. *Johns Hopkins Med J* 149:145, 1981.
20. Powell AL, Cummings JL, Hill MA, Benson DF: Speech and language alterations in multi-infarct dementia. *Neurology* 38:717, 1988.
21. Mesulam M-M: Slowly progressive aphasia without generalized dementia. *Ann Neurol* 11:592, 1982.
22. Chawluk JB, Mesulam M-M, Hurtig H, Kushner M, Wientraub S, Saykin A, Rubin N, Alavi A, Reivich M: Slowly progressive aphasia without generalized dementia: Studies with positron emission tomography. *Ann Neurol* 19:68, 1986.
23. Dal Pan G, Stern Y, Sano M, Mayeux R: Clock-drawing in neurological disorders. *Behav Neurol* (in press).
24. Crystal HA, Horoupian DS, Katzman R, Jotkowitz S: Biopsy-proved Alzheimer's disease presenting as a right parietal syndrome. *Ann Neurol* 12:186, 1982.
25. Reifler BV, Larson E, Hanley R: Coexistence of cognitive impairment and depression in geriatric outpatients. *Am J Psychiatry* 139:623, 1982.
26. Stern Y, Mayeux R, Hesdorffer D, Sano M: Measurement and prediction of functional capacity in Alzheimer's disease *Ann Neurol* 38:248, 1988.
27. Devanand DP, Sackeim HA, Mayeux R: Psychosis, behavioral disturbance, and the use of neuroleptics in dementia. *Compr Psychiatry* 29:387, 1988.
28. Folstein MF, Folstein SE, McHugh PR: "Mini-mental state": A practical method for grading the cognitive state of patients for the clinician. *J Psychiatr Res* 12:189, 1975.

29. Katzman R, Brown T, Fuld P, Peck A, Schecter R, Schimmel H: Validation of a short Orientation-Memory-Concentration test of cognitive impairment. *Am J Psychiatry* 140:734, 1983.

30. Rosen WG, Mohs RC, Davis KL: A new rating scale for Alzheimer's disease. *Am J Psychiatry* 141:1356, 1984.

31. Hughes CP, Berg L, Danziger WL, Coben LA, Martin RL: A new clinical scale for the staging of dementia. *Br J Psychiatry* 140:566, 1982.

32. Wade JPH, Mirsen TR, Hackinski VC et al: The clinical diagnosis of Alzheimer's disease. *Arch Neurol* 44:24, 1987.

33. Boller F, Mizutani T, Roessmann U, Gambetti P: Parkinson's disease, dementia, Alzheimer's disease: Clinicopathological correlations. *Ann Neurol* 1:329, 1980.

34. Huff FJ, Boller F, Lucchelli F, Querriera R, Beyer J, Belle S: The neurologic examination in patients with probable Alzheimer's disease. *Arch Neurol* 44:924, 1987.

35. Mayeux R, Stern Y, Spanton S: Heterogeneity in dementia of the Alzheimer type: Evidence of subgroups. *Neurology* 35:453, 1985.

36. Stern Y, Mayeux R, Sano M, Hauser A, Bush T: Predictors of disease course in patients with probable Alzheimer's disease. *Neurology* 37:1649, 1987.

37. Ditter SM, Mirra SS: Neuropathologic and clinical features of Parkinson's disease in Alzheimer's disease patients. *Neurology* 37:754, 1987.

38. Jacob H: Muscular twitchings in Alzheimer's disease, in Wolstenholme GEW, O'Connor M (eds): *Alzheimer's Disease and Related Conditions.* London, Churchill, 1970, pp 75–93.

39. Hauser WA, Morris ML, Heston LL, Anderson VE: Seizures and myoclonus in patients with Alzheimer's disease. *Neurology* 36:1226, 1986.

40. Chui HC, Teng EL, Henderson VW, Moy AC: Clinical subtypes of dementia of the Alzheimer type. *Neurology* 35:1544, 1985.

41. Nerl C, Mayeux R, O'Neill GJ: HLA-linked complement markers in Alzheimer's and Parkinson's disease: C4 variant (C4B2) a possible marker for senile dementia of the Alzheimer type. *Neurology* 34:310, 1984.

42. Blass JP, Zemcov A: Alzheimer's disease: A metabolic systems degeneration? *Neurochem Pathol* 2:103, 1984.

43. Zubenko GZ, Cohen BM, Boller F, Malinkova I, Keffe N, Chojnacki B: Platelet membrane abnormality in Alzheimer's disease. *Ann Neurol* 22:237, 1987.

44. Hammerstrom DC, Zimmer B: The role of lumbar puncture in the evaluation of dementia: The University of Pittsburgh Study. *J Am Geriatr Soc* 33:397, 1985.

45. Larson EB, Reifler BV, Sumi SM, Canfield CG, Chinn NM: Diagnostic tests in the evaluation of dementia: A prospective study of 200 elderly outpatients. *Arch Intern Med* 146:1917, 1986.

46. Duara R, Grady C, Haxby J, Sundaram M, Cutler NR, Heston L, Moore A, Schlageter N, Larson S, Rapport SI: Positron emission tomography in Alzheimer's disease. *Neurology* 36:876, 1986.

47. DeKosky ST, Shin WJ, Coupal J, Kirkpatric C: Role of single photon emission computed tomography (SPECT) in the diagnosis of Alzheimer's disease. *Neurology* 37:159, 1987.

48. Hagberg B, Ingvar DH: Cognitive reduction in presenile dementia related to regional abnormalities of the cerebral blood flow. *Br J Psychiatry* 128:209, 1976.

49. Prohovnik I, Mayeux R, Sackeim HA, Smith G, Stern Y, Alderson PO: Cerebral perfusion as a diagnostic marker of early Alzheimer's disease. *Neurology* 38:931, 1988.

50. Pedley TA, Miller JA: Clinical neurophysiology of aging and dementia, in Mayeux R, Rosen W (eds): *The Dementias.* New York, Raven Press, 1983, pp 31–49.

51. Rae-Grant A, Blume W, Lau C, Hachinski VC, Fishman M, Merskey H: The electroencephalogram in Alzheimer-type dementia. *Arch Neurol* 44:50, 1987.

52. Duffy FH, Albert MS, McAnulty G: Brain electrical activity in patients with presenile and senile dementia of the Alzheimer's type. *Ann Neurol* 16:439, 1984.

53. Rocca WA, Luigi AA, Schoenberg BS. Epidemiology of clinically diagnosed Alzheimer's disease. *Ann Neurol* 19:415, 1986.

54. Molsa PK, Marttila RJ, Rinne UK: Epidemiology of dementia in a Finnish population. *Acta Neurol Scand* 65:541, 1982.

55. Broe GA, Akhtar AJ, Andrews GR et al: Neurological disorders in the elderly at home. *J Neurol Neurosurg Psychiatry* 39:362, 1976.

56. Treves T, Korczyn A, Zilber N et al: Presenile dementia in Israel. *Arch Neurol* 43:26, 1986.

57. Schoenberg BS, Anderson DW, Haerer AF: Severe dementia, prevalence and clinical features in a bi-racial U.S. population. *Arch Neurol* 42:740, 1985.

58. Sluss TK, Gruenberg EM, Kramer M: The use of longitudinal studies in the investigation of risk factors for senile dementia—Alzheimer type, in Mortimer JA, Schuman IM (eds): *Epidemiology of Dementia.* New York, Oxford, 1984, pp 132–154.

59. Henderson AS: The epidemiology of Alzheimer's disease. *Br Med Bull* 42:3, 1986.

60. Heston LL, Mastri AR, Anderson VE, White J: Dementia of the Alzheimer type: Clinical genetics, natural history, and associated conditions. *Arch Gen Psychiatry* 38:1085, 1981.

61. Heyman A, Wilkinson WE, Stafford JA, Heims MJ, Sigmon AH, Wienberg T: Alzheimer's disease: A study of epidemiological aspects. *Ann Neurol* 34:335, 1984.

62. Wisnieski KE, Wisnieski HM, Wen GY: Occurrence of neuropathological changes and dementia of Alzheimer's disease in Down's syndrome. *Ann Neurol* 17:278, 1985.

63. Breitner JCS, Silverman JM, Mohs RC, Davis KL: Familial aggregation in Alzheimer's disease: Comparison of risk among relatives of early- and late-onset cases, and among male and female relatives in successive generations. *Neurology* 38:207, 1988.

64. St. George-Hyslop PH, Tanzi RE, Polinsky RJ, Haines JL, Nee L, Watkins PC, Myers RH, Feldman RG: The genetic defect causing familial Alzheimer's disease maps to chromosome 21. *Science* 235:885, 1987.

65. Khachaturian ZS: Diagnosis of Alzheimer's disease. *Arch Neurol* 42:1097, 1985.

66. Perry EK, Tomlinson BE, Blessed G, Bergmann K, Gibson PH, Perry RH: Correlation of cholinergic abnormalities with senile plaques and mental test scores in senile dementia. *Br Med J* 2:1457, 1978.

67. Selkoe DJ, Ihara Y, Salazar FJ: Alzheimer's disease: In-

solubility of partially purified paired helical filaments in sodium dodecyl sulfate and urea. *Science* 215:1243, 1982.

68. Kosik KS, Duffy LK, Dowling MM: Microtubule-associated protein 2: Monoclonal antibodies demonstrate the selective incorporation of certain epitopes into Alzheimer neurofibrillary tangles. *Proc Natl Acad Sci USA* 81:7941, 1984.

69. Ponte P, Gonzalez-DeWhitt P, Schilling J, Miller J, Hsu D, Greenberg G, Davis K, Wallace W, Lieberberg I, Fuller F, Cordell B: A new A4 amyloid mRNA contains a domain homologous to serine proteinase inhibitors. *Nature* 331:525, 1988.

70. Tanzi RE, McClatchey AI, Lamperti ED, Villa-Komaroff L, Gusella JF, Neve RI: Protease inhibitor domain encoded by an amyloid protein precursor in mRNA associated with Alzheimer's disease. *Nature* 331:528, 1988.

71. Kitaguchi N, Takahashi Y, Tokushima Y, Shiojiri S, Hirataka I: Novel precursor of amyloid protein shows protease inhibitory activity. *Nature* 311:530, 1988.

72. Candy JM, Klinowski J, Perry RH, Perry EK: Alumino-silicates and senile plaque formation in Alzheimer's disease. *Lancet* 1:354, 1986.

73. Tanzi R, Gusella JF, Watkins PC, Burns GAP, St. George-Hyslop P, Van Keuren ML, Patterson D, Pagan S, Kurnit G, Neve RL: Amyloid B protein gene: cDNA, mRNA distribution and genetic linkage near the Alzheimer locus. *Science* 235:880, 1987.

74. Cork LC, Sternberger NW, Sternberger MF, Casanova MF, Struble RG, Price DL: Phosphorylated neurofilament antigens in neurofibrillary tangles in Alzheimer's disease. *J Neuropathol Exp Neurol* 45:56, 1986.

75. Kosik KS, Joachim CLK, Selkoe DJ: Microtubule-associated protein tau is a major antigenic component of paired helical filaments in Alzheimer's disease. *Proc Natl Acad Sci USA* 83:4044, 1986.

76. Dammerman M, Goldstein M, Yen S-HC, Shafti-Zagardo B: Isolation and characterization of cDNA clones encoding epitopes shared with Alzheimer neurofibrillary tangles. *J Neurosci Res* 19:43, 1988.

77. Sternberger NH, Sternberger LA, Ulrich J: Aberrant neurofilament phosphorylation in Alzheimer's disease. *Proc Natl Acad Sci USA* 82:4274, 1985.

78. Emory CR, Ala TA, Frey WH: Ganglioside monoclonal antibody (A2B5) labels Alzheimer's neurofibrillary tangles. *Neurology* 37:768, 1987.

79. Masters CL, Multhaup G, Simms G, Potgiesser J, Martins RN, Beyreuther J: Tau protein. *Eur Mol Biol Org* 4:2757, 1987.

80. Goedert M, Wischik CM, Crowther RA, Walker JE, Klug A: Cloning and sequencing of the cDNA encoding a core protein of the paired helical filament of Alzheimer's disease: Identification as the microtubule-associated protein, tau. *Proc Natl Acad Sci USA* 85:4051, 1988.

81. Wong CW, Quaranta U, Glenner GG: Neuritic plaques and cerebrovascular amlyoid in Alzheimer's disease are antigenically related. *Proc Natl Acad Sci USA* 82:8729, 1985.

82. Whitehouse PJ, Price DL, Struble RG, Clark AW, Coyle JT, DeLong MR: Alzheimer's disease and senile dementia: Loss of neurons in the basal forebrain. *Science* 215:12379, 1982.

83. Whitehouse PJ, Price DL, Clark AW: Alzheimer's disease: Evidence for selective loss of cholinergic neurons in the nucleus basalis. *Ann Neurol* 10:122, 1981.

84. Marcyniuk B, Mann DMA, Yates PO: Loss of cells from locus ceruleus in Alzheimer's disease is topographically arranged. *Neurosci Lett* 64:247, 1986.

85. Mann DMA, Yates PO, Marcyniuk B: Dopaminergic neurotransmitter systems in Alzheimer's disease and in Down's syndrome at middle age. *J Neurol Neurosurg Psychiatry* 50:341, 1987.

86. Mann DMA, Yates PO, Marcyniuk B: Alzheimer's presenile dementia, senile dementia of Alzheimer type and Down's syndrome in middle age form an age-related continuum of pathological changes. *Neuropathol Appl Neurobiol* 10:185, 1984.

87. Carcio CA, Kemper T: Nucleus raphe dorsalis in dementia of the Alzheimer type: Neurofibrillary changes and neuronal packing density. *J Neuropathol Exp Neurol* 43:359, 1984.

88. Price DL, Whitehouse PJ, Struble RG: Cellular pathology in Alzheimer's and Parkinson's disease. *Trends Neurosci* 29, 1986.

89. Whitehouse P, Hedreen JC, White C, DeLong M, Price DL: Basal forebrain neurons in the dementia of Parkinson's disease. *Ann Neurol* 13:243, 1983.

90. Ruberg M, Aloska A, Javoy-Agid F, Agid Y: Muscarinic binding and choline acetyltransferase activity in Parkinsonism subjects with reference to dementia. *Brain Res* 232:129, 1982.

91. Bartus RT, Dean RL, Beer B, Lippa AS: The cholinergic hypothesis of geriatric memory dysfunction. *Science* 217:408, 1982.

92. Price DL, Whitehouse PJ, Struble RG: Alzheimer's disease. *Annu Rev Med* 36:349, 1985.

93. Francis PT, Palmer AM, Sims NR, Bowen DM et al: Neurochemical studies of early-onset Alzheimer's disease. *N Engl J Med* 313:7, 1985.

94. Davies P, Katzman R, Terry RD: Reduced somatostatin-like immunoreactivity in cerebral cortex from cases of Alzheimer's disease and Alzheimer senile dementia. *Nature* 288:279, 1980.

95. Davies P, Terry RD: Cortical somatostatin-like immunoreactivity in cases of Alzheimer's disease and senile dementia of the Alzheimer type. *Neurobiol Aging* 2:9, 1981.

96. Rossor MN, Emson PC, Mountjoy CQ, Roth M, Iversen LL: Reduced amounts of immunoreactive somatostatin in the temporal cortex in senile dementia of Alzheimer type. *Neurosci Lett* 20:373, 1980.

97. Taminga CA, Foster NL, Chase TN: Reduced brain somatostatin levels in Alzheimer's disease. *N Engl J Med* 313:1294, 1985.

98. Bissette G, Reynolds GP, Kitts CD, Widerlov E, Nemeroff CB: Corticotropin-releasing factor-like immunoreactivity in senile dementia of the Alzheimer type. *JAMA* 254:3067, 1985.

99. De Sousa EB, Whitehouse PJ, Kuhar MJ, Price DL, Vale WW: Reciprocal changes in corticotropin-releasing factor (CRF)-like immunoreactivity and CRF receptors in cerebral cortex of Alzheimer's disease. *Nature* 319:593, 1986.

100. Rossor MN, Iversen LL, Roth M, Hawthorn J, Arg VY, Jentan JS: Arginine vasopressin and choline acetyltransferase in brains of patients with Alzheimer type senile dementia. *Lancet* 2:1367, 1980.

101. Beal MF, Mazurek MF, Chattha GK, Svendsen CN, Bird ED, Martin JB: Neuropeptide Y immunoreactivity is reduced in cerebral cortex in Alzheimer's disease. *Ann Neurol* 20:489, 1986.

102. Crystal HA, Davies P: Cortical substance P-like immunoreactivity in cases of Alzheimer's disease and senile dementia of the Alzheimer type. *J Neurochem* 38:1782, 1982.

103. Beal MF, Martin JB: Neuropeptides in neurological disease. *Ann Neurol* 20:547, 1986.

104. Chu DCM, Penny JB, Young AB: Cortical GABA$_B$ and GABA$_A$ receptors in Alzheimer's disease: A quantitative autoradiographic study. *Neurology* 37:1454, 1987.

105. Sasaki H, Muramoto O, Kanazawa I, Arai H, Kosaka K, Iizuka R: Regional distribution of amino acid transmitters in postmortem brains of presenile dementia of the Alzheimer-type dementia. *Ann Neurol* 19:263, 1986.

106. Greenamyre JT, Penny JB, Young AB, D'Amato CJ, Hicks SP, Shoulson I: Alterations in L-glutamate binding in Alzheimer's and Huntington's diseases. *Science* 227:1496, 1985.

107. Whitehouse PJ, Martino Am, Antuono PG: Nicotinic acetylcholine binding sites in Alzheimer's disease. *Brain Res* 371:146, 1986.

108. Nordberg A, Alafuzoff I, Winblad B: Reduced number of [³H]nicotine and [³H]acetylcholine binding sites in frontal cortex of Alzheimer brains. *Neurosci Lett* 72:15, 1986.

109. Shimohama S, Taniguchi T, Fujiwara M, Kameyama M: Changes in nicotinic and muscarinic cholinergic receptors in Alzheimer-type dementia. *J Neurochem* 46:28, 1986.

110. D'Amato RJ, Zweig RM, Whitehouse PJ, Wenk TL, Singer HS, Mayeux R, Price DL, Snyder SH: Aminergic systems in Alzheimer's disease and Parkinson's disease. *Ann Neurol* 22:229, 1987.

111. Drachman DA, Leavitt J: Human memory and the cholinergic system: A relationship to aging? *Arch Neurol* 30:113, 1974.

112. Davies P: Neurotransmitter-related enzymes in senile dementia of the Alzheimer type. *Brain Res* 171:319, 1979.

113. Cohen EL, Wurtman RJ: Brain acetylcholine: Control by dietary choline. *Science* 191:561, 1976.

114. Wurtman RJ, Hirsch MJ, Growdon J: Lecithin consumption raises serum-free-choline levels. *Lancet* 2:68, 1977.

115. Canter NL, Hallet M, Growdon JH: Lecithin does not affect EEG spectral analysis or P300 in Alzheimer's disease. *Neurology* 32:1260, 1982.

116. Pomara N, Block R, Moore N, Rhiew HP, Berchou R, Stanley M, Gerson S: Combined piracetam and cholinergic precursor treatment for primary degenerative dementia. *IRCS Med Sci* 12:388, 1984.

117. Ferris SH, Reisberg B, Frfiedman E et al: Combination choline/piracetam treatment of senile dementia. *Psychopharmacol Bull* 18:96, 1982.

118. Smith RC, Uroalis G, Johnson R, Morgan R: Compari-

119. son of therapeutic response to long-term treatment with lecithin versus piracetam plus lecithin in patients with Alzheimer's disease. *Psychopharmacol Bull* 20:542, 1984.

119. Thal LJ, Fuld PA, Masur DM, Sharpless NS: Oral physostigmine and lecithin improve memory in Alzheimer's disease. *Ann Neurol* 13:491, 1983.

120. Mohs RC, Davis BM, Johns CA, Mathe AA, Greenwald BS, Morvath TB, Davis KL: Oral physostigmine treatment of patients with Alzheimer's disease. *Am J Psychiatry* 142:28, 1985.

121. Peters BH, Levin HS: Memory enhancement after physostigmine treatment in the amnestic syndrome. *Arch Neurol* 34:215, 1977.

122. Davis KL, Mohs RC: Enhancement of memory processes in Alzheimer's disease with multiple-dose intravenous physostigmine. *Am J Psychiatry* 139:1421, 1982.

123. Beller SA, Overall JE, Swann AC: Efficacy of oral physostigmine in primary degenerative dementia. *Psychopharmacology* 87:147, 1985.

124. Caltagirone C, Gainotti C, Masullo O: Oral administration of chronic physostigmine does not improve cognitive or amnestic performances in Alzheimer's presenile dementia. *Int J Neurosci* 16:247, 1982.

125. Stern Y, Sano M, Mayeux R: Effects of oral physostigmine in Alzheimer's disease. *Ann Neurol* 22:306, 1987.

126. Muramato O, Sugishita M, Kazuya H et al: Cholinergic system and constructional apraxis: A further study of physostigmine in Alzheimer's disease. *J Neurol Neurosurg Psychiatry* 47:485, 1984.

127. Mayeux R, Albert M, Jenike MA: Physostigmine induced myoclonus in Alzheimer's disease. *Neurology* 37:345, 1987.

128. Summers WK, Majovski LV, Marsch GM, Tachiki K, Kling A: Oral tetrahydroaminoacridine in long-term treatment of senile dementia Alzheimer's disease. *N Engl J Med* 315:1241, 1986.

129. Summers WK, Viesselman JO, Marsh GM, Candelora K: Use of THA in the treatment of Alzheimer-like dementia: Pilot study in twelve patients. *Biol Psychol* 16:145, 1981.

130. Brinkman SD, Gershon S: Measurement of cholinergic drug effects on memory in Alzheimer's disease. *Neurobiol Aging* 4:139, 1983.

131. Davis KL, Mohs RC: Cholinergic drugs in Alzheimer's disease. *N Engl J Med* 315:1286, 1986.

132. Stern Y, Sano M, Mayeux R: Long term administration of oral physostigmine in Alzheimer's disease. *Neurology* 38:1837, 1988.

133. Christie JE, Shering A, Ferguson J, Glen AIM: Physostigmine and arecoline: Effects of intravenous infusions in Alzheimer presenile dementia. *Br J Psychiatry* 138:46, 1981.

134. Wettstein A, Spiegel R: Clinical trials with the cholinergic drug RS86 in Alzheimer's disease (AD) and senile dementia of the Alzheimer type (SDAT). *Psychopharmacology* 84:572, 1984.

135. Fleischbacker WW, Buchgeher A, Schubert A: Menatire in the treatment of senile dementia of the Alzheimer type. *Prog Neuropsychopharmacol Biol Psychiatry* 10:87, 1986.

136. Davous P, Lamour Y: Bethenechol decreases reaction

time in senile dementia of the Alzheimer type. *J Neurol Neurosurg Psychiatry* 48:1297, 1985.

137. Harbaugh RE, Roberts DW, Coombs DW, Saunders RL, Reeder TM: Preliminary report: Intracranial cholinergic drug infusion in patients with Alzheimer's disease. *Neurosurgery* 15:514, 1984.

138. Penn RD, Martin EM, Wilson RS, Fox JH, Savoy SM: Intraventricular bethanechol infusion for Alzheimer's disease: Results of double-blind and escalating-dose trials. *Neurology* 38:219, 1988.

139. Ferris SH, Sathananthon G, Gershon S, Clark C, Moshinsky J: Cognitive effects of ACTH 4-10 in the elderly. *Pharmacol Biochem Behav* 5:73, 1976.

140. Reisberg B, Ferris SH, Anand R, Mir P, Geibel V, DeLeon MJ, Roberts E: Effects of naloxone in senile dementia: A double-blind trial. *N Engl J Med* 308:721, 1983.

141. Steiger NA, Medelson M, Jenkins T, Smith M, Gay R: Effects of naloxone in treatment of senile dementia. *J Am Geriatr Soc* 33:155, 1985.

142. Soininen H, Koskinen T, Helkala E-L, Pigache R, Riekkinen PJ: Treatment of Alzheimer's disease with a synthetic ACTH 4-9 analog. *Neurology* 35:1348, 1985.

143. Peabody CA, Davis H, Berger PA, Tinklenberg JR: Desamino-D-arginine-vasopressin (DDAVP) in Alzheimer's disease. *Neurobiol Aging* 7:301, 1986.

144. McDonald RJ: Hydergine: A review of 26 clinical studies. *Pharmacopsychiatry* 12:407, 1979.

145. Devenand DP, Sackeim HA, Brown RP, Mayeux R: Haloperidol treatment of psychosis and behavioral disturbance in Alzheimer's disease. *Arch Neurol* (in press).

146. Risse SC, Barnes R: Pharmacologic treatment of agitation associated with dementia. *J Am Geriatr Soc* 34:368, 1986.

147. Gilleard CJ, Morgan K, Wade BE: Patterns of neuroleptic use among the institutionalized elderly. *Acta Psychiatr Scand* 68:419, 1983.

148. Prien Y, Haber PA, Caffey EM: The use of psychoactive drugs in elderly patients with psychiatric disorders: Survey conducted in twelve Veterans Administration hospitals. *J Am Geriatr Soc* 23:104, 1975.

149. Helms PM: Efficacy of antipsychotics in the treatment of the behavioral complications of dementia. *J Am Geriatr Soc* 33:206, 1985.

Chapter 93

LESS COMMON DEMENTIAS

Peter J. Whitehouse and Douglas J. Lanska

Alzheimer's disease (Chap. 92), related common degenerative disorders such as Parkinson's disease (Chap. 94), and multi-infarct dementia (Chap. 91) account for perhaps 80 percent of all cases of dementia. The less common dementias are, however, important because some are treatable or at least partially reversible.[1] These dementias include intellectual impairment associated with systemic illnesses and may present as delirium rather than dementia (Chap. 90). In this chapter, we will review briefly some of these rarer dementias and refer the reader to chapters that discuss the pathophysiology of the underlying disease. We will include infectious dementias (Chap. 98), metabolic dementias (Chap. 90), psychiatric disease associated with dementia (Chap. 102 and 103), and a miscellaneous category dealing primarily with illnesses that alter cerebrospinal fluid (CSF) dynamics and disrupt structural integrity of the brain, including brain tumor (Chap. 101), head trauma (Chap. 99), and normal pressure hydrocephalus (Table 93-1).

INFECTIOUS DEMENTIAS

Many cases of progressive memory impairment caused by infections are potentially treatable, although the success of treatment often depends on rapid diagnosis and initiation of appropriate therapy.[2] Although not every elderly individual with dementia requires a lumbar puncture, patients with an early age of onset, short duration of disease, rapid course, history of systemic infections, immunosuppression, unexplained fever, and meningeal symptoms or focal neurological signs should be considered for lumbar puncture after computed tomography (CT) or magnetic resonance imaging (MRI).

VIRAL CAUSES OF DEMENTIA

Several types of DNA and RNA viruses invade the brain and can present with a subacute dementia syndrome.[3]

The forms of brain damage can include meningitis, encephalitis, demyelination, or noninflammatory cortical neuronal degeneration due either to a direct effect of the infectious agent or as a result of an immunological response of the host. In this section, we will review some selective viral causes of dementia.

Herpes Simplex

In the elderly, psychiatric manifestations may precede focal neurological signs, such as amnesia or aphasia. Type I herpes simplex virus is the usual cause, unassociated with systemic illness. Brain biopsy is still recommended in many institutions prior to treatment with acyclovir since other disorders with different treatments can present the same clinical picture and serological tests on CSF or blood are inconclusive.[4,5]

Slow Virus Infections

Creutzfeldt-Jakob disease is the prototypical slow virus infection, so-called because of the prolonged incubation time.[6] Clinically, this rare disorder is characterized by rapid progression of dementia, often associated with other neurological symptoms including myoclonus and visual, corticospinal, or cerebellar abnormalities. An EEG demonstrating characteristic periodic bursts of slow waves can be helpful in diagnosis. The nature of the infectious agent is uncertain; some have proposed it may not include nucleic acids.

Acquired Immune Deficiency Syndrome

Dementia occurs eventually in a majority of patients with acquired immune deficiency syndrome (AIDS) and can occasionally be the presenting complaint.[7] The human immunodeficiency virus (HIV) agent can directly invade brain and cause an encephalopathy which pro-

TABLE 93-1

Disease	Cardinal Features	Diagnostic Tests	References
Infectious	Systemic signs (fever)	Lumbar puncture	Chap. 98
	Subacute meningial signs	Serology	Refs. 3–8
Metabolic	Clinical history	Serum chemistries	Chap. 90
	Systemic signs	Endocrine tests	Refs. 9–11
	Often delirium	Drug screens	
Psychiatric	Affect and psychotic features	Mental status	Chap. 102 and 103
	Family history		Refs. 12, 13
	Fluctuation		
Normal pressure hydrocephalus (NPH)	Early gait and urinary difficulties	Imaging Lumbar puncture	Ref. 14
Head injury	History		Chap. 99 Ref. 15
Neoplasia	Systemic signs	Imaging	Chap. 101
	Headache		
	Focal signs		
Demyelinating	Visual and motor signs	Imaging	Ref. 16
	History of dissemination in time and space		
Epilepsy	History	Imaging, EEG Drug levels	Ref. 17
Rare Degenerative diseases	History Associated motor signs	Imaging	

duces dementia. Opportunistic infections such as toxoplasmosis and cytomegalovirus can also present as progressive cognitive impairment.

CHRONIC MENINGITIS

Chronic meningitis is caused by bacteria such as *Listeria monocytogenes*, *Brucella*, Lyme disease, *Leptospira*, *Borrelia*, mycoplasmal pneumonia, *Legionella*, *Actinomyces endocardia*, syphilis, and tuberculosis and fungi, including histoplasmosis, aspergillosis coccidioidomycosis, candidiasis, and, particularly, *Cryptococcus*.[8] Diagnosis is frequently made serologically by change in serum titers. The incidence of primary syphilis is on the rise again, and more cases of partially treated late-stage syphilis may be seen. Late-stage syphilis may present as a meningovascular form or as a meningoencephalitis (paretic) form. Tuberculous meningitis is more common in less developed countries than in industrialized nations and in children rather than in older adults.

BRAIN ABSCESS

Abscesses are usually seen in the setting of other illnesses, either infectious processes in the ears or mastoids, hematogenous spread from other systemic infections, or head injury. Subdural empyema and septic venous thrombosis should also be considered in these same settings.

OTHER INFECTIONS

Many other infectious processes can present with dementia and need to be considered in the appropriate clinical circumstances. Subacute bacterial endocarditis does not need to present as stroke with focal findings. Dementia can be a prominent early finding in Whipple's disease.[9]

METABOLIC DEMENTIAS

Cognitive function is dependent on adequate metabolic support from other body systems and can be dramatically impaired by endogenous or exogenous toxins.[10] The differentiation of dementia due to metabolic causes from delirium is often uncertain. Acute withdrawal of metabolic support to the brain often results in rapid onset of delirium; whereas, a slowly progressive metabolic problem may present more as a progressive dementia.

SYSTEMIC ILLNESSES

Failure of any of the major body systems can result in encephalopathy and cognitive dysfunction. Electrolyte abnormalities usually present as acute confusional states. Anoxic injury due to any cause can lead to residual amnesia or full dementia. A delayed postanoxic encephalopathy may be associated with motor system abnormalities. Hepatic failure can lead to a slowly developing dementia due to inadequate clearance of toxic metabolites as well as, more rarely, acquired hepatocerebral degeneration. Renal failure can present as a dementia in slowly developing uremia. Other associated dementias relate to complications of dialysis or drug toxicity. Several endocrine system abnormalities need to be considered in the differential diagnosis of dementia in the elderly including panhypopituitary disease, both hypo- and hyperthyroid and hypo- and hyperparathyroidism. Moreover, Addison's and Cushing's diseases can both present as subacute cognitive impairment. Several connective tissue and related disorders can present with dementia, although delirium, psychiatric symptoms, peripheral neuropathies, and vascular events can also occur. Cognitive changes are especially common in granulomatous angiitis, frequent in systemic lupus erythematosus and polyarteritis nodosa, but can occur in almost any of the other collagen vascular syndromes. Dementia is rare in subacute combined degeneration of the spinal cord but may be the presenting complaint. Pellagra (niacin deficiency) can present with dementia and diarrhea.

EXOGENOUS TOXINS

Numerous over-the-counter and prescribed medications can cause cognitive impairment which may present as a delirium or dementia in the elderly.[11] Particularly notable are sedatives and psychotropic compounds, especially those with anticholinergic properties. Moreover, antihypertensive agents may cause either depression or dementia. Alcohol abuse needs to be considered in every case of dementia and may present either as a pure memory impairment (Wernicke-Korsakoff) or as a dementia syndrome. Heavy metals and other kinds of industrial exposures can also cause cognitive impairment.

METABOLIC ABNORMALITIES

In children, several metabolic abnormalities, often genetic in nature, can present as a progressive dementia. Some of these disorders can present in later life and need to be considered in the appropriate clinical circumstances. Some illnesses are associated with peripheral neuropathy, such as Leigh disease, Fabry's disease, and forms of porphyria. Storage diseases can occasionally present in later life (although usually in young adults), including GM_2 gangliosidosis (adult Tay-Sachs), adult Gaucher's disease (type III), Niemann-Pick disease, cerebrotendinous xanthomatosis, and neurocerolipofuscinosis (Kufs' disease).

If abnormal movements and psychiatric symptoms occur, Wilson's disease, a treatable autosomal recessive abnormality in copper metabolism, needs to be considered as does Huntington's disease.

PSYCHIATRIC DISEASES ASSOCIATED WITH DEMENTIA

DEPRESSION

The relationships between depression and dementia are complex.[12,13] Depression can present with primary cognitive symptoms (so-called pseudodementia). The earliest manifestations of what proves to be a dementia syndrome may be changes in mood and affect. Finally, depression and dementia can coexist in the same patient. Several criteria are useful to distinguish the reversible dementia of depression and irreversible degenerative dementia. These include more frequent complaints of memory problems, family history of depression, and fluctuating deficits, especially in attention, in the depressed patient. Since depression is treatable, even in situations where the diagnosis is not clear, vigorous attempts should be made to treat the depression before concluding that the impairment is irreversible.

SCHIZOPHRENIA

Renewed attention has been paid to cognitive impairment in schizophrenia (formerly known as "dementia praecox").[12] The dementia relates to the so-called negative symptoms—apathy and social withdrawal—and, perhaps in some cases, to chronic institutionalization. Patients with chronic schizophrenia do show evidence of structural brain changes on brain imaging tests as well as cognitive impairments on neuropsychological tests. Schizophrenia usually presents in early life, but some authors believe that a rarer, late-onset schizophrenia does exist, which is characterized by prominent delusions and hallucinations, especially of a paranoid nature.

HYSTERICAL DEMENTIA

Hysterical dementia is a relatively rare condition in which patients' complaints of cognitive impairment are often inconsistent and incongruous with observed behavior. Occasionally, answers to questions are obviously confabulated. As in other situations, hysteria often occurs in the setting of actual structural disease.

MISCELLANEOUS CAUSES OF DEMENTIA

Several causes of dementia relate to changes in brain structure or CSF dynamics.

NORMAL PRESSURE HYDROCEPHALUS

Normal pressure hydrocephalus (NPH) is characterized by dementia, gait disturbance, and urinary incontinence in the setting of large ventricles out of proportion to the degree of cortical atrophy seen on brain imaging.[14] The diagnosis of NPH has become somewhat uncertain as time has progressed and fewer patients are being referred for neurosurgical shunting. Clinical improvement produced by the withdrawal of a small amount of fluid by spinal tap, the presence of typical clinical signs in a patient with a known cause for hydrocephalus (e.g., subarachnoid hemorrhage) and short duration of disease may be the best predictors for a response to a ventricular shunt.

HEAD INJURY

Older individuals are more at risk for falling and may sustain head injuries that may produce cognitive impairment. Assessment of the severity of the head injury is based on physical evidence as well as the duration of any impaired consciousness. The mechanisms by which head injuries produce cognitive impairment are many, including direct injury to brain tissue or secondary effects of hemorrhage such as hematomas or hydrocephalus.[15]

NEOPLASIA

Brain tumors may present with dementia and without other neurological symptoms. This picture is most likely to occur in the setting of a slowly progressive, often surgically treatable tumor of frontal or temporal lobes such as a meningioma or slow-growing glioma. Carcinomous meningitis and paraneoplastic phenomena such as limbic encephalitis can also present as cognitive impairment and need also to be considered in appropriate circumstances.

DEMYELINATING DISEASES

Demyelinating diseases are divided into either myelinoclastic, in which normal myelin is destroyed by a disease process, or dysmyelinating diseases, in which the myelin is never formed normally. Both may cause cognitive impairment.[16] Dysmyelinating diseases such as adrenoleukodystrophy and metachromatic leukodystrophy can usually be differentiated by their signs of white matter abnormalities (spasticity, blindness, ataxia). Dysmyelinating diseases usually present earlier in life. Multiple sclerosis is the most common myelinoclastic disorder; probably 75 percent of cases present before age 40. In older adults, the symptoms of the initial attack occurring in years previously may have been forgotten. Evidence of lesions in white matter disseminated in time and space is characteristic of multiple sclerosis.

EPILEPSY

The associations between epilepsy and cognitive impairment are complex.[17] In patients with seizures due to

identified brain diseases, the underlying disorder may be the cause of the dementia (e.g., Alzheimer's disease). Some patients with active temporal lobe seizures may present with acute confusional state. Epileptics, particularly older individuals, treated with phenobarbital or other anticonvulsants are more at risk for the cognitive side effects of these medications.

LESS COMMON DEGENERATIVE DEMENTIAS

Degenerative dementias are defined as idiopathic progressive incurable illnesses primarily occurring in the elderly and characterized neuropathologically by neuronal loss. Alzheimer's disease and Parkinson's disease are discussed elsewhere as is motor neuron disease which can be associated with cognitive impairment. Several rarer degenerative dementias can present in the elderly in association with involuntary motor system abnormalities. Lewy body dementia usually occurs in a setting of clinical parkinsonism. Progressive supranuclear palsy can be mistaken for Parkinson's disease. Bulbar signs such as abnormalities in vertical eye movements and swallowing difficulties, as well as axial rigidity, usually allow differentiating progressive supranuclear palsy from Parkinson's disease. Huntington's disease can present in late life. In this fully penetrant autosomal dominant condition, dementia and psychiatric symptoms may precede motor abnormalities such as chorea. Some of the spinal cerebellar degeneration syndromes are characterized by dementia especially type III (with visual loss, supranuclear palsy) and type V (with parkinsonism and ophthalmoplegia). Pick's disease frequently occurs under age 65. Prominent frontal lobe (personality change, disinhibition) and language disturbance accompanied by asymmetrical atrophy on CT and normal EEG late in the course may allow discrimination of Pick's disease from Alzheimer's disease in life. Other rare degenerative dementias ("simple" atrophy, cortical atrophy with swollen chromalytic neurons, progressive subcortical gliosis, thalamic dementias) are often difficult to differentiate clinically from Alzheimer's disease.

REFERENCES

1. Larson EB et al: Dementia in elderly outpatients: A prospective study. *Ann Intern Med* 100:417, 1984.
2. Clarfield AM: The reversible dementias: Do they reverse? (Review) *Ann Intern Med* 109:476, 1988.
3. McArthur J et al: Viruses and dementia, in Whitehouse PJ (ed): *Dementia*. Philadelphia, Davis, in press.
4. Sawyer J et al: To biopsy or not to biopsy in suspected herpes simplex encephalitis. *Med Decis Making* 8:95, 1988.
5. Hanley DF et al: Yes, brain biopsy should be a prerequi-

site for herpes simplex encephalitis treatment. *Arch Neurol* 144:1289, 1987.

6. Brown P et al: Creutzfeldt-Jakob disease: Clinical analyses of a consecutive series of 230 neuropathologically verified cases. *Ann Neurol* 20:597, 1986.

7. Johnson RT, McArthur JC: AIDS and the brain. *Trends Neurosci* 9:1, 1986.

8. Ellner J, Bennett J: Chronic meningitis. *Medicine* 55:344, 1976.

9. Fleming JL et al: Whipple's disease: Clinical, biochemical, and histopathologic features and assessment of treatment in 29 patients. *Mayo Clin Proc* 63:539, 1988.

10. Feldmann E, Plum F: Metabolic dementia, in Whitehouse PJ (Ed): *Dementia*. Philadelphia, Davis, in press.

11. Larson EB et al: Adverse drug reactions associated with global cognitive impairment in elderly persons. *Ann Intern Med* 107:169, 1987.

12. Rabins P et al: Psychiatric disorders that mimic dementia, in Whitehouse PJ (ed): *Dementia*. Philadelphia, Davis, in press.

13. Reifler BV et al: Dementia of the Alzheimer's type and depression. *J Am Geriatr Soc* 34:855, 1986.

14. Hakim S, Adams RD: The special clinical problem of symptomatic hydrocephalus with normal cerebrospinal fluid pressure. Observations on cerebrospinal fluid hydrodynamics. *J Neurol Sci* 2:307, 1965.

15. Lishman WA: The psychiatric sequelae of head injury: A review. *Psychol Med* 3:304, 1973.

16. Rao SM: Neuropsychology of multiple sclerosis: A critical review. *J Clin Exp Neuropsychol* 8:503, 1986.

17. Lesser RP et al: Mental deterioration in epilepsy. *Epilepsia* 27:S105, 1986.

Chapter 94

PARKINSON'S DISEASE

Lucien J. Cote and Margaret Henly

Parkinson's disease was described formally as a medical disorder in 1817 by James Parkinson in a monograph entitled "An Essay on the Shaking Palsy."[1] Undoubtedly, the disorder existed much before that time. Galen, an ancient Greek physician, did refer to a tremor at rest in some of his medical writings, and Sauvage, a French physician in the eighteenth century, described the festination gait seen in some parkinsonian patients. In Rembrandt's sketch of the "Good Samaritan" the innkeeper has a stooped posture, flexed arms across his body, and semiflexed fingers, all suggestive of Parkinson's disease. However, it was James Parkinson who established Parkinson's disease as a specific medical entity, and his description of the clinical manifestations of this malady is amazingly accurate and perceptive; the disease is appropriately named after him.

The classical features of Parkinson's disease are tremor at rest, cogwheel-like rigidity, paucity of movements (bradykinesia), gait impairment and postural reflex impairment. However, one or more of these features can be seen with many neurological disorders that involve the same area of the brain as is affected in Parkinson's disease. Thus, the term *Parkinson's disease* (primary parkinsonism, paralysis agitans) applies specifically to the entity described by James Parkinson, while all other disorders with one or more of these symptoms are referred to as secondary parkinsonism or symptomatic parkinsonism (Table 94-1).

This chapter focuses on Parkinson's disease, the most common disorder in neurology after stroke, Alzheimer's disease, and epilepsy. About half a million Americans have the disease, that is, 1 percent of the population over age 50. This degenerative disease begins most frequently between the ages of 50 and 65 and hence is a disease of the late middle age. Less than 15 percent of patients have their first symptom before age 40. The annual incidence rate is 20 per 100,000; the prevalence rate is 200 per 100,000. The prevalence is increasing as the population is getting older.[2] Parkinson's disease has a similar prevalence in all countries with good statistical records, and the incidence of the malady has not changed for the past 100 years.[3] The incidence of Parkinson's disease is nearly equal in both sexes, all ethnic groups, and all socioeconomic classes.

Although 10 to 15 percent of patients with Parkinson's disease report that they have a first-degree relative

TABLE 94-1
Classification of Parkinsonism

Primary

Parkinson's disease (paralysis agitans)

Secondary (Symptomatic)

Infections
  Encephalitis lethargica (von Economo's encephalitis)
  Encephalitis (coxsackie B, Japanese B, St. Louis, and others)
Drug-induced
  Phenothiazines, thioxanthenes, butyrophenones, reserpine
Toxic agents
  Carbon monoxide, carbon disulfide, manganese, MPTP (N-methyl-4-phenyl-1,2,3,6-tetrahydropyridine)
Metabolic
  Hypoparathyroidism, anoxic states
Vascular
  Arteriosclerosis (pseudoparkinsonism)
Miscellaneous
  Tumor, arteriovenous malformation, head trauma
Degenerative disorders
  Parkinson-dementia complex of Guam
  Striatonigral degeneration
  Progressive supranuclear palsy (Steele-Richardson-Olszewski syndrome)
  Olivopontocerebellar atrophy
  Corticodentatonigral degeneration
  Multisystem atrophy (Shy-Drager syndrome)
  Neuroaxonal dystrophy (Hallervorden-Spatz syndrome)
  Alzheimer's disease with basal ganglia involvement

Supported in part by the Parkinson's Disease Foundation in New York.

with the disease, the evidence suggests that it is not genetically determined. Neuroepidemiologists believe that the prevalence of Parkinson's disease is such that at least half of these cases in relatives could occur by chance and that many of the remaining cases are misdiagnosed and are actually disorders mimicking Parkinson's disease. A study of 65 pairs of twins with one member with Parkinson's disease uncovered only two pairs with both members afflicted with the disease.[4]

CLINICAL FEATURES

The diagnosis of Parkinson's disease is obvious when the cardinal features of tremor at rest, ratchetlike rigidity, and slowness with paucity of movements are present. However, often the disease is insidious in onset and presents minimal, if any, objective signs. Often it goes undiagnosed, or misdiagnosed, for a considerable period of time. In a study by Snider et al.,[5] 43 percent of patients with early, undiagnosed Parkinson's disease sought medical attention because they experienced in the involved areas sensory symptoms such as pain, tingling, numbness, or a burning sensation. Often the diagnosis of bursitis, tendonitis, or arthritis was suggested to the patient, and Parkinson's disease was not recognized until several months later.

The symptoms associated with Parkinson's disease are numerous, and they involve all motor functions. Characteristically, the tremor, which is present in about two-thirds of patients with Parkinson's disease, is most noticeable when the involved part is at rest, and it increases with stress and in cold weather. The tremor is abated with action of the involved part, and in sleep. The rate of the tremor varies from 4 to 8 beats per second. Tremor with a slower rate (i.e., 4 beats per second) tends to be most severe at rest and is reduced with action, while the tremor with a faster rate (i.e., 8 beats per second) is not as rhythmic and is more persistent with action.

In about 15 percent of patients with Parkinson's disease there is present also essential tremor, which should not be confused with the rest tremor of Parkinson's disease (see Table 94-2). Essential tremor is intensified with action, such as raising a cup to drink or to pour the contents into another cup. Essential tremor does not respond to antiparkinsonian drugs, but it is often reduced by a nonselective β-adrenergic blocker such as propanolol or by a barbiturate derivative such as primidone (Mysoline). It is important to differentiate these two types of tremor since their origins and their modes of treatment are different. Occasionally a patient with essential tremor will develop Parkinson's disease, usually mild in nature and late in life. Essential tremor is referred to sometimes as senile tremor or familial tremor because it usually progresses with age and is commonly seen in several members of a family. It is a relatively common condition with an incidence rate of 5.5 per 1000.[6] The pathogenesis of essential tremor is obscure.

The type of muscular rigidity seen in parkinsonian patients is unique in that it is characterized by increased resistance to passive movement throughout the entire range of motion but with rhythmic release of the rigidity. Hence, this type of muscular rigidity is referred to as cogwheel- or ratchet-like in character, and it is related almost surely to the parkinsonian tremor which, even if not visible, alters rhythmically the degree of rigidity. In those parkinsonian patients in whom rigidity is not found clinically, it can often be brought out by having the patient perform a synkinetic movement with the contralateral extremity, such as tapping with one hand while the muscle tone in the other hand and wrist is assessed.

Difficulty initiating a movement (akinesia) and slowness in movement (bradykinesia) are primary and disabling symptoms of Parkinson's disease. The range of movement at a joint is reduced in Parkinson's disease,

TABLE 94-2
Differential Diagnosis of Essential Tremor and Parkinsonian Tremor

Features	*Essential Tremor*	*Parkinsonian Tremor*
Family history	Positive in >60%	Usually none
Age of onset	Young adult	>50 years old
Type of tremor	Postural; with action	At rest, less with action
Location	Hands, head, face, voice	Any part of the body
Effect of alcohol	Markedly reduced	Usually no effect
Course	Variable, may progress	Progressive
Bradykinesia	Never	Usually
Rigidity	Never	Usually
Balance impairment	Never	Commonly
Gait impairment	Never	Commonly
Treatment	Propanolol	Levodopa/carbidopa
	Primidone	Anticholinergics
		Bromocriptine
		Pergolide

and with a repetitive motor act such as tapping the thumb with the index finger there is a progressive decrease or a trailing in the range of motion. Parkinsonian patients with bradykinesia often complain of weakness of the part of the body involved, in spite of having more than adequate muscular power when tested. Bradykinesia in Parkinson's disease is often associated with a shuffling gait, micrographia, difficulty getting into and out of a chair or car, reduced voice volume, slowness in feeding, and so on. Although the tremor seen in Parkinson's disease is disturbing to the patient, bradykinesia is much more disabling because it involves all motor functions.

Gait and postural reflex impairment develop commonly in patients with Parkinson's disease, usually in the more advanced stages of the disease. The neurophysiologic mechanisms involved in the maintenance of posture and locomotion are extremely complex and poorly understood. Massive inputs from higher centers such as the basal ganglia and related nuclei (extrapyramidal motor system) are needed to maintain a normal posture in the face of changing external forces, as well as in locomotion. Normally these events are automatic and finely orchestrated, but in Parkinson's disease they are involved, leading to impaired gait and postural reflexes. The parkinsonian patient develops a shuffling gait (festination) with propulsion (i.e., involuntary stepping forward) and at times inability to move ("freezing"). Occasionally, a patient will show impaired gait and postural reflexes without other features of Parkinson's disease, raising the possibility that it is a variant form of the disorder, especially since these symptoms do not usually respond well to dopamine agonists. Parkinsonian patients with gait or postural reflex impairment, but not both together, usually avoid falling; however, when both symptoms are present together, patients are highly prone to falling and to sustaining serious injuries. These patients require constant assistance when walking.

OTHER CLINICAL FEATURES

There are numerous other symptoms that parkinsonian patients may experience beside those of tremor, rigidity, bradykinesia, gait impairment, and postural reflex impairment. These other symptoms are often overlooked or minimized by physicians and caregivers, yet they can be disturbing and disabling to parkinsonian patients.

MENTAL CHANGES

Mental changes are common in patients with Parkinson's disease. Parkinsonian patients often lose their drive, initiative, and motivation. They become passive, withdrawn, and disinterested in outside activities. They are often accused of being self-centered by their loved ones.

About 40 percent of the parkinsonian patients are depressed, with most of them having a dysthymic type of depression.[7] The degree of depression is not related to the severity of the motor symptoms, and it may even precede the clinical manifestations of Parkinson's disease. Mayeux et al.[7] showed that parkinsonian patients who are depressed have significantly lower levels of 5-hydroxyindoleacetic acid (5-HIAA) in their cerebrospinal fluids than those parkinsonian patients who are not depressed. When these depressed parkinsonian patients are given 5-hydroxytryptophan, the direct precursor of serotonin, they show a significant improvement in mood. The level of 5-HIAA in the cerebrospinal fluid normalizes as mood improves.

Parkinsonian patients often complain that they forget for a few seconds the name of a person they know well or a thought they want to express in a conversation. This "tip of the tongue" phenomenon is very disturbing to the patient, and it often leads to withdrawal from society. It is not evidence of dementia, but rather of diminished vigilance. Stern et al.[8] have linked this phenomenon to an alteration in brain norepinephrine as manifested by a change in 3-methoxy-4-hydroxyphenylglycol (MHPG), the main metabolite of norepinephrine, in the cerebrospinal fluid.

The prevalence of dementia in parkinsonian patients is estimated to be 15 percent; however, in some studies it has been reported to be as high as 50 percent.[9,10] This discrepancy is due to several reasons, including a bias in the selection of patients, who were often from a hospital- or clinic-based population. The criteria used for dementia varied in some of these studies and did not take into consideration that many patients with Parkinson's disease have selective intellectual impairment which is not dementia, such as impaired vigilance and delayed motor reaction. Most parkinsonian patients are on several medications which may affect their mental performance. Lastly, it is true that with the advent of levodopa (Sinemet) and other dopamine agonists, parkinsonian patients can live a full life span, and that in the later phase of the disease they may become demented. Further studies are needed to assess this possibility.

A few parkinsonian patients have visual illusions and hallucinations, but auditory hallucinations are quite rare. Visual illusions and hallucinations usually occur in older patients, and in some cases they can be linked to the medications patients are taking. However, it is not uncommon that even when all medications are stopped, patients may continue indefinitely to experience visual illusions and hallucinations.

Parkinsonian patients often complain of not sleeping through the night, presumably because the sleep cycle is altered. Usually they have no difficulty falling asleep, but they wake up in 2 to 3 hours, feeling wide awake and unable to go back to sleep for several hours. These restless nights take their toll in that patients roam around most of the night, in danger of falling and injuring themselves. During the day they are tired and fall asleep easily, and overall the parkinsonian symptoms intensify. A small dose of amitriptyline (e.g., 10 to 25 mg) at bedtime often helps to improve the sleep cycle.

SKIN

Many parkinsonian patients develop an oily skin, especially over the forehead and along the nasal folds. Other skin surfaces can become dry and scaly. Seborrheic dermatitis of the scalp is often a chronic problem. The eyelids and conjunctivae are chronically irritated, and excessive tearing or dryness of the eyes is noted.

MUSCULOSKELETAL SYSTEM

The musculoskeletal system can show many changes. Usually parkinsonian patients maintain a stooped posture when standing or walking and lose the associated movements of the uppper extremities when walking. Sometimes they lean abnormally to one side when sitting or standing. Some patients complain of ill-defined aches and pains, usually in the more severely involved areas of the body. Deep muscular aching is a troublesome symptom for some patients, and it is most often seen in those patients taking large amounts of levodopa (Sinemet).

SPEECH

Some parkinsonian patients develop a soft, monotonous voice. The vocal cords and the musculature for articulation are involved in this change, and it is also due to decreased air volume in the lungs because parkinsonian patients breathe shallowly. Some patients develop a stammering-like speech (palilalia) manifested by a tendency to repeat a syllable in a word two or more times. This phenomenon resembles the stuttering gait seen in some parkinsonian patients; the two symptoms are often seen in the same patient.

CARDIOVASCULAR SYSTEM

Some parkinsonian patients develop orthostatic hypotension, which may be intensified by some of the drugs taken for the treatment of their symptoms. Swelling of the ankles, which can be severe, is not uncommonly seen in parkinsonian patients. The exact causes are not known, but the swelling is partially due to lack of activity of the legs. Parkinsonian patients sit for hours with their legs in the same position.

GASTROINTESTINAL SYSTEM

Sialorrhea (drooling) is a common symptom in parkinsonian patients because they swallow less often than normal and because they maintain their heads flexed, causing the saliva to come forward. There is no evidence that more saliva is produced by parkinsonian patients. In general, parkinsonian patients have excellent appetites, although they may not be physically active. They often develop a sweet tooth, especially for chocolates and ice cream. In spite of that, most parkinsonian patients gradually lose weight, a process which can start early in the course of the illness. This loss of weight frequently causes concern, leading to an extensive medical workup to rule out thyroid disease, malignancy, and so on.

Constipation is one of the most common complaints from parkinsonian patients. They become preoccupied with their bowel function. Constipation exists for several reasons. Parkinsonian patients are physically less active, and because they feel weak they have difficulty bearing down hard enough to adequately increase the intraabdominal pressure. The antiparkinsonian drugs that patients take reduce bowel mobility, which in Parkinson's disease may already be less than normal.

GENITOURINARY SYSTEM

Some patients with Parkinson's disease experience urinary frequency and urgency, but they rarely have incontinence. Urodynamic studies in these patients reveal uninhibited, spontaneous, involuntary bladder contractions.

In general, there is a reduction in sexual drive associated with Parkinson's disease, but it depends a great deal on how well the parkinsonian symptoms are controlled with medications. It is uncommon for women with Parkinson's disease to be still menstruating; however, when they are, their responses to levodopa vary during the menstrual cycle. They tend to have more severe abnormal involuntary movements just prior to menstruation.

PATHOLOGY

In Parkinson's disease there is a profound loss of pigmented neurons in the brain stem, such as those in the substantia nigra, locus ceruleus, and dorsal nucleus of the vagus. Macroscopically, these structures in the brain stem are visibly pale, and by light microscopy the pigmented neurons are severely depleted. Electron microscopy studies[11] suggest that there is a partial loss of the very dense component of the melanin granules within the remaining pigmented neurons with exposure of the underlying lipofuscin matrix. In addition, there are spherical eosinophilic inclusions (Lewy bodies) found in the involved areas which are intracytoplasmic filamentous structures often adjacent to melanin granules. The origin of Lewy bodies is unclear. There are no other consistent macroscopic or histologic changes seen in the other areas of the brain in Parkinson's disease.

PATHOGENESIS

The etiology of Parkinson's disease is unknown. The fact that the pigmented neurons are primarily involved in Parkinson's disease suggests that the underlying cause of the disorder is linked to neuromelanin. Curiously, the large amount of neuromelanin in the substantia nigra, locus ceruleus, and dorsal nucleus of the vagus is found only in higher primates, with the greatest amount seen in humans. Normally, the pigment is first seen during the first year of life, and it accumulates until age 40 to 50, when the bodies of the pigmented cells are filled with pigment. The function of neuromelanin is obscure. It has been suggested that it may be a way to remove toxic substances formed in these neurons, such as metabolites of dopamine in the substantia nigra or metabolites of norepinephrine in the locus ceruleus. Interestingly, the activities of tyrosine hydroxylase and dopa decarboxylase, enzymes needed to synthesize dopamine and norepinephrine, show rapid decreases with age so that by ages 40 to 50 more than three-quarters of the activities are lost.[12,13] The changes in the activities of these enzymes appear to be inversely related to the increase in neuromelanin. Mann and Yates[14] have reported that when the amount of neuromelanin reaches about 25 percent of the volume of the bodies of the neurons, there is a profound decrease in the nucleolar and cytoplasmic RNA and thus in the ability to synthesize proteins. It remains to be determined if these changes are interrelated.

Regardless of the basic, underlying cause of Parkinson's disease, the fact remains that dopamine is profoundly reduced in the basal ganglia of patients with Parkinson's disease, and, to a lesser degree, norepinephrine and serotonin are reduced as well. When dopamine is replenished by the administration of levodopa, most of the parkinsonian symptoms are ameliorated significantly. In a broader sense, this avenue of therapy was made possible based on our prior knowledge that dopamine is reduced in Parkinson's disease. It is the first example of using a precursor to a neurotransmitter as a drug in the treatment of a disease.

LABORATORY STUDIES

The diagnosis of Parkinson's disease is based on the clinical symptoms and findings. Routine cerebrospinal fluid studies are normal. However, special studies on the cerebrospinal fluid such as the measurement of homovanillic acid (HVA), the main metabolite of dopamine, and of 5-hydroxyindoleacetic acid (5-HIAA), the main metabolite of serotonin, can be informative. Normally the HVA and 5-HIAA values are both above 40 ng/dl of cerebrospinal fluid. In Parkinson's disease they are reduced by at least 50 percent.

Routine blood and urine studies are normal. The electroencephalogram (EEG) is not revealing. Computed tomography (CT) of the head is normal in Parkinson's disease, but most clinicians recommend that it be done at least once early in the course of the disease to rule out other disorders which might parade as or be masked by the clinical features of Parkinson's disease. Magnetic resonance imaging (MRI) is useful in patients in whom the physician suspects multiple small infarcts in the basal ganglia, and elsewhere, producing parkinson-like symptoms. Also, it has been noted on MRI that in some patients there is increased iron "signal" in the basal ganglia, suggesting metabolic changes in these structures in Parkinson's disease. However, this finding is not diagnostic of Parkinson's disease, and further studies are needed to explain its significance.

MANAGEMENT OF PARKINSON'S DISEASE

The overall goal in treating Parkinson's disease is to maintain the patient as asymptomatic and functional as possible. The approach is multifaceted, which means use of antiparkinsonian medications along with a program of physical, speech, and occupational therapy, as well as psychotherapy. The therapeutic program must be individualized to meet the specific needs of the patient. The successful management of a parkinsonian patient hinges on establishing a good rapport with the patient and with those closest to the patient. From early on in the disease, parkinsonian patients are anxious about their symptoms and deeply concerned about their future. They need to be informed and reassured, since much of their anxiety stems from lack of knowledge about the disease and the common hearsay about Parkinson's disease as a progressive, debilitating disease.

ANTICHOLINERGIC DRUGS

The medical treatment of Parkinson's disease has vastly improved in the past 20 years. For many years prior to that, the only medications available for the treatment of Parkinson's disease were anticholinergic drugs. At first, only the naturally occurring anticholinergics, i.e., scopolamine and belladonna, were available. In the early 1950s, many synthetic anticholinergics were introduced.

Some of these anticholinergics are still available, and they can play an important role in the treatment of Parkinson's disease, especially in mild, early cases and in combination with dopamine agonists. These anticholinergics include trihexyphenidyl (Artane), benztropine (Cogentin), biperiden (Akineton), procyclidine (Kemadrin), ethopropazine (Parsidol), and others that are less commonly used. In general, all anticholinergic drugs produce about the same degree of improvement when given at their optimal doses. They act for 4 to 6 hours, and they are usually given two to three times a day. They are most effective against tremor and rigidity, but only minimally helpful for bradykinesia, postural impairment, and gait impairment.

Unfortunately, anticholinergic drugs can cause many unpleasant side effects, including dryness of the mouth, blurring of vision, reduced sweating, decreased emptying time of the stomach, constipation, mental changes, and difficulty voiding, especially in men with prostatic hypertrophy. The mental effects of anticholinergics can be troublesome, and they include impaired recent memory, visual illusions, and hallucinations. These mental symptoms occur more frequently and are more severe as the dosage is increased, especially in elderly patients who already show mental changes.

If an anticholinergic drug is stopped suddenly, the parkinsonian patient may experience in 2 to 3 days a withdrawal effect manifested by a worsening of parkinsonian symptoms for several days. It is important to recognize that this withdrawal phase may occur, since the patient (and physician) may conclude erroneously that the drug was more helpful to the patient than was previously appreciated. It is best to slowly taper off these drugs, if possible.

In 1968, amantadine (Symmetrel), an antiviral agent, was serendipitously found to be helpful in the treatment of Parkinson's disease. A parkinsonian patient who took amantadine to prevent the flu noted a significant improvement in her parkinsonian symptoms. Because amantadine was found to be helpful at about the same time that levodopa was discovered, amantadine was largely overlooked. Amantadine can be beneficial in about two-thirds of parkinsonian patients. It is usually well-tolerated, but the beneficial effects can be lost after only a few weeks to a few months.

The mode of action of amantadine is complex; it appears to augment the synthesis and release of dopamine, and it has anticholinergic properties. The duration of action of amantadine is about 6 to 8 hours. The side effects of amantadine include livedo reticularis, ankle swelling, and anticholinergic side effects. Livedo reticularis is a purplish mottling of the skin, usually of the legs but occasionally of other parts of the body, due to engorgement of the small veins of the skin. It is a benign and a totally reversible phenomenon. Ankle swelling

due to amantadine can be severe and may require discontinuing the drug. The anticholinergic side effects are usually mild and are similar to those listed above. Although younger parkinsonian patients can usually tolerate amantadine in doses of 300 mg/day, older patients should take only 200 mg/day or less. Higher doses can cause confusion, with visual illusions and hallucinations.

LEVODOPA

The approach to treating patients with Parkinson's disease was revolutionized with the advent of levodopa (L-dopa: L-3, 4-dihydroxyphenylalanine). This milestone followed several major scientific breakthroughs that occurred in the late 1950s and early 1960s. At that time, dopamine was found to be highly localized in some portions of the human extrapyramidal motor system (caudate, putamen, and substantia nigra), the areas involved in Parkinson's disease.[15] Subsequently, it was found that the substantia nigra was the seat for most of the dopaminergic neurons in the brain and that about 80 percent of their axons projected to the caudate and putamen (striatum), forming the nigrostriatal pathway.[16] Hornykiewicz[15] found that dopamine was profoundly reduced in the basal ganglia of patients who died with Parkinson's disease. Although he observed that norepinephrine and serotonin were reduced also, dopamine was the most drastically reduced of these biogenic amines in Parkinson's disease. Birkmayer and Hornykiewicz[17] reasoned that patients with Parkinson's disease might improve if the level of dopamine could be restored. With that in mind, they administered intravenously the amino acid DOPA, the precursor to dopamine, to patients with Parkinson's disease. They predicted that, unlike dopamine, DOPA would cross the blood-brain barrier and be converted to dopamine in the brain. Indeed, they observed a remarkable remission of symptoms that lasted a few hours. Thus, based on recently acquired scientific knowledge, a new approach to the treatment of Parkinson's disease was introduced. In a broader sense, it was the beginning of a new concept in therapy, that is, using a precursor amino acid to a neurotransmitter to correct a deficiency in that neurotransmitter and ameliorate symptoms.

From the time that intravenous DOPA was shown to reverse the symptoms of Parkinson's disease, it took more than 7 years before Cotzias et al. in 1967[18] demonstrated the beneficial effects of DOPA administered orally. Looking back, the long delay was mainly due to reports of several negative clinical trials with oral DOPA. These negative trials were later shown to be due to several errors, including inadequate amount of DOPA being given and patients being kept on large doses of pyridoxine (vitamin B_6) while taking DOPA orally, causing the rapid destruction of DOPA before it could reach the brain. Also, in some negative studies the patients probably had secondary parkinsonism due to long-term treatment with antipsychotic drugs such as phenothiazines. Cotzias et al. chose only patients with primary parkinsonism (Parkinson's disease), and they excluded other medications, including pyridoxine. They were first to document the benefits of orally administered DL-dopa. It soon followed that L-dopa (levodopa), the active isomer, became available for human use.

A few years later, carbidopa was combined with levodopa (Sinemet); the former blocks the peripheral destruction of levodopa and reduces the amount of levodopa needed. The mechanism of action of carbidopa depends on the fact that it is an excellent inhibitor of the enzymes DOPA decarboxylase and DOPA transaminase, the two main enzymes that metabolize DOPA. Carbidopa cannot cross the blood-brain barrier; therefore, carbidopa protects levodopa outside the brain, but it does not interfere with the metabolism of levodopa in the brain.

There are many factors affecting the action of orally administered levodopa. The absorption of levodopa from the intestine depends on the gastric content and on the rate at which the content is passed on to the small intestine. Carbohydrates shorten the emptying time of the stomach, while proteins lengthen it. Once in the duodenum and proximal portion of the jejunum, levodopa is actively transported across the intestinal mucosa into the circulation, sharing the transport mechanism with other large neutral amino acids, such as tyrosine, phenylalanine, tryptophan, valine, leucine, and isoleucine.[19] From the blood stream, levodopa is actively transported into the brain, again sharing the transport mechanism for large neutral amino acids.

Clearly, the type of food ingested can affect the amount of levodopa that reaches the brain. It may not be fortuitous that parkinsonian patients have a sweet tooth and naturally avoid large protein meals, such as those with steak, roast beef, and so on. On the other hand, extreme control of protein intake, such as no protein-containing foods during the day but with dinner only, as suggested by Pincus,[20] is unnecessary except in a very few patients. Moderate protein intake, i.e., 30 to 40 g/50 kg per day, is recommended. To enhance the absorption of levodopa, it should be taken 30 to 60 minutes before meals; however, this is not usually possible for patients who have just started to take levodopa because of nausea and emesis. Most patients who have taken levodopa for more than a year can take it before meals without experiencing nausea or emesis. On the other hand, for some patients a moderate amount of gastric content is good, in that it helps to slow down the rate of absorption of levodopa, avoiding sharp peaks and valleys in the amount that reaches the brain. In spite of careful control of the diet and the amount of levodopa taken,

there is still a marked variation in the plasma level of levodopa from day to day, within the same patient and between patients. This wide variation, which can be only partially reduced by fasting before taking levodopa, is poorly understood. Carbidopa given with levodopa does not alter this wide daily variation, although it does reduce nausea and emesis. Pyridoxine (vitamin B_6), which profoundly affects the metabolism of levodopa, is not involved either, since carbidopa blocks the effects of pyridoxine.

The peak plasma level of levodopa is reached between $\frac{1}{2}$ and 2 hours after intake, and only traces can be found 6 to 8 hours later. Curiously, the clinical response to levodopa, with or without carbidopa, does not correlate well with the plasma level of levodopa. This strongly suggests that patients, some more than others, can store levodopa and dopamine in the brain for a considerable period of time. This suggestion is consistent with the observation that the symptoms of Parkinson's disease can be improved significantly in 2 to 3 hours after a single dose of levodopa, but the benefits of levodopa can remain for several days after discontinuing the drug.

Side effects from levodopa were noted soon after it was introduced as a therapeutic agent. The most common side effects are nausea and emesis, abnormal involuntary movements, "wearing-off" and "on-off" phenomena, decreased benefit with time, and mental disturbances. Early on in the treatment with levodopa most parkinsonian patients experience, soon after taking the drug, nausea and sometimes emesis. For this reason, it is recommended that it be taken after meals to avoid a sudden high plasma level of levodopa. Carbidopa in combination with levodopa (Sinemet) has markedly reduced this problem; however, it may still occur unless the amount of carbidopa/levodopa (Sinemet) taken is small initially and then slowly increased. Sinemet (10/100) refers to 10 mg of carbidopa and 100 mg of levodopa, while Sinemet (25/100) contains 25 mg of carbidopa with 100 mg of levodopa. Usually the patient is started on either Sinemet (10/100) or Sinemet (25/100), one-half to one tablet taken after each of the three meals of the day. Slowly, over a period of 2 months, or longer if necessary, the amount of Sinemet is increased until the patient experiences optimal benefit without side effects. If nausea and emesis continue to be troublesome, an antiemetic drug such as diphenidol (Vontrol), 25 mg taken 20 to 30 minutes before Sinemet, can usually eliminate the problem. It is prudent to maintain the dose of Sinemet at a minimum and to adhere to three doses a day, with meals. Although there are still not enough data to support this notion, patients who do the best on Sinemet are those able to stay on relatively small doses and take it only at meal time (within a 12-hour period out of a 24-hour day). Studies are needed to assess the notion that the more frequently Sinemet is taken, day and night, the sooner the late-onset complications appear. These late-onset complications include abnormal involuntary movements, wearing-off and on-off phenomena, loss of benefit, and mental disturbances.

Dyskinesia, or abnormal involuntary movements associated with levodopa (Sinemet), limits the amount of the drug that the patient can take. These movements are varied and include myoclonic jerks, chorea, athetosis, and dystonia. At first these abnormal movements usually occur at the peak of the benefit from levodopa and on the side of the body most involved with Parkinson's disease. Eventually, these abnormal involuntary movements may follow a different pattern: they occur within a few minutes after taking levodopa (Sinemet), last only a few minutes, and are followed by improvement of the parkinsonian symptoms for 2 to 3 hours; then the abnormal involuntary movements resurface and last for 1 to 2 hours. This pattern is sometimes referred to as dyskinesia-improvement-dyskinesia (D.I.D.). The dyskinesias that occur at the end of the dose are usually the most violent and dramatic abnormal movements seen with levodopa therapy. If the dose of levodopa (Sinemet) is increased, this phenomenon may improve for a short while, but eventually the problem is made worse. There is no good solution to this complication associated with levodopa therapy. The best hope is for the patient to tolerate a very slow, gradual reduction of Sinemet over a period of several weeks to months until these abnormal movements are reduced. Although the patient may experience more parkinsonian symptoms, eventually he or she is better off. At times, a dopamine agonist such as bromocriptine (Parlodel) can be added at a small dose (i.e., 1.25 to 2.5 mg) with each dose of Sinemet and achieve some improvement without intensifying the abnormal, involuntary movements.

The wearing-off and the on-off phenomena are probably one and the same except that the latter is at the extreme end of the spectrum. The wearing-off or "end of the dose" effect is seen usually after 2 or more years on levodopa. Typically, the parkinsonian patient enjoys the benefits of levodopa (Sinemet) for 2 to 3 hours and then acutely becomes impaired due to a worsening of the parkinsonian symptoms. This "withdrawal" period lasts 20 to 30 minutes, and then the symptoms are partially ameliorated even without another dose of levodopa. If the dose of levodopa is increased, or the drug is given more frequently in an effort to overcome these periods, the problem may transiently improve, but eventually the situation worsens with more severe wearing-off and on-off periods, during which the patient becomes totally disabled for a period of time. In some patients the addition of a small dose of bromocriptine, given with Sinemet, helps to improve the situation.

Some patients on levodopa for 5 or more years will notice a gradual loss of benefit from the drug. Dopamine

agonists such as bromocriptine will not significantly improve the situation. Presumably the dopamine receptors have degenerated to the degree that they can no longer be stimulated, or some other unknown change has occurred.

In the past, patients suffering from severe manifestations of the late-onset complications of levodopa were hospitalized for the purpose of stopping levodopa for 7 to 10 days (a so-called drug holiday). The notion was that the dopamine receptors were profoundly altered by levodopa and that a holiday from levodopa corrected the problem. During the withdrawal period these patients showed severe worsening of their parkinsonian symptoms, often requiring nasogastric feeding, intensive physical and chest therapy to avoid pneumonia, and deep vein thrombophlebitis. Although these patients usually showed a significant improvement when levodopa was resumed, the benefit of the holiday was temporary; in fact, it rarely lasted for more than a few weeks.[21] This approach to the problem has been abandoned.

DIRECT-ACTING DOPAMINE AGONISTS

Bromocriptine (Parlodel) is the only direct dopamine agonist approved for human use in the United States. Bromocriptine can be helpful, as stated above, in combination with levodopa (Sinemet). Although it has been recommended by some that bromocriptine be used initially for the treatment of Parkinson's disease instead of levodopa, in most cases it is not adequate when used alone. Some investigators have argued that it is wise to delay the use of levodopa as long as possible in order to postpone the late-onset complications of levodopa therapy. As stated above, many clinical investigators feel that the judicious use of levodopa from the outset can significantly delay, and possibly avoid, the appearance of the late-onset complications of levodopa therapy.

Pergolide (Permax) is another direct dopamine agonist which will soon be available for use in the United States. Pergolide is an ergot derivative similar to bromocriptine. Some patients do better with pergolide than with bromocriptine, but others show no significant difference in response to use of one drug over the other.

PHYSICAL THERAPY

A well-designed exercise program for patients with Parkinson's disease is essential to maintain good muscle tone and function. Parkinsonian patients tend to become inactive, and often they do not appreciate the importance of exercise. Relatively few parkinsonian patients will faithfully carry out a daily exercise program unless they are continuously encouraged and supervised. For this reason it is wise to encourage parkinsonian patients to participate in a group exercise program guided by an experienced physical therapist who understands the fundamental neuromuscular changes encountered in Parkinson's disease.

Patients with parkinsonism have reduction in the range of motion that decreases even more on repetitive movements. One of the goals of exercise is to have patients overcome this problem by doing full range-of-motion exercises frequently during the day. Parkinsonian patients fatigue easily, and therefore it is better for them to exercise for short periods, i.e., 5 to 10 minutes several times a day, than to exercise for a long period once a day. Frequent, short periods of exercises help to keep muscle rigidity down to minimum.

Gait difficulty and postural reflex impairment in parkinsonian patients are major disabilities that unfortunately respond poorly to all antiparkinsonian medications. In fact, in some patients, increasing the dose of levodopa (Sinemet) or direct dopamine agonists can accentuate the problem. On the other hand, an experienced physical therapist can significantly help these patients, and this kind of therapy is the best avenue of treatment for gait and balance difficulty.

In parkinsonian patients the overall speed of gait is reduced, as is the forward progression of the body. The stride length and the mean speed are reduced, while the duration of each cycle is increased. Although the velocity is greatly diminished, the work-per-unit distance in a parkinsonian patient is close to that of normal individuals. Both hip and knee excursions during the cycle are shortened because flexion normally occurring at the beginning of the swing and extension at the end of the swing are reduced in parkinsonian patients. The initial contact of the foot, normally occurring with the heel, almost invariably occurs with the foot flat or on the ball of the foot. This is partially the result of inadequate extension of the knee in the terminal swing. During stance, the hips and knees remain flexed, but at the end of the stance the knee does not flex enough to gain the momentum the limb needs to initiate swing. Trunk rotation and arm swing are also diminished. Festination, or the tendency to take smaller and smaller steps while increasing forward propulsion, is in part due to the system trying unsuccessfully to control the forward progression of the body and the unsuccessful weight shift onto the stance limb during the advancement of the swing limb. A properly selected program of physical therapy can increase weight shift, encourage unilateral weight bearing, facilitate postural reactions, and increase trunk rotation. Thus, exercise to improve these motor functions is critical in patients with gait and postural reflex impairment. Group activities often accomplish these goals while providing emotional support, decreasing social isolation, and encouraging competition.

RECENT DEVELOPMENTS IN THE TREATMENT OF PARKINSON'S DISEASE

Continuous Release of Levodopa/Carbidopa (Sinemet CR)

Soon after Sinemet was introduced it was suggested that a continuous-release form of the drug could give an even delivery of levodopa to the brain and thus possibly smooth out the effects of levodopa. Several preparations of Sinemet CR have been tried with mixed results. One of the problems related to continuous-release Sinemet is to find the proper matrix needed to release the drug in the appropriate portion of the small bowel. Recent data suggest that this goal may be reached in the near future. Whether Sinemet CR will help to reduce the late-onset complications of levodopa remains to be determined.

Monoamine Oxidase Inhibitor of the B Form

Deprenyl selectively inhibits monoamine oxidase of the B form (MAO_B), allowing dopamine to accumulate in the brain. Unfortunately, Deprenyl is not available in the United States yet. All MAO inhibitors that are approved for clinical use in the United States inhibit both forms of the enzyme, MAO_A and MAO_B, and as such they cannot be used with Sinemet. Deprenyl does enhance the effects of levodopa (Sinemet) by as much as 20 to 30 percent. Deprenyl is a mild mood elevator, and many patients feel that it increases their level of energy.

In addition, Birkmayer et al.[22] have reported that Deprenyl may slow down the progression of Parkinson's disease. In a long-term (9-year) retrospective study of 564 parkinsonian patients on Deprenyl plus all other antiparkinsonian drugs normally used compared with 377 patients on no Deprenyl but on all other antiparkinsonian drugs, those on Deprenyl did better in that their disabilities were significantly less and their life expectancy increased. The study concluded that Deprenyl prevents or retards the degeneration of nigrostriatal dopaminergic neurons. If so, Deprenyl is the first antiparkinsonian drug with the ability to retard or prevent further progression of the disease. These observations need to be retested in a prospective study, which is currently being done.

Surgical Approach to the Treatment of Parkinson's Disease

Several surgical approaches to alleviate the symptoms of Parkinson's disease have been attempted for the past several decades. Lesions produced stereotactically in the ventrolateral nucleus of the thalamus can relieve contralateral tremor and rigidity; however, bradykinesia, gait impairment, and postural impairment are not improved. With the advent of levodopa in 1967, this approach has been all but discontinued.

Surgical Autologous Adrenal Medullary Transplantation

In 1987, Madrazo et al.[23] reported improvement in all parkinsonian symptoms following the transplantation of the adrenal medulla from the patient to the caudate nucleus. Based on this report, over 200 patients have undergone this procedure throughout the United States. The results have been disappointing, and the procedure has been all but discontinued. However, selective areas of improvement in some of these patients have been noted. For instance, patients tend to have fewer wearing-off and on-off periods. Goetz et al.[24] have concluded that the widespread use of adrenal medullary transplantation to treat Parkinson's disease is not warranted, but further research is indicated.

Fetal Substantia Nigra Implantation

Several clinical research centers in Europe and elsewhere have begun to implant fetal substantia nigra into the basal ganglia of patients with severe Parkinson's disease. So far, it is too soon to know the outcome of this potentially exciting new approach to the treatment of Parkinson's disease.

CONCLUSIONS

Parkinson's disease is a progressive, disabling illness which has been at the forefront of research in neurology for many years. In recent years, major advances have been made both in our understanding of the disease process and in our therapeutic approaches. However, the treatment of Parkinson's disease is still far from its ultimate goal of uncovering the cause of the disease and correcting it before the symptoms become irreversible.

REFERENCES

1. Parkinson J: An essay on the shaking palsy. Sherwood, Neely and Jones, 1817. Reprinted in *Medical Classics* 2:964, 1938.
2. Calne DB: *Parkinsonism: Physiology, Pharmacology and Treatment.* Baltimore, Williams & Wilkins, 1970.
3. Martilla RJ: Diagnosis and epidemiology of Parkinson's disease. *Neurologica Scand (suppl)* 95:9, 1983.
4. Ward CD, Duvoisin RC, Ince SE, Nutt JD, Eldridge R, Calne DB: Parkinson's disease in 65 pairs of twins and in a set of quadruplets. *Neurology* 35:841, 1985.
5. Snider SR, Fahn S, Cote LJ, Isgreen WP: Primary sensory symptoms in Parkinson's disease, in Birkmayer W, Hornykiewicz O (eds): *Advances in Parkinsonism.* Basle, Roche Scientific Service, 1976, pp 367–376.
6. Haerer AF, Anderson UW, Schoenberg BS: Prevalence of essential tremor. *Arch Neurol* 39:750, 1982.
7. Mayeux R, Stern Y, Cote L, Williams JBW: Altered serotonin metabolism in depressed patients with Parkinson's disease. *Neurology* 34:642, 1984.
8. Stern Y, Mayeux R, Cote LJ: Reaction time and vigilance in Parkinson's disease: Possible role of altered norepinephrine metabolism. *Arch Neurol* 41:1086, 1984.
9. Mayeux R: Depression and dementia in Parkinson's disease, in Marsden CD, Fahn S (eds): *Movement Disorders.* London, Butterworth, 1982, pp 75–95.
10. Bronx RG, Marsden CD: How common is dementia in Parkinson's disease. *Lancet* 1262, 1984.
11. Duffy PE, Tennyson VM: Phase and electron microscopic observations of Lewy bodies and melanin granules in the sustantia nigra and locus caeruleus in Parkinson's disease. *J Neuropathol Exp Neurol* 24:398, 1965.
12. McGeer EG, McGeer PL: Age changes in the human for some enzymes associated with metabolism of catecholamines, GABA, acetylcholine, in Ordy JM, Brizzee KR (eds): *Neurobiology of Aging: Advances in Behavioral Biology,* vol 16. New York, Raven Press, 1975, pp 287–305.
13. Cote LJ, Kremzner LT: Biochemical changes in normal aging in human brain, in Mayeux R, Rosen WG (eds): *Advances in Neurology, The Dementias.* New York, Raven Press, 1982, pp 19–30.
14. Mann DMA, Yates PO: Possible role of neuromelanin in the pathogenesis of Parkinson's disease. *Mech Ageing Dev* 21:193, 1983.
15. Hornykiewicz O: Brain transmitter changes in Parkinson's disease, in Marsden CD, Fahn S (eds): *Neurology, II. Movement Disorders.* London, Butterworth, 1982, pp 41–58.
16. Anden NE, Carlsson A, Dahstrom A, Fuxe K, Hillary NA, Larsson K: Demonstration and mapping out of nigro-neostriatal dopamine neurons. *Life Sci* 3:523, 1964.
17. Birkmayer W, Hornykiewicz O: Der L-3, 4-Dioxyphenylalanine (=DOPA)-Effekt bei der Parkinson-Akinese. *Wien Klin Wochenschr* 73:787, 1961.
18. Cotzias GC, Van Woert MH, Schiffer LM: Aromatic amino acids and modification of Parkinsonism. *N Engl J Med* 276:374, 1967.
19. Nutt JG, Woodward WR, Hammerstad JP, Carter JH, Anderson JL: The "on-off" phenomenon in Parkinson's disease: Relation to levodopa absorption and transport. *N Engl J Med* 310:483, 1984.
20. Pincus JH, Barry K: Influence of dietary protein on motor fluctuations in Parkinson's disease. *Arch Neurol* 44:270, 1987.
21. Mayeux R, Stern Y, Mulvey K, Cote LJ: Reappraisal of temporary levodopa withdrawal ("drug holiday") in Parkinson's disease. *N Engl J Med* 313:724, 1985.
22. Birkmayer W, Knoll J, Riederer P, Youdim MBH, Hars V, Marton J: Increased life expectancy resulting from addition of L-Deprenyl to madopar treatment in Parkinson's disease: A longterm study. *J Neurol Trans* 64:113, 1985.
23. Madrazo I, Drucker-Colin R, Diaz V et al: Open microsurgical autograft of adrenal medulla to the right caudate nucleus in two patients with intractable Parkinson's disease. *N Engl J Med* 316:831, 1987.
24. Goetz CG, Olanow W, Koller WC et al: Multicenter study of autologous adrenal medullary transplantation to the corpus striatum in patients with advanced Parkinson's disease. *N Engl J Med* 320:337, 1989.

Chapter 95

OTHER DEGENERATIVE DISORDERS OF THE NERVOUS SYSTEM

John P. Blass and Donald L. Price

This chapter deals with several degenerative disorders of the nervous system that are discussed in other chapters from other viewpoints or are not discussed elsewhere in this volume. The topics discussed here are pure autonomic failure; multiple system degenerations, including Shy-Drager syndrome, nigrostriatal degeneration, olivopontocerebellar atrophies, and amyotrophy-parkinsonian complex; and motor neuron diseases (amyotrophic lateral sclerosis, ALS).

PURE AUTONOMIC FAILURE

The subject of autonomic failure has been fully reviewed in a recent multiauthor volume.[1] Diagnostic classifications of disorders associated with autonomic failure has been somewhat confusing in part because this syndrome occurs in a variety of settings. When autonomic failure is associated with a well-characterized disease entity (e.g., diabetes) in which aspects of the pathology and pathophysiology have been identified, then the autonomic failure is classified as secondary (e.g., "diabetic autonomic neuropathy"). Other patients, in whom the etiology of the autonomic failure is unknown, are considered to have "pure autonomic failure." These patients include those who have a familial disorder, since no gene for familial autonomic failure has as yet been identified. The term *pure autonomic failure* (PAF) has been chosen to replace the earlier form "idiopathic orthostatic hypotension" (IOH). The word "pure" in PAF does not imply either pathological or pathophysiological homogeneity among these patients, nor similarity or dissimilarity to other syndromes in which autonomic failure occurs. "Pure" simply implies the absence of other recognized

clinical abnormalities in these individuals. The syndromes associated with autonomic failure are summarized in Table 95-1. Aspects of autonomic failure associated with general medical illnesses are discussed in the appropriate chapters (e.g., Chap. 71 on diabetes).

The syndrome of pure autonomic failure is recognized clinically when alterations in autonomic function cross a threshold and begin causing clinical disability in the affected patient. Autonomic function tends to decrease with aging even in otherwise healthy individuals. Several mechanisms appear to contribute to the age-associated effects, including adaptive mechanisms. Levels of circulating catecholamines appear to increase with age. The *affinity* of adrenergic receptors for their physiological ligands appears not to be altered by age, while data implicating a decrease in receptor *number* is controversial.[2] The functional efficiency of the responses mediated by adrenergic receptors appears in general to decrease with age in both humans and experimental animals, whether measured by such physiological parameters as the response of isolated mesenteric arterioles or aortic strips[2] or by chemical determinations of the generation of intracellular second messengers such as adenyl cyclase.[2,3] It has been proposed that some of these changes in the efficiency of adrenergic receptor functioning represent changes in the membranes in which these receptors are embedded. With aging, degenerative changes and neuronal cell loss characteristically occur in both central and peripheral neural structures mediating autonomic responses (see Chap. 88), including central nuclei characteristically involved in multiple system atrophy (see below). Elderly patients with autonomic failure characteristically have, however, an *increased* response to pressors and other medications

TABLE 95-1
Syndromes of Autonomic Failure

   I. Due to primary disease of the nervous system
      1. Pure autonomic failure (previously called idiopathic orthostatic hypotension)
      2. Autonomic failure with multiple system atrophy, including Shy-Drager syndrome and the syndromes of nigrostriatal degeneration (NSD) and olivopontocerebellar atrophy (OPCA)
      3. Autonomic failure with Parkinson's disease
      4. Autonomic failure with spinal cord lesions
      5. Autonomic failure with brain lesions, including hypothalamic mass lesions
  II. Due to general disorders
      1. Diabetic
      2. Associated with other metabolic disorders (porphyria, Fabry's disease, Tangier disease, Vitamin B_{12} and B_1 deficiency
      3. Amyloid
      4. Autoimmune (including collagen-vascular disorders)
      5. Carcinomatous
      6. Infections (HIV, syphilis, Chagas disease, botulism, herpes zoster)
      7. Renal failure
 III. Pharmacologically induced, by
      1. Alcohol
      2. Phenothiazines
      3. Barbiturates
      4. Antidepressants, including tricylic and MAO inhibitors
      5. Antihypertensives (vasodilator, centrally active antihypertensives, adrenergic and ganglionic blockers, ACE inhibitors)

SOURCE: Modified from Bannister, p. 8.[1]

which act on adrenergic systems.[4] Their increased sensitivity to these agents is usually attributed to *denervation sensitivity*, despite their characteristically elevated levels of circulating catecholamines. Bannister[1] makes a distinction between "primary autonomic failure" and "postural hypotension of the elderly,"[5] although the pathological and pathophysiological changes appear to be part of a continuum. Symptomatic postural hypotension may be more common in the elderly because the superposition of even relatively mild changes of disease on top of changes associated with aging may lead to effects which cross the threshold into clinical symptoms.

Clinically, the most frequent reason that patients with pure autonomic failure seek medical attention is postural hypotension.[1] The earliest symptoms are, however, characteristically referable to the genitourinary system. In men, impotence and loss of libido are common. They are typically manifested by decreasing ability to achieve erection, sometimes following a period of increased erectile activity, and later by failure of ejaculation. In both men and women, urinary disturbances,

including incontinence, are common early signs. Various combinations of symptoms and signs can occur, linked to particular types of physiological disturbances. Uninhibited detrusor activity tends to lead to urgency, frequency, and nocturia. Incontinence can be due to either sphincter weakness or to an atonic bladder. Bladder weakness can lead to a weak or interrupted stream and even to a total inability to urinate. These symptoms in men are similar to those occurring with prostate disease, and it is frequently important to differentiate these conditions to prevent unnecessary surgery. Bowel function is affected less commonly. Decreased sweating is an important, common, and early manifestation of autonomic failure. In warm climates, where the ability to perspire is important to prevent syndromes of hyperthermia, the first manifestation of pure autonomic failure may be heat intolerance.

Postural hypotension is discussed in detail in Chaps. 48 and 109. The pathophysiology involves pooling of blood in the lower limbs due to impaired vasoconstriction. Generally, postural hypotension manifests itself clinically as dizziness or light-headedness developing over a period of seconds to a minute or so, although sudden "drop attacks" also often occur. Warning symptoms may include a severe ache in the neck or visual symptoms. The latter can include scotomata, hallucinations, or tunnel vision. Symptoms characteristically occur after the patient arises from a recumbent or sitting position. Circumstances which lead to an unfavorable distribution of blood volume characteristically exacerbate symptoms. Thus, symptoms are more likely to occur in hot weather, in the mornings, after exercise, and characteristically after a meal (post-cibal hypotension). Lying flat typically leads to recovery from all symptoms within a few minutes.

Tests for autonomic failure are based on the known physiology and pharmacology of the autonomic system, and these have been extensively reviewed.[1] Common clinical tests monitor cardiovascular function (maintenance of blood pressure on standing, presence or absence of sinus arrhythmia on deep breathing, startle or other stress response leading to hypertension and tachycardia, maintenance of blood pressure, and transient tachycardia after Valsalva maneuver). Other bedside tests include sweating (in response to heat or pilocarpine) and pupillary responses (to adrenaline, cocaine, or methanochol). More detailed discussions of detection of disordered autonomic responses in these and other organ systems, including the genitourinary system, are presented in other chapters. As yet, direct electrophysiological monitoring of neural activity remains a research technique.

The *prognosis* in pure autonomic failure is relatively good. Permanent sequelae are rare. Although falls in blood pressure to as low as 60 mm systolic can occur, they rarely precipitate frank strokes. While arrhythmias may occur, due in part perhaps to impaired autonomic function in the heart, permanent cardiac consequences are also rare. A few patients who have been treated with bed rest for postural hypotension have developed persistent recumbent hypertension, probably due mainly to loss of baroreceptor reflexes. The prognosis of autonomic failure associated with another disease is no better than that of the disease with which it is associated. For instance, when autonomic failure is the first manifestation of multiple system atrophy, the prognosis is usually poor (see below).

Therapy of autonomic failure is discussed in the chapters which deal with the particular organ systems involved. A general principle is to treat disability but to avoid treating asymptomatic physiological abnormalities. A number of pharmacological and physiological approaches are available for the therapy of postural hypotension, but, as emphasized by Bannister and Mathias,[6] the first lines of treatment are counseling of the patient and caregivers and the use of the head-up position while sleeping at night (Table 95-2).

MULTIPLE SYSTEM ATROPHY

The term *multiple system atrophy (MSA)* has come into increasing use to refer to a group of overlapping syndromes, some of which have previously been described

TABLE 95-2
Approach to Treatment of Postural Hypotension

Education of the patient and caregiver
  Techniques include the need to arise slowly and carefully while holding on to a support, after being supine or sitting, or after a large meal; avoiding factors which exacerbate the condition, including inappropriate drugs; effects of a warm environment; tendency of blood pressure to be lowest in the morning and to rise during the day.
Head-up tilt at night
  Sleeping with head-up tilt at night tends to increase body water by well-characterized mechanisms and is often adequate to control symptoms for years.
External support
  Support hose or more specific fitted garments, which prevent pooling of blood in the legs on arising.
Cardiac pacing
  Generally less effective in patients with more severe lesions.
Medications
  Vasoconstrictors, blockers of vasodilatations (such as propranolol), medications preventing postprandial hypotension (including caffeine), cardiotonic medications, and plasma expanders (including fludrocortisone).

SOURCE: Modified from Bannister and Mathias.[6]

as separate diseases. As discussed in Chap. 94, these overlap with variant forms of parkinsonism. The MSAs include a group of disorders, themselves complex and overlapping, referred to as the "olivopontocerebellar atrophies" (OPCAs). The OPCAs are part of a larger group of degenerative disorders of the nervous system called the "spinocerebellar degenerations" (SCDs) or "hereditary ataxias." The various forms of MSAs, including specifically the OPCAs (and in fact the SCDs in general), typically affect the motor system as well as other parts of the nervous system. Since motor function, including coordination, has been relatively well mapped topographically in the nervous system, and since the classical neurological examination gives detailed information about motor function, it has been possible to classify these patients clinically into a wide variety of subgroups on the basis of clinical and pathological patterns.[7] Refsum and Skre[8] have pointed out that there are nearly as many classifications of these disorders as there are classifiers. The discussion below uses the classification recently put forward by Fahn,[9] as well as the formulations of Bannister.[1]

The full syndrome of MSA involves the symptoms and signs of PAF as well as other neurological manifestations. These include weakness and spasticity; rigidity; rest tremor; cog-wheeling; intention tremor and loss of skill in rapid succession movements; gait disturbances, including frank ataxia; pupillary disturbances, including Horner's syndrome; alternating anisocoria and abnormal responses to drugs; muscle wasting; disorders of breathing, including gasping respiration and sleep apnea; and laryngeal stridor with accompanying hypoxia. The neurological manifestations can be linked to the particular systems involved pathologically: weakness and spasticity (upper motor neuron disease); parkinsonian signs, including rigidity and tremor (basal ganglia); ataxia (cerebellum and inferior olivary nuclei); pupillary disturbances and disorders of respiration (nuclei of the basis ponti); autonomic failure (preganglionic sympathetic neurons in the thoracic cord); and weakness and muscle wasting (damage to spinal motor neurons). Studies of the age incidence of MSA suggest that it is primarily a disease of those over 60 years of age.

Four syndromes which are now classified as parts of the spectrum of MSA are the Shy-Drager syndrome, olivopontocerebellar atrophy, the parkinsonism-amyotrophy syndrome, and nigrostriatal degeneration.

The Shy-Drager syndrome represents that part of the spectrum in which autonomic failure is prominently associated with a disorder of coordination, related to disease of either the basal ganglia or the cerebellum.[9] The onset of this form of MSA is typically in the fifth to the seventh decade of life. The two most common clinical forms are autonomic failure with parkinsonism and autonomic failure plus ataxia. Pathologically, there is a characteristic loss of neurons in the intermediolateral horns and of the preganglionic sympathetic neurons. Degeneration of the substantia nigra correlates with the parkinsonian syndrome, lesions of the cerebellum are related to ataxia, and damage to the striatum is associated with the lack of a therapeutic response to L-DOPA. The original patients of Shy and Drager[10] also had reduced numbers of anterior horn cells, with resultant weakness, fasciculations, muscle wasting, and evidence of denervation on electromyography and muscle biopsy. A characteristic finding in Shy-Drager syndrome is normal levels of plasma norepinephrine when the patient is recumbent, with a failure of plasma norepinephrine to rise when the patient stands.[9]

The phenotype in the MSA spectrum represented by the combination of cerebellar and extrapyramidal disease is classified as OPCA. The pathology is that of Shy-Drager syndrome without involvement of the intermediolateral horns and thus with less prominent autonomic involvement. Ataxia, often including truncal ataxia, may be the most disabling symptom. It should be noted that OPCA syndromes can also occur at a younger age and in familial forms, but the extensive discussion of OPCAs and of other SCDs falls outside the scope of a book on geriatrics and gerontology.[7,11]

The parkinsonism-amyotrophy syndrome, a relatively rare entity, is that part of the MSA spectrum in which prominent damage is restricted to the anterior horn cells and the nigrostriatal complex. It manifests itself clinically as expected in a combination of weakness, muscle wasting, fasciculations, and evidence for denervation on muscle biopsy and electromyography (due to the anterior horn cell lesion) and of parkinsonian signs and symptoms (due to nigrostriatal damage).

Nigrostriatal degeneration is that part of the MSA spectrum in which nerve cell loss and gliosis are predominantly in the nigra- and neostriatum. The symptoms are those of parkinsonism, but without tremor and with poor response to L-DOPA (since the striatal cells are severely damaged). If associated with cerebellar damage and cerebellar ataxia—or if such cerebellar damage develops during the course of the disease—the condition would be classified as a form of OPCA.

As the above discussion indicates, patients afflicted with these disorders are part of a spectrum. The diagnostic category which is appropriate for a particular patient may change as the disease progresses. For instance, patients with OPCA and nigrostriatal degeneration typically do not have fasciculations but do have evidence of damage to lower motor neurons on electromyographic investigation and muscle biopsy. If these manifestations become more prominent as the disorder progresses, the classification of that patient may have to change.

Laboratory tests can assist in the diagnosis of MSA. The anatomic nature of the brain damage in these pa-tients can now be documented with newer scanning techniques. Magnetic resonance imaging (MRI) provides a better image of subcortical structures and particularly of the brain stem than was possible with at least the older CT scanners. Brain stem auditory evoked potentials (BAERs) are also characteristically abnormal in patients with MSA.[12]

The etiology of the MSAs is not known. One form of MSA is associated with a deficiency of the enzyme glutamate dehydrogenase.[13] In the rat, the form of enzyme which is deficient appears to be concentrated in glia surrounding nuclei analogous to those which degenerate in MSA in the human syndrome.[14] The speculation has been made that the enzyme may be involved in removing the excitotoxin glutamate, and that the presence of elevated amounts of glutamate over protracted periods may lead to premature degeneration of those neurons receiving glutamatergic innervation. Other studies have suggested that mitochondrial abnormalities may be a common underlying feature in these disorders, with the damage again mediated through a glutamatergic, excitotoxic effect.[7]

The *prognosis* and *response to treatment* in the MSAs vary with the specific syndromes but can be disappointing. Treatment is directed to the manifestations of autonomic failure. Treatment of the symptoms and signs related to disease of the basal ganglia is often disappointing. Indeed, failure of response to L-DOPA or to Sinemet is a characteristic finding of some forms of these disorders.

As the above discussion documents, the MSAs remain a confusing clinical area, even for the specialist. Optimal diagnosis and care of patients with these disorders requires consultation with a qualified neurologist.

MOTOR NEURON DISEASES

The group of patients who suffer from selective dysfunction and death of cells mediating voluntary motor function are described as suffering from motor neuron disease. These are particularly disorders of older age, and the incidence may increase linearly with age from middle age onward.[15]

The defining characteristic of this syndrome is involvement of the voluntary motor system *without* clinically significant involvement of other parts of the nervous system. At the onset of the disease, findings may be primarily of weakness, spasticity, and hyperreflexia with extensor plantar responses, associated with damage to upper motor neurons in the cerebral cortex, or they may be associated primarily with weakness, muscle wasting, and fasciculation due to damage to lower motor neurons in the spinal cord and brain stem. The syndrome in which disability is due primarily to damage to upper motor neurons is "primary lateral sclerosis," whereas that in which clinical signs and symptoms are due primarily to damage to lower motor neurons is "progressive muscular atrophy." In most cases, within a year or two, signs of and symptoms of both upper and lower motor neuron disease are, however, evident, and lead to the classic syndrome of amyotrophic lateral sclerosis (ALS).

Clinically, the first signs and symptoms depend on the degree of damage to upper and lower motor neurons. Munsat[15] suggests that the presenting signs are slightly more often referable to loss of neurons in the cervical cord (e.g., weakness and fasciculations in the hands—38 percent) than abnormalities in the lumbar cord (26 percent) or medulla (27 percent). In the remaining 9 percent of patients the exact nature of the presenting manifestations is mixed. Problems with gait, with limb weakness, or with speaking or eating are common early complaints. As with other degenerative diseases of the nervous system, the abnormalities may start asymmetrically, but the process rapidly becomes symmetrical.

On physical examination, the diagnostic hallmarks of motor neuron diseases are weakness, atrophy, and fasciculations. The latter are visible twitches believed to be due to the spontaneous firing of single giant motor units secondary to the loss of other motor neurons. Fasciculations can sometimes be elicited, when they are not evident spontaneously, by tapping a muscle once briskly with a reflex hammer and then observing it for a minute or so. Weakness, atrophy, and fasciculations in the tongue are other common physical signs of the motor neuron diseases. Whether reflexes are increased or decreased depends on the relative balance of abnormalities of upper motor neurons (spasticity and hyperreflexia) and lower motor neurons (flaccid weakness and atrophy). Other neurological functions are characteristically spared. Voluntary eye movements and the control of urinary and other sphincters are typically normal, as is sensation. Intellect is characteristically normal, although uncommon syndromes have been reported in which upper and lower motor neuron disease accompanies more extensive brain damage and is associated with dementia.

Laboratory tests document the presence of a subacute denervating process. If abnormalities of lower motor neurons are prominent, the electromyogram (EMG) shows evidence of denervation and renervation. If upper motor neuron disease predominates, EMG findings may not be prominent. Motor nerve conduction velocities, and sometimes those of sensory nerves as well, tend to be slowed. Muscle biopsy can be a useful procedure to document lesions of lower motor neurons, even in the early stages of the disorder. Elevations of creatine phosphokinase correlate with the degree of weakness but not with the duration or rate of progression

of the disease. Other clinical laboratory tests tend to be normal.

Patients should be screened for causes of multiple nerve root compression as in cervical spondylosis or in compressing or other mass lesions, which are potentially more treatable. MRI or CT scan are now used in preference to myelography. They should also be carried out in patients with upper motor neuron signs in both legs, again to rule out a treatable mass lesion. Other routine investigations in these patients should be for lead toxicity and for paraproteinemias, both of which can cause motor neuron syndromes.

The *pathology* of this disorder is consistent with degeneration of motor neurons, both in the cortex and in the spinal cord. It appears that spinal motor neurons do not die suddenly in these disorders, but rather develop functional abnormalities associated with structural changes.[16] These include the accumulation of filaments proximally and their relative depletion distally, consistent with a defect in axonal transport. Since axonal transport is sensitive to a variety of insults to the cell, this finding unfortunately does not give a clear clue to fundamental etiology. Loss of axons and secondary demyelination lead to thinning and pallor of the motor nerve roots, particularly when compared to the (posterior) sensory roots. Loss of axons of upper motor neurons is associated with pallor in the corticospinal tracts.

The *etiology* of the motor neuron diseases is not known. Analogies to poliomyelitis have made viral theories of interest, and the recognition of "post-polio" syndromes has encouraged speculations about possible roles of antecedent viral disorders. There is, however, no evidence for a viral etiology of the common forms of motor neuron diseases in older individuals. Lead toxicity can lead to a similar syndrome, but attempts to link toxins, including heavy metals, to the common forms of this disorder have not provided convincing evidence. In about 10 to 15 percent of adult patients, the disorder appears to be familial. Rarely, motor neuron disease is a variant manifestation of a hexosaminadase deficiency,[17] but these patients are a very small fraction of the total suffering from these disorders. As noted above, abnormalities of motor neurons can be a part of more widespread neurological disorders, including MSA. By definition, disorders which involve but are not limited to motor neurons are not called motor neuron disease. Some of these other disorders, in which motor neurons as well as other parts of the neuraxis are involved, have a clear genetic etiology.

The *prognosis* in motor neuron diseases is variable but tends to be poor. Death typically occurs in over 70 percent of patients within 5 years after both upper and lower motor neurons are clearly involved.[15,16] The prognosis tends to be better in patients in whom involvement remains limited to either upper motor neurons (primary lateral sclerosis or familial spastic paraparesis) or to lower motor neurons (progressive muscular atrophy). If only upper or only lower motor neurons appear involved after 2 years, extension appears relatively unlikely and the prognosis therefore better. Indeed, familial spastic paraparesis appears usually not to be a life-shortening condition. On the other hand, if bulbar involvement is prominent (progressive bulbar palsy), the prognosis tends to be poorer. The poorer prognosis appears to reflect not so much more rapid progression of the disease as the critical nature of the functions of bulbar neurons. A particular danger to patients with prominent bulbar involvement is aspiration. Motor neuron disease appears to be tolerated more poorly in older patients, perhaps because of their general frailty. The immediate cause of death is typically pulmonary disease, as is often true in chronic degenerative disorders of the nervous system. The immediate causes can include respiratory failure or pneumonia related to aspiration or failure to clear secretions.

Treatment of motor neuron diseases is symptomatic. No medical therapy is known to alter the outcome. On the other hand, antispastic medications, such as baclofen or benzodiazepines, can make a patient more comfortable and more functional. Anticholinergics can help with excessive salivation (trihexyphenidyl, amitriptyline, or atropine). Tracheotomy can prolong life, but it should be undertaken only when the patient and family understand and agree to the implications. As in patients with other chronic diseases, the patient and family require from the physician both realism and compassion.

REFERENCES

1. Bannister R (ed): *Autonomic Failure*, 2d ed. New York, Oxford University Press, 1988.
2. Kelly J, O'Malley K: Adrenoreceptor function and ageing. *Clin Sci* 66:590, 1984.
3. Narayan N, Derby JA: Alterations in the properties of beta-adrenergic receptors of myocardial membranes in ageing: Impairments in agonist-receptor interactions and guanine nucleotide regulation accompanying diminished catecholamine responsiveness of adenylate cylclase. *Mech Ageing Develop* 19:127, 1982.
4. Bannister R, Davies IB, Holly E, Rosenthal T, Sever PS: Defective cardiovascular reflexes and supersensitivity to sympathomimetic drugs in autonomic failure. *Brain* 102:163, 1979.
5. Robinson BJ, Johnson RH, Lambie DG, Palmer KT: Do elderly patients with an excessive fall in blood pressure on standing have evidence of autonomic failure? *Clin Sci* 64:587, 1983.
6. Bannister R, Mathias C: Management of postural hypotension, in Bannister R, (ed): *Autonomic Failure*. New York, Oxford University Press, pp 569–595, 1988.
7. Blass JP, Sheu KFR, Cedarbaum JM: Energy metabolism in disorders of the nervous system. *Rev Neurol* 144:543, 1988.
8. Refsum S, Skre H: Neurological approaches to the hereditary ataxias. *Adv Neurol* 21:1, 1978.
9. Fahn S: Parkinson's disease and other basal ganglion disorders, in Asbury AK, McKhann GM, McDonald WII, (eds): *Diseases of the Nervous System*. Philadelphia, Saunders, p 1225, 1986.
10. Shy GM, Drager GA: A neurological syndrome associated with orthostatic hypotension. *Arch Neurol* 2:511, 1960.
11. Berciano J: Olivopontocerebellar atrophy. *J Neurol Sci* 53:253, 1982.
12. Prasher DK, Bannister R: Brainstem auditory evoked potentials in patients with multiple system atrophy with progressive autonomic failure (Shy-Drager syndrome). *J Neurol Neurosurg Psychiatry* 49:278, 1986.
13. Plaitakis A, Berl S, Yahr MD: Abnormal glutamate metabolism in an adult-onset degenerative neurological disorder. *Science* 216:193, 1982.
14. Aoki K, Milner TA, Sheu KFR, Blass JP, Pickel VM: Regional distribution of astrocytes with intense immunoreactivity for glutamate dehydrogenase in rat brain: Implications for neuron-glia interactions in glutamate transmission. *J Neurosci* 7:2214, 1987.
15. Munsat TL: Adult motor neuron diseases, in Rowland LP (ed): *Merritts Textbook of Neurology*, 7th ed. Philadelphia, Lea & Febiger, pp 548–552, 1984.
16. Price DL, Griffin WJ, Hoffman PN, Cork LC, Spencer PS: The response of motor neurons to injury and disease, in Dyck PJ, Thomas PK, Lambert EH, Bunge R, (eds): *Peripheral Neuropathy*, vol 1. Philadelphia, Saunders, pp 732–759, 1984.
17. Johnson WG: The clinical spectrum of hexosaminidase deficiencies. *Neurology* 31:1453, 1981.

Chapter 96

SPINE DISEASE

John C. Morris

Diseases of the spine and related structures are extremely prevalent. Over 5 million Americans are disabled each year by low back problems,[1] and 80 percent of all Americans will experience at least one lifetime episode of acute back pain.[2] In spite of this frequent occurrence, the clinical diagnosis of spine disorders can be difficult because the resultant motor and sensory symptoms often are variable and ill-defined. In elderly persons in particular, there may be a tendency to dismiss complaints as simply those of "rheumatism" or "old age." It is imperative, however, to recognize promptly and accurately the causes of back pain in older adults because age-associated conditions such as lumbar stenosis, spondylotic radiculopathy, osteoporotic vertebral fracture, and metastatic tumor may have potentially severe consequences. The diagnostic features and management of these and other important geriatric spine disorders are discussed in this chapter.

FUNCTIONAL ANATOMY OF THE SPINE

The spinal column consists of 33 vertebrae: 7 cervical, 12 thoracic, 5 lumbar, 5 sacral, and 4 coccygeal. The sacral and coccygeal vertebrae often are fused to form a solid wedge between the pelvis, with which they articulate via the synovial sacroiliac joints. Each bony vertebra has a cylindrical body anteriorly and a posterior arch which is formed by the pedicles, lamina, and spinous processes. The stacked vertebral bodies, which increase in size from above down in relation to their weight-bearing function, are separated by fibrocartilaginous intervertebral discs. The discs consist of an outer ring (the annulus fibrosus) and a gelatinous central nucleus pulposus which acts as an efficient mechanical shock absorber. The posterior arches form a bony canal protecting the spinal cord and cauda equina; nerve roots exit the canal through intervertebral foramina, which are bounded by the vertebral bodies, discs, and articular processes of the

pedicles of each superior and inferior vertebra comprising an apophyseal joint on either side (Fig. 96-1). Although in a fetus the spinal cord terminates at the coccyx, skeletal growth exceeds that of the neural elements and by adult life the cord generally ends at the lower border of the first lumbar vertebra. As a result, the lumbar and sacral roots, together comprising the cauda equina, pass down the spinal canal until they reach the appropriate intervertebral foramen.

The normal spine assumes a dorsal kyphosis and a lumbar lordosis to accommodate the stress involved in transmitting the weight of the body to the hips. Spine stability is conferred by the tension-bearing anterior and posterior longitudinal ligaments which connect the vertebral bodies and, particularly in the lower back, by powerful muscles which attach to the posterior arches, especially the spinous processes. The intervertebral discs and apophyseal joints provide flexibility. Although only limited movement is possible between each vertebra, relatively large ranges of motion are achieved by summation of the individual movements, especially in the cervical and lumbar regions where discs are thicker and the splinting effect of ribs is absent. The facet joints between the superior and inferior articular processes of adjacent vertebrae allow flexion and extension but only limited rotation. Pain-sensitive spinal structures include the annulus fibrosus, the longitudinal ligaments, the paraspinal muscles, and the facet and sacroiliac joints.

GENERAL APPROACH TO THE PATIENT WITH BACK PAIN

An accurate history is essential for the proper diagnosis of spine disorders, partly because the spine is not readily accessible to physical or laboratory assessment and partly because pain is the cardinal manifestation of spine disease; objective findings may be absent.[3] Hence, the mode and circumstances of the onset of pain, the pain's

FIGURE 96-1
Anatomy of intervertebral disc and lumbar vertebrae. *(Copyright 1983. CIBA-GEIGY Corporation. Reproduced with permission from the CIBA Collection of Medical Illustrations by Frank H. Netter, M.D. All rights reserved.)*

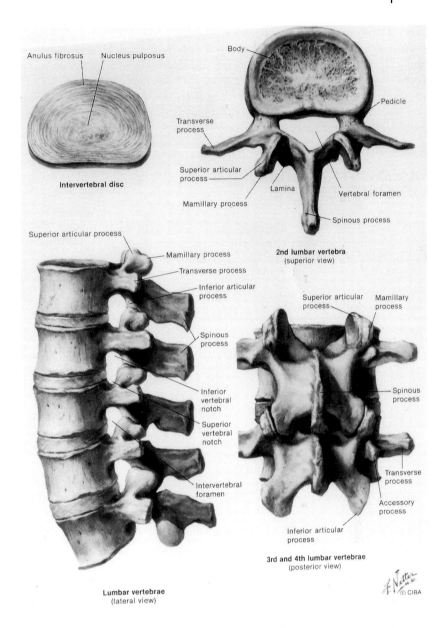

Anulus fibrosus   Nucleus pulposus

Intervertebral disc

Body
Pedicle
Transverse process
Superior articular process
Mamillary process
Lamina
Vertebral foramen
Spinous process

2nd lumbar vertebra
(superior view)

Superior articular process
Mamillary process
Transverse process
Inferior articular process
Spinous process
Inferior vertebral notch
Superior vertebral notch
Intervertebral foramen

Superior articular process
Mamillary process
Spinous process
Transverse process
Accessory process
Inferior articular process

3rd and 4th lumbar vertebrae
(posterior view)

Lumbar vertebrae
(lateral view)

quality and distribution, and the identification of provocative and palliative factors help determine whether the pain originates in the vertebrae, discs, articulations, nerve roots, or supporting elements (i.e., ligaments and muscles). Psychosocial factors and the possibility of secondary gain (e.g., compensation) should be explored, particularly when apparently excessive disability results from an injury. Examination of the spine should be performed while the patient assumes various positions and motions, including walking and flexion, extension, and lateral rotation of the spine. Abnormal curvatures or deviations, muscle tenderness or spasm on palpation, and percussion-induced tenderness of the spinous processes should be noted. Motor, sensory, and reflex changes in the trunk and extremities, when present, are important in localizing spinal lesions. Examination of the abdomen, rectum, and pelvis may uncover visceral or

vascular diseases (e.g., neoplasm, aneurysm of the abdominal aorta) associated with pain referred to the back. Thus, a complete history and physical examination should be the first step in the evaluation of each patient with back pain.[4]

Plain radiographs of the spine provide diagnostic information in many instances of spine disease, but the depiction of soft structures (i.e., intervertebral discs, ligaments, and muscles) in addition to bone has become possible with computed tomography (CT) and magnetic resonance imaging (MRI). When combined with intrathecal administration of water-soluble contrast agents, CT can demonstrate intradural and extradural lesions and so has gradually replaced conventional myelography using oil-based contrast media. Improved spatial resolution has allowed the inherent soft-tissue contrast sensitivity of MRI to be utilized increasingly for the evaluation of the spine.[5] Given equal availability, MRI is preferred for identification of suspected disc herniation and CT myelography is indicated for the depiction of spondylosis and spinal stenosis.[6] Particularly for nerve root entrapment syndromes, nerve conduction studies and electromyography are useful for diagnostic purposes and to monitor recovery after definitive therapy.[7]

DIAGNOSTIC CATEGORIES OF SPINE DISEASE

This chapter focuses on disorders of the spine and its contents which are likely to occur in the geriatric population (Table 96-1). Other diseases (e.g., multiple sclero-

TABLE 96-1
Causes of Geriatric Spine Disease

Myelopathic Disorders

Tumors
  Malignant:
    Primary tumors (e.g., multiple myeloma)
    Secondary tumors (extradural metastasis or extension)
      Carcinoma of lung, breast, prostate, or kidney
      Lymphoma
  Benign:
    Intradural (e.g., meningioma, neurofibroma)
    Extradural (e.g., Paget's disease)
Infections
  Directly involving bone (e.g., tuberculosis, pyogenic osteomyelitis)
  Extension to extradural space (e.g., epidural pyogenic abscess)
Degenerative
  Spondylotic spinal stenosis
  Central disc herniation

Nerve Root Entrapment Disorders

Degenerative (e.g., spondylosis)
Trauma (e.g., lateral disc herniation)
Leptomeningeal metastasis

Vertebral Disorders

Metabolic (e.g., osteoporosis)
Inflammatory (e.g., osteoarthritis)
Trauma (e.g., compression fracture)

Mechanical Disorders

Articulatory
Trauma:
  Facet syndrome
  Spondylolisthesis
Inflammatory (e.g., sacroiliac involvement by ankylosing spondylitis)
Muscular trauma (e.g., acute and chronic strain)

sis, subacute combined degeneration of the spinal cord, and diabetic radiculopathy) also can affect older adults and cause similar patterns of neurologic impairment, but these diseases do not directly involve the musculoskeletal spinal structures and thus are not discussed here. The diagnostic categories of spine disease are organized in relation to the principal site of dysfunction: contents of the spinal canal (myelopathy), intervertebral foramina (radiculopathy), the bony vertebrae, and mechanical disorders of connecting structures (facet joints, paraspinal muscles). Discussion in each category is limited to representative disorders and/or those having the greatest clinical impact. Additional information is available in several excellent reviews (e.g., see Refs. 1, 8, and 9).

MYELOPATHY

The constellation of neck or back pain, weakness of an extremity, and sphincter dysfunction should prompt immediate consideration of damage to the spinal cord or cauda equina. A similar clinical picture is produced by several age-associated conditions that may result in myelopathy, including tumor, infection, ischemia,[10] and mechanical compression due to degenerative disc disease. Weakness is prominent (frequent falling may be the presenting symptom) and is often accompanied by heightened reflex activity in the affected extremities. Sensory complaints are more variable, ranging from poorly localized dull pain, numbness, or stiffness affecting the spine and extremities to bandlike paresthesias around the trunk. Below the level of the lesion, there may be a consistent reduction or loss in the perception of pain and temperature (sensory level). Bladder, bowel, and sexual dysfunction are sensitive indicators of myelopathy. The degree of sensorimotor and autonomic impairment depends upon the extent of the disease and may be associated with nonmyelopathic features (e.g., radicular pain due to coexistent nerve root compression). A careful search, however, usually reveals information sufficient for localization to the spinal cord or cauda equina. Sensory deficits often are helpful in this regard; for example, a sensory level at the nipples or umbilicus suggest a cord lesion at the fourth (T4) or tenth (T10) thoracic vertebra, respectively. Pain in a saddle distribution over the buttocks indicates damage to the second, third, and fourth sacral roots in the cauda equina. The type of bladder dysfunction also has important localizing value: cord compression usually results in a spastic bladder, whereas compression of the cauda equina produces a flaccid bladder with urinary retention and overflow incontinence.

Acute myelopathy is a true neurologic emergency and usually represents compression of the contents of the spinal canal by epidural mass lesions, generally tumor[11] or abscess,[12] extending from a primary focus in the vertebral body. Antecedent backache with continuous pain during recumbancy (e.g., at night) suggests vertebral involvement by tumor, whereas back pain with associated fever is a common feature of vertebral osteomyelitis.[8] In older adults, the responsible event usually is metastasis from carcinoma of the lung, breast, prostate, or kidney to one or more vertebral bodies, with subsequent invasion of the epidural space; lymphoma and multiple myeloma also may produce this syndrome. Acute spinal cord compression may be the presenting sign of the tumor, although a history of known primary or metastatic neoplasm is more common. The initial myelopathic symptoms may be the gradual onset of pain and asymmetric weakness, but progression within days to months to complete paraplegia and sphincteric paralysis occurs if the compression is not relieved. Examination of spine films (for widening of the spinal canal or bony destruction) and myelography (for obliteration of cerebrospinal fluid space at the site of the lesion) help to establish the diagnosis.[13] Because the degree of clinical improvement is dependent on the extent and duration of the spinal block, treatment should be instituted as quickly as possible.[14] In combination with high-dose corticosteroids and specific antineoplastic agents, directed radiation is the mainstay of therapy, although surgical decompression may be required in some instances.

Spondylotic myelopathy is caused by age-associated changes that reduce the size of the spinal canal (spinal stenosis). This degenerative process, termed spondylosis, occurs uniformly after middle life and is compounded by changes induced by osteoarthritis and trauma. The initial alteration is degeneration of the intervertebral disc, particularly in regions with the greatest freedom of movement (i.e., cervical and lumbar spine.) Fibrocartilage gradually replaces the mucoid material of the nucleus pulposus, reducing flexibility and narrowing the disc space such that the cumulative loss in height approaches 2 to 3 cm (the discs normally contribute as much as 25 percent of the length of the vertebral column).[15] The loss of disc height moves the facets into closer apposition, forcing them to become weight-bearing and potentially pain-producing (Fig. 96-2). Infolding of ligaments, increased vertebral angulation, narrowing

of the intervertebral foramina, and muscle strain also may occur in relation to disc space narrowing. The effects of gravity, maximal at the L4–L5 and L5–S1 interspaces, compress the degenerated disc with resultant bulging of the weakened annulus. Bony overgrowth of the bulging disc material and at articular cartilages forms osteophytes at the posterior margins of the vertebral bodies and the facet joints, with reduction in the size of the spinal canal. These changes, which may be demonstrated radiographically in asymptomatic persons, occur almost uniformly in older adults. Thus, clinical judgment is necessary before ascribing specific dysfunction to these ubiquitous findings.

A relatively distinct subtype of spondylotic myelopathy is *lumbar spinal stenosis.* Occurring primarily in men aged 50 years or more, this syndrome is caused by compression of the lumbosacral nerve roots in the cauda equina at multiple levels in the narrowed spinal canal; maximal involvement is usually between L3 and L5 (Fig. 96-3). The major symptom is severe and chronic low back pain, with or without patchy radicular manifestations. In approximately one-third of patients, walking or other exercise may precipitate pain in the buttocks, hips, and thighs in a pattern similar to that produced by arteriosclerotic claudication. The variable amount of exercise required for symptoms to appear, relief of pain by forward flexion of the spine (a posture which may be assumed more or less permanently by the patient), back stiffness at rest, and integrity of peripheral pulses are features distinguishing the spondylotic pseudoclaudication syndrome from that of ischemia. The absence of a positive straight leg-raising test and the exacerbation of symptoms by hyperextension of the spine help to differentiate lumbar stenosis from acute disc herniation, although radiographic studies may be necessary for definite diagnosis. Similar to the management of back pain caused by herniated disc or lumbar strain, conservative treatment (i.e., absolute bed rest and analgesic medication, followed by a regimen of back exercises) generally is indicated for lumbar stenosis (see below). Less commonly, chronic and/or severe disability may occur and require decompressive laminectomy.[16]

Cervical spondylosis may present as a predomi-

FIGURE 96-2

Spondylotic disease with loss of disc height affects the normal spacing of lumbar vertebra (shown on the left) and results in subluxation of the articular processes and narrowing of the intervertebral foramen (shown on the right). *(Copyright 1986. CIBA-GEIGY Corporation. Reproduced with permission from the CIBA Collection of Medical Illustrations by Frank H. Netter, M.D. All rights reserved.)*

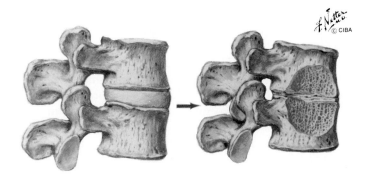

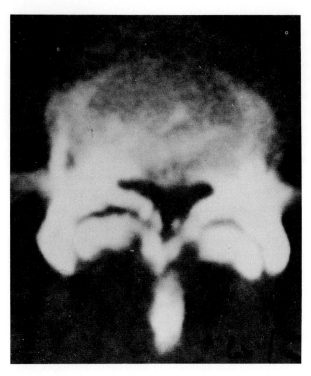

FIGURE 96-3
CT scan at L4–L5 interspace showing spinal stenosis due to central bulging of the disc and hypertrophic bony changes at the facet joints. *(Courtesy of Mokhtar Gado, M.D.)*

nantly myelopathic disorder, although coexistent involvement of cervical nerve roots occurs frequently.[17] Large osteophytic cervical bars, most frequently affecting the C5–C7 interspaces, reduce the anterior-posterior diameter of the spinal canal (normally averaging 17 mm) to 11 mm or less[18] and produce dysfunction of both long tracts (spastic paraparesis, ataxia, bladder dysfunction) and roots (atrophic weakness of the upper extremities with absent or diminished biceps or triceps reflexes), with or without associated radicular pain. Nonsurgical treatment is appropriate for most patients with cervical spondylosis. Although often cited etiologically, the role of cervical spondylosis in producing headaches is controversial.[19]

RADICULOPATHY

Nerve root entrapment syndromes in elderly persons generally are caused by the same conditions (e.g., discopathy, spondylosis, osteoarthritis, trauma) that produce spinal stenosis. Thus, overlapping features of radiculopathy and myelopathy frequently are present in the same patient. Unless there is concurrent compression of the spinal cord or cauda equina, the basic management of radiculopathic pain is conservative (see below).

Although relatively uncommon in older adults, *acute disc herniation* is a classic cause of radiculopathy. It occurs most often in the lumbosacral spine (especially

at the L4–L5 and L5–S1 interspaces). Cervical (usually C5–C6 or C6–C7) and thoracic disc herniations also occur in the elderly and may produce lower-extremity symptoms of seemingly obscure origin. Protrusion of the nucleus pulposus into the spinal canal typically results from acute trauma (major or minor) superimposed upon an annulus fibrosus weakened from degenerative factors or prior insults. The ruptured disc fragments move along the point of least resistance through rents in the annulus posteriolaterally into the spinal canal, where they impinge on one or more nerve roots (Fig. 96-4); centrally protruding discs (producing spinal stenosis) occur less commonly. The characteristic features of acute disc herniation include monoradicular pain with weakness, numbness, and diminished reflexes in the affected limb and stiffness of the back or neck. The distribution of pain suggests the specific root affected: pain in the buttocks, posterior thigh and calf, plantar foot surface, and fourth and fifth toes indicates S1 involvement, whereas L5 lesions produce pain in the hip, posteriolateral thigh, dorsum of the foot, and great toe. Reproduction of the pain with maneuvers such as straight leg–raising that increase nerve root tension is a helpful diagnostic sign, particularly if the pain is provoked on the affected side by elevation of the contralateral leg. Not surprisingly, sciatica (pain in the distribution of the sciatic nerve, arising from the L4–S3 nerve roots) is aggravated by spine flexion and alleviated by reducing root tension (e.g., lying with knees and hips flexed).[1] Nerve root entrapment by cervical disc herniation is associated with unilateral arm pain, diminished reflexes in the appropriate nerve root distri-

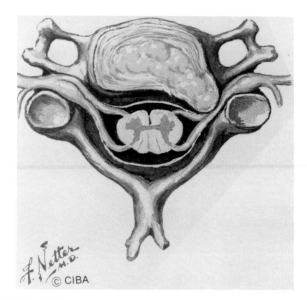

FIGURE 96-4
Posteriolateral disc herniation with nerve root compression. *(Copyright 1986. CIBA-GEIGY Corporation. Reproduced with permission from the CIBA Collection of Medical Illustrations by Frank H. Netter, M.D. All rights reserved.)*

bution, and limited neck motion to protect against exacerbation of pain. *Spondylotic radiculopathy*, a much more common cause of nerve root compression in elderly persons than disc herniation, results from foraminal encroachment by bony overgrowth incited by degenerative and osteoarthritic changes; except for the absent history of a precipitating traumatic event, the clinical syndrome is very similar to that produced by disc protrusion.

VERTEBRAL DISEASE

Osteoporosis represents a decrease in mineralized bone mass (osteopenia) due to a failure in bone matrix deposition. Multiple factors, many of them age-related (see Chap. 77), appear to influence the development of osteoporosis,[20] which is the most common metabolic bone disorder of elderly persons. A lower peak bone mass in women and the greater decline for women in sex hormone production with age probably accounts for its well-known female preponderance. Because vertebral bodies are weight-bearing and consist primarily of cancellous bone, they are among the first bones to show osteoporotic changes, namely, decreased bone density and strength. Acute vertebral collapse as a result of injury (sometimes trivial) can be associated with severe back pain that may be aggravated by muscle spasm. However, most patients with osteoporosis (usually postmenopausal white women) and collapsed vertebra are asymptomatic. Generalized osteoporotic loss of anterior vertebral body height results in a smooth kyphosis ("dowager's hump"), whereas an angular kyphosis, or gibbus, is seen with a more isolated vertebral compression fracture. X rays of the spine show reduced vertebral body density in addition to the vertebral fractures. Osteoporotic management includes the correction of deficiencies in sex hormones, calcium intake, and activity levels to prevent further bone loss, although after substantial bone loss has occurred these modalities may be of little benefit.[21]

By far the most frequent arthritic disease, *osteoarthritis* is nearly universal in older adults, although only in a small percentage is it alone a major cause of spine disease. Inflammatory changes are relatively mild; degeneration of the articular cartilage, particularly affecting the facet joints, is the primary causative mechanism ("wear and tear" syndrome). The salient clinical features are back stiffness and pain, aggravated by movement. There may be little or no relation to radiographic findings. Episodic symptomatic treatment is recommended.

MECHANICAL DISORDERS

Degeneration of the articular facets, in combination with their oblique alignment in the lumbar spine, may result in subluxation of the facet joint (Fig. 96-2). Low back pain exacerbated by twisting or turning (the *facet syndrome*) may occur in relation to relatively minor injury.[22] *Spondylolisthesis* is the anterior displacement of a vertebral body relative to the body below (typically, L4 or L5); the posterior vertebral elements are left behind. The degree of anterior slippage is graded from I to IV.[23] In association with a potential genetic predisposition, mechanical stresses (maximal at L4 and L5) may cause a fatigue fracture of the pars interarticularis (i.e., the juncture of the pedicle and the lamina). When bilateral, this defect permits the development of isthmic spondylolisthesis and produces the characteristic "Scotty dog" appearance on oblique radiography of the lumbar spine.[9] Neurologic damage is generally absent in both the facet syndrome and spondylolisthesis, although the latter may cause root irritation. When symptomatic, these disorders produce back pain that usually responds to conservative management.

Involvement of the *sacroiliac joints* by inflammatory conditions (e.g., ankylosing spondylitis) may be associated with troublesome back pain and stiffness but is rarely seen as an isolated disorder in elderly individuals. Much more frequent is *acute or chronic lumbar strain*, commonly termed *lumbago*. Multiple factors contribute to the occurrence of this syndrome, including poor muscle tone and poor posture. When subjected to varying degrees of strain, nonneuropathic back pain results with severe discomfort typically centered in the low back and buttocks. Absolute bed rest combined with heat therapy is the indicated treatment.

MANAGEMENT OF BACK PAIN

Because the syndromes causing acute back pain generally are self-limited, initial therapy consists of short-term bed rest supplemented with nonnarcotic medications as needed for effective analgesia. An individualized but intensive physical therapy program incorporating back-training exercises also may be beneficial. Because prolonged bed rest leads to muscle deconditioning and thus aggravates the factors responsible for lumbago, back-training exercises should be instituted as soon as possible[24] and early mobilization should be promoted once back pain improves.[25] Resolution of pain occurs for most patients within 4 to 6 weeks, even those with intense sciatica; only a small percentage (about 10 percent) have persistent disability[26] which ultimately may require nerve root decompression.

REFERENCES

1. Frymoyer JW: Back pain and sciatica. *N Engl J Med* 318:291, 1988.
2. Newton PA: Chronic pain, in Cassel CK, Walsh JR (eds): *Geriatric Medicine*, vol 2. New York, Springer-Verlag, 1984, pp 236–274.

3. Adams RD, Victor M: Pain in the back, neck, and extremities, in *Principles of Neurology*, 3d ed. New York, McGraw-Hill, 1985, pp 149–172.

4. Waddell G: Clinical assessment of lumbar impairment. *Clin Orthop* 221:110, 1987.

5. Lee SH et al: Magnetic resonance imaging of degenerative disk disease of the spine. *Radiol Clin North Am* 26:949, 1988.

6. Gado M: The spine, in Lee KT, Sagal S, Stanley RJ (eds): *Computed Body Tomography*, 2d ed. New York, Raven Press, 1988, pp 991–1063.

7. Leblhuber F et al: Diagnostic value of different electrophysiological tests in cervical disk prolapse. *Neurology* 38:1879, 1988.

8. Hadler NM: *Medical Management of the Regional Musculoskeletal Diseases: Backache, Neckache, Disorders of the Upper and Lower Extremities*. Orlando, FL, Grune and Stratton, 1984.

9. Keim HA, Kirkaldy-Willis WH: Low back pain. *Clin Symp* 32(6):2, 1980.

10. Hughes JT, Brownell B: Spinal cord ischemia due to arteriosclerosis. *Arch Neurol* 15:189, 1966.

11. Gilbert RW et al: Epidural spinal cord compression from metastatic tumor: Diagnosis and treatment. *Ann Neurol* 3:40, 1978.

12. Baker AS et al: Spinal epidural abscess. *N Engl J Med* 293:463, 1975.

13. Rodichok LD et al: Early detection and treatment of spinal epidural metastases: The role of myelography. *Ann Neurol* 20:696, 1986.

14. Portenoy RK et al: Back pain in the cancer patient: An algorithm for evaluation and management. *Neurology* 37:134, 1987.

15. Netter FH: *Nervous System, Part I: Anatomy and Physiology*. West Caldwell, NJ, CIBA Pharmaceutical, 1983, pp 11–20.

16. Weir B, deLeo R: Lumbar stenosis: Analysis of factors affecting outcome in 81 surgical cases. *Can J Neurol Sci* 8:295, 1981.

17. Gregorius FK et al: Cervical spondylotic radiculopathy and myelopathy. *Arch Neurol* 33:618, 1976.

18. Netter FH: *Nervous System, Part II: Neurologic and Neuromuscular Disorders*. West Caldwell, NJ, CIBA Pharmaceutical, 1986, pp 181–201.

19. Edmeads J: The cervical spine and headache. *Neurology* 38:1874, 1988.

20. Raisz LG: Local and systemic factors in the pathogenesis of osteoporosis. *N Engl J Med* 318:818, 1988.

21. Resnick NM, Greenspan SL: "Senile" osteoporosis reconsidered. *JAMA* 261:1025, 1989.

22. Mooney V, Robertson J: The facet syndrome. *Clin Orthop* 116:149, 1976.

23. Wiltse LL et al: Classification of spondylosis and spondylolisthesis. *Clin Orthop* 117:23, 1976.

24. Manniche C et al: Clinical trial of intensive muscle training for chronic low back pain. *Lancet* ii:1473, 1988.

25. Deyo RA et al: How many days of bed rest for acute low back pain? *N Engl J Med* 315:1064, 1986.

26. Nachemson AL: Advances in low-back pain. *Clin Orthop* 200:266, 1985.

Chapter 97

PERIPHERAL NEUROPATHIES

Reid Taylor and Walter G. Bradley

With improvement in medical care and subsequent survival of patients into the eighth and ninth decades, the incidence of both symptomatic and asymptomatic peripheral nervous system dysfunction rises. Asymptomatic patients may demonstrate reduction in strength with mild distal atrophy; a decrease in vibratory, light touch, or pain sensation; reduced deep tendon reflexes; and slowed nerve conduction velocities. With the prolonged survival of patients with metabolic disease, such as diabetes, chronic renal failure, cancer, and deficiency states, the incidence of symptomatic nervous system dysfunction rises. In the geriatric population the patient may have one or more disorders associated with peripheral neuropathy. Although peripheral nerve disease is only rarely the immediate cause of death, it can be a significant contributor to patient morbidity and reduction of quality of life.

The symptomatic patient typically presents with symptoms such as numbness or weakness caused by loss of function of the peripheral nerves. At times there may be positive symptoms such as paresthesiae, a feeling of tightness around the limbs, or burning or shooting pain. The most common pattern at any age is a distal symmetric polyneuropathy with gradually worsening motor and sensory function of the feet and legs that eventually spreads to the hands. In mononeuropathy, the abnormality may lie in the anatomic distribution of a single peripheral nerve or root. In multiple mononeuropathy (mononeuritis multiplex), several nerves have focal abnormalities.

Peripheral nervous system disease typically includes motor and sensory dysfunction and the tendon reflexes are usually lost. It is the pattern of these symptoms and signs which localizes the problem to the peripheral rather than the central nervous system. Localization of the disease process is very important, but differentiation between any of the multiple etiologies of peripheral neuropathies can be difficult.

ANATOMY OF THE PERIPHERAL NERVES

Within a peripheral nerve there are different populations of axons which have specialized functions. On the sensory side, the small unmyelinated fibers convey pain and temperature sensation, whereas the large myelinated nerve fibers convey light touch, joint position, and vibration sensation. On the motor side, large myelinated motor fibers innervate the extrafusal fibers of muscle, and the small myelinated fibers innervate the intrafusal fibers. Fibers of the postganglionic sympathetic nervous system are unmyelinated and innervate blood vessels and sweat glands.

Within the nerve the fibers are separated into groups of fasciculi surrounded by the perineurium. The perineurium is a functional barrier which prevents the access of potentially harmful substances into the nerve. The fasciculi interconnect within the nerve. This complex interweaving is clinically important when nerves are repaired after injury. The closer the repair approximates corresponding fascicles, the higher the chance of recovery.

The nerve and axon have evolved to convey an electrical impulse from one part of the body to another. The speed of transmission is proportional to the diameter of the axon and in unmyelinated fibers that impulse travels at about 1 m/s. Myelinated fibers, however, are covered by the spiraled plasma membrane of Schwann cells, the myelin sheath. The junction between each Schwann cell is a node of Ranvier, and the nerve impulse jumps from node to node in its passage along myelinated fibers. This saltatory transmission enables the speed of conduction in the largest myelinated fibers to increase to 60 to 80 m/s. All axons, whether myelinated or unmyelinated, are surrounded by Schwann cells throughout their length in the peripheral nerve, but a myelin sheath is not formed around all axons. This close relationship between the axons and their supporting cells, the Schwann cells, underlie the two main disease processes seen in peripheral nerves.

PERIPHERAL NERVES: DISEASE PROCESSES

Two major disease processes underlie all cases of peripheral nerve disease. In axonal degeneration, some disruption of the axon occurs and the distal part of the fiber degenerates. Axonal degeneration occurs in many inherited and toxic neuropathies. In focal nerve trauma or infarction, the integrity of the axon is disrupted and the distal part subsequently degenerates. This distal degeneration after injury is known as *wallerian degeneration* after its first description by Waller in the 1850s.

As Waller described, axonal degeneration of myelinated fibers is followed by secondary degeneration and digestion of the myelin sheath. If the nerve cell body and the proximal axon remain intact, there may be regeneration with sprouting and eventually reconnection of the previously innervated peripheral structures. This typically occurs at a rate of 1 to 2 mm/day.

The second main process occurring in peripheral neuropathies is segmental demyelination. The primary damage is to the myelin sheath of the Schwann cells which leads to degeneration and digestion of the myelin with preservation of the axon. Although peripheral structures still maintain normal innervation, conduction along the axon is frequently blocked by such a process. This damage to the Schwann cells is often patchy, and if the disease process is mild or limited, the Schwann cells may remyelinate with restitution of normal nerve conductions.

It should be emphasized that the major disease processes are not mutually exclusive and that mild nerve injury may produce segmental demyelination, whereas severe injury can cause axonal degeneration.

INVESTIGATION OF THE PATIENT WITH PERIPHERAL NEUROPATHY

As in most disease processes, the information which is most helpful in deciding the etiology of a peripheral neuropathy is revealed by taking a careful history from the patient and by the clinical examination. The rate of progression, distribution of involvement, and description of peripheral nerve impairment are helpful in defining the group of etiologies to be considered. A history of toxic exposure through work or hobby, the institution of new medications, a recent viral illness, similar symptoms in family or other people in the same environment, pertinent medical disorders, and alcohol use are information of great importance.

Physical examination should include documentation of muscle bulk and strength, any abnormalities of sensation and recordings of blood pressure and pulse in both the supine and erect positions to evaluate autonomic involvement. As important as specialized neurologic tests to quantify the extent of the peripheral neuropathy is a thorough general physical examination. Peripheral neuropathies are associated with systemic diseases which may be discovered on physical examination. Abnormalities such as splenomegaly, blood in the stool or stigmata of toxin exposure, if noted early, could hasten the discovery of the etiology of a peripheral neuropathy. Repeated investigations have demonstrated that a thorough history, negative physical examination including pelvic and rectal examination, and chest x ray obviate the need for further radiologic or invasive procedures in the search for malignancy unless a specific organ system or area has been implicated.

A tailored laboratory screen should be undertaken looking for vitamin B_{12} deficiency, for diabetes mellitus, and for liver, kidney, or thyroid disease. In addition, evaluation for vasculitis or paraproteinemias may include an erythrocyte sedimentation rate, antinuclear antibody, rheumatoid factor, and serum and urine immunoelectrophoresis. Evaluation of cerebral spinal fluid is rarely indicated, although an elevation of CSF protein without pleocytosis may be seen in chronic inflammatory demyelinating polyneuropathy.

Electrophysiologic studies are always indicated in the evaluation of a neuropathy. The widely available electrophysiologic tests of the peripheral nervous system are nerve conduction studies and electromyography. In general, the size or amplitude of the motor response to nerve stimulation reflects the health of the axons of the nerve fiber, whereas slowing to less than 60 percent of normal conduction velocity suggests demyelination. In both motor and sensory nerve conduction studies only the largest and fastest nerve fibers are analyzed, so that the study may be normal if only small fibers are affected. In electromyography, if there has been axonal damage, there may be fibrillation potentials or positive waves consistent with acute denervation. If denervation has been chronic and there has been time for sprouting and reinnervation, chronic neurogenic changes consisting of high-amplitude prolonged-duration polyphasic motor units may be seen.

A nerve biopsy is occasionally of help in the diagnosis of a peripheral neuropathy. Typically, the sural nerve is biopsied from the lateral side of the ankle and evaluated by specialized techniques. An area of numbness will be created over the ankle and outer portion of the foot which usually shrinks with time, although this may be accompanied by painful dysesthesiae. Every nerve biopsy should be evaluated by light microscopy, morphometry to evaluate differential involvement of large versus small fibers, fiber teasing to estimate the degree of axonal versus myelin involvement, and electron microscopy to examine the ultrastructure of the nerve. The experience of the pathologist and technologist is vital to the quality of information gained from a nerve biopsy. Although toxic neuropathies are typically axonal and chronic inflammatory demyelinating polyneuropathy may demonstrate abnormalities of myelin, only rarely is a specific etiologic diagnosis made via nerve biopsy. The nerve biopsy may demonstrate the changes of a vasculopathy as in polyarteritis nodosa and may also be diagnostic in metachromatic leukodystrophy, amyloidosis, leprosy, or sarcoidosis. Therefore, although a nerve biopsy should be performed only after noninvasive studies are completed and in centers where there is established experience, a specific treatable diagnosis can be found in some cases. Table 97-1 outlines the evaluation of patients with peripheral neuropathy.

CLASSIFICATION AND DIAGNOSIS OF PERIPHERAL NEUROPATHIES

Clues to the etiology of the disease may frequently be found in the history and physical examination of patients with peripheral neuropathies. Damage to large myelinating fibers with subsequent ataxia and loss of superficial sensation along with motor denervation is seen more frequently in toxic neuropathies and inherited neuronal degenerations. Abnormalities of pain and temperature sensation with derangement of autonomic dysfunction imply small-fiber neuropathies, and the clinician should consider amyloidosis, diabetes, or inherited acrodystrophic neuropathy.

Pain may be associated with peripheral neuropathies and, if severe or prolonged, may help define the etiology. Dysesthesiae are unpleasant sensations of the skin which may be due to an imbalance between the large- and small-fiber sensory input to the spinal cord. Actual pain is more clearly a feature of nerve compression perhaps due to entrapment, local pressure by tumor

TABLE 97-1
Diagnostic Evaluation of Peripheral Neuropathy

History, including family history
Complete physical examination, including rectal and pelvic
   examination
Biochemical studies, CBC, differential, sedimentation rate,
   creatinine, blood urea nitrogen, electrolytes, liver function
   tests, vitamin B_{12}, thyroid function tests, serum and urine
   protein electrophoresis, and immunoelectrophoresis
Electrophysiology
Chest x ray
Cerebrospinal fluid examination
Nerve biopsy

or aneurysm, or nerve infiltration. Partial lesions of the large nerve trunks can give rise to severe, continuous pain known as causalgia which can be associated with trophic skin changes and autonomic dysfunction. Soreness of the calves and burning feet may be seen in vitamin deficiencies, malabsorption, diabetes, and carcinoma.

Nerve impairment may have a specific distribution which can help define the etiology. For example, abnormalities within the distribution of a single peripheral nerve or several individual peripheral nerves (multiple mononeuropathy) point to local processes. Common anatomic sites of nerve entrapments are the carpal tunnel, fibular head, and ulnar groove. Local damage to multiple nerves can occur in vasculitis. The more common distal symmetrical polyneuropathy indicates a diffuse disease process.

If the primary disturbance of the neuropathy is motor function, then postinfectious polyneuropathy (Guillain-Barré syndrome), diphtheria, acute intermittent porphyria, and inherited neuropathies should be considered. Sensory neuropathies may be inherited or may be seen in association with carcinoma, metabolic diseases, toxic exposures, and diabetes. Nerve hypertrophy can be seen in some of the familial forms of nerve disease as well as the chronic immunologically mediated polyneuropathies. These clinical clues to the source of the condition provide a classification which is outlined in Table 97-2. Review of the clinical presentation in comparison with the table may help to pinpoint the diagnosis.

DIFFERENTIAL DIAGNOSIS OF PERIPHERAL NERVE DAMAGE

ACUTE INFLAMMATORY POLYRADICULOPATHY

The rapid recognition of acute, potentially fatal, disease is important. Viral hepatitis, lymphoma, acute intermittent porphyria, sarcoidosis, uremia, macroglobulinemia, toxic exposure, and diphtheria can be associated with geriatric neuropathies of acute onset. However, the most common cause is acute inflammatory polyradiculopathy (Guillain-Barré syndrome). About two-thirds of affected patients give a history of recent upper respiratory infection followed by weakness, usually of proximal muscles. Weakness progresses until a nadir is reached. The time to maximal weakness averages 17 days, and 90 percent of patients stop progressing by the end of 3 weeks. Areflexia is very common and moderate glove and stocking sensory changes are sometimes seen. Autonomic abnormalities including ileus, tachycardia, and labile blood pressure may be present.

TABLE 97-2
Classification of Peripheral Neuropathies

Clinical Classification	Distribution	Etiology
Acute polyneuropathies	Proximal or diffuse	Guillain-Barré syndrome, acute intermittent porphyria, diphtheria
Mononeuropathy or Mononeuropathy multiplex	Proximal / Any distribution	Diabetic amyotrophy, neuralgia amyotrophy / Trauma, entrapment, vasculitis, nerve tumor
Symmetric polyneuropathy	Distal	Toxic, metabolic, inherited, paraneoplastic, deficiency states
Recurrent or hypertrophic polyneuropathy	Usually distal	Hereditary hypertrophic neuropathies, chronic inflammatory demyelinating polyradiculopathy

SOURCE: After AK Asbury, 1967 (personal communication).

The Miller Fisher variant of Guillain-Barré syndrome consists of areflexia, ophthalmoplegia, and ataxia.

Although the course of the Guillain-Barré syndrome may be prolonged, functional recovery is the rule, with mortality less than 5 percent despite the potential requirement of intubation and complications of pneumonia, pulmonary embolism, dysautonomia, etc. The diagnosis rests on clinical course, and the acute nerve conduction studies may be normal with some evidence of demyelination. Raised CSF protein without pleocytosis is helpful but not essential for diagnosis. Old age is a poor prognostic feature in acute inflammatory polyradiculopathy.

NERVE TRAUMA

Mononeuropathy or multiple mononeuropathy can have several causes. However, *nerve trauma* due to compression or damage by penetrating injuries and focal entrapment by existing anatomic structures are relatively common. If a nerve is subjected to prolonged pressure due to immobility or pressure from a crutch or cast, there may be focal demyelination which can be associated with localized loss of nerve function. The term *neurapraxia* refers to local demyelination, which has an excellent prognosis with recovery over 3 to 6 weeks. More severe nerve injury leads to axonal damage with distal degeneration. Recovery depends on regenerating axonal sprouts which grow at a rate of 1 to 2 mm/day. Such an injury,

termed *axonotmesis*, has a poorer prognosis the more proximal the injury occurs. Penetrating nerve damage is associated with disruption of the nerve itself and is termed *neurotmesis*. This type of injury has the worst prognosis.

Although external compression is always a danger, compression of nerves as they course within tight anatomic channels can also cause significant dysfunction. The carpal tunnel is a structure bordered by the flexor retinaculum of the wrist on one side and the wrist bones on the other. The median nerve runs within that tunnel along with the tendons of the flexors of the fingers. If there is inflammation of the flexor tendons as in tendonitis, encroachment on the tunnel by adjacent arthritis, or infiltration of the surrounding tissues as in myxedema, the median nerve may be compressed. This produces a syndrome of pain in the wrist and numbness of the thumb and first two fingers with weakness of the thenar muscles. Other mononeuropathies may be related to repeated episodes of trauma such as leaning on the elbows in ulnar neuropathy. A systemic vasculitis can be associated with mononeuropathy or mononeuritis multiplex due to focal infarction of nerves.

NEURALGIC AMYOTROPHY

The syndrome of *neuralgic amyotrophy* consists of severe pain in the shoulder or elbow lasting for several days followed by atrophy of one or more muscles supplied by the brachial plexus. Diagnosis is made by clinical course and electrophysiologic studies. The pain typically resolves within a month and atrophy begins. Recovery may be prolonged for up to 2 years.

POSTHERPETIC NEURALGIA

Postherpetic neuralgia is a syndrome of pain localized to one or more dermatomes previously affected by a cutaneous outbreak of herpes zoster. Rarely, this syndrome occurs without cutaneous manifestations ("herpes sine zoster").

DIABETES MELLITUS

The metabolic neuropathies typically cause distal symmetric polyneuropathies although diabetes mellitus can be associated with mononeuropathies, multiple mononeuropathy, or distal polyneuropathy. The syndrome of *diabetic amyotrophy* consists of severe pain in the hip or thigh associated with progressive weakness and atrophy of the proximal muscles of the legs, generally the quadriceps, along with absence of the knee jerk. Although there may be an associated symmetric distal polyneuropathy with mild sensory loss, sensory loss is not a major component of diabetic amyotrophy. Usually, weight loss and poor diabetic control are associated with this syndrome. Improvement in pain and recovery of strength occurs over months.

The chronic distal sensory polyneuropathy of diabetes mainly affects the legs. The symptoms are numbness and paresthesiae of the toes and feet which may be described as burning in the feet and tenderness of the calves. The distal reflexes are depressed or absent. Typically, abnormalities of the hands are not seen until the lower extremity abnormalities have progressed to the level of the knee. Autonomic neuropathy may be seen in diabetes causing postural hypotension, diarrhea, bladder dysfunction, and impotence.

HYPOTHYROIDISM AND ACROMEGALY

Hypothyroidism and acromegaly can be associated with a sensory polyneuropathy. This is typically a mild, distal, symmetrical predominantly sensory neuropathy and is more common in patients with severe myxedema. Accumulation of myxedema material in the carpal tunnel and other areas may lead to focal neuropathies.

UREMIC NEUROPATHIES

In the past, patients with *uremia* had a distal, symmetrical sensory and motor polyneuropathy only as a terminal feature. However, with renal dialysis, clinically apparent polyneuropathies have become more frequent. About two-thirds of patients requiring renal dialysis had dysesthesiae, restless legs, mild distal wasting, impaired sensation, and absent ankle jerks. The duration and severity of the renal failure, but not its cause, are related to the severity of the neuropathy. The symptoms improve with dialysis, and are cured by renal transplantation. Uremic neuropathies usually are not seen until the blood urea nitrogen level exceeds 100 mg/dl and creatinine clearance falls below 5 ml/min. Additionally, renal failure can be associated with toxic levels of a medication because the drug is normally excreted by the kidneys. It is important to consider this possibility in the patient who presents with uremia and a neuropathy.

PARANEOPLASTIC NEUROPATHIES

Neoplasms may have effects which are remote from the local invasion and damage which they produce (paraneoplastic syndromes). Syndromes of hormone secretion and generalized weight loss have been well described. The peripheral nervous system can also be affected by certain carcinomas, particularly those of the bronchus, ovary, breast, and stomach. The leukemias, lymphomas, and dysproteinemic syndromes such as multiple myeloma and macroglobulinemia are also associated with peripheral neuropathies. The peripheral neuropathy may precede a diagnosis of cancer by years, and removal of the carcinoma may both help the neuropathy as well as potentially cure the patient. An elderly patient with a neuropathy should have a thorough screening for malignancy consisting of history, physical examination, chest x ray and appropriate laboratory studies. Invasive procedures and more extensive radiologic investigations are often not necessary. However, because the neuropathy may precede the diagnosis of cancer by several years, periodic rescreening of the patients is indicated.

TOXINS

The potential of many *toxins* to damage the peripheral nerve system is well known. The general pattern is of a sensorimotor or predominantly sensory distal symmetric polyneuropathy with axonal degeneration as the primary pathologic substrate. In the geriatric population, as in those who are younger, careful inquiry into occupational history, hobbies, or exposure to chemicals may be important to define the etiology of a peripheral neuropathy. Metals such as lead, arsenic, and thallium can produce polyneuropathies. Industrial solvents, insecticides, and herbicides can also cause neuropathies. Alcohol can damage the peripheral nervous system; additionally its chronic abuse typically exists with dietary deficiencies, malabsorption of vitamins, and liver disease.

The geriatric population typically is exposed to more medication, but therapeutic drugs have been reported to cause peripheral nerve damage in only a few instances. Neuropathy can be seen with isoniazid therapy and can be prevented with concomitant treatment with pyridoxine. Vincristine is used as a chemotherapeutic agent in leukemia and certain solid tumors and causes a neuropathy.

VITAMIN DEFICIENCIES

Several *vitamin deficiency* syndromes can be associated with neuropathy. Vitamin B_{12} deficiency in the elderly population may be due to the autoimmune loss of intrinsic factor (pernicious anemia), blind loop syndromes, or ileal resection. In addition to macrocytic anemia, the patients develop peripheral neuropathy which may be associated with central nervous system dysfunction. Intramuscular injections of vitamin B_{12} are necessary to improve this neuropathy, although the central nervous system dysfunction, once developed, may remain. Thiamine deficiency is associated with a severe distal sensorimotor neuropathy due to axonal degeneration. An adequate diet is necessary for recovery, which may take months.

CHRONIC INFLAMMATORY POLYRADICULOPATHY

Chronic inflammatory polyradiculopathy is an immune-mediated process in which lymphocytic infiltration and segmental demyelination lead to chronic or recurrent symptoms of polyneuropathy. Segmental demyelination is the primary pathologic substrate.

INHERITED NEUROPATHIES

There are many *inherited* neuropathies. Familial neuropathies such as Charcot-Marie-Tooth disease, inherited sensory neuropathy, or familial amyloid neuropathy may present in the geriatric population. Evaluation of family members may be necessary to confirm the diagnosis. The absence of the usually associated skeletal deformities like pes cavus may indicate that the disease began after growth had ceased.

IDIOPATHIC NEUROPATHIES

Unfortunately, in the geriatric population, as in all patients with neuropathies, the largest group is the chronic distal sensorimotor polyneuropathy which, despite extensive investigation, have no specific etiology determined. In one intensive study by Dyck and others of a group of 205 *idiopathic* polyneuropathies, an etiologic diagnosis was made in 76 percent of the cases. The largest category was the inherited polyneuropathies (42 percent). Careful questioning of the patient about affected family members and review of medical records is important since 35 of 86 cases of inherited neuropathy (41 percent) could be diagnosed without examination of family members. In 51 of 86 inherited neuropathies (59 percent), the diagnosis could not be made by history or review of medical records. Physical examination, electrophysiologic studies, and, in some cases, nerve biopsy were utilized to detect an abnormal family member in 24 of 51 cases. The remaining inherited neuropathies were so classified because of characteristic phenotype, natural history, or specific pathologic or biochemical abnormality. In 43 of the 205 patients (21 percent), a diagnosis of inflammatory demyelinating polyradiculoneuropathy was made, and 27 of the 205 patients (13 percent) had various acquired neuropathies including leprosy, heavy-metal intoxication, and neuropathies associated with diabetes, myxedema, carcinoma, multiple myeloma, and monoclonal gammopathy. After intensive study, 49 of 205 patients remained undiagnosed.

TREATMENT OF GERIATRIC PERIPHERAL NEUROPATHIES

The treatment of the acute severe neuropathies require support of nutrition and ventilation while the etiology is determined. Plasmapheresis in Guillain-Barré syndrome shortens the course of the disease. Treatment of the underlying disorder such as cancer, diabetes, or renal fail-

ure may improve an associated neuropathy. Clinical experience has demonstrated that strict management of glucose can be associated with more rapid improvement of the diabetic amyotrophy and an improvement of the symmetric distal polyneuropathy. Conservative care of entrapment mononeuropathies makes use of splinting, padding, and, in some cases, injection of corticosteroids into the area of entrapment. Surgical decompression may be necessary.

In chronic inflammatory demyelinating polyradiculopathy and neuropathies associated with vasculitis, immunosuppression may be necessary. Glucocorticoids are usually tried initially and must be given at a high-enough dose and long enough, such as 60 mg/day prednisone for 3 months, for an adequate trial. Since long-term use of corticosteroids is associated with significant side effects, sometimes immunosuppression with azathioprine or cyclophosphamide is instituted. This allows lower doses of corticosteroids to be used with comparable efficacy.

The idiopathic neuropathies, genetic neuropathies, and neuropathies unresponsive to improvement of the systemic disease are treated symptomatically. Weakness may require bracing or aids for walking designed to prevent falls. In the geriatric group, medical intervention should be performed carefully. Some of the burning dysesthesiae and pain of peripheral neuropathy can be treated with tricyclic antidepressants, phenytoin, or carbamazepine. A very low initial dose, followed by gradual increase to a therapeutic dose, is used to avoid unnecessary side effects. An adequate trial of tricyclic antidepressants should last 3 months. Drug levels confirming effective therapeutic levels of phenytoin and carbamazepine allow discontinuation if no benefit is achieved within a month. These medications are not successful in every case and different doses or drug types may be necessary for different patients.

GENERAL READING

Asbury AK, Gilliat RW: *Peripheral Nerve Disorders.* London, Butterworth, 1984.

Bradley WG: *Disorders of Peripheral Nerves.* Oxford, Blackwell Scientific, 1974.

Dyck PJ, Oviatt KF, Lambert EH: Intensive evaluation of referred unclassified neuropathies yields improved diagnosis. *Ann Neurol* 10:222, 1981.

Dyck PJ, Thomas PK, Lambert EH, Bunge R: *Peripheral Neuropathy*, 2d ed. Philadelphia, Saunders, 1984.

Katzman R, Terry RD: *The Neurology of Aging.* Philadelphia, Davis, 1983.

Steward JD: *Focal Peripheral Neuropathies.* New York, Elsevier, 1987.

Sunderland S: *Nerves and Nerve Injuries*, 2d ed. Edinburgh, Churchill Livingstone, 1978.

Chapter 98

CENTRAL NERVOUS SYSTEM INFECTIONS

William G. Gardner and Joseph P. Myers

Central nervous system infections in the geriatric population are serious, often life-threatening problems that present difficult challenges in diagnosis and treatment. A wide variety of central nervous system infections and pathogens may occur in the elderly. The discussion in this chapter will include three specific problems: (1) bacterial meningitis, (2) herpes simplex encephalitis, and (3) central nervous system syphilis. In addition, two other important infections, tuberculous meningitis and brain abscess, will be briefly mentioned.

BACTERIAL MENINGITIS

Bacterial meningitis in the geriatric population presents three important problems that make it different from meningitis in the pediatric or younger adult age groups. First, in the elderly there is a wider array of potential pathogens often related to coexistent or underlying disease. Second, the presentation is often subacute, rather than the very acute presentation commonly seen in younger individuals. Third, because of the wide spectrum of potential pathogens, the presence of underlying disease, and the nonspecific clinical presentation, the diagnosis of bacterial meningitis in the elderly is often difficult.

The majority of cases of community-acquired bacterial meningitis occur in individuals less than 60 years of age. In Finland's series only 24 percent of cases occurred after age 60. In Geisler's series only 7 percent of cases were in persons over age 40. In contrast, hospital-acquired bacterial meningitis commonly involves the elderly. The morbidity and mortality of both community- and hospital-acquired meningitis is higher in the elderly, possibly because of coexistent underlying disease and difficulty in making the diagnosis.

PATHOGENESIS

Bacterial meningitis usually occurs by one of two mechanisms. First, bacteria may reach the subarachnoid space by the hematogenous route, as often occurs with *Streptococcus pneumoniae* or *Neisseria meningitidis*, which colonize the nasopharynx and then become bacteremic. Staphylococci or gram-negative bacilli causing infection at another body site may also spread to the central nervous system by the hematogenous route. Secondly, these same bacteria can cause meningitis by direct spread to the subarachnoid space from a contiguous infection following a neurosurgical procedure or trauma to the cranial bones resulting in a dural tear. With either mechanism, once bacteria reach the cerebrospinal fluid (CSF) there are inadequate host defenses to prevent bacterial replication and infection.

ETIOLOGY

Determining the bacterial etiology of meningitis in the elderly is often more difficult than the same task in younger age groups. Yet, establishing the etiology is important because early treatment with an appropriate antimicrobial agent is a key factor in achieving a favorable outcome. Two key factors influence bacterial etiology. First, the age of the individual is important. *Haemophilus influenzae*, a common cause of meningitis in children, is rare in adults over 60 years of age. In contrast, *S. pneumoniae* is more common in the older adult. Second, the presence of underlying disease or clinical condition will influence etiology. Infrequent causes of bacterial meningitis, such as *Staphylococcus aureus*, gram-negative bacilli, or *Listeria*, are usually associated with an underlying disease or condition that alters the host defenses. Several conditions with pathogens to consider in each condition are listed in Table 98-1.

TABLE 98-1
Etiology of Acute and Subacute Meningitis in Relation to
Underlying Disease or Condition

Disease or Condition	Microbial Pathogens
Diabetes mellitus	Pneumococcus, gram-negative bacilli, staphylococci, *Cryptococcus*
Alcoholism	Pneumococcus
Neutropenia or inadequate neutrophil function	*Pseudomonas aeruginosa,* Enterobacteriaceae, *Candida* species
Impaired cell-mediated immunity (lymphoma, corticosteroid therapy)	*Listeria monocytogenes, Cryptococcus, Mycobacterium tuberculosis*
Cerebrospinal fluid rhinorrhea	Pneumococcus
Open skull fracture or craniotomy	Gram-negative bacilli, staphylococci

CLINICAL FEATURES

The clinical course of bacterial meningitis in the elderly may be either acute or subacute. In acute bacterial meningitis the onset is abrupt, with symptoms present in less than 24 hours. The course is rapidly progressive, and the mortality rate approaches 50 percent. In contrast, subacute bacterial meningitis has a more insidious onset, with symptoms present in from 1 to 7 days. The progression is slower, and the mortality rate is much lower. Infection due to *S. aureus* or *S. pneumoniae* usually follows an acute course, whereas infection due to *Listeria* or the gram-negative bacilli is often subacute. Nosocomial meningitis in the elderly often follows a subacute course, adding to the difficulty in diagnosis.

Clinical findings in the patient with bacterial meningitis include fever, severe headache, altered mental status, and nuchal rigidity. However, any or all of these findings may be absent in the elderly. Altered mental status occurs in at least 80 percent of cases. Temperature is often markedly elevated but may be normal or subnormal in the chronically ill or severely septic patient. Nuchal rigidity may be present secondary to conditions other than meningitis such as cervical spine disease or Parkinson's disease. On the other hand, the neck may be supple in the presence of meningitis, a poor prognostic sign. Thus, the clinical findings are of limited value, and examination of the CSF is essential in establishing the diagnosis.

DIAGNOSIS

The hallmark of diagnosis of bacterial meningitis is examination of the CSF obtained by lumbar puncture. This is especially true in elderly patients, who often have a nonspecific clinical presentation. The typical findings include a CSF pleocytosis, an elevated protein level, and a low glucose level. Two-thirds of patients with bacterial meningitis will have a CSF cell count of over 1000 per mm^3 with a predominance of polymorphonuclear leukocytes. A predominance of mononuclear cells may be seen in partially treated meningitis or with *Listeria* meningitis. The CSF glucose is usually less than 40 percent of the simultaneous blood glucose. In the diabetic patient a CSF glucose to blood glucose ratio of 0.31 or less is consistent with meningitis. A Gram's stain of the CSF smear may be helpful in identifying a microorganism; however, it may be negative in patients with subacute disease or in those who have received prior antimicrobial therapy, both common situations in the elderly. Special studies of the CSF, such as counterimmunoelectrophoresis (CIE) or latex agglutination to detect bacterial antigen, may be helpful in the patient with pneumococcal or meningococcal meningitis but are of no value with *Listeria*, gram-negative bacilli, or *Staphylococcus*. Routine cultures of the CSF will be positive in over 90 percent of cases of bacterial meningitis. Blood cultures are also frequently positive and should always be done prior to starting therapy.

TREATMENT

Specific antimicrobial therapy of bacterial meningitis will depend on the infecting pathogen, but certain general principles will apply in all cases. The most important principle of treatment is the prompt administration of an appropriate antimicrobial agent. The initial therapy must be started as soon as the diagnosis is made and often before a specific bacterial etiology is confirmed. Cultures of blood, CSF, and other potential sites of infection should be obtained prior to beginning therapy. Initial choice of antimicrobial agent is based on several factors, including the age of the individual, the suspected bacterial pathogen, the CSF Gram's stain, and the clinical setting (including underlying diseases that would predispose to a particular pathogen). Additional considerations include the penetration of the drug into the CSF, the dosage required to achieve adequate serum and CSF concentrations, and the dosage interval. The antimicrobial agent should be given intravenously for the entire course of therapy. There is no role for oral therapy in the treatment of bacterial meningitis. When aminoglycosides are used to treat gram-negative meningitis, intrathecal administration is indicated in addition to intravenous administration.

Another important aspect of therapy is good supportive care. Protection of the airway, adequate ventilation, intravenous fluids to correct dehydration, and good general nursing care are important in preventing complications. The patient should be observed for the development of complications, including convulsions, which may occur in up to one-third of cases. In severe cases the use of intracranial pressure (ICP) monitoring may be helpful in reducing intracranial pressure and improving the outcome. However, routine use of ICP monitoring is not indicated and does carry a small risk of complications. In cases where the bacterial etiology is in doubt, serious underlying disease is present, or complications such as convulsions occur, consultation with specialists in the fields of infectious diseases and/or neurology should be obtained.

HERPES SIMPLEX ENCEPHALITIS

EPIDEMIOLOGY

Herpes simplex encephalitis is the most common cause of fatal sporadic encephalitis in the United States. Overall, however, encephalitis due to herpes simplex is uncommon, with an estimated incidence of 2.3 cases per million persons per year. Cases occur throughout the year, in contrast to the seasonal occurrence of arbovirus or enterovirus encephalitis. The age distribution tends to be biphasic, with most cases occurring between 5 and 30 years of age and above 50 years of age. Most cases in older adults are due to *Herpesvirus hominis* type I (HSV-I). The mortality of untreated cases exceeds 70 percent, and survivors often have severe neurologic sequelae. Morbidity and mortality, however, are greatly reduced by early diagnosis and specific antiviral therapy.

PATHOGENESIS

The pathogenesis of herpes encephalitis is not entirely understood. In children and young adults encephalitis may result from primary infection in which virus travels from the periphery to the brain by a neurotrophic route by way of the olfactory bulb. However, older adults often have serologic evidence of prior HSV infection, suggesting reactivation of latent virus in the trigeminal ganglion. Reactivated virus then enters the brain by nerves innervating the middle cranial fossa. Other possible mechanisms include reactivation of latent virus that entered the brain during primary infection years earlier or exogenous reinfection with a different strain of herpesvirus. HSV has a predilection for the temporal lobes, resulting in a necrotizing, hemorrhagic encephalitis.

CLINICAL PRESENTATION

The clinical presentation of HSV encephalitis often includes a prodrome of fever, malaise, headache, and upper respiratory symptoms occurring one to several days prior to the onset of neurologic signs. However, the clinical hallmark of HSV encephalitis is the acute onset of high fever, severe headache, and focal neurologic signs often suggesting a temporal lobe lesion. Alteration of consciousness, mentation, and behavior are common findings, and untreated patients progress to stupor and coma. Seizures are seen in over 50 percent of adults with HSV encephalitis, in contrast to their uncommon occurrence in other forms of viral encephalitis. Over 75 percent of patients will exhibit localizing neurologic signs, including seizures, hemiplegia, cranial nerve palsies, aphasia, and unilateral Babinski's sign.

DIAGNOSIS

The early diagnosis of HSV encephalitis requires a clinical suspicion in the patient with severe headache and fever, with or without mental status changes. A complete neurologic examination looking for focal signs is essential. If focal neurologic signs are present, further studies to exclude a mass lesion must be done before proceeding with lumbar puncture. The technetium brain scan will be abnormal in 50 percent of cases of HSV encephalitis, the computed tomography (CT) scan in 60 percent, and the electroencephalogram (EEG) in 80 percent. However, any of these tests may be abnormal while the others are normal, so each may be helpful in diagnosis. Typically these studies will suggest a localized encephalopathy, usually in the temporal lobe. No single EEG pattern is indicative of the diagnosis.

If no focal signs are present or the studies mentioned are normal, a lumbar puncture should be performed to evaluate the CSF. In HSV encephalitis the CSF typically contains 50 to 500 white blood cells per mm^3, predominantly lymphocytes. Red blood cells are usually present, reflecting the necrotizing nature of the process. The CSF protein level is moderately increased, and the glucose level is usually normal. These findings do not differentiate herpes from other forms of viral encephalitis. The CSF should be cultured for bacteria, fungi, and mycobacteria. Herpes cultures of the CSF are rarely positive.

A presumptive diagnosis of HSV encephalitis may be made on the basis of the above findings. Brain biopsy should be considered to exclude the wide range of conditions that may have a clinical presentation similar to herpes encephalitis. Included in the differential diagnosis are (1) bacterial brain abscess, especially in the early cerebritis stage; (2) tumor; (3) vascular disease; (4) tuberculosis; (5) cryptococcosis; (6) toxoplasmosis; and (7) other viral encephalitides, including coxsackievirus, Epstein-Barr virus, St. Louis encephalitis, and post-influenza encephalitis.

THERAPY

The treatment of choice for HSV encephalitis is intravenous acyclovir 30 mg/kg daily for 10 days. Acyclovir has been shown to be superior to vidarabine and less toxic. The dosage of acyclovir must be modified if there is renal impairment. Outcome is related to level of consciousness at the start of therapy, making early treatment essential. Therapy should be started as soon as a presumptive diagnosis is made and should not be delayed for brain biopsy. Neurologic and infectious diseases specialists should be consulted as soon as a central nervous system infection is suspected. Other important aspects of therapy to consider include adequate hydration and nutrition, maintenance of airway if comatose, prevention of skin breakdown, control of seizure activity, and control of increased intracranial pressure.

NEUROSYPHILIS

Infection due to *Treponema pallidum* continues to be a worldwide health problem. There has been a recent increase in the incidence of syphilis in the United States and, therefore, a subsequent increase in the incidence of neurosyphilis should be anticipated.

ETIOLOGY AND PATHOGENESIS

Neurosyphilis is the result of the systemic dissemination of the spirochete, *T. pallidum*, and its invasion of cerebral blood vessels, meninges, and brain parenchyma. Syphilis of the central nervous system may occur at any stage of the disease and CSF findings may be completely normal.

EPIDEMIOLOGY

Syphilis is usually transmitted by sexual contact or kissing, but it may also be transmitted through the placenta, by transfusion of fresh infected blood, or by direct innoculation of the skin with contaminated blood or other laboratory specimens. The five stages of syphilis are the incubation period, primary syphilis, secondary (disseminated) syphilis, latent syphilis, and tertiary (late) syphilis. Because of the relatively young age at which syphilis is usually contracted and the short time period between exposure to *T. pallidum* and the development of the neurologic manifestations in primary and secondary syphilis, the central nervous system manifestations of these stages are not usually seen in the elderly. The most common neurosyphilitic syndromes in the elderly are general paresis and tabes dorsalis.

SEROLOGY

The serologic tests for syphilis are divided into treponemal and nontreponemal tests. The nontreponemal tests check the ability of the patient's serum to flocculate a suspension of cardiolipin-lecithin antigen. Many infectious and noninfectious illnesses may cause positive nontreponemal tests in the absence of true infection by *T. pallidum*. These false-positive tests may be caused by such diverse conditions as connective tissue disorders, pregnancy, rheumatic fever, tuberculosis, "old age," and many others. The two most commonly used nontreponemal tests are the Venereal Disease Research Laboratory (VDRL) test and the Rapid Plasma Reagin (RPR) test. Treponemal tests detect specific antibody directed against *T. pallidum*. The treponemal tests include the *T. pallidum* immobilization (TPI) test, the fluorescent treponemal antibody absorbed (FTA-ABS) test, the microhemagglutination assay for *T. pallidum* (MHA-TP), and the *T. pallidum* hemagglutination assay (TPHA). Nontreponemal serologic tests are positive in 75 percent of patients with documented neurosyphilis, and treponemal tests are positive in 95 to 100 percent.

CLINICAL FEATURES AND DIAGNOSIS

Asymptomatic Neurosyphilis

Asymptomatic neurosyphilis implies the presence of CSF abnormalities and the absence of neurologic signs or symptoms. Examination of the CSF is an absolute requirement for making this diagnosis. Asymptomatic neurosyphilis accounted for over 30 percent of the cases of central nervous system syphilis in the preantibiotic era. CSF abnormalities are most likely to occur from 12 to 18 months after the initial infection. Because of this and because of the relatively young age at which syphilis is usually acquired, this form of neurosyphilis is not usually seen in the elderly. However, untreated asymptomatic neurosyphilis may progress to other forms of central nervous system syphilis, so asymptomatic neurosyphilis is more than just a curiosity for the gerontologist.

Acute Syphilitic Meningitis

Acute syphilitic meningitis most commonly affects young adults and usually presents within 2 years of the initial infection with *T. pallidum*. Occasionally (in 10 percent of cases) it occurs concomitantly with the rash of secondary syphilis. The most common signs and symptoms are headache, confusion, and meningismus. There may be abnormalities of the cranial nerves; the seventh and eighth cranial nerves are most commonly affected. Syphilitic meningitis often resolves without antimicrobial therapy. It may later progress to general paresis or tabes dorsalis.

Meningovascular Syphilis

Meningovascular syphilis is due to syphilitic endarteritis and the resultant infarction of areas of the central nervous system supplied by the inflamed arteries. It may affect the cerebrum, brainstem, spinal cord, or meninges. Almost all patients with meningovascular syphilis are between 30 and 50 years of age. The usual latency period between primary syphilitic infection and the onset of neurologic symptoms is 7 years (range: 3 months to 12 years). The most common presenting manifestations are the result of vascular insufficiency of the brain and include hemiparesis or hemiplegia (83%), aphasia (31%), and seizure disorder (14%). The CSF is always abnormal, showing a lymphocytic pleocytosis (>60%), an elevated protein level (66%), and a positive CSF-VDRL (81%). The symptoms related to vascular damage in meningovascular syphilis are usually more slowly progressive than those seen with thrombotic or embolic stroke. Indeed, the progression may be over a period of days rather than over a period of minutes or hours. Undiagnosed and/or untreated meningovascular syphilis may result in the subsequent development of paretic or tabetic neurosyphilis in late adulthood.

Parenchymatous Neurosyphilis

GENERAL PARESIS General paresis develops over many years and usually produces symptoms in middle-aged to elderly adults. The time from initial infection to the onset of symptoms averages 15 to 20 years (range: 3 to 30 years). In the early stages of paretic neurosyphilis, signs and symptoms include generalized irritability, personality changes, memory loss, decreased ability to concentrate, poor personal hygiene and appearance, headache, and insomnia. In the later stages defective judgment, emotional lability, lack of insight, confusion, disorientation, delusions of grandeur, paranoia, and seizure disorder are predominant. The psychiatric manifestations may mimic almost any psychiatric illness. The diagnosis is made by the presence of a positive serologic test for syphilis, as well as an abnormal CSF. The CSF usually shows a lymphocytic pleocytosis (90%), a normal or moderately reduced glucose level, an elevated protein level (75%), and a positive CSF-VDRL (almost 100%). The likelihood of reversing the central nervous system findings with appropriate therapy is related to the degree of damage present at the time of initiation of antimicrobial therapy: the longer the period of time between the onset of symptoms and the initiation of therapy, the less likely the reversibility of the neurologic damage.

TABES DORSALIS Tabes dorsalis was the most common clinical form of neurosyphilis in the preantibiotic era, accounting for 30 percent of all patients with neurosyphilis. Tabes usually occurs in the fifth or sixth decade of life and, therefore, is the form of neurosyphilis most commonly seen in the geriatric population. It usually develops after a latency period averaging 20 to 25 years (range: 5 to 50 years). It is characterized by a triad of symptoms (lightning pains, dysuria, and ataxia) and a triad of signs (Argyll Robertson pupils, areflexia, and loss of proprioceptive sensation). Lightning pains are severe, paroxysmal, stabbing pains of sudden onset which last for a few minutes at a time; these pains occur mainly in the lower extremities and persist for variable periods of time. They occur at some time in as many as 90 percent of patients with tabetic neurosyphilis. Argyll Robertson pupils are characterized by (1) a light-sensitive retina (i.e., the patient is not blind); (2) small, fixed pupils which do not react to a strong light stimulus; (3) normally convergent and accommodative pupils; (4) the lack of pupillary dilatation by mydriatic substances; and (5) nondilatation of the pupil upon painful stimulation. Other symptoms may occur as the disease progresses: a broad-based, stamping gait; optic atrophy with decreased visual acuity; Charcot's joints; and painless penetrating trophic ulcers on the plantar surfaces of the foot at the base of the toes. The serum VDRL may be negative in as many as 40 percent of patients. All patients have a positive specific serum antibody test. The CSF findings are less abnormal than in other neurosyphilis syndromes. In fact, the CSF may be normal in patients with tabes dorsalis who have either been appropriately treated or who have a "burned-out" case of the disease. The most common CSF abnormalities are a lymphocytic pleocytosis (50%), an elevated protein concentration (50%), and a positive CSF-VDRL (72%). After treatment the CSF findings may return to normal, but the neurologic abnormalities may persist at the level of function present at the onset of therapy.

ATYPICAL PRESENTATIONS OF NEUROSYPHILIS

Some patients may have atypical and/or antibiotic-modified neurosyphilis with one of the following sets of clinical findings: (1) blurring of the vision, CSF changes, and Argyll Robertson pupils; or (2) bilateral oculomotor nerve paresis, minimal CSF pleocytosis, and positive serologic findings in both blood and CSF; or (3) the sudden onset of deafness, tinnitus, and dizziness, with positive VDRL and FTA-ABS reactions in both blood and CSF. The various forms of neurosyphilis may also exist as mixed clinical syndromes.

THERAPY AND ASSESSMENT OF RESPONSE TO THERAPY

Parenteral penicillin G continues to be the treatment of choice for all types of neurosyphilis. The treatment schedules currently recommended by the Centers for Disease Control are listed in Table 98-2. Recent reports of relapsing neurosyphilis in patients with concomitant infection with the human immunodeficiency virus suggest that regimens requiring a higher dosage and longer duration of penicillin G may be required in these patients. Because of scientifically sound data showing that benzathine penicillin G has almost no penetration into the CSF, we recommend one of the aqueous penicillin G regimens. If the patient in question has some type of immunodeficiency, we recommend the intravenous aqueous crystalline penicillin G regimen for at least 14 days.

Repeat examination of the CSF should be done weekly during antibiotic therapy and every 6 months for 2 years after the completion of antimicrobial therapy or until the CSF is normal. Adequate therapy is defined as documentation of a normal CSF cell count with a falling protein at least 6 months after the start of therapy. In most cases, the CSF-VDRL should become negative 5 years after the initiation of therapy, although some individuals remain positive ("serofast") indefinitely in the absence of any clinical signs of neurosyphilitic progression. Any increase in the CSF cell count is an indication for retreatment.

TUBERCULOUS MENINGITIS

Tuberculous meningitis is an important infection to consider in the elderly patient who presents with an insidious onset of headache, lethargy, mentation changes, and fever. The infection usually evolves over a period of weeks. Meningeal signs are often present. The CSF typically contains 100 to 500 leukocytes per mm^3 with a predominance of lymphocytes. The CSF glucose level is usually depressed but may be normal. The CSF protein level is between 100 and 500 mg/dl. Acid-fast bacilli are seen in initial specimens of CSF sediment in only one-third of cases, but the yield increases with repeated CSF examinations. Seventy-five percent of patients will have associated active or inactive extrameningeal tuberculosis. However, up to one-half will initially have a negative intermediate tuberculin skin test. Cranial nerve deficits caused by involvement of the nerves passing through the inflammatory exudate in the subarachnoid space at the base of the brain are common. This basilar exudative response may also lead to obstruction of CSF flow and resultant hydrocephalus in undiagnosed cases. Hyponatremia is a common finding and an important diagnostic

TABLE 98-2
Treatment Regimens for Neurosyphilis

Non-Penicillin-Allergic Patients

1. Aqueous crystalline penicillin G, 2.0–4.0 million units intravenously, every 4 hours for 10 days, followed by benzathine penicillin G, 2.4 million units intramuscularly weekly for 3 doses
2. Aqueous procaine penicillin G, 2.4 million units intramuscularly daily plus probenecid, 500 mg orally 4 times daily, both for 10 days, followed by benzathine penicillin G, 2.4 million units intramuscularly weekly for 3 doses
3. Benzathine penicillin G, 2.4 million units intramuscularly weekly for 3 doses

Penicillin-Allergic Patients

1. Tetracycline hydrochloride, 500 mg orally 4 times daily for 30 days
2. Erythromycin, 500 mg orally 4 times daily for 30 days
3. Chloramphenicol, 1 gram intravenously 4 times daily for 14 days

clue. Early diagnosis and specific therapy is important since delay leads to an increase in neurologic morbidity and mortality. Treatment should be instituted with isoniazid, 10 mg/kg, and rifampin, 600 mg/day, and continued for 1 year. Corticosteroids have been advocated for patients with significant neurologic signs.

BRAIN ABSCESS

Brain abscess should be considered in the elderly patient who presents with fever, headache, lethargy, and focal neurologic deficits. These findings, however, are not always present, making the diagnosis difficult. Brain abscess in the adult occurs either as a result of direct extension of bacteria into the brain from an adjacent focus of infection in the mastoid or paranasal sinuses or by hematogenous spread of bacteria to the brain from a condition with a distant site of infection, such as endocarditis, pneumonia, or lung abscess. The presentation is often subacute with signs and symptoms suggesting a mass lesion. The differential diagnosis includes tumor, cerebral infarction, focal encephalitis, or other mass lesions such as tuberculoma. The microbial etiology varies with the underlying cause. Common microorganisms include aerobic and anaerobic streptococci, S. *aureus*, *Bacteroides* species, and *Actinomyces*. Gram-negative bacilli are occasionally involved. The diagnosis should be considered when clinical findings suggest a mass lesion. The CT scan of the head will demonstrate a mass lesion (or lesions) with a hypodense center and an outer rim that enhances with contrast. Lumbar puncture may precipitate clinical deterioration and should be avoided. Cerebral angiography will help differentiate abscess from tumor, but in most cases surgical exploration and biopsy is preferred. Surgical drainage is necessary unless the abscess is very small or is discovered during the early cerebritis phase before necrosis occurs. Antimicrobial therapy given parenterally for 4 to 6 weeks is indicated in addition to surgery. The antimicrobial agent should be selected for its activity against the suspected or proven pathogen and its penetration into brain tissue.

GENERAL READING

Bacterial Meningitis

Berk SL, McCabe WR: Meningitis caused by gram-negative bacilli. *Ann Intern Med* 93:253, 1980.

Cherubin CE, Marr JS, Sierra MF, Becker S: *Listeria* and gram-negative bacillary meningitis in New York City, 1972–1979. *Am J Med* 71:199, 1981.

Finland M, Barnes MW: Acute bacterial meningitis at Boston City Hospital during 12 selected years, 1935–1972. *J Infect Dis* 136:400, 1977.

Geisler PJ, Nelson KE, Levin S, Reddi KT, Moses VK: Community-acquired purulent meningitis: A review of 1,316 cases during the antibiotic era, 1954–1976. *Rev Infect Dis* 2:725, 1980.

Hodges GR, Perkins RL: Acute bacterial meningitis: An analysis of factors influencing prognosis. *Am J Med Sci* 270:427, 1975.

Hodges GR, Perkins RL: Hospital-associated bacterial meningitis. *Am J Med Sci* 271:335, 1976.

Powers WJ: Cerebrospinal fluid to serum glucose ratios in diabetes mellitus and bacterial meningitis. *Am J Med* 71:217, 1981.

Quagliariello VJ, Scheld WM: Review: Recent advances in the pathogenesis and pathophysiology of bacterial meningitis. *Am J Med Sci* 292:306, 1986.

Romer FK: Difficulties in the diagnosis of bacterial meningitis. *Lancet* 2:345, 1977.

Herpes Simplex Encephalitis

Barza M, Pauker SG: The decision to biopsy, treat, or wait in suspected herpes encephalitis. *Ann Intern Med* 92:641, 1980.

Corey L, Spear PG: Infections with herpes simplex viruses. *N Engl J Med* 314:749, 1986.

Elian M: Herpes simplex encephalitis: Prognosis and long term follow up. *Arch Neurol* 32:39, 1975.

Illis LS, Taylor FM: The electroencephalogram in herpes simplex encephalitis. *Lancet* 1:718, 1972.

Johnson KP, Rosenthal MS, Lerner PI: Herpes simplex encephalitis, the course in five virologically proven cases. *Arch Neurol* 27:103, 1972.

Koskiniemi M, Vaheri A, Taskinen E: Cerebrospinal fluid alterations in herpes simplex virus encephalitis. *Rev Infect Dis* 6:608, 1984.

Skoldenberg B, Alestig K, Burman L: Acyclovir versus vidarabine in herpes simplex encephalitis. *Lancet* 2:707, 1984.

Whitley RJ, Alford CA, Hirsch MS: Vidarabine versus acyclovir therapy in herpes simplex encephalitis. *N Engl J Med* 314:144, 1986.

Neurosyphilis

Felman YM: Lumbar puncture in asymptomatic neurosyphilis. *Arch Intern Med* 145:422, 1985.

Lukehart SA, Hook EW III, Baker-Zander SA, Collier AC, Critchlow CW, Handsfield HH: Invasion of the central nervous system by *Treponema pallidum:* Implications for diagnosis and treatment. *Ann Intern Med* 109:855, 1988.

Musher DM: Syphilis. *Infect Dis Clin North Am* 1:83, 1987.

Musher DM: Evaluation and management of an asymptomatic patient with a positive VDRL reaction, in Remington JS, Swartz MN (eds): *Current Clinical Topics in Infectious Diseases,* 9. New York, McGraw-Hill, 1988, pp 147–157.

Musher DM: How much penicillin cures early syphilis? *Ann Intern Med* 109:849, 1988.

Simon RP: Neurosyphilis. *Arch Neurol* 42:606, 1985.

Swartz MN: Neurosyphilis, in Holmes KK, Mardh PA, Sparling PF, Wiesner PJ (eds): *Sexually Transmitted Diseases.* New York, McGraw-Hill, 1984, pp 318–334.

Tramont EC: *Treponema pallidum* (syphilis), in Mandell GL, Douglas RG Jr, Bennett JE (eds): *Principles and Practice of Infectious Diseases,* 2d ed. New York, Wiley, 1985, p 1323.

Tramont EC: Syphilis in the AIDS era. *N Engl J Med* 316:1600, 1987.

Tuberculous Meningitis

Barrett-Connor E: Tuberculous meningitis in adults. *South Med J* 60:1061, 1967.

Haas EJ, Madhavan T, Quinn EL: Tuberculous meningitis in an urban general hospital. *Arch Intern Med* 137:1518, 1977.

Kennedy DH, Fallon RJ: Tuberculous meningitis. *JAMA* 241:264, 1979.

Brain Abscess

Brewer NS, MacCarty CS, Wellman WE: Brain abscess: A review of recent experience. *Ann Intern Med* 82:571, 1975.

Yang SH: Brain abscess: A review of 400 cases. *J Neurosurg* 55:794, 1981.

Chapter 99

HEAD INJURY (INCLUDING SUBDURAL HEMATOMA)

Dennis G. Vollmer and Howard M. Eisenberg

Because trauma is the leading cause of death of individuals less than 45 years of age,[1,11,37] it is generally considered to be an affliction of the young. It should be remembered, however, that injuries rank fifth among causes of death for adults 65 years of age or older; 25 percent of all trauma fatalities occur in this age group, which comprises only about 11 percent of the population.[7,38,48] Furthermore, nearly one-third of the annual health care resources available for the treatment of trauma are expended on the elderly.[45] Serious trauma is not more frequent in the geriatric population, but when it occurs, it has a greater likelihood of producing a fatal outcome.[48] Within this context, traumatic brain injury is particularly important because of its high toll in mortality and serious morbidity. It has been increasingly well appreciated that even a relatively mild head injury may produce prolonged sequelae.[10,19,25,50,55,56] Survivors of more severe brain trauma often suffer significant disability. Many such patients have severe neuropsychological deficits despite the absence of gross neurologic or physical sequelae.[31,41,56,64]

In the geriatric age group, mortality rates following severe brain trauma approach 90 percent.[28,29,32,35,49,51,52,66,67] Elderly survivors tend to have more prolonged hospitalizations and are left with more severe sequelae.[28] The elderly also appear to have a lesser ability to recover from neurologic insult so that milder injuries are less well tolerated.[9,10,29,60] Despite the serious implications of head injury in the older adult, relatively few studies have concentrated primarily on the problem of head injury in this age group.[13,29,53,54] It is clear however, that with the aging of the population in most developed countries and with the rapidly escalating cost of medical care, the issue of traumatic brain injury in the geriatric patient will be of ever-increasing interest and importance. In this chapter, we will focus upon head injury in the elderly, examining epidemiology, pathophysiology, and treatment.

EPIDEMIOLOGIC CONSIDERATIONS

The overall incidence of head injury in the United States is estimated to be in the range of 200 per 100,000 persons per year.[37] Considerable differences are observed however, when age-specific incidence rates are examined (Fig. 99-1). Most studies have demonstrated a peak incidence for young adults in the 15 to 25 age range with a secondary rise in incidence rates in the elderly.[1,12,28,37] For individuals age 65 or over, the incidence has been estimated to approximate the overall national rate.[37] Males are well known to experience a greater risk of head injury than females (Fig. 99-2).[12,34,37] In most studies this gender effect is observed into the extremes of old age. For example, Cooper et al. have shown a twofold or greater incidence of head injury for males older than 65 than for females in this same age group.[12] The causes for male predominance in geriatric head injury are less clear than for younger age groups. Many of the factors usually blamed for injuries in the elderly would appear to affect both sexes similarly. The changing sex ratio observed in the population over age 65, however, acts to obscure somewhat the sex-related differences in incidence. Based upon census data from 1982, there are 1.5 females for each male in the population 65 and older.[7] This has the result that hospital-based studies of head injury may report equal numbers of elderly males and females treated.[53]

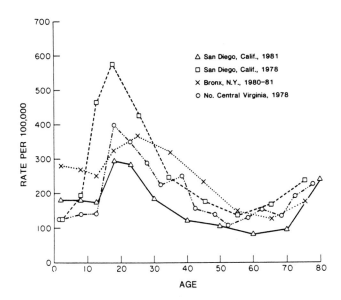

FIGURE 99-1
Age-specific incidence rates for head injury. Note the rise in incidence after age 60. (*From Kraus,[41] with permission.*)

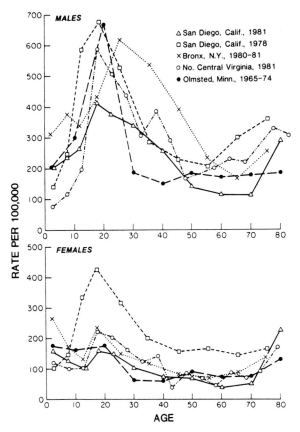

FIGURE 99-2
Age-specific incidence rates of head injury for males (upper) and females (lower). The incidence rate for males is approximately twice that for females for all age groups. (*From Kraus,[41] with permission.*)

The distribution of causes observed for head injuries varies depending upon numerous factors. The characteristics of the population under study—e.g., urban versus rural, higher versus lower socioeconomic status, differences in racial composition—will all influence the relative frequency of the different causes observed.[37] In addition, the cause of injury varies with severity, i.e., studies of severe injuries have higher frequencies of vehicular accidents, whereas falls are more common in minor injuries. Age is also a key determinant of the cause of head trauma. In a preliminary analysis of data on severe head injury from the National Institutes of Health—Traumatic Coma Data Bank,*,[43] the cause of injury was clearly associated with the age of the patient (Fig. 99-3).[68] Older adults tended to have much higher rates of falls and assaults, whereas the likelihood of injury to a vehicular passenger decreased with age. Pedestrian injuries were more common in older age groups as well.

The significance of fall injuries in the elderly is well known.[2,27,44] It has been noted that 35 to 40 percent of all individuals over age 65 suffer at least one fall each year and that the risk increases sharply with advancing age.[62] It is not surprising then, that older patients with a head injury are more likely to have had a fall as the causative event. The reasons for the greater risk of falling in the elderly are also well described.[2,14,59] Decreased vision, limitations in other sensory modalities, medical problems such as orthostatic hypotension, muscle weakness, and impaired balance from numerous causes have all been cited as contributing to higher rates of falling in

the elderly. Many of these same factors increase the risk for pedestrian injury as well.

CLINICAL PATHOLOGY

The age of a patient appears to influence the frequency with which specific brain disease is encountered after head injury. For example, it is recognized that patients with subdural hematomas are older on average than patients with other disease processes.[40,61] The reasons for this observation are clearly multiple. It has been well documented both by laboratory and clinical study that a fall injury is more likely to result in biomechanical forces which favor the production of an acute subdural hematoma.[24] On the other hand, the biomechanics of motor vehicle accidents appear more likely to result in a so-called diffuse axonal shearing injury. In a clinical series, Gennarelli et al. noted that falls and assaults caused a disproportionate number of acute subdural hematomas (72 percent), whereas the cause of diffuse axonal shearing injury was vehicular in 89 percent of cases.[23] It therefore stands to reason that the elderly, who have a higher incidence of falling, would also have a greater

---

*Medical College of Virginia, University of California San Diego, University of Texas Medical Branch at Galveston, and the University of Virginia.

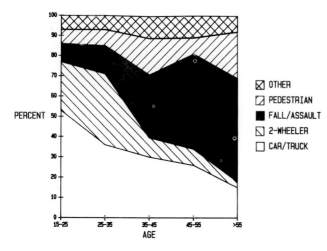

FIGURE 99-3
Mechanism of injury according to age for 540 patients analyzed in the National Institutes of Health—Traumatic Coma Data Bank. Note the increase in injuries due to falls and assaults in the older patients with the reciprocal decline in vehicular accidents.

chance of sustaining an acute subdural hematoma. Other factors also appear to predispose elderly patients to the development of acute subdural hematoma. Brain atrophy, which occurs with age, places the parasagittal bridging veins on a greater degree of stretch, making them more prone to rupture after an impact. Similarly, in the setting of brain atrophy, a given degree of angular acceleration is likely to produce more brain movement because there is more space. Changes in the viscoelastic properties of the brain parenchyma and the vascular elements brought on by the aging process may also play a role.[22,24]

The acute subdural hematoma is the most lethal of the mass lesions and of all abnormalities is associated with the greatest risk of dying. Mortality rates above 60 percent are frequently reported.[5,20,23,52] In the National Institutes of Health—Traumatic Coma Data Bank there was a strong association of age and dying in those patients with severe injuries and subdural hematoma; so that patients younger than 40 years had less than a 40 percent chance of dying (the lowest rate yet reported in large series), whereas those older than age 40 years had a 70 percent chance (unpublished data).

In contrast to acute subdural hematoma, the incidence of epidural hematoma appears to decrease with age, although skull fractures seem to be just as common in the elderly as in younger patients.[30,68] The greater adherence of the dura to the inner table of the skull in older individuals likely impedes the development of an extradural collection.

In the National Institutes of Health—Traumatic Coma Data Bank series, the overall frequency of acute intraparenchymal hematomas did not change with age. The syndrome of delayed traumatic intracerebral hema-

toma, however, does appear to occur more frequently in older patients.[70] The clinical hallmark of this entity is the relatively abrupt neurologic deterioration of a patient several days after a head injury which often was only of mild or moderate severity. The lesions in delayed traumatic intracerebral hematoma tend to develop in areas of contusion.[70] Neurologic deterioration may not be readily apparent in patients who are initially comatose, however; thus a low threshold for repeat computed tomographic (CT) scanning particularly in patients who have elevated intracranial pressure must be maintained.

CHRONIC SUBDURAL HEMATOMA

Chronic subdural hematoma is a distinct clinicopathologic entity which differs significantly in its manner of presentation, treatment, and prognosis from acute subdural hematoma discussed previously.[8,42,54,69] This entity largely affects patients who are middle-aged or older with increasing incidence associated with advancing age. It is generally felt that brain atrophy with the associated tethering of the parasagittal bridging veins results in a propensity for the formation of chronic subdural hematomas. It is further reasoned that the decreased cerebral volume in this situation allows for larger hematomas to accumulate without significant symptoms. Trauma is generally thought to be the precipitating factor in the formation of these lesions, although the injury may be mild. A clear history of head injury may be absent in 20 to 50 percent of patients.[8,40] Patients with chronic subdural hematomas, by definition, present 3 or more weeks after injury.[40] Hematomas presenting earlier after trauma have been traditionally termed subacute subdural hematomas. This distinction is somewhat arbitrary. From a practical point of view, patients who present with slowly progressive signs and symptoms, with a liquid clot in the subdural space, are comparable regardless of the exact history of trauma.[7]

The presentation of chronic subdural hematoma is quite variable.[8,40,54] Signs and symptoms tend to be insidious and slowly progressive. Although focal neurologic deficits may prompt a search for an intracranial mass lesion, patients with chronic subdural hematoma often present with nonspecific signs and symptoms such as headache, nausea and vomiting, apathy, alteration in level of consciousness, personality changes, or overt dementia. The lack of a clear relationship of this deterioration with antecedent trauma further complicates the diagnosis. Because chronic subdural hematoma commonly affects the elderly, who are at risk for a great many other neurologic and systemic disorders, the diagnosis is often delayed.

CT scanning is presently the diagnostic method of choice for patients suspected of harboring a chronic subdural hematoma.[42] In the majority of cases, the lesions are hypodense crescentic collections over the convexity of the cerebral hemispheres. There is frequently associated mass effect with shift of compression of the ventricular system. Occasionally the CT scan appearance is less straightforward with the lesions demonstrating multiple densities within the collection or with layering of hyperdense material posteriorly. In some cases, the hematomas may be isodense with normal brain, and in these cases the radiographic signs of an intracranial mass, as well as the obliteration of the cortical sulci, should raise the question of a chronic subdural hematoma. When there is doubt, contrast enhancement can help establish the diagnosis. Magnetic resonance imaging (MRI) scans also show these lesions to good advantage and may eventually supplant CT scanning as the preferred diagnostic modality.[62]

Chronic subdural hematomas, being largely liquid, are often amenable to a much less extensive surgical treatment than acute subdural hematomas. Although numerous variations in treatment have been advocated, drainage of the collection using burr holes or a small twist drill craniostomy with closed system drainage appear to be the methods most commonly employed.[8,42,47,54,57,69]

The prognosis for chronic subdural hematoma is significantly better than for acute subdural hematoma. Mortality rates in most series have generally been lower than 15 percent.[69] Higher mortality and morbidity seem to occur in patients whose level of neurologic function is more severely impaired prior to treatment. In addition, elderly or debilitated patients tend to fare worse, both in terms of mortality and morbidity.[54] Recurrence of the collection requiring further treatment is not uncommon and may occur in as many as 20 percent of patients.[69]

MINOR HEAD INJURY

A head injury is considered minor when it produces a transient loss of consciousness, usually 20 minutes or less in duration, with a relatively rapid return to full alertness. Patients present for evaluation with a Glasgow Coma Scale (GCS) score of 13 or better. In a series of 1248 consecutive head injury patients seen at the University of Virginia, such minor head injuries accounted for 55 percent of the total.[55] Patients age 60 years or older accounted for 4 percent of this series. In a subsequent series of minor head injuries studied at the same institution, 81 of 1216 patients were 60 years of age or older (6.7 percent).[10,19] In these studies it does not appear that the geriatric population is predisposed to head injuries of this severity. However, these data are not population-based so that strict conclusions about the epidemiology of minor head injury in the elderly cannot be made.

In recent years it has become more apparent that minor head injuries can and do result in sequelae which persist for a considerable length of time. Rimel et al. reported a series of patients examined 3 months after minor head injury.[55] While only 2 percent manifested positive findings on neurologic examination, the majority of patients tested ($n = 69$) showed substandard scores on a battery of neuropsychological tests. Furthermore, 34 percent of patients gainfully employed prior to a mild head injury remained unemployed 3 months after the injury. Other studies have described similar results.[15,26,41,50] Although the duration of subsequent impairment continues to be debated, most investigators agree that minor head injury produces significant, objective neuropsychological deficits. None of the studies alluded to have specifically examined the effects of minor head injury on the elderly patient. It seems logical to assume that similar sequelae might be seen in the aged, but the question as to whether these effects are more severe cannot be answered with confidence. Colohan et al., however, performed a linear multiple regression analysis of factors associated with hospital stay and return to normal social activity after minor head injury.[10] In each instance, advanced age proved to be a highly significant, independent predictor of a poorer outcome.

OUTCOME

It is well known that the prognosis following a closed head injury worsens significantly with increasing age.[6,9,11,28,32,67,68] Figure 99-4 shows outcome data according to age for patients entered into the National Institutes of Health—Traumatic Coma Data Bank between January 1984 and September 1986. Mortality increases with age for all levels of severity of injury studied. Vegetative survival, however, appears to be relatively constant in all age groups approximating 5 percent.

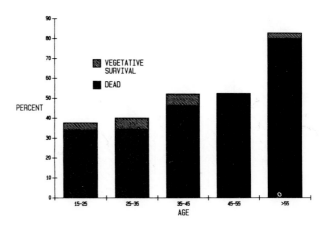

FIGURE 99-4
Outcome following severe head injury according to age. Percent dead or surviving in a vegetative state for 540 patients entered into the National Institutes of Health—Traumatic Coma Data.

Although a relatively large number of patients were studied in the National Institutes of Health—Traumatic Coma Data Bank, it is not possible to accurately assess whether the age-related risk of mortality after head injury increases in a linear fashion or whether there are increments of risk at various age thresholds. In the International Data Bank,* a continuous relationship was found between age and outcome,[66] whereas other studies have suggested that inflections in the age-outcome curve may occur at 20, 40, and 60 years of age.[6,28]

The causes of the adverse effect of age on the outcome of head injury are also unclear. Several authors have attributed the higher rates of mortality to the greater frequency of prior systemic illness or secondary medical complications seen in the elderly.[3,9] Others have suggested that events primary to the central nervous system may be involved.[19,68] Furthermore, the greater frequency of intracranial hematomas in the elderly may play a role since the mortality associated with these lesions remains high. Interestingly, in the International Data Bank, older patients who did not have an intracranial hematoma did not fare any better than the cohort of those who did.[32]

In the National Institutes of Health—Traumatic Coma Data Bank, the primary cause of death was determined for 236 patients (Fig. 99-5). No age-related increase in extracerebral causes for death was noted.[68] These findings contrast sharply with those of Carlsson et al. who attributed excess mortality associated with increasing age to extracranial complications.[9] Interestingly, however, in Carlsson's series, cases with "surgically oriented complications such as intracranial hematoma, depressed fracture, lacerations of the brain,

*University of Glasgow, Universities of Rotterdam and Groningen, and the University of Southern California.

and localized space-occupying cerebral contusion" were not included. In the National Institutes of Health—Traumatic Coma Data Bank in which CT scans were utilized, elderly patients demonstrating none of these complications comprised a very small minority (5 percent). Hypotension or hypoxemia are well known to increase the chances of mortality after head injury.[17] In the National Institutes of Health—Traumatic Coma Data Bank, neither of these abnormalities were more common in the older groups of patients (Fig. 99-6), but multiple injuries were less frequent in older patients. This is not surprising when the cause of injury is taken into account, since multiple injuries are more common after vehicular trauma (Fig. 99-7). Multiple injuries in the elderly, however, result in particularly poor outcome.

In addition to having a higher overall mortality rate after head injury, geriatric patients also continue to die further along in their hospital course (Fig. 99-8). Of patients admitted to the hospital who ultimately die of

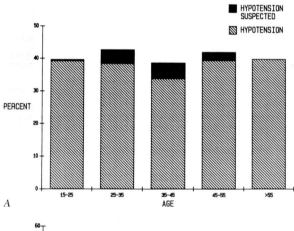

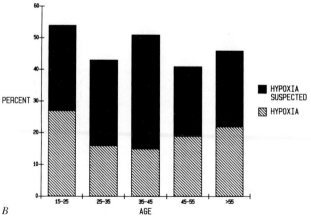

FIGURE 99-6
Hypotension and hypoxia in severe injury. **A.** Percentage of 539 patients with hypotension, defined as systolic blood pressure lower than 100 mmHg (upper). **B.** Percentage of 524 patients exhibiting hypoxia defined as PaO₂ less than 60 mmHg. No significant differences were observed for the different age groups. (*From the National Institutes of Health—Traumatic Coma Data Bank.*)

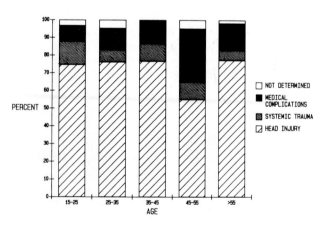

FIGURE 99-5
Primary cause of death as determined by the medical team caring for 236 patients. No significant differences or trends observed according to age. (*From National Institutes of Health—Traumatic Coma Data Bank.*)

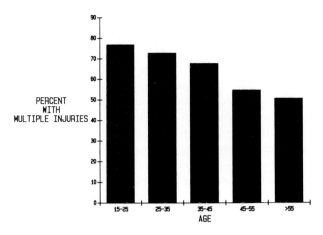

FIGURE 99-7
Percent of 540 patients with severe head injury who have multiple injuries, defined as an associated injury scale greater than 1. The decline in multiple injuries according to older age group was statistically significant. (*From the National Institutes of Health—Traumatic Coma Data Bank.*)

their injuries, 60 percent age 55 years or older die later than 48 hours after injury. In contrast, 61 percent of patients younger than 55 who ultimately die do so within 48 hours of injury.[68] The implication is that older patients may be dying from different causes than their younger counterparts. Further study is required to determine these causes as well as to possibly define subsets within the elderly head-injured population whose prognosis is substantially better (or worse) than the age group as a whole.

Age has also been shown to be a powerful predictor of outcome in statistical models that considered multiple variables and their interactions. Jennett, Teasdale, and their co-workers[4,33,65] demonstrated that accurate prediction of outcome with a high level of confidence could be made using information from the International Data Bank in models employing a sequential Bayes method. Using this technique and data from 305 patients admitted to the Netherland centers, Braakman and his associates ranked the order of variables that best fitted the

model. On admission, the rank order of best predictors were age, pupillary responses, and the eye and motor score (from the GCS). At different times after injury, the relative importance of these variables change within the model, but age always ranked highly. Narayan, Stablein, and their coworkers[46,63] applied a logistic regression model to analyze their data from patients admitted in acute traumatic coma. The rank order of the 12 most important variables is shown in Table 99-1.

There is a relative paucity of information regarding the functional outlook for elderly survivors of head injury. Pazzaglia et al. showed a decreasing quality of survival with increasing age for patients after coma-producing head injury.[52] Similarly, the study of mild head injury reported by Colohan et al. demonstrated that age was an independent predictor both for longer hospital stay, as well as later return to baseline social functioning.[10] On the other hand, in a series of 26 head-injured, elderly patients admitted to a rehabilitation unit, 85 percent were noted to return to a home setting, with over half being independent in activities of daily living.[13] Thus, a uniformly pessimistic attitude does not appear to be justified.

EVALUATION AND TREATMENT

In principle, the evaluation and treatment of the elderly, head-injured patient differs little from that of the younger adult[18]; the primary goal is the prevention of secondary brain damage. Initial attention, as in all trauma patients, should be directed to the airway, respiratory function, and hemodynamic status. Because the injured brain is more susceptible to the effects of hypoxia and ischemia, intubation and ventilatory support should be considered early in the management of severe head injury. It has been shown that longer times from injury to intubation correlate with poorer outcomes.[25] Furthermore, hypoxia is common in head injuries even in the absence of apparent respiratory difficulty.[21] Aggressive

FIGURE 99-8
Survival rates according to age for severely head-injured patients. Note that survival rates within the first 24 hours are similar for all age groups. Older patients continue to die later in their hospital course. (*From the National Institutes of Health—Traumatic Coma Data Bank.*)

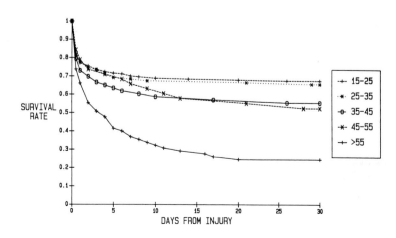

TABLE 99-1
Statistical Importance of 12 Variables*

Ranking of Factors in Order of Prognostic Importance	Regression Coefficients (Mean ± SEM)	Asymptomatic Z Test
1. Requirement for surgical decompression	-2.55 ± 0.98	-2.60
2. Age	-0.06 ± 0.02	-2.56
3. Po_2, ≤ 65; $Pco_2 > 45$; systolic blood pressure, ≤ 90; hematocrit, ≤ 30	-2.72 ± 1.18	-2.32
4. Motor response	-3.57 ± 1.59	-2.24
5. Pupil light response	-2.59 ± 1.31	-1.97
6. Interaction between motor response and presence of mass lesion	3.23 ± 1.71	1.89
7. Mass lesion presence on CT scan	-1.81 ± 1.01	-1.80
8. Eye opening to pain	-1.63 ± 1.01	-1.62
9. Pupil size	-1.75 ± 1.24	-1.41
10. Sex	1.18 ± 0.91	1.29
11. Oculocephalic response	1.46 ± 1.26	1.16
12. Verbal response	0.785 ± 0.99	0.80

*The regression coefficient for the intercept term is $a = 6.23 \pm 1.54$.
SOURCE: From Stablein et al.[63]

fluid resuscitation may be necessary to maintain adequate cerebral perfusion, especially when there are associated extracranial injuries.

Associated cervical spine injuries should be assumed to be present until ruled out by appropriate radiographic examination. The patient should therefore be immobilized. Degenerative and inflammatory arthritides and osteopenia, more common in the elderly, may increase the risk of associated spine fractures in this age group. One should be cognizant of the occurrence of central cord syndrome following a hyperextension injury in patients with congenital or spondylotic cervical spinal stenosis. This syndrome is most commonly observed in an elderly male patient who has suffered a fall and is immediately rendered quadriparetic, most severely in the upper extremities often with significant preservation of lower-extremity function.

The baseline neurologic assessment is performed during the initial resuscitation. This evaluation should not be exhaustive and time-consuming but should rather focus upon the patient's level of consciousness, the presence of lateralizing deficits and the status of brainstem reflex function. The specific aspects of the examination must be tailored to the patient's status.

The GCS provides a reproducible means of objectively quantifying the level of consciousness by examining verbal, eye-opening, and motor responses. It has

been shown to correlate well with outcome and has become a standard means for quantifying the severity of injury in head trauma literature. While the GCS[32,51,65] is a useful tool for the evaluation of head-injured patients, there are limitations to its use. The GCS may overestimate brain injuries in patients who are hypoxemic, postictal or intoxicated or who are in shock.[18] Born et al. have examined the importance of examining brainstem function in severe head injury, and have found, as have others, that this assessment adds significantly to prognostic accuracy.[4,6,39,46] This part of the examination should assess the pupillary light reflex, spontaneous eye movements, oculocephalic or oculovestibular responses, the response to corneal stimulation, the presence of gag and cough reflexes, and the respiratory rate and pattern. The motor examination is incorporated in part in the GCS, but attention should also be directed to the presence of lateralizing findings such as a hemiparesis or hemiplegia. These abnormalities often indicate the presence of an expanding intracranial mass lesion particularly when coupled with a fixed or dilated pupil. When present, a unilaterally dilated pupil is ipsilateral to a mass lesion in more than 95 percent of cases. Although it is usually contralateral to a mass, hemiplegia is occasionally ipsilateral to a lesion. This seems to occur most often in mass lesions which develop rapidly.

In the assessment of elderly patients following head injury, one must be careful to consider the possibility of other confounding diseases. For example, a head injury sustained in a fall may have been precipitated by a syncopal episode or cerebral ischemia. Similarly, a motor vehicle accident may be the cause, or the result, of an intracerebral hemorrhage in an elderly motorist. While these scenarios may occur in patients of any age, they are most apt to occur in the geriatric patient with the greater incidence of underlying disease.

SUMMARY AND CONCLUSIONS

Head injury in the elderly adult is not uncommon and may affect more than 200 per 100,000 population per year in the United States. The magnitude of the problem is further compounded when the excessive rates of mortality and morbidity for patients in this age group are examined. The mortality rate after severe head injury rises continuously with increasing age and exceeds 75 percent in the older age groups. Morbidity in terms of both neurologic and nonneurologic complications also appears to increase with advancing age.

Falls are the leading cause of head injury in the geriatric age group. Older individuals are also at greater risk for pedestrian injury. Age-related differences in the incidence of intracranial mass lesions are also observed. The elderly have higher rates of acute and chronic subdural hematomas and delayed traumatic intracerebral hemorrhage. Epidural hematoma is less frequently seen in elderly head-injured patients.

Further study of clinical head injury in the elderly as well as of the basic neurobiology of aging is required to fully understand the age-related differences in outcome. An improved understanding of the pathophysiology involved may lead to more effective treatment.

The excessive incidence of adverse outcome in the head-injured elderly patient remains a difficult challenge for modern health care. For the present, it would appear that the greatest reductions in mortality and morbidity might be achieved through efforts directed at the prevention of injury. As suggested by the data on cause of injury in the elderly, measures which can reduce the likelihood of falling or the likelihood of sustaining a head injury if a fall occurs should receive a high priority.

REFERENCES

1. Annegers JF, Grabor JD, Kurland LT, Laws ER Jr: The incidence, causes, and secular trends of head trauma in Olmsted County, Minnesota, 1935–1974. *Neurology* 30:912, 1980.
2. Baker SP, Harvey AH: Fall injuries in the elderly. *Clin Geriatr Med* 1:501, 1985.
3. Becker DP, Miller JD, Ward JD, Greenberg RP, Young HF, Sakalas R: The outcome from severe head injury with early diagnosis and intensive management. *J Neurosurg* 47:491, 1977.
4. Born JD, Albert A, Hans P, Bonnal J: Relative prognostic value of best motor response and brain stem reflexes in patients with severe head injury. *Neurosurgery* 16(5):595, 1985.
5. Bowers SA, Marshall LF: Outcome in 200 consecutive cases of severe head injury treated in San Diego County: A prospective analysis. *Neurosurgery* 6(3):237, 1980.
6. Braakman R, Gelpke GJ, Habbema JDF, Maas AIR, Minderhoud JM: Systemic selection of prognostic features in patients with severe head injury. *Neurosurgery* 6(4):362, 1980.
7. Brody JA, Brock DB, Williams TF: Trends in the health of the elderly population. *Ann Rev Public Health* 8:211, 1987.
8. Cameron MM: Chronic subdural haematoma: A review of 114 cases. *J Neurol Neurosurg Psychiatry* 41:834, 1978.
9. Carlsson C-A, Von Essen C, Lofgren J: Factors affecting the clinical course of patients with severe head injuries. Part 1. Influence of biological factors. Part 2. Significance of post-traumatic coma. *J Neurosurg* 29:242, 1968.
10. Colohan ART, Alves WM, Rimel RW, O'Leary T, Jane JA: Factors influencing outcome after mild head injury. Paper presented at the Congress of Neurological Surgeons Meeting, Hawaii, September 1985.
11. Conroy C, Kraus JF: Survival after brain injury; cause of death, length of survival and prognostic variables in a cohort of brain-injured people. *Neuroepidemiology* 7:13, 1988.
12. Cooper KD, Tabaddor K, Hauser WA, Shulman K, Feiner C, Factor PR: The epidemiology of head injury in the Bronx. *Neuroepidemiology* 2:70, 1983.
13. Davis CS, Action P: Treatment of the elderly brain-injured patient; experience in a traumatic brain injury unit. *J Am Geriatr Soc* 36:225, 1988.
14. Degutis LC, Baker CC: Trauma in the elderly: A statewide perspective. *Conn Med* 51:161, 1987.
15. Dikmen S, McLean A, Temkin N: Neuropsychological and psychosocial consequences of minor head injury. *J Neurol Neurosurg Psychiatry* 49:1227, 1986.
16. Edna T-H: Risk factors in traumatic head injury. *Acta Neurochir* 69:15, 1983.
17. Eisenberg H, Cayard C, Papanicolaou A, Weiner R, Franklin D, Jane J, Grossman R, Tabaddor K, Becker DP, Marshall LF, Kunitz S: The effects of three potentially preventable complications on outcome after severe closed head injury, in Ishii S, Nagai H, Brock M (eds): *Intracranial Pressure V*. New York, Springer-Verlag, 1983, p 549.
18. Eisenberg HM, Weiner RL, Tabaddor K: Emergency care: Initial evaluation, in Cooper PR (ed): *Head Injury*, 2d ed. Baltimore, Williams & Wilkins, 1987, p 20.
19. Farmer JP, Colohan ART, Comair Y, Jane JA: Less than severe head injury—An overview. *Acta Anesth Belg* 38:427, 1987.
20. Fell DA, Fitzgerald S, Moiel RH, Caram P: Acute subdural hematomas. Review of 144 cases. *J Neurosurg* 42:37, 1975.
21. Frost EAM, Arancibia CM, Shulman K: Pulmonary shunt as a prognostic indicator in head injury. *J Neurosurg* 50:768, 1979.
22. Gennarelli TA: Head injury in brain and experimental animals: Clinical aspects. *Acta Neurochir (Suppl)* 32:1, 1983.
23. Gennarelli, TA, Spielman GM, Langfitt TW, Gildenberg PL, Harrington T, Jane JA, Marshall LF, Orilles JD, Pitts LH: Influence of the type of intracranial lesion on outcome from severe head injury. *J Neurosurg* 56:26, 1982.
24. Gennarelli TA, Thibault LB: Biomechanics of acute subdural hematoma. *J Trauma* 22:680, 1982.
25. Gildenberg PL, Makela M: Effect of early intubation and ventilation on outcome following head trauma, in Dacey RG Jr et al (eds): *Trauma Central Nervous System*. New York, Raven Press, 1985, p 79.
26. Gronwall D, Wrightson P: Delayed recovery of intellectual function after minor head injury. *Lancet* 2:605, 1974.
27. Hadley E, Radebaugh TS, Suzman R: Falls and gait disorders among the elderly: A challenge for research. *Clin Geriatr Med* 1:497, 1985.
28. Heiskanen O, Sipponen P: Prognosis of severe brain injury. *Acta Neurol Scand* 46:343, 1970.
29. Hernesniemi J: Outcome following head injury in the aged. *Acta Neurochir* 49:67, 1979.
30. Jamieson KG, Yelland JDN: Extradural hematoma. Report of 167 cases. *J Neurosurg* 29:13, 1968.
31. Jennett B, Teasdale G: *Management of Head Injuries*. Philadelphia, Davis, 1981.
32. Jennett B, Teasdale G, Braakman R, Minderhoud J, Heiden J, Kurze T: Prognosis of patients with severe head injury. *Neurosurgery* 4:283, 1979.
33. Jennett B, Teasdale G, Braakman R, Minderhoud J,

Knill-Jones R: Predicting outcome in individual patients after severe head injury. *Lancet* 1:1031, 1976.

34. Klonoff H, Thompson GB: Epidemiology of head injuries in adults: A pilot study. *Can Med Assoc J* 100:235, 1969.

35. Klun B, Fettich M: Factors determining prognosis in acute subdural hematoma. *Acta Neurochir (Suppl)* 28:134, 1979.

36. Kraus JF: The relationship of family income to the incidence, external causes, and outcomes of serious brain injury, San Diego County, California. *Am J Public Health* 76(11):1345, 1986.

37. Kraus JF: Epidemiology of head injury, in Cooper PR (ed): *Head Injury*, 2d ed. Baltimore, Williams & Wilkins, 1987.

38. Lauer AR: Age and sex in relation to accidents. *Traffic Safety Res Rev* 3:21, 1959.

39. Levati A, Farina ML, Vecchi G, Rossanda M, Marrubini MB: Prognosis of severe head injuries. *J Neurosurg* 57:779, 1982.

40. McKissock W, Richardson A, Bloom WH: Subdural hematoma: A review of 389 cases. *Lancet* 1:1365, 1960.

41. McLean A Jr, Dikmen S, Temkin N, Wyler AR, Gale JL: Psychosocial functioning at one month after head injury. *Neurosurgery* 14:393, 1984.

42. Markwaler TM: Chronic subdural hematomas: A review. *J Neurosurg* 54:637, 1981.

43. Marshall LF, Becker DP, Eisenberg HM, Grossman RG, Jane JA, Tabaddor K, Bowers SA, Gross CR, Kunitz SC: The National Traumatic Coma Data Bank. Part I. Design, purpose, goals and results. *J Neurosurg* 59:279, 1983.

44. Morse JM: Computerized evaluation of a scale to identify the fall-prone patient. *Can J Public Health* 77 (Suppl) 1:21, 1986.

45. Mueller MS, Gibson RM: Age difference in health care spending. *Soc Secur Bull* 39(6):18, 1976.

46. Narayan RK, Greenberg RP, Miller JD, Freas CG, Choi SC, Kishore PRS, Selhorst JB, Lutz HA, Becker DP: Improved confidence of outcome prediction in severe head injury. *J Neurosurg* 54:751, 1981.

47. Oku Y, Takimoto N, Yamamoto K, Onishi T: Trial of a new operative method for recurrent chronic subdural hematoma. *J Neurosurg* 61:269, 1984.

48. Oreskovich MR, Howard JD, Copass MK, Carrico J: Geriatric trauma: Injury patterns and outcome. *J Trauma* 24:565, 1984.

49. Orosz E: Factors influencing the outcome of coma in severely injured patients. *Acta Neurochir (Suppl)* 28:137, 1979.

50. O'Shaughnessy EJ, Fowler RS, Reid V: Sequelae of mild closed head injuries. *J Fam Pract* 18(3):391, 1984.

51. Overgaard J, Hvid-Hansen O, Land AM, Pedesen KK, Christensen S, Haase J, Hein O, Tweed WA: Prognosis after head injury based on early clinical examination. *Lancet* 2:631, 1973.

52. Pazzaglia P, Frank G, Frank F, Gaist G: Clinical course and prognosis of acute post-traumatic coma. *J Neurol Neurosurg Psychiatry* 38:149, 1975.

53. Pentland B, Jones PA, Roy CW, Miller JD: Head injury in the elderly. *Age Ageing* 15:193, 1986.

54. Raskind R, Glover B, Weiss SR: Chronic subdural hematoma in the elderly: A challenge in diagnosis and treatment. *J Am Geriatr Soc* 20:330, 1972.

55. Rimel RW, Giordani B, Barth JT, Boll TJ, Jane JA: Disability caused by minor head injury. *Neurosurgery* 9:221, 1981.

56. Rimel RW, Giordani B, Barth JT, Jane JA: Moderate head injury: Completing the clinical spectrum of brain trauma. *Neurosurgery* 11:344, 1982.

57. Robinson RG: Chronic subdural hematoma: Surgical management in 133 patients. *J Neurosurg* 61:263, 1984.

58. Rowe JW: Falls, in Rowe JW, Besdine RW (eds): *Health and Disease in Old Age*. Boston, Little, Brown, 1982, p 393.

59. Rubenstein LZ, Robbins AS, Schulman BL, Rosado J, Osterweil D, Josephson KR: Falls and instability in the elderly. *J Am Geriatr Soc* 36:266, 1988.

60. Russell WR: Cerebral involvement in head injury: A study based on the examination of two hundred cases. *Brain* 55:549, 1932.

61. Seelig JM, Becker DP, Miller JD, Greenberg RP, Ward JD, Choi SC: Traumatic acute subdural hematoma; major mortality reduction in comatose patients treated within four hours. *New Engl J Med* 304:1511, 1981.

62. Sipponen JT, Sipponen RE, Sirula A: Chronic subdural hematoma: Demonstration by magnetic resonance. *Radiology* 150:79, 1984.

63. Stablein DM, Miller JD, Choi SC, Becker DP: Statistical methods for determining prognosis in severe head injury. *Neurosurgery* 6(3):243, 1980.

64. Tabaddor K, Mattis S, Zazula T: Cognitive sequelae and recovery course after moderate and severe head injury. *Neurosurgery* 14:701, 1984.

65. Teasdale G, Jennett B: Assessment and prognosis of coma after head injury. *Acta Neurochir* 34:45, 1976.

66. Teasdale G, Skene A, Parker L, Jennett B: Age and outcome of severe head injury. *Acta Neurochir (Suppl)* 28:140, 1979.

67. Teasdale G, Skene A, Spiegelhalter D, Murray L: Age, severity and outcome of head injury, in Grossman RG, Gildenberg PL (eds): *Head Injury: Basic and Clinical Aspects*. New York, Raven Press, 1982, p 213.

68. Vollmer DG, Torner JC, Charlebois D, Sadovnic B, Jane JA: Age and outcome following traumatic coma: Why do older patients fare worse? Presented at the Annual Meeting of the American Association of Neurological Surgeons, Dallas, May 1987.

69. Weir BKA: Results of burr hole and open or closed suction drainage for chronic subdural hematomas in adults. *Can J Neurol Sci* 10:22, 1983.

70. Young HA, Gleave JRW, Schmidek HH, Gregory S: Delayed traumatic intracerebral hematoma: Report of 15 cases operatively treated. *Neurosurgery* 14:22, 1984.

Chapter 100

SEIZURES
AND EPILEPSY

John W. Miller and James A. Ferrendelli

Seizures are the clinical manifestation of sudden abnormal and excessive discharges of electrical activity in populations of neurons in the brain. *Epilepsy* is the condition where seizures recur chronically. Seizures are common with an annual incidence of 75 per 100,000 in an American urban population, and epilepsy has an incidence of 48 per 100,000 and a prevalence of 5.5 per 1000.[1] The incidence of epilepsy is greatest in infancy, somewhat lower in childhood, and lowest in adolescence and during most of adult life.[1] However, it increases greatly in those over 60 with a rate of 82 per 100,000 per year.[1] This chapter will review the principles of the clinical assessment and treatment of geriatric patients with seizures including the differentiation of epileptic seizures from other phenomena which cause transient neurological disturbance, investigation, definition and treatment of underlying causes, and management.

CLASSIFICATION OF SEIZURE TYPES

Accurate seizure classification is an essential prerequisite for correct decisions in evaluation and management. Modern classification is based on both clinical and electroencephalographic criteria.[2] The major distinction is between *partial* seizures, which clinically and electrographically appear to originate focally in a specific region of the cerebral cortex, and *generalized* seizures, which involve most of the brain bilaterally and symmetrically at their onset.

PARTIAL SEIZURES

Partial seizures are subdivided into *simple partial seizures*, when consciousness is not impaired; *complex partial seizures*, when it is impaired; and *secondarily generalized tonic-clonic seizures*, when a partial seizure spreads to generate a generalized convulsion. Simple partial seizures have diverse manifestations, including motor, sensory, affective, autonomic, or elaborate psychic symptoms. The signs or symptoms of these seizures reflect the normal function of the area of the cortex in which the seizure occurs.[3] Complex partial seizures most commonly arise in the temporal or frontal lobes. Many of their symptoms are assumed to result from incorporation of deeper limbic and diencephalic structures in the seizure. In most cases of complex partial seizures, loss of awareness is accompanied by amnesia for at least a portion of the clinical event. Clinical evidence of a focal onset for secondarily generalized tonic-clonic convulsions is not always available from the history or even from observation of the seizure. In many cases a focal onset for generalized convulsions may be deduced from the presence of focal abnormalities on neurological examination, imaging studies, or the EEG.

GENERALIZED SEIZURES

This category includes a variety of convulsive and nonconvulsive seizures with the first clinical and electrographic changes indicating involvement of both cerebral hemispheres simultaneously.[2] Usual nonconvulsive seizures are *absence seizures*, which are brief periods of unawareness and staring without loss of posture or postictal symptoms. Absence seizures are associated with trains of generalized spike-and-wave or multispike-and-wave EEG discharges. Generalized tonic-clonic convulsions may also have a bilaterally symmetric electrographic onset consisting of low-voltage fast activity or rapid generalized spiking.[2] It is occasionally difficult to distinguish absence from complex partial seizures and primary from secondarily generalized convulsions on clinical grounds alone. The EEG is then the most useful test for making this distinction.

ETIOLOGY OF SEIZURES

Definition of seizure etiology is also essential for rational and successful treatment. A patient may suffer from a single or a few seizures as a result of some transient cerebral dysfunction caused by metabolic or toxic disturbances including hyponatremia, hypoglycemia, rapid withdrawal from sedative/hypnotic drugs, and intoxication with agents such as theophylline or penicillin. Cerebral infarction and intracranial infections or bleeding may also produce transient seizures. Epilepsy, i.e., chronic recurrent seizures, is usually a consequence of some chronic cerebral abnormality which may be static or progressive. Epilepsy may be a result of congenital/genetic factors, *primary epilepsy,* or of an acquired cerebral abnormality, *secondary epilepsy.* It is assumed that most individuals with primary epilepsy have some abnormality of neurotransmission mechanisms which lowers seizure threshold. Most, if not all, secondary epilepsies are a consequence of some injury to cerebral cortex, most often from head trauma, cerebral infarctions, intracranial infection, or brain tumor. Patients with primary epilepsy most often suffer from nonconvulsive or convulsive generalized seizures. Partial seizures and/or secondarily generalized convulsions are the usual clinical manifestations of patients with secondary epilepsies.

Newly diagnosed epilepsy in an elderly patient should always be considered to be secondary since essentially all patients with primary epilepsy begin having seizures during childhood or adolescence. However, one must realize that infrequently some patients with primary epilepsy may continue to have seizures into old age. Since most elderly patients have secondary epilepsy it is not surprising that the cause of their seizures can often be defined. For example, in a recent study in a geriatric Scandinavian population[4] 75 percent of patients had an identifiable cause for their seizures, with previous cerebral infarct the cause in 32 percent and tumors being the cause in 14 percent. Other causes included prior severe head trauma, alcohol and drug abuse, dementing illnesses, and metabolic disorders including hypoglycemia and hyponatremia. These results are confirmed by other recent studies of geriatric patients.[5-7]

EVALUATION OF SEIZURES

The first step in the assessment of a patient with new spells is to confirm that they are actually seizures rather than some other type of transient disturbance in neurological function such as syncope, migraine, or transient ischemic attack or if they have a psychiatric cause. If the patient indeed has epileptic seizures, the next step is to classify them using the history and laboratory evaluation. The final step is to determine, if possible, their etiology taking care to exclude reversible causes.

The history should reconstruct, moment by moment, experiences during typical episodes and include interviews with witnesses. It should be noted whether there are any apparent precipitating factors or postictal confusion, memory disturbance, or dysphasia. With complex partial or generalized tonic-clonic seizures, one should also inquire whether the patient also has simple partial seizures preceding those seizures or whether simple partial seizures occur at other times. It should be inquired whether there is a history of seizures during childhood or in other family members or whether there is past severe head trauma, risk factors for neoplasm or cerebrovascular disease, or a history of any other neurological symptoms or diseases.

A careful neurological examination should be performed. A focal deficit may indicate an underlying structural lesion, or it may be a postictal deficit from a recent partial seizure. If the patient is on antiepileptic drugs, it should be noted whether there is evidence of toxicity. The general physical examination should look for clues of underlying etiology such as evidence of cardiac, cerebrovascular, or neoplastic disease.

Especially in the elderly, a cranial CT scan with contrast or a magnetic resonance imaging study and an EEG are essential. With appropriate activation techniques such as hyperventilation, photic stimulation, and sleep, abnormalities with a specific association with seizures such as spikes, sharp waves, or generalized spike-and-wave complexes may be seen in about 50 percent of initial EEG studies and in up to 90 percent of patients after multiple EEGs.[8] The finding of interictal epileptiform activity confirms that a patient's spells are seizures and helps to distinguish between partial seizures and seizures that are generalized from onset. If the nature of a patient's spells are unclear after careful clinical and laboratory evaluation, the most useful diagnostic test is an extended EEG which records typical spells, preferably with video taping of behavior.

TREATMENT OF SEIZURES

GENERAL PRINCIPLES

Treatment should be directed at both controlling seizures and, if possible, correcting the underlying disease or disorder producing them. For those patients with a single or a few seizures from some transient disorder such as drug intoxication, withdrawal from alcohol or sedative/hypnotic drugs, hyponatremia, or hypoglycemia, antiepileptic drugs may be unnecessary or may be necessary only briefly. Patients who have recurrent seizures secondary to a treatable neurological disease such as brain tumor or intracranial infection should be treated with antiepileptic drugs and should also receive treatment for the underlying problem. In many patients the cause of seizures is undefined or is a static process such as completed cerebral infarction or brain contusion secondary to head injury. In these patients treatment with antiepileptic drugs is the only possible therapy.

Regardless of etiology, all patients with chronic recurrent seizures should be treated with antiepileptic drugs. There is much controversy, however, as to whether antiepileptic drug treatment should be begun after a single first seizure. It has been argued[9] that, since many of these patients will not have a second seizure in several years of follow-up, there is no justification in beginning antiepileptic drugs and subjecting the patients to possible side effects. For example, in one retrospective study,[10] only 60 percent of patients had a second seizure in 5 years. However, this view has been challenged[11] primarily because, overall, patients with recurrent seizures are far more common than those with single seizures,[12] and the majority of the patients in retrospective studies of the prognosis of a single seizure[10] were in fact treated with antiepileptic drugs. In any case, antiepileptic drug treatment should be considered in at least some patients after a first seizure, especially when further seizures may be especially dangerous, because of individual circumstances. It should also be noted that the risk of seizure recurrence is higher in patients with generalized spike-and-wave EEG activity, but relatively low in patients who have been seizure-free 6 months or more after the first one.[10]

Treatment with antiepileptic drugs should follow certain basic principles. Therapy should be started with a single suitable agent. For partial and secondarily generalized seizures, appropriate drugs are carbamazepine, phenytoin, primidone, or phenobarbital; the first two are more desirable because of the sedating and behavioral side effects[13] of phenobarbital and primidone. For primary generalized tonic-clonic seizures valproate, phenytoin, and carbamazepine are the most appropriate agents. Absence seizures are best treated with valproate or ethosuximide. A fundamental principle of antiepileptic drug treatment is that seizure control should be achieved, if possible, by increasing the dosage of the single initial agent rather than by adding a second one. Dosage changes should be guided by the patient's clinical response rather than by drug levels, with inadequate seizure control indicating the need for raising the dose, unless toxicity has appeared. Levels are usually not needed in patients with good seizure control on a well-tolerated medication. They can be useful under some circumstances, for example, when inadequate seizure control or toxicity is present especially in a patient on more than one medication. Levels may also be useful in understanding drug interactions, where the level of one drug is altered by concomitant administration of another antiepileptic drug or other agent. This is usually due to competition for, or induction of, enzymatic systems for drug metabolism or to altered binding to plasma proteins.

If seizure control cannot be achieved with the first medication, a second alternate agent should be considered. Two or more antiepileptic drugs used in combination should be avoided whenever possible, and treatment with multiple antiepileptic drugs is only appropriate in patients who fail monotherapy with two or more single drugs. It should be recognized that simultaneous treatment with several antiepileptic drugs is more likely to cause toxicity and often does not produce better control than a single agent. With chronically intractable seizures, it is usually counterproductive to continually add new antiepileptic drugs. A better approach is to reevaluate the patient to be sure that the spells are indeed epileptic seizures and that the initial impressions regarding seizure type and cause are correct. For a select subgroup of patients with intractable, disabling partial seizures, evaluation for epilepsy surgery may be considered. Surgical excision of an epileptic focus requires careful electrographic recording of the patient's typical seizures, usually with epidural, cortical, or depth electrodes, to document a consistent site of seizure origin which is accessible to removal without unacceptable risk of significant neurological deficits.

Therapy with antiepileptic drugs is often compromised by adverse drug effects. All the antiepileptic drugs produce dose-related neurotoxicity, most commonly impairment of cognition, sedation, and incoordination. All of these are particularly disabling in the elderly and should be avoided by treating geriatric patients with the lowest effective dosage and with the fewest drugs possible. Idiosyncratic reactions usually occur within the first 6 weeks to 6 months of therapy and include allergic reactions, severe leukopenia, aplastic anemia, and hepatotoxicity. All can be serious or even fatal, but fortunately occur very infrequently. An idiosyncratic reaction requires immediate cessation of the offending drug. Several side effects occur with each of the anticonvulsant drugs and include gingival hyperplasia, changes in appetite and weight, reversible leukopenia, and elevation of liver enzymes to mention only a few. Treatment of side effects may or may not require lowering the dose or discontinuation of the drug, depending on the side effect and the drug involved.

STATUS EPILEPTICUS

Convulsive status epilepticus is a condition where repeated generalized convulsions occur for at least 30 minutes without recovery of consciousness.[14] This is a medical emergency. Without prompt treatment it leads to irreversible neurological damage, progressive metabolic disturbance, and death. The causes of status epilepticus are diverse but include abrupt withdrawal of antiepileptic drugs, withdrawal of alcohol, barbiturates or benzodiazepines, trauma, cerebrovascular disease, CNS infection, and hypoxia.[15]

In treating status, the initial and most important step is to support vital functions.[14–17] The airway should be protected as needed, and oxygenation maintained. As intravenous access is obtained, blood should be sent for determination of glucose, electrolyte, and antiepileptic drug levels. At that time 50 ml of 50% glucose and 100 mg of thiamine should be given. If the pH is less than 7.2, bicarbonate should be given and fluid and electrolyte disturbances corrected.

There are various acceptable approaches to anticonvulsant administration in status.[14,16,17] Whatever approach is chosen, it should be initiated promptly, adequate loading doses should be administered, and preparations should be made to support respirations if depressed by these medications.

A reasonable way to initiate therapy is with intravenous benzodiazepines, either 10 mg of diazepam over 2 minutes or 4 mg of lorazepam monitoring for respiratory depression and hypotension. Immediately afterward an intravenous phenytoin infusion of 15 to 25 mg/kg should be given no faster than 50 mg/min to reduce the risk of hypotension and bradycardia. Phenytoin cannot be mixed with dextrose, and intramuscular administration should be avoided. Since phenytoin is rapidly acting, an additional medication should be given if seizures do not stop by the end of the infusion. Phenobarbital may be given at a rate of 100 mg/min to a loading dose of 5 to 10 mg/kg.[14,16] Ventilatory support may be needed by this point.

If seizures are not controlled, care should be taken to ensure that possible metabolic or structural causes have been addressed. Many drugs, including lidocaine, paraldehyde, valproic acid, and continuous infusions of diazepam, have been used in intractable status epilepticus. One reasonable approach at this stage is to administer general anesthesia with a short-acting barbiturate such as pentobarbital.[16] The efficacy of such treatment has been demonstrated using a loading dose of 15 mg/kg of pentobarbital over 1 hour, a maintenance infusion of 1 to 2 mg/h, and use of dopamine as needed for hypotension.[18] This requires EEG monitoring to maintain a state of burst suppression, intubation, ventilation, and monitoring of hemodynamics with an arterial line and a central venous pressure or Swan-Ganz catheter.

ANTIEPILEPTIC DRUGS[14,19]

BARBITURATES Phenobarbital and primidone are inexpensive, safe, and effective for partial and generalized tonic-clonic seizures, but have substantial undesirable sedative and behavioral effects. Phenobarbital has an oral half-life of 3 to 5 days; 1 to 4 mg/kg can be given as a single daily dose preferably at bedtime. Primidone has a half-life of 3 to 12 hours and can be given in 2 or 3 doses per day for a total of 10 to 20 mg/kg. Since primidone is metabolized partially to phenobarbital, these two drugs should not be given together.

PHENYTOIN This is effective for partial and generalized tonic-clonic seizures. Typical adult doses are 200 to 400 mg in one or two divided doses per day. At lower serum concentrations the half-life is 15 to 24 hours; however, at high concentrations saturation of elimination mechanisms occurs, leading to a longer half-life. For this reason large increases in doses should be avoided. Dose-related neurotoxicity usually begins at levels of 20 to 30 μg/ml and includes nystagmus, ataxia, and lethargy as the concentration increases. Possible chronic side effects include osteomalacia, gum hypertrophy, and mild peripheral neuropathy.

CARBAMAZEPINE This is also used for generalized tonic-clonic convulsions and partial, particularly complex partial seizures. The dose is 7 to 15 mg/(kg)(day) in three divided doses and the half-life is 8 to 36 hours. Dose-dependent neutropenia is not uncommon but idiosyncratic aplastic anemia is very rare. With a neutrophil count of 1200 or less, carbamazepine should be discontinued or the dose reduced. Hyponatremia is another potentially serious side effect. Diplopia and ataxia are the most common neurotoxic symptoms with high doses.

VALPROATE This is most effective for seizures that are generalized from onset, and may be a useful adjunct medication for partial seizures. It should be administered in the enteric-coated slow-release form, sodium divalproex, in a dose of 10 to 60 mg/kg in 3 or 4 divided daily doses. It has a half life of 8 to 12 hours. Neurological toxicity is usually minor, with tremor being the most common. Common side effects include gastrointestinal upset, and increased appetite and weight gain. The most serious adverse effect is idiosyncratic hepatic failure, which is rare and which usually occurs in children who are also taking other antiepileptic drugs.[20]

REFERENCES

1. Hauser WA, Kurland LT: The epidemiology of epilepsy in Rochester Minnesota 1935 through 1967. *Epilepsia* 16:1, 1975.

2. Commission on Classification and Terminology of the International League Against Epilepsy: Proposal for revised clinical and electroencephalographic classification of epileptic seizures. *Epilepsia* 22:489, 1981.

3. Penfield W, Jasper H: *Epilepsy and the Functional Anatomy of the Human Brain*. Boston, Little, Brown, 1954.

4. Lühdorf K et al: Etiology of seizures in the elderly. *Epilepsia* 27:458, 1986.

5. Roberts MA et al: Epileptic seizures in the elderly: Etiology and type of seizure. *Aging* 11:24, 1982.

6. Lopez JLP et al: Late onset epileptic seizures: A retrospective study of 250 patients. *Acta Neurol Scand* 72:380, 1985.

7. Dam AM et al: Late onset epilepsy: Etiologies, type of seizure, and value of clinical investigations, EEG and computerized tomography scan. *Epilepsia* 26:227, 1985.

8. Salinski M et al: Effectiveness of multiple EEGs in supporting the diagnosis of epilepsy: An operational curve. *Epilepsia* 28:231, 1987.

9. Hauser WA: Should people be treated after a first seizure? *Arch Neurol* 43:1287, 1986.

10. Annegers JF et al: Risk of recurrence after an initial unprovoked seizure. *Epilepsia* 27:45, 1986.

11. Hart RG, Easton JD: Seizure recurrence after a first, unprovoked seizure. *Arch Neurol* 43:1289, 1986.

12. Goodridge DM, Shorvon SD: Epileptic seizures in a population of 6000: II. Treatment and prognosis. *Br Med J* 287:645, 1983.

13. Mattson RH et al: Comparison of carbamazepine, phenobarbital, phenytoin and primidone in partial and secondarily generalized tonic-clonic seizures. *N Engl J Med* 313:145, 1985.

14. Dodson WE, Ferrendelli JA: Convulsive disorders and their management, in Wirth FP, Ratcheson RA (eds): *Neurosurgical Critical Care*, vol 1: *Concepts in Neurosurgery*. New York, Williams & Wilkins, 1987, p 169.

15. Aiminoff MJ, Simon RP: Status epilepticus. Causes, clinical features and consequences in 98 patients. *Am J Med* 69:657, 1980.

16. Simon RP: Management of status epilepticus, in Pedley TA, Medrum BS (eds): *Recent Advances in Epilepsy*, Number Two. New York, Churchill Livingstone, 1985.

17. Delgado-Escueta AV et al: Management of status epilepticus. *N Engl J Med* 306:1537, 1982.

18. Lowenstein DH et al: Barbiturate anesthesia in the treatment of status epilepticus: Clinical experience with 14 patients. *Neurology* 38:395, 1988.

19. Woodbury DM et al: *Antiepileptic Drugs*, 2d ed. New York, Raven Press, 1982.

20. Dreifuss FE et al: Valproic acid hepatic fatalities: A retrospective review. *Neurology* 37:379, 1987.

Chapter 101

INTRACRANIAL NEOPLASMS

Jerome B. Posner

Intracranial tumors affect all ages. Some evidence indicates that the incidence increases throughout adult life until age 60, with an actual decline after age 75[1]; other data suggest that the incidence increases with increasing age throughout the life span.[2] Furthermore, intracranial malignancies may be actually increasing in frequency in the elderly.[3,4] In general, the same types of intracranial tumors occur throughout adult life, but those in the elderly are more likely to be malignant.[5] The elderly also differ from their younger counterparts in that some of the classic symptoms and signs of brain tumor (i.e., headache and papilledema) occur less frequently; instead, elderly patients often present with cognitive dysfunction suggesting dementia rather than a tumor. Even if a correct diagnosis is made, the treatment may be more complicated in the elderly than in younger people: Patients may suffer from systemic disease which may make surgery dangerous. In addition, the elderly brain tolerates radiation and chemotherapy less well than does the younger brain. Thus even if treatment of the tumor is successful, the patient may suffer long-term side effects of the treatment which may equal in disability the tumor itself.

This chapter discusses the classification and epidemiology of intracranial tumors, diagnostic considerations, and treatment. Recent reviews of the topic can also be found elsewhere.[6–8]

CLASSIFICATION AND EPIDEMIOLOGY

Table 101-1 classifies the major intracranial tumors encountered in the elderly population (over 65) and gives approximate percentages of each.[1] The data are taken from a national survey of discharges from short-term hospitals conducted in 1973 and 1974. The major findings of the study are that both primary and metastatic intracranial neoplasms increase in incidence throughout adulthood until approximately age 60 when there is a leveling off. There is a decline in incidence after age 75. The same decline is apparent in another epidemiologic study from Rochester, Minnesota,[2] where only those intracranial neoplasms diagnosed prior to death are considered. However, if autopsy data are included, there is an increase in incidence of intracranial tumors throughout the life span. Some of the tumors undiagnosed in the elderly before death are asymptomatic meningiomas, but others are gliomas in which an incorrect diagnosis of cerebral vascular disease or dementia was made. "Inapparent" brain tumors are found in approximately 1 percent of elderly patients at autopsy.

A recent report examining U.S. mortality data from 1968 to 1983 indicates an 8 percent annual rise in primary brain malignancy mortality of white men in the

TABLE 101-1
Intracranial Tumors in the Elderly

Primary	39%		
Gliomas		49%	
Glioblastoma			50%
Other gliomas			50%
Meningioma		34%	
Adenoma		6%	
Neurinoma		10%	
Lymphoma		?	
Metastatic CNS tumors	61%		
Lung		45%	
Breast		15%	
Gastrointestinal		13%	
Genitourinary		11%	
Unspecified and others		16%	

SOURCE: Modified from Walker.[1]

1004

65-to-84 age group and women in the 75-to-84 age group.[3] The increased incidence began in the late 1960s and has continued to the present time. Most of the data were collected before widespread use of the computed tomographic (CT) scan, making it unlikely that the increased incidence is simply due to better diagnostic tests.[3,4] These same dramatic increases in incidence do not appear in the younger age group. With increasing age, low-grade astrocytomas become less common and more malignant gliomas, particularly glioblastoma multiforme, become more common.[1,5] Malignant gliomas appear to be more malignant in the elderly.[5] Anaplastic astrocytomas comprise 46 percent of malignant gliomas encountered in patients under the age of 40, 14 percent in patients age 40 to 60, and only 7 percent of those over the age of 60.[5] Median survivals in the elderly are shorter even when controlled for the histologic type of glioma. Meningiomas and probably pituitary adenomas also increase in incidence with increasing age. Primary lymphomas of the nervous system, which are thought to represent less than 1 percent of primary brain tumors, also appear to be increasing in frequency, particularly in the elderly—even those not obviously immunosuppressed.

In the elderly, metastatic brain tumors are more common than primary tumors.[1] Clinical evidence suggests that two-thirds to three-quarters of metastatic brain tumors are symptomatic during life,[9] but they generally occur in patients already known to have cancer and usually do not represent a major diagnostic problem.

DIAGNOSIS

CLINICAL PRESENTATION

Table 101-2 lists some of the symptoms of brain tumor and compares symptoms in patients over 60 years of age with those who are younger.[10] The differences in symptoms between older and younger people probably result

TABLE 101-2
Some Significant Differences in Symptoms of Intracranial Tumor by Age

	548 Patients over 60 years, %	2005 Patients under 60 years, %
Headaches	48.9	63.1
Disturbances of gait	28.3	21.5
Personality changes	25.2	18.4
Disturbances of memory	19.3	15.1
Confusion	15.5	7.4
Speech disorders	21.0	12.2
Epileptic attacks	17.9	25.0

SOURCE: Modified from Schirmer and Bock.[10]

from loss of normal brain substance, which occurs with aging. This allows tumors to grow larger in the elderly without raising intracranial pressure. As a result, headache is less common and papilledema is rare. The absence of papilledema probably results not only from lower intracranial pressure but also from fibrosis of the optic nerve sheath with aging so that intracranial pressure, even when elevated, is less likely to be transmitted to the optic nerve head. Mental changes, including personality change (often mimicking depression),[11] disturbance of memory, and confusion are more common in the elderly than in the young. Seizures are less common. Focal findings such as hemiparesis and visual field defects are not significantly different.

Symptoms of brain tumor usually present and progress insidiously. However, in some patients either an apoplectic onset or paroxysmal symptoms may dominate the clinical picture. As many as 10 percent of patients with malignant glioma may have a sudden or paroxysmal onset of symptoms. An apoplectic onset may be caused by hemorrhage or vascular obstruction, but in most instances the cause is not known. Paroxysmal symptoms appear to result from seizures originating from the cerebral cortex surrounding the tumor. Unlike typical epileptic focal or generalized seizures in which positive symptoms (e.g., tonic and clonic movement of extremities) are common, paroxysmal symptoms in patients with brain tumors are often negative[12] (e.g., aphasia, paralysis, episodic confusion) and may last hours rather than the usual few minutes.

Thus, the diagnosis of brain tumors in the elderly may be difficult. When the symptoms begin insidiously as confusion or personality change but without headache or papilledema, the physician may suspect psychiatric disease (e.g., depression) or a degenerative disorder (e.g., Alzheimer's disease). If a careful neurologic examination yields focal motor or sensory changes, one should suspect a brain tumor but, particularly, if the tumor is in the frontal lobe, there may be no such changes. When the symptoms are apoplectic, the physician is more likely to suspect cerebrovascular disease which is usually apoplectic in onset and much more common than brain tumor. Progression of neurologic symptoms after apoplectic onset suggests tumor and warrants careful imaging studies. Paroxysmal neurologic symptoms mimic transient ischemic attacks and also suggest vascular disease. However, paroxysmal symptoms in brain tumors tend to last longer[13] and present more complex abnormalities (i.e., apraxias and confusion in addition to the usual hemiparesis and aphasia of transient ischemic attacks). Despite these clinical clues, the diagnosis of a brain tumor can often be differentiated from the more common dementing illnesses or vascular diseases of the elderly only if the physician suspects the presence of a tumor and does appropriate diagnostic tests.

DIAGNOSTIC EVALUATION[14]

Brain Imaging

The diagnosis of intracranial tumors in all age groups has been revolutionized first by computed tomography (CT) and, more recently, magnetic resonance imaging (MRI). If the physician suspects an intracranial neoplasm, MRI is the best diagnostic test. MRI is more sensitive than CT in detecting parenchymal neoplasms and is particularly sensitive early in the evolution of a glioma when the CT scan may be normal. One exception is a small meningioma that, because of its isodensity with brain, may be difficult to distinguish from normal brain on MRI but is apparent on CT by its intense contrast enhancement. The paramagnetic substance gadolinium serves the same function as iodinated contrast material for CT scan and easily identifies meningiomas. If MRI is not available or if the patient is claustrophobic or too restless to tolerate longer scan time, CT may be preferable. CT should be performed both before and after the injection of contrast material.

Although extremely sensitive for detection of brain lesions, neither CT nor MRI specifically proves that an abnormality is a neoplasm or, if it is a neoplasm, its type. In the appropriate clinical context, lesions identified by CT or MRI that occupy space and are surrounded by edema are likely to be tumors rather than infarcts, abscesses, or inflammatory lesions. Certain other clues help identify the nature of the tumor: Multiple lesions within the substance of the brain, particularly if they possess contrast-enhancing rings on CT scan or if they are each surrounded by extensive edema, suggest metastatic disease. Even single lesions in the cerebellum in the elderly suggest metastatic disease since primary tumors of the cerebellum are uncommon in the elderly. A single lesion with a contrast-enhancing ring of irregular size and shape suggests a malignant glioma. A glioma can also appear as an area of hypodensity in the white matter which does not contrast-enhance and is sometimes confused with a cerebral infarct. Such an appearance suggests a low-grade glioma, but high-grade tumors may also fail to contrast-enhance, whereas some low-grade tumors do contrast-enhance (although such tumors appear to have a worse prognosis than low-grade tumors that do not contrast-enhance).[15] A densely and uniformly contrast-enhancing lesion[16] deep in the white matter surrounding the ventricular system suggests primary lymphoma. Primary lymphomas are often multicentric (about 30 percent), whereas primary gliomas are monocentric (95 percent); exceptions exist. Lesions on the surface of the brain (attached to the dura) that uniformly contrast-enhance suggest meningioma although dural-based metastases from carcinomas of the breast, prostate, and other tumors may appear similar.

Metastatic brain tumors are more common than pri-

mary brain tumors in the elderly.[1] Metastases are multiple in 50 percent of patients so that an elderly patient with more than one brain lesion should be judged as harboring a metastasis until proved otherwise. However, extensive metastatic workup is often not revealing.[17] If examination of the chest (by plain x ray or CT) or the kidneys (CT or renal sonogram) is negative, and if the patient's general physical examination (including rectal examination, stool guaiac test, and breast examination) is negative, it is unlikely that a more extensive search will identify a primary lesion.[17] One should consider proceeding directly to biopsy.

Other diagnostic tests may also yield information of value. Examination of the CSF may reveal malignant cells particularly in primary lymphomas of the nervous system or metastatic tumors that have invaded the leptomeninges.[18] Lumbar puncture should not be performed until MRI or CT rules out a large space-occupying lesion which might cause herniation after an inappropriate lumbar puncture. Tumor markers in both blood and spinal fluid may give clues as to the presence of a systemic cancer and whether the tumor has invaded the central nervous system.[19]

Arteriography can help differentiate vascular disease from tumor. If the external carotid artery is injected, the arteriogram will determine whether a tumor is fed by the external carotid circulation, a characteristic feature of meningiomas and dural-based metastases. In both meningiomas and highly malignant gliomas, the vasculature is often abnormal (tumor blush). However, despite the fact that it sometimes aids in diagnosis, cerebral angiograms are invasive. In most instances, when a brain tumor is suspected on the basis of CT or MRI, arteriography does not add substantially to the diagnostic information and is not worth the risk.

Biopsy

If CT or MRI reveals a space-occupying lesion suspected of being a tumor, surgical resection or biopsy is the next step. A patient with known cancer and typical metastatic lesions(s) of the brain on scan need not be biopsied, but the physician should consider that other brain lesions (e.g., meningiomas) can coexist with systemic cancer. Generally speaking, tumors that can be, should be surgically resected; a craniotomy with removal of the tumor both establishes the diagnosis and treats the disease. This approach holds true for most meningiomas, pituitary adenomas, neurinomas, and gliomas. However, there is no evidence that malignant lymphomas benefit by surgical removal[16] and often a patient's neurologic symptoms are worsened by attempted removal. The same is true of patients with multiple metastatic tumors or surgically inaccessible gliomas. In those instances, because the CT or MRI lesion may not be a tumor and because both the treatment of tumor and its prognosis depend in part on histologic type, an attempt should be made to establish a histologic diagnosis. This can usually be done by stereotactic needle biopsy under CT or MRI control.[20] The procedure can be done either under local or general anesthesia and carries a morbidity of under 2 percent, the primary complication being hemorrhage into the tumor site. A definitive diagnosis can be made in most instances, distinguishing primary from metastatic tumors and both of those from infectious or inflammatory processes that may mimic tumors.

TREATMENT

GENERAL CONSIDERATIONS

For the most part, treatment of intracranial tumors is dictated by the tumor type and not by the age of the patient. With some qualification this holds true in the elderly. One study shows a slightly lower perioperative mortality in patients over 60 years of age than in those who are younger and a slightly lower incidence of worsened neurologic condition on discharge in the older patients.[10] However, at any age, the overall health of the patient is a consideration in determining specific treatment. This is especially true in the elderly since coincident coronary artery disease, hypertension, diabetes, chronic obstructive pulmonary disease, venous insufficiency and other common general medical problems may limit the therapeutic options. With those caveats the usual brain tumor treatments of adrenal corticosteroids (steroids), surgical extirpation, radiation therapy, chemotherapy, and immunotherapy are available to both the young and the elderly.

Adrenal Corticosteroids (Steroids)

Steroids have been used in the treatment of brain tumors for over 30 years. Their beneficial effects result from decreasing the edema which invariably surrounds malignant glial tumors, metastatic brain tumors, and rapidly growing meningiomas. The salutary effect on edema appears to be a result of "closing" the blood-brain barrier which has broken down both within and immediately surrounding the tumor.[21] Some symptomatic improvement is observed in the majority of patients usually within 24 to 48 hours of beginning treatment. The symptoms most likely to respond are those which reflect generalized brain dysfunction (headache, confusion, gait difficulty) due to cerebral edema, increased intracranial pressure, and brain shifts. Focal signs and symptoms (hemiparesis, aphasia) generally respond less favorably, but are improved in many instances. The most widely used steroid preparation, because of its minimal miner-

alocorticoid activity, is dexamethasone; it also appears less likely to cause mental changes than other steroids. The standard starting dose is 16 mg dexamethasone a day in divided doses with increasing doses being used if patients do not respond to the lower dose. The elderly respond as well to steroids as the younger patients.[22] Only 5 percent of elderly patients suffer major side effects which include psychosis, hyperglycemia, and perforated ulcers.[22] However, long-term use of steroids leads to osteoporosis and hypertension, and we have observed severe oral candidiasis and herpes zoster as complications of steroid therapy in the elderly. Thus, although steroids are effective in ameliorating the symptoms of brain tumor, they should be used at the lowest-possible dose and tapered as soon as definitive therapy permits.

Surgery

Surgical extirpation is the treatment of choice for most intracranial neoplasms. The goal is either to remove the tumor completely, thus obviating recurrence (meningiomas, pituitary adenomas, single metastases) or to remove as much of the lesion as possible (debulk) in order to allow additional therapy (i.e., radiation and chemotherapy) to be more effective. When a surgical procedure is undertaken, the surgeon should attempt to remove as much of the tumor as possible: There is no increase in postoperative morbidity in patients who undergo major resections compared with those who undergo small resections or biopsies.[23] In fact, the incidence of postoperative herniation is higher in those patients who have had small resections.[23] Furthermore, survival is substantially better in those patients with malignant gliomas who have little or no residual tumor identifiable on CT scan after surgery when compared with those patients in whom substantial residual tumor remains.[24]

Not all elderly patients in whom a brain tumor is identified require surgery. A small meningioma found either incidentally or after a seizure can be followed or treated with anticonvulsants. The growth rate may be so slow as not to require surgery before the patient lives out the natural life span. Small, single metastatic lesions in elderly patients with widespread cancer are probably best-treated by radiation therapy (see below) since it is often possible to control these tumors beyond the time that the systemic disease incapacitates or kills the patient.

Radiation Therapy

Radiation therapy is a primary treatment for lymphomas of the brain (where radiation therapy should probably be combined with chemotherapy), multiple metastatic brain tumors, and certain pituitary adenomas. Radiation therapy is indicated following surgery in patients with malignant gliomas, meningiomas that cannot be totally resected and probably after resection of a single intracerebral metastasis.[25] However, radiation therapy is not without its complications, and there is some evidence that chronic radiation damage to the nervous system is more severe in the older age group than in patients of younger age who have received similar radiation therapy.[26] Multiple small daily doses (hyperfractionation) are safer to the normal brain than are larger doses; however, small doses take more time, and in patients with systemic cancer who have a very limited life span, larger fractions may be more appropriate. Side effects of radiation therapy are classified as immediate (acute), early delayed, and late delayed. (1) Acute complications include headache, fever, lethargy, and increase in preexisting neurologic signs; these complications respond to steroids. (2) Early delayed complications occur after a delay of weeks with exacerbation of preexisting symptoms and lethargy often responding to steroids or resolving spontaneously. (3) Late side effects appear months to a few years after treatment and are characterized by dementia with or without focal signs[27]; they are usually irreversible, and steroids may provide transient symptomatic improvement or none at all.

When radiation therapy is prescribed for an elderly patient, the physician and the radiation oncologist should work together to identify the smallest total dose to the smallest brain volume which will control the tumor effectively.

Chemotherapy

Chemotherapy may be an important treatment for patients with primary lymphomas of the brain.[16] Many centers now utilize systemic chemotherapy prior to radiation therapy to treat CNS lymphomas. There is some evidence that metastatic brain tumors may respond to chemotherapy independent of the response to radiation therapy.[28] Chemotherapy added to surgery and radiation therapy appears to prolong the survival of some patients with malignant brain tumors.[29] The elderly tend to tolerate chemotherapy somewhat less well than do younger people, and doses may have to be adjusted to decrease toxicity in the elderly.

TREATMENT OF SPECIFIC TUMORS
Malignant Gliomas

The current conventional treatment of malignant gliomas, whether in young or elderly, is a maximally feasible resection of the tumor followed by radiation with the whole brain receiving approximately 40 gray (Gy)(4000 rad) and the tumor site approximately 60 Gy.[29] Concomitant chemotherapy with carmustine (BCNU) in a dose of 200 mg/m^2 every 8 weeks does not appear to significantly increase median survival in elderly patients, but does increase the long-term survival in some.

Low-Grade Gliomas

Low-grade gliomas are uncommon in the elderly. When the tumors are symptomatic, conventional treatment involves maximally feasible resection followed by radiation therapy, approximately 55 Gy to the tumor. Whole brain radiation is not given. There is no evidence that chemotherapy helps.

Metastatic Tumors

Single metastasis in patients who are either free of systemic disease as a result of treatment or whose disease appears to be under control respond better if the brain tumor is extirpated than if they receive radiation therapy alone.[30] Radiation therapy after the tumor is removed appears to increase the time to recurrence and thus is probably indicated.[25] For multiple metastatic tumors, radiation therapy is the treatment of choice.[9] If the cancer is widespread, radiation should be delivered in large fractions over a short period of time (e.g., 3 Gy × 10 days). However, if the patient's systemic disease is under control and it is likely that the patient will live longer than 6 months to a year, smaller fractions (e.g., 2 Gy × 20 days) will decrease some of the late delayed effects of radiation therapy. In those patients whose tumors are chemosensitive (for example, carcinoma of the breast), one might consider the use of chemotherapy either in addition to or independent of radiation therapy.[28]

Lymphoma

Primary lymphoma of the central nervous system is sensitive to both radiation and chemotherapy. A significant number of tumors disappear when they are treated with corticosteroids only, often leaving the surgeon nothing to biopsy but giving the oncologist valuable diagnostic information. Despite this sensitivity, the tumors almost invariably recur usually within a year to 14 months and are fatal. Most current protocols now call for the use of chemotherapy either with CHOP (cyclophosphamide, adriamycin, vincristine, prednisone) or high-dose methotrexate followed by whole brain radiation, 45 to 50 Gy.[16] Some investigators believe that intrathecal methotrexate is also indicated to irradicate leptomeningeal tumor. Postradiation chemotherapy with another drug, such as cytosine arabinoside, is also being utilized.

Meningiomas

Surgical resection is the treatment of choice for meningiomas. When surgical resection is complete, no further therapy is necessary. If the surgical resection is incomplete or if the tumor recurs despite an apparent complete resection, radiation therapy is indicated at the time of recurrence.[31] The radiation should be delivered in doses of about 50 Gy to a focal portal encompassing the tumor. There is no chemotherapy for this neoplasm.

Neurinomas

The most common neurinoma in both the young and the elderly is the acoustic nerve neurinoma. The treatment is surgical resection. With modern techniques of surgery and particularly with early detection of acoustic neurinomas, removal may allow preservation of both facial muscle function and hearing. Only large tumors are associated with morbidity involving the central nervous system.

Pituitary Adenomas

Symptomatic adenoma of the pituitary can be treated with a high cure rate and low morbidity by transphenoidal resection of the tumor.[32] If the tumor cannot be completely resected or if it is invasive, postoperative radiation therapy is indicated. Bromocriptine may be the treatment of choice in patients with prolactin-secreting tumors, particularly if the patient is a poor surgical or radiation therapy candidate.[32] Asymptomatic pituitary tumors can be followed.

REFERENCES

1. Walker EA et al: Epidemiology of brain tumors. *Neurology* 35:219, 1985.
2. Codd MB, Kurland LT: Descriptive epidemiology of primary intracranial neoplasms. *Prog Exp Tumor Res* 29:1, 1985.
3. Davis LD, Schwartz J: Trends in cancer mortality: US white males and females, 1968–83. *Lancet* 633, 1988.
4. Bharucha NE et al: Primary malignant nervous system neoplasms. Birth cohort effect in the elderly. *Arch Neurol* 42:1061, 1985.
5. Chang CH et al: Comparison of postoperative radiotherapy and combined postoperative radiotherapy and chemotherapy in the multidisciplinary management of malignant gliomas. *Cancer* 52:997, 1983.
6. Cairncross J, Posner JB: Brain tumors in the elderly, in Albert ML (ed): *Clinical Neurology of Aging.* New York, Oxford University Press, 1984, p 445.
7. Werner MH, Schold SC: Primary intracranial neoplasms in the elderly. *Clin Geriatr Med* 3:765, 1987.
8. Caird FI: Intracranial tumours in the elderly: Diagnosis and treatment. *Age Ageing* 13:152, 1984.
9. Cairncross JG et al: Radiation therapy of brain metastases. *Ann Neurol* 7:29, 1980.
10. Schirmer M, Bock WJ: Intracranial tumors in advanced age. *Adv Neurosurg* 12:145, 1984.
11. Meyers BS: Increased intracranial pressure and depression in the elderly. *J Am Geriatr Soc* 936.
12. Fisher CM: Transient paralytic attacks of obscure nature: The question of non-convulsive seizure paralysis. *Can J Neurol Sci* 5:267, 1978.
13. Levy DE: How transient are transient ischemic attacks? *Neurology* 38 (suppl 1):108, 1988.
14. Zawadski-Brant M et al: Primary intracranial tumor imaging. A comparison of magnetic resonance and CT. *Radiology* 150:435, 1984.
15. Piepmeier JM: Observations on the current treatment of low-grade astrocytic tumors of the cerebral hemispheres. *J Neurosurg* 67:177, 1987.
16. Deangelis LM et al: Primary central nervous system lymphoma: Managing patients with spontaneous and AIDS-related lymphomas. *Oncology* 1:52, 1987.
17. Voorhies RM et al: The single supratentorial lesion. *J Neurosurg* 53:364, 1980.
18. Wasserstrom WR et al: Diagnosis and treatment of leptomeningeal metastases from solid tumors: Experience with 90 patients. *Cancer* 49:759, 1982.
19. Malkin MG, Posner JB: Cerebrospinal fluid tumor markers for the diagnosis and management of leptomeningeal metastases. A Review. *Eur J Cancer Clin Oncol* 23(1):1, 1987.
20. Bullard DE: Role of Stereotaxic biopsy in the management of patients with intracranial lesions. *Neurol Clin* 3:817, 1985.
21. Delattre J-Y et al: High dose versus low dose dexamethasone in experimental epidural spinal cord compression. *Neurosurgery* 22:1005, 1988.
22. Graham K, Caird FI: High-dose steroid therapy of intracranial tumour in the elderly. *Age Ageing* 7:146, 1978.
23. Fadul C et al: Morbidity and mortality of craniotomy for excision of supratentorial gliomas. *Neurology* (in press) 1989.
24. Wood JR et al: The prognostic importance of tumor size in malignant gliomas: A computed tomographic scan study by the Brain Tumor Cooperative Group. *J Clin Oncol* 6:338, 1988.
25. Deangelis LM et al: The role of post-operative radiotherapy after resection of brain metastases. *Neurosurgery* (in press) 1989.
26. Stylopoulos LA et al: Longitudinal CT study of parenchymal brain changes in glioma survivors. *Am J Neuroradiol* 9:517, 1988.
27. Delattre J-Y, Posner JB: Neurological complications of chemotherapy and radiation therapy, in Aminoff (ed): *Neurology and General Medicine.* New York, Churchill Livingstone, 1989.
28. Rosner D et al: Chemotherapy induces regression of brain metastases in breast carcinoma. *Cancer* 58:832, 1986.
29. Shapiro WR: Therapy of adult malignant brain tumors: What have the clinical trials taught us? *Sem Oncol* 13:38, 1986.
30. Patchell RA et al: Surgery plus radiation versus radiation alone in the treatment of single brain metastases. *Neurology* 36:447, 1986.
31. Barbaro NM et al: Radiation therapy in the treatment of partially resected meningiomas. *Neurosurgery* 20:525, 1987.
32. Ciric I: Pituitary tumors. *Neurol Clin* 3:751, 1985.

Chapter 102

DEPRESSION

Dan Blazer

The themes of aging and depression often coalesce. Simone de Beauvoir, in her book *The Coming of Age*, tells of Prince Siddhartha on one of his frequent visits from his protected palace.[1] On this particular day he encounters a tottering, wrinkled, white-haired, decrepit old man who is stooped and mumbling incomprehensibly while making his way along a road with a stick to improve his balance. The sight of the old man disturbs the young prince, and Siddhartha informs his charioteer, "It is the world's pity that we as ignorant beings, drunk with the vanity of youth, do not behold old age. Let us hurry back to the palace. What is the use of pleasures . . . since I myself am the future dwelling-place of old age?" It is tempting to perceive disorders of mood as being on a continuum, with mood declining as age increases owing to the inevitable physical disabilities and mental incapacitation associated with aging.

Such a perception, however, is of little value in the clinical management of the depressed older adult. Precise boundaries cannot be identified between a normal depressed mood and the extremes of depressive illness.[2] Nevertheless, most clinical investigators do not perceive depression as phenomenologically homogeneous. For this reason, the *Diagnostic and Statistical Manual of Mental Disorders* categorizes the depressive disorders as a group of distinct entities or independent syndromes presenting with a depressed mood, analogous to the different disease entities that might contribute to the symptoms and signs of an anemia.[3] Therapy of depression can therefore be selected based upon a thorough diagnostic workup. Given the availability of excellent, but at times expensive and potentially dangerous, biological therapies, the categorical approach is accepted by most geriatric psychiatrists.

Supported by the Clinical Research Center for the Study of Psychopathology in the Elderly (CRC/PE) grant number P50 MH40159 from the National Institute of Mental Health, Center for the Study of Aging and Mental Health.

EPIDEMIOLOGY

Mood disorders are among the most common psychiatric disorders of adulthood. Nevertheless, the prevalence of major depression is lower than in late adulthood.[4-6] The prevalence of major depression in community populations in the Epidemiologic Catchment Area (ECA) project range from less than 1 to 3 percent.

In contrast, the prevalence of depressive symptoms in the elderly remains relatively high. For example, Blazer and Williams reported significant dysphoria in almost 15 percent of a community-based sample of older adults.[4] Gurland et al. found 13 percent of the 65-and-over age group to have "pervasive depression."[7] In a recent study, 27 percent of adults in the community reported depressive symptoms, with 8 percent suffering from significant depressive symptoms associated with physical problems.[5]

Depression is more common in institutional settings. Folks and Ford diagnosed major depression in 26 percent of subjects in a medical/surgical inpatient unit.[8] Meador et al. found major depression in 15 percent of 130 consecutive men 70 years of age and over admitted to a medical and neurologic service of a large teaching hospital.[9] Teeter et al., in a survey of a skilled nursing facility, found depressive neurosis in 21.6 percent of the sample, and psychotic depression in 4 percent.[10] Depressive symptoms are therefore common among older adults, and major depression is a frequent problem encountered in acute- and chronic-care facilities. The prevalence of major or clinical depression in community populations, however, is not as great as has been previously described.

Despite the relative decrease in frequency of severe depression in community-dwelling elders, suicide rates are positively correlated with age. This correlation is exclusively explained by the increase in suicide rates among white males over the age of 60.[11] No adequate explanation is forthcoming for this trend that has been recognized throughout the twentieth century in most Western countries. Nevertheless, the association of suicide with medical illness, decreased impulse control (which is occasionally associated with decreased cognitive functioning), social isolation, and loss of a loved one may contribute to the elevated risk of suicide among a group of older adults who may be more alienated emotionally—namely, the widowed white male who has survived his friends and grown apart from his family.

ETIOLOGY

Etiologic theories of mood disorders include biological, psychological, and psychosocial hypotheses. No single causal agent has been identified for any mood disorder, and therefore the onset of depression in late life undoubtedly involves a web of causation, with contributions from each of these domains intermixed in unique ways in each individual suffering from a depressive disorder.

Disregulation of chemical messengers, hormonal feedback mechanisms, and circadian rhythms are most often implicated in the pathophysiology of mood disorders. These disregulated systems derive in part from a genetic predisposition, but the association of the majority of mood disorders in late life with a clear mode of inheritance has not been demonstrated. Norepinephrine and serotonin are the neurotransmitters most often thought to contribute to the pathophysiology of mood disorders. Robinson et al. found the concentrations of both these neurotransmitters to decrease with age; but the metabolic product of serotonin, 5-hydroxyindoleacetic acid (5-HIAA), and the enzyme monoamine oxidase (MAO) were found to increase with age.[12] More recent studies have been equivocal. No convincing evidence exists that significant neurotransmitter abnormalities increase with advancing age.

Disregulation of the hypothalamic-pituitary-adrenal (HPA) axis has also been implicated as associated with depression. The finding of increased secretion of cortisol in many depressed patients led to the adaptation of the dexamethasone suppression test (DST) as a laboratory marker of melancholic depression.[13,14] Rosenbaum et al., in a study of the DST across the life cycle, found a positive relationship between age and cortisol levels after administration of dexamethasone.[15] For example, 4 percent of subjects under 65 years of age had a cortisol level of 5 μg/dl after the test, whereas 12.5 percent of those subjects over the age of 65 were nonsuppressors. Each was physically healthy and not depressed. In general, however, there has been no overwhelming evidence of a propensity for older persons to suffer disregulation of the HPA axis significantly greater than persons in midlife, at least up until the age of 75.

Desynchronization of circadian rhythms has also been implicated in the onset of major depression. Abnormalities of sleep architecture are among the most robust biological markers of depression. The major abnormality identified is a decrease in REM latency (the time between falling asleep and the first REM period).[16] Disruption of normal sleep with increasing age suggests the possibility of circadian abnormalities contributing to the etiology of late-life depression. As age increases, there is a gradual diminution in overall sleep time, a decrease in sleep continuity, and a decreased REM latency.[17]

The psychological contribution to depression includes at least three predisposing factors. The first, and most intuitive, is loss of a valued object. Older persons generally experience fewer stressful life events, but the majority of these events are *exit events*. Freud postulated that the ambivalent introjection of the lost object into the ego leads to typical depressive symptoms derived from a lack of energy available to the ego. Guilt ensues when the individual cannot express anger externally toward the lost object, and the depressed person then internalizes this anger. Though older persons experience loss frequently, the loss is generally an "on-time" experience. For example, the older married female anticipates that she will outlive her husband and has rehearsed widowhood. Therefore, adaptation to the death of her spouse is more easily facilitated.

According to cognitive theories, depression results from negative distortions of life experiences, negative self-evaluation, pessimism, and hopelessness. For example, automatic thoughts resulting from an event lead to depressive symptoms. Depressed older adults may view the absence of a phone call from a child as an overt statement devaluing the parent for past failures. In reality, the reasons for not contacting the parent may relate to an overbooked schedule or even the inability to contact the parent because of the parent's busy schedule.

The third putative theory for the etiology of depression in late life derives from Erikson's eighth stage of man, i.e., integrity versus despair. Late life is a time for "the acceptance of one's one and only life cycle and of the people who have become significant to it as something that had to be and that, by necessity, permitted of no substitutions."[18] If one fails to integrate one's life, to link one's life to both past heritage and future generations, then despair ensues. "Time is short, too short for the attempt to start another life and to try out alternative roads to integrity."[18]

Social factors may also contribute to the onset of depression in the elderly. Pfifer and Murrell found that health and social support played both an additive and an interactive role in the onset of depressive symptoms.[19] Life events themselves had only weak effects, and sociodemographic factors, overall, did not contribute to depression onset. However, a weak support network and the presence of poor physical health placed older persons at especial risk for the onset of depression.

DIAGNOSIS AND DIFFERENTIAL DIAGNOSIS

The Differential Diagnosis of Depressive Symptoms in Late Life (*DSM-III-R*) lists many of the symptoms as criteria symptoms for major depression (see Table 102-1). Older persons suffering from major depression do not differ significantly from persons at earlier stages of the life cycle in the distribution of these symptoms, except that they are less likely to express feelings of worthless-

TABLE 102-1
The Diagnosis of Major or Clinical Depression in Late Life

Diagnostic Criteria

Depressed mood and/or loss of interest or pleasure, plus four of the following (three if both depressed mood and loss of interest or pleasure):
- Weight loss or weight gain (more common)
- Insomnia or hypersomnia
- Psychomotor agitation or retardation
- Fatigue or loss of energy
- Feelings of worthlessness or of guilt (less common)
- Difficulty concentrating
- Recurrent thoughts of death or suicidal ideation

Diagnostic Distinctions of Importance

Melancholic/endogenous (at least five of the following) versus nonmelancholic:
- Loss of interest or pleasure
- Lack of reactivity to pleasurable stimuli
- Symptoms worse in morning
- Psychomotor agitation or retardation
- Significant weight loss
- Previous response to somatic therapies
- Previous episodes with remission
- Psychotic (delusions and/or hallucinations) versus nonpsychotic: Psychotic depression relatively more prevalent in late life
- Single episode versus recurrent (especially rapid cycling)
- Seasonal (recurrence in winter months with full remission in summer months; atypical symptoms such as excessive sleep and weight gain) versus sporadic
- Pseudodementia versus mixed depression and dementia: Pseudodementia is not common
- Retarded depression versus agitated depression (mixed depression/anxiety)
- Pure major depression versus double depression (major depression plus dysthymia)
- Treatment-sensitive versus treatment-resistant: Elders more likely to be resistant to tricyclic antidepressants

ness or guilt overtly and more likely to suffer from weight loss.[20] Though the older adult may be reticent to report a depressed mood or dysphoria spontaneously, once asked about depression, he or she is no less likely to report such a mood than persons at earlier stages of the life cycle. Though older persons do not report more difficulty concentrating (contrary to traditional beliefs about the frequency of self-reported cognitive dysfunction in late life when compared to persons in midlife), they in fact do suffer more symptoms of cognitive impairment. The association of depression and dementia is far more common than the masking of depression as dementia, i.e., pseudodementia.[21]

The determination that an individual is suffering from a major or clinical depression (as compared with a less severe presentation of depressive symptoms) is the important first step in the diagnostic process. Regardless of etiology, major depression deserves careful evaluation by the clinician, for it must be disaggregated in order to prescribe the most appropriate therapy.

To assist in disaggregating major depression in the elderly, a series of diagnostic distinctions are of importance (Table 102-1). First, melancholic depression must be distinguished from nonmelancholic depression. Melancholic depression is more responsive to biological intervention, and nonmelancholic depression is more responsive to psychosocial intervention. Persons suffering from a melancholic depression deserve at least a trial on a pharmacotherapeutic agent. The second distinction of importance is psychotic versus nonpsychotic depression. Psychotic depression is more common in late life, is more resistant to pharmacologic intervention, but is responsive to electroconvulsive therapy (ECT).[22]

Psychiatrists have become more aware in recent years of the problem of recurrent depressions. In fact, most episodes of major depression tend to recur. Fortunately, these recurrences are few and separated by many years. In some cases, however, depression in late life becomes rapidly recurrent, i.e., *rapid cycling*. This rapid-cycling variant may reflect an underlying bipolar disorder but may never manifest itself in overt manic episodes. Rapid-cycling depression usually requires intervention with lithium or carbamazepine along with an antidepressant medication. Older persons may also suffer seasonal affective disorders, a variant of rapid-cycling depression, with recurrence of depression meeting criteria for major depression during the winter months with a full remission in the summer. Most persons suffering from a seasonal affective disorder report atypical symptoms of depression, such as excessive sleep and weight gain.

Depression is often associated with symptoms of anxiety or agitation. Phenomenologically, depression may therefore be divided into a retarded depression versus an agitated depression (or mixed depression-anxiety syndrome). Agitated depression is associated with a poor prognosis and often requires the use of multiple pharmacologic agents, such as the combined prescription of an antianxiety medication along with an antidepressant medication. Though the symptoms of depression may remit over time, the symptoms of anxiety are often chronic.

The differential diagnosis of depression is complex and is presented in Table 102-2. Within the mood disorders, an episode of major depression may reflect unipolar depression (single episode or recurrent), a bipolar depressive episode, or an atypical bipolar disorder—now classified as a mood disorder NOS (not otherwise specified). Older persons are not immune to bipolar disorder and may experience the first onset of a manic episode in late life. Even if this episode meets *DSM-III-R* criteria for a manic episode, it is often atypical. Those who have worked with elderly bipolar patients describe a "dysphoric" manic episode. Agitation, decreased sleep, increased energy, increased irritability, angry outbursts, and paranoid ideation often predominate the clinical picture. In other situations, older adults may

TABLE 102-2
The Differential Diagnosis of Depressive Symptoms in Late Life (*DSM-III-R*)

Mood Disorders

- Major depression (single episode or recurrent)
- Dysthymia (or depressive neurosis)
- Bipolar disorder, depressed
- Depressive disorder NOS (i.e., atypical depression or mild biogenic depression)

Adjustment Disorders

- Adjustment disorder with depressed mood
- Uncomplicated bereavement

Organic Mental Disorders

- Primary degenerative dementia with associated major depression
- Organic mood disorder, depressed:
  - Secondary to physical illness (e.g., hypothyroidism, stroke, carcinoma of the pancreas)
  - Secondary to pharmacologic agents (e.g., methyldopa, propranolol)

Psychoactive Substance-Use Disorders

- Alcohol abuse and/or dependence
- Sedative, hypnotic, or anxiolytic abuse and/or dependence

Somatoform Disorders

- Hypochondriasis
- Somatization disorder

experience periodic and definitive episodes of major depression that are intermixed with episodes of hypomania. During these latter episodes, the older person exhibits increased activity, some decreased sleep, an exaggerated sense of well-being, and may profusely praise the clinician for his miraculous cure. Such patients must be monitored carefully, for these hypomanic symptoms can lead to behaviors that are potentially damaging, though the person may not evidence overt psychotic behavior. The antidepressant medications, especially the monoamine oxidase inhibitors, can precipitate hypomanic and even overt manic episodes in a previously depressed older adult.

Adjustment disorders account for many of the depressive symptoms exhibited by older adults. As noted above, depressive symptoms frequently ensue as a reaction to a chronic or painful physical illness, especially an illness that decreases functional capacity. Other stressors for older adults include retirement, marital problems (which can derive from increased contact), difficulty with children, loss of a social role, or an ill-advised change of residence. The most frequent stressor, however, is a physical illness.

In the study by Reiffler and colleagues, approximately 20 percent of all subjects suffering from primary degenerative dementia who were evaluated in a dementia clinic were concurrently suffering from a major depressive episode.[21] When treated with antidepressant medications, the depressive symptoms remitted but the dementia persisted. This combined clinical presentation is much more common than pseudodementia, i.e., a pure depressive episode which masks as a cognitive dysfunction.

Several physical illnesses and pharmacologic agents can induce a depressed mood. The association between depression and hypothyroidism has been well established. Symptoms of myxedema include constipation, cold intolerance, psychomotor retardation, decreased exercise tolerance, and cognitive changes along with the depressed affect. A low tetraiodothyroxine (T4) and elevated serum thyroid-stimulating hormone (TSH) usually confirm the diagnosis. Left-sided stroke is also associated with depression and catastrophic responses manifested by episodes of profuse crying, feelings of despair, hopelessness, anger, and self-depreciation. These symptoms may derive from damage to structures in the left hemisphere as opposed to the right hemisphere. A number of medications have been implicated in the etiology of depression, including frequently used antihypertensive agents and sedative-hypnotic or anxiolytic agents. Alcohol dependence often is disguised as a depression.

Hypochondriasis is another confounder of the differential diagnosis of the depressed older adult. Depressed mood is common in hypochondriacal elders, though the essential feature of hypochondriasis is an unrealistic interpretation of physical signs or sensations as abnormal, which in turn leads to a preoccupation with fear or to the belief that one is suffering from a serious illness.[3] The prevalence of hypochondriacal symptoms is increased among the depressed elderly, though the course of the disorder and response to usual therapeutic intervention should differentiate the two conditions. Concurrence of depressive symptoms and hypochondriacal symptoms may increase the risk for suicide.

DIAGNOSTIC EVALUATION

The clinical interview is fundamental to the diagnostic evaluation of depressed elders. Both the older adult patient and family members should be included in this interview process. Length of the current depressive episode, history of previous episodes, history of drug and alcohol abuse, response to previous therapeutic interventions for depressive illness, family history of depression, suicidal ideations or attempts, and the level of physical functioning of the depressed elder can be determined by eliciting and combining information from both patient and family. The severity of the depressive symptoms, including risks for suicide, should be established regardless of the differential diagnosis in order to decide whether the depressed elder is to be hospitalized. A number of severity rating scales are available to assist the clinician, including the Hamilton Depression Rating Scale, the Montgomery-Asberg Depression Rating Scale, and the Global Assessment Scale. Scores on these operationalized ratings of severity also provide the clinician with a tool for tracking improvement during therapy.

The mental status examination of a patient assists in determining the quality of mood and affect, perceptual distortions that may result from depression (such as delusions and hallucinations), and psychomotor agitation or retardation. A thorough evaluation of cognitive status assists the clinician in distinguishing depression from a mixed depression/dementia syndrome. Orientation, memory, judgment, insight, and ability to abstract are key ingredients in the cognitive assessment. A number of formal scales are available to the clinician, such as the Mini-Mental State Examination and the Blessed Dementia Rating Scale.

Physical examination should include a neurologic evaluation to determine the presence of soft neurologic signs, such as frontal release signs or laterality. Weight loss and psychomotor retardation may precipitate peroneal palsy because of sitting with crossed legs. Both lying and standing blood pressures should be recorded, for postural hypotension frequently is exacerbated by antidepressant medication.

The laboratory diagnostic workup of the depressed older adult is outlined in Table 102-3. Though no definitive laboratory test for depression has emerged, the pattern of laboratory findings across a number of diagnostic

TABLE 102-3
The Laboratory Diagnostic Workup of the Depressed Older Adult

Routine Laboratory Studies

- Clinical blood count and differential (B_{12} and/or folate deficiency)
- Urinalysis
- Chest x ray (to rule out cancer of lung)
- Electrocardiogram (baseline before beginning antidepressant therapy)
- Blood chemistries (to screen for dehydration secondary to severe depression or hypokalemia)

Endocrinologic Studies

- Dexamethasone suppression test, or DST (may be most valuable in predicting outcome)
- Thyroid panel and TSH (adequate for assessment of thyroid status)
- Thyrotropine-releasing hormone (TRH)/TSH stimulation test (used by some as a diagnostic test)

Polysomnography

- Sleep EEG, ECG, EMG, etc. (diagnostic test that complements the DST; patient must be drug-free if the test is to be effective; screens for sleep apnea syndrome)

Experimental or Less Frequently Used Diagnostic Studies

- Magnetic resonance imaging, or MRI (depressed elderly exhibit increased leukoencephalopathy)
- Tritiated imipramine binding in platelets (may be more specific for melancholic depression in late life than in midlife)
- Urinary MHPG and 5-HIAA (of questionable value in differential diagnosis or selection of pharmacologic agents)
- Platelet monoamine oxidase inhibition (if tested before and after prescription of MAOI, provides evidence of peripheral effectiveness of the drug)

Psychological Tests and Rating Scales

- Standardized diagnostic interviews: Schedule for Affective Disorders and Schizophrenia (SADS), Diagnostic Interview Schedule (DIS), Geriatric Mental Status (GMS)
- Personality inventories: Structured Interview for DSM-III—Personality Disorders (SID-P), Millon, Dysfunctional Attitude Scale, Attributional Style Questionnaire
- Clinical assessment scales of severity: Hamilton Rating Scale for Depression, Montgomery-Asberg Depression Scale, Global Assessment Scale
- Self-rated assessment scales of severity: Center for Epidemiologic Studies—Depression Scale (CES-D), Zung SDS, Beck Depression Inventory, Geriatric Depression Scale

tests not only rules out physical illness as the cause of depressive symptoms but also delineates depressive illness that is in part biologically determined. Baseline laboratory values, such as the electrocardiogram, are important in monitoring the impact of medication. The dexamethasone suppression test has been extensively described as a diagnostic procedure, but its value is debated frequently. Cortisol levels at 3 P.M. and 10 P.M. greater than 5 μg/dl on the day following nighttime administration of 1 mg dexamethasone are abnormal in approximately 50 percent of depressed patients and are no different for older adults, at least to the age of 75. The DST is not specific for depression, and the reading may be abnormal especially in patients with severe organic mental disorders. The greatest value of the test, however, may be in tracking the progress of treatment. If a positive test returns to a negative value and remains negative, this bodes well for short-term outcome.

COURSE AND PROGNOSIS

The risk for suicide in the depressed older adult has been described above. Depression, however, may lead to other adverse outcomes. The all-cause mortality among depressed older adults evaluated in psychiatric facilities has been shown in a number of studies to be higher in depressed elders when compared with general population groups of the same age.[23,24] Though these depressed elders, at baseline, experience poor physical health, poor health alone does not explain the increased mortality rate. Older persons are thought to experience loss of meaningful roles and emotional support through retirement, widowhood, death of friends, low economic and material well-being, and increased isolation. These factors are known to contribute to increased mortality in the elderly and may in turn interact with depressive symptoms. In addition, depressed elders may be less willing to care for themselves physically, and poor health practices contribute to increased mortality.

There is evidence to support the impression that older adults are less likely to recover from a depressive episode than middle-aged adults. Combined results from a number of outcome studies suggest that approximately 25 percent of depressed elders recover from an index episode of depression within 1 year and maintain recovery. Thirty to fifty percent do not recover from the episode, and an additional 20 to 30 percent recover but experience a relapse.[25–27] Even those individuals who recover suffer symptoms at follow-up.[25] That is, older adults who recover from an episode do not recover entirely (compared to persons in midlife) but experience residual depressive symptoms.

Approximately 2 percent of depressed elders suffer from a dysthymic disorder (depressive neurosis). By def-

inition, these individuals must experience mild to moderate depressive symptoms (but symptoms not meeting criteria for a major depressive episode) for at least 2 years. Some of these persons will suffer intermittent episodes of major depression. Therefore, when they are treated with pharmacologic agents (or even electroconvulsive therapy), they exhibit significant recovery from the major depression yet remain dysthymic. Some studies suggest that persons with dysthymic disorder with concurrent major depression (i.e., double depression) have a poor prognosis for major depression, but this finding has not been validated for older adults.[28]

CLINICAL MANAGEMENT

The clinical management of depression in late life is four-pronged: psychotherapy, pharmacotherapy, electroconvulsive therapy, and family therapy. Cognitive-behavioral therapy, along with interpersonal therapy (a cognitive-behavioral orientation to improving interpersonal relationships), has been developed specifically to treat depressive illness.[29,30] Cognitive-behavioral therapy has been used in treating depressed older adults and has been demonstrated to be effective.[31,32] These therapies are based upon cognitive theories of depression, with a goal of changing behavior and modes of thinking. Change is accomplished through behavioral interventions such as weekly activity schedules, graded task assignments, and logs of mastery or pleasure. Negative cognitions are restructured and automatic thoughts are challenged by testing empirical reality, examining distortions such as overgeneralizations, and generating new ways of viewing one's life. Such therapies are especially attractive to clinicians treating the depressed elder for they are directive (and therefore culturally more suited to older adults), time-limited (usually requiring between 10 and 25 sessions), and educational. The depressed elder who views self as inadequate and defective (and therefore interprets experiences as being caused by problems with self) is challenged to rethink the course of events that led to a negative cognition. When negative or disturbing events occur, the elder can mobilize new means of interpreting these events that preclude the onset of feelings of worthlessness, helplessness, and hopelessness.

Pharmacotherapy of the depressed elder is indicated in cases where depressive symptoms are severe and/or where clear symptoms of a melancholic or endogenous depression are evident. Tricyclic antidepressants (TCAs) remain the agents of choice, despite the marketing of new antidepressants in recent years. A list of pharmacologic agents used in the treatment of depression in late life and characteristics of these agents appears in Table 102-4. Medications which are relatively free of

TABLE 102-4
Characteristics of Pharmacologic Agents Used in the Treatment of Depression in Late Life

Generic Name	Starting Daily Dose	Sedative Effect	Relative Anticholinergic Effect	Therapeutic Blood Level
Tricyclic tertiary amines				
Doxepin (Sinequan, Adapin)	50–75 mg	+++	+++	>100 ng/dl
Tricyclic secondary amines				
Nortriptyline (Pamelor, Aventyl)	25–50 mg	++	++	50–150 ng/dl
Desipramine (Norpramin)	25–50 mg	+	+	>125 ng/dl
Heterocyclic agents				
Amoxapine (Asendin)	75–100 mg	++	++	NA
Trazodone (Desyrel)	100–150 mg	+++	0	NA
Fluoxetine (Prozac)	20 mg	0	+	NA
Monoamine oxidase inhibitors				
Tranylcypromine (Parnate)	20 mg	+	++	≥80% reduction of MAO activity in platelets
Lithium				
Lithium carbonate	150–300 mg	++	0	0.4–0.7 mmol/liter
Psychostimulants				
Methylphenidate	5–10 mg	0	0	NA
Potentiating agents				
T_3 (Cytomel)	25 μg	0	0	NA

SOURCE: Adapted in part from Jenike MA: *Handbook of Geriatric Psychopharmacology*. Littleton, MA, PSG Publishing, 1985.

side effects (especially cardiovascular side effects) and yet effective are preferred. Among the TCAs, nortriptyline, desipramine, and doxepin are the most popular agents for treating major depression.

Dosing tricyclic antidepressants must be case-specific. The daily dose will usually be less for elders than for persons in midlife. For example, 25 to 50 mg nortriptyline PO qhs or 25 mg bid desipramine are commonly prescribed doses for relieving depressive symptoms in older adults. The heterocyclic agents have been less used. Nevertheless, in some circumstances these agents are preferred. Trazodone is virtually free of anticholinergic effects and would appear to be an ideal agent for treating depressed elders. Unfortunately, the drug is not free of side effects, especially sedative effects and occasional priapism. Monoamine oxidase inhibitors are not tolerated better than TCAs. When symptoms are atypical, however, such as increased sleep and increased appetite along with associated significant symptoms of anxiety, an MAO inhibitor may be indicated. Jenike recommends the less used MAO inhibitor tranylcypromine.[33] When a depressive episode is severe and ECT is considered to be a viable treatment where subjects fail to respond to an antidepressant medication, the clinician must remember that a monoamine oxidase inhibitor (MAOI) precludes initiation of ECT until 10 days to 2 weeks following discontinuance of the drug. Such a delay, coupled with Medicare constraints upon psychiatric hospital days, renders the use of an MAOI in the hospital less desirable.

The administration of low-dose stimulants, such as methylphenidate in the morning, or augmentation of TCAs with T_3 (Cytomel) may improve mood in the apathetic older adult. The effect of these augmentating medications, however, has yet to be conclusively demonstrated among the depressed elderly. Stimulants are generally safe in low dosage, and rarely does withdrawal lead to significant side effects. In some patients suffering from rapid-cycling depression, even if no manic episodes emerge in the clinical picture, the use of lithium carbonate is indicated. If lithium is not effective, other agents that have been tried experimentally, including carbamazepine and clonazepam, may be used.

For the severe and pharmacologically resistant major depressive episodes in late life, electroconvulsive therapy (ECT) is the treatment of choice. Despite the adverse publicity that has been associated with ECT, the number of persons being treated has increased in recent years across the life cycle, especially among the elderly. In most general psychiatric units, nearly 50 percent of subjects who receive ECT are over the age of 60. Reasons for the frequent use of ECT in late life include the probable (though not documented) increased number of pharmacologically resistant cases, the effectiveness of ECT in pharmacologically resistant patients, and the relative lack of side effects. Even persons suffering from moderately severe cardiovascular disease can undergo ECT, usually at less risk than taking antidepressant medications.

ECT is not without problems. Even the use of unilateral, nondominant electrode placement does not eliminate the transient memory loss that accompanies treatment. Though recent and remote memory generally return to normal, the amnestic period during treatment is disturbing to the depressed elder. Older adults in the midst of a depressive episode who express concern regarding their cognitive capacities are especially at risk for agitation and worry about the memory loss that accompanies ECT. Persons who are suffering combined depression and dementia, a syndrome that is not always readily identified during an index episode of depression requiring ECT, may exhibit sustained confusion and memory difficulties for several weeks following ECT. If the depression recurs (ECT does not prevent the recurrence of depression but only relieves an existing episode), the clinician will have difficulty disaggregating the memory difficulties secondary to depression from the memory difficulties secondary to ECT. Six to ten treatments are usually required for effective therapy and should be performed in the hospital under the care of a psychiatrist experienced in the administration of ECT.

The depressed older adult cannot be treated in isolation. Family members usually initiate the depressed elder's visit to the clinician's office or to the hospital. Severely depressed elders are often incapable of making decisions regarding treatment, yet will listen to family members who advise. Clinicians should make an effort to ally with family members from at least two generations, usually the spouse and a child. In some situations, a sibling or a grandchild may also provide significant support and assistance during the course of treating severe depression. Most depressed elders do not resist ongoing interaction between the clinician and family members. Not only can valuable information be derived from diagnostic interviews with family members, but families must be instructed as to the nature of depressive illness, its course, and the potential for adverse outcomes—especially suicide. Such preventive measures early in the care of the depressed elder render care much more effective.

REFERENCES

1. de Beauvoir S: *The Coming of Age.* Paris, Editions Gallimard, 1970.
2. Blazer D et al: Depressive symptoms and depressive diagnoses in a community population: Use of a new procedure for analysis of psychiatric classification. *Arch Gen Psychiatry* (in press).
3. *Diagnostic and Statistical Manual of Mental Disorders,* 3d ed (rev). Washington, American Psychiatric Association, 1987.
4. Blazer D, Williams CD: Epidemiology of dysphoria and depression in an elderly population. *Am J Psychiatry* 137:439, 1980.
5. Blazer D et al: The epidemiology of depression in an elderly community population. *Gerontologist* 27:281, 1987.
6. Myers JK et al: Six-month prevalence of psychiatric disorders in three communities: 1980 to 1982. *Arch Gen Psychiatry* 41:959, 1984.
7. Gurland BJ et al: The epidemiology of depression and dementia in the elderly: The use of multiple indicators of these conditions, in Coles JO, Barrett JE (eds): *Psychopathology of the Aged.* New York, Raven Press, 1980.
8. Folks DG, Ford CV: Psychiatric disorders in geriatric medical/surgical patients. *South Med J* 78:239, 1985.
9. Meador KG et al: Detection and treatment of major depression in older medically ill hospitalized patients. *Int J Psychiatry Med* (in press).
10. Teeter RB et al: Psychiatric disturbances of aged patients in skilled nursing homes. *Am J Psychiatry* 133:1430, 1976.
11. Blazer DG et al: Suicide in late life: Review and commentary. *J Am Geriatr Soc* 34:519, 1986.
12. Robinson DS et al: Relation of sex and aging to monoamine oxidase activity of human plasma and platelets. *Arch Gen Psychiatry* 24:536, 1971.
13. Sachar EJ: Neuroendocrine abnormalities in depressive illness, in Sachar EJ (ed): *Topics in Psychoendocrinology.* New York, Grune & Stratton, 1975.
14. Carroll BJ et al: A specific laboratory test for the diagnosis of melancholia: Standardization, validity, and clinical utility. *Arch Gen Psychiatry* 38:15, 1981.
15. Rosenbaum AH et al: The DST in normal control subjects: A comparison of two assays and the effects of age. *Am J Psychiatry* 141:1550, 1984.
16. Kupfer DJ et al: Sleep EEG and motor activity as indicators in affective states. *Neuropsychobiology* 1:296, 1975.
17. Kupfer DJ: Neuropsychological markers: EEG sleep measures. *J Psychiatr Res* 18:467, 1984.
18. Erikson EH: *Identity, Youth, and Crisis.* New York, Norton, 1968.
19. Pfifer JF, Murrell SA: Etiologic factors in the onset of depressive symptoms in older adults. *J Abnorm Psychol* 95:282, 1986.
20. Blazer D et al: Major depression with melancholia: A comparison of middle-aged and elderly adults. *J Am Geriatr Soc* 35:927, 1987.
21. Reiffler BV et al: Coexistence of cognitive impairment and depression in geriatric outpatients. *Am J Psychiatry* 39:623, 1982.
22. Meyers BS et al: Late-onset delusional depression: A distinct clinical entity? *J Clin Psychiatry* 45:347, 1984.
23. Murphy E et al: Increased mortality rates in late-life depression. *Br J Psychiatry* 152:347, 1988.
24. Rabins PV et al: High fatality rates of late-life depression associated with cardiovascular disease. *J Affective Disord* 9:165, 1985.
25. Blazer D et al: Follow-up of hospitalized depressed patients. An age comparison. Unpublished data, 1987.
26. Murphy E: The prognosis of depression in old age. *Br J Psychiatry* 142:111, 1983.
27. Post F: The management and nature of depressive illness in late life: A follow-through study. *Br J Psychiatry* 121:393, 1972.
28. Keller MB, Shapiro RW: Major depressive disorder: Initial results from a one-year prospective naturalistic follow-up study. *J Nerv Ment Dis* 169:761, 1981.
29. Beck AT et al: *Cognitive Therapy of Depression.* New York, Guilford Press, 1979.

30. Klerman GL et al: *Interpersonal Psychotherapy of Depression.* New York, Basic Books, 1984.

31. Gallagher D, Thompson LW: Differential effectiveness of psychotherapies for the treatment of major depressive disorder in older adults. *Psychother Theor Res Pract* 19:42, 1982.

32. Steuer JL et al: Cognitive-behavioral and psychodynamic group psychotherapy in treatment of geriatric depression. *J Consult Clin Psychol* 52:180, 1984.

33. Jenike MA: *Handbook of Geriatric Psychopharmacology.* Littleton, MA, PSG Publishing, 1985.

Chapter 103

PARAPHRENIAS AND OTHER PSYCHOSES

Leila B. Laitman and Kenneth L. Davis

Paraphrenia and other late-onset psychoses are poorly understood; nonetheless, as many as 15 to 33 percent of schizophrenic patients have an onset after age 40, and 5 to 14 percent after age 50.[1] The prevalence of primary psychoses in psychiatric patients with onset of illness of 60 years of age or older has been reported as anywhere from 2 to 3 percent[2,3] to 10 percent.[4,5] In a general population sample of subjects aged 65 or older, 0.1 percent were found to have some form of late-onset psychosis.[6] As high as these figures are, they do not include psychoses which are secondary to other illnesses, such as dementia, delirium, or affective disorder. Yet very little systematic research has been done on this group of late-life psychotic states.

One obstacle to the rigorous investigation of paraphrenia and related conditions is that the terminology has changed continually for more than 100 years. The terms *paranoia, paraphrenia,*[7] *late paraphrenia,*[4] *senile schizophrenia,*[8] *paranoid disorder,*[9] *delusional disorder,*[10] *paranoid hallucinosis,*[11] *schizophreniform psychosis,*[11,12] *schizophrenic syndrome,*[11] *reactive psychosis,*[12] *paranoid psychosis, paranoiac psychosis,*[13] and *late-onset paranoid schizophrenia*[10] have all been used to describe late-onset psychoses. Many diagnostic categories overlap, and there are no universally accepted diagnostic criteria for the late-onset psychoses. Indeed, the term *paraphrenia* does not even appear in the *Diagnostic and Statistical Manual of Mental Disorders*, Third Edition, Revised (DSM III-R), the major American diagnostic resource which revised and replaced DSM III. The intent of this chapter is (1) to discuss these nosologic issues in an attempt to clarify the terminology which has confounded research and treatment efforts for so long and (2) to raise a few implications for future research.

DEFINITION OF TERMS

The two primary paranoid psychoses found in the elderly—paraphrenia and delusional (paranoid) disorder—will be the focus of this chapter. In the early twentieth century, Kraepelin defined *paranoia* as a state in which there were completely systematized delusions of a jealous or persecutory nature, without the presence of hallucinations. He devised the term "paraphrenia" for the state characterized by paranoia and hallucinations. In both conditions, patients' symptoms remained essentially unchanged over the course of the illness. The later onset of symptoms and nondeteriorating course set paraphrenic patients apart from those with "dementia praecox," which is now called schizophrenia.[7]

In the 1930s, doubt was cast on the unchanging nature of Kraepelin's patients. Kolle and Mayer-Gross followed Kraepelin's paraphrenic group and learned that in the majority the diagnosis had been changed to schizophrenia.[14,15] Thus, whether paraphrenia was a true diagnostic entity or was simply a variant of schizophrenia or some other diagnosis in the elderly remained unclear. As a consequence, the term was discarded by the psychiatric community, and elderly patients with paranoid symptoms were considered to have arteriosclerosis, senile dementia, or an "involutional" diagnosis.

In 1955, the term *paraphrenia* was reintroduced by Roth[4] to describe schizophrenia of late onset. Roth found that about 10 percent of all first-admission elderly psychiatric patients were schizophrenic and usually paranoid. These patients had no evidence of dementia or serious affective illness. He called them "late paraphrenics" because they fit the clinical picture of paraphrenia described by Kraepelin but had a late onset of illness. Subsequently, Kay and Roth[16] described late paraphrenia more fully as a psychiatric disorder of late onset (usually after age 60) involving paranoid delusions and possibly hallucinations (including auditory, visual, tactile, and olfactory) without evidence of dementia or primary affective disorder. The patient's overall personality does not change in late paraphrenia as it does in schizophrenia. There is little, if any, looseness of association, affective incongruity, blunting, loss of volition, or other classical negative symptoms of schizophrenia.

In essence, paraphrenia is somewhat of an intermediate state between paranoia, as Kraepelin described it, and paranoid schizophrenia, as defined by DSM III.[9] In paranoia, hallucinations could not accompany the paranoid delusions, whereas in paraphrenia they could. Paranoid schizophrenia, too, is characterized by both paranoid delusions and hallucinations; however, the course is one of deterioration in level of functioning and change in overall personality. So paraphrenia develops later in life and is unassociated with many symptoms frequently found in paranoid schizophrenia, yet meets DSM III criteria for schizophrenia except for age of onset.

Paraphrenia is a primary paranoid psychosis of late onset by its very definition. Delusional (paranoid) disorder, however, is a primary paranoid psychosis that can appear for the first time in late life, although it more frequently appears in younger patients. Paranoia as Kraepelin described it is considered by DSM III to be one of the "paranoid disorders," the others being "shared paranoid disorder" and "acute paranoid state." The paranoid disorders are defined by DSM III as states in which there is an insidiously developing delusional system in the presence of otherwise clear and orderly thinking. The delusions are of a persecutory or jealous nature. There is no age-of-onset cutoff. Hallucinations would exclude patients from this diagnosis. There is no evidence of organic, affective, or schizophrenic illness.[9]

So paraphrenia differs from paranoid disorder in two ways: (1) hallucinations may be present in paraphrenia but not in paranoid disorders, and (2) age of onset of paraphrenia is generally over age 60, whereas there is no minimum age of onset for paranoid disorder.

It is interesting to note that paraphrenia is not represented at all in DSM III. It is listed in the index, where readers are referred to a discussion of paranoid disorder. Bizarre delusions and prominent auditory hallucinations are exclusion criteria for paranoid disorder, and criteria for schizophrenia could not accommodate onset after age 45. Thus true paraphrenia could only be classified as an "atypical psychosis" in DSM III.

In the recent revision of DSM III (DSM III-R), the paranoid disorders are renamed as delusional (paranoid) disorders. In this new diagnostic category, delusions are no longer confined to those of persecution and jealousy but now include the following subtypes: erotomanic, grandiose, jealous, persecutory, somatic, and unspecified.[10] Thus many more patients can be classified as having this diagnosis, and, as a consequence, far fewer patients with late-life psychoses are classified as "atypical" cases. The former subtypes of paranoid disorder in DSM III, "paranoia," "shared paranoid disorder," and "acute paranoid disorder," have been eliminated in DSM III-R and subsumed in other categories. In the new category of delusional (paranoid) disorders, patients may have hallucinations if the hallucinations are not prominent. It is thus conceivable that some patients with late paraphrenia as described by Roth can now be classified in DSM III-R as having delusional (paranoid) disorder. Indeed, paraphrenia still does not appear as a diagnostic category in DSM III-R. If delusions are very bizarre or if hallucinations are quite prominent, DSM III-R provides for a late-onset schizophrenia which develops after age 45.

VALIDATORS OF DSM III-R

DSM III-R has chosen to avoid the term *paraphrenia*, but allows for later-life-onset schizophrenia. Therefore, the patient who has onset of primary psychosis in old age can be diagnosed as having either delusional (paranoid) disorder or paranoid schizophrenia, late onset. However, the question that must be asked is whether this nosologic system is correct. Is paraphrenia a separate entity from delusional disorder or late-life schizophrenia? Is it even possible that paraphrenia or delusional disorder in the elderly are subtypes of affective illness? These and similar queries speak to the issue of diagnostic validity.

To address the validity of these diagnostic categories, the available data will be organized into three categories: (1) antecedent validators, (2) concurrent validators, and (3) predictive validators. Antecedent validators include family history, premorbid personality, demographic factors, and precipitating events. Concurrent validators are symptoms and biological markers. Predictive validators encompass diagnostic consistency over time, outcome data, and therapeutic response. These data must be viewed with some reservation as the terminology and methodology are not consistent across studies from which information on validity was extracted. For example, the data on delusional (paranoid) disorder derives from patients below age 60.

ANTECEDENT VALIDATORS
Family History

Europeans view paraphrenia as being part of a spectrum of schizophrenia-like disorders. Data from family history studies have indicated increased incidence of schizophrenia in the first-degree relatives of late-onset paranoid patients, as compared to incidence of schizophrenia in the general population.[7,11,17] However, the expectancy rate of 2.5 percent for schizophrenia in the siblings of paraphrenics is significantly less than the 7.4 percent expectancy rate for schizophrenia among the siblings of younger schizophrenics.[17]

Other data indicate that relatives of elderly paranoid patients have an increased overall expectancy for any psychosis of the same magnitude as that found in first-degree relatives of schizophrenics and manic-depressives.[16,17] There is mildly increased expectancy for personality disorders, as compared to expectancy for the community at large.[18] Thus, paraphrenia differs in genetic pattern from schizophrenia. Familial linkage does seem to exist, but to be any more specific than linkage to psychoses is difficult to establish.

The familial relationship between delusional (paranoid) disorder and schizophrenia is also rather weak. Some data have shown an increased prevalence of schizophrenia (but not significantly increased) in relatives of patients with paranoid psychoses similar to Kraepelin's concept of "paranoia" when compared to controls.[19] Most reports, however, have found no increased risk of schizophrenia in the first-degree relatives of paranoid psychotic probands.[17,20,21] Affective disorder, as well, seems to be unrelated to delusional disorder from family history data.[17,22]

The family history of the delusional disorder patient shows major chronic psychiatric illness in excess of normal expectations, if anything. The illness is similar in kind to the illness in the proband. This suggests a qualitative difference from nonparanoid schizophrenia in that the delusional disorder "breeds true."[23] Still, family studies do not demonstrate that delusional disorder clusters strongly in families.[24]

Thus, paraphrenia has been compared to schizophrenia and to affective illness through family history studies. A direct comparison with delusional disorder has not been done, nor has delusional disorder been studied in the elderly. The family history data point to paraphrenia being a condition distinct from schizophrenia and affective illness. The data tentatively suggest that delusional disorder is a separate entity from schizophrenia and affective disorder, and from paraphrenia as well.

Premorbid Personality

The retrospective determination of premorbid personality carries with it many methodological difficulties and must be viewed with caution. The premorbid personality of paraphrenia seems to be predominantly paranoid and schizoid in type. Common traits are jealousy, suspiciousness, arrogance, egocentricity, emotional coldness, and extreme solitariness.[16,18]

A particular type of premorbid personality has not been established for delusional disorder patients. Compared to schizophrenics, they are less likely to be schizoid, introverted, or submissive, and more likely to have inferiority feelings[24] and to be hypersensitive.[13]

The premorbid personality data add little to the validity of the diagnosis of paraphrenia. The specific familial link to marked inferiority feelings in delusional disorder patients can be interpreted to mean that the personality prone to delusional disorder is different from that prone to schizophrenia. Beyond that, premorbid personality has not been a helpful validator for the diagnosis of delusional disorder.

Demographic and Precipitating Factors

In paraphrenia, females predominate over males in the ratio of about 7:1. Paraphrenic patients of both sexes are unlikely to be married or to have children. As compared with affective disorder patients, significantly more paraphrenics were living alone and were socially isolated at the time they became ill (40 percent of paraphrenics vs. 12 percent of affective disorder patients).[16] Interestingly, deafness seems to play a large part in the isolation. An association between acquired deafness and paranoid illness in the elderly has been demonstrated.[2,16,25] Paraphrenic patients also have significantly more cataracts and far vision problems than do affective disorder patients.[26]

Age-at-onset data suggest that paraphrenia is separate from schizophrenia but may be part of a continuum in late life.[1,4,13,27] Most schizophrenics emerge as such before age 30. While catatonic and hebephrenic conditions generally emerge in the twenties, paranoid schizophrenic conditions invariably emerge later. Data has shown that most schizophrenics with onset after 40 are paranoid and that patients with the older-age-of-onset and late-onset psychoses are for the most part paranoid.

It is not clear whether delusional disorder patients are more likely to be male or female.[13,28] Marriage rates were significantly higher in delusional disorder patients than in schizophrenics.[13,29] Delusional disorder patients have been reported to be more socially isolated and to have more "conflicts of conscience" than schizophrenics. They are more likely to have a precipitating factor, such as immigration, than are schizophrenics, who often have none.[30] Age-at-onset data show delusional disorder patients to be older than schizophrenics at time of onset of illness.[13,14,24,28,29]

So, paraphrenia has later age of onset than schizophrenia, but not distinctly so. Delusional disorder patients have onset at older ages than typical schizophrenics. Social isolation and sensory loss are strong premorbid factors in both delusional disorder and paraphrenia as compared to schizophrenia and affective disorder. The distinctness of the diagnoses of paraphrenia and delusional disorder is supported weakly by these data.

CONCURRENT VALIDATORS

Symptoms

The typical paraphrenic is similar to the schizophrenic, except for the absence of thought disorder and the fact that personality remains basically unchanged from the premorbid state.[16] Paranoid delusions and hallucinations (including auditory, visual, tactile, and olfactory) may be present together, or the delusions may occur alone. Delusions may be as bizarre as they are in schizophrenia, including delusions of influence and passivity. Frequent themes involve sexual molestation, poisoning, or other bodily harm. Paraphrenics may believe that lethal gases are being pumped into their homes or that their food and water are poisoned. They complain of being stabbed, cut, irradiated, or otherwise bodily manipulated by persons in distant settings. They feel controlled by demonic instruments or machines. Hallucinations may be voices communicating about the patient in the third person. While incoherence of speech and even neologisms occur, they are unusual except in cases of long duration. In general there is initially no looseness of association and only mild affective incongruity, affective blunting, or loss of volition.[16,18] Studies that examined diagnostic criteria for late paraphrenia found them compatible with DSM III criteria for paranoid schizophrenia except that age of onset is over age 45.[31,32]

Delusional disorder commonly manifests itself by delusions concerning marriage, plots, and being unfairly treated. Delusions of reference, jealousy, and persecution are common. Delusions in schizophrenia and in paraphrenia are typically more bizarre than in delusional disorder. Delusional disorder in DSM III differs from schizophrenia in that patients do not hallucinate or have thought disorder along with their delusions.[23]

In DSM III-R, the age-45 cutoff for onset has been removed from paranoid schizophrenia, and a late-onset subcategory now exists. Late paraphrenia as a diagnosis is now compatible with a late-onset schizophrenia from the symptomatic point of view. The symptomatology of delusional (paranoid) disorder in DSM III-R has been expanded to include persecutory, jealous, erotomanic, somatic, grandiose, and other types of delusions. Hallucinations may be present if they are not prominent. No thought disorder is present. Some paraphrenics might meet these criteria as well. Thus, diagnostic criteria for paraphrenia continue to overlap with both late-onset schizophrenia, paranoid type, and delusional (paranoid) disorder in DSM III-R. From a symptomatic point of

view, delusional disorder is distinct from schizophrenia but not from paraphrenia.

Biological Markers

There have been little (if any) biological data using techniques of modern biological psychiatry to validate either the diagnosis of paraphrenia or delusional disorder.

PREDICTIVE VALIDATORS

Diagnostic Consistency Over Time

Kraepelin originally believed that paraphrenia was a chronic, unremitting condition that did not progress to a state in which patients could no longer function, think clearly, or take care of themselves.[7] Follow-up of his paraphrenic group, however, showed that in most cases the diagnosis had been changed to schizophrenia. Most data agree that the clinical changes seen over time in patients diagnosed with paraphrenia are the same as those seen in schizophrenia. At least 40 percent of paraphrenic patients progress to paranoid schizophrenia. However, the pronounced deterioration of intellect, personality, and habits that occurs in some chronic schizophrenic patients is not usual in paraphrenics. Paraphrenic patients, for the most part, remain clean, tidy, and generally well-conducted.[14,15,16] Paraphrenics are often able to survive well in noninstitutional settings because they can carry on the activities of daily living quite adeptly. Younger schizophrenics, however, more often require some kind of institutionalization even after active symptoms have subsided as they have a marked disintegration of previous personality and ability to care for themselves.[11,22]

In delusional disorder, there seems to be longitudinal diagnostic consistency.[17,33] Only a small portion (3 to 22 percent) of patients eventually develop schizophrenia. No more than 6 percent of delusional disorder patients evolve into affective disorder patients.[24] Thus, on this parameter, the validity of the delusional disorder diagnosis is established. The paraphrenia diagnosis is not as durable over time. It is not consistently possible to separate paraphrenia from schizophrenia based on these data.

Outcome Data

The outcome of paraphrenia was originally regarded as poor. This may have been due to the fact that data existed only on hospitalized patients. Many paraphrenics, however, never require hospitalization and never come to medical attention. Another factor implicating poor outcome for paraphrenia was that much of the original data was collected before the advent of the use of neuroleptics. Efforts at psychological therapy are usually unrewarding, although situational or environmental manipulation can sometimes produce symptomatic response.[34] Electroconvulsive therapy (ECT) has been tried, but it is usually helpful only in cases in which there are significant affective symptoms.[35] Outcome, however, is not as poor as it once seemed. Neuroleptics and community-based therapeutic programs have allowed many paraphrenics to lead independent lives, free from hospitalization.

In general, the outcome of delusional disorder patients is good in that most are discharged from hospitals back to the community, with fewer rehospitalizations than occur with schizophrenics.[13,23] Paraphrenics and delusional disorder patients are equally able to function occupationally and socially despite their symptoms, whereas schizophrenics are not. Thus, a distinction from schizophrenia is apparent.

Therapeutic Response

Treatment of paraphrenic symptoms with adequate initial and maintenance neuroleptic therapy has been shown to lead to the disappearance or attenuation of symptoms. There is striking improvement in the long-term outcome of paraphrenia with neuroleptic treatment. Factors predicting a good outcome for patients were (1) immediate response to treatment, (2) insight gained secondary to treatment, (3) success in maintaining a longer period of drug treatment, (4) marriage, (5) younger age, and (6) good premorbid relationships predicting cooperation during maintenance treatment.[11] Outpatients often have poor compliance with taking oral medication. It has been found that giving an extremely low dose of a long-acting depot intramuscular neuroleptic preparation can be an effective and safe treatment when "crisis intervention" for the paraphrenic is necessary.[36]

Delusional disorder is most often treated with neuroleptics as well. No placebo control studies have been done. Neuroleptics seem helpful initially, but results are not dramatic. Patients remain symptomatic but able to function socially. Psychotherapy had similar effects. The effect of ECT is not delineated.[23,24] Neuroleptics are nonspecific treatments, and thus the validity of neither paraphrenia nor delusional disorders can be established on this parameter. Nonetheless, some similarity with schizophrenia is suggested by the parallel in responsivity to the same class of drugs.

SUMMARY

Let us now attempt to answer a series of critical questions regarding the paraphrenias and other late-life psychoses.

Are the DSM III-R diagnostic categories of delusional (paranoid) disorder and paranoid schizophrenia, late onset, sufficient to give a diagnosis to all patients who have onset of primary psychosis in old age that is not a nosologic afterthought?

The answer is a qualified yes. Looking purely at the majority of concurrent validating data on symptoms, there is a consensus that the illness called "late paraphrenia" in Europe is compatible with a late-onset schizophrenia. The problem with DSM-III was that there was an age cutoff for schizophrenia of age 45. Now that a subcategory or late-onset type exists in DSM III-R, the diagnosis should no longer be classified as "atypical" psychosis. The elderly onset psychotic patient can also be diagnosed as having delusional (paranoid) disorder if hallucinations are not prominent and there is no thought disorder. According to DSM III-R criteria, delusions can be persecutory, jealous, erotomanic, somatic, grandiose, or "other."

Is paraphrenia a separate entity from delusional (paranoid) disorder and schizophrenia?

This question of diagnostic validity is still difficult to answer. Paraphrenia has been compared with schizophrenia and with affective illness. A direct comparison with delusional disorder has not been done, nor has delusional disorder been studied in the elderly. The antecedent validator of family history points to paraphrenia being distinct from schizophrenia. Family studies suggest that delusional disorder is not closely related to schizophrenia but does have a familial link to inferiority feelings. Thus, there are tentative data that paraphrenia seems to be a separate entity from schizophrenia and delusional disorder.

Premorbid personality does not conclusively separate paraphrenia from schizophrenia, although paraphrenics seem to be more hypersensitive premorbidly. The typical paraphrenic has a schizoid or paranoid premorbid personality. Delusional disorder patients differ from schizophrenics in that they have more inferiority feelings than do schizophrenics and are less schizoid, submissive, and introverted. The question of delineation of paraphrenia from delusional disorder cannot be answered from these data.

Paraphrenia has later age of onset than schizophrenia, but the older the age of onset of schizophrenia, the more likely it is to be of a paranoid variety. So it is not clear whether paraphrenia is merely a very late onset schizophrenia or a distinct entity based on available data. Delusional disorder patients have onset at older ages than do typical schizophrenics.

Social isolation and sensory loss seem to be strong premorbid factors in both delusional disorder and paraphrenia, as compared to schizophrenia and affective illness. Thus, paraphrenia and delusional disorder can be separated from schizophrenia on these parameters but not from each other.

The symptoms of paraphrenia overlap with both delusional disorder and schizophrenia. No consistent diagnostic criteria exist for paraphrenia. It is not possible to differentiate paraphrenia from delusional disorder or schizophrenia based on symptomatology.

There have been virtually no biological investigations of the molecular or cellular basis for paraphrenia or delusional disorder as there have been for schizophrenia and affective illness. Whether these illnesses can be differentiated on biological measures from each other or from illnesses which display early onset of symptoms demands investigation.

The predictive validator of longitudinal diagnostic consistency points to paraphrenia being some type of schizophrenia. Delusional disorder seems to remain diagnostically consistent over time. Outcome, however, is better for both paraphrenics and delusional disorder patients than it is for schizophrenics. Paraphrenics and delusional disorder patients also are less likely to be chronically institutionalized than are schizophrenics. Although paraphrenics respond to treatment as schizophrenics do, neuroleptics are nonspecific treatments. The symptoms of delusional disorder patients do not seem to respond as well to treatment, but the patients can still function. Thus, the parameter of treatment response does not separate paraphrenia from delusional disorder or schizophrenia.

Could paraphrenia or delusional disorder in the elderly be subtypes of affective illness?

Neither illness seems to be related to affective disorder. This is borne out by all validators, although delusional disorder has not been studied in the elderly.

Until DSM III-R, American psychiatry had been lumping too many diagnoses together into "atypical" categories. The addition of a late-onset category in schizophrenia and the acceptance of the Kraepelinian description of paranoia, with subtypes of persecutory, jealous, erotomanic, somatic, grandiose, and "other" for delusional (paranoid) disorder, are major steps in recognizing diagnostic realities that have been evident for years in European literature.

FINAL THOUGHTS

Now that a clearer nosology exists, it would be useful to launch an epidemiological study to determine the incidence and prevalence of these late-life paranoid states. Additional family studies must be done to clarify the genetic relationship, if any, to schizophrenia or affective disorder, and to determine if these conditions "breed

true." Modern biological methodology must be applied to these patients. The areas of personality integration, sensory loss, and life expectancy are also underinvestigated and might yield a great deal of data on the process of schizophrenia and of aging. Finally, rigorous psychopharmacological treatment studies need to be conducted. Until these kinds of data are collected, it will not be possible to know conclusively if late-onset psychoses are merely subtypes of illnesses that appear in the young or are unique entities in themselves.

REFERENCES

1. Larson C, Nyman G: Age of onset in schizophrenia. *Hum Hered* 20:241, 1970.
2. Leuchter AF, Spar JE: The late-onset psychoses: Clinical and diagnostic features. *J Nerv Ment Dis* 173:488, 1985.
3. Fish F: Senile schizophrenia. *J Ment Sci* 106:938, 1960.
4. Roth M: The natural history of mental disorder in old age. *J Ment Sci* 101:281, 1955.
5. Blessed G, Wilson ID: The contemporary natural history of mental disorder in old age. *Br J Psychiatry* 141:59, 1982.
6. Kay DWK et al: Old age mental disorders in Newcastle-upon-Tyne. *Br J Psychiatry* 110:146, 1964.
7. Kraepelin E: *Dementia Praecox and Paraphrenia*, reprint of 1919 ed. New York, Krieger, 1971.
8. Fish F: Senile schizophrenia. *J Ment Sci* 106:938, 1960.
9. American Psychiatric Association: *Diagnostic and Statistical Manual of Mental Disorders*, 3d ed. Washington, American Psychiatric Association, 1980.
10. American Psychiatric Association: *Diagnostic and Statistical Manual of Mental Disorders*, 3d ed, revised. Washington, American Psychiatric Association, 1987.
11. Post F: *Persistent Persecutory States of the Elderly*. Oxford, Pergamon Press, 1966.
12. Langfeldt G: The prognosis in schizophrenia and the factors influencing the course of the disease. *Acta Psychiatr Neurol Scand* (suppl 13):1, 1937.
13. Retterstol N: *Paranoid and Paranoiac Psychoses*. Springfield, Ill, Charles C. Thomas, 1966.
14. Kolle K: *Die Primare Verrucktheit*. Leipzig, Thieme, 1931.
15. Mayer-Gross W: *Die Schizophrenie*. Berlin, Springer, 1932.
16. Kay DWK, Roth M: Environmental and hereditary factors in the schizophrenia of old age ("late paraphrenia") and their bearing on the general problem of causation in schizophrenia. *J Ment Sci* 107:649, 1961.
17. Funding T: Genetics of paranoid psychoses of later life. *Acta Psychiatr Scand* 37:267, 1961.
18. Herbert ME, Jacobson S: Late paraphrenia. *Br J Psychiatry* 113:461, 1967.
19. Debray Q: A genetic study of chronic delusions. *Neuropsychobiology* 1:313, 1975.
20. Watt JAG et al: Paranoid states of middle life: Familial occurrence and relationship to schizophrenia. *Acta Psychiatr Scand* 61:413, 1980.
21. Kendler K, Hays P: Paranoid psychoses (delusional dis-

order) and schizophrenia: A family history study. *Arch Gen Psychiatry* 38:547, 1981.

22. Bridge TP, Wyatt JW: Paraphrenia: Paranoid states of late life. II. American research. *J Am Geriatr Soc* 28:201, 1980.

23. Winokur G: Delusional disorder (paranoia). *Compr Psychiatry* 18:511, 1977.

24. Kendler K: The nosologic validity of paranoia (simple delusional disorder). *Arch Gen Psychiatry* 37:699, 1980.

25. Cooper AF et al: Hearing loss in paranoid and affective psychoses of the elderly. *Lancet* 1:851, 1974.

26. Cooper AF, Porter R: Visual acuity and ocular pathology in the paranoid and affective psychoses of later life. *J Psychosom Res* 20:107, 1976.

27. Astrup C et al: *Prognosis in Functional Psychoses.* Springfield, Ill, Charles C. Thomas, 1962.

28. Rimón R et al.: A sociopsychiatric study of paranoid psychoses. *Acta Psychiatr Scand* 40(suppl 180):335, 1964.

29. Bonner H: The problem of diagnosis in paranoiac disorder. *Am J Psychiatry* 107:677, 1951.

30. Eitinger L: The symptomatology of mental disease among refugees in Norway. *J Ment Sci* 106:947, 1960.

31. Grahame PS: Schizophrenia in old age (late paraphrenia) *Br J Psychiatry* 145:493, 1984.

32. Craig TJ, Bregman Z: Late onset schizophrenia-like illness. *J Am Geriatr Soc* 36:104, 1988.

33. Retterstol N: Jealousy-paranoiac psychoses. *Acta Psychiatr Scand* 43:75, 1968.

34. Raskind M: Paranoid syndromes in the elderly, in Eisdorfer C, Fann WE (eds): *Treatment of Psychopathology in the Aging.* New York, Springer, 1982, p 184.

35. Bridge TP, Wyatt JW: Paraphrenia: Paranoid states of late life. I. European research. *J Am Geriatr Soc* 28:193, 1980.

36. Raskind M: Fluphenazine enanthate in the outpatient treatment of late paraphrenia. *J Am Geriatr Soc* 27:459, 1979.

Chapter 104

AGING OF THE CHRONICALLY NEUROPSYCHOLOGICALLY IMPAIRED

Steven R. Gambert

DEFINING THE PROBLEM

Despite a decline in the incidence of birth defects over the past few decades, many persons are alive today who were born with disabilities affecting proper growth and development and lifelong functioning. Although both inherited and congenital disabilities may affect numerous aspects of functioning, this chapter will focus only on those persons with chronic neuropsychological impairments (CNI), often referred to as *mental retardation*.

Mental retardation has been defined by any one or a combination of the following: IQ test score, social adaptability, neurological functioning, and behavioral competence. The most widely accepted classification refers to a general intellectual functioning that is significantly below average and exists concurrently with deficits in adaptive behavior; changes must have manifested during the developmental period. While some prefer four categories of mental retardation, (mild, moderate, severe, and profound) others use only two (mild and severe). Mild retardation is defined as an IQ of less than 70 or two standard deviations below the mean with a concurrent impairment in adaptive behavior; severe retardation is defined as an IQ below 50. Modern medicine has improved our capacity to provide preventive health care and treat problems early in their course. Even those limited by some genetic defect are living longer than ever before, and the life span for many persons with CNI now approaches that of the general population.

Those with CNI are often grouped epidemiologically with persons with other developmental disabilities, including chronic epilepsy, autism, and cerebral palsy.

Although each has its own set of distinct problems, many similarities exist. Full independence throughout life is often difficult in all groups especially during later life after a decline in primary family support. Because of considerable overlap between these disorders, there is great difficulty in ensuring exactly how many persons exist in each category.

In the 1980 census, 150,000 persons over the age of 60 were listed as having a lifelong neuropsychological impairment. Most agree that this number greatly underestimates those with CNI. Lubin reported the prevalence of older adults with CNI to be 4.5 per 1000 general population or 1.5 million persons over the age of 60.[1] As an overall estimate of persons with mental retardation, the Association for Retarded Citizens has historically used 3.0 percent of the general population. This is in contrast to 0.4 percent of the population with chronic epilepsy and 0.3 percent with cerebral palsy. Stratification of data by age, however, is less certain. Although data regarding the prevalence of persons with severe mental retardation is easier to find and reports range from 3 to 5 per 1000 general population, identifying persons with mild mental retardation is more difficult. Many escape recognition until later in life when aged parents can no longer provide the structured environment necessary to meet daily needs. Many persons with mild CNI perform minor tasks in order to maintain financial independence. This may become increasingly more difficult as age-related disorders couple with underlying CNI to prevent continued employment; economic loss may force one to seek public assistance or even institutional living.

LIFE EXPECTANCY

Recent decades have seen a dramatic rise in the average life expectancy of the general population. Although those with CNI share in this increase, they continue to have higher age-specific mortality rates. As a group, average life expectancy for persons with CNI is 59.1 years. Those with Down's syndrome, or trisomy 21, can expect to live, on average, 54.0 years. This is no small achievement since Down's syndrome babies could expect to live only 9 years in 1929, 12 to 15 years in 1947, and 18.3 years in 1961. While most of this change has been attributed to the decline in childhood mortality resulting from improved preventive health care, immunization programs, and a philosophy of active intervention, changes have also been noted after maturity. While genetic defects may be difficult to resolve, i.e., increased amyloid deposits in the brains of persons with Down's syndrome, persons with CNI resulting from problems such as cerebral anoxia should not be expected to live any less than the general population. Unfortunately, mental retardation is not a pure entity and coexisting problems are common. Such problems include, among other disorders, nutritional abnormalities and increased risk of infections, especially in those living in institutional settings. Crowding and closed environments may lead to a high exposure to infectious diseases, including *Neisseria* meningitis, influenza, tuberculosis, and hepatitis. Diets may be less than optimal, especially for those with limited attention spans requiring individualized feeding programs. Mass cooking practices may also result in suboptimal nutrition. Efforts to deinstitutionalize those persons with CNI have already realized benefits and should continue to increase life span. Although many factors have historically been associated with the decision to institutionalize a given person, including severity of disability, gender, ethnicity, associated handicaps, and availability of community services, current trends favor deinstitutionalization whenever possible.

DOWN'S SYNDROME

The most commonly identified genetic abnormality is Down's syndrome, or trisomy 21. Despite the fact that few persons with Down's syndrome live beyond their fifties, this entity has long fascinated gerontologists. It has been reported that nearly all individuals with Down's syndrome over the age of 40 have neuropathological changes consistent with Alzheimer's disease, i.e., neurofibrillary tangles, plaques, and nucleovascuolar degeneration.[2,3] Recent data identifying a genetic defect on chromosome 21 in familial cases of Alzheimer's disease lend further support to the hypothesis linking these

two disorders.[4] Despite neuropathological findings suggestive of an Alzheimer-type dementia in almost all persons over 40 with Down's syndrome, however, a diagnosis of clinical dementia cannot be made to the same degree of certainty in this population. Limited attention span may interfere with one's ability to properly assess mental status. When a change in cognition is identified, however, coexisting dementia must be considered. Changes in behavior, increased regressive tendencies, or loss of learned behavior may be suggestive of degenerative changes. It is equally as important, however, not to blame all changes on a presumed diagnosis of Alzheimer's disease. As with all cases of dementia, all treatable causes must be considered, especially in a population at risk for trauma, infections, drug toxicities, nutritional abnormalities, etc.

COEXISTING MEDICAL CONDITIONS

Persons with CNI often have coexisting medical problems and physical disabilities, factors which are particularly pronounced during later life. Poor health screening and lack of preventive measures may result in an accelerated aging process; diseases may occur at an earlier age than in the general population. Table 104-1 lists problems more commonly noted in adult persons with CNI as compared to the general population.

Scoliosis may progress and result in frequent muscular strain and backaches. Advanced disease may eventually compromise normal respiratory function leading to decreased pulmonary reserve and infection. Down's syndrome patients frequently have poor ligamentous support for the cervical spine. This can result in a subluxation of the cervical spine that may lead to paraplegia and even quadriplegia. Radiological monitoring of this problem is advised; cervical collars and even cervical spine fusion are well-recognized preventive measures.

TABLE 104-1
Problems More Commonly Found in Persons with CNI

1. Scoliosis
2. Cervical spine subluxation
3. Hip dislocation
4. Dental caries and gingivitis
5. Nutritional deficiency states
6. Obesity
7. Visual abnormalities
8. Hearing deficits
9. Seizure disorders
10. Medication toxicity
11. Emotional disorders (including "institutional behavior")
12. Dementia

Untreated hip dislocation can lead to loss of mobility; this may greatly hamper one's ability to be independent and may accelerate other changes including demineralization of the bones and reduced muscular and cardiovascular fitness.

One of the most common findings in adult persons with Down's syndrome is poor dentition and gingival disease. This often leads to loss of teeth, discomfort, and difficulty in chewing. When coupled with poor attention span, nutritional problems may become significant. Dentures are rarely accepted by persons with CNI, and few dentists are willing to take the extra time and effort needed to fit them properly. Lifelong attention to good dental hygiene is the best way to prevent dental and gingival disease in this population. A program ensuring proper brushing and flossing prior to bedtime is a minimal necessity when twice daily oral care is not possible. Regular visits to the dentist and fluoride treatments during early life also help maintain a healthy oral environment.

As stated above, nutritional problems are frequently encountered. In certain cases diets may contain excessive quantities of calories, salt, and fats, especially for those living within institutional settings. This increases the risk of developing atherosclerotic cardiovascular disease, hypertension, obesity, and even cancer late in life. Obesity, further exacerbated by diminished physical activity, may accelerate articular changes in weight-bearing joints and may also increase the risk of developing type 11 diabetes. Dietary deficiencies in calcium, minerals, and vitamins may also be noted. The use of dietary supplements may be necessary if certain nutrients are not being consumed on a regular basis. Multiple small, but well-balanced, meals are often better tolerated. An adequate intake of protein (0.8 g/kg body weight) is essential.

Regular screening to detect changes in hearing is advised. Congenital hearing deficits are not uncommon in this population, and age-related changes may result in a functional disturbance earlier than otherwise expected. Isolation, apathy, declining cognition, and impaired communication may be the only signs of hearing impairment. Any change in daily care pattern or ability to interact with others must be explored and hearing deficits carefully evaluated. Although newer hearing aids are capable of selectively increasing certain frequency sounds, thus improving functional hearing, many persons with CNI lack the interest or capacity to wear an assistive device. For this reason, care providers and health professionals must speak slowly and use amplifying devices whenever a hearing problem exists. Since neurosensory hearing loss may make discrimination of sounds more difficult, extraneous sounds should be reduced as much as possible and attempts should be made to use an FM amplifier with individual headsets to improve direct communication.

Although congenital vision problems are common, age-related changes and age-prevalent diseases affecting vision may further compromise function. Keratoconus, glaucoma, and cataracts usually present at a more advanced stage due to difficulty in eliciting vision changes in this population. Screening programs that hopefully detect and treat problems early are encouraged.

Regardless of the severity of mental retardation, emotional disorders must be anticipated and recognized. Loss of loved ones, family, roommates, and care providers may precipitate an emotional crisis; an atypical presentation may be the only warning. All attempts should be made to limit changes in environmental surroundings and anticipate stressful situations. An impaired judgment in social situations may require that help be given to form new friendships despite an advanced age. Once formed, however, bonding is usually strong even in those with severe mental retardation. Social interactions are important in promoting self-esteem and avoiding feelings of isolation. Institutionalization is thought to decrease feelings of self-reliance. The least restrictive, yet safe, environment should be chosen.

Much like the general aging population, feelings of loss, loneliness, and depression may be noted. While emotional disorders may be reactive to specific handicaps, at times no specific cause can be found. In either case, a careful review of medications and assessment of physical well-being is advised in order that treatable problems be dealt with as early as possible. Changes in function such as ability to conduct one's activities of daily living, interest in attending group activities and workshops, sleep/wake cycles, or sexual behavior may indicate a deeper emotional disorder in need of investigation and treatment.

A decline in cognition or "dementia" is often difficult to detect until gross changes have been noted. Depending on underlying pathology and baseline functioning, subtle changes in behavior may be the only warning sign that a dementia exists. Although persons with Down's syndrome have a greater chance of developing dementia of the Alzheimer type after age 40, other causes of dementia should be considered and ruled out prior to making a definitive diagnosis. Antiseizure medications should be continually evaluated and monitored and attempts made to discontinue therapy under close supervision as indicated. These medications have a significant potential for interacting with other medications, and the physician must watch carefully for toxicities. The long-term use of phenytoin, for example, has been associated with osteomalacia, ataxia, and gingival hyperplasia; early recognition of these problems may reduce morbidity.

With advancing age and decreased reserve capability, falls from seizures may increase the risk of fractures from direct trauma and cerebral, cardiac, and renal damage from transient hypotension and cerebral anoxia. Care providers should be advised as to what precautions are necessary. In those instances where seizures do not respond to pharmacological therapy, protective head gear and joint padding may be essential.

The prevalence of medical conditions in elderly persons with CNI is somewhat different from age-matched cognitively intact individuals. Although many of the problems listed in Table 104-1 occur more frequently in persons with CNI than in the general population, they do not necessarily represent the most commonly noted problems. Table 104-2 lists in order those conditions found most commonly in a geriatric assessment program.[5]

AGING AND CNI

While Down's syndrome is the most frequent genetic cause of CNI, it is responsible for less than 30 percent of cases of CNI in those over 50 years of age and less than 5 percent of cases in those over 65. Cerebral anoxia at birth appears to be the major cause of CNI in this elderly population. A variety of other genetic and environmental causes may also be responsible.

Elderly persons with CNI are indeed at double jeopardy. Advanced age and mental retardation may result in problems not encountered in either population when considered separately. Health professionals must consider not only those conditions associated with normal aging and age-prevalent disease, but also problems related to circumstances surrounding the CNI. In many cases, elderly persons with CNI have spent time within an institutional setting. Although recent decades have seen major changes in the ability to care for the disabled and although individual rights and freedoms are protected, the elderly person with CNI has lived in less illustrious times and can often bear witness to societal

and family abandonment. Despite advances, many problems still exist. In an attempt to provide structured activities for persons with CNI, those living in federally funded homes are required to continue to attend "workshop" activities comparable to going to work—regardless of advanced age. There is no option to "retire" unless physical ailments preclude activities. Even then, group homes find it increasingly difficult to keep those persons who do not leave the residence during the day—budgets simply do not allow for the increase in required staff. Many elderly persons with CNI, therefore, are facing premature dismissal from community residences to more restricted settings including nursing homes.

Although future generations of persons with CNI will most likely be living longer and leading more functional lives thanks to preventive health measures, the present cohort of elderly persons with CNI must still be considered at great risk of developing premature functional impairments. Deinstitutionalization throughout life, regular screening by a team of health professionals, and active intervention when necessary, including updating immunizations, can help maintain function throughout life.[5]

A comprehensive geriatric assessment program should be integrated with ongoing care. Despite little change in function, community-dwelling elderly persons with CNI are often thought to be in need of nursing home placement earlier than is necessary.[6] The perception of caregivers may be clouded by their inability to recognize and even care for many age-prevalent disorders. IQ and social adaptive age have not been shown to correlate with functional status, and ongoing individual assessment is necessary. An evaluation team combining individuals with expertise in both geriatric health care and CNI can impact greatly on clinical outcome and help maintain the older person with CNI in the community.

TABLE 104-2
Prevalence of Medical Conditions Noted in Elderly Persons with CNI Following Geriatric Assessment

1. Hearing deficit	80%
2. Dental problem	70%
3. Cardiovascular disease	60%
4. Gerontourinary problem	50%
5. Infectious disease	50%
6. Visual impairment	40%
7. Gastrointestinal disorder	40%
8. Endocrine disorder	40%
9. Rheumatologic problem	30%
10. Obesity	30%
11. Cerebrovascular disease	20%
12. Dermatologic condition	10%

REFERENCES

1. Lubin RA et al: Projected impact of the functional definition of developmental disabilities: The categorically disabled population and service eligibility. *Am J Ment Defic* 87:73, 1982.
2. Malanuid N: Neuropathology, in Stevens HA, Heba R (eds): *Mental Retardation*. Chicago, University of Chicago Press, 1964, p 429.
3. Mozar HN et al: Perspectives on the etiology of Alzheimer's disease. *JAMA* 257:1503, 1987.
4. St. George-Hyslop PH et al: The genetic defect causing familial Alzheimer's disease maps on chromosome 21. *Science* 235:885, 1987.
5. Gambert SR et al: Lifelong Preventive health care for elderly persons with disabilities. *J Assoc Persons Severe Handicaps* 12:292, 1987.
6. Gambert SR et al: Geriatric assessment of the mentally retarded elderly. *NY Med Q* 8:144, 1988.

Chapter 105

CHEMICAL DEPENDENCY IN THE ELDERLY

Patricia P. Barry

DEFINITIONS AND DIAGNOSTIC CRITERIA

As defined by the American College of Physicians, *chemical dependence* encompasses both alcohol and drug addiction and includes dependence upon three types of drugs: (1) social drugs, such as alcohol, (2) licit drugs, both prescription and nonprescription, and (3) illicit drugs. Additionally, in the absence of dependence, problem use may occur, including abuse, misuse, and overuse.[1] This chapter will specifically address the problems of chemical dependence upon alcohol, licit, and illicit drugs in the elderly.

The Revised Third Edition of the *Diagnostic and Statistical Manual of Mental Disorders* of the American Psychiatric Association, known as the *DSM III-R*, describes criteria for both psychoactive substance abuse and psychoactive substance dependence. *Abuse* includes "a maladaptive pattern of psychoactive substance use" and symptoms persistent for longer than 1 month or occurring repeatedly, but not meeting the criteria for dependence. *Dependence* includes at least three of the following: (1) substance taken in greater amounts or for longer than intended, (2) persistent desire or inability to control use, (3) considerable time spent obtaining, taking, or recovering from the drug, (4) frequent intoxication or withdrawal symptoms when expected to fulfill major obligations, (5) reduced social, occupational, or recreational activities, (6) continued use despite persistent problems, (7) marked tolerance, (8) characteristic withdrawal symptoms, (9) substance taken to avoid withdrawal. In addition, dependence requires some symptoms persisting for at least 1 month or occurring repeatedly. The *DSM III-R* also notes that psychoactive substance abuse and dependence often involve more than one substance.[2]

Several other organizations have described criteria for the diagnosis of alcoholism, including the World Health Organization and the National Council on Alcoholism.[3,4] Blazer and Pennybacker have noted that studies of alcoholism in the elderly have used such diverse criteria as quantity and frequency of consumption; social problems or problems in role performance, tolerance, and withdrawal; and physical health problems.[5] As a result, many descriptive studies, as well as evaluations of treatment programs, may not be comparable if different criteria have been used.

CHARACTERISTICS

Although some observers have noted a decreasing prevalence of alcoholism with increasing age, this finding is controversial. Drew reviewed cross-sectional studies and concluded that alcoholism appeared to be a self-limited disease which tended to "disappear with increasing age." He proposed three possible explanations[6]:

1. Morbidity and mortality resulting in death or chronic institutionalization and, therefore, a decreased prevalence in the general population, probably accounting for a significant part of the decrease
2. Beneficial effects of treatment, probably an unlikely explanation
3. "Spontaneous recovery"

A 1979 report of alcohol use in 1041 adults in the general population also showed decreased consumption in the cohort over age 60, compared with cohorts aged 50 to 59 or 18 to 49. The author postulated that chronic alcohol abusers may be dead or institutionalized by old age and thus not be found in the general population.[7]

A 1981 cross-sectional study of 928 older Bostonians also reported that those over 75 were less likely to drink than those 60 to 75. However, the "very old" reported different lifelong drinking habits, parental drinking habits, and attitudes about alcohol and health, suggesting that there may be significant cohort differences. These authors also proposed that chronic alcoholics may be underrepresented in the very old due to increased mortality at a younger age.[8]

Recent results from the Normative Aging Study tend to support the hypothesis that cohort differences confound cross-sectional studies. Longitudinal assessment of the effects of birth cohort and aging on mean alcohol consumption level, prevalence of drinking problems, and frequency of alcohol consumption indicated that there was no tendency for men to reduce their consumption over time or to have fewer drinking problems. The authors concluded that generational or attitudinal factors may be more important than age as determinants of drinking behavior.[9]

If the prevalence of alcohol problems is indeed related to cohort factors, then we might expect to see an increase in the proportion of elderly alcoholics in the future, as those cohorts with a higher alcohol consumption grow older. Although premature morbidity and mortality might remove some of these elderly alcoholics from the general population by institutionalization or death, a significant number would no doubt remain in the community and require the attention of health care providers.

Other factors may also contribute to a decrease in consumption of alcohol by the elderly. A cross-sectional study by Vestal and his associates, using ethanol infusions in 21- to 81-year-old volunteers, demonstrated a significant increase in peak blood ethanol concentration with age. The authors believed that a smaller volume of distribution and reduced lean body mass affected drug distribution and explained the higher peak concentrations in the elderly.[10] A 1984 study of social drinkers age 19 to 63 also reported higher blood alcohol levels in older subjects consuming a higher dose. In addition, impairment of task performance increased significantly with age, suggesting that increased behavioral effects might lead older persons to decrease their alcohol intake in social situations.[11] If the results of these studies of nonalcoholics are extrapolated to elderly alcoholics, it is possible that frequency and quantity of consumption may be reduced in alcoholics as well. Thus, using these parameters as identification criteria would tend to underestimate the prevalence of alcoholism in the elderly.

Two populations of elderly alcoholics have been proposed by Rosin and Glatt: those with long-standing alcohol problems who have simply grown old and those with emerging alcohol abuse exacerbated by the stresses of aging, such as retirement, bereavement, and loneli-

ness.[12] Gaitz and Baer described most of the 100 elderly alcoholics admitted to their psychiatric screening ward as having begun abuse in early adulthood.[13] However, Schuckit concluded that alcoholics in the elderly population include a substantial proportion who began abuse late in life, with a resulting increase in their medical problems. He estimated the prevalence of alcoholism in the general elderly population to be 2 to 10 percent, with 10 percent of all alcoholics being over age 60.[14]

A 1981 Swedish study of over 400 seventy-year-old men, examined at 5-year intervals, found a 10 percent prevalence of alcohol abuse or heavy consumption in this group, as well as in a comparison group of 489 men in a cohort 5 years younger.[15] Brody estimates the prevalence at 1 to 5 percent in the general population over age 65, with a prevalence of 10 to 15 percent in those seeking medical attention.[16] Solomon has stated that alcoholism is the second leading cause for admission of the elderly to psychiatric institutions and that it is a major factor in 15 to 20 percent of nursing home admissions, 5 to 15 percent of medical outpatient visits, and 10 percent of hospital admissions of the elderly. He estimates that there are approximately 1.5 million alcoholics aged 65 and older in the United States.[17] It is evident that the prevalence of alcoholism in the elderly population is not exactly known, but probably lies between 5 and 10 percent.

Simon and associates reported a prevalence of alcoholism of 28 percent in their study of 534 first-admission psychiatric patients over age 60,[18] and Gaitz and Baer found that 44 percent of 100 elderly psychiatric patients were alcoholics.[13] These studies, as well as those cited previously, strongly suggest that the prevalence of alcoholism in the ill elderly seeking medical or psychiatric care is much higher than among the well elderly residing in the community.

Even less information is available about the elderly who are addicted to narcotics. Schuckit notes that an estimated 1 percent of those in methadone maintenance programs are over 60 yeras of age; slightly more may be in hospital treatment programs. Many of these have prior arrests and a history of previous treatment. An average of 35 years of past abuse exists by the age of 60. With increasing age there is a decrease in income and a tendency to decrease the frequency and dose of drugs. In addition, he notes that elderly addicts often shift their abuse from "street" drugs, such as heroin, to the abuse of "legal" narcotics, such as Dilaudid, morphine, or codeine, tend to be medically "sicker" than their younger counterparts, and may also abuse alcohol and ancillary drugs.[14]

A 1970 New Orleans study described 38 male addicts not in treatment, with an average age of 58.9 and a median of three past imprisonments. Drugs used most often were Dilaudid, heroin, morphine, and codeine;

sources were most commonly pushers, less commonly physicians or friends. These men were typically withdrawn; all but one lived alone. Reduced intake was described as being due to decreased income.[19]

The aging of cohorts in which drug abuse has a much higher prevalence is likely to result in increasing numbers of elderly addicts, although the increased mortality due to the AIDS epidemic among intravenous drug users could adversely affect survival. The National Institute on Drug Abuse (NIDA) has noted that although "there is currently no reliable documentation of the nature and extent of illicit drug abuse among the elderly, . . . the use of illicit drugs among the elderly cannot be ignored . . . [and] is likely to increase over the next two decades." NIDA noted the need for more basic research as well as evaluation of prevention and treatment programs.[20]

SCREENING AND DETECTION

When compared with younger alcoholics, elderly alcoholics are less likely to have problems such as criminal and antisocial behavior, divorce, bankruptcy, violence, and motor vehicle accidents.[17] Thus they are less likely to be identified and referred into treatment by the legal system. This "hidden" abuse is also characteristic of elderly drug addicts. As has been noted, studies suggest that elderly alcoholics are more likely to be found among those seeking medical or psychiatric attention; thus, case finding might be conducted through the health care system. However, Solomon notes that the diagnosis of alcoholism in the elderly is often missed by clinicians due to a low index of suspicion, concealment by patients and families, and attribution of symptoms to advancing age.[17] Elderly alcoholics who seek medical attention rarely complain of their alcoholism, due to their denial, and physicians either fail to recognize or ignore the problem.[2] Patients also tend to underreport alcohol consumption, even when questioned directly by physicians.[21]

In order to facilitate identification of alcohol dependence, both psychosocial and biochemical markers, or a combination of the two, have been utilized. The most widely evaluated psychosocial instrument is the Michigan Alcoholism Screening Test (MAST), consisting of 25 true/false items, reasonably valid in distinguishing alcoholics from nonalcoholics.[22] The CAGE items (asking whether the patient feels the need to Cut down on drinking, is Annoyed by criticism, feels Guilty about drinking, and ever has an Eye-opener) are easy to use as a screening test and are quite specific.[23] Other rapid, inexpensive and reasonable screening instruments exist, which are somewhat simple and obvious.[3] Although usefulness in the elderly has not been specifically addressed in the development or evaluation of these instruments,

they are presumably of value if positive. However, they may lack sufficient sensitivity to detect alcoholism in elderly patients whose drinking patterns may be different from those of younger alcoholics. In addition, they are directed toward the late stages of alcoholism, and may not be helpful in detecting earlier stages.[23] Further evaluation is needed to demonstrate the usefulness of these psychosocial indicators in the detection of alcoholism in the elderly.

Numerous clinical symptoms and signs also suggest the diagnosis of alcoholism to the informed clinician. Liver and pancreatic disease, unexplained trauma, neurologic problems, sleep disturbances, and classic skin lesions may be associated with chronic alcohol problems.[23] However, in many instances such findings occur only in the later stages of alcoholism, and thus may not be useful for early detection. In addition, diagnosis of substance abuse in the elderly may be complicated by the presence of other diseases, including psychiatric disorders such as depression and dementia.

Biochemical markers such as elevations of alanine aminotransferase, aspartine aminotransferase, alkaline phosphatase, and others may be a useful adjunct in differentiating alcoholics from nonalcoholics.[24]

If the prevalence of substance abuse is higher among those elderly who present for medical and psychiatric care, then efforts at screening should be most productive when conducted in this population by personnel affiliated with such services. By combining a reasonable index of suspicion, psychosocial screening instruments, careful examination for symptoms and signs of chemical dependence, and evaluation of biochemical markers, the clinician may appropriately diagnose substance abuse and enable referral of the patient to the treatment system.

CONSEQUENCES

A recent study of 270 healthy, independent community-residing men and women over age 65[25] found that 8 percent drank over 30 g/day (classified as "heavy drinkers") and 48 percent consumed some alcohol daily. Increased alcohol intake did not appear to be associated with decreased cognitive, psychological, or social status in this functional population. Among psychiatric patients, however, alcoholics have been frequently noted to have organic brain syndromes,[13,18] usually at a younger age than nonalcoholics. Alcoholism may also be a frequent factor in admission of the elderly to psychiatric institutions, nursing homes, and hospitals.[17]

One consequence of alcoholism in the community-residing elderly may be the so-called "senile squalor" syndrome: squalor and self-neglect without dementia or other chronic illness.[26] Seventy-two cases of this syndrome were originally described in persons aged 60 to

92, most commonly women living alone. Twenty-eight were found to have significant alcohol use; in most of these subjects, alcoholism preceded squalor.[27]

In the Swedish study by Mellstrom and his associates,[15] elderly alcoholics had higher morbidity and mortality, they required more care, and they had lower functional ability in cognition, muscle strength, gonadal and pulmonary function, visual acuity, walking ability, and skeletal density. The medical consequences of alcoholism in the elderly include sleep disturbances, diminished sexual performance, cirrhosis of the liver, pancreatitis, myopathy, Korsakoff's psychosis, nutritional and vitamin deficiencies, Wernicke's encephalopathy, and drug interactions.[28]

Elderly abusers of illegal drugs are susceptible to the same difficulties as younger addicts,[20] including poverty, isolation, and arrest.[19] In the elderly population, chemical dependence may also contribute to difficulties in management of other medical conditions, by affecting the patient's ability to seek appropriate care, comply with medications and other treatment modalities, keep appointments for medical care and other therapy, and maintain the social and supportive interactions necessary for community residence.

TREATMENT

Treatment of chronic alcoholism can result in long-term improvement (abstinence over 1 year) in approximately 25 percent of all alcoholics in the general population. The usual approach includes nonjudgmental confrontation and detoxification, followed by intense inpatient or outpatient educational and therapeutic experiences, including introduction into Alcoholics Anonymous.[29]

Elderly persons should be expected to have recovery rates at least equal to those of the general population, if they can be brought into treatment. Mishara and Kastenbaum reviewed the available literature and emphasize that although studies are limited, elderly alcoholics appear to have a good response to treatment in standard programs. They point out that since studies use different criteria for defining alcoholism and consider different populations of alcoholics, the results are not always comparable. They also note that criteria for successful treatment vary, and may include total abstinence, abstinence with improved functioning, or overall improved function without abstinence.[30] Schuckit points out that elderly opiate addicts are unlikely to give up drug abuse but will often enter treatment voluntarily, perhaps due to health or financial considerations.

DRUG TREATMENT

Drug treatment includes the use of psychotropic drugs as an adjunct for problems such as anxiety and depression. Evidence is lacking for the efficacy of such therapy, and there are risks involved in the use of such drugs in the elderly.[30] In addition to psychotropic drugs, disulfiram (Antabuse), which causes a marked toxic response to ingested alcohol, has been used in younger alcoholics, but should be used only with extreme caution in the elderly, due to its severe physical effects.[31]

Methadone maintenance is the drug treatment available for narcotic addicts, but little information is available regarding its efficacy in the elderly. Pascarelli and Fischer described elderly addicts in methadone maintenance programs and noted that they are least likely to request detoxification, that they are dissatisfied with dosage changes, and that they may abuse alcohol to produce euphoria.[32] Treatment of narcotic addiction does not appear as promising as that of alcohol alone, but more studies are needed.

PSYCHOSOCIAL THERAPY

Individual psychotherapy and counseling is usually behavior-oriented and addresses the defense mechanism of denial.[31] Problems may exist with the negative attitudes of therapists and the reluctance of the elderly to seek this kind of therapy.[30] The elderly may also have problems with the financing of individual psychotherapy, which is often poorly reimbursed by third-party payors. Group therapy is usually less expensive and may be helpful in promoting insight, especially when the group is composed of other elderly alcoholics,[31] although this is not always possible. Alcoholics Anonymous (AA) provides the opportunity for continuation of treatment beyond the institutional setting and is essentially free of cost. The AA network tends to combat the isolation of the alcoholic and provides understanding and support, using a group therapy concept.[31] Although AA encourages members of all ages, the elderly are not always well-represented. For opiate addicts, Narcotics Anonymous (NA) provides a parallel program, but members may be even younger than in AA.

Inpatient programs provide the opportunity to initiate treatment in a controlled, structured setting, with detoxification as the first concern. However, many programs have admission screening policies, usually regarding medical diagnoses, which may make it difficult for the elderly to gain admission.[30] In addition, unless they are subsidized, inpatient programs are very expensive and thus may be limited to those clients with insurance or private funds. The literature does not indicate whether in- or outpatient programs are more effective for the elderly.[31]

Evaluations of specific programs for the elderly with chemical dependence have not been conducted, and thus information is not readily available concerning the effectiveness of various types of treatment. Controversy exists as to whether the elderly need special programs, due to their special characteristics and problems. A recommendation was made to the National Institute on Alcohol Abuse and Alcoholism (NIAAA) in 1976 to develop special programs for the aged alcoholic within existing services.[30] However, a Scottish study compared alcoholics over age 60 with sex-matched younger alcoholics. Except for an increased prevalence of organic brain syndrome in the elderly, few differences were found between the two groups: the elderly consumed less alcohol than younger alcoholics, they were more likely to be widowed, they were less likely to experience loss of control, and their onset of alcoholism occurred at a later age. The author concluded that elderly alcoholics can be treated along with younger ones, except for those with organic brain syndromes, who may do better with psychogeriatric services.[33]

This conclusion was supported by an analysis of data from the National Alcoholism Program Information System, which represents 550 alcoholism treatment programs. All 3163 patients over age 60 followed for 180 days were compared with 3190 patients aged 21 to 59. Dependent variables included drinking characteristics before treatment, type of treatment received, and outcome measures. No significant differences were found between the two groups for treatment or outcome variables, except for slightly poorer outcomes in the age group 40 to 59. These authors concluded that there is little evidence to suggest that elderly alcoholics need special treatment programs once they have been identified and brought into the treatment system.[34]

The NIAAA Fifth Report stated that many alcoholics do not find a good match with available treatment programs, especially such groups as women, ethnic minorities, the disabled, and the elderly; access to treatment may be impaired by financial constraints, cultural barriers, and program design. However, specific problems related to the elderly were not discussed further.[4] Indeed, one might postulate that problems which the elderly encounter may be more in the nature of access to programs rather than their actual structure. Financial limitations, transportation difficulties, physical access problems, and safety and security concerns may pose real obstacles to the elderly person's ability to enter into treatment.

Treatment of chemical dependence in the elderly must also involve family members, who may be providing important caregiving services for the dependent person. Although studies are lacking, some benefit is likely from referral to Al-Anon, Nar-Anon, and Alateen, the specific programs for families of alcoholics and narcotic addicts. In addition, Adult Children of Alcoholics groups have evolved from Al-Anon, and may be particularly appropriate for "adult-child" caregivers. Family therapy may also provide support for the patient and caregivers during critical periods of treatment.

The role of the physician has been clearly expressed by the American College of Physicians, stating that recognizing and treating chemical dependence requires knowledge of the symptoms of chronic and excessive drug use and increased sensitivity to and awareness of behavior associated with such problem use."[1] Once the diagnosis is suspected, nonthreatening and nonjudgmental confrontation is appropriate. Senay[4] suggests obtaining a substance-abuse history, including age of first use; period of heaviest lifetime use (dose per unit of time); classes of drugs abused; recent patterns of use (frequency and dose); development of tolerance (need for increasing dose); development of dependence (withdrawal symptoms); benefits of drug use; and history of convulsions, hallucinations, confusion, delirium, and/or overdosage. In addition, questions regarding the effect of abuse on family, job, and social functioning are appropriate.[1]

The physician should be knowledgeable about the different treatment modalities available for both acute detoxification and chronic management, and should be prepared to follow the patient long-term. Referral for chronic treatment may be appropriate, and should include community resources such as AA or NA, which may be integrated into other rehabilitation programs.

CONCLUSION

Chemical dependence is a significant, and probably underestimated, problem in the elderly. Although prevalence of abuse probably does decrease with age, this may not occur to the extent previously surmised. Elderly alcoholics and narcotic addicts tend to be more reclusive and less visible in the community. Elderly alcoholism has been more thoroughly studied than elderly narcotic addiction, and treatment appears to be more successful among alcoholics. Physicians and other health care providers should be able to diagnose chemical dependence and make appropriate referrals for treatment.

Appropriate care of the chemically dependent elderly requires consideration of their special needs, and must take into account those characteristics which distinguish this group. In addition, research is needed to address questions regarding prevalence, characteristics, and treatment and program evaluation, in order to design and implement necessary and effective interventions.

REFERENCES

1. "Chemical Dependence." A position paper of the American College of Physicians. Philadelphia, American College of Physicians, 1984.

2. American Psychiatric Association (APA): *Diagnostic and Statistical Manual of Mental Disorders*, 3d ed (rev). Washington, American Psychiatric Association, 1987.

3. National Institute on Alcohol Abuse and Alcoholism (NIAAA): *Fifth Special Report to the U.S. Congress on Alcohol and Health*. Washington, Government Printing Office, 1983.

4. Senay EC: *Substance Abuse Disorders in Clinical Practice*. Boston, John Wright, 1983.

5. Blazer DG, Pennybacker MR: Epidemiology of alcoholism in the elderly, in Hartford JT, Samorajski T (eds): *Alcoholism in the Elderly: Social and Biochemical Issues*. New York, Raven Press, 1984.

6. Drew H: Alcoholism as a self-limited disease. *Q J Stud Alcohol* 29:956, 1968.

7. Barnes GM: Alcohol use among older persons: Findings from a western New York state general population survey. *J Am Geriatr Soc* 27:244, 1979.

8. Meyers AR et al: Evidence for cohort or generational differences in the drinking behavior of older adults. *Int J Aging Human Dev* 14:31, 1981.

9. Glynn RJ et al: Aging and generational effects on drinking behaviors in men: Results from the Normative Aging Study. *Am J Public Health* 75:1413, 1985.

10. Vestal RE et al: Aging and ethanol metabolism. *Clin Pharmacol Ther* 21:343–354, 1977.

11. Vogel-Sprott M, Barret P: Age, drinking habits, and the effects of alcohol. *J Stud Alcohol* 45:517, 1984.

12. Rosin AJ, Glatt MM: Alcohol excess in the elderly. *Q J Stud Alcohol* 32:53, 1971.

13. Gaitz CM, Baer PE: Characteristics of elderly patients with alcoholism. *Arch Gen Psychiatry* 24:372, 1971.

14. Schuckit MA: Geriatric alcoholism and drug abuse. *Gerontologist* 17:168, 1977.

15. Mellstrom D et al: Previous alcohol consumption and its consequences for ageing, morbidity and mortality in men aged 70–75. *Age Ageing* 10:277, 1981.

16. Brody JA: Aging and alcohol abuse. *J Am Geriatr Soc* 30:123, 1982.

17. Solomon DH: Alcoholism and aging, pp 411–412 in West LJ, moderator: Alcoholism. *Ann Intern Med* 100:405, 1984.

18. Simon A et al: Alcoholism in the geriatric mentally ill. *Geriatrics* 23(10):125, 1968.

19. Capel WC et al: The aging narcotic addict: An increasing problem for the next decades. *J Gerontol* 27:102, 1972.

20. Glantz MD et al (eds): *Drugs and the Elderly Adult*, Research Issues no 32. Rockville, MD, National Institute on Drug Abuse, 1983.

21. Skinner HA et al: Early identification of alcohol abuse: 1: Critical issues and psychosocial indicators for a composite index. *Can Med Assoc J* 124:1141, 1981.

22. Selzer ML: The Michigan Alcoholism Screening Test: The quest for a new diagnostic instrument. *Am J Psychiatry* 127:1653, 1971.

23. Holt S et al: Early identification of alcohol abuse: 2: Clinical and laboratory indicators. *Can Med Assoc J* 124:1279, 1981.

24. Ryback RS et al: Biochemical and hematologic correlates of alcoholism and liver disease. *JAMA* 248:2261, 1982.

25. Goodwin JS et al: Alcohol intake in a healthy elderly population. *Am J Public Health* 77:173, 1987.

26. Kafetz K, Cox M: Alcohol excess and the senile squalor syndrome. *J Am Geriatr Soc* 30:706, 1982.

27. Macmillan D, Shaw P: Senile breakdown in standards of personal and environmental cleanliness. *Br Med J* 2:1032, 1966.

28. Hartford JT, Samorajski T: Alcoholism in the geriatric population. *J Am Geriatr Soc* 30:18, 1982.

29. West LJ: Some treatment issues in chronic alcoholism, pp 412–414, in West LJ, moderator: Alcoholism. *Ann Intern Med* 100:405, 1984.

30. Mishara BL, Kastenbaum R: Treatment of problem drinking among the elderly, in *Alcohol and Old Age*. New York, Grune & Stratton, 1980.

31. Hartford JT, Thienhaus OJ: Psychiatric aspects of alcoholism in geriatric patients, in Hartford JT, Samorajski T (eds): *Alcoholism in the Elderly: Social and Biomedical Issues*. New York, Raven Press, 1984.

32. Pascarelli EF, Fischer W: Drug dependence in the elderly. *Int J Aging Hum Dev* 5(4):347, 1974.

33. Rix KJB: Elderly alcoholics in the Edinburgh psychiatric services. *J R Soc Med* 75:177, 1982.

34. Janik SW, Dunham RG: A nationwide examination of the need for specific alcoholism treatment programs for the elderly. *J Stud Alcohol* 44:307, 1983.

Chapter 106

PERSONALITY DISORDERS IN THE ELDERLY

Jacobo E. Mintzer, Margarita Lermo, and Carl Eisdorfer

Personality disorders involve long-standing patterns of maladaptive behavior and, as such, rarely develop in later life. Nevertheless, it is possible that the problems which challenge the aged individual may cause relatively mild habitual maladaptive behavior patterns to become exacerbated or to manifest themselves during the later years of life. The reasons for the emergence and manifestation of behavioral disturbances among the elderly are broad. Sometimes there are changes in a patient's social or physical supports, and the patient is deprived of behavioral patterns that have been a standard way of obtaining care and support over the years. Events ranging from the loss of a spouse or close confidant to the onset of a debilitating physical disease compound the problem. The emergence of other psychopathologic syndromes may also highlight the presence of an underlying chronic personality disorder.[1,50] Biological changes observed in normal aging which can compromise certain capacities[2] may also be of significance in limiting a person's standard behavioral repertoire and leading to a new pattern of responses which may be maladaptive. Frustration may lead to anger and passive aggressivity or to learned helplessness and chronic depression.[3,51]

DESCRIPTION AND CLINICAL COURSE OF PERSONALITY DISORDERS IN THE ELDERLY

Personality disorders are defined as long-term patterns of behavior that cause significant impairment in social or occupational functioning or that cause subjective distress. These disorders have been divided into three general types, called clusters, in the American Psychiatric Association's revised *Diagnostic and Statistical Manual of Mental Disorders*, Third Edition (DSM III-R), published in 1988.[4] Cluster A includes patterns such as para-

noid personality disorder, schizoid personality disorder, and schizotypal personality disorder. Cluster B consists of disorders involving control of impulses, e.g., antisocial personality disorder. Cluster C includes patterns that involve problems of control and/or dependency, such as passive-aggressive personality or dependent personality disorders.

CLUSTER A: PARANOID PERSONALITY DISORDER, SCHIZOID PERSONALITY DISORDER, AND SCHIZOTYPAL PERSONALITY DISORDER

Paranoid personality disorders are characterized by suspiciousness and lack of trust of people. The most prominent feature of this disorder in an individual is a wide-ranging tendency to interpret other people's actions as deliberately demeaning or threatening to him or her. Almost invariably the individual expects to be harmed or manipulated by others for some purpose. Such individuals will question the loyalty of friends or colleagues and make accusations without fact; they interpret relatively innocent or innocuous data as "proof" of their beliefs. Often such persons are pathologically jealous, and they question without justification the fidelity of their loved ones. These patients frequently use the mechanism of projection, that is, they attribute to others impulses and thoughts that they are unable to accept in themselves. Ideas of reference and logically defended illusions are common; for example, a patient may believe that the judicial system or revenue system has singled him or her out for "special" treatment.

Paranoid patients show a narrower emotional range than nonparanoid people do and may appear to be totally unemotional. They take pride in being rational and objective when in fact they have trouble expressing feelings. They lack warmth, and they are impressed with

1036

and pay close attention to social structure, i.e., power and rank. Since they are very dependent upon an external organization for their own adaptation, they express disdain for those who are considered to be weak or impaired. In social situations, persons with paranoid personality disorder may appear businesslike and efficient, but often they generate fear or conflict because they seem so lacking in warmth and humanity.

Schizoid personality disorder is associated with a lifelong pattern of social isolation and is characterized by introversion, discomfort with people, and a bland, narrow affect. Schizoid personalities typically appear to be eccentric, isolated, lonely, or, on occasion, bizarre.

Schizoid personalities may give an impression of being cold or aloof and uninvolved with everyday events, including the concerns of others. They pursue their lives with remarkably little need or apparent longing for emotional ties with others. Their lives reflect solitary interests, and they often hold noncompetitive jobs that others might find difficult to tolerate. A schizoid person's sexual life may exist exclusively in fantasy. Schizoid persons usually reveal a lifelong inability to express anger. They are able to invest enormous energy in nonhuman interests, such as physics or mathematics, and they may be very attached to objects or pets. Often they can become engrossed in philosophical movements, especially those that require no personal involvement.

Schizoid personalities show no loss of capacity to recognize reality. Aggression is an unusual response, and threats (real or imagined) are dealt with by a fantasy of omnipotence or of resignation. At times, schizoid personalities are able to conceive and develop genuinely original, creative ideas, although they may shun any accompanying publicity and recognition if the acclaim involves much socialization.

Other people often label persons with *schizotypal personality disorder* "strange." Magical thinking, peculiar ideas, ideas of reference, and illusions are part of their everyday world. The schizotypal personality disorder is characterized by a disturbance in the patterns of thinking and communication. Persons with schizotypal personalities may not be aware of the nature of their own feelings, yet they are exquisitely sensitive to the feelings of others and especially sensitive in detecting negative feelings, such as anger. Further, the inner world of the schizotypal patient may be filled with imaginary relationships and fears, and the patient may believe that he or she has special powers and insight. Although a frank thought disorder is absent, the patient's conversations may often be difficult to follow. The speech of a schizotypal patient may seem peculiar and may have meaning only to the patient, who is responding to a nonconventional reality. Schizotypal patients show difficulties with interpersonal relationships and may act inappropriately; as a result, they are often isolated and have few friends. According to DSM III-R, these patients may show features of borderline personality disorder, and, indeed, both diagnoses can be made. Under stress, schizotypal patients may decompensate and have psychiatric symptoms, but these episodes are usually of brief duration. In extreme cases, severe depression may occur.

There is a lack of definitive data, but Cluster A personality disorders are likely to become exacerbated as the individual grows older. Paranoid individuals will probably become more suspicious with increasing age.[5,45,46,52] Their previous behavior may be facilitated by underlying memory disorders or visual and/or hearing deficits, leading to a state of relative sensory deprivation that can be blamed on others and can challenge the individual's ability to accurately test reality.[45,46,47,48,52] Schizoid individuals may become more eccentric as they grow older, evidencing increased use of magical thinking. The schizoid individual may be viewed by a benign or uncaring society as "just the old eccentric."[6] The emergence with age of other psychopathology, such as depression, also can increase social withdrawal,[7] giving the clinical impression of a general worsening of any pre-existing personality disorders.

When discussing this group of personality disorders in the elderly, it is important to consider the changes in environment and social support which may occur in an aging individual's world.[1] So-called eccentric behavior previously tolerated in one setting may be seen as inappropriate behavior requiring intervention in another setting. The basic behavioral pattern of the individual may be unchanged, but the tolerance for this marginal behavior may be reduced. The patient's behavior is now considered to be inappropriate, manifesting deterioration of his or her previous personality. Finally, loneliness and a state of disaffection leading to isolation can occur, particularly with the loss of supportive systems, as in the case of widowhood.[1,8,9] The social isolation in turn leads to the appearance of psychiatric symptoms. In the elderly patient, the clinician should be looking for a change in the personality pattern or a deterioration in previous level of function.

Clinical management for this group of personality disorders in the elderly involves careful evaluation to determine the need for antipsychotic medication when severe impairment in reality testing is observed and the need for antidepressants in the case of mood disturbances. Personality disorders require more of a social and psychological approach, rather than a pharmacological approach. Even when reality testing is impaired, the use of environmental manipulation is indicated. Finally, psychotherapy aimed at enhancing the patient's feelings of support and awareness of reality can be used. (A detailed description of the different treatment techniques can be found in the "Treatment" section of this chapter.)

CLUSTER B: ANTISOCIAL PERSONALITY DISORDER, BORDERLINE PERSONALITY DISORDER, NARCISSISTIC PERSONALITY DISORDER, AND HISTRIONIC PERSONALITY DISORDER

The second cluster of personality disorders, Cluster B, includes those disorders which involve impaired impulse control. Such disorders are antisocial personality disorder, borderline personality disorder, narcissistic personality disorder, and histrionic personality disorder.

The person with an *antisocial personality disorder* is characteristically antisocial and may be involved in criminal acts. He or she shows an inability to conform to social norms, rather than a studied criminality. Persons with antisocial personalities often present a normal and even pleasant exterior. By history, however, they have long-standing problems involving lying, truancy, thefts, fights, drug abuse, and the like. Persons with antisocial personalities impress some people with their colorful personalities, but others see them as manipulative and demanding. Suicide threats and somatic preoccupations may be reported. Delusions and other signs of irrational thinking are absent; in fact, these individuals often impress observers as being intelligent and observant.

Persons with antisocial personalities are highly manipulative and are often able to talk others into participating in activities that involve easy ways to make money or to achieve notoriety. In the main, such schemes lead to social embarrassment or financial ruin. Antisocial personalities often do not tell the truth and cannot be trusted to carry out their responsibilities, but since they do not adhere to any conventional standard of morality they can appear to be sincere even when they are lying. Behaviors such as promiscuity and spouse or child abuse are often observed in these individuals, who show a lack of remorse and a lack of empathy for others. Simply put, such an individual appears to lack a conscience.

Borderline personality disorder patients may be difficult to diagnose. They are at the border of personality disorders and psychosis and are characterized by an unstable affect, marginal behavior, poor interpersonal relationships, and an impaired self-image. The borderline disorder has also been called "ambulatory schizophrenia" because patients with the disorder may slip into psychotic states so readily. Borderline individuals constantly appear to be in a state of emergency, and mood swings are common: they may be angry at one moment and sad at the next, or else have no feelings at all.

While borderline individuals suffer from short-lived psychotic episodes, the episodes are almost always limited in time or easily treated. Behavior management of these individuals is complicated since behavior is characterized by unpredictability. They rarely achieve up to the level of their abilities, and their lives seem to show repetitive self-destructive acts.

Individuals with borderline personalities have tumultuous interpersonal dealings; intense anger at one moment because of frustration can quickly switch into expressions of great affection. Generally these patients do not tolerate being alone, and they are often involved in a frantic search for companionship, no matter how unsatisfactory. In order to assuage loneliness, they can become promiscuous. Also, they may rapidly become very close to total strangers. They lack a sense of identity and complain about emptiness and boredom.

Persons with a *narcissistic personality disorder* are characterized by a prominent sense of self-importance and grandiosity. These individuals consider themselves to be special and, as a consequence, expect to be treated as special. They handle criticism poorly and may become enraged at anyone who dares to criticize them. Narcissistic individuals demand their own way and are frequently very ambitious. They upset others because they typically ignore the conventional rules of behavior. Their distorted sense of superiority leads them to believe that they are justified in deviating from accepted rules. However, despite what appear to be grandiose feelings, these patients are in fact quite fragile and are prone to depression. They are unable to show real compassion or sympathy and predictably have difficulties with others, frequently causing problems which produce rejection that they then have trouble handling.

Individuals with a *histrionic personality disorder* manifest dramatic and extroverted behavior. They come across as outgoing and warm persons; however, their inability to maintain strong, long-lasting attachments and their frequent attention-seeking behavior shows up their problems. They will have temper tantrums, tears, and histrionic behavior of all sorts when they are not the center of attention. Seductive behavior is very common, as are (unfulfilled) sexual fantasies about persons with whom they are involved. They are flirtatious but rather commonly have a psychosexual dysfunction. Their interpersonal relationships tend to be superficial, although their dependency needs may make them too trusting of others. Disassociation and repression are their most frequent defense mechanisms, so that patients are unaware of their true feelings and are unable to explain their motivations.

In summary, personality disorders in Cluster B reflect two common problems: poor impulse control and trouble delaying gratification. Despite the lack of data regarding age-related changes in this type of personality disorder, some speculations are warranted based upon the nature of the behavior patterns. It has been suggested that individuals seem to improve their impulse control with age. Thus the prognosis for the person with a Cluster B personality disorder seems to be for improving adaptation. For example, individuals rarely commit violent crimes for the first time after age forty[11]; however, other issues may mediate this behavior, including an age-related tendency toward more passive strategies for handling stress[6] and a relative decrease in energy associated with later life.[12] Finally, there is a reported decrease in aggressivity, especially among older men.[13]

While control related to the external world seems to increase, there seems to be a counter-balanced increase in the older individual's aggressive impulses toward his or her own self.[14] This is manifested as an increase in bodily symptoms, suicidal thoughts, and depressive symptoms. The treatment of this type of personality disorder includes psychotherapy, psychotropic medications for psychotic symptoms, and antidepressant medications for the treatment of diagnosed mood disorders. Recently, certain antidepressant medications, particularly those enhancing serotonin levels and drugs such as lithium, have been reported to have a positive effect impulse control, but currently these data are still preliminary and to our knowledge no relevant studies have been conducted on elderly patients.

CLUSTER C: AVOIDANT PERSONALITY DISORDER, DEPENDENT PERSONALITY DISORDER, OBSESSIVE-COMPULSIVE PERSONALITY DISORDER, AND PASSIVE-AGGRESSIVE PERSONALITY DISORDER

The third class of personality disorders, Cluster C, includes disorders that focus on issues of dependency and control. This cluster includes avoidant personality disorder, dependent personality disorder, obsessive-compulsive personality disorder, and passive-aggressive personality disorder.

Persons with *avoidant personality disorder* show an extreme sensitivity to rejection, which may lead the individual to defend himself or herself by minimizing all social contacts. Such individuals are not asocial or antisocial, but they are shy, even though they have a great desire for companionship. Persons with avoidant personalities need very strong assurances of uncritical acceptance before they attempt any social contact. They are so uncertain and lacking in self-confidence that they are apt to misinterpret harmless comments as derogatory or ridiculing. The refusal of any of their requests can result in feelings of hurt and withdrawl.

Persons with this type of personality avoid the exercise of authority; instead, they often seem eager to please those in control. Because they require an unusually strong guarantee of uncritical acceptance, they often have few, if any, close friends or confidants.

Persons with *dependent personality disorder* get others to assume responsibility for major areas in their lives. They are so lacking in self-confidence as to distrust their ability to make any important decisions.

The dependent personality is characterized by a pervasive pattern of submissive behavior. People with this disorder become anxious if asked to assume a leadership role. They find it difficult to persevere at tasks and tend simply to let things happen.

In general, persons with dependent personality disorder are most secure in the presence of persons they can depend upon, and their relationships are thus distorted by this need to be supported. In the rare condition of *folie a deux* (a shared delusional disorder) of two persons, one member of the pair is usually suffering from a dependent personality disorder, and this submissive partner takes on the delusional system of the more aggressive, assertive partner on whom he or she is dependent.

Persons with *obsessive-compulsive personality disorder* show emotional constriction, a demand for orderliness, and perseverance. One of the major features of this disorder is a pervasive pattern of perfectionism and inflexibility. Persons with obsessive-compulsive personality disorder are preoccupied with rules, regulations, order, neatness, details, and the achievement of perfection. They are formal, serious, and often intolerant. They insist that rules be followed rigidly and laws be strictly enforced. They are unable to tolerate inaccurate statements or vague directions.

Obsessive-compulsive persons have limited interpersonal skills. They alienate people because they never compromise, always insisting that others submit to their needs and to the exact letter of the rule. They respect power, but because of their fear of making mistakes, they may become indecisive when it comes to making decisions in situations requiring flexibility. Although with this disorder stable marriage and occupational adequacy is common, obsessive-compulsive persons usually have few friends since their anxiety is evoked by changes in routine and disruptive events.

The *passive-aggressive personality disorder* is characterized by covert obstructionism, procrastination, stubbornness, and inefficiency. Such behavior is felt to be a manifestation of underlying aggression, which is expressed passively. Persons with this disorder constantly find excuses; however, they never show open opposition since they lack assertiveness, and they are not direct about their own needs or wishes. They therefore control a situation by failing to do what is required or by doing it wrong. This patient purposely fails to ask questions necessary to perform the requested task, in order to lay the groundwork for failure.

While persons with passive-aggressive personalities try to maneuver themselves into dependent relationships, their behavior is so exasperating to others as to generate anger and social isolation. The clinician may become caught up in a patient's many claims of unjust treatment or in simply trying to get the patient to do something as basic as taking medication. Passive-aggressive personalities are rarely tranquil or happy. Since they are not able to express what it is that gives them pleasure, they cannot enjoy themselves. People with this disorder are typically pessimistic. Elderly patients with this personality cluster will most likely have a difficult time, since family and clinicians alike find them so difficult to manage.

As discussed earlier, data suggest an increase in passive coping among the aged. These findings are in agreement with studies on elderly response to major natural disasters. These data show that elderly subjects are more dependent on external help for rehabilitation and recovery after a disaster.[20] Such data suggest an increase in dependency traits with age and a potential for the worsening with age of personality disorders with dependent traits. Life events commonly observed late in life, such as retirement and loss of spouse, further enhance the dependency needs of these individuals.

The clinical importance of these dependent behavioral tendencies is widespread. A dependent or a passive-aggressive patient will be less likely to take prescribed medication or to follow medical advice (e.g., to avoid salt in the diet). These patients will be less likely to request help and more likely to make mistakes in self-care. Closer supervision of these persons is likely to be required, but caring for them is frustrating and provokes anger in the clinician. In these patients, the appropriate manipulation of the environment is crucial. The adequate support of social services and the active role of a clinician can make the difference between a successful outcome or a poor outcome of treatment. The need to turn suspiciousness into trust and passivity and dependency into a treatment tool through the building of a successful patient-physician relationship is a challenge that all geriatricians will have to confront.

OTHER PERSONALITY DISORDERS

A group of disorders identified as *personality disorders not otherwise specified* includes personality disturbances that cannot be classified as any specific personality disorder. A person may have features of more than one personality disorder and yet not meet the required criteria for any particular one, despite significant impairment in social or occupational functioning or subjective distress. This category can also be used when the clinician judges that a specific personality disorder is not included in any of the preceding categories or, for that matter, is not part of the official DSM III-R nomenclature. Other categories like self-defeating and sadistic personality disorders may be included here.

ETIOLOGY OF PERSONALITY DISORDERS

During the past decade a number of longitudinal studies of personality in adulthood have reported stability of personality patterns during the life cycle as demonstrated by substantial levels of retest stability in personality patterns over periods of up to 12 years.[28-31] These investigations have been widely confirmed using self-administered as well as projective tests.[32,33] One example of such research is the recent study by Costa and McCrae of 93 men and women ages 25 to 90 using the Holtzman Inkblot Technique (HIT). This study found high-stability coefficiencies and concluded that HIT measures are moderately stable in adulthood.[34] Despite these findings of stability in personality patterns over life, it is possible that behavioral changes within personality patterns may occur with increasing age.

Indeed, several factors seem to point toward the possibility of changes in behavior as they relate to personality patterns in old age. For example, loneliness is a common, unpleasant psychological state, caused by a lack of satisfying social networks and intimate relationships. It reflects a mix of both internal and external factors.[9] Loneliness has been found in association with the loss of someone close, as with widowhood, divorce, or loss of friends; however, it is compounded by inadequacy of social networks or by such structural barriers to social contact as a dangerous neighborhood or inadequate transportation.[1] Loneliness also can occur as a result of behaviors which keep people away. These changes include feelings of hopelessness, emptiness, defeat, or anger.[35,36] In addition, loneliness is associated with poor social skills and a long-term tendency toward social isolation.[37-40]

Another factor to be considered when studying personality changes in the elderly is change in the ways used to overcome anxiety-provoking situations. Gutman et al.[41-44] have conducted a series of studies based on both literate and preliterate societies. Using primarily male participants and relying on interview material and dream content, Gutman concluded that there are age-related shifts in men's mastery styles. As they grow older, males are said to shift from active to passive mastery and finally go to magical mastery.[41-43,49] Older men in primitive cultures go from hunter, to storyteller (a varied role), to religious leader or priest. In his writings, Gutman suggests that this movement from active to passive mastery may represent a regression and the renewal of the use of less effective primitive psychological defense mechanisms. Although these studies must be evaluated further, such changes should be considered when studying the long-term prognosis of those personality trends which are characterized by a tendency toward active coping but which present clinical difficulties in impulse control, such as borderline personality disorders or antisocial personality disorders.

Personality disorders such as the schizotypal personality could be influenced by an increase in the use of magical thinking as a coping strategy; thus, as ability drops, fantasy could increase and exacerbate the personality pattern. Finally, several studies have been published which demonstrate the importance of social support as a buffer between life events and personality-dependent coping styles, when psychological distress or psychiatric impairment is used as a dependent variable.[17,18,44] The role of social support seems to be of special relevance when such problems as physical illness are considered as the stressor life event.[19] In such situations, personality disorders with trends to passive coupling or dependency will have a better or poorer prognosis with advancing age that is related to the availability of others in the environment willing to help.

DIFFERENTIAL DIAGNOSIS

The criteria for diagnosis of personality disorders in the elderly are not different from those used to diagnose young adults. For the diagnosis of personality disorders, we will follow the criteria of the DSM III-R of the American Psychiatric Association. Several considerations need to be taken into account when diagnosing personality disorders in the elderly, including stereotyping, other disorders, previous personality patterns, and support networks.

A stereotype of older people in our society has repeatedly been shown to be held strongly by health and mental professionals.[21] Adherence to a stereotype may easily contribute to misdiagnosis. For example, if dependency is believed to be a stereotypical personality trait in older people, then the dependent behavior of an older patient may not be identified as being pathological or part of an underlying personality disorder; likewise, if older persons are felt to be rigid, then diagnosis of compulsive disorders may be missed. Conversely, because of stereotyping the clinician may attribute such traits to patients even when they are present only in a modest degree.

The differential diagnosis between personality disorders and medical disease always needs to be considered. Several medical disorders, such as hyperthyroidism and urinary tract infection, may present as personality changes in elderly patients. For example, symptoms of suspiciousness, leading to the diagnosis of a psychotic episode due to steroid therapy or a septic episode, could be ambiguous in an individual considered to suffer from a paranoid personality disorder.

Among the disorders known to cause manifestations frequently misdiagnosed as personality disorders are thyroid disease, adrenocortical or parathyroid disease, brain tumors, Parkinson's disease, Alzheimer's disease, multi-infarct dementia, and infectious diseases. In order to differentiate between personality disorders and medical disease, the clinician should focus on two major issues: changes in previous personality patterns and exaggeration/exacerbation of previous personality traits. For this purpose, a careful history of the patient's behavioral patterns and response to stress is important, particularly his or her reaction to difficult situations, such as the death of a spouse or friend, or economic problems. A history of the patient's previous interpersonal relations also needs to be considered. Any change in longstanding patterns needs to be seen as a warning sign and should be an indication for a complete medical evaluation. Such an evaluation should also include an assessment of the available family and community support networks. Who is living with the patient? Who is responsible for the patient? What is available if needed? Answers to these questions will give important information for the patient's management.

In summary, although the criteria for the diagnosis of personality disorders in the elderly do not differ substantially from those used for young adults, several points merit careful consideration by the physician treating an elderly patient:

1. Personal and community stereotypes
2. Presence of concurrent medical and psychiatric disorders
3. Evaluation of previous personality patterns
4. Evaluation of changes in or exaggerations of previous personality patterns
5. Evaluation of community and family networks

TREATMENT

The treatment of personality disorders in the elderly patient, as in the young patient, is often difficult and prolonged. The techniques for the treatment of these disorders are broad and range from pharmacotherapy to psychotherapeutic techniques.

PHARMACOTHERAPY

Pharmacological treatments are inefficient and usually contraindicated in the modification of lifelong behavioral patterns such as personality traits. Medication can be useful in the treatment of severe psychiatric symptoms commonly observed with personality disorders in the elderly, including the psychotic symptoms which may emerge in patients suffering from borderline personality disorders, or in the treatment of severe anxiety symptoms observed in patients suffering from dependent and obsessive-compulsive personality disorders.[22]

Antipsychotic Medication

The use of antipsychotic medication should be restricted to patients presenting with psychotic symptoms, such as impairment in reality testing, delusions, ideas of reference, or hallucinations. Although the selection of antipsychotic drugs is large, in the treatment of elderly patients we select those with the lowest anticholinergic and sedative side effects.[15] Special attention should be paid in these patients to the onset of symptoms of orthostatic hypotension, which increase the risk for falls.[15] Low doses are invariably indicated at least at the outset of treatment.

Anxiolytic Medication

The use of anxiolytics in the elderly is controversial. Some specialists will prefer to avoid the usage of these medications for fear of inducing increased cognitive defects, which are commonly observed in the elderly with the use of these medications.[15] In our opinion this risk should be clinically weighed against the importance of the rapid and effective relief of anxiety symptoms in these patients. Barbiturates and other drugs like meprobamate are not recommended in elderly patients. The diazepines are the most commonly used medication in this class. The choice of long-acting versus short-acting agents is also controversial. While the former offers the advantages of rapid metabolism of the drug in the case of severe medication side effects, the first provides a stable blood level of the medications, avoiding fluctuation of blood levels and therapeutic effects during the day. If the clinician chooses to use a long-acting drug, diazepam (Valium) and alprazolam (Xanax) have been shown to be effective in the relief of anxiety symptoms. Recently buspirone, a non-benzodiazepine anxiolytic drug that lacks the problems of tolerance and withdrawal observed with other anxiolytics like barbiturates and benzodiazepine, has been proposed as an effective treatment for anxiety symptoms in the elderly. This drug lacks cross-tolerance with alcohol, barbiturates, and benzodiazepines.[23] The major disadvantage is the lag between the intake of the medication and the start of the therapeutic effects. This lag may range from 1 to 3 weeks.[23]

ENVIRONMENTAL MANIPULATION

Changes in a patient's social environment resulting from the death of a spouse, loss of friends, retirement, or moving are frequent precipitating causes of psychiatric consultations, in elderly patients.[16] The relocation of an elderly patient to a living situation with a very structured environment, such as an adult congregate living facility (ACLF), may be an appropriate strategy for anxiety symptoms or difficulties in adjustment. Resocialization, including such activities as volunteering for charity work or joining a community center or starting occupational therapy, may be enough to improve substantially the patient's quality of life and, therefore, improve the patient's symptoms. The number of community options increases every day, and it is an obligation of the clinical geriatrician to know about the presence of these facilities in the community in which he or she practices.[1,53]

Other factors to be considered when using treatment techniques of environmental manipulation are individual and cultural differences. Alternatives such as moving parents into their children's homes may be a natural and appropriate alternative for some patients and families, while for others it is a terrible mistake.

PSYCHOTHERAPY

Psychotherapy, ranging from psychoanalytically oriented psychotherapy to cognitive techniques, is one of the most effective ways to treat personality disorders at any age.[24] The use of psychoanalytic/psychotherapeutic techniques in the elderly had been a subject of controversy over the years.[25] Some clinicians considered that prolonged psychological treatments were not appropriate for elderly patients. These issues are now resolved. In a healthy, highly educated, psychologically oriented, and highly functional patient with intact cognitive functions, the use of psychodynamic psychotherapy should be seriously considered for the treatment of some personality disorders. These techniques include long-term psychoanalytically oriented psychotherapy, as well as short-term psychotherapy using techniques such as those developed by Mann[26] and Malan.[27]

For patients that do not meet the criteria of this restricted group, other therapeutic approaches, such as individual or group supportive or cognitive therapies, should be considered. The goals of supportive techniques are to enhance adequate perceptions of reality and maximize the patient's level of functioning. These goals are accomplished by strengthened adaptive behaviors, through advice, environmental restructuring, and problem solving. Cognitive psychotherapy identifies and alters behavioral distortions that maintain symptoms. This treatment may include the use of assigned readings, homework, and identification of attitudes and beliefs underlying partly successful patterns of behavior.

CONCLUSION

The onset of personality disorders is not common in the elderly. However, lifelong behavioral traits may be modified with age and the various changes which accompany aging. The clinical geriatrician should be aware of these disorders, not only for the need of their prompt diagnosis and treatment but also because several systemic disorders may mimic personality disorders in their presentation. Differential diagnosis will be of critical importance in the treatment of the underlying disorder, and ongoing personality disorders play a crucial role in the patient's management.

REFERENCES

1. Jones WH, Cavert C, Snider R, Bruce T: Relational stress: An analysis of situations and events associated with loneliness, in Duck S, Perlman D (eds): *Sage Series on Personal Relationships*. Beverly Hills, CA, Sage, 1985.
2. Sapolsky RM, Krey LC, McEwen BS: The neuroendocrinology of stress and aging: The glucocorticoid cascade hypothesis. *Endocrinol Rev* 7(1):284, 1986.
3. Holmes S: *Adaptive Behavior and Health Change*. Medical thesis, University of Washington, Seattle, 1970.
4. American Psychiatric Association: *Diagnostic and Statistical Manual of Mental Disorders*, 3d ed, revised. Washington, American Psychiatric Association, 1987.
5. Clow H, Allen E: Manifestations of psychoneuroses occuring in later life. *Geriatrics* 6:31, 1951.
6. Gutman D: An exploration of ego configurations in middle and later life, in Neugarten B et al (eds): *Personality in Middle and Late Life*. New York, Atherton Press, 1964.
7. Sinnott JD: Stress, health, and mental health symptoms of older women and men. *Int J Aging Hum Dev* 20(2):123, 1984–85.
8. Silverman PR: Widowhood and preventive intervention. *Fam Coord* 21:95, 1972.
9. Hansson RO, Jones WH, Carpenter BN, Remondet JH: Loneliness and adjustment to old age. *Int J Aging Hum Dev* 24(1):41, 1986–87.
10. Cicero: On old age (44 BC), in *Selected Works* (trans M Grant). Baltimore, Penguin, 1960, pp 213–247.
11. Robbins, Murphy GE: Drug use in a normal population of young Negro men. *Am J Public Health* 57(9):1580, 1967.
12. Ciompi L: Follow-up studies on the evolution of former neurotic and depressive states in old age. *J Geriatr Psychiatry* 3:90, 1969.
13. Gutman D, Grunes J, Giffin B: The clinical psychology of later life. Developmental paradigms presented at the 32nd Annual Meeting of the Gerontological Society, Washington, November 29, 1979.
14. Fenichel O: *The Psychoanalytic Theory of Neurosis*. New York, Norton, 1945.
15. Olsen E, Guterman A, Lowenstein D, Mintzer J: *The Older Patient, Depression in the Older Patient—Common but Complex*, vol 2, no 2, pp 12–18.
16. Simons RL, West GE: Life changes, coping resources, and health among the elderly. *Int J Aging Hum Dev* 20(3):173, 1984–85.
17. Cohen E, Poulshock S: Societal response to mass dislocation of the elderly. *Gerontologist* 17:262, 1977.
18. Friedsam H: Reactions of older persons to disaster-caused losses: An hypothesis of relative deprivation. *Gerontologist* 1:34, 1961.
19. Bolin R, Klenow DJ: Older people in disaster: A comparison of black and white victims. *Int J Aging Hum Dev* 26(1):29, 1988.
20. Moore H, Friedsam H: Reported emotional stress following a disaster. *Soc Forces* 38:135, 1959.
21. Luken PC: Social identity in later life: A situational approach to understanding old age stigma. *Int J Aging Hum Dev* 25(3):177, 1987.
22. Eisdorfer C, Fann W (eds): *Psychopharmacology in the Aging*. New York, Plenum, 1973.
23. Eison AS, Temple DL: Busiprone: Review of its pharmacology and current perspectives on its mechanism of action. *Am J Med* 80(suppl 3B):1, 1986.
24. Moore JT, Christenson R: Significance of premorbid adjustment and psychotherapy in selected case studies. *Int J Aging Hum Dev* 26(2):117, 1988.
25. Butler RN, Lewis MI: *Aging and Mental Health: Positive Psychosocial Approaches*. New York, Mosby, 1977.
26. Mann J: *The Limited Psychotherapy*. Cambridge, Harvard University Press, 1973.
27. Malan DH: *The Frontier of Brief Psychotherapy*. New York, Plenum, 1978.
28. McCrae RR, Costa PT Jr: *Emerging Lives, Enduring Dispositions: Personality in Adulthood*. Boston, Little, Brown, 1984.
29. Costa PT Jr, McCrae RR: Age differences in personality structure revisited: Studies in validity, stability and change. *Aging Hum Dev* 8:261, 1977.
30. Douglas K, Arenberg D: Age changes, cohort differences, and cultural change on the Guilford-Zimmerman temperament survey. *J Gerontol* 33:737, 1978.
31. Siegler IC, George LK, Okun MA: Cross-sequential analysis of adult personality. *Dev Psychobiol* 15:350, 1979.
32. Block J: Some enduring and consequential structures of personality, in Rabin AI (ed): *Further Explorations in Personality*. New York, Wiley-Interscience, 1981.
33. McCrae RR, Costa PT Jr: Self-concept and the stability of personality: Cross-sectional comparisons of self-reports and ratings. *J Pers Soc Psychol* 43:1282, 1982.
34. Costa PT Jr, McCrae RR: Age, personality, and the Holtzman inkblot technique. *Int J Aging Hum Dev* 23(2):115, 1986.
35. Russell D, Peplau LA, Ferguson M: Developing a measure of loneliness. *J Pers Assess* 42:190, 1978.
36. Perlman D, Gerson AC, Spinner B: Loneliness among senior citizens: An empirical report. *Essence* 2:239, 1978.
37. Russell D, Peplau LA, Cutrona CE: The revised UCLA loneliness scale: Concurrent and discriminant validity. *J Pers Social Psychol* 39:472, 1980.
38. Jones WH, Freemon JA, Goswick RA: The persistence of loneliness: Self and other determinants. *J Pers* 49:27, 1981.
39. Jones WH, Hobbs SA, Hockenbury D: Loneliness and social skill deficits. *J Pers Social Psychol* 42:682, 1982.
40. Jones WH: Loneliness and social behavior, in Peplau LA, Perlman D (eds): *Loneliness: A Sourcebook of Current Theory, Research and Therapy*. New York, Wiley-Interscience, 1982.
41. Gutman D: Mayan aging: A comparative T.A.T. study. *Psychiatry* 29:246, 1966.

42. Gutman D: Aging among the highland Maya. *J Pers Social Psychol* 7:28, 1967.
43. Gutman D: Alternatives to disengagement: The old men of the highland Druze, in Levine RA (ed): *Culture and Personality: Contemporary Readings.* Chicago, Aldine, 1974.
44. Gutman D: Impact and recovery: A comparison of black and white disaster victims. Paper presented at the meetings of the American Sociological Association, San Antonio, Texas, 1984.
45. Menninger K: *The Vital Balance: The Life Process in Mental Health and Illness.* New York, Viking Press, 1963.
46. Haan N: *Coping and Defending.* New York, Academic Press, 1977.
47. Shenfeld ME: The developmental course of defense mechanisms in later life. *Int J Aging Hum Dev* 19(1):55, 1984–85.
48. Pfeiffer E: Psychopathology and social pathology, in Birren J, Schaie K (eds): *Handbook on the Psychology of Aging.* New York, Litton, 1977.
49. Gutman D: *Reclaimed Powers.* New York, Basic Books, 1987.
50. Neugarten BL: Personality and psychosocial patterns of aging, in Bergener M, Ermini M, Stahelin HB (eds): *Crossroads in Aging.* San Diego, Academic Press, 1988, pp 205–219.
51. Shanan J: Coping style, personality type and aging, in Bergener M, Ermini M, Stahelin HB (eds): *Crossroads in Aging.* San Diego, Academic Press, 1988, pp 221–232.
52. Eastwood R, Corbin S, Reed M: Hearing impairment and paraphrenia. *J Otolaryngol* 10(4):306, 1981.
53. Cohen D, Hegarty J, Eisdorfer C: The desk directory of social resources: A physician reference guide to social and community services for the aged. *J Am Geriatr Soc* 31:38, 1983.

Chapter 107

PSYCHOTHERAPY AND PSYCHOPHARMACOLOGY

Kimberly A. Sherrill and Burton V. Reifler

The psychiatrist is less likely than the primary care practitioner to provide mental health services for the elderly.[1–5] According to one estimate, the elderly with mental disorders make about 4.3 visits per year to primary care providers, compared to only 1.7 visits per year to mental health specialists.[6] In addition, primary care practitioners are by far the largest prescribers of psychotropic medications in the elderly.[7]

One useful and relevant principle is that psychological issues rarely exist independent from physical ones. This applies to treatment as well, for psychopharmacology and psychotherapy are interrelated when the individual patient is considered. In fact, psychological factors may have more influence on health behavior than physical symptoms. For example, the stigma often associated with mental illness may lead a patient to cover up problems such as depression or cognitive disturbance, thus delaying recognition and treatment.

We will discuss principles of both the theory and practice of psychotherapy and psychopharmacologic therapy. These two areas span a broad range of therapeutic options available to the physician caring for the mental and emotional needs of the geriatric patient.

PRINCIPLES OF PSYCHOTHERAPY

Psychotherapy, whether practiced as office counseling by the primary care physician, or as psychoanalytic psychotherapy by the psychiatrist, derives from theory, without which it would be a hit or miss venture. Unfortunately the elderly are conspicuously absent from most psychodynamic theories. Freud was not the only one, but perhaps the boldest, to express pessimistic assumptions about the elderly.[8] He wrote, "older people are no longer educable," and felt that late in life "the mass of material to be dealt with would prolong treatment indefinitely."[9] Fortunately, theoretical perspectives are emerging which acknowledge the value of psychotherapeutic work in the elderly.[10–13] The following sections address two major contributions to theory, namely, psychoanalytic concepts and newer concepts based on stage theory, and concludes with a discussion of psychotherapeutic modalities useful in work with the elderly.

PSYCHOANALYTIC CONCEPTS

Early Life Experiences

One of Freud's important contributions was the illumination of the significance of early years in shaping personality, a notion which is central to psychoanalytic theory. The importance of this concept for clinical work derives from the fact that events from early years may influence behavior as much as, or even more than, current events do. Nonpsychiatrists may focus exclusively on current events in their elderly patients, or may ask only about immediate stressors, without seeking out the circumstances of early childhood such as birth, school years, or adolescence. Patients may have experienced significant losses or disruptions in their formative years which affect their attitudes toward health behaviors, illnesses, physicians, and other aspects of the health care system. Early life experiences may have beneficial effects on patients' attitudes toward health care, e.g., a patient whose favorite aunt was a nurse, or they may have negative effects, e.g., the patient who is taught that illness is a punishment for misdeeds. In this latter example, old conflicts may be stirred by the onset of illness, such as the need to be taken care of versus the fear that some imagined misdeed will be discovered. Yet another reason for learning about a patient's younger years is that unknown strengths may be found. A demented patient who studied piano as a young girl may be able to enjoy using her musical skills in spite of failing cognitive abilities.

Mechanisms of Defense

Defense mechanisms may be thought of as the different ways an individual copes with daily emotional demands. For example, in order to keep attention focused on driving safely, one might make an effort to exclude distressing thoughts about a family member's illness, using the defense mechanism of suppression. Other common defense mechanisms include denial, rationalization, regression, projection, reaction formation, and intellectualization.[14]

Under many circumstances the use of defense mechanisms is quite appropriate, and the physician may safely support their use. For example, a patient may refer to an antidepressant as a "sleeping pill" in order to make it more psychologically palatable. In general, as long as the defense mechanism promotes healthy behavior, it may be considered appropriate. At other times, when stress exceeds a person's coping abilities, the use of defense mechanisms may become harmful. One example is the use of denial by a patient who knows or suspects that he or she is ill but refuses to see a physician.

Denial is a common defense mechanism because of fears aroused by the possibility or actuality of illness, for example, fear of loss of independent functioning, fear of becoming a burden to others, or fear of death. This may explain why elderly patients sometimes omit important bits of information and why physicians must inquire specifically, directly, and systematically about symptoms.

Transference and Countertransference

Transference and countertransference may be thought of as similar to stereotyping. When the patient unconsciously stereotypes the physician, the process is called *transference*, an example being the elderly patient who views the physician as a son or daughter. Like defense mechanisms, transference may be harmless or even helpful. In the example given above, the patient's ability to relate warmly to the physician may be enhanced by a positive son or daughter transference. On the other hand, negative transference can interfere with the therapeutic aspects of the patient-doctor relationship. An elderly patient who expects the physician to behave as an idealized son or daughter might make unrealistic demands or become unreasonably angry at perceived slights.

Countertransference is essentially the same process, but operates in the opposite direction, i.e., the physician stereotypes the patient. Although countertransference may also contribute positively to the relationship, problems can arise if the stereotypes are negative. For example, older patients are sometimes insensitively referred to as "gomers," or physicians may

fail to ask elderly patients about sexual issues because of stereotypes which label older adults as asexual. The tenacity of many such stereotypes arises in part from their role as defense mechanisms in protecting physicians (and others) from issues and conflicts that may be uncomfortable for them to face, such as awareness of aging, illness, and the growing sense of inevitability of one's own death; loss of physical function and compromised independence; changes in sexual drive and function; retirement; and growing independence of and separation from children.[10,15,16]

STAGES AND TASKS OF ADULT DEVELOPMENT

Erikson's theoretical formulations were among the first to extend beyond puberty.[17,18] He postulated a series of developmental stages, two of which are relevant to the geriatric population: adulthood and maturity. Each stage is characterized by a unique psychosocial crisis. For the stage of adulthood, the crisis is "generativity versus stagnation," and involves the need to find satisfying goals, motivation, and meaning in one's work and relationships. The stage of maturity is characterized by the crisis of "ego integrity versus despair" during which one reflects back on life's accomplishments in an evaluative way.

More recent theoretical work suggests that the notion of stages may focus too much on chronological time. Since important life events do not necessarily fall in the same order for each adult, a more fitting approach might be one which considers the specific tasks themselves, regardless of chronological age.[10] This "task" rather than "stage" focus allows for more flexibility in theoretical and clinical approaches.

THERAPEUTIC APPROACHES

Some of the major types of therapy which are potentially useful with elderly patients are described next.

Supportive Therapy

Office counseling is one type of supportive therapy which is an important part of clinical practice with the elderly. Support is widely held to benefit physical and psychological health.[19–21] The one-on-one, or confidant, relationship may be particularly important to the older adult, perhaps even more so than interaction with family and friends.[22] A physician may be in the position of a confidant for elderly patients, thus serving as an important source of support.

Three principles guide supportive therapeutic work: (1) the clinician acts as an "external ego," providing for coping mechanisms which are weak or absent in the patient; (2) the approach focuses on a specific problem which the patient helps identify; and (3) the clinician is explicit and direct, giving advice and voicing opinions about what he or she thinks is best in a given situation.[23] In this way the patient can "borrow" helpful ideas from the clinician. Being supportive may include touching or making special efforts to overcome communication blocks such as impaired vision or hearing. The physician may need to sit nearer the older person than he or she would for other adults.[24] Support may entail acknowledgment of religious values, which are an important coping resource for many elderly people, particularly those who are seriously or terminally ill.[25–29] Finally, support may mean confronting maladaptive behaviors.

Behavioral Techniques

Conditioning techniques, such as systematically reinforcing desirable behaviors while ignoring undesirable ones, may benefit certain patients who are unable to respond to other therapeutic approaches or who require a multifaceted approach. For example, a severely demented patient with incontinence may be helped by a toileting program at regular intervals. Or a severely depressed unmotivated patient may benefit from positive reinforcement to help reengage the person in social activities.

Some researchers have suggested that older adults may be harder to treat through behavioral techniques because of increased resistance to conditioning and decline of retention of learned responses.[8,30] However, if tasks are kept simple and rewards are reinforced regularly, these age-related changes may not stand in the way of therapeutic benefits. For example, simple muscle relaxation techniques which are easy to learn and apply[31] can help a patient suffering from anxiety.

Group Therapy

Fundamental to all types of group therapy are the goals of decreasing alienation and social isolation. Encouragement of autonomy and control may be one of the major determinants of successful adaptation in old age.[32] For this reason, different group approaches can be beneficial to elderly patients with all kinds of psychiatric impairment. A depressed, withdrawn patient may find new interests through the socialization of a group, while a demented patient may find needed stimulation and models for appropriate behaviors.

Family Therapy

Family interventions can be important for many frail or ill elderly people. Families operate as systems, so that changes in one element of the system affect all other system components.[33,34] Caregivers themselves may be suffering from depression or other stress-related illnesses due to the strain of dealing with their parents' health or mental health problems.[35,36] Family members of patients with Alzheimer's disease can benefit from support groups such as those sponsored by the Association for Alzheimer's and Related Disorders Association.[35]

Elements of a useful educational approach to family interventions are discussed in detail elsewhere.[37] However, general principles include: (1) avoiding blaming or expressing critical attitudes toward any individual family member; (2) acknowledging the caregiver's burden; (3) encouraging involvement of all family members in important decisions, even if they are not involved with daily care responsibilities; (4) encouraging the letting go of old sources of bitterness, allowing relationships to grow through time and understanding; and (5) emphasizing that caring for an elderly family member can be mutually rewarding and satisfying.[37,38]

PRINCIPLES OF PSYCHOPHARMACOLOGY

Judicious use of psychotropic medication can benefit elderly patients greatly. Unfortunately, psychotropics also present potential hazards, the most common ones arising from unnecessary use of multiple drugs, failure to monitor side effects, and lack of understanding of the major physiologic vulnerabilities of the elderly.[39–46] The following section presents guidelines for the use of psychotropic medications in the elderly, including physiologic, nonphysiologic, and drug-specific considerations.

PHYSIOLOGIC CONSIDERATIONS
Absorption

A number of variables such as absorptive surface, splanchnic blood flow, gastric pH, and altered gastrointestinal motility change with age, resulting in delayed absorption. Absorption may also be slowed by excess use of antacids, or by antihistamines which slow intestinal motility and gastric emptying.[41–44]

Distribution

Changes in lean body mass, total body water, and total body fat lead to increased sensitivity to psychotropic drugs. The clinical implications of these changes include a potential for prolonged action of fat-soluble psychotropics (all psychotropics except lithium), lowering of the effective milligram per kilogram body weight dose of fat-soluble drugs, and decreases in the dose of lithium required to achieve therapeutic levels.

Metabolism

All commonly prescribed psychotropic drugs are metabolized in the liver except lithium, which relies on renal clearance. While several age-related liver changes such as decreased blood flow and changes in microsomal enzymes may lead to clinically relevant effects, the evidence is conflicting, and changes are thought to be somewhat unpredictable.[43,44]

Excretion

Age-related changes in the kidney lead to prolonged drug elimination times. Accordingly, drugs may be effective at half the dose (or less) used in younger adults, and they pose a risk for side effects at low dosages.

Tissue Sensitivity

Increased target-organ sensitivity brought about by changes in receptor number and sensitivity occurs with age.[43] Such changes add to the drug sensitivity of the geriatric patient. For all the reasons noted above, drug blood levels must be interpreted conservatively in this age group.

NONPHYSIOLOGIC CONSIDERATIONS

Diagnosis

Accurate diagnosis is fundamental to safe and appropriate use of psychotropics.[7,39–43,47] Unfortunately, demented patients may not be able to give a good history, while depressed or frightened patients may omit a great deal. The physician often must inquire about symptoms very specifically and directly or turn to family members or friends for information.[24]

Compliance

Several factors potentially lead to poor medical compliance.

LEARNING PROBLEMS The ability to retain newly learned patterns is lower in the elderly, so that acquiring a new behavior such as taking a medicine regularly may be more difficult. For depressed patients who have difficulty concentrating, the potential for problems is greater. Physicians can help by reinforcing the prescribed regimen each time the patient is seen and by educating the caregiver.

FEARS In addition to cognitive problems, psychological elements such as difficulty acknowledging the need for medication and the accompanying fear of loss of independent functioning can stand in the way of successful medical compliance. Inappropriate fear of addiction may lead to underuse of certain psychotropics. Acknowledgment of such concerns and education about the nature of specific medications will often relieve patients' fears.

POLYPHARMACY Adverse side effects increase with the use of multiple drugs.[48] In particular, the sedative effects of multiple medications are cumulative, and occur more often than other kinds of drug-drug interactions. The implications of these findings for patient care are twofold: first, the number of prescribed drugs in elderly patients needs to be kept at the minimum effective level; and second, whenever possible, clinicians should strive to avoid prescribing a second drug to counteract the side effects of another, such as the use of an antipsychotic to counteract confusion due to a benzodiazepine. A safer strategy is to decrease or discontinue the offending drug.

A related complicating factor in drug compliance is treatment by more than one physician. Because of the potential for inappropriate polypharmacy, it is good practice to ask specifically whether patients are receiving care from other physicians.

CHRONICITY Many elderly patients suffer from chronic illnesses which require preventive or suppressive measures as opposed to time-limited drug therapy to alleviate specific symptoms. As a result, patients may be less motivated to comply with treatment. Antidepressants may fall into the category of preventive or suppressive agents in the treatment of chronic or recurrent depression. As many as two-thirds of depressed elderly patients may have a chronic course even when the patient has strong social supports.[49] It may be especially important to ensure good medical compliance in those individuals since social factors may have less influence. To enhance compliance, family members can be mobilized to assist; frequent follow-up can be instituted; and drugs can be carefully monitored, for example, by pill counts.

DRUG CLASSES

While the following section considers each of the major psychotropic drug classes, several overall recommendations can be made. First, drug doses should generally start at one-half to one-third the usual adult dose, and increases should be made cautiously. Second, drug regimens should be reviewed frequently, and therapeutic benefits weighed against side effects so that the number of drugs and the level of dosages used may be kept to a minimum. Finally, physicians should frequently discuss the therapeutic and adverse effects of medications frequently with both patients and their family members.

Antianxiety Agents

Antianxiety agents are useful for the short-term management of severe anxiety,[40,50] defined as anxiety which significantly interferes with the patient's ability to function in daily activities. Patients most likely to benefit from antianxiety agents are those with good cognitive abilities and no history of alcohol or drug abuse.

Three primary concerns arise from the use of these drugs in the elderly: (1) toxic effects due to accumulation of long-half-life drugs, the most worrisome effects being orthostatic hypotension and oversedation; (2) anticholinergic side effects, resulting in dry mouth, blurred vision, urinary retention, constipation, sexual dysfunction, confusion, or psychosis; and (3) idiosyncratic responses such as the paradoxical excitement sometimes seen with the use of benzodiazepines. Table 107-1 lists the half-lives of commonly prescribed benzodiazepines.

Chloral hydrate, diphenhydramine, and hydroxyzine are alternatives to the benzodiazepines for treatment of both anxiety and insomnia. However, care must be taken in using them since anticholinergic side effects can occur. Barbiturates are now rarely used to treat anxiety or insomnia because of the high potential for addiction. Other adverse effects such as suppression of REM sleep and rebound nightmares make these drugs poorly suited for use in the elderly.[42]

In terms of drug-drug interactions, antianxiety agents can add to the effects of other centrally active drugs such as other psychotropics, alcohol, narcotics, antihistamines, and antihypertensives to cause excess sedation, confusion, and increased risk of falling.[44]

Antidepressants

Antidepressant medication is useful for the treatment of major depression, particularly when symptoms interfere with daily functioning or when the patient is delusional or suicidal (in such cases inpatient treatment may be necessary). In milder cases, such as a patient who is not suicidal and is able to function adequately, a more conservative approach of supportive psychotherapy and behavioral management may be tried initially. If improvement is not seen over a 1- or 2-month period, antidepressant medication may prove useful.[51]

Unlike most of the other psychotropic medications, antidepressants may require 10 days to 2 weeks before having an effect, although minor symptoms such as sleeplessness may be helped immediately by sedative side effects. Because of this delayed action, compliance is particularly important in order to ensure an adequate trial.

Two major groups of antidepressants are in common use: the tricyclics and related compounds and the monoamine oxidase inhibitors (MAOIs). In spite of major chemical differences, a number of generalizations regarding potential harmful effects can be made.

Choice of antidepressants is primarily guided by knowledge of previous effective treatments and drug side effects. In general, those with strong anticholinergic side effects are less preferred, except where the patient has responded well to such a drug in the past or where the sedative effects of a strongly anticholinergic drug are desired for an agitated or sleepless patient.

The most common adverse side effects of concern are related to anticholinergic properties. Table 107-2 shows the relative strength of anticholinergic and sedative effects for the major tricyclics and related drugs.[26] Desipramine and nortryptyline are often the favored drugs in the older patient because of weaker side-effect profiles.

The MAOIs may be used when a patient does not respond to or cannot tolerate tricyclic antidepressants. MAOIs generally have little anticholinergic activity, with the exception of phenelzine.[52] Other serious side

TABLE 107-1
Half-Lives of Selected Benzodiazepines

Drug	Half-life, h
Alprazolam	12
Chlordiazepoxide	18
Clorazepate dipotassium	100
Diazepam	60
Lorazepam	15
Oxazepam	8
Flurazepam hydrochloride	72
Temazepam	11
Triazolam	2

SOURCE: From Baldessarini RJ: Antianxiety drugs, in *Chemotherapy in Psychiatry: Principles and Practice.* Cambridge, Harvard University Press, 1985.

TABLE 107-2
Selected Antidepressants: Pharmacologic Factors of Special Relevance to the Elderly

Agent	Relative Anticholinergic Effects	Relative Sedative Effects
Amitriptyline	6 +	5 +
Doxepin	3 +	6 +
Imipramine	4 +	3 +
Nortriptyline	3 +	2 +
Desipramine	1 +	2 +
Maprotiline	3 +	3 +
Amoxapine	3 +	3 +
Trazodone	1 +	3 +

SOURCE: From Thompson IL II et al: Psychotropic drug use in the elderly [second of 2 parts]. *N Engl J Med* 308:194, 1983.

effects result from interactions with tyramine which is present in certain aged foods. Although they may be quite effective in some patients, the dietary restrictions required for their safe use may be difficult for depressed or cognitively impaired elderly people to remember and apply, and therefore the MAOIs should probably be used with caution.[50]

Tricyclic antidepressants may cause cardiac effects including prolonging the PR interval and the QRS duration. Although these quinidinelike effects may actually benefit some patients with arrhythmias, electrocardiography is recommended in patients with heart disease,[53] with particular attention to conduction defects.

In terms of drug-drug interactions, the antihypertensives guanethidine, bethanidine, and debrisoquin may decrease the therapeutic effects of antidepressants. Centrally active drugs, including other psychotropics, alcohol, and pain medications, increase the risk of confusion, falling, and orthostatic hypotension. Over-the-counter drugs such as antihistamines also increase the risk for anticholinergic effects.[46]

Some authors[54] have advocated the use of psychostimulants such as methylphenidate as an antidepressant in certain patients who are unable to tolerate other antidepressants or who have medical illnesses which contraindicate their use. However, no large-scale controlled studies have been conducted in support of these case reports.

Antipsychotics

Antipsychotics are most commonly used in the treatment of acute or chronic psychosis or for agitation in the demented patient. For example, in low dosage, antipsychotics can reduce or even eliminate paranoid delusions. However, when using antipsychotic drugs, it is important to seek underlying organic illness which may be causing or contributing to the psychosis.

Like the antidepressants, choice of antipsychotics is largely empirical. If a patient has benefited from a certain drug before, it should be tried first; otherwise, drug choices may be individualized according to desirable versus undesirable side effects.

The antipsychotics have three major types of side effects: (1) sedative and anticholinergic effects, (2) extrapyramidal symptoms (EPS), and (3) tardive dyskinesia. The more potent (on a milligram-for-milligram basis) antipsychotics, e.g., haloperidol and fluphenazine, have the highest incidence of EPS and the lowest incidence of anticholinergic side effects. The reverse (low EPS, high anticholinergic activity) is true for the low-potency drugs such as chlorpromazine and thioridazine. Drugs with an intermediate range of side effects include trifluoperazine and thiothixene. In situations where sedation may be needed such as for an agitated elderly patient, the low-

potency drugs may serve best, but the trade-off is a greater risk of adverse anticholinergic effects. Conversely, where delirium or psychosis is the most pressing concern, a high-potency drug is a good choice, given that greater care must be taken to watch for EPS. All antipsychotics have long half-lives and so accumulate over time. Once-a-day or every-other-day administration may be the best approach for the geriatric patient.

The syndrome of motor restlessness, known as *akathisia*, is a common type of EPS. A second type is *parkinsonism*, with the classic shuffling gait, muscle rigidity, and blank face. While the best treatment for these two syndromes is either a reduction in antipsychotic dosage or a change to a less potent antipsychotic, at times an antiparkinson agent such as amantadine may be useful. A final type of EPS commonly seen is the dystonic reaction, or syndrome of fixed muscle spasm.[45] For acute dystonic reactions benztropine or diphenhydramine provide almost immediate relief. The physician can then lower the antipsychotic dose, switch to a less potent drug, or discontinue the antipsychotic altogether.

Tardive dyskinesia is a severe, potentially irreversible side effect of neuroleptic treatment characterized by involuntary movements primarily involving the oral-facial or neck muscles. The extremities may be involved, and occasionally swallowing can be affected.[52] In the early stages, the signs may be easily overlooked as normal movements. Of concern in the geriatric population is that the risk for tardive dyskinesia increases markedly with age.[53] The treatment of choice, discontinuation of the neuroleptic, may lead to a temporary worsening, but spontaneous remissions are known to occur.

Important drug-drug interactions include an increased risk for orthostatic hypotension when antipsychotics are combined with antihypertensives. In addition, centrally active drugs such as pain medicines, alcohol, and other psychotropics can cause confusion and oversedation. Heavy use of antacids may interfere with absorption,[43] and antihistamines may add anticholinergic side effects.[44]

Lithium

Lithium is primarily indicated for the treatment of mania which, though it is uncommon, may present as an initial episode in late life. Depressed patients who cannot tolerate antidepressants may respond to lithium alone, or lithium may be added as a second drug in treatment-resistant cases.

Side effects and toxicity are more likely to occur in the elderly than in other adults, and they occur at lower blood levels.[45] Low starting doses are recommended, and blood levels should be monitored weekly at first, then as frequently as every 3 months for maintenance therapy, depending on the details of the particular case.

Blood levels are usually therapeutic at lower levels than for younger adults, a reasonable range being 0.3–0.7 meq/liter. Signs of toxicity include nausea and vomiting, hand tremor, and confusion. Patients may appear to be "drunk." Common effects, which may fade away after the first few weeks of treatment, include dry mouth, increased urination, and mild hand tremor. Less commonly, thyroid supresion or loss of renal concentrating ability may occur, so that thyroid function, creatinine, and electrolytes should be assessed prior to beginning treatment and regularly thereafter. Both thyroid and renal effects are thought to be reversible by lowering the dose or discontinuing the drug.

The most important drug-drug interactions include raising of blood levels caused by concomitant use of sodium-depleting diuretics. Inadequate diet or dehydration may lead to toxicity.[46] Patients should be advised to avoid skipping meals and to take precautions if they expect to be outdoors for long on a hot day. The diuretic effect of alcohol may similarly cause problems, particularly when combined with excess evaporative loss. Finally, use with other centrally active drugs may lead to greater risk of confusion or sedation.[48]

CONCLUSION

This summary of the two major treatment strategies for psychiatric disorders emphasizes the importance of the primary care practitioner in providing services to the mentally ill elderly patient. A variety of effective treatment approaches are available, not only for those with mild illness who may benefit greatly from relatively simple interventions, but also for patients suffering from chronic or debilitating illnesses who can be helped through an approach that combines medical and psychotherapeutic modalities. While the psychiatrist can be called on as needed for his or her expertise, primary care physicians can incorporate many of these strategies into their own practices.

REFERENCES

1. Regier DA et al: The de facto US mental health services system. *Arch Gen Psychiatry* 35:685, 1978.
2. German PS et al: Detection and management of mental health problems of older patients by primary care providers. *JAMA* 257:489, 1987.
3. Group for the Advancement of Psychiatry: *Toward a Public Policy on Mental Health Care of the Elderly.* New York, Report no 79, 1970.
4. Shapiro S et al: Utilization of health and mental health services. *Arch Gen Psychiatry*, 41:971, 1984.
5. George LK et al: Psychiatric disorders and mental health service use in later life: Evidence from the Epidemiologic Catchment Area program, in Brody J, Maddox G (eds): *Epidemiology and Aging.* New York, Springer, 1987.
6. Goldstrom ID et al: Mental health services use by elderly adults in a primary care setting. *J Gerontol* 42:147, 1987.
7. Larson DB et al: Psychotropics prescribed to the U.S. elderly in 1980 and 1981: Prescribing patterns of primary care practitioners, psychiatrists, and other physicians. (Submitted for review.)
8. Larson DB et al: Geriatrics, in Wolman BB (ed): *The Therapist's Handbook: Treatment Methods of Mental Disorders,* 2d ed. New York, Van Nostrand Reinhold, 1983, p 343.
9. Freud S: On psychotherapy (1906), in Jones E (ed): *Collected Papers,* London RJ (translator). London, Hogarth Press, vol I, 1942.
10. Colarusso CA, Nemiroff RA: Clinical implications of adult developmental theory. *Am J Psychiatry* 144:1263, 1987.
11. Blank ML: Raising the age barrier to psychotherapy. *Geriatrics* 29:141, 1974.
12. Nemiroff RA, Colarusso CA: *The Race against Time: Psychotherapy and Psychoanalysis in the Second Half of Life.* New York, Plenum, 1985.
13. Butler RN, Lewis MI: *Aging and Mental Health: Positive Psychosocial Approaches.* St. Louis, Mosby, 1977.
14. White RB, Gilliland RM: *Elements of Psychopathology: The Mechanisms of Defense.* New York, Grune & Stratton, 1975.
15. Gurian BS: The myth of the aged as asexual: Countertransference issues in therapy. *Hosp Community Psychiatry* 37:345, 1986.
16. Ray DC et al: Ageism in psychiatrists: Associations with gender, certification, and theoretical orientation. *Gerontologist* 25:496, 1985.
17. Erikson EH: *Childhood and Society,* 2d ed. New York, Norton, 1963.
18. Meissner WW: Theories of personality and psychopathology: Classical psychoanalysis, in Kaplan HI, Sadock BJ (eds): *Comprehensive Textbook of Psychiatry/IV,* 4th ed. Baltimore, Williams & Wilkins, 1985.
19. House JS, Kahn RL: Measures and concepts of social support, in Cohen S, Syme SL (eds): *Social Support and Health.* Orlando, FL, Academic Press, 1985, p 83.
20. House JS et al: The association of social relationships and activities with mortality: Prospective evidence from the Tecumseh community health study. *Am J Epidemiol* 116:123, 1982.
21. Thoits PA: Social support and psychological well-being: Theoretical possibilities, in Sarason IG, Sarason BR (eds): *Social Support: Theory, Research and Applications.* Boston, Martinus Nijhoff, 1985, p 51.
22. Strain LA, Chappel NL: Confidants: Do they make a difference in quality of life? *Res Aging* 4:479, 1982.
23. Werman DS: *The Practice of Supportive Psychotherapy.* New York, Brunner/Mazel, 1984.
24. Blazer DG: Techniques for communicating with your elderly patient. *Geriatrics* 33:79, 1978.
25. Moberg DO: Religiosity in old age. *Gerontologist* 5:78, 1965.
26. Blazer D, Palmore E: Religion and aging in a longitudinal panel. *Gerontologist* 16:82, 1976.
27. Hadaway CK: Life satisfaction and religion: A reanalysis. *Soc Forces* 57:636, 1978.

28. Vastayan EA: Spiritual aspects of the care of cancer patients, in Holleb AI et al (eds): *Ethics and Cancer.* New York, American Cancer Society, 1986.

29. Suchman AL, Matthews DA: What makes the patient-doctor relationship therapeutic? Exploring the connexional dimensional of medical care. *Ann Intern Med* 108:125, 1988.

30. Soumireu-Mourat B: Experimental studies of ageing: Behavioural and physiological correlates. *Gerontology* 32 (suppl):24, 1986.

31. Ferguson JA et al: A script for deep muscle relaxation. *Dis Nerv System* 38:703, 1977.

32. Rowe JW, Kahn RL: Human aging: Usual and successful. *Science* 237:143, 1987.

33. Minuchin S: *Families and Family Therapy.* Cambridge, Harvard University Press, 1974.

34. Miller JG, Miller JL: General living systems theory, in Kaplan HI, Sadock BJ (eds): *Comprehensive Textbook of Psychiatry/IV,* 4th ed. Baltimore, Williams and Wilkins, chap. 1.2, 1985.

35. Gallagher DE: Intervention strategies to assist caregivers of frail elders: Current research status and future directions, in Lawton MP, Maddox G (eds): *Annual Review of Gerontology and Geriatrics.* New York, Springer, 1985, vol 5, p 249.

36. Mace NL, Rabins PV: *The 36-Hour Day: A Family Guide to Caring for Persons with Alzheimer's Disease, Related Dementing Illnesses, and Memory Loss in Later Life.* Baltimore, Johns Hopkins University Press, 1981.

37. Couper DP, Sheehan NW: Family dynamics for caregivers: An educational model. *Fam Rel* 16:181, 1987.

38. Silverstone B, Hyman HK: *You and Your Aging Parents.* New York, Pantheon Books, 1982.

39. Vestal RE: Pharmacology and aging. *J Am Geriatr Soc* 30:191, 1982.

40. Beardsley RS et al: Prescribing of psychotropics in elderly nursing home patients. *J Am Geriatr Soc* 37:327, 1989.

41. Ouslander JG: Drug therapy in the elderly. *Ann Intern Med* 95:711, 1981.

42. Thompson TL II et al: Psychotropic drug use in the elderly, I. *N Engl J Med* 308:134, 1983.

43. Ouslander JG, Tamai I: Drug treatment for elderly patients. *Compr Ther* 13:62, 1987.

44. Salzman C: Key concepts in geriatric psychopharmacology. *Psychiatr Clin North Am* 5:181, 1982.

45. Salzman C: A primer on geriatric psychopharmacology. *Am J Psychiatry* 139:67, 1982.

46. Lippmann S: Geriatric aspects of psychopharmacology, pt A. *J Ky Med Assoc* 85:285, 1987.

47. Burns BJ, Kamerow DB: Psychotropic drug prescriptions for nursing home residents. *J Fam Pract* 26:155, 1988.

48. Larson EB, et al: Adverse drug reactions associated with global cognitive impairment in elderly persons. *Ann Intern Med* 107:169, 1987.

49. Murphy E: The prognosis of depression in old age. *Br J Psychiatry* 142:111, 1983.

50. Salzman C: Geriatric psychopharmacology. *Ann Rev Med* 36:217, 1985.

51. Reifler BV, Borson S: Geriatric psychiatry, in Cavenar JO Jr (ed): *Psychiatry.* Philadelphia, Lippincott, 1985, vol 2, chap 119.

52. Baldessarini RJ: *Chemotherapy in Psychiatry: Principles and Practice.* Cambridge, Harvard University Press, 1985.

53. Thompson TL II et al: Psychotropic drug use in the elderly, II. *N Engl J Med* 308:194, 1983.

54. Katon W, Raskind M: Treatment of depression in the medically ill elderly with methylphenidate. *Am J Psychiatry* 137:963, 1980.

Part Four

GERIATRIC SYNDROMES AND SPECIAL PROBLEMS

Chapter 108

APPROACH TO THE DIAGNOSIS AND TREATMENT OF THE INFECTED OLDER ADULT

Thomas T. Yoshikawa

EPIDEMIOLOGY

PREVALENCE OF IMPORTANT INFECTIONS

When compared to young adults, older adults—particularly those who are 75 years and older—are at greater risk for acquiring an infection.[1] Currently available data indicate that this increased susceptibility with old age is limited to select infectious diseases (Table 108-1).[2] However, several of these infections are those that are the most frequently encountered by physicians in their clinical practice, i.e., pneumonia, urinary tract infection, sepsis, intraabdominal infections, and soft-tissue infections.

Some of the important infections of the older adult (pneumonia, tuberculosis, and herpes zoster) are reviewed in depth elsewhere in this book and, therefore, will not be discussed in any detail in this chapter. Pneumonia occurs at a higher rate—up to 60 percent of all cases—in individuals 65 years or older compared to younger patients.[3] The prevalence of urinary tract infection as well as asymptomatic bacteriuria increases significantly with advancing age, both in males and females.[4] This prevalence varies from 10 to 50 percent, depending on the patient's residential status, functional limitations,

The author gratefully acknowledges the Department of Veterans Affairs for support of programs in aging and Mr. Jerry Sproul for typing of the manuscript.

underlying genitourinary disorders, and gender. Urinary tract infections alone account for 30 to 50 percent of all cases of bacteremia and sepsis in the older adult regardless of the setting.[5–8] Bacteremia and sepsis, especially gram-negative bacillary sepsis, occur predominantly in the elderly population, and they account for 40 to 60 percent of all cases.[8,9] Acute diverticulitis and cholecystitis are important intraabdominal infections that are more common in the older adult.[10] Although acute appendicitis is primarily a surgical disease of the young, it does occur in approximately 5 percent of adults aged 60 and older.[11] Its importance in the older adult consists of the fact that the diagnosis is only infrequently considered in this age group, with resulting diagnostic and therapeutic delays; thus, morbidity and mortality are extremely high. In the preantibiotic era, infective endocarditis occurred predominantly in young adults. However, over the past 20 years, the demography of infective endocarditis has changed to involve more older adults with several studies reporting a mean age of the patients of approximately 55 years.[12] This rise in age reflects the fact that infective endocarditis involves valves with degenerative or atherosclerotic changes.[13] Tuberculosis is evolving into an infection that is dominated by the aging population including nursing home patients.[14,15] Septic arthritis is a particularly important problem in the aged because of the high prevalence of preexisting joint disease (e.g., osteoarthritis, rheumatoid arthritis, gout, and

TABLE 108-1
Important Infectious Diseases of Older Adults

Infections	Comments
Pneumonia	Leading cause of death due to infection in the elderly
Urinary tract infection	Most common cause of bacteremia and sepsis in older adults
Intraabdominal infections	Gangrene of appendix and gallbladder is highest in elderly; diverticulitis occurs primarily in older adults
Soft-tissue infection	Pressure sores (decubitus ulcers) and postoperative wound infections most common in older age group
Bacteremia/sepsis	Of all cases, 40 percent occur in elderly; responsible for 60 percent of deaths in the older adult
Infective endocarditis	Increased prevalence with old age
Tuberculosis	Disproportionately high number of cases in the elderly including nursing home residents
Septic arthritis	Previous joint disease increases risk in the older adult
Tetanus	Of all U.S. cases, 60% occur in older adults
Herpes zoster (shingles)	Prevalence increases with age; postherpetic neuralgia occurs primarily in elderly

pseudogout) as well as the common occurrence of prosthetic joints.[16,17] Of the various soft-tissue infections, infected pressure sores (decubitus ulcers) occur most commonly in the elderly patient,[18,19] with a frequency that varies from 5 to 10 percent. Because of waning immunity and lack of adequate immunization in the older patient, 60 percent of tetanus cases in the United States occur in persons 60 years and older.[20] Finally, herpes zoster (shingles) increases in frequency with old age,[21,22] most likely related to the decline in cell-mediated immunity that is associated with senescence. More importantly, the dreaded complication of postherpetic neuralgia is seen primarily in individuals over the age of 60.[21,22]

MORTALITY RELATED TO INFECTIONS

The elderly are at increased risk for more serious infections as well as more severe complications including death.[23] Several factors related to aging contribute to poorer outcomes of older adults with infections[24]: (1) limited physiologic reserve capacities in response to

stress; (2) alterations in host defense mechanisms; (3) presence of chronic and debilitating illnesses; (4) greater exposure to nosocomial pathogens; (5) delays in diagnosis and treatment; (6) higher frequency of complications from diagnostic and therapeutic procedures; (7) delayed response to chemotherapy; and (8) higher incidence of adverse reaction to antimicrobial drugs.

When comparative studies or data are available, the difference in mortality between the young and older adult is striking. The following are several examples. The mortality for hospitalized elderly patients with pneumonia is 12.8 per 100 hospital discharges compared to 1.5 per 100 hospital discharges for younger patients.[25] Elderly persons with acute appendicitis experience death at rates 10 to 15 times that of young adults.[10] Gram-negative bacillary sepsis is associated with a mortality that is two to three times higher in older adults.[26] Similar mortality figures are found when comparing bacterial meningitis and infective endocarditis in the young versus older adult.[27,28]

AGING AND RISK FACTORS TO INFECTION

Since the topic of immunity and aging is reviewed elsewhere in this book, the discussion here will focus on other factors that appear to place the older adult at greater risk or susceptibility to infectious diseases.

ENVIRONMENTAL FACTORS

The elderly not only are hospitalized more frequently but the duration of their hospitalization is generally longer than younger patients.[29] This places the older adult at greater risk for acquisition of nosocomial infections. When age alone is considered, the nosocomial infection rate in the elderly is significantly higher than in adults under 65 years old.[30] Similarly, the very old provide the highest census in long-term care facilities. In both the acute care hospital setting and long-term care facility, urinary tract infection, pneumonia, soft-tissue infections, and bacteremia are the dominant infectious diseases.[30–33] Moreover, the attack rate for each of these infections is two to five times higher in the very old compared to young adults.[30,31] Unfortunately, under these circumstances, gram-negative bacilli are the most frequently isolated etiologic pathogens. They are often resistant to several antibiotics, and tend to infect individuals with poor host resistance. They cause bacteremia and are associated with high mortality.

HOST FACTORS

THE PHYSIOLOGIC CHANGES OF AGING Physiologic changes include a variety of anatomic and functional alterations in tissues and organs. For example, diminished blood perfusion, degenerative processes, alterations in permeability, decreased cough reflex, loss of cells, calcification, thinning of skin, and altered gastric motility are biological changes that might increase the risk to infection.[1]

CHRONIC DISEASES These diseases are common in older adults, and many of these disorders increase the susceptibility of the individual to infection. For example, dementia and strokes are associated with higher frequency of pneumonia, urinary tract infection, and pressure sores because these neurologic problems cause motor dysfunction, immobility, incontinence, poor personal hygiene, poor cough and swallowing reflexes, and diminished cognition. Similarly, tumors and cancers cause anatomic changes, obstruction and altered blood flow, as well as compromised host defense mechanisms either from the disease or the associated therapy—all of which predispose the patient to infections.

ABERRATION OF HOST DEFENSE MECHANISM Changes in host defense mechanism occur more frequently in the elderly, either from the aging process or chronic underlying diseases.[1,23] Although aging alone may not be associated with dramatic changes in phagocytosis by neutrophils and macrophages and in complement function,[34] it is likely that some of the chronic diseases that are seen in the elderly do impact on these host defense mechanisms. Moreover, there is increasing evidence that neutrophil functions as part of the inflammation process are significantly influenced or regulated by various cytokines (which are part of the immune system).[35] With the finding of functional impairments of cell-mediated immunity with aging, the association of aging and phagocytic dysfunction may become more apparent in the future.

CLINICAL FEATURES OF INFECTIONS

Although the topic of altered presentations of diseases in the elderly is discussed in another chapter (Chap. 22), it is worthwhile to review some important aspects of the clinical manifestations of infection in the older adult.

FEVER

Fever, whether elicited by history or determined by physical examination, is a cardinal characteristic of most infectious diseases. Although fever in children or young adults is frequently caused by relatively benign illnesses (e.g., pharyngitis, otitis media, viral syndrome), the rapid development of an elevated body temperature in an older adult is almost invariably due to a serious infec-

tious disease, e.g., pneumonia, urinary tract infection, intraabdominal sepsis.[36] It is imperative, therefore, that the clinician carefully evaluate the febrile elderly patient for a potential serious infectious disease before being released from the clinic, office, or emergency room as simply having a benign illness.

In older adults who have prolonged fever of undetermined origin (FUO), infections have been found to be the cause of FUO in approximately 40 percent of cases.[37] Neoplasms and connective tissue diseases account for the remaining cases of FUO.

Although the presence of fever in the aged person heralds a serious underlying problem, the elderly when compared to younger adults more often fail to show a temperature elevation despite having a serious infectious disease.[38] In comparative studies of fever in younger adults versus older adults with bacteremia,[39,40] pneumonia,[41] infective endocarditis,[28] and tuberculosis,[15] the lack of a fever response occurred two to three times more often in the elderly.

OTHER FEATURES

In addition to a blunted fever response, other clinical manifestations of an infection may be atypical or nonspecific in the older adult. Like many illnesses that affect the elderly, such nonspecific symptoms as anorexia, fatigue, and weight loss as well as atypical complaints of incontinence, falls, or mental confusion may be the primary clinical manifestation of an infection.

DIAGNOSTIC APPROACH

DIFFERENTIAL DIAGNOSIS

In older adults who present with typical clinical manifestations of a particular infection (e.g., fever, dysuria, frequency, and urgency for urinary tract infection), the diagnostic approach is straightforward and uncomplicated. However, in those elderly individuals who manifest only nonspecific symptoms or who have atypical complaints within a short period, an infectious disease must always be considered in the differential diagnosis.[1]

It is not practical or cost-effective to initiate an extensive diagnostic evaluation for an infectious disease in patients in whom the most likely type of infection is not clinically apparent. Certainly, determining which underlying diseases are present is often helpful in suspecting which infection and/or microorganisms might be the most probable cause. For example, chronic obstructive lung disease is most frequently complicated by pneumonia; prostatic enlargement is complicated by urinary tract infection; gallstones are complicated by bacillary sepsis; and leukemia is complicated by gram-negative bacillary sepsis.

Alternatively, a reasonably reliable differential diagnosis of various infectious diseases in the elderly can be made based on functional status or level of care. A differential diagnostic approach is summarized in Table 108-2. A healthy, functionally independent older adult living at home most frequently acquires respiratory tract infections (especially bacterial pneumonia), urinary tract infection, or intraabdominal sepsis (usually biliary sepsis, diverticulitis, or appendicitis). Less frequently, infective endocarditis, tuberculosis, septic arthritis, and meningitis cause infections in this group. Elderly patients in the hospital are at greater risk for urinary tract infection, aspiration pneumonia, and surgical wound infection,[30,31] and less often develop septic thrombophlebitis (local intravenous site). Noninfectious disorders may cause a fever or simulate an infectious disease, and these include pulmonary emboli, drug reactions, and hepatitis (viral or toxic reaction). Patients in chronic care facilities or nursing homes are most commonly transferred to an acute-care hospital because of fever or an infection.[42,43] The most frequent infections are pneumonia, urinary tract infection, and infected pressure sores.[32,33] These three infections account for 80 percent of proven cases of bacteremia in long-term care facilities.[44] Tuberculosis and gastroenteritis are also common in nursing homes and are associated with major outbreaks.

TABLE 108-2
Differential Diagnosis of Infection in Older Adults by Functional Status or Level of Care

Functional Status or Level of Care	Types of Infection	
	Primary Considerations	Secondary Considerations
Independent, healthy individual living in community	Bacterial pneumonia and other respiratory tract infections Urinary tract infection Intraabdominal infections (cholecystitis, diverticulitis, appendicitis)	Infective endocarditis Tuberculosis Septic arthritis Meningitis
Hospital patient	Urinary tract infection Pneumonia Surgical wound infections	Septic thrombophlebitis Drug reactions* Pulmonary emboli* Hepatitis
Nursing home resident	Pneumonia Urinary tract infection Decubitus ulcer	Tuberculosis Drug reactions* Intraabdominal infection Gastroenteritis

*Noninfectious disorders simulating an infection or causing fever.

LABORATORY TESTS

In the current modern practice of medicine, clinicians have availability of highly technical diagnostic procedures and tests that can diagnose or exclude, with reasonable accuracy, serious diseases or disease processes. However, many of these "high tech" procedures are expensive. With the enormous cost of medical care that currently exists as well as the restrictions in health expenditures imposed by the diagnosis-related group (DRG) system of payment through Medicare, the clinicians who care for older adults must be able to judiciously select diagnostic tests. Such factors as risk versus benefits, cost versus benefits, and impact (of the test) on management must be seriously considered whenever diagnostic tests and procedures are contemplated for a geriatric patient.

As previously discussed, based on clinical assessment, a reasonably accurate differential diagnosis for an infectious disease process can be established (see Table 108-2). The following are suggestions and guidelines for which diagnostic tests to order in older patients with a possible infection.

ALL PATIENTS WITH SUSPECTED INFECTION If the physician suspects infection, he or she should have the following tests and evaluations performed: blood cultures (at least two sets), complete blood count, urinalysis with culture, chest x ray, and renal function tests.

URINARY TRACT INFECTION Tests for urinary tract infection should be evaluated with urinalysis and culture, prostate examination, prostatic fluid culture (for recurrent urinary infections in males), residual urine volume, and possibly intravenous pyelogram or renal ultrasound (for genitourinary structure and size). More invasive procedures such as cystoscopy should be individualized.

PULMONARY INFECTIONS Pulmonary infections are difficult to evaluate in older patients because the elderly frequently are unable to cough or they are too frail to withstand a diagnostic procedure. Nevertheless, an expectorated sputum should be obtained whenever possible for staining (Gram's stain, acid-fast stain) and culture (bacterial, mycobacterial, and fungal), realizing the limited diagnostic value of these specimens for bacterial isolation because of contamination by mouth flora. Chest x rays that include a lateral view as well as special views (e.g., apical lordotic for possible tuberculosis) should be ordered. Pleural fluid should be obtained for anaerobic and aerobic bacterial cultures (and Gram's stain) and for mycobacterial and fungal studies. Skin tests for tuberculous and fungal infections are recommended in older patients with a pulmonary lesion in whom a bacterial infection is an unlikely cause. Flexible bronchoscopy should be reserved for older patients in whom a cause is not determined after preliminary tests or in whom a malignancy is considered as part of the differential diagnosis. Transtracheal aspiration is generally recommended only for patients with multiple potential microbial etiologies who have failed to respond to initial chemotherapy for their pulmonary lesion.

ABDOMINAL INFECTIONS These infections are best assessed by initially doing an ultrasonogram, which is then followed by an abdominal computed tomographic scan. If these tests reveal nothing of significance, radionuclide scans such as a gallium-67 scintigraph may be helpful in localizing a septic focus (e.g., abscess).

ANTIBIOTICS: SPECIAL CONSIDERATIONS

Antimicrobial therapy and antibiotic usage in older patients require special considerations. Many factors and circumstances influence the approach to the selection, administration, and monitoring of antibiotics in the elderly.

LIMITATIONS IN COLLECTION OF DIAGNOSTIC SPECIMENS

Collection of body fluids or tissue for microbiological studies is frequently not feasible in the older patient, particularly the very old and frail elderly. Many are unable to expectorate sputum or to spontaneously void urine. In addition, invasive procedures (e.g., thoracentesis) are often not possible because the elderly patient is unable to cooperate or cannot tolerate the test. Hence, it is more difficult to make a precise etiologic diagnosis in older patients with an infection.

ETIOLOGIC HETEROGENEITY

The most common infections that occur in all age groups are respiratory infection, urinary tract infection, skin/soft-tissue infections, and intraabdominal sepsis. These infections involve a variety of bacterial pathogens, including aerobic (facultative anaerobic) and obligate anaerobic strains. Moreover, etiologic diversity is greater in the elderly compared to younger adults with the same infection. For example, pneumonia in the general population is predominantly (60 to 80 percent) caused by *Streptococcus pneumoniae*. In contrast, the elderly population will experience a lower frequency of *S. pneumoniae* (40 to 60 percent) and a higher rate of such other pathogens as *Haemophilus influenzae*, gram-negative

bacilli, *Staphylococcus aureus*, and *Branhamella catarrhalis*.[1]

ANTIBIOTIC PHARMACOLOGY

A detailed discussion of aging and pharmacokinetics is beyond the scope of this chapter (see Chap. 21, Clinical Pharmacology). In terms of antibiotics, age-related changes in gastrointestinal absorption, volume distribution, and hepatic metabolism probably have little impact on the selection, administration, and dosing of these drugs.[45] However, associated with the age-related decline in renal function is a greater risk for higher serum and tissue concentration of antibiotics.[45] Antibiotics that are associated with dose-related toxicity should therefore be avoided or should be given in reduced dosages in elderly patients. The aminoglycosides are particularly relevant under these circumstances since the elderly, who already experience age-related losses in hearing and renal function, are at greatest risk for oto- and nephrotoxicity of these drugs.

COSTS OF ANTIBIOTIC THERAPY

Traditionally, the cost of antibiotic therapy has been equated to the purchasing cost of a specific drug. This is primarily the reason why physicians are reluctant to use newer and more expensive antibiotics. However, antimicrobial therapy costs include not only the acquisition cost but also the expenses related to preparation and administration of the drugs (materials and labor), and costs accrued from drug monitoring.[46] Another cost that should be (but is not) calculated as part of antibiotic costs is the added cost of adverse effects.

Drugs that are administered more frequently are often more costly because of the added staff time required. Thus, although the purchasing cost may be high for a drug, it may be less expensive to administer than another drug with a cheaper purchasing price but may require more frequent dosing. In addition, drugs which require frequent laboratory monitoring or which are associated with high incidence of adverse effects become more expensive (e.g., aminoglycosides).

DIAGNOSIS-RELATED GROUPS

With the implementation of the diagnosis-related group (DRG) system of reimbursement for hospital costs and physician fees, it becomes imperative that elderly patients with a potential infection are diagnosed early and treated promptly. Moreover, the traditional approach to managing infectious diseases, i.e., determining a specific etiology and treating with a narrow-spectrum antibiotic, is frequently not feasible in frail, ill elderly patients who cannot provide clinical specimens. Thus, the clinician has a greater chance of making errors in the initial choice of chemotherapy. These errors in diagnosis and treatment prolong hospital stay. Thus, in severely ill older patients in whom a precise etiologic diagnosis cannot be made before culture data return, therapy should be initiated with a *broad-spectrum* antibiotic agent (or combination thereof). When the specific cause is determined, a more narrow-spectrum agent may be substituted.

With the increasing availability of oral antibiotics, it becomes more feasible to treat the older patient with infection as an outpatient. This will limit the number of patients who will require hospitalization as well as permit patients to be discharged from the hospital sooner. Despite many newer oral antibiotics having high retail purchasing costs (to the patient), outpatient antimicrobial chemotherapy with oral drugs is always less expensive than inpatient care.

RECOMMENDATIONS

Based on the above conditions and circumstances, the following recommendations are made regarding antibiotic therapy in older adults:

1. Empirical antibiotic therapy should be considered earlier and more often in older patients (compared with younger patients) who appear ill or functionally incapacitated by a potential infectious disease process. Empirical therapy should be initiated only *after* all available clinical specimens for microbiological studies have been obtained.
2. Empirical therapy should be begun with a broad-spectrum antimicrobial agent that will be effective against the most likely pathogens responsible for the infection. Generally, β-lactam antibiotics, particularly the cephalosporins, will be the agent(s) of choice in older patients because of their proven efficacy, broad spectrum, safety, and favorable dosing regimens.
3. A specific narrow-spectrum antibiotic should be administered only after a precise etiologic diagnosis is made and only after determining that the causative pathogen is highly susceptible to this drug.
4. If parenteral therapy is initiated, it should be continued until the patient has clinically improved and relevant microbiological studies (e.g., cultures) have shown elimination of the causative pathogen. The patient should then be changed to oral antibiotics as soon as possible. Generally, for most serious infections, parenteral therapy will be continued for 3 to 7 days in uncomplicated infections (older patients without severe underlying diseases or disabilities) and 7 to 10 days in elderly patients who are critically ill, who have immunocompromised status or other debilitating disease, and/or who fail to respond to

treatment within the first 3 to 4 days. Of course, certain infections such as infective endocarditis, brain abscess, acute osteomyelitis, and abscesses will require parenteral therapy for a prolonged period regardless of the patient's age or underlying health status.
5. Aminoglycoside antibiotics for the elderly patients should be reserved for select circumstances, i.e., patients with septic shock without a specific etiologic diagnosis (the risk of death under these conditions is far greater than the risk of aminoglycoside toxicity); patients with serious *Pseudomonas aeruginosa* infection (endocarditis, osteomyelitis, meningitis, etc.); patients infected with an organism susceptible only to an aminoglycoside; and patients with infective endocarditis caused by a pathogen that is eradicated optimally by the principle of synergistic therapy (aminoglycoside added to a primary antibiotic).

PREVENTION

The topic of prevention of infectious diseases in the older adult is broad and beyond the scope and limitations of this chapter. However, it should be stated that immunoprophylaxis of the elderly with influenza vaccine (yearly), pneumococcal vaccine (one dose only, except repeat dose in 6 years for patients at high risk for sepsis—e.g., asplenia—or who have rapid fall in antibodies to pneumococci—e.g., immunosuppression), and tetanus toxoid (three primary series followed by booster every 10 years) is an important aspect of geriatric care. Influenza-related deaths occur predominantly in the elderly[47]; pneumococcal pneumonia and bacteremia occur most frequently and are associated with the highest mortality in persons over the age of 60 years[48]; and, as stated earlier, 60 percent of tetanus cases in the United States occur in persons over the age of 60.[20] However, the immune response or clinical efficacy of these vaccines in the elderly has been quite variable and inconsistent.[49–52]

REFERENCES

1. Yoshikawa TT, Norman DC (eds): *Aging and Clinical Practice: Infectious Diseases. Diagnosis and Treatment.* New York, Igaku-Shoin, 1987.
2. Yoshikawa TT: Important infections in elderly persons. *West J Med* 135:441, 1981.
3. National Center for Health Statistics, Graves EJ: Utilization of short-stay hospitals, United States, 1983 Annual Summary. *Vital and Health Statistics*, ser 13, no 83, DHHS (PHS) 85-1744. Washington, Public Health Service, Government Printing Office, 1985.

4. Yoshikawa TT: Unique aspects of urinary tract infection in the geriatric population. *Gerontology* 30:339, 1984.
5. Bryan CS, Reynolds KL: Hospital-acquired bacteremic urinary tract infection: Epidemiology and outcome. *J Urol* 132:494, 1984.
6. Setia U et al: Bacteremia in a long-term care facility. Spectrum and mortality. *Arch Intern Med* 144:1633, 1984.
7. Esposito AL et al: Community-acquired bacteremia in the elderly: Analysis of one hundred consecutive episodes. *J Am Geriatr Soc* 28:315, 1980.
8. McCue JD: Gram-negative bacillary bacteremias in the elderly: Incidence, etiology, and mortality. *J Am Geriatr Soc* 35:213, 1987.
9. Holloway WJ: Management of sepsis in the elderly. *Am J Med* 80(suppl 6B):143, 1986.
10. Norman DC, Yoshikawa TT: Intraabdominal infection: Diagnosis and treatment in the elderly patient. *Gerontology* 30:327, 1984.
11. Norman DC, Yoshikawa TT: Acute appendicitis in the elderly, in Meakins J, McClaron J (eds): *Surgical Care of the Elderly*. Chicago, Year Book Medical Publishers (in press).
12. Cantrell M, Yoshikawa TT: Aging and infective endocarditis. *J Am Geriatr Soc* 31:216, 1983.
13. Atkinson JB, Virmani B: Infective endocarditis: Changing trends and general approach for examination. *Human Path* 18(6):603, 1987.
14. Stead WN et al: Tuberculosis as an endemic and nosocomial infection among the elderly in nursing homes. *N Engl J Med* 312:1483, 1985.
15. Alvarez S et al: Pulmonary tuberculosis in elderly men. *Am J Med* 82:602, 1987.
16. Norman DC, Yoshikawa TT: Responding to septic arthritis. *Geriatrics* 38:83, 1983.
17. McGuire NM, Kauffman CA: Septic arthritis in the elderly. *J Am Geriatr Soc* 33:170, 1985.
18. Manley MT: Incidence, contributory factors and costs of pressure sores. *S Afr Med J* 53:217, 1978.
19. Kostuik JB, Fernie G: Pressure sores in elderly patients. *J Bone Joint Surg* 67(B):1, 1985.
20. Centers for Disease Control: *Tetanus—United States, 1985–1986*. MMWR 36(29):477, July 31, 1987.
21. Loeser JD: Herpes zoster and post herpetic neuralgia. *Pain* 25:149, 1986.
22. Watson PN, Evans RJ: Postherpetic neuralgia: A review. *Arch Neurol* 43:836, 1986.
23. Garibaldi RA, Nurse BA: Infections in the elderly. *Am J Med* 81(suppl 1A):53, 1986.
24. Yoshikawa TT: Impact of aging on host response to infectious disease, In Wood WG, Strong R (eds): *Geriatric Clinical Pharmacology*. New York, Raven Press, 1987, p 107.
25. Utilization of short-stay hospitals. United States 1981, Annual Summary. National Center for Health Statistics, Data from the National Health Survey, ser 13, no 72 DHSS (PHS)83-1733. Washington, Government Printing Office, 1983.
26. Hodgin UG, Sanford JP: Gram-negative rod bacteremia: An analysis of 100 patients. *Am J Med* 39:952, 1965.
27. Gorse GJ et al: Bacterial meningitis in the elderly. *Arch Intern Med* 144:1603, 1984.
28. Terpenning MS et al: Infective endocarditis: Clinical features in young and elderly patients. *Am J Med* 83:626, 1987.
29. Campion EW et al: Why acute-care hospitals must undertake long-term care. *N Engl J Med* 308:71, 1983.
30. Saviteer SM, Samsa GP, Rutale WA: Nosocomial infections in the elderly. Increased risk per hospital day. *Am J Med* 84:661, 1988.
31. Haley RW et al: Nosocomial infections in U.S. hospitals, 1975–1976. Estimated frequency of selected characteristics of patients. *Am J Med* 70:947, 1981.
32. Norman DC et al: Infections in the nursing home. *J Am Geriatr Soc* 35:796, 1987.
33. Alvarez S et al: Nosocomial infections in long-term facilities. *J Gerontol* 43:179, 1988.
34. Yoshikawa TT et al: Infections in the aging population. *J Am Geriatr Soc* 33:496, 1985.
35. Movat HZ et al: Acute inflammation in gram-negative infection: Endotoxin, interleukin 1, tumor necrosis factor, and neutrophils. *Fed Proc* 46:97, 1987.
36. Keating HJ III et al: Effect of aging on the clinical significance of fever in ambulatory adult patients. *J Am Geriatr Soc* 32:282, 1984.
37. Esposito AL, Gleckman RA: Fever of unknown origin in the elderly. *J Am Geriatr Soc* 26:498, 1978.
38. Norman DC et al: Fever and aging. *J Am Geriatr Soc* 33:859, 1985.
39. Gleckman R, Hibert D: Afebrile bacteremia: A phenomenon in geriatric patients. *JAMA* 243:1478, 1981.
40. Finklestein MS et al: Pneumococcal bacteremia in adults. Age-dependent differences in presentation and in outcome. *J Am Geriatr Soc* 31:19, 1983.
41. Marrie TJ et al: Community-acquired pneumonia requiring hospitalization. Is it different in the elderly? *J Am Geriatr Soc* 38:671, 1985.
42. Irvine PW et al: Causes for hospitalization of nursing home residents: The role of infection. *J Am Geriatr Soc* 32:103, 1984.
43. Tresch DD et al: Relationship of long-term and acute-care facilities. The problem of patient transfer and continuity of care. *J Am Geriatr Soc* 33:819, 1985.
44. Setia U et al: Bacteremia in a long-term care facility. Spectrum and mortality. *Arch Intern Med* 144:1633, 1984.
45. Lundberg B, Nilsson-Ehle I: Pharmacokinetics of antimicrobial agents in the elderly. *Rev Infect Dis* 9:250, 1987.
46. McCue JD et al: Hospital charges for antibiotics. *Rev Infect Dis* 7:643, 1985.
47. Immunization Practices Advisory Committee: Prevention and control of influenza. *MMWR* 38(17):297, 1989.
48. Immunization Practices Advisory Committee: Pneumococcal polysaccharide vaccine. *MMWR* 38(5):64, 1989.
49. Levine M et al: Characterization of the immune response to trivalent influenza vaccine in elderly men. *J Am Geriatr Soc* 35:607, 1987.
50. Sims RV et al: The clinical effectiveness of pneumococcal vaccine in the elderly. *Ann Intern Med* 108:653, 1988.
51. Simberkoff MS et al: Efficacy of pneumococcal vaccine in high-risk patients: Results of a Veterans Administration Cooperative Study. *N Engl J Med* 315:1318, 1986.
52. Carbon PY et al: Serum levels of antibody to toxoid during tetanus and after specific immunization of patients with tetanus. *J Infect Dis* 145:278, 1982.

Chapter 109

DIZZINESS AND SYNCOPE

Palmi V. Jonsson and Lewis A. Lipsitz

This chapter deals with dizziness and syncope, two very important geriatric syndromes that produce falls and their morbid consequences.[1] Dizziness and syncope may be due to cardiovascular abnormalities, in which case they differ only quantitatively, according to the degree of cerebral ischemia experienced by the patient during a cardiovascular event. However, dizziness and syncope may also differ qualitatively, dizziness being due to primary abnormalities in the central or peripheral nervous system and syncope due to cardiovascular disorders. For practical purposes, the two symptoms will be discussed separately; however, areas of overlap in their etiology, evaluation, and treatment will be highlighted.

DIZZINESS

"Dizziness" is one of several terms that patients use to describe an unpleasant sensation of insecure balance. *Dizziness* has a different meaning to different people and has multiple underlying causes. Dizziness can be separated by history into four broad categories which are useful in guiding the clinical evaluation[2]:

1. *Vertigo (spinning):* Distortion of orientation or erroneous perception of motion. Vertigo indicates a vestibular system disorder, but lack of a spinning sensation does not exclude a vestibular disorder (see Ref. 2). The vertigo may be continuous or positional only, as well as acute or chronic.[3]
2. *Dysequilibrium (unsteadiness, imbalance):* The feeling of an imminent fall. This feeling usually indicates a neurologic disorder but may also reflect a vestibular disorder.

Supported by the Hebrew Rehabilitation Center for Aged, and by Grant #AG06443 and an NIA Teaching Nursing Home Award, AG04390, from the U.S. Public Health Service. Dr. Lipsitz was supported in part by a National Institute on Aging Academic Award, AG00213.

3. *Near-syncope (fainting, light-headedness):* The feeling of impending loss of consciousness. This feeling usually indicates a cardiovascular disorder and is best approached in a way similar to the diagnostic approach for syncope (see "Syncope").
4. *Non-specific dizziness:* A psychogenic disease is likely when there is a vague history lacking any of the three symptom characteristics above, coupled with the presence of psychiatric symptoms and absence of known patterns of organic disease.

EPIDEMIOLOGY

The complaint of dizziness is common, but studies of its incidence and prevalence in the total population are scanty. One study of symptom prevalence in the elderly[4] showed a steady increase in dizziness complaints with age for both men and women, rising from 4 to 9 percent in people in their late sixties to about 20 percent in people above the age of 84.

PATHOPHYSIOLOGY

The pathophysiology of dizziness due to cardiovascular abnormalities is discussed later, under "Syncope." Maintenance of balanced posture is accomplished through several mechanisms.[5] Continuous afferent input from the eyes, vestibular labyrinths, muscles, and joints is processed centrally and produces the adaptive movements necessary to maintain equilibrium.

The vestibular system has several components: the vestibular labyrinth, the vestibular nerve, and the central connections. The vestibular labyrinths are spatial proprioceptors that are stimulated by gravity and rotational movement. Because the vestibular labyrinth (which is a spatial proprioceptor) and the cochlea (which is a sound receptor) lie adjacent to each other and their nerves run together to the central connections, diseases causing dizziness usually affect both balance and hearing. Visual impulses are coordinated with impulses from the vestibular labyrinths and the neck to stabilize gaze during movements of the head and body. Proprioceptive receptors around the facet joints of the cervical spine and large joints of the shoulders, hips, knees, and ankles are similarly important and lead to reflex changes in posture. Visual, proprioceptive, and labyrinthine mechanisms can generally compensate for one another to maintain balance, unless there are simultaneous defects in any two of these three sensory systems. Additionally, there is important psychophysiologic input from the cortex which modifies the interpretation of afferent stimuli. Vertigo or dysequilibrium therefore may be induced by psychological stimulation, by pathologic dysfunction in any of the sensory systems, or by impaired central processing.[3]

AGE-RELATED CHANGES

Many age-related changes have been identified within the balance system which alone or in combination with diseases of older age may result in impaired perception of where the head or the body are in space. These changes may partially explain the high prevalence of dizziness among the elderly. Some of these changes (see Table 109-1) are diminished perception of various visual stimuli,[6] increased thresholds for vestibular[7] and proprioceptive sensory organ responses,[8] and loss of sensory receptors such as the proprioceptive receptors of the cervical spine (mechanoreceptors).[9]

DISEASE-RELATED CHANGES

Degenerative diseases of the special sensory organs are well-known accompaniments of aging. The prevalences of cataracts, glaucoma, and macular degeneration and acquired vestibular dysfunction increase with age. Peripheral neuropathy from diabetes, alcoholism, vitamin deficiency, and idiopathic causes may produce dizziness. Cervical spondylosis, which is common in advanced age,

TABLE 109-1
Age-Related Changes Affecting the Special Senses

I. Vision
  Focal
    Reduced glare tolerance
    Reduced nocturnal acuity
  Ambient
    Reduced ability to perceive contrast
    Reduced ability to fixate accurately
II. Vestibular
  Increased threshold of response
  Reduction in hair cell population
III. Peripheral proprioception
  Increased threshold of response
  Degeneration of cervical mechanoreceptors

may impair cervical mechanoreceptor function or cause cervical myelopathy with associated impairment of spacial orientation.

ETIOLOGY

Table 109-2 shows the principal diseases that cause dizziness, which can be divided into peripheral or central neurologic causes, systemic diseases, psychiatric disorders, and contributions of multiple sensory deficits. Drachman and Hart[2] found that 38 percent of dizzy patients had peripheral neurologic disorders, 11 percent had central neurologic disorders, 8 percent had systemic diseases, 32 percent had psychiatric illness, 13 percent had multiple sensory deficits, and 9 percent had uncertain diagnoses.

Neurologic Disorders

PERIPHERAL NERVOUS SYSTEM (PNS) DISORDERS Vertigo generally indicates a PNS disorder, but rarely may be due to a central lesion. PNS disorders can also present less dramatically as dysequilibrium or

TABLE 109-2
Etiology of Dizziness

Neurologic
Peripheral (labyrinth or vestibulocochlear nerve):
  Benign paroxysmal positional vertigo
  Vestibulopathy
  Meniere's disease
  Acoustic neuroma
  Medication toxic effects: aminoglycosides, diuretics, chincona alkaloids (quinidine), salicylates
  Post-traumatic
Central (brain stem, cerebellum, and cerebrum):
  Ischemia, infarcts, bleeding
  Demyelination (multiple sclerosis, postinfectious, paraneoplastic)
  Tumors (meningioma, metastasis)
  Seizures (temporal lobe)
  Medication/toxic effects: phenytoin, lithium, benzodiazepines

Systemic
Cardiac, hypotension (see Table 109-4)
Toxins (lead, arsenic)
Metabolic (diabetes, hypothyroidism)
Other

Psychiatric
Anxiety, psychotic, and affective disorders

Multiple Pathology
Combined visual, vestibular, and peripheral proprioceptive deficits

unsteadiness. Central and peripheral disorders generally can be distinguished by the characteristics of nystagmus induced by a rapid head-hanging maneuver (Nylen-Barany maneuver) as described later, under "Evaluation" (see Table 109-3). Peripheral disorders[10] are characterized by a latency time of 3 to 45 seconds until the onset of vertigo or nystagmus, brief nystagmus for less than a minute, and fatigue of the response on repeated testing. In central disorders[11] there is no latency, the vertigo and nystagmus lasts more than a minute, and there is no fatigue on repeated testing.

Benign Paroxysmal Positional Vertigo (BPPV)

BPPV, the most common peripheral nervous system disorder, is about twice as common as any other vestibular disorder, occurring in 10 to 20 percent of patients reporting dizziness. BPPV can be due to a specific etiology (40 percent), such as head injury or ear disease, but it is more commonly idiopathic (60 percent). The diagnostic criteria are as follows[12]: (1) a history of episodic vertigo occurring *only* with a change in position, (2) nystagmus elicited in a head-hanging position with the Nylen-Barany maneuver, and (3) normal caloric (oculovestibular) responses (i.e., symmetric nystagmus is induced).

The pathophysiology of BPPV probably involves the labyrinth. Schuknecht[13] hypothesized that labyrinthine degeneration causes a mass of particles (otoconia) to form within the posterior semicircular canal on one side, thus making the endolymph heavier on that side than on the opposite side. This would cause an asymmetric vestibular response with posture change.

Clinically, the episodes of vertigo in BPPV are of short duration and occur when the patient turns from

TABLE 109-3
Characteristics of Positionally Induced Vertigo and Nystagmus (the Nylen-Barany Maneuver)

	Peripheral	Central
Latency (time to onset of vertigo or nystagmus)	3–45 s	No latency
Duration	Less than 1 min	More than 1 min
Fatigability (signs and symptoms decrease after onset and on repetition of stimulus)	Yes	No
Direction of nystagmus	Same	May change
Intensity of symptoms and signs	Severe	Mild
Reproducibility	Inconsistent	More consistent
Associated symptoms or signs	Auditory	Neurologic

side to side in bed, gets out of bed, bends the head back, or moves the head rapidly horizontally or vertically. Vertigo may be associated with nausea, and the patient may complain about unsteadiness and nausea between episodes.

The incidence of BPPV peaks after age 60. The female-to-male ratio is 2:1. Most often the symptoms subside over a period of 6 months to a year, but they have been documented to last as long as 10 years.

Vestibulopathy (Vestibular Neuronitis): Acute or Recurrent

Vestibulopathy is a distinctive vestibular disturbance characterized by the sudden onset of severe vertigo continuing over 5 to 24 hours and associated with a unilateral decrease in caloric response and spontaneous nystagmus in the *absence* of auditory or other neurologic abnormalities.[14] Nausea and vomiting/retching can be severe. In the recovery phase, vertigo can become positional. Vestibulopathy is a benign disorder that may occur as a single episode or be recurrent. It is thought to be due to a virus affecting the vestibular nerve between the labyrinth and the brain. It is probably less common in the elderly than in the young and middle-aged, but reliable data in the elderly are not available.

Meniere's Disease

Meniere's disease is a vestibulocochlear disorder.[15] It is associated with distension of the endolymphatic space within the cochlea and leads to degeneration of the cochlear cells. Meniere's disease is diagnosed when there is a recurrent peripheral vestibulopathy accompanied by tinnitus and hearing loss. The hearing loss has a *cochlear* sensorineural pattern, which is characterized by partial loss of perception of high-pitched sounds that can be compensated somewhat by increasing loudness (loudness recruitment). There is relative preservation of speech discrimination (i.e., the ability to distinguish similar sounds). The attacks of vertigo are typically abrupt and last minutes to hours. Nausea, vomiting, and a feeling of fullness in the ear are present to a varying degree. Attacks may vary in frequency and severity. Recurrent attacks often give rise to mild chronic states of dysequilibrium. Caloric testing may or may not disclose an impairment on the involved side. Hearing loss usually begins before the first attack, fluctuates, and worsens with each attack. The disease is bilateral in 10 to 30 percent of cases. The sexes are affected equally, and the onset is most often in the fifth and sixth decades. The course of Meniere's disease is characterized by remissions and relapses.

Acoustic Neuroma

Acoustic neuroma is uniformly associated with hearing loss and should be suspected in any patient with progressive unilateral hearing loss.[16] Early symptoms are tinnitus and mild sensorineural hearing loss of the *retrocochlear* type, characterized by a partial loss of high-frequency sound perception that cannot be compensated by increasing loudness (i.e., lack of loudness recruitment). There is also diminished speech discrimination that is out of proportion to the hearing loss. Caloric testing indicates decreased vestibular response on the affected side. A small number of patients will complain about vertigo early on; later on it can resemble vertigo in Meniere's disease due to the associated hearing loss. The vertigo is rarely positional. Most often patients complain about dysequilibrium. Continued tumor growth may lead to frank ataxia and other associated neurologic findings, including disturbance of taste, sensory loss over the face, gait abnormality, and unilateral ataxia of the limbs.

Medication Toxicity Although medication ototoxicity is not specific to the elderly, preexisting inner-ear pathology and the high prevalence of medication use in this population increase the risk. Impaired renal function in advanced age is the dominant risk factor for ototoxicity from medications which are cleared by the kidney. Medication ototoxicity is often an overlooked cause of hearing and balance problems.[17]

The known toxic medications include antibiotics (e.g., aminoglycosides, vancomycin, and erythromycin), diuretics (e.g., ethacrynic acid and furosemide), salicylates, and quinine. *Aminoglycosides* pass the blood-perilymph barrier and bind to the sensory epithelium in the inner ear, to the hair cells, and to the striae vascularis of both the cochlea and the vestibular portions of the labyrinth. Ototoxic *diuretics* inhibit the enzyme adenosine triphosphatase, causing an increase in sodium concentration in the inner ear. Direct hair-cell toxicity may also occur. *Salicylates* may cause constriction of small cochlear blood vessels, and *quinine* is believed to affect the spiral ganglion. Concurrent use of more than one toxic drug, for example, use of both gentamicin and furosemide, increases the probability of toxicity.

Gentamicin is now the principal offending toxic agent, since streptomycin and kanamycin are rarely used. It is twice as toxic to the vestibular apparatus as to the cochlear, resulting in a higher incidence of balance impairment than hearing impairment. Since a serum level above 10 μg/ml is associated with ototoxicity, peak and trough serum levels should be obtained, and the dose should be adjusted to avoid toxic levels.

CENTRAL NERVOUS SYSTEM (CNS) DISORDERS
Cerebrovascular Disease Basilar artery insufficiency is a cerebrovascular disease in which dizziness is one of the cardinal symptoms.[18] Dizziness also can be seen in posterior cerebral artery insufficiency but is rare in association with anterior cerebral circulatory disturbances. Dizziness can present alone as a symptom of transient

ischemic attack (TIA), but it is usually associated with other neurologic symptoms such as dysarthria, numbness of the face, hemiparesis, headache, and diplopia (in order of decreasing frequency). When a TIA presents as dizziness alone, an arrhythmia should be suspected.

When dizziness is due to a stroke, accompanying neurologic signs are almost always present. These signs are most frequently diplopia, dysarthria, weakness, headache, numbness of the face or limbs, ataxia of gait, cerebellar ataxia of the limbs, and visual impairment. In rare cases, sudden deafness (with or without other brain stem signs) is due to anterior inferior cerebellar artery or internal auditory artery vascular occlusion. A rotatory feeling (vertigo) is present in only 22 percent of patients with dizziness of central vascular origin in contrast to its presence in 90 percent of dizzy patients with peripheral causes.[18] Episodes of dizziness that are associated with vestibulocochlear nerve manifestations alone are highly unlikely to be vascular in origin. Episodes of dizziness that continue for more than 6 weeks without neurologic accompaniments are also rarely vascular in nature. Positional vertigo is rarely ever the result of cerebrovascular disease.

Cerebellar Disorders Cerebellar strokes (particularly those involving the flocculonodular complex and the vestibular connections of the cerebellum) can present as vertigo, unsteadiness, nausea, vomiting, nystagmus, and truncal ataxia. Therefore, these cerebellar strokes may mimic vestibular labyrinthine disease, such as acute vestibular neuronitis or Meniere's disease.[19] Truncal ataxia is a distinguishing feature of dizziness due to cerebellar stroke. A computed tomography (CT) scan or magnetic resonance imaging (MRI) of the head with attention to the posterior fossa is an urgent test in any patient with sudden onset of these symptoms and associated ataxia.

Other Disorders Complaints of dizziness and postural instability while standing and walking are common among patients with Parkinson's disease.[20] Objective findings of vestibular dysfunction, such as reduced caloric responses, correlate highly with severity of balance impairment. These patients are diagnosed by the parkinsonian tremor, the increase in neuromuscular tone, and the typical shuffling gait.

Direct effects of medications on the CNS (as distinguished from ototoxicity) are an important cause of dizziness that often can be detected by noting the presence of a particular medication history coupled with the presence of multidirectional nystagmus. Lithium and phenytoin (Dilantin) are two good examples of drugs that cause dizziness and nystagmus. Benzodiazepines, neuroleptics, and antidepressants often cause dysequilibrium but are not associated with nystagmus.

Many other CNS diseases, such as tumors, metabolic and demyelinating disorders, can cause dizziness. They are detected by associating features of the history and physical examination with results from appropriate laboratory tests.

Systemic Causes

The major systemic causes of dizziness are the same as those that predispose to syncope and are discussed later, under "Syncope." Transient arrhythmias[21] and hypotension are the two most common causes; only rarely will an endocrine disorder such as hypothyroidism underlie the complaint of dizziness.

Psychiatric Disease

Psychiatric disorders are the cause of dizziness in about 20 to 33 percent of all cases. This is a diagnosis made by exclusion of other potential causes, but it is suspected when the complaint of dizziness does not fit any particular recognized disease pattern.

Multiple Pathology

Drachman and Hart[2] found that multiple sensory deficits account for 13 percent of cases of dizziness. They maintain that any two or more deficits of the visual, vestibular, or somatosensory systems may cause dizziness.

EVALUATION

The evaluation of dizziness is best accomplished by a systematic approach (see Fig. 109-1) in which the history and physical examination guide the selection of tests.[22] The *history* should begin with an exact description of what the patient means by dizziness. Provocative factors should be sought. A spinning sensation in response to movement of the head and neck may indicate BPPV, carotid sinus syndrome, or cervical spondylosis. Faintness precipitated by standing and relieved by lying down may indicate orthostatic hypotension. Dizziness on straining at stool may indicate a posterior fossa lesion, a foramen magnum lesion, or hypotension secondary to the Valsalva maneuver. Lack of provocative factors may indicate TIAs or cardiac arrhythmias. Mode of onset of symptoms (gradual vs. sudden), frequency and duration of symptoms (constant vs. episodic), and symptoms between attacks all give valuable clues. When the dizziness is acute, it is more likely due to traumatic, vascular, or inflammatory causes. When it is chronic, neoplasia, demyelinating disorders, and psychiatric conditions are more likely. If symptoms are felt in the legs and there is difficulty standing and walking due to limb ataxia or dys-

metria, a cerebellar lesion or a proprioceptive disorder may be the cause. Temporal-lobe seizures can present as dizziness and are suggested by automatism and amnesia. Tinnitus, hearing impairment, and fullness or pain in the ear indicate inner ear dysfunction. Nausea and vomiting are nonspecific, but when severe and sudden they may suggest a labyrinthine disorder (Meniere's disease or vestibular neuronitis) or a serious CNS disorder such as a cerebellar hemorrhage. Finally, detailed medication and toxic exposure history is important.

The *physical examination* includes postural vital signs, a cardiovascular examination, carotid sinus massage (see "Syncope"), and a careful ear and neurologic examination. Special emphasis needs to be placed on testing of the cranial nerves (e.g., hearing, corneal reflex, facial sensation, taste, eye control, spontaneous nystagmus, and swallowing), cerebellar examination (dysmetria and truncal ataxia), and gait and balance testing (Romberg and turning while walking). Deafness, hemifacial paresthesia, and unilateral limb ataxia suggest a cerebellopontine angle tumor. Diplopia, dysarthria, dysphagia, numbness of the face, weakness, and visual deficits suggest posterior circulation (vascular) causes. Any cranial nerve or brain stem sign suggests a vestibular nerve (as opposed to vestibular labyrinth) or a central cause of dizziness. If the basic evaluation is negative, psychiatric symptoms are present, and symptoms are reproduced with hyperventilation, a psychiatric disturbance is likely.

If pure tone hearing is impaired, as evidenced by reduced capacity to hear the sound of fingers rubbing together or a watch ticking, hearing should be assessed clinically with the time-honored tests of Rinne and Weber.

The *Nylen-Barany provocative maneuver*[23] is a test indicated in all patients. For this maneuver, the patient is seated on the examining table, with the head first turned 45 degrees to one side, then quickly lowered to a position with the head hanging over the edge of the table 30 degrees below horizontal. The test is repeated with the head turned 45 degrees in the opposite direction and again with the head in the straight-forward position. In each position, the patient is observed for the appearance and character of nystagmus. In a peripheral nervous system disorder, such as BPPV, there is (1) a latency period of 5 to 15 seconds before nystagmus occurs, (2) a decrease in intensity of the nystagmus after 2 to 30 seconds, (3) frequent reversal of the direction of nystagmus with assumption of the sitting position, and (4) fatigability of the nystagmus and vertigo when the subject is repeatedly put in the provocative head-hanging position. These findings are contrasted with those of a CNS disorder in Table 109-3.

The *minicaloric test* of vestibular function, modified by Nelson,[24] is a simple screening test that can be done

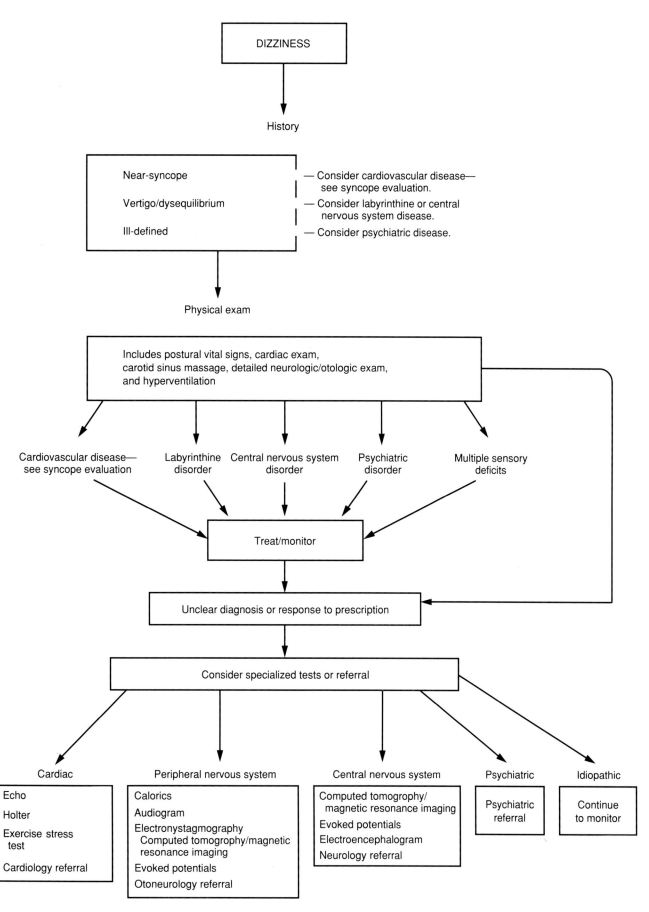

FIGURE 109-1
Algorithm for the diagnostic evaluation of the elderly dizzy patient.

in any outpatient setting. A tuberculin syringe is filled with ice water and 0.2 cc of the water is instilled into the ear canal with the patient supine and the patient's head positioned at approximately a 30-degree angle to the table. After the patient's head is turned to midline, the eyes are observed for nystagmus. A repeatedly negative response, i.e., the absence of induced nystagmus, indicates the presence of peripheral disease on that side.

Symptoms and signs found during history and physical examination and simple maneuvers either make the diagnosis or guide further evaluation and selection of *specialized testing*. If a peripheral vestibular disorder is suspected but cannot be confirmed clinically, caloric tests supplemented by electronystagmography (ENG) and a detailed audiometric evaluation are usually helpful. Depending on the results of these more advanced ENG studies, a CT or a MRI study may be required. When there are accompanying neurologic symptoms and signs in the initial evaluation that suggest a CNS lesion, a CT or MRI scan, an electroencephalogram (EEG), and auditory evoked potentials can help elucidate the etiology.

THERAPEUTIC ISSUES

Therapy for dizziness depends on the underlying disorder identified. The therapy is surgical for some diseases (e.g., acoustic neuroma). Symptomatic therapy with antihistamines or sedatives is only marginally effective, and the probability of side effects, such as falls or confusion, is markedly increased in the elderly.

If BPPV is identified, desensitization exercises involving a series of positional movements can be helpful.[25] After the head-position change that elicits the symptom of vertigo is identified, the patient repeats the provocative maneuver five times a day until the condition improves. Elderly patients have had very satisfying results with this approach, albeit the therapeutic effect develops more slowly and is less complete than in younger patients. Use of assistive devices such as a cane or a walker can be of major benefit to the elderly patient with multiple sensory deficits. Attention to a treatable eye disease, such as cataracts, or the use of a hearing device may also benefit the patient. Finally, periodic review and support is important in the management of this prevalent and often disabling symptom.

SYNCOPE

Syncope is defined as transient loss of consciousness accompanied by loss of postural tone, with spontaneous recovery that does not require resuscitation. This common problem has multiple underlying causes and suggests an increased risk of sudden death if the etiology is cardiac. Irrespective of etiology, syncope can cause adverse consequences, such as falls, fractures, subdural hematomas, and loss of independent function.

EPIDEMIOLOGY

The information on incidence and prevalence of syncope is fragmented. Studies of young people show a prevalence of syncope as high as 47 percent, which is primarily due to benign causes such as vasovagal reactions.[26] Data from the Framingham study show an increase in prevalence of syncope with age.[27] One percent of emergency ward visits and up to three percent of admissions to hospitals are for the evaluation of syncope. Most of these hospital visits are by elderly patients. A study of very elderly residents of a nursing home revealed a 10-year prevalence of 23 percent and a 1-year incidence of 6 percent. The recurrence rate for syncope is about 30 percent.[28] Patients with cardiac causes for syncope are at the highest risk for death, having a 40 percent 2-year mortality. Patients with noncardiac causes for syncope have a 20 percent 2-year mortality, which is similar to that of syncope of unknown cause.[29,30] Although syncope is associated with a high mortality rate, this high rate is probably due to the underlying diseases that cause syncope, rather than to an independent relationship between syncope and death. Recurrent syncope that remains unexplained after thorough initial evaluation is not associated with excess mortality.[28,31]

PATHOPHYSIOLOGY

Syncope results from inadequate energy substrate delivery to the brain. The major energy substrates are oxygen and glucose. Significant hypoglycemia tends to result in coma rather than syncope, and a prolonged cessation of oxygen delivery results in death. Thus, transient cerebral hypoxia from decreased cerebral blood flow is the final common pathway in most cases of syncope. Generalized hypoxemia from cardiac or pulmonary diseases and decreased oxygen-carrying capacity of the blood from anemia are risk factors for syncope, particularly in the elderly, but are rarely the sole cause. Infrequently, focal stenosis of arteries supplying critical areas of the brain causes syncope.

Blood pressure is determined by the product of cardiac output and peripheral arterial resistance. A reduction in either variable without an increase in the other will lower blood pressure and potentially result in syncope. Cardiac output may fall because of a reduction in stroke volume or because of extreme heart rates, either fast or slow. Reduced stroke volume may result from an obstruction to flow within the heart or pulmonary vasculature, myocardial pump failure, or a reduction in venous return. Venous return may decrease as a result of venous blood pooling or hypovolemia. Impaired arterial resistance can result from autonomic failure or medication-related effects. Cardiovascular reflexes may cause syncope by decreasing vascular resistance and/or cardiac output.

AGE- AND DISEASE-RELATED CHANGES PREDISPOSING TO SYNCOPE IN THE ELDERLY

One of the characteristics of elderly people that predisposes them to syncope is the presence of multiple clinical abnormalities.[32] Additive age- and disease-related conditions that threaten cerebral blood flow or reduce oxygen content in the blood may bring oxygen delivery close to the threshold needed to maintain consciousness. A situational stress that further reduces blood pressure, such as posture change, or a Valsalva maneuver during voiding, may reduce cerebral oxygen delivery below the critical threshold and result in syncope.

Several homeostatic mechanisms that normally preserve blood pressure and cerebral oxygen delivery in the face of stress become impaired with age. These mechanisms include cerebral autoregulation,[33] baroreflexes,[34] myocardial diastolic relaxation,[35] and renal sodium conservation.[36]

Cerebral blood flow declines with normal aging.[33] In hypertension, which often accompanies advancing age, the threshold for cerebral autoregulation is shifted to higher levels of blood pressure, making elderly hypertensives more vulnerable to cerebral ischemia from relatively small degrees of hypotension. Baroreflex sensitivity is also impaired with advanced age. This impaired sensitivity can be demonstrated by a blunted bradycardiac response to hypertensive stimuli and diminished tachycardiac response to blood pressure reduction. At the bedside, this reduced sensitivity is evident in the absent or very modest cardioacceleration associated with posture change in the elderly patient.

The elderly are particularly vulnerable to the hypotensive effects of a rapid heart rate that results in a decreased stroke volume. Due to progressive myocardial stiffness, impaired diastolic relaxation, and reduced early diastolic ventricular filling with advancing age, the aged heart becomes more dependent on atrial contraction to fill the ventricle and maintain cardiac output. A rapid heart rate reduces ventricular filling and therefore threatens cardiac output. In atrial fibrillation, the loss of atrial contraction further reduces cardiac output. This combination of diminished stroke volume and loss of atrial contraction makes rapid atrial fibrillation particularly dangerous in the elderly patient.

Declines in basal and stimulated plasma renin and aldosterone concentrations with advancing age predispose to volume depletion. Furthermore, many elderly persons have an impaired thirst response to hyperosmolality and therefore may not consume a sufficient quantity of fluids to prevent dehydration[37] and hypovolemia.

ETIOLOGY

Multiple studies have shown that 20 to 30 percent of syncopal episodes have cardiac causes, 10 to 20 percent have noncardiac causes, and 30 to 50 percent remain unexplained in spite of extensive evaluation.[38,39] Table 109-4 shows the common causes of syncope in the elderly.

TABLE 109-4
Causes of Syncope

Cardiac disease (decreased cardiac output)
  Structural (mechanical obstruction to flow)
    Aortic stenosis
    Mitral stenosis
    Atrial myxoma
    Cardiomyopathy
    Pulmonary embolism
  Myocardial
    Acute myocardial infarction
  Electrical
    Tachyarrhythmias
    Bradyarrhythmias
    (Conduction disturbance, sinus node dysfunction)
Hypotension (decreased volume or peripheral vascular resistance)
  Orthostatic hypotension
    Prolonged inactivity
    Medications (vasodilator, antihypertensives, antidepressants, neuroleptics, diuretics)
    Central nervous system disease (Shy-Drager, Parkinson's disease)
    Peripheral autonomic neuropathies (diabetes, alcoholism, amyloidosis)
    Idiopathic
  Postprandial hypotension
  Volume depletion (fluid or blood loss)
Reflex (decreased cardiac output or peripheral vascular resistance)
  Vasovagal
  Defecation
  Micturition
  Cough
  Swallowing
  Carotid sinus syndrome
Abnormal blood composition (reduced energy substrates)
  Hypoxemia
  Hypoglycemia
  Acute anemia
Central nervous system disease
  Seizures
  Cerebrovascular insufficiency

Structural Heart Disease

The three main structural heart diseases that cause syncope in the elderly are aortic stenosis, hypertrophic cardiomyopathy, and mitral regurgitation. They all feature systolic murmurs that need to be distinguished from those attributable to the more prevalent, but benign, aortic sclerosis. About 30 percent of people over 65 years of age and 60 percent of people over 80 years of age have systolic murmurs.[40] The distinguishing features of these murmurs are often absent, making the clinical assessment difficult in the elderly.

AORTIC VALVE DISEASE Hemodynamically significant aortic stenosis is present in approximately 5 percent of elderly patients with a systolic murmur. Congenitally, bicuspid valves are the principal cause in the 60- to 70-year-old age group, while degenerative calcification of an otherwise normal tricuspid aortic valve is the most frequent cause of aortic stenosis in the very old.[41] Rheumatic heart disease is now an infrequent cause of aortic stenosis in the elderly. Most often aortic stenosis will present insidiously as congestive heart failure, but angina and syncope are still frequent manifestations.[42] The mechanism of syncope is either arrhythmia or reflex vasodilatation secondary to stimulation of ventricular vagal afferent fibers by a powerful ventricular contraction,[43] superimposed upon the structural impediment to left ventricular outflow.

HYPERTROPHIC CARDIOMYOPATHY (HCM) HCM is commonly overlooked in elderly patients, despite the fact that as many as 33 percent of patients with idiopathic HCM are over 60 years of age.[44] Hypertensive HCM has recently been described in the elderly and appears to be most common in black women.[45] HCM can present with angina, dyspnea, or syncope.[44] Syncope is due either to left ventricular outflow obstruction or to tachyarrhythmias.[46] Most patients with HCM have diastolic dysfunction characterized by impaired isovolumic relaxation, slow filling during the rapid-filling phase of diastole, and an excessive dependence on atrial systole to optimize ventricular volume.[47] Echocardiography is the diagnostic test of choice. It is important to think of HCM because it is exacerbated by commonly used ionotrophic and vasodilating medications.

MITRAL REGURGITATION (MR) Mitral valve prolapse, papillary muscle dysfunction, idiopathic calcification of the mitral valve annulus, and rheumatic disease are the common causes of MR. MR usually presents with congestive heart failure, but can also cause syncope.

Electrical Heart Disease

Syncope is frequently the result of electrical heart disease, such as asystole, bradycardia, or tachyarrhythmia.

Myocardial infarction may produce syncope via any of these mechanisms and is a common cause of syncope in the elderly.[28] Because arrhythmias are common in elderly people, their presence between syncopal attacks may be coincidental. Routine 24-hour ambulatory monitoring does not commonly show correlations between symptoms and rhythm disturbances.[48] A syncopal episode can be attributed to an arrhythmia only if the arrhythmia is found on an electrocardiogram at the time of the event, or if it is associated with symptoms of dizziness, near-syncope, or syncope during ambulatory monitoring. Ambulatory cardiac monitoring should be performed under the same conditions in which the syncopal episode occurred.

RHYTHM ABNORMALITIES Ventricular and supraventricular tachy- or bradyarrhythmias may produce syncope, but these rhythm abnormalities are also common in asymptomatic elderly persons.[49] In the Baltimore Longitudinal Study on Aging, 13 percent of healthy people 60 to 85 years of age showed asymptomatic paroxysmal atrial tachycardia and 50 percent showed complex ventricular arrhythmias, including multiform ventricular premature contractions in 35 percent, couplets in 11 percent, and ventricular tachycardia in 4 percent.[50] Seriousness of ventricular ectopy correlates closely with the degree of impaired left ventricular function, with persistent ST-segment elevation, and with the extent of obstructive coronary vascular disease.[51] Thus, ventricular ectopic activity in the absence of structural or ischemic heart disease is associated with a good prognosis.[52]

CONDUCTION DISTURBANCES Conduction disturbances are common in the elderly and are thought to be markers for transient heart block and associated syncope. First-degree heart block is never causally related to syncope.[53] On the other hand, second- and third-degree atrioventricular (AV) block are often seen in the elderly and may be associated with syncope, either directly through progression to complete heart block or through their close association with coexistent ventricular arrhythmias. Complete heart block is most commonly due to degenerative sclerosis of the conduction system, rather than to coronary artery disease.[54] The development of syncope in a patient with complete heart block (Stokes-Adams attack) is associated with increased mortality and should be treated with cardiac pacing.[55]

The prevalence of left bundle-branch block in population-based studies ranges from 0.6 percent to 2.5 percent; right bundle-branch block prevalence ranges from 1.9 percent to 3.5 percent.[56] In the absence of symptoms, these forms of bundle-branch block alone do not have predictive value for syncope. Bifascicular or trifascicular conduction disease in association with syncope is of greater concern.[57] Several large studies[56,58] have shown that in asymptomatic patients with these findings, the risk of progression to high-degree AV block is low. However, in patients with transient unexplained neurologic symptoms and bi- or trifascicular block, the finding of a His-ventricular interval greater than 70 ms in an electrophysiological study was associated with significantly greater progression to second- or third-degree AV block on follow-up. Therefore, prophylactic pacemaker implantation has been recommended in such patients for control of symptoms.[59] Syncope in patients with bifascicular block, however, is often due to causes other than heart block and does not in itself predict sudden death. Pacemaker insertion does not prevent sudden death, which presumably is due to ventricular arrhythmias, but may prevent serious morbidity associated with syncopal falls, if heart block is the cause of syncope.

SINUS NODE DISEASE Sinus bradycardia alone in an elderly patient may be a normal finding that does not imply cardiac disease and has no effect on mortality.[60,61] However, sinus node disease (i.e., "sick sinus syndrome"), characterized by sinus bradycardia in association with paroxysmal supraventricular tachyarrhythmias, is a common cause of syncope in old people. Conduction disturbances are also common in sick sinus syndrome, occurring in approximately 50 percent of patients.[62,63] One of the major causes of syncope in sick sinus syndrome is prolonged asystole after abrupt cessation of an associated supraventricular tachycardia. Although there is potential morbidity from dizziness, falls, and syncope, the mortality rate associated with sick sinus syndrome is quite low. In one study, an 80 percent 5-year survival was found, which is similar to that for a normal age- and sex-matched population.[64] Pacemaker implantation is therefore indicated for control of symptoms and not for the prolongation of life.

Hypotension

Due to age-related abnormalities in blood pressure homeostasis, as well as superimposed conditions which reduce intravascular volume and/or peripheral vascular resistance, hypotensive syndromes are common in elderly patients.

ORTHOSTATIC HYPOTENSION Orthostatic hypotension, defined as a systolic blood pressure decline of 20 mmHg or more on assumption of an upright posture, has been reported to occur in 20 to 30 percent of community-dwelling elderly.[65,66] However, recent studies suggest that this may be due to hypertension, rather than age. Many elderly patients have marked variability in orthostatic blood pressure, which may be due to impaired baroreflex function.[67] These elderly patients have normal elevations in plasma norepinephrine in response to posture change.

The major pathologic causes of orthostatic hypoten-

sion are shown in Table 109-4. Autonomic dysfunction is commonly accompanied by a fixed heart rate, visual difficulty, incontinence, constipation, inability to sweat, heat intolerance, impotence, and fatigability.[68]

Central and peripheral autonomic insufficiency can be differentiated on the basis of plasma norepinephrine levels. Patients with idiopathic orthostatic hypotension (peripheral) have lower basal plasma norepinephrine levels while supine,[69] no increase in norepinephrine levels with standing, a lower threshold for the pressor response to infused norepinephrine, and lower plasma norepinephrine levels in response to tyramine despite a greater pressor response to the drug.[70] These findings suggest that in idiopathic orthostatic hypotension there is depletion of norepinephrine from sympathetic nerve endings with resultant postsynaptic denervation supersensitivity. In central autonomic insufficiency, circulating norepinephrine and the response to infused norepinephrine and tyramine are normal,[70] but plasma norepinephrine levels also fail to increase with standing. This syndrome is associated with degeneration of neurons in the CNS.

POSTPRANDIAL HYPOTENSION Postprandial hypotension is a recently identified abnormality in blood pressure homeostasis.[71] Institutionalized and healthy community-dwelling elderly have an average 11-mmHg decline in blood pressure by 1 hour after a meal. While in most older people this is an asymptomatic, age-related abnormality, individuals with postprandial syncope have more profound declines in blood pressure that are probably responsible for their fainting episodes.[72] Postprandial hypotension may be related to an inability to compensate for splanchnic blood pooling during digestion.

VOLUME DEPLETION The elderly are at increased risk for dehydration and associated orthostatic hypotension due to an age-related impairment in renal salt and water conservation[36] and to any disease that threatens access to fluids or results in volume loss.

Abnormal Cardiovascular Reflexes

VASOVAGAL SYNCOPE Vasovagal syncope is the most common form of syncope in the younger population. It is also seen in the elderly but appears to be relatively less common. Syncope without an apparent cause is often inappropriately labeled "vasovagal." The exact prevalence is unknown. There is often a precipitant such as a painful or unpleasant experience (e.g., phlebotomy), surgical manipulation, or trauma. It is commonly associated with hunger, fatigue, crowding, or warmth. There are often premonitory signs and symptoms of intense autonomic nervous system stimulation, such as marked weakness, sweating, pallor, epigastric discomfort, nausea, yawning, sighing, hyperventilation, blurred vision, impaired hearing, a feeling of unawareness, and mydriasis.[26] Most often these symptoms occur while standing and are aborted by lying down. The circulatory changes preceding vasovagal syncope are biphasic, with initial increase in heart rate, blood pressure, total systemic resistance, and cardiac output. These changes are followed by peripheral vasodilatation, an increase in muscle blood flow, and a decrease in venous return to the heart.[73] The prognosis is good in true vasovagal syncope.

CAROTID SINUS SYNDROME Carotid sinus hypersensitivity is a common abnormality of reflex blood pressure regulation that in its pathologic extreme may result in syncope. A hypersensitive carotid sinus reflex, defined by a sinus slowing of greater than 50 percent (cardioinhibitory) or systolic blood pressure decline (vasodepressor) of over 50 mmHg or to hypotensive levels during carotid sinus massage, may identify a predisposition for syncope but does not prove that it is responsible for a given episode. When carotid sinus hypersensitivity is associated with syncope, it is designated the carotid sinus syndrome.[74] A number of patients with undiagnosed syncope may have the carotid sinus syndrome. Unfortunately, many physicians may overlook the carotid sinus syndrome by not doing carotid sinus massage on patients with syncope.

DEFECATION,[75] MICTURITION,[76] SWALLOWING,[77,78] AND COUGH SYNCOPE[79,80] Syncope may occur in response to any of these activities. The mechanism of syncope may be decreased venous return during the activities, an intermittent conduction disturbance or arrhythmia, or reflex-induced bradycardia or vasodilatation. Patients with syncope during these activities may develop syncope later under different conditions. The prognosis depends on the underlying pathophysiologic mechanism.

Abnormal Blood Composition

The maintenance of consciousness depends not only on delivery of blood to the brain, but also on adequate levels of glucose and oxygen in the blood in order to support oxidative cerebral metabolism. Thus, hypoxemia due to respiratory failure, anemia, and hypoglycemia may predispose to syncope.[32]

Central Nervous System Disease

Syncope can be attributed to CNS disease or cerebrovascular insufficiency only if transient and focal neurologic deficits are associated with the episode. The new onset of a seizure disorder may present as syncope. Conversely, syncope from other causes may be associated with seizure activity.[26]

EVALUATION

The history is the most important part of the evaluation of syncope, providing a diagnosis in up to 50 percent of cases where a cause is found. The physical examination makes the diagnosis in another 20 percent of cases.[81]

The *history* includes four key questions.[82] First, was there an obvious precipitant? Emotional stress, pain, cough, micturition, defecation, swallowing, effort (aortic stenosis), neck turning (carotid sinus syndrome), change in position, recent meal, or medication are all important clues. Second, were there any associated symptoms? Hunger, sweating, odd behavior, or slow onset and recovery may suggest hypoglycemia. Paresthesias may suggest hypocalcemia or hyperventilation. Flushing on recovery may suggest a Stokes-Adams attack. Palpitations, dyspnea, or chest pain may suggest pulmonary embolism, angina pectoris, or myocardial infarction. Focal neurologic symptoms suggest a neurologic disorder. Third, could medications have been responsible? Various antihypertensive and antianginal medications can cause hypotension. Digoxin and various antiarrhythmic medications can paradoxically cause arrhythmias. Fourth, how long did the symptoms last? If the symptoms last for more than 15 minutes, the physician should consider transient ischemic attack, seizure, hypoglycemia, or hysteria.

Physical examination should focus on postural vital signs, cardiovascular and neurologic systems, and a search for trauma. Blood pressure and heart rate are measured after at least a 5-minute rest in the supine position, then again after 1 minute of standing and 3 minutes of standing. If the patient cannot stand, sitting will suffice but may lead to failure to diagnose orthostatic hypotension. A symptomatic blood pressure drop focuses further evaluation on the causes of orthostatic hypotension. In the young patient, excessive acceleration of the pulse in response to posture change suggests that volume depletion, bleeding, or medications may be the cause of orthostatic hypotension. However, this finding is often absent in the elderly patient with baroreflex impairment. If pulse rate does not accelerate, autonomic dysfunction may also be the cause.

Careful evaluation of the carotid pulsations for contour, amplitude, and sound is important. Although the carotid upstroke is characteristically delayed in aortic stenosis, a normal upstroke does not rule out the diagnosis of aortic stenosis in the elderly patient because of an age-related increase in vascular rigidity which increases the rate of rise of the carotid pulse. When aortic stenosis develops, the rate of rise falls, but to an amplitude that may feel normal for a younger patient.[83] Also, a diminished carotid pulse or bruit may be suggestive of cerebrovascular disease, but its absence does not rule out a diagnosis of cerebral ischemia. In patients with severe aortic stenosis, simultaneous palpation of the carotid and apical impulses yields a palpable lag time between the two, which may suggest severe aortic stenosis.[84]

Cardiopulmonary examination focuses on detection of obstructive cardiovascular disorders such as aortic stenosis, hypertrophic cardiomyopathy, and pulmonary embolism. Unfortunately, cardiac murmurs become exceedingly common with advanced age, and significant murmurs in the elderly may be atypical in character or location.[85] Thus, associated clinical symptoms, such as congestive heart failure or angina pectoris, or signs, such as a diminished second aortic sound or left ventricular hypertrophy, should heighten the suspicion of hemodynamically significant conditions and stimulate further studies (e.g., a Doppler echocardiogram). Stools should be checked for blood. A careful neurologic examination should include a search for focal deficits that may signify cerebral infarction, hemorrhage, or tumor.

Carotid sinus massage[86] is an important test in the evaluation if cerebrovascular disease or cardiac conduction disturbances are not present. With the electrocardiogram running and the head slightly extended and rotated to the opposite side, the carotid sinus is massaged for 5 seconds. The blood pressure is taken before and immediately after the procedure. Two to three minutes later the procedure is repeated on the other side. Only symptomatic bradycardia or hypotension can be considered truly positive responses indicating carotid sinus hypersensitivity. However, there is general agreement that a systolic blood pressure decline of more than 50 mmHg (or an absolute value less than 90 mmHg) or a sinus pause of 3 seconds or longer is sufficient to produce syncope, particularly if the patient was in an upright position at the time of the syncopal event.

An *electrocardiogram* is indicated in all patients presenting with syncope, since it can provide diagnostic clues for myocardial infarction, ischemia, or transient tachy- or bradyarrhythmias. Multifocal and frequent atrial and ventricular ectopic beats are an indication for prolonged cardiac monitoring. A short PR interval may indicate an accessory pathway.[87] QT prolongation is associated with ventricular tachycardia and fibrillation.[88] Sinoatrial pauses or inappropriate sinus bradycardia may indicate a sinus node disorder. The presence of AV conduction abnormalities or bundle-branch block hints at transient heart block as the etiology of syncope.

Tests of autonomic function are indicated in any patient with orthostatic or postprandial hypotension. The simplest tests are deep breathing and the Valsalva maneuver.[89] The cold pressor and pharmacologic tests are poorly tolerated, potentially dangerous, and usually unnecessary in elderly patients.

Since electrical cardiac disease is so common in elderly patients, telemetry is usually indicated, even without cues from the electrocardiogram, unless noncardiac causes are positively identified. Ambulatory cardiac monitoring is only indicated in those syncope patients who are still suspected, after initial evaluation and/or telemetry monitoring, to have a symptomatic and safely treatable arrhythmia or conduction disturbance. Ambulatory monitoring should be performed during the patient's usual daily activities to increase the diagnostic yield. When monitored for 24 to 48 hours, 10 to 40 percent of patients will have transient symptoms. In these patients, an etiology based on an arrhythmia can be confirmed or excluded in 50 to 75 percent.[90]

Laboratory tests are generally of low yield but nevertheless are useful in the elderly syncopal patient without apparent etiology on history and physical examination, since syncope may be the atypical presentation of several conditions evident only on laboratory testing. Cardiac enzymes should be obtained if there is any associated chest pain or electrocardiographic change, both of which raise the suspicion of myocardial infarction. It is important to evaluate the volume status with electrolytes, blood urea nitrogen, and creatinine and to identify abnormalities that predispose to arrhythmias. Testing of arterial blood gases is indicated if there are pulmonary symptoms. A hematocrit is helpful to rule out anemia. Blood sugar values should be obtained to look for hypoglycemia and marked hyperglycemia, both of which may present with syncope in the elderly patient. Drug levels of anticonvulsants, antiarrhythmics, digoxin, or bronchodilators are useful to detect toxicity or undertreatment of a prior condition known to produce syncope.

Echocardiography is an invaluable study when structural heart disease is suspected. Recently, Doppler echocardiography has been shown to identify patients with significant aortic valve gradients. Doppler echocardiography correlates well with invasive cardiac catheterization, particularly when combined with 2-D echo.[91,92]

An *electroencephalogram* and a *CT scan of the head* should be obtained in the presence of focal neurologic abnormalities on physical examination or signs and symptoms of seizures.[30] More invasive studies such as cerebral or coronary angiography are only indicated to confirm specific clinical diagnoses.

Electrophysiologic studies of the heart are indicated in patients with cardiovascular disease and recurrent syncope in whom there is a high suspicion of sinus node dysfunction, conduction disease, or life-threatening arrhythmias. The overall incidence of findings (sinus node dysfunction, complete AV block, or ventricular tachycardia) considered to be positively related to syncope ranges from 18 to 69 percent. Most investigators find possible causes in approximately 50 percent and an even higher yield in patients with structural heart disease.[93] During follow-up, between 70 and 90 percent of those patients who received therapy on the basis of positive electrophysiologic findings remained asymptomatic. Although these results are impressive, it should also be noted that an average of 50 percent of patients not specifically treated also remained free of recurrent syncope.

Predictors for a positive electrophysiologic study include[94] a left ventricular ejection fraction of less than 0.40, presence of bundle-branch block, coronary artery disease, remote myocardial infarction, use of type 1 antiarrhythmic drugs, injury related to loss of consciousness, and male sex. Predictors for a negative study were an ejection fraction of greater than 0.40, absence of structural heart disease, a normal electrocardiogram, and normal ambulatory electrocardiographic monitoring. The benefits of any invasive procedure should be balanced against the risk and cost of the procedure and the potential adverse effects of therapy (including surgery and medications). The diagnostic approach to the elderly syncope patient is summarized in Fig. 109-2.

THERAPEUTIC ISSUES

The purpose of treating an elderly patient who presents with syncope is to prevent the morbidity and mortality associated with recurrent episodes. When the cause of a syncopal episode is readily apparent, specific therapy should be planned if the potential morbidity of the treatment is less than that of recurrent syncope. Because therapeutic interventions may be toxic to elderly patients, such interventions should be instituted with cautious attention to age- and disease-related physiologic changes that may affect response to a treatment. No person should be denied therapy on the basis of age alone.

When the cause of a syncopal episode is not clear, the therapy should be directed toward minimizing the risk of recurrent syncope by correcting predisposing conditions and eliminating drugs that may incrementally contribute to a syncopal event.[32] For example, the risk of syncope in an older person may be substantially reduced by treating anemia with a blood transfusion, correcting hypoxemia with supplemental oxygen, improving cardiac ischemia with nitrates (while observing for orthostatic hypotension), or preventing orthostatic hypotension with a high salt intake (while observing for congestive heart failure) and support stockings. The mainstay of therapy for autonomic insufficiency is fludrocortisone and salt loading, but new pharmacologic approaches are being investigated (e.g., the use of caffeine, ergotamine, and somatostatin).[95]

Before prescribing pharmacologic or surgical therapy for a diagnosed condition, the available safe, simple and commonsense treatments should be implemented. Such treatments include discontinuing use of potentially harmful drugs, such as digoxin, propranolol, or alpha methyldopa, which may predispose to carotid sinus hypersensitivity or suppress the sinus node; avoiding extreme neck rotation and tight collars when there is evidence of carotid sinus hypersensitivity; arising from the supine position slowly and dorsiflexing the feet a few minutes before standing (for persons prone to postural hypotension); maintaining adequate intravascular volume through regular fluid intake (for cognitively impaired or acutely ill patients); and urinating while sitting down (for men with micturition syncope). Often a simple behavioral change or drug elimination is the only therapy necessary to prevent recurrent syncopal episodes.

Antiarrhythmic medications should be prescribed only for *symptomatic* rhythm disturbances and initially at one-half the usual dose, due to the medications' prolonged half-lives and their increased toxicity in elderly patients.[96] Clinically significant adverse reactions are seen in up to half of young patients treated with antiarrhythmic medications, with major reactions noted in one-third.[97] Proarrhythmic effects (i.e., worsening of arrhythmia as a result of therapy) are now an appreciated complication of antiarrhythmic medications in up to one-third of patients. When the high incidence of serious side effects is coupled with the fact that no controlled studies have conclusively proven that patients with arrhythmia benefit from antiarrhythmic drug therapy, a high level of reluctance for initiating this kind of therapy in the very elderly is justifiable. Basic monitoring of medication levels, electrolytes, the electrocardiographic QT interval, and arrhythmia frequency on the ambulatory cardiac monitor is important when antiarrhythmic medications are prescribed.

Pacemakers[98] are generally indicated for the amelioration of symptoms due to bradyarrhythmias. Only in Stokes-Adams attacks do pacemakers improve longevity.[60] The most common indications for permanent pacemakers are third-degree AV block and sick sinus syndrome. Symptomatic second-degree AV block, symptomatic bi- or trifascicular block, and carotid sinus syndrome are also indications for a permanent pacemaker. A single-chamber ventricular pacemaker is generally adequate, but in the elderly patient who is dependent on atrial contraction to generate an adequate cardiac output, a dual-chamber pacemaker should be considered. Indications for antiarrhythmic medications, pacemakers, and electrophysiologic studies are continually being reassessed, and the latest consensus should be sought and carefully considered prior to making such a prescription for an elderly patient.

Invasive therapy such as aortic valve repair, balloon valvuloplasty, coronary angioplasty, and coronary artery bypass surgery has been shown to be feasible and effective in the elderly patient and to have an acceptable (low) mortality rate in patients who are otherwise well. Recent experience with balloon valvuloplasty for aortic stenosis suggests that this procedure may be of particular benefit to the symptomatic elderly patient who is at high surgical risk.[99]

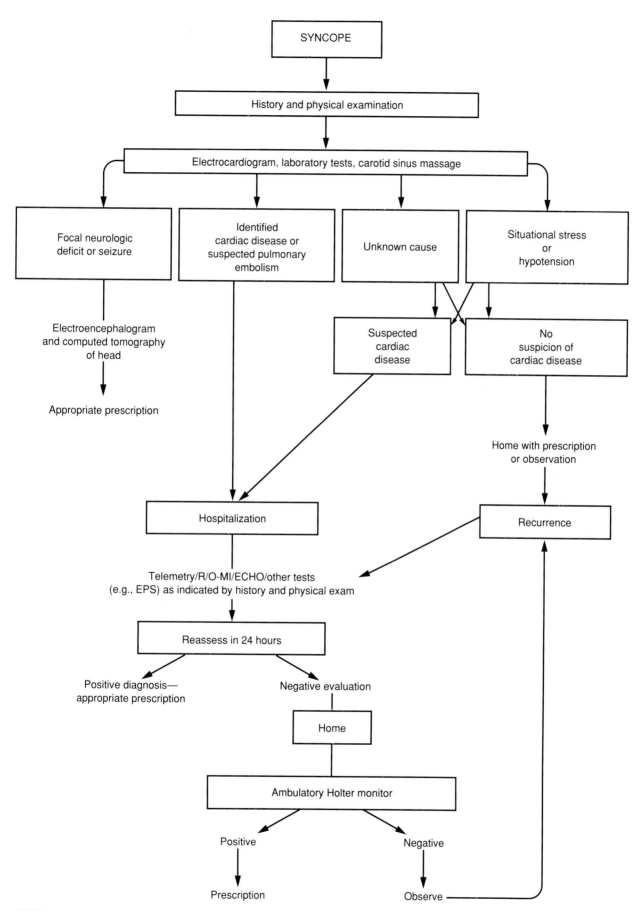

FIGURE 109-2
Algorithm for the diagnostic evaluation of the elderly syncope patient.

CONCLUSION

Age-related physiologic changes and disease-related abnormalities predispose the elderly patient to syncope. Syncope may be the atypical manifestation of diseases or situational stresses that are usually not expected to present with syncopal episodes. Attention to situational stresses, such as posture change, meals, or drug ingestion, is likely to increase the diagnostic yield and lead to simple therapy that can reduce the morbidity and potential mortality of recurrent episodes. Therapy should be directed toward minimizing multiple risks for syncope, avoiding toxic interventions, and treating specific symptomatic diseases, while basing treatment on underlying disease rather than on age per se.

REFERENCES

1. Blumenthal MB, Davie JW: Dizziness and falling in elderly psychiatric outpatients. *Am J Psychiatry* 137:203, 1980.
2. Drachman DA, Hart CW: An approach to the dizzy patient. *Neurology* 22:323, 1972.
3. Brandt TB, Daroff RB: The multisensory physiological and pathological vertigo syndromes. *Ann Neurol* 7:195, 1980.
4. Hale HE et al: Symptom prevalence in the elderly. An evaluation of age, sex, disease, and medication use. *J Am Geriatr Soc* 34:333, 1986.
5. Adams RD, Victor M: Dizziness and vertigo, in *Principles of Neurology*, 3d ed. New York, McGraw-Hill, 1985, p 218.
6. Cohn TE, Lasley DJ: Visual depth illusion and falls in the elderly. *Clin Geriatr Med* 1:601, 1985.
7. Lebowitz H et al: The independence of dynamic spatial orientation from luminance and refractive error. *Percept Psychophysiol* 25:75, 1979.
8. Koken E et al: Quantitative evaluation of joint motion sensation in an aging population. *J Gerontol* 33:62, 1978.
9. Wyke B: Cervical articular contributions to posture and gait: Their relation to senile dysequilibrium. *Age Ageing* 8:251, 1979.
10. Stanle J, Tenino J: Paroxysmal positional nystagmus: An electronystagmographic and clinical study. *Ann Otol* 74:69, 1965.
11. Cawthorne TE, Hinchcliffe R: Positional nystagmus of the central type as evidence of subtentorial metastases. *Brain* 84:415, 1961.
12. Baloh RW et al: Benign positional vertigo: Clinical and oculographic features in 240 cases. *Neurology* 37:371, 1987.
13. Schuknecht H: Cupulolithiasis. *Arch Otolaryngol* 90:765, 1969.
14. Rutka JA, Barber HO: Recurrent vestibulopathy: Third review. *J Otolaryngol* 15:105, 1986.
15. Arenberg IK: Symposium on Meniere's disease. *Otolaryngol Clin North Am* 135:4, 1984.
16. Hart R et al: Acoustic tumors: Atypical features and recent diagnostic tests. *Neurology* 33:211, 1983.
17. Hybels RL: Drug toxicity of the inner ear. *Med Clin North Am* 63:309, 1979.
18. Fisher CM: Vertigo in cerebrovascular disease. *Arch Otolaryngol* 85:529, 1967.
19. Huang C, Yu Y: Small cerebellar strokes may mimic labyrinthine lesions. *J Neurol Neurosurg Psychiatry* 48:263, 1985.
20. Reichert WH et al: Vestibular dysfunction in Parkinson's disease. *Neurology* 32:1133, 1982.
21. Van Durme JP: Tachyarrhythmias and transient cerebral ischemic attacks. *Am Heart J* 85:538, 1975.
22. Vemma N: Dizziness, falling, and fainting: Differential diagnosis in the aged, Part II. *Geriatrics* 41(7):31, 1986.
23. Dix MR, Hallpike C: The pathology, symptomatology and diagnosis of certain common disorders of the vestibular system. *Proc R Soc Med* 45:341, 1952.
24. Nelson JR: The minimal ice water caloric test. *Neurology* 19:577, 1969.
25. Norre ME, Beckers A: Benign paroxysmal positional vertigo in the elderly. Treatment by habituation exercises. *J Am Geriatr Soc* 36:425, 1988.
26. Wayne HH: Syncope: Physiological considerations and an analysis of the clinical characteristics in 510 patients. *Am J Med* 30:418, 1961.
27. Savage DD et al: Epidemiologic features of isolated syncope: The Framingham Study. *Stroke* 16:626, 1985.
28. Lipsitz LA et al: Syncope in an elderly, institutionalized population: prevalence, incidence, and associated risk. *Q J Med* 216:45, 1985.
29. Kapoor WN et al: Syncope in the elderly. *Am J Med* 80:419, 1986.
30. Day SC et al: Evaluation and outcome of emergency room patients with transient loss of consciousness. *Am J Med* 73:15, 1982.
31. Kapoor WN et al: Diagnostic and prognostic implications of recurrences in patients with syncope. *Am J Med* 83:700, 1987.
32. Lipsitz LA: Syncope in the elderly. *Ann Intern Med* 99:92, 1983.
33. Kety SS: Human cerebral blood flow and oxygen consumption as related to aging. *J Chron Dis* 3:478, 1956.
34. Minaker KL et al: Impaired cardiovascular adaptation to vasodilation in the elderly. *Gerontologist* 20(part II):163, 1980.
35. Iskandrian AS, Hakki AH: Age-related changes in left ventricular diastolic performance. *Am Heart J* 112:75, 1986.
36. Duthie EH et al: Evaluation of the systolic murmur in the elderly. *J Am Geriatr Soc* 29:498, 1981.
37. Fish LC et al: Altered thirst threshold during hypertonic stress in aging man. *Gerontologist* 25:118, 1985.
38. Kapoor WN et al: Syncope of unknown origin: The need for a more cost-effective approach to its diagnostic evaluation. *JAMA* 247:2687, 1982.
39. Silverstein MD et al: Patients with syncope admitted to medical intensive care units. *JAMA* 248:1185, 1982.
40. Pomerance A: Cardiac pathology in the elderly, in Noble RJ, Rothbaum DA (eds): *Geriatric Cardiology*. Philadelphia, Davis, 1981, pp 28–29.
41. Pomerance A: Pathogenesis of aortic stenosis and its relation to age. *Br Heart J* 34:569, 1972.
42. Finegan RE et al: Aortic stenosis in the elderly. *N Engl J Med* 279:225, 1968.

43. Mark AL: The Bezold-Jarisch reflex revisited: Clinical implications of inhibitory reflexes originating in the heart. *J Am Coll Cardiol* 1:90, 1983.

44. Krasnow N, Stein RA: Hypertrophic cardiomyopathy in the aged. *Am Heart J* 96:326, 1978.

45. Topol EJ et al: Hypertensive hypertrophic cardiomyopathy of the elderly. *N Engl J Med* 312:277, 1985.

46. Cookson H: Fainting and fits in cardiac infarction. *Br Heart J* 4:163, 1942.

47. Betocchi S et al: Isovolumic relaxation period in hypertrophic cardiomyopathy: Assessment by radionuclide angiography. *J Am Coll Cardiol* 7:74, 1986.

48. Gibson TC, Hertzman MR: Diagnostic efficacy of 24-hour electrocardiographic monitoring for syncope. *Am J Cardiol* 5:398, 1984.

49. Rasmussen J et al: Premature ventricular beats in healthy adult subjects 20 to 79 years of age. *Eur Heart J* 6:335, 1985.

50. Fleg JL, Kennedy HL: Cardiac arrhythmias in a healthy elderly population. Detection by 24 hour ambulatory electrocardiography. *Chest* 81:302, 1982.

51. Horan MJ, Kennedy HL: Ventricular ectopy. History, epidemiology and clinical implications. *JAMA* 251:380, 1984.

52. Kennedy HL et al: Long-term follow-up of asymptomatic healthy subjects with frequent and complex ventricular ectopy. *N Engl J Med* 312:193, 1985.

53. Mymin D et al: The natural history of primary first-degree heart block. *N Engl J Med* 315:1183, 1986.

54. Leu M: Anatomic basis for atrioventricular block. *Am J Med* 37:742, 1964.

55. Dunst M: Cardiac pacemakers. *Med Clin N Am* 57:1515, 1973.

56. McAnulty JH et al: Natural history of "high-risk" bundle-branch block. Final report of a prospective study. *N Engl J Med* 307:137, 1982.

57. Ezri M et al: Electrophysiologic evaluation of syncope in patients with bifascicular block. *Am Heart J* 106:693, 1983.

58. Dhingra RC et al: Syncope in patients with chronic bifascicular block. Significance, causative mechanisms, and clinical implications. *Ann Intern Med* 81:302, 1974.

59. Scheinman MM et al: Prognostic value of infranodal conduction time in patients with chronic bundle branch block. *Circulation* 56:240, 1977.

60. Agruss NS et al: Significance of chronic sinus bradycardia in elderly people. *Circulation* 46:924, 1972.

61. Gann D et al: Electrophysiologic evaluation of elderly patients with sinus bradycardia. A long-term follow-up study. *Ann Intern Med* 90:24, 1979.

62. Obel IWP et al: Chronic symptomatic sinoatrial block: A review of 34 patients and their treatment. *Chest* 65:397, 1974.

63. Moss AJ, Davis RJ: Brady-tachy syndrome. *Prog Cardiovasc Dis* 16:439, 1974.

64. Shaw DB et al: Survival in sinoatrial disorder (sick-sinus syndrome). *Br Med J* 280:139, 1980.

65. Johnson RH et al: Effect of posture on blood pressure in the elderly. *Lancet* 1:731, 1965.

66. Caird FI et al: Effect of posture on blood pressure in the elderly. *Br Heart J* 35:527, 1973.

67. Lipsitz LA et al: Intraindividual variability in postural blood pressure in the elderly. *Clin Sci* 69:337, 1985.

68. Ziegler MG: Postural hypotension. *Annu Rev Med* 31:239, 1980.

69. Ziegler MC et al: The sympathetic nervous system defect in primary orthostatic hypotension *N Engl J Med* 296:293, 1977.

70. Polinsky RJ et al: Pharmacologic distinction of different orthostatic hypotension syndromes. *Neurology* 31:1, 1981.

71. Lipsitz LA et al: Postprandial reduction in blood pressure in the elderly. *N Engl J Med* 309:81, 1983.

72. Lipsitz LA et al: Cardiovascular and norepinephrine responses after meal consumption in elderly (older than 75 years) persons with postprandial hypotension and syncope. *Am J Cardiol* 58:810, 1986.

73. Engel GL: Psychologic stress, vasodepressor (vasovagal) syncope, and sudden death. *Ann Intern Med* 89:403, 1978.

74. Lown B, Levine SA: The carotid sinus. Clinical value of its stimulation. *Circulation* 23:766, 1961.

75. Kapoor WW et al: Defecation syncope a symptom with multiple etiologies. *Arch Intern Med* 146:2377, 1986.

76. Kapoor WW et al: Micturition syncope: A reappraisal *JAMA* 253:796, 1985.

77. Levin B, Posner JB: Swallow syncope. Report of a case and review of the literature. *Neurology* 22:1086, 1972.

78. Kadish AH et al: Swallowing syncope: Observations in the absence of conduction system or esophageal disease. *Am J Med* 81:1098, 1986.

79. Sharpey-Schafer EP: The mechanism of syncope after coughing. *Br Med J* 2:860, 1953.

80. Strauss MJ et al: Case report, atypical cough syncope. *JAMA* 251:1731, 1984.

81. Kudenchuk PJ, McAnulty JH: Syncope: Evaluation and treatment. *Mod Conc Cardiovasc Dis* 54:25, 1985.

82. Ormerod AD: Syncope. *Br Med J* 288:1219, 1984.

83. Flohr KH et al: Diagnosis of aortic stenosis in older age groups using external carotid pulse recording and phonocardiography. *Br Heart J* 45:577, 1981.

84. Chun PKC, Dunn BE: Clinical clues of severe aortic stenosis. Simultaneous palpation of the carotid and apical impulses. *Arch Intern Med* 142:2284, 1982.

85. Pomerance A: Cardiac pathology and systolic murmurs in the elderly. *Br Heart J* 30:687, 1968.

86. Schweitzer P, Teichholz LE: Carotid sinus massage: Its diagnostic and therapeutic value in arrhythmia. *Am J Med* 78:645, 1985.

87. Wellens HJJ et al: The management of preexcitation syndrome. *JAMA* 257:2325, 1987.

88. Moss AJ: Prolonged QT interval syndrome. *JAMA* 256:2985, 1986.

89. Henrich WL: Autonomic insufficiency. *Arch Intern Med* 142:339, 1982.

90. Kapoor WN: Evaluation of syncope in the elderly. *J Am Geriatr Soc* 35:826, 1987.

91. Yaeger M et al: Comparison of doppler-derived pressure gradient to that determined at cardiac catheterization in adults with aortic valve stenosis: Implications for management. *Am J Cardiol* 57:644, 1986.

92. Zoghbi WA et al: Accurate noninvasive quantification of stenotic aortic valve area of doppler echocardiography. *Circulation* 73:452, 1986.

93. DiMarco JP: Electrophysiologic studies in patients with unexplained syncope. *Circulation* 75(suppl III):140, 1987.

94. Krol RB et al: Electrophysiologic testing in patients with unexplained syncope: Clinical and noninvasive predictors of outcome. *J Am Coll Cardiol* 10:358, 1987.

95. Cunha UV: Management of orthostatic hypotension in the elderly. *Geriatrics* 42:61, 1987.

96. Everitt DE, Avorn J: Drug prescribing for the elderly. *Arch Intern Med* 146:2393, 1986.

97. Woosley RL: Risk/benefit considerations in antiarrhythmic therapy. *JAMA* 256:82, 1986.

98. Ludmer PL, Goldschlager N: Cardiac pacing in the 1980s. *N Engl J Med* 311:1671, 1984.

99. McKay RG et al: Balloon dilatation of calcific aortic stenosis in elderly patients: Postmortem, intraoperative, and percutaneous valvuloplasty studies. *Circulation* 74:119, 1986.

Chapter 110

DISORDERS OF FLUID AND ELECTROLYTE BALANCE

Kenneth M. Davis and Kenneth L. Minaker

Disorders of water balance occur more frequently in elderly patients than in young adults. Dehydration is the most common fluid and electrolyte problem accompanying acute illnesses in old age and is caused by one or more of the following mechanisms: excess losses of water, failure to recognize the need to increase water intake, or impaired water ingestion. The electrolyte disorder classically associated with water loss is hypernatremia, which occurs in 1.1 to 1.6 percent of all acute hospital admissions in the elderly.[1] More common is isotonic dehydration, which is associated with a diverse array of illnesses. The mortality of hospitalized patients with dehydration is seven times that of age-matched patients without dehydration and ranges between 40 and 70 percent.[2]

Because the incidence and morbidity of dehydration increases with age, there is a strong belief that aging itself may predispose to abnormalities of hydration. In this chapter, current understanding of the age-related alterations in the homeostatic mechanisms regulating the volume and composition of extracellular fluid will be reviewed. Following this, an overview of the common illnesses predisposing to dehydration will be discussed. Finally, current therapy for dehydration will be outlined.

PHYSIOLOGIC REGULATION OF EXTRACELLULAR FLUID VOLUME IN THE ELDERLY

In the normal young adult, neurohypophyseal-pituitary-renal axis capacity far exceeds the ordinary demands for water conservation and excretion.[3] While the functional reserve of the system is substantially diminished in old age, in healthy elderly persons adequate regulation of the volume and composition of extracellular fluid re-

mains.[4] Thus, basal levels of sodium, osmolality, and vasopressin are unchanged with age, indicating adequate basal organ function. During extremes of physiologic stress or in the course of common illness, however, clinical abnormalities of water balance frequently occur. A spectrum of significant alterations in the central, renal, and neurohumoral mechanisms supporting the normal maintenance of water balance occur progressively with advancing age.

The central nervous system (CNS) control of fluid balance involves both vasopressin and thirst. Under ordinary physiologic conditions, vasopressin modulates water balance, and thirst functions to repair water deficits.[5] The major physiologic stimulus for vasopressin secretion in humans is plasma osmolality. Studies of the plasma vasopressin response of young subjects (22 to 48 years old) and older subjects (52 to 66 years old) during hypertonic saline infusions show that the threshold for vasopressin release is not influenced by the age (to this age, at least) and that vasopressin responses are enhanced in the older group.[6] During water deprivation, greater elevations of vasopressin have been observed in older subjects, albeit with somewhat greater accompanying hyperosmolarity.[7] Other stimuli for vasopressin release result in distinctly different vasopressin responses with age. Volume-pressure stimulation is less likely to result in vasopressin release with age.[8]

When vasopressin and renal capacity to maintain water balance have been overwhelmed, thirst supervenes, stimulating the ingestion of water, which reduces the systemic hyperosmolarity. Following water deprivation, subjective measures of thirst and objective measures of drinking behavior in the 2 hours following water deprivation are decreased in the elderly.[7] The mechanisms for these phenomena are currently unclear. Thirst and drinking are stimulated by cellular dehydration in the central brain osmoreceptors located in a region extending from the preoptic area of the hypothalamus and including tissue surrounding the anterocentral part of the third ventricle to the zona incerta posteriorly.[9] The renin-angiotensin system and cardiac receptors stimulate drinking when extracellular fluid volume depletion occurs. Oropharyngeal factors, including taste and gastric distention, are also modulators of drinking behavior. Substantial variability in the level of osmolality producing thirst is observed in young subjects. Thirst threshold has not yet been carefully examined in elderly subjects, but similar variability is likely.[10] Of potential importance to the renally mediated thirst response is the well-established age-related decrease in basal and stimulated renin levels, as well as the decrease in angiotensin levels.[11]

Changes in intrarenal vasculature and glomeruli that occur with age are associated with generally linear, progressive declines in renal plasma flow. Studies of water deprivation in healthy males reveal that young subjects can decrease urine flow markedly to a minimum of 0.5 ± 0.03 ml/min and increase urine osmolality to a maximum of 1100 ± 22 mosm/kg.[4] Elderly subjects are only able to decrease urine flow to 1.0 ± 0.1 ml/min and increase urine osmolality to a maximum of 882 ± 49 mosm/kg. Correction of the changes in urine flow for the age-related decline in glomerular filtration rate does not alter the highly significant effect of age on urine flow rate. While Lindemann et al. were unable to demonstrate an age-related decline with age in response to submaximal vasopressin (Pitressin) infusion, Miller and Shock have shown a clear diminution of maximal urinary osmolality during high-dose Pitressin infusions in older subjects.[12,13]

A modest age-related impairment in the maximal excretion of free water after water loading has been demonstrated.[13,14] Minimal urinary concentration (urinary/plasma osmolality) rises from 0.247 in younger persons to 0.418 in the elderly.[14,15] Finally, significant delays in adaptation to salt restriction have been documented in older subjects.[15,16]

These age-related changes in the regulation of the volume and composition of extracellular fluid can be viewed as increasing the likelihood and severity of dehydration during the course of an illness. When combined with diminishing reserve capacity of the cardiac, pulmonary, hepatic, and renal systems, the clinical sequelae of dehydration are likely to be more severe in the elderly.

COMMON ILLNESSES PREDISPOSING TO DEHYDRATION IN THE ELDERLY

In addition to the normal aging-related changes, superimposed illnesses may result in a further diminution of the homeostatic capacity to regulate fluid balance. A re-

cent study by Snyder[1] of 15,187 consecutive admissions of patients over 60 years old revealed that 162 (1.1 percent) had serum sodium levels greater than 148 meq/l. Only 43 percent of these patients were hypernatremic on admission; the majority developed an elevated serum sodium during hospitalization, one-half of them within the first 8 days. Patients that presented with hypernatremia on admission had higher sodium levels but a lower mortality rate (29 percent vs. 52 percent) than those developing hypernatremia during acute hospitalization.

Table 110-1 lists the factors most commonly associated with (or causing) hypernatremia. Forty-four percent of patients had three or more factors contributing to their hypernatremic states. This is consistent with the fact that multiple factors usually contribute to dehydration in the elderly patient. No matter what the illness, the evaluation must assess for excessive fluid loss or decreased fluid intake (Tables 110-2 and 110-3).

INCREASED FLUID LOSSES

Acute infections, such as pneumonia and urinary tract infections, are common in the elderly, accounting for up to 20 percent of acute hospitalizations in this population. The associated fever results in increased insensible water loss from sweating, tachypnea, and increased cellular catabolism. Infection of the upper urinary tract may specifically result in reduction of the renal concentrating ability that may persist for weeks following resolution of the infection.

Excessive urinary losses of water and sodium are very common in the sick elderly patient. Continuation of diuretic drug therapy in the elderly dehydrated patient is an unfortunate yet common and preventable problem. As many as 10 percent of hospitalized elderly in the United Kingdom are admitted with diuretic side effects such as dehydration. In addition to pharmacologic diure-

TABLE 110-1
Factors Associated with Hypernatremia

Factor	Percentage of Patients
Febrile illness	70
Infirmity	40
Surgery	21
Nutritional supplementation	20
Intravenous solutes	18
Diabetes mellitus	15
Diarrhea	11
Gastrointestinal bleeding	9
Diuretics	9
Diabetes insipidus	7
Dialysis-related	3

SOURCE: Data from Ref. 1.

TABLE 110-2
Causes of Increased Fluid Loss in the Elderly

Chronic or acute infections
Excessive urinary losses
   Diuretic misuse
   Glycosuria
   Hypercalciuria
   Mannitol
   Radiographic contrast agents
   Elevated blood urea nitrogen
   Diabetes insipidus
      Central (pituitary)
      Nephrogenic
   Hypoaldosteronism
      Addison's disease
      Hyporeninemic hypoaldosteronism
   Suppressed vasopressin
      Phenytoin
      Ethanol
      Postatrial tachyarrhythmia
   Postobstructive diuresis
Gastrointestinal losses
   Upper GI
      Vomiting
      Nasogastric drainage
   Lower GI (diarrhea)
      Laxative abuse/bowel preps
      Infectious/secretory
      Surgical bypass/fistulas
      Ischemic bowel
      Colectomy
Excessive blood loss
Environment-related fluid loss
   Heat wave
   Hypothermia
Compartmental fluid shifts
   Hypoalbuminemia
   Pancreatitis
   Ascites
   Anaphylaxis
   Burns
   Hypertonic peritoneal dialysate

TABLE 110-3
Causes of Decreased Fluid Intake in the Elderly

Limited access to fluids
   Physical restraints
   Mobility restriction
   Poor visual acuity
Fluid restriction
   Pre-procedure
   Prevention of incontinence/nocturia/aspiration
   Therapy for edema or hyponatremia
Altered sensorium
   Decreased consciousness level
      Sedatives, neuroleptics, narcotics
      Structural and metabolic CNS insults
      Febrile illness
   Decreased level of awareness
      Dementia, delirium
      Mania, psychosis, depression
Gastrointestinal disorders
   Swallowing disorders
   Bowel obstruction
      Mechanical
      Metabolic
      Ischemic
   Anticholinergic medication
Alteration in thirst mechanism
   Primary adipsia
   Medication-related
      Cardiac glycosides
      Amphetamines
   Associated with focal CNS pathology

sis, obligate diuresis is common to many prevalent illnesses in the elderly. These include the glycosuria of diabetes mellitus, hypercalciuria of malignancy and hyperparathyroidism, and the use of intravenous mannitol and radiographic contrast agents. An obligate diuresis may result from renal absorption of excessive blood urea nitrogen (BUN) generated by increased protein catabolism in the gut in the setting of gastrointestinal bleeding or high-protein enteral tube feedings.[17,18]

Central diabetes insipidus is not a common disease in the elderly, but nephrogenic diabetes insipidus is frequently seen in association with drugs such as lithium, demeclocycline, and methoxyflurane anesthesia. Hypoaldosteronism occurs in the setting of Addison's disease

with inadequate mineralocorticoid replacement, as well as in the hyporeninemic state associated with normal aging. This hypoaldosteronism results in impairment in the urinary salvage of sodium and water during periods of dehydration. Drugs such as phenytoin and ethanol cause a suppression in the release of vasopressin, resulting in a decrease in tubular reabsorption of water. Alcohol abuse contributing to dehydration is frequently underrecognized in the elderly patient.

Urinary tract obstruction is a common affliction in the elderly male with prostatic hypertrophy (often exacerbated by anticholinergic medication). In the elderly female, postoperative urinary retention is a frequently unrecognized cause of obstructive uropathy. The postobstructive diuresis associated with relief of urinary obstruction is physiologically similar to nephrogenic diabetes insipidus with inadequate renal responsiveness to vasopressin.

Gastrointestinal losses of fluid occur with vomiting, nasogastric drainage, diarrhea, and bleeding. In addition to the commonly recognized etiology of diarrhea, laxative abuse is often present but unreported in the elderly. As many as 40 to 60 percent of the elderly use laxatives regularly, and the elderly patient may experience unrecognized continuation of regularly ordered laxatives and stool softeners in the setting of diarrhea. Older patients are often victimized by aggressive bowel cleansing regimens before radiographic study of the bowel or kidney. A patient with previous intestinal bypass or colectomy is at further risk for dehydration due to reduced gastrointestinal water absorptive capacity.

The elderly are especially prone to heat-related fluid loss from excessive sweating with inadequate volume replacement. The excess mortality seen during prolonged summer heat waves disproportionately affects the elderly. Many older persons have inadequate social and physical protective mechanisms to avoid excessive heat exposure. These same people may suffer from limited access to (or recognition of the need for) salt and water and therefore do not compensate for the increased insensible fluid loss.

Compartmental fluid shifts from conditions such as hypoalbuminemia and pancreatitis often result in a relative intravascular dehydration without clinically obvious sources of fluid loss.

DECREASED FLUID INTAKE

Often underappreciated in the elderly are conditions resulting in inadequate fluid intake (Table 110-3). Patients with physical restraints, restricted mobility, and poor vision may not have free access to fluids. Most frequently underrecognized as being at risk for fluid access problems are patients presenting with deteriorating mobility, vision, or level of consciousness who were independent in their fluid access prior to becoming ill.

Iatrogenic oral fluid deprivation is commonly ordered before diagnostic or surgical procedures or, inappropriately, for edema, renal insufficiency, or hyponatremia. Self- or caregiver-imposed fluid restriction is common in the older person prone to urinary incontinence, nocturia, or pulmonary aspiration. Acute and chronic alterations in sensorium are prevalent in the ill elderly patient, with a resulting decrease in the perception of the need for, and access to, appropriate fluids.

Gastrointestinal problems, such as swallowing disorders, bowel obstruction, and the underrecognized side effects of medication (nausea, vomiting, early satiety), often preclude adequate oral fluid intake. A common yet infrequently diagnosed cause of bowel obstruction in the elderly is ischemic bowel disease. This condition is exacerbated by dehydration, resulting in a vicious cycle of dehydration and ischemic bowel injury.

A further decrease in thirst perception in the elderly can be precipitated by drugs such as cardiac glycosides and amphetamines.[19] Finally, a syndrome of primary adipsia has been described in patients with a remote history of cerebal vascular accidents.[20]

THERAPY FOR DEHYDRATION

Prevention and early intervention are the most effective therapies for dehydration. This strategy can be accomplished by education of patients, families, and health care workers to appreciate the need for early intervention with fluid therapy in the elderly patient prone to dehydration. Specific fluid prescriptions in home, nursing home, or acute care hospital settings can be very helpful toward this end.

For the dehydrated patient, it is essential to establish the causes of fluid loss with history, physical examination, and appropriate laboratory studies and to direct therapy accordingly. Dehydration may be classified as either isotonic or hypertonic. Isotonic dehydration is characterized by loss of equimolar amounts of sodium and water, with resulting dehydration but without change in serum osmolarity. Hypertonic (hypernatremic) dehydration is seen in conditions of primary loss of free water more than sodium and is characterized by hypernatremia and hyperosmolarity.

The severity of fluid loss must be estimated by evaluation of blood pressure, orthostasis, skin turgor (though less useful in the elderly), and urine output. Very useful is a careful measurement of weight to compare to a baseline weight determined before the most recent illnesses. The serum osmolarity can be measured or estimated within ±10 mosm/l by the following formula:

$$\text{Serum osmolarity} = 2\,(\text{Na}) + \frac{\text{Glucose}}{18} + \frac{\text{BUN}}{2.8}$$

where Na is measured in meq/l and glucose and BUN are measured in mg/dl. If measured osmolarity is significantly greater than the calculated value, the presence of abnormal unmeasured solutes such as ethanol, isopropanol, ethylene glycol, methanol, or mannitol should be considered.

The magnitude of fluid deficits with primarily free water loss (hypernatremic dehydration) can be estimated by the following calculation:

Fluid deficit (l) = desired TBW − current TBW
Current TBW = 0.5 × body weight (kg)

$$\text{Desired TBW} = \frac{\text{measured serum sodium}}{140} \times \frac{\text{current}}{\text{TBW}}$$

where TBW is the total body water in liters. In the young, water comprises 60 percent of the body weight as compared to only 50 percent in the elderly male and 45 percent in the elderly female. This proportional decrease in water is due to the increase in fat and decrease in lean body mass with aging.[21] Three methods of fluid replacement (oral, subcutaneous, and intravenous) may be used singly or in combination, depending on the care setting and the severity of the condition. Oral rehydration is preferred; administration of free water or oral electrolyte solutions developed for use in third world countries is encouraged. Subcutaneous fluids may be very effective, safe, and easily administered, especially in the home or in nursing home settings.[22] Three liters of isotonic fluid per day may be delivered through two subcutaneous infusion sites, each dispensing 60 cc per hour. The addition of hyaluronidase (Wydase, Wyeth) may facilitate fluid absorption. The abdomen and upper outer aspect of the thighs are the preferred infusion sites. Intravenous fluid replacement is best reserved for the acute care setting where the dehydrated patient can be closely monitored.

The first step in the therapy of hypernatremic dehydration is correction of hemodynamic collapse, manifested by hypotension, orthostasis, and decreased urine output. Rapid infusions of isotonic saline until these parameters of volume status stabilize constitute initial therapy. The hemodynamically stable patient should have replacement of one-half of the fluid deficit over the first 24 hours, with the remaining volume replaced over the next 48 to 72 hours. A goal during rapid fluid replacement is to reduce serum osmolarity to 300 at a rate of no greater than 1 meq/l per hour, followed by gradual infusion to correct the total osmolar deficit over the next 48 to 72 hours. The replacement fluid for these patients during this phase will be 5% dextrose in ½ normal saline. Patients with isotonic dehydration (normal or low serum sodium) should have isotonic saline as replacement fluid. In addition to correction of the fluid deficit, ongoing fluid losses must be replaced. These losses average 2 to 3 liters per day in the healthy person and may be significantly greater in illness. Continued reassessment of fluid status, including measurement of intake and output, weight, blood pressure, pulse, serum chemistries, and osmolarities, must be done periodically to assure appropriate fluid replacement.

Overzealous rehydration, such as replacement of the entire fluid deficit over 24 hours, may result in death from cerebral edema. Dehydration of brain cells is prevented by the generation of osmotically active solute ("idiogenic osmoles"), thereby setting up an osmotic gradient to retain intracellular water in the face of systemic hyperosmolarity. If plasma hyperosmolarity is corrected too rapidly, there may be excessive movement of water into brain cells, resulting in cerebral edema.[23] The fluid deficits of dehydration may be safely corrected over 72 hours, yet the associated mental status changes may persist for as long as two weeks.

REFERENCES

1. Snyder NA, Feigal DW, Arieff AI: Hypernatremia in elderly patients. *Ann Intern Med* 107:309, 1987.
2. Lavizzo-Mourey RJ: Dehydration in the elderly: A short review. *J Natl Med Assoc* 79:1033, 1987.
3. Shannon RP, Minaker KL, Rowe JW: The influence of age on water balance in man. *Semin Nephrol* 4:346, 1984.
4. Rowe JW, Shock NW, Defronzo RA: The influence of age on the renal response to water deprivation in man. *Nephron* 17:270, 1976.
5. Helderman JH: The impact of normal aging on the hypothalamic-neurohypophyseal-renal axis, in Korenman SG (ed): *Endocrine Aspects of Aging*. New York, Elsevier Biomedical, 1982, p 9.
6. Helderman JH, Vestal RE, Rowe JW, Tobin JD, Andres RA, Robertson GL: The response of arginine vasopressin to intravenous ethanol and hypertonic saline in man: The impact of aging. *J Gerontol* 33:39, 1978.
7. Phillips PA, Rolls BJ, Ledingham JGG, Forsling ML, Morton JJ, Crowe MJ, Wollner L: Reduced thirst after water deprivation in healthy elderly men. *N Engl J Med* 12:753, 1984.
8. Rowe JW, Minaker KL, Robertson GL: Age-related failure of volume-pressure mediated vasopressin release in man. *J Clin Endocrinol Metab* 54:661, 1982.
9. Rolls BJ, Rolls ET: The control of drinking. *Br Med Bull* 37(2):127, 1981.
10. Robertson GL: Vasopressin function in health and disease. *Recent Prog Horm Res* 33:333, 1977.
11. Crane MG, Hornis JJ: Effect of age on renin activity and aldosterone secretion. *J Lab Clin Med* 87:947, 1976.
12. Lindemann RD, Van Buren HC, Raisz LG: Osmolar renal concentrating ability in healthy young men and hospitalized patients without renal disease. *N Engl J Med* 262:1396, 1960.
13. Miller JH, Shock NW: Age differences in the renal tubular response to antidiuretic hormone. *J Gerontol* 8:446, 1953.
14. Dontas AS, Karkeros S, Papanayioutou P: Mechanisms of real tubular defects in old age. *Postgrad Med J* 48:295, 1972.
15. Crowe MJ, Forsling ML, Rolls BJ, Phillips PA, Ledingham JGG, Smith RF: Altered water excretion in healthy elderly men. *Age Ageing* 16:285, 1987.
16. Epstein M, Hollenberg NK: Age as a determinant of renal sodium conservation in normal man. *J Lab Clin Med* 87:411, 1976.
17. Berenyl M, Straus B: Hyperosmolar states in the chronically ill. *J Am Geriatr Soc* 17(7):648, 1968.
18. Rodes J, Arroyo V, Bordas JM, Bruguera M: Hypernatremia following gastrointestinal bleeding in cirrhosis and ascites. *Am J Dig Dis* 20:127, 1975.
19. Hays RM, Levine SO: Pathophysiology of water metabolism, in Brenner B, Rector FC Jr (eds): *The Kidney*. Philadelphia, Saunders, 1980, pp 105–130.
20. Miller P, Krebs R, Neal B, McIntyre D: Hypodipsia in geriatric patients. *Am J Med* 73:354, 1982.
21. Weitzman RE, Keeman CR: The clinical physiology of water metabolism. Part 1: The physiologic regulation of arginine vasopressin secretion and thirst. *West J Med* 13(5):373, 1979.
22. Berger EY: Nutrition by hypodermoclysis. *J Am Geriatr Soc* 32(3):199, 1984.
23. Arieff AI, Guisado R, Lazarowitz VC: Pathophysiology of hyperosmolar states, in Andreoli TE, Grantham JJ, Rector FC Jr (eds): *Disturbances in Body Fluid Osmolality*. Bethesda, MD, American Physiological Society, 1977, p 227.

Chapter 111

DISORDERS OF TEMPERATURE REGULATION

Itamar B. Abrass

Temperature dysregulation in the elderly demonstrates the narrowing of homeostatic mechanisms that occurs with advancing age. Elderly persons are less able to adjust to extremes of environmental temperatures. Hypo- and hyperthermic states are predominantly disorders of the elderly. Despite underreporting of these disorders, there is evidence that morbidity and mortality increase during particularly hot or cold periods, especially among ill elderly.[1-3] Much of this illness is caused by an increased incidence of cardiovascular disorders (myocardial infarct and stroke) or infectious diseases (pneumonia) during periods of temperature extremes.

HYPOTHERMIA

EPIDEMIOLOGY

Studies in the United Kingdom reveal that hypothermia is a common finding among the elderly during the winter, when homes are usually heated below 70°F.[2] As might be expected, there is a similar seasonal occurrence in the United States and Canada.[4] In Britain, as many as 3.6 percent of all patients older than 65 admitted to the hospital are hypothermic.[5] In a population study, 10 percent of elderly people living at home were found to be on the borderline of hypothermia, with a deep body temperature of less than 35.5°C.[6]

PATHOPHYSIOLOGY

Hypothermia is defined as a core temperature (rectal, esophageal, tympanic) below 34°C. Susceptibility of the elderly to hypothermia is related to both disease and physiologic change.

The thermoregulatory center maintains body temperature through control of sweating, vasoconstriction and vasodilation, chemical thermogenesis, and shivering. Diminished sensation of cold and impaired sensitivity to change in temperature are associated with poor thermoregulation in the elderly[2,7,8] and can lead to maladaptive behavior in cold environments. In older adults, shivering is often observed to be less intense, despite greater loss of core temperature.[2,9-11] Since maximal shivering increases heat production three- to fivefold above the resting level,[12,13] those elderly with a less efficient or reduced shivering process are at increased risk for hypothermia.

The mechanisms by which adrenergic deficits contribute to hypothermia in the elderly have not been defined. However, abnormal autonomic vasoconstrictor response to cold[2,11,14,15] is a key factor in temperature dysregulation associated with aging. This autonomic dysregulation is also manifest as a higher incidence of orthostatic hypotension in those at risk for hypothermia.[2,15] Diminished thermogenesis is another key factor in temperature dysregulation in the elderly. The metabolic rate is lower in older people due to a decrease in lean body mass,[16] thus contributing to the risk of hypothermia in these individuals. Since body fat contributes to insulation against heat loss,[13] thin elderly with decreased fat mass also are at increased risk.

Besides actual exposure to cold, there are a host of factors predisposing to hypothermia.[13,17] Disorders associated with decreased heat production include hypothyroidism, hypoglycemia, starvation, and malnutrition. The most common endocrinopathy associated with hypothermia is myxedema, a condition in which as many as 80 percent of patients will have low body temperatures due to the marked depression of metabolic rate and calorigenesis.[17] Hypoglycemia reduces shivering, probably by a central effect.[18] Hypothermia may occur in 50 percent or more of patients with hypoglycemia.[19] Starvation and malnutrition may contribute to the risk of hypothermia by a decrease in lean body mass and energy stores for calorigenesis, as well as by a loss of body fat and its insulating effect. Immobility and decreased activity due to such disorders as stroke, arthritis, and parkinsonism also may lead to decreased heat production. Autonomic dysfunction in Parkinson's disease may also contribute to temperature dysregulation.

Thermoregulatory impairment may occur due to hypothalamic and central nervous system dysfunction or may be drug-induced. Trauma, hypoxia, tumor, or cerebrovascular disease may impair central regulation of temperature. The drugs most commonly associated with hypothermia are ethanol, barbiturates, phenothiazines, benzodiazepines, and anesthetic agents and narcotics.[13,17,20] Ethanol predisposes to this problem by being a vasodilator, a central nervous system depressant, an anesthetic, a cause of hypoglycemia, and a risk factor for trauma and environmental exposure. Phenothiazines inhibit shivering by a peripheral curarizing effect.

Hypothermia in sepsis reflects an alteration in the hypothalamic set-point and overwhelmed host defenses. In cardiovascular disease, the circulatory system may not be able to respond to the stress of changes in body temperature or to the demands of such counterregulatory mechanisms as shivering.

Particularly in the elderly, lack of central heating, failure to use heating (whatever the type), and dementia or confusion are associated with increased risk for hypothermia.[21] In one survey of the elderly, only 1 elderly person in 10 was aware of the dangers of accidental hypothermia.[22]

CLINICAL PRESENTATION

As stated above, hypothermia is defined as a core temperature below 35°C. Essential to the diagnosis is early recognition with a low-recording thermometer. Ordinary thermometers will not serve. Because early signs are nonspecific and subtle, a high index of suspicion must exist to allow an early diagnosis. A history of known or potential exposure is helpful, but elderly patients can become hypothermic at modest temperatures. Early signs which occur at core temperatures of 32–35°C include fatigue, weakness, slowness of gait, apathy, slurred speech, confusion, and cool skin. Patients may complain of the sensation of cold and may be shivering. As hypothermia progresses (28–30°C), the skin becomes cold. Hypopnea and cyanosis are present, at first due to decreased metabolic demands and later due to depression of the central respiratory drive. Bradycardia, atrial and ventricular arrhythmias, and hypotension occur. Semicoma or coma and muscular rigidity are present. Consciousness is commonly lost at brain temperature between 32° and 30°C.[23] Reflexes are slowed and pupils are poorly reactive. Generalized edema and polyuria or

oliguria may be present. Cold exposure is associated with both a water and osmotic diuresis. Volume contraction occurs due to diuresis and also some degree of extra- and intracellular water shifts.[24]

As core temperature falls below 28°C, the skin becomes very cold, and individuals become unresponsive, rigid, and areflexive and have fixed and dilated pupils. Apnea and ventricular fibrillation are present. Patients may sometimes be mistaken for dead. Case reports reveal patients who have survived after being discovered without respiration and pulse.

The most significant early complications of severe hypothermia are arrhythmias and cardiorespiratory arrest. Later complications include bronchopneumonia and aspiration pneumonia. The cough reflex is depressed by hypothermia, and cold results in the production of large quantities of thick, tenacious bronchial secretions, predisposing the patient to the above-mentioned complications. Pulmonary edema may occur, especially in those with prior cardiovascular disease. Pancreatitis and gastrointestinal bleeding are frequent complications, although massive hemorrhage is unusual. Acute tubular necrosis may occur. Intravascular thrombosis is a complication of hemoconcentration and the temperature-induced changes in viscosity.

Electrocardiogram (ECG) abnormalities are common.[25] The most specific ECG finding is the J wave (Osborn wave) following the QRS complex. This abnormality disappears as temperature returns to normal. Other common abnormalities include bradycardia and prolonged PR interval, QRS complex, and QT segment, as well as atrial fibrillation, premature ventricular contractions, and ventricular fibrillation.

Frequently the most difficult differential diagnosis in hypothermia is hypothyroidism. A previous history of thyroid disease, a neck scar from previous thyroid surgery, and a delay in the relaxation phase of the deep tendon reflexes may assist in the diagnosis of hypothyroidism.

TREATMENT

In the field, the hypothermic person should be immediately removed from the cold environment, windy areas, and contact with cold objects. Wet clothing should be removed to prevent further heat loss. Top and bottom blankets should be used (covers may need to be preheated to avoid a drain of heat from the victim). The patient should be moved carefully, since the cold, bradycardic heart is extremely irritable, and even minor stimuli can precipitate ventricular fibrillation or asystole.[26] Cardiac monitoring should be started as soon as possible. Patients with detectable heartbeat who are breathing spontaneously, no matter how slowly, should not be subjected to unnecessary procedures such as chest compression or placement of a pacemaker. Patients in asystole or ventricular fibrillation should be resuscitated, but the cold heart may be relatively unresponsive to drugs or electrical stimulation. Intravenous fluids, preferably D$_5$ normal saline without potassium, should be warmed before being used.[26]

In the hospital, general supportive therapy for severe hypothermia consists of intensive care management of complicated multisystem dysfunctions. Every attempt should be made to assess and treat any contributing medical disorder (e.g., hypothyroidism or hypoglycemia). If myxedema is suspected, the patient should be treated with 0.5 mg levothyroxine IV and corticosteroids. While patients should have continuous ECG monitoring, central lines should be avoided if possible because of myocardial irritability. Because there is delayed metabolism, most drugs have little effect on a severely hypothermic patient, but they may cause problems once the patient is rewarmed. Arrhythmias are resistant to cardioversion and drug therapy. Insulin is ineffective below 30°C[13] and should be avoided in the hyperglycemic hypothermic patient. If given during hypothermia, insulin may cause hypoglycemia as the patient is rewarmed. Insulin resistance will improve spontaneously as core body temperature rises. In chronic hypothermia (lasting longer than 12 hours), volume depletion may be great, and volume repletion may be needed as rewarming occurs.[17] Blood gases should be followed to assess respiratory function. Oxygen therapy, suctioning, and endotracheal intubation may be required. Serious arrhythmias, acidosis, and fluid and electrolyte disorders will usually respond to therapy only after rewarming has been accomplished. It is preferable to stabilize the patient and immediately undertake specific rewarming techniques.

Passive rewarming with insulating material and placement of the patient in a warm environment (>70°F) is generally adequate for those with mild (>32°C) hypothermia.[17,27] Active external rewarming (electric blankets, warm mattresses and bottles, submersion in a warm water bath) is a more rapid technique of rewarming than passive procedures.[27] However, active external rewarming has been associated with increased morbidity and mortality[28] because cold blood may suddenly be shunted to the core, further decreasing core temperature, and because peripheral vasodilation can precipitate hypovolemic shock by decreasing circulatory blood volume.[17]

For more severe hypothermia (<32°C), core rewarming is necessary. Several techniques for core rewarming have been used, but positive results have been reported only from small, uncontrolled studies. Mediastinal lavage is effective, but it is a major surgical procedure.[29] Extracorporeal circulation is a rapid method for rewarming, but this procedure requires a special hospital unit; also, there is a risk for hypotension and a risk of bleeding from the use of heparin.[30,31] In gastric lavage, balloons are placed in the stomach and filled with water.[32] With this method, a smaller area is rewarmed than in peritoneal dialysis, and local pharyngeal irritation may precipitate an arrhythmia. Peritoneal dialysis and inhalation rewarming may be the most practical techniques in most institutions. However, inhalation therapy may not be as effective in moderate-to-severe hypothermia as it is in mild hypothermia. Peritoneal dialysis (40°C) implies little risk for the patient, is easy to perform, requires simple equipment, and may be performed in every hospital.[33] Dialysis with two liters of a potassium-free solution and rapid installation and immediate removal is preferred.[17] Normothermia is usually accomplished within six to eight exchanges. Enemas are little used but can be used in conjunction with dialysis.

In dogs, radio wave–induced regional hyperthermia has been shown to be superior to inhalation and peritoneal lavage in the treatment of experimental hypothermia.[34,35] However, controlled studies of the treatment of hypothermia still need to be performed in humans.[36]

Mortality is usually greater than 50 percent for severe hypothermia. It increases with age and is particularly related to underlying disease.[37,38]

HYPERTHERMIA

EPIDEMIOLOGY

In the United States, approximately 5000 deaths occur annually as a direct result of heatstroke, and two-thirds of the victims are over 60 years old.[39] Hyperthermia often contributes to increased morbidity and mortality from various cardiovascular diseases in the elderly.[40] In the past, a significant number of deaths during heat waves occurred in nursing home residents.[41] Increased awareness of the problem has probably benefited this group of elderly. During the New York heat wave of 1984, the death rate for those over 75 years of age increased by almost 50 percent, but the increase was limited almost exclusively to noninstitutionalized elderly.[42]

Women appear to be more prone to the lethal effects of heatstroke. In the New York heat wave, mortality increased by 66 percent for women, compared to 39 percent for men.[42] A similar sex distribution was seen in the St. Louis and Georgia heat waves of 1983, when 77 percent of excess deaths occurred in women.[1]

PATHOPHYSIOLOGY

Heatstroke is defined as an acute failure to maintain normal body temperature in the setting of a warm environment.[43] The elderly usually present with nonexertional heatstroke due to impaired heat loss and failure of homeostatic mechanisms.[44] As with hypothermia, susceptibility of the elderly to heatstroke is related to both disease and physiologic changes.

Impairment of the thermoregulatory system by diminished or absent sweating is an important cause of heat exhaustion and heatstroke in hot conditions.[16] Deaths of the elderly during heat waves can usually be ascribed to heart disease and cardiovascular disease exacerbated by heat stress.[45] However, some disease is directly related to primary thermoregulatory failure.[45] The sweating response to thermal and neurochemical stimulation in most elderly has been found to be reduced as compared with that in younger adults.[46,47] There is also a significantly higher core-temperature threshold at which sweating can be initiated.[2] Delayed development of vasodilation with heating may also interfere with heat loss.[16] Impaired sensitivity to change in temperature[2] may lead to maladaptive behavior in warm environments. Acclimatization to heat may be less likely to occur in the elderly, as compared with the young,[16] and may thus contribute to the physiologic deficits.

Inability to take appropriate measures such as removing heavy clothing, moving to a cooler environment, and increasing fluid intake increases the risk of heatstroke in elderly individuals with limited mobility. Living alone and confusion add to this risk. Elderly individuals with cardiovascular disease may not be able to adequately increase their cardiac output in response to heat stress. Congestive heart failure, diabetes mellitus, obesity, and obstructive lung disease have been associated with increased risk of death in heatstroke victims.[48] Other risk factors for death from heatstroke are alcoholism, use of tranquilizers and anticholinergics, and reduction in physical activity.[49] The elderly are more likely to be taking multiple drugs, some of which may impair the response to a warm environment. Anticholinergics, phenothiazines, and antidepressants lead to hypohidrosis. Diuretics may be associated with hypovolemia and hypokalemia, and beta-blockers may depress myocardial function.

CLINICAL PRESENTATION

Heatstroke is characterized by a core temperature of greater than 40.6°C (105°F), severe central nervous system dysfunction (psychosis, delirium, coma), and anhidrosis (hot, dry skin). Earlier manifestations of heat exhaustion are nonspecific and include dizziness, weakness, sensation of warmth, anorexia, nausea, vomiting, headache, and dyspnea.

Complications of heatstroke include congestive heart failure and a host of cardiac arrhythmias, cerebral edema with seizures and diffuse and focal neurological deficits, hepatocellular necrosis with jaundice and liver failure, hypokalemia, respiratory alkalosis and metabolic acidosis, and hypovolemia and shock. Rhabdomyolysis, disseminated intravascular coagulation, and acute renal failure are less frequent in elderly than in younger patients with exertional heatstroke.[49] The ultimate complication, death, occurs in as many as 80 percent of patients once the full syndrome of heatstroke is manifest.

TREATMENT

The key to treatment is rapid cooling. It should be started immediately in the field, and core body temperature should be brought to 102°F within the first hour. The duration of hyperthermia is the major determinant of ultimate outcome. Ice packs and ice water immersion are superior to convection cooling with alcohol sponge baths or electric fans. Complications require intensive multisystem care.

CONCLUSIONS

Prevention appears to be the most appropriate approach to management of temperature dysregulation in the elderly. Education of older adults about their susceptibility to hypo- and hyperthermia in extremes of environmental temperature, education about appropriate behavior in such conditions, and close monitoring of the most vulnerable elderly should help reduce the morbidity and mortality from these disorders.

REFERENCES

1. Hope W et al: Illness and death due to environmental heat: Georgia and St. Louis, 1983. Leads from the MMWR. *JAMA* 252:209, 1984.
2. Collins KJ et al: Accidental hypothermia and impaired temperature homeostasis in the elderly. *Br Med J* 1:353, 1977.
3. Rango N: Exposure-related hypothermia mortality in the United States, 1970–79. *Am J Public Health* 74:1159, 1984.
4. Danzl DF et al: Multicenter hypothermia survey. *Ann Emerg Med* 16:1042, 1987.
5. Goldman A et al: A pilot study of low body temperature in old people admitted to hospital. *J R Coll Physicians Lond* 11:291, 1977.
6. Fox RH et al: Body temperature in the elderly: A national study of physiological, social and environmental conditions. *Br Med J* 1:200, 1963.
7. Watts AJ: Hypothermia in the aged: A study of the role of cold sensitivity. *Environ Res* 5:119, 1972.
8. Collins KJ et al: Urban hypothermia: Preferred temperature and thermal perception in old age. *Br Med J* 282:175, 1981.
9. Collins KJ et al: Shivering thermogenesis and vasomotor

responses with convective cooling in the elderly. *J Physiol* 320:76, 1981.

10. Horvath SM et al: Metabolic responses of old people to a cold environment. *J Appl Physiol* 8:145, 1965.

11. MacMillan AL et al: Temperature regulation in survivors of accidental hypothermia of the elderly. *Lancet* 2:165, 1967.

12. Hemingway A: Shivering. *Physiol Rev* 43:397, 1963.

13. Matz R: Hypothermia: Mechanisms and countermeasures. *Hosp Pract* 21:45, 1986.

14. Wagner JA et al: Age and temperature regulation of humans in neutral and cold environments. *J Appl Physiol* 37:562, 1974.

15. Collins KJ et al: Functional changes in autonomic nervous responses with ageing. *Age Ageing* 9:17, 1980.

16. Collins KJ, Exton-Smith AN: Thermal homeostasis in old age. *J Am Geriatr Soc* 31:519, 1983.

17. Reuler JB: Hypothermia: Pathophysiology, clinical settings, and management. *Ann Intern Med* 89:519, 1978.

18. Freinkel N et al: The hypothermia of hypoglycemia. *N Engl J Med* 287:841, 1972.

19. Strauch BS et al: Hypothermia in hypoglycemia. *JAMA* 210:345, 1969.

20. Lonning PE et al: Accidental hypothermia: Review of the literature. *Acta Anaesthesiol Scand* 30:601, 1986.

21. Dawson JA: A case control study of accidental hypothermia in the elderly in relation to social support and social circumstances. *Community Med* 9:141, 1987.

22. Avery CE, Pestle RE: Hypothermia and the elderly: Perceptions and behaviors. *Gerontologist* 27:523, 1987.

23. Anderson KL: Thermogenetic mechanisms involved in men's fitness to resist cold exposure. *Hum Evolut* 2:117, 1973.

24. Lennquist S et al: Fluid balance and physical work capacity in humans exposed to cold. *Arch Environ Health* 29:241, 1974.

25. Trevino A et al: The characteristic electrocardiogram of accidental hypothermia. *Arch Intern Med* 127:470, 1971.

26. Treatment of hypothermia. *Med Lett Drugs Ther* 28:123, 1986.

27. Collins ML et al: Accidental hypothermia: An experimental study of practical rewarming methods. *Aviat Space Environ Med* 48:625, 1977.

28. Gregory RT, Doolittle WH: Accidental hypothermia. II. Clinical implications of experimental studies. *Alaska Med* 15:48, 1973.

29. Linton AI, Ledingham IM: Severe hypothermia with barbiturate intoxication. *Lancet* 1:24, 1966.

30. Davies DM et al: Accidental hypothermia treated by extracorporeal warming. *Lancet* 1:1036, 1967.

31. Maresca L, Vasko JS: Treatment of hypothermia by extracorporeal circulation and internal rewarming. *J Trauma* 27:89, 1987.

32. Barnard CN: Hypothermia: A method of intragastric cooling. *Br J Surg* 44:269, 1956.

33. Bristow G: Treatment of accidental hypothermia with peritoneal dialysis. *Can Med Assoc J* 118:764, 1978.

34. White JD et al: Controlled comparison of radio wave regional hyperthermia and peritoneal lavage rewarming after immersion hypothermia. *J Trauma* 25:989, 1985.

35. White JD et al: Rewarming in accidental hypothermia: Radio wave versus inhalation therapy. *Ann Emerg Med* 16:50, 1987.

36. Chinard FP: Hypothermia treatment needs controlled studies. *Ann Intern Med* 90:990, 1979.

37. Hudson LD, Conn RD: Accidental hypothermia: Associated diagnoses and prognosis in a common problem. *JAMA* 227:37, 1974.

38. O'Keeffe KM: Accidental hypothermia: A review of 62 cases. *JACEP* 6:491, 1977.

39. Halle A, Repasy A: Classic heatstroke: A serious challenge for the elderly. *Hosp Pract* 22:26, 1987.

40. Fish PD et al: Heatwave morbidity and mortality in old age. *Age Ageing* 14:243, 1985.

41. Levine JA: Heat stroke in the aged. *Am J Med* 47:251, 1969.

42. Heat-associated mortality—New York City. *MMWR* 33:430, 1984.

43. Krochel JP, Dallas MD: Environmental heat illness: An eclectic review. *Arch Intern Med* 133:841, 1974.

44. Wheeler M: Heat stroke in the elderly. *Med Clin North Am* 60:1289, 1976.

45. Ellis FP: Mortality from heat illness and heat-aggravated illness in the United States. *Environ Res* 5:1, 1972.

46. Foster KL et al: Sweat responses in the aged. *Age Ageing* 5:91, 1976.

47. Anderson RK, Kenney WL: Effect of age on heat-activated sweat gland density and flow during exercise in dry heat. *J Appl Physiol* 63:1089, 1987.

48. Kilbourne EM et al: Risk factors for heat stroke: A case-control study. *JAMA* 247:3332, 1982.

49. Curley FJ, Irwin RS: Disorders of temperature control: I. Hyperthermia. *J Intensive Care* 1:5, 1986.

Chapter 112

SYNDROMES OF ALTERED MENTAL STATE

Marshal F. Folstein and Susan E. Folstein

The term *altered mental state* means "a change in the patient's usual premorbid state of mind." Although it is sometimes used to mean delirium or dementia, the definition used here includes alterations in *emotions* and *behavior*, as well as in *cognition*. To diagnose an altered mental state, it is necessary to establish the patient's premorbid mental state and the nature and associations of any change. This requires that a history be taken from both the patient and another informant and that the patient's mental state be examined. Neurological and physical examinations, appropriate laboratory tests, and sometimes repeated examinations over a period of months are needed to complete the diagnostic process.

This chapter emphasizes a psychiatric approach to the patient with an altered mental state. The standard procedures for psychiatric examination usually covered in medical school courses are repeated here because there is ample evidence that many physicians in medical inpatient and outpatient settings do not routinely assess mental state and, consequently, fail to recognize altered mental states.[1,2] Since disorders presenting as alterations of mental state are so common, affecting 25 to 30 percent of medical inpatients and 90 percent of nursing home residents, and are more frequent in the elderly, the general physician and geriatrician must be able to diagnose and treat them.[3,4]

DIAGNOSTIC PROCEDURES

The aims of the psychiatric history and mental state examination are (1) the documentation of the onset, pro-

The preparation of this chapter was supported in part by NINCDS-1637 (Huntington's Disease Center Without Walls), NIA AG-05146 (Alzheimer's Disease Research Center), T32 AG00149 (Research Training in the Dementias of Aging), and by Meridian Healthcare Systems.

gression, and current state of abnormal cognition, mood, and behaviors and (2) the identification of these signs and symptoms with recognizable syndromes and disease entities. The case is formulated so that the symptoms, syndromes, and diseases are viewed in relation to the individual patient, taking into account the patient's particular vulnerabilities and situation. Out of this formulation emerges the prognosis and treatment plan. The treatment plan may include a rational therapy or, if none is known, empirical and empathic approaches to the patient and his or her family. For the geriatric patient, the treatment plan may range from definitive therapy to palliative pharmacotherapy to advice about living circumstances, competence, and finances.[5]

PSYCHIATRIC HISTORY TAKING

The history is taken from the patient first, even though he or she may have a cognitive impairment. Patients may have different points of view about their symptoms than their families or caretakers have, and asking patients for their views will enhance their self-respect and increase their willingness to cooperate with the examination. By examining the patient in a quiet room and by maintaining a helping attitude, the physician can further improve the patient's cooperation. After introducing himself or herself, the physician explains the purpose of the examination: "In order to find out what is causing your memory trouble (pain, etc.), I would like to ask you some questions. Is that all right?"

The physician begins by asking "What is your major problem?" or "Why are you here?" in order to elicit the patient's perception of the chief complaint, and then proceeds on the basis of the reply. The nature of the patient's account, vague and disconnected or clear and sequential, will give clues to the presence of cognitive impairment. The physician then asks the patient about his or her personal history. This has two purposes. First, assessment of the patient's education, occupation, and family life supplies a baseline of expected general knowledge and sophistication, as well as current social supports. Second, the clarity of the account is useful in assessing the presence of cognitive impairment. The physician should question the patient about a history of illnesses in other family members, including Alzheimer's disease ("the patient may say memory trouble," "died in a nursing home," "didn't recognize people," "couldn't dress self"), stroke, and depression. The medical history includes an accurate account of all current medications (ask families to bring all medications to the clinic) since these alone could be responsible for cognitive impairment or depression. When inquiring about past treatments, include treatment for psychiatric disorders.

A similar history should be taken from a family member or friend who knows the patient well. This second version of the history is essential if the patient is cognitively impaired, but provides valuable information for every patient assessed for an alteration in mental state. The impact of cognitive or emotional impairment on social function can be estimated by asking the informant about the patient's ability to function in daily activities, relative to his or her normal baseline. Patients tend to underestimate their disability or may be unaware of it. Examples of such questions are: Can the patient still function adequately at work? balance a checkbook? find the way home when driving or walking? Does the patient leave pots on the stove when cooking or forget to turn off the gas? Can the patient use the telephone and remember previously familiar phone numbers? dress himself or herself? recognize family members? eat if food is placed in front of him or her? remember how to use the bathroom?

ASSESSMENT OF DISABILITY

It is useful to distinguish impairment from disability. Impairment is the defect of a part, function, or organ; for example, a patient may have a visual or motor or cognitive impairment. A disability is the incapacity of an individual with an impairment to function in a particular environment. Impairments may or may not be associated with disability in a particular environment. The assessment of the ability to function in daily life, or its opposite, disability, is an aspect of history taking that has been the subject of numerous attempts at quantification.

As with other components of the diagnostic process, a disability assessment is not, on its own, a diagnostic procedure. Impairments of cognition, emotion, perception, or mobility may all lead to an incapacity to perform tasks in the same social environments. Thus, a patient may be unable to climb stairs because of apraxia, blindness, or arthritis. Disabilities can range in severity from an incapacity to perform a high-level job or manage the complex finances of a large corporation to being unable to survive unsupported because of inability to feed oneself. Since disabilities are defined in terms of environments, the same impairment can be more or less disabling in various settings. A microbiologist who develops a mild cognitive impairment may be able to function well at home but may not be able to work. A change of job might even remove the occupational disability. On the other hand, cognitive impairments that appear to be mild on formal testing may be associated with severe disability. For example, individuals with Pick's disease, which afflicts the frontal lobes, may score normally on an intelligence test but be unable even to care for themselves because of apathy and inertia.

Disability should also be distinguished from incompetence. Disability is the inability to perform certain functions because of any one of a variety of impairments. Incompetence is a term assigned by the legal system to limit certain individuals' freedom and rights to manage themselves and their property. While a person judged to be incompetent is ordinarily disabled in one or more ways, disabled persons are not necessarily incompetent to manage their affairs.

Disability scales are useful adjuncts to history taking and are also used in research and in the assessment of payments for social security and nursing home reimbursement. Many scales are available, and they can be divided into two general types. One is the pure disability scale (Powell, Katz), which assesses instrumental activities (e.g., the capacity to use a telephone or checkbook) or activities of daily living (the capacity to dress, bathe, and feed oneself).[6,7] This type of scale makes it possible to systematize one aspect of history taking and to study the effects of cognition, emotion, or physical mobility on the ability to function. In the other type of scale, the assessment of disability is mixed with other dimensions such as cognition, mood, and personality. Examples of this type are the Blessed Dementia Scale, which correlates with the numbers of plaques and tangles in Alzheimer's disease, and the Psychogeriatric Dependency Rating Scale (PGDRS), which predicts the amount of nursing time needed for nursing home patients.[8,9]

THE MENTAL STATE EXAMINATION

This part of the medical examination assesses the patient's mental experience and capacity at the time of the examination. It is thus distinguished from history taking, which covers distressing mental experiences or behavior that have taken place in the past. The history and the manner in which it is related can give clues about the patient's current mental state, but a separate procedure is needed to determine and document the present mental state per se. This procedure includes an examination of the patient's appearance, talk, mood, and cognitive state and a determination of the presence of delusions, hallucinations, phobias, and obsessions.

The mental state examination is introduced by an explanation of the necessity for an examination and a request for the patient's permission and cooperation. For example, the physician asks, "As a routine part of the examination, I would like to ask you some questions about how you feel and how you think." The examination is conducted in a supportive manner, but direct questions are asked in order to elicit the patient's experiences. For example, the patient may be asked, "Do you hear voices?" Ambiguous or uncertain responses are followed with further questioning to determine whether the patient is reporting on an experience that meets the definition of the phenomenon, for example, "Are the voices as clear as mine? Do you hear through your ears?" The cognitive examination must also be conducted supportively in order to avoid emotional responses to failure (catastrophic reactions), which in themselves can worsen performance. In particular, if the patient gives an incorrect response, do not correct him or her. If the patient fails to respond at all, go to another topic (after having ascertained that the patient heard the question).

The mental state examination is conventionally divided into the following sections:

Appearance: The patient's dress and grooming are assessed with attention to evidence of self-neglect or inability to dress, perhaps due to apraxia. The physician notes the patient's level of activity, e.g., agitation or motor slowing, and notes whether the patient walks normally, is wearing hearing aids and glasses, or appears lethargic, as in delirium or confusional states.

Talk: The physician listens for the form of talk and notes whether the patient's talk is normally coherent; whether it is fast (as in mania) or slow (as in depression or dementia); whether speech is clear or slurred (as in dysarthria secondary to stroke or parkinsonism); and whether there is evidence of trouble with naming or the appearance of jargon words (as in aphasia due to stroke or Alzheimer's disease).

Mood: The physician asks the patient questions like "How are your spirits?" or "How is your mood?" followed, if necessary, by questions about whether the patient feels depressed, hopeless, worthless, or guilty, or, alternatively, unduly cheerful, optimistic, or overconfident. Mood-associated disturbances of appetite and sleep are determined at this point. A sense of dread or impending doom, as seen in attacks of panic or anxiety, may also be queried. In the elderly, apathy, an empty feeling, or a nonspecific irritability can be prominent features of a depressed mood. Suicidal thoughts and intentions must be assessed in depressed elderly persons since suicide rates are high, particularly in elderly males

with physical impairments who are also depressed. The physician asks, "Have you thought of harming yourself or doing away with yourself?" If the patient indicates the presence of suicidal thinking, an inquiry is made into the patient's plans. Psychiatric hospitalization is indicated for the depressed patient with suicidal thoughts.

Delusions: Delusions are false, fixed, idiosyncratic, and preoccupying beliefs. The physician may ask questions such as "Is anyone harassing you or trying to harm you?" and inquire also about delusions of poverty or delusions that someone is stealing from the patient or poisoning the patient's food.

Delusions as they occur in late-life schizophrenia or paraphrenia should be distinguished from overvalued ideas which may be expressed as a hobby that preoccupies a person's life to the exclusion of other activities; they should also be distinguished from culturally determined beliefs such as religious, superstitious, or magical ideas that, while not widely held, are part of the patient's immediate culture. Delusions should be distinguished also from obsessions or hypochondriacal preoccupations which are not idiosyncratic and which appear to arise from obsessive character traits.

Obsessions or compulsions: Obsessions are recurrent, unwanted thoughts that the patient tries unsuccessfully to resist. Compulsions are recurrent, unwanted behaviors, such as constant hand washing. The physician should ask, "Do you have thoughts that keep coming back that you can't get out of your mind? Are the thoughts sensible or do they seem foolish?"

Hallucinations: Hallucinations are false perceptions in the visual, auditory, olfactory, or touch realms. The physician asks such questions as: "Do you see visions of people?" "Is there any buzzing or ringing in your ears?" "Are there voices talking about you?" "Are they as clear as my voice?" "Do you smell anything unusual?" "Do you feel things crawling on your skin?" Hallucinations are prominent in delirium, dementia, and schizophrenia and may occur in late-life depression and occasionally in bereavement.

Phobias: Phobias are irrational fears of particular places, things, or situations that are severe enough to cause the person to avoid them. For example, the patient may stay in the house because of a fear of going out or avoid high buildings because of a fear of elevators. In the elderly the appearance of phobias, as well as obsessions and compulsions, can be the first signs of a severe depression, but they often occur with anxiety and a sense of impending doom and are associated with autonomic signs of palpitations, trouble swallowing, or trouble breathing.

Cognition: Cognition is the capacity to think in order to know the world. The level of cognition produced by disease is related to premorbid intelligence, and it can be assessed only in an alert state of consciousness (as opposed to drowsiness, stupor, or coma). Assessment of cognition traditionally involves testing orientation, attention, memory, and language functions. Cognition is best tested through a quantitative procedure, such as the one described below, that ensures a systematic assessment and the clear documentation of change due to illness or its treatment.

Screening Tests

The clinical mental state examination can be supplemented with quantified procedures that are also useful for patient follow-up or case finding in the hospital, clinic, or community. In some cases these quantified aids to the examination can be used to buttress a clinical opinion that an impairment exists.

Extensive batteries of neuropsychological tests are part of the psychologist's armamentarium. These tests are designed to quantify specific cognitive functions along a dimension. That is, they do not make a diagnosis but rather quantify the severity of impairment of particular cognitive functions. Briefer quantified measures are available, however, for use at the bedside by physicians, nurses, social workers, or technicians. These brief measures are also used as dimensional measures but, in addition, have established specificities and sensitivities so that they can be used for case detection in the hospital or community. If physicians review the results of brief screening tests administered by technicians, their recognition of emotional and cognitive disorders improves, and their practice is altered—they are more likely to further evaluate any detected cognitive impairment and to discuss emotional problems with the patient and family and make any appropriate referrals.

MINI-MENTAL STATE EXAMINATION (MMSE) The MMSE (Fig. 112-1) is one of several quantified measures that can be used to screen for cognitive disorders in the elderly.[10] The MMSE has been found to be reliable and valid in field studies and hospital settings. Of elderly community-dwelling subjects over age 65, 95 percent score 24 or higher out of a total of 30 possible points on this test. Scores below 24 occur in delirium or dementia; they can also occur in severe depression in the elderly and in mental retardation. Although the MMSE has adequate sensitivity and specificity to detect dementia in elderly community or hospital populations, many additional persons with no diagnosable medical conditions also attain low scores. The reasons for these low scores are not understood at this time, but *they do not necessarily indicate a medical diagnosis.* In general, individuals who have had little education score lower; race and sex do not appear to influence scores if level of education is taken into account.[11,12]

GENERAL HEALTH QUESTIONNAIRE (GHQ)

Emotional disorders can be detected through the use of brief, quantified screening methods such as the GHQ.[13] The GHQ is a self-rated questionnaire derived from the Cornell Medical Index. It is designed to detect emotional disturbances of all sorts and has been extensively tested in general practitioners' offices, in outpatient settings, and in field surveys that have included large numbers of elderly individuals.[14] A score of 5 or above on the 30-item version indicates emotional disturbance.

Pitfalls

There are two commonly encountered pitfalls in the use of the mental state examination. First, physicians often attribute observations of cognitive or emotional impairment to a particular cause before completely evaluating the observations. For example, a low MMSE score may be attributed to aging or to a lack of education, prematurely excluding the possibility of a dementia syndrome from diagnostic consideration. Observations of a depressed mood in an isolated elderly person may be interpreted as an understandable, meaningful response to a sad situation before consideration is given to the possible relationship of the mood to a concurrent stroke or parkinsonism, both of which are associated with high rates of depression. Depressed mood, combined with cognitive impairment, is frequently ascribed to old age, and often the physician fails to ask about a family or personal history of affective disorder which may be a treatable cause of the patient's symptoms.

The second inappropriate use of the mental state examination results from the belief that the result of any single examination, such as a screening test or a laboratory test, implies a particular diagnosis. For example, psychological test results indicating impairment or a computed tomography (CT) scan showing atrophy are often used to make a diagnosis of Alzheimer's disease. Diagnosis requires the combining of all sources of information, including the frequency of particular disorders in particular settings, and should rarely depend on only one examination or test.

Physical and neurological examinations and laboratory tests are covered in other chapters, but a few points should be emphasized. First, elderly individuals often suffer from several diseases, so a complete examination is needed in every case, even though the major cause of the altered mental state may be apparent in the first minutes of the interview. Laboratory tests should be carried out initially, but are often not as helpful in the diagnostic process as the clinical examination. Second, repeated history and physical examinations at follow-up visits are useful to determine the reliability of initial findings and, in cases such as Alzheimer's disease, to assess the validity of the diagnosis, which is often uncer-

FIGURE 112-1
Mini-Mental State Examination.

Patient's Name_____

Date Administered_____

Maximum   Patient
 Score   Score

                             Orientation

  5   ____   What is the (year) (season) (date) (day) (month)?

  5   ____   Where are we: (state) (county) (town) (hospital) (floor)?

                             Registration

  3   ____   Name three objects - 1 second to say each. Then ask the patient all three after you have said them.

                             Give one point for each correct answer. Then repeat them until patient learns all three. Count trials and record.

                                    Number of Trials ____

                             Attention and Calculation

  5   ____   Serial sevens. One point for each correct. Stop after five answers. If subject refuses, spell "WORLD" backwards.

                             Recall

  3   ____   Ask for three objects repeated above. Give one point for each correct.

                             Language

  9   ____   Name a pencil and watch. (2 points)

                             Repeat the following: "No ifs, ands, or buts." (1 point)

                             Follow a three-stage command: "Take a paper in your right hand, fold it in half, and put in on the floor." (3 points)

                             Read and obey the following: "Close your eyes." (1 point)

                             Write a sentence. (1 point)

                             Copy design. (1 point)

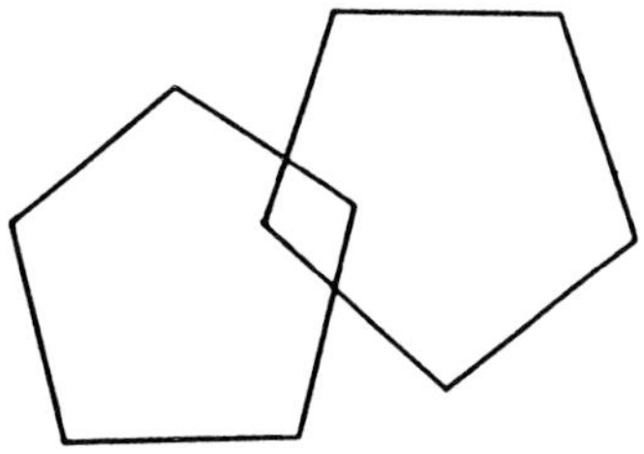

____
 30
Maximum   Patient
 Score   Total

ASSESS level of consciousness along a continuum.

_____

Alert   Drowsy   Stupor   Coma

tain early in the disease course. Patients and families are also reassured by repeated examinations, even in cases in which the diagnosis is clear. Third, a precipitous decline in the mental state of a patient with stroke or Alzheimer's disease can be caused by some other treatable conditions; repeated examination will aid in the prompt detection and prescription of appropriate treatment.

The conditions that commonly present with altered mental state can be divided into two broad categories: disorders of cognition and disorders of mood. These conditions will be briefly summarized here and are considered in more detail in other chapters.

COGNITIVE SYNDROMES

DELIRIUM

Delirium is a global decline in cognitive function, accompanied by alteration in consciousness. The term *delirium* is used here to cover those altered mental states sometimes called "acute confusional states," "metabolic encephalopathy," or "twilight states."[15,16,17]

Delirium is frequent in the emergency room, inpatient services, and the recovery room. Many nursing home patients are delirious from prescribed medications. Some 10 to 15 percent of elderly surgical patients and one-third of elderly medical inpatients are delirious.[18,19] The onset may be insidious and the course chronic, as in the patient who gradually becomes intoxicated from overmedication, or the onset may be acute and the course short-lived, as in patients with drug-withdrawal syndromes. Risk factors for delirium include age, drug or alcohol abuse and withdrawal, excessive dosage of certain prescribed drugs, seizures, and metabolic disorders. Structural brain injury due to stroke, Alzheimer's disease, trauma, and infections also predispose to delirium. Delirious patients can recover fully if the underlying cause is reversible, but the mortality rate is high since many delirious patients suffer from irreversible organ failure.

The diagnosis of delirium rests on the recognition of an altered state of consciousness. Despite the difficulty in precisely defining it, consciousness can be reliably assessed.[20] Patients who are delirious may be either somnolent or hypervigilant and agitated, but they always have a decreased ability to focus attention on relevant stimuli and to remain accessible to environmental demands. The patient may appear alert and coherent one minute and confused and drowsy the next. The MMSE score is above 23 in 30 percent of delirious patients in our practice, but even such higher-scoring patients may report feeling clouded in the mind or feeling drugged. Mildly delirious patients often have disturbed sleep and a mild tachycardia. In more severe delirium, the patient becomes disoriented and unable to follow even the simple request to write his or her name. Maintenance of a handwriting chart is a useful way to measure daily change in the patient's condition.

In addition to cognitive impairment, other mental phenomena are frequently prominent. These include illusions (such as shadows on the wall or folds of drapery appearing to be a face or other figure), delusions (patients may believe that the staff of the hospital is mistreating them or conspiring against them), or hallucinations (which are commonly visual or tactile, unlike those of schizophrenia or manic depressive illness, which are typically auditory). These experiences can be frightening to patients and have led to suicide in the midst of delirium. Delirious patients are frequently anxious and depressed, even in the absence of delusions and hallucinations.

Physical signs of delirium include tachycardia, autonomic instability with either hypertension or hypotension, and diaphoresis. These symptoms are particularly common in the delirium of alcohol or sedative withdrawal, delirium tremens. Asterixis or "liver flap" can be seen in delirium due to many different causes in addition to hepatic encephalopathy. It results from the patient's inability to maintain a fixed posture. When the patient is asked to extend the arms and hands for a period of a few seconds, an intermittent lapse in posture is seen, which appears as a flap or wave of the hand. Patients may also display tremor, myoclonus (repetitive, random, single muscle jerks), or purposeless movements such as picking at clothing.

The single most useful laboratory test for delirium is the electroencephalogram (EEG), which will often reveal generalized slowing. In schizophrenia, with which delirium is often confused, the EEG is normal.[21] However, several provisos must be kept in mind. First, the patient's baseline EEG alpha frequency is usually unknown. Therefore, an EEG with an alpha frequency in the low end of the normal range does not exclude delirium, since it may represent a fall from a higher baseline (for instance from a frequency of 12 to 8 per second, both of which are within normal limits). Second, slow EEGs can be present in the absence of delirium in cognitively impaired patients with Alzheimer's disease or other diffuse cortical disorders. Finally, some forms of agitated delirium—such as those caused by alcohol or sedative withdrawal—may be unaccompanied by EEG slowing. Nevertheless, the EEG remains a useful confirmatory test for the presence of delirium.

The specific diagnostic workup will depend on the patient's clinical presentation and the most likely etiologies. Delirium often reflects abnormal central nervous system (CNS) function secondary to systemic infection; secondary to metabolic disorders associated with drug toxicity, drug or alcohol withdrawal, or electrolyte abnormalities; or secondary to cardiac, pulmonary, renal, or hepatic disease. Laboratory evaluation usually includes electrolytes, blood urea nitrogen (BUN), creatinine, blood glucose, complete blood count (c.b.c.) with differential, erythrocyte sedimentation rate (ESR), calcium (and possibly magnesium) level, liver function tests, blood culture and other cultures (if appropriate), blood or urine levels of alcohol and any medications which can be measured, and other specific tests as suggested by the history. Drugs frequently contributing to delirium in geriatric patients include sedatives, benzodiazepines, and medications with anticholinergic effects.[22] A lumbar puncture should be done if there is fever or nuchal rigidity, since delirium may also be caused by meningitis or encephalitis.

Treatment of delirium includes treatment of the underlying cause of the delirium and the symptomatic management of the delirious state until recovery occurs. Whenever possible, treatment of the underlying cause should include discontinuation, or at least reduction, of the dosage of psychoactive medications. In particular, medications with high anticholinergic activity, such as cimetidine, ranitidine, and tricyclic antidepressants or neuroleptics, should be reduced or discontinued if possible. Management of the delirious state includes maintenance of adequate nutrition, surveillance of fluid and electrolyte balance, and the provision of a well-lighted, predictable environment. The nursing staff and family will need to provide frequent reorientation, and the medical staff should provide simple explanations of any procedures or confusing stimuli. Since patients with delirium often have abnormal sleep–wake cycles, they should be encouraged to stay awake during the day to increase their chances of sleeping at night. If a patient is agitated, hallucinating, or deluded, he or she may require treatment with low doses of a neuroleptic that has low anticholinergic activity, such as haloperidol (beginning at 0.5 to 2 mg per day). Except for delirium caused by alcohol or sedative withdrawal, benzodiazepines are generally second-line drugs for sedation in delirium and frequently exacerbate delirium. If delirious patients are not closely observed, they frequently suffer falls, and physical restraint may be necessary to prevent patients from falling out of bed, wandering, or harming themselves when agitated. Obviously, constant observation by family or personnel is preferable to restraint. Not only is this more humane, but physical restraints often make patients more agitated because they cannot understand why their liberty has been restricted.

Recovery from delirium may be slow, and confusion and EEG slowing may be present for some time *after* the primary cause has been attended to. Improvement can be followed by serial mental status examinations and serial EEGs. After a delirium, patients often need a period of recuperation because they feel weak and lethargic. During this period adequate support is needed to avoid secondary complications of falls, dehydration, and malnutrition. Most patients have little memory of the delirious episode, but some retain islands of memories and remain convinced of the veracity of the delusions and misperceptions that they experienced during the delirious period.

DEMENTIA

Dementia is a form of altered mental state characterized by a decline in multiple cognitive functions which occurs in clear consciousness.[23] Dementia is a syndrome defined by a group of psychological impairments and does *not* refer to a particular brain disease, such as Alzheimer's disease, or to aging itself. In Baltimore, 6.1 percent of the community-dwelling population over the age of 65 suffers from a dementia syndrome.[12] In nursing homes, more than 50 percent of the patients suffer from dementia.[4] The onset may be acute or insidious, and the course may be reversible or irreversible, depending on the etiology. The most common diseases causing dementia are Alzheimer's disease and stroke, together accounting for more than two-thirds of cases.

Dementia syndromes can be classified into two general types, cortical and subcortical.[23] These categories are not always mutually exclusive, but can be used as a framework for thinking about the underlying diseases. Cortical dementias include Alzheimer's disease, Jakob-Creutzfeldt disease, Pick's disease, and, often, stroke. Cortical dementias are characterized by prominent *amnesia* (memory loss), *aphasia* (inability to use language), *apraxia* (inability to perform skilled movements), and *agnosia* (inability to recognize visual stimuli), and, in Alzheimer's disease, the preservation of fine motor movement and gait until late in the course. (See below for a description of specific cognitive defects.) The presence of all these symptoms indicates dysfunction of wide areas of cerebral cortex. In contrast, subcortical dementias are characterized by amnesia, slowness of thought, apathy, and lack of initiative in all aspects of cognition, but without prominent aphasia, apraxia, or agnosia.[24] Disorders of movement and gait are prominent early in the course of subcortical dementias, and depression of mood is frequent. This constellation of symptoms is seen in diseases affecting subcortical structures that have direct connections to the frontal cortex and association areas: Parkinson's disease, Huntington's disease, and hydrocephalus.

The diagnosis of a patient with dementia requires two steps: (1) the documentation of a decline in cognition from a previous level and (2) the delineation of the process causing the decline. The first step requires a history and examination of the patient's cognition. The history reveals a decline from a previous level, and the mental state examination indicates that the patient is alert, although cognitively impaired. An individual with dementia has multiple cognitive impairments, not just memory loss. The documentation of decline can be difficult in a person who has a low level of premorbid functioning, who has no close relatives or friends who can provide a history, or who reports cognitive decline but has mild or absent findings on examinations. In such cases, longitudinal examinations may be needed to decide whether a cognitive decline is taking place.

For the second step, a history and examination of factors associated with neurological diseases are documented. The onset and course of symptoms will provide clues to the etiology. A sudden onset suggests stroke; a subacute course over weeks and months suggests a tumor or Jakob-Creutzfeldt disease. The early appearance of a gait disorder suggests a subcortical disorder, such as hydrocephalus or Parkinson's disease, or a focal lesion of the cortex, such as stroke or tumor. A dementia which increases in the weeks following a head trauma suggests a subdural hematoma. The insidious onset of cognitive decline in the absence of early motor signs and progression to severe dementia suggests Alzheimer's disease.

The delineation of the cause of a cognitive decline may not be unequivocal. The most common dilemma is caused by finding minor neurological signs or a small stroke on CT scan. This always raises the question of whether the stroke caused the patient's cognitive impairment or is an incidental finding.

Although dementia is defined by cognitive features, other psychiatric symptoms may also be present, such as delusions, hallucinations, and abnormalities of mood, as well as abnormal behaviors such as insomnia, wandering, incontinence, irritability, and occasionally violence. These symptoms and behaviors cause distress to patients and their families and require psychological, social, and psychopharmacological management.

Physical signs that may accompany dementia are helpful in identifying the underlying disease. In Alzheimer's disease, no abnormal motor or sensory signs are present during the first years of illness. After 3 to 4 years, patients develop abnormalities of tone and gait, eventually becoming unable to move. Pathological reflexes such as suck and grasp reflexes appear in the middle to late stages of the disease, and myoclonus and seizures are late-appearing signs in a minority of patients. In stroke-related dementia, asymmetrical motor signs, such as a unilateral extensor plantar response, occur early. In subcortical dementias such as hydrocephalus, Parkinson's disease, and Huntington's disease, abnormal involuntary movements, bradykinesia, and disturbances of gait appear early in the illness.

Laboratory tests in the evaluation of dementia are covered elsewhere in detail. Specific tests that are par-

ticularly useful in the differential diagnosis of the more common dementias will be mentioned here. The EEG usually becomes slow in Alzheimer's disease after the first year of illness. This test is useful in differentiating Alzheimer's disease from depression, schizophrenia, and sometimes Pick's disease, in which the EEG is normal. The CT scan and magnetic resonance imaging (MRI) are useful for detecting stroke and other focal lesions. Repeated CT or MRI examinations may reveal increasing atrophy in Alzheimer's disease. Single photon emission computed tomography (SPECT scan) is a promising method for the diagnosis of Alzheimer's disease, since temporal-parietal hypometabolism is seen, as it is in positron emission tomography (PET) scans, during the first years of illness.

Specific causes of dementia require specific treatments, but some general principles apply to all groups. First, management of the patient in all settings is made easier if any noncognitive symptoms are identified and treated. Pharmacological treatments for depression, hallucinations, or sleep disturbances must be carefully monitored because of the susceptibility of demented patients to delirium. Thus, it is safer to use small dosages of neuroleptics and antidepressants and to arrange frequent follow-up to monitor both efficacy and side effects. Second, families benefit from explanations about the nature of amnesia, aphasia, agnosia, and apraxia and the disabilities they cause. For example, families can be taught to ask the patient to do only one thing at time; to assist effectively with dressing, bathing, and eating; to avoid catastrophic reactions by arranging activities within the patient's ability and by avoiding confrontations. Third, families benefit from a discussion of diplomatic ways to gradually decrease, and eventually eliminate, the patient's access to a car, heavy machinery, and some kitchen appliances. Fourth, patients gradually become unable to concentrate and calculate, and different arrangements for financial management may need to be made; the family may need to consult a lawyer about these and other financial issues. Fifth, the patient will remain calmer if the family organizes a structured weekly schedule that includes predictable, planned activities for the patient. When patients begin to have difficulty with continence, families and caregivers can be taught to toilet the patient every 2 to 4 hours during waking hours to prevent incontinence. If the patient has a gradually worsening dementia, such as Alzheimer's disease, the family needs help at each stage to organize social supports appropriate to the patient's changing needs. This may include day care, help at home for the spouse, and eventually 24-hour nursing care at home or in a nursing home.

The prognosis of dementia depends on the underlying cause. Some dementias, as for example those due to hypothyroidism or cerebral infections, are reversible. In others, such as Alzheimer's disease, the symptoms gradually worsen over a period of years with death occurring 7 years, on average, after the onset of memory loss. The prognosis of multi-infarct disease is relatively uncertain and probably varies with the severity and cause of the underlying vascular disease.

FOCAL COGNITIVE SYNDROMES

Focal cognitive syndromes involve relatively isolated deficits of memory, language, and other cognitive functions occurring in clear consciousness. These focal syndromes are to be distinguished from the multiple cognitive deficits that define dementia or mental retardation.

Amnesia, the loss of memory or the inability to learn new verbal or spatial information, occurs as a focal syndrome caused by bilateral lesions of the medial temporal cortex, particularly in the hippocampal formations, or by bilateral lesions of diencephalic structures with temporal lobe connections, such as mediodorsal thalamus or mammillary bodies. Another type of amnesia, the inability to learn new procedures such as mirror writing, is of uncertain localization but might be related to lesions of the basal ganglia and cerebellum. The physician may test for amnesia by asking the patient to learn, and then to recall, word lists (as in the MMSE) and to learn and recall diagrams or figures such as those in the Benton Visual Retention Test. Etiologies include hypotension or anoxia, to which hippocampal pyramidal cells are particularly susceptible. Amnesic syndromes can also be caused by thiamine deficiency, usually in the context of alcohol abuse (Korsakoff's syndrome), bilateral herpes encephalitis, head trauma, and bilateral stroke.[25]

Aphasia is the loss of the ability to use language. It is to be distinguished from difficulties in the articulation of speech such as dysarthria or stammering. Aphasia may be divided into fluent (Wernicke's) or nonfluent (Broca's) forms. Fluent aphasia is characterized by impaired comprehension of language, but continued production of fluent speech. However, on closer listening, the speech is frequently empty of content and contains word selection errors. Such paraphasic errors consist of substitutions either in sound or sense for the intended meaning. Patients with Broca's aphasia, by contrast, are able to understand language relatively well, but have difficulty in its production. Speech is effortful, sparse, and may appear telegraphic—containing just a few nouns with high semantic content. When testing language, it is important to examine language production in both verbal and written forms, language comprehension (by asking the patient to follow commands), and word repetition (as in repeating the phrase "no ifs, ands, or buts"). Word repetition is thought to require the abilities to both comprehend and produce language. There are many causes of aphasia, but the most common is left-middle cerebral artery infarction. Left-hemisphere stroke usually produces a mixed aphasia. However, left anterior lesions often cause a Broca's aphasia associated with facial apraxia and a right hemiparesis, while left posterior lesions often produce a Wernicke's aphasia with variable motor signs.[26]

Apraxia is loss of the ability to perform learned motor acts. This is tested by asking patients to perform such behaviors as miming brushing their teeth or combing their hair. Patients should be able to perform these behaviors as if the proper instrument were in their hands (e.g., patients should not rub the fingers against the teeth, but should leave room for the handle of an imaginary toothbrush). Another test for praxis is to have the patient mime putting a key in a lock, turning it, and opening a door using the doorknob. Apraxia generally results from damage to the right parietal lobe, usually caused by stroke.

A less common focal deficit is *agnosia*, or a patient's inability to recognize specific visual stimuli although not afflicted by visual impairment or aphasia. It may be caused by lesions, such as tumors, in the visual association areas.

The importance of cognitive screening is underlined in patients with focal cognitive deficits since such deficits may be missed entirely if the clinician is not alert to them. Some individuals with severe memory impairment would be judged cognitively normal because of their spared ability to perform certain complex procedural tasks such as typing, playing the piano, or even playing cards. Such areas of intact functioning are the hallmark of the focal deficits.

SCHIZOPHRENIA

Schizophrenia in the elderly is an infrequent cause of altered mental state, but when it occurs it is often responsive to treatment with phenothiazines; thus, it should be considered in the differential diagnosis of every case with prominent delusions and hallucinations.[27,28] The characteristic presentation is an elderly person who develops intense auditory hallucinations and, sometimes, passivity experiences in association with delusions of persecution. The presentation of late-life-onset schizophrenia differs from schizophrenia that begins early in life. When the onset is late in life, thought disorder does not occur, and there is preservation of the personality, i.e., there are no so-called negative symptoms such as apathy and coarsening of relationships with other people (Chap. 103). Although the cause is not known, late-onset schizophrenia occurs in hearing-impaired individuals more often than expected. Several cases have been reported in association with parietal stroke in the nondominant hemisphere.[29]

MENTAL RETARDATION

Mental retardation should be considered in the differential diagnosis of an abnormal mental state because many mentally retarded individuals now live into old age and present with cognitive impairment that can be misdiagnosed as a change in mental state. They may also present with a truly altered mental state since the retarded are vulnerable to psychological and physiological environmental changes that will affect their behavior.

Many cognitively impaired elderly individuals in the community suffer from a lifelong impairment of unknown cause; the exact prevalence is unknown. Two to three percent of all adults are thought to suffer from mental retardation, as defined by an IQ of less than 70.[30] However, 10 to 15 percent of adults in a survey of three Baltimore communities suffered from cognitive impairment as measured by a MMSE score of less than 24 and had no diagnosable medical condition after psychiatric and neurological examinations. These individuals had often been reared in impoverished environments in the early 1900s and had attended school for only brief periods in a system that did not provide special educational classes. Most would be classified as having below average intelligence rather than mental retardation, and many were illiterate. Despite the high prevalence of such individuals, no studies have been published that identify the specific risk factors for their impairment. The roles of genetics, prenatal and postnatal environments, and educational opportunity remain unexplored.[12] Furthermore, no studies exist of the prevalence of psychiatric disorder in the elderly retarded, but in younger mentally retarded individuals the rate is high relative to children with normal intelligence living in the same community.

Somewhat more is known about the mental state in elderly individuals with Down's syndrome. The neuropathology of Alzheimer's disease occurs in all cases of Down's syndrome after the age of 35, although not all cases appear to deteriorate clinically before death.[31] Individuals with Down's syndrome are particularly sensitive to anticholinergic agents and therefore susceptible to delirium.[32] Depression has been reported, but the rates have not yet been established.

EMOTIONAL SYNDROMES

Elderly individuals present to medical clinics with changes in emotional state as well as in cognitive state. These changes are often unrecognized by physicians who attempt to treat the patients' somatic complaints symptomatically with an accumulation of analgesics, antispasmodics, and sedatives that can produce increasing lethargy, somatic preoccupation, and sometimes delirium. The emotional syndromes of the elderly can be classified into those that are understandable reactions to the environment, called adjustment disorders by the DSM-IIIR classification, and those that occur on a genetic or other somatic basis, most commonly affective disorders. The latter can be divided into primary affective disorders and affective disorders that are symptomatic of, or secondary to, somatic conditions such as stroke, parkinsonism, or medication with antihypertensive agents. Physicians can screen for emotional disorders in the elderly with the GHQ or other scales, such as the Center for Epidemiological Studies Depression Scale (CES-D) or the Yesavage Depression Scale.[33,34] These brief questionnaires were originally developed for research, but they are also useful clinical tools. They are self-rated and require that the patient have the cognitive capacity to complete them. If the patient is cognitively impaired, the physician can complete the Hamilton Depression Scale or the Montgomery Asberg Scale based on an interview with the patient and, if necessary, an informant.[35,36]

REACTIVE SYNDROMES

Reactive syndromes, or adjustment disorders, are the most common emotional disorders in the elderly and rank second only to cognitive disorders in prevalence.[37] Reactive syndromes can be viewed as resulting from certain personality traits that cause an individual to be vulnerable to particular environmental stressors.[38] For example, individuals with dependent traits who were able to function in the setting of a marriage may become symptomatic when they are widowed and when their children live too far away to provide support. The symptoms vary but may appear as prolonged and unresolved grief, fears and anxieties leading to insomnia or gastrointestinal complaints, or simply demoralization and discouragement from failure to master a changing environment. Individuals who are obsessional and perfectionistic may become preoccupied with minor aches and pains and make frequent appointments to see physicians from whom they request (demand) medications to relieve their symptoms. Such patients accumulate many unnecessary medicines that can cause other symptoms.

The management of these conditions is based on an individual formulation of each case. A detailed review of a patient's personal history will improve the physician's ability to make such a formulation. In addition, the interest shown in the patient by the physician by this detailed review will improve the patient's trust in the physician. In the context of this relationship a conversation can emerge which will help the patient put his or her symptoms into perspective and will redirect the patient's goals and tactics. Most importantly, the relationship will convey an attitude of hope and support.

AFFECTIVE DISORDERS

Major affective disorder (bipolar or unipolar affective disorder) occurs in the elderly as a continuation of a process of recurrent mood disorders which began earlier in life. Occasionally the disorder begins in old age, but there is usually a history of previous episodes and often a family history of depression.[37] There are two characteristic symptoms of depressive disorder: *a change in mood and self attitude*, with feelings of hopelessness and worthlessness, and *a change in the vital sense*.[39] Patients report a new and unpleasant sensation in the body, with a draining of energy and interest. These phenomena, which appear to afflict the person like a dark cloud, usually appear out of the blue but are sometimes precipitated by life events. The symptoms are accompanied by a change in appetite, bowel function, and sleep pattern. There is sometimes a diurnal variation, with the mood lightening in the afternoon or evening. This syndrome is sometimes accompanied by delusions of poverty, guilt, or persecution, congruent with the patient's low mood, or by feelings of worthlessness and guilt. The person may believe he or she is being persecuted because of some indiscretion or other blameworthy act. The patient's unpleasant bodily sensations and constipation can lead to a preoccupation with somatic symptoms and the belief that he or she has a blocked bowel, cancer, or rotting organs. These thoughts can lead to suicide. Elderly males with primary depression complicated by physical illness present the highest suicide risk.

The depressive syndrome usually occurs alone, but it may alternate with periods of mania, a feeling of elation or irritability accompanied by inflation of self attitude. The patient may feel that he or she has special talents or powers, and the patient's thoughts and behaviors reflect this belief. Buying sprees, increased alcohol intake, sleeplessness, overtalkativeness, and overactivity are common.

The management of affective disorder is based on an empathic relationship with the patient which elicits the patient's cooperation. This is necessary to enable the patient to relate painful suicidal thoughts and to develop trust in the doctor, which will increase the likelihood that the patient will cooperate with the treatment plan. The empathic relationship is built as the physician spends time listening to the details of the patient's life story. The traditional medical/psychiatric history-taking framework can be used to systematically survey aspects of the patient's life ranging from birth to parental relationships to the present.

Pharmacological management of affective disorder includes tricyclic antidepressants, lithium, and neuroleptics. Electroconvulsive therapy (ECT) may be necessary for patients who are unresponsive to more conservative treatment. Elderly patients often suffer from conditions that complicate the use of antidepressants, which have anticholinergic potential. These conditions include glaucoma, prostatic hypertrophy, chronic constipation, gait disorder, and some cardiac arrhythmias. Patients with cerebral disorders, such as stroke or Alzheimer's disease, may develop delirium when treated with psychoactive medications. Because of these side effects, such patients require frequent checkups by the physician and small doses of medication. Psychiatric consultation and often psychiatric hospitalization are needed for these cases, and ECT may be necessary if pharmacological treatment causes too many difficulties.

SECONDARY OR SYMPTOMATIC DEPRESSION

The syndrome of depression occurs frequently as a consequence of neurological disease. The symptoms are similar to those of primary affective disorder, but they may be difficult to elicit because of the patient's compromised ability to remember or to clearly describe his or her mental state because of the presence of amnesia, aphasia, or dysarthria. However, with the assistance of family members the physician can elicit the usual symptoms of depression or irritability, the associated changes in self attitude, and the vegetative symptoms of insomnia, anorexia, and loss of energy. Affective disorder associated with neurological disease might or might not be precipitated by environmental events in the life of the injured person.

A depressive syndrome occurs in perhaps 30 percent of stroke patients who have lesions in the left anterior hemisphere, 20 percent of patients with Alzheimer's disease, 40 percent of patients with Huntington's disease, and 40 to 60 percent of patients with Parkinson's disease. Although the mechanism of the depression is not understood, all of these conditions interfere with catecholaminergic pathways originating in the brain stem.[40] Patients with Alzheimer's disease who had been depressed during life had, on autopsy, fewer neurons in the locus coeruleus than patients who had not suffered from a depressive syndrome.[41] Patients with Parkinson's disease associated with depression were found to have lower levels of catechol metabolites in the cerebrospinal fluid than Parkinson's disease patients without depression.[42]

Few clinical trials have been carried out to test the usefulness of antidepressants for depression associated with neurological disorders. Stroke patients with anterior left hemisphere lesions and patients with Alzheimer's disease have been shown to respond to tricyclic antidepressants at therapeutic levels better than to placebo administered in a double-blind trial. Case reports indicate that patients with Parkinson's disease respond to ECT, and clinical experience suggests that patients with Huntington's disease respond to tricyclics and ECT.

The prognosis of depression in neurological disease is not well studied. Clinical experience suggests that depression, even if untreated, occurs in episodes. This has been demonstrated by prospective study for stroke and by retrospective chart review for Huntington's disease.

In patients with neurological disease, the depressive syndrome is to be distinguished from other disturbances of mood such as emotional lability, pathological emotion, and catastrophic reactions. The depressive syndrome is characterized by a sustained change in mood that lasts from weeks to months, compared to the short-lived, even fleeting, changes of mood characteristics of these other conditions. Emotional lability describes a short-lived change in emotion that lasts from seconds to hours and is sometimes precipitated by thoughts or circumstances. Pathological emotion is an involuntary emotional outburst that is often ego-dystonic. The patient does not know why he is laughing or crying and often does not have a congruent mood, as if the motor component of emotion but not the sensory component were released from control. Pathological emotion occurs in patients with pseudobulbar palsy, which is caused by bilateral lesions of the corticobulbar pathways, usually due to stroke in the elderly and sometimes by multiple sclerosis in younger patients. Catastrophic reactions are emotional outbursts caused by task failure and are clearly related in time to some frustrating or confusing aspect of the patient's environment.

CONCLUSION

An elderly patient who presents to a physician with an altered mental state is likely to have either a cognitive syndrome, most commonly a delirium or a dementia, or an emotional disorder, most commonly depression.

A diagnosis can usually be reached by taking a careful history from the patient and another informant and carrying out a detailed examination of the patient's mental state, followed by selected laboratory procedures and longitudinal follow-up. Elderly patients may have several coexisting conditions that act together to alter mental state, so a thorough evaluation is important even when there is a clear primary diagnosis.

REFERENCES

1. Mayer-Gross W et al: *Clinical Psychiatry*, 3d ed. London, Balliere Tindall, 1977, pp 41–56.
2. Rocca RP et al: Dementia among medical inpatients. *Arch Intern Med* 146(10):1923, 1986.
3. Knights EB, Folstein MF: Unsuspected emotional and cognitive disturbance in medical patients. *Ann Intern Med* 87:723, 1977.
4. Rovner BW et al: The prevalence of mental illness in a community nursing home. *Am J Psychiatry* 143(11):1446, 1986.
5. Folstein MF, McHugh PR: Phenomenological approach to the treatment of organic psychiatric syndromes, in Wolman BB (ed): *The Therapist Handbook: Treatment Methods of Mental Disorders.* New York, Van Nostrand Reinhold, 1976, pp 279–286.
6. Lawton MP, Brody EM: Assessment of older people: Self-maintaining and instrumental activities of daily living. *Gerontologist* 9:179, 1969.
7. Katz et al: Studies of illness in the aged. The index of ADL: A standardized measure of biological and psychological functions. *JAMA* 185:914, 1963.
8. Blessed G et al: Blessed Dementia Scale. *Br J Psychiatry* 114:797, 1986.
9. Wilkinson IM, Graham-White J: Psychogeriatric Dependency Rating Scale (PGDRS): A method of assessment for use by nurses. *Br J Psychiatry* 137:558, 1980.
10. Folstein MF et al: "Mini-Mental State." A practical method for grading the cognitive state of patients for the clinician. *J Psychiatr Res* 12:189, 1975.
11. Folstein MF et al: Meaning of cognitive impairment in the elderly. *J Am Geriatr Soc* 33(4):228, 1985.
12. Anthony JC et al: Limits of the mini-mental state as a screening test for dementia and delirium among hospital patients. *Psychol Med* 12:397, 1982.
13. Goldberg DP: *The Detection of Psychiatric Illness by Questionnaire.* New York, Oxford University Press, 1972.
14. German PS et al: The detection and management of mental health problems of older patients by primary care providers. *JAMA* 257(4):489, 1987.
15. Bonhoeffer C: Exogenic psychoses, in Hirsch S, Sheppard M (eds): *Themes and Variations in European Psychiatry.* Bristol, John Right and Sons, 1974, pp 47–63.
16. Wolf HG, Curran D: Nature of delirium in allied states: The dysergastic reaction. *Arch Neurol Psychiatry* 33:175, 1935.
17. Plum F, Posner JB: The pathologic physiology of signs and symptoms of coma, in *The Diagnosis of Stupor and Coma*, 3d ed. Philadelphia, F. A. Davis Company, 1982, pp 1–86.
18. Folstein MF et al: Cognitive assessment of cancer patients. *Cancer* 53:2250, 1984.
19. Tune LE, Folstein MF: Post-operative delirium. *Adv Psychosom Med* 15:15, 1986.
20. Leresche AJ et al: Screening for delirium on a general medical ward: The tachistoscope and a global accessibility rating. *Gen Hosp Psychiatry* 7:36, 1985.
21. Engel GL, Romano J: A syndrome of cerebral insufficiency. *J Chronic Dis* 9:260, 1959.
22. Tune L et al: Association of postoperative delirium with raised serum levels of anticholinergic drugs. *Lancet* 8248(2):651, 1981.
23. McHugh PR, Folstein MF: Organic mental disorders, in Cavenar, JO (ed): *Psychiatry.* New York, J. B. Lippincott, 1988.
24. McHugh PR, Folstein MF: Psychiatric syndromes of

Huntington's chorea: A clinical and phenomenologic study, in Benson DF, Blumer D (eds): *Psychiatric Aspects of Neurologic Disease*. New York, Grune and Stratton, 1975, pp 267–286.

25. Butters N, Milotis P: Amnesia, in Heilman KM, Valenstein E (eds): *Clinical Neuropsychology*. New York, Oxford, 1985, pp 403–439.

26. Benson F: Aphasia, in Heilman KM, Valenstein E (eds): *Clinical Neuropsychology*. New York, Oxford, 1985, pp 17–40.

27. Post F: *Persistent Persecutory States of the Elderly*. London, Pergamon Press, 1966.

28. Rabins P et al: Increased ventricle-to-brain ratio in late-onset schizophrenia. *Am J Psychiatry* 144(9):1216, 1987.

29. Peroutka SJ et al: Hallucinations and delusions following a right temporoparietooccipital infarction. *Johns Hopkins Med J* 151:181, 1982.

30. Adams RD, Victor M: Disorders contingent upon deviations in development of the nervous system. *Princ Neurol* 24:381, 1977.

31. Wisniewski KE et al: Alzheimer's disease in Down's syndrome: Clinicopathologic studies. *Neurology* 35(7):957, 1985.

32. Victor A: Personal communication.

33. Comstock GW, Helsing KJ: Symptoms of depression in two communities. *Psychol Med* 6:551, 1976.

34. Savage JA et al: The geriatric depression rating scale in comparison with other self report and psychiatric rating scales, in Crook T, Fairs S, Bartess R (eds): *Assessment and Geriatric Psychopharmacology*. New Canaan, CT, Mark Powley Associates, 1983.

35. Hamilton MA: A rating scale for depression. *J Neurol Neurosurg Psychiatry* 23:56, 1960.

36. Montgomery SA, Asberg M: A new depression designed to be sensitive to change. *Br J Psychiatry* 134:382, 1979.

37. Slater E, Roth M: *Clinical Psychiatry*, 3d ed. Baltimore, Williams and Wilkins, 1977.

38. McHugh P, Slavney P: *Perspectives of Psychiatry*. Baltimore, Johns Hopkins University Press, 1983.

39. Schneider K: *General Psychopathology*. New York, Grune & Stratton, 1959.

40. Folstein MF et al: Depression in neurological disorders: New treatment opportunities for elderly depressed patients. *J Affective Disord* 1:11, 1985.

41. Zweig R et al: The neuropathology of aminergic nuclei in Alzheimer's disease. *Ann Neurol* 24(2):233, 1988.

42. Mayeux R et al: Clinical and biochemical features of depression in Parkinson's disease. *Am J Psychiatry* 143(6):756, 1986.

Chapter 113

FATIGUE, FAILURE TO THRIVE, WEIGHT LOSS, AND CACHEXIA

Roy B. Verdery

A progressive and apparently irreversible decrease in functional body mass is common with increasing age. This decrease frequently is discovered at a late stage when low weight may prompt a referral for evaluation. Another example of this phenomenon is an elderly nursing home resident who gradually loses weight, is switched to enteral feeding, becomes bed-bound, develops decubitus ulcers, and eventually dies. Though this syndrome is common, it has been poorly studied from either a clinical or a mechanistic, biological perspective.

The result of the processes which will be discussed is cachexia or malnutrition.[1,2] Malnutrition in this sense, however, is a general descriptive term that does not provide insight into pathogenesis or treatment. The inexorable decline preceding cachexia is failure to thrive. In common with failure to thrive in children, failure to thrive in the elderly can be divided into "organic" failure to thrive (OFTT) and "nonorganic" failure to thrive (NOFTT) on the basis of etiology.[3,4] The quotation marks indicate the artificiality and potential for misapplication of such a distinction when rigidly applied. Table 113-1 is a partial list of causes of OFTT and Table 113-2 is a partial list of causes of NOFTT. The importance of OFTT is underscored by the prevalence of chronic infections, such as tuberculosis[5] and occult cancer,[6] in the elderly. The importance of NOFTT and its prevalence, while unstudied, are hinted at by the popularity, importance, and increase in senior citizen feeding programs. When it appears alone as the major problem, the symptom of fatigue, common in primary care medicine, is more indicative of NOFTT than OFTT.[7]

EPIDEMIOLOGY

There have been few studies of the prevalence and natural history of failure to thrive and the relationship of failure to thrive to age, sex, race, and socioeconomic condition. If this syndrome is identified with malnutrition, estimates of prevalence vary widely depending on the definition and the population being studied. Among nursing home residents, prevalence ranges from 10 to 25 percent, although it may be as high as 50 to 60 percent among persons newly admitted.[8-14] From studies of cancer cachexia it can be estimated that elderly people with failure to thrive due to causes other than cancer are about equal in number and older on average than those with cancer cachexia.[15-17]

The colloquialism "little old man" (or "little old lady") suggests that decreased weight and size are more common in older than in younger individuals. Although the weight associated with minimum mortality increases with age[18,19] (Chap. 72), cross-sectional and longitudinal studies show that average weight decreases after age 60 to 70 in both men and women.[20] This observation, combined with the observation that muscle mass decreases with age[21-24] and the clinical impressions of those who care for the elderly, suggests that the prevalence and incidence of cachexia increase with age. Therefore, the syndrome is more common in the very old (75 to 85 years old) and oldest old (>85 years old). The paucity of quantitative studies of this syndrome is in all likelihood due to the paucity of studies of the very old and oldest old in general.

TABLE 113-1
Etiologies of Organic Failure to Thrive (OFTT) in the Elderly

Malignancy
Tuberculosis
Heart failure
Uremia
Cirrhosis
Emphysema/chronic obstructive pulmonary disease
Inflammatory bowel disease
Hypo/hyper thyroidism
Diabetes mellitus
Cushing's disease
Addison's disease
Connective tissue disease
Mechanical gastrointestinal dysfunction
Maldigestion/malabsorption

The natural history of OFTT varies with the underlying disease. In cancer, profound loss of fat and muscle mass often occurs with minimal tumor burden.[25,26] Cancer cachexia in the absence of large tumor mass is due to changes in host metabolism caused by a variety of effectors discussed below. In patients with a large tumor burden, cachexia may also be due to gastrointestinal obstruction. In cardiac cachexia, a condition known since the time of Hippocrates,[27] progressive loss of muscle and fat mass occurs, although the exact cause is unknown.[28] In Alzheimer's disease and multi-infarct dementia, patients often have low weight in spite of adequate energy and protein intake.[29] In general, weight loss in dementing illness indicates poor prognosis. Such weight loss occurs in supportive institutional environments where food is provided and enteral feeding is commonly instituted. Thus, there may be an organic basis for weight loss in dementing illness.

Lack of prospective studies of cachexia among the elderly makes it difficult to ascertain the consequences of changes in body composition occurring in the absence of pathology. In nursing home patients, however, decreased visceral mass including decreased albumin and

TABLE 113-2
Etiologies of Nonorganic Failure to Thrive (NOFTT) in the Elderly

Neglect
Abuse
Immobility*
Dementia*
Depression*
Psychosis*
Polypharmacy
Anorexia nervosa
Poor dentition

* Possibly also "organic" in origin

cholesterol levels is associated with increased risk of death.[30–33] Among healthy, free-living elderly, a cellular marker of cachexia, decreased lymphocyte number, is also associated with increased risk of death.[34,35] Decreased visceral and cellular mass occur independently of decreased body mass.[36] Decreased body mass per se, however, is also associated with increased risk of death.[37] Thus, it appears that all of these signs of cachexia are indicators of poor prognosis.

CHANGES IN FUNCTIONAL BODY MASS

Cachectic individuals are usually recognized by their decreased functional body mass. Thus *weak* is almost synonymous with *cachectic*. Visceral mass including circulating blood cells and plasma protein also decreases in cachexia. As mentioned above, however, these findings, as a constellation, do not give insight into the mechanisms leading to the observed deficits or the means of treating them.

Whether measured by creatinine excretion, by hydrodensitometry, or by determining maximum aerobic capacity, muscle mass decreases with age.[22–24,38] Recent studies suggest that the decline in muscle function with age is due to the decline in the maximum capacity of muscle to extract oxygen and is not due to the decline in cardiovascular reserve.[39] With the decline in muscle function, there is a concomitant decrease in strength, an independent predictor of mortality.[40,41] Loss of muscle mass also can be measured by anthropometric methods, but age-adjusted standards must be used.[42–44]

In addition to decreased somatic mass, decreased visceral mass is seen in cachexia. Markers of decreased visceral mass include low levels of circulating plasma proteins, albumin, and retinol-binding protein, low levels of lipoproteins (and low levels of cholesterol), and low numbers of blood cells and lymphocytes.[30–36,45] The combination of hypoalbuminemia, hypocholesterolemia, and anemia is common in cachexia.[46]

It is difficult to distinguish changes in body mass due to aging from changes due to disease. One advantage of longitudinal studies of aging, such as the Baltimore Longitudinal Study on Aging (BLSA), the Framingham Study, and the Gothenburg Study, is their ability to track individuals over a period of time, accumulating data about disease as well as aging in an attempt to distinguish these processes.[47–49] In BLSA subjects, changes in muscle and fat mass, as well as changes in levels of circulating proteins and numbers of circulating blood cells, occur in absence of disease.[47] For most measurements of plasma constituents, however, the interrelation between cross-sectional, time-series, and longitudinal changes makes it impossible to distinguish changes due to aging from changes due to cohort or secular environmental (disease) influence.[50]

Whether due to age or disease, it may be hypothesized that decreased functional body mass leads to decreased tolerance for environmental stress. Environmental stress, in turn, may exacerbate changes due to aging or cause disease and further reduce functional body mass. This chain of events can give rise to a vicious circle culminating in death.[51] Whether this circle occurs and, if so, whether it can be broken, is an important clinical concern and matter for further research.

TASTE AND APPETITE

Declining food intake and subsequent cachexia can be attributed to anorexia and an altered perception of satiety. Appetite clearly involves endocrinologic considerations, since it is affected by gastrointestinal hormones, including cholecystokinin; systemic hormones, including insulin; and central mediators, including endorphins and serotonin.[52–54] The serotonin receptor blocker, cyproheptadine,[55] and hydrazine, a drug which inhibits glycolysis,[56] improve appetite in some individuals.

Altered taste and a diminished sense of smell also contribute to anorexia and subsequent cachexia. Older individuals have higher smell thresholds for detecting odors, and flavor enhancement can increase food intake.[57–59] Altered taste, dysgeusia, is also common in the elderly, due to drug intake or to primary changes in the sensory organs or nervous system.[60] Dysgeusia is associated with decreased energy intake,[61] but treatment of anosmia or dysgeusia in cachectic individuals has not been studied.

Social isolation and depression may also cause anorexia, failure to thrive, cachexia, and death; company and pleasant eating circumstances, as well as good-tasting and attractive food, are thought to be important in preventing this syndrome. Programs such as Meals-on-Wheels, geriatric feeding centers, and protective housing reverse deficits in this area.

The mechanical and enzymatic requirements of eating and digestion are also important. Mobility and dexterity are required to get food to the mouth. Teeth or dentures must be in good enough condition for chewing, or food must be mechanically prepared. Swallowing must not be impaired by neuromuscular dysfunction, and the mechanical, exocrine, and endocrine functions of the stomach and the rest of the gastrointestinal system must be intact. All of these components of the gastrointestinal system are subject to age-associated changes, as described in other chapters, and dysfunction of even one component may cause cachexia.

CONTROL MECHANISMS

ENDOCRINOLOGIC CONSIDERATIONS

The control of somatic and visceral mass is regulated by classic anabolic and catabolic hormones. These include growth hormone, the sex hormones, and insulin[62,63] (Chap. 69). In men, levels of both growth hormone and testosterone decrease with age, and there are age-associated decreases in the magnitude of pulsatile release of these hormones.[64,65] In women, levels of growth hormone and estrogen decrease with age, and there is a change from estradiol to estrone as the major estrogen.[66] Whether these age-associated changes ultimately cause decreases in function is uncertain. It has been hypothesized, however, that decreased levels of growth hormone are responsible for decreased mass of several organs.[67] In aging rats, administration of exogenous growth hormone reverses the age-related decrease in protein synthesis[68]; and growth hormone treatment of elderly men increases the levels of insulin-like growth factor II (somatomedin C), the primary anabolic effector of growth hormone.[69] In cancer cachexia, sex hormones are decreased.[70] Administration of androgens or estrogens reverses cancer cachexia in some instances.[71,72] Insulin resistance increases with age[62,73]; it also occurs with cancer and starvation, two processes associated with cachexia.[74,75] For cancer cachexia, administration of insulin (along with aggressive feeding) has been proposed as a possible treatment, although its efficacy is doubtful.[75–77] It is not known whether administration of growth hormone, androgens, estrogens, or insulin would be effective in treating cachexia in the elderly.

HUMORAL MECHANISMS OF CONTROL

Mass of fat, muscle, and other organs including bone is controlled by specific growth factors, in addition to the classic hormones discussed above.[78] These growth factors regulate the proliferation of specific cells in specific organs.[79,80] Proliferation of circulating blood cells is also controlled by levels of cell-type specific growth factors.[81] Synthesis of albumin, transferrin, prealbumin, lipoproteins, and other plasma proteins is also specifically regulated.[82,83]

Fat mass is regulated by energy intake, expenditure, and activities of lipoprotein lipase and hormone-sensitive lipase. These enzyme activities are, in turn, regulated by fat intake and levels of insulin and catecholamines.[84,85] Resistance to insulin and beta-adrenergic stimulation occurring with age therefore contributes to the changes in body composition seen with both aging and cachexia. In addition, since tumor necrosis factor (cachectin) and other cytokines directly affect the activity of lipoprotein lipase, changes in the immune system occurring with age may lead to changes in body composition.[86-90]

Muscle mass is regulated by levels of growth hormone and androgens as well as by habitual aerobic activity.[91] It is probable that a sedentary lifestyle causes a decline in muscle mass and contributes to the decline in function and the increased prevalence of cachexia seen in the very old and oldest old.[92]

Regulation of blood cell levels in the elderly has been intensively studied. The number of circulating red cells in healthy elderly declines only slightly with age (Chaps 64 and 65). However, elderly individuals, particularly the very old and oldest old, are susceptible to rapidly developing anemia under a variety of mild stressors, and this anemia may be less readily reversed in the elderly than in the young.[93,94] The mechanism for this decline is unknown, but it may be caused by decreased erythropoietin levels or decreased response of bone marrow to erythropoietin. The mechanism for the decrease in lymphocyte number occurring prior to death[35] is also unknown, although with age there is a decline in the number of T cells which can be stimulated to proliferate by a nonspecific stimulus such as phytohemagglutinin.[95] Thus, these markers of cachexia may be caused by both decreased levels of growth factors and decreased target cell response.

Levels of circulating plasma proteins also decline with age.[96-99] Decreases in levels of plasma proteins during stress are more pronounced in the elderly than in the young; and low albumin levels in the very old and oldest old do not respond to nutritional supplementation as well as they do in younger individuals.[100] The significance of decreased lipoprotein (and cholesterol) levels in the elderly is unknown. However, cholesterol levels decrease to a greater extent in the elderly than in the young during stress or trauma, and low cholesterol levels indicate poor prognosis.[30-33,46]

OTHER POSSIBLE MECHANISMS

In cancer cachexia, tumors which rely on glycolysis for energy may deplete circulating glucose, increase gluconeogenesis, and cause protein loss.[101] The drug hydrazine blocks glycolysis, thus forcing aerobic metabolism of glucose and sometimes reverses cancer cachexia.[102] The use of this drug in conditions other than cancer has not been studied.

Tumor necrosis factor (TNF), also called cachectin, has been implicated in cachexia due to chronic infection and cancer.[103] TNF may cause cachexia by inhibiting lipoprotein lipase and, hence, energy utilization.[86-90] TNF levels are decreased in cachectic nursing home patients.[104] Secretion of interleukin-2, another cytokine, decreases with age,[105] and it can be hypothesized that TNF secretion also changes with age. Other catabolic

hormones have been detected in cancer patients. These include anemia-inducing substance (AIS) and various toxohormones.[106,107] These substances are not well understood in cancer, and their role in cachexia in the elderly is unknown.

POSSIBILITIES FOR TREATMENT

Treatment of failure to thrive and cachexia depends on determining its etiology. Access to good food must be provided. The second step is to maximize desire for and intake of food. The use of flavor enhancers or enteral feeding may have a role here.[59] The detection of organic causes for weight loss and failure to thrive is equally important. Diabetes can be readily treated, and treatment may reverse most of the abnormalities. Diagnosis of cancer, although it may not lead to simple treatment, is also important, because it may lead to appropriate limitation of treatment modalities.

Neuropsychiatric problems, including depression, psychosis, and dementia, also cause failure to thrive by a variety of mechanisms, and both depression and psychosis are treatable. However, drugs used for treating depression and psychosis may change taste and affect food intake by themselves.[60] Use of other drugs, including growth hormone, anabolic steroids, estrogens, and hydrazine, is experimental.

FUTURE AVENUES OF RESEARCH

Cachexia in the elderly appears to be most prevalent in the very old and the oldest old. Because of this, the occurrence of failure to thrive will increase as the population in this age range increases. The incidence, prevalence, and natural history of this syndrome need to be better studied. In particular, it is important to determine the prevalence of reversible causes of failure to thrive and a method by which individuals with irreversible failure to thrive may be identified.

The functional correlates of changes in somatic and visceral body mass need to be further explored. For example, are there adverse effects of the decrease in cholesterol level (or other measurements of somatic or visceral mass) which are seen with age? Although hypocholesterolemia in nursing home residents indicates poor prognosis,[30-33] cachexia due to chronic infection is associated with decreased atherosclerosis, perhaps due to lower cholesterol levels.[108,109] Endocrinologic aspects of cachexia need to be further explored and the use of anabolic hormones in reversing cachexia needs to be studied. Taste, smell, and anorexia need to be studied from chemosensory and neurologic perspectives, as well as from the perspective of their relationship to depression and psychosis. From a cell biological perspective, the changes with age in growth factor levels and the response of target cells need to be further studied. Finally, the role of catabolic hormones such as TNF in causing cachexia in the absence of infection and cancer remains to be studied.

REFERENCES

1. Clark NG, Blackburn GL: Enteral nutrition—Part 2: Nutritional assessment and support of the elderly patient. *Am J Intraven Ther Clin Nutr* 10:7, 1983.
2. Friedman PJ, Campbell AJ, Caradoc-Davies TH: Prospective trial of a new diagnostic criterion for severe wasting malnutrition in the elderly. *Age Ageing* 14:149, 1984.
3. Homer C, Ludwig S: Categorization of etiology of failure to thrive. *Am J Dis Child* 135:848, 1981.
4. Powell GF, Low JF, Speers MA: Behavior as a diagnostic aid in failure-to-thrive. *J Dev Behav Pediatr* 8:18, 1987.
5. Narain JP, Lofgren JP, Warren E, Stead WW: Epidemic tuberculosis in a nursing home: A retrospective study. *J Am Geriatr Soc* 33:258, 1985.
6. Hardy C, Wallace C, Khansur T, Vance RB, Thigpen JT, Balducci L: Nutrition, cancer, and aging: An annotated review. II. Cancer cachexia and aging. *J Am Geriatr Soc* 34:219, 1986.
7. Kroenke K, Wood DR, Mangelsdorff AD, Meier MJ, Powell JB: Chronic fatigue in primary care: Prevalence, patient characteristics, and outcome. *JAMA* 260:929, 1988.
8. Sahyoun NR, Otradovec CL, Hartz SC, Jacob RA, Peters H, Russell RM, McGandy RB: Dietary intakes and biochemical indicators of nutritional status in an elderly, institutionalized population. *Am J Clin Nutr* 47:524, 1988.
9. Banerjee AK, Brocklehurst JC, Swindell R: Protein status in long-stay geriatric in-patients. *Gerontology* 27:161, 1981.
10. Lipschitz DA: Protein calorie malnutrition in the hospitalized elderly. *Prim Care* 9:531, 1982.
11. Vir SC, Love AHG: Nutritional status of institutionalized and non-institutionalized aged in Belfast, Northern Ireland. *Am J Clin Nutr* 32:1934, 1979.
12. Bienia R, Ratcliff S, Barbour GL, Kummer M: Malnutrition in the hospitalized geriatric patient. *J Am Geriatr Soc* 30:433, 1982.
13. Morley JE, Silver AJ, Fiatarone M, Mooradian AD: Geriatric grand rounds: Nutrition and the elderly, University of California, Los Angeles. *J Am Geriatr Soc* 34:823, 1986.
14. Thomas D, Kant A, Gardner LB, Lindsay J, Verdery RB: High prevalence of malnutrition in patients newly admitted to a nursing home. *J Am Geriatr Soc* 1989 (in press).
15. Eden E, Edstrom S, Bennegard K, Schersten T, Lundholm K: Glucose flux in relation to energy expenditure in malnourished patients with and without cancer during periods of fasting and feeding. *Cancer Res* 44:1718, 1984.
16. Lindmark L, Bennegard K, Eden E, Ekman L, Schersten T, Svaninger G, Lundholm K: Resting energy expenditure in malnourished patients with and without cancer. *Gastroenterology* 87:402, 1984.
17. Lindmark L, Eden E, Ternell M, Bennegard K, Svaninger G, Lundholm K: Thermic effect and substrate oxidation in response to intravenous nutrition in cancer patients who lose weight. *Ann Surg* 204:628, 1986.
18. Andres R: Mortality and obesity: The rationale for age-specific height-weight tables, in Andres R, Bierman EL, Hazzard WR (eds): *Principles of Geriatric Medicine.* New York, McGraw-Hill, 1985, p 311.
19. Manson JE, Stampfer MJ, Hennekens CH, Willett WC: Body weight and longevity: A reassessment. *JAMA* 257:353, 1987.
20. Najjar MF, Rowland M: Anthropometric reference data and prevalence of overweight. *Vital Health Stat* 238:1, 1987.
21. McGandy RB, Barrows CH, Spanias A, Meredith A, Stone JL, Norris AH: Nutrient intakes and energy expenditure in men of different ages. *J Gerontol* 21:581, 1966.
22. Shock NW: Energy metabolism, caloric intake, and physical activity in the aging, in Carlson LA (ed): *Nutrition in Old Age X.* Symposium Swedish Nutrition Foundation, Uppsala, Almquist and Wiksell, 1972.
23. Munro H: Nutrition and ageing. *Br Med Bull* 37:83, 1981.
24. Rossman I: Anatomic and body changes with aging, in Finch CE, Hayflick L, Brody H, Rossman I, Sinex FM (eds): *Handbook of the Biology of Aging.* New York, Van Nostrand Reinhold, 1977, p 189.
25. Theologides A: Pathogenesis of cachexia in cancer. *Cancer,* 29:484, 1972.
26. Theologides A: Anorexins, asthenins, and cachectins in cancer. *Am J Med* 81:696, 1986.
27. Katz AM, Katz PB: Diseases of the heart in the works of Hippocrates. *Br Heart J* 24:256, 1962.
28. Ansari A: Syndromes of cardiac cachexia and the cachectic heart: Current perspective. *Prog Cardiovasc Dis* 30:45, 1987.
29. Sandman P-O, Adolfsson R, Nigren C, Hallman G, Winblad B: Nutritional status and dietary intake in institutionalized patients with Alzheimer's disease and multiifarct dementia. *J Am Geriatr Soc* 35:31, 1987.
30. Verdery RB, Rogers E, Goldberg A: Metabolic profile and body composition predict decubiti and death in elderly nursing home residents. *J Am Geriatr Soc* 35:87, 1987.
31. Rudman D, Mattson DE, Nagraj HS, Caindec N, Rudman IW, Jackson DL: Antecedents of death in the men of a Veterans Administration nursing home. *J Am Geriatr Soc* 35:496, 1987.
32. Rudman D, Feller AG, Nagraj HS, Jackson DL, Rudman IW, Mattson DE: Relation of serum albumin concentration to death rate in nursing home men. *JPEN J Parenter Enteral Nutr* 11:360, 1987.
33. Rudman D, Dale MD, Mattson E, Nagraj HS, Axel MD, Feller G, Jackson DL, Caindec N, Rudman IW: Prognostic significance of serum cholesterol in nursing home men. *JPEN J Parenter Enteral Nutr* 12:155, 1988.
34. Proust J, Rosenzweig P, Debouzy C, Moulias R: Lymphopenia induced by acute bacterial infections in the

elderly: A sign of age-related immune dysfunction of major prognostic significance. *Gerontology* 31:178, 1986.

35. Bender BS, Nagel JE, Adler WH, Andres R: A sixteen year longitudinal study of the absolute peripheral blood lymphocyte count and subsequent mortality of elderly men. *J Am Geriatr Soc* 34:649, 1986.

36. Kergoat M-J, Leclerc BS, PetitClerc C, Imbach A: Discriminant biochemical markers for evaluating the nutritional status of elderly patients in long-term care. *Am J Clin Nutr* 46:849, 1987.

37. Dwyer JT, Coleman KA, Krall E, Yang GA, Scanlan M, Galper L, Winthrop E, Sullivan P: Changes in relative weight among institutionalized elderly adults. *J Gerontol* 42:246, 1987.

38. Heath GW, Hagberg JM, Ehansi AA, Holloszy JO: A physiological comparison of young and older endurance athletes. *J Appl Physiol* 51:634, 1981.

39. Lakatta EG, Mitchell JH, Pomerance A, Rowe GG: Human aging: Changes in structure and function. *J Am Coll Cardiol* 10(suppl A):42A, 1987.

40. Phillips P: Grip strength, mental performance and nutritional status as indicators of mortality risk among female geriatric patients. *Age Ageing* 15:53, 1986.

41. Pearson MB, Bassey EJ, Bendall MJ: The effects of age on muscle strength and anthropometric indices within a group of elderly men and women. *Age Ageing* 14:230, 1985.

42. Vir SC, Love AHG: Anthropometric measurements in the elderly. *Gerontology* 26:1, 1980.

43. Frisancho AR: New standards of weight and body composition by frame size and height for assessment of nutritional status of adults and the elderly. *Am J Clin Nutr* 40:808, 1984.

44. Latin RW, Johnson SC, Ruhling RO: An anthropometric estimation of body composition of older men. *J Gerontol* 42:24, 1987.

45. Kemm JR, Allcock J: The distribution of supposed indicators of nutritional status in elderly patients. *Age Ageing* 13:21, 1984.

46. Verdery RB, Rogers E, Goldberg AP: Age and sex variations in predictors of death in nursing home residents. Unpublished observations, 1988.

47. Shock NW, Greulich RC, Andres R, Arenberg D, Costa PT, Lakatta EG, Tobin JD (eds): *Normal Human Aging: The Baltimore Longitudinal Study of Aging.* Washington, Government Printing Office, 1984.

48. Gordon T, Castelli WP, Hjortland MC, Kannel WB, Dawver TR: High density lipoprotein as a protective factor against coronary heart disease: The Framingham study. *Am J Med* 62:707, 1977.

49. Svanborg A: The Gothenburg longitudinal study of 70-year-olds: Clinical reference values in the elderly, in Bergener M, Ermini M, Stahelin HB (eds): *The 1984 Sandoz Lectures in Gerontology, Thresholds in Aging.* Orlando, Academic Press, 1985, p 231.

50. Elahi VK, Elahi D, Andres R, Tobin JD, Butler MG, Norris AH: A longitudinal study of nutritional intake in men. *J Gerontol* 38:162, 1983.

51. Verdery RB: Weight loss and cachexia, in Kelley WN (ed): *Textbook of Internal Medicine.* New York, J. B. Lippincott, 1988.

52. Porte D, Woods SC: Regulation of food intake and body weight by insulin. *Diabetologia* 20:274, 1981.

53. Rampal P: Les mechanismes de controle de l'appetit. *Presse Med* 15:23, 1986.

54. Silverstone T, Goodall E: Serotoninergic mechanisms in human feeding: The pharmacological evidence. *Appetite* 7(suppl):85, 1986.

55. Silverstone T, Schuyler D: The effect of cyproheptadine on hunger, calorie intake and body weight in man. *Psychopharmacologia* 40:335, 1975.

56. Chlebowski RT, Bulcavage L, Grosvenor M, Tsunokai R, Block JB, Heber D, Scrooc M, Chlebowski JS, Chi J, Oktay E, Akman S, Ali I: Hydrazine sulfate in cancer patients with weight loss, a placebo-controlled clinical experience. *Cancer* 59:406, 1987.

57. Schiffman SS: Mechanisms of disease, taste and smell in disease. Part I. *N Engl J Med* 308:1275, 1983.

58. Schiffman SS: Mechanisms of disease, taste and smell in disease. Part II. *N Engl J Med* 308:1337, 1983.

59. Schiffman SS: Diagnosis and treatment of smell and taste disorders. *West J Med* 146:471, 1987.

60. Bartoshuk LM, Rifkin B, Marks LE, Bars P: Taste and aging. *J Gerontol* 41:51, 1986.

61. Mattes-Kulig DA, Henkin RI: Energy and nutrient consumption of patients with dysgeusia. *J Am Diet Assoc* 85:822, 1985.

62. Andres R, Tobin JD: Aging and disposition of glucose. *Adv Exp Med Biol* 61:239, 1979.

63. Blackman MR: Pituitary hormones and aging. *Endocrinol Metab Clin North Am* 16:981, 1987.

64. Florini JR, Prinz PN, Vitiello MV, Hintz RL: Somatomedin-C levels in healthy young and old men: Relationship to peak and 24-hour integrated levels of growth hormone. *J Gerontol* 40:2, 1985.

65. Sonntag WE: Hormone secretion and action in aging animals and man. *Rev Biol Res Aging* 3:299, 1987.

66. Ho KY, Evans WS, Blizzard RM, Veldhuis JD, Merriam GR, Samojlik E, Furlanetto R, Rogol AD, Kaiser DL, Thorner MO: Effects of sex and age on the 24-hour profile of growth hormone secretion in man: Importance of endogenous estradiol concentrations. *J Clin Endocrinol Metab* 64:51, 1987.

67. Rudman D: Growth hormone body composition, and aging. *J Am Geriatr Soc* 33:800, 1985.

68. Sonntag WE, Hylka VW, Meites J: Growth hormone restores protein synthesis in skeletal muscle of old male rats. *J Gerontol* 40:689, 1985.

69. Johanson AJ, Blizzard RM: Low somatomedin-C levels in older men rise in response to growth hormone administration. *Johns Hopkins Med J* 149:115, 1981.

70. Chlebowski RT, Heber D: Hypogonadism in male patients with metastatic cancer prior to chemotherapy. *Cancer Res* 42:2495, 1982.

71. Chlebowski RT, Herrold J, Ali I, Oktay E: Influence of nandrolone decanoate on weight loss in advanced non-small cell cancer. *Cancer* 58:183, 1986.

72. Tchekmedyian NS, Tait N, Moody M, Aisner J: High-dose megestrol acetate: A possible treatment for cachexia. *JAMA* 257:1195, 1987.

73. Chen M, Halter JB, Porte D: The role of dietary carbohydrate in the decreased glucose tolerance of the elderly. *J Am Geriatr Soc* 35:417, 1987.

74. Cahill GF, Herrera MG, Morgan AP, Soeldner JS,

Steinke J, Levy PL, Reichard GA, Kipnis DM: Hormone-fuel interrelationships during fasting. *J Clin Invest* 45:1751, 1966.

75. Schein PS, Kisner D, Haller D, Belcher M, Hamosh M: Cachexia of malignancy: Potential role of insulin in nutritional management. *Cancer* 43:2070, 1979.

76. Moley JF, Morrison SD, Norton JA: Preoperative insulin reverses cachexia and decreases mortality in tumor-bearing rats. *J Surg Res* 43:21, 1987.

77. Svaninger G, Drott C, Lundholm K: Role of insulin in development of cancer cachexia in nongrowing sarcoma-bearing mice: Special reference to muscle wasting. *JNCI* 78:943, 1987.

78. Goustin AS, Leof EB, Shipley GD, Moses HL: Growth factors and cancer. *Cancer Res* 46:1015, 1986.

79. Ross R: Platelets, platelet-derived growth factor, growth control, and their interactions with vascular wall. *J Cardiovasc Pharmacol* 7(suppl 3):S186, 1985.

80. Levi-Montalcini R: The nerve growth factor 35 years later. *Science* 237:1154, 1987.

81. Sieff CA: Hematopoietic growth factors. *J Clin Invest* 79:1549, 1987.

82. Birch HE, Schreiber G: Transcriptional regulation of plasma protein synthesis during inflammation. *J Biol Chem* 261:8077, 1986.

83. Baumann H, Richards C, Gauldie J: Interaction among hepatocyte stimulating factors, interleukin 1, and glucocorticoids for regulation of acute phase plasma proteins in human hepatoma (HepG2) cells. *J Biol Chem* 139:4122, 1987.

84. Taskinen MR: Lipoprotein lipase in diabetes. *Diabetes Metab Rev* 3:551, 1987.

85. Sacks FM, Dzau VJ: Adrenergic effects on plasma lipoprotein metabolism: Speculation on mechanisms of action. *Am J Med* 80:71, 1986.

86. Kawakami M, Pekala PH, Lane MD, Cerami A: Lipoprotein lipase suppression in 3T3-L1 cells by an endotoxin-induced mediator from exudate cells. *Proc Natl Acad Sci USA* 79:912, 1982.

87. Torti FM, Dieckmann B, Beutler B, Cerami A, Ringold GM: A macrophage factor inhibits adipocyte gene expression. An in vitro model of cachexia. *Science* 229:867, 1985.

88. Price SR, Olivecrona T, Pekala PH: Regulation of lipoprotein lipase by synthesis by recombinant tumor necrosis factor—the primary regulatory role of the hormone in 3T3-L1 adipocytes. *Arch Biochem Biophys* 251:738, 1986.

89. Old LJ: Tumor necrosis factor. *Sci Am* 258:59, 1988.

90. Beutler BA, Cerami A: Recombinant interleukin 1 suppresses lipoprotein lipase activity in 3T3L1 cells. *J Immunol* 135:3961, 1985.

91. McIntyre JG: Growth hormone and athletes. *Sports Med* 4:129, 1987.

92. Gerstenblith G, Renlund DG, Lakatta EG: Cardiovascular response to exercise in younger and older men. *Fed Proc* 46:1834, 1987.

93. Hyams DE: The blood, in Brocklehurst JC (ed): *Textbook of Geriatric Medicine and Gerontology*. New York, Churchill Livingston, 1985, p 835.

94. Lipschitz DA, Udupa KB, Milton KY, Thompson CO: Effect of age on hematopoiesis in man. *Blood* 63:502, 1984.

95. Adler WH, Nagel JE: Studies of immune function in a human population, in Serge D, Smith L (eds): *Immunological Aspects of Aging*. New York, Marcel Dekker, 1981, p 296.

96. MacLennan WJ, Martin P, Mason BJ: Protein intake and serum albumin levels in the elderly. *Gerontology* 23:360, 1977.

97. Herschkopf RJ, Elahi D, Andres R, Baldwin HL, Raizes GS, Schocken DD, Tobin JD: Longitudinal changes in serum cholesterol in man: An epidemiological search for an etiology. *J Chron Dis* 35:101, 1982.

98. Curb JD, Reed DM, Yano K, Kautz JA, Albers JJ: Plasma lipids and lipoproteins in elderly Japanese-American men. *J Am Geriatr Soc* 34:773, 1986.

99. National Center for Health Statistics: Trends in serum cholesterol levels among US adults aged 20 to 74 years. *JAMA* 257:937, 1987.

100. Misra DP, Loudon JM, Staddon GE: Albumin metabolism in elderly patients. *J Gerontol* 30:304, 1975.

101. Chlebowski RT, Heber D, Richardson B, Block JB: Influence of hydrazine sulfate on abnormal carbohydrate metabolism in cancer patients with weight loss. *Cancer Res* 44:857, 1984.

102. Gold J: Hydrazine sulfate: A current perspective. *Nutr Cancer* 9:59, 1987.

103. Balkwill F, Burke F, Talbot D, Tavernier J, Osborne R, Naylor S, Durbin H, Fiers W: Evidence for tumour necrosis factor/cachectin production in cancer. *Lancet* ii:1229, 1987.

104. Verdery RB, Winchurch RA, Adler WH: Tumor necrosis factor-cachectin levels in nursing home residents are correlated with interleukin 2 response of CTLL2 cells but not with endotoxin levels. *Clin Res* 37:19a, 1989.

105. Nagel JE, Chopra RK, Chrest FJ, McCoy MT, et al: Decreased proliferation, interleukin 2 synthesis, and interleukin 2 receptor expression are accompanied by decreased mRNA expression in phytohemagglutinin-stimulated cells from elderly donors. *J Clin Invest* 81:1096, 1988.

106. Ishiko O, Sugawa T, Tatsuta I, Shimura K, Naka K, Deguchi M, Umsaki N: Anemia-inducing substance (AIS) in advanced cancer: Inhibitory effect of AIS on the function of erythrocytes and immunocompetent cells. *Jpn J Cancer Res* 78:596, 1987.

107. Masuno H, Yoshimura H, Ogawa N, Okuda H: Isolation of a lipolytic factor (toxohormone-L) from ascites fluid of patients with hepatoma and its effect on feeding behavior. *Eur J Cancer Clin Oncol* 20:1177, 1984.

108. Eilersen P, Faber M: The human aorta. VI. The regression of atherosclerosis in pulmonary tuberculosis. *Arch Path* 70:117, 1960.

109. Wilens SL, Dische MR, Henderson D: The low incidence of terminal myocardial infarction and the reversibility of cardiac hypertrophy in cachexia. *Am J Med Sci* 253:651, 1967.

Chapter 114

DISORDERED SLEEP IN THE ELDERLY

Edward F. Haponik

Recognition that abnormalities occurring during sleeping hours can produce considerable morbidity manifest during wakefulness has been one of the major recent advances in medicine. Such alterations may considerably alter the quality of life and, in some individuals, are life-threatening. In addition, there has been enhanced appreciation of secondary deleterious effects upon sleep by diverse acute and chronic illnesses and of untoward effects of disordered sleep upon these diseases. Nowhere is the clinical relevance of such interactions more important than in care for the elderly. Although many uncertainties regarding sleep and its disorders in this group remain, it is increasingly clear that familiarity with these conditions and with pragmatic approaches to their management is an essential component of comprehensive geriatric patient care.

Primary clinical considerations in elderly patients with sleep-related complaints are summarized in Table 114-1; they are similar to basic principles delineated in preceding chapters. First, the clinician must attempt to differentiate disease from normal changes accompanying aging. This distinction is the focus of major ongoing clinical investigations; it is often difficult to determine whether a patient's sleep-related complaints truly reflect disease. Nevertheless, the chronicity and severity of complaints and, most importantly, of their impact upon the patient's functional status provide useful determinants of whether evaluation and intervention are necessary or appropriate. Second, it must be recognized that symptoms which are present during wakefulness might have originated in a primary disorder of sleep. In particular, excessive somnolence interfering with daytime activities might reflect profound alterations of normal sleep structure by disordered breathing. Moreover, symptoms and signs less clearly related to sleep may originate in such conditions: systemic hypertension, cor pulmonale, altered neurologic function, cardiac arrhythmias, and

erythrocytosis may all be sequelae of sleep apnea. Third, the clinician must exclude deleterious secondary effects upon the quality and quantity of sleep that are due to diverse systemic diseases, psychiatric illnesses, or social problems confronting the elderly patient. Acute and chronic pain, nocturia, paroxysmal dyspnea, bereavement, retirement, or institutionalization commonly exert profound effects upon sleep. Failure to recognize their central role as the causes of an inability to fall asleep or of complaints of frequent nocturnal awakenings might lead to misdiagnosis and mismanagement. Fourth, one must attempt to identify treatable disease or those potentially reversible elements of what are often chronic, generally progressive conditions. For example, appreciation that sleep apnea is a potentially curable, life-threatening disorder underscores the importance of its recognition. Early morning awakening might signal a major depressive illness, which might be ameliorated pharmacologically. Finally, and perhaps most importantly, the clinician must avoid iatrogenic illness in the vulnerable elderly population. Medications prescribed by physicians are one of the most common causes of sleep-related complaints in the elderly. Furthermore, drugs administered because of such complaints are too often expedient substitutes for systematic diagnosis and therapy. In this chapter, the alterations of sleep that ac-

TABLE 114-1
Clinical Considerations in Elderly Patients with Sleep Complaints

1. Differentiate disease from normal changes with aging.
2. Recognize symptoms during wakefulness that originate in sleep.
3. Exclude secondary dysfunction due to systemic diseases, psychologic factors, and social factors.
4. Identify treatable/reversible conditions.
5. Minimize iatrogenic illness.

company aging, the major sleep disorders, and the evaluation and management of elderly patients with disturbed sleep are reviewed.

SLEEP ALTERATIONS IN THE ELDERLY

A spectrum of subjective and objective changes in sleep occurs with aging.[1–17] Epidemiologic surveys of elderly persons residing at home or in extended-care facilities demonstrate that from 15 to 75 percent of these individuals are dissatisfied with either the duration or the quality of their noctural sleep.[1,1a,3–7] Hoch and coworkers have found that healthy elderly women have subjectively more troubled sleep than men.[8,9] Reviews have consistently identified the following subjective complaints: elderly persons report that although they spend relatively more total time in bed (often resting without attempting to sleep, napping, or else unable to fall asleep), their total sleep time is reduced from what it was during younger years.[1–2a] In addition, sleep latency, the time it takes to fall asleep, is increased. Importantly, aged individuals very commonly report that they awaken after the onset of sleep and the number of daytime naps tends to increase as they get older. Objective testing of patients in sleep laboratory settings and, to a lesser extent, in less artificial environments has confirmed these subjective observations (Table 114-2). Perhaps the most striking characteristic is the polygraphic confirmation of wakefulness after sleep onset. Reynolds and coworkers[10,11] evaluated 40 healthy individuals aged 58 to 82 years and found that men were unable to maintain sleep as well as women, and had reduced Stage 3 sleep (see below). Increased wakefulness during sleep was most notable during the early morning hours, i.e., the last 2 hours of recording.

Patients' perceptions of differences in sleep have been substantiated by the objective demonstration that fundamental changes in sleep structure accompany aging.[1–3a,10,17] Although there is considerable variation among individuals and within the environments in which their sleep alterations have been studied, such objectively measured alterations of sleep can be usefully summarized, as in Table 114-2, Table 114-3, and Fig. 114-1. Electrophysiologic and behavioral criteria (established, for the most part, in younger populations) describe three states of active brain function: wakefulness, non-rapid eye movement (NREM) sleep, and rapid eye movement (REM) sleep.[18] NREM, or "quiet sleep," is characterized by four stages. Stage 1 sleep is a transitional period of drowsiness during which electroencephalographic (EEG) activity slows, muscles relax, and slow rolling eye movements occur. This period is followed by Stage 2, during which well-characterized sleep spindles and K complexes can be identified. Stage 3 and Stage 4 NREM, or "deep sleep," is characterized by profound EEG slowing and high amplitude delta waves. This "slow wave sleep" is the stage believed to be particularly important for the restorative functions of sleep.[2] REM sleep resembles wakefulness and is associated with increased autonomic activity and dreaming. Wide variations of heart rate, systemic blood pressure, and respiratory frequency occur. Voluntary muscle tone (including that of accessory respiratory muscles) is reduced or absent, except for the characteristic extraocular muscle activity. There is usually a normal transition from wakefulness through the four stages of NREM sleep, followed by the onset of initial REM sleep. This is followed subsequently by alternating NREM and REM periods (Fig. 114-1). Thus, sleep can be described by the absolute and relative durations of these stages and the distribution of cycles between NREM and REM sleep (Table 114-3).

This sleep structure is altered in elderly persons. With increased age there is a striking increase of Stage 1 sleep and a decrease of slow wave sleep.[1–3] Reductions of both the number and amplitude of delta waves have been observed. The increase of Stage 1 sleep provides a practical measure of the fragmentation or disruption of

TABLE 114-2
Altered Sleep in the Elderly

	Subjective Reports	Objective Monitoring
Total time in bed	Increased	Increased
Total sleep time	Decreased	Variable (usually decreased)
Sleep latency	Increased	Variable (usually increased)
Wakefulness after sleep onset	Increased	Increased
Daytime naps	Increased	Variable
Sleep efficiency	Decreased	Decreased

TABLE 114-3
Changes in Sleep Structure with Aging

Sleep Stage	Polysomnographic Findings
Non-rapid eye movement (NREM)	
Stage 1	Increased*
Stage 2	Variable (usually decreased)
Stage 3	Decreased
Stage 4	Decreased*
Rapid eye movement (REM)	
Quantity	Decreased
Distribution	Early onset; trend toward period of equal duration (rather than progressive lengthening)

*Common, major changes

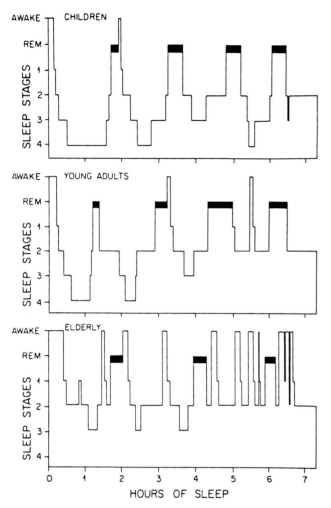

FIGURE 114-1
The structure of sleep in the elderly is characterized by increases in Stage 1 and Stage 2 sleep with marked reductions of Stage 3 and Stage 4 in NREM sleep. In addition, multiple awakenings occur, and the amount and duration of REM sleep are reduced. (*Reproduced from Refs. 18 and 18A.*)

sleep structure. The consistently observed reduction of deep sleep presumably has major deleterious effects upon the restorative functions of sleep. It is likely that sleep is disturbed even more profoundly, since conventional sleep-scoring systems do not take into account very brief arousals, which are prevalent in the aged.[3] Some of the latter are due to identifiable systemic illnesses (e.g., congestive heart failure), while others have no apparent precipitant. The precise effects of such effective sleep deprivation in the elderly are unclear. However, fatigue, irritability, impaired cognitive function, incoordination, and hallucinations have been associated with sleep deprivation.[2]

The differences with age in sleep structure and, in particular, the increased Stage 1 sleep, decreased Stage 4 sleep, and increased wakefulness after sleep onset are more prominent in men than in women and have been thought to represent an exaggeration of gender differ-

ences observed in younger individuals.[2] The absolute amount of REM sleep is reduced in the elderly, although its percentage of total sleep time is similar to that of young individuals.[3] The distribution of REM sleep also changes, with REM periods tending to occur earlier and to be more equal in their duration, in contrast to their progressive prolongation in younger individuals. Reduced REM sleep has been associated with organic brain syndromes and alterations of cerebral blood flow.

The ubiquity of clinical complaints and physiologic alterations of sleep in the elderly supports the notion that these represent expected changes, but the extent to which these truly represent normal physiologic alterations or subtle manifestations of disease is unknown. Further assessment of these areas and, in particular, longitudinal studies of their evolution are needed. In one recent longitudinal study, 19 healthy older subjects (ages 60 to 82) were found to have increased but otherwise stable objective measures of EEG sleep and its quality over a 2.2-year period.[9]

The similarity of EEG alterations commonly observed during sleep and wakefulness in the elderly to those found in aged persons who have senile dementia of the Alzheimer's type (or other chronic brain syndromes) suggests that this altered electrical activity represents degenerative changes of the central nervous system.[1,3] Several authors have shown sleep structure to be fragmented severely in such individuals. Feinberg found that patients with dementia had reduced total sleep time, Stage 4 sleep, REM sleep, and eye-movement rates as compared with age-matched controls; decreased REM sleep correlated with psychometric scores.[19,20] Allen and coworkers performed continuous 72-hour polygraphic recordings in elderly patients (mean age >80) hospitalized in a geriatric unit.[21] Individuals with dementia (Alzheimer's disease, multi-infarct dementia, and mixed/undefined dementia) had less Stage 2 and REM sleep and less total sleep time than did nondemented controls. The study found no differences among the dementia subgroups, nor any differences between nondemented control patients and dementia patients with regard to their REM–NREM cycles. In contrast to patterns in healthy elderly individuals, no gender difference was seen in demented patients. Only 3 of 30 demented patients experienced more daytime than nighttime sleep. The contributions of altered cerebral blood flow and focal or systemic metabolic derangements to these changes require further investigation.

MAJOR SLEEP DISORDERS

One important consequence of the recent dynamic study of sleep has been the more systematic description of sleep disorders. Although some overlap is seen in its application to clinical presentations of elderly persons, the classification promulgated by the Association of Sleep Disorder Centers in 1979 is not only comprehensive but also useful in a practical way.[22] Major sleep disorders of the elderly include disturbances of initiating and maintaining sleep (DIMS), disorders of excessive somnolence (DOES), disorders of the sleep-wake cycle, and abnormal sleep behaviors (parasomnias).[1,18,22–24] These heterogeneous conditions are summarized in Table 114-4. Preliminary estimates of their relative frequencies have been derived, for the most part, from sleep laboratory evaluations and from a limited number of ambulatory studies performed in apparently healthy elderly volunteers.[1,10,17] Clearly, such relative frequencies of these conditions will vary considerably with the reporting center and the characteristics of the population evaluated and will be modified with increasing experience. Differences would be expected according to whether patients represent referrals to a sleep disorders center or are evaluated by a neurologist, psychiatrist,

pulmonologist, or primary care physician. Although more comprehensive epidemiologic information is needed, clinical experience suggests that sleep disorders are common problems whose prevalence is underestimated. In a study by Reynolds et al. of 27 elderly patients evaluated in a sleep center because of either daytime hypersomnolence or chronic insomnia, all were found to have organic disorders: 19 of these individuals had DIMS, and two-thirds had either depression or persistent psychophysiologic insomnia. This investigation confirmed the diversity of sleep disturbances in the symptomatic elderly patient and both the need for and feasibility of accurate characterization of illness.[10]

DISORDERS OF INITIATING AND MAINTAINING SLEEP

Disorders of initiating and maintaining sleep (DIMS)[22] are characterized by the primary complaint of insomnia. Sleep apnea ("central" sleep apnea in particular) and sleep-related myoclonus (period leg movements [PLM]) are important primary sleep disorders. PLM are repetitive, stereotypical, unilateral or bilateral sudden leg movements.[1,22,25] When this abnormal motor activity is associated with complete arousals from sleep, the patient complains of insomnia; when associated with only partial arousals, this condition leads to sleep fragmentation and the clinical complaint of hypersomnolence. Common conditions to be differentiated from PLM are "restless legs" (uncomfortable dysthesias experienced during sleep), nocturnal leg cramps, manifestations of peripheral neuropathy or myelopathy, and folate or iron deficiency.

A variety of emotional conflicts and stresses are psychophysiologic causes of insomnia that would be expected to have an effect on elderly persons who characteristically have impaired homeostasis. Major psychiatric illness (in particular, depression) often leads to early morning awakening and might be manifest by either insomnia or hypersomnia. Endogenous depression may be associated with the early onset of REM sleep (REM sleep latency) and if recognized might be improved dramatically by the appropriate initiation of antidepressant therapy. The patient might also be awakened repetitively by unrelieved pain (e.g., pain due to arthritis or malignancy), nocturia, occult thyroid, hepatic or renal disease, paroxysmal nocturnal dyspnea caused by congestive heart failure, or nocturnal exacerbations of obstructive airway disease. Chronic brain syndromes are often associated with insomnia. Individuals with parkinsonism may exhibit disturbed sleep characterized by their awakening 2 to 3 hours into the night despite having retired at their normal hour. Patients with Alzheimer's dementia often awaken in the middle of the night, with subsequent efforts at sedation sometimes resulting

TABLE 114-4
Major Sleep Disorders of the Elderly

ASDC Classification*	Clinical Problem	Estimated Frequency
Disorders of Initiating and Maintaining Sleep	Sleep apnea	16–18%
	Nocturnal myoclonus	0–33%
	Restless legs	5%
	Psychophysiologic problem	21–31%
	Psychiatric problem	18–47%
	Drugs/alcohol	21%
	Symptoms of organic disease (e.g., arthritic pain, nocturia, nocturnal dyspnea, chronic brain syndrome)	Common; exact frequency unknown
Disorders of Excessive Sleepiness	Sleep apnea	28–71%
	Nocturnal myoclonus	16%
	Narcolepsy	11–29%
	Drugs	Common
	Miscellaneous (e.g., post infection fatigue, chronic brain syndrome)	?Common
Disrupted Sleep-wake Cycle	Early morning arousal, evening drowsiness	?Common
Parasomnias	Abnormal sleep behaviors (e.g., nocturnal confusion, wandering, seizures)	?Less common

*Association of Sleep Disorders Classification (see Ref. 22).
SOURCE: Derived from Refs. 1, 10, 11, and 17.

in paradoxical excitement. Alcohol may cause insomnia, and other drugs often disrupt sleep. Corticosteroids, theophylline preparations, and beta-blockers are common offenders. Concurrent treatment with stimulants and either the withdrawal from or the development of tolerance to chronically administered sedative hypnotic agents are other causes to be sought. The latter agents are administered typically in efforts to calm a patient whose awakening has disrupted the institutional or home routine.

DISORDERS OF EXCESSIVE SOMNOLENCE

Disorders of excessive somnolence (DOES)[22] are characterized by pathologic sleepiness which interferes with activities during wakefulness. The severity of the sleepiness, its onset during inappropriate times, and its interference with activities are characteristics to seek in assessing its clinical importance. Obstructive sleep apnea and nocturnal myoclonus (PLM) are the major primary sleep disorders which may lead to hypersomnolence. Ancoli-Israel et al. performed home portable sleep recordings in 145 randomly selected, healthy volunteers 65 years of age and older.[26,27] The authors found that 18 percent of these individuals had sleep apnea as defined by conventional criteria, 34 percent had PLM during sleep (with myoclonus indices exceeding 5), and 10 percent of individuals had both; thus, over one-half of these asymptomatic individuals had evidence of sleep disorders. Comprehensive evaluations of 83 symptomatic patients age 60 or older referred to the Stanford Sleep-Wake Disorders Clinic demonstrated sleep apnea in 39 percent and PLM in 18 percent of individuals.[1] These conditions occurred significantly more often than in patients less than 60 years of age. In addition, elderly patients more often had objective evidence of disturbed sleep: there was more wake time present after sleep onset and longer, more frequent awakenings; fewer patients had Stage 4 sleep. Kales et al.[23,24] have reported that 20 to 30 percent of people over the age of 65 have either sleep apnea or nocturnal myoclonus or a combination of the two. Thus, these primary sleep disorders are common in both asymptomatic and symptomatic elderly. Narcolepsy is infrequently a newly found cause of sleepiness among the elderly; this condition characteristically has an onset during childhood or adolescence, and therefore the diagnosis is usually already established.[24]

Drug effects, particularly the residual or "carry-over" effects of sedative hypnotics, are perhaps the most common and also the most underrecognized causes of hypersomnolence in the elderly. Metabolism of these agents may be altered substantially in elderly individuals, who are particularly vulnerable to their hazardous effects.[1] Despite the paucity of data substantiating benefits of their chronic use and insufficient information regarding their particular benefits and risks in the elderly, sleeping pills are prescribed regularly (and in disproportionately high numbers) to this population.[1,28,28a] It has been noted that from 13 to 48 percent of noninstitutionalized elderly persons and 26 to 94 percent of institutionalized elderly persons receive sedative hypnotic agents regularly.[1] Although precise information regarding their impact on performance, motor coordination, and balance (particularly if the patient is required to awaken during the night) is unavailable, it seems likely that these agents contribute to the major morbidity incurred through falls.[1] Respiratory suppression by these drugs potentiates the effects of underlying pulmonary diseases or intrinsic disorders of respiratory control. In one recent study of nonobese, healthy elderly volunteers (mean age 73.3), benzodiazepines, alcohol, and sleep deprivation all increased the frequency of apneic events during sleep.[29] Thus, efforts either to control the patient, impose conformity to a schedule, or treat real or perceived problems with sedative hypnotics may cause considerable morbidity. Other commonly used drugs, such as antihistamines, major and minor tranquilizers, methyldopa, and tricyclic antidepressants, also may cause excessive sleepiness. This major iatrogenic problem is reviewed in further detail in Chapter 21.

SLEEP-WAKE CYCLE DISTURBANCES

It seems likely that disruption of the sleep-wake cycle and disturbances of the circadian rhythm will prove to be important problems in the elderly, but more information is necessary to appraise their extent and impact. Prototypical examples of such disorders are represented by time-zone changes, work-shift changes, irregular sleep-wake schedules, non–24-hour schedules, and both advanced and delayed sleep phase syndromes.[2,22,30,30a] While the sleep-wake cycle is a dominant rhythm, its relationship to other homeostatic rhythms (and potential disruptive effects upon them) may have a profound functional impact. Despite the importance of the maintenance of stable interactions among circadian rhythms and overall homeostasis, and a general impression that threats to such rhythms by internal and external stresses increase with age, there is little definitive information in this area. A shortening of the period of sleep-wake rhythms has been observed with increasing age,[2] but it has not yet been established whether such changes in circadian rhythm occur universally. The relationship of internal circadian rhythms to external environmental stimuli and to age-related alterations of other rhythms (e.g., reduced amplitudes of neuroendocrine rhythms and body temperature swings) also requires further study. Changes such as an advanced position of the "circadian oscillator" relative to the environment probably account for early morning wakefulness commonly observed in healthy elderly individuals.[2] It has been suggested that the order imposed on elderly, institutionalized patients contributes to more regular synchronous rhythms.[1] Alternatively, if the imposed schedule does not coincide with the patient's intrinsic schedule, disturbed sleep might result.

PARASOMNIAS

Parasomnias, such as somnambulism and night terrors, typically have their onset in childhood and often resolve with maturity.[22,23] A variety of abnormal behaviors during sleep, however, have been observed in the elderly.[3] These heterogeneous problems include nocturnal confusion, wandering, seizure disorders, decompensation of cardiovascular disease, enuresis, and gastroesophageal reflux. Further study and elucidation of these conditions are necessary.

SLEEP APNEA: A PROTOTYPICAL SLEEP PROBLEM IN THE ELDERLY

Recently, enhanced awareness of abnormal sleep in younger people has been extended to the elderly, with recognition of a spectrum of conditions of major clinical importance.[24,31,37] Diverse sleep-related breathing disorders (Table 114-5) merit particular emphasis because of their prevalence, their potential reversibility, and the morbidity of unrecognized disease.

PREVALENCE AND DEFINITIONS

Sleep apnea is defined by the cessation of airflow at the nose and mouth for at least a 10-second duration. Characteristically, patients with clinically important sleep apnea have repetitive episodes permeating sleep and resulting in major alterations of its structure. The prevalence of disordered breathing during sleep in the aged has varied considerably with patient ascertainment and

TABLE 114-5
Common Sleep-Related Breathing Disorders in the Elderly

Sleep apnea
  Central (failure of rhythmnogenesis)
  Obstructive (upper airway occlusion)
  Mixed
Hypopnea
Snoring
Respiratory disease with deterioration during sleep
  Hemoglobin oxygen desaturation with:
    Chronic obstructive pulmonary disease (COPD)
    Interstitial lung disease
    Nocturnal exacerbation of COPD
Nocturnal aspiration
Paroxysmal nocturnal dyspnea (cardiogenic)

definitions of the presence of a breathing disorder. Diagnoses have been based arbitrarily upon the presence of more than five episodes per hour of sleep, but this "apneic index" is frequently exceeded in healthy elderly persons. While the frequency with which potentially clinically important breathing disorders might vary among reports, it has been noted consistently that the frequency of apneas and hypopneas during sleep increases with age.[26,27,32–42] In one early study, Carskadon and Dement found that eight men (45.4 percent) and seven women (31.8 percent) had more than five disordered breathing events per hour of sleep.[39] There appeared to be an age-related increase in respiratory disturbances among women, most notably during the eighth decade. Disordered breathing events were associated with EEG arousals, clearly a disruption of the pattern of nocturnal sleep and potentially a cause of symptoms. Kriger compared 20 elderly individuals with 20 medical students and identified frequent hypopneas and apneas in the elderly group.[41] Niafeh et al., in a similar comparative study, also found that sleep apnea and hypopnea were more frequent (55 percent vs. 8 percent) in older subjects (>60 years old).[43] Changes in sleep structure (brief arousals) accompanied these episodes of abnormal breathing. Ancoli-Israel evaluated 358 randomly selected elderly volunteers (mean age 72.4) and found that 17 percent had obstructive sleep apnea, 6 percent had central apnea, and 1 percent had mixed events.[26,27,32,33] As in younger populations, sleep apnea was found more commonly among men. In individuals with obstructive apnea, there was a significant correlation of apnea frequency with age, an observation confirmed recently.[38,45] Bixler and coworkers found that asymptomatic older patients often had greater "sleep apnea activity" in comparison with controls: approximately one-fourth of subjects older than age 50 had such activity, while it was present in only 8.7 percent of younger individuals.[36] Interestingly, only one person satisfied commonly used criteria for the presence of sleep apnea (a frequency of 30 or more apneic episodes during the night of sleep). By contrast, McGinty and coworkers found that 62 percent of healthy men (age range 55 to 70) had at least 12 disordered breathing episodes per hour of sleep.[42]

Three basic patterns of apnea are recognized, and their distinction has therapeutic implications. Central apnea results from the periodic cessation of respiratory muscle activity and is associated primarily with neurologic diseases such as bulbar poliomyelitis, encephalitis, brain stem infarction, neoplasms, cervical cordotomy, spinal surgery, and idiopathic alveolar hypoventilation. Central apnea results from recurrent interruption of drive to ventilator muscles, and complete EEG arousals associated with these events typically lead to insomnia.

By contrast, obstructive apnea is characterized by the occlusion of the upper airway despite continued and often accentuated diaphragmatic movements. In individuals with mixed apnea, the initial phase of the event is central, followed by a predominant obstructive pattern. The pharyngeal occlusion which characterizes obstructive apnea is caused by an imbalance of forces tending to collapse the airway (negative pharyngeal pressure) and those which dilate it (pharyngeal muscle contraction). Alterations of upper airway motor tone occur with changes in sleep state, and reductions of tone have been documented during apneic episodes. Occlusion appears to be passive, due to the lack of normal, rhythmic activation of upper airway respiratory muscles. Anatomic narrowing of the upper airway is an important predisposition to its occlusion. Activation of pharyngeal muscles follows EEG arousal and is associated with the loud, resuscitative snore (indicating opening of the airway and restoration of airflow) that characterizes obstructive apnea. Ultimately, however, it is likely that both primary and secondary dysfunction of respiratory centers are responsible for these alterations.

Although hemoglobin oxygen saturation (Sa_{O_2}) is normally well-maintained during sleep, Sa_{O_2} falls during apnea. The lower baseline Pa_{O_2} of elderly individuals makes them even more likely to desaturate hemoglobin during apnea. Such repetitive hypoxemic events may have numerous sequelae, including systemic hypertension, nocturnal cardiac arrhythmias (especially in individuals with preexisting cardiac disease), angina, stroke, and sudden death. Less often, pulmonary hypertension, cor pulmonale, left-ventricular failure, and erythrocytosis may ensue. Hypercapnia in individuals with severe disease (particularly in combination with chronic obstructive pulmonary disease) may result in morning headache. EEG arousal is associated with abnormal motor activity during sleep as the patient unknowingly struggles to open an occluded airway. Repetitive EEG arousals lead to a disproportionate increase in Stage 1 and Stage 2 NREM sleep, with major reductions in slow wave sleep. Thus, excessive daytime somnolence and unrefreshing sleep are major presenting complaints. Intellectual deterioration and personality changes are other prominent alterations attributed to combined effects of hypoxemia and sleep fragmentation. Because of the high prevalence of sleep apnea now recognized in asymptomatic elderly persons, unrecognized apnea may account for some of the changes of sleep structure previously attributed to aging in studies which did not exclude individuals with clinically unsuspected breathing disorders.

TRANSITIONS FROM HEALTH TO DISEASE

Gradations in the severity of sleep-related breathing disorders suggest that there is a transition from health to disease (Fig. 114-2). These suspicions have been supported by epidemiologic and physiologic investigations, and they are particularly important to the evaluation of elderly persons. It seems likely that subclinical, physiologic abnormalities progress to clinically recognizable stages identified by symptoms of increasing severity and/or life-threatening events. Because this course may progress insidiously through stages spanning decades, concerns about its importance in the elderly are well-founded. These are supported by recent investigations documenting sleep apnea to be a common finding in healthy elderly persons and reporting its association with common diseases of aging. Genetically determined alterations of upper airway structure and neurologic controls of breathing, and changes in these factors with increasing age, are important in the pathogenesis of sleep apnea.[46] In one study of 26 healthy men ages 55 to 70, greater than 12 sleep-disordered breathing events per hour of sleep occurred in 16.[47] These individuals were found to have reduced ventilatory responses to hypercapnia and elevated nasal airway resistance, suggesting that both anatomic abnormalities of the upper airways and altered central nervous system control of breathing had predisposed to their breathing disorders. Snoring, an upper airway occlusive event, has an important, although incompletely understood role in this transition. Lugaresi has shown that approximately 60 percent of men and 45 percent of women over the age of 60

FIGURE 114-2
It is likely that there is a dynamic evolution of breathing disorders, from normal variations of breathing within the states of sleep through transitional periods of progressively severe abnormalities until a clinically recognizable obstructive sleep apnea syndrome is present. (*Reproduced from Ref. 46.*)

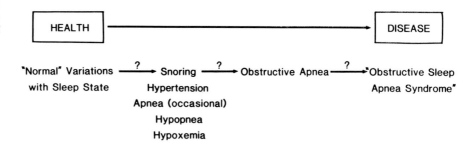

SLEEP DISORDERED BREATHING:

PROPOSED TRANSITION FROM HEALTH TO DISEASE

snore.[53,54] Snoring has been associated with systemic hypertension, coronary disease, neurophysiologic deterioration, and embolic stroke.

As noted earlier, it has not been resolved whether sleep apnea activity represents disease or is a normal concomitant of aging. As depicted in Fig. 114-3, it seems likely that there is a large population of persons who have subclinical physiologic changes which progress with age and a much smaller group who develop the sleep apnea syndrome with its full constellation of manifestations. Also noted are a clinical diagnostic threshold (when physiologic changes become manifest by recognizable functional impairment apparent to the patient and, more often, to family members) and a therapeutic threshold at which intervention is necessary.[46] The optimum points at which clinical diagnosis and intervention are either appropriate or necessary need further clarification. Resolution of this dilemma will require considerably improved understanding about the natural history of sleep apnea and, in particular, about its significance in the aged.

SLEEP APNEA AND SUDDEN NOCTURNAL DEATH

Associations of sleep apnea with cardiac arrhythmias and anecdotal reports of sudden death support clinical suspicions that sleep apnea is a lethal illness, but the extent to which sleep apnea represents a life-threatening problem in the elderly is unknown. In one major study of elderly persons evaluated for up to 12 years, the presence of greater than 10 apneic and hypopneic episodes per hour of sleep was associated with an elevated risk of death (2.7).[44] However, this relationship could not be confirmed in multivariate analysis because of the confounding effects of age. In a recent retrospective analysis, individuals with more than 20 obstructive sleep apneic events per hour of sleep were found to have a higher mortality than those with fewer episodes; surprisingly, however, patients who were 50 years old and older did not differ from younger individuals with regard to mortality.[48]

Other intriguing observations suggest that sleep-disordered breathing contributes to sudden nocturnal death. Obstructive sleep apnea is typically recognized during the fifth and sixth decades and characteristically occurs in overweight men and postmenopausal women. The relationship of sleep-disordered breathing to male gender has received considerable attention but has not been explained completely. Block found that 12 of 20 postmenopausal women had numerous sleep-disordered breathing episodes and accompanying hemoglobin oxygen desaturation, a finding that was rare in premenopausal women; postmenopausal women resembled men with regard to their breathing during sleep.[49] Responses to hypoxia and hypercapnia are reduced in the elderly, and such diminished sensitivity to these stimuli during sleep is especially prominent in men.[46,50,51] Whether or not the increased prevalence of sleep apnea in men (15–20:1) is a significant factor in the well-appreciated sex differential of mortality has not been established.[54]

Chronobiologic studies underscore the hazards of the early morning hours,[1,26,52,55,56] when the likelihood of cardiac death is particularly increased. Most deaths occur during nocturnal sleep, peaking immediately prior to morning arousal (6:00 a.m.). This timing coincides with the periods during which REM sleep occurs and during which responsiveness to a variety of physiologic stimuli is attenuated. Moreover, there is diminished accessory respiratory muscle use during these periods, a factor which may exacerbate the effects of underlying obstructive airways disease or interstitial lung disease. Disordered breathing events such as sleep apnea tend to be more prolonged, and accompanying hypoxemia (and

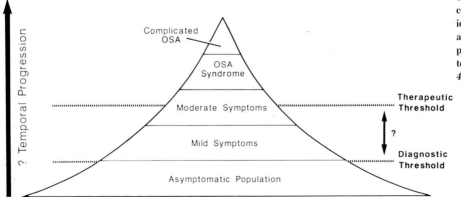

Potential Relationships of Clinical Course to Diagnosis and Treatment of Sleep Apnea

FIGURE 114-3
Sleep-disordered breathing appears to become worse with age, and the optimum diagnostic and therapeutic thresholds are continuing to evolve. The problem of identifying these thresholds is accentuated in elderly persons, who have a high prevalence of subclinical or mildly symptomatic disease. (*Reproduced from Ref. 46.*)

associated hemodynamic responses) is exaggerated, potentially predisposing the patient to sudden death.

SLEEP APNEA, DEMENTIA, AND DEPRESSION

Sleep apnea often accompanies degenerative diseases such as Alzheimer's disease, multi-infarct dementia, and depression.[47,57–59] The extent to which sleep apnea may either exacerbate these conditions and/or be caused by them is unclear. It seems likely that such interactions are important clinically, but establishing their precise relationships has been difficult. Findings derived from several recent studies are particularly interesting. Smallwood and coworkers performed sleep studies in patients without sleep complaints or medical problems other than Alzheimer's disease and found that elderly men had more frequent apneic and hypopneic episodes than either elderly women or young men.[46] However, the mean frequencies of apneas and numbers of individuals with more than five episodes of apnea per hour were no higher in the Alzheimer's patients than in age- and sex-matched controls. By contrast, Reynolds et al. found that sleep apnea (greater than five episodes per hour of sleep) occurred in 42.9 percent of patients with probable Alzheimer's disease, significantly more often than in healthy, elderly controls or in elderly patients with depression.[58] Interestingly, these authors found that there was a significant association between sleep apnea and Alzheimer's dementia in women, but not in men, and that the severity of dementia correlated with the frequency of apneic events. Yesavage et al. have correlated impaired performance on neuropsychological tests with the presence of sleep-related respiratory disorders in 41 nondemented men (mean age 69.5).[59] It has not been established whether such impairment, presumably due to "deficits in vigilance or cortical insult" from repetitive nocturnal hypoxemic events, identifies individuals who are likely to progress to more severe dementia.[59]

Hoch et al. reported that sleep apnea occurred in 41.7 percent of subjects with Alzheimer's dementia, significantly more often than in healthy controls (5.5 percent), subjects with depression (11.4 percent), and individuals with symptoms of both depression and cognitive impairment (16.7 percent). In Alzheimer's patients apnea was particularly prominent during NREM sleep, and the frequency of apneic events correlated with the severity of dementia as graded by the Blessed dementia rating scale. Erkinjuntti et al. found more than 10 disordered breathing events per hour of sleep in nearly one-half of patients with multi-infarct dementia and Alzheimer's disease, and in one-fifth of elderly controls.[57] In addition, nearly one-half of the patients with multi-infarct dementia and Alzheimer's disease had nocturnal restlessness, compared with only 10.2 percent of con-

trols. Apneas and hypopneic events occurred more often in patients with multi-infarct dementia than in those with Alzheimer's disease, and the frequency of the events varied with the severity of dementia.

CLINICAL EVALUATION OF THE PATIENT WITH SLEEP COMPLAINTS

Clinical evaluation of the elderly patient with sleep complaints requires comprehensive, firsthand assessment, and enlists the integrated efforts of all members of the health care team. As in other settings, maximizing the yield from history, physical examination, and other noninvasive sources is essential, with particular attention placed upon the identification of possible offending drugs, chronic diseases known to disrupt sleep, and clinical signs of the major primary sleep disorders (especially sleep apnea and nocturnal myoclonus).

HISTORICAL CLUES

Elements of a detailed history are summarized in Table 114-6 and should be reviewed not only with the patient,

TABLE 114-6
Evaluation of Elderly Patients with Sleep-Related Complaints

Seek historical clues
    Determine characteristics of sleep:
        Time required to fall asleep (sleep latency)
        Times of retiring and awakening
        Total sleep time
        Number and duration of nocturnal awakenings
        Quality of sleep (restorative and refreshing?)
        Level of daytime alertness (hypersomnolent?)
        Napping pattern
        Recent changes in pattern of sleep
        Previous history of sleep problems/treatment
        History of snoring, periodic breathing, abnormal motor
            activity
    Exclude potential external factors:
        Use of drugs, alcohol, caffeine
        Diets
        Levels of activity; patterns of exercise
        Presence of symptoms of dysfunction of other organ
            systems
        Evidence of inciting situational stresses
    Assess Impact of the Problem
        Duration of sleep disturbances
        Degree of functional impairment by symptoms
Perform complete physical examination
Observe patient during sleep
Obtain objective physiologic testing
    Polysomnography
    Other monitoring studies (oximetry, Holter monitoring)
    Multiple Sleep Latency Test (MSLT)

but also with all potential observers, including bed partners, family members, or, in extended-care settings, other medical personnel.[1,3] In obtaining histories from significant others, it should be appreciated that this information might be tinctured heavily by the possible disruptive effects of the patient's sleep pattern upon the lifestyle of the person helping with the history. Inquiries in these areas can be incorporated readily into a routine review of systems. A portrait of the characteristics of the patient's sleep and how it either coincides with or disrupts the patient's daily routine should be obtained. Besides the quantity and distribution of sleep, the quality of sleep is also extremely important: Does the patient feel refreshed upon awakening in the morning? In addition, the level of daytime alertness and the presence, number, and duration of awakenings from sleep must be assessed.

The history should also be directed at the numerous external factors which might disrupt sleep, since these are often more easily treatable than internal ones. The use of prescribed and nonprescribed medications, alcohol, and caffeine is particularly important; these agents are, for many, common and removable causes. In addition, the presence of cardiopulmonary or urologic symptoms might directly implicate an etiology of troubled sleep. Heavy snoring interrupted by long pauses may be diagnostic of obstructive apnea.

Because of the vulnerability of sleep to physiologic, psychological, and social problems, present alone or in combination in the aged, this aspect of the history must be underscored. Alterations of the time cues and rituals that have been familiar to the patient throughout life or altered environments due to shifts of residence commonly occur.[3] Increased napping might reflect major changes in activity, exercise tolerance, or mere boredom, rather than a result of pathologic hypersomnolence. Changes or threats to the patient's overall sense of well-being that are imposed by retirement or adjustments of sleep-wake schedules (such as the need to conform to work-shift changes, the schedules of an extended-care facility, or children's household routines) must all be sought. Because of the importance of the continuity of sleep, such factors exert major deleterious impact upon elderly patients. The clinician must appreciate the life stresses impacting upon the patient and his or her family. Alterations of support systems (for example, the death of or separation from family members or shifts to unfamiliar surroundings) often alter sleep profoundly.

In this careful appraisal, the clinician's estimate of the impact of the problem is the primary determinant of the vigor with which further evaluations are pursued. Thus, the duration of the sleep disturbance and, most importantly, the degree of functional impairment it causes are essential data. The "normal changes" of sleep in the elderly are not known to lead to perceptible functional impairment. Thus, severe sleep-related complaints must not be dismissed as being due to old age alone; they must be explained. Pathologic hypersomnolence, which interferes with daily function, is caused by the reduced quality of total sleep time and the interruption of the continuity of sleep; it is most often due to an underlying sleep disorder and/or drugs.

OBJECTIVE ASSESSMENT

A complete physical examination and, when appropriate, laboratory tests directed at particular organ systems (e.g., thyroid function studies, electrocardiogram, chest roentgenogram, pulmonary function tests) will usually help to identify conditions which secondarily disrupt sleep. The nocturnal observation of a sleeping patient is a particularly important source of information that is too often deleted or delegated. The direct observation of nocturnal wheezing, repetitive stereotypic leg movements, Cheyne-Stokes respirations, or characteristic obstructive apneic episodes may be diagnostic. In the latter instance, the brief bedside observation of periodic breathing, paradoxical thoracoabdominal movement indicative of upper airway obstruction, and apneic events terminated by loud resuscitative snoring has an extraordinarily high positive predictive value for obstructive sleep apnea.[60] Thus, merely watching the patient sleep may provide definitive information in a cost-effective manner.

When a major sleep disorder is likely to be present or when detailed history and physical examination fail to provide a definitive diagnosis, objective physiologic testing is usually needed to clarify management options. Polysomnography, the simultaneous recording of multiple physiologic parameters during sleep, is the gold standard for evaluation of sleep and its disorders.[1,2,20] During such studies performed in sleep laboratories, a limited EEG, electro-oculogram, and chin electromyogram (EMG) characterize sleep and its stages. Recordings of the leg EMG (to detect abnormal movements such as myoclonus), electrocardiogram (to detect cardiac arrhythmias), nasal and oral thermistors (to monitor airflow), thoracic and abdominal strain gauges or an esophageal balloon (to assess breathing efforts), and an ear oximeter (to noninvasively record Sa_{O_2}) are included in typical studies. These tests may be tailored further to evaluate problems applicable to a particular patient (e.g., assessments of nocturnal seizure activity, esophageal pH, or nocturnal penile tumescence). The degree of sleepiness also can be evaluated objectively by means of multiple sleep latency testing (MSLT), during which the time it takes the patient to fall asleep (i.e., the time from "lights out" until sleep is electroencephalographically confirmed) in a quiet, darkened room is measured.[2,61-63]

Such tests have shown an increased sleepiness in elderly individuals with sleep-disordered breathing, but not in aged individuals without breathing disorders.[2]

Comprehensive evaluations are available at an increasing number of multidisciplinary sleep disorder centers. More recently, the expansion of facilities at community hospitals has made the detailed evaluation of sleep accessible to most patients. There are, however, important limitations which must be recognized in the use of these facilities. The need to perform these evaluations in carefully controlled laboratory environments might hinder their applications to relatively immobile, fragile elderly patients. Pressman and Fry have reviewed practical caveats for the interpretation of sleep studies in the elderly, addressing potentially confounding methodologic problems and some of the biases in the standard scoring criteria which might underestimate the degree of sleep impairment.[3] How representative sleep in the laboratory is of that in familiar home surroundings is an especially important issue. Night-to-night and subject-to-subject variability is well recognized. The artificial laboratory environment itself disrupts sleep; because of a "first night effect," a single initial night's evaluation is often not representative of a patient's typical sleep. In one recent investigation, conclusions about the presence and severity of sleep apnea and PLM based upon a single nocturnal test were found to be often erroneous.[64] Thus, studies performed during several successive nights are preferable; in many instances complete 24- to 72-hour recordings are necessary to characterize a disorder completely. Whether or not the apnea index (the frequency of apneic events during sleep) is sufficient for diagnosis of the sleep apnea syndrome is controversial because of the common observations of apneic events in normal aging individuals. In the elderly, the widely used threshold of five apneic events per hour of sleep as a diagnostic criterion of sleep apnea neither correlates with hypersomnolence nor appears to have reliable prognostic import at present.[35] Another practical issue is posed by the high financial cost of complete sleep studies (e.g., $2000 to $3000) that may make appropriate evaluation unfeasible for elderly patients with limited economic resources. Development of streamlined, less costly tests is necessary for their optimal availability.

Although complete polysomnography remains the gold standard for comprehensive evaluation, rapid progress in computer technology has resulted in development of units suitable for reliable outpatient recording. Such portable monitoring systems have already been used successfully in evaluation of elderly persons at home and in extended-care facilities.[33] It is likely that validation of these advances will have a major impact on applications of sleep testing in the elderly, enhancing the feasibility of assessing individuals with impaired mobility in familiar surroundings. Thus, the timely, con-

venient, and cost-effective evaluation of patients with sleep complaints should become even more available to clinicians.

TREATMENT OF ELDERLY PERSONS WITH SLEEP PROBLEMS

The therapy of sleep problems in elderly individuals is necessarily conservative, with emphasis upon minimizing what is done *to* the patient. As in other settings, decisions must be predicated on careful risk-benefit assessments, with recognition that potential benefits are time-limited, that any interventions are potentially harmful, and that maintenance of the patient's functional status is the prime objective. Manipulation of the environment (and potential external causes of the problem) rather than of the patient is the preferred approach.

With these caveats in mind, the basic elements of therapy are summarized in Table 114-7. First, potential offending drugs are discontinued, which necessarily requires the critical reappraisal of the indications for which they were initially administered. When complete discontinuation of a pharmacologic agent is not feasible, selection of alternative agents less likely to disrupt sleep is necessary. In general, the physician should avoid introducing other drugs; this may be quite difficult in view of frequent patient (and family) expectations for "a prescription in hand." In the absence of proven benefits of sedative hyponotic agents in the elderly, formulating reasonable general recommendations for their use is difficult. When selected for their limited, short-term use, however, short-acting preparations should be prescribed in low dosages (e.g., triazolam 0.125–0.25 mg, temazepam 15–30 mg) and regarded as adjunctive therapy only.

Counseling the patient and establishing a number of hygienic sleep practices may lessen the perceived need for medications considerably. Some patients and families will benefit greatly just from the physician's confirmation

TABLE 114-7
Treatment of Sleep Problems in the Elderly

1. Discontinue offending drugs; avoid introducing others.
2. Establish hygienic sleep practices.
3. Treat specific primary sleep disorders.
   Nocturnal myoclonus: muscle relaxants (short-acting benzodiazepines)
   Obstructive sleep apnea: weight loss (when indicated), nasal CPAP, tracheostomy, uvulopalatopharyngoplasty
   Central sleep apnea: rocking bed, diaphragmatic pacing, oxygen
4. Treat conditions secondarily disrupting sleep.
5. Monitor therapeutic responses objectively.

that minor changes in sleep (for example, earlier morning wakening, reduction of total sleep time, increased napping), when not disruptive to the patient's usual activities, are part of normal expectations with aging. This approach not only might relieve pressures to intervene but also might result in improved sleep by reducing stress in the patient. Sleep should be attempted in a comfortable environment and on a regular schedule. Although sleep onset may be appropriate following alcohol ingestion, awakening may occur hours later and persist. A patient should avoid concerted attempts to "force" himself or herself to fall asleep; this approach will generally be unsuccessful and may lead to a form of "learned insomnia."

Kales et al. have recently reviewed the major components of a regular sleep program, with emphasis upon adjustments of activities schedules and environmental factors.[23] These include standardizing times of rising and retiring, eliminating daytime naps, increasing daytime exercise and meaningful activities, avoiding large meals before bedtime, avoiding alcohol and caffeine, and having arguments or problem solving discussions early in the day (*not* right before bedtime). Such behavioral therapy may be exceedingly effective and is best achieved through the integrated efforts of family members and other support systems, as well as through education of the patient.

When evaluation identifies primary sleep disorders as the cause of the patient's complaints, effective therapy is available. Nocturnal myoclonus may be treated with short-acting benzodiazepines with expectations of a good response. Obstructive sleep apnea is also treatable, but there are a number of unresolved controversies regarding the optimal therapy available. Whether or not intervention is necessary or appropriate in asymptomatic individuals with subclinical breathing abnormalities has not been established. Thus, for practical purposes, evaluation and treatment (other than weight loss for the patient with hypertension, for instance) should be reserved for symptomatic patients. The potential deleterious effects of available therapies for sleep apnea in elderly patients also require careful assessments of the risks and benefits of such interventions. The application of nasal continuous positive airway pressure (CPAP) is the current treatment of choice. With this safe, noninvasive approach, continuous airway pressure delivered by means of a mask during sleep effectively stents open the upper airway; the pharynx remains patent, oxygenation is well maintained, and the sequelae of hypoxemia and sleep fragmentation are avoided. This approach, well tolerated by even elderly individuals, avoids the potential morbidity of tracheostomy and upper airway surgery (uvulopalatopharyngoplasty). Tracheostomy is reserved for those patients with severe potential life-threatening sequelae of sleep apnea requiring urgent management or

in whom nasal CPAP either cannot be tolerated or is unsuccessful. While oxygen and a variety of medications have been used for treatment of mild obstructive apnea, clinical responses are quite variable and do not support a general recommendation for use. Protriptyline, a nonsedating tricyclic antidepressant useful in selected younger individuals with mild apnea, is less often helpful in elderly individuals because of its anticholinergic side effects and its cardiac arrhythmogenic potential. Patients with central sleep apnea may benefit from mechanical devices (cuirass ventilation), diaphragmatic pacing, oxygen, or respiratory stimulants.

Treatment of nocturnal angina, congestive heart failure, exacerbated obstructive airways disease, depression, and other conditions which secondarily disrupt sleep often leads to dramatic improvement in sleep. For example, sleep problems due to depression, a common problem, may respond rapidly following the initiation of a tricyclic antidepressant, and this response may be prognostically helpful. Management in such circumstances should be focused on these primary disorders, rather than on the sleep complaints themselves.

In all of these instances, responses to therapy should be monitored objectively. Effective follow-up may range from interested counseling during an office visit, to home visits by the nurse practitioner, to repeat polysomnographic documentation of the effects of treatment. The levels of intensity and technology required are adjusted readily on an individual basis according to the severity of dysfunction and the risks of therapy. In general, objective documentation of the response to therapy of the primary sleep disorders is necessary. Such serial evaluations of sleep disorders are usually both well-tolerated and informative.

CONCLUSIONS

Troubled sleep is a common problem of the elderly. Primary sleep disorders, depression, iatrogenic illness, and effects of chronic diseases and life stresses may, alone or in combination, disrupt sleep. Major epidemiologic studies will have substantial implications for practitioners as the prevalence of these conditions, their relationships to normal changes with aging, and their effects upon a patient's overall functional status become better understood. In the meantime, the systematic approach to sleep disorders can and should be incorporated within comprehensive management programs; it is too often neglected. Unprecedented technologic facilities for the objective study of sleep are currently available, and further modifications will enhance their usefulness. Careful, personal attention to the needs of each patient and the selective use of the available tools permit effective design of hygienic approaches to normal sleep and therapeutic programs for sleep disorders by the practicing geriatrician.

REFERENCES

1. Dement WC, Miles LE, Carskadon MA: "White paper" on sleep and aging. *J Am Geriatr Soc* 30:25, 1982.

1a. Bliwise DL: Normal aging, in Kryger MH, Roth T, Dement WC (eds): *Principles and Practice of Sleep Medicine.* Philadelphia, Saunders, 1989.

2. Dement WC, Richardson G, Prinz P, Carskadon MA, Kripke D, Czeisler C: Changes of sleep and wakefulness with age, in Finch CE, Schneider EL (eds): *Handbook of the Biology of Aging.* NY, Van Nostrand Reinhold, 1985.

2a. Ancoli-Israel S: Epidemiology of sleep disorders. *Clin Geriatr Med* 5:347, 1989.

3. Pressman MR, Fry JM: What is normal sleep in the elderly? *Clin Geriatr Med* 4:71, 1988.

3a. Webb WB: Age-related changes in sleep. *Clin Geriatr Med* 5:275, 1989.

4. Thornby J, Karacan I, Searle R et al: Subjective reports of sleep disturbance in a Houston metropolitan healthy survey. *Sleep Res* 6:180, 1977.

5. Gerard P, Collins K, Dore C et al: Subjective characteristics of sleep in the elderly. *Age Ageing* 7(suppl):55, 1978.

6. Karacan I, Thornby J, Anch M et al: Prevalence of sleep disturbance in a primarily urban Florida county. *Soc Sci Med* 10:239, 1976.

7. McGhie A, Russell S: The subjective assessment of normal sleep patterns. *J Ment Sci* 108:642, 1962.

8. Hoch CC, Reynolds CF, Kupfer DJ, Berman SR, Houck PR, Stack JA: Empirical note: Self-reported versus recorded sleep in healthy seniors. *Psychophysiology* 24:293, 1987.

9. Hoch CC, Reynolds CF, Kupfer DJ, Berman SR: Stability of EEG sleep and sleep quality in healthy seniors. *Sleep* 11:521, 1988.

10. Reynolds CF, Cable PA, Black RS, Holzer B, Carroll R, Kupfer DJ: Sleep disturbances in a series of elderly patients: Polysomnographic findings. *J Am Geriatr Soc* 28:164, 1980.

11. Reynolds CF III, Kupfer DJ, Taska LS, Hock CC, Sewitch DE, Spiker DG: Sleep of healthy seniors: A revisit. *Sleep* 8:30, 1985.

12. Hayashi Y, Otomo E, Endo S et al: The all-night polygraphies for healthy aged persons. *Sleep Res* 8:122, 1979.

13. Hayashi Y, Endo S: All-night sleep polygraphic recordings of healthy aged persons: REM and slow-wave sleep. *Sleep* 5:183, 1982.

14. Kales A, Wilson T, Kales JD et al: Measurements of all-night sleep in normal elderly persons: Effects of aging. *J Am Geriatr Soc* 15:405, 1967.

15. Miles LE, Dement WC: Sleep and aging. *Sleep* 3:1, 1980.

16. Prinz P, Raskind M: Aging and sleep disorders, in Williams R, Karacan I (eds): *Sleep Disorders: Diagnosis and Treatment.* New York, John Wiley and Sons, 1978, p 303.

17. Coleman RM, Miles LE, Guilleminault CC, Zarcone VP Jr, van den Hoed J, Dement WC: Sleep-wake disorders in the elderly: Polysomnographic analysis. *J Am Geriatr Soc* 29:289, 1981.

18. Baker TL: Introduction to sleep and sleep disorders, in Thawley SE (ed): *Med Clin North Am,* 69:1123, 1985.

18a. Kales A, Kales J: Sleep disorders: Recent findings in the diagnosis and treatment of disturbed sleep. *N Engl J Med* 290:487, 1974.

19. Feinberg I, Koreska R, Heller N: EEG sleep patterns as a function of normal and pathological aging in man. *J Psychiatr Res:* 5:107, 1967.

20. Feinburg I: The ontogenesis of human sleep and the relationship of sleep variables to intellectual function in the aged. *Compr Psychiatry* 9:138, 1968.

21. Allen SR, Seiler WO, Stahelin HB, Spiegel R: Seventy-two hour polygraphic and behavioral recording of wakefulness and sleep in a hospital geriatric unit: Comparison between demented and nondemented patients. *Sleep* 10:143, 1987.

22. Association of Sleep Disorders Centers: Diagnostic Classification of Sleep and Arousal Disorders, First Edition, prepared by the Sleep Disorders Classification Committee, HP Roffwarg, Chairman. *Sleep* 2:1, 1979.

23. Kales A, Soldatos CR, Kales JD: Sleep disorders: Insomnia, sleepwalking, night terrors, nightmares, and enuresis. *Ann Intern Med* 106:582, 1987.

24. Kales A, Vela-Bueno A, Kales JD: Sleep disorders: Sleep apnea and narcolepsy. *Ann Intern Med* 106:434, 1987.

25. Ekbom K: Restless legs syndrome. *Neurology* 10:868, 1960.

26. Ancoli-Israel S, Kripke DF, Mason W, Messin S: Sleep apnea and nocturnal myoclonus in a senior population. *Sleep* 4:349, 1981.

27. Ancoli-Israel S, Kripke DF, Mason W, Kaplan OJ: Sleep apnea and periodic movements in an aging sample. *J Gerontol* 40:419, 1985.

28. Kripke DF, Simons R, Garfinkel L et al: Short and long sleep and sleeping pills. *Arch Gen Psychiatry* 36:103, 1979.

28a. Roehrs TA, Roth T: Drugs, sleep disorders, and aging. *Clin Geriatr Med* 5:395, 1989.

29. Guilleminault C, Silverstri R, Mondini S, Coburn S: Aging and sleep apnea: Action of benzodiazepine, acetazolamide, alcohol, and sleep deprivation in a healthy elderly group. *J Gerontol* 39:655, 1984.

30. Smolensky MH, D'Alonzo G: Biologic rhythms and medicine. *Am J Med* 85(suppl 1B):34, 1988.

30a. Monk TH: Circadian rhythm. *Clin Geriatr Med* 5:331, 1989.

31. Guilleminault C, Tilkian A, Dement W: The sleep apnea syndromes. *Annu Rev Med* 27:465, 1976.

32. Ancoli-Israel S, Kripke DF, Mason W: Characteristics of obstructive and central sleep apnea in the elderly: An interim report. *Biol Psychiatry* 22:741, 1987.

33. Ancoli-Israel S, Kripke DF, Mason W, Messin S: Comparisons of home sleep recordings and polysomnograms in older adults with sleep disorders. *Sleep* 4:283, 1981.

34. Block AJ et al: Sleep apnea, hypopnea and oxygen desaturation in normal subjects. *N Engl J Med* 300:513, 1978.

35. Berry DTR, Phillip BA, Cook YR et al: Sleep-disordered breathing in healthy aged persons: Possible daytime sequelae. *J Geronotol* 42(6):620, 1987.

36. Bixler EO, Kales A, Cadieux RJ, Vela-Bueno A, Jacoby

JA, Soldatos CR: Sleep apneic activity in older healthy subjects. *J Appl Physiol* 58:1597, 1985.

37. Kripke DF, Ancoli-Israel S, Okudaira N: Sleep apnea and nocturnal myoclonus in the elderly. *Neurobiol Aging* 3:329, 1982.

38. Bliwise DL, Feldman DE, Bliwise NG et al: Risk factors for sleep disordered breathing in heterogeneous geriatric populations. *J Am Geriatr Soc* 35:132, 1987.

39. Carskadon MA, Dement WC: Respiration during sleep in the aged human. *J Gerontol* 36:420, 1981.

40. Hoch CC, Reynolds CF III, Kupfer DJ, Houck PR, Berman S, Stack JA: Sleep-disordered breathing in normal and pathologic aging. *J Clin Psychiatry* 47:499, 1986.

41. Kriger J, Turlot JC, Mangin P, Kurtz D: Breathing during sleep in normal young and elderly subjects: Hypopneas, apneas, and correlated factors. *Sleep* 6:108, 1983.

42. McGinty D, Littner M, Beahm E, Ruiz-Primo E, Yound E, Sowers J: Sleep-related breathing disorders in older men: A search for underlying mechanisms. *Neurobiol Aging* 3:337, 1982.

43. Naifeh KH, Severinghaus JW, Kamiya J: Effect of aging on sleep-related changes in respiratory variables. *Sleep* 10:160, 1987.

44. Smallwood RG, Vitello MV, Giblin EC, Prinz PN: Sleep apnea: Relationship of sleep apnea to age, sex, and Alzheimer's dementia. *Sleep* 6:16, 1983.

45. Bliwise DL, Bliwise NG, Partinen M, Pursley AM, Dement WC: Sleep apnea and mortality in an aged cohort. *Am J Public Health* 78:544, 1988.

46. Haponik EF, Summer WR: Obstructive sleep apnea: Current diagnostic dilemmas. *Am Rev Respir Dis* (submitted).

47. Littner M, Yound E, McGinty D, Beahm E, Riege W, Sowers J: Awake abnormalities of control of breathing and of the upper airway: Occurrence in healthy older men with nocturnal disordered breathing. *Chest* 86:573, 1984.

48. He J, Kryger MH, Zorick RJ, Conway W, Roth T: Mortality and apnea index in obstructive sleep apnea: Experience in 385 male patients. *Chest* 94:9, 1988.

49. Block AJ, Wynne JW, Boysen PG: Sleep-disordered breathing and nocturnal oxygen desaturation in postmenopausal women. *Am J Med* 69:75, 1980.

50. Kronenberg RC, Drage CW: Attenuation of the ventilatory and heart rate responses to hypoxia and hypercapnia with aging in normal men. *J Clin Invest* 52:1812, 1973.

51. Douglas NJ, White DP, Weil JV et al: Hypoxic ventilatory response decreases during sleep in normal men. *Am Rev Respir Dis* 125:286, 1982.

52. Lugaresi E, Coccagna G, Cirignotta F: Snoring and its clinical implications, in Guilleminault C, Dement W (eds): *Sleep Apnea Syndromes*. New York, Alan R. Liss, 1978.

53. Lugaresi E, Cirignotta F, Coccagna G, Piana C: Some epidemiological data on snoring and cardiocirculatory disturbances. *Sleep* 3:221, 1980.

54. Lavie P: Sleep apnea syndrome: Is it a contributing factor to the sex diffferential in mortality? *Med Hypotheses* 21:273, 1986.

55. Mitler MM, Hajdukovic RM, Shafor R, Hahn PM, Kripke DF: When people die: Cause of death versus time of death. *Am J Med* 82:266, 1987.

56. Marshall J: Diurnal variation in occurrence of strokes. *Stroke* 8:230, 1977.

57. Erkinjuntti T, Partinen M, Sulkava R, Telakivi T, Salmmi T, Tilvis R: Sleep apnea in multiinfarct dementia and Alzheimer's disease. *Sleep* 10:419, 1987.

58. Reynolds CF III, Kupfer DJ, Taska LS, Hoch CC et al: Sleep apnea in Alzheimer's dementia: Correlation with mental deterioration. *J Clin Psychiatry* 46:257, 1985.

59. Yesavage J, Bliwise D, Guilleminault C, Carskadon J, Dement W: Preliminary communication: Intellectual deficit and sleep-related respiratory disturbance in the elderly. *Sleep* 8:40, 1985.

60. Haponik EF, Smith PL, Meyers DA et al: Evaluation of sleep disordered breathing: Is polysomnography necessary? *Am J Med* 77:671, 1984.

61. Carskadon MA, Brown ED, Dement WC: Sleep fragmentation in the elderly: Relationship to daytime sleep tendency. *Neurobiol Aging* 3:321, 1982.

62. Carskadon MA, Van De Hoed JO, Dement WC: Sleep and daytime sleepiness in the elderly. *J Geriatr Psychiatry* 13:131, 1980.

63. Carskadon M: Nocturnal sleep and daytime alertness in the aged: A pilot study. *Sleep Res* 8:120, 1979.

64. Mosko SS, Dickel MJ, Ashurst J: Night-to-night variability in sleep apnea and sleep-related periodic leg movements in the elderly. *Sleep* 11:340, 1988.

Chapter 115

URINARY INCONTINENCE

Joseph G. Ouslander

Incontinence is a common, disruptive, and potentially disabling condition in the elderly. It is defined as the involuntary loss of urine in sufficient amount or frequency to be a social and/or health problem. The prevalence of urinary incontinence increases with age, is slightly higher in females, and is more common in the elderly in acute care hospitals and nursing homes than in those dwelling in the community (Fig. 115-1).[1–5] Incontinence is a very heterogeneous condition, ranging in severity from occasional episodes of dribbling small amounts of urine to continuous urinary incontinence with concomitant fecal incontinence.

Physical health, psychological well-being, social status, and the costs of health care can all be adversely affected by incontinence.[6–10] Urinary incontinence is curable in many elderly patients, especially those who have adequate mobility and mental functioning. Even when not curable, incontinence can always be managed in a manner that will keep patients comfortable, make life easier for caregivers, and minimize costs of caring for the condition and its complications. Since many elderly patients are embarrassed and frustrated by their incontinence and either deny it or do not discuss it with a health professional, it is essential for specific questions about incontinence to be included in periodic assessments and for incontinence to be noted as a problem when detected in institutional settings. This chapter briefly reviews the pathophysiology of incontinence in the elderly and provides detailed information on the evaluation and management of this condition.

NORMAL URINATION

Continence requires effective functioning of the lower urinary tract, adequate cognitive and physical functioning, motivation, and an appropriate environment (Table 115-1). Thus, the pathophysiology of incontinence in the elderly can relate to the anatomy and physiology of the lower urinary tract, as well as to functional, psychological, and environmental factors. At the most basic level, urination is governed by a reflex centered in the sacral micturition center. Afferent pathways (via somatic and autonomic nerves) carry information on bladder volume to the spinal cord as the bladder fills. Motor output is adjusted accordingly (Fig. 115-2). Thus, as the bladder fills, sympathetic tone closes the bladder neck, relaxes the dome of the bladder, and inhibits parasympathetic tone; somatic innervation maintains tone in the pelvic floor musculature (including striated muscle around the urethra). When urination occurs, sympathetic and somatic tone diminish, and parasympathetic cholinergically mediated impulses cause the bladder to contract. All these processes are under the influence of higher centers in the brain stem, cerebral cortex, and cerebel-

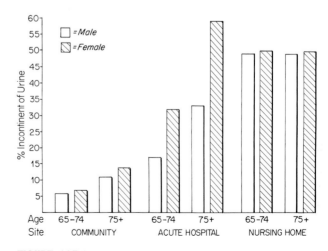

FIGURE 115-1
Prevalence of urinary incontinence by age and site. (*Reprinted with permission from Kane RL et al.*[23])

TABLE 115-1
Requirements for Continence

Effective lower urinary tract function
  Storage:
    Accommodation by bladder of increasing volumes of
      urine under low pressure
    Closed bladder outlet
    Appropriate sensation of bladder fullness
    Absence of involuntary bladder contractions
  Emptying:
    Bladder capable of contraction
    Lack of anatomic obstruction to urine flow
    Coordinated lowering of outlet resistance with bladder
      contractions
Adequate mobility and dexterity to use toilet or toilet sub-
  stitute and manage clothing
Adequate cognitive function to recognize toileting needs and
  find a toilet or toilet substitute
Motivation to be continent
Absence of environmental and iatrogenic barriers such as
  restraints and bed rails, inaccessible toilets or toilet substitutes, unavailable caregivers, or drug side effects

SOURCE: From Kane RL et al.,[23] with permission.

lum. This is a very simplified description of a very complex process, and the neurophysiology of urination remains incompletely understood.[11] It appears, however,
that the cerebral cortex exerts a predominantly inhibi-

tory influence and the brain stem facilitates urination.
Thus, loss of the central cortical inhibiting influences
over the sacral micturition center from diseases such as
dementia, stroke, and parkinsonism can produce incontinence in elderly patients. Disorders of the brain stem
and suprasacral spinal cord can interfere with the coordination of bladder contractions and lower urethral resistance, and interruptions of the sacral innervation can
cause impaired bladder contraction and problems with
continence.

Normal urination is a dynamic process, requiring
the coordination of several physiological processes. Figure 115-3 depicts a simplified schematic diagram of the
pressure–volume relationships in the lower urinary
tract, similar to measurements made in urodynamic
studies (which are discussed later in this chapter). Under
normal circumstances, as the bladder fills, pressure remains low (<15 cm H$_2$O). The first urge to void is variable, but generally occurs between 150 and 350 ml, and
normal bladder capacity is 300 to 600 ml. When normal
urination is initiated, true detrusor pressure (bladder
pressure minus intraabdominal pressure) increases until
it exceeds urethral resistance, and urine flow occurs. If
at any time during bladder filling total intravesical pressure (which includes intraabdominal pressure) exceeds
outlet resistance, urinary leakage will occur. This will
happen if, for example, intraabdominal pressure rises
without a rise in true detrusor pressure by coughing or
sneezing in someone with low outlet or urethral sphincter weakness. This would be defined as *genuine stress
incontinence* in urodynamic terminology. Alternatively,
the bladder can contract involuntarily and cause urinary
leakage. This would be defined as *detrusor motor instability*, or *detrusor hyperreflexia* in patients with neurological disorders.[12]

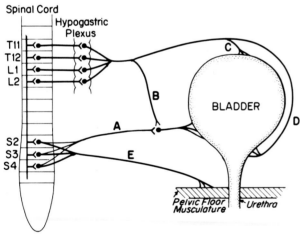

	TYPE OF NERVE	FUNCTION
A	PARASYMPATHETIC CHOLINERGIC (Nervi Erigentes)	Bladder contraction
B	SYMPATHETIC	Bladder relaxation (by inhibition of parasympathetic tone)
C	SYMPATHETIC	Bladder relaxation (β adrenergic)
D	SYMPATHETIC	Bladder neck and urethral contraction (α adrenergic)
E	SOMATIC (Pudendal nerve)	Contraction of pelvic floor musculature

FIGURE 115-2
Peripheral nerves involved in micturition. (*Reprinted with permission
from Kane RL et al.*[23])

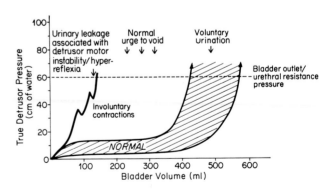

FIGURE 115-3
Simplified schematic diagram of pressure–volume relationships during bladder filling depicting the normal relationship and involuntary
contractions (detrusor motor instability or hyperreflexia). True
detrusor pressure is measured by subtracting intraabdominal pressure from total intravesical pressure, as would be done during a
multichannel cystometrogram. (*Reprinted with permission from
Kane RL et al.*[23])

CAUSES AND TYPES OF INCONTINENCE

BASIC CAUSES

There are four basic categories of causes for urinary incontinence in the elderly: urologic, neurological, psychological, and functional (including iatrogenic and environmental factors). Determining the cause or causes is essential to proper management. It is very important to distinguish between urologic and neurological disorders that cause incontinence and other problems (such as diminished mobility and/or mental function, inaccessible toilets, and psychological problems) that can cause or contribute to the condition. As is the case for a number of other common geriatric problems, multiple disorders often interact to cause urinary incontinence.

Aging alone does not cause urinary incontinence. Several age-related changes can, however, contribute to its development.[13] In general, bladder capacity declines with age, residual urine increases, and involuntary bladder contractions become more common. These contractions are found in 40 to 75 percent of elderly incontinent patients and in 10 to 20 percent of elderly people with no or minimal urinary symptoms.[14,15] Combined with impaired mobility, these contractions may account for a substantial proportion of incontinence in elderly functionally disabled patients.

Aging is also associated with a decline in bladder outlet and urethral resistance pressure in females. This decline, which is related to diminished estrogen influence and laxity of pelvic structures in females associated with prior childbirths, surgeries, and deconditioned muscles, predisposes to the development of stress incontinence. Decreased estrogen can also cause atrophic vaginitis and urethritis, which can, in turn, cause symptoms of dysuria and urgency and predispose to the development of urinary infection and urge incontinence. In men, prostatic enlargement is associated with decreased urine flow rates and detrusor motor instability and can lead to urge and/or overflow types of incontinence (see below).

ACUTE (REVERSIBLE) VERSUS PERSISTENT URINARY INCONTINENCE

The distinction between acute, reversible forms of incontinence and persistent incontinence is clinically important. Acute incontinence refers to those situations in which the incontinence is of sudden onset, usually related to an acute illness or an iatrogenic problem, and subsides once the illness or medication problem has been resolved. Persistent incontinence refers to incontinence that is unrelated to an acute illness and persists over time.

Acute Incontinence

The causes of acute and reversible forms of urinary incontinence can be remembered using the acronym DRIP (Table 115-2). Because of urinary frequency and urgency, many elderly persons, especially those limited in mobility, carefully arrange their schedules (and may even limit social activities) in order to be close to a toilet. Thus, an acute illness (e.g., pneumonia, cardiac decompensation, stroke, lower-extremity fracture) can precipitate incontinence by disrupting this delicate balance. Hospitalization, with its attendant environmental barriers (such as bed rails and poorly lit rooms), and the immobility that often accompanies acute illnesses in the elderly can contribute to acute incontinence. Acute incontinence in these situations is likely to resolve with resolution of the underlying acute illness. Unless an indwelling or external catheter is necessary to record urine output accurately, this type of incontinence should be managed by environmental manipulations, scheduled toiletings, the appropriate use of toilet substitutes and pads, and careful attention to skin care. In a substantial proportion of patients, incontinence may persist for several weeks after hospitalization and should be evaluated as for persistent incontinence (see below).[5]

Fecal impaction is a common problem in both acutely and chronically ill elderly patients. Its role in and mechanism of producing urinary incontinence are unclear. Possibilities include mechanical obstruction of the bladder outlet with overflow-type incontinence and reflex bladder contractions induced by rectal distension. Whatever the underlying mechanism, relief of a fecal impaction can lead to resolution of the urinary incontinence.

Urinary retention with overflow incontinence should be considered in any patient who suddenly develops urinary incontinence. Immobility; anticholinergic, narcotic, and beta-adrenergic drugs; and fecal impaction can all precipitate overflow incontinence in an elderly patient. In addition, this condition may be a manifestation of an underlying process causing spinal cord compression presenting acutely.

TABLE 115-2
Causes of Acute and Reversible Forms of Urinary Incontinence

D	Delirium
R	Restricted mobility, retention
I	Infection,* inflammation,* impaction (fecal)
P	Polyuria,† pharmaceuticals‡

*Acute symptomatic urinary tract infection, atrophic vaginitis/urethritis
†Hyperglycemia, volume-expanded states causing excessive nocturia (e.g., congestive heart failure, venous insufficiency)
‡See Table 115-3.
SOURCE: From Kane RL et al.,[23] with permission.

Although the relationship of bacteriuria and pyuria to the pathogenesis of incontinence is unclear (see below), any acute inflammatory condition in the lower urinary tract that causes frequency and urgency can precipitate incontinence. Thus, treatment of an acute cystitis or urethritis can help to restore continence.

Diuretics (especially the rapid-acting loop diuretics) and conditions that cause polyuria, including hyperglycemia and hypercalcemia, can precipitate acute incontinence. Patients with volume-expanded states, such as congestive heart failure and lower-extremity venous insufficiency, may have polyuria at night, which can contribute to nocturia and nocturnal incontinence. As is the case in many other conditions in geriatric patients, a wide variety of medications can play a role in the development of incontinence in elderly patients (Table 115-3). Whether the incontinence is acute or persistent, the potential role of these medications in causing or contributing to a patient's incontinence should be considered. When feasible, stopping the medication, switching to an alternative, or modifying the dosage schedule can be an important component (and possibly the only one necessary) of the treatment for incontinence.

Persistent Incontinence

The clinical definitions and common causes of persistent urinary incontinence are shown in Table 115-4. These types can overlap with each other and an individual patient may have more than one type simultaneously. While this classification is not in complete agreement

TABLE 115-3
Medications That Can Potentially Affect Continence

Type of Medication	Potential Effects on Continence
Diuretics	Polyuria, frequency, urgency
Anticholinergics	Urinary retention, overflow incontinence, impaction
Psychotropics:	
Antidepressants	Anticholinergic actions, sedation
Antipsychotics	Anticholinergic actions, sedation, rigidity, immobility
Sedatives/Hypnotics	Sedation, delirium, immobility, muscle relaxation
Narcotic analgesics	Urinary retention, fecal impaction, sedation, delirium
Alpha-adrenergic blockers	Urethral relaxation
Alpha-adrenergic agonists	Urinary retention
Beta-adrenergic agonists	Urinary retention
Calcium channel blockers	Urinary retention
Alcohol	Polyuria, frequency, urgency, sedation, delirium, immobility

SOURCE: From Kane RL et al.,[23] with permission.

with others described in the literature[16–18] and does not include all of the neurophysiologic abnormalities associated with incontinence (such as reflex incontinence), it is helpful in approaching the clinical assessment and treatment of incontinence in the elderly.

Three of these types of incontinence—stress, urge, and overflow—result from one or a combination of two basic abnormalities in lower genitourinary tract function:

1. Failure to store urine, caused by a hyperactive or poorly compliant bladder or by diminished outflow resistance
2. Failure to empty the bladder, caused by a poorly contractile bladder or by increased outflow resistance

Stress incontinence is common in elderly women, especially in ambulatory clinic settings.[19–21] It may be infrequent and involve very small amounts of urine and need no specific treatment in women who are not bothered by it. On the other hand, it may be so severe and/or bothersome that it requires surgical correction. It is most often associated with weakened supporting tissues surrounding the bladder outlet and urethra caused by lack of estrogen and/or previous vaginal deliveries or surgery. Obesity and chronic coughing can also contribute. Stress incontinence is unusual in men, but it can occur after transurethral surgery and/or radiation therapy for lower urinary tract malignancy when the anatomic sphincters are damaged.

Urge incontinence can be caused by a variety of lower genitourinary and neurological disorders (Table 115-4). It is most often, but not always, associated with detrusor motor instability or detrusor hyperreflexia (Fig. 115-3). Some patients have a poorly compliant bladder without involuntary contractions (e.g., in conditions of radiation or interstitial cystitis, both unusual in the elderly). Other patients have symptoms of urge incontinence but do not exhibit detrusor motor instability on urodynamic testing. This is sometimes termed "sensory instability" or "hypersensitive bladder"; it is likely that some of these patients do have detrusor motor instability in their everyday lives which is not documented at the time of the urodynamic study. On the other hand, there are some patients with neurological disorders who do have detrusor hyperreflexia on urodynamic testing but may not have urgency; they may instead have incontinence without any warning symptoms. Almost all of the patients described above are generally treated as if they have urge incontinence if they empty their bladders and do not have other correctable genitourinary pathology (see below). Recently, a subgroup of very elderly incontinent patients with detrusor hyperreflexia has been described who also have impaired bladder contractility, emptying less than one-third of their bladder volume

TABLE 115-4
Basic Types and Causes of Persistent Urinary Incontinence

Type	Definition	Common Causes
Stress	Involuntary loss of urine (usually small amounts) with increases in intraabdominal pressure (e.g., cough, laugh, or exercise)	Weakness and laxity of pelvic floor musculature Bladder outlet or urethral sphincter weakness

Urge	Leakage of urine (usually larger volumes) because of inability to delay voiding after sensation of bladder fullness is perceived	Detrusor motor and/or sensory instability, isolated or associated with one or more of the following:
		  Local genitourinary condition such as cystitis, urethritis, tumors, stones, diverticuli, or outflow obstruction
		  Central nervous system disorders such as stroke, dementia, parkinsonism, suprasacral spinal cord injury, or disease*

Overflow	Leakage of urine (usually small amounts) resulting from mechanical forces on an overdistended bladder or from other effects of urinary retention on bladder and sphincter function	Anatomic obstruction by prostate, stricture, cystocele Acontractile bladder associated with diabetes mellitus or spinal cord injury Neurogenic (detrusor-sphincter dyssynergy), associated with multiple sclerosis and other suprasacral spinal cord lesions
Functional	Urinary leakage associated with inability to toilet because of impairment of cognitive and/or physical functioning, psychological unwillingness, or environmental barriers	Severe dementia and other neurological disorders Psychological factors such as depression, regression, anger, and hostility

*When detrusor motor instability is associated with a neurologic disorder, it is termed "detrusor hyperreflexia" by the International Continence Society.
SOURCE: From Kane RL et al.,[23] with permission.

with involuntary contractions on urodynamic testing.[22] The implications of this urodynamic finding for the pathophysiology and treatment of incontinence in the elderly are unclear and currently under investigation.

Urinary retention with overflow incontinence can result from anatomic or neurogenic outflow obstruction, a hypotonic or acontractile bladder, or both. The most common causes include prostatic enlargement, diabetic neuropathic bladder, and urethral stricture. Low spinal cord injury and anatomic obstruction in females (caused by pelvic prolapse and urethral distortion) are less common causes of overflow incontinence. Several types of drugs can also contribute to this type of persistent incontinence (Table 115-3). Some patients with suprasacral spinal cord lesions (e.g., multiple sclerosis) develop detrusor–sphincter dyssynergy and consequent urinary retention, which must be treated in a similar manner as is overflow incontinence; in some instances a sphincterotomy is necessary.

Stress, urge, and overflow incontinence can occur in combination. Thus, a woman with stress incontinence or a man with obstruction may also have urge incontinence and detrusor motor instability or hyperreflexia. The coexistence of these disorders can have important therapeutic implications (see below).

Functional incontinence results when an elderly person is unable or unwilling to reach a toilet on time.

Distinguishing this type of incontinence from other types of persistent incontinence is critical to appropriate management. Factors that cause functional incontinence (such as inaccessible toilets and psychological disorders) can also exacerbate other types of persistent incontinence. Patients with incontinence that appears to be predominantly related to functional factors may also have abnormalities of the lower genitourinary tract, such as detrusor hyperreflexia. In some patients it can be very difficult to determine whether the functional factors or the genitourinary factors predominate without a trial of specific types of treatment.

EVALUATION

In patients with the sudden onset of incontinence (especially when associated with an acute medical condition and hospitalization), the causes of acute incontinence (Table 115-2) can be ruled out by a brief history, a physical examination, and basic laboratory studies (urinalysis, culture, serum glucose, or calcium, if indicated).

Table 115-5 shows the basic components of the evaluation of persistent urinary incontinence. Detailed descriptions of the history and physical examination can be found elsewhere.[23] The history should focus on the characteristics of the incontinence, on current medical prob-

TABLE 115-5
Basic Components of the Diagnostic Evaluation of
Persistent Urinary Incontinence

All patients:
  History
  Physical examination
  Urinalysis
  Urine culture
  Simple tests of lower urinary tract function (see Tables
  115-6 and 115-7)
Selected patients*
  Gynecologic evaluation
  Urologic evaluation
    Cystoscopy
    Voiding cystourethrography
  Urodynamic tests
    Urine flowmetry
    Cystometrogram
    Pressure flow study
    Urethral pressure profilometry
    Sphincter electromyography

*See text and Table 115-7.
SOURCE: From Kane RL et al.,[23] with permission.

lems and medications, and on the impact of the incontinence on the patient and caregivers. The incontinence should be carefully characterized in terms of onset; frequency, timing, and amount of leakage; bladder sensation; symptoms of urge versus stress incontinence; and associated genitourinary symptoms such as dysuria, hematuria, and symptoms of voiding difficulty (including hesitancy, intermittent stream, and straining to void). Although these symptoms are generally not specific for the different types of incontinence, a careful history is essential in targeting the important parts of the evaluations and treatment. This history must be taken carefully; for example, women who actually have stress incontinence may report "leaking on the way to the toilet" after they stand up, which may sound on superficial questioning like urge incontinence. Reliably reported symptoms of voiding difficulty, especially if confirmed on clinical assessment, are an indication to consider referral for further evaluation (see below). Bladder records such as those shown in Fig. 115-4 (for outpatients) and 115-5 (for institutionalized patients[24]) can be helpful in characterizing symptoms, as well as in following the response to treatment.

Physical examination should focus on abdominal, rectal, and genital examinations, as well as an evaluation of lumbosacral innervation. During the history and physical examination, special attention should be given to factors such as mobility, mental status, medications, and accessibility of toilets that may either be causing the incontinence or interacting with urologic and neurological disorders to worsen the condition.

Urinalysis and urine culture are the next steps in the evaluation of incontinence—although there is controversy about how this is best done and how the results relate to incontinence. The following considerations are important:

1. Clean urine specimens are often difficult to obtain, especially in elderly women. The risk of inducing infection by a single sterile catheterization is small, probably less than 2 percent[25]; because catheterization yields a clean bladder specimen and minimizes false-positives, and because other valuable information can be obtained with the catheter in place, it is probably worth the risk.

2. Although there is a clear relationship between acute symptomatic urinary tract infection and incontinence, the relationship between "asymptomatic" bacteriuria and incontinence is controversial. Because the prevalence of bacteriuria and incontinence roughly parallel each other in the elderly,[26] and because the bacteriuria may resolve spontaneously and does not appear to be related to symptoms (at least in patients with minimal incontinence[27]), it is difficult to make clear recommendations. In addition, recent controlled studies of treating asymptomatic bacteriuria (including patients with incontinence), especially in nursing home settings, have not favored treatment.[28–30] Although hard data are lacking, it would still seem reasonable, when evaluating persistent incontinence in an individual patient, to eradicate the bacteriuria once and observe the effect on the incontinence.

3. Catheterization, in addition to yielding a clean urine specimen, allows other information to be obtained by performing the simple tests of lower urinary tract function described below.

Most authors do not recommend that all incontinent elderly patients undergo a urologic, gynecologic, or complex urodynamic evaluation as listed in Table 115-5.[17,18,21,31,32] Complex urodynamic testing as outlined in Table 115-5, cystoscopy, and radiologic evaluations should be reserved for patients with specific indications, for whom irreversible therapy (i.e., surgical intervention) is being contemplated and for whom these evaluations will alter the treatment approach.

Several algorithms have been described which attempt to determine the appropriate treatment approach without the need for more complex evaluations and identify patients who would benefit from further evaluation.[31,33–35] Some of these strategies depend on clinical history and physical examination alone; others include bladder catheterizations or simplified urodynamic procedures. None has been tested prospectively in large enough populations of elderly incontinent patients to make definitive recommendations about the most cost-effective diagnostic strategy.

FIGURE 115-4
Example of a Bladder Record for ambulatory care settings. (*Reprinted with permission from Kane RL et al.*[23])

BLADDER RECORD

Day:_____   Date:_____/_____.
                                                    month   day

1NSTRUCTIONS:

1) In the 1st column make a mark every time during the 2—hour period you urinate into the toilet

2) Use the 2nd column to record the amount you urinate (if you are measuring amounts)

3) In the 3rd or 4th column, make a mark every time you accidentally leak urine

Time Interval	Urinated in Toilet	Amount	Leaking Accident	*or*	Large Accident	Reason for Accident *
6–8 am						
8–10 am						
2–4 pm						
4–6 pm						
6–8 pm						
8–10 pm						
10–12 pm						
Overnight						

Number of pads used today: _____

* For example, if you coughed and have a leaking accident, write "cough".
If you had a large accident after a strong urge to urinate, write "urge".

A series of simplified tests of lower urinary tract function which can be carried out in a clinic, hospital, nursing home, or even home setting can be used in conjunction with information obtained from the history and physical examination and a series of criteria for referral for further evaluation in the initial assessment of incontinent elderly patients. The tests, which are outlined in Table 115-6, are generally easy to perform and interpret after becoming experienced in a few patients with different types of incontinence. They take 15 to 20 minutes to complete and can in many patients be performed by a single examiner (although an extra pair of hands is usually helpful). The tests require less than $10 to $15 of equipment. Bladder capacity and stability, as determined by the procedure outlined in Table 115-7, have been shown to be highly correlated with results of formal multichannel cystometrograms.[32] In some settings, relatively inexpensive simple cystometric equipment and noninvasive methods of measuring urine flow rate may be available which can enhance the accuracy of the assessment. The bladder-filling procedure may not be necessary for making a reasonable treatment plan for some patients, such as women who have sterile urine, have no atrophic vaginitis, and meet none of the criteria in Table 115-7, and who, in addition, either (1) reliably give a history of leakage with stress maneuvers without irritative or obstructive voiding symptoms and completely empty their bladder (they can be treated for stress-type incontinence), or (2) reliably give a history of urge incontinence without symptoms of stress incontinence, voiding difficulty, or incomplete bladder emptying (they can be treated for urge-type incontinence).

The criteria for referral for further evaluation in Table 115-7 have in preliminary studies been shown to be reasonably sensitive but not very specific for identifying patients who require further evaluation for appropriate treatment.

Figure 115-6 summarizes the above outlined approach to the diagnostic evaluation of incontinent elderly patients.

MANAGEMENT

Several therapeutic modalities are used in managing incontinent patients (Table 115-8). Although few of them have been studied in well-controlled trials in the elderly population, they can be especially helpful if specific di-

INCONTINENCE MONITORING RECORD

INSTRUCTIONS: EACH TIME THE PATIENT IS CHECKED:
1) Mark *one* of the circles in the BLADDER section at the hour closest to the time the patient is checked.
2) Make an X in the BOWEL section if the patient has had an incontinent or normal bowel movement.

✒ = Incontinent, small amount	∅ = Dry	X = Incontinent BOWEL
● = Incontinent, large amount	△̸ = Voided correctly	X = Normal BOWEL

PATIENT NAME _____ ROOM # _____ DATE _____

	BLADDER				BOWEL			
	INCONTINENT OF URINE		DRY	VOIDED CORRECTLY	INCONTINENT X	NORMAL X	INITIALS	COMMENTS
12 am	●	●	○	△ cc ____				
1	●	●	○	△ cc ____				
2	●	●	○	△ cc ____				
3	●	●	○	△ cc ____				
4	●	●	○	△ cc ____				
5	●	●	○	△ cc ____				
6	●	●	○	△ cc ____				
7	●	●	○	△ cc ____				
8	●	●	○	△ cc ____				
9	●	●	○	△ cc ____				
10	●	●	○	△ cc ____				
11	●	●	○	△ cc ____				
12 pm	●	●	○	△ cc ____				
1	●	●	○	△ cc ____				
2	●	●	○	△ cc ____				
3	●	●	○	△ cc ____				
4	●	●	○	△ cc ____				
5	●	●	○	△ cc ____				
6	●	●	○	△ cc ____				
7	●	●	○	△ cc ____				
8	●	●	○	△ cc ____				
9	●	●	○	△ cc ____				
10	●	●	○	△ cc ____				
11	●	●	○	△ cc ____				

TOTALS:

FIGURE 115-5

Example of a record to monitor bladder and bowel function in institutional settings. This type of record is especially useful for implementing and following the results of various training procedures and other treatment protocols. (*Reprinted with permission from Regents of the University of California.*)

1130

TABLE 115-6

Procedures for Simple Tests of Lower Urinary Tract Function

Procedure	Observations	Interpretation
1. Stress maneuvers If possible, start the tests when the patient feels his or her bladder is full. Ask the patient to cough forcefully 3 times in the standing position with a small pad over the urethral area.	a. Timing (coincident or after stress) and amount (drops or larger volumes) of any leakage	Leakage of urine coincident with stress manuever confirms presence of stress incontinence.
2. Normal voiding The patient is asked to void privately in his or her normal fashion into a commode containing a measuring "hat" after a standard prep for clean urine specimen collection.	a. Signs of voiding difficulty (hesitancy, straining, intermittent stream) b. Voided volume	Signs of voiding difficulty may indicate obstruction or bladder contractility problem.
3. Post-void residual determination A 14 French straight catheter is inserted into the bladder using sterile technique within 5–10 minutes of the patient voiding.	a. Ease of catheter passage b. Post-void residual volume	If there is great difficulty passing the catheter, obstruction may be present. If the residual volume is elevated (e.g., over 100 ml) after a normal void, obstruction or a bladder contractility problem may be present.
4. Bladder filling For females, position a fracture pan under their buttocks, and for males, have a urinal available to measure any leakage during filling. A 50-ml catheter tip syringe without the piston is attached to the catheter and used as a funnel to fill the bladder. The bladder is filled with room temperature sterile water, 50 ml at a time, by holding the syringe so that it is approximately 15 cm above the pubic symphysis (bladder pressure should not normally exceed 15 cm of water during filling) until the patient feels the urge to void; then water is instilled in 25-ml increments until bladder capacity is reached (an involuntary contraction, or "I would rush to the toilet now, I can't hold anymore"). The catheter is then removed.	a. First urge to void ("I'm starting to feel a little full") b. Presence or absence of involuntary bladder contractions, detected by continuous upward movement of the fluid column (sometimes accompanied by leaking around or expulsion of the catheter) in the absence of abdominal straining, which the patient cannot inhibit c. Amount lost with involuntary contraction and subsequent bladder emptying d. Bladder capacity—amount instilled before either an involuntary contraction or the strong urge to void is perceived	Involuntary contractions or severe urgency at relatively low bladder volume (e.g., <250–300 ml) suggests urge incontinence, especially if consistent with the patient's presenting symptoms.
5. Repeat stress maneuvers The patient is asked to cough forcefully 3 times in the supine and standing positions.	a. Timing (coincident or after stress) and amount (drops or larger volumes) of any leakage	See interpretation above for stress maneuvers. Stress maneuvers with a full bladder are more sensitive for detecting stress incontinence.
6. Bladder emptying The patient is asked to empty his or her bladder again privately into the commode with the measuring "hat."	a. Signs of voiding difficulty (see above) b. Voided volume c. Calculated post-void residual (amount instilled minus amount voided)	See interpretation above for normal voiding. Calculated post-void residual may be more valid if patient did not feel full at beginning of tests.

SOURCE: From Kane RL et al.,[23] with permission.

TABLE 115-7
Criteria for Referral of Elderly Incontinent Patients for Urologic, Gynecologic, or Urodynamic Evaluation

Criteria	Definition	Rationale
History		
Recent history of lower urinary tract or pelvic surgery or irradiation	Surgery or irradiation involving the pelvic area or lower urinary tract within the past 6 months	A structural abnormality relating to the recent procedure should be sought.
Relapse or rapid recurrence of a symptomatic urinary tract infection	Onset of dysuria, new or worsened irritative voiding symptoms, fever, suprapubic or flank pain associated with growth of $>10^5$ colony forming units of a urinary pathogen; symptoms and bacteriuria return within 4 weeks of treatment	A structural abnormality or pathologic condition in the urinary tract predisposing to infection should be excluded.
Physical examination		
Marked pelvic prolapse*	Pronounced uterine descensus to or through the introitus, or a prominent cystocele that descends the entire height of the vaginal vault with coughing during speculum examination	Anatomic abnormality may underlie the pathophysiology of the incontinence and may require surgical repair.
Stress incontinence*,†	Stress incontinence demonstrated standing or supine; urine leaks, generally drops or small volumes, coincident with increasing abdominal pressure by vigorous coughing	Bladder neck suspension procedures are generally well tolerated and successful in properly selected elderly women who have stress incontinence that respond poorly to more conservative measures.
Marked prostatic enlargement and/or suspicion of cancer	Gross enlargement of the prostate on digital exam; prominent induration or asymmetry of the lobes	An evaluation to exclude prostate cancer that requires curative or palliative therapy should be undertaken.
Severe hesitancy, straining, and/or interrupted urinary stream	Straining to begin voiding and a dribbling or intermittent stream at a time the patient's bladder feels full	Signs are suggestive of obstruction or poor bladder contractility.
Post-void residual		
Difficulty passing a 14 French straight catheter	Catheter passage is impossible or requires considerable force, or a larger, more rigid catheter	Anatomic blockage of the urethra or bladder neck may be present.
Post-void residual volume >100 ml	Volume of urine remaining in the bladder within 5–10 minutes after the patient voids spontaneously in as normal a fashion as possible‡	Anatomic or neurogenic obstruction or poor bladder contractility may be present.
Urinalysis		
Hematuria	Greater than five red blood cells per high power field on microscopic exam in the absence of infection	A pathologic condition in the urinary tract should be excluded.
Uncertain diagnosis	After the history, physical exam, simple tests of lower urinary tract function, and urinalysis, none of the other referral criteria are met, and the results are not consistent with predominantly functional, urge, and/or stress incontinence	A formal urodynamic evaluation may help better define and reproduce the symptoms associated with the patient's incontinence and target treatment.

*If medical conditions precluded surgery, or if the patient is adamantly opposed to considering surgical intervention, the patient should not be referred.
†Stress incontinence that is a prominent, bothersome symptom which has not responded to nonsurgical treatment.
‡For patients who cannot void at the time of the evaluation, post-void residual can be calculated after filling the bladder (see Table 115-6).
SOURCE: From Kane RL et al.,[23] with permission.

FIGURE 115-6
Summary of assessment of geriatric urinary incontinence (see referenced tables and text for details). (*Reprinted with permission from Kane RL et al.*[23])

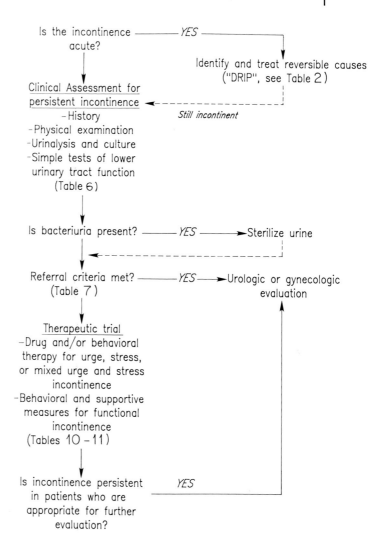

agnoses are made and attention is paid to all factors that may be contributing to the incontinence in a given patient. Even when cures are not possible, the comfort and satisfaction of both patients and caregivers can almost always be enhanced.

Special attention should be given to the management of acute forms of incontinence, which are most common in elderly patients in acute care hospitals. These forms of incontinence are often transient if managed appropriately; on the other hand, inappropriate management may lead to a permanent problem. The most common approach to elderly incontinent patients in acute hospitals is indwelling catheterization. In some instances, this practice is justified by the necessity for accurate measurement of urine output during the acute phase of an illness. In many instances, however, it is unnecessary and poses a substantial and unwarranted risk of catheter-induced infection. Although it may be more difficult and time-consuming, making toilets and toilet substitutes accessible and combining this accessibility with some form of scheduled toileting is probably a more appropriate approach in patients who do not really

require indwelling catheterization. Newer launderable or disposable and highly absorbent bed pads and undergarments may also be helpful in managing these patients. These products may be more costly than catheters, but will probably result in less morbidity (and therefore overall cost) in the long run. All of the factors that can cause or contribute to a reversible form of incontinence (Table 115-2) should be attended to in order to maximize the potential for regaining continence.

Supportive measures are critical in managing all forms of incontinence and should be used in conjunction with other, more specific treatment modalities. A positive attitude, environmental manipulations, appropriate use of toilet substitutes, avoidance of iatrogenic contributions to incontinence, modifications of diuretic and fluid intake patterns, and good skin care are all important.[36]

Specially designed incontinence undergarments and pads can be very helpful in many patients, but they must be used appropriately. They are now being marketed on television and are readily available in retail stores. Although they can be effective, several caveats should be raised:

TABLE 115-8
Treatment Options for Geriatric Urinary Incontinence

Drugs (see Table 115-10)
  Bladder relaxants
  Alpha agonists
  Estrogen
  Others
Training procedures (see Table 115-11)
  Pelvic floor exercises
  Biofeedback, behavioral training
  Bladder retraining (see Table 115-12)
  Toileting procedures
Surgery
  Bladder neck suspension
  Removal of obstruction or pathologic lesion
Mechanical/electrical devices
  Artificial sphincters
  Intravaginal electrical stimulation
  Anal electrical stimulation
Catheters (for overflow incontinence) (see Tables 115-13 and 115-14)
  Intermittent
  Indwelling
Nonspecific supportive measures
  Toilet substitutes (e.g., commodes and urinals)
  Environmental manipulations
  Modifications of drug regimens and fluid intake pattern
  External collection devices
  Incontinence undergarments and pads
  Chronic indwelling catheters

SOURCE: From Kane RL et al.,[23] with permission.

TABLE 115-9
Primary Treatments for Different Types of Geriatric Urinary Incontinence

Type of Incontinence	Primary Treatments
Stress	Pelvic floor (Kegel) exercises
	Alpha adrenergic agonists
	Estrogen
	Biofeedback, behavioral training
	Surgical bladder neck suspension
Urge	Bladder relaxants
	Estrogen (if vaginal atrophy present)
	Training procedures (e.g., biofeedback, behavioral therapy)
	Surgical removal of obstructing or other irritating pathologic lesions
Overflow	Surgical removal of obstruction
	Intermittent catheterization (if practical)
	Indwelling catheterization
Functional	Behavioral therapies (e.g., habit training, scheduled toileting)
	Environmental manipulations
	Incontinence undergarments and pads
	External collection devices
	Bladder relaxants (selected patients)*
	Indwelling catheters (selected patients)†

*Many patients with functional incontinence also have detrusor hyperreflexia and some may benefit from bladder relaxant drug therapy (see text).
† See Table 115-13.
SOURCE: From Kane RL et al.,[23] with permission.

1. Garments and pads are a nonspecific treatment. They should not be used as the first response to incontinence or before some type of diagnostic evaluation is done.
2. Many patients are curable if treated with specific therapies, and some have potentially serious factors underlying their incontinence which must be diagnosed and treated.
3. Pants and pads can interfere with attempts at certain types of behaviorally oriented therapies designed to restore a normal pattern of voiding and continence (see below).

To a large extent the optimal treatment of persistent incontinence depends upon identifying the type or types. Table 115-9 outlines the primary treatments for the basic types of persistent incontinence in the geriatric population. Each treatment modality is briefly discussed below.

DRUG TREATMENT

Table 115-10 lists the drugs used to treat various types of incontinence. The efficacy of drug treatment has not been as well studied in the elderly as it has been in younger populations,[37] but for many patients, especially those with urge or stress incontinence, drug treatment may be very effective. Drug treatment can be prescribed in conjunction with one or more of the behaviorally oriented training procedures discussed in the section that follows. There are no data on the relative efficacy of drug versus behavioral versus combination treatment in the elderly. Thus, until controlled trials are conducted, treatment decisions should be individualized and will depend in large part on the characteristics and preferences of the patient and the preferences of the health care professional.

For urge incontinence, drugs with anticholinergic and bladder smooth-muscle-relaxant properties are used. All of these drugs can have bothersome systemic anticholinergic side effects, especially dry mouth, and they can precipitate urinary retention in some patients. Men with some degree of outflow obstruction, diabetics, and patients with impaired bladder contractility[22] may be at the highest risk for developing urinary retention and should be followed carefully when these drugs are prescribed. Patients with Alzheimer's disease must be followed for the development of drug-induced delirium,

TABLE 115-10
Drugs Used to Treat Urinary Incontinence

Drugs	Dosages	Mechanisms of Action	Types of Incontinence	Potential Adverse Effects
Anticholinergic/anti-spasmodic agents:				
Oxybutynin (Ditropan)	2.5–5.0 mg tid	Increase bladder capacity	Urge or stress with detrusor instability or hyperreflexia	Dry mouth, blurry vision, elevated intraocular pressure, delirium, constipation
Propantheline (Pro-Banthine)	15–30 mg tid			
Dicyclomine (Bentyl)	10–20 mg tid	Diminish involuntary bladder contractions		
Flavoxate (Urispas)	100–200 mg tid			
Imipramine (Tofranil)	25–50 mg tid			Above effects plus postural hypotension, cardiac conduction disturbances
Alpha-adrenergic agonists:				Headache, tachycardia, elevation of blood pressure
Pseudoephedrine (Sudafed)	30–60 mg tid	Increase urethral smooth muscle contraction	Stress incontinence with sphincter weakness	
Phenylpropanol-amine (Ornade)	75 mg bid			
Imipramine (Tofranil)	25–50 mg tid			All effects listed above
Conjugated estrogens:* Oral (Premarin)	0.625 mg/day	Increase periurethral blood flow Strengthen periurethral tissues	Stress incontinence Urge incontinence associated with atrophic vaginitis	Endometrial cancer, elevated blood pressure, gallstones
Topical	0.5–1.0 g/application			
Cholinergic agonists:†				
Bethanechol (Urecholine)	10–30 mg tid	Stimulate bladder contraction	Overflow incontinence with atonic bladder	Bradycardia, hypotension, bronchoconstriction, gastric acid secretion
Alpha-adrenergic antagonist: Prazosin (Minipress)‡	1–2 mg tid	Relax smooth muscle of urethra and prostatic capsule	Overflow or urge incontinence associated with prostatic enlargement	Postural hypotension

*With prolonged use, cyclical administration with a progestational agent should be considered. Transdermal preparations are also available, but have not been studied for treating incontinence.
†The efficacy of chronic bethanechol therapy is controversial (see text).
‡May provide some symptomatic relief in patients who are unwilling or unable to undergo prostatectomy (see text).
SOURCE: From Kane RL et al.,[23] with permission.

although it is unusual. Oxybutynin, starting in half the usual recommended dose (i.e., 2.5 mg three times per day), may offer some advantage over other drugs with more pronounced systemic anticholinergic side effects[38] and does not have the potentially serious effects on blood pressure and cardiac conduction of imipramine. The latter drug has also been associated with hip fractures in the elderly,[39] possibly due to the side effect of postural hypotension. Calcium channel blockers have been used for urge incontinence in Europe, but none have been studied or are approved for this indication as yet in the United States. Several studies suggest that cognitive and physical functional impairment are associated with poor responses to bladder relaxant drug therapy.[40–43] The results of these studies should not, however, preclude a treatment trial in this patient population. Some patients may respond, especially in conjunction with scheduled toileting or prompted voiding (see below). The goal of treatment in these patients may not be to cure the incontinence, but to reduce its severity and prevent discomfort and complications.

For stress incontinence, drug treatment involves a combination of an alpha-agonist and estrogen. Drug treatment is appropriate for motivated patients who (1) have mild to moderate degrees of stress incontinence, (2) do not have a major anatomic abnormality (e.g., large cystocele), and (3) do not have any contraindications to these drugs. These patients may also respond to behavioral treatments (see below), and preliminary data suggest the two treatment modalities are roughly equivalent, with about three-fourths of patients reporting improvement[44]; a combination would also be a reasonable approach for some patients. Estrogen alone is not as effective as in combination with an alpha-agonist for stress incontinence. If either oral or vaginal estrogen is used for a prolonged period of time (more than a few months), cyclic administration and the addition of a progestational agent should be considered.[45] Estrogen is also used, either chronically or on an intermittent basis (i.e., one- to two-month courses), for the treatment of irritative voiding symptoms and urge incontinence in women with atrophic vaginitis and urethritis.

Drug treatment for chronic overflow incontinence using a cholinergic agonist or an alpha-adrenergic antagonist is usually not highly efficacious. Bethanechol may be helpful when given for a brief period subcutaneously in patients with persistent bladder contractility problems after an overdistention injury, but the drug is generally not effective when given orally and long term.[46] Alpha-adrenergic blockers may be helpful in relieving symptoms associated with outflow obstruction in some patients, but they are probably not efficacious for long-term treatment of overflow incontinence in the elderly.[47]

Many elderly women have symptomatically and urodynamically a combination of both urge and stress incontinence. A combination of estrogen and imipramine would, at least in theory, be appropriate for these patients, because imipramine has both anticholinergic and alpha-adrenergic effects. If urge incontinence is the predominant symptom, a combination of estrogen and oxybutynin would be appropriate. Behavioral training procedures are also a reasonable approach for women with mixed incontinence (see below).

BEHAVIORALLY ORIENTED TRAINING PROCEDURES

Many types of behavioral training procedures have been described for the management of urinary incontinence.[48,49] The nosology of these procedures has been somewhat confusing, and much of the literature has used the term *bladder training* to encompass a wide variety of techniques. It is very important to distinguish between procedures that are patient-dependent (i.e., require adequate function and motivation of the patient), in which the goal is to restore a normal pattern of voiding and continence, and procedures that are caregiver-dependent and can be used for functionally disabled patients, in which the goal is to keep the patient and the environment dry. Six of these procedures are discussed below according to the techniques used, the types of incontinence they are used for, and the characteristics of the patients for whom the techniques are most useful. This information is summarized in Table 115-11. All of the patient-dependent procedures generally involve the patient's continuous, self-monitoring use of a record such as the one depicted in Fig. 115-4, and the caregiver-dependent procedures usually involve a record such as the one in Fig. 115-5.

Pelvic floor (Kegel) exercises are used to treat stress incontinence in women and are also used occasionally in men. These exercises consist of repetitive contractions of the pelvic floor muscles. This procedure is taught by having the patient interrupt voiding to get a sense of the muscles being used or by having a woman patient squeeze the examiner's fingers during a vaginal exam (without doing a Valsalva maneuver, which is opposite of the intended effect). Once learned, the exercises should be practiced many times throughout the day, both during voiding and at other times. Pelvic floor exercises may be done in conjunction with biofeedback procedures and can be especially helpful for women who bear down (increasing intraabdominal pressure) when attempting to contract pelvic floor muscles.

Biofeedback procedures involve the use of bladder, rectal, or vaginal pressure or electrical activity recordings to train patients to contract pelvic floor muscles and relax the bladder. Studies have shown that these techniques can be very effective for managing both stress and urge incontinence, even in the elderly.[50] The use of biofeedback techniques may be limited by their requirements for equipment and trained personnel; in addition, some of these techniques are relatively invasive and require the use of bladder or rectal catheters, or both. Electrical stimulation, introduced either vaginally or rectally, has also been used to help train muscles in the management of both stress and urge incontinence. Electrical stimulation techniques are not acceptable to many patients and have been not well-studied or used to any great degree in the elderly in this country.

Other forms of patient-dependent training procedures include behavioral training and bladder retraining. Behavioral training involves the educational components taught during biofeedback, without the use of biofeedback equipment. Patients are taught pelvic floor

TABLE 115-11
Examples of Behaviorally Oriented Training Procedures for Urinary Incontinence

Procedure	Definition	Types of Incontinence	Comments
Patient-dependent:			
Pelvic floor (Kegel) exercises	Repetitive contraction of pelvic floor muscles	Stress	Requires adequate function and motivation May be done in conjunction with biofeedback
Biofeedback	Use of bladder, rectal, or vaginal pressure recordings to train patients to contract pelvic floor muscles and relax bladder	Stress and urge	Requires equipment and trained personnel Relatively invasive Requires adequate cognitive and physical function and motivation
Behavioral training	Use of educational components of biofeedback, bladder records, pelvic floor and other behavioral exercises	Stress and urge	Requires trained therapist, adequate cognitive and physical functioning, and motivation
Bladder retraining*	Progressive lengthening or shortening of intervoiding interval, with adjunctive techniques,† intermittent catheterization used in patients recovering from overdistension injuries with persistent retention	Acute (e.g., postcatheterization with urge or overflow, poststroke)	Goal is to restore normal pattern of voiding and continence Requires adequate cognitive and physical function and motivation
Caregiver dependent:			
Scheduled toileting/prompted voiding	Fixed toileting schedule with prompted voiding; adjunctive techniques may also be used	Urge and functional	Goal is to prevent wetting episodes Can be used in patients with impaired cognitive or physical functioning Requires staff/caregiver availability and motivation
Habit training	Variable toileting schedule with positive reinforcement and adjunctive techniques†	Urge and functional	Goal is to prevent wetting episodes Can be used in patients with impaired cognitive or physical functioning Requires staff/caregiver availability and motivation

*See Table 115-12.
†Techniques to trigger voiding (running water, stroking thigh, suprapubic tapping), completely empty bladder (bending forward, suprapubic pressure), and alterations of fluid or diuretic intake patterns.
SOURCE: From Kane RL et al.,[23] with permission.

exercises and strategies to manage urgency and are taught to use bladder records regularly. There is some evidence that these techniques are as effective as biofeedback in a selected group of functional, motivated elderly patients.[51] Bladder retraining as described here is similar to "bladder drill," which as been used successfully to treat urge incontinence in young women. An example of a bladder-retraining protocol is shown in Table 115-12. This protocol is also applicable to patients who have had an indwelling catheter for monitoring of urinary output during a period of acute illness or for treatment of urinary retention with overflow incontinence. Such catheters should always be removed as soon as possible, and this type of bladder-retraining protocol should enable most indwelling catheters to be removed from patients in acute care hospitals as well as some in

TABLE 115-12
Example of a Bladder Retraining Protocol

Objective: To restore a normal pattern of voiding and continence after the removal of an indwelling catheter.*

1. Remove the indwelling catheter (clamping the catheter before removal is not necessary).
2. Treat urinary tract infection if present.†
3. Initiate a toileting schedule. Begin by toileting the patient:
   a. upon awakening
   b. every 2 hours during the day and evening
   c. before getting into bed
   d. every 4 hours at night
4. Monitor the patient's voiding and continence pattern with a record‡ that allows for the recording of:
   a. Frequency, timing, and amount of continent voids
   b. Frequency, timing, and amount of incontinence episodes
   c. Fluid intake pattern
   d. Post-void or intermittent catheter volume
5. If the patient is having difficulty voiding (complete urinary retention or very low urine outputs, e.g., <240 cc in an 8-hour period while fluid intake is adequate):
   a. Perform in and out catheterization, recording volume obtained, every 6 to 8 hours until residual values are <100 cc§
   b. Instruct the patient on techniques to trigger voiding (e.g., running water, stroking inner thigh, suprapubic tapping) and to help completely empty bladder (e.g., bending forward, suprapubic pressure, double voiding)
6. If the patient is voiding frequently (i.e., more often than every 2 hours):
   a. Perform post-void residual determination to ensure the patient is completely emptying the bladder
   b. Encourage the patient to delay voiding as long as possible and instruct him to use techniques to help completely empty bladder (above)
7. If the patient continues to have frequency and nocturia, with or without urgency and incontinence, in the absence of infection:
   a. Rule out other reversible causes (e.g., medication effects, hyperglycemia, congestive heart failure)
   b. Consider urologic referral to rule out bladder instability (unstable bladder, detrusor hyperreflexia)

---

*Indwelling catheters should be removed from all patients who do not have an indication for their acute or chronic use (see text and Table 115-13). Clamping routines have never been shown to be helpful and are not appropriate for patients who have had overdistended bladders.
†Significant bacteriuria with pyuria (>10 white blood cells per high power field on a spun specimen).
‡See Fig. 115-5.
§In patients who have been in urinary retention, it may take days or weeks for the bladder to regain normal function. If residuals remain high, urologic consultation should be considered before committing the patient to a chronic indwelling catheter.
SOURCE: From Kane RL et al.,[23] with permission.

long-term care settings. A patient who continues to have difficulty voiding after 1 to 2 weeks of such a bladder-retraining protocol should be examined for other potentially reversible causes of voiding difficulties, such as those mentioned in the section above on acute incontinence. When difficulties persist, a urologic referral should be considered in order to rule out correctable lower-genitourinary pathology.

The goal of caregiver-dependent procedures such as habit training and scheduled toileting is to prevent incontinence episodes, rather than restore normal pattern of voiding and complete continence. Such procedures have also been referred to as "habit retraining," "prompted voiding," and "contingency management techniques." In its simplest form, scheduled toileting or prompted voiding involves putting the patient on the toilet at regular intervals, usually every 2 hours during the day and every 4 hours during the evening and night. Habit training involves a schedule of toiletings or prompted voidings that is modified according to the patient's pattern of continent voids and incontinence episodes, as demonstrated by a monitoring record such as that shown in Fig. 115-5. Positive reinforcement is offered for continent voids, and neutral reinforcement employed when incontinence occurs. Adjunctive techniques to prompt voiding (e.g., running of tap water, stroking of the inner thigh, or suprapubic tapping) and to help empty the bladder completely (e.g., bending forward after completion of voiding) may be helpful in some patients. The success of habit training and scheduled toileting procedures is largely dependent on the knowledge and motivation of the caregivers who are implementing them, rather than on the physical functional and mental status of the incontinent patient. These techniques may not be feasible in home settings without available caregivers. In order for these types of training procedures to be feasible and cost-effective in the nursing home setting, the amount of time generally spent by the nursing staff in changing patients after incontinence episodes should not be exceeded by the time and effort necessary to implement such training procedures.[52] Targeting these procedures to selected patients, such as those with less frequent voiding and larger bladder capacities or voided volumes, may enhance their cost-effectiveness.[53]

SURGERY

Surgery should be considered for elderly women with stress incontinence that continues to be bothersome after attempts at nonsurgical treatment and for women with a significant degree of pelvic prolapse. As with many other surgical procedures, patient selection and the experience of the surgeon are critical to success. Any woman being considered for surgical therapy should have a thorough evaluation, including urodynamic tests, by an experienced surgeon before undergoing the procedure. Women with mixed stress incontinence and detrusor motor instability may also benefit from surgery,[54] especially if the clinical history and urodynamic findings suggest that stress incontinence is the predominant problem. In some patients this may be difficult to determine, and a trial of medical therapy as discussed above would be appropriate. Newly modified techniques of bladder neck suspension can be done with minimal risks and are highly successful in achieving continence.[55] Urinary retention can occur after surgery, but it is usually transient and can be managed by intermittent catheterization.

Surgery may be indicated in men in whom incontinence is associated with anatomically and/or urodynamically documented outflow obstruction. Men who have experienced an episode of complete urinary retention are likely to have another episode within a short period of time and should have a prostatic resection, as should men with incontinence associated with enough residual urine to be causing recurrent symptomatic infections or hydronephrosis. The decision about surgery in men who do not meet these criteria must be an individual one, weighing carefully the degree to which the symptoms bother the patient, the potential benefits of surgery (obstructive symptoms often respond better than irritative symptoms), and the risks of surgery (which may be minimal with newer prostate resection techniques). Several recent articles discuss these issues in detail,[56–58] and a Veterans Administration Cooperative Study involving a randomized trial of surgical versus medical follow-up for men with moderately symptomatic prostatic hyperplasia is currently underway.

A small number of elderly patients, especially men who have stress incontinence related to sphincter damage due to previous transurethral surgery, may benefit from the surgical implantation of an artificial urinary sphincter.

CATHETERS AND CATHETER CARE

Three basic types of catheters and catheterization procedures are used for the management of urinary incontinence: external catheters, intermittent straight catheterization, and chronic indwelling catheterization. External catheters generally consist of some type of condom connected to a drainage system. Improvements in design and observance of proper procedure and skin care when applying the catheter will decrease the risk of skin irritation, as well as the frequency with which the catheter falls off. Studies of complications associated with the use of these devices have been limited. Existing data suggest that patients with external catheters are at increased risk

of developing symptomatic infection.[59] External catheters should only be used to manage intractable incontinence in male patients who do not have urinary retention and who are extremely physically dependent. As with incontinence undergarments and padding, these devices should not be used as a matter of convenience, since they may foster dependency. Contrary to popular belief, urine specimens can be collected from male patients with external catheters that accurately reflect bladder urine by simply cleaning the penis with povidone-iodine (Betadine), applying a new catheter, and collecting the first urine the patient voids.[60] Using this simple technique will avoid false-positive cultures and the discomfort of straight catheterization in patients suspected of having an infection. An external catheter for use in female patients is now commercially available, but its safety and effectiveness have not been well documented in the elderly.

Intermittent catheterization can help in the management of patients with urinary retention and overflow incontinence. The procedure can be carried out by either the patient or a caregiver and involves straight catheterization two to four times daily, depending on residual urine volumes. In the home setting, the catheter should be kept clean (but not necessarily sterile). Studies conducted largely among younger paraplegics have shown that this technique is practical and reduces the risk of symptomatic infection as compared with the risk associated with chronic catheterization. Self-intermittent catheterization has also been shown to be feasible for elderly female outpatients who are functional and willing and able to catheterize themselves.[61] However, studies carried out in young paraplegics and elderly female outpatients cannot automatically be extrapolated to an elderly male or institutionalized population. The technique may be useful for certain patients in acute care hospitals or nursing homes, such as women who have undergone bladder neck suspension; it may also be useful following removal of an indwelling catheter in a bladder-retraining protocol (Table 115-12). However, the practicality and safety of this procedure in a long-term care setting have never been documented. Elderly nursing home patients, especially men, may be difficult to catheterize, and the anatomic abnormalities commonly found in elderly patients' lower urinary tracts may increase the risk of infection due to repeated straight catheterizations. In addition, using this technique in an institutional setting (which may have an abundance of organisms relatively resistant to many commonly used antimicrobial agents) may yield an unacceptable risk of nosocomial infections, and using sterile catheter trays for these procedures would be very expensive; thus it may be extremely difficult to implement such a program in a typical nursing home setting.

TABLE 115-13
Indications for Chronic Indwelling Catheter Use

Urinary retention that:
   Is causing persistent overflow incontinence, symptomatic infections, or renal dysfunction
   Cannot be corrected surgically or medically
   Cannot be managed practically with intermittent catheterization
Skin wounds, pressure sores, or irritations that are being contaminated by incontinent urine
Care of terminally ill or severely impaired for whom bed and clothing changes are uncomfortable or disruptive
Preference of patient or caregiver when patient has failed to respond to more specific treatments

SOURCE: From Kane RL et al.,[23] with permission.

TABLE 115-14
Key Principles of Chronic Indwelling Catheter Care

Maintain sterile, closed, gravity drainage system.

Avoid breaking the closed system.

Use clean techniques in emptying and changing the drainage system; wash hands between patients in institutionalized setting.

Secure the catheter to the upper thigh or lower abdomen to avoid perineal contamination and urethral irritation due to movement of the catheter.

Avoid frequent and vigorous cleaning of the catheter entry site; washing with soapy water once per day is sufficient.

Do not routinely irrigate.

If bypassing occurs in the absence of obstruction, consider the possibility of a bladder spasm, which can be treated with a bladder relaxant.

If catheter obstruction occurs frequently, increase the patient's fluid intake and acidify the urine if possible.

Do not routinely use prophylactic or suppressive urinary antiseptics or antimicrobials.

Do not do routine surveillance cultures to guide management of individual patients because all chronically catheterized patients have bacteriuria (which is often polymicrobial) and the organisms change frequently.

Do not treat infection unless the patient develops symptoms; symptoms may be nonspecific and other possible sources of infection should be carefully excluded before attributing symptoms to the urinary tract.

If a patient develops frequent symptomatic urinary tract infections, a genitourinary evaluation should be considered to rule out pathology such as stones, periurethral or prostatic abscesses or chronic pyelonephritis.

SOURCE: From Kane RL et al.,[23] with permission.

Chronic indwelling catheterization is overused in some settings, and when used for periods of up to 10 years has been shown to increase the incidence of a number of other complications, including chronic bacteriuria, bladder stones, periurethral abscesses, and even bladder cancer. Elderly nursing home patients managed by this technique, especially men, are at relatively high risk of developing symptomatic infections.[62,63] Given these risks, it seems appropriate to recommend that the use of chronic indwelling catheters be limited to certain specific situations (Table 115-13). When indwelling catheterization is used, certain principles of catheter care should be observed in order to attempt to minimize complications (Table 115-14).

REFERENCES

1. Mohide EA: The prevalence and scope of urinary incontinence. *Clin Geriatr Med* 2:639, 1986.
2. Harris T: Aging in the eighties: Prevalence and impact of urinary problems in individuals age 65 years and over. National Center for Health Statistics, Advance Data No. 121, 1986.
3. Diokno AC, Brock BM, Brown MB, Herzog AR: Prevalence of urinary incontinence and other urological symptoms in the non-institutionalized elderly. *J Urol* 136:1022, 1986.
4. Ouslander JG, Kane RL, Abrass IB: Urinary incontinence in elderly nursing home patients. *JAMA* 248:1194, 1982.
5. Sier H, Ouslander JG, Orzeck S: Urinary incontinence among geriatric patients in an acute care hospital. *JAMA* 257:1767, 1987.
6. Ory MG, Wyman JF, Yu L: Psychosocial factors in urinary incontinence. *Clin Geriatr Med* 2:657, 1986.
7. Wyman JF, Harkins SW, Choi SC, Taylor JR, Fantl JA: Psychosocial impact of urinary incontinence in women. *Obstet Gynecol* 70(3):378, 1987.
8. Gartley C: *Managing Incontinence: A Guide to Living with the Loss of Bladder Control.* Ottowa, Illinois, Jameson Books, 1985.
9. Hu TW: The economic impact of urinary incontinence. *Clin Geriatr Med* 2:673, 1986.
10. Ouslander JG, Kane RL: The costs of urinary incontinence in nursing homes. *Med Care* 22:69, 1984.
11. Wein AJ: Lower urinary tract function and pharmacologic management of lower urinary tract dysfunction. *Urol Clin North Am* 14:273, 1987.
12. Abramsi P, Blaivas JG, Stanton SL, Anderson, JT: Standardization of terminology of lower urinary tract function. *Neurourology and Urodynamics* 7:403, 1988.
13. Ouslander JG, Bruskewitz RC: Micturition in the aging patient, in Stollerman GH (ed): *Advances in Internal Medicine*, Vol. 34. Chicago, Year Book, pp 165–190, 1989.
14. Leach GE, Yip CM: Urologic and urodynamic evaluation of the elderly population. *Clin Geriatr Med* 2:731, 1986.
15. Staskin DR: Age-related physiologic and pathologic

changes affecting lower urinary tract function. *Clin Geriatr Med* 2:701, 1986.

16. Wein AJ: Classification of neurogenic voiding dysfunction. *J Urol* 125:605, 1981.

17. Williams ME, Pannill PC: Urinary incontinence in the elderly. *Ann Intern Med* 97:895, 1982.

18. Resnick NM, Yalla SV: Management of urinary incontinence in the elderly. *N Engl J Med* 313:800, 1985.

19. Ouslander JG, Raz S, Hepps K, Su HL: Genitourinary dysfunction in a geriatric outpatient population. *J Am Geriatr Soc* 34:507, 1986.

20. Wells TJ, Brink CA, Diokno A et al: Urinary incontinence in elderly women: Clinical findings. *J Am Geriatr Soc* 35:933, 1987.

21. Diokno AC, Wells TJ, Brink CA: Urinary incontinence in elderly women: Urodynamic evaluation. *J Am Geriatr Soc* 35:940, 1987.

22. Resnick NM, Yalla SV: Detrusor hyperactivity with contractile function: An unrecognized but common cause of incontinence in elderly patients. *JAMA* 257:3076, 1987.

23. Kane RL, Ouslander JG, Abrass IB: *Essentials of Clinical Geriatrics*, 2d ed. New York, McGraw-Hill, 1989.

24. Ouslander JG, Uman GC, Urman HN: Development and testing of an incontinence monitoring record. *J Am Geriatr Soc* 34:83, 1986.

25. Kunin CM: *Detection, Prevention and Management of Urinary Tract Infections*. Philadelphia, Lea and Febiger, 1987.

26. Boscia JA, Kobasa WD, Knight RA, Abrutyn E, Levison ME, Kaye D: Epidemiology of bacteriuria in an elderly ambulatory population. *Am J Med* 80:208, 1986.

27. Boscia JA, Kobasa WD, Levison ME, Kaplan JE, Kaye D: Lack of association between bacteriuria and symptoms in the elderly. *Am J Med* 81:979, 1986.

28. Boscia JA, Kobasa WD, Knight RA, Abrutyn E, Levison ME, Kaye D: Therapy vs. no therapy for bacteriuria in elderly ambulatory nonhospitalized women. *JAMA* 257:1067, 1987.

29. Nicolle LE, Bjornson J, Harding GMK et al: Bacteriuria in elderly institutionalized men. *N Engl J Med* 309:1420, 1983.

30. Nicolle LE, Mayhew JW, Bryan L et al: Prospective randomized comparison of therapy and no therapy for asymptomatic bacteriuria in institutionalized elderly women. *JAMA* 83:27, 1987.

31. Abrams P, Fenely R, Torrens M: *Urodynamic*. New York, Springer-Verlag, 1983.

32. Ouslander JG, Leach G, Abelson S, Staskin D, Blaustein J, Raz S: Simple vs. multichannel cystometry in the evaluation of bladder function in an incontinent geriatric population. *J Urol* 140:1482, 1988.

33. Hilton P, Staton SL: Algorithmic method for assessing urinary incontinence in elderly women. *Br Med J* 282:940, 1981.

34. Resnick NM, Yalla SV, Laurino E: An algorithmic approach to urinary incontinence in the elderly. *Clin Res* 34:832A, 1986.

35. Ouslander JG: Diagnostic evaluation of geriatric urinary incontinence. *Clin Geriatr Med* 2:715, 1986.

36. Brink CA, Wells TJ: Environmental support for geriatric incontinence: Toilets, toilet supplements and external equipment. *Clin Geriatr Med* 2:829, 1986.

37. Ouslander JG, Sier HC: Drug therapy for geriatric incontinence. *Clin Geriatr Med* 2:789, 1986.

38. Ouslander JG, Blaustein J, Connor A, Yong C: Pharmacokinetics and clinical effects of oxybutynin in geriatric patients. *J Urol* 140:47, 1988.

39. Ray WA, Griffin MR, Schaffner W et al: Psychotropic drug use and the risk of hip fracture. *N Engl J Med* 316:363, 1987.

40. Castleden CM, Duffin HM, Ashner MJ, Yeomason CW: Factors influencing outcome in elderly patients with urinary incontinence and detrusor instability. *Age Ageing* 14:303, 1985.

41. Zorzitto ML, Jewett MAS, Fernie GR, Holliday RJ, Bartlett S: Effectiveness of propantheline bromide in the treatment of geriatric patients with detrusor instability. *Neurourology and Urodynamics* 5:133, 1986.

42. Tobin GW, Brocklehurst JC: The management of urinary incontinence in local authority residential homes for the elderly. *Age Ageing* 15:292, 1986.

43. Ouslander JG, Blaustein J, Connor A, Pitt A: Habit training and oxybutynin for incontinence in nursing home patients. *J Am Geriatr Soc* 36:40, 1988.

44. Wells T, Brink C, Diokno A, Gillis G: Pelvic muscle exercise for stress urinary incontinence in elderly women. *Gerontologist* (special issue):244A, 1987.

45. Lufkin EG, Carpenter PC, Ory SJ, Malkasian GD, Edmonson JH: Estrogen replacement therapy: Current recommendations. *Mayo Clin Proc* 63:453, 1988.

46. Finkbeiner AE: Is bethanechol chloride clinically effective in promoting bladder emptying? A literature review. *J Urol* 134:443, 1985.

47. Caine M: The present role of alpha-adrenergic blockers in the treatment of benign prostatic hypertrophy. *J Urol* 136:1, 1986.

48. Burgio KL, Burgio LD: Behavior therapies for urinary incontinence in the elderly. *Clin Geriatr Med* 2:809, 1986.

49. Hadley E: Bladder training and related therapies for urinary incontinence in older people. *JAMA* 256(3):372, 1986.

50. Burgio KL, Whitehead WE, Engel BT: Urinary incontinence in elderly—bladder-sphincter biofeedback and toilet skills training. *Ann Intern Med* 104:507, 1985.

51. Burton JR, Pearch KL, Burgio KL, Engle BT, Whitehead WE: Behavioral training for urinary incontinence in elderly patients. *J Am Geriatr Soc* 36:693, 1988.

52. McCormick KA, Scheve AAS, Leahy E: Nursing management of urinary incontinence in geriatric inpatients. *Nurs Clin North Am* 23(1):231, 1988.

53. Schnelle JF, Sowell VA, Hu TW, Traughber B: Reduction of urinary incontinence in nursing homes: Does it reduce or increase costs? *J Am Geriatr Soc* 36:34, 1988.

54. McGuire EJ, Savastano JA: Stress incontinence and detrusor instability/urge incontinence. *Neurourology and Urodynamics* 4:313, 1985.

55. Schmidbauer CP, Chiang H, Raz S: Surgical treatment for female geriatric incontinence. *Clin Geriatr Med* 2:759, 1986.

56. Barry MJ, Mulley AG, Fowler FJ, Wennberg JW: Watchful waiting vs. immediate transurethral resection for symptomatic prostatism. *JAMA* 259:3010, 1988.

57. Fowler FJ, Wennberg JE, Timothy RP, Barry MJ, Mul-

ley AG, Hanley D: Symptom status and quality of life following prostatectomy. *JAMA* 259:3018, 1988.

58. Wennberg JE, Mulley AG, Hanley D, Timothy RP et al: An assessment of prostatectomy for benign urinary tract obstruction. *JAMA* 259(20):3027, 1988.

59. Ouslander JG, Greengold BA, Chen S: External catheter use and urinary tract infections among male nursing home patients. *J Am Geriatr Soc* 35:1063, 1987.

60. Ouslander JG, Greengold BA, Silverblatt FJ, Garcia JP: An accurate method to obtain urine for culture in men with external catheters. *Arch Intern Med* 147:286, 1987.

61. Bennett CJ, Diokno AC: Clean intermittent self-catheterization in the elderly. *Urology* 24:43, 1984.

62. Ouslander JG, Greengold BA, Chen S: Complications of chronic indwelling urinary catheters among male nursing home patients: A prospective study. *J Urol* 138:1191, 1987.

63. Warren JW, Damron D, Tenney JH, Hoopes JM, Deforge B, Muncie HL: Fever, bacteremia, and death as complications of bacteriuria in women and long-term urethral catheters. *J Infect Dis* 155(6):1151, 1987.

Chapter 116

FECAL INCONTINENCE

Lawrence J. Cheskin and Marvin M. Schuster

Incontinence is the inability to consistently maintain voluntary control of the act of defecation. Fecal and urinary incontinence together constitute the second most common reason for institutionalizing elderly persons. In economic terms, over $400 million is spent each year in the United States on adult diapers. Compared to urinary incontinence, with which it often coexists, fecal incontinence is a greater social stigma in this country and makes greater demands on the patient and/or the caregivers of the patient who is so handicapped. A 1977 national survey found that 35 percent of nursing home residents had difficulty controlling either their bowels or both their bladders and their bowels. Among nursing home residents who are constipated, 55 percent are also incontinent of stool. Fecal incontinence is reported to occur in 10 to 25 percent of hospitalized elderly patients. The true prevalence among noninstitutionalized elderly is difficult to assess, because of both patient under-reporting and discrepancies in whether minor or occasional soiling is reported as incontinence.

With regard to the patient with only rare episodes of incontinence, it is important to recognize that even the individual with normal anorectal function can become incontinent temporarily when the normal mechanisms which maintain continence are overwhelmed. This may occur, for example, with massive diarrhea. When stool of normal consistency cannot be controlled, this is defined as major incontinence. Minor incontinence is defined as incontinence for diarrheal stool or rare soiling with small quantities of stool.

Normal fecal continence is aided by a number of factors, some of which may be affected by normal aging or diseases which accompany aging. The first factor is intact neuromuscular function. The external anal sphincter, which is composed of striated muscle and is under voluntary control, must be competent. The internal anal sphincter, which is not under voluntary control, shows a gradual drop-off in resting tone both in men and women over the age of 50. A crude indication of a tendency to

fecal incontinence is provided by the ability to retain barium during a barium enema examination. In one study, only 2 percent of patients with good resting sphincter tone were incontinent during a barium enema, while 90 percent of those with poor tone were incontinent under those circumstances. Inability to retain barium increased in frequency precipitously in men after age 50. In women, an increase occurs in the third decade and accelerates after age 50. The early onset in women may be related to trauma during parturition. Other causes of injury to the anal sphincters include posttraumatic or postsurgical damage, usually after hemorrhoidectomy. Damage to the innervation of these muscles has the same effect as direct muscular injury and may be caused by spinal cord injuries, neurologic diseases such as multiple sclerosis, and peripheral neuropathies such as diabetic neuropathy.

A second mechanism aiding normal continence is distensibility of the rectum, the ability to accommodate to an increased volume without an increase in pressure. Diseases which impair rectal distensibility include inflammatory conditions such as inflammatory bowel disease, mechanical impairment of distension such as may be caused by rectal carcinomas or adhesions related to surgery or pelvic disease, or fibrosis of the rectum related to radiation treatments or connective tissue diseases. With aging, loss of muscular elasticity resulting from ischemia and subsequent fibrosis may also contribute to a loss of normal distensibility. Thus, resting rectal pressures are somewhat elevated in the elderly, and a given volume of stool may cause a larger increase in pressure than in younger people. Thus, there effectively is a decreased rectal capacity and a greater stimulation of the anorectal reflex with rectal filling. A smaller degree of distension may therefore be sufficient to stimulate the urge to defecate.

A third factor important in maintaining continence is sensory-cognitive. As stool is propelled into the rectum from the sigmoid colon, distension of the rectum causes reflex relaxation of the internal anal sphincter and concomitant contraction of the external anal sphincter. At this point normal sensory pathways make us aware of an urge to defecate. We can then choose to answer Nature's call or not. If we choose to wait, an accommodation to the rectal distension occurs with relaxation and reduction of pressure in the rectum. This diminishes the sensory stimulus, and we no longer feel the urge to defecate, at least until more stool or gas enters the rectum.

Thus, intact sensory pathways and a conscious act are both involved in maintaining continence. One study[1] revealed that about a quarter of patients with fecal incontinence had a defect in the sensation of rectal filling. Others can sense rectal distension but have learned to ignore it until it reaches urgent levels. At that point they may not have time to get to the bathroom since their external anal sphincter tone may be poor. In addition, voluntary contraction of the external sphincter in the face of increased rectal pressure can be maintained only for about a minute in normal subjects. Mobility is often impaired in the elderly, decreasing the likelihood that they will make it to the bathroom in time to avoid incontinence. Those incontinent patients who have abnormal sensation can often be retrained to recognize the sensory stimulus and respond appropriately.

EVALUATION

A careful history can be most useful in the evaluation of a fecally incontinent elderly person. The time course and the circumstances of onset are important in deciding whether there is an acute event which is contributing to incontinence. Thus, incontinence in the form of liquid stools in a patient with a prior history of normally formed stools or constipation suggests an acute diarrheal illness or fecal impaction. In such cases, treatment of the underlying illness or disimpaction may "cure" the incontinence. On the other hand, incontinence of normally formed stools is more likely to be caused by an irreversible anatomic or neurologic condition. The questioning should focus on the neurologic, surgical, traumatic, obstetric, and gastrointestinal histories.

The degree of incontinence can be described in terms of frequency, type and quantity of material expelled (gas, liquid, or solid stool), and special circumstances which may result in an episode of incontinence. For example, some elderly patients with poor resting anal tone but no other deficits in continence mechanisms may experience fecal soiling only when exerting themselves physically or coughing, so-called "stress incontinence."

Perhaps the most important thing to be learned from the history is what the effects of the incontinence are on the patient's lifestyle. Patients may be reluctant to discuss such issues as soiling of bedding or clothing if the physician is not sensitive to these problems. Many ambulatory patients will shun activities which they would otherwise do (working, socializing, or even leaving their homes) for fear of embarrassment.

The physical examination should focus on the neurologic examination to exclude central or peripheral neuropathies and should include examination of the anus and rectum. Perianal skin excoriation is good evidence of fecal incontinence or pruritus ani. Look for surgical scars or evidence of anal trauma. Digital anal and rectal examination may reveal anal fissures or fistulae or a rectal mass. Asking the patient to squeeze in the anal sphincter during digital examination will give an indication both of the general degree of sphincter strength and any asymmetry of contraction.

Assessment of the rectosigmoid mucosa, either with a rigid or flexible sigmoidoscope, should be performed to exclude inflammatory or neoplastic conditions of the distal colon and rectum. Pathology proximal to the reach of a sigmoidoscope will rarely be the cause of fecal incontinence. Nonetheless, examination of the entire colon, either by colonoscopy or a barium enema, may be indicated when there are symptoms or signs, such as weight loss, abdominal pain, diarrhea, or blood in the stools, in addition to fecal incontinence.

Further studies to assess the causes of fecal incontinence in the elderly may be useful but are available only at specialized centers. At such centers, evaluation usually includes a test of anorectal motility. One validated technique consists of the insertion of a triple-balloon catheter so that the most proximally placed balloon can be used to transiently distend the rectum. The middle balloon measures reflex inhibition of internal anal sphincter contraction, and the distal balloon measures contraction of the external anal sphincter and neighboring pelvic floor muscles in response to rectal distension. The threshold of rectal sensation can also be assessed with this technique by transiently distending the rectal balloon with progressively smaller volumes of air, until a volume is reached which cannot be felt by the patient. The amplitude of the external anal sphincter response to rectal distension is measured, and the presence or absence of an internal anal sphincter inhibitory reflex is noted. One group[1] reports that the amount of time it takes a patient to report noticing rectal distension after insufflation of the rectal balloon with a volume just above their sensory threshold (the "sensory delay") is an important measure. Patients with a sensory delay of more than 2 seconds were found to respond well to retraining with biofeedback. Individuals without fecal incontinence and individuals with incontinence who do not tend to have a good response to biofeedback training had sensory delays of less than 2 seconds.

Radiographic tests may be of value in the assessment of fecal incontinence. The anorectal angle is maintained by the anal sphincter and puborectalis muscles. This angle has been found to measure 105.6 ± 20.8 degrees at rest, 96.8 ± 24.8 degrees during squeeze, and 133.7 ± 17.9 degrees during attempted defecation in normal subjects. Incontinent subjects tend to have flatter angles during squeeze, 115 ± 28 degrees, although there is clearly substantial overlap between the two groups. This angle, as well as abnormal pelvic descent or mucosal prolapse, can be assessed via barium proctography, either static or dynamic (videoproctogram), in which the patient is asked to defecate barium.

TREATMENT

Once the underlying mechanism has been assessed, a rational treatment approach can be devised. Clearly, those patients in whom diarrhea or fecal impaction is contributing to incontinence will be helped by treatment of the diarrhea or by disimpaction and treatment of constipation, respectively. In diarrhea of unclear etiology, nonspecific treatment may be worthwhile. In this case, loperamide may be useful, both because of its antidiarrheal action and because it has been shown to increase anal sphincter pressures.[2]

Biofeedback therapy of fecal incontinence has been shown to be quite useful in geriatric patients.[3] The training involves feedback to the patient when the appropriate response is elicited, coupled with exercises to increase the strength of the external anal sphincter. A triple-balloon catheter (described above) is inserted into the anorectum, and the rectal balloon is distended with progressively smaller volumes of air. The patient is able to see a tracing of the resulting external anal sphincter response and is encouraged to mimic a normal response, i.e., strong external sphincter contraction beginning soon after rectal distension, lasting about 10 seconds, and not accompanied by increases in rectal pressure indicative of contraction of the abdominal wall muscles. It is important that this response be synchronous with reflex relaxation of the internal sphincter, and the biofeedback training is designed to shape this response. Patients as old as 97 years of age have learned to control gross incontinence by this technique. Often only one or two sessions lasting 30 to 45 minutes each are required. In one study,[3] 13 incontinent patients age 65 to 92 who had failed to regain continence with medical therapy (treatment of constipation) and habit training (attempting to defecate right after breakfast each day) were provided sphincter biofeedback therapy. Anal sphincter exercises alone did not significantly increase sphincter strength or reduce the frequency of incontinence, but when biofeedback training was added, 10 out of 13 patients showed greater than 75 percent decreases in the fre-

quency of incontinence. Follow-up showed these improvements were maintained in 50 percent of patients at 6 months and in 42 percent at 1 year without further biofeedback sessions. Relapse was associated with progressive physical illness in most cases. Other groups have found comparable improvements in continence with biofeedback either in the form of pressure measurements or muscle impulses measured by electromyography. Thus, biofeedback training can be expected to result in sustained improvements in the frequency of incontinence in most elderly patients. Patients who are severely cognitively impaired, however, are poor candidates for biofeedback.

If medical and biofeedback treatments fail, surgery remains a viable treatment option in selected cases. Incontinence due to anal sphincter injury resulting from surgery, childbirth, or trauma is particularly amenable to surgical cure. A popular technique is the overlapping sphincteroplasty in which the sphincter muscles are cut, overlapped, and tightened. Good to excellent results are reported in about 75 percent of cases with this operation. In instances where gross rectal prolapse is associated with incontinence, surgical repair of the prolapse restores continence in many patients.

While it is seldom discussed by elderly patients, fecal incontinence is a prevalent and important problem for geriatrics. Fortunately, there are now diagnostic tools and therapeutic options available which make it a treatable problem for a substantial majority of elderly persons who suffer from this physically unpleasant and emotionally traumatic condition.

REFERENCES AND GENERAL READING

1. Buser WD, Miner PB: Delayed rectal sensation with fecal incontinence. *Gastroenterology* 91:1186, 1986.

2. Read M, Read NW, Barber DC et al: Effects of loperamide on anal sphincter function in patients complaining of chronic diarrhea with fecal incontinence and urgency. *Dig Dis Sci* 27:807, 1982.

3. Whitehead WE, Ur KL, Engel BT: Biofeedback treatment of fecal incontinence in geriatric patients. *J Am Geriatr Soc* 33:320, 1985.

Fang DT, Nivatvongs S, Bermeulen FD et al: Overlapping sphincteroplasty for acquired anal incontinence. *Dis Colon Rectum* 27:72, 1984.

Leigh RJ, Turnberg LA: Fecal incontinence: The unvoiced symptom. *Lancet* 1:1349, 1982.

MacLeod JH: Management of anal incontinence by biofeedback. *Gastroenterology* 93:291, 1987.

Wald A, Tunerguntla AK: Anorectal sensorimotor dysfunction in fecal incontinence and diabetes. *N Engl J Med* 310:1282, 1984.

Chapter 117

IMPOTENCE

Stanley G. Korenman

Impotence is principally a disorder of older men. In their landmark study of human sexual inadequacy, Masters and Johnson emphasized the psychological problems of premature ejaculation in disease-free younger men, which served to impede investigation of the organic causes of impotence in the older population.[1] While impotence is only one of numerous sexual dysfunctions, it is quite common, generally of organic origin, and, as will be seen, amenable to therapy.

DEFINITIONS

What is impotence? Impotence is one of the sexual dysfunctions conventionally defined as an inability to attain an erection of sufficient rigidity for vaginal penetration in 75 percent or more of attempts. Secondary impotence occurs after a period of normal sexual functioning. Since the disorder is usually progressive in men over the age of 50, it is appropriate to consider those with a lesser degree of disability as candidates for therapy. Other sexual dysfunctions associated with impotence include loss of libido, loss of ability to sustain an erection, and failure of ejaculation. Loss of libido characterizes severely hypogonadal men, whether the hypogonadism is due to testicular or to hypothalamic-pituitary failure. Intercurrent illness, drugs, and psychiatric problems may also be associated with a markedly reduced libido.

Early ejaculation often presages the development of full-blown impotence, so this symptom should not be attributed to an altered psychological state in men who have had previously normal erectile duration. In many instances sexual dysfunction results in patient withdrawal from sexual activities. Such patients should be considered as impotent. Ejaculatory capability tends to be preserved in almost all cases of penile impotence.

EPIDEMIOLOGY

There have only been a few studies attempting to determine the age-dependent prevalence of impotence in the population. Of these, only the study of Kinsey dealt with men who were not identified through a medical source, although other small prevalence studies exist.[2-4] As shown in Fig. 117-1, impotence (including an absence of sexual activity) increases rapidly after age 50. Conservative estimates of the prevalence of impotence are 5 to 10 percent in the sixth decade, 20 percent in the seventh, 30 to 40 percent in the eighth, and greater than 50 percent in the ninth.

MEDICAL DISEASES CONTRIBUTING TO OR CAUSING IMPOTENCE

A substantial level of impotence has been reported in association with certain medical disorders (Table 117-1). Unfortunately, the analyses underlying the reports did not compare the prevalence in disease groups with age-matched controls. In one important study, however, it was demonstrated that in medical outpatients the age-dependent prevalence of erectile dysfunction in hypertensives did not differ from normotensive patients, while

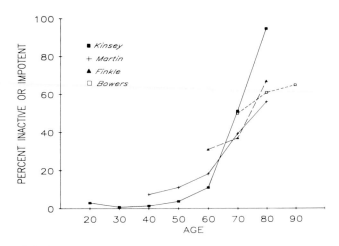

FIGURE 117-1

Reported prevalence of impotence and sexual inactivity in population studies.

1146

TABLE 117-1
Incidence of Impotence in Various Diseases

Disorder Type	Disorder	Number	% Impotent
Genetic	Diabetes mellitus	541	35
	Hemachromatosis	41	22
	Cystic fibrosis	30	30
	Coeliac disease	26	19
Metabolic	Uremia	256	68
	Uremia + transplant	24	21
	Alcoholism	120	69
	Graves' disease	7	56
Vascular	Hypertension		25
	Aorto-iliac disease	413	53
	Coronary heart disease	131	64
Neurologic	Stroke	78	70
	Multiple sclerosis	258	71
	Postconcussion	19	58
Inflammatory	Obstructive pulmonary	20	35
	Bowel disease	9	11
	Abdominal perineal resection	7	55
	Rectal anastomosis	5	40
Neoplastic	Prostate postoperatively	152	47
	Penis postirradiation	36	28
	Testis after cure	74	25
	Rectal postoperatively	41	5
	Hodgkin's after therapy	41	58
Psychiatric	Schizophrenia on neuroleptics	26	54

the prevalence of impotence in diabetics was much greater than in other groups.[5] This high prevalence was almost entirely due to impotence in long-standing insulin-dependent diabetes mellitus (IDDM).

UREMIA

Uremia is associated with a high prevalence of impotence, but the mechanism is not fully understood. Refractory tissue hypogonadism, elevated prolactin levels, and zinc depletion are thought to be contributors in addition to the vascular disease characterizing the underlying process in so many of these patients.[6]

NEUROLOGIC DISEASES

Neurologic diseases and pelvic surgery presumably affect potency by interrupting the autonomic fibers of the nervi erigentes that control the erectile process (see below). In the past 3 years those pathways have been traced in humans so that even radical prostatectomy may be carried out with preservation of potency in 70 percent or more of cases.[7]

DIABETES MELLITUS

Impotence in diabetics has been attributed to endocrinopathy, neuropathy, and vascular disease.[8] The evidence of several large series suggests that the prevalence of erectile impotence is about 50 percent in unselected diabetics, rising steadily with age to reach 98 percent in a geriatric diabetes clinic. Impotence does not appear to be related to duration of the diabetes but rather seems to precede the development of other complications.[9] In our studies, IDDM in insulin-requiring patients diagnosed under the age of 40 results in impotence several to many years after diagnosis and is often associated with normal penile blood pressure. In contrast, in noninsulin-dependent diabetes mellitus (NIDDM), impotence is discovered at a variable time, from before the diagnosis to several years thereafter, depending inversely on the age at onset of the diabetes. Once developed, it appears to be permanent. Nocturnal penile tumescence (NPT) is almost invariably abnormal in impotent diabetics whether compared with that of normals or of potent diabetics.[10]

Hypogonadism was implicated in the pathogenesis of impotence in early studies of diabetics. Therapy of those under age 40 with human chorionic gonadotropin (HCG) and testosterone was deemed successful. A number of other studies followed which failed to confirm a decline in hypothalamic or testicular function in diabetic impotence and demonstrated a failure of androgen therapy. The issue was revived recently by reports suggesting that inhibition of gonadotropin releasing hormone (Gn-RH) on a neuropathic basis, infiltration of the testicular interstitial matrix with collagen-like material, and abnormal seminiferous tubules characterized diabetic impotence.[11] The strongest evidence for a contribution of hypogonadism appears to be in young patients with IDDM.

Neurogenic factors in diabetic impotence were proposed in a demonstration that showed peripheral and bladder neuropathy to be much more frequent (an 80 percent incidence) in impotent patients than in potent diabetics.[12] That result was not readily confirmed. A recent study employing newer technologies to evaluate both autonomic and peripheral nerves demonstrated that slowed motor-nerve conduction velocity correlated best with secondary impotence. Clinical evidence to neuropathy, age, treatment modality, or quality of control could not distinguish the groups.[13] It is of some importance to determine the prevalence of abnormal nerve conduction velocity in nondiabetic impotent subjects, which in our series reached 35 percent due at least in part to alcohol and tobacco abuse. Measurement of the conduction velocity of the dorsal nerve of the penis may provide a more direct measure of penile sensory function, which may be more closely related to the development of impotence.[14]

The major pathogenetic role of vascular disease in diabetic impotence has come to be widely appreciated.[15–17] In patients with severe vascular disease, twice as many of the diabetic subjects were impotent as compared with nondiabetic patients. The use of the penile-brachial pressure index (PBPI) (see below) provides a simple, moderately sensitive test with considerable specificity to evaluate the vascular contribution to impotence. In our experience, the prevalence of an abnormal PBPI was greater in NIDDM (73 percent) than in IDDM (47 percent). Also in an extensive analysis it was found that the PBPI was significantly lower in those with two or more positive cardiovascular risk factors (diabetes, smoking, hypertension, hyperlipidemia).[18] Thus, diabetics have multiple risk factors for impotence that result in a much higher than expected prevalence for age.

HYPERTENSION

Hypertension has long been thought to be associated with an increased incidence of impotence. In one study 20 percent of hypertensives were found to be impotent prior to initiation of therapy and impotence rates of greater than 30 percent were seen in all drug-treated groups.[19] There is evidence that the age-specific incidence of impotence in hypertensives does not differ from that of the remainder of the population receiving medical care.[5] Impotence has generally been attributed to antihypertensive agents. Central and peripheral autonomic agents were especially implicated, but all agents,

including diuretics, β-blockers, angiotensin-converting enzyme inhibitors, and calcium channel blockers, have been reported to result in impotence. There is some evidence that reduction of the arterial blood pressure and reduced resistance in nonpenile vascular beds may accentuate the reduction in flow rate associated with an obstructive lesion in the hypogastric-penile arterial tree, so that the process of controlling the blood pressure may result in reduced penile filling.[20] It is essential to deal honestly with the problem of potency in hypertensives when initiating therapy to avoid a lack of compliance.

ALCOHOLISM

Alcoholism is associated with a high prevalence of impotence. Among the risk factors involved are hypogonadism with estrogen excess, autonomic neuropathy, and vascular disease associated with the smoking that almost invariably accompanies alcohol excess. A significant number of alcoholics will respond to very high doses of androgens, suggesting that, in many, a refractory form of hypogonadism is the main problem.[21]

HYPOGONADISM

Hypogonadism is not uncommon with increasing age. Its origin is not usually obvious, although testicular trauma, irradiation, and chemical exposure are sometimes etiologically involved. Treatment with estrogens, Gn-RH, cimetidine, and metoclopramide, as well as ethanol, often affect androgen availability. In older men, in many cases, establishment of the hypogonadal state is difficult because there are low androgen levels without a compensatory hypothalamic-pituitary response.[22,23] Furthermore, there is evidence of reduced tissue concentration of androgens with aging.[24] In severe cases of hypogonadism with impotence there is a gratifying response to testosterone therapy.[25,26] However, the vast majority of trials with androgens demonstrated very little success, probably because treatment solely with androgens, when vasculogenic impotence also was present, was doomed to failure.

VASCULAR DISEASE

There is growing agreement that the majority of cases of secondary impotence are due to the complications of atherosclerosis.[5,8,9,15–18,27–29] There are no reports, however, relating impotence to angina, myocardial infarction, or stroke, although there is evidence that penile blood pressure falls with the presence of an increasing number of cardiovascular risk factors and that low penile blood pressure significantly predicts cardiovascular events.[18,30]

MECHANISM OF ERECTION

Normal sexual function depends upon the interaction of libido and potency. Libido consists of desires (drives), thoughts (fantasies), and satisfactions (pleasures). Potency involves pelvic congestion leading to erection and orgasmic contractions leading to ejaculation. Androgens appear to play an important role in libido and the frequency of nonerotic or "reflex" erections, including NPT, and are required for normal seminal fluid volume. Androgens do not seem to be involved acutely in erections associated with erotic stimuli.[25]

The neural, vascular, and muscular events responsible for the erectile process have come to be much better understood over the past few years. The central nervous system (CNS) responds in a complex fashion to erotic signals, at least in part by reversing tonic suppression of the thoracolumbar and sacral erection centers that activate the nervi erigentes.[31] The nervi erigentes are parasympathetics that branch into cavernosal nerves whose postsynaptic terminals operate through an unknown neurotransmitter(s), possibly vasoactive intestinal peptide (VIP), to relax corpus cavernosal arterial and sinusoidal smooth muscle.[32,33] A doubling of the corporal arterial diameter provides a large increase of blood flow into the cavernosal sinuses.[34] The penetrating veins that drain most of the body of the penis through the tunica albuginea are compressed severely, inhibiting venous outflow.[35] The increased influx and inhibited venous drainage produce erectile firmness. Contraction of the ischiocavernosus muscles just prior to ejaculation results in very high intracavernosal pressures and maximal erectile strength.[34]

Nocturnal erections and reflex erections that are maintained even with spinal cord injury are stimulated by pudendal nerve afferents. NPT occurs primarily during REM sleep resulting in 2 to 8 full erections per night lasting up to 40 minutes each.[36] Detumescence is usually a consequence of α_2-sympathetic vasoconstrictor activity. Ejaculation occurs via both CNS and reflex arcs terminating in sympathetic nerve terminals in the testes, in the seminal vesicles and prostate, and in pelvic smooth muscle structures.

With aging, "sexy" sensations are reduced in frequency, and spontaneous pelvic swelling becomes much less frequent. Latency to erection is increased, and erotogenic stimuli must be of greater intensity; also, penile filling is slower, and there is increased venous drainage resulting in less firm maximal erection.[1] Often, time to ejaculation is prolonged, enhancing the quality of coitus. There is an increased absolute refractory period to the next erection. NPT declines in frequency, duration and rigidity with age.[36] In many patients there is a decrease in penile sensation.

THE CLINICAL PROBLEM

The loss of erectile capacity has a debilitating psychological effect on many men that permeates their entire lives. If impotence is associated with a divorce or other loss of a spouse, then the man may experience social isolation, with its attendant ills. In the typical clinical scenario, secondary impotence begins slowly with loss of erectile duration during intercourse, followed by diminished erectile quality, inability to achieve a full erection, loss of spontaneous morning erections, and, ultimately, inability to achieve any erection at all. The onset of impotence is frequently associated with a major medical event such as thoracic or abdominal surgery or with initiation of drug therapy for a medical condition. In some instances a long period of sexual abstinence will be followed by impotence.

In most cases of impotence, the sexual partners react predictably. The man slowly withdraws from sexual activity, and the conjugal bed is transformed into a place of anxiety. There is a loss of intimacy. The female partner may first feel unattractive and guilty, then angry at possible infidelities. Depending on the quality of the dyadic interaction, impotence can result in dissolution of the relationship, a tension-filled truce, or a determination to resolve the problem. In our experience, the impotent man's sexual partner can be either sexually demanding or satisfied with restoration of intimacy without penile penetration. It is important to understand the feelings and wishes of both partners by insisting on seeing them together and frankly discussing the problem and all the diagnostic and therapeutic alternatives.

DIAGNOSTIC EVALUATION

HISTORY

The sexual history should determine whether erectile difficulty is indeed the problem and focus on erection duration, progression, and characteristics. We determine the extent of current sexual activity, the percent of time vaginal entry can be accomplished, partner universality or selectivity, the presence of spontaneous (morning) erections, and the quality and duration of best erections (full, partial, absent) and their usability for coitus. The present state should be compared with patient's best and recent normal years and the importance of sex in his life. The ejaculatory capacity and presence of spontaneous ejaculations should be recorded.

It is important to determine the level of libido, expressed as interest in sex, thoughts or fantasies of a sexual nature, and the presence of spontaneous or erotogenic pelvic sensations in relation to the patient's historical norm. A substantial decline in libido suggests the possibility of hypogonadism.

It should be possible from the history to determine the extent and progression of impotence and to surmise as to whether it is organic or psychogenic. The importance of erectile potency to the individual, the prior level of satisfaction, and the impact on self-image will help to ascertain the urgency of diagnostic and therapeutic maneuvers.

Impotence is a couple's problem. Successful therapy will depend to a great degree on partner availability, interest, and health. The integrity of the female partner's sexual tissues will often depend on that partner's menopausal state and its therapy. There are women, particularly in the geriatric age group, who are not prepared for a resurgence of erectile capability in their mate. It is mandatory in the history taking to include the partner and discuss the erectile problem with her and determine her view of sex and of the various therapeutic alternatives.

Impotence may be the harbinger of serious medical illness or a consequence thereof.[30] A complete medical evaluation is mandatory, including a psychiatric history and a careful assessment of substance abuse, as well as occupational and medicative exposure to chemicals and drugs. Evidence of atherosclerosis, hypertension, and diabetes would suggest a vascular etiology, while certain chemical agents or drugs might produce a neuropathy inhibition of autonomic function or result in hypogonadism.

PHYSICAL EXAMINATION

The physical examination should place special emphasis on evidence of hypogonadism, including axillary and pubic hair loss, gynecomastia, and reduced testicular volume and density. Autonomic nervous system function should be tested by evaluating postural hypotension and heart rate responses to deep breathing. Penile size and shape, plaque or fibrous tissue formation, and prostate size and characteristics round out the genital examination. A careful neurologic examination, especially in the sacral area and for peripheral neuropathy, is useful.

LABORATORY TESTING

The appropriate laboratory testing for impotence is somewhat controversial. For patients who are not under medical care there should be a full evaluation for unsuspected medical illness. The endocrine assessment should include measurements of follicle-stimulating hormone (FSH), luteinizing hormone (LH), testosterone (T), and loosely bound or bioavailable testosterone (BT) on at least two occasions, as well as measurements of prolactin, thyroid-stimulating hormone (TSH), and thy-

roxine. Both hyper- and hypothyroidism may be associated with impotence and are difficult to diagnose on clinical grounds, particularly in the geriatric population. The diagnosis of hypogonadism in the older male by hormone assay may be extremely difficult. If there is increased T-binding to sex hormone-binding globulin there may be a very low concentration of BT in the presence of a normal total T level. If the gonadotropins are elevated, then a presumptive diagnosis of hypogonadism may be made, but a significant proportion of older men will have low BT levels with normal to low gonadotropins, suggesting hypogonadotropic hypogonadism. However, the possibility that these men may have a pituitary adenoma and require a computed tomography (CT) scan is remote. Normal prolactin, TSH, and thyroxine levels and a normal response to Gn-RH help to rule out pituitary tumor.

OTHER DIAGNOSTIC TESTS

NOCTURNAL PENILE TUMESCENCE

The erections occurring during sleep (NPT) are measured directly in a sleep laboratory employing penile strain gauges and continuous monitoring of penile diameter and sleep stage,[33] and a technician assesses rigidity visually. The procedure is time-consuming and expensive. Recently, the Rigiscan monitor was developed, which registers penile diameter and rigidity continuously during sleep, utilizing penile strain gauges to produce a record of the number and quality of erectile episodes throughout the night. The equipment for this procedure is expensive, requiring a $10,000 device and a computer. Simple techniques such as the stamp test, in which a ring of stamps is placed around the flaccid penis at bedtime and a broken ring indicates that at least one episode of rigidity has taken place, and the Dacomed snap gauge, which responds to three different levels of nocturnal tumescence with the rupture of thin plastic strips, are inexpensive measures of tumescence, but they determine only whether a single episode reaching sufficient diameter and rigidity to break the band has occurred.[37,38]

NPT evaluation was first developed to distinguish organic from psychogenic impotence. It was considered to be the gold standard until recent demonstrations showed that men with normal vasculature may have abnormal NPT because of disturbed sleep and that normal NPT may be consistent with organic impotence associated with a pelvic steal. Furthermore, there is a poor correlation between nocturnal erections and those due to erotic stimuli. For these reasons, the effectiveness of NPT evaluation as a test has come under skeptical scrutiny.[39,40] In our series, over 90 percent of men over the age of 50 with impotence had abnormal NPT. We employ NPT testing only occasionally, primarily in patients with a normal PBPI (see below) who claim to have no full erections.

PENILE-BRACHIAL BLOOD PRESSURE INDEX

A major advance in the evaluation of impotence was the development of a simple, noninvasive method of evaluating penile arterial integrity by comparing the penile and the brachial systolic pressure.[41-43] This method has been shown to be quite specific but not very sensitive.[44,45] Our version of the test will be described in detail because it can be done in every physician's office. To measure the penile BP, use a portable mercury manometer connected to a 2.5-cm-wide infant cuff. Employ an inexpensive hand-held 10-mHz doppler instrument and listen for the systolic BP at 10 o'clock and 2 o'clock on the penile shaft to get right- and left-sided corporal artery values. Brachial and penile pressure measurements are carried out after 5 minutes in the supine position and repeated after 5 minutes of standing; the patient is then asked to lie down. After 5 minutes in a supine position, the patient is asked to perform bicycling motions with his legs in the air for 2 minutes or as long as possible. Immediately after cessation of the exercise the blood pressure measurements are repeated. The PBPI is composed of a total of six ratios, the ratio of penile to brachial blood pressure on each side in each of three positions. The criteria for abnormal responses are not well-established because early investigations were trying to establish values below which penile erection was impossible. We consider the following to be appropriate criteria for an abnormal response:

1. One of the six determinations is ≤0.6.
2. A mean of the six ratios is ≤0.65.
3. A ≥0.15 decline in ratio between the supine and exercise PBPI exists, indicating a pelvic steal syndrome.
4. A mean of the six determinations is ≤.75, indicating a probable vascular risk factor for impotence.

DIAGNOSTIC PAPAVERINE INJECTION

The diagnostic papaverine injection test is employed to confirm the existence of vascular impotence, assess the probability of major venous leakage, and determine whether a series of injections or self-injections will have a high probability of success in restoring erectile function.[46,47] It is probably indicated only if the patient is interested in the possibility of therapeutic injections or corrective surgery. The injections carry a risk of priapism (about 1 percent of injections), hematoma (3 to 10 percent of injections), infection (rare), and local pain

(usual). The patients are asked to stop taking aspirin 5 days prior to each injection to avoid subcutaneous hematoma formation. The quality of the erection obtained helps determine the degree of vascular insufficiency. A normal sustained erection suggests minimal arterial and venous disease. A sustained but soft erection (often seen) suggests that arterial disease may be present and that papaverine therapy may be successful. A weak erection suggests either severe arterial insufficiency or substantial venous leakage and also suggests the utility of further diagnostic tests if the patient would be willing to have surgery for the problem.

INVASIVE AND COMPLEX DIAGNOSTICS

ELECTROMYOGRAPHY

Electromyographic analysis of peripheral nerves is a time-consuming and painful technique designed to diagnose peripheral neuropathy, bulbocavernosus reflex latency, and sacral- and genitocerebral-evoked potentials.[48] Evidence is provided as to the integrity of the neural circuits tested but not as to whether those circuits play a role in the impotence. Dorsal penile nerve conduction velocity measurement is directed at the penile sensory system. Demonstration of a delay of conduction velocity below 40 m/sec indicates that a portion of the penile innervation is abnormal.[14] There is no substantiation, however, that sensory defects affect potency. Many investigators believe that a careful neurologic history and physical examination suffices to determine whether there is a neurogenic component of the sexual dysfunction.

DUPLEX SCANNING

Duplex scanning of penile arteries before and after papaverine-induced erection is an important new diagnostic procedure that can determine whether corporal arterial diameters are reduced and whether they dilate after papaverine.[20] It predicts to some extent whether there will be a good response to therapeutic papaverine. It does not evaluate for pelvic steal. The duplex scanning procedure requires the use of expensive ultrasound equipment.

PHALLOARTERIOGRAPHY

Arteriography of the penile arteries and corpora cavernosa before and after papaverine-induced erection identifies arterial spasm and obstructive disease. It would be especially useful if efficacious and lasting surgical reconstruction were reliable.[49]

CAVERNOSOGRAPHY

Cavernosography and cavernosometry after pretreatment using vasodilators are essential for identification of venous leaks.[50] Saline is injected into a corpus cavernosum to achieve an erection. Cavernosal pressure is measured on the other side. Normally, an erection occurs at about 20 mmHg pressure. If not, venous insufficiency is suggested. Cavernosography with diluted contrast medium will then demonstrate veno-occlusive incompetence (venous leaks). There is a high prevalence of such leaks, especially in older men. These procedures result in a significant number of local hematomas.

THERAPEUTIC INTERVENTIONS

Therapeutic initiatives in impotence should be undertaken only after thorough discussion with the couple involved. It is important for the physician to develop an understanding of the acceptability to them of the various alternatives and the risks they are willing to take. Management should be based on a risk-factor approach, since (1) the presence of hypogonadism does not rule out vascular impotence, (2) combined arterial and veno-occlusive incompetence are not uncommon, and (3) psychogenic factors, when present, do not preclude other diagnoses.

INTRACORPOREAL PHARMACOTHERAPY

Vasculogenic impotence may be treated with intracorporeal papaverine or papaverine-phentolamine combinations either as a short series of physician-administered doses or by self-administration (after appropriate education and training) when sex is desired.[51] The short series may produce long-term erectile improvement in about 30 percent of patients. The self-injection protocols are effective in a much higher percentage of patients but may result in corporeal fibrosis.

VASCULAR SURGERY

Venous leaks may be treated surgically by ligation and by fluoroscopically directed sclerosis, but the results are not clear. Arterial revascularization has been tried extensively, with unconvincing results thus far.

PENILE PROSTHESIS

Penile prostheses were the first effective universal treatment modality for impotence and have been a godsend for many thousands of men. Their properties have been reviewed recently.[52] Prostheses with rigid or semirigid rods have the disadvantage of always being erect. Those with a scrotal or abdominal reservoir are more complex and have a significant incidence of pump failure. Those with a corporal reservoir produce erections of rather limited quality. In all cases the corporal sinusoids are permanently destroyed, and there is a significant incidence of tissue breakdown, particularly in diabetics.

EXTERNAL VACUUM DEVICES

External vacuum devices have been available for about a decade. They can be considered to provide vascular pump assistance and can be employed regardless of the etiology of the impotence.[53,54] They produce an erection by creating a vacuum around the penis that causes an increase of blood flow sufficient for a good erection. Venous drainage is inhibited by the use of constricting bands. After the patient learns how to use them, these devices are a very satisfactory solution to the problem. The erection is present only when needed. Tissues are not adversely affected. The usual coital pattern may be restored. In patients with normal sensation, excessive negative pressure is prevented by pain. The principal complications are reversible hematomas seen in a few patients, discomfort from the bands, and the cold temperature of the erect penis.

ANDROGEN THERAPY

Hypogonadism should be treated with androgens. In older men, who have a very high incidence of vascular disease, androgen therapy alone should not be expected to normalize erectile function. However, androgens improve energy, mood, and sense of well-being. The use of the available oral preparations is not warranted because of hepatic complications. A long-acting T ester such as testosterone enanthate or testosterone cypionate should be given, usually at a dose of 200 mg intramuscularly every 2 weeks. Although a hyperphysiological level of T and BT is produced for several days, and values may fall below normal before the next injection, these are the best available preparations. The principal complication of this treatment is polycythemia, sometimes requiring phlebotomy. Concerns regarding stimulation of benign prostatic hyperplasia and prostatic carcinoma have not been supported experimentally, nor have they been subjected to rigorous scrutiny.

SEX THERAPY

Sex therapy techniques seem to be particularly effective in patients with primary sexual dysfunction and in those with early ejaculation problems. These techniques may offer consolation and improvement of sexual attitudes to those with organic impotence. Sex therapy should focus on the couple. Unrealistic expectations must be dealt with and the characteristics of a more satisfactory sex life defined. Sequential goals of the couple should include (1) frequent getting together, with clarity about who is to initiate, (2) showering or bathing together, (3) spending time touching each other without genital contact, (4) sharing genital touching without focus on intercourse, and (5) intercourse without pressure toward orgasm.

CONCLUSION

Recent advances in understanding the scientific basis of impotence and the development of new diagnostic tests and therapeutic alternatives have made it possible to provide the vast majority of dysfunctional couples with an opportunity to restore sexual intimacy. Alleviation of this vexing emotionally and socially destructive problem provides a more vital and satisfying life to couples of all ages and particularly to the elderly. It is mandatory for geriatricians to direct attention to sexual dysfunction.

REFERENCES

1. Masters WH, Johnson VE: *Human Sexual Inadequacy.* Boston, Little, Brown, 1970.
2. Kinsey AC, Pomeroy WB, Martin CF: *Sexual Behavior in the Human Male.* Philadelphia, W. B. Saunders, 1948.
3. Finkle AL, Moyers TG, Tobenkin MI, Karg SJ: Sexual potency and aging males. *JAMA* 170:1391, 1959.
4. Bowers LM, Cross RR Jr, Lloyd FA: Sexual function and urologic disease in the elderly male. *J. Am Geriatr Soc* 11:647, 1963.
5. Newman HF, Marcus H: Erectile dysfunction in diabetes and hypertension. *Urology* 26:135, 1985.
6. Antoniou LD, Shalhoub RJ, Sudhakar T, Smith JC Jr: Reversal of uraemic impotence by zinc. *Lancet* 2:895, 1977.
7. Walsh PC, Mostwin JL: Radical prostatectomy and cystoprostatectomy with preservation of potency: Results using a new nerve-sparing technique. *Br J Urol* 56:694, 1984.
8. Kaiser FE, Korenman SG: Impotence in diabetic men. *Am J Med* 85(suppl 5a):147, 1988.
9. McCulloch K, Young RJ, Prescott RJ, Campbell IW, Clarke BF: The natural history of impotence in diabetic men. *Diabetologia* 26:437, 1984.
10. Schiavi RC, Fisher C, Quadland M, Glover A: 1985 Nocturnal penile tumescent evaluation of erectile function in insulin-dependent diabetic men. *Diabetologia* 28:90, 1985.
11. Murray FT, Wyss HU, Thomas RG et al: Gonadal dysfunction in diabetic men with organic impotence. *J Clin Endocrinol Metab* 65:127, 1987.
12. Ellenberg M: Impotence in diabetes: The neurological factor. *Ann Intern Med* 75:213, 1971.
13. Palmer JDK, Fink S, Burger RH: Diabetic secondary impotence: Neuropathic factor as measured by peripheral motor nerve conduction. *Urology* 28:197, 1986.
14. Lin JT, Bradley WE: Penile neuropathy in insulin-dependent diabetes mellitus. *J Urol* 133:213, 1985.
15. Herman A, Adar R, Rubinstein Z: Vascular lesions associated with impotence in diabetic and nondiabetic arterial occlusive disease. *Diabetes* 27:975, 1978.
16. Lehman TP, Jacobs JA: Etiology of diabetic impotence. *J Urol* 129:291, 1983.
17. Jevtich MJ, Edson M, Jarmon WD, Herrera HH: Vascular factor in erectile failure among diabetics. *Urology* 19:163, 1982.
18. Virag R, Bouilly P, Frydman D: Is impotence an arterial disorder? *Lancet* 1:181, 1985.
19. Bulpitt CJ, Dollery CT: Side effects of hypotensive agents evaluated by a self-administered questionnaire. *Br Med J* 3:485, 1973.
20. Lue TF, Hricak H, Marich KW, Tanagho EA: Vasculogenic impotence evaluated by high resolution ultrasonography and pulsed doppler spectrum analysis. *Radiology* 155:778, 1985.
21. Van Thiel DH, Gavaler JS, Sanghvi A: Recovery of sexual function in abstinent alcoholic men. *Gastroenterology* 84:677, 1982.
22. Kaiser FE, Viosca SP, Mooradian AD, Morley JE, Korenman SG: Impotence and aging: Alterations in hormonal secretory patterns with age. Proceedings of the 70th Annual Meeting of the Endocrine Society, 1988, p 215.
23. Tenover JS, Matsumoto AM, Plymate SR et al: The effects of aging in normal men on bioavailable testosterone and luteinizing hormone secretion: Response to clomiphene citrate. *J Clin Endocrinol Metab* 65:1118, 1987.
24. Deslypere JP, Vermeulen A: Influence of age on steroid concentrations in skin and striated muscle in women and in cardiac muscle and lung tissue in men. *J Clin Endocrinol Metab* 61:648, 1985.
25. Davidson JM, Camargo CA, Smith ER: Effects of androgen on sexual behavior in hypogonadal men. *J Clin Endocrinol Metab* 48:955, 1979.
26. Kwan M, Greenleaf WJ, Mann J et al: The nature of androgen action on male sexuality: A combined laboratory-self-report study on hypogonadal men. *J Clin Endocrinol Metab* 57:557, 1983.
27. Davis SS, Viosca S, Guralnik M et al: Evaluation of impotence in older men. *West J Med* 142:499, 1985.
28. Slag MF, Morley JE, Elson MK et al: Impotence in medical clinic outpatients. *JAMA* 249:1736, 1983.
29. Kaiser FE, Viosca SP, Morley JE, Mooradian AD, Davis SS, Korenman SG: Impotence and aging: Clinical and hormonal factors. *J Am Geriatr Soc* 36:511, 1988.
30. Morley JE, Korenman SG, Kaiser FE, Mooradian AD, Viosca S: Relationship of penile brachial pressure index to myocardial infarction and cerebrovascular accidents in older men. *Am J Med* 84:445, 1988.
31. Lue TF, Zeinah SJ, Schmidt RA, Tanagho EA: Neuroanatomy of penile erection: Its relevance to iatrogenic impotence. *J Urol* 131:273, 1984.
32. Gu J, Lazarides M, Pryor JP et al: Decrease of vasoactive intestinal polypeptide (VIP) in the penises from impotent men. *Lancet* 2:315, 1984.
33. Lincoln J, Crowe R, Blacklay PF et al: Changes in the vipergic, cholinergic, and adrenergic innervation of

human penile tissue in diabetic and nondiabetic impotent males. *J Urol* 137:1053, 1987.

34. Lue TF, Tanagho EA: Physiology of erection and pharmacological management of impotence. *J Urol* 137:829, 1987.

35. Aboseif SR, Lue TF: Hemodynamics of penile erection. *Urol Clin North Am* 15:1, 1988.

36. Karacan I, Williams RL, Thornby JI, Salis PJ: Sleep-related tumescence as a function of age. *Am J Psychiatry* 132:932, 1975.

37. Anders EK, Bradley WE, Krane RJ: Nocturnal penile rigidity measured by the snap gauge band. *J Urol* 130:964, 1983.

38. Bertini J, Boileau MA: Evaluation of nocturnal penile tumescence with potentest. *Urology* 27:492, 1986.

39. Marshall P, Morales A, Surridge D: Unreliability of nocturnal penile tumescence recording and MMPI profiles in assessment of impotence. *Urology* 17:1369, 1982.

40. Condra M, Morales A, Surridge DH, Owen JA, Marshall P, Fenemore J: The unreliability of nocturnal penile tumescence as an outcome measurement in the treatment of organic impotence. *J Urol* 135:280, 1986.

41. Gaskell P: The importance of penile blood pressure in cases of impotence. *CMA J* 105:1047, 1971.

42. Abelson D: Diagnostic value of the penile pulse and blood pressure: A doppler study of impotence in diabetics. *J Urol* 113:636, 1975.

43. Blaivas JG, O'Donnell TF, Gottlieb P, Labib KB: Comprehensive laboratory evaluation of impotent men. *J Urol* 124:201, 1980.

44. Metz P, Christensen J, Mathiesen FR, Ostri P: Ultrasonic Doppler pulse wave analysis versus penile blood pressure measurement in the evaluation of arteriogenic impotence. *Vasa* 12:363, 1983.

45. Chiu RCJ, Lidstone D, Blundell PE: Predictive power of penile/brachial index in diagnosing male sexual impotence. *J Vasc Surg* 4:251, 1986.

46. Virag R, Frydman D, Legman, Virag H: Intracavernous injection of papaverine as a diagnostic and therapeutic method in erectile failure. *Angiology* 35:79, 1984.

47. Buvat J, Lemaire A, Buvat-Herbaut M, Dehaene JL, Lemaire A: Is intracavernous injection of papaverine a reliable screening test for vascular impotence? *J Urol* 135:476, 1986.

48. Mehta AJ, Viosca SP, Korenman SG et al: Peripheral nerve conduction studies and bulbocavernosus reflex in the investigation of impotence. *Arch Phys Med Rehabil* 67:332, 1986.

49. Bookstein JJ, Valji K, Parson, L, Kessler W: Pharmaco-arteriography in the evaluation of impotence. *J Urol* 137:333, 1987.

50. Lue TF, Hricak H, Schmidt RA, Tanagho EA: Functional evaluation of penile veins by cavernosography in papaverine-induced erection. *J Urol* 134:479, 1985.

51. Zorgniotti AW, Lefleur R: Auto-injection of the corpus cavernosum with a vasoactive drug combination for vasculogenic impotence. *J Urol* 133:39, 1985.

52. Krane RJ: Penile prosthesis. *Urol Clin North Am* 15:103, 1988.

53. Wiles PG: Successful non-invasive management of erectile impotence in diabetic men. *Br Med J* 296:161, 1988.

54. Korenman SG, Viosca S, Griner B: Use of the Erecaid[R] in the management of impotence. Proceedings of the 70th Annual Meeting of the Endocrine Society 1988, p 206.

Chapter 118

EATING AND SWALLOWING DISORDERS

Donald O. Castell

IMPORTANCE OF DYSPHAGIA IN THE ELDERLY

Dysphagia, or difficulty in swallowing, can present at any age due to a variety of disorders. Advanced age excludes none of the possibilities, and a few conditions are more likely to be seen in elderly patients. In addition, eating disorders may frequently result from defects not associated with the gastrointestinal tract, such as cognitive problems or physical disability of the upper limbs. Recognition of the etiology of a patient's inability to maintain adequate nutrition is crucial, since it has been shown that eating and swallowing disorders are associated with a particularly bad prognosis in the elderly.[1] This chapter will primarily cover diagnostic considerations in the patient with dysphagia, with special emphasis on the importance of understanding and clarifying the unique historical features of the diverse abnormalities producing this symptom.

CLINICAL PRESENTATION AND CLASSIFICATION OF DYSPHAGIA

In 1959, Schatzki suggested that a strong suspicion of the right diagnosis could be obtained from a careful history in up to 85 percent of patients with dysphagia.[2] That emphatic statement helps to emphasize the critical importance of the medical history in clarifying the cause of this symptom.

The term *dysphagia* is derived from Greek (*dys*, "with difficulty," and *phagia*, "to eat"). It describes difficulty in swallowing and should not be confused with odynophagia (painful swallowing). The two symptoms may appear together, but dysphagia is usually not associated with pain. The patient with true dysphagia will describe either difficulty initiating a swallow or a sensation of food stopping or "sticking" somewhere behind the sternum or at the suprasternal notch. When a patient complains of true difficulty with swallowing, i.e., food not passing into the stomach in the normal way, it almost always indicates some kind of organic lesion, rather than a functional problem.

Another important diagnostic distinction is that dysphagia should not be confused with globus hystericus. Globus hystericus is the frequent feeling (sometimes a constant sensation) of a lump, fullness, or tickle in the throat that typically does not interfere with swallowing and may even be relieved by swallows. It also implies, often inaccurately, that patients with the symptom have hysterical personalities. The diagnosis of globus hystericus should never be made without a thorough investigation for a lesion in the pharynx or neck and for organic esophageal disease such as reflux or a hypertensive upper esophageal sphincter. In fact, globus hystericus has been described in patients with each of of these conditions.[3,4] Thus, it is essentially a diagnosis of exclusion.

Dysphagia is usually divided clinically into two types: oropharyngeal (pre-esophageal) and esophageal.[5] A number of specific symptoms discussed below are likely to help identify the different types and causes of dysphagia. An algorithm for the more typical symptom presentations of patients with some of the more common causes of dysphagia is illustrated in Fig. 118-1.

OROPHARYNGEAL DYSPHAGIA

Dysphagia secondary to a lesion above or proximal to the esophagus is called oropharyngeal dysphagia. This ab-

1155

DYSPHAGIA

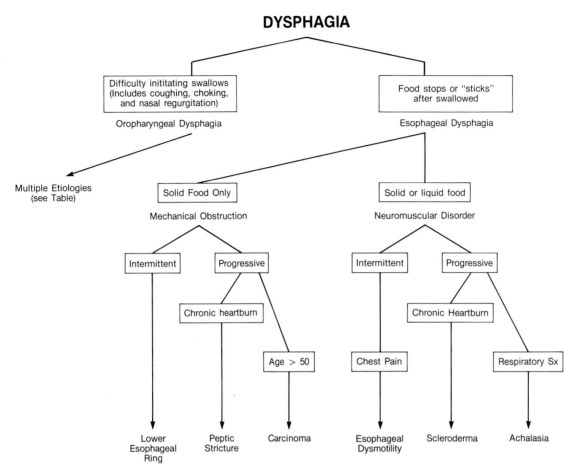

FIGURE 118-1
Diagnostic algorithm for the symptomatic assessment of patients with dysphagia. Important symptoms are included within the boxes.

normality is also called transfer dysphagia because the patient has trouble voluntarily transferring food from the mouth into the esophagus to initiate the involuntary phase of swallowing. Normal swallowing is accomplished by a series of finely coordinated neural and muscular phenomena, modulated through the swallowing center in the brain stem. The food bolus must be moved to the back of the mouth, and the nasopharynx must be closed so that food does not go up into the nasal passages and the vocal cords must close and the epiglottis tilt downward to prevent food from entering the airway. Coordinated relaxation of the upper esophageal sphincter must occur to allow unimpeded bolus passage. All these phenomena occur in appropriate sequence within approximately one second during each swallow. In the elderly it is appropriate to also include a subdivision most appropriately termed *oral dysphagia*. Neurologic or neuromuscular degenerative disorders can produce such profound weakness of the tongue and facial muscles that the patient is unable to move food to the back of the mouth. Defects of this type which exacerbate other swallowing impairments are more likely to occur in stroke patients.

A great variety of conditions can cause dysphagia in

the region of the oropharynx, before a swallowed bolus enters the esophagus.[5,6] These early aspects of swallowing are produced by striated muscle, as opposed to the smooth muscle in the esophagus and the rest of the gastrointestinal tract. Thus, the lesions that cause difficulty in this region are different from those that cause esophageal dysphagia. Anything that might affect the swallowing center in the brain stem or the nerves that modulate the process—the fifth, seventh, ninth, tenth, and twelfth cranial nerves—can cause oropharyngeal dysphagia. In addition, a disorder of the striated muscles of the oropharynx, such as myasthenia gravis, or local abnormalities, such as tumors, thyroiditis, or a retropharyngeal abscess, can cause this symptom. The upper esophageal sphincter's relaxation may be incomplete or delayed, or its closure may be premature. In the patient with a Zenker's diverticulum, the pouch may fill with food and may either obstruct the esophagus by compression or result in regurgitation of previously eaten food some time following a meal.

Table 118-1 lists the numerous conditions that may cause oropharyngeal dysphagia. Particularly relevant in the elderly are strokes, degenerative neuromuscular dis-

TABLE 118-1
Abnormalities Causing Oropharyngeal Dysphagia

Neuromuscular Diseases

Central nervous system (CNS)
  Cerebral vascular accident (brain stem or pseudobulbar
    palsy)
  Parkinson's disease
  Wilson's disease
  Multiple sclerosis
  Amyotrophic lateral sclerosis
  Brain stem tumors
  Tabes dorsalis
  Miscellaneous congenital and degenerative disorders of
    CNS
Peripheral nervous system
  Bulbar poliomyelitis
  Peripheral neuropathies (diphtheria, botulism, rabies, dia-
    betes mellitus)
Motor end plate
  Myasthenia gravis
Muscle
  Muscular dystrophies
  Primary myositis
  Metabolic myopathy (thyrotoxicosis, myxedema, steroid
    myopathy)
  Amyloidosis
  Systemic lupus erythematosus

Local Structural Lesions

Inflammatory (pharyngitis, abscess, tuberculosis, syphilis)
Neoplastic
Congenital webs
Plummer-Vinson syndrome (sideropenic dysphagia)
Extrinsic compression (thyromegaly, cervical spine hyperos-
  tosis, lymphadenopathy).
Surgical resection of the oropharynx

Motility Disorders of the Upper Esophageal Sphincter (UES)

Hypertensive UES ("globus," "spasm")
Hypotensive UES (esophagopharyngeal regurgitation)
Abnormal UES relaxation
  Incomplete relaxation (cricopharyngeal achalasia, CNS
    lymphoma, cricopharyngeal bar)
  Premature closure (Zenker's diverticulum?)
  Delayed relaxation (familial dysautonomia)

ease, tumors, cervical spine hyperostosis, surgical resection of the oropharynx, and hyperthyroidism. Aside from specifically treatable disorders such as thyroid disease, retropharyngeal abscess, or myasthenia gravis, therapy for oropharyngeal dysphagia is usually disappointing. In some patients, the best treatment may be rehabilitation to reteach the patient how to swallow.

Patients with oropharyngeal dysphagia usually describe trouble initiating a swallow, that is, difficulty transferring food back into the esophagus. Associated phenomena include nasal regurgitation, coughing during swallowing, dysarthria, or nasal speech due to weakness of palatal muscles. Other possibly associated clinical features of central nervous system defects may represent important diagnostic clues. These features include the presence of a speech disorder or evidence of any cranial nerve defects, limb weakness, or changes in sleep pattern, including sleep apnea or recent onset of snoring. Dysphagia is usually only part of the total symptom complex in oropharyngeal dysphagia; the primary diagnosis is usually quite apparent, such as a recent stroke or some form of muscular disease. In contrast, esophageal lesions often produce no symptoms other than dysphagia, and diagnosis of the cause may be more difficult. Oropharyngeal dysphagia is also more likely to affect the patient's ability to swallow liquids, while esophageal dysphagia can be expected to primarily affect the swallowing of solid foods. These distinctions are not absolutes, however, and many combinations exist.

Motility abnormalities affecting the hypopharynx are usually mild or moderate and are due to progressive weakness of the functions of mouth and pharynx combined with atrophy of the musculature. They are usually compensated, except when labial spill of saliva may occur during sleeping. Upon questioning, the patient may admit to fatigue. Gradually progressive pharyngeal dysphagia resulting from progressive impairment of motility in this area may lead to a shift in dietary preference or prolonging of meals. Weakness of the palatal muscles may cause snoring. Many symptoms in these patients are frequently not recognized as related to the swallowing difficulty and may be subtle even in the presence of significant dysphagia.[6]

ESOPHAGEAL DYSPHAGIA

Esophageal dysphagia describes difficulty with the transport of food down the esophagus once the bolus has been successfully transferred. Normally, food is cleared from the esophagus quickly, the peristaltic wave taking approximately 8 seconds to travel from top to bottom. When liquid is swallowed while a person stands upright, the liquid will traverse the esophagus in 2 or 3 seconds. Solids take longer and may require a series of peristaltic waves (primary followed by secondary peristalsis) to clear the esophagus. Normally the transport is quite efficient, and the waves sweep the esophagus clean of retained food.

Any difficulty with the coordinated contractions of the esophagus (motility disorder) or any kind of mechanical obstruction may cause abnormal transport. The patient will most often describe a sensation of food "hanging up" somewhere behind the sternum.[7] If the symptom is localized to the lower part of the sternum or the epigastric area, the lesion is most likely in the distal esophagus. The symptom is often referred, however, and the patient may locate the level of dysphagia at the lower part of the neck.[8] For example, a patient with a carcinoma of the distal end of the esophagus will sometimes indicate that he or she feels food stop at the suprasternal notch.

To better understand and define specific symptom components of esophageal dysphagia, three questions are most crucial: (1) What type of food causes the symptoms? (2) Is the dysphagia intermittent or progressive? (3) Does the patient have heartburn? These concerns are illustrated in Fig. 118-1.

When a patient reports that dysphagia occurs with both solids and liquids, and that even water sometimes seems to stop, he or she most likely has a motility disorder or primary neuromuscular abnormality of the esophagus. In contrast, if dysphagia occurs only after swallowing a fairly large piece of meat or other solid food (and not when ingesting any kind of beverage), the physician should think immediately of a mechanical obstruction. Therefore, asking what kind of food causes the problem should be the initial step in sorting out the correct diagnosis.

MECHANICAL OBSTRUCTION

Features of the three most likely lesions and of a few other lesions related to mechanical obstruction are described below. An important feature is whether the dysphagia is progressive or intermittent.

Lower Esophageal Ring

In patients with a lower esophageal ring, dysphagia only occurs intermittently, when the patient is swallowing a fairly large piece of meat or bread. This pattern may persist for years, and it may happen most often when the patient is under unusual tension. This is a typical history of a lower esophageal (Schatzki) ring. The symptom pattern should strongly suggest this diagnosis, and barium radiographic studies should confirm it. The latter will define the ring and determine the luminal diameter and the necessity for dilatation, as well as show concomitant esophagitis or other pathology. It may be necessary to give a solid bolus (such as a pill or a marshmallow) during the barium study to completely identify the ring.

Because the dysphagia is intermittent, a physician who is not especially attuned to patterns of dysphagia produced by different lesions may have the impression that the symptom is psychological. A physician's positive diagnosis of an esophageal ring may be quite satisfying to some patients because many of these patients have been told that their symptoms are all "in their head" and oth-

ers are worried about cancer. Effective therapy may require nothing more than allaying their apprehensions and teaching them to chew their food better. If the ring is less than 13 mm in diameter, dilatation is often required.

Carcinoma

A diagnosis of carcinoma should be suspected in an older patient with dysphagia only for solid foods and usually of relatively short duration (less than 6 months). The swallowing disorder will progressively worsen, occurring more frequently and resulting in inability to swallow almost any kind of solid food unless it is well chewed. There is typically no trouble swallowing liquids until the last stages, when the esophageal lumen is closed by the constricting lesion. Carcinoma of the esophagus occurs frequently in this country. The older the patient, the more the physician should suspect carcinoma. Other features that point to this diagnosis are a history of heavy alcohol use and a well-established smoking habit. Excessive weight loss (greater than 15 pounds) associated with dysphagia in the elderly is an ominous sign of malignancy.

Peptic Stricture

The other lesion that might cause progressive dysphagia is peptic stricture. Most patients with this lesion have a history of chronic heartburn and/or chronic antacid use of some years' duration, but this is not always the case. The age group of patients with peptic stricture is often similar to that of patients with esophageal carcinoma. There is, however, no evidence that patients who have chronic reflux and chronic esophagitis are especially likely to develop carcinoma except in the setting of a Barrett's esophagus, i.e., metaplastic epithelial changes from squamous to columnar cell types.

Other Lesions Likely to Cause Mechanical Obstruction

VASCULAR CAUSES Dysphagia may be caused by vascular anomalies producing compression of the esophagus. The more common lesions are congenital aortic arch abnormalities, with dysphagia presenting early in childhood. Occasionally, symptoms can present in adulthood. Dysphagia aortica is a disorder of the elderly and is due to compression of the esophagus either by a large thoracic aortic aneurysm or by an atherosclerotic, rigid aorta posteriorly and the heart or esophageal hiatus anteriorly.

MEDIASTINAL ADENOPATHY Adenopathy produced by lung cancer, lymphoma, tuberculosis, or sarcoid can cause dysphagia by compression of the esophagus.

CERVICAL HYPERTROPHIC OSTEOARTHROPATHY

In the elderly, cervical osteoarthritis can result in dysphagia from esophageal compression due to hypertrophic spurs. Patients can present with solid food dysphagia, odynophagia, or simply discomfort in the throat. Barium-swallow radiography is usually diagnostic, but intraluminal pathology should be ruled out endoscopically.

NEUROMUSCULAR (MOTILITY) DISORDERS

When a patient has dysphagia for both solids and liquids (i.e, most likely a motility disorder), the next question is whether it is progressive or intermittent. Features of the three most likely lesions are described below.

Spasm

Intermittent dysphagia for all kinds of food suggests the presence of diffuse esophageal spasm.[9] Sometimes it may be helpful to ask whether the dysphagia occurs only with particularly hot or cold foods, pills, or carbonated beverages. Another clue is the presence of intermittent chest pain which may mimic angina pectoris, even with relief from nitroglycerine. Pain of this type may result from diffuse spasm, particularly if it is associated with eating.

Achalasia

Patients with achalasia usually describe difficulty swallowing all kinds of food for considerably longer than 6 months. It is often not clear to the patient exactly when the dysphagia started, but it becomes slowly and progressively worse. The situation becomes more critical clinically with the onset of nocturnal coughing. This description is a classic history of achalasia, in which nocturnal pulmonary symptoms may be due to aspiration from an enlarged fluid-filled esophagus.[9] Occasionally these patients present initially with aspiration pneumonia, and the esophageal abnormality is only identified through careful questioning and radiographic studies. The progressive dysphagia in achalasia is often so indolent in its development that patients will adapt to it. One recent study has indicated that the average duration of symptoms prior to initial treatment in patients with achalasia was greater than 8 years.[10]

Scleroderma

Esophageal involvement with progressive systemic sclerosis is characterized by progressive dysphagia for solids and liquids and a history of chronic heartburn. Other manifestations may include skin tightness and/or Raynaud's phenomenon. In fairly advanced scleroderma, the esophagus may be involved in 70 or 80 percent of cases, with connective tissue in the wall of the esophagus squeezing out and replacing the smooth muscle. Patients so affected lose tone in the lower esophageal sphincter and also lose esophageal peristaltic contraction. Severe heartburn often develops, and complicated reflux esophagitis occurs in patients who have scleroderma esophagus. The presence of chronic heartburn and regurgitation in the patient with progressive dysphagia may help to differentiate scleroderma from achalasia, although this distinction is not an absolute rule. In contrast to scleroderma, achalasia is characterized by a strongly contracted lower esophageal sphincter with poor relaxation; therefore, reflux is highly unlikely. Some patients with achalasia, however, do describe a burning sensation similar to heartburn, believed to be due to esophageal dilatation and chronic stasis of food. An alternative explanation might be the acid pH potentially resulting from fermentation of retained food in the distal esophagus.[11]

GASTROESOPHAGEAL (GE) REFLUX

Although the typical symptoms of GE reflux are heartburn and acid regurgitation, a number of other symptoms, both esophageal and nonesophageal, may be present in these patients. Dysphagia is not commonly present, but it does occur in patients with chronic GE reflux. The genesis of dysphagia may be an obstructing lesion (edema or peptic stricture) and/or a motility abnormality secondary to disordered peristalsis commonly found in patients with severe reflux disease.

As mentioned previously, a globus sensation has also been described as secondary to reflux. This clinical belief may possibly be attributed to some patients with GE reflux referring their symptoms to the region of the suprasternal notch. It is also possible that a globus symptom occurs when contents of the upper esophagus are displaced upward against the undersurface of the upper sphincter. As a result, the sphincter may contract vigorously to protect the pharynx from regurgitation of esophageal contents, causing intraluminal pressure in the sphincter segment to increase. Such a sudden contraction of the cricopharyngeal muscle might become symptomatic and result in a globus sensation.

DIAGNOSTIC CONSIDERATIONS

This discussion has emphasized the importance of a systematic approach to the patient with a history of dysphagia. Here and elsewhere it has been emphasized that the careful taking of a concise history of a patient's symptoms can lead to a strong suspicion of a diagnosis in the majority of cases. Some of the symptoms are directly related to the site of abnormality along the swallowing tract; others are indirect manifestations of dysphagia, such as compensation efforts, the results of complications, or a complete breakdown of swallow coordination. Aside from the major complaints, other important historical features include voice changes, sleep disorders, alterations in eating habits, respiratory malfunctions, effects of medication on swallowing functions, previous illnesses, systemic diseases, surgery, and irradiation. In one form or another, effects of these extraneous events, past or present, may adversely influence, or compound existing problems with the swallowing process.

A thorough examination of the mouth and neck structures is essential. Also important is a complete neurological exam, particularly of the cranial nerves.

Barium radiographic studies of the swallowing mechanism (both pharyngeal and esophageal) should be considered the initial screening procedure in all patients with dysphagia. It is important to remember that patients with dysphagia only for solids may require a solid bolus challenge (a marshmallow or a pill) to demonstrate the obstructing lesion. For patients with oropharyngeal dysphagia, videotaping swallows in both the anterior and lateral aspects may be required to identify abnormalities of the rapid sequence of contractions in the pharynx. If the barium study shows an obstructing lesion, endoscopy and biopsy is usually required to establish a diagnosis. On the other hand, if the barium study suggests a motility disorder or is normal, an esophageal motility study is indicated. This approach should provide a clear understanding of the diagnosis in most patients with dysphagia.

REFERENCES

1. Siebens H, Trupe E, Siebens A et al: Correlates and consequences of eating dependency in institutionalized elderly. *J Am Geriatr Soc* 34:192, 1986.
2. Schatzki R: Panel discussion on diseases of the esophagus. *Am J Gastroenterol* 31:117, 1959.
3. Freeland AP, Ardran GM, Emrys-Roberts E: Globus hystericus and reflux oesophagitis. *J Laryngol Otol* 88:1025, 1974.
4. Cattau EL, Castell DO: Symptoms of esophageal dysfunction, in Stollerman GH (ed): *Advances in Internal Medicine*, vol 27. Chicago, Year Book Medical Publishers, 1982.
5. Hurwitz AL, Newlson JA, Haddad JK: Oropharyngeal dysphagia. *Am J Dig Dis* 20:313, 1975.
6. Bosma JF: Sensorimotor examination of the mouth and pharynx. *Frontiers of Oral Physiology* 2:78, 1976.
7. Pope CE: Symptoms of esophageal disease, in Sleisenger MH, Fordtran JS (eds): *Gastrointestinal Disease*, 3d ed. Philadelphia, WB Saunders, 1983.
8. Edwards DA: Discriminatory value of symptoms in the differential diagnosis of dysphagia. *Clin Gastroenterol* 5:49, 1976.
9. Castell DO: Dysphagia. *Gastroenterology.* 76:1015, 1979.
10. Goulbourne IA, Walbaum PR: Long term results of Heller's operation for achalasia. *J R Coll Surg Edinb* 30:101, 1985.
11. Smart HL, Foster PN, Evans DF, Slevin B, Atkinson M: Twenty-four-hour oesophageal acidity in achalasia before and after pneumatic dilatation. *Gut* 28:883, 1987.

Chapter 119

CONSTIPATION

Lawrence J. Cheskin and Marvin M. Schuster

Constipation is a major problem for elderly persons in developed countries. This is evidenced by the rise in the use of laxatives with age. One British study found that 16 percent of persons between the ages of 10 and 59 used laxatives more frequently than once weekly while 30 percent of those over age 60 were regular laxative users.[1] A recent survey in the United States of community-dwelling elderly persons over age 65 found that 30 percent of the males and 29 percent of the females considered themselves constipated. Twenty-four percent of the men and 20 percent of the women had used laxatives in the month before the survey.[2] The largest study reported to date found that 21 to 35 percent (depending on age) of 1888 women over age 65 and 9 to 26 percent of 1110 men in an ambulatory health screening program reported recurrent constipation.[3]

DEFINITION

There is an important discrepancy between what physicians and elderly patients define as constipation. Many patients consider themselves constipated even if they have a bowel movement each day, particularly if defecation is difficult and associated with excessive straining, while the medical profession tends to define constipation solely by frequency of stooling and consistency of the stool. In one study, 52 percent of elderly men and 65 percent of elderly women who were constipated by self-report had a bowel movement at least once a day.[2]

In contrast to subject self-reports, the few studies of stooling frequency available have not documented differences in frequency of bowel movements[1] or whole gut transit times[4] between elderly and young populations. This kind of evidence has led some investigators to conclude that aging is not associated with an increasing prevalence of constipation. The regularity many older people achieve, however, may be a result of laxative use. What these laxative users' bowel frequency would be were they to stop using laxatives is not known. Other

indirect evidence in support of an association between increasing age and decreasing frequency of bowel movements comes from the survey of community-dwelling elderly persons mentioned previously. Thirty-six percent of male and 21 percent of female respondents reported being more constipated as they grew older.[2]

Since frequency of stooling is the most easily measured parameter of bowel function, constipation is usually defined as a frequency of fewer than three bowel movements per week. However, it is probably not advisable to work up or treat elderly patients merely because they report fewer than three bowel movements per week. Even one bowel movement per week is acceptable if it is not associated with symptoms such as painful defecation or bloating and does not represent a recent change in the patient's normal bowel habits.

LAXATIVE USE

Another issue which is difficult to assess is whether laxatives are necessary in many of the elderly who use them and believe they need them. Almost all laxatives are available without prescription, and there are over 700 different products sold in this country at an annual cost of $400 million. Today's elderly were raised during an era in which an undue emphasis was placed on the virtues of daily or more frequent bowel movements. It becomes difficult to determine whether laxatives were indicated in the first place, since chronic use of laxatives may lead to destruction of neurons in the enteric nervous sytem, with resulting impairment of motility, dilatation of the colon, worsening constipation, and diminished effectiveness of laxatives.[5] Except for those with underlying diseases such as colorectal carcinoma or volvulus, which may cause a fairly sudden change in bowel habits, most elderly patients who are constipated will report being constipated for years and report a gradual, almost imperceptible shift toward constipation and increased laxative use.

ASSOCIATED FACTORS

Factors which are probably associated with constipation in the elderly include impaired general health status, increasing number of medications other than laxatives, and diminished mobility and physical activity. It is unclear what the effect of diet is on bowel habit. There is epidemiologic evidence from developing countries that greater amounts of crude dietary fiber are associated with a lesser prevalence of various gastrointestinal disorders, including diverticular disease, colorectal cancer, and constipation, but there may be intervening variables which account for these differences. Studies in which fiber was added to the diet have shown an increase in stool weight but have not shown a consistent change in whole gut transit times, one group finding no change,[6] another a speeding of transit,[7] and a third a speeding of transit when the baseline was slow but no change or even a slowing when the baseline was rapid transit.[8,9]

Regarding the interaction of psychological illness and constipation, in one study psychological illness was significantly related to self-reported constipation in both elderly men and elderly women but not related to average stool frequency.[2] This suggests that constipation may be among the symptoms which depressed or anxious patients are likely to exaggerate. Aside from this, patients who are being treated with antidepressants may suffer constipation as a side effect of these medications.

In summary, the increased prevalence of self-reported constipation and laxative use in the elderly results from a complex interaction between age-related changes in lifestyle and health status. When organic causes of constipation, including unnecessary laxative use, have been ruled out, there may be little contribution from biological aging per se.

EVALUATION

Unlike constipation in young or middle-aged adults, which is usually due to spastic haustral contractions associated with the irritable bowel syndrome, most constipation in the elderly is associated with decreased motility of the colon. This may be generalized colorectal smooth muscle dysmotility or decreased motility restricted to the anorectum. The latter is termed *dyschezia* and refers to a failure of the defecation mechanism, often due to failure of the striated muscles of the pelvic floor to relax during defecation. This is sometimes described as a functional outlet obstruction. While the processes of absorption and secretion are important in determining the consistency of the stool, hard stools are not due to excessively active absorption, but are a consequence of increased exposure time of the stool to normal absorptive processes because of impaired colonic motility or dyschezia.

HISTORY

When an elderly patient complains of constipation, a careful history is the most important part of the evaluation. As noted, not all self-defined constipation is abnormal, and reassurance that there is a broad range of normal bowel frequency may be all the treatment needed in many cases. Symptoms of disorders which can impair the motility of the large bowel should be sought. These include hypothyroidism, hyperparathyroidism, scleroderma, and neurologic disorders such as Parkinson's disease, strokes, or diabetic neuropathy. Drugs, including opiates, anticholinergics, antidepressants, and calcium- or aluminum-containing antacids may also impair gut motility (see Table 119-1).

Localized colorectal diseases, such as tumors or other constricting lesions, which may cause constipation are often accompanied by other symptoms in addition to constipation. Thus, the history should include questions about abdominal pain and bleeding per rectum. In idiopathic, dietary, or drug-related constipation, there are usually no symptoms other than constipation, although a complaint of abdominal bloating sensation is common with severe constipation.

PHYSICAL EXAMINATION

The general physical examination of the elderly patient with constipation in most cases will be of no value in determining etiology or deciding on treatment. Exceptions include the detection of a localized mass on abdominal examination and local anorectal lesions which may contribute to constipation, such as anal fissures, fistulae, strictures, cancer, or hemorrhoids. Digital rectal exami-

TABLE 119-1
Drugs Causing Constipation

Antacids
  Aluminium hydroxide
  Calcium carbonate
Anticholinergics
Antidepressants
  Tricyclics
  Lithium
Antihypertensive/antiarhythmics
  Calcium channel blockers, especially verapamil
Metals
  Bismuth
  Iron
  Heavy metals
Narcotic analgesics
Nonsteroidal anti-inflammatory compounds
Sympathomimetics
  Pseudoephedrine

nation is sensitive in detecting these anal lesions, though fissures and hemorrhoids, unless they are thrombosed or large, are found more reliably with anoscopy. Thus, anoscopy should be performed routinely in newly constipated elderly persons. Digital examination of the anal canal and rectum is also useful in assessing the tone of the internal anal sphincter and the strength of the external anal sphincter and puborectalis muscles. Occasionally, the anal canal, which is normally contracted, will be lax or asymmetrically contracted. This may be seen with neurologic disorders, especially strokes, peripheral neuropathies, spinal cord trauma, or postoperative scarring. The constipation in such cases is due to failure of the defecation mechanism. The amount and the consistency of stool felt in the rectum may indicate the type of constipation present. Patients with a failure of the defecation mechanism will tend to have much stool in the rectal vault, while those with colonic atony or irritable bowel syndrome will have little or no stool in the rectum between defecations.

SPECIAL STUDIES

The chief value of endoscopic or radiographic examinations of the colorectum in constipated elderly patients is in excluding life-threatening causes, especially carcinoma of the colon. The extent of the diagnostic evaluation must be individualized. Although for screening purposes it is probably justified to obtain a flexible or rigid sigmoidoscopy in all elderly patients because of the high incidence of colorectal carcinoma and premalignant lesions, examining the entire colon via colonoscopy or barium enema should be reserved for patients who have occult or gross rectal bleeding, or who complain of recent (within a year or two) change in bowel habits or who complain of abdominal pain or other symptoms in addition to constipation.

Other lesions which may be diagnosed by barium enema or colonoscopy include megacolon, sigmoid or cecal volvulus, and benign strictures, usually ischemic in nature. Endoscopic examination of the colon in chronically constipated elderly patients sometimes reveals a spotty or diffuse dark pigmentation of the colonic mucosa, known as melanosis coli. This is caused by chronic use of certain laxatives, especially the anthracenes such as cascara, senna, and aloe. It subsides within a year of discontinuing the offending laxatives.[10]

Additional studies which may be useful in the evaluation of constipation are tests of colonic transit and colonic motility. Transit time tests use solid radiopaque markers (Sitzmarks) which are usually enclosed 20 to a capsule and taken orally. Single abdominal radiographs are then taken 5 and 7 days after ingestion of these markers and the number and location of those remaining in

the colon noted. Eighty percent of the markers are normally excreted by day 5 and all by day 7. The retention of markers in the colon or rectum is indicative of significant constipation. In addition, the pattern of retention gives information about mechanism in that holdup of markers in the rectum indicates a failure of expulsion, while holdup throughout the colon indicates generalized inertia. A refinement of this technique utilizes daily ingestion of 24 markers until a steady state is reached, at which point a single radiograph is taken; the number of markers remaining is equal to the transit time in hours.[11]

Colonic motility testing is performed only in specialized centers and involves the recording of pressure activity in the distal colon and rectum using a water-perfused or solid state catheter introduced into the lumen via the anus. It can be used to identify different patterns of colonic activity, for example, phasic contractions (spasms) associated with the irritable bowel syndrome or the decreased response to distension seen in the atonic colon. An empiric approach to the evaluation of constipation in the elderly is diagrammed in Fig. 119-1.

COMPLICATIONS OF CONSTIPATION

Although for most elderly patients constipation is just an annoyance, in a minority it has more serious consequences. Patients who are institutionalized, especially the bedridden, are most susceptible to complications.

Fecal impaction is the result of prolonged exposure of accumulated stool to the absorptive forces of the colon and rectum. The stool may become rocklike in consistency in the rectum (70 percent), sigmoid colon (20 percent), or proximal colon (10 percent).[12] Symptoms of crampy lower abdominal and lower back pain are common. Diarrhea may paradoxically succeed the constipation which led to the impaction as watery material makes its way around the impacted mass of stool. The impaction can sometimes be evacuated by the patient after oral administration of 2 liters of a nonabsorbed solution containing polyethylene glycol (Golytely) daily for 2 days.[13] Usually, however, manual disimpaction will need to be performed. With this technique, the impacted mass is fragmented with the examining finger by pressing it against the posterior rectal wall, and the pieces are then removed. This may have to be repeated over a period of days in severe cases.

Stercoral ulcer is often an incidental finding at autopsy in the bedbound elderly[14] and is usually asymptomatic. It is caused by pressure necrosis of the rectal or sigmoid mucosa due to a fecal mass. In some cases the ulcer may present as rectal bleeding, and perforation can occur, though rarely.[15]

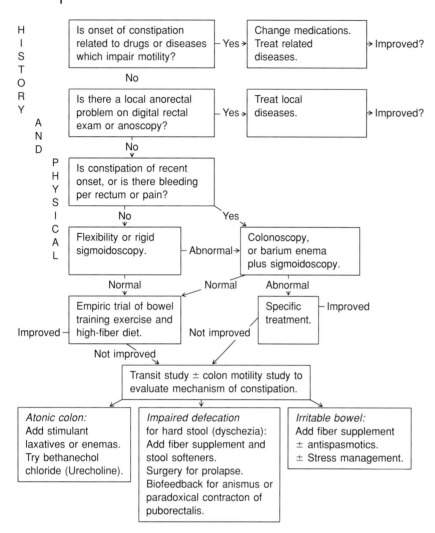

FIGURE 119-1
Evaluation of constipation in the elderly.

Anal fissures may result when excessive straining at stool produces tears or passive congestion of tissues near the dentate margin. The irritating effect of hard stools and toilet paper further magnify the problem. Intraabdominal pressures of up to 300 mmHg are generated during straining. Excessive straining at stool may cause prolapse of the anal mucosa, venous distension, and external and internal hemorrhoids.

Megacolon, while sometimes due to a congenital absence of the myenteric plexus of the colon (Hirschsprung's disease) in young patients, is almost always idiopathic when seen in elderly patients. Chronic use of cathartics over a period of many years may lead to an acquired degeneration of the colonic myenteric plexus.[5] The diagnosis of megacolon is made on a plain abdominal radiograph or barium enema, with associated findings of typanitic distension on abdominal examination and often complaints of constipation or diarrhea and fecal incontinence.

Treatment is difficult and is aimed at preventing buildup of stool and further distension of the already impaired colon by administering enemas regularly. Such patients are susceptible to bacterial overgrowth, which may require antibiotics, and to another complication of constipation, volvulus of the colon.

Volvulus, especially of the sigmoid colon, occurs most commonly in institutionalized, bedbound elderly patients and has a high mortality once the blood supply of the bowel is compromised. Although usually intermittent, the presentation may be quite insidious, and therefore a high index of suspicion is required to make an early diagnosis. Signs and symptoms include abdominal distension of variable degree, abdominal cramping, and constipation. A plain abdominal radiograph is often diagnostic. Urgent reduction of the loop is indicated, and this can be accomplished by the passage of a flexible endoscope in 85 percent of cases. In many cases, however, operative intervention is necessary.[16]

Finally, there is some evidence that chronic constipation is a risk factor for the development of carcinoma of the colon and rectum, particularly in women.[17] This might be related to increased exposure time of susceptible mucosa to potentially carcinogenic substances.

TREATMENT OF CONSTIPATION

Ideally, the treatment of constipation is based on accurate knowledge of the underlying cause or causes. Often, it is not warranted to perform an exhaustive evaluation of constipation, especially in a debilitated elderly patient. In the simplest circumstance, there will be an underlying disease process associated with constipation which can be controlled (hypothyroidism, for example) or a constipating medication which can be substituted with another drug or stopped. The use of laxatives when there is an easily corrected cause is both unnecessary and potentially harmful in that the patient may become laxative-dependent or suffer side effects from the specific laxatives prescribed.

When the cause of the constipation is not obvious or readily identified, and life-threatening causes such as colorectal carcinoma have been ruled out, a phased-in approach to treatment is advisable, especially in a frail, elderly patient. These phases are essentially treatment trials, beginning with lifestyle interventions such as bowel retraining and dietary adjustments and proceeding, if necessary, to progressively more potent laxative treatment.

BOWEL TRAINING

Even in cognitively impaired elderly persons, it is worthwhile to impose a regular schedule of attempts at defecation. In patients who already have a regular time of day when they attempt to stool, it is best to continue on their schedule, advising the patient to make an undistracted attempt for 10 minutes only, each day, even if they do not feel the urge to defecate. When no regular schedule has been established by the patient, the best times to recommend are after breakfast and after the evening meal, to take advantage of the postprandial gastrocolic response.

The importance of establishing a regular bowel "habit" in the elderly stems also from the frequency of diminished sensation of rectal distension. With a less readily recognized signal in such patients, it is easy to ignore an urge. Such a pattern may lead to retention as the rectum accommodates to progressively greater amounts of distension. Reestablishing a logical and regular time for stooling is thus the first step in treatment.

EXERCISE

Competitive runners, including elderly athletes, rarely become constipated. Bedfast patients are at great risk of constipation and often respond poorly to treatment. While the role of physical activity in the treatment of constipation in the elderly is unclear, patients seem often to respond favorably to a regular program of mild exercise such as walking.

DIET

In most cases of constipation in the elderly, dietary manipulations are helpful, though they may not in isolation be sufficient treatment. Bowel training, dietary management, and regular exercise when feasible should be undertaken together as the first phase of treatment. Although certain patients may find specific foods of value as laxatives, it is not necessary to recommend, to use the most famous example, prunes to all one's constipated elderly patients. If the patient is already using a favorite "natural" laxative, however, and is convinced it is beneficial, there is usually no need to stop it.

The dietary adjustment which can be recommended to nearly all constipated elderly who are not obstructed is increased consumption of fiber. There are misconceptions, however, among patients and caregivers about which foods are high in fiber content. Most raw fruits and vegetables, for example, are not especially high in dietary fiber, are expensive, and are often poorly tolerated by elderly persons with functional bowel disorders or poor dentition. For instance, to provide 10 g of total dietary fiber, a minimally effective supplementary amount for constipation, the elderly person would have to eat a low-fiber diet plus two heads of lettuce, or six bananas, or four servings of string beans daily. The few truly high-fiber foods are listed in Table 119-2. As a practical matter, it may be more efficient in many elderly patients, particularly the institutionalized, to provide additional dietary fiber in the form of supplements. Numerous preparations are available which provide 3.4–6.0 g of total dietary fiber per dose. For the best tolerance, each dose should be taken with liberal amounts of fluid, at least 8 ounces, and the total daily dose increased over a couple of weeks to minimize the transient bloating which occurs frequently. Ten grams is often a sufficient dose, although many patients require 20–30 g a day. By comparison, some African tribes consume upwards of 50 g of total dietary fiber daily. Idiopathic constipation is not reported to be a big problem for them. Although fiber is traditionally not prescribed for patients with atonic constipation, it is worth a try in all except those with severe megacolon or mechanical obstructions.

Finally, it should be recognized that a poor state of hydration may exacerbate constipation in elderly

TABLE 119-2
Very High-Fiber Foods

Type	Total Dietary Fiber per Serving, g
100% bran cereal	8.4
Beans (baked, kidney, lima, navy)	8.5–10.0
Peas (canned)	6.0
Raspberries	4.6
Broccoli	3.2

patients, particularly those who are institutionalized, demented, or receiving diuretics or nasogastric tube feedings.

LAXATIVES

When the lifestyle changes described in the initial phases of treatment fail or do not produce a sufficient improvement in symptoms, the clinician must resort to pharmacologic treatments which have a greater risk of side effects. Because almost all laxatives and enemas are available without prescription and they represent a "quick fix" for constipation, their use is rampant and often unnecessary. Often one will find the most difficult treatment question to be which laxatives to discontinue rather than which one to start. It is also common to encounter patient resistance to stopping his or her laxatives.

Traditionally, laxatives have been divided into five categories: bulk, emollient, saline, hyperosmotic, and stimulant laxatives. Bulk laxatives include the various fiber-containing preparations and are thought to act in two ways. They are hydrophilic, so tend to increase stool mass and soften its consistency. In addition, while not digestible by pancreatic enzymes, they are acted upon by colonic bacteria, producing osmotically potent metabolites. They are the safest laxatives and are generally well-tolerated by elderly patients when introduced gradually. They are contraindicated in patients with partial mechanical obstruction of any portion of the gastrointestinal tract, since there have been rare reports of complete obstruction secondary to bulk agents in patients with esophageal as well as intestinal strictures.

Emollients, or stool softeners, include mineral oil, as well as the newer docusate salts such as dioctyl sodium sulfosuccinate (Colace). Mineral oil may impair absorption of fat-soluble vitamins and may be aspirated by patients with impaired swallowing or gag reflex, with resulting lipid pneumonitis or pleuritis. It is generally not recommended since safer, effective agents are available. The newer agents work by lowering surface tension, allowing water to enter the stool more readily. They are generally well-tolerated and may be particularly useful in bedbound elderly patients who are at risk for fecal impaction. They are also a useful adjunct to bulk preparations in elderly patients. For idiopathic constipation, these agents are the next step in a phased-in treatment trial after bulk agents.

Saline laxatives and enemas are salts of magnesium and sodium. Those in most common use are oral milk of magnesia, oral magnesium citrate, and sodium phosphate (Fleet's) enemas. All function as hyperosmolar agents and cause net secretion of fluid into the colon. There is also evidence that colonic motility is increased by these agents via release of the hormone cholecystokinin. Chronic use of magnesium-containing saline laxa-

tives in the elderly may contribute to hypermagnesemia when there is impaired renal function (known or unsuspected). The phosphate-containing preparations may induce hypocalcemia when high doses are used, even in patients with normal renal function. The phosphate-containing enemas have been reported to cause damage to the rectum, both traumatic from the plastic nozzle of the enema and as a direct toxic effect of the hypertonic solution on the rectal mucosa.[18] It is advisable to use saline laxatives and enemas not as a chronic medication but as an "escape" medication when earlier phases of treatment are being tried. For example, during bowel training or a trial of fiber supplementation, one may allow the patient to take a phosphate enema after the morning attempt at stooling if no bowel movement has occurred on the trial regimen for more than 2 consecutive days. The other common use for saline laxatives is in preparing the bowels for radiographic or endoscopic examinations.

Hyperosmolar laxatives, notably lactulose, exert their effect primarily by drawing water into the gut lumen. Lactulose is a semisynthetic disaccharide which cannot be digested by pancreatic or intestinal enzymes but is metabolized by colonic bacteria to hydrogen and organic acids. This acidifies the colon and, in addition to an osmotic effect, may alter electrolyte transport and colonic motility. Lactulose is usually well-tolerated but may cause transient bloating. It is used to treat hepatic encephalopathy and has also been shown to be useful in treating constipation in the elderly.[19] Lactulose is not commonly used in the United States in the treatment of constipation. As with most laxatives, there are no data on effectiveness compared to other agents.

Stimulant laxatives are in very common use in the elderly. They are very effective but, unfortunately, may have the worst toxic consequences. They exert their effects primarily through direct stimulation of the myenteric plexuses of the colon, thereby increasing motility. Specific agents include the anthraquinone derivatives cascara, senna, and aloe, which are absorbed then excreted via the enterohepatic circulation into the colon, where they are converted to an active metabolite, emodine. These agents, as noted, may lead to melanosis coli and may also do permanent damage to the myenteric plexus. Phenolphthalein is a fat-soluble stimulant which may therefore have a prolonged duration of action. It has been associated with dermatitis, photosensitivity reactions, and the Stevens–Johnson syndrome.[20] Abuse of laxatives containing this substance can be demonstrated by noting a red color upon alkalinizing a stool specimen.

Castor oil, nominally but inaccurately classed with the stimulant laxatives, has as its active ingredient ricinoleic acid. It inhibits glucose and sodium absorption and stimulates water and electrolyte secretion via inhibition of Na-K-ATPase and increases in cellular cAMP. Its use can lead to fluid and electrolyte disturbances, and it generally cannot be recommended with safer agents available. Bisacodyl (Ducolax) tablets or suppositories are not absorbed but exert a stimulant effect directly on the myenteric plexus. Bisacodyl is a popular agent and probably has less toxicity than the other stimulant laxatives mentioned. All, however, affect electrolyte balance, so may precipitate hypokalemia, fluid and salt overload, or diarrhea. This category of laxatives, because of its potential for significant side effects, should be considered only after adequate trial of the categories of laxatives described earlier.

SURGICAL PROCEDURES

Finally, in selected cases of intractable constipation, a variety of surgical procedures have been attempted ranging from left hemicolectomy to subtotal colectomy with ileoproctostomy.[21] Surgery is rarely needed in the treatment of constipation in the elderly, and can in general be recommended only when there is an obstructing lesion of the colorectum, or recurrent volvulus due to congenital or acquired megacolon.

Thus, the treatment of constipation in the elderly should first be directed at remediable medical and surgical conditions and the cessation of constipating medications (Fig. 119-1). When the constipation is believed to be idiopathic or related to the elderly patient's diet, mobility, dyschezia, or atonic colon, a phased-in series of treatment trials should be instituted, starting with lifestyle changes alone and adding progressively more potent laxatives over a period of weeks to months until a satisfactory outcome is achieved. Ideally, the phased-in approach will not be rigidly followed but will be adapted to the underlying pathophysiology and symptoms of the individual elderly patient. Once an effective treatment regimen is arrived at in this manner, particularly if laxatives with potentially dangerous side effects are being utilized, an attempt should be made to reduce dosages to the minimally effective range. The laxatives needed to break the cycle of severe constipation are often more potent than those needed to maintain adequate bowel movement. Thus, it may not be necessary to use more than dietary changes ultimately in most of the elderly suffering from this common condition.

REFERENCES

1. Connell AM et al: Variations in bowel habit in two population samples. *Br Med J* 1:1095, 1965.
2. Whitehead WE et al: Constipation and laxative use in the elderly living at home: Prevalence and relationship to exercise and dietary fiber. *J Am Geriatr Soc*, in press.
3. Hale WE et al: Symptom prevalence in the elderly: An evaluation of age, sex, disease, and medication use. *J Am Geriatr Soc* 34:333, 1986.
4. Eastwood HDH: Bowel transit studies in the elderly. Radio-opaque markers in the investigation of constipation. *Geront Clin* 14:154, 1972.
5. Smith B: The effect of irritant purgatives on the myenteric plexus in man and mouse. *Gut* 9:139, 1968.
6. Eastman MA et al: Effects of dietary supplements of wheat bran and cellulose on faeces and bowel function. *Br Med J* 4:392, 1973.
7. Cummings JH et al: Measurement of the mean transit time of dietary residue through the human gut. *Gut* 17:210, 1976.
8. Harvey RF et al: Effects of increased dietary fiber on intestinal transit. *Lancet* 1:1278, 1973.
9. Payler DK et al: The effect of wheat bran on intestinal transit. *Gut* 16:209, 1975.
10. Fine KD et al: Diarrhea, in Sleisenger MH, Fordtran JS (eds): *Gastrointestinal Disease*, 4th ed. Philadelphia, Saunders, 1988, p 307.
11. Metcalf AM et al: Simplified assessment of segmental colonic transit. *Gastroenterology* 91:1186, 1986.
12. Kaufman SA, Karin H: Fecaloma of the sigmoid flexure. *Dis Colon Rectum* 9:133, 1966.
13. Puxty JA, Fox RA: Golytely: A new approach to fecal impaction in old age. *Age Ageing* 15:182, 1982.
14. Grinvalsky HT, Bowerman CI: Stercoraceous ulcers of the colon. *JAMA* 171:1941, 1959.
15. Gekas P, Schuster MM: Stercoral perforation of the colon: Case report and review of the literature. *Gastroenterology* 80:1054, 1981.
16. Anderson JR, Lee D: The management of acute sigmoid volvulus. *Br J Surg* 68:117, 1981.
17. Vobecky J et al: A case-control study of risk factors for large bowel carcinoma. *Cancer* 51:1958, 1983.
18. Pietsch JB et al: Injury by hypertonic phosphate enema. *Can Med J* 116:1169, 1977.
19. Wesselius-DeCasparis A et al: Treatment of chronic constipation with 'lactulose' syrup. Results of a double-blind study. *Gut* 9:84, 1968.
20. Sekas G: *Prac Gastroenterol* 1:33, 1987.
21. Gilbert K et al: Surgical treatment of constipation. *West J Med* 140:569, 1984.

Chapter 120

DIARRHEA IN THE ELDERLY

William B. Greenough III and Richard G. Bennett

Diarrheal diseases in the elderly are a significant problem. However, little research has been done to document the epidemiology of these illnesses beyond identifying gastroenteritis as a common problem in nursing homes. Heretofore, no textbooks of geriatric medicine have discussed this common problem in depth. Diarrheal diseases have serious consequences and hence deserve investigation and consideration. Diarrhea causes incontinence, disability, and even death. In this chapter we will discuss the epidemiology of diarrheal diseases in the elderly as it is now understood; the causes of diarrhea, with a particular emphasis on those agents which affect the elderly preferentially; the mechanisms which result in diarrhea; host factors in the elderly which predispose to diarrheal disease; and rational treatment and preventive considerations for gastroenteritis based on an understanding of these mechanisms.

SCOPE AND NATURE OF THE PROBLEM

In 1970 an outbreak of *Salmonella* enteritis resulted in the deaths of 24 individuals in a Baltimore nursing home.[1] This outbreak attracted national attention and resulted in congressional hearings; it was responsible, in part, for ushering in many needed changes in the process of nursing home accreditation and licensure. In the years since this tragedy, little progress has been made in our understanding of diarrheal diseases in nursing home patients, and recently a similar tragedy occurred in a Canadian facility where 19 people died from an outbreak of vero toxin–producing *Escherichia coli.*[2] Nationally, diarrheal diseases are among the four most common causes of infection in nursing homes,[3–5] and there is an 8 percent annual incidence rate of diarrheal outbreaks in Maryland nursing homes.[6] Despite the magnitude of this problem, there are no reports on the epidemiology of infectious diarrhea in nursing homes, and the causes of more than 80 percent of the outbreaks in Maryland are never identified.[6] Furthermore, oral rehydration therapy (ORT), the mainstay of treatment of diarrheal diseases throughout the world for more than 10 years, is rarely used to treat elderly patients with diarrhea in the United States.[7] Recently a publication from the American Association of Retired Persons has focused on the importance of ORT.[8] Thus, although current advances are not being applied to diagnose and treat elderly patients with diarrhea, awareness is beginning to improve.

Diarrhea is usually self-limited (24 to 48 hours), but significant fluid losses can occur in a short time. In healthy individuals, such losses are partially corrected by hormonally mediated urinary concentration and by increased drinking in response to thirst. If appropriate fluids are taken, no serious consequences ensue. When fluid losses occur in the elderly, however, a different situation exists. Maximal urinary concentration in response to dehydration is less with old age. Although the mechanisms underlying decreased renal capacity are not fully understood, the ability of the kidney to respond to disturbances in volume is diminished in the elderly. More importantly, the normal mechanism whereby hyperosmolarity from volume depletion leads to thirst may decrease with age. The perception of thirst is impaired in patients with dementia, as may be their ability to obtain fluids. Thus, dehydration from diarrhea may not be translated into a desire or opportunity to drink, and the losses of fluid may remain uncorrected. The frail elderly, particularly those confined in nursing homes, may have difficulty with ambulation and communication. Even if thirst is present, these individuals may be unable to replace losses because of their physical disabilities.

The loss of circulating fluid volume in the elderly has consequences far more severe than such a loss in younger individuals. Silent atherosclerosis which results in partial occlusion of blood vessels to vital organs is common, and drugs which induce salt and potassium losses, as well as block cardiac and circulatory reflexes, are frequently prescribed. The combination of silent atherosclerosis and drug therapy increases the vulnerability to infarctions and arrhythmias. Small decrements in intravascular volume in an old person with atherosclerosis can lead directly to hypoperfusion of vital organs or the portions of vital organs served by atherosclerotic arteries. Worsening renal failure, congestive heart failure, or a decline in mental status occurring after a benign episode of gastroenteritis may not be thought to be related. The important physiologic differences between the young and the old make diarrhea a life-threatening illness in the elderly. This has been seen in Japan, where individuals over the age of 75 have a 400-fold increased mortality rate from gastrointestinal infections,[9] and it was also evident in the 1970 nursing home outbreak in Baltimore, in which patients generally did not die immediately of acute dehydration or sepsis but succumbed after a week or more from the secondary effects of myocardial, cerebral, or renal damage.[1]

Identifying the significance of volume depletion in the elderly is important. Most of the parameters used in pediatric and adult populations are not helpful since age itself results in poor skin turgor, sunken eyes, and a dry tongue. About the only clinical sign of diagnostic value in the elderly is orthostatic change in the blood pressure. However, by the time measurable orthostasis occurs, as much as 6 to 10 percent of the intravascular volume has been lost, and serious hypoperfusion of a vital organ may have occurred. The serum electrolytes only identify changes in the concentration of sodium or potassium in relation to water and other solutes. Electrolyte determination tells little of the absolute status of the intravascular and extracellular fluid volume. A useful parameter which is measurable is total plasma protein or plasma specific gravity. To date no studies have been reported using these measurements to estimate fluid loss in the elderly, but we believe they would prove to be as useful in these patients as they have been in younger patients.[10]

Unfortunately, a typical scenario which occurs when a nursing home patient has diarrhea is that enteral feedings are discontinued and orders are written to encourage fluids, but the type of fluids are not specified. Since both salts and water are lost with diarrhea, if too little fluid is given, both hypovolemia and hypernatremia occur. If volume depletion is treated by fluids low in salt, then hyponatremia accompanies volume depletion. This scenario can lead to anuria, delirium, or seizures. Inadequate replacement of volume may lead to infarc-

tions of vital organs. Such events typically end when the patient is transferred to an acute hospital for emergency treatment or else expires. It is now 10 years since an editorial in *Lancet* declared that ORT was perhaps the most important advance in medicine during the twentieth century.[11] Many lessons have been learned in developing countries over the last two decades. ORT is a simple and inexpensive treatment for dehydration from diarrhea. ORT can be employed early (when diarrhea first strikes) and without any complicated technology. It can be administered by mouth in those who can drink or through enteral feeding tubes.[12] However, ORT is rarely used for adults in the United States, and there are no reports to our knowledge of its use in the elderly in any setting. We believe that appropriate use of ORT in nursing homes and in the community could avert many hospitalizations and prevent serious damage to vital organs, especially the brain, heart, and kidneys.

Since it has recently been well-documented that malnutrition is a common and serious problem among nursing home patients,[13] and it is perhaps a problem among those living in the community as well, then any diseases which accelerate malnutrition deserve highest attention. There is also a sufficiency of information that indicates that in both residents of developing countries and travelers to such countries an apparently trivial bout of acute diarrhea can be accompanied by rather prolonged malabsorption and anorexia.[14] It is not uncommon for travelers or long-term visitors to developing countries to experience significant weight loss as a consequence of diarrhea. To our knowledge, the relationship between gastroenteritis and malnutrition among the elderly in this country has not been explored. As in poor countries, it can be expected that diarrhea may be important in the malnutrition of the elderly.

The principal change in management of diarrhea during the past 20 years has arisen from the repeated documentation that continued and early feeding, even during the acute illness, is associated with less severe disease, shorter disease course, and more rapid recovery.[15] The use of early feeding and ORT in children has prevented prolonged weight loss and has accelerated a return to a normal growth curve. It is to be expected that in the elderly, such an approach would result in prevention of accelerated malnutrition and the disorders which accompany this state (e.g., pressure sores that do not heal, anorexia, lethargy, edema, and loss of strength and muscle mass).

CAUSES

There are no thorough studies of sporadic or epidemic diarrhea in either institutionalized or community-dwelling elderly in which the currently available technology for the diagnosis or cause of diarrhea has been applied. In settings in which this technology has been used, it is possible to identify two-thirds of the causes of an episode of severe acute diarrhea.[16] Table 120-1 indicates some of the noninfectious and infectious causes of diarrhea that are of signal importance in the elderly. The evaluation of patients with diarrheal illness should be directed at excluding the noninfectious causes and identifying infectious agents. Among the common noninfectious causes are laxative use and abuse, complications of prescribed medications, supplemental and tube feedings of high osmolarity, and gastrointestinal syndromes such as partial bowel obstruction, mesenteric vascular insufficiency, and certain neoplasms.

TABLE 120-1
Common Causes of Diarrheal Disease in the Elderly

Noninfectious Causes

Iatrogenesis
  Dietary supplements
  Antacids
  Bulk and osmotically active laxatives (e.g., Colace, milk of
    magnesia)
  Miscellaneous drugs (e.g., digoxin, quinidine, methyl-
    dopa)
Neoplasia
  Obstructive lesions
  Secretory adenomas
  Hormone-secreting tumors
Gastrointestinal disease
  Malabsorption
  Mesenteric atherosclerosis
  Portal hypertension
Systemic illness
  Thyrotoxicosis
  Uremia
Miscellaneous (Impaction)

Infectious Agents

Bacteria
  S. aureus
  Salmonella sp.*
  *C. difficile**
  *C. perfringens**
  *E. coli**
  Campylobacter sp.
  Shigella sp.
  Vibrio sp.
Viruses
  Norwalk agent*
  Astrovirus*
  Calcivirus*
Parasites
  Cryptosporidium
  Giardia

*Each of these agents has been reported as the cause of outbreaks of diarrhea in nursing homes.

Of the infectious diarrheas, there are three broad categories. The first of these is acute food poisoning, in which an individual consumes preformed toxins in foods contaminated by bacteria. The most common illness of this type is associated with *Staphylococcus aureus* enterotoxins. This is an explosive illness which occurs within 2 to 8 hours of eating contaminated food and is characterized principally by vomiting.[17]

The second category of infectious diarrheal diseases is acute watery diarrhea. These syndromes are caused by bacteria which produce several potent enterotoxins. The most dramatic of these diseases is cholera, mediated by the *Vibrio cholerae* exotoxin.[18] A number of other gram-negative bacteria also produce a cholera-like exotoxin, and there are several other toxins capable of producing similar diseases which are less severe and prolonged. The heat-stable toxin (ST) and heat-labile toxin (LT) of *E. coli* are examples of such toxins. Acute watery diarrhea is also caused in the absence of exotoxin production by adherence of bacteria such as enteroadherent *E. coli* to cells of the small intestine.

The third main category of infectious diarrhea is invasive or tissue-destructive diseases mediated by inflammation. The organisms which cause these illnesses also often produce enterotoxins. Among this group are the viral diarrheas. Many viral gastroenterities, initially identified in infants and young children, have now been implicated in nursing home outbreaks of diarrhea. These include Norwalk agent, calicivirus, and astrovirus. Other enteroviruses, no doubt, will continue to be identified. The most characteristic cause of inflammatory diarrhea is *Shigella* sp., in which a dysentery-like syndrome occurs, accompanied by fever and systemic illness; however, *Salmonella* sp. is a more common cause in the United States. With both shigellosis and salmonellosis it is not uncommon for young adults and children to have a dysenteric or tissue-destructive phase preceded by an acute bout of watery diarrhea, since both groups of bacteria possess enterotoxins capable of triggering a mechanism that causes acute watery diarrhea. More common than either *Shigella* or *Salmonella* in this country, and of special note in the elderly, is an inflammatory diarrhea caused by *Clostridium difficile*. This syndrome often follows the administration of antibiotics, and recent studies in nursing homes have indicated that antibiotic-associated *C. difficile* diarrhea is very common.[19] *C. difficile* is among the invasive group of organisms in that it produces a potent cytotoxin which produces necrosis of the lining cells of the colon (and perhaps the terminal ileum) and results in severe inflammation. This inflammation can be recognized as pseudomembranous colitis either proctoscopically or by special scanning studies such as an indium white cell scan, in which affected areas of the colon and terminal ileum can be seen by their concentration of labeled white blood cells. The nuclear medicine study is particularly useful for frail individuals who may not tolerate colonscopy, and an example of a study in a patient with pseudomembranous colitis is shown in Fig. 120-1.

Although carriage of *C. difficile* is not common in the general population, we have observed that colonization is very common in nursing home residents. Colonization may also be sustained over long periods of time, but more worrisome is the observation that colonization is associated with an increase in the likelihood of death.[19] In experimental animals, particularly the hamster, death due to *C. difficile* infection is usually not accompanied by diarrhea, but it is associated with a severe and occult caecitis which might lead to systemic intoxication by *C. difficile* toxins A and B. We have seen cases in which nursing home patients without diarrhea died and *C. difficile* colitis was found at autopsy. Although we are concerned about the possibility of systemic intoxication, proof of systemic effects remains to be elucidated.

MECHANISMS

Through studies on cholera, mechanisms which underlie bacterial and viral diarrhea have been clarified over the last two decades.[17] The final common pathway for secretion in the intestines operates through the cells of the villus crypts. These cells are influenced directly by enterotoxins and neural signals, as well as by hormones, including prostaglandins, vasoactive intestinal peptides, gastrin, and others. The final stage for secretion is a chloride secretory mechanism which is linked to intracellular signals which also decrease absorption of sodium chloride at the villus tips. Thus, to a greater or lesser extent, in instances of diarrhea mediated either directly by toxins or indirectly through humoral signals accompanying inflammation, crypt cells secrete and villus tip cells fail to absorb fluids. The ensuing fluid accumulation which takes place principally in the duodenum and jejunum overwhelms the absorptive capacity of the ileum and colon and results in watery diarrhea.[18]

The mechanisms by which the adherence of bacteria to intestinal epithelium produces diarrhea are not as clearly defined as are those for enterotoxin-mediated diarrhea. However, it is expected that bacterial products trigger endogenous humoral signals which precipitate a secretory and nonabsorptive state of the upper intestine. Such a state, in fact, is a partial defense mechanism and operates nicely as long as the host has fluid replacement adequate to sustain the gastrointestinal fluid losses. What is in essence a flushing mechanism acts to remove the pathogens from the upper gut and allow normal endogenous flora to become reestablished. The precise mechanisms of invasive diarrheas are less fully studied; however, it is clear that organisms which invade possess potent substances which damage cells and allow bacterial entrance into the cells. The best studied of these factors is the verotoxin produced by *Shigella* and *E. coli*.[20]

HOST FACTORS

In humans, diarrhea is the single most common cause of death before the reproductive years begin.[7] Even so, evolutionary biology has endowed humans with very effective host defenses against enteric infection. We are not aware of studies to date which investigate the change in the defense mechanism against enteric infection with age. Since diarrhea is common and disabling in the elderly, certainly this is an important area for investigation. Clearly the most important defense against enteric infection is the intelligence of the human brain, which has gathered knowledge and created technologies to prepare food and water free of parasites and microorganisms. However, especially in poor countries and institutional settings, systems preventing enteric pathogens from entering food or water often break down, engendering a risk of diarrheal diseases.

The next line of defense lies in the nose and in the mouth. The olfactory sense can detect spoiled food and

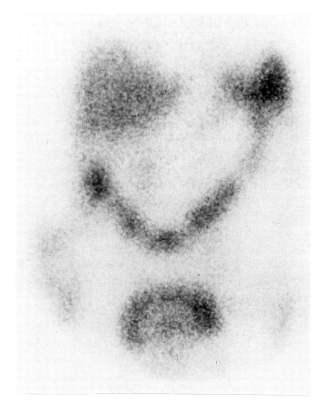

FIGURE 120-1
A photograph of an indium-labeled white blood cell scan in a patient with *C. difficile* diarrhea showing accumulation of the radioactively labeled cells in the colon.

will produce an avoidance from eating it. Unfortunately, some enteric pathogens can proliferate in food without producing noxious odors or tastes; also, age reduces the ability of smell. The next major defense is gastric acid. Both in experimental animals and humans, the loss or diminution of gastric acid results in much higher susceptibility to all kinds of enteric infections and diarrheal diseases. Quantitative examples of this in young adults are available from research on cholera in volunteer studies. In subjects with full gastric acid, nearly a millionfold more organisms were required to create disease than in those in whom gastric acid had been neutralized.[21] Production of gastric acid may decline with age, although it is not clear whether this is a normal part of aging. Certain infections, principally *Campylobacter pylori*, cause gastritis and a reduction of gastric acid and may predispose for diarrhea. The integrity of the gastric acid barrier in the elderly warrants study. Many elderly patients take histamine (H_2) receptor–blocking drugs and antacids. It would be expected that these medications would predispose individuals to developing diarrhea, particularly if they are institutionalized, or if they travel to countries where fecal-oral contamination is common. Thus, the gastric acid has importance in that it can be regulated by medicines.

The next line of defense is reflexive elimination from the gut by vomiting or diarrhea. The vomiting reflex occurs when certain contaminated substances are taken into the stomach and then rejected. This is particularly common with food poisonings but also occurs in other infections. Diarrhea can result from the secretory response by the upper gut which accelerates the propulsion of infecting materials to the colon and expulsion from the anus. Diarrhea is a defense mechanism which causes disability and death when fluids are not replaced.

The most distal defense is the normal microbial flora. The anaerobic conditions of the caecum and internal ileum created by the close symbiotic relationship of intestinal microflora with these organs is a strong defense against enteric pathogens. The most striking experimental demonstration of this defense has been done using mice. A millionfold more salmonella are required to generate a fatal bloodstream infection when normal intestinal flora are present as compared to when antibiotics are used to destroy the intestinal flora.[22] This underscores the risks of disturbing gut microflora and permits an understanding of why infection by *C. difficile* and *C. perfringens* are such problems in the institutionalized elderly.[19,23] This knowledge also leads to therapeutic approaches which aim to reestablish normal intestinal microflora. At the present time we are not aware of definitive studies of microfloral changes as they occur with aging. It is clear that very young infants (neonates) and very old persons have certain infections in common, among them *C. difficile*. Further information on evolution of gut microflora with age will be important to an understanding of susceptibility to invasive diarrheal diseases.

Finally, the intestine has an extremely talented and effective local immune system. Antigens passing through the gut from the earliest days of childhood are monitored by sensor cells located in the Peyer's patches. Antibodies are formed locally at the surface of the intestine where infecting organisms adhere or invade. Defense against viral and bacterial diarrheal diseases is principally through the local immune system of the intestinal tract.[24] Those growing up in countries or situations where fecal-oral pollution is great acquire a high level of resistance to most of the diarrheal diseases and enteric infections at a very young age. Few studies of the local immune system of the gut with aging are available,[25] but intestinal immunity would be expected to remain intact along with other components of the immune system except in the case of disease, severe malnutrition, immune compromising infections, or immunosuppressive therapy. An understanding of the gut immune system is important, as all of the currently effective experimental vaccines directed against enteric pathogens are administered orally. The prototypical oral vaccine is the oral polio virus vaccine. Polio virus enters the system through the gut, and the gut is the principal site of immune defense. Long-lasting immunity is engendered by oral polio vaccine. This also appears to be true of immunity induced by other enteric vaccines.[24]

TREATMENT

Treatment of diarrhea is very straightforward. Since acute watery diarrhea is more common than inflammatory dysentery, and since most cases are self-limited and last from 2 to 5 days, the only requirement for avoiding any complications is to replace all gastrointestinal losses with fluids of appropriate volume and composition.[7,8] Losses must be replaced early before vascular complications occur. Therapy should be initiated from the onset of the first loose stool. Although a great deal of information has been gathered on the composition of diarrheal stools in children and young adults, we are not aware of any data in the elderly. It is unlikely that there will be major differences with aging in the composition of secretory diarrhea. Although most oral solutions have been designed for use in children, and none has been developed based on studies of diarrheal losses in older individuals, those solutions listed in Table 120-2 are appropriate for use in the elderly. Except for the rice-based formula, these solutions are commercially available.

ORT is now the standard and best treatment for all diarrheal diseases. Neither technology nor a specialized health-provider is required for the administration of

TABLE 120-2
Analysis of Three Commercially Available Glucose-Based Oral Rehydration Therapy Solutions
and a Prepared Rice-Based Solution

Oral Rehydration Therapy Solution	Analysis/Liter					
	Na (meq)	K (meq)	Cl (meq)	Base* (meq)	Carbohydrate† (g)	Calorie
Pedialyte (Ross)	45	20	35	30	25	96
Resol (Wyeth)	50	20	50	34	20	80
ORS‡ (Jianas Bros.)	90	20	80	30	20	80
Rice-based§	90	20	80	30	80	320

*HCO_3^- or citrate
†Pedialyte, Resol, and ORS contain glucose.
‡This is the WHO/UNICEF formula.
§Rice-based ORT can be made from precooked instant rice cereal, e.g., Gerber's "Rice Cereal for Baby."

ORT. What is necessary is an individual capable of offering sips of the solution to the affected patient frequently, at least every 3 to 5 minutes in patients with severe losses, and also capable of roughly estimating the volume of the diarrheal losses. The simplest rules for knowing when enough ORT has been given are that urine will be passed every 3 to 4 hours and the specific gravity of the urine will be less than 1.015. If there is concern about urinary retention, it may be necessary in debilitated patients to temporarily insert a urinary catheter to insure that adequate replacement has been achieved. Except in patients with anuria from end-stage renal disease, urine output is the best guide to therapy. Thirst is a helpful index for guiding ORT in children and young adults, but some studies have shown the thirst mechanism to be abnormal in the elderly, and cognitive impairment limits the usefulness of this symptom as a guide for monitoring repletion in many nursing home patients.

More precise measurements of fluid losses and gains can be carried out by accurate measurement of plasma specific gravity or plasma protein. Such measurements, however, are only necessary under metabolic study conditions. They are not needed as a guide to therapy in general practice. Careful measurements of intake and output would be ideal, but they are not usually obtainable either in the community setting or in nursing home settings. The principal physical finding in relation to volume loss is orthostatic hypotension. It is essential not to allow sufficient depletion to occur such that orthostasis is present. ORT should always be administered before orthostasis occurs and in quantities sufficient to ensure that blood volume never decreases to the point of circulatory compromise.

There are risks of ORT that are greater in the elderly than in the younger age groups. The principal risk is that many older people have impaired cardiac function, and overhydration can result in congestive heart failure. Therefore it is important to observe the patient with diarrhea who is being treated with ORT and watch for signs of failure, including rales at the lung bases, jugular vein distension, and sacral or peripheral edema. In protracted illness, body weights can be measured daily, and serial weights can be used as a rough index of the state of hydration.

Feeding should accompany rehydration early in diarrheal illness. It is important, however, to avoid feedings containing a high osmolarity. Digestive enzymes of the intestinal tract are generally present in excess during diarrheal illness. Thus, proteins and starches may be given during the diarrheal illness. In fact, it can be expected that as these are degraded to component amino acids and monosaccharides, enhanced transport of sodium and absorption of water from the intestinal lumen to the blood stream will result. Indeed, "advanced" oral rehydration therapy solutions are made with proteins and starches, or malti-dextrins. These solutions are characteristically lower in osmolality than the present standard ORS (Table 120-2) containing glucose and have been shown to shorten the duration of diarrhea and reduce fluid losses in young adults.[7]

From studies of food absorption in diarrheal disease, it is clear that fat is the most poorly digested food component before, during, and after diarrhea. Impairment of protein digestion and absorption is next. Carbohydrate absorption is almost unimpaired in most diarrheal illnesses.[14] An additional safety factor in using large carbohydrate molecules or polymers in ORT is that any molecules not digested and absorbed will not worsen diarrhea because the osmotic activity of solutions of large molecules and polymers is low as compared to solutions of simple sugars and monomers. The intestine is a very permeable membrane, and any differences in physical or osmotic pressures equilibrate extraordinarily rapidly.

When there is an inflammatory colitis, as in shigellosis, salmonellosis, *Campylobacter* infection, or *C. difficile* disease, antibiotics may be indicated. However, the effect of antibiotics in salmonella disease is controversial and disappointing, and at present antibiotics are felt to be contraindicated in this condition. Shigellosis is caused by an organism that possesses a high degree of resistance, and appropriate antibiotic therapy demands knowledge of the resistance pattern of the organism from the area where it was acquired. Treatment of *C. difficile* disease with antibiotics has been very disappointing.[26] Relapses are frequent, and failure to eradicate toxin from the stool is not uncommon. For these reasons, investigations at a number of centers are currently being carried out which would rely on microbial competition and restoration of normal gut flora to combat colonization by *C. difficile* and formation of its toxin.[27] Finally, a recent investigation of an outbreak of dysentery-like diarrhea caused by *E. coli* in a nursing home in Toronto found that either the prior ingestion of antibiotics or the prescription of antibiotics during diarrhea significantly increased morbidity and mortality.[2] Hence the physician must proceed with great caution in treating any diarrheal illness with antibiotics.

In most instances, watery diarrhea requires no further treatment than replacement of fluid losses with ORT. In view of the risks of antibiotic therapy in the elderly, unless there is clearly infection with an invasive organism, antibiotics are contraindicated. The risk of postantibiotic diarrhea of a more serious nature than that of the acute watery diarrhea being treated outweighs the benefit of the antibiotic. Furthermore, there are available several potentially useful antisecretory drugs that are of low cost and have few side effects. The most available of these is bismuth subsalicylate (Pepto-Bismol). This very interesting remedy combines some microbicidal activity together with the antisecretory activity inherent in the salicylate moiety.[28] Except in cholera, most diarrheal diseases have a component of inflammation, which causes fluid losses through secretion of prostaglandins and other substances. Therefore, compounds which inhibit the arachidonic acid cascade can sharply reduce fluid losses in diarrhea and decrease duration of illness. This has been nicely demonstrated in the case of traveler's diarrhea, and further studies are underway in the elderly and in populations in poor countries with this agent. At present, it can be recommended that bismuth subsalicylate be given in doses of 30 ml every hour for up to eight doses, or until diarrhea stops, followed by a maintenance dose of 60 ml four times a day. This regimen can be prescribed without risk of toxicity and with the possibility of increasing patient comfort and shortening illness duration. Other agents which are commonly used, e.g., adsorbents like Kaopectate, charcoal, etc., have not been shown to be of significant benefit in treating diarrheal diseases. Antimotility drugs can decrease the duration of diarrhea but do not affect the amount of fluid loss. They also can have adverse effects in that they allow pooling of infected material within the intestine, delaying its expulsion from the body; they have been shown to increase the severity and duration of invasive diarrheal diseases. We presently would recommend the use of ORT in all cases of diarrhea at the earliest possible time, as well as prescription of bismuth subsalicylate and avoidance of all other antidiarrheal drugs.

In approaching all cases of diarrhea in the elderly, it is important to recognize that instances of intestinal obstruction, appendicitis, diverticulitis, and vascular insufficiency all are more common in older age groups. Each of these conditions may require surgical intervention. Except in the instance of intestinal ileus, it is still safe to administer ORT while observing the patient and carrying out further necessary investigations. It is also important to review orders and ensure that laxatives or other diarrhea-causing drugs or diets have not been introduced immediately prior to the onset of diarrhea. It is likely that many cases of diarrhea in nursing home patients are related to medications. Thus, the only indicated therapy aside from replacement of fluid would be cancellation or modification of prescribed drugs.

PREVENTIVE CONSIDERATIONS

The principal consideration in prevention of diarrheal illness is ensuring that water and food supplies are not contaminated with fecal organisms. This means proper refrigeration, proper preparation of foods with adequate cooking, and careful handling of food by dietary workers who have been screened for carriage of enteric pathogens. Even in a wealthy and advanced society, breakdowns occur regularly in food processing, food handling, and water supplies. This can be particularly true in feeding large numbers of people in institutions where food handling may be contracted out or managed with insufficient budgets and under adverse conditions. Since malnutrition is so common in the elderly and in nursing home residents,[13,29] clearly a much greater emphasis needs to be placed not only on proper handling of food to avoid enteric infections but also on improving diets so as to make catering to individual tastes possible and ensuring that individuals are fed under pleasant conditions that encourage adequate food intake. Water supplies may be clean and safe coming into an institution, but the containers in which water is placed can become contaminated if left standing for a long time. Thus, attention to the proper management of water provided to patients is essential.

Avoidance of prescription of excessive laxatives and of drugs which cause diarrhea can prevent many instances of diarrhea in the nursing home setting. Use of antibiotics only under clear indication is perhaps the single most important concern in preventing serious and disabling diarrhea related to *C. difficile* and other organisms which may multiply if the normal gut flora is disturbed. When outbreaks occur, observing basic enteric precautions of hand-washing and proper handling of soiled bed linens becomes essential to avoid spread across an entire institution. The single most important measure, however, is hand-washing with soap and water by all health-providers. When hand-washing has been instituted even under the most adverse circumstances, there has been a marked reduction in spread of enteric infection.[30,31] Thus, education and attention to this measure deserves the greatest emphasis.[32] It is also likely, of course, that many other diseases spread by contact in handling could also be avoided in this way.

At present, there are no immunizations indicated to prevent enteric infection in the elderly, although it is possible that in the next half decade this may change, as several successful field trials have been carried out for vaccines which prevent both invasive and secretory diarrhea.[33] Further investigations on the role of gastric acid as a defense against diarrheal disease in the elderly are essential since there is such widespread use of antacids and H_2-blocking agents, and studies are needed to determine the overall morbidity and mortality of patients taking these drugs routinely. Finally, treatment regimens based on microbial replacement hold promise, and ongoing studies may provide new therapies for ameliorating and preventing infectious diarrheas.

CONCLUSION

Diarrheal diseases are very common and are an important source of morbidity and perhaps mortality in the elderly. We have little or no information on the role they play in illness in those living at home; however, in nursing homes there is evidence that a significant problem exists. Treatment measures are available which are simple and low in cost but which require knowledge of their use. To be effective, fluid replacement therapies must be initiated at the earliest possible time and continued until diarrhea is over. Oral rehydration therapy (ORT) is the standard treatment of diarrheal diseases the world over and should be employed both at home and in institutional settings in the United States. In the elderly, special considerations in administering ORT exist because heart failure is often present and the hazard of fluid overload exists to a greater extent than in healthy young children and adults. Although there are few useful adjunctive agents to ORT, bismuth subsalicylate holds promise and should be used. Antimicrobial therapy in general has been shown to be hazardous, to result in higher death rates, and to be a predisposing cause for serious diarrheal diseases in the elderly. Prescription of antibiotics must be approached with great caution. Monitoring laxatives and diarrhea-causing drugs can reduce the incidence of diarrhea in older patients. The use of gastric acid–inhibiting drugs such as H_2-blocking agents and antacids may predispose toward diarrheal illness and should be used only when clearly indicated. *C. pylori* infection needs to be studied in older people as a possible predisposing cause, both for gastritis and diarrheal diseases. *C. difficile* is a prevalent infection in nursing homes and is associated with an excess mortality rate. Current treatment methods for *C. difficile* are not satisfactory, and this is a specific infection for which health care providers should maintain a high index of suspicion. Preventive measures for diarrhea are relatively simple and are not costly. The most important is hand-washing with soap and water by all health-providers and all food-handlers.

REFERENCES

1. Farber RE, Solomon N, Garber HJ et al: Salmonellosis—Baltimore, Maryland. *MMWR* 19:314, 1970.
2. Carter AO, Borczyk AA, Carlson JAK et al: A severe outbreak of *Escherichia coli* 0157:H7-associated hemorrhagic colitis in a nursing home. *N Engl J Med* 317:1496, 1987.
3. Garibaldi RA, Brodine S, Matsumiya A: Infections among patients in nursing homes: Policies, prevalence, and problems. *N Engl J Med* 305:731, 1981.
4. Nicolle LE, McIntyre M, Zacharias H, MacDonell JA: Twelve-month surveillance of infections in institutionalized elderly men. *J Am Geriatr Soc* 32:513, 1984.
5. Farber BF, Brennen C, Puntereri AJ, Brody JP: A prospective study of nosocomial infections in a chronic care facility. *J Am Geriatr Soc* 32:499, 1984.
6. Lin FYC, Gnores H, Wasserman BP et al: Gastroenteritis outbreaks in nursing homes. *Abst Annu Mtg Am Soc Microbiol* 350, 1988.
7. Taylor CE, Greenough WB III: *Annu Rev Public Health* 10:221, 1989.
8. Greenough WB III: Diarrhea: Etiology and treatment with oral rehydration therapy. *Am Assoc Retired Persons* 2(3):1, 1988.
9. World Health Statistic Annual: I. Vital statistics and cause of death. Geneva, World Health Organization, 1975.
10. Carpenter CCJ: Cholera diagnosis and treatment. *Bull NY Acad Med* 47:1191, 1971.
11. Editorial: Water, sugar and salt. *Lancet* ii:300, 1978.
12. Nalin DR, Cash RA: Oral or nasogastric maintenance therapy for diarrhea of unknown etiology resembling cholera. *Trans R Soc Trop Med Hyg* 64(5):769, 1970.
13. Lipschitz DA: Protein calorie malnutrition in the hospitalized elderly. *Primary Care* 9:531, 1982.
14. Molla AM, Sarker SA, Khatoon M, Rahaman MM: Food intake during and after recovery from diarrhea, in Chen L, Schrimsaw N (eds): *Diarrhea and Malnutrition*. New York, Plenum, 1983.

15. Santosham M, Foster S, Reid R et al: Role of soy-based lactose-free formula during treatment of acute diarrhea. *Pediatrics* 76:292, 1985.

16. Stoll BJ, Glass RI, Hug MI et al: Surveillance of patients attending a diarrhoeal disease hospital in Bangladesh. *Br J Med* 285:1185, 1982.

17. Moriarty KJ, Turnberg LA: Bacterial toxins and diarrhoea. *Clin Gastroenterol* 15(3):529, 1986.

18. Rabbani GH: Cholera. *Clin Gastroenterol* 15(3):507, 1986.

19. Bender BS, Bennett R, Laughon B et al: Is *Clostridium difficile* endemic in chronic-care facilities? *Lancet* i:11, 1986.

20. O'Brien, Holmes RK: Shiga and Shiga-like toxins. *Microbiol Rev* 51:206, 1987.

21. Hornick RB, Music SI, Wnezel R et al: The Broad Street Pump revisited: Response of volunteers to ingested cholera vibrios. *Bull NY Acad Med* 47:1181, 1971.

22. Bonhoff M, Miller CP, Martin WR: Resistance of the mouse's intestinal tract to experimental *Salmonella* infection I and II. *J Exp Med* 120:805, 1964.

23. Williams R, Piper M, Borriello P et al: Diarrhoea due to enterotoxigenic *Clostridium perfringens:* Clinical features and management of a cluster of cases. *Age Ageing* 14:296, 1985.

24. Pierce NF, Cray WC Jr, Sircar BK: Induction of a mucosal antitoxin response and its role in immunity to experimental canine cholera. *Infect Immun* 21:185, 1978.

25. Schmucker DL, Daniels CK: Aging, gastrointestinal infections, and mucosal immunity. *J Am Geriatr Soc* 34:377, 1986.

26. Aronsson B, Mollby R, Nord CE: Antimicrobial agents and *Clostridium difficile* in acute enteric disease: Epidemiological data from Sweden, 1980–1982. *J Infec Dis* 151:476, 1985.

27. Elmer GW, McFarland L: Suppression by *Saccharomyces boulardii* of toxigenic *Clostridium difficile* overgrowth after vancomycin treatment in hamsters. *Antimicrob Agents Chemother* 31:129, 1987.

28. Ericsson CD, Dupont HL, Johnson PC: Non-antibiotic therapy for traveler's diarrhea. *Rev Infect Dis* 8(suppl 12):S202, 1986.

29. Rudman D, Feller AG: Protein-calorie undernutrition in the nursing home. *J Am Geriatr Soc* 37:173, 1989.

30. Black RE, Dykes AC, Anderson KE et al: Handwashing to prevent diarrhoea in day care centers. *Am J Epidemiol* 113:445, 1981.

31. Khan MU: Interruption of shigellosis by hand-washing. *Trans R Soc Trop Med Hyg* 76:164, 1982.

32. Otherson MJ, Otherson HB Jr: *A History of Hand-washing: Seven Hundred Years at a Snails's Pace.* The Pharos, Spring, 1987, pp 23–27.

33. Clements JD, El Morshidy S: Construction of a potential live oral bivalent vaccine for typhoid fever and cholera–*Escherichia coli* related diarrheas. *Infec Immun* 46:564, 1984.

Chapter 121

HERPES ZOSTER

Arthur K. Balin

Herpes zoster, commonly referred to as "shingles," is caused by the varicella zoster virus, *Herpesvirus varicellae*. Varicella zoster belongs to the family of herpes viruses which also includes the Epstein-Barr virus, cytomegalic virus, and herpes simplex virus. It is a DNA virus composed of double-stranded DNA, a nucleocapsid with icosahedral symmetry, and an outer lipid envelope. The virus is approximately 200 nm in size and has a molecular mass of 80 million daltons. Replication occurs within infected cell nuclei, and intranuclear inclusions can be seen on stained preparations.

Chicken pox, or varicella, is caused by acute infection with this virus. Herpes zoster is due to reactivation of latent varicella zoster virus which was deposited in sensory dorsal root or cranial nerve ganglia during a prior acute infection.

Chicken pox is highly contagious, with acute infection developing in 90 percent of susceptible individuals exposed to the virus. It is transmitted mostly by droplet infection from the upper respiratory tract, although blister fluid does contain infectious particles. Approximately 50 percent of the reported cases occur in children ages 5 to 9, and the incubation period usually ranges from 10 to 21 days after exposure. Infection can be transmitted approximately 48 hours before the typical vesicular eruption develops and up until all lesions are crusted.

Herpes zoster can occur only in individuals previously infected with varicella, and its incidence increases as a person ages,[1] with more than 60 percent of the cases occurring in people over the age of 45. The highest incidence of disease occurs during the fifth to seventh decades[2] and is approximately 5 to 10 cases per 1000 people per year in this age group. Men and women are equally affected. Ten to twenty percent of all people will be affected by herpes zoster during their lifetime.

The mechanism for reactivation of the varicella zoster virus that results in herpes zoster is not fully known. Immunosuppression may contribute to reactivation by depression of cell-mediated immunity. Zoster has been reported to develop from pressure on nerve roots due to tumor, after minor trauma to the skin or cornea, or after direct injury to nerves or the vertebrae.[3] Onset of herpes zoster after trauma ranges from 1 day to 3 weeks after injury. Radiation therapy has been reported to activate latent virus in the ganglion of nerves supplying the treated dermatome.[4,5]

Although specific mechanisms determining viral reactivation are unknown, some systemic diseases are associated with an increased incidence of herpes zoster. Herpes zoster occurs more frequently in patients with lymphoproliferative malignancies such as Hodgkin's disease, acute lymphocytic leukemia, and chronic lymphocytic leukemia[5,6] than in the general population. Other disease states in which the incidence of zoster is higher include systemic lupus erythematosus, rheumatoid arthritis, and diabetes. Patients who have cancer or are immunocompromised due to immunosuppressive drug therapy or X-irradiation are especially prone to developing zoster. Whereas herpes zoster in cancer patients usually occurs in previously diagnosed advanced cancer or in those actively undergoing therapy, zoster in those with the human immunodeficiency virus infection may actually be the presenting sign of the HIV infection.[7–9] There is not sufficient evidence, however, to suggest that otherwise healthy patients with zoster are at an increased risk of having or developing a malignancy.[10] Recurrent herpes zoster occurs in approximately 2 percent of healthy individuals, whereas immunosuppressed individuals have about a fivefold increase in the frequency of recurrent zoster. In 50 percent of recurrent cases of zoster, lesions occur in the same dermatome as the first episode.

CLINICAL FEATURES

Clinically, the first signs of localized zoster are malaise and pain and tenderness of the skin in the involved area. Some patients may experience burning pain, itching, shooting pains, or dysesthesias. Pain may vary from mild to severe, although children and young adults may experience no pain at all. Zoster begins after this 3- to 4-day prodrome as grouped erythematous papules occurring unilaterally in the cutaneous distribution of a sensory nerve, or dermatome (Fig. 121-1). Lesions usually appear posteriorly and progress to the anterior and peripheral distribution of the involved nerve (Fig. 121-2). Vesicles or blisters develop in the area and new ones may continue to appear for a few days. In an uncomplicated case the vesicles become purulent due to the accumulation of leukocytes, and then they dry up, form crusts, and begin to heal (Fig. 121-3). In the elderly, lesions may become necrotic and heal with scarring. Secondary bacterial infection can lead to delayed healing and scar formation at any age (Figs. 121-4 and 121-5).

Characteristically, lesions develop in a continuous or interrupted band in one or more dermatomes. Mucous membranes within the affected dermatomes are also involved. The affected dermatomes are usually hyperesthetic. In about 15 percent of cases the pain and skin lesions develop simultaneously. Lymph nodes draining the involved area may become swollen and tender. Occasionally, especially in immunocompromised patients, two or three adjacent dermatomes may be involved. Painful herpes zoster can be present without a rash developing. This has been called "zoster sine herpete" or "zoster sine erupcion."

The affected dermatomes are located in the thoracic area in 50 percent of cases, in the cervical area in 20 percent of cases, and in 15 and 10 percent of cases in the trigeminal and lumbosacral areas, respectively. Herpes zoster of the ophthalmic branch of the trigeminal nerve occurs with an increased incidence in old age. When branches of the trigeminal nerve are affected, lesions erupt on the face, mouth, eye, or tongue. Lesions on the tip of the nose (Hutchinson's sign) indicate involvement of the

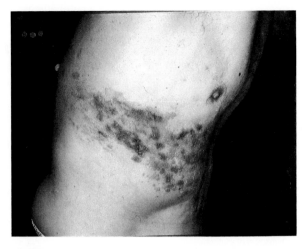

FIGURE 121-2
Herpes zoster. Typical appearance of dermatomal distribution (T-7 or T-8) of herpes zoster. Grouped vesicles evolve into crusts on a brightly erythematous base.

nasociliary nerve and have been found to correlate with eye involvement, which includes intraocular disease. Complications occur in about 50 percent of patients with ophthalmic zoster, which is manifested by a red swollen conjunctiva and a superficial or deep keratitis. Argyll Robertson pupil can result from involvement of the ciliary ganglia.[11] Zoster of the maxillary division of the trigeminal nerve produces vesicles on the uvula and tonsillar area. When the mandibular division of the trigeminal nerve is involved, vesicles appear on the anterior part of the tongue, the floor of the mouth, and the buccal mucous membrane. The Ramsay Hunt syndrome, manifested by vesicular lesions of the pinna, auditory canal, and anterior two-thirds of the tongue, is associated with Bell's palsy, tinnitus, deafness, vertigo, decreased taste, decreased hearing, and meningitis. This syndrome is

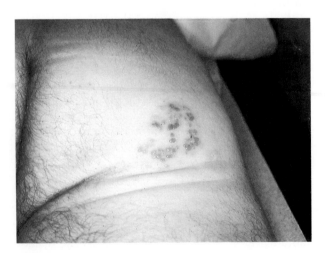

FIGURE 121-1
Herpes zoster. Grouped vesicles on an erythematous base. In this early lesion vesicles are filled with clear to serosanguinous fluid.

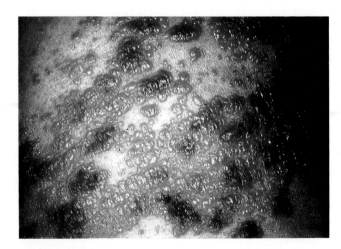

FIGURE 121-3
Herpes zoster. Close-up view of older confluent intact vesicles, filled with yellow turbid fluid, on erythematous skin. Several vesicles have a dusky gray appearance.

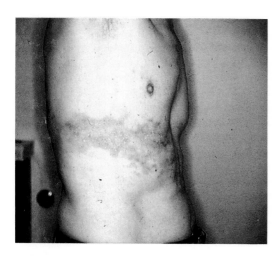

FIGURE 121-4
Herpes zoster. Six weeks after onset of zoster demonstrating the amount of resolution that can be expected. Some crusts are still evident, and the skin remains erythematous to violaceous. This is the same patient shown in Fig. 121-2.

due to involvement of the sensory branch of the facial nerve and possibly the geniculate ganglion. In orofacial zoster toothache may be the presenting symptom.[12]

Patients with zoster may develop scattered lesions outside of the involved dermatome. These lesions represent hematogenous dissemination probably due to circulating monocytes.[13] The frequency of cutaneous dissemination reported in the literature is 2 to 5 percent.[1,14] Dissemination occurs more frequently in elderly individuals and in immunosuppressed patients, reflecting an inability of the host's immune system to keep the infection in check. Cutaneous dissemination develops in about 40 percent of patients with Hodgkin's and non-Hodgkin's lymphoma. Evidence for dissemination oc-

curs within 4 to 6 days after the appearance of the initial zoster lesions. The skin lesions which develop as a result of dissemination usually heal within 3 to 5 days. Dissemination may be accompanied by systemic signs of viremia with fever, prostration, and lymphadenopathy.

DIFFERENTIAL DIAGNOSIS

The diagnosis of herpes zoster can usually be made on clinical grounds. The presence of pain and unilateral grouped vesicles in a dermatomal distribution are most helpful in making the diagnosis. In general lesions of herpes zoster do not cross the midline of the body. An exception to this rule, however, can be observed when, due to local extension of virus through the skin rather than nerves, lesions cross the midline by 0.5 to 1.0 cm. Early lesions and zoster without a rash may create diagnostic dilemmas.

Distinguishing herpes simplex from herpes zoster can sometimes be difficult, as recurrent simplex occasionally produces grouped vesicles in a band-like pattern resembling a dermatome. Tzanck preparations from the base of blisters in both conditions show similar findings, with multinucleated epithelial giant cells, nuclear margination of chromatin, and intranuclear inclusions (Fig. 121-6). The Tzanck procedure can be helpful in distinguishing simplex and zoster from other vesicular conditions such as allergic contact dermatitis and bullous impetigo. Histopathologic examination by light microscopy also shows identical findings in the skin lesions of both simplex and zoster. Helpful differential points include a history of recurrent lesions in the same area, which is usual for herpes simplex but rare in herpes zoster, and the presence or absence of pain in the distribution of the

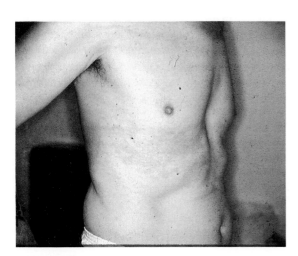

FIGURE 121-5
Herpes zoster. Six months after onset of zoster demonstrating persistent erythema at the site of the zoster eruption. This is the same patient shown in Figs. 121-2 and 121-4.

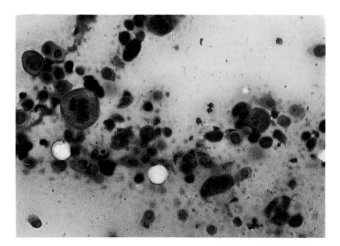

FIGURE 121-6
Tzanck smear. A Giemsa-stained preparation of a scraping of the base of a viral vesicle. Many acantholytic multinucleated giant cells are present.

rash. The pain associated with zoster can be mistaken for visceral diseases such as myocardial ischemia, renal colic, or cholecystitis. Rarely, herpes simplex and coxsackievirus infections can be a cause of dermatomal vesicular lesions. Diagnostic virology, including viral cultures and viral antibody titers, can be important in assuring the proper diagnosis. Direct immunofluorescence of a cytologic smear of a vesicle using a monoclonal antibody to the varicella zoster virus can provide an immediate definitive diagnosis.

HISTOPATHOLOGY

Histologically, skin biopsy specimens show intracellular edema of epidermal cells with "ballooning" degeneration and multinucleated epithelial giant cells containing as many as 15 nuclei[15] (Fig. 121-7). The presence of intercellular edema contributes to formation of the viral vesicle. Pathologic changes in the ganglia and nerves affected by the varicella zoster virus include inflammation and neuronal destruction in the posterior nerve roots and ganglia with lymphocytic infiltration, hemorrhage, and nuclear inclusions. Viral particles are present in involved ganglia and nerves and have been identified in the trigeminal nerve and ganglion[16] and in dorsal root ganglia.[17] There is degeneration of sensory nerves linking the affected skin and the central nervous system and subsequent fibrosis of nerves and ganglia.[18] Nerve damage often occurs early in the course of the illness. Degeneration of nerve fibers in the middle and lower dermis occurs and may be responsible for postherpetic neuralgia, which persists for months to years.[19,20]

SEQUELAE

Although herpes zoster usually resolves in nonimmunocompromised hosts without sequelae, several important complications may occur, especially in the elderly. Postherpetic neuralgia, one of the most intractable pain disorders, is the most common sequela of zoster and is defined as pain persisting for 1 month or more after the rash has healed. Whereas postherpetic neuralgia lasting more than a year occurs in less than 10 percent of patients less than 50 years old, it occurs in 35 to 50 percent of patients over 60 years of age.[21] The cause of this higher incidence of postherpetic neuralgia in the elderly might be explained by lowered cellular immunity to varicella zoster virus[22] or to decreased ability to repair damaged tissue and nerve structures.

Ocular disease, including blindness, may complicate involvement of the ophthalmic branch of the trigeminal nerve. Zoster of the eyelids can lead to scarring with ectropion, lid retraction, and corneal damage. Conjunctivitis occurs frequently. Other ocular complications

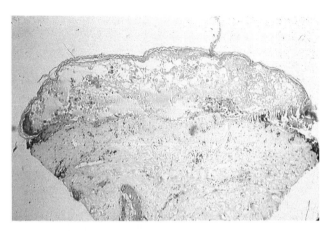

FIGURE 121-7
Histologic section of viral vesicle in herpes zoster. This hematoxylin-and eosin-stained section is characterized by epidermal edema, vesiculation, and ballooning degeneration of epidermal cells. The pathologic changes in this section can be caused by herpes simplex or varicella zoster virus.

include episcleritis, dendritic keratopathy, and iritis. The syndrome of acute retinal necrosis has been attributed to reactivation of varicella zoster virus.[23] This syndrome is characterized by retinal arteritis and retinitis with retinal detachment and has led to legal blindness in 64 percent of patients diagnosed. Transient ocular muscle palsies develop in approximately 13 percent of cases of ophthalmic zoster, and facial palsies occur in 7 percent of cases.[24] Several cases of contralateral hemiparesis following herpes zoster ophthalmicus due to either thrombosis[25] or vasculitis have been reported in the literature.

Other neurologic complications of zoster include Bell's palsy, which is rarely permanent, and leg weakness or foot drop resulting from motor nerve damage during lumbosacral zoster. Zoster involving the sacral or anogenital area can produce abnormalities in bowel function and urination.[26] Persistent encephalitis with progressive encephalopathy is seen in immunocompromised patients following zoster.[27]

Zoster in immunosuppressed individuals is usually more severe, prolonged, and more likely to disseminate. Patients with cutaneous dissemination have a 5 to 10 percent increased risk of serious complications such as encephalitis, hepatitis, and pneumonitis. Pneumonitis is the leading cause of death in patients with zoster. With recent advances in antiviral therapy, disseminated zoster is rarely fatal even in immunocompromised patients. Mortality rates have been estimated in the range of 4 to 15 percent in immunocompromised patients with disseminated disease.[28]

TREATMENT

Zoster responds to intravenous acyclovir,[29] and progression of the infection can be halted in the immunosuppressed patient.[30] Oral acyclovir is also useful, particularly if started early. While 200 mg five times daily is adequate therapy for herpes simplex, higher doses are more useful in zoster.[31] One useful treatment approach for zoster that does not involve the ophthalmic nerve employs oral acylovir 400 mg five times daily for 7 days, then 200 mg five times daily for an additional 7 to 14 days, depending upon the severity of the outbreak. Acyclovir has not been shown to reduce or prevent postherpetic neuralgia.

Rest and analgesics are sufficient for mild attacks of zoster. Topical application of acyclovir is useful, and secondary bacterial infection can be treated with systemic and topical antibacterial preparations.

Corticosteroids given during the acute stage of zoster suppress the inflammatory changes and may reduce the incidence and duration of postherpetic neuralgia in otherwise healthy patients. Five double-blind, placebo-controlled studies have been performed that were found methodologically adequate for meta-analysis.[32] One study, which found no benefit, employed adrenocorticotropic hormone (ACTH).[33] A well-designed study with 37 people treated with prednisolone and 41 controls found that acute pain was lessened in the treatment group, but there was no difference in the incidence of postherpetic neuralgia.[34] Three other double-blind studies employing prednisone,[35] prednisolone,[36] or triamcinolone[37] demonstrated that corticosteroid administration was helpful in preventing postherpetic neuralgia. These studies were relatively small, and the utility of corticosteroids is not completely resolved. A typical dose would be 40 mg prednisone daily for 10 days, followed by a 3-week taper of the steroid. Dissemination of infection due to systemic steroids is a major risk in immunocompromised patients but is not usually a problem in healthy patients.

Postherpetic neuralgia can be treated with topical capsaicin.[38] Narcotic analgesics may be required but should be avoided if at all possible.[39] Amitriptyline can be helpful for hyperaesthesia and burning pain[40] and carbamazepine or other anticonvulsants for stabbing pain.[41] In the elderly, doses should be low and increased every few days as required. Transcutaneous electrical nerve stimulation can provide temporary relief of pain for some patients.[42]

REFERENCES

1. Ragozzino MW, Melton LJ III, Kurland LT, Chu CP, Perry HO: Population-based study of herpes zoster and its sequelae. *Medicine (Baltimore)* 61:310, 1982.
2. Burgoon CF, Burgoon JS, Baldridge GD: The natural history of herpes zoster. *JAMA* 164:264, 1957.
3. Klauder JV: Herpes zoster appearing after trauma. *JAMA* 134:245, 1949.
4. Ellis F, Stoll BA: Herpes zoster after irradiation. *Br Med J* 2:1323, 1949.
5. Mazur MH, Dolin R: Herpes zoster at the NIH: A 20 year experience. *Am J Med* 65:738, 1978.
6. Goffinet DR, Glatstein EJ, Merigan TC: Herpes zoster-varicella infections and lymphoma. *Ann Intern Med* 76:235, 1972.
7. Cone LA, Schiffman MA: Herpes zoster and the acquired immunodeficiency syndrome. *Ann Intern Med* 252:462, 1984.
8. Friedman-Kien AE, Lafleur FL, Gendler E et al: Herpes zoster: A possible early clinical sign for development of acquired immunodeficiency syndrome in high-risk individuals. *J Am Acad Dermatol* 14:1023, 1986.
9. Colebunders R, Mann JM, Francis H et al: Herpes zoster in African patients: A clinical predictor of human immunodeficiency virus infection. *J Infect Dis* 157:314, 1988.
10. Ragozzino MW, Melton LJ, Kurland LT, Chu CP, Perry HO: Risk of cancer after herpes zoster. *N Engl J Med* 307:393, 1982.
11. Becker FT: Herpes zoster ophthalmicus. Its therapy with convalescent blood. *Arch Dermatol Syphil* 58:265, 1948.
12. Nally F, Ross IH: Herpes zoster of the oral and facial structures. *Oral Surg* 32:221, 1971.
13. Twomey JJ, Gyorkey F, Norris SM: The monocyte disorder with herpes zoster. *J Lab Clin Med* 83:768, 1974.
14. Merselis JG, Kaye D, Hook EW: Disseminated herpes zoster. *Arch Intern Med* 113:679-686, 1964.
15. Barski G, Robinson R: Evolution of herpes simplex cellular lesions observed in vitro by phase contrast microcinematography. *Proc Soc Exp Biol Med* 101:632, 1959.
16. Esiri MM, Tomlinson AH: Herpes zoster: Demonstration of virus in trigeminal nerve and ganglion by immunofluorescence and electron microscopy. *J Neurol* (in press).
17. Bastian FO et al: Herpes virus varicellae: Isolated from human dorsal root ganglia. *Arch Pathol* 97:331, 1974.
18. Head H, Campbell AW: The pathology of herpes zoster and its bearing on sensory localization. *Brain* 23:353, 1900.
19. Muller SA, Winkelmann RK: Cutaneous nerve changes in zoster. *J Invest Derm* 52:71, 1969.
20. Ebert MH: Histologic changes in sensory nerves of the skin in herpes zoster. *Arch Derm Syphil* 60:641, 1949.
21. Moragas JM, Kierland RR: The outcome of patients with herpes zoster. *Arch Derm* 75:193, 1957.
22. Burke BL et al: Immune responses to varicella zoster in the aged. *Arch Intern Med* 142:291, 1982.
23. Culbertson WW et al: Varicella zoster virus is a cause of acute retinal necrosis syndrome. *Ophthalmology* 93:559, 1986.
24. Juel-Jensen BE, MacCallum FO: *Herpes Simplex, Varicella and Zoster.* London, Heinemann, 1972.
25. Eidelberg D et al: Thrombotic cerebral vasculopathy associated with herpes zoster. *Ann Neurol* 19:7, 1986.
26. Fugelso PD, Reed WB, Newman SB et al: Herpes zoster of the anogenital area affecting urination and defaecation. *Br J Derm* 89:285, 1973.
27. Horten B, Price RW, Jimenez D: Multifocal varicella-zoster virus leukoencephalitis temporally remote from herpes zoster. *Ann Neurol* 9:251, 1981.
28. Strauss SE et al: Varicella zoster virus infections. *Ann Intern Med* 108:221, 1988.
29. Bean B et al: Acyclovir therapy for acute herpes zoster. *Lancet* 2:118, 1982.
30. Balfour HH: Acyclovir halts progression of herpes zoster

in immunocompromised patients. *N Engl J Med* 308:1448, 1983.

31. McKendrick MW et al: Oral acyclovir for herpes zoster. *Lancet* 2:925, 1984.

32. Schmader KE, Studenski S: Are current therapies useful for the prevention of postherpetic neuralgia? A critical analysis of the literature. *J Gen Intern Med* 4:83, 1989.

33. Clemmemsen OJ, Andersen KE: ACTH verus placebo in herpes zoster treatment. *Clin Exp Dermatol* 9:557, 1984.

34. Esmann V, Kroon S, Peterslund NA: Prednisolone does not prevent post-herpetic neuralgia. *Lancet* 2:126, 1987.

35. Elliot FA: Treatment of herpes zoster with high doses of prednisone. *Lancet* 2:610, 1964.

36. Keczkes K, Basheer AM: Do corticosteroids prevent post-herpetic neuralgia? *Br J Dermatol* 102:551, 1980.

37. Eaglstein WH, Katz R, Brown JA: The effects of early corticosteroid therapy on the skin eruption and pain of herpes zoster. *JAMA* 211:1681, 1970.

38. Bernstein JE, Bickers DR, Dahl MV et al: Treatment of chronic post-herpetic neuralgia with topical capsaicin. *J Am Acad Dermatol* 17:93, 1987.

39. Portenoy RK, Dama C, Foley KM: Acute herpetic and postherpetic neuralgia: Clinical review and current management. *Ann Neurol* 20:651, 1986.

40. Watson CP, Evans RJ, Reed K: Amitriptyline versus placebo in post-herpetic neuralgia. *Neurology* 32:671, 1982.

41. Killian JM, Fromm GH: Carbamazepine in the treatment of neuralgia. *Arch Neurol* 19:129, 1968.

42. Nathan PW, Wall PD: Treatment of post-herpetic neuralgia by prolonged electrical stimulation. *Br Med J* 3:645, 1974.

Chapter 122

GAIT DISORDERS

William C. Koller and Sander L. Glatt

A crucial determinant of the quality of life in the elderly is their ability to walk. Inability to safely ambulate causes loss of independence and may lead to nursing home placement. Immobility is associated with a series of serious medical complications, including deep venous thrombosis, respiratory infection, and the development of decubitus ulcers. Immobility and disorders of gait are second only to cognitive dysfunction as the most frequent neurological concomitants of the aging process.[1] These difficulties may relate to "normal aging" as well as to specific disease processes.

GAIT MECHANISMS

Mobility is achieved through a neurological servomechanism that insures mechanical stability in all postures and positions required by a person's daily activity. In the upright posture, mobility and stability are complicated by the small base of support between the feet, as compared to a person's height. There are a number of requirements for normal locomotion. These include (1) antigravity support in the upright posture, (2) balance control, and (3) forward-stepping movements.[2]

In the upright posture the center of gravity is located just anterior and superior to the second sacral vertebra.[3] The hips are slightly anterior and the knees and ankles are slightly posterior to a line drawn from the center of gravity perpendicular to the ground. The musculoskeletal system provides antigravity support by fixing the major joints, which minimizes the motor activity required to maintain the upright posture. Such a posture requires little energy to maintain balance while standing. Mechanical stability is maintained as long as the line of gravity passes within the base of support between the feet. Movement may perturb the line of gravity off the support base. Postural stability requires these movements to be perceived and the gravitational forces on the body part to be calculated in order to perform compensatory maneuvers to place the center of gravity back over the feet.[4] Walking depends on a series of reciprocal flexion–extension movements of the legs, alternating between support in extension and advancement in flexion.[5] Gait has been classically studied in terms of the walking cycle, which is the time interval between successive floor contacts of each foot. It is further divided into stance and swing phases. The stance phase occurs when the foot is in contact with the floor, and the swing phase occurs when the foot is advancing to take the next position. During each walking cycle there are two periods of single-limb support and two brief periods of double-limb support while the legs alternate between postures.[5]

The impetus to forward locomotion is achieved by pushing off on the leg in the stance phase while swinging the other leg forward. This motion is associated with fixation and elevation of the pelvis by the hip abductors as well as with tilting the body towards the supporting limb, allowing the swinging leg to fall in a line directly anterior to the stance leg. The movement of the pelvis allows for maintenance of mechanical stability by integration of the line of gravity such that it falls through the foot of the stance leg. The swing leg is flexed and externally rotated slightly at the hip, flexed at the knee, and dorsiflexed at the foot. After the heel of the swing leg strikes the floor, the hip and knee extend. This phase ends as external rotation and dorsiflexion of the stance leg shifts the center of gravity forward.[5] Rotatory movements of the upper body arms and shoulders are used to counter balance the movements of the pelvis and lower extremity in order to maintain lateral stability despite alterations in the legs providing support. Lateral movement of the center of gravity is minimized since the swing leg ends its journey directly in line with the stance leg. Movement is generated by a combination of muscular and gravitational forces. The rear stance leg pushes the body forward off its base of support so forward body momentum aided by gravity propels the body. The swing leg then hurries forward to catch the body as the forward stance leg. Mobility derives from the controlled instability of the body in the direction of desired movement. A mundane activity such as walking is simple only because of the exquisitely fine control exerted by a very complicated neurological servomechanism with highly sensitive input, complex central integration, and finely graded motor effort.

Locomotor programs to direct walking originate in central pattern generators located in the spinal cord. These areas are under the control of locomotor centers located in the midbrain and brain stem regions, which in turn are responsible to cerebellar, basal ganglionic, and cortical control. Postural adjustments are directed by a variety of neurological reflexes and responses such as vestibular and vestibulo-ocular reflexes, positive and negative supportive reactions, and placing, stepping, and long loop stretch reflexes.[6] These are combined in a complicated scenario to produce the desired output in a preprogrammed manner which depends on previous experience with the environment. These programs are readily modifiable by somatesthetic, visual, and vestibular input. Malfunction in any of these areas can be reflected in abnormalities in gait and posture.

MOBILITY AND NORMAL SENESCENCE

Considering the stress put on this rather complicated system by activities required by the elderly for daily living, it is not surprising that abnormalities associated with both normal aging and pathological disease processes may impact on their function. Decrements in physical function are generally noted in athletes within their fourth decade. The safety factor built into the neurological servomechanism which directs mobility is sufficient such that difficulties are frequently not noted until focal diseases or a combination of less obvious clinical deficits develop. Even with "normal aging," however, decrements in function may be measured. Postural stability, as measured by a balance platform or ataxiameter, markedly declines with age.[7,8] Functional concomitants may be seen in tests involving standing on one foot with the eyes closed.[9]

Abnormalities in gait are obvious as well. In one study, older men showed shorter step lengths, decreased excursion of hip and ankle joints, and decreased movement in the upper extremity at the shoulder and elbow. Decreased elevation of the toe in swing phase also occurs with age, which may have obvious functional effects. There is increased out-toeing of the foot to increase the base of support. Rather than resembling a pathological gait, the older person's gait seems more like

a guarded or restrained type of walking, as if the person is walking in darkness without visual or sensory information.[10] While the automatic gait pattern program appears to be intact, there is increased variability in both stride width and the double-limb support time, suggesting increasing difficulties with balance control.[11] Deficits in the long-latency reflex arcs have been noted with increased latencies and inconsistent motor responses to postural perturbation.[12]

It has been suggested that the most important cause of these locomotion difficulties may be the marked change in vibratory threshold in the lower extremities with increasing age. Measures of deficits in lower extremities somesthesia have been correlated with decreased postural stability with aging. Such deficits have not generally resulted in significant functional disability in the elderly except for the marked rise in accidental falls. Up to one-half of community-based elderly will experience a fall. Among ambulatory nursing home patients there are approximately 700 falls per 1000 patient-beds per year. Six percent of the elderly who fall will sustain a fracture, and 12 percent will sustain a significant soft tissue injury.[13] Twenty-five percent of the elderly who fall will die within the year. Most falls in the elderly are related to systemic pathology rather than to obvious environmental hazards. This pathology is reflected in abnormalities of gait and balance.[14]

A large variety of diseases may cause significant gait disability. It has been suggested that this disability frequently may be caused by subclinical disease in a variety of systems resulting in a multifactorial gait disturbance with etiology of the difficulties not obvious. However, a recent study of 50 patients presenting with gait disorder revealed that 56 percent could be assigned to one specific diagnosis; only 24 percent had a specific therapy available.[15] Diseases identified included myelopathy (16%), Parkinson's disease (10%), hydrocephalus (4%), multiple cerebral infarcts (16%), cerebellar atrophy (8%), sensory deficits (18%), and senile gait disorder (14%). The physician is responsible for an accurate diagnosis in order to direct therapy and counsel with regard to prognosis.

EXAMINATION OF STATION AND GAIT

Difficulties in gait may reflect pathologic injuries to multiple regions of the neuroaxis. Therefore, evaluation involves a detailed history and complete neurological examination. Special emphasis in the history should be given to the mode of onset and concrete examples of functional disability related to changes in activities of daily living. The patient should be asked about accidental falls and other problems with movement such as turning in bed, sitting in a low chair, or entering a car.

In general the patients' descriptions of their difficulties will be much less incisive than actual observation of gait and station. Station is defined as the patient's attitude or posture on quiet standing. The patient's stance or foot placement should be noted, as well as his or her ability to stand straight in the erect posture with head upright. Skeletal deformities such as kyphosis, scoliosis, or lordosis, and postural abnormalities involving limb, head, and shoulders, should be noted. Patients should be asked to stand with their feet together with eyes open and then closed. A positive Romberg test occurs when patients can stand quite normally with eyes open but sway seriously or fall when eyes are closed. This effect is related to loss of proprioceptive input from the lower extremities and is referred to as a sensory ataxia. In cerebellar disease, swaying may occur both with eyes open and with eyes closed, and the patient stands with a broad base. Patients with hysterical gait problems will usually have large excursions of sway at their hips but maintain the upright posture. A useful test will be to ask patients to perform certain tasks with their hands, such as the finger-to-nose test, while standing. Patients with sensory ataxia will have increased unsteadiness, while patients with hysteria may be quite steady.[16]

The gait examination should begin as soon as the physician is introduced to the patient. The patient should be observed on walking into the room and to the examination table. The patient should be asked to walk forward, backward, and around obstacles and should also be asked to walk on his or her toes and heels, tandem walk, walk rapidly, turn, and climb stairs. Gait should be tested with eyes open and eyes closed. The physician should note the body posture; the movements of the arms, shoulders, pelvis, and head; and the width of the base of support. Gait should be scored for bradykinesia, step size, ability to advance steps, and associated movements, as well as for regularity, rhythm, and speed. Occasionally, as in a case of Parkinson's disease, a gait disorder will be so characteristic that diagnosis may be made on initial observation. Listening to the cadence of the gait and examining worn areas of the shoes can be helpful; in the case of a hemiparetic gait, the physician may hear the scraping of the front of the shoe, as documented by excessive wear on the front of the shoe's sole. A complete neurologic evaluation should include assessment of sensation in the lower extremity, motor strength, reflexes, cerebellar function, and extrapyramidal function. Mechanical disturbances should be ruled out by examination of joint mobility as well as by examination for painful lesions. The examination of station and gait in the elderly provides information about multiple subsystems in the neuroaxis in a simple and rapid manner.

NEUROLOGIC DISORDERS OF GAIT

FRONTAL APRAXIA

Associated with the behavioral disturbance of frontal lobe disease, manifested by the apathetic abulic syndrome, there is a motor syndrome that occurs in the context of normal strength and sensory function. Luria describes this as the "deautomatization" of complex motor tasks and the revival of elementary automatisms, with an interruption of "kinetic melodies."[17] This interruption is manifested in difficulty in moving from one aspect of a complex motor task to another. Denny-Brown has described the motor difficulties associated with frontal lobe lesions as being due to a limb kinetic apraxia with perseveration of motor tasks.[18] This is reflected by the grasp reflex of the hand and the foot grasp which is elicited when the affected foot contacts the floor. The lower limb stiffens and becomes glued to the floor, and steps, made with difficulty, are small and may resemble a shuffle.[18] When these disorders are bilateral, coordinated movements such as walking may be severely impaired. This impairment has been described as the "slipping clutch," which is characterized by a rapid shuffling of feet before a step may be made. This inability to inhibit the grasping response of the feet is the cause of a "magnetic apraxia."[18] Frontal lobe apraxic gait is associated with poor postural reflexes, gegenhalten or paratonic rigidity, and prominent frontal release signs.[19] Particularly noted is difficulty on initiation of gait. The clinical syndrome suggests defective supraspinal modulation of the automatic gait programs since step size, which is normally constant for a given walking speed, is variable.

NORMAL PRESSURE HYDROCEPHALUS

Communicating "normal pressure" hydrocephalus presents in the elderly with a distinctive triad of a gait disturbance, dementia, and incontinence.[20] Initial enthusiasm for surgical shunting procedures has been tempered by the relatively poor results. While excellent results have been seen in up to one-fourth of patients so treated, there has been a high frequency of nonresponders and an appreciable incidence of perioperative complications. The gait disorder includes elements of a gait apraxia with a magnetic short-stepped gait, poor balance control, and difficulty with turning.[21] Corticospinal abnormalities have been reported, with extensor-plantar responses and frontal release signs, as well as difficulty with fine-motor control in the upper extremity and turning in bed. Recent analysis of the gait of such patients revealed that there is decreased velocity and stride length with increased sway and double-limb support time. There is a marked reduction in step height, decreased associated shoulder movements, and continuous activity in limb antigravity musculature with cocontracture instead of the normal phasic activities seen in the gait cycle.[22] Paradoxically, leg movements while lying down are performed with normal agility. Even gait movements may be imitated. It has been suggested that stimulation of the dorsum of foot leads to a stiffening reaction of the lower extremity similar to motor perseveration of the upper extremity due to frontal lobe lesions. Perseveration of this reflex impairs automatic gait programs.[18] The remarkable similarity to patients with frontal lobe lesions has been noted, and it has been suggested that because the leg fibers lie in the medial portion of the frontal hemispheres they are most susceptible to compression by the enlarging frontal horns.[20]

A subcortical dementia with a dilapidation of mental processes and increased apathy and inattention has been associated with the motor findings. Urinary incontinence is a frequent concomitant and generally improves with cerebrospinal fluid drainage. Diagnosis is dependent on the recognition of the clinical triad. However, similar signs have been seen in vascular dementia and dementia of the Alzheimer type. Various procedures have been used to aid with differential diagnosis, including transmission computed tomography (CT), radioisotope cisternography, and magnetic resonance imaging (MRI). It was hoped that MRI would be particularly incisive since periventricular edema secondary to transependymal fluid flow can be readily recognized by a periventricular rim of high density, on proton density, and T2 weighted images. However, similar abnormalities have been reported both in cerebrovascular disease and in Alzheimer's disease. It has been suggested that the best clinical indicator is the presence of a gait dyspraxia with the appropriate CT, MRI, and cisternography findings in a patient who is mentally normal or only mildly demented. Therapeutic procedures include ventricular peritoneal and lumboperitoneal shunts.

BASAL GANGLIA DISORDERS

Parkinson's Disease

Parkinson's disease is a common degenerative disease of the nervous system.[23] The average incidence is 20 cases out of every 100,000 people. It is estimated that half a million to 1 million people suffer with the disease in this country. The average age of onset of Parkinson's disease is approximately 60 years old, and the prevalence increases with age. Parkinson's disease is a symptom complex consisting of resting tremor, bradykinesia, rigidity, and impaired postural reflexes. The pathologic basis is degeneration of the substantia nigra with the resultant neurochemical abnormality of decreased striatal dopa-

mine. Gait abnormalities are very common. James Parkinson, in his essay on the Shaking Palsy in 1817, clearly described the parkinsonian gait. The clinical manifestations are distinctive. The trunk of the parkinsonian patient is frequently bent forward (simian posture). The arms do not swing (loss of associated movements). In hemiparkinsonism an important early sign is lack of arm swing on one side of the body. Rigidity is evident while walking, as the legs are stiff and bend at the knees. Parkinsonian patients often have great difficulty with the initiation of gait (start hesitation). The steps are short, and the feet appear barely to clear the floor (marche à petits pas). The patient shuffles forward. Dragging of one leg is a common initial symptom. Sometimes there is an involuntary acceleration of walking (festination). The upper part of the body often advances ahead of the lower part, as if trying to catch up with the center of gravity. Once walking, the patient may do fairly well; however, turning is often difficult. The individual turns with many small steps and moves the trunk in a rigid manner (en bloc turning). Interestingly, the resting tremor is often exacerbated during walking. Some patients appear to get stuck while walking, unable to move at doorways or other enclosed spaces. This is referred to as freezing phenomenon. Falling is common in Parkinson's disease. Bradykinesia, rigidity, gait disturbances, and postural instability all appear to contribute to falling. Objective measurements of the parkinsonian gait reveal a reduced speed of walking due primarily to diminished stride length. There is decreased angular excursion in both hip and knee, with agonist-antagonist cocontracture superimposed on a normal phasic pattern of muscular activation.[24]

Hyperkinesias

Abnormal gaits may be associated with hyperkinetic movement disorders. Choreoathetosis is a dyskinesia characterized by arrhythmic, involuntary movements that intrude in a sudden, brief, nonrepetitive fashion. Laypersons often call individuals with this dyskinesia "fidgety." Chorea is a symptom that can be caused by neurodegenerative disorders, endocrine and immunologic disease, structural insults to the brain, and various drugs. Chorea can be limited to certain body parts, such as the face, or be more generalized. The choreic gait consists of continuous irregular movements affecting the limbs and trunk. Each step may appear different because the chorea is irregular and affects different body parts. The legs may advance slowly with seemingly poor coordination and superimposed hyperkinesia. Chorea is a major symptom in Huntington's disease, a hereditary form of chorea associated with mental changes. A prominent gait disorder occurs in Huntington's disease, unrelated to the chorea.[25] This gait has parkinsonian features, as well as several unusual features. Dystonia is a symptom defined by spasms or twisting movements which result in an abnormal posture. Dystonia may be focal, affecting one body part, or generalized, as with torsion dystonia. Dystonic posturing such as inversion of the foot may disturb walking. Spasms of the arms and trunk, such as opisthotonus, also alter the normal gait pattern. The trunk may assume a lordotic or scoliotic position. Some patients have action dystonia so that dystonia only occurs during movement, as when walking. Tics are abnormal movements in which an abrupt, jerky, repetitive movement occurs which involves discrete muscle groups. Tics can often be temporarily suppressed by will power. The movements may be focal, as in the facial muscles (e.g., eye blinking), or more generalized. Tics are most often a childhood affliction, as in Tourette's syndrome, in which both vocal and motor tics occur. A variety of complex movements can disturb gait, such as walking backward, kneeling, turning in circles, squatting, and jumping. Myoclonus is a dyskinesia defined as irregular or regular muscle jerks which originate in the central nervous system. These quick movements can also interfere with normal walking.

CEREBELLAR DISEASE

The cerebellum is one of the three basic subdivisions of the brain (the other divisions are the cerebral hemispheres and the brain stem). The anatomical components of the cerebellum consist of two hemispheres and a midline structure termed the *vermis*. The cerebellar hemispheres are concerned with movement of the extremities. Each hemisphere subserves function for the ipsilateral arm and leg. The vermis subserves function of the trunk and lower extremities. Abnormalities of standing and walking are common clinical signs of cerebellar dysfunction. Structural lesions (e.g., stroke or tumor), primary neurodegenerative disorders, and drugs may cause cerebellar dysfunction. Lesions of the midline structures often result in disturbances of stance and gait. Alcoholic cerebellar degeneration characteristically affects these structures and causes substantial gait changes, often without other cerebellar signs. Quantitative studies have documented a 3-Hz postural tremor in the anterior-posterior direction.[26]

Patients with cerebellar disease complain of walking with a staggering gait as if they were drunk. The stance is wide-based. While walking the patient may totter, reel, and tip forward then backward, appearing at each moment to lose his or her balance and fall. Control over trunk and legs is greatly impaired. Individuals tend to lurch from one side to the other and often veer irresistibly to one side. The feet are often lifted too high and placed either too widely apart or too closely together in an irregular sequence, causing successive steps to be

spaced irregularly. The physician's ability to study gait dysfunction can be enhanced by various examination techniques. Having the patient walk in tandem (the successive placement of the heel of the foot in line and contact with the bone of the other foot) may disclose an inability to walk on a narrow base or a tendency to fall toward one side. Having the patient walk on the heels or toes, or backward, may elicit subtle deficits in gait due to cerebellar disease. Besides gait ataxia, postural abnormalities may be present, particulary in long-standing disease of the cerebellar hemispheres. Truncal instability may be decreased slightly by visual cues. However, there is no major change in the inclination to fall when the eyes are closed. The Romberg test cannot be applied to assess position sense in these patients.

SENILE GAIT

MacDonald Critchley[27] first called attention to what he termed "senile disorders of gait," noting that the aged often had disturbances of movement and ambulation unassociated with paralysis or weakness of the lower limbs. He described the gradual appearance of a broad-based gait with small steps associated with a diminished arm swing, a stooped posture, flexion of the hips and knees, uncertainty and stiffness in turning, occasional difficulty getting started, and a tendency toward falling. However, the clinical picture of senile gait is quite variable. Gait characteristics, along with other aspects of the neurologic examination in the elderly, remain controversial. Senile gait may at times be difficult to distinguish from parkinsonism, yet at other times may be totally different in appearance. It is stated that the inability to walk tandem seems universal in the very old. A broad-based gait is often present in elderly patients. The general neurologic examination may reveal some minimal alteration in deep tendon reflexes in the lower extremity and some loss of vibratory sense in the feet. No neurologic abnormalities of major neuroanatomic systems are present to adequately explain the disturbance in walking. It is common clinical experience that elderly patients often will complain of gait difficulty and examination will reveal no evidence of gait or motor abnormalities.

There is little agreement or definite knowledge regarding the basic underlying cause and anatomical basis of the senile gait. Critchley suggested that the gait of the elderly was a manifestation of extrapyramidal dysfunction.[27] It has been further hypothesized that disordered movements seen in senescence result from defective striatal dopaminergic mechanism. Disease of the mesial frontal lobes produces a gait apraxia. Alternatively, it has been suggested that senile gait is attributable to cerebellar disease. In recent studies of CT scans in the elderly it was found that the cerebellar vermis selectively atrophies with age.[28] Yet other studies indicate that ataxia in the elderly may correlate with sensory abnormalities and a loss of nerve fibers in the dorsal column. Adams and Victor[29] hypothesized that the peculiar gait of the aged is due to a combined frontal-lobe–basal-ganglion degeneration. Fischer has offered a new and controversial hypothesis regarding the pathophysiology of senile gait.[21] He suggested that the unexplained unsteady gait in late life was caused by hydrocephalus and that gait instability could be reversed by cerebrospinal fluid shunting procedures. Fifty patients with senile gait were found in his study to have an increase in the size of the lateral ventricle as compared to that of controls. He speculated that senile gait is an early and sole manifestation of normal-pressure hydrocephalus. It is evident that not all patients with the syndrome respond to shunting. No single clinical syndrome or group of diagnostic tests (e.g., CT scan or RISA cisternography) can reliably identify which patients are most likely to improve with cerebrospinal fluid in shunting.[30] We believe that many such patients may have ventriculomegaly secondary to diffuse neurodegenerative and cerebrovascular lesions. Shunt placement should only be considered in patients fulfilling strict clinical criteria with early onset of gait difficulty as described above.

PYRAMIDAL GAIT DISORDERS

Hemiplegia

The corticospinal tract originates in the precentral cortical gyrus, and its fiber tracts descend to synapse in the anterior horn of the spinal cord. The most common cause of gait disorders in the elderly relating to supraspinal control is cerebrovascular disease. There are over 1.7 million stroke survivors in the United States. The incidence increases exponentially from ages 45 to 85. The most common clinical syndrome, which is associated with hemispheral involvement in the distribution of the middle cerebral artery, is a hemiparesis. Spastic hemiplegia frequently involves the upper extremity, which is held in flexion and adduction at the shoulder and flexion at the elbow, wrist, and interphalangeal joints.[16] The lower extremity is held in extension at the hip and knee, with plantar flexion of the foot. On walking, the arm is held in flexion with markedly decreased association movements, and there is circumduction of the lower extremity with hip abductor weakness. There may be dragging or scraping of that foot which may result in abnormal wear on the sole of one shoe, most obvious at the toes. Larger intracerebral lesions may involve more extensive middle cerebral artery distribution, as well as the anterior cerebral artery territory which supplies the cortical area–controlling distal portion of the lower extremity. With larger lesions initial flaccidity frequently occurs with the development of increased tone and spas-

ticity over the several weeks that follow. Examination reveals hyperflexia, increased flexor tone in the arm, and extensor tone in the leg and extensor plantar responses. Despite the relatively poor return of voluntary motor control, patients are frequently able to walk because of the development of marked extensor tonus in their lower extremity. Electrophysiologic abnormalities in spasticity have been noted with lowered stretch reflex threshold, decreased muscle activation at appropriate intervals, and coactivation of agonist-antagonist groups.[31] Electromyographic studies reveal that there are abnormalities involving both timing and extent of phasic muscular activity. The relative preservation of ability to execute stepping movements reflects the integrity of the central locomotor centers. Impaired supraspinal mechanisms are demonstrated by abnormalities in spinal reflex inhibition and activation of long loop polysynaptic reflex patterns required for rapid balance adjustment.[32]

Spastic Paraparesis

The presence of bilateral spasticity in the elderly may be seen with a variety of disorders of the spinal cord. The most common and clinically perplexing situation involves myelopathy due to cervical spondylosis. It has been estimated that greater than 50 percent of the population over the age of 50 would have radiographic findings of cervical spondylosis with anterior and posterior osteophytes. The overwhelming majority of these people are asymptomatic. The development of symptoms is related to preexisting spinal column stenosis. Cervical stenosis with spondylosis may present with symptoms of radiculopathy and myelopathy. Patients with myelopathy will frequently have a history of radicular symptoms and the insidious development of a spastic paraparesis, one leg usually being more affected than the other. Extensor hypertonus will be present on examination in the lower extremities. There is a stiff, shuffling gait, with circumduction of each leg. Hyperadduction of the thighs may result in a scissors gait, compounding balance problems by forcing patients to maneuver on a narrow base. The indications for surgical intervention remain controversial because of the relatively poor results and frequent complications involved with the surgical procedures.

Ambulatory difficulty in patients with upper motor neuron signs may be seen in other degenerative processes in the elderly. Amyotrophic lateral sclerosis may present with disorders of gait and balance. Elements of the upper and lower motor neuron disease with a steppage gait and foot drop as well as spastic paraplegic symptoms may be encountered. Widespread muscle fasciculation may be noted with atrophy and hyperreflexia. Diagnosis may be confirmed by electromyographic examination. At present there is no effective therapy.

MOTOR NEURON AND PERIPHERAL NERVE DYSFUNCTION

The lower motor neuron system is comprised of the anterior horn cell, the nerve root, and the peripheral nerves. Weakness caused by lesions of these motor neurons can result in gait disturbances. While polio is a historically important disease of the anterior horn cell, the degenerative disease amyotrophic lateral sclerosis is currently the most commonly encountered motor neuron disease. This condition also affects the upper motor pyramidal pathway. Nerve root or radicular disease is often due to compressive lesions such as with tumors or disc disease. There are many causes of peripheral nerve dysfunction, including diabetes, alcohol, immunologic diseases, heredity disorders, and drugs. A common gait disturbance is the steppage gait in association with a foot drop, caused by weakness of dorsiflexion of the foot and/ or the toes. The patient may drag his or her foot or, to compensate for the foot drop, lift the foot as high as possible to keep the toes from scraping the floor. There is exaggerated flexion at the hip and the knee. The foot may be thrown forward, with the toe flopping down with a characteristic sound. The patient is unable to stand on his or her heels. Steppage gait may be unilateral or bilateral and may be due to peroneal nerve dysfunction. A shuffling gait may result from paresis of the gastrocnemius and soleus muscles. These patients are unable to stand on their toes and the heel strikes first while walking. With paresis of the hamstring there is weakness of flexion at the knee. Weakness of the quadriceps results in paresis of extension at the knee. The patient has difficulty extending the knee and climbing stairs. Sciatic nerve lesions cause varying types of gait abnormalities. In paresis of the superficial peroneal nerve there is loss of eversion, and the patient walks on the outer aspect of the foot.

MUSCLE DISORDERS

Disorders of muscle may result in gait disturbances. The musular dystrophies, such as Duchenne's, are primarily diseases of childhood. Gait is often severely affected, and patients may become wheelchair-bound. Adult-onset muscle disease, such as polymyositis, often interferes with normal ambulation. Muscle disorders almost always affect proximal musculature, such as the limb-girdle muscles. The patient may have a marked lordosis and with walking there is marked waddling because of difficulty with fixing the pelvis. There is an exaggerated rotation of the pelvis and rolling of the hips with each step. The patient has marked difficulty climbing stairs because of proximal muscle weakness. Muscular dystrophy children have problems getting up from a lying or seated position and must assist themselves by climbing up on

themselves, placing their hands first on their knees and then on their hips to brace themselves (Gower's maneuver).

SENSORY ATAXIA

A gait disorder resembling that seen with cerebellar disease is caused by loss of kinesthetic sensibility from the lower extremity. Patients walk with a wide-based, unsteady gait, with small irregular steps and eyes directed toward their feet. They fling out their feet and strike the ground abruptly, first with their heel and then their toes, producing the foot-slapping gait. In some patients gait may be nearly normal with visual input but may become markedly abnormal when they walk in the dark. This is reflected by a positive Romberg test in which patients who can stand normally on a narrow base fall when they close their eyes. It has been suggested that gait and balance difficulties in the elderly may well relate to the progressive loss of posterior column functions associated with aging. The most marked changes with aging among measures of neurologic function have been observed in vibratory sensibility.[9] Correlations have been noted between the vibratory sensibility and postural sway in a normal aging population. Abnormalities of stance, mimicking that of patients with structural cerebellar disease, have been documented in patients with sensory loss.[33] Loss of kinesthetic sensibility has proven to be more critical than all other sensory modalities for the maintenance of normal posture and balance.[12]

Sensory ataxia may be caused by either peripheral nerve dysfunction or spinal cord disease involving the posterior columns. A variety of peripheral neuropathies have been noted in the elderly. Most common is the sensory disorder associated with a diabetic polyneuropathy. Patients may present with painful dysesthesias and balance difficulty. Pernicious anemia results in combined systems disease with involvement of both the cortical spinal tract and the posterior columns. This disease, which is related to inadequate absorption of vitamin B_{12}, may result in a spastic ataxic gait with elements of balance control deficits due to spasticity, as well as sensory ataxia resulting in a highly unstable gait.

NONNEUROLOGIC GAIT DISORDERS

GENERAL MEDICAL PROBLEMS

Medical diseases which do not affect the nervous system can also cause disturbances of gait. Diseases of the bone and orthopedic problems often interfere with walking.[34] Sometimes in conditions in which both the orthopedic and neurologic systems are involved it may be difficult to know to which system to attribute the dysfunction. This is often the case with cerebral palsy. The gait in this disorder may be due to mechanical and/or neurologic problems. A variety of pathologic processes may prevent the hip from functioning in normal walking. The painful hip (antalgic gait) and the dislocated hip cause the patient to bend the trunk. A limp which results can be helped by using a cane on the normal side. The knee joint is also important for walking. The knee is flexed during the swing phase of gait. If the knee is held extended, the pelvis must be elevated by exaggerated plantar flexion of the opposite ankle or by circumduction of the entire leg to provide toe clearance. Loss of knee motion also greatly slows gait speed. Disturbances of the ankle joint and the foot also affect walking. It is also important to remember that medical illnesses by themselves can alter gait by causing pain or by local disturbances. Infections of the groin area and even the vagina can be responsible for severly abnormal gaits.

PSYCHIATRIC DISEASE

Various gait changes may be associated with major affective disorders. The depressed patient may be stooped over and move and walk slowly because of psychomotor retardation. This gait may appear somewhat parkinsonian. The manic patient, on the other hand, is erect and may be overactive. In schizophrenia various abnormalities can occur. Abnormal postures and various stereotypes and mannerisms may affect walking. Hysterical gaits are quite distinctive. These disorders may result from conversion reactions or malingering. The gait is often bizarre and not characteristic of neurologic gait syndromes. Walking is irregular and changeable. There may be marked swaying from one side to another. There is a theatrical nature to the walking which often demonstrates great coordination in order to perform the many movements associated with the hysterical gait. The patient appears to fall but will rarely do so if unattended. Falling often takes the form of sliding down a wall so that injury is avoided. The term *astasia-abasia* has been used to describe the hysterical gait, but since it literally means "an inability to walk" the use of the term is best avoided. The motor, cerebellar, reflex, and sensory examinations are normal in individuals with this gait disorder. Diagnosis is usually not difficult.

REFERENCES

1. Drachman D: An approach to the neurology of aging, in Birren J, Sloan R (eds): *Handbook of Mental Health and Aging.* Englewood Cliffs, Prentice-Hall, 1980, p 501.
2. Martin JP: *The Basal Ganglia and Posture.* Philadelphia, J. B. Lippincott, 1967.
3. Horenstein S: Managing gait disorders. *Geriatrics* 29:86, 1974.
4. Martin JP: A short essay on posture and motion. *J Neurol Neurosurg Psychiatry* 40:25, 1977.
5. Murray MP: Gait as a total pattern of movement. *Am J Phys Med* 46:290, 1967.
6. Brooks VB: *The Neural Basis of Motor Control.* New York, Oxford, 1986.
7. Overstall PW et al: Falls in the elderly related to postural imbalance. *Br Med J* 1:261, 1977.
8. Murray MP et al: Center of gravity, center of pressure and supportive forces during human activity. *J Appl Physiol* 23:831, 1967.
9. Potvin AR et al: Human neurologic function and the aging process. *J Am Geriatr Soc* 28:1, 1980.
10. Murray MP et al: Walking patterns in healthy old men. *J Gerontol* 24:169, 1969.
11. Gabell A et al: The effect of age on variability in gait. *J Gerontol* 39:662, 1984.
12. Woollacott ML: Gait and postural control in the aging adult, in Bles W, Brandt TH (eds): *Disorders of Posture and Gait.* Amsterdam, Elsevier, 1986, p 325.
13. Gryfe CI: Longitudinal study of falls in an elderly population: Incidence and morbidity. *Age Ageing* 6:201, 1977.
14. Nickens H: Intrinsic factors in falling among the elderly. *Arch Intern Med* 145:1089, 1985.
15. Sudarsky L et al: Gait disorders among elderly patients. *Arch Neurol* 40:740, 1983.
16. De Jong RH: *The Neurology Examination.* Hagerstown, Harper & Row, 1979.
17. Luria AR: Frontal lobe syndromes, in Vinken PJ, Bruyn GW (eds): *Handbook of Clinical Neurology*, vol 2, *Localization in Clinical Neurology.* Amsterdam, North Holland Publishing Company, 1969, p 725.
18. Denny-Brown D: The nature of apraxia. *J Nerv Ment Dis* 216:9, 1958.
19. Meyer JS et al: Apraxia of gait: A clinico-pathological study. *Brain* 83:261, 1960.
20. Adams RD et al: Symptomatic occult hydrocephalus with "normal" cerebrospinal fluid pressure (a treatable syndrome). *N Engl J Med* 273:117, 1965.
21. Fisher CM: Hydrocephalus as a cause of disturbance of gait in the elderly. *Neurology* 32:1358, 1982.
22. Sudarsky L, Simon S: Gait disorder in late-life hydrocephalus. *Arch Neurol* 44:263, 1987.
23. Koller WC: *Handbook of Parkinson's Disease.* New York, Marcel Dekker, 1988.
24. Knutsson E, Martensson A: Posture and gait in parkinsonian patients, in Bles W, Brandt TH (eds): *Disorders of Posture and Gait.* Amsterdam, Elsevier, 1986, p 217.
25. Koller WC, Trimble J: The gait abnormality of Huntington's Disease. *Neurology* 35:1450, 1985.
26. Mauritz KH et al: Quantitative analysis of stance in late cortical cerebellar of the anterior lobe and other forms of cerebellar ataxia. *Brain* 102:461, 1982.
27. Critchley M: Senile disorders of gait including the so-called "senile paraplegia." *Geriatrics* 3:364, 1948.
28. Koller WC, Glatt S, Wilson R, Huckman MS, Fox JH: Cerebellar atrophy: Relationship to aging and cerebral atrophy. *Neurology* 23:405, 1981.
29. Adams RD, Victor M: *Principles of Neurology*, 4th ed. New York, McGraw-Hill, 1989.
30. Katzman R: *Normal Pressure Hydrocephalus in Dementia.* Philadelphia, Davis, 1977, p 69.

31. Knutsson E: Analysis of gait and isokinetic movements for evaluation of antispastic drugs or physical therapy, in Desmedt JG (ed): *Motor Control Mechanisms in Health and Disease*. New York, Raven, 1983, p 1013.

32. Berger W et al: Spastic paresis: Impaired spinal reflexes and intact motor programs. *J Neurol Neurosurg Psychiatry* 51:568, 1988.

33. Kotaka S et al: Somatosensory ataxia, in Bles W, Brandt TH (eds): *Disorders of Posture and Gait*. Amsterdam, Elsevier, 1986, p 177.

34. Inman VT, Ralston HJ, Todd F: *Human Walking*. Baltimore, Williams and Wilkins, 1981.

Chapter 123

FALLS

Mary E. Tinetti

Falling is a common and potentially preventable source of mortality, morbidity, and suffering in elderly patients. While some falls have an overwhelming intrinsic cause, such as syncope (discussed in Chap. 109), or an overwhelming extrinsic cause, such as being hit by a bus, most falls by elderly patients are multifactorial in origin, resulting from an interaction between stability-impairing characteristics of the host and hazards or demands of the environment.

Falls by institutionalized and community-dwelling persons are considered separately in this chapter because of significant differences in levels of impairment, as well as in environmental demands and hazards. The topics discussed in this chapter include prevalence, morbidity, risk factors, and possible preventive strategies.

FALLS AMONG COMMUNITY-LIVING ELDERLY PERSONS

PREVALENCE

According to several community-based surveys, about 30 percent of persons over age 65 fall each year.[1-3] About one-half of these fallers have multiple falling episodes. The likelihood of falling increases with age.[1-4] Results have been contradictory as to whether older women fall more frequently than older men. Both frail elderly persons and healthy elderly persons fall, suggesting that falling is not merely a nonspecific marker of functional decline.

MORBIDITY

Accidents are the sixth leading cause of death in persons over age 65.[5] The majority of these accident-related deaths are attributed to falls. The number of deaths directly resulting from falls is difficult to estimate because on the one hand, falls are missed as the inciting event in

This work was supported by NIA academic award KO8 AG00292.

many cases, and on the other hand, falling may be a manifestation of deterioration due to other causes.

Perhaps the most feared morbid outcome of falling is a fractured hip, suffered by over 200,000 Americans every year, most of whom are elderly women.[5] Hip fractures are discussed in Chap. 124. While injury to any bone may result from a fall, humeral, wrist, pelvic, and hip fractures are the most common age-related fractures, resulting from the combined effects of osteoporosis and falling.[6] Serious soft tissue injuries, such as hemarthroses, sprains, and strains, may also result from falls.[1,3] Fortunately, the most serious injuries, such as subdural hematomas and cervical fractures, are rare. Certainly, the majority of falls do not result in serious physical injury. An estimated 1 percent of falls result in a hip fracture, 5 percent in other fractures, and an additional 5 percent in serious soft tissue injuries.[1,3]

Women appear to have a greater risk of both fracture and nonfracture injuries than men.[1] There is also some evidence that healthier, more active elderly persons are at greater risk of injury per fall than are frailer individuals.[1] Risk of injury has been postulated to result from the combined effect of impaired protective responses of the faller and greater force of impact of the fall.[6] However, characteristics distinguishing the faller at high risk of injury are not yet known.

Restriction in activity because of fear of falling is another important fall-related morbidity. Up to one-half of fallers admit to being afraid, and one-quarter report that due to fear they avoid even essential activities such as mobility within the home, bathing, and dressing.[3] Family and friends may become anxious as well. Overprotectiveness may lead to unwarranted restriction in independence and mobility. Falling is mentioned as one reason for institutionalization in up to 40 percent of admissions.[7]

RISK FACTORS

The risk factors associated with falling include both chronic risk factors that predispose to falling and situational factors that are present at the time of falls.

Predisposing Risk Factors

Predisposing risk factors are best understood by considering that stability requires input from sensory, central integrative, cognitive, and musculoskeletal components in a highly integrated manner. Diseases and disabilities impacting on these components often are superimposed on age-related physiologic changes. Furthermore, cardiac, respiratory, metabolic, and other systemic disorders may compromise the functioning of any (or all) of these components. Gait disorders (Chap. 122) are especially important contributors to the risk of falling in the elderly. Therefore, it is the cumulative effect of multiple age-related changes, diseases, and disabilities that appears to predispose to falling.

SENSORY Vision, hearing, vestibular function, and proprioception are the major sensory modalities related to stability. Age-related visual changes are discussed in Chap. 42. Falling has been associated with both structural diseases of the eye, such as cataracts, and functional impairments in visual perception and acuity.[1–4,8] The question of age-related changes in the vestibular system remains unresolved. Certainly, benign positional vertigo is seen more frequently in older persons. Factors predisposing to vestibular dysfunction, including previous ear infections, ear surgery, aminoglycosides, quinidine, and furosemide, are common among elderly patients.[9] Peripheral neuropathy and cervical degenerative disease probably are the most common causes of proprioceptive dysfunctions in elderly patients.[10] Almost one-third of elderly patients have abnormal position sense when tested clinically.[11]

CENTRAL NERVOUS SYSTEM Sensory inputs are integrated in the central nervous system and appropriate signals are then sent to the effector components of the musculoskeletal system. Therefore, any altered central nervous system process will predispose to falling. Falling has been associated with many central nervous system diseases, including stroke, Parkinson's disease, and normal-pressure hydrocephalus.

COGNITIVE Dementia has been associated with an increased risk of falling in several studies.[1–4,12] Dementia may be an especially important risk factor for falling among patients with other impairments because of greater need for problem-solving ability.

MUSCULOSKELETAL The effector component of stability includes the efferent peripheral nervous system, bones, joints, and muscles. Patients with lower-extremity disabilities such as severe arthritis or weakness have a several-fold increase in risk of fall.[3] The feet are an often unrecognized source of morbidity in elderly patients.

Thick nails, callouses, bunions, and toe deformities, as well as ill-fitting shoes, may give misleading proprioceptive information.[13]

OTHER PREDISPOSING RISK FACTORS In several community studies, depression has been associated with an increased risk of falling. This risk appears to be independent of medication effect or other diseases. Postural hypotension has been postulated as a fall risk factor as well. However, recent studies have found a lower prevalence of this condition among community-dwelling elderly than had previously been thought to exist and have found no association with falling.[3,14] Unfortunately, the lack of blood pressure measurements at the time of the fall is a major limitation in determining the contribution of postural hypotension to falls in community-dwelling persons.

Medications appear to be a major predisposing risk factor for falls. Several studies have shown that sedatives such as benzodiazepines, phenothiazines, and antidepressants increase risk of falling, independent of the effect of the dementia or depression for which they are usually prescribed.[1–4] There is evidence suggesting a dose–response relationship, and the risk appears to be greater for the longer-acting medications.[15] The independent role of other medications that may impair postural regulation of blood pressure, such as antihypertensives or cardiac medications, is not yet clear.

The results of studies concerning the role of alcohol have been contradictory, with some studies showing an association with falls and injury and others showing no such association. One problem is that the self-report of alcohol consumption may not be reliable in older patients.

Situational Factors

Patients who are predisposed to falling because of the above characteristics do so only intermittently. Therefore, in understanding fall etiology, it is also necessary to identify factors that may precipitate falls.

ACTIVITY The majority of falls occur during only mildly or moderately displacing activities such as walking, stepping up or down, or changing position. Only a minority of falls, probably about 5 percent, occur during clearly hazardous activities such as climbing on ladders or chairs.[3] However, there is an increased incidence of falls among elderly persons who participate in more physical activity and exercise, probably because of exposure to severe displacement and hazards.

ENVIRONMENT More than 70 percent of falls occur at home. Perhaps 10 percent of falls occur on stairs, with descending being more hazardous than ascending. Environmental hazards may be present in over one-half of all falls. Most commonly, these hazards are objects that are tripped over, such as cords, furniture, and small objects left on the floor. The role of other potential environmental hazards such as poor lighting, improperly fitting shoes, and surfaces with glare are more difficult to assess. A recent area of research in environmental hazards concerns optical patterns on escalators, stairs, and floor surfaces that may be important contributors to falls because of visual perceptual problems in the elderly.[16]

ACUTE HOST FACTORS Dizziness and syncope, other obvious causes of falls, are discussed in Chap. 109. Acute illnesses or exacerbations of chronic illnesses are known to precipitate falls. In fact, falling is a well-recognized nonspecific presentation for illnesses such as pneumonias, urinary tract infections, and congestive heart failure among elderly patients.

PREVENTION

While results of controlled studies of fall prevention in community-dwelling elderly persons are not yet available, potential preventive strategies can be recommended based on knowledge of fall etiology as discussed above. Preventive strategies should address both the predisposing and the precipitating factors and should also address both intrinsic and environmental factors.

Identifying Predisposing Risk Factors

Because elderly fallers are predisposed to fall based on the cumulative effects of multiple disabilities, the primary aim of the clinical evaluation is to identify the modifiable factors. The optimal fall evaluation involves assessing sensory, neurologic, musculoskeletal, and systemic processes in order to identify all possible contributors in individual patients (Table 123-1). The evaluation should include observing directly the patient's balance and gait (Table 123-2).

Because risk of falling increases with the number of impairments, the clinician can estimate risk of falling based on the results of the routine clinical evaluation suggested in Table 123-1. More importantly, if risk of falling increases with the number of disabilities, risk may be minimized by ameliorating or eliminating even a few contributing factors.

As shown in Table 123-1, potential interventions may be medical, surgical, rehabilitative, or environmental. In most cases, the treatment of identified risk factors should include components of each of these types of intervention. Examples include surgery for cataracts; recommendations concerning good lighting; podiatric care, adaptive footwear, or surgery for foot problems; and physical therapy, exercise programs, and appropriate walking aids for musculoskeletal problems. Several in-

TABLE 123-1
Predisposing Risk Factors and Potential Interventions

Risk Factor	Potential Interventions
Sensory	
Vision: close-range and distance perception, dark adaptation	Appropriate refraction; surgery; medications; good lighting
Hearing	Cerumen removal; hearing aid
Vestibular	
Drugs, previous infections, surgery, benign positional vertigo	Avoidance of toxic drugs; surgery; balance exercises; good lighting
Proprioceptive	
Peripheral nerves, spinal cord	Treatment of underlying disease; good lighting; appropriate walking aid and footwear
Cervical: arthritis, spondylosis	Balance exercises; surgery
Central neurologic	
Any central nervous system disease impairing problem solving and judgment	Treatment of underlying disease; supervised, structured, safe environment
Musculoskeletal	
Arthritides, especially lower extremities	Medical and possibly surgical treatment of underlying disease
Muscle weakness, contractures	Strengthening exercises; balance and gait training; appropriate adaptive devices
Foot disorders: bunions, calluses, deformities	Podiatry; appropriate footwear
Systemic diseases	
Postural hypotension	Hydration; lowest effective dosage of necessary medications; reconditioning exercises; elevation of head of bed; stockings
Cardiac, respiratory, metabolic diseases	Treatment of underlying diseases
Depression	Careful consideration to risk-benefit of antidepressant medication
Medications	
All—especially sedating medications	Lowest effective dosage of essential medications, starting low and increasing slowly
Environment	Environmental hazard checklist; appropriate adaptations and manipulations

vestigators have seen benefit from balance exercises for vestibular or proprioceptive problems.[17,18] Further ex-

TABLE 123-2
Performance-Oriented Evaluation of Balance and Gait

Abnormal Maneuver	Possible Etiologies*	Possible Therapeutic or Rehabilitative Measures†	Possible Preventive or Adaptive Measures†
Difficulty arising from chair	Proximal muscle weakness (many causes) Arthritides (especially involving hip and knees) Parkinson's syndrome Hemiparesis or paraparesis Deconditioning	Treatment of specific disease states (e.g., with steroids, L-dopa) Hip and quadricep exercises Transfer training	High, firm chair with arms Raised toilet seats Ejection chairs
Instability on first standing	Postural hypotension Cerebellar disease Multisensory deficits Lower-extremity weakness or pain Foot pain causing reduced weight bearing	Treatment of specific diseases (e.g., adequate salt and fluid status, flucortisone) Jobst stockings Hip and knee exercises Correct foot problems	Arise slowly Head of bed on blocks Supportive aid (e.g., walker, quadcane)
Instability with nudge on sternum	Parkinson's syndrome Back problems Normal pressure hydrocephalus ? Peripheral neuropathy Deconditioning	Treatment of specific diseases (e.g., with L-dopa, shunt) ? Back exercises Analgesia ? Balance exercises (e.g., Frankel's)	Obstacle-free environment Appropriate walking aid (cane, walker) Night-lights (less likely to fall if bump into object) Close observation with acute illness (high risk of falling) Avoid slippers
Instability with eyes closed (stable with eyes open)	Multisensory deficits Reduced proprioception, position sense (e.g., B_{12} deficiency, diabetes mellitus, etc.)	Treatment of specific diseases (e.g., B_{12}) Correct visual, hearing problem ? Balance exercises	Bright lights Night-lights Cane
Instability on neck turning or extension	Cervical arthritis Cervical spondylosis Vertebral-basilar insufficiency	? Antiarthritic medication ? Cervical collar ? Neck exercises	Avoid quick turns Turn body, not just head Store objects in home low enough to avoid need to look up
Instability on turning	Cerebellar disease Hemiparesis Visual field cut Reduced proprioception Mild ataxia	Gait training ? Proprioceptive exercises	Appropriate walking aid Obstacle-free environment Properly fitting shoes
Unsafeness on sitting down (misjudges distance or falls into chair)	Reduced vision Proximal myopathies Apraxia	Treatment of specific diseases ? Coordination training Leg-strengthening exercises	High, firm chairs with arms, in good repair Transfer training Avoid throw rugs
Decreased step height and length (bilateral)‡	Parkinson's syndrome Pseudobulbar palsy Myelopathy (usually spastic gait) Normal pressure hydrocephalus Advanced Alzheimer's disease (frontal lobe gait) Compensation for reduced vision or proprioception Fear of falling Habit	Treatment of specific diseases (e.g., with L-dopa) Correct vision Gait training (correct problems, suggest compensations, increase confidence)	Good lighting Proper footwear (good fit, not too much friction or slipperiness) Appropriate walking aid

*This is not an exhaustive list.
†Most of these measures have not been subjected to clinical trials; evidence for effectiveness is usually anecdotal at best.
‡There will often be a flexed posture with all of these conditions.
SOURCE: From Ref. 19.

amples of recommended interventions for fall-related impairments are listed in Table 123-1 and are described elsewhere.[1,13,19,20] Obviously, all interventions need to be considered within the context of overall health and not merely fall prevention. Furthermore, the risk and benefit of each intervention needs to be considered because of possible opposing effects. For example, while depression is associated with an increased risk of falling, evidence does not suggest that treatment decreases risk. In fact, there is mounting evidence that antidepressants are associated with an increased risk of falling.

Medications need to be carefully assessed. In an evaluation of an individual's risk of falling, the use of sedative drugs, tranquilizers, and antidepressants requires particular attention because of strong evidence supporting the role of such drugs in causing falls. Recommendations concerning medications and their contribution to falling include careful review of risks and benefits of each medication, consideration of the combination of drugs consumed, maintenance of the lowest dose possible, and frequent review of the continued need for each medication.

The complex relationship between activity level and falling highlights the opposing goals of independence and safety in health care of the elderly. On the one hand, regular exercise can lead to improved musculoskeletal strength, flexibility, and endurance.[21] On the other hand, those who regularly engage in more strenuous activity are at increased risk of falling and at increased risk of injury during a fall. Given these conflicting effects, educational emphasis should be on avoiding clearly hazardous and probably unnecessary activities such as climbing on stools or chairs. Other activities, such as climbing stairs or exercising, while increasing risk of falling, probably should be encouraged given their contributions to functional independence and overall health.

Observing Balance and Gait

Directly observing how the patient performs the position changes and movements used during daily activity has the dual purpose of identifying how the disabilities and impairments described above impact on mobility and identifying the situations under which the patient is at risk of falling. Clinically useful tests for this purpose have been developed that require no equipment and little expertise.[11,17,22] These tests involve observing the patient perform position changes and movements such as getting up from and sitting down in a chair, turning, reaching up, and bending over. Gait observations include initiation, step height, length, continuity, and symmetry, as well as path deviation, usual walking speed, and the ability to pick up walking speed. Again, potential fall situations and preventive measures can be identified by using these observations. For example, the individual who has difficulty getting up from a chair is at risk for falling during this maneuver. Possible interventions include leg-strengthening exercises, balance training, and the use of high, firm chairs with arms. Further examples are included in Table 123-2 and in Chap. 122.

Addressing Situational Factors

Preventive strategies need to address factors present at the time of the fall, as well as the chronic predisposing factors discussed above. Situational factors may be intrinsic to the individual or related to the activity engaged in at the time of the fall, or they may represent hazards within the environment. A careful review of the fall situation may identify interventions aimed at preventing recurrence.[13] If the activity was an essential one, such as walking, performing a basic activity of daily living, changing positions, or climbing up or down stairs, the preventive strategy should be to ensure that these activities are performed in a safer, more effective manner. A short course in balance and gait training by a physical therapist may be effective for this purpose. As noted above, only if the activity was clearly hazardous, such as climbing on stools or chairs, should avoidance of the activity be recommended.

Environmental hazard assessment is an integral part of any fall-prevention strategy. Potential hazards can be identified through the use of environmental hazard checklists.[23] These checklists, developed for use at home, include assessment of floor surfaces and lighting and the presence of obstacles, as well as careful review of high-risk areas such as bathrooms and stairs. These checklists can be completed by home health nurses or therapists and perhaps by patients and families themselves. Specific environmental recommendations follow from the environmental assessments. Because of reluctance in some elderly people to making even minor environmental changes (such as removing throw rugs), careful education and close follow-up are needed to improve compliance with recommendations. In addition to an environmental hazard assessment, environmental contributors to individual falls should be ascertained using both open- and closed-ended questions. The closed-ended questions assure thoroughness, while an open-ended approach, that is, asking patients to identify the environmental hazards themselves, has an important advantage in that compliance with recommended environmental changes may be higher if the faller identifies the environmental hazards as contributing to the fall.[18]

FALLS AMONG INSTITUTIONALIZED ELDERLY

PREVALENCE

Over one-half of ambulatory nursing home patients fall each year. Estimated annual incidence is 1600 falls per 1000 beds.[13] The higher frequency of falling among institutionalized elderly persons probably results both from the greater frailty of these patients as compared with community-living elderly and from the better reliability of fall reporting because of closer observation. The evidence is conflicting concerning fall frequency in women versus men.

MORBIDITY

As with community-living elderly, about 5 percent of falls by institutionalized persons result in fracture. Another 10 percent of falls result in serious soft tissue injuries and 20 percent in minor soft tissue injuries such as lacerations or abrasions.[24,25] Women are more likely than men to suffer a serious injury. Other factors associated with an increased risk of injury during a fall are lower-extremity weakness, greater independence in activities of daily living, and a history of fewer falls.[25] These factors suggest that both components of injury, namely, increased force of impact of the fall and impaired protective responses of the faller, contribute to likelihood of injury.[6]

Clustering of falls, that is, a sudden increase in number over a short time, is associated with a high 6-month mortality.[24] Most likely, this clustering of falling is a marker for decline rather than a direct cause of death.

RISK FACTORS

Predisposing and Situational Intrinsic Risk Factors

As with falls experienced by community-living elderly, the majority of falls in institutionalized elderly are multifactorial. Only about 3 percent of falls experienced by institutionalized elderly result from an overwhelming intrinsic event such as syncope, seizure, or stroke. The chronic disabilities and impairments predisposing the institutionalized elderly to falls are similar to those of community-living elderly. Dementia, visual and hearing impairments, musculoskeletal and neurologic disorders, postural instability, and depression have all been associated with falling in institutionalized elderly persons.[1,26,27] The proportion of institutionalized elderly who fall increases with the number of these risk factors present.

Acute problems are more readily identified in institutionalized elderly who are often observed at or near the time of the fall. About 5 percent of falls occur during acute illnesses such as pneumonias, other febrile illnesses, urinary tract infections, or exacerbations of chronic diseases such as congestive heart failure. Acute medication toxicities are identified as the cause of about 8 percent of falls. In addition to the acute effect of medications, the chronic use of sedatives, tranquilizers, and antidepressants increases the risk of falling.[26,28] Risk increases with the number of these medications con-

sumed. Postural hypotension related to deconditioning, dehydration, cardiovascular disease, and medications probably contributes to some falls. Postural hypotension should especially be considered in falls occurring upon arising or after meals.[29]

Environmental Risk Factors

Fall etiology appears to be predominantly intrinsic among institutionalized elderly persons, with less contribution from environmental factors than among community-dwelling elderly. The reasons for this difference are several. First, their greater frailty and larger number of disabilities predispose institutionalized elderly persons to fall under situations where healthier, more functional community-dwelling elderly persons would not. Second, institutions in general are safer environments with many of the fall hazards already identified and removed. Furthermore, institutionalized elderly have fewer opportunities and lesser need to engage in hazardous activities such as climbing on ladders or walking on ice.

Although perhaps less important than in community-dwellers' falls, environmental contributors to falls in the institutionalized elderly do exist. These environmental hazards may be more subtle, such as ill-fitting shoes, untied shoe laces, long pants, or a floor slippery from water or urine.[13] Furniture may constitute a hazard. Beds that are too high or too short, bed rails that can be climbed over, and chairs that are too low and soft are responsible for some falls by institutionalized patients. Walking aids may also contribute to falls. Canes and walkers may be tripped over. Wheelchairs may be a hazard if not locked when getting in or out and footrests may be tripped over.

The contribution of staffing patterns remains unclear. Some studies show a higher fall incidence during shift change or during hours of lower staff-to-patient ratios, while other studies show no such effect.

PREVENTION

As in community-dwelling elderly, the first step in fall prevention in institutionalized elderly is establishing appropriate goals. In nursing homes where persons are more closely observed, where prevalence of falling, but not injury, is higher, and where personal mobility may be an important index of remaining autonomy, perhaps the primary goal should be preventing injury rather than preventing falls.

Identification of Intrinsic Risk Factors

A thorough clinical evaluation aimed at identifying all contributing risk factors is the cornerstone of the evaluation in nursing home residents. As with community-living elderly, risk of falling increases with number of disabilities, suggesting again that ameliorating or eliminating as many risk factors as possible may decrease risk.[26]

Directly observing balance and gait has proved to be effective in identifying residents at risk for falling. As discussed earlier, this direct observation has the added benefit of identifying potential causes of problems, as well as potential interventions within the resident and in the environment.

Interventions aimed at minimizing chronic predisposing factors can be recommended based on results of the evaluation. Exercise programs may increase strength and flexibility or improve balance. Careful review of medications should ensure the use of the least number of drugs at the lowest effective dose. Balance and gait training should target problem maneuvers such as getting in and out of chairs or turning while walking.

A careful review of fall situations may identify problem situations to be avoided in the future. The patient who falls during acute illnesses needs closer observation during future episodes. Falls soon after meals or upon getting up suggest postural hypotension. Remedies include advising the resident to rise more slowly and having companions available to help during these high-risk times. For subjects with persistent hypotension, sleeping with the head of the bed elevated, wearing support stockings, and avoiding exacerbating medications may be helpful.

Environmental Prevention

General environmental measures include assuring adequate lighting without glare and dry, nonslippery floors which are free of obstacles (and urine). High, firm chairs and beds at appropriate levels for individual residents (feet should touch the floor with the knees bent at 90 degrees) and raised toilet seats are preventive measures appropriate for all residents.

Footwear that fits properly and has soles that are neither too slippery nor too high in friction are simple fall prevention measures. Pant legs should not be long enough or loose enough to trip over.

Given the contribution of walking aids to falls, ensuring that the patient has the appropriate walking aid and uses it correctly is very important. This education should be an ongoing process.

Use of Restraints

Restraints are perhaps the most frequently used fall prevention measure in nursing homes. Restraints include side rails in bed, geriatric chairs that residents cannot get out of alone, and vest and waist restraints. Although restraint use is frequent enough to be considered almost routine, no study has ever shown a decrease in falls, or, more importantly, injuries, with restraint use. Potential complications of restraints include strangulation, vascular and neurologic damage, and skin tears. Complications occur when the restraints are applied inappropriately, when the incorrect type of restraint is used, or when the resident is not observed closely. Falls and injuries do occur with restraints when the resident slips out of or removes the restraints. A resident may tip over a chair or wheelchair while wearing restraints. The role of restraints in fall and injury prevention remains undefined. Restraints should not take the place of close supervision and attention to the risk factors discussed in this chapter.

SUMMARY

In summary, falling is a common and potentially morbid problem among community-living and institutionalized elderly persons. Potential morbidity includes fractures, other physical injuries, and restriction of activity because of fear or discouragement from care-providers. The risk factors include predisposing factors and situational factors present at the time of the fall. The goal of preventive strategies should be to minimize risk of falls and injuries without compromising autonomy and mobility. Preventive strategies include a combination of medical, surgical, rehabilitative, social, and environmental components.

REFERENCES

1. Kennedy TE, Coppard LC (eds): The prevention of falls in later life. *Dan Med Bull* 34(suppl 4):1, 1987.
2. Campbell AJ et al: Falls in old age: A study of frequency and related clinical factors. *Age Ageing* 10:264, 1981.
3. Tinetti ME, Speechley M, Ginter SF: Risk factors for falls among elderly persons living in the community. *N Engl J Med* 319:1701, 1988.
4. Nevitt MC et al: Risk factors for recurrent falls in older persons. *JAMA* (in press).
5. Baker SP, Harvey AH: Fall injuries in the elderly. *Clin Geriatr Med* 1:501, 1985.
6. Melton LJ, Riggs BL: Risk factors for injury after a fall. *Clin Geriatr Med* 1:525, 1985.
7. Smallegan M: How families decide on nursing home admission. *Geriatr Consultant* 2:21, 1983.
8. Tobis JS et al: Visual perception dominance of fallers among community-dwelling adults. *J Am Geriatr Soc* 33:330, 1985.
9. Hazell JWP: Vestibular problems of balance. *Age Ageing* 8:258, 1979.
10. Wyke B: Cervical articular contributions to posture and gait: Their relation to senile disequilibrium. *Age Ageing* 8:251, 1979.

11. Tinetti ME, Ginter SF: Identifying mobility dysfunctions in elderly patients. *JAMA* 259:1190, 1988.

12. Buchner DM, Larson EB: Falls and fractures in patients with Alzheimer-type dementia. *JAMA* 257:1492, 1987.

13. Rubenstein LZ et al: Falls and instability in the elderly. *J Am Geriatr Soc* 36:266, 1988.

14. Mader SL et al: Low prevalence of postural hypotension among community-dwelling elderly. *JAMA* 258:1511, 1987.

15. Ray WA et al: Psychotropic drug use and the risk of hip fracture. *N Engl J Med* 316:363, 1987.

16. Archea JC: Environmental factors associated with stair accidents by the elderly. *Clin Geriatr Med* 1:555, 1985.

17. Norré ME, Beckers A: Benign positional vertigo in the elderly: Treatment by habituation exercises. *J Am Geriatr Soc* 36:425, 1988.

18. Kottke FJ: Exercises to develop neuromuscular coordination, in Kottke FJ, Stillwell GK, Lehmann JF (eds): *Krusens Handbook of Physical Medicine and Rehabilitation.* Philadelphia, Saunders, 1982, p 403.

19. Tinetti ME: Performance-oriented assessment of mobility problems in elderly patients. *J Am Geriatr Soc* 34:119, 1986.

20. Isaacs B: Clinical and laboratory studies of falls in old people: Prospects for prevention. *Clin Geriatr Med* 1:513, 1985.

21. Stelmach CE, Worringham CJ: Sensorimotor deficits related to postural stability: Implications for falling in the elderly. *Clin Geriatr Med* 1:679, 1985.

22. Mathias S et al: Balance in elderly patients: The "Get Up and Go" test. *Arch Phys Med Rehabil* 67:387, 1986.

23. Tideiksaar R: Preventing falls: Home hazard checklists to help older patients protect themselves. *Geriatrics* 41:26, 1986.

24. Gryfe CI et al: A longitudinal study of falls in an elderly population. I. Incidence and morbidity. *Age Ageing* 6:201, 1977.

25. Tinetti ME: Factors associated with serious injury during falls by ambulatory nursing home residents. *J Am Geriatr Soc* 35:644, 1987.

26. Tinetti ME et al: Fall risk index for elderly patients based on number of chronic disabilities. *Am J Med* 80:429, 1986.

27. Wolfson L: Falls and the elderly: Gait and balance in the elderly. *Clin Geriatr Med* 1:649, 1985.

28. Granek E et al: Medications and diagnoses in relation to falls in a long term care facility. *J Am Geriatr Soc* 35:503, 1987.

29. Lipsitz LA: Syncope in the elderly. *Ann Intern Med* 99:92, 1983.

Chapter 124

HIP FRACTURES

Thomas W. Jackson and Kenneth W. Lyles

Hip fracture is a major problem in the elderly as evidenced by the 219,000 fractures that occurred in persons over age 65 in 1985.[1] After age 65, the incidence of hip fractures rises dramatically with age so that by age 80 a white woman has a 1 to 2 percent annual risk of suffering a hip fracture. About 15 percent of white women will suffer from hip fracture at sometime in their lives. The occurrence of hip fractures is lower in black women and much lower in males of all races because of a much lower incidence of osteoporosis in these groups than in white women. Hip fractures are a major cause of hospital admission and are estimated to account for $6.1 billion in medical costs yearly.[2] Mortality after fracture is 12 to 20 percent in the first year. Significant morbidity occurs, including the 15 to 25 percent chance that previously independent patients will require nursing home care for at least 1 year.[3]

ANATOMY

Hip fractures are more accurately referred to as fractures of the proximal femur. They can be divided into two types: subcapital fractures, occurring in one-third of cases, and trochanteric fractures occurring in the remaining two-thirds.

Subcapital fractures (cervical neck fractures) occur directly underneath the femoral head, in the neck of the femur. These fractures are intracapsular (inside the ligamentous capsule of the hip joint) and may cause impaired blood supply to the proximal fragment. This often leads to nonunion and post-traumatic degenerative joint disease secondary to avascular necrosis or damage to cartilage. Five percent of subcapital fractures are impacted and are thus relatively stable and have a relatively low complication rate.

This work was supported in part by grants from the Charles A. Dana Foundation and the Andrew W. Mellon Foundation.

The other type of hip fractures are extracapsular and involve the trochanteric area of the femur. The trochanteric fractures are further classified into intertrochanteric and subtrochanteric types. The blood supply to the trochanteric area is abundant, and avascular necrosis is not the problem: bleeding is. This fracture site is prone to instability and deformity. Surgical repair of these fractures can be technically difficult, especially in older patients or in those with comminuted fractures.

While younger persons can suffer hip fractures, theirs are usually sustained from major trauma, and uneventful recovery is the rule. Elderly patients, however, usually suffer from hip fracture as the result of minor trauma, and occasionally a spontaneous collapse of weakened bone occurs without any trauma present. Recent work by Cummings[4] suggests that although the bone mineral content of the proximal femur is an important determinant of fracture potential, many other factors are also important contributors. Cummings argues that by age 80 almost all people have a reduced bone mineral content of the proximal femur and are at risk for fracture.

ETIOLOGY

The problems leading to increased injury susceptibility are multifactorial. They include osteoporosis, unsteady gait, decreased vision, weakened muscles, decreased body fat, medications, substance abuse, and a predisposition towards falling. Recent studies have suggested that elderly fallers have decreased reaction time and thus fail to restore equilibrium in time to prevent a fall[5] (see Chap. 123). Patients with moderately slowed reaction times often are still able to break a fall with an outstretched hand, thus risking a Colles' fracture. Persons with even slower reaction times may not be able to move their arms quickly enough to break a fall and may land directly on the unprotected hip.

Because of the difficulties with treating hip fracture, prevention by reducing risk factors for hip fracture, as outlined in Table 124-1, is of prime importance. Modification of osteoporosis and osteomalacia risk factors has been described in Chaps. 77 and 78, respectively. Patients who already have osteoporosis can derive benefits from modifying risk factors for falling (see Chap. 123).

SURGICAL MANAGEMENT

Surgical management of hip fractures, described in orthopedic textbooks, will not be described here. The surgical procedure and type of hardware for fracture stabilization is best decided by the orthopedist.

TABLE 124-1
Risk Factors and Protective Factors for Osteoporosis and Hip Fracture

Well-Established Risk Factors

Advanced age
Female sex
White race
Thin
Bilateral oophorectomy
>2 alcoholic drinks/day
Chronic corticosteroid use
Severe rheumatoid arthritis
Previous hip fracture
Psychotropic drugs
Cigarette smoking

Poorly Established Risk Factors

Family history of osteoporosis
Early natural menopause
Pregnancies and breast-feeding
Asian race
Low-calcium diet
Caffeine intake
Moderate use of alcohol
High-protein diet
Thyroid supplements (replacement doses)
Use of antacids
Diabetes
Mild-to-moderate rheumatoid arthritis
Sedentary lifestyle
Scoliosis

Protective Factors

Long-term estrogen use
Black, Latin race
Obesity

SOURCE: After SR Cummings: *Epidemiology of Osteoporotic Fractures,* from the American Geriatric Society meeting presentation, April 22, 1988.

Immediate care in the emergency room after the patient has presented with hip fracture should be directed at ascertaining the history of the fall and nature of circumstances after the fall. Hypothermia and dehydration should be suspected and ruled out or addressed. Hypovolemic shock from bleeding into the fracture site is not uncommon. Other injuries should also be searched for.

Intravenous access should be established and two to four units of blood typed and cross matched. Underlying medical problems will need to be addressed, and immediate consultation with an orthopedic surgeon is indicated. The key to successful treatment of hip fractures is early surgery with prompt postoperative ambulation.

Surgical repair of hip fracture is the only workable therapeutic option in the elderly. Treatment with traction requires prolonged bed rest, with all its complications, and is tolerated poorly in the elderly. Indeed, the surgical literature suggests that delaying surgery for more than 48 hours beyond the time of injury significantly increases mortality. This applies even if medical problems cannot be optimized within 48 hours. Surgical repair also permits ambulation the following day, thus minimizing the dangers of prolonged bed rest.

The type of surgery used is less important than the skill with which it is performed. This same principle applies to the anesthesia method selected. While there is some literature to support spinal anesthesia in medically compromised patients,[6] the studies are not conclusive. The surgeon and anesthesiologist should use the techniques with which they are most comfortable and successful, rather than attempting to use the textbook "best" technique.

MEDICAL MANAGEMENT

Conceptually there are two types of older patients who suffer hip fracture. One is the basically healthy person who has had an accident, and the other is the slowly failing person whose decline manifests itself with a fracture. Clearly, the healthier the patient originally, the better the outcome and the shorter the hospital stay. However, both types of patient are susceptible to the same complications and poor outcome if postfracture care is not optimally managed to deal with the complex set of problems and needs the healing fracture produces. A coordinated approach to patient care among orthopedics, geriatrics, physical therapy, occupational therapy, and social work can improve the chances for successful recovery.

Just such a coordinated approach has been taken by the Geriatric Orthopedic Unit in Nottingham, England.[7] Care is provided by members of a multidisciplinary team. Members of the care team include a geriatric physician, an orthopedic surgeon, a physical therapist, an occupational therapist, and members of the nursing staff.

The care is directed at persons with average or somewhat-less-than-average levels of function prior to injury. The fit elderly and the severely disabled are excluded. A fixed time limit of 6 weeks for response to rehabilitation is used. Over 1000 patients have been seen since the unit opened. During this time, the length of stay decreased by 27 percent, from 66 days to 48 days. The mortality rate is 5 percent, and the rate of discharge to home or family is 69 percent. These figures are not directly comparable to American practice, but the magnitude of potential improvement shown is suggestive of future directions for hip fracture care.

COMPLICATIONS

A key to the successful postoperative and postdischarge management of hip fracture patients is to anticipate complications that might interfere with rehabilitation or even prove life-threatening. The most common major complications are listed in Table 124-2. Not specifically included in the table as complications, but very possible nevertheless, are exacerbations of existing medical problems, e.g., myocardial infarction in patients whose coronary artery disease was previously silent but has been unmasked by the stress of surgery.

The complication most associated with hip fracture is deep venous thrombosis (DVT), occurring in 16 to 50 percent of patients. 14 percent of hip fracture fatalities are due to pulmonary embolism.[8] Hip fracture creates a set of circumstances highly favorable to DVT. The injury releases large amounts of blood over a raw tissue surface, activating the clotting cascade. Other factors that predispose to DVT include immobility, either from pain or from enforced bed rest. Occasionally, direct vascular damage occurs during the injury, contributing to intravascular clot formation. Only full-dose anticoagulation is adequate to counteract these various factors; however, full-dose anticoagulation causes excessive bleeding and

TABLE 124-2
Complications of Hip Fracture

Deep venous thrombosis
Decubitus ulcers
Wound infections
Urinary tract infections
Pulmonary infections
Separation of bone fragments
Subluxation of prosthesis
Osteomyelitis
Aseptic necrosis
Myositis ossificans
Bursitis
Septic arthritis

is not commonly used. Prophylactic use of mini-dose heparin or dextran, with or without antiplatelet drugs,[9] is only partially effective.

Because of the lack of effective prophylaxis, DVT and pulmonary embolism should always be high on the differential diagnosis index anytime a patient is deteriorating for unknown reasons. Clouding the diagnostic picture further is the frequent occurrence of pneumonia and congestive heart failure simultaneously, both of which can mask pulmonary embolism.

A hip fracture complication that is easier to diagnose is the development of pressure sores. Decubitus ulcers occur in up to 42 percent of hip fracture patients and consume up to 40 percent of nursing time spent on affected patients. Pressure sores tend to develop in the first 2 weeks after hospital admission, with approximately 15 percent of the sores being preexistent. Decubiti are known to greatly prolong length of hospital stay and to increase the mortality of affected patients. Prevention is the best treatment (see Chap. 125).

Prophylactic use of pressure-distributing mattresses is recommended for patients with hip fracture. If possible, protective padding should be used during surgery as well. Daily skin checks for redness are important, as is keeping the skin dry. Sliding patients in bed can tear fragile skin and should be avoided. Attention should also be paid to maintaining the nutritional status of all hip fracture patients to promote healing and prevent complications.

Most hip fractures occur in women, and Foley catheters are frequently used to prevent soiling. This use leads to urinary tract infection as another frequent complication. The catheter should be removed as quickly as possible, unless frequent wetting of injured skin is deemed a greater hazard than urinary tract infection. Antibiotic therapy should be based on known sensitivities of causative bacteria.

Another major complication of hip fracture is prosthetic joint infection. Approximately 50 percent of these infections occur within the first year after prosthetic surgery and may be considered the product of surgical seeding, while the remaining 50 percent are thought to occur mainly as the result of hematogenous seeding from other sites. Early infections have been reduced by the use of prophylactic antibiotics and gentamicin-impregnated bone cement. Staphylococci predominate in over one-half of infections, with *Staphylococcus epidermidis* as the predominant species. The balance of the infections are caused by various gram-negative organisms and anaerobic bacteria.

A small percentage of infections are from hematogenous seeding from overt oral infections, but the number of infections due to normal dental work is unknown. The major problems of joint infection have led to the use of antibiotic prophylaxis for routine dental work in all patients who have hip prostheses, despite a lack of proven need and lack of standardized drug regimens. Infections of surgical pins and similar hardware are rare and do not require prophylactic antibiotics.

Many hospitalized elderly patients develop confusion during hospitalization. Confused patients tend not to cooperate with therapists and nursing staff. Confusion should be prevented if possible, since understanding and cooperation are essential for successful rehabilitation. Therefore, the avoidance of sedatives and the judicious use of pain medications are essential as well. The early use of night-lights and frequent reality orientation of patients may prove beneficial.

DISCHARGE PLANNING

Discharge planning should be started soon after hospital admission. Realistic assessments of the patient's progress and motivation and arrangements for support systems that will be available upon discharge should be made early in the hospital stay. The family and patient should be educated about reasonable expectations and made a part of the planning process before it is time for the patient to leave the hospital.

Family members and other visitors should be encouraged to give a patient as much independence as both parties can handle. Overzealous attempts to do things for a patient will lead to increased dependence and lack of progress. Patients who are recovering slowly should be considered for early discharge to a rehabilitation center, while nursing home placement should be advised for persons who remain severely disabled while showing no progress at all.

Care after discharge should take into consideration the mortality rate of 12 to 20 percent in the first year. This rate is due to late complications, such as pulmonary embolism, as well as worsening of underlying medical problems. Good follow-up of multiple underlying diseases is essential, as is maintaining a high index of suspicion for likely medical and social complications.[7]

Social complications are numerous. Many patients require several months of regular home health visits. They may be physically unable to get out of the house to purchase food and medicines. A significant number of patients who are physically recovered from a fall may develop a disabling fear of falling and thus may limit all outside activities. This isolation contributes to depression and lack of activity and sets the patient up for a declining course. Inquiries should be made of the patient, family, and home health workers about these problems so that the problems can be corrected before the patient has adverse consequences from them. Another area that should be monitored is the patient's progress with outpatient physical and occupational therapy, since restoring the patient's strength, gait, and independence are essential to recovery.

SUMMARY

Hip fractures are a major problem in the elderly, with high mortality and significant long-term morbidity. This poor outcome is greatly contributed to by coexisting disease and disability. A team approach to these multiple medical and social problems is needed to maximize recovery. This approach includes optimal treatment of medical problems and good rehabilitation. Complications should be anticipated, given the known natural history of the disease, and their impact minimized. Medications, as well as environmental and social risk factors for repeat injury, should be minimized as much as possible before and after hospital discharge. Frequent follow-up after discharge, with attention to medical, social, and rehabilitation injuries, is vital for a successful outcome.

REFERENCES

1. National Center for Health Statistics: *1985 Summary, National Hospital Discharge Survey; Advance Data from Vital and Health Statistics*, no 127. DHHS (PHS) 86-1250. Hyattsville, MD, Sept. 25, 1986.
2. Riggs BL, Melton LB III: Involutional osteoporosis. *N Engl J Med* 314:1676, 1986.
3. Cummings SR et al: Epidemiology of osteoporosis and osteoporotic fractures. *Epidemiol Rev* 7:178, 1985.
4. Cummings SR: Are patients with hip fractures more osteoporotic? Review of the evidence. *Am J Med* 78:487, 1985.
5. Kelsey JL, Hoffman S: Risk factors for hip fracture. *N Engl J Med* 316:404, 1987.
6. Davis FM, Laurenson VG: Spinal anesthesia or general anaesthesia for emergency hip surgery in elderly patients. *Anaesth Intensive Care* 9:352, 1981.
7. Boyd RV et al: The Nottingham orthogeriatric unit after 1000 admissions. *Injury* 15:193, 1983.
8. Holmberg S et al: Mortality after cervical hip fracture. 3002 patients followed for 6 years. *Acta Orthop Scand* 57:8, 1986.
9. Sautter RD et al: Aspirin-sulfinpyrazone in prophylaxis of deep venous thrombosis in total hip replacement. *JAMA* 250:2649, 1983.

Chapter 125

PRESSURE ULCERS

Richard M. Allman

EPIDEMIOLOGY

PREVALENCE AND INCIDENCE

Pressure ulcers are a common and serious problem for older people suffering from immobility. They may present as nonblanchable erythema over a bony prominence or as areas of epithelial loss, skin breakdown, or skin necrosis manifested by eschar formation. Synonymous terms include *pressure sores*, *decubitus ulcers*, and *bedsores*, but since pressure is the primary pathophysiologic factor in the development of these lesions, *pressure ulcer* has become the preferred term. The term *decubitus ulcer* implies that the lesions occur only when a person is lying down, but some of the most severe pressure-induced cutaneous injury may occur as a result of prolonged sitting.

The prevalence of pressure ulcers among patients in acute care hospitals ranges from 3 to 11 percent, and the incidence is between 1 percent and 3 percent. Among patients expected to be confined to bed or chair for at least 1 week, the prevalence is as high as 28 percent, and the incidence within 3 weeks is 7.7 percent.[1] Pressure ulcers generally occur within the first 2 weeks of hospitalization; 60 percent of all patients with an ulcer develop the ulcer in the hospital. More than 50 percent of pressure ulcers occur in persons over age 70.[2]

Pressure ulcers are more common in persons with spinal cord injuries than in the general hospital population. After a spinal cord injury, 40 percent of persons develop a pressure ulcer during initial hospitalization. Pressure ulcers are a persistent problem for 20 to 30 percent of spinal cord injury patients 1 to 5 years after injury.[3] The prevalence of pressure ulcers in nursing homes is very similar to that reported in acute care hospitals.[4,5] As many as 21 percent of patients admitted to nursing homes from acute care hospitals have a pressure ulcer.[6]

COMPLICATIONS

Sepsis is the most serious complication of pressure ulcers. One study found that there were 3.5 episodes of pressure ulcer–associated bacteremia per 10,000 discharges among four major hospitals. The rates of bacteremic episodes per 10,000 discharges were 12.1 in a teaching Veterans Administration hospital, 4.6 in a teaching municipal hospital, and 1.0 and 0.2, respectively, in two nonteaching community hospitals. Of the episodes of pressure ulcer–associated bacteremia, the pressure ulcer met criteria for being the probable source in 49 percent of the cases. Among bacteremic patients with a pressure ulcer as the probable source of infection, the in-hospital mortality was 56.9 percent. Sixty-two percent of the deaths were attributed to the infection in these cases.[7] In another study, transient bacteremia occurred after débridement of pressure ulcers in 50 percent of subjects.[8]

Other infectious complications of pressure ulcers include local infection, cellulitis, and osteomyelitis. Infected pressure ulcers were the most common infection found in a survey of seven skilled nursing facilities and were found in 6 percent of the patients.[9] Among patients with nonhealing pressure ulcers, one study found that 26.3 percent of ulcers had underlying bone pathology consistent with osteomyelitis.[10] Infected pressure ulcers may be deeply undermined and may lead to pyarthrosis or penetrate into the abdominal cavity. Secondary amyloidosis can also be a complication of chronic suppurative pressure ulcers.[11] Infected pressure ulcers also can serve as reservoirs for nosocomial infections with antibiotic-resistant bacteria.[12]

Pressure ulcers are associated with prolonged and expensive hospitalizations. The mean length of stay for hospitalized patients with pressure ulcers was nearly five times that noted for other patients in one study. After adjusting for other factors associated with increased length of stay, the association remained significant.[1]

Because of the underlying disease severity of persons suffering from pressure ulcers it is not clear that the association of pressure ulcers with length of stay is causal, but is has been suggested that one-fourth of the costs of care for patients with spinal cord injury is for treatment of pressure ulcers.[13]

MORTALITY

Pressure ulcers also are associated with increased mortality. About a fourfold increased risk of death has been noted in elderly patients who develop pressure ulcers.[14,15] In addition, failure of an ulcer to heal has been associated with nearly a six times higher rate of death in nursing home patients.[6] In-hospital death rates for patients with pressure ulcers range from 23 to 36 percent.[1,16] Most of these deaths are in patients with severe underlying disease, so the contribution of the pressure ulcers themselves to the outcome is difficult to define.

RISK FACTORS

Many factors have been suggested as risk factors for the development of pressure ulcers, but any disease process leading to immobility, whether a spinal cord injury, dementia, Parkinson's disease, severe congestive heart failure, or lung disease, increases the risk of pressure ulcers. In one study of elderly patients, spontaneous nocturnal movements were counted using a device attached to the patients' mattresses. No patient with 51 or more spontaneous movements during the night developed a pressure ulcer, but 90 percent of patients with 20 or fewer spontaneous movements developed an ulcer.[17]

One cross-sectional study of hospitalized patients found that hypoalbuminemia, fecal incontinence, the use of urinary catheters, decreased body weight, and the presence of a fracture were more common among patients with pressure ulcers than among immobilized patients without ulcers. After adjusting for fecal incontinence, hypoalbuminemia, and fractures, the other factors were no longer significant. Among 78 patients who were at risk for development of a pressure ulcer because they were expected to be confined to bed or chair for at least 1 week, fecal incontinence and fractures were more common and serum albumin tended to be lower in the patients who subsequently developed pressure ulcers.[1] The functional impairment associated with the age-related increase in disease prevalence may explain the association of age with increased risk of pressure ulcers in part, but age-related changes in the skin (see Chap. 40) may predispose the elderly to pressure-induced cutaneous injury independent of immobility.

In addition to hypoalbuminemia, fecal incontinence, fractures, and age, other factors may increase the risk of pressure ulcers independent of immobility. Vitamin C–deficient guinea pigs have been shown to be more susceptible to pressure-induced muscle injury than are normal animals.[18] Other nutritional deficiencies and loss of subcutaneous tissues may also increase risk (see Chap. 113). Urinary incontinence also may play a role in predisposing persons to pressure ulcers, but larger prospective studies of at-risk subjects are needed to confirm incontinence as a risk factor.

PATHOGENESIS AND PATHOPHYSIOLOGY

ROLE OF PRESSURE

Four factors have been implicated in the pathogenesis of pressure ulcers: pressure, shearing forces, friction, and moisture. Animal studies have repeatedly shown that muscles and subcutaneous tissues are more sensitive to pressure-induced injury than is the epidermis.[19] Contact pressure of 60 to 70 mmHg for 1 to 2 hours leads to degeneration of muscle fibers. Pressure can also lead to subepidermal blister formation.[20]

Depending on the methodology used, pressures measured under bony prominences such as the sacrum and greater trochanter can be as high as 100 to 150 mmHg when a subject is lying on a regular hospital mattress.[13,21] The pressures obtained are sufficient to decrease the transcutaneous oxygen tension to nearly zero.[22] Although the magnitude of these pressures may not be sufficient to cause full-thickness tissue injury without prolonged exposure to pressure, other factors can lower the pressure or time required to cause the cutaneous injury observed clinically. A loss of subcutaneous tissue may be one factor that lowers the threshold for skin breakdown due to pressure.[19]

ROLE OF SHEARING FORCES, FRICTION, AND MOISTURE

Shearing forces lower the amount of pressure required to cause damage to the epidermis. Shearing forces are tangential forces that are exerted when a person is seated or the head of the bed is elevated and the person slides toward the floor or the foot of the bed. The sacral skin is held in place by friction while the gluteal vessels are stretched and angulated.[23] Such forces decrease the amount of pressure required to occlude blood vessels and are likely important in the development of deep tissue injury.[24] One study found that the shearing forces of seated elderly and paraplegic patients are threefold greater than these forces in other individuals and blood flow is about one-third that of healthy young adults, even though the contact pressures are similar.[25]

In experimental studies, friction has been shown to cause intraepidermal blisters.[26] When unroofed, these lesions result in superficial erosions. Repeated exposures to friction lowers the amount of pressure required to induce skin injury.[27] This kind of injury can occur if a patient is pulled across a sheet or if a patient has repetitive movements that expose a bony prominence to such frictional forces. Intermediate degrees of moisture increase the amount of friction produced at the rubbing interface, while extremes of moisture or dryness decrease the frictional forces between two surfaces rubbing against each other.[28]

In addition to its impact on frictional forces, skin moisture may lead to maceration and epidermal injury. One prospective study showed that the incidence of pressure ulcers was 5.5 times greater with incontinence, but urinary and fecal incontinence were not examined separately.[29] Fecal incontinence may be more important than urinary incontinence in the development of skin breakdown because of the toxins and bacteria in stool.[1]

RELATIVE IMPORTANCE OF PATHOPHYSIOLOGIC FACTORS

The effects of pressure on tissues overlying bony prominences are likely due to ischemia associated with the occlusion of blood and lymphatic vessels (rather than to mechanical injury), since exposure to cold prevents pressure-induced injury in some animal models.[30] Injury due to pressure alone will typically begin in deeper tissues and spread toward the skin surface.[19] If pressure is relieved, the normal response to the pressure is hyperemia, but if pressure is allowed to persist, pressure-induced ischemia leads to endothelial swelling and vessel leak. As plasma leaks into the interstitium, diffusing distances between the cellular elements of skin and blood vessels increase. Ultimately, hemorrhage will occur and lead to nonblanchable erythema of the skin.[20] In bacteremic experimental animals, bacteria will be deposited at sites of pressure-induced injury and set up a deep suppurative process.[19] This may explain the occurrence of deep pressure ulcers with normal-appearing overlying skin or simply a draining sinus. The accumulation of edema fluid, blood, inflammatory cells, toxic wastes, and possibly bacteria ultimately and progressively leads to muscle death, subcutaneous tissue death, and, finally, epidermal death. The damage caused by shearing forces probably is mediated by pressure-induced ischemia in deep tissues, as well as by direct mechanical injury to subcutaneous tissue.[23] Friction and moisture are most important in the development of superficial lesions, but their effects are likely to be greatest when excessive pressures are also present. Since the most severe lesions are caused by pressure, and the effects of shearing and frictional forces could not occur without pressure, prevention of pressure ulcers should focus on ways to reduce the possibility of pressure-induced cutaneous injury.

PREVENTION

REPOSITIONING

Frequent repositioning historically has been the primary method of preventing pressure ulcers. The standard practice of repositioning persons every 2 hours has not been established in randomized, controlled trials, but the observations in animals of microscopic changes in tissues exposed to pressure after such time intervals have been given as the rationale for the practice.[18,31,32] The frequency of repositioning required to prevent pressure-induced injury is likely to be dependent on the risk status of the patient, the frequency of spontaneous movement, and whether a support surface that decreases pressure on the bony prominence is used or not.

Repositioning should be performed so that a person at risk is positioned without pressure on vulnerable bony prominences. Most of these sites are avoided by positioning patients with the back at a 30° angle to the support surface, alternatively from the right to left sides and the supine position. At-risk patients should never be repositioned with the back at a 90° angle to the support surface because such a position exposes the greater trochanter and lateral malleolus to excessive pressure. The use of pillows between the legs, behind the back, and supporting the arms will aid in maintaining optimal positioning.[22] If a person with limited ability to change position needs to sit in a chair or to have the head of the bed elevated, he or she should not remain in the chair for more than 2 hours at a time and the head of the bed should not be elevated at more than a 30° angle. This will decrease exposure of the sacral area to shearing forces that may predispose to deep tissue injury.

ANTIPRESSURE DEVICES

Despite nurses' best efforts, the use of proper repositioning techniques frequently is not sufficient or possible, and pressure ulcers occur. While one should not rely on a pressure-relieving device to substitute for good nursing care, such a mattress or support surface is indicated for persons at high risk for pressure ulcers. Unfortunately, no controlled trials have been performed in the United States to test which available products are most effective for the prevention of pressure ulcers. One randomized, controlled trial in Europe showed that the use of water mattresses or alternating air mattresses decreased the incidence of pressure ulcers by more than one-half compared with the use of conventional hospital mattresses.[33] The comparability of these devices to those used in the United States is uncertain.

A number of products and devices are marketed for the prevention and treatment of pressure ulcers in the United States. Sheepskins and 2-inch convoluted foam pad products are very popular and relatively inexpensive. Unfortunately, they do not have the capability to decrease pressure enough to eliminate risk of cutaneous injury. Alternating air mattresses consist of interconnecting air cells that are alternately inflated and deflated with a bedside pump. Alternating air mattresses are prone to mechanical breakdowns and may unreliably lower pressure under bony prominences. The alternating air mattresses shown to be effective in Europe have larger diameter air cells than devices marketed in the United States have. Some air mattresses have interconnecting air cells that may deflate or inflate when a person changes position on them and thus do not require a bedside pump. These air mattresses and some thicker foam products with different configurations or densities than the typical "egg crate" foam mattress are reportedly capable of decreasing skin pressures to below capillary filling pressure under most bony prominences. Water mattresses are heavy; they can leak; and they theoretically increase the risk of maceration since they are made of impermeable materials. Moreover, nursing tasks are difficult to perform on a patient on a water mattress. The use of specialized heel and elbow protectors, foam-padded chairs, stretchers, and wheelchairs also may be helpful in lowering the incidence of pressure ulcers. Donut cushions should not be used because they decrease blood flow to the skin in the center of the cushion.[22,32] In most cases, air-fluidized and low air-loss beds are probably not indicated for the prevention of pressure ulcers (but they may be indicated for treatment, as discussed later).

OTHER PREVENTION STRATEGIES

Studies are needed to determine the most effective and most cost-effective methods to prevent pressure ulcers. Effective prevention programs may include the appropriate assessment and management of incontinence (Chaps. 115 and 116) with the goal of keeping patients clean and dry. Treatment of spasticity may lower the risk of friction-induced cutaneous injury.[32] Educational programs aimed at physicians, nurses, and other caregivers, including family members and at-risk patients themselves, are likely to be important. Multidisciplinary teams have been able to reduce dramatically the incidence of pressure ulcers in acute care hospitals.[34] One study has suggested that when physicians ordered preventive measures for high-risk patients, the incidence of pressure ulcers was one-half that observed among simi-

lar patients for which such orders were not written.[35] This emphasizes the need for physicians to do their part as a team member caring for the elderly patient with multiple impairments. Close attention to the nutritional status of patients also may be important in preventing pressure ulcers.

ASSESSMENT OF PATIENTS

GENERAL ASSESSMENT

The appropriate management of patients with pressure ulcers requires assessment and treatment of underlying diseases and conditions that have put the person at risk for development of a pressure ulcer and may prevent the lesion from healing. Nutritional assessment is particularly important (see Chaps. 5 and 113).

The size, number, location, and wound character of pressure ulcers should be recorded. The most common sites for pressure sores are the sacrum, the buttocks over the ischium, the trochanters, heels, and lateral malleoli. Eighty percent of pressure ulcers occur at these sites.[2] The most severe ulcers are generally found in the pelvic area. Surrounding erythema may indicate cellulitis, while purulent drainage suggests that the wound is infected. The presence of necrotic tissue or a darkly pigmented eschar identifies a wound that is unlikely to heal without débridement. Sinograms may be required to delineate the extent of pressure ulcers associated with a sinus tract.[32]

Clinical staging of pressure ulcers helps guide management decisions. Stage 1 lesions present as nonblanchable erythema of intact skin; lesions extending into the epidermis or dermis are stage 2. These superficial lesions may heal in days to weeks without scarring. Deep lesions include stage 3 ulcers that extend into the subcutaneous tissues and to the deep fascia; these lesions typically show undermining. Stage 4 lesions involve muscle and/or bone.[36] Full-thickness injury manifested by eschar frequently involves muscle and bone. Deep lesions require weeks to months to heal and may require surgical correction to close them. Pressure-induced subepidermal blisters typically occur on the heels. Their depth cannot be determined by clinical examination. Serial color photographs can be very helpful in monitoring the progress of pressure ulcers.

ASSESSMENT OF ASSOCIATED INFECTIONS

Bacterial counts of greater than 100,000 colonies per gram of tissue in pressure ulcers correlate well with poor wound healing and wound graft failure.[37] In particular, *Pseudomonas aeruginosa*, *Providencia* and *Proteus* species, and anaerobic bacteria have been reported to be associated with poorly healing ulcers.[38,39] Despite this association, bacteriologic studies are probably not indicated unless there is evidence for sepsis, osteomyelitis, or cellulitis. When performed, bacteriologic studies of infected pressure ulcers often identify multiple organisms. The most common isolates include gram-negative aerobic rods such as *Proteus mirabilis, Escherichia coli, Klebsiella, Enterobacter, P. aeruginosa,* and *Providencia.* These accounted for 45 percent of isolates in one study of sepsis due to pressure ulcers. Gram-positive aerobic cocci also were frequent and accounted for 39 percent of isolates. *Staphylococcus aureus* accounted for 16 percent of isolates, but *Staphylococcus epidermidis,* group A streptococci, enterococci, and other streptococci represented 23 percent of isolates. *Bacteroides* species were the most common anaerobic isolates, accounting for 16 percent of the total. This study also found that isolation of *Bacteroides,* the presence of multiple pressure ulcers, and surgical débridement were associated with having a pressure ulcer as the probable source of the bacteremia.[7] The frequency of polymicrobial sepsis in patients with bacteremia due to a pressure ulcer ranges from 19.6 to 38 percent.[7,40] Foul-smelling lesions are very likely to be infected with anaerobic organisms, but the absence of odor does not exclude infection with anaerobes. Deep lesions also are more likely to be infected with anaerobes.[41]

Underlying osteomyelitis may also lead to a nonhealing pressure ulcer. The diagnosis of osteomyelitis beneath a pressure ulcer can be difficult because there may be pressure-induced radiographic changes in the underlying bone that may mimic changes seen in osteomyelitis. Moreover, while technetium bone scans are extremely sensitive, they give a large number of false-positives in the study of bones underlying pressure ulcers. A negative scan excludes the diagnosis, but a positive scan should be followed by a bone biopsy to confirm involvement of the bone.[10]

TREATMENT

SYSTEMIC MEASURES

Systemic measures are critical in the management of patients with pressure ulcers. Nutritional factors seem to be particularly important. In one randomized, placebo-controlled trial of vitamin C at a dose of 500 mg PO bid, the patients receiving vitamin C showed an 84 percent reduction of pressure ulcer surface area, while those receiving placebo showed only a 43 percent reduction in ulcer area ($p < 0.005$).[42] In another study, protein intake was one of the most important predictors of pressure ulcer improvement, while an elevated leukocyte count was associated with failure to improve.[16] This suggests that protein intake, underlying infection, and catabolic

stress are important variables in wound healing. Although zinc therapy has been shown to improve wound healing in young men after excision of pilonidal cysts,[43] as well as in zinc-deficient subjects with venous stasis ulcers,[44] the one study examining the use of zinc sulfate for pressure ulcers in elderly patients was too small to detect an effect.[45] Nevertheless, some experts suggest the use of zinc sulfate 220 mg tid for the treatment of recalcitrant ulcers.[46]

Systemic antibiotics are indicated for patients with sepsis, cellulitis, and osteomyelitis, and for the prevention of bacterial endocarditis in persons with valvular heart disease who require débridement of a pressure ulcer. A first generation cephalosporin, cefazolin, does not penentrate into the tissue surrounding pressure ulcers,[47] while clindamycin and gentamicin do.[47,48] Because of the high mortality of sepsis associated with pressure ulcers despite appropriate antibiotics,[7,40] broad-spectrum coverage for aerobic gram-negative rods, gram-positive cocci, and anaerobes is indicated pending culture results in patients with suspected bacteremia. In septic patients, vigorous surgical débridement of necrotic tissue is necessary to remove the source of the bacteremia.[32]

SPECIALIZED BEDS AND MATTRESSES

Treatment of pressure ulcers includes the use of preventive measures such as frequent repositioning and the use of pressure-relieving support surfaces. Some of the air or foam products used for prevention probably are adequate for many patients with pressure ulcers, but some patients may benefit from the use of one of the more expensive, specialized beds available.

One such specialized device is the air-fluidized bed. Air-fluidized beds contain microspheres of ceramic glass. Warm, pressurized air is forced up through the glass beads so that they take on the characteristics of a fluid. The beads are covered by a filter sheet that allows air to escape but not the beads. Patients float on the beads with pressures reduced under bony prominences.

Air-fluidized bed therapy was compared with conventional therapy (repositioning every 2 hours on a regular bed covered with an alternating air mattress and foam pad) for the treatment of pressure ulcers in one randomized, controlled trial. In that study, pressure ulcers showed a decrease in surface area on air-fluidized therapy and an increase in size on conventional therapy. The effect of treatment was greater for pressure ulcers that were 7.8 cm^2 or larger. After adjusting for other factors associated with a masked assessment of improvement, air-fluidized therapy was associated with a greater than fivefold increase in the odds of pressure sore improvement, as compared with conventional therapy. Although air-fluidized therapy increased the odds of improvement, only 13 percent of patients using such therapy achieved healing of all pressure ulcers. About 25 percent of affected patients died in-hospital, regardless of pressure ulcer treatment, and improved pressure ulcer outcome did not result in a significantly shorter hospital stay.[16]

While these data suggest that air-fluidized therapy is more effective than conventional therapy for treatment of pressure ulcers, the clinical impact of this difference in effectiveness may be limited by the underlying disease severity of patients hospitalized with pressure ulcers. On the other hand, failure of a pressure sore to improve was associated with a fourfold increased risk of death. An effective treatment may lower this risk for some pressure ulcer patients.

Other specialized beds are available for treatment of patients with pressure ulcers. Low air-loss beds consist of large fabric cushions that are constantly inflated with air. In contrast to air-fluidized beds, the cushions of low air-loss beds are fitted on a regular hospital bed frame. This allows the head of these beds and the beds themselves to be raised or lowered. These features facilitate patient transfer and eliminate the difficulties associated with trying to keep a patient's head elevated when the patient is on an air-fluidized bed. The effectiveness of low air-loss beds has not been compared with that of air-fluidized beds, but both types of devices are capable of lowering pressure under bony prominences to below capillary filling pressure. It is possible that they are similarly effective for treating patients for pressure ulcers and protecting persons with other types of cutaneous injuries. Air-fluidized bed therapy is more expensive than low air-loss bed therapy and does have a drying effect on tissues that may or may not be desired in certain clinical situations.

Other specialized beds have been developed that automatically reposition immobilized subjects. A low air-loss bed with this capability is available, and there are also other devices that automatically turn patients from side to side on a more traditional support surface. These beds are generally more expensive than both the air-fluidized and regular low air-loss beds. Without more data to suggest that these beds with automatic repositioning capability improve clinical outcome, there appears to be little justification to use them for treatment or prevention of pressure-induced cutaneous injury. On the other hand, they may be useful in preventing the pulmonary complications of immobility, particularly in spinal cord injury patients.

LOCAL WOUND CARE

The role of topical antibiotics and antiseptics is controversial. One controlled trial reported greater healing with topical gentamicin than with saline gauze dress-

ings.[49] Another study showed that silver sulfadiazine, normal saline, and povidone-iodine all are able to lower pressure ulcer bacterial counts but suggested that silver sulfadiazine was significantly better than povidone-iodine but not saline. Clinical outcome seemed to reflect changes in bacterial counts.[50] Buffered hypochlorite solutions, with pH adjusted to between 8.5 and 9.0 with sodium bicarbonate and ranging in concentration from 0.52% and 0.13% (modified Dakin's solution), may be used to lower wound bacterial counts over a 7-day period. If more prolonged use is anticipated, then the lowest concentration should be used because of potential for inhibiting wound healing.[51] Iodine compounds may cause systemic toxicity if applied to large ulcers. Enzymatic agents such as collagenase, fibrinolysin and desoxyribonuclease, streptokinase, and streptodornase may be helpful in aiding débridement but should not be used when an ulcer bed becomes clean and begins to granulate. The débridement of moist, exudative wounds may be augmented by using hydrophilic polymers like dextranomer.[46] Other authors have reported dramatic results with use of granulated sugar for grossly infected wounds.[52] In general, the use of surgical débridement augmented with wet-to-dry dressings using normal saline is sufficient to remove necrotic tissue in a pressure ulcer and thereby lower bacterial counts and allow healing to occur. Superficial ulcers infrequently require the use of any specific topical therapy. Additional randomized, controlled trials are needed to determine the precise role for topical agents.

Once an ulcer is clean and granulation or epithelialization begins to occur, a moist wound environment should be maintained without disturbing the healing tissue. Superficial lesions heal by migration of epithelial cells from the borders of an ulcer, while deep lesions heal as granulation tissue fills the base of the wound. Two controlled trials have suggested that the use of an occlusive, vapor-permeable dressing improves healing of superficial pressure ulcers, but the trials did not adjust for baseline differences in nutritional factors.[53,54] The dressings may remain in place for several days and may allow a layer of serous exudate to form underneath the dressing, presumably facilitating epithelial migration. Such occlusive dressings have not proved helpful for deep ulcers. Clean, deep ulcers may be dressed with gauze dressing kept moistened with normal saline. Some reports have suggested that the use of Ringer's lactated solution may stimulate healing.[55] Moist dressings should be kept off surrounding intact skin to avoid macerating normal tissues.

SURGERY

Many surgical procedures are available for the treatment of pressure ulcers. These include primary closure, skin grafts and myocutaneous flaps, and removal of underlying bony prominences.[56] Radical procedures such as amputation and hemicorporectomy are sometimes required in complicated and extensively infected pressure ulcers. Removal of ischial tuberosities can be complicated by urethral fistula formation. Most of these procedures have been attempted primarily in young spinal cord injury patients, so the exact role in elderly patients is not clear. Recurrences of pressure ulcers are common, and the surgeries are complicated and frequently require prolonged hospitalization. Surgical consultation should be obtained for those older persons for whom such interventions would be appropriate after considering their rehabilitative potential and their ability to tolerate a surgical procedure.

POTENTIAL OR EXPERIMENTAL TREATMENTS

Multitudes of treatments have been advocated for the treatment of pressure ulcers without sufficient data to support their use.[57,58] Such treatments include the use of hyperbaric oxygen and the use of electrical stimulation of wound margins. Some reports have advocated the use of topical nutrient solutions. A number of topical agents are being developed that may stimulate wound healing. Lasers, whirlpool therapy, or use of a dental irrigating device may facilitate débridement. Despite the potential development of more effective treatments in the future, the best approach to pressure ulcers will continue to be prevention.[59]

REFERENCES

1. Allman RM et al: Pressure sores among hospitalized patients. *Ann Intern Med* 105:337, 1986.
2. Peterson NC, Bittman S: The epidemiology of pressure sores. *Scand J Plast Reconstr Surg* 5:62, 1971.
3. Young JS, Burns PE: Pressure sores and the spinal cord injured, in Young JS et al (eds): *Spinal Cord Injury Statistics: Experience of the Regional Spinal Cord Injury Systems.* Phoenix, Good Samaritan Medical Center, 1982, p 95.
4. Hing E: *Characteristics of Nursing Home Residents, Health Status, and Care Received: National Nursing Home Survey,* United States, National Center for Health Statistics, 1977, p 48.
5. Scheckler WE, Peterson PJ: Infections and infection control among residents of eight rural Wisconsin nursing homes. *Arch Intern Med* 146:1981, 1986.
6. Reed JW: Pressure ulcers in the elderly: Prevention and treatment utilizing the team approach. *Md State Med J* 30:45, 1981.
7. Bryan LS et al: Bacteremia associated with decubitus ulcers. *Arch Intern Med* 143:2093, 1983.
8. Glenchor H et al: Transient bacteremia associated with débridement of decubitus ulcers. *Milit Med* 146:432, 1981.
9. Garibaldi RA et al: Infections among patients in nursing homes: Policies, prevalence, and problems. *N Engl J Med* 305:731, 1981.
10. Sugarman B: Pressure sores and underlying bone infection. *Arch Intern Med* 147:553, 1987.
11. Dalton JJ et al: Amyloidosis in the paraplegic: Incidence and significance. *J Urol* 93:553, 1965.
12. Haley RW et al: The emergence of methicillin-resistant *Staphylococcus aureus* infections in United States hospitals: Possible role of the housestaff-patient transfer circuit. *Ann Intern Med* 97:297, 1982.
13. Houle RJ: Evaluation of seat devices designed to prevent ischemic ulcers in paraplegic patients. *Arch Phys Med Rehabil* 50:587, 1969.
14. Norton et al: A study of factors concerned in the production of pressure sores and their prevention, in *An Investigation of Geriatric Nursing Problems in Hospital,* 2d ed. Edinburgh, Churchill Livingstone, 1975, p 194.
15. Michocki RJ, Lamy PP: The problem of pressure sores in a nursing home population: Statistical data. *J Am Geriatr Soc* 24:323, 1976.
16. Allman RM et al: Air-fluidized beds or conventional therapy for pressure sores: A randomized trial. *Ann Intern Med* 107:641, 1987.
17. Exton-Smith AN, Sherwin RW: The prevention of pressure sores: Significance of spontaneous bodily movements. *Lancet* 2:1124, 1961.
18. Husain T: An experimental study of some pressure effects on tissues, with reference to the bed-sore problem. *J Pathol Bacteriol* 66:347, 1953.
19. Daniel RK et al: Etiologic factors in pressure sores: An experimental model. *Arch Phys Med Rehabil* 62:492, 1981.
20. Witkowski JA, Parish LC: Histopathology of the decubitus ulcer. *J Am Acad Dermatol* 6:1014, 1982.
21. Lindan O: Etiology of ducubitus ulcers: An experimental study. *Arch Phys Med Rehabil* 42:774, 1961.
22. Seiler WO, Stahelin HB: Decubitus ulcers: Preventive techniques for the elderly patient. *Geriatrics* 40:53, 1985.
23. Reichel SM: Shearing force as a factor in decubitus ulcers in paraplegics. *JAMA* 11:762, 1958.
24. Bennett L et al: Shear vs pressure as causative factors in skin blood flow occlusion. *Arch Phys Med Rehabil* 60:309, 1969.
25. Bennett L et al: Skin stress and blood flow in sitting paraplegic patients. *Arch Phys Med Rehabil* 65:186, 1984.
26. Hunter JAA et al: Light and electron microscopic studies of physical injury to the skin: II. Friction. *Br J Dermatol* 90:491, 1974.
27. Dinsdale SM: Decubitus ulcers: Role of pressure and friction in causation. *Arch Phys Med Rehabil* 55:147, 1974.
28. Sulzberger MB: Studies on blisters produced by friction: I. Results of linear rubbing and twisting technics. *J Invest Dermatol* 47:456, 1966.
29. Lowthian PT: Underpads in the prevention of decubiti, in Kenedi RM et al (eds): *Bedsore Biomechanics: Proceedings of a Seminar on Tissue Viability and Clinical Applications.* Baltimore, University Park Press, 1976, p 141.
30. Brooks B, Duncan GW: Effects of pressure on tissues. *Arch Surg* 40:696, 1940.

31. Kosiak M: Etiology and pathology of ischemic ulcers. *Arch Phys Med Rehabil* 40:62, 1959.
32. Reuler JB, Cooney TG: The pressure sore: Pathophysiology and principles of management. *Ann Intern Med* 94:661, 1981.
33. Anderson KE et al: Decubitus prophylaxis: A prospective trial on the efficiency of alternating-pressure air-mattresses and water-mattresses. *Acta Derm Venereol (Stockh)* 63:227, 1982.
34. Ameis A et al: Management of pressure sores: Comparative study in medical and surgical patients. *Postgrad Med* 67:177, 1980.
35. Dornbrand L et al: Prevention of pressure sores: Who cares? *Clin Res* 31:232A, 1983. (Abstract)
36. Shea JD: Pressure sores: Classification and management. *Clin Orthop* 112:89, 1975.
37. Robson MC, Heggers JP: Bacterial quantification of open wounds. *Milit Med* 134:19, 1969.
38. Seller WO, Stähelin HB: Recent findings on decubitus ulcer pathology: Implications for care. *Geriatrics* 41:47, 1986.
39. Daltrey DC et al: Investigation into the microbial flora of healing and non-healing decubitus ulcers. *J Clin Pathol* 34:701, 1981.
40. Galpin JE et al: Sepsis associated with decubitus ulcers. *Am J Med* 61:346, 1976.
41. Sapico FL et al: Quantitative microbiology of pressure sores in different stages of healing. *Diagn Microbiol Infect Dis* 5:31, 1986.
42. Taylor TV et al: Ascorbic acid supplementation in the treatment of pressure sores. *Lancet* 2:544, 1974.
43. Pores WJ et al: Acceleration of wound healing in man with zinc sulphate given by mouth. *Lancet* 1:121, 1967.
44. Hallbook T, Lanner E: Serum-zinc and healing of venous leg ulcers. *Lancet* 2:780, 1972.
45. Norris JR, Reynolds RE: The effect of oral zinc sulfate therapy on decubitus ulcers. *J Am Geriatr Soc* 19:793, 1971.
46. Judson R: Pressure sores. *Med J Aust* 1:417, 1983.
47. Berger SA et al: Penetration of antibiotics in decubitus ulcers. *J Antimicrob Chemother* 7:193, 1981.
48. Berger SA et al: Penetration of clindamycin into decubitus. *Antimicrob Agents Chemother* 14:498, 1978.
49. Bendy RH et al: Relationship of quantitative wound bacterial counts to healing of decubiti: Effect of topical gentamicin. *Antimicrob Agents Chemother* 4:147, 1965.
50. Kucan JO et al: Comparison of silver sulfadiazine, povidone-iodine and physiologic saline in the treatment of chronic pressure ulcers. *J Am Geriatr Soc* 29:232, 1981.
51. Como JA, Smith PJ (eds): Sodium hypochlorite solutions, in *Drug Information Bulletin*, vol 21. Birmingham, University of Alabama at Birmingham, 1987.
52. Trouillet JL et al: Use of granulated sugar in treatment of open mediastinitis after cardiac surgery. *Lancet* 1:180, 1985.
53. Oleske DM et al: A randomized clinical trial of two dressing methods for the treatment of low-grade pressure ulcers. *J Enterostom Ther* 13:90, 1986.
54. Sebern MD: Pressure ulcer management in home health care: Efficacy and cost effectiveness of moisture vapor permeable dressing. *Arch Phys Med Rehabil* 67:726, 1986.
55. Seiler WO, Stähelin HB: Decubitus ulcers: Treatment through five therapeutic principles. *Geriatrics* 40:30, 1985.
56. Vasconez et al: Pressure sores, in Ravitch MM et al (eds): *Current Problems in Surgery*. Chicago, Year Book Medical Publishers, 1977, p 6.
57. Morgan JE: Topical therapy of pressure ulcers. *Surg Gynecol Obstet* 141:945, 1975.
58. David JA: Pressure sore treatment: A literature review. *Int J Nurs Stud* 19:183, 1982.
59. Allman RM: Pressure ulcers among the elderly. *N Engl J Med* 320:850, 1989.

Chapter 126

PREDICTING FUNCTIONAL OUTCOME IN OLDER PEOPLE

Mark E. Williams and Thomas V. Jones

Predicting an older person's ability to function is a primary goal of geriatric care[1] because ability to function may indicate an older person's ability to cope in a particular environment. Decrease in the ability to function independently requires a patient to adapt in one or more ways: accept the limitation; develop new strategies to overcome the disability; move to a less demanding environment; or increase reliance on support systems such as family, friends, health care workers, social agencies, and nursing homes.

Clinically, a prediction of the ability to function will determine the *prognosis*, a judgment of the probable course and outcome of a disease or condition. In younger people, prognosis implies longevity and the likelihood of full recovery. In older people, who often have multiple chronic ailments and may not return to a disease-free state, a prognosis implies the likelihood of a patient's maintaining independent functioning.

It is appropriate that this chapter on functional outcome concludes this book since the conditions discussed in the preceeding chapters are all factors which affect the development of a prognosis of functional ability. This chapter will summarize the research on predictors associated with institutionalization in populations of older people and then review studies concerning predictors of use in the clinical setting. Disease-specific measures of predicting function will not be addressed, but research on a measure of manual function and its efficacy in predicting the future care needs of individual older persons, which is a critical clinical issue, will be described in detail.

PREDICTING FUNCTION IN POPULATIONS OF ELDERLY PEOPLE

Many population-based geriatric studies equate predicting function with predicting future use of long-term care services. Several investigations of risk factors for use of home care and institutionalization in nursing homes have employed multivariate analysis to develop models for predicting patient outcomes. These studies have had limited success in clarifying which elderly persons will live at home without formal services and which will need home services or need to be placed in nursing homes.

Palmore followed a sample of community-residing elderly volunteers to their deaths. He found greater utilization of nursing home care among those who were white, affluent, female, unmarried, and living alone.[2] Nielson et al. found that elderly persons who lived alone and did not receive home care services were more likely to be institutionalized.[3] Zarit used univariate analysis to identify characteristics of day-care participants that predicted future need for total care in institutional settings.[4] Patients who subsequently needed total care were more likely than other patients to be severely cognitively impaired, to require more assistance with home tasks, to have a positive viewpoint about receiving care in a protective setting at the beginning of care, and to have been receiving more home assistance. These studies used univariate statistical analysis, so the relationships between various factors cannot be confidently interpreted.

Vicente et al. determined that persons who were older than age 75, unmarried, and living alone were more likely to have been placed in a nursing home. Being white, having a low income, and reporting health problems were additional factors associated with nursing home stays of 6 months or more.[5] Greenberg and Gin found that institutionalized elderly persons were more likely to be widowed or unmarried women without living children and to have more medical conditions than elderly persons who weren't institutionalized. In general, such institutionalized persons were functionally dependent, had no help from relatives, were unable to take medications, were unable to make decisions, had good financial resources, and preferred to live in an institutional setting.[6] McCoy and Edwards found that advanced age, white racial background, household isolation, presence of nonrelatives in the living situation, and functional impairment were associated with a greater probability of institutionalization.[7]

Several studies have used a prospective, multivariate research design to overcome the limitations of univariate and retrospective research. Branch and Jette determined that advanced age, use of assistive devices for ambulation, mental disorientation, living alone, and need of assistance for performing basic activities of daily living were all significantly related to institutionalization.[8] Weinberger et al., controlling for age, sex, race, and education, found that self-reported poor health was associated with nursing home placement.[9] Pearlman and Ryan-Dykes identified certain status predictors of future nursing home placement, including the need for assistance in financial management, meal preparation, walking, and traveling beyond walking distance; use of a walker was another specific predictor they identified. Their study also found that changes such as initiation of wheelchair use and decreased telephone conversations also predicted institutionalization.[10] Shapiro examined predictors of home care use by community-residing elderly persons. In a home care program based solely on professionally assessed need, age and difficulty performing instrumental activities of daily living were strong determinants of subsequent use of home care.[11]

Other investigations have sought to identify predictors of future use of home care and institutionalization in elderly persons who are in day-care programs or acute care hospitals. Kane and Matthias used multivariate analysis to develop a model for predicting discharge to a nursing home following hospitalization.[12] Factors associated with institutionalization included being an older female, having a diagnosis of mental disease, and having undergone recent orthopedic surgery. However, when the model was applied to samples in other geographic areas, age was the only consistently strong predictor. Roudot-Thoraval et al. found that among elderly patients admitted to an acute care hospital, family opinion was the only significant predictor of subsequent transfer to a long-term care facility.[13] Additional studies have attempted to identify predictors of future nursing home care in elderly persons seen in the context of comprehensive geriatric assessment units. Rubenstein et al., using discriminant analysis, found several factors that when present in a patient upon admission to a geriatric evaluation unit were related to discharge status.[14] Patients who were admitted for a "medical" problem (rather than for a "geriatric" problem or for "rehabilitation"), who were not expected by their referring physicians to be able to go home, who had lower functional and mental status, and who required more intense nursing care were all more likely to be discharged to a nursing home. The model was developed with the first 98 patients and then validated with the next 101 admissions. Martin et al. used a prospective, multivariate design to identify predictors of institutionalization in elderly patients seen at a community-based geriatric assessment unit.[15] The strongest predictors were a history of falls or unstable gait, dementia, caregiver strain, lack of support services, and moderate-to-severe impairment of ability to perform activities of daily living.

Contrary to conclusions drawn from previous studies, in these investigations, sex, race, marital status, financial resources, and mental status were not shown to characterize the risk of institutionalization. Moreover, none of the factors studied in the previous investigations has consistently differentiated elderly persons who subsequently receive home care or are institutionalized from those who remain at home without formal services. With a few exceptions,[12,14] the models derived from these studies have not been validated in populations independent of the original sample used to develop the model. Notably, in the two instances in which investigators did attempt to validate their models,[12,14] the results were mixed.

There are several possible explanations for the lack of consistency among these studies. Many variables and factors were not considered in the analytic strategies, as is evident by the modest amount of the variance in home care use or institutionalization explained by the models. Many studies were based on self-reports, which may not have been totally accurate. Specific disease measures were not included in some studies. Studies which look at elderly persons residing in the community face the inevitable difficulty of predicting events likely to occur in the distant future. Most of the studies have not considered possible interactions among several variables. Additional variance might have been explained if studies had placed greater emphasis on the availability and quality of long-term care services and the attitudes of patients and families towards home care and nursing home care.

In summary, these investigations have increased our understanding of several factors, such as advanced age, which may predict the need for home care and institutionalization in large populations of older persons. However, population-based predictors are not always helpful or relevant in the clinical setting where the management of a specific case is the focus. For example, while age is a risk factor in functional decline, most elderly people remain functionally independent. What is needed is a measure that accurately predicts an older individual's current and future need for assistance.

PREDICTING FUNCTION IN OLDER INDIVIDUALS

Over the past decade a series of studies has evaluated a promising method for identifying individuals at risk for changes in function. This approach measures the time required by older persons to perform simple manual tasks which are chosen to reflect certain skills necessary to carry out basic daily activities. These studies suggest that the time required to perform simple manual tasks may represent a kind of "vital sign of functioning" analo-

gous to the classical physical vital signs. This research has suggested that persons who demonstrate difficulty with manual performance will eventually need additional help to function as they grow older. Those with both behavioral difficulties and inefficient manual skills are especially vulnerable. This section will address the technique of measuring timed manual performance (TMP) and summarize the studies using this methodology.

MEASURING MANUAL PERFORMANCE

The TMP evaluation takes approximately 15 minutes and is conducted in two parts. The first part evaluates opening and closing a variety of fasteners, such as a screen door latch, a bolt-action lock, and a padlock. These fasteners are mounted in a 3 by 3 array on a 2- × 3-ft plywood panel (Fig. 126-1) that attaches to a card table (Fig. 126-2). Subjects sit in front of the panel and are timed with a stopwatch while they attempt to undo each fastener. The fasteners are opened and closed in a numerical sequence, using the following format, which is read to the individual by the tester: "This is door number _____. It is fastened by a _____. It is opened in this

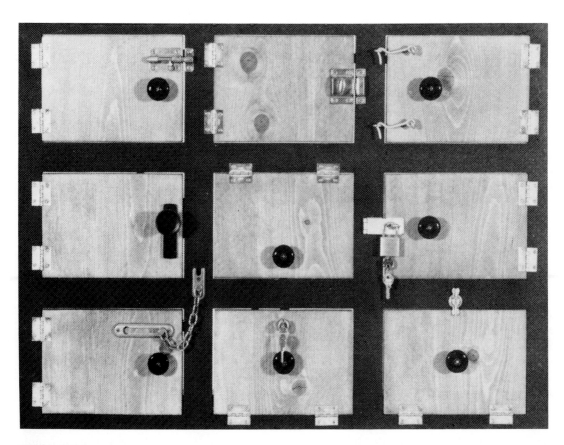

FIGURE 126-1
Plywood panel for testing manual ability. Manual performance was measured by timing each study participant as she opened and closed the panel door.

FIGURE 126-2
Plywood panel mounted on card table for testing manual performance.

manner (demonstration of how fasteners are undone and how the door opens). Do you have any questions about how to open door number _____? Place your hands on the table, please. When I say 'go,' open door number _____. Ready? Go!"

The timing begins from the last word "go" and ends when the opened door is perpendicular to the front of the panel. A similar protocol is used to time the closing of the fasteners.

The second part of the manual assessment consists of performing a series of simulated daily activities with the dominant and nondominant hands. These tasks, modified from Jebsen's test of hand function,[16] include writing a short sentence; turning over 3 × 5 index cards (to simulate page turning); picking up two paper clips, pennies, and bottle caps and placing them in a container; stacking four checkers; and transferring four kidney beans from one container to another using a spoon (to simulate eating). Each of these tasks is timed for the nondominant and dominant hands following Jebsen's structured format.

The manual assessment yields 27 discrete measurements for each individual: opening compartments (nine measurements), closing compartments (eight measurements), dominant-hand skills (five measurements), and

nondominant-hand skills (five measurements). These 27 measurements are added together to produce a manual skill time. Individuals with missing values on any particular hand function are given a penalty score for that item. This score is calculated as the mean plus two standard deviations of all individuals who can perform that task.

Predictions using this approach are based on whether the person can complete all items on the testing protocol and on the amount of time required to do so. Times of less than 350 seconds predict little use of long-term care services over the next year, while times of 350 or more seconds identify persons likely to require long-term care services within that interval.

MANUAL PERFORMANCE AND CURRENT NEEDS FOR CARE

In 1979 a pilot survey was performed to assess the usefulness of basic musculoskeletal skills as potential markers for functional dependency.[17] Two groups of elderly women were evaluated: inpatients of an intermediate-care nursing home and members of a retirement organization living independently. The TMP approach was used in both groups. Table 126-1 summarizes the find-

TABLE 126-1
Time Taken to Perform Hand Function Skills: A Comparison Between Nursing Home Patients and Independent Individuals*

Skill	Nursing Home Group (n = 17)	Independent Group (n = 11)
Opening fasteners		
Cupboard latch	14.0 + 13.6	2.3 + 0.9
Padlock	61.8 + 39.2	12.1 + 3.3
Drawer	29.8 + 15.1	7.5 + 1.7
Turn buckle	8.2 + 5.4	3.2 + 1.0
Closing fasteners		
Cupboard latch	8.8 + 11.1	2.1 + 0.5
Padlock	50.2 + 30.1	13.7 + 5.3
Drawer lock	17.5 + 9.3	4.2 + 2.4
Turn buckle	5.1 + 2.9	2.2 + 0.6
Dominant hand skills		
Writing	52.5 + 21.1	17.1 + 5.0
Card turning	28.2 + 16.8	5.3 + 0.9
Picking up small objects	23.2 + 11.1	7.1 + 1.0
Stacking checkers	10.7 + 5.2	2.2 + 0.7
Simulated eating	29.4 + 15.8	9.9 + 2.4
Non-dominant hand skills		
Writing	87.5 + 27.6	40.0 + 10.4
Card turning	37.7 + 25.0	6.5 + 1.5
Picking up small objects	30.9 + 17.5	7.7 + 1.1
Stacking checkers	14.6 + 6.8	2.4 + 0.6
Simulated eating	41.2 + 14.7	12.7 + 3.0

*All differences between the nursing home group and the independent group are significant ($p < 0.01$). All times are given in seconds (mean + 1 S.D.).

ings. TMP skills clearly distinguished between those two separate groups of elderly women—the women residing independently at home were consistently quicker at performing the TMP tasks.

To follow up this potentially important observation, a comprehensive cross-sectional study was designed to look for markers associated with the need for social supports.[18] The specific research aim was to compare TMP evaluation with traditional measures of function, such as activities of daily living, to see which approach would best reflect an individual's needs for care.

To encompass a broad range of care requirements, 56 elderly women, competent in all activities of daily living, were randomly selected from three settings. The most dependent group consisted of nursing home inpatients, an intermediate group was made up of women receiving nutritional assistance but able to perform all other daily activities, and an independent group, receiving no support, was chosen from the subscription list of a local senior citizens' newsletter. By design, the participants were all white, affluent, and well-educated. All underwent an initial evaluation consisting of a structured 30-minute interview, a 15-minute physical examination, and a 15-minute assessment of manual ability. The structured interview measured the following: demographic trends, morale, ability to perform instrumental activities of daily living, strength of the social network, mental status, and past and present medical problems, including use of medications. The physical examination focused on the upper extremity and included a complete neurologic and rheumatologic evaluation. TMP was measured by the technique described previously, and remarkable timing differences among the three groups were readily apparent (see Table 126-2). Multivariate analysis quantified the role of specific clinical observations as markers of care needs (Table 126-3). The manual skill index (derived by multiplying the times of three manual tasks) was by far the most powerful marker. Even the least sensitive of the 27 timed manual measurements was better than the best traditional measure, the mental status score.

TABLE 126-2
Time* Needed to Open Selected Compartments of the Hand Skill Panel

	Group		
Type of Fastener	*Independent (n = 20)*	*Intermediate (n = 16)*	*Dependent (n = 20)*
Cupboard latch	1.3 + 0.3	2.9 + 1.5	4.1 + 2.3
Padlock	12.3 + 2.2	20.6 + 9.9	50.6 + 29.7
Drawer lock	8.2 + 3.3	13.7 + 8.9	31.3 + 19.7
Turn buckle	2.4 + 0.9	5.8 + 4.9	8.8 + 4.0

*Values are given in seconds (mean + 1 S.D.).

TABLE 126-3
Contribution of Individual Variables as Markers of Dependency

Independent Variables	*F value**	*R^2†*
Manual skill index	143.86	0.86
Least sensitive manual skill	19.67	0.43
Mental status score	16.87	0.39
Total number of drugs	14.08	0.34
Number of medical problems	8.9	0.25
Level of education	8.7	0.25
Morale score	4.07	0.13

*The F value tests how well the independent variable in question accounts for the dependent variable's behavior.
†The R^2 measures how much variation in the dependent variable can be explained by each independent variable.

To validate these findings, an additional cross-sectional survey was performed in Rochester, New York. Frail older people ($n = 356$) were evaluated using the manual function instrument. Four groups of persons over age 65, representing a range of people with increasing need of community and institutional support, were selected. Group 1 included 95 people living independently in the community. Group 2 ($n = 86$) consisted of all persons referred over a 1-year period to a geriatric evaluation clinic because of declines in function. Group 3 ($n = 60$) included individuals living in an intermediate level nursing home. Group 4, the most disabled group, consisted of 52 persons receiving active inpatient geriatric rehabilitation. Table 126-4 summarizes the findings. The four groups differed in the proportion of persons who could complete the simple tasks, in the average number of test items completed, and in the average amount of time required for the tasks.

MANUAL PERFORMANCE AND FUTURE NEEDS FOR CARE

To test whether changes in manual performance precede the need for care, a random sample of 40 residents receiving intermediate-level nursing home care was tested. Predictions of a person's need for "skilled nursing care" (a more intensive level of care) during the following year were based on the time taken to complete the manual test. Times of less than 350 seconds were chosen to predict stable care needs, and times of 350 seconds or more predicted increasing needs for care. Two experienced nurses involved in the care of the study's subjects were asked to make similar predictions of care needs for the coming year. Of the original sample of 40, 4 subjects withdrew. The remaining 36 patients' records were reviewed 1 year later.

The association between initial hand-function times and ultimate care requirements of participants is shown

TABLE 126-4
A Comparison of Demographic and Functional Measures in Four Groups of Elderly People

	Average Age (Range)	% Female	No. of Participants Completing Protocol	No. of Items Completed: Mean + 1 S.D. (Range)	Total Time in Seconds: Mean + 1 S.D.
Independent (n = 95)	75.5 (65–93)	81.1%	84 (88.4%)	26.8 + 0.75 (21–27)	218.5 + 69.0
Clinic (n = 86)	78.0 (65–100)	76.7%	37 (43.0%)	23.8 + 4.4 (10–27)	433.4 + 215.3
Intermediate nursing home (n = 60)	74.7 (47–98)	83.3%	25 (41.6%)	24.8 + 3.2 (12–27)	536.5 + 220.7
Acute rehabilitation (n = 52)	72.6 (66–91)	51.9%	14 (26.9%)	23.3 + 3.7 (9–27)	600.8 + 244.8

in Fig. 126-3. A highly significant association was observed between the predicted and actual outcomes (see Table 126-5). The predictions of the two experienced nurses were not confirmed. Thus, TMP evaluation proved to be a sensitive and specific predictor of subsequent care requirements and proved to be more reliable than a clinical assessment in this study.

COMBINING MANUAL PERFORMANCE WITH OTHER PERFORMANCE MEASURES

To integrate TMP with other indices of functional performance, a study was performed to test the utility of upper- and lower-extremity performance, grip strength, and mental status as predictors of stability or chronic deterioration in a cohort of frail older persons.[19] The study population consisted of a random sample of 40 patients selected from an intermediate-level care facility. Demographic information, manual ability, mental status, grip strength, mobility, active and resolved medical problems, medications, and a health care professional's estimate of each participant's likelihood of requiring skilled nursing care were obtained within 2 weeks after identifying the sample. Manual ability, mental status, grip strength, and mobility were included in a Performance Index to predict functional ability. Study participants were followed for 2 years to observe which individuals remained at the intermediate care level and which persons required transfer to the level of skilled nursing care.

Of the 27 persons who completed the study, 21 persons remained stable (Group 1) and 6 individuals were transferred to skilled nursing care (Group 2). Comparisons of group mean values for each category revealed statistically significant differences for age, manual per-

FIGURE 126-3
The relation between initial hand-function times and care requirements 1 year later in 36 institutionalized elderly people. Labeling is as follows: individuals discharged to home, "Improved"; individuals who suffered acute irreversible events, "Acute"; individuals who maintained their care needs, "Stable"; and individuals requiring skilled nursing care, "Chronic deterioration." See text for a discussion of the hand-function measurements.

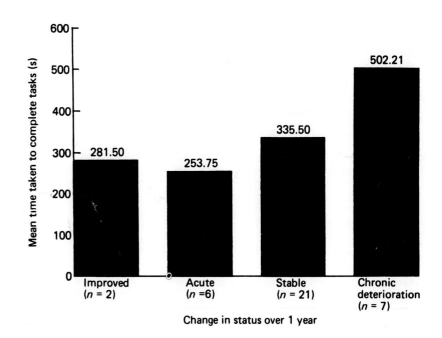

TABLE 126-5
Comparison between Predictions (Based on Hand-Function Times) and Actual Outcomes for 36 Elderly People Receiving Intermediate-Level Nursing Home Care

	Actual Need for Care	
Prediction	No Change	Increasing Care
No change (23)	22	1
Increasing care (13)	7	6
Total	29	7
Descriptive statistics:		
Sensitivity	75.3	
Specificity	85.7	
Positive predictive value	95.7	
Negative predictive value	46.2	
$\chi^2 = 10.1$, $p < 0.005$		

formance, and the Performance Index (Table 126-6). The Performance Index was a statistically significant predictor of increasing dependency ($p < 0.005$). Within Group 1, no patients had a performance score which predicted a poor outcome; only one person in Group 2 had a prediction of a favorable outcome. Professional judgment correctly predicted the outcome for 16 of the 21 persons in Group 1 but for only 2 of the 6 persons in Group 2.

PREDICTING CARE NEEDS FOR OLDER PERSONS RECEIVING OUTPATIENT CARE

Eighty-six persons undergoing outpatient geriatric evaluation over a 1-year period underwent manual skills testing.[20] Predictions of a person's need for long-term care services were made during the initial evaluation and were based on the TMP test (whether it could be completed and, if so, whether the TMP time was greater than or less than 350 seconds). Outcomes were determined approximately 1 year later via telephone inter-

views (see Tables 126-7, 126-8, and 126-9). Review of the data in Table 126-7 does not suggest any discriminating historical or diagnostic features relating to these outcomes. However, TMP scores proved to be highly predictive of outcome.

Of the twelve clinic individuals who completed the protocol but used additional services (Table 126-8), seven were subsequently institutionalized, while five received services in their homes. Eleven of these twelve persons had major psychiatric problems, noted on the physician's initial assessment as moderately severe or severe. Seven of the eleven persons with psychiatric disease were also noted by the physician to have problems with alcohol abuse. The one individual who did not have psychiatric disease had a spouse with a dementing illness, and a review of the medical record suggested that the additional services were targeted for the spouse.

Fifteen persons unable to complete the protocol did not require additional long-term care services. Only four of these fifteen people were noted to have limited financial and family resources. One-way analysis of variance for persons surviving the follow-up interval confirmed that the mean times were significantly different (F = 2.6, $p < 0.05$). Thus assessment of function, of which TMP is a central component, is also useful in the ambulatory setting in predicting individual survival, need for additional service, and level of care.

CONCLUSION

The results of these studies show that timing manual performance in vulnerable older persons allows prospective identification of individuals likely to require additional long-term care services. Older people who cannot complete the TMP or who take an excessive amount of time to do so (more than 350 seconds) subsequently require more long-term care services. Other health observations such as increasing age, sex, type or number of

TABLE 126-6
A Comparison of Functional and Clinical Observations for Two Groups of Institutionalized Older Persons

Observations	Group 1 Stable Care Needs (n = 21)			Group 2 Increasing Care Needs (n = 6)		
	Mean	Standard Deviation	Range	Mean	Standard Deviation	Range
Age (yr)*	77.9	7.0	68.0– 92.0	84.5	3.9	81.0– 92.0
Number of drugs	5.7	2.2	1.0– 9.0	7.8	4.3	2.0– 14.0
Number of diagnoses	4.9	1.6	1.0– 8.0	5.5	2.6	2.0– 10.0
Manual ability (s)*	127.8	44.3	66.0–252.5	175.7	44.8	104.0–226.0
Mental status	7.1	2.0	1.0– 9.0	5.3	2.1	2.0– 8.0
Ambulation (s)	9.2	6.7	2.0– 25.0	14.6	6.2	5.5– 22.3
Grip strength (mmHg)	80.4	28.9	7.0–135.0	62.7	21.0	35.0– 87.0
Performance Index*	2.5	1.8	0.2– 6.4	10.2	6.2	1.8– 18.8

*$p < 0.05$

TABLE 126-7
Comparison of Initial Medical Characteristics and Outcomes for 86 Outpatients Receiving Geriatric Evaluation*

Medical Characteristics	No Additional Services (n = 40)	Home Services (n = 16)	Domicile (n = 4)	Institutionalized (n = 18)	Dead (n = 8)
Average age (range)	76.9 (65–90)	75.8 (67–92)	81.3 (69–87)	80.2 (66–91)	80.8 (69–96)
Average number of medications (range)	2.3 (0–14)	2.8 (0–10)	4.0 (1–6)	1.3 (0–3)	2.7 (0–9)
Behavioral problems	.82†	.80	.75	1.0	.78
Weight loss‡	.41	.14	.25	.18	.38
Fall within 3 months	.38	.31	0	.35	.63
Alcohol problem	.42	.44	.25	.50	.14
Hypertension	.31	.46	0	.18	.38
Cardiac disease	.36	.36	.25	.33	.43
Stroke	.10	.19	.25	.28	.25
Neurologic disease	.13	.13	.25	.28	.13
Rheumatic disease	.41	.25	.25	.33	.63
Psychiatric illness (including dementia)	.44	.50	.75	.67	.63

*Determined from the physician's evaluation as part of a formal geriatric assessment.
†Numbers are the proportion in each group.
‡Over 3 kg in 6 months.

medical problems, and medication use do not seem to be as discriminating as TMP evaluation.

How could these risks for long-term care be estimated for an individual? Timing the performance of manual skills appears to provide important information regarding whether an older person's need for assistance will relate to his or her physical limitations. Persons with efficient manual skills who require additional services often have clear-cut psychiatric and behavioral conditions. Conversely, individuals with or without psychiatric illness who demonstrate difficulty with physical activities usually need additional support to maintain themselves. Those with family or financial resources may receive such services in their own homes, while individuals without these resources are likely to enter an institutional setting.

Further studies are needed to define risk factors for chronic deterioration. Identification of older persons likely to undergo a decline in ability to function can allow specific interventions, such as comprehensive interdisciplinary geriatric assessment, to be targeted selectively for high-risk groups. Moreover, identification of risk factors for declines in function may stimulate the development of strategies to reverse or prevent deterioration.

Improved measures of function may suggest changes in referral patterns for elderly people. For example, practitioners may refer high-risk individuals for a comprehensive, team-oriented geriatric assessment on

TABLE 126-8
Predictions of Need for Additional Care Based on Completing the Testing Protocol Compared to Actual Use of Additional Long-Term Care Services

Prediction	No Additional Services Used	Additional Services Used	Total
	Actual Outcome		
No additional services required (completed protocol)	25	12	37
Services required (could not complete protocol)	15	34	49
Total	40	46	86

TABLE 126-9
Comparison between Predictions of Older Person's Need for Additional Services, Based on Rate of Functional Performance and Actual Outcome

Prediction	Number Who Required Additional Services	Number Who Required No Additional Services
	Actual Outcome	
Total		
No services required (completed testing in less than 350 seconds)	25	15
Services required (took longer than 350 seconds to complete testing)	15	31

$\chi^2 = 6.4$, $p < 0.05$

the basis of the outcome of tests of simple tasks of function. In addition, professional attention may be shifted toward such areas as manual ability, foot care, or behavioral problems wherein disability can produce significant morbidity and dependency.

The impact of musculoskeletal dysfunction on the lives of older people is considerable, and every effort must be made to reduce the burden of this disability. The findings from manual performance tests suggest several potential interventions. Firstly, the value of musculoskeletal rehabilitation should be tested to see if conditioning, analgesics, and restorative techniques actually reduce an increasing dependency in older persons with poor manual performance. Even in the presence of significant rheumatic disease, manual performance testing may also reflect poor cognitive problem-solving skills. Interventions to improve mental performance, e.g., repetitive exercises, pharmacological agents, or adaptive training, may also reduce the risk of functional dependency. Secondly, studies to quantify other performance parameters, such as lower-extremity functioning or transferring skills, would add to our present knowledge of factors influencing patient movement from independent to dependent settings. This additional knowledge would also permit further refinement of predictive models and greater specificity of intervention strategies.

The effective reduction of disability and improvement in functioning depends on special knowledge and on the clinician's willingness to evaluate each patient's environment carefully and formulate a care plan tailored specifically to the individual's needs. The accumulation and constant refinement of these skills is the essence of geriatric medicine. This clinical approach requires time and a fundamental concern for each patient's welfare, and reflects both the clinical maturity and scientific grounding of the geriatric practitioner.

REFERENCES

1. Williams ME, Hadler NM: The illness as the focus of geriatric medicine. *N Engl J Med* 308:1357, 1983.
2. Palmore E: Total chance of institutionalization among the aged. *Gerontologist* 16:504, 1976.
3. Nielson M, Blenker M, Bloom M et al: Older persons after hospitalization: A controlled study of home aide service. *Am J Public Health* 62:1094, 1972.
4. Zarit SH: Predictors of outcome among day care participants. *Long-Term Care and Health Serv Admin Q* 2:150, 1978.
5. Vicente L, Wiley JA, Carrington RA: The risk of institutionalization before death. *Gerontologist* 19:361, 1979.
6. Greenberg JN, Ginn A: A multivariate analysis of the predictors of long-term care placement. *Home Health Serv Q* 1:75, 1979.
7. McCoy JL, Edwards BE: Contextual and socio-demographic antecedents of institutionalization among aged welfare recipients. *Med Care* 19:907, 1981.
8. Branch LG, Jette AM: A prospective study of long-term care institutionalization among the aged. *Am J Public Health* 72:1373, 1982.
9. Weinberger M, Darnell JC, Tierney WM et al: Self-rated health as a predictor of hospital admission and nursing home placement in elderly public housing tenants. *Am J Public Health* 76:457, 1986.
10. Pearlman RA, Ryan-Dykes M: The vulnerable elderly. *J Gerontol Nurs* 12:15, 1986.
11. Shapiro E: Patterns and predictors of home care use by the elderly when need is the sole basis for admission. *Home Health Serv Q* 7:29, 1986.
12. Kane RL, Matthias R: From hospital to nursing home: The long-term care connection. *Gerontologist* 24:604, 1984.
13. Roudot-Thoraval F, Boubert M, Fourestie V et al: Social future of elderly admitted to acute care hospital: Opinion of patient or family as predictive factor of subsequent transfer to long-term care. *Br Med J* 294:608, 1987.
14. Rubenstein LZ, Wieland D, English P et al: The Sepulveda VA Geriatric Evaluation Unit: Data on four-year outcomes and predictors of improved patient outcomes. *J Am Geriatr Soc* 32:503, 1984.
15. Martin DC, Morycz RK, McDowell J et al: Community-based geriatric assessment. *J Am Geriatr Soc* 33:602, 1985.
16. Jebsen RH, Taylor N, Trieschmann RB et al: An objective and standardized test of hand function. *Arch Phys Med Rehabil* 50:311, 1969.
17. Williams ME, Hadler NM: Musculoskeletal components of decrepitude. *Semin Arthritis Rheum* 11:284, 1981.
18. Williams ME, Hadler NM, Earp JAL: Manual ability as a marker of dependency in geriatric women. *J Chronic Dis* 35:115, 1982.
19. Williams ME, Hornberger JC: A quantitative method of identifying older persons at risk for increasing long-term care services. *J Chronic Dis* 37:705, 1984.
20. Williams ME: Identifying the older person likely to require long-term care services. *J Am Geriatr Soc* 35:761, 1987.

INDEX

Page numbers in italics indicate figures; page numbers followed by t indicate tabular material.

A

A4 peptide, in Alzheimer's disease, 940
AA (*see* Alcoholics Anonymous)
Abdominal infections, laboratory studies in, 1059
Abrasions, corneal, 426
Abscess:
  of brain, 988–989
    dementia and, 950
  hepatic, pyogenic, 634
Absence seizures, 999
Absorption:
  of drugs, 203–204
    psychopharmacology and, 1047
  by small intestine, aging and, 598, 599
Abuse, definition of, 1030
Accreditation, of nursing education programs, 305
ACE (*see* Angiotensin converting enzyme)
Acetaminophen, 287, 291
  hepatotoxicity of, 632
  in osteoarthritis, 886
  pain and, in dying patients, 356, 357
Acetanilid, liver function and, 604
Acetyl coenzyme A (acetyl-CoA), 908
Acetylcholine, 908
Acetylcholinesterase (AChE), 908
Achalasia, 613–614
  esophageal dysphagia and, 1159
Achlorhydria, 596
Achondroplasia, paternal age and, 32
Acid-base parameters, 557
Acid-base status, in chronic renal failure, 576
Acidosis, metabolic, in chronic renal failure, 576
Acid perfusion test, in gastroesophageal reflux disease, 610

Acid phosphatase:
  in prostate, 582–583
  serum, prostate carcinoma and, 588
Acoustic neuroma, dizziness and, 1064–1065
Acquired immune deficiency syndrome (AIDS), dementia and, 949–950
Acromegaly, 714
  peripheral neuropathy and, 981
ACTH (*see* Adrenocorticotropic hormone)
Actinic keratoses, 399–403, *400, 401*
  progression from carcinoma in situ to invasive squamous cell carcinoma, *401,* 401–402, *402*
  treatment of, *402,* 402–403
Active life expectancy (ALE), 179
Activities of daily living (ADL):
  caregiving and, 233
  functional loss and, 178t, 178–179
  home assistance with, 349–350
  home care and, 317
  instrumental (IADL):
    caregiving and, 233
    comprehensive functional assessment and, 220, 221
    functional loss and, 178t, 178–179
    home assistance with, 350
  physical functioning and, 153–154
Activity (*see* Physical activity)
Acute abdomen, presentation of, 216
Acute hospital care, 247–252
  gerontological nurses in, 305–306
  prevention of iatrogenesis and, 251–252
    comprehensive functional assessment and, 251–252
    quality of care and, 252
  stress of, 249–251, *250*
  treatment and environment and, 248t, 248–249, *249*
Acute myocardial infarction (AMI):
  presentation of, 214
  stroke and, 931

Acute renal failure (*see* Renal failure, acute)
Acute respiratory failure (ARF), 531
Acyclovir:
  in herpes simplex encephalitis, 986
  in herpes zoster, 1180–1181
AD (*see* Alzheimer's disease)
Addison's disease, 716
Adenocarcinoma:
  of bile ducts, 637
  esophageal, 617
  of gallbladder, 636–637
  gastric, 626–627
  of prostate, 586
Adenomas:
  in hyperparathyroidism, 837, 838
  pituitary, 1005
    treatment of, 1008, 1009
  toxic, hyperthyroidism due to, 725–726
Adenopathy, mediastinal, esophageal dysphagia and, 1158–1159
Adenylate cyclase activators, platelet function and, 690
ADH (*see* Antidiuretic hormone)
Adjustment disorders, 1098
  depression and, 1013
ADL (*see* Activities of daily living)
Adrenal glands:
  aging and, 708
  disorders of, 716
Adrenal hormones, 708
  (*See also specific hormones*)
Adrenal insufficiency, 716
Adrenal medullary transplantation, in Parkinson's disease, 963
Adrenergic agents, in asthma, 527
Adrenocorticotropic hormone (ACTH), 707–708
  aging and, 708
  characterization and actions of, 707
  feedback inhibition and, 708
  physiologic secretion of, 707
    neurotransmitter control of, 707

Adriamycin, with primary lymphoma of central nervous system, 1008

Adult development, psychotherapy and, 1046

Adult respiratory distress syndrome (ARDS), distinguishing from cardiogenic pulmonary edema, 536

Advance care directives, 373–374, 373–376t, 377
(*See also* Living wills; Power of attorney)

Adverse drug reactions, 202
anorexia and, 50
(*See also specific drugs and drug types*)

Aerobic exercise, 98

Aerobic exercise capacity:
central versus peripheral determinants of, 87
effects of aerobic exercise training in sedentary older people and, 88, 88–90, 89, 91
in elderly, 86, 86–91
physiologic adaptation in aerobically conditioned older athletes and, 87–88, 88

Aesthetic concerns, dying patients and, 360

Affective disorders, 1099
(*See also specific disorders*)

Afterload, resting, 447–448

Age:
chronological versus biological, 5–6
difficulties in determining, extreme old age and, 142–145
parental, mutation and, 32–33
as risk factor, for morbidity and mortality, 126, 127

Ageism, diagnosis and, 213

Age-related changes:
atherogenesis and, 461–462
biological, rehabilitation and, 321
dizziness and, 1063, 1063t
in lifestyle, 445
in lipoproteins, 768–770
clinical significance of, 769–770
in industrialized communities, 768–769
in nonindustrialized communities, 769, 770
predisposing to syncope, 1069
psychological, rehabilitation and, 321
as risk factors for infection, 1056–1057

Age-related changes (*Cont.*):
in skin (*see* Skin, age-related changes in)
social, rehabilitation and, 322

Aging:
anorexia of, 50t, 50–51
basal metabolic rate and, 296–297
biological (*see* Biological aging)
cancer and, 74, 74–76, 75t
characteristics of, 6
comparative studies on, 15–20
confusion among dying and disease and, 5
continuities of life course and, 119–121
death and, 5
definition of, 5
demography of, 146–147, 147t
dependency ratio and, 148, 148t
education and, 147
geographic distribution and, 149–150
institutionalization and, 148–149, 149
labor force participation and income and, 147–148
marital status and living arrangements and, 148, 149t
race distribution and, 147
sex distribution and, 147
diversity in, 116–119
macrosocial effects and, 116–117
mesosocial effects and, 117–119
microsocial effects and, 119
effects of, compared with effects of protein-calorie malnutrition, 51, 52, 52t
epidemiology of, 150, 150, 151t
mortality and morbidity and, 150, 150, 151t
as epiphenomenon, 3
evolutionary thought on, 5
modifiability of processes of, 121–122, 122t
normal, 138, 175–176
nutrition and, 48t, 48–58
pathologic, 138
physiologic aging related to, 140, 140
personality and, 101–106
primary versus secondary, 121
rate of, 16
maximum life span and, 8
research on, 3–4
sexuality and, 108–113

Aging (*Cont.*):
sociology of, 115–124
successful, 138–140
carbohydrate metabolism and, 139
osteoporosis and, 140, 140
usual aging and, 138–139
theories of, 3–4
usual, successful aging and, 138–139

Agnosia, 1097
in dementia, 1095

Agranulocytosis, 669

AIDS (*see* Acquired immune deficiency syndrome)

Air-bone gap, 437

Airway obstruction, in chronic obstructive pulmonary disease, 529

Airway secretions, in dying patients, 358

AIS (*see* Anemia-inducing substance)

Akathisia, antipsychotics and, 1050

Akinesia, in Parkinson's disease, 955

Akineton (*see* Biperiden)

Albumin, serum concentration of, drug distribution and, 204

Alcohol:
drug interactions of, 1050, 1051
falls and, 1193
hepatotoxicity of, 632
hypothermia and, 1085
peripheral neuropathy and, 981
platelet function and, 690
preventive gerontology and, 169–170
protective effect of, 169–170
sleep disorders and, 1113

Alcoholics Anonymous (AA), 1033

Alcoholism:
characteristics of, 1030–1031
consequences of, 1032–1033
depression and, 1013
disease prevention and, 195–196
esophagus and, 617
impotence and, 1148
pancreatitis and, 642
screening for, 1032
treatment of, 1033–1034
drugs in, 1033
psychosocial therapy in, 1033–1034

Aldosterone:
in chronic renal failure, 575
syncope and, 1069

ALDs (*see* Assistive listening devices)

ALE (*see* Active life expectancy)

Alertness, disorder of, in delirium, 922

Alginic acid, in gastroesophageal reflux disease, 611–612

Alkaline phosphatase:
in chronic renal failure, 576
occult disease and, 243
in Paget's disease, 845–846

Alkalosis, metabolic, in hypercapnic respiratory failure, 534

Alkylating agents, in chronic lymphocytic leukemia, 674

ALL (*see* Leukemia, acute lymphoblastic)

Allele, 23
mutant, 23

Allergic conjunctivitis, 425–426

Allergy:
photocontact, 393, 395
role in host defense and immune reaction, 64

Allopurinol, in gout, 893

Alpha-adrenergic antagonists, in urinary incontinence, 1136

Alpha$_1$-antitrypsin locus, genetic variation for, 23

Alprazolam (Xanax):
anxiety and, in dying patients, 359
in personality disorders, 1042

ALS (*see* Amyotrophic lateral sclerosis)

Altered mental state, 1089–1100
cognitive syndromes and, 1094–1098
diagnostic procedures and, 1089–1094
assessment of disability and, 1090
history in, 1089–1090
mental state examination in, 1090–1092
emotional syndromes and, 1098–1100
(*See also* Cognitive function; Psychiatric disorders)

Aluminum hydroxide, in chronic renal failure, 576

Alveolitis:
fibrosing, rheumatoid arthritis and, 874
in interstitial lung disease, 538

Alzheimer's disease (AD), 909, 934–944, 1096
biochemistry of, 909, 911t, 941–942
cachexia in, 1103
clinical diagnosis of, 934–935, 935t, 936t
cognitive and behavioral manifestations of, 935–937, 937
corticotropin-releasing hormone in, 708–709

Alzheimer's disease (AD) (*Cont.*):
dementia of, 29
depression in, 1099
Down's syndrome related to, 901–902, 939, 939
epidemiology of, 938t, 938–939, 939t
familial (FAD), 31, 901
gait and, 1186
gene expression in, 901–902
laboratory studies in, 937–938
management of, 942–944
experimental therapies in, 942–943
practical, 943–944
nutritional support and, 299
overlap between Parkinson's disease and, 941
pathology of, 940, 940–941
physical manifestations of, 937
relationship with cerebral amyloid, 901
risk factors for, 939, 939, 939t
sleep disorders and, 1112–1113, 1117
somatostatin in, 908
weight loss and, 51

Alzheimer's Disease Rating Scale, 937

Amantadine (Symmetrel):
in influenza, 513
in Parkinson's disease, 959
in pneumonia, 516

Amaurosis fugax, 422

American Cancer Society:
cervical cancer detection guidelines of, 77
early detection guidelines of, 76, 76t
screening guidelines of, 76

American Geriatric Society, on distribution of resources, 370

American Medical Association, statement on euthanasia, 372

American Nurses' Association:
certification by, 305
Council on Gerontological Nursing of, 304
standards of care of, 309

AMI (*see* Acute myocardial infarction)

Amiloride, hyperkalemia and, 562

Amino acids, decline in levels of, 52

Aminoglycosides, 1060
acute bacterial pyelonephritis and, 571
acute tubular necrosis and, 574
dizziness and, 1065

Aminoglycosides (*Cont.*):
pharmacology of, 1059
in pneumonia, 514

Aminophylline, in hypercapnic respiratory failure, 534

Amitriptyline, 291–292
in motor neuron diseases, 968
pain and:
in dying patients, 357
in postherpetic neuralgia, 1181
in Parkinson's disease, 957

AML (*see* Leukemia, acute myelogenous)

Amnesia, 1097
in dementia, 1095

Amphetamines, 291
side effects of, 292

Amphotericin B, acute tubular necrosis and, 574

Ampicillin:
acute bacterial pyelonephritis and, 571
platelet function and, 690

Ampullary disequilibrium, of aging, 443

Amputation:
occlusive peripheral vascular disease and, 267
rehabilitation and, 328

Amylase, serum levels of, in acute pancreatitis, 641

Amyloid, 897–902
aging and, 900, 900–901
in Alzheimer's disease, 940
cerebral, 901–902
Alzheimer's disease and, 901–902
gene expression in, 901–902
classification and clinical characteristics of, 898, 899
dialysis-related amyloidosis and, 899
light chain-related amyloidosis and, 899–900
secondary or reactive amyloidosis and, 899
genetic aspects of, 897–898
nature of, 897, 898t
origin and dynamics of, 897
(*See also* Amyloidosis)

Amyloid β protein deposition, in Alzheimer's disease, 941

Amyloidosis:
cardiac, senile, 898, 901
dialysis-related, 899
hereditary, 30–31

Amyloidosis (*Cont.*):
  light chain–related, 899–900
  nephrotic syndrome and, 570
  primary, 67
  rheumatoid arthritis and, 875
  secondary (reactive), 898, 899
  time and aging and, 902
Amyotrophic lateral sclerosis (ALS), gait and, 1188
Amyotrophy:
  diabetic, 980–981
  neuralgic, 980
Anabolic steroids (*see* Androgens; Steroids, anabolic)
Anaerobic bacteria, pneumonia and, 511–512
Anal fissures, constipation and, 1164
Analgesia, postoperative, anesthesia and, 276
Analgesic nephropathy, 572
Analgesics:
  adjuvant, 287
    in dying patients, 357
  guidelines for rational use of, 286, 287t
  guidelines for use of, 287, 288t, 289–294
  mild, 287
  narcotic, in dying patients, 357
  nonnarcotic, dying patients and, 356–357
  opioid, 289, 290t
    strong, 287
  pharmacodynamics of, 286
  pharmacokinetics of, 286, 289–290
  (*See also specific drugs*)
Anchorin CII, in cartilage, 851
Androgen(s):
  aging and, 715–716
  in impotence, 1152
  lipoproteins and, 45–46
  male sexual senescence and, 109–110
  sex therapy in men with, 113
  in women, 112–113
Androgen ablation, in prostate carcinoma, 589
Androstenedione, menopause and, 779
Anemia, 662–667
  of chronic disease, 666
  evaluation of, 663–664, 664t, *665*
  hemolytic, 667
    autoimmune, 667
    congenital, 667
    microangiopathic, 667

Anemia (*Cont.*):
  hypoproliferative, 664, 666
  ineffective erythropoiesis and, 666–667
  macrocytic, in hypothyroidism, 729–730
  nutrition and, 662–663
  pernicious, 666
  prevalence of, 662–663, 663t
  refractory (RA), 671, 672t
    with excess blasts (RAEB), 671, 672, 672t
    with excess blasts in transformation (RAEBT), 671, 672, 672t
    with ring sideroblasts (RARS), 671, 672t
  sideroblastic, 667
  (*See also* Bone marrow, failure of)
Anemia-inducing substance (AIS), in cancer cachexia, 1105
Anesthesia, 270–278
  blood replacement and, 277
  choice of general anesthetic agent for, 275
  consultation and, 277–278
  hypotension and postoperative renal failure and, 276t, 276–277
  informed consent and, 277
  monitoring and, 277
    electrocardiographic, 277
    pulse oximetry and, 277
  obvious anesthetic risk and, 271–272, *272*
  operative risk and, 270t, 270–271
  perioperative hypertension and, 275, 275–276
  postoperative analgesia and, 276
  postoperative hypothermia and, 276
  postoperative somnolence or confusion and, 275
    premedication and, 275
    relative overdose and, 275
  regional versus general, 273–275
    acute postoperative somnolence and, 274
    anesthetic failure and, 274
    blood loss and, 274
    cardiac complications and, 274
    deep venous thrombosis and pulmonary embolism and, 273–274
    hemodynamic changes and, 273
    mortality and, 273, 274t
    prolonged postoperative somnolence or confusion and, 274
    pulmonary complications and, 274

Anesthesia: regional versus general (*Cont.*):
    wound complications and, 274
  subtle anesthetic risk and, 272–273
Aneuploidy, maternal age and, 32–33
Aneurysms:
  in arteriosclerosis obliterans, 477–479
    ancillary diagnostic aids and, 479
    clinical evaluation of, 478–479
    clinical features of, 478
    treatment of, 480
  berry, in stroke, 929
  in pulmonary hypertension, 545
Angina, in hyperthyroidism, 720
Angina pectoris, 467–468
  coronary angioplasty in, 468
  pharmacologic therapy of, 467–468
Angiography:
  pulmonary, pulmonary embolism and, 546
  (*See also* Arteriography)
Angiokeratomas, of scrotum, 397, *397*
Angioplasty, in angina pectoris, 468
Angiotensin converting enzyme (ACE), hyperkalemia and, 562
Angiotensin converting enzyme (ACE), inhibitors:
  hypertension and, 493
  interference with renal autoregulation and, 574
Anomia, in Alzheimer's disease, 935
Anorectal function, aging and, 600–601, *601*
Anorexia:
  of aging, 50t, 50–51
  causes of, 49–50
  depression and, 49–50
  drug side effects as cause of, 50
  in dying patients, 358
  sensory function and, 416–417
  zinc deficiency and, 54
  (*See also* Cachexia)
Anorexia nervosa, in elderly patients, 50
Antabuse (*see* Disulfiram)
Antacids:
  in chronic gastritis, 620
  in gastroesophageal reflux disease, 611–612
  interactions of, 204, 1050
  peptic ulcer and, 623
Antianxiety agents (*see* Anxiolytic agents)
Antiarrhythmic agents, 471–472, *472*
  in syncope, 1074

Antibiotics:
  acute bacterial pyelonephritis and, 571
  acute tubular necrosis and, 574
  costs of, 1059
  in diarrhea, 1174
  dizziness and, 1065
  interstitial lung disease caused by, 541
  pharmacology of, 1059
  platelet function and, 690
  pressure ulcers and, 1208
  prophylactic, pneumonia and, 516
  urinary tract infections and, 360
  (*See also specific drugs*)
Antibodies:
  anti-idiotype, 68
  autoimmune, 23, 67–68
Antibody responses, specific, 67
Anticholinergic agents:
  in asthma, 528
  hyperthermia and, 1087
  interactions of, 204
  in motor neuron diseases, 968
    in Parkinson's disease, 958–959
    side effects of, 959
  (*See also specific drugs*)
Anticholinesterase inhibitors, in Alzheimer's disease, 942–943
Anticoagulants:
  circulating, 693–694
  in stroke, 928–929, 931
  in transient ischemic attack, 930–931
  in venous thrombotic disorders, 700–702
  (*See also specific drugs*)
Anticonvulsants:
  nutrient interactions of, 57
  pain management and, 291
  in postherpetic neuralgia, 1181
  (*See also specific drugs*)
Antidepressants, 1049–1050
  in affective disorders, 1099
  in dementia, 1096
  in depression, 1012, 1015–1016
    secondary, 1099, 1100
  dizziness and, 1065
  drug interactions of, 1050
  hyperthermia and, 1087
  interactions of, 204
  monoamine oxidase inhibitors as, 1049t, 1049–1050
  pain and, 291–292
    in dying patients, 357
  pharmacokinetics of, 226

Antidepressants (*Cont.*):
  tricyclic, 1049, 1050
    in depression, 1015–1016
    in dying patients, 359
    pain management and, 291–292
    in peripheral neuropathy, 982
    sleep disorders and, 1113
  (*See also specific drugs*)
Antidiuretic hormone (ADH):
  in congestive heart failure, 470
  (*See also* Syndrome of inappropriate antidiuretic hormone secretion)
Antiemetic therapy, cancer chemotherapy and, 82
Antiepileptic drugs:
  seizures and, 1001–1002
  side effects of, 1001
  (*See also specific drugs*)
Antigens, in hypersensitivity pneumonitis, 543
Antigeroid syndromes, 31–32
Antihistamines, 291
  drug interactions of, 1050
  sleep disorders and, 1113
Antihypertensive agents:
  depression and, 1013
  drug interactions of, 1050
  efficacy of, 488–491
    isolated systolic hypertension and, 490
    systolic-diastolic hypertension and, 489t, 489–490, 490t
  in renovascular disease, 566
  (*See also specific drugs*)
Anti-idiotype antibodies, 68
Antimalarial drugs, in rheumatoid arthritis, 877
Antimicrobial agents:
  in bacterial meningitis, 984
  in bacterial pneumonia, 512
  platelet function and, 690
  in pneumonia, 514
  (*See also* Antibiotics; *specific drugs*)
Antioncogenes, 75
Antiplatelet agents, in stroke, 932
Antipressure devices, prevention of pressure ulcers and, 1206–1207
Antipsychotics, 1050
  drug interactions of, 1050
  in personality disorders, 1042
  side effects of, 1050
  (*See also specific drugs*)
Antipyrine, hepatic metabolism of, 205
Antirheumatic drugs, in rheumatoid arthritis, 876–877

Antisocial personality disorder, 1038
Antispastic drugs, in motor neuron diseases, 968
Antithrombotic therapy:
  for arterial thrombosis, 683–685
    aspirin in, 683–684
    dietary omega-3 fatty acids in, 685
    dipyridamole in, 684
    ticlopidine in, 684–685
  in venous thrombotic disorders, 700–703
    anticoagulants in, 700–702
    fibrinolytic agents in, 702
    management and, 702–703
    prevention and, 703
  (*See also specific drugs*)
Antithyroid drugs, thioamide, 725
Antitumor agents:
  interstitial lung disease caused by, 541
  (*See also specific drugs*)
Anxiety:
  in dying patients, 359
  menopause and, 781
Anxiolytic agents, 1049, 1049t
  depression and, 1013
  in personality disorders, 1042
Aortic aneurysm, surgery for, 267
Aortic stenosis, 472–473
Aortic valve disease, syncope and, 1070
Aortoiliac occlusive disease, surgery for, 267
Apathy, in Alzheimer's disease, 935
Aphasia, 1097
  in Alzheimer's disease, 935
  Broca's nonfluent, 927, 1097
  in dementia, 1095
  in stroke, 927
  Wernicke's, 927, 1097
Apnea, sleep (*see* Sleep apnea)
Apocrine sweat glands, age-related changes in, 387
Apolipoproteins, 45
Appearance, in mental state examination, 1091
Appendicitis:
  acute, 1055
  presentation of, 216–217
  surgery for, 264
Appetite:
  in hyperthyroidism, 720
  in Parkinson's disease, 957
  (*See also* Anorexia; Cachexia)
Apraxia, 1097
  in dementia, 1095
  frontal, gait and, 1185

Aqueous humor, 423
Ara-C (*see* Cytosine arabinoside)
Arcus senilis, 182
ARDS (*see* Adult respiratory distress syndrome)
ARF (*see* Acute respiratory failure; Renal failure, acute)
Aristotle, 3
Arrhythmias:
  antiarrhythmic therapy and, 471–472, *472*
  dizziness and, 1066
Arsenic, in Bowen's disease, 403, *403*
Artane (*see* Trihexyphenidyl)
Arterial blood gases:
  in hypercapnic respiratory failure secondary to mismatch of ventilation and perfusion, 533
  lung cancer and, 550
Arterial disease:
  extracranial, 481–483
    clinical presentation of, 481–482
    diagnosis of, 482–483
    pathogenesis of, 481
    therapy of, 483
  occlusive, below inguinal ligament, surgery for, 267–268
Arterial wall, cell biology of, atherogenesis and, 461
Arteriography:
  intracranial neoplasms and, 1006
  in renovascular disease, 566
Arteriosclerosis:
  nonatheromatous, 458–459
  (*See also* Atherosclerosis)
Arteriosclerosis obliterans, 476–481
  clinical features of, 477–479
  pathogenesis and disease patterns in, 476
  pathophysiology of arterial obstruction in, 476–477
  treatment of, 479–481
Arteriovenous fistulas, autogenous, construction in elderly patients, 578
Arteriovenous oxygen difference, maximal oxygen consumption and, 87
Arteritis:
  giant cell (*see* Giant cell arteritis)
  temporal, 431
Artery(ies):
  age-related changes in, 448
  thrombosis and (*see* Thrombosis, arterial)
  (*See also specific arteries*)

Arthritis:
  gouty (*see* Gout)
  rheumatoid (*see* Rheumatoid arthritis)
  septic, 1055–1056
  (*See also* Osteoarthritis)
Arthroscopy, in osteoarthritis, 887
Articular disturbances (*see* Joint(s); *specific joint disturbances*)
Artificial feeding (*see* Nutritional support)
Artificial hydration:
  ethical issues related to, 374–376
  (*See also* Oral rehydration therapy)
Asbestos, lung cancer and, 548
Asbestosis, 538
Ascites, in hypothyroidism, 729
Aspiration pneumonia, 510, 511
  anaerobic bacteria and, 512
Aspirin, 287, 291
  arterial thrombosis and, 683–684
  myocardial infarction and, 684
  pain and, in dying patients, 356
  platelet function and, 690
  in stroke, 932
  in transient ischemic attack, 931
Assessment:
  of cardiovascular function, surgery and, 257t, 257–259, 258t, 259
  comprehensive (*see* Comprehensive functional assessment)
  of dying patients, medical, 354
    psychosocial aspects of, 355
  education of team members on, 187
  of human sexuality, 108–109
  of immune function, 64–68, 65t, 68t, 69
  neuropsychiatric (*see* Neuropsychiatric assessment)
  in nursing process, 308
  nutritional, 49
  of operative risk, 256
  of pain (*see* Pain, clinical assessment of)
  of personality, 101
  of pulmonary function, surgery and, *260*, 260–261
  of renal function, surgery and, 261
  of wound healing, surgery and, 262–263
Assisted ventilation, in hypercapnic respiratory failure, 534–535
Assistive aids, 323
Assistive listening devices (ALDs), 441–442

Astasia-abasia, 1190
Asthma, 526–528
  clinical presentation of, 526–527
  gastroesophageal reflux disease associated with, 610
  hypercapnic respiratory failure and, secondary to mismatch of ventilation and perfusion, 532
  laboratory studies in, 527
  prevalence and etiology of, 526, 527t
  prognosis of, 528
  treatment of, 527–528
Astigmatism, 431
Astrocytomas, 1005
Atarax (*see* Hydroxyzine)
Ataxia:
  in hypothyroidism, 728
  sensory, gait and, 1189
  vestibular, of aging, 443
Ataxia telangiectasia, 28–29
Atenolol, in hyperthyroidism, 725
Atheroembolic disorders, renal, 566–567
Atherosclerosis, 458–464
  in diabetes mellitus, 748
  exercise and, 96
  in Hutchinson-Guilford syndrome, 28
  in hypothyroidism, 729
  life span and, 92
  natural history of, 458, *459*
  pathogenesis of, 461–462
  prevention of, 464
  preventive gerontology and, 169
  reversibility and regression and, 463–464
    in animals, 463
    in humans, 463–464
  risk factors for, 459t, 459–461
    pathobiology and, 462–463
  sex differential in, 41–47, *42–45*
  silent, diarrhea and, 1169
  surgery for, 267
"Atherosclerotic dementia," stroke and, 931
Athletes, aerobically conditioned, physiologic adaptations in, 87–88, *88*
Athlete's foot, 394, 395
Ativan (*see* Lorazepam)
ATN (*see* Tubular necrosis, acute)
Atrial fibrillation, in hyperthyroidism, 720
Atrial septal defect, 473
Atrophic vaginitis, 111

Atropine:
  in asthma, 528
  in chronic obstructive pulmonary disease, 530
  intestinal obstruction and, in dying patients, 358
  in motor neuron diseases, 968
  premedication with, surgery and, 275
Attention, 914
  global disorder of, in delirium, 922
Attorney, value of consulting, 362, 363
Audiography, 436, *437*
Audiologic evaluation, 436–437, *437*
  test interpretation and, 437–438
Audiometer, screening, 436
Audioscope, 436, *436*
Auranofin, in rheumatoid arthritis, 877
Authority to treat, 362–364
Autoimmune theory of aging, 67–68
Autoimmunity:
  autoimmune antibodies and, 67–68
    heritability of longevity and, 23
  in chronic lymphocytic leukemia, 674
Autonomic function, tests of, syncope and, 1073
Autonomy, ethical dilemmas and, 369
  withdrawing and withholding life-sustaining therapies and, 373
Avoidant personality disorder, 1039
Awareness, disorder of, in delirium, 922
Axonal degeneration, in peripheral neuropathy, 978
Axonotmesis, peripheral neuropathy and, 980
Azathioprine (Imuran):
  in peripheral neuropathy, 982
  in polymyositis/dermatomyositis, 867
  in rheumatoid arthritis, 877–878
Azotemia, prerenal, 573

B

Back pain:
  management of, 975
  in osteoporosis, diagnostic evaluation of, 819
  patient approach and, 970–972
Baclofen, in motor neuron diseases, 968
Bacon, Francis, 3

Bacon, Roger, 3
Bacteria:
  anaerobic, pneumonia and, 511–512
  (*See also specific organisms*)
Bacterial conjunctivitis, 425
Bacterial endophthalmitis, 428
Bacterial meningitis (*see* Meningitis, bacterial)
Bacteriuria:
  asymptomatic, 1055
  urinary incontinence and, 1126
Balance, 442
  (*See also* Falls)
Bank accounts, joint, 366
Barbiturates, 1049
  in older patients, 208
  (*See also specific drugs*)
Barium enema, in constipation, 1163
Barium esophagram, in gastroesophageal reflux disease, 610
Baroreflex sensitivity, syncope and, 1069
Barrett's esophagus, in gastroesophageal reflux disease, 612–613
Basal ganglia disorders, gait and, 1186–1187
Basal metabolic rate (BMR), impact of age on, 296–297
BCDDP (*see* Breast Cancer Detection Demonstration Project)
B cells, 62
  augmentation of activity of, 69
  evaluation of function of, 67
  immune response initiation and, 63
BCNU (*see* Bischloroethylnitrosurea)
Bed:
  air-fluidized, prevention of pressure ulcers and, 1208–1209
  (*See also* Mattresses)
Bedsores (*see* Pressure ulcers)
Behavior:
  of disease, 177–179
    active life expectancy and, 179
    chronicity of disease and, 178
    functional loss and, 178t, 178–179
    multiple disease processes and, 177t, 177–178
    relationship of function and disease and, 179
  during illness, 176–177
    of patient, 176
    symptom underreporting and, 176–177
  (*See also* Altered mental state)
Behavioral techniques, 1047

Behavioral techniques (*Cont.*):
  in urinary incontinence, 1136–1138, 1137t, 1138t
Behçet's disease, esophagus and, 617
Bell's palsy, herpes zoster and, 1180
Benadryl (*see* Diphenhydramine)
Beneficence, ethical dilemmas and, 369
Benign adrenal neoplasia, 716
Benign migraine equivalent, 930
Benign monoclonal gammopathy, 67
Benign paroxysmal positional vertigo (BPPV), 1064
  treatment of, 1068
Benign prostatic hyperplasia (BPH), 583–585
  diagnostic tests in, 585
  etiology of, 583–584
  incidence of, 583, *584*
  pathogenesis of, 584
  physical examination in, 584–585
  symptoms of, 584
  treatment of, 585
Benzodiazepines:
  in Alzheimer's disease, 943
  anxiety and, in dying patients, 359
  dizziness and, 1065
  hepatic metabolism of, 205
  in management of nausea and vomiting, 82
  in motor neuron diseases, 968
  seizures and, 1002
  sleep disorders and, 1113, 1120
Benztropine (Cogentin), in Parkinson's disease, 959
Bereavement, 360
Bernstein test, in gastroesophageal reflux disease, 610
Berry aneurysms, in stroke, 929
Beta-adrenergic blockers, in Parkinson's disease, 955
Beta-adrenergic stimulation, cardiovascular response to, 453, *454*
Beta-blockers:
  in angina pectoris, 468
  hypertension and, 493
  in hyperthyroidism, 725
  sleep disorders and, 1113
Beta-carotene, 57
Beta lactam derivatives, tubulointerstitial nephritis and, 571
Bethanechol (Urecholine):
  in Alzheimer's disease, 942–943
  in gastric emptying disorders, 624
  side effects of, 293

Bethanidine, drug interactions of, 1050
BFU-E (*see* Burst-forming unit erythroid)
Bile acids, oral administration of, gallstone dissolution with, 635
Bile ducts:
  adenocarcinoma of, 637
  common:
    aging and, 602
    stones in, 636
Biliary tract:
  aging and, 634–637
    acute cholelithiasis and, 635
    adenocarcinoma and, 637
    choledocholithiasis and, 635–636
    cholelithiasis and, 634
    silent gallstones and, 634–635
  disease of, surgery for, 263–264
Biofeedback procedures:
  in fecal incontinence, 1145
  in urinary incontinence, 1136
Biological age, chronological age versus, 5–6
Biological aging, 5
  autoimmune theory of, 67–68
  cellular basis of, 11–12
  cross-linking theory of, 8
  error theory of, 7–8, 26
  exercise and, 85–98, *86*
  free radical theory of, 10–11
  genetics of, 22–26
  immunological theory of, 9–10
  intrinsic mutagenesis theory of, 9
  muscle structure and function with, *91*, 91–92
  neuroendocrine theories of, 8–9
  rate of, 16
  somatic mutation theory of, 6–7
  survivorship kinetics of, 5
  in vivo and in vitro, 12
Biological markers, in paraphrenias, 1022
Biopsy:
  of bone, in osteomalacia, 830–831
  breast cancer diagnosis and, 794
  core-needle, in prostate carcinoma, 586–587
  fine-needle aspiration, in prostate carcinoma, 587
  in gastroesophageal reflux disease, 611
  of iliac bone crest (BX), in osteoporosis, 816, 818
  intracranial neoplasms and, 1006–1007

Biopsy (*Cont.*):
  of muscle, in polymyositis/dermatomyositis, 867
  of nerves, in peripheral neuropathy, 978–979
  of temporal arteries, in giant cell arteritis, 862
  transperineal, in prostate carcinoma, 587
Biopsychosocial model, for patient assessment, 218
  synthesis with functional model, 220t, 220–221, 221t
Biperiden (Akineton), in Parkinson's disease, 959
Biphosphonates:
  in osteoporosis, 822–823
  in Paget's disease, 847
Bisacodyl (Ducolax), in constipation, 1167
Bischloroethylnitrosurea (BCNU), 81
Bismuth sodium tartrate (Pepto-Bismol), peptic ulcer and, 623
Bladder, "hypersensitive," 1126
Bladder retraining, in urinary incontinence, 1137–1138
Bladder training, in urinary incontinence, 1136–1138, 1137t, 1138t
Blast crisis, in chronic granulocytic leukemia, 675
Bleeding:
  coagulation factor defects and, 692–698
    acquired and complex, 693–698
    hereditary, 692–693
  in diverticular disease, 647–648
  gastrointestinal, 625–626
  in liver disease, management of, 695–696
  upper gastrointestinal, in Mallory-Weiss syndrome, 615
  (*See also* Hemorrhage)
Bleomycin, interstitial lung disease caused by, 541
Blepharitis, 424
Blepharochalasis, 424
Blepharoptosis, 423, *424*
Blepharospasm, 423–424
Blessed Dementia Rating Scale, 936, 1014, 1090
Blood:
  abnormal composition of, syncope and, 1072
  loss of:
    anemia and, 664, 666

Blood: loss of (*Cont.*):
    regional versus general anesthesia and, 274
    (*See also* Bleeding; Hemorrhage)
  (*See also* Anemia)
Blood cells, cachexia and, 1105
Blood component therapy, in bleeding disorders, 693
Blood flow, renal (RBF), aging changes in, 556
Blood pressure:
  estrogen and, 783, 784t
  isometric exercise and, 92
  sex differences in, 42
  syncope and, 1068–1069
  (*See also* Hypertension; Hypotension)
Blood sugar levels, sex differences in, 42
Blood tests:
  in interstitial lung disease, 539–540
  (*See also* Laboratory studies)
Blood transfusion, 277
  massive, 698
Bloom's syndrome, 27
BMR (*see* Basal metabolic rate)
Body composition:
  drug distribution and, 204
  maximal oxygen consumption and, 87
  measurement of, 297
Body fat, distribution of, 764–765
Body mass index, computation of, 760
Bone:
  biopsy of, in osteomalacia, 830–831
  calcium metabolism and, 801
  cortical, 803–804, *804*
  density of:
    genetic influences on, 810–811
    regulation of, 805, 807–810
  loss of:
    contributors to, 140
    estrogen deficiency and, 782
    osteoporosis and, 814, 815
    trabecular, 804
  Paget's disease of (*see* Paget's disease)
  remodeling of:
    osteoporosis and, 814
    regulation of, 805, 807–808
  resorption of:
    osteoporosis and, 814–815
    pathological impaired coupling and, 809
  trabecular, 804, *804*
  (*See also* Musculoskeletal system)

Bone marrow:
    cancers metastatic to, 676
    drug effects on, 669–670
    drug-induced damage to, 686t, 686–687
    failure of, anemia and, 666
    normal function of, 655–657, *656*
        aging and, 657–658
    transplantation of, in chronic granulocytic leukemia, 676
    (*See also* Hematopoietic system)
Bone marrow reserve, chemotherapy and, 81
Bone mass, in osteomalacia, 831
Bone metabolism, 803–811
    bone cells and, 804–805
    bone structure and, 803–804, *804*
    regulation of bone remodeling and bone density and, 805, 807–811
Bone minerals, aging, physical activity, and metabolism of, 96–97
Bone scan:
    in lung cancer, 551
    in osteomalacia, 831
    in Paget's disease, 845
    in prostate carcinoma, 588
Borderline personality disorder, 1038
Boston University Hospital, community-based long-term care services at, 351
Bowel training, in constipation, 1165
Bowen's disease, *403*, 403–404
BPH (*see* Benign prostatic hyperplasia)
BPPV (*see* Benign paroxysmal positional vertigo)
Braces, in stroke rehabilitation, 326
Bradycardia, sinus, 471
Bradykinesia, in Parkinson's disease, 955, 956
Brain:
    acetylcholine in, 908
    age-related diseases of, 909
    aging in, 905–906
        chemical constituents and, 906–907
        morphological considerations and, 905–906
        pre- and postmortem considerations and, 907
    amyloid in, 901–902
    atrophy of, head injury and, 992
    catecholamines and serotonin in, 907–908
    gamma aminobutyric acid and glutamic acid decarboxylase in, 908

Brain (*Cont.*):
    neuropeptides in, 908–909
    neurotransmitter biology and, 907
    tumors metastatic to, 1005
        brain imaging and, 1006
        of lung cancer, 553
        treatment of, 1007–1008
    (*See also* Central nervous system)
Brain abscess, 988–989
    dementia and, 950
Brain imaging:
    in Alzheimer's disease, 937–938
    intracranial neoplasms and, 1006
Breast:
    cancer of (*see* Cancer, of breast)
    cysts of, 794
    examination of, 182
Breast Cancer Detection Demonstration Project (BCDDP), 793
Breast diseases, 789–796
    background physiology and, 789–791, *790*, *791*
    estrogen and, 784, 784t
    pathology of, 791–792, 792t
Breathing:
    control of, 502
    work of, in chronic obstructive pulmonary disease, 530
    (*See also headings beginning with terms* Pulmonary *and* Respiratory)
Broca's aphasia, 927, 1097
Bromocriptine (Parlodel), in Parkinson's disease, 961
Bronchitis, chronic, 528, 529
Bronchoalveolar lavage, in interstitial lung disease, 540, 542
Bronchodilators:
    in chronic obstructive pulmonary disease, 530
    in hypercapnic respiratory failure, 533–534
Bronchopulmonary symptoms, in gastroesophageal reflux disease, 609–610
Bruit, asymptomatic, stroke and, 931–932
Brush-border enzymes, aging and, 598–599
Bullous pemphigoid, 406–407
Buprenorphine, 289
Burst-forming unit erythroid (BFU-E), 655, 657–658
Buspirone, in personality disorders, 1042

Busulfan:
    interstitial lung disease caused by, 541
    marrow damage induced by, 686
Butorphanol, 289
BX (*see* Biopsy, of iliac bone crest)

C

Cachectin (*see* Tumor necrosis factor)
Cachexia, 1102–1106, 1103t
    changes in functional body mass and, 1103–1104
    control mechanisms in, 1104–1105
        endocrinologic, 1104
        humoral, 1104–1105
    epidemiology of, 1102–1103
    future research directions for, 1105–1106
    taste and appetite and, 1104
    treatment of, 1105
CAH (*see* Hepatitis, chronic, active)
Calcitonin (Calcimar):
    calcium metabolism and, 803
    human, in Paget's disease, 846
    in osteoporosis, 815, 822
    salmon, in Paget's disease, 846–847
Calcitrol (*see* Vitamin D)
Calcium, 56
    absorption of, in small intestine, 600
    deficiency of:
        in females, 808–810
        in males, 810
    metabolism of, 799–811
        in chronic renal failure, 576
        serum calcium regulation and, *800*, 800–803
    in osteoporosis, 821
    postoperative, in hyperparathyroidism, 841
    urinary excretion of, in hyperparathyroidism, 840
Calcium blockers, in stroke, 929
Calcium carbonate, in chronic renal failure, 576
Calcium channel antagonists, in angina pectoris, 468
Calcium channel blockers:
    in achalasia, 613–614
    hypertension and, 493
    in urinary incontinence, 1135
Calcium pyrophosphate dihydrate crystal deposition disease (*see* Chrondrocalcinosis)

Calculus (i):
  renal, in gout, 893
  (*See also* Gallstones)
Callahan, Daniel, on distribution of resources, 371
Caloric restriction:
  free radical theory of aging and, 10–11
  life span and, 48, 70
Cancer, 72–82, *73*
  biologic behavior of tumors in elderly and, 78–79
  of breast:
    age differences in, 78, 79
    chemotherapy in, 82
    clinical presentation of, 793t, 793–794
    diagnosis and treatment of, 794–796, *795*, 795t
    estrogen-receptor-positive, 79
    factors interfering with early diagnosis of, 77–78
    incidence of, 73, 789, 790t
    management of, 79
    screening for, 197
  cachexia and, 1103, 1104, 1105
  as cause of death, 152
  cervical, screening for, 197
  chemotherapy in (*see* Chemotherapy)
  colorectal, 648–651
    clinical features of, 650
    constipation and, 1164
    epidemiology and pathogenesis of, 648–650
    incidence of, 72–73
    screening for, 197, 651
    surgery for, 265
    treatment of, 650–651
  ectopic hormone production in association with, weight loss and, 111–113
  endometrial, estrogen and, 785, 822
  estrogen and, 46
  factors interfering with early diagnosis of, 77–78
  hormonal therapy in, 81–82
  immune function and, 75–76
  incidence of, 72–74
  initial presentation of, 77–78, 78t
  of lung (*see* Lung cancer)
  management of, 79, 79–80
  menopause and, 780
  oral, 418
  pain of, 281
    extent of disease and, 284

Cancer (*Cont.*):
  pancreatic, 642–643
  preventive gerontology and, 169
  probability of, 17, *17*
  radiation therapy in (*see* Radiation therapy)
  relationship of aging and, *74*, 74–76, 75t
  risk factors for, 133–134
    diet as, 134
    selenium and, 55
    smoking as, *133*, 133–134
  screening in asymptomatic patients and, 76t, 76–77
  of skin, ultraviolet light and, 400
  supportive care in, 82
  surgical treatment of, 80
  in Werner's syndrome, 27
  (*See also* Carcinoma; Leukemia)
Cancer genes (*see* Oncogenes)
Cancer suppressor genes, 75
Candidiasis:
  esophageal, 616
    anorexia and, 50
  oral, in dying patients, 359
Canes:
  hip fractures and, 327
  in rheumatoid arthritis, 878
Cannabinols, in management of nausea and vomiting, 82
CAPD (*see* Continuous ambulatory peritoneal dialysis)
Capsaicin, in postherpetic neuralgia, 1181
Captopril, interference with renal autoregulation and, 574
Carbamazepine (Tegretol), 291
  in depression, 1012
  in peripheral neuropathy, 982
  in postherpetic neuralgia, 1181
  seizures and, 1001, 1002
    in dying patients, 359
Carbenicillin, platelet function and, 690
Carbidopa (Sinemet), in Parkinson's disease, 960–962
Carbohydrates, 53
  absorption of, in small intestine, 599
  metabolism of, aging and, 139
Carcinoembryonic antigen (CEA), serum levels of, in colorectal cancer, 650–651
Carcinogenesis, *74*, 74–76, 75t
Carcinoid, gastric, 621

Carcinoma:
  basal cell:
    of eyelid, 424, *425*
    of skin, *404*, 404–405, *405*
  of colon, constipation and, 1164
  esophageal dysphagia and, 1158
  in multinodular goiter, 734
  parathyroid, in hyperparathyroidism, 837, 838
  of prostate (*see* Prostate, carcinoma of)
  squamous cell:
    esophageal, 616–617
    of eyelid, 424, *425*
    of prostate, 586
    of skin, *401–403*, 401–404
  thyroid, 736–737
    radiation-associated, 737
    surgical removal versus suppression therapy of cold nodules and, 736–737
  transitional cell, of prostate, 586
Cardiac cachexia, 1103
Cardiac complications:
  in hyperthyroidism, 720
  in polymyositis/dermatomyositis, 866
  regional versus general anesthesia and, 274
  of rheumatoid arthritis, 874
Cardiac disease:
  stroke and, 931
  surgery for, 268, 268t
Cardiac examination, 182
Cardiac monitoring, hypothermia and, 1085–1086
Cardiac output:
  maximal oxygen consumption and, 86–87
  nutritional support and, 300
Cardiac rhythm abnormalities, syncope and, 1070
Cardiomyopathy, hypertrophic, syncope and, 1070
Cardiopulmonary examination, syncope and, 1073
Cardiopulmonary resuscitation, decision making regarding, 373–374, 373–376t
Cardiovascular disorders:
  as cause of death, 92
  hyperparathyroidism and, 839
  hyperthermia and, 1087
  in hypothyroidism, 729
  (*See also specific disorders*)

Cardiovascular function:
  in Parkinson's disease, 957
  sex steroids and, 46
  surgery and, 256–259
    evaluation and management of, 257t, 257–259, 258t, 259
    pathophysiology of, 256–257
Cardiovascular mortality, sex differences in, 43, *43*
Cardiovascular reflexes, abnormal, syncope and, 1071–1072
Cardiovascular response, to isometric exercise, 92
Cardiovascular risk factors, sex differences in, 43–44
Caregivers, 232–236
  adult children as, 234
    demographic developments and, 234–235
    women in labor force and, 235
  impact of behavioral disorders on, 230
  spouses as, 234
Care needs:
  manual performance and, current needs and, 1215–1217, 1215–1217t
    future needs and, 1216–1217, *1217*, 1218t
    predicting, for outpatients, 1218, 1219t
Care plan, individualized, comprehensive functional assessment and, 221
Caries, dental, 414–415
Carotid bruits, in physical examination, 182
Carotid endarterectomy, in transient ischemic attack, 931
Carotid pulses, syncope and, 1072–1073
Carotid sinus massage, syncope and, 1073
Carotid sinus syndrome, syncope and, 1072
Carrel, Alexis, 11
Cartilage of diarthroidal joints, 849–855
  aging in, 851
  biochemistry of, *850*, 850–851
  evolution of osteoarthritis and, 851t, 851–855
  mechanical properties of, 851
"Cascade of disasters," rehabilitation and, 320

Cascade of illness, in acute care hospital, frail patients and, 249–251, *250*
Case finding, disease prevention and, 198
Castor oil in constipation, 1166–1167
CAT (*see* Choline acetyltransferase)
Cataract, 426–427
"Catastrophic" insurance, 163
Catecholamines, 907–908
  cardiovascular response to, 453, *454*
Catechol-*o*-methyltransferase (COMT), 907
Cathartics, constipation and, in dying patients, 358
Catheterization:
  hip fracture and, 1202
  in urinary incontinence, 360, 1137, 1139–1140, 1140t
Caucasus, longevity in, 144
Cavernosography, in impotence, 1152
Cefamandole, in pneumonia, 514
Cefuroxime, in pneumonia, 514
Cell (s):
  aging of, 11–12
  of immune system (*see* Immunology)
  somatic, 22
  tumor, 74
Cellular immunity, aging and, 503
Cementum, 414
Center for Epidemiological Studies Depression Questionnaire (CES-D), 1098
Central nervous system (CNS):
  age changes in, neuropsychiatric assessment and, 224–225
  control of fluid balance by, 1079
  disorders of:
    dizziness and, 1065
    syncope and, 1072
  dysfunction of, hypothermia and, 1085
  falls and, 1193
  in hypothyroidism, 728
  infections of, 938–939
  treatment of, in acute lymphoblastic leukemia, 673
  (*See also* Brain)
Cephalosporins:
  in pneumonia, 514
  third-generation, acute bacterial pyelonephritis and, 571
Cephalothin, platelet function and, 690
Cerebellar disorders:
  dizziness and, 1065
  gait and, 1187

Cerebellar function, in hypothyroidism, 728
Cerebrospinal fluid (CSF)
  in bacterial meningitis, 984
  in herpes simplex encephalitis, 985
  intracranial neoplasms and, 1006
  in neurosyphilis, 986
Cerebrovascular disease, dizziness and, 1065
Certification, of gerontological nurses, 305
Cerumen, 433
Cervical cancer:
  age differences in, 78
  detection of, 77
  screening for, 197
Cervical collar, in rheumatoid arthritis, 878
Cervical spine:
  injuries of, head injury and, 996
  rheumatoid arthritis in, 873
Cervical spondylosis, 973–974
CES-D (*see* Center for Epidemiological Studies Depression Questionnaire)
CFA (*see* Comprehensive functional assessment)
CFU-E (*see* Colony-forming unit erythroid)
CFU-S (*see* Colony-forming unit spleen)
Chalazion, 424, *425*
CHD (*see* Coronary heart disease)
Chemical dependency (*see* Alcoholism; Drug addiction)
Chemical senses, reduction in, anorexia and, 50
Chemical toxicity, cutaneous, 394
Chemotherapy, 81–82
  acute tubular necrosis and, 574
  in breast cancer, 796
  in chronic lymphocytic leukemia, 674
  combination, 81
    in acute myelogenous leukemia, 672–673
    in chronic lymphocytic leukemia, 674
  with intracranial neoplasms, 1008
  in lung cancer, 553
  management of nausea and vomiting with, 82
  toxicity and, 81
  underdosing in, 81–82
Chenodeoxycholic acid (Chenodiol), gallstone dissolution with, 635

Cherry angiomas, 397, *397*
Chest pain:
  in diffuse esophageal spasm, 614
  in gastroesophageal reflux disease, 609
  noncardiac, in esophageal motor disorders, 614
Chest wall, interaction with lung, aging and, 500–501, *501*
Chest x ray:
  in hypercapnic respiratory failure, secondary to mismatch of ventilation and perfusion, 533
  intrathoracic metastases and, 551–552
  lung cancer and, 550, 551
  pulmonary embolism and, 546
Chickenpox (*see* Herpes zoster infection)
Childhood, "progeria of," 27
Chloral hydrate, 1049
Chlorambucil, in chronic lymphocytic leukemia, 674
Chloramphenicol, marrow damage induced by, 686
Chlorazepate, hepatic metabolism of, 205
Chlordiazepoxide:
  absorption of, 204
  hepatic metabolism of, 205
Chlormethiazole, absorption of, 204
Chlorpromazine (Thorazine), hallucinations and, in dying patients, 359
Chlorthalidone, hypokalemia and, 563
Cholecystectomy, 634
Cholecystitis, 1055
  acalculous, 635
  acute, 635
    as surgical emergency, 263
Cholecystography, oral, 634
Cholecystokinin, anorexia and, 51
Choledocholithiasis, 635–636
Cholelithiasis, 634
Cholera, diarrhea and, 1170
Cholesterol:
  age-related changes in, 768–769, *769*
  in gallstones, 634
  as index of nutritional status, 49
  reference ranges for, 242–243
  sex differences in, 42
  total serum:
    disease prevention and, 196
    as risk factor, 129–130
  [*See also* Lipoprotein(s)]

Cholesterol emboli, renal, 566–567
Cholestyramine, interactions of, 204
Choline acetyltransferase (CAT), 908
Choline magnesium trisalicylate, 287
Cholinergic agonists, in urinary incontinence, 1136
Chondrocalcinosis, 893–895
  clinical presentation of, 894–895
  diagnosis of, 895
  disorders associated with, 894
  gout differentiated from, 893–894
  lanthanic, 895
  prognosis and management of, 895
  pseudoneuropathic, 895
Chondroitin sulfate (CS), in cartilage, 850, 851
Chorea, gait and, 1186–1187
Choreoathetosis, gait and, 1186–1187
Chromium, 55–56
  deficiency of, changes associated with, 55–56
  recommended daily allowance for, 56
  functioning and, 153, 153t
Chronicity, psychopharmacology and, compliance with, 1048
Chronic neuropsychological impairment (*see* Mental retardation)
Chronic obstructive pulmonary disease (COPD), 528–531
  diagnosis of, 529
  epidemiology of, 528
  etiology of, 528–529
  hypercapnic respiratory failure and, secondary to mismatch of ventilation and perfusion, 532
  hypercapnic respiratory failure secondary to, management of, 533–535
  laboratory studies in, 529–530
  pathophysiology and clinical correlates of, 529
  patient approach in, 506
  treatment of, 530–531
  weight loss and, 50
Chronological age, biological age versus, 5–6
Chylomicronemia, pancreatitis and, 642
Chylomicrons, 767
Cigarette smoking (*see* Smoking)
Cimetidine:
  in gastroesophageal reflux disease, 612
  in hypercapnic respiratory failure, 534

Cimetidine (*Cont.*):
  interactions of, 206
  interstitial nephritis and, 572
  peptic ulcer and, 623
Circadian rhythms, desynchronization of, in depression, 1011
Circulation, 445–455, *446*
  cardiovascular response to stress and, 451–455
    beta-adrenergic stimulation and, 453, *454*
    dynamic exercise stress and, *452*, 452–453, *453*
    physical work capacity and, 454–455
    postural stress and, 451
    pressor stress and, 451
  cardiovascular structure and function at rest and, *446*, 446–451, *447*
    afterload and impedance to ejection and, 447–448, *448*, *449*
    contractile behavior of heart and, 448–450, *449*
    coronary flow and, 450
    heart rate and, 446–447
    preload or filling and, 447, *447*
  (*See also* Vascular disorders; *specific disorders*)
Circulatory failure, liver in, 633–634
Cirrhosis, 633
  primary biliary (PBC), 633
Cisapride, in gastric emptying disorders, 625
Citric acid mouthwashes, dry mouth and, in dying patients, 359
CK (*see* Creatine kinase)
Claudication, arteriosclerosis obliterans and, 478–479
Clearance, of lung, 503
Climacteric:
  female, 110
    (*See also* Menopause)
  male, 110
Clindamycin, in bacterial pneumonia, 512
Clinical Dementia Rating Scale, 937
Clinical evaluation, 175–182
  behavior during illness and, 176–177
    patient behavior and, 176
    symptom underreporting and, 176–177
  behavior of disease and, 177–179
    active life expectancy and, 179
    chronicity of disease and, 178
    functional loss and, 178t, 178–179

Clinical evaluation: behavior of disease and (*Cont.*):
multiple disease processes and, 177t, 177–178
relationship of function and disease and, 179
patient examination and, 179–182
history and, 180–181
physical examination and, 181–182
setting for, 179–180
Clinical nurse specialist (CNS), 305–306
CLL (*see* Leukemia, chronic lymphocytic)
Clonidine, menopause and, 786
Clostridium difficile, diarrhea and, 1170–1171
Clotrimazole (Mycelex), oral thrush and, in dying patients, 359
Cluster designation numbers, 66
CMML (*see* Leukemia, chronic myelomonocytic)
CNI (*see* Mental retardation)
CNS (*see* Central nervous system; Clinical nurse specialist)
Coagulability, alterations in, deep venous thrombosis and, 546
Coagulation factor defects:
bleeding disorders due to, 692–698
acquired and complex, 693–698
hereditary, 692–693
Coagulation factor inhibitors:
lupuslike, 694
specific factor, 694
Cobalt, 56
Codeine, 289
pain and, in dying patients, 357
Cogentin (*see* Benztropine)
Cognitive-behavioral therapy, in depression, 1015
Cognitive function, 154, 913–917
age-related changes in, rehabilitation and, 321
attention and, 914
conceptualization and, 916, *916*
disease-related changes in, rehabilitation and, 322
disorder of, in Alzheimer's disease, 935–937, *937*
falls and, 1193
general intelligence and, 916–917, *917*
global disorder of, in delirium, 921–922

Cognitive function (*Cont.*):
language and, 914–915, *915*
memory and, 915–916, *916*
in mental state examination, 1091–1092
methodological issues in study of, 913–914
rehabilitation assessment of, 325
visuospatial ability and, 916
(*See also* Altered mental state)
Cognitive scales, useful in Alzheimer's disease, 936–937
Cohort(s), continuities in life course and, 120–121
Cohort-sequential design, in study of cognitive function, 913
Colace (*see* Dioctyl sodium sulfosuccinate)
Colchicine:
in chondrocalcinosis, 895
in gout, 892
Cold intolerance, in hypothyroidism, 728
Collagen:
in cartilage, 850–851
cross-linking in, 8
Collagenase, pressure ulcers and, 1209
Collagen vascular disorders:
dementia and, 951
interstitial lung disease associated with, 541
Colles' fractures, 92
osteoporosis and, 96
Colon:
cancer of (*see* Cancer, colorectal)
disorders of, surgery for, 265, 265–266
diverticular disease of, 645–648
clinical features of, 646–648
epidemiology and pathogenesis of, 645–646
function of, aging and, 600
Colonic motility test, in constipation, 1163
Colonic transit test, in constipation, 1163
Colonoscopy, in constipation, 1163
Colony-forming unit erythroid (CFU-E), 655, 657–658
Colony-forming unit spleen (CFU-S), 655–656
aging and, 656–657
Colorectal cancer (*see* Cancer, colorectal)
Coma:
myxedema, 728, 730

Coma (*Cont.*):
nonketotic, hyperosmolar, 754–755, 755t
(*See also* Unconsciousness)
Comfort, A., 3
Common bile duct:
aging and, 602
stones in, 636
Communication:
hearing loss and, 433
informed consent and, 370
team approach and, 189
withdrawing or withholding life-sustaining therapies and, 373–374
(*See also* Hearing impairment; Speech)
Community:
long-term care in (*see* Long-term care, community-based)
(*See also* Home; Home care)
Compazine (*see* Prochlorperazine)
Competence, ethical issues related to, 376–377
Complete blood count, lung cancer and, 551
Compliance:
with drug regimens, 202–203
psychopharmacology and, 1048
(*See also* Noncompliance)
"Compositional heterogeneity," of cartilage, 850
Comprehensive functional assessment (CFA), 218–222
in acute care hospital, frail patients and, 251–252
biopsychosocial model and, 218
clinical applications of, 221, 222–223t
cost effectiveness of, 221–222
functional model and, 218–219
definition of function and, 219
usefulness of, 219–220
synthesis of biopsychosocial and functional models in, 220t, 220–221, 221t
Comprehensive Geriatric Model, 79, 80
Compulsions:
in obsessive-compulsive personality disorder, 1039
in mental state examination, 1091
Computed tomography (CT):
in Alzheimer's disease, 1096
dizziness and, 1068

Computed tomography (*Cont.*):
  gait disorders and, 1186
  in head injury, 993
  intracranial neoplasms and, 1006
  in lung cancer, 550
  in neuropsychiatric assessment, 228
  in osteoporosis, 816–818, 817t
  in spine disease, 971, 972
  in stroke, 927–928
  syncope and, 1073
COMT (*see* Catechol-*o*-methyltransferase)
Conceptualization, 916, *916*
Conduction disturbances, syncope and, 1070–1071
Conflict management, team approach and, 189–190
Confusion:
  hip fracture and, 1203
  postoperative:
    premedication and, 275
    prolonged, 274
    relative overdose and, 275
  (*See also* Delirium)
Congestive heart failure (CHF), 469–470
  chronic, liver and, 634
  in hyperthyroidism, 720
  in hypothyroidism, 729
  pathophysiology of, *469*, 469–470
  stroke and, 931
  treatment of, 470
Congo red, amyloid affinity for, 897
Conjugation reactions, hepatic, 604
Conjunctivitis, 424–426
  allergic, 425–426
  bacterial, 425
  inclusion, 425
  viral, 425
Conn's syndrome, 716
Conscientiousness, health status and, 105
Consciousness:
  global disorder of, in delirium, 922
  (*See also* Coma; Unconsciousness)
Consent:
  implied, 363
  informed, 369–370
  withdrawal or changes of, 363
Conservatorships, 366
Constipation, 1161–1167
  analgesics and, 293
  cancer chemotherapy and, 82
  in chronic renal failure, 575
  complications of, 1163–1164

Constipation (*Cont.*):
  definition of, 1161
  in dying patients, 358–359
  evaluation of, 1162
  factors associated with, 1162
  history in, 1162, 1162t
  in hypothyroidism, 729
  laxative use and, 1161
  in Parkinson's disease, 957
  physical examination in, 1162–1163
  special studies in, 1163, *1164*
  treatment of, 1165–1167
    bowel training in, 1165
    diet in, 1165t, 1165–1166
    exercise in, 1165
    laxatives in, 1166–1167
    surgical, 1167
Consultation, anesthesia and, 277–278
"Contingency management techniques," in urinary incontinence, 1138
Continuous ambulatory peritoneal dialysis (CAPD):
  in end-stage renal disease, 578
  morbidity associated with, 579
Continuous cyclic peritoneal dialysis, in end-stage renal disease, 578
Continuous positive airway pressure (CPAP):
  in respiratory failure, 536
  in sleep apnea, 1120
Continuous positive pressure ventilation (CPPV), in respiratory failure, 536
Contractures:
  prevention of, in rheumatoid arthritis, 878
  rehabilitation and, 320
COPD (*see* Chronic obstructive pulmonary disease)
Copper, 56
Core-needle biopsy, in carcinoma of prostate, 586–587
Core rewarming, in hypothermia, 1086
Cornea:
  abrasions of, 426
  edema of, 426
  herpes keratitis and, 426
  ulcers of, 426
Coronary angioplasty, in angina pectoris, 468
Coronary artery disease, 85
  asymptomatic, presentation of, 214
  diagonal earlobe crease and, 397
  exercise in prevention of, 97

Coronary artery disease (*Cont.*):
  hemodialysis and, 578
  presentation of, 213–214
  stroke and, 931
Coronary bypass surgery, in myocardial infarction, 469, 469t
Coronary flow, 450
Coronary heart disease (CHD):
  estrogen and, 132, 784, 784t
  hypertension and, 487
    antihypertensive therapy and, 490–491
    diuretics and, 492–493
  lipoproteins as risk factors for, 768, 769
  personality and, 105
  risk factors for, 129, 129t
  sex differential in longevity and, 41
Corticosteroids:
  adrenal, with intracranial neoplasms, 1007
  in herpes zoster, 1181
  in hypothermia, 1086
  in idiopathic pulmonary fibrosis, 541
  in interstitial lung disease, 542
  in rheumatoid arthritis, 878
  sleep disorders and, 1113
  in tuberculosis, 524
  (*See also* Glucocorticoids; *specific corticosteroids*)
Corticotropin-releasing hormone (CRH):
  in Alzheimer's disease, 708–709
  characterization and actions of, 707
Cortisol, 708
  depression and, 1015
Cost(s):
  of antibiotic therapy, 1059
  defined, 159
  of health care, quality versus, 165
Cost effectiveness, of comprehensive functional assessment, 221–222
"Cotton wool" appearance, in Paget's disease, 845, *845*
Cough:
  in asthma, 527
  in dying patients, 358
Cough reflex, aging and, 503
Cough syncope, 1072
Coumadin (*see* Sodium warfarin)
Council on Gerontological Nursing, 304
Counseling:
  chemical dependency and, 1033
  sexual, 113
Countertransference, psychotherapy and, 1046

Coupling:
  bone density and, 808–810
    pathological impaired coupling and, 808–810, *809*
    physiologically appropriate impaired coupling and, 808
  bone remodeling and, 807–808
Cowdry, E.V., 4
CPAP (*see* Continuous positive airway pressure)
CPPD crystal deposition disease (*see* Chondrocalcinosis)
CPPV (*see* Continuous positive pressure ventilation)
Cranial nerve abnormalities, in stroke, 927
Creatine kinase (CK), in polymyositis/dermatomyositis, 867
Creatinine clearance:
  chronic renal failure and, 577
  fall in, 556–557
Credentialing, of gerontological nurses, 305
Crescendo TIAs, 930
Creutzfeldt-Jakob disease, dementia and, 949
CRH (*see* Corticotropin-releasing hormone)
Crohn's disease, presentation of, 217
Cross-linking theory of aging, 8
Cross-sectional studies, of cognitive function, 913
"Crush type" fractures, osteoporosis and, 96
Crystalline lens, 423
CS (*see* Chondroitin sulfate)
CSF (*see* Cerebrospinal fluid)
CT (*see* Computed tomography)
Cupulolithiasis, of aging, 443
Cushing's syndrome, 716
Cyclophosphamide:
  in chronic lymphocytic leukemia, 674
  in idiopathic pulmonary fibrosis, 541–542
  in peripheral neuropathy, 982
  with primary lymphoma of central nervous system, 1008
  in rheumatoid arthritis, 877–878
Cyst(s), of breast, 794
Cystourethroscopy, benign prostatic hyperplasia and, 585
Cytomegalovirus retinitis, 429, *429*
Cytomel (*see* Triiodothyronine)
Cytopenia, cancer chemotherapy and, 82

Cytosine arabinoside (ara-C):
  combination, 672–673
  with primary lymphoma of central nervous system, 1008

D

Dacryocystitis, acute, 426
Daniels, Norman, on distribution of medical resources, 371
Daunorubicin, in acute myelogenous leukemia, 672–673
Day care, 352
  medical, 352
  social, 352
DCC (*see* Dopa decarboxylase)
Death:
  aesthetic concerns and, 360
  aging and, 5
  bereavement and, 360
  causes of, 6, 72, 92
  confusion among aging and disease and, 5
  distinction between life and, 367–368
  at home, 360
  nocturnal, sudden, 1116–1117
  principal causes of, in elderly, 150, 151t, 152
  probability of, 5
  of spouse, 105
  (*See also* Dying patients; Mortality)
Death rate, decline in, 146, 147
Debrisoquin, drug interactions of, 1050
Decision making:
  dying patients and, 355–356
    artificial feeding and, 356
    resuscitation and, 355
  team approach and, 189
DECO (*see* "Decreasing oxygen consumption hormone")
Deconditioning, rehabilitation and, 329
"Decreasing oxygen consumption hormone" (DECO), 9
Decubitus ulcers (*see* Pressure ulcers)
Deep venous thrombosis (DVT):
  hip fractures and, 1202
  regional versus general anesthesia and, 273–274
Defecation syncope, 1072
Defense mechanisms, psychotherapy and, 1046

Dehydration, 53, 1079
  in hyperosmolar nonketotic coma, 755
  illnesses predisposing to, 1080t, 1080–1082, 1081t
    decreased fluid intake and, 1082
    increased fluid losses and, 1080–1082
  therapy for, 1082–1083
Delayed hypersensitivity skin reaction, assessment of immune function and, 65
Delirium, 920–924, 1094–1095
  course and outcome of, 922–923
  definition of, 920
  diagnosis and differential diagnosis of, 923–924
  disordered sleep-wake cycle in, 922
  disorder of psychomotor behavior in, 922
  etiology of, 923
  features associated with, 922
  frequency and importance of, 920–921
  global disorder of attention and consciousness in, 922
  global disorder of cognition in, 921–922
  management of, 924
  onset of, 921
  pathogenesis of, 923
  physical signs of, 1094
  treatment of, 1095
Delusions:
  in Alzheimer's disease, 936
  in mental state examination, 1091
  paranoid, 1020
  in paraphrenias, 1022
Dementia, 1095–1097
  of Alzheimer type (*see* Alzheimer's disease)
  "atherosclerotic," stroke and, 931
  demyelinating diseases and, 952
  depression and, 1013
  diagnosis of, 1095–1097
  dialysis, 578
  epilepsy and, 952
  head injury and, 952
  Huntington's disease and, 952
  in hypothyroidism, 727
  hysterical, 951
  infectious, 949–950
    in acquired immune deficiency syndrome, 949–950
    brain abscess and, 950

Dementia: infectious (*Cont.*):
in chronic meningitis, 950
viral causes of, 949
Lewy body, 952
mental retardation and, 1028
metabolic, 950–951
exogenous toxins and, 951
metabolic abnormalities and, 951
systemic illness and, 950–951
multi-infarct:
cachexia in, 1103
stroke and, 931
neoplasia and, 952
normal pressure hydrocephalus and, 951–952
in Parkinson's disease, 956
physical signs of, 1096
Pick's disease and, 952
prognosis of, 1096–1097
progressive supranuclear palsy and, 952
psychiatric diseases associated with, 951
rehabilitation and, 322
senile, Alzheimer's type, 29
sleep apnea and, 1117
spinal cerebellar degeneration syndromes and, 952
treatment of, 1096
weight loss and, 51
"Dementia syndrome of depression," 229
Demerol (*see* Meperidine)
Demethylation, liver function and, 604
Demyelinating diseases, dementia and, 952
Denial, psychotherapy and, 1046
Dental caries, 414–415
Dental disease, 196
Dental pulp, 414
Dentin, 414
Dentures, cachexia and, 1104
Deoxyribonucleic acid (DNA):
ability to repair, 7–9
methylation of, 9, 26
Dependence, definition of, 1030
Dependency ratio, demographics of aging and, 148, 148t
Dependent personality disorder, 1039
Deprenyl, in Parkinson's disease, 962
Depression, 1010–1017, 1099
in Alzheimer's disease, 935
bipolar, 1013
atypical, 1013
as cause of malnutrition, 49–50

Depression (*Cont.*):
clinical management of, 1015–1017, 1016t
course and prognosis of, 1015
dementia associated with, 951
diagnosis and differential diagnosis of, 225, 1012–1014t, 1012–1015
in dying patients, 359
endogenous, sleep disorders and, 1112
epidemiology of, 1010–1011
etiology of, 1011–1012
hearing loss and, 433
lithium and, 1050
"masked," 225
melancholic versus nonmelancholic, 1012
menopause and, 781
in Parkinson's disease, 956
psychotic versus nonpsychotic, 1012
rapid cycling, 1012
rehabilitation and, 322
retarded versus agitated, 1012–1013
secondary (symptomatic), 1099–1100
sleep apnea and, 1117
stability of personality and, 104
stroke rehabilitation and, 326
unipolar, 1013
Dermabrasion, actinic keratoses and, 402
Dermal-epidermal cohesion, age-related changes in, 388
Dermatitis, 393
seborrheic, 393, 393, 394, 408
stasis, 407, 407
Dermatomyositis (*see* Polymyositis/dermatomyositis)
Dermis, age-related changes in, 385–387
Dermopathy, in diabetes mellitus, 396
Desalkylflurazepam, hepatic metabolism of, 205
Desensitization, dizziness and, 1068
Desipramine, in depression, 1016
Desmethyldiazepam, hepatic metabolism of, 205
Desoxyribonuclease, pressure ulcers and, 1209
Detrusor hyperreflexia, 1124
Detrusor motor instability, 1124
Development:
adult, psychotherapy and, 1046
gene action and, 25
Development-genetic theories of aging, 8–11

Dexamethasone:
with intracranial neoplasms, 1007
pain and, in dying patients, 357
Dexamethasone suppression test (DST), in depression, 1011, 1015
Dexedrine (*see* Dextroamphetamine sulfate)
Dextrans, platelet function and, 690
Dextroamphetamine sulfate (Dexedrine), 291
Diabetes insipidus:
fluid losses and, 1081
hyperparathyroidism and, 839
Diabetes mellitus, 85, 739–756
acute emergencies in, 754–755
arteriosclerosis obliterans and, 478, 479
treatment of, 480
atherosclerosis and, 462–463
classification of, 745–747
complications of, 748–749
dermopathy in, 396
diagnostic criteria for, 743–744, 744t
fasting plasma glucose and, 744
oral glucose tolerance test and, 744–745, 746
esophagus and, 617
exercise and, 94
gestational, 747
glucose intolerance in older people and, 739–740, 740t
pathophysiology of, 740–742, 741, 742t
implications for older populations, 747–748
impotence and, 1147–1148
insulin-dependent (IDDM), 745–746
management of, 749–754, 750t
compliance to diet and exercise in, 751–752
dietary guidelines for, 750–751
drug therapy in 752t, 752–754
exercise in, 751
non-insulin-dependent (NIDDM), 739
non-insulin-dependent ketosis-resistant, 739
pancreatitis and, 642
peripheral neuropathy and, 980–981
prevalence in older populations, 742–743
retinopathy in, 430, 430
risk of stroke and, 133

Diabetes mellitus (*Cont.*):
  secondary to other diseases or drugs, 747, 747t
  sex differences in longevity and, 43
  skin tags and, 397
  stroke and, 931
  weight loss and exercise and, 93
Diabetic ketoacidosis, 754
Diagnosis-related groups (DRGs):
  infections and, 1059–1060
  rehabilitation and, 315
Diagnostic and Statistical Manual of Mental Disorders, Third Edition, Revised (*DSM III-R*):
  chemical dependency and, 1030
  paraphrenia and, 1019–1024
  personality disorders and, 1036
Dialysis:
  in chronic renal failure, indications for, 577
  in end-stage renal disease, 577–579
  in hypothermia, 1086
  peritoneal, in end-stage renal disease, 578–579
"Dialysis dementia," 578
Diarrhea, 1168–1175
  causes of, 1169–1171, 1170t, *1171*
  as defense against enteric infection, 1172
  host factors in, 1171–1172
  mechanisms of, 1171
  nutritional support and, 300–301
  prevention of, 1174–1175
  scope and nature of problem of, 1168–1169
  treatment of, 1172–1174, 1173t
Diarthroidal joints, aging and, 849–856
  articular cartilage and, 849–855
  meniscus and, 856
  synovial fluid and, 856
  synovial membrane and, 855, 855t
Diazepam (Valium):
  anxiety and, in dying patients, 359
  hepatic metabolism of, 205
  in personality disorders, 1042
  seizures and, 1002
    in dying patients, 359
Diazepines:
  in personality disorders, 1042
  pharmacokinetics of, 225
DIC (*see* Disseminated intravascular coagulation)
Dichloralphenazone, interactions of, 206
D.I.D. (*see* Dyskinesia-improvement-dyskinesia)

Didronel (*see* EHDP)
Diet:
  calcium in, in chronic renal failure, 576
  cancer risk and, 134
  colorectal cancer and, 649
  in constipation, 1165t, 1165–1166
  in diabetes mellitus, 750–751
    compliance with, 751–752
  disease prevention and, 195
  in gastroesophageal reflux disease, 611
  hypertension and, 492
  immune function and, 70
  lipoprotein metabolism and, 96
  monoamine oxidase inhibitors and, 1050
  obesity and, 772–773
  pharmacokinetics and, 206
  phosphorus in, in chronic renal failure, 576
  protein in, in chronic renal failure, 576
  purine free, in gout, 892–893
  sodium in, in chronic renal failure, 575
  vitamins in, in chronic renal failure, 576
Diet history, 181
Diflusinal, 287
DiGeorge syndrome, 70
Digitalis:
  in congestive heart failure, 470
  pharmacokinetics of, 225
Digoxin:
  absorption of, 204
  in antiarrhythmic therapy, 471
  chronic renal failure and, 577
  in congestive heart failure, 470
Di Guglielmo's syndrome, 667
Dilantin (*see* Phenytoin)
Dilaudid (*see* Hydromorphone)
Dioctyl sodium sulfosuccinate (Colace), in constipation, 1166
Diphenhydramine (Benadryl), 1049
  anxiety and, in dying patients, 359
  in chronic gastritis, 620
  oral thrush and, in dying patients, 359
  pruritus and, in dying patients, 359
Diphenoxylate hydrochloride:
  intestinal obstruction and, in dying patients, 358
Diplopia, 422
Dipyridamole:
  myocardial infarction and, 684
  platelet function and, 690

Disability:
  in altered mental states, assessment of, 1090
  community versus institutional living and, 118
  definitions of, 319, 884
  demographics of, 319–320
Discharge planning, hip fractures and, 1203
Disc herniation, acute, 974, *974*
Disease(s):
  behavior of (*see* Behavior, of disease)
  chronic:
    anemia of, 666
    behavior of, 178
    as risk factor for infection, 1057
    confusion among aging and dying and, 5
    contributing to or causing impotence, 1146–1148, 1147t
    education of team members on, 187
    function related to, 179
    medical, gain and, 1189–1190
    occult, laboratory data and, 243–244
    personality disorders and, 1041
    physical, neuropsychiatric assessment and, 226
    predisposing to dehydration, 1080t, 1080–1082, 1081t
      decreased fluid intake and, 1082
      increased fluid losses and, 1080–1082
    presentation of, 212–217
      problems in making diagnoses and, 212–213
    prevention of, 192–198, 194t
      case finding and, 198
      health habits and, 195–196
      primary and secondary, 192, 193, 196–197
      recommendations for, 193–195
      settings and approaches for, 193
      tertiary, 192, 193, 198
    skin and, 396–397, *396–398*
Disease-related changes:
  biological, rehabilitation and, 322
  dizziness and, 1063
  predisposing to syncope, 1069
  psychological, rehabilitation and, 322
  social, rehabilitation and, 322–323
Disequilibrium:
  ampullary, of aging, 443
  definition of, 1062
  macular, of aging, 443

Disodium etidronate, in Paget's disease, 846, 847
Disseminated intravascular coagulation (DIC), 696–698
  diseases associated with, 697
  laboratory diagnosis of, 696–697
  management of, 697–698
  pathogenesis of, 696, *696*
Disulfiram (Antabuse), in alcoholism treatment, 1033
Diuresis, obligate, 1081
Diuretics:
  in chronic renal failure, 575
  in congestive heart failure, 470
  dizziness and, 1065
  drug interactions of, 1051
  in hypercapnic respiratory failure, 534
  hyperkalemia and, 562
  hypertension and, 492–494
  hyperthermia and, 1087
  hypokalemia and, 563
  nutrient interactions of, 58
  urinary incontinence and, 1126
Diverticula:
  epiphrenic, 615
  esophageal, 615
  midthoracic, 615
  traction, 615
  Zenker's, 615
Diverticular disease, 645–648
  aging and, 600
  clinical features of, 646–648
  epidemiology and pathogenesis of, 645–646
  painful, 645
  (*See also specific disorders*)
Diverticulitis, 645
  acute, 1055
  clinical features of, 646–647
  surgery for, 265–266
Diverticulosis, 645
Dizziness, 1062–1068
  age-related changes and, 1063, 1063t
  disease-related changes and, 1063
  epidemiology of, 1062
  etiology of, 1063t, 1063–1066
    multiple pathology in, 1066
    neurologic disorders in, 1063–1066
    psychiatric disease in, 1066
    systemic causes in, 1066
  evaluation of, 1066, *1067*, 1068
  nonspecific, definition of, 1062
  pathophysiology of, 1062–1063
  therapeutic issues in, 1068

DLco (*see* Single-breath carbon monoxide diffusing capacity)
DNA (*see* Deoxyribonucleic acid)
Documentation, of nursing home care, 339–340
Domperidone, in gastric emptying disorders, 625
Donnatal, in chronic gastritis, 620
"Do Nothing" order, 355
"Do Not Resuscitate" (DNR) orders, 355
  decision making regarding, 373–374, *373*–376t
Dopa decarboxylase (DCC), 907
Dopamine, 907–908
  in Parkinson's disease, 958
  regulation of, 705–706
  seizures and, 1002
Dopamine agonists, direct-acting, in Parkinson's disease, 961
Dopaminergic receptors, 907–908
Down's syndrome, 29, 32–33, 1027
  Alzheimer's disease associated with, 939, *939*, 1027
  coexisting medical conditions and, 1028
  life expectancy and, 1027
  relationship with Alzheimer's disease, 901–902
Doxepin:
  in depression, 1016
  pain and, in dying patients, 357
Doxycycline, esophageal injury induced by, 616
DPA (*see* Dual-photon absorptiometry)
Drains, percutaneous placement of, in gallbladder adenocarcinoma, 636
Drooling, in Parkinson's disease, 957
Drowsiness, analgesics and, 292
Drug(s):
  absorption of, 203–204
    psychopharmacology and, 1047
  acute tubular necrosis and, 574
  administration route for, dying patients and, 356
  adverse reactions to, 202
    anorexia and, 50
  causing hypercalcemia, 840
  chronic renal failure and, 577
  in delirium, 924
  depression induced by, 1013
  diet, smoking, and drug interactions and, 206
  distribution of, 204

Drug(s): distribution of (*Cont.*):
    psychopharmacology and, 1047
  dizziness and, 1065
  dosing schedule for, dying patients and, 356
  effects on bone marrow, 669–670
  epidemiology of use of, 201–202
    adverse drug reactions and, 202
    demographic trends and, 201
    patterns of use and prescribing and, 201–202
  esophageal injury induced by, 616
  excretion of, psychopharmacology and, 1048
  expenditures for, 201
  falls and, 1193
  gastroesophageal reflux disease and, 611
  general principles of geriatric prescribing and, 206–209, 207t, 208t
  gynecomastia and, 715
  hepatic injury induced by, 632
  hepatic metabolism of, 205
  hyperkalemia and, 562
  hyperprolactinemia and, 714
  hypersensitivity induced by, tubulointerstitial nephritis and, 571–572
  hypothermia and, 1085
  in hypothyroidism, 730
  influence on laboratory data, 244
  interactions of, 206
    in diabetes mellitus, 750
  interstitial lung disease caused by, 541
  marrow damage caused by, 686t, 686–687
  neuropsychiatric assessment and, 225–226
  pancreatitis and, 642
  patient compliance and, 202–203
  peripheral neuropathy and, 981
  platelet function defects and, 689–690
  psychopharmacology and (*see* Psychopharmacology)
  renal excretion of, 205–206
  sleep disorders and, 1113
  (*See also* Pharmacodynamics; Pharmacokinetics; *specific drugs and drug types*)
Drug addiction:
  characteristics of, 1031–1032
  consequences of, 1033
  treatment of, 1033–1034

Drug history, 181

Drug–nutrient interactions, 57–58

Drug reactions, cutaneous, 397, *398*

Drug therapy:

  in achalasia, 613–614

  in angina pectoris, 467–468

  in depression, 1015–1016, 1016t

  in diabetes mellitus, 752t, 752–754

  in impotence, 1152

  in Paget's disease, 846t, 846–847

  in personality disorders, 1041–1042

  in rheumatoid arthritis, 876

  in urinary incontinence, 1134–1136, 1135t

Dry eyes, 426

Dry mouth, in dying patients, 359

DSM III-R (see Diagnostic and Statistical Manual of Mental Disorders, Third Edition, Revised)

DST (*see* Dexamethasone suppression test)

Dual-photon absorptiometry (DPA), in osteoporosis, 816–818, 817t

Ducolax (*see* Bisacodyl)

Duodenal ulcer, 622

  (*See also* Ulcers, peptic)

Duplex scanning, in impotence, 1151

Durable power of attorney, 355, 365

  for health care, 365, 377

DVT (*see* Deep venous thrombosis)

Dying patients, 354–360

  aesthetic concerns and, 360

  bereavement and, 360

  death at home and, 360

  decision making and, 355–356

    artificial feeding and, 356

    resuscitation and, 355

  designing care for comfort of, 356

  doctor-patient relationship and, 354

  gastrointestinal problems in, 358–359

  genitourinary tract disorders in, 360

  identifying, 354

  medical assessment of, 354

  mental status changes in, 359

  pain in, 356–358, 357t

    adjuvant analgesic drugs and, 357

    narcotics and, 357

    nonnarcotic analgesics and, 356–357

    physical measures and, 357–358

  psychosocial aspects of assessment of, 355

  pulmonary symptoms in, 358

Dying patients (*Cont.*):

  seizures in, 359–360

  skin disorders in, 359

  team approach and, 355

  (*See also* Death)

Dynamic exercise stress, cardiovascular response to, *452*, 452–453, *453*

Dynorphin, anorexia and, 51

Dyschezia, 1162

Dyskinesia, in Parkinson's disease, 961

Dyskinesia-improvement-dyskinesia (D.I.D), in Parkinson's disease, 961

Dysphagia, 1155–1160

  in achalasia, 613

  clinical presentation and classification of, 1155, *1156*

  diagnosis of, 1159–1160

  in diffuse esophageal spasm, 614

  esophageal, 1157–1159

    mechanical obstruction and, 1158–1159

    neuromuscular disorders and, 1159

  in esophageal carcinoma, 616

  in gastroesophageal reflux disease, 609

  importance of, 1155

  oral, 1156

  oropharyngeal, 609, 1155–1157, 1157t

  transfer, 1156

Dyspnea:

  in asthma, 527

  in chronic obstructive pulmonary disease, 529

  in dying patients, 358

  in interstitial lung disease, 542

  patient approach in, 506

  in pulmonary hypertension, 545

Dysproteinemia, 67

Dysthymic disorder, 1015

Dystonia, gait and, 1187

E

Ear:

  external, hearing loss and, 433–434

  inner, hearing loss and, 434–435

  middle, hearing loss and, 434

  (*See also* Hearing aids; Hearing impairment; Vestibular dysfunction)

Earlobe, diagonal crease in, coronary artery disease and, 397

Early life experiences, psychotherapy and, 1045

Eating (*see* Dysphagia; Swallowing)

Eating circumstances, cachexia and, 1104

EBV (*see* Epstein-Barr virus)

Eccrine sweat glands, age-related changes in, 387

ECG (*see* Electrocardiography)

Echocardiography, syncope and, 1073

Economic resources, rehabilitation assessment of, 325

Economic strain, caregiving and, 235

ECT (*see* Electroconvulsive therapy)

Ectropion, 423, *424*

Ecuador, longevity in, 142–144

Edema:

  corneal, 426

  macular, cystoid, 429

Education:

  demographics of aging and, 147

  of gerontological nurses, 304–305

    accreditation of programs and, 305

    generalists and, 304–305

    specialists and, 305

  of team members (*see* Team approach, education of team members and)

EEG (*see* Electroencephalography)

EHDP (Didronel), in osteoporosis, 822

Eighth (VIIIth) nerve function, in hypothyroidism, 728

Ejaculation, 109

  early, impotence and, 1146

Ejection, impedance to, 447–448

Elastic tissue, of dermis, age-related changes in, 385, 385t

Elastin, cross-linking in, 8

Electrocardiography (ECG):

  anesthesia and, 277

  hypothermia and, 1085

  pulmonary embolism and, 546

  syncope and, 1073

Electroconvulsive therapy (ECT):

  in affective disorders, 1099

  in depression, 1016–1017

    secondary, 1099–1100

  in paraphrenias, 1023

Electroencephalography (EEG), 230

  in Alzheimer's disease, 938, 1096

  in delirium, 1094

  dizziness and, 1068

  in herpes simplex encephalitis, 985

Electroencephalography (EEG) (*Cont.*):
  seizures and, 1000
  sleep disorders and, 1111
  syncope and, 1073
Electrolytes:
  in hypercapnic respiratory failure, 534
  renal handling of, hypertension and, 486
  renal, in hypothyroidism, 729
  (*See also* Dehydration)
Electromyography (EMG):
  in impotence, 1151
  in motor neuron diseases, 968
  in peripheral neuropathy, 978
  in polymyositis/dermatomyositis, 867
Electronystagmography (ENG), 442
  dizziness and, 1068
Electrophysiology, cardiac, 230
  in peripheral neuropathy, 978
  syncope and, 1073–1074
EMB (*see* Ethambutol)
Embolectomy, pulmonary, 547
Embolism:
  pulmonary (*see* Pulmonary embolism)
  stroke and, 926
  (*See also* Thromboembolism)
Emmetropia, 431
Emotional disorders:
  altered mental states and, 1098–1100
  mental retardation and, 1028
  (*See also* Psychiatric disorders)
Enalapril, interference with renal autoregulation and, 574
Enamel, 414
Encephalitis, herpes simplex, 985–986
  clinical presentation of, 985
  diagnosis of, 985
  epidemiology of, 985
  pathogenesis of, 985
  therapy of, 986
Endocarditis, infective, 1055
  valvular pathology and, 473
Endocrine system:
  aging of, 705–716, *706*
    growth hormone and, 709–712
    hypothalamic-pituitary-adrenal axis and, *706*, 706–709
    hypothalamic-pituitary-testicular axis and, *712*, 712–713
    neurotransmitter regulation and, 705–706
  disorders of, 713–716

Endocrine system: disorders of (*Cont.*):
    adrenal, 716
    hypothalamic-pituitary, 714–715
    testicular, 715–716
    [*See also* Hormone(s); *specific hormones*]
Endometrial cancer:
  estrogen and, 46, 785, 822
  menopause and, 779
Endophthalmitis, bacterial, 428
End-organ damage, hypertension and, 491
Endoscopic retrograde cholangiopancreatography (ERCP), 640
Endoscopy:
  in constipation, 1163
  in gastroesophageal reflux disease, 611
Endotracheal tube, in hypercapnic respiratory failure, 534
Energy expenditure, for physical activities, 98
ENG (*see* Electronystagmography)
Enteral alimentation (*see* Nutritional support)
Entropion, 423, *423*
Environment:
  of acute care hospital, 248t, 248–249, *249*
  adaptation and, in rehabilitation, 320
  falls and, 1193–1194
    risk factors for, 1197, 1198
  manipulation of, in personality disorders, 1042
  physical, 238
  rehabilitation and, 323
  risk factors for infection in, 1056
  social, 238–239
EPESE (*see* Established Populations for Epidemiologic Studies in the Elderly)
Epidermal-dermal cohesion, age-related changes in, 388
Epidermis, age-related changes in, 383-385
Epidermolysis bullosa, esophagus and, 617
Epilepsy:
  definition of, 999
  dementia and, 952
  primary, 1000
  secondary, 1000
  (*See also* Seizures)
Epinephrine, cardiovascular response to, 453

Epiphrenic diverticulum, 615
Epstein-Barr virus (EBV), in rheumatoid arthritis, 870
Equianalgesic dose, 291
Equipment, for patient examination, 180
ERCP (*see* Endoscopic retrograde cholangiopancreatography)
Erectile capacity, 109
Erection:
  mechanism of, 1149
  (*See also* Impotence)
Error theory of aging, 7–8, 26
Erythrocyte sedimentation rate (ESR):
  in interstitial lung disease, 540
  in polymyalgia rheumatica and giant cell arteritis, 862
Erythromycin:
  in hypercapnic respiratory failure, 534
  in legionellosis, 513
  in pneumonia, 514
Erythropoiesis, ineffective, 666–667
Erythropoietin, 657–658
Escherichia coli, diarrhea and, 1170
Esophageal candidiasis, anorexia and, 50
Esophageal disorders, 609–617
  infectious, 615–616
  motor, 613t, 613–614
    noncardiac chest pain in, 614
  neoplastic, 616–617
  (*See also specific disorders*)
Esophageal dysphagia, 1157–1159
  mechanical obstruction and, 1158–1159
  neuromuscular disorders and, 1159
Esophageal ring, of lower esophagus, 614–615, 1158
Esophageal spasm, diffuse, 614
Esophageal webs, cervical, 614
Esophagus, "nutcracker," 614
ESRD (*see* Renal disease, end-stage)
Essential tremor, in Parkinson's disease, 955
Established Populations for Epidemiologic Studies in the Elderly (EPESE), 153
Estradiol:
  lipoproteins and, 45–46
  menopause and, 777–779
Estrogen (Premarin):
  blood pressure and, 783, 784t
  bone resorption and, 815, 820
  breast disease and, 784, 784t

Estrogen (Premarin) (*Cont.*):
  cachexia and, 1104
  coronary heart disease and, 132, 784, 784t
  endometrial cancer and, 785
  female sexual function and, 111, 112
  gallbladder disease and, 784, 784t
  lipid profiles and, 783–784, 784t
  lipoproteins and, 45–46
  menopause and, 777–779
    hot flushes and, 780–781
  pathological impaired coupling and, 809, *809*
  prostate and, 583
  in urinary incontinence, 1136
  in osteoporosis, 781–783, 782, 782t, 783, 822
Estrogen-receptor-positive breast cancer, 79
Estrone, menopause and, 779
ESWL (*see* Extracorporeal shock wave lithotripsy)
Ethacrynic acid, in chronic renal failure, 575
Ethambutol (EMB), in tuberculosis, 521, 523
Ethanol (*see* Alcohol; Alcoholism)
Ethical issues, 367–377
  equitable distribution of resources and, 370–371
  informed consent and, 369–370
  in institutional setting, 377
  mental incapacitation and, 376–377
  nursing home care and, 346, 346t
  physician values and, 371–372
  reasoning about dilemmas and, 368–369
  withdrawing and withholding life-sustaining procedures and, 372–376
    artificial hydration and nutrition and, 374–376
    CPR and DNR orders and, 373–374, 373–376t
    general recommendations about, 373
Ethopropazine (Parsidol), in Parkinson's disease, 959
Euthanasia:
  active, 372
  passive, 372
Euthyroid hyperthyroxinemia, 723
Euthyroid sick syndrome, 723
  hypothyroidism versus, 731
Evaluation, in nursing process, 308–309

Excretory capacity, laboratory data and, 241–242
Exercise(s), 85–98, *86*
  aerobic (*see* Aerobic exercise; Aerobic exercise capacity)
  in constipation, 1165
  in diabetes mellitus, 749–751
    compliance with, 751–752
  disease prevention and, 195
  dynamic exercise stress and, *452*, 452–453, *453*
  exercise prescription for older people and, 97–98
  free radical theory of aging and, 11
  isometric exercise capacity in elderly and, 91–92
  maximal aerobic capcity in elderly and, *86*, 86–91
  metabolic function in elderly and, 92–97
  in osteoporosis, 823
  pelvic floor, in urinary incontinence, 1136
  in polymyositis/dermatomyositis, 867
  in prevention of coronary artery disease, 97
Exercise capacity, 502–503
  aerobic (*see* Aerobic exercise capacity)
Exercise prescription, for elderly people, 97–98
Exercise studies, in interstitial lung disease, 539
Expenditures:
  defined, 159
  for drugs, 201
  for health care:
    distribution of, 160
    future trend in, 160–161
    increasing, causes of, *159*, 159–160
  [*See also* Cost(s)]
External vacuum devices, in impotence, 1152
Extracellular fluid loss, 54
Extracellular fluid volume, physiologic regulation of, 1079–1080
Extracorporeal shock wave lithotripsy (ESWL), 635
Eye(s), 422–431
  anatomy and physiology of, 423
  dry, 426
  in hyperthyroidism, 720
  optical defects of, 431
  routine examination of, 422–423

Eye(s): routine examination of (*Cont.*):
    by general physician, 422–423
    history in, 422
  (*See also* Visual impairment)
Eye diseases, 423–431
  conjunctival, 424–426
  corneal, 426
  diabetic, 430, *430*
  eyelids and, 423–424, *423–425*
  of lacrimal apparatus, 426
  of orbit, 431
  retinal, *428*, 428–429, *429*
  uveal, 427–428, *428*
  (*See also specific diseases*)
Eyelids, diseases of, 423–424, *423–425*

F

Face sheet, format for, 339, *340*
Facet syndrome, 975
FAD (*see* Familial Alzheimer's disease)
Failure to thrive (*see* Cachexia)
Falls, 1192–1198
  among community-living elderly persons, 1192–1196
    morbidity and, 1192
    prevalence of, 1192
    prevention of, 1194–1196
    risk factors for, 1192–1194
  head injury and, 996
  among institutionalized elderly persons, 1196–1198
    morbidity and, 1197
    prevalence of, 1196–1197
    prevention of, 1197–1198
    risk factors for, 1197
  osteoporosis and, 813–814
  risk factors for, 134
Familial Alzheimer's disease (FAD), 31, 901
Familial cervical lipodysplasia, 29
Familial hypercholesterolemia, 29–30, 43
Family, 232–239
  chemical dependency treatment and, 1034
  doctor's relationship with, 236
  effects of caregiving on, 235–236
  guidance regarding home care and, 317
  impact of behavioral disorders on, 230
  institutionalization and, 238
  interdependence of members of, 233

Family (*Cont.*):
   lack of, 236
   role of, 232–234
   training of, in rehabilitation, 321
   treatment of dementia and, 1096
Family history, paraphrenias and, 1020–1021
Family therapy, 1047
Famotidine:
   in gastroesophageal reflux disease, 612
   peptic ulcer and, 623
Fasciculations, in motor neuron diseases, 968
Fat(s), absorption of, in small intestine, 599
Fatigue:
   menopause and, 781
   (*See also* Cachexia)
Fatty acids, omega-3, arterial thrombosis and, 685
Favre-Racouchot syndrome, 396, *396*
Fears:
   in mental state examination, 1091
   psychopharmacology and, compliance with, 1048
Fecal continence:
   factors aiding, 1143–1144
Fecal impaction:
   constipation and, 1163
   urinary incontinence and, 1125
Fecal incontinence, 1143–1145
   evaluation in, 1144–1145
   treatment of, 1145
Feedback inhibition:
   of adrenocorticotropic hormone, 708
   growth hormone and, 710, 711
   hypothalamic-pituitary-adrenal axis and, 708
   hypothalamic-pituitary-testicular axis and, 712–713
Feeding tubes, gastric placement of, 298
Feet, rheumatoid arthritis in, 873
Felty's syndrome, rheumatoid arthritis and, 875
Females:
   aging, sexuality in, 110–113
   androgen and sexuality in, 112–113
   effects of menopause in, 111
   hormonal factor in sexuality of, 111–113
   ischemic heart disease in, 43
   osteoporosis and, 92, 96
   Pap test in, 77

Females (*Cont.*):
   pathological impaired coupling in, 808–810, *809*
   (*See also* Sex differences)
Fenoprofen, interference with renal autoregulation and, 574
Fertility, decline in, 146
"Fetalization," 25
Fetal substantia nigra implantation, in Parkinson's disease, 963
Fever, infection and, 216, 1057
Fever of undetermined origin (FUO), 1057
FHH (*see* Hypercalcemia, familial hypocalciuria)
Fiber, dietary, 53
   in constipation, 1165
Fibrinogen, in stroke, 932
Fibrin(ogen)olytic degradation products, 689
Fibrinolysin, pressure ulcers and, 1209
Fibrinolytic agents, in venous thrombotic disorders, 702
Fibrosis:
   interstitial, in interstitial lung disease, 538
   pulmonary, idiopathic, 541–542
Filling, left-ventricular, resting, 447, *447*
Filter, venal caval, in venous thrombotic disorders, 703
Fine-needle aspiration, in carinoma of prostate, 587
"First Revolution in Health," 121
Five-factor model of personality, 101–102, 102t, 105
Floaters, 422
Flow cytometers, assessment of immune function and, 66
Fluid(s):
   in hypercapnic respiratory failure, 534
   (*See also* Dehydration)
Fluid intake, decreased, 1082
Fluid losses, in diarrhea, 1168–1169
   oral rehydration therapy and, 1168, 1172–1174
Fluid replacement:
   in hyperosmolar nonketotic coma, 755
   (*See also* Hydration)
5-Fluorouracil, actinic keratoses and, 402, *402*
Flurazepam, anxiety and, in dying patients, 359

FMLP (*see* Formyl-methyl-leucine-phenylalanine)
Focal cognitive syndromes, 1097
Folacin, 56
Folate deficiency, 57
   anemia and, 667
   neutropenia and, 670
Folie à deux, 1039
Follicle-stimulating hormone (FSH):
   hypothalamic-pituitary-testicular axis and, 712
   menopause and, 778
Follicular hyperkeratosis, vitamin A and, 57
Follow-up, neuropsychiatric, 230
Food:
   drug interactions of, 204
   (*See also* Diet; Nutrition)
Food impaction, esophagus and, 617
Food poisoning, diarrhea and, 1170
Foot drop, 1189
Formyl-methyl-leucine-phenylalanine (FMLP), neutrophil function and, 659
Fractures:
   of hip (*see* Hip fractures)
   in osteoporosis, 815–816
      diagnostic evaluation of, 819
   osteoporosis and, 92, 96
   risk factors for, 134–135
   spinal compression, treatment of, 819–820
   (*See also* Osteoporosis)
Frailty, acute hospital care and, 247–252
   cascade of illness and functional decline and, 249–251, *250*
   description of frail patient and, 247–248
   prevention of iatrogenesis and, 251–252
   treatment and environment and, 248t, 248–249, *249*
Francis Scott Key Medical Center, community-based long-term care services at, 351
FRC (*see* Functional residual capacity)
Freeman, Joseph, 3
Free radical theory of aging, 10–11
Friction, pressure ulcers and, 1205–1206
Friedländer's pneumonia, 511
FSH (*see* Follicle-stimulating hormone)
Function:
   definition of, 219

Function (*Cont.*):
 functional loss and, 178t, 178–179
Functional decline, in acute care hospital, frail patients and, 249–251, *250*
Functional model, for patient assessment, 218–219
 synthesis with biopsychosocial model, 220t, 220–221, 221t
Functional outcome, predicting, 1212–1220
 in older individuals, 1214–1219
 in populations of elderly persons, 1212–1214
Functional residual capacity (FRC), aging and, 500
Functioning, 153–154
 chronic conditions and, 153, 153t
 cognitive, 154
 in neuropsychiatric assessment, 230
 physical, 153–154
 relationship of disease and, 179
 (*See also* Comprehensive functional assessment)
Fundamentalist theories of aging, 3
Funduscopic examination, 182
FUO (*see* Fever of undetermined origin)
Furosemide:
 in chronic renal failure, 575
 dizziness and, 1065

G

GABA (*see* Gamma aminobutyric acid)
GAD (*see* Glutamic acid decarboxylase)
GAG (*see* Glycosaminoglycans)
Gait:
 hysterical, 1190
 observing, falls and, 1196
 in Parkinson's disease, 956
 senile, 1187–1188
Gait disorders, 1183–1190
 examination of station and gait in, 1184–1185
 gait mechanisms and, 1183–1184
 neurologic, 1185–1189
 nonneurologic, 1189–1190
 normal senescence and, 1184
 pyramidal, 1188
Galen, 3
Gallbladder, aging and, 602–603, 634–637
 acute cholecystitis and, 635

Gallbladder, aging and (*Cont.*):
 adenocarcinoma and, 636–637
 choledocholithiasis and, 635–636
 cholelithiasis and, 634
 silent gallstones and, 634–635
Gallbladder disease, estrogen and, 784, 784t
Gallium 67 lung scan, in interstitial lung disease, 540, 542
Gallstones, 634–636
 choledocholithiasis and, 635–636
 pancreatitis and, 641
 silent, 634–635
Gamma aminobutyric acid (GABA), 908
Gastrectomy, gastric emptying disorders following, 624
Gastric acid output, aging and, 596
Gastric disorders, surgery for, 264–265
Gastric emptying:
 aging and, 595–596, *596*
 disorders of, 624–625
 clinical concerns in, 624
 treatment of, 624–625
Gastric function, aging and, 595–597, *596*
Gastric lavage, in hypothermia, 1086
Gastric mucosa, aging and, 597
Gastric stasis syndromes, 624
Gastric ulcer, 622
 surgery for, 264
 (*See also* Peptic ulcers)
Gastrin, serum levels of, aging and, 596–597
Gastritis, 619–621
 acute, 619–620
 atrophic, 597
 chronic, 620–621
 antral, 620
 clinical concerns in, 620
 complications of, 621
 fundal, 620
 treatment of, 620–621
 hypertrophic, 621
Gastroesophageal reflux, 609–613, 1159
 complications of, 612–613
 diagnosis of, *610*, 610–611
 24-hour pH monitoring in, 611
 acid perfusion test in, 610
 barium esophagram in, 610
 endoscopy with biopsies in, 611
 esophageal manometry in, 611
 pathophysiology of, 609
 symptoms of, 609–610

Gastroesophageal reflux (*Cont.*):
 treatment of, 611t, 611–612
 antacids and alginic acid in, 611–612
 histamine-H$_2$ blockers in, 612
 lifestyle modifications in, 611
 promotility drugs in, 612
 sucralfate in, 612
 surgical, 612
Gastrointestinal disorders:
 bleeding and, 625–626
 hyperparathyroidism and, 839
 in hyperthyroidism, 720
 in hypothyroidism, 729
 (*See also specific disorders*)
Gastrointestinal system:
 aging of, 593–604, 594t
 anorectal function and, 600–601, 601
 colonic function and, 600
 gastric function and, 595–597, *596*
 hepatobiliary function and, 602–604, *603*
 pancreatic function and, 601–602
 pharyngoesophageal function and, 593–595
 small-intestinal function and, 597–600
 fluid losses from, 1081–1082
 in Parkinson's disease, 957
Gastroparesis, 624
Gastrostomy, 299
GAUs (*see* Geriatric assessment units)
GCA (*see* Giant cell arteritis)
GCS (*see* Glasgow Coma Scale)
Gene(s):
 cancer suppressor, 75
 "longevity assurance," 5, 25–26
 longevity-determinant, 20
Gene action, aging and, 25–26
Gene expression, in cerebral amyloid and Alzheimer's disease, 901–902
General Health Questionnaire (GHQ), 1092
Genetic factors:
 aging and, 22–26
 development-genetic theories of, 8–11
 amyloid and, 897–898
 bone density and, *810*, 810–811
 in diabetes mellitus, 741–742
 osteoarthritis and, 883
Genetic loci, number involved in human aging, 23–24

Genetic polymorphisms, heritability of longevity and, 23

Genetic syndromes, modulating aspects of senescent phenotype, 26–32

Genital examination, 182

Genital vasocongestion, assessment of, 108

Genitourinary system, in Parkinson's disease, 957

Gentamicin:
    dizziness and, 1065
    pressure ulcers and, 1209

Geographic distribution, demographics of aging and, 149–150

Geriatric assessment units (GAUs), 220

Geriatrician, 324
    complex roles of, 190
    role of, overlap with physiatrist's role, 323

Geriatrics:
    definition of, 4n
    preventive, preventive gerontology distinguished from, 170
    stability of personality and, 104

Germ line, 22

Gerontological nurse practitioners (GNP), in primary care, 307

Gerontological nursing, 304–310
    in acute care, 305–306
    ancillary personnel and, 309–310
    credentialing and, 305
    education for, 304–305
        generalist and, 304–305
        specialist and, 305
    history of, 304
    in home care, 307
    interdisciplinary collaboration and, 310
    in long-term care, 306
    nursing process and, 308–309
    in primary care, 306–307
    standards of care and, 309
    supply and demand for, 307–308

Gerontology:
    definition of, 4n
    preventive (see Preventive gerontology)
    stability of personality and, 104

Gerontology Research Center, 4

GF (see Growth factors)

GFR (see Glomerular filtration rate)

GH (see Growth hormone)

GHQ (see General Health Questionnaire)

GHRH (see Growth hormone-releasing hormone)

Giant cell arteritis (GCA), 861–863
    clinical features of, 861–862
    differential diagnosis of, 862–863
    pathogenesis of, 863
    pathology and laboratory features of, 862
    treatment and course of, 863

Gingival disease, mental retardation and, 1028

Gingivitis, 414

Glasgow Coma Scale (GCS), 993, 996

Glaucoma, 427, 427
    open-angle, 427
    primary angle-closure, 427

Glioblastoma multiforme, 1005

Gliomas:
    low-grade, treatment of, 1008
    malignant, 1005
        brain imaging and, 1006
        clinical presentation of, 1005
        treatment of, 1008

Global Assessment Scale, 1014

Globulins, elevation of, 243–244

Globus hystericus, 1155

Glomerular diseases, 567–570
    clinical presentation of, 568
    prevalence of, 567–568
    (See also specific diseases)

Glomerular filtration, nutritional support and, 300

Glomerular filtration rate (GFR), aging changes in, 556–557

Glomerulonephritis:
    acute, 568t, 568–569
        clinical manifestations of, 568–569
        diagnosis of, 569
        pathologic findings in, 569
        prognosis of, 569
        treatment of, 569
    membranous, prognosis of, 570
    minimal-change, prognosis of, 570

Glucocorticoids:
    control of adrenocorticotropic hormone by, 708
    excess of, 716
    in minimal-change glomerulonephritis, 570
    in peripheral neuropathy, 982
    in polymyositis/dermatomyositis, 867
    secretion of, aging and, 708
    in subacute thyroiditis, 734–735

Glucose:
    metabolism of:

Glucose: metabolism of (Cont.):
        aging and physical activity and, 93–94, 94, 95
        decline in, 92
    plasma, fasting levels of, 744

Glucose clamp technique, 740–741

Glucose intolerance, 739–747, 740t
    pathophysiology of, 740–742, 741, 742t
    (See also Diabetes mellitus)

Glucose threshold, renal, 557

Glucose tolerance:
    nutritional support and, 300
    (See also Glucose intolerance)

Glucose tolerance test:
    intravenous (IVGTT), 745
    oral (OGTT), 744–745, 746
    in older populations, 740

Glucose transport, renal, 557

Glutamic acid decarboxylase (GAD), 908

Glutethimide, interactions of, 206

Glycerine, dry mouth and, in dying patients, 359

Glycoproteins, platelet adhesion and, 679–680

Glycopyrrolate, premedication with, surgery and, 275

Glycosaminoglycans (GAG), in cartilage, 850, 851

GNP (see Gerontological nurse practitioners)

GnRH (see Gonadotropin-releasing hormone)

Goiter, 732–734
    differential diagnosis of, 733
    diffuse (simple), 732–733
    multinodular, carcinoma in, 734
    recognition of, 733
    treatment of, 733–734

Gold salts:
    interstitial lung disease caused by, 541
    in rheumatoid arthritis, 877

Golytely (see Polyethylene glycol)

Gonadal failure, 715

Gonadal hormones, hypothalamic-pituitary-testicular axis and, 712

Gonadotropin-releasing hormone (GnRH), hypothalamic-pituitary-testicular axis and, 712, 713

Gout, 889–893
    chondrocalcinosis differentiated from, 893–894
    classification of, 892–893

Gout (*Cont.*):
 diagnosis of, 891
 disorders associated with, 890–891
 hyperuricemia and, 890
 treatment of, 892
Graft-versus-host disease, esophagus and, 617
Gram-negative bacilli, pneumonia and, 511
Granulocytes, immune function and, 61, 63–64, 68
Granulocytic leukemia, chronic (CGL), 675–676
Granulovacuolar degeneration, in Alzheimer's disease, 941
Graves' disease:
 antithyroid drugs in, 725
 presentation of, 215
Greenfield filter, pulmonary embolism and, 547
Group therapy, 1047
Growth factors (GF), osteoblasts and, 804
Growth hormone (GH), 709–712
 aging and, 710
 cachexia and, 1104
 characterization and actions of, 709, *709*
 feedback inhibition and, 710, 711
 neurotransmitter control of, 709–710
 peripheral effects and, 711
 physiologic secretion of, 709, 710
Growth hormone-releasing hormone (GHRH):
 hypothalamus and, 710
 pituitary responsiveness to, 711
Guaifenesin syrup, cough and, in dying patients, 358
Guanethidine, drug interactions of, 1050
Guardian ad litem, 366
Guardianships, 366
Guillain-Barré syndrome, 979–980
Gynecomastia, 715

H

H$_2$ blockers:
 in gastroesophageal reflux disease, 612
 peptic ulcer and, 623
HA (*see* Hyaluronate)
"Habit retraining," in urinary incontinence, 1138

Haemophilus influenzae, bacterial meningitis and, 983
 pneumonia and, 512
Hair:
 age-related changes in, 387
 graying of, 385, 393
 premature, 396
 growth of, 387
 menopause and, 780
Hairy cell leukemia, 675
Haldol (*see* Haloperidol)
Hallucinations:
 in Alzheimer's disease, 936
 in dying patients, 359
 in mental state examination, 1091
 in paranoia, 1020
 in paraphrenias, 1022
 in Parkinson's disease, 956
Haloperidol (Haldol):
 in Alzheimer's disease, 943
 in delirium, 924
 hallucinations and, in dying patients, 359
 nausea and vomiting and, in dying patients, 358
 pain and, in dying patients, 357
Halothane, hepatotoxicity of, 632
Hamilton Depression Rating Scale, 1098, 1014
Hand(s), rheumatoid arthritis in, 873
Handicap, definition of, 319, 884
Hardy-Weinberg equation, heritability of longevity and, 23
"Hayflick Limit," 25
HCG (*see* Human chorionic gonadotropin)
HCM (*see* Hypertrophic cardiomyopathy)
HDL [*see* Lipoprotein(s), high-density]
Head, in physical examination, 182
Head injury, 990–997
 cervical spine injuries associated with, 996
 chronic subdural hematoma and, 992–993
 clinical pathology of, 991–992
 dementia and, 952
 epidemiology of, 990–991, *991*, *992*
 evaluation and treatment of, 995–996
 minor, 993–995
 outcome of, 993–995, *993–995*, 996t
 mortality and, 990, 994–995, *995*

Health:
 caregiving and, 235
 education of team members on, 186–187
 rehabilitation assessment of, 325
 self-perception of, 176
Health behavior, sex differential in longevity and, 40
Health care:
 allocation of, 165
 cost-quality trade-offs and, 165
 costs of, 159–161
 causes of increasing expenditures and, *159*, 159–160
 distribution of expenditures and, 160
 future trend in, 160–161
 durable power of attorney for, 365
 financing of, *161*, 161–164
 personnel and organization of, 164–165
 preventive (*see* Disease, prevention of)
 program development and, 190
 quality of, 165
 service provision and, education of team members on, 187
Health care utilization, 157–159, *158*, 158t
Health expectancy, 117
Health habits, disease prevention and, 195–196
 alcohol abuse and, 195–196
 diet and, 195
 exercise and, 195
 sleep and, 196
 smoking and, 195
Health promotion [*see* Disease(s), prevention of]
Hearing aids, 438–441, *439*
 behind-the-ear, 439, *439*
 body, *439*, 440
 candidacy for, 440
 eyeglass, 439, *439*
 in-the-canal, *439*, 440
 in-the-ear, *439*, 439–440
 prognostic factors for, 440–441
Hearing Handicap Inventory for the Elderly (HHIE), 436
Hearing impairment, 432–442
 anatomic-physiologic correlates of, 433–435
 external ear and, 433–434
 inner ear and, 434–435
 middle ear and, 434

Hearing impairment (*Cont.*):
  clinical evaluation of, 435–438
    audiologic, 436–437, *437*
      audiologic test interpretation and, 437–438
      identification of hearing loss and, 435–436, *436*
    conductive, 437, *438*
    general considerations in, 432–433
    history taking and, 212
    in hypothyroidism, 728
    mental retardation and, 1028
    mixed, 438, *439*
    patient examination and, 180
    prevention of, 197
    psychosocial implications of, 433
    rehabilitation of, 438–442
      assistive listening devices and, 441–442
      hearing aid amplification and, 438–441, *439*
      speech reading/auditory training and, 441, 441t
    sensorineural, 437, *438*
Heart attacks, as cause of death, 92
Heartburn, in gastroesophageal reflux disease, 609
Heart, contractile behavior of, 448–450, *449*
Heart disease, 466–473
  amyloid, 900–901
  as cause of death, 152
  electrical, syncope and, 1070–1071
  electrophysiology and, 470–472, 471t
  ischemic, 466–467, *467*, 467t
  structural, syncope and, 1070
  valvular, 472–473
    aortic valve and, 472–473
    atrial septal defect and, 473
    mitral valve and, 472
  (*See also specific disorders*)
Heart murmurs, aortic valve disease and, 473
Heart rate:
  exercise and, 97, 98
  resting, 446–447
  syncope and, 1069
Heat intolerance, in hyperthyroidism, 719
Heatstroke (*see* Hyperthermia)
Heavy-chain disease, 67
Height, as nutritional indicator, 49
Height-weight tables, age-specific, 759–765

Height-weight tables, age-specific (*Cont.*):
  analysis of actuarial data and, 762–764, *763*, *764*, 764t
  computation of body mass index and, 760
  distribution of body fat and, 764–765
  effect of body weight on mortality and, 760–762
  standards of normal weight and, 759–760
Hematological disorders, in hypothyroidism, 729–730
Hematoma:
  epidural, head injury and, 992
  intraparenchymal, head injury and, 992
  subdural, head injury and, 992–993
Hematopoietic system, aging of, 655–660
  colony-forming unit spleen and, 656–657
  in humans, 658, 658t, *659*
  in mice, 657–658
  neutrophil function in humans and, 658–660, *660*
  normal bone marrow function and, 655–657, *656*
Hemiparesis, in stroke, 927
Hemiplegia, gait and, 1188
Hemochromatosis, in cirrhosis, 633
Hemodialysis, in end-stage renal disease, 578
Hemodynamic function:
  hypertension and, 486
  isometric exercise and, 92
  regional versus general anesthesia and, 273
Hemoglobin, glycosylated, in diabetes mellitus, 745
Hemophilia, 692
  diagnosis of, 693
  management of, 693
Hemorrhage:
  gastrointestinal, surgery for, 264
  intracerebral, 929
  in stroke, 929, 929t
  subarachnoid, 929
Hemostatic plug formation (*see* Platelets, hemostatic plug formation and)
Heparin:
  in disseminated intravascular coagulation, 698
  platelet function and, 690
  pulmonary embolism and, 546–547

Heparin (*Cont.*):
  in stroke, 928–929
  in venous thrombotic disorders, 700–703
Hepatic enzymes, "protective," 604
Hepatic triglyceride lipase (HTGL), 45–46
Hepatitis:
  alcoholic, 632
  chronic, 633
    active (CAH), 633
    viral, 633
  isoniazid, 632
  non-A, non-B, 633
  viral, 632–633
Hepatitis B, 633
Hepatobiliary disorders, 631–637
  gallbladder and biliary tract aging and, 634–637
  hepatic aging and, 631–634
  (*See also* Biliary tract; Gallbladder; Liver)
Hepatobiliary function, aging and, 602–604, *603*
Hereditary amyloidosis, 30–31
Hereditary diseases, gout and, 890
Hereditary keratitis, 426
Herpes simplex:
  dementia caused by, 949
  differential diagnosis of, *1179*, 1179–1180
  esophageal, 616
Herpes simplex encephalitis (*see* Encephalitis, herpes simplex)
Herpes zoster infection, 1056, 1177–1181
  clinical features of, 1177–1179, *1178*, *1179*
  cutaneous, 406
  differential diagnosis of, *1179*, 1179–1180
  histopathology of, 1180, *1180*
  ophthalmic, 1178
  sequelae of, 1180
  treatment of, 1180–1181
  of trigeminal nerve, 1178
Heterogameticity, 24
HHIE (*see* Hearing Handicap Inventory for the Elderly)
5-HIAA (*see* 5-Hydroxyindolacetic acid)
High-density lipoproteins (HDL), 43–46, 53
  aging, physical activity, and metabolism of, 94–96
  as risk factor, 130

Hip dislocation, mental retardation and, 1028
Hip fractures, 92, 1200–1203
  anatomy and, 1200
  etiology of, 1200–1201, 1201t
  extracapsular, 1200
  medical management of, 1201–1203
    complications and, 1202t, 1202–1203
    discharge planning for, 1203
  mortality and, 316
  rehabilitation and, 315–317, 327
  subcapital, 1200
  surgical management of, 1201
Hippocampus, control of adrenocorticotropic hormone by, 708
Hirano body, in Alzheimer's disease, 941
History, 180–181
  barriers to eliciting, 212
  in constipation, 1162, 1162t
  diet, 181
  dizziness and, 1066
  drug, 181
  in impotence, 1149–1150
  in neuropsychiatric assessment, 226–227
  occupational, in interstitial lung disease, 541
  of pain complaints, 284
  psychiatric, taking of, 1089–1090
  in routine eye examination, 422
  sexual, 181
  sleep disorders and, 1117t, 1117–1118
  social, 180–181
  syncope and, 1072
Histrionic personality disorder, 1038
HIT (*see* Holtzman Inkblot Technique)
Hoarseness, in pulmonary hypertension, 545
Hodgkin's disease:
  chemotherapy in, 81
  incidence of, 73–74
Holtzman Inkblot Technique (HIT), personality disorders and, 1040
Home:
  dying in, 360
  rehabilitation in, 324
Home care:
  definition of, 349
  of frail elderly, 349–350
  gerontological nurses in, 307
  following rehabilitation, 317
Home health care agencies, rehabilitation provided by, 315

Home modification, 323
Homeostasis, laboratory data and, 242
Homogameticity, 24
  sex differences in longevity and, 25
Homovanillic acid (HVA), in Parkinson's disease, 958
Hordeolum, 424
Hormonal therapy for cancer, 81–82
  of prostate, 589
Hormone(s):
  adrenal, 708
  benign prostatic hyperplasia and, 583–584
  bone resorption and, 814–815
  cachexia and, 1104
  calcium metabolism and, 801–803
  "decreasing oxygen consumption," 9
  ectopic production in association with neoplasms, weight loss and female sexuality and, 111–113
  gonadal, hypothalamic-pituitary-testicular axis and, 712
  laboratory data and, 242
  pituitary, neuroendocrine theory of aging and, 9
  sex (*see* Sex hormones)
  (*See also* Corticosteroids; Glucocorticoids; Steroids; *specific hormones*)
Hormone replacement therapy, in testicular disorders, 715–716
Hospice care, 354
Hospitals:
  acute:
    interface with nursing homes, 344–346
    rehabilitation in, 314–315, 317, 324
  physician's role in, 237
  pressure ulcers and, 1204–1205
  rehabilitation, 314–315, 324
    specialization in, 324
  urinary incontinence and, 1125
Host defense system (*see* Immunology; Immune system)
Host factors:
  diarrhea and, 1171–1172
  falls and, 1194
  as risk factors for infection, 1056–1057
    aberration of host defense mechanism and, 1057
    chronic defenses and, 1057
    physiologic changes of aging and, 1056–1057

Hot flush, menopause and, 780
  estrogen treatment of, 780–781
Housing, 238–239
HPA (*see* Hypothalamic-pituitary-adrenal axis)
HPRT (*see* Hypoxanthine guanine phosphoribosyltransferase)
HTGL (*see* Hepatic triglyceride lipase)
Human chorionic gonadotropin (HCG), in impotence, 1147
Humoral immunity, aging and, 503
"Hungry bones" (*see* Osteitis fibrosa cystica)
Huntington's disease, 31, 952
  depression in, 1099
Hutchinson-Guilford syndrome, 25, 27–28
Hutchinson's sign, 1178
HVA (*see* Homovanillic acid)
Hyaluronate (HA), in cartilage, 850, 851
Hydralazine:
  in hypertension, 494
  nutrient interactions of, 57
Hydration:
  artificial, ethical issues related to, 374–376
  in constipation, 1165–1166
  oral rehydration therapy and, 1168, 1169, 1172–1174
Hydrazine, in cancer cachexia, 1105
Hydrocephalus, normal pressure:
  dementia and, 951–952
  gait and, 1185–1186
Hydrocodeine syrup, cough and, in dying patients, 358
Hydromorphone (Dilaudid), pain in, in dying patients, 357
Hydroxychloroquine, in rheumatoid arthritis, 877–878
5-Hydroxyindolacetic acid (5-HIAA), in Parkinson's disease, 958
Hydroxyproline, urinary excretion of, in Paget's disease, 846
Hydroxyzine (Atarax; Vistaril), 291, 1049
  anxiety and, in dying patients, 359
  pain and, in dying patients, 357
  pruritus and, in dying patients, 359
Hyperactivity, in delirium, 922
Hyperalphalipoproteinemia:
  familial, 773
  neonatal, 32
Hypercalcemia:
  in chronic renal failure, 576

Hypercalcemia (*Cont.*):
  differential diagnosis of, 840, 840t
  familial hypocalciuria (FHH), 840
Hypercalcemic crisis, 841
Hypercalcemic nephropathy, 572
Hypercalciuria, in osteomalacia, 832
Hypercapnia, respiratory failure and
    (*see* Respiratory failure, hyper-
    capnic)
Hypercholesterolemia:
  atherosclerosis and, 460
  diagnosis of, 773, 774t
  familial, 29–30, 43
  management of, 773–775, 775t
Hyperglycemia, 748
  atherosclerosis and, 460, 462–463
  chromium deficiency and, 55–56
  stroke and, 928
Hyperinflation, in asthma, 527
Hyperinsulinemia, postprandial, aging
    and, 139
Hyperkalemia, 558, 562
  in chronic renal failure, 575–576
Hyperkeratosis, follicular, vitamin A
    and, 57
Hyperkinesias, gait and, 1186–1187
Hyperlipidemia, 773–775
  atherosclerosis and, 460–461, 463
  pancreatitis and, 641–642
  weight loss and exercise and, 93
Hyperlipoproteinemia, pancreatitis
    and, 642
Hypernatremia, water metabolism
    and, 561–562
Hyperopia, 431
Hyperparathyroidism, 837–841
  background of, 837
  in chronic renal failure, 576
  dementia and, 951
  diagnosis of, 839–840
  differential diagnosis of, 840, 840t
  etiology and pathology of, 837–838
  signs and symptoms of, 838, 838–
    839, 839
  therapy of, 840–841
Hyperphosphatemia, in chronic renal
    failure, 575
Hyperplasia, in hyperparathyroidism,
    837, 838
Hyperprolactinemia, 714–715
Hypersensitivity, drug-induced, tubu-
    lointerstitial nephritis and, 571–
    572
Hypersensitivity pneumonitis, 542–
    544, 543t

Hypersensitivity pneumonitis (*Cont.*):
  clinical features of, 543
  diagnosis of, 544
  therapy and prognosis of, 544
Hypertension, 485–494
  atherosclerosis and, 460, 462
  diagnostic approach to, 491–492
  in hypothyroidism, 729
  impotence and, 1148
  isolated systolic (ISH), 485
    efficacy of antihypertensive ther-
      apy in, 490
  malignant, in renal atheroembolic
    diseases, 566
  perioperative, anesthesia and, 275,
    275–276
  physiology of, 485–486, 487t
  prevalence and risk for, 486–487
  prevention of, 197
  pulmonary (*see* Pulmonary hyper-
    tension)
  in renal atheroembolic diseases, 566
  in renal thromboembolic disorders,
    566
  in renovascular disease, 565
  as risk factor, 130–131
  stroke and, 132–133, 928
  syncope and, 1069
  systolic-diastolic (SDH), 485
    efficacy of antihypertensive ther-
      apy in, 489t, 489–490, 490t
  therapy in, 492–494
    angiotensin converting enzyme
      inhibitors in, 493
    beta-blockers in, 493
    calcium channel blockers in, 493
    coronary heart disease and, 490–491
    diuretics in, 492–493
    efficacy of, 488–491
    isolated systolic hypertension and,
      490
    risk/benefit ratio of, 487–488
    systolic-diastolic hypertension
      and, 489t, 489–490, 490t
Hyperthermia, 1086–1087
  clinical presentation of, 1087
  epidemiology of, 1086
  pathophysiology of, 1086–1087
  treatment of, 1087
Hyperthyroidism, 719–726
  apathetic, 723–724
  "apathetic," presentation of, 215
  dementia and, 951
  due to toxic adenoma, radioactive
    iodide therapy of, 725–726

Hyperthyroidism (*Cont.*):
  incidence in elderly, 719
  iodide-induced thyrotoxicosis and,
    724
  laboratory tests in diagnosis of, 720–
    722
    general, 720–721
    radioiodide uptake, 722
    results of, 722–723
    standard thyroid function tests
      and, 721
    TSH and TRH, 721–722
  lympocytic "silent" or "painless"
    thyroiditis and, 724
  masked, 723
    presentation of, 215
  presentation of, 215
  symptoms and signs of, 719–720
    cardiac, 720
    constitutional, 719
    gastrointestinal, 720
    neuromuscular, 719–720
    ocular, 720
    thyroid, 720
  therapy of, 724–726
    adjunctive therapy with β-
      blockers and iodide in, 725
    radioactive iodide in, 725–726
    thioamide antithyroid drugs in,
      725
  weight loss and, 50
Hyperthyroxinemia, euthyroid, 723
Hypertriglyceridemia, 775
  atherosclerosis and, 460
  pancreatitis and, 642
Hypertrophic cardiomyopathy (HCM),
    syncope and, 1070
Hyperuricemia, gout and, 890
Hypnotics:
  depression and, 1013
  sleep disorders and, 1113
Hypoactivity, in delirium, 922
Hypoaldosteronism:
  in chronic renal failure, 575
  fluid losses and, 1081
Hypobetalipoproteinemia, familial, 773
  neonatal, 32
Hypocalcemia:
  in osteomalacia, 828
  vitamin D therapy and, in osteoma-
    lacia, 836
Hypochlorite, pressure ulcers and,
    1209
Hypochondriasis, 105
  depression and, 1013–1014

Hypodipsia, 53–54
Hypoglycemia:
  hypothermia and, 1084
  sulfonylureas and, 753
  syncope and, 1068
Hypoglycemic agents, oral, in diabetes mellitus, 752
Hypogonadism:
  impotence and, 1147–1148
  treatment of, 1152
Hypokalemia, 558, 562–563
Hyponatremia:
  nutritional support and, 300
  water metabolism and, 561
Hypoparathyroidism:
  dementia and, 951
  permanent, 841
Hypoperfusion, renal, acute tubular necrosis and, 574
Hypophosphatemia, in osteomalacia, 830, 832, 833
Hypopituitarism, 714
"Hypostatic pneumonia," 513
Hypotension:
  in acute tubular necrosis, 574
  dizziness and, 1066
  orthostatic, syncope and, 1071
  postoperative renal failure and, anesthesia and, 276t, 276–277
  postprandial, syncope and, 1071
  postural, in pure autonomic failure, 965
  regional anesthesia and, 273
Hypothalamic dysfunction, hypothermia and, 1085
Hypothalamic-pituitary-adrenal (HPA) axis, 706, 706–709
  adrenocorticotropic hormone and, 707–708
    characterization and actions of, 707
    feedback inhibition and, 708
    neurotransmitter control of, 707
    physiologic secretion of, 707
  aging and, 708–709
  corticotropin-releasing hormone and, 707
  in depression, 1011
  neuroendocrine theory of aging and, 8–9
Hypothalamic-pituitary-testicular axis, 712, 712–713
  aging and, 713
  feedback inhibition and, 712–713
  gonadotropin-releasing hormone and, 712

Hypothalamic-pituitary-testicular axis (Cont.):
  gonadotropins and gonadal hormones and, 712
  neurotransmitter control and, 712
Hypothermia, 1084–1086
  clinical presentation of, 1085
  epidemiology, 1084
  pathophysiology of, 1084–1085
  postoperative, anesthesia and, 276
  treatment of, 1085–1086
Hypothyroidiśm, 726–733
  ablation-related, 726
  causes of, 726
  clinical presentation of, 727
    in young versus elderly individuals, 727–730
  dementia and, 951
  depression and, 1013
  euthyroid sick syndrome versus, 731
  hyperprolactinemia and, 714
  laboratory diagnosis of, 730–731
    TSH elevation and, 730–731
  myxedema versus, 727
  peripheral neuropathy and, 981
  presentation of, 214–215
  therapy of, 731–733
    follow-up of, 726
Hypovolemic shock, diabetic ketoacidosis and, 754
Hypoxanthine guanine phosphoribosyltransferase (HPRT), Lesch-Nyhan disease and, 890
Hypoxemia:
  in chronic obstructive pulmonary disease, 530
  in hypercapnic respiratory failure, 532
  syncope and, 1068
Hypoxia, respiratory failure and, 535t, 535–536
Hysterical dementia, 951
Hysterical gait, 1190

I

IADL (see Activities of daily living, instrumental)
Iatrogenesis, in acute care hospital, prevention of, 251–252
Ibuprofen, 291
  interference with renal autoregulation and, 574
IDDM (see Diabetes mellitus, insulin-dependent)

IDH (see Hypertension, isolated systolic)
IDL (see Lipoprotein(s), intermediate-density)
α-IFN, in chronic granulocytic leukemia, 676
IIT (see Thyrotoxicosis, iodide-induced)
IL-2 (see Interleukin 2)
Illness:
  physical, depression and, 1013
  systemic, metabolic dementia and, 950–951
  [See also Diseases(s)]
Imipenem, in pneumonia, 514
Imipramine, in urinary incontinence, 1136
Immobility, rehabilitation and, 329
Immobilization, effects of, 85
Immune-cell differentiation, factors inducing, 63, 63t
Immune function:
  cancer and, 75–76
  wound healing and (see Wound healing, immune function and nutrition and)
Immune neutropenia, 670–671
Immune reaction, time required for, 61
Immune regulation, sex differential in longevity and, 39–40
Immune response:
  initiation of, 63
  measurement of, 297
Immune system, as defense against enteric infection, 1172
Immunity:
  cellular, aging and, 503
  humoral, aging and, 503
Immunization, 196
  against influenza and pneumococci, 516
Immunoglobulins, 64, 67
Immunological theory of aging, 9–10
Immunology, 60–70
  assessment of immune function in elderly and, 64–68, 65t, 68t, 69
  augmentation of immune response and, 68–70
  normal immune function and host defense mechanisms and, 62t, 62–64, 63t
  organization of immune system and, 61–62
Immunosuppression, 68–69

Immunosuppressive agents:
  in peripheral neuropathy, 982
  in polymyositis/dermatomyositis, 867
  in rheumatoid arthritis, 877
Imodium, intestinal obstruction and, in
    dying patients, 358
Impairment, definition of, 319, 884
Implied consent, 363
Impotence, 1146–1153
  clinical problem of, 1149
  definitions in, 1146
  diagnosis of, 1149–1152
    cavernosography in, 1152
    duplex scanning in, 1151
    electromyography in, 1151
    history in, 1149–1150
    laboratory testing in, 1150
    nocturnal penile tumescence in,
      1150–1151
    papaverine injection in, 1151
    penile-brachial blood pressure
      index in, 1151
    phalloarteriography in, 1151
    physical examination in, 1150
  mechanism of erection and, 1149
  medical diseases causing or contrib-
    uting to, 1146–1148, 1147t
  secondary, 1146
  therapeutic interventions in, 1152–
    1153
    androgens in, 1152
    external vacuum devices and, 1152
    intracorporeal pharmacotherapy
      as, 1152
    penile prostheses in, 1152
    sex therapy and, 1152–1153
    surgical, 1152
Imuran (see Azathioprine)
Inbreeding, somatic theory of aging
    and, 7
Inclusion conjunctivitis, 425
Income:
  demographics of aging and, 148
  of elders, 238
  health care financing and, 163
  international comparisons of, 117–119
Incontinence (see Fecal incontinence;
    Urinary incontinence)
Individual differences:
  health status and, 105
  in personality, stability of, 103–104
  stability of, 104
Individualized care plan, comprehen-
    sive functional assessment and,
    221

Indomethacin, interference with renal
    autoregulation and, 574
Infections, 1055–1060
  antibiotics in, 1059–1060
    costs of therapy with, 1059
    diagnosis-related groups and,
      1059–1060
    etiologic heterogeneity and, 1059
    pharmacology of, 1059
    specimen collection and, 1059
  of central nervous system, 983–989
  in chronic lymphocytic leukemia,
    674–675
  clinical features of, 1057
  diabetic ketoacidosis and, 754
  diagnostic approach to, 1057–1058
    differential diagnosis and, 1057–
      1058, 1058t
    laboratory tests and, 1058–1059
  epidemiology of, 1055–1056
    mortality and, 1056
    prevalence of important infections
      and, 1055–1056, 1056t
  esophageal, 615–616
  fluid losses and, 1080
  nosocomial, 515–516, 1056
  presentation of, 215–216
  pressure ulcers and, 1204
    assessment of, 1207–1208
  prevention of, 1060
  risk factors for, 1056–1057
    environmental, 1056
    host factors as, 1056–1057
Infectious dementias (see Dementias,
    infectious)
Inflammation, hypoproliferative ane-
    mia and, 666
Inflammatory responses, age-related
    changes in, 390
Influenza:
  immunization against, pneumonia
    and, 516
  pneumonia and, 510, 513
Influenza immunization, 196
Informed consent, 363, 369–370
  anesthesia and, 277
INH (see Isoniazid)
Inhibin, hypothalamic-pituitary-testic-
    ular axis and, 712, 713
Initiation stage of cancer development,
    74
Injury, risk of, exercise and, 98
Institutionalization:
  demographics of aging and, 148–
    149, *149*

Institutionalization (*Cont.*):
  factors affecting, 118
  family and, 238
  physician's role in, 237–238
  self-care and, 119
Instrumental activities of daily living
    (see Activities of daily living,
    instrumental)
Insulin:
  cachexia and, 1104
  chronic renal failure and, 577
  in diabetes mellitus, 752, 753
  in diabetic ketoacidosis, 754
  in hyperosmolar nonketotic coma,
    755
  in hypothermia, 1086
Insurance:
  "catastrophic," 163
  eligibility for, 364
  Medigap, 162
  private, 162–163
Integrity versus despair, in depression,
    1011
Intelligence, 916–917, *917*
  (See also Cognitive function)
Intelligent noncompliance, with drug
    regimens, 202–203
Intensity of service, 159
Interdisciplinary team:
  dying patients and, 355
  gerontological nurses on, 310
  in rehabilitation, 321
Interleukin 2 (IL-2), 66
  augmentation of T-cell activity and,
    69
  in cancer cachexia, 1105
  vaccines and, 69–70
Intermittent peritoneal dialysis (IPD),
    in end-stage renal disease, 578
International Workshop of Human
    Leukocyte Differentiation Anti-
    gens, assessment of immune
    function and, 66
Interstitial lung disease, 538–542
  blood tests in, 539–540
  bronchoalveolar lavage and gallium
    67 lung scans in, 540
  clinical manifestations of, 538–539
  general approach to patients with,
    541–542
  pulmonary functions in, 539, 539t
  radiography in, 539m, *540*
  treatment of, 542
Interstitial nephritis (see Tubulointers-
    titial nephritis)

Intervention, in nursing process, 308
Intervertebral discs, aging and, 857
Inter vivos trusts, 365
Intestinal ischemia, anorexia and, 50
"Intestinal metaplasia," 620
Intestinal obstruction, in dying patients, 358
Intraocular tension, measurement of, 423
Intrinsic mutagenesis theory of aging, 9, 26
Iodide:
    radioactive (*see* Radioiodide)
    thyrotoxicosis induced by, 724
Iodide therapy, in hyperthyroidism, 725
Iodine compounds, pressure ulcers and, 1209
Ionizing radiation, somatic mutation theory of aging and, 6–7
IPD (*see* Intermittent peritoneal dialysis)
iPTH (*see* Parathyroid hormone, immunoreactive)
Iritis, 427–428
Iron, 56
    absorption of, in small intestine, 600
    recommended daily allowance for, 56
Iron deficiency, anemia and, 664, 666
Irritability, menopause and, 781
Ischemia:
    in arteriosclerosis obliterans, 477
        treatment of, 479–480
    intestinal, anorexia and, 50
    myocardial (*see* Myocardial ischemia)
    silent, in diabetes mellitus, 749
    in stroke, 928–929
Ischemic heart disease, 466–467, *467*, *467t*
    menopause and, 43
Isoimmune regulation, sex differential in longevity and, 39
Isometric exercise, 98
Isometric exercise capacity:
    cardiovascular response and, 92
    in elderly, 91–92
    muscle structure and function with aging and, *91*, 91–92
Isoniazid (INH):
    hepatotoxicity of, 632
    nutrient interactions of, 57
    peripheral neuropathy and, 981
    side effects of, 525
    in tuberculosis, 521, 523

Isoproterenol:
    cardiovascular response to, 453
    pharmacodynamics of, 206
IVGTT (*see* Glucose tolerance test, intravenous)

J

Jaundice, 631–632
    in choledocholithiasis, 635–636
    due to septicemia, 634
    postoperative, 634
Joint(s):
    calcification within (See Chondrocalcinosis)
    hyperparathyroidism and, 839
    prosthetic, infection of, 1202–1203
    range of motion of, in Parkinson's disease, 955–956
    rheumatoid arthritis and (*see* Rheumatoid arthritis)
    sacroiliac, disease of, 975
    total replacement of, in osteoarthritis, 887
    (*See also specific articular disorders*)
Joint bank accounts, 366
Josiah Macy Foundation, 4

K

Kegel exercises, in urinary incontinence, 1136
Kemadrin (*see* Procyclidine)
Keratinocytes, age-related changes in, 383–384, 384t
Keratin sulfate (KS), in cartilage, 850, 851
Keratitis, herpes, 426
Keratoses:
    actinic, 399–403, *400*, *401*
        progression from carcinoma in situ to invasive squamous cell carcinoma, *401*, 401–402, *402*
        treatment of, *402*, 402–403
    seborrheic, 398–399, *399*
Ketoacidosis, diabetic, 754
Ketoconazole (Nizoral), oral thrush and, in dying patients, 359
Kidneys:
    calcium metabolism and, 801
    drug excretion and, 205–206
    hypertension and, 486

Kidneys (*Cont.*):
    phosphate metabolism in, in osteomalacia, 830
    (*See also entries beginning with term* Renal)
Klebsiella pneumoniae, 511
Kleinfelter syndrome, 29
Knee:
    osteoarthritis of, obesity and, 883
    rheumatoid arthritis in, 873
KS (*see* Keratin sulfate)

L

Labetolol:
    absorption of, 204
    in hypertension, 494
Laboratory studies, 241–245
    in Alzheimer's disease, 937–938
    in asthma, 527
    in chronic obstructive pulmonary disease, 529–530
    depression and, 1014–1015
    difficulty in obtaining, 213
    in disseminated intravascular coagulation, 696–697
    in hyperthyroidism, 720–722
        general, 720–721
        radioiodide uptake, 722
        results of, 722–723
        standard thyroid function tests and, 721
        TSH and TRH, 721–722
    in impotence, 1150
    infections and, 1058–1059
    in motor neuron diseases, 968
    in multiple system atrophy, 967
    in neuropsychiatric assessment, 228
    in osteomalacia, 832–833
    in Parkinson's disease, 958
    in polymyositis/dermatomyositis, 866–867
    reference ranges for, 241
        appropriate in geriatric practice, 244
        clinically significant, 245, 245t
        homeostasis and, 242
        hormonal effects on, 242
        influence of medication on, 244
        limited excretory capacity and, 241–242
        nutrient intake and, 243
        occult disease and, 243–244
        in old age, 241

Laboratory studies: reference ranges for (*Cont.*):
    selective effects of mortality and, 242–243
      serum protein changes and, 242
    in rheumatoid arthritis, 875
    in stroke, 927–928, 928t
    syncope and, 1073
Labor force participation, demographics of aging and, 147–148
Lacrimal apparatus, disorders of, 426
Lactulose, in constipation, 1166
Lagophthalmos, 423
Langerhans' cells, age-related changes in, 384
Language ability, 914–915, *915*
    disorder of, in Alzheimer's disease, 935
Laryngeal symptoms, in gastroesophageal reflux disease, 609–610
Lawyer, value of consulting, 362
Laxatives, 1161
    abuse of, fluid losses and, 1081–1082
    in constipation, 1166–1167
LCAT (*see* Lecithin-cholesterol acyltransferase)
LDL [*see* Lipoprotein(s), low-density]
Leadership, team approach and, 189
Learning problems, psychopharmacology and, compliance with, 1048
Lecithin-cholesterol acyltransferase (LCAT), 96
Left-ventricular failure, in pulmonary hypertension, 544
Legal issues, 362–366
    informed consent and authority to treat and, 362–364
    insurance and Medicare/Medicaid eligibility and, 364
    legal tools and procedures and, 365–366
Legionella pneumophila, pneumonia and, 512–513
Leiomyomas, gastric, 627
LES (*see* Lower esophageal sphincter)
Lesch-Nyhan disease, gout and, 890
Leser-Trélat sign, 399
Leukemia, *671*, 671–676
    acute lymphoblastic (ALL), 673
    acute myelogenous (AML), 671–673
    acute myelogenous, following myelodysplastic syndromes, 672
    acute nonlymphocytic, 81
    acute promyelocytic, disseminated intravascular coagulation and, 697

Leukemia (*Cont.*):
    biphenotypic, 673
    chronic granulocytic (CGL), 675–676
    chronic lymphocytic (CLL), 74, 673–674
      B-cell, 674t, 674–675
      hairy cell, 675
      prolymphocytic, 675
      T-cell, 675
    chronic myelomonocytic (CMML), 671, 672, 672t
    Di Guglielmo's syndrome and, 667
    incidence of, 74
    myelodysplastic syndromes and, 671–672, 672t
Leukocytes, assessment of immune function and, 65
Levodopa (Sinemet):
    in Parkinson's disease, 956–962
    side effects of, 960–961
Levorphanol, pharmacokinetics of, 289–290
Levothyroid (*see* Thyroxine)
Levothyroxine, in hypothermia, 1086
Lewy body dementia, 952
Lexical knowledge, 915
Leydig cells, decline in, 713
Libido, 108
    in aging males, 109
    loss of, impotence and, 1146
Licensed practical nursing, education for, 304
Licensure, of gerontological nurses, 305
Lidocaine, absorption of, 204
Life expectancy:
    active, 179
    end-stage renal disease and, 578
    international comparisons of, 116
    quality-adjusted, 117
Life span expectancy, 15, *16*
Life span, natural limit of, 145
Lifestyle:
    age-related changes in, 445
    caregiving and, 235
    diabetes mellitus and, 742
    modifications of, in gastroesophageal reflux disease, 611
    sedentary, effects of aerobic exercise training and, 88, *88–90*, 89, 91
    Spartan, life span and, 48
    of women, changing, 41
Life sustaining procedures, withdrawing and witholding, 372–376

Linear accelerator, for radiation therapy, 80–81
Lipase, serum levels of, in acute pancreatitis, 641
Lipids, 52–53
    in brain, 906–907
    estrogen and, 783–784, 784t
    as risk factor, 129–130
    sex differences in, 42
Lipodysplasia, cervical, familial, 29
Lipoprotein(s), 767–775
    age-related changes in, 768–770
      clinical significance of, 769–770
      in industrialized communities, 768–769
      in nonindustrialized communities, 769, 770
    aging and metabolism of, 771–773
    diet and obesity and, 772–773
    high-density (HDL):
      age-related changes in, 769
      metabolism of, 771
    hyperlipidemia and, 773–775
    hypertriglyceridemia and, 775
    intermediate-density (IDL), 767
    longevity syndromes and, 773
    low-density (LDL), 43–46, 52, 767–775
      aging, physical activity, and metabolism of, 94–96
      in familial hypercholesterolemia, 29
      as risk factor, 130
      metabolism of, 771–772, 772
    metabolism of, 767–768
      aging and physical activity and, 94–96
      decline in, 92
    as risk factors, 129–130
      for coronary disease, 768, 769
    very low density (VLDL), 767
      metabolism of, 771
Lipoprotein lipase (LPL), 96
Lip reading, 441
Lips, venous lakes of, 397
Lisinopril, interference with renal autoregulation and, 574
Listeria, bacterial meningitis and, 983, 984
Lithium carbonate, 1050–1051
    in affective disorders, 1099
    in depression, 1012, 1016
    distribution of, 1047
    dizziness and, 1065
    drug interactions of, 1051

Lithium carbonate (*Cont.*):
metabolism of, 1048
side effects of, 1050–1051
Liver:
aging and, 603–604, 631–634
alcohol-induced injury and, 632
chronic hepatitis and, 633
circulatory failure and, 633–634
cirrhosis and, 633
drug-induced injury and, 632
jaundice and, 631–632
pyogenic liver abscess and sepsis
and, 634
viral hepatitis and, 632–633
drug metabolism by, 205
Liver disease:
dementia and, 951
hemostatic disorders and, 695–696
platelets and, 689
Living arrangements, demographics of
aging and, 148, 149t
Living trusts, 365
Living wills, 365–366, 374
Lomotil, intestinal obstruction and, in
dying patients, 358
Loneliness, personality disorders and,
1040
Longevity:
comparative studies on, 15–20
evolutionary perspective of, 15–21
evolution of, in primates, 18–20,
19t, *20*
heritability of, 22–23
sex differences in, 24–25, 37, 37t,
37–47, *38*, *40*, 41t, *42–45*
in the wild and in captivity, 16–18,
17, 17t
"Longevity assurance genes," 5, 25–26
Longevity syndromes, lipoproteins
and, 773
Longevity-determinant genes, 20
Longitudinal studies, of cognitive function, 913
Long-lived populations, 142–145, *143*
Long-term care:
community-based, 349–352
day and respite care and, 352
evaluation of, 351–352
frail elderly living at home and,
349–350
policy questions and, 350–351
public programs and, 350
definition of, 349
gerontological nurses in, 306
Long-term memory, 915

Loperamide hydrochloride, intestinal
obstruction and, in dying patients, 358
Lorazepam (Ativan):
anxiety and, in dying patients, 359
in management of nausea and vomiting, 82
seizures and, 1002
in dying patients, 359
Losses, in depression, 1011
Low-density lipoprotein [*see* Lipopro-
tein(s), low-density]
Lower esophageal sphincter (LES),
aging and, 594–595
LPL (*see* Lipoprotein lipase)
Lumbago, 975
Lumbar spinal stenosis, 973, *974*
Lumbar strain, acute and chronic, 975
Lung:
aging, pathophysiology of, 499–503,
500t
arterial O_2 tension and, 501–502
defense mechanisms of, 503
diffusing capacity of, 501
interaction with chest wall, aging
and, 500–501, *501*
Lung cancer, 548–553
age differences in, 78, 79
chemotherapy in, 81
detection of, 77
diagnosis of, 549t, 549–552
chest x ray evidence of intrathoracic metastases and, 551–552
negative chest x ray and, 551
solitary pulmonary nodule and, 551
epidemiology of, 548–549, 549t
incidence of, 72
management of, 79
metastases of, 549
to brain, 553
intrathoracic, 551–552
non-small-cell (NSCLC)
epidemiology of, 548–549
prognosis of, 553
prognosis of, 553
radiation therapy in, 81
screening for, 548
sex differential in longevity and, 41
small-cell, prognosis of, 553
surgery for, 268
therapy of, 552–553
Lung disease, interstitial (*see* Interstitial lung disease)
Lung irradiation, interstitial lung disease caused by, 541

Lung scan:
gallium 67, in interstitial lung disease, 540, 542
perfusion, pulmonary embolism and,
546
Luteinizing hormone (LH):
hypothalamic-pituitary-testicular
axis and, 712
menopause and, 778
Luteinizing hormone releasing hormone (LHRH) agonists, in benign prostatic hyperplasia, 585
Lymphadenectomy, pelvic, in prostate
carcinoma, 588
Lymph nodes, immune function and,
62
Lymphoblastic leukemia, acute (ALL),
673
Lymphocyte count, as index of nutritional status, 49
Lymphocytic leukemia, chronic (CLL)
(*see* Leukemia, chronic lymphocytic)
Lymphoid cells, assessment of immune
function and, 65
Lymphomas:
gastric, 628
non-Hodgkin's (*see* Non-Hodgkin's
lymphoma)
primary, of nervous system, 1005–
1008
Lysosomal theory, of atherogenesis,
462

M

Macromolecules:
cross-linking in, 8
platelets and, 689
Macronutrients, 51–53
Macrophages, immune function and,
68
Macular degeneration, 422
age-related, 429, *429*
Macular disequilibrium, of aging, 443
Macular edema, cystoid, 429
"Magic Mouthwash," oral thrush and,
in dying patients, 359
Magnesium citrate, in constipation,
1166
Magnetic resonance imaging (MRI):
in Alzheimer's disease, 1096
dizziness and, 1068
gait disorders and, 1186

Magnetic resonance imaging (MRI) (*Cont.*):
  in head injury, 993
  intracranial neoplasms and, 1006
  in neuropsychiatric assessment, 228
  in Parkinson's disease, 958
  in spine disease, 971–972
Maintenance, gene action and, 25–26
Major histocompatibility complex, immunological theory of aging and, 9, 10
Males:
  aging, sexuality in, 109–110
  androgen levels and sexual senescence in, 109–110
  causes of sexual decline in, 110
  paternal age and point mutation and, 32
  pathological impaired coupling in, 810
  (*See also* Sex differences)
Malignancies:
  in Paget's disease, 844
  in polymyositis/dermatomyositis, 866
  skin of Leser-Trélat and, 396–397
Malignant hypertension, in renal atheroembolic diseases, 566
Malignant melanoma:
  age differences in, 78–79
  of uvea, 428, *428*
Mallory-Weiss syndrome, 615
Malnutrition:
  diarrhea and, 1169
  hypothermia and, 1084–1085
  stroke rehabilitation and, 326
  would healing and (*see* Wound healing, immune function and nutrition and)
  (*See also* Protein-calorie malnutrition)
Mammalian species:
  life span of, 15
  maximum life span potential for, 18, 19
Mammography, 792–793
Manganese deficiency, changes associated with, 56
Mannitol, in stroke, 928, 929
Manometry, in gastroesophageal reflux disease, 611
Manual performance:
  combining with other performance measures, 1217–1218, 1218t
  current needs for care and, 1215–1217, 1215–1217t

Manual performance (*Cont.*):
  future needs for care and, 1216–1217, *1217*, 1218t
  measuring, *1214*, 1214–1215, *1215*
MAO (*see* Monoamine oxidase)
MAOIs (*see* Monoamine oxidase inhibitors)
Marital status, demographics of aging and, 148, 149t
MAST (*see* Michigan Alcoholism Screening Test)
Mast cells, of dermis, age-related changes in, 386
Mastectomy, pain syndrome following, 284
Master's tables of average weight, 49
Maternal age, aneuploidy and, 32–33
Mattresses:
  alternating air, 1207
  pressure-reducing, 359, 1202, 1206–1209
Maximal cardiac output, maximal oxygen consumption and, 86–87
Maximum life span, aging rate and, 8
Maximum life span potential (MLSP):
  aging rate and, 16
  as constitutional feature of speciation, 22
  evolution of longevity in primates and, 18–20, 19t, *20*
  in the wild and in captivity, 16–18, *17*, 17t
  (*See also* Longevity)
Maximum oxygen consumption ($Vo_{2\ max}$):
  aerobic exercise capacity and, *86*, 86–89, *88–90*, 91
  aging and, 454–455, 502–503
M-components (*see* Monoclonal immunoglobulins)
MDS (*see* Myelodysplastic syndromes)
Mechanical stress, osteoarthritis and, 882–883
Mediastinal adenopathy, esophageal dysphagia and, 1158–1159
Medicaid, 162
  day care services coverage under, 352
  eligibility for, 364
  long-term care under, 350
  Medicare coverage compared with, 364
  nursing home care reimbursement under, 335
Medical care, personality stability and, 105

Medical director, role in nursing home care, 339
Medicare:
  "catastrophic" insurance under, 163
  eligibility for, 364
  expenditures under, 159, *159*
  long-term care under, 350
  Medicaid coverage compared with, 364
  nursing home care reimbursement under, 335
  Part A of, 161
  Part B of, 161–162
  rehabilitation and, 323
  rehabilitation coverage under, 315, 324
  reimbursement of nurse practitioners and, 307
  reimbursement structure of, 160
Medigap insurance, 162
Medroxyprogesterone acetate (Provera):
  lipoproteins and, 46
  menopause and, 786
Megacolon, constipation and, 1164
Megakaryocytes, platelets and, 685
Megavoltage equipment, for radiation therapy, 80
Megestrol, menopause and, 786
Meissner's corpuscles, age-related changes in, 386
Melanocytes, age-related changes in, 384–385
Melanoma, malignant (*see* Malignant melanoma)
Melanosis coli, 1163
Mellaril (*see* Thioridazine)
Melphalan:
  in amyloidosis, 570
  marrow damage induced by, 686
Memory, 915–916, *916*
  amnesia and, 1097
  in dementia, 1095
  disorder of, in Alzheimer's disease, 934
  in delirium, 921
  primary (short-term), 915
  secondary (long-term), 915
  sensory, 915
Meniere's disease, dizziness and, 1064
Meningiomas, 1005
  brain imaging and, 1006
  treatment of, 1009
Meningitis:
  bacterial, 983–985
  clinical features of, 984

Meningitis: bacterial (*Cont.*):
  diagnosis of, 984
  etiology of, 983, 984t
  pathogenesis of, 983
  treatment of, 984–985
 chronic, dementia and, 950
 syphilitic, acute, 986–987
 tuberculous, 520, 988
Meniscus, of diarthroidal joints, 856
Menopausal syndrome, 780
Menopause:
 effects of, 111
 endocrine changes during, 777–779, 778, 779, 779t
 estrogen therapy and, breast disease and, 784
   cardiovascular effects of, 783–784, 784t
   endometrial cancer and, 785
   gallbladder disease and, 784
   osteoporosis and, 781–783, 782, 782t, 783
 ischemic heart disease and, 43
 laboratory data and, 242
 osteoporosis and, 815
 psychological symptoms of, 781
 structural and physiological changes associated with, 779–780
 therapeutic recommendations for, 785–786
 vasomotor symptoms and genitourinary changes of, 780–781, 781
Mental changes, in Parkinson's disease, 956
Mental disorders, age differences in, neuropsychiatric assessment and, 225
Mental illness, risk factors for, age differences in, 225
Mental incompetency, ethical issues related to, 376–377
Mental retardation, 1026–1029, 1098
 aging and, 1029
 coexisting medical conditions and, 1027t, 1027–1029, 1029t
 Down's syndrome and, 1027
 life expectancy and, 1027
Mental state, altered (*see* Altered mental state)
Mental status examination, 228, 229
 in altered mental states, 1090–1092
 depression and, 1014
 pitfalls of, 1092, 1094
Meperidine (Demerol):
 in gout, 892

Meperidine (Demerol) (*Cont.*):
 side effects of, 293
Mesenteric ischemia, acute, surgery for, 266
Metabolic acidosis, in chronic renal failure, 576
Metabolic alkalosis, in hypercapnic respiratory failure, 534
Metabolic complications, of nutritional support, 300–301
Metabolic dementias (*see* Dementias, metabolic)
Metabolic function:
 aging, physical activity, and bone mineral metabolism and, 96–97
 aging, physical activity, and glucose metabolism and, 93–94, 94, 95
 aging, physical activity, and lipoprotein metabolism and, 94–96
 in elderly, 92–97
Metabolism:
 of lipoproteins, 767–768
 rate of:
   basal, impact of age on, 296–297
   free radical theory of aging and, 9, 10
 reduced, in delirium, 923
Metaclopramide (Reglan), nausea and vomiting and, in dying patients, 358
Metals, peripheral neuropathy and, 981
Metamorphopsia, 422
Metastases, of lung cancer, 549
 to brain, 553
 intrathoracic, 551–552
Metchnikoff, Elie, 3
Methadone maintenance, 1033
Methadone, pharmacokinetics of, 289–290
Methicillin, tubulointerstitial nephritis and, 571
Methotrexate:
 in polymyositis/dermatomyositis, 867
 in rheumatoid arthritis, 877
 toxicity of, 81
Methyl-CCNU, toxicity of, 81
Methyl-dopa, sleep disorders and, 1113
Methylphenidate (Ritalin), 1050
 depression and, 1016
   in dying patients, 359
 side effects of, 292
Methyl tert-butyl ether (MTBE), gallstone dissolution with, 635

Methysergide, interstitial lung disease caused by, 541
Metoclopramide:
 in gastric emptying disorders, 624–625
 in gastroesophageal reflux disease, 612
 in management of nausea and vomiting, 82
Metoprolol, absorption of, 204
Metropolitan Life Insurance Tables, 49
Michigan Alcoholism Screening Test (MAST), 1032
Microbial flora, intestinal, normal, 1172
Microcirculation, of dermis, age-related changes in, 386, 386t
Microcytosis, 663–664
Micronutrients, aging and, 297
Microscopy, breast cancer diagnosis and, 794
Microsomal enzyme activity, liver function and, 604
Microvascular disease, in diabetes mellitus, 748
Micturition syncope, 1072
Midarm muscle circumference, as index of muscle loss, 49
"Midlife crisis," 102, 104
Midthoracic diverticulum, 615
Migraine, differential diagnosis of, 930
Milk of magnesia, in constipation, 1166
Minerals:
 absorption of, in small intestine, 599–600
 deficiency of, skin disorders and, 395–396
Mineralocorticoids, excess of, 716
Mineral oil:
 in constipation, 1166
 nutrient interactions of, 57
Minicaloric test, dizziness and, 1066, 1068
Mini-Mental State Examination (MMSE), 936, 1092, 1093
 in delirium, 1094
 depression and, 1014
 in mental retardation, 1098
Mintox, oral thrush and, in dying patients, 359
Minute ventilation, decreased, hypercapnic respiratory failure secondary to, 532
Mithramycin (*see* Plicamycin)
Mitral regurgitation (MR), syncope and, 1070

Mitral stenosis, 472
  in pulmonary hypertension, 544
Mitral valve prolapse, 472
MLSP (*see* Maximum life span potential)
MMSE (*see* Mini-Mental State Examination)
Moisture, pressure ulcers and, 1205–1206
Mönckeberg's sclerosis, 458–459
Monitoring, anesthesia and, 277
Monoamine oxidase (MAO), 907
Monoamine oxidase inhibitors (MAOIs), 1049t, 1049–1050
  B form, in Parkinson's disease, 962
  in depression, 1016
  side effects of, 1049, 1049t
Monoclonal antibodies, assessment of immune function and, 66
Monoclonal gammopathy, 67
Monoclonal gammopathy of uncertain significance, 67
Monoclonal hypothesis, of atherogenesis, 461–462
Monoclonal immunoglobulins (M-components), 67
Monocytes, immune function and, 68
Monocytic cells, immune function and, 64
Montgomery-Asberg Depression Rating Scale, 1014, 1098
Mood disorder not otherwise specified, 1013
Mood, in mental state examination, 1091
Morbidity:
  associated with continuous ambulatory peritoneal dialysis, 579
  epidemiology of, 150
  falls and, 1192, 1197
  operative, 270t, 270–271
  risk factors for (*see* Risk factors, for morbidity and mortality)
  surgical, 254–256, 255t
Morphine:
  administration schedule for, 291
  pain and, in dying patients, 357
  respiratory depression and, 292
  respiratory symptoms and, in dying patients, 358
Mortality:
  in acute cholecystitis, surgery and, 635
  aortic aneurysm and, 267
  body weight and, 760–762
  breast cancer and, 794–795
  in choledocholithiasis, surgery and, 636

Mortality (*Cont.*):
  depression and, 1015
  diabetic ketoacidosis and, 754
  epidemiology of, 150, *150*, 151t
  gastrointestinal surgery and, 264
  in head injury, 994–995, *995*
  head injury and, 990
  hemodialysis and, 578
  hip fractures and, 316
  in hypercapnic respiratory failure, 535
  infection and, 1056
  intestinal ischemia and, 266
  intracranial neoplasms and, 1004–1005
  lung cancer and, 548
  operative, 270t, 270–271
    breast cancer and, 794
    in polymyositis/dermatomyositis, 867–868
  pressure ulcers and, 1205
  pulmonary embolism and, 545–546
  regional versus general anesthesia and, 273, 274t
  renal transplantation and, 579
  risk factors for (*see* Risk factors, for morbidity and mortality)
  risk for, pulmonary function tests and, 504, *505, 506*
  selective effects of, laboratory data and, 242–243
  surgical, 254t, 254–256, 255t
    appendicitis and, 264
    cardiac disease and, 268
    thoracotomies and, 268
  (*See also* Death; Dying patients)
Motility disorders:
  esophageal dysphagia and, 1159
  oropharyngeal dysphagia and, 1157
Motivation, rehabilitation and, 322
Motor function, of oral cavity, 418–419
Motor neuron diseases, 967–969
Motor neuron dysfunction, gait and, 1189
MPD (*see* Myofascial pain dysfunction syndrome)
MR (*see* Mitral regurgitation)
MRI (*see* Magnetic resonance imaging)
MSA (*see* Multiple system atrophy)
MTBE (*see* Methyl tert-butyl ether)
Mucosa:
  gastric, aging and, 597
  oral, 417–418
  of small intestine, aging and, 598
  vaginal, menopause and, 779–780

Multidisciplinary team, in rehabilitation, 321
Multi-infarct dementia, stroke and, 931
Multiple myeloma, 67
  incidence of, 74
  interstitial nephritis and, 572–573
Multiple system atrophy (MSA), 966–967
Murmurs, aortic valve disease and, 473
Muscarinic cholinergic agonists, in Alzheimer's disease, 943
Muscle(s):
  of eye, 423
  skeletal:
    aging and, 856–857
    pharyngoesophageal function and, 593–594
    smooth, pharyngoesophageal function and, 594
Muscle biopsy, in polymyositis/dermatomyositis, 867
Muscle mass, cachexia and, 1103, 1105
Muscle strength:
  aging and, 856
  rehabilitation and, 320
  (*See also* Muscle weakness)
Muscle structure and function, with aging, *91*, 91–92
Muscle tone, in Alzheimer's disease, 937
Muscle weakness:
  in hyperthyroidism, 720
  in motor neuron diseases, 968
  in osteomalacia, 833
  in polymyositis/dermatomyositis, 865–866, 866t
Muscular dystrophies, gait and, 1189
Muscular rigidity, in Parkinson's disease, 955
Musculoskeletal disorders:
  falls and, 1193
  gait and, 1189
  in hypothyroidism, 728–729
Musculoskeletal system:
  aging and, 849–857
    diarthrodial joints and, 849–856
    intervertebral discs and, 857
    skeletal muscle and, 856–857
    tendons and, 857
  in Parkinson's disease, 957
  [*See also* Bone; Muscle(s)]
Mutation:
  intrinsic mutagenesis theory of aging and, 26
  malignancy and, 75

Mutation (*Cont.*):
  mutant alleles and, 23
  parental age and, 32–33
  somatic, aging and, 6–7
Mycelex (*see* Clotrimazole)
Myc-like oncogenes, 75
Mycobacterium tuberculosis, 518
  isolation of, 520
Mycolog cream, pruritus and, in dying
    patients, 359
Mycostatin (*see* Nystatin)
Myelodysplasia, platelets and, 689
Myelodysplastic syndromes (MDS),
    671–672, 672t
Myelogenous leukemia, acute (AML),
    672–673
Myeloma, multiple (*see* Multiple mye-
    loma)
Myelopathy, 972–974, *973*, *974*
  acute, 972–973
  due to cervical spondylosis, gait and,
    1188
  spondylitic, *973*, *973*
Myelophthisis, 676
Myocardial hypertrophy, 448, *448*
Myocardial infarction (MI), 468–469
  acute:
    presentation of, 214
    stroke and, 931
  aspirin and, 684
  coronary bypass surgery in, 469,
    469t
  estrogen and, 46
  silent:
    in diabetes mellitus, 749
    presentation of, 214
  thrombolytic therapy of, 468t, 468–
    469
Myocardial ischemia, asymptomatic,
    presentation of, 214
Myoclonus:
  in Alzheimer's disease, 937
  multifocal, analgesics and, 293
  nocturnal (PLM), 1113
    treatment of, 1120
  sleep-related, 1112
Myofascial pain dysfunction (MPD)
    syndrome, 419
Myopathy, in hypothyroidism, 729
Myopia, 431
Myotonic dystrophy, 29
Mysoline (*see* Primidone)
Myxedema:
  depression and, 1013
  hypothermia and, 1084, 1086

Myxedema (*Cont.*):
  hypothyroidism versus, 727
Myxedema coma, 730
  in hypothyroidism, 728

N

Nail(s), white, of old age, 396
Nail growth, age-related changes in,
    388
Nalbuphine, 289
Naloxone (Narcan):
  menopause and, 786
  respiratory depression and, 292
  respiratory distress and, in dying
    patients, 358
Naproxen, 287
  interference with renal autoregula-
    tion and, 574
Narcan (*see* Naloxone)
Narcissistic personality disorder, 1038
Narcotics:
  addiction to, 1031–1032
  epidural, 276
  intestinal obstruction and, in dying
    patients, 358
  pain and, in dying patients, 357
  respiratory distress from, in dying
    patients, 358
Nasoenteral tubes, 298
National Diabetes Data Group
    (NDDG), diagnostic criteria of,
    744
National Heart Institute, 4
National Institute on Aging, 4
National Institutes of Health, 4
National League for Nursing:
  Accreditation Criteria for Programs
    in Nursing of, 304
  accreditation of nursing education
    programs by, 305
Natural Death Acts, 374
Natural killer (NK) cells, 63, 68
Nausea:
  analgesics and, 292–293
  in cancer patient, management of, 82
  in dying patients, 358
NDDG (*see* National Diabetes Data
    Group)
Near-syncope, definition of, 1062
Neck, in physical examination, 182
Necrosis, tubular (*see* Tubular necrosis)
Negotiation, team approach and, 189–
    190

Neonatal familial hyperalphalipopro-
    teinemia, 32
Neonatal familial hypobetalipoprotein-
    emia, 32
"Neonatal progeroid syndrome," 28
Neoplasms [*see* Cancer; Carcinoma;
    Tumor(s)]
Nephritis, tubulointerstitial (*see*
    Tubulointerstitial nephritis)
Nephrolithiasis, hyperparathyroidism
    and, 839
Nephrotic syndrome, 569–570
  clinical manifestations of, 569–570
  diagnosis of, 570
  incidence in the elderly, 569
  pathologic findings in, 570
  prognosis of, 570
  treatment of, 570
Nephrotoxic drugs, chronic renal fail-
    ure and, 577
Nerve(s):
  biopsy of, in peripheral neuropathy,
    978–979
  of dermis, age-related changes in,
    386–387, 387t
  of eye, 423
Nerve blocks, pain and, in dying pa-
    tients, 357
Nerve trauma, peripheral neuropathy
    and, 980
Neuralgia:
  postherpetic, 980, 1180
  treatment of, 1181
Neuralgic amyotrophy, 980
Neurapraxia, 980
Neurinoma, acoustic nerve, treatment
    of, 1009
Neuroendocrine theories of aging, 8–9
Neurofibrillary tangles, in Alzheimer's
    disease, 940–941
Neurofibromatosis, mutation and, 32
Neuroleptics:
  in affective disorders, 1099
  in Alzheimer's disease, 943–944
  in dementia, 1096
  dizziness and, 1065
  in paraphrenias, 1023
  side effects of, 943–944
Neurologic complications, of rheuma-
    toid arthritis, 874–875
Neurologic disorders:
  dizziness and, 1063–1066
  impotence and, 1147
Neurologic examination, 182, 229
  pain and, 284

Neuroma, acoustic, dizziness and, 1064–1065

Neuromuscular disorders:
esophageal dysphagia and, 1159
hyperparathyroidism and, 839
in hyperthyroidism, 719–720
in hypothyroidism, 728
oropharyngeal dysphagia and, 1157

Neuronal degeneration, vestibular dysfunction and, 443

Neuronal loss:
aging and, 906
in Alzheimer's disease, 941

Neuronitis, vestibular, 1064

Neuropathy:
diabetic, arteriosclerosis obliterans and, 480
distal, rheumatoid arthritis and, 874
entrapment, rheumatoid arthritis and, 874–875

Neuropeptides, 908–909

Neuropsychiatric assessment, 224–230
electrophysiology and, 230
family members and caregivers and, 230
follow-up, 230
general principles of, 224–226
age-associated mental disorders and, 225
central nervous system changes and, 224–225
coexisting physical illness and, 226
pharmacokinetics and polypharmacy and, 225–226
symptom presentation and, 225
history in, 226–227
imaging and, 230
laboratory tests and, 228–229
physical examination and, 228
purpose of, 224
screening and, 227–228
specialized, 229–230
functional status and social support network and, 230
neurologic, 229
neuropsychological, 229–230
psychiatric, 229
speech and language assessment and, 230

Neuropsychological evaluation, 229–230

Neurosis, depressive, 1015

Neurosyphilis, 986–988
acute syphilitic meningitis and, 986–987

Neurosyphilis (*Cont.*):
asymptomatic, 986
atypical presentations of, 987
epidemiology of, 986
etiology and pathogenesis of, 986
meningovascular syphilis and, 987
parenchymatous, 987
serology of, 986
therapy of, 988, 988t

Neurotensin, 909

Neuroticism, health status and, 105

Neurotmesis, peripheral neuropathy and, 980

Neurotransmitters, 907–909
in Alzheimer's disease, 909, 911t, 941–942
biology of, 907
control of adrenocorticotropic hormone by, 707
in depression, 1011
growth hormone control by, 709–710
hypothalamic-pituitary-testicular axis and, 712
modulatory, 907
regulation of, 705–706

Neutropenia:
drug-induced, 669
immune, 670–671
nutritional deficiencies and, 670

Neutrophil function, aging and, 658–660, *660*

NIDDM (*see* Diabetes mellitus, non-insulin-dependent)

Nigrostriatal degeneration, 967

Nimodipine, in stroke, 929

Nitrates:
in achalasia, 613–614
in angina pectoris, 467–468

Nitrofurantoin, interstitial lung disease caused by, 541

Nitrogen balance studies, nutritional support and, 299

Nizatidine:
in gastroesophageal reflux disease, 612
peptic ulcer and, 623

Nizoral (*see* Ketoconazole)

NK (*see* Natural killer cells)

Nocturnal penile tumescence (NPT), 108
in impotence, 1150–1151

Nodules:
pulmonary, solitary, lung cancer and, 551

Nodules (*Cont.*):
rheumatoid, rheumatoid arthritis and, 874

Noncompliance:
with drug regimens, 202–203
intelligent, 202–203
with tuberculosis therapy, 523

Non-Hodgkin's lymphoma, chemotherapy in, 81

Nonmaleficence, ethical dilemmas and, 369

"Nonorganic" failure to thrive (*see* Cachexia)

Nonspecific esophageal motor disorders, 614

Nonsteroidal anti-inflammatory drugs (NSAIDs), 287, 289
in chondrocalcinosis, 895
chronic renal failure and, 577
hyperkalemia and, 562
interference with renal autoregulation and, 574
in osteoarthritis, 885
pain and, in dying patients, 356–357
peptic ulcer and, 623
platelet function and, 690
in rheumatoid arthritis, 876
side effects of, 885–886, 886t
tubulointerstitial nephritis and, 572

Norepinephrine:
cardiovascular response to, 453, *454*
in depression, 1011
in hypertension, 486
regulation of, 706

Normal pressure hydrocephalus (NPH), dementia and, 951–952

Norms, team approach and, 189

Nortriptyline, in depression, 1016

Nosocomial infections, 1056

Nosocomial pneumonia, 515–516

NPH (*see* Normal pressure hydrocephalus)

NPT (*see* Nocturnal penile tumescence)

NSAIDs (*see* Nonsteroidal anti-inflammatory drugs)

NSCLC (*see* Lung cancer, non-small-cell)

Nucleic acids, in brain, 906

Nurse(s), role in nursing home care, 338

Nurse practitioners:
in nursing homes, 344
in primary care, 306–307

Nursing assistants, 309

Nursing diagnosis, 308

Nursing home(s), 331–332, 332t

Nursing home(s) (*Cont.*):
  advance care policies and, 374, 375t
  ethical issues in, 377
  interface with acute-care hospital, 344–346
  monitoring in, 341
  preventive health practices in, 341, 344
  rehabilitation in, 324
  residents of, 332, 332–333, 333
    role in care, 339–340
  yearly reevaluation in, 340–341
Nursing home care, 331–346
  clinical aspects of, 333–334, 334t, 335t
  ethical issues in, 346, 346t
  goals of, 333, 333t
  process of, 334–335, 336–338t, 338–339
  strategies to improve, 339–341, *340*, 341–344t, 344, *345*
"Nursing home pneumonia," 513
Nursing process, 308–309
"Nutcracker esophagus," 614
Nutrient intake, laboratory data and, 243
Nutrients, role in disease pathogenesis, 48, 48t
Nutrition:
  aging and, 48t, 48–58
  anemia and, 662–663
  drug–nutrient interactions and, 57–58
  iron deficiency and, 664
  liver function and, 604
  macronutrients and, 51–53
  needs of elderly and, 296–297, 297t
  pressure ulcers and, 1208
  trace elements and, 54–56
  vitamins and, 56–57
  water and, 53–54
  white blood cell disorders and, 670
  wound healing and (*see* Wound healing, immune function and nutrition and)
Nutritional assessment, 49, 297t, 297–298
Nutritional problems, mental retardation and, 1028
Nutritional support, 298–300, 298–300t
  case studies and, 301–302
  of dying patients, decision making about, 356
  ethical issues related to, 374–376
  metabolic complications of, 300–301

Nylen-Barany provocative maneuver, dizziness and, 1064, 1066
Nystatin (Mycostatin), oral thrush and, in dying patients, 359

O

OA (*see* Osteoarthritis)
Obesity:
  atherosclerosis and, 459–460, 462
  diet and, 772–773
  disease prevention and, 195
  life span and, 48, 53
  lipoprotein metabolism and, 95
  osteoarthritis and, 883
  preventive gerontology and, 168–169
  as risk factor, 131–132
Obligate diuresis, 1081
Obsessions, in mental state examination, 1091
Obsessive-compulsive personality disorder, 1039
Obstructive uropathy, acute renal failure and, 474–475
Occult blood testing, colorectal cancer and, 651
Occupational exposures, lung cancer and, 548
Occupational history, in interstitial lung disease, 541
Ocular complications, of rheumatoid arthritis, 874
Ocular disease, herpes zoster and, 1178, 1180
OGTT (*see* Glucose tolerance test, oral)
Old age, extreme, 142–145, *143*
Older Americans Act, long-term care under, 350
Olfaction, changes in, anorexia and, 50
"Olivopontocerebellar atrophies" (OPCAs), 966, 967
Oncogenes, 74–75
  antioncogenes and, 75
  ras-like and myc-like, 75
  recessive, 75
Oncology (*see* Cancer)
On Lok Senior Health Services, community-based long-term care services provided by, 351
Onychomycosis, 394, *395*
OPCAs (*see* "Olivopontocerebellar atrophies")

Openness to Experience, health status and, 105
Ophthalmoscopy, direct, 423
Opioids:
  hypothalamic-pituitary-testicular axis and, 713
  regulation of, 706
Oral cavity, 413–419
  dentition and periodontium and, 413–415, 414t
  motor function and, 418–419
  oral mucosa and, 417–418
  in physical examination, 182
  radiation therapy to, 81
  salivary glands and, 415t, 415–416
  sensory function and, 416–417
Oral mucosa, 417–418
Oral pharynx, radiation therapy to, 81
Oral rehydration therapy (ORT), in diarrhea, 1168, 1169, 1172–1174
Oral thrush, in dying patients, 359
Orbit, disorders of, 431
"Organic" failure to thrive (*see* Cachexia)
Orgasm, in males, 109
Orientation-Memory-Concentration test, 936–937
Oropharyngeal dysphagia, 609, 1155–1157, 1157t
ORT (*see* Oral rehydration therapy)
Osmolar therapy, stroke and, 928
Osteitis fibrosa cystica, in hyperparathyroidism, 838, 841
Osteoarthritis (OA), 880–887
  articular cartilage and, 849–850
  cartilage biochemistry and, 851t, 851–855
    chondrocyte cultures and, 852–853
    chondrocyte longevity and donor age and, 853
    explant cultures and, 852
    markers of chondrocyte phenotype in vitro and, 853–855, 854t
  clinical management of, 883–884
  etiology and pathogenesis of, 882–883
  histology and biochemistry of, 881–882
  in hypothyroidism, 728–729
  osteoporosis and, 883
  prevalence of, 880–881, *881*
  treatment of, 884–887, 885t
    nonsurgical, 885–887, 886t
    surgical, 887

Osteoarthritis (*Cont.*):
  vertebral, 975
Osteoarthropathy, hypertrophic, cervical, esophageal dysphagia and, 1159
Osteoblasts, 804–805
  interaction with osteoclasts, 805, *807*
  in Paget's disease, 843
Osteoclasts, 805
  interaction with osteoblasts, 805, *807*
  proliferation of, in Paget's disease, 843
Osteocytes, 805, *806*
Osteogenesis imperfecta, mutation and, 32
Osteomalacia, 96, 826–836
  bone biopsy findings in, 830–831
  bone mass and bone scan findings in, 831
  causes of, 826, 826t
  clinical findings in, 833
    illustrative case history and, *833*, 833–834, *834*
  definition of, 826
  differential diagnosis of, 834–835
  disorders of phosphate metabolism in, 830, *830*
  disorders of vitamin D metabolism in, 829, 829–830
  general considerations in, 826, 826t, 827
  laboratory findings in, 832–833
  osteoporosis distinguished from, 834
  pathogenesis of, 826–829, *828*
  treatment of, 835–836
  x-ray findings in, 831, *832*
Osteomyelitis, pressure ulcers and, 1208
Osteopenia, 92, 96–97
  skeletal, 813
    treatment of, 820, 820t, *821*
Osteoporosis, 92, 96–97, 813–824, 814t
  aging and, 140, *140*
  clinical presentation of, 815–816
  definition of, 813
  diagnosis of, 816–819
    at-risk patients and, 818
    back pain and, 819
    bone mass quantity and quality measurement and, 816–817
    fractures and, 819
    indications for noninvasive techniques in, 818
  epidemiology of, 813

Osteoporosis (*Cont.*):
  estrogen therapy and, 781–783, *782*, 782t, *783*
  hyperparathyroidism and, 838–839
  osteoarthritis and, 883
  osteomalacia distinguished from, 834
  pathogenesis of, *813*, 813–815, *814*
  preventive gerontology and, 169
  risk factors for, 134–135, 815, 816t
  transparent skin and, 396
  treatment of, 819–823
    anabolic steroids in, 823
    biphosphonates in, 822–823
    bone mass deficiency and, 820, 820t, *821*
    calcitonin in, 822
    calcium in, 821
    estrogens in, 822
    exercise in, 823
    general recommendations for, 823
    monitoring response to, 824
    secondary osteoporosis and, 823–824
    sodium fluoride in, 823
    symptomatic, 819–820
    vitamin D in, 822
  vertebral, 975
Osteoporosis circumscripta, 844, *845*
Outpatient(s), predicting care needs for, 1218, 1219t
Outpatient rehabilitation, 315, 324
Ovariectomy, unilateral, Down's syndrome and, 32–33
Ovary, menopause and, 779
Oxybutynin, in urinary incontinence, 1135
Oxycodone, 289
Oxygen:
  arterial tension and, 501–502
  in hypercapnic respiratory failure, secondary to chronic obstructive lung disease, 533
  in pulmonary hypertension, 545
  (*See also* Maximum oxygen consumption)

P

Pacemakers, 472, *472*
  in syncope, 1074
Pacinian corpuscles, age-related changes in, 386
PAF (*see* Pure autonomic failure)

Paget's disease, 843–848
  biochemistry of, 845–846
  clinical manifestations and complications of, 844, 844t
  epidemiology of, 843
  etiology of, 843–844, 844t
  pathology of, 843
  radiology in, 844–845, *845*
  treatment of, 845–848
    drug therapy in, 846t, 846–847
    general considerations and indications for, 846, 846t
    surgical, *847*, 847–848
Pain, 281–294
  in back (*see* Back pain)
  in chest (*see* Chest pain)
  clinical assessment of, 283–286
    alternative methods of control during, 285, 285–286t
    believing patients' complaints and, 283
    diagnostic procedures and, 284
    extent of disease and, in cancer, 284
    history and, 284
    medical and neurologic examination and, 284
    psychosocial status and, 284
    reassessment and, 285–286
    treatment and, 284–285
  deafferentation, 282
  in dying patients, 356–358, 357t
    adjuvant analgesic drugs and, 357
    narcotics and, 357
    nonnarcotic analgesics and, 356–357
    physical measures and, 357–358
  epidemiology of, 281–282
  neuropathic, 291
  in Paget's disease, 844
  perception of, 386–387
  in peripheral neuropathies, 979
  in postherpetic neuralgia, 1181
  in pulmonary hypertension, 545
  skeletal, in osteomalacia, 833
  somatic or nociceptive, 282
  temporal aspects of, 282
  thresholds for, 281–282
  types of patients with, 282–283, 283t
  visceral, 282
Pain management, 286–294
  analgesics in, 287, 288t, 289–294
    administration schedule for, 291
    caution against placebos and, 294
    combination therapy with, 291–292

Pain management: analgesics in (*Cont.*):
  equianalgesic dose and route of administration of, 291
  pharmacology and, 289–290, 290t
  route of administration and, 292
  side effects of, 292–293
  specific drugs for specific types of pain and, 289, 290t
  tolerance and, 293–294
  clinical pharmacologic considerations in, 286, 287t
Pain medications, drug interactions of, 1050
Pain syndromes, 283, 291
  post-mastectomy, 284
  post-thoracotomy, 284
Pakistan, longevity in, 144
Palilalia, in Parkinson's disease, 957
Palpitations, in hyperthyroidism, 720
Pancreas:
  aging and, 640
  cancer of, 642–643
Pancreatic enzyme replacement, in pancreatitis, 642
Pancreatic function, aging and, 601–602
Pancreatitis:
  acute, 641–642
    drugs and, 642
    gallstone, 641
    general considerations in, 642
    hemorrhagic, disseminated intravascular coagulation and, 697
    hyperlipidemia and, 641–642
  chronic, 642
Pancytopenia, 666
  drug-induced, 669
Papaverine, diagnostic injection of, in impotence, 1151
Pap test, 77
Para-aminosalicylic acid (PAS), in tuberculosis, 521
Paralysis:
  gait and, 1188
  in parenchymatous neurosyphilis, 987
  in stroke, 927
  Todd's, 928, 930
Paraneoplastic neuropathies, 981
Paranoia, 1037
  definition of, 1019
  hallucinations in, 1020
Paranoid personality disorder, 1036–1037
Paranoid schizophrenia, 1020

Paraparesis, spastic, gait and, 1188
Paraphrenias, 1019–1024
  definition of terms and, 1019–1020
  validators of *DSM III-R* and, 1020–1023
    antecedent, 1020–1022
    concurrent, 1022
    predictive, 1022–1023
Paraproteinemia, 67
Parasomnias, 1114
Parathyroidectomy, in hypercalcemia, 841
Parathyroid hormone (PTH):
  calcium metabolism and, 801–802
  in chronic renal failure, 576
  in hyperparathyroidism, 837
  immunoreactive (iPTH), bone resorption and, 815
  measurement of, in hyperparathyroidism, 839–840
Parental age, mutation and, 32–33
Parenteral alimentation (*see* Nutritional support)
Paresis (*see* Paralysis)
Paresthesia, in hypothyroidism, 728
Parkinsonism:
  antipsychotics and, 1050
  sleep disorders and, 1112
Parkinsonism-amyotrophy syndrome, 967
Parkinson's disease, 909, 954–963, 954t
  biochemical abnormalities in, 909, 910t
  classification of, 954, 954t
  clinical features of, 955t, 955–957
  depression in, 1099
  dizziness and, 1065
  gait and, 1186
  laboratory studies in, 958
  management of, 958–963
    anticholinergic drugs in, 958–959
    continuous release of levodopa/carbidopa in, 962
    direct-acting dopamine agonists in, 961
    fetal substantia nigra implantation in, 963
    levodopa in, 959–961
    monoamine oxidase inhibitor of B form in, 962
    physical therapy in, 961–962
    recent surgical, 962–963
  overlap between Alzheimer's disease and, 941

Parkinson's disease (*Cont.*):
  pathogenesis of, 958
  pathology of, 957–958
  rehabilitation and, 328–329
Parlodel (*see* Bromocriptine)
Parsidol (*see* Ethopropazine)
PAS (*see Para*-aminosalicylic acid)
Passive-aggressive personality disorder, 1039–1040
Paternal age, point mutation and, 32
Patient-specific differences, rehabilitation and, 321–323
  age-related, 321–322
  disease-related, 322–323
Patterson-Kelly syndrome, 614
PBC (*see* Cirrhosis, primary biliary)
PBPI (*see* Penile-brachial pressure index)
PEEP (*see* Positive end-expiratory pressure)
Pelvic examination, 182
Pelvic floor exercises, in urinary incontinence, 1136
Pemphigoid:
  bullous, 406–407
  esophagus and, 617
Penicillamine, in rheumatoid arthritis, 877
Penicillin(s):
  acute bacterial pyelonephritis and, 571
  in pneumonia, 512, 514
Penicillin G:
  in neurosyphilis, 988, 988t
  platelet function and, 690
Penile-brachial pressure index (PBPI), in impotence, 1148, 1151
Penile prostheses, in impotence, 1152
Penis:
  mechanism of erection and, 1149
  (*See also* Impotence)
Pentazocine, 289
Pepsin, secretion of, aging and, 596
Peptic strictures:
  esophageal dysphagia and, 1158
  in gastroesophageal reflux disease, 612
Peptic ulcers (*see* Ulcers, peptic)
Pepto-Bismol (*see* Bismuth sodium tartrate)
Perception, disorder of, in delirium, 921
Percutaneous absorption, age-related changes in, 388–389
Performance, measures of (*see* Manual performance)

Perfusion lung scan, pulmonary embolism and, 546
Perfusion, mismatch of ventilation and, hypercapnic respiratory failure secondary to, 532–533
Pergolide (Permax), in Parkinson's disease, 961
Periodontal disease, 196, 415
Periodontitis, 414
Periodontium, 414
Peripheral nerve dysfunction, gait and, 1189
Peripheral nervous system (PNS):
　disorders of, dizziness and, 1063–1065, 1064t
　in hypothyroidism, 728
Peripheral neuropathies, 977–982
　classification and diagnosis of, 979, 980t
　differential diagnosis of, 979–982
　esophagus and, 617
　idiopathic, 982
　inherited, 982
　paraneoplastic, 981
　patient evaluation and, 978–979, 979t
　peripheral nerve anatomy and, 977–978
　toxins and, 981
　treatment of, 982
　uremic, 981
　vitamin deficiencies and, 981
Peripheral vascular disease, 476–483
　extracranial, 481–483
　　clinical presentation of, 481–482
　　diagnosis of, 482–483
　　pathogenesis of, 481
　　therapy of, 483
　surgery for, 267–268
Peritoneal dialysis:
　in end-stage renal disease, 578–579
　in hypothermia, 1086
Permax (see Pergolide)
Permeability, of skin, age-related changes in, 388–389
Pernicious anemia, 666
Personality, 101–106
　change in, in Alzheimer's disease, 935
　definition of, 101–102
　five-factor model of, 101–102, 102t, 105
　implications of stability of, 104–105
　premorbid, paraphrenias and, 1021
　stability versus change in, with aging, 102–104

Personality disorders, 1036–1043
　antisocial, 1038
　avoidant, 1039
　borderline, 1038
　dependent, 1039
　description and clinical course of, 1036
　differential diagnosis of, 1041
　etiology of, 1040–1041
　histrionic, 1038
　narcissistic, 1038
　not otherwise specified, 1040
　obsessive-compulsive, 1039
　paranoid, 1036–1037
　passive-aggressive, 1039–1040
　schizoid, 1037
　schizotypal, 1037
　stability of personality and, 104
　treatment of, 1041–1042
　　drugs in, 1041–1042
　　environmental manipulation in, 1042
　　psychotherapeutic, 1042
Personality traits, 101
　mean-level differences in, 102–103, 103
Person–milieu interaction, aging and, 119–120
PET (see Positron emission tomography)
PG (see Proteoglycans)
PGDRS (see Psychogeriatric Dependency Rating Scale)
Phalloarteriography, in impotence, 1151
Pharmacodynamics, 206
　of analgesics, 286
Pharmacokinetics, 203t, 203–206
　of analgesics, 286, 289–290
　definition of, 203
　neuropsychiatric assessment and, 225–226
Pharyngoesophageal function, aging and, 593–595
Phenazopyridine (Pyridium), urinary tract infections and, 360
Phenobarbital:
　seizures and, 1001, 1002
　in dying patients, 359
Phenolphthalein, in constipation, 1166
Phenothiazines:
　hyperthermia and, 1087
　hypothermia and, 1085
　in management of nausea and vomiting, 82
Phenytoin (Dilantin), 291

Phenytoin (Dilantin) (Cont.):
　distribution of, 204
　dizziness and, 1065
　interactions of, 206
　interstitial lung disease caused by, 541
　in peripheral neuropathy, 982
　seizures and, 1001, 1002
　　in dying patients, 359
Phlebectasis, 397
pH monitoring, in gastroesophageal reflux disease, 611
Phobias, in mental state examination, 1091
Phonologic knowledge, 915
Phosphate:
　deficiency of, in osteomalacia, 836
　metabolism of, disorders of, in osteomalacia, 830, 830
　serum levels of, in hyperparathyroidism, 840
Phosphodiesterase inhibitors, platelet function and, 690
Phosphorus metabolism, in chronic renal failure, 576
Photoaging, of skin, 385, 385t
Photocontact allergy, 393, 395
Photosensitivity reactions, 393–394, 395
Physiatrist, 324
　role of, overlap with geriatrician's role, 323
Physical activity:
　disease risk and, 131
　falls and, 1193
　weight-bearing:
　　hip fractures and, 327
　　osteoporosis and, 97
Physical dependence:
　on analgesics, 293–294
　on narcotics, in dying patients, 357
Physical environment, 238
Physical examination, 181–182
　benign prostatic hyperplasia and, 584–585
　in carcinoma of prostate, 586
　in constipation, 1162–1163
　depression and, 1014
　dizziness and, 1066
　in fecal incontinence, 1144
　in impotence, 1150
　in neuropsychiatric assessment, 228
　problems in performing, 213
　syncope and, 1072–1073
　in urinary incontinence, 1128

Physical functioning, 153–154
Physical therapy:
 in osteoarthritis, 886
 in Parkinson's disease, 961–962
Physical work capacity, aging and, 454–455
Physicians:
 distribution of resources and, 370–371
 Medicare reimbursement of, 160
 relationship with dying patient, 354
 relationship with family, 236
 responsibility of, team approach and, 185
 role in nursing home care, 335, 338
 role in planning, 236–238
  goals and, 237
  hospitalization and, 237
  institutionalization and, 237–238
  referral for formal services and, 237
 role in rehabilitation, 317
  decision making and, 317–318
  team goal setting and, 186
 values of, 371–372
 withdrawing and withholding life-sustaining therapies and, 373
Physicians' assistants, in nursing homes, 344
Physiologic change:
 age-related, rehabilitation and, 321
 disease-related, rehabilitation and, 322
Physostigmine, 275
 in Alzheimer's disease, 942
Pick's disease, 952
Pigment nephropathy, acute tubular necrosis and, 574
Pindolol, in hyperthyroidism, 725
Piracetam, in Alzheimer's disease, 942
Pituitary, aging and, 708
Pituitary hormones:
 neuroendocrine theory of aging and, 9
 secretion of, 909
Placebos, pain management and, 294
Planning:
 in nursing process, 308
 physician's role in (*see* Physician, role in planning)
Plasma cell dyscrasia, 67
Plasma, in hemophilia B, 693
Plastic deformities, in osteomalacia, 827, 831
Platelets:
 activation of, markers of, 682

Platelets (*Cont.*):
 destruction of, 685–686, 686t
  immune, 686
 hemostatic plug formation and, 679–685, *680*
  antithrombotic therapy for arterial thrombosis and, 683–685
  pathogenesis of arterial thrombus formation and, 682–683, 683t
  regulation of, *681*, 681–682
 ineffective production of, 685
 qualitative disorders of, 687–690, 688t, *687*
  drugs and, 689–690
  fibrin(ogen)olytic degradation products and, 689
  liver disease and, 689
  macromolecules and, 689
  myelodysplasia and, 689
  uremia and, 688–689
  von Willebrand disease and, 687–688
 quantitative disorders of, 685–687, 686t
Pleural effusions, rheumatoid arthritis and, 874
Pleuropulmonary complications, of rheumatoid arthritis, 874
Plicamycin (mithramycin), in Paget's disease, 847
PLM (*see* Myoclonus, nocturnal)
Plummer-Vision syndrome, 614
PM/DM (*see* Polymyositis/dermatomyositis)
PMR (*see* Polymyalgia rheumatica)
Pneumococcal pneumonia, immunization against, 196
Pneumococci, immunization against, pneumonia and, 516
Pneumonia, 509–516, 1055
 aspiration, anaerobic bacteria and, 512
 "aspiration," 511
 epidemics of, 516
 etiologic agents in, 510–513
 Friedländer's, 511
 "hypostatic," 513
 incidence and prognosis of, 509–510
 management of, 513–515, 515t
 nosocomial, 509–510, 515–516
 "nursing home," 513
 predisposing factors for, 510
 prevention of, 515–516
 "walking," 513
Pneumonitis, hypersensitivity (*see* Hypersensitivity pneumonitis)

PNS (*see* Peripheral nervous system)
Polyarteritis nodosa, 567
Polycythemia, stroke and, 931
Polyethylene glycol (Golytely), in constipation, 1163
Polymyalgia rheumatica (PMR), 861–863
 clinical features of, 861–862
 differential diagnosis of, 862–863
 pathogenesis of, 863
 pathology and laboratory features of, 862
 treatment and course of, 863
Polymyositis/dermatomyositis (PM/DM), 865–868
 classification of, 865, 866t
 clinical characteristics of, 865–866, 866t
 laboratory features of, 866–867
 pathogenesis of, 867
 prognosis of, 867–868
 treatment of, 867
Polyp(s):
 adenomatous:
  colorectal cancer and, 648
  gastric, 627
 hyperplastic:
  colorectal cancer and, 648
  gastric, 627
Polypharmacy:
 neuropsychiatric assessment and, 225–226
 psychopharmacology and, compliance with, 1048
Polyradiculopathy:
 acute inflammatory, 979–980
 chronic inflammatory, 981–982
Pontiac fever, 513
Positive end-expiratory pressure (PEEP), in respiratory failure, 536
Positron emission tomography (PET), in Alzheimer's disease, 937–938, 1096
Postherpetic neuralgia, 980
Postoperative management, importance of, 270–271
Postthrombotic syndrome, 481
Postural reflex impairment, in Parkinson's disease, 956
Postural stress, cardiovascular response to, 451
Potassium metabolism:
 aging changes in, 558
  clinical consequences of, 562–563
 in chronic renal failure, 575–576

Potency, sexual, 108, 109
(See also Impotence)
Povidone-iodine, pressure ulcers and, 1209
Power of attorney, 363, 365
durable, 355, 365
Practolol, in hyperthyroidism, 725
Prazepam, hepatic metabolism of, 205
Prazosin:
absorption of, 204
in hypertension, 494
Prednisolone, in herpes zoster, 1181
Prednisone:
in amyloidosis, 570
in herpes zoster, 1181
in polymyalgia rheumatica and giant cell arteritis, 863
with primary lymphoma of central nervous system, 1008
Preleukemia, 671–672, 672t
Preload, resting, 447
Premarin (see Estrogen)
Premedication, postoperative confusion and somnolence and, 275
Prerenal azotemia, 573
Presbycusis, 432, 434–435
conductive, cochlear, 435
neural, 434
patient examination and, 180
sensory, 434
strial, 434–435
(See also Hearing impairment)
"Presbyesophagus" 595
Presbyopia, 431
President's Commission for the Study of Ethical Problems in Medicine and Biomedical and Behavioral Research, 373
Pressor stress, cardiovascular response to, 451
Pressure ulcers, 1204–1210
in dying patients, 359
epidemiology of, 1204–1205
complications and, 1204–1205
mortality and, 1205
prevalence and incidence and, 1204
risk factors and, 1205
hip fractures and, 1202
infected, 1056
pathogenesis and pathophysiology of, 1205–1206
relative importance of pathophysiologic factors in, 1206
role of pressure in, 1205

Pressure ulcers: pathogenesis and pathophysiology of (Cont.):
role of shearing forces, friction, and moisture in, 1205–1206
patient assessment and, 1207–1208
associated infections and, 1207–1208
general, 1207
in physical examination, 181–182
prevention of, 1206–1207
antipressure devices in, 1206–1207
repositioning in, 1206
rehabilitation and, 320
treatment of, 1208–1210
experimental, 1210
local wound care in, 1209
specialized beds and mattresses in, 1208–1209
surgical, 1209–1210
systemic measures in, 1208
zinc deficiency and, 54
Presynaptic cholinergic markers, loss of, in Alzheimer's disease, 941–942
Prevention:
of diarrhea, 1174–1175
of falls:
among community-living elderly persons, 1194–1196
among institutionalized elderly persons, 1197–1198
of infections, 1060
of pressure ulcers, 1206–1207
antipressure devices in, 1206–1207
repositioning in, 1206
primary:
of atherosclerosis, 464
of disease (see Disease, prevention of)
secondary:
of atherosclerosis, 464
of disease (see Disease, prevention of)
of stroke, 931t, 931–932
of venous thrombosis, 703
Preventive geriatrics, preventive gerontology distinguished from, 170
Preventive gerontology, 167–170, 168t
alcohol and, 169–170
atherosclerosis and, 169
cancer and, 169
obesity and, 168–169

Preventive gerontology (Cont.):
osteoporosis and, 169
preventive geriatrics distinguished from, 170
smoking and, 168
Primary care, gerontological nurses in, 306–307
Primary memory, 915
Primates, evolution of longevity in, 18–20, 19t, 20
Primidone (Mysoline):
in Parkinson's disease, 955
seizures and, 1001, 1002
seizures and, in dying patients, 359
Private insurance, 162–163
"Private markers":
in hereditary amyloidosis, 30–31
heritability of longevity and, 23
Prochlorperazine (Compazine):
nausea and vomiting and, in dying patients, 358
pain and, in dying patients, 357
Procyclidine (Kemadrin), in Parkinson's disease, 959
Progeria, "of childhood," 27
Progeroid syndromes, 26–31
segmental, 26–29
unimodal, 29–31
Progesterone, female sexual function and, 111, 112
Progestins:
lipoproteins and, 46
menopause and, 786
Progression stage of cancer development, 74–75
Progressive supranuclear palsy, 952
Progressive systemic sclerosis, esophageal, 617
Prolactin, hypothalamic-pituitary-testicular axis and, 713
Prolymphocytic leukemia, 675
Promoters of cancer, 74
Promotility drugs, in gastroesophageal reflux disease, 612
Promotion stage of cancer development, 74
"Prompted voiding," in urinary incontinence, 1138
Propoxyphene, 289
Propranolol:
absorption of, 204
in angina pectoris, 468
in hyperthyroidism, 725
interstitial lung disease caused by, 541

Propranolol (*Cont.*):
  menopause and, 786
  in Parkinson's disease, 955
  pharmacodynamics of, 206
Proptosis, 431
Prostaglandin synthetase inhibitors, interference with renal autoregulation and, 574
Prostanoid synthesis, drugs influencing, platelet function and, 690
Prostate, 582–589
  carcinoma of, 586–589
    diagnosis of, 586–587
    etiology of, 586
    incidence of, 72, 586
    pathogenesis of, 586
    physical examination in, 586
    screening test for, 585
    staging classification of, 587, *587*
    staging evaluation of, 587–588
    symptoms of, 586
    treatment of, 588, *588*–589
  hyperplastic (*see* Benign prostatic hyperplasia)
  normal, *582*, 582–583, *583*
    anatomy of, 582
    biochemistry of, 583, *583*
    physiology of, 582–583
Prostatectomy:
  in benign prostatic hyperplasia, 585
  in prostate carcinoma, 588, *588*–589
Prostate-specific antigen (PSA), prostate carcinoma and, 588
Prostheses:
  amputation and, 328
  hip fractures and, 327
Protein(s), 51–52
  in brain, 906
  dietary intake of, in chronic renal failure, 576
  plasma levels of, in cachexia, 1105
  recommended daily allowance for, 51–52
  serum levels of, laboratory data and, 242
  synthesis of:
    aging and, 297
    total-body, liver function and, 604
  visceral concentration of, nutritional support and, 299
Protein-calorie malnutrition, 49–51
  anorexia of aging and, 50t, 50–51
  effects of, compared with effects of aging, 51, 52, 52t
  nutritional assessment and, 49

Protein-calorie malnutrition (*Cont.*):
  pathological causes of weight loss in elderly and, 51, *51*
  treatable causes of, 49–50, 50t
Protein intake:
  in Parkinson's disease, 960
  pressure ulcers and, 1208
Proteinuria, tubulointerstitial nephritis and, 573
Proteoglycans (PG), in cartilage, 850, *850*, 851
Protriptyline, in sleep apnea, 1120
Provera (*see* Medroxyprogesterone acetate)
Pruritus, 407–408
  in dying patients, 359
PSA (*see* Prostate-specific antigen)
Pseudo-arthritis, 895
"Pseudodementia" syndrome, 229
Pseudofractures, in osteomalacia, 831, 832, 833
Pseudogout (*see* Chondrocalcinosis)
Pseudohypertension, 491
Pseudo-rheumatoid arthritis, 894–895
Psychiatric disorders:
  dizziness and, 1066
  gait and, 1190
  in hypothyroidism, 727
  (*See also specific disorders*)
Psychiatric evaluation, 101, 229
Psychiatric history taking, 1089–1090
Psychiatric social workers, responsibility of, team approach and, 185
Psychiatry, 101
  personality stability and, 104–105
Psychodiagnostic instruments, age differences in performance on, 225
Psychogeriatric Dependency Rating Scale (PGDRS), 1090
Psychogeriatric nursing, 306
Psychological illness, constipation and, 1162
Psychological symptoms, in hypothyroidism, 727
Psychomotor behavior, disordered, in delirium, 922
Psychopharmacology, 1047–1051
  drug classes and, 1048–1051
  nonphysiologic considerations in, 1048
  physiologic considerations in, 1047–1048
Psychoses (*see* Paraphrenias; Schizophrenia)

Psychosocial function:
  hearing loss and, 433
  pain and, 284
Psychosomatic medicine, 105
Psychotherapy, 1045–1047
  chemical dependency and, 1033
  in depression, 1015
  in paraphrenias, 1023
  in personality disorders, 1037, 1042
  psychoanalytic concepts and, 1045–1046
    defense mechanisms and, 1046
    early life experiences and, 1045
    transference and countertransference and, 1046
    stages and tasks of adult development and, 1046
  therapeutic approaches of, 1046–1047
    behavioral, 1047
    family therapy and, 1047
    group therapy and, 1047
    supportive, 1046–1047
Psychotropic drugs, in alcoholism treatment, 1033
Pterygium, 426
Public policy:
  disability and health care utilization and, 118
  importance of, 122–124
  long-term care and, 350–351
Pulmonary disorders (*see* Respiratory disorders)
Pulmonary edema, cardiogenic, distinguishing adult respiratory distress syndrome from, 536
Pulmonary embolism, 545–546
  clinical features of, 546
  diagnosis of, 546
  regional versus general anesthesia and, 273–274
  treatment of, 546–547
Pulmonary examination, 182
Pulmonary fibrosis, idiopathic, 541–542
Pulmonary function(s):
  in interstitial lung disease, 539, 539t
  surgery and, 259–261
    evaluation and management of, *260*, 260–261
    pathophysiology of, 259–260
Pulmonary function tests, 503–505
  assessment of risk for morbidity and mortality and, 504, *505*, *506*
  assessment of type and extent of pulmonary disorder by, 504t, 504–505

Pulmonary function tests (*Cont.*):
  in chronic obstructive pulmonary disease, 529
  initial assessment of normality and, 503–504
Pulmonary hypertension, 544–545
  clinical findings in, 545
  etiology of, 544–545
  therapy of, 545
Pulmonary infections, laboratory studies in, 1058–1059
Pulmonary nodule, solitary, lung cancer and, 551
Pulmonary sarcoidosis, 542
Pulmonary thromboembolism, in pulmonary hypertension, 544
Pulmonary vascular disease, 544–547
Pulmonary vasoconstriction, in pulmonary hypertension, 545
Pulse(s), carotid, syncope and, 1072–1073
Pulse oximetry, anesthesia and, 277
"Punched out" appearance, in gout, 891
Pure autonomic failure (PAF), 964–966, 965t, 966t
Pyelonephritis, bacterial, acute, 571
Pyoderma, 394
Pyrazinamide (PZA), in tuberculosis, 521, 523
Pyridium (*see* Phenazopyridine)
Pyridoxine (*see* Vitamin B$_6$)
Pyrosis (*see* Heartburn)
Pyuria, urinary incontinence and, 1126
PZA (*see* Pyrazinamide)

Q

Quality-adjusted life expectancy, 117
Quality of care, 165
  cost versus, 165
  for hospitalized frail older patients, 252
Quality of life:
  dialysis and, 578
  physician values and, 371–372
Quality-adjusted life expectancy, 117
Quinidine, in antiarrhythmic therapy, 472
Quinine, dizziness and, 1065

R

RA (*see* Anemia, refractory; Rheumatoid arthritis)

Race:
  demographics of aging and, 147
  osteoarthritis and, 882
Radiation:
  ionizing, somatic theory of aging and, 6–7
  thyroid carcinoma associated with, 737
Radiation therapy, 80–81
  breast cancer and, 795–796
  in chronic lymphocytic leukemia, 674
  interstitial lung disease caused by, 541
  with intracranial neoplasms, 1007–1008
  in lung cancer, 552–553
  palliative, 80
  in prostate carcinoma, 589
  side effects of, 81, 1008
  technology for 80–81
Radiculopathy, *974*, 974–975
  spondylitic, 974–975
Radiography:
  in fecal incontinence, 1144–1145
  in interstitial lung disease, 539, *540*
  in osteomalacia, 831, 832
  in osteoporosis, 816–817
  in Paget's disease, 844–845, *845*
  in rheumatoid arthritis, 875
  (*See also* Bone scan; Chest x ray; Computed tomography; Magnetic resonance imaging; Positron emission tomography; Single photon emission computed tomography)
Radioiodide (RaI):
  ablation-related hypothyroidism and, 726
  in goiter, 734
  in hyperthyroidism, 725–726
Radioiodide uptake (RaIU) tests, thyroidal, in hyperthyroidism, 722
Radioiodinated contrast agents, acute tubular necrosis and, 574
Radioisotopes:
  in Paget's disease, 845
  (*See also* Bone scan)
RAEB (*see* Anemia, refractory, with excess blasts)
RAEBT (*see* Anemia, refractory, with excess blasts in transformation)
RaI (*see* Radioiodide)
RaIU (*see* Radioiodide uptake tests)
Ramsay Hunt syndrome, 1178–1179

Range of motion, in Parkinson's disease, 955–956
Ranitidine:
  in gastroesophageal reflux disease, 612
  peptic ulcer and, 623
RARS (*see* Anemia, refractory, with ring sideroblasts)
Rash, in polymyositis/dermatomyositis, 866
Ras-like oncogenes, 75
Rauwolfia derivatives, pharmacokinetics of, 226
RBF (*See* Blood flow, renal)
Reaction to injury hypothesis, of atherogenesis, 461
Reactive syndromes (*see* Adjustment disorders)
Recessive oncogenes, 75
Rectal examination, 182
Reference groups, role expectations and, team approach and, 187
Reference ranges, for laboratory tests (*see* Laboratory studies)
Reflexes, cardiovascular, syncope and, 1071–1072
Reglan (*see* Metaclopramide)
Regurgitation, in gastroesophageal reflux disease, 609
Rehabilitation, 312–329
  amputation and, 328
  assessment for, 325
  care needs and, 317–318
    physician's role in decision making and, 317–318
  care sites and, 324
  components of, 320–321
  deconditioning/immobility and, 329
  definition of, 319
  environment-specific differences and, 323
  goal-specific differences and, 324
  goals in, 314–317
    rehabilitation site and, 314–315
  of hearing loss, 438–442
    assistive listening devices and, 441–442
    hearing aid amplification and, 438–441, *439*
    speech reading/auditory training and, 441, 441t
  hip fractures and, 315–317, 327
  Parkinson's disease and, 328–329
  patient-specific differences and, 321–323

Rehabilitation: patient-specific differences and (*Cont.*):
  age-related, 321–322
  disease-related, 322–323
  in polymyositis/dermatomyositis, 867
  provider-specific differences and, 323
  in rheumatoid arthritis, 878
  stroke and, 312–313, 325–327
    acute phase in, 326
    chronic phase in, 326–327
    patient evaluation and, 313–314
    predictive factors and, 312–313
    rehabilitation phase in, 326
  team approach to, 321
Rehabilitation hospitals, 314–315, 324
  specialization in, 324
Relaxed selection, 33
Renal autoregulation, interference with, 574
Renal blood flow (*see* Blood flow, renal)
Renal disease, end-stage (ESRD), 577–579
  dialysis in, 577–578
  hemodialysis in, 578
  peritoneal dialysis in, 578–579
  transplantation in, 579
Renal diseases, 565–579
  glomerular, 567–570
    clinical presentation of, 568
    prevalence of, 567–568
  vascular, 565–567
    atheroembolic, 566–567
    thromboembolic, 566
  (*See also specific diseases*)
Renal failure:
  acute (ARF), 573–575
    acute tubular necrosis and, 573–574
    nonsteroidal anti-inflammatory agents and, 886
    obstructive urography and, 574–575
    prerenal azotemia and, 573
    renal autoregulation and, 574
  chronic, 575–577
    acid-base status and, 576
    calcium and phosphorus metabolism and, 576
    dietary protein intake and, 576
    dietary vitamins and, 576
    drug dosages and, 577
    indications for dialysis in, 577
    potassium homeostasis and, 575–576

Renal failure: chronic (*Cont.*):
    sodium and water and, 575
    systemic complications of, 577
  dementia and, 951
  postoperative, hypotension and, 276t, 276–277
Renal function:
  aging changes in, 555–563
    anatomic, 555–556
    clinical consequences of, 560–562
    glomerular filtration rate and, 556–557
    potassium homeostasis and, 558, 562–563
    renal blood flow and, 556
    sodium handling and, 557–558, 560
    tubular, 557
    water homeostasis and, 558–562
  fluid balance and, 1080
  nutritional support and, 300
  surgery and, 261
    evaluation and management of, 261
    pathophysiology of, 261
Renin-aldosterone axis, sodium metabolism and, 558
Renin-angiotensin system, in hypertension, 486
Renin, plasma concentration of, syncope and, 1069
Renovascular disease, 565–566
Repositioning, prevention of pressure ulcers and, 1206
Research, on aging, 3–4
Reserpine, in hypertension, 494
Residual volume (RV), aging and, 501
Resource allocation, 165, 368, 370–371
  differential, aging and, 116
Respiratory burst, neutrophil function and, 659
Respiratory depression:
  analgesics and, 292
  from narcotics, in dying patients, 358
Respiratory disorders:
  patient approach and, 505–507, 507t
  in polymyositis/dermatomyositis, 866
  pulmonary function tests and, 504t, 504–505
  regional versus general anesthesia and, 274
Respiratory distress:
  adult respiratory distress syndrome and, 536
  in dying patients, 358

Respiratory failure, 531–536
  acute (ARF), 531
  hypercapnic, 531t, 531–532
    secondary to chronic obstructive lung disease, management of, 533–535
    secondary to decreased minute ventilation, 532
    secondary to mismatch of ventilation and perfusion, 532–533
  hypoxic, 535t, 535–536
  pathogenesis of, 526, 536t
Respiratory function, in hypothyroidism, 728
Respiratory system, aging of, 499–507
  pathophysiology of, 499–503, 500t
  pulmonary function tests and, 503–505
Respite care, 352
Rest, in rheumatoid arthritis, 876
Restraints, fall prevention and, 1198
Resuscitation, of dying patients, decision making about, 355
Reticulocyte index, in anemia, 664
Retina, 423
  detachment of, 429–430
  disorders of, *428*, 428–429, *429*
  metabolism of, zinc and, 55
Retinal artery, central, occlusion of, 428, *428*
Retinal vein, central, occlusion of, 428–429, *429*
Retinitis, 429, *429*
Retinopathy, diabetic, 430, *430*
Reversible ischemic neurological deficit (RIND), clinical presentation of, 482
Rewarming, in hypothermia, 1086
Rheumatic disease, mitral disease and, 472
Rheumatic disorders, in hypothyroidism, 728–729
Rheumatoid arthritis (RA), 869–879, *870*
  clinical features of, 871–873, 872t
  complications of, 873–875
    articular, 873
    extraarticular, 873–875
  diagnosis of, 871, 872t
  differential diagnosis of, 876
  epidemiology of, 871
  etiology and pathogenesis of, 869–871, *870*
  interstitial lung disease associated with, 541

Rheumatoid arthritis (RA) (*Cont.*):
  (RA), laboratory evaluation in, 875, 875t
    radiographic evaluation in, 875
  transparent skin and, 396
  treatment of, 876–878
    corticosteroids in, 878
    immunosuppressives in, 877–878
    medications in, 876
    rehabilitation in, 878
    second-line therapy in, 876–877
    surgical, 878
Rheumatoid factor, in rheumatoid arthritis, 870
Rheumatoid nodules, rheumatoid arthritis and, 874
Rhinophyma, 393, 395
Riboflavin (*see* Vitamin B$_{12}$)
Rifampin (RIF):
  interactions of, 206
  in tuberculosis, 521, 523
RIND (*see* Reversible ischemic neurological deficit)
Risk(s):
  anesthetic, 271, 271–273
    obvious, 271–272, 272
    subtle, 272–273
  surgical (*see* Surgery, risks of)
Risk factors:
  for Alzheimer's disease, 939, 939, 939t
  for atherosclerosis, 459t, 459–461
    pathobiology and, 462–463
  continuities in life course and, 120–121
  for coronary heart disease, lipoproteins as, 768, 769
  definition of, 125
  for falls:
    identifying, 1194t, 1194–1198
    among community-living elderly persons, 1192–1194
    among institutionalized elderly persons, 1197
  in hypertension, 486–487
  for infection, 1056–1057
    environmental, 1056
    host factors as, 1056–1057
  for mental illness, age differences in, 225
  for morbidity and mortality, 125
    age as, 126, 127
    cancer and, 133–134
    coronary heart disease and, 129, 129t

Risk factors: for morbidity and mortality (*Cont.*):
    estrogen use and, 132
    falls and, 134
    hypertension and, 130–131
    lipids and lipoproteins and, 129–130
    obesity and, 131–132
    osteoporosis and fractures and, 134–135
    physical activity and, 131
    pulmonary function tests and, 504, 505, 506
    sex as, 126, 128, 129
    smoking and, 130
    stroke and, 132, 132t, 132–133
  for osteoporosis, 782, 815, 816t
  for pressure ulcers, 1205
  for stroke, 931t, 931–932
  for venous thrombotic disorders, 699–700, 700
Risk-taking behavior, sex differential in longevity and, 40
Ritalin (*see* Methylphenidate)
Role ambiguity, team approach and, 188
Role conflict, team approach and, 188
Role expectations, team approach and, 187–189
    behavioral roles and, 188–189
    externally imposed, 187
    factors contributing to, 188
    internally generated, 188
Role overload, team approach and, 188
Romberg test, 1185
Rosacea, 393, 394
RV (*see* Residual volume)

S

Sacroiliac joints, disease of, 975
Salicylates:
  dizziness and, 1065
  in gout, 893
  nutrient interactions of, 57–58
  in osteoarthritis, 885
  (*See also* Aspirin)
Saline, pressure ulcers and, 1209
Saliva:
  artificial (Salivart), dry mouth and, 359
  role in maintenance of oral health, 415, 415t
  whole, 415

Salivary glands, 415t, 415–416
Salmonellosis, diarrhea and, 1170
"Salt and pepper" appearance, in hyperparathyroidism, 838, 839
Sarcoidosis, pulmonary, 542
Sarcomas, squamous cell, 586
SBN$_2$ (*see* Single-breath nitrogen washout technique)
Schatzki ring, 614–615
Schizoid personality disorder, 1037
Schizophrenia, 1097
  dementia associated with, 951
  paranoid, 1020
Schizotypal personality disorder, 1037
Scleritis, rheumatoid arthritis and, 874
Scleroderma, esophageal dysphagia and, 1159
Scleromalacia perforans, rheumatoid arthritis and, 874
Scoliosis, mental retardation and, 1027
Scopolamine, premedication with, surgery and, 275
Screening:
  for cancer, 76t, 76–77
    of breast, 197, 792–793
    cervical, 197
    colorectal, 197
    of lung, 548
    prostatic, 585
  for chemical dependency, 1032
  cognitive function and, 651, 1092
  for congenital bleeding disorders, 692–693
  neuropsychiatric, 227–228
Scrotum, angiokeratomas of, 397, 397
SDH (*see* Hypertension, systolic-diastolic)
Sebaceous glands:
  age-related changes in, 387
  of external ear, atrophy of, 433–434
Seborrheic dermatitis, 393, 393, 394, 408
Seborrheic keratoses, 398–399, 399
Secondary memory, 915
Second Revolution in Health, 121–122
Sedation, analgesics and, 292
Sedatives:
  depression and, 1013
  falls and, 1193
  menopause and, 786
  sleep disorders and, 1113
Sedentary lifestyle, effects of aerobic exercise training and, 88, 88–90, 89, 91
Segmental demyelination, in peripheral neuropathy, 978

Segmental progeroid syndromes, 26–29

Seip syndrome, 29

Seizures, 999–1002
  absence, 999
  in Alzheimer's disease, 937
  analgesics and, 293
  classification of, 999–1000
  in dying patients, 359–360
  etiology of, 1000
  evaluation of, 1000
  generalized, 999–1000
  in herpes simplex encephalitis, 985
  intracranial neoplasms and, 1005
  mental retardation and, 1028–1029
  partial, 999
    complex, 999
    simple, 999
  Todd's paralysis and, 928, 930
  tonic-clonic, secondarily generalized, 999
  treatment of, 1000–1002
    barbiturates in, 1002
    carbamazepine in, 1002
    general principles of, 1000–1002
    phenytoin in, 1002
    status epilepticus and, 1002
    valproate in, 1002

Selection, relaxed, 33

Selenium, 55
  deficiency of, changes associated with, 55

Self-assessment inventories, for hearing impairment, 436

Self-care, institutionalization and, 119

Self-determination, ethical dilemmas and, 369

Self Help for Hard of Hearing People (SHHH), 441

Self-help groups, for hearing impaired persons, 441

Self-perception, of health, 176

Self-report instruments, personality assessment and, 101

Senescence, definition of, 5n

Senescent phenotype, genetic syndromes modulating aspects of, 26–32

Senile gait, 1187–1188

Senile (neuritic) plaques, 901
  in Alzheimer's disease, 940, *940*

"Senile squalor" syndrome, 1032–1033

Sensory ataxia, gait and, 1189

Sensory degeneration, vestibular dysfunction and, 442–443

"Sensory instability," urinary incontinence and, 1126

Sensory memory, 915

Sepsis:
  gout distinguished from, 891
  hepatic, 634
  hypothermia and, 1085
  pressure ulcers and, 1204

Serotonin, 907–908
  in depression, 1011
  regulation of, 706

Sertoli cells, decline in, 713

Serum albumin, 49
  proteins and, 52

Serum chemistries, lung cancer and, 551

Serum glutamic-oxaloacetic transaminase (SGOT), in tuberculosis, 524

Setting:
  for disease prevention, 193
  for patient examination, 179–180

Sex:
  demographics of aging and, 147
  as risk factor, for morbidity and mortality, 126, *128*, 129

Sex differences:
  in longevity, 24–25, 37, 37t, 37–47, 38, *40*, 41t, *42–45*
  in osteoarthritis, 882
  in paraphrenias, 1021

Sex hormones, 113
  cardiovascular effects of, 46
  lipoprotein levels and, 44–47

Sex therapy, in impotence, 1152–1153

Sexual history, 181

Sexuality, 108–113
  in aging females, 110–113
  in aging males, 109–110
  analysis and assessment of, 108–109
  therapy and, 113

SGOT (*see* Serum glutamic-oxaloacetic transaminase)

Shearing forces, pressure ulcers and, 1205–1206

SHHH (*see* Self Help for Hard of Hearing People)

Shigellosis, diarrhea and, 1170

Shingles (*see* Herpes zoster)

Shivering, surgery and, 276

Shock, Nathan W., 4

Shock, hypovolemic, diabetic ketoacidosis and, 754

Short-term memory, 915

Shy-Drager syndrome, 966–967

SIADH (*see* Syndrome of inappropriate antidiuretic hormone secretion)

Sialorrhea, in Parkinson's disease, 957

Sicca syndrome, rheumatoid arthritis and, 874

Sideroblastic anemia, 667

Sigmoidoscopy, in constipation, 1163

Silicon, 56

Silicosis, 538

Silver sulfadiazine, pressure ulcers and, 1209

Sinemet (*see* Carbidopa)

Single-breath carbon monoxide diffusing capacity (DLco), 501

Single-breath nitrogen (SBN$_2$) washout technique, 501

Single-photon absorptiometry (SPA):
  in osteomalacia, 831
  in osteoporosis, 816, 817

Single photon emission computed tomography (SPECT), in Alzheimer's disease, 937–938, 1096

Sinus node disease, syncope and, 1071

Sjögren's syndrome:
  rheumatoid arthritis and, 873–874
  salivary glands and, 416

Skeletal muscle [*see* Muscle(s), skeletal]

Skilled nursing facilities, rehabilitation in, 315, 317

Skin:
  age-related changes in, 383–388
    apocrine sweat glands and, 387
    dermal-epidermal cohesion and, 388
    dermis and, 385–387
    eccrine sweat glands and, 387
    inflammatory responses and, 390
    permeability and, 388–389
    physical appearance and, 408, 408t, 409t
    sebaceous glands and, 387
    stratum corneum and, 383, 384t
    subcutaneous tissue and, 387
    viable epidermis and, 383–385
    vitamin D synthesis and, 390–391
    wound healing and, 389–390, 390t
  breakdown of (*see* Pressure ulcers)
  cancer of:
    progression from carcinoma in situ to invasive squamous cell carcinoma, *401*, 401–402, *402*
    ultraviolet radiation and, 400
  collagen of, menopause and, 781
  in gout, 891
  in hypothyroidism, 728
  internal disorders and, 396–397, *396–398*

Skin (*Cont.*):
Leser-Trélat sign and, 396–397, 399
in Parkinson's disease, 957
in physical examination, 181–182
transparent, disorders associated with, 396
Skin disorders, 391–397, 398–408
expression of, 393–395, 393–396
prevalence in elderly, 391t, 391–393, 392t
(*See also specific disorders*)
Skin tags, 397
Skin testing:
as indicator of nutritional status, 49
for tuberculosis, 520
Sleep:
disease prevention and, 196
menopause and, 781
Sleep apnea, 1112, 1114t, 1114–1117
dementia and depression and, 1117
in hypothyroidism, 728
obstructive, 1113
prevalence and definitions of, 1114–1115
sudden nocturnal death and, 1116–1117
transitions from health to disease in, 1115, 1115–1116, 1116
treatment of, 1120
Sleep disorder(s), 1109t, 1109–1121
aging and, 1110t, 1110–1111, 1111
clinical evaluation of, 1117–1119
history in, 1117t, 1117–1118
objective assessment in, 1118–1119
major, 1111–1112, 1112t
excessive somnolence and, 1113
initiating and maintaining sleep and, 1112–1113
parasomnias and, 1114
sleep-wake cycle disturbances and, 1113–1114
treatment of, 1119t, 1119–1120
(*See also* Sleep apnea)
Sleep disorder centers, 1119
Sleep-wake cycle disturbances, 1113–1114
in delirium, 922
in Parkinson's disease, 956–957
SM (*see* Streptomycin)
Small intestine:
aging and, 597–600
calcium metabolism and, 800–801, 801
bone and, 803
vitamin D and, 802

Smell:
cachexia and, 1104
as defense against enteric infection, 1171–1172
Smoking:
atherosclerosis and, 463
cancer risk and, 133, 133–134
chronic obstructive pulmonary disease and, 528–529
in diabetes mellitus, 752
disease prevention and, 195
effect of body weight on mortality and, 762
gastroesophageal reflux disease and, 611
lung cancer and, 548
menopause and, 777
pharmacokinetics and, 206
preventive gerontology and, 168
as risk factor, 130
sex differential in longevity and, 40–41
Smooth muscles, pharyngoesophageal function and, 594
Snellen chart, 422
SOAP (Subjective, Objective, Assessment, Plan) format, 339, 341t
Social environment, 238–239
Social factors:
anorexia and, 50
in depression, 1011–1012
Social function:
age-related changes in, rehabilitation and, 322
disease-related changes in, rehabilitation and, 322
rehabilitation assessment of, 325
Social history, 180–181
Social isolation, hearing loss and, 433
Social security, policy and, 122
Social Security Act:
Title XIX of (*see* Medicaid)
Title XX of (*see* Medicare)
Social Service Block Grants, long-term care under, 350
Social support network, in neuropsychiatric assessment, 230
Social ties, epidemiology of aging and, 154
Social worker, responsibility of, team approach and, 185
Socioeconomic status, aging and, 116–117, 117t
Sociology of aging, 115–124
SOD (*see* Superoxide dismutase)

Sodium:
metabolism of:
aging changes in, 557–558
in chronic renal failure, 575
clinical consequences of, 560
restriction of:
in chronic renal failure, 575
hypertension and, 492
urinary losses of, 1080–1081
Sodium fluoride, in osteoporosis, 823
Sodium phosphate, in constipation, 1166
Sodium polystyrene sulfonate (Kayexalate), in chronic renal failure, 576
Sodium warfarin (Coumadin), in pneumonia, 514
Solar keratoses (*see* Actinic keratoses)
Somatic cells, 22
Somatic mutation theory of aging, 6–7
Somatomedin C, as index of nutritional status, 49
Somatostatin, 908
hypothalamus and, 710–711
pituitary responsiveness to, 711
Somnolence, postoperative:
acute, 274
premedication and, 275
prolonged, 274
relative overdose and, 275
SPA (*see* Single-photon absorptiometry)
Spasm, esophageal dysphagia and, 1159
Speciation, longevity and, 20
Specimen collection, infections and, 1059
SPECT (*see* Single photon emission computed tomography)
Speech:
in mental state examination, 1091
in Parkinson's disease, 957
(*See also* Aphasia)
Speech and language assessment, 230
Speech discrimination test, 437–438
Speech reading, 441
Speech Reception Threshold (SRT), 436–437
Sphincterotomy, endoscopic, in choledocholithiasis, 636
Spinal cerebellar degeneration syndromes, 952
Spinal compression fractures, treatment of, 819–820
Spinal electrical stimulator, pain and, in dying patients, 358

Spinal epidural morphine pump, pain and, in dying patients, 358
Spinal stenosis, lumbar, 973, *974*
Spine:
  cervical:
    injuries of, head injury and, 996
    rheumatoid arthritis in, 873
  functional anatomy of, 970, *971*
Spine disease, 970–975
  back pain and:
    general approach to patient with, 970–972
    management of, 975
  diagnostic categories of, 972t, 972–975
  mechanical, 975
  vertebral, 975
Spirometry, lung cancer and, 550
Spironolactone, hyperkalemia and, 562
Spleen, sequestration of neutrophils in, 671
Splenectomy, in hairy cell leukemia, 675
Splints, in rheumatoid arthritis, 878
Spondylitic myelopathy, 973, *973*
Spondylitic radiculopathy, 974–975
Spondylolisthesis, 975
Spondylosis, cervical, 973–974
  gait and, 1188
"Springing powers," 365
Sputum bacteriology, in pneumonia, 514
Sputum cytology, lung cancer and, 550
Staging, of breast cancer, 796
Staging:
  of prostate carcinoma, 587, 587–588
  TNM system for:
    lung cancer and, 549
    prostate carcinoma and, 587
Standards of care, 309
Stanozolol, lipoproteins and, 45–46
Staphylococcus aureus:
  bacterial meningitis and, 983, 984
  diarrhea and, 1170
  pneumonia and, 512
Staphylococcus pneumoniae, bacterial meningitis and, 983, 984
Starvation, hypothermia and, 1084–1085
Stasis dermatitis, 407, *407*
Stasis ulcers, 407, *407*
Station, examination of, 1185
Status epilepticus, treatment of, 1002
Steatorrhea, pancreatitis and, 642
Steinert disease (*see* Myotonic dystrophy)

Stents, endoscopic placement of, in gallbladder adenocarcinoma, 636
Stercoral ulcer, constipation and, 1163
Stereotypes, personality disorders and, 1041
Steroids:
  anabolic, in osteoporosis, 823
  in asthma, 527–528
  in chronic obstructive pulmonary disease, 530
  in management of nausea and vomiting, 82
  pain and, in dying patients, 357
  pruritus and, in dying patients, 359
  (*See also* Corticosteroids; Glucocorticoids; *specific steroids*)
Stimulants, in depression, 1016
Stochastic theories of aging, 6–8
Stomach:
  adenocarcinoma of, 626–627
  benign tumors of, 627–628
  lymphomas of, 628
  (*See also entries beginning with term* Gastric)
Stool softeners:
  in constipation, 1166–1167
  in dying patients, 358
Stool specimens, lung cancer and, 550
Stratum corneum, age-related changes in, 383, 384t
Strength, decline in, 91
Streptococcus pneumoniae, 1059
  pneumonia and, 511
Streptodornase, pressure ulcers and, 1209
Streptokinase:
  pressure ulcers and, 1209
  pulmonary embolism and, 547
  in stroke, 929
  in venous thrombotic disorders, 702
Streptomycin (SM), in tuberculosis, 521, 523
Stress:
  cardiovascular response to, 451–455
    beta-adrenergic stimulation and, 453, *454*
    dynamic exercise stress and, *452*, 452–453, *453*
    physical work capacity and, 454–455
    postural stress and, 451
    pressor stress and, 451
  dynamic exercise, cardiovascular response to, *452*, 452–453, *453*
  in etiology of delirium, 923

Stress (*Cont.*):
  mechanical, osteoarthritis and, 882–883
Stress activation, hypothalamic-pituitary-adrenal axis and, 708
Stress incontinence, 1124, 1126
Stroke, 926–932
  background for, 926t, 926–927
  cerebellar, dizziness and, 1065
  clinical presentation of, 482
  depression and, 1013
  deteriorating, 926
    management of, 929
  diagnosis of, 482–483
  evaluation in, 927–928
    differential diagnosis and, 928
    history in, 927
    laboratory studies in, 927–928, 928t
    physical examination in, 927
  gait and, 1188
  hemorrhagic, 926
  hypertension and, 487
  ischemic, 926
  major, 926
    management of, 928–929
  management of, 928–931
    general principles of, 928, 928t
  minor, 926
    management of, 929–931, 930t
  multi-infarct dementia and, 931, 931t
  pathogenesis of, 481
  prevention of, 931t, 931–932
  rehabilitation and, 312–313, 325–327
    in acute phase, 326
    in chronic phase, 326–327
    patient evaluation and, 313–314
    predictive factors and, 312–313
    in rehabilitation phase, 326
  risk factors for, *132*, 132t, 132–133
    diabetes as, 133
    hypertension as, 132–133
  therapy of, 483
  ticlopidine and, 684–685
  young, 927
  (*See also* Transient ischemic attack)
Stye, 424
Subcutaneous tissue, age-related changes in, 387
Substantia nigra implantation, in Parkinson's disease, 963
Sucralfate:
  in gastroesophageal reflux disease, 612

Sucralfate (*Cont.*):
  peptic ulcer and, 623
Sulfonylureas:
  in diabetes mellitus, 752t, 752–753
    problems associated with, 753
  drug interactions of, 750
Sunlight (*see* Ultraviolet radiation)
Superoxide dismutase (SOD), in Down's syndrome, 29
Superoxide, free radical theory of aging and, 9, 10
Support environment, rehabilitation assessment of, 325
Supportive care, for cancer, 82
Supportive therapy, 1046–1047
Supraventricular premature beats, 471, 471t
Surgery, 254–268
  in acute cholecystitis, 635
  in adenocarcinoma of bile ducts, 637
  anesthesia and (*see* Anesthesia)
  for appendicitis, 264
  benign prostatic hyperplasia and, 585
  for biliary tract disease, 263–264
  for breast cancer, operative mortality and, 794
  for cancer, 80
  for cardiac disease, 268, 268t
  cardiovascular abnormalities and, 256–259
    evaluation and management of, 257t, 257–259, 258t, 259
    pathophysiology of, 256–257
  in choledocholithiasis, 636
  for colonic disorders, 265, 265–266
  in fecal incontinence, 1145
  gastric adenocarcinoma and, 627
  for gastric disorders, 264–265
  in gastroesophageal reflux disease, 612
  in goiter, 734
  hip fractures and, 1201
  in hypercalcemia, 841
  in impotence, 1152
  with intracranial neoplasms, 1007, 1009
  in lung cancer, 552
  in motor neuron diseases, 968
  in osteoarthritis, 887
  in Paget's disease, *847*, 847–848
  in pancreatic cancer, 643
  in Parkinson's disease, 962–963
  for peripheral vascular disease, 267–268

Surgery (*Cont.*):
  pressure ulcers and, 1209–1210
  pulmonary abnormalities and, 259–261
    evaluation and management of, *260*, 260–261
    pathophysiology of, 259–260
  renal abnormalities and, 261
    evaluation and management of, 261
    pathophysiology of, 261
  in renovascular disease, 566
  in rheumatoid arthritis, 878
  risks of, 254–256, 270t, 270–271
    assessment of, 256
    morbidity and mortality and, 254t, 254–256, 255t
  in syncope, 1074
  thyroid nodules and, cold, 736–737
  in tuberculosis, 524
  in urinary incontinence, 1138–1139
  wound healing, immune function, and nutrition and, 261–263, *262*
    evaluation and management of, 262–263
    pathophysiology of, 261–262
  wound healing and, 389, 390t
  (*See also specific procedures*)
Surrogate:
  designation of, 374
  dying patients and, 355
  withdrawing and withholding life-sustaining therapies and, 373
Surrogate authority, 363
Survival curve, 15, *16*
Survivorship kinetics of biological aging, 5
Swallowing, 419
  aging and, 593–595
  cachexia and, 1104
  (*See also* Dysphagia; Gastroesophageal reflux)
Swallowing syncope, 1072
Sweat glands:
  apocrine, age-related changes in, 387
  eccrine, age-related changes in, 387
Sweating:
  fluid losses and, 1082
  hyperthermia and, 1087
Sweden, incomes in, 117–118
Symmetrel (*see* Amantadine)
β-Sympathomimetics, in hypercapnic respiratory failure, 533–534
Symptoms, underreporting of, 176–177

Syncope, 1068–1076
  age- and disease-related factors predisposing to, 1069
  cough, 1072
  defecation, 1072
  definition of, 1068
  epidemiology of, 1068
  etiology of, 1069t, 1069–1072
    abnormal blood composition in, 1072
    abnormal cardiovascular reflexes in, 1071–1072
    central nervous system disease in, 1072
    electrical heart disease in, 1070–1071
    hypotension in, 1071
    structural heart disease in, 1070
  evaluation of, 1072–1074, *1075*
  micturition, 1072
  pathophysiology of, 1068–1069
  swallowing, 1072
  therapeutic issues in, 1074
  vasovagal, 1071–1072
Syndrome of inappropriate antidiuretic hormone secretion (SIADH):
  water metabolism and, 561
  water restriction in, 54
Synovial fluid, of diarthroidal joints, 856
Synovial membrane, of diarthroidal joints, 855, 855t
Syntactic knowledge, 915
Synthases, 908
Synthyroid (*see* Thyroxine)
Syphilis:
  dementia and, 950
  meningovascular, 987
  (*See also* Neurosyphilis)
Systemic necrotizing vasculitis, 567

T

T cell(s), 62, 62t, 66
  assessment of immune function and, 65–66
  augmentation of activity of, 69
  immune response initiation and, 63
T-cell function, zinc and, 54–55
T-cell system, thymic involution and, 61
T$_3$ (*see* Triiodothyronine)
T$_3$RU (*see* Triiodothyronine resin uptake)

T₄ (*see* Thyroxine)

Tabes dorsalis, in parenchymatous neurosyphilis, 987

Tachycardia:
in hyperthyroidism, 720
ventricular, 471

Talk (*see* Speech)

Tardive dyskinesia, antipsychotics and, 1050

Taste:
cachexia and, 1104
oral health and, 416–417

Taste buds, reduction in, anorexia and, 50

TBC-NAA (*see* Total body calcium by neutron activation analysis)

TDB (*see* Tripotassium dicitrato bismuthate)

TDDs (*see* Telephone devices for the deaf)

Team approach, 184–191
administrative and organizational problems and, 190–191
complex role of geriatrician and, 190
health system challenges and, 190–191
program development and, 190
communication patterns and, 189
conflict management and negotiation and, 189–190
controversy and, 185–186
professional responsibility and, 185
team composition and membership and, 185t, 185–186, 186t
team format and, 1185
decision making and, 189
to dying patients, 355
education of team members and, 186–187
on comprehensive assessment, 187
on diseases and problems of old age, 187
on health, 186–187
on health care service provision, 187
on team approach, 187
extended organizational teams and, 190
gerontological nurses and, 310
goals and objectives and, 186
leadership and, 189
norms and, 189

Team approach (*Cont.*):
in rehabilitation, 321
role expectations and, 187–189
behavioral roles and, 188–189
externally imposed, 187
factors contributing to, 188
internally generated, 188
settings for, 190
special program teams and, 190
specific clinical care teams and, 190
team concept and, 184–185

Tear secretion, decreased, 426

Technological advances, ethical issues and, 367–368

Teeth, 414
cachexia and, 1104
dental caries and, 414–415
disease of, 196
loss of, 196, 413–414, 414t
mental retardation and, 1028

Tegretol (*see* Carbamazepine)

Telephone devices for the deaf (TDDs), 442

Temperature regulation disorders (*see* Hyperthermia; Hypothermia)

Temporal arteries:
biopsy of, in giant cell arteritis, 862
in physical examination, 182

Temporal arteritis, 431

Temporomandibular joint (TMJ), 419

Tendons, aging and, 857

Tessalon, cough and, in dying patients, 358

Testicular disorders, endocrine, 715–716

Testicular function, aging and, 713

Testosterone:
apocrine sweat glands and, 387
cachexia and, 1104
female sexual function and, 112
hypothalamic-pituitary-testicular axis and, 712, 713
male sexual function and, 109–110
impotence and, 1147, 1150, 1152
prostate and, 583, 583
pathological impaired coupling and, 810

Tetanus, 1056
immunization for, 196

Tetracycline:
assessment of mineralization and, 831
esophageal injury induced by, 616
fungating tumors and, in dying patients, 359
nutrient interactions of, 57

Tetrahydroaminoacridine, in Alzheimer's disease, 942–943

Tetraiodothyroxine (T₄), depression and, 1013

TH (*see* Tyrosine hydroxylase)

Thalassemia, 667

Theophylline:
in asthma, 527
in chronic obstructive pulmonary disease, 530
in hypercapnic respiratory failure, 534
sleep disorders and, 1113

Thiamine (*see* Vitamin B₁)

Thioridazine (Mellaril):
in Alzheimer's disease, 943
hallucinations and, in dying patients, 359

Thirst, fluid balance and, 1079–1080

Thoracotomy:
with lobectomy, respiratory reserve adequate for, 550–551
operative mortality and, 268
pain syndrome following, 284

Thorazine (*see* Chlorpromazine)

Thought, disorder of, in delirium, 921

Thrombin, hemostatic plug formation and, *680*, 680–682

Thrombocytopenia, drug-induced, 686t, 686–687

Thromboembolism:
pulmonary, in pulmonary hypertension, 544
renal, 566

Thrombolytic agents:
in myocardial infarction, 468t, 468–469
pulmonary embolism and, 547
in stroke, 929

Thrombosis:
arterial, risk factors for, 683, 683t
deep venous, 546
regional versus general anesthesia and, 273–274
estrogen and, 46
stroke and, 926
venous, 698–703, *699*
antithrombotic agents and, 700–702
antithrombotic therapy and, 702–703
risk factors for, 699–700, *700*

Thrombus(i):
arterial:
antithrombotic therapy for, 683–685

Thrombus(i): arterial, antithrombotic therapy for (*Cont.*):
  pathogenesis of formation of, 682–683, 683t
  "white," 682
Thymic involution, immune function and, 60–61, 66, 69
Thyroid:
  carcinoma of, 736–737
    age differences in, 78
    radiation-associated, 737
    surgical removal versus suppression therapy of cold nodules and, 737
  deliberate ablation of, 725
  diseases of, presentation of, 214–215
  enlargement of, in hyperthyroidism, 720
  (*See also* Hyperthyroidism; Hypothyroidism)
Thyroiditis:
  lymphocytic, "silent" or "painless," hyperthyroidism due to, 724
  subacute (granulomatous; de Quervain's), therapy of, 734–735
Thyroid nodules, 735–736
  cancerous, 735
  clinical approach to, 735–736
  cold, suppression therapy of, 736
Thyroid-stimulating hormone (TSH):
  depression and, 1013
  in impotence, 1150
Thyrotoxicosis, iodide-induced (IIT), 724
Thyrotropin (TSH), serum:
  in hyperthyroidism, 721
  in hypothyroidism, 730–731
Thyrotropin-releasing hormone (TRH), in hyperthyroidism, 721
Thyroxine (Levothyroid; Synthyroid; T₄):
  blood levels of, in hyperthyroidism, 722–723
    nonhyperthyroid elevation of, 723
  cardiac contraction and, 450
  in hypothyroidism, 731–732
    ablation-related, 726
  serum levels of, in hyperthyroidism, 721
  thyroid nodules and, 736
TIA (*see* Transient ischemic attack)
Ticarcillin, platelet function and, 690
Ticlopidine:
  myocardial infarction and, 684–685
  in stroke, 932

Ticlopidine (*Cont.*):
  stroke and, 684–685
  in transient ischemic attack, 931
Time, required for immune reaction, 61
Timed manual performance (*see* Manual performance)
Timolol:
  in angina pectoris, 468
  in hyperthyroidism, 725
Tissue plasminogen activator (tPA):
  pulmonary embolism and, 547
  in stroke, 929
  in venous thrombotic disorders, 702
Tissue sensitivity, psychopharmacology and, 1048
TMJ (*see* Temporomandibular joint)
TNF (*see* Tumor necrosis factor)
TNM system:
  lung cancer and, 549
  prostate carcinoma and, 587
Tocopherols, 57
Todd's paralysis, 928, 930
Tolectin (*see* Tolmetin sodium)
Tolerance:
  analgesics and, 293–294
  to narcotics, in dying patients, 357
Tolmetin sodium (Tolectin), interference with renal autoregulation and, 574
Total body calcium by neutron activation analysis (TBC-NAA), in osteoporosis, 816, 818
Total body water, 558
Total joint replacement:
  of hip:
    in osteoarthritis, 887
    in Paget's disease, 847, 847
  in osteoarthritis, 887
Toxins:
  exogenous, dementias and, 951
  peripheral neuropathy and, 981
tPA (*see* Tissue plasminogen activator)
Trace elements, 54–56
Tracheobronchial secretions, in hypercapnic respiratory failure, 534
Tracheostomy, in hypercapnic respiratory failure, 534–535
Tracheotomy, in motor neuron diseases, 968
Trachoma, 425
Traction diverticulum, 615
Tranquilizers, sleep disorders and, 1113

Transcutaneous nerve stimulation:
  in dying patients, 357–358
  in postherpetic neuralgia, 1181
Transference, psychotherapy and, 1046
Transferrin, absorption of, in small intestine, 600
Transfusion, 277
  massive, 698
Transient ischemic attack (TIA):
  clinical presentation of, 482
  crescendo, 930–931
  definition of, 926
  diagnosis of, 482–483
  dizziness and, 1065
  management of, 929–931, 930t
  pathogenesis of, 481
  therapy of, 483
Transperineal biopsy, in carcinoma of prostate, 587
Transplantation:
  adrenal medullary, in Parkinson's disease, 963
  of bone marrow, in chronic granuloytic leukemia, 676
  renal:
    in end-stage renal disease, 579
    mortality associated with, 579
Transthyrin, in hereditary amyloidosis, 30
Trazodone, in depression, 1016
Treatment, refusal or withdrawal of, 363–364
Treponema pallidum (*see* Neurosyphilis; Syphilis)
Tretinoin, actinic keratoses and, 402–403
TRH (*see* Thyrotropin-releasing hormone)
Triamcinolone, in herpes zoster, 1181
Triamterene, hyperkalemia and, 562
Trichiasis, 424
Triglyceride:
  metabolism of, 771
  plasma, age-related changes in, 769, 770
Triglycerides:
  physical activity and, 94–96
  sex differences in, 42
    cardiovascular disease and, 44
Trihexyphenidyl (Artane):
  in motor neuron diseases, 969
  in Parkinson's disease, 959
Triiodothyronine (Cytomel; T₃):
  blood levels of, in hyperthyroidism, 722–723

Triiodothyronine (Cytomel: T₃) (Cont.):
  in depression, 1016
  thyroid nodules and, 736
Triiodothyronine resin uptake (T₃RU), in hyperthyroidism, 721
Trimethoprim-sulfamethoxazole, in pneumonia, 514
Tripotassium dicitrato bismuthate (TDB), peptic ulcer and, 623
Trisomy 21 (see Down's syndrome)
Trusts, inter vivos or living, 365
TSH (see Thyrotropin)
Tuberculosis, 518–525, 1055
  clinical, 519
  disseminated, 520
  etiology, transmission, and pathogenesis of, 518–519
  extrapulmonary, 524
    prognosis of, 524
  pleural disease and, 519–523
    diagnosis of, 519–520
    treatment of, 521, 522t, 523
  presentation of, 216
  prevention of, 525
  primary infection in, 519
  pulmonary, chronic, 519
  special problems in elderly with, 524–525
Tuberculous meningitis, 988
Tuberous sclerosis, mutation and, 32
Tubular necrosis, acute (ATN), 573–574
Tubules, renal, aging changes in, 556, 557
Tubulointerstitial nephritis, 570–573
  acute, 571–572
    bacterial, 571–572
    drug-induced, 571–572
  age-associated, 573
  chronic, 572
    analgesic-induced, 572
    hypercalcemic, 572
  of elderly, 573
  functional defects in, 571
  neoplastic diseases associated with, 572–573
Tumor(s):
  adrenal, benign, 716
  associated with interstitial nephritis, 572–573
  cutaneous, iatrogenic, 405–406
  dementia and, 952
  esophageal, 616–617
  fungating, in dying patients, 359

Tumor(s) (Cont.):
  gastric, 626–628
    benign, 627–628
  intracranial, 1004–1009
    classification and epidemiology of, 1004t, 1004–1005
    clinical presentation of, 1005, 1005t
    diagnostic evaluation of, 1006–1007
    mortality and, 1004–1005
    treatment of, 1007–1009
  of lacrimal apparatus, 426
  malignant, in Paget's disease, 844
  monoclonal B-cell, 67
  peripheral neuropathy and, 981
  thyroid, 735–737
  (See also Cancer; Carcinoma)
Tumor cells, 74
Tumor necrosis factor (TNF):
  in cancer cachexia, 1105
  weight loss and, 51
Turner syndrome, 29, 32
Type A behavior, coronary heart disease and, 105
Tyramine, monoamine oxidase inhibitor interactions with, 1050
Tyrosine hydroxylase (TH), 907
Tzanck procedure, 1179, *1179*

U

Ulcers:
  corneal, 426
  decubitus (see Pressure ulcers)
  peptic, 621–624
    clinical manifestations of, 217, 622–623
    diagnosis of, 623
    duodenal, 622
    gastric, 622
    treatment of, 623–624
  pressure (see Pressure ulcers)
  stasis, 407, *407*
  stercoral, constipation and, 1163
Ultrasound (US):
  in benign prostatic hyperplasia, 585
  gallstones and, 634
  in osteoporosis, 816, 818
  transrectal, prostate carcinoma and, 587–588
Ultraviolet radiation:
  actinic keratoses and, 399–403, *400, 401*

Ultraviolet radiation (Cont.):
  basal cell carcinoma and, 404
  damage caused to skin by, 384
  protection against, 406
Unconsciousness:
  stroke and, patient approach and, 927
  (See also Coma)
Underdosing, in cancer chemotherapy, 81–82
Undernutrition, 195
Underweight, life span and, 48
Unimodal progeroid syndromes, 29–31
Unit-bases assessment, 220
United States:
  incomes in, 117–118
  longevity in, 144
Urecholine (see Bethanechol chloride)
Uremia, 688–689
  impotence and, 1147
  peripheral neuropathy and, 981
Urethra, menopause and, 780
Urge incontinence, 1126–1127
Uric acid, production of, in gout, 892
Urinalysis, in urinary incontinence, 1128
Urinary incontinence, 1123t, 1123–1140
  acute, 1125t, 1125–1126, 1126t
  basic causes of, 1125
  in dying patients, 360
  evaluation of, 1127–1129, 1128t, *1129, 1130,* 1131t, 1132t, *1133*
  functional, 1127
  gait and, 1186
  management of, 1129, 1133–1140, 1134t
    behaviorally oriented training procedures in, 1136–1138, 1137t, 1138t
    catheters in, 1139–1140, 1140t
    drug treatment in, 1134–1136, 1135t
    surgery in, 1138–1139
  overflow, 1125
  persistent, 1126–1127, 1127t
  stress, 1124, 1126
  urge, 1126–1127
Urinary obstruction, benign prostatic hyperplasia and, 585
Urinary retention, analgesics and, 293
Urinary tract infection, 1055
  in dying patients, 360
  laboratory studies in, 1058
Urinary tract obstruction, fluid losses and, 1081

Urination:
normal, 1123–1124, *1124*, 1124t
(*See also* Urinary incontinence)
Urine:
bacteriuria and:
asymptomatic, 1055
incontinence and, 1126
concentration of, 558–560
Urine culture, in urinary incontinence, 1128
Urine specimens, lung cancer and, 550
Urokinase:
pulmonary embolism and, 547
in venous thrombotic disorders, 702
Uropathy, obstructive, acute renal failure and, 574–575
Ursodeoxycholic acid, gallstone dissolution with, 635
US (*see* Ultrasound)
Uterine cancer, age differences in, 78
Uvea, disorders of, 427–428, *428*
Uveitis, anterior, acute, 427–428

V

Vo$_{2max}$ (*see* Maximum oxygen consumption)
Vagina, structure and function of, 111
Vaginitis, atrophic, 111, 781
Valium (*see* Diazepam)
Valproate, seizures and, 1002
Values, of medical practitioners, 368, 369, 371–372
Valvular heart disease, 472–473
aortic valve and, 472–473
atrial septal defect and, 473
mitral valve and, 472
Vascular disorders:
collagen:
dementia and, 951
interstitial lung disease associated with, 541
esophageal dysphagia and, 1158
impotence and, 1148
peripheral (*see* Peripheral vascular disease)
pulmonary (*see* Pulmonary vascular disease)
renal, 556, 565–567
atheroembolic, 566–567
thromboembolic, 566
Vascular endothelial injury, deep venous thrombosis and, 546

Vasculitis:
necrotizing, systemic (*see* Systemic necrotizing vasculitis)
rheumatoid arthritis and, 875
Vasoactive intestinal peptide (VIP), 909
Vasoconstriction, pulmonary, in pulmonary hypertension, 545
Vasodilators:
in hypertension, 494
in pulmonary hypertension, 545
Vasopressin (Pitressin):
fluid balance and, 1079–1080
gastric bleeding and, 264–265
responsiveness to, 559
Vasovagal syncope, 1071–1072
Veins:
thrombotic disorders and (*see* Thrombotic disorders, venous)
(*See also specific veins*)
Vena caval devices:
pulmonary embolism and, 547
in venous thrombotic disorders, 703
Venous lakes, of lips, 397
Venous stasis, deep venous thrombosis and, 546
Venous thrombosis, deep, 546
Ventilation:
assisted, in hypercapnic respiratory failure, 534–535
distribution of, 501
mismatch of perfusion and, hypercapnic respiratory failure secondary to, 532–533
Ventilation scan, lung cancer and, 551
Ventricular ectopic beats, multiform, 471
Ventricular premature beats, 471, 471t
Ventricular tachycardia, 471
Verapamil, pharmacodynamics of, 206
Verbal fluency, 915
Vertebral disease, 975
Vertigo, 442
definition of, 1062
falls and, 1193
Vestibular ataxia, of aging, 443
Vestibular dysfunction, 442–443
anatomic and physiologic correlates of, 442–443
clinical evaluation of, 442
dizziness and, 1062–1063
falls and, 1193
general considerations in, 442
Vestibular neuronitis, 1064
Vestibulopathy, acute or recurrent, 1064

Vigilance, disorder of, in delirium, 922
Vincristine:
peripheral neuropathy and, 981
with primary lymphoma of central nervous system, 1008
VIP (*see* Vasoactive intestinal peptide)
Viral conjunctivitis, 425
Viral oncogenes (*see* Oncogenes)
Viruses:
dementia caused by, 949
diarrhea and, 1170
hepatitis and, 632–633
Paget's disease and, 843–844
in polymyositis/dermatomyositis, 867
Visceral mass, cachexia and, 1103
Vistaril (*see* Hydroxyzine)
Visual field defects, 422
testing for, 182
Visual illusions, in Parkinson's disease, 956
Visual impairment:
falls and, 1193
history taking and, 212
mental retardation and, 1028
patient examination and, 180
Visuospatial ability, 916
in Alzheimer's disease, 935, 937
Vital capacity, nutritional support and, 300
Vital sign(s), in physical examination, 181
"Vital sign of functioning," 1215
Vitamin(s), 56–57
aging and, 297
dietary intake of, in chronic renal failure, 576
fat-soluble, small-intestinal absorption of, 599
recommended daily allowance for, 56, 296
water-soluble, small-intestinal absorption of, 599
Vitamin A, 56–57
toxicity of, 57
Vitamin B$_1$, 57
Vitamin B$_6$, 56, 57
Vitamin B$_{12}$, 56, 57
deficiency of:
neutropenia and, 670
peripheral neuropathy and, 981
malabsorption of, pernicious anemia and, 666
Vitamin C, 56, 56t
megadoses of, 56
pressure ulcers and, 1208

Vitamin C (*Cont.*):
    withdrawal of, 56
Vitamin D (Calcitrol), 56
    calcium metabolism and, 800, *802,* 802–803, 803t
    in chronic renal failure, 576
    deficiency of:
        in osteomalacia, 833, 835–836
        skin disorders and, 395–396
    laboratory data and, 243
    metabolism of, disorders of, in osteomalacia, 829, 829–830
    in osteomalacia, 832–835
    in osteoporosis, 815, 822
    postoperative, in hyperparathyroidism, 841
    synthesis of, age-related changes in, 390–391
Vitamin D intoxication, hypercalcemia caused by, 840
Vitamin E, 56, 57
Vitamin K, 57
    foods containing, drug interactions of, 58
    hemostatic disorders and, 694–695, *695*
VLDL [*see* Lipoprotein(s), very low density]
Volume depletion:
    sodium metabolism and, 560
    syncope and, 1071
Volvulus:
    constipation and, 1164
    sigmoid, surgery for, 266
    surgery for, 266
Vomiting:
    analgesics and, 292–293
    in cancer patient, management of, 82
    as defense against enteric infection, 1172
    in dying patients, 358
Von Willebrand's disease (vWD), 687–688, 692
    diagnosis of, 693
    management of, 693

W

Waldenström's macroglobulinemia, 67
Walker, hip fractures and, 327
"Walking pneumonia," 513
Wallerian degeneration, in peripheral neuropathy, 978

Warfarin:
    drug interactions of, 701
    in venous thrombotic disorders, 701–703
Water:
    hypodipsia and, 53–54
    urinary losses of, 1080–1081
Water brash, in gastroesophageal reflux disease, 609
Water metabolism:
    aging changes in, 558–560
        clinical consequences of, 560–562
    in chronic renal failure, 575
    renal, hypertension and, 486
Water prescription, 54
WBC [*see* White blood cell(s)]
Weight:
    life span and, 48
    measurement of, in physical examination, 181
    as nutritional indicator, 49
    sex differences in, 42
        cardiovascular disease and, 44
    (*See also* Height-weight tables; Obesity)
Weight-bearing activity:
    hip fractures and, 327
    osteoporosis and, 97
Weight gain:
    sex differences in, 42–43
    (*See also* Obesity)
Weight loss:
    causes of, 49–50
    in diabetes mellitus, 749, 751
    in elderly, pathological causes of, 51, *51*
    gastroesophageal reflux disease and, 611
    glucose metabolism and, 93
    hypertension and, 492
    in hyperthyroidism, 719
    as nutritional indicator, 49
    in Parkinson's disease, 957
    (*See also* Cachexia)
Werner's syndrome, 26–27
Wernicke's aphasia, 927, 1097
White blood cell(s) (WBC), 669–676, 670t
    assessment of immune function and, 65
    increased destruction of, 670–671
    lack of production of, 669–670
        drugs and toxins and, 669–670, *670*
        nutritional deficiency and, 670

White blood cell(s) (WBC) (*Cont.*):
    neoplastic diseases and, *671,* 671–676
        metastases to bone marrow and, 676
        qualitative defects of, 676
        splenic sequestration of, 671
White blood cell (WBC) count, infection and, 216
"White nails of old age," 396
"White thrombus," 682
Whitmore staging system, prostate carcinoma and, 587, *587*
WHO (*see* World Health Organization)
Widowhood, caregiving and, 234
Wills, living, 365–366, 374
Withdrawal, analgesics and, 293
Women, in labor force, caregiving and, 235
"Women-in-the-middle," 235–236
Work capacity (*see* Maximum oxygen consumption)
World Health Organization (WHO), International Classification of Impairments, Disabilities, and Handicaps of, 884
Wound care, pressure ulcers and, 1209
Wound complications, regional versus general anesthesia and, 274
Wound healing:
    age-related changes in, 389–390, 390t
    immune function and nutrition and, 261–263, *262*
        evaluation and management of, 262–263
        pathophysiology of, 261–262
    zinc deficiency and, 54

X

X chromosomes, sex differences in longevity and, 24–25
X ray (*see* Chest x ray; Radiography)
X-ray densitometry (XD), in osteoporosis, 816–818, 817t
Xanax (*see* Alprazolam)
Xeroderma pigmentosum, 32
    skin cancer and, 400
Xerosis, 408
XX genotype, sex differential in longevity and, 39
Xylocaine, oral thrush and, in dying patients, 359

Y

Y chromosomes, sex differences in longevity and, 25
Yesavage Depression Scale, 1098

Z

Zenker's diverticulum, 615
Zinc, 54t, 54–55, 55
  deficiency of:

Zinc: deficiency of (*Cont.*):
  abnormalities associated with, 54
  anorexia and, 50
  in prostate, 582
  recommended daily allowance for, 54
  toxicity of, 55
Zinc therapy, pressure ulcers and, 1208